The
Complete
Word Study
New Testament

King James Version

Presented to

from

occasion

date

The
Complete
Word Study
New Testament

King James Version

The Complete Word Study New Testament

King James Version

Words in the text numerically coded to Strong's Greek
dictionary, Introduction to each book, Exegetical Notes,
Grammatical Codes on the text, Lexical Aids,
Greek Concordance, Translational Reference Index,
and Strong's Greek dictionary.

Compiled and edited by
Spiros Zodhiates, Th.D.

AMG PUBLISHERS
CHATTANOOGA, TN 37422, U.S.A.

ISBN 0-89957-651-6

June 1991
The Complete Word Study New Testament
King James Version

AMG PUBLISHERS

PREFACE

You are holding in your hands one of the most useful reference works available for in-depth study of the New Testament. It is an excellent tool that will help the English reader to properly understand the full meaning of God's Word as it was originally recorded in the Greek language. Each word in the Greek New Testament is represented by a number and a grammatical code that are printed above the English text. The number corresponds to the original Greek word in Strong's *Dictionary of the Greek Testament* and the Lexical Aids (both of which appear in the Study Helps section at the back). The grammatical codes identify the forms (case, tense, gender, etc.) of the Greek word and are explained in the Study Helps section.

Another great study help which we have included is the Translational Reference Index. With this index it is possible to find all the Greek words that a particular English word represents in the King James Version of the New Testament. The Greek words are identified by the numbers which correspond to Strong's Dictionary. These Greek words can then be looked up in the Lexical Aids section for detailed explanations. The Greek Concordance, which also appears in the Study Helps section of this book, will enable you to find the other occurrences of these words in the New Testament.

I would like to express my thanks to those who worked so hard to make this unique New Testament possible:

Rev. George A. Hadjiantoniou, Ph.D., who has taught theology, Greek grammar, and exegesis in higher institutions of learning. He is responsible for assigning the grammatical codes for the Greek words.

Mrs. Ruth Peters, the librarian at AMG International, who prepared the Translational Reference Index contained in this volume.

The staff of AMG's Special Projects Department under the direction of Warren Baker: Jim and Gertrude Gee, Joel Kletzing, Trevor Overcash, Amy Turner, Sam Wallace, Todd Williams, and Mark Oshman who worked to place the Strong's numbers on the text. These men and women are responsible for the research and preparation of this project.

Although we have labored tediously to make this work free from error, we are not infallible. If you should find a mistake, whatever it may be, please let us know.

SPIROS ZODHIATES

EXPLANATION OF GENERAL FORMAT

THE COMPLETE WORD STUDY NEW TESTAMENT

PLACEMENT OF NOTATIONS AND NUMBERS
In most cases, grammatical notations associated with a word are placed directly before the Strong's number representing that word. This is not the case, however, when conjunctions and other grammatical particles occur because these are not assigned notations. In addition, non-declinable proper nouns are listed with only the Strong's number. These notations and numbers are placed directly above the word they designate (whenever possible) or are placed as close as possible above the word(s) with which they are associated.

When two English words placed next to each other represent a single Greek word, the grammatical notation and number of that Greek word are placed above the two English words and between them (for procedures adopted when three or more adjacent English words are used to translate a single Greek word, see Word Clusters, below).

On occasion, words which appear in the Greek text are not translated into English. This frequently occurs with double negatives which are acceptable in Greek grammar but are not so in English. Such words are depicted by having their corresponding notations and numbers placed in parentheses above the text in the position that the English translation best allows.

When a word, or group of words, is carried over from one line to the line below it, the grammatical notation has often been placed above one line and the Strong's number is placed above the line below.

When particles such as *an* (302), *eán* (1437), or *men* (3303) seem to be associated with words that express uncertainty (in the first two cases) or contrast (in the case of "men"), the numbers for these words have been placed after the word with an intervening virgule (e.g., art3588/3303).

The Greek word *hóti* (3754) is often untranslated when used to introduce direct discourse (e.g., Acts 26:31). In such instances, the number of *hóti* has not been placed over the text. When not used in direct discourse and not translated in English, however, the Strong's number has been placed over the text in parentheses (e.g., Acts 24:21).

WORD CLUSTERS are groups of three or more adjacent English words which are connected with each other. These have been set off by asterisks between each word in that cluster. Asterisks have been placed after the first word in the cluster, before the last word in the cluster, and between intervening words. Word clusters have been used in the following instances:

To demonstrate where three or more English words have been used to translate one Greek word (e.g., *mépote* has been rendered as "lest*at*any*time" [Heb. 2:1]).

To show where an English word(s) has been placed between two or more English words associated with a single Greek word (e.g., in the phrase "they gathered*them*together" [John 6:13], the supplied word *"them"* is placed between "gathered . . . together" which, in Greek, is the word *sunégagon*

[4863]). If the intervening word itself possessed a grammatical notation and Strong's number, a virgule (slash) would be used to separate the respective notations and numbers (e.g., aina4863/ppro846). The first notation and number would represent the first word appearing in the English translation.

To render Greek idioms according to their English equivalents (e.g., "found with child" in Matt. 1:18 is literally 'found to be having in belly' in Greek. Therefore, it is presented as "found*with*child" to reflect the translation of this expression).

QUOTATIONS OF AND ALLUSIONS TO THE OLD TESTAMENT within the body of the text have been underlined with the OT references placed at the end of the verse. Where two or more verses in the NT contain a quote from the same OT verse(s), the latter citation is given at the end of the last verse containing that quotation.

Often, one NT verse will contain more than one OT reference. Where certain portions of such verses are underlined, the OT verses will respectively apply to each underlined section and will be found at the end of the verse(s). Thus the OT references may not be in chronological order.

INTRODUCTIONS to each book of the New Testament cover Bible history, archaeology, and customs that are important in understanding the significance of the book in relationship to the whole Bible.

FOOTNOTES explain the exegetical, theological, historical, and geographical significance of certain passages. A key (☛) in the text informs the reader that there is a note at the bottom of the page that discusses that verse, and perhaps several of the verses that follow.

STUDY HELPS appear after the Book of Revelation. They include:

THE GRAMMATICAL CODES and their explanation. The letters over the English text of the New Testament refer to the grammatical structure of the Greek word(s). These codes are also listed on the bookmark that accompanied this product.

THE LIST OF IRREGULAR ADVERBS records the occasions where adverbs function as prepositions. Where this has occurred in the text, these adverbs have been assigned an *ad** notation. It must be remembered that even though these words may play the role of prepositions, they are still classified as adverbs.

GUIDE TO TRANSLITERATION of Greek with helps for modern pronunciation.

LEXICAL AIDS TO THE NEW TESTAMENT which provides additional material for selected words from the Greek New Testament. They are indexed according to the numbering system found in James Strong's *Dictionary of the Greek Testament* located at the end of this book.

A GREEK CONCORDANCE of the New Testament which lists the occurrences of almost every word in the Greek New Testament.

A TRANSLATIONAL REFERENCE INDEX of the New Testament which lists almost every word of the King James Text followed by the Strong's numbers for all the Greek words that are translated by each English word.

A SCRIPTURE INDEX which is designed to aid the reader in locating all the Scripture references found in the Footnotes and Introductions.

How to Use the Complete

The First Epistle of

PETER

The Apostle Peter was the most prominent disciple during the ministry of Jesus and had a tremendous impact on the early church. The first twelve chapters of Acts are devoted to his ministry and to the development of the church in the East where he was the dominant figure. Paul mentioned him in 1 Corinthians (1 Cor. 1:12; 3:22; 9:5; 15:5) and Galatians (Gal. 1:18; 2:7–9, 11, 14), and he wrote two New Testament books. This first letter is addressed to the five Roman provinces in Asia Minor (modern-day Turkey) north of the Taurus Mountains (1 Pet. 1:1).

AN INTRODUCTION is given for each book.

This letter was written to encourage the believers to endure the intense persecution that was prevalent in the area and to prepare the readers for the difficult times ahead them. The first empire-wide persecution of Christians did not come until A.D. 249 under the brutal emperor Decius, but local persecutions many times were quite severe. One in particular took place early in the second century in Bithynia, one of the provinces to which Peter wrote (1 Pet. 1:1). A letter was sent from Pliny, governor of Bithynia, to the Roman emperor Trajan, in A.D. 112. He explained that he had been executing people who confessed that they were Christians. Trajan's reply expressed his approval of Pliny's policy but instructed him to set free those Christians who would renounce their faith and worship the Roman gods. Since 1 Peter was most likely written in the A.D. 60's, persecution of the severest kind was yet to come. Peter used Jesus' own suffering as the cornerstone of his exhortation. Likewise, Peter admonished believers to suffer as "Christians," not as lawbreakers.

KEYS indicate explanatory notes at the bottom of the page.

1
an,nn4074   an,nn652   an,nn2424 an,nn5547   an,ajn3927   an,nn1290
Peter, an apostle of Jesus Christ, to the strangers scattered throughout
an,nn4195   an,nn1053   an,nn2587   an,nn773   2532   an,nn978
Pontus, Galatia, Cappadocia, Asia, and Bithynia,
an,aj1588   pre2596   an,nn4268   an,nn2316   an,nn3962   pre1722
2 Elect according to the foreknowledge of God the Father, through
an,nn38   an,nn4151 pre1519 an,nn5218   2532   an,nn4473   an,nn129   an,nn2424
sanctification of the Spirit, unto obedience and sprinkling of the blood of Jesus
an,nn5547 an,nn5485   ppro5213 2532 an,nn1515   opt4129
Christ: Grace unto you, and peace, be multiplied.

> ### Heaven Is Worth Suffering For

SUBJECT HEADINGS are provided throughout the text.

pr/an,aj2128   art3588   nn2316   2532   an,nn3962   ppro2257 art,nn2962 an,nn2424   an,nn5547
3 Blessed *be* the God and Father of our Lord Jesus Christ, which

1:2 See note on Ephesians 1:4, 5.

LETTERS above a word refer to the grammatical structure of the Greek word and are explained in the Grammatical Notations section.

NUMBERS above the words are Strong's reference numbers for the corresponding Greek words. These numbers can be used to find the Greek words in the Study Helps section where further study material is available.

Word Study New Testament

pre2596   ppro848   art,aj4183   an,nn1656   art,apta313/ppro2248   pre1519   pap2198   an,nn1680
according to his abundant mercy hath (begotten*us*again) unto a lively hope
pre1223   an,nn386   an,nn2424   an,nn5547   pre1537   an,ajn3498
by the resurrection of Jesus Christ from the dead,
          pre1519   an,nn2817   an,aj862   2532   an,aj283   2532
4 To   an   inheritance   incorruptible,   and   undefiled,   and
          an,aj263   pfpp5083   pre1722 an,nn3772 pre1519 ppro2248
that*fadeth*not*away, reserved in heaven for you,
                   art,ppmp5432   pre1722   an,nn1411   an,nn2316   pre1223   an,nn4102 pre1519 an,nn4991   an,aj2092
☞ 5 Who*are*kept by the power of God through faith unto salvation ready
          aifp601   pre1722   an,aj2078 an,nn2540
to be revealed in the last time.
          pre1722/repro3739   pinm21   ad737   an,ajn3641   1487 pap1163/pin2076
6 Wherein ye greatly rejoice, though now for a season, if need be, ye
          aptp3076   pre1722   an,aj4164   an,nn3986
are*in*heaviness through manifold temptations:
          2443   art3588   nn1383   ppro5216 art,nn4102   an,ajn4183   pred·an,aj5093   an,nn5553
☞ 7 That [the trial of your faith,] being much more precious than of gold
art,ppmp622   1161   ppmp1381 pre1223 an,nn4442   asbp2147 pre1519 an,nn1868   2532
that perisheth, though it be tried with fire, might be found unto praise and
an,nn5092 2532 an,nn1391 pre1722   an,nn602   an,nn2424   an,nn5547
honor and glory at the appearing of Jesus Christ:

       (Job 23:10; Ps. 66:10; Prov. 17:3; Is. 48:10; Zech. 13:9; Mal. 3:3)
          repro3739   3756   apta1492   pin25   pre1519 repro3739   ad737   pap3708
8 Whom having not seen, ye love; in whom, though now ye see *him*
3361   1161   pap4100   pinm21   an,nn5479   an,aj412   2532   pfpp1392
not, yet believing, ye rejoice with joy unspeakable and full*of*glory:
          ppmp2865   art3588 nn5056   ppro5216 art,nn4102   an,nn4991   an,nn5590
9 Receiving the end of your faith, *even* the salvation of *your* souls,
          pre4012 repro3739   an,nn4991   an,nn4396   aina1567   2532   aina1830
10 Of which salvation the prophets have inquired and searched diligently,
          art,apta4395   pre4012 art3588   nn5485   pre1519 ppro5209
who prophesied of the grace (*that should come*) unto you:
          pap2045   (pre1519) inpro5101   2228   an,aj4169   an,nn2540 art3588   nn4151   an,nn5547
11 Searching   what, or what manner of time the Spirit of Christ
          pre1722 ppro846   ipf1213   ppmp4303   art3588   nn3804   pre1519
which was in them did signify, when it testified beforehand the sufferings of
an,nn5547 2532 art3588 nn1391   pre3326/depro5023
Christ, and the glory that*should* follow.   *(Ps. 22:1-31; Is. 53:1-12)*
          repro3739   ainp601   3754 3756   rxpro1438   1161   ppro2254
12 Unto whom it was revealed, that not unto themselves, but unto us

---

☞ **1:5** The phrase "who are kept by the power of God" refers to believers (1 Pet. 1:3). These also
have become heirs of a resurrection body (1 Pet. 1:4), and their inheritance is reserved in heaven. The
sense in which the perfect participle, *tetērēménēn* (meaning "reserved," and derived from *tereō* [5083]),
is used denotes that the act was made possible by Christ sometime in the past and is now being kept
by Him until the proper time of delivery. Also, the purpose of the protection indicated in verse five is
related to the believer's future liberation noted in the phrase, "kept by the power of God . . . unto
salvation" (Rom. 8:23; 13:11).
☞ **1:7, 13** See note on 1 Thessalonians 2:19.

ASTERISKS in the text indicate word clusters, which are discussed in the Explanation of General Format.

UNDERLINING identifies quotations from or allusions to the Old Testament. References are at the end of the verse.

ITALICS are used in the text to indicate words which are not found in the Greek but implied by it.

PARENTHESES around a notation and/or a number indicate that the corresponding Greek word has not been translated into English.

NOT ILLUSTRATED: ADVERBS sometimes function as prepositions. In such cases the grammatical notation *ad** has been placed above the English text. All such occurrences can be found in the List of Irregular Adverbs.

ABBREVIATIONS

abl.	=	ablative	masc.	=	masculine
acc.	=	accusative	mid.	=	middle
act.	=	active	Mod.	=	Modern
adj.	=	adjective	MS	=	manuscript
adv.	=	adverb	MSS	=	manuscripts
ant.	=	antonym	MT	=	Masoretic text
aor.	=	aorist [2 aor. for second aorist]	neg.	=	negative
art.	=	article	neut.	=	neuter
attrib.	=	attributive	nom.	=	nominative
ca.	=	approximately	NT	=	New Testament
cf.	=	compare	obj.	=	object, objective(ly)
chap.	=	chapter	opp.	=	opposite, opposition
Class.	=	Classical	opt.	=	optative
coll.	=	collective	Or	=	An alternate translation
comp.	=	compound	OT	=	Old Testament
conj.	=	conjunction	p.	=	page, past
dat.	=	dative	part.	=	participle
def.	=	definite	pass.	=	passive
deriv.	=	derivative, derivation	perf.	=	perfect
e.g.	=	for example	pl.	=	plural
Eng.	=	English	poss.	=	possessive
etc.	=	and so forth	pp.	=	pages
f.	=	following	prep.	=	preposition
fem.	=	feminine	pres.	=	present
ff.	=	following in the plural	priv.	=	privative
fut.	=	future	pron.	=	pronoun
gen.	=	genitive	Rom.	=	Roman
Gr.	=	Greek	Sept.	=	Septuagint
Hebr.	=	Hebrew	sing.	=	singular
imper.	=	imperative	subj.	=	subject, subjective
imperf.	=	imperfect	subst.	=	substantive
indef.	=	indefinite	syn.	=	synonym, synonymous
indic.	=	indicative	TR	=	Textus Receptus
inf.	=	infinitive	trans.	=	transitive
intens.	=	intensive	UBS	=	United Bible Society
intrans.	=	intransitive	v.	=	verse
KJV	=	King James Version	voc.	=	vocative
Lat.	=	Latin	vv.	=	verses

THE BOOKS OF THE BIBLE

THE OLD TESTAMENT

Book	Abbrev.	Book	Abbrev.
Genesis	Gen.	Ecclesiastes	Eccl.
Exodus	Ex.	Song of Solomon	Song
Leviticus	Lev.	Isaiah	Is.
Numbers	Num.	Jeremiah	Jer.
Deuteronomy	Deut.	Lamentations	Lam.
Joshua	Josh.	Ezekiel	Ezek.
Judges	Judg.	Daniel	Dan.
Ruth	Ruth	Hosea	Hos.
1 Samuel	1 Sam.	Joel	Joel
2 Samuel	2 Sam.	Amos	Amos
1 Kings	1 Kgs.	Obadiah	Obad.
2 Kings	2 Kgs.	Jonah	Jon.
1 Chronicles	1 Chr.	Micah	Mic.
2 Chronicles	2 Chr.	Nahum	Nah.
Ezra	Ezra	Habakkuk	Hab.
Nehemiah	Neh.	Zephaniah	Zeph.
Esther	Esth.	Haggai	Hag.
Job	Job	Zechariah	Zech.
Psalms	Ps.	Malachi	Mal.
Proverbs	Prov.		

THE NEW TESTAMENT

Book	Abbrev.	Book	Abbrev.
The Gospel According to:		2 Thessalonians	2 Thess.
Matthew	Matt.	1 Timothy	1 Tim.
Mark	Mark	2 Timothy	2 Tim.
Luke	Luke	Titus	Titus
John	John	Philemon	Phile.
The Acts	Acts	Hebrews	Heb.
Romans	Rom.	James	James
1 Corinthians	1 Cor.	1 Peter	1 Pet.
2 Corinthians	2 Cor.	2 Peter	2 Pet.
Galatians	Gal.	1 John	1 John
Ephesians	Eph.	2 John	2 John
Philippians	Phil.	3 John	3 John
Colossians	Col.	Jude	Jude
1 Thessalonians	1 Thess.	Revelation	Rev.

CONTENTS

THE NEW TESTAMENT

STUDY HELPS

MATTHEW

Matthew, whose name means "gift of Jehovah," left his occupation of gathering taxes (Matt. 9:9–13) in order to follow Jesus. In Luke 5:27–32, Matthew gave a banquet for Jesus before becoming one of the Twelve Apostles (Matt. 10:3). He was an eyewitness of Jesus' entire ministry.

The four Gospels (Matthew, Mark, Luke, and John) form a unique kind of written document. They present four complementary views of the life of Jesus. Aside from these four Gospels, there are only a few writings in the contemporary historians, Josephus and Tacitus, which discuss the life and activities of Jesus. Several scholars suggest that they were written down, under the inspiration of the Holy Spirit, because the number of surviving eyewitnesses to Jesus' life were dwindling.

From early times, Matthew's book has been placed at the beginning of the New Testament. The approximate date for its writing is A.D. 58–68. There is some evidence that it was originally written in Hebrew or that Matthew made one copy in Hebrew and one in Greek.

The large number of Old Testament quotations used in the book seem to indicate that Matthew directed his primarily writing toward a Jewish audience. He lays great stress on the Old Testament passages which show that Jesus was the Messiah (Christ), the long-awaited King of Israel. For the most part, the narrative is chronological, though certain portions of the material are grouped according to subject matter (e.g., the Sermon on the Mount, chaps. 5—7, and the parables in chap. 13). In Matthew's presentation of the life of Jesus, the central theme is that He is the King of the long-awaited kingdom of God.

Of the fifteen parables and twenty miracles recorded in the Book of Matthew, ten of the parables and three of the miracles are not mentioned in the other Gospels. In addition, the account of the saints who came back to life at Christ's resurrection (Matt. 27:51, 52), the sealing of Jesus' tomb, and the posting of the Roman guard outside it (Matt. 27:62–66) are exclusively recorded in the Gospel of Matthew.

Genealogy of Jesus (Luke 3:23-28)

1 The book of the generation of Jesus Christ, the son of David, the son of Abraham.

2 Abraham begat Isaac; and Isaac begat Jacob; and Jacob begat Judas and his brethren;

1161   an,nn2455 aina1080   5329   2532 2196 pre1537   2283   1161   5329   aina1080   2074

3 And Judas begat Phares and Zara of Thamar; and Phares begat Esrom;

1161   2074   aina1080   689

and Esrom begat Aram;

1161   689   aina1080   284   1161   284   aina1080   3476   1161   3476

4 And Aram begat Aminadab; and Aminadab begat Naasson; and Naasson

aina1080   4533

begat Salmon;

1161   4533   aina1080   1003   pre1537   4477   1161   1003   aina1080   5601   pre1537   4503

5 And Salmon begat Boaz of Rachab; and Boaz begat Obed of Ruth;

1161   5601   aina1080   2421

and Obed begat Jesse;

1161   2421   aina1080   1138   art3588   nn935   1161   1138   art3588   nn935   aina1080   art,nn4672   pre1537

6 And Jesse begat David the king; and David the king begat Solomon of

art3588   art,nn3774

her *that had been the wife* of Urias;

1161   an,nn4672   aina1080   4497   1161   4497   aina1080   7   1161   7   aina1080

7 And Solomon begat Roboam; and Roboam begat Abia; and Abia begat

760

Asa;

1161   760   aina1080   2498   1161   2498   aina1080   2496   1161   2496   aina1080

8 And Asa begat Josaphat; and Josaphat begat Joram; and Joram begat

art,nn3604

Ozias;

1161   an,nn3604   aina1080   2488   1161   2488   aina1080   881   1161   881   aina1080

9 And Ozias begat Joatham; and Joatham begat Achaz; and Achaz begat

art,nn1478

Ezekias;

1161   an,nn1478   aina1080   art,nn3128   1161   an,nn3128   aina1080   300   1161   300

10 And Ezekias begat Manasses; and Manasses begat Amon; and Amon

aina1080   art,nn2502

begat Josiah;

1161   an,nn2502   aina1080   art,nn2423   2532   ppro846   art,nn80   pre1909   art3588

11 And Josiah begat Jechoniah and his brethren, about the

nn3350   an,nn897

time*they*were*carried*away to Babylon:

(2 Kgs. 24:12-16; 2 Chr. 36:10; Jer. 27:20)

1161   pre3326   art3588   nn350   an,nn897   an,nn2423   aina1080   4528   1161

12 And after they were brought to Babylon, Jechoniah begat Salathiel; and

4528   aina1080   2216

Salathiel begat Zorobabel;

1161   2216   aina1080   10   1161   10   aina1080   1662   1161   1662

13 And Zorobabel begat Abiud; and Abiud begat Eliakim; and Eliakim

aina1080   107

begat Azor;

1161   107   aina1080   4524   1161   4524   aina1080   885   1161   885   aina1080

14 And Azor begat Sadoc; and Sadoc begat Achim; and Achim begat

1664

Eliud;

1161   1664   aina1080   1648   1161   1648   aina1080   3157   1161   3157

15 And Eliud begat Eleazar; and Eleazar begat Matthan; and Matthan

aina1080   2384

begat Jacob;

1161   2384   aina1080   2501   art3588   nn435   an,nn3137   pre1537   repro3739   ainp1080

16 And Jacob begat Joseph the husband of Mary, of whom was born

an,nn2424   art3588   ppmp3004   an,nn5547

Jesus, who is called Christ.

3767   an,aj3956   art3588   nn1074   pre575   11   ad2193   1138   nu1180

17 So all the generations from Abraham to David *are* fourteen

an,nn1074   2532   pre575   1138   ad2193   art3588   nn3350   an,nn897   nu1180

generations; and from David until the carrying away into Babylon *are* fourteen

an,nn1074   2532   pre575   art3588   nn3350   an,nn897   ad2193   art,nn5547   nu1180

generations; and from the carrying away into Babylon unto Christ *are* fourteen

an,nn1074

generations.

The Birth of Jesus (Luke 2:1-7)

1161   art3588   nn1083   art,nn2424   an,nn5547   ipf2258   ad3779   1063   ppro846   art,nn3384

18 Now the birth of Jesus Christ was on*this*wise: When as his mother

an,nn3137   aptp3423   2501   ad4250   ppro846   aifp4905

Mary was espoused to Joseph, before they came together, she was

ainp2147/pap2192/pre1722/an,nn1064 pre1537   an,aj40   an,nn4151

found*with*child of the Holy Ghost.

1161   2501   ppro846   art,nn435   pap5607   pr/an,aj1342   2532   3361   pap2309

19 Then Joseph her husband, being a just *man,* and not willing to

ainf3856/ppro846   ainp1014   ainf630/ppro846   ad2977

make*her*a*public*example, was minded to put*her*away privily.

1161   ppro846   aptp1760   depro5023   2400   an,nn32   an,nn2962

20 But while he thought on these things, behold, the angel of the Lord

ainp5316   ppro846   pre2596   an,nn3677   pap3004   2501   an,nn5207   1138   aosi5399   3361

appeared unto him in a dream, saying, Joseph, thou son of David, fear not

ainf3880   3137   ppro4675   art,nn1135   1063   art,aptp1080   pre1722   ppro846   pin2076

to take unto thee Mary thy wife; for that*which*is*conceived in her is

pre1537   an,aj40   an,nn4151

of the Holy Ghost.

1161   fm5088   an,nn5207   2532   ft2564   ppro846   art,nn3686   an,nn2424

21 And she shall bring forth a son, and thou shalt call his name JESUS:

1063   epn846   ft4982   ppro848   art,nn2992   pre575   ppro846   art,nn266

for he shall save his people from their sins.

1161   an,aj3650   depro5124   pfi1096   2443   asbp4137   art3588   aptp4483

22 Now all this was done, that it might be fulfilled which was spoken

pre5259   art3588   nn2962   pre1223   art3588   nn4396   pap3004

of the Lord by the prophet, saying,

2400   art,nn3933   ft2192/pre1722/an,nn1064   2532   fm5088   an,nn5207   2532

23 Behold, a virgin shall be*with*child, and shall bring forth a son, and

ft2564   ppro846   art,nn3686   1694   repro3739   pr/ppmp3177   pin2076   art,nn2316   pre3326

they shall call his name Emmanuel, which being interpreted is, God with

ppro2257

us.   *(Is. 7:14)*

24 Then Joseph being raised from sleep did as the angel of the Lord had bidden him, and took unto him his wife:

☞ 25 And knew her not till she had brought forth her firstborn son: and he called his name JESUS.

The Visit of the Magi

2 Now when Jesus was born in Bethlehem of Judea in the days of Herod the king, behold, there came wise men from the east to Jerusalem,

2 Saying, Where is he*that*is*born King of the Jews? for we have seen his star in the east, and are come to worship him. *(Num. 24:17)*

3 When Herod the king had heard *these things,* he was troubled, and all Jerusalem with him.

4 And when he had gathered all the chief priests and scribes of the people together, he demanded of them where Christ should be born.

5 And they said unto him, In Bethlehem of Judea: for thus it is written by the prophet,

6 And thou Bethlehem, *in* the land of Judah, art not the least among the princes of Judah: for out of thee shall come a Governor, that shall rule my people Israel. *(Mic. 5:2)*

7 Then Herod, when he had privily called the wise men, inquired*of*them*diligently what time the star appeared.

8 And he sent them to Bethlehem, and said, Go and search diligently

☞ **1:25** See note on Colossians 1:15.

pre4012 art3588   nn3813   1161 ad1875   asba2147   aima518/ppro3427   3704
for the young child; and when ye have found *him*, bring*me*word*again, that

epn2504   apta2064   asba4352   ppro846
I may come and worship him also.

1161   art3588   apta191 art3588 nn935   ainp4198   2532 2400 art3588 nn792 repro3739
9 When they had heard the king, they departed; and, lo, the star, which

aina1492 pre1722 art13588   nn395   ipf4254   ppro846 ad2193 apta2064   aina2476 ad*1883 ad3757
they saw in the east, went before them, till it came and stood over where

art3588   nn3813   ipf2258
the young child was.

1161   apta1492 art3588 nn792   aina5463   ad4970 an,aj3173 an,nn5479
10 When they saw the star, they rejoiced with exceeding great joy.

2532   apta2064 pre1519 art3588 nn3614   aina1492 art3588   nn3813
11 And when they were come into the house, they saw the young child

pre3326 an,nn3137 ppro846 art,nn3384 2532 apta4098   aina4352   ppro846 2532
with Mary his mother, and fell down, and worshiped him: and when they

apta455   ppro848   art,nn2344   aina4374   ppro846 an,nn1435 an,nn5557 2532
had opened their treasures, they presented unto him gifts; gold, and

an,nn3030   2532 an,nn4666
frankincense, and myrrh.   *(Ps.72:10,11,15; Is. 60:6)*

2532   aptp5537   pre2596 an,nn3677   3361 ainf344
12 And being warned*of*God in a dream that they should not return

pre4314 an,nn2264   aina402   pre1519 ppro848   art,nn5561 (pre1223) an,aj243 an,nn3598
to Herod, they departed into their own country another way.

God Warns Joseph

1161   ppro846   apta402   2400   an,nn32   an,nn2962
13 And when they were departed, behold, the angel of the Lord

pinp5316   2501 pre2596 an,nn3677 pap3004 aptp1453   aima3880 art3588   nn3813   2532
appeareth to Joseph in a dream, saying, Arise, and take the young child and

ppro846   art,nn3384   2532 pim5343 pre1519 an,nn125 2532 pim2468   ad1563   ad2193(302)
his mother, and flee into Egypt, and be thou there until I

asba2036/ppro4671   1063 an,nn2264 pin3195 pinf2212 art3588   nn3813   infg622   ppro846
bring*thee*word: for Herod will seek the young child to destroy him.

1161   art3588 aptp1453   aina3880 art3588   nn3813   2532 ppro846 art,nn3384   an,nn3571
14 When he arose, he took the young child and his mother by night,

2532   aina402   pre1519 an,nn125
and departed into Egypt:

2532   ipf2258 ad1563 ad2193 art3588   nn5054   an,nn2264 2443   asbp4137   art3588
15 And was there until the death of Herod: that it might be fulfilled which

aptp4483   pre5259 art3588 nn2962 pre1223 art3588   nn4396   pap3004   pre1537   an,nn125
was spoken of the Lord by the prophet, saying, Out of Egypt have I

aina2564 ppro3450 art,nn5207
called my son.   *(Hos. 11:1)*

ad5119   an,nn2264   apta1492 3754   ainp1702 pre5259 art3588   nn3097
16 Then Herod, when he saw that he was mocked of the wise men,

ainp2373/ad3029   2532   apta649   2532 aina337 an,aj3956 art3588   nn3816   art3588
was*exceeding*wroth, and sent forth, and slew all the children that were

pre1722 965 2532 pre1722 an,aj3956 art3588 nn3725 ppro846 pre575 an,ajn1332 2532

in Bethlehem, and in all the coasts thereof, from two*years*old and

ad2736 pre2596 art3588 nn5550 repro3739 aina198 pre3844 art3588

under, according to the time which he had diligently inquired of the

nn3097

wise men.

ad5119 ainp4137 art,aptp4483 pre5259 an,nn2408 art3588 nn4396

17 Then was fulfilled that*which*was*spoken by Jeremiah the prophet,

pap3004

saying,

pre1722 4471 an,nn5456 ainp191 an,nn2355 2532 an,nn2805 2532

18 In Ramah was there a voice heard, lamentation, and weeping, and

an,aj4183 an,nn3602 4478 pap2799 ppro848 art,nn5043 2532 ipf2309 3756 aifp3870

great mourning, Rachel weeping *for* her children, and would not be comforted,

3754 pin1526 3756

because they are not. *(Jer. 31:15)*

1161 art,nn2264 apta5053 2400 an,nn32 an,nn2962 pinp5316 pre2596

19 But when Herod was dead, behold, an angel of the Lord appeareth in

an,nn3677 2501 pre1722 an,nn125

a dream to Joseph in Egypt,

pap3004 aptp1453 aima3880 art3588 nn3813 2532 ppro846 art,nn3384 2532 pim4198 pre1519

20 Saying, Arise, and take the young child and his mother, and go into

an,nn1093 2474 1063 pfi2348 art,pap2212 art3588 nn3813 art,nn5590

the land of Israel: for they are dead which sought the young child's life.

1161 art3588 aptp1453 aina3880 art3588 nn3813 2532 ppro846 art,nn3384 2532 aina2064

21 And he arose, and took the young child and his mother, and came

pre1519 an,nn1093 2474

into the land of Israel.

1161 apta191 3754 an,nn745 pin936 pre1909 art,nn2449 pre473

22 But when he heard that Archelaus did reign in Judea in*the*room of

ppro846 art,nn3962 an,nn2264 ainp5399 ainf565 ad1563 1161

his father Herod, he was afraid to go thither: notwithstanding, being

aptp5537 pre2596 an,nn3677 aina402 pre1519 art3588 nn3313 art,nn1056

warned*of*God in a dream, he turned aside into the parts of Galilee:

2532 apta2064 aina2730 pre1519 an,nn4172 ppmp3004 3478 3704

23 And he came and dwelt in a city called Nazareth: that it might be

asbp4137 art,aptp4483 pre1223 art3588 nn4396 fp2564 an,aj3480

fulfilled which*was*spoken by the prophets, He shall be called a Nazarene.

The Preaching of John (Mark 1:1-8; Luke 3:1-9, 15-17; John 1:19-28)

pre1722 depro1565 art,nn2250 pinm3854 an,nn2491 art3588 nn910 pap2784 pre1722 art3588 ajn2048

3 In those days came John the Baptist, preaching in the wilderness

art,nn2449

of Judea,

2532 pap3004 pim3340 1063 art3588 nn932 art,nn3772 pfi1148

2 And saying, Repent ye: for the kingdom of heaven is*at*hand.

1063   depro3778 pin2076   art,aptp4483   pre5259 art3588   nn4396   an,nn2268 pap3004

3 For   this   is   he*that*was*spoken*of   by   the   prophet   Isaiah,   saying,

an,nn5456   pap994 pre1722 art3588   ajn2048   aima2090   art3588 nn3598   an,nn2962

The voice of one crying in   the wilderness, Prepare ye the way of the Lord,

pim4160 ppro846 art,nn5147 pr/an,aj2117

make his paths straight.   *(Is. 40:3)*

1161   epn846   art,nn2491 ipf2192 ppro848   art,nn1742 pre575   an,nn2574 an,nn2359 2532   an,aj1193

4 And the same John had his raiment of camel's hair, and a leathern

an,nn2223 pre4012 ppro846 art,nn3751 1161 ppro848 art,nn5160 ipf2258 pr/an,nn200 2532 an,aj66 pr/an,nn3192

girdle about his loins; and his meat was locusts and wild honey.

ad5119   ipf1607   pre4314 ppro846   an,nn2414   2532   an,aj3956 art,nn2449   2532 an,aj3956 art3588

5 Then went out   to   him Jerusalem, and   all   Judea, and   all   the

nn4066   art,nn2446

region*round*about Jordan,

2532   ipf907   pre5259 ppro846 pre1722 art,nn2446   ppmp1843   ppro848 art,nn266

6 And were baptized of him in Jordan, confessing their sins.

1161   apta1492 an,aj4183 art3588   nn5330   2532   an,nn4523   ppmp2064 pre1909 ppro846

7 But when he saw many of the Pharisees and Sadducees come to   his

art,nn908   aina2036   ppro846   an,nn1081   an,nn2191 inpro5101   aina5263 ppro5213

baptism, he said unto them, O generation of vipers, who hath warned you to

ainf5343 pre575 art3588   nn3709   pap3195

flee from the wrath to come?

aima4160   3767   an,nn2590 an,aj514   art,nn3341

8 Bring forth therefore fruits meet for repentance:

2532   aosi1380   3361   pinf3004 pre1722   rxpro1438   pin2192   11

9 And think not to   say within yourselves, We have Abraham to *our*

an,nn3962 1063   pin3004   ppro5213 3754 art,nn2316 pinm1410 pre1537 depro5130 art,nn3037   ainf1453

father: for I say unto you, that God is able of these stones to raise up

an,nn5043   11

children unto Abraham.

1161   ad2235   2532 art3588 nn513   pinm2749 pre4314 art3588 nn4491   art3588   nn1186   3767

10 And now also the axe is laid unto the root of the trees: therefore

an,aj3956 an,nn1186   pap4160/3361   an,nn2590   pinp1581   2532 pinp906 pre1519

every tree which bringeth*not*forth good fruit is hewn down, and cast into the

an,nn4442

fire.

epn1473   3303   pin907   ppro5209 pre1722 an,nn5204 pre1519   an,nn3341   1161

☞ 11 I   indeed baptize you with water unto repentance: but

art,ppmp2064   ad*3694 ppro3450 pin2076 pr/an,aj2478   ppro3450 repro3739 art,nn5266 pin1510 3756

he*that*cometh after me is mightier than I, whose shoes I am not

pr/an,aj2425   ainf941 epn846   ft907 ppro5209 pre1722 an,aj40 an,nn4151 2532   an,nn4442

worthy to bear: he shall baptize you with the Holy Ghost, and *with* fire:

repro3739 art,nn4425   pre1722 ppro846 art,nn5495 2532   ft1245   ppro848 art,nn257

12 Whose fan *is* in his hand, and he will throughly purge his floor,

2532   ft4863 ppro848 art,nn4621 pre1519 art3588   nn596   1161   ft2618   art3588 nn892

and gather his wheat into the garner; but he will burn up the chaff with

an,aj762   an,nn4442

unquenchable fire.

☞ **3:11** See notes on Acts 1:5.

Jesus Is Baptized by John (Mark 1:9-11; Luke 3:21,22)

ad5119   pinm3854   art,nn2424   pre575   art,nn1056   pre1909   art,nn2446   pre4314   art,nn2491   infg907

13 Then cometh Jesus from Galilee to Jordan unto John, to be baptized

pre5259 ppro846

of him.

1161   art,nn2491   ipf1254   ppro846   pap3004   epn1473   pin2192   an,nn5532   aifp907   pre5259

14 But John forbade him, saying, I have need to be baptized of

ppro4675   2532   pinm2064   epn4771   pre4314   ppro3165

thee, and comest thou to me?

1161   art,nn2424   aptp611   aina2036   pre4314   ppro846   aima863   ad737   1063

15 And Jesus answering said unto him, Suffer *it to be so* now: for

ad3779   (pin2076)   pr/an,ajn4241   ppro2254   ainf4137   an,aj3956   an,nn1343   ad5119   pin863

thus it becometh us to fulfill all righteousness. Then he suffered

ppro846

him.

2532   art,nn2424   aptp907   aina305   ad2117   pre575   art3588

16 And Jesus, when he was baptized, went up straightway out of the

nn5204   2532   2400   art3588   nn3772   ainp455   ppro846   2532   aina1492   art3588   nn4151

water: and, lo, the heavens were opened unto him, and he saw the Spirit of

art,nn2316   pap2597   ad5616   an,nn4058   2532   ppmp2064   pre1909   ppro846

God descending like a dove, and lighting upon him:

2532   2400   an,nn5456   pre1537   art,nn3772   pap3004   pr/depro3778   pin2076   ppro3450   art,aj27   art,nn5207

17 And lo a voice from heaven, saying, This is my beloved Son,

pre1722   repro3739   aina2106

in whom I am*well*pleased.   *(Ps. 2:7; Is. 42:1)*

Jesus Is Tempted By the Devil (Mark 1:12,13; Luke 4:1-13)

ad5119   art,nn2424   ainp321   pre5259   art3588   nn4151   pre1519   art3588   ain2048   aifp3985

4 Then was Jesus led up of the spirit into the wilderness to be tempted

pre5259   art3588   ajn1228

of the devil.

2532   apta3522   nu5062   an,nn2250   2532   nu5062   an,nn3571

2 And when he had fasted forty days and forty nights, he

aina3983/ad5305

was*afterward*hungry.

2532   art3588   pap3985   apta4334   ppro846   aina2036   1487   pin1488   pr/an,nn5207

3 And when the tempter came to him, he said, If thou be the Son of

art,nn2316   aima2036   2443   depro3778   art,nn3037   asbm1096   pr/an,nn740

God, command that these stones be made bread.

1161   art3588   aptp611   aina2036   pfip1125   an,nn444   3756   fm2198   pre1909   an,nn740

4 But he answered and said, It is written, Man shall not live by bread

an,aj3441   235   pre1909   an,aj3956   an,nn4487   ppmp1607   pre1223   an,nn4750   an,nn2316

alone, but by every word that proceedeth out of the mouth of God.

                                                     (Deut. 8:3)

ad5119   art3588   ajn1228   pin3880/ppro846   pre1519 art3588 an,aj40   nn4172   2532   pin2476   ppro846 pre1909

5 Then the devil taketh*him*up into the holy city, and setteth him on a

art,nn4919   art3588   nn2411

pinnacle of the temple,

2532   pin3004   ppro846 1487   pin1488 pr/an,nn5207   art,nn2316 aima906 rxpro4572   ad2736   1063

6 And saith unto him, If thou be the Son of God, cast thyself down: for it

pfip1125   fm1781/ppro848/art,nn32   pre4012   ppro4675   2532   pre1909

is written, He shall give*his*angels*charge concerning thee: and in *their*

an,nn5495   ft142/ppro4571   3379   asba4350 ppro4675 art,nn4228   pre4314

hands they shall bear*thee*up, lest*at*any*time thou dash thy   foot against a

an,nn3037

stone.   *(Ps. 91:11,12)*

art,nn2424 aina5346   ppro846   pfip1125   ad3825   3756   ft1598   an,nn2962

7 Jesus said unto him, It is written again, Thou shalt not tempt the Lord

ppro4675 art,nn2316

thy God.   *(Deut. 6:16)*

ad3825   art3588   ajn1228   pin3880/ppro846   pre1519   ad3029   an,aj5308   an,nn3735   2532

8 Again, the devil taketh*him*up into an exceeding high mountain, and

pin1166   ppro846 an,aj3956 art3588   nn932   art3588   nn2889   2532 art3588   nn1391   ppro846

showeth him   all   the kingdoms of the world, and the glory of them;

2532   pin3004   ppro846 an,ajn3956   depro5023   ft1325 ppro4671 1437

9 And saith unto him, All these things will I give thee, if thou wilt

apta4098   asba4352   ppro3427

fall down and worship me.

ad5119   pin3004 art,nn2424   ppro846   aima5217   an,nn4567 1063   pfip1125

10 Then saith Jesus unto him, Get*thee*hence, Satan: for it is written, Thou

ft4352   an,nn2962 ppro4675 art,nn2316 2532 epn846 an,aj3441   ft3000

shalt worship the Lord thy God, and him only shalt thou serve. *(Deut. 6:13)*

ad5119   art3588   ajn1228   pin863   ppro846   2532   2400   an,nn32   aina4334 2532   ipf1247

11 Then the devil leaveth him, and, behold, angels came and ministered

ppro846

unto him.

Jesus Teaches the People (Mark 1:14,15; Luke 4:14,15)

1161   art,nn2424   apta191   3754 an,nn2491   ainp3860

12 Now when Jesus had heard that John was cast*into*prison, he

aina402   pre1519   art,nn1056

departed into Galilee;

2532   apta2641   3478   apta2064   aina2730   pre1519   2584

13 And leaving Nazareth, he   came and dwelt in   Capernaum,

art,aj3864   pre1722   an,nn3725   2194   2532   3508

which*is*upon*the*sea*coast, in the borders of Zebulun and Naphtali:

2443   asbp4137   art3588   aptp4483   pre1223 an,nn2268 art3588   nn4396

14 That it might be fulfilled which was spoken by Isaiah the prophet,

pap3004

saying,

an,nn1093   2194   2532   an,nn1093   3508   an,nn3598

15 The land of Zebulun, and the land of Naphthali, *by* the way of the

an,nn2281   ad4008   art,nn2446   an,nn1056   art3588   nn1484

sea, beyond Jordan, Galilee of the Gentiles;

art3588　　nn2992　　　art3588　ppmp2521　pre1722　　an,nn4655　　aina1492　　an,aj3173　an,nn5457　　2532

16 The people which   sat   in   darkness saw great light; and to

art,ppmp2521　　　pre1722　　　an,nn5561　　2532　　an,nn4639　　　an,nn2288　an,nn5457　　　　aina393

them*which*sat in the region and shadow of death light is sprung up.

(Is. 9:1,2)

pre575　　　　ad5119　　　art,nn2424　　aom756　　　pinf2784　　2532　　　pinf3004　　pim3340　　1063　art3588

17 From that time Jesus began to preach, and to say, Repent: for the

nn932　　　　art,nn3772　　　pfi1448

kingdom of heaven is*at*hand.

Jesus Calls Four Fishermen (Mark 1:14-20; Luke 5:1-11)

1161　　art,nn2424　　　pap4043　　pre3844　art3588　nn2281　　　　art,nn1056　　aina1492　nu1417　　　an,nn80　　　an,nn4613

18 And Jesus, walking by the sea of Galilee, saw two brethren, Simon

art,ppmp3004　an,nn4074　　2532　　an,nn406　　ppro846　　art,nn80　　pap906　　　an,nn293　pre1519 art3588　nn2281　1063

called Peter, and Andrew his brother, casting a net into the sea: for they

ipf2258　　pr/an,nn231

were fishers.

2532　　　pin3004　　　　　ppro846　　ad1205　　(ad*3694) ppro3450　2532　　　　　ft4160　　ppro5209　pr/an,nn231

19 And he saith unto them, Follow   me, and I will make you fishers of

an,nn444

men.

1161　　art3588　　　ad2112　　　apta863　　art,nn1350　　　aina190　　ppro846

20 And they straightway left *their* nets, and followed him.

2532　　apta4260　　　　　ad1564　　　aina1492　an,aj243　nu1417　　an,nn80　　an,nn2385　art3588

21 And going on from thence, he saw other two brethren, James the son

art,nn2199　　2532　an,nn2491　ppro846　　art,nn80　　pre1722　art,nn4143　pre3326　an,nn2199　　ppro846　art,nn3962

of Zebedee, and John his brother, in a ship with Zebedee their father,

pap2675　　ppro848 art,nn1350　2532　　aina2564　　ppro846

mending their nets; and he called them.

1161　　　　art,apta863/ad2112　　　art3588 nn4143　2532　ppro848　art,nn3962　2532　　aina190　　ppro846

22 And they*immediately*left the ship and their father, and followed him.

Jesus Ministers to a Great Multitude

2532　art,nn2424　　ipf4013　　an,aj3650　art,nn1056　　pap1321　　pre1722　ppro846　　art,nn4864　　2532

23 And Jesus went about all Galilee, teaching in their synagogues, and

pap2784　　art3588　　nn2098　　art3588　　　nn932　　2532　　pap2323　　an,aj3956　　　an,nn3554　　2532

preaching the gospel of the kingdom, and healing all manner of sickness and

an,aj3956　　　　　an,nn3119　　pre1722　art3588　　nn2992

all manner of disease among the people.

2532　ppro846 art,nn189　aina565　　　pre1519　　an,aj3650 art,nn4947　2532　　　　aina4374　　　ppro846

24 And his fame went throughout all Syria: and they brought unto him

an,aj3956　　art,pap2192/ad2560　　　　　ppmp4912　　　an,aj4164　　an,nn3554　　2532　　an,nn931　　2532

all sick people that were taken with divers diseases and torments, and

ppmp1139　　　　　　　2532　　　　　ppmp4583　　　　　　2532

those*which*were*possessed*with*devils, and those*which*were*lunatic, and

an,ajn3885　　　2532　　aina2323　　ppro846

those*that*had*the*palsy; and he healed them.

2532   aina190   ppro846 an,aj4183   an,nn3793   pre575   art,nn1056 2532

25 And there followed him great multitudes*of*people from Galilee, and *from*

an,nn1179   2532   an,nn2414   2532   an,nn2449   2532   ad4008   art,nn2446

Decapolis, and *from* Jerusalem, and *from* Judea, and *from* beyond Jordan.

The Sermon on the Mount: The Beatitudes (Luke 6:20-26)

1161   apta1492   nn3793   nn3793   aina305   pre1519   art,nn3735   2532

5 ☞And seeing the multitudes, he went up into a mountain: and when

ppro846   apta2523 ppro846 art,nn3101   aina4334   ppro846

he was set, his disciples came unto him:

2532   apta455   ppro848 art,nn4750   ipf1321   ppro846   pap3004

2 And he opened his mouth, and taught them, saying,

pr/an,aj3107   art3588 ajn4434   art,nn4151 3754 epn846 pin2076 art3588   nn932   art,nn3772

3 Blessed *are* the poor in spirit: for theirs   is   the kingdom of heaven.

pr/an,aj3107   art,pap3996   3754 epn846   fp3870

4 Blessed *are* they*that*mourn: for they shall be comforted.   *(Is. 61:2)*

pr/an,aj3107   art,ajn4239 3754 epn846   ft2816 art3588 nn1093

5 Blessed *are* the meek: for they shall inherit the earth.   *(Ps. 37:11)*

pr/an,aj3107   art,pap3983   2532 pap1372   art,nn1343   3754

6 Blessed *are* they*which*do*hunger and thirst after righteousness: for

epn846   fp5526

they shall be filled.

☞ **5:1–12** The Greek word translated "blessed" is *makárioi* (3107), which means to be "fully satisfied." In Classical Greek, the word referred to a state of blessedness in the hereafter. In the NT, however, the term is used of the joy that comes from salvation (cf. Ps. 51:12). This satisfaction is not the result of favorable circumstances in life. It comes only from being indwelt by Christ. Therefore, it would be wrong to translate *makárioi* as "happy" (derived from the English word "hap") because it is connected with luck or favorable circumstances.

Blessedness is not static, but progressive. This progress depends upon the fulfillment of the conditions set down in these Beatitudes: (1) "The poor in spirit . . ." (*ptōchoís* [4434], v. 3) indicates a "helpless" person as opposed to *pénēs* (3993) which means "poor, but able to help oneself." The first step toward blessedness is a realization of one's own spiritual helplessness. (2) "They that mourn . . ." (v. 4) are those who sorrow for their sins and the sins of others. (3) The "meek" ones are willing to see themselves as they really are (v. 5). This concept they have of themselves is evidenced in their submission to God and His Word, as well as in their dealings with others. (4) "They which do hunger . . ." (v. 6; from the Greek, *hoi peinóntes* [3983]) could be better rendered "the hungering ones." This indicates a constant and recurrent satisfaction with God's righteousness; the nourishment received from being filled is expended in hungering anew for another filling. (5) The "merciful" are characterized by a caring attitude for those who are in misery (v. 7). They take the heartaches of others and make them their own. (6) "Purity of heart" can only be acquired through the continuous cleansing that believers experience when they have fulfilled the previous conditions of blessedness (v. 8). The purer a person becomes, the more clearly he can see God. (7) A "peacemaker" is not simply someone who tries to stop the feuding between nations and people (v. 9). It is a believer that has experienced the peace of God and who brings that peace to his fellow human beings. (8) Being "persecuted for righteousness' sake" causes a person to reach the highest level of the satisfaction of blessedness (v. 10).

This state of blessedness begins the very moment that a person believes on Jesus Christ for salvation. This is demonstrated by the fact that the promises concerning the kingdom of heaven in verses three and ten are in the present tense. While in this life one may enjoy the results of implementing these truths, the ultimate condition of blessedness will be experienced in heaven (v. 12).

pr/an,aj3107   art3588   ajn1655   3754   epn846   fp1653

☞ 7 Blessed *are* the merciful: for they shall obtain mercy.

pr/an,aj3107   art3588 ajn2513   art,nn2588 3754 epn846   fm3700 art,nn2316

8 Blessed *are* the pure in heart: for they shall see God.   *(Ps. 24:3,4)*

pr/an,aj3107   art3588   ajn1518   3754   epn846   fp2564   an,nn5207

9 Blessed *are* the peacemakers: for they shall be called the children of

an,nn2316

God.

pr/an,aj3107   art,pfpp1377   ad*1752/an,nn1343   3754

☞ 10 Blessed *are* they*which*are*persecuted for*righteousness'*sake: for

pr/epn846 pin2076 art3588   nn932   art,nn3772

theirs is the kingdom of heaven.

pr/an,aj3107   pin2075   ad3752   asba3679 ppro5209 2532   asba1377   2532

11 Blessed are ye, when *men* shall revile you, and persecute *you*, and

asba2036   an,aj3956/an,aj4190/an,nn4487   pre2596   ppro5216   ppmp5574   ad*1752/epn1700

shall say all*manner*of*evil against you falsely, for*my*sake.

pim5463   2532   pim21   3754 pr/an,aj4183   ppro5216 art,nn3408 pre1722   art,nn3772

12 Rejoice, and be*exceeding*glad: for great *is* your reward in heaven:

1063 ad3779   aina1377   art3588   nn4396   art3588   pre4253   ppro5216

for so persecuted they the prophets which were before you.

Salt and Light (Mark 9:50; Luke 14:34,35)

epn5210 pin2075 art3588 pr/nn217   art13588   nn1093   1161   1437 art13588   nn217   asbp3471

13 Ye are the salt of the earth: but if the salt have lost*his*savor,

pre1722/inpro5101   fp233   ad2089 pin2480 pre1519 an,ajn3762   1508   aifp906

wherewith shall it be salted? it is thenceforth good for nothing, but to be cast

ad1854 2532   pip2662   pre5259 art,nn444

out, and to be trodden*under*foot of men.

epn5210 pin2075 art3588 pr/nn5457   art3588   nn2889   an,nn4172   ppmp2749 ad*1883   an,nn3735

14 Ye are the light of the world. A city that is set on a hill

pinm1410/3756   aifp2928

cannot be hid.

3761   pin2545   an,nn3088   2532 pin5087 ppro846 pre5259   art,nn3426   235   pre1909

15 Neither do men light a candle, and put it under a bushel, but on a

art,nn3087   2532   pin2989   an,ajn3956 art3588   pre1722 art3588   nn3614

candlestick; and it giveth light unto all that are in the house.

ppro5216 art,nn5457 ad3779 aima2989   ad*1715   art,nn444   3704   asba1492 ppro5216 art,aj2570

16 Let your light so shine before men, that they may see your good

an,nn2041   2532   asba1392 ppro5216 art,nn3962   art3588   pre1722   art,nn3772

works, and glorify your Father which is in heaven.

Teaching About the Law

aosi3543   3361   3754   aina2064   ainf2647   art3588   nn3551   2228 art3588   nn4396

17 Think not that I am come to destroy the law, or the prophets: I am

3756 aina2064   ainf2647   235   ainf4137

not come to destroy, but to fulfill.

☞ **5:7** See note on James 2:12, 13.
☞ **5:10** See note on 2 Timothy 2:12, 13.

1063   281   pin3004   ppro5213 ad2193 art,nn3772   2532 art,nn1093 asba3928 nu1520 an,nn2503 2228 nu3391

18 For verily I say unto you, Till heaven and earth pass, one jot or one

an,nn2762   efn3364   asba3928 pre575 art3588 nn3551 ad2193 an,aj3956   asbm1096

tittle shall in*no*wise pass from the law, till   all be fulfilled.

repro3739/1437   3767   asba3089 nu3391   depro5130 art,aj1646   art,nn1785

19 Whosoever therefore shall break one of these least commandments,

2532   asba1321 art,nn444 ad3779   fp2564   an,aj1646 pre1722 art3588   nn932

and shall teach men so, he shall be called the least in   the kingdom of

art,nn3772   1161   repro3739/302   asba4160 2532 asba1321   depro3778   fp2564

heaven: but whosoever shall do and teach *them,* the same shall be called

an,aj3173 pre1722 art3588   nn932   art,nn3772

great in the kingdom of heaven.

1063   pin3004   ppro5213 3754 3362 ppro5216   art,nn1343   asba4052/ad4119

20 For I say unto you, That except your righteousness shall exceed *the*

art3588   nn1122   2532   an,nn5330   efn3364   asba1525 pre1519 art3588

righteousness of the scribes and Pharisees, ye shall in*no*case enter into the

nn932   art,nn3772

kingdom of heaven.

Teaching About Anger

aina191   3754   ainp4483   art,ajn744   3756

21 Ye have heard that it was said by them*of*old*time, Thou shalt not

ft5407 1161   repro3739/302   asba5407   fm2071 pr/an,aj1777   art3588   nn2920

kill; and whosoever shall kill shall be in danger of the judgment:

(Ex. 20:13; Deut. 5:17)

1161   epn1473 pin3004   ppro5213   3754   an,aj3956   art,ppmp3710   ppro848   art,nn80

☞ 22 But   I   say unto you, That whosoever is angry with his brother

ad1500   fm2071   pr/an,aj1777   art3588   nn2920   1161   repro3739/302   asba2036

without*a*cause shall be in danger of the judgment: and whosoever shall say

ppro848   art,nn80   4469   fm2071   pr/an,aj1777   art3588   nn4892   1161   repro3739/302

to his brother, Raca, shall be in danger of the council: but whosoever

asba2036   an,ajn3474   fm2071   pr/an,aj1777   pre1519 art,nn1067 art,nn4442

shall say, Thou fool, shall be in danger of   hell   fire.

3767   1437   psa4374 ppro4675 art,nn1435 pre1909 art3588   nn2379   ad2546

23 Therefore if   thou bring thy   gift   to   the altar, and there

asbp3415   3754 ppro4675 art,nn80 pin2192 idpro5100   pre2596   ppro4675

rememberest that thy brother hath aught against thee;

aima863   ad1563   ppro4675 art,nn1435 ad*1715 art3588   nn2379   2532   aima5217   nu,ajn4412

24 Leave there thy   gift before the altar, and go*thy*way; first be

aipp1259   ppro4675 art,nn80   2532 ad5119 apta2064   aima4374 ppro4675 art,nn1435

reconciled to thy brother, and then come and offer thy gift.

pim2468/pap2132   ppro4675   art,nn476   an,ajn5035   ad2193 (repro3757) pin1488 pre1722 art3588 nn3598

25 Agree with thine adversary quickly, while thou   art in   the way

pre3326 ppro846   3379   art3588   nn476   asba3860 ppro4571   art3588 nn2923 2532 art3588

with him; lest*at*any*time the adversary deliver thee to the judge, and the

nn2923 asba3860 ppro4571 art3588 nn5257 2532   fp906 pre1519 an,nn5438

judge deliver thee to the officer, and thou be cast into prison.

☞ 5:22, 29, 30 See note on Matthew 8:11, 12.

281   pin3004   ppro4671   efn3364   asba1831   ad1564

26 Verily I say unto thee, Thou shalt by*no*means come out thence,

ad2193/302   asba591 art3588   aj2078   an,nn2835

till thou hast paid the uttermost farthing.

Sin Begins in the Heart

aina191   3754   ainp4483   art,ajn744   3756

☞ 27 Ye have heard that it was said by them*of*old*time, Thou shalt not

ft3431

commit adultery: *(Ex. 20:14; Deut. 5:18)*

1161   epn1473 pin3004   ppro5213   3754   an,aj3956   art,pap991   an,nn1135   aipr1937

28 But I say unto you, That whosoever looketh on a woman to lust

ppro846   aina3431   ppro846   ad2235   pre1722 ppro848 art,nn2588

after her hath committed adultery with her already in his heart.

1161   1487 ppro4675 art,aj1188 art,nn3788   pin4624   ppro4571   aima1807/ppro846   2532   aima906   pre575   ppro4675

☞ 29 And if thy right eye offend thee, pluck*it*out, and cast *it* from thee:

1063   pin4861   ppro4671 2443 nu1520   ppro4675   art,nn3196   asbm622   2532   3361

for it is profitable for thee that one of thy members should perish, and not *that*

ppro4675 an,aj3650 art,nn4983   asbp906 pre1519 an,nn1067

thy whole body should be cast into hell.

2532   1487 ppro4675 art,aj1188 an,nn5495   pin4624   ppro4571   aima1581/ppro846   2532   aima906   pre575   ppro4675

30 And if thy right hand offend thee, cut*it*off, and cast *it* from thee:

1063   pin4851   ppro4671 2443 nu1520   ppro4675   art,nn3196   asbm622   2532   3361

for it is profitable for thee that one of thy members should perish, and not *that*

ppro4675 an,aj3650 art,nn4983   asbp906 pre1519 an,nn1067

thy whole body should be cast into hell.

Divorce (Matt. 19:9; Mark 10:11,12; Luke 16:18; Rom. 7:1-3; 1 Cor. 7:10-15)

(1161)   ainp4483   repro3739/302   asba630   ppro848 art,nn1135   aima1325

☞ 31 It hath been said, Whosoever shall put away his wife, let him give

ppro846   an,nn647

her a writing*of*divorcement: *(Deut. 24:1)*

1161   epn1473 pin3004   ppro5213   3754   repro3739/302   asba630   ppro848 art,nn1135

32 But I say unto you, That whosoever shall put away his wife,

ad*3924   an,nn3056   an,nn4202   pin4160   ppro846   pip3429   2532

saving for the cause of fornication, causeth her to commit adultery: and

repro3739/1437   asba1060   pfpp630   pinm3429

whosoever shall marry her*that*is*divorced committeth adultery.

☞ **5:27–32** The person who "keeps on looking" (v. 28, from the Greek, *ho blépōn* [991]) is guilty of adultery in his heart. If a person continues to place himself in a position where he knows he will be tempted to sin, he will most likely continue in it.

☞ **5:31, 32** A more literal translation of these two very difficult verses would be "And it was said, 'Whosoever dismisses his wife, let him give her a bill of divorcement.' But I say unto you that whosoever dismisses his wife except for reason of fornication [while she is his wife] commits adultery against her, and whosoever marries one who is unjustifiably dismissed is considered as committing adultery." See note on Matthew 19:3–9.

Oaths

ad3825   aina191   3754   ainp4483   art,ajn744

33 Again, ye have heard that it hath been said by them*of*old*time, Thou

3756   ft1964   1161   ft591   art3588 nn2962 ppro4675 art,nn3772

shalt not forswear thyself, but shalt perform unto the Lord thine oaths:

(Lev. 19:12; Num. 30:2; Deut. 23:21)

1161 epn1473 pin3004   ppro5213 ainf3660   3361   ad3654   3383   pre1722 art,nn3772   3754   pin2076

34 But I say unto you, Swear not at all; neither by heaven; for it is

art,nn2316 pr/an,nn2362

God's throne:

3383   pre1722 art3588   nn1093   3754   pin2076 ppro846 pr/an,nn5286/art,nn4228   3383   pre1519   an,nn2414

35 Nor by the earth; for it is his footstool: neither by Jerusalem;

3754   pin2076   pr/an,nn4172   art3588 an,aj3173   nn935

for it is the city of the great King.   *(Is. 66:1; Ps. 48:2)*

3383   aosi3660   pre1722 ppro4675 art,nn2776   3754   pinm1410   3756

36 Neither shalt thou swear by thy head, because thou canst not

ainf4160 nu3391 an,nn2359 an,aj3022 2228 an,aj3189

make one hair white or black.

1161   ppro5216   art,nn3056   pim2077   3483   3483   3756   3756   1161

37 But let your communication be, Yea, yea; Nay, nay: for

art,aj4053   depro5130   pin2076   pre1537 art,ajn4190

whatsoever*is*more than these cometh of evil.

Retaliation (Luke 6:29,30)

aina191   3754   ainp4483   an,nn3788 pre473   an,nn3788 2532

38 Ye have heard that it hath been said, An eye for an eye, and a

an,nn3599 pre473   an,nn3599

tooth for a tooth: *(Ex. 21:24; Lev. 24:20; Deut. 19:21)*

1161   epn1473   pin3004   ppro5213   ainf436   3361 art,ajn4190   235   repro3748

39 But I say unto you, That ye resist not evil: but whosoever

ft4474   ppro4571 pre1909 ppro4675 art,aj1188   an,nn4600 aima4762   ppro846 art3588 ajn243   2532

shall smite thee on thy right cheek, turn to him the other also.

2532   art,pap2309   aifp2919/ppro4671   2532   ainf2983   ppro4675 art,nn5509

40 And if any*man*will sue*thee*at*the*law, and take away thy coat, let

ppro846 aima863   art,nn2440 2532

him have *thy* cloak also.

2532   repro3748   ft29/ppro4571   nu1520 an,nn3400 aima5217   pre3326 ppro846

41 And whosoever shall compel*thee*to*go a mile, go with him

nu,ajn1417

twain.

pim1325   art,pap154   ppro4571 2532   art,pap2309   aifm1155   pre575 ppro4675

42 Give to him*that*asketh thee, and from him*that*would borrow of thee

aosi654/3361

turn*not*thou*away.

Enemies (Luke 6:27,28,32-36)

aina191   3754   ainp4483   ft25   ppro4675   art,ad4139
43 Ye have heard that it hath been said, Thou shalt love thy neighbor,

2532   ft3404   ppro4675   art,ajn2190
and hate thine enemy.   (Lev. 19:18)

1161   epn1473   pin3004   ppro5213   pim25   ppro5216   an,ajn2190   pim2127   art,ppmp2672   ppro5209
44 But I say unto you, Love your enemies, bless them*that*curse you,

pim4160   ad2573   art,pap3404   ppro5209   2532   pim4336   pre5228   art,pap1908
do good to them*that*hate you, and pray for them*which*despitefully*use

ppro5209   2532   pap1377   ppro5209
you, and persecute you;

3704   asbm1096   pr/an,nn5207   ppro5216   art,nn3962   art3588   pre1722   an,nn3772   3754
45 That ye may be the children of your Father which is in heaven: for

ppro848   art,nn2246   pin393   pre1909   an,ajn4190   2532   an,ajn18   2532   pin1026
he maketh his sun to rise on the evil and on the good, and sendeth rain

pre1909   an,ajn1342   2532   an,ajn94
on the just and on the unjust.

1063   1437   asba25   art,pap25   ppro5209   inpro5101   an,nn3408   pin2192   pin4160   3780
46 For if ye love them*which*love you, what reward have ye? do not

2532   art3588   nn5057   art3588   ppro846
even the publicans the same?

2532   1437   asbm782   ppro5216   art,nn80   an,ajn3440   inpro5101   pin4160   an,ajn4053
47 And if ye salute your brethren only, what do ye more than others?

pin4160   3780   2532   art3588   nn5057   ad3779
do not even the publicans so?

fm2071   epn5210   3767   pr/an,aj5046   ad5618   ppro5216   art,nn3962   art3588   pre1722   art,nn3772
48 Be ye therefore perfect, even as your Father which is in heaven

pin2076   pr/an,aj5046
is perfect.   (Lev. 19:2; Deut. 18:13)

The Proper Manner of Almsgiving

pim4337   pinf4160   3361   ppro5216   art,nn1654   ad*1715   art,nn444   aipr2300   ppro846
6 Take heed that ye do not your alms before men, to be seen of them:

1490   pin2192   3756   an,nn3408   pre3844   ppro5216   art,nn3962   art3588   pre1722   art,nn3772
otherwise ye have no reward of your Father which is in heaven.

3767   ad3752   psa4160   an,nn1654   3361   aosi4537   ad*1715
2 Therefore when thou doest thine alms, do not sound*a*trumpet before

ppro4675   ad5618   art3588   nn5273   pin4160   pre1722   art3588   nn4864   2532   pre1722   art3588   nn4505   3704
thee, as the hypocrites do in the synagogues and in the streets, that

asbp1392   pre5259   art,nn444   281   pin3004   ppro5213   pin568   ppro848
they may have glory of men. Verily I say unto you, They have their

art,nn3408
reward.

1161   ppro4675   pap4160   an,nn1654   3361   ppro4675   art,ajn710   aima1097   inpro5101   ppro4675
3 But when thou doest alms, let not thy left hand know what thy

art,ajn1188   pin4160
right hand doeth:

^{3704   ppro4675 art,nn1654   psa5600 pre1722   art,ajn2927   2532   ppro4675   art,nn3962   art,pap991   pre1722}

4 That thine alms may be   in secret: and thy Father which seeth in

^{art,ajn2927   epn848   ft591   ppro4671 pre1722/art,ajn5318}

secret himself shall reward thee   openly.

Prayer (Luke 11:2-4)

^{2532   ad3752   psa4336   3756   fm2071 ad5618 art3588   nn5273   3754}

5 And when thou prayest, thou shalt not be   as the hypocrites *are*: for

^{pin5368   pifm4336   pfp2476   pre1722 art3588   nn4864   2532 pre1722 art3588   nn1137   art3588}

they love to pray standing in the synagogues and in the corners of the

^{ajn4113   3704   asba5316/302   art,nn444   281   pin3004   ppro5213   pin568}

streets, that they may be   seen of men. Verily I say unto you, They have

^{ppro848   art,nn3408}

their reward.

^{1161   epn4771   ad3752   psa4336   aima1525 pre1519 ppro4675 art,nn5009   2532}

6 But thou, when thou prayest, enter into thy closet, and when thou hast

^{apta2808 ppro4675 art,nn2374 aipm4336   ppro4675 art,nn3962   art3588   pre1722   art,ajn2927   2532 ppro4675 art,nn3962}

shut thy door, pray to thy Father which is in   secret; and thy Father

^{art,pap991   pre1722 art,ajn2927   ft591   ppro4671 pre1722/art,ajn5318}

which seeth in secret shall reward thee   openly.

^{1161   ppmp4336   aosi945/3361   ad5618 art3588 ajn1482   1063}

7 But when ye pray, use*not*vain*repetitions, as the heathen *do*: for they

^{pin1380 3754   fp1522 pre1722 ppro848   art,nn4180}

think that they shall be heard for their much speaking.

^{3361   3767   aosi3666   ppro846   1063   ppro5216   art,nn3962   pin1492}

8 Be not ye therefore like unto them: for your Father knoweth

^{repro3739   pin2192 an,nn5532   ppro5209 aip154 ppro846}

what things ye have need of, before ye ask him.

^{ad3779   3767   pim4336 epn5210 ppro2257 an,nn3962   art3588   pre1722}

9 After*this*manner therefore pray ye: Our Father which art in

^{art,nn3772   aipp37   ppro4675 art,nn3686}

heaven, Hallowed be thy name.   *(Ezek. 36:23)*

^{ppro4675   art,nn932   aima2064   ppro4675 art,nn2307   aipp1096 pre1909 art,nn1093 ad5613   pre1722}

10 Thy kingdom come. Thy will be done in earth, as *it is* in

^{an,nn3772}

heaven.

^{aima1325 ppro2254   ad4594   ppro2257 art,aj1967   art,nn740}

11 Give us this day our daily bread.

^{2532   aima863   ppro2254 ppro2257 art,nn3783 ad5613 epn2249   pin863   ppro2257   art,nn3781}

12 And forgive us   our debts, as we forgive our debtors.

^{2532   aosi1533 ppro2248 3361 pre1519   an,nn3986   235   aipm4506   ppro2248 pre575 art,aj4190 3754}

☞ 13 And lead us   not into temptation, but deliver us   from evil: For

^{epn4675 pin2076 art3588   nn932   2532 art3588   nn1411   2532 art3588   nn1391   pre1519/art,nn165   281}

thine is the kingdom, and the power, and the glory, forever. Amen.

☞ **6:13** Why did the Lord teach His disciples to pray, ". . . lead us not into temptation . . ."? Does this in fact mean that God tempts people? When God allows one of His children to be tempted, it is for the purpose of proving to His child that he can rely on God's wisdom and strength. It is God's desire to

(continued on next page)

1063 1437   asba863 art,nn444 ppro846   art,nn3900   ppro5216 art,aj3770   art,nn3962   2532

14 For if ye forgive men their trespasses, your heavenly Father will also

ft863   ppro5213

forgive you:

1161 1437   asba863 3361 art,nn444 ppro846   art,nn3900   3761   ppro5216 art,nn3962

15 But if ye forgive not men their trespasses, neither will your Father

ft863 ppro5216   art,nn3900

forgive your trespasses.

Fasting

1161   ad3752   psa3522 pim1096 3361 ad5618 art3588   nn5273

16 Moreover when ye fast, be not, as the hypocrites, of a

pr/an,aj4659   1063   pin853 ppro848 art,nn4383 3704   asba5316

sad countenance: for they disfigure their faces, that they may appear unto

art,nn444 pap3522 281   pin3004   ppro5213   pin568 ppro848 art,nn3408

men to fast. Verily I say unto you, They have their reward.

1161 epn4471   pap3522 aipm218 ppro4675 art,nn2776 2532 aipm3538 ppro4675 art,nn4383

17 But thou, when thou fastest, anoint thine head, and wash thy face;

3704   asbm5316 3361   art,nn444 pap3522 235   ppro4675 art,nn3962   art3588

18 That thou appear not unto men to fast, but unto thy Father which is

pre1722 art,ajn2927 2532 ppro4675 art,nn3962   art,pap991   pre1722 art,ajn2927   ft591   ppro4671

in secret: and thy Father, which seeth in secret, shall reward thee

pre1722/art,ajn5318

openly.

Treasures in Heaven (Luke 12:33,34)

pim2343/3361   ppro5213   an,nn2344 pre1909 art,nn1093 ad3699 an,nn4597 2532 an,nn1035

19 Lay*not*up for yourselves treasures upon earth, where moth and rust

pin853 2532 ad3699 an,nn2812   pin1358   2532 pin2813

doth corrupt, and where thieves break through and steal:

1161 impro5101 pim2343   ppro5213   an,nn2344 pre1722 an,nn3772 ad3699   3777

20 But lay up for yourselves treasures in heaven, where neither

an,nn4597 3777 an,nn1035   pin853 2532 ad3699 an,nn2812   3756   pin1358   3761

moth nor rust doth corrupt, and where thieves do not break through nor

pin2813

steal:

1063 ad3699 ppro5216 art,nn2344 pin2076 ad1563   ppro5216 art,nn2588 fm2071 2532

21 For where your treasure is, there will your heart be also.

(continued from previous page)

give him victory over the temptation and at the same time make him more experienced in the tactics of spiritual warfare against the devil. It is crucial to remember, however, that the actual enticement to sin is never generated by God; hence, no one can ever truthfully say that God has tempted him to sin.

The Light of the World (Luke 11:34,36)

art3588 nn3088   art3588 nn4983 pin2076 art3588 nn3788 1437   3767   ppro4675 art,nn3788 psa5600 pr/an,aj573

22 The light of the body is the eye: if therefore thine eye be single,

ppro4675 an,aj3650 art,nn4983   fm2071   pr/an,aj5460

thy whole body shall be full*of*light.

1161   1437   ppro4675 art,nn3788 psa5600 pr/an,aj4190 ppro4675 an,aj3650 art,nn4983   fm2071

23 But if thine eye be evil, thy whole body shall be

pr/an,aj1652   1487   3767   art3588 nn5457 art3588 pre1722 ppro4671 pin2076 pr/an,nn4655   an,aj4214

full*of*darkness. If therefore the light that is in thee be darkness, how great

art,nn4655

is that darkness!

Put God's Kingdom First (Luke 12:22-34; 16:13)

an,ajn3762   pinm1410 pinf1398 nu1417 an,nn2962   1063   2228   ft3404 art3588 nu,ajn1520 2532

24 No man can serve two masters: for either he will hate the one, and

ft25 art3588 ajn2087   2228   fm472   nu,ajn1520 2532 ft2706 art3588 ajn2087

love the other; or else he will hold to the one, and despise the other. Ye

pinm1410/3756 pinf1398 an,nn2316 2532   an,nn3126

cannot serve God and mammon.

pre1223/depro5124 pin3004   ppro5213   pim3309/3361   ppro5216 art,nn5590 inpro5101

25 Therefore I say unto you, Take*no*thought for your life, what ye shall

asba5315 2532 inpro5101   asba4095   3366   ppro5216 art,nn4983 inpro5101   asbm1746 pin2076

eat, or what ye shall drink; nor yet for your body, what ye shall put on. Is

3780 art3588 nn5590 pr/an,aj4119   art,nn5160 2532 art3588 nn4983   art,nn1742

not the life more than meat, and the body than raiment?

aima1689/pre1519 art3588 nn4071   art3588 nn3772 3754   pin4687 3756   3761   pin2325

26 Behold the fowls of the air: for they sow not, neither do they reap,

3761   pin4863   pre1519 an,nn596   2532 ppro5216   art,aj3770   art,nn3962   pin5142   ppro846

nor gather into barns; yet your heavenly Father feedeth them.

pin1308/epn5210/3756/ad3123   ppro846

Are*ye*not*much*better than they?

(1161)   pre1537 ppro5216   pap3309   pinm1410 ainf4369 nu1520 an,nn4083 pre1909 ppro848

27 Which of you by taking thought can add one cubit unto his

art,nn2244

stature?

2532 inpro5101   pin3309   pre4012 an,nn1742   aima2648 art3588 nn2918   art3588 nn68

28 And why take*ye*thought for raiment? Consider the lilies of the field,

ad4459   pin837   pin2872 3756   3761   pin3514

how they grow; they toil not, neither do they spin:

1161   pin3004   ppro5213 3754   3761   an,nn4672   pre1722 an,aj3956 ppro848 art,nn1391

29 And yet I say unto you, That even Solomon in all his glory was

aom4016   ad5613 nu1520   depro5130

not arrayed like one of these.   (1 Kgs. 10; 2 Chr. 9)

1161   1487 art,nn2316 ad3779   pin294 art3588 nn5528   art3588   nn68   ad4594 pap5607

30 Wherefore, if God so clothe the grass of the field, which today is,

2532   ad839   ppmp906 pre1519   an,nn2823   3756 an,ajn4183 ad3123   epn5209

and tomorrow is cast into the oven, shall he not much more clothe you, O

an,ajn3640

ye*of*little*faith?

3767   aosi3309/3361   pap3004   inpro5101   asba5315 2228 inpro5101

31 Therefore take*no*thought, saying, What shall we eat? or, What shall

asba4095 2228   inpro5101   asbm4016

we drink? or, Wherewithal shall we be clothed?

1063   an,aj3956   depro5023   art3588   nn1484   pin1934   1063 ppro5216   art,aj3770

32 (For after   all   these things do the Gentiles seek:) for your heavenly

art,nn3962   pin1492   3754   pin5535   an,ajn537   depro5130

Father knoweth that ye have need of all   these things.

1161   pim2212   nu,ajn4412 art3588   nn932   art,nn2316 2532 ppro846   art,nn1343   2532

33 But seek ye first   the kingdom of God, and his righteousness; and

an,aj3956   depro5023   fp4369   ppro5213

all   these things shall be added unto you.

aosi3309/3767/3361   pre1519 art3588   ad839   1063 art3588   ad839

34 Take*therefore*no*thought for   the   morrow: for   the   morrow shall

ft3309   art3588   rxpro1438   pr/an,ajn713   art3588 nn2250   art3588 nn2548   ppro846

take thought for the things of itself. Sufficient unto the day *is* the evil thereof.

Judging Others (Luke 6:37,38,41,42)

pim2919   3361   2443   3361   asbp2919

7 Judge not, that ye be not judged.

1063   pre1722 repro3739   an,nn2917   pin2919   fp2919   2532

2 For with what judgment ye judge, ye shall be judged: and

pre1722 repro3739   an,nn3358   pin3354   fp484/ppro5213

with what measure ye mete, it shall be measured*to*you*again.

1161   inpro5101   pin991   art3588   nn2595 art3588   pre1722 ppro4675   art,nn80   artnn3788 1161

3 And why beholdest thou the mote that is in   thy brother's eye, but

pin2657   3756 art3588   nn1385   pre1722   art,popro4674 an,nn3788

considerest not the beam that *is* in   thine own eye?

2228   ad4459   ft2046   ppro4675   art,nn80   aima863   asba1544   art3588 nn2595   pre575

4 Or how wilt thou say to thy   brother, Let me pull out the mote out of

ppro4675 art,nn3788 2532   2400   art,nn1385 pre1722   ppro4675   art,nn3788

thine eye; and, behold, a beam is in thine own eye?

an,nn5273   nu,ajn4412   alma1544   art3588   nn1385   pre1537   ppro4675   art,nn3788 2532

5 Thou hypocrite, first   cast out the beam out of thine own eye; and

ad5119   ft1227   ainf1544   art3588   nn2595   pre1537 ppro4675   art,nn80   art,nn3788

then shalt thou see clearly to cast out the mote out of thy brother's eye.

aosi1325 3361   art,ajn40   art3588   nn2965   3366   aosi906   ppro5216 art,nn3135

6 Give not that*which*is*holy unto the dogs, neither cast ye your pearls

ad*1715   art,nn5519   3379   asba2662   ppro846   pre1722   ppro848 art,nn4228 2532   apta4762   asba4486

before swine, lest they trample them under their feet, and turn again and rend

ppro5209

you.

Seeking God's Help (Luke 11:9-13)

pim154   532   fp1325 ppro5213 pim2212 2532   ft2147   pim2925 2532

7 Ask, and it shall be given you; seek, and ye shall find; knock, and it shall

fp455   ppro5213

be opened unto you:

1063   an,ajn3956   art,pap154   pin2983   2532   art,pap2212   pin2147   2532

8 For every one that asketh receiveth; and he*that*seeketh findeth; and to

art,pap2925   fp455

him*that*knocketh it shall be opened.

2228 inpro5101 an,nn444 pin2076   pre1537 ppro5216 repro3739 1437 ppro846 art,nn5207 asba154   an,nn740

9 Or what man is there of you, whom if his son ask bread, will he

ft1929 ppro846 (3361) an,nn3037

give him a stone?

2532 1437   asba154   an,nn2486   ft1929 ppro846   an,nn3789

10 Or if he ask a fish, will he give him a serpent?

1487 epn5210   3767   pap5607 pr/an,aj4190 pin1492   pinf1325 an,aj18   an,nn1390   ppro5216

11 If ye then, being evil, know how to give good gifts unto your

art,nn5043   an,aj4214   ad3123   ppro5216 art,nn3962   art3588   pre1722 art,nn3772   ft1325

children, how much more shall your Father which is in heaven give

an,ajn18   art,pap154   ppro846

good things to them*that*ask him?

3767   an,ajn3956   an,ajn3745/302   psa2309   2443   art,nn444   psa4160   ppro5213

12 Therefore all things whatsoever ye would that men should do to you,

pim4160 epn5210 2532 ad3779   ppro846   1063 pr/depro3778 pin2076 art3588 nn3551 2532 art3588   nn4396

do ye even so to them: for this is the law and the prophets.

The Narrow Way (Luke 13:24)

aima1525   pre1223   art3588 an,aj4728   nn4439   3754 pr/an,aj4116   art3588   nn4439   2532 pr/an,aj2149

13 Enter ye in at the strait gate: for wide is the gate, and broad is

art3588   nn3598   art,pap520   pre1519   art,nn684   2532   an,aj4183   pin1526   art,ppmp1525

the way, that leadeth to destruction, and many there be which*go*in

pre1223/ppro846

thereat:

3754   pr/an,aj4728   art3588   nn4439   2532   pr/pfpp2346   art3588   nn3598   art3588   pap520   pre1519

14 Because strait is the gate, and narrow is the way, which leadeth unto

art,nn2222 2532 an,aj3641   pin1526   art,pap2147   ppro846

life, and few there be that find it.

Behavior and Belief (Luke 6:43,44)

(1161)   pim4337   pre575   art,nn5578   repro3748   pinm2064   pre4314 ppro5209 pre1722   an,nn4263

15   Beware of false prophets, which come to you in sheep's

an,nn1742   1161   ad2081   pin1526   pr/an,aj727   pr/an,nn3074

clothing, but inwardly they are ravening wolves.

fm1921   ppro846 pre575 ppro846 art,nn2590   (3385)   pin4816   an,nn4718   pre575   an,nn173

16 Ye shall know them by their fruits. Do men gather grapes of thorns,

2228 an,nn4810 pre575   an,nn5146

or figs of thistles?

ad3779   an,aj3956   an,aj18   an,nn1186   pin4160   an,aj2570 an,nn2590 1161   art,aj4550   an,nn1186

17 Even so every good tree bringeth forth good fruit; but a corrupt tree

pin4160   an,aj4190 an,nn2590

bringeth forth evil fruit.

an,aj18   an,nn1186   pinm1410/3756   pinf4160   an,aj4190 an,nn2590   3761   an,aj4550   an,nn1186

18 A good tree cannot bring forth evil fruit, neither *can* a corrupt tree

pinf4160   an,aj2570 an,nn2590

bring forth good fruit.

an,aj3956   an,nn1186   pap4160/3361   an,aj2570 an,nn2590   pinp1581   2532 pinp906

19 Every tree that bringeth*not*forth good fruit is hewn down, and cast

pre1519   an,nn4442

into the fire.

686   pre575 ppro846 art,nn2590   fm1921   ppro846

20 Wherefore by their fruits ye shall know them.

"I Never Knew You" (Luke 13:25-27)

     3756   an,ajn3956   art,pap3004   ppro3427   an,nn2962   an,nn2962   fm1525   pre1519 art3588

☞ 21 Not every one that saith unto me, Lord, Lord, shall enter into the

nn932   art,nn3772   235   art,pap4160   art3588   nn2307   ppro3450   art,nn3962   3588   pre1722

kingdom of heaven; but he*that*doeth the will of my Father which is in

an,nn3772

heaven.

an,ajn4183   ft2046   ppro3427   pre1722   depro1565   art,nn2250   an,nn2962   an,nn2962   3756

22 Many will say to me in that day, Lord, Lord, have we not

aina4395   art,popro4674 an,nn3686   2532   art,popro4674 an,nn3683   aina1544   an,nn1140   2532

prophesied in thy name? and in thy name have cast out devils? and in

art,popro4674 an,nn3686 aina4160 an,aj4183   an,nn1411

thy name done many wonderful works?   *(Jer. 14:14; 27:15)*

2532   ad5119   ft3670   ppro846   ad3762   aina1097 ppro5209   pim672   pre575 ppro1700

23 And then will I profess unto them, I never knew you: depart from me,

art,ppmp2038   art,nn458

ye*that*work iniquity.   *(Ps. 6:8)*

Build on a Firm Foundation (Luke 6:47-49)

      3767   an,aj3956/repro3748   pin191   depro5128   art,nn3056   ppro3450   2532   pin4160   ppro846

24 Therefore whosoever heareth these sayings of mine, and doeth them, I

ft3666   ppro846   an,aj5429 an,nn435   repro3748 aina3618 ppro848 art,nn3614   pre1909   art,nn4073

will liken him unto a wise man, which built his house upon a rock:

2532   art3588   nn1028   aina2597   2532   art3588   nn4215   aina2064   2532   art3588   nn417   aina4154

25 And the rain descended, and the floods came, and the winds blew,

2532   aina4363   depro1565 art,nn3614   2532   aina4098   3756   1063   plpf2311   pre1909   art,nn4073

and beat upon that house; and it fell not; for it was founded upon a rock.

2532   an,ajn3956   art,pap191   depro5128   art,nn3056   ppro3450   2532   pap4160   ppro846   3361

26 And every one that heareth these sayings of mine, and doeth them not,

fp3666   an,aj3474   an,nn435   repro3748 aina3618 ppro848 art,nn3614   pre1909 art3588   nn285

shall be likened unto a foolish man, which built his house upon the sand:

☞ **7:21–23** See note on Matthew 8:11, 12.

2532 art3588 nn1028   aina2597   2532 art3588 nn4125   aina2064   2532 art3588 nn417   aina4154
27 And the rain descended, and the floods came, and the winds blew,

2532   aina4350   depro1565 art,nn3614   2532   aina4098 2532 pr/an,aj3173 ipf2258 art3588 nn4431   ppro846
and beat upon that house; and it fell: and great was the fall of it.

2532   aom1096   ad3753   art,nn2424   aina4931   depro5128   art,nn3056   art3588
28 And it came*to*pass, when Jesus had ended these sayings, the

nn3793   ipf1605   pre1909 ppro846   art,nn1322
people were astonished at his doctrine:

1063   ipf2258/pap1321   ppro846   ad5613   pap2192   an,nn1849   2532   3756 ad5613 art3588
29 For he taught them as *one* having authority, and not as the

nn1122
scribes.

Jesus Heals Leprosy (Mark 1:40-45; Luke 5:12-16)

1161   ppro846   apta2597   pre575 art3588   nn3735   an,aj4183   an,nn3793   aina190
8 When he was come down from the mountain, great multitudes followed

ppro846
him.

2532   2400   apta2064   an,nn3015   ipf4352   ppro846   pap3004 an,nn2962 1437
2 And, behold, there came a leper and worshiped him, saying, Lord, if

psa2309   pinm1410   ainf2511/ppro3165
thou wilt, thou canst make*me*clean.

2532 art,nn2424   apta1614   art,nn5495   aom680   ppro846   pap3004   pin2309
3 And Jesus put forth *his* hand, and touched him, saying, I will;

aipp2511   2532   ad2112   ppro846 art,nn3014   ainp2511
be*thou*clean. And immediately his leprosy was cleansed.

2532 art,nn2424 pin3004   ppro846 pim3708   aosi2036 an,ajn3367 235   aima5217   aima1166
4 And Jesus saith unto him, See thou tell no man; but go*thy*way, show

rxpro4572   art3588   nn2409   2532 aima4374 art3588 nn1435 repro3739 an,nn3475   aina4367   pre1519
thyself to the priest, and offer the gift that Moses commanded, for a

an,nn3142   ppro846
testimony unto them.   *(Lev. 14:2, 4-32)*

Healing A Centurion's Servant (Luke 7:1-10; John 4:43-54)

1161   art,nn2424   apta1525 pre1519   2584   aina4334   ppro846
5 And when Jesus was entered into Capernaum, there came unto him

an,nn1543   pap3870   ppro846
a centurion, beseeching him,

2532   pap3004 an,nn2962 ppro3450 art,nn3816   pfip906 pre1722 art,nn3614   an,ajn3885
6 And saying, Lord, my servant lieth at home sick*of*the*palsy,

ad1171   ppmp928
grievously tormented.

2532 art,nn2424 pin3004   ppro846 epn1473   apta2064   ft2323 ppro846
7 And Jesus saith unto him, I will come and heal him.

(2532)art3588   nn1543   aptp611   aina5346 an,nn2962   pin1510 3756 pr/an,aj2425 2443
8 The centurion answered and said, Lord, I am not worthy that thou

shouldest come under my roof: but speak the word only, and my servant
shall be healed.

9 For I am a man under authority, having soldiers under me: and I say to this *man,* Go, and he goeth; and to another, Come, and he cometh; and to my servant, Do this, and he doeth *it.*

10 When Jesus heard *it,* he marveled, and said to them*that*followed, Verily I say unto you, I have not found so great faith, no, not in Israel.

☞ 11 And I say unto you, That many shall come from the east and west, and shall sit down with Abraham, and Isaac, and Jacob, in the kingdom of heaven.

(Ps. 107:3)

☞ **8:11, 12** Jesus has just commended the great faith of the Roman centurion, a Gentile, who came seeking healing for his servant. The "children of the kingdom" in this instance, refers to unrepentant Jews who thought that their ancestry automatically entitled them to the kingdom of God (see John 8:31–59). In reality, however, these were false children of the kingdom (Matt. 7:21–23; 13:38; Luke 13:22–30). Those who come "from the east and west" are Gentiles who, like this centurion, exercise personal faith in Jesus Christ. The Jews thought that they were assured of special favor by God, but the Lord reminded them that they could be "last" in the kingdom of God while those who thought themselves "last," such as publicans and prostitutes, would be "first" if they exercised faith in Him (Matt. 21:31). Furthermore, the unrepentant Jews would be "cast out" because of their hypocritical claim that they were the children and followers of Abraham. Abraham was the father of the faithful, and although these men were physical descendants of him, they were not part of the family of faith.

The expression "outer darkness" occurs three times in the Bible (Matt. 8:12; 22:13; 25:30) and is always preceded by the definite article in Greek. It seems to have denoted an area outside a well-illuminated banquet hall where there was darkness (see the parable of the wedding feast in Matt. 22:1–14). The person who managed to sneak into the banquet hall without the proper garment was cast into "outer darkness," separated from the ongoing feast. In the first two instances, "outer darkness" refers to the place of suffering for the unbelievers and is in contrast to the light where the believers dwell (see 1 John 1:5–7). Unbelievers will be thrown into the furnace of fire, whereas believers will shine as the sun in the kingdom of the Father (Matt. 13:42, 43). The "outer darkness" in Matthew 8:12 and 22:13 is referring to *Géenna* (1067), the "place of burning" (Matt. 5:22, 29, 30; 10:28; 18:9, cf. note on Josh. 15:8).

The expression "outer darkness" in Matthew 25:30 occurs at the end of the parable of the talents which emphasizes the necessity of serving Christ faithfully. However, the "outer darkness" of Matthew 25:30 may not refer to *Géenna.* Those who say that it does refer to the "place of burning" are persuaded that the servants mentioned here are members of the visible church, and therefore are not necessarily believers. Hence, those wicked servants who "hide their talents," are in fact unbelievers, who are cast into hell (John 15:6; James 2:14–26). Others say that this parable does not refer at all to unbelievers or hypocrites but to the believers who neglect to exercise their God-given talents. The Lord calls such a servant *ponēré* (4190), "wicked" (Matt. 25:26), and *hoi katēraménoi* (2672), "cursed" (Matt. 25:41), despite the fact that he is one of the Lord's servants. This is similar to the instance where the Lord called Peter "Satan" (Matt. 16:23). Hence, these terms may also be applied to believers who have failed the Lord in their service. The words of Paul in 1 Corinthians 3:10–15 are in full support of the fact that the works of faith as servants will be tried as by fire. Therefore, in this instance, the

(continued on next page)

1161 art3588   nn5207   art3588   nn932   fp1544   pre1519 art,aj1857 art,nn4655
12 But the children of the kingdom shall be cast out into outer darkness:
ad1563   fm2071 pr/art,nn2805 2532 pr/art,nn1030   art,nn3599
there shall be weeping and gnashing of teeth.
           2532 art,nn2424 aina2036   art3588   nn1543   aima5217   2532 ad5613
13 And Jesus said unto the centurion, Go*thy*way; and as thou hast
aina4100   aipp1096   ppro4671 2532 ppro846 art,nn3816   ainp2390 pre1722
believed, *so* be it done unto thee. And his servant was healed in
depro1565   art,nn5610
the selfsame hour.

Peter's Mother-in-law Is Healed (Mark 1:29-34; Luke 4:38-41)

        2532   art,nn2424   apta2064 pre1519 an,nn4074 art,nn3614   aina1492 ppro846
14 And when Jesus was come into Peter's house, he saw his
art,nn3994   pfpp906 2532   pap4445
wife's mother laid, and sick*of*a*fever.
           2532   aom680   ppro846 art,nn5495 2532 art3588   nn4446 aina863 ppro846 2532   ainp1453 2532
15 And he touched her hand, and the fever left her: and she arose, and
ipf1247   ppro846
ministered unto them.
        1161   an,nn3798   aptm1096   aina4374   ppro846 an,ajn4183
16 When the even was come, they brought unto him many that were
ppmp1139   2532   aina1544 art3588 nn4151   an,nn3056 2532 aina2323
possessed*with*devils: and he cast out the spirits with *his* word, and healed
an,aj3956   art,pap2192/ad2560
all that*were*sick:

(continued from previous page)
"outer darkness" may be a reference to a place or position of far less rewards for the servants who proved themselves less diligent than those who used and exercised their talents to the fullest. The expression would then refer to the degrees of the enjoyment of heaven rather than referring to hell. This teaching of varied rewards is part and parcel of the inherent doctrine in the NT that neither heaven nor hell are experienced equally by all because this would annul the justice of God. Entrance into heaven is gained by accepting Christ's sacrifice for justification, but a person's rewards in heaven will be determined by what he did for Christ on earth (Matt. 5:3–12; 7:21–23; 10:15; Luke 6:20–26; 12:47, 48; Acts 10:4, 31; Rom. 2:1–16; 14:10–23; 1 Cor. 3:13; 4:5; 2 Cor. 5:10; 1 John 4:17; Rev. 20:11–15). The Christian's faithfulness to his tasks and responsibilities in the world is considered of such paramount importance that the same metaphor, the "outer darkness," that was used by the Lord to indicate the punishment of the unbeliever for his rejection of God's salvation is used of the believer who does not live in obedience to the light he has received. In the case of the non-believer, it will be a punishment of fire and burning (Matt. 13:30; John 15:6). In the case of the believer, it will be weeping or expressing sorrow over not having used the opportunities God provided. Though his tears will be wiped away (Rev. 7:17; 21:4), he will nonetheless suffer a loss of reward. The phrase "gnashing of teeth" indicates anger at oneself for ignoring the marvelous opportunities that he had on earth. The same emotional attitude will be expressed by the unbeliever, but in his case, he will be weeping about the lost opportunity of genuine and true repentance followed by the works of repentance. "Gnashing of teeth," in the case of the unbeliever, refers to being angry at oneself because he did not decide to go through the narrow gate and live in the straight way when he had the opportunity.

17 That it might be fulfilled which*was*spoken by Isaiah the prophet, saying, Himself took our infirmities, and bare *our* sicknesses.   *(Is. 53:4)*

Following Jesus (Luke 9:57-62)

18 Now when Jesus saw great multitudes about him, he gave commandment to depart unto the other side.

19 And a certain scribe came, and said unto him, Master, I will follow thee whithersoever thou goest.

20 And Jesus saith unto him, The foxes have holes, and the birds of the air *have* nests; but the Son of man hath not where to lay *his* head.

21 And another of his disciples said unto him, Lord, suffer me first to go and bury my father.

22 But Jesus said unto him, Follow me; and let the dead bury their dead.

Calming a Storm (Mark 4:35-41; Luke 8:22-25)

23 And when he was entered into a ship, his disciples followed him,

24 And, behold, there arose a great tempest in the sea, insomuch that the ship was covered with the waves: but he was asleep.

25 And his disciples came to *him* and awoke him, saying, Lord, save us: we perish.

26 And he saith unto them, Why are ye fearful, O ye*of*little*faith? Then he arose, and rebuked the winds and the sea; and there was a great calm.

27 But the men marveled, saying, What*manner*of*man is this, that even the winds and the sea obey him!

Healing the Demon-Possessed at Gergesenes (Mark 5:1-20; Luke 8:26-39)

_{2532   ppro846   apta2064 pre1519 art3588   ad4008   pre1519 art3588   nn5561   art3588}
28 And when he was come to the other side into the country of the
_{ajn1086   aina5221 ppro846 nu,ajn1417   ppmp1139   ppmp1831 pre1537   art3588}
Gergesenes, there met him two possessed*with*devils, coming out of the
_{nn3419   ad3029   an,aj5467   ad5620   3361 idpro5100 pinf2480 ainf3928 pre1223 depro1565 art,nn3598}
tombs, exceeding fierce, so that no man might pass by that way.
_{2532   2400   aina2896   pap3004   inpro5101/epn2254/epn4671}
29 And, behold, they cried out, saying, What*have*we*to*do*with*thee,
_{an,nn2424   an,nn5207   art,nn2316   aina2064   ad5602   ainf928   ppro2248   pre4253}
Jesus, thou Son of God? art thou come hither to torment us before the
_{an,nn2540}
time?
_{1161   ipf2258   ad3112   pre575   ppro846   an,nn34   an,aj4183   an,nn5519}
30 And there was a*good*way*off from them an herd of many swine
_{ppmp1006}
feeding.
_{1161 art3588   nn1142   ipf3870   ppro846   pap3004   1487   pin1544/ppro2248   aima2010 ppro2254}
31 So the devils besought him, saying, If thou cast*us*out, suffer us to
_{ainf565   pre1519 art3588   nn34   art,nn5519}
go away into the herd of swine.
_{2532   aina2036   ppro846   aima5217   1161   art,apta1831}
32 And he said unto them, Go. And when they*were*come*out, they
_{aina565   pre1519 art3588   nn34   art,nn5519   2532   2400   art3588   an,aj3956   nn34   art,nn5519}
went into the herd of swine: and, behold, the whole herd of swine
_{aina3729   pre2596   art,nn2911   pre1519 art3588 nn2281 2532   aina599   pre1722 art3588   nn5204}
ran violently down a steep place into the sea, and perished in the waters.
_{1161   art,pap1006   aina5343 2532   apta565   pre1519 art3588 nn4172   2532}
33 And they*that*kept them fled, and went*their*ways into the city, and
_{aina518   an,ajn3956   2532   art3588   art3588   ppmp1139}
told every thing, and what*was*befallen to the possessed*of*the*devils.
_{2532   2400   art,3588 an,aj3956   nn4172   aina1831   pre1519/an,nn4877 art,nn2424 2532}
34 And, behold, the whole city came out to meet Jesus: and when they
_{apta1492 ppro846   aina3870   3704   asba3327   pre575   ppro846   art,nn3725}
saw him, they besought *him* that he would depart out of their coasts.

Jesus Heals a Crippled Man (Mark 2:1-12; Luke 5:17-26)

_{2532   apta1684   pre1519   art,nn4143   aina1276   2532 aina2064 pre1519   art,aj2398}
9 And he entered into a ship, and passed over, and came into his own
_{an,nn4172}
city.
_{2532   2400   ipf4374   ppro846   an,ajn3885   pfpp906 pre1909}
2 And, behold, they brought to him a man*sick*of*the*palsy, lying on a
_{an,nn2825 2532 art,nn2424 apta1492 ppro846 art,nn4102 aina2036   art3588   ajn3885   an,nn5043}
bed: and Jesus seeing their faith said unto the sick*of*the*palsy; Son,
_{pim2293   ppro4675 art,nn266 pfip863   ppro4671}
be*of*good*cheer; thy sins be forgiven thee.

²⁵³² ²⁴⁰⁰ ^{idpro5100} ^{art3588} ⁿⁿ¹¹²² ^{aina2036} ^{pre1722} ^{rxpro1438} ^{depro3778}
3 And, behold, certain of the scribes said within themselves, This *man*
^{pin987}
blasphemeth.

²⁵³² ^{art,nn2424} ^{apta1492} ^{ppro846} ^{art,nn1761} ^{aina2036} ^{inpro2444} ^{pinm1760} ^{epn5210} ^{an,ajn4190} ^{pre1722}
4 And Jesus knowing their thoughts said, Wherefore think ye   evil   in
^{ppro5216} ^{art,nn2588}
your hearts?

¹⁰⁶³ ^{inpro5101} ^{pin2076} ^{pr/an,aj2123} ^{ainf2036} ^{art,nn266} ^{pfip863} ^{ppro4671} ²²²⁸ ^{ainf2036}
5 For whether is easier, to say, *Thy* sins be forgiven thee; or to say,
^{aipm1453} ²⁵³² ^{pim4043}
Arise, and walk?

¹¹⁶¹ ²⁴⁴³ ^{asba1492} ³⁷⁵⁴ ^{art3588} ⁿⁿ⁵²⁰⁷ ^{art,nn444} ^{pin2192} ^{an,nn1849} ^{pre1909} ^{art,nn1093}
6 But that ye may know that the Son of man hath power on earth to
^{pinf863} ^{an,nn266} ^{ad5119} ^{pin3004} ^{art3588} ^{ajn3885} ^{aptp1453} ^{aima142} ^{ppro4675}
forgive sins, (then saith he to the sick*of*the*palsy,) Arise, take up thy
^{art,nn2825} ²⁵³² ^{aina5217} ^{pre1519} ^{ppro848} ^{art,nn3624}
bed, and go unto thine house.

²⁵³² ^{aptp1453} ^{aina565} ^{pre1519} ^{ppro848} ^{art,nn3624}
7 And he arose, and departed to   his house.

¹¹⁶¹ ^{art3588} ⁿⁿ³⁷⁹³ ^{apta1492} ^{aina2296} ²⁵³² ^{aina1392} ^{art,nn2316}
8 But when the multitudes saw *it,* they marveled, and glorified God,
^{art,apta1325} ^{an,aj5108} ^{an,nn1849} ^{art,nn444}
which*had*given such power unto men.

Jesus Calls Matthew (Mark 2:13-17; Luke 5:27-32)

²⁵³² ^{art,nn2424} ^{pap3855} ^{ad1564} ^{aina1492} ^{an,nn444} ^{ppmp3004} ^{an,nn3156}
9 And as Jesus passed forth from thence, he saw a man, named Matthew,
^{ppmp2521} ^{pre1909} ^{art3588} ⁿⁿ⁵⁰⁵⁸ ²⁵³² ^{pin3004} ^{ppro846} ^{pim190} ^{ppro3427} ²⁵³²
sitting at the receipt*of*custom: and he saith unto him, Follow me. And he
^{apta450} ^{aina190} ^{ppro846}
arose, and followed him.

²⁵³² ^{aom1096} ^{ppro846} ^{ppmp345} ^{pre1722} ^{art3588} ⁿⁿ³⁶¹⁴ ⁽²⁵³²⁾ ²⁴⁰⁰
10 And it came*to*pass, as Jesus sat*at*meat in the house, behold,
^{an,aj4183} ^{an,nn5057} ²⁵³² ^{an,ajn268} ^{apta2064} ^{ipf4873} ^{art,nn2424} ²⁵³² ^{ppro846} ^{art,nn3101}
many publicans and sinners came and sat down with him and his disciples.

²⁵³² ^{art3588} ⁿⁿ⁵³³⁰ ^{apta1492} ^{aina2036} ^{ppro846} ^{art,nn3101} ^{pre,inpro1302}
11 And when the Pharisees saw *it,* they said unto his disciples, Why
^{pin2068} ^{ppro5216} ^{art,nn1320} ^{pre3326} ^{art,nn5057} ²⁵³² ^{an,ajn268}
eateth your Master with publicans and sinners?

¹¹⁶¹ ^{art,nn2424} ^{apta191} ^{aina2036} ^{ppro846} ^{art,pap2480}
12 But when Jesus heard *that,* he said unto them, They*that*be*whole
^{pin2192/an,nn5532} ³⁷⁵⁶ ^{an,nn2395} ²³⁵ ^{art,pap2192/ad2560}
need   not a physician, but they*that*are*sick.

¹¹⁶¹ ^{aptp4198} ^{aima3129} ^{inpro5101} ^{pin2076} ^{pin2309} ^{an,nn1656} ²⁵³² ³⁷⁵⁶
13 But go ye and learn what *that* meaneth, I will have mercy, and not
^{an,nn2378} ¹⁰⁶³ ³⁷⁵⁶ ^{aina2064} ^{ainf2564} ^{an,ajn1342} ²³⁵ ^{an,ajn268} ^{pre1519}
sacrifice: for I am not come to call the righteous, but sinners to
^{an,nn3341}
repentance.   *(Hos. 6:6)*

Fasting (Mark 2:18-22; Luke 5:33-39)

ad5119   pinm4334   ppro846 art3588   nn3101   an,nn2491 pap3004   pre,inpro1302   epn2249 2532 art3588

14 Then came to him the disciples of John, saying, Why do we and the

nn5330   pin3522 an,ajn4183 1161 ppro4675   art,nn3101   pin3522   3756

Pharisees fast oft, but thy disciples fast not?

2532   art,nn2424 aina2036   ppro846   pinm1410(3361) art3588   nn5207   art3588   nn3567

15 And Jesus said unto them,   Can   the children of the bridechamber

pinf3996   pre1909/an,ajn3745 art3588   nn3566   pin2076 pre3326 ppro846   1161   an,nn2250   fm2064

mourn, as*long*as the bridegroom is with them? but the days will come,

ad3752 art3588   nn3566   fp522   pre575 ppro846 2532   ad5119   ft3522

when the bridegroom shall be taken from them, and then shall they fast.

(1161)   an,ajn3762   pin1911   an,nn1915   an,aj46 an,nn4470 pre1909   an,aj3820 an,nn2440   1063

16 No man putteth a piece of new cloth unto an old garment, for

art,nn4138/ppro846   pin142 pre575 art3588   nn2440   2532   an,nn4978 pinm1096

that*which*is*put*in*to*fill*it*up taketh from the garment, and the rent   is

pr/an,aj5501

made worse.

3761   pin906 an,aj3501 an,nn3631 pre1519 an,aj3820   nn779   1490 art3588 nn779   pinm4486

17 Neither do men put new wine into old bottles: else the bottles break,

2532 art3588   nn3631   pinm1632   2532 art3588   nn779   fm622   235   pin906 an,aj3501 an,nn3631 pre1519

and the wine runneth out, and the bottles perish: but they put new wine into

an,aj2537 an,nn779   2532 an,ajn297   pinm4933

new bottles, and both are preserved.

Jesus Raises Jarius' Daughter (Mark 5:21-43; Luke 8:40-56)

ppro846 pap2980   depro5023   ppro846   2400   apta2064   nu1520

18 While he spake these things unto them, behold, there came a certain

an,nn758   2532   ipf4352   ppro846   pap3004 ppro3450 art,nn2364   aina5053/ad737   235   apta2064

ruler, and worshiped him, saying, My daughter is*even*now*dead: but come

2532 aima2007 ppro4675 art,nn5495 pre1909 ppro846 2532   fm2198

and lay thy hand upon her, and she shall live.

2532 art,nn2424 aptp1453   aina190 ppro846 2532   ppro846 art,nn3101

19 And Jesus arose, and followed him, and so did his disciples.

2532   2400   an,nn1135   pap131

20 And, behold, a woman, which was diseased*with*an*issue*of*blood

nu1427 an,nn2094 apta4334 ad3693   aom680 art3588 nn2899   ppro846 art,nn2440

twelve years, came behind him, and touched the hem of his garment:

1063   ipf3004   pre1722 rxpro1438 1437   an,ajn3440 asbm680 ppro846 art,nn2440

21 For she said within herself, If I may but touch his garment, I shall

fp4982

be whole.

1161   art,nn2424   aptp1994   2532   apta1492 ppro846 aina2036 an,nn2364

22 But Jesus turned*him*about, and when he saw her, he said, Daughter,

pim2293   ppro4675 art,nn4102   pfi4982/ppro4571   2532   art3588   nn1135

be*of*good*comfort; thy faith hath made*thee*whole. And the woman was

ainp4982   pre575 depro1565 art,nn5610

made whole from that hour.

23 And when Jesus came into the ruler's house, and saw the minstrels
and the people making*a*noise,

24 He said unto them, Give place: for the maid is*not*dead, but sleepeth.
And they laughed*him*to*scorn.

25 But when the people were put forth, he went in, and took her by the
hand, and the maid arose.

26 And the fame hereof went abroad into all that land.

Jesus Heals Two Blind Men

27 And when Jesus departed thence, two blind men followed him, crying,
and saying, *Thou* son of David, have mercy on us.

28 And when he was come into the house, the blind men came to him:
and Jesus saith unto them, Believe ye that I am able to do this? They said
unto him, Yea, Lord.

29 Then touched he their eyes, saying, According to your faith be it unto
you.

30 And their eyes were opened; and Jesus straitly charged them, saying,
See *that* no man know *it*.

31 But they, when they were departed, spread*abroad*his*fame in all
that country.

Jesus Heals a Mute

32 As they went out, behold, they brought to him a dumb man
possessed*with*a*devil.

2532   art3588 nn1140   aptp1544 art3588 ajn2974 aina2980 2532 art3588   nn3793

33 And when the devil was cast out, the dumb spake: and the multitudes

aina2296   pap3004   ad3762   ad3779 aom5316 pre1722   2474

marveled, saying, It was never so seen in Israel.

1161   art3588   nn5330   ipf3004   pin1544   art,nn1140   pre1722   art3588   nn758

34 But the Pharisees said, He casteth out devils through the prince of

art3588   nn1140

the devils.

Jesus' Compassion

2532   art,nn2424   ipf4013   an,aj3956 art3588   nn4172   2532   art,nn2968   pap1321   pre1722 ppro846

35 And Jesus went about all the cities and villages, teaching in their

art,nn4864   2532   pap2784   art3588   nn2098   art3588   nn932   2532   pap2323   an,aj3956

synagogues, and preaching the gospel of the kingdom, and healing every

an,nn3554   2532 an,aj3956   an,nn3119 pre1722 art3588   nn2992

sickness and every disease among the people.

1161   apta1492 art3588   nn3793   ainp4697   pre4012

36 But when he saw the multitudes, he was moved*with*compassion on

ppro846   3754   ipf2258/pfpp1590 2532   pfpp4496   ad5616 an,nn4263 pap2192 3361

them, because they fainted, and were scattered abroad, as sheep having no

an,nn4166

shepherd.   (Num. 27:17; Ezek. 34:5; Zech. 10:2)

ad5119   pin3004   ppro848 art,nn3101   art3588   nn2326   3303   pr/an,aj4183   1161

37 Then saith he unto his disciples, The harvest truly is plenteous, but

art3588   nn2040   pr/an,aj3641

the laborers are few;

aipp1189   3767   art3588 nn2962   art3588   nn2326   3704   asba1544

38 Pray ye therefore the Lord of the harvest, that he will send forth

an,nn2040   pre1519 ppro848 art,nn2326

laborers into his harvest.

Jesus Chooses Twelve Apostles (Mark 3:13-19; 6:7-13; Luke 6:12-16; 9:1-6)

2532   aptm4341   ppro848   nu1427   art,nn3101

10

☞ And when he had called unto him his twelve disciples, he

aina1325   ppro846   an,nn1849   an,aj169   an,nn4151 5620   pinf1544/ppro846

gave them power against unclean spirits, to cast*them*out,

2532   pinf2323   an,aj3956   an,nn3554   2532   an,aj3956   an,nn3119

and to heal all manner of sickness and all manner of disease.

☞ **10:1–15** This concerns the special commission of the Twelve Apostles. They were given special instructions and they were to focus their ministry on the Jews. What was said to these disciples at this time should not be assumed applicable to those who are commissioned by the Lord at other times. For instance, in Luke 22:36, the Lord sent his disciples on an extended mission to the Gentiles and gave them instructions that were in direct opposition to those He gave here in Matthew chapter ten. In addition to this, only certain of the general principles of the ministry that were given to Christ's disciples can be applied to the commissioning of believers in this day. For example, the gifts of healing and raising the dead (v. 8) were only given to some (1 Cor. 12:28, 29), not to all. See note on 1 Corinthians 12:31.

2 Now the names of the twelve apostles are these; The first, Simon,

who*is*called Peter, and Andrew his brother; James the son of Zebedee, and

John his brother;

3 Philip, and Bartholomew; Thomas, and Matthew the publican; James

the son of Alphaeus, and Lebbaeus whose*surname*was Thaddaeus;

4 Simon the Canaanite, and Judas Iscariot, who*also*betrayed him.

5 These twelve Jesus sent forth, and commanded them, saying, Go not

into the way of the Gentiles, and into *any* city of the Samaritans enter ye

not:

6 But go rather to the lost sheep of the house of Israel.   (*Jer. 50:6*)

7 And as ye go, preach, saying, The kingdom of heaven is*at*hand.

8 Heal the sick, cleanse the lepers, raise the dead, cast out devils: freely

ye have received, freely give.

9 Provide neither gold, nor silver, nor brass in your purses,

10 Nor scrip for *your* journey, neither two coats, neither shoes, nor yet

staves: for the workman is worthy of his meat.

11 And into whatsoever city or town ye shall enter, inquire who in

it is worthy; and there abide till ye go thence.

12 And when ye come into a house, salute it.

13 And if   the house be worthy, let your peace come upon it: but

if*it*be*not worthy, let your peace return to you.

14 And whosoever shall not receive you, nor hear your words, when ye

depart out of that house or city, shake off the dust of your feet.

15 Verily I say unto you, It shall be more tolerable for the land of

Sodom and Gomorrah in the day of judgment, than for that city.

(*Gen. 18:20—19:28*)

The Disciples Should Expect Persecution (Mark 13:9-13; Luke 21:12-17)

2400 epn1473 pin649/ppro5209 ad5613 an,nn4263 pre1722 an,ajn3319 an,nn3074 pim1096

16 Behold, I send*you*forth as sheep in the midst of wolves: be

3767 pr/an,aj5429 ad5613 art,nn3789 2532 pr/an,aj185 ad5613 art,nn4058

ye therefore wise as serpents, and harmless as doves.

1161 pim4337 pre575 art,nn444 1063 ft3860/ppro5209 pre1519 an,nn4892

17 But beware of men: for they will deliver*you*up to the councils,

2532 ft3146 ppro5209 pre1722 ppro848 art,nn4864

and they will scourge you in their synagogues;

2532 (1161) fp71 pre1909 an,nn2232 2532 an,nn935 ad*1752/ppro1700 pre1519

18 And ye shall be brought before governors and kings for*my*sake, for a

an,nn3142 ppro846 2532 art3588 nn1484

testimony against them and the Gentiles.

1161 ad3752 psa3860/ppro5209 aosi3309/3361 ad4459 2228 inpro5101

19 But when they deliver*you*up, take*no*thought how or what

asba2980 1063 fp1325 ppro5213 pre1722 depro1565 art,nn5610 inpro5101

ye shall speak: for it shall be given you in that same hour what ye shall

ft2980

speak.

1063 pin2075 3756 epn5210 pr/art,pap2980 235 art3588 nn4151 ppro5216 art,nn3962

20 For it is not ye that speak, but the Spirit of your Father

art,pap2980 pre1722 ppro5213

which speaketh in you.

1161 an,nn80 ft3860 an,nn80 pre1519 an,nn2288 2532 an,nn3962

21 And the brother shall deliver up the brother to death, and the father

an,nn5043 2532 an,nn5043 fm1881 pre1909 an,nn1118 2532

the child: and the children shall rise up against *their* parents, and

ft2289/ppro846

cause*them*to*be*put*to*death.   (Mic. 7:6)

2532 fm2071 ppmp3404 pre5259 an,ajn3956 pre1223/ppro3450/art,nn3686 1161

22 And ye shall be hated of all *men* for*my*name's*sake: but

art,apta5278 pre1519 an,nn5056 (depro3778) fp4982

he*that*endureth to the end shall be saved.

1161 ad3752 psa1377 ppro5209 pre1722 depro5026 art,nn4172 pim5343 pre1519 art,ajn243

23 But when they persecute you in this city, flee ye into another:

1063 281 pin3004 ppro5213 efn3364 asba5055 art3588 nn4172 2474

for verily I say unto you, Ye shall not have gone over the cities of Israel,

ad2193/302 art3588 nn5207 art,nn444 asba2064

till the Son of man be come.

an,nn3101 pin2076 3756 pre5228 art,nn1320 3761 an,ajn1401 pre5228 ppro848

24 The disciple is not above *his* master, nor the servant above his

art,nn2962

lord.

pr/an,aj713 art3588 nn3101 2443 asbm1096 ad5613 ppro846 art,nn1320

25 It is enough for the disciple that he be as his master,

2532 art3588 ajn1401 ad5613 ppro846 art,nn2962 1487 aina2564 art3588

and the servant as his lord. If they have called the

nn3617 954 an,ajn4214 ad3123

master*of*the*house Beelzebub, how much more *shall* *they* *call*

art,nn3165/ppro846

them*of*his*household?

Admonitions Against Fear (Luke 12:2-7)

aosi5399 ppro846 3361   3767   1063   pin2076 an,ajn3762 pfpp2572 repro3739   3756
26 Fear them not therefore: for there is nothing covered, that shall not
fp601   2532 an,ajn2927 repro3739   3756   fp1097
be revealed; and hid, that shall not be known.

repro3739   pin3004   ppro5213   pre1722   art,nn4653   aima2036
27 What   I   tell   you   in   darkness,   *that*   speak   ye
pre1722 art,nn5457 2532 repro3739   pin191 pre1519 art3588 nn3775   aima2784   pre1909 art3588   nn1430
in light: and what ye hear in the ear, *that* preach ye upon the housetops.

2532 aosi5399 3361(pre575)   art,pap615   art3588   nn4983   1161   3361 ppmp1410   ainf615 art3588
☞ 28 And fear   not them*which*kill the body, but are not able to kill the
nn5590 1161 ad3123 aipp5399   art,ppmp1410   ainf622   2532 an,nn5590 2532 an,nn4983 pre1722
soul: but rather fear him*which*is*able to destroy both soul and body in
an,nn1067
hell.

3780 nu1417 an,nn4765 pinp4453   an,nn787   2532 nu1520 pre1537 ppro846   3756
29 Are not two sparrows sold for a farthing? and one of them shall not
fm4098 pre1909 art3588   nn1093   ad*427   ppro5216 art,nn3962
fall on the ground without your Father.

1161 art3588 2532   nn2359   epn5216 art,nn2776 pin1526 an,aj3956   pr/pfpp705
30 But the very hairs of your head are all numbered.
aosi5399   3361   3767   epn5210   pin1308   an,aj4183   an,nn4765
31 Fear ye not therefore, ye are*of*more*value than many sparrows.

Confessing Christ Before Men (Luke 12:8,9)

an,ajn3956/repro3748   3767   ft3670(pre1722) ppro1698   ad*1715   art,nn444(pre1722) ppro846
32 Whosoever therefore shall confess me before men, him will
epn2504/ft3670   ad*1715 ppro3450 art,nn3962 art3588   pre1722 art,nn3772
I*confess*also before my Father which is in heaven.
1161   repro3748/302   asbm720 ppro3165   ad*1715 art,nn444 ppro846   epn2504 fm720
33 But whosoever shall deny me before men, him will I also deny
ad*1715 ppro3450 art,nn3962   art3588   pre1722 art,nn3772
before my Father which is in heaven.

Change Brings Conflict (Luke 12:51-53; 14:26,27)

aosi3543 3361 3754   aina2064   ainf906 an,nn1515 pre1909 art,nn1093 aina2064 3756
34 Think not that I am come to send peace on earth: I came not to
ainf906 an,nn1515 235   an,nn3162
send peace, but a sword.
1063   aina2064   ainf1369/an,nn444   pre2596 ppro848 art,nn3962 2532
35 For I am come to set*a*man*at*variance against his father, and the

---

☞ **10:28** See note on Matthew 8:11, 12.

^{an,nn2364} ^{pre2596} ^{ppro848} ^{art,nn3384} ²⁵³² ^{an,nn3565} ^{pre2596} ^{ppro848}
daughter against her mother, and the daughter-in-law against her
^{art,nn3994}
mother-in-law.

²⁵³² ^{art,nn444} ^{an,ajn2190} ^{art,nn3615/ppro846}
36 And a man's foes *shall be* they*of*his*own*household. *(Mic. 7:6)*

^{art,pap5368} ^{an,nn3962} ²²²⁸ ^{an,nn3384} ^{pre5228} ^{ppro1691} ^{pin2076} ³⁷⁵⁶ ^{pr/an,aj514}
37 He*that*loveth father or mother more than me is not worthy of
^{ppro3450} ²⁵³² ^{art,pap5368} ^{an,nn5207} ²²²⁸ ^{an,nn2364} ^{pre5228} ^{ppro1691} ^{pin2076} ³⁷⁵⁶ ^{pr/an,aj514}
me: and he*that*loveth son or daughter more than me is not worthy of
^{ppro3450}
me.

²⁵³² ^{repro3739} ^{pin2983} ³⁷⁵⁶ ^{ppro848} ^{art,nn4716} ²⁵³² ^{pin190} ^{ad*3694} ^{ppro3450} ^{pin2076} ³⁷⁵⁶
38 And he that taketh not his cross, and followeth after me, is not
^{pr/an,aj514} ^{ppro3450}
worthy of me.

^{art,apta2147} ^{ppro848} ^{art,nn5590} ^{ft622} ^{ppro846} ²⁵³² ^{art,apta622} ^{ppro848} ^{art,nn5590}
39 He*that*findeth his life shall lose it: and he*that*loseth his life
^{ad*1752/ppro1700} ^{ft2147} ^{ppro846}
for*my*sake shall find it.

Rewards for Service (Mark 9:41)

^{art,ppmp1209} ^{ppro5209} ^{pinm1209} ^{epn1691} ²⁵³² ^{art,ppmp1209} ^{epn1691}
40 He*that*receiveth you receiveth me, and he*that*receiveth me
^{pinm1209} ^{art,apta649} ^{ppro3165}
receiveth him*that*sent me.

^{art,ppmp1209} ^{an,nn4396} ^{pre1519} ^{an,nn3686} ^{an,nn4396} ^{fm2983}
41 He*that*receiveth a prophet in the name of a prophet shall receive a
^{an,nn4396} ^{an,nn3408} ²⁵³² ^{art,ppmp1209} ^{an,ajn1342} ^{pre1519} ^{an,nn3686}
prophet's reward; and he*that*receiveth a righteous man in the name of a
^{an,ajn1342} ^{fm2983} ^{an,ajn1342} ^{an,nn3408}
righteous man shall receive a righteous man's reward.

²⁵³² ^{repro3739/1437} ^{asba4222} ^{nu1520} ^{depro5130} ^{art,ajn3398} ^{an,nn4221}
42 And whosoever shall give*to*drink unto one of these little ones a cup
^{an,ajn5593} ^{an,ajn3440} ^{pre1519} ^{an,nn3686} ^{an,nn3101} ²⁸¹ ^{pin3004} ^{ppro5213}
of cold *water* only in the name of a disciple, verily I say unto you, he shall
^{efn3364} ^{asba622} ^{ppro848} ^{art,nn3408}
in*no*wise lose his reward.

Messengers from John the Baptist (Luke 7:18-23)

²⁵³² ^{aom1096} ^{ad3753} ^{art,nn2424} ^{aina5055} ^{pap1299}
11 And it came*to*pass, when Jesus had made*an*end of commanding
^{ppro848} ^{nu1427} ^{art,nn3101} ^{aina3327} ^{ad1564} ^{infg1321} ²⁵³² ^{infg2784}
his twelve disciples, he departed thence to teach and to preach
^{pre1722} ^{ppro846} ^{art,nn4172}
in their cities.

¹¹⁶¹ ^{art,nn2491} ^{apta191} ^{pre1722 art3588} ⁿⁿ¹²⁰¹ ^{art3588} ⁿⁿ²⁰⁴¹ ^{art,nn5547} ^{apta3992}

2 Now when John had heard in the prison the works of Christ, he sent

^{nut1417} ^{ppro848} ^{art,nn3101}

two of his disciples,

^{aina2036} ^{ppro846 pin1488 epn4771} ^{art,pmpp2064} ²²²⁸ ^{pin4328}

3 And said unto him, Art thou he*that*should*come, or do we look for

^{an,ajn2087}

another?   (Mal. 3:1)

^{(2532) art,nn2424} ^{aptp611} ^{aina2036} ^{ppro846} ^{aptp4198} ^{aima518/an,nn2491}

4   Jesus answered and said unto them,   Go   and show*John*again

^{repro3739} ^{pin191 2532} ^{pin991}

those things which ye do hear and see:

^{an,ajn5185} ^{pin308} ²⁵³² ^{an,ajn5560} ^{pin4043} ^{an,ajn3015}

5 The blind receive*their*sight, and the lame walk, the lepers are

^{pinp2511} ²⁵³² ^{an,ajn2974} ^{pin191} ^{an,ajn3498} ^{pinp1453} ²⁵³² ^{an,ajn4434}

cleansed, and the deaf hear, the dead are raised up, and the poor

^{pinm2097}

have*the*gospel*preached*to*them.   (Is. 35:5,6; 42:18; 61:1)

²⁵³² ^{pr/an,aj3107} ^{pin2076} ^{repro3739/1437} ³³⁶¹ ^{asbp4624} ^{pre1722 ppro1698}

6 And blessed is he, whosoever shall not be offended in me.

Jesus Commends John (Luke 7:24-35)

¹¹⁶¹ ^{depro5130} ^{ppmp4198} ^{art,nn2424} ^{aom756} ^{pinf3004} ^{art3588} ⁿⁿ³⁷⁹³

7 And as they departed, Jesus began to say unto the multitudes

^{pre4012} ^{an,nn2491} ^{inpro5101} ^{aina1831} ^{pre1519 art3588} ^{ajn2048} ^{aifm2300} ^{an,nn2563}

concerning John, What went*ye*out into the wilderness to see? A reed

^{ppmp4531} ^{pre5259} ^{an,nn417}

shaken with the wind?

²³⁵ ^{inpro5101} ^{aina1831} ^{ainf1492} ^{an,nn444} ^{pfpp294} ^{pre1722 an,aj3120} ^{an,nn2440}

8 But what went*ye*out for to see? A man clothed in   soft raiment?

²⁴⁰⁰ ^{art,pap5409} ^{art,ajn3120} ^{pin1526 pre1722 art,nn935} ^{art,nn3624}

behold, they*that*wear soft clothing are in kings' houses.

²³⁵ ^{inpro5101} ^{aina1831} ^{ainf1492} ^{an,nn4396} ³⁴⁸³ ^{pin3004} ^{ppro5213 2532}

9 But what went*ye*out for to see? A prophet? yea, I say unto you, and

^{an,ajn4055} ^{an,nn4396}

more than a prophet.

¹⁰⁶³ ^{depro3778 pin2076} ^{pre4012 repro3739} ^{pfip1125} ²⁴⁰⁰ ^{epn1473} ^{pin649} ^{ppro3450}

10 For this is he, of whom it is written, Behold, I send my

^{art,nn32} ^{pre4253} ^{ppro4675 an,nn4383} ^{repro3739} ^{ft2680} ^{ppro4675 art,nn3598} ^{ad*1715} ^{ppro4675}

messenger before thy face, which shall prepare thy   way before thee.

                                                        (Mal. 3:1)

²⁸¹ ^{pin3004} ^{ppro5213} ^{pre1722} ^{an,ajn1084} ^{an,nn1135}

11 Verily I say unto you, Among them*that*are*born of women there hath

³⁷⁵⁶ ^{pfip1453} ^{cd/an,aj3187} ^{an,nn2491 art3588} ⁿⁿ⁹¹⁰ ¹¹⁶¹ ^{art,ajn3398}

not risen a greater than John the Baptist: notwithstanding he*that*is*least

^{pre1722 art3588} ⁿⁿ⁹³² ^{art,nn3772} ^{pin2076} ^{pr/cd/an,aj3187} ^{ppro846}

in the kingdom of heaven is greater than he.

1161   pre575   art3588   nn2250   an,nn2491   art3588   nn910   ad2193   ad737   art3588   nn932

12 And from the days of John the Baptist until now the kingdom of

art,nn3772   pinp971   2532   an,nn973   pin726/ppro846

heaven suffereth violence, and the violent take*it*by*force.

1063   an,aj3956   art3588   nn4396   2532   art3588   nn3551   aina4395   ad2193   an,nn2491

13 For all the prophets and the law prophesied until John.

2532   1487   pin2309   aifm1209   epn846   pin2076   pr/an,nn2243   art,pap3195   pifm2064

14 And if ye will receive *it,* this is Elijah, which was for to come.

art,pap2192   an,nn3775   pinf191   pim191

15 He*that*hath ears to hear, let him hear.

1161   inpro5101   asba3666   depro5026   art,nn1074   pin2076   pr/an,anj3664   an,nn3808

16 But whereunto shall I liken this generation? It is like unto children

ppmp2521   pre1722   an,nn58   2532   pap4377   ppro848   art,nn2083

sitting in the markets, and calling unto their fellows,

2532   pin3004   aina832   ppro5213   2532

17 And saying, We have piped unto you, and ye have

3756   aom3738   aina2354   ppro5213   2532   3756   aom2875

not danced; we have mourned unto you, and ye have not lamented.

1063   an,nn2491   aina2064   3383   pap2068   3383   pap4095   2532   pin3004   pin2192

18 For John came neither eating nor drinking, and they say, He hath a

an,nn1140

devil.

art3588   nn5207   art,nn444   aina2064   pap2068   2532   pap4095   2532   pin3004   2400   an,nn444

19 The Son of man came eating and drinking, and they say, Behold a man

an,nn5314   2532   an,nn3630   an,ajn5384   an,nn5057   2532   an,ajn268   2532   art,nn4678

gluttonous, and a winebibber, a friend of publicans and sinners. But wisdom is

ainp1344   pre575   ppro848   art,nn5043

justified of her children.

Jesus Condemns Certain Cities (Luke 10:13-15)

ad5119   aom756   pinf3679   art3588   nn4172   pre1722/repro3739   art,aj4118   ppro846

20 Then began he to upbraid the cities wherein most of his

an,nn1411   aom1096   3754   aina3340   3756

mighty works were done, because they repented not:

3759   ppro4671   5523   3759   ppro4671   966   3754   1487   art3588

21 Woe unto thee, Chorazin! woe unto thee, Bethsaida! for if the

nn1411   art,aptp1096   pre1722   ppro5213   aom1096   pre1722   an,nn5184   2532   an,nn4605

mighty works, which*were*done in you, had been done in Tyre and Sidon,

aina3340   ad3819   pre1722   an,nn4526   2532   an,nn4700

they would have repented long ago in sackcloth and ashes.

(Is. 23:1-8; Ezek. 26-28; Joel 3:4-8; Amos 1:9,10; Zech. 9:2-4)

4133   pin3004   ppro5213   fm2071   pr/cd/an,aj414   an,nn5184   2532   an,nn4605   pre1722

22 But I say unto you, It shall be more tolerable for Tyre and Sidon at

an,nn2250   an,nn2920   2228   ppro5213

the day of judgment, than for you.

2532   epn4771   2584   art,aptp5312   ad2193   art,nn3772

23 And thou, Capernaum, which*art*exalted unto heaven, shalt be

fp2601   ad2193 an,nn86   3754 1487 art3588   nn1411   art,aptp1096   pre1722

brought down to hell: for if the mighty works, which*have*been*done in

ppro4671   ainp1096 pre1722 an,nn4670   aina3306   ad3360 art,ad4594

thee, had been done in Sodom, it would have remained until this day.

(Is. 14:13,15; Gen. 19:24-28)

              4133   pin3004   ppro5213   3754   fm2071   pr/cd/an,aj414   an,nn1093

24 But I say unto you, That it shall be more tolerable for the land of

an,nn4670   pre1722   an,nn2250   an,nn2920   2228   ppro4671

Sodom, in the day of judgment, than for thee.

Rest in Jesus (Luke 10:21,22)

        pre1722 depro1565 art,nn2540 art,nn2424 aptp611   aina2036   pinm1843 ppro4671   an,nn3962   an,nn2962

25 At that time Jesus answered and said, I thank thee, O Father, Lord

art,nn3772   2532   art,nn1093   3754   aina613   depro5023   pre575   an,ajn4680 2532

of heaven and earth, because thou hast hid these things from the wise and

an,ajn4908   2532   aina601   ppro846   an,ajn3516

prudent, and hast revealed them unto babes.

              3483   art,nn3962   3754 ad3779   aom1096   pr/an,nn2107   ad*1715/ppro4675

26 Even so, Father: for so it seemed good in*thy*sight.

              an,ajn3956   ainp3860   ppro3427 pre5259 ppro3450   art,nn3962   2532   an,ajn3762

27 All things are delivered unto me of my Father: and no man

pin1921   art3588 nn5207 1508 art3588   nn3962   3761   pin1921   idpro5100   art3588   nn3962   1508

knoweth the Son, but the Father; neither knoweth any man the Father, save

art3588 nn5207 2532   repro3739/1437   art3588 nn5207 psmp1014   ainf601

the Son, and *he* to whomsoever the Son will reveal *him.*

        ad1205   pre4314 ppro3165 an,aj3956   art,pap2782   2532   pfpp5412   epn2504

28 Come unto me, all *ye* that labor and are*heavy*laden, and I will

ft373/ppro5209

give*you*rest.   *(Jer. 6:16)*

        aima142 ppro3450 art,nn2218   pre1909 ppro5209   2532   aima3129 pre575 ppro1700 3754   pin1510 pr/an,aj4235 2532

29 Take my yoke upon you, and learn of me; for I am meek and

pr/an,aj5011   art,nn2588 2532   ft2147 an,nn372   ppro5216 art,nn5590

lowly in heart: and ye shall find rest unto your souls.

        1063   ppro3450 art,nn2218   pr/an,aj5543 2532 ppro3450 art,nn5413 pin2076 pr/an,aj1645

30 For my yoke *is* easy, and my burden is light.

Jesus Is Lord Over the Sabbath Day (Mark 2:23-28; Luke 6:1-5)

12

        pre1722 depro1565 art,nn2540 art,nn2424 ainp4198   art3588   nn4521   pre1223   art3588   ajn4702

At that time Jesus went on the sabbath day through the corn;

        2532 ppro846   art,nn3101   aina3983   2532   aom756   pinf5089   an,nn4719

and his disciples were hungry, and began to pluck the ears*of*corn,

2532   pinf2068

and to eat.   *(Deut. 23:24,25)*

¹¹⁶¹   ^{art3588}   ⁿⁿ⁵³³⁰   ^{apta1492}   ^{aina2036}   ^{ppro846}   ²⁴⁰⁰   ^{ppro4675}

2 But when the Pharisees saw *it,* they said unto him, Behold, thy

^{art,nn3101}   ^{pin4160}   ^{repro3739}   ^{pin1832/3756}   ^{pinf4160}   ^{pre1722}   ^{an,nn4521}

disciples do that which is*not*lawful to do upon the sabbath day.

(Ex. 20:10; Deut. 5:14)

¹¹⁶¹   ^{art3588}   ^{aina2036}   ^{ppro846}   ³⁷⁵⁶   ^{aina314}   ^{inpro5101}   ¹¹³⁸   ^{aina4160}   ^{ad3753}   ^{epn846}

3 But he said unto them, Have ye not read what David did, when he

^{aina3983}   ²⁵³²   ^{art3588}   ^{pre2236 ppro846}

was hungry, and they that were with him;

^{ad4459}   ^{aina1525}   ^{pre1519}   ^{art3588}   ⁿⁿ³⁶²⁴   ^{art,nn2316}   ²⁵³²   ^{aina5315}   ^{art3588}   ^{nn740/art,nn4286}

4 How he entered into the house of God, and did eat the shewbread,

^{repro3739}   ^{ipf2258}   ³⁷⁵⁶   ^{pap1832}   ^{ppro846}   ^{ainf5315}   ³⁷⁶¹   ^{art3588}   ^{pre3326 ppro846}

which was not lawful for him to eat, neither for them which were with him,

¹⁵⁰⁸   ^{an,aj3441}   ^{art3588}   ⁿⁿ²⁴⁰⁹

but only for the priests?   *(1 Sam. 21:1-6; Lev. 24:5-9)*

²²²⁸   ³⁷⁵⁶   ^{aina314}   ^{pre1722}   ^{art3588}   ⁿⁿ³⁵⁵¹   ³⁷⁵⁴   ^{art3588}   ⁿⁿ⁴⁵²¹   ^{art3588}

5 Or have ye not read in the law, how that on the sabbath days the

ⁿⁿ²⁴⁰⁹   ^{pre1722 art3588}   ⁿⁿ²⁴¹¹   ^{pin953}   ^{art3588}   ⁿⁿ⁴⁵²¹   ^{2532 pin1526}   ^{pr/an,aj338}

priests in the temple profane the sabbath, and are blameless?

(Num. 28:9,10)

¹¹⁶¹   ^{pin3004}   ^{ppro5213}   ³⁷⁵⁴   ^{ad5602}   ^{pin2076}   ^{cd/an,ajn3187}   ^{art3588}   ⁿⁿ²⁴¹¹

6 But I say unto you, That in*this*place is *one* greater than the temple.

¹¹⁶¹   ¹⁴⁸⁷   ^{plpf1097}   ^{inpro5101}   ^{pin2076}   ^{pin2309}   ^{an,nn1656}   ²⁵³²   ³⁷⁵⁶

7 But if ye had known what *this* meaneth, I will have mercy, and not

^{an,nn2378}   ³⁷⁵⁶   ^{aina2613}   ^{art3588}   ^{ajn338}

sacrifice, ye would not have condemned the guiltless.   *(Hos.6:6)*

¹⁰⁶³   ^{art3588 nn5207}   ^{art,nn444}   ^{pin2076}   ^{pr/an,nn2962}   ²⁵³²   ^{art3588}   ⁿⁿ⁴⁵²¹

8 For the Son of man is Lord even of the sabbath day.

Jesus Heals a Man With a Withered Hand (Mark 3:1-6; Luke 6:6-11)

²⁵³²   ^{apta3327}   ^{ad1564}   ^{aina2064}   ^{pre1519}   ^{ppro846}   ^{art,nn4864}

9 And when he was departed thence, he went into their synagogue:

²⁵³²   ²⁴⁰⁰   ^{ipf2258}   ^{an,nn444}   ^{pap2192}   ^{art,nn5495}   ^{an,aj3584}   ²⁵³²

10 And, behold, there was a man which had *his* hand withered. And they

^{aina1905}   ^{ppro846}   ^{pap3004(1487)}   ^{pin1832}   ^{pinf2323}   ^{art3588}   ⁿⁿ⁴⁵²¹   ²⁴⁴³

asked him, saying, Is*it*lawful to heal on the sabbath days? that they might

^{asba2723}   ^{ppro846}

accuse him.

¹¹⁶¹   ^{art3588}   ^{aina2036}   ^{ppro846}   ^{inpro5101}   ^{an,nn444}   ^{fm2071}   ^{pre1537}   ^{ppro5216}   ^{repro3739}

11 And he said unto them, What man shall there be among you, that

^{ft2192}   ^{nu1520}   ^{an,nn4263}   ²⁵³²   ¹⁴³⁷   ^{depro5124}   ^{asba1706}   ^{pre1519}   ^{an,nn999}   ^{art3588}   ⁿⁿ⁴⁵²¹

shall have one sheep, and if it fall into a pit on the sabbath day, will he

³⁷⁸⁰   ^{ft2902}   ^{ppro846 2532}   ^{ft1453}

not lay hold on it, and lift*it*out?

an,ajn4214   3767   pin1308/an,nn4444   an,nn4263   5620   pin1832
12 How much then is*a*man*better than a sheep? Wherefore it is lawful to
pinf4160 ad2573   art3588   nn4521
do well on the sabbath days.

ad5119   pin3004   art3588   nn444   aima1614   ppro4675 art,nn5495   2532
13 Then saith he to the man, Stretch forth thine hand. And he
aina1614   2532   ainp600   pr/an,aj5199 ad5613 art3588 ajn243
stretched*it*forth; and it was restored whole, like as the other.

1161   art3588   nn5330   apta1831   aina2983   an,nn4824 pre2596 ppro846   3704
14 Then the Pharisees went out, and held a council against him, how they
asba622   ppro846
might destroy him.

God's Servant

1161   art,nn2424 apta1097   aina402   ad1564   2532 an,aj4183
15 But when Jesus knew it, he withdrew himself from thence: and great
an,nn3793   aina190   ppro846 2532   aina2323   ppro846 an,aj3956
multitudes followed him, and he healed them all;

2532   aina2008   ppro846   2443   3361 asba4160 ppro846 pr/an,aj5318
16 And charged them that they should not make him known:

3704   asbp4137   art,aptp4483   pre1223 an,nn2268 art3588   nn4396
17 That it might be fulfilled which*was*spoken by Isaiah the prophet,
pap3004
saying,

2400   ppro3450 art,nn3816 repro3739   aina140   ppro3450 art,ajn27   pre1519 repro3739
18 Behold my servant, whom I have chosen; my beloved, in whom
pre1519 art,nn5590   aina2106   ft5087 ppro3450 art,nn4151 pre1909 ppro846 2532   ft518
my soul is*well*pleased: I will put my spirit upon him, and he shall show
an,nn2920   art3588   nn1484
judgment to the Gentiles.

3756   ft2051   3761   ft2905   3761   idpro5100   ft191   ppro846 art,nn5456 pre1722
19 He shall not strive, nor cry; neither shall any man hear his voice in
art3588   ajn4113
the streets.

pfpp4937 an,nn2563   3756   ft2608   2532 ppmp5188   an,nn3043   3756
20 A bruised reed shall he not break, and smoking flax shall he not
ft4370   ad2193/302   asba1544 art,nn2920 pre1519 an,nn3534
quench, till he send forth judgment unto victory.

2532   pre1722 ppro846 art,nn3686   an,nn1484   ft1679
21 And in his name shall the Gentiles trust.   (Is. 42:1-4)

The Power of God Over the Devil (Mark 3:20-30; Luke 11:14-23; 12:10)

ad5119   ainp4374   ppro846   ppmp1139   an,ajn5185 2532
22 Then was brought unto him one*possessed*with*a*devil, blind, and
an,ajn2974 2532   aina2323 ppro846   ad5620   art3588 ajn5185 2532 an,ajn2974 2532   pinf2980 2532
dumb: and he healed him, insomuch that the blind and dumb both spake and
pinf191
saw.

2532 an,aj3956 art3588 nn3793   ipf1839   2532   ipf3004 pin2076 3385 depro3778 art3588 pr/nn5207

23 And all the people were amazed, and said, Is not this the son of
1138
David?

1161   art3588   nn5330   apta191   aina2036 depro3778   3756

24 But when the Pharisees heard *it,* they said, This *fellow* doth not
pin1544   art,nn1140 1508 pre1722   954   an,nn758   art3588   nn1140

cast out devils, but by Beelzebub the prince of the devils.

1161 art,nn2424 apta1492 ppro846   art,nn1761   aina2036   ppro846   an,aj3956   an,nn932

25 And Jesus knew their thoughts, and said unto them, Every kingdom
aptp3307   pre2596   rxpro1438   pinp2049   2532   an,aj3956   an,nn4172 2228   an,nn3614

divided against itself is brought*to*desolation; and every city or house
aptp3307   pre2596   rxpro1438   3756   fp2476

divided against itself shall not stand:

2532   1487 art,nn4567   pin1544   art,nn4567   ainp3307   pre1909   rxpro1438   ad4459

26 And if Satan cast out Satan, he is divided against himself; how shall
3767 ppro846   art,nn932   fp2476

then his kingdom stand?

2532   1487 epn1473 pre1722   954   pin1544   art,nn1140 pre1722 inpro5101   ppro5216 art,nn5207

27 And if I by Beelzebub cast out devils, by whom do your children
pin1544   pre1223/depro5124 epn846   fm2071 ppro5216 pr/an,nn2923

cast**them*out? therefore they shall be your judges.

1161   1487 epn1473   pin1544   art,nn1140 pre1722   an,nn4151   an,nn2316   686   art3588   nn932

28 But if I cast out devils by the Spirit of God, then the kingdom of
art,nn2316   aina5348   pre1909 ppro5209

God is come unto you.

2228   ad4459 pinm1410 idpro5100 ainf1525 pre1519   art,ajn2478   art,nn3614   2532 ainf1283 ppro846

29 Or else how can one enter into a strong man's house, and spoil his
art,nn4632   3362   nu,ajn4412 asba1210 art3588   ajn2478   2532   ad5119   ft1283   ppro846

goods, except he first bind the strong man? and then he will spoil his
art,nn3614

house.   *(Is. 49:24)*

art,pap5607   3361   pre3326 ppro1700 pin2076   pre2596   ppro1700   2532   art,pap4863   3361

30 He*that*is not with me is against me; and he*that*gathereth not
pre3326 ppro1700   pin4650

with me scattereth abroad.

pre1223/depro5124   pin3004   ppro5213   an,aj3956   an,nn266 2532   an,nn988

☞ 31 Wherefore I say unto you, All manner of sin and blasphemy shall be
fp863   art,nn444 1161 art3588   nn988   art3588   nn4151   3756

forgiven unto men: but the blasphemy *against* the *Holy* Ghost shall not be
fp863   art,nn444

forgiven unto men.

2532   repro3739/302   asba2036   an,nn3056   pre2596   art3588 nn5207   art,nn444

32 And whosoever speaketh a word against the Son of man, it shall be
fp863   ppro846 1161   repro3739/302   asba2036   pre2596 art3588   aj40   art,nn4151   3756

forgiven him: but whosoever speaketh against the Holy Ghost, it shall not be
fp863   ppro846   3777   pre1722 depro5129 art,nn165   3777   pre1722 art3588   pap3195

forgiven him, neither in this world, neither in the *world* to come.

☞ **12:31, 32** See notes on Mark 3:28, 29 and Hebrews 6:1–6.

A Tree Is Known By Its Fruit (Luke 6:43-45)

₂₂₂₈ _{aima4160} _{art3588} _{nn1186} _{an,aj2570} ₂₅₃₂ _{ppro846} _{art,nn2590} _{an,aj2570} ₂₂₂₈ _{aima4160} _{art3588} _{nn1186}

33 Either make the tree good, and his fruit good; or else make the tree

_{an,aj4550} ₂₅₃₂ _{ppro846} _{art,nn2590} _{an,aj4550} ₁₀₆₃ _{art3588} _{nn1186} _{pinp1097} _{pre1537} _{art,nn2590}

corrupt, and his fruit corrupt: for the tree is known by *his* fruit.

_{an,nn1081} _{an,nn2191} _{ad4459} _{pinm1410} _{pap5607} _{pr/an,aj4190} _{pinf2980} _{an,ajn18}

34 O generation of vipers, how can ye, being evil, speak good things?

₁₀₆₃ _{pre1537} _{art3588} _{nn4051} _{art3588} _{nn2588} _{art3588} _{nn4750} _{pin2980}

for out of the abundance of the heart the mouth speaketh.

_{art,aj18} _{an,nn444} _{pre1537} _{art3588} _{aj18} _{an,nn2344} _{art3588} _{nn2588} _{pin1544}

35 A good man out of the good treasure of the heart bringeth forth

_{art,ajn18} ₂₅₃₂ _{art,aj4190} _{an,nn444} _{pre1537} _{art3588} _{aj4190} _{an,nn2344} _{pin1544}

good things: and an evil man out of the evil treasure bringeth forth

_{an,ajn4190}

evil things.

₁₁₆₁ _{pin3004} _{ppro5213} ₃₇₅₄ _{an,aj3956} _{an,aj692} _{an,nn4487} _{repro3739/1437} _{art,nn444} _{asba2980}

36 But I say unto you, That every idle word   that   men shall speak,

_{ft591} _{an,nn3056} _{pre4012/ppro846} _{pre1722} _{an,nn2250} _{an,nn2920}

they shall give account thereof in the day of judgment.

₁₀₆₃ _{pre1537} _{ppro4675} _{art,nn3056} _{fp1344} ₂₅₃₂ _{pre1537} _{ppro4675} _{art,nn3056}

37 For by thy words thou shalt be justified, and by   thy words thou

_{fp2613}

shalt be condemned.

The Desire for Signs Is Rebuked (Mark 8:11,12; Luke 11:29-32)

_{ad5119} _{idpro5100} _{art3588} _{nn1122} ₂₅₃₂ _{an,nn5330} _{ainp611} _{pap3004}

38 Then certain of the scribes and of the Pharisees answered, saying,

_{an,nn1320} _{pin2309} _{ainf1492} _{an,nn4592} _{pre575} _{ppro4675}

Master, we would see a sign from thee.

₁₁₆₁ _{art3588} _{aptp611} _{aina2036} _{ppro846} _{an,aj4190} ₂₅₃₂ _{an,nn3428}

39 But he answered and said unto them, An evil and adulterous

_{an,nn1074} _{pin1934} _{an,nn4592} ₂₅₃₂ _{3756 an,nn4592} _{fp1325} _{ppro846} ₁₅₀₈

generation seeketh after a sign; and there shall no sign be given to it, but

_{art3588 nn4592} _{art3588} _{nn4396} _{an,nn2495}

the sign of the prophet Jonah:

₁₀₆₃ _{ad5618} _{an,nn2495} _{ipf2258} _{nu5140} _{an,nn2250} ₂₅₃₂ _{nu5140} _{an,nn3571} _{pre1722 art3588} _{nn2785} _{art,nn2836}

40 For as Jonah was three days and three nights in   the whale's belly;

_{ad3779} _{art3588 nn5207} _{art,nn444} _{fm2071} _{nu5140} _{an,nn2250} ₂₅₃₂ _{nu5140} _{an,nn3571} _{pre1722 art3588} _{nn2588}

so shall the Son of man be three days and three nights in   the heart of

_{art3588} _{nn1093}

the earth.   *(Jon. 1:17)*

_{an,nn435} _{an,ajn3536} _{fm450} _{pre1722} _{art,nn2920} _{pre3326 depro5026} _{art,nn1074} ₂₅₃₂

41 The men of Nineveh shall rise in judgment with this generation, and

_{ft2632} _{ppro846} ₃₇₅₄ _{aina3340} _{pre1519 art3588} _{nn2782} _{an,nn2495} ₂₅₃₂

shall condemn it: because they repented at the preaching of Jonah; and,

₂₄₀₀ _{cd/an,ajn4119} _{an,nn2495} _{ad5602}

behold, a greater than Jonah *is* here.   *(Jon. 3:5,8)*

an,nn938   an,nn3558   fp1453   pre1722 art3588   nn2920   pre3326 depro5026
42 The queen of the south shall rise up in the judgment with this
art,nn1074   2532   ft2632 ppro846 3754   aina2064 pre1537 art3588   nn4009
generation, and shall condemn it: for she came from the uttermost parts of
art3588 nn1093   ainf191 art3588   nn4678   an,nn4672   2532   2400   cd/an,ajn4119
the earth to hear the wisdom of Solomon; and, behold, a greater than
an,nn4672   ad5602
Solomon *is* here.   *(1 Kgs. 10:1-10; 2 Chr. 9:1-12)*

The Unclean Spirit Returns (Luke 11:24-26)

(1161) ad3752 art3588 an,aj169   nn4151   asba1831 pre575   art,nn444   pinm1330   pre1223 an,aj504
43   When the unclean spirit is gone out of a man, he walketh through dry
an,nn5117   pap2212   an,nn372 2532 pin2147   3756
places, seeking rest, and findeth none.
ad5119   pin3004   ft1994 pre1519 ppro3450 art,nn3624   ad3606   aina1831
44 Then he saith, I will return into my house from whence I came out;
2532   apta2064   pin2147   pap4980   pfpp4563   2532   pfpp2885
and when he is come, he findeth *it* empty, swept, and garnished.
ad5119   pinm4198   2532   pin3880   pre3326   rxpro1438   nu2033   an,aj2087 an,nn4151
45 Then goeth he, and taketh with himself seven other spirits
an,aj4191   rxpro1438 2532   apta1525   pin2730 ad1563 2532 art3588 ajn2078
more wicked than himself, and they enter in and dwell there: and the last *state*
depro1565 art,nn444 pinm1096 pr/cd/an,aj5501   art3588 nu,ajn4413 ad3779   fm2071 2532   depro5026
of that man is   worse than the first. Even so shall it be also unto this
art,aj4190   art,nn1074
wicked generation.

The True Family of Jesus (Mark 3:31-35; Luke 8:19-21)

1161   ppro846 ad2089 pap2980   art3588   nn3793   2400   art,nn3384   2532 ppro846
46 While he yet talked to the people, behold, *his* mother and his
art,nn80   pipf2476   ad1854   pap2212   ainf2980   ppro846
brethren stood without, desiring to speak with him.
1161   idpro5100 aina2036   ppro846   2400   ppro4675 art,nn3384 2532 ppro4675   art,nn80
47 Then one said unto him, Behold, thy mother and thy brethren
pfi2476   ad1854   pap2212   ppro4671
stand without, desiring to speak with thee.
1161 art3588   aptp611   aina2036   art,apta2036   ppro846 inpro5101 pin2076 ppro3450
48 But he answered and said unto him*that*told him, Who is   my
pr/art,nn3384 2532 inpro5101 pin1526 ppro3450   pr/art,nn80
mother? and who are my brethren?
2532   apta1614   ppro848 art,nn5495 pre1909   ppro848   art,nn3101   aina2036
49 And he stretched forth his hand toward his disciples, and said,
2400 ppro3450 art,nn3384   2532 ppro3450   art,nn80
Behold my mother and my brethren!
1063   repro3748   asba4160 art3588 nn2307   ppro3450 art,nn3962 art3588   pre1722 an,nn3772
50 For whosoever shall do the will of my Father which is in heaven,
epn846   pin2076 ppro3450 pr/an,nn80   2532 pr/an,nn79 2532 pr/an,nn3384
the same is   my brother, and sister, and mother.

The Parable of the Sower (Mark 4:1-9; Luke 8:4-8)

13 (1161 pre1722)   depro1565   art,nn2250   apta1831   art,nn2424   pre575   art3588   nn3614   2532
The   same   day   went   Jesus   out   of   the   house,   and

ipf2521 pre3844 art3588   nn2281
sat   by   the   sea side.

2532   an,aj4183   an,nn3793   ainp4863   pre4314   ppro846   5620   ppro846
2 And   great   multitudes   were   gathered   together   unto   him,   so that   he

apta1684 pre1519   art,nn4143   aifp2521 2532 art3588 an,aj3956   nn3793   pipf2476 pre1909 art3588   nn123
went into   a   ship,   and   sat;   and   the   whole   multitude   stood   on   the   shore.

2532   aina2980   an,ajn4183   ppro846   pre1722   an,nn3850   pap3004   2400
3 And   he   spake   many   things   unto   them   in   parables,   saying,   Behold,   a

art,pap4687   aina1831   infg4687
sower   went   forth   to sow;

2532   ppro846   aie4687   repro3739/3303   aina4098 pre3844 art3588   nn3598   2532 art3588
4 And when   he   sowed,   some   *seeds*   fell   by   the   way   side,   and   the

nn4071   apta2064 2532   aina2719/ppro846
fowls came and devoured*them*up:

(1161) an,ajn243   aina4098   pre1909   art,ajn4075   ad3699   ipf2192   3756   an,aj4183   an,nn1093   2532
☞ 5   Some   fell   upon   stony   places,   where   they   had   not   much   earth: and

ad2112   aina1816   aid2192 3361   an,nn899   an,nn1093
forthwith they sprung up,   because they had   no   deepness   of earth:

1161   an,nn2246   apta393   ainp2739   2532   aid2192
6 And   when   the   sun   was   up,   they   were   scorched;   and because   they   had

3361 an,nn4491   ainp3583
no   root,   they   withered away.

1161   an,ajn243   aina4098   pre1909   art,nn173   2532   art3588   nn173   aina305   2532   aina638
7 And   some   fell   among   thorns;   and   the   thorns   sprung   up,   and   choked

ppro846
them:

1161   an,ajn243   aina4098   pre1909   art,aj2570   art,nn1093   2532   ipf1325   an,nn2590   repro3739/3303
8 But   other   fell   into   good   ground,   and   brought   forth   fruit,   some

nu,ajn1540 (1161)   repro3739 nu,ajn1835 (1161) repro3739   nu,ajn5144
a hundredfold,   some   sixtyfold,   some   thirtyfold.

art,pap2192   an,nn3775   pinf191   pim191
9 Who   hath   ears   to hear,   let him hear.

The Reason for Parables (Mark 4:10-12; Luke 8:9,10)

2532   art3588   nn3101   apta4334   aina2036   ppro846   pre,inpro1302   pin2980
☞ 10 And   the   disciples   came,   and   said   unto   him,   Why   speakest thou unto

ppro846 pre1722   an,nn3850
them   in   parables?

☞ **13:5–7** See note on Luke 8:13.
☞ **13:10–17** The key to understanding this difficult passage is found in Jesus' motive for using parables. Since the parables were given to explain spiritual truths, those who had already rejected Jesus did not have divinely enlightened minds with which to perceive these truths, and no amount of explanation
(continued on next page)

(1161) art3588   aptp611   aina2036   ppro846   3754   pfip1325   epn5213

11   He answered and said unto them, Because it is given unto you to

ainf1097 art3588 nn3466   art3588   nn932   art,nn3772 1161 depro1565   3756 pfip1325

know the mysteries of the kingdom of heaven, but to them it is not given.

1063   repro3748   pin2192   ppro846   fp1325   2532

12 For whosoever hath, to him shall be given, and he shall

fp4052   1161   repro3748   pin2192   3756   pre575   ppro846

have*more*abundance: but whosoever hath not, from him shall be

fp142   2532 repro3739   pin2192

taken away even that he hath.

pre1223/depro5124 pin2980   ppro846 pre1722 an,nn3850   3754   pap991 pin991 3756

13 Therefore speak I to them in parables: because they seeing see not;

2532   pap191   pin191 3756   3761   pin4920

and hearing they hear not, neither do they understand.

2532   pre1909 ppro846   pinp378 art3588   nn4394   an,nn2268   art,pap3004

14 And in them is fulfilled the prophecy of Isaiah, which saith, By

an,nn189   ft191   2532   efn3364   asba4920   2532   pap991   ft991 2532

hearing ye shall hear, and shall not understand; and seeing ye shall see, and

efn3364   asba1492

shall not perceive:

1063   depro5127   art,nn2992 art,nn2558   ainp3975   2532   art,nn3775

15 For   this   people's   heart is waxed gross, and *their* ears

aina191/ad917   2532 ppro848 art,nn3788   aina2576   3379

are*dull*of*hearing, and their eyes they have closed; lest*at*any*time they

asba1492   art,nn3778 2532 asba191   art,nn3775 2532   asba4920

should see with *their* eyes, and hear with *their* ears, and should understand

art,nn2588 2532   asba1994   2532   fm2390 ppro846

with *their* heart, and should be converted, and I should heal them.

(Is. 6:9,10)

1161   pr/an,aj3107   epn5216 art,nn3778 3754   pin991 2532 ppro5216 art,nn3775 3754   pin191

16 But blessed *are* your eyes, for they see: and your ears, for they hear.

1063   281   pin3004   ppro5213 3754 an,aj4183 an,nn4396 2532 an,ajn1342

17 For verily I say unto you, That many prophets and righteous *men* have

aina1937   ainf1492   repro3739   pin991 2532   3756 aina1492   2532   ainf191

desired to see *those things* which ye see, and have not seen *them*; and to hear

repro3739   pin191 2532   3756 aina191

those things which ye hear, and have not heard *them*.

(continued from previous page)
would make them understand (1 Cor. 1:27; 2:14, cf. Rom. 7:13). They could watch and hear Jesus with their physical eyes and ears, but they were not capable of understanding the truth in their heart because they had rejected Him (2 Cor. 4:3, 4). Verse twelve simply explains the principle that those who accept the true light they have been given will receive even more light, while those who turn away from the light will continue to be increasingly shrouded in darkness. The word "for" at the beginning of verse fifteen should be understood as having the same meaning as "because." In other words, the people do not hear and see because their heart is full of wickedness; consequently, they fail to understand the truth that has been given them. They are so opposed to God's message that they harden themselves against it lest they should happen to understand it and ask forgiveness of God. Once they reject Jesus, they also reject the possibility of understanding the parables that Jesus told (Is. 55:6–8).

The Parable of the Sower Explained (Mark 4:13-20; Luke 8:11-15)

aima191 epn5210   3767   art3588   nn3850   art3588   pap4687

18 Hear ye therefore the parable of the sower.

an,ajn3956   pap191   art3588   nn3056   art3588   nn932   2532   pap4920

19 When any one heareth the word of the kingdom, and understandeth *it*

3361   pinm2064   art3588   ajn4190   2532   pin726   art,pfpp4687

not, then cometh the wicked *one,* and catcheth away that*which*was*sown

pre1722 ppro846 art,nn2588 depro3778 pin2076   pr/art,aptp4687   pre3844 art3588   nn3598

in his heart. This is he*which*received*seed by the way side.

1161   art,aptp4687   pre1909   art,ajn4075   depro3778   pin2076

20 But he*that*received*the*seed into stony places, the same is

pr/art,pap191   art3588 nn3056   2532   ad2117 pre3326 an,nn5479   pap2983   ppro846

he*that*heareth the word, and anon with joy receiveth it;

1161   pin2192   3756 an,nn4491 pre1722 rxpro1438   235   pin2076/pr/an,aj4340   1161

21 Yet hath he not root in himself, but endureth*for*a*while: for when

an,nn2347   2228   an,nn1375   aptm1096   pre1223   art3588   nn3056   ad2117

tribulation or persecution ariseth because of the word, by*and*by he is

pinp4624

offended.

art,aptp4687/1161   pre1519   art3588 nn173(depro3778) pin2076   pr/art,pap191

22 He*also*that*received*seed among the thorns is he*that*heareth

art3588   3056   2532 art3588 nn3308   depro5127 art,nn165 2532 art3588   nn539   art,nn4149   pin4846

the word; and the care of this world, and the deceitfulness of riches, choke

art3588   nn3056 2532   pinm1096   pr/an,aj175

the word, and he becometh unfruitful.

1161   art,aptp4687   pre1909 art3588 aj2570   art,nn1093 pin2076   pr/art,pap191

23 But he*that*received*seed into the good ground is he*that*heareth

art3588   nn3056   2532   pr/pap4920   repro3739 1211   pin2592   2532   pin4160

the word, and understandeth *it*; which also beareth fruit, and bringeth forth,

art3588 (3303)   nu,ajn1540(1161)   art3588 nu,ajn1835(1161) art3588 nu,ajn5144

some a hundredfold some sixty, some thirty.

The Wheat and Tares

an,aj243   an,nn3850   aina3908   ppro846   pap3004   art3588   nn932

☞ 24 Another parable put*he*forth unto them, saying, The kingdom of

art,nn3772   ainp3666   an,nn444   apta4687 an,aj2570 an,nn4690 pre1722 ppro848 art,nn68

heaven is likened unto a man which sowed good seed in his field:

1161   art,nn444   aie2518   ppro846 art,ajn2190 aina2064   2532   aina4687   an,nn2215 pre303/an,ajn3319 art3588

25 But while men slept, his enemy came and sowed tares among the

nn4621   2532   aina565

wheat, and went*his*way.

1161   3753   art3588   nn5528   aina985   2532   aina4160   an,nn2590   ad5119

26 But when the blade was sprung up, and brought forth fruit, then

ainp5316   art3588 nn2215   2532

appeared the tares also.

☞ **13:24–30** Compare this parable with the parable of the fish (Matt. 13:47–50).

1161 art3588 ajn1401 art3588 nn3617 apta4334 aina2036 ppro846 an,nn2962
27 So the servants of the householder came and said unto him, Sir, didst

3780 aina4687 an,aj2570 an,nn4690 pre1722 popro4674 art,nn68 ad4159 3767 pin2192 art,nn2215
not thou sow good seed in thy field? from whence then hath it tares?

(1161) art3588 aina5346 ppro846 (an,nn444) an,aj2190 aina4160 depro5124 art3588 ajn1401 aina2036
28 He said unto them, An enemy hath done this. The servants said

ppro846 pin2309 3767 apta565 2532 asba4816/ppro846
unto him, Wilt thou then that we go and gather*them*up?

1161 art3588 aina5346 3756 3379 pap4816 art3588 nn2215 asba1610
29 But he said, Nay; lest while ye gather up the tares, ye root up also

art3588 nn4621 ad*260 ppro846
the wheat with them.

aima863 an,ajn297 pifm4885 ad3360 art3588 nn2326 2532 pre1722 art3588 nn2540 art,nn2326
30 Let both grow together until the harvest: and in the time of harvest

ft2046 art3588 nn2327 aima4816 nu,ajn4412 art3588 nn2215 2532 aima1210 ppro846
I will say to the reapers, Gather*ye*together first the tares, and bind them

pre1519 an,nn1197 aipr2618 ppro846 1161 aima4863 art3588 nn4621 pre1519 ppro3450 art,nn596
in bundles to burn them: but gather the wheat into my barn.

A Mustard Seed (Mark 4:30-32; Luke 13:18,19)

an,aj243 an,nn3850 aina3908 ppro846 pap3004 art3588 nn932
☞ 31 Another parable put*he*forth unto them, saying, The kingdom of

art,nn3772 pin2076 pr/an,ajn3664 an,nn2748 an,nn4615 repro3739 an,nn444 apta2983 2532 aina4687 pre1722
heaven is like to a grain of mustard seed, which a man took, and sowed in

ppro846 art,nn68
his field:

repro3739 3303 pin2076 pr/cd/an,aj3398 an,aj3956 art,nn4690 1161 ad3752 asbp837
32 Which indeed is the least of all seeds: but when it is grown, it

pin2076 pr/cd/an,aj3187 art,nn3001 2532 pinm1096 pr/an,nn1186 5620 art3588 nn4071 art3588
is the greatest among herbs, and becometh a tree, so that the birds of the

nn3772 ainf2064 2532 pinf2681 pre1722 art3588 nn2798 ppro846
air come and lodge in the branches thereof.

(Ps. 104:12, Ezek. 17:23; 31:6; Dan. 4:12,21)

Leaven (Luke 13:20,21)

an,aj243 an,nn3850 aina2980 ppro846 art3588 nn932 art,nn3772 pin2076
33 Another parable spake he unto them; The kingdom of heaven is

pr/an,ajn3664 an,nn2219 repro3739 an,nn1135 apta2983 2532 aina1470 pre1519 nu5140 an,nn4568 an,nn224
like unto leaven, which a woman took, and hid in three measures of meal,

ad2193 (repro3739) an,ajn3650 ainp2220
till the whole was leavened.

☞ **13:31, 32** The analogy of the mustard seed vividly contrasts the size of the seed with the great results it produces. In these verses, Jesus was explaining that even though at that time the influence of the kingdom of heaven seemed small and insignificant, it would eventually have far reaching effects just like the tree that grows from a mustard seed.

Parables Explained (Mark 4:33,34)

an,aj3956   depro5023   aina2980 art,nn2424   art3588   nn3793   pre1722   an,nn3850   2532

☞ 34 All these things spake Jesus unto the multitude in parables; and

ad*5565   an,nn3850   ipf2980   3756   ppro846

without a parable spake he not unto them:

3704   asbp4137   art,aptp4483   pre1223 art3588   nn4396

35 That it might be fulfilled which*was*spoken by the prophet,

pap3004   ft455   ppro3450 art,nn4750 pre1722 an,nn3850   fm2044

saying, I will open my mouth in parables; I will utter

pfpp2928   pre575   an,nn2602   an,nn2889

things*which*have*been*kept*secret from the foundation of the world.

(Ps. 78:2)

The Parable of the Wheat and Weeds Explained

ad5119 art,nn2424   apta863/art3588/nn3793   aina2064 pre1519 art3588   nn3614   2532

36 Then Jesus sent*the*multitude*away, and went into the house: and

ppro846 art,nn3101 aina4334   ppro846 pap3004   aima5419   ppro2254 art3588   nn3850   art3588

his disciples came unto him, saying, Declare unto us the parable of the

nn2215   art3588   nn68

tares of the field.

(1161) art3588   aptp611   aina2036   ppro846   art,pap4687   art3588 an,aj2570

37 He answered and said unto them, He*that*soweth the good

nn4690 pin2076 art3588 pr/nn5207 art,nn444

seed is the Son of man;

(1161) art3588   nn68 pin2076 art3588 pr/nn2889 art3588 an,aj2570 nn4690 (depro3778)pin1526 art3588 pr/nn5207   art3588

☞ 38 The field is the world; the good seed are the children of the

nn932   1161 art3588   nn2215 pin1526 art3588 pr/nn5207   art3588   ajn4190

kingdom; but the tares are the children of the wicked one;

(1161) art3588   ajn2190   art,apta4687 ppro846 pin2076 art3588 pr/ajn1228 art3588   nn2326   pin2076

39 The enemy that sowed them is the devil; the harvest is the

pr/an,nn4930   art3588 nn165 2532 art3588   nn2327   pin1526   pr/an,nn32

end of the world; and the reapers are the angels.

ad5618   3767   art3588 nn2215   pinp4816   2532   pinp2618   an,nn4442 ad3779

40 As therefore the tares are gathered and burned in the fire; so shall it

fm2071 pre1722 art3588 nn4930   depro5127 art,nn165

be in the end of this world.

art3588   nn5207   art,nn444   ft649   ppro846 art,nn32   2532   ft4816

41 The Son of man shall send forth his angels, and they shall gather

pre1537 ppro848 art,nn932   an,aj3956   art,nn4625 2532   art,pap4160   art,nn458

out of his kingdom all things that offend, and them*which*do iniquity;

2532   ft906 ppro846 pre1519 art,nn2575   art,nn4442 ad1563   fm2071 art,nn2805   2532

☞ 42 And shall cast them into a furnace of fire: there shall be wailing and

art,nn1030   art,nn3599

gnashing of teeth.

☞ **13:34, 35** See note on Matthew 13:10–17.
☞ **13:38, 42, 43** See note on Matthew 8:11, 12.

ad5119   art3588   ajn1342   ft1584   ad5613 art3588 nn2246 pre1722 art3588   nn932

43 Then shall the righteous shine forth as the sun in the kingdom of

ppro848 art,nn3962   art,pap2192 an,nn3775   pinf191   pim191

their Father. Who hath ears to hear, let him hear.   *(Dan. 12:3)*

A Buried Treasure

ad3825   art3588   nn932   art,nn3772 pin2076 pr/an,ajn3664   an,nn2344   pfpp2928 pre1722   art,nn68

44 Again, the kingdom of heaven is like unto treasure hid in a field;

repro3739   an,nn444   apta2147   aina2928   2532 pre575 art,nn5479 ppro846   pin5217 2532

the which when a man hath found, he hideth, and for joy thereof goeth and

pin4453 an,ajn3956 an,ajn3745   pin2192 2532   pin59   depro1565 art,nn68

selleth all that he hath, and buyeth that field.   *(Prov. 2:4)*

The Pearl of Great Price

ad3825   art3588   nn932   art,nn3772 pin2076 pr/an,aj3664   an,nn1713 an,nn444 pap2212

45 Again, the kingdom of heaven is like unto a merchant man, seeking

an,aj2570 an,nn3135

goodly pearls:

repro3739   apta2147 nu1520 an,nn3135   an,aj4186   apta565   pfi4097 an,aj3956

46 Who, when he had found one pearl of great price, went and sold all

an,ajn3745   ipf2192 2532 aina59 ppro846

that he had, and bought it.

A Large Net

ad3825   art3588   nn932   art,nn3772 pin2076 pr/an,ajn3664   an,nn4522   aptp906 pre1519

☞ 47 Again, the kingdom of heaven is like unto a net, that was cast into

art3588 nn2281 2532   apta4863   pre1537 an,aj3956 an,nn1085

the sea, and gathered of every kind:

repro3739   ad3753   ainp4137   apta307 pre1909 art,nn123 2532   apta2523

48 Which, when it was full, they drew to shore, and sat down, and

aina4816 art3588 ajn2570 pre1519 an,nn30   1161 aina906 art3588 ajn4550 ad1854

gathered the good into vessels, but cast the bad away.

ad3779   frm2071 pre1722 art3588 nn4930   art3588   nn165   art3588   nn32   fm1831

49 So shall it be at the end of the world: the angels shall come forth,

2532 ft873 art3588 ajn4190   pre1537 an,ajn3319 art3588 ajn1342

and sever the wicked from among the just,

☞ **13:47–50** This is similar to the parable of the wheat and the tares (Matt. 13:24–30). The separation of the wicked from among the righteous will ultimately be done by the angels, not by believers. Until that time, the true believers will co-exist, perhaps unknowingly, with unbelievers in the visible church here on earth.

2532   ft906   ppro846   pre1519 art3588   nn2575   art,nn4442   ad1563   fm2071   art,nn2805

50 And shall cast them into the furnace of fire: there shall be wailing

2532   art,nn1030   art,nn3559

and gnashing of teeth.

The Householder's Treasure

art,nn2424   pin3004   ppro846   aina4920   an,aj3956   depro5023

51 Jesus saith unto them, Have ye understood all these things? They

pin3004   ppro846   3483   an,nn2962

say unto him, Yea, Lord.

1161   aina2036 art3588   ppro846   pre1223/depro5124   an,aj3956   an,nn1122   aptp3100

52 Then said he unto them, Therefore every scribe *which is* instructed

pre1519 art3588   nn932   art,nn3772   pin2076   pr/an,aj3664   an,nn444   an,nn3617   repro3748

unto the kingdom of heaven is like unto a man *that is* a householder, which

pin1544   pre1537   ppro848   art,nn2344   an,aj2537 2532 an,ajn3820

bringeth forth out of his treasure *things* new and old.

Jesus Rejected at Nazareth (Mark 6:1-6; Luke 4:16-30)

2532   aom1096   ad3753   art,nn2424   aina5055   depro5025   art,nn3850

53 And it came*to*pass, *that* when Jesus had finished these parables, he

aina3332   ad1564

departed thence.

2532   apta2064   pre1519   ppro848   art,nn3968   ipf1321   ppro846   pre1722

54 And when he was come into his own country, he taught them in

ppro846   art,nn4864   5620   ppro846   pifm1605   2532   pinf3004   ad4159

their synagogue, insomuch that they were astonished, and said, Whence hath

depro5129   depro3778   art,nn4678   2532   art,nn1411

this *man* this wisdom, and *these* mighty works?

pin2076   3756   depro3778 art3588   nn5045   pr/art,nn5207   3780   ppro846   art,nn3384   pinp3004   3137

☞ 55 Is not this the carpenter's son? is not his mother called Mary?

2532   ppro846   art,nn80   an,nn2385   2532   an,nn2500   2532   an,nn4613   2532   an,nn2455

and his brethren, James, and Joses, and Simon, and Judas?

2532   ppro846   art,nn79   pin1526   3780   an,aj3956   pre4314   ppro2248   ad4159   3767   depro5129

56 And his sisters, are they not all with us? Whence then hath this

an,aj3956   depro5023

man all these things?

2532   ipf4624   pre1722 ppro846   1161   art,nn2424 aina2036   ppro846   an,nn4396

57 And they were offended in him. But Jesus said unto them, A prophet

pin2076   3756   pr/an,aj820   1508   pre1722   ppro848   art,nn3968   2532   pre1722   ppro848

is not without honor, save in his own country, and in his own

art,nn3614

house.

☞ **13:55** See the introduction to the Book of Jude.

2532   aina4160 3756 an,aj4183   an,nn1411   ad1563   pre1223   ppro846 art,nn570

58 And he did not many mighty works there because of their unbelief.

The Death of John the Baptist (Mark 6:14-29; Luke 9:7-9)

pre1722 depro1565 art,nn2540 an,nn2264 art3588   nn5076   aina191   art3588   nn189

14 At   that   time   Herod   the   tetrarch   heard   of   the   fame   of

an,nn2424

Jesus,

2532 aina2036   ppro848 art,nn3816   depro3778 pin2076 pr/an,nn2491 art3588   nn910   ppro846   ainp1453

2 And said unto his servants, This is   John the Baptist; he is risen

pre575 art3588 ajn3498   2532   pre1223/depro5124   art,nn1411   pin1754   pre1722

from the dead; and therefore mighty works do show forth themselves in

ppro846

him.

1063 art,nn2264   apta2902   art,nn2491   aina1210   ppro846   2532   aom5087   pre1722

3 For Herod had laid*hold*on John, and bound him, and put *him* in

an,nn5438   pre1223/an,nn2266   ppro846 art,nn80   an,nn5376 art,nn1135

prison for*Herodias'*sake, his brother Philip's wife.

1063 art,nn2491 ipf3004   ppro846   pin1832/3756   ppro4671   pinf2192 ppro846

4 For John said unto him, It is*not*lawful for thee to have her.

(Lev. 18:16)

2532   pap2309   ainf615/ppro846   ainp5399 art3588   nn3793

5 And when he would have put*him*to*death, he feared the multitude,

3754   ipf2192   ppro846 ad5613   an,nn4396

because they counted him as a prophet.

1161   art,nn2264   an,nn1077   ppmp71 art3588   nn2364   art,nn2266   aom3738

6 But when Herod's birthday was kept, the daughter of Herodias danced

pre1722/art,ajn3319   2532 aina700 art,nn2264

before them, and pleased Herod.

3606   aina3670   pre3326   an,nn3727   ainf1325 ppro846   repro2729/1437

7 Whereupon he promised with an oath to give her whatsoever she would

asbm154

ask.

1161   art3588   aptp4264   pre5259 ppro848 art,nn3384 pin5346 aima1325 ppro3427 ad5602

8 And she, being before instructed of her mother, said, Give me here

an,nn2491 art,nn910 art,nn2776 pre1909   an,nn4094

John Baptist's head in a charger.

2532 art3588   nn935   ainp3076   1161   pre1223/art3588/nn3727   2532

9 And the   king was sorry: nevertheless for*the*oath's*sake, and

art,ppmp4973   aina2753   aifp1325

them*which*sat*with*him*at*meat, he commanded *it* to be given *her*.

2532   apta3992   aina607   art,nn2491 pre1722 art3588   nn5438

10 And he sent, and beheaded John in   the prison.

2532 ppro846 art,nn2776   ainp5342   pre1909   an,nn4094   2532 ainp1325   art3588   nn2877

11 And his head was brought in a charger, and given to the damsel:

2532   aina5342   ppro846 art,nn3384

and she brought *it* to her mother.

2532   ppro846   art,nn3101   apta4334   aina142   art3588   nn4983   2532   aina2290   ppro846   2532
12 And his disciples came, and took up the body, and buried it, and

apta2064   aina518 art,nn2424
went and told Jesus.

Jesus Feeds the Five Thousand (Mark 6:30-44; Luke 9:10-17; John 6:1-14)

2532   art,nn2424   apta191   aina402   ad1564   pre1722 an,nn4143 pre1519   an,aj2048
13 When Jesus heard *of it,* he departed thence by ship into a desert

an,nn5117 pre2596/an,ajn2398 2532   art3588   nn3793   apta191   aina190   ppro846
place apart: and when the people had heard *thereof,* they followed him

an,ajn3979   pre575   art3588   nn4172
on foot out of the cities.

2532   art,nn2424   apta1831   aina1492   an,aj4183   an,nn3793   2532
14 And Jesus went forth, and saw a great multitude, and was

ainp4697   pre1909   ppro846 2532   aina2323   pro846 art,ajn732
moved*with*compassion toward them, and he healed their sick.

1161   aptm1096   an,nn3798 ppro846 art,nn3101   aina4334   ppro846 pap3004
15 And when it was evening, his disciples came to him, saying, This

pin2076   pr/an,aj2048 art,nn5117 2532 art3588 nn5610   ad2235 aina3928   aima630/art3588/nn3793   2443
is a desert place, and the time is now past; send* the*multitude*away, that

apta565 pre1519 art3588   nn2968   2532 asba59   rxpro1438   an,nn1033
they may go into the villages, and buy themselves victuals.

1161 art,nn2424 aina2036   ppro846   pin2192/an,nn5532 3756   ainf565   aima1325 epn5210 ppro846
16 But Jesus said unto them, They need not depart; give ye them to

ainf5315
eat.

1161   art3588   pin3004   ppro846   pin2192(3756) ad5602   1508 nu4002 an,nn740 2532 nu1417
17 And they say unto him, We have here but five loaves, and two

an,nn2486
fishes.

(1161) art3588 aina2036 aima5342 ppro846   ad5602   ppro3427
18 He said, Bring them hither to me.

2532   apta2753   art3588   nn3793   aifp347   pre1909 art3588   nn5528   2532 apta2983
19 And he commanded the multitude to sit down on the grass, and took

art3588 nu4002   nn740   2532 art3588 nu1417   nn2486   apta308   pre1519 art,nn3772   aina2127
the five loaves, and the two fishes, and looking up to heaven, he blessed,

2532   apta2806   2532 aina1325 art3588   nn740   art,nn3101 1161 art3588 nn3101   art3588
and broke, and gave the loaves to *his* disciples, and the disciples to the

nn3793
multitude.

2532   an,ajn3956 aina5315 2532   ainp5526   2532   aina142   art3588
20 And they did all eat, and were filled: and they took up of the

nn2801   art,pap4052   nu1427 an,nn2894 an,aj4134
fragments that remained twelve baskets full.

1161   art,pap2068   ipf2258 ad5616   nu4000   an,nn435 ad*5565   an,nn1135
21 And they*that*had*eaten were about five thousand men, beside women

2532   an,nn3813
and children.

Walking on Water (Mark 6:45-52; John 6:16-21)

2532   ad2112   art,nn2424   aina315   ppro848   art,nn3101   ainf1684 pre1519   art,nn4143

22 And straightway Jesus constrained his disciples to get into a ship,

2532   pinf4254   ppro846   pre1519   art3588   ad4008   ad2193/repro3739

and   to   go   before   him   unto   the   other   side,   while   he

asba630/art3588/nn3793

sent*the*multitudes*away.

2532   apta630/art3588/nn3793   aina305   pre1519

23 And when he had sent*the*multitudes*away, he went up into a

an,nn3735   pre2596/an,ajn2398   aifm4336   1161   an,nn3798   aptm1096   ipf2258   ad1563

mountain   apart   to pray: and when the evening was come, he was there

pr/an,aj3441

alone.

1161   art3588   nn4143   ipf2258   ad2235   an,ajn3319   art3588   nn2281   ppmp928   pre5259   art,nn2949   1063

24 But the ship was now in the midst of the sea, tossed with waves: for

art3588   nn417   ipf2258   pr/an,aj1727

the wind was contrary.

1161   nu,aj5067   an,nn5438   art3588   nn3571   art,nn2424   aina565   pre4314   ppro846   pap4043

25 And in the fourth watch of the night Jesus went unto them, walking

pre1909 art3588 nn2281

on the sea.

2532   art3588   nn3101   apta1492 ppro846   pap4043   pre1909 art3588   nn2281

26 And when the disciples saw him walking on the sea, they were

ainp5015   pap3004   pin2076   pr/an,nn5326 2532   aina2896   pre575 art,nn5401

troubled, saying, It is a spirit; and they cried out for fear.

1161   ad2112   art,nn2424   aina2980   ppro846   pap3004   pim2293

27 But straightway Jesus spake unto them, saying, Be*of*good*cheer;

pin1510 epn1473   pim5399/3361

it is I; be*not*afraid.

1161   art,nn4074   aptp611   ppro846   aina2036   an,nn2962   1487   pin1488   pr/epn4771   aima2753   ppro3165

28 And Peter answered him and said, Lord, if it be thou, bid   me

ainf2064   pre4314 ppro4571 pre1909 art3588   nn5204

come unto thee on the water.

1161   art3588   aina2036   aima2064   2532   art,nn4074   apta2597   pre575   art3588   nn4143

29 And he said, Come. And when Peter was come down out of the ship,

aina4043   pre1909 art3588   nn5204   ainf2064   pre4314 art,nn2424

he walked on the water, to go to Jesus.

1161   pap991 art3588   nn417   an,aj2478   ainp5399   2532   aptm756

30 But when he saw the wind boisterous, he was afraid; and beginning to

pifm2670   aina2896   pap3004   an,nn2962   aima4982 ppro3165

sink, he cried, saying, Lord, save me.

1161   ad2112   art,nn2424   apta1614   art,nn5495   aom1949   ppro846   2532

31 And immediately Jesus stretched forth *his* hand, and caught him, and

pin3004   ppro846   an,ajn3640   pre1519/inpro5101   aina1365

said unto him, O thou*of*little*faith, wherefore didst thou doubt?

2532   ppro846   apta1684 pre1519 art3588 nn4143 art3588   nn417   aina2869

32 And when they were come into the ship, the wind ceased.

1161   art3588   pre1722 art3588 nn4143 apta2064   aina4352   ppro846   pap3004

33 Then they that were in the ship came and worshiped him, saying,

ad230   pin1488   pr/an,nn5207   an,nn2316

Of*a*truth thou art the Son of God.

Jesus Heals the Sick at Gennesaret (Mark 6:53-56)

2532   apta1276   aina2064   pre1519   art3588   nn1093

34 And when they were gone over, they came into the land of
1082

Gennesaret.

2532   art3588   nn435   depro1565 art,nn5117   apta1921   ppro846   aina649

35 And when the men of that place had knowledge of him, they sent out
pre1519   an,aj3650   depro1565   art,nn4066   2532   aina4374   ppro846   an,aj3956

into all that country*round*about, and brought unto him all
art,pap2192/ad2560

that*were*diseased;

2532   ipf3870   ppro846   2443   an,ajn3440   asbm680   art3588   nn2899   ppro846

☞ 36 And besought him that they might only touch the hem of his
art,nn2440   2532   an,ajn3745   aom680   ainp1295

garment: and as*many*as touched were made*perfectly*whole.

God's Command Or Man's Tradition? (Mark 7:1-23)

ad5119   pinm4334   art,nn2424   art,nn1122   2532   an,nn5330   art3588   pre575   an,nn2414

15 Then came to Jesus scribes and Pharisees, which were of Jerusalem,
pap3004

saying,

pre,inpro1302   ppro4675   art,nn3101   pin3845   art3588   nn3862   art3588   ajn4245   1063

2 Why do thy disciples transgress the tradition of the elders? for they
pinm3538 3756 ppro848 art,nn5495   ad3752   psa2068   an,nn740

wash not their hands when they eat bread.

1161   art3588   aptp611   aina2036   ppro846   pre,inpro1302   epn5210   2532   pin3845

3 But he answered and said unto them, Why do ye also transgress
art3588   nn1785   art,nn2316 pre1223 ppro5216   art,nn3862

the commandment of God by your tradition?

1063   art,nn2316   aom1781   pap3004   pin5091   ppro4675 art,nn3962   2532   art,nn3384   2532

4 For God commanded, saying, Honor thy father and mother: and,
art,pap2551   an,nn3962 2228   an,nn3384   pim5053   an,nn2288

He*that*curseth father or mother, let him die the death.

(Ex. 20:12; Deut. 5:16; Ex. 21:17; Lev. 20:9)

1161   epn5210 pin3004   repro3739/302   asba2036   art,nn3962 2228   art,nn3384

5 But ye say, Whosoever shall say to *his* father or *his* mother, *It is* a
an,nn1435   repro3739/1437   asbp5623   pre1537 ppro1700

gift, by whatsoever thou mightest be profited by me;

2532   asba5091 efn3364 ppro848 art,nn3962 2228 ppro848   art,nn3384   2532

6 And honor not his father or his mother, *he shall be free.* Thus have ye
aina208/art3588/nn1785/art,nn2316   pre1223 ppro5216   art,nn3862

made*the*commandment*of*God*of*none*effect by your tradition.

☞ **14:36** See note on Philippians 2:6–8.

an,nn5273   ad2573   an,nn2268   aina4395   pre4012 ppro5216 pap3004

7 *Ye* hypocrites, well did Isaiah prophesy of you, saying,

depro3778   art,nn2992   pin1448   ppro3427   ppro848   art,nn4750   2532   pin5091

8 This people draweth nigh unto me with their mouth, and honoreth

ppro3165   art,nn5491 1161 ppro846 art,nn2588 pin568 ad4206 pre575 ppro1700

me with *their* lips; but their heart is far from me.

1161   ad3155   pinm4576   ppro3165   pap1321   an,nn1319

9 But in vain they do worship me, teaching *for* doctrines the

an,nn1778   an,nn444

commandments of men.   *(Is. 29:13 [Sept.])*

2532   aptm4341   art3588   nn3793   aina2036   ppro846   pim191   2532

10 And he called the multitude, and said unto them, Hear, and

pim4920

understand:

3756   art,ppmp1525   pre1519   art3588   nn4750   pin2840   art,nn444   235

11 Not that*which*goeth into the mouth defileth a man; but

art,ppmp1607   pre1537   art3588   nn4750   depro5124   pin2840   art,nn444

that*which*cometh out of the mouth, this defileth a man.

ad5119   apta4334   ppro846   art,nn3101   aina2036   ppro846   pin1492   3754   art3588

12 Then came his disciples, and said unto him, Knowest thou that the

nn5330   ainp4624   apta191   art,nn3056

Pharisees were offended, after they heard this saying?

1161   art3588   aptp611   aina2036   an,aj3956   an,nn5451 repro3739 ppro3450   art,aj3770   art,nn3962

13 But he answered and said, Every plant, which my heavenly Father

3756   aina5452   fp1610

hath not planted, shall be rooted up.

aima863/ppro846   pin1526 an,aj5185 pr/an,nn3595   an,aj5185 1161 1437   an,aj5185

14 Let*them*alone: they be blind leaders of the blind. And if the blind

psa3594   an,ajn5185 an,ajn297   fm4098 pre1519   an,nn999

lead the blind, both shall fall into the ditch.

1161   aptp611   art,nn4074   aina2036   ppro846   aima5419   ppro2254 depro5026

15 Then answered Peter and said unto him, Declare unto us this

art,nn3850

parable.

1161   art,nn2424 aina2036 pin2075 epn5210 2532   ad188   pr/an,aj801

16 And Jesus said, Are ye also yet without understanding?

ad3768   pin3539   3754   an,aj3956   art,ppmp1531   pre1519   art3588

17 Do*not*ye*yet understand, that whatsoever entereth in at the

nn4750   pin5562 pre1519 art3588   nn2836   2532   pinp1544   pre1519   an,nn856

mouth goeth into the belly, and is cast out into the draught?

1161   art,ppmp1607   pre1537 art3588   nn4750   pinm1831   pre1537 art3588

18 But those*things*which*proceed out of the mouth come forth from the

nn2588   depro2548   pin2840 art3588   nn444

heart; and they defile the man.

1063   pre1537   art3588   nn2588   pinm1831   an,aj4190   an,nn1261   an,nn5408   an,nn3430

19 For out of the heart proceed evil thoughts, murders, adulteries,

an,nn4202   an,nn2829   an,nn5577   an,nn988

fornications, thefts, false witness, blasphemies:

depro5023   pin2076   pr/art,pap2840   art,nn444 1161   ainf5315   an,aj449

20 These are *the things* which defile a man: but to eat with unwashen

an,nn5495   pin2840   3756   art,nn444

hands defileth not a man.

The Faith of a Gentile Woman (Mark 7:24-30)

21 Then Jesus went thence, and departed into the coasts of Tyre and Sidon.

22 And, behold, a woman of Canaan came out of the same coasts, and cried unto him, saying, Have mercy on me, O Lord, *thou* son of David; my daughter is grievously vexed*with*a*devil.

23 But he answered her not a word. And his disciples came and besought him, saying, Send*her*away; for she crieth after us.

24 But he answered and said, I am not sent but unto the lost sheep of the house of Israel.

25 Then came she and worshiped him, saying, Lord, help me.

26 But he answered and said, It is not meet to take the children's bread, and to cast *it* to dogs.

27 And she said, Truth, Lord: yet the dogs eat of the crumbs which fall from their masters' table.

28 Then Jesus answered and said unto her, O woman, great *is* thy faith: be it unto thee even as thou wilt. And her daughter was made whole from that very hour.

Jesus Heals Many

29 And Jesus departed from thence, and came nigh unto the sea of Galilee; and went up into a mountain, and sat down there.

30 And great multitudes came unto him, having with them *those that were* lame, blind, dumb, maimed, and many others, and cast*them*down at Jesus' feet; and he healed them:

5620   art3588   nn3793   ainf2296   pap991   an,ajn2974

31 Insomuch that the multitude wondered, when they saw the dumb to

pap2980   an,ajn2948   an,aj5199   an,ajn5560   pap4043   2532   an,ajn5185   pap991   2532

speak, the maimed to be whole, the lame to walk, and the blind to see: and

aina1392   art3588 nn2316   2474

they glorified the God of Israel.

Jesus Feeds Four Thousand (Mark 8:1-10)

1161   art,nn2424 aptm4341 ppro848 art,nn3101   aina2036   pinm4697

32 Then Jesus called his disciples *unto him,* and said, I have compassion

pre1909 art1388   nn3793   3754   pin4357   ppro3427 ad2235 nu5140 an,nn2250 2532 pin2192

on the multitude, because they continue with me now three days, and have

inpro5101/3756   asba5315 2532   pin2309 3756   ainf630/ppro846   an,aj3523   3379   asbp1590 pre1722 art3588

nothing to eat: and I will not send*them*away fasting, lest they faint in the

nn3598

way.

2532   ppro846   art,nn3101   pin3004   ppro846   ad4159   ppro2254   an,aj5118

33 And his disciples say unto him, Whence should we have so much

an,nn740 pre1722   an,nn2047   5620   ainf5526 an,aj5118   an,nn3793

bread in the wilderness, as to fill so great a multitude?

2532 art,nn2424 pin3004   ppro846   an,aj4214   an,nn740 pin2192   1161   art3588 aina2036

34 And Jesus saith unto them, How many loaves have ye? And they said,

nu,ajn2033   2532   an,aj3641   an,nn2485

Seven, and a few little fishes.

2532   aina2753   art3588   nn3793   ainf377   pre1909 art3588   nn1093

35 And he commanded the multitude to sit down on the ground.

2532   apta2983 art3588   nu2033   nn740   2532 art3588   nn2486   2532   apta2168

36 And he took the seven loaves and the fishes, and gave thanks, and

aina2806   2532 aina1325   ppro848   art,nn3101   1161 art3588   nn3101   art3588   nn3793

broke *them,* and gave to his disciples, and the disciples to the multitude.

2532   an,ajn3956 aina5315 2532   ainp5526   2532   aina142   art3588

37 And they did all eat, and were filled: and they took up of the

nn2801   art,pap4052   nu2033   an,nn4711 an,aj4134

broken *meat* that*was*left seven baskets full.

1161   art,pap2068   ipf2258   nu5070   pr/an,nn435   ad*5565   an,nn1135   2532

38 And they*that*did*eat were four thousand men, beside women and

an,nn3813

children.

2532   apta630   art3588   nn3793   aina1684/pre1519/art,nn4143 2532 aina2064 pre1519 art3588

39 And he sent away the multitude, and took ship, and came into the

nn3725   3093

coasts of Magdala.

Understanding the Times (Mark 8:11-13; Luke 12:54-56)

(2532) art3588   nn5330   2532   an,nn4523   apta4334   pap3985

16

The Pharisees also with the Sadducees came, and tempting

aina1906 ppro846   ainf1925 ppro846   an,nn4592 pre1537 art,nn3772

desired him that he would show them a sign from heaven.

_{(1161) art3588}   _{aptp611}   _{aina2036}   _{ppro846}   _{aptm1096}   _{an,nn3798}   _{pin3004}

2   He answered and said unto them, When it is evening, ye say,

_{an,nn2105}   _{1063 art3588 nn3772}   _{pin4449}

It will be fair weather: for the sky is red.

₂₅₃₂   _{ad4404}   _{an,nn5494}   _{ad4594}   _{1063 art3588 nn3722}   _{pin4449}

3 And in*the*morning, *It will be* foul weather today: for the sky is red

₂₅₃₂   _{pap4768}   _{an,nn5273}   _{pin1097}   _{pinf1252}   _{art3588(3303) nn4383}   _{art3588 nn3772} _{1161 pinm1410}

and lowering. O *ye* hypocrites, ye can discern   the   face of the sky; but can

₃₇₅₆   _{art3588 nn4592}   _{art3588}   _{nn2540}

ye not *discern* the signs of the times?

_{an,aj4190}   ₂₅₃₂   _{an,nn3428}   _{an,nn1074}   _{pin1934}   _{an,nn4592}   ₂₅₃₂

4 A wicked and adulterous generation seeketh after a sign; and there shall

_{3756 an,nn4592}   _{fp1325}   _{ppro846} _{1508 art3588 nn4592}   _{art3588}   _{nn4396}   _{an,nn2495}   ₂₅₃₂   _{apta2641}

no sign be given unto it,   but the sign of the prophet Jonah. And he left

_{ppro846}   _{aina565}

them, and departed.   *(Jon. 1:17)*

Pharisees and Sadducees, and Their Influence (Mark 8:14-21)

₂₅₃₂   _{ppro846}   _{art,nn3101}   _{apta2064} _{pre1519 art3588}   _{ad4008}

5 And when his disciples were come to   the other side, they had

_{aom1950}   _{ainf2983}   _{an,nn740}

forgotten to take bread.

₁₁₆₁   _{art,nn2424 aina2036}   _{ppro846}   _{pim3708}   ₂₅₃₂   _{pim4337}   _{pre575 art3588}   _{nn2219}

6 Then Jesus said unto them, Take heed and beware of the leaven of

_{art3588}   _{nn5330}   ₂₅₃₂   _{an,nn4523}

the Pharisees and of the Sadducees.

₁₁₆₁   _{art3588}   _{ipf1260}   _{pref722}   _{rxpro1438}   _{pap3004}   ₃₇₅₄

7 And they reasoned among themselves, saying, *It is* because we have

_{aina2983} ₃₇₅₆ _{an,nn740}

taken no bread.

₁₁₆₁   _{art,nn2424}   _{apta1097}   _{aina2036}   _{ppro846}   _{an,ajn3640}

8 *Which* when Jesus perceived, he said unto them, O ye*of*little*faith,

_{inpro5101} _{pinm1260}   _{pre1722}   _{rxpro1438}   ₃₇₅₄   _{aina2983}   ₃₇₅₆ _{an,nn740}

why reason ye among yourselves, because ye have brought no bread?

_{ad3768}   _{pin3539}   ₃₇₆₁   _{pin3421}   _{art3588} _{nu4002}   _{nn740}   _{art3588}

9 Do ye not yet understand, neither remember the five loaves of the

_{nu,ajn4000}   ₂₅₃₂   _{an,aj4214}   _{an,nn2894}   _{aina2983}

five thousand, and how many baskets ye took up?

₃₇₆₁   _{art3588} _{nu2033}   _{nn740}   _{art3588}   _{nu,ajn5070}   ₂₅₃₂   _{an,aj4214}   _{an,nn4711}

10 Neither the seven loaves of the four thousand, and how many baskets

_{aina2983}

ye took up?

_{ad4459}   ₃₇₅₆   _{pin3539}   ₃₇₅₄   _{aina2036}   ₃₇₅₆   _{ppro5213}

11 How is it that ye do not understand that I spake *it* not to you

_{pre4012}   _{an,nn740}   _{pinf4337}   _{pre575 art3588}   _{nn2219}   _{art3588}   _{nn5330}   ₂₅₃₂

concerning bread, that ye should beware of the leaven of the Pharisees and

_{an,nn4523}

of the Sadducees?

ad5119   aina4920   3754   aina2036   3756   pinf4337   pre575 art3588
12 Then understood they how that he bade *them* not beware of the

nn2219   nn740   235 pre575 art3588   nn1322   art3588   nn5330   2532   an,nn4523
leaven of bread, but of the doctrine of the Pharisees and of the Sadducees.

Jesus Is the Messiah (Mark 8:27-30; Luke 9:18-21)

1161   art,nn2424 apta2064 pre1519 art3588   nn3313   an,nn2542   art,nn5376   ipf2065 ppro848
13 When Jesus came into the coasts of Caesarea Philippi, he asked his

art,nn3101 pap3004 inpro5101 art,nn444 pin3004   ppro3165 art3588 nn5207   art,nn44 pinf1511
disciples, saying, Whom do men say that   I   the Son of man am?

1161   art3588   aina2036   art3588   (3303)   an,nn2491 art3588   nn910(1161)   an,ajn243 an,nn2243
14 And they said, Some *say that thou art* John the Baptist: some, Elijah;

1161 an,ajn2087   an,nn2408   2228 nu1520   art3588   nn4396
and others, Jeremias, or one of the prophets.

pin3004   ppro846   1161   inpro5101 pin3004 epn5210   ppro3165 pinf1511
15 He saith unto them, But whom say ye that   I   am?

1161   an,nn4613 an,n4074 aptp611   aina2036 epn4771 pin1488 art3588   pr/nn5547   art3588 pr/nn5207
16 And Simon Peter answered and said, Thou art the Christ, the Son of

art,pap2198   art,nn2316
the living God.

2532   art,nn2424   aptp611   aina2036   ppro846   pr/an,aj3107   pin1488   an,nn4613
17 And Jesus answered and said unto him, Blessed art thou, Simon

an,nn920   3754 an,nn4561 2532   an,nn129   3756   aina601   ppro4671   235 ppro3450 art,nn3962
Bar–jona: for flesh and blood hath not revealed *it* unto thee, but my Father

art3588   pre1722   art,nn3772
which is in heaven.

1161   epn2504/pin3004   ppro4671   3754   epn4771 pin1488 pr/an,nn4074 2532   pre1909 depro5026 art,nn4073
☞ 18 And I*say*also unto thee, That thou art Peter, and upon this rock I

ft3618 ppro3450 art,nn1577   2532   an,nn4439   an,nn86   3756   ft2729   ppro846
will build my church; and the gates of hell shall not prevail against it.

2532   ft1325   ppro4671 art3588   nn2807   art3588   nn932   art,nn3772   2532
19 And I will give unto thee the keys of the kingdom of heaven: and

---

☞ **16:18, 19** A more accurate translation of verse nineteen from the Greek is, "And I will give thee the keys of the kingdom of the heavens. And whatever thou shalt bind on the earth shall be as having been bound in the heavens; and whatever thou shalt loose on the earth shall be as having been loosed in the heavens." Before these verses can be correctly understood, a distinction must be made between the "church" (v. 18) and the kingdom of the heavens (v. 19). The Church is representative of the body of believers here on earth while the kingdom of the heavens is made up of both the earthly and heavenly realms. The teaching here is that those things which are conclusively decided by God in the kingdom of heaven, having been so decided upon, are emulated by the Church on earth. The Church is made up of true believers who acknowledge the deity of Jesus Christ as Peter did. Christ is the "Rock" upon which the Church is built (1 Cor. 3:11). There is no reference made here to the binding or loosing of persons. One can note that this speaks exclusively of things because of the neuter gender of the indefinite pronouns *hó* (3739), "whatever," in verse nineteen, and *hósa* (3745), "whatever," in Matthew 18:18. Believers can never make conclusive decisions about things, but can only confirm those decisions which have already been made by God Himself as conclusive in the general context of His kingdom both on earth and in heaven. The two verbs, *dedeménon* (from *déō* [1210]) and *leluménon* (from *lúō* [3089]), are both perfect passive participles which should have been translated respectively as "having been bound" and "having been loosed" already in the heavens.

repro3739/1437   asba1210   pre1909   art,nn1093   fm2071   pfpp1210   pre1722   art,nn3772   2532

whatsoever thou shalt bind on earth shall be bound in heaven: and

repro3739/1437   asba3089   pre1909   art,nn1093   fm2071   pfpp3089   pre1722   art,nn3772

whatsoever thou shalt loose on earth shall be loosed in heaven.

       ad5119   aom1291   ppro848   art,nn3101   2443   asba2036   an,ajn3367   3752   epn846

20 Then charged he his disciples that they should tell no man that he

pin2076 pr/an,nn2424 art3588   pr/nn5547

was Jesus the Christ.

Jesus Must Die (Mark 8:31—9:1; Luke 9:22-27)

      pre575   ad5119   aom756   art,nn2424   pinf1166   ppro848   art,nn3101

21 From that*time*forth began Jesus to show unto his disciples, how

3754   ppro846 pin1163 ainfp565 pre1519   an,nn2414   2532   aifp3958   an,ajn4183   pre575 art3588   ajn4245   2532

that he must go unto Jerusalem, and suffer many things of the elders and

   an,nn749   2532   an,nn1122   2532   aifp615   2532   aifp1453   art3588 nu,aj5154 nn2250

chief priests and scribes, and be killed, and be raised again the third day.

      2532   art,nn4074 aptm4355 ppro846   aom756   pinf2008   ppro846 pap3004   an,aj2436

22 Then Peter took him, and began to rebuke him, saying, Be*it*far from

ppro4671 an,nn2962 depro5124   efn3364 fm2071   ppro4671

thee, Lord: this shall not be unto thee.

     1161   art3588   aptp4762   aina2036   art,nn4074   aima5217   ad*3694   ppro3450   an,nn4567

23 But he turned, and said unto Peter, Get thee behind me, Satan: thou

pin1488   pr/an,nn4625   ppro3450 3754   pin5426   3756   art3588   art,nn2316   235

art an offense unto me: for thou savorest not the things that be of God, but

art3588   art,nn444

those that be of men.

      ad5119   aina2036 art,nn2424   ppro848   art,nn3101   idpro1536   pin2309 ainf2064 ad*3694 ppro3450

24 Then said Jesus unto his disciples, If any *man* will come after me, let

aipm533   rxpro1438   2532   aima142   ppro848 art,nn4716   2532   pim190   ppro3427

him deny himself, and take up his cross, and follow me.

      1063   repro3739/302   psa2309 ainf4982 ppro848 art,nn5590   ft622   ppro846   1161   repro3739/302

25 For whosoever will save his life shall lose it: and whosoever will

asba622 ppro848 art,nn5590   ad*1752/ppro1700   ft2147 ppro846

lose his life for*my*sake shall find it.

     1063   inpro5101   an,nn444   pinm5623   1437   asba2770 art3588   an,aj3650   nn2889   2532   asbp2210

26 For what is a man profited, if he shall gain the whole world, and lose

ppro848   art,nn5590 2228 inpro5101   an,nn444 ft1325   an,nn465   ppro848 art,nn5590

his own soul? or what shall a man give in exchange for his soul?

     1063   art3588   nn5207   art,nn444 pin3195 pifm2064 pre1722 art3588   nn1391   ppro848   art,nn3962   pre3326 ppro848

27 For the Son of man shall come in the glory of his Father with his

art,nn32   2532   ad5119   ft591   an,ajn1538   pre2596   ppro848 art,nn4234

angels; and then he shall reward every man according to his works.

                                 (Ps. 28:1; 62:12; Prov. 24:12; Jer. 17:10)

     281   pin3004   ppro5213   pin1526 idpro5100   art,pfp2476   ad5602   repro3748   efn3664

28 Verily I say unto you, There be some standing here, which shall not

fm1089   an,nn2288 ad2193/302   asba1492 art3588 nn5207   art,nn444 ppmp2064   pre1722 ppro848   art,nn932

taste of death, till they see the Son of man coming in his kingdom.

The Transfiguration (Mark 9:2-13; Luke 9:28-36)

17
2532 pre3326 nu1803 an,nn2250 art,nn2424 pin3880 art,nn4074 (2532) an,nn2385 2532 an,nn2491
And after six days Jesus taketh Peter, James, and John
ppro846 art,nn80 2532 pin399/ppro846 pre1519 an,aj5308 an,nn3735
his brother, and bringeth*them*up into a high mountain
pre2596/an,ajn2398
apart,

2532 ainp3339 ad*1715 ppro846 2532 ppro846 art,nn4383 aina2989 ad5613 art3588 nn2246
2 And was transfigured before them: and his face did shine as the sun,
1161 ppro846 art,nn2440 aom1096 pr/an,aj3022 ad5613 art3588 nn5457
and his raiment was white as the light.

2532 2400 ainp3700 ppro846 an,nn3475 2532 an,nn2243 pap4814 pre3326
3 And, behold, there appeared unto them Moses and Elijah talking with
ppro846
him.

1161 aptp611 art,nn4074 aina2036 art,nn2424 an,nn2962 pin2076 pr/an,aj2570 ppro2248
4 Then answered Peter, and said unto Jesus, Lord, it is good for us
pinf1511 ad5602 1487 pin2309 aosi4160 ad5602 nu5140 an,nn4633 nu,ajn3391 ppro4671
to be here: if thou wilt, let us make here three tabernacles; one for thee,
2532 nu,ajn3391 an,nn3475 2532 nu,ajn3391 an,nn2243
and one for Moses, and one for Elijah.

ppro846 ad2089 pap2980 2400 an,aj5460 an,nn3507 aina1982 ppro846 2532
5 While he yet spake, behold, a bright cloud overshadowed them: and
2400 an,nn5456 pre1537 art3588 nn3507 pap3004 depro3778 pin2076 ppro3450 art,aj27 pr/art,nn5207
behold a voice out of the cloud, which said, This is my beloved Son,
pre1722 repro3739 aina2106 pin191 epn846
in whom I am*well*pleased; hear ye him. _(Ps. 2:7; Deut. 18:15)_

2532 art3588 nn3101 apta191 aina4098 pre1909 ppro848 an,nn4383 2532
6 And when the disciples heard _it_, they fell on their face, and
ainp5399/ad4970
were*sore*afraid.

2532 art,nn2424 apta4334 aom680 ppro846 2532 aina2036 aipp1453 2532 pin5399/3361
7 And Jesus came and touched them, and said, Arise, and be*not*afraid.

1161 apta1869 ppro848 art,nn3788 aina1492 an,ajn3762 1508 art,nn2424
8 And when they had lifted up their eyes, they saw no man, save Jesus
an,aj3441
only.

2532 ppro846 pap2597 pre575 art3588 nn3735 art,nn2424 aom1781 ppro846 pap3004
9 And as they came down from the mountain, Jesus charged them, saying,
aosi2036 art3588 nn3705 an,aj3367 ad2193/302 art3588 nn5207 art,nn444 asba450 pre1537
Tell the vision to no man, until the Son of man be risen again from the
an,ajn3498
dead.

2532 ppro846 art,nn3101 aina1905 ppro846 pap3004 inpro5101 3767 pin3004 art3588 nn1122 3754
10 And his disciples asked him, saying, Why then say the scribes that
an,nn2243 pin1163 nu,aj4412 ainf2064
Elijah must first come? _(Mal. 4:5)_

1161 art,nn2424 aptp611 aina2036 ppro846 an,nn2243 3303 nu,aj4412 pinm2064
11 And Jesus answered and said unto them, Elijah truly shall first come,
2532 ft600 an,ajn3956
and restore all things. _(Mal. 4:6)_

1161   pin3004   ppro5213   3754   an,nn2243   aina2064   ad2235   2532   aina1921   ppro846

12 But I say unto you, That Elijah is come already, and they knew him

3756   235   aina4160 pre1722 ppro846   an,ajn3745   aina2309   ad3779   pin3195   2532   art3588

not, but have done unto him whatsoever they listed. Likewise shall also the

nn5207   art,nn444   pinf3958   pre5259   ppro846

Son of man suffer of them.

ad5119   art3588   nn3101   aina4920   3754   aina2036   ppro846   pre4012 an,nn2491 art3588

13 Then the disciples understood that he spake unto them of John the

nn910

Baptist.

Jesus Heals a Boy Possessed With a Demon (Mark 9:14-29; Luke 9:37-43)

2532   ppro846   apta2064   pre4314 art3588   nn3793   aina4334   ppro846

14 And when they were come to the multitude, there came to him a

an,nn444   pap1120   ppro846 2532   pap3004

certain man, kneeling down to him, and saying,

an,nn2962   aima1653   ppro3450 art,nn5207 1063   pinm4583   2532   ad2560   pin3958   3754

15 Lord, have mercy on my son: for he is lunatic, and sore vexed: for

ad4178   pin4098   pre1519 art3588   nn4442   2532   ad4178 pre1519 art3588   nn5204

ofttimes he falleth into the fire, and oft into the water.

2532   aina4374   ppro846   ppro4675   art,nn3101   2532   ainp1410 3756 ainf2323 ppro846

16 And I brought him to thy disciples, and they could not cure him.

1161   art,nn2424   aptp611   aina2036 5599   an,aj571   2532   pfpp1294   an,nn1074

17 Then Jesus answered and said, O faithless and perverse generation,

ad2193/ad4219   fm2071 pre3326 ppro5216 ad2193/ad4219   fm430   ppro5216 pim5342 ppro846   ad5602

how long shall I be with you? how long shall I suffer you? bring him hither to

ppro3427

me.   *(Deut. 32:5,20)*

2532   art,nn2424   aina2008   ppro846   2532 (art,nn1140)   aina1831   pre575   ppro846 2532 art3588

18 And Jesus rebuked the devil; and he departed out of him: and the

nn3816   ainp2323   pre575   depro1565   art,nn5610

child was cured from that very hour.

ad5119   apta4334 art3588   nn3101   art,nn2424 pre2596/an,ajn2398   aina2036 pre,inpro1302 ainp1410 3756

19 Then came the disciples to Jesus apart, and said, Why could not

epn2249   ainf1544/ppro846

we cast*him*out?

1161   art,nn2424 aina2036   ppro846   pre1223   ppro5216   art,nn570   1063   281   pin3004

20 And Jesus said unto them, Because of your unbelief: for verily I say

ppro5213 1437   psa2192 an,nn4102 ad5613   an,nn2748   an,nn4615   ft2046

unto you, If ye have faith as a grain of mustard seed, ye shall say unto

depro5129   art,nn3735   aipp3327   ad1782   ad1563   2532   fm3327   2532

this mountain, Remove hence to yonder place; and it shall remove; and

an,ajn3762   ft101   ppro5213

nothing shall be impossible unto you.

1161   depro5124 art,nn1085   pinm1607/3756   1508 pre1722 an,nn4335   2532   an,nn3521

21 Howbeit this kind goeth*not*out but by prayer and fasting.

Jesus Prophesies of His Death and Resurrection (Mark 9:30-32; Luke 9:43-45)

1161   ppro846 ppmp390 pre1722 art,nn1056 art,nn2424 aina2036   ppro846 art3588 nn5207

22 And while they abode in Galilee, Jesus said unto them, The Son of

art,nn444 pin3195   pip3860   pre1519   an,nn5495   an,nn444

man shall be betrayed into the hands of men:

2532   ft615 ppro846 2532 art3588 nu,aj5154 an,nn2250   fp1453

23 And they shall kill him, and the third day he shall be raised again.

2532   ainp3076/ad4970

And they were*exceeding*sorry.

Tax Money in the Mouth of a Fish

1161   ppro846   apta2064 pre1519   2584   art,pap2983   art,nn1323

24 And when they were come to Capernaum, they*that*received <u>tribute</u>

aina4334 art,nn4074 2532 aina2036   3756 ppro5216 art,nn1320 pin5055 art,nn1323

<u>money</u> came to Peter, and said, Doth not your master pay tribute?

(Ex. 30:13; 38:26)

pin3004   3483   2532   ad3753   aina1525 pre1519 art3588   nn3614 art,nn2424

25 He saith, Yes. And when he was come into the house, Jesus

aina4399   ppro846 pap3004 inpro5101 pin1380   ppro4671 an,nn4613 pre575 inpro5101   art3588   nn935

prevented him, saying, What thinkest thou, Simon? of whom do the kings of

art3588 nn1093 pin2983 an,nn5056 2228 an,nn2778 pre575   ppro848   art,nn5207 2228 pre575 art,ajn245

the earth take custom or tribute? of their own children, or of strangers?

art,nn4074 pin3004   ppro846 pre575 art,ajn245   art,nn2424 aina5346   ppro846   686   pin1526

26 Peter saith unto him, Of strangers. Jesus saith unto him, Then are

art3588   nn5207   pr/an,aj1658

the children free.

1161   3363   asba4624 ppro846 aptp4198   pre1519 art3588

27 Notwithstanding, lest we should offend them, go thou to the

nn2281   aima906 an,nn44 2532 aima142   an,nn2486 nu,ajn4413 art,apta305 2532

sea, and cast a hook, and take up the fish that first cometh up; and when

apta455   pro846 art,nn4750   ft2147   an,nn4715   depro1565 apta2983 2532

thou hast opened his mouth, thou shalt find a piece*of*money: that take, and

aima1325   ppro846 pre473 ppro1700 2532 ppro4675

give unto them for me and thee.

Humble Yourself as a Little Child (Mark 9:33-37; Luke 9:46-48)

pre1722   depro1565   art,nn5610 aina4334 art3588   nn3101   art,nn2424 pap3004 inpro5101 (686)

18 At the same time came the disciples unto Jesus, saying, Who

pin2076   pr/cd/an,ajn3187 pre1722 art3588   nn932   art,nn3772

is the greatest in the kingdom of heaven?

2532   art,nn2424 aptm4341   an,nn3813   2532   aina2476 ppro846 pre1722   an,ajn3319
2 And Jesus called a little child unto him, and set him in the midst of
pppro846
them,

2532   aina2036   281   pin3004   ppro5213   3362   asbp4762   2532   asbm1096
3 And said, Verily I say unto you, Except ye be converted, and become
ad5613   pr/art,nn3813   efn3364 asba1525 pre1519 art3588   nn932   art,nn3772
as little children, ye shall not enter into the kingdom of heaven.

repro3748   3767   asba5013   rxpro1438   ad5613 depro5124   art,nn3813
4 Whosoever therefore shall humble himself as this little child,
depro3778   pin2076 pr/cd/art,ajn3187 pre1722 art3588   nn932   art,nn3772
the same is greatest in the kingdom of heaven.

2532   repro3739/1437   asbm1209   nu1520 an,aj5108   an,nn3813   pre1909 ppro3450 art,nn3686   pinm1209
5 And whoso shall receive one such little child in my name receiveth
epn1691
me.

Stumblingblocks (Mark 9:42-48; Luke 17:1,2)

1161   repro3739/302   asba4624 nu1520   depro5130   art,ajn3398   art,pap4100   pre1519 ppro1691
6 But whoso shall offend one of these little ones which believe in me, it
pin4851   ppro846 2443   an,nn3458/an,aj3684   asbp2910   pre1909 ppro846 art,nn5137 2532
were better for him that a millstone were hanged about his neck, and *that* he
asbp2670   pre1722 art3588   nn3989   art3588 nn2281
were drowned in the depth of the sea.

3759   art3588   nn2889   pre575   art,nn4625   1063   pin2076/an,nn318
7 Woe unto the world because of offenses! for it must*needs*be that
art,nn4625   ainf2064   4133   3759   depro1565 art,nn444 pre1223 repro3739 art3588   nn4625   pinm2064
offenses come; but woe to that man by whom the offense cometh!

1161   1487 ppro4675 art,nn5495 2228   ppro4675 art,nn4228   pin4624   ppro4571   aima1581/ppro846   2532
8 Wherefore if thy hand or thy foot offend thee, cut*them*off, and
aima906   pre575   ppro4675   pin2076 pr/cd/an,ajn2570   ppro4671   ainf1525   pre1519 art,nn2222 an,ajn5560 2228
cast *them* from thee: it is better for thee to enter into life halt or
an,ajn2948   2228   pap2192 nu1417 an,nn5495 2228 nu1417 an,nn4228   aifp906 pre1519   art,aj166
maimed, rather than having two hands or two feet to be cast into everlasting
art,nn4442
fire.

2532   1487   ppro4675   art,nn3788   pin4624   ppro4571   aima1807/ppro846   2532   aima906
☞ 9 And if thine eye offend thee, pluck*it*out, and cast *it*
pre575 ppro4675   pin2076 pr/cd/an,ajn2570   ppro4671   ainf1525   pre1519 art,nn2222   an,ajn3442   2228
from thee: it is better for thee to enter into life with one eye, rather
pap2192   nu1417 an,nn3788   aifp906 pre1519 art,nn1067 art,nn4442
than having two eyes to be cast into hell fire.

☞ **18:9, 12** See note on Matthew 8:11, 12.

Parable of a Lost Sheep (Luke 15:3-7)

pim3708 aosi2706 3361 nu1520 depro5130 art,ajn3398 1063 pin3004

10 Take heed that ye despise not one of these little ones; for I say unto

ppro5213 3754 pre1722 an,nn3772 ppro846 art,nn32 pre1223/an,ajn3956 pin991 art3588 nn4383 ppro3450 art,nn3962

you, That in heaven their angels do always behold the face of my Father

art3588 pre1722 an,nn3772

which is in heaven.

1063 art3588 nn5207 art,nn444 aina2064 ainf4982 art,pfp622

11 For the Son of man is come to save that*which*was*lost.

inpro5101 pin1380 ppro5213 1437 idpro5100 an,nn444 asbm1096 nu1540 an,nn4263 2532 nu1520 pre1537 ppro846

☞ 12 How think ye? if a man have a hundred sheep, and one of them

asbp4105 3780 apta863 art3588 nu,ajn1768 aptp4198 pre1909 art3588

be gone astray, doth he not leave the ninety*and*nine, and goeth into the

nn3735 2532 pin2212 art,ppmp4105

mountains, and seeketh that*which*is*gone*astray?

2532 1437 asbm1096 ainf2147 ppro846 281 pin3004 ppro5213 (3754) pin5463

13 And if so be that he find it, verily I say unto you, he rejoiceth

cd/an,ajn3123 pre1909 ppro846 2228 pre1909 art3588 nu,ajn1768 art,pfpp4105/3361

more of that *sheep,* than of the ninety*and*nine which*went*not*astray.

ad3779 pin2076 3756 pr/an,nn2307 ad*1715 ppro5216 art,nn3962 art3588 pre1722 an,nn3772

14 Even so it is not the will of your Father which is in heaven,

2443 nu1520 depro5130 art,ajn3398 asbm622

that one of these little ones should perish.

When One Brother Sins Against Another (Luke 17:3)

1161 1437 ppro4675 art,nn80 asba264 pre1519 ppro4571 aima5217 2532

☞ 15 Moreover if thy brother shall trespass against thee, go and

aima1651/ppro846 ad*3342 ppro4675 2532 ppro846 an,aj3441 1437 asba191 ppro4675

tell*him*his*fault between thee and him alone: if he shall hear thee, thou hast

aina2770 ppro4675 art,nn80

gained thy brother.   *(Lev. 19:17)*

1161 1437 3361 asba191 aima3880 pre3326 ppro4675 nu,ajn1520 2228 nu,ajn1417 ad2089

16 But if he will not hear *thee, then* take with thee one or two more,

2243 pre1909 an,nn4720 nu1417 2228 nu5140 an,nn3144 an,aj3956 an,nn4487

that in the mouth of two or three witnesses every word may be

asbp2476

established.   *(Deut. 19:15)*

1161 1437 asba3878 ppro846 aima2036 art3588 nn1577 1161 1437

17 And if he shall neglect*to*hear them, tell *it* unto the church: but if

asba3878 art3588 nn1577 pim2077 ppro4671 ad5618 pr/art,ajn1482 2532

he neglect*to*hear the church, let him be unto thee as a heathen man and a

pr/art,nn5057

publican.

281 pin3004 ppro5213 an,ajn3745/1437 asba1210 pre1909 art,nn1093 fm2071

18 Verily I say unto you, Whatsoever ye shall bind on earth shall be

---

☞ **18:15–17** See note on 1 Timothy 1:20.

pr/pfpp1210 pre1722 art,nn3772 2532 an,ajn3745/1437   asba3089 pre1909 art,nn1093   fm2071 pr/pfpp3089

bound in heaven: and whatsoever ye shall loose on earth shall be loosed

pre1722 art,nn3772

in heaven.

ad3825   pin3004   ppro5213 3754 1437 nu1417 ppro5216   asba4856 pre1909 art,nn1093

19 Again I say unto you, That if two of you shall agree on earth as

pre4012 an,aj3956 an,nn4229 repro3739/1437   asbm154   fm1096   ppro846 pre3844 ppro3450

touching any thing that they shall ask, it shall be done for them of my

art,nn3962 art3588 pre1722 art,nn3772

Father which is in heaven.

1063   repro3757 nu,ajn1417 2228 nu,ajn1540 pin1526   pr/pfpp4863   pre1519 popro1699 art,nn3686

20 For where two or three are gathered together in my name,

ad1563 pin1510 pre1722 an,ajn3319 ppro846

there am I in the midst of them.

Forgiving Others

ad5119 apta4334 art,nn4074 ppro846   aina2036 an,nn2962 ad4212   ppro3450 art,nn80

21 Then came Peter to him, and said, Lord, how oft shall my brother

ft264 pre1519 ppro1691 2532 ft863 ppro846 ad2193 nu,ad2034

sin against me, and I forgive him? till seven times?

art,nn2424 pin3004   ppro846 pin3004 3756   ppro4671 ad2193

22 Jesus saith unto him, I say not unto thee, Until

nu,ad2034   ad2193 nu,ad1441 nu2033

seven times: but, Until seventy times seven.

pre1223/depro5124 art3588 nn932 art,nn3772 ainp3666 an,nn444/an,nn935

23 Therefore is the kingdom of heaven likened unto a certain king,

repro3739 aina2309 ainf4868 an,nn3056 pre3326 ppro848 art,ajn1401

which would take account of his servants.

1161 ppro846 aptm756 pinf4868 nu,ajn1520 ainp4374 ppro846

24 And when he had begun to reckon, one was brought unto him, which

an,nn3781 nu3463 an,nn5007

owed him ten thousand talents.

1161 ppro846 pap2192 3361 ainf591 ppro846 art,nn2962 aina2753 ppro846

25 But forasmuch as he had not to pay, his lord commanded him to be

aifp4097 2532 ppro846 art,nn1135 2532 art,nn5043 2532 an,aj3956 (an,ajn3745) ipf2192 2532

sold, and his wife, and children, and all that he had, and

aifp591

payment*to*be*made.

art3588 ajn1401 3767 apta4098 ipf4352 ppro846 pap3004 an,nn2962

26 The servant therefore fell down, and worshiped him, saying, Lord,

aima3114 pre1909 ppro1698 2532 ft591 ppro4671 an,ajn3956

have patience with me, and I will pay thee all.

1161 art3588 nn2962 depro1565 art,ajn1401 aptp4697 aina630

27 Then the lord of that servant was moved*with*compassion and loosed

ppro846 2532 aina863 ppro846 art3588 nn1156

him, and forgave him the debt.

1161 art3588 depro1565 ajn1401 apta1831 aina2147 nu1520 ppro846 art,nn4889

28 But the same servant went out, and found one of his fellowservants,

repro3739   ipf3784   pppro846   nu1540   an,nn1220   2532   apta2902   pppro846
which owed him a hundred pence: and he laid hands on him, and

        ipf4155   pap3004   aima591 pppro3427 repro3748   pin3784
took*him*by*the*throat, saying, Pay me that thou owest.

    3767   pppro846   art,nn4889   apta4098   pre1519 pppro846 art,nn4228   ipf3870   pppro846
29 And his fellowservant fell down at his feet, and besought him,

pap3004   aima3114   pre1909 pppro1698 2532   ft591 ppro4671 an,ajn3956
saying, Have patience with me, and I will pay thee all.

        1161   art3588   ipf2309   3756   235   apta565   aina906 pppro846 pre1519   an,nn5438   ad2193   (repro3757)
30 And he would not: but went and cast him into prison, till he should

asba591 art3588 ppmp3784
pay the debt.

        1161   pppro846   art,nn4889   apta1492   art,aptm1096
31 So when his fellowservants saw what*was*done, they

ainp3076/ad4970   2532 apta2064   aina1285   pppro848 art,nn2962 an,aj3956   art,aptm1096
were*very*sorry, and came and told unto their lord all that*was*done.

        ad5119   pppro846 art,nn2962   aptm4341   pppro846 pin3004   pppro846
32 Then his lord, after that he had called him, said unto him, O thou

an,aj4190   an,ajn1401   aina863   ppro4671 an,aj3956 depro1565 art,nn3782   1893   aina3870   pppro3165
wicked servant, I forgave thee all that debt, because thou desiredst me:

        ipf1163   3756 ppro4571 2532   ainf1653   ppro4675   art,nn4889
33 Shouldest not thou also have had compassion on thy fellowservant,

2532   ad5613 epn1473   aina1653   ppro4571
even as I had pity on thee?

        2532   pppro846 art,nn2962   aptp3710   aina3860   pppro846   art3588   nn930   ad2193
34 And his lord was wroth, and delivered him to the tormentors, till

(repro3739)   asba591 an,aj3956   art,ppmp3784   pppro846
he should pay all that*was*due unto him.

            ad3779   ppro3450   art,aj2032   art,nn3962   ft4160   2532   ppro5213 3362   pre575
35 So likewise shall my heavenly Father do also unto you, if ye from

pppro5216 art,nn2588   asba863   3362   an,ajn1538   pppro848   art,nn80   pppro846   art,nn3900
your hearts forgive not every one his brother their trespasses.

Divorce *(Matt. 5:27-32; Mark 10:1-12; Luke 16:18; Rom. 7:1-3; 1 Cor. 7)*

            2532   aom1096   ad3753   art,nn2424   aina5055   depro5128   art,nn3056
19 And it came*to*pass, *that* when Jesus had finished these sayings,

            aina3332   pre575   art,nn1056   2532   aina2064   pre1519 art3588   nn3725   art,nn2449
he departed from Galilee, and came into the coasts of Judea

ad*4008   art,nn2446
beyond Jordan;

    2532   an,aj4183   an,nn3793   aina190   pppro846 2532   aina2323   pppro846   ad1563
2 And great multitudes followed him; and he healed them there.

    art3588   nn5330   2532   aina4334   pppro846   pap3985   pppro846   2532   pap3004
☞ 3 The Pharisees also came unto him, tempting him, and saying

---

☞ **19:3–9** It is assumed many times when these and similar verses (Matt. 5:32; Luke 16:18) are read that the one who is divorced should not remarry. However, in the situations that Jesus dealt with, the person that was put away was innocent. Jesus was addressing the issue here of a spouse divorcing a

(continued on next page)

ppro846 (1487)   pin1832   an,nn444   ainf630   ppro848 art,nn1135 pre2596 an,aj3956   an,nn156
unto   him,   Is*it*lawful for a man to put away   his   wife   for every cause?

1161   art3588   aptp611   aina2036   ppro846   3756   aina314   3754
4 And   he   answered and   said   unto them, Have ye not read, that

art,apta4160   pre575   an,nn746   aina4160 ppro846 an,nn730 2532   an,nn2338
he*which*made *them* at the beginning made them male and female,

(Gen. 1:24; 5:2)

2532   aina2036   ad*1752/depro5127   an,nn444   ft2641   art,nn3962 2532   art,nn3384 2532
5 And said, For*this*cause shall a man leave father and mother, and shall

fp4347   ppro848 art,nn1135 2532   art,nu,ajn1417   fm2071 pr/nu3391 (pre1519) an,nn4561
cleave to his wife: and they twain shall be   one   flesh?   *(Gen. 2:24)*

5620   pin1526   ad3765   pr/hu,ajn1417 235 pr/hu3391 an,nn4561 repro3739   3767
6 Wherefore they are no more twain, but one   flesh. What therefore

art,nn2316   aina4801   3361 an,nn444   pim5563
God hath joined together, let not man put asunder.

pin3004   ppro846 inpro5101   an,nn3475   3767   aom1781   ain1325   an,nn975
7 They say unto him, Why did Moses then command to give a writing of

an,nn647   2532   ainf630/ppro846
divorcement, and to put*her*away?   *(Deut. 24:1)*

pin3004   ppro846   an,nn3475   pre4314   art3588   nn4641/ppro5216
8 He saith unto them, Moses because of the hardness*of*your*hearts

aina2010   ppro5213   ainf630   ppro5216 art,nn1135 1161 pre575   an,nn746 pfi1096 3756 ad3779
suffered you to put away your wives: but from the beginning it was not so.

1161   pin3004   ppro5213   repro3739/302   asba630   ppro848 art,nn1135   1508
9 And I say unto you, Whosoever shall put away his   wife, except *it be*

pre1909   an,nn4202   2532   asba1060   an,ajn243   pinm3429   2532
for fornication, and shall marry another, committeth adultery: and

art,apta1060   pfpp630   pinm3429
whoso marrieth her*which*is*put*away doth commit adultery.

ppro846   art,nn3101 pin3004   ppro846 1487 art3588 nn156   art3588 nn444 pin2076 ad3779 pre3326
10 His disciples say unto him, If the case of the man be   so with *his*

art,nn1135   pin4851/3756   ainf1060
wife, it is*not*good to marry.

1161 art3588 aina2036   ppro846 an,ajn3956   pin5562/3756   depro5126 art,nn3056   235
11 But he said unto them, All *men* cannot receive this saying, save *they*

repro3739   pfip1325
to whom it is given.

(continued from previous page)
mate with the mere excuse that the desire to be married to that particular person was gone. The only just cause for divorce is fornication. Consequently, anyone who was unjustly divorced acquired the false stigma that they were guilty of moral misconduct. For this reason, the Lord insisted that the OT provision (Deut. 24:1–4) be adhered to: the person that unjustly dismisses an innocent mate ought to clear them of guilt by providing them with a bill of divorcement. In the case that the dismissed spouse was guilty of fornication, the Mosaic Law required that he or she be stoned (Deut. 22:21), making a bill of divorcement unnecessary. Divorce papers issued by a judge in today's society should not be equated with the OT bill of divorcement.

A careful reading of two passages in the OT will reveal how the Lord determined who was the guilty party (Num. 5; Deut. 22). The Lord concerns Himself only with the innocent party and not with one who is merely able to secure a legal divorce. It is important to remember that Jesus never forbad the innocent party to remarry. In fact, Jesus accepted that this person might remarry because He stated in Matthew 5:32 that the spouse who initiated the divorce causes the innocent one to commit adultery (i.e., marry someone else).

1063   pin1526   pr/an,nn2135 repro3748   ad3779 aina1080 pre1537   an,nn3384
12 For there are some eunuchs, which were so born from *their* mother's

an,nn2836   2532   pin1526   pr/an,nn2135 repro3748   ainp2134   pre5259 art,nn444
womb: and there are some eunuchs, which were made eunuchs of men:

2532   pin1526   pr/an,nn2135   repro3748   aina2134/rxpro1438
and there be eunuchs, which have made*themselves*eunuchs

pre1223/art3588/nn932/art,nn3772   art,ppmp1410   pinf5562
for*the*kingdom*of*heaven's*sake. He*that*is*able to receive *it,* let him

pim5562
receive *it.*

Who Will Enter God's Kingdom? (Mark 10:13-16; Luke 18:15-17)

ad5119   ainp4336   ppro846   an,nn3813   2443   asba2007
13 Then were there brought unto him little children, that he should put

art,nn5495   ppro846   2532 asbm4374 1161 art3588   nn3101   aina2008   ppro846
his hands on them, and pray: and the disciples rebuked them.

1161   art,nn2424 aina2036   aima863   art,nn3813   2532 pim2967 ppro846 3361   ainf2064 pre4314
14 But Jesus said, Suffer little children, and forbid them not, to come unto

ppro3165 1063   pr/art,ajn5108 pin2076 art3588   nn932   art,nn3772
me: for of such is the kingdom of heaven.

2532   apta2007   art,nn4595   ppro846   ainp4198   ad1564
15 And he laid *his* hands on them, and departed thence.

The Rich Young Man (Mark 10:17-31; Luke 18:18-20)

2532   2400   nu,ajn1520 apta4334   aina2036   ppro846 an,aj18   an,nn1320   inpro5101
16 And, behold, one came and said unto him, Good Master, what

an,ajn18   asba4160 2443   psa2192 an,aj166 an,nn2222
good thing shall I do, that I may have eternal life?

1161   art3588 aina2036   ppro846 inpro5101 pin3004   ppro3165 pr/an,ajn18   an,ajn3762
17 And he said unto him, Why callest thou me good? *there is* none

an,aj18   1508 nu,ajn1520   art,nn2316 1161 1487   pin2309 ainf1525 pre1519 art,nn2222 aima5083 art3588
good but one, *that is,* God: but if thou wilt enter into life, keep the

nn1785
commandments.   *(Ps. 14:1 106:1; Lev. 18:5)*

pin3004   ppro846 an,ajn4169 art,nn2424 aina2036   (art3588)   fr5407/3756
18 He saith unto him, Which? Jesus said, Thou shalt do*no*murder, Thou

3756   ft3431   3756   ft2813
shalt not commit adultery, Thou shalt not steal, Thou shalt not

ft5576
bear*false*witness,

pim5091   ppro4675 art,nn3962   2532   art,nn3384   ft25   ppro4675 art,ad4139
19 Honor thy father and *thy* mother: and, Thou shalt love thy neighbor

ad5613 rxpro4572
as thyself.   *(Ex. 20:12-16; Deut. 5:16-20; Lev. 19:18)*

art3588   nn3495   pin3004   ppro846 an,aj3956   depro5023   aom5442   pre1537
20 The young man saith unto him, All these things have I kept from

ppro3450 an,nn3503   inpro5101 pin5302   ad2089
my youth up: what lack I yet?

art,nn2424 aina5346   pppro846 1487   pin2309 pinf1511   pr/an,aj5046   aima5217   aima4453
21 Jesus said unto him, If thou wilt be perfect, go *and* sell

art,pap5224/ppro4675   2532   aima1325   an,ajn4434   2532   ft2192   an,nn2344   pre1722
that*thou*hast, and give to the poor, and thou shalt have treasure in

an,nn3772   2532   ad1204   pim190   ppro3427
heaven: and come *and* follow me.

1161   art3588   nn3495   apta191   art,nn3056   aina565   ppmp3076
22 But when the young man heard that saying, he went away sorrowful:

1063   ipf2258/pap2192 an,aj4183   an,nn2933
for he had great possessions.

1161   aina2036 art,nn2424   pppro848   art,nn3101   281   pin3004   ppro5213   3754
23 Then said Jesus unto his disciples, Verily I say unto you, That a

an,ajn4145   ad1423   fm1525   pre1519 art3588   nn932   art,nn3772
rich man shall hardly enter into the kingdom of heaven.

1161   ad3825   pin3004   ppro5213   pin2076   pr/cd/an,ajn2123   an,nn2574   ainf1330   pre1223
24 And again I say unto you, It is easier for a camel to go through

an,nn5169   an,nn4476   2228   an,ajn4145   ainf1525 pre1519 art3588   nn932   art,nn2316
the eye of a needle, than for a rich man to enter into the kingdom of God.

1161   ppro846   art,nn3101   apta191   ad4970   ipf1605   pap3004
25 When his disciples heard *it,* they were exceedingly amazed, saying,

inpro5101 686   pinm1410   aifp4982
Who then can be saved?

1161   art,nn2424   apta1689   aina2036   ppro846   pre3844   an,nn444   depro5124 pin2076
26 But Jesus beheld *them,* and said unto them, With men this is

pr/an,aj102   1161   pre3844 an,nn2316   an,ajn3956   pin2076   pr/an,aj1415
impossible; but with God all things are possible.

(Gen. 18:14; Job 42:2; Jer. 32:17)

ad5119   aptp611   art,nn4074   aina2036   ppro846   2400   epn2249   aina863
☞ 27 Then answered Peter and said unto him, Behold, we have forsaken

an,ajn3956 2532   aina190   ppro4671 pr/inpro5101   epn2254 fm2071   686
all, and followed thee; what shall we have therefore?

1161   art,nn2424 aina2036   ppro846   281   pin3004   ppro5213   3754   ppro5210
28 And Jesus said unto them, Verily I say unto you, That ye

art,apta190   ppro3427 pre1722 art3588   nn3824   ad3752 art3588 nn5207   art,nn444
which*have*followed me, in the regeneration when the Son of man shall

asba2523 pre1909   an,nn2362   ppro848 an,nn1391   epn5210 2532   fm2523   pre1909   nu1427   an,nn2362
sit in the throne of his glory, ye also shall sit upon twelve thrones,

pap2919   art3588   nu1427   nn5443   2474
judging the twelve tribes of Israel.   *(Dan. 7:9,10)*

2532   an,ajn3956   repro3739   aina863   an,nn3614   2228   an,nn80   2228   an,nn79   2228
29 And every one that hath forsaken houses, or brethren, or sisters, or

an,nn3962 2228   an,nn3384   2228 an,nn1135 2228   an,nn5043   2228   an,nn68   ad*1752/ppro3450/art,nn3686
father, or mother, or wife, or children, or lands, for*my*name's*sake, shall

fm2983   nu,ajn1542   2532   ft2816   an,aj166   an,nn2222
receive a hundredfold, and shall inherit everlasting life.

1161   an,ajn4183   nu,ajn4413   fm2071 pr/an,aj2078 2532   an,ajn2078   pr/nu,aj4413
30 But many *that are* first shall be last; and the last *shall be* first.

☞ **19:27** See note on Matthew 20:1–16.

The Parable of the Laborers

20   ☞For the kingdom of heaven is like unto a man *that is* a
<small>1063   art3588   nn932   art,nn3772   pin2076   pr/an,aj3664   an,nn444</small>

householder, which went out early*in*the*morning to hire laborers
<small>an,nn3617   repro3748   aina1831   ad260/ad4404   aifm3409   an,nn2040</small>

into his vineyard.
<small>pre1519 ppro848   art,nn290</small>

2 And when he had agreed with the laborers for a penny a day, he sent
<small>1161   apta4856   pre3326 art3588   nn2040   pre1537   an,nn1220   art,nn2250   aina649</small>

them into his vineyard.
<small>ppro846   pre1519 ppro848   art,nn290</small>

3 And he went out about the third hour, and saw others standing idle
<small>2532   apta1831   pre4012 art3588   nu,ajn5154 an,nn5610   aina1492   an,ajn243   pfp2476   an,aj692</small>

in the marketplace,
<small>pre1722 art3588   nn58</small>

4 And*said*unto*them; Go ye also into the vineyard, and whatsoever
<small>depro2548/aina2036   aima5217 epn5210   2532   pre1519 art3588   nn290   2532   repro3739/1437</small>

is right I will give you. And they went*their*way.
<small>psa5600 pr/an,aj1342   ft1325 ppro5213   1161   art3588   aina565</small>

5 Again he went out about the sixth and ninth hour, and did likewise.
<small>ad3825   apta1831   pre4012   an,nu,aj1622 and2532 an,nu,aj1766 an,nn5610   aina4160   ad5615</small>

6 And about the eleventh hour he went out, and found others standing
<small>1161   pre4012   art3588   nu,aj1734   an,nn5610   apta1831   aina2147   an,ajn243   pfp2476</small>

idle, and saith unto them, Why stand ye here all the day idle?
<small>pr/an,aj692 2532   pin3004   ppro846   inpro5101   pfi2476   ad5602 an,aj3650 art3588 nn2250 pr/an,aj692</small>

7 They say unto him, Because no man hath hired us. He saith unto
<small>pin3004   ppro846   3754   an,ajn3762   aom3409 ppro2248   pin3004</small>

them, Go ye also into the vineyard; and whatsoever is right, *that* shall ye
<small>ppro846   aima5217 epn5210   2532   pre1519 art3588   nn290   2532   repro3739/1437   psa5600 pr/an,aj1342</small>

receive.
<small>fm2983</small>

8 So when even was come, the lord of the vineyard saith unto his
<small>1161   an,nn3798   aptm1096   art3588   nn2962   art3588   nn290   ppro848</small>

☞ **20:1–16** The meaning of this parable is related to Peter's question in Matthew 19:27. The lesson that Jesus is teaching with this parable hinges upon the distinction between those laborers who were hired (vv. 1, 2), and those who were not (vv. 3–7). The first group of workers was hired to do twelve hours of work (6 a.m. to 6 p.m.) for a specific sum of money. All the others were not hired, but called with a promise from the householder that he would reward them justly according to his own estimation. The translation of verse nine causes a serious misunderstanding of this parable because the word "hired" is inserted. It should be translated: "And those having come about the eleventh hour each received one *dēnárion*." A *dēnárion* (1220) was a coin that denoted the regularly accepted pay for a normal twelve-hour day of work. Those who agreed to earn one *dēnárion* for twelve hours of work set their own price for their work and that is what they received. The Lord wants His servants (Christians) to follow the example of the other workers. Those who serve the Lord and leave the size of the reward up to Him will always be given far more than if they insist on knowing how much they will receive before they begin. It is significant that Jesus did not refer to the hired man as a "dear friend" which would have been indicated by *philós* (5384). Instead He called him *hetaíros* (2083) which is used to describe a comrade or acquaintance. Jesus called Judas *hetaíros* in Gethsemane just before He was arrested (Matt. 26:50; see 11:16; 22:12).

art,nn2012 aima2564 art3588 nn2040 2532 aima591 ppro846 art,nn3408 aptm756 pre575 art3588 ajn2078

steward, Call the laborers, and give them *their* hire, beginning from the last

ad2193 art3588 nu,ajn4413

unto the first. *(Lev. 19:13; Deut. 24:15)*

2532 apta2064 art3588 pre4012 art3588 nu,aj1734 an,nn5610

9 And when they came that *were hired* about the eleventh hour, they

aina2983 pre303 an,nn1220

received every man a penny.

1161 art3588 nu,ajn4413 apta2064 aina3543 3754

10 But when the first came, they supposed that they should have

fm2983 an,ajn4119 2532 epn846 2532 aina2983 pre303 an,nn1220

received more; and they likewise received every man a penny.

1161 apta2983 ipf1111 pre2596 art3588

11 And when they had received *it,* they murmured against the

nn3617

goodman*of*the*house,

pap3004 depro3778 art,ajn2078 aina4160 nu3391 an,nn5610 2532

12 Saying, These last have wrought *but* one hour, and thou hast

aina4160 ppro846 pr/an,aj2470 ppro2254 art,apta941 art3588 nn922 2532 art,nn2742 art3588

made them equal unto us, which*have*borne the burden and heat of the

nn2250

day.

1161 art3588 aptp611 nu1520 ppro846 aina2036 an,nn2083 pin91/ppro4571/3756

13 But he answered one of them, and said, Friend, I do*thee*no*wrong:

3780 aina4856 ppro3427 an,nn1220

didst not thou agree with me for a penny?

aima142 art,popro4674 2532 aima5217 (1161) pin2309 ainf1325 depro5129 art,ajn2078

14 Take *that* thine *is,* and go*thy*way: I will give unto this last,

2532 ad5613 epn4671

even as unto thee.

pin1832/3756 ppro3427 ainf4160 repro3739 pin2309 pre1722 art,popro1699 (1487) pin2076

15 Is*it*not*lawful for me to do what I will with mine own? Is

ppro4675 art,nn3788 pr/an,aj4190 3754 epn1473 pin1510 pr/an,aj18

thine eye evil, because I am good?

ad3770 art3588 ajn2078 fm2071 pr/an,aj4413 2532 art3588 nu,ajn4413 pr/an,aj2078 1063 an,ajn4183 pin1526 pr/an,aj2822

16 So the last shall be first, and the first last: for many be called,

1161 an,aj3641 pr/an,aj1588

but few chosen.

Jesus Will Rise From the Dead (Mark 10:32-34; Luke 18:31-34)

2532 art,nn2424 pap305 pre1519 an,nn2414 aina3880 art3588 nu1427 nn3101 pre2596/an,aj2398

17 And Jesus going up to Jerusalem took the twelve disciples apart

pre1722 art3588 nn3598 2532 aina2036 ppro846

in the way, and said unto them,

2400 pin305 pre1519 an,nn2414 2532 art3588 nn5207 art,nn444

18 Behold, we go up to Jerusalem: and the Son of man shall be

fp3860   art3588   nn749   2532   an,nn1122   2532   ft2632
betrayed unto the chief priests and unto the scribes, and they shall condemn

pppro846   an,nn2288
him to death,

2532   ft3860   pppro846   art3588   nn1484   aies1702   2532   aies3146   2532
19 And shall deliver him to the Gentiles to mock, and to scourge, and to

aies4717   2532 art3588 nu,aj5154 an,nn2250   fm450
crucify *him*: and the third day he shall rise again.

The Request of the Mother of James and John (Mark 10:35-45)

ad5119   aina4334   pppro846 art3588   nn3384   an,nn2199   art,nn5207   pre3326 pppro848 art,nn5207
20 Then came to him the mother of Zebedee's children with her sons,

pap4352   2532   pap154   idpro5100   pre3844 pppro846
worshiping *him,* and desiring a certain thing of him.

1161   art3588 aina2036   pppro846 inpro5101 pin2309   pin3004   pppro846 aima2036   2443
21 And he said unto her, What wilt thou? She saith unto him, Grant that

depro3778 pppro3450 nu1417 art,nn5207   asba2523   an,nu,ajn1520 pre1537 pppro4675   an,ajn1188   2532   an,nu,ajn1520
these my two sons may sit, the one on thy right hand, and the other

pre1537   an,ajn2176 pre1722 pppro4675   art,nn932
on the left, in thy kingdom.

1161   art,nn2424   aptp611   aina2036   pin1492   3756   inpro5101   pinm154   pinm1410
22 But Jesus answered and said, Ye know not what ye ask. Are*ye*able

ainf4095   art3588 nn4221 repro3739 epn1473 pin3195 pinf4095   2532   aifp907   art3588
to drink of the cup that I shall drink of, and to be baptized with the

nn908   repro3739 epn1473   aifp907   pin3004   pppro846   pinm1410
baptism that I am baptized with? They say unto him, We are able.

2532   pin3004   pppro846   ft4095   3303   pppro3450 art,nn4221 2532
23 And he saith unto them, Ye shall drink indeed of my cup, and be

fp907   art3588   nn908   repro3739 epn1473   pinp907   1161   art,ainf2523 pre1537 pppro3450
baptized with the baptism that I am baptized with: but to sit on my

an,ajn1188   2532   pre1537 pppro3450 an,ajn2176 pin2076 3756 an,popro1699   ainf1325   235
right hand, and on my left, is not mine to give, but *it shall be given to*

repro3739   pfip2090   pre5259 pppro3450 art,nn2962
them for whom it is prepared of my Father.

2532   art3588   nu,ajn1176   apta191   aina23
24 And when the ten heard *it,* they were moved*with*indignation

pre4012   art3588 nu1417   nn80
against the two brethren.

1161   art,nn2424 aptm4341   pppro846   aina2036   pin1492   3754 art3588   nn758
25 But Jesus called them *unto him,* and said, Ye know that the princes of

art3588   nn1484   pin2634   pppro846   2532   art,ajn3173
the Gentiles exercise dominion over them, and they*that*are*great

pin2715   pppro846
exercise authority upon them.

1161   3756 fm2071 ad3779 pre1722 pppro5213 235   repro3739/1437 psa2309 aifm1096 pr/an,aj3173
26 But it shall not be so among you: but whosoever will be great

pre1722 pppro5213   pim2077 pppro5216 pr/an,nn1249
among you, let him be your minister;

2532   repro3739/1437   psa2309   pinf1511   pr/nu,ajn4413   pre1722   ppro5213   pim2077   ppro5216

27 And whosoever will be chief among you, let him be your

pr/an,ajn1401

servant:

ad5618   art3588   nn5207   art,nn444   aina2064   3756   aifp1247   235

28 Even as the Son of man came not to be ministered unto, but to

ainf1247   2532   ainf1325 ppro848 art,nn5590   an,nn3083   pre473 an,ajn4183

minister, and to give his life a ransom for many.

Jesus Heals Two Blind Men (Mark 10:46-52; Luke 18:35-43)

2532   ppro846   ppmp1607   pre575   2410   an,aj4183   an,nn3793   aina190   ppro846

29 And as they departed from Jericho, a great multitude followed him.

2532   2400   nu1417   an,ajn5185   ppmp2521 pre3844 art3588   nn3598   apta191

30 And, behold, two blind men sitting by the way side, when they heard

3754   an,nn2424   pin3855   aina2896   pap3004   aima1653   ppro2248   an,nn2962

that Jesus passed by, cried out, saying, Have mercy on us, O Lord, *thou*

an,nn5207   1138

son of David.

1161   art3588   nn3793   aina2008   ppro846   2443

31 And the multitude rebuked them, because they should

asba4623   1161   art3588   ipf2896   cd/an,ajn3185 pap3004   aima1653   ppro2248

hold*their*peace: but they cried the more, saying, Have mercy on us, O

an,nn2962   an,nn5207   1138

Lord, *thou* son of David.

2532   art,nn2424   apta2476   aina5455 ppro846   2532 aina2036 inpro5101 pin2309

32 And Jesus stood still, and called them, and said, What will ye that I

asba4160   ppro5213

shall do unto you?

pin3004   ppro846 an,nn2962 2443 ppro2257 art,nn3788   asbp455

33 They say unto him, Lord, that our eyes may be opened.

1161   art,nn2424   aptp4697   aom680   ppro846   art,nn3788   2532

34 So Jesus had compassion *on them*, and touched their eyes: and

ad2112   ppro846 art,nn3788   aina308   2532   aina190   ppro846

immediately their eyes received sight, and they followed him.

Jesus Enters Jerusalem (Mark 11:1-11; Luke 19:28-38; John 12:12-19)

2532   ad3753   aina1448   pre1519   an,nn2414   2532   aina2064 pre1519

21
And when they drew nigh unto Jerusalem, and were come to

967   pre4314 art3588   nn3735   art,nn1636   ad5119 aina649 art,nn2424 nu1417

Bethphage, unto the mount of Olives, then sent Jesus two

an,nn3101

disciples,

pap3004   ppro846 aipp4198 pre1519 art3588   nn2968   art,ad*561   ppro5216   2532

2 Saying unto them, Go into the village over against you, and

ad2112   ft2147   an,nn3688 pfpp1210 2532 an,nn4454 pre3326 ppro846 apta3089   aima71

straightway ye shall find an ass tied, and a colt with her: loose *them,* and bring

ppro3427

them unto me.

2532   1437 idpro5100   asba2036 idpro5100   ppro5213   ft2046 art3588 nn2962 pin2192
3 And if any *man* say aught unto you, ye shall say, The Lord hath

an,nn5532   ppro846 2532   ad2112   ft649   ppro846
need of them; and straightway he will send them.

(1161) an,aj3650 depro5124   pfi1096   2443   asbp4137   art,aptp4483   pre1223
4   All   this was done, that it might be fulfilled which*was*spoken by

art3588   nn4396 pap3004
the prophet, saying,

aima2036   art3588   nn2364   4622   2400   ppro4675 art,nn935 pinm2064   ppro4671
5 Tell ye the daughter of Zion, Behold, thy king cometh unto thee,

an,aj4239 2532 pfp1910 pre1909 an,nn3688 2532 an,nn4454   an,nn5207   an,nn5268
meek, and sitting upon an ass, and a colt the foal of an ass.

(Is. 62:11; Zech. 9:9)

1161 art3588   nn3101   aptp4198   2532 apta4160 ad2531 art,nn2424   aina4367   ppro846
6 And the disciples went, and did as Jesus commanded them,

aina71   art3588 nn3688 2532 art3588 nn4454 2532 aina2007 ad*1883 ppro846 ppro848 art,nn2440
7 And brought the ass, and the colt, and put on them their clothes,

2532   aina1940   ad*1883/ppro846
and they set *him* thereon.

1161   art,aj4118   an,nn3793   aina4766 rxpro1438 art,nn2440 pre1722 art3588 nn3598(1161)
8 And a very great multitude spread their garments in the way;

an,ajn243 ipf2875   an,nn2798 pre575 art3588 nn1186 2532 ipf4766   pre1722 art3588 nn3598
others cut down branches from the trees, and strewed *them* in the way.

1161 art3588   nn3793   art,pap4254   2532   art,pap190   ipf2896 pap3004
9 And the multitudes that*went*before, and that followed, cried, saying,

5614   art3588 nn5207   1138   pr/pfpp2127 art,pmpp2064   pre1722   an,nn3686
Hosanna to the son of David: Blessed *is* he*that*cometh in the name of the

an,nn2962   5614   pre1722 art3588 ajn5310
Lord; Hosanna in the highest.   *(Ps. 118:26)*

2532   ppro846   apta1525 pre1519   an,nn2414   an,aj3956 art3588 nn4172   ainp4579
10 And when he was come into Jerusalem, all the city was moved,

pap3004   pr/inpro5101 pin2076 depro3778
saying, Who is this?

1161 art3588   nn3793   ipf3004 depro3778 pin2076 pr/an,nn2424 art3588   nn4396 art,pre575   3478
11 And the multitude said, This is Jesus the prophet of Nazareth of

art,nn1056
Galilee.

Jesus Cleanses the Temple (Mark 11:15-19; Luke 19:45-48; John 2:13-22)

2532 art,nn2424 aina1525 pre1519 art3588   nn2411   art,nn2316 2532   aina1544 an,aj3956
12 And Jesus went into the temple of God, and cast out all

art,pap4453   2532   pap59 pre1722 art3588   nn2411   2532   aina2690   art3588 nn5132
them*that*sold and bought in the temple, and overthrew the tables of

art3588   nn2855   2532 art3588 nn2515   art,pap4453   art,nn4058
the moneychangers, and the seats of them*that*sold doves,

2532 pin3004   ppro846   pfip1125 ppro3450 art,nn3624   fp2564   an,nn3624
13 And said unto them, It is written, My house shall be called the house

an,nn4335   1161 epn5210   aina4160 ppro846 an,nn4693   an,nn3027

of prayer; but ye have made   it   a den of thieves.   *(Is. 56:7; Jer. 7:11)*

2532   an,ajn5185 2532   an,ajn5560 aina4334   ppro846 pre1722 art3588 nn2411   2532

14 And the blind and the lame came to him   in   the temple; and he

aina2323 ppro846

healed them.

1161   art3588   nn749   2532   art,nn1122 apta1492 art3588   ajn2297   repro3739

15 And when the chief priests and scribes saw the wonderful things that

aina4160 2532 art3588   nn3816   pap2896 pre1722 art3588   nn2411   2532   pap3004   5614   art3588

he did, and the children crying in   the temple, and saying, Hosanna to the

nn5207   1138   aina23

son of David; they were sore displeased,

2532   aina2036   ppro846   pin191   inpro5101 depro3778 pin3004 2532 art,nn2424 pin3004

16 And said unto him, Hearest thou what these say? And Jesus saith unto

ppro846   3483   ad3762   aina314   pre1537   an,nn4750   an,ajn3516 2532   pap2337

them, Yea; have ye never read, Out of the mouth of babes and sucklings thou

aom2675   an,nn136

hast perfected praise?   *Ps. 8:2 [Sept.])*

2532   apta2641   ppro846   aina1831 ad1854   art3588 nn4172 pre1519 an,nn963   2532

17 And he left them, and went out of the city into Bethany; and he

ainp835   ad1563

lodged there.

Jesus and the Unfruitful Fig Tree (Mark 11:12-14,20-24)

1161   an,nn4405   pap1877 pre1519 art3588 nn4172   aina3983

☞ 18 Now in the morning as he returned into the city, he hungered.

2532   apta1492 nu3391 an,nn4808 pre1909 art3588 nn3598   aina2064 pre1909 ppro846 2532

19 And when he saw   a fig tree in   the way, he came to it, and

aina2147 an,ajn3762 pre1722/ppro846 1508 an,nn5444 an,ajn3440 2532 pin3004   ppro846   an,nn2590 asbm1096

found nothing thereon, but leaves only, and said unto it, Let no fruit grow

pre1537 ppro4675   ad3371   pre1519/art,nn165 2532   ad3916   art3588   nn4808   ainp3583

on thee henceforward forever. And presently the fig tree withered away.

2532   art3588   nn3101   apta1492   aina2296   pap3004   ad4459   ad3916

20 And when the disciples saw *it,* they marveled, saying, How soon is

art3588   nn4808   ainp3583

the fig tree withered away!

(1161) art,nn2424 aptp611   aina2036   ppro846   281   pin3004   ppro5213 1437   psa2192

21 Jesus answered and said unto them, Verily I say unto you, If ye have

an,nn4102 2532 asbp1252 3361   3756 an,ajn3440 ft4160 art3588   art3588   nn4808

faith, and doubt not, ye shall not only do this *which is done* to the fig tree,

---

☞ **21:18–22** The Lord did not curse the barren tree because it failed to provide food for His hunger, but because it had leaves and no fruit. Fig trees in that area yield fruit in both June and August and it is normal for the figs to hang on the trees through the winter. New fruit grows right over the old and out of the old shoots. Consequently, fruit can normally be found on the trees all year round. This particular fig tree is symbolic of Israel which produced leaves, but bore no fruit (Is. 63:7; 64:12; 65:3–7). The Lord was entering Jerusalem where He would experience his final public rejection by Israel. Despite the fact that Jesus had adequately demonstrated that He was indeed God incarnate, they still refused to accept Him as such (vv. 21, 22). The withering of the fig tree illustrates the result of the Jews as a people rejecting Christ as their Messiah.

235   2579   asba2036   depro5129   art,nn3735   aipp142   2532
but also if ye shall say unto this mountain, Be thou removed, and be thou
aipp906 pre1519 art3588 nn2281   fm1096
cast into the sea; it shall be done.

2532   an,aj3956   an,ajn3745/302   asba154 pre1722 art,nn4335   pap4100
22 And all things, whatsoever ye shall ask in prayer, believing, ye shall
fm2983
receive.

The Chief Priests Inquire About Jesus' Authority
(Mark 11:27-33; Luke 20:1-8)

2532   pproo846   apta2064 pre1519 art3588   nn2411   art3588   nn749   2532 art3588
23 And when he was come into the temple, the chief priests and the
ajn4245   art3588   nn2992   aina4334   pproo846   pap1321   pap3004 pre1722 an,aj4169
elders of the people came unto him as he was teaching, and said, By what
an,nn1849   pin4160   depro5023   2532 inpro5101 aina1325 ppro4671 depro5026   art,nn1849
authority doest thou these things? and who gave thee this authority?

1161 art,nn2424   aptp611   aina2036   ppro846   epn2504   ft2065 ppro5209 nu1520 an,nn3056
24 And Jesus answered and said unto them, I also will ask you one thing,
repro3739 1437   asba2036 ppro3427   epn2504   ft2046 ppro5213 pre1722 an,aj4169   an,nn1849   pin4160
which if ye tell me, I*in*likewise will tell you by what authority I do
depro5023
these things.

art3588   nn908   an,nn2491   ad4159   ipf2258   pre1537   an,nn3772   2228 pre1537 an,nn444   1161
25 The baptism of John, whence was it? from heaven, or of men? And
art3588   ipf1260   pre3844   rxpro1438   pap3004   1437   asba2036 pre1537 an,nn3772
they reasoned with themselves, saying, If we shall say, From heaven; he will
ft2046   ppro2254 pre,inpro1302   3756   3767   aina4100   ppro846
say unto us,   Why did ye not then believe him?

1161   1437   asba2036 pre1537 an,nn444   pinm5399 art3588   nn3793   1063 an,ajn3956 pin2192
26 But if we shall say, Of men; we fear the people; for   all   hold
art,nn2491 ad5613   pr/an,nn4396
John as a prophet.

2532   aptp611   art,nn2424   aina2036   pin1492/3756   2532 epn846 aina5346
27 And they answered Jesus, and said, We cannot tell. And he said unto
ppro846   3761   pin3004 epn1473 ppro5213 pre1722 an,aj4169   an,nn1849   pin4160   depro5023
them, Neither tell   I   you by what authority I do these things.

The Parable of the Two Sons

1161   inpro5101 pin1380 ppro5213   an,nn444 ipf2192 nu1417 an,nn5043 2532   apta4334   art3588
28 But what think ye? A *certain* man had two sons; and he came to the
nu,ajn4413   aina2036 an,nn5043 aima5217 pim2038   ad4594 pre1722 ppro3450 art,nn290
first, and said, Son, go work today in my vineyard.

art3588   aptp611   aina2036   pin2309   3756   1161   ad5305   aptp3338
29 He answered and said, I will not: but afterward he repented, and
aina565
went.

2532   apta4334   art3588   nu,ajn1208   aina2036   ad5615   1161   art3588   aptp611
30 And he came to the second, and said likewise. And he answered and
aina2036 epn1473   an,nn2962 2532   aina565   3756
said, I *go,* sir: and went not.

inpro5101   pre1537   art3588   nu,ajn1417 aina4160 art3588   nn2307   art,nn3962   pin3004
31 Whether of them twain did the will of *his* father? They say unto
ppro846   art3588   nu,ajn4413 art,nn2424 pin3004   ppro846   281   pin3004   ppro5213   3754   art3588
him, The first. Jesus saith unto them, Verily I say unto you, That the
nn5057   2532 art3588   nn4204   pin4254/pre1519/art3588/nn932/art,nn2316   ppro5209
publicans and the harlots go*into*the*kingdom*of*God*before you.

1063   an,nn2491   aina2064   pre4314 ppro5209 pre1722   an,nn3598   an,nn1343   2532
32 For John came unto you in the way of righteousness, and ye
aina4100   ppro846   3756   1161 art3588   nn5057   2532 art3588   nn4204   aina4100   ppro846 1161 epn5210
believed him not; but the publicans and the harlots believed him: and ye, when
apta1492   ainp3338   3756   ad5305   infg4100   ppro846
ye had seen *it,* repented not afterward, that ye might believe him.

The Wicked Husbandmen (Mark 12:1-12; Luke 20:9-19)

aima191   an,aj243   an,nn3850   ipf2258   idpro5100   (an,nn444) an,nn3617   repro3748
33 Hear another parable: There was a certain householder, which
aina5452   an,nn290   2532   aina4060/ppro846/an,nn5418   2532   aina3736   an,nn3025   pre1722
planted a vineyard, and hedged*it*round*about, and digged a winepress in
ppro846 2532 aina3618   an,nn4444   2532 aom1554/ppro846   an,nn1092   2532   aina589
it, and built a tower, and let*it*out to husbandmen, and went*into*a*far*country:

(Is. 5:1,2)

1161   ad3753   art3588   nn2540   art3588   nn2590   aina1448   aina649 ppro848   art,ajn1401   pre4314
34 And when the time of the fruit drew near, he sent his servants to
art3588   nn1092   ainf2983   art3588   nn2590   ppro846
the husbandmen, that they might receive the fruits of it.
2532   art3588   nn1092   apta2983 ppro846   art,ajn1401   aina1194 repro3739/303 1161 aina615
35 And the husbandmen took his servants, and beat one, and killed
repro3739   1161   aina3036   repro3739
another, and stoned another.
ad3825   aina649 an,aj243   an,ajn1401   cd/an,aj4119   art3588 nu,ajn4413 2532   aina4160
36 Again, he sent other servants more than the first: and they did unto
ppro846   ad5615
them likewise.
1161   ad5305   aina649 pre4314 ppro846 ppro848 art,nn5207 pap3004   fm1788
37 But last of all he sent unto them his son, saying, They will reverence
ppro3450 art,nn5207
my son.
1161   art3588   nn1092   apta1492 art3588 nn5207   aina2036   pre1722   rxpro1438
38 But when the husbandmen saw the son, they said among themselves,
depro3778 pin2076 art3588 pr/nn2818   ad1205   aosi615   ppro846 2532   aosi2722   ppro846
This is the heir; come, let us kill him, and let us seize on his
art,nn2817
inheritance.

39 And they caught him, and cast *him* out of the vineyard, and slew

him.

40 When the lord therefore of the vineyard cometh, what will he do unto those husbandmen?

41 They say unto him, He will miserably destroy those wicked men, and will let out *his* vineyard unto other husbandmen, which shall render him the fruits in their seasons.

42 Jesus saith unto them, Did ye never read in the Scriptures, The stone which the builders rejected, the same is become the head of the corner: this is the Lord's doing, and it is marvelous in our eyes?

(Ps. 118:22,23)

43 Therefore say I unto you, The kingdom of God shall be taken from you, and given to a nation bringing forth the fruits thereof.

44 And whosoever*shall*fall on this stone shall be broken: but on whomsoever it shall fall, it will grind*him*to*powder. *(Dan. 2:34,35,44,45)*

45 And when the chief priests and Pharisees had heard his parables, they perceived that he spake of them.

46 But when they sought to lay hands on him, they feared the multitude, because they took him for a prophet.

The Wedding Banquet (Luke 14:15-24)

22 ☞And Jesus answered and spake unto them again by parables, and said,

2 The kingdom of heaven is*like*unto a certain king, which made a marriage for his son.

☞ **22:1–14** See note on Matthew 8:11, 12.

2532   aina649   ppro848   art,ajn1401   ainf2564   art,pfpp2564   pre1519 art3588
3 And sent forth his servants to call them*that*were*bidden to the

nn1062   2532   ipf2309   3756   ainf2064
wedding: and they would not come.

ad3825   aina649   an,aj243   an,ajn1401   pap3004   aima2036   art,pfpp2564
4 Again, he sent forth other servants, saying, Tell them*which*are*bidden,

2400   aina2090   ppro3450 art,nn712   ppro3450 art,nn5022 2532   art,nn4619   pr/pfpp2380 2532
Behold, I have prepared my dinner: my oxen and *my* fatlings *are* killed, and

an,ajn3956   pr/an,aj2092 ad1205   pre1519 art3588   nn1062
all things *are* ready: come unto the marriage.

1161   art3588   apta272   aina565   art3588/3303 pre1519 art,aj2398 an,nn68
5 But they made*light*of *it,* and went*their*ways, one to his farm,

(1161)art3588/3303 pre1519 ppro848   art,nn1711
another to his merchandise:

1161   art3588 ajn3062   apta2902 ppro846   art,ajn1401   aina5195   2532
6 And the remnant took his servants, and entreated**them**spitefully, and

aina615
slew *them.*

1161   art3588 nn935 apta191   ainp3710   2532   apta3992   ppro848
7 But when the king heard *thereof,* he was wroth: and he sent forth his

art,nn4753   aina622   depro1565 art,nn5406 2532   aina1714   ppro846 art,nn4172
armies, and destroyed those murderers, and burned up their city.

ad5119   pin3004   ppro848   art,ajn1401   art3588   nn1062(3303)   pin2076   pr/an,aj2092 1161
8 Then saith he to his servants, The wedding is ready, but

art,pfpp2564   ipf2258 3756   pr/an,aj514
they*which*were*bidden were not worthy.

pim4198   3767   pre1909 art3588 nn1327/art,nn3598 2532   an,ajn3745/302   asba2147 aima2564
9 Go ye therefore into the highways, and as*many*as ye shall find, bid

pre1519 art3588   nn1062
to the marriage.

2532 depro1565   art,ajn1401   apta1831   pre1519 art3588   nn3598   aina4863
10 So those servants went out into the highways, and gathered together

an,aj3956   an,ajn3745   aina2147   5037 an,ajn4190   2532   an,ajn18   2532 art3588   nn1062
all as*many*as they found, both bad and good: and the wedding was

ainp4130   ppmp345
furnished with guests.

1161   art3588 nn935   apta1525   aifm2300 art3588   ppmp345   aina1492 ad1563   an,nn444
11 And when the king came in to see the guests, he saw there a man

pfpp1746/3756   an,nn1062   an,nn1742
which had*not*on a wedding garment:

2532   pin3004   ppro846 an,nn2083   ad4459   aina1525   ad5602 3361 pap2192
12 And he saith unto him, Friend, how camest thou in hither not having a

an,nn1062   an,nn1742   1161   art3588   ainp5392
wedding garment? And he was speechless.

ad5119   aina2036 art3588 nn935   art3588   nn1249   apta1210 ppro846 an,nn5495 2532 an,nn4228
13 Then said the king to the servants, Bind him hand and foot, and

aima142/ppro846   2532   aima1544   pre1519 art,aj1857   art,nn4655   ad1563   fm2071   art,nn2805
take*him*away, and cast *him* into outer darkness; there shall be weeping

2532   art,nn1030   art,nn3599
and gnashing of teeth.

1063 an,ajn4183 pin1526 pr/an,aj2822 1161 an,ajn3641   pr/an,aj1588
14 For many are called, but few *are* chosen.

Jesus and Taxes *(Mark 12:13-17; Luke 20:20-26)*

ad5119 aptp4198 art3588   nn5330   2532 aina2983 an,nn4824   3704   asba3802

15 Then went the Pharisees, and took counsel how they might entangle

ppro846 pre1722   an,nn3056

him in *his* talk.

2532   pin649   ppro846 ppro848   art,nn3101   pre3326 art3588   ajn2265   pap3004

16 And they sent out unto him their disciples with the Herodians, saying,

an,nn1320   pin1492   3754   pin1488 pr/an,aj227 2532   pin1321   art3588 nn3598   art,nn2316 pre1722 an,nn225

Master, we know that thou art true, and teachest the way of God in truth,

2532/3756   pin3199   ppro4671   pre4012 an,ajn3762   1063   pin991   3756   (pre1519)   an,nn4383

neither carest thou for any *man*: for thou regardest not the person of

an,nn444

men.

aima2036 ppro2254   3767   inpro5101   pin1380   ppro4671   pin1832   ainf1325 an,nn2778

17 Tell us therefore, What thinkest thou? Is*it*lawful to give tribute unto

an,nn2541 2228 3756

Caesar, or not?

1161   art,nn2424   apta1097   ppro846   art,nn4189   aina2036 inpro5101 pin3985   ppro3165

18 But Jesus perceived their wickedness, and said, Why tempt ye me, *ye*

an,nn5273

hypocrites?

aima1925 ppro3427 art3588   nn2778   art,nn3546   1161 art3588   aina4374   ppro846 an,nn1220

19 Show me the tribute money. And they brought unto him a penny.

2532   pin3004   ppro846 inpro5101   depro3778 pr/art,nn1504 2532   pr/art,nn1923

20 And he saith unto them, Whose *is* this image and superscription?

pin3004   ppro846   an,nn2541   ad5119   pin3004   ppro846

21 They say unto him, Caesar's. Then saith he unto them,

aima591   3767   an,nn2541   art3588   an,nn2541   2532   art,nn2316

Render therefore unto Caesar the things which are Caesar's; and unto God the

art3588   an,nn2316

things that are God's.

(2532)   apta191   aina2296   2532 apta863 ppro846

22 When they had heard *these words,* they marveled, and left him, and

aina565

went*their*way.

Questions Concerning the Resurrection *(Mark 12:18-27; Luke 20:27-40)*

(pre1722)   depro1565 art,nn2250 aina4334   ppro846   an,nn4523   art,pap3004

23 The same day came to him the Sadducees, which say that there

pinf1511 3361   an,nn386   2532 aina1905 ppro846

is no resurrection, and asked him,

pap3004   an,nn1320   an,nn3475 aina2036 1437   idpro5100 asba599 pap2192 3361   an,nn5043   ppro848

24 Saying, Master, Moses said, If a man die, having no children, his

art,nn80   ft1918 ppro846 art,nn1135 2532   ft450   an,nn4690   ppro848   art,nn80

brother shall marry his wife, and raise up seed unto his brother.

(Gen. 38:8; Deut. 25:5)

25 Now there were with us seven brethren: and the first, when he had married*a*wife, deceased, and, having no issue, left his wife unto his brother:

26 Likewise the second also, and the third, unto the seventh.

27 And last of all the woman died also.

28 Therefore in the resurrection whose wife shall she be of the seven? for they all had her.

29 Jesus answered and said unto them, Ye do err, not knowing the Scriptures, nor the power of God.

30 For in the resurrection they neither marry, nor are given*in* marriage, but are as the angels of God in heaven.

31 But as touching the resurrection of the dead, have ye not read that*which*was*spoken unto you by God, saying,

32 I am the God of Abraham, and the God of Isaac, and the God of Jacob? God is not the God of the dead, but of the living. *(Ex. 3:6,15,16)*

33 And when the multitude heard *this,* they were astonished at his doctrine.

The Great Commandment (Mark 12:28-34; Luke 10:25-28)

34 But when the Pharisees had heard that he had put*the*Sadducees*to*silence, they were gathered together.

35 Then one of them, *which was* a lawyer, asked *him a question,* tempting him, and saying,

36 Master, which *is* the great commandment in the law?

37 Jesus said unto him, Thou shalt love the Lord thy God with all

ppro4675 art,nn2588 2532 pre1722 an,aj3650 pppro4675 art,nn5590 2532 pre1722 an,aj3650 pppro4675 art,nn1271

thy heart, and with all thy soul, and with all thy mind. *(Deut. 6:5)*

depro3778 pin2076   pr/an,nu,aj4413 2532 pr/an,aj3173   an,nn1785

38 This is the first and great commandment.

1161   an,nu,ajn1208   pr/an,ajn3664   pppro846   ft25   pppro4675   art,ad4139   ad5613

39 And the second *is* like unto it, Thou shalt love thy neighbor as

rxpro4572

thyself.   *(Lev. 19:18)*

pre1722 depro5025 nu1417   art,nn1785   pinm2910 an,aj3650 art3588 nn3551 2532 art3588   nn4396

40 On these two commandments hang all the law and the prophets.

David's Lord (Mark 12:35-37; Luke 20:41-44)

1161   art3588   nn5330   pfpp4863   art,nn2424 aina1905 pppro846

41 While the Pharisees were gathered together, Jesus asked them,

pap3004   inpro5101 pin1380 pppro5213 pre4012 art,nn5547 inpro5101 pr/an,nn5207 pin2076   pin3004

42 Saying, What think ye of Christ? whose son is he? They say

pppro846   1138

unto him, *The son* of David.

pin3004   pppro846   ad4459   3767   1138   pre1722 an,nn4151 pin2564 pppro846 an,nn2962

43 He saith unto them, How then doth David in spirit call him Lord,

pap3004

saying,

art3588   nn2962 aina2036   pppro3450 art,nn2962 pim2521   pre1537 pppro3450   an,ajn1188   ad2193

44 The LORD said unto my Lord, Sit thou on my right hand, till I

asba5087 pppro4675 art,ajn2190   pppro4675 an,nn5286/art,nn4228

make thine enemies thy footstool?   *(Ps. 110:1)*

1487   1138   3767 pin2564 pppro846 an,nn2962 ad4459 pin2076   pppro846 pr/an,nn5207

45 If David then call him, Lord, how is he his son?

2532   an,ajn3762   ipf1410   aifp611   pppro846   an,nn3056   3761   aina5111 idpro5100

46 And no man was able to answer him a word, neither durst any *man*

pre575 depro1565 art,nn2250   ainf1905 pppro846   ad3765

from that day forth ask him any more *questions.*

Jesus Condemns the Scribes and Pharisees (Mark 12:38-40; Luke 11:37-52; 20:45-47)

ad5119   aina2980 art,nn2424   art3588   nn3793   2532   pppro848   art,nn3101

23 Then spake Jesus to the multitude, and to his disciples,

pap3004   art3588 nn1122 2532 art3588   nn5330   aina2523 pre1909 an,nn3475 art,nn2515

2 Saying, The scribes and the Pharisees sit in Moses' seat:

an,aj3956   3767   an,ajn3745/302   asba2036 pppro5213   pinf5083   pim5083   2532

3 All therefore whatsoever they bid you observe, *that* observe and

pim4160 1161 pim4160 3361   pre2596 pppro846 art,nn2041 1063   pin3004 2532 pin4160 3756

do; but do not ye after their works: for they say, and do not.

1063   pin1195 an,aj926   an,nn5413 2532   an,aj1419   2532 pin2007

4 For they bind heavy burdens and grievous*to*be*borne, and lay *them*

pre1909   art,nn444   art,nn5606   1161   pin2309   3756   ainf2795   ppro846

on men's shoulders; but they *themselves* will not move them with

ppro848   art,nn1147

one*of*their fingers.

         1161   an,aj3956   ppro848   art,nn2041   pin4160   aipr2300   art,nn444   (1161)   pin4115

5 But all their works they do for to be seen of men: they make broad

ppro848   art,nn5440   2532   pin3170   art3588   nn2899   ppro848   art,nn2440

their phylacteries, and enlarge the borders of their garments,

(Ex. 13:9; Num. 15:38,39; Deut. 6:8; 11:18)

   5037   pin5368 art3588   nn4411   pre1722   art,nn1173   2532   art3588   nn4410   pre1722 art3588

6 And love the uppermost rooms at feasts, and the chief seats in the

nn4864

synagogues,

       2532   art,nn783   pre1722 art3588   nn58   2532   pip2564   pre5259 art,nn444   4461   4461

7 And greetings in the markets, and to be called of men, Rabbi, Rabbi.

    1161   3361   epn5210   aosi2564   4461   1063   pr/nu,ajn1520 pin2076 ppro5216   art,nn2519   art,nn5547

8 But be not ye called Rabbi: for one is your Master, *even* Christ;

1161 an,aj3956 ppro5210 pin2075   pr/an,nn80

and all ye are brethren.

       2532   aosi2564 3361   ppro5216   an,nn3962   pre1909   art3588   nn1093   1063   pr/nu,ajn1520 pin2076 ppro5216

9 And call no *man* your father upon the earth: for one is your

art,nn3962   art3588   pre1722   art,nn3772

Father, which is in heaven.

      3366   aosi2564   an,nn2519   1063   pr/nu,ajn1520   pin2076 ppro5216   art,nn2519

10 Neither be ye called masters: for one is your Master, *even*

art,nn5547

Christ.

      1161   cd/art,aj3187   ppro5216   fm2071 ppro5216   pr/an,nn1249

11 But he*that*is*greatest among you shall be your servant.

      1161   repro3748   ft5312   rxpro1438   fp5013   2532   repro3748

12 And whosoever shall exalt himself shall be abased; and he that shall

ft5312   rxpro1438   fp5312

humble himself shall be exalted.   *(Job 22:29; Prov. 29:23; Ezek. 21:26)*

     1161   3759   ppro5213   an,nn1122   2532   an,nn5330   an,nn5273   3754   pin2808

13 But woe unto you, scribes and Pharisees, hypocrites! for ye shut up

art3588   nn932   art,nn3772   ad*1715   art,nn444 1063 epn5210   3756   pinm1525   3761

the kingdom of heaven against men: for ye neither go in *yourselves,* neither

pin863   art,ppmp1525   ainf1525

suffer ye them*that*are*entering to go in.

   (1161)   3759   ppro5213   an,nn1122   2532   an,nn5330   an,nn5273   3754   pin2719

14   Woe unto you, scribes and Pharisees, hypocrites! for ye devour

art,nn5503   art,nn3614   2532   an,nn4392   ppmp4336/an,ajn3117   pre1223/depro5124

widows' houses, and for a pretence make*long*prayer: therefore ye shall

fm2983   cd/an,ajn4056   an,nn2917

receive the greater damnation.

     3759   ppro5213   an,nn1122   2532   an,nn5330   an,nn5273   3754   pin4013   art,nn2281

15 Woe unto you, scribes and Pharisees, hypocrites! for ye compass sea

2532   art,nn3584   ainf4160   nu1520   an,nn4339   2532   ad3752   asbm1096   pin4160   ppro846

and land to make one proselyte, and when he is made, ye make him

cd/an,aj1362   an,nn5207   an,nn1067   ppro5216

twofold more the child of hell than yourselves.

16 Woe unto you, *ye* blind guides, which say, Whosoever shall swear by the temple, it is nothing; but whosoever shall swear by the gold of the temple, he is*a*debtor!

17 *Ye* fools and blind: for whether is greater, the gold, or the temple that sanctifieth the gold?

18 And, Whosoever shall swear by the altar, it is nothing; but whosoever sweareth by the gift that is upon it, he is guilty.

19 *Ye* fools and blind: for whether *is* greater, the gift, or the altar that sanctifieth the gift?   *(Ex. 29:37)*

20 Whoso*therefore*shall*swear by the altar, sweareth by it, and by all things thereon.

21 And whoso*shall*swear by the temple, sweareth by it, and by him*that*dwelleth*therein.   *(Ps. 26:8)*

22 And he*that*shall*swear by heaven, sweareth by the throne of God, and by him*that*sitteth thereon.

23 Woe unto you, scribes and Pharisees, hypocrites! for ye pay tithe of mint and anise and cummin, and have omitted the weightier *matters* of the law, judgment, mercy, and faith: these ought ye to have done, and not to leave the other undone.   *(Lev. 27:30)*

24 *Ye* blind guides, which strain at a gnat, and swallow a camel.

25 Woe unto you, scribes and Pharisees, hypocrites! for ye make clean the outside of the cup and of the platter, but within they are full of extortion and excess.

26 *Thou* blind Pharisee, cleanse first that *which is* within the cup and platter, that the outside of them may be clean also.

27 Woe unto you, scribes and Pharisees, hypocrites! for ye are*like*unto

<small>pfpp2867   an,nn5028   repro3748   3303   pinp5316   pr/an,aj5611   ad1855   1161   pin1073/ad2081</small>
whited sepulchers, which indeed appear beautiful outward, but are*within*full

<small>an,aj3498   an,nn3747   2532   an,aj3956   an,nn167</small>
of dead *men's* bones, and of   all   uncleanness.

<small>   ad3779   epn5210   2532   ad1855 (3303)   pinp5316   pr/an,aj1342   art,nn444   1161   ad2081</small>
28 Even so ye   also outwardly appear righteous unto men, but within ye

<small>pin2075 pr/an,aj3324   an,nn5272   2532   an,nn458</small>
are   full   of hypocrisy and iniquity.

<small>   3759   ppro5213   an,nn1122   2532   an,nn5330   an,nn5273   3754   pin3618 art3588</small>
29 Woe unto you, scribes and Pharisees, hypocrites! because ye build the

<small>nn5028   art3588   nn4396   2532   pin2885 art3588   nn3419   art3588   ajn1342</small>
tombs of the prophets, and garnish the sepulchers of the righteous,

<small>   2532   pin3004 1487   ipf2258 pre1722 art3588 nn2250   ppro2257   art,nn3962   3756</small>
30 And say, If we had been in   the days of our fathers, we would not

<small>   ipf2258/302   pr/an,ajn2844   ppro846 pre1722 art3588   nn129   art3588   nn4396</small>
have been partakers with them in   the blood of the prophets.

<small>   5620   pin3140   rxpro1438   3754   pin2075   pr/an,nn5207</small>
31 Wherefore ye be witnesses unto yourselves, that ye are the children of

<small>art,apta5407   art3588   nn4396</small>
them*which*killed the prophets.

<small>   aima4137/epn5210   2532   art3588   nn3358   ppro5216   art,nn3962</small>
32 Fill*ye*up then the measure of your fathers.

<small>   an,nn3789   an,nn1081   an,nn2191   ad4459   asba5343 (pre575)   art3588</small>
33 *Ye* serpents, *ye* generation of vipers, how can ye   escape   the

<small>nn2920   art,nn1067</small>
damnation of hell?

<small>   pre1223/depro5124   2400   epn1473 pin649 pre4314 ppro5209   an,nn4396   2532   an,ajn4680   2532</small>
34 Wherefore, behold,   I   send unto you prophets, and wise men, and

<small>an,nn1122   2532   pre1537 ppro846   ft615 2532   ft4717   2532   pre1537 ppro846</small>
scribes: and *some* of them ye shall kill and crucify; and *some* of them shall

<small>ft3146   pre1722 ppro5216   art,nn4864   2532   ft1377   pre575 an,nn4172 pre1519 an,nn4172</small>
ye scourge in your synagogues, and persecute *them* from city to   city:

<small>   3704   pre1909 ppro5209   asba2064 an,aj3956   an,aj1342   an,nn129 ppmp1632 pre1909 art3588</small>
35 That upon you may come   all   the righteous blood shed upon the

<small>nn1093   pre575 art3588   nn129   art,aj1342   6   ad*2193 art3588   nn129   an,nn2197   an,nn5207</small>
earth, from the blood of righteous Abel unto the blood of Zechariah son of

<small>an,nn914   repro3739   aina5407   ad*3342   art3588   nn3485   2532 art3588 nn2379</small>
Barachias, whom ye slew between the temple and the altar.

(Gen. 4:8; 2 Chr. 24:20,21)

<small>   281   pin3004   ppro5213 an,aj3956   depro5023   ft2240   pre1909 depro5026</small>
36 Verily I say unto you, All these things shall come upon this

<small>art,nn1074</small>
generation.

Christ Weeps Over Jerusalem (Luke 13:34,35)

<small>   2419   2419   art,pap615   art3588   nn4396   2532</small>
37 O Jerusalem, Jerusalem, *thou* that killest the prophets, and

<small>pap3036   art,pfpp649   pre4314   ppro846   ad4212   aina2309</small>
stonest them*which*are*sent unto   thee, how often would I have

ainf1996/ppro4675/art,nn5043   repro3739/an,nn5158   an,nn3733   pin1996   rxpro1438   art,nn3556   pre5259

gathered*thy*children*together, even as a hen gathereth her chickens under

art,nn4420   2532   aina2309   3756

her wings, and ye would not!

2400   ppro5216   art,nn3624   pinp863   ppro5213   an,aj2048

38 Behold, your house is left unto you desolate.

(1 Kgs. 9:7,8; Jer. 12:7; 22:5)

1063   pin3004   ppro5213   efn3364 asba1492 ppro3165   pre575/ad737   ad2193/302

39 For I say unto you, Ye shall not see me henceforth, till ye shall

asba2036   pr/pfpp2127   art,ppmp2064   pre1722   an,nn3686   an,nn2962

say, Blessed *is* he*that*cometh in the name of the Lord.   *(Ps. 118:26)*

The Destruction of the Temple And the Last Days (Mark 13:1,2; Luke 21:5,6)

2532   art,nn2424   apta1831   ipf4198   pre575 art3588   nn2411   2532 ppro846   art,nn3101

24 And Jesus went out, and departed from the temple: and his disciples

aina4334   ainf1925 ppro846 art3588   nn3619   art3588   nn2411

came to *him* for to show him the buildings of the temple.

1161   art,nn2424 aina2036   ppro846   pin991   3756   an,aj3956   depro5023   281   pin3004

2 And Jesus said unto them, See ye not all these things? verily I say

ppro5213   efn3364   asbp863   ad5602   an,nn3037/pre1909/an,nn3037   repro3739

unto you, There shall not be left here one*stone*upon*another, that shall

efn3364   fp2647

not be thrown down.

Coming Woes (Mark 13:3-13; Luke 21:7-19)

1161   ppro846 ppmp2521 pre1909 art3588   nn3735   art,nn1636   art3588   nn3101   aina4334

☞ 3 And as he sat upon the mount of Olives, the disciples came unto

ppro846 pre2596/an,ajn2396   pap3004   aina2036 ppro2254 ad4129   depro5023   fm2071 2432 inpro5101

him privately, saying, Tell us, when shall these things be? and what *shall be*

art3588 nn4592   art,popro4674   an,nn3952   2532   art3588 nn4930   art3588   nn165

the sign of thy coming, and of the end of the world?

2532   art,nn2424   aptp611   aina2036   ppro846   pim991   3361 idpro5100

☞ 4 And Jesus answered and said unto them, Take heed that no man

asba4105   ppro5209

deceive you.

☞ **24:3** See note on 1 Thessalonians 2:19.

☞ **24:4—25:46** This passage is known as the Olivet Discourse. Jesus begins this discourse in response to the disciples' questions in verse three. Their first inquiry was an attempt to ascertain when the destruction of the temple in Jerusalem, of which Christ had spoken (Matt. 24:3, cf. vv. 1, 2), would take place.

(continued on next page)

5 For many shall come in my name, saying, I am Christ; and shall deceive many.

6 And ye shall hear of wars and rumors of wars: see that ye be not troubled: for all *these things* must come*to*pass, but the end is not yet.

7 For nation shall rise against nation, and kingdom against kingdom: and there shall be famines, and pestilences, and earthquakes, in divers places.

8 All these *are* the beginning of sorrows.

9 Then shall they deliver*you*up to be afflicted, and shall kill you: and ye shall be hated of all nations for*my*name's*sake.

10 And then shall many be offended, and shall betray one another, and shall hate one another.

11 And many false prophets shall rise, and shall deceive many.

12 And because iniquity shall abound, the love of many shall wax cold.

13 But he*that*shall*endure unto the end, the same shall be saved.

14 And this gospel of the kingdom shall be preached in all the world for a witness unto all nations; and then shall the end come.

(continued from previous page)

Their second query concerned Christ's Second Coming and the end of the world. Some scholars feel that Jesus only responded to this second question.

There are two different views on how this passage relates to end time events. Some theologians suggest that this entire portion of Matthew relates exclusively to eschatological events. They propose that chapter twenty-four should be divided into four parts: the first half of the Great Tribulation (vv. 4–14), the second half of the Tribulation (vv. 15–28), the signs of Christ's coming (vv. 29–31), and the illustrations of the sudden end of the world (vv. 32–51). They also suggest that chapter twenty-five is an exhortation to God's people to be watchful for the coming of the events previously mentioned in chapter twenty-four.

On the other hand, there are those who believe that not all of the things Christ mentioned in these two chapters necessarily refer to eschatological events. These people suggest that chapter twenty-four opens with a general description of the events that will mark the end of the world (vv. 4–14), revealing the deceit and rampant sin that will be evident on the earth. Then, they propose that Christ sets forth the signs that will precede the end of the world (vv. 15–28). These "signs" are divided into two categories: Jerusalem's destruction (vv. 15–22) and God's restrained judgment on the earth during the Church Age (vv. 23–28). This chapter closes with the fulfillment of the events that take place marking the end of the world, as well as Christ's gathering of His people and the Battle of Armageddon (vv. 29–44, cf. Rev. 19:11–21). The proponents of this view also hold that Matthew 24:45—25:46 gives the details regarding the future judgment of the visible church (24:45–51) and of mankind (25:1–46).

The Great Tribulation (Mark 13:14-23; Luke 21:20-24)

☞ 15 When ye therefore shall see the abomination of desolation, spoken of by Daniel the prophet, stand in the holy place, (whoso readeth, let him understand:) *(Dan. 9:27; 11:31; 12:11)*

16 Then let them which be in Judea flee into the mountains:

17 Let him which is on the housetop not come down to take any thing out of his house:

18 Neither let him which is in the field return back to take his clothes.

19 And woe unto them*that*are*with*child, and to them*that*give*suck in those days!

20 But pray ye that your flight be not in the winter, neither on the sabbath day:

21 For then shall be great tribulation, such as was not since the beginning of the world to this time, no, nor ever shall be.

(Dan. 12:1; Joel 2:2)

☞ 22 And except those days should be shortened, there should no flesh be saved: but for*the*elect's*sake those days shall be shortened.

23 Then if any man shall say unto you, Lo, here is Christ, or there; believe it not.

24 For there shall arise false Christs, and false prophets, and shall show great signs and wonders; insomuch that, if it were possible, they shall deceive the very elect.

25 Behold, I have told*you*before.

☞ 24:15 See notes on 2 Thessalonians 2:3–8 and Revelation 13:1–18.
☞ 24:22, 31 See notes on Ephesians 1:4, 5 and 1 Thessalonians 2:19.

3767   1437   asba2036   ppro5213   2400   pin2076 pre1722 art3588   ajn2048
26 Wherefore if they shall say unto you, Behold, he is   in   the desert;
aosi1831/3361   2400   pre1722 art3588   nn5009   aosi4100   3361
go*not*forth: behold, *he is*   in   the secret chambers; believe *it* not.

1063   ad5618 art3588   nn796   pinm1831   pre575   an,nn395   2532   pinm5316   ad2193
27 For as the lightning cometh out of the east, and shineth even unto the
an,nn1424 ad3779   2532 art3588   nn3952   art3588 nn5207   art,nn444 fm2071
west; so shall also the coming of the Son of man be.

1063   ad3699/1437   art3588   nn4430   psa5600   ad1563   art3588   nn105
28 For   wheresoever   the   carcass   is,   there   will   the   eagles   be
fp4863
gathered together.

Christ's Second Coming (Mark 13:24-27; Luke 21:25-28)

(1161)   ad2112   pre3326 art3588   nn2347   depro1565 art,nn2250   art3588 nn2246
29   Immediately after the tribulation of those days shall the sun be
fp4654   2532 art3588   nn4582   3756   ft1325 ppro848 art,nn5338 2532 art3588   nn792   fm4098 pre575
darkened, and the moon shall not give her light, and the stars shall fall from
art,nn3772   2532 art3588   nn1411   art3588   nn3772   fp4531
heaven, and the powers of the heavens shall be shaken:

(Is. 13:10; 34:4; Ezek. 32:7; Joel 2:10,31; 3:15; Hag. 2:6,21)

2532   ad5119   fm5316   art3588 nn4592   art3588 nn5207   art,nn444   pre1722   art,nn3772   2532
30 And then shall appear the sign of the Son of man   in   heaven: and
ad5119   an,aj3956 art3588   nn5443   art3588 nn1093   fm2875   2532   fm3700 art3588 nn5207
then shall   all   the tribes of the earth mourn, and they shall see the Son of
art,nn444   ppmp2064   pre1909 art3588   nn3507   art,nn3772   pre3326 an,nn1411   2532 an,aj4183 an,nn1391
man coming   in   the clouds of heaven with power and great glory.

(Zech. 12:10; Dan. 7:13,14)

2532   ft649   ppro846 art,nn32   pre3326   an,aj3173 an,nn5456   an,nn4536   2532
☞ 31 And he shall send his angels with a great sound of a trumpet, and they
ft1996   ppro848 art,ajn1588 pre1537 art3588 nu5064   nn417   pre575   an,nn206   an,nn3772
shall gather together his elect from the four winds, from one end of heaven
ad2193   an,nn206 (ppro846)
to the other.   *(Zech. 2:6)*

The Lesson of the Fig Tree (Mark 13:28-31; Luke 21:29-33)

1161   aima3129   art,nn3850 pre575 art3588   nn4808   ad3752 ppro846 art,nn2798 asbm1096 ad2235
32 Now learn a parable of   the fig tree; When his branch is   yet
pr/an,aj527   2532   psa1631   art,nn5444   pin1097 3754   art,nn2330   pr/ad1451
tender, and putteth forth leaves, ye know that summer *is* nigh:
ad3779   2532 epn5210 ad3752   asba1492 an,aj3956   depro5023   pim1097   3754
33 So likewise ye, when ye shall see   all   these things, know that it
pin2076 pr/ad1451   pre1909   an,nn2374
is near, *even* at the doors.

²⁸¹   pin3004   ppro5213 depro3778   art,nn1074   efn3364   asba3928   ad2193/302   an,aj3956

34 Verily I say unto you, This generation shall not pass, till all

depro5023   asbm1096

these things be fulfilled.

art,nn3772   2532 art,nn1093   fm3928   1161 ppro3450 art,nn3056   efn3364   asbm3928

35 Heaven and earth shall pass away, but my words shall not pass away.

The Time of Christ's Coming Is Unknown (Mark 13:32-37; Luke 17:26-30,34-36)

1161   pre4012 depro1565 art,nn2250 2532   art,nn5610   pin1492   an,ajn3762   3761 art3588   nn32

☞ 36 But of that day and hour knoweth no *man,* no, not the angels of

art,nn3772   1508 ppro3450 art,nn3962 an,aj3441

heaven, but my Father only.

1161   ad5618 art3588   nn2550   3575   ad3779   2532 art3588   nn3952   art3588 nn5207

37 But as the days of Noah *were,* so shall also the coming of the Son of

art,nn444 fm2071

man be.   *(Gen. 6:9-12)*

1063   ad5618 pre1722 art3588 nn2250 art3588   pre4253 art3588 nn2627   ipf2258 pap5176   2532

38 For as in the days that were before the flood they were eating and

pap4095   pap1060   2532   pap1547   ad891   an,nn2250 repro3739   3575   aina1525

drinking, marrying and giving*in*marriage, until the day that Noah entered

pre1519 art3588 nn2787

into the ark,

2532   aina1097   3756   ad2193 art3588   nn2627   aina2064   2532   aina142/an,ajn537   ad3779

39 And knew not until the flood came, and took*them*all*away; so shall

2532 art3588   nn3952   art3588 nn5207   art,nn444   fm2071

also the coming of the Son of man be.   *(Gen. 7:21-23)*

ad5119   nu,ajn1417 fm2071 pre1722 art3588   nn68   art3588 nu,ajn1520   pinp3880   2532   art3588

40 Then shall two be in the field; the one shall be taken, and the

nu,ajn1520 pinp863

other left.

nu,ajn1417   pap229   pre1722 art3588   nn3459   an,nu,ajn3391   pinp3880

41 Two *women shall be* grinding at the mill; the one shall be taken,

2532   an,nu,ajn3391 pinp863

and the other left.

pim1127   3767   3754   pin1492   3756 an,aj4169 an,nn5610 ppro5216 art,nn2962   pinm2064

42 Watch therefore: for ye know not what hour your Lord doth come.

1161   pim1097 depro1565   3754   1487 art3588   nn3617   ipf1492   an,aj4169

43 But know this, that if the goodman*of*the*house had known in what

an,nn5438   art3588 nn2812   pinm2064   aina1127/302   2532   3756

watch the thief would come, he would have watched, and would not have

aina1439/302   ppro848 art,nn3614   aifp1358

suffered his house to be broken up.

pre1223/depro5124 pim1096 epn5210 2532   pr/an,aj2092 3754   repro3739   an,nn5610   pin1380 3756 art3588

44 Therefore be ye also ready: for in such an hour as ye think not the

nn5207   art,nn444   pinm2064

Son of man cometh.

☞ **24:36** See note on Philippians 2:6–8.

Faithful and Unfaithful Servants (Luke 12:41-48)

inpro5101　　686　　pin2076　　　　art,aj4103　　　2532　　an,aj5429　　pr/an,ajn1401　　repro3739　　ppro846　art,nn2962
45 Who　then　　is　　a　faithful　and　wise　servant,　whom　his　　lord　hath

aina2525　　pre1909　ppro848　　art,nn2322　　　　infg1325　ppro846　art,nn5160　pre1722　　an,nn2540
made ruler　over　his　household,　to　give　them　meat　in　due season?

pr/an,aj3107　depro1565　　art,ajn1401　　repro3739　ppro846　art,nn2962　　　　　　　apta2064　　　　　　ft2147
46 Blessed　*is*　that　servant,　whom　his　　lord　when　he　cometh　shall　find

ad3779　pap4160
so　doing.

281　　pin3004　　ppro5213　3754　　　　　　ft2525/ppro846　　pre1909　an,aj3956　ppro848
47 Verily I　say　unto　you,　That　he　shall make*him*ruler　over　　all　　his

art,pap5224
goods.

1161　　1437　depro1565　art,aj2556　　an,ajn1401　　　　asba2036　pre1722　ppro848　art,nn2588　ppro3450　art,nn2962
48 But and　if　that　evil　servant　shall　say　in　his　heart,　My　lord

pin5549　　　　ainf2064
delayeth his coming;

2532　　　fm756　　　pinf5180　　art,nn4889　　1161　　pinf2068　2532
49 And　shall　begin　to　smite　*his*　fellowservants,　and　to　eat　and

pinf4095　pre3326 art3588　pap3184
drink with the drunken;

art3588　nn2962　　depro1565　art,ajn1401　　ft2240　pre1722　an,nn2250 repro3739　　pin4328　3756
50 The lord of　that　servant shall come　in　a　day　when he looketh not

2532　pre1722　an,nn5610 repro3739　　3756　pin1097
for *him,* and　in　an hour　that　he is not aware of,

2532　　ft1371/ppro846　　2532　　ft5087　　ppro846　art,nn3313　pre3326 art3588
51 And　shall　cut*him*asunder,　and　appoint　*him*　his　portion　with　the

nn5273　　ad1563　　fm2071 art,nn2805　2532　art,nn1030　　art,nn3599
hypocrites: there shall be　weeping and gnashing of teeth.

The Parable of the Ten Virgins

　　　　ad5119　　art3588　　nn932　　art,nn3772　　　　fp3666　　nu1176　an,nn3933
25 Then shall the kingdom of heaven be likened unto ten virgins,

repro3748　apta2963　ppro848　art,nn2985　　　　aina1831　pre1519/an,nn529　art3588
which　took　their　lamps,　and　went　forth　to　meet　the

nn3566
bridegroom.

1161 nu4002 pre1537 ppro846 ipf2258 pr/an,aj5429 2532 art,nu,ajn4002　　pr/an,aj3474
2 And five　of　them were wise,　and　five　*were* foolish.

repro3748　　an,ajn3474 apta2983 rxpro1438 art,nn2985　　aina2983 3756 an,nn1637 pre3326 rxpro1438
3 They　that *were* foolish took their lamps, and took no　oil　with them:

1161 art3588　ajn5429 aina2983 an,nn1637 pre1722 ppro848　art,nn30　pre3326 ppro848 art,nn2985
4 But the wise took　oil　in　their vessels with their lamps.

1161　art3588　　nn3556　　pap5549　　an,ajn3956　aina3573　2532 ipf2518
5 While the bridegroom tarried, they　all　slumbered and slept.

1161　an,aj3319/an,nn3571　　an,nn2906 pfi1096　2400　art3588　　nn3566
6 And at　midnight　there was a　cry　made, Behold, the bridegroom

pinm2064　　pim1831　pre1519/an,nn529 ppro846
cometh; go*ye*out to meet him.

ad5119 an,aj3956 depro1565 art,nn3933 ainp1453 2532 aina2885 ppro848 art,nn2985
7 Then all those virgins arose, and trimmed their lamps.

1161 art3588 ajn3474 aina2036 art3588 ajn5429 aima1325 ppro2254 pre1537 ppro5216 art,nn1637 3754 ppro2257
8 And the foolish said unto the wise, Give us of your oil; for our

art,nn2985 pinm4570
lamps are gone out.

1161 art3588 ajn5429 ainp611 pap3004 3379 asba714/3756
9 But the wise answered, saying, *Not so*; lest there be*not*enough for

ppro2254 2532 ppro5213 1161 pim4198 ad3123 pre4314 art,pap4453 2532 aima59
us and you: but go ye rather to them*that*sell, and buy for

rxpro1438
yourselves.

1161 ppro846 ppmp565 ainf59 art3588 nn3566 aina2064 2532
10 And while they went to buy, the bridegroom came; and

art,ajn2092 aina1525 pre3326 ppro846 pre1519 art3588 nn1062 2532 art3588 nn2374
they*that*were*ready went in with him to the marriage: and the door was

ainp2808
shut.

(1161) ad5305 pinm2064 2532 art3588 an,aj3062 nn3933 pap3004 an,nn2962 an,nn2962 aima455
11   Afterward came also the other virgins, saying, Lord, Lord, open to

ppro2254
us.

1161 art3588 aptp611 aina2036 281 pin3004 ppro5213 pin1492 ppro5209 3756
12 But he answered and said, Verily I say unto you, I know you not.

pim1127 3767 3754 pin1492 3756 art3588 nn2250 3761 art3588 nn5610 pre1722/repro3739
13 Watch therefore, for ye know neither the day nor the hour wherein

art3588 nn5207 art,nn444 pinm2064
the Son of man cometh.

The Talents (Luke 19:11-27)

1063 ad5618 an,nn444 pap589
☞ 14 For *the kingdom of heaven is* as a man traveling*into*a*far*country,

aina2564 art,aj2398 an,ajn1401 2532 aina3860 ppro846 ppro848 art,pap5224
who called his own servants, and delivered unto them his goods.

2532 repro3739/3303 aina1325 nu4002 an,nn5007 (1161) repro3739 nu,ajn1417 1161 repro3739
15 And unto one he gave five talents, to another two, and to another

nu,ajn1520 an,ajn1538 pre2596 art,aj2398 an,nn1411 2532 ad2112
one; to every man according to his several ability; and straightway

aina589
took*his*journey.

1161 art,apta2983 art3588 nu4002 nn5007 aptp4198 2532 aom2038 pre1722
16 Then he*that*had*received the five talents went and traded with

ppro846 2532 aina4160 an,aj243 nu4002 an,nn5007
the same, and made *them* other five talents.

2532 ad5615 art3588 art,nu,ajn1417 epn846 2532 aina2770 an,aj243
17 And likewise he that *had received* two, he also gained other

nu,ajn1417
two.

☞ **25:14–30** See notes on Matthew 8:11, 12 and Luke 19:11–27.

₁₁₆₁ _{art,apta2983} _{art,nu,ajn1520} _{apta565} _{aina3736} _{pre1722} _{art3588} _{nn1093} ₂₅₃₂

18 But he*that*had*received one went and digged in the earth, and

_{aina613} _{ppro848} _{art,nn2962} _{art,nn694}

hid his lord's money.

₍₁₁₆₁₎ _{pre3326} _{an,aj4183} _{an,nn5550} _{art3588} _{nn2962} _{depro1565} _{art,ajn1401} _{pinm2064} ₂₅₃₂ _{pin4868/an,nn3056}

19 After a long time the lord of those servants cometh, and reckoneth

_{pre3326} _{ppro846}

with them.

₂₅₃₂ _{art,apta2983} _{(art3588)nu4002} _{nn5007} _{apta4334} _{aina4374} _{an,aj243}

20 And so he*that*had*received five talents came and brought other

_{nu4002} _{an,nn5007} _{pap3004} _{an,nn2962} _{aina3860} _{ppro3427} _{nu4002} _{an,nn5007} _{aima2396}

five talents, saying, Lord, thou deliveredst unto me five talents: behold, I have

_{aina2770} _{pre1909} _{ppro846} _{nu4002} _{an,nn5007} _{an,aj243}

gained beside them five talents more.

₍₁₁₆₁₎ _{ppro846} _{art,nn2962} _{aina5346} _{ppro846} _{ad2095} _{an,aj18} ₂₅₃₂ _{an,aj4103} _{an,ajn1401}

21 His lord said unto him, Well done, *thou* good and faithful servant: thou

_{ipf2258} _{pr/an,aj4103} _{pre1909} _{an,ajn3641} _{ft2525/ppro4571} _{pre1909} _{an,ajn4183}

hast been faithful over a few things, I will make*thee*ruler over many things:

_{aima1525} _{pre1519} _{art3588} _{nn5479} _{ppro4675} _{art,nn2962}

enter thou into the joy of thy lord.

₍₁₁₆₁₎ _{art,apta2983/2532} _{art,nu1417} _{nn5007} _{apta4334} _{aina2036} _{an,nn2962}

22 He*also*that*had*received two talents came and said, Lord, thou

_{aina3860} _{ppro3427} _{nu1417} _{an,nn5007} _{aima2396} _{aina2770} _{nu1417} _{an,aj243} _{an,nn5007}

deliveredst unto me two talents: behold, I have gained two other talents

_{pre1909} _{ppro846}

beside them.

_{ppro846} _{art,nn2962} _{aina5346} _{ppro846} _{ad2095} _{an,aj18} ₂₅₃₂ _{an,aj4103} _{an,ajn1401}

23 His lord said unto him, Well done, good and faithful servant; thou hast

_{ipf2258} _{pr/an,aj4103} _{pre1909} _{an,ajn3641} _{ft2525/ppro4571} _{pre1909} _{an,ajn4183}

been faithful over a few things, I will make*thee*ruler over many things:

_{aima1525} _{pre1519} _{art3588} _{nn5479} _{ppro4675} _{art,nn2962}

enter thou into the joy of thy lord.

₁₁₆₁ _{art,pfp2983} _{art3588} _{nu1520} _{nn5007} _{(2532)apta4334} _{aina2036} _{an,nn2962}

24 Then he*which*had*received the one talent came and said, Lord, I

_{aina1097} _{ppro4571} ₃₇₅₄ _{pin1488} _{pr/an,aj4642} _{an,nn444} _{pap2325} _{ad3699} ₃₇₅₆ _{aina4687}

knew thee that thou art a hard man, reaping where thou hast not sown,

₂₅₃₂ _{pap4863} _{ad3606} ₃₇₅₆ _{aina1287}

and gathering where thou hast not strewed:

₂₅₃₂ _{aptp5399} _{apta565} _{aina2928} _{ppro4675} _{art,nn5007} _{pre1722} _{art3588} _{nn1093} _{aima2396}

25 And I was afraid, and went and hid thy talent in the earth: lo,

_{pin2192} _{art,popro4674}

there thou hast *that is* thine.

₍₁₁₆₁₎ _{ppro846} _{art,nn2962} _{aptp611} _{aina2036} _{ppro846} _{an,aj4190} ₂₅₃₂ _{an,aj3636}

26 His lord answered and said unto him, *Thou* wicked and slothful

_{an,ajn1401} _{ipf1492} ₃₇₅₄ _{pin2325} _{ad3699} _{aina4687} ₃₇₅₆ ₂₅₃₂ _{pin4863} _{ad3606}

servant, thou knewest that I reap where I sowed not, and gather where I have

₃₇₅₆ _{aina1287}

not strewed:

_{ppro4571} _{ipf1163} ₃₇₆₇ _{ainf906} _{ppro3450} _{art,nn694} _{art3588} _{nn5133}

27 Thou oughtest therefore to have put my money to the exchangers,

₂₅₃₂ _{apta2064} _{epn1473} _{aom2865/302} _{art,popro1699} _{pre4862} _{an,nn5110}

and *then* at my coming I should have received mine own with usury.

aima142   3767   art3588   nn5007   pre575   ppro846   2532   aima1325   art,pap2192

28 Take therefore the talent from him, and give *it* unto him*which*hath

nu1176   art,nn5007

ten talents.

1063   an,ajn3956   art,pap2192   fp1325   2532

29 For unto every one that hath shall be given, and he shall

fp4052   1161   pre575   art3588   pap2192 3361   fp142   (pre575 ppro846)2532

have abundance: but from him that hath not shall be taken away   even   that

repro3739   pin2192

which he hath.

2532   pim1544   art3588   an,aj888   ajn1401   pre1519 art,aj1857   art,nn4655   ad1563

30 And cast ye the unprofitable servant into outer darkness: there shall

fm2071   art,nn2805   2532   art,nn1030   art,nn3599

be weeping and gnashing of teeth.

Concerning the Future Judgment

(1161)   ad3752   art3588   nn5207   art,nn444   asba2064   pre1722   ppro848   art,nn1391   2532   an,aj3956   art3588   an,aj40

31   When the Son of man shall come in his glory, and all the holy

nn32   pre3326   ppro846   ad5119   ft2523   pre1909   an,nn2362   ppro848   an,nn1391

angels with him, then shall he sit upon the throne of his glory: *(Zech. 14:5)*

2532   ad*1715   ppro846   fp4863   an,aj3956   art,nn1484   2532   ft873

32 And before him shall be gathered all   nations: and he shall separate

ppro846   rcpro240/pre575   ad5618   art,nn4166   pin863   art,nn4263   pre575   art3588   nn2056

them one*from*another, as a shepherd divideth *his* sheep from the goats:

(Ezek. 34:17)

2532   ft2476 art3588 (3303)nn4263 pre1537 ppro848   an,ajn1188   1161   art3588   nn2055   pre1537

33 And he shall set the sheep on his right hand, but the goats on the

an,ajn2176

left.

ad5119   art3588   nn935   ft2046   art3588   pre1537   ppro848   an,ajn1188   ad1205

34 Then shall the King say unto them on his right hand, Come, ye

art,pfpp2127   ppro3450   art,nn3962   aima2816   art3588   nn932   pfpp2090   ppro5213   pre575

blessed of my Father, inherit the kingdom prepared for you from the

an,nn2602   an,nn2889

foundation of the world:

1063   aina3983   2532   aina1325   ppro3427   ainf5315   aina1372   2532

35 For I was hungry, and ye gave me meat: I was thirsty, and ye

aina4222/ppro3165   ipf2252   pr/an,ajn3581   2532   aina4863/ppro3165

gave*me*drink: I was a stranger, and ye took*me*in:

pr/an,aj1131   2532   aina4016   ppro3165   aina770   2532   aom1980   ppro3165   ipf2252 pre1722

36 Naked, and ye clothed me: I was sick, and ye visited me: I was in

an,nn5438   2532   aina2064   pre4314   ppro3165

prison, and ye came unto me.

ad5119   art3588   ajn1342   fp611   ppro846   pap3004   an,nn2962   ad4219   aina1492

37 Then shall the righteous answer him,, saying, Lord, when saw we

ppro4571   pap3983   2532 aina5142   2228   pap1372   2532   aina4222

thee hungry, and fed *thee*? or thirsty, and gave*thee*drink?

38   When saw we thee a stranger, and took**thee***in? or naked, and

clothed *thee?*

39 Or when saw we thee sick, or in prison, and came unto thee?

40 And the King shall answer and say unto them, Verily I say unto you,

Inasmuch as ye have done *it* unto one of the least of these my brethren, ye

have done *it* unto me.

41 Then shall he say also unto them on the left hand, Depart from me,

ye cursed, into everlasting fire, prepared for the devil and his angels:

42 For I was hungry, and ye gave me no meat: I was thirsty, and ye

gave*me*no*drink:

43 I was a stranger, and ye took*me*not*in: naked, and ye clothed me

not: sick, and in prison, and ye visited me not.

44 Then shall they also answer him, saying, Lord, when saw we thee

hungry, or athirst, or a stranger, or naked, or sick, or in prison, and did

not minister unto thee?

45 Then shall he answer them, saying, Verily I say unto you,

Inasmuch as ye did *it* not to one of the least of these, ye did *it* not to me.

46 And these shall go away into everlasting punishment: but the

righteous into life eternal.

The Leaders Plot to Kill Jesus (Mark 14:1,2; Luke 22:1,2; John 11:45-53)

26 And it came*to*pass, when Jesus had finished all these sayings, he said unto his disciples,

2 Ye know that after two days is *the feast of* the passover, and the

Son of man is betrayed to be crucified.   *(Ex. 12:1-27)*

ad5119   ainp4863   art3588   nn749   2532 art3588   nn1122   2532 art3588

3 Then assembled together the chief priests, and the scribes, and the

ajn4245   art3588   nn2992   pre1519 art3588   nn833   art3588   nn749   art,ppmp3004

elders of the people, unto the palace of the high priest, who*was*called

an,nn2533

Caiaphas,

2532   aom4823   2443   asba2902 art,nn2424   an,nn1388   2532 asba615

4 And consulted that they might take Jesus by subtlety, and kill *him*.

1161   ipf3004   3361 pre1722 art3588 nn1859   3363   asbm1096   an,nn2351   pre1722

5 But they said, Not on the feast *day,* lest there be an uproar among

art3588   nn2992

the people.

Jesus Anointed at Bethany (Mark 14:3-9; John 12:1-8)

1161   art,nn2424 aptm1096 pre1722   an,nn963   pre1722   an,nn3614   an,nn4613 art3588

6 Now when Jesus was in Bethany, in the house of Simon the

ajn3015

leper,

aina4334   ppro846   an,nn1135   pap2192   an,nn211   an,aj927

7 There came unto him a woman having an alabaster box of very precious

an,nn3464   2532   ipf2708   pre1909 ppro846 art,nn2776   ppmp345

ointment, and poured it on his head, as he sat *at meat.*

1161   ppro846   art,nn3101   apta1492   aina23   pap3004   pre1519

8 But when his disciples saw *it,* they had indignation, saying, To

inpro5101   depro3778   art,nn684

what purpose *is* this waste?

1063   depro5124   art,nn3464   ipf1410   aifp4097   an,ajn4183   2532   aifp1325

9 For this ointment might have been sold for much, and given to the

an,ajn4434

poor.

1161   art,nn2424   apta1097   aina2036   ppro846   inpro5101 pin3930/an,nn2873   art3588

10 When Jesus understood *it,* he said unto them, Why trouble ye the

nn1135   1063   aom2038   an,aj2570 an,nn2041 pre1519 ppro1691

woman? for she hath wrought a good work upon me.

1063   pin2192 art3588 ajn4434   ad3842   pre3326 rxpro1438 1161 epn1691   pin2192 3756   ad3842

11 For ye have the poor always with you; but me ye have not always.

(Deut. 15:11)

1063   depro3778   apta906   depro5124   art,nn3464   pre1909 ppro3450 art,nn4983   aina4160

12 For in that she hath poured this ointment on my body, she did *it*

ppro3165   aipr1779

for my burial.

281   pin3004   ppro5213   ad3699/1437   depro5124 art,nn2098   asbp2784   pre1722

13 Verily I say unto you, Wheresoever this gospel shall be preached in

art3588 an,aj3650   nn2889   2532 repro3739   depro3778   aina4160   fp2980 pre1519

the whole world, *there* shall also this, that this woman hath done, be told for a

an,nn3422   ppro846

memorial of her.

Judas Agrees to Betray Jesus (Mark 14:10,11; Luke 22:3-6)

ad5119 nu1520   art3588   nu,ajn1427   art,ppmp3004   an,nn2455   an,ajn2469   aptp4198   pre4314   art3588

14 Then one of the twelve, called Judas Iscariot, went unto the

nn749

chief priests,

aina2036   inpro5101 pin2309   ainf1325 ppro3427   epn2504   ft3860   ppro846

15 And said *unto them*, What will ye give me, and I will deliver him unto

ppro5213 1161 art3588   aina2476   ppro846   nu5144   an,nn694

you? And they covenanted with him for thirty pieces*of*silver.   (*Zech. 11:12*)

2534   pre575   ad5119   ipf2212   an,nn2120   2443 asba3860 ppro846

16 And from that time he sought opportunity to betray him.

Jesus Eats the Passover With His Disciples (Mark 14:12-21; Luke 22:7-14,21-23; John 13:21-30)

1161   art3588 nu,ajn4413   art3588   ajn106   art3588   nn3101   aina4334

17 Now the first *day* of the *feast of* unleavened bread the disciples came

art,nn2424 pap3004   ppro846   ad4226 pin2309   asba2090   ppro4671   ainf5315

to Jesus, saying unto him, Where wilt thou that we prepare for thee to eat

art3588   3957

the passover?   (*Ex. 12:14-20*)

1161 art3588 aina2036 aima5217 pre1519 art3588 nn4172 pre4314   art,ajn1170   2532 aima2036   ppro846

18 And he said, Go into the city to such*a*man, and say unto him,

art3588   nn1320   pin3004   ppro3450 art,nn2540 pin2076 pr/ad1451   pin4160 art3588   3957   pre4314

The Master saith, My time is at hand; I will keep the passover at

ppro4571   pre3326 ppro3450   art,nn3101

thy house with my disciples.

2532   art3588   nn3101   aina4160 ad5613 art,nn2424   aina4929   ppro846   2532

19 And the disciples did as Jesus had appointed them; and they

aina2090   art3588   3957

made ready the passover.

1161   an,nn3798   aptm1096   ipf345   pre3326 art3588 nu,ajn1427

20 Now when the even was come, he sat down with the twelve.

2532   ppro846   pap2068   aina2036   281   pin3004   ppro5213 3754 nu1520 pre1537 ppro5216

21 And as they did eat, he said, Verily I say unto you, that one of you

ft3860   ppro3165

shall betray me.

2532   ppmp3076/ad4970   aom756 an,ajn1538   ppro846

22 And they were*exceeding*sorrowful, and began every one of them to

pinf3004   ppro846 an,nn2962(3385) pin1510   epn1473

say unto him, Lord, is it I?

1161   art3588   aptp611   aina2036   art,apta1686   art,nn5495 pre3326 ppro1700 pre1722

23 And he answered and said, He*that*dippeth *his* hand with me   in

art3588 nn5165   depro3778   ft3860   ppro3165

the dish, the same shall betray me.   (*Ps. 41:9*)

art3588 nn5207   art,nn444 pin5217 ad2531 (3303)   pfip1125   pre4012 ppro846   1161   3759   depro1565

24 The Son of man goeth as it is written of him. but woe unto that

art,nn444 pre1223 repro3739 art3588 nn5207   art,nn444   pinp3860   ipf2258 an,ajn2570 (ppro846) depro1565 art,nn444

man by whom the Son of man is betrayed! it had been good ˙for that man

1487   3756   ainp1080

if he had not been born.   *(Ps. 22:7,8,16-18; Is. 53:9)*

1161   an,nn2455   art,pap3860   ppro846   aptp611   aina2036 4461(3385) pin1510

25 Then Judas, which betrayed him, answered and said, Master, is it

epn1473   pin3004   ppro846 epn4771   aina2036

I? He said unto him, Thou hast said.

The Lord's Supper (Mark 14:22-26; Luke 22:15-20; 1 Cor. 11:23-25)

1161   ppro846   pap2068 art,nn2424 apta2983 art,nn740 2532 apta2127   aina2806

26 And as they were eating, Jesus took bread, and blessed *it,* and broke *it,*

2532 ipf1325   art3588   nn3101   2532 aina2036 aima2983 aima5315 depro5124 pin2076 ppro3450 pr/art,nn4983

and gave *it* to the disciples, and said, Take, eat; this is my body.

2532   apta2983 art3588 nn4221 2532   apta2168   aina1325   ppro846   pap3004

27 And he took the cup, and gave thanks, and gave *it* to them, saying,

aima4095   an,ajn3956 pre1537 ppro846

Drink ye all of it;

1063 depro5124 pin2076 ppro3450 pr/art,nn129 (art3588) art3588 aj2537 an,nn1242   art,ppmp1632   pre4012

28 For this is my blood of the new testament, which*is*shed for

an,ajn4183 pre1519   an,nn859   an,nn266

many for the remission of sins.   *(Ex. 24:8; Jer. 31:31; Zech. 9:11)*

1161   pin3004   ppro5213   efn3364 asba4095 pre575/ad737 pre1537 depro5127 art,nn1081   art3588

29 But I say unto you, I will not drink henceforth of this fruit of the

nn288   ad2193 depro1565 art,nn2250 ad3752   psa4095 ppro846 an,aj2537 pre3326 ppro5216 pre1722 ppro3450 art,nn3962

vine, until that day when I drink it new with you in my Father's

art,nn932

kingdom.

2532   apta5214   aina1831   pre1519 art3588   nn3735

30 And when they had sung*a*hymn, they went out into the mount of

art,nn1636

Olives.   *(Ps. 113—118)*

Prediction About Peter's Denial (Mark 14:27-31; Luke 22:31-34; John 13:36-38)

ad5119   pin3004 art,nn2424   ppro846 an,aj3956 ppro5210   fp4624   pre1722

31 Then saith Jesus unto them, All ye shall be offended because of

ppro1698 (pre1722) depro5026 art,nn3571 1063   pfip1125   ft3960 art3588   nn4166   2532 art3588 nn4263

me   this night: for it is written, I will smite the shepherd, and the sheep

art3588 nn4167   fp1287

of the flock shall be scattered abroad.   *(Zech. 13:7)*

1161   ppro3165   aime1453   ft4254   ppro5209 pre1519 art,nn1056

32 But after I   am risen again, I will go before you into Galilee.

(1161) art,nn4074   aptp611   aina2036   ppro846   1499   an,ajn3956

33 Peter answered and said unto him, Though all *men* shall be

fp4624   pre1722   ppro4671   epn1473   ad3762   fp4624

offended because of thee, *yet* will I never be offended.

art,nn2424   aina5346   ppro846   281   pin3004   ppro4671   3754(pre1722) depro5026 art,nn3571   ad4250

34 Jesus said unto him, Verily I say unto thee, That this night, before

an,nn220   ainf5455   fm533   ppro3165   nu,ad5151

the cock crow, thou shalt deny me thrice.

art,nn4074   pin3004   ppro846   2579   ppro3165   psa1163   ainf599   pre4862   ppro4671   efn3364

35 Peter said unto him, Though I should die with thee, yet will I not

fm533   ppro4571   ad3668   2532   aina2036 an,aj3956 art3588   nn3101

deny thee. Likewise also said all the disciples.

Jesus Prays in Gethsemane (Mark 14:32-42; Luke 22:39-46)

ad5119   pinm2064   art,nn2424   pre3326   ppro846   pre1519   an,nn5564   ppmp3004   1068   2532

36 Then cometh Jesus with them unto a place called Gethsemane, and

pin3004   art3588   nn3101   aima2523   ad847   ad2193/repro3739   apta565   asbm4336   ad1563

saith unto the disciples, Sit ye here, while I go and pray yonder.

2532   apta3880   art,nn4074   2532 art3588 nu1417 nn5207   an,nn2199   aom756

37 And he took with him Peter and the two sons of Zebedee, and began to

pim3076   2532   pinf85

be sorrowful and very heavy.

ad5119   pin3004   ppro846   ppro3450   art,nn5590   pin2076   pr/an,aj4036

38 Then saith he unto them, My soul is exceeding sorrowful,

ad2193   an,nn2288 aima3306   ad5602   2532   pim1127   pre3326 ppro1700

even unto death: tarry ye here, and watch with me.   *(Ps. 42:5,11; 43:5)*

2532   apta4281   an,ajn3397   aina4098 pre1909 ppro848 an,nn4383   ppmp4336(2532)

39 And he went a little farther, and fell on his face, and prayed,

pap3004   ppro3450   an,nn3962   1487   pin2076   pr/an,ajn1415   depro5124 art,nn4221 aipp3928   pre575   ppro1700

saying, O my Father, if it be possible, let this cup pass from me:

4133   3756 ad5613 epn1473 pin2309   235   ad5613 epn4771

nevertheless not as I will, but as thou *wilt*.

2532   pinm2064   pre4314 art3588   nn3101   2532   pin2147   ppro846   pap2518   2532   pin3004

40 And he cometh unto the disciples, and findeth them asleep, and saith

art,nn4074   ad3779   aina2480   3756   ainf1127   pre3326 ppro1700 nu3391 an,nn5610

unto Peter, What, could ye not watch with me one hour?

pim1127   2532   pim4336   2443   asba1525   3361 pre1519   an,nn3986   art3588   nn4151   3303

41 Watch and pray, that ye enter not into temptation: the spirit indeed *is*

pr/an,aj4289   1161 art3588 nn4561   pr/an,aj772

willing, but the flesh *is* weak.

apta565   ad3825   (pre1537)   nu,ajn1208   aom4336   pap3004   ppro3450

42 He went away again the second time, and prayed, saying, O my

an,nn3962   1487 depro5124 art,nn4221 pinm1410 3756   ainf3928   pre575 ppro1700   3362   asba4095 ppro846 ppro4675

Father, if this cup may not pass away from me, except I drink it, thy

art,nn2307   aipp1096

will be done.

2532   apta2064   pin2147   ppro846   pap2518   ad3825   1063   ppro846   art,nn3788   ipf2258

43 And he came and found them asleep again: for their eyes were

pfpp916

heavy.

2532   apta863   ppro846   apta565   ad3825   aom4336   (pre1537)   nu,ajn5154
44 And he left them, and went away again, and prayed the third time,

apta2036   art3588   ppro848   an,nn3056
saying the same words.

ad5119   pinm2064   pre4314   ppro848   art,nn3101   2532   pin3004   ppro846   pim2518
45 Then cometh he to his disciples, and saith unto them, Sleep on

art,ajn3063   2532   pim373   2400   art3588   nn5610   pfi1448   2532   art3588   nn5207   art,nn444
now, and take*your*rest: behold, the hour is*at*hand, and the Son of man is

pinp3860   pre1519   an,nn5495   an,ajn268
betrayed into the hands of sinners.

pim1453   pim71   2400   pfi1448   art,pap3860   ppro3165
46 Rise, let us be going: behold, he is*at*hand that*doth*betray me.

Jesus Is Arrested (Mark 14:43-50; Luke 22:47-53; John 18:3-12)

2532   ppro846 ad2089   pap2980   2400 an,nn2455   nu1520   art3588   nu,ajn1427   aina2064   2532   pre3326
47 And while he yet spake, lo, Judas, one of the twelve, came, and with

ppro846   an,aj4183   an,nn3793   pre3326   an,nn3162   2532   an,nn3586   pre575   art3588   nn749   2532
him a great multitude with swords and staves, from the chief priests and

an,ajn4245   art3588   nn2992
elders of the people.

1161   art,pap3860   ppro846 aina1325 ppro846   an,nn4592   pap3004   repro3739/302
48 Now he*that*betrayed him gave them a sign, saying, Whomsoever I

asba5368   pr/epn846   pin2076   aima2902/ppro846
shall kiss, that same is he: hold*him*fast.

2532   ad2112   apta4334   art,nn2424   aina2036 pim5463   4461   2532   aina2705
49 And forthwith he came to Jesus, and said, Hail, master; and kissed

ppro846
him.

1161   art,nn2424   aina2036   ppro846   an,nn2083   pre1909/repro3739   pin3918   ad5119
50 And Jesus said unto him, Friend, wherefore art thou come? Then

apta4334   aina1911 art,nn5495 pre1909 art,nn2424   2532 aina2902 ppro846
came they, and laid hands on Jesus, and took him.

2532   2400   nu1520   art3588   pre3326 an,nn2424   apta1614
51 And, behold, one of them which were with Jesus stretched out *his*

art,nn5495   aina645 ppro848 art,nn3162   2532 apta3960   art,ajn1401   art3588   nn749
hand, and drew his sword, and struck a servant of the high priest's, and

aina851   ppro846 art,nn5621
smote off his ear.

ad5119   pin3004 art,nn2424   ppro846   aima654   pre4675 art,nn3162 pre1519 ppro846 art,nn5117   1063
52 Then said Jesus unto him, Put*up*again thy sword into his place: for

an,aj3956   art,apta2983   an,nn3162   ft622   pre1722   an,nn3162
all they*that*take the sword shall perish with the sword.   *(Gen. 9:6)*

(2228)   pin1380   3754   pinm1410/3756 ad737   ainf3870   ppro3450   art,nn3962   2532
53   Thinkest thou that I cannot now pray to my Father, and he shall

ft3936   ppro3427 cd/an,aj4119   2228   nu427   an,nn3003   an,nn32
presently give me more than twelve legions of angels?

ad4459   3767   art3588   nn1124   asbp4137   3754   ad3779   pin1163 aifm1096
54 But how then shall the Scriptures be fulfilled, that thus it must be?

pre1722   depro1565   art,nn5610   aina2036   art,nn2424   art3588   nn3793   aina1831

55 In that same hour said Jesus to the multitudes, Are ye come out

ad5613   pre1909   an,nn3027   pre3326   an,nn3162   2532   an,nn3586   ainf4815 ppro3165   ipf2516 pre2596/an,nn2250

as against a thief with swords and staves for to take me? I sat   daily

pre4314 ppro5209   pap1321   pre1722 art3588   nn2411   2532   aina2902/3756   ppro3165

with you teaching in the temple, and ye laid*no*hold on me.

              1161   an,aj3650 depro5124   pfi1096   2443 art3588   nn1124   art3588   nn4396

56 But all this was done, that the Scriptures of the prophets might be

       asbp4137   ad5119   an,aj3956 art3588   nn3101   apta863   ppro846   aina5343

fulfilled. Then all the disciples forsook him, and fled.

Jesus Is Brought Before Caiaphas (Mark 14:53-65; Luke 22:54,55,63-71; John 18:12-14,19-24)

              1161   art,apta2902   art,nn2424   aina520   pre4314   an,nn2533   art3588

57 And they*that*had*laid*hold on Jesus led*him*away to Caiaphas the

nn749   ad3699 art3588   nn1122   2532 art3588 ajn4245   ainp4863

high priest, where the scribes and the elders were assembled.

              1161   art,nn4074   ipf190   ppro846 pre575/ad3113 ad2193 art3588   nn749   art,nn833   2532   apta1525

58 But Peter followed him afar off unto the high priest's palace, and went

ad2080   ipf2521 pre3326 art3588   nn5257   ainf1492 art3588 nn5056

in, and sat with the servants, to see the end.

              1161   art3588   nn749   2532   art,ajn4245   2532   an,aj3650   art3588   nn4892   ipf2212

59 Now the chief priests, and elders, and all the council, sought

an,nn5577   pre2596   art,nn2424 3704   asba2289/ppro846

false witness against Jesus, to put*him*to*death;

         2532   aina2147   3756   2532   an,aj4183   an,nn5575   apta4334   aina2147

60 But found none: yea, though many false witnesses came, yet found they

3756   (1161)ad5305   apta4334 nu1417   an,nn5575

none. At*the*last came two false witnesses,

              aina2036 depro3778   aina5346   pinm1410   ainf2647 art3588   nn3485   art,nn2316

61 And said, this fellow said, I am able to destroy the temple of God,

2532   ainf3618 ppro846 pre1223 nu5140 an,nn2250

and to build it   in three days.

              2532 art3588   nn749   apta450   aina2036   ppro846   pinm611   an,ajn3762

62 And the high priest arose, and said unto him, Answerest thou nothing?

inpro5101   depro3778   pin2649   ppro4675

what is it which these witness against thee?

              1161   art,nn2424   ipf4623   2532 art3588   nn749   aptp611   aina2036

63 But Jesus held*his*peace. And the high priest answered and said unto

ppro846   pin1844   ppro4571 pre2596 art3588 pap2198 art,nn2316 2443   asba2036 ppro2254 1487   epn4771 pin1488

him, I adjure thee by the living God, that thou tell us whether thou be

art3588   pr/nn5547   art3588 pr/nn5207   art,nn2316

the Christ, the Son of God.   (Is. 53:7)

              art,nn2424   pin3004   ppro846 epn4771   aina2036   4133   pin3004   ppro5213

64 Jesus saith unto him, Thou hast said: nevertheless I say unto you,

pre575/ad737   fm3700 art3588 nn5207   art,nn444 ppmp2521 pre1537   an,ajn1188   art,nn1411

Hereafter shall ye see the Son of man sitting on the right hand of power,

2532   ppmp2064   pre1909 art3588   nn3507   art,nn3772

and coming in the clouds of heaven.   (Ps. 110:1; Dan. 7:13) ad5119   art3588   nn749   aina1284   ppro848   art,nn2440   pap3004

☞ 65 Then the high priest rent his clothes, saying, He hath

aina987   inpro5101   ad2089   an,nn5532   pin2192   an,nn3144   aima2396   ad3568

spoken blasphemy; what further need have we of witnesses? behold, now ye

aina191   ppro846   art,nn988

have heard his blasphemy.

inpro5101   pin1380   ppro5213(1161)   art3588   aptp611   aina2036   pin2076   pr/an,aj1777   an,nn2288

66 What think ye? They answered and said, He is guilty of death.

(Lev. 24:16)

ad5119   aina1716   pre1519   ppro846   art,nn4383   2532   aina2852   ppro846   1161   art3588

67 Then did they spit in his face, and buffeted him; and others

aina4474

smote*him*with*the*palms*of*their*hands,   *(Is. 50:6;53:5)*

pap3004   aima4395   ppro2254   an,nn5547   pr/inpro5101   pin2076   art,apta3817   ppro4571

68 Saying, Prophesy unto us, thou Christ, Who is he*that*smote thee?

Peter Denies Jesus (Mark 14:66-72; Luke 22:56-62; John 18:15-18,25-27)

1161   art,nn4074   ipf2521   ad1854   pre1722   art3588   nn833   2532   nu3391   an,nn3814   aina4334

69 Now Peter sat without in the palace: and a damsel came unto

ppro846   pap3004   epn4771   2532   ipf2258   pre3326   an,nn2424   art,aj1057

him, saying, Thou also wast with Jesus of Galilee.

1161   art3588   aom720   ad*1715   an,ajn3956   pap3004   pin1492   3756   inpro5101   pin3004

70 But he denied before *them* all, saying, I know not what thou sayest.

1161   ppro846   apta1831   pre1519   art3588   nn4440   an,ajn243   aina1492   ppro846

71 And when he was gone out into the porch, another *maid* saw him,

2532   pin3004   art3588   ad1563   depro3778   ipf2258   2532   pre3326   an,nn2424

and said unto them that were there, This *fellow* was also with Jesus of

art,nn3480

Nazareth.

2532   ad3825   aom720   pre3326   an,nn3728   3756   pin1492   art3588   nn444

72 And again he denied with an oath, I do not know the man.

1161   pre3326   an,ajn3397   apta4334   art,pfp2476   aina2036   art,nn4074

73 And after a while came unto *him* they*that*stood*by, and said to Peter,

ad230   epn4771   2532   pin1488   pre1537   ppro846   1063   ppro4675   art,nn2981   pin4160/an,aj1212   ppro4571

Surely thou also art *one* of them; for thy speech betrayeth thee.

ad5119   aom756   pinf2653   2532   pinf3660   pin1492   3756   art3588   nn444

74 Then began he to curse and to swear, *saying*, I know not the man.

2532   ad212   an,nn220   aina5455

And immediately the cock crew.

2532   art,nn4074   ainp3415   art3588   nn4487   art,nn2424   pfp2046   ppro846

75 And Peter remembered the word of Jesus, which said unto him,

ad4250   an,nn220   ainf5455   fm533   ppro3165   nu,ad5151   2532   apta1831   ad1854

Before the cock crow, thou shalt deny me thrice. And he went out, and

aina2799   ad4090

wept bitterly.

☞ **26:65, 66** See note on Mark 3:28, 29.

Jesus Is Brought Before Pilate (Mark 15:1; Luke 23:1,2; John 18:28-32)

1161 an,nn4405 aptm1096 an,aj3956 art3588 nn749 2532 art,ajn4245

27 When the morning was come, all the chief priests and elders of
art3588 nn2992 aina2983 an,nn4824 pre2596 art,nn2424 5620 ainf2289/ppro846

the people took counsel against Jesus to put*him*to*death:

2532 apta1210 ppro846 aina520 2532 aina3860 ppro846

2 And when they had bound him, they led*him*away, and delivered him to
an,nn4194 an,nn4091 art3588 nn2232

Pontius Pilate the governor.

The Death of Judas (Acts 1:18,19)

ad5119 an,nn2455 art,pap3860 ppro846 apta1492 3754

3 Then Judas, which*had*betrayed him, when he saw that he was
ainp2632 aptp3338 aina654 art3588 nu5144 nn694

condemned, repented himself, and brought again the thirty pieces*of*silver to
art3588 nn749 2532 art,ajn4245

the chief priests and elders,

pap3004 aina264 apta3860 an,aj121 an,nn129 1161

4 Saying, I have sinned in that I have betrayed the innocent blood. And
art3588 aina2036 inpro5101 pre4314 ppro2248 fm3700 epn4771

they said, What is that to us? see thou to that.

2532 apta4496 art3588 nn694 pre1722 art3588 nn3485 aina402

5 And he cast down the pieces*of*silver in the temple, and departed,
2532 apta565 aom519

and went and hanged himself.

1161 art3588 nn749 apta2983 art3588 nn694 aina2036 pin1832/3756

6 And the chief priests took the silver pieces, and said, It is*not*lawful for
ainf906 ppro846 pre1519 art3588 nn2878 1893 pin2076 pr/an,nn5092 an,nn129

to put them into the treasury, because it is the price of blood.

1161 apta2983 an,nn4824 aina59 pre1537 ppro846 art3588 nn2763 art,nn68

7 And they took counsel, and bought with them the potter's field, to
pre1519/an,nn5027/art,nn3581

bury*strangers*in.

pre,repro1352 depro1565 art,nn68 ainp2564 an,nn68 an,nn129 ad2193 art,ad4594

8 Wherefore that field was called, The field of blood, unto this day.

ad5119 ainp4137 art3588 aptp4483 pre1223 an,nn2408 art3588 nn4396

9 Then was fulfilled that which was spoken by Jeremiah the prophet,

---

27:9, 10 Although Matthew states that he is quoting the prophet Jeremiah, actually the prophet Zechariah wrote these words. Some suggest that in fact Jeremiah did make a prophecy in regards to the purchase of a field for a certain amount of money, but their efforts are supported only by speculation. Others have suggested that since Jewish traditions holds that Zechariah prophesied "in the spirit of Jeremiah," it is possible that Matthew was supporting that idea when he mentioned this prophecy. Although Jeremiah could have been spoken these words without writing them down, they were in fact spoken and written by Zechariah. Another view that is suggested by scholars is that in the older method of dividing the books of the OT the third section contained the books of the prophets beginning with the Book of Jeremiah. Since Zechariah's prophecy is found within this section, it is possible that Matthew was referring to a prophecy within that particular division of the OT. In any event, it is clear that the one who made this prophecy accurately accounted of the events that occurred between the death of Christ and His burial.

pap3004　　2532　　aina2983　art3588　nu5144　　nn694　　art3588　nn5092

saying, And they took the thirty pieces*of*silver, the price of

art,pfpp5091　　repro3739　pre575　an,nn5207　2474　aom5091

him*that*was*valued, whom they of the children of Israel did value;

2532　aina1325　ppro846　pre1519　art3588　nn2763　art,nn68　ad2505　an,nn2962　aina4929　ppro3427

10 And gave them for the potter's field, as the Lord appointed me.

(Jer. 32:6-9; Zech. 11:12,13)

Jesus Is Before Pilate Again (Mark 15:2-5; Luke 23:3-5; John 18:33-38)

1161　art,nn2424　aina2476　ad*1715　art3588　nn2232　2532　art3588　nn2232　aina1905　ppro846

11 And Jesus stood before the governor: and the governor asked him,

pap3004　pin1488　epn4771　art3588　pr/nn935　art3588　nn2453　1161　art,nn2424　aina5346　ppro846　epn4771

saying, Art thou the King of the Jews? And Jesus said unto him, Thou

pin3004

sayest.

2532　　ppro846　　aie2723　pre5259　art3588　nn749　2532　art,ajn4245

12 And when he was accused of the chief priests and elders, he

aom611　an,ajn3762

answered nothing.　　　　　　　　　　　　　　　　　　　*(Is. 53:7)*

ad5119　pin3004　art,nn4091　ppro846　pin191　3756　an,ajn4214

13 Then said Pilate unto him, Hearest thou not how*many*things they

pin2649　ppro4675

witness against thee?

2532　　ainp611(3756)　ppro846　pre4314　3761　nu1520　an,nn4487　5620　art3588

14 And he answered him to never a word; insomuch that the

nn2232　pinf2296　ad3029

governor marveled greatly.　　　　　　　　　　　　　　　*(Is. 53:7)*

Jesus Sentenced to Death (Mark 15:6-15; Luke 23:13-25; John 18:39—19:16)

1161　pre2596　an,nn1859　art3588　nn2232　plpf1486　pinf630　art3588　nn3793

15 Now at *that* feast the governor was wont to release unto the people

nu1520　an,ajn1198　repro3739　ipf2309

a prisoner, whom they would.

1161　ipf2192　ad5119　an,aj1978　an,ajn1198　ppmp3004　an,nn912

16 And they had then a notable prisoner, called Barabbas.

3767　ppro846　pfpp4863　art,nn4091　aina2036　ppro846

17 Therefore when they were gathered together, Pilate said unto them,

inpro5101　pin2309　asba630　ppro5213　an,nn912　2228　an,nn2424　art,ppmp3004

Whom will ye that I release unto you? Barabbas, or Jesus which*is*called

an,nn5547

Christ?

1063　ipf1492　3754　pre1223　an,nn5355　aina3860　ppro846

18 For he knew that for envy they had delivered him.

1161　ppro846　ppmp2521　pre1909　art3588　nn968　ppro846　art,nn1135　aina649　pre4314

19 When he was set down on the judgment seat, his wife sent unto

ppro846   pap3004   an,ajn3367/ppro4671   depro1565   art,ajn1342   1063

him, saying, Have*thou*nothing*to*do with that just man: for I have

aina3958   an,ajn4183   ad4594   pre2596   an,nn3677   pre1223   ppro846

suffered many things this day in a dream because of him.

1161   art3588   nn749   2532   art,ajn4245   aina3982   art3588   nn3793   2443

20 But the chief priests and elders persuaded the multitude that they should

asbm154   art,nn912   1161   asba622   art,nn2424

ask Barabbas, and destroy Jesus.

(1161)art3588   nn2232   aptp611   aina2036   ppro846   inpro5101   pre575 art3588 nu,ajn1417

21   The governor answered and said unto them, Whether of the twain

pin2309   asba630   ppro5213(1161)   art3588   aina2036   an,nn912

will ye that I release unto you? They said, Barabbas.

art,nn4091   pin3004   ppro846   inpro5101   asba4160   3767   an,nn2424

22 Pilate saith unto them,, What shall I do then with Jesus

art,ppmp3004   an,nn5547   an,ajn3956 pin3004   ppro846   aipp4717

which*is*called Christ? *They* all say unto him, Let him be crucified.

1161   art3588   nn2232   aina5346   1063   inpro5101 an,ajn2556   aina4160   1161   art3588

23 And the governor said, Why, what evil hath he done? But they

ipf2896   ad4057   pap3004   aipp4717

cried out the more, saying, Let him be crucified.

1161   art,nn4091   apta1492   3754   pin5623   an,ajn3762   235   ad3123   an,nn2351

24 When Pilate saw that he could prevail nothing, but *that* rather a tumult

pinm1096   apta2983   an,nn5204   aom633   art,nn5495   ad*561   art3588   nn3793   pap3004

was made, he took water, and washed *his* hands before the multitude, saying, I

pin1510   pr/an,aj121   pre575 art3588   nn129   depro5127   art,ajn1342   fm3700 epn5210

am innocent of the blood of this just person: see ye *to it.*

(Deut. 21:6-9; Ps. 26:6)

2532   aptp611   an,aj3956 art3588   nn2992   aina2036 ppro846 art,nn129   pre1909 ppro2248   2532

25 Then answered all the people, and said, His blood *be* on us, and

pre1909 ppro2257   art,nn5037

on our children.

(Ezek. 33:5)

ad5119   aina630   art,nn912   ppro846   1161   apta5417

26 Then released he Barabbas unto them: and when he had scourged

art,nn2424   aina3860   2443   asbp4717

Jesus, he delivered *him* to be crucified.

Jesus Is Mocked by the Soldiers (Mark 15:16-20; John 19:2,3)

ad5119 art3588   nn4757   art3588   nn2232   apta3880 art,nn2424 pre1519 art3588   nn4232

27 Then the soldiers of the governor took Jesus into the common hall, and

aina4863   pre1909 ppro846 art3588 an,aj3650   nn4686

gathered unto him the whole band *of soldiers.*

2532   apta1562   ppro846   aina4060 ppro846   an,aj2847   an,nn5511

28 And they stripped him, and put on him a scarlet robe.

2532   apta4120   an,nn4735 pre1537   an,nn173   aina2007   pre1909 ppro846

29 And when they had plaited a crown of thorns, they put *it* upon his

art,nn2776   2532   an,nn2563 pre1909 ppro846   art,ajn1188   2532   apta1120   ad*1715

head, and a reed in his right hand: and they bowed*the*knee before

ppro846   ipf1702   ppro846   pap3004   pim5463 art,nn935   art3588   nn2453

him, and mocked him, saying, Hail, King of the Jews!

2532   apta1716 pre1519 ppro846   aina2983 art3588 nn2563 2532 ipf5180   ppro846 pre1519 art3588
30 And they spit upon him, and took the reed, and smote him on the

nn2776
head.   *(Is. 50:6)*

2532   ad3753   aina1702 ppro846   aina1562 art3588 nn5511 aina1562 ppro846
31 And after that they had mocked him, they took the robe off from him,

2532 aina1746   ppro846   art,nn2440   ppro846 2532   aina520/ppro846   aies4717
and put his own raiment on him, and led*him*away to crucify *him.*

Jesus' Crucifixion (Mark 15:21-32; Luke 23:26-43; John 19:17-27)

1161   ppmp1831   aina2147 an,nn444   an,aj2956   an,nn4613   an,nn3686
32 And as they came out, they found a man of Cyrene, Simon by name:
depro5126   aina29   2443 asba142 ppro846 art,nn4716
him they compelled to bear his cross.

2532   apta2064 pre1519 an,nn5117 ppmp3004   1115   repro3739 pin2076
33 And when they were come unto a place called Golgotha, that is to
ppmp3004 an,nn5117   an,nn2898
say, a place of a skull,

aina1325 ppro846 an,nn3690   ainf4095 pfpp3396   pre3326 an,nn5521 2532
34 They gave him vinegar to drink mingled with gall: and when he had
aptm1089   ipf2309 2756 ainf4095
tasted *thereof,* he would not drink.   *(Ps. 69:21)*

1161   apta4717 ppro846   aom1266 ppro846 art,nn2440   pap906 an,nn2819 2443
35 And they crucified him, and parted his garments, casting lots: that it
asbp4137   art,aptp4483   pre5259 art3588   nn4396   aom1266   ppro3450
might be fulfilled which*was*spoken by the prophet, They parted my
art,nn2440   rxpro1438 2532 pre1909 ppro3450 art,nn2441   aina906 an,nn2819
garments among them, and upon my vesture did they cast lots. *(Ps. 22:18)*

2532   ppmp2521   ipf5083   ppro846 ad1563
36 And sitting down they watched him there;   *(Ps. 22:17)*

2532   aina2007 ad*1883 ppro846 art,nn2776 ppro846   art,nn156   pfpp1125 depro3778 pin2076 pr/an,nn2424
37 And set up over his head his accusation written, THIS IS JESUS
art3588   nn935   art3588   nn2453
THE KING OF THE JEWS.

ad5119   nu1417 an,nn3027 pinp4717   pre4862 ppro846 nu,ajn1520 pre1537
38 Then were there two thieves crucified with him, one on the
an,ajn1188   2532 nu,ajn1520 pre1537   an,ajn2176
right hand, and another on the left.   *(Is. 53:12)*

1161   art,ppmp3899   ipf987 ppro846 pap2795 ppro848 art,nn2776
39 And they*that*passed*by reviled him, wagging their heads,

(Ps. 22:7; 109:25)

2532 pap3004   art,pap2647   art3588 nn3485 2532 pap3618   pre1722 nu5140
40 And saying, Thou*that*destroyest the temple, and buildest *it* in three
an,nn2250 aima4982 rxpro4572 1487   pin1488 pr/an,nn5207 art,nn2316 aipp2597   pre575 art3588
days, save thyself. If thou be the Son of God, come down from the
nn4716
cross.

41 Likewise also the chief priests mocking *him,* with the scribes and elders, said,

42 He saved others; himself he cannot save. If he be the King of Israel, let him now come down from the cross, and we will believe him.

43 He trusted in God; let him deliver him now, if he will have him: for he said, I am the Son of God. *(Ps. 22:8)*

44 The thieves also, which*were*crucified*with him, cast*the*same*in*his*teeth.

Jesus' Death *(Mark 15:33-41; Luke 23:44-49; John 19:28-30)*

45 Now from the sixth hour there was darkness over all the land unto the ninth hour. *(Amos 8:9)*

46 And about the ninth hour Jesus cried with a loud voice, saying, Eli, Eli, lama sabachthani? that*is*to*say, My God, my God, why hast thou forsaken me? *(Ps. 22:1)*

47 Some of them*that*stood there, when they heard *that,* said, This *man* calleth for Elijah.

48 And straightway one of them ran, and took a sponge, and filled *it* with vinegar, and put *it* on a reed, and gave*him*to*drink.

49 The rest said, Let be, let us see whether Elijah will come to save him.

50 Jesus, when he had cried again with a loud voice, yielded up the ghost.

51 And, behold, the veil of the temple was rent in twain from the top to the bottom; and the earth did quake, and the rocks rent; *(Ex. 26:31-35)*

52 And the graves were opened; and many bodies of the saints which slept arose,

2532   apta1831   pre1537 art3588   nn3419   pre3326 ppro846   art,nn1454   aina1525 pre1519 art3588
53 And came out of the graves after his resurrection, and went into the

an,aj40 nn4172 2532   ainp1718   an,ajn4183
holy city, and appeared unto many.

1161   art3588   nn1543   2532   art3588   pre3326 ppro846   pap5083
54 Now when the centurion, and they that were with him, watching

art,nn2424 apta1492 art3588   nn4578   2532   art,aptm1096   ainp5399
Jesus, saw the earthquake, and those*things*that*were*done, they feared

ad4970   pap3004 ad230 depro3778 ipf2258   pr/an,nn5207   an,nn2316
greatly, saying, Truly this was the Son of God.

1161   an,aj4183 an,nn1135 ipf2258 ad1563   pap2334   pre575/ad3113 repro3748   aina190   art,nn2424
55 And many women were there beholding afar off, which followed Jesus

pre575 art,nn1056   pap1247   ppro846
from Galilee, ministering unto him:

pre1722   repro3739 ipf2258 an,nn3137   art,aj3094   2532   an,nn3137 art3588   nn3384   art,nn2385
56 Among which was Mary Magdalene, and Mary the mother of James

2532 an,nn2500 2532 art3588   nn3384   an,nn2199   art,nn5207
and Joses, and the mother of Zebedee's children.

The Burial of Jesus (Mark 15:42-47; Luke 23:50-56; John 19:38-42)

1161   an,nn3798   aptm1096   aina2064   an,aj4145 an,nn444 pre575   an,nn707
57 When the even was come, there came a rich man of Arimathaea,

art,nn5122   2501   repro3739 2532   epn846   aina3100/art,nn2424
named Joseph, who also himself was*Jesus'*disciple:

depro3778 apta4334   art,nn4091   aom154 art3588   nn4983   art,nn2424   ad5119   art,nn4091
58 He went to Pilate, and begged the body of Jesus. Then Pilate

aina2753   art3588 nn4983   aifp591
commanded the body to be delivered.   (Deut. 21:22,23)

2532   2501   apta2983 art3588   nn4983   aina1794   ppro846   an,aj2513
59 And when Joseph had taken the body, he wrapped it in a clean

an,nn4616
linen cloth,

2532   aina5087 ppro846 pre1722 ppro848   art,aj2537 an,nn3419 repro3739   aina2998 pre1722 art3588
60 And laid it in his own new tomb, which he had hewn out in the

nn4073 2532   apta4351 an,aj3173 an,nn3037   art3588   nn2374 art3588   nn3419   aina565
rock: and he rolled a great stone to the door of the sepulcher, and departed.

1161   ad1563   ipf2258 an,nn3137   art,aj3094   2532   art3588   aj243   an,nn3137 ppmp2521
61 And there was Mary Magdalene, and the other Mary, sitting

ad*561   art3588   nn5028
over against the sepulcher.

1161   art3588   ad1887   repro3748 pin2076/pre3326   art3588   nn3904   art3588
62 Now the next day, that followed the day of the preparation, the

nn749   2532   art,nn5330   ainp4863   pre4314 an,nn4091
chief priests and Pharisees came together unto Pilate,

pap3004 an,nn2962   ainp3415   3754 depro1565 art,nn4108 aina2036 ad2089
63 Saying, Sir, we remember that that deceiver said, while he was yet

pap2198 pre3326 nu5140 an,nn2250   pinm1453
alive, After three days I will rise again.

aima2753   3767   art3588   nn5028   aifp805   ad2193 art3588 nu,aj5154
64 Command therefore that the sepulcher be made sure until the third

an,nn2250 3379 ppro846 art,nn3101 apta2064   an,nn3571   asba2813/ppro846   2532 asba2036   art3588
day, lest his disciples come by night, and steal*him*away, and say unto the

nn2992   ainp1453 pre575 art3588 ajn3498 2532 art3588 aj2078 an,nn4106   fm2071 pr/cd/an,aj5501   art3588
people, He is risen from the dead: so the last error shall be worse than the

nu,ajn4413
first.

(1161) art,nn4091   aina5346   ppro846   pin2192   an,nn2892   aima5217
65   Pilate   said   unto   them, Ye   have   a   watch: go*your*way,

aipm805   ad5613   pin1492
make*it*as*sure as ye can.

1161 art3588 aptp4198   aom805/art3588/nn5028   apta4972 art3588 nn3037   2532
66 So they went, and made*the*sepulcher*sure, sealing the stone, and

pre3326/art,nn2892
setting*a*watch.

Jesus Is Risen (Mark 16:1-8; Luke 24:1-12; John 20:1-10)

(1161) ad*3796   an,nn4521   art,pap2020   pre1519   au,ajn3391
28 In*the*end of the sabbath, as it began*to*dawn toward the first

an,nn4521 aina2064 an,nn3137   art,aj3094   2532 art3588   aj243   an,nn3137
day of the week, came Mary Magdalene and the other Mary to

ainf2334 art3588   nn5028
see the sepulcher.

2532   2400   aom1096   an,aj3173   an,nn4578   1063   an,nn32   an,nn2962
2 And, behold, there was a great earthquake: for the angel of the Lord

apta2597   pre1537 an,nn3772   apta4334   aina617   art3588 nn3037   pre575 art3588 nn2374
descended from heaven, and came and rolled back the stone from the door,

2532 ipf2521 ad*1883 ppro846
and sat upon it.

(1161) ppro846   art,nn2397   ipf2258 ad5613   pr/an,nn796   2532 ppro846   art,nn1742   pr/an,aj3022 ad5616
3   His countenance was like lightning, and his raiment white as

an,nn5510
snow:

1161 pre575 art,nn5401   ppro846 art3588   pap5083   ainp4579 2532 aom1096 ad5616 pr/an,ajn3498
4 And for fear of him the keepers did shake, and became as dead

men.

1161 art3588 nn32   aptp611   aina2036   art3588   nn1135   pim5399 3361 epn5210 1063
5 And the angel answered and said unto the women, Fear not ye: for I

pin1492   3754   pin2212 an,nn2424   art,pfpp4717
know that ye seek Jesus, which*was*crucified.

pin2076 3756   ad5602   1063   ainp1453 ad2531   aina2036   ad1205 aima1492 art3588 nn5117
6 He is not here: for he is risen, as he said. Come, see the place

ad3699 art3588 nn2962 ipf2749
where the Lord lay.

2532 aptp4198 an,ajn5035   aima2036 ppro846 art,nn3101   3754   ainp1453 pre575 art3588 ajn3498
7 And go quickly, and tell his disciples that he is risen from the dead;

_{2532   2400   pin4254   ppro5209 pre1519 art,nn1056   ad1563   fm3700 ppro846 2400}
and, behold, he goeth before you into Galilee; there shall ye see him: lo, I
_{aina2036 ppro5213}
have told you.

_{2532   apta1831   an,ajn5035 pre575 art3588   nn3419   pre3326 an,nn5401 2532 an,aj3173 an,nn5479}
8 And they departed quickly from the sepulcher with fear and great joy;
_{aina5143   ainf518/ppro846/art,nn3101}
and did run to bring*his*disciples*word.

_{1161   ad5613   ipf4198   ainf518 ppro846 art,nn3101   2400(2532)   art,nn2424 aina528   ppro846}
9 And as they went to tell his disciples, behold, Jesus met them,
_{pap3004   pim5463   1161 art3588 apta4334   aina2902 ppro846   art3588   nn4228   2532   aina4352}
saying, All hail. And they came and held him by the feet, and worshiped
_{ppro846}
him.

_{ad5119   pin3004 art,nn2424   ppro846   pim5399/3361   aima5217 aima518 ppro3450   art,nn80   2443}
10 Then said Jesus unto them, Be*not*afraid: go tell my brethren that
_{asba565 pre1519 art,nn1056   ad2546   fm3700 ppro3165}
they go into Galilee, and there shall they see me.

_{1161   ppro846   ppmp4198   2400   idpro5100   art3588   nn2892   apta2064 pre1519 art3588}
11 Now when they were going, behold, some of the watch came into the
_{nn4172   aina518   art3588   nn749   an,aj537   art,aptm1096}
city, and showed unto the chief priests all the*things*that*were*done.
_{2532   aptp4863   pre3326 art3588   ajn4245   5037   apta2983}
12 And when they were assembled with the elders, and had taken
_{an,nn4824   aina1325 an,aj2425 an,nn694   art3588   nn4757}
counsel, they gave large money unto the soldiers,
_{pap3004   aima2036   ppro846 art,nn3101 apta2064   an,nn3571   aina2813 ppro846}
13 Saying, Say ye, His disciples came by night, and stole him *away* while
_{ppro2257 ppmp2837}
we slept.
_{2532   1437 depro5124   asbp191/pre1909/art,nn2232   epn2249   ft3982   ppro846}
14 And if this come*to*the*governor's*ears, we will persuade him,
_{2532 ft4160/an,aj275 ppro5209}
and secure you.
_{1161 art3588 apta2983 art3588   nn694   aina4160 ad5613   ainp1321   2532 depro3778}
15 So they took the money, and did as they were taught: and this
_{art,nn3056   ainp1310   pre3844   an,nn2453 ad3360   art,ad4594}
saying is commonly reported among the Jews until this day.

The Great Commission (Mark 16:14-18; Luke 24:36-49; John 20:19-23; Acts 1:9-11)

_{1161   art3588   nu1733   nn3101   ainp4198   pre1519 art,nn1056 pre1519   art,nn3735}
16 Then the eleven disciples went away into Galilee, into a mountain
_{repro3757 art,nn2424   aom5021   ppro846}
where Jesus had appointed them.
_{2532   apta1492 ppro846   aina4352   ppro846 1161   art3588   aina1365}
17 And when they saw him, they worshiped him: but some doubted.

2532   art,nn2424 apta4334   aina2980   ppro846   pap3004   an,aj3956 an,nn1849   ainp1325
18 And Jesus came and spake unto them, saying, <u>All</u> power is given unto
ppro3427 pre1909 an,nn3772   2532   pre1722 an,nn1093
me   in heaven and in   earth.   *(Dan. 7:14)*

              aptp4198   3767   aima3100 an,aj3956   art,nn1484   pap907   ppro846 pre1519 art3588
☞ **19** Go   ye therefore, and teach   all   nations, baptizing them in   the
nn3686   art3588   nn3962   2532   art3588 nn5207 2532   art3588 an,aj40   nn4151
name of the Father, and of the Son, and of the Holy Ghost:

            pap1321   ppro846   pinf5083   an,aj3956   an,ajn3745   aom1781
20 Teaching them to observe all things whatsoever I have commanded
ppro5213 2532 2400 epn1473 pin1510 pre3326 ppro5216 an,aj3956/art,nn2250   ad2193 art3588 nn4930   art3588   nn165
you: and, lo, <u>I   am with you</u>   always,   *even* unto the end of the world.
281
Amen.   *(Hag. 1:13)*

☞ **28:19** See notes on Mark 16:16 and 1 Corinthians 10:2.

MARK

The name Mark is actually a surname, his common name being John (Acts 12:12; 13:5; 2 Tim. 4:11). Since he was related to Barnabas (Col. 4:10), Mark may have been a Levite (Acts 4:36).

Mark traveled with the Apostle Paul and Barnabas on their first missionary journey (Acts 12:25), but he turned back (Acts 13:13). For this reason, Paul refused to consider taking him along on the second missionary journey (Acts 15:36–39). Paul and Barnabas had such a strong disagreement about the matter that they decided to go different directions, Paul with Silas and Barnabas with Mark. Later Paul and Mark were reconciled (Col. 4:10; Phile. 1:24), and Paul came to regard Mark as one who was "profitable . . . for the ministry" (2 Tim. 4:11).

The contents of the book and extra-biblical sources indicate that Mark's Gospel was written for the benefit of those who lived outside Palestine. These people who had not witnessed the events of Jesus life would profit most from Mark's emphasis on the supernatural power of Jesus. His actions, rather than His words, are given the most attention, particularly the miracles He performed which demonstrated His divinity. The narrative moves swiftly from one stirring scene of Jesus' ministry to another without interruption. The rapid pace can be seen in the frequent use of the transitional Greek word *euthéos* (2117), meaning "immediately" or "straightway" (used 40 times).

It is generally accepted and supported by the writings of the church historians that Peter was Mark's source for the information contained in his Gospel. Since the book was probably written from Rome immediately after Peter's death, the date for its writing is presumed to be A.D. 67 or 68. The Book of Mark, being written earlier than the other Gospels, has about ninety-three percent of its material repeated in Matthew and Luke, many times using the same words. The details that Mark gives in his brief account, however, are more graphic than in the other accounts.

The Preaching of John the Baptist (Matt. 3:1-12; Luke 3:1-9, 15-17; John 1:19-28)

1
    an,nn746   art3588   nn2098   an,nn2424 an,nn5547   an,nn5207   art,nn2316

The beginning of the gospel of Jesus Christ, the Son of God;

    ad5613   pfip1125   pre1722 art3588   nn4396   2400   epn1473 pin649 ppro3450   art,nn32

2 As it is written in the prophets, Behold, I send my messenger

pre4253 ppro4675 an,nn4383 repro3739   ft2680   ppro4675 art,nn3598 pre*1715 ppro4675

before thy face, which shall prepare thy way before thee. *(Mal. 3:1)*

        an,nn5456   pap994   pre1722 art3588 ajn2048   aima2090   art3588 nn3598

3 The voice of one crying in the wilderness, Prepare ye the way of the

an,nn2962 pim4160 ppro846 art,nn5147 pr/an,aj2117

Lord, make his paths straight. *(Is. 40:3)*

4 John did baptize in the wilderness, and preach the baptism of repentance for the remission of sins.

5 And there went out unto him all the land of Judea, and they*of*Jerusalem, and were all baptized of him in the river of Jordan, confessing their sins.

6 And John was clothed with camel's hair, and with a girdle of a skin about his loins; and he did eat locusts and wild honey;

7 And preached, saying, There cometh one mightier than I after me, the latchet of whose shoes I am not worthy to stoop down and unloose.

8 I indeed have baptized you with water: but he shall baptize you with the Holy Ghost.

Jesus Is Baptized (Matt. 3:13-17; Luke 3:21,22)

9 And it came*to*pass in those days, that Jesus came from Nazareth of Galilee, and was baptized of John in Jordan.

10 And straightway coming up out of the water, he saw the heavens opened, and the Spirit like a dove descending upon him:

11 And there came a voice from heaven, *saying,* Thou art my beloved Son, in whom I am*well*pleased.   *(Ps. 2:7)*

Jesus Is Tempted by the Devil (Matt. 4:1-11; Luke 4:1-13)

12 And immediately the Spirit driveth him into the wilderness.

13 And he was there in the wilderness forty days, tempted of Satan; and was with the wild beasts; and the angels ministered unto him.

1:8 See note on Acts 1:5.

Jesus Begins His Ministry in Galilee (Matt. 4:12-17; Luke 4:14,15)

_{1161   art,nn2491   aime3860   aina2064   aina2064   pre1519   art,nn1056}

14 Now after that John was put*in*prison, Jesus came into Galilee,

_{pap2784   art3588   nn2098   art3588   nn932   art,nn2316}

preaching the gospel of the kingdom of God,

_{2532   pap3004   art3588   nn2540   pfip4137   2532   art3588   nn932   art,nn2316   pfi1448}

15 And saying, The time is fulfilled, and the kingdom of God is*at*hand:

_{pim3340   2532   pim4100   (pre1722) art3588   nn2098}

repent ye, and believe   the gospel.

Jesus Calls Four Fishermen (Matt. 4:18-22; Luke 5:1-11)

_{1161   pap4043   pre3844 art3588   nn2281   art,nn1056   aina1492   an,nn4613   2532   an,nn406}

16 Now as he walked by the sea of Galilee, he saw Simon and Andrew

_{ppro846   art,nn80   pap906   an,nn293 pre1722 art3588   nn2281   1063   ipf2258   pr/an,nn231}

his brother casting a net into the sea: for they were fishers.

_{2532   art,nn2424 aina2036   ppro846   ad1205   ad*3694 ppro3450   2532   ft4160   ppro5209}

17 And Jesus said unto them, Come ye after me, and I will make you to

_{aifp1096   pr/an,nn231   an,nn444}

become fishers of men.

_{2532   ad2112   apta863   ppro848 art,nn1350 2532   aina190   ppro846}

18 And straightway they forsook their nets, and followed him.

_{2532   apta4260   an,ajn3641   ad1564   aina1492 an,nn2385 art3588}

19 And when he had gone a little farther thence, he saw James the *son* of

_{art,nn2199   2532   an,nn2491 ppro846   art,nn80   epn846   2532   pre1722 art3588   nn4143   pap2675}

Zebedee, and John his brother, who also were in the ship mending their

_{art,nn1350}

nets.

_{2532   ad2112   aina2564   ppro846   2532   apta863   ppro848   art,nn3962   art,nn2199}

20 And straightway he called them: and they left their father Zebedee

_{pre1722 art3588   nn4143   pre3326 art3588   nn3411   2532   aina565   ad*3694 ppro846}

in the ship with the hired servants, and went after him.

The Man With an Unclean Spirit (Luke 4:31-37)

_{2532   pinp1531 pre1519   2584   2532   ad2112   art3588   nn4521}

21 And they went into Capernaum; and straightway on the sabbath day he

_{apta1525   pre1519 art3588   nn4864   ipf1321}

entered into the synagogue, and taught.

_{2532   ipf1605   pre1909 ppro846   art,nn1322   1063   ipf2258/pap1321   ppro846 ad5613}

22 And they were astonished at his doctrine: for he taught them as

_{pap2192   an,nn1849   2532   3756 ad5613 art3588   nn1122}

one that had authority, and not as the scribes.

_{2532   ipf2258 pre1722 ppro846   art,nn4864   an,nn444 pre1722   an,aj169   an,nn4151   2532}

23 And there was in their synagogue a man with an unclean spirit; and he

_{aina349}

cried out,

pap3004   pim1436   inpro5101/ppro2254/2532/ppro4671   an,nn2424
24 Saying, Let*us*alone; what*have*we*to*do*with*thee, thou Jesus of
an,aj3479   aina2064   ainf622   ppro2248   pin1492 ppro4571 pr/inpro5101   pin1488 art3588
Nazareth? art thou come to destroy us? I know thee who thou art, the
ajn40   art,nn2316
Holy One of God.

        2532   art,nn2424   aina2008   ppro846   pap3004   aipp5392   2532   aima1831   pre1537
25 And Jesus rebuked him, saying, Hold*thy*peace, and come out of
ppro846
him.

        2532   art3588   art,aj169   nn4151   apta4682 ppro846 2532 apta2896   an,aj3173 an,nn5456
26 And when the unclean spirit had torn him, and cried with a loud voice,
aina1831   pre1537 ppro846
he came out of him.

        2532   an,ajn3956   ainp2284   5620   pinf4802   pre4314
27 And they were   all   amazed, insomuch that they questioned among
ppro848   pap3004   pr/inpro5101   pin2076 depro5124 pr/inpro5101 art,aj2537 art,nn1322   depro3778 3754
themselves saying, What thing is   this? what new doctrine is this? for
pre2596 an,nn1849   pin2004   2532 art3588 art,aj169   nn4151   2532   pin5219
with authority commandeth he even the unclean spirits, and they do obey
ppro846
him.

        1161   ad2117   ppro846 art,nn189   aina1831   pre1519   an,aj3650 art3588
28 And immediately his fame spread abroad throughout all   the
nn4066   art,nn1056
region*round*about Galilee.

Jesus Heals Many (Matt. 8:14-17; Luke 4:38-41)

        2532   ad2112   apta1831   pre1537 art3588   nn4864
29 And forthwith, when they were come out of the synagogue, they
aina2064   pre1519 art3588 nn3614   an,nn4613 2532   an,nn406   pre3326 an,nn2385 2532 an,nn2491
entered into the house of Simon and Andrew, with James and John.

        1161   an,nn4613   art,nn3994   ipf2621   pap4445   2532   ad2112   pin3004 ppro846
30 But Simon's wife's mother lay sick*of*a*fever, and anon they tell him
pre4012 ppro846
of her.

        2532   apta4334   apta2902 ppro846   art3588   nn5495   aina1453/ppro846   2532
31 And he came and took her by the hand, and lifted*her*up; and
ad2112   art3588 nn4446 aina863 ppro846 2532   ipf1247   ppro846
immediately the fever left her, and she ministered unto them.

        1161   an,nn3798/aptp1096   ad3753   art3588 nn2246   aina1416   ipf5342   pre4314 ppro846 an,aj3956
32 And at even, when the sun did set, they brought unto him all
art,pap2192/ad2560   2532   art,ppmp1139
that*were*diseased, and them*that*were*possessed*with*devils.

        2532   an,aj3650 art3588 nn4172 ipf2258   pr/pfpp1996   pre4314 art3588   nn2374
33 And all   the city was gathered together at the door.

        2532   aina2323   an,aj4183   pap2192/ad2560   an,aj4164   an,nn3554   2532   aina1544
34 And he healed many that were sick of divers diseases, and cast out
an,aj4183 an,nn1140 2532   ipf863   3756 art3588   nn1140   pinf2980   3754   ipf1492 ppro846
many devils; and suffered not the devils to speak, because they knew him.

Jesus Ministers in All of Galilee (Luke 4:42-44)

35 And in*the*morning, rising up a*great*while*before*day, he went out,
and departed into a solitary place, and there prayed.

36 And Simon and they that were with him followed after him.

37 And when they had found him, they said unto him, All *men* seek for thee.

38 And he said unto them, Let us go into the next towns, that I may preach there also: for therefore came*I*forth.

39 And he preached in their synagogues throughout all Galilee, and cast out devils.

Jesus Cleanses a Leper (Matt. 8:1-4; Luke 5:12-16)

40 And there came a leper to him, beseeching him, and kneeling down to him, and saying unto him, If thou wilt, thou canst make*me*clean.

41 And Jesus, moved*with*compassion, put forth *his* hand, and touched him, and saith unto him, I will; be*thou*clean.

42 And, as soon as he had spoken, immediately the leprosy departed from him, and he was cleansed.

43 And he straitly charged him, and forthwith sent*him*away;

44 And saith unto him, See thou say nothing to any man: but go*thy*way, show thyself to the priest, and offer for thy cleansing those things which Moses commanded, for a testimony unto them.   *(Lev. 14:2-32)*

45 But he went out, and began to publish *it* much, and to blaze abroad the matter, insomuch that Jesus could no more openly enter into the city, but was without in desert places: and they came to him from*every*quarter.

Jesus Heals a Crippled Man (Matt. 9:1-8; Luke 5:17-26)

2 And again he entered into Capernaum after *some* days; and it was noised that he was in the house.

2 And straightway many were gathered together, insomuch that there was no*room*to*receive *them,* no, not*so*much*as about the door: and he preached the word unto them.

3 And they come unto him, bringing one*sick*of*the*palsy, which was borne of four.

4 And when they could not come nigh unto him for the press, they uncovered the roof where he was: and when they had broken*it*up, they let down the bed wherein the sick*of*the*palsy lay.

5 When Jesus saw their faith, he said unto the sick*of*the*palsy, Son, thy sins be forgiven thee.

6 But there were certain of the scribes sitting there, and reasoning in their hearts,

7 Why doth this *man* thus speak blasphemies? who can forgive sins but God only?

8 And immediately when Jesus perceived in his spirit that they so reasoned within themselves, he said unto them, Why reason ye these things in your hearts?

9 Whether is it easier to say to the sick*of*the*palsy, *Thy* sins be forgiven thee; or to say, Arise, and take up thy bed, and walk?

10 But that ye may know that the Son of man hath power on earth to forgive sins, (he saith to the sick*of*the*palsy,)

11 I say unto thee, Arise, and take up thy bed, and go*thy*way into thine house.

2532   ad2112   ainp1453   apta142   art3588   nn2895   2532   aina1831   ad*1726
12 And immediately he arose, took up the bed, and went forth before them
an,ajn3956   5620   an,ajn3956   pifm1839   2532   pinf1392   art,nn2316 pap3004
all;   insomuch that they were   all   amazed, and glorified God, saying, We
ad3762   aina1492   ad3779
never saw it on*this*fashion.

Jesus Calls Levi (Matt. 9:9-13; Luke 5:27-32)

2532   aina1831   ad3825   pre3844 art3588   nn2281   2532   an,aj3956 art3588   nn3793
13 And he went forth again by the sea side; and all   the multitude
ipf2064   pre4314 ppro846   2532   ipf1321   ppro846
resorted unto him, and he taught them.
2532   pap3855   aina1492 an,nn3018 art3588   art,nn256   ppmp2521 pre1909 art3588
14 And as he passed by, he saw Levi the *son* of Alphaeus sitting at the
nn5058   2532   pin3004   ppro846   pim190   ppro3427 2532   apta450   aina190
receipt*of*custom, and said unto him, Follow me. And he arose and followed
ppro846
him.
2532   aom1096   (pre1722) ppro846   aie2621   pre1722 ppro846 art,nn3614
15 And it came*to*pass, that, as Jesus sat*at*meat in   his house,
an,aj4183   an,nn5057   2532 an,ajn268   ipf4873/2532   art,nn2424   2532 ppro846   art,nn3101
many publicans and sinners sat*also*together*with Jesus and his disciples:
1063   ipf2258 an,ajn4183 2532   aina190   ppro846
for there were many, and they followed him.
2532   art3588   nn1122   2532   art,nn5330   apta1492 ppro846 pap2068 pre3326   art,nn5057   2532
16 And when the scribes and Pharisees saw him eat with publicans and
an,ajn268   ipf3004   ppro846   art,nn3101   inpro5101   3754   pin2068   2532   pin4095
sinners, they said unto his disciples, How*is*it that he eateth and drinketh
pre3326   art,nn5057   2532   an,ajn268
with publicans and sinners?
2532   art,nn2424 apta191   pin3004   ppro846   art,pap2480   pin2192 3756
17 When Jesus heard *it,* he saith unto them, They*that*are*whole have no
an,nn5532   an,nn2395   235   art,pap2192/ad2560   aina2064 3756   ainf2564   an,ajn1342
need of the physician, but they*that*are*sick: I came not to call the righteous,
235   an,ajn268   pre1519   an,nn3341
but sinners to repentance.

Jesus' Teaching on Fasting (Matt. 9:14-17; Luke 5:33-39)

2532 art3588   nn3101   an,nn2491 2532 (art3588) art3588   nn5330   ipf2258/pap3522   2532
18 And the disciples of John and of the Pharisees used*to*fast: and they
pinm2064   2532   pin3004   ppro846   pre,inpro1302   art3588   nn3101   an,nn2491   2532 (art3588) art3588
come and say unto him, Why do the disciples of John and of   the
nn5330   pin3522 1161 ppro4671 art,nn3101   pin3522 3756
Pharisees fast, but thy disciples fast not?
2532 art,nn2424 aina2036   ppro846 pinm1410 (3361) art3588   nn5207   art3588   nn3567
19 And Jesus said unto them, Can   the children of the bridechamber

pinf3522 pre1722/repro3739 art3588   nn3566   pin2076 pre3326   ppro846   an,aj3745   (an,nn5550) pin2192 art3588

fast,   while   the bridegroom   is   with   them? as*long*as   they   have   the

nn3566   pre3326 rxpro1438   pinm1410/3756 pinf3522

bridegroom with them, they cannot fast.

1161   an,nn2250   fm2064   ad3752   art3588   nn3566   asbp522

20 But the days will come, when the bridegroom shall be taken away

pre575 ppro846 2532 ad5119   ft3522 pre1722 depro1565 art,nn2250

from them, and then shall they fast in those days.

an,ajn3762   2532   pin1976   an,nn1915   an,aj46 an,nn4470 pre1909   an,aj3820   an,nn2440   1490

21 No man also seweth a piece of new cloth on an old garment: else

art3588   ajn2537   art,nn4138/ppro846   pin142   art3588 ajn3820 2532   an,nn4978

the new piece that*filled*it*up taketh away from the old, and the rent

pinp1096 pr/an,aj5501

is made worse.

2532   an,ajn3762   pin906   an,aj3501 an,nn3631 pre1519 an,aj3820   an,nn779   1490 art3588 aj3501 art,nn3631

22 And no man putteth new wine into old bottles: else the new wine

pin4486 art3588   nn779   2532 art3588 nn3631   pinp1632   2532 art3588   nn779   fp622

doth burst the bottles, and the wine is spilled, and the bottles will be marred:

235 an,aj3501 an,nn3631   an,ajn992 pre1519 an,aj2537   an,nn779

but new wine must be put into new bottles.

Jesus Is Lord Over the Sabbath Day (Matt. 12:1-8; Luke 6:1-5)

2532   aina1096   ppro846 pinm3899   pre1223   art3588   nn4702   pre1722 art3588

23 And it came*to*pass, that he went through the corn fields on the

nn4521   2532   ppro846   art,nn3101   aom756   pinf4160/an,nn3598   pap5089   art3588

sabbath day; and   his   disciples began,   as*they*went, to pluck the

nn4719

ears*of*corn.   (Deut. 23:25)

2532 art3588   nn5330   ipf3004   ppro846 aima2396 inpro5101 pin4160   pre1722 art3588   nn4521

24 And the Pharisees said unto him, Behold, why do they on the sabbath

repro3739   pin1832/3756

day that which is*not*lawful?

2532 epn846 ipf3004   ppro846   ad3762 aina314 inpro5101 1138 aina4160 ad3753

25 And he said unto them, Have ye never read what David did, when he

aina2192 an,nn5532 2532   aina3983   epn846 2532 art3588   pre3326 ppro846

had need, and was hungry, he, and they that were with him?

ad4459   aina1525 pre1519 art3588   nn3624   art,nn2316 pre1909   8   art3588

26 How he went into the house of God in the days of Abiathar the

nn749   2532   aina5315 art3588 nn740/art,nn4286 repro3739   pin1832/3756   ainf5315 1508

high priest, and did eat the shewbread, which is*not*lawful to eat but for

art3588   nn2409   2532 aina1325 2532   art,pap5607   pre4862 ppro846

the priests, and gave also to them*which*were with him?

                                                (1 Sam. 21:1-6; Lev. 24:5-9)

2532   ipf3004   ppro846 art3588   nn4521   aom1096 pre1223 art,nn444   3756 art,nn444

27 And he said unto them, The sabbath was made for man, and not man

pre1223 art3588   nn4521

for the sabbath:

5620   art3588 nn5207   art,nn444 pin2076 pr/an,nn2962 2532   art3588   nn4521

28 Therefore the Son of man is   Lord also of the sabbath.

Jesus Heals a Man on the Sabbath Day (Matt. 12:9-14; Luke 6:6-11)

2532   aina1525   ad3825 pre1519 art3588   nn4864   2532   ipf2258   an,nn444 ad1563
3 And he entered again into the synagogue; and there was a man there
pap2192   pfpp3583 art,nn5495
which had a withered hand.

2532   ipf3906   ppro846   1487   ft2323 ppro846 art3588   nn4521
2 And they watched him, whether he would heal him on the sabbath day;
2443   asba2723 ppro846
that they might accuse him..

2532   pin3004   art3588   nn444   pap2192 art3588 pfpp3583   art,nn5495 aima1453
3 And he saith unto the man which had the withered hand, Stand
pre1519/art,ajn3319
forth.

2532   pin3004   ppro846   pin1832   ainf15   art3588   nn4521   2228
4 And he saith unto them, Is*it*lawful to do good on the sabbath days, or
ainf2554   ainf4982 an,nn5590 2228   ainf615 1161 art3588   ipf4623
to do evil? to save life, or to kill? But they held*their*peace.

2532   aptp4017   ppro846 pre3326 an,nn3709
5 And when he had looked*round*about on them with anger, being
ppmp4818 pre1909 art3588   nn4457   ppro846 art,nn2588   pin3004   art3588 nn44   aima1614
grieved for the hardness of their hearts, he saith unto the man, Stretch forth
ppro4675 art,nn5495 2532   aina1614   2532 ppro846 art,nn5495   ainp600   pr/an,aj5199 ad5613
thine hand. And he stretched*it*out: and his hand was restored whole as
art3588   ajn243
the other.

2532 art3588   nn5330   apta1831   ad2112   ipf4160/an,nn4824 pre3326 art3588
6 And the Pharisees went forth, and straightway took counsel with the
nn2265   pre2596 ppro846 3704   asba622 ppro846
Herodians against him, how they might destroy him.

A Multitude Follows Jesus by the Sea

2532 art,nn2424   aina402   pre3326 ppro848 art,nn3101   pre4314 art3588 nn2281 2532   an,aj4183
7 But Jesus withdrew himself with his disciples to the sea: and a great
an,nn4128   pre575 art,nn1056 aina190   ppro846 2532 pre575 art,nn2449
multitude from Galilee followed him, and from Judea,

2532   pre575   an,nn2414   2532 pre575   art,nn2401 2532   ad4008 art,nn2446   2532
8 And from Jerusalem, and from Idumea, and *from* beyond Jordan; and
art3588   pre4012 an,nn5184 2532 an,nn4605   an,aj4183   an,nn4128   apta191
they about Tyre and Sidon, a great multitude, when they had heard
an,ajn3745   ipf4160 aina2064 pre4314 ppro846
what*great*things he did, came unto him.

2532   aina2036   ppro848 art,nn3101   2443   an,nn4142   psa4342 ppro846
9 And he spake to his disciples, that a small ship should wait on him
pre1223   art3588   nn3793   3363   psa2346 ppro846
because of the multitude, lest they should throng him.

10 For he had healed many; insomuch that they pressed upon him for to touch him, as*many*as had plagues.

11 And unclean spirits, when they saw him, fell*down*before him, and cried, saying, Thou art the Son of God.

12 And he straitly charged them that they should not make him known.

Jesus Chooses Twelve Apostles (Matt. 10:1-4; Luke 6:12-16)

13 And he goeth up into a mountain, and calleth *unto him* whom he would: and they came unto him.

14 And he ordained twelve, that they should be with him, and that he might send*them*forth to preach,

15 And to have power to heal sicknesses, and to cast out devils:

16 And Simon he surnamed Peter;

17 And James the *son* of Zebedee, and John the brother of James; and he surnamed them Boanerges, which is, The sons of thunder:

18 And Andrew, and Philip, and Bartholomew, and Matthew, and Thomas, and James the *son* of Alphaeus, and Thaddaeus, and Simon the Canaanite,

19 And Judas Iscariot, which also betrayed him: and they went into a house.

Jesus and Beelzebub (Matt. 12:22-32; Luke 11:14-23)

20 And the multitude cometh together again, so that they could not so*much*as eat bread.

21 And when his friends heard *of it*, they went out to lay*hold*on him: for they said, He is*beside*himself.

22 And   the   scribes   which*came*down   from   Jerusalem   said,   He   hath
Beelzebub, and   by   the   prince   of   the   devils   casteth*he*out   devils.

23 And   he   called   them   *unto   him,*   and   said   unto   them   in   parables,   How
can   Satan   cast   out   Satan?

24 And   if   a   kingdom   be   divided   against   itself,   that   kingdom   cannot
stand.

25 And   if   a   house   be   divided   against   itself,   that   house   cannot   stand.

26 And   if   Satan   rise   up   against   himself,   and   be   divided,   he   cannot   stand,
but   hath   an   end.

27 No   man   can   enter   into   a   strong   man's   house,   and   spoil   his   goods,
except   he   will   first   bind   the   strong   man;   and   then   he   will   spoil   his   house.

☞ 28 Verily   I   say   unto   you,   All   sins   shall   be   forgiven   unto   the   sons   of
men,   and   blasphemies   wherewith   soever   they   shall   blaspheme:

☞ **3:28, 29** Christ is here answering the accusation that had been made against Him that the miracle He performed (the casting out a demon) was done by the power of Beelzebub, who was the chief of the demons (see Matt. 12:22–30; Mark 3:20–27). In doing so, these men were calling the Holy Spirit a "devil" or "an unclean spirit" (vv. 22, 30). In fact, the work of the devil is designed to counter the work done by the Holy Spirit (John 16:8). The attitude of these scribes revealed their complete rejection of Christ's power and authority as the Son of God.

The "blasphemy against the Holy Spirit" to which Christ referred in verse twenty-nine was said to be unforgivable (Matt. 12:31, 32 and Luke 12:10). Matthew 12:32 says, "It shall not be forgiven him, neither in this age, neither in the world to come." The verb *ouk aphethēsetai,* translated "shall not be forgiven," is in the passive punctiliar future, which means that it will not be forgiven by God, and in particular by Jesus Christ, at any specific time in the future. Matthew says, "shall not be forgiven him," which might better be stated "will not be removed from him." Stated positively, it means it will be counted against him, hindering him from entrance into heaven.

Of the three passages in the Gospels where this is discussed, only Mark 3:29 has the concluding phrase, ". . . but is in danger of eternal damnation." Literally, the Greek text says, ". . . but he is guilty of eternal judgment." The Greek word is *enochós* (1777), meaning "something that is held fast or bound." Therefore, *enochós* means that one is deserving of the punishment (see Matt. 26:66; Mark 14:64). One should observe that the verb *estín* (from *eimí,* [1510]) is in the present tense, meaning that this guilt is always upon the man who does not recognize the Holy Spirit as the power behind the work of Christ. The last phrase of Mark 3:29, in the TR, is *aiōníou* which means "eternal judgment or condemnation." In other manuscripts, instead of *kríseōs,* "judgment," the word *hamartēmatos* is used connoting the "individual sin or the result of sin." This agrees with the meaning of *hamartēmata* found in verse twenty-eight in the phrases "all sins" and "whatever blasphemies." The adjective *aiōníou* (166) refers to the eternal judgment, namely that judgment that will take effect in the future, especially in the "age" to come (see 2 Thess. 1:9; Jude 1:7).

The Holy Spirit represented the manifestation of the power that Christ possessed. By denying this
(continued on next page)

29 But   he   that   shall   blaspheme against   the   Holy Ghost hath
never forgiveness, but is *in*danger of eternal damnation:

30 Because they said, He hath an unclean spirit.

Jesus' Mother and Brothers (Matt. 12:46-50; Luke 8:19-21)

31 There came then his brethren and his mother, and, standing without,
sent unto him, calling him.

32 And the multitude sat about him, and they said unto him, Behold,
thy mother and thy brethren without seek for thee.

33 And he answered them, saying, Who is my mother, or my
brethren?

34 And he looked round about on them*which*sat about him, and said,
Behold my mother and my brethren!

35 For whosoever shall do the will of God, the same is my brother,
and my sister, and mother.

The Parable of the Sower (Matt. 13:1-9; Luke 8:4-8)

4 And he began again to teach by the sea side: and there was gathered
unto him a great multitude, so that he entered into a ship, and
sat in the sea; and the whole multitude was by the sea on the land.

2 And he taught them many things by parables, and said unto them in
his doctrine,

(continued from previous page)
power, these scribes were guilty of a sin for which there was no forgiveness. See note on Hebrews
10:26, 27.

^{pim191}   ²⁴⁰⁰   ^{aina1831}   ^{art,pap4687}   ^{infg4687}

3 Hearken; Behold, there went out a sower to sow:

²⁵³²   ^{aom1096}   ^{aie4687}   ^{repro3739/3303} ^{aina4098} ^{pre3844} ^{art3588}   ⁿⁿ³⁵⁹⁸   ²⁵³²

4 And it came*to*pass, as he sowed, some fell by the way side, and

^{art3588} ⁿⁿ⁴⁰⁷¹   ^{art3588} ⁿⁿ³⁷⁷² ^{aina2064} ²⁵³²   ^{aina2719/ppro846}

the fowls of the air came and devoured*it*up.

¹¹⁶¹   ^{an,ajn243}   ^{aina4098} ^{pre1909}   ^{art,ajn4075}   ^{ad3699}   ^{ipf2192} ³⁷⁵⁶ ^{an,aj4183} ^{an,nn1093}   ²⁵³²

5 And some fell on stony ground, where it had not much earth; and

^{ad2112}   ^{aina1816}   ^{aid2192} ³³⁶¹ ^{an,nn899}   ^{an,nn1093}

immediately it sprang up, because it had no depth of earth:

¹¹⁶¹   ^{an,nn2246}   ^{apta393}   ^{ainp2739}   ²⁵³²   ^{aid2192} ³³⁶¹

6 But when the sun was up, it was scorched; and because it had no

^{an,nn4491}   ^{ainp3583}

root, it withered away.

²⁵³² ^{an,ajn243} ^{aina4098} ^{pre1519}   ^{art,nn173}   ²⁵³² ^{art3588}   ⁿⁿ¹⁷³   ^{aina305}   ²⁵³²   ^{aina4846}   ^{ppro846}

7 And some fell among thorns, and the thorns grew up, and choked it,

²⁵³²   ^{aina1325}   ³⁷⁵⁶ ^{an,nn2590}

and it yielded no fruit.

²⁵³²   ^{an,ajn243} ^{aina4098} ^{pre1519} ^{art,aj2570}   ^{art,nn1093}   ²⁵³²   ^{ipf1325}   ^{an,nn2590}   ^{pap305}   ²⁵³²

8 And other fell on good ground, and did yield fruit that sprang up and

^{pap837}   ²⁵³²   ^{ipf5342}   ^{nu,ajn1520}   ^{nu,ajn5144}   ²⁵³²   ^{nu,ajn1520}   ^{nu,ajn1835}   ²⁵³²   ^{nu,ajn1520}

increased; and brought forth, some thirty, and some sixty, and some

^{nu,ajn1540}

a hundred.

²⁵³²   ^{ipf3004}   ^{ppro846}   ^{art,pap2192}   ^{an,nn3775}   ^{pinf191}   ^{pim191}

9 And he said unto them, He*that*hath ears to hear, let him hear.

Why Jesus Taught in Parables (Matt. 13:10-17; Luke 8:9,10)

¹¹⁶¹   ^{ad3753}   ^{aom1096}   ^{pre,an,ajn2651} ^{art3588}   ^{pre4012} ^{ppro846} ^{pre4862} ^{art3588} ^{nu,ajn1427}

☞ 10 And when he was alone, they that were about him with the twelve

^{ipf2065}   ^{ppro846} ^{art3588}   ⁿⁿ³⁸⁵⁰

asked of him the parable.

²⁵³²   ^{ipf3004}   ^{ppro846}   ^{epn5213}   ^{pfip1325}   ^{ainf1097} ^{art3588}   ⁿⁿ³⁴⁶⁶

11 And he said unto them, Unto you it is given to know the mystery of

^{art3588}   ⁿⁿ⁹³²   ^{art,nn2316} ¹¹⁶¹   ^{depro1565} ^{art3588}   ^{ad1854}   ^{art,ajn3956}

the kingdom of God: but unto them that are without, all*these*things are

^{pinm1096} ^{pre1722}   ^{an,nn3850}

done in parables:

²⁴⁴³   ^{pap991}   ^{psa991}   ²⁵³²   ³³⁶¹   ^{asba1492}   ²⁵³²   ^{pap191}

12 That seeing they may see, and not perceive; and hearing they may

^{psa191}   ²⁵³² ³³⁶¹   ^{psa4920}   ³³⁷⁹   ^{asba1994}   ²⁵³²

hear, and not understand; lest*at*any*time they should be converted, and *their*

^{art,nn265}   ^{asbp863}   ^{ppro846}

sins should be forgiven them.   *(Is. 6:9,10)*

☞ **4:10–12** See note on Matthew 13:10–17.

Explanation of the Parable of the Sower (Matt. 13:18-23; Luke 8:11-15)

13 And he said unto them, Know ye not this parable? and how then will ye know all parables?

14 The sower soweth the word.

15 And these are they by the way side, where the word is sown; but when they have heard, Satan cometh immediately, and taketh away the word that*was*sown in their hearts.

16 And these are they*likewise*which*are*sown on stony ground; who, when they have heard the word, immediately receive it with gladness;

17 And have no root in themselves, and so endure*but*for*a*time: afterward, when affliction or persecution ariseth for*the*word's*sake, immediately they are offended.

18 And these are they*which*are*sown among thorns; such*as* hear the word,

19 And the cares of this world, and the deceitfulness of riches, and the lusts of other things entering in, choke the word, and it becometh unfruitful.

20 And these are they*which*are*sown on good ground; such as hear the word, and receive it, and bring*forth*fruit, some thirtyfold, some sixty, and some a hundred.

A Light Under a Bushel (Luke 8:16-18)

21 And he said unto them, Is a candle brought to be put under a bushel, or under a bed? and not to be set on a candlestick?

1063   pin2076 3756/idpro5100 pr/an,ajn2927 repro3739   (3362)   asbp5319   3761

22 For there is nothing hid, which shall not be manifested; neither

aom1096   pr/an,ajn614   235   2443   asba2064 pre1519/an,ajn5318

was any*thing*kept*secret, but that it should come abroad.

idpro1536   pin2192 an,nn3775   pinf191   pim191

23 If*any*man have ears to hear, let him hear.

2532   ipf3004   ppro846   pim991   inpro5101   pin191   pre1722 repro3739   an,nn3358

24 And he said unto them, Take heed what ye hear: with what measure ye

pin3354   ip3354   ppro5213   2532   epn5213   art,pap191

mete, it shall be measured to you: and unto you that hear shall

fp4369

more*be*given.

1063   repro3739/302   psa2192   ppro846   fp1325   2532 repro3739   pin2192   3756

25 For he that hath, to him shall be given: and he that hath not,

pre575 ppro846   fp142   2532   repro3739   pin2192

from him shall be taken even that which he hath.

The Parable of the Growth of the Seed

2532   ipf3004 ad3779 pin2076 art3588   nn932   art,nn2316 ad5613 1437   an,nn444   asba906

26 And he said, So is the kingdom of God, as if a man should cast

art,nn4703 pre1909 art3588   nn1093

seed into the ground;

2532   psa2518   2532 psmp1453 an,nn3571 2532   an,nn2250 2532 art3588   nn4703

27 And should sleep, and rise night and day,, and the seed should

psa985   2532   psmp3373 epn846   pin1492   3756 ad5613

spring and grow up, he knoweth not how.

1063 art3588   nn1093   pin2592   an,ajn844   an,ajn4412   an,nn5528 ad1534

28 For the earth bringeth*forth*fruit of herself; first the blade, then the

an,nn4719 ad1534   art3588 an,aj4134 nn4621 pre1722 art3588 nn4719

ear, after that the full corn in the ear.

1161   ad3752 art3588 nn2590   asba3860   ad2112   pin649   art3588 nn1407

29 But when the fruit is brought forth, immediately he putteth in the sickle,

3754   art3588   nn2326   pfi3936

because the harvest is come.   (Joel 3:13)

The Parable of the Mustard Seed (Matt. 13:31,32; Luke 13:18,19)

2532   ipf3004   inpro5101   asba3666 art3588   nn932   art,nn2316 2228 pre1722

30 And he said, Whereunto shall we liken the kingdom of God? or with

inpro4169   an,nn3850   asba3846   ppro846

what comparison shall we compare it?

ad5613   pr/an,nn2848   an,nn4615   repro3739 ad3752   asbp4687 pre1909 art3588

31 It is like a grain of mustard seed, which, when it is sown in the

nn1093 pin2076 pr/an,aj3398   an,aj3956 art3588 nn4690 art3588   pre1909 art3588   nn1093

earth, is less than all the seeds that be in the earth:

2532   ad3752   asbp4687   pin305   2532   pinm1096 pr/cd/an,aj3187   an,aj3956

32 But when it is sown, it groweth up, and becometh greater than all

art,nn3001   2532   pin4160   an,aj3173   an,nn2798   5620   art3588   nn4071   art3588 nn3772 pifm1410

herbs, and shooteth out great branches; so that the fowls of the air may

pinf2681   pre5259 art3588   nn4639   ppro846

lodge under the shadow of it.   *(Ezek. 17:23; 31:6; Dan. 4:12,21)*

Jesus' Use of Parables (Matt. 13:34,35)

2532   an,aj4183 an,aj5108   an,nn3850   ipf2980   art3588   nn3056   ppro846   ad2531

33 And with many such parables spake he the word unto them, as they

ipf1410   pinf191

were able to hear *it.*

1161   ad*5565   an,nn3850   ipf2980   3756   ppro846   1161

34 But without a parable spake he not unto them: and when

pre2596/an,ajn2398   ipf1956   an,ajn3956   ppro848   art,nn3101

they*were*alone, he expounded all things to his disciples.

Jesus Calms a Storm (Matt. 8:23-27; Luke 8:22-25)

2532   (pre1722) depro1565 art,nn2250   an,nn3798   aptp1096   pin3004   ppro846

35 And the same day, when the even was come, he saith unto them, Let

aosi1330   pre1519 art3588   ad4008

us pass over unto the other side.

2532   apta863   art3588   nn3793   pin3880 ppro846   ad5613

36 And when they had sent away the multitude, they took him even as he

ipf2258 pre1722 art3588 nn4143   1161   ipf2258   2532   pre3326 ppro846 an,aj243   an,nn4142

was in the ship. And there were also with him other little ships.

2532   pinm1096   an,aj3173 an,nn2978   an,nn417   1161   art3588   nn2949   ipf1911 pre1519 art3588

37 And there arose a great storm of wind, and the waves beat into the

nn4143   5620   ppro846   pifm1072/ad2235

ship, so that it was*now*full.

2532   epn846 ipf2258 pre1909 art3588   nn4403   pap2518   pre1909   art,nn4344   2532

38 And he was in the hinder*part*of*the*ship, asleep on a pillow: and

pin1326   ppro846   2532 pin3004   ppro846   an,nn1320   pin3199 ppro4671 3756   3754   pinp622

they awake him, and say unto him, Master, carest thou not that we perish?

2532   aptp1326   aina2008   art3588   nn417   2532 aina2036   art3588 nn2281   pim4623

39 And he arose, and rebuked the wind, and said unto the sea, Peace, be

pfimm5392 2532 art3588 nn417   aina2869   2532   aom1096   an,aj3173 an,nn1055

still. And the wind ceased, and there was a great calm.

2532   aina2036   ppro846   inpro5101 pin2075   ad3779   pr/an,aj1169   ad4459   pin2192

40 And he said unto them, Why are ye so fearful? how is it that ye have

3756 an,nn4102

no faith?

2532   ainp5399   an,aj3173/an,nn5401   2532   ipf3004   rcpro240/pre4314

41 And they feared exceedingly, and said one*to*another,

inpro5101   pin2076   pr/depro3778   3754   2532   art3588   nn417   2532   art3588   nn2281   pin5219

What*manner*of*man is this, that even the wind and the sea obey

ppro846

him?

Healing the Gadarene Demoniac (Matt. 8:28-34; Luke 8:26-39)

2532   aina2064   pre1519   art3588   ad4008

5 And they came over unto the other side of

art3588 nn2281 pre1519 art3588   nn5561   art3588   nn1046

the sea, into the country of the Gadarenes.

2532   ppro846   apta1831   pre1537 art3588 nn4143   ad2112   aina528 ppro846

2 And when he was come out of the ship, immediately there met him

pre1537 art3588 nn3419   an,nn444 pre1722   an,aj169   an,nn4151

out of the tombs a man with an unclean spirit,

repro3739 ipf2192   art,nn2731   pre1722 art3588   nn3419   2532   an,ajn3762 ipf1410 ainf1210 ppro846

3 Who had *his* dwelling among the tombs; and no man could bind him, no,

3777   an,nn254

not with chains:

ppro846   ad4178   aid1210   an,nn3976   2532   an,nn254   2532   art3588

4 Because that he had been often bound with fetters and chains, and the

nn254   aid1288   pre5259 ppro846 2532 art3588   nn3976   aid4937

chains had been plucked asunder by him, and the fetters broken*in*pieces:

2532   ipf2480 an,ajn3762   ainf1150 ppro846

neither could any *man* tame him.

2532   pre,an,ajn1275 an,nn3571 2532 an,nn2250   ipf2258 pre1722 art3588   nn3735   2532 pre1722 art3588

5 And always, night and day, he was in the mountains, and in the

nn3418   pap2896   2532   pap2629   rxpro1438   an,nn3037

tombs, crying, and cutting himself with stones.

1161   apta1492 art,nn2424 pre575/ad3113   aina5143 2532   aina4352   ppro846

6 But when he saw Jesus afar off, he ran and worshiped him,

2532   apta2896   an,aj3173 an,nn5456   pin2036   inpro5101/ppro1698/2532/ppro4671

7 And cried with a loud voice, and said, What*have*I*to*do*with*thee,

an,nn2424   an,nn5207 art3588   aj5310   art,nn2316   pin3726 ppro4571   art,nn2316

Jesus, *thou* Son of the most high God? I adjure thee by God, that thou

aosi928   ppro3165 3361

torment me not.

1063   ipf3004   ppro846 aima1831   pre1537 art3588   nn444   art,aj169 art,nn4151

8 For he said unto him, Come out of the man, *thou* unclean spirit.

2532   ipf1905   ppro846 pr/inpro5101   ppro4671 an,nn3686   2532   pinp611   pap3004   ppro3427

9 And he asked him, What *is* thy name? And he answered, saying, My

an,nn3686   an,nn3003   3754   pin2070 pr/an,aj4183

name *is* Legion: for we are many.

2532   ipf3870   ppro846 ad4183   2443   3361   asba649/ppro846   ad1854

10 And he besought him much that he would not send*them*away out of

art3588   nn5561

the country.

1161   ipf2258   ad1563   pre4314   art3588   nn3735   an,aj3173 an,nn34   an,nn5519

11 Now there was there nigh unto the mountains a great herd of swine

ppmp1006

feeding.

2532 an,aj3956 art3588   nn1142   aina3870   ppro846   pap3004   aima3992 ppro2248 pre1519 art3588   nn5519

12 And all the devils besought him, saying, Send us into the swine,

2443   asba1525 pre1519 ppro846

that we may enter into them.

2532   ad2112   art,nn2424   aina2010/ppro846   2532   art3588   aj169   art,nn4151

13 And forthwith Jesus gave*them*leave. And the unclean spirits

apta1831   2532   aina1525   pre1519 art3588   nn5519   2532 art3588   nn34   aina3729   pre2596
went out, and entered into the swine: and the herd ran violently down a

art,nn2911   pre1519 art3588 nn2281   (1161)   ipf2258   ad5613   pr/nu,ajn1367   2532   ipf4155
steep place into the sea, (they were about two thousand;) and were choked

pre1722 art3588 nn2281
in   the sea.

1161   art,pap1006   art3588   nn5519   aina5343   2532 aina312   pre1519 art3588   nn4172   2532   pre1519
14 And they*that*fed the swine fled, and told *it* in   the city, and   in

art3588   nn68   2532   aina1831   ainf1492 pr/inpro5101   pin2076   art,pfp1096
the country. And they went out to see   what it was that*was*done.

2532   pinm2064   pre4314   art,nn2424   2532   pin2334
15 And   they   come   to   Jesus,   and   see   him*that*was*

art,ppmp1139   art,pap2192 art3588   nn3003   ppmp2521   2532   pfpp2439
possessed*with*the*devil, and   had   the   legion, sitting, and   clothed,

2532   pap4993   2532   ainp5399
and in*his*right*mind: and they were afraid.

2532   art,apta1492   aom1334   ppro846   ad4459   aom1096
16 And   they*that*saw   *it*   told   them   how   it   befell   to

art,ppmp1139   2532   pre4012   art3588   nn5519
him*that*was*possessed*with*the*devil, and *also* concerning the swine.

2532   aom756   pinf3870 ppro846   ainf565   pre575   ppro846   art,nn3725
17 And they began to pray him to depart out of their coasts.

2532   ppro846   pap1684   pre1519   art3588   nn4143
18 And   when   he   was   come   into   the   ship,

art,aptp1139   ipf3870   ppro846   2443   psa5600
he*that*had*been*possessed*with*the*devil prayed him that he might   be

pre3326 ppro846
with him.

1161   art,nn2424   aina863   ppro846   3756   235   pin3004   ppro846   aima5217
19 Howbeit Jesus   suffered   him   not,   but   saith   unto   him,   Go

pre1519/ppro4675/art,nn3624/pre4314/art,popro4674 2532 aima312 ppro846   an,ajn3745   art3588   nn2962   pfi4160
home*to*thy*friends,   and tell them how*great*things the Lord hath done

ppro4671 2532   aina1653   ppro4571
for thee, and hath had compassion on thee.

2532   aina565   2532   aom756   pinf2784   pre1722   art,nn1179   an,ajn3745
20 And he departed, and began to publish   in   Decapolis how*great*things

art,nn2424   aina4160   ppro846 2532 an,ajn3956   ipf2296
Jesus had done for him: and   all   *men* did marvel.

Jesus Raises Jarius' Daughter (Matt. 9:18-26; Luke 8:40-56)

2532   art,nn2424   apta1276   ad3825 pre1722 art,nn4143 pre1519 art3588   ad4008
21 And when Jesus was passed over again by   ship unto the other side,

an,aj4183 an,nn3793   ainp4863   pre1909 ppro846 2532   ipf2258   pre3844   art3588 nn2281
much people gathered unto him: and he was nigh unto the sea.

2532   2400   pinm2064   nu1520   art3588   nn752   an,nn2383
22 And, behold, there cometh one of the rulers*of*the*synagogue, Jairus

an,nn3686 2532   apta1492 ppro846   pin4098 pre4314 ppro846 art,nn4228
by name; and when he saw him, he fell   at   his   feet,

2532   ipf3870   ppro846   an,ajn4183   pap3004   ppro3450   art,nn2365
23 And   besought   him   greatly,   saying,   My   little   daughter

pin2192/ad2079   (2443)   apta2064   asba2007   art,nn5495   ppro846   3704
lieth*at*the*point*of*death: *I pray thee,* come and lay thy hands on her, that

asbp4982   2532   fm2198
she may be healed; and she shall live.

2532   aina565   pre3326 ppro846   2532   an,aj4183   an,nn3793   ipf190   ppro846   2532   ipf4918
24 And *Jesus* went with him; and much people followed him, and thronged

ppro846
him.

2532   idpro5100   an,nn1135   pap5607 (pre1722) an,nn4511   an,nn129   nu1427   an,nn2094
25 And a certain woman, which had   an   issue of blood twelve years,

2532   apta3958   an,ajn4183   pre5259 an,aj4183   an,nn2395   2532   apta1159
26 And had suffered many things of   many physicians, and had spent

an,ajn3956/art,pre3844/rxpro1438   2532   an,ajn3367   aptp5623   235   ad3123   apta2064/pre1519/art,ajn5501
all*that*she*had, and was nothing bettered, but rather grew worse,

apta191   pre4012 art,nn2424   apta2064   pre1722 art3588   nn3793   ad3693
27 When she had heard of Jesus, came   in   the press behind, and

aom680   ppro846   art,nn2440
touched his garment.

1063   ipf3004 2579   asbm680   ppro846   art,nn2440   fp4982
28 For she said, If I may touch but his clothes, I shall be whole.

2532   ad2112   art3588   nn4077   ppro846 art,nn129   ainp3583   2532   aina1097
29 And straightway the fountain of her blood was dried up; and she felt in

art,nn4983 3754   pfip2390   pre575   art,nn3148
her body that she was healed of that plague.

2532   art,nn2424   ad2112   apta1921   pre1722 rxpro1438   art,nn1411   apta1831
30 And Jesus, immediately knowing   in   himself that virtue had gone

pre1537   ppro846   aptp1994   pre1722 art3588   nn3793   2532   ipf3004   inpro5101   aom680
out of him, turned*him*about   in   the press, and said, Who touched

ppro3450 art,nn2440
my clothes?

2532   ppro846   art,nn3101   ipf3004   ppro846   pin991   art3588   nn3793   pap4918
31 And his disciples said unto him, Thou seest the multitude thronging

ppro4571 2532   pin3004   inpro5101   aom680   ppro3450
thee, and sayest thou, Who touched me?

2532   ipf4017   ainf1492   art,apta4160   depro5124
32 And he looked*round*about to see her*that*had*done this thing.

1161   art3588   nn1135   aptp5399   2532   pap5141   pap1492   repro3739   pfi1096   pre1909
33 But the woman fearing and trembling, knowing what was done   in

ppro846 aina2064 2532   aina4363   ppro846 2532 aina2036 ppro846 an,aj3956 art3588   nn225
her, came and fell*down*before him, and told him all the truth.

1161   art3588 aina2036   ppro846   an,nn2364   ppro4675 art,nn4102   pfi4982/ppro4571
34 And he said unto her, Daughter, thy faith hath made*thee*whole;

aima5217 pre1519 an,nn1515   2532 aima2468 pr/an,aj5199 pre575 ppro4675   art,nn3148
go   in peace, and be whole of thy plague.

ppro846 ad2089 pap2980   pinm2064 pre575 art3588   nn752
35 While he yet spake, there came from the ruler*of*the*synagogue's *house*

pap3004 ppro4675   art,nn2364   aina599   inpro5101   pin4660   art3588   nn1320
certain which said, Thy daughter is dead: why troublest thou the Master

ad2089
any further?

⁽¹¹⁶¹⁾ _{ad2112}   _{art,nn2424}   _{apta191} _{art3588}   _{nn3056}   _{ppmp2980}   _{pin3004}   _{art3588}

36   As*soon*as Jesus heard the word that was spoken, he saith unto the

_{nn752}   _{pim5399/3361}   _{ad3440}   _{pim4100}

ruler*of*the*synagogue, Be*not*afraid, only believe.

₂₅₃₂   _{aina863}   _{an,ajn3762}   _{ainp4870}   _{ppro846}   ₁₅₀₈   _{an,nn4074}   ₂₅₃₂   _{an,nn2385}   ₂₅₃₂

37 And he suffered no man to follow him, save Peter, and James, and

_{an,nn2491} _{art3588}   _{nn80}   _{an,nn2385}

John the brother of James.

₂₅₃₂   _{pinm2064}   _{pre1519} _{art3588}   _{nn3624}   _{art3588}   _{nn752}   ₂₅₃₂

38 And he cometh to   the house of the ruler*of*the*synagogue, and

_{pin2334}   _{an,nn2351}   _{pap2799} ₂₅₃₂   _{pap214}   _{ad4183}

seeth the tumult, and them that wept and wailed greatly.

₂₅₃₂   _{apta1525}   _{pin3004}   _{ppro846}   _{inpro5101}

39 And   when   he   was   come   in,   he   saith   unto   them,   Why

_{pinm2350}   ₂₅₃₂ _{pin2799} _{art3588}   _{nn3813}   _{aina599/3756}   ₂₃₅   _{pin2518}

make*ye*this*ado, and weep? the damsel is*not*dead, but sleepeth.

₂₅₃₂   _{ipf2606/ppro846}   ₁₁₆₁   _{art3588}   _{apta1544/an,ajn537}

40 And they laughed*him*to*scorn. But when   he   had   put*them*all*out,

_{pin3880} _{art3588}   _{nn3962}   ₂₅₃₂ _{art3588}   _{nn3384}   _{art3588}   _{nn3813}   ₂₅₃₂ _{art3588}   _{pre3326}

he taketh the father and the mother of the damsel, and them that were with

_{ppro846} ₂₅₃₂   _{pin1531}   _{ad3699} _{art3588}   _{nn3813}   _{ipf2258} _{ppmp345}

him, and entereth in where the damsel was lying.

₂₅₃₂   _{apta2902} _{art3588}   _{nn3813}   _{art3588}   _{nn5495}   _{pin3004}   _{ppro846}   ₅₀₀₈   ₂₈₉₁

41 And he took the damsel by the hand, and said unto her, Talitha cumi;

_{repro3739} _{pin2076}   _{ppmp3177}   _{art,nn2877}   _{pin3004}   _{epn4671} _{aima1453}

which is, being interpreted, Damsel, I say unto thee, arise.

₂₅₃₂   _{ad2112}   _{art3588}   _{nn2877}   _{aina450}   ₂₅₃₂   _{ipf4043}   ₁₀₆₃   _{ipf2258}

42 And straightway the damsel arose, and walked; for she was *of the age* of

_{pr/nu1427} _{an,nn2094}   _{aina1839}   _{an,aj3173}   _{an,nn1611}

twelve years. And they were astonished with a great astonishment.

₂₅₃₂   _{aom1291}   _{pprp846}   _{an,ajn4183}   ₂₄₄₃   _{an,ajn3367}   _{asba1097} _{depro5124}   ₂₅₃₂

43 And he charged them straitly that no man should know   it;   and

_{aina2036}   _{aifp1325} _{ppro846}   _{ainf5315}

commanded that something should be given her to eat.

Jesus Is Rejected in His Own Home Town (Matt. 13:53-58; Luke 4:16-30)

₂₅₃₂   _{aina1831}   _{ad1564}   ₂₅₃₂ _{aina2064} _{pre1519}   _{ppro848}   _{art,nn3968}   ₂₅₃₂ _{ppro846}

6 And he went out from thence, and came into his own country; and his

_{art,nn3101}   _{pin190}   _{ppro846}

disciples follow him.

₂₅₃₂   _{an,nn4521}   _{aptp1096}   _{aom756}   _{pinf1321} _{pre1722} _{art3588}

2 And when the sabbath day was come, he began to teach in   the

_{nn4864}   ₂₅₃₂ _{an,aj4183}   _{pap191}   _{ipf1605}   _{pap3004}   _{ad4159}

synagogue: and many hearing *him* were astonished, saying, From whence hath

_{depro5129}   _{depro5023}   ₂₅₃₂ _{inpro5101} _{art,nn4678}   _{art,apta1325}   _{ppro846}   ₃₇₅₄

this *man* these things? and what wisdom *is* this*which*is*given unto him, that

₂₅₃₂ _{an,aj5108}   _{an,nn1411}   _{pinp1096}   _{pre1223} _{ppro846} _{art,nn5495}

even such mighty works are wrought by his hands?

pin2076 3756 depro3778 art3588   pr/nn5045   art3588 nn5207   an,nn3137 (1161) an,nn80   an,nn2385

☞ 3 Is not this the carpenter, the son of Mary, the brother of James,

2532 an,nn2500 2532 an,nn2455 2532 an,nn4613 2532 pin1526 3756 ppro846 art,nn79 ad5602 pre4314 ppro2248

and Joses, and of Juda, and Simon? and are not his sisters here with us?

2532   ipf4624   pre1722 ppro846

And they were offended at him.

1161 art,nn2424 ipf3004   ppro846   an,nn4396 pin2076 3756   pr/an,820   1508 pre1722

4 But Jesus said unto them, A prophet is not without honor, but in

ppro848   art,nn3968 2532 pre1722   art,nn4773 2532 pre1722 ppro848 art,nn3614

his own country, and among his own kin, and in his own house.

2532   ipf1410 ad1563 ainf4160 3756 (an,aj3762) an,nn1411   1508

5 And he could there do no mighty work, save that he

apta2007 art,nn5495   an,aj3641 an,ajn732   aina2323

laid*his*hands*upon a few sick folk, and healed *them.*

2532   ipf2296   pre1223   ppro846 art,nn570 2532   ipf4013   an,nn2945

6 And he marveled because of their unbelief. And he went round about

art3588 nn2968   pap1321

the villages, teaching.

The Mission of the Twelve (Matt. 10:1, 5-15; Luke 9:1-6)

2532   pinm4341   art3588 nu,ajn1427 2532 aom756   pinf649/ppro846

7 And he called *unto him* the twelve, and began to send*them*forth

nu,ajn1417/nu,ajn1417 2532 ipf1325 ppro846 an,nn1849   art,aj169 art,nn4151

by two*and*two; and gave them power over unclean spirits;

2532 aina3853   ppro846 2443   psa142 an,ajn3367 pre1519   an,nn3598

8 And commanded them that they should take nothing for *their* journey,

1508 an,nn4464 ad3440 3361 an,nn4082 3361 an,nn740 3361 an,nn5475 pre1519   art,nn2223

save a staff only; no scrip, no bread, no money in *their* purse;

235 pfmp5265   an,nn4547 2532 3361 aifm1746 nu1417 an,nn5509

9 But *be* shod with sandals; and not put on two coats.

2532   ipf3004   ppro846   ad3699/1437   asba1525 pre1519 an,nn3614

10 And he said unto them, In*what*place*soever ye enter into a house,

ad1563 pim3306 ad2193/302 asba1831   ad1564

there abide till ye depart from*that*place.

2532 an,ajn3745/302   3361 asbm1209 ppro5209 3366 asba191 ppro5216   ppmp1607

11 And whosoever shall not receive you, nor hear you, when ye depart

ad1564 aima1621 art3588 nn5522 art,ad*5270 ppro5216 art,nn4228 pre1519   an,nn3142   ppro846

thence, shake off the dust under your feet for a testimony against them.

281 pin3004 ppro5213   fm2071   ad414   an,nn4670 2228 an,nn1116

Verily I say unto you, It shall be more tolerable for Sodom and Gomorrah

pre1722 an,nn2250 an,nn2920 2228 depro1565 art,nn4172

in the day of judgment, than for that city.

2532 apta1831 aina2784 2443   asba3340

12 And they went out, and preached that men should repent.

☞ **6:3** See general remarks in the introduction to the Book of Jude.

2532   ipf1544   an,aj4183   an,nn1140   2532   ipf218   an,nn1637   an,aj4183

13 And they cast out many devils, and anointed with oil many

an,ajn732   2532   ipf2323

that*were*sick, and healed *them.*

Herod is Confused About Jesus (Matt. 14:1-12; Luke 9:7-9)

2532   art,nn935   an,nn2264   aina191   1063   ppro846   art,nn3686   aom1096/pr/an,aj5318   2532

14 And king Herod heard *of him*; (for his name was*spread*abroad:) and

ipf3004   3754   an,nn2491   art3588   pap907   ainp1453   pre1537   an,ajn3498   2532   pre1223/depro5124

he said, That John the Baptist was risen from the dead, and therefore

art,nn1411   pin1754   pre1722 ppro846

mighty works do show forth themselves in him.

an,ajn243   ipf3004   3754   pin2076 pr/an,nn2243   1161   an,ajn243   ipf3004   3754   pin2076   pr/an,nn4396

15 Others said, That it is Elijah. And others said, That it is a prophet,

2228 ad5613 pr/nu1520   art3588   nn4396

or as one of the prophets.

1161   art,nn2264   apta191   aina2036 depro3778 pin2076 pr/an,nn2491 repro3739 epn1473

16 But when Herod heard *thereof,* he said, It is John, whom I

aina607   epn846   ainp1453   pre1537   an,ajn3498

beheaded: he is risen from the dead.

1063   art,nn2264   epn846   apta649   2532   aina2902   art,nn2491   2532   aina1210

17 For Herod himself had sent forth and laid*hold*upon John, and bound

ppro846   pre1722   art,nn5438   pre1223/an,nn2266   ppro848   art,nn80   an,nn5376   art,nn1135   3754

him in prison for*Herodias'*sake, his brother Philip's wife: for he had

aina1060   ppro846

married her.

1063   art,nn2491   ipf3004   art,nn2264   pin1832/3756   ppro4671   pinf2192 ppro4675

18 For John had said unto Herod, It is*not*lawful for thee to have thy

art,nn80   art,nn1135

brother's wife.   *(Lev. 18:16)*

1161   art,nn2266   ipf1758   ppro846   2532   ipf2309   ainf615

19 Therefore Herodias had*a*quarrel*against him, and would have killed

ppro846   2532   ipf1410   3756

him; but she could not:

1063   art,nn2264   ipf5399   art,nn2491   pap1492   ppro846   an,aj1342 pr/an,nn435   2532   an,aj40

20 For Herod feared John, knowing that he was a just man and a holy,

2532   ipf4933   ppro846   2532   apta191   ppro846   ipf4160   an,ajn4183   2532   ipf191

and observed him; and when he heard him, he did many things, and heard

ppro846   ad2234

him gladly.

2532   an,aj2121   an,nn2250   aptp2064   ad3753   an,nn2264   ppro848   art,nn1077

21 And when a convenient day was come, that Herod on his birthday

ipf4160   an,nn1173   ppro848 art,nn3175 (2532)   art,nn5506   2532 art,nu,ajn4413   art,nn1056

made a supper to his lords,   high captains, and chief *estates* of Galilee;

2532   art3588   nn2364   ppro846   art,nn2266   apta1525   2532   aptp3738   2532

22 And the daughter of the said Herodias came in, and danced, and

apta700   art,nn2264   2532   art,ppmp4873   art3588   nn935   aina2036   art3588   nn2877

pleased Herod and them*that*sat*with him, the king said unto the damsel,

aima154   ppro3165   repro3739/1437   psa2309   2532   ft1325   ppro4671

Ask of me whatsoever thou wilt, and I will give *it* thee.

²⁵³²   ^{aina3660}   ^{ppro846}   ^{repro3739/1437}   ^{asba154}   ^{ppro3165}   ^{ft1325}

23 And he sware unto her, Whatsoever thou shalt ask of me, I will give *it*

^{ppro4671} ^{ad2193}   ^{an,nn2255}   ^{ppro3450}   ^{art,nn932}

thee, unto the half of my kingdom.

¹¹⁶¹   ^{art3588}   ^{apta1831}   ^{aina2036}   ^{ppro848} ^{art,nn3384} ^{inpro5101}   ^{fm154}   ¹¹⁶¹

24 And she went forth, and said unto her mother, What shall I ask? And

^{art3588} ^{aina2036} ^{art3588} ⁿⁿ²⁷⁷⁶   ^{an,nn2491} ^{art3588}   ⁿⁿ⁹¹⁰

she said, The head of John the Baptist.

²⁵³²   ^{apta1525}   ^{ad2112}   ^{pre3326} ^{an,nn4710} ^{pre4314}   ^{art3588}   ⁿⁿ⁹³⁵   ^{aom154}

25 And she came in straightway with haste unto the king, and asked,

^{pap3004}   ^{pin2309}   ²⁴⁴³   ^{asba1325} ^{ppro3427}   ^{ad1824}   ^{pre1909}   ^{an,nn4094}   ^{art3588} ⁿⁿ²⁷⁷⁶   ^{an,nn2491}

saying, I will that thou give me by*and*by in a charger the head of John

^{art3588}   ⁿⁿ⁹¹⁰

the Baptist.

²⁵³²   ^{art3588} ⁿⁿ⁹³⁵   ^{aptp1096}   ^{pr/an,aj4036}   ^{pre1223/art,nn3727}   ²⁵³²

26 And the king was exceeding sorry; *yet* for*his*oath's*sake, and for their

^{art,ppmp4873}   ^{aina2309} ³⁷⁵⁶   ^{ainf114} ^{ppro846}

sakes which*sat*with him, he would not reject her.

²⁵³²   ^{ad2112}   ^{art3588}   ⁿⁿ⁹³⁵   ^{apta649}   ^{an,nn4688}   ^{aina2004}   ^{ppro846}

27 And immediately the king sent an executioner, and commanded his

^{art,nn2776}   ^{aifp5342}   ¹¹⁶¹ ^{art3588} ^{apta565}   ^{aina607}   ^{ppro846} ^{pre1722} ^{art3588}   ⁿⁿ⁵⁴³⁸

head to be brought: and he went and beheaded him in the prison,

²⁵³²   ^{aina5342}   ^{ppro846} ^{art,nn2776} ^{pre1909}   ^{an,nn4094}   ²⁵³² ^{aina1325} ^{ppro846}   ^{art3588}   ⁿⁿ²⁸⁷⁷

28 And brought his head in a charger, and gave it to the damsel:

²⁵³² ^{art3588}   ⁿⁿ²⁸⁷⁷   ^{aina1325} ^{ppro846}   ^{ppro848} ^{art,nn3384}

and the damsel gave it to her mother.

²⁵³²   ^{ppro846}   ^{art,nn3101}   ^{apta191}   ^{aina2064} ²⁵³²   ^{aina142}   ^{ppro846} ^{art,nn4430}

29 And when his disciples heard *of it*, they came and took up his corpse,

²⁵³² ^{aina5087} ^{ppro846} ^{pre1722}   ^{art,nn3419}

and laid it in a tomb.

The Feeding of the Five Thousand (Matt. 14:13-21; Luke 9:10-17; John 6:1-14)

²⁵³² ^{art3588}   ⁿⁿ⁶⁵²   ^{pinm4863}   ^{pre4314} ^{art,nn2424} ²⁵³² ^{aina518}

30 And the apostles gathered*themselves*together unto Jesus, and told

^{ppro846} ^{an,ajn3956}   ²⁵³² ^{an,ajn3745}   ^{aina4160} ²⁵³² ^{an,ajn3745}   ^{aina1321}

him all things, both what they had done, and what they had taught.

²⁵³²   ^{aina2036}   ^{ppro846}   ^{ad1205} ^{epn5210}   ^{ppro846}   ^{pre2596/an,ajn2398} ^{pre1519}   ^{an,aj2048}

31 And he said unto them, Come ye yourselves apart into a desert

^{an,nn5117} ²⁵³² ^{aima373}   ^{an,ajn3641}   ¹⁰⁶³   ^{ipf2258} ^{an,aj4183} ^{art,ppmp2064} ²⁵³² ^{art,pap5217}   ²⁵³²

place, and rest a while: for there were many coming and going, and they

^{ipf2119/3761}   ^{ainf5315}

had*no*leisure*so*much*as to eat.

²⁵³²   ^{aina565}   ^{pre1519}   ^{an,aj2048} ^{an,nn5117}   ^{art,nn4143} ^{pre2596/an,ajn2398}

32 And they departed into a desert place by ship privately.

²⁵³² ^{art3588}   ⁿⁿ³⁷⁹³ ^{aina1492} ^{ppro846}   ^{pap5217}   ²⁵³² ^{an,ajn4183} ^{aina1921} ^{ppro846} ²⁵³² ^{aina4936}

33 And the people saw them departing, and many knew him, and ran

ad3979   ad1563   pre575   an,aj3956   art,nn4172   2532   aina4281   ppro846   2532   aina4905   pre4314
afoot thither out of all   cities, and outwent them, and came together unto
ppro846
him.

2532   art,nn2424   apta1831   aina1492   an,aj4183   an,nn3793   2532
34 And Jesus, when he came out, saw much people, and was
ainp4697   pre1909   ppro846   3754   ipf2258   ad5613   pr/an,nn4263   3361
moved*with*compassion toward them, because they were as sheep not
pap2192   an,nn4166   2532   aom756   pinf1321 ppro846   an,ajn4183
having a shepherd: and he began to teach them many things.   (Ezek. 34:8)

2532   ad2235/aptp1096/an,aj4183/an,nn5610   ppro846   art,nn3101   apta4334   ppro846
35 And when the day*was*now*far*spent, his disciples came unto him,
pin3004   pin2076   pr/an,aj2048 art,nn5117 2532   ad2235   pr/an,aj4183/an,nn5610
and said, This is a desert place, and now the time*is*far*passed:

aima630/ppro846   2443   apta565   pre1519 art3588   nn68   an,nn2945
36 Send*them*away, that they may go into the country round about,
2532   an,nn2968   asba59   rxpro1438   an,nn740   1063   pin2192   3756/inpro5101
and into the villages, and buy themselves bread: for they have nothing to
asba5315
eat.

(1161) art3588   aptp611   aina2036   ppro846 aima1325 epn5210 ppro846   ainf5315   2532
37   He answered and said unto them, Give ye them to eat. And they
pin3004   ppro846   apta565   asba59   nu1250   an,nn1220   an,nn740   2532
say unto him, Shall we go and buy two hundred pennyworth of bread, and
asba1325 ppro846   ainf5315
give them to eat?

(1161) art3588 pin3004   ppro846   an,aj4214   an,nn740 pin2192   aima5217 2532 aima1492 2532
38   He saith unto them, How many loaves have ye? go and see. And
apta1097   pin3004 nu,ajn4002 2532 nu1417 an,nn2486
when they knew, they say, Five, and two fishes.

2532   aina2004   ppro846   ainf347/an,ajn3956   an,nn4849/an,nn4849 pre1909 art3588
39 And he commanded them to make*all*sit*down by companies upon the
an,aj5515   nn5528
green grass.

2532   aina377   an,nn4237/an,nn4237   pre303/nu,ajn1540   2532   pre303/nu,ajn4004
40 And they sat down in ranks, by hundreds, and by fifties.

2532   apta2983 art3588   nu4002   nn740   2532 art3588 nu1417   nn2486
41 And when he had taken the five loaves and the two fishes, he
apta308   pre1519   art,nn3772   aina2127   2532 aina2622 art3588   nn740   2532 ipf1325
looked up to heaven, and blessed, and broke the loaves, and gave them to
ppro848 art,nn3101   2443   asba3908   ppro846   2532 art3588 nu1417 nn2486   aina3307
his disciples to set before them; and the two fishes divided he among them
an,ajn3956
all.

2532   an,ajn3956 aina5315 2532   ainp5526
42 And they did all   eat, and were filled.

2532   aina142 nu1427   an,nn2894 an,aj4134   an,nn2801   2532 pre575 art3588
43 And they took up twelve baskets full of the fragments, and of the
nn2486
fishes.

2532   art,apta5315   art3588   nn740   ipf2258   ad5616   pr/nu4000   an,nn435
44 And they*that*did*eat of the loaves were about five thousand men.

Jesus Walks on Water (Matt. 14:22-33; John 6:16-21)

45 And straightway he constrained his disciples to get into the ship, and to go*to*the*other*side before unto Bethsaida, while he sent away the people.

46 And when he had sent*them*away, he departed into a mountain to pray.

47 And when even was come, the ship was in the midst of the sea, and he alone on the land.

48 And he saw them toiling in rowing; for the wind was contrary unto them: and about the fourth watch of the night he cometh unto them, walking upon the sea, and would have passed by them.

49 But when they saw him walking upon the sea, they supposed it had been a spirit, and cried out:

50 For they all saw him, and were troubled. And immediately he talked with them, and saith unto them, Be*of*good*cheer: it is I; be*not*afraid.

51 And he went up unto them into the ship; and the wind ceased: and they were sore amazed in themselves beyond measure, and wondered.

52 For they considered not *the miracle* of the loaves: for their heart was hardened.

Jesus Heals in Gennesaret (Matt. 14:34-36)

53 And when they had passed over, they came into the land of Gennesaret, and drew*to*the*shore.

54 And when they were come out of the ship, straightway they knew him,

^{aina4063} ^{depro1565} ^{an,aj3650} ^{art,nn4066} ^{aom756}

55 And ran through that whole region*round*about, and began to

^{pinf4064} ^{pre1909} ^{art,nn2895} ^{art,pap2192/ad2560} ^{ad3699} ^{ipf191} ⁽³⁷⁵⁴⁾ ^{pin2076(ad1563)}

carry about in beds those*that*were*sick, where they heard he was.

²⁵³² ^{ad3699/302} ^{ipf1531} ^{pre1519} ^{an,nn2968} ²²²⁸ ^{an,nn4172} ²²²⁸ ^{an,nn68}

56 And whithersoever he entered, into villages, or cities, or country, they

^{ipf5087} ^{art3588} ^{pap770} ^{pre1722} ^{art3588} ⁿⁿ⁵⁸ ²⁵³² ^{ipf3870} ^{ppro846} ²⁴⁴³ ^{asbm680}

laid the sick in the streets, and besought him that they might touch

²⁵⁷⁹ ^{art3588} ⁿⁿ²⁸⁹⁹ ^{ppro846} ^{art,nn2440} ²⁵³² ^{an,ajn3745/302} ^{ipf680} ^{ppro846}

if*it*were*but the border of his garment: and as*many*as touched him were

^{ipf4982}

made whole.

God's Command Or Man's Tradition? (Matt. 15:1-20)

²⁵³² ^{pinm4863} ^{pre4314} ^{ppro846} ^{art3588} ⁿⁿ⁵³³⁰ ²⁵³² ^{idpro5100} ^{art3588} ⁿⁿ¹¹²²

7 Then came together unto him the Pharisees, and certain of the scribes,

^{apta2064} ^{pre575} ^{an,nn2414}

which came from Jerusalem.

²⁵³² ^{apta1492} ^{idpro5100} ^{ppro846} ^{art,nn3101} ^{pap2068} ^{an,nn740} ^{an,aj2839}

2 And when they saw some of his disciples eat bread with defiled,

^{depro,pin5123} ^{an,aj449} ^{an,nn5495} ^{aom3201}

that*is*to*say, with unwashen, hands, they found fault.

¹⁰⁶³ ^{art3588} ⁿⁿ⁵³³⁰ ²⁵³² ^{an,aj3956} ^{art3588} ⁿⁿ²⁴⁵³ ³³⁶² ^{asbm3538} ^{art,nn5495}

3 For the Pharisees, and all the Jews, except they wash *their* hands

^{an,nn4435} ^{pin2068} ³⁷⁵⁶ ^{pap2902} ^{art3588} ⁿⁿ³⁸⁶² ^{art3588} ^{ajn4245}

oft, eat not, holding the tradition of the elders.

²⁵³² ^{pre575} ^{an,nn58} ³³⁶² ^{asbm907} ^{pin2068} ³⁷⁵⁶

4 And *when they come* from the market, except they wash, they eat not.

²⁵³² ^{an,aj4183} ^{an,ajn243} ^{pin2076} ^{repro3739} ^{aina3880} ^{pinf2902}

And many other things there be, which they have received to hold, *as* the

^{an,nn909} ^{an,nn4221} ²⁵³² ^{an,nn3582} ⁽²⁵³²⁾ ^{an,nn5473} ²⁵³² ^{an,nn2825}

washing of cups, and pots, brazen vessels, and of tables.

^{ad1899} ^{art3588} ⁿⁿ⁵³³⁰ ²⁵³² ^{art,nn1122} ^{pin1905} ^{ppro846} ^{pre,inpro1302} ^{pin4043} ³⁷⁵⁶ ^{ppro4675}

5 Then the Pharisees and scribes asked him, Why walk not thy

^{art,nn3101} ^{pre2596} ^{art3588} ⁿⁿ³⁸⁶² ^{art3588} ^{ajn4245} ²³⁵ ^{pin2068} ^{art,nn740}

disciples according to the tradition of the elders, but eat bread with

^{an,aj449} ^{an,nn5495}

unwashen hands?

⁽¹¹⁶¹⁾ ^{art3588} ^{aptp611} ^{aina2036} ^{ppro846} ^{ad2573} ^{an,nn2268} ^{aina4395} ^{pre4012}

6 He answered and said unto them, Well hath Isaiah prophesied of

^{ppro5216} ^{art,nn5273} ^{ad5613} ^{pfip1125} ^{depro3778} ^{art,nn2992} ^{pin5091} ^{ppro3165} ^{art,nn5491}

you hypocrites, as it is written, This people honoreth me with *their* lips,

¹¹⁶¹ ^{ppro846} ^{art,nn2588} ^{pin468/ad4206} ^{pre575} ^{ppro1700}

but their heart is far from me.

¹¹⁶¹ ^{ad3155} ^{pinm4576} ^{ppro3165} ^{pap1321} ^{an,nn1319}

7 Howbeit in vain do they worship me, teaching *for* doctrines the

^{an,nn1778} ^{an,nn444}

commandments of men.   *(Is. 29:13 [Sept.])*

8 For laying aside the commandment of God, ye hold the tradition of men,

as the washing of pots and cups: and many other such like things ye do.

9 And he said unto them, Full well ye reject the commandment of God,

that ye may keep your own tradition.

10 For Moses said, Honor thy father and thy mother; and,

whoso curseth father or mother, let him die the death:

(Ex. 20:12; Deut. 5:16; Ex. 21:17)

11 But ye say, If a man shall say to his father or mother, *It is* Corban,

that*is*to*say, a gift, by whatsoever thou mightest be profited by me; *he*

shall be free.

12 And ye suffer him no more to do aught for his father or his

mother;

13 Making*the*word*of*God*of*none*effect through your tradition, which

ye have delivered: and many such like things do ye.

Evil Comes From the Heart

14 And when he had called all the people *unto him,* he said unto them,

Hearken unto me every one *of you,* and understand:

15 There is nothing from without a man, that entering into him can

defile him: but the things*which*come out of him, those are they*that*defile

the man.

16 If*any*man have ears to hear, let him hear.

17 And when he was entered into the house from the people, his

disciples asked him concerning the parable.

18 And he saith unto them, Are ye   so without understanding also? Do ye

3756   pin3539   3754   an,aj3956   art,ad1855   ppmp1531   pre1519 art3588   nn444

not perceive, that whatsoever thing from without entereth into the man, *it*

pinm1410/3756   ainf2840   ppro846

cannot defile him;

                    3754   pinp1531   3756 pre1519 ppro846 art,nn2588   235   pre1519 art3588 nn2836   2532

19 Because it entereth not into his heart, but into the belly, and

pinp1607   pre1519 art3588   nn856   pap2511   an,aj3956   art,nn1033

goeth out into the draught, purging all meats?

        1161   ipf3004 (3754)   art,ppmp1607   pre1537 art3588 nn444 depro1565 pin2840 art3588

20 And he said,   That*which*cometh out of the man, that defileth the

nn444

man.

        1063   ad2081   pre1537 art3588 nn2588   art,nn444 pinp1607 art,aj2556 art,nn1261

21 For from within, out of the heart of men, proceed evil thoughts,

an,nn3430   an,nn4202   an,nn5408

adulteries, fornications, murders,

        an,nn2829   an,nn4124   an,nn4189   an,nn1388   an,nn766   an,aj4190

22 Thefts, covetousness, wickedness, deceit, lasciviousness, an evil

an,nn3788   an,nn988   an,nn5243   an,nn877

eye, blasphemy, pride, foolishness:

        an,aj3956 depro5023   art,ajn4190   pinp1607   ad2081   2532 pin2840 art3588 nn444

23 All these evil things come from within, and defile the man.

Jesus Honors a Syrophoenician Woman's Faith (Matt. 15:21-28)

        2532   ad1564   apta450   aina565 pre1519 art3588   nn3181   an,nn5184 2532

24 And from thence he arose, and went into the borders of Tyre and

an,nn4605 2532   apta1525 pre1519 art,nn3614   ipf2309   an,ajn3762 ainf1097   2532   ainm1410

Sidon, and entered into a house, and would have no man know *it*, but he could

3756   aifp2990

not be hid.

        1063   an,nn1135   repro3739 (ppro848)   art,nn2365   ipf2192   an,aj169   an,nn4151

25 For a *certain* woman, whose   young daughter had an unclean spirit,

apta191 pre4012 ppro846   apta2064   aina4363 pre4314 ppro846 art,nn4228

heard of him, and came and fell at his feet:

        (1161)art3588   nn1135   ipf2258   pr/an,nn1674   an,nn4949   art,nn1085   2532

26   The woman was a Greek, a Syrophenician by nation; and she

ipf2065   ppro846 2443   asba1544 art3588 nn1140 pre1537 ppro848 art,nn2364

besought him that he would cast forth the devil out of her daughter.

        1161 art,nn2424 aina2036   ppro846 aima863 art3588   nn5043   nu,ajn4412 aifp5526 1063   pin2076 3756

27 But Jesus said unto her, Let the children first be filled: for it is not

pr/an,ajn2570   ainf2983 art3588   nn5043   art,nn740 2532   ainf906   art3588 nn2952

meet to take the children's bread, and to cast *it* unto the dogs.

        1161   art3588   ainp611   2532 pin3004   ppro846   3483 an,nn2962 1063 (2532) art3588 nn2952

28 And she answered and said unto him, Yes, Lord: yet   the dogs

ad*5270 art3588 nn5132 pin2068 pre575 art3588   nn3813   art,nn5589

under the table eat of the children's crumbs.

        2532   aina2036   ppro846 pre1223 depro5126 art,nn3056   aima5217   art3588 nn1140   pfi1831

29 And he said unto her, For this saying go*thy*way; the devil is gone

pre1537 ppro4675   art,nn2364

out of thy daughter.

2532   apta565   pre1519 ppro848 art,nn3624   aina2147 art3588 nn1140   pfp1831
30 And when she was come to her house, she found the devil gone out,
2532   art,nn2364   pfpp906 pre1909 art3588 nn2825
and her daughter laid upon the bed.

Jesus Heals a Deaf and Dumb Man

2532   ad3825   apta1831   pre1537 art3588   nn3725   an,nn5184 2532   an,nn4605   aina2064 pre4314
31 And again, departing from the coasts of Tyre and Sidon, he came unto
art3588 nn2281   art,nn1056   pre303   an,ajn3319   art3588   nn3725   an,nn1179
the sea of Galilee, through the midst of the coasts of Decapolis.

2532   pin5342   ppro846   an,ajn2974
32 And   they   bring   unto   him   one*that*was*deaf,   and
                an,ajn3424   2532   pin3870   ppro846   2443
had*an*impediment*in*his*speech;   and   they   beseech   him   to
put*his*hand*upon him.
asba2007/art,nn5495   ppro846

2532   apta618 ppro846 pre2596/an,ajn2398 pre575 art3588   nn3793   aina906 ppro848 art,nn1147
33 And he took him   aside   from the multitude, and put his fingers
pre1519 ppro846 art,nn3775 2532   apta4429   aom680   ppro846 art,nn1100
into his ears, and he spit, and touched his tongue;

2532   apta308   pre1519 art,nn3772   aina4727   2532 pin3004   ppro846   2188
34 And looking up to heaven, he sighed, and saith unto him, Ephphatha,
repro,pin3603   aipp1272
that is, Be opened.

2532   ad2112   ppro846 art,nn189   ainp1272   2532 art3588   nn1199   ppro846 art,nn1100
35 And straightway his ears were opened, and the string of his tongue
ainp3089   2532   ipf2980   ad3723
was loosed, and he spake plain.

2532   aom1291   ppro846   2443   asba2036 an,ajn3367 1161 an,ajn3745 epn846
36 And he charged them that they should tell no man: but the more he
ipf1291   ppro846   ad3123   an,ajn4054   ipf2784
charged them, so*much*the*more a*great*deal they published *it*;

2532   ad5249   ipf1605   pap3004   pfi4160   an,ajn3956
37 And were beyond measure astonished, saying, He hath done all things
ad2573   pin4160   2532 art3588 ajn2974   pinf191 2532 art3588 ajn216   pinf2980
well: he maketh both the deaf to hear, and the dumb to speak.

Jesus Feeds the Four Thousand (Matt. 15:32-39)

pre1722 depro1565 art,nn2250   an,nn3793   pap5607   pr/an,aj3827   2532   pap2192   3361/inpro5101
8 In those days the multitude being very great, and having nothing to
asba5315 art,nn2424 aptp4341 ppro848 art,nn3101   2532 pin3004   ppro846
eat, Jesus called his disciples *unto him,* and saith unto them,

pinm4697   pre1909 art3588   nn3793   3754   ad2235 pin4357
2 I have compassion on the multitude, because they have now been with
ppro3427 nu5140 an,nn2250 2532 pin2192 3756/inpro5101   asba5315
me three days, and have nothing to eat:

2532 1437   asba630/ppro846   an,nn3523 pre1519 ppro848   an,nn3624   fp1590

3 And if I send*them*away fasting to their own houses, they will faint

pre1722 art3588 nn3598 1063 idpro5100   ppro846 pfi2240   ad3113

by the way: for divers of them came from far.

2532 ppro846   art,nn3101   ainp611   ppro846   ad4159   fm1410 idpro5100 ainf5526 depro5128

4 And his disciples answered him, From whence can a man satisfy these

an,nn740 ad5602 pre1909   an,nn2047

men with bread here in the wilderness?

2532   ipf1905 ppro846 an,aj4214   an,nn740 pin2192   1161 art3588 aina2036 nu,ajn2033

5 And he asked them, How many loaves have ye? And they said, Seven.

2532   aina3853   art3588   nn3793   ainf377 pre1909 art3588   nn1093   2532   apta2983

6 And he commanded the people to sit down on the ground: and he took

art3588 nu2033   nn740   apta2168   aina2806 2532 ipf1325   ppro848   art,nn3101   2443

the seven loaves, and gave thanks, and broke, and gave to his disciples to

psa3908   2532   aina3908   art3588   nn3793

set before *them*; and they did set*them*before the people.

2532   ipf2192 an,aj3641   an,nn2485   2532   apta2127   aina2036

7 And they had a few small fishes: and he blessed, and commanded to

pinf3908/epn846/2532

set*them*also*before *them*.

1161   aina5315 2532   ainp5526 2532   aina142   an,nn2801

8 So they did eat, and were filled: and they took up of the broken *meat*

an,nn4051   nu2033 an,nn4711

that*was*left seven baskets.

1161   art,apta5315   ipf2258   ad5613   pr/nu,ajn5070   2532

9 And they*that*had*eaten were about four thousand: and he

aina630/ppro846

sent*them*away.

2532   ad2112   apta1684   pre1519 art,nn4143 pre3326 ppro848 art,nn3101

10 And straightway he entered into a ship with his disciples, and

aina2064 pre1519 art3588 nn3313   1148

came into the parts of Dalmanutha.

The Pharisees Demand a Sign (Matt. 16:1-4)

2532 art3588   nn5330   aina1831   2532 aom756   pinf4802   ppro846

11 And the Pharisees came forth, and began to question with him,

pap2212 pre3844 ppro846 an,nn4592 pre575 art,nn3772   pap3985   ppro846

seeking of him a sign from heaven, tempting him.

2532   apta389   ppro848 art,nn4151 2532 pin3004 inpro5101   depro3778

12 And he sighed deeply in his spirit, and saith, Why doth this

art,nn1074   pin1834   an,nn4592   281   pin3004   ppro5213   (1487)   an,nn4592

generation seek after a sign? verily I say unto you, There shall no sign be

fp1325   depro5026   art,nn1074

given unto this generation.

2532   apta863 ppro846   apta1684 pre1519 art3588 nn4143 ad3825   aina565   pre1519 art3588

13 And he left them, and entering into the ship again departed to the

ad4008

other side.

The Leaven of the Pharisees and of Herod (Matt. 16:5-12)

2532   aom1950   ainf2983   an,nn740   3756   ipf2192   pre1722

14 Now *the disciples* had forgotten to take bread, neither had they   in
art3588 nn4143 pre3326 rxpro1438   1508   nu1520 an,nn740

the ship with them more than one loaf.
2532   ipf1291   ppro846 pap3004   pim3708   pim991   pre575 art3588   nn2219

15 And he charged them, saying, Take heed, beware of the leaven of
art3588   nn5330   2532   art3588   nn2219   an,nn2264

the Pharisees, and *of* the leaven of Herod.
2532   ipf1260   pre4314/rcpro240   pap3004   3754   pin2192

16 And they reasoned among themselves, saying, *It is* because we have
3756 an,nn740

no bread.
2532   art,nn2424 apta1097   ppro846 inpro5101 pinm1260   3754

17 And when Jesus knew *it,* he saith unto them, Why reason ye, because
pin2192 3756   an,nn740 pin3539   ad3768   3761   pin4920   pin2192   ppro5216

ye have no bread? perceive ye not yet, neither understand? have ye your
art,nn2588 ad2089   pfpp4456

heart yet hardened?
pap2192   an,nn3788 pin991   3756 2352 pap2192 an,nn3775 pin191   3756 2532   3756

18 Having eyes, see ye not? and having ears, hear ye not? and do ye not
pin3421

remember?   *(Jer. 5:21; Ezek. 12:2)*
ad3753   aina2806 art3588 nu4002   nn740   pre1519   art,nu,ajn4000   an,aj4214   an,nn2894

19 When I broke the five loaves among five thousand, how many baskets
an,aj4134   an,nn2801   aina142   pin3004   ppro846   nu,ajn1427

full of fragments took*ye*up? They say unto him, Twelve.
1161   ad3753   art3588 nu,ajn2033   pre1519   art,nu,ajn5070   an,aj4214   an,nn4711 an,nn4138

20 And when the seven among four thousand, how many baskets full of
an,nn2801   aina142   1161   art3588 aina2036 nu,ajn2033

fragments took*ye*up? And they said, Seven.
2532   ipf3004   ppro846 ad4459   3756   pin4920

21 And he said unto them, How is it that ye do not understand?

Jesus Heals a Blind Man at Bethsaida

2532   pinm2064 pre1519   966   2532   pin5342   an,ain5185   ppro846 2532

22 And he cometh to Bethsaida: and they bring a blind man unto him, and
pin3870   ppro846 2443 asbm680 ppro846

besought him to touch him.
2532   apta1949 art3588   ajn5185   art3588 nn5495   aina1806 ppro846 ad1854   art3588 nn2968

23 And he took the blind man by the hand, and led him out of the town;
2532   apta4429 pre1519 ppro846 art,nn3659   apta2007/art,nn5495   ppro846   ipf1905

and when he had spit on his eyes, and put*his* hands*upon him, he asked
ppro846   idpro1536/pin991

him if*he*saw*aught.
2532   apta308   ipf3004 pin991 art,nn444 ad5613 an,nn1186 (pin3708) pap4043

24 And he looked up, and said, I see men as trees,   walking.

ad1534   aina2007   art,nn5495   ad3825   pre1909 ppro846 art,nn3788   2532   aina4160 ppro846

25 After that he put *his* hands again upon his eyes, and made him

ainf308   2532   ainp600   2532 aina1689   an,ajn537   ad5081

look up: and he was restored, and saw every man clearly.

2532   aina649/ppro846   pre1519 ppro846 art,nn3624 pap3004   3366   aosi1525 pre1519 art3588

26 And he sent*him*away to his house, saying, Neither go into the

nn2968   3366 aosi2036   idpro5100 pre1722 art3588   nn2968

town, nor tell *it* to any in the town.

Peter's Declaration That Jesus Is the Messiah (Matt. 16:13-20; Luke 9:18-21)

2532 art,nn2424   aina1831   2532 ppro846   art,nn3101   pre1519 art3588   nn2968   art,nn2542

27 And Jesus went out, and his disciples, into the towns of Caesarea

art,nn5376   2532 pre1722 art3588 nn3598   ipf1905   ppro846   art,nn3101   pap3004   ppro846 pr/inpro5101

Philippi: and by the way he asked his disciples, saying unto them, Whom do

art,nn444 pin3004   ppro3165 pinf1511

men say that I   am?

1161 art3588   ainp611   an,nn2491 art3588   art,nn910   2532 an,ajn243   an,nn2243   1161 an,ajn243

28 And they answered, John the Baptist: but some *say*, Elijah; and others,

nu1520   art3588   nn4396

One of the prophets.

2532 epn846 pin3004   ppro846   1161 pr/inpro5101 pin3004 epn5210   ppro3165 pinf1511 1161 art,nn4074

29 And he saith unto them, But whom say ye that I   am? And Peter

aptp611   pin3004   ppro846 epn4771 pin1488 art3588 pr/nn5547

answereth and saith unto him, Thou art the Christ.

2532   aina2008   ppro846   2443   psa3004 an,ajn3367   pre4012 ppro846

30 And he charged them that they should tell no man of him.

Jesus Predicts His Death and Resurrection (Matt. 16:21-28; Luke 9:22-27)

2532   aom756   pinf1321 ppro846   3754 art3588   nn5207   art,nn444   pin1163   ainf3958

31 And he began to teach them, that the Son of man must suffer

an,ajn4183   2532   aifp593   pre575 art3588 ajn4245   2532   an,nn749   2532

many things, and be rejected of the elders, and *of* the chief priests, and

an,nn1122   2532   aifp615   2532 pre3326 nu5140 an,nn2250   ainf450

scribes, and be killed, and after three days rise again.

2532   ipf2980   art,nn3056   an,nn3954   2532 art,nn4074 aptp4355 ppro846   aom756

32 And he spake that saying openly. And Peter took him, and began to

ainf2008 ppro846

rebuke him.

1161   art3588   aptp1994   2532   apta1492   ppro848   art,nn3101

33 But when he had turned about and looked on his disciples, he

aina2008   art,nn4074   pap3004 aima5217   ad*3694   ppro3450 an,nn4567   3754   pin5426   3756

rebuked Peter, saying, Get thee behind me, Satan: for thou savorest not

art3588   art,nn2316 235   art3588   art,nn444

the things that be of God, but the things that be of men.

2532   aptp4341 art3588 nn3793   pre4862 ppro848 art,nn3101

34 And when he had called the people *unto him* with his disciples also, he

aina2036   ppro846   repro3748   pin2309 pinf2064 ad⁺3694 ppro3450   aipm533 rxpro1438 2532

said unto them, Whosoever will come after me, let him deny himself, and

aima142   ppro846 art,nn4716 2532   pim190   ppro3427

take up his cross, and follow me.

1063   repro3739/302   psa2309 ainf4982   ppro848   art,nn5590   ft622   ppro846   1161

35 For   whosoever   will   save   his   life   shall   lose   it;   but

repro3739/302   asba622 ppro848 art,nn5590   ad⁺1752/ppro1700   2532 art3588   nn2098   depro3778

whosoever shall lose his   life   for*my*sake and the   gospel's, the same shall

ft4982   ppro846

save it.

1063   inpro5101   ft5623   an,nn444 1437   asba2770 art3588   an,aj3650   nn2889

36 For what shall it profit a man, if he shall gain the   whole world,

2532 asbp2210   ppro848   art,nn5590

and lose his own soul?

2228 inpro5101   an,nn444 ft1325   an,nn465   ppro848 art,nn5590

37 Or what shall a man give in exchange for his   soul?

repro3739/302   1063   asbp1870   ppro3165 2532   popro1699 art,nn3056 pre1722

38 Whosoever therefore shall be ashamed of me and of my words in

depro5026   art,nn3428   2532 an,aj268   art,nn5026   ppro846 2532   art3588 nn5207   art,nn444

this adulterous and sinful generation; of him also shall the Son of man be

fp1870   ad3752   asba2064   pre1722 art3588   nn1391   ppro848 art,nn3962 pre3326 art3588 aj40   art,nn32

ashamed, when he cometh in   the glory of his Father with the holy angels.

2532   ipf3004   ppro846   281   pin3004   ppro5213 3754   pin1526 idpro5100

9 And he said unto them, Verily I say unto you, That there be some of

art,pfp2476   ad5602   repro3748   efn3364 asbm1089   an,nn2288 ad2193/302

them*that*stand here, which shall not taste of death, till they

asba1492 art3588   nn932   art,nn2316 pfp2064 pre1722 an,nn1411

have seen the kingdom of God come with power.

The Transfiguration (Matt. 17:1-13; Luke 9:28-36)

2532   pre3326 nu1803 an,nn2250 art,nn2424   pin3880   art,nn4074   2532   art,nn2385   2532 art,nn2491

2 And after six days Jesus taketh *with him* Peter, and James, and John,

2532   pin399/ppro846   pre1519   an,aj5308   an,nn3735   pre2596/an,ajn2398/an,aj3441   2532

and leadeth*them*up into a high mountain apart*by*themselves: and he was

ainp3339   ad⁺1715   ppro846

transfigured before them.

2532   ppro846   art,nn2440   aom1096   pr/pap4744   ad3029   pr/an,aj3022 ad5613 an,nn5510 repro3634 3756

3 And his raiment became shining, exceeding white as snow; so as no

an,nn1102 pre1909 art,nn1093 pinm1410 ainf3021

fuller on earth can white them.

2532   ainp3700   ppro846   an,nn2243 pre4862   an,nn3475   2532   ipf2258

4 And there appeared unto them Elijah with Moses: and they were

pap4814   art,nn2424

talking with Jesus.

2532　art,nn4074　　aptp611　　　　pin3004　art,nn2424　4461　　　pin2076　pr/an,ajn2570　ppro2248

5 And Peter answered and said to Jesus, Master, it is　good for　us　to

pinf1511　ad5602　2532　　　　aosi4160　nu5140　an,nn4633　nu,ajn3391　epn4671　2532　nu,ajn3391

be　here: and let us make three tabernacles;　one　for thee, and　one　for

an,nn3475　2532　nu,ajn3391　an,nn2243

Moses, and　one　for Elijah.

1063　　ipf1492　3756　inpro5101　asba2980　1063　　ipf2258　pr/an,aj1630

6 For he wist not what to say; for they were sore afraid.

2532　　　aom1096　an,nn3507　　　　pap1982　　　ppro846　2532　　an,nn5456　aina2064

7 And there was a cloud that overshadowed them: and a voice came

pre1537　art3588　nn3507　pap3004　pr/depro3778　pin2076 ppro3450　art,aj27　art,nn5207　pim191　apn846

out of the cloud, saying, <u>This　is　my　beloved Son: hear him.</u>

(Ps. 2:7; Deut. 18:15)

2532　　ad1819　　　　　　　　　　aptm4017　　　　　　　aina1492　an,ajn3762

8 And suddenly, when they had looked*round*about, they saw no man

ad3765　　235　art,nn2424　an,aj3440　pre3326　rxpro1438

any more, save Jesus only with themselves.

1161　　ppro846　　pap2597　　pre575　art3588　　nn3735　　aom1291　ppro846　2443

9 And as they came down from the mountain, he charged them that they

asbm1334　an,ajn3367　repro3739　　　aina1492　1508/ad3752 art3588 nn5207　art,nn444

should　tell　no man what things they had seen,　till　the Son of man were

asba450　pre1537　an,ajn3498

risen from the dead.

2532　　　　aina2902　　　　art,nn3056　　pre4314　　　rxpro1438

10 And　they　kept　that　saying　with　themselves,

pap4802　　　　pr/inpro5101 art3588　ainf450　pre1537　an,ajn3498　　pin2076

questioning*one*with*another　what　the rising from the dead should mean.

2532　　ipf1905　ppro846　pap3004　　pin3004 art3588　nn1122　3754　an,nn2243　pin1163

11 And they asked him, saying, Why say the scribes that Elijah must

nu,ajn4412　ainf2064

first come?

1161　art3588　　aptp611　　　aina2036　ppro846　an,nn2243　3303　apta2064　nu,ajn4412

12 And　he　answered and told　them,　Elijah verily cometh first,　and

pin600　　an,ajn3956　2532　ad4459　　pfip1125　pre1909 art3588　nn5207　art,nn444　2443

restoreth all things; and how it is written of　the Son of man, that he must

asba3958　an,ajn4183　2532　　asbp1847

suffer many things, and be set*at*naught.

235　pin3004　ppro5213　3754　an,nn2243　　2532　pfi2064　2532　　　aina4160

13 But I say unto you, That Elijah is indeed come, and they have done

ppro846　an,ajn3745　　aina2309　ad2531　pfip1125　pre1909 ppro846

unto him whatsoever they listed,　as　it is written　of　him.

Jesus Heals a Boy With an Unclean Spirit (Matt. 17:14-20; Luke 9:37-43)

2532　　　apta2064　pre4314　art,nn3101　aina1492　an,aj4183　an,nn3793　pre4012

14 And when he came to *his* disciples, he saw a great multitude about

ppro846　2532　art3588　nn1122　pap4802　　ppro846

them, and the scribes questioning with them.

15 And straightway all the people, when they beheld him, were greatly amazed, and running to *him* saluted him.

16 And he asked the scribes, What question ye with them?

17 And one of the multitude answered and said, Master, I have brought unto thee my son, which hath a dumb spirit;

18 And wheresoever he taketh him, he teareth him: and he foameth, and gnasheth with his teeth, and pineth away: and I spake to thy disciples that they should cast*him*out; and they could not.

19 He answereth him, and saith, O faithless generation, how long shall I be with you? how long shall I suffer you? bring him unto me.

20 And they brought him unto him: and when he saw him, straightway the spirit tore him; and he fell on the ground, and wallowed foaming.

21 And he asked his father, How*long*is*it*ago since this came unto him? And he said, Of*a*child.

22 And ofttimes it hath cast him into the fire, and into the waters, to destroy him: but if*thou*canst*do*any*thing, have compassion on us, and help us.

23 Jesus said unto him, If thou canst believe, all things *are* possible to him*that*believeth.

24 And straightway the father of the child cried out, and said with tears, Lord, I believe; help thou mine unbelief.

25 When Jesus saw that the people came*running*together, he rebuked the foul spirit, saying unto him, *Thou* dumb and deaf spirit, I charge thee, come out of him, and enter no more into him.

26 And *the spirit* cried, and rent him sore, and came out of him: and he was as one dead; insomuch that many said, He is dead.

1161 art,nn2424 apta2902 ppro846   art3588   nn5495   aina1453/ppro846   2532   aina450

27 But Jesus took him by the hand, and lifted*him*up; and he arose.

2532   ppro846   apta1525 pre1519   an,nn3624 ppro846 art,nn3101 ipf1905 ppro846

28 And when he was come into the house, his disciples asked him

pre2596/an,aj2318   3754   ainm1410 3756 epn2249   ainf1544/ppro846

privately, Why could not we cast*him*out?

2532   aina2036   ppro846 depro5124 art,nn1085 pinm1410   ainf1831   pre1722 an,ajn3762   1508

29 And he said unto them, This kind can come forth by nothing, but

pre1722 an,nn4335   2532   an,nn3521

by prayer and fasting.

Jesus Predicts His Death and Resurrection (Matt. 17:22,23; Luke 9:43-45)

2532   apta1831   ad1564   ipf3899   pre1223   art,nn1056   2532   ipf2309

30 And they departed thence, and passed through Galilee; and he would

3756 2443   idpro5100   asba1097

not that any man should know it.

1063   ipf1321   ppro848 art,nn3101   2532 ipf3004   ppro846 art3588 nn5207   art,nn444

31 For he taught his disciples, and said unto them, The Son of man is

pinp3860   pre1519   an,nn5495   an,nn444 2532   ft615 ppro846 2532

delivered into the hands of men, and they shall kill him; and after that he is

aptp615   fm450 art3588 nu,aj5154 nn2250

killed, he shall rise the third day.

1161   art3588   ipf50   art,nn4487   2532   ipf5399   ainf1905 ppro846

32 But they understood not that saying, and were afraid to ask him.

The Greatness of Humility (Matt. 18:1-5; Luke 9:46-48)

2532   aina2064 pre1519   2584   2532 aptm1096 pre1722 art3588   nn3614   ipf1905 ppro846

33 And he came to Capernaum: and being in the house he asked them,

inpro5101   ipf1260   pre4314   rxpro1438   pre1722 art3588 nn3598

What was it that ye disputed among yourselves by the way?

1161 art3588   ipf4623   1063 pre1722 art3588 nn3598   ainp1256   pre4314

34 But they held*their*peace: for by the way they had disputed among

rcpro240   inpro5101   pr/cd/an,ajn3187

themselves, who should be the greatest.

2532   apta2523   aina5455 art3588 nu,ajn1427 2532 pin3004   ppro846

35 And he sat down, and called the twelve, and saith unto them,

idpro1536   pin2309   pinf1511 pr/nu,aj4413   fm2071 pr/an,aj2078 an,ajn3956 2532 an,nn1249

If*any*man desire to be first, the same shall be last of all, and servant

an,ajn3956

of all.

2532   apta2983   an,nn3813   aina2476 ppro846 pre1722 art3588 ajn3319   ppro846   2532

36 And he took a child, and set him in the midst of them: and when he

aptm1723/ppro846   aina2036   ppro846

had taken*him*in*his*arms, he said unto them,

repro3739/1437   asbm1209 nu1520   art,aj5108   an,nn3813 pre1909 ppro3450 art,nn3686

37 Whosoever shall receive one of such children in my name,

pin1209   epn1691   2532   repro3739/1437   asbm1209   epn1691   pin1209   3756   epn1691   235

receiveth me: and whosoever shall receive me, receiveth not me, but

art,apta649   ppro3165

him*that*sent me.

Others Who Work in Christ's Name (Luke 9:49,50)

1161   art,nn2491   ainp611   ppro846   pap3004   an,nn1320   aina1492 idpro5100   pap1544

38 And John answered him, saying, Master, we saw one casting out

an,nn1140   pre1722 ppro4675 art,nn3686   repro3739   pin191   3756 ppro2254   2532   aina2967   ppro846

devils in thy name, and he followeth not us: and we forbade him,

3754   pin191   3756 ppro2254

because he followeth not us.

1161   art,nn2424 aina2036 pim2967   ppro846 3361 1063   pin2076 an,ajn3762 repro3739   ft4160

39 But Jesus said, Forbid him not: for there is no man which shall do a

an,nn1411   pre1909 ppro3450 art,nn3686   2532 fm1410 ad5035   ainf2551   ppro3165

miracle in my name, that can lightly speak evil of me.

1063   repro3739   pin2076 3756   pre2596   ppro5216 pin2076   pre5228/ppro5216

40 For he that is not against us is on*our*part.

1063   repro3739/302   asba4222/ppro5209/an,nn4221/an,nn5204   pre1722 ppro3450 art,nn3686

41 For whosoever shall give*you*a*cup*of*water*to*drink in my name,

3754   pin2075   an,nn5547   281   pin3004   ppro5213   efn3364 asba622 ppro848

because ye belong to Christ, verily I say unto you, he shall not lose his

art,nn3408

reward.

Entrapments (Matt. 18:6-9; Luke 17:1,2)

2532   repro3739/302   asba4624   nu1520   art,ajn3398   art,pap4100   pre1519

42 And whosoever shall offend one of these little ones that believe in

ppro1691   pin2076 pr/an,ajn2570   ppro846 (ad3123) 1487   an,nn3037/an,aj3457   pinp4029   pre4012 ppro846 art,nn5137

me, it is better for him   that a millstone were hanged about his neck,

2532   pfim906 pre1519 art3588 nn2281

and he were cast into the sea.

2532   1437 ppro4675 art,nn5495   psa4624   ppro4571   aima609/ppro846   pin2076   pr/an,aj2570   ppro4671

43 And if thy hand offend thee, cut*it*off: it is better for thee to

ainf1525 pre1519 art,nn2222   an,ajn2948   2228   pap2192   nu1417 art,nn5495   ainf565 pre1519 art,nn1067 pre1519 art3588 nn4442

enter into life maimed, than having two hands to go into hell, into the fire

art,aj762

that never*shall*be*quenched:

ad3699   ppro846 art,nn4663 pin5053   3756   2532 art3588 nn4442   3756   pinp4570

44 Where their worm dieth not, and the fire is not quenched.   *(Is. 66:24)*

2532   1437 ppro4675 art,nn4228   psa4624   ppro4571   aima609/ppro846   pin2076   pr/an,ajn2570   ppro4671

45 And if thy foot offend thee, cut*it*off: it is better for thee to

ainf1525 an,ajn5560 pre1519 an,nn2222   2228   pap2192 nu1417 art,nn4228   aifp906 pre1519 art,nn1067 pre1519 art3588 nn4442

enter halt into life, than having two feet to be cast into hell, into the fire

art,aj762

that never*shall*be*quenched:

ad3699   ppro4675 art,nn4663 pin5053   3756   2532 art3588 nn4442   3756   pinp4570

46 Where their worm dieth not, and the fire is not quenched.   *(Is. 66:24)*

47 And if thine eye offend thee, pluck*it*out: it is better for thee to enter into the kingdom of God with one eye, than having two eyes to be cast into hell fire:

48 Where their worm dieth not, and the fire is not quenched. *(Is. 66:24)*

49 For every one shall be salted with fire, and every sacrifice shall be salted with salt.

50 Salt *is* good: but if the salt have lost*his*saltness, wherewith will ye season it? Have salt in yourselves, and have peace one*with*another.

Divorce (Matt. 5:27-32; 19:1-12; Luke 16:18; Rom. 7:1-3; 1 Cor. 7:10-17)

10 And*he*arose*from*thence, and cometh into the coasts of Judea by the farther side of Jordan: and the people resort unto him again; and, as he was wont, he taught them again.

2 And the Pharisees came to him, and asked him, Is*it*lawful for a man to put away *his* wife? tempting him.

3 And he answered and said unto them, What did Moses command you?

4 And they said, Moses suffered to write a bill of divorcement, and to put*her*away. *(Deut. 24:1,3)*

5 And Jesus answered and said unto them, For the hardness*of*your*heart he wrote you this precept.

6 But from the beginning of the creation God made them male and female. *(Gen. 1:27; 5:2)*

7 For*this*cause shall a man leave his father and mother, and cleave to his wife;

8 And they twain shall be one flesh: so then they are no more twain, but one flesh.   *(Gen. 2:24)*

9 What therefore God hath joined together, let not man put asunder.

10 And in the house his disciples asked him again of the same *matter.*

11 And he saith unto them, Whosoever shall put away his wife, and marry another, committeth adultery against her.

12 And if a woman shall put away her husband, and be married to another, she committeth adultery.

Who Will Enter God's Kingdom? (Matt. 19:13-15; Luke 18:15-17)

13 And they brought young children to him, that he should touch them: and *his* disciples rebuked those*that*brought *them.*

14 But when Jesus saw *it,* he was much displeased, and said unto them, Suffer the little children to come unto me, and forbid them not: for of such is the kingdom of God.

15 Verily I say unto you, Whosoever shall not receive the kingdom of God as a little child, he shall not enter therein.

16 And he took*them*up*in*his*arms, put *his* hands upon them, and blessed them.

The Rich Man Tested (Matt. 19:16-30; Luke 18:18-30)

17 And when he was gone forth into the way, there came one running, and kneeled to him, and asked him, Good Master, what shall I do that I may inherit eternal life?

1161   art,nn2424   aina2036   ppro846   inpro5101   pin3004   ppro3165   pr/an,aj18   an,ajn3762

18 And Jesus said unto him, Why callest thou me good? *there is* none

pr/an,aj18   1508   nu,ajn1520   art,nn2316

good but one, *that is,* God.

pin1492   art3588   nn1785   3361   asba3431   3361

19 Thou knowest the commandments, Do not commit adultery, Do not

asba5407   3361   asba2813   3361   asba5576   asba650   3361   pim5091   ppro4675

kill, Do not steal, Do not bear*false*witness, Defraud not, Honor thy

art,nn3962   2532   art,nn3384

father and mother.   *(Ex. 20:12-16; Deut. 5:16-20)*

1161   art3588   aptp611   aina2036   ppro846   an,nn1320   an,aj3956   depro5023

20 And he answered and said unto him, Master, all these have I

aom5442   pre1537   ppro3450   an,nn3503

observed from my youth.

1161   art,nn2424   apta1689   ppro846   aina25   ppro846   2532   aina2036   ppro846   nu,ajn1520

21 Then Jesus beholding him loved him, and said unto him, One thing

ppro4671   pin5302   aima5217   aima4453   an,ajn3745   pin2192   2532   aima1325   art3588   ajn4434

thou lackest: go*thy*way, sell whatsoever thou hast, and give to the poor,

2532   ft2192   an,nn2344   pre1722   an,nn3772   2532   ad1204   apta142   art3588   nn4716

and thou shalt have treasure in heaven: and come, take up the cross, and

pim190   ppro3427

follow me.

1161   art3588   apta4768   pre1909   art,nn3056   aina565   ppmp3076   1063

22 And he was sad at that saying, and went away grieved: for he

ipf2258/pap2192 an,aj4183   an,nn2933

had great possessions.

2532   art,nn2424   aptp4017   pin3004   ppro848   art,nn3101   ad4459

23 And Jesus looked*round*about, and saith unto his disciples, How

ad1423   art,pap2192   art,nn5536   fm1525   pre1519 art3588   nn932   art,nn2316

hardly shall they*that*have riches enter into the kingdom of God!

1161   art3588   nn3101   ipf2284   pre1909   ppro846   art,nn3056   1161   art,nn2424

24 And the disciples were astonished at his words. But Jesus

aptp611   ad3825   pin3004   ppro846   an,nn5043   ad4459   pr/an,ajn1422   pin2076

answereth again, and saith unto them, Children, how hard is it for

art,pfp3982   pre1909 art,nn5536   ainf1525   pre1519 art3588   nn932   art,nn2316

them*that*trust in riches to enter into the kingdom of God!

pin2076 pr/an,ajn2123   an,nn2574   ainf1525   pre1223   art3588 nn5168   art,nn4476   2228

25 It is easier for a camel to go through the eye of a needle, than for a

an,ajn4145   ainf1525   pre1519 art3588   nn932   art,nn2316

rich man to enter into the kingdom of God.

1161   art3588   ipf1605   ad4057   pap3004   pre4314   rxpro1438

26 And they were astonished out*of*measure, saying among themselves,

inpro5101   2532   pinm1410   aifp4982

Who then can be saved?

1161   art,nn2424   apta1689   ppro846   pin3004   pre3844   an,nn444   an,ajn102   235   3756

27 And Jesus looking upon them saith, With men *it is* impossible, but not

pre3844 art,nn2316 1063   pre3844 art,nn2316   an,ajn3956   pin2076   pr/an,an1415

with God: for with God all things are possible.

2532   art,nn4074   aom756   pinf3004   ppro846   2400   epn2249   aina863 an,ajn3956   2532

28 Then Peter began to say unto him, Lo, we have left all, and have

aina190   ppro4671

followed thee.

1161 art,nn2424 aptp611 aina2036 281 pin3004 ppro5213 pin2076
29 And Jesus answered and said, Verily I say unto you, There is

an,ajn3762 aina863 an,nn3614 2228 an,nn80 2228 an,nn79 2228 an,nn3962 2228 an,nn3384 2228
no man that hath left house, or brethren, or sisters, or father, or mother, or

an,nn1135 2228 an,nn5043 2228 an,nn68 ad*1752/ppro1700 2532 art3588 art,nn2098
wife, or children, or lands, for*my*sake, and the gospel's,

1437/3361 asba2983 nu,ajn1542 ad3568 pre1722 depro5129 art,nn2540 an,nn3614 2532
30 But he shall receive a hundredfold now in this time, houses, and

an,nn80 2532 an,nn79 2532 an,nn3384 2532 an,nn5043 2532 an,nn68 pre3326 an,nn1375
brethren, and sisters, and mothers, and children, and lands, with persecutions;

2532 pre1722 art3588 nn165 art,ppmp2064 an,aj166 an,nn2222
and in the world to come eternal life.

1161 an,ajn4183 nu,ajn4413 fm2071 pr/an,aj2078 2532 art3588 ajn2078 pr/nu,aj4413
31 But many that are first shall be last; and the last first.

Jesus Will Rise From the Dead (Matt. 20:17-19; Luke 18:31-34)

1161 ipf2258 pre1722 art3588 nn3598 pap305 pre1519 an,nn2414 2532 art,nn2424
32 And they were in the way going up to Jerusalem; and Jesus

ipf2258/pap4254 ppro846 2532 ipf2284 2532 pap190
went before them: and they were amazed; and as they followed, they

ipf5399 2532 apta3880 ad3825 art3588 nu,ajn1427 aom756 pinf3004 ppro846
were afraid. And he took again the twelve, and began to tell them

art,pap3195 pinf4819 ppro846
what*things*should happen unto him,

2400 pin305 pre1519 an,nn2414 2532 art3588 nn5027 art,nn444
33 Saying, Behold, we go up to Jerusalem; and the Son of man shall be

fp3860 art3588 nn749 2532 art3588 nn1122 2532 ft2632
delivered unto the chief priests, and unto the scribes; and they shall condemn

ppro846 an,nn2288 2532 ft3860 ppro846 art3588 nn1484
him to death, and shall deliver him to the Gentiles:

2532 ft1702 ppro846 2532 ft3146 ppro846 ft1716
34 And they shall mock him, and shall scourge him, and shall spit upon

ppro846 2532 ft615 ppro846 2532 art3588 nu,aj5154 art,nn2250 fm450
him, and shall kill him: and the third day he shall rise again.

James and John Request Special Positions (Matt. 20:20-28)

2532 an,nn2385 2532 an,nn2491 art3588 nn5207 an,nn2199 pinm4365 ppro846 pap3004
35 And James and John, the sons of Zebedee, come unto him, saying,

an,nn1320 pin2309 2443 asba4160 ppro2254 repro3739/1437
Master, we would that thou shouldest do for us whatsoever we shall

asba154
desire.

1161 art3588 aina2036 ppro846 inpro5101 pin2309 ppro3165 ainf4160
36 And he said unto them, What would ye that I should do for

ppro5213
you?

(1161) art3588 aina2036 ppro846 aima1325 ppro2254 2443 asba2523 nu,ajn1520
37 They said unto him, Grant unto us that we may sit, one

pre1537 ppro4675   an,ajn1188   2532   an,nu,ajn1520 pre1537 ppro4675   an,ajn2176   pre1722 ppro4675 art,nn1391

on   thy right hand, and the other   on   thy left hand, in   thy glory.

1161 art,nn2424 aina2036   ppro846   pin1492 3756 inpro5101 ,   pinm154 pinm1410   ainf4095

38 But Jesus said unto them, Ye know not what ye ask: can ye drink of

art3588 nn4221 repro3739 epn1473 pin4095   2532   aifp907   art3588   nn908   repro3739 epn1473

the cup that   I   drink of? and be baptized with the baptism that   I   am

pinp907

baptized with?

1161 art3588 aina2036   ppro846   pinm1410 1161 art,nn2424 aina2036   ppro846

39 And they said unto him, We can. And Jesus said unto them, Ye shall

3303   fm4095   art3588 nn4221 repro3739 epn1473 pin4095   2532   art3588 nn908   repro3739 epn1473

indeed drink of the cup that   I   drink of; and with the baptism that   I   am

pinp907   fp907

baptized withal shall ye be baptized:

1161   art,ainf2523 pre1537 ppro3450 an,ajn1188   2532 pre1537 ppro3450 an,ajn2176 pin2076 3756 popro1699

40 But to sit   on my right hand and on my left hand is not mine

ainf1325 235   repro3739   pfip2090

to give; but *it shall be given to them* for whom it is prepared.

2532   art3588 nu,ajn1176 apta191   aom756   pinf23   pre4012

41 And when the ten heard *it*, they began to be*much*displeased with

an,nn2385 2532 an,nn2491

James and John.

1161 art,nn2424 aptm4341 ppro846   pin3004   ppro846   pin1492 3754

42 But Jesus called them *to him,* and saith unto them, Ye know that

art,pap1380   pinf757 art3588 nn1484   pin2634   ppro846

they*which*are*accounted to rule over the Gentiles exercise lordship over them;

2532 ppro846 art,ajn3173   pin2715   ppro846

and their great ones exercise authority upon them.

1161 ad3779   3756 fm2071 pre1722 ppro5213 235   repro3739/1437 psa2309 aifm1096 pr/an,ajn3173

43 But so shall it not be among you: but whosoever will be   great

pre1722 ppro5213   fm2071 ppro5216 pr/an,nn1249

among you, shall be your minister:

2532   repro3739/302   ppro5216 psa2309 aifm1096   pr/nu,ajn4413   fm2071 pr/an,ajn1401

44 And whosoever of you will be the chiefest shall be servant of

an,ajn3956

all.

1063   2532   art3588 nn5207 art,nn444 aina2064 3756   aifp1247   235

45 For even the Son of man came not to be ministered unto, but to

ainf1247   2532   ainf1325 ppro848 art,nn5590   an,nn3083 pre473 an,ajn4183

minister, and to give his life a ransom for many.

The Healing of Blind Bartimaeus (Matt. 20:29-34; Luke 18:35-43)

2532   pinm2064 pre1519 2410   2532   ppro846 ppmp1607 pre575 2410   2532 ppro846

46 And they came to Jericho: and as he went out of Jericho with his

art,nn3101   2532   an,aj2425   an,nn3793 art,aj5185 an,nn924   an,nn5207

disciples and a great number of people, blind Bartimaeus, the son of

an,nn5090 ipf2521 pre3844 art3588   nn3598   pap4319

Timaeus, sat by the highway side begging.

2532   apta191   3754   pin2076   pr/an,nn2424   art,aj3480   aom756

47 And when he heard that it was Jesus of Nazareth, he began to

pinf2896   2532   pinf3004   an,nn2424   art,nn5207   1138   aima1653   ppro3165

cry out, and say, Jesus, *thou* son of David, have mercy on me.

2532   an,ajn4183   ipf2008   ppro846   2443   asba4623   1161 art3588   ipf2896

48 And many charged him that he should hold*his*peace: but he cried the

an,aj4183   ad3123   an,nn5207   1138   aima1653   ppro3165

more a*great*deal, *Thou* son of David, have mercy on me.

2532   art,nn2424   apta2476   aina2036   ppro846   aima5455   2532   pin5455

49 And Jesus stood still, and commanded him to be called. And they call

art3588   ajn5185   pap3004   ppro846   pim2293   aima1453   pin5455   ppro4571

the blind man, saying unto him, Be*of*good*comfort, rise; he calleth thee.

1161   art3588   apta577   ppro848   art,nn2440   apta450   aina2064   pre4314   art,nn2424

50 And he, casting away his garment, rose, and came to Jesus.

2532   art,nn2424   aptp611   pin3004   ppro846   inpro5101   pin2309

51 And Jesus answered and said unto him, What wilt thou that I should

asba4160   ppro4671   (1161)   art3588   ajn5185   aina2036   ppro846   4462   2443

do unto thee?   The blind man said unto him, Lord, that I might

asba308

receive*my*sight.

1161   art,nn2424   aina2036   ppro846   aima5217   ppro4675   art,nn4102

52 And Jesus said unto him, Go*thy*way; thy faith hath

pfi4982/ppro4571   2532   ad2112   aina308   2532   ipf190   art,nn2424

made*thee*whole. And immediately he received*his*sight, and followed Jesus

pre1722 art3588   nn3598

in the way.

Jesus Enters Jerusalem (Matt. 21:1-11; Luke 19:28-40; John 12:12-19)

11

2532   ad3753   pin1448   pre1519   an,nn2419   pre1519   967   2532

And when they came nigh to Jerusalem, unto Bethphage and

an,nn963   pre4314 art3588   nn3735   art,nn1636   pin649   nu1417   ppro848

Bethany, at the mount of Olives, he sendeth forth two of his

art,nn3101

disciples,

2532   pin3004   ppro846   aima5217   pre1519 art3588   nn2968   art,ad*2713   ppro5216

2 And saith unto them, Go*your*way into the village over against you:

2532   ad2112   ppmp1531   pre1519 ppro846   ft2147   an,nn4454 pfpp1210 pre1909/an,ajn3739

and as*soon*as ye be entered into it, ye shall find a colt tied, whereon

an,ajn3762 an,nn444 pfi2523 apta3089 ppro846   aima71

never man sat; loose him, and bring *him.*

2532   1437   idpro5100   asba2036   ppro5213 inpro5101 pin4160   depro5124 aima2036   3754   art3588

3 And if any man say unto you, Why do ye this? say ye that the

nn2962   pin2192   nn5532   ppro846   2532   ad2112   ft649   ppro846   ad5602

Lord hath need of him; and straightway he will send him hither.

1161   aina565   2532   aina2147   art3588   nn4454   pfpp1210   pre4314   art3588   nn2374   ad1854

4 And they went*their*way. and found the colt tied by the door without

pre1909   art,nn296   2532   pin3089 ppro846

in a place*where*two*ways*met; and they loose him.

²⁵³² ^{idpro5100} ^{art,pfp2476} ^{ad1563} ^{ipf3004} ^{ppro846} ^{inpro5101} ^{pin4160}
5 And certain of them*that*stood there said unto them, What do ye,
^{pap3089} ^{art3588} ⁿⁿ⁴⁴⁵⁴
loosing the colt?

¹¹⁶¹ ^{art3588} ^{aina2036} ^{ppro846} ^{ad2531} ^{art,nn2424} ^{aom1781} ²⁵³²
6 And they said unto them even as Jesus had commanded: and they
^{aina863/ppro846}
let*them*go.

²⁵³² ^{aina71} ^{art3588} ⁿⁿ⁴⁴⁵⁴ ^{pre4314} ^{art,nn2424} ²⁵³² ^{aina1911} ^{ppro848} ^{art,nn2440} ^{ppro846}
7 And they brought the colt to Jesus, and cast their garments on him;
²⁵³² ^{aina2523} ^{pre1909} ^{ppro846}
and he sat upon him.

¹¹⁶¹ ^{an,ajn4183} ^{aina4766} ^{ppro848} ^{art,nn2440} ^{pre1519} ^{art3588} ⁿⁿ³⁵⁹⁸ ¹¹⁶¹ ^{an,ajn243} ^{ipf2875}
8 And many spread their garments in the way: and others cut down
^{an,nn4746} ^{pre1537} ^{art3588} ⁿⁿ¹¹⁸⁶ ²⁵³² ^{ipf4766} ^{pre1519} ^{art3588} ⁿⁿ³⁵⁹⁸
branches off the trees, and strewed *them* in the way.

²⁵³² ^{art,pap4254} ²⁵³² ^{art,pap190} ^{ipf2896} ^{pap3004}
9 And they*that*went*before, and they*that*followed, cried, saying,
⁵⁶¹⁴ ^{pr/pfpp2127} ^{art,ppmp2064} ^{pre1722} ^{an,nn3686} ^{an,nn2962}
Hosanna; Blessed *is* he*that*cometh in the name of the Lord:

(Ps. 118:25,26)

^{pr/pfpp2127} ^{art3588} ⁿⁿ⁹³² ^{ppro2257} ^{art,nn3962} ¹¹³⁸ ^{ppmp2064} ^{pre1722}
10 Blessed *be* the kingdom of our father David, that cometh in the
^{an,nn3686} ^{an,nn2962} ⁵⁶¹⁴ ^{pre1722} ^{art3588} ^{ajn5310}
name of the Lord: Hosanna in the highest.

²⁵³² ^{art,nn2424} ^{aina1525} ^{pre1519} ^{an,nn2414} ²⁵³² ^{pre1519} ^{art3588} ⁿⁿ²⁴¹¹ ²⁵³²
11 And Jesus entered into Jerusalem, and into the temple: and when he
^{aptp4017} ^{an,ajn3956} ²⁵³² ^{ad2235} ^{art3588} ⁿⁿ⁵⁶¹⁰ ^{pap5607/pr/an,aj3798}
had looked*round*about upon all things, and now the eventide was come, he
^{aina1831} ^{pre1519} ^{an,nn963} ^{pre3326} ^{art3588} ^{nu,ajn1427}
went out unto Bethany with the twelve.

The Fruitless Fig Tree (Matt. 21:18,19)

²⁵³² ^{art3588} ^{ad1887} ^{ppro846} ^{aina1831} ^{pre575} ^{an,nn963}
12 And on the morrow, when they were come from Bethany, he
^{aina3983}
was hungry:

²⁵³² ^{apta1492} ^{an,nn4808} ^{ad3113} ^{pap2192} ^{an,nn5444} ^{aina2064} ¹⁴⁸⁷ ⁶⁸⁶
13 And seeing a fig tree afar off having leaves, he came, if haply he might
^{ft2147} ^{idpro5100} ^{pre1722/ppro846} ²⁵³² ^{apta2064} ^{pre1909} ^{ppro846} ^{aina2147} ^{an,ajn3762} ¹⁵⁰⁸
find anything thereon: and when he came to it, he found nothing but
^{an,nn5444} ¹⁰⁶³ ^{an,nn2540} ^{an,nn4810} ^{ipf2258} ³⁷⁵⁶
leaves; for the time of figs was not *yet*.

²⁵³² ^{art,nn2424} ^{aptp611} ^{aina2036} ^{ppro846} ^{an,ajn3367} ^{opt5315} ^{an,nn2590} ^{pre1537} ^{ppro4675}
14 And Jesus answered and said unto it, No man eat fruit of thee
^{ad3371} ^{pre1519/art,nn165} ²⁵³² ^{ppro846} ^{art,nn3101} ^{ipf191}
hereafter forever. And his disciples heard *it*.

Jesus Cleanses the Temple (Matt. 21:12-17; Luke 19:45-48; John 2:13-22)

₂₅₃₂   _{pinm2064 pre1519}   _{an,nn2414}   _{2532   art,nn2424   apta1525   pre1519   art3588   nn2411}

15 And they come to Jerusalem: and Jesus went into the temple, and

_{aom756}   _{pinf1544}   _{art,pap4453}   _{2532   pap59   pre1722 art3588   nn2411   2532   aina2690}

began to cast out them*that*sold and bought in the temple, and overthrew

_{art3588   nn5132   art3588   nn2855   2532 art3588   nn2515   art,pap4453   art,nn4058}

the tables of the moneychangers, and the seats of them*that*sold doves;

_{2532   3756   ipf863   2443   idpro5100   asba1308   an,nn4632   pre1223   art3588}

16 And would not suffer that any man should carry *any* vessel through the

_{nn2411}

temple.

_{2532   ipf1321   pap3004   ppro846   3756   pfip1125   ppro3450 art,nn3624}

17 And he taught, saying unto them, Is it not written, My house shall be

_{fp2564   an,aj3956   art,nn1484   an,nn3624   an,nn4335   1161   epn5210   aina4160 ppro846   an,nn4693}

called of all nations the house of prayer? but ye have made it a den of

_{an,nn3027}

thieves.   *(Isa. 56:7; Jer. 7:11)*

_{2532   art3588   nn1122   2532   art,nn749   aina191   2532   ipf2212   ad4459}

18 And the scribes and chief priests heard *it,* and sought how they might

_{asba622   ppro846 1063   ipf5399   ppro846   3754   an,aj3956   art3588   nn3793   ipf1605}

destroy him: for they feared him, because all the people was astonished

_{pre1909 ppro846   art,nn1322}

at his doctrine.

_{2532   ad3753   ad3796   aom1096   ipf1607   ad1854   art3588   nn4172}

19 And when even was come, he went out of the city.

"Have Faith in God" (Matt. 21:20-22)

_{2532   ad4404   ppmp3899   aina1492 art3588   nn4808   pfpp3583}

20 And in*the*morning, as they passed by, they saw the fig tree dried up

_{pre1537   an,nn4491}

from the roots.

_{2532   art,nn4074   aptp363   pin3004   ppro846   4461   aima2396}

21 And Peter calling*to*remembrance saith unto him, Master, behold,

_{art3588   nn4808   repro3739   ainm2672   pfip3583}

the fig tree which thou cursedst is withered away.

_{2532   an,nn2424   aptp611   pin3004   ppro846   pim2192 an,nn4102   an,nn2316}

22 And Jesus answering saith unto them, Have faith in God.

_{1063   281   pin3004   ppro5213   3754   repro3739/302   asba2036   depro5129}

23 For verily I say unto you, That whosoever shall say unto this

_{art,nn3735   aipp142   2532   aipp906 pre1519 art3588   nn2281   2532   3361}

mountain, Be thou removed, and be thou cast into the sea; and shall not

_{asbp1252 pre1722 ppro848 art,nn2588   235   asba4100   3754   repro3739   pin3004}

doubt in his heart, but shall believe that those things which he saith shall

_{pinm1096   ppro846   fm2071   repro3739/1437   asba2036}

come*to*pass; he shall have whatsoever he saith.

pre1223/depro5124   pin3004   ppro5213   an,ajn3956/an,ajn3745/302   pinm154

24 Therefore I say unto you, What*things*soever ye desire, when ye

ppmp4336 pim4100   3754   pin2983   2532 ppro5213   fm2071

pray, believe that ye receive *them,* and ye shall have *them.*

2532   ad3752   psa4739   ppmp4336   pim863   1487   pin2192 idpro5100 pre2596 idpro5100

25 And when ye stand praying, forgive, if ye have aught against any:

2443 ppro5216 art,nn3962 2532 art3588   pre1722 art,nn3772   asba863   ppro5213 ppro5216   art,nn3900

that your Father also which is in heaven may forgive you your trespasses.

1161   1487 epn5210   3756   pin863   3761   ppro5216 art,nn3962   art3588   pre1722

26 But if ye do not forgive, neither will your Father which is in

art,nn3772   ft863   ppro5216   art,nn3900

heaven forgive your trespasses.

Where Did Christ's Authority Come From? (Matt. 21:23-27; Luke 20:1-8)

2532   pinm2064 ad3825 pre1519   an,nn2414   2532   ppro846   pap4043 pre1722 art3588

27 And they come again to Jerusalem: and as he was walking in the

nn2411   pinm2064 pre4314 ppro846 art3588   nn749   2532 art3588   nn1122   2532 art3588

temple, there come to him the chief priests, and the scribes, and the

ajn4245

elders,

2532   pin3004   ppro846 pre1722 an,aj4169   an,nn1849   pin4160   depro5023   2532

28 And say unto him, By what authority doest thou these things? and

inpro5101 aina1325 ppro4671 depro5026   art,nn1849   2443 psa4160   depro5023

who gave thee this authority to do these things?

1161 art,nn2424   aptp611   aina2036   ppro846   epn2504/ft1905   ppro5209 nu1520

29 And Jesus answered and said unto them, I*will*also*ask of you one

an,nn3056   2532 aipp611   ppro3427 2532   ft2046 ppro5213 pre1722 an,aj4169   an,nn1849   pin4160

question, and answer me, and I will tell you by what authority I do

depro5023

these things.

art3588   nn908   an,nn2491 ipf2258   pre1537   an,nn3772   2228 pre1537 an,nn444   aipp611   ppro3427

30 The baptism of John, was *it* from heaven, or of men? answer me.

2532   ipf3049   pre4314   rxpro1438   pap3004   1437   asba2036   pre1537

31 And they reasoned with themselves, saying, If we shall say, From

an,nn3772   ft2046 pre,inpro1302 3767   3756   aina4100   ppro846

heaven; he will say, Why then did ye not believe him?

235   1437   asba2036 pre1537 an,nn444   ipf5399   art3588   nn2992   1063 an,ajn537

32 But if we shall say, Of men; they feared the people: for all *men*

ipf2192   art,nn2491 3754   ipf2258   pr/an,nn4396   ad3689

counted John, that he was a prophet indeed.

2532   aptp611   pin3004   art,nn2424   pin1492/3756   2532 art,nn2424

33 And they answered and said unto Jesus. We cannot tell. And Jesus

aptp611   pin3004   ppro846   3761   epn1473 pin3004 ppro5213 pre1722 an,aj4169   an,nn1849   pin4160

answering saith unto them, Neither do I tell you by what authority I do

depro5023

these things.

The Parable of the Vineyard And the Tenants (Matt. 21:33-46; Luke 20:9-19)

                    2532   aom756   pinf3004   ppro846 pre1722   an,nn3850   an,nn444
12 And he began to speak unto them by parables. A *certain* man
                    aina5452   an,nn290   2532   aina4060/an,nn5418   2532   aina3736
planted a vineyard, and set*an*hedge*about *it,* and digged *a place*
       an,nn5276   2532   aina3618   an,nn4444   2532 aom1554/ppro846   an,nn1092   2532
for the wine vat, and built a tower, and let*it*out to husbandmen, and
       aina589
went*into*a*far* country.   *(Is. 5:1,2)*

       2532   art3588   nn2540   aina649 pre4314 art3588   nn1092   an,ajn1401   2443
2 And at the season he sent to the husbandmen a servant, that he might
asba2983   pre3844 art3588   nn1092   pre575 art3588 nn2590   art3588   nn290
receive from the husbandmen of the fruit of the vineyard.

       1161 art3588   apta2983   aina1194 ppro846 2532   aina649   an,aj2756
3 And they caught *him,* and beat him, and sent*him*away*empty.

       2532   ad3825   aina649 pre4314   ppro846   an,aj243   an,ajn1401   depro2548
4 And again he sent unto them another servant; and*at*him they
       apta3036   aina2775   2532   aina649
cast stones, and wounded*him*in*the*head, and sent*him*away
       pfpp821
shamefully handled.

       2532   ad3825   aina649   an,ajn243   depro2548   aina615 2532 an,aj4143 an,ajn243
5 And again he sent another; and him they killed, and many others;
   pap1194 art3588/3303 1161 pap615   art3588
beating some, and killing some.

       pap2192 ad2089   3767   nu1520 an,nn5207 ppro848   an,ajn27   aina649 epn846 2532 an,aj2078
6 Having yet therefore one son, his well-beloved, he sent him also last
pre4314 ppro846 pap3004   fm1788   ppro3450 art,nn5207
unto them, saying, They will reverence my son.

       1161   depro1565   art,nn1092   aina2036 pre4314   rxpro1438   pr/depro3778 pin2076 art3588 nn2818
7 But those husbandmen said among themselves, This is the heir;
ad1205   aosi615 ppro846 2532 art3588   nn2817   fm2071 epn2257
come, let us kill him, and the inheritance shall be ours.

       2532   apta2983 ppro846   aina615   2532 aina1544   ad1854   art3588   nn290
8 And they took him, and killed *him,* and cast *him* out of the vineyard.

       inpro5101   3767   art3588 nn2962   art3588   nn290   ft4160   fm2064 2532
9 What shall therefore the lord of the vineyard do? he will come and
ft622   art3588   nn1092   2532   ft1325 art3588   nn290   an,ajn243
destroy the husbandmen, and will give the vineyard unto others.

       3761   aina314 depro5026 art,nn1124   an,nn3037 repro3739 art3588 pap3618
10 And have ye not read this Scripture; The stone which the builders
aina593   (depro3778) ainp1096 (pre1519) an,nn2776   an,nn1137
rejected is become the head of the corner:

       depro3778 aom1096   pre3844/an,nn2962   2532   pin2076   pr/an,aj2298 pre1722 ppro2254 an,nn3788
11 This was the Lord's doing, and it is marvelous in our eyes?

                                                                (Ps. 118:22,23)

       2532   ipf2212   ainf2902   ppro846 2532 aina5399 art3588   nn3793   1063
12 And they sought to lay*hold*on him, but feared the people: for they

aina1097   3754   aina2036   art3588   nn3850   pre4314   ppro846   2532   apta863 ppro846

knew that he had spoken the parable against them: and they left him, and

aina565

went*their*way.

Jesus and Taxes (Matt. 22:15-22; Luke 20:20-26)

2532   pin649   pre4314   ppro846   idpro5100   art3588   nn5330   2532   art3588

13 And they send unto him certain of the Pharisees and of the

nn2265   2443 asba64 ppro846   an,nn3056

Herodians, to catch him in *his* words.

1161   art3588   apta2064   pin3004   ppro846   an,nn1320   pin1492 3754

14 And when they were come, they say unto him, Master, we know that

pin1488   pr/an,aj227 2532 (3756) pin3199/ppro4671 pre4012 an,ajn3762 1063   pin991   3756 (pre1519)

thou art true, and carest for no man: for thou regardest not the

an,nn4383   an,nn444   235   pin1321   art3588 nn3598   art,nn2316 pre1909 an,nn225   pin1832   ainf1325

person of men, but teachest the way of God in truth: Is*it*lawful to give

an,nn2778   an,nn2541 2228 3756

tribute to Caesar, or not?

aosi1325 2228   3361 aosi1325 1161 art3588 pfp1492   ppro846   art,nn5272

15 Shall we give, or shall we not give? But he, knowing their hypocrisy,

aina2036   ppro846 inpro5101 pin3985   ppro3165 pim5342 ppro3427   an,nn1220   2443   asba1492

said unto them, Why tempt ye me? bring me a penny, that I may see *it*.

1161 art3588   aina5342   2532   pin3004   ppro846   pr/inpro5101   depro3778

16 And they brought *it*. And he saith unto them, Whose *is* this

art,nn1504 2532   art,nn1923   1161   art3588 aina2036   ppro846   an,nn2541

image and superscription? And they said unto him, Caesar's.

2532 art,nn2424   aptp611   aina2036   ppro846   aima591   an,nn2541   art3588

17 And Jesus answering said unto them, Render to Caesar the things that

an,nn2541   2532   art,nn2316   art3588   art,nn2316 2532   aina2296   pre1909

are Caesar's, and to God the things that are God's. And they marveled at

ppro846

him.

Life After the Resurrection (Matt. 22:23-33; Luke 20:27-40)

2532   pinm2064   pre4314   ppro846   an,nn4523   repro3748 pin3004   pinf1511 3361

18 Then come unto him the Sadducees, which say there is no

an,nn386   2532   ipf1905 ppro846 pap3004

resurrection; and they asked him, saying,

an,nn1320   an,nn3475   aina1125   ppro2254 1437 idpro5100   an,nn80   asba599 2532 asba2641

19 Master, Moses wrote unto us, If a man's brother die, and leave *his*

an,nn1135   2532 asba863 3361   an,nn5043   2443 ppro848 art,nn80   asba2983 ppro846

wife *behind him,* and leave no children, that his brother should take his

art,nn1135 2532   asba1817   an,nn4690   ppro846   art,nn80

wife, and raise up seed unto his brother.   *(Gen. 38:8; Deut. 25:5)*

ipf2258   nu2033   an,nn80   2532 art3588 nu,ajn4413 aina2983   an,nn1135 2532   pap599

20 Now there were seven brethren: and the first took a wife, and dying

aina863 3756 an,nn4690

left no seed.

2532   art3588   nu,ajn1208 aina2983 ppro846 2532   aina599   (2532) 3761 aina863 epn846   an,nn4690 2532 art3588

21 And the second took her, and died, neither left he any seed: and the

nu,ajn5154   ad5615

third likewise.

2532   art3588 nu,ajn2033 aina2983 ppro846 2532 aina863 3756 an,nn4690 an,aj2078   an,ajn3956 art3588   nn1135

22 And the seven had her, and left no seed: last of   all   the woman

aina599 2532

died also.

pre1722 art3588   nn386   3767   ad3752   asba450 inpro5101 pr/an,nn1135

23 In the resurrection therefore, when they shall rise, whose wife shall

fm2071   ppro846   1063 art3588 nu,ajn2033 aina2192 ppro846   an,nn1135

she be of them? for the seven had her to wife.

2532   art,nn2424   aptp611   aina2036   ppro846   3756 pre1223/depro5124 pin4105

24 And Jesus answering said unto them, Do ye not therefore err, because

pfp1492 3361 art3588   nn1124   3366   art3588   nn1411   art,nn2316

ye know not the Scriptures, neither the power of God?

1063   ad3752   asba450 pre1537   an,ajn3498   3777   pin1060   3777

25 For when they shall rise from the dead, they neither marry, nor are

pinp1061   235 pin1526 ad5613   pr/an,nn32   art3588   pre1722 art,nn3772

given*in*marriage; but are as the angels which are in heaven.

1161   pre4012   art3588 ajn3498   3754   pinm1453   3756 aina314 pre1722 art3588

26 And as touching the dead, that they rise: have ye not read in the

nn976   an,nn3475   ad5613 pre1909 art3588 nn942 art,nn2316 aina2036   ppro846 pap3004 epn1473   art3588

book of Moses, how in the bush God spake unto him, saying, I *am* the

pr/hn2316   11   2532 art3588 pr/nn2316   2464 2532 art3588 pr/nn2316   2384

God of Abraham, and the God of Isaac, and the God of Jacob?

(Ex. 3:6,15,16)

pin2076 3756 art3588 pr/nn2316   an,ajn3498 235   pr/an,nn2316   an,pap2198 epn5210

27 He is not the God of the dead, but the God of the living: ye

3767   an,ajn4183 pinm4105

therefore do greatly err.

The Great Commandment (Matt. 22:34-40; Luke 10:25-28)

2532   nu1520   art3588   nn1122   apta4334   apta191   ppro846

28 And one of the scribes came, and having heard them

pap4802   pfp1492   3754   ainp611   ppro846 ad2573 aina1905

reasoning together, and perceiving that he had answered them well, asked

ppro846 pr/an,ajn4169 pin2076   nu,aj4413   an,nn1785   an,ajn3956

him, Which is the first commandment of all?

1161   art,nn2424   aina611   nu,aj4413 an,ajn3956 art3588   nn1785

29 And Jesus answered him, The first of all   the commandments *is,*

pim191   2474   an,nn2962 ppro2257 art,nn2316 pin2076 pr/nu1520 an,nn2962

Hear, O Israel; The Lord our God is one Lord:

2532   ft25   an,nn2962 ppro4675 art,nn2316 pre1537 an,aj3650 ppro4675 art,nn2588 2532 pre1537

30 And thou shalt love the Lord thy God with all thy heart, and with an,aj3650 ppro4675 art,nn5590 2532 pre1537 an,aj3650 ppro4675 art,nn1271 2532 pre1537 an,aj3650 ppro4675 art,nn2479 pr/depro3778

all   thy soul, and with all   thy mind, and with all   thy strength: this

an,nu,aj4413   an,nn1785

is the first commandment.   *(Deut. 6:4,5; Josh. 22:5)*

2532   an,nu,ajn1208 pr/an,aj3664   pr/depro3778   ft25 ppro4675 art,ad4139

31 And the second *is* like, *namely* this, Thou shalt love thy neighbor

ad5613   rxpro4572   pin2076   3756   an,aj243   an,nn1785   cd/an,aj3173

as   thyself. There   is   none other commandment greater than

depro5130

these.   *(Lev. 19:18)*

2532 art3588 nn1122 aina2036   ppro846 ad2573 an,nn1320   aina2036 (pre1909) an,nn225

32 And the scribe said unto him, Well, Master, thou hast said the truth:

3754   pin2076 pr/nu,ajn1520 art,nn2316 2532   pin2076 3756 an,ajn243 4133 ppro846

for there is   one God; and there is none other but he:

2532   art,pinf25 ppro846 pre1537 an,aj3650 art3588 nn2588 2532 pre1537 an,aj3650 art3588   nn4907

33 And to love him with all   the heart and with all   the understanding,

2532 pre1537 an,aj3650 art3588 nn5590 2532 pre1537 an,aj3650 art3588   nn2479   2532 art,pinf25   art,ad4139

and with all   the soul, and with all   the strength, and to love *his* neighbor

ad5613 rxpro1438   pin2076 cd/an,aj4119   an,aj3956   art,nn3646   2532   art,nn2378

as himself, is more than all   whole*burnt*offerings and sacrifices.

(Deut. 6:4,5; Lev. 19:18; Hos. 6:6)

2532   art,nn2424 apta1492 (ppro846) 3754   ainp611   ad3562   aina2036

34 And when Jesus saw   that he answered discreetly he said unto

ppro846   pin1488 3756 ad3112 pre575 art3588   nn932   art,nn2316 2532 an,ajn3762   ad3765   ipf5111

him, Thou art not far from the kingdom of God. And no man after that durst

ainf1905 ppro846

ask him *any question.*

David's Lord (Matt. 22:41-46; Luke 20:41-44)

2532 art,nn2424   aptp611   ipf3004   pap1321 pre1722 art3588   nn2411   ad4459

35 And Jesus answered and said, while he taught in the temple, How

pin3004 art3588 nn1122   3754 art,nn5547 pin2076   pr/an,nn5207   1138

say the scribes that Christ is the son of David?

1063   1138   epn846   aina2036 pre1722 art3588 aj40   art,nn4151 art3588 nn2962 aina2036 ppro3450

36 For David himself said by the Holy Ghost, the LORD said to my

art,nn2962 pim2521   pre1537 ppro3450   an,ajn1188   ad2193/302   asba5087 ppro4675 art,ajn2190

Lord, Sit thou on my right hand, till I make thine enemies

an,nn5286/ppro4675/art,nn4228

thy footstool.   *(Ps. 110:1)*

1138   3767   epn846   pin3004 ppro846 an,nn2962 2532 ad4159 pin2076   ppro846

37 David therefore himself calleth him Lord; and whence is he *then* his

an,nn5207 2532 art3588   an,aj4183   nn3793   ipf191 ppro846 ad2234

son? And the common people heard him gladly.

Jesus Denounces the Scribes (Matt. 23:1-36; Luke 20:45-47)

2532   ipf3004   ppro846 pre1722 ppro848   art,nn1322   pim991   pre575 art3588   nn1122

38 And he said unto them in his doctrine, Beware of the scribes,

art,pap2309   pinf4043   pre1722   nn4749   2532   an,nn783   pre1722 art3588

which love to go in long clothing, and *love* salutations in the
nn58

marketplaces,
2532   an,nn4410   pre1722 art3588   nn4864   2532   an,nn4411

39 And the chief seats in the synagogues, and the uppermost rooms
pre1722 art,nn1173

at feasts:
art,pap2719   art,nn5503   art,nn3614   2532   an,nn4392   ppmp4336/an,ajn3117

40 Which devour widows' houses, and for a pretence make*long*prayers:
depro3778   fm2983   cd/an,aj4055   an,nn2917

these shall receive greater damnation.

The Widow's Offering (Luke 21:1-4)

2532   art,nn2424 apta2523   ad*2713   art3588   nn1049   ipf2334   ad4459   art3588

41 And Jesus sat over against the treasury, and beheld how the
nn3793   pin906   an,nn5475 pre1519 art3588   nn1049   2532 an,aj4183   an,ajn4145   ipf906

people cast money into the treasury: and many that were rich cast in
an,ajn4183

much.
2532   apta2064   nu3391   an,aj4434 an,nn5503   aina906   nu1417 an,nn3016

42 And there came a certain poor widow, and she threw in two mites,
repro,pin3603   pr/an,nn2835

which make a farthing.
2532   apta4341   ppro848   art,nn3101   aina3004   ppro846   281   pin3004

43 And he called *unto him* his disciples, and saith unto them, Verily I say
ppro5213   3754   depro3778 art,aj4434 art,nn5503   aina906/an,ajn4119   an,aj3956

unto you, That this poor widow hath cast*more*in, than all
art,pap906   pre1519 art3588   nn1049

they*which*have*cast into the treasury:
1063 an,ajn3956   aina906 pre1537 ppro846   art,pap4052   1161 depro3778 pre1537 ppro848 art,nn5304

44 For all *they* did cast in of their abundance; but she of her want
aina906   an,aj3956 an,ajn3745   ipf2192   an,aj3650 ppro848 art,nn979

did cast in all that she had, *even* all her living.

The Destruction of the Temple And the Last Days (Matt. 24:1,2; Luke 21:5,6)

2532   ppro846 ppmp1607 pre1537 art3588   nn2411   nu1520   ppro846 art,nn3101 pin3004

13 And as he went out of the temple, one of his disciples saith unto
ppro846   an,nn1320   aina2396   an,aj4217   an,nn3037   2532 an,aj4217   an,nn3619

him, Master, see what manner of stones and what buildings

are here!
2532   art,nn2424   aptp611   aina2036   ppro846   pin991   depro5025 an,aj3173   art,nn3619

2 And Jesus answering said unto him, Seest thou these great buildings?

efn3364   asbp863   an,nn3037/pre1909/an,nn3037   repro3739   efn3364

there shall not be left one*stone*upon*another, that shall not be

asbp2647

thrown down.

Forthcoming Woes (Matt. 24:3-14; Luke 21:7-19)

2532   ppro846 ppmp2521   pre1519 art3588   nn3735   art,nn1636   ad*2713   art3588   nn2411

3 And as he sat upon the mount of Olives over against the temple,

an,nn4074 2532 an,nn2385 2532 an,nn2491 2532   an,nn406   ipf1905   ppro846 pre2596/an,ajn2398

Peter and James and John and Andrew asked him privately,

aima2036 ppro2254 ad4219   depro5023   fm2071 2532 inpro5101   art3588 nn4592 ad3752

4 Tell us, when shall these things be? and what *shall be* the sign when

an,aj3956   depro5023   psa3195   pip4931

all these things shall be fulfilled?

1161   art,nn2424   aptp611   ppro846   aom756   pinf3004   pim991   3361 idpro5100

5 And Jesus answering them began to say, Take heed lest any *man*

asba4105   ppro5209

deceive you:

1063 an,ajn4183   fm2064   pre1909 ppro3450 art,nn3686 pap3004 epn1473 pin1510   2532

6 For many shall come in my name, saying, I am *Christ*; and shall

ft4105   an,ajn4183

deceive many.

1161   ad3752   asba191   an,nn4171 2532   an,nn189   an,nn4171   3361   pim2360

7 And when ye shall hear of wars and rumors of wars, be ye not troubled:

1063   pin1163   aifm1096 235 art3588 nn5056   ad3768

for *such things* must needs be; but the end *shall* not*be*yet.

1063 an,nn1484   fp1453   pre1909   an,nn1484 2532   an,nn932   pre1909   an,nn932   2532

8 For nation shall rise against nation, and kingdom against kingdom: and

fm2071   an,nn4578   pre2596/an,nn5117 2532   fm2071 an,nn3042   2532

there shall be earthquakes in divers places, and there shall be famines and

an,nn5016   depro5023   an,nn746   an,nn5604

troubles: these *are* the beginnings of sorrows.   (Is. 19:2)

1161 (epn5210)   pim991   rxpro1438   1063   ft3860/ppro5209   pre1519

9 But take heed to yourselves: for they shall deliver*you*up to

an,nn4892   2532 pre1519   an,nn4864   fp1194   2532   fp2476

councils; and in the synagogues ye shall be beaten: and ye shall be brought

pre1909 an,nn2232 2532 an,nn935   ad*1752/ppro1700   pre1519   an,nn3142   ppro846

before rulers and kings for*my*sake, for a testimony against them.

2532 art3588   nn2098   pin1163 nu,ajn4412   aifp2784   pre1519 an,aj3956 art,nn1484

10 And the gospel must first be published among all nations.

1161   ad3752   asba71   ppro5209   pap3860

11 But when they shall lead *you,* and deliver*you*up,

pim4305/3361   inpro5101   asba2980   3366   pim3191

take*no*thought*beforehand what ye shall speak, neither do ye premeditate:

35   repro3739/1437   asbp1325 ppro5213 pre1722 depro1565 art,nn5610 depro1565 pim2980   1063   pin2075

but whatsoever shall be given you in that hour, that speak ye: for it is

3756 epn5210 pr/art,pap2980 235 art3588 aj40   art,nn4151

not ye that speak, but the Holy Ghost.

1161   an,nn80   ft3860   an,nn80 pre1519 an,nn2288 2532   an,nn3962

12 Now the brother shall betray the brother to death, and the father the

an,nn5043 2532   an,nn5043   fm1881   pre1909   an,nn1118   2532

son; and children shall rise up against *their* parents, and shall

ft2289/ppro846

cause*them*to*be*put*to*death.

2532   fm2071 ppmp3404 pre5259 an,ajn3956   pre1223/ppro3450/art,nn3686   1161

13 And ye shall be hated of all *men* for*my*name's*sake: but

art,apta5278   pre1519   an,nn5056 depro3778   fp4982

he*that*shall*endure unto the end, the same shall be saved.

The Great Tribulation (Matt. 24:15-28; Luke 21:20-24)

1161 ad3752   asba1492 art3588   nn946   art,nn2050   art,aptp4483 pre5259

14 But when ye shall see the abomination of desolation, spoken of by

1158 art3588   nn4396   pfp2476   ad3699   pin1163 3756   art,pap314

Daniel the prophet, standing where it ought not, (let him*that*readeth

pim3539 ad5119   art3588   pre1722 art,nn2449 pim5343 pre1519 art3588   nn3735

understand,) then let them that be in Judea flee to the mountains:

(Dan. 9:27; 11:31; 12:11)

1161   art3588   pre1909 art3588   nn1430   3361   aima2597 pre1519 art3588   nn3614

15 And let him that is on the housetop not go down into the house,

3366   aima1525   ainf142 idpro5100 pre1537 ppro848 art,nn3614

neither enter *therein,* to take any thing out of his house:

2532   art,pap5607   pre1519 art3588   nn68   3361   aima1994   pre1519/art,ad3694

16 And let him*that*is in the field not turn back again for to

ainf142 ppro848 art,nn2440

take up his garment.

1161 3759   art,pap2192/pre1722/an,nn1064   2532   art,pap2337   pre1722

17 But woe to them*that*are*with*child, and to them*that*give*suck in

depro1565 art,nn2250

those days!

1161 pim4336   2443 ppro5216 art,nn5437 asbm1096 3361   an,nn5494

18 And pray ye that your flight be not in the winter.

1063   depro1565 art,nn2250   fm2071 an,nn2347   repro3634 pfi1096 3756 (pr/depro5108) pre575

19 For *in* those days shall be affliction, such as was not from the

an,nn746   an,nn2937   repro3739 art,nn2316 aina2936   ad2193   art,ad3568 (2532) efn3364

beginning of the creation which God created unto this time, neither shall

asbm1096

be.   (Dan. 12:1)

2532 1508   an,nn2962   aina2856   art,nn2250 an,aj3956/3756 an,nn4561

20 And except that the Lord had shortened those days, no flesh should

ainp4982/302 235   pre1223/art3588/ajn1588   repro3739   aom1586   aina2856

be saved: but for*the*elect's*sake, whom he hath chosen, he hath shortened

art3588 nn2250

the days.

2532 ad5119 1437 idpro5100   asba2036   ppro5213 2400 ad5602 art,nn5547 2228 2400

21 And then if any man shall say to you, Lo, here *is* Christ; or, lo, *he is*

ad1563   pim4100   3361

there; believe *him* not:

1063   an,nn5580   2532   an,nn5578   fp1453 2532   ft1325 an,nn4592 2532
☞ 22 For false Christs and false prophets shall rise, and shall show signs and
an,nn5059   aipr635   1487   pr/an,ajn1415   2532 art3588 ajn1588
wonders, to seduce, if *it were* possible, even the elect.

1161   pim991/epn5210   2400   pfi4280   ppro5213   an,ajn3956
23 But take*ye*heed: behold, I have foretold you all things.

Christ Is Coming Again (Matt. 24:29-31; Luke 21:25-28)

235   pre1722 depro1565 art,nn2250 pre3326 depro1565   art,nn2347   art3588 nn2246   fp4654
24 But in those days, after that tribulation, the sun shall be darkened,
2532 art3588   nn4582   3756 ft1325 ppro848 art,nn5338
and the moon shall not give her light,

2532   art3588   nn792   art,nn3772   (fm2071) pr/pap1601 2532 art3588   nn1411   art3588   pre1722
25 And the stars of heaven shall fall, and the powers that are in
art,nn3772   fp4531
heaven shall be shaken.   *(Isa. 13:10; 34:4; Ezek. 32:7,8; Joel 2:10,31; 3:15)*

2532 ad5119   fm3700 art3588 nn5207   art,nn444 ppmp2064 pre1722   an,nn3507 pre3326
26 And then shall they see the Son of man coming in the clouds with
an,aj4183 an,nn1411 2532 an,nn1391
great power and glory.   *(Dan. 7:13,14)*

2532 ad5119   ft649 ppro848 art,nn32 2532   ft1996   ppro848 art,ajn1588
27 And then shall he send his angels, and shall gather together his elect
pre1537 art3588   nu5064   nn417   pre575   an,nn206   an,nn1093 ad2193
from the four winds, from the uttermost part of the earth to the
an,nn206   an,nn3772
uttermost part of heaven.   *(Deut. 30:4; Zech. 2:6)*

The Parable of the Fig Tree (Matt. 24:32-35; Luke 21:29-33)

1161   aima3129   art,nn3850   pre575 art3588   nn4808   3752   ppro846   art,nn2798 asbm1096 ad2235
28 Now learn a parable of the fig tree; When her branch is yet
pr/an,aj527 2532   psa1631   art,nn5444   pin1097 3754 art,nn2330 pin2076 pr/ad1451
tender, and putteth forth leaves, ye know that summer is near:

ad3779 epn5210   2532   ad3752   asba1492   depro5023
29 So ye in*like*manner, when ye shall see these things
ppmp1096   pim1097 3754   pin2076 pr/ad1451   pre1909   an,nn2374
come*to* pass, know that it is nigh, *even* at the doors.

281   pin3004   ppro5213   3754 depro3778   art,nn1074   efn3364 asba3928
30 Verily I say unto you, that this generation shall not pass,
ad3360 (repro3739) an,aj3956   depro5023   asbm1096
till   all these things be done.

art,nn3772   2532 art,nn1093   fm3928   1161 ppro3450 art,nn3056   efn3364
31 Heaven and earth shall pass away: but my words shall not
fm3928
pass away.

☞ **13:22, 32** See note on Philippians 2:6–8.

Time of Christ's Coming Unknown (Matt. 24:36-44)

1161 pre4012 depro1565 art,nn2250 2532 art,nn5610 pin1492 an,ajn3762 ad3761 art3588 nn32
☞ 32 But of that day and *that* hour knoweth no man, no, not the angels
art3588 pre1722 an,nn3772 ad3761 art3588 nn5207 1508 art3588 nn3962
which are in heaven, neither the Son, but the Father.

pim991 pim69 2532 pim4336 1063 pin1492 3756 ad4219 art3588 nn2540 pin2076
33 Take*ye*heed, watch and pray: for ye know not when the time is.

ad5613 an,nn444 an,aj590 apta863 ppro848
34 *For the Son of man is* as a man taking*a*far*journey, who left his
art,nn3614 2532 apta1325 art,nn1849 ppro848 art,ajn1401 2532 an,ajn1538 ppro848 art,nn2041 2532
house, and gave authority to his servants, and to every man his work, and
aom1781 art3588 nn2377 2443 psa1127
commanded the porter to watch.

pim1127 3767 1063 pin1492 3756 ad4219 art3588 nn2962 art3588 nn3614
35 Watch ye therefore: for ye know not when the master of the house
pinm2064 ad3796 2228 an,nn3317 2228 an,nn219 2228 ad4404
cometh, at even, or at midnight, or at the cockcrowing, or in*the*morning:

3361 apta2064 ad1810 asba2147 ppro5209 pap2518
36 Lest coming suddenly he find you sleeping.

1161 repro3739 pin3004 ppro5213 pin3004 an,ajn3956 pim1127
37 And what I say unto you I say unto all, Watch.

The Plot to Kill Jesus (Matt. 26:1-5; Luke 22:1,2; John 11:45-53)

(1161) pre3326 nu1417 an,nn2250 ipf2258 art3588 3957 2532
14 After two days was *the feast of* the passover, and of
art,ajn106 2532 art3588 nn749 2532 art3588 nn1122 ipf2212
unleavened bread: and the chief priests and the scribes sought
ad4459 apta2902 ppro846 pre1722 an,nn1388 asba615
how they might take him by craft, and put*him*to*death.   (*Ex. 12:1-27*)
1161 ipf3004 3361 pre1722 art3588 nn1859 3379 fm2071 an,nn2351 art3588
2 But they said, Not on the feast *day,* lest there be an uproar of the
nn2992
people.

The Anointing of Jesus at Bethany (Matt. 26:6-13; John 12:1-8)

2532 (ppro846) pap5607 pre1722 an,nn963 pre1722 art3588 nn3614 an,nn4613 art3588 ajn3015 ppro846
3 And   being in Bethany in the house of Simon the leper, as he
ppmp2621 aina2064 an,nn1135 pap2192 an,nn211 an,nn3464
sat*at*meat, there came a woman having an alabaster box of ointment of
an,aj4101/an,nn3487 an,aj4185 2532 apta4937 art3588 nn211 ipf2708 pre2596 ppro846
spikenard very precious; and she broke the box, and poured *it* on his
art,nn2776
head.

1161   ipf2258   idpro5100   pr/pap23   pre4314   rxpro1438   2532

4 And there were some that had indignation within themselves, and

pap3004 (pre1519) inpro5101   depro3778 art,nn684   art3588   nn3464   pfi1096

said,   Why was this waste of the ointment made?

1063   depro5124   ipf1410 aifp4097   ad*1883   nu5145   an,nn1220   2532

5 For it might have been sold for more than three hundred pence, and

aifp1325   art3588 ajn4434   2532   ipf1690   ppro846

have been given to the poor. And they murmured against her.

1161   art,nn2424 aina2036   aima863/ppro846   inpro5101 pin3930/an,nn2873   ppro846   aom2038

6 And Jesus said, Let*her*alone; why trouble ye her? she hath wrought

an,aj2570 an,nn2041 pre1519 ppro1691

a good work on me.

1063   pin2192   art3588   ajn4434   pre3326 rxpro1438   ad3842   2532   ad3752

7 For ye have the poor with you always, and whensoever ye

psa2309   pinm1410 ainf4160 ppro846   ad2095 1161 epn1691   pin2192 3756   ad3842

will ye may do them good: but me ye have not always.

aina4160 repro3739 depro3778 aina2192   aina4301   ainf3462 ppro3450

8 She hath done what she could: she is come aforehand to anoint my

art,nn4983 pre1519 art3588   nn1780

body to the burying.

281   pin3004   ppro5213   ad3699/302   depro5124 art,nn2098   asbp2784

9 Verily I say unto you, Wheresoever this gospel shall be preached

pre1519   art3588   an,aj3650   nn2889   2532 repro3739 depro3778   aina4160   fp2980

throughout the whole world, this also that she hath done shall be spoken of

pre1519   an,nn3422   ppro846

for a memorial of her.

Judas Agrees on a Price to Betray Jesus (Matt. 26:14-16; Luke 22:3-6)

2532 art,nn2455 art,aj2469   nu1520   art3588   nu,ajn1427   aina565   pre4314 art3588   nn749   2443

10 And Judas Iscariot, one of the twelve, went unto the chief priests, to

asba3860 ppro846   ppro846

betray him unto them.

1161   art3588 apta191   ainp5463   2532 aom1861   ainf1325 ppro846

11 And when they heard it, they were glad, and promised to give him

an,nn694 2532   ipf2212 ad4459   ad2122   asba3860 ppro846

money. And he sought how he might conveniently betray him.

Jesus Eats the Passover With His Disciples (Matt. 26:17-25; Luke 22:7-14,21-23; John 13:21-30)

2532 art3588 nu,aj4413 nn2250   art,ajn106   ad3753   ipf2380 art3588   3957

12 And the first day of unleavened bread, when they killed the passover,

ppro846 art,nn3101   pin3004   ppro846 ad4226 pin2309   apta565   asba2090 2443

his disciples said unto him, Where wilt thou that we go and prepare that thou

asba5315 art3588   3957

mayest eat the passover?   (Ex. 12:6,14-20)

2532   pin649   nu1417   ppro848   art,nn3101   2532   pin3004   ppro846 aima5217

13 And he sendeth forth two of his disciples, and saith unto them, Go ye

pre1519 art3588   nn4172   2532   ft528   ppro5213   an,nn444   pap941   an,nn2765   an,nn5204

into the city, and there shall meet you a man bearing a pitcher of water:

aima190 ppro846

follow him.

2532   ad3699/1437   asba1525   aima2036   art3588

14 And wheresoever he shall go in, say ye to the

nn3617   art3588   nn1320   pin3004   ad4226   pin2076 art3588   nn2646

goodman*of*the*house, The Master saith, Where is the guestchamber,

ad3699   asba5315 art3588   3957   pre3326 ppro3450   art,nn3101

where I shall eat the passover with my disciples?

2532   epn846   ft1166   ppro5213   an,aj3173   an,nn508   pfpp4766   an,aj2092

15 And he will show you a large upper room furnished and prepared:

ad1563   aima2090   ppro2254

there make ready for us.

2532   ppro846   art,nn3101   aina1831   2532   aina2064 pre1519 art3588 nn4172   2532   aina2147 ad2531

16 And his disciples went forth, and came into the city, and found as he

aina2036   ppro846   2532   aina2090   art3588   3957

had said unto them: and they made ready the passover.

2532   an,nn3798   (ppmp1096) pinm2064   pre3326 art3588 nu,ajn1427

17 And in the evening he cometh with the twelve.

2532   ppro846 ppmp345 2532   pap2068 art,nn2424 aina2036   281   pin3004   ppro5213 nu1520

18 And as they sat and did eat, Jesus said, Verily I say unto you, One

pre1537 ppro5216   art,pap2068   pre3326 ppro1700   ft3860   ppro3165

of you which eateth with me shall betray me.   (Ps. 41:9)

1161   art3588   aom756   pifm3076   2532   pinf3004   ppro846   nu,ajn,pre,nu,ajn1527

19 And they began to be sorrowful, and to say unto him one* by*one,

(3385)   epn1473 2532   an,ajn243   (3385)   epn1473

Is it I? and another said, Is it I?

1161   art3588   aptp611   aina2036   ppro846   nu1520 pre1537 art3588   nu,ajn1427

20 And he answered and said unto them, It is one of the twelve,

art,ppmp1686   pre3326 ppro1700 pre1519 art3588 nn5165

that dippeth with me in the dish.

art3588 nn5207   art,nn444   3303   pin5217 ad2531   pfip1125   pre4012 ppro846 1161   3759

21 The Son of man indeed goeth, as it is written of him: but woe to

depro1565 art,nn444 pre1223 repro3739 art3588 nn5207   art,nn444   ainp3860   pr/an,ajn2570 ipf2258 (ppro846)   depro1565

that man by whom the Son of man is betrayed! good were it for that

art,nn444 1487   3756   ainp1080

man if he had never been born.

The Lord's Supper (Matt. 26:26-30; Luke 22:15-20; 1 Cor. 11:23-25)

2532   ppro846   pap2068 art,nn2424 apta2983   an,nn740   apta2127   aina2806   2532

22 And as they did eat, Jesus took bread, and blessed, and broke it, and

aina1325   ppro846   2532 aina2036 aima2983 aima5315 pr/depro5124 pin2076 ppro3450 art,nn4983

gave to them, and said, Take, eat: this is my body.

23 And he took the cup, and when he had given thanks, he gave *it* to them: and they all drank of it.

24 And he said unto them, This is my blood of the new testament, which*is*shed for many.   *(Ex. 24:8; Zech. 9:11)*

25 Verily I say unto you, I will drink no more of the fruit of the vine, until that day that I drink it new in the kingdom of God.

26 And when they had sung*a*hymn, they went out into the mount of Olives.

Jesus Predicts Peter's Denial (Matt. 26:31-35; Luke 22:31-34; John 13:36-38)

27 And Jesus saith unto them, All ye shall be offended because of me this night: for it is written, I will smite the shepherd, and the sheep shall be scattered.   *(Zech. 13:7)*

28 But after that I am risen, I will go before you into Galilee.

29 But Peter said unto him, Although all shall be offended, yet *will* not I.

30 And Jesus saith unto him, Verily I say unto thee, That this day, *even* in this night, before the cock crow twice, thou shalt deny me thrice.

31 But he spake the more vehemently, If I should die with thee, I will not*deny*thee*in*any*wise.   Likewise also said they all.

Jesus in Gethsemane (Matt. 26:36-46; Luke 22:39-46)

32 And they came to a place which was named Gethsemane: and he saith to his disciples, Sit ye here, while I shall pray.

2532   pin3880   pre3326   rxpro1438 art,nn4074   2532   art,nn2384   2532   an,nn2491   2532   aom756

33 And he taketh with him Peter and James and John, and began to

pip1568   2532   pinf85

be*sore*amazed, and to be*very*heavy;

2532   pin3004   ppro846   ppro3450 art,nn5590 pin2076   pr/an,aj4036   ad2193   an,nn2288

34 And saith unto them, My soul is exceeding sorrowful unto death:

aima3306   ad5602   2532   pim1127

tarry ye here, and watch.

2532   apta4281   an,ajn3397   aina4098 pre1909 art3588 an,nn1093   2532   ipf4336

35 And he went forward a little, and fell on the ground, and prayed

2443 1487   pin2076   pr/an,ajn1415 art3588 nn5610   asba3928 pre575 ppro846

that, if it were possible, the hour might pass from him.

2532   ipf3004   5   art,nn3962 an,ajn3956   pr/an,aj1415   ppro4671 aima3911

36 And he said, Abba, Father, all things *are* possible unto thee; take away

depro5124 art,nn4221 pre575 ppro1700   235   3756 inpro5101 epn1473 pin2309 235 inpro5101 epn4771

this cup from me: nevertheless not what I will, but what thou wilt.

2532   pinm2064   2532   pin2147   ppro846   pap2518   2532 pin3004   art,nn4074

37 And he cometh, and findeth them sleeping, and saith unto Peter,

an,nn4613   pin2518   aina2480   3756   ainf1127 nu3391 an,nn5610

Simon, sleepest thou? couldest not thou watch one hour?

pim1127   2532 pim4336 3363 asba1525 pre1519 an,nn3986   art3588 nn4151 3303

38 Watch ye and pray, lest ye enter into temptation. The spirit truly *is*

pr/an,aj4289 1161 art3588 nn4561   pr/an,aj772

ready, but the flesh *is* weak.

2532 ad3825   apta565   aom4336   apta2036 art3588 epn846   nn3056

39 And again he went away, and prayed, and spake the same words.

2532   apta5290   aina2147 ppro846   pap2518 ad3825   1063 ppro846 art,nn3778

40 And when he returned, he found them asleep again, (for their eyes

ipf2258 pr/ppmp916 2532/3756 ipf1492   inpro5101 asbp611   ppro846

were heavy,) neither wist they what to answer him.

2532   pinm2064 art3588 nu,ajn5154 2532 pin3004   ppro846   pim2518 art,ajn3063 2532

41 And he cometh the third time, and saith unto them, Sleep on now, and

pim373   pin566   art3588 nn5610   aina2064 2400 art3588 nn5207 art,nn444

take*your*rest; it is enough, the hour is come; behold, the Son of man is

pinp3860 pre1519 art3588 nn5495   art,nn268

betrayed into the hands of sinners.

pim1453   psa71 2400   art,pap3860   ppro3165 pfi1448

42 Rise up, let us go; lo, he*that*betrayeth me is*at*hand.

They Arrest Jesus (Matt. 26:47-56; Luke 22:47-53; John 18:2-12)

2532   ad2112   ppro846 ad2089 pap2980   pinm3854 an,nn2455 (pap5607) pr/nu1520 art3588

43 And immediately, while he yet spake, cometh Judas, one of the

nu,ajn1427 2532 pre3326 ppro846 an,aj4183 an,nn3793 pre3326 an,nn3162 2532 an,nn3586 pre3844 art3588

twelve, and with him a great multitude with swords and staves, from the

nn749   2532 art3588 nn1122 2532 art3588 ajn4245

chief priests and the scribes and the elders.

1161   art,pap3860   ppro846   plpf1325   ppro846   an,nn4953 pap3004

44 And he*that*betrayed him had given them a token, saying,

repro3739/302   asba5368   pr/epn846   pin2076   aima2902   ppro846   2532

Whomsoever I shall kiss, that same is he; take him, and

aima520/ad806

lead*him*away*safely.

2532   apta2064   apta4334   ad2112   ppro846   pin3004

45 And as soon as he was come, he goeth straightway to him, and saith,

4461   4461   2532   aina2705   ppro846

Master, master; and kissed him.

1161   art3588   aina1911   ppro848   art,nn5495   pre1909   ppro846   2532   aina2902   ppro846

46 And they laid their hands on him, and took him.

1161   (idpro5100)   nu1520   art,pfp3936   aptm4685   art,nn3162   aina3817   art,ajn1401

47 And   one of them*that*stood*by drew a sword, and smote a servant

art3588   nn749   2532   aina851   ppro846 art,nn5621

of the high priest, and cut off his ear.

2532   art,nn2424   aptp611   aina2036   ppro846   aina1831   ad5613   pre1909

48 And Jesus answered and said unto them, Are ye come out, as against

an,nn3027 pre3326 an,nn3162   2532   an,nn3586   ainf4815 ppro3165

a thief, with swords and *with* staves to take me?

ipf2252   pre2596/an,nn2250   pre4314   ppro5209 pre1722 art3588   nn2411   pap1321   2532   aina2902 ppro3165

49 I was daily with you in the temple teaching, and ye took me

3756   235   (2443) art3588   nn1124   asbp4137

not: but the Scriptures must be fulfilled.

2532   an,ajn3956   apta863   ppro846   aina5343

50 And they all forsook him, and fled.

2532   aina190   ppro846 nu1520 idpro5100   an,nn3495   pfpp4016   an,nn4616

☞ 51 And there followed him a certain young man, having a linen cloth

pre1909   an,ajn1131   2532 art3588   nn3495   pin2902   ppro846

cast about *his* naked *body*; and the young men laid*hold*on him:

1161   art3588 apta2641 art3588   nn4616   aina5343 pre575 ppro846 an,aj1131

52 And he left the linen cloth, and fled from them naked.

Jesus Is Brought Before Caiaphas (Matt. 26:57-68; Luke 22:54,63-71; John 18:13,14,19-24)

2532   aina520/art,nn2424   pre4314 art3588   nn749   2532   ppro846

53 And they led*Jesus*away to the high priest: and with him were

pinm4905   an,aj3956 art3588   nn749   2532 art3588   ajn4245   2532 art3588   nn1122

assembled all the chief priests and the elders and the scribes.

2532   art,nn4074   aina190   ppro846   pre575/ad3113   ad2193   (ad2080)   pre1519 art3588   nn833   art3588

54 And Peter followed him afar off, even into the palace of the

nn749   2532   ipf2258/ppmp4775 pre3326 art3588   nn5257   2532   ppmp2328   pre4314 art3588

high priest: and he sat with the servants, and warmed himself at the

nn5457

fire.

1161 art3588   nn749   2532 an,aj3650 art3588   nn4894   ipf2212   an,nn3141   pre2596

55 And the chief priests and all the council sought for witness against

art,nn2424   aies2289/ppro846   2532   ipf2147   3756

Jesus to put*him*to*death; and found none.

☞ **14:51, 52** Some scholars feel that the young man mentioned here is Mark himself.

¹⁰⁶³　^{an,ajn4183}　^{ipf5576}　^{pre2596}　^{ppro846}　²⁵³²　^{ppro846}　^{art,nn3141}

56 For many bare*false*witness against him, but their witness

^{ipf2258/3756/pr/an,aj2470}

agreed*not*together.

²⁵³²　^{apta450}　^{idpro5100}　^{ipf5576}　^{pre2596}　^{ppro846}　^{pap3004}

57 And there arose certain, and bare*false*witness against him, saying,

^{epn2249}　^{aina191}　^{ppro846}　^{pap3004}　^{epn1473}　^{ft2647}　^{depro5126}　^{art,nn3485}

☞ 58 We heard him say, I will destroy this temple that is

^{art,aj5499}　²⁵³²　^{pre1223}　^{nu5140}　^{an,nn2250}　^{ft3618}　^{an,ajn243}

made*with*hands, and within three days I will build another

^{an,aj886}

made*without*hands.

²⁵³²　³⁷⁶¹　^{ad3779}　^{ppro846}　^{art,nn3141}　^{ipf2258/pr/an,aj2470}

59 But neither so did their witness agree together.

²⁵³²　^{art3588}　ⁿⁿ⁷⁴⁹　^{apta450}　^{pre1519}　^{art3588}　^{ajn3319}　^{aina1905}　^{art,nn2424}

60 And the high priest stood up · in the midst, and asked Jesus,

^{pap3004 (3756)}　^{pinp611}　^{an,ajn3762}　^{inpro5101}　^{depro3778}　^{pin2649}

saying, Answerest thou nothing? what is it which these witness against

^{ppro4675}

thee?

¹¹⁶¹　^{art3588}　^{ipf4623}　²⁵³²　^{aom611}　^{an,aj3762}　^{ad3825}　^{art3588}　ⁿⁿ⁷⁴⁹

61 But he held*his*peace, and answered nothing. Again the high priest

^{ipf1905}　^{ppro846}　²⁵³²　^{pin3004}　^{ppro846}　^{pin1488}　^{epn4771}　^{art3588}　^{pr/nn5547}　^{art3588}　^{pr/nn5207}　^{art3588}

asked him, and said unto him, Art thou the Christ, the Son of the

^{ajn2128}

Blessed?　　　　　　　　　　　　　　　　　　　　　　*(Is. 53:7)*

¹¹⁶¹　^{art,nn2424}　^{aina2036}　^{epn1473}　^{pin1510}　²⁵³²　^{fm3700}　^{art3588}　ⁿⁿ⁵²⁰⁷　^{art,nn444}　^{ppmp2521}　^{pre1537}

62 And Jesus said, I am: and ye shall see the Son of man sitting on

^{an,ajn1188}　^{art,nn1411}　²⁵³²　^{ppmp2064}　^{pre3326}　^{art3588}　ⁿⁿ³⁵⁰⁷　^{art,nn3772}

the right hand of power, and coming in the clouds of heaven.

(Ps. 110:1; Dan. 4:13)

¹¹⁶¹　^{art3588}　ⁿⁿ⁷⁴⁹　^{apta1284}　^{ppro848}　^{art,nn5509}　^{pin3004}　^{inpro5101}　^{pin2192/an,nn5532}

63 Then the high priest rent his clothes, and saith, What need we

^{ad2089}　^{an,nn3144}

any further witnesses?

^{aina191}　^{art3588}　ⁿⁿ⁹⁸⁸　^{inpro5101}　^{pinm5316}　^{ppro5213}　¹¹⁶¹　^{art3588}　^{an,ajn3956}

☞ 64 Ye have heard the blasphemy: what think ye? And they all

^{aina2632}　^{ppro846}　^{pinf1511}　^{pr/an,aj1777}　^{an,nn2288}

condemned him to be guilty of death.　　　　　　　*(Lev. 24:16)*

²⁵³²　^{idpro5100}　^{aom756}　^{pinf1716}　^{ppro846}　²⁵³²　^{pinf4028}　^{ppro846}　^{art,nn4383}　²⁵³²　^{pinf2852}

65 And some began to spit on him, and to cover his face, and to buffet

^{ppro846}　²⁵³²　^{pinf3004}　^{ppro846}　^{aima4395}　²⁵³²　^{art3588}　ⁿⁿ⁵²⁵⁷　^{aina906}　^{ppro846}

him, and to say unto him, Prophesy: and the servants did strike him with the

^{an,nn4475}

palms*of*their*hands.

☞ **14:58** See note on 2 Corinthians 5:1.
☞ **14:64** See note on Mark 3:28, 29.

Peter Denies Jesus (Matt. 26:69-75; Luke 22:54-62; John 18:15-18,25-27)

2532   art,nn4074   pap5607   ad2736   pre1722 art3588   nn833   pinm2064 nu3391   art3588

66 And as Peter was beneath in the palace, there cometh one of the

nn3814   art3588   nn749

maids of the high priest:

2532   apta1492 art,nn4074   ppmp2328   apta1689   ppro846

67 And when she saw Peter warming himself, she looked upon him, and

pin3004 2532 epn4771   ipf2258   pre3326 an,nn2424   art,aj3479

said, And thou also wast with Jesus of Nazareth.

1161   art3588   aom720   pap3004   pin1492   3756   3761   pinm1987   inpro5101 epn4771

68 But he denied, saying, I know not, neither understand I what thou

pin3004   2532   aina1831 ad1854 pre1519 art3588   nn4259   2532   an,nn220 aina5455

sayest. And he went out into the porch; and the cock crew.

2532   art,nn3814 apta1492 ppro846   ad3825   aom756   pinf3004   art,pfp3936

69 And a maid saw him again, and began to say to them*that*stood*by,

depro3778 pin2076   pre1537   epn846

This is *one* of them.

1161   art3588   ipf720   ad3825   2532   an,ajn3397   pre3326   art,pfp3936   ipf3004

70 And he denied it again. And a little after, they*that*stood*by said

ad3825   art,nn4074   ad230   pin1488   pre1537   epn846   1063   (2532)   pin1488   pr/an,ajn1057   2532

again to Peter, Surely thou art *one* of them: for thou art a Galilaean, and

ppro4675 art,nn2981   pin3662

thy speech agreeth *thereto.*

1161   art3588   aom756   pinf332   2532   pinf3660   pin1492   3756 depro5126 art,nn444

71 But he began to curse and to swear, *saying,* I know not this man of

repro3739   pin3004

whom ye speak.

2532   (pre1537)   nu,ajn1208   an,nn220 aina5455   2532   art,nn4074   ainp363   art3588

72 And the second time the cock crew. And Peter called*to*mind the

nn4487 repro3739 art,nn2424 aina2036   ppro846   ad4250   an,nn220 ainf5455   nu,ad1364   fm533

word that Jesus said unto him, Before the cock crow twice, thou shalt deny

ppro3165 nu,ad5151   2532   apta1911   ipf2799

me thrice. And when he thought thereon, he wept.

Jesus Is Brought to Pilate (Matt. 27:1,2,11-14; Luke 23:1-5; John 18:28-38)

2532　ad2112　pre1909　art3588　ad4404　art3588　nn749　apta4160

15 And straightway in the morning the chief priests held a

an,nn4824　pre3326　art3588　ajn4245　2532　an,nn1122　2532　art3588　an,aj3650　nn4892

consultation with the elders and scribes and the whole council,

apta1210　art,nn2424　aina667　2532　aina3860　art,nn4091

and bound Jesus, and carried*him*away, and delivered *him* to Pilate.

2532　art,nn4091　aina1905　ppro846　pin1488　epn4771　art3588　pr/nn935　art3588　nn2453　1161　art3588

2 And Pilate asked him, Art thou the King of the Jews? And he

aptp611　aina2036　ppro846　epn4771　pin3004

answering said unto him, Thou sayest *it*.

2532　art3588　nn749　ipf2723　ppro846　an,ajn4183　1161　art3588　aom611

3 And the chief priests accused him of many things: but he answered

an,ajn3762

nothing.

1161　art,nn4091　ipf1905　ppro846　ad3825　pap3004　pinp611　(3756)　an,ajn3762　aima2396

4 And Pilate asked him again, saying, Answerest thou nothing? behold

an,ajn4214　pin2649　ppro4675

how*many*things they witness against thee.

1161　art,nn2424　ad3765　ainp611　an,ajn3762　5620　art,nn4091　pinf2296

5 But <u>Jesus yet answered nothing; so that Pilate marveled.</u>   *(Is. 53:7)*

Jesus Sentenced to Death (Matt. 27:15-26; Luke 23:13-25; John 18:39—19:16)

1161　pre2596　an,nn1859　ipf630　ppro846　nu1520　an,ajn1198　repro4007

6 Now at *that* feast he released unto them one prisoner, whomsoever

ipf154

they desired.

1161　ipf2258　art,ppmp3004　an,nn912　pfpp1210　pre3326

7 And there was *one* named Barabbas, *which* *lay* bound with

art,nn4955　repro3748　plpf4160　an,nn5408　pre1722

them*that*had*made*insurrection*with him, who had committed murder in

art3588　nn4714

the insurrection.

2532　art3588　nn3793　apta310　aom756　pinf154　ad2531

8 And the multitude crying aloud began to desire *him to do* as he had

ad104　ipf4160　ppro846

ever done unto them.

1161　art,nn4091　ainp611　ppro846　pap3004　pin2309　asba630　ppro5213　art3588

9 But Pilate answered them, saying, Will ye that I release unto you the

nn935　art3588　nn2453

King of the Jews?

1063　ipf1097　3754　art3588　nn749　plpf3960　ppro846　pre1223　an,nn5355

10 For he knew that the chief priests had delivered him for envy.

1161　art3588　nn749　aina383　art3588　nn3973　2443　ad3123　asba630

11 But the chief priests moved the people, that he should rather release

art,nn912　ppro846

Barabbas unto them.

^{1161 art,nn4091   aptp611   aina2036   ad3825   ppro846   inpro5101 pin2309   3767}

12 And Pilate answered and said again unto them, What will ye then that I

^{asba4160   repro3739   pin3004 art3588 nn935   art3588   nn2453}

shall do *unto him* whom ye call the King of the Jews?

^{1161 art3588   aina2896   ad3825   aima4717   ppro846}

13 And they cried out again, Crucify him.

^{1161   art,nn4091 ipf3004   ppro846   1063   inpro5101 an,ajn2556   aina4160   1161   art3588}

14 Then Pilate said unto them, Why, what evil hath he done? And they

^{aina2896   ad4056   aima4717   ppro846}

cried out the*more*exceedingly, Crucify him.

^{1161   art,nn4091   ppmp1410   ainf4160/art,nn2425 art3588   nn3793   aina630   art,nn912}

15 And *so* Pilate, willing to   content   the people, released Barabbas

^{ppro846   2532   aina3860   art,nn2424   apta5417   2443}

unto them, and delivered Jesus, when he had scourged *him,* to be

^{asbp4717}

crucified.

The Soldiers Mock Jesus (Matt. 27:27-31; John 19:2,3)

^{1161   art3588   nn4757   aina520/ppro846   ad*2080 art3588   nn833   repro,pin3603   pr/an,nn4232   2532}

16 And the soldiers led*him*away into the hall, called Praetorium; and

^{pin4779   art3588 an,aj3650   nn4686}

they call together the whole band.

^{2532   pin1746/ppro846   an,nn4209 2532   apta4120   an,nn4735   an,aj174}

17 And they clothed*him*with purple, and platted a crown of thorns, and

^{pin4060   ppro846}

put*it*about his *head,*

^{2532   aom756   pifm782   ppro846 pim5463 an,nn935   art3588 nn2453}

18 And began to salute him, Hail, King of the Jews!

^{2532   ipf5180   ppro846   art3588 nn2776   an,nn2563 2532   ipf1716   ppro846}

19 And they smote him on the head with a reed, and did spit upon him,

^{2532   pap5087   art,nn1119   ipf4352   ppro846}

and bowing *their* knees worshiped him.

^{2532   ad3753   aina1702   ppro846   aina1562   art3588   nn4209   ppro846}

20 And when they had mocked him, they took off the purple from him,

^{2532   aina1746/art,aj2398/art,nn2440   ppro846 2532   pin1806/ppro846   2443 asba4717   ppro846}

and put*his*own*clothes*on him, and led*him*out to crucify him.

Jesus Is Crucified (Matt. 27:32-44; Luke 23:26-43; John 19:17-27)

^{2532   pin29   idpro5100   an,nn4613   an,aj2956   pap3855   ppmp2064}

21 And they compel one Simon a Cyrenian, who passed by, coming

^{pre575   an,nn68   art3588 nn3962   an,nn223   2532 an,nn4504 2443 asba142 ppro846 art,nn4716}

out of the country, the father of Alexander and Rufus, to bear his cross.

^{2532   pin5342   ppro846 pre1909   an,nn5117   1115   repro,pin3603}

22 And they bring him unto the place Golgotha, which is, being

^{ppmp3177   pr/an,nn5117   an,nn2898}

interpreted, The place of a skull.

2532   ipf1325 ppro846   ainf4095 an,nn3631   pfpp4669   1161 art3588

23 And they gave him to drink wine mingled*with*myrrh: but he

aina2983   3756

received *it* not.

2532   apta4717 ppro846   pinm1266 ppro846 art,nn2440   pap906

24 And when they had crucified him, they parted his garments, casting

an,nn2819 pre1909 ppro846   inpro5101/inpro5101   asba142

lots upon them, what*every*man should take.   *(Ps. 22:18)*

1161   ipf2258   pr/an,nu,aj5154 an,nn5610 2532   aina4717 ppro846

25 And it was the third hour, and they crucified him.

2532 art3588   nn1923   ppro846 art,nn156   ipf2258   pr/pfpp1924   art3588

26 And the superscription of his accusation was written over, THE

nn935   art3588   nn2453

KING OF THE JEWS.

2532 pre4862 ppro846   pin4717 nu1417 an,nn3027   nu,ajn1520 pre1537   an,ajn1188

27 And with him they crucify two thieves; the one on his right hand,

2532   nu,ajn1520 pre1537 ppro846 an,nn2176

and the other on his left.

2532 art3588   nn1124   ainp4137   art,pap3004   2532   ainp3049

28 And the Scripture was fulfilled, which saith, And he was numbered

pre3326   an,ajn459

with the transgressors.   *(Is. 53:12)*

2532   art,ppmp3899   ipf987 ppro846 pap2795 ppro848 art,nn2776 2532 pap3004

29 And they*that*passed*by railed on him, wagging their heads, and saying,

3758   art,pap2647   art3588 nn3485 2532   pap3618 pre1722 nu5140 an,nn2250

Ah, thou*that*destroyest the temple, and buildest *it* in three days,

(Ps. 22:7; 109:25; Lam. 2:15)

aima4982 rxpro4572 2532   aima2597   pre575 art3588 nn4716

30 Save thyself, and come down from the cross.

(1161) ad3668   2532 art3588   nn749   pap1702 ipf3004 pre4314   rcpro240   pre3326

31 Likewise also the chief priests mocking said among themselves with

art3588 nn1122   aina4982 an,ajn243 rxpro1438   pinm1410/3756 ainf4982

the scribes, He saved others; himself he cannot save.

art,nn5547 art3588 nn935   2474   aima2597 ad3568 pre575 art3588 nn4716 2443

32 Let Christ the King of Israel descend now from the cross, that we may

asba1492 2532 asba4100   2532   art,pfpp4957   ppro846 ipf3679 ppro846

see and believe. And they*that*were*crucified*with him reviled him.

The Death of Jesus (Matt. 27:45-56; Luke 23:44-49; John 19:28-30)

1161   an,nu,aj1622 an,nn5610   aptm1096 aom1096 an,nn4655 pre1909 art3588

33 And when the sixth hour was come, there was darkness over the

an,aj3650 nn1093 ad2193   an,nu,aj1766 an,nn5610

whole land until the ninth hour.

2532   art3588 nu,aj1766 art,nn5610 art,nn2424 aina994   an,aj3173 an,nn5456 pap3004 1682 1682

34 And at the ninth hour Jesus cried with a loud voice, saying, Eloi, Eloi,

²⁹⁸²   ⁴⁵¹⁸   ^{repro,pin3603}   ^{ppmp3177}   ^{ppro3450 art,nn2316 ppro3450 art,nn2316 (pre1519) inpro5101}
lama sabachthani? which is, being interpreted, My God, my God,   why
          ^{aina1459}   ^{ppro3165}
hast thou forsaken me?   *(Ps. 22:1)*

        ²⁵³²   ^{idpro5100}   ^{art,pfp3936}   ^{apta191}   ^{ipf3004}   ²⁴⁰⁰
   35 And some of them*that*stood*by, when they heard *it,* said, Behold, he
^{pin5455}   ^{an,nn2243}
calleth Elijah.

        ¹¹⁶¹   ^{nu,ajn1520} ^{apta5143} ²⁵³²   ^{apta1072/an,nn4697}   ^{an,nn3690} ⁵⁰³⁷   ^{apta4060}
   36 And   one   ran and filled*a*sponge*full of vinegar, and put*it*on a
^{an,nn2563} ²⁵³²   ^{ipf4222/ppro846}   ^{pap3004}   ^{aima863}   ^{aosi1492} ¹⁴⁸⁷ ^{an,nn2243}
reed, and gave*him*to*drink, saying, Let alone; let us see whether Elijah will
^{pinm2064}   ^{ainf2507/ppro846}
come to take*him*down.   *(Ps. 69:21)*

        ¹¹⁶¹ ^{art,nn2424} ^{apta863}   ^{an,aj3173} ^{an,nn5456}   ^{aina1606}
   37 And Jesus cried with a loud voice, and gave*up*the*ghost.

        ²⁵³² ^{art3588}   ⁿⁿ²⁶⁶⁵   ^{art3588}   ⁿⁿ³⁴⁸⁵   ^{ainp4977} ^{pre1519} ^{nu,ajn1417} ^{pre575}   ^{ad509}   ^{ad2193}
   38 And the veil of the temple was rent in twain from the top to
^{ad2736}
the bottom.

        ¹¹⁶¹   ^{art3588}   ⁿⁿ²⁷⁶⁰   ^{art,pfp3936}   ^{pre1537/an,ajn1727} ^{ppro846} ^{apta1492} ³⁷⁵⁴
   39 And when the centurion, which stood over against him, saw that he
^{ad3779}   ^{apta2896}   ^{aina1606}   ^{aina2036}   ^{ad230} ^{depro3778} ^{art,nn444} ^{ipf2258}
so cried out, and gave*up*the*ghost, he said, Truly this man was the
^{pr/an,nn5207}   ^{an,nn2316}
Son of God.

        ⁽¹¹⁶¹⁾   ^{ipf2258} ²⁵³²   ^{an,nn1135}   ^{pap2334}   ^{pre575/ad3113}   ^{pre1722} ^{repro3739} ^{ipf2258} ^{an,nn3137}
   40 There were also women looking on afar off: among whom was Mary
^{art,aj3094}   ²⁵³²   ^{an,nn3137} ^{art3588}   ⁿⁿ³³⁸⁴   ^{art,nn2385} ^{art3588} ^{aj3398} ²⁵³²   ^{an,nn2500}   ²⁵³²
Magdalene, and Mary the mother of James the less and of Joses, and
^{an,nn4539}
Salome;

        ^{repro3739} ²⁵³²   ^{ad3753}   ^{ipf2258} ^{pre1722} ^{art,nn1056}   ^{ipf190} ^{ppro846} ²⁵³²   ^{ipf1247}
   41 (Who also, when he was in Galilee, followed him, and ministered unto
^{ppro846} ²⁵³² ^{an,aj4183}   ^{an,ajn243}   ^{art,apta4872}   ^{ppro846} ^{pre1519}   ^{an,nn2414}
him;) and many other women which*came*up*with him unto Jerusalem.

Joseph of Arimathea (Matt. 27:57-61; Luke 23:50-56; John 19:38-42)

        ²⁵³²   ^{ad2235}   ^{an,nn3798}   ^{aptm1096}   ¹⁸⁹³   ^{ipf2258}   ^{pr/an,nn3904}
   42 And now when the even was come, because it was the preparation,
^{repro,pin3603}   ^{pr/an,nn4315}
that is, the day*before*the*sabbath,

        ²⁵⁰¹   ^{art,pre575}   ^{an,nn707}   ^{an,aj2158}   ^{an,nn1010}   ^{repro3739} ^(epn846)   ²⁵³²
   43 Joseph   of Arimathaea, an honorable counselor, which   also
^{ipf2258/ppmp4327} ^{art3588}   ⁿⁿ⁹³²   ^{art,nn2316} ^{aina2064}   ^{aina1525} ^{apta5111} ^{pre4314} ^{an,nn4091}   ²⁵³²
waited for the kingdom of God, came, and went in boldly unto Pilate, and
^{aom154}   ^{art3588} ⁿⁿ⁴⁹⁸³   ^{art,nn2424}
craved the body of Jesus.

1161   art,nn4091   aina2296   1487   pfi2348/ad2235   2532   aptm4341

44 And Pilate marveled if he were*already*dead: and calling *unto him*

art3588   nn2760   aina1905 ppro846   1487   aina599/ad3819

the centurion, he asked him whether he had been*any*while*dead.

2532   apta1097   pre575 art3588   nn2760   aom1433 art3588   nn4983

45 And when he knew *it* of the centurion, he gave the body to

2501

Joseph.

2532   apta59   an,nn4616   2532   apta2507/ppro846   aina1750

46 And he bought fine linen, and took*him*down, and wrapped*him*in

art3588 nn4616   2532 aina2698 ppro846 pre1722   an,nn3419   repro3739 ipf2258 pr/pfpp2998   pre1537   an,nn4073 2532

the linen, and laid him in a sepulcher which was hewn out of a rock, and

aina4351   an,nn3037 pre1909 art3588 nn2374   art3588   nn3419

rolled a stone unto the door of the sepulcher.   (Is. 53:9)

1161   art,nn3137   art,aj3094   2532 an,nn3137   an,nn2500   ipf2334   ad4226

47 And Mary Magdalene and Mary *the mother* of Joses beheld where he

pinp5087

was laid.

Jesus Is Risen (Matt. 28:1-8; Luke 24:1-12; John 20:1-10)

2532   art3588   nn4521   aptp1230 an,nn3137   art,aj3094   2532   an,nn3137 art3588

16 And when the sabbath was past, Mary Magdalene, and Mary the

art,nn2385   2532   an,nn4539   aina59   an,nn759   2443

mother of James, and Salome, had bought sweet spices, that they

apta2064   asba218   ppro846

might come and anoint him.

2532   ad3029   ad4404   art3588 nu,ajn3391   art3588   nn4521   pinm2064

2 And very early*in*the*morning the first *day* of the week, they came

pre1909 art3588   nn3419   apta393   art3588 nn2246

unto the sepulcher at the rising of the sun.

2532   ipf3004   pre4314   rxpro1438   inpro5101   ft617/ppro2254   art3588   nn3037

3 And they said among themselves, Who shall roll*us*away the stone

pre1537 art3588 nn2374   art3588   nn3419

from the door of the sepulcher?

2532   apta308   pin2334 3754 art3588   nn3037   pfip617   1063

4 And when they looked, they saw that the stone was rolled away: for it

ipf2258   ad4970 pr/an,aj3173

was very great.

2532   apta1525   pre1519 art3588   nn3419   aina1492   an,nn3495   ppmp2521 pre1722 art3588

5 And entering into the sepulcher, they saw a young man sitting on the

ajn1188   pfpp4016   an,nn4749/an,aj3022   2532   ainp1568

right side, clothed in a long*white*garment; and they were affrighted.

1161   art3588 pin3004   ppro846   3361   pim1568   pin2212 an,nn2424   art,aj3479

6 And he saith unto them, Be not affrighted: Ye seek Jesus of Nazareth,

art,pfpp4717   ainp1453   pin2076 3756 ad5602   aima2396 art3588   nn5117   ad3699

which*was*crucified: he is risen; he is not here: behold the place where they

aina5087 ppro846

laid him.

235   aima5217   aima2036   ppro846   art,nn3101   2532   art,nn4074   3754   pin4254

7 But go*your*way, tell his disciples and Peter that he goeth before

ppro5209 pre1519   art,nn1056   ad1563   fm3700 ppro846 ad2531   aina2036   ppro5213

you into Galilee: there shall ye see him, as he said unto you.

     2532   apta1831   ad5035   aina5343   pre575   art3588   nn3419   1161   ppro846

8 And they went out quickly, and fled from the sepulcher; for they

an,nn5156/ipf2192 2532   an,nn1611   2532   aina2036   an,ajn3762   an,ajn3762   1063

trembled and were amazed: neither said they any thing to any *man*; for they

ipf5399

were afraid.

Jesus Appears to Mary Magdalene (Matt. 28:1-10; John 20:11-18)

     1161   apta450   ad4404   nu,ajn4413   an,nn4521   ainp5316

9 Now when *Jesus* was risen early the first *day* of the week, he appeared

an,ajn4412   an,nn3137   art,aj3094   pre575   repro3739   plpf1544   nu2033   an,nn1140

first to Mary Magdalene, out of whom he had cast seven devils.

       depro1565   aptp4198   aina518   art,aptm1096   pre3326   ppro846

10 *And* she went and told them*that*had*been with him, as they

pap3996   2532   pap2799

mourned and wept.

      depro2548   apta191   3754   pin2198   2532   ainp2300

11 And they, when they had heard that he was alive, and had been seen

pre5259 ppro846   aina569

of her, believed not.

The Appearance to Two Disciples (Luke 24:13-35)

    (1161) pre3326   depro5023   ainp5319   pre1722   an,aj2087   an,nn3444   nu1417 pre1537 ppro846

12 After that he appeared in another form unto two of them, as they

pap4043   ppmp4198 pre1519   an,nn68

walked, and went into the country.

      depro2548   apta565   aina518   art3588   ajn3062   3761   aina4100

13 And they went and told *it* unto the residue: neither believed they

depro1565

them.

The Great Commission (Matt. 28:16-20; Luke 24:36-49; John 20:19-23; Acts 1:6-8)

      ad5305   ainp5319   art3588   nu,ajn1733   epn846   ppmp345   2532

14 Afterward he appeared unto the eleven as they sat*at*meat, and

aina3679   ppro846   art,nn570   2532   an,nn4641   3754

upbraided them with their unbelief and hardness*of*heart, because they

aina4100   3756   art,aptm2300   ppro846   pfpp1453

believed not them*which*had*seen him after he was risen.

2532   aina2036   ppro846 apta4198   pre1519 an,aj537 art3588   nn2889   aima2784 art3588

15 And he said unto them, Go ye into all the world, and preach the

nn2098   an,aj3956   art,nn2937

gospel to every creature.

art,apta4100   2532   an,aptp907   fp4982   1161

☞ 16 He*that*believeth and is baptized shall be saved; but

art,apta569   fp2632

he*that*believeth*not shall be damned.

1161   depro5023 an,nn4592   ft3877   art3588   apta4100   pre1722 ppro3450 art,nn3686

☞ 17 And these signs shall follow them that believe; In my name shall they

ft1544   an,nn1140   ft2980   an,aj2537   an,nn1100

cast out devils; they shall speak with new tongues;

ft142   an,nn3789   2579   asba4095 adpro5100   an,ajn2286

18 They shall take up serpents; and if they drink any deadly thing, it shall

efn3364   ft984   ppro846   ft2007   an,nn5495   pre1909   an,ajn732   2532

not hurt them; they shall lay hands on the sick, and they shall

ft2192/ad2573

recover.

The Ascension of Jesus (Luke 24:50-53; Acts 1:9-11)

3767   3303   art3588   nn2962   aime2980   ppro846   ainp353   pre1519

19 So then after the Lord had spoken unto them, he was received up into

art,nn3772   2532 aina2523 pre1537   an,ajn1188   art,nn2316

heaven, and sat on the right hand of God.

1161   depro1565   apta1831   aina2784   ad3837   art3588   nn2962

20 And they went forth, and preached every where, the Lord

pap4903   2532   pap950   art3588 nn3056 pre1223 art,nn4592 pap1872   281

working with *them,* and confirming the word with signs following. Amen.

☞ **16:16** The word "believeth" is *pisteúsas* (from *pisteúō* [4100]), an aorist participle referring to one who has believed at some time in the past. Also, *baptistheís* (907), translated "is baptized," is an aorist participle but in the passive voice. This form refers to an act of outward obedience, in this case, baptism. Therefore, the correct translation here should be stated, "He who believed and who was baptized shall be saved." However, the Lord adds, ". . . but he that believeth not shall be damned." It should be noted that this negative statement does not include a reference to baptism, making it clear that what saves a person is living faith in Jesus Christ. This is made clear in Ephesians 2:8, "For by grace are ye saved through faith . . . ." The word "saved" is translated from the Greek word *sesōsménoi*, which is a perfect passive participle. It means that this salvation took place at some point in the past and is continuing on in the present, being accomplished by Jesus Christ Himself. If baptism were necessary for salvation, Ephesians 2:8 and many others verses should have been translated "ye are saved through faith and baptism." There are examples in the NT of people who were baptized for selfish reasons, rather than for the purpose of demonstrating their inner, saving faith in Christ (Luke 3:7–9, the Pharisees; Acts 8:9–25, Simon). Baptism is a distinct act of obedience apart from salvation. This is clarified by the order in which the words "believe" and "baptize" occur in the text (cf. Matt. 28:19 [note here that the word "teaching" precedes the mentioning of "baptism"]; Acts 2:38; 10:44–48).

☞ **16:17** The verb "believe" in Greek is in the aorist tense *pisteúsasi* (4100) which refers to those who did believe, not those who would believe at that time or in the future. See note on 1 Corinthians 14:1–3.

LUKE

There is little doubt that the author of this book is Luke, "the beloved physician" (Col. 4:14). He was a Gentile who is thought to have been a native of Antioch. He accompanied the Apostle Paul from Troas on his second missionary journey but remained in Philippi until Paul returned there on his last known missionary expedition (Acts 20:6). They seem to have been close companions up until Paul's death (2 Tim. 4:11). Paul referred to him as his "fellow-worker" in Philemon 1:24. The introductory remarks (Mark 1:1–4) indicate that there were other written accounts of the events surrounding Jesus' life, death, and resurrection that existed at the time this book was written. Apparently, as Luke gathered a wealth of information from "eye-witnesses" that he had come in contact with while traveling with Paul, the Holy Spirit burdened his heart with the need to compose another narrative.

Indeed, Luke does provide a more complete history than the other Gospels. He records twenty miracles of Jesus, more than any other Gospel, as well as twenty-three parables, eighteen of which appear only in his account.

The Book of Luke also gives special attention to prayer. The combined Gospels record that Christ prayed a total of fifteen different times. Luke records eleven of these instances (each of the other Gospels include four or less [some of the prayers are repeated]) as well as a significant portion of Christ's teaching on prayer that is not recorded in the other Gospels.

The book is thought to have been written sometime between the years A.D. 58 and 60. It is generally agreed that Luke intended his Gospel to be available to the public, particularly the Greek public, even though it was initially written to Theophilus (Luke 1:3). The information that is included and the way that the material is presented indicates that Luke was appealing to the Greek mindset. The vocabulary and style are so refined that Luke's Gospel has been compared to various writings of Classical Greek.

Jesus is portrayed in the Gospel of Luke as the long-awaited Messiah, the Savior of all mankind. Special emphasis is placed upon the kindness of Jesus toward women, the weak and poor, outcasts, and those who were suffering.

1
1895   an,ajn4183   aina2021   aifm392   an,nn1335
Forasmuch as many have taken*in*hand to set*forth*in*order a declaration
pre4012   art,nn4229   pfpp4135   pre1722   ppro2254
of those things which are most*surely*believed among us,

ad2531   aina3860   ppro2254   art,aptm1096/pre575,an,nn746
2 Even as they delivered them unto us, which*from*the*beginning*were
pr/an,nn845   2532   pr/an,nn5257   art3588   nn3056
eyewitnesses, and ministers of the word;

_{aina1380}   _{epn2504}   _{ad199}   _{pfp3877}

3 It seemed good to me also, having had perfect understanding of
_{an,ajn3956}   _{ad509}   _{ainf1125}   _{ppro4671}   _{ad2517}   _{an,aj2903}

all things from*the*very*first, to write unto thee in order, most excellent
_{an,nn2321}

Theophilus,
          ₂₄₄₃   _{asba1921} _{art3588}   _{nn803}   _{an,nn3056}   _{pre4012/repro3739}

4 That thou mightest know the certainty of those things, wherein thou
          _{ainp2727}

hast been instructed.

The Birth of John the Baptist

          _{aom1096} _{pre1722} _{art3588}   _{nn2250}   _{an,nn2264}   _{art3588}   _{nn935}   _{art,nn2449}   _{idpro5100}   _{an,nn2409}

5 There was in the days of Herod, the king of Judea, a certain priest
_{an,nn3686}   _{an,nn2197}   _{pre1537}   _{an,nn2183}   ₇   ₂₅₃₂   _{ppro846} _{art,nn1135}   _{pre1537} _{art3588}

named Zacharias, of the course of Abijah: and his wife *was* of the
          _{nn2364}   ₂   ₂₅₃₂   _{ppro846 art,nn3686}   _{pr/1665}

daughters of Aaron, and her name *was* Elisabeth.   *(1 Chr. 24:10)*
          ₁₁₆₁   _{ipf2258}   _{an,ajn297}   _{pr/an,aj1342}   _{ad*1799}   _{art,nn2316}   _{ppmp4198}   _{pre1722} _{an,aj3956}   _{art3588}

6 And they were both righteous before God, walking in all the
          _{nn1785}   ₂₅₃₂   _{an,nn1345}   _{art3588} _{nn2962}   _{an,aj273}

commandments and ordinances of the Lord blameless.
          ₂₅₃₂   _{ipf2258/ppro846} ₃₇₅₆ _{an,nn5043}   ₂₅₃₀   ₁₆₆₅   _{ipf2258} _{pr/an,aj4723} ₂₅₃₂

7 And they had no child, because that Elisabeth was barren, and they
_{an,ajn297} _{ipf2258}   _{pr/pfp4260}   _{pre1722 (ppro846)} _{art,nn2250}

both were *now* well stricken in years.
          ₁₁₆₁   _{aom1096}   _{ppro846}   _{aie2407}   _{ad*1725}

8 And it came*to*pass, that while he executed*the*priest's*office before
_{art,nn2316} _{pre1722 art3588}   _{nn5010}   _{ppro848} _{art,nn2183}

God in the order of his course,
          _{pre2596}   _{art3588}   _{nn1485}   _{art3588}   _{nn2405}   _{aina2975}

9 According to the custom of the priest's office, his lot was to
_{infg2370}   _{apta1525} _{pre1519 art3588}   _{nn3485}   _{art3588} _{nn2962}

burn incense when he went into the temple of the Lord.
          ₂₅₃₂   _{art3588} _{an,aj3956}   _{nn4128}   _{art3588} _{nn2992} _{ipf2258} _{ppmp4336}   _{ad1854}   _{art3588}

10 And the whole multitude of the people were praying without at the
_{nn5610}   _{art,nn2368}

time of incense.
          ₁₁₆₁   _{ainp3700}   _{ppro946}   _{an,nn32}   _{an,nn2962}   _{pfp2476}   _{pre1537}

11 And there appeared unto him an angel of the Lord standing on the
_{an,ajn1188}   _{art3588 nn2379}   _{art,nn2368}

right side of the altar of incense.
          ₂₅₃₂   _{an,nn2197}   _{apta1492}   _{ainp5015}   ₂₅₃₂ _{an,nn5401} _{aina1968} _{pre1909}

12 And when Zacharias saw *him,* he was troubled, and fear fell upon
_{ppro846}

him.
          ₁₁₆₁ _{art3588}   _{nn32}   _{aina2036}   _{pre4314} _{ppro846} _{pim5399}   ₃₃₆₁   _{an,nn2197}   ₁₃₆₀ _{ppro4675} _{art,nn1162}

13 But the angel said unto him, Fear not, Zacharias: for thy prayer is

ainp1522   2532 ppro4675 art,nn1135   1665   ft1080 ppro4671   an,nn5207 2532   ft2564 ppro846
heard; and thy wife Elisabeth shall bear thee a son, and thou shalt call his
art,nn3686 an,nn2491
name John.

2532 ppro4671   fm2071 an,nn5479 2532   an,nn20   2532 an,ajn4183   fm5463   pre1909 ppro846
14 And thou shalt have joy and gladness; and many shall rejoice at   his
art,nn1083
birth.

1063   fm2071 pr/an,aj3173   ad*1799   art3588 nn2962 2532   asba4095   efn3364
15 For he shall be   great in*the*sight of the Lord, and shall drink neither
an,nn3631 2532   an,nn4608   2532   fp4130   an,aj40 an,nn4151 ad2089 pre1537
wine nor strong drink; and he shall be filled with the Holy Ghost, even from
ppro848 an,nn3384 an,nn2836
his mother's womb.   *(Num. 6:3)*

2532 an,ajn4183   art3588   nn5207   2474   ft1994 pre1909   an,nn2062 ppro846
16 And many of the children of Israel shall he turn to   the Lord their
art,nn2316
God.

2532 epn846   fm4281 ad*1799 ppro846   an,nn4151 2532 an,nn1411   an,nn2243   ainf1994
17 And he shall go before him in the spirit and power of Elijah, to turn
an,nn2588   an,nn3962 pre1909   an,nn5043 2532   an,ajn545   pre1722
the hearts of the fathers to the children, and the disobedient to   the
an,nn5428   an,ajn1342   ainf2090   an,nn2992 pipp2860   an,nn2962
wisdom of the just; to make ready a people prepared for the Lord.

(Mal. 4:5,6)

2532   an,nn2197   aina2036 pre4314 art3588   nn32   pre2596/inpro5101   fm1097 depro5124 1063 epn1473
18 And Zacharias said unto the angel, Whereby shall I know this? for   I
pin1510   pr/an,nn4246 2532 ppro3450 art,nn1135 pfp4260   pre1722 (ppro848) art,nn2250
am an old man and my   wife well stricken in   years.

2532 art3588   nn32   aptp611   aina2036   ppro846 epn1473 pin1510   pr/1043   art,pfp3936
19 And the   angel answering said unto him,   I   am Gabriel, that stand
ad*1799   art,nn2316 2532   ainp649   ainf2980 pre4314 ppro4571   2532
in*the*presence of God; and am sent to speak unto thee, and to
aifm2097/ppro4671/depro5023
show*thee*these*glad*tidings.

2532   2400   fm2071 pr/pap4623 2532 3361 ppmp1410   ainf2980   ad891   (repro3739)
20 And, behold, thou shalt be dumb, and not able to speak, until the
an,nn2250   depro5023   asbm1096   pre473 (repro3739) aina4100   3756 ppro3450
day that these things shall be performed, because thou believest not my
art,nn3056 repro3748   fp4137 pre1519 ppro848 art,nn2540
words, which shall be fulfilled in   their season.

2532 art3588   nn2992   ipf2258/pap4328   art,nn2197   2532   ipf2296   ppro846
21 And the   people waited for Zacharias, and marveled that he
aie5549   pre1722 art3588   nn3485
tarried*so*long in   the temple.

1161   apta1831   ipf1410 3756 ainf2980   ppro846 2532
22 And when he came out, he could not speak unto them: and they
aina1921   3754   pfi3708   an,nn3701 pre1722 art3588   nn3485   2532 ppro846 ipf2258/pap1269
perceived that he had seen a vision in the temple: for he beckoned unto
ppro846 2532   ipf1265   pr/an,aj2974
them, and remained speechless.

23 And it came*to*pass, that, as*soon*as the days of his ministration were accomplished, he departed to his own house.

24 And after those days his wife Elisabeth conceived, and hid herself five months, saying,

25 Thus hath the Lord dealt with me in the days wherein he looked on *me,* to take away my reproach among men.

The Angel Appears to Mary

26 And in the sixth month the angel Gabriel was sent from God unto a city of Galilee, named Nazareth,

27 To a virgin espoused to a man whose name was Joseph, of the house of David; and the virgin's name *was* Mary.

28 And the angel came in unto her, and said, Hail, *thou that art* highly favored, the Lord *is* with thee: blessed *art* thou among women.

29 And when she saw *him,* she was troubled at his saying, and cast*in*her*mind what manner of salutation this should be.

30 And the angel said unto her, Fear not, Mary: for thou hast found favor with God.

31 And, behold, thou shalt conceive in thy womb, and bring forth a son, and shalt call his name JESUS.   (Is. 7:14)

32 He shall be great, and shall be called the Son of the Highest: and the Lord God shall give unto him the throne of his father David:

(2 Sam. 7:12)

33 And he shall reign over the house of Jacob forever; and of his kingdom there shall be no end.   (2 Sam. 7:13; Dan. 2:44)

1161 aina2036 3137 pre4314 art3588 nn32 ad4459 depro5124 fm2071 1893 pin1097 3756

34 Then said Mary unto the angel, How shall this be, seeing I know not

an,nn435

a man?

2532 art3588 nn32 aptp611 aina2036 ppro846 an,aj40 an,nn4151 fm1904

35 And the angel answered and said unto her, The Holy Ghost shall come

pre1909 ppro4571 2532 an,nn1411 an,ajn5310 ft1982 ppro4671 pre,repro1352

upon thee, and the power of the Highest shall overshadow thee: therefore

2532 art,ajn40 ppmp1080 pre1537 ppro4675 fp2564 pr/an,nn5207

also that holy thing which shall be born of thee shall be called the Son of

an,nn2316

God.

2532 2400 ppro4675 art,ajn4773 1665 epn846 2532 pfp4815 an,nn5207

36 And, behold, thy cousin Elisabeth, she hath also conceived a son

pre1722 ppro848 an,nn1094 2532 depro3778 pin2076 pr/an,nu,aj1622 an,nn3376 ppro846 art,ppmp2564

in her old age: and this is the sixth month with her, who*was*called

pr/an,aj4723

barren.

3754 pre3844 art,nn2316 an,aj3956/an,nn4487/3756 ft101

37 For with God nothing shall be impossible.   *(Gen. 18:14)*

1161 3137 aina2036 2400 art3588 nn1399 an,nn2962 opt1096 ppro3427

38 And Mary said, Behold the handmaid of the Lord; be it unto me

pre2596 ppro4675 art,nn4487 2532 art3588 nn32 aina565 pre575 ppro846

according to thy word. And the angel departed from her.

Mary Visits Elisabeth

1161 3137 apta450 pre1722 depro5025 art,nn2250 ainp4198 pre1519 art3588 ajn3714 pre3326

39 And Mary arose in those days, and went into the hill country with

an,nn4710 pre1519 an,nn4172 2448

haste, into a city of Judah;

2532 aina1525 pre1519 art3588 nn3624 an,nn2197 2532 aom782 1665

40 And entered into the house of Zacharias, and saluted Elisabeth.

2532 aom1096 ad5613 1665 aina191 art3588 nn783

41 And it came*to*pass, that, when Elisabeth heard the salutation of

art,nn3137 art3588 nn1025 aina4640 pre1722 ppro846 art,nn2836 2532 1665 ainp4130

Mary, the babe leaped in her womb; and Elisabeth was filled with the

an,aj40 an,nn4151

Holy Ghost:

2532 aina400 an,aj3173 an,nn5456 2532 aina2036 pr/pfpp2127 epn4771 pre1722

42 And she spake out with a loud voice, and said, Blessed *art* thou among

an,nn1135 2532 pr/pfpp2127 art3588 nn2590 ppro4675 art,nn2836

women, and blessed *is* the fruit of thy womb.

2532 ad4159 depro5124 ppro3427 2443 art3588 nn3384 ppro3450 art,nn2962 asba2064

43 And whence *is* this to me, that the mother of my Lord should come

pre4314 ppro3165

to me?

1063 2400 ad5613 art3588 nn5456 ppro4675 art,nn783 aom1096 pre1519 ppro3450

44 For, lo, as*soon*as the voice of thy salutation sounded in mine

art,nn3775 art3588 nn1025 aina4640 pre1722 ppro3450 art,nn2836 pre1722 an,nn20

ears, the babe leaped in   my womb for joy.

2532   pr/an,aj3107   art,apta4100   3754   fm2071   an,nn5050
45 And blessed *is* she*that*believed for there shall be a performance of
art,pfpp2980   ppro846 pre3844   an,nn2962
those*things*which*were*told her from the Lord.

Mary's Song of Praise

2532   3137   aina2036 ppro3450 art,nn5590   pin3170   art3588   nn2962
46 And Mary said, My soul doth magnify the Lord,
2532   ppro3450 art,nn4151   aina21   pre1909 art,nn2316 ppro3450 art,nn4990
47 And my spirit hath rejoiced in God my Savior.   *(1 Sam. 2:1)*

3754   aina1914   (pre1909) art3588   nn5014   ppro848   art,nn1399   1063   2400
☞ 48 For he hath regarded   the low estate of his handmaiden: for, behold,
pre575   art,ad3568   an,aj3956   art,nn1074   ft3106/ppro3165
from henceforth all generations shall call*me*blessed.

3754   art,ajn1415   aina4160   ppro3427   an,nn3167   2532   pr/an,aj40   ppro846
49 For he*that*is*mighty hath done to me great things; and holy *is* his
art,nn3686
name.

2532   ppro846   art,nn1656   art,ppmp5399   ppro846   pre1519   an,nn1074
50 And his mercy *is* on them*that*fear him from generation to
an,nn1074
generation.   *(Ps. 103:17)*

aina4160   an,nn2904   pre1722 ppro848 an,nn1023   aina1287   an,ajn5244
51 He hath showed strength with his arm; he hath scattered the proud in
an,nn1271   ppro846   an,nn2588
the imagination of their hearts.

aina2507   an,nn1413   pre575   an,nn2362   2532   aina5312
52 He hath put down the mighty from *their* seats, and exalted
an,ajn5011
them*of*low*degree.

aina1705   an,pap3983   an,ajn18   2532   an,pap4147
53 He hath filled the hungry with good things; and the rich he
aina1821/an,aj2756
hath sent*empty*away.   *(Ps. 107:9)*

☞ **1:48** This verse contains one of the most misunderstood words of the NT. It is the word *makários* which is used repeatedly in the Beatitudes. The verb form that corresponds to the adjective *makários*, "blessed" (*makarízō* [3106]), is used here. The translation says "all generations shall call me blessed," but the Greek says *makarioúsi*, the future of *makarízō*, which in reality means "they shall bless me." In James 5:11, the verb *makarízō* is totally mistranslated as ". . . we count them happy which endure . . . ." Happiness has absolutely nothing to do with *makariótēs*, "blessedness," an inner quality granted by God. The Greek words for "happiness," in the Classic writings, *eudaímōn* and *eutuchés*, "lucky," never occur in the NT. The Lord never promised good luck or favorable circumstances to the believer, but *makariótēs*, "blessedness." See note on Matthew 5:1–12.

One should note that the word translated "blessed" in verse forty-two is not *makária*, but is a totally different word, *eulogēménē* (2127), which in its literal meaning is "eulogized, well spoken of." When one blesses (*eulogéō*) God, he is speaking well of Him, which is equal to praising or thanking Him. When, however, a person asks God to bless another, he is not asking Him to approve the plans that have been made, but to use providence and the work of the Holy Spirit to affect his heart and life.

^{aom482} ^{ppro848} ^{an,nn3816} ²⁴⁷⁴ ^{aifp3415} ^{an,nn1656}

54 He hath helped his servant Israel, in remembrance of *his* mercy;

^{ad2531} ^{aina2980} ^{pre4314} ^{ppro2257} ^{art,nn3962} ¹¹ ²⁵³² ^{ppro846} ^{art,nn4690}

55 As he spake to our fathers, to Abraham, and to his seed

^{pre1519/art,nn165}

forever.

¹¹⁶¹ ³¹³⁷ ^{aina3306} ^{pre4862} ^{ppro846} ^{ad5616} ^{nu5140} ^{an,nn3376} ²⁵³² ^{aina5290} ^{pre1519}

56 And Mary abode with her about three months, and returned to

^{ppro848} ^{art,nn3624}

her own house.

John Is Born

¹¹⁶¹ ¹⁶⁶⁵ ^{art,nn5550} ^{ainp4130} ^{ppro846} ^{infg5088} ²⁵³²

57 Now Elisabeth's full time came that she should be delivered; and she

^{aina1080} ^{an,nn5207}

brought forth a son.

²⁵³² ^{ppro848} ^{art,nn4040} ²⁵³² ^{art,ajn4773} ^{aina191} ³⁷⁵⁴ ^{an,nn2962}

58 And her neighbors and her cousins heard how the Lord had

^{aina3170/ppro848/art,nn1656} ^{pre3326} ^{ppro846} ²⁵³² ^{ipf4796} ^{ppro846}

showed*great*mercy upon her; and they rejoiced with her.

²⁵³² ^{aom1096} ^{pre1722} ^{art3588} ^{nu,aj3590} ^{an,nn2250} ^{aina2064}

59 And it came*to*pass, that on the eighth day they came to

^{ainf4059} ^{art3588} ⁿⁿ³⁸¹³ ²⁵³² ^{ipf2564} ^{ppro846} ^{an,nn2197} ^{pre1909} ^{art3588} ⁿⁿ³⁶⁸⁶ ^{ppro846}

circumcise the child; and they called him Zacharias, after the name of his

^{art,nn3962}

father.   *(Lev. 12:3)*

²⁵³² ^{ppro846} ^{art,nn3384} ^{aptp611} ^{aina2036} ³⁷⁸⁰ ²³⁵ ^{fp2564}

60 And his mother answered and said, Not *so*; but he shall be called

^{an,nn2491}

John.

²⁵³² ^{aina2036} ^{pre4314} ^{ppro846} ^{pin2076} ^{an,ajn3762} ^{pre1722} ^{ppro4675} ^{art,nn4772} ^{repro3739}

61 And they said unto her, There is none of thy kindred that is

^{pinp2564} ^{depro5129} ^{art,nn3686}

called by this name.

²⁵³² ^{ipf1770} ^{ppro846} ^{art,nn3962} ^{art,inpro5101} ^{opt2309/302} ^{ppro846} ^{pip2564}

62 And they made signs to his father, how he would have him called.

²⁵³² ^{apta154} ^{an,nn4093} ^{aina1125} ^{pap3004} ^{ppro846} ^{art,nn3686} ^{pin2076}

63 And he asked for a writing table, and wrote, saying, His name is

^{pr/an,nn2491} ²⁵³² ^{aina2296} ^{an,ajn3956}

John. And they marveled all.

¹¹⁶¹ ^{ppro846} ^{art,nn4750} ^{ainp455} ^{ad3916} ²⁵³² ^{ppro846} ^{art,nn1100} ²⁵³²

64 And his mouth was opened immediately, and his tongue *loosed,* and he

^{ipf2980} ^{pap2127} ^{art,nn2316}

spake, and praised God.

²⁵³² ^{an,nn5401} ^{aom1096} ^{pre1909} ^{an,aj3956} ^{art,pap4039} ^{ppro846} ²⁵³² ^{an,aj3956}

65 And fear came on all that*dwelt*round*about them: and all

^{depro5023} ^{art,nn4487} ^{ipf1255} ^{pre1722} ^{an,aj3650} ^{art3588} ^{ajn3714} ^{art,nn2449}

these sayings were noised abroad throughout all the hill country of Judea.

66 And   all   they*that*heard *them* laid*them*up   in   their hearts, saying,
What manner of   child shall   this   be! And the hand of the Lord was with him.

The Prophecy of Zacharias

67 And   his   father Zacharias   was   filled   with   the   Holy   Ghost,   and
prophesied, saying,

68 Blessed *be* the Lord   God   of Israel; for he hath visited and redeemed
his people,   *(Ps. 41:13; 72:18; 106:4; Is. 63:9; Zech. 10:3)*

69 And hath raised up a   horn   of salvation for   us   in   the house of his
servant David;   *(Ps. 18:2; 132:17)*

70 As   he   spake   by   the mouth of   his   holy prophets, which have been
since*the*world*began:

71 That we   should   be   saved from   our   enemies, and from the   hand of
all   that hate   us;   *(Ex. 3:8; 2 Kgs. 17:39; Is. 33:22)*

72 To   perform   the   mercy *promised*   to   our   fathers, and to remember
his holy covenant;   *(Ps. 106:45)*

73 The   oath   which he sware   to   our   father Abraham,

74 That he   would   grant unto   us,   that we being delivered out of the hand
of our enemies might serve him without fear,

75 In   holiness   and   righteousness before   him,   all   the   days   of   our
life.

76 And thou, child, shalt be called the prophet of the Highest: for thou shalt
go   before   the   face   of the Lord to prepare   his   ways;   *(Is. 40:3; Mal. 3:1)*

77 To   give   knowledge   of salvation unto   his   people   by   the   remission of
their sins,

^{pre1223}   ^{an,nn4698/an,nn1656}   ^{ppro2257 an,nn2316}   ^{pre1722/repro3739}   ^{an,nn395}   ^{pre1537}

78 Through the tender mercy of our God; whereby the dayspring from

^{an,nn5311}   ^{aom1980}   ^{ppro2248}

on high hath visited us,

^{ainf2014}   ^{art,ppmp2521}   ^{pre1722}   ^{an,nn4655}   ²⁵³²   ^{an,nn4639}

79 To give light to them*that*sit in darkness and *in* the shadow of

^{an,nn2288}   ^{infg2720 ppro2257 art,nn4228 pre1519}   ^{an,nn3598}   ^{an,nn1515}

death, to guide our feet into the way of peace.   *(Is. 9:2; 58:8; 60:1,2)*

¹¹⁶¹   ^{art3588}   ⁿⁿ³⁸¹³   ^{ipf837}   ²⁵³²   ^{ipf2901}   ^{an,nn4151}   ²⁵³²   ^{ipf2258 pre1722 art3588}

80 And the child grew, and waxed strong in spirit, and was in the

^{ajn2048}   ^{ad2193}   ^{an,nn2250}   ^{ppro846}   ^{an,nn323}   ^{pre4314}   ²⁴⁷⁴

deserts till the day of his showing unto Israel.

The Birth of Jesus (Matt. 1:18-25)

¹¹⁶¹   ^{aom1096}   ^{pre1722 depro1565 art,nn2250}   ^{aina1831}   ^{an,nn1378}   ^{pre3844}

2 And it came*to*pass in those days, that there went out a decree from

^{an,nn2541}   ^{an,nn828}   ^{an,aj3956 art3588 nn3625}   ^{pip583}

Caesar Augustus, that all the world should be taxed.

^{depro3778}   ^{art,nn582}   ^{nu,aj4413 aom1096}   ^{an,nn2598}   ^{pap2230}

2 (*And* this taxing was first made when Cyrenius was governor of

^{art,nn4947}

Syria.)

^{2532 an,ajn3956 ipf4198}   ^{pip583}   ^{an,ajn1538}   ^{pre1519}   ^{art,aj2398}   ^{an,nn4172}

3 And all went to be taxed, every one into his own city.

¹¹⁶¹   ²⁵⁰¹   ²⁵³²   ^{aina305}   ^{pre575}   ^{art,nn1056}   ^{pre1537}   ^{an,nn4172}   ³⁴⁷⁸   ^{pre1519}

4 And Joseph also went up from Galilee, out of the city of Nazareth, into

^{art,nn2449}   ^{pre1519}   ^{an,nn4172}   ¹¹³⁸   ^{repro3748}   ^{pinp2564}   ⁹⁶⁵   ^{ppro846}   ^{aid1511}

Judea, unto the city of David, which is called Bethlehem; (because he was

^{pre1537}   ^{an,nn3624 2532}   ^{an,nn3965}   ¹¹³⁸

of the house and lineage of David:)

^{aifm583}   ^{pre4862}   ³¹³⁷   ^{ppro846}   ^{art,pfpp3423}   ^{art,nn1135 pap5607}   ^{pr/an,aj1471}

5 To be taxed with Mary his espoused wife, being great*with*child.

¹¹⁶¹   ^{aom1096}   ^{ppro846 aie1511}   ^{ad1563}   ^{art3588 nn2250}   ^{ainp4130}

6 And so it was, that, while they were there, the days were accomplished

^{ppro846}   ^{infg5088}

that she should be delivered.

²⁵³²   ^{aina5088}   ^{ppro848}   ^{art,aj4416}   ^{art,nn5207}   ²⁵³²

☞ 7 And she brought forth her firstborn son, and

^{aina4683/ppro846}   ^{2532 aina347 ppro846 pre1722}   ^{art,nn5336}   ¹³⁶⁰

wrapped*him*in*swaddling*clothes, and laid him in a manger; because there

^{ipf2258 3756 an,nn5117}   ^{ppro846 pre1722 art3588 nn2646}

was no room for them in the inn.

The Shepherds and the Angels

²⁵³²   ^{ipf2258 pre1722 art3588 ppro846}   ^{art,nn5561}   ^{an,nn4166}   ^{pap63}   ⁽²⁵³²⁾

8 And there were in the same country shepherds abiding*in*the*field,

^{pap5442}   ^{an,nn5438 pre1909 ppro848 art,nn4167}   ^{art,nn3571}

keeping watch over their flock by night.

☞ **2:7** See note on Colossians 1:15–18.

2532 2400   an,nn32   an,nn2962   aina2186   ppro846 2532   an,nn1391
9 And, lo, the angel of the Lord came upon them, and the glory of the

an,nn2962   aina4034   ppro846 2532   ainp5399/an,aj3173/an,nn5401
Lord shone*round*about them: and they were*sore*afraid.

2532 art3588 nn32 aina2036   ppro846 pim5399 3361 1063   2400
10 And the angel said unto them, Fear not: for, behold, I

pinm2097/ppro5213 an,aj3173 an,nn5479 repro3748   fm2071   an,aj3956 art,nn2992
bring*you*good*tidings of great joy, which shall be to all people.

3754   ppro5213   ainp5088 ad4594 pre1722 an,nn4172 1138   an,nn4990 repro3739
11 For unto you is born this day in the city of David a Savior, which

pin2076 pr/an,nn5547   an,nn2962
is Christ the Lord.

2532   pr/depro5124   art,nn4592   ppro5213   ft2147   an,nn1025
12 And this *shall be* a sign unto you; Ye shall find the babe

pfpp4683   ppmp2749 pre1722 art,nn5336
wrapped*in*swaddling*clothes, lying in a manger.

2532   ad1810   aom1096 pre4862 art3588 nn32   an,nn4128   an,aj3770
13 And suddenly there was with the angel a multitude of the heavenly

an,nn4756 pap134 art,nn2316 2532   pap3004
host praising God, and saying,

an,nn1391   an,nn2316 pre1722   an,ajn5310 2532 pre1909 an,nn1093 an,nn1515 an,nn2107   pre1722
14 Glory to God in the highest, and on earth peace, good will toward

an,nn444
men.

2532   aom1096   ad5613 art3588   nn32   aina565   pre575 ppro846 pre1519
15 And it came*to*pass, as the angels were gone away from them into

art,nn3772 (art,nn444) art3588 nn4166 aina2036 rcpro240/pre4314   aosi1330 1211 ad2193
heaven, the shepherds said one*to*another, Let us now go even unto

965   2532 aosi1492 depro5124 art,nn4487   art,pfp1096   repro3739 art3588 nn2962
Bethlehem, and see this thing which*is*come*to*pass, which the Lord hath

aina1107   ppro2254
made known unto us.

2532   aina2064   apta4692 2532 aina429 (5037) 3137 2532   2501   2532 art3588 nn1025
16 And they came with haste, and found Mary, and Joseph, and the babe

ppmp2749 pre1722   art,nn5336
lying in a manger.

1161   apta1492   aina1232 (pre4012) art3588 nn4487
17 And when they had seen *it*, they made*known*abroad the saying

art,apta2980   ppro846   pre4012   depro5127 art,nn3813
which*was*told them concerning this child.

2532   an,aj3956   art,apta191   aina2296   pre4012
18 And all they*that*heard *it* wondered at

art,apta2980   ppro846 pre5259 art3588   nn4166
those*things*which*were*told them by the shepherds.

1161   3137   ipf4933 an,aj3956 depro5023 art,nn4487   pre1722 ppro848 art,nn2588
19 But Mary kept all these things, and pondered *them* in her heart.

2532 art3588   nn4166   aina1994   pap1392 2532 pap134 art,nn2316 pre1909 an,ajn3956
20 And the shepherds returned, glorifying and praising God for all the

repro3739   aina191 2532 aina1492 ad2531   ainp2980 pre4314 ppro846
things that they had heard and seen, as it was told unto them.

2532   ad3753 nu3638 an,nn2250   ainp4130   infg4059   art3588
21 And when eight days were accomplished for the circumcising of the

nn3813   (2532) ppro846 art,nn3686   ainp2564   an,nn2424   art,aptp2564   pre5259 art3588   nn32
child,   his name was called JESUS, which*was*so*named   of   the angel

pre4253 ppro846   infg4815   pre1722 art3588   nn2836
before he   was conceived in   the womb.   *(Lev. 12:3)*

Jesus Is Dedicated in the Temple

2532   ad3753   art3588   nn2250   ppro846   art,nn2512   pre2596   art3588 nn3551   an,nn3475
22 And when the days of her purification according to the law of Moses

ainp4130   aina321   ppro846 pre1519   an,nn2414   ainf3936   art3588
were accomplished, they brought him   to   Jerusalem, to present *him* to the

nn2962
Lord;   *(Lev. 12:6)*

ad2531   pfip1125   pre1722   an,nn3551   an,nn2962 an,aj3956 an,nn730   pap1272
23 (As it is written in   the   law of the Lord Every male that openeth the

an,nn3388   fp2564   an,aj40   art3588 nn2962
womb shall be called holy to the Lord;)   *(Ex. 13:2,12,15)*

2532   infg1325   an,nn2378   pre2596   art,pfpp2046   pre1722   an,nn3551
24 And to offer a sacrifice according to that*which*is*said in   the   law of

an,nn2962   an,nn2201   an,nn5167   2228 nu1417 an,nn3502   an,nn4058
the Lord, A pair of turtledoves, or two young pigeons.   *(Lev. 12:8)*

2532   2400   ipf2258   an,nn444 pre1722   2419   repro3739 an,nn3686
25 And, behold, there was a man in   Jerusalem, whose name *was*

pr/4826   2532   depro3778   art,nn444   pr/an,aj1342 2532   pr/an,aj2126   pr/ppmp4327   an,nn3874
Simeon; and the same man *was*   just   and devout, waiting for the consolation

2474   2532   an,aj40   an,nn4151 ipf2258 pre1909 ppro846
of Israel: and the Holy Ghost was upon him.   *(Is. 40:1; 49:13)*

2532   ipf2258   pfpp5537   ppro846 pre5259 art3588   aj40   art,nn4151   3361
26 And it was revealed unto him by   the Holy Ghost, that he should not

ainf1492 an,nn2288   ad4250   asba1492   an,nn2962 art,nn5547
see death, before he had seen the Lord's Christ.

2532   aina2064 pre1722 art3588   nn4151   pre1519 art3588   nn2411   2532   art3588   nn1118
27 And he came by   the Spirit into the temple: and when the parents

aie1521   art3588 nn3813   an,nn2424   infg4160 pre4012 ppro846 pre2596 art3588   pfpp1480   art3588 nn3551
brought in the child Jesus, to   do   for him after the custom of the law,

2532   aom1209/ppro846/ppro846   pre1519 ppro848   art,nn43   2532   aina2127   art,nn2316 2532 aina2036
28 Then took*he*him*up in   his arms, and blessed God, and said,

an,nn1203   ad3588   ppro4675   art,ajn1401   pin630   pre1722 an,nn1515   pre2596
29 Lord, now lettest thou thy   servant depart in   peace, according to

ppro4675 art,nn4487
thy word:

3754   ppro3450 art,nn3778   aina1492 ppro4675   art,ajn4992
30 For mine eyes have seen thy salvation,

repro3739   aina2090   pre2596   an,nn4383   an,aj3956   art,nn2992
31 Which thou hast prepared before the face of   all   people;

an,nn5457 pre1519   an,nn602   an,nn1484   2532   an,nn1391   ppro4675 an,nn2992   2474
32 A light   to lighten the Gentiles, and the glory of thy people Israel.

(Is. 42:6; 46:13; 49:6)

33 And   Joseph   and   his   mother   marveled   at

those*things*which*were*spoken of him.

34 And Simeon blessed them, and said unto Mary his mother, Behold,

this *child* is set for the fall and rising again of many in Israel; and for a

sign which shall be spoken against;   *(Is. 8:14)*

35 (Yea,   a   sword shall pierce through thy own soul also,) that the

thoughts of many hearts may be revealed.

36 And there was one Anna, a prophetess, the daughter of Phanuel, of

the tribe of Asher: she was*of*a*great*age, and had lived with a husband

seven years from her virginity;

37 And she *was* a widow of about fourscore*and*and*four years, which

departed not from the temple, but served *God* with fastings and prayers night

and day.

38 And she coming in*that*instant gave thanks likewise unto the Lord,

and spake of him to all them*that*looked*for redemption in Jerusalem.

(Is. 52:9)

The Return to Nazareth

39 And when they had performed all things according to the law of the

Lord, they returned into Galilee, to their own city Nazareth.

40 And the child grew, and waxed strong in spirit, filled with wisdom: and

the grace of God was upon him.

Jesus Speaks With the Leaders in the Temple

41 Now his parents went to Jerusalem every year at the feast of the

passover.   *(Ex. 12:24-27; 23:14,15; Deut. 16:1-8)*

42 And when he was twelve*years*old, they went up to Jerusalem after the custom of the feast.

43 And when they had fulfilled the days, as they returned, the child Jesus tarried behind in Jerusalem; and Joseph and his mother knew not *of it.*

44 But they, supposing him to have been in the company, went a day's journey; and they sought him among *their* kinsfolk and acquaintance.

45 And when they found him not, they turned*back*again to Jerusalem, seeking him.

46 And it came*to*pass, that after three days they found him in the temple, sitting in the midst of the doctors, both hearing them, and asking*them*questions.

47 And all that heard him were astonished at his understanding and answers.

48 And when they saw him, they were amazed: and his mother said unto him, Son, why hast thou thus dealt with us? behold, thy father and I have sought thee sorrowing.

49 And he said unto them, How is it that ye sought me? wist ye not that I must be about my Father's business?

50 And they understood not the saying which he spake unto them.

51 And he went down with them, and came to Nazareth, and was subject unto them: but his mother kept all these sayings in her heart.

52 And Jesus increased in wisdom and stature, and in favor with God and man.

(1 Sam. 2:26; Prov. 3:4)

John the Baptist Preaches (Matt. 3:1-12; Mark 1:1-8; John 1:19-28)

1161 pre1722   an,nu,aj4003   an,nn2094   art3588   nn2231   an,nn5086   an,nn2541   an,nn4194

3 Now in the fifteenth year of the reign of Tiberius Caesar, Pontius

an,nn4091   pap2230   art,nn2449   2532   an,nn2264   pap5075   art,nn1056

Pilate being governor of Judea, and Herod being tetrarch of Galilee,

1161   ppro846   art,nn80   an,nn5376   pap5075   art,nn2484   2532   an,nn5561   an,aj5139

and his brother Philip tetrarch of Ituraea and of the region of Trachonitis,

2532   an,nn3078   pap5075   art,nn9

and Lysanias the tetrarch of Abilene,

an,nn452   2532   an,nn2533   pre1909/an,nn749   an,nn4487   an,nn2316   aom1096

2 Annas and Caiaphas being*the*high*priests, the word of God came

pre1909 an,nn2491 art3588 nn5207   art,nn2197   pre2197 art3588   ajn2048

unto John the son of Zacharias in the wilderness.

2532   aina2064 pre1519 an,aj3956 art3588   nn4066   art,nn2446   pap2784   an,nn908

3 And he came into all the country about Jordan, preaching the baptism

an,nn3341   pre1519   an,nn859   an,nn266

of repentance for the remission of sins;

ad5613   pfip1125   pre1722   an,nn976   an,nn3056   an,nn2268 art3588   nn4396

4 As it is written in the book of the words of Isaiah the prophet,

pap3004   an,nn5456   pap994   pre1722 art3588   ajn2048   aima2090   art3588 nn3598

saying, The voice of one crying in the wilderness, Prepare ye the way of the

an,nn2962 pim4160 ppro846 art,nn5147 pr/an,aj2117

Lord, make his paths straight.

an,aj3956   an,nn5327   fp4137   2532   an,aj3956   an,nn3735   2532   an,nn1015

5 Every valley shall be filled, and every mountain and hill shall be

fp5013   2532 art3588   ajn4646   fm2071 (pre1519)   an,ajn2117   2532 art3588   ajn5138

brought low; and the crooked shall be made straight, and the rough ways

(pre1519 an,nn3598)   an,aj3006

shall be made smooth;

2532   an,aj3956 an,nn4561   fm3700 art3588   ajn4992   art,nn2316

6 And all flesh shall see the salvation of God.   *(Is. 40:3-5)*

3767   ipf3004   an,nn3793   art,ppmp1607   aifp907   pre5259 ppro846

7 Then said he to the multitude that*came*forth to be baptized of him, O

an,nn1081   an,nn2191   inpro5101   aina5263   ppro5213   ainf5343 pre575 art3588   nn3709   an,pap3195

generation of vipers, who hath warned you to flee from the wrath to come?

(Zeph. 1:14,15)

aima4160   3767   an,nn2590   an,aj514   art,nn3341   2532   aosi756   3361   pinf3004

8 Bring forth therefore fruits worthy of repentance, and begin not to say

pre1722   rxpro1438   pin2192   11   an,nn3962   1063   pin3004   ppro5213   3754

within yourselves, We have Abraham to *our* father: for I say unto you, That

art,nn2316   pinm1410   pre1537 depro5130 art,nn3037   ainf1453   an,nn5043   11

God is able of these stones to raise up children unto Abraham.

1161   ad2235   2532   art3588   nn513   pinm2749 pre4314 art3588   nn4491   art3588   nn1186   an,aj3956   an,nn1186

9 And now also the axe is laid unto the root of the trees: every tree

3767   pap4160/3361   an,aj2570 an,nn2590   pinp1581   2532   pinp906 pre1519

therefore which bringeth*not*forth good fruit is hewn down, and cast into the

an,nn4442

fire.

10 And the people asked him, saying, What shall we do then?

11 He answereth and saith unto them, He*that*hath two coats, let him impart to him*that*hath none; and he*that*hath meat, let him do likewise.

12 Then came also publicans to be baptized, and said unto him, Master, what shall we do?

13 And he said unto them, Exact no more than that*which*is*appointed you.

14 And the soldiers likewise demanded of him, saying, And what shall we do? And he said unto them, Do violence to no man, neither accuse*any*falsely; and be content with your wages.

15 And as the people were*in*expectation, and all men mused in their hearts of John, whether*he*were*the*Christ,*or*not;

☞ 16 John answered, saying unto *them* all, I indeed baptize you with water; but one mightier than I cometh, the latchet of whose shoes I am not worthy to unloose: he shall baptize you with the Holy Ghost and with fire:

17 Whose fan *is* in his hand, and he will thoroughly purge his floor, and will gather the wheat into his garner; but the chaff he will burn with fire unquenchable.

18 And many other things in his exhortation preached he unto the people.

19 But Herod the tetrarch, being reproved by him for Herodias his brother Philip's wife, and for all the evils which Herod had done,

20 Added yet this above all, that he shut up John in prison.

☞ **3:16** See note on Acts 1:5.

John Baptizes Jesus (Matt. 3:13-17; Mark 1:9-11)

1161   an,aj537 art3588   nn2992   aie907   aom1096   an,nn2424
21 Now when all the people were baptized, it came*to*pass, that Jesus
2532   aptp907 2532   ppmp4336 art3588   nn3772   aifp455
also being baptized, and praying, the heaven was opened,

2532   an,nn5456 aifm1096 art,nn4151   ainf2597   an,aj4984 an,nn1491 ad5616   an,nn4058 pre1909 ppro846
22 And the Holy Ghost descended in a bodily shape like a dove upon him,
2532   an,nn5456 aifm1096 pre1537 an,nn3772   pap3004 epn4771 pin1488 ppro3450   art,aj27   pr/art,nn5207 pre1722
and a voice came from heaven, which said, Thou art my beloved Son; in
epn4671   aina2106
thee I am*well*pleased.   *(Ps. 2:7; Is. 42:1)*

The Genealogy of Jesus (Matt. 1:1-17)

2532   art,nn2424 epn846   ppmp756   ipf2258   ad5616   pr/nu5144/an,nn2094   pap5607 ad5613
23 And Jesus himself began to be about thirty*years*of*age being (as was
ipf3543   pr/an,nn5207 2501   2242
supposed) the   son   of Joseph, which was *the son* of Heli,
3158   3018
24 Which was *the son* of Matthat, which was *the son* of Levi, which was *the*
3197   2388   2501
son of Melchi, which was *the son* of Janna, which was *the son* of Joseph,
art,nn3161   301
25 Which was *the son* of Mattathias, which was *the son* of Amos, which was
3486   2069   3477
the son of Naum, which was *the son* of Esli, which was *the son* of Nagge,
3092   art,nn3161
26 Which was *the son* of Maath, which was *the son* of Mattathias, which
4584   2501   art,nn2455
was *the son* of Semei, which was *the son* of Joseph, which was *the son* of Judah,
2490   4488
27 Which was *the son* of Joanna, which was *the son* of Rhesa, which was *the*
2216   4528   3518
son of Zorobabel, which was *the son* of Salathiel, which was *the son* of Neri,
3197   78
28 Which was *the son* of Melchi, which was *the son* of Addi, which was *the*
2973   1678   2262
son of Cosam, which was *the son* of Elmodam, which was *the son* of Er,
2499   1663
29 Which was *the son* of Jose, which was *the son* of Eliezer, which was *the*
2497   3158   3018
son of Jorim, which was *the son* of Matthat, which was *the son* of Levi,
4826   art,nn2455
30 Which was *the son* of Simeon, which was *the son* of Judah, which was *the*
2501   2494   1662
son of Joseph, which was *the son* of Jonan, which was *the son* of Eliakim,
3190   3104
31 Which was *the son* of Melea, which was *the son* of Menan, which was *the*
3160   3481   1138
son of Mattatha, which was *the son* of Nathan, which was *the son* of David,

32 Which was *the son* of Jesse, which was *the son* of Obed, which was *the son* of Boaz, which was *the son* of Salmon, which was *the son* of Naasson,

33 Which was *the son* of Aminadab, which was *the son* of Aram, which was *the son* of Esrom, which was *the son* of Phares, which was *the son* of Judah,

34 Which was *the son* of Jacob, which was *the son* of Isaac, which was *the son* of Abraham, which was *the son* of Thara, which was *the son* of Nachor,

35 Which was *the son* of Saruch, which was *the son* of Ragau, which was *the son* of Phalec, which was *the son* of Heber, which was *the son* of Sala,

36 Which was *the son* of Cainan, which was *the son* of Arphaxad, which was *the son* of Shem, which was *the son* of Noah, which was *the son* of Lamech,

37 Which was *the son* of Methuselah, which was *the son* of Enoch, which was *the son* of Jared, which was *the son* of Maleleel, which was *the son* of Cainan,

38 Which was *the son* of Enos, which was *the son* of Seth, which was *the son* of Adam, which was *the son* of God.

The Devil Tempts Jesus (Matt. 4:1-11; Mark 1:12,13)

4 And Jesus being full of the Holy Ghost returned from Jordan, and was led by the Spirit into the wilderness,

2 Being forty days tempted of the devil. And in those days he did eat nothing: and when they were ended, he afterward hungered.

3 And the devil said unto him, If thou be the Son of God, command this stone that it be made bread.

4 And Jesus answered him, saying, It is written, That man shall not live by bread alone, but by every word of God.   *(Deut. 8:3)*

5 And the devil, taking*him*up into a high mountain, showed unto him all the kingdoms of the world in a moment of time.

6 And the devil said unto him, All this power will I give thee, and the glory of them: for that is delivered unto me; and to whomsoever I will I give it.

7 If thou therefore wilt worship me, all shall be thine.

8 And Jesus answered and said unto him, Get thee behind me, Satan: for it is written, Thou shalt worship the Lord thy God, and him only shalt thou serve. *(Deut. 6:13,14)*

9 And he brought him to Jerusalem, and set him on a pinnacle of the temple, and said unto him, If thou be the Son of God, cast thyself down from hence:

10 For it*is*written, He shall give*his*angels*charge over thee, to keep thee:

11 And in *their* hands they shall bear*thee*up, lest*at*any*time thou dash thy foot against a stone. *(Ps. 91:11,12)*

12 And Jesus answering said unto him, It is said, Thou shalt not tempt the Lord thy God. *(Deut. 6:16)*

13 And when the devil had ended all the temptation, he departed from him for*a*season.

Jesus Teaches the Scriptures (Matt. 4:12-17; Mark 1:14,15)

14 And Jesus returned in the power of the Spirit into Galilee: and there went out a fame of him through all the region*round*about.

15 And he taught in their synagogues, being glorified of all.

Jesus' Rejection at Nazareth (Matt. 13:53-58; Mark 6:1-6)

2532   aina2064   pre1519   3478   repro3757   ipf2258   pfpp5142   2532   pre2596

16 And he came to Nazareth, where he had been brought up: and, as

ppro846   art,pfp1486   aina1525   pre1519   art3588   nn4864   pre1722   art3588   nn4521   art,nn2250   2532

his custom was, he went into the synagogue on the sabbath day, and

aina450   ainf314

stood up for to read.

2532   ainp1929   ppro846   an,nn975   art3588   nn4396   an,nn2268   2532

17 And there was delivered unto him the book of the prophet Isaiah. And

apta380   art3588   nn975   aina2147   art3588   nn5117   repro3757   ipf2258   pfpp1125

when he had opened the book, he found the place where it was written,

an,nn4151   an,nn2962   pre1909   ppro1691   repro3757/ad˙1752   aina5548   ppro3165

18 The Spirit of the Lord *is* upon me, because he hath anointed me to

pifm2097   an,ajn4434   pfi649   ppro3165   aifm2390   art3588   pfpp4937/art,nn2588

preach*the*gospel to the poor; he hath sent me to heal the brokenhearted,

ainf2784   an,nn859   an,nn164   2532   an,nn309   an,ajn5185

to preach deliverance to the captives, and recovering*of*sight to the blind, to

ainf649   pre1722   an,nn859   an,pfpp2352

set at liberty them*that*are*bruised,

ainf2784   an,aj1184   an,nn1763   an,nn2962

19 To preach the acceptable year of the Lord.   *(Is. 58:6; 61:1,2)*

2532   apta4428   art3588   nn975   apta591   art3588   nn5257

20 And he closed the book, and he gave*it*again to the minister, and

aina2523   2532   art3588   nn3788   an,ajn3956   pre1722   art3588   nn4864   ipf2258

sat down. And the eyes of all them that were in the synagogue were

pap816   ppro846

fastened on him.

1161   aom756   pinf3004   pre4314   ppro846   ad4594   depro3778   art,nn1124   pfip4137

21 And he began to say unto them, This day is this Scripture fulfilled

pre1722 ppro5216 art,nn3775

in your ears.

2532   an,ajn3956   ipf3140/ppro846   2532   ipf2296   pre1909 art3588   nn5485   art,nn3056

22 And all bare*him*witness, and wondered at the gracious words

art,ppmp1607   pre1537   ppro846   art,nn4750   2532   ipf3004   pin2076   3756   depro3778   2501

which proceeded out of his mouth. And they said, Is not this Joseph's

pr/art,nn5207

son?

2532   aina2036   pre4314   ppro846   ad3843   ft2046   ppro3427   depro5026   art,nn3850

23 And he said unto them, Ye will surely say unto me this proverb,

an,nn2395   aina2323   rxpro4572   an,ajn3745   aina191   aptm1096   pre1722   2584   aima4160

Physician, heal thyself: whatsoever we have heard done in Capernaum, do

2532   ad5602   pre1722 ppro4675   art,nn3968

also here in thy country.

1161   aina2036   281   pin3004   ppro5213 an,aj3762   an,nn4396   pin2076   pr/an,aj1184   pre1722

24 And he said, Verily I say unto you, No prophet is accepted in

ppro848   art,nn3968

his own country,

1161   pin3004 ppro5213 pre1909   an,nn225   an,aj4183   an,nn5503   ipf2258   pre1722   2474   pre1722 art3588 nn2250

25 But I tell you of a truth, many widows were in Israel in the days

an,nn2243   ad3753   art3588   nn3772   ainp2008   (pre1909)   nu5140   an,nn2094   2532   nu1803   an,nn3376   ad5613

of Elijah, when the heaven was shut up   three years and six months, when

an,aj3173 an,nn3042 aom1096   pre1909   an,aj3956 art3588 nn1093
great famine was throughout all the land;   *(1 Kgs. 17:1,7)*

        2532 pre4314 an,ajn3762   pppro846   an,nn2243 ainp3992 1508 pre1519 an,nn4558
26 But unto none of them was Elijah sent, save unto Sarepta, *a city* of

art,nn4605 pre4314 an,nn1135   an,nn5503
Sidon, unto a woman *that was* a widow.   *(1 Kgs. 17:9)*

        2532 an,aj4183 an,nn3015 ipf2258 pre1722   2474   pre1909   an,nn1666 art3588   nn4396
27 And many lepers were in Israel in*the*time of Elisha the prophet;

2532 an,ajn3762   pppro846   ainp2511   1508   3497   art3588 aj4948
and none of them was cleansed, saving Naaman the Syrian.   *(2 Kgs. 5:1-4)*

        2532 an,ajn3956   pre1722 art3588   nn4864   pap191   depro5023
28 And all they in the synagogue, when they heard these things, were

ainp4130   an,nn2372
filled with wrath,

        2532   apta450   aina1544 pppro846 ad*1854 art3588 nn4172 2532 aina71 pppro846 ad2193 art3588
29 And rose up, and thrust him out of the city, and led him unto the

nn3790   art3588   nn3735   pre1909/repro3739 pppro846 art,nn4172   pipf3618
brow of the hill whereon their city was built, that they might

     aies2630/pppro846
cast*him*down*headlong.

        1161 epn846   apta1330   pre1223   an,ajn3319   pppro846   ipf4198
30 But he passing through the midst of them went*his*way,

The Man With an Unclean Spirit (Mark 1:21-28)

        2532   aina2718   pre1519   2584   an,nn4172 art,nn2056 2532 ipf2258/pap1321 pppro846
31 And came down to Capernaum, a city of Galilee, and taught them

pre1722 art3588   nn4521
on the sabbath days.

        2532   ipf1605   pre1909 pppro846   art,nn1322   3754 pppro846 art,nn3056 ipf2258 pre1722
32 And they were astonished at his doctrine: for his word was with

an,nn1849
power.

        2532 pre1722 art3588   nn4864   ipf2258   an,nn444   pap2192   an,nn4151
33 And in the synagogue there was a man, which had a spirit of an

an,aj169 an,nn1140 2532   aina349   an,aj3173 an,nn5456
unclean devil, and cried out with a loud voice,

       pap3004   pim1436   inpro5101/epn2254/2532/epn4671   an,nn2424
34 Saying, Let*us*alone; what*have*we*to*do*with*thee, *thou* Jesus of

an,aj3479   aina2064   ainf622 pppro2248 pin1492 pppro4571 pr/inpro5101   pin1488 art3588
Nazareth? art thou come to destroy us? I know thee who thou art; the

ajn40   art,nn2316
Holy One of God.

        2532 art,nn2424   aina2008   pppro846 pap3004   aipp5392   2532 aina1831 pre1537 pppro846
35 And Jesus rebuked him, saying, Hold*thy*peace, and come out of him.

2532   art3588 nn1140   apta4496 pppro846 pre1519 art3588 ajn3319   aina1831   pre575 pppro846 2532
And when the devil had thrown him in the midst, he came out of him, and

apta984 pppro846 an,ajn3367
hurt him not.

        2532   (pre1909)   an,ajn3956 an,nn2285/aom1096 2532   ipf4814   pre4314   rcpro240   pap3004
36 And they were all amazed, and spake among themselves, saying,

_{inpro5101} _{art,nn3056} _{pr/depro3778} ₃₇₅₄ _{pre1722} _{an,nn1849} ₂₅₃₂ _{an,nn1411} _{pin2004} _{art3588}
What a word *is* this! for with authority and power he commandeth the
_{an,aj169} _{nn4151} ₂₅₃₂ _{pinm1831}
unclean spirits, and they come out.

₂₅₃₂ _{an,nn2279} _{pre4012} _{ppro846} _{ipf1607} _{pre1519} _{an,aj3956} _{an,nn5117} _{art3588}
37 And the fame of him went out into every place of the
_{nn4066}
country*round*about.

Jesus Heals Many (Matt. 8:14-17; Mark 1:29-34)

₁₁₆₁ _{apta450} _{pre1537} _{art3588} _{nn4864} _{aina1525} _{pre1519} _{an,nn4613} _{art,nn3614}
38 And he arose out of the synagogue, and entered into Simon's house.
₁₁₆₁ _{art,nn4613} _{art,nn3994} _{ipf2258} _{ppmp4912} _{an,aj3173} _{an,nn4446} ₂₅₃₂ _{aina2065}
And Simon's wife's mother was taken with a great fever; and they besought
_{ppro846} _{pre4012} _{ppro846}
him for her.

₂₅₃₂ _{apta2186} _{ad*1883} _{ppro846} _{aina2008} _{art3588} _{nn4446} ₂₅₃₂ _{aina863} _{ppro846} ₁₁₆₁
39 And he stood over her, and rebuked the fever; and it left her: and
_{ad3916} _{apta450} _{ipf1247} _{ppro846}
immediately she arose and ministered unto them.

₁₁₆₁ _{art3588} _{nn2246} _{pap1416} _{an,aj3956} _{an,ajn3745} _{ipf2192} _{pap770}
40 Now when the sun was setting, all they that had any sick with
_{an,aj4164} _{an,nn3554} _{aina71} _{ppro846} _{pre4314} _{ppro846} ₁₁₆₁ _{art3588} _{apta2007/art,nn5495} _{an,aj1538} _{nu1520}
divers diseases brought them unto him; and he laid*his*hands*on every one of
_{ppro846} _{aina2323} _{ppro846}
them, and healed them.

₁₁₆₁ _{an,nn1140} ₂₅₃₂ _{ipf1831} _{pre575} _{an,ajn4183} _{pap2896} ₂₅₃₂ _{pap3004} _{epn4771} _{pin1488}
41 And devils also came out of many, crying out, and saying, Thou art
_{pr/art,nn5547} _{art3588} _{pr/nn5207} _{art,nn2316} ₂₅₃₂ _{pap2008} _{ipf1439} _{ppro846} ₃₇₅₆ _{pinf2980}
Christ the Son of God. And he rebuking *them* suffered them not to speak:
₃₇₅₄ _{ipf1492} _{epn846} _{pinf1511} _{pr/art,nn5547}
for they knew that he was Christ.

Jesus Preaches in the Synagogues of Galilee (Mark 1:35-39)

₁₁₆₁ _{aptm1096} _{an,nn2250} _{apta1831} _{ainp4198} _{pre1519} _{an,aj2048} _{an,nn5117} ₂₅₃₂
42 And when it was day, he departed and went into a desert place: and
_{art3588} _{nn3793} _{ipf2212} _{ppro846} ₂₅₃₂ _{aina2064} _{ad*2193} _{ppro846} ₂₅₃₂ _{ipf2722} _{ppro846}
the people sought him, and came unto him, and stayed him, that he should
₃₃₆₁ _{infg4198} _{pre575} _{ppro846}
not depart from them.

₁₁₆₁ _{art3588} _{aina2036} _{pre4314} _{ppro846} _{ppro3165} _{pin1163} _{ainf2097} _{art3588} _{nn932} _{art,nn2316}
43 And he said unto them, I must preach the kingdom of God to
_{art,aj2087} _{an,nn4172} ₂₅₃₂ ₃₇₅₄ _{pre1519/depro5124} _{pfip649}
other cities also: for therefore am I sent.

₂₅₃₂ _{ipf2258/pap2784} _{pre1722} _{art3588} _{nn4864} _{art,nn1056}
44 And he preached in the synagogues of Galilee.

Jesus Calls His Disciples (Matt. 4:18-22; Mark 1:16-20)

5 And it came*to*pass, that, as the people pressed upon him to hear the word of God, he stood by the lake of Gennesaret,

2 And saw two ships standing by the lake: but the fishermen were gone out of them, and were washing *their* nets.

3 And he entered into one of the ships, which was Simon's, and prayed him that he would thrust out a little from the land. And he sat down, and taught the people out of the ship.

4 Now when he had left speaking, he said unto Simon, Launch out into the deep, and let down your nets for a draught.

5 And Simon answering said unto him, Master, we have toiled all the night, and have taken nothing: nevertheless at thy word I will let down the net.

6 And when they had this done, they enclosed a great multitude of fishes: and their net broke.

7 And they beckoned unto *their* partners, which were in the other ship, that they should come and help them. And they came, and filled both the ships, so that they began to sink.

8 When Simon Peter saw *it*, he fell down at Jesus' knees, saying, Depart from me; for I am a sinful man, O Lord.

9 For he was astonished, and all that were with him, at the draught of the fishes which they had taken:

10 And so *was* also James, and John, the sons of Zebedee, which were partners with Simon. And Jesus said unto Simon, Fear not; from henceforth thou shalt catch men.

2532   apta2609   art,nn4143 pre1909 art,nn1093   apta863   an,ajn537

11 And when they had brought their ships to land, they forsook all, and

aina190   ppro846

followed him.

Jesus Cleanses a Leper (Matt. 8:1-4; Mark 1:40-45)

2532   aom1096   ppro846 aie1511 pre1722   nu3391   art,nn4172 (2532)   2400

12 And it came*to*pass, when he was in a certain   city,   behold a

an,nn435 an,aj4134   an,nn3014   (2532) apta1492 art,nn2424 apta4098 pre1909   an,nn4383   ainp1189   ppro846

man full of leprosy: who seeing Jesus fell   on *his* face, and besought him,

pap3004   an,nn2962 1437   psa2309   pifm1410   ainf2511/ppro3165

saying, Lord, if thou wilt, thou canst make*me*clean.

2532   apta1614   art,nn5495   aom680   ppro846   apta2036   pin2309

13 And he put forth *his* hand, and touched him, saying, I will:

aipp2511   2532   ad2112   art3588   nn3014   aina565   pre575 ppro846

be*thou*clean. And immediately the leprosy departed from him.

2532 epn846 aina3853   ppro846 ainf2036   an,ajn3367   235 apta565   aima1166   rxpro4572   art3588

14 And he charged him to tell no man: but go, and show thyself to the

nn2409   2532 aima4374 pre4012 ppro4675 art,nn2512   ad2531   an,nn3475   aina4367   pre1519

priest, and offer for thy cleansing, according as Moses commanded, for a

an,nn3142   ppro846

testimony unto them.   *(Lev. 14:2-32)*

1161   ad3123   ipf1330/art,nn3056   pre4012 ppro846 2532 an,aj4183

15 But so*much*the*more went*there*a*fame*abroad of him: and great

an,nn3793   ipf4905   pinf191   2532   pip2323   pre5259 ppro846 pre575   ppro848

multitudes came together to hear, and to be healed by him of their

art,nn769

infirmities.

1161   epn846 ipf2258/pap5298   pre1722 art3588   ajn2048   2532   ppmp4336

16 And he withdrew himself into the wilderness, and prayed.

Jesus Heals a Paralytic (Matt. 9:1-8; Mark 2:1-12)

2532   aom1096   pre1722   nu3391 art,nn2250 (2532) ppro846 ipf2258   pap1321   2532

17 And it came*to*pass on a certain day, as he was teaching, that there

ipf2258   an,nn5330   2532   an,nn3547   ppmp2521   repro3739 ipf2258   pfp2064   pre1537

were Pharisees and doctors*of*the*law sitting by, which were come out of

an,aj3956 an,nn2968   art,nn1056   2532   an,nn2449   2532   2419   2532   an,nn1411   an,nn2962

every town of Galilee, and Judea, and Jerusalem: and the power of the Lord

ipf2258   aies2390 ppro846

was *present* to heal them.

2532   2400   an,nn435   pap5342   pre1909   an,nn2825   an,nn444 repro3739   ipf2258

18 And, behold, men brought in a bed a man which was

pr/pfpp3886   2532   ipf2212   ainf1533/ppro846   2532   ainf5087

taken*with*a*palsy: and they sought *means* to bring*him*in, and to lay *him*

ad*1799   ppro846

before him.

2532   3361 apta2147 ppro1223 an,ajn4169   asba1533/ppro846

19 And when they could not find   by   what *way* they might bring*him*in

pre1223   art3588   nn3793   apta305 pre1909 art3588   nn1430   2532   aina2524/ppro846

because of the multitude, they went upon the housetop, and let*him*down

pre1223   art3588 nn2766 pre4862   art,nn2826 pre1519 art3588 ajn3319   ad⁺1715 art,nn2424

through the tiling with *his* couch into the midst before Jesus.

2532   apta1492 ppro846 art,nn4102   aina2036   ppro846 an,nn444 ppro4675 art,nn266

20 And when he saw their faith, he said unto him, Man, thy sins are

pfip863   ppro4671

forgiven thee.

2532   art3588   nn1122   2532 art3588   nn5330   aom756   pifm1260   pap3004   pr/inpro5101 pin2076

21 And the scribes and the Pharisees began to reason, saying, Who   is

depro3778 repro3739 pin2980   an,nn988   inpro5101 pinm1410   pinf863   an,nn266 1508 art,nn2316 an,aj3441

this which speaketh blasphemies? Who can forgive sins, but God alone?

1161   art,nn2424 apta1921   ppro846   art,nn1261   aptp611   aina2036   pre4314

22 But when Jesus perceived their thoughts, he answering said unto

ppro846 inpro5101 pinm1260   pre1722 ppro5216 art,nn2588

them, What reason ye in your hearts?

inpro5101   pin2076 pr/an,aj2123   ainf2036 ppro4675 art,nn266   pfip863   ppro4671 2228   ainf2036

23 Whether is   easier, to say, Thy sins be forgiven thee; or to say,

aipm1453   2532   pim4043

Rise up and walk?

1161   2443   asba1492 3754 art3588 nn5207   art,nn444 pin2192 an,nn1849 pre1909 art,nn1093

24 But that ye may know that the Son of man hath power upon earth to

pinf863   an,nn266   aina2036   art3588   pfpp3886   pin3004   epn4671 aipm1453   2532

forgive sins, (he said unto the sick*of*the*palsy,) I say unto thee, Arise, and

apta142   ppro4675 art,nn2826   2532 pim4198 pre1519 ppro4675 art,nn3624

take up thy couch, and go into thine house.

2532   ad3916   apta450   ad⁺1799 ppro846   apta142   pre1909/repro3739

25 And immediately he rose up before them, and took up that whereon he

ipf2621   aina565   pre1519 ppro848   art,nn3624   pap1392   art,nn2316

lay, and departed to his own house, glorifying God.

2532   an,ajn1611/aina2983/an,ajn537   2532   ipf1392   art,nn2316 2532   ainp4130

26 And they were*all*amazed, and they glorified God, and were filled with

an,nn5401   pap3004   aina1492   an,ajn3861   ad4594

fear, saying, We have seen strange things today.

Jesus Calls Levi (Matt. 9:9-13; Mark 2:13-17)

2532   pre3326   depro5023   aina1831   2532 aom2300   an,nn5057   an,nn3686   3018

27 And after these things he went forth, and saw a publican, named Levi,

ppmp2421 pre1909 art3588   nn5058   2532   aina2036   ppro846   pim190   ppro3427

sitting at the receipt*of*custom: and he said unto him, Follow me.

2532   apta2641 an,ajn537   apta450   aina190   ppro846

28 And he left   all,   rose up, and followed him.

2532   3018   aina4160 ppro846   an,aj3173 an,nn1403 pre1722   ppro848   art,nn3614   2532   ipf2258

29 And Levi made him a great feast in his own house: and there was a

an,aj4183   an,nn3793   an,nn5057   2532   an,ajn243 repro3739 ipf2258/ppmp2621 ppre3326 ppro846

great company of publicans and of others that sat down with them.

2532   ppro846   art,nn1122   2532   art,nn5330   ipf1111   pre4314   ppro846   art,nn3101

30 But their scribes and Pharisees murmured against his disciples,

pap3004   pre,inpro1302   pin2068 2532 pin4095 pre3326   an,nn5057   2532   an,ajn268

saying, Why do ye eat and drink with publicans and sinners?

2532 art,nn2424   aptp611   aina2036   pre4314 ppro846   art,pap5198   pin2192/an,nn5532

31 And Jesus answering said unto them, They*that*are*whole need

3756   an,nn2395   235   art,pap2192/ad2560

not a physician: but they*that*are*sick

        pfi2064   3756   ainf2564   an,ajn1342   235   an,ajn268 pre1519   an,nn3341

32 I came not to call the righteous, but sinners to repentance.

The Question Concerning Fasting (Matt. 9:14-17; Mark 2:18-22)

        1161   art3588 aina2036 pre4314 ppro846 pre,inpro1302   art3588   nn3101   an,nn2491 pin3522 an,ajn4437 2532

33 And they said unto him, Why do the disciples of John fast often, and

pinm4160   an,nn1162   2532   ad3668   (art3588)   art3588   nn5330   1161 art,popro4674 pin2068 2532

make prayers, and likewise the disciples of the Pharisees; but thine eat and

pin4095

drink?

        1161   art3588   aina2036   pre4314   ppro846   pinm1410   (3361) ainf4160 art3588   nn5207   art3588

34 And he said unto them, Can ye make the children of the

        nn3567   pinf3522 pre1722/repro3739 art3588   nn3566   pin2076 pre3326 ppro846

bridechamber fast, while the bridegroom is with them?

        1161   an,nn2250   fm2064   (2532) ad3752 art3588   nn3566   asbp522

35 But the days will come, when the bridegroom shall be taken away

pre575   ppro846   ad5119   ft3522 pre1722 depro1565 art,nn2250

from them, and then shall they fast in those days.

        1161   ipf3004   2532   an,nn3850   pre4314 ppro846   an,ajn3762   pin1911   an,nn1915

36 And he spake also a parable unto them; No man putteth a piece of a

an,aj2537   an,nn2440   pre1909   an,aj3820   (an,nn2440)   1490   2532 art3588   aj2537

new garment upon an old; if otherwise, then both the new

        pin4977   2532 art3588   nn1915   art3588   pre575 art3588 ajn2537   pin4856   3756

maketh*a*rent, and the piece that was taken out of the new agreeth not with

art3588 ajn3820

the old.

        2532   an,ajn3762   pin906   an,aj3501 an,nn3631 pre1519 an,aj3820   an,nn779   1490 art3588 aj3501 art,nn3631

37 And no man putteth new wine into old bottles; else the new wine

ft4486 art3588   nn779   2532 (epn846) fp1632   2532 art3588   nn779   fm622

will burst the bottles, and be spilled, and the bottles shall perish.

        235   an,aj3501   an,nn3631   an,ajn992 pre1519 an,aj2537   an,nn779   2532 an,ajn297

38 But new wine must be put into new bottles; and both are

pinm4933

preserved.

        an,ajn3762   2532   apta4095 an,aj3820   ad2112   pin2309 an,ajn3501 1063

39 No man also having drunk old wine straightway desireth new: for he

pin3004   art3588 ajn3820 pin2076 pr/cd/an,aj5543

saith, The old is better.

Jesus Is Lord Over the Sabbath (Matt. 12:1-8; Mark 2:23-28)

6
1161   aom1096   pre1722   an,nu,aj,an,aj1207/an,nn4521   ppro846
And it came*to*pass on the second*sabbath*after*the*first, that he
pifm1279   pre1223   art3588   ajn4702   2532   ppro846   art,nn3101   ipf5089   art3588
went through the corn fields; and his disciples plucked the
nn4719   2532   ipf2068   pap5597   art,nn5495
ears*of*corn, and did eat, rubbing *them* in *their* hands.   *(Deut. 23:25)*

1161   idpro5100   art3588   nn5330   aina2036   ppro846   inpro5101 pin4160   repro3739
2 And certain of the Pharisees said unto them, Why do ye that which
pin1832/3756   pinf4160 pre1722 art3588   nn4521
is*not*lawful to do   on the sabbath days?   *(Ex. 31:14,15)*

2532   art,nn2424   aptp611 (pre4314)   ppro846   aina2036   3761/aina314   depro5124
3 And Jesus answering them said, Have ye not*read*so*much*as this,
repro3739   1138   aina4160   ad3698   epn846   aina3983   2532   art,pap5607   pre3326 ppro846
what David did, when himself was hungry, and they*which*were with him;

ad5613   aina1525   pre1519 art3588   nn3624   art,nn2316   2532   aina2983   2532 aina5315 art3588
4 How he went into the house of God, and did take and eat the
nn740/art,nn4286   2532 aina1325   2532   art3588   pre3326 ppro846   repro3739   pin1832/3756
shewbread, and gave also to them that were with him; which it is*not*lawful to
ainf5315 1508   art3588   nn2409   an,aj3441
eat but for the priests alone?   *(1 Sam. 21:1-6; Lev. 24:5-9)*

2532   ipf3004   ppro846   3754   art3588 nn5207   art,nn444 pin2076 pr/an,nn2962 2532   art3588
5 And he said unto them, That the Son of man is Lord also of the
nn4521
sabbath.

The Man With a Withered Hand (Matt. 12:9-14; Mark 3:1-6)

1161   aom1096   2532 pre1722   an,aj2087   an,nn4521   ppro846 ainf1525   pre1519
6 And it came*to*pass also on another sabbath, that he entered into
art3588   nn4864   2532   pinf1321   2532   ad1563   ipf2258   an,nn444 (2532)   ppro846 art,aj1188 art,nn5495 ipf2258
the synagogue and taught: and there was a   man   whose right hand was
pr/an,aj3584
withered.

1161   art3588   nn1122   2532   art,nn5330   ipf3906   ppro846   1487   ft2323 pre1722
7 And the scribes and Pharisees watched him, whether he would heal on
art3588   nn4521   2443   asba2147   an,nn2724   ppro846
the sabbath day; that they might find an accusation against him.

1161   epn846   ipf1492   ppro846   art,nn1261   2532   aina2036   art3588   nn444   art,pap2192
8 But he knew their thoughts, and said to the man which had the
an,aj3584   art,nn5495   aipm1453   2532   aima2476   pre1519 art3588 ajn3319   1161   art3588   apta450
withered hand, Rise up, and stand forth in the midst. And he arose and
aina2476
stood forth.

3767   aina2036 art,nn2424 pre4314   ppro846   ft1905 ppro5209   idpro5101   pin1832
9 Then said Jesus unto them, I will ask you one thing; Is*it*lawful on
art3588   nn4521   ainf15   2228   ainf2554   ainf4982 an,nn5590 2228   ainf622
the sabbath days to do good, or to do evil? to save life, or to destroy *it*?

2532   aptm4017   ppro846 an,aj3956   aina2036   art3588   nn444
10 And looking*round*about*upon them all, he said unto the man,

aima1614   pp4675 art,nn5495   1161 art3588 aina4160 ad3779 2532 ppro846 art,nn5495   ainp600   an,aj5199

Stretch forth thy hand. And he did so: and his hand was restored whole

ad5613 art3588   ajn243

as the other.

1161   epn846   ainp4130   an,nn454   2532   ipf1255   rcpro240/pre4314

11 And they were filled with madness; and communed one*with*another

inpro5101   opt4160/302   art,nn2424

what they might   do   to Jesus.

Jesus Chooses the Twelve Disciples (Matt. 10:1-4; Mark 3:13-19)

1161   aom1096   pre1722 depro5025 art,nn2250   aina1831   pre1519   art,nn3735

12 And it came*to*pass in those days, that he went out into a mountain

aifm4336 2532   ipf2258/pap1273   pre1722 art,nn4335   art,nn2316

to pray, and continued*all*night in   prayer to God.

2532   ad3753   aom1096 an,nn2250   aina4377   ppro848 art,nn3101   2532 pre575 ppro846

13 And when it was day, he called *unto him* his disciples: and of them

aptm1586   nu,ajn1427 repro3739 2532   aina3687   an,nn652

he chose twelve, whom also he named apostles;

an,nn4613   repro3739   2532   aina3687   an,nn4074   2532   an,nn406 ppro846   art,nn80   an,nn2385

14 Simon, (whom he also named Peter,) and Andrew his   brother, James

2532 an,nn2491 an,nn5376 2532   an,nn918

and John, Philip and Bartholomew,

an,nn3156   2532   an,nn2381   an,nn2385 art3588   art,nn256   2532 an,nn4613 art,ppmp2564

15 Matthew and Thomas, James the *son* of Alphaeus, and Simon called

an,nn2208

Zelotes,

an,nn2455   an,nn2385 2532 an,nn2455 an,aj2469   repro3739 2532 aom1096

16 And Judas *the brother* of James, and Judas Iscariot, which also was the

pr/an,nn4273

traitor.

Jesus Ministers to a Great Multitude (Matt. 4:23-25)

2532   apta2597   pre3326 ppro846   aina2476 pre1909   an,aj3977/an,nn5117 2532

17 And he came down with them, and stood in the   plain,   and the

an,nn3793   ppro846   an,nn3101   2532   an,aj4183   an,nn4128   art,nn2992   pre575 an,aj3956 art,nn2449

company of his disciples, and a great multitude of people out of all   Judea

2532   2419   2532   art3588   ajn3882   an,nn5184 2532 an,nn4605 repro3739 aina2064   ainf191

and Jerusalem, and from the sea coast of Tyre and Sidon, which came to hear

ppro846 2532   aifp2390   pre575 ppro848   art,nn3554

him, and to be healed of their diseases;

2532   art,ppmp3791   pre5259 an,aj169   an,nn4151   2532   ipf2323

18 And they*that*were*vexed with unclean spirits: and they were healed.

2532   art3588   an,aj3956   nn3793   ipf2212   pifm680   ppro846   3754

19 And   the   whole multitude sought to touch him: for there

ipf1831/an,nn1411   pre3844 ppro846 2532   ipf2390   an,ajn3956

went*virtue*out of him, and healed *them* all.

Blessings and Woes (Matt. 5:1-12)

2532 ppro846   apta1869   ppro848 art,nn3788 pro1519 ppro846   art,nn3101   ipf3004   pr/an,aj3107
20 And he lifted up his eyes on his disciples, and said, Blessed *be ye*

art,ajn4434 3754 pr/popro5212 pin2076 art3588   nn932   art,nn2316
poor: for yours is the kingdom of God.

pr/an,aj3107   art,pap3983   ad3568   3754   fp5526   pr/an,aj3107
21 Blessed *are ye* that hunger now: for ye shall be filled. Blessed *are ye*

art,pap2799   ad3568   3754   ft1070
that weep now: for ye shall laugh.

pr/an,aj3107   pin2075   ad3752   art,nn444   asba3404 ppro5209   2532   ad3752
22 Blessed are ye, when men shall hate you, and when they shall

asba873   ppro5209   2532   asba3679   2532   asba1544   ppro5216
separate you *from their company,* and shall reproach *you,* and cast out your

art,nn3686 ad5613 an,aj4190   ad*1752/art3588/nn5207/art,nn444
name as evil, for*the*Son*of*man's*sake.

pim5463   pre1722 depro1565 art,nn2250 2532   aima4640   1063   2400   ppro5216 art,nn3408
23 Rejoice ye in that day, and leap*for*joy: for, behold, your reward *is*

pr/an,aj4183   pre1722   art,nn3772   1063   pre2596/depro5024   ipf4160   ppro846   art,nn3962   art3588
great in heaven: for in*the*like*manner did their fathers unto the

nn4396
prophets.

4133   3759   ppro5213   art,ajn4145 3754   pin568   ppro5216
24 But woe unto you that are rich! for ye have received your

art,nn3874
consolation.

3759   ppro5213   art,pfpp1705   3754   ft3983   3759   ppro5213
25 Woe unto you that*are*full for ye shall hunger. Woe unto you

art,pap1070   ad3568   3754   ft3996   2532   ft2799
that laugh now! for ye shall mourn and weep.

3759   ppro5213   ad3752   an,aj3956 art,nn444   asba2036   ad2573   ppro5209 1063 pre2596/depro5024
26 Woe unto you, when all men shall speak well of you! for so

ipf4160 ppro846 art,nn3962   art3588   nn5578
did their fathers to the false prophets.

Love Your Enemies (Matt. 5:38-48; 7:12)

235   pin3004   ppro5213   art,pap191   pim25   ppro5216   art,ajn2190   pim4160   ad2573
27 But I say unto you which hear, Love your enemies, do good to

art,pap3404   ppro5209
them*which*hate you,

pim2127   art,ppmp2672   ppro5213 2532 pim4336 pre5228   art,pap1908
28 Bless them*that*curse you, and pray for them*which*despitefully*use

ppro5209
you.

art,pap5180   ppro4571 pre1909 art3588   nn4600   pin3930   2532   art3588
29 And unto him*that*smiteth thee on the *one* cheek offer also the

ajn243   2532 (pre575)   art,pap142   ppro4675 art,nn2440 aosi2967   3361
other; and him*that*taketh*away thy cloak forbid not *to take thy*

art,nn5509   2532
coat also.

30   (1161) pim1325   an,ajn3956   art,pap154   ppro4571 2532 pre575   art,pap142
Give to every man that asketh of thee; and of him*that*taketh*away
art,popro4674   pim523/3361
thy goods ask*them*not*again.

2532   ad2531   pin2309   2443 art,nn444   psa4160   ppro5213 pim4160 epn5210 2532   ppro846
31 And as ye would that men should do to you, do ye also to them
ad3668
likewise.

2532   1487   psa25   art,pap25   ppro5209 an,aj4169 an,nn5485 pin2076 ppro5213 1063   art,ajn268
32 For if ye love them*which*love you, what thank have ye? for sinners
2532   pin25   art,pap25   ppro846
also love those*that*love them.

2532   1437   psa15   art,pap15   ppro5209 an,aj4169 an,nn5485 pin2076
33 And if ye do good to them*which*do*good to you, what thank have
ppro5213 1063 art,ajn268   2532 pin4160   2532 art3588   epn846
ye? for sinners also do even the same.

2532   1437   psa1155   pre3844 repro3739   pin1679   ainf618   an,aj4169 an,nn5485 pin2076
34 And if ye lend *to them* of whom ye hope to receive, what thank have
ppro5213 1063 art,ajn268   2532 pin1155   an,ajn268 2443   asba615   art,ajn2470
ye? for sinners also lend to sinners, to receive as*much*again.

4133   pim25   ppro5216 art,ajn2190   2532   pim15   2532   pim1155
35 But love ye your enemies, and do good, and lend,
pap560/an,ajn3367   2532 ppro5216 art,nn3408   fm2071 pr/an,aj4183 2532   fm2071
hoping*for*nothing*again; and your reward shall be great, and ye shall be the
pr/an,nn5207   art3588   ajn5310   3754 epn846 pin2076 pr/an,aj5543 pre1909 art3588   ajn884   2532
children of the Highest: for he is kind unto the unthankful and *to* the
an,ajn4190
evil.   (Neh. 9:17; Jer. 9:24)

pim1096   3767   pr/an,aj3629 ad2531 ppro5216 art,nn3962 2532 pin2076 pr/an,aj3629
36 Be ye therefore merciful, as your Father also is merciful.

(Ex. 34:6; Joel 2:13)

Judging Others (Matt. 7:1-5)

(2532) pim2919 3361 2532   efn3364   asba2919   pim2613   3361 2532   efn3364
37   Judge not, and ye shall not be judged: condemn not, and ye shall not
asbp2613   pim630   2532   fp630
be condemned: forgive, and ye shall be forgiven:

pim1325   2532   fp1325   ppro5213 an,aj2570   an,nn3358   pfpp4085   2532
38 Give, and it shall be given unto you, good measure, pressed down, and
pfpp4531   2532   ppmp5240   ft1325 pre1519 ppro5216 art,nn2859 1063
shaken together, and running over, shall men give into your bosom. For with
art3588 epn846   nn3358   repro3739   pin3354   fp488/ppro5213
the same measure that ye mete withal it shall be measured*to*you*again.

1161   aina2036   an,nn3850   ppro846 pinm1410   an,ajn5185 pinf3594   an,ajn5185
39 And he spake a parable unto them, Can the blind lead the blind? shall
3780 an,ajn297 fm4098 pre1519   an,nn999
they not both fall into the ditch?

an,nn3101   pin2076   3756   pre5228   ppro848   art,nn1320   1161   an,ajn3956   pr/pfpp2675

40 The disciple is not above his master: but every one that is perfect

fm2071 ad5613 ppro846   art,nn1320

shall be as his master.

1161   inpro5101   pin991   art3588   nn2595   art3588   pre1722 ppro4675   art,nn80   art,nn3788   1161

41 And why beholdest thou the mote that is in thy brother's eye, but

pin2657   3756 art3588   nn1385   art3588   pre1722   art,aj2398   an,nn3788

perceivest not the beam that is in thine own eye?

2228   ad4459 pinm1410   pinf3004   ppro4675   art,nn80   an,nn80   aima863   asba1544

42 Either how canst thou say to thy brother, Brother, let me pull out

art3588   nn2595   art3588   pre1722 ppro4675 art,nn3788   epn846   pap991   3756 art3588   nn1385

the mote that is in thine eye, when thou thyself beholdest not the beam

art3588   pre1722   ppro4675   art,nn3788   an,nn5273   aima1544   nu,ajn4412 art3588   nn1385   pre1537

that is in thine own eye? Thou hypocrite, cast out first the beam out of

ppro4675   art,nn3788   2532   ad5119   ft1227   ainf1544   art3588   nn2595   art3588

thine own eye, and then shalt thou see clearly to pull out the mote that is

pre1722 ppro4675   art,nn80   art,nn3788

in thy brother's eye.

Bearing Fruit (Matt. 7:17-20; 12:34,35)

1063   an,aj2570   an,nn1186   pin2076/3756/pap4160   an,aj4550   an,nn2598   3761

43 For a good tree bringeth*not*forth corrupt fruit; neither doth a

an,aj4550   an,nn1186   pap4160   an,aj2570 an,nn2590

corrupt tree bring forth good fruit.

1063   an,aj1538   an,nn1186   pinp1097   pre1537   art,aj2398   an,nn2590   1063   pre1537   an,nn173

44 For every tree is known by his own fruit. For of thorns men do

3756   pin4816   an,nn4810 3761 pre1537   an,nn942   pin5166   an,nn4718

not gather figs, nor of a bramble bush gather they grapes.

art,aj18   an,nn444 pre1537   art3588   an,aj18   nn2344   ppro848 art,nn2588   pin4393

45 A good man out of the good treasure of his heart bringeth forth

art,aj18   2532   art,aj4190 an,nn444 pre1537   art3588 an,aj4190   nn2344   ppro848 art,nn2588

that*which*is*good; and an evil man out of the evil treasure of his heart

pin4393   art,ajn4190   1063 pre1537 art3588   nn4051   art3588   nn2588   ppro846

bringeth forth that*which*is*evil: for of the abundance of the heart his

art,nn4750   pin2980

mouth speaketh.

The Two Foundations (Matt. 7:24-27)

1161   inpro5101   pin2564   ppro3165   an,nn2962   an,nn2962   2532   pin4160   3756   repro3739

46 And why call ye me, Lord, Lord, and do not the things which I

pin3004

say?

an,aj3956   art,ppmp2064   pre4314   ppro3165   2532   pap191   ppro3450   art,nn3056   2532   pap4160

47 Whosoever cometh to me, and heareth my sayings, and doeth

ppro846   ft5263   ppro5213   inpro5101   pin2076 pr/an,ajn3664

them, I will show you to whom he is   like:

pin2076 pr/an,ajn3664   an,nn444   pap3618   an,nn3614 (repro3739) aina4626   aina900   2532 aina5087

48 He is   like   a man which built a house, and digged deep, and laid

an,nn2310   pre1909   art,nn4073 1161   an,nn4132   aptm1096   art3588   nn4215

the foundation on   a rock: and when the   flood arose, the stream

aina4366   depro1565 art,nn3614 2532 aina2480   3756 ainf4531 ppro846 1063

beat*vehemently*upon that house, and could not shake it: for it was

plpf2311   pre1909   art,nn4073

founded upon a rock.

1161   art,apta191   2532   apta4160   3361   pin2076   pr/an,ajn3664   an,nn444

49 But he*that*heareth, and doeth not, is   like   a man that

ad*5565   an,nn2310   apta3618   an,nn3614   pre1909   art3588   nn1093

without   a   foundation   built   a   house   upon   the   earth;

aina4366/repro3739/art3588/nn4215   2532   ad2112   aina4098 2532

against*which*the*stream*did*beat*vehemently, and immediately it fell; and

art3588 nn4485   depro1565 art,nn3614 aom1096 pr/an,aj3173

the ruin of that house was great.

Jesus Heals the Centurion's Servant (Matt. 8:5-13; John 4:43-54)

1161   ad1893   aina4137 an,aj3956 ppro848 art,nn4487 pre1519 art3588   nn189   art3588

7 Now when he had ended all   his sayings in   the audience of the

nn2992   aina1525   pre1519   2584

people, he entered into Capernaum.

1161   idpro5100   an,nn1543   an,ajn1401   repro3739 ipf2258 pr/an,aj1784   ppro846   pap2192/ad2560

2 And a certain centurion's servant, who was dear unto him, was sick,

ipf3195   pinf5053

and ready to die.

1161   apta191   pre4012 art,nn2424   aina649 pre4314 ppro846   an,ajn4245   art3588   nn2453

3 And when he heard of Jesus, he sent unto him the elders of the Jews,

pap2065   ppro846 3704   apta2064 2532 asba1295 ppro846   art,ajn1401

beseeching him that he would come and heal his servant.

1161   art3588 aptm3854 pre4314 art,nn2424   ipf3870   ppro846   ad4709   pap3004

4 And when they came to Jesus, they besought him instantly, saying,

3754   pin2076 pr/an,aj514   repro3739   ft3930 depro5124

That he was worthy for whom he should do this:

1063   pin25   ppro2257 art,nn1484 2532 epn846   aina3618 ppro2254   art,nn4864

5 For he loveth our nation, and he hath built us a synagogue.

1161   art,nn2424   ipf4198   pre4862 ppro846   1161   ppro846 pap568 ad2235 3756 ad3112 pre575 art3588

6 Then Jesus went with them. And when he was now not far from the

nn3614   art3588   nn1543   aina3992 an,ajn5384 pre4314 ppro846 pap3004   ppro846 an,nn2962 pim4660   3361

house, the centurion sent friends to him, saying unto him, Lord, trouble not

1063   pin1510 3756 pr/an,aj2425 2443   asba1525 pre5259 ppro3450 art,nn4721

thyself: for I am not worthy that thou shouldest enter under my roof:

pre,repro1352   3761   aina515/rxpro1683   ainf2064 pre4314 ppro4571 235

7 Wherefore neither thought*I*myself*worthy to come unto thee: but

aima2036   an,nn3056 2532 ppro3450 art,nn3816   fp2390

say in a word, and my servant shall be healed.

1063   epn1473   2532 pin1510   pr/an,nn444 ppmp5021 pre5259   an,nn1849   pap2192 pre5259 rxpro1683

8 For   I   also am a   man   set under authority, having under me

an,nn4757   2532   pin3004   depro5129 aipp4198 2532   pinm4198   2532   an,ajn243   pim2064   2532
soldiers, and I say unto one, Go, and he goeth; and to another, Come, and he

pinm2064   2532   ppro3450 art,ajn1401   aima4160 depro5124 2532   pin4160
cometh; and to my servant, Do this, and he doeth *it*.

1161   art,nn2424   apta191   depro5023   aina2296   ppro846   2532
9 When Jesus heard these things, he marveled at him, and

aptp4762   aina2036   art3588   nn3793   pap190   ppro846   pin3004
turned*him*about, and said unto the people that followed him, I say unto

ppro5213   aina2147   an,aj5118   an,nn4102   3761 pre1722   2474
you, I have not found so great faith, no, not in Israel.

2532   art,aptp3992   apta5290   pre1519 art3588   nn3624   aina2147 art3588   ajn1401
10 And they*that*were*sent, returning to the house, found the servant

pr/pap5198   art,pap770
whole that*had*been*sick.

The Raising of the Widow's Son at Nain

2532   aom1096   (pre1722) art3588   ad1836   ipf4198 pre1519   an,nn4172 ppmp2564
11 And it came*to*pass   the day after, that he went into a city called

3484   2532 an,aj2425   ppro846   art,nn3101   ipf4848   ppro846 2532   an,aj4183   an,nn3793
Nain; and many of his disciples went with him, and much people.

1161   ad5613   aina1448   art3588 nn4439   art3588 nn4172 (2532)   2400
12 Now when he came nigh to the gate of the city,   behold, there was a

pfp2348   ipf1580   an,aj3439 an,nn5207   ppro848   art,nn3384   2532 depro3778 ipf2258   pr/an,nn5503
dead man carried out, the only son of his mother, and she was a widow:

2532 an,aj2425   an,nn3793   art3588 nn4172 ipf2258 pre4862 ppro846
and much people of the city was with her.

2532   art3588   nn2962   apta1492 ppro846   ainp4697   pre1909 ppro846 2532 aina2036
13 And when the Lord saw her, he had compassion on her, and said unto

ppro846 pim2799   3361
her, Weep not.

2532   apta4334   aom680   art3588   nn4673   1161   art,pap941   aina2476
14 And he came and touched the bier: and they*that*bare *him* stood still.

2532   aina2036   an,nn3495   pin3004   epn4671   aipp1453
And he said, Young man, I say unto thee, Arise.

2532   art,ajn3498   aina339   2532   aom756   pinf2980   2532   aina1325
15 And he*that*was*dead sat up, and began to speak. And he delivered

ppro846   ppro846   art,nn3384
him to his mother.

1161   an,nn5401/aina2983   an,ajn537 2532   ipf1392   art,nn2316 pap3004   3754
16 And there came*a*fear on all: and they glorified God, saying, That a

an,aj3173   an,nn4396   pfip1453   pre1722   ppro2254   2532   3754 art,nn2316   aom1980   ppro848
great prophet is risen up among us; and, That God hath visited his

art,nn2992
people.

2532   depro3778   art,nn3056   pre4012 ppro846   aina1831   pre1722   an,aj3950   art,nn2449   2532
17 And this rumor of him went forth throughout all Judea, and

pre1722   an,aj3956 art3588   nn4066
throughout all the region*round*about.

John Asks About Jesus (Matt. 11:2-6)

2532 art3588 nn3101 an,nn2491 aima518 ppro846 pre4012 an,aj3956 depro5130
18 And the disciples of John showed him of all these things.

2532 art,nn2491 aptm4341 (idpro5100) nu1417 ppro848 art,nn3101 aina3992 pre4314 art,nn2424
19 And John calling *unto him* two of his disciples sent *them* to Jesus,

pap3004 pin1488 epn4771 pr/art,ppmp2064 2228 pin4328 an,ajn243
saying, Art thou he*that*should*come? or look*we*for another? *(Mal. 3:1)*

1161 art3588 nn435 apta3854 pre4314 ppro846 aina2036 an,nn2491 art,nn910 pfi649
20 When the men were come unto him, they said, John Baptist hath sent

ppro2248 pre4314 ppro4571 pap3004 pin1488 epn4771 pr/art,ppmp2064 2228 pin4328
us unto thee, saying, Art thou he*that*should*come? or look*we*for

an,ajn243
another? *(Mal. 3:1)*

1161 pre1722 epn846 art,nn5610 aina2323 an,ajn4183 pre575 an,nn3554
21 And in that same hour he cured many of *their* infirmities

2532 an,nn3184 2532 an,aj4190 an,nn4151 2532 an,aj4183 an,ajn5185 aom5483
and plagues, and of evil spirits; and unto many *that were* blind he gave

art,pinf991
sight.

2532 art,nn2424 aptp611 aina2036 ppro846 aptp4198 aima518 an,nn2491
22 Then Jesus answering said unto them, Go*your*way, and tell John

repro3739 aina1492 2532 aina191 3754 an,ajn5185 pin308 an,ajn5560 pin4043
what things ye have seen and heard; how that the blind see, the lame walk,

an,nn3015 pinp2511 an,ajn2974 pin191 an,ajn3498 pinp1453 an,ajn4434
the lepers are cleansed, the deaf hear, the dead are raised, to the poor

pinm2097
the*gospel*is*preached. *(Is. 35:5; 61:1)*

2532 pr/an,aj3107 pin2076 repro3739/1437 3361 asbp4624 pre1722 ppro1698
23 And blessed is *he,* whosoever shall not be offended in me.

Jesus Talks About John the Baptist (Matt. 11:7-19)

1161 art3588 nn32 an,nn2491 apta565 aom756 pinf3004
24 And when the messengers of John were departed, he began to speak

pre4314 art3588 nn3793 pre4012 an,nn2491 inpro5101 pfi1831 pre1519 art3588 ajn2048
unto the people concerning John, What went*ye*out into the wilderness for to

aifm2300 an,nn2563 ppmp4531 pre5259 an,nn417
see? A reed shaken with the wind?

235 inpro5101 pfi1831 ainf1492 an,nn444 pfpp294 pre1722 an,aj3120 an,nn2440
25 But what went*ye*out for to see? A man clothed in soft raiment?

2400 art3588 pre1722/an,aj1741/an,nn2441 2532 pap5225 an,nn5172 pin1526 pre1722
Behold, they which are gorgeously appareled, and live delicately, are in

art,nn933
kings' courts.

235 inpro5101 pfi1831 ainf1492 an,nn4396 3483 pin3004 ppro5213
26 But what went*ye*out for to see? A prophet? Yea, I say unto you,

2532 cd/an,ajn4055 an,nn4396
and much more than a prophet.

pr/depro3778   pin2076   pre4012   repro3739   pfip1125   2400   epn1473   pin649   ppro3450
27 This   is   *he,*   of whom it is written, Behold,   I   send   my

art,nn32   pre4253 ppro4675 an,nn4383 repro3739   ft2680   ppro4675 art,nn3598 ad·1715 ppro4675
messenger before thy face, which shall prepare thy   way before thee.

(Is. 40:3; Mal. 3:1)

        1063   pin3004   ppro5213 pre1722   an,ajn1084   an,nn1135   pin2076
28 For I say unto you, Among those*that*are*born of women there is

an,aj3762   pr/cd/an,aj3187   an,nn4396   an,nn2491 art3588   nn910   1161   cd/art,ajn3398   pre1722 art3588
not a greater prophet than John the Baptist: but he*that*is*least in the

       nn932   art,nn2316 pin2076 pr/cd/an,aj3187   ppro846
kingdom of God is greater than he.

           2532 an,aj3956 art3588   nn2992   apta191   2532 art3588   nn5057   aina1344 art,nn2316
29 And all the people that heard *him,* and the publicans, justified God,

   aptp907   art3588   nn908   an,nn2491
being baptized with the baptism of John.

      1161 art3588   nn5330   2532   art,nn3544   aina114   art3588   nn1012   art,nn2316 pre1519
30 But the Pharisees and lawyers rejected the counsel of God against

rxpro1438   3361   aptp907   pre5259 ppro846
themselves, being not baptized of him.

      1161   art3588   nn2962   aina2036   inpro5101   3767   ft3666   art3588 nn444   depro5026
31 And the Lord said, Whereunto then shall I liken the men of this

art,nn1074   2532   inpro5101 pin1526   pr/an,ajn3664
generation? and to what are they like?

         pin1526   pr/an,ajn3664   an,nn3813 ppmp2521 art,pre1722   an,nn58   2532   pap4377
32 They are like unto children sitting   in   the marketplace, and calling

rcpro240   2532   pap3004   aina832   ppro5213 2532   3756
one*to*another, and saying, We have piped unto you, and ye have not

aom3738   aina2354   ppro5213 2532   3756 aina2799
danced; we have mourned to you, and ye have not wept.

      1063 an,nn2491 art3588   nn910   pfi2064   3383   pap2068 an,nn740   3383   pap4095   an,nn3631 2532
33 For John the Baptist came neither eating bread nor drinking wine; and

pin3004   pin2192   an,nn1140
ye say, He hath a devil.

      art3588   nn5207   art,nn444   pfi2064   pap2068   2532   pap4095   2532   pin3004   2400
34 The Son of man is come eating and drinking; and ye say, Behold a

an,nn5314   an,nn444 2532   an,nn3630   an,ajn5384   an,nn5057   2532   an,ajn268
gluttonous man, and a winebibber, a friend of publicans and sinners!

       2532   art,nn4678   ainp1344   pre575 an,aj3956 ppro848   art,nn5043
35 But wisdom is justified of   all   her children.

Jesus Forgives a Sinful Woman

         1161 idpro5100 art3588   nn5330   ipf2065   ppro846   2443   asba5315 pre3326 ppro846
36 And one of the Pharisees desired him that he would eat with him.

2532   apta1525 pre1519 art3588   nn5330   art,nn3614   2532   ainp347
And he went into the Pharisee's house, and sat*down*to*meat.

         2532   2400   an,nn1135   pre1722 art3588 nn4172 repro3748 ipf2258   pr/an,ajn268
37 And, behold, a woman in the city, which was a sinner, when she

knew that *Jesus* sat*at*meat in the Pharisee's house, brought an alabaster box of ointment,

38 And stood at his feet behind *him* weeping, and began to wash his feet with tears, and did wipe *them* with the hairs of her head, and kissed his feet, and anointed *them* with the ointment.

39 Now when the Pharisee which*had*bidden him saw *it,* he spake within himself, saying, This man, if he were a prophet, would have known who and what manner of woman *this is* that toucheth him: for she is a sinner.

40 And Jesus answering said unto him, Simon, I have somewhat to say unto thee. And he saith, Master, say on.

41 There was a certain creditor which had two debtors: the one owed five hundred pence, and the other fifty.

42 And when they had nothing to pay, he frankly forgave them both. Tell me therefore, which of them will love him most?

43 Simon answered and said, I suppose that *he,* to whom he forgave most. And he said unto him, Thou hast rightly judged.

44 And he turned to the woman, and said unto Simon, Seest thou this woman? I entered into thine house, thou gavest me no water for my feet: but she hath washed my feet with tears, and wiped *them* with the hairs of her head.

45 Thou gavest me no kiss: but this woman since the time I came in hath not ceased to kiss my feet.

46 My head with oil thou didst not anoint: but this woman hath anointed my feet with ointment.

47 Wherefore I say unto thee, Her sins, which are many, are forgiven;

3754   aina25   an,ajn4183 1161   repro3739 an,ajn3641   pinp863   pin25   an,ajn3641
for she loved much: but to whom little is forgiven, *the same* loveth little.

1161   aina2036   ppro846 ppro4675 art,nn266   pfip863
48 And he said unto her, Thy sins are forgiven.

2532   art,ppmp4873   aom756   pinf3004 pre1722   rxpro1438
49 And they*that*sat*at*meat*with him began to say within themselves,

pr/inpro5101 pin2076 depro3778 repro3739   pin863   an,nn266 2532
Who is this that forgiveth sins also?

1161   aina2036 pre4314 art3588   nn1135   ppro4675 art,nn4102   pfi4982 ppro4571 pim4198 pre1519
50 And he said to the woman, Thy faith hath saved thee; go in

an,nn1515
peace.

2532   aom1096   pre1722/art,ad2517 2532 epn846   ipf1353   pre2596/an,nn4172 2532
8 And it came*to*pass afterward, that he went throughout every city and

an,nn2968   pap2784   2532   ppmp2097   art3588   nn932   art,nn2316
village, preaching and showing*the*glad*tidings of the kingdom of God:

2532 art3588 nu,ajn1427   pre4862 ppro846
and the twelve *were* with him,

2532   idpro5100   an,nn1135   repro3739   ipf2258   pr/pfpp2323 pre575 an,aj4190 an,nn4151 2532
2 And certain women, which had been healed of evil spirits and

an,nn769   an,nn3137 art,ppmp2564   an,aj3092   pre575 repro3739 plpf1831 nu2033 an,nn1140
infirmities, Mary called Magdalene, out of whom went seven devils,

2532   an,nn2489   an,nn1135   an,nn5529   an,nn2264   an,nn2012 2532   an,nn4677   2532 an,aj4183
3 And Joanna the wife of Chuza Herod's steward, and Susanna, and many

an,ajn2087 repro3748   ipf1247   ppro846 pre575 ppro846   art,pap5224
others, which ministered unto him of their substance.

The Parable of the Sower (Matt. 13:1-9; Mark 4:19)

1161   an,aj4183   an,nn3793   pap4896   2532   art,ppmp1975 pre4314
4 And when much people were gathered together, and were come to

ppro846   pre2596/an,nn4172   aina2036 pre1223   an,nn3850
him out*of*every*city, he spake by a parable:

art,pap4687   aina1831   infg4687 ppro848 art,nn4703 2532   ppro846 aie4687 repro3739/3303 aina4098
5 A sower went out to sow his seed: and as he sowed, some fell

pre3844 art3588   nn3598   2532   ainp2662   2532 art3588   nn4071   art3588   nn3772
by the way side; and it was trodden down, and the fowls of the air

aina2719   ppro846
devoured it.

2532   an,ajn2087 aina4098 pre1909   art,nn4073 2532   aptp5453
6 And some fell upon a rock; and as soon as it was sprung up, it

ainp3583   aid2192/3361   an,nn2429
withered away, because it lacked moisture.

2532   an,ajn2087 aina4098 pre1722/an,ajn3319 art,nn173 2532 art3588   nn173   aptp4855
7 And some fell among thorns; and the thorns sprang*up*with it, and

aina1970 ppro846
choked it.

2532   an,ajn2087 aina4098 pre1909 art,aj18   art,nn1093   2532   aptp5453   an,nn2590

☞ 8 And other fell on good ground, and sprang up, and bare fruit

an,aj1542   pap3004   depro5023   ipf5455   art,pap2192

a hundredfold. And when he had said these things, he cried, He*that*hath

an,nn3775   pinf191   pim191

ears to hear, let him hear.

The Reason for Parables (Matt. 13:10-17; Mark 4:10-12)

1161 ppro846 art,nn3101   ipf1905 ppro846 pap3004 pr/inpro5101   depro3778 art,nn3850 opt1498

9 And his disciples asked him, saying, What might this parable be?

1161   art3588 aina2036   epn5213   pfip1325   ainf1097 art3588   nn3466   art3588

10 And he said, Unto you it is given to know the mysteries of the

nn932   art,nn2316 1161   art,ajn3062 pre1722 an,nn3850   2443   pap991   3361   psa991

kingdom of God: but to others in parables; that seeing they might not see,

2532   pap191   3361   psa4920

and hearing they might not understand.   *(Is. 6:9,10)*

Explanation of the Parable of the Sower (Matt. 13:18-23; Mark 4:13-20)

1161   art3588   nn3850   pin2076 pr/depro3778 art3588   nn4703 pin2076 art3588 pr/nn3056   art,nn2316

☞ 11 Now the parable is   this: The seed is   the word of God.

(1161) art3588   pre3844 art3588   nn3598   pin1526   pr/art,pap191   ad1534   pinm2064 art3588 ajn1228

12   Those by the way side are they*that*hear; then cometh the devil,

2532   pin142   art3588 nn3056   pre575 ppro846 art,nn2588 3363   apta4100

and taketh away the word out of their hearts, lest they should believe and be

asbp4982

saved.

(1161) art3588   pre1909 art3588 nn4073   repro3739   ad3752   asba191   pinm1209 art3588 nn3056

☞ 13   They on the rock *are they,* which, when they hear, receive the word

pre3326 an,nn5479 2532 depro3778 pin2192 3756 an,nn4491 repro3739 pre4314   an,nn2540   pin4100   2532 pre1722 an,nn2540

with joy; and these have no root, which for a while believe, and in   time of

an,nn3986   pinm868

temptation fall away.

☞ **8:8, 11** See note on Matthew 13:10–17.

☞ **8:13** There is a category of people who would be confused with the true believers. These are those who appear to have be saved and be a child of God, but have reverted to the world and continue in its ways. For instance, the phrase ". . . which, when they hear, receive the word with joy; and these have no root; which for a while believe . . ." denotes a different meaning for the word "believe." It should not be confused as the exercise of true faith in Jesus Christ which transforms a person's life. This "belief" is merely an intellectual assent. Not simply giving reference to a repentant heart, but to an obedient heart toward God which causes them to do righteousness and to hate sin (Rom. 5:19). These who have no deep roots are the ones who profess faith, but do not possess Christ. See notes on 2 Thessalonians 2:3; Hebrews 6:1–6; and 1 John 3:6–9.

1161   art,apta4098   pre1519   art,nn173(depro3778) pin1526
14 And that*which*fell among   thorns   are they, which, when they have

pr/art,apta191   ppmp4198   2532   pinm4846   pre5259 an,nn3308 2532 an,nn4149 2532   an,nn2237
heard, go forth, and are choked with cares and riches and pleasures of *this*

art,nn979 2532   pin5052/3756
life, and bring*no*fruit*to*perfection.

1161 art3588 pre1722 art3588 aj2570   an,nn1093 (depro3778) pin1526 pr/repro3748   pre1722   an,aj2570   2532
15 But that on the good ground   are they, which in an honest and

an,aj18   an,nn2588   apta191   art3588   nn3056   pin2722   2532   pin2592   pre1722
good heart, having heard the word, keep *it,* and bring*forth*fruit with

an,nn5281
patience.

A Light Hidden (Matt. 5:15; Mark 4:21-25)

(1161)   an,ajn3762   apta681   an,nn3088   pin2572 ppro846   an,nn4632
16   No man, when he hath lighted a candle, covereth it   with a vessel,

2228   pin5087   ad*5270   an,nn2825 235   pin2007   pre1909   an,nn3087   2443
or putteth *it* under a bed; but setteth *it* on   a   candlestick, that

art,ppmp1531   psa991 art3588   nn5457
they*which*enter*in may see the light.

1063   3756   pin2076 pr/an,ajn2927 repro3739   3756   fm1096   pr/an,aj5318   3761
17 For nothing   is secret, that shall not be made manifest; neither *any*

an,ajn614 repro3739   3756   fp1097   2532   asba2064 pre1519/an,ajn5318
thing hid,   that shall not be known and come abroad.

pin991   3767   ad4459   pin191 1063   repro3739/302   psa2192   ppro846
18 Take heed therefore how ye hear: for whosoever hath, to him shall be

fp1325   2532   repro3739/302   psa2192   3361   pre575 ppro846   fp142   2532   repro3739
given; and whosoever hath not, from him shall be taken even that which he

pin1380   pinf2192
seemeth to have.

Jesus' Mother and Brothers (Matt. 12:46-50; Mark 3:31-35)

1161   aom3854 pre4314 ppro846   art,nn3384 2532 ppro846   art,nn80   2532 ipf1410 3756
19 Then came to him *his* mother and his brethren, and could not

ainf4940   ppro846 pre1223 art3588   nn3793
come at him for the press.

2532   ainp518 ppro846   pap3004 ppro4675 art,nn3384 2532 ppro4675
20 And it was told him *by certain* which said, Thy mother and thy

art,nn80   pfi2476   ad1854   pap2309   ainf1492 ppro4571
brethren stand without, desiring to see thee.

1161   art3588   aptp611   aina2036 pre4314 ppro846 ppro3450 art,nn3384   2532 ppro3450   art,nn80
21 And he answered and said unto them, My mother and my brethren

pin1526 pr/depro3778   art,pap191   art3588   nn3056   art,nn2316 2532 pap4160 ppro846
are these which hear the word of God, and do it.

Jesus Calms a Storm (Matt. 8:23-27; Mark 4:35-41)

2532   aom1096   pre1722   nu3391   art,nn2250   (2532) epn846 aina1684 pre1519   an,nn4143
22 Now it came*to*pass on a certain day, that he went into a ship
(2532) ppro846 art,nn3101   2532   aina2036 pre4314   ppro846   aosi1330 pre1519 art3588   ad4008
with his disciples: and he said unto them, Let us go over unto the other side
art3588 nn3041   2532   ainp321
of the lake. And they launched forth.

        1161   ppro846 pap4126   aina879   2532   aina2597   an,nn2978   an,nn417
23 But as they sailed he fell asleep: and there came down a storm of wind
pre1519 art3588 nn3041   2532   ipf4845   2532   ipf2793
on the lake; and they were filled *with water,* and were*in*jeopardy.

        1161   apta4334   aina1326   ppro846 pap3004   an,nn1988   an,nn1988
24 And they came to him, and awoke him, saying, Master, master, we
pinm622   1161 art3588 apta1453   aina2008   art3588   nn417   2532 art3588   nn2830   art3588   nn5204
perish. Then he arose, and rebuked the wind and the raging of the water:
2532   aom3973   2532   aom1096   an,nn1055
and they ceased, and there was a calm.

        1161   aina2036   ppro846   ad4226   pin2076 ppro5216 art,nn4102 1161   aptp5399
25 And he said unto them, Where is your faith? And they being afraid
aina2296   pap3004   rcpro240/pre4314   pr/inpro5101 (686)   pin2076 depro3778 3754
wondered, saying one*to*another, What*manner*of*man is this! for he
pin2004   2532   art3588   nn417   2532 art,nn5204 2532   pin5219 ppro846
commandeth even the winds and water, and they obey him.

Jesus Heals the Gadarene Demoniac (Matt. 8:28-34; Mark 5:1-20)

        2532   aina2668   pre1519 art3588   nn5561   art3588   ajn1046   repro3748   pin2076
26 And they arrived at the country of the Gadarenes, which is
ad*495   art,nn1056
over against Galilee.

        1161   ppro846   apta1831   pre1909 art,nn1093   aina5221 ppro846 pre1537 art3588 nn4172
27 And when he went forth to land, there met him out of the city a
idpro5100 an,nn435 repro3739 ipf2192 an,nn1140(pre1537) an,aj2425/an,nn5550 2532   ipf1737   3756 an,nn2440 2532/3756
certain man, which had devils long time, and wore no clothes, neither
ipf3306 pre1722   an,nn3614   235 pre1722 art3588   nn3418
abode in *any* house, but in the tombs.

        (1161)   apta1492 art,nn2424   apta349   2532   aina4363   ppro846 2532
28 When he saw Jesus, he cried out, and fell*down*before him, and with a
an,aj3173 an,nn5456 aina2036   inpro5101/epn1698/2532/epn4671   an,nn2424   an,nn5207   art,nn2316
loud voice said, What*have*I*to*do*with*thee, Jesus, *thou* Son of God
art,aj5310   pinm1189   ppro4675 aosi928   ppro3165 3361
most high? I beseech thee, torment me not.
        1063   aina3853   art3588   aj169   art,nn4151   ainf1831   pre575 art3588 nn444   1063
29 (For he had commanded the unclean spirit to come out of the man. For
an,aj4183/an,nn5550 plpf4884   ppro846 2532   ppmp5442   ipf1196   an,nn254   2532   an,nn3976
oftentimes it had caught him: and he was kept bound with chains and in fetters;
2532   pap1284 art3588   nn1199   ipf1643   pre5259 art3588   nn1142 pre1519 art3588   ajn2048
and he broke the bands, and was driven of the devil into the wilderness.)

30 And Jesus asked him, saying, What is thy name? And he said,

Legion: because many devils were entered into him.

31 And they besought him that he would not command them to go out into the deep.

32 And there was there an herd of many swine feeding on the mountain: and they besought him that he would suffer them to enter into them. And he suffered them.

33 Then went the devils out of the man, and entered into the swine: and the herd ran violently down a steep place into the lake, and were choked.

34 When they*that*fed *them* saw what*was*done, they fled, and went and told *it* in the city and in the country.

35 Then they went out to see what*was*done; and came to Jesus, and found the man, out of whom the devils were departed, sitting at the feet of Jesus, clothed, and in*his*right*mind: and they were afraid.

36 They*also*which*saw *it* told them by*what*means he*that*was*possessed*of*the*devils was healed.

37 Then the whole multitude of the country*of*the*Gadarenes*round*about besought him to depart from them; for they were taken with great fear: and he went up into the ship, and returned*back*again.

38 Now the man out of whom the devils were departed besought him that he might be with him: but Jesus sent*him*away, saying,

39 Return to thine own house, and show how*great*things God hath done unto thee. And he went*his*way, and published throughout the whole city how*great*things Jesus had done unto him.

Jesus Raises Jairus' Daughter (Matt. 9:18-26; Mark 5:21-43)

1161   aom1096   aie5290   art3588   nn3793
40 And it came*to*pass, that, when Jesus was returned, the people *gladly*
aom588   ppro846 1063   ipf2258 an,ajn3956   pap4328   ppro846
received him: for they were   all   waiting for him.

2532   2400   aina2064   an,nn435 (repro3739) an,nn3686   an,nn2383 2532 epn846 ipf5225
41 And, behold, there came a man   named Jairus, and he was a
pr/an,nn758   art3588   art,nn4864   2532   apta4098   pre3844 art,nn2424 art,nn4228   ipf3870   ppro846
ruler of the synagogue: and he fell down at Jesus' feet, and besought him
ainf1525 pre1519 ppro848 art,nn3624
that he would come into his house:

3754   ppro846 ipf2258   an,aj3439   an,nn2364   ad5613   nu1427   an,nn2094   2532 depro3778
42 For he had one only daughter, about twelve years*of*age, and she
ipf599 1161   ppro846 aie5217 art3588   nn3793   ipf4846   ppro846
lay a dying. But as he went the people thronged him.

2532   an,nn1135 pap5607 (pre1722) an,nn4511   an,nn129 (pre575) nu1427   an,nn2094 repro3748
43 And a woman having   an   issue of blood   twelve years, which had
apta4321 an,aj3650   art,nn979 pre1519 an,nn2395   3756   aina2480   aifp2323 pre5259 an,ajn3762
spent all her living upon physicians, neither could be healed of any,

apta4334   ad3693   aom680   art3588   nn2899   ppro846   art,nn2440   2532
44 Came behind *him,* and   touched   the   border of his   garment: and
ad3916   ppro846 art,nn4511   art,nn129   aina2476
immediately her issue of blood stanched.

2532 art,nn2424 aina2036 inpro5101 art,aptm680 ppro3450 1161   an,ajn3956 ppmp720 art,nn4074 2532 art3588
45 And Jesus said, Who touched me? When   all   denied, Peter and they
pre3326 ppro846 aina2036 an,nn1988   art3588   nn3793   pin4912   ppro4571 2532   pin598
that were with him said, Master, the multitude throng thee and press *thee,*
2532   pin3004   inpro5101 art,aptm680   ppro3450
and sayest thou, Who touched me?

1161   art,nn2424 aina2036   idpro5100   aom680   ppro3450 1063 epn1473   aina1097
46 And Jesus said, Somebody hath touched me: for I   perceive that
an,nn1411   apta1831 pre575 ppro1700
virtue is gone out of me.

1161   art3588   nn1135   apta1492 3754   3756 aina2990   aina2064   pap5141
47 And when the woman saw that she was not hid, she came trembling,
2532   apta4363   ppro846   aina518   ppro836   ad*1799 an,aj3956 art3588   nn2992
and falling*down*before him, she declared unto him before all the people
pre1223 repro3739 an,nn156   aom680   ppro846 2532 ad5613   ainp2390   ad3916
for what cause she had touched him, and how she was healed immediately.

1161   art3588 aina2036   ppro846   an,nn2364   pim2293   ppro4675 art,nn4102
48 And he said unto her, Daughter, be*of*good*comfort: thy faith hath
pfi4982/ppro4571   pim4198 pre1519 an,nn1515
made*thee*whole; go in peace.

ppro846   ad2089   pap2980   pinm2064   idpro5100   pre3844   art3588
49 While   he   yet   spake,   there   cometh   one   from   the
nn752   pap3004   ppro846 ppro4675 art,nn2364   pfi2348   pim4660
ruler*of*the*synagogue's *house,* saying to him, Thy daughter is dead; trouble
3361 art3588   nn1320
not the Master.

1161   art,nn2424   apta191   ainp611   ppro846   pap3004   pim5399   3361   pim4100

50 But when Jesus heard *it,* he answered him, saying, Fear not: believe

an,aj3440 2532   fp4982

only, and she shall be made whole.

1161   apta1525 pre1519 art3588   nn3614   aina863   3756/an,ajn3762   ainf1525   1508

51 And when he came into the house, he suffered no man to go in, save

an,nn4074   2532   an,nn2385   2532   an,nn2491   2532   art3588   nn3962   2532   art3588   nn3816

Peter, and James, and John, and the father and the mother of the maiden.

1161   an,ajn3956   ipf2799   2532   ipf2875   ppro846   1161   art3588   aina2036   pim2799   3361

52 And   all   wept,   and   bewailed   her: but   he   said,   Weep not;   she

aina599/3756   235   pin2518

is*not*dead, but sleepeth.

2532   ipf2606/ppro846   pfp1492   3754   aina599

53 And they laughed*him*to*scorn, knowing that she was dead.

1161   ppro846 apta1544   an,ajn3956   ad1854   2532   apta2902 ppro846   art3588   nn5495   aina5455

54 And   he   put them   all   out, and took   her   by the hand, and called,

pap3004   art,nn3816   pim1453

saying, Maid, arise.

2532   ppro846   art,nn4151   aina1994   2532   aina450   ad3916   2532

55 And   her   spirit   came   again,   and   she   arose   straightway: and   he

aina1299   aifp1325 ppro846   ainf5315

commanded to give her meat.

2532   ppro846   art,nn1118   aina1839   1161   art3588   aina3853   ppro846

56 And   her   parents   were   astonished: but   he   charged   them   that   they

ainf2036   an,ajn3767   art,pfp1096

should tell no man what*was*done.

The Twelve Apostles (Matt. 10:5-15; Mark 6:7-13)

1161   aptm4779/ppro848/nu1427/art,nn3101   aina1325 ppro846 an,nn1411   2532

9 Then he called*his*twelve*disciples*together, and gave them power and

an,nn1849   pre1909 an,aj3956 art,nn1140   2532   pinf2323   an,nn3554

authority over all devils, and to cure diseases.

2532   aina649 ppro846   pinf2784   art3588   nn932   art,nn2316   2532   pifm2390 art3588 pap770

2 And he sent them to preach the kingdom of God, and to heal the sick.

2532   aina2036 pre4314   ppro846   pim142   an,ajn3367   pre1519   art,nn3598   3383   an,nn4464

3 And he said unto them, Take nothing for *your* journey, neither staves,

3383 an,nn4082   3383   an,nn740   3383   an,nn694   3383   pinf2192 nu1417 an,nn5509   pre303

nor scrip, neither bread, neither money; neither have two coats apiece.

2532   repro3739/302   an,nn3614   asbp1525 pre1519   ad1563   pim3306   2532   ad1564   pim1831

4 And whatsoever house ye enter into, there abide, and thence depart.

2532   an,ajn3745/302   3361   asbm1209   ppro5209   ppmp1831   pre575   depro1565 art,nn4172

5 And whosoever will not receive you, when ye   go   out   of   that   city,

aima660   art3588   2532   nn2868   pre575 ppro5216 art,nn4228 pre1519   an,nn3142   pre1909   ppro846

shake off the very dust from your feet for a testimony against them.

1161   ppmp1831   ipf1330   pre2596   art3588   nn2968   ppmp2097

6 And they departed, and went through the towns, preaching*the*gospel,

2532   pap2323   ad3837

and healing everywhere.

Herod Disturbed (Matt. 14:1-12; Mark 6:14-29)

1161   an,nn2264 art3588   nn5076   aina191   an,aj3956   art,ppmp1096   pre5259 ppro846 2532

7 Now Herod the tetrarch heard of all that*was*done by him: and he

ipf1280   aid3004 pre5259 idpro5100   3754 an,nn2491   pfip1453 pre1537

was perplexed, because that it was said of some, that John was risen from

an,ajn3498

the dead;

1161   pre5259 idpro5100   3754 an,nn2243   ainp5316   1161   an,ajn243   3754 nu1520   art3588

8 And of some, that Elijah had appeared; and of others, that one of the

an,ajn744   nn4396   aina450

old prophets was risen again.

2532   art,nn2264 aina2036 an,nn2491   epn1473   aina607   1161 inpro5101 pin2076 pr/depro3778 pre4012

9 And Herod said, John have I beheaded: but who is this, of

repro3739 epn1473 pin191   an,ajn5108   2532   ipf2212   ainf1492 ppro846

whom I hear such things? And he desired to see him.

Jesus Feeds the Five Thousand (Matt. 14:13-21; Mark 6:30-44; John 6:1-14)

2532 art3588   nn652   apta5290   aom1334 ppro846 an,ajn3745

10 And the apostles, when they were returned, told him all that they had

aina4160   2532   apta3880 ppro846   aina5298   pre2596/an,ajn2398 pre1519   an,aj2048 an,nn5117

done. And he took them, and went aside privately into a desert place belonging

an,nn4172 ppmp2564   966

to the city called Bethsaida.

1161   art3588   nn3793   apta1097   aina190   ppro846 2532   aptm1209

11 And the people, when they knew it, followed him: and he received

ppro846   ipf2980   ppro846   pre4012   art3588   nn932   art,nn2316 2532   ipf2390

them, and spake unto them of the kingdom of God, and healed

art,pap2192   an,nn5532   an,nn2322

them*that*had need of healing.

1161   art3588 nn2250   aom756   pinf2827   1161   apta4334 art3588   nu,ajn1427

12 And when the day began to wear away, then came the twelve, and

aina2036   ppro846   aima630/art3588/nn3793   2443   apta565 pre1519 art3588   nn2968

said unto him, Send*the*multitude*away, that they may go into the towns

2532   art,nn68   an,nn2945   asba2647   2532 asba2147 an,nn1979   3754   pin2070 ad5602 pre1722

and country round about, and lodge, and get victuals: for we are here in a

an,aj2048   an,nn5117

desert place.

1161   aina2036 pre4314   ppro846 aima1325 epn5210 ppro846   ainf5315 1161   art3588 aina2036 ppro2254

13 But he said unto them, Give ye them to eat. And they said, We

pin1526 3756 cd/an,ajn4119 2228 nu4002 an,nn740   2532 nu1417 an,nn2486   1509   epn2249   aptp4198

have no more but five loaves and two fishes; except we should go and

asba59 an,nn1033 pre1519 an,aj3956 depro5126   art,nn2992

buy meat for all this people.

1063   ipf2258   ad5616   nu4000   an,nn435 1161   art3588 aina2036 pre4314 ppro848

14 For they were about five thousand men. And he said to his

art,nn3101   ppro846   aima2625   pre303 nu,ajn4004   an,nn2828

disciples, Make them sit down by fifties in a company.

2532   aina4160 ad3779 2532   an,ajn537   aina347
15 And they did so, and made them all sit down.

1161   apta2983 art3588 nu4002 nn740   2532 art3588 nu1417   nn2486   apta308   pre1519
16 Then he took the five loaves and the two fishes, and looking up to

art,nn3772   aina2127   pppro846 2532   aina2622 2532   ipf1325   art3588   nn3101   ainf3908
heaven, he blessed them, and broke, and gave to the disciples to set before

art3588   nn3793
the multitude.

2532   aina5315 2532   an,ajn3956 ainp5526 2532   ainp142
17 And they did eat, and were all filled: and there was taken up of

an,nn2801   art,apta4052   pppro846 nu1427   an,nn2894
fragments that remained to them twelve baskets.

Peter's Confession (Matt. 16:13-19; Mark 8:27-29)

2532   aom1096   pppro846 aie1511 pre,an,nn2651 ppmp4336   art,nn3101
18 And it came*to*pass, as he was alone praying, his disciples

ipf4895   pppro846 2532   aina1905   pppro846   pap3004 pr/inpro5101 pin3004 art3588   nn3793   pppro3165
were with him: and he asked them, saying, Whom say the people that I

pinf1511
am?

(1161) art3588   aptp611   aina2036 an,nn2491 art3588   nn910   1161 an,ajn243   an,nn2243 1161
19 They answering said, John the Baptist; but some *say,* Elijah; and

an,ajn243   3754 idpro5100   art3588 an,ajn744   nn4396   aina450
others *say,* that one of the old prophets is risen again.

(1161)   aina2036   pppro846 1161 pr/inpro5101 pin3004 epn5210   pppro3165 pinf1511 (1161) art,nn4074
20 He said unto them, But whom say ye that I am? Peter

aptp611   aina2036 art3588 nn5547   art,nn2316
answering said, The Christ of God.

Jesus Predicts His Death and Resurrection (Matt. 16:20-28; Mark 8:30—9:1)

1161 art3588   apta2008   pppro846   aina3853   ainf2036 an,ajn3367
21 And he straitly charged them, and commanded *them* to tell no man

depro5124
that thing;

apta2036   art3588 nn5207   art,nn444 pin1163 aifp3958   an,ajn4183   2532   aifp593   pre575
22 Saying, The Son of man must suffer many things, and be rejected of

art3588 ajn4245   2532   an,nn749   2532 an,nn1122 2532   aifp615 2532   aifp1453 art3588 nu,aj5154
the elders and chief priests and scribes, and be slain, and be raised the third

nn2250
day.

1161   ipf3004 pre4314   an,ajn3956 1487 idpro5100   pin2309 ainf2064 ad*3694 pppro3450
23 And he said to *them* all, If any *man* will come after me, let him

aipp533 rxpro1438 2532   aima142   pppro848 art,nn4716 pre2596/an,nn2250 2532 pim190 pppro3427
deny himself, and take up his cross daily, and follow me.

1063   repro3739/302   psa2309 ainf4982 ppro848 art,nn5590   ft622   ppro846   1161   repro3739/302

24 For whosoever will save his   life   shall lose it: but whosoever will

asba622 ppro848 art,nn5590   ad*1752/ppro1700   depro3778   ft4982 ppro846

lose his   life for*my*sake, the same shall save it.

1063   inpro5101   an,nn444   pinm5623   apta2770 art3588 an,aj3650   nn2889   1161 apta622

☞ 25 For what is a man advantaged, if he gain the whole world, and lose

rxpro1438   2228   aptp2210

himself, or be cast away?

1063   repro3739/302   asbp1870   ppro3165 2532   art,popro1699 an,nn3056   depro5126

26 For whosoever shall be ashamed of me and of my   words, of him

art3588 nn5207   art,nn444   fp1870   ad3752   asba2064 pre1722 ppro848 art,nn1391 2532

shall the Son of man be ashamed, when he shall come in his own glory, and

art,nn3962   2532   art3588 an,aj40   nn32

in his Father's, and of the holy angels.

1161   pin3004 ppro5213   ad230   pin1526 idpro5100 art,pfp2476   ad5602 repro3739

27 But I tell you of*a*truth, there be some standing here, which shall

efn3364 fm1089   an,nn2288 ad2193/302   asba1492 art3588   nn932   art,nn2316

not taste of death, till   they see the kingdom of God.

The Transfiguration of Jesus (Matt. 17:1-8; Mark 9:2-8)

1161   aom1096   ad5616   nu3638 an,nn2250 pre3326 depro5128   art,nn3056   (2532) apta3880

28 And it came*to*pass about eight days after these sayings, he took

art,nn4074 2532 an,nn2491 2532 an,nn2385   aina305   pre1519   art,nn3735   aifm4336

Peter and John and James, and went up into a mountain to pray.

2532   (aom1096) ppro846 aie4336   art3588   nn1491   ppro846   art,nn4383   pr/an,aj2087

29 And as   he prayed, the fashion of his countenance was altered,

2532 ppro846 art,nn2441   pr/an,aj3022   pr/pap1823

and his raiment was white and glistering.

2532   2400   ipf4814   ppro846 nu1417 an,nn444 repro3748 ipf2258 pr/an,nn3475 2532

30 And, behold, there talked with him two men, which were Moses and

pr/an,nn2243

Elijah:

repro3739   aptp3700   pre1722 an,nn1391   ipf3004   ppro846   art,nn1841   repro3739   ipf3195

31 Who appeared in glory, and spake of his decease which he should

pinf4137   pre1722   2419

accomplish at Jerusalem.

1161 art,nn4074 2532 art3588   pre4862 ppro846 ipf2258   pfpp916   an,nn5258 1161

32 But Peter and they that were with him were heavy with sleep: and when

apta1235   aina1492 ppro846 art,nn1391 2532 art3588 nu1417   nn444   art,pfp4921

they were awake, they saw his glory, and the two men that*stood*with

ppro846

him.

2532   aom1096   ppro846   aie1316   pre575 ppro846 art,nn4074 aina2036 pre4314

33 And it came*to*pass, as they departed from him, Peter said unto

art,nn2424   an,nn1988   pin2076 pr/an,aj2570 ppro2248   pinf1511 ad5602   2532   aosi4160   nu5140

Jesus, Master, it is   good for us to be here: and let us make three

---

☞ 9:25 See note on Hebrews 6:1–6.

an,nn4633   nu,ajn3391   ppro4671   2532   nu,ajn3391   an,nn3475   2532   nu,ajn3391   an,nn2243   3361

tabernacles; one for thee, and one for Moses, and one for Elijah: not

pfp1492   repro3739   pin3004

knowing what he said.

(1161)   ppro846 depro5023 pap3004   aom1096   an,nn3507   2532   aina1982   ppro846

34 While he thus spake, there came a cloud, and overshadowed them:

1161   ainp5399   depro1565 aie1525   pre1519 art3588   nn3507

and they feared as they entered into the cloud.

2532   aom1096   an,nn5456   pre1537 art3588   nn3507   pap3004   depro3778 pin2076 ppro3450

35 And there came a voice out of the cloud, saying, This is my

art,aj27   pr/art,nn5207 pim191 epn846

beloved Son: hear him.   *(Ps. 2:7; Is. 42:1)*

2532   art3588   nn5456   aie1096 art,nn2424   ainp2147   an,aj3440   2532   epn846

36 And when the voice was past, Jesus was found alone. And they

aina4601   2532 aina518 an,ajn3762 pre1722 depro1565 art,nn2250   an,aj3762   repro3739

kept*it*close, and told no man in those days any*of*those*things which they

pfp3708

had seen.

Jesus Heals a Boy With an Unclean Spirit (Matt. 17:14-18; Mark 9:14-27)

1161   aom1096   pre1722 art3588 ad1836   nn2250   ppro846

37 And it came*to*pass, that on the next day, when they were

apta2718   pre575 art3588 nn3735 an,aj4183   an,nn3793 aina4876 ppro846

come down from the hill, much people met him.

2532   2400   an,nn435 pre575 art3588   nn3793   aina310   pap3004 an,nn1320

38 And, behold, a man of the company cried out, saying, Master, I

pinm1189   ppro4675 aima1914 pre1909 ppro3450 art,nn5207 3754   pin2076 ppro3427   pr/an,aj3439

beseech thee, look upon my son: for he is mine only child.

2532   2400   an,nn4151 pin2983   ppro846   2532   ad1810   pin2896   2532

39 And, lo, a spirit taketh him, and he suddenly crieth out; and it

pin4682   ppro846   pre3326/an,nn876   2532 pap4937   ppro846 ad3425   pin672   pre575

teareth him that he foameth again, and bruising him hardly departeth from

ppro846

him.

2532   ainp1189   ppro4675 art,nn3101   2443   psa1544/ppro846   2532   ainp1410

40 And I besought thy disciples to cast*him*out; and they could

3756

not.

1161   art,nn2424   aptp611   aina2036 5599   an,aj571   2532   pfpp1294   an,nn1074

41 And Jesus answering said, O faithless and perverse generation,

ad2193/ad4219   fm2071 pre4314 ppro5209 2532 fm430 ppro5216 aima4317 ppro4675 art,nn5207 ad5602

how long shall I be with you, and suffer you? Bring thy son hither.

1161   ppro846   ad2089 ppmp4334 art3588 nn1140   aina4486/ppro846   2532 aina4952

42 And as he was yet a coming, the devil threw*him*down, and tore *him*.

1161   art,nn2424   aina2008 art3588   aj169   art,nn4151   2532 aom2390   art3588   nn3816   2532

And Jesus rebuked the unclean spirit, and healed the child, and

aina591/ppro846   ppro846 art,nn3962

delivered*him*again to his father.

Jesus Again Foretells His Death (Matt. 17:22,23; Mark 9:30-32)

43 And they were all amazed at the mighty power of God. But while they wondered every one at all things which Jesus did, he said unto his disciples,

44 Let these sayings sink down into your ears: for the Son of man shall be delivered into the hands of men.

45 But they understood not this saying, and it was hid from them, that they perceived it not: and they feared to ask him of that saying.

Jesus Sets a Child Before His Disciples (Matt. 18:1-5; Mark 9:33-37)

46 Then there arose a reasoning among them, which of them should be greatest.

47 And Jesus, perceiving the thought of their heart, took a child, and set him by him,

48 And said unto them, Whosoever shall receive this child in my name receiveth me: and whosoever shall receive me receiveth him*that*sent me: for he*that*is least among you all, the same shall be great.

Others Who Work in Christ's Name (Mark 9:38-40)

49 And John answered and said, Master, we saw one casting out devils in thy name; and we forbade him, because he followeth not with us.

50 And Jesus said unto him, Forbid him not: for he that is not against us is for us.

A Samaritan Village Refuses to Receive Jesus

₁₁₆₁ _{aom1096} _{art3588} _{nn2250} _{aie4845} ₂₅₃₂ _{ppro846}
51 And it came*to*pass, when the time was come that he should be
_{art,nn354} _{epn846} _{aina4741} _{ppro848 art,nn4383} _{infg4198 pre1519} ₂₄₁₉
received up, he steadfastly set his face to go to Jerusalem,

₂₅₃₂ _{aina649} _{an,nn32} _{pre4253} _{ppro848 an,nn4383} ₂₅₃₂ _{aptp4198} _{aina1525}
52 And sent messengers before his face: and they went, and entered
_{pre1519} _{an,nn2968} _{an,ajn4541} ₅₆₂₀ _{ainf2090} _{ppro846}
into a village of the Samaritans, to make ready for him.

₂₅₃₂ ₃₇₅₆ _{aom1209} _{ppro846} ₃₇₅₄ _{ppro846 art,nn4383 ipf2258}
53 And they did not receive him, because his face was as though he would
_{pomp4198 pre1519} ₂₄₁₉
go to Jerusalem.

₁₁₆₁ _{ppro846} _{art,nn3101} _{an,nn2385} ₂₅₃₂ _{an,nn2491 apta1492} _{aina2036 an,nn2962 pin2309}
54 And when his disciples James and John saw *this*, they said, Lord, wilt
_{asba2036} _{an,nn4442} _{ainf2597} _{pre575} _{art,nn3772} ₂₅₃₂ _{ainf355} _{ppro846}
thou that we command fire to come down from heaven, and consume them,
₂₅₃₂ _{ad5613 an,nn2243 aina4160}
even as Elijah did?   *(2 Kgs. 1:10,12)*

₁₁₆₁ _{aptp4762} _{aina2008} _{ppro846} _{2532 aina2036} _{pin1492 3756} _{repro3634}
55 But he turned, and rebuked them, and said, Ye know not what manner
_{an,nn4151 epn5210 pin2075}
of spirit ye are of.

₁₀₆₃ _{art3588 nn5207} _{art,nn444} ₃₇₅₆ _{aina2064} _{ainf622} _{an,nn444 an,nn5590} ₂₃₅ _{ainf4982}
56 For the Son of man is not come to destroy men's lives, but to save
₂₅₃₂ _{ainp4198 pre1519} _{an,aj2087} _{an,nn2968}
them. And they went to another village.

God's Kingdom Must Be First (Matt. 8:19-22)

₁₁₆₁ _{aom1096} _{ppro846} _{ppmp4198 pre1722 art3588} _{nn3598} _{idpro5100}
57 And it came*to*pass, that, as they went in the way, a certain *man*
_{aina2036 pre4314} _{ppro846 an,nn2962} _{ft190} _{ppro4671} _{ad3699/302} _{psa565}
said unto him, Lord, I will follow thee whithersoever thou goest.

₂₅₃₂ _{art,nn2424 aina2036} _{ppro846 art,nn258} _{pin2192} _{an,nn5454} ₂₅₃₂ _{art,nn4071} _{art3588 nn3772}
58 And Jesus said unto him, Foxes have holes, and birds of the air *have*
_{an,nn2682} ₁₁₆₁ _{art3588 nn5207} _{art,nn444} _{pin2192 3756} _{ad4226} _{psa2827} _{art,nn2776}
nests; but the Son of man hath not where to lay *his* head.

₁₁₆₁ _{aina2036 pre4314} _{an,ajn2087} _{pim190} _{ppro3427} ₁₁₆₁ _{art3588 aina2036} _{an,nn2962 aima2010 ppro3427}
59 And he said unto another, Follow me. But he . said, Lord, suffer me
_{nu,ajn4412} _{apta565} _{ainf2290 ppro3450} _{art,nn3962}
first to go and bury my father.

₍₁₁₆₁₎ _{art,nn2424 aina2036} _{ppro846 aima863 art3588 ajn3498} _{ainf2290 rxpro1438 art,ajn3498} _{1161 apta565 epn4771}
60   Jesus said unto him, Let the dead bury their dead: but go thou and
_{pim1229} _{art3588} _{nn932} _{art,nn2316}
preach the kingdom of God.

₁₁₆₁ _{an,ajn2087} ₂₅₃₂ _{aina2036 an,nn2962} _{ft190} _{ppro4671} _{1161 aima2010 ppro3427 nu,ajn4412}
61 And another also said, Lord, I will follow thee; but let me first go
_{ainf657} _{art3588} _{pre1519 ppro3450 art,nn3624}
bid*them*farewell, which are at home at my house.

1161   art,nn2424 aina2036 pre4314 ppro846   an,ajn3762   apta1911 ppro848 art,nn5495 pre1909

62 And Jesus said unto him, No man, having put his hand to the

an,nn723   2532   pap991   pre1519/art,ad3694 pin2076 pr/an,aj2111 pre1519 art3588   nn932   art,nn2316

plough, and looking back, is fit for the kingdom of God.

Jesus Sends the Seventy

(1161) pre3226   depro5023   art3588 nn2962   aina322   an,aj2087 nu,ajn1440 2532 2532

10
After these things the Lord appointed other seventy also, and

aina649 ppro846   pre303/nu,ajn1417   pre4253 ppro848 an,nn4383 pre1519 an,aj3956 an,nn4172 2532

sent them two*and*two before his face into every city and

an,nn5117 repro3757   ppro846   ipf3195   pifm2064

place, whither he himself would come.

3767   ipf3004   pre4314 ppro846   art3588   nn2326   3303   pr/an,aj4183 1161 art3588

2 Therefore said he unto them, The harvest truly *is* great, but the

nn2040   pr/an,aj3641 aipp1189   3767   art3588 nn2962   art3588 nn2326   3704

laborers *are* few: pray ye therefore the Lord of the harvest, that he would

psa1544   an,nn2040 pre1519 ppro848 art,nn2326

send forth laborers into his harvest.

aima5217   2400   epn1473   pin649/ppro5209   ad5613   an,nn704   pre1722/an,ajn3319

3 Go*your*ways: behold, I send*you*forth as lambs among

an,nn3074

wolves.

pim941   3361   an,nn905   3361 an,nn4082 3366 an,nn5266 2532 aosi782   an,ajn3367 pre2596 art3588

4 Carry neither purse, nor scrip, nor shoes: and salute no man by the

nn3598

way.

1161   pre1519   repro373/302   an,nn3614   psmp1525 nu,ajn4412 pim3004 an,nn1515   depro5129

5 And into whatsoever house ye enter, first say, Peace *be* to this

art,nn3614

house.

2532   1437 (3303) art3588 nn5207   an,nn1515 psa5600 ad1563 ppro5216 art,nn1515   fm1879 pre1909 ppro846

6 And if the son of peace be there, your peace shall rest upon it:

1490   ft344/pre1909/ppro5209

if not, it shall turn*to*you*again.

1161   pre1722 art3588 epn846   nn3614   pim3306   pap2068   2532   pap4095

7 And in the same house remain, eating and drinking

art3588/pre3844/ppro846   1063 art3588 nn2040 pin2076 pr/an,aj514 ppro848 art,nn3408 pim3327 3361

such*things*as*they*give: for the laborer is worthy of his hire. Go not

pre1537 an,nn3614 pre1519 an,nn3614

from house to house.

2532   pre1519 (1161) repro3739/302 an,nn4172 psmp1525 2532   psmp1209 ppro5209 pim2068

8 And into whatsoever city ye enter, and they receive you, eat

art,ppmp3908   ppro5213

such*things*as*are*set*before you:

2532 pim2323 art3588 ajn772   pre1722/ppro846 2532 pim3004   ppro846 art3588 nn932

9 And heal the sick that are therein, and say unto them, The kingdom of

art,nn2316   pfi1448   pre1909 ppro5209

God is come nigh unto you.

10 But into   whatsoever city ye enter, and they receive you not,
go*your*ways*out into the streets of the same, and say,

11 Even the very dust of your city, which cleaveth on us, we do
wipe off against you: notwithstanding be*ye*sure of this, that the kingdom of
God is come nigh unto you.

12 But I say unto you, that it shall be more tolerable in that day for
Sodom, than for that city.

Woes to Unrepentant Cities (Matt. 11:20-24)

13 Woe unto thee, Chorazin! woe unto thee, Bethsaida! for if the
mighty works had been done in Tyre and Sidon, which*have*been*done in
you, they had a*great*while*ago repented, sitting in sackcloth and ashes.

14 But it shall be more tolerable for Tyre and Sidon at the judgment,
than for you.   *(Is. 23:1-18; Ezek. 26:2-28:23; Joel 3:4-8)*

15 And thou, Capernaum, which*art*exalted to heaven, shalt be
thrust down to hell.   *(Is. 14:13,15)*

16 He*that*heareth you heareth me; and he*that*despiseth you
despiseth me; and he*that*despiseth me despiseth him that sent me.

The Return of the Seventy

17 And the seventy returned again with joy, saying, Lord, even the
devils are subject unto us through thy name.

18 And he said unto them, I beheld Satan as lightning fall from
heaven.   *(Is. 14:12)*

19 Behold, I give unto you power to tread on serpents and scorpions,

2532 pre1909 an,aj3956 art3588   nn1411   art3588   ajn2190   2532   an,ajn3762   efn3364   asba91

and over all the power of the enemy: and nothing shall by*any*means hurt
ppro5209

you.   *(Ps. 91:13)*

                   4133   pre1722 depro5129   pim5463   3361   3754 art3588   nn4151   pinp5293

20 Notwithstanding in this rejoice not, that the spirits are subject unto
ppro5213 1161   ad3123   pim5463   3754   ppro5216 art,nn3686   ainp1125 pre1722 art,nn3772

you; but rather rejoice, because your names are written in   heaven.

Jesus Praises God *(Matt. 11:25-27; 13:16,17)*

            pre1722 ppro846 art,nn5610 art,nn2424   aom21   art,nn4151   2532   aina2036   pinm1843   ppro4671

21 In that hour Jesus rejoiced in spirit, and said, I thank thee, O
an,nn3962   an,nn2962   art,nn3772   2532   art,nn1093   3754   aina613   depro5023   pre575

Father, Lord of heaven and earth, that thou hast hid these things from the
an,ajn4680 2532   an,ajn4908   2532   aina601   ppro846   an,ajn3516   3483   art,nn3962   3754

wise and prudent, and hast revealed them unto babes: even so, Father; for
ad3779   aom1096   pr/an,nn2107   ad*1715/ppro4675

so it seemed good in*thy*sight.

                 an,ajn3956   ainp3860   ppro3427 pre5259 ppro3450 art,nn3962   2532   an,ajn3762   pin1097

22 All things are delivered to me   of   my Father: and no man knoweth
inpro5101 art3588 pr/nn5207 pin2076 1508 art3588   nn3962   2532 inpro5101 art3588 pr/hn3962 pin2076 1508 art3588 nn5207 2532

who the Son is, but the Father; and who the Father is, but the Son, and
           repro3739/1437 art3588 nn5207 psmp1014   ainf601

he to whom the Son will reveal *him*.

           2532   aptp4762   pre4314   art,nn3101   aina2036 pre2596/an,ajn2398 pr/an,aj3107

23 And he turned him unto *his* disciples, and said privately, Blessed *are*
art3588 nn3788   art,pap991   repro3739   pin991

the eyes which see the things that ye see:
          1063   pin3004 ppro5213 3754 an,aj4183   an,nn4396   2532   an,nn935   aina2309   ainf1492

24 For I tell you, that many prophets and kings have desired to see those
          repro3739 epn5210 pin991   2532   3756 aina1492   2532   ainf191   repro3739

things which ye see, and have not seen *them*; and to hear those things which
          pin191   2532   3756 aina191

ye hear, and have not heard *them*.

A Good Samaritan

           2532   2400   idpro5100   an,nn3544   aina450   pap1598   ppro846 (2532)   pap3004

25 And, behold, a certain lawyer stood up, and tempted him,   saying,
art,nn1320 inpro5101   apta4160   ft2816   an,aj166   an,nn2222

Master, what shall I do to inherit eternal life?
      (1161) art3588 aina2036 pre4314 ppro846 inpro5101   pfip1125   pre1722 art3588 nn3551   ad4459   pin314

26   He said unto him, What is written in the law? how readest thou?

27 And he answering said, Thou shalt love the Lord thy God with all thy heart, and with all thy soul, and with all thy strength, and with all thy mind; and thy neighbor as thyself.   *(Lev. 18:5; Deut. 6:5)*

28 And he said unto him, Thou hast answered right: this do, and thou shalt live.

29 But he, willing to justify himself, said unto Jesus, And who is my neighbor?

30 And Jesus answering said, A certain *man* went down from Jerusalem to Jericho, and fell among thieves, which stripped him of his raiment, and wounded *him*, and departed, leaving *him* half dead.

31 And by chance there came down a certain priest that way: and when he saw him, he passed*by*on*the*other*side.

32 And likewise a Levite, when he was at the place, came and looked *on him*, and passed*by*on*the*other*side.

33 But a certain Samaritan, as he journeyed, came where*he*was: and when he saw him, he had compassion *on him*,

34 And went to *him*, and bound up his wounds, pouring in oil and wine, and set him on his own beast, and brought him to an inn, and took care of him.

35 And on the morrow when he departed, he took out two pence, and gave *them* to the host, and said unto him, Take care of him; and whatsoever thou spendest more, when I come again, I will repay thee.

36 Which now of these three, thinkest thou, was neighbor unto him*that*fell among the thieves?

37 And he said, He*that*showed mercy on him. Then said Jesus unto him, Go, and do thou likewise.

Visiting Martha and Mary

1161   aom1096   ppro846   aie4198   (2532)   epn846   aina1525   pre1519   idpro5100

38 Now it came*to*pass, as they went, that he entered into a certain

an,nn2968   1161   idpro5100   an,nn1135   an,nn3686   an,nn3136   aom5264   ppro846   pre1519   ppro848   art,nn3624

village: and a certain woman named Martha received him into her house.

2532   depro3592   ipf2258   an,nn79   ppmp2564   an,nn3137   repro3739   2532   apta3869   pre3844   art,nn2424   art,nn4228

39 And she had a sister called Mary, which also sat at Jesus' feet, and

ipf191   ppro846   art,nn3056

heard his word.

1161   art,nn3136   ipf4049   pre4012   an,aj4183   an,nn1248   1161   apta2186

40 But Martha was cumbered about much serving, and came to him, and

aina2036   an,nn2962   pin3199/3756/ppro4671   3754   ppro3450   art,nn79   aina2641   ppro3165   pinf1247   an,aj3440

said, Lord, dost*thou*not*care that my sister hath left me to serve alone?

aima2036   ppro846   3767   2443   asbm4878   ppro3427

bid her therefore that she help me.

1161   art,nn2424   aptp611   aina2036   ppro846   an,nn3136   an,nn3136

41 And Jesus answered and said unto her, Martha, Martha, thou

pin3309   2532   pinp5182   pre4012   an,ajn4183

art careful and troubled about many things:

1161   nu,ajn1520   pin2076   pr/an,nn5532   1161   an,nn3137   aom1586   art,aj18   an,nn3310

42 But one thing is needful: and Mary hath chosen that good part,

repro3748   3756   fp851   pre575   ppro846

which shall not be taken away from her.

Jesus Teaches the Disciples How to Pray (Matt. 6:9-15; 7:7-11)

2532   aom1096   ppro846   aie1511   ppmp4336   pre1722   idpro5100

11 And it came*to*pass, that, as he was praying in a certain

an,nn5117   ad5613   aom3974   idpro5100   ppro846   art,nn3101   aina2036   pre4314   ppro846

place, when he ceased, one of his disciples said unto him,

an,nn2962   aima1321   ppro2248   pifm4336   ad2531   an,nn2491   2532   aina1321   ppro848   art,nn3101

Lord, teach us to pray, as John also taught his disciples.

1161   aina2036   ppro846   ad3752   psmp4336   pim3004   ppro2257   an,nn3962   art3588   pre1722

☞ 2 And he said unto them, When ye pray, say, Our Father which art in

art,nn3772   aipp37   ppro4675   art,nn3686   ppro4675   art,nn932   aima2064   ppro4675   art,nn2307   aipp1096   ad5613

heaven, Hallowed be thy name. Thy kingdom come. Thy will be done, as

pre1722   an,nn3772   2532   pre1909   art,nn1093

in heaven, so in earth.

pim1325   ppro2254   art,pre2596/an,nn2250   ppro2257   art,aj1967   art,nn740

3 Give us day*by*day our daily bread.

2532   aima863   ppro2254   ppro2257   art,nn266   1063   epn846   2532   pin863   an,aj3956

4 And forgive us our sins; for we also forgive every one that is

pap3784   ppro2254   2532   aosi1533   ppro2248   3361   pre1519   an,nn3986   235   aipm4506   ppro2248   pre575

indebted to us. And lead us not into temptation; but deliver us from

art,ajn4190

evil.

☞ **11:2–4** See the note on Matthew 6:13.

☞ 5 And he said unto them, Which of you shall have a friend, and shall go unto him at midnight, and say unto him, Friend, lend me three loaves;

6 For a friend of mine in his journey is come to me, and I have nothing to set before him?

7 And he from within shall answer and say, Trouble*me*not: the door is now shut, and my children are with me in bed; I cannot rise and give thee.

8 I say unto you, Though he will not rise and give him, because he is his friend, yet because of his importunity he will rise and give him as*many*as he needeth.

☞ 9 And I say unto you, Ask, and it shall be given you; seek, and ye shall find; knock, and it shall be opened unto you.

10 For every one that asketh receiveth; and he*that*seeketh findeth; and to him*that*knocketh it shall be opened.

11 If a son shall ask bread of any of you that is a father, will he give him a stone? or if he ask a fish, will he for a fish give him a serpent?

12 Or if he shall ask an egg, will he offer him a scorpion?

13 If ye then, being evil, know how to give good gifts unto your

---

☞ **11:5–13** This parable deals with the responsibility of the Christian. When someone comes at midnight and asks for bread, the believer should not be indifferent. The Lord spoke this parable to teach Christians that they should earnestly pray on behalf of others and their needs. God wants to satisfy those prayers through them and give them the joy of being intercessors for others.

☞ **11:9** The word that is translated "ask" is *aiteíte* (from *aitéō* [154]). This is the word that the Lord uses when He asks for something from His Father (John 14:16). In the same context, when it comes to the disciples asking something from the Father, the verb *aitéō* is used (Luke 11:13, 14)."Asking in prayer" means coming to the Lord as would a beggar to a generous person. One should not demand anything from God. If God's children will only trust Him for their needs, God will give them their request. Many times, however, people ask for things that are not according to His will. Christians must realize that He will only give the things that are "good" (agathón [18]) in light of eternity and His plan and timetable for the whole world (Eccl. 3:11). "Good" for the believer may not be what he desires, but it is that which God has established as the thing which will execute His plan and bring the believer into a closer relationship with Him. See note on James 5:14, 15.

art,nn5043   an,aj4214   ad3123   pre1537/art,nn3772 art,nn3962 ft1325   an,aj40 an,nn4151
children: how much more shall *your* heavenly Father give the Holy Spirit to
art,pap154   ppro846
them*that*ask him?

Jesus and Beelzebub (Matt. 12:22-30; Mark 3:30-27)

              2532   ipf2258   pap1544   an,nn1140 2532 epn846 ipf2258 pr/an,aj2974 1161
☞ 14 And he was casting out a devil, and it was dumb. And it
       aom1096   art3588 nn1140   apta1831 art3588 ajn2974 aina2980 2532 art3588 nn3793
came*to*pass, when the devil was gone out, the dumb spake; and the people
aina2296
wondered.
        1161   idpro5100 pre1537 ppro846 aina2036   pin1544   art,nn1140 pre1722   954
15 But some of them said, He casteth out devils through Beelzebub the
an,nn758   art3588   nn1140
chief of the devils.
        1161   an,ajn2087 pap3985   ipf2212 pre3844 ppro846 an,nn4592 pre1537 an,nn3772
16 And others, tempting *him,* sought of him a sign from heaven.
        1161 epn846 pfp1492 ppro846 art,nn1270 aina2036   ppro846 an,aj3956   an,nn932
17 But he, knowing their thoughts, said unto them, Every kingdom
aptp1266   pre1909 rxpro1438   pinp2049   2532 an,nn3624   pre1909
divided against itself is brought*to*desolation; and a house *divided* against a
an,nn3624   pin4098
house falleth.
          (1161)1487 art,nn4567 2532   ainp1266   pre1909   rxpro1438 ad4459   ppro846 art,nn932 fp2476
18   If Satan also be divided against himself, how shall his kingdom stand?
3754   pin3004   ppro3165 pinf1544 art,nn1140 pre1722   954
because ye say that   I   cast out devils through Beelzebub.
        1161   1487 epn1473 pre1722   954   pin1544 art,nn1140 pre1722 inpro5101   ppro5216 art,nn5207
19 And if   I   by Beelzebub cast out devils, by whom do your sons
pin1544   pre1223/depro5124   epn846 fm2071 ppro5216 pr/an,nn2923
cast**them**out? therefore shall they be your judges.
        1161 1487   pre1722   an,nn1147   an,nn2316 pin1544 art,nn1140   686   art3588   nn932
20 But if I with the finger of God cast out devils, no doubt the kingdom
art,nn2316   aina5348 pre1909 ppro5209
of God is come upon you.
          ad3752   art,ajn2478 pfpp2528 psa5442 rxpro1438 art,nn833 ppro846 art,nn5224 pin2076 pre1722
21 When a strong man armed keepeth his palace, his goods are in
an,nn1515
peace:
          1161   ad1875   cd/art,ajn2478   ppro846   apta1904   asba3528
22 But when a stronger than he shall come upon him, and overcome
ppro846   pin142   art,nn3833/ppro846 pre1909/repro3739 plpf3982 2532 pin1239 ppro846
him, he taketh from him all*his*armor wherein he trusted, and divideth his
art,nn4661
spoils.

─────────────────────────────────────

☞ 11:14–32 See note on Mark 3:28, 29.

art,pap5607   3361 pre3326 ppro1700 pin2076   pre2596 ppro1700 2532   art,pap4863   3361

23 He*that*is not with me   is against me: and he*that*gathereth not

pre3326 ppro1700   pin4650

with me scattereth.

The Return of the Unclean Spirit (Matt. 12:43-45)

ad3752 art3588   an,aj169   nn4151   asba1831 pre575   art,nn444   pinm1330   pre1223   an,aj504

24 When the unclean spirit is gone out of a man, he walketh through dry

an,nn5117 pap2212 an,nn372 2532 pap2147   3361   pin3004   ft5290 pre1519 ppro3450 art,nn3624

places, seeking rest; and finding none, he saith, I will return unto my house

ad3606 aina1831

whence I came out.

2532   apta2064   pin2147   pfpp4563 2532   pfpp2885

25 And when he cometh, he findeth *it* swept and garnished.

ad5119   pinm4198   2532   pin3880   nu2033 an,aj2087 an,nn4151   cd/an,aj4191

26 Then goeth he, and taketh *to him* seven other spirits more wicked than

rxpro1438   2532   apta1525   2532 pin2730 ad1563   2532 art3588 ajn2078   depro1565 art,nn444

himself; and they enter in, and dwell there: and the last *state* of that man

pinm1096 pr/cd/an,aj5501   art3588 nu,ajn4413

is worse than the first.

True Blessedness

1161   aom1096   ppro846 aie3004   depro5023   idpro5100 an,nn1135 pre1537

27 And it came*to*pass, as he spake these things, a certain woman of

art3588   nn3793   apta1869   an,nn5456   aina2036   ppro846 pr/an,aj3107   art3588   nn2836

the company lifted up her voice, and said unto him, Blessed *is* the womb

art,apta941   ppro4571 2532   an,nn3149 repro3739   aina2337

that bare thee, and the paps which thou hast sucked.

1161 epn846 aina2036   3304   pr/an,aj3107   art,pap191   art3588 nn3056   art,nn2316

28 But he said, Yea rather, blessed *are* they*that*hear the word of God,

2532 pap5442 ppro846

and keep it.

The Demand for a Sign (Matt. 12:38-42; Mark 8:12)

1161   art3588   nn3793   ppmp1865   aom756   pinf3004

29 And when the people were gathered*thick*together, he began to say,

depro3778 pin2076   an,aj4190 pr/art,nn1074   pin1934   an,nn4592 2532   3756 an,nn4592

This is an evil generation: they seek a sign; and there shall no sign be

fp1325 ppro846 1508 art3588 nn4592   an,nn2495 art3588   nn4396

given it, but the sign of Jonah the prophet.

1063 ad2531 an,nn2495 aom1096 pr/an,nn4592   art,nn444   ajn3536   ad3779   2532 art3588 nn5207

30 For as Jonah was a sign unto the Ninevites, so shall also the Son

art,nn444 fm2071   depro5026   art,nn1074

of man be to this generation.

an,nn938   an,nn3558   fp1453   pre1722 art3588   nn2920   pre3326 art3588   nn435

31 The queen of the south shall rise up in the judgment with the men of

depro5026   art,nn1074   2532   ft2632   ppro846   3754   aina2064 pre1537 art3588   nn4009

this generation, and condemn them: for she came from the utmost parts of

art3588   nn1093   ainf191 art3588   nn4678   an,nn4672   2532   2400   pr/cd/an,aj4119

the earth to hear the wisdom of Solomon; and, behold, a greater than

an,nn4672   ad5602

Solomon *is* here.   *(1 Kgs. 10:1-10; 2 Chr. 9:1-12)*

an,nn435   3535   fm450   pre1722 art3588   nn2920   pre3326 depro5026

32 The men of Nineveh shall rise up in the judgment with this

art,nn1074   2532   ft2632   ppro846 3754   aina3340   pre1519 art3588   nn2782

generation, and shall condemn it: for they repented at the preaching of

an,nn2495   2532   2400   pr/cd/an,aj4119   an,nn2495   ad5602

Jonah; and, behold, a greater than Jonah *is* here.   *(Jon. 3:8,10)*

Light Should Not Be Hidden *(Matt. 5:15; 6:22,23)*

(1161)   an,ajn3762   apta681   an,nn3088   pin5087   pre1519   an,ajn2927

33   No man, when he hath lighted a candle, putteth *it* in a secret place,

3761   pre5259   art,nn3426   235 pre1909   art,nn3087   2443   art,ppmp1531

neither under a bushel, but on a candlestick, that they*which*come*in may

psa991 art3588 nn5338

see the light.

art3588 pr/nn3088   art3588   nn4983   pin2076 art3588   nn3788   3767   ad3752   ppro4675 art,nn3788 psa5600

34 The light of the body is   the eye: therefore when thine eye   is

pr/an,aj573 ppro4675 an,aj3650 art,nn4983 2532 pin2076   pr/an,aj5460   1161   ad1875   psa5600 pr/an,aj4190

single, thy whole body also is full*of*light; but when *thine eye* is   evil,

ppro4675 art,nn4983 2532   pr/an,aj4652

thy body also *is* full*of*darkness.

pim4648   3767   art3588   nn5457   art3588   pre1722 ppro4671 pin2076   3361

35 Take heed therefore that the light which is in thee be not

pr/an,nn4655

darkness.

1487   ppro4675 an,aj3650 art,nn4983   3767   pr/an,aj5460   pap2192   3361/idpro5100 an,nn3313

36 If   thy whole body therefore *be* full*of*light, having no part

an,aj4652   an,aj3650   fm2071   pr/an,aj5460   ad5613 ad3752 art3588   nn796   art,nn3088

dark, the whole shall be full*of*light, as when the bright shining of a candle

psa5461/ppro4571

doth give*thee*light.

Jesus Denounces the Pharisees and Lawyers *(Matt. 23:1-36; Mark 12:38-40; Luke 20:45-47)*

1161   aie2980   idpro5100   an,nn5330   ipf2065   ppro846 3704 asba709 pre3844 ppro846

37 And as he spake, a certain Pharisee besought him to dine with him:

1161   apta1525   aina377

and he went in, and sat*down*to*meat.

1161   art3588   nn5330   apta1492   aina2296   3754   3756 nu,ajn4412

38 And when the Pharisee saw *it,* he marveled that he had not first

aina907   pre4253   art,nn712

washed before dinner.

1161 art3588 nn2962 aina2036 pre4314 ppro846 ad3568   epn5210 art,nn5330   pin2511   art3588

39 And the Lord said unto him, Now do ye Pharisees make clean the

ad1855   art3588 nn4221 2532 art3588   nn4094   1161 ppro5216   art,ad2081   pin1073   an,nn724   2532

outside of the cup and the platter; but your inward part is full of ravening and

an,nn4189

wickedness.

an,ajn878   3756   art,apta4160   art3588   ad1855   aina4160 art3588

40 *Ye* fools, did not he*that*made that which is without make that which is

ad2081   2532

within also?

4133   aima1325 an,nn1654   art,pap1751   2532   2400   an,ajn3956

41 But rather give alms of such*things*as*ye*have; and, behold, all things

pin2076 pr/an,aj2513   ppro5213

are clean unto you.

235   3759   ppro5213 art,nn5330   3754   pin586 art,nn2238 2532 art,nn4076   2532

42 But woe unto you, Pharisees! for ye tithe mint and rue and

an,aj3956   an,nn3001 2532   pinm3928 art,nn2920 2532 art3588 nn26   art,nn2316 depro5023 ipf1163

all manner of herbs, and pass over judgment and the love of God: these ought

ainf4160   depro2548/3361/pinf863

ye to have done, and*not*to*leave*the*other undone.   *(Lev. 27:30)*

3759   ppro5213   art,nn5330   3754   pin25 art3588   nn4410   pre1722 art3588

43 Woe unto you, Pharisees! for ye love the uppermost seats in the

nn4864   2532   art,nn783   pre1722 art3588   nn58

synagogues, and greetings in the markets.

3759   ppro5213 an,nn1122 2532   an,nn5330   an,ajn5273   3754   pin2075 ad5613

44 Woe unto you, scribes and Pharisees, hypocrites! for ye are as

pr/art,nn3419   art,aj82   2532 art3588 nn444   art,pap4043   ad*1883   pin1492/3756

graves which*appear*not, and the men that walk over *them* are*not*aware *of*

them.

1161   aptp611   idpro5100 art3588   nn3544   pin3004   ppro846 an,nn1320 depro5023

45 Then answered one of the lawyers, and said unto him, Master, thus

pap3004   pin5195   epn2248 2532

saying thou reproachest us also.

1161 art3588 aina2036 3759   epn5213 2532   art,nn3544 3754   pin5412 art,nn444

46 And he said, Woe unto you also, *ye* lawyers! for ye lade men with

an,nn5413   an,aj1419   2532   epn846   pin4379 3756 art3588   nn5413

burdens grievous*to*be*borne, and ye yourselves touch not the burdens with

'nu1520   ppro5216 art,nn1147

one of your fingers.

3759   ppro5213 3754   pin3618 art3588   nn3419   art3588   nn4396   1161 ppro5216

47 Woe unto you! for ye build the sepulchers of the prophets, and your

art,nn3962 aina615   ppro846

fathers killed them.

686   pin3140   2532   pin4909 art3588   nn2041   ppro5216 art,nn3962 3754 epn846

48 Truly ye bear witness that ye allow the deeds of your fathers: for they

3303   aina615   ppro846 1161 epn5210 pin3618 ppro846   art,nn3419

indeed killed them, and ye build their sepulchers.

pre1223/depro5124　2532　aina2036　art3588　　nn4678　　　　art,nn2316　　　　ft649 (pre1519)　ppro846　　an,nn4396

49 Therefore also said the wisdom of God, I will　send　them prophets

2532　an,nn652　2532　　　　pre1537　ppro846　　　　　ft615　2532　　ft1559

and apostles, and *some* of them they shall slay and persecute:

2553　art3588　　nn129　　an,aj3956　art3588　　nn4396　　　art,ppmp1632　　　pre575

50 That the blood of all the prophets, which*was*shed from the

an,nn2602　　　　　an,nn2889　　　　asbp1567　pre575 depro5026　art,nn1074

foundation of the world, may be required of this generation;

pre575　art3588　nn129　　6　ad*2193 art3588　nn129　　an,nn2197　　　art,aptp622

51 From the blood of Abel unto the blood of Zacharias, which perished

ad*3342　art3588　nn2379　2532 art3588　nn3624　　3483　pin3004　　ppro5213　　　fp1567

between the altar and the temple: verily I say unto you, It shall be required

pre575 depro5026　art,nn1074

of this generation.　　　　　　　　*(Gen. 4:8; 2 Chr. 24:20,21)*

3759　　　ppro5213　art,nn3544　3754　　　　　aina142　art3588　nn2807　　art,nn1108

52 Woe unto you, lawyers! for ye have taken away the key of knowledge:

aina1525/3756　epn846　　2532　　　art,ppmp1525　　　aina2967

ye entered*not*in yourselves, and them*that*were*entering*in ye hindered.

1161　　ppro846　pap3004　　depro5023　pre4314　ppro846　art3588　nn1122　2532　art3588

53 And as he said these things unto them, the scribes and the

nn5330　aom756　pinf1758　　ad1171　2532　　　pinf653/ppro846　　pre4012

Pharisees began to urge *him* vehemently, and to provoke*him*to*speak of

cd/an,ajn4119

many things:

pap1748　　ppro846　2532　pap2212　　ainf2340　　idpro5100　　pre1537　ppro846　art,nn4570

54 Laying wait for him, and seeking to catch something out of his mouth,

2443　　　asba2723　ppro846

that they might accuse him.

Hypocrisy Will Be Revealed

pre1722/repro3739　　　　　　　　　　aptp1996

12 In*the*mean*time, when there were gathered together an

art,nn3461　　　　　art,nn3793　　5620　　　pinf2662

innumerable multitude of people, insomuch that they trode

rcpro240　　　aom756　pinf3004 pre4314 ppro848　art,nn3101　nu,ajn4412　pim4337

one*upon*another, he began to say unto his disciples first*of*all, Beware

rxpro1438 pre575 art3588　nn2219　art3588　nn5330　repro3748 pin2076　pr/an,nn5272

ye of the leaven of the Pharisees, which is hypocrisy.

1161　pin2076　an,ajn3762　pr/pfpp4780　repro3739　3756　　fp601　　2532　an,ajn2927

2 For there is nothing covered, that shall not be revealed; neither hid,

repro3739　3756　　fp1097

that shall not be known.

pre473/repro3739　an,ajn3745　　aina2036　pre1722　art,nn4653　　fp191　pre1722

3 Therefore whatsoever ye have spoken in darkness shall be heard in

art3588　nn5457　2532　repro3739　aina2980　pre4314 art3588 nn3775 pre1722　art,nn5009

the light; and that which ye have spoken in the ear in closets shall be

fp2784　pre1909 art3588　nn1430

proclaimed upon the housetops.

Fear God (Matt. 10:28-31)

 1161   pin3004   ppro5213 ppro3450 art,ajn5384   aosi5399/3361   pre575   art,pap615   art3588
4 And I say unto you   my friends, Be*not*afraid of them*that*kill the
 nn4983   2532 pre3326 depro5023 pap2192 3361 idpro5100/cd/an,ajn4055   ainf4160
body, and after that have no   more   that they can do.
 1161   ft5263   ppro5213 inpro5101   asbp5399 aipp5399
5 But I will forewarn you whom ye shall fear: Fear him, which after he
 aime615 art,pap2192 an,nn1849 ainf1685 pre1519 art,nn1067 3483 pin3004   ppro5213 aipp5399 depro5126
hath killed hath power to cast into hell; yea, I say unto you, Fear him.
      3780 nu4002 an,nn4765   pin4453 nu1417   an,nn787   2532 3756 nu1520 pre1537 ppro846 pin2076
6 Are not five sparrows sold for two farthings, and not one of them is
 pfpp1950   ad*1799 art,nn2316
forgotten before God?
      235   2532 art3588   nn2359   ppro5216 art,nn2776   an,aj3956   pfi705   pim5399 3361
7 But even the very hairs of your head are all numbered. Fear not
 3767   pin1308   an,aj4183   an,nn4765
therefore: ye are*of*more*value than many sparrows.

Confessing Christ Before Men (Matt. 10:19,20,32,33; 12:32)

 1161   pin3004   ppro5213 an,ajn3956/repro3739/302   asba3670 (pre1722) ppro1698 ad*1715 art,nn444 (pre1722)
8 Also I say unto you, Whosoever shall confess   me before   men,
ppro846   art3588 nn5207 art,nn444 2532   ft3670   ad*1715 art3588   nn32   art,nn2316
him shall the Son of man also confess before the angels of God:
 1161   art,aptm720   ppro3165 ad*1799 art,nn444   fp533   ad*1799 art3588   nn32
9 But he*that*denieth me before men shall be denied before the angels
 art,nn2316
of God.
      2532 an,ajn3956/repro3739   ft2046   an,nn3056 pre1519 art3588 nn5207   art,nn444
☞ 10 And whosoever shall speak a word against the Son of man, it shall be
 fp863   ppro846 1161   art,apta987   pre1519 art3588 aj40 an,nn4151
forgiven him: but unto him*that*blasphemeth against the Holy Ghost it shall
 3756   fp863
not be forgiven.
      1161   ad3752   psa4374 ppro5209 pre1909 art3588   nn4864   2532   art,nn746
11 And when they bring you unto the synagogues, and *unto* magistrates,
 2532   art,nn1849   pim3309/3361   ad4459 2228 inpro5101   asbm626   2228 inpro5101
and powers, take*ye*no*thought how or what thing ye shall answer, or what
      asba2036
ye shall say:
      1063 art3588 an,aj40   nn4151   ft1321 ppro5029 pre1722 art3588 epn846 nn5610 repro3739   pin1163
12 For the Holy Ghost shall teach you in the same hour what ye ought
 ainf2036
to say.

☞ **12:10** See notes on Mark 3:28, 29.

A Prosperous Farmer

13 And one of the company said unto him, Master, speak to my brother, that he divide the inheritance with me.

14 And he said unto him, Man, who made me a judge or a divider over you?

15 And he said unto them, Take heed, and beware of covetousness: for a man's life consisteth not in*the*abundance of the*things*which*he* possesseth.

16 And he spake a parable unto them, saying, The ground of a certain rich man brought*forth*plentifully:

17 And he thought within himself, saying, What shall I do, because I have no room where to bestow my fruits?

18 And he said, This will I do: I will pull down my barns, and build greater; and there will I bestow all my fruits and my goods.

19 And I will say to my soul, Soul, thou hast much goods laid up for many years; take*thine*ease, eat, drink, and be merry.

20 But God said unto him, Thou fool, this night thy soul shall be required of thee: then whose shall those things be, which thou hast provided?

21 So is he that layeth*up*treasure for himself, and is*not*rich toward God.

Christ Warns Against Earthly Anxiety (Matt. 6:19-21, 24-34)

22 And he said unto his disciples, Therefore I say unto you, Take*no*thought for your life, what ye shall eat; neither for the body, what ye shall put on.

art3588 nn5590 pin2076 pr/cd/an,aj4119   art,nn5160   2532 art3588 nn4983   art,nn1742
23 The life   is   more   than meat, and the body *is more* than raiment.
    aima2657   art3588   nn2876   3754   3756   pin4687 3761 pin2325 repro3739   3756
24 Consider the ravens: for they neither sow nor reap; which neither
pin2076   an,nn5009   3761   an,nn596   2532 art,nn2316 pin5142 ppro846   an,ajn4214   ad3123
have storehouse nor barn; and God feedeth them: how much more
    pin1308/epn5210   art3588   nn4071
are*ye*better than the fowls?   *(Ps. 147:9)*

    1161 inpro5101 pre1537 ppro5216   pap3309   pinm1410 ainf4369 pre1909 ppro848 art,nn2244 nu1520
25 And which of you with taking thought can add to his stature one
an,nn4083
cubit?

    1487   3767   pinm1410/3777   cd/an,ajn1646   inpro5101
26 If   ye   then   be*not*able   to   do   that*thing*which*is*least,   why
    pin3309   pre4012 art3588 ajn3062
take*ye*thought for the rest?

    aima2657   art3588 nn2918   ad4459   pin837   pin2872 3756   pin3514 3761 1161
27 Consider the lilies how they grow: they toil not, they spin not; and yet
    pin3004   ppro5213   an,nn4672   pre1722 an,aj3956 ppro848 art,nn1391   3761   aom4016   ad5613 nu1520
I say unto you, that Solomon in all his glory was not arrayed like one of
depro5130
these.

    (1161) 1487   art,nn2316 ad3779   pin294 art3588   nn5528   pap5607 ad4594 pre1722 art3588   nn68
28   If then God   so clothe the grass, which is today in the field,
    2532   ad839   ppmp906 pre1519   an,nn2823   an,ajn4214   ad3123   epn5209
and tomorrow is cast into the oven; how much more *will he clothe* you, O
    an,ajn3640
ye*of*little*faith?

    2532 pim2212 3361 epn5210 inpro5101   asba5315 2228 inpro5101   asba4095 2532/3361
29 And seek not ye what ye shall eat, or what ye shall drink, neither
    pim3349
be*ye*of*doubtful*mind.

    1063 an,aj3956   depro5023   art3588 nn1484   art3588 nn2889   pin1934   1161 epn5216
30 For all these things do the nations of the world seek after: and your
art,nn3962   pin1492   3754   pin5536   depro5130
Father knoweth that ye have need of these things.

    4133   pim2212 art3588   nn932   art,nn2316 2532 an,aj3956   depro5023
31 But rather seek ye the kingdom of God; and all these things shall be
fp4369   ppro5213
added unto you.

    pim5399   3361   art,aj3398 an,nn4168   3754   aina2106/ppro5216/art,nn3962   ainf1325
32 Fear not, little flock; for it is*your*Father's*good*pleasure to give
ppro5213 art3588   nn932
you the kingdom.

    aima4453   ppro5216/art,pap5224   2532 aima1325 an,nn1654   aima4160   rxpro1438   an,nn905
33 Sell that*ye*have, and give alms; provide yourselves bags which
ppmp3822/3361   an,nn2344   pre1722 art3588   nn3772   an,aj413   ad3699 3756 an,nn2812
wax*not*old, a treasure in the heavens that faileth not, where no thief
    pin1448   3761 an,nn4597   pin1311
approacheth, neither moth corrupteth.

    1063   ad3699 ppro5216 art,nn2344 pin2076 ad1563   ppro5216 art,nn2588 fm2071 2532
34 For where your treasure is, there will your heart be also.

Watchful Servants (Matt. 24:45-51)

ppro5216 art,nn3751 aima2077   pr/pfpp4024   2532   art,nn3088 pr/ppmp2545

35 Let your loins be girded about, and *your* lights burning;

2532   epn5210   pr/an,ajn3664   an,nn444   ppmp4327 rxpro1438 art,nn2962   ad4219

36 And ye yourselves like unto men that wait for their lord, when he will

ft360   pre1537 art3588   nn1062   2443   apta2064   2532   apta2925   asba455

return from the wedding; that when he cometh and knocketh, they may open

ppro846   ad2112

unto him immediately.

pr/an,aj3107   depro1565   art,ajn1401   repro3739 art3588 nn2962   apta2064   ft2147

37 Blessed *are* those servants, whom the lord when he cometh shall find

pap1127   281   pin3004   ppro5213   3754   fm4024   2532   ppro846

watching: verily I say unto you, that he shall gird himself, and make them to

ft347   2532   apta3928   ft1247   ppro846

sit*down*to*meat, and will come forth and serve them.

2532   1437   asba2064 pre1722 art3588   nu,aj1208   an,nn5438   2532 asba2064 pre1722 art3588 nu,aj5154

38 And if he shall come in the second watch, or come in the third

an,nn5438   2532 asba2147   ad3779 pr/an,aj3107 pin1526 depro1565   art,ajn1401

watch, and find *them* so, blessed are those servants.

1161   depro5124 pim1097   3754 1487 art3588   nn3617   ipf1492   an,aj4169

39 And this know, that if the goodman*of*the*house had known what

an,nn5610 art3588   nn2812   pinm2064   aina1127/302   2532   3756   aina863/302

hour the thief would come, he would have watched, and not have suffered

ppro848 art,nn3624   aifp1358

his house to be broken through.

pim1096 epn5210   3767   pr/an,aj2092   2532   3754 art3588 nn5207 art,nn444 pinm2064 (repro3739)

40 Be ye therefore ready also: for the Son of man cometh   at   an

an,nn5610   pin1380   3756

hour when ye think not.

Do What God Expects of You

1161   art,nn4074 aina2036   ppro846 an,nn2962   pin3004   depro5026 art,nn3850   pre4314 epn2248

41 Then Peter said unto him, Lord, speakest thou this parable unto us,

2228   2532   pre4314 an,ajn3956

or even to   all?

1161 art3588   nn2962   aina2036   pr/inpro5101   686   pin2076   art,aj4103   2532 an,aj5429   an,nn3623

42 And the Lord said, Who then is that faithful and wise steward,

repro3739   art,nn2962   ft2525   pre1909 ppro848   art,nn2322   infg1325

whom *his* lord shall make ruler over his household, to give *them their*

art,nn4620   pre1722   an,nn2540

portion*of*meat in due season?

pr/an,aj3107   depro1565   art,ajn1401   repro3739 ppro846 art,nn2962   apta2064   ft2147

43 Blessed *is* that servant, whom his   lord when he cometh shall find

ad3779   pap4160

so doing.

ad230   pin3004   ppro5213   3754   ft2525/ppro846   pre1909 an,aj3956

44 Of*a*truth I say unto you, that he will make*him*ruler over   all

art,pap5224/ppro848

that*he*hath.

45 But and if that servant say in his heart, My lord delayeth his coming; and shall begin to beat the menservants and maidens, and to eat and drink, and to be drunken;

46 The lord of that servant will come in a day when he looketh*not* for *him,* and at an hour when he is*not*aware, and will cut*him*in*sunder, and will appoint him his portion with the unbelievers.

47 And that servant, which knew his lord's will, and prepared not *himself,* neither did according to his will, shall be beaten with many *stripes.*

48 But he*that*knew not, and did commit things worthy of stripes, shall be beaten with few *stripes.* For unto whomsoever much is given, of him shall be much required: and to whom men have committed much, of him they will ask the more.

No Compromise (Matt. 10:34-36)

49 I am come to send fire on the earth; and what will I, if it be already kindled?

50 But I have a baptism to be baptized with; and how am I straitened till it be accomplished!

51 Suppose ye that I am come to give peace on earth? I tell you, Nay; but rather division:

52 For from henceforth there shall be five in one house divided, three against two, and two against three.

53 The father shall be divided against the son, and the son against the father; the mother against the daughter, and the daughter against the mother;

⌐ **12:47, 48** See note on Matthew 8:11, 12.

an,nn3994   pre1909   ppro848   art,nn3565   2532   an,nn3565   pre1909

the mother in law against her daughter in law, and the daughter in law against

ppro848   art,nn3994

her mother in law. *(Mic. 7:6)*

Discerning the Time (Matt. 16:2,3)

1161   ipf3004 2532   art3588   nn3793   ad3752   asba1492 art,nn3507 pap393   pre575

54 And he said also to the people, When ye see a cloud rise out of the

an,nn1424   ad2112   pin3004   pinm2064   an,nn3655 2543 ad3779 pinm1096

west, straightway ye say, There cometh a shower; and so it is.

2532   ad3752   an,nn3558   pap4154   pin3004   fm2071 an,nn2742 2532

55 And when *ye see* the south wind blow, ye say, There will be heat; and

pinm1096

it cometh*to*pass.

an,nn5273   pin1492 pinf1381 art3588 nn4383   art3588 nn3772 2532   art3588   nn1093

56 *Ye* hypocrites, ye can discern the face of the sky and of the earth;

1161 ad4459   3756   pin1381   depro5126 art,nn2540

but how is it that ye do not discern this time?

Being Reconciled With Your Accuser (Matt. 5:25,26)

1161 inpro5101 2532 pre575   rxpro1438   pin2919   3756   art,ajn1342

57 Yea, and why even of yourselves judge ye not what*is*right?

(1063) ad5613   pin5217 pre3326 ppro4675 art,nn476   pre1909   an,nn758

58 When thou goest with thine adversary to the magistrate, *as thou art*

pre1722 art3588 nn3598 aima1325   an,nn2039   pfin525   pre575 ppro846 3379

in the way, give diligence that thou mayest be delivered from him; lest he

asba2694 ppro4571 pre4314 art3588   nn2923 2532 art3588 nn2923 asba3860 ppro4571   art3588   nn4233   2532 art3588

hale thee to the judge, and the judge deliver thee to the officer, and the

nn4233   psa906 ppro4571 pre1519 an,nn5483

officer cast thee into prison.

pin3004 ppro4671   efn3364 asba1831   ad1564   ad*2193 (repro3739) asba591 art3588 2532

59 I tell thee, thou shalt not depart thence, till thou hast paid the very

aj2078 an,nn3016

last mite.

A Call to Repentance

(1161)   ipf3918   pre1722 ppro846 art,nn2540 idpro5100   pap518 ppro846 pre4012

13 There were present at that season some that told him of

art3588   ajn1057   repro3739 art,nn129 an,nn4091   aina3396 pre3326 ppro846 art,nn2378

the Galilaeans, whose blood Pilate had mingled with their sacrifices.

13:1–5 The Jews of the first century believed that all suffering was a result of God's judgment on sin. This concept is shared by many Christians today when they ask, "Why do the righteous suffer?" The Scripture teaches that God allows temporal disasters to happen for various reasons—one

(continued on next page)

_{2532   art,nn2424   aptp611   aina2036   ppro846   pin1380   3754   depro3778   art,ajn1057}

2 And Jesus answering said unto them, Suppose ye that these Galilaeans

_{aom1096   pr/an,ajn268   pre3844   an,aj3956 art3588   ajn1057   3754   pfi3958   an,ajn5108}

were sinners above   all   the Galilaeans, because they suffered such things?

_{pin3004 ppro5213   3780   235   1437/3361   psa3340   an,ajn3956   ad5615   fm622}

3 I tell you, Nay: but, except ye repent, ye shall   all   likewise perish.

_{2228   depro1565   art,nu1176/2532/nu,ajn3638   pre1909   repro3739   art3588   nn4444   pre1722   4611   aina4098   2532   aina615}

4 Or those   eighteen,   upon whom the tower   in   Siloam fell, and slew

_{ppro846   pin1380   3754   depro3778   aom1096   pr/an,nn3781   pre3844   an,aj3956   an,nn444   art,pap2730   pre1722}

them, think ye that they were sinners above   all   men that dwelt   in

₂₄₁₉

Jerusalem?

_{pin3004 ppro5213   3780   235   1437/3361   psa3340   an,ajn3956   ad3668   fm622}

5 I tell you, Nay: but, except ye repent, ye shall   all   likewise perish.

The Parable of the Barren Fig Tree

_{ipf3004   1161   depro5026   art,nn3850   idpro5100   ipf2192   an,nn4808   pfpp5452   pre1722}

6 He spake also   this   parable; A certain *man* had a fig tree planted   in

_{ppro848   art,nn290   2532   aina2064   pap2212   an,nn2590 pre1722/ppro846   2532   aina2147   3756}

his   vineyard; and he came and sought fruit thereon, and found none.

_{1161   aina2036   pre4314 art3588   nn289   2400   nu5140}

7 Then said he unto the dresser*of*his*vineyard, Behold, these three

_{an,nn2094   pinm2064   pap2212   an,nn2590 pre1722 depro5026   art,nn4808   2532   pin2147   3756   aima1581/ppro846}

years I come seeking fruit   on   this   fig tree, and find none: cut*it*down;

_{inpro2444 (2532)   pin2673   art3588   nn1093}

why   cumbereth it the ground?

_{1161   art3588   aptp611   pin3004   ppro846   an,nn2962   aima863/ppro846   depro5124   art,nn2094   2532}

8 And he answering said unto him, Lord, let*it*alone   this   year   also,

_{ad2193   (repro3755)   asba4626   pre4012   ppro846   2532   asba906/an,nn2874}

till I shall   dig   about it, and   dung   *it*:

_{2579   (3303)   asba4160   an,nn2590   1490   pre1519/an,ajn3195}

9 And if   it   bear fruit, *well*: and*if*not,   *then*   after that   thou shalt

_{ft1581/ppro846}

cut*it*down.

The Healing of a Crippled Woman on the Sabbath

_{1161   ipf2258   pap1321   pre1722 nu3391   art3588   nn4864   pre1722 art3588   nn4521}

10 And he was teaching   in   one of the synagogues on   the sabbath.

_{2532   2400   ipf2258   an,nn1135   pap2192   an,nn4151   an,nn769}

11 And, behold, there was a woman which had a spirit of infirmity

_{nu1176/2532/nu3638 an,nn2094   2532   ipf2258   pr/pap4794   2532   ppmp1410 3361/pre1519/art,ajn3838   ainf352}

eighteen   years, and was bowed together, and could in*no*wise lift up *herself*.

(continued from previous page)
of which is to lead people to repentance. Although God may punish sin with suffering some suffering
may, it is often a testing or learning process.

1161　　　　　　art,nn2424　apta492　ppro846　　　　　aina4377　　　　　　　　　　　2532　aina2036　　　　　　　ppro846

12 And when Jesus saw her, he called *her to him*, and said unto her,

an,nn1135　　　　　　pfip630　　　　ppro4675　art,nn769

Woman, thou art loosed from thine infirmity.

2532　　aina2007　art,nn5495　ppro846　2532　　　ad3916　　　　　　　　　　ainp461

13 And he laid *his* hands on her: and immediately she was made straight,

2532　ipf1392　art,nn2316

and glorified God.

1161　art3588　　　　　　nn752　　　　　aptp611　　　　　　　　pap23　　　　3754

14 And the ruler*of*the*synagogue answered with indignation, because that

art,nn2424　　aina2323　art3588　　　nn4521　　　　ipf3004　　　art3588　　nn3793　　　　pin1526

Jesus had healed on the sabbath day, and said unto the people, There are

nu1803　an,nn2250　pre1722　repro3739　　　pin1163　　pinf2038　pre1722 depro5025　　3767　ppmp2064　2532

six days in which men ought to work: in them therefore come and be

pin2323　2532　3361　art3588　nn4521　art,nn2250

healed, and not on the sabbath day.

art3588　nn2962　3767　ainp611　ppro846　2532　aina2036　　　an,nn5273　　　3756

15 The Lord then answered him, and said, *Thou* hypocrite, doth not

an,ajn1538　ppro5216　art3588　nn4521　pin3089　ppro848 art,nn1016　2228　art,nn3688 pre575 art3588 nn5336

each one of you on the sabbath loose his ox or *his* ass from the stall,

2532　apta520　　　　　pin4222

and lead*him*away to watering?

1161　ipf1163　3756　depro5026　　pap5607　pr/an,nn2364　　11　repro3739 art,nn4567

16 And ought not this woman, being a daughter of Abraham, whom Satan

aina1210　2400　nu1176/2532/hu3638　an,nn2094　aifp3089　pre575 depro5127 art,nn1199　art3588

hath bound, lo, these eighteen years, be loosed from this bond on the

nn4521　art,nn2250

sabbath day?

2532　ppro846　pap3004　depro5023　an,aj3956 ppro846　art,ppmp480

17 And when he had said these things, all his adversaries were

ipf2617　2532　an,aj3956 art3588　nn3793　ipf5463　pre1909 an,aj3956 art3588　ajn1741

ashamed: and all the people rejoiced for all the glorious things

art,ppmp1096　pre5259 ppro846

that*were*done by him.

The Parables of the Mustard Seed and the Leaven
(Matt. 13:31-33; Mark 4:30-32)

1161　ipf3004　　　inpro5101 pin2076 art3588　nn932　art,nn2316 pr/an,ajn3664　2532

18 Then said he, Unto what is the kingdom of God like? and

inpro5101　　asba3666　ppro846

whereunto shall I resemble it?

pin2076 pr/an,nn3664　an,nn2848　　an,nn4615　repro3739 an,nn444 apta2983　aina906 pre1519

19 It is like a grain of mustard seed, which a man took, and cast into

rxpro1438 an,nn2779　2532　aina837　2532　aom1096　(pre1519) an,aj3173 an,nn1186 2532 art3588 nn4071　art3588

his garden; and it grew, and waxed a great tree; and the fowls of the

nn3772　aina2681　pre1722 art3588　nn2798　ppro846

air lodged in the branches of it.　　　*(Ezek. 17:23; 31:6; Dan. 4:12,21)*

2532　ad3825　aina2036　inpro5101　　asba3666 art3588　nn932　art,nn2316

20 And again he said, Whereunto shall I liken the kingdom of God?

pin2076 pr/an,ajn3664 an,nn2219 repro3739 an,nn1135 apta2983 aina1470 pre1519 nu5140
21 It   is   like   leaven, which a woman took and hid in three
an,nn4568   an,nn224 ad2193 (repro3739) an,aj3650   ainp2220
measures of meal, till   the   whole was leavened.

The Strait Gate (Matt. 7:13,14,21-23)

2532   ipf1279   pre2596   an,nn4172 2532 an,nn2968 pap1321 2532 ppmp4160/an,nn4197
22 And he went through the cities and villages, teaching, and journeying
pre1519   2419
toward Jerusalem.

1161   aina2036 idpro5100   ppro846 an,nn2962 (1487)   pr/an,aj3641 art,ppmp4982 1161
23 Then said one unto him, Lord, are there few that*be*saved? And
art3588 aina2036 pre4314 ppro846
he said unto them,

pim75   ainf1525   pre1223 art3588 aj4728 an,nn4439 3754 an,ajn4183 pin3004   ppro5213
24 Strive to enter in at the strait gate: for many, I say unto you, will
ft2212   ainf1525 2532   3756   ft2480
seek to enter in, and shall not be able.

pre575/repro3739/302 art3588   nn3617   asbp1453 2532   asba608 art3588
25 When once the master*of*the*house is risen up, and hath shut to the
nn2374 2532   asbm756   pfin2476 ad1854 2532 pinf2925 art3588 nn2374 pap3004 an,nn2962
door, and ye begin to stand without, and to knock at the door, saying, Lord,
an,nn2962 aima455   ppro2254 2532   aptp611   ft2046   ppro5213 pin1492 ppro5209 3756
Lord, open unto us; and he shall answer and say unto you, I know you not
ad4159   pin2075
whence ye are:

ad5119   fm756   pinf3004   aina5315 2532 aina4095   ad*1799/ppro4675
26 Then shall ye begin to say, We have eaten and drunk in thy presence,
2532   aina1321 pre1722 ppro2257 art,ajn4113
and thou hast taught in our streets.

2532   ft2046 pin3004 ppro5213 pin1492 ppro5209 3756 ad4159   pin2075 aima868
☞ 27 But he shall say, I tell you, I know you not whence ye are; depart
pre575 ppro1700 an,aj3956   art,nn2040   art,nn93
from me, all ye workers of iniquity.   (Ps. 6:8)

ad1563   fm2071 art,nn2805 2532   art,nn1030   art,nn3599 ad3752   asbm3700
28 There shall be weeping and gnashing of teeth, when ye shall see
11   2532   2464 2532   2384 2532 an,aj3956 art3588   nn4396 pre1722 art3588   nn932
Abraham, and Isaac, and Jacob, and all the prophets, in the kingdom of
art,nn2316 1161 epn5209   ppmp1544 ad1854
God, and you yourselves thrust out.

2532   ft2240 pre575 an,nn395 2532   an,nn1424 2532 pre575
29 And they shall come from the east, and from the west, and from the
an,nn1005 2532   an,nn3558 2532   fp347 pre1722 art3588 nn932 art,nn2316
north, and from the south, and shall sit down in the kingdom of God.

(Ps. 107:3)

☞ 13:27–30 See notes on Matthew 8:11, 12 and 2 Thessalonians 2:3.

2532   2400   pin1526 pr/an,ajn2078   repro3739   fm2071 pr/nu,aj4413   2532   pin1526

30 And, behold, there are   last   which shall be   first, and there are

pr/nu,ajn4413 repro3739   fm2071 pr/an,aj2078

first which shall be   last.

Jesus Laments over Jerusalem (Matt. 23:37-39)

(pre1722) epn846 art,nn2250   aina4334 idpro5100   an,nn5330   pap3004   ppro846

31 The same day there came certain of the Pharisees, saying unto him,

aima1831   2532 pim4198   ad1782   3754 an,nn2264 pin2309 ainf615 ppro4571

Get*thee*out, and depart hence: for Herod will kill thee.

2532   aina2036   ppro846 aptp4198   aima2036 depro5026 art,nn258   2400

32 And he said unto them, Go ye, and tell   that   fox, Behold, I

pin1544   an,nn1140 2532 pin2005 an,nn2392 ad4594 2532   ad839   2532 art3588 nu,ajn5154

cast out devils, and I do cures today and tomorrow, and the third day I shall

pinm5048

be perfected.

4133   ppro3165 pin1163 pifm4198 ad4594   2532   ad839   2532 art3588

33 Nevertheless   I   must walk today, and tomorrow, and the day

ppmp2192   3754   pinm1735/3756   an,nn4396   aifm622 ad*1854   2419

following: for it cannot be that a prophet perish out of Jerusalem.

2419   2419   art,pap615   art3588   nn4396   2532   pap3036

34 O Jerusalem, Jerusalem, which killest the prophets, and stonest

art,pfpp649   pre4314   ppro846   ad4212   aina2309

them*that*are*sent   unto   thee; how   often   would   I   have

ainf1996/4675/art,nn5043   repro3739/an,nn5158   an,nn3733   rxpro1438   art,nn3555

gathered*thy*children*together,   as   a   hen doth gather her brood

pre5259   art,nn4420 2532   aina2309   3756

under her wings, and ye would not!

2400   ppro5216 art,nn3624   pinp863   ppro5213 an,aj2048   1161   281   pin3004

35 Behold, your house is left unto you desolate: and verily I say unto

ppro5213   efn3364 asba1492 ppro3165 ad2193/302   asba2240 ad3753   asba2036 pr/pfpp2127

you, Ye shall not see me, until the time come when ye shall say, Blessed is

art,ppmp2064   pre1722   an,nn3686   an,nn2962

he*that*cometh in the name of the Lord.   (Ps. 118:26)

Jesus Heals a Dropsical Man on the Sabbath Day

2532   aom1096   ppro846 aie2064 pre1519   an,nn3624   idpro5100   art3588

14 And it came*to*pass, as he went into the house of one of the

nn758   art,nn5330   ainf5315 an,nn740   an,nn4521   2532 ppro846 ipf2258/ppmp3906

chief Pharisees to eat bread on the sabbath day, that they watched

ppro846

him.

2532   2400   ipf2258   idpro5100   an,nn444   ad*1715   ppro846

2 And, behold, there was   a   certain man before him

an,aj5203

which*had*the*dropsy.

²⁵³² ^{art,nn2424} ^{aptp611} ^{aina2036} ^{pre4314} ^{art3588} ⁿⁿ³⁵⁴⁴ ²⁵³² ^{an,nn5330} ^{pap3004 (1487)}

3 And Jesus answering spake unto the lawyers and Pharisees, saying,

^{pin1832} ^{pinf2323} ^{art3588} ⁿⁿ⁴⁵²¹

Is*it*lawful to heal on the sabbath day?

¹¹⁶¹ ^{art3588} ^{aina2270} ²⁵³² ^{aptm1949} ^{aom2390} ^{ppro846} ²⁵³²

4 And they held*their*peace. And he took *him,* and healed him, and

^{aina630}

let*him*go;

²⁵³² ^{aptp611} ^(pre4314) ^{ppro846} ^{aina2036} ^{inpro5101} ^{ppro5216} ^{an,nn3688} ²²²⁸

5 And answered them, saying, Which of you shall have an ass or an

^{an,nn1016} ^{fm1706} ^{pre1519} ^{an,nn5421} ²⁵³² ³⁷⁵⁶ ^{ad2112} ^{ft385/ppro846} ^{pre1722 art3588} ⁿⁿ⁴⁵²¹

ox fallen into a pit, and will not straightway pull*him*out on the sabbath

^{art,nn2250}

day?

²⁵³² ^{aina2480} ³⁷⁵⁶ ^{aifp470/ppro846} ^{pre4314} ^{depro5023}

6 And they could not answer*him*again to these things.

Jesus Teaches Humility

¹¹⁶¹ ^{ipf3004} ^{an,nn3850} ^{pre4314} ^{art,pfpp2564}

7 And he put forth a parable to those*which*were*bidden, when he

^{pap1907} ^{ad4459} ^{ipf1586} ^{art3588} ⁿⁿ⁴⁴¹¹ ^{pap3004} ^{pre4314} ^{ppro846}

marked how they chose out the chief rooms; saying unto them,

^{ad3752} ^{asbp2564} ^{pre5259} ^{idpro5100} ^{pre1519} ^{an,nn1062} ^{aosi2625/3361} ^{pre1519}

8 When thou art bidden of any *man* to a wedding, sit*not*down in

^{art3588} ⁿⁿ⁴⁴¹¹ ³³⁷⁹ ^{cd/an,ajn1784} ^{ppro4675} ^{psa5600} ^{pfpp2564} ^{pre5259 ppro846}

the highest room; lest a more*honorable*man than thou be bidden of him;

²⁵³² ^{art,apta2564} ^{ppro4571} ^{2532 ppro846} ^{apta2064} ^{ft2046} ^{ppro4671} ^{aima1325} ^{depro5129}

9 And he*that*bade thee and him come and say to thee, Give this man

^{an,nn5117} ^{2532 (ad5119)} ^{fm756} ^{pre3326} ^{an,nn152} ^{pinf2722 art3588} ^{aj2078} ^{an,nn5117}

place; and thou begin with shame to take the lowest room. *(Prov. 25:6,7)*

²³⁵ ^{ad3752} ^{asbp2564} ^{apta4198} ^{aima377} ^{pre1519 art3588} ^{aj2078} ^{an,nn5117}

10 But when thou art bidden, go and sit down in the lowest room;

²⁴⁴³ ^{ad3752} ^{art,pfp2564} ^{ppro4571} ^{asba2064} ^{asba2036} ^{ppro4671} ^{an,ajn5384} ^{aipp4320}

that when he bade thee cometh, he may say unto thee, Friend, go up

^{cd/an,ajn511} ^{ad5119} ^{ppro4671} ^{fm2071} ^{an,nn1391} ^{ad*1799}

higher: then shalt thou have worship in*the*presence of

^{art,ppmp5013} ^{ppro4671}

them*that*sit*at*meat*with thee.

³⁷⁵⁴ ^{an,aj3956} ^{art,pap5312} ^{rxpro1438} ^{fp5013} ²⁵³² ^{art,pap5013}

11 For whosoever exalteth himself shall be abased; and he*that*humbleth

^{rxpro1438} ^{fp5312}

himself shall be exalted.

¹¹⁶¹ ^{ipf3004} ²⁵³² ^{art,pfp2564} ^{ppro846} ^{ad3752} ^{psa4160} ^{an,nn712} ²²²⁸

12 Then said he also to him*that*bade him, When thou makest a dinner or

^{an,nn1173} ^{pim5455 3361} ^{ppro4675} ^{art,ajn5384} ³³⁶⁶ ^{ppro4675} ^{art,nn80} ³³⁶⁶ ^{ppro4675} ^{art,ajn4773} ³³⁶⁶

a supper, call not thy friends, nor thy brethren, neither thy kinsmen, nor

an,aj4145   an,nn1069   3379 epn846 2532   asba479/ppro4571   2532   an,nn468   asbm1096
thy rich neighbors; lest they also bid*thee*again, and a recompense be made
ppro4671
thee.

235   ad3752   psa4160 an,nn1403 pim2564   an,ajn4434   an,ajn376   an,ajn5560
13 But when thou makest a feast, call the poor, the maimed, the lame, the
an,ajn5185
blind:

2532   fm2071 pr/an,aj3107 3754   pin2192/3756   ainf467   ppro4671 1063 ppro4671
14 And thou shalt be blessed; for they cannot recompense thee: for thou
fp467   pre1722 art3588   nn386   art3588 ajn1342
shalt be recompensed at the resurrection of the just.

The Parable of the Great Banquet (Matt. 22:1-10)

1161   idpro5100   art,ppmp4873   apta191   depro5023
15 And when one of them*that*sat*at*meat*with him heard these things,
aina2036   ppro846   pr/an,aj3107   repro3739   fm5315 an,nn740 pre1722 art3588   nn932
he said unto him, Blessed *is* he that shall eat bread in the kingdom of
art,nn2316
God.

1161 aina2036 art3588   ppro846   idpro5100 an,nn444 aina4160   an,aj3173   an,nn1173   2532 aina2564
16 Then said he unto him, A certain man made a great supper, and bade
an,ajn4183
many:

2532   aina649   ppro848   art,ajn1401   art,nn1173   art,nn5610   ainf2036
17 And   sent   his   servant   at   supper   time   to   say   to
art,pfpp2564   pim2064   3754   an,ajn3956   pin2076 ad2235 pr/an,aj2092
them*that*were*bidden, Come; for all things are now ready.

2532   an,ajn3956   pre575   nu,ajn3391   aom756   pifm3868   art3588 nu,ajn4413
18 And they   all   with   one   *consent* began to make excuse. The first
aina2036   ppro846   aina59   an,nn68   2532   pin2192 an,nn318 ainf1831 2532
said unto him, I have bought a piece*of*ground, and I must needs go and
ainf1492 ppro846   pin2065 ppro4571 pim2192 ppro3165   pfpp3868
see it: I pray thee have me excused.

2532   an,ajn2087   aina2036   aina59   nu4002 an,nn2201   an,nn1016   2532   pinm4198   ainf1381
19 And another said, I have bought five yoke of oxen, and I go to prove
ppro846   pin2065 ppro4571 pim2192 ppro3165   pfpp3868
them: I pray thee have me excused.

2532   an,ajn2087   aina2036   aina1060   an,nn1135   2532   pre1223/depro5124   pinm1410/3756
20 And another said, I have married a wife, and therefore I cannot
ainf2064
come.

2532   depro1565   art,ajn1401   aptp3854   aina518   ppro848 art,nn2962   depro5023   ad5119   art3588
21 So that servant came, and showed his lord these things. Then the
nn3617   aptp3710   aina2036   ppro848   art,ajn1401   aima1831   ad5030   pre1519 art3588
master*of*the*house being angry said to his servant, Go out quickly into the
ajn4113   2532   an,nn4505   art3588 nn4172   2532   aima1521   ad5602   art3588 ajn4434   2532   an,ajn376
streets and lanes of the city, and bring in hither the poor, and the maimed,
2532   an,ajn5560 2532   an,ajn5185
and the halt, and the blind.

2532 art3588 ajn1401 aina2036 an,nn2962   pfi1096 ad5613   aina2004 2532

22 And the servant said, Lord, it is done as thou hast commanded, and

ad2089   pin2076 an,nn5117

yet there is room.

2532 art3588 nn2962 aina2036 pre4314 art3588 ajn1401   aima1831 pre1519 art3588   nn3598 2532

23 And the lord said unto the servant, Go out into the highways and

an,nn5418 2532 aima315   ainf1525 2443 ppro3450 art,nn3624   asbp1072

hedges, and compel *them* to come in, that my house may be filled.

1063   pin3004   ppro5213 3754 an,ajn3762   depro1565 art,nn435   art,pfpp2564

24 For I say unto you, That none of those men which*were*bidden shall

fm1089   ppro3450   art,nn1173

taste of my supper.

Love Jesus More Than Yourself

1161   ipf4848/an,aj4183/an,nn3793   ppro846 2532   aptp4762   aina2036

☞ 25 And there went*great*multitudes*with him: and he turned, and said

pre4314 ppro846

unto them,

idpro1536   pinm2064 pre4314 ppro3165 2532 pin3404 3756 rxpro1438 art,nn3962 2532 art,nn3384 2532

26 If any *man* come to me, and hate not his father, and mother, and

art,nn1135 2532 art,nn5043 2532 art,nn80 2532 art,nn79 (ad2089) 1161 rxpro1438 art,nn5590 2532

wife, and children, and brethren, and sisters, yea, and his own life also, he

pinm1410/3756 pinf1511 ppro3450 pr/an,nn3101

cannot be my disciple.

2532   repro3748   3756 pin941 ppro848 art,nn4716 2532 pinm2064 ad*3694 ppro3450 pinm1410/3756

27 And whosoever doth not bear his cross, and come after me, cannot

pinf1511 ppro3450 pr/an,nn3101

be my disciple.

1063 inpro5101 pre1537 ppro5216   pap2309   ainf3618 an,nn4444   apta2523/3780   nu,ajn4412

28 For which of you, intending to build a tower, sitteth*not*down first,

pin5585   art3588 nn1160 1487   pin2192   art,pre4314/an,nn535

and counteth the cost, whether he have *sufficient* to finish *it*?

3379   (2443) ppro846   apta5087   an,nn2310 2532 pap2480/3361   ainf1615

29 Lest haply, after he hath laid the foundation, and is*not*able to finish

an,aj3956 art,pap2334   asbm756   pinf1702 ppro846

it, all that behold *it* begin to mock him,

pap3004   depro3778 art,nn444 aom756   pinf3618 2532 aina2480/3756   ainf1615

30 Saying, This man began to build, and was*not*able to finish.

2228 inpro5101 an,nn935 ppmp4198   ainf4820/pre1519/an,nn4171   an,aj2087 an,nn935

31 Or what king, going to make war against another king,

☞ **14:25–33** In light of Matthew 10:37, the word "hate" in verse twenty-six should be understood as loving one's relatives less than the Lord. The phrase, "that forsaketh not" (v. 33), does not refer to the abandonment of one's belongings, but the proper prioritization of them. The Greek word is *apotássetai* ([657], the middle voice of *apotássō*, from *apó* (575), "from," and *tássō* (5021), "to properly arrange." It refers to believers who are worthy of Christ and know how to properly arrange their life so that Christ is given the preeminence.

apta2523/3780   nu,ajn4412 2532   pinm1011   1487   pin2076 pr/an,aj1415 pre1722 nu1176

sitteth*not*down first, and consulteth whether he be able with ten

an,nn5505   ainf528   art,ppmp2064   pre1909 ppro846 pre3326 nu1501 an,nn5505

thousand to meet him*that*cometh against him with twenty thousand?

     1490   ppro846   pap5607 ad2089   ad4206   apta649

32 Or else, while the other is yet a great*way*off, he sendeth

an,nn4242   pin2065   art3588   pre4314 an,nn1515

ambassadors, and desireth conditions of peace.

  3767 ad3779   an,ajn3956   pre1537 ppro5216 repro3739   pinm657 3756 an,aj3956

33 So likewise, whosoever he be of you that forsaketh not all

art,pap5224/rxpro1438   pinm1410/3756 pinf1511 ppro3450 pr/an,nn3101

that*he*hath, he cannot be my disciple.

Salt (Matt. 5:13; Mark 9:50)

     art,nn217 pr/an,aj2570 1161 1437 art3588 nn217   asbp3471   pre1722/inpro5101

34 Salt *is* good: but if the salt have lost*his*savor, wherewith shall it be

fp741

seasoned?

     pin2076 3777 pr/an,aj2111 pre1519 an,nn1093 3777 pre1519 an,nn2874

35 It is neither fit for the land, nor yet for the dunghill; *but* men

pin906 ppro846 ad1854 art,pap2192 an,nn3775 pinf191   pim191

cast it out. He*that*hath ears to hear, let him hear.

The Lost Sheep (Matt. 18:12-14)

    1161 ipf2258/pap1448   ppro846 an,aj3956 art3588   nn5057 2532 art,ajn268

15 Then drew near unto him all the publicans and sinners for to

pinf191 ppro846

hear him.

  2532 art3588   nn5330 2532 art,nn1122 ipf1234   pap3004 depro3778 pinm4327

2 And the Pharisees and scribes murmured, saying, This man receiveth

an,ajn268 2532   pin4906   ppro846

sinners, and eateth with them.

  1161   aina2036 depro5026 art,nn3850 pre4314 ppro846 pap3004

3 And he spake this parable unto them, saying,

  inpro5101 an,nn444 pre1537 ppro5216 pap2192 nu1540 an,nn4263 2532 apta622 nu1520 pre1537 ppro846

4 What man of you, having a hundred sheep, if he lose one of them,

  3756 pin2641 art3588 nu1768   pre1722 art3588 ajn2048   2532 pinm4198 pre1909

doth not leave the ninety*and*nine in the wilderness, and go after

  art,pfp622 ad2193 asba2147 ppro846

that*which*is*lost, until he find it?   *(Ezek. 34:11,16)*

  2532   apta2147   pin2007 pre1909 rxpro1438 art,nn5606 pap5463

5 And when he hath found *it*, he layeth *it* on his shoulders, rejoicing.

  2532   apta2064 (pre1519) art,nn3624   pin4779   art,ajn5384 2532

6 And when he cometh home, he calleth together *his* friends and

art,nn1069 pap3004   ppro846 aima4796 ppro3427 3754 aina2147 ppro3450 art,nn4263

neighbors, saying unto them, Rejoice with me; for I have found my sheep

art,pfpp622

which*was*lost.

_{pin3004}   _{ppro5213} ₃₇₅₄   _{ad3779}   _{an,nn5479}   _{fm2071} _{pre1722} _{art,nn3772}   _{pre1909} _{nu1520} _{an,ajn268}

7 I say unto you, that likewise joy shall be in heaven over one sinner

_{pap3340}   ₂₂₂₈ _{pre1909}   _{nu1768}   _{an,ajn1342}   _{repro3748} _{pin2192/an,nn5532}

that repenteth, more than over ninety*and*nine just persons, which   need

₃₇₅₆   _{an,nn3341}

no repentance.

The Lost Coin

₂₂₂₈   _{inpro5101} _{an,nn1135}   _{pap2192} _{nu1176}   _{an,nn1406}   ₁₄₃₇   _{asba622} _{nu3391} _{an,nn1406}

8 Either what woman having ten pieces*of*silver, if she lose one piece,

₃₇₈₀ _{pin681}   _{an,nn3088}   ₂₅₃₂ _{pin4563} _{art3588} _{nn3614}   ₂₅₃₂ _{pin2212}   _{ad1960}   _{ad2193} _(repro3755)

doth not light a candle, and sweep the house, and seek diligently till   she

_{asba2147}

find it?

₂₅₃₂   _{apta2147}

9 And   when   she   hath   found   it,   she

_{pinm4779/art,ajn5384/2532/art,nn1069}   _{pap3004}   _{aima4796}   _{ppro3427}

calleth*her*friends*and*her*neighbors*together,   saying,   Rejoice   with   me;

₃₇₅₄   _{aina2147} _{art3588} _{nn1406} _{repro3739}   _{aina622}

for I have found the piece which I had lost.

_{ad3779}   _{pin3004}   _{ppro5213}   _{pinm1096} _{an,nn5479}   _{ad*1799}   _{art3588}

10 Likewise, I say unto you, there   is   joy in*the*presence of the

_{nn32}   _{art,nn2316} _{pre1909} _{nu1520} _{an,ajn268}   _{pap3340}

angels of God over one sinner that repenteth.

The Lost Son

₁₁₆₁   _{aina2036}   _{idpro5100} _{an,nn444} _{ipf2192} _{nu1417} _{an,nn5207}

11 And he said, A certain man had two sons:

₂₅₃₂ _{art3588}   _{ajn3501}   _{ppro846} _{aina2036}   _{art,nn3962}   _{an,nn3962} _{aima1325} _{ppro3427} _{art3588}

12 And the younger of them said to his father, Father, give   me   the

_{nn3313}   _{art,nn3776}   _{pap1911}   ₂₅₃₂   _{aina1244}   _{ppro846}   _{art,nn979}

portion of goods that falleth to me. And he divided unto them his living.

₂₅₃₂   ₃₇₅₆ _{an,aj4183} _{an,nn2250} _{pre3326} _{art3588}   _{an,aj3501}   _{nn5207}   _{apta4863/an,ajn537}

13 And not many days after the younger son gathered*all*together, and

_{aina589}   _{pre1519} _{an,aj3117} _{an,nn5561}   ₂₅₃₂   _{ad1563}   _{aina1287} _{ppro848}   _{art,nn3776}

took*his*journey into a far country, and there wasted his substance with

_{ad811}   _{pap2198}

riotous living.   (Prov. 29:3)

₁₁₆₁   _{ppro846}   _{apta1159} _{an,ajn3956}   _{aom1096}   _{an,aj2478} _{an,nn3042} _{pre2596} _{depro1565}

14 And when he had spent all, there arose a mighty famine in   that

_{art,nn5561} ₂₅₃₂ _{epn846} _{aom756}   _{pifm5302}

land; and he began to be*in*want.

₂₅₃₂   _{apta4198}   _{ainp2853}   _{nu1520} _{art,nn4177}   _{depro1565}   _{art,nn5561}   ₂₅₃₂

15 And he went and joined himself to   a   citizen of that country; and he

_{aina3992} _{ppro846} _{pre1519} _{ppro848} _{art,nn68}   _{pinf1006} _{an,nn5519}

sent him into his fields to feed swine.

₂₅₃₂   _{ipf1937}   _{ainf1072} _{ppro848} _{art,nn2836} _{pre575} _{art3588}   _{nn2769} _{repro3739} _{art3588}   _{nn5519}

16 And he would fain have filled his belly with the husks that the swine

_{ipf2068} ₂₅₃₂ _{an,ajn3762} _{ipf1325}   _{ppro846}

did eat: and no man gave unto him.

1161   apta2064 pre1519 rxpro1438   aina2036   an,aj4214   an,ajn3407
17 And when he came to himself, he said, How many hired servants of

ppro3450 art,nn3962   pifm4052/an,nn740   1161 epn1473 pinm622   an,nn3042
my father's have*bread*enough*and*to*spare, and   I   perish with hunger!

          apta450   fm4198 pre4314 ppro3450 art,nn3962   2532   ft2046   ppro846 an,nn3962
18 I will arise and go to my father, and will say unto him, Father, I

aina264   pre1519 art,nn3772   2532   ad*1799 ppro4675
have sinned against heaven, and before thee,

          2532   pin1510   ad3765   pr/an,aj514   aifp2564   ppro4675 an,nn5207 aima4160 ppro3165 ad5613 nu1520
19 And am no more worthy to be called thy son: make me   as one of

ppro4675   art,ajn3407
thy hired servants.

          2532   apta450   aina2064   pre4314 rxpro1438   art,nn3962   1161   ppro846
20 And he arose, and came to his father. But when   he

pap568/ad2089/ad3112   ppro846 art,nn3962 aina1492 ppro846   2532   ainp4697   2532 apta5143
was*yet*a*great*way*off, his father saw him, and had compassion, and ran,

aina1968 pre1909 ppro846 art,nn5137 2532   aina2705   ppro846
and fell on his neck, and kissed him.

          1161 art3588 nn5207 aina2036   ppro846   an,nn3962   aina264   1519   art,nn3772   2532
21 And the son said unto him, Father, I have sinned against heaven, and

ad1799/ppro4675   2532 pin1510   ad3765   pr/an,ajn514   aifp2564 ppro4675 an,nn5207
in*thy*sight, and am no more worthy to be called thy son.

          1161 art3588   nn3962   aina2036 pre4314 ppro848   art,ajn1401   aima1627   art3588 nu,aj4413 art,nn4749 2532
22 But the father said to his servants, Bring forth the best robe, and

aima1746   ppro846 2532 aima1325   an,nn1146 pre1519 ppro846 art,nn5495 2532   an,nn5266 pre1519   art,nn4228
put*it*on him; and put a ring on his hand, and shoes on his feet:

          2532   apta5342   art3588   aj4618   art,nn3448   aima2380   2532   apta5315
23 And bring hither the fatted calf, and kill it; and let us eat, and

aosi2165
be merry:

          3754 depro3778 ppro3450 art,nn5207 ipf2258 pr/an,aj3498 2532   aina326   ipf2258 pr/pfp622 2532
24 For this my   son was dead, and is*alive*again; he was lost, and is

ainp2147 2532   aom756   pifm2165
found. And they began to be merry.

          1161   ppro846 art,aj4245 art,nn5207 ipf2258 pre1722   an,nn68   2532   ad5613   ppmp2064
25 Now his elder son was in the field: and as he came and

aina1448   art3588   nn3614   aina191 an,nn4858 2532   an,nn5525
drew nigh to the house, he heard music and dancing.

          2532   aptm4341 nu1520   art3588   nn3816   2532 ipf4441 inpro5101   pr/depro5023   opt1498
26 And he called one of the servants, and asked what these things meant.

          1161 art3588 aina2036   ppro846 ppro4675   art,nn80   pin2240 2532 ppro4675 art,nn3962
27 And he said unto him, Thy brother is come; and thy father hath

aina2380 art3588 aj4618 art,nn3448   3754   aina618   ppro846   pap5198
killed the fatted calf, because he hath received him safe*and*sound.

          1161   ainp3710   2532   ipf2309   3756   ainf1525   3767
28 And he was angry, and would not go in: therefore

apta1831/ppro846/art,nn3962   2532   ipf3870   ppro846
came*his*father*out, and entreated him.

1161   art3588   aptp611   aina2036   art,nn3962   2400   an,aj5118   an,nn2094   pin1398

29 And he answering said to *his* father, Lo, these many years do I serve

ppro4671   2532   aina3928   ad3762   ppro4675   an,nn1785   2532

thee, neither transgressed I at*any*time thy commandment: and yet thou

ad3762   aina1325 epn1698   an,nn2056 2443   asbp2165   pre3326 ppro3450 art,ajn5384

never gavest me a kid, that I might make merry with my friends:

          1161   ad3753   depro3778 ppro4675 art,nn5207   aina2064   art,apta2719

☞ 30 But as*soon*as this   thy   son was come, which*hath*devoured thy

art,nn979 pre3326 an,nn4204   aina2380   ppro846 art3588   aj4618   art,nn3448

living with harlots, thou hast killed for him the fatted calf.

          1161   art3588 aina2036   ppro846 an,nn5043 epn4771 pin1488   ad3842   pre3326 ppro1700   2532   an,aj3956

31 And he   said unto him, Son, thou art ever with me, and all

art,popro1699   pin2076 popro4674

that*I*have is thine.

          (1161)   ipf1163   aifp2165   2532   aifp5463   3754 depro3778 ppro4675

32 It was meet that we should make merry, and be glad: for this   thy

art,nn80   ipf2258 pr/an,aj3498 2532   aina326   2532 ipf2258 pr/pfp622 2532   ainp2147

brother was dead, and is*alive*again; and was lost, and is found.

The Parable of the Unrighteous Servant

               1161   ipf3004 2532 pre4314 ppro846   art,nn3101   ipf2258   idpro5100   pr/an,aj4145

16 ☞ And he said also unto his disciples, There was a certain rich

an,nn444 repro3739 ipf2192 an,nn3623 2532   depro3778   ainp1225   ppro846

man, which had a steward; and the same was accused unto him

ad5613   pap1287   ppro848 art,pap5224

that he had wasted his goods.

☞ **15:30** The elder son would not accept his younger brother because he thought his brother had associated himself with harlots, although he repented. In the case of such prodigal sons and daughters, Christians today sometimes act like the "older son," when they should follow the example of the father.

☞ **16:1–13** To understand this parable, two words must be understood. The word *dieblḗthē*, translated as "accused," should actually be translated "falsely accused" (v. 1). It is derived from *diabállō* (1225), from which the word *diabólos* (1228), "devil," is derived. The other important word is *metastathṓ*, translated "put out of" (from *methístēmi* [3179]), which was a word used by the Greeks to denote one's removal from this world to the next (see Acts 13:22 where the word "removed" is the same as "taken away"). In view of his "metastasis" (his removal from this earth), he must engage in the declaration of the forgiveness of debts (sins). This declaration of forgiveness of sins is the most important thing that any believer can receive in during his life of faith before his departure from earth (death). Furthermore, Jesus declares what will happen when this believer, here presented as the business manager (see 1 Cor. 4:1), is finally removed from his job on this earth as the steward of God. The business manager collected at least part of the debts due to his master, who would have otherwise received nothing, thus pleasing his master. This also pleased the debtors, who were unable to pay the full debt that they owed, and they became good friends with the business manager. This business manager knew that when he became needy, after being dismissed from his job, these debtors would be hospitable and take him into their homes.

In verse eight, the words "wisely" and "wiser" are translations of the Greek word *phronímōs* (5430) and its derivative *phronimṓtepoi* (5429). This word must be distinguished from *sophós* (4680), a Greek word that is translated "wise." Both words refer to the use of intelligence and the wise use of one's means to accomplish something. The difference lies in the ends which one is attempting to accomplish. The word *sophós* is used only when the thing that will be accomplished is good, but the word *phronímōs* is most often used when the end that will be accomplished is evil.

2532   apta5455   ppro846   aina2036   ppro846 inpro5101   pin191   depro5124 pre4012

2 And he called him, and said unto him, How is it that I hear this of

ppro4675   aima591   art,nn3056   ppro4675   art,nn3622   1063   fm1410

thee? give an account of thy stewardship; for thou mayest

pinf3621/3756/ad2089

be*no*longer*steward.

1161   art3588   nn3623   aina2036   pre1722   rxpro1438   inpro5101   asba4160   3754 ppro3450 art,nn2962

3 Then the steward said within himself, What shall I do? for my lord

pinm851   pre575 ppro1700 art3588   nn3622   pin2480/3756 pinf4626   pinf1871   pinm153

taketh away from me the stewardship: I cannot dig; to beg I am ashamed.

aina1097   inpro5101   asba4160   2443   ad3752   asbp3179   art3588   nn3622

4 I am resolved what to do, that, when I am put out of the stewardship,

asbm1209   ppro3165 pre1519 ppro848   art,nn3624

they may receive me into their houses.

2532   aptm4341   an,ajn1538 nu1520   rxpro1438 art,nn2962   art,nn5533   ipf3004

5 So he called every one of his lord's debtors unto him, and said unto

art3588 nu,ajn4413   an,ajn4214   pin3784   ppro3450 art,nn2962

the first, how much owest thou unto my lord?

1161   art3588 aina2036   nu1540   an,nn943   an,nn1637 2532   aina2036   ppro846

6 And he said, A hundred measures of oil. And he said unto him,

aipm1209 ppro4675 art,nn1121 2532 apta2523   ad5030   aima1125 nu,ajn4004

Take thy bill, and sit down quickly, and write fifty.

ad1889   aina2036   an,ajn2087   1161   an,ajn4214   pin3784   epn4771   1161   art3588 aina2036

7 Then said he to another, And how much owest thou? And he said,

nu1540   an,nn2884   an,nn4621   2532   pin3004   ppro846 aipm1209 ppro4675 art,nn1121 2532

A hundred measures of wheat. And he said unto him, Take thy bill, and

aima1125   nu,ajn3589

write fourscore.

2532   art3588   nn2962   aina1867   art3588   nn93   art,nn3623   3754   aina4160

8 And the lord commended the unjust steward, because he had done

ad5430   3754 art3588   nn5207   depro5127 art,nn165 pin1526 pre1519 art,rxpro1438   art,nn1074   pr/an,aj5429 pre5228

wisely: for the children of this world are in their generation wiser than

art3588   nn5207   art,nn5457

the children of light.

epn2504   pin3004   ppro5213   aina4160   rxpro1438   an,ajn5384 pre1537 art3588   nn3126

9 And I say unto you, Make to yourselves friends of the mammon of

art,nn93   2443   ad3752   asba1587   asbm1209   ppro5209 pre1519   art,aj166

unrighteousness; that, when ye fail, they may receive you into everlasting

an,nn4633

habitations.

art,ajn4103   pre1722   an,ajn1646   pin2076 pr/an,ajn4103 2532 pre1722 an,ajn4183

10 He*that*is*faithful in that*which*is*least is faithful also in much:

2532   art,ajn94   pre1722   an,ajn1646 pin2076 pr/an,ajn94 2532 pre1722 an,ajn4183

and he*that*is*unjust in the least is unjust also in much.

1487   3767   3756 aom1096 pr/an,ajn4103 pre1722 art3588   an,aj94   nn3126

11 If therefore ye have not been faithful in the unrighteous mammon,

inpro5101   ft4100/ppro5213   art3588 ajn228

who will commit*to*your*trust the true riches?

2532   1487   3756 aom1096 pr/an,ajn4103 pre1722   art,ajn245

12 And if ye have not been faithful in that*which*is*another*man's,

inpro5101   ft1325 ppro5213   art,popro5212

who shall give you that*which*is*your*own?

_{an,aj3762 an,nn3610 pinm1410 pinf1398 nu1417 an,nn2962 1063 2228   ft3404 art3588 nu,ajn1520}

13 No servant can serve two masters: for either he will hate the one,

_{2532 ft25 art3588 ajn2087   2228   fm472   an,nu,ajn1520 2532   ft2706 art3588 ajn2087}

and love the other; or else he will hold to the one, and despise the other. Ye

_{pinm1410/3756 pinf1398 an,nn2316 2532   an,nn3126}

cannot serve God and mammon.

_{1161 art3588   nn5330   2532   pap5225   pr/an,ajn5366   ipf191 an,aj3956   depro5023}

14 And the Pharisees also, who were covetous, heard all these things:

_{2532   ipf1592   ppro846}

and they derided him.

_{2532   aina2036   ppro846 epn5210 pin2075   art,pap1344   rxpro1438   ad*1799}

15 And he said unto them, Ye are they*which*justify yourselves before

_{art,nn444 1161 art,nn2316   pin1097   ppro5216 art,nn2588   3754   art,ajn5308}

men; but God knoweth your hearts: for that*which*is*highly*esteemed

_{pre1722 an,nn444 pin2076 pr/an,nn946   ad*1799   art,nn2316}

among men is abomination in*the*sight of God.

The Law and the Kingdom of God

_{art3588 nn3551 2532 art3588   4396   ad*2193 an,nn2491 pre575   ad5119   art3588   nn932}

16 The law and the prophets *were* until John: since that time the kingdom

_{art,nn2316   pinm2097   2532 an,ajn3956   pinm971   pre1519 ppro846}

of God is preached, and every man presseth into it.

_{1161   pin2076 pr/cd/an,aj2123   art,nn3772   2532 art,nn1093 ainf3928   2228 nu3391 an,nn2762   art3588}

17 And it is easier for heaven and earth to pass, than one tittle of the

_{nn3551   ainf4098}

law to fail.

Divorce (Matt. 5:27-32; 19:1-12; Mark 10:1-12; Rom. 7:1-3; 1 Cor. 7:10-17)

_{an,aj3956   art,pap630   ppro848 art,nn1135   2532   pap1060   an,ajn2087}

☞ 18 Whosoever putteth away his wife, and marrieth another,

_{pin3431   2532   an,aj3956   pap1060   art,pfpp630   pre575}

committeth adultery: and whosoever marrieth her*that*is*put*away from *her*

_{an,nn435   pin3431}

husband committeth adultery.

The Rich Man and Lazarus

_{(1161) ipf2258 idpro5100 an,aj4145 an,nn444 (2532)   ipf1737   an,nn4209 2532}

☞ 19 There was a certain rich man, which was clothed in purple and

_{an,nn1040   ppmp2165   ad2988   pre2596/an,nn2250}

fine linen, and fared sumptuously every day:

☞ **16:18** See note on Matthew 19:3–9.

☞ **16:19–31** See note on 2 Corinthians 12:1–10.

¹¹⁶¹ ^{ipf2258} ^{idpro5100} ^{an,ajn4434} ^{an,nn3686} ^{an,nn2976} ^{repro3739} ^{plpf906} ^{pre4314}
20 And there was a certain beggar named Lazarus, which was laid at
^{ppro846} ^{art,nn4440} ^{pfpp1669}
his gate, full*of*sores,

²⁵³² ^{pap1937} ^{aifp5526} ^{pre575} ^{art3588} ⁿⁿ⁵⁵⁸⁹ ^{art,pap4098} ^{pre575} ^{art3588}
21 And desiring to be fed with the crumbs which fell from the
^{ajn4145} ^{art,nn5132} ^{235/2532} ^{art3588} ⁿⁿ²⁹⁶⁵ ^{ppmp2064} ^{ipf621} ^{ppro846} ^{art,nn1668}
rich man's table: moreover the dogs came and licked his sores.

¹¹⁶¹ ^{aom1096} ^{art3588} ^{ajn4434} ^{ainf599} ²⁵³² ^(ppro846) ^{aifp667}
22 And it came*to*pass, that the beggar died, and was carried
^{pre5259} ^{art3588} ⁿⁿ³² ^{pre1519} ¹¹ ^{art,nn2859} ⁽¹¹⁶¹⁾ ^{art3588} ^{ajn4145} ²⁵³² ^{aina599} ²⁵³²
by the angels into Abraham's bosom: the rich man also died, and was
^{ainp2290}
buried;

²⁵³² ^{pre1722} ^{art,nn86} ^{apta1869} ^{ppro848} ^{art,nn3788} ^{pap5225} ^{pre1722} ^{an,nn931} ^{pin3704}
23 And in hell he lifted up his eyes, being in torments, and seeth
¹¹ ^{pre575/ad3113} ²⁵³² ^{an,nn2976} ^{pre1722} ^{ppro846} ^{art,nn2859}
Abraham afar off, and Lazarus in his bosom.

²⁵³² ^{ppro846} ^{apta5455} ^{aina2036} ^{an,nn3962} ¹¹ ^{aima1653} ^{ppro3165} ²⁵³²
24 And he cried and said, Father Abraham, have mercy on me, and
^{aima3992} ^{an,nn2976} ²⁴⁴³ ^{asba911} ^{art3588} ⁿⁿ²⁰⁶ ^{ppro848} ^{art,nn1147} ^{an,nn5204} ²⁵³² ^{asba2711} ^{ppro3450}
send Lazarus, that he may dip the tip of his finger in water, and cool my
^{art,nn1100} ³⁷⁵⁴ ^{pinm3600} ^{pre1722} ^{depro5026} ^{art,nn5395}
tongue; for I am tormented in this flame.

¹¹⁶¹ ¹¹ ^{aina2036} ^{an,nn5043} ^{aipp3415} ³⁷⁵⁴ ^{epn4771} ^{pre1722} ^{ppro4675} ^{art,nn2222}
25 But Abraham said, Son, remember that thou in thy lifetime
^{aina618} ^{ppro4675} ^{art,ajn18} ²⁵³² ^{ad3668} ^{an,nn2976} ^{art,ajn2556} ¹¹⁶¹ ^{ad3568} ^{repro3592}
receivedst thy good things, and likewise Lazarus evil things: but now he is
^{pinp3870} ¹¹⁶¹ ^{epn4771} ^{pinp3600}
comforted, and thou art tormented.

²⁵³² ^{pre1909} ^{an,aj3956} ^{depro5125} ^{ad*3342} ^{ppro2257} ²⁵³² ^{ppro5216} ^{an,aj3173} ^{an,nn5490}
26 And beside all this, between us and you there is a great gulf
^{pfip4741} ^{ad3704} ^{art,pap2309} ^{ainf1224} ^{ad1782} ^{pre4314} ^{ppro5209} ^{psmp1410/3361} ³³⁶⁶
fixed: so that they*which*would pass from hence to you cannot; neither can
^{psa1276} ^{pre4314} ^{ppro2248} ^{art,ad1564}
they pass to us, that *would come* from thence.

¹¹⁶¹ ^{aina2036} ^{pin2065} ^{ppro4571} ³⁷⁶⁷ ^{an,nn3962} ²⁴⁴³ ^{asba3992}
27 Then he said, I pray thee therefore, father, that thou wouldest send
^{ppro846} ^{pre1519} ^{ppro3450} ^{art,nn3962} ^{art,nn3624}
him to my father's house:

¹⁰⁶³ ^{pin2192} ^{nu4002} ^{an,nn80} ³⁷⁰⁴ ^{psa1263} ^{ppro846} ³³⁶³ ^{epn846} ²⁵³²
28 For I have five brethren; that he may testify unto them, lest they also
^{asba2064} ^{pre1519} ^{depro5126} ^{art,nn5117} ^{art,nn931}
come into this place of torment.

¹¹ ^{pin3004} ^{ppro846} ^{pin2192} ^{an,nn3475} ²⁵³² ^{art3588} ⁿⁿ⁴³⁹⁶
29 Abraham saith unto him, They have Moses and the prophets; let them
^{aima191} ^{ppro846}
hear them.

¹¹⁶¹ ^{art3588} ^{aina2036} ³⁷⁸⁰ ^{an,nn3962} ¹¹ ²³⁵ ¹⁴³⁷ ^{idpro5100} ^{asbp4198} ^{pre4314} ^{ppro846} ^{pre575}
30 And he said, Nay, father Abraham: but if one went unto them from
^{an,ajn3498} ^{ft3340}
the dead, they will repent.

1161   aina2036   ppro846   pin191   3756   an,nn3475   2532   art3588   nn4396

31 And he said unto him, If they hear not Moses and the prophets,

3756   fp3982   3761/1437   idpro5100   asba450   pre1537   an,ajn3498

neither will they be persuaded, though one rose from the dead.

Always Forgive (Matt. 18:6,7,21,22; Mark 9:42)

1161   aina2036   pre4314 art3588   nn3101   pin2076   pr/an,ajn418   3361   art,nn4625

17 Then said he unto the disciples, It is impossible but that offences

infg2064   1161   3759   pre1223   repro3739   pinm2064

will come: but woe *unto him,* through whom they come!

pin3081   ppro846   1487   an,nn3458/an,aj3684   pinm4029   pre4012   ppro846

2 It were better for him that a millstone were hanged about his

art,nn5137   2532   pfip4496   pre1519 art3588   nn2281   2228   2443   asba4624   nu1520   depro5130

neck, and he cast into the sea, than that he should offend one of these

art,ajn3398

little ones.

pim4337   rxpro1438   (1161) 1437 ppro4675   art,nn80   asba264   pre1519   ppro4571   aima2008

3 Take heed to yourselves: If thy brother trespass against thee, rebuke

ppro846   2532 1437   asba3340   aima863   ppro846

him; and if he repent, forgive him.

2532   1437   asba264   pre1519   ppro4571   nu,ad2034   art,nn2250   2532   nu,ad2034

4 And if he trespass against thee seven times in a day, and seven times in

art,nn2250   asba1994   pre1909 ppro4571   pap3004   pin3340   ft863   ppro846

a day turn again to thee, saying, I repent; thou shalt forgive him.

2532 art3588   nn652   aina2036   art3588   nn2962   aima4369   ppro2254 an,nn4102

5 And the apostles said unto the Lord, Increase our faith.

1161   art3588   nn2962   aina2036 1487   pin2192 an,nn4102 ad5613   an,nn2848   an,nn4615

6 And the Lord said, If ye had faith as a grain of mustard seed, ye

ipf3004/302   depro5026   art,nn4807   aipp1610   2532

might say unto this sycamine tree, Be thou plucked*up*by*the*root, and

aipp5452   pre1722 art3588 nn2281   2532   aina5219/302 ppro5213

be thou planted in the sea; and it should obey you.

1161   inpro5101   pre1537 ppro5216   pap2192   an,ajn1401   pap722   2228   pap4165   (repro3739)

7 But which of you, having a servant plowing or feeding cattle,   will

ft2046   ad2112   apta1525   pre1537   art3588   nn68   apta3928

say unto him by*and*by, when he is come from the field, Go and

aipm377

sit*down*to*meat?

235   3780   ft2046   ppro846   aima2090   inpro5101   asba1172   2532

8 And will not rather say unto him, Make ready wherewith I may sup, and

aptm4024   pim1247   ppro3427 ad2193   asba5315   2532   asba4095   2532   pre3326/depro5023

gird thyself, and serve me, till I have eaten and drunken; and afterward

epn4771   fm5315 2532   fm4095

thou shalt eat and drink?

pin2192/3361/an,nn5485   depro1565   art,ajn1401   3754   aina4160

9 Doth*he*thank   that   servant   because   he   did

art,aptp1299   ppro846   pin1380   3756

the*things*that*were*commanded him? I think not.

ad3779   (2532)   epn5210   ad3752   asba4160   an,aj3956
10 So   likewise   ye,   when   ye   shall   have   done   all
art,aptp1299   ppro5213 pim3004   an,aj888   pr/an,ajn1401
those*things*which*are*commanded you, say, We are unprofitable servants:
(3754)   pfi4160   repro3739   ipf3784   ainf4160
we have done that which was*our*duty to do.

Jesus Cleanses Ten Lepers

         2532   aom1096   ppro846 aie4198 pre1519   2419   2532 epn846   ipf1330
11 And it came*to*pass, as he went to Jerusalem, that he passed
pre1223   an,ajn3319   an,nn4540 2532   an,nn1056
through the midst of Samaria and Galilee.
         2532   ppro846   ppmp1525   pre1519   idpro5100   an,nn2968   aina528 ppro846 nu1176 an,nn435
12 And as he entered into a certain village, there met him ten men that
an,aj3015   repro3739 aina2476   ad4207
were lepers, which stood afar off:
         2532   epn846   aina142   an,nn5456   pap3004 an,nn2424   an,nn1988   aima1653
13 And they lifted up *their* voices, and said, Jesus, Master, have mercy on
ppro2248
us.
         2532   apta1492   aina2036   ppro846 aptp4198 aima1925   rxpro1438
14 And when he saw *them,* he said unto them, Go show yourselves unto
art3588 nn2409   2532   aom1096   ppro846 aie5217   ainp2511
the priests. And it came*to*pass, that, as they went, they were cleansed.

                                                           (Lev. 14:2,3)
         1161   nu1520 pre1537 ppro846   apta1492 3754   ainp2390   aina5290
15 And one of them, when he saw that he was healed, turned back, and
pre3326 an,aj3173 an,nn5456   pap1392   art,nn2316
with a loud voice glorified God,
         2532   aina4098   pre1909   an,nn4383 pre3844 ppro846 art,nn4228   pap2168/ppro846   2532 epn846
16 And fell down on *his* face at his feet, giving*him*thanks: and he
ipf2258   pr/an,ajn4541
was a Samaritan.
         1161   art,nn2424   aptp611   aina2036   3780 art,nu,ajn1176   ainp2511   1161   ad4226
17 And Jesus answering said, Were there not   ten   cleansed? but where
art3588 nu,ajn1767
are the nine?
              3756   ainp2147   apta5290   ainf1325 an,nn1391   art,nn2316 1508   depro3778
18 There are not found that returned to give glory to God, save this
art,ajn241
stranger.
         2532   aina2036   ppro846   apta450   pim4198   ppro4675 art,nn4012
19 And he said unto him, Arise, go*thy*way: thy faith hath
pfi4982/ppro4571
made*thee*whole.

The Kingdom of God (Matt. 24:23-28,37-41)

¹¹⁶¹

20 And when he was demanded of the Pharisees, when the kingdom of
^{art,nn2316   pinm2064   ainp611   ppro846   2532   aina2036 art3588   nn932   art,nn2316   pinm2064}

God should come, he answered them and said, The kingdom of God cometh
^{3756   pre3326   an,nn3907}

not with observation:
³⁷⁶¹

21 Neither shall they say, Lo here! or, lo there! for, behold, the kingdom
^{art,nn2316 pin2076   ad1787   ppro5216}

of God is within you.
^{1161   aina2036   pre4314 art3588   nn3101   an,nn2250   fm2064   ad3753}

22 And he said unto the disciples, The days will come, when ye shall
^{ft1937   ainf1492 nu3391   art3588 nn2250   art3588 nn5207   art,nn444 2532   3756 fm3700}

desire to see one of the days of the Son of man, and ye shall not see *it.*
^{2532   ft2046   ppro5213 2400   ad5602   2228   2400   ad1563   aosi565/3361}

23 And they shall say to you, See here; or, see there: go*not*after *them,*
^{3366   aosi1377}

nor follow *them.*

When Jesus Comes Again

^{1063   ad5618   art3588   nn796   pap797   pre1537   art3588   pre5259}

24 For as the lightning, that lighteneth out of the one *part* under
^{an,nn3772   pin2989   pre1519   art3588   pre5259   an,nn3772   ad3779   2532 art3588 nn5207}

heaven, shineth unto the other *part* under heaven; so shall also the Son of
^{art,nn444   fm2071   pre1722 ppro848 art,nn2250}

man be in his day.
^{1161   nu,ajn4412   pin1163   ppro846   ainf3958   an,ajn4183   2532   aifp593   pre575   depro5026}

25 But first must he suffer many things, and be rejected of this
^{art,nn1074}

generation.
^{2532   ad2531   aom1096 pre1722 art3588   nn2250   3575   ad3779   fm2071   2532   pre1722 art3588}

26 And as it was in the days of Noah, so shall it be also in the
^{nn2250   art3588 nn5207   art,nn444}

days of the Son of man.   *(Gen. 6:5-12)*
^{ipf2068   ipf4095   ipf1060}

27 They did eat, they drank, they married wives, they were
^{ipf1547   ad891   (repro3739) an,nn2250   3575   aina1525   pre1519 art3588 nn2787 2532 art3588}

given*in*marriage, until the day that Noah entered into the ark, and the
^{nn2627   aina2064   2532   aina622   an,ajn537}

flood came, and destroyed them all.
^{ad3668   2532   ad5613   aom1096 pre1722 art3588   nn2250   3091   ipf2068}

28 Likewise also as it was in the days of Lot; they did eat, they
^{ipf4095   ipf59   ipf4453   ipf5452   ipf3618}

drank, they bought, they sold, they planted, they builded;   *(Gen. 19:24,25)*
^{1161   repro3739   an,nn2250   3091   aina1831   pre575   an,nn4670   aina1026   an,nn4442 2532}

29 But the same day that Lot went out of Sodom it rained fire and
^{an,nn2303   pre575   an,nn3772   2532   aina622   an,ajn537}

brimstone from heaven, and destroyed *them* all.

pre2596/depro5024   fm2071 (repro3739) an,nn2250   art3588 nn5207   art,nn444   pinm601

30 Even thus shall it be in the day when the Son of man is revealed.

pre1722 depro1565 art,nn2250   repro3739   fm2071 pre1909 art3588   nn1430   2532 ppro846 art,nn4632

31 In that day, he which shall be upon the housetop, and his stuff

pre1722 art3588   nn3614   3361   aima2597   ainf142/ppro846   2532 art3588   pre1722

in the house, let him not come down to take*it*away: and he that is in

art3588   nn68   ad3668   3361   aima1994 pre1519/art,ad3694

the field, let him likewise not return   back.

pim3421   3091   art,nn1135

32 Remember Lot's wife.   *(Gen. 19:26)*

repro3739/1437   asba2212   ainf4982 ppro848 art,nn5590   ft622 ppro846 2532 repro3739/1437

33 Whosoever shall seek to save his   life   shall lose it; and whosoever

asba622 ppro848   ft2225   ppro846

shall lose his life shall preserve it.

pin3004 ppro5213   depro5026 art,nn3571   fm2071 nu,ajn1417   pre1909 nu3391 an,nn2825 art3588

34 I tell you, in that night there shall be   two *men* in one bed; the

nu,ajn1520   fp3880   2532 art3588 ajn2087   fp863

one shall be taken, and the other shall be left.

nu,ajn1417   fm2071 pap229   pre1909/ppro846 art3588 nu,ajn3391   fp3880   2532

35 Two *women* shall be grinding together; the one shall be taken, and

art3588 ajn2087   fp863

the other left.

nu,ajn1417   fm2071 pre1722 art3588   nn68   art3588 nu,ajn1520   fp3880   2532 art3588

36 Two *men* shall be in the field; the one shall be taken, and the

ajn2087   fp863

other left.

2532   aptp611   pin3004   ppro846   ad4226   an,nn2962   1161   art3588 aina2036

37 And they answered and said unto him, Where, Lord? And he   said

ppro846   ad3699   art3588   nn4483   ad1563   art3588   nn105

unto them, Wheresoever the body *is*, thither will the eagles be

fp4873

gathered together.

The Importunate Widow: A Lesson in Prayer

1161   ipf3004   (2532)   an,nn3850   ppro846   aipr1163

18 And he spake a parable unto them *to this end,* that men ought

ad3842   pifm4336 2532 3361   pinf1573

always to pray, and not to faint;

pap3004   ipf2258 pre1722 (idpro5100) an,nn4172 (idpro5100) an,nn2923   ppmp5399 3361 art,nn2316

2 Saying, There was in   a   city   a   judge, which feared not God,

2532/3361   ppmp1788 an,nn444

neither regarded man:

1161   ipf2258   an,nn5503 pre1722 depro1565 art,nn4172 2532   ipf2064 pre4314 ppro846 pap3004

3 And there was a widow   in   that city; and she came unto him, saying,

aima1556 ppro3165 pre575 ppro3450   art,nn476

Avenge me   of mine adversary.

2532   aina2309   3756   pre1909/an,nn5550   1161   pre3326/depro5023   aina2036   pre1722   rxpro1438

4 And he would not for*a*while: but afterward he said within himself,

1499   pinm5399 3756 art,nn2316 2532/3756 pinm1788 an,nn444

Though I fear not God, nor regard man;

1065   depro5026 art,nn5503 aid3930/an,nn2873 ppro3427   ft1556   ppro846 3363
5 Yet because this widow troubleth me, I will avenge her, lest by her

pre1519/an,nn5056 ppmp2064   psa5299 ppro3165
continual coming she weary me.

1161 art3588 nn2962 aina2036 aima191 inpro5101 art3588 art,nn93   nn2923   pin3004
6 And the Lord said, Hear what the unjust judge saith.

1161   efn3364 art,nn2316 asba4160/art,nn1557 ppro848 art,ajn1588 art,pap994 an,nn2250 2532 an,nn3571
☞ 7 And shall not God avenge his own elect, which cry day and night

pre4314 ppro846   2532   pap3114   pre1909 ppro846
unto him, though he bear long with them?

pin3004 ppro5213 3754   ft4160/art,nn1557 ppro846 pre1722/an,nn5034   4133   art3588
8 I tell you that he will avenge them speedily. Nevertheless when the

nn5207 art,nn444 apta2064 (687)   ft2147 art,nn4102 pre1909 art3588   nn1093
Son of man cometh, shall he find faith on the earth?

The Parable of the Pharisee and the Tax Collector

1161   aina2036 (2532) depro5026 art,nn3850 pre4314 idpro5100   art,pfp3982   pre1909   rxpro1438
9 And he spake   this parable unto certain which trusted in themselves

3754   pin1526 pr/an,aj1342 2532 pap1848   art,ajn3062
that they were righteous, and despised others:

nu1417 an,nn444 aina305   pre1519 art3588 nn2411   aifm4336 art3588 nu,ajn1520   pr/an,nn5330 2532
10 Two men went up into the temple to pray; the one a Pharisee, and

art3588 ajn2087   pr/an,nn5057
the other a publican.

art3588   nn5330 aptp2476   ipf4336 depro5023 pre4314 rxpro1438 art,nn2316   pin2168 ppro4671
11 The Pharisee stood and prayed thus with himself, God, I thank thee,

3754   pin1510 3756 ad5618 art,ajn3062 art,nn444   an,nn727   an,ajn94   an,nn3432 2228 2532
that I am not as other men are, extortioners, unjust, adulterers, or even

ad5613 depro3778   art,nn5057
as this publican.

pin3522 nu,ad1364 art3588   nn4521   pin586   an,ajn3956 an,ajn3745   pinm2932
12 I fast twice in the week, I give tithes of all that I possess.

2532 art3588   nn5057   pfp2476   ad3113   ipf2309 3756 ainf1869   3761
13 And the publican, standing afar off, would not lift up so*much*as his

art,nn3778 pre1519 art,nn3772 235 ipf5180 pre1519 ppro848 art,nn4738 pap3004 art,nn2316 aipp2433
eyes unto heaven, but smote upon his breast, saying, God be merciful to

ppro3427 art,ajn268
me a sinner.   (Ps. 51:1)

pin3004 ppro5213 depro3778 aina2597   pre1519 ppro848 art,nn3624 pfpp1344   2228
14 I tell you, this man went down to his house justified rather than

depro1565   3754   an,aj3956   art,pap5312   rxpro1438   fp5013   1161
the other: for every one that exalteth himself shall be abased; and

art,pap5013   rxpro1438   fp5312
he*that*humbleth himself shall be exalted.

☞ 18:7 See note on Ephesians 1:4, 5.

Jesus Blesses Little Children (Matt. 19:13-15; Mark 10:13-16)

15 And they brought unto him also infants, that he would touch them: but when *his* disciples saw *it,* they rebuked them.

16 But Jesus called them *unto him,* and said, Suffer little children to come unto me, and forbid them not: for of such is the kingdom of God.

17 Verily I say unto you, Whosoever shall not receive the kingdom of God as a little child shall in*no*wise enter therein.

How to Inherit Eternal Life (Matt. 19:16-30; Mark 10:17-31)

18 And a certain ruler asked him, saying, Good Master, what shall I do to inherit eternal life?

19 And Jesus said unto him, Why callest thou me good? none *is* good, save one, *that is,* God.

20 Thou knowest the commandments, Do not commit adultery, Do not kill, Do not steal, Do not bear*false*witness, Honor thy father and thy mother.   *(Ex. 20:12-16; Deut. 5:16-20)*

21 And he said, All these have I kept from my youth up.

22 Now when Jesus heard these things, he said unto him, Yet lackest thou one thing: sell   all   that thou hast, and distribute unto the poor, and thou shalt have treasure in heaven: and come, follow me.

23 And when he heard this, he was very sorrowful: for he was very rich.

24 And when Jesus saw that he was very sorrowful, he said, How hardly shall they*that*have riches enter into the kingdom of God!

25 For it is   easier for a camel to go through a needle's eye, than for a rich man to enter into the kingdom of God.

¹¹⁶¹   art,apta191   aina2036 inpro5101 2532 pinm1410   aifp4982
26 And they*that*heard *it* said, Who then can be saved?

¹¹⁶¹ art3588 aina2036   art,ajn102   pre3844 an,nn444 pin2076 pr/an,aj1415
27 And he said, The*things*which*are*impossible with men are possible

pre3844 art,nn2316
with God.   *(Gen. 18:14)*

¹¹⁶¹   art,nn4074 aina2036 2400 epn2249   aina863 an,ajn3956 2532   aina190   ppro4671
28 Then Peter said, Lo, we have left all, and followed thee,

¹¹⁶¹ art3588 aina2036   ppro846   281   pin3004   ppro5213   pin2076   pr/an,ajn3762
29 And he said unto them, Verily I say unto you, There is no man

repro3739   aina863   an,nn3614 2228 an,nn1118 2228   an,nn80   2228 an,nn1135 2228   an,nn5043
that hath left house, or parents, or brethren, or wife, or children,

pre1752/art3588/nn932/art,nn2316
for*the*kingdom*of*God's*sake,

repro3739   efn3364   asba618   an,ajn4179   pre1722 depro5129   art,nn2540   2532 pre1722
30 Who shall not receive manifold more in this present time, and in

art3588 nn165   art,ppmp2064 an,nn2222   an,aj166
the world to come life everlasting.

Jesus Foretells His Resurrection (Matt. 20:17-19; 10:32-34)

¹¹⁶¹   apta3880   art3588   nu,ajn1427   aina2036 pre4314 ppro846   2400
31 Then he took *unto him* the twelve, and said unto them, Behold, we

pin305 pre1519   an,nn2414   2532   an,aj3956   art,pfpp1125   pre1223 art3588   nn4396
go up to Jerusalem, and all things that*are*written by the prophets concerning

art3588 nn5207 art,nn444   fp5055
the Son of man shall be accomplished.

¹⁰⁶³   fp3860   art3588   nn1484   2532   fp1702   2532
32 For he shall be delivered unto the Gentiles, and shall be mocked, and

fp5195   2532   fp1716
spitefully entreated, and spitted on:

2532   apta3146   ft615/ppro846   2532 art3588 nu,aj5154 art,nn2250
33 And they shall scourge *him,* and put*him*to*death: and the third day

fm450
he shall rise again.

2532 epn846   aina4920   an,ajn3762   depro5130   2532 depro5124 art,nn4487 ipf2258 pfpp2928
34 And they understood none of these things: and this saying was hid

pre575 ppro846   2532/3756 ipf1097   art,ppmp3004
from them, neither knew they the*things*which*were*spoken.

Jesus Heals a Blind Beggar Near Jericho (Matt. 20:29-34; Mark 10:46-52)

¹¹⁶¹   aom1096   ppro846   aie1448   pre1519   2410
35 And it came*to*pass, that as he was come nigh unto Jericho, a

idpro5100   an,ajn5185   ipf2521 pre3844 art3588   nn3598   pap4319
certain blind man sat by the way side begging:

¹¹⁶¹ apta191   an,nn3793   ppmp1279   ipf4441 inpro5101 depro5124 opt1498
36 And hearing the multitude pass by, he asked what it meant.

37 And they told him, that Jesus of Nazareth passeth by.

38 And he cried, saying, Jesus, *thou* son of David, have mercy on me.

39 And they*which*went*before rebuked him, that he should hold*his*peace: but he cried so much the more, *Thou* son of David, have mercy on me.

40 And Jesus stood, and commanded him to be brought unto him: and when he was come near, he asked him,

41 Saying, What wilt thou that I shall do unto thee? And he said, Lord, that I may receive*my*sight.

42 And Jesus said unto him, Receive*thy*sight: thy faith hath saved thee.

43 And immediately he received*his*sight, and followed him, glorifying God: and all the people, when they saw *it,* gave praise unto God.

The Conversion of Zacchaeus

19 And *Jesus* entered and passed through Jericho.

2 And, behold, *there was* a man named Zacchaeus, which was the chief*among*the*publicans, and he was rich.

3 And he sought to see Jesus who he was; and could not for the press, because he was little of stature.

4 And he ran before, and climbed up into a sycamore tree to see him: for he was to pass that *way.*

5 And when Jesus came to the place, he looked up, and saw him, and said unto him, Zacchaeus, make haste, and come down; for today I must abide at thy house.

2532   apta4692   aina2597   2532   aom5264   ppro846   pap5463

6 And he made haste, and came down, and received him joyfully.

2532   apta1492   an,ajn537   ipf1234   pap3004   3754   aina1525

7 And when they saw *it*, they all murmured, saying, That he was gone

ainf2647   pre3844   an,nn435   an,aj268

to be guest with a man that is a sinner.

1161   an,nn2195   aptp2476   aina2036   pre4314   art3588   nn2962   2400   an,nn2962   art3588   ajn2255

8 And Zacchaeus stood, and said unto the Lord; Behold, Lord, the half

ppro3450   art,pap5224   pin1325   art3588   ajn4434   2532   1487

of my goods I give to the poor; and if I have

aina4811/idpro5100/idpro5100   pin591   an,ajn5073

taken*any*thing*from*any*man*by*false*accusation, I restore *him* fourfold.

(Ex. 22:1)

1161   art,nn2424   aina2036   pre4314   ppro846   ad4594   an,nn4991   aom1096   depro5129   art,nn3624

9 And Jesus said unto him, This day is salvation come to this house

2530   epn846   2532   pin2076   pr/an,nn5207   11

forsomuch as he also is a son of Abraham.

1063   art3588   nn5207   art,nn444   aina2064   ainf2212   2532   ainf4982

10 For the Son of man is come to seek and to save

art,pfp622

that*which*was* lost.   *(Ezek. 34:11,16)*

The Parable of the Ten Pounds *(Matt. 25:14-30)*

1161   ppro846   pap191   depro5023   apta4369   aina2036   an,nn3850

☞ 11 And as they heard these things, he added and spake a parable, because

ppro846   aid1511   ad*1451   2419   2532   ppro846   pinf1380   3754   art3588   nn932

he was nigh to Jerusalem, and because they thought that the kingdom of

art,nn2316   pin3195   ad3916   pifm398

God should immediately appear.

aina2036   3767   idpro5100   an,aj2104   an,nn444   ainp4198   pre1519   an,aj3117   an,nn5561

12 He said therefore, A certain noble man went into a far country to

ainf2983   rxpro1438   an,nn932   2532   ainf5290

receive for himself a kingdom, and to return.

1161   apta2564   rxpro1438   nu1176   an,ajn1401   aina1325   ppro846   nu1176   an,nn3414   2532

13 And he called his ten servants, and delivered them ten pounds, and

aina2036   pre4314   ppro846   aipm4231   ad2193   pinm2064

said unto them, Occupy till I come.

☞ **19:11–27** The contrast between this parable and the parable of the talents in Matthew 25:14–30 is in Luke's parable, the nobleman gave equally one pound to each person. But in the parable of the talents in Matthew, He bestowed unequal endowments. He expects the proper yield proportionate to His endowment. This is in confirmation of Paul's statement in 1 Corinthians 4:7: ". . . and what hast thou that thou didst not receive? now if thou didst receive it, why dost thou glory as if thou hadst not received it?" All things have been received from God. None can say that he has received nothing. No matter how much or how little one has, it must always be remembered that it has come from God, and that he is responsible to Him for the way he uses what the Lord has given.

1161   ppro846   art,nn4177   ipf3404   ppro846   2532   aina649   an,nn4242   ad*3694   ppro846   pap3004

14 But his citizens hated him, and sent a message after him, saying, We

3756   pin2309   depro5126   ainf936   pre1909   ppro2248

will not have this *man* to reign over us.

2532   aom1096   ppro846   aie1880   apta2983

15 And it came*to*pass, that when he was returned, having received

art3588   nn932   2532   aina2036   depro5128   art,ajn1401   aifp5455   ppro848

the kingdom, then he commanded these servants to be called unto him, to

repro3739   aina1325 art3588   nn694   2443   asba1097   inpro5101   idpro5100

whom he had given the money, that he might know how much every man had

aom1281

gained*by*trading.

1161   aom3854   art3588   nu,ajn4413   pap3004   an,nn2962   ppro4675   art,nn3414   aom4333   nu1176

16 Then came the first, saying, Lord, thy pound hath gained ten

an,nn3414

pounds.

2532   aina2036   ppro846   ad2095   an,aj18   an,ajn1401   3754

17 And he said unto him, Well, thou good servant: because thou hast

aom1096   pr/an,aj4103   pre1722   cd/an,ajn1646   aima2468/pap2192   an,nn1849   ad*1883 nu1176 an,nn4172

been faithful in a very little, have thou authority over ten cities.

2532   art3588   nu,ajn1208   aina2064   pap3004   an,nn2962   ppro4675   art,nn3414   aina4160   nu4002

18 And the second came, saying, Lord, thy pound hath gained five

an,nn3414

pounds.

1161   aina2036   2532   depro5129 pim1096 epn4771   2532   ad*1883 nu4002 an,nn4172

19 And he said likewise to him, Be thou also over five cities.

2532   an,ajn2087   aina2064   pap3004   an,nn2962   2400   ppro4675   art,nn3414   repro3739

20 And another came, saying, Lord, behold, *here is* thy pound, which I

ipf2192   ppmp606   pre1722   an,nn4676

have kept laid up in a napkin:

1063   ipf5399   ppro4571   3754   pin1488   pr/an,aj840   an,nn444   pin142

21 For I feared thee, because thou art an austere man: thou takest up

repro3739   aina5087/3756   2532   pin2325   repro3739   3756   aina4687

that thou laidst*not*down, and reapest that thou didst not sow.

1161   pin3004   ppro846 pre1537   ppro4675   art,nn4750   ft2919   ppro4571

22 And he saith unto him, Out of thine own mouth will I judge thee, *thou*

an,aj4190   an,ajn1401   ipf1492   3754   epn1473 pin1510   pr/an,aj840   an,nn444   pap142   repro3739

wicked servant. Thou knewest that I was an austere man, taking up that I

aina5087/3756   2532   pap2325   repro3739   3756   aina4687

laid*not*down, and reaping that I did not sow:

pre,inpro1302   2532   aina1325   3756   ppro3450   art,nn694   pre1909 art3588   nn5132   2532   epn1473

23 Wherefore then gavest not thou my money into the bank, that at my

apta2064   aina4238/302   ppro846   pre4862   an,nn5110

coming I might have required mine own with usury?

2532   aina2036   art,pfp3936   aima142   pre575   ppro846 art3588   nn3414   2532

24 And he said unto them*that*stood*by, Take from him the pound, and

aima1325   art,pap2192   nu1176   art,nn3414

give *it* to him*that*hath ten pounds.

2532   aina2036   ppro846 an,nn2962   pin2192 nu1176   an,nn3414

25 (And they said unto him, Lord, he hath ten pounds.)

1063   pin3004   ppro5213   3754   an,aj3956   art,pap2192   fp1325

26 For I say unto you, That unto every one which hath shall be given;

1161   pre575   art,pap2192   3361   2532   repro3739   pin2192   fp142   pre575   ppro846
and from him*that*hath not, even that he hath shall be taken away from him.

          4133   depro1565 ppro3450   art,ajn2190   art,apta2309   3361   ppro3165   aifp936   pre1909
    27 But those mine enemies, which would not that   I   should reign over

ppro846   aima71   ad5602   2532 aima2695   ad*1715   ppro3450
them, bring hither, and slay *them* before me.

Jesus Enters Jerusalem (Matt. 21:1-11; Mark 11:1-11; John 12:12-19)

          2532   depro5023   apta2036   ipf4198   ad1715   pap305   pre1519
    28 And when he had thus spoken, he went before, ascending up to
an,nn2414
Jerusalem.

          2532   aom1096   ad5613   aina1448   pre1519   967   2532
    29 And it came*to*pass, when he was come nigh to Bethphage and
an,nn963   pre4314 art3588   nn3735   art,ppmp2564   an,nn1636   aina649 nu1417   ppro848
Bethany, at the mount called *the mount* of Olives, he sent two of his
art,nn3101
disciples,

          apta2036   aima5217   pre1519 art3588   nn2968   ad2713   pre1722   repro3739
    30 Saying, Go ye into the village over against *you*; in the which at your
ppmp1531   ft2147   an,nn4454 pfpp1210 pre1909/repro3739 ad4455/an,ajn3762 an,nn444 aina2523 apta3089 ppro846
entering ye shall find a colt tied, whereon yet never man sat: loose him, and
aima71
bring *him hither.*

          2532   1437   idpro5100   pin2065 ppro5209 pre,inpro1302   pin3089   ad3779   ft2046
    31 And if any man ask you, Why do ye loose *him*? thus shall ye say
ppro846   3754   art3588 nn3962 pin2192 an,nn5532   ppro846
unto him, Because the Lord hath need of him.

          1161   art,pfpp649   apta565   aina2147   ad2531
    32 And they*that*were*sent went*their*way, and found even as he had
aina2036   ppro846
said unto them.

          1161   ppro846   pap3089 art3588 nn4454 art3588   nn2962   ppro846 aina2036 pre4314 ppro846
    33 And as they were loosing the colt, the owners thereof said unto them,
inpro5101   pin3089   art3588 nn4454
Why loose ye the colt?

          1161   art3588 aina2036 art3588   nn2962   pin2192 an,nn5532   ppro846
    34 And they said, The Lord hath need of him.

          2532   aina71   ppro846 pre4314 art,nn2424   2532   apta1977 rxpro1438   art,nn2440   pre1909
    35 And they brought him to Jesus: and they cast their garments upon
art3588 nn4454   aina1913/art,nn2424
the colt, and they set*Jesus*thereon.

          1161   ppro846 ppmp4198   ipf5291   ppro848 art,nn2440 pre1722 art3588   nn3598
    36 And as he went, they spread their clothes in the way.

          1161   ppro846   pap1448   ad2235   pre4314 art3588   nn2600   art3588
    37 And when he was come nigh, even now at the descent of the
nn3735   art,nn1636 art3588 an,aj537   nn4128   art3588   nn3101   aom756   pap5463
mount of Olives, the whole multitude of the disciples began to rejoice and

pinf134   art,nn2316   an,aj3173 an,nn5456 pre4012 an,aj3956   an,nn1411   repro3739

praise God with a loud voice for all the mighty works that they had
aina1492

seen;

pap3004   pr/pfpp2127   art3588   nn935   ppmp2064 pre1722   an,nn3686   an,nn2962

38 Saying, Blessed *be* the King that cometh in the name of the Lord:
an,nn1515 pre1722 an,nn3772   2532 an,nn1391 pre1722   an,ajn5310

peace in heaven, and glory in the highest.   *(Ps. 118:26)*

2532   idpro5100   art3588   nn5330   pre575   art3588   nn3793   aina2036 pre4314 ppro846

39 And some of the Pharisees from among the multitude said unto him,
an,nn1320   aima2008   ppro4675   art,nn3101

Master, rebuke thy disciples.

2532   aptp611   aina2036   ppro846   pin3004 ppro5213 3754 1437 depro3778

40 And he answered and said unto them, I tell you that, if these should
asba4623   art3588   nn3037   fm2896

hold*their*peace, the stones would immediately cry out.

2532   ad5613   aina1448   apta1492 art3588 nn4172   aina2799 pre1909 ppro846

41 And when he was come near, he beheld the city, and wept over it,
pap3004   1487   aina1097   2532   epn4771   2532/1065   pre1722 depro5026 ppro4675 art,nn2250

42 Saying, If thou hadst known, even thou, at least in this thy day,
art3588   pre4314 ppro4675 an,nn1515 1161 ad3568   ainp2928 pre575 ppro4675

the things *which belong* unto thy peace! but now they are hid from thine
art,nn3788

eyes.

3754   an,nn2250   ft2240 pre1909 ppro4571 2532 ppro4675 art,ajn2190

43 For the days shall come upon thee, that thine enemies shall
ft4016/an,nn5482   ppro4571 2532   ft4033/ppro4571   2532   ft4912/ppro4571

cast*a*trench*about thee, and compass*thee*round, and keep*thee*in
ad3840

on*every*side,

2532   ft1474/ppro4571   2532 ppro4675 art,nn5043   pre1722

44 And shall lay*thee*even*with*the*ground, and thy children within
ppro4671 2532   3756 ft863 pre1722 ppro4671   an,nn3037/pre1909/an,nn3037   pre473/repro3739

thee; and they shall not leave in thee one*stone*upon*another; because thou
aina1097   3756 art3588 nn2540   ppro4675   art,nn1984

knewest not the time of thy visitation.

The Cleansing of the Temple (Matt. 21:12-17; Mark 11:15-19; John 2:13-22)

2532   apta1525 pre1519 art3588   nn2411   aom756   pinf1544   art,pap4453

45 And he went into the temple, and began to cast out them*that*sold
pre1722/ppro846 2532   pap59

therein, and them*that*bought;

pap3004   ppro846   pfip1125   ppro3450 art,nn3624 pin2076   pr/an,nn3624   an,nn4335

46 Saying unto them, It is written, My house is the house of prayer:
1161 epn5210   aina4160 ppro846   an,nn4693   an,nn3027

but ye have made it a den of thieves.   *(Is. 56:7; Jer. 7:11)*

2532   ipf2258/pap1321 art,pre2596/an,nn2250 pre1722 art3588   nn2411   1161 art3588   nn749   2532

47 And he taught daily in the temple. But the chief priests and
art3588   nn1122   2532 art3588 nu,ajn4413   art3588   nn2992   ipf2212   ainf622   ppro846

the scribes and the chief of the people sought to destroy him,

     2532   3756   ipf2147   art,inpro5101   asba4160   1063   an,aj537   art3588   nn2992

48 And could not find what they might do: for all the people

ipf1582   pap191   ppro846

were*very*attentive to hear him.

Jesus' Authority Questioned (Matt. 21:23-27; Mark. 11:27-33)

           2532   aom1096   pre1722 nu3391   depro1565 art,nn2250   ppro846   pap1321

20 And it came*to*pass, *that* on one of those days, as he taught

    art3588   nn2992   pre1722   art3588   nn2411   2532   ppmp2097   art3588

   the people in the temple, and preached*the*gospel, the

nn749   2532 art3588   nn1122   aina2186   pre4862 art3588 aj4245

chief priests and the scribes came upon *him* with the elders,

    2532   aina2036   pre4314 ppro846   pap3004   aima2036 ppro2254 pre1722 an,aj4169   an,nn1849   pin4160

2 And spake unto him, saying, Tell us, by what authority doest thou

depro5023   2228 inpro5101 pin2076 pr/art,apta1325 ppro4671 depro5026 art,nn1849

these things? or who is he*that*gave thee this authority?

   1161   aptp611   aina2036 pre4314   ppro846   epn2504/ft2065   ppro5209 nu1520 an,nn3056

3 And he answered and said unto them, I*will*also*ask you one thing;

2532   aima2036 ppro3427

and answer me:

   art3588   nn908   an,nn2491 ipf2258   pre1537   an,nn3772   2228 pre1537 an,nn444

4 The baptism of John, was it from heaven, or of men?

   1161 art3588 aom4817   pre4314   rxpro1438   pap3004   1437   asba2036 pre1537

5 And they reasoned with themselves, saying, If we shall say, From

an,nn3772   ft2046 pre,inpro1302 3767   aina4100   ppro846 3756

heaven; he will say, Why then believed ye him not?

   1161   1437   asba2036 pre1537 an,nn444 an,aj3956 art3588   nn2992   ft2642   ppro2248 1063

6 But and if we say, Of men; all the people will stone us: for they

pin2076   pr/pfpp3982   an,nn2491 pinf1511   pr/an,nn4396

be persuaded that John was a prophet.

   2532   pinp611   3361 pinf1492 ad4159

7 And they answered, that they could not tell whence *it was.*

   2532 art,nn2424 aina2036   ppro846   3761   pin3004 epn1473 ppro5213 pre1722 an,aj4169   an,nn1849

8 And Jesus said unto them, Neither tell I you by what authority I

pin4160   depro5023

do these things.

The Parable of the Husbandmen (Matt. 21:33-46; Mark 12:1-12)

   1161   aom756   pinf3004   pre4314 art3588   nn2992 depro5026 art,nn3850   idpro5100

9 Then began he to speak to the people this parable; A certain

an,nn444   aina5452   an,nn290   2532   aom1554/ppro846   an,nn1092   2532

man planted a vineyard, and let*it*forth to husbandmen, and

       aina589   an,aj2425 an,nn5550

went*into*a*far*country for a long time.   *(Is. 5:1)*

²⁵³² ^{pre1722}   ^{an,nn2540}   ^{aina649}   ^{an,ajn1401}   ^{pre4314} ^{art3588}   ⁿⁿ¹⁰⁹²   ²⁴⁴³

10 And   at   the season he sent a servant   to   the husbandmen, that they

^{asba1325} ^{ppro846} ^{pre575} ^{art3588} ⁿⁿ²⁵⁹⁰   ^{art3588}   ⁿⁿ²⁹⁰   ¹¹⁶¹ ^{art3588}   ⁿⁿ¹⁰⁹²   ^{apta1194} ^{ppro846}

should give him of the fruit of the vineyard: but the husbandmen beat him,

^{aina1821}   ^{an,aj2756}

and sent*him*away empty.

²⁵³²   ^{aom4369/ainf3992}   ^{an,aj2087}   ^{an,ajn1401}   ¹¹⁶¹ ^{art3588} ^{apta1194}   ^{depro2548}   ²⁵³²

11 And   again*he*sent another servant: and they beat him also, and

^{apta818}   ^{aina1821}   ^{an,aj2756}

entreated*him*shamefully, and sent*him*away empty.

²⁵³²   ^{aom4369/ainf3992}   ^{nu,ajn5154} ¹¹⁶¹ ^{art3588}   ^{apta5135}   ^{depro5126}   ²⁵³²

12 And   again*he*sent a   third: and they wounded   him   also, and

^{aina1544}

cast*him*out.

¹¹⁶¹   ^{aina2036} ^{art3588} ⁿⁿ²⁹⁶²   ^{art3588}   ⁿⁿ²⁹⁰   ^{inpro5101}   ^{asba4160}

13 Then   said   the   lord   of   the   vineyard, What   shall   I   do?   I   will

^{ft3992}   ^{ppro3450} ^{art,aj27}   ^{art,nn5207}   ^{ad2481}   ^{fm1788}

send   my   beloved   son: it*may*be they will reverence   him   when they

^{apta1492} ^{depro5126}

see   him.

¹¹⁶¹   ^{art3588}   ⁿⁿ¹⁰⁹²   ^{apta1492} ^{ppro846}   ^{ipf1260}   ^{pre4314}

14 But   when   the   husbandmen   saw   him,   they   reasoned   among

^{rxpro1438}   ^{pap3004}   ^{depro3778} ^{pin2076} ^{art3588} ^{pr/nn2818} ^{ad1205}   ^{aosi615} ^{ppro846} ²⁴⁴³ ^{art3588}

themselves, saying, This   is   the   heir: come, let us   kill   him, that the

ⁿⁿ²⁸¹⁷   ^{asbm1096} ^{ppro2254}

inheritance may   be   ours.

²⁵³²   ^{apta1544} ^{ppro846} ^{ad1854} ^{art3588}   ⁿⁿ²⁹⁰   ^{aina615}   ^{inpro5101}   ³⁷⁶⁷

15 So they cast him out of the vineyard, and killed *him*. What therefore

^{art3588} ⁿⁿ²⁹⁶²   ^{art3588}   ⁿⁿ²⁹⁰   ^{ft4160}   ^{ppro846}

shall the lord of the vineyard do unto them?

^{fm2064}   ²⁵³²   ^{ft622}   ^{depro5128}   ^{art,nn1092}   ²⁵³²

16 He   shall   come   and   destroy   these   husbandmen,   and   shall

^{ft1325} ^{art3588}   ⁿⁿ²⁹⁰   ^{an,ajn243} ¹¹⁶¹   ^{apta191}   ^{aina2036}   ^{opt1096/3361}

give the vineyard to others. And when they heard *it,* they said, God forbid.

¹¹⁶¹ ^{art3588}   ^{apta1689} ^{ppro846}   ^{aina2036} ^{pr/inpro5101} ^{pin2076} ^{depro5124} ³⁷⁶⁷   ^{art,pfpp1125}

17 And   he   beheld them, and said, What   is   this   then that*is*written,

^{an,nn3037} ^{repro3739} ^{art3588} ^{pap3618}   ^{aina593}   ^{depro3778}   ^{ainp1096} ^(pre1519) ^{an,nn2776}

The stone which the builders rejected, the same is become   the   head of the

^{an,nn1137}

corner?   *(Ps. 118:22)*

^{an,aj3956}   ^{art,apta4098} ^{pre1909} ^{depro1565} ^{art,nn3037}   ^{fp4917}   ¹¹⁶¹ ^{pre1909}

18 Whosoever shall   fall   upon   that   stone shall   be   broken;   but   on

^{repro3739/302}   ^{asba4098}   ^{ft3039/ppro846}

whomsoever it shall fall, it will grind*him*to*powder.

²⁵³² ^{art3588}   ⁿⁿ⁷⁴⁹   ²⁵³² ^{art3588} ⁿⁿ¹¹²² ^(pre1722) ^{epn846} ^{art,nn5610} ^{aina2212}   ^{ainf1911}

19 And the chief priests and the scribes   the same hour sought to lay

^{art,nn5495} ^{pre1909} ^{ppro846} ²⁵³²   ^{aina5399} ^{art3588}   ⁿⁿ²⁹⁹²   ¹⁰⁶³   ^{aina1097}   ³⁷⁵⁴

hands   on   him; and they feared the people: for they perceived that he had

^{aina2036} ^{depro5026} ^{art,nn3850} ^{pre4314} ^{epn846}

spoken this parable against them.

Paying Tribute (Matt. 22:15-22; Mark 12:13-17)

20 And they watched *him*, and sent forth spies, which should feign themselves   just men, that they might take hold of his words, that so they might deliver him unto the power and authority of the governor.

21 And they asked him, saying, Master, we know that thou sayest and teachest rightly, neither acceptest thou the person *of any*, but teachest the way of God   truly:

22 Is*it*lawful for   us   to give tribute unto Caesar, or no?

23 But he perceived their craftiness, and said unto them, Why tempt ye me?

24 Show   me   a penny. Whose image and superscription hath it? They answered and said, Caesar's.

25 And he   said unto them, Render therefore unto Caesar the things which be Caesar's and unto God the things which be God's.

26 And they could not take hold of his words before the people: and they marveled at   his answer, and held*their*peace.

Is There a Resurrection? (Matt. 22:23-33; Mark 12:18-27)

27 Then came to *him* certain of the Sadducees, which deny that there is any resurrection: and they asked him,

28 Saying, Master, Moses wrote unto us, If any man's brother die, having a wife, and he   die without children, that his brother should take his wife, and raise up seed unto his brother.   *(Deut. 25:5)*

29 There were therefore seven brethren: and the first took a wife, and died without children.

2532 art3588 nu,ajn1208 aina2983   art,nn1135 2532 depro3778 aina599   an,aj815

30 And the second took her to wife, and   he   died childless.

2532 art3588 nu,ajn5154 aina2983 ppro846 1161   ad5615   art3588 nu,ajn2033   2532

31 And the third took her; and in*like*manner the seven also: and they

aina2641 3756   an,nn5043   2532   aina599

left no children, and died.

(1161) ad5305   an,ajn3956 art3588   nn1135   aina599 2532

32   Last of   all   the woman died also.

3767   pre1722 art3588   nn386   inpro5101 an,nn1135   ppro846   pinm1096 1063 art,nu,ajn2033

33 Therefore in   the resurrection whose wife of them is she? for seven

aina2192 ppro846   art,nn1135

had her to wife.

2532 art,nn2424 aptp611   aina2036   ppro846 art3588   nn5207   depro5127 art,nn165

34 And Jesus answering said unto them, The children of this   world

pin1060 2532   pinp1548

marry, and are given*in*marriage:

1161   art,aptp2661   ainf5177   depro1565 art,nn165   2532

35 But they*which*shall*be*accounted*worthy to obtain that world, and

art3588   nn386   art,pre1537   an,ajn3498   3777   pin1060   3777   pinp1548

the resurrection from the dead, neither marry, nor are given*in*marriage:

(1063)   3777   pinm1410   ainf599   ad2089   1063   pin1526   pr/an,aj2465

36   Neither can they die any more: for they are equal*unto*the*angels;

2532 pin1526   pr/an,nn5207   art,nn2316 pap5607   pr/an,nn5207   art3588   nn386

and are the children of God, being the children of the resurrection.

1161   3754 art3588 ajn3498   pinp1453   2532   an,nn3475   aina3377 pre1909 art3588   nn942

37 Now that the dead are raised, even Moses showed   at   the bush,

ad5613   pin3004   an,nn2962 art3588 nn2316   11   2532 art3588 nn2316   2464   2532 art3588

when he calleth the Lord the God of Abraham, and the God of Isaac, and the

nn2316   2384

God of Jacob.   (Ex. 3:2,6)

1161   pin2076 3756   an,nn2316   an,ajn3498   235   an,pap2198 1063 an,ajn3956 pin2198

38 For he is not a God of the dead, but of the living: for all   live unto

epn846

him.

1161   idpro5100   art3588   nn1122   aptp611   aina2036   an,nn1320   ad2573

39 Then certain of the scribes answering said, Master, thou hast well

aina2036

said.

1161   ipf5111 ad3765 pinf1905 ppro846 an,ajn3762

40 And after that they durst not ask him any question at all.

David's Lord (Matt. 22:41-46; Mark 12:35-37)

1161   aina2036 pre4314   ppro846   ad4459 pin3004   art,nn5547 pinf1511   1138   pr/an,nn5207

41 And he said unto them, How say they that Christ is David's son?

2532   1138   epn846   pin3004 pre1722   an,nn976   an,nn5568 art3588 nn2962 aina2036

42 And David himself saith in   the book of Psalms, The Lord said unto

ppro3450 art,nn2962 pin2521   pre1537 ppro3450   an,ajn1188

my Lord, Sit thou on my right hand,

ad2193/302   asba5087   pppro4675   art,ajn2190   pppro4675 an,nn5286/art,nn4228
43 Till I make thine enemies thy footstool.   *(Ps. 110:1)*

1138   3767   pin2564   pppro846 an,nn2962 ad4459 pin2076   2532   pppro846 pr/an,nn5207
44 David therefore calleth him Lord, how is he then his son?

Jesus Denounces the Scribes (Matt. 23:1-36; Mark 12:38-40; Luke 11:37-54)

1161   pap191   an,aj3956 art3588   nn2992   aina2036   pppro848   art,nn3101
45 Then in the audience of all the people he said unto his disciples,

pim4337   pre575 art3588   nn1122   art,pap2309   pinf4043 pre1722   an,nn4749   2532 pap5368
46 Beware of the scribes, which desire to walk in long robes, and love

an,nn783   pre1722 art3588   nn58   2532   an,nn4410   pre1722 art3588   nn4864   2532
greetings in the markets, and the highest seats in the synagogues, and the

an,nn4411   pre1722 art,nn1173
chief rooms at feasts;

repro3739   pin2719   art,nn5503   art,nn3614   2532   an,nn4392   pinm4336/an,ajn3117
47 Which devour widows' houses, and for a show make*long*prayers:

depro3778   fm2983   cd/an,aj4055   an,nn2917
the same shall receive greater damnation.

The Widow's Offering (Mark 12:41-44)

1161   apta308   aina1492 art3588   ajn4145   pap906   pppro848 art,nn1435
21 ☞ And he looked up, and saw the rich men casting their gifts

pre1519 art3588   nn1049
into the treasury.

1161   aina1492 2532   idpro5100 an,aj3998 an,nn5503   pap906   ad1563 nu1417 an,nn3016
2 And he saw also a certain poor widow casting in thither two mites.

2532   aina2036   ad230   pin3004   pppro5213 3754 depro3778 art,aj4434 art,nn5503
3 And he said, Of*a*truth I say unto you, that this poor widow hath

aina906 cd/an,ajn4119   an,ajn3956
cast in more than they all:

1063   an,aj537 depro3778   pre1537 pppro846   art,pap4052   aina906   pre1519 art3588   nn1435
4 For all these have of their abundance cast in unto the offerings of

art,nn2316 1161 epn3778 pre1537 pppro848 art,nn5303   aina906 an,aj537 art3588   nn979 repro3739   ipf2192
God: but she of her penury hath cast in all the living that she had.

The Temple Will Be Destroyed (Matt. 24:1,2; Mark 13:1,2)

2532   idpro5100 pap3004   pre4012 art3588   nn2411   3754   pfip2885   an,aj2570
5 And as some spake of the temple, how it was adorned with goodly

an,nn3037 2532 an,nn334   aina2036
stones and gifts, he said,

☞ **21:1–38** See note on Matthew 24:4—25:46 concerning the Olivet Discourse.

depro5023   repro3739   pin2334   an,nn2250   fm2064   pre1722   repro3739
6 *As for* these things which ye behold, the days will come,   in the which

3756   fp863   an,nn3037/pre1909/an,nn3037   repro3739   3756
there shall not be left one*stone*upon*another,   that shall not be

fp2647
thrown down.

Signs and Persecutions (Matt. 24:3-14; Mark 13:3-13)

1161   aina1905 ppro846 pap3004   an,nn1320   ad4219   (3767)   depro5023   fm2071
7 And they asked him, saying, Master, but when shall these things be?

2532 inpro5101 art,nn4592   ad3752   depro5023   psa3195   pifm1096
and what sign *will there be* when these things shall come*to*pass?

1161   art3588 aina2036   pim991   3361   asbp4105   1063 an,ajn4183   fm2064
8 And he said, Take heed that ye be not deceived: for many shall come

pre1909 ppro3450 art,nn3686   pap3004   epn1473 pin1510   2532 art3588 nn2540   pfi1448   aosi4198
in my name, saying, I am *Christ*; and the time draweth near: go ye

3361   3767   ad*3694 ppro846
not therefore after them.

1161   ad3752   asba191   an,nn4171 2532   an,nn181   3361   aosi4422   1063
9 But when ye shall hear of wars and commotions, be not terrified: for

depro5023   pin1163 nu,ajn4412   aifm1096   235 art3588 nn5056   3756   ad2112
these things must first come*to*pass; but the end *is* not by*and*by.

ad5119 ipf3004   ppro846 an,nn1484   fp1453 pre1909 an,nn1484 2532   an,nn932
10 Then said he unto them, Nation shall rise against nation, and kingdom

pre1909 an,nn932
against kingdom:

5037   an,aj3173   an,nn4578   fm2071   pre2596/an,nn5117   2532   an,nn3042   2532
11 And great earthquakes shall be in divers places, and famines, and

an,nn3061   5037   an,nn5400   2532 an,aj3173 an,nn4592   fm2071 pre575 an,nn3772
pestilences; and fearful sights and great signs shall there be from heaven.

1161   pre4253 an,aj537 depro5130   ft1911   ppro848 art,nn5495 pre1909 ppro5209 2532
12 But before all these, they shall lay their hands on you, and

ft1377   pap3860   pre1519   an,nn4864   2532   an,nn5438
persecute *you*, delivering*you*up to the synagogues, and into prisons, being

ppmp71   pre1909 an,nn935 2532 an,nn2232   pre1752/ppro3450/art,nn3686
brought before kings and rulers for*my*name's*sake.

1161   fm576   ppro5213 pre1519   an,nn3142
13 And it shall turn to you for a testimony.

aipm5087   3767   pre1519 ppro5216 art,nn2588 3361   pinf4304
14 Settle *it* therefore in your hearts, not to meditate before what ye shall

aifp626
answer:

1063 epn1473   ft1325 ppro5213   an,nn4750 2532   an,nn4678   repro3739 an,aj3956 ppro5213   art,ppmp480
15 For I will give you a mouth and wisdom, which all your adversaries

3756   fm1410   ainf471   3761   ainf436
shall not be able to gainsay nor resist.

1161   fp3860   2532   pre5259   an,nn1118   2532   an,nn80   2532
16 And ye shall be betrayed both by parents, and brethren, and

an,ajn4773   2532   an,ajn5384   2532   pre1537   ppro5216

kinsfolks,   and   friends;   and   *some*   of   you   shall   they

ft2289

cause*to*be*put*to*death.

     2532   fm2071 ppmp3404 pre5259 an,ajn3956   pre1223/ppro3450/art,nn3686

17 And ye shall be hated of   all   *men* for*my*name's*sake.

     2532   efn3364   an,nn2539 pre1537 ppro5216 art,nn2776   asbp622

18 But there shall not a hair of your head perish.

   pre1722 ppro5216 art,nn5281   aipm2932   ppro5216 art,nn5590

19 In your patience possess ye your souls.

The Destruction of Jerusalem Foretold (Matt. 24:15-21; Mark 13:14-19)

   1161   ad3752   asba1492   2419   ppmp2944 pre5259 an,nn4760 ad5119 aima1097

20 And when ye shall see Jerusalem compassed with armies, then know

3754 art3588   nn2050   ppro846   pfi1448

that the desolation thereof is nigh.

    ad5119   art3588   pre1722 art,nn2449 pim5343 pre1519 art3588   nn3735   2532

21 Then let them which are in Judea flee to the mountains; and let

art3588   pre1722   an,ajn3319   ppro848   pim1633   2532   3361   art3588

them which are in the midst of it depart out; and let not them that are

pre1722 art3588   nn5561   pim1525   pre1519/ppro846

in the countries enter thereinto.

     3754   depro3778   pin1526   pr/an,nn2250   an,nn1557   an,aj3956

22 For these be the days of vengeance, that all things

art,pfpp1125   infg4137

which*are*written may be fulfilled.   *(Deut. 32:35; Hos. 9:7; Joel 1:15)*

     1161   3759   art,pap2192/pre1722/an,nn1064   2532   art,pap2337

23 But woe unto them*that*are*with*child, and to them*that*give*suck,

pre1722 depro1565 art,nn2250 1063   fm2071 an,aj3173 an,nn318 pre1909 art3588 nn1093   2532 an,nn3709

in those days! for there shall be great distress in the land, and wrath

pre1722 depro5129 art,nn2992

upon this people.

     2532   fm4098   an,nn4750   an,nn3162   2532

24 And they shall fall by the edge of the sword, and shall be

fp163   pre1519 an,aj3956 art,nn1484 2532   2419   fm2071 ppmp3961   pre5259

led*away*captive into all nations: and Jerusalem shall be trodden down of

  an,nn1484   ad891   an,nn2540   an,nn1484   asbp4137

the Gentiles, until the times of the Gentiles be fulfilled.

Jesus Will Return (Matt. 24:29-31; Mark 13:24-27)

    2532   fm2071 an,nn4592 pre1722   an,nn2246 2532   an,nn4582   2532

25 And there shall be signs in the sun, and in the moon, and in the

an,nn798 2532 pre1909 art3588 nn1093   an,nn4928   an,nn1484 pre1722   an,nn640   an,nn2281 2532

stars; and upon the earth distress of nations, with perplexity; the sea and the

an,nn4535   pap2278

waves roaring;   *(Is. 13:10; Joel 2:30,31)*

an,nn444   pap674   pre575 an,nn5401   2532   an,nn4329
26 Men's   hearts*failing*them   for   fear,   and   for   looking   after
art,ppmp1904   art3588 nn3625 1063 art3588 nn1411   art,nn3772
those*things*which*are*coming*on the earth: for the powers of heaven shall
fp4531
be shaken.   *(Hag. 2:6,21)*

2532   ad5119   fm3700 art3588 nn5207   art,nn444 ppmp2064 pre1722   an,nn3507 pre3326
27 And then shall they see the Son of man coming in a cloud with
an,nn1411 2532 an,aj4183 an,nn1391
power and great glory.

1161   depro5130   ppmp756   pifm1096   aima352   2532
28 And when these things begin to come*to*pass, then look up, and
aima1869 pppro5216 art,nn2778 1360 pppro5216   art,nn629   pin1448
lift up your heads; for your redemption draweth nigh.

The Parable of the Fig Tree (Matt. 24:32-35; Mark 13:28-31)

2532   aina2036   ppro846   an,nn3850   aima1492   art3588   nn4808   2532 an,aj3956 art3588
29 And he spake to them a parable; Behold the fig tree, and all   the
nn1186
trees;

ad3752   ad2235   asba4261   pap991   pin1097 pre575   rxpro1438
30 When they now shoot forth, ye see and know of your*own*selves
3754 art,nn2330 pin2076 ad2235   pr/ad1451
that summer is now nigh*at*hand.

2532   ad3779   epn5210 ad3752   asba1492   depro5023   ppmp1096   pim1097
31 So likewise ye, when ye see these things come*to* pass, know ye
3754 art3588   nn932   art,nn2316 pin2076   pr/ad1451
that the kingdom of God is nigh*at*hand.

281   pin3004   ppro5213 (3754) depro3778   art,nn1074   efn3364   asba3928   ad2193/302
32 Verily I say unto you,   This generation shall not pass away,   till
an,ajn3956   asbm1096
all be fulfilled.

art,nn3772   2532 art,nn1093   fm3928   1161 ppro3450 art,nn3056   efn3364
33 Heaven and earth shall pass away: but my words shall not
asba3928
pass away.

Be Watchful

1161   pim4337   rxpro1438   3379   pppro5216 art,nn2588
34 And take heed to yourselves, lest*at*any*time your hearts be
asbp925   pre1722   an,nn2897   2532   an,nn3178   2532 an,nn3308   an,aj982 2532
overcharged with surfeiting, and drunkenness, and cares of this life, and *so*
depro1565 art,nn2250 asba2186 pre1909 ppro5209   an,aj160
that day come upon you unawares.

1063   ad5613   an,nn3803   fm1904 pre1909 an,aj3956   art,ppmp2521   pre1909   an,nn4383
35 For as a snare shall it come on   all them*that*dwell on the face
art3588 an,aj3956   nn1093
of the whole earth.

pim69   3767   ppmp1189   pre1722/an,aj3956/an,nn2540   2443

36 Watch ye therefore, and pray always, that ye may be

asbp2661   ainf1628   an,ajn3956   depro5023   art,pap3195   pifm1096   2532

accounted worthy to escape all these things that shall come*to*pass, and to

aifp2476   ad⁺1715   art3588   nn5207   art,nn444

stand before the Son of man.

1161   art3588   nn2250   ipf2258   pap1321   pre1722   art3588   nn2411   1161   art,nn3571

37 And in the daytime he was teaching in the temple; and at night he

ppmp1831   ipf835   pre1519   art3588   nn3735   art,ppmp2564   an,nn1636

went out, and abode in the mount that*is*called *the mount* of Olives.

2532   an,aj3956   art3588   nn2992   ipf3719   pre4314   ppro846   pre1722   art3588

38 And all the people came*early*in*the*morning to him in the

nn2411   pinf191   ppro846

temple, for to hear him.

Passover Is Near (Matt. 26:1-5,14-16; Mark 14:1,2,10,11; John 11:45-55)

1161   art3588   nn1859   art,ajn106   ipf1448   art,ppmp3004

22 Now the feast of unleavened bread drew nigh, which*is*called the

3957

Passover.   *(Ex. 12:1-27)*

2532   art3588   nn749   2532   art,nn1122   ipf2212   art,ad4459   asba337   ppro846   1063

2 And the chief priests and scribes sought how they might kill him; for

ipf5399   art3588   nn2992

they feared the people.

1161   aina1525   art,nn4567   pre1519   an,nn2455   art,ppmp1941   an,ajn2469   pap5607   pre1537   art3588   nn706

3 Then entered Satan into Judas surnamed Iscariot, being of the number

art3588   nu,ajn1427

of the twelve.

2532   apta565   aina4814   art3588   nn749   2532

4 And he went*his*way, and communed with the chief priests and

art,nn4755   art,ad4459   asba3860   ppro846   ppro846

captains, how he might betray him unto them.

2532   aina5463   2532   aom4934   ainf1325   ppro846   an,nn694

5 And they were glad, and covenanted to give him money.

2532   aina1843   2532   ipf2212   an,nn2120   infg3860   ppro846   ppro846

6 And he promised, and sought opportunity to betray him unto them

pre817   an,nn3793

in*the*absence*of the multitude.

The Preparation of the Passover (Matt. 26:17-25; Mark 14:12-21)

1161   aina2064   art3588   nn2250   art,ajn106   pre1722/repro3739   art3588   3957   ipf1163

7 Then came the day of unleavened bread, when the passover must be

pifm2380

killed.   *(Ex. 12:6)*

2532   aina649   an,nn4074 2532 an,nn2491 apta2036 aptp4198   aima2090 ppro2254 art3588

8 And he sent Peter and John, saying, Go and prepare us the

3957   2443   asba5315

passover, that we may eat.

1161 art3588 aina2036   ppro846 ad4226 pin2309   asba2090

9 And they said unto him, Where wilt thou that we prepare?

1161 art3588 aina2036   ppro846 2400   ppro5216   apta1525 pre1519 art3588 nn4172

10 And he said unto them, Behold, when ye are entered into the city,

an,nn444 ft4876 ppro5213 pap941 an,nn2765   an,nn5204 aima190 ppro846 pre1519 art3588

there shall a man meet you, bearing a pitcher of water; follow him into the

nn3614 repro3757   pinm1531

house where he entereth in.

2532   ft2046   art3588 nn3617   art3588 nn3614 art3588 nn1320 pin3004

11 And ye shall say unto the goodman of the house, The Master saith unto

ppro4671 ad4226 pin2076 art3588   nn2646   ad3699   asba5315 art3588 3957 pre3326

thee, Where is the guestchamber, where I shall eat the passover with

ppro3450 art,nn3101

my disciples?

depro2548   ft1166 ppro5213 an,aj3173   an,nn508   pfpp4766 ad1563

12 And he shall show you a large upper room furnished: there

aima2090

make ready.

1161   apta565   aina2147 ad2531   pfi2046   ppro846 2532

13 And they went, and found as he had said unto them: and they

aina2090 art3588 3957

made ready the passover.

The True Meaning of the Passover Meal (Matt. 26:26-30; Mark 14:22-26; 1 Cor. 11:23-25)

2532 ad3753 art3588 nn5610   aom1096   aina377 2532 art3588 nu1427 nn652

14 And when the hour was come, he sat down, and the twelve apostles

pre4862 ppro846

with him.

2532   aina2036 pre4314 ppro846   an,nn1939   aina1937 ainf5315 depro5124

15 And he said unto them, With desire I have desired to eat this

3957 pre3326 ppro5216   ppro3165 aip3958

passover with you before I suffer:

1063 pin3004   ppro5213 (3754) efn3364 ad3765 asba5315 pre1537/ppro846 ad2193 (repro3755)

16 For I say unto you, I will not any more eat thereof, until it be

asbp4137 pre1722 art3588 nn932 art,nn2316

fulfilled in the kingdom of God.

2532 aptm1209 an,nn4221   apta2168   aina2036 aima2983 depro5124 2532 aima1266

17 And he took the cup, and gave thanks, and said, Take this, and divide

rxpro1438

it among yourselves:

1063 pin3004   ppro5213 (3754) efn3364 asba4095 pre575 art3588 nn1081   art3588 nn288 ad2193 (repro3755)

18 For I say unto you, I will not drink of the fruit of the vine, until

art3588 nn932 art,nn2316   asba2064

the kingdom of God shall come.

2532   apta2983   an,nn740   apta2168   aina2806   2532   aina1325

19 And he took bread, and gave thanks, and broke *it,* and gave unto

ppro846   pap3004   depro5124 pin2076 ppro3450 pr/art,nn4983   pre5228 ppro5216 depro5124 pim4160 pre1519

them, saying, This is my body which*is*given for you: this do in

art,nn364   popro1699

remembrance of me.

ad5615   2532 art3588   nn4221   aime1172   pap3004   depro5124   art,nn4221 art3588   aj2537

20 Likewise also the cup after supper, saying, This cup *is* the new

pr/an,nn1242   pre1722 ppro3450 art,nn129   art,ppmp1632   pre5228 ppro5216

testament in my blood, which*is*shed for you.

(Ex. 24:8; Jer. 31:31; Zech. 9:11)

4133   2400   art3588   nn5495   art,pap3860   ppro3165   pre3326 ppro1700 pre1909 art3588

21 But, behold, the hand of him*that*betrayeth me *is* with me on the

nn5132

table.

(Ps. 41:9)

2532   3303   art3588   nn5207   art,nn444   pinm4198   pre2596   art,pfpp3724   4133   3759

22 And truly the Son of man goeth, as it was determined: but woe

depro1565 art,nn444 pre1223 repro3739   pinp3860

unto that man by whom he is betrayed!

2532   epn846   aom756   pinf4802   pre4314   rxpro1438   (art3588) inpro5101 (686) pre1537 ppro846

23 And they began to inquire among themselves, which of them it

opt1498   art,pap3195   pinf4238   depro5124

was that should do this thing.

Who Is The Greatest?

1161   aom1096 2532   an,nn5379   pre1722   ppro846   art,inpro5101   ppro846

24 And there was also a strife among them, which of them should be

pin1380   (pinf1511) pr/cd/an,ajn3187

accounted the greatest.

1161   art3588   aina2036   ppro846   art3588   nn935   art3588   nn1484

25 And he said unto them, The kings of the Gentiles

pin2961   ppro846 2532   art,pap1850   ppro846

exercise*lordship*over them; and they*that*exercise*authority*upon them are

pinp2564   an,nn2110

called benefactors.

1161   epn5210   3756   ad3779   235   cd/art,ajn3187   pre1722 ppro5213

26 But ye *shall* not *be* so: but he*that*is*greatest among you, let him

aipm1096 ad5613 art3588 pr/cd/ajn3501 2532   art,ppmp2233   ad5613   pr/art,pap1247

be as the younger; and he*that*is*chief, as he*that*doth*serve.

1063   inpro5101   pr/cd/an,aj3187   art,ppmp345   2228   art,pap1247

27 For whether *is* greater, he*that*sitteth*at*meat, or he*that*serveth?

3780   art,ppmp345   1161   epn1473   pin1510   pre1722/an,ajn3319 ppro5216   ad5613

is not he*that*sitteth*at*meat? but I am among you as

art,pap1247

he*that*serveth.

22:24–34 See note on 1 Peter 2:17.

(1161) epn5210 pin2075   pr/art,pfp1265   pre3326 ppro1700 pre1722 ppro3450   art,nn3986

28   Ye are they*which*have*continued with me   in   my temptations.

epn2504   pinm1303   ppro5213   an,nn932   ad2531 ppro3450 art,nn3962   aom1303

29 And I appoint unto you a kingdom, as   my Father hath appointed unto

ppro3427

me;

2443   psa2068   2532   psa4095   pre1909 ppro3450 art,nn5132 pre1722 ppro3450   art,nn932   2532

30 That ye may eat and drink   at   my   table   in   my kingdom, and

asbm2523 pre1909 an,nn2362   pap2912 art3588   nu1427   nn5443   2474

sit   on thrones judging the twelve tribes of Israel.

Peter's Denial Foretold (Matt. 26:31-35; Mark 14:27-31; John 13:36-38)

1161   art3588   nn2962 aina2036   an,nn4613   an,nn4613   2400   art,nn4567   aom1809

31 And the Lord said, Simon, Simon, behold, Satan hath desired *to have*

ppro5209   infg4617   ad5613 art,nn4621

you, that he may sift *you* as wheat:

1161   epn1473   ainp1189   pre4012 ppro4675   2443 ppro4675 art,nn4102 asba1587 3361   2532   ad4218

32 But   I   have prayed for thee, that thy   faith   fail   not: and when

epn4771   apta1994   aima4741   ppro4675   art,nn80

thou art converted, strengthen thy brethren.

1161   art3588 aina2036   ppro846 an,nn2962   pin1510 pr/an,aj2092   pifm4198 pre3326 ppro4675   2532   pre1519

33 And he said unto him, Lord, I am ready to go with thee, both into

an,nn5438   2532 pre1519 an,nn2288

prison, and to death.

1161   art3588 aina2036   pin3004 ppro4671 an,nn4074   an,nn220   efn3364   ft5455   ad4594

34 And he said, I tell thee, Peter, the cock shall not crow this day,

ad4250   (2228)   nu,ad5151 fm533   (3361)   pinf1492   ppro3165

before that thou shalt thrice deny that thou knowest me.

Christ's Servants Will Lack Nothing

2532   aina2036   ppro846 ad3753   aina649 ppro5209 pre817   an,nn905 2532 an,nn4082

35 And he said unto them, When I sent you without purse, and scrip,

2532 an,nn5266 (3361) aina5302   idpro5100   1161 art3588 aina2036 an,ajn3762

and shoes,   lacked ye any thing? And they said, Nothing.

3767 aina2036   ppro846 235   ad3568   art,pap2192   an,nn905   aima142

36 Then said he unto them, But now, he*that*hath a purse, let him take

2532   ad3668   (2532) an,nn4082 2532   art,pap2192   3361   aima4453 ppro848

it, and likewise *his* scrip: and he*that*hath no sword, let him sell his

art,nn2440   2532 aima59 (an,nn3162)

garment, and buy one.

1063   pin3004   ppro5213   3754   depro5124   art,pfpp1125   pin1163   ad2089

37 For I say unto you,   that this that*is*written must yet be

aifp5055   pre1722 ppro1698 (art3588)   2532   ainp3049   pre3326   an,ajn459

accomplished in me,   And he was reckoned among the transgressors:

1063 (2532)   art3588   pre4012   ppro1700 pin2192   an,nn5056

for   the things concerning me have an end.   *(Is. 53:12)*

^{1161   art3588 aina2036 an,nn2962   2400   ad5602   nu1417 an,nn3162   1161 art3588 aina2036}
38 And they said, Lord, behold, here *are* two swords. And he said unto
^{ppro846   pin2076 pr/an,ajn2425}
them, It is enough.

Jesus' Prayer on the Mount of Olives (Matt. 26:36-46; Mark 14:32-42)

^{2532   apta1831   ainp4198   pre2596/art,nn1485   pre1519 art3588   nn3735}
39 And he came out, and went, as*he*was*wont, to the mount of
^{art,nn1636   1161 ppro846 art,nn3101   2532   aina190   ppro846}
Olives; and his disciples also followed him.
^{1161   aptm1096 pre1909 art3588   nn5117   aina2036   ppro846   pim4336}
40 And when he was at the place, he said unto them, Pray that ye
^{ainf1525 3361 pre1519   an,nn3986}
enter not into temptation.
^{2532   epn846   ainp645   pre575   ppro846   ad5616   an,nn3037   an,nn1000   2532}
41 And he was withdrawn from them about a stone's cast, and
^{apta5087/art,nn1119   ipf4336}
kneeled down, and prayed,
^{pap3004   an,nn3962   1487   pinm1014   aima3911   depro5124 art,nn4221   pre575 ppro1700}
42 Saying, Father, if thou be willing, remove this cup from me:
^{4133   3361 ppro3450 art,nn2307 235 art,popro4674   aipm1096}
nevertheless not my will, but thine, be done.
^{1161   ainp3700   an,nn32   ppro846 pre575   an,nn3772   pap1765}
43 And there appeared an angel unto him from heaven, strengthening
^{ppro846}
him.
^{2532   aptm1096 pre1722   an,nn74   ipf4336   cd/an,aj1617   1161 ppro846 art,nn2402}
44 And being in an agony he prayed more earnestly: and his sweat
^{aom1096   ad5616   pr/an,nn2361   an,nn129   pap2597   pre1909 art3588   nn1093}
was as*it*were great drops of blood falling down to the ground.
^{2532   apta450   pre575 art,nn4335   apta2064 pre4314   art,nn3101}
45 And when he rose up from prayer, and was come to his disciples, he
^{aina2147 ppro846   ppmp2837   pre575 art,nn3077}
found them sleeping for sorrow,
^{2532 aina2036   ppro846 inpro5101 pin3518   apta450   pim4336   3363   asba1525 pre1519}
46 And said unto them, Why sleep ye? rise and pray, lest ye enter into
^{an,nn3986}
temptation.

Judas Betrays the Lord (Matt. 26:47-56; Mark 14:43-50; John 18:3-11)

^{1161   ppro846 ad2089 pap2980   2400   an,nn3793   2532   art,ppmp3004}
47 And while he yet spake, behold a multitude, and he*that*was*called
^{an,nn2455 nu1520   art3588 nu,ajn1427   ipf4281   ppro846 2532   aina1448   art,nn2424   ainf5368}
Judas, one of the twelve, went before them, and drew near unto Jesus to kiss
^{ppro846}
him.

1161   art,nn2424 aina2036   pppro846 an,nn2455   pin3860   art3588 nn5207   art,nn444

48 But Jesus said unto him, Judas, betrayest thou the Son of man with a

an,nn5370

kiss?

1161   art3588   pre4012 pppro846 apta1492   art,fptm2071   aina2036

49 When they which were about him saw what*would*follow, they said

pppro846 an,nn2962   (1487)   ft3960 pre1722   an,nn3162

unto him, Lord, shall we smite with the sword?

2532(idpro5100) nu1520 pre1537 pppro846   aina3960 art3588   ajn1401   art3588   nn749   2532

50 And one of them smote the servant of the high priest, and

aina851   pppro846 art,aj1188 art,nn3775

cut off his right ear.

1161   art,nn2424 aptp611   aina2036 pim1439   ad*2193/depro5127 2532   aptm680   pppro846

51 And Jesus answered and said, Suffer ye thus far. And he touched his

art,nn5621   aom2390 pppro846

ear, and healed him.

1161   art,nn2424 aina2036 pre4314   an,nn749   2532   an,nn4755   art3588   nn2411   2532

52 Then Jesus said unto the chief priests, and captains of the temple, and

an,ajn4245   art,aptm3854   pre1909 pppro846   pfi1831   ad5613 pre1909   an,nn3027

the elders, which*were*come to him, Be ye come out, as against a thief,

pre3326 an,nn3162   2532   an,nn3586

with swords and staves?

pppro3450 pap5607   pre2596/an,nn2250   pre3326   pppro5216 pre1722 art3588   nn2411

53 When I was daily with you in the temple, ye

aina1614   3756 art,nn5495 pre1909   pppro1691 235 depro3778 pin2076 pppro5216 pr/art,nn5610 2532 art3588 pr/nn1849

stretched forth no hands against me: but this is your hour, and the power

art,nn4655

of darkness.

Peter's Denial of Jesus (Matt. 26:57,58,69-75; Mark 14:53,54,66-72; John 18:12-18,25-27)

1161   apta4815   pppro846   aina71   2532 aina1521   pppro846 pre1519 art3588

54 Then took they him, and led *him,* and brought him into the

nn749   art,nn3624 1161 art,nn4074 ipf190   ad3113

high priest's house. And Peter followed afar off.

1161   pppro846   apta681   an,nn4442 pre1722   an,ajn3319   art3588 nn833   2532

55 And when they had kindled a fire in the midst of the hall, and were

apta4776   art,nn4074   ipf2521   pre1722/an,ajn3319 pppro846

set*down*together, Peter sat down among them.

1161   idpro5100 an,nn3814 apta1492 pppro846   ppmp2521 pre4314 art3588 nn5457   2532

56 But a certain maid beheld him as he sat by the fire, and

apta816   pppro846   aina2036 depro3778 ipf2258 2532 pre4862 pppro846

earnestly looked upon him, and said, This man was also with him.

1161   art3588 aom720   pppro846 pap3004   an,nn1135   pin1492 pppro846 3756

57 And he denied him, saying, Woman, I know him not.

2532 pre3326   an,ajn1024   an,ajn2087 apta1492 pppro846   aina5346 epn4771 pin1488 2532 pre1537

58 And after a little while another saw him, and said, Thou art also of

pppro846 1161 art,nn4074 aina2036 an,nn444   pin1510 3756

them. And Peter said, Man, I am not.

2532   ad5616   apta1339/nu3391/an,nn5610   (idpro5100)   an,ajn243   ipf1340

59 And about the*space*of*one*hour*after   another confidently affirmed,

pap3004   pre1909/an,nn225   depro3778   2532   ipf2258 pre3326 ppro846 1063   pin2076 (2532)   pr/an,ajn1057

saying, Of*a*truth this *fellow* also was with him: for he is   a Galilaean.

1161   art,nn4074 aina2036   an,nn444   pin1492   3756 repro3739   pin3004   2532   ad3916

60 And Peter said, Man, I know not what thou sayest. And immediately,

ppro846 ad2089   pap2980 art3588 nn220   aina5455

while he yet spake, the cock crew.

2532 art3588 nn2962   apta4762   aina1689   art,nn4074   2532 art,nn4074   ainp5279

61 And the Lord turned, and looked upon Peter. And Peter remembered

art3588   nn3056   art3588   nn2962   ad5613   aina2036   ppro846   ad4250   an,nn220 ainf5455

the word of the Lord, how he had said unto him, Before the cock crow, thou

fm533   ppro3165 nu,ad5151

shalt deny me thrice.

2532 art,nn4074 apta1831 ad1854   aina2799   ad4090

62 And Peter went out, and wept bitterly.

Mocking and Beating of Jesus (Matt. 26:67,68; Mark 14:65)

2532 art3588 nn435   art,pap4912 art,nn2424   ipf1702   ppro846   pap1194

63 And the men that held Jesus mocked him, and smote him.

2532   apta4028   ppro846   ipf5180   ppro846   art3588 nn4383 2532

64 And when they had blindfolded him, they struck him on the face, and

ipf1905 ppro846   pap3004   aima4395   inpro5101 pin2076   pr/art,apta3817   ppro4571

asked him, saying, Prophesy, who is it that smote thee?

2532 an,aj4183   an,ajn2087   pap987   ipf3004   pre1519   ppro846

65 And many other things blasphemously spake they against him.

Jesus Before the Council (Matt. 26:59-66; Mark 14:55-64; John 18:19-24)

2532   ad5613   aom1096 an,nn2250 art3588   nn4244   art3588   nn2992   5037

66 And as*soon*as it was day, the elders of the people and the

an,nn749   2532   an,nn1122   ainp4863   2532 aina321 ppro846 pre1519 rxpro1438   art,nn4892

chief priests and the scribes came together, and led him into their council,

pap3004

saying,

(1487) pin1488 epn4771 art3588   pr/nn5547 aima2036 ppro2254 1161   aina2036   ppro846 1437   asba2036 ppro5213

67 Art thou the Christ? tell us. And he said unto them, If I tell you,

efn3364   asba4100

ye will not believe:

1161   1437   2532 asba2065   efn3364   asbp611   ppro3427 2228   asba630

68 And if I also ask *you,* ye will not answer me, nor let*me*go.

pre575/art,ad3568 (fm2071) art3588 nn5207   art,nn444 ppmp2521 pre1537   an,ajn1188   art3588   nn1411

69 Hereafter shall the Son of man sit   on the right hand of the power

art,nn2316

of God.   *(Ps. 110:1)*

1161   aina2036   an,ajn3956 pin1488 epn4771 3767 art3588 pr/nn5207   art,nn2316 1161   art3588 aina5346

70 Then said they all, Art thou then the Son of God? And he said

pre4314   ppro846 epn5210 pin3004 3754 epn1473 pin1510

unto them, Ye say that I am.

1161   art3588 aina2036 inpro5101 pin2192/an,nn5532   ad2089   an,nn3141   1063

71 And they said, What   need   we any further witness? for we

epn846   aina191 pre575 ppro846   art,nn4750

ourselves have heard of his own mouth.

Jesus Brought Before Pilate (Matt. 27:1,2,11-14; Mark 15:1-5; John 18:28-38)

2532 art3588 an,aj537   nn4128   ppro846 apta450   aina71 ppro846 pre1909 art,nn4091

23 And the whole multitude of them arose, and led him unto Pilate.

1161   aom756   pinf2723 ppro846 pap3004   aina2147 depro5126

2 And they began to accuse him, saying, We found this *fellow*

pap1294   art3588   nn1484   2532   pap2967   pinf1325 an,nn5411   an,nn2541 pap3004

perverting the nation, and forbidding to give tribute to Caesar, saying that he

rxpro1438 pinf1511 pr/an,nn5547 pr/an,nn935

himself is Christ a King.

1161   art,nn4091 aina1905 ppro846 pap3004   pin1488 epn4771 art3588 pr/nn935   art3588   nn2453   1161 art3588

3 And Pilate asked him, saying, Art thou the King of the Jews? And he

aptp611   ppro846   aina5346 epn4771 pin3004

answered him and said, Thou sayest *it.*

1161   aina2036 art,nn4091 pre4314 art3588   nn749   2532   art3588   nn3793   pin2147 an,aj3762

4 Then said Pilate to the chief priests and *to* the people, I find no

an,nn158 pre1722 depro5129 art,nn444

fault in this man.

1161   art3588   ipf2001   pap3004   pin383   art3588   nn2992

5 And they were*the*more*fierce, saying, He stirreth up the people,

pap1321   pre2596 an,aj3650 art,nn2449 aptm756   pre575 art,nn1056 ad*2193 ad5602

teaching throughout all Jewry, beginning from Galilee to this place.

Jesus Before Herod

1161   an,nn4091 apta191   an,nn1056   aina1905   1487 art3588 nn444   pin2076

6 When Pilate heard of Galilee, he asked whether the man were a

pr/an,ajn1057

Galilaean.

2532   apta1921 3754   pin2076/pre1537   an,nn2264   art,nn1849

7 And as soon as he knew that he belonged unto Herod's jurisdiction, he

aina375 ppro846 pre4314 an,nn2264   epn846 2532 pap5607 pre1722   an,nn2414   pre1722 depro5025 art,nn2250

sent him to Herod, who himself also was at Jerusalem at that time.

1161   art,nn2264 apta492 art,nn2424   aina5463/ad3029   1063   ipf2258

8 And when Herod saw Jesus, he was*exceeding*glad: for he was

pap2309 ainf1492 ppro846 pre1537 an,ajn2425   aid191   an,ajn4183

desirous to see him of a long *season,* because he had heard many things

pre4012 ppro846 2532   ipf1679   ainf1492 idpro5100 an,nn4592 ppmp1096 pre5259 ppro846

of him; and he hoped to have seen some miracle done by him.

¹¹⁶¹ ^{ipf1905} ^{ppro846 pre1722 an,aj2425} ^{an,nn3056} ^{1161 epn846} ^{aom611} ^{ppro846}

9 Then he questioned with him in many words; but he answered him

^{an,ajn3762}

nothing.

^{1161 art3588} ⁿⁿ⁷⁴⁹ ^{2532 art,nn1122} ^{plpf2476} ^{ad2159} ^{pap2723} ^{ppro846}

10 And the chief priests and scribes stood and vehemently accused him.

¹¹⁶¹ ^{art,nn2264 pre4862 ppro848} ^{art,nn4753} ^{apta1848/ppro846} ²⁵³² ^{apta1702}

11 And Herod with his men*of*war set*him*at*naught, and mocked *him,*

^{apta4016} ^{ppro846} ^{an,aj2986} ^{an,nn2066} ^{aina375/ppro846} ^{art,nn4091}

and arrayed him in a gorgeous robe, and sent*him*again to Pilate.

^{1161 (pre1722)} ^{epn846} ^{art,nn2250 (repro3739 5037) art,nn4091} ^{2532 art,nn2264} ^{aom1096 pr/an,ajn5384}

12 And   the same day   Pilate and Herod were made friends

^{pre3326/rcpro240 1063} ^{ipf4391} ^{pap5607 pre1722 an,nn2189} ^{pre4314} ^{rxpro1438}

together: for before they were at enmity between themselves.

Jesus Sentenced to Die (Matt. 27:15-26; Mark 15:6-15; John 18:39—19:16)

¹¹⁶¹ ^{an,nn4091} ^{aptm4779} ^{art3588} ⁿⁿ⁷⁴⁹ ^{2532 art3588}

13 And Pilate, when he had called together the chief priests and the

ⁿⁿ⁷⁵⁸ ^{2532 art3588} ⁿⁿ²⁹⁹²

rulers and the people,

^{aina2036 pre4314} ^{ppro846} ^{aina4374} ^{depro5126 art,nn444} ^{ppro3427 ad5613}

14 Said unto them, Ye have brought this man unto me, as one that

^{pap654} ^{art3588} ⁿⁿ²⁹⁹² ²⁵³² ²⁴⁰⁰ ^{epn1473} ^{apta350} ^{ad*1799 ppro5216}

perverteth the people: and, behold, I, having examined *him* before you, have

^{aina2147} ^{an,aj3762 an,nn158 pre1722 depro5129 art,nn444} ^{repro3739} ^{pin2723} ^(pre2596)

found no fault in this man touching those things whereof ye accuse

^{ppro846}

him:

⁽²³⁵⁾ ^{ad3761} ^{an,nn2264} ¹⁰⁶³ ^{aina375 ppro5209 pre4314 ppro846} ²⁵³² ²⁴⁰⁰ ^{an,ajn3762} ^{an,aj514}

15 No, nor yet Herod: for I sent you to him; and, lo, nothing worthy of

^{an,nn2288 pin2076 pfpp4238} ^{ppro846}

death is done unto him.

³⁷⁶⁷ ^{apta3811} ^{ppro846} ^{ft630}

16 I will therefore chastise him, and release *him.*

¹¹⁶¹ ^{an,nn318} ^{ipf2192} ^{pinf630} ^{nu,ajn1520} ^{ppro846 pre2596} ^{an,nn1859}

17 (For of necessity he must release one unto them at the feast.)

¹¹⁶¹ ^{aina349} ^{ad3826} ^{pap3004} ^{pim142} ^{depro5126} ¹¹⁶¹

18 And they cried out all*at*once, saying, Away with this *man,* and

^{aima630} ^{ppro2254} ^{art,nn912}

release unto us Barabbas:

^{repro3748 pre1223} ^{idpro5100} ^{an,nn4714} ^{aptm1096 pre1722 art3588} ⁿⁿ⁴¹⁷² ²⁵³² ^{an,nn5408} ^{ipf2258}

19 (Who for a certain sedition made in the city, and for murder, was

^{pfpp906 pre1519} ^{an,nn5438}

cast into prison.)

^{art,nn4091} ³⁷⁶⁷ ^{pap2309} ^{ainf630} ^{art,nn2424} ^{aina4377/ad3825}

20 Pilate therefore, willing to release Jesus, spake*again*to*them.

¹¹⁶¹ ^{art3588} ^{ipf2019} ^{pap3004} ^{aima4717} ^{aima4717} ^{ppro846}

21 But they cried, saying, Crucify *him,* crucify him.

1161   art3588 aina2036 pre4314 ppro846   an,nu,ajn5154   1063   inpro5101 an,ajn2556   depro3778
22 And he   said unto them the third time, Why, what evil hath he

aina4160   aina2147 an,aj3762 an,nn158   an,nn2288 pre1722 ppro846   3767   apta3811   ppro846
done? I have found   no   cause of death in   him: I will therefore chastise him,

2532   ft630
and let*him*go.

1161   art3588   ipf1945   an,aj3173 an,nn5456   ppmp154   ppro846
23 And they were instant with loud voices, requiring that   he   might be

aifp4717   2532 art3588   nn5456   ppro846 2532   art3588   nn749   ipf2729
crucified. And the voices of them and of the chief priests prevailed.

1161   art,nn4091   aina1948   aifm1096   ppro846/art,nn155
24 And Pilate gave sentence that it should   be as they required.

1161   aina630   ppro846   pre1223 an,nn4714   2532   an,nn5408
25 And he released unto them him that   for   sedition and murder

art,pfpp906   pre1519 art,nn5438 repro3739   ipf154   1161   aina3860 art,nn2424 ppro846
was cast into prison, whom they had desired; but he delivered Jesus to their

art,nn2307
will.

The Way to the Cross (Matt. 27:32-44; Mark 15;21-32; John 19:17-27)

2532   ad5613   aina520/ppro846   aptm1949   idpro5100   an,nn4613
26 And   as   they led*him*away, they laid*hold*upon   one   Simon, a

an,ajn2956   art,ppmp2064   pre575   an,nn68   ppro846   aina2007 art3588   nn4716
Cyrenian, coming out of the country, and on him they laid the cross, that he

pinf5342   ad*3693   art,nn2424
might bear it after Jesus.

1161   ipf190   ppro846   an,aj4183   an,nn4128   art,nn2992   2532   an,nn1135
27 And there followed him a great company of people, and of women,

repro3739 2532   ipf2875   2532   ipf2354   ppro846
which also bewailed and lamented him.

1161   art,nn2424 aptp4762 pre4314 ppro846 aina2036   an,nn2364   2419   pim2799 3361
28 But Jesus turning unto them said, Daughters of Jerusalem, weep not

pre1909 ppro1691 4133 pim2799 pre1909   rxpro1438   2532 pre1909 ppro5216 art,nn5043
for me, but weep for yourselves, and for your children.

3754   2400   an,nn2250   pinm2064   pre1722   repro3739   ft2046
29 For, behold, the days are coming, in   the which they shall say,

pr/an,aj3107   art3588   ajn4723   2532   an,nn2836 repro3739   3756   aina1080 2532   an,nn3149 repro3739
Blessed are the barren, and the wombs that never bare, and the paps which

3756   aina2337
never gave suck.

ad5119   fm756   pinf3004   art3588   nn3735   aima4098 pre1909 ppro2248 2532
30 Then shall they begin to say to the mountains, Fall   on   us; and to

art3588 nn1015 aima2572 ppro2248
the hills, Cover us.   (Hos. 10:8)

3754 1487   pin4160   depro5023   pre1722   art,aj5200 an,nn3586 inpro5101   asbm1096 pre1722
31 For if they do these things in a green tree, what shall be done   in

art3588 ajn3584
the dry?

32 And there were also two other, malefactors, led with him to be put*to*death.

33 And when they were come to the place, which*is*called Calvary, there they crucified him, and the malefactors, one on the right hand, and the other on the left. *(Is. 53:12)*

34 Then said Jesus, Father, forgive them; for they know not what they do. And they parted his raiment, and cast lots. *(Ps. 22:18)*

35 And the people stood beholding. And the rulers also with them derided *him,* saying, He saved others; let him save himself, if he be Christ, the chosen of God. *(Ps. 22:7,8)*

36 And the soldiers also mocked him, coming to him, and offering him vinegar, *(Ps. 69:21)*

37 And saying, If thou be the king of the Jews, save thyself.

38 And a superscription also was written over him in letters of Greek, and Latin, and Hebrew, THIS IS THE KING OF THE JEWS.

39 And one of the malefactors which were hanged railed on him, saying, If thou be Christ, save thyself and us.

40 But the other answering rebuked him, saying, Dost not thou fear God, seeing thou art in the same condemnation?

41 And we indeed justly; for we receive the due reward of our deeds: but this man hath done nothing amiss.

42 And he said unto Jesus, Lord, remember me when thou comest into thy kingdom.

☛ 43 And Jesus said unto him, Verily I say unto thee, Today shalt thou be with me in paradise.

☛ **23:43** See note on 2 Corinthians 12:1–10.

The Death of Jesus (Matt. 27:45,46; Mark 15:33-41; John 19:28-30)

1161   ipf2258   ad5616   an,nu,aj1622 an,nn5610 2532   aom1096   an,nn4655   pre1909 an,aj3650

44 And it was about the sixth hour, and there was a darkness over all

art3588   nn1093   ad2193   an,nu,aj1766 an,nn5610

the earth until the ninth hour.

2532   art3588 nn2246   pap4654   2532 art3588 nn2665   art3588   nn3485   ainp4977

45 And the sun was darkened, and the veil of the temple was rent in the

an,ajn3319

midst.   (Ex. 26:31-33; 36:35)

2532   art,nn2424   apta5455   an,aj3173 an,nn5456   aina2036   an,nn3962   pre1519 ppro4675

46 And when Jesus had cried with a loud voice, he said, Father, into thy

an,nn5495   fm3908   ppro3450 art,nn4151 2532   apta2036 depro5023   aina1606

hands I commend my spirit: and having said thus, he gave*up*the*ghost.

(Ps. 31:5)

1161   art3588   nn1543   apta1492   art,aptm1096   aina1392   art,nn2316

47 Now when the centurion saw what*was*done, he glorified God,

pap3004   ad3689   depro3778 ipf2258   pr/an,aj1342   art,nn444

saying, Certainly this was a righteous man.

2532   an,aj3956 art3588   nn3793   aptm4836   pre1909 depro5026 art,nn2335   pap2334

48 And all the people that came together to that sight, beholding

art,aptm1096   pap5180 rxpro1438 art,nn4738   ipf5290

the*things*which*were*done, smote their breasts, and returned.

1161   an,aj3956 ppro846   art,ajn1110   2532   an,nn1135   art,apta4870   ppro846 pre575

49 And all his acquaintance, and the women that followed him from

art,nn1056   plpf2476   ad3113   pap3708   depro5023

Galilee, stood afar off, beholding these things.

The Burial of Jesus (Matt. 27:57-61; Mark 15:42-47; John 19:38-42)

2532   2400   an,nn435 an,nn3686   2501   (pap5225)   pr/an,nn1010

50 And, behold, *there was* a man named Joseph, a counselor; *and he*

an,aj18 an,nn435 2532   an,aj1342

was a good man, and a just:

depro3778   ipf2258 3756   pfpp4784   art3588   nn1012   2532 art,nn4234   ppro846

51 (The same had not consented to the counsel and deed of them;) *he was*

pre575   an,nn707   an,nn4172   art3588 nn2453 repro3739 2532 epn846   ipf4327   art3588   nn932

of Arimathaea, a city of the Jews: who also himself waited for the kingdom

art,nn2316

of God.

depro3778   apta4334   art,nn4091   aom154 art3588 nn4983   art,nn2424

52 This *man* went unto Pilate, and begged the body of Jesus.

2532   apta2507/ppro846   aina1794   ppro846   an,nn4616   2532 aina5087 ppro846 pre1722

53 And he took*it*down, and wrapped it in linen, and laid it in a

an,nn3418   an,aj2991   repro3757 ad3762/an,ajn3764   (3756) ipf2258 ppmp2749

sepulcher that was hewn*in*stone, wherein never man before was laid.

2532   an,nn2250 ipf2258   an,nn3904   2532   an,nn4521   ipf2020

54 And that day was the preparation, and the sabbath drew on.

1161   an,nn1135   2532   repro3748   ipf2258/pr/pfp4905   ppro846   pre1537   art,nn1056

55 And the women also, which came with him from Galilee,

apta2628   aom2300 art3588   nn3419   2532   ad5613 ppro846 art,nn4983   ainp5087

followed after, and beheld the sepulcher, and how his body was laid.

1161   apta5290   aina2090   an,nn759   2532   an,nn3464   2532   aina2270 art3588

56 And they returned, and prepared spices and ointments; and rested the

(3303)   nn4521   pre2596   art3588   nn1785

sabbath day according to the commandment. *(Ex. 12:16; 20:10; Deut. 5:14)*

The Resurrection of Jesus (Matt. 28:1-10; Mark 16:1-8; John 20:1-10)

1161   art3588 nu,aj3391   art3588   nn4521   an,aj901/an,nn3722

24 Now upon the first *day* of the week, very*early*in*the*morning,

aina2064 pre1909 art3588   nn3418   pap5342   an,nn759 repro3739

they came unto the sepulcher, bringing the spices which they had

aina2090   2532   idpro5100   pre4862   ppro846

prepared, and certain *others* with them.

1161   aina2147 art3588   nn3037   pfpp617   pre575 art3588   nn3419

2 And they found the stone rolled away from the sepulcher.

2532   apta1525   aina2147 3756 art3588 nn4983   art3588 nn2962 an,nn2424

3 And they entered in, and found not the body of the Lord Jesus.

2532   aom1096   ppro846   aie1280   pre4012/depro5127   (2532)

4 And it came*to*pass, as they were*much*perplexed thereabout,

2400   nu1417 an,nn435   aina2186   ppro846 pre1722   pap797   an,nn2067

behold, two men stood by them in shining garments:

1161   ppro846 aptm1096 pr/an,aj1719 2532   pap2827   art,nn4383 pre1519 art3588   nn1093

5 And as they were afraid, and bowed down *their* faces to the earth, they

aina2036 pre4314   ppro846 inpro5101 pin2212   art3588 pap2198   pre3326   art3588 ajn3498

said unto them, Why seek ye the living among the dead?

pin2076 3756 ad5602   235   ainp1453   aipp3415   ad5613   aina2980   ppro5213

6 He is not here, but is risen: remember how he spake unto you when

pap5607 ad2089 pre1722   art,nn1056

he was yet in Galilee,

pap3004   art3588 nn5207   art,nn444 pin1163   aifp3860   pre1519   an,nn5495   an,aj268 an,nn435

7 Saying, the Son of man must be delivered into the hands of sinful men,

2532   aifp4717   2532 art3588 nu,aj5154 nn2250   ainf450

and be crucified, and the third day rise again.

2532   ainp3415   ppro846 art,nn4487

8 And they remembered his words,

2532   apta5290   pre575 art3588   nn3419   aina518 an,ajn3956   depro5023   art3588

9 And returned from the sepulcher, and told all these things unto the

nu,ajn1733   2532   an,aj3956 art3588 ajn3062

eleven, and to all the rest.

(1161)   ipf2258 an,nn3137   art,aj3094   2532   an,nn2489   2532   an,nn3137   an,nn2385

10 It was Mary Magdalene and Joanna, and Mary *the mother* of James,

2532   art,aj3062   pre4862   ppro846   repro3739   ipf3004   depro5023   pre4314 art3588

and other *women that were* with them, which told these things unto the

nn652

apostles.

11 And their words seemed to them as idle tales, and they believed*them*not.

12 Then arose Peter, and ran unto the sepulcher; and stooping down, he beheld the linen clothes laid by themselves, and departed, wondering in himself at that*which*was*come*to*pass.

The Road to Emmaus (Mark 16:12,13)

13 And, behold, two of them went that same day to a village called Emmaus, which was from Jerusalem *about* threescore furlongs.

14 And they talked together of all these things which*had*happened.

15 And it came*to*pass, that, while they communed *together* and reasoned, Jesus himself drew near, and went with them.

16 But their eyes were holden that they should not know him.

17 And he said unto them, What manner of communications *are* these that ye have one*to*another, as ye walk, and are sad?

18 And the one of them, whose name was Cleopas, answering said unto him, Art*thou*only*a*stranger in Jerusalem, and hast not known the*things*which*are*come*to*pass there in these days?

19 And he said unto them, What things? And they said unto him, Concerning Jesus of Nazareth, which was a prophet mighty in deed and word before God and all the people:

20 And how the chief priests and our rulers delivered him to be condemned to death, and have crucified him.

21 But we trusted that it had been he which should have redeemed Israel: and beside all this, today is the third day since these things were done.

235   idpro5100   an,nn1135   2532   pre1537   ppro2257   aina1839/ppro2248

22 Yea, and certain women also of our company made*us*astonished, which

aptm1096 pr/an,aj3721 pre1909 art3588   nn3419

were early   at   the sepulcher;

2532   apta2147   3361   ppro846   art,nn4983   aina2064   pap3004

23 And when they found not his body, they came, saying, that they had

2532   pfin3708   an,nn3701   an,nn32   repro3739 pin3004   ppro846   pinf2198

also seen a vision of angels, which said that he was alive.

2532   idpro5100   art3588   pre4862 ppro2554 aina565 pre1909 art3588   nn3419

24 And certain of them which were with us went to the sepulcher,

2532   aina2147   2532   ad3779 ad2531 art3588   nn1135   aina2036 1161 epn846   aina1492 3756

and found it even so as the women had said: but him they saw not.

2532   epn846 aina2036 pre4134   ppro846   5599 an,ajn453   2532 an,ajn1021   art,nn2588   infg4100   (pre1909)

25 Then he said unto them, O fools, and slow of heart to believe

an,aj3956 repro3739 art3588   nn4396   aina2980

all   that the prophets have spoken:

ipf1163   3780   art,nn5547   ainf3958   depro5023   2532   ainf1525 pre1519 ppro848

26 Ought not Christ to have suffered these things, and to enter into his

art,nn1391

glory?

2532   aptm756   pre575 an,nn3475   2532 (pre575) an,aj3956 art3588   nn4396   ipf1329

27 And beginning at Moses and   all the prophets, he expounded unto

ppro846 pre1722 an,aj3956 art3588   nn1124   art3588   pre4012   rxpro1438

them in   all   the Scriptures the things concerning himself.

2532   aina1448   pre1519 art3588   nn2968   repro3757   ipf4198   2532   epn846

28 And they drew nigh unto the village, whither they went: and he

ipf4364   pifm4198   ad4208

made*as*though he would have gone further.

2532   aom3849   ppro846   pap3004   aima3306 pre3326 ppro2257 3754   pin2076   pre4314

29 But they constrained him, saying, Abide with us: for it is toward

an,nn2073   2532 art3588 nn2250   pfi2827   2532   aina1525   infg3306 pre4862   ppro846

evening, and the day is*far*spent. And he went in to tarry with them.

2532   aom1096   ppro846   aie2625   pre3326 ppro846   apta2983 art,nn740

30 And it came*to*pass, as he sat*at*meat with them, he took bread, and

aina2127   2532   apta2806   ipf1929   ppro846

blessed it, and broke, and gave to them.

1161   epn846 art,nn3788   ainp1272   2532   aina1921   ppro846   2532   epn846 aom1096/pr/an,aj855

31 And their eyes were opened, and they knew him; and he vanished

pre575/ppro846

out*of*their*sight.

2532   aina2036   rcpro240/pre4314   3780 ppro2257 art,nn2588 ipf2258/ppmp2545 pre1722   ppro2254

32 And they said one*to*another, Did not our heart burn   within us,

ad5613   ipf2980   ppro2254 pre1722 art3588   nn3598   2532   ad5613   ipf1272   ppro2254 art3588

while he talked with us   by the way, and while he opened to us   the

nn1124

Scriptures?

2532   apta450   art3588   epn846   nn5610   aina5290   pre1519   2419   2532

33 And they rose up the same hour, and returned to Jerusalem, and

aina2147 art3588 nu,ajn1733   pfpp4867   2532   art3588   pre4862 ppro846

found the eleven gathered together, and them that were with them,

pap3004   art3588 nn2962   ainp1453   ad3689   2532   ainp3700   an,nn4613

34 Saying, The Lord is risen indeed, and hath appeared to Simon.

²⁵³² ^{epn846} ^{ipf1834}   ^{art3588}   ^{pre1722} ^{art3588} ⁿⁿ³⁵⁹⁸ ²⁵³² ^{ad5613}

35 And they told what things *were done* in the way, and how he was

^{ainp1097}   ^{ppro846} ^{pre1722}   ^{art,nn2800}   ^{art,nn740}

known of them in breaking of bread.

Jesus Appears to the Disciples (Matt. 28:16-20; Mark 16:14-18; John 20:19-23; Acts 1:6-8)

     ¹¹⁶¹   ^{ppro846} ^{depro5023} ^{pap2980} ^{art,nn2424} ^{epn846}   ^{aina2476} ^{pre1722}   ^{an,ajn3319}   ^{ppro846}

36 And as they thus spake, Jesus himself stood in the midst of them,

²⁵³² ^{pin3004}   ^{ppro846} ^{an,nn1515}   ^{ppro5213}

and saith unto them, Peace *be* unto you.

     ¹¹⁶¹   ^{aptp4422}   ²⁵³² ^{aptm1096/pr/an,aj1719}   ^{ipf1380}

37 But they were terrified and affrighted, and supposed that they had

^{pinf2334} ^{an,nn4151}

seen a spirit.

     ²⁵³²   ^{aina2036}   ^{ppro846} ^{inpro5101} ^{pin2075}   ^{pr/pfpp5015}   ²⁵³² ^{pre,inpro1302}   ^{an,nn1261}

38 And he said unto them, Why are ye troubled? and why do thoughts

^{pin305} ^{pre1722} ^{ppro5216} ^{art,nn2588}

arise in your hearts?

     ^{aima1492}   ^{ppro3450} ^{art,nn5495} ²⁵³² ^{ppro3450} ^{art,nn4228} ³⁷⁵⁴   ^{pin1510} ^{epn1473}   ^{pr/epn846}   ^{aima5584}   ^{ppro3165}

39 Behold my hands and my feet, that it is I myself: handle me,

²⁵³² ^{aina1492} ³⁷⁵⁴   ^{an,nn4151} ^{pin2192} ³⁷⁵⁶ ^{an,nn4561} ²⁵³²   ^{an,nn3747} ^{ad2531}   ^{pin2334} ^{epn1691} ^{pap2192}

and see; for a spirit hath not flesh and bones, as ye see me have.

     ²⁵³²   ^{depro5124} ^{apta2036}   ^{aina1925}   ^{ppro846}   ^{art,nn5495} ²⁵³²

40 And when he had thus spoken, he showed them *his* hands and *his*

^{art,nn4228}

feet.

     ¹¹⁶¹   ^{ppro846} ^{ad2089}   ^{pap569}   ^{pre575} ^{art,nn5479} ²⁵³²   ^{pap2296}   ^{aina2036}

41 And while they yet believed not for joy, and wondered, he said unto

^{ppro846} ^{pin2192}   ^{ad1759} ^{idpro5100} ^{an,ajn1034}

them, Have ye here any meat?

     ¹¹⁶¹ ^{art3588} ^{aina1921} ^{ppro846}   ^{an,nn3313}   ^{an,aj3702} ^{an,nn2486} ²⁵³² ^{pre575}   ^{an,aj3193/an,nn2781}

42 And they gave him a piece of a broiled fish, and of a honeycomb.

     ²⁵³²   ^{apta2983}   ^{aina5315} ^{ad*1799}   ^{ppro846}

43 And he took *it,* and did eat before them.

     ¹¹⁶¹   ^{aina2036}   ^{ppro846} ^{pr/depro3778}   ^{art3588}   ⁿⁿ³⁰⁵⁶ ^{repro3739}   ^{aina2980} ^{pre4314} ^{ppro5209}

44 And he said unto them, These *are* the words which I spake unto you,

          ^{pap5607} ^{ad2089} ^{pre4862} ^{ppro5213} ³⁷⁵⁴   ^{an,ajn3956}   ^{pin1163}   ^{aifp4137}   ^{art,pfpp1125}

while I was yet with you, that all things must be fulfilled, which*were*written

^{pre1722} ^{art3588} ⁿⁿ³⁵⁵¹   ^{an,nn3475}   ²⁵³²   ^{an,nn4396}   ²⁵³²   ^{an,nn5568}   ^{pre4012}

in the law of Moses, and *in* the prophets, and *in* the psalms, concerning

^{ppro1700}

me.   *(Deut. 18:15; Ps. 22:1-18; Is. 9:6,7; 53:2-12)*

      ^{ad5119}   ^{aina1272}   ^{ppro846}   ^{art,nn3563}   ^{infg4920}   ^{art3588}

45 Then opened he their understanding, that they might understand the

ⁿⁿ¹¹²⁴

Scriptures,

^{2532 aina2036}   ^{ppro846 ad3779}   ^{pfip1125 2532 ad3779}   ^{ipf1163   art,nn5547}

46 And said unto them, Thus it is written, and thus it behooved Christ to

^{aifp3958 2532   ainf450 pre1537   an,ajn3498 art3588 nu,aj5154 an,nn2250}

suffer, and to rise from the dead the third day:

^{2532   an,nn3341   2532   an,nn859   an,nn266}   ^{aifp2784   pre1909 ppro846}

47 And that repentance and remission of sins should be preached in   his

^{art,nn3686   pre1519 an,aj3956 art,nn1484   aptm756   pre575   2419}

name among all nations, beginning at Jerusalem.

^{1161 epn5210 pin2075 pr/an,nn3144   depro5130}

48 And ye are witnesses of these things.

^{2532   2400   epn1473 pin649 art3588   nn1860   ppro3450 art,nn3962   pre1909 ppro5209 1161 aima2523}

49 And, behold, I send the promise of my Father upon you: but tarry

^{epn5210 pre1722 art3588 nn4172   2419   ad2193 (repro3739) asbm1746   an,nn1411 pre1537   an,nn5311}

ye in the city of Jerusalem, until ye be endued with power from on high.

The Ascension of Jesus (Mark 16:19,20; Acts 1:9-11)

^{1161   aina1806 ppro846 ad1854   ad2193   pre1519   an,nn963   2532   apta1869   ppro848}

50 And he led them out as*far*as to Bethany, and he lifted up his

^{art,nn5495   aina2127   ppro846}

hands, and blessed them.

^{2532   aom1096   ppro846 aie2127   ppro846   aina1339   pre575}

51 And it came*to*pass, while he blessed them, he was parted from

^{ppro846 2532   ipf399   pre1519 art,nn3772}

them, and carried up into heaven.

^{2532 epn846   apta4352   ppro846   aina5290   pre1519   2419   pre3326 an,aj3173}

52 And they worshiped him, and returned to Jerusalem with great

^{an,nn5472}

joy:

^{2532   ipf2258   pre,an,ajn1275   pre1722 art3588   nn2411   pap134   2532   pap2127   art,nn2316}

53 And were continually in the temple, praising and blessing God.

²⁸¹

Amen.

JOHN

The Apostle John is believed to have written this book about the year A.D. 90 in the city of Ephesus in Asia. John's name is never mentioned in the book, but it is assumed that he is referring to himself when he speaks of the disciple "whom Jesus loved" and who leaned against the bosom of Jesus (John 13:23; 20:2). He and the Apostle James were the sons of Zebedee, but Jesus surnamed them the "sons of thunder" (Mark 3:17) and included them in the "inner circle" of apostles (Matt. 17:1; Mark 5:37; Luke 8:51). Jesus also entrusted His aged mother to John (John 19:26, 27). John was the first of the disciples to believe that Jesus rose from the dead (John 20:8) and the first to recognize Him on the shore of the Sea of Galilee (John 21:1–7).

This account of Jesus' life is very different from the Synoptic Gospels (Matthew, Mark, and Luke). The purpose of this Gospel, stated near the end of the book (John 20:30, 31), is to present the signs and wonders that Jesus performed so that those who read it will believe that He is "the Christ, the Son of God." Each of the incidents recorded in the Book of John is specifically included to prove that Jesus is indeed the Son of God.

The literary style is simple and easy to understand. Each incident and discourse of Jesus is treated as an isolated event or statement, rather than being incorporated into an overall framework. The same majestic truths that appear in the other Gospels are repeated in intricate parallelisms.

Several miracles mentioned in the Book of John are not mentioned in the other Gospels: Jesus' turning the water into wine (John 2:1–12); the healing of the nobleman's son (John 4:46–54); the healing of the paralytic at the pool of Bethesda (John 5:1–9); the healing of the blind man (John 9:1–7); the raising of Lazarus (John 11:38–44); and the second drought of fishes (John 21:4–6).

The Gospel of John allows us to determine the approximate length of Jesus' public ministry (about three and a half years) by the number of times that Passover was celebrated (John 2:23; 6:4; 11:55).

The Book of John may be divided into the following chronological portions: the pre-existence of Christ (John 1:1–18); His first year of ministry (John 1:19—4:54); His popularity during the second year (chap. 5); the opposition against Him in His third year of ministry (John 6:1—12:11); the passion week (John 12:12—19:42); and the forty days following His resurrection (chaps. 20; 21).

The Word Became Flesh

1
pre1722   an,nn746   ipf2258 art3588   nn3056   2532 art3588   nn3056 ipf2258 pre4314 art,nn2316 2532
In the beginning was the Word, and the Word was with God, and

art3588 nn3056 ipf2258 pr/an,nn2316
the Word was God.

depro3778   ipf2258 pre1722   an,nn746   pre4314 art,nn2316
2 The same was in the beginning with God.

an,ajn3956   aom1096 pre1223 epn846 2532   ad*5565   ppro846   3761   nu,ajn1520   aom1096
3 All things were made by him; and without him was not any thing made

repro3739   pfi1096
that was made.

pre1722 ppro846 ipf2258 an,nn2222 2532 art3588 nn2222 ipf2258 art3588 pr/nn5457   art,nn444
4 In him was life; and the life was the light of men.

2532   art3588 nn5457   pin5316   pre1722   art,nn4653   2532   art3588   nn4563   aina2638
5 And the light shineth in darkness; and the darkness comprehended

ppro846 3756
it not.

aom1096   an,nn444 pfpp649 pre3844 an,nn2316 ppro846 an,nn3686   pr/an,nn2491
6 There was a man sent from God, whose name *was* John.

depro3778   aina2064 pre1519   an,nn3141   2443   asba3140   pre4012 art3588   nn5457   2443
7 The same came for a witness, to bear witness of the Light, that

an,ajn3956   pre1223   ppro846   asba4100
all *men* through him might believe.

depro1565 ipf2258 3756   pr/art,nn5457 235   2443   asba3140   pre4012   art,nn5457
8 He was not that Light, but *was sent* to bear witness of that Light.

ipf2258 art3588 aj228 pr/art,nn5457 repro3739   pin5461   an,aj3956 an,nn444   ppmp2064   pre1519
9 *That* was the true Light, which lighteth every man that cometh into

art3588 nn2889
the world.   *(Is. 49:6)*

ipf2258 pre1722 art3588   nn2889   2532 art3588   nn2889   aom1096 pre1223 ppro846 2532 art3588
10 He was in the world, and the world was made by him, and the

nn2889 aina1097 epn846 3756
world knew him not.

1:1–17 John is the only writer who begins his story of Jesus Christ with His eternal existence rather than the time He appeared on earth. *Lógos* (3056), the word given to describe His existence at the beginning, is the "intelligence." He is said to have originated everything that is, and then He became the Word, which is the expression that explains that Intelligence which is undiscoverable except through the revelation of God and the Scriptures (Rom. 1:20).

There are two main verbs throughout this passage that serve to contrast what Jesus had always been and what He became at His incarnation. There is *ēn*, the imperfect of *eimí* (1510), "to be," which in this context could have been better translated as "had been." Thus, a paraphrase of the first verse would be: "Before there was any beginning, the Word had been, and the Word has been toward the God, and God had been the Word." This verb *ēn* is found in every instance in this context where the Person of Jesus Christ is referred to in His eternal state of being (vv. 1, 2, 4, 8, 9, 10, 15). See notes on Philippians 2:6–8 and 1 John 1:5–10. The second verb is *egéneto* (the aorist form of *gínomai* [1096]), "to become." It refers to becoming something that one was not before. Thus, in verse fourteen John says, "And the Word *became* flesh . . . ." The Lord Jesus, at a particular time in the past, became that which He was not before, a physical being. This verb is in the aorist, *egéneto* (John 1:3, 6, 10, 14, 17) and is also found in the perfect, *gégone* (John 1:3, 15). The aorist usage refers to some historical time in the past as the beginning of this new state. The perfect tense also implies a continuing existence in a new state.

1:9 See notes on Matthew 13:10–17 and Hebrews 6:1–6.

11 He came unto his own, and his own received him not.

☞ 12 But as*many*as received him, to them gave he power to become the sons of God, *even* to them*that*believe on his name:

13 Which were born, not of blood, nor of the will of the flesh, nor of the will of man, but of God.

14 And the Word was made flesh, and dwelt among us, (and we beheld his glory, the glory as of the only begotten of the Father,) full of grace and truth.

15 John bare witness of him, and cried, saying, This was he of whom I spake, He*that*cometh after me is preferred before me: for he was before me.

16 And of his fullness have all we received, and grace for grace.

17 For the law was given by Moses, *but* grace and truth came by Jesus Christ. *(Ex. 20:1)*

☞ 18 No man hath seen God at*any*time; the only begotten Son, which is in the bosom of the Father, he hath declared *him*. *(Ex. 20:1)*

The Testimony of John the Baptist (Matt. 3:1-12; Mark 1:7,8; Luke 3:15-17)

19 And this is the record of John, when the Jews sent priests and Levites from Jerusalem to ask him, Who art thou?

☞ **1:12** See note on Hebrews 6:1–6.

☞ **1:18** In the Greek NT, this verse begins with the word "God" (*Théon* [2316]), without the definite article. It therefore refers to God in His essence as Spirit (John 4:24). John is declaring that no created being has ever seen God in His essence as Spirit. This first statement is to be connected with verse one, which also speaks of Jesus Christ in His self-existence as an eternal and infinite Spirit. Then, to show the very special relationship of the Son to the Father, He is called *monogenēs* (3439). The word is translated "only begotten," thus giving the false idea that, in His eternal state, He was generated by

(continued on next page)

2532   aina3670   2532   aom720   3756 2532   aina3670   epn1473 pin1510 3756 art3588

☞ 20 And he confessed, and denied not; but confessed, I am not the

pr/hn5547

Christ.

2532   aina2065 ppro846 inpro5101   3767   pin1488 ppro4771 pr/an,nn2243 2532   pin3004   pin1510

21 And they asked him, What then? Art thou Elijah? And he saith, I am

3756 pin1488 ppro4771   pr/art,nn4396   2532   ainp611   3756

not. Art thou that Prophet? And he answered, No.

(Mal. 4:5,6; Deut. 18:15,16)

3767   aina2036   ppro846 pr/inpro5101 pin1488   2443   .asba1325

22 Then said they unto him, Who art thou? that we may give an

an,nn612   art,apta3992   ppro2248 inpro5101   pin3004   pre4012 rxpro4572

answer to them*that*sent us. What sayest thou of thyself?

aina5346   epn1473   pr/an,nn5456   pap994   pre1722 art3588   ajn2048

23 He said, I am the voice of one crying in the wilderness,

aima2116   art3588 nn3598   an,nn2962 ad2531 aina2036 art3588   nn4396   an,nn2268

Make straight the way of the Lord, as said the prophet Isaiah.   (Is. 40:3)

2532   art,pfpp649   ipf2258 pre1537 art3588   nn5330

24 And they*which*were*sent were of the Pharisees.

2532   aina2065 ppro846 2532 aina2036   ppro846 inpro5101   pin907   3767 1487

25 And they asked him, and said unto him, Why baptizest thou then, if

epn4771 pin1488 3756   pr/art,nn5547 3777 pr/an,nn2243   3777   pr/art,nn4396

thou be not that Christ, nor Elijah, neither that prophet?

art,nn2491   ainp611   ppro846   pap3004 epn1473   pin907   pre1722 an,nn5204 1161

26 John answered them, saying, I baptize with water: but there

pfi2476   an,aj3319 ppro5216 repro3739 epn5210 pin1492 3756

standeth one among you, whom ye know not;

epn846   pin2076 art,ppmp2064 ad*3694 ppro3450 (repro3739)   pfi1096   ad*1715 ppro3450 repro3739

27 He it is, who coming after me is   preferred before me, whose

art,nn5266 art,nn2438 epn1473 pin1510 3756 pr/an,aj514 2443 asba3089 (ppro846)

shoe's latchet I am not worthy to unloose.

depro5023   aom1096 pre1722 an,nn962   ad4008   art,nn2446   ad3699 an,nn2491

28 These things were done in Bethabara beyond Jordan, where John

ipf2258   pap907

was baptizing.

(continued from previous page)

the Father. The second part of verse eighteen declares that this unique Son, or "unique God" (as some manuscripts have it), who has always been in the bosom of the Father, manifested the Godhead and made Him understood. This second declaration of verse eighteen agrees with verse fourteen which speaks of the incarnation of the Lógos, the "Word." See note on Colossians 1:15–18.

☞ 1:20, 21 In these verses, the priests and Levites wanted to know whether or not John the Baptist was the Messiah, a reincarnation of the prophet Elijah, or "that Prophet." The Jews understood, according to Scripture, that a prophet would come and speak of delivering the people of Israel from all their oppression (see notes on Deut. 18:15–19 and Mal. 4:1–6). The fact that John the Baptist denied being Elijah is significant because the Jews believed that Elijah would be the forerunner of the Messiah. John's appearance certainly resembled Elijah's, and even the angel Gabriel that appeared to Zechariah, John's father, pointed out that he would come "in the spirit and power of Elijah" (Luke 1:17). However, John's answer to the priests and Levites was intended to show them that he was simply a messenger of God, not a reincarnation of Elijah or any other prophet.

The Lamb of God

^{art3588} ^{ad1887} ^{art,nn2491} ^{pin991} ^{art,nn2424} ^{ppmp2064} ^{pre4314} ^{ppro846} ²⁵³² ^{pin3004} ^{aima2396}

29 The next day John seeth Jesus coming unto him, and saith, Behold

^{art3588} ⁿⁿ²⁸⁶ ^{art,nn2316} ^{art,pap142} ^{art3588} ⁿⁿ²⁶⁶ ^{art3588} ⁿⁿ²⁸⁸⁹

the Lamb of God, which*taketh*away the sin of the world.   *(Is. 53:6,7)*

^{pr/depro3778} ^{pin2076} ^{pre4012} ^{repro3739} ^{ppro1473} ^{aina2036} ^{ad*3694} ^{ppro3450} ^{pinm2064} ^{an,nn435} ^{repro3739}

30 This is he of whom I said, After me cometh a man which is

^{pfi1096} ^{ad*1715} ^{ppro3450} ³⁷⁵⁴ ^{ipf2258} ^{pr/nu,ajn4413} ^{ppro3450}

preferred before me: for he was before me.

^{epn2504} ^{ipf1492} ^{ppro846} ³⁷⁵⁶ ²³⁵ ²⁴⁴³ ^{asbp5319} ²⁴⁷⁴

31 And I knew him not: but that he should be made manifest to Israel,

^{pre1223/depro5124} ^{epn1473} ^{aina2064} ^{pap907} ^{pre1722} ^{art,nn5204}

therefore am I come baptizing with water.

²⁵³² ^{an,nn2491} ^{aina3140} ^{pap3004} ^{pfip2300} ^{art3588} ⁿⁿ⁴¹⁵¹ ^{pap2597} ^{pre1537}

32 And John bare record, saying, I saw the Spirit descending from

^{an,nn3772} ^{ad5616} ^{an,nn4058} ²⁵³² ^{aina3306} ^{pre1909} ^{ppro846}

heaven like a dove, and it abode upon him.

^{epn2504} ^{ipf1492} ^{ppro846} ³⁷⁵⁶ ²³⁵ ^{art,apta3992} ^{ppro3165} ^{pinf907} ^{pre1722} ^{an,nn5204}

☞ 33 And I knew him not: but he*that*sent me to baptize with water,

^{depro1565} ^{aina2036} ^{ppro3427} ^{pre1909} ^{repro3739/302} ^{asba1492} ^{art3588} ⁿⁿ⁴¹⁵¹ ^{pap2597}

the same said unto me, Upon whom thou shalt see the Spirit descending,

²⁵³² ^{pap3306} ^{pre1909} ^{ppro846} ^{depro3778} ^{pin2076} ^{pr/art,pap907} ^{pre1722} ^{an,aj40}

and remaining on him, the same is he*which*baptizeth with the Holy

^{an,nn4151}

Ghost.

^{epn2504} ^{pfi3708} ²⁵³² ^{pfi3140} ³⁷⁵⁴ ^{depro3778} ^{pin2076} ^{art3588} ^{pr/nn5207} ^{art,nn2316}

34 And I saw, and bare record that this is the Son of God.

The First Disciples

^{ad3825} ^{art3588} ^{ad1887} ^{art,nn2491} ^{plpf2476} ²⁵³² ^{nu1417} ^{pre1537} ^{ppro846} ^{art,nn3101}

35 Again the next*day*after John stood, and two of his disciples;

²⁵³² ^{apta1689} ^{art,nn2424} ^{pap4043} ^{pin3004} ^{aima2396} ^{art3588} ⁿⁿ²⁸⁶

36 And looking upon Jesus as he walked, he saith, Behold the Lamb of

^{art,nn2316}

God!

²⁵³² ^{art3588} ^{nu1417} ⁿⁿ³¹⁰¹ ^{aina191} ^{ppro846} ^{pap2980} ²⁵³² ^{aina190} ^{art,nn2424}

37 And the two disciples heard him speak, and they followed Jesus.

¹¹⁶¹ ^{art,nn2424} ^{aptp4762} ²⁵³² ^{aptm2300} ^{ppro846} ^{pap190} ^{pin3004} ^{ppro846}

38 Then Jesus turned, and saw them following, and saith unto them,

^{inpro5101} ^{pin2212} ⁽¹¹⁶¹⁾ ^{art3588} ^{aina2036} ^{ppro846} ⁴⁴⁶¹ ^{repro3739} ^{pinp3004}

What seek ye? They said unto him, Rabbi, (which is to say, being

^{ppmp2059} ^{an,nn1320} ^{ad4226} ^{pin3306}

interpreted, Master,) where dwellest thou?

^{pin3004} ^{ppro846} ^{pim2064} ²⁵³² ^{aima1492} ^{aina2064} ²⁵³² ^{aina1492} ^{ad4226}

39 He saith unto them, Come and see. They came and saw where he

^{pin3306} ²⁵³² ^{aina3306} ^{pre3844} ^{ppro846} ^{depro1565} ^{art,nn2250} ¹¹⁶¹ ^{ipf2258} ^{ad5613} ^{pr/an,nu,aj1182} ^{an,nn5610}

dwelt, and abode with him that day: for it was about the tenth hour.

☞ **1:33** See note on Acts 1:5.

nu1520   pre1537   art3588   nu,ajn1417   art,apta191   an,nn2491   2532   apta190   ppro846   ipf2258

40 One   of   the   two   which heard John *speak,* and followed him, was

pr/an,nn406   an,nn4613   an,nn4074   art,nn80

Andrew, Simon Peter's brother.

depro3778 nu,ajn4413   pin2147   art,aj2398   art,nn80   an,nn4613   2532   pin3004   ppro846

41   He   first findeth his own brother Simon, and saith unto him, We have

pfi2147   art3588   nn3323   repro,pin3603   ppmp3177   art3588   pr/nn5547

found the Messiah, which is, being interpreted, the Christ.

2532   aina71   ppro846   pre4314 art,nn2424   1161   art,nn2424   apta1689   ppro846   aina2036

42 And he brought him   to   Jesus. And when Jesus beheld him, he said,

epn4771   pin1488   pr/an,nn4613   art3588   nn5207   an,nn2495   epn4771   fp2564   an,nn2786   repro3739

Thou   art   Simon   the   son of Jona: thou shalt be called Cephas, which

pinp2059   an,nn4074

is*by*interpretation, A stone.

Jesus Calls Philip and Nathanael

art3588   ad1887   art,nn2424   aina2309   ainf1831   pre1519   art,nn1056   2532   pin2147   an,nn5376

43 The day following Jesus would go forth into Galilee, and findeth Philip,

2532   pin3004   ppro846   pim190   ppro3427

and saith unto him, Follow me.

1161   art,nn5376   ipf2258 pre575   966   (pre1537) art3588 nn4172   an,nn406   2532   an,nn4074

44 Now Philip was of Bethsaida,   the city of Andrew and Peter.

art,nn5376   pin2147   3482   2532   pin3004   ppro846   pfi2147

45 Philip findeth Nathanael, and saith unto him, We have found him, of

repro3739   an,nn3475   pre1722 art3588   nn3551 2532 art3588   nn4396   aina1125 an,nn2424 art,pre575   3478

whom Moses in   the law, and the prophets, did write, Jesus   of   Nazareth,

art3588 nn5207   2501

the son of Joseph.   *(Deut. 18:18; Is. 7:14; 9:6; Ezek. 34:23)*

2532   3482   aina2036   ppro846 pinm1410   idpro5100   an,ajn18   pinf1511   pre1537

46 And Nathanael said unto him, Can there any good thing come out of

3478   an,nn5376 pin3004   ppro846 pim2064 2532 aima1492

Nazareth? Philip saith unto him, Come and see.

art,nn2424 aina1492   3482   ppmp2064 pre4314 ppro846   2532   pin3004 pre4012 ppro846   aima2396

47 Jesus saw Nathanael coming to   him, and saith of   him, Behold an

an,ajn2475   ad230   pre1722 repro3739 pin2076 3756 an,nn1388

Israelite indeed, in whom is no guile!

3482   pin3004   ppro846   ad4159   pin1097   ppro3165 art,nn2424   ainp611

48 Nathanael saith unto him, Whence knowest thou me? Jesus answered

2532   aina2036   ppro846   an,nn5376 aip5455 ppro4571   pap5607 pre5259 art3588

and said unto him, Before that Philip called thee, when thou wast under the

nn4808   aina1492 ppro4571

fig tree, I saw thee.

3482   ainp611   2532 pin3004   ppro846   4461   epn4771 pin1488 art3588 pr/nn5207

49 Nathanael answered and saith unto him, Rabbi, thou art the Son of

art,nn2316 epn4771 pin1488 art3588 pr/nn935   2474

God; thou art the King of Israel.

an,nn2424   ainp611   2532 aina2036   ppro846   3754   aina2036   ppro4671   aina1492

50 Jesus answered and said unto him, Because I said unto thee, I saw

ppro4571 ad*5270 art3588   nn4808   pin4100   fm3700   cd/an,ajn3187

thee under the fig tree, believest thou? thou shalt see greater things than

depro5130

these.

2532   pin3004   pppro846   281   281   pin3004   pppro5213   pre575/ad737

51 And he saith unto him, Verily, verily, I say unto you, Hereafter ye shall

fm3700 art,nn3772 pfp455 2532 art3588   nn32   art,nn2316 pap305   2532   pap2597   pre1909 art3588

see heaven open, and <u>the angels of God ascending and descending</u> upon the

nn5207   art,nn444

Son of man.   *(Gen. 28:12)*

The First Miracle

2532   art3588 nu,aj5154 art,nn2250   aom1096   an,nn1062   pre1722   2580   art,nn1056   2532 art3588

2 And the third day there was a marriage in Cana of Galilee; and the

nn3384   art,nn2424 ipf2258 ad1563

mother of Jesus was there:

1161   2532 art,nn2424   ainp2564 2532 pppro846 art,nn3101 pre1519 art3588   nn1062

2 And both Jesus was called, and his disciples, to the marriage.

2532   apta5302 an,nn3631 art3588   nn3384   art,nn2424 pin3004 pre4314 pppro846

3 And when they wanted wine, the mother of Jesus saith unto him, They

pin2192 3756 an,nn3631

have no wine.

art,nn2424   pin3004   pppro846   an,nn1135   inpro5101/epn1698/2532/epn4671   pppro3450

4 Jesus saith unto her, Woman, what*have*I*to*do*with*thee? mine

art,nn5610   ad3768   pin2240

hour is not yet come.

pppro846   art,nn3384 pin3004   art3588   nn1249   repro3748/302   psa3004   pppro5213

5 His mother saith unto the servants, Whatsoever he saith unto you,

aima4160

do *it*.

1161   ipf2258   ppmp2799   ad1563   nu1803   an,nn5201   an,aj3035   pre2596 art3588

6 And there were set there six waterpots of stone, after the

nn2512   art3588 nn2453   pap5562   nu1417 2228 nu5140 an,nn3355 pre303

manner*of*the*purifying of the Jews, containing two or three firkins apiece.

art,nn2424 pin3004   pppro846 aima1072 art3588   nn5201   an,nn5204 2532   aina1072

7 Jesus saith unto them, Fill the waterpots with water. And they filled

pppro846 ad2193   ad507

them up to the brim.

2532   pin3004   pppro846   aima501   ad3568 2532   pim5342   art3588

8 And he saith unto them, Draw out now, and bear unto the

nn755   2532   aina5342

governor*of*the*feast. And they bare *it*.

(1161) ad5613 art3588   nn755   aom1089 art3588 nn5204   pfpp1096

9 When the ruler*of*the*feast had tasted the water that was made

pr/an,nn3631 2532 ipf1492 3756   ad4159   pin2076 1161 art3588 nn1249   art,pfp501 art3588 nn5204

wine, and knew not whence it was: (but the servants which drew the water

ipf1492 art3588   nn755   pin5455 art3588   nn3566

knew;) the governor*of*the*feast called the bridegroom,

2532   pin3004   ppro846 an,aj3956 an,nn444   nu,ajn4412   pin5087   art,aj2570
10 And saith unto him, Every man at*the*beginning doth set forth good

an,nn3631 2532   ad3752   asbp3184   ad5119   cd/art,aj1640   epn4771
wine; and when men have well drunk, then that*which*is*worse: *but* thou hast

pfi5083 art3588 aj2570 an,nn3631 ad2193   ad737
kept the good wine until now.

depro5026   art,nn746   art,nn4592   aina4160 art,nn2424 pre1722   2580   art,nn1056   2532
11 This beginning of miracles did Jesus in Cana of Galilee, and

aina5319   ppro848 art,nn1391 2532 ppro846   art,nn3101   aina4100   pre1519 ppro846
manifested forth his glory; and his disciples believed on him.

pre3326   depro5124   aina2597   pre1519   2584   epn846 2532 ppro846   art,nn3384   2532
12 After this he went down to Capernaum, he, and his mother, and

ppro846   art,nn80   2532 ppro846   art,nn3101   2532   aina3306   ad1563   3756 an,aj4183 an,nn2250
his brethren, and his disciples: and they continued there not many days.

Jesus Goes to the Temple *(Matt. 21:12,13; Mark 11:15-18; Luke 19:45,46)*

2532   art3588   nn2453   3957   ipf2258   pr/ad1451   2532   art,nn2424   aina305   pre1519
13 And the Jews' passover was at hand, and Jesus went up to

an,nn2414
Jerusalem,

2532   aina2147 pre1722 art3588   nn2411   art,pap4453   an,nn1016 2532 an,nn4263 2532 an,nn4058
14 And found in the temple those*that*sold oxen and sheep and doves,

2532 art3588   nn2773   ppmp2521
and the changers*of*money sitting:

2532   apta4160   an,nn5416   pre1537   an,nn4979   aina1544
15 And when he had made a scourge of small cords, he drove them

an,ajn3956   pre1537 art3588   nn2411   5037 art3588   nn4263   2532 art3588   nn1016   2532   ipf1632   art3588
all out of the temple, and the sheep, and the oxen; and poured out the

nn2855   art,nn2772   2532   aina390   art3588   nn5132
changers' money, and overthrew the tables;

2532   aina2036   art,pap4453   art,nn4058   aima142   depro5023   ad1782   pim4160
16 And said unto them*that*sold doves, Take these things hence; make

3361 ppro3450 art,nn3962   art,nn3624   an,nn3624   an,nn1712
not my Father's house a house of merchandise.

1161   ppro846   art,nn3101   ainp3415   3754   pin2076   pfpp1125   art3588 nn2205   ppro4675
17 And his disciples remembered that it was written, The zeal of thine

art,nn3624   aina2719/ppro3165
house hath eaten*me*up.   *(Ps. 69:7)*

3767   ainp611   art3588   nn2453   2532 aina2036   ppro846 inpro5101 an,nn4592   pin1166
18 Then answered the Jews and said unto him, What sign showest thou

ppro2254   3754   pin4160   depro5023
unto us, seeing that thou doest these things?

art,nn2424   ainp611   2532 aina2036   ppro846   aima3089   depro5126   art,nn3485   2532 pre1722
19 Jesus answered and said unto them, Destroy this temple, and in

nu5140 an,nn2250   ft1453/ppro846
three days I will raise*it*up.

20 Then said the Jews, Forty*and*six years was*this*temple*in*building, and wilt thou rear*it*up in three days?

21 But he spake of the temple of his body.

22 When therefore he was risen from the dead, his disciples remembered that he had said this unto them; and they believed the Scripture, and the word which Jesus had said.

23 Now when he was in Jerusalem at the passover, in the feast *day,* many believed in his name, when they saw the miracles which he did.

☞ 24 But Jesus did not commit himself unto them, because he knew all *men,*

25 And needed not that any should testify of man: for he knew what was in man.

Nicodemus

3 There was a man of the Pharisees, named Nicodemus, a ruler of the Jews:

☞ 2 The same came to Jesus by night, and said unto him, Rabbi, we know

---

☞ 2:24 Christ was performing many miracles in Jerusalem, and as a result, many people believed on Him. The phrase "did not commit himself to them" is significant because it reveals that only Christ knew if these people were sincere. Most commentators agree that this verse speaks of those who believed on Christ, yet because Christ knew their true intentions, He saw the hypocrisy and shallowness of their faith. The word "commit" would be better understood if it were translated "trust." Evidently, Christ was sorrowful at the knowledge of the hypocrisy of their faith. Others feel that these people were in fact unbelievers who only accepted those things that they had seen with their eyes. A good example of people like this is, found in Christ's "Parable of the sower," represented by the seed that fell on stony ground. See notes on Luke 8:13 and 1 John 3:6–9.

☞ 3:2 The question that arises from an examination of this verse is why Nicodemus came to Christ at night. Some scholars suggest that Nicodemus was a timid man, and because he was a religious leader among the Pharisees, he was afraid to be seen with Jesus for fear that his associates would criticize him. Others say that this view lacks substantiation because it was too early in Christ's ministry for Him to have received such opposition as to warrant Nicodemus' speaking with Him at night. They propose

(continued on next page)

3754   an,nn1320   pfi2064   pre575 an,nn2316 1063   an,ajn3762 pinm1410 pinf4160 depro5023 art,nn4592
that thou art a teacher come from God: for no man can   do these miracles

repro3739 epn4771 pin4160   3362   art,nn2316 psa5600 pre3326 ppro846
that thou doest, except God be with him.

art,nn2424   ainp611   2532   aina2036   ppro846   281   281   pin3004   ppro4671
3 Jesus answered and said unto him, Verily, verily, I say unto thee,

3362   idpro5100   asbp1080   ad509   pinm1410/3756 ainf1492 art3588   nn932   art,nn2316
Except a man be born again, he cannot see the kingdom of God.

art,nn3530   pin3004   pre4314 ppro846 ad4459 pinm1410   an,nn444   aifp1080   pap5607
4 Nicodemus saith unto him, How can a man be born when he   is

pr/an,nn1088 pinm1410   (3361) ainf1525   an,nu,ajn1208   pre1519 ppro848   art,nn3384   art,nn2836   2532
old? can he   enter the second time into his mother's womb, and be

aifp1080
born?

art,nn2424   ainp611   281   281   pin3004   ppro4671   3362   idpro5100   asbp1080
5 Jesus answered, Verily, verily, I say unto thee, Except a man be born

pre1537 an,nn5204 2532   an,nn4151   pinm1410/3756 ainf1525 pre1519 art3588   nn932   art,nn2316
of water and of the Spirit, he cannot enter into the kingdom of God.

art,pfpp1080   pre1537 art3588 nn4561 pin2076 pr/an,nn4561 2532   art,pfpp1080   pre1537
6 That*which*is*born of the flesh is flesh; and that*which*is*born of

art3588   nn4151   pin2076 pr/an,nn4151
the Spirit is spirit.

aosi2296   3361 3754   aina2036   ppro4671 ppro5209 pin1163   aifp1080   ad509
7 Marvel not that I said unto thee, Ye must be born again.

art3588   nn4151   pin4154   ad3699   pin2309 2532   pin191   art3588   nn5456   ppro846
8 The wind bloweth where it listeth, and thou hearest the sound thereof,

235   pin1492/3756   ad4159   pinm2064   2532   ad4226   pin5217 ad3779 pin2076   an,aj3956
but canst*not*tell whence it cometh, and whither it goeth: so is every one

art,pfpp1080   pre1537 art3588   nn4151
that*is*born of the Spirit.   (Eccl. 11:5)

an,nn3530   ainp611   2532   aina2036   ppro846   ad4459 pinm1410   depro5023   aifm1096
9 Nicodemus answered and said unto him, How can these things be?

art,nn2424   ainp611   2532   aina2036   ppro846 pin1488 epn4771   pr/art,nn1320   2474   2532
10 Jesus answered and said unto him, Art thou a master of Israel, and

pin1097   3756   depro5023
knowest not these things?

281   281   pin3004   ppro4671 (3754) pin2980 repro3739   pin1492   2532
11 Verily, verily, I say unto thee, We speak that we do know, and

pin3140   repro3739   pfi3708   2532   pin2983 3756 ppro2257 art,nn3141
testify that we have seen; and ye receive not our witness.

1487   aina2036 ppro5213   art,ajn1919   2532   pin4100   3756   ad4459
12 If I have told you earthly things, and ye believe not, how shall ye

ft4100   1437 asba2036 ppro5213   art,ajn2032
believe, if I tell you of heavenly things?

(continued from previous page)
that Christ was simply too busy during the day to have made time to meet with Nicodemus. Still another view suggests that Nicodemus was the one who was busy during the day, being a member of the Sanhedrin, and he would have only had time to meet with Jesus at night. Whatever his motive was for coming to Christ when he did, Nicodemus later confessed Jesus before the other Pharisees and leaders of the Jews (John 7:50, 51).

13 And no man hath ascended up to heaven, but he*that*came*down from heaven, *even* the Son of man which is in heaven.   *(Prov. 30:4)*

14 And as Moses lifted up the serpent in the wilderness, even so must the Son of man be lifted up: *(Num. 21:9)*

☞ 15 That whosoever believeth in him should not perish, but have eternal life.

16 For God so loved the world, that he gave his only begotten Son, that whosoever believeth in him should not perish, but have everlasting life.

17 For God sent not his Son into the world to condemn the world; but that the world through him might be saved.

18 He*that*believeth on him is not condemned: but he*that*believeth not is condemned already, because he hath not believed in the name of the only begotten Son of God.

☞ 19 And this is the condemnation, that light is come into the world, and men loved darkness rather than light, because their deeds were evil.

20 For every one that doeth evil hateth the light, neither cometh to the light, lest his deeds should be reproved.

21 But he*that*doeth truth cometh to the light, that his deeds may be made manifest, that they are wrought in God.

Jesus Is Greater Than John

22 After these things came Jesus and his disciples into the land of Judea; and there he tarried with them, and baptized.

☞ **3:15, 16** See notes on Ephesians 1:4, 5 and Hebrews 6:1–6.
☞ **3:19** See note on 1 John 1:5–10.

1161 an,nn2491 2532 ipf2258 pr/pap907 pre1722 137 ad1451 4530 3754
23 And John also was baptizing in Aenon near to Salim, because there

ipf2258 an,aj4183 an,nn5204 ad1563 2532 ipf3854 2532 ipf907
was much water there: and they came, and were baptized.

1063 art,nn2491 ipf2258 ad3768 pfpp906 pre1519 art,nn5438
24 For John was not yet cast into prison.

3767 aom1096 an,nn2214 pre1537 an,nn2491 art,nn3101 pre3326
25 Then there arose a question between *some* of John's disciples and the

an,nn2453 pre4012 an,nn2512
Jews about purifying.

2532 aina2064 pre4314 art,nn2491 2532 aina2036 ppro846 4461 repro3739 ipf2258 pre3326
26 And they came unto John, and said unto him, Rabbi, he that was with

ppro4675 ad4008 art,nn2446 repro3739 epn4771 pfi3140 aima2396 depro3778
thee beyond Jordan, to whom thou barest witness, behold, the same

pin907 2532 an,ajn3956 pinm2064 pre4314 ppro846
baptizeth, and all *men* come to him.

an,nn2491 ainp611 2532 aina2036 an,nn444 pinm1410 (3756) pinf2983 an,ajn3762 3362
27 John answered and said, A man can receive nothing, except it

psa5600 pr/pfpp1325 ppro846 pre1537 art,nn3772
be given him from heaven.

epn5210 ppro846 pin3140/ppro3427 3754 aina2036 epn1473 pin1510 3756 art3588 pr/nn5547
28 Ye yourselves bear*me*witness, that I said, I am not the Christ,

235 3754 pin1510 pr/pfpp649 ad*1715 depro1565
but that I am sent before him.   *(Mal. 3:1)*

art,pap2192 art3588 nn3565 pin2076 pr/an,nn3566 1161 art3588 ajn5384 art3588
29 He*that*hath the bride is the bridegroom: but the friend of the

nn3566 art,pfp2476 2532 pap191 ppro846 pin5463 an,nn5479 pre1223 art3588
bridegroom, which standeth and heareth him, rejoiceth greatly because of the

nn3566 art,nn5456 depro3778 popro1699 art,nn5479 3767 pfip4137
bridegroom's voice: this my joy therefore is fulfilled.

depro1565 pin1163 pinf837 1161 epn1691 pifm1642
30 He must increase, but I *must* decrease.

art,ppmp2064 ad509 pin2076 ad*1883 an,ajn3956 art,pap5607 pre1537 art3588
31 He*that*cometh from above is above all: he*that*is of the

nn1093 pin2076 pre1537/art,nn1093 2532 pin2980 pre1537 art3588 nn1093 art,ppmp2064 pre1537 art,nn3772
earth is earthly, and speaketh of the earth: he*that*cometh from heaven

pin2076 ad*1883 an,ajn3956
is above all.

2532 repro3739 pfi3708 2532 aina191 depro5124 pin3140 2532 an,ajn3762
32 And what he hath seen and heard, that he testifieth; and no man

pin2983 ppro846 art,nn3141
receiveth his testimony.

art,apta2983 ppro846 art,nn3141 aina4972 3754 art,nn2316
33 He*that*hath*received his testimony hath set*to*his*seal that God

pin2076 pr/an,aj227
is true.

1063 repro3739 art,nn2316 aina649 pin2980 art3588 nn4487 art,nn2316 1063 art,nn2316
34 For he whom God hath sent speaketh the words of God: for God

pin1325 3756 art3588 nn4151 pre1537 an,nn3358
giveth not the Spirit by measure *unto him*.

art3588 nn3962 pin25 art3588 nn5207 2532 pfi1325 an,ajn3956 pre1722 ppro846 art,nn5495
35 The Father loveth the Son, and hath given all things into his hand.

art,pap4100   pre1519 art3588 nn5207 pin2192   an,aj166   an,nn2222 1161
36 He*that*believeth on   the   Son   hath everlasting   life: and

art,pap544   art3588 nn5207   3756 fm3700 an,nn2222 235 art3588 nn3709   art,nn2316 pin3306
he*that*believeth not the Son shall not see life; but the wrath of God abideth

pre1909 ppro846
on him.

A Samaritan Woman

ad5613   3767   art3588 nn2962 aina1097 3754 art3588   nn5330   aina191 3754 an,nn2424
4 When therefore the Lord knew how the Pharisees had heard that Jesus

pin4160 2532   pin907   cd/an,aj4119 an,nn3101   2228 an,nn2491
made and baptized more disciples than John,

2544   an,nn2424 epn846   ipf907   3756 235 ppro846   art,nn3101
2 (Though Jesus himself baptized not, but his disciples,)

aina863 art,nn2449 2532   aina565   ad3825 pre1519 art,nn1056
3 He left Judea, and departed again into Galilee.

1161   ppro846   ipf1163   pifm1330   pre1223   art,nn4540
4 And he must needs go through Samaria.

3767   pinm2064   pre1519 an,nn4172   art,nn4540   ppmp3004   4965   ad4139
5 Then cometh he to a city of Samaria, which is called Sychar, near to

art3588   nn5564   repro3739 2384 aina1325   ppro848 art,nn5207 2501
the parcel*of*ground that Jacob gave to his son Joseph.

1161   2384   pr/an,nn4077 ipf2258 ad1563 art,nn2424   3767   pfp2872   pre1537
6 Now Jacob's well   was there. Jesus therefore, being wearied with *his*

art,nn3597 ipf2516 ad3779 pre1909 art3588 nn4077   ipf2258 ad5616   pr/an,nu,aj1622 an,nn5610
journey, sat thus on the well: *and* it was about the   sixth   hour.

pinm2064   an,nn1135 pre1537 art,nn4540   ainf501   an,nn5204 art,nn2424 pin3004
7 There cometh a woman of Samaria to draw water: Jesus saith unto

ppro846 aima1325 ppro3427   ainf4095
her, Give me to drink.

1063 ppro846 art,nn3101   plpf565   pre1519 art3588 nn4172 2443 asba59 an,nn5160
8 (For his disciples were gone away unto the city to buy meat.)

3767 pin3004 art3588   nn1135   art,aj4542   ppro846 ad4459   epn4771 pap5607
9 Then saith the woman of Samaria unto him, How is it that thou, being a

pr/an,nn1135 pin154 ainf4095 pre3844 ppro1700   pap5607 pr/an,nn1135   an,aj4542 1063   an,nn2453
Jew, askest drink of me, which am a woman of Samaria? for the Jews

pinm4798/3756   an,nn4541
have*no*dealings with the Samaritans.   *(Ezra 4:3; 9:1-10,44)*

an,nn2424   ainp611   2532 aina2036   ppro846 1487   ipf1492   art3588 nn1431 art,nn2316
☞ 10 Jesus answered and said unto her, If thou knewest the gift of God,

---

☞ **4:10** The important idea to glean from this verse is the meaning of the phrase, "the gift of God." Some believe that the gift refers to the statement by Christ that follows: "and who it is that saith to thee . . . ." They suggest that the word translated "and" should in fact be translated "namely," which would define the "gift of God" as the knowledge of who Jesus is and His reason for coming to earth. For the believer, this would provide the basis for the benefits that Christ gives to him and would reveal His willingness to meet all the believer's needs. Other scholars propose that the "gift" is the "living water" that Jesus was offering to the Samaritan woman. They suggest that there is a two-fold purpose

(continued on next page)

2532　inpro5101　　pin2076　　pr/art,pap3004　　　ppro4671　aima1325　ppro3427　　ainf4095　epn4771
and who it is that saith to thee, Give me to drink; thou wouldest have

aina154/302　　ppro846　2532　　　　　　　　　　aina1325/302 ppro4671 pap2198　an,nn5204
asked of him, and he would have given thee living water.

　　　art3588　nn1135　pin3004　　　　ppro846 an,nn2962　　pin2192　3777　　an,nn502　　　　2532
11 The woman saith unto him, Sir, thou hast nothing to draw with, and

art3588 nn5421 pin2076 pr/an,aj901　　ad4159　　3767　pin2192　　art,pap2198　art,nn5204
the well is deep: from whence then hast thou that living water?

　　　pin1488　epn4771(3361) pr/cd/an,aj3187　　ppro2257 art,nn3962　2384　repro3739 aina1325 ppro2254 art3588 nn5421
12 Art thou greater than our father Jacob, which gave us the well,

2532　aina4095　pre1537/ppro846　epn846　2532 ppro846　art,nn5207　2532 ppro846 art,nn2353
and drank thereof himself, and his children, and his cattle?

　　　art,nn2424　ainp611　2532 aina2036　　ppro846　an,aj3956　art,pap4095　pre1537 depro5127
13 Jesus answered and said unto her, Whosoever drinketh of this

art,nn5204　ft1372　ad3825
water shall thirst again:

　　　1161　repro3739/302　asba4095　pre1537 art3588　nn5204　repro3739 epn1473　ft1325 ppro846
14 But whosoever drinketh of the water that I shall give him shall

efn3364/pre1519/art,nn165 asba1372　235 art3588　nn5204 repro3739　　ft1325 ppro846　fm1096 pre1722 ppro846
never thirst; but the water that I shall give him shall be in him a

pr/an,nn4077　an,nn5204　ppmp242　pre1519　an,aj166　an,nn2222
well of water springing up into everlasting life.

　　　art3588　nn1135　pin3004　pre4314 ppro846 an,nn2962 aima1325 ppro3427 depro5124 art,nn5204　2443　psa1372
15 The woman saith unto him, Sir, give me this water, that I thirst

3361　3366　psmp2064　ad1759　pinf501
not, neither come hither to draw.

　　　art,nn2424 pin3004　　ppro846 aima5217 aima5455 ppro4675　art,nn435　2532 aima2064　ad1759
16 Jesus saith unto her, Go, call thy husband, and come hither.

　　　art3588　nn1135　ainp611　2532 aina2036　pin2192 3756　an,nn435　art,nn2424 pin3004
17 The woman answered and said, I have no husband. Jesus said unto

ppro846　　　ad2573 aina2036　pin2192 3756　an,nn435
her, Thou hast well said, I have no husband:

　　　1063　aina2192 nu4002　an,nn435　2532　repro3739　ad3568 pin2192 pin2076 3756
18 For thou hast had five husbands; and he whom thou now hast is not

ppro4675　pr/an,nn435　depro5124　pfi2046　an,aj227
thy husband: in that saidst thou truly.

　　　art3588　nn1135　pin3004　ppro846 an,nn2962　pin2334　3754 epn4771 pin1488　pr/an,nn4396
19 The woman saith unto him, Sir, I perceive that thou art a prophet.

　　　ppro2257 art,nn3962　aina4352　pre1722 depro5129 art,nn3735　2532 epn5210 pin3004　3754　pre1722
20 Our fathers worshiped in this mountain; and ye say, that in

an,nn2414　pin2076 art3588 nn5117　ad3699　pin1163　pinf4352
Jerusalem is the place where men ought to worship.

(Deut. 11:29; Josh. 8:33; 2 Chr. 7:12; Ps. 122:1-5)

(continued from previous page)
to this water: first, it can refer to the spiritual, everlasting water for the soul (John 4:14, "eternal life"), while also applying to the literal water found in the well from which the Samaritan woman was going to draw. Yet a third view states that the "gift" is in fact Christ Himself. This idea is seen in the freeness with which the offer was made to the woman. Christ said, "If thou knewest . . . who it is that saith to thee . . . thou wouldest have asked of him." Christ did not come to earth because God felt that He owed something to mankind. This final view seems to be the most consistent since it shows the Person of Christ as the focal point of the gift, not anything that He brought with Him.

art,nn2424 pin3004   pppro846 an,nn1135 aima4100 ppro3427 (3754)   an,nn5610 pinm2064 ad3753

21 Jesus saith unto her, Woman, believe me, the hour cometh, when

3777 pre1722 depro5129 art,nn3735 3777 pre1722 an,nn2414 ft4352 art3588

ye shall neither in this mountain, nor yet at Jerusalem, worship the

nn3962

Father.

epn5210 pin4352   pin1492 3756 repro3739 epn2249 pin1492 repro3739   pin4352 3754

22 Ye worship ye know not what: we know what we worship: for

art,nn4991 pin2076 pre1537 art3588 nn2453

salvation is of the Jews.

235 an,nn5610 pinm2064 2532 pr/ad3568 pin2076 ad3753 art3588 aj228 an,nn4353

23 But the hour cometh, and now is, when the true worshipers shall

ft4352 art3588 nn3962 pre1722 an,nn4151 2532 an,nn225 1063 art3588 nn3962 (2532) pin2212 an,aj5108

worship the Father in spirit and in truth: for the Father seeketh such to

art,pap4352 ppro846

worship him.

art,nn2316   pr/an,nn4151 2532   art,pap4352 ppro846 pin1163 pinf4352 pre1722

24 God is a Spirit: and they*that*worship him must worship him in

an,nn4151 2532 an,nn225

spirit and in truth.

art3588 nn1135 pin3004 ppro846 pin1492 3754 an,nn3323 pinm2064

25 The woman saith unto him, I know that Messiah cometh,

art,ppmp3004 an,nn5547 ad3752 depro1565 asba2064 ft312 ppro2254 an,ajn3956

which*is*called Christ: when he is come, he will tell us all things.

(Deut. 18:15)

art,nn2424 pin3004 ppro846 epn1473 pr/art,pap2980 ppro4671 pin1510

26 Jesus saith unto her, I that speak unto thee am he.

2532 pre1909 depro5129 aina2064 ppro846 art,nn3101 2532 aina2296 3754 ipf2980 pre3326

27 And upon this came his disciples, and marveled that he talked with

an,nn1135 3305 an,ajn3762 aina2036 inpro5101 pin2212 2228 inpro5101 pin2980 pre3326

the woman: yet no man said, What seekest thou? or, Why talkest thou with

ppro846

her?

art3588 nn1135 3767 aina863 ppro848 art,nn5201 2532 aina565 pre1519 art3588 nn4172

28 The woman then left her waterpot, and went*her*way into the city,

2532 pin3004 art3588 nn444

and saith to the men,

ad1205 aima1492 an,nn444 repro3739 aina2036 ppro3427 an,aj3956 an,ajn3745 aina4160 pin2076 3385

29 Come, see a man, which told me all things that ever I did: is not

depro3778 art3588 pr/nn5547

this the Christ?

3767 aina1831 pre1537 art3588 nn4172 2532 ipf2064 pre4314 ppro846

30 Then they went out of the city, and came unto him.

(1161) pre1722 art3588 ad3342 art,nn3101 ipf2065 ppro846 pap3004 4461 aima5315

31 In the mean while his disciples prayed him, saying, Master, eat.

1161 art3588 aina2036 ppro846 epn1473 pin2192 an,nn1035 ainf5315 repro3739 epn5210 pin1492 3756

32 But he said unto them, I have meat to eat that ye know not of.

3767 ipf3004 art3588 nn3101 rcpro240/pre4314 idpro3387 aina5342

33 Therefore said the disciples one*to*another, Hath any man brought

ppro846 ainf5315

him *aught* to eat?

34 Jesus saith unto them, My meat is to do the will of him*that*sent me, and to finish his work.

35 Say not ye, There are yet four months, and *then* cometh harvest? behold, I say unto you, Lift up your eyes, and look on the fields; for they are white already to harvest.

36 And he*that*reapeth receiveth wages, and gathereth fruit unto life eternal: that both he*that*soweth and he*that*reapeth may rejoice together.

37 And herein is that saying true, One soweth, and another reapeth.

38 I sent you to reap that whereon ye bestowed*no*labor: other men labored, and ye are entered into their labors.

39 And many of the Samaritans of that city believed on him for the saying of the woman, which testified, He told me all that ever I did.

40 So when the Samaritans were come unto him, they besought him that he would tarry with them: and he abode there two days.

41 And many more believed because of his own word;

42 And said unto the woman, Now we believe, not because of thy saying: for we have heard *him* ourselves, and know that this is indeed the Christ, the Savior of the world.

Jesus Heals an Official's Son

43 Now after two days he departed thence, and went into Galilee.

44 For Jesus himself testified, that a prophet hath no honor in his own country.

45 Then when he was come into Galilee, the Galilaeans received him, having

pfp3708   an,ajn3956   repro3739   aina4160   pre1722   an,nn2414   pre1722 art3588   nn1859   1063   epn846   2532

seen all*the*things that he did at Jerusalem at the feast: for they also

aina2064   pre1519 art3588   nn1859

went unto the feast.

     3767   art,nn2424   aina2064   ad3825   pre1519   2580   art,nn1056   ad3699   aina4160 art3588   nn5204

46 So Jesus came again into Cana of Galilee, where he made the water

pr/an,nn3631   2532   ipf2258   idpro5100   an,ajn937   repro3739   art,nn5207   ipf770   pre1722

wine. And there was a certain nobleman, whose son was sick at

  2584

Capernaum.

    depro3778   aina191   3754   an,nn2424   ipf2240   pre1537   art,nn2449 pre1519   art,nn1056

47 When he heard that Jesus was come out of Judea into Galilee, he

aina565   pre4314 ppro846   2532   ipf2065   ppro846   2443   asba2597   2532   asbm2390 ppro846

went unto him, and besought him that he would come down, and heal his

art,nn5207 1063   ipf3195/pinf599

son: for he was*at*the*point*of*death.

     3767   aina2036 art,nn2424 pre4314 ppro846   3362   asba1492 an,nn4592   2532   an,nn5059

48 Then said Jesus unto him, Except ye see signs and wonders, ye will

efn3364   asba4100

not believe.

     art3588   ajn937   pin3004   pre4314 ppro846 an,nn2962   aima2597   ad4250 ppro3450 art,nn3813 ainf599

49 The nobleman saith unto him, Sir, come down ere my child die.

    art,nn2424   pin3004   ppro846   pim4198   ppro4675 art,nn5207   pin2198   2532   art3588   nn444

50 Jesus saith unto him, Go*thy*way; thy son liveth. And the man

aina4100   art3588   nn3056   repro3739 an,nn2424   aina2036   ppro846   2532   ipf4198

believed the word that Jesus had spoken unto him, and he went*his*way.

     1161   ppro846   ad2235   pap3597   ppro846   art,ajn1401   aina528 ppro846   2532   aina518

51 And as he was now going down, his servants met him, and told him,

pap3004   ppro4675 art,nn3816   pin2198

saying, Thy son liveth.

     3767   aina4441   pre3844   ppro846   art3588   nn5610   pre1722/repro3739   aina2192/cd/an,ajn2866

52 Then inquired he of them the hour when he began*to*amend.

2532   aina2036   ppro846   ad5504   an,nu,aj1442   an,nn5610 art3588   nn4446   aina863 ppro846

And they said unto him, Yesterday at the seventh hour the fever left him.

     3767   art3588   nn3962   aina1097   3754   pre1722   depro1565   art,nn5610 pre1722   repro3739

53 So the father knew that *it was* at the same hour, in the which

art,nn2424 aina2036   ppro846 ppro4675 art,nn5207   pin2198   2532   epn846   aina4100   2532 ppro846   an,aj3650

Jesus said unto him, Thy son liveth: and himself believed, and his whole

art,nn3614

house.

    depro5124   ad3825   an,nu,aj1208   an,nn4592   art,nn2424 aina4160   apta2064

54 This *is* again the second miracle *that* Jesus did, when he was come

pre1537   art,nn2449 pre1519   art,nn1056

out of Judea into Galilee.

Jesus Heals a Sick Man on the Sabbath Day

     pre3326   depro5023   ipf2258   an,nn1859   art3588   nn2453   2532 art,nn2424   aina305   pre1519

5 After this there was a feast of the Jews; and Jesus went up to

an,nn2414

Jerusalem.   *(Lev. 23:2)*

2 Now there is at Jerusalem by the sheep *market* a pool,
which*is*called in*the*Hebrew*tongue Bethesda, having five porches.

3 In these lay a great multitude of impotent folk, of blind, halt,
withered, waiting for the moving of the water.

4 For an angel went down at*a*certain*season into the pool, and troubled
the water: whosoever then first after the troubling of the water stepped in
was made whole of whatsoever disease he had.

5 And a certain man was there, which had an infirmity thirty*and*eight
years.

6 When Jesus saw him lie, and knew that he had been now a long
time *in that case,* he saith unto him, Wilt thou be made whole?

7 The impotent man answered him, Sir, I have no man, when the
water is troubled, to put me into the pool: but while I am coming,
another steppeth down before me.

8 Jesus saith unto him, Rise, take up thy bed, and walk.

9 And immediately the man was made whole, and took up his bed, and
walked: and on the same day was the sabbath.

10 The Jews therefore said unto him*that*was*cured, It is the
sabbath day: it is*not*lawful for thee to carry *thy* bed. *(Ex. 20:10)*

11 He answered them, He*that*made me whole, the same said unto
me, Take up thy bed, and walk.

12 Then asked they him, What man is that*which*said unto thee,
Take up thy bed, and walk?

13 And he*that*was*healed wist not who it was: for Jesus had
conveyed*himself*away, a multitude being in *that* place.

14 Afterward Jesus findeth him in the temple, and said unto him,

aina2396   pfi1096   pr/an,aj5199 pim264   ad3371   3363   pr/an,ajn5501 idpro5100 asbm1096

Behold, thou art made whole: sin no more, lest a worse thing come unto
ppro4671

thee.

art3588   nn444   aina565   2532   aina312 art3588   nn2453   3754   pin2076   an,nn2424

15 The man departed, and told the Jews that it was Jesus,
pr/art,apta4100   ppro846 pr/an,aj5199

which*had*made him whole.

2532   pre1223/depro5124   art3588   nn2453   ipf1377   art,nn2424   2532   ipf2212   ainf615 ppro846

16 And therefore did the Jews persecute Jesus, and sought to slay him,
3754   ipf4160   depro5023   pre1722   an,nn4521

because he had done these things on the sabbath day.

1161 art,nn2424   aom611   ppro846 ppro3450 art,nn3962   pinm2038   ad2193/ad737 epn2504 pinm2038

17 But Jesus answered them, My Father worketh hitherto, and I work.

pre1223/depro5124 (3767) art3588   nn2453   ipf2212   ad3123   ainf615 ppro846   3754   3756

18 Therefore   the Jews sought the more to kill him, because he not
an,ajn3440   ipf3089 art3588   nn4521   235   ipf3004 2532   art,nn2316   an,aj2398 an,nn3962

only had broken the sabbath, but said also that God was his Father,
pap4160   rxpro1438 pr/an,aj2470 art,nn2316

making himself equal with God.

The Father and the Son

3767   aom611   art,nn2424 2532 aina2036   ppro846   281   281   pin3004

19 Then answered Jesus and said unto them, Verily, verily, I say unto
ppro5213 art3588 nn5207 pinm1410 (3756) pinf4160 an,ajn3762 pre575 rxpro1438   3362 idpro5100   psa991 art3588 nn3962

you, The Son can   do nothing of himself, but what he seeth the Father
pap4160 1063   repro3739/302   depro1565 psa4160 depro5023 2532 pin4160 art3588 nn5207   ad3668

do: for what*things*soever he doeth, these also doeth the Son likewise.

1063   art3588   nn3962   pin5368 art3588 nn5207 2532   pin1166 ppro846   an,aj3956 repro3739

20 For the Father loveth the Son, and showeth him all things that
epn846   pin4160 2532   ft1166 ppro846 cd/an,aj3187 an,nn2041   depro5130 2443 epn5210

himself doeth: and he will show him greater works than these, that ye may
psa2296

marvel.

1063 ad5618 art3588   nn3962   pin1453   art3588 ajn3498 2532   pin2227   ad3779

21 For as the Father raiseth up the dead, and quickeneth *them*; even so
art3588 nn5207 (2532)   pin2227   repro3739   pin2309

the Son   quickeneth whom he will.

1063 (3761) art3588   nn3962   pin2919 an,ajn3762 235   pfi1325 an,aj3956 art,nn2920

22 For   the Father judgeth no man, but hath committed all judgment
art3588 nn5207

unto the Son:

2443 an,ajn3956   psa5091 art3588 nn5207 ad2531   pin5091 art3588 nn3962

23 That all *men* should honor the Son, even as they honor the Father.
art,pap5091   3361 art3588 nn5207   pin5091   3756   art3588   nn3962

He*that*honoreth not the Son honoreth not the Father
art,apta3992   ppro846

which*hath*sent him.

281   281   pin3004   ppro5213 (3754) art,pap191   ppro3450 art,nn3056 2532

24 Verily, verily, I say unto you, He*that*heareth my word, and

pap4100   art,apta3992   ppro3165 pin2192   an,aj166   an,nn2222 2532   3756 pinm2064 pre1519
believeth on him*that*sent me, hath everlasting life, and shall not come into

an,nn2920   235   pfi3327   pre1537 art,nn2288 pre1519 art,nn2222
condemnation; but is passed from death unto life.

281   281   pin3004   ppro5213 (3754) an,nn5610   pinm2064   2532 pr/ad3568 pin2076   ad3753
25 Verily, verily, I say unto you, The hour is coming, and now is, when

art3588   ajn3498   fm191 art3588 nn5456   art3588 nn5207   art,nn2316 2532   art,apta191
the dead shall hear the voice of the Son of God: and they*that*hear shall

fm2198
live.

1063 ad5618 art3588   nn3962   pin2192 an,nn2222 pre1722   rxpro1438   ad3779   aina1325 (2532) art3588
26 For as the Father hath life in himself; so hath he given to the

nn5207   pinf2192 an,nn2222 pre1722   rxpro1438
Son to have life in himself;

2532   aina1325 ppro846   an,nn1849   pinf4160   an,nn2920   2532   3754
27 And hath given him authority to execute judgment also, because he

pin2076   pr/an,nn5207   art,nn444
is the Son of man.   *(Dan. 7:13)*

pim2296   3361   depro5124 3754   an,nn5610   pinm2064 pre1722   repro3739 an,aj3956 art3588
28 Marvel not at this: for the hour is coming, in the which all that are

pre1722 art3588   nn3419   fm191 ppro846 art,nn5456
in the graves shall hear his voice,

2532   fm1607   art,apta4160   art,ajn18   pre1519   an,nn386
29 And shall come forth; they*that*have*done good, unto the resurrection

an,nn2222 1161   art,apta4238   art,ajn5337 pre1519   an,nn386   an,nn2930
of life; and they*that*have*done evil, unto the resurrection of damnation.

                                                                    (Dan. 12:2)

epn1473 pinm1410 (3756) pre575   rxpro1683   pinf4160 an,ajn3762   ad2531   pin191   pin2919   2532
30 I can of mine*own*self do nothing: as I hear, I judge: and

art,popro1699   art,nn2920   pin2076 pr/an,aj1342   3754   pin2212 3756   art,popro1699 art,nn2307 235 art3588 nn2307
my judgment is just; because I seek not mine own will, but the will of

art3588   nn3962   apta3992 ppro3165
the Father which hath sent me.

1437 epn1473   pin3140   pre4012 rxpro1683   ppro3450 art,nn3141   pin2076 3756 pr/an,aj227
31 If I bear witness of myself, my witness is not true.

pin2076   an,aj243   pr/art,pap3140   pre4012 ppro1700 2532   pin1492 3754 art3588
32 There is another that*beareth*witness of me; and I know that the

nn3141   repro3739   pin3140   pre4012 ppro1700 pin2076 pr/an,aj227
witness which he witnesseth of me is true.

epn5210 pfi649   pre4314 an,nn2491 2532   pfi3140   art3588   nn225
33 Ye sent unto John, and he bare witness unto the truth.

1161   epn1473   pin2983   3756   art,nn3141   pre3844 an,nn444 235   depro5023   pin3004 2443
34 But I receive not testimony from man: but these things I say, that

epn5210   asbp4982
ye might be saved.

depro1565 ipf2258   art,ppmp2545   2532   pap5316 pr/art,nn3088 1161 epn5210   aina2309 pre4314
35 He was a burning and a shining light: and ye were willing for a

an,nn5610   aifp21   pre1722 ppro846 art,nn5457
season to rejoice in his light.

1161 epn1473 pin2192 cd/an,aj3187   art,nn3141   art,nn2491 1063 art3588   nn2041   repro3739
36 But I have greater witness than *that* of John: for the works which

art3588   nn3962   aina1325   ppro3427   2443   asba5048   (ppro846)   epn846   art,nn2041   repro3739   epn1473   pin4160

the Father hath given me to finish, the same works that I do,

pin3140   pre4012 ppro1700   3754   art3588   nn3962   pfi649   ppro3165

bear witness of me, that the Father hath sent me.

2532   art3588   nn3962   epn846   art,apta3992   ppro3165   pfi3140   pre4012

37 And the Father himself, which*hath*sent me, hath borne witness of

ppro1700   3777   pfi191   ppro846 an,nn5456   ad4455   3777   pfi3708 ppro846 an,nn1491

me. Ye have neither heard his voice at*any*time, nor seen his shape.

2532   pin2192   3756   ppro846 art,nn3056   pap3306   pre1722 ppro5213 3754   repro3739 depro1565   aina649

38 And ye have not his word abiding in you: for whom he hath sent,

depro5129 epn5210   pin4100   3756

him ye believe not.

pim2045   art3588   nn1124   3754   pre1722 ppro846 epn5210   pin1380   pinf2192   an,aj166   an,nn2222

39 Search the Scriptures; for in them ye think ye have eternal life:

2532   depro1565 pin1526   pr/art,pap3140   pre4314 ppro1700

and they are they*which*testify of me.

2532   pin2309 3756   ainf2064   pre4314 ppro3165   2443   psa2192 an,nn2222

40 And ye will not come to me, that ye might have life.

pin2983   3756   an,nn1391   pre3844   an,nn444

41 I receive not honor from men.

235   pfi1097   ppro5209   3754   pin2192   3756   art3588   nn26   art,nn2316 pre1722 rxpro1438

42 But I know you, that ye have not the love of God in you.

epn1473   pfi2064   pre1722   ppro3450   art,nn3962   art,nn3686   2532   pin2983   ppro3165   3756   1437

☞ 43 I am come in my Father's name, and ye receive me not: if

an,ajn243   asba2064   pre1722   art,aj2398   art,nn3686   depro1565   fm2983

another shall come in his own name, him ye will receive.

ad4459   pinm1410 epn5210   ainf4100   pap2983   an,nn1391   rcpro240/pre3844   2532   pin2212

44 How can ye believe, which receive honor one*of*another, and seek

3756   art3588   nn1391   art3588   pre3844 an,nn2316 art,aj3441

not the honor that *cometh* from God only?

3361   pim1380   3754   epn1473   ft2723   ppro5216 pre4314 art3588   nn3962   pin2076

45 Do not think that I will accuse you to the Father: there is *one*

art,pap2723   ppro5216   an,nn3475   pre1519 repro3739 epn5210   pfi1679

that accuseth you, *even* Moses, in whom ye trust.   *(Deut. 31:26,27)*

1063   (1487)   ipf4100   an,nn3475   ipf4100/302   epn1698   1063   depro1565

46 For had ye believed Moses, ye would have believed me: for he

aina1125   pre4012 epn1700

wrote of me.   *(Deut. 18:15)*

1161   1487   pin4100   3756   depro1565   art,nn1121   ad4459   ft4100   art,popro1699

47 But if ye believe not his writings, how shall ye believe my

an,nn4487

words?

Jesus Feeds the Five Thousand (Matt. 14:13-21; Mark 6:30-44; Luke 9:10-17)

pre3326   depro5023   art,nn2424   aina565   ad4008   art3588 nn2281   art,nn1056

6 After these things Jesus went over the sea of Galilee, which is *the sea*

art,nn5085

of Tiberias.

☞ **5:43** See note on Revelation 13:1–18.

2532   an,aj4183   an,nn3793   ipf190   ppro846   3754   ipf3708   ppro846   art,nn4592
2 And a great multitude followed him, because they saw his miracles

repro3739   ipf4160 pre1909   art,pap770
which he did   on   them*that*were*diseased.

1161   art,nn2424   aina424   pre1519   art,nn3735   2532   ad1563   ipf2521   pre3326   ppro848
3 And Jesus went up into a mountain, and there he sat with his

art,nn3101
disciples.

1161   art3588   3957   art,nn1859   art3588   nn2453   ipf2258   pr/ad1451
4 And the passover, a feast of the Jews, was nigh.

(Ex. 12:16; Lev. 23:5; Num. 28:16)

art,nn2424   3767   apta1869   art,nn3788   2532   aptm2300   (3754)   an,aj4183   an,nn3793   pinm2064
5 When Jesus then lifted up *his* eyes, and saw   a   great company come

pre4314   ppro846   pin3004   pre4314   art,nn5376   ad4159   ft59   an,nn740   2443   depro3778
unto him, he saith unto Philip, Whence shall we buy bread, that these may

asba5315
eat?

1161   depro5124   ipf3004   pap3985   ppro846   1063   epn846   ipf1492   inpro5101   ipf3195
6 And this he said to prove him: for he himself knew what he would

pinf4160
do.

an,nn5376   ainp611   ppro846   nu1250   an,nn1220   an,nn740
7 Philip   answered   him,   Two   hundred   pennyworth   of   bread

pin714/3756   ppro846   2443   an,ajn1538   ppro846   asba2983 idpro5100/an,ajn1024
is*not*sufficient for them, that every one of them may take   a little.

nu1520   pre1537   ppro846   art,nn3101   an,nn406   an,nn4613   an,nn4074   art,nn80   pin3004
8 One   of   his   disciples, Andrew, Simon Peter's brother, saith unto

ppro846
him,

pin2076   nu1520   an,nn3808   ad5602   repro3739   pin2192   nu4002   an,aj2916   an,nn740   2532   nu1417
9 There   is   a   lad   here, which hath five barley loaves, and two

an,nn3795   235   pr/inpro5101 pin2076 depro5023   pre1519   an,ajn5118
small fishes: but what are they among so many?

1161   art,nn2424   aina2036   aima4160   art3588   nn444   ainf377   1161   ipf2258
10 And   Jesus   said,   Make   the   men   sit   down.   Now   there   was

an,aj4183   an,nn5528   pre1722   art3588   nn5117   3767   art3588   nn435   aina377   art,nn706   ad5616
much   grass   in   the   place. So the men sat down, in number about

nu,ajn4000
five thousand.

1161   art,nn2424   aina2983   art3588   nn740   2532   apta2168
11 And Jesus took the   loaves;   and when he had given thanks, he

aina1239   art3588   nn3101   2532   art3588   nn3101   art,ppmp345
distributed to the disciples, and the disciples to them*that*were*set*down;

2532   ad3668   pre1537 art3588   nn3795   an,ajn3745   ipf2309
and likewise of the fishes as*much*as they would.

(1161) ad5613   ainp1705   pin3004   ppro848   art,nn3101   aima4863   art3588
12   When they were filled, he said unto his disciples, Gather up the

nn2801   apta4052   2443   idpro5100/3361   asbm622
fragments that remain, that nothing be lost.

3767   aina4863   2532   aina1072   nu1427   an,nn2894
13 Therefore they gathered*them*together, and filled twelve baskets with

an,nn2801   pre1537 art3588 nu4002 art,aj2916   nn740   repro3739   aina4052

the fragments of the five barley loaves, which remained*over*and*above unto

art,pfp977

them*that*had*eaten.

3767   art,nn444   apta1492   an,nn4592 repro3739 art,nn2424 aina4160 ipf3004

14 Then those men, when they had seen the miracle that Jesus did, said,

depro3778 pin2076   ad230   pr/art,nn4396   art,ppmp2064   pre1519 art3588   nn2889

This   is of*a*truth that prophet that*should*come into the world.

(Deut. 18:15,18)

an,nn2424   3767   apta1097   3754   pin3195   pifm2064   2532

15 When Jesus therefore perceived that they would come and

pinf726/ppro846   2443 asba4160 ppro846   pr/an,nn935   aina402   ad3825 pre1519   art,nn3735

take*him*by*force, to make him a king, he departed again into a mountain

epn846   an,aj3441

himself alone.

Jesus Walks on Water (Matt. 14:22-33; Mark 6:45-52)

1161   ad5613   an,nn3798   aom1096 ppro846   art,nn3101   aina2597   pre1909 art3588

16 And when even was *now* come, his disciples went down unto the

nn2281

sea,

2532   apta1684   pre1519 art,nn4143   ipf2064 ad4008 art3588 nn2281   pre1519   2584

17 And entered into a ship, and went over the sea toward Capernaum.

2532   plpf1096 ad2235 an,nn4653 2532 art,nn2424   3756 plpf2064 pre4314 ppro846

And it was now dark, and Jesus was not come to them.

5037 (repro3739) an,nn2281 ipf1326   an,aj3173 an,nn417   pap4154

18 And the   sea arose by reason of a great wind that blew.

3767   pfp1643   ad5613   nu4002/nu1501   2228   nu5144   an,nn4712

19 So when they had rowed about five*and*twenty or thirty furlongs, they

pin2334 art,nn2424   pap4043   pre1909 art3588 nn2281   2532   ppmp1096   pr/ad1451   art3588 nn4143   2532

see Jesus walking on the sea, and drawing nigh unto the ship: and they

ainp5399

were afraid.

1161 art3588 pin3004   ppro846   pin1510 pr/epn1473   pim5399/3361

20 But he saith unto them, It is   I; be*not*afraid.

3767   ipf2309   ainf2983   ppro846 pre1519 art3588 nn4143   2532   ad2112   art3588

21 Then they willingly received him into the ship: and immediately the

nn4143 aom1096 pre1909 art3588 nn1093 pre1519/repro3739   ipf5217

ship was at the land whither they went.

art3588   ad1887   art3588 nn3793   art,pfp2476   ad4008

22 The day following, when the people which stood on*the*other*side of

art3588 nn2281 apta1492   3754   ipf2258   3756 an,aj243 an,nn4142 ad1563   1508   depro1565 nu,ajn1520

the sea saw that there was none other boat there, save that one

pre1519/repro3739 ppro848   art,nn3101   aina1684   2532 3754 art,nn2424   aina4897/3756   ppro846

whereinto his disciples were entered, and that Jesus went*not*with his

art,nn3101   pre1519 art3588 nn4142   235   ppro846   art,nn3101   aina565   an,aj3441

disciples into the boat, but *that* his disciples were gone away alone;

1161   aina2064 an,aj243 an,nn4142 pre1537 an,nn5085   ad1451   art3588 nn5117

23 (Howbeit there came other boats from Tiberias nigh unto the place

ad3699   aina5315 art,nn740   art3588 nn2962   apta2168

where they did eat bread, after that the Lord had given thanks:)

ad3753 art3588   nn3793   3767   aina1492 3754 an,nn2424 pin2076 3756 ad1563 3761   ppro846

24 When the people therefore saw that Jesus was not there, neither his

art,nn3101   epn846 2532 aina1684 pre1519/art,nn4143 2532 aina2064 pre1519   2584   pap2212

disciples, they also took shipping, and came to Capernaum, seeking for

art,nn2424

Jesus.

Everlasting Food: Jesus Is the Bread of Life

2532   apta2147 ppro846   ad4008   art3588 nn2281   aina2036

25 And when they had found him on*the*other*side of the sea, they said

ppro846 4461   ad4219   pfi1096   ad5602

unto him, Rabbi, when camest thou hither?

art,nn2424 ainp611   ppro846 2532 aina2036 281   281   pin3004   ppro5213   pin2212

26 Jesus answered them and said, Verily, verily, I say unto you, Ye seek

ppro3165 3756   3754   aina1492   an,nn4592 235   3754   aina5315 pre1537 art3588

me, not because ye saw the miracles, but because ye did eat of the

nn740   2532   ainp5526

loaves, and were filled.

pim2038   3361   art3588   nn1035   art,ppmp622   235   art,nn1035

27 Labor not for the meat which perisheth, but for that meat

art,pap3306   pre1519   an,aj166   an,nn2222 repro3739 art3588 nn5207   art,nn444   ft325

which endureth unto everlasting life, which the Son of man shall give unto

ppro5213 1063 depro5126   art,nn2316 art3588   nn3962   aina4972

you: for him hath God the Father sealed.

3767   aina2036   pre4314 ppro846 inpro5101   psa4160 2443   psmp2038 art3588

28 Then said they unto him, What shall we do, that we might work the

nn2041   art,nn2316

works of God?

art,nn2424   ainp611   2532 aina2036   ppro846 depro5124 pin2076 art3588 pr/nn2041   art,nn2316 2443

29 Jesus answered and said unto them, This is the work of God, that

asba4100   pre1519   repro3739 depro1565   aina649

ye believe on him whom he hath sent.

aina2036   3767   ppro846 inpro5101 an,nn4592   pin4160   epn4771 3767   2443

30 They said therefore unto him, What sign showest thou then, that we

asba1492 2532   asba4100   ppro4671 inpro5101   pinm2038

may see, and believe thee? what dost thou work?

ppro2257 art,nn3962   aina5315   3131   pre1722 art3588 ajn2048   ad2531   pin2076 pr/pfpp1125

31 Our fathers did eat manna in the desert; as it is written, He

aina1325 ppro846 an,nn740 pre1537 art,nn3772   ainf5315

gave them bread from heaven to eat.   (Ex. 16:14,15; Num. 11:7-9; Ps. 78:24)

3767 art,nn2424 aina2036   ppro846   281   281   pin3004   ppro5213 an,nn3475 pfi1325

32 Then Jesus said unto them, Verily, verily, I say unto you, Moses gave

ppro5213 3756   art,nn740 pre1537 art,nn3772   235 ppro3450 art,nn3962 pin1325 ppro5213 art3588 aj228 art,nn740

you not that bread from heaven; but my Father giveth you the true bread

pre1537   art,nn3772

from heaven.

1063   art3588   nn740   art,nn2316 pin2076   pr/art,pap2597   pre1537   art,nn3772   2532

33 For the bread of God   is   he*which*cometh*down from heaven, and

pap1325 an,nn2222   art3588   nn2889

giveth life   unto the world.

3767   aina2036   pre4314 ppro846 an,nn2962   ad3842   aima1325 ppro2254 depro5126 art,nn740

34 Then said they unto him, Lord, evermore give   us   this bread.

1161   art,nn2424   aina2036   ppro846   epn1473 pin1510 art3588   pr/nn740   art,nn2222

35 And Jesus   said   unto them,   I   am   the   bread of   life:

art,ppmp2064   pre4314 ppro3165   efn3364   asba3983   2532   art,pap4100   pre1519

he*that*cometh to   me   shall never hunger; and he*that*believeth on

ppro1691   efn3364/ad4455 asba1372

me shall never thirst.

235   aina2036   ppro5213 3754   2532   pfi3708 ppro3165 2532   pin4100   3756

36 But I said unto you, That ye also have seen me, and believe not.

an,aj3956 repro3739 art3588   nn3962   pin1325   ppro3427   ft2240   pre4314 ppro1691   2532

37 All   that   the Father giveth   me   shall   come   to   me;   and

art,ppmp2064   pre4314 ppro3165   efn3364   asba1544 ad1854

him*that*cometh to   me I will in*no*wise cast out.

3754   pfi2597   pre1537 art,nn3772   3756 2443 psa4160   art,popro1699 art,nn2307 235 art3588 nn2307

38 For I came down from heaven, not to   do mine own will, but the will

art,apta3992   ppro3165

of him*that*sent me.

1161   depro5124 pin2076 art3588   nn3962   pr/art,nn2307   apta3992 ppro3165 2443   an,aj3956

39 And this   is   the Father's   will   which hath sent me, that of all

repro3739   pfi1325   ppro3427   (3361)   asba622 pre1537/ppro846 235   asba450/ppro846

which he hath given me I should lose nothing, but should raise*it*up*again

pre1722 art3588 aj2078 an,nn2250

at the last day.

1161   depro5124 pin2076 art3588 pr/nn2307   art,apta3992   ppro3165   2443   an,aj3956

40 And this   is   the   will   of him*that*sent me, that every one

art,pap2334   art3588 nn5207   2532   pap4100   pre1519 ppro846   psa2192   an,aj166   an,nn2222 2532

which seeth the Son, and believeth on   him, may have everlasting life: and

epn1473   ft450/ppro846   art3588 aj2078 an,nn2250

I will raise*him*up at the last day.

art3588   nn2453   3767   ipf1111   pre4012 ppro846   3754   aina2036 epn1473 pin1510 art3588

41 The Jews then murmured at him, because he said,   I   am   the

pr/nn740   art,apta2597   pre1537 art,nn3772

bread which*came*down from heaven.

2532   ipf3004 pin2076 3756 depro3778 pr/an,nn2424 art3588 pr/nn5207   2501   repro3739 art,nn3962

42 And they said, Is not this Jesus, the son of Joseph, whose father

2532   art,nn3384 epn2249 pin1492 ad4459   3767   depro3778 pin3004   pfi2597   pre1537

and mother we   know? how is it then that he   saith, I came down from

art,nn3772

heaven?

art,nn2424   3767   ainp611   2532 aina2036   ppro846   pim1111   3361   pre3326

43 Jesus therefore answered and said unto them, Murmur not among

rcpro240

yourselves.

an,ajn3762 pinm1410 ainf2064 pre4314 ppro3165   3362   art3588   nn3962   art,apta3992   ppro3165

44 No man can   come   to   me, except the   Father which*hath*sent me

asba1670 ppro846 2532 epn1473   ft450/ppro846   art3588 aj2078 an,nn2250

draw him: and   I   will raise*him*up at the last day.

pin2076   pr/pfpp1125   pre1722 art3588   nn4396   2532   fm2071   an,ajn3956   pr/an,aj1318
45 It   is   written   in   the   prophets,   And they shall be   all   taught of

art,nn2316   an,aj3956   3767   art,apta191   2532   apta3129   pre3844   art3588
God. Every   man   therefore   that*hath*heard,   and   hath   learned   of   the

nn3962   pinm2064   pre4314   ppro3165
Father, cometh   unto   me.   *(Is. 54:13)*

3756   3754   idpro5100   pfi3708 art3588   nn3962   1508   art,pap5607   pre3844   art,nn2316
46 Not that   any   man hath   seen   the   Father,   save   he*which*is   of   God,

depro3778   pfi3708   art3588   nn3962
he   hath seen the   Father.

281   281   pin3004   ppro5213   art,pap4100   pre1519   ppro1691   pin2192
47 Verily,   verily,   I   say   unto   you,   He*that*believeth   on   me   hath

an,aj166   an,nn2222
everlasting   life.

epn1473 pin1510   pr/art,nn740   art,nn2222
48 I   am that bread of life.

ppro5216   art,nn3962   aina5315 (art3588)   3131   pre1722 art3588   ajn2048   2532   aina599
49 Your fathers did eat   manna   in   the   wilderness, and are dead.

depro3778 pin2076 art3588 pr/nn740   art,pap2597   pre1537 art,nn3772   2443   idpro5100
50 This   is   the bread which*cometh*down from heaven, that a man may

asba5315 pre1537/ppro846 2532 3361 asba599
eat   thereof, and not die.

epn1473 pin1510 art3588 pap2198 pr/art,nn740   art,apta2597   pre1537 art,nn3772   1437   idpro5100
51 I   am the living bread which*came*down from heaven: if any man

asba5315 pre1537 depro5127 art,nn740   fm2198 pre1519/art,nn165 1161 art3588 nn740   repro3739 epn1473   ft1325
eat   of   this   bread, he shall live forever: and the bread that   I   will give

pin2076 ppro3450 pr/art,nn4561 repro3739 epn1473   ft1325 pre5228 art3588 nn2222   art3588   nn2889
is   my   flesh, which   I   will give for the life of the world.

art3588   nn2453   3767   ipf3164   pre4314   rcpro240   pap3004   ad4459   pinm1410
52 The Jews   therefore   strove   among   themselves,   saying,   How   can

depro3778   ainf1325 ppro2254   art,nn4561   ainf5315
this man give   us   *his* flesh to eat?

3767   art,nn2424 aina2036   ppro846   281   281   pin3004   ppro5213   3362
53 Then Jesus said unto them, Verily, verily, I say unto you, Except ye

asba5315 art3588 nn4561   art3588 nn5207   art,nn444 2532 asba4095 ppro846 art,nn129   pin2192 3756 an,nn2222 pre1722
eat   the flesh of the Son of man, and drink his blood, ye have no   life   in

rxpro1438
you.

art,pap5176   ppro3450 art,nn4561   2532   pap4095   ppro3450 art,nn129   pin2192   an,aj166   an,nn2222
54 Whoso eateth   my   flesh, and   drinketh   my   blood, hath eternal life;

2532 epn1473   ft450/ppro846   art3588 aj2078 an,nn2250
and   I   will raise*him*up at the last day.

1063 ppro3450 art,nn4561 pin2076 pr/an,nn1035 ad230   2532 ppro3450 art,nn129 pin2076 pr/an,nn4213 ad230
55 For my flesh   is   meat indeed, and my blood is   drink indeed.

art,pap5176   ppro3450 art,nn4561 2532   pap4095   ppro3450 art,nn129   pin3306   pre1722 epn1698
56 He*that*eateth   my   flesh, and drinketh   my   blood, dwelleth   in   me,

epn2504 pre1722 ppro846
and I   in   him.

ad2531 art3588 an,pap2198   nn3962   aina649 ppro3165 epn2504 pin2198 pre1223 art3588   nn3962   2532
57 As the living Father hath sent me, and I live   by   the Father: so

art,pap5176   ppro3165 depro2548   fm2198 pre1223 epn1691
he*that*eateth me, even he shall live   by   me.

depro3778 pin2076   pr/art,nn740   art,apta2597   pre1537 art,nn3772   3756 ad2531 ppro5216

58 This is that bread which*came*down from heaven: not as your

art,nn3962   aina5315 (art3588) 3131   2532   aina599   art,pap5176   depro5126 art,nn740

fathers did eat   manna, and are dead: he*that*eateth of this bread shall

fm2198 pre1519/art,nn165

live forever.

depro5023   aina2036   pre1722   an,nn4864   pap1321   pre1722

59 These things said he in the synagogue, as he taught in

2584

Capernaum.

Many Disciples Desert Jesus

an,aj4183   3767   pre1537 ppro846   art,nn3101   apta191   aina2036

60 Many therefore of his disciples, when they had heard *this,* said,

depro3778 pin2076   pr/an,aj4642 art,nn3056 inpro5101 pinm1410 pinf191 ppro846

This is a hard saying; who can hear it?

1161   art,nn2424   pfp1492 pre1722   rxpro1438   3754   ppro846   art,nn3101   pin1111   pre4012 depro5127

61 When Jesus knew in himself that his disciples murmured at it, he

aina2036   ppro846   depro5124 pin4624 ppro5209

said unto them, Doth this offend you?

3767 1437   psa2334 art3588 nn5207   art,nn444   pap305   ad3699   ipf2258

62 *What* and if ye shall see the Son of man ascend up where he was

art,ajn4386

before?

pin2076 art3588   nn4151   pr/art,pap2227   art3588   nn4561   (3756)   pin5623   an,ajn3762   art3588

63 It is the spirit that quickeneth; the flesh   profiteth nothing: the

nn4487   repro3739 epn1473 pin2980   ppro5213   pin2076 pr/an,nn4151 2532   pin2076 pr/an,nn2222

words that I speak unto you, *they* are spirit, and *they* are life.

235   pin1526 idpro5100 pre1537 ppro5216 repro3739   pin4100   3756   1063 art,nn2424 ipf1492   pre1537

64 But there are some of you that believe not. For Jesus knew from

an,nn746   inpro5101   pin1526   pr/art,pap4100   3361 2532 inpro5101   pin2076   pr/art,fpta3860 ppro846

the beginning who they were that believed not, and who should betray him.

2532   ipf3004   pre1223/depro5124 pfi2046   ppro5213 3754   an,ajn3762 pinm1410 ainf2064   pre4314

65 And he said, Therefore said I unto you, that no man can come unto

ppro3165   3362   psa5600 pr/pfpp1325   ppro846 pre1537 ppro3450   art,nn3962

me, except it were given unto him of my Father.

pre1537   depro5127   an,ajn4183   ppro846   art,nn3101   aina565   pre1519/art,ad3694   2532   ipf4043

66 From that *time* many of his disciples went   back,   and walked

ad3765   pre3326 ppro846

no more with him.

3767   aina2036 art,nn2424   art3588   nu,ajn1427 pin2309 (3361) epn5210 2532   ainf5217

67 Then said Jesus unto the twelve, Will   ye also go away?

3767   an,nn4613   an,nn4074   ainp611   ppro846 an,nn2962 pre4314 inpro5101   fm565

68 Then Simon Peter answered him, Lord, to whom shall we go? thou

pin2192   an,nn4487   an,aj166   an,nn2222

hast the words of eternal life.

2532   epn2249   pfi4100   2532   pfi1097   3754   epn4771 pin1488   pr/art,nn5547 art3588   pr/nn5207

69 And we believe and are sure that thou art that Christ, the Son of

art3588   pap2198 art,nn2316

the living God.

art,nn2424   ainp611   ppro846   3756 epn1473 aom1586   ppro5209 art,nu,ajn1427 2532 nu1520 pre1537

70 Jesus answered them, Have not I chosen you twelve, and one of

ppro5216 pin2076   pr/an,ajn1228

you is a devil?

   (1161)   ipf3004   art,nn2455   an,ajn2469   an,nn4613   1063 depro3778

71 He spake of Judas Iscariot *the son* of Simon: for he it was that

ipf3195   pinf3860   ppro846   pap5607 pr/nu1520 pre1537 art3588   nu,ajn1427

should betray him, being one of the twelve.

Jesus at the Feast of Tabernacles

   (2532)   pre3326   depro5023   art,nn2424 ipf4043   pre1722   art,nn1056 1063   ipf2309 3756 pinf4043

7 After these things Jesus walked in Galilee: for he would not walk

pre1722 art,nn2449   3754   art3588 nn2453   ipf2212   ainf615 ppro846

in Jewry, because the Jews sought to kill him.

   1161   art3588   nn2453   art,nn1859   art,nn4634   ipf2258   pr/ad1451

2 Now the Jews' feast of tabernacles was at hand.   *(Lev. 23:34)*

    ppro846   art,nn80   3767   aina2036   pre4314 ppro846   aima3327   ad1782   2532 aima5217

3 His brethren therefore said unto him, Depart hence, and go

pre1519 art,nn2449 2443 ppro4675 art,nn3101   2532   asba2334 (ppro4675) art3588 nn2041   repro3739

into Judea, that thy disciples also may see the works that thou

pin4160

doest.

    1063   an,ajn3762   pin4160   idpro5100   pre1722 an,ajn2927 2532 epn846

4 For *there is* no man *that* doeth any thing in secret, and he himself

pin2212   pinf1511   pre1722/an,nn3954   1487   pin4160   depro5023   aima5319 rxpro4572   art3588

seeketh to be known openly. If thou do these things, show thyself to the

nn2889

world.

   1063   3761   ppro846 art,nn80   ipf4100 pre1519 ppro846

5 For neither did his brethren believe in him.

   3767   art,nn2424 pin3004   ppro846 art,popro1699 art,nn2540   ad3768   pin3918   1161 art,popro5212

6 Then Jesus said unto them, My time is not yet come: but your

art,nn2540 pin2076   ad3842   pr/an,aj2092

time is always ready.

   art3588   nn2889 pinm1410/3756 pinf3404 epn5209 1161 epn1691   pin3404   3754   epn1473 pin3140 pre4012

7 The world cannot hate you; but me it hateth, because I testify of

ppro846 3754 art3588   nn2041   ppro846   pin2076 pr/an,aj4190

it, that the works thereof are evil.

    aima305/epn5210   pre1519 depro5026 art,nn1859 epn1473   pin305/ad3768   pre1519 depro5026 art,nn1859 3754

8 Go*ye*up unto this feast: I go*not*up*yet unto this feast; for

art,popro1699 art,nn2540   ad3768   pfip4137

my time is not yet full come.

   1161   apta2036 depro5023   ppro846   aina3306   pre1722 art,nn1056

9 When he had said these words unto them, he abode *still* in Galilee.

   1161 ad5613 ppro846 art,nn80   aina305 ad5119   aina305/epn846/2532   pre1519 art3588

10 But when his brethren were gone up, then went*he*also*up unto the

nn1859 3756 ad5320 235   ad5613   pre1722 an,ajn2927

feast, not openly, but as*it*were in secret.

　　　3767　　art3588　nn2453　　　ipf2212　　ppro846 pre1722 art3588　　nn1859　　2532　　ipf3004　　ad4226　pin2076 depro1565

11 Then the Jews sought him at the feast, and said, Where is he?

　　2532　　　　　　ipf2258　an,aj4183　　　an,nn1112　　pre1722　art3588　　nn3793　　　pre4012　　ppro846　1063

12 And there was much murmuring among the people concerning him: for

art3588/3303 ipf3004　　pin2076　　pr/an,aj18　　(1161)　an,ajn243 ipf3004　3756　235　　　　pin4105　　art3588

some said, He is a good man:　　others said, Nay; but he deceiveth the

nn3793

people.

　　　3305　an,ajn3762　ipf2980　an,nn3954　pre4012 ppro846 pre1223 art,nn5401　　art3588　nn2453

13 Howbeit no man spake openly of him for fear of the Jews.

　　1161　ad2235　　an,pap3322　art3588　nn1859　art,nn2424　　aina305　pre1519 art3588　　nn2411　2532

14 Now about the midst of the feast Jesus went up into the temple, and

ipf1321

taught.

　　2532　art3588　nn2453　　ipf2296　　pap3004　ad4459　pin1492　depro3778　an,nn1121

15 And the Jews marveled, saying, How knoweth this man letters, having

3361　　pfp3129

never learned?

　　art,nn2424　ainp611　ppro846　2532　aina2036 art,popro1699　an,nn1322　pin2076　3756 pr/popro1699　235

16 Jesus answered them, and said, My doctrine is not mine, but

art,apta3992　ppro3165

his*that*sent me.

　　1437　　idpro5100　psa2309 pinf4160 ppro846 art,nn2307　　　　fm1097　pre4012 art3588　　nn1322

17 If any man will do his will, he shall know of the doctrine,

an,ajn4220　pin2076 pre1537 art,nn2316 2228　　epn1473 pin2980 pre575 rxpro1683

whether it be of God, or *whether* I speak of myself.

　　　　art,pap2980　　pre575　rxpro1438　pin2212　　　art,aj2398　art,nn1391　1161

18 He*that*speaketh of himself seeketh his own glory: but

art,pap2212　art,nn1391　art,apta3992 ppro846　depro3778　pin2076 pr/an,aj227　2532　3756

he*that*seeketh his glory that sent him, the same is true, and no

an,nn93　　pin2076 pre1722 ppro846

unrighteousness is in him.

　　　3756　an,nn3475　pfi1325 ppro5213 art3588　nn3551　2532　　an,ajn3762 pre1537 ppro5216　pin4160　art3588

19 Did not Moses give you the law, and *yet* none of you keepeth the

nn3551 inpro5101　　pin2212　　ainf615 ppro3165

law? Why go*ye*about to kill me?　　　　　　　　　　(*Deut. 4:44,45*)

　　art3588　nn3793　ainp611　2532 aina2036　　pin2192　an,nn1140 inpro5101　pin2212

20 The people answered and said, Thou hast a devil: who goeth about to

ainf615 ppro4571

kill thee?

　　art,nn2424　ainp611　2532 aina2036　　ppro846　　aina4160 nu1520 an,nn2041　2532

21 Jesus answered and said unto them, I have done one work, and ye

an,ajn3956　pin2296

all marvel.

　　an,nn3475 pre1223/depro5124 pfi1325　ppro5213　art,nn4061　　3756　3754　pin2076 pre1537

22 Moses therefore gave unto you circumcision; (not because it is of

art,nn3475　235 pre1537 art3588　nn3962　　2532　pre1722　an,nn4521　　pin4059　an,nn444

Moses, but of the fathers;) and ye on the sabbath day circumcise a man.

　　　　　　　　　　　　　　　　　　(*Lev. 12:3; Gen. 17:10-13*)

　　1487　an,nn444 pre1722　　an,nn4521　　pin2983　an,nn4061　　2443 art3588 nn3551

23 If a man on the sabbath day receive circumcision, that the law of

an,nn3475   3361   asbp3089   pin5520   ppro1698   3754   aina4160

Moses should not be broken; are*ye*angry at me, because I have made a
an,nn444   an,aj3650   pr/an,aj5199 pre1722   an,nn4521

man every whit whole on the sabbath day?
        pim2919   3361   pre2596   an,nn3799   235   aima2919 art,aj1342   an,nn2920

24 Judge not according to the appearance, but judge righteous judgment.

(Is. 11:3,4)

Divisions Concerning Who Christ Is

        3767   ipf3004 idpro5100 pre1537   art,ajn2415   pin2076 3756 depro3778   pr/repro3739

25 Then said some of them*of*Jerusalem, Is not this he, whom they
pin2212   ainf615

seek to kill?
        2532 aima2396   pin2980   an,nn3954   2532   pin3004 an,ajn3762   ppro846 (3379) art3588

26 But, lo, he speaketh boldly, and they say nothing unto him. Do the
nn758   aina1097   ad230   3754 depro3778 pin2076 art3588 ad230   pr/nn5547

rulers know indeed that this   is   the very Christ?
        235   pin1492   depro5126   ad4159   pin2076 1161   ad3752   art,nn5547   psa2064

27 Howbeit we know this man whence he is: but when Christ cometh,
an,ajn3762   pin1097   ad4159   pin2076

no man knoweth whence he is.
        3767   aina2896 art,nn2424 pre1722 art3588   nn2411   pap1321 (2532) pap3004

28 Then   cried Jesus in   the   temple as he taught,   saying, Ye
epn2504/pin1492   2532   pin1492   ad4159   pin1510 2532   3756   pfi2064   pre575   rxpro1683

both*know*me, and ye know whence I am: and I am not come of myself,
235   art,apta3992   ppro3165 pin2076 pr/an,aj228 repro3739 epn5210 pin1492   3756

but he*that*sent me is true, whom ye know not.
        1161 epn1473 pin1492 ppro846 3754   pin1510 pre3844 ppro846 depro2548   aina649 ppro3165

29 But I   know him: for I am from him, and he hath sent me.
        3767   ipf2212   ainf4084 ppro846   2532   an,ajn3762   aina1911 art,nn5495 pre1909 ppro846

30 Then they sought to take him: but no man laid hands on him,
3754   ppro846 art,nn5610   ad3768   plpf2064

because his hour was not yet come.
        1161 an,ajn4183 pre1537 art3588   nn3793   aina4100   pre1519 ppro846   2532   ipf3004   ad3752   art,nn5547

31 And many of the people believed on him, and said, When Christ
asba2064   (3385)   ft4160 cd/an,aj4119 an,nn4592   depro5130 repro3739 depro3778   aina4160

cometh, will he do more miracles than these which this *man* hath done?

Officers Sent to Arrest Jesus

        art3588   nn5330   aina191   art3588   nn3793   pap1111   depro5023   pre4012

32 The Pharisees heard that the people murmured such things concerning
ppro846 2532 art3588   nn5330   2532 art3588   nn749   aina649 an,nn5257 2443 asba4084 ppro846

him; and the Pharisees and the chief priests sent officers to take him.
        3767   aina2036 art,nn2424   ppro846   ad2089   an,aj3398 an,nn5550 pin1510   pre3326 ppro5216 2532

33 Then said Jesus unto them, Yet a little while am I with you, and *then*
pin5217 pre4314   art,apta3992   ppro3165

I go unto him*that*sent me.

ft2212 ppro3165 2532 3756 ft2147 2532 ad3699 epn1473 pin1510
34 Ye shall seek me, and shall not find *me*: and where I am, *thither*

epn5210 pinm1410/3756 ainf2064
ye cannot come.

3767 aina2036 art3588 nn2453 pre4314 rxpro1438 ad4226 pin3195 depro3778 pifm4198 3754
35 Then said the Jews among themselves, Whither will he go, that

epn2249 3756 ft2147 ppro846 pin3195 (3371) pifm4198 pre1519 art3588 nn1290 art3588 nn1672
we shall not find him? will he go unto the dispersed among the Gentiles,

2532 pinf1321 art3588 nn1672
and teach the Gentiles?

pr/inpro5101 art,nn3056 pin2076 depro3778 repro3739 aina2036 ft2212 ppro3165 2532
36 What *manner of* saying is this that he said, Ye shall seek me, and

3756 ft2147 2532 ad3699 epn1473 pin1510 epn5210 pinm1410/3756 ainf2064
shall not find *me*: and where I am, *thither* ye cannot come?

"Rivers of Living Water"

(1161) pre1722 art3588 aj2078 an,nn2250 art,aj3173 art3588 nn1859 art,nn2424 plpf2476 2532 aina2896
37 In the last day, that great *day* of the feast, Jesus stood and cried,

pap3004 1437 idpro5100 psa1372 pim2064 pre4314 ppro3165 2532 pim4095
saying, If any man thirst, let him come unto me, and drink.

(Lev. 23:36; Is. 55:1)

art,pap4100 pre1519 ppro1691 ad2531 art3588 nn1124 aina2036 pre1537 ppro846
38 He*that*believeth on me, as the Scripture hath said, out of his

art,nn2836 ft4482 an,nn4215 pap2198 an,nn5204
belly shall flow rivers of living water. *(Prov. 18:4; Is. 58:11)*

1161 depro5124 aina2036 pre4012 art3588 nn4151 repro3739 art,pap4100 pre1519 ppro846
39 (But this spake he of the Spirit, which they*that*believe on him

ipf3195 pinf2983 1063 an,aj40 an,nn4151 ipf2258 ad3768 3754 art,nn2424
should receive: for the Holy Ghost was not yet *given*; because that Jesus was

ad3764 ainp1392
not yet glorified.)

Division Among the People

an,ajn4183 pre1537 art3588 nn3793 3767 apta191 art,nn3056 ipf3004
40 Many of the people therefore, when they heard this saying, said,

ad230 depro3778 pin2076 art3588 pr/nn4396
Of*a*truth this is the Prophet. *(Deut. 18:15)*

an,ajn243 ipf3004 depro3778 pin2076 art3588 pr/nn5547 1161 an,ajn243 ipf3004 (1063 3361) art,nn5547 pinm2064
41 Others said, This is the Christ. But some said, Shall Christ come

pre1537 art,nn1056
out of Galilee?

3780 art3588 nn1124 aina2036 3754 art,nn5547 pinm2064 pre1537 art3588 nn4690
42 Hath not the Scripture said, That Christ cometh of the seed of

1138 2532 pre575 art3588 nn2968 965 ad3699 1138 ipf2258
David, and out of the town of Bethlehem, where David was? *(Mic. 5:2)*

3767   aom1096   an,nn4978   pre1722 art3588   nn3793   pre1223   ppro846

43 So there was a division among the people because of him.

1161   dpro5100 pre1537 ppro846   ipf2309   ainf4084 ppro846   235   an,ajn3762   aina1911 art,nn5495 pre1909

44 And some of them would have taken him; but no man laid hands on

ppro846

him.

Unbelieving Rulers

3767   aina2064 art3588   nn5257   pre4314 art3588   nn749   2532   an,nn5330   2532 depro1565

45 Then came the officers to the chief priests and Pharisees; and they

aina2036   ppro846   pre,inpro1302   3756   aina71   ppro846

said unto them, Why have ye not brought him?

art3588   nn5257   ainp611   ad3762   an,nn444 aina2980   (ad3779) ad5613 depro3778 art,nn444

46 The officers answered, Never man spake   like this man.

3767   ainp611   ppro846 art3588   nn5330   (3361) epn5210 2532   pfip4105

47 Then answered them the Pharisees, Are ye also deceived?

idpro3387 pre1537 art3588   nn758   2228 pre1537 art3588   nn5330   aina4100   pre1519 ppro846

48 Have any of the rulers or of the Pharisees believed on him?

235   depro3778 art,nn3793   art,pap1097   3361 art3588 nn3551 pin1526 pr/an,aj1944

49 But this people who knoweth not the law are cursed.

an,nn3530   pin3004 pre4314   ppro846   art,apta2064   pre4314 ppro846   an,nn3571   pap5607

50 Nicodemus saith unto them, (he*that*came to Jesus by night, being

pr/nu1520 pre1537   ppro846

one of them,)

ppro2257 art,nn3551 (3361)   pin2919   art,nn444 an,ajn4386/3362   asba191 (pre3844) ppro846 2532 asba1097

51 Doth our law   judge *any* man, before it hear   him, and know

inpro5101   pin4160

what he doeth?

ainp611   2532   aina2036   ppro846 pin1488 (3361) epn4771   2532   pre1537   art,nn1056

☞ 52 They answered and said unto him, Art   thou also of Galilee?

aima2045   2532 aima1492   3754   pre1537   art,nn1056   pfip1453   3756   an,nn4396

Search, and look: for out of Galilee ariseth no prophet.

2532   an,ajn1538   ainp4198 pre1519   ppro848   art,nn3624

53 And every man went unto his own house.

A Woman Taken in Adultery

(1161) an,nn2424 ainp4198 pre1519 art3588   nn3735   art,nn1636

8 Jesus went unto the mount of Olives.

1161   an,nn3722   aom3854 ad3825 pre1519 art3588   nn2411   2532

2 And early*in*the*morning he came again into the temple, and

an,aj3956 art3588   nn2992   ipf2064   pre4314 ppro846 2532   apta2523   ipf1321   ppro846

all the people came unto him; and he sat down, and taught them.

☞ **7:52** The Pharisees were challenging the statement that the people made in verse forty concerning Christ being "the Prophet." The Pharisee's argument was based on the assumption that in all of Scripture,

(continued on next page)

3 And the scribes and Pharisees brought unto him a woman taken in adultery; and when they had set her in the midst,

4 They say unto him, Master, this woman was taken in adultery, in*the*very*act.

5 Now Moses in the law commanded us, that such should be stoned: but what sayest thou?   *(Lev. 20:10; Deut. 22:22)*

6 This they said, tempting him, that they might have to accuse him. But Jesus stooped down, and with *his* finger wrote on the ground, *as though he heard them not.*

7 So when they continued asking him, he lifted up himself, and said unto them, He*that*is*without*sin among you, let him first cast a stone at her.

(Deut. 17:7)

8 And again he stooped down, and wrote on the ground.

9 And they*which*heard *it,* being convicted by *their own* conscience, went out one*by*one, beginning at the eldest, *even* unto the last: and Jesus was left alone, and the woman standing in the midst.

10 When Jesus had lifted up himself, and saw none but the woman, he said unto her, Woman, where are those thine accusers? hath no man condemned thee?

11 She said, No man, Lord. And Jesus said unto her, Neither do I condemn thee: go, and sin no more.

(continued from previous page)
no prophets ever came out of Galilee. When Nicodemus entreated the other Pharisees to consider Christ's words before determining whether or not He spoke the truth, they sought to confuse the issue and discredit Christ's ministry. However, their arguments were faulty. First of all, Christ did not grow up in Galilee, but He was born in Bethlehem of Judah. The Pharisees probably made this assumption because Christ's followers were mostly from Galilee. Another mistake that they made was that they told Nicodemus to search the Scriptures; they had forgotten that there was a prophet that came from the area of Galilee. Jonah was called by God to go to Nineveh from the city of Gath-hepher (1 Kgs. 14:25).

Jesus Is the True Light

3767 aina2980 art,nn2424 ad3825 pproc846 pap3004 epn1473 pin1510 art3588 pr/nn5457 art3588
12 Then spake Jesus again unto them, saying, I am the light of the
nn2889 art,pap190 ppro1698 efn3364 ft4043 pre1722 art,nn4653 235 ft2192 art3588
world: he*that*followeth me shall not walk in darkness, but shall have the
nn5457 art,nn2222
light of life.

art3588 nn5330 3767 aina2036 ppro846 epn4771 pin3140 pre4012
13 The Pharisees therefore said unto him, Thou bearest record of
rxpro4572 ppro4675 art,nn3141 pin2076 3756 pr/an,aj227
thyself; thy record is not true.

an,nn2424 ainp611 2532 aina2036 ppro846 2579 epn1473 pin3140 pre4012
14 Jesus answered and said unto them, Though I bear record of
rxpro1683 ppro3450 art,nn3141 pin2076 pr/an,aj227 3754 pin1492 ad4159 aina2064 2532 ad4226
myself, *yet* my record is true: for I know whence I came, and whither I
pin5217 1161 epn5210 pin1492/3756 ad4159 pinm2064 2532 ad4226 pin5217
go; but ye cannot tell whence I come, and whither I go.

epn5210 pin2919 pre2596 art3588 nn4561 epn1473 pin2919 an,ajn3762
15 Ye judge after the flesh; I judge no man.

2532 1161 1437 epn1473 psa2919 art,popro1699 art,nn2920 pin2076 pr/an,aj227 3754 pin1510 3756 pr/an,aj3441
16 And yet if I judge, my judgment is true: for I am not alone,
235 epn1473 2532 art3588 nn3962 art,apta3992 ppro3165
but I and the Father that sent me.

(2532) 1161 pfip1125 pre1722 art,popro5212 art,nn3551 3754 art3588 nn3141 nu1417 an,nn444 pin2076
17 It is also written in your law, that the testimony of two men is
pr/an,aj227
true.   *(Deut. 17:6; 19:15)*

epn1473 pin1510 pr/art,pap3140 pre4012 rxpro1683 2532 art3588 nn3962 art3588 apta3992
18 I am one*that*bear*witness of myself, and the Father that sent
ppro3165 pin3140 pre4012 ppro1700
me beareth witness of me.

3767 ipf3004 ppro846 ad4226 pin2076 ppro4675 art,nn3962 art,nn2424 ainp611
19 Then said they unto him, Where is thy Father? Jesus answered, Ye
3777 pin1492 epn1691 3777 ppro3450 art,nn3962 1487 ipf1492 epn1691
neither know me, nor my Father: if ye had known me, ye should have
ipf1492/302 ppro3450 art,nn3962 2532
known my Father also.

depro5023 art,nn4487 aina2980 art,nn2424 pre1722 art3588 nn1049 pap1321 pre1722 art3588
20 These words spake Jesus in the treasury, as he taught in the
nn2411 2532 an,ajn3762 aina4084 ppro846 3754 ppro846 art,nn5610 ad3768 plpf2064
temple: and no man laid*hands*on him; for his hour was not yet come.

3767 aina2036 art,nn2424 ad3825 ppro846 epn1473 pin5217 2532 ft2212
21 Then said Jesus again unto them, I go*my*way, and ye shall seek
ppro3165 2532 fm599 pre1722 ppro5216 art,nn266 ad3699 epn1473 pin5217 epn5210 pinm1410/3756 ainf2064
me, and shall die in your sins: whither I go, ye cannot come.

3767 ipf3004 art3588 nn2453 (3385) ft615 rxpro1438 3754 pin3004 ad3699
22 Then said the Jews, Will he kill himself? because he saith, Whither
epn1473 pin5217 epn5210 pinm1410/3756 ainf2064
I go, ye cannot come.

8:12 See note on 1 John 1:5–10.

2532 aina2036   ppro846 epn5210 pin2075 pre1537 art,ad2736 epn1473 pin1510 pre1537 art,ad507

23 And he said unto them, Ye are from beneath; I am from above:

epn5210 pin2075 pre1537 depro5127 art,nn2889 epn1473 pin1510 3756 pre1537 depro5127 art,nn2889

ye are of this world; I am not of this world.

aina2036 3767   ppro5213 3754   fm599 pre1722 ppro5216 art,nn266 1063 1437

24 I said therefore unto you, that ye shall die in your sins: for if ye

asba4100 3361 3754 epn1473 pin1510   fm599 pre1722 ppro5216 art,nn266

believe not that I am *he,* ye shall die in your sins.

3767 ipf3004   ppro846 pr/inpro5101 pin1488 epn4771 2532 art,nn2424 aina2036   ppro846

25 Then said they unto him, Who art thou? And Jesus saith unto them,

2532   repro3748 pin2980 ppro5213 art3588 nn746

Even *the same* that I said unto you from the beginning.

pin2192 an,ajn4183 pinf2980 2532 pinf2919 pre4012 ppro5216 235 art,apta3992

26 I have many things to say and to judge of you: but he*that*sent

ppro3165 pin2076 pr/an,aj227 epn2504 pin3004 pre1519 art3588 nn2889   depro5023   repro3739   aina191

me is true; and I speak to the world those things which I have heard

pre3844 ppro846

of him.

aina1097 3756 3754   ipf3004   ppro846 art3588 nn3962

27 They understood not that he spake to them of the Father.

3767 aina2036 art,nn2424   ppro846 ad3752   asba5312 art3588 nn5207 art,nn444

28 Then said Jesus unto them, When ye have lifted up the Son of man,

ad5119   fm1097 3754 epn1473 pin1510 2532   pin4160 an,ajn3762 pre575 rxpro1683 235 ad2531

then shall ye know that I am *he,* and *that* I do nothing of myself; but as

ppro3450 art,nn3962   aina1321 ppro3165 pin2980 depro5023

my Father hath taught me, I speak these things.

2532 art,apta3992   ppro3165 pin2076 pre3326 ppro1700 art3588 nn3962   3756 aina863 ppro3165

29 And he*that*sent me is with me: the Father hath not left me

pr/an,aj3441 3754 epn1473 pin4160 ad3842   art,ajn701   ppro846

alone; for I do always those*things*that*please him.

ppro846 pap2980 depro5023 an,ajn4183 aina4100 pre1519 ppro846

30 As he spake these words, many believed on him.

The Truth Frees You

3767 ipf3004 art,nn2424 pre4314   art,nn2453   pfp4100   ppro846 1437 epn5210

☞ 31 Then said Jesus to those Jews which believed on him, If ye

asba3306 pre1722 art,popro1699 art,nn3056 pin2075 ppro3450 pr/art,nn3101 ad230

continue in my word, *then* are ye my disciples indeed;

2532   fm1097 art3588 nn225 2532 art3588 nn225   ft1659/ppro5209

32 And ye shall know the truth, and the truth shall make*you*free.

ainp611   ppro846   pin2070   11   pr/an,nn4690 2532

33 They answered him, We be Abraham's seed, and

pfi1398/ad4455   an,ajn3762 ad4459 pin3004 epn4771   fm1096

were*never*in*bondage to any man: how sayest thou, Ye shall be made

pr/an,aj1658

free?

☞ **8:31, 32** See notes on Hebrews 6:1–6 and 1 John 3:6–9.

art,nn2424   ainp611   ppro846   281   281   pin3004   ppro5213   an,aj3956

34 Jesus answered them, Verily, verily, I say unto you, Whosoever

art,pap4160   art,nn266 pin2076   pr/an,ajn1401   art,nn266

committeth sin is the servant of sin.

1161   art3588   ajn1401   pin3306   3756   pre1722 art3588   nn3614   pre1519/art,nn165   art3588   nn5207

35 And the servant abideth not in the house forever: *but* the Son

pin3306   pre1519/art,nn165

abideth ever.

1437   art3588   nn5207   3767   asba1659/ppro5209   fm2071   pr/an,aj1658

36 If the Son therefore shall make*you*free, ye shall be free

ad3689

indeed.

pin1492   3754   pin2075   11   pr/an,nn4690   235   pin2212   ainf615 ppro3165   3754

37 I know that ye are Abraham's seed; but ye seek to kill me, because

art,popro1699 art,nn3056   pin5562/3756   pre1722 ppro5213

my word hath*no*place in you.

epn1473   pin2980   repro3739   pfi3708   pre3844 ppro3450   art,nn3962   2532 epn5210 pin4160

38 I speak that which I have seen with my Father: and ye do that

repro3739   (3767)   pfi3708   pre3844 ppro5216   art,nn3962

which ye have seen with your father.

ainp611   2532   aina2036   ppro846   pr/11   pin2076 ppro2257   art,nn3962   art,nn2424

39 They answered and said unto him, Abraham is our father. Jesus

pin3004   ppro846 1487   ipf2258   11   pr/an,nn5043   ipf4160/302 art3588   nn2041

saith unto them, If ye were Abraham's children, ye would do the works of

11

Abraham.

1161   ad3568   pin2212   ainf615 ppro3165   an,nn444 repro3739   pfi2980 ppro5213 art3588   nn225

40 But now ye seek to kill me, a man that hath told you the truth,

repro3739   aina191   pre3844 art,nn2316 depro5124 aina4160 3756   11

which I have heard of God: this did not Abraham.

epn5210 pin4160 art3588   nn2041   ppro5216   art,nn3962   3767   aina2036   ppro846 epn2249   3756

☞ 41 Ye do the deeds of your father. Then said they to him, We be not

pfip1080 pre1537   an,nn4202   pin2192 nu1520   an,nn3962   art,nn2316

born of fornication; we have one Father, *even* God.

(Deut. 32:6; Is. 63:16; 64:8)

art,nn2424 aina2036   ppro846 1487 art,nn2316 ipf2258 ppro5216 pr/an,nn3962   ipf25/302 epn1691

42 Jesus said unto them, If God were your Father, ye would love me:

1063 epn1473   aina1831   2532 pin2240 pre1537 art,nn2316 (1063)   3761 pfi2064   pre575 rxpro1683   235

for I proceeded forth and came from God; neither came I of myself, but

depro1565 aina649 ppro3165

he sent me.

pre,inpro1302   3756   pin1097   art,popro1699   art,nn2981   3754   pinm1410/3756

43 Why do ye not understand my speech? *even* because ye cannot

pinf191 art,popro1699 art,nn3056

hear my word.

☞ **8:41** These people believed they were God's "spiritual" children because they were Abraham's physical children. Christ stated that if the works that they were supposedly doing for God were genuine, they would have readily accepted Christ who was also performing God's work (cf. John 8:42). The truth was that their works were done deceitfully, revealing them to be children of the devil (John 8:44).

44 Ye are of *your* father the devil, and the lusts of your father ye will do. He was a murderer from the beginning, and abode not in the truth, because there is no truth in him. When he speaketh a lie, he speaketh of his own: for he is a liar, and the father of it.

45 And because I tell *you* the truth, ye believe me not.

46 Which of you convinceth me of sin? And if I say the truth, why do ye not believe me?

47 He*that*is of God heareth God's words: ye therefore hear *them* not, because ye are not of God.

48 Then answered the Jews, and said unto him, Say we not well that thou art a Samaritan, and hast a devil?

49 Jesus answered, I have not a devil; but I honor my Father, and ye do dishonor me.

50 And I seek not mine own glory: there is one*that*seeketh and judgeth.

51 Verily, verily, I say unto you, If a man keep my saying, he shall never see death.

52 Then said the Jews unto him, Now we know that thou hast a devil. Abraham is dead, and the prophets; and thou sayest, If a man keep my saying, he shall never taste of death.

53 Art thou greater than our father Abraham, which is dead? and the prophets are dead: whom makest thou thyself?

54 Jesus answered, If I honor myself, my honor is nothing: it is my Father that honoreth me; of whom ye say, that he is your God:

55 Yet ye have not known him; but I know him: and if I should say, I

pin1492　ppro846　3756　　　　　fm2071　pr/an,nn5583　pr/an,ajn3664　ppro5216　235　　pin1492　ppro846　2532　pin5083

know him not, I shall be a　liar　like unto you: but I know him, and keep

ppro846　art,nn3056

his saying.

　　　ppro5216　art,nn3962　　　11　　　aom21　　2443　asba1492　art,popro1699　art,nn2250　2532　　aina1492　　　2532

56 Your father Abraham rejoiced to　see　my　day: and he saw it, and

aina5463

was glad.

　　　　3767　aina2036　art3588　nn2453　pre4314　ppro846　　　pin2192　ad3768　nu4004　an,nn2094　2532

57 Then said the Jews unto him, Thou art not yet fifty years old, and hast

pfi3708　　11

thou seen Abraham?

　　art,nn2424　aina2036　　ppro846　281　　281　　pin3004　　ppro5213　ad4250　　11

58 Jesus said unto them, Verily, verily, I say unto you, Before Abraham

aifm1096　epn1473　pin1510

was,　I　am.　　　　　　　　　　　　　　　　　　　　　　　　(Ex. 3:14)

　　3767　　　aina142　　an,nn3037　2433　asba906　pre1909　ppro846　1161　an,nn2424　ainp2928

59 Then took*they*up stones to cast　at　him: but Jesus　hid　himself,

2532　aina1831　pre1537　art3588　nn2411　apta1330　pre1223　an,ajn3319　ppro846　2532　ad3779

and went out of the temple, going through the midst of them, and so

ipf3855

passed by.

A Man Born Blind

　　2532　　　　　　pap3855　　aina1492　an,nn444　　pr/an,aj5185　pre1537　an,nn1079

9 And as Jesus passed by, he saw a man which was blind from his birth.

　　　2532　ppro846　art,nn3101　aina2065　ppro846　pap3004　4461　inpro5101　aina264　depro3778

　　2 And his disciples asked him, saying, Master, who did sin, this man,

2228 ppro846　art,nn1118　2443　　asbp1080 pr/an,aj5185

or his parents, that he was born blind?　　　　　(Ex. 20:5; Ezek.18:20)

　　art,nn2424　ainp611　　3777　　depro3778　aina264　3777　ppro846　art,nn1118　235

3 Jesus answered, Neither hath this man sinned, nor　his　parents: but

2443 art3588　nn2041　art,nn2316　　　asbp5319　pre1722 ppro846

that the works of God should be made manifest　in　him.

epn1691　pin1163　pifm2038 art3588　nn2041　art,apta3992　ppro3165 ad2193　pin2076 an,nn2250

4　I　must work the works of him*that*sent me, while it is　day: the

an,nn3571　pinm2064　ad3753　an,ajn3762　pinm1410 pifm2038

night cometh, when no man　can　work.

　　　ad3752　　psa5600 pre1722 art3588　nn2889　pin1510　pr/an,nn5457　art3588　nn2889

5 As*long*as I am　in　the world, I am the　light　of the world.

　　　　　　　　　　　　　　　　　　　　　　　　　　　　(Is. 49:6)

　　　depro5023　apta2036　　aina4429　　ad5476　　2532 aina4160 an,nn4081 pre1537

6 When he had　thus　spoken, he spat on*the*ground, and made　clay　of

art3588　nn4427　2532　aina2025　art3588　nn3788　art3588　ajn5185　art3588　nn4081

the spittle, and he anointed the eyes of the blind man with the clay,

　　2532　aina2036　　ppro846　aima5217　aipm3538　pre1519 art3588　nn2861　　4611　　repro3739

7 And　said　unto　him,　Go,　wash　in　the　pool of Siloam, (which

pin2059　　　　pfpp649　　　　aina565　　　　3767　　2532　aom3538　2532
is*by*interpretation, Sent.) He went*his*way therefore, and washed, and
aina2064　　pap991
came seeing.

art3588　　nn1069　　3767　　2532　　art,ajn4386　　pap2334 ppro846 3754
8 The neighbors therefore, and they*which*before had seen him that he
ipf2258 pr/an,ajn5185 ipf3004 pin2076 3756 depro3778　pr/art,ppmp2521　2532　pr/pap4319
was blind, said, Is not this he*that*sat and begged?
　　　　　　an,ajn243　　ipf3004　pr/depro3778 pin2076 (1161)　an,ajn243　　　　pin2076 pr/an,ajn3664 ppro846　　depro1565
9 Some said, This　is he: others *said,* He is　like　him: *but* he
ipf3004 epn1473 pin1510
said, I　am *he.*
　　　　　3767　　ipf3004　　　　ppro846 ad4459　　　ppro4675 art,nn3788　　ainp455
10 Therefore said they unto him, How were thine eyes opened?
depro1565　　ainp611　　2532　aina2036　　an,nn444　　　ppmp3004 an,nn2424 aina4160　an,nn4081 2532
11 He answered and said, A man that is called Jesus made clay, and
aina2025　ppro3450 art,nn3788 2532 aina2036　　ppro3427 aima5217 pre1519 art3588 nn2861　　4611　2532
anointed mine eyes, and said unto me, Go　to　the pool of Siloam, and
aipm3538 1161 apta565 2532 aptm3538 2532　　aina308
wash: and I went and washed, and I received sight.
　　　　3767　aina2036　　　　ppro846 ad4226 pin2076 depro1565　　pin3004　pin1492 3756
12 Then said they unto him, Where is　he? He said, I know not.
　　　　pin71　pre4314 art3588　nn5330　ppro846　　ad4218　　pr/art,aj5185
13 They brought to　the Pharisees him that aforetime was blind.
　　1161　ipf2258　　an,nn4521　ad3753 art,nn2424 aina4160 art3588 nn4081 2532　aina455 ppro846
14 And it was the sabbath day when Jesus made the clay, and opened his
art,nn3788
eyes.
　　3767　ad3825　art3588　　nn5330　2532　ipf2065　ppro846 ad4459
15 Then again the Pharisees also asked him how he had
aina308　(1161) art3588 aina2036　ppro846　aina2007 an,nn4081 pre1909 ppro3450 art,nn3788 2532
received*his*sight. He said unto them, He put clay upon mine eyes, and
aom3538 2532　pin991
I washed, and do see.
　　3767　ipf3004 idpro5100 pre1537 art3588　nn5330　depro3778 art,nn444 pin2076 3756 pre3844
16 Therefore said some of the Pharisees, This man is not of
art,nn2316 3754　pin5083 3756 art3588　nn4521　an,ajn243 ipf3004 ad4459 pinm1410
God, because he keepeth not the sabbath day. Others said, How can a
an,nn444　an,aj268 pinf4160 an,aj5108 an,nn4592 2532　ipf2258 an,nn4978 pre1722
man that is a sinner do such miracles? And there was a division among
ppro846
them.
　　pin3004　art3588　ajn5185　ad3825 inpro5101 pin3004 epn4771 pre4012 ppro846 3754
17 They say unto the blind man again, What sayest thou of him, that he
aina455 ppro4675 art,nn3788 (1161) art3588 aina2036　pin2076 pr/an,nn4396
hath opened thine eyes? He said, He is a prophet.
　　3767 art3588　nn2453　3756 aina4100　pre4012 ppro846 3754　ipf2258
18 But the Jews did not believe concerning him, that he had been
pr/an,aj5185 2532　aina308　ad2193 (repro3755) aina5455 art3588 nn1118　ppro846
blind, and received*his*sight, until they called the parents of him
art,apta308
that*had*received*his*sight.

2532   aina2065   ppro846   pap3004   pin2076 depro3778 ppro5216 pr/art,nn5207 repro3739 epn5210 pin3004 (3754)

19 And they asked them, saying, Is this your son, who ye say was

ainp1080 pr/an,aj5185 ad4459   3767   ad737 pin991

born blind? how then doth he now see?

ppro846   art,nn1118   ainp611   ppro846 2532   aina2036   pin1492   3754 depro3778 pin2076 ppro2257

20 His parents answered them and said, We know that this is our

pr/art,nn5207 2532   3754   ainp1080 pr/an,aj5185

son, and that he was born blind:

1161   ad4459   ad3568   pin991   pin1492   3756 2228 inpro5101   aina455

21 But by*what*means he now seeth, we know not; or who hath opened

ppro846 art,nn3788   epn2249   pin1492 3756 epn846   pin2192/an,nn2244 aima2065   epn846   epn846   ft2980   pre4012

his eyes, we know not: he is*of*age; ask him: he shall speak for

ppro848

himself.

depro5023   aina2036 ppro846 art,nn1118   3754   ipf5399 art3588 nn2453   1063

22 These *words* spake his parents, because they feared the Jews: for

art3588 nn2453   plpf4934   ad2235   2443   1437   idpro5100   asba3670   ppro846

the Jews had agreed already, that if any man did confess that he was

an,nn5547   asbm1096   pr/an,ajn656

Christ, he should be put*out*of*the*synagogue.

pre1223/depro5124 aina2036 ppro846 art,nn1118   pin2192/an,nn2244 aima2065 epn846

23 Therefore said his parents, He is*of*age; ask him.

3767   pre1537/nu,ajn1208 aina5455   art3588 nn444 repro3739 ipf2258 pr/an,aj5185 2532 aina2036   ppro846

24 Then again called they the man that was blind, and said unto him,

aima1325 art,nn2316   an,nn1391 epn2249 pin1492 3754 depro3778 art,nn444 pin2076   pr/an,ajn268

Give God the praise: we know that this man is a sinner.

depro1565   ainp611 (3767) 2532 aina2036   1487   pin2076 pr/an,ajn268   pin1492   3756

25 He answered and said, Whether he be a sinner *or no,* I know not:

nu,ajn1520   pin1492 3754   pap5607 pr/an,aj5185 ad737   pin991

one thing I know, that, whereas I was blind, now I see.

1161   aina2036   ppro846 ad3825   inpro5101 aina4160   ppro4671 ad4459   aina455

26 Then said they to him again, What did he to thee? how opened he

ppro4675 art,nn3788

thine eyes?

ainp611   ppro846   aina2036 ppro5213   ad2235   2532   3756 aina191

27 He answered them, I have told you already, and ye did not hear:

inpro5101   pin2309   pinf191   ad3825 pin2309 (3361) epn5210 2532 aifm1096 ppro846 pr/an,nn3101

wherefore would ye hear *it* again? will ye also be his disciples?

3767   aina3058   ppro846 2532 aina2036 epn4771 pin1488 depro1565 pr/an,nn3101 1161 epn2249 pin2070

28 Then they reviled him, and said, Thou art his disciple; but we are

art,nn3475   pr/art,nn3101

Moses' disciples.

epn2249 pin1492   3754 art,nn2316 pfi2980   an,nn3475   (1161) depro5126   pin1492

29 We know that God spake unto Moses: *as for* this *fellow,* we know

3756   ad4159   pin2076

not from whence he is.

art3588   nn444   ainp611   2532 aina2036   ppro846   1063 pre1722/depro5129 pin2076

30 The man answered and said unto them, Why herein is a

pr/an,ajn2298   3754 epn5210 pin1492 3756   ad4159   pin2076 2532

marvelous thing, that ye know not from whence he is, and *yet* he hath

aina455   ppro3450 art,nn3788

opened mine eyes.

31 Now we know that God heareth not sinners: but if any man be a worshiper*of*God, and doeth his will, him he heareth.

(Ps. 66:18; Is. 1:15; Ps. 34:15; Prov. 15:29)

32 Since*the*world*began was it not heard that any man opened the eyes of one*that*was*born blind.

33 If this man were not of God, he could do nothing.

34 They answered and said unto him, Thou wast altogether born in sins, and dost thou teach us? And they cast him out.   *(Ps. 51:5)*

35 Jesus heard that they had cast him out; and when he had found him, he said unto him, Dost thou believe on the Son of God?

36 He answered and said, Who is he, Lord, that I might believe on him?

37 And Jesus said unto him, Thou hast both seen him, and it is he that talketh with thee.

38 And he said, Lord, I believe. And he worshiped him.

☞ 39 And Jesus said, For judgment I am come into this world, that they*which*see not might see; and that they*which*see might be made blind.

40 And *some* of the Pharisees which were with him heard these words and said unto him, Are we blind also?

41 Jesus said unto them, If ye were blind, ye should have no sin: but now ye say, We see; therefore your sin remaineth.

☞ **9:39** Christ came into the world to open the spiritual eyes of some and to close others. The Jews were given the true light of Christ's message, but they chose to reject it. As a result, the message was later sent to the Gentiles. The Jews thought that simply because they were God's chosen people, they had no spiritual duties. They took pride in their ancestry and totally disregarded their own spiritual need. In this way, those who thought they saw the truth were made blind by the coming of the Messiah (see 1 Cor. 1:18–31).

Jesus Is the Good Shepherd

10 ☞ ²⁸¹ ²⁸¹ ^{pin3004} ^{ppro5213} ^{art,ppmp1525} ³³⁶¹ ^{pre1223} ^{art3588}
Verily, verily, I say unto you, He*that*entereth not by the

ⁿⁿ²³⁷⁴ ^{pre1519} ^{art3588} ^{nn833/art,nn4263} ²³⁵ ^{pap305} ^{ad237}
door into the sheepfold, but climbeth up some*other*way,

^{depro1565} ^{pin2076} ^{pr/an,nn2812} ²⁵³² ^{pr/an,nn3027}
the same is a thief and a robber.

¹¹⁶¹ ^{art,ppmp1525} ^{pre1223} ^{art3588} ⁿⁿ²³⁷⁴ ^{pin2076} ^{art3588} ^{pr/an,nn4166} ^{art3588}
2 But he*that*entereth*in by the door is the shepherd of the

ⁿⁿ⁴²⁶³
sheep.

^{depro5129} ^{art3588} ⁿⁿ²³⁷⁷ ^{pin455} ²⁵³² ^{art3588} ⁿⁿ⁴²⁶³ ^{pin191} ^{ppro846} ^{art,nn5456} ²⁵³²
3 To him the porter openeth; and the sheep hear his voice: and he

^{pin2564} ^{art,aj2398} ^{an,nn4263} ^{pre2596} ^{an,nn3686} ²⁵³² ^{pin1806/ppro846}
calleth his own sheep by name, and leadeth*them*out.

²⁵³² ^{ad3752} ^{asba1544} ^{art,aj2398} ^{an,nn4263} ^{pinm4198} ^{ad*1715} ^{ppro846} ²⁵³²
4 And when he putteth forth his own sheep, he goeth before them, and

^{art3588} ⁿⁿ⁴²⁶³ ^{pin190} ^{ppro846} ³⁷⁵⁴ ^{pin1492} ^{ppro846} ^{art,nn5456}
the sheep follow him: for they know his voice.

¹¹⁶¹ ^{an,ajn245} ^{efn3364} ^{asba190} ²³⁵ ^{fm5343} ^{pre575} ^{ppro846} ³⁷⁵⁴
5 And a stranger will they not follow, but will flee from him: for they

^{pin1492} ³⁷⁵⁶ ^{art3588} ⁿⁿ⁵⁴⁵⁶ ^{art,ajn245}
know not the voice of strangers.

^{depro5026} ^{art,nn3942} ^{aina2036} ^{art,nn2424} ^{ppro846} ¹¹⁶¹ ^{depro1565} ^{aina1097} ³⁷⁵⁶
6 This parable spake Jesus unto them: but they understood not

^{pr/inpro5101} ^{ipf2258} ^{repro3739} ^{ipf2980} ^{ppro846}
what things they were which he spake unto them.

³⁷⁶⁷ ^{aina2036} ^{art,nn2424} ^{ppro846} ^{ad3825} ²⁸¹ ²⁸¹ ^{pin3004} ^{ppro5213} ⁽³⁷⁵⁴⁾
7 Then said Jesus unto them again, Verily, verily, I say unto you,

^{epn1473} ^{pin1510} ^{art3588} ^{pr/nn2374} ^{art3588} ⁿⁿ⁴²⁶³
I am the door of the sheep.

^{an,aj3956} ^{an,ajn3745} ^{aina2064} ^{pre4253} ^{ppro1700} ^{pin1526} ^{pr/an,nn2812} ²⁵³² ^{pr/an,nn3027} ²³⁵ ^{art3588}
8 All that ever came before me are thieves and robbers: but the

ⁿⁿ⁴²⁶³ ³⁷⁵⁶ ^{aina191} ^{ppro846}
sheep did not hear them. *(Jer. 23:1,2; Ezek. 34:2,3)*

^{epn1473} ^{pin1510} ^{art3588} ^{pr/nn2374} ^{pre1223} ^{epn1700} ¹⁴³⁷ ^{idpro5100} ^{asba1525} ^{fp4982} ²⁵³²
9 I am the door: by me if any man enter in, he shall be saved, and

^{fm1525} ²⁵³² ^{fm1831} ²⁵³² ^{ft2147} ^{an,nn3542}
shall go in and out, and find pasture. *(Ps. 118:20)*

^{art3588} ⁿⁿ²⁸¹² ^{pinm2064} ³⁷⁵⁶ ¹⁵⁰⁸ ²⁴⁴³ ^{asba2813} ²⁵³² ^{asba2380} ²⁵³² ^{asba622} ^{epn1473}
10 The thief cometh not, but for to steal, and to kill, and to destroy: I

^{aina2064} ²⁴⁴³ ^{psa2192} ^{an,nn2222} ²⁵³² ^{psa2192}
am come that they might have life, and that they might have *it*

^{an,ajn4053}
more abundantly.

☞ **10:1–21** See note on Mark 3:28, 29.

epn1473 pin1510 art3588 aj2570 pr/art,nn4166   art3588 aj2570   art,nn4166   pin5087 ppro846 art,nn5590 pre5228

11   I   am the good shepherd: the good shepherd giveth his life for

art3588   nn4263

the sheep.   *(Ps. 23:1; Is. 40:11; Ezek. 34:15)*

1161   art,nn3411   2532 3756 (pap5607) pr/an,nn4166   repro3729 pr/an,aj2398 art3588

12 But he*that*is*a*hireling, and not   the   shepherd, whose   own   the

nn4263 pin1526 3756 pin2334 art3588 nn3074 ppmp2064   2532   pin863 art3588 nn4263   2532   pin5343   2532

sheep are not, seeth the wolf coming, and leaveth the sheep, and fleeth: and

art3588 nn3074   pin726   ppro846   2532   pin4650   art3588   nn4263

the wolf catcheth them, and scattereth the sheep.

(1161) art3588   nn3411   pin5343   3754   pin2076   pr/an,nn3411 2532   pin3199 (ppro846) 3756 pre4012

13   The hireling fleeth, because he is a hireling, and careth   not for

art3588 nn4263

the sheep.   *(Zech. 11:16)*

epn1473 pin1510 art3588 aj2570 pr/art,nn4166 2532 pin1097 art,popro1699   2532   pinp1097

14   I   am the good shepherd, and know   my   *sheep,* and am known

pre5259 art,popro1699

of mine.

ad2531 art3588   nn3962   pin1097 ppro3165 epn2504/pin1097   art3588   nn3962   2532

15 As   the Father knoweth me, even*so*know*I the Father: and I

pin5087   ppro3450 art,nn5590 pre5228 art3588   nn4263

lay down my life for the sheep.

2532 an,aj243 an,nn4263   pin2192 repro3739 pin2076 3756 pre1537 depro5026 art,nn833   depro2548 ppro3165

16 And other sheep I have, which are not of   this   fold: them also   I

pin1163 ainf71   2532   ft191 ppro3450 art,nn5456 2532   fm1096 nu3391 an,nn4167

must bring, and they shall hear my voice; and there shall be one fold, *and*

nu1520   an,nn4166

one shepherd.   *(Is. 56:8; Ezek. 34:23; 37:24)*

pre1223/depro5124   art,nn3962 pin25 ppro3165   3754   epn1473   pin5087   ppro3450 art,nn5590

17 Therefore doth my Father love me, because   I   lay down my   life,

2443   asba2983 ppro846 ad3825

that I might take   it   again.

an,ajn3762   pin142   ppro846 pre575 ppro1700   235   epn1473 pin5087/ppro846   pre575   rxpro1683   pin2192

18 No man taketh it from me, but I lay*it*down of myself. I have

an,nn1849   ainf5087/ppro846   2532   pin2192   an,nn1849   ainf2983 ppro846 ad3825   depro5026

power to lay*it*down, and I have power to take it again. This

art,nn1785   aina2983   pre3844 ppro3450 art,nn3962

commandment have I received of   my Father.

aom1096   an,nn4978   3767   ad3825   pre1722 art3588 nn2453 pre1223 depro5128

19 There was a division therefore again among the Jews for these

art,nn3056

sayings.

1161 an,ajn4183 pre1537 ppro846 ipf3004   pin2192 an,nn1140   2532 pinm3105 inpro5101 pin191

20 And many of them said, He hath a devil, and is mad; why hear ye

ppro846

him?

an,ajn243   ipf3004 depro5023 pin2076 3756 art3588 nn4487   an,ppmp1139   pinm1410

21 Others said, These are not the words of him*that*hath*a*devil. Can

(3361) an,nn1140 pinf455   an,nn3788   an,ajn5185

a devil open the eyes of the blind?

The Believer's Assurance

_{1161   aom1096   pre1722   art,nn2414   art3588   nn1456   2532   ipf2258}
☞ 22 And it was at Jerusalem the feast*of*the*dedication, and it was
_{an,nn5494}
winter.

_{2532   art,nn2424   ipf4043   pre1722 art3588   nn2411   pre1722   art,nn4672   art,nn4745}
23 And Jesus walked in the temple in Solomon's porch.

_{3767   aina2944/art3588/nn2453   ppro846 2532 ipf3004   ppro846   ad2193/ad4219}
24 Then came*the*Jews*round*about him, and said unto him, How long dost
_{pin142/ppro2257/art,nn5590   1487 epn4771 pin1488 art3588   pr/nn5547   aina2036 ppro2254   an,nn3954}
thou make*us*to*doubt? If thou be the Christ, tell us plainly.

_{art,nn2424   ainp611   ppro846   aina2036 ppro5213 2532   pin4100   3756 art3588   nn2041   repro3739}
25 Jesus answered them, I told you, and ye believed not: the works that
_{epn1473 pin4160 pre1722 ppro3450   art,nn3962   art,nn3686 depro5023   pin3140   pre4012 ppro1700}
I do in my Father's name, they bear witness of me.

_{235   epn5210   pin4100   3756   1063   pin2075 3756 pre1537 art,popro1699 art,nn4263   ad2531   aina2036}
26 But ye believe not, because ye are not of my sheep, as I said
_{ppro5213}
unto you.

_{art,popro1699 art,nn4263   pin191 ppro3450 art,nn5456 epn2504   pin1097   ppro846   2532   pin190   ppro3427}
27 My sheep hear my voice, and I know them, and they follow me:

_{epn2504   pin1325   ppro846   an,aj166   an,nn2222 2532   efn3364/pre1519/art,nn165   asbm622}
28 And I give unto them eternal life; and they shall never perish,
_{2532/3756   idpro5100   ft726   ppro846   pre1537   ppro3450 art,nn5495}
neither shall any *man* pluck them out of my hand.

_{ppro3450   art,nn3962   repro3739   pfi1325   ppro3427 pin2076 pr/cd/an,aj3187   an,ajn3956 2532   an,ajn3762}
☞ 29 My Father, which gave *them* me, is greater than all; and no
_{pinm1410   pinf726   pre1537 ppro3450 art,nn3962   art,nn5495}
man is able to pluck *them* out of my Father's hand.

_{epn1473 2532   art,nn3962 pin2070 pr/nu,ajn1520}
30 I and *my* Father are one.

_{3767   art3588   nn2453   aina941   an,nn3037   ad3825 2443 asba3034 ppro846}
31 Then the Jews took up stones again to stone him.

_{art,nn2424   ainp611   ppro846   an,aj4183 an,aj2570 an,nn2041   aina1166   ppro5213 pre1537}
32 Jesus answered them, Many good works have I showed you from
_{ppro3450 art,nn3962   pre1223 an,aj4169   ppro846 an,nn2041   pin3034 ppro3165}
my Father; for which of those works do ye stone me?

_{art3588   nn2453   ainp611   ppro846   pap3004   pre4012 an,aj2570 an,nn2041   pin3034 ppro4571 3756}
33 The Jews answered him, saying, For a good work we stone thee not;

☞ **10:22** The Feast of Dedication was a ceremony of great importance to the Jewish people. It originated at the dedication of the temple after its desecration by Antiochus Epiphanes (see note on Ezek. 43:13–27). The Jews underwent severe persecution by this ruler. A number of years later, a priest named Mattathias led a revolt, later continued by his son Maccabeus, that ended this persecution. Following this victory, the temple in Jerusalem was cleansed, and a ceremony was held to mark its rededication. Jewish tradition records that the oil lamps that were lit as part of this celebration had only one day's supply of oil, but burned for eight days. This annual feast was marked by the lighting of candles and the chanting of the Hallel (Ps. 113—118), as well as the waving of palm branches. Since the Feast of Dedication was intended as a time of great rejoicing, all fasting and public mourning were prohibited.
☞ **10:29–39** See note on Philippians 2:6–8.

235   pre4012   an,nn988   2532   3754   epn4771 pap5607   pr/an,nn444 pin4160   rxpro4572

but for blasphemy; and because that thou, being a man, makest thyself

pr/an,nn2316

God.   *(Lev. 24:16)*

       art,nn2424   ainp611   ppro846 pin2076   3756   pr/pfpp1125 pre1722 ppro5216 art,nn3551 epn1473 aina2036

34 Jesus answered them, Is it not written in your law, I said, Ye

pin2075 pr/an,nn2316

are gods?   *(Ps. 82:6)*

       1487   aina2036 depro1565 an,nn2316 pre4314   repro3739 art3588 pr/nn3056   art,nn2316   aom1096   2532 art3588

35 If he called them gods, unto whom the word of God came, and the

nn1124   pinm1410/3756   aifp3089

Scripture cannot be broken;

       pin3004 epn5210   repro3739 art3588   nn3962   aina37   2532 aina649 pre1519 art3588

36 Say ye of him, whom the Father hath sanctified, and sent into the

nn2889   pin987   3754   aina3004   pin1510   pr/an,nn5207   art,nn2316

world, Thou blasphemest; because I said, I am the Son of God?

       1487   pin4160 3756 art3588   nn2041   ppro3450 art,nn3962   pim4100   ppro3427 3361

37 If I do not the works of my Father, believe me not.

       1161   1487   pin4160   2579   psa4100   3361 epn1698 aima4100 art3588 nn2041   2443

38 But if I do, though ye believe not me, believe the works: that ye may

asba1097   2532   asba4100   3754 art3588   nn3962   pre1722 ppro1698 ppro2504 pre1722 ppro846

know, and believe, that the Father *is* in me, and I in him.

       3767   ipf2212   ad3825   ainf4084 ppro846 2532   aina1831   pre1537   ppro846

39 Therefore they sought again to take him: but he escaped out of their

art,nn5495

hand,

       2532   aina565   ad3825   ad4008   art,nn2446 pre1519 art3588   nn5117   ad3699   an,nn2491 art,nu,ajn4412

40 And went away again beyond Jordan into the place where John at first

ipf2258/pap907 2532 ad1563   aina3306

baptized; and there he abode.

       2532 an,ajn4183   aina2064   pre4314 ppro846   2532 ipf3004 an,nn2491 aina4160 an,aj3762   an,nn4592   1161

41 And many resorted unto him, and said, John did no miracle: but

an,ajn3956   an,ajn3745 an,nn2491 aina2036 pre4012   depro5127   ipf2258 pr/an,aj227

all things that John spake of this man were true.

       2532 an,ajn4183   aina4100   pre1519 ppro846   ad1563

42 And many believed on him there.

Lazarus Dies

          1161   idpro5100   ipf2258 pr/pap770   an,nn2976   pre575   an,nn963   (pre1537)

11 Now a certain *man* was sick, *named* Lazarus, of Bethany,

          art3588 nn2968   an,nn3137 2532 ppro846 art,nn79   an,nn3136

the town of Mary and her sister Martha.

       (1161) ipf2258   an,nn3137   pr/art,apta218   art3588   nn2962   an,nn3464   2532 pr/apta1591

2 (It was *that* Mary which anointed the Lord with ointment, and wiped

ppro846 art,nn4228   ppro848 art,nn2359 repro3739   art,nn80   an,nn2976   ipf770

his feet with her hair, whose brother Lazarus was sick.)

          3767   art,nn79   aina649 pre4314 ppro846 pap3004 an,nn2962 aima2396   repro3739

3 Therefore his sisters sent unto him, saying, Lord, behold, he whom thou

pin5368   pin770

lovest is sick.

1161   art,nn2424   apta191   aina2036 depro3778   art,nn769   pin2076 pre3756 pre4314 an,nn2288   235

4 When Jesus heard *that,* he said, This sickness is not unto death, but

pre5228 art3588 nn1391   art,nn2316 2443 art3588 nn5207   art,nn2316   asbp1392   pre1223/ppro846

for the glory of God, that the Son of God might be glorified thereby.

1161 art,nn2424   ipf25   art,nn3136   2532 ppro846 art,nn79 2532   art,nn2976

5 Now Jesus loved Martha, and her sister, and Lazarus.

ad5613   aina191   3767   3754   pin770   ipf3306 (3303) nu1417 an,nn2250 ad5119

6 When he had heard therefore that he was sick, he abode   two days still

pre1722   repro3739 an,nn5117   ipf2258

in the same place where he was.

ad1899   pre3326 depro5124 pin3004   art,nn3101   psa71 pre1519 art,nn2449 ad3825

7 Then after that saith he to *his* disciples, Let us go into Judea again.

art,nn3101   pin3004   ppro846   4461   art3588 nn2453   ad3568   ipf2212   aina3034

8 *His* disciples say unto him, Master, the Jews of late sought to stone

ppro4571 2532 pin5217   ad1563   ad3825

thee; and goest thou thither again?

art,nn2424   ainp611   pin1526   3780   nu1427   an,nn5610   art3588 nn2250 1437 idpro5100

9 Jesus answered, Are there not twelve hours in the day? If any man

psa4043 pre1722 art3588 nn2250   pin4350   3756   3754   pin991 art3588 nn5457   depro5127

walk in the day, he stumbleth not, because he seeth the light of this

art,nn2889

world.

1161 1437 idpro5100 psa4043 pre1722 art3588   nn3571   pin4350   3754   pin2076 3756

10 But if a man walk in the night, he stumbleth, because there is no

art,nn5457 pre1722 ppro846

light in him.

depro5023   aina2036   2532 pre3326 depro5124   pin3004   ppro846 ppro2257 art,ajn5384

11 These things said he: and after that he saith unto them, Our friend

an,nn2976   pfip2837   235   pinm4198 2443   asba1852/ppro846

Lazarus sleepeth; but I go, that I may awake*him*out*of*sleep.

3767   aina2036 ppro846 art,nn3101 an,nn2962 1487   pfip2837   fp4982

12 Then said his disciples, Lord, if he sleep, he shall do well.

1161   art,nn2424 plpf2046 pre4012 ppro846 art,nn2288 1161 depro1565 aina1380   3754

13 Howbeit Jesus spake of his death: but they thought that he had

pin3004   pre4012   art,nn2838   art,nn5258

spoken of taking*of*rest in sleep.

ad5119   (3767) aina2036 art,nn2424   ppro846 an,nn3954 an,nn2976   aina599

14 Then   said Jesus unto them plainly, Lazarus is dead.

2532   pin5453   pre1223/ppro5209   3754 ipf2252 3756 ad1563   2443

15 And I am glad for*your*sakes that I was not there, to*the*intent ye

asba4100   235   psa71 pre4314 ppro846

may believe; nevertheless let us go unto him.

3767   aina2036 an,nn2381   art,ppmp3004   an,ajn1324   art,nn4827

16 Then said Thomas, which*is*called Didymus, unto his fellow disciples,

epn2249 2532 psa71 2443   asba599 pre3326 ppro846

Let us also go, that we may die with him.

3767   art,nn2424 apta2064 aina2147 (ppro846) pap2192   pre1722 art3588 nn3419 nu5064

17 Then when Jesus came, he found that he had *lain* in the grave four

an,nn2250 ad2235

days already.

1161   art,nn963 ipf2258   ad1451   art,nn2414   ad5613 nu1178 an,nn4712 pre575

18 Now Bethany was nigh unto Jerusalem, about fifteen furlongs off:

2532   an,ajn4183 pre1537 art3588 nn2453 plpf2064 pre4314 (art,pre4012) an,nn3136   2532   an,nn3137 2443   asbm3888

19 And many of the Jews came to   Martha and Mary, to comfort

ppro846   pre4012   ppro846   art,nn80

them concerning their brother.

3767   art,nn3136   ad5613   aina191   3754 art,nn2424   pinm2064

20 Then Martha, as*soon*as she heard that Jesus was coming, went and

aina5221 ppro846 1161 an,nn3137 ipf2516   pre1722 art3588   nn3624

met him: but Mary sat *still* in the house.

3767   aina2036 art,nn3136 pre4314 art,nn2424 an,nn2962 1487   ipf2258   ad5602 ppro3450

21 Then said Martha unto Jesus, Lord, if thou hadst been here, my

art,nn80   3756 plpf2348/302

brother had not died.

235   pin1492   3754 2532 ad3568   an,ajn3745   asbm154/302   art,nn2316 art,nn2316

22 But I know, that even now, whatsoever thou wilt   ask of God, God

ft1325   ppro4671

will give *it* thee.

art,nn2424 pin3004   ppro846 ppro4675 art,nn80   fm450

23 Jesus saith unto her, Thy brother shall rise again.

an,nn3136 pin3004   ppro846   pin1492 3754   fm450   pre1722 art3588

24 Martha saith unto him, I know that he shall rise again   in   the

nn386   pre1722 art3588 aj2078 an,nn2250

resurrection at the last day.   (*Dan. 12:2*)

art,nn2424 aina2036   ppro846 epn1473 pin1510 art3588   pr/nn386   2532   art3588 pr/nn2222

25 Jesus   said   unto her,   I   am   the   resurrection, and   the   life:

art,pap4100   pre1519 ppro1691 2579   asba599   fm2198

he*that*believeth in   me, though he were dead, yet shall he live:

2532   an,aj3956 art,pap2198 2532 pap4100   pre1519 ppro1691 efn3364/pre1519/art,nn165 asba599

26 And whosoever liveth and believeth in   me shall   never   die.

pin4100   depro5124

Believest thou this?

pin3004   ppro846 3483 an,nn2962 epn1473 pfi4100   3754 epn4771 pin1488 art3588 pr/nn5547

27 She saith unto him, Yea, Lord: I believe that thou art the Christ,

art3588 pr/nn5207 art,nn2316   art,ppmp2064   pre1519 art3588 nn2889

the Son of God, which*should*come into the world.

2532   depro5023 apta2036   aina565   2532 aina5455 an,nn3137 ppro848

28 And when she had   so   said, she went*her*way, and called Mary her

art,nn79   ad2977   apta2036 art3588 nn1320   pin3918 2532 pin5455   ppro4571

sister secretly, saying, The Master is come, and calleth for thee.

ad5613   depro1565 aina191   pinm1453 an,ajn5035   2532 pinm2064 pre4314 ppro846

29 As*soon*as she heard *that,* she arose quickly, and came unto him.

1161   art,nn2424   ad3768   plpf2064 pre1519 art3588   nn2968   235 ipf2258 pre1722   art,nn5117

30 Now Jesus was not yet come into the town, but was in that place

ad3699   art,nn3136 aina5221 ppro846

where Martha met him.

art3588   nn2453 3767   art,pap5607   pre3326 ppro846 pre1722 art3588   nn3614   2532   ppmp3888

31 The Jews then which were with her in the house, and comforted

ppro846   apta1492 art,nn3137 3754   aina450   ad5030   2532   aina1831   aina190

her, when they saw Mary, that she rose up hastily and went out, followed

ppro846   pap3004   pin5217 pre1519 art3588 nn3419 2443 asba2799 ad1563

her, saying, She goeth unto the grave to weep there.

3767   ad5613 art,nn3137   aina2064   ad3699 art,nn2424 ipf2258   apta1492 ppro846

32 Then when Mary was come where Jesus was, and saw him, she

aina4098   pre1519 ppro846 art,nn4228   pap3004   ppro846 an,nn2962 1487   ipf2258 ad5602 ppro3450

fell down   at his feet, saying unto him, Lord, if thou hadst been here, my

art,nn80   3756 aina599/302

brother had not died.

ad5613   an,nn2424   3767   aina1492 ppro846   pap2799   2532 art3588 nn2453   pap2799

33 When Jesus therefore saw her weeping, and the Jews also weeping which

apta4905 ppro846   aom1690 art3588 nn4151 2532   aina5015 (rxpro1438)

came with her, he groaned in the spirit, and was troubled.

2532 aina2036   ad4226   pfi5087 ppro846   pin3004   ppro846 an,nn2962 pim2064

34 And said, Where have ye laid him? They said unto him, Lord, come

2532 aima1492

and see.

art,nn2424 aina1145

35 Jesus wept.

3767 ipf3004 art3588 nn2453 aima2396 ad4459   ipf5368 ppro846

36 Then said the Jews, Behold how he loved him!

1161 idpro5100 pre1537 ppro846 aina2036 ipf1410 3756 depro3778   art,apta455   art3588 nn3788

37 And some of them said, Could not this man, which opened the eyes of

art3588 ajn5185   ainf4160   2443 2532 depro3778   3361   asba599

the blind, have caused that even this man should not have died?

Jesus Brings Lazarus Back to Life

an,nn2424   3767   ad3825 ppmp1690 pre1722 rxpro1438 pinm2064 pre1519 art3588 nn3419 (1161)

38 Jesus therefore again groaning in himself cometh to the grave. It

ipf2258   an,nn4693 2532   an,nn3037 ipf1945 pre1909 ppro846

was a cave, and a stone lay upon it.

art,nn2424 pin3004   aima142   art3588   nn3037   an,nn3136 art3588   nn79

39 Jesus said, Take*ye*away   the   stone. Martha,   the sister of

art,pfp2348   pin3004   ppro846 an,nn2962 ad2235   pin3605   1063

him*that*was*dead, saith unto him, Lord, by*this*time he stinketh: for he hath

pin2076   pr/nu,ajn5066

been *dead* four days.

art,nn2424 pin3004   ppro846 aina2036 3756   ppro4671 3754 1437

40 Jesus saith unto her, Said I not unto thee, that, if thou wouldest

asba4100   fm3700 art3588 nn1391   art,nn2316

believe, thou shouldest see the glory of God?

3767   aina142   art3588 nn3037   repro3757 art3588 pfp2348 ipf2258

41 Then they took away the stone *from the place* where the dead was

ppmp2749 1161 art,nn2424 aina142 ad507 art,nn3788 2532 aina2036 an,nn3962 pin2168 ppro4671 3754

laid. And Jesus lifted up *his* eyes, and said, Father, I thank thee that thou hast

aina191 ppro3450

heard me.

1161 epn1473 ipf1492 3754   pin191   ppro3450 ad3842   235   pre1223   art3588

42 And I knew that thou hearest me always: but because of the

nn3793   art,pfp4026   aina2036 2443   asba4100 3754 epn4771 aina649

people which*stand*by I said *it,* that they may believe that thou hast sent

ppro3165

me.

2532   depro5023 apta2036 aina2905   an,aj3173 an,nn5456 an,nn2976

43 And when he thus had spoken, he cried with a loud voice, Lazarus,

ad1204 ad1854

come forth.

2532 art,pfp2348   aina1831 pfpp1210 art,nn5495 2532 art,nn4228

44 And he*that*was*dead came forth, bound hand and foot with

an,nn2750 2532 ppro846 art,nn3799 plpf4019   an,nn4676 art,nn2424 pin3004

graveclothes: and his face was bound about with a napkin. Jesus saith unto

ppro846 aima3089 ppro846 2532 aima863 pinf5217

them, Loose him, and let him go.

3767 an,ajn4183 pre1537 art3588 nn2453 art,apta2064 pre4314 art,nn3137 2532 aptm2300

45 Then many of the Jews which came to Mary, and had seen the things

repro3739 art,nn2424 aina4160 aina4100 pre1519 ppro846

which Jesus did, believed on him.

1161 idpro5100 1537 ppro846   aina565   pre4314 art3588 nn5330 2532 aina2036 ppro846

46 But some of them went*their*ways to the Pharisees, and told them

repro3739 art,nn2424 aina4160

what things Jesus had done.

The Pharisees Take Counsel Against Jesus

3767 aina4863 art3588 nn749 2532 art3588 nn5330 an,nn4892 2532 ipf3004

47 Then gathered the chief priests and the Pharisees a council, and said,

inpro5101 pin4160 3754 depro3778 art,nn444 pin4160 an,aj4183 an,nn4592

What do we? for this man doeth many miracles.

1437   asba863/ppro846/ad3779 an,ajn3956   ft4100 pre1519 ppro846 2532 art3588

48 If we let*him*thus*alone, all *men* will believe on him: and the

nn4514   fm2064 2532 ft142 2532 ppro2257 art,nn5117 2532 art,nn1484

Romans shall come and take away both our place and nation.

1161 (idpro5100) nu1520 pre1537 ppro846 an,nn2533 pap5607   pr/an,nn749

49 And one of them, *named* Caiaphas, being the high priest

depro1565 art,nn1763 aina2036 ppro846 epn5210 pin1492 (3756) an,ajn3762

that same year, said unto them, Ye know nothing*at*all,

3761 pinm1260 3754 pin4851   ppro2254 2443 nu1520 an,nn444   asba599 pre5228

50 Nor consider that it is expedient for us, that one man should die for

art3588 nn2992 2532 art3588 an,aj3650 nn1484 asbm622 3361

the people, and that the whole nation perish not.

1161 depro5124 aina2036 3756 pre575 rxpro1438 235 pap5607 pr/an,nn749 depro1565 art,nn1763

51 And this spake he not of himself: but being high priest that year, he

aina4395 3754 art,nn2424 ipf3195 pinf599 pre5228 art,nn1484

prophesied that Jesus should die for that nation;

2532 3756 pre5228 art,nn1484 an,ajn3440 235 2443 2532   asba4863

52 And not for that nation only, but that also he should gather together

pre1519 nu,ajn1520 art3588 nn5043 art,nn2316   pfpp1287

in one the children of God that were scattered abroad. *(Is. 49:6)*

3767 pre575 depro1565 art,nn2250   aom4823   2443

53 Then from that day forth they took*counsel*together for to

asba615/ppro846

put*him*to*death.

an,nn2424 3767 ipf4043 3756 ad2089 an,nn3954 pre1722 art3588 nn2453 235 aina565

54 Jesus therefore walked no more openly among the Jews; but went

ad1564   pre1519   art,nn5561   ad1451   art3588   ajn2048   pre1519   an,nn4172 ppmp3004   2187
thence unto a country near to the wilderness, into a city called Ephraim,

ad2546   ipf1304   pre3326 ppro846   art,nn3101
and there continued with his disciples.

1161   art3588   nn2453   3957   ipf2258   pr/ad1451   2532   an,ajn4183
55 And   the   Jews'   passover   was   nigh*at*hand: and   many

aina305/pre1537/art3588/nn5561   pre1519   an,nn2414   pre4253 art3588   3957   2443   asba48
went*out*of*the*country*up   to   Jerusalem before the passover, to purify

rxpro1438
themselves.   (2 Chr. 30:17)

3767   ipf2212   art,nn2424   2532   ipf3004   pre3326   rcpro240
56 Then sought they for Jesus, and spake among themselves, as they

pfp2476 pre1722 art3588   nn2411   inpro5101 pin1380 ppro5213 3754   efn3364 asba2064 pre1519 art3588   nn1859
stood in the temple, What think ye, that he will not come to the feast?

1161   2532   art3588   nn749   2532   art3588   nn5330   plpf1325
57 Now both the chief priests and the Pharisees had given a

an,nn1785   2443   1437   idpro5100   asba1097   ad4226   pin2076   asba3377
commandment, that, if any man knew where he were, he should show it,

3704   asba4084 ppro846
that they might take him.

Mary Anoints Jesus at Bethany (Matt. 26:6-13; Mark 14:3-9)

3767   art,nn2424 nu1803 an,nn2250   pre4253 art3588   3957   aina2064 pre1519   an,nn963   ad3699
12 Then Jesus six days before the passover came to Bethany, where

an,nn2976   ipf2258   art,pfp2348   repro3739   aina1453 pre1537   an,ajn3498
Lazarus was which*had*been*dead, whom he raised from the dead.

(3767) ad1563   aina4160 aina4160   an,nn1173   2532   art,nn3136   ipf1247   1161   art,nn2976   ipf2258
2   There they made him a supper; and Martha served: but Lazarus was

pr/nu1520   art,ppmp4873   ppro846
one of them*that*sat*at*the*table*with him.

3767   apta2983 art,nn3137   an,nn3046   an,nn3464   an,aj4101/an,nn3487   an,aj4186
3 Then took Mary a pound of ointment of spikenard, very costly, and

aina218   art3588 nn4228   art,nn2424   2532   aina1591 ppro846 art,nn4228   ppro848 art,nn2359 1161 art3588   nn3614
anointed the feet of Jesus, and wiped his feet with her hair: and the house

ainp4137 pre1537 art3588   nn3744   art3588   nn3464
was filled with the odor of the ointment.

3767   pin3004 nu1520   pre1537   ppro846   art,nn3101   an,nn2455   an,aj2469   an,nn4613
4 Then saith one of his disciples, Judas Iscariot, Simon's son,

art,pap3195   pinf3860   ppro846
which should betray him,

pre,inpro1302   3756 depro5124   art,nn3464   ainp4097   nu5145   an,nn1220   2532   ainp1325
5 Why was not this ointment sold for three hundred pence, and given

an,ajn4434
to the poor?

(1161) depro5124   aina2036 3756   3754   ppro846   ipf3199 pre4012 art3588   ajn4434   235   3754   ipf2258
6   This he said, not that he cared for the poor; but because he was a

pr/an,nn2812 2532 ipf2192 art3588 nn1101   2532   ipf941   art,ppmp906
thief, and had the bag, and bare what*was*put therein.

7 Then said Jesus, Let*her*alone: against the day of my burying hath she kept this.

8 For the poor always ye have with you; but me ye have not always.

(Deut. 15:11)

9 Much people of the Jews therefore knew that he was there: and they came not for*Jesus'*sake only, but that they might see Lazarus also, whom he had raised from the dead.

10 But the chief priests consulted that they might put*Lazarus*also*to*death;

11 Because that by*reason*of him many of the Jews went away, and believed on Jesus.

Jesus' Triumphal Entry Into Jerusalem (Matt. 21:1-11; Mark 11:1-11; Luke 19:28-40)

12 On the next day much people that*were*come to the feast, when they heard that Jesus was coming to Jerusalem,

13 Took branches of palm trees, and went forth to meet him, and cried, Hosanna: Blessed *is* the King of Israel that cometh in the name of the Lord.

(Ps. 118:25,26)

14 And Jesus, when he had found a young ass, sat thereon; as it is written,

15 Fear not, daughter of Zion; behold, thy King cometh, sitting on an ass's colt.

(Zech. 9:9)

16 These things understood not his disciples at*the*first: but when Jesus was glorified, then remembered they that these things were written of him, and *that* they had done these things unto him.

art3588   nn3793   3767   art,pap5607 pre3326 ppro846 ad3753   aina5455 art,nn2976 pre1537

17 The people therefore that was with him when he called Lazarus out of

art,nn3419 2532 aina1453 ppro846 pre1537   an,ajn3498   ipf3140

his grave, and raised him from the dead, bare record.

pre1223   depro5124   art3588   nn3793   2532 aina5221 ppro846 3754   aina191   ppro846

18 For this cause the people also met him, for that they heard that he

pfin4160 depro5124 art,nn4592

had done this miracle.

art3588   nn5330   3767   aina2036   pre4314   rxpro1438   pin2334   3754

19 The Pharisees therefore said among themselves, Perceive ye how ye

pin5623 (3756)   an,ajn3762   aima2396 art3588 nn2889   aina565 ad*3694 ppro846

prevail   nothing? behold, the world is gone after him.

Christ's Final Discourse to the People

1161   ipf2258   idpro5100   an,nn1672   pre1537   art,pap305   2443 asba4352

20 And there were certain Greeks among them*that*came*up to worship

pre1722 art3588   nn1859

at the feast:

depro3778   aina4334   3767   an,nn5376   art3588   pre575   966

21 The same came therefore to Philip, which was of Bethsaida of

art,nn1056   2532   ipf2065   ppro846 pap3004 an,nn2962   pin2309   ainf1492 art,nn2424

Galilee, and desired him, saying, Sir, we would see Jesus.

an,nn5376   pinm2064   2532   pin3004   art,nn406   2532   ad3825   an,nn406   2532 an,nn5376 pin3004

22 Philip cometh and telleth Andrew: and again Andrew and Philip tell

art,nn2424

Jesus.

1161 art,nn2424   aom611   ppro846   pap3004 art3588 nn5610   pfi2064   2443 art3588 nn5207

23 And Jesus answered them, saying, The hour is come, that the Son of

art,nn444   asbp1392

man should be glorified.

281   281   pin3004   ppro5213   3362   art,nn2848   art,nn4621 apta4098 pre1519 art3588

24 Verily, verily, I say unto you, Except a corn of wheat fall into the

nn1093   asba599 ppro846 pin3306 pr/an,aj3441 1161 1437 asba599   pin5342   an,aj4183 an,nn2590

ground and die, it abideth alone: but if it die, it bringeth forth much fruit.

art,pap5368   ppro848 art,nn5590   ft622 ppro846 2532   art,pap3404   ppro848 art,nn5590

25 He*that*loveth his   life shall lose it; and he*that*hateth his   life

pre1722 depro5129 art,nn2889   ft5442 ppro846 pre1519 an,nn2222   an,aj166

in this world shall keep it   unto life eternal.

1437   idpro5100   psa1247 epn1698   pim190 epn1698 2532   ad3699 epn1473 pin1510 ad1563

26 If any man serve me, let him follow me; and where   I   am, there

2532   art,popro1699 art,nn1249 fm2071 (2532) 1437   idpro5100   psa1247 epn1698 ppro846

shall also   my   servant   be: if any man serve me, him will *my*

art,nn3962   ft5091

Father honor.

ad3568   ppro3450 art,nn5590 pfip5015   2532 inpro5101   asba2036 an,nn3962 aima4982 ppro3165

27 Now is my   soul troubled; and what shall I say? Father, save me

pre1537 depro5026 art,nn5610 235   pre1223/depro5124   aina2064   pre1519 depro5026 art,nn5610

from this hour: but for*this*cause came I unto this hour.

28 Father, glorify thy name. Then came there a voice from heaven, *saying,*
I have both glorified *it,* and will glorify *it* again.

29 The people therefore, that*stood*by, and heard *it,* said that it
thundered: others said, An angel spake to him.

30 Jesus answered and said, This voice came not because of me, but
for*your*sakes.

31 Now is the judgment of this world: now shall the prince of this
world be cast out.

32 And I, if I be lifted up from the earth, will draw all *men* unto
me.

33 This he said, signifying what death he should die.

34 The people answered him, We have heard out of the law that Christ
abideth forever : and how sayest thou, The Son of man must be lifted up?
who is this Son of man? *(Ps. 89:4,36; 110:4; Is. 9:7; Dan. 7:14)*

☞ 35 Then Jesus said unto them, Yet a little while is the light with you.
Walk while ye have the light, lest darkness come upon you: for
he*that*walketh in darkness knoweth not whither he goeth.

36 While ye have light, believe in the light, that ye may be the
children of light. These things spake Jesus, and departed, and did hide himself
from them.

Many People Believe, But Are Afraid

37 But though he had done so many miracles before them, yet they
believed not on him:

☞ 12:35 See note on 1 John 1:5–10.

38 That the saying of Isaiah the prophet might be fulfilled, which he

spake, Lord, who hath believed our report? and to whom hath the arm of the

Lord been revealed?   *(Is. 53:1)*

39 Therefore they could not believe, because that Isaiah said again,

40 He hath blinded their eyes, and hardened their heart; that they should

not see with *their* eyes, nor understand with *their* heart, and be converted,

and I should heal them.   *(Is. 6:10)*

41 These things said Isaiah, when he saw his glory, and spake of

him.   *(Is. 6:1)*

42 Nevertheless among the chief rulers also many believed on him; but

because of the Pharisees they did not confess *him,* lest they should be

put*out*of*the*synagogue:

43 For they loved the praise of men more than the praise of God.

44 Jesus cried and said, He*that*believeth on me, believeth not on

me, but on him*that*sent me.

45 And he*that*seeth me seeth him*that*sent me.

46 I am come a light into the world, that whosoever believeth on

me should not abide in darkness.

47 And if any man hear my words, and believe not, I judge him not:

for I came not to judge the world, but to save the world.

48 He*that*rejecteth me, and receiveth not my words, hath

one*that*judgeth him: the word that I have spoken, the same shall judge him

in the last day.

49 For I have not spoken of myself; but the Father which sent me,

he gave me a commandment, what I should say, and what I should speak.

50 And I know that his commandment is life everlasting:

repro3739   epn1473   pin2980   3767   ad2531   art3588   nn3962   pfi2046   ppro3427   ad3779

whatsoever   I   speak therefore,   even as   the   Father   said   unto   me,   so   I

pin2980

speak.

Jesus Washes His Disciples' Feet

1161   pre4253 art3588 nn1859   art3588   3957   art,nn2424 pfp1492   3754   ppro846

13 Now before the feast of the passover, when Jesus knew that his

art,nn5610   pfi2064   2443   asba3327   pre1537 depro5127 art,nn2889 pre4314 art3588

hour was come that he should depart out of this world unto the

nn3962   apta25   art,ajn2398   art3588   pre1722 art3588   nn2889   aina25   ppro846   pre1519

Father, having loved his own which were in the world, he loved them unto

an,nn5056

the end.

2532   an,nn1173   aptm1096 art3588 ajn1228   ad2235   pfp906 pre1519 art3588   nn2588

2 And supper being ended, the devil having now put into the heart of

an,nn2455   an,aj2469   an,nn4613   2443 asba3860 ppro846

Judas Iscariot, Simon's *son,* to betray him;

art,nn2424 pfp1492   3754 art3588   nn3962   pfi1325   an,ajn3956   pre1519 ppro846 art,nn5495   2532

3 Jesus knowing that the Father had given all things into his hands, and

3754   aina1831 pre575 an,nn2316 2532 pin5217 pre4314 art,nn2316

that he was come from God, and went to God;

pinm1453   pre1537 art,nn1173   2532   pin5087   art,nn2440   2532 apta2983   an,nn3012

4 He riseth from supper, and laid aside his garments; and took a towel, and

aina1241   rxpro1438

girded himself.

ad1534   pin906   an,nn5204 pre1519 art,nn3537   2532   aom756   pinf3538 art3588

5 After that he poureth water into a basin, and began to wash the

nn3101   art,nn4228 2532   pinf1591   art3588 nn3012   repro3739   ipf2258 pfpp1241

disciples' feet, and to wipe *them* with the towel wherewith he was girded.

3767   pinm2064   pre4314 an,nn4613 an,nn4074 2532 depro1565 pin3004   ppro846 an,nn2962

6 Then cometh he to Simon Peter: and Peter saith unto him, Lord, dost

epn4771 pin3538 ppro3450 art,nn4228

thou wash my feet?

art,nn2424   ainp611   2532 aina2036   ppro846 repro3739 epn1473 pin4160 epn4771   pin1492   3756

7 Jesus answered and said unto him, What I do thou knowest not

ad737   1161   fm1097   pre3326/depro5023

now; but thou shalt know hereafter.

an,nn4074 pin3004   ppro846   efn3364/pre1519/art,nn165 asba3538 ppro3450 art,nn4228 art,nn2424

☞ 8 Peter saith unto him, Thou shalt   never   wash   my   feet. Jesus

ainp611   ppro846 3362 asba3538 ppro4571 3756   pin2192 3756 an,nn3313 pre3326 ppro1700

answered him, If I wash thee not, thou hast no part with me.

☞ **13:8** There are three major viewpoints that deal with Jesus' statement in this verse. First, it has been suggested that in refusing to have Christ wash his feet, Peter was rejecting salvation from his sins. This opinion is based on the definition of the word translated "wash." It has been suggested that the "washing" represents free forgiveness or pardon from sin, the "newness of life," or both.

Another view proposes that Peter sought physical cleansing as opposed to spiritual. In focusing

(continued on next page)

an,nn4613 an,nn4074 pin3004   ppro846 an,nn2962 3361 ppro3450 art,nn4228 an,ajn3440 235 2532

9 Simon Peter saith unto him, Lord, not my feet only, but also *my*

art,nn5495 2532   art,nn2776

hands and *my* head.

art,nn2424 pin3004   ppro846   art,pfpp3068   pin2192/an,nn5532 3756   2228   aifm3538

10 Jesus saith to him, He*that*is*washed needeth not save to wash *his*

art,nn4228 235 pin2076 pr/an,aj2513   an,aj3650   2532 epn5210 pin2075 pr/an,aj2513 235   3780 an,ajn3956

feet, but is clean every whit: and ye are clean, but not all.

1063   ipf1492   art,pap3860   ppro846 pre1223/depro5124 aina2036   pin2075 3780

11 For he knew who*should*betray him; therefore said he, Ye are not

an,ajn3956 pr/an,aj2513

all clean.

3767 ad3753   aina3538 ppro846 art,nn4228 2532   aina2983 ppro848 art,nn2440

12 So after he had washed their feet, and had taken his garments, and

apta377 ad3825 aina2036   ppro846 pin1097   inpro5101   pfi4160   ppro5213

was set down again, he said unto them, Know ye what I have done to you?

epn5210 pin5455 ppro3165 art,nn1320 2532 art,nn2962 2532   pin3004 ad2573 1063   pin1510

13 Ye call me Master and Lord: and ye say well; for *so* I am.

1487 epn1473 3767   art,nn2962 2532   art,nn1320   aina3538 ppro5216 art,nn4228 epn5210 2532

14 If I then, *your* Lord and Master, have washed your feet; ye also

pin3784   pinf3538   rcpro240   art,nn4228

ought to wash one another's feet.

1063   aina1325 ppro5213   an,nn5262 2443 epn5210 (2532) psa4160 ad2531 epn1473

15 For I have given you an example, that ye should do as I have

aina4160   ppro5213

done to you.

281   281   pin3004   ppro5213   an,ajn1401 pin2076 3756 pr/cd/an,aj3187   ppro848

16 Verily, verily, I say unto you, The servant is not greater than his

art,nn2962 3761   an,nn652   pr/cd/an,aj3187   art,apta3992   ppro846

lord; neither he*that*is*sent greater than he*that*sent him.

1487   pin1492   depro5023   pr/an,aj3107 pin2075   1437   psa4160 ppro846

17 If ye know these things, happy are ye if ye do them.

pin3004   3756 pre4012 ppro5216 an,aj3956 epn1473 pin1492 repro3739   aom1586 235 2443

18 I speak not of you all: I know whom I have chosen: but that

art3588   nn1124   asbp4137   art,pap5176   art,nn740 pre3326 ppro1700   aina1869

the Scripture may be fulfilled, He*that*eateth bread with me hath lifted up

ppro848 art,nn4418 pre1909 ppro1691

his heel against me.   *(Ps. 41:9)*

pre575/ad737   pin3004 ppro5213 pre4253   aip1096 2443 ad3752   asbm1096

19 Now I tell you before it come, that, when it is come*to*pass, ye

asba4100 3754 epn1473 pin1510

may believe that I am *he*.

(continued from previous page)

on himself for this "cleansing," Peter missed the whole point to Christ's illustration—that is, humility.

A third interpretation of this passage reflects two particular perspectives on this verse. In the first place it states that Jesus was warning Peter that he would be disobeying the Lord if he did not allow Him to wash his feet. In other words, Peter would be standing apart from Christ, renouncing Him as Lord. It also emphasizes the importance of a person being washed spiritually. A person cannot enjoy the blessings which result from a close, personal walk with Jesus Christ without being spiritually cleansed. This last interpretation is supported best by the text because obedience to Christ is not the focus of the verses in context.

281   281   pin3004   ppro5213   art,pap2983   idpro5100/1437

20 Verily, verily, I say unto you, He*that*receiveth whomsoever

asba3992   pin2983   epn1691   1161   art,pap2983   epn1691   pin2983   art,apta3992

I send receiveth me; and he*that*receiveth me receiveth him*that*sent

ppro3165

me.

Jesus Foretells His Betrayal (Matt. 26:20-25; Mark 14:17-21; Luke 22:21-23)

art,nn2424   depro5023   apta2036   ainp5015   art,nn4151   2532

21 When Jesus had thus said, he was troubled in spirit, and

aina3140   2532 aina2036   281   281   pin3004   ppro5213 3754 nu1520 pre1537 ppro5216   ft3860

testified, and said, Verily, verily, I say unto you, that one of you shall betray

ppro3165

me.

3767   art3588   nn3101   ipf991   rcpro240/pre1519   ppmp639   pre4012   inpro5101

22 Then the disciples looked one*on*another, doubting of whom he

pin3004

spake.

1161   ipf2258 ppmp345   pre1722 art,nn2424 art,nn2859 nu1520 pre1537 ppro846   art,nn3101   repro3739

23 Now there was leaning on Jesus' bosom one of his disciples, whom

art,nn2424   ipf25

Jesus loved.

an,nn4613   an,nn4074   3767   pin3506   depro5129   aifm4441 inpro5101

24 Simon Peter therefore beckoned to him, that he should ask who it

opt1498/302 pre4012 repro3739   pin3004

should be of whom he spake.

depro1565   1161   apta1968 pre1909 art,nn2424 art,nn4738 pin3004   ppro846 an,nn2962 inpro5101 pin2076

25 He then lying on Jesus' breast saith unto him, Lord, who is it?

art,nn2424   pinp611   depro1565   pin2076   repro3739 epn1473   ft1929   art,nn5596

26 Jesus answered, He it is, to whom I shall give a sop, when I

apta911   2532   apta1686 art3588 nn5596   pin1325   an,nn2455 an,aj2469

have dipped it. And when he had dipped the sop, he gave it to Judas Iscariot,

an,nn4613

the son of Simon.

2532   pre3326 art3588 nn5596 (ad5119) art,nn4567   aina1525   pre1519 depro1565   3767   pin3004 art,nn2424

27 And after the sop Satan entered into him. Then said Jesus unto

ppro846 repro3739   pin4160   aima4160   cd/an,aj5032

him, That thou doest, do quickly.

1161   an,ajn3762   art,ppmp345   aina1097 pre4314   inpro5101   aina2036 depro5124

28 Now no man at*the*table knew for what intent he spake this unto

ppro846

him.

1063   idpro5100   ipf1380   1893   art,nn2455 ipf2192 art3588 nn1101 3754 art,nn2424

29 For some of them thought, because Judas had the bag, that Jesus had

pin3004   ppro846 aima59   repro3739   pin2192 an,nn5532   pre1519 art3588 nn1859 2228

said unto him, Buy those things that we have need of against the feast; or,

2443   asba1325 idpro5100   art3588 ajn4434

that he should give something to the poor.

depro1565   3767   apta2983   art3588 nn5596   aina1831/ad2112   1161   ipf2258

30 He   then having received the   sop went*immediately*out: and it was

an,nn3571

night.

"Love One Another"

ad3753   aina1831   art,nn2424 pin3004   ad3568   art3588 nn5207   art,nn444

31 Therefore, when he was gone out, Jesus said, Now is the Son of man

ainp1392   2532 art,nn2316   ainp1392   pre1722 ppro846

glorified, and God is glorified in him.

1487 art,nn2316   ainp1392   pre1722 ppro846 art,nn2316   2532   ft1392   ppro846 pre1722   rxpro1438

32 If God be glorified in   him, God shall also glorify him   in   himself,

2532   ad2117   ft1392   ppro846

and shall straightway glorify him.

an,nn5040   ad2089   an,ajn3397   pin1510 pre3326 ppro5216   ft2212   ppro3165 2532

33 Little children, yet a little while I am with you. Ye shall seek me: and

ad2531   aina2036   art3588   nn2453   ad3699   epn1473 pin5217 epn5210 pinm1410/3756   ainf2064   2532   ad737   pin3004

as I said unto the Jews, Whither   I   go,   ye   cannot come; so now I say

epn5213

to you.

an,aj2537   an,nn1785   pin1325   ppro5213 2443   pim25   rcpro240   ad2531

34 A new commandment I give unto you, That ye love one another; as I

aina25   ppro5209 2443 epn5210 2532   pim25   rcpro240

have loved you, that ye also love one another.

pre1722 depro5129   an,ajn3956   fm1097   3754   pin2075 popro1698   pr/an,nn3101   1437   psa2192

35 By this shall   all   men know that ye are   my   disciples, if ye have

an,nn26   rcpro240/pre1722

love one*to*another.

Peter's Denial Predicted (Matt. 26:31-35; Mark 14:27-31; Luke 22:31-34)

an,nn4613 an,nn4074 pin3004   ppro846 an,nn2962   ad4226   pin5217   art,nn2424   ainp611

36 Simon Peter said unto him, Lord, whither goest thou? Jesus answered

ppro846   ad3699   pin5217   pinm1410 3756   ainf190 ppro3427 ad3568   1161   ft190   ppro3427

him, Whither I go, thou canst not follow me now; but thou shalt follow me

an,ajn5305

afterwards.

art,nn4074 pin3004   ppro846 an,nn2962   pre,inpro1302 pinm1410/3756   ainf190 ppro4671 ad737

37 Peter said unto him, Lord,   why   cannot I follow thee now? I will

ft5087   ppro3450 art,nn5590   pre5228/ppro4675

lay down my   life for*thy*sake.

art,nn2424   ainp611   ppro846   ft5087   ppro4675 art,nn5590   pre5228/ppro1700

38 Jesus answered him, Wilt thou lay down thy   life   for* my*sake?

281   281   pin3004   ppro4671   an,nn220   efn3364   ft5455   ad2193   (repro3739)

Verily, verily, I say unto thee, The cock shall not crow, till thou hast

asbm533   ppro3165 nu,ad5151

denied me thrice.

"I Go to Prepare a Place"

14 Let not your heart be troubled: ye believe in God, believe also in me.

2 In my Father's house are many mansions: if*it*were*not so, I would have told you. I go to prepare a place for you.

3 And if I go and prepare a place for you, I will come again, and receive you unto myself; that where I am, *there* ye may be also.

4 And whither I go ye know, and the way ye know.

5 Thomas saith unto him, Lord, we know not whither thou goest; and how can we know the way?

6 Jesus saith unto him, I am the way, the truth, and the life: no man cometh unto the Father, but by me.

7 If ye had known me, ye should have known my Father also: and from henceforth ye know him, and have seen him.

8 Philip saith unto him, Lord, show us the Father, and it sufficeth us.

9 Jesus saith unto him, Have I been so long time with you, and yet hast thou not known me, Philip? he*that*hath*seen me hath seen the Father; and how sayest thou *then,* Show us the Father?

10 Believest thou not that I am in the Father, and the Father in me? the words that I speak unto you I speak not of myself: but the Father that dwelleth in me, he doeth the works.

11 Believe me that I *am* in the Father, and the Father in me: or else believe me for*the*very*works'*sake.

12 Verily, verily, I say unto you, He*that*believeth on me, the works that I do shall he*do*also; and greater *works* than these shall he do; because I go unto my Father.

13 And whatsoever ye shall ask in my name, that will I do, that the Father may be glorified in the Son.

14 If ye shall ask any thing in my name, I will do it.

The Holy Spirit Will Come

15 If ye love me, keep my commandments.

16 And I will pray the Father, and he shall give you another Comforter, that he may abide with you forever;

17 *Even* the Spirit of truth; whom the world cannot receive, because it seeth him not, neither knoweth him: but ye know him; for he dwelleth with you, and shall be in you.

18 I will not leave you comfortless: I will come to you.

19 Yet a little while, and the world seeth me no more; but ye see me: because I live, ye shall live also.

20 At that day ye shall know that I *am* in my Father, and ye in me, and I in you.

21 He*that*hath my commandments, and keepeth them, he it is that loveth me: and he*that*loveth me shall be loved of my Father, and I will love him, and will manifest myself to him.

22 Judas saith unto him, not Iscariot, Lord, how is it that thou wilt manifest thyself unto us, and not unto the world?

23 Jesus answered and said unto him, If a man love me, he will keep my words: and my Father will love him, and we will come unto him, and make our abode with him.

14:13–16 See note on Luke 11:9.

art,pap25   pppro3165   3361   pin5083   3756   pppro3450   art,nn3056   2532   art3588   nn3056   repro3739

24 He*that*loveth me not keepeth not my sayings: and the word which

pin191   pin2076   3756   pr/popro1699   235   an,nn3962   art,apta3992   pppro3165

ye hear is not mine, but the Father's which sent me.

depro5023   pfi2980   pppro5213   pap3306   pre3844 epn5213

25 These things have I spoken unto you, being*yet*present with you.

1161   art3588   nn3875   art3588   aj40   art,nn4151   repro3739 art3588   nn3962

26 But the Comforter, *which is* the Holy Ghost, whom the Father will

ft3992   pre1722   pppro3450   art,nn3686   depro1565   ft1321   pppro5209   an,ajn3956   2532

send in my name, he shall teach you all things, and

ft5279/an,aj3956/pppro5209   repro3739   aina2036   pppro5213

bring*all*things*to*your*remembrance, whatsoever I have said unto you.

an,nn1515   pin863   pppro5213 art,popro1699 an,nn1515   pin1325   pppro5213   3756   ad2531 art3588

27 Peace I leave with you, my peace I give unto you: not as the

nn2889   pin1325   pin1325 epn1473   pppro5213   3361 pppro5216 art,nn2588   pim5015   3366

world giveth, give I unto you. Let not your heart be troubled, neither let it

pim1168

be afraid.

aina191   3754   epn1473 aina2036   pppro5213   pin5217   2532   pinm2064

☞ 28 Ye have heard how I said unto you, I go away, and come *again*

pre4314 pppro5209 1487   ipf25   pppro3165   aina5463/302   3754   aina2036   pinm4198 pre4314 art3588

unto you. If ye loved me, ye would rejoice, because I said, I go unto the

nn3962   3754 pppro3450 art,nn3962 pin2076 pr/cd/an,aj3187   pppro3450

Father: for my Father is greater than I.

2532   ad3568   pfi2046 pppro5213   ad4250   aifm1096   2443   ad3752

29 And now I have told you before it come*to*pass, that, when it is

asbm1096   asba4100

come*to*pass, ye might believe.

ad2089   3756   ft2980 an,ajn4183 pre3326 pppro5216 1063 art3588   nn758   depro5127 art,nn2889

30 Hereafter I will not talk much with you: for the prince of this world

pinm2064   2532   pin2192 (3756)   an,ajn3762   pre1722 pppro1698

cometh, and hath   nothing in me.

235   2443   art3588   nn2889   asba1097   3754   pin25   art3588   nn3962   2532   ad2531   art3588

31 But that the world may know that I love the Father; and as the

nn3962   aom1781/pppro3427   ad3779   pin4160 pim1453   psa71   ad1782

Father gave*me*commandment, even so I do. Arise, let us go hence.

Jesus Is the True Vine

15

epn1473 pin1510 art3588   aj228   pr/art,nn288 2532 pppro3450   art,nn3962 pin2076 art3588   pr/nn1092

I am the true vine, and my Father is the husbandman.

(Is. 5:1; Ezek. 19:10)

an,aj3956   an,nn2814   pre1722   pppro1698   pap5342   3361   an,nn2590   pin142 (pppro846)   2532

2 Every branch in me that beareth not fruit he taketh away: and

an,aj3956   art,pap5342   an,nn2590   pin2508   pppro846   2443   psa5342   cd/an,aj4119

every *branch* that beareth fruit, he purgeth it, that it may bring forth more

an,nn2590

fruit.

☞ **14:28** See note on Philippians 2:6–8.

ad2235   epn5210   pin2075   pr/an,aj2513   pre1223   art3588   nn3056   repro3739   pfi2980
3 Now   ye   are   clean   through   the   word   which   I   have   spoken   unto
ppro5213
you.

aima3306   pre1722   ppro1698   ppro2504   pre1722   ppro5213   ad2531   art3588   nn2814   pinm1410/3756   pinf5342   an,nn2590   pre575
☞ 4 Abide   in   me,   and   I   in   you.   As   the   branch   cannot   bear   fruit   of
rxpro1438   3362   asba3306   pre1722   art3588   nn288   3761   ad3779   epn5210   3362   asba3306   pre1722
itself,   except   it   abide   in   the   vine;   no   more   can   ye,   except   ye   abide   in
ppro1698
me.

epn1473   pin1510   art3588   pr/nn288   epn5210   art3588   pr/nn2814   art,pap3306   pre1722   ppro1698
5   I   am   the   vine,   ye   *are*   the   branches: He*that*abideth   in   me,
ppro2504   pre1722   ppro846   depro3778   pin5342   an,aj4183   an,nn2590   3754   ad*5565   ppro1700
and   I   in   him,   the   same   bringeth   forth   much   fruit: for   without   me   ye
pinm1410 (3756)   pinf4160   an,ajn3762
can   do   nothing.

3362/idpro5100/asba3306   pre1722   ppro1698   ainp906   ad1854   ad5613   art,nn2814   2532
6   If*a*man*abide*not   in   me,   he   is   cast   forth   as   a   branch,   and   is
ainp3583   2532   pin4863   ppro846   2532   pin906   pre1519   an,nn4442   2532
withered;   and   men   gather   them,   and   cast   *them*   into   the   fire,   and   they   are
pinp2545
burned.

1437   asba3306   pre1722   ppro1698   2532   ppro3450   art,nn4487   asba3306   pre1722   ppro5213   fm154
☞ 7 If   ye   abide   in   me,   and   my   words   abide   in   you,   ye   shall   ask
repro3739/1437   psa2309   2532   fm1096   ppro5213
what   ye   will,   and   it   shall   be   done   unto   you.

pre1722/depro5129   ppro3450   art,nn3962   ainp1392   2443   psa5342   an,aj4183   an,nn2590   2532
8   Herein   is   my   Father   glorified,   that   ye   bear   much   fruit;   so   shall   ye
fm1096   popro1698   art,nn3101
be   my   disciples.

ad2531   art3588   nn3962   aina25   ppro3165   epn2504/aina25   ppro5209   aima3306   pre1722
9   As   the   Father   hath   loved   me,   so*have*I*loved   you: continue   ye   in
art,popro1699   art,nn26
my   love.

1437   asba5083   ppro3450   art,nn1785   ft3306   pre1722   ppro3450   art,nn26
10   If   ye   keep   my   commandments,   ye   shall   abide   in   my   love;
ad2531   epn1473   pfi5083   ppro3450   art,nn3962   art,nn1785   2532   pin3306   pre1722   ppro846
even   as   I   have   kept   my   Father's   commandments,   and   abide   in   his
art,nn26
love.

☞ **15:4, 5, 7** The phrase, "abide in me," has been interpreted in several different ways, but all arrive at the same conclusion. Some feel that Christ was referring to the power that He would grant to those who would remain "in Christ." According to this view, the meaning of the phrase is seen in verses seven and nine. Christ desired that His disciples continue to obey the words that He had spoken to them so that their lives would be full of joy.

Another view continues the meaning of this phrase, suggesting that it reflects one's dependence on Christ, communion with Him, and obedience to Him. Remaining in these things will result in one's life becoming fruitful for Christ. For the believer, Christ alone can provide the grace and provision of needs in life. Thus, he must remain faithful to his service for the Lord and to the study of the Scriptures in order to bear fruit.

depro5023   pfi2980   ppro5213   2443   art,popro1699 art,nn5479   asba3306
11 These things have I spoken unto you, that my   joy   might remain

pre1722 epn5213 2532   ppro5216 art,nn5479   asbp4137
in you, and *that* your   joy   might be full.

pr/depro3778 pin2076 art,popro1699   art,nn1785   2443   psa25   rcpro240   ad2531
12 This   is   my   commandment, That ye love one another, as I have

aina25   ppro5209
loved you.

cd/an,aj3187 an,nn26 pin2192 an,ajn3762   depro5026 2443   idpro5100   asba5087   ppro848 art,nn5590
13 Greater love hath no man than this, that a man lay down his   life

pre5228 ppro848   art,ajn5384
for his friends.

epn5210 pin2075 ppro3450 pr/an,ajn5384 1437   psa4160   an,ajn3745   epn1473   pinm1781   ppro5213
14 Ye are my friends, if ye do whatsoever I   command you.

ad3765/pin3004/ppro5209   an,ajn1401   3754 art3588   ajn1401   pin1492   3756 inpro5101
15 Henceforth*I*call*you*not servants; for the servant knoweth not what

ppro846 art,nn2962 pin4160 1161   pfi2046 epn5209 an,ajn5384   3754   an,ajn3956 repro3739   aina191
his lord doeth: but I have called you friends; for all things that I have heard

pre3844 ppro3450 art,nn3962   aina1107   ppro5213
of   my Father I have made known unto you.

epn5210   3756 aom1586 ppro3165 235 epn1473   aom1586 ppro5209 2532 aina5087   ppro5209
16 Ye have not chosen me, but   I   have chosen you, and ordained you,

2443 epn5210   psa5217 2532   psa5342   an,nn2590 2532   ppro5216 art,nn2590   psa3306
that ye should go and bring forth fruit, and *that* your fruit should remain:

2443   repro3748/302   asba154 art3588   nn3962   pre1722 ppro3450 art,nn3686   asba1325
that whatsoever ye shall ask of the Father in   my   name, he may give it

ppro5213
you.

depro5023   pinm1781   ppro5213 2443   psa25   rcpro240
17 These things I command you, that ye love one another.

The Disciple of Christ Should Expect Persecution

1487 art3588   nn2889   pin3404 epn5209   pin1097   3754   pfi3404   epn1691 nu,ajn4412
18 If the world hate you, ye know that it hated me before *it hated*

ppro5216
you.

1487   ipf2258   pre1537 art3588   nn2889   art3588   nn2889   ipf5368/302   art,ajn2398   1161
19 If ye were of   the world, the world would   love his own: but

3754   pin2075 3756 pre1537 art3588   nn2889   235 epn1473   aom1586 ppro5209 pre1537 art3588
because ye are not of   the world, but   I   have chosen you out of the

nn2889   pre1223/depro5124 art3588   nn2889   pin3404 ppro5209
world, therefore the world hateth you.

pim3421   art3588   nn3056 repro3739 epn1473 aina2036   ppro5213   an,ajn1401 pin2076 3756
20 Remember the word that   I   said unto you, The servant is not

pr/cd/an,aj3187   ppro848 art,nn2962 1487   aina1377   epn1691   2532   ft1377
greater than his lord. If they have persecuted me, they will also persecute

epn5209 1487   aina5083 ppro3450 art,nn3056   ft5083 art,popro5212 2532
you; if they have kept my saying, they will keep yours also.

21 But all these things will they do unto you for*my*name's*sake, because they know not him*that*sent me.

22 If I had not come and spoken unto them, they had not had sin: but now they have no cloak for their sin.

23 He*that*hateth me hateth my Father also.

24 If I had not done among them the works which none other man did, they had not had sin: but now have they both seen and hated both me and my Father.

25 But *this cometh to pass,* that the word might be fulfilled that*is*written in their law, They hated me without*a*cause.   *(Ps. 35:19; 69:4)*

26 But when the Comforter is come, whom I will send unto you from the Father, *even* the Spirit of truth, which proceedeth from the Father, he shall testify of me:

27 And ye also shall bear witness, because ye have been with me from the beginning.

16

These things have I spoken unto you, that ye should not be offended.

2 They shall put you out*of*the*synagogues: yea, the time cometh, that whosoever killeth you will think that he doeth God service.   *(Is. 66:5)*

3 And these things will they do unto you, because they have not known the Father, nor me.

4 But these things have I told you, that when the time shall come, ye may remember that I told you of them. And these things I said not unto you at the beginning, because I was with you.

The Work of the Holy Spirit

1161   ad3568   pin5217   pre4313   art,apta3992   ppro3165   2532   an,ajn3762 pre1537 ppro5216
5 But now I go*my*way to him*that*sent me; and none of you
pin2065 ppro3165 ad4226   pin5217
asketh me, Whither goest thou?

235   3754   pfi2980   depro5023   ppro5213 art,nn3077   pfi4137 ppro5216
6 But because I have said these things unto you, sorrow hath filled your
art,nn2588
heart.

235   epn1473 pin3004 ppro5213 art3588   nn225   pin4851   ppro5213 2443 epn1473
☞ 7 Nevertheless I tell you the truth; It is expedient for you that I
asba565   1063 1437   asba565/3361   art3588   nn3875   3756   fm2064 pre4314 ppro5209 1161 1437
go away: for if I go*not*away, the Comforter will not come unto you; but if I
asbp4198   ft3992 ppro846 pre4314 ppro5209
depart, I will send him unto you.

2532   depro1565   apta2064   ft1651   art3588   nn2889   pre4012 an,nn266 2532 pre4012
8 And when he is come, he will reprove the world of sin, and of
an,nn1343   2532 pre4012   an,nn2920
righteousness, and of judgment:

pre4012 an,nn266 (3303)   3754   pin4100   3756 pre1519 ppro1691
9 Of sin,   because they believe not on me;
(1161) pre4012   an,nn1343   3754   pin5217 pre4314 ppro3450 art,nn3962   2532   pin2334 ppro3165
☞ 10   Of righteousness, because I go to my Father, and ye see me
3756 ad2089
no more;

(1161) pre4012   an,nn2920   3754   art3588   nn758   depro5127 art,nn2889   pfip2919
11   Of judgment, because the prince of this world is judged.
pin2192 ad2089   an,ajn4183   pinf3004   ppro5213 235   pinm1410/3756 pinf941
12 I have yet many things to say unto you, but ye cannot bear them
ad737
now.

1161   ad3752 depro1565 art3588 nn4151   art,nn225   asba2064   ft3594 ppro5209 pre1519
13 Howbeit when he, the Spirit of truth, is come, he will guide you into
an,aj3956 art,nn225 1063   3756   ft2980 pre575 rxpro1438   235   an,ajn3745/302   asba191
all truth: for he shall not speak of himself; but whatsoever he shall hear,
ft2980   2532   ft312 ppro5213   art,ppmp2064
that shall he speak: and he will show you things*to*come.

depro1565   ft1392 epn1691 3754   fm2983   pre1537 art,popro1699 2532   ft312
14 He shall glorify me: for he shall receive of mine, and shall show *it*
ppro5213
unto you.

an,aj3956   an,ajn3745 art3588   nn3962   pin2192 pin2076 pr/popro1699 pre1223/depro5124 aina2036   3754
15 All things that the Father hath are mine: therefore said I, that he
fm2983 pre1537 art,popro1699 2532   ft312   ppro5213
shall take of mine, and shall show *it* unto you.

☞ **16:7–15** See note on Mark 3:28, 29.

☞ **16:10** It has been suggested that the world being reproved of righteousness (John 16:8) means that the message of the need for accepting God's grace will be made known by the convicting power of the Holy Spirit (John 16:13). Along with the coming of the Holy Spirit, the ascension of Christ itself proves that He had finished the work He had set out to do.

16 A little while, and ye shall not see me: and again, a little while, and ye shall see me, because I go to the Father.

17 Then said *some* of his disciples among themselves, What is this that he saith unto us, A little while, and ye shall not see me: and again, a little while, and ye shall see me: and, Because I go to the Father?

18 They said therefore, What is this that he saith, A little while? we cannot tell what he saith.

19 Now Jesus knew that they were desirous to ask him, and said unto them, Do ye inquire among yourselves of that I said, A little while, and ye shall not see me: and again, a little while, and ye shall see me?

20 Verily, verily, I say unto you, That ye shall weep and lament, but the world shall rejoice: and ye shall be sorrowful, but your sorrow shall be turned into joy.

21 A woman when she is*in*travail hath sorrow, because her hour is come: but as*soon*as she is delivered of the child, she remembereth no more the anguish, for joy that a man is born into the world.

22 And ye now therefore have sorrow: but I will see you again, and your heart shall rejoice, and your joy no man taketh from you.

23 And in that day ye shall ask me nothing. Verily, verily, I say unto you, Whatsoever ye shall ask the Father in my name, he will give *it* you.

24 Hitherto have ye asked nothing in my name: ask, and ye shall receive, that your joy may be full.

Jesus Will Return to Heaven

depro5023   pfi2980   ppro5213 pre1722   an,nn3942   235   an,nn5610

25 These things have I spoken unto you in proverbs: but the time

pinm2064   ad3753   3756 ad2089   ft2980   ppro5213 pre1722   an,nn3942   235   ft312

cometh, when I shall no more speak unto you in proverbs, but I shall show

ppro5213 an,nn3954 pre4012 art3588   nn3962

you plainly of the Father.

pre1722 depro1565 art,nn2250   fm154 pre1722 ppro3450 art,nn3686   2532   pin3004 3756   ppro5213

26 At that day ye shall ask in my name: and I say not unto you,

3754 epn1473   ft2065 art3588   nn3962   pre4012 ppro5216

that I will pray the Father for you:

1063 art3588   nn3962   epn846   pin5368   ppro5209   3754   epn5210   pfi5368 epn1691 2532

27 For the Father himself loveth you, because ye have loved me, and

pfi4100   3754 epn1473   aina1831   pre3844 art,nn2316

have believed that I came out from God.

aina1831   pre3844 art3588   nn3962   2532   pfi2064   pre1519 art3588   nn2889   ad3825

28 I came forth from the Father, and am come into the world: again, I

pin863 art3588   nn2889   2532 pinm4198 pre4314 art3588   nn3962

leave the world, and go to the Father.

ppro846   art,nn3101   pin3004   ppro846 aima2396 ad3568   pin2980   an,nn3954   2532

29 His disciples said unto him, Lo, now speakest thou plainly, and

pin3004   an,ajn3762   an,nn3942

speakest no proverb.

ad3568   pin1492   3754   pin1492   an,ajn3956   2532 pin2192/an,nn5532 3756   2443

30 Now are*we*sure that thou knowest all things, and needest not that

idpro5100   psa2065 ppro4571 pre1722 depro5129   pin4100   3754   aina1831   pre575

any man should ask thee: by this we believe that thou camest forth from

an,nn2316

God.

art,nn2424   ainp611   ppro846   ad737   pin4100

31 Jesus answered them, Do ye now believe?

2400   an,nn5610   pinm2064   2532   ad3568   pfi2064   2443

32 Behold, the hour cometh, yea, is now come, that ye shall be

asbp4650   an,ajn1538   pre1519   art,ajn2398   2532   asba863 epn1691 pr/an,aj3441 2532

scattered, every man to his own, and shall leave me alone: and yet

pin1510 3756 pr/an,aj3441   3754   art3588   nn3962   pin2076 pre3326 ppro1700

I am not alone, because the Father is with me.   *(Zech. 13:7)*

depro5023   pfi2980   ppro5213 2443   pre1722 epn1698   psa2192

☞ 33 These things I have spoken unto you, that in me ye might have

an,nn1515 pre1722 art3588   nn2889   ft2192   an,nn2347   235   pim2293   epn1473

peace. In the world ye shall have tribulation: but be*of*good*cheer; I have

pfi3528   art3588   nn2889

overcome the world.

☞ **16:33** See note on 2 Timothy 1:12.

Jesus' Intercessory Prayer

17
depro5023   aina2980 art,nn2424 2532   aina1869   ppro848 art,nn3788 pre1519   art,nn3772
These words spake Jesus, and lifted up his eyes to heaven,
2532 aina2036 an,nn3962 art3588 nn5610   pfi2064   aima1392 ppro4675 art,nn5207 2443   ppro4675
and said, Father, the hour is come; glorify thy Son, that thy
art,nn5207 2532   asba1392 ppro4571
Son also may glorify thee:

ad2531   aina1325 ppro846 an,nn1849   an,aj3956 an,nn4561 2443   asba1325
2 As thou hast given him power over all flesh, that he should give
an,aj166 an,nn2222 an,aj3956/repro3739   pfi1325 ppro846
eternal life to as*many*as thou hast given him.

1161 depro3778 pin2076 pr/art,nn2222 an,aj166   2443   psa1097 epn4571 art3588 aj3441 an,aj228
3 And this is life eternal, that they might know thee the only true
an,nn2316 2532 an,nn2424 an,nn5547 repro3739   aina649
God, and Jesus Christ, whom thou hast sent.

epn1473   aina1392 ppro4571 pre1909 art3588 nn1093   aina5048 art3588 nn2041 repro3739
4 I have glorified thee on the earth: I have finished the work which
pfi1325 ppro3427 2443 asba4160
thou gavest me to do.

2532 ad3568 an,nn3962 aima1392 epn4771 ppro3165 pre3844   rxpro4572   art,nn1391
☞ 5 And now, O Father, glorify thou me with thine*own*self with the glory
repro3739 ipf2192 pre3844 ppro4671 pre4253 art3588 nn2889   aip1511
which I had with thee before the world was.

aina5319 ppro4675 art,nn3686   art3588 nn444 repro3739   pfi1325 ppro3427
6 I have manifested thy name unto the men which thou gavest me
pre1537 art3588 nn2889 pr/popro4674   ipf2258 2532   pfi1325 ppro846 epn1698 2532
out of the world: thine they were, and thou gavest them me; and they have
pfi5083 ppro4675 art,nn3056
kept thy word.   *(Ps. 22:22)*

ad3568   pfi1097 3754 an,ajn3956   an,ajn3745   pfi1325 ppro3427
7 Now they have known that all things whatsoever thou hast given me
pin2076 pre3844 epn4675
are of thee.

3754   pfi1325   ppro846 art3588 nn4487 repro3739   pfi1325 ppro3427 2532 epn846
8 For I have given unto them the words which thou gavest me; and they
aina2983   2532   aina1097   ad230 3754   aina1831 pre3844 epn4675 2532
have received *them,* and have known surely that I came out from thee, and
aina4100   3754 epn4771   aina649 ppro3165
they have believed that thou didst send me.

epn1473 pin2065 pre4012 epn846   pin2065 3756 pre4012 art3588 nn2889   235 pre4012   repro3739
9 I pray for them: I pray not for the world, but for them which thou
pfi1325 ppro3427 3754   pin1526 pr/popro4674
hast given me; for they are thine.

2532 an,aj3956 art,popro1699 pin2076 pr/popro4674 2532 art,popro4674   pr/an,popro1699 2532   pfip1392
10 And all mine are thine, and thine are mine; and I am glorified
pre1722 ppro846
in them.

☞ **17:5, 11, 21, 22** See note on Philippians 2:6–8.

☞ 11 And now I am no more in the world, but these are in the world,

and I come to thee. Holy Father, keep through thine own name those

whom thou hast given me, that they may be one, as we *are.*

☞ 12 While I was with them in the world, I kept them in thy name:

those that thou gavest me I have kept, and none of them is lost, but the

son of perdition; that the Scripture might be fulfilled.   *(Ps. 41:9; 109:4,5,7,8)*

13 And now come I to thee; and these things I speak in the world,

that they might have my joy fulfilled in themselves.

14 I have given them thy word; and the world hath hated them,

because they are not of the world, even as I am not of the world.

15 I pray not that thou shouldest take them out of the world, but that thou

shouldest keep them from the evil.

16 They are not of the world, even as I am not of the world.

17 Sanctify them through thy truth: thy word is truth.

18 As thou hast sent me into the world, even so have I also sent them

into the world.

19 And for*their*sakes I sanctify myself, that they also might be

sanctified through the truth.

20 Neither pray I for these alone, but for them*also*which*shall*believe

on me through their word;

☞ 21 That they all may be one; as thou, Father, *art* in me, and I

in thee, that they also may be one in us: that the world may believe

that thou hast sent me.

22 And the glory which thou gavest me I have given them; that they

may be one, even as we are one:

☞ **17:12** See note on 2 Thessalonians 2:3.

epn1473 pre1722 ppro846   2532 epn4771 pre1722 epn1698 2443   psa5600   pr/pfpp5048   pre1519

23 I   in them, and thou in me, that they may be made perfect in

nu,ajn1520 2532   2443 art3588 nn2889   psa1097 3754 epn4771   aina649 ppro3165 2532   aina25

one; and that the world may know that thou hast sent me, and hast loved

ppro846 ad2531   aina25 epn1691

them, as thou hast loved me.

an,nn3962   pin2309 2443   depro2548   repro3739   pfi1325 ppro3427 psa5600 pre3326 epn1700

24 Father, I will that they also, whom thou hast given me, be with me

ad3699   epn1473 pin1510 2443   psa2334 art,popro1699 art,nn1391 repro3739   aina1325 ppro3427

where I am; that they may behold my   glory, which thou hast given me:

3754   aina25 ppro3165 pre4253   an,nn2602   an,nn2889

for thou lovedst me before the foundation of the world.

an,aj1342   an,nn3962 (2532) art3588 nn2889   3756 aina1097 ppro4571 1161 epn1473

25 O righteous Father,   the world hath not known thee: but I   have

aina1097 ppro4571 2532 depro3778   aina1097 3754 epn4771   aina649 ppro3165

known thee, and these have known that thou hast sent me.

2532   aina1107   ppro846 ppro4675 art,nn3686 2532   ft1107   2443 art3588

26 And I have declared unto them thy name, and will declare it: that the

nn26   repro3739   aina25 ppro3165   psa5600 pre1722 epn846 epn2504 pre1722 ppro846

love wherewith thou hast loved me may be in them, and I in them.

Jesus Taken in the Garden (Matt. 26:47-56; Mark 14:43-50; Luke 22:47-53)

artnn2424   apta2036   depro5023   aina1831   pre4862 ppro846

18 When Jesus had spoken these words, he went forth with his

art,nn3101   ad4008 art3588 nn5493   2748   ad3699 ipf2258 an,nn2779 pre1519

disciples over the brook Cedron, where was a garden, into

repro3739 epn846 aina1525 2532 ppro846 art,nn3101

the which he entered, and his disciples.

1161 an,nn2455 2532   art,pap3860   ppro846 ipf1492 art3588 nn5117 3754 art,nn2424 ad4178

2 And Judas also, which betrayed him, knew the place: for Jesus ofttimes

ainp4863   ad1563 pre3326 ppro846 art,nn3101

resorted thither with his disciples.

art,nn2455 3767   apta2983   art,nn4686   2532 an,nn5257 pre1537 art3588

3 Judas then, having received a band of men and officers from the

nn749   2532 an,nn5330   pinm2064 ad1563 pre3326 an,nn5322 2532 an,nn2985 2532

chief priests and Pharisees, cometh thither with lanterns and torches and

an,nn3696

weapons.

an,nn2424   3767   pfp1492 an,aj3956   art,ppmp2064   pre1909 ppro848

4 Jesus therefore, knowing all things that*should*come upon him,

apta1831   aina2036 ppro846 inpro5101 pin2212

went forth, and said unto them, Whom seek ye?

ainp611 ppro846 an,nn2424 art,aj3480 art,nn2424 pin3004 ppro846 epn1473 pin1510

5 They answered him, Jesus of Nazareth. Jesus saith unto them, I   am

1161 an,nn2455 2532   art,pap3860 ppro846 plpf2476 pre3326 ppro846

he. And Judas also, which betrayed him, stood with them.

ad5613/3767   aina2036   ppro846   epn1473 pin1510   aina565

6 As*soon*then*as he had said unto them, I am *he,* they went

pre1519/art,ad3694 2532 aina4098   ad5476

backward, and fell to*the*ground.

3767   aina1905   ppro846   ad3825   inpro5101   pin2212   1161   art3588 aina2036 an,nn2424

7 Then asked he them again, Whom seek ye? And they said, Jesus of

art,aj3480

Nazareth.

art,nn2424   ainp611   aina2036 ppro5213 3754 epn1473 pin1510   1487   3767   pin2212

8 Jesus answered, I have told you that I am *he*: if therefore ye seek

epn1691 aima863 depro5128   pinf5217

me, let these go*their*way:

2443 art3588   nn3056   asbp4137   repro3739   aina2036 pre1537 ppro846 repro3739

9 That the saying might be fulfilled, which he spake, Of them which thou

pfi1325 ppro3427 (3756) aina622 an,ajn3762

gavest me have I lost none.

3767   an,nn4613 an,nn4074 pap2192   an,nn3162 aina1670 ppro846 2532 aina3817 art3588

10 Then Simon Peter having a sword drew it, and smote the

nn749   art,ajn1401   2532   aina609 ppro846 art,aj1188 art,nn5621 (1161) art3588   ajn1401   an,nn3686 ipf2258

high priest's servant, and cut off his right ear. The servant's name was

pr/an,nn3124

Malchus.

3767 aina2036 art,nn2424   art,nn4074 alma906 ppro4675 art,nn3162 pre1519 art3588 art,nn2336 art3588

11 Then said Jesus unto Peter, Put up thy sword into the sheath: the

nn4221 repro3739   art,nn3962   pfi1325 ppro3427   efn3364 asba4095 ppro846

cup which my Father hath given me, shall I not drink it?

Jesus Before the High Priest (Matt. 26:57, 58; Mark 14:53,54; Luke 22:54)

3767   ar13588 nn4686 2532 art3588   nn5506 2532 art,nn5257   art3588 nn2453 aina4815 art,nn2424

12 Then the band and the captain and officers of the Jews took Jesus,

2532 aina1210 ppro846

and bound him,

2532   aina520/ppro846 pre4314 an,nn452 nu,ajn4412 1063   ipf2258   pr/an,nn3995

13 And led*him*away to Annas first; for he was father in law to

art,nn2533   repro3739 ipf2258   pr/an,nn749   depro1565   art,nn1763

Caiaphas, which was the high priest that same year.

1161   an,nn2533   ipf2258 art3588   pr/art,apta4823   art3588 nn2453   3754

14 Now Caiaphas was he, which*gave*counsel to the Jews, that it

pin4851   nu1520 an,nn444   aifm622 pre5228 art3588   nn2992

was expedient that one man should die for the people.

Peter Denies Jesus (Matt. 26:69, 70; Mark 14:66-68; Luke 22:55-57)

1161 an,nn4613 an,nn4074 ipf190   art,nn2424 2532   an,aj243   an,nn3101 (1161) depro 1565

15 And Simon Peter followed Jesus, and *so did* another disciple: that

art,nn3101   ipf2258   pr/an,aj1110   art3588   nn749   2532   aina4897   art,nn2424 pre1519 art3588
disciple was known unto the high priest, and went*in*with Jesus into the

nn833   art3588   nn749
palace of the high priest.

1161   art,nn4074   plpf2476   pre4314 art3588   nn2374   ad1854   3767   aina1831   art,aj243
16 But Peter stood at the door without. Then went out that other

art,nn3101   repro3739   ipf2258   pr/an,aj1110   art3588   nn749   2532   aina2036
disciple, which was known unto the high priest, and spake unto

art,nn2377   2532   aina1521   art,nn4074
her*that*kept*the*door, and brought in Peter.

3767   pin3004 art3588   nn3814   art,nn2377   art,nn4074 pin1488 3361 epn4771
17 Then saith the damsel that kept*the*door unto Peter, Art not thou

2532   pre1537 depro5127 art,nn444   art,nn3101 depro1565 pin3004   pin1510 3756
also one of this man's disciples? He saith, I am not.

1161   art3588   ajn1401   2532   art,nn5257   plpf2476   pfp4160
18 And the servants and officers stood there, who had made a

an,nn439   3754   ipf2258 an,nn5592 2532   ipf2328   1161 art,nn4074
fire*of*coals; for it was cold: and they warmed themselves: and Peter

ipf2258/pr/pap2476 pre3326 ppro846   2532 pr/ppmp2328
stood with them, and warmed himself.

The High Priest Questions Jesus (Matt. 26:59-66; Mark 14:55-64; Luke 22:66-71)

art3588   nn749   3767   aina2065 art,nn2424 pre4012 ppro846   art,nn3101   2532   pre4012 ppro846
19 The high priest then asked Jesus of his disciples, and of his

art,nn1322
doctrine.

art,nn2424   ainp611   ppro846 epn1473 aina2980 an,nn3954   art3588   nn2889   epn1473 ad3842   aina1321
20 Jesus answered him, I spake openly to the world; I ever taught

pre1722 art3588   nn4864   2532 pre1722 art3588   nn2411   ad3699   art3588 nn2453   ad3842 pinm4905   2532
in the synagogue, and in the temple, whither the Jews always resort; and

pre1722 an,ajn2927   aina2980   an,ajn3752
in secret have I said nothing.

inpro5101 pin1905   aima1905 aina1905   art,pfp191   inpro5101   aina2980
21 Why askest thou me? ask them*which*heard me, what I have said

ppro846   aima2396   depro3778 pin1492 repro3739 epn1473 aina2036
unto them: behold, they know what I said.

1161   ppro846   depro5023 apta2036 nu1520   art3588   nn5257   pfp3933
22 And when he had thus spoken, one of the officers which stood by

aina1325/art,nn2424/an,nn4475   apta2036   pinm611   art3588
struck*Jesus*with*the*palm*of*his*hand, saying, Answerest thou the

nn749   ad3779
high priest so?   (Is. 50:6)

art,nn2424   ainp611   ppro846 1487   aina2980   ad2560   aima3140   pre4012 art3588 ajn2556
23 Jesus answered him, If I have spoken evil, bear witness of the evil:

1161 1487 ad2573 inpro5101   pin1194   ppro3165
but if well, why smitest thou me?

art,nn452   aina649 ppro846 pfpp1210 pre4314 an,nn2533 art3588   nn749
24 Now Annas had sent him bound unto Caiaphas the high priest.

Peter Denies Jesus Again (Matt. 26:71-75; Mark 14:69-72; Luke 22:58-62)

25 And Simon Peter stood and warmed himself. They said therefore unto him, Art not thou also *one* of his disciples? He denied *it,* and said, I am not.

26 One of the servants of the high priest, being *his* kinsman whose ear Peter cut off, saith, Did not I see thee in the garden with him?

27 Peter then denied again: and immediately the cock crew.

Jesus Is Brought to Pilate (Matt. 27:1,2,11-14; Mark 15:1-5; Luke 23:1-5)

28 Then led they Jesus from Caiaphas unto the hall*of*judgment: and it was early; and they themselves went not into the judgment hall, lest they should be defiled; but that they might eat the passover.

29 Pilate then went out unto them, and said, What accusation bring ye against this man?

30 They answered and said unto him, If he were not a malefactor, we would not have delivered*him*up unto thee.

31 Then said Pilate unto them, Take ye him, and judge him according to your law. The Jews therefore said unto him, It is* not*lawful for us to put*any*man*to*death:

32 That the saying of Jesus might be fulfilled, which he spake, signifying what death he should die.

33 Then Pilate entered into the judgment hall again, and called Jesus, and said unto him, Art thou the King of the Jews?

34 Jesus answered him, Sayest thou this thing of thyself, or did others tell it thee of me?

35 Pilate answered, Am I a Jew? Thine own nation and the chief priests have delivered thee unto me: what hast thou done?

36 Jesus answered, My kingdom is not of this world: if my kingdom were of this world, then would my servants fight, that I should not be delivered to the Jews: but now is my kingdom not from hence.

(Is. 9:6)

37 Pilate therefore said unto him, Art thou a king then? Jesus answered, Thou sayest that I am a king. To this end was I born, and for this cause came I into the world, that I should bear witness unto the truth. Every one that is of the truth heareth my voice.

Jesus Sentenced to Die (Matt. 27:15-31; Mark 15:6-20; Luke 23:13-25)

38 Pilate saith unto him, What is truth? And when he had said this, he went out again unto the Jews, and saith unto them, I find in him no fault *at all.*

39 But ye have a custom, that I should release unto you one at the passover: will ye therefore that I release unto you the King of the Jews?

40 Then cried they all again, saying, Not this man, but Barabbas. Now Barabbas was a robber.

Jesus Is Sent to Die on the Cross

19 Then Pilate therefore took Jesus, and scourged *him.* 2 And the soldiers plaited a crown of thorns, and put*it*on his head, and they put on him a purple robe,

_{2532   ipf3004   pim5463   art,nn935   art588   nn2453   2532}
3 And   said,   Hail,   King   of   the   Jews!   and   they
_{ipf1325/ppro846/an,nn4475}
smote*him*with*their*hands.

_{art,nn4091   3767   aina1831   ad1854   ad3825   2532   pin3004   ppro846   aima2396   pin71}
4 Pilate therefore went forth again, and saith unto them, Behold, I bring
_{ppro846   ad1854   ppro5213   2443   asba1097   3754   pin2147 an,aj3762 an,nn156 pre1722 ppro846}
him forth to you, that ye may know that I find   no   fault   in   him.

_{3767   aina1831   art,nn2424   ad1854   pap5409   art3588   nn4735   an,aj174   2532   art3588   an,aj4210}
5 Then came Jesus forth, wearing the crown of thorns, and the purple
_{nn2440   2532   pin3004   ppro846   aima2396   art3588   nn444}
robe. And *Pilate* saith unto them, Behold the man!

_{ad3753   art3588   nn749   3767   2532   art,nn5257   aina1492   ppro846   aina2905}
6 When the chief priests therefore and officers saw him, they cried out,
_{pap3004   aima4717   aima4717   art,nn4091   pin3004   ppro846   aima2983   epn5210 ppro846   2532}
saying, Crucify *him,* crucify *him.* Pilate saith unto them, Take ye him, and
_{aima4717   1063 epn1473 pin2147 3756 an,nn156 pre1722 ppro846}
crucify *him*: for   I   find no fault   in   him.

_{art3588   nn2453   ainp611   ppro846 epn2249 pin2192   an,nn3551   2532   pre2596 ppro2257 art,nn3551   pin3784}
7 The Jews answered him, We have a law, and by   our   law he ought
_{ainf599   3754   aina4160   rxpro1438   pr/an,nn5207   art,nn2316}
to die, because he made himself the   Son   of God.   *(Lev. 24:16)*

_{ad3753   art,nn4091   3767   aina191   depro5126   art,nn3056   ainp5399/ad3123}
8 When Pilate therefore heard that saying, he was*the*more*afraid;

_{2532   aina1525   ad3825   pre1519 art3588   nn4232   2532   pin3004   art,nn2424   ad4159}
9 And went again into the judgment hall, and saith unto Jesus, Whence
_{pin1488 epn4771   1161   art,nn2424 aina1325 ppro846 3756   an,nn612}
art thou? But Jesus gave him no answer.   *(Is. 53:7)*

_{3767   pin3004   art,nn4091   ppro846   pin2980   3756   epn1698   pin1492}
10 Then saith Pilate unto him, Speakest thou not unto me? knowest
_{3756   3754   pin2192   an,nn1849   ainf4717   ppro4571   2532   pin2192   an,nn1849   ainf630}
thou not that I have power to crucify thee, and have power to release
_{ppro4571}
thee?

_{art,nn2424   ainp611   (3756)   ipf2192   an,aj3762   an,nn1849   pre2596   ppro1700}
11 Jesus answered, Thou couldest have   no   power *at all* against me,
_{1487/3361   ipf2258   pr/pfpp1325 ppro4571   ad509   pre1223/depro5124   art,pap3860   ppro3165}
except it were given thee from above: therefore he*that*delivered me unto
_{ppro4571 pin2192   cd/an,aj3187 an,nn266}
thee hath the greater sin.

_{pre1537   depro5127   art,nn4091   ipf2212   ainf630   ppro846   1161   art3588   nn2453}
12 And from thenceforth Pilate sought to release him: but the Jews
_{ipf2896   pap3004   1437   asba630/depro5126   pin1488   3756   art,nn2541   pr/an,ajn5384}
cried out, saying, If thou let*this*man*go, thou art not Caesar's friend:
_{an,aj3956   art,pap4160   ppro848   pr/art,nn935   pin483   art,nn2541}
whosoever maketh himself a   king   speaketh against Caesar.

_{art,nn4091   3767   apta191   depro5126   art,nn3056   aina71   art,nn2424   ad1854   2532}
13 When Pilate therefore heard that saying, he brought Jesus forth, and
_{aina2523   pre1909 art3588   nn968   pre1519   an,nn5117   ppmp3004   an,ajn3038   1161}
sat down in   the judgment seat   in   a place that is called the Pavement, but
_{ad1447   1042}
in*the*Hebrew, Gabbatha.

1161   ipf2258   an,nn3904   art3588   3957   1161   ad5616   pr/an,nu,ajn1622
14 And it was the preparation of the passover, and about the   sixth

an,nn5610 2532   pin3004   art3588   nn2453   aima2396   ppro5216 art,nn935
hour: and he saith unto the Jews, Behold your King!

1161 art3588   aima2905   aima142   aima142   aima4717   ppro846 art,nn4091
15 But they cried out, Away with *him,* away with *him,* crucify him. Pilate

pin3004   ppro846   asba4717   ppro5216 art,nn935 art3588   nn749   ainp611
saith unto them, Shall I crucify your King? The chief priests answered, We

pin2192 3756 an,nn935 1508   an,nn2541
have no king but Caesar.

ad5119   aina3860   ppro846   3767   ppro846   asbp4717   1161
16 Then delivered he him therefore unto them to be crucified. And they

aina3880 art,nn2424 2532   aina520
took Jesus, and led*him*away.

Jesus on the Cross (Matt. 27:32-44; Mark 15:21-32; Luke 23:26-43)

2532   pap941   ppro848 art,nn4716   aina1831   pre1519   an,nn5117 art,ppmp3004
17 And he bearing his cross went forth into a place called *the place* of a

an,nn2898 repro3739   pinp3004   ad1447   1115
skull, which is called in*the*Hebrew Golgotha:

ad3699   aina4717   ppro846 2532 nu1417 pl/an,ajn243 pre3326 ppro846   ad1782/2532/ad1782
18 Where they crucified him, and two other with him, on*either*side*one,

1161 art,nn2424   an,aj3319
and Jesus in the midst.

1161   art,nn4091   aina1125   an,nn5102 2532 aina5087   pre1909 art3588   nn4716   1161   pr/an,pfpp1125
19 And Pilate wrote a title, and put *it* on the cross. And the writing

ipf2258   art,nn2424   art,aj3480   art3588   nn935   art3588   nn2453
was, JESUS OF NAZARETH THE KING OF THE JEWS.

depro5126 art,nn5102 3767 aina314 an,ajn4183   art3588 nn2453 3754 art3588 nn5117   ad3699   art,nn2424
20 This title then read many of the Jews: for the place where Jesus was

ainp4717   ipf2258   pr/ad1451 art3588 nn4172 2532   ipf2258 pr/pfpp1125   ad1447   ad1676
crucified was nigh to the city: and it was written in Hebrew, *and* Greek, *and*

ad4515
Latin.

3767   ipf3004 art3588   nn749   art3588 nn2453   art,nn4091 pim1125   3361 art3588 nn935
21 Then said the chief priests of the Jews to Pilate, Write not, The king of

art3588 nn2453 235   3754 depro1565 aina2036 pim1510 pr/an,nn935   art3588 nn2453
the Jews; but that   he   said, I am King of the Jews.

art,nn4091   ainp611   repro3739   pfi1125   pfi1125
22 Pilate answered, What I have written I have written.

3767 art3588   nn4757   ad3753   aina4717   art,nn2424 aina2983 ppro846   art,nn2440
23 Then the soldiers, when they had crucified Jesus, took his garments,

2532 aina4160 nu5064 an,nn3313   an,aj1538 an,nn4757 an,nn3313 2532   art,nn5509 1161 art3588 nn5509
and made four parts, to every soldier a part; and also *his* coat: now the coat

ipf2258   pr/an,aj729   pr/an,aj5307 pre1537 art3588 ad509   pre1223/an,ajn3650
was without seam, woven from the top throughout.

aina2036   3767   pre4314   rcpro240   3361 aosi4977 ppro846 235
24 They said therefore among themselves, Let us not rend it, but

aosi2975   pre4012   pppro846   inpro5101   fm2071   2443   art3588   nn1124   asbp4137

cast lots for   it,   whose it shall be: that the Scripture might be fulfilled,

art,pap3004   aom1266   pppro3450   art,nn2440   rxpro1438   2532   pre1909 pppro3450   art,nn2441

which saith, They parted my raiment among them, and for my vesture they

aina906 an,nn2819   depro5023   3767   (3303) art3588   nn4757   aina4160

did cast lots. These things therefore   the soldiers did.   *(Ps. 22:18)*

1161   plpf2476 pre3844 art3588   nn4716   art,nn2424 pppro846   art,nn3384 2532 pppro846

25 Now there stood by   the cross of Jesus his   mother, and his

art,nn3384   art,nn79   an,nn3137 art3588   art,nn2832   2532 an,nn3137   art,aj3094

mother's sister, Mary the *wife* of Cleophas, and Mary Magdalene.

an,nn2424   3767   apta1492   art,nn3384   2532   art3588   nn3101

26 When Jesus therefore   saw   his   mother, and the   disciple

pfp3936   repro3739   ipf25   pin3004   pppro848 art,nn3384   an,nn1135   2400   pppro4675

standing by, whom he loved, he saith unto his mother, Woman, behold thy

art,nn5207

son!

ad1534   pin3004   art3588   nn3101   2400   pppro4675   art,nn3384   2532   pre575 depro1565

27 Then saith he to the disciple, Behold thy mother! And from that

art,nn5610   art,nn3101   aina2983 pppro846 pre1519 art,ajn2398

hour that disciple took her unto his own *home.*

The Death of Jesus (Matt. 27:45-56; Mark 15:33-41; Luke 23:44-49)

pre3326   depro5124 art,nn2424   pfp1492   3754   an,ajn3956   ad2235   pfip5055

28 After this, Jesus knowing that all things were now accomplished,

2443 art3588   nn1124   asbp5048   pin3004   pin1372

that the Scripture might be fulfilled, saith, I thirst.   *(Ps. 22:15)*

3767   ipf2749   an,nn4632 an,ajn3324   an,nn3690   1161   art3588   apta4130

29 Now there was set a vessel full of vinegar: and they filled a

an,nn4699   an,nn3690   2532   apta4060   an,nn5301   2532 aina4374   pppro846 art,nn4750

sponge with vinegar, and put*it*upon hyssop, and put it to his mouth.

(Ps. 69:21)

ad3753   art,nn2424   3767   aina2983   art3588   nn3690   aina2036   pfip5055

30 When Jesus therefore had received the vinegar, he said, It is finished:

2532   apta2827   art,nn2776   aima3860   art3588   nn4151

and he bowed his head, and gave up the ghost.

art3588 nn2453   3767   1893   ipf2258   an,nn3904   2443 art3588   nn4983

31 The Jews therefore, because it was the preparation, that the bodies should

3361   asba3306   pre1909 art3588 nn4716   pre1722 art3588   nn4521   1063 depro1565 art,nn4521 art,nn2250 ipf2258

not remain upon the cross on the sabbath day, (for that sabbath day was a

pr/an,aj3173   aina2065 art,nn4091 2443 pppro846 art,nn4628   asbp2608   2532

high day,) besought Pilate that their legs might be broken, and *that* they might

asbp142

be taken away.   *(Deut. 21:22,23)*

3767   aina2064 art3588   nn4757   2532 aina2608 art3588 nn4628   art3588 nu,ajn4413 2532   art3588

32 Then came the soldiers, and broke the legs of the first, and of the

ajn243   art,aptp4957   pppro846

other which*was*crucified*with him.

33 But when they came to Jesus, and saw that he was dead already, they broke not his legs:

34 But one of the soldiers with a spear pierced his side, and forthwith came*there*out blood and water.

35 And he*that*saw *it* bare record, and his record is true: and he knoweth that he saith true, that ye might believe.

36 For these things were done, that the Scripture should be fulfilled, A bone of him shall not be broken.   *(Ex. 12:46; Num. 9:12; Ps. 34:20)*

37 And again another Scripture saith, They shall look on him whom they pierced.   *(Zech. 12:10)*

The Burial of Jesus (Matt. 27:57-61; Mark 15:42-47; Luke 23:50-56)

38 And after this Joseph of Arimathaea, being a disciple of Jesus, but secretly for fear of the Jews, besought Pilate that he might take away the body of Jesus: and Pilate gave*him*leave. He came therefore, and took the body of Jesus.

39 And there came also Nicodemus, which*at*the*first*came to Jesus by night, and brought a mixture of myrrh and aloes, about a hundred pound *weight.*

40 Then took they the body of Jesus, and wound it in linen clothes with the spices, as the manner of the Jews is to bury.

41 Now in the place where he was crucified there was a garden; and in the garden a new sepulcher, wherein was never*man*yet laid.

42 There laid they Jesus therefore because of the Jews' preparation *day*; for the sepulcher was nigh*at*hand.

Jesus' Resurrection (Matt. 28:1-10; Mark 16:1-8; Luke 24:1-12)

(1161) art3588 nu,ajn3391 art3588 nn4521 pinm2064 an,nn3137 art,aj3094 ad4404

20 The first *day* of the week cometh Mary Magdalene early,

pap5607 ad2089 pr/an,nn4653 pre1519 art3588 nn3419 2532 pin991 art3588

when it was yet dark, unto the sepulcher, and seeth the

nn3037 pfpp142 pre1537 art3588 nn3419

stone taken away from the sepulcher.

3767 pin5143 2532 pinm2064 pre4314 an,nn4613 an,nn4074 2532 pre4314 art3588 an,aj243

2 Then she runneth, and cometh to Simon Peter, and to the other

an,nn3101 repro3739 art,nn2424 ipf5368 2532 pin3004 ppro846 aina142 art3588

disciple, whom Jesus loved, and saith unto them, They have taken away the

nn2962 pre1537 art3588 nn3419 2532 pin1492 3756 ad4226 aina5087 ppro846

Lord out of the sepulcher, and we know not where they have laid him.

art,nn4074 3767 aina1831 2532 art,aj243 an,nn3101 2532 ipf2064 pre1519 art3588

3 Peter therefore went forth, and that other disciple, and came to the

nn3419

sepulcher.

1161 ipf5143 art,nu,ajn1417 ad3674 2532 art3588 an,aj243 nn3101 aina4390/ad5032 art,nn4074,

4 So they ran both together: and the other disciple did outrun Peter

2532 aina2064 nu,aj4413 pre1519 art3588 nn3419

and came first to the sepulcher.

2532 apta3879 pin991 art3588 nn3608 ppmp2749 3305

5 And he stooping down, *and looking in,* saw the linen clothes lying; yet

aina1525/3756

went*he*not*in.

3767 pinm2064 an,nn4613 an,nn4074 pap190 ppro846 2532 aina1525 pre1519 art3588 nn3419

6 Then cometh Simon Peter following him, and went into the sepulcher,

2532 pin2334 art3588 nn3608 ppmp2749

and seeth the linen clothes lie,

2532 art3588 nn4676 repro3739 ipf2258 pre1909 ppro846 art,nn2776 3756 ppmp2749 pre3326 art3588

7 And the napkin, that was about his head, not lying with the

nn3608 235 pfpp1794 pre1519 nu1520 an,nn5117 ad5565

linen clothes, but wrapped together in a place by itself.

ad5119 aina1525 2532 (3767) art,aj243 an,nn3101 art,apta2064 nu,aj4413 pre1519 art3588

8 Then went in also that other disciple, which came first to the

nn3419 2532 aina1491 2532 aina4100

sepulcher, and he saw, and believed.

1063 ad3764/plpf1492 art3588 nn1124 3754 ppro846 pin1163 ainf450 pre1537

9 For as*yet*they*knew*not the Scripture, that he must rise again from

an,ajn3498

the dead. *(Ps. 16:10; 49:15)*

3767 art3588 nn3101 aina565 ad3825 pre4314 rxpro1438

10 Then the disciples went away again unto their*own*home.

Jesus Appears to Mary Magdelene (Mark 16:9-11)

1161 an,nn3137 plpf2476 ad1854 pre4314 art3588 nn3419 pap2799 3767 ad5613

11 But Mary stood without at the sepulcher weeping: and as she

ipf2799 aina3879 pre1519 art3588 nn3419

wept, she stooped down, *and looked* into the sepulcher,

2532   pin2334   nu1417   an,nn32   pre1722 an,ajn3022   ppmp2516   an,nu,ajn1520 pre4314 art3588   nn2776   2532

12 And seeth two angels in white sitting, the one at the head, and

an,nu,ajn1520 pre4314 art3588   nn4228   ad3699   art3588   nn4983   art,nn2424   ipf2749

the other at the feet, where the body of Jesus had lain.

2532   depro1565 pin3004   ppro846   an,nn1135   inpro5101   pin2799   pin3004

13 And they say unto her, Woman, why weepest thou? She saith unto

ppro846   3754   aina142   ppro3450 art,nn2962   2532   pin1492   3756   ad4226

them, Because they have taken away my Lord, and I know not where they

aina5087 ppro846

have laid him.

2532   depro5023 apta2036   ainp4762   pre1519/art,ad3694   2532   pin2334

14 And when she had thus said, she turned herself back, and saw

art,nn2424   pfp2476   2532   ipf1492   3756   3754   pin2076   pr/art,nn2424

Jesus standing, and knew not that it was Jesus.

art,nn2424 pin3004   ppro846   an,nn1135   inpro5101   pin2799   inpro5101   pin2212

15 Jesus saith unto her, Woman, why weepest thou? whom seekest thou?

depro1565   pap1380   (3754)   pin2076 art3588   pr/nn2780   pin3004   ppro846 an,nn2962 1487 epn4771

She, supposing him to be the gardener, saith unto him, Sir, if thou have

aina941   ppro846   aima2036   ppro3427   ad4226   aina5087   ppro846   epn2504

borne him hence, tell me where thou hast laid him, and I will

ft142/ppro846

take*him*away.

art,nn2424 pin3004   ppro846   an,nn3137   depro1565 aptp4762   pin3004   ppro846

16 Jesus saith unto her, Mary. She turned herself, and saith unto him,

4462   repro3739/pinp3004   an,nn1320

Rabboni; which*is*to*say, Master.

art,nn2424 pin3004   ppro846   pim680   ppro3450   3361   1063   ad3768   pfi305   pre4314

☞ **17** Jesus saith unto her, Touch me not; for I am not yet ascended to

ppro3450   art,nn3962   1161 pim4198 pre4314 ppro3450   art,nn80   2532 aima2036   ppro846   pin305   pre4314

my Father: but go to my brethren, and say unto them, I ascend unto

ppro3450   art,nn3962   and ppro5216 an,nn3962   2532   ppro3450 an,nn2316 2532 ppro5216 an,nn2316

my Father, and your Father; and to my God, and your God.

an,nn3137   art,aj3094   pinm2064   pap518 art3588   nn3101   3754   pfi3708 art3588

18 Mary Magdalene came and told the disciples that she had seen the

nn2962   2532   aina2036   depro5023   ppro846

Lord, and *that* he had spoken these things unto her.

Jesus Appears to the Disciples (Matt. 28:16-20; Mark 16:14-18; Luke 24:36-49)

3767   art3588 depro1565 nn2250   an,nn3798 pap5607 art3588 pr/nu,ajn3391   art3588   nn4521

19 Then the same day at evening, being the first *day* of the week,

---

☞ **20:17** The verb *háptou*, the present imperative of *haptómai* (680), should be translated "do not continue touching me." The significance of Christ mentioning this statement is related to the fact that He had not ascended to His Father. Some suggest that Mary was attempting to show Christ that she desired for Him to remain in the world and not go to His Father. Christ's command to her to stop touching Him was His explanation to her that His life now would not be the same as it was before His death. In this view, it has been stated that Christ would be ascending to His Father, which would complete His resurrected state. Others go a step further to say that this woman reflected the feelings of all of Christ's followers who desired to have Christ set up an earthly kingdom. This statement by the Lord was a reminder of His earlier statements about His ascension to His Father (cf. John 14).

2532   art3588   nn2374   pfpp2808   ad3699   art3588   nn3101   ipf2258   pr/pfpp4863   pre1223   art,nn5401

when the doors were shut where the disciples were assembled for fear of

art3588   nn2453   aina2064   art,nn2424   2532   aina2476   pre1519   art3588   ajn3319   2532   pin3004   ppro846   an,nn1515

the Jews, came Jesus and stood in the midst, and saith unto them, Peace be

ppro5213

unto you.

         2532   depro5124   apta2036   aina1166   ppro846   art,nn5495   2532   ppro848

20 And when he had so said, he showed unto them *his* hands and his

art,nn4125   3767   aina5463/art3588/nn3101   apta1492 art3588   nn2962

side. Then were*the*disciples*glad, when they saw the Lord.

         3767   aina2036   art,nn2424   ppro846   ad3825   an,nn1515   ppro5213   ad2531   art,nn3962

21 Then said Jesus to them again, Peace be unto you: as *my* Father hath

pfi649   ppro3165   epn2504/pin3992   ppro5209

sent me, even*so*send*I you.

         2532   apta2036   depro5124   aina1720   2532   pin3004   ppro846

☞ 22 And when he had said this, he breathed on *them,* and saith unto them,

aima2983   an,aj40   an,nn4151

Receive ye the Holy Ghost:

         idpro5100/302   art,nn266   asba863   pinp863   ppro846

☞ 23 Whose soever sins ye remit, they are remitted unto them; *and*

         idpro5100/302   psa2902   pfip2902

whose soever *sins* ye retain, they are retained.

Thomas' Unbelief

         1161   an,nn2381   nu1520   pre1537 art3588   nu,ajn1427   art,ppmp3004   an,ajn1324   ipf2558   3756   pre3326   ppro846

24 But Thomas, one of the twelve, called Didymus, was not with them

ad3753   art,nn2424   aina2064

when Jesus came.

         art3588   an,aj243   nn3101   3767   ipf3004   ppro846   pfi3708   art3588   nn2962

25 The other disciples therefore said unto him, We have seen the Lord.

1161   art3588   aina2036   ppro846   3362   asba1492 pre1722 ppro846 art,nn5495 art3588   nn5179   art3588

But he said unto them, Except I shall see in his hands the print of the

nn2247   2532 asba906 ppro3450 art,nn1147 pre1519 art3588   nn5179   art3588   nn2247   2532   asba906   ppro3450 art,nn5495 pre1519

nails, and put my finger into the print of the nails, and thrust my hand into

ppro856   art,nn4125   efn3364   ft4100

his side, I will not believe.

         2532   pre3326   nu3638   an,nn2250   ad3825   ppro846   art,nn3101   ipf2258   ad2080   2532   an,nn2381   pre3326

26 And after eight days again his disciples were within, and Thomas with

ppro846   pinm2064   art,nn2424   art3588   nn2374   pfpp2808   2532   aina2476 pre1519 art3588   ajn3319   2532

them: *then* came Jesus, the doors being shut, and stood in the midst, and

aina2036   an,nn1515   ppro5213

said, Peace, *be* unto you.

☞ **20:22** This was one of the many times that God "breathed," gave, or filled His people with the Holy Spirit. This giving or filling of the Holy Spirit should not be confused with the baptism in the Holy Spirit (see note on Acts 1:5) and the special advent of the Holy Spirit at Jerusalem, Caesarea, and Ephesus (Acts 2:1–13; 11:15–18; 19:1–7). See also note on 1 Corinthians 12:13.

☞ **20:23** See note on Matthew 16:18, 19.

ad1534 pin3004   art,nn2381   pim5342   ad5602   ppro4675 art,nn147   2532   aima1492 ppro3450
27 Then saith he to Thomas, Reach hither thy finger, and behold my

art,nn5495 2532 pim5342   ppro4675 art,nn5495 2532   aima906   pre1519 ppro3450 art,nn4125 2532 pim1096 3361
hands; and reach hither thy hand, and thrust *it* into my side: and be not

pr/an,aj571   235   pr/an,aj4103
faithless, but believing.

2532   art,nn2381   ainp611   2532 aina2036   ppro846 ppro3450 art,nn2962 2532 ppro3450 art,nn2316
28 And Thomas answered and said unto him, My Lord and my God.

art,nn2424 pin3004   ppro846   an,nn2381   3754   pfi3708 ppro3165
29 Jesus saith unto him, Thomas, because thou hast seen me, thou hast

pfi4100   pr/an,aj3107   art,apta1492/3361   2532   apta4100
believed: blessed *are* they*that*have*not*seen, and *yet* have believed.

The Purpose of the Book

2532   an,aj4183   an,aj243   an,nn4592   3303   aina4160 art,nn242   ad1799   ppro848
30 And many other signs truly did Jesus in*the*presence of his

art,nn3101   repro3739 pin2076 3756 pr/pfpp1125 pre1722 depro5129 art,nn975
disciples, which are not written in this book:

1161 depro5023   pfip1125   2443   asba4100   3754 art,nn2424 pin2076 art3588   pr/nn5547
31 But these are written, that ye might believe that Jesus is the Christ,

art3588 pr/hn5207   art,nn2316 2532 2443   pap4100   psa2192 an,nn2222 pre1722   ppro846 art,nn3686
the Son of God; and that believing ye might have life through his name.

Jesus Appears in Galilee

pre3326   depro5023   art,nn2424 aina5319   rxpro1438 ad3825   art3588   nn3101   pre1909
21 After these things Jesus showed himself again to the disciples at

art3588 nn2281   art,nn5085   1161   ad3779   aina5319
the sea of Tiberias; and on*this*wise showed he *himself.*

ipf2258   ad3674   an,nn4613 an,nn4074   2532 an,nn2381 art,ppmp3004 an,ajn1324   2532
2 There were together Simon Peter, and Thomas called Didymus, and

3482   art,pre575 2580   art,nn1056   2532 art3588   art,nn2199   2532 nu1417 an,aj243 pre1537
Nathanael of Cana in Galilee, and the *sons* of Zebedee, and two other of

ppro846 art,nn3101
his disciples.

an,nn4613 an,nn4074 pin3004   ppro846   pin5217   pinf232   pin3004   ppro846 epn2249
☞ 3 Simon Peter saith unto them, I go a fishing. They say unto him, We

2532 pinm2064 pre4862 ppro4671   aina1831   2532 aina305 pre1519 art,nn4143   ad2117
also go with thee. They went forth, and entered into a ship immediately:

2532 (pre1722) depro1565 art,nn3571   aina4084   an,ajn3762
and   that night they caught nothing.

☞ **21:3** Some have suggested that Peter's statement about going fishing is significant in that it marks his departure from service to the Lord back to his old profession as a fisherman. They say this was a result of his confusion about the circumstances that had previously transpired (i.e., Christ's death). Others, however, suggest that Peter and the other disciples had to have some form of livelihood until the power that Christ promised came on them.

1161   an,nn4405   ad2235   aptm1096 art,nn2424 aina2476 pre1519 art3588   nn123   3305

4 But when the morning was now come, Jesus stood on the shore: but

art3588   nn3101   ipf1492   3756 3754   pin2076 pr/an,nn2424

the disciples knew not that it was Jesus.

3767   art,nn2424   pin3004   ppro846   an,nn3813   pin2192   idpro3387   an,nn4371

5 Then Jesus saith unto them, Children, have ye any meat? They

ainp611   ppro846   3756

answered him, No.

1161   art3588 aina2036   ppro846   aima906 art3588 nn1350 pre1519 art3588 an,aj1188 nn3313   art3588 nn4143

6 And he said unto them, Cast the net on the right side of the ship,

2532   ft2147   aina906   3767   2532 ad2089   aina2480/3756   ainf1670

and ye shall find. They cast therefore, and now they were*not*able to draw

ppro846 pre575 art3588   nn4128   art,nn2486

it for the multitude of fishes.

3767   depro1565   art,nn3101   repro3739 art,nn2424 ipf25   pin3004   art,nn4074   pin2076

7 Therefore that disciple whom Jesus loved saith unto Peter, It is

art3588   pr/hn2962   3767   an,nn4613   an,nn4074 apta191   3754   pin2076 art3588 pr/nn2962

the Lord. Now when Simon Peter heard that it was the Lord, he

aom1241   art,nn1903   1063   ipf2258 pr/an,aj1131 2532   aina906 rxpro1438 pre1519

girt *his* fisher's coat *unto him,* (for he was naked,) and did cast himself into

art3588 nn2281

the sea.

1161   art3588 an,aj243   nn3101   aina2064   art,nn4142   1063   ipf2258   3756

8 And the other disciples came in a little ship; (for they were not

ad3112   pre575 art,nn1093   235   ad5613 (pre575) nu1250   an,nn4083   pap4951   art3588 nn1350

far from land, but as*it*were two hundred cubits,) dragging the net with

art,nn2486

fishes.

ad5613/3767   aina576   pre1519 art,nn1093   pin991   an,nn439

9 As*soon*then*as they were come to land, they saw a fire*of*coals

(ppmp2749) 2532 an,nn3795   ppmp1945   2532 an,nn740

there, and fish laid thereon, and bread.

art,nn2424 pin3004   ppro846   aima5342 pre575 art3588 nn3795 repro3739   ad3568   aina4084

10 Jesus saith unto them, Bring of the fish which ye have now caught.

an,nn4613   an,nn4074   aina305   2532   aina1670 art3588 nn1350 pre1909 art,nn1093 pr/an,aj3324   an,aj3173

11 Simon Peter went up, and drew the net to land full of great

an,nn2486   nu1540/nu4004/nu5140   2532   pap5607   pr/an,aj5118

fishes, a*hundred*and*fifty*and*three: and for all there were so many, yet

3756 art3588 nn1350   ainp4977

was not the net broken.

art,nn2424 pin3004   ppro846   ad1205   aima709 1161 an,aj3762   art3588   nn3101   ipf5111

12 Jesus saith unto them, Come *and* dine. And none of the disciples durst

ainf1833 ppro846 pr/inpro5101 pin1488 epn4771   pfp1492   3754   pin2076 art3588 pr/nn2962

ask him, Who art thou? knowing that it was the Lord.

art,nn2424 3767   pinm2064   2532   pin2983   art,nn740   2532   pin1325   ppro846   2532 art,nn3795

13 Jesus then cometh, and taketh bread, and giveth them, and fish

ad3668

likewise.

depro5124   ad2235   nu,ajn5154   art,nn2424 ainp5319   ppro848   art,nn3101

14 This is now the third time that Jesus showed himself to his disciples,

aptp1453 pre1537   an,ajn3498

after that he was risen from the dead.

Do You Love Me?

3767   ad3753   aina709   art,nn2424 pin3004   art,nn4613   an,nn4074   an,nn4613

15 So when they had dined, Jesus saith to Simon Peter, Simon, *son* of

an,nn2495   pin25   ppro3165 cd/an,ajn4119   depro5130   pin3004   ppro846   3483 an,nn2962 epn4771

Jonah, lovest thou me   more than these? He saith unto him, Yea, Lord; thou

pin1492   3754   pin5368 ppro4571   pin3004   ppro846 pim1006 ppro3450 art,nn721

knowest that I love thee. He saith unto him, Feed my lambs.

pin3004   ppro846 ad3825   nu,ajn1208   an,nn4613   an,nn2495   pin25

16 He saith to him again the second time, Simon, *son* of Jonah, lovest thou

ppro3165   pin3004   ppro846   3483   an,nn2962 epn4771   pin1492   3754   pin5368 ppro4571   pin3004

me? He saith unto him, Yea, Lord; thou knowest that I love thee. He saith

ppro846 pim4165 ppro3450 art,nn4263

unto him, Feed my sheep.

pin3004   ppro846 art3588   nu,ajn5154   an,nn4613   an,nn2495   pin5368

17 He saith unto him the third time, Simon, *son* of Jonah, lovest thou

ppro3165 art,nn4074   ainp3076   3754   aina2036   ppro856 art3588   nu,ajn5154   pin5368

me? Peter was grieved because he said unto him the third time, Lovest thou

ppro3165   2532   aina2036   ppro846 an,nn2962 epn4771   pin1097   an,ajn3956   epn4771   pin1492   3754

me? And he said unto him, Lord, thou knowest all things; thou knowest that I

pin5368 ppro4571 art,nn2424 pin3004   ppro846 pim1006 ppro3450 art,nn4263

love thee. Jesus saith unto him, Feed my sheep.

281   281   pin3004   ppro4671   ad3753   ipf2258 pr/cd/an,aj3501   ipf2224

18 Verily, verily, I say unto thee, When thou wast young, thou girdedst

rxpro4572   2532   ipf4043   ad3699   ipf2309   1161   ad3752   asba1095

thyself, and walkedst whither thou wouldest: but when thou shalt be old, thou

ft1614   ppro4675 art,nn5495   2532   an,ajn243   ft2224 ppro4571 2532   ft5342

shalt stretch forth thy hands, and another shall gird thee, and carry *thee*

ad3699   pin2309   3756

whither thou wouldest not.

(1161) depro5124   aina2036   pap4591   an,aj4169 an,nn2288   ft1392 art,nn2316 2532

19   This spake he, signifying by what death he should glorify God. And

apta2036 depro5124   pin3004   ppro846 pim190 ppro3427

when he had spoken this, he saith unto him, Follow me.

1161   art,nn4074   aptp1994   pin991 art3588   nn3101   repro3739 art,nn2424 ipf25

20 Then Peter, turning about, seeth the disciple whom Jesus loved

pap190   repro3739   2532   aina377   pre1909 ppro846 art,nn4738   pre1722   art,nn1173   2532 aina2036 an,nn2962

following; which also leaned on his breast at supper, and said, Lord,

inpro5101 pin2076   pr/art,pap3860   ppro4571

which is he*that*betrayeth thee?

art,nn4074 apta1492 depro5126 pin3004   art,nn2424 an,nn2962 1161 inpro5101   depro3778

21 Peter seeing him saith to Jesus, Lord, and what *shall* this man *do*?

art,nn2424   pin3004   ppro846 1437 psa2309   ppro846 pinf3306 ad2193   pinm2064 inpro5101

22 Jesus saith unto him, If I will that he tarry till I come, what *is that*

pre4314 ppro4571 pim190 epn4771 ppro3427

to thee? follow thou me.

3767   aina1831/depro3778/art,nn3056   pre1519 art3588   nn80   3754 depro1565 art,nn3101

23 Then went*this*saying*abroad among the brethren, that that disciple

3756 pin599 2532 art,nn2424 aina2036 3756   ppro846   (3754)   3756 pin599   235   1437 psa2309

should not die: yet Jesus said not unto him, He shall not die; but, If I will that

ppro846 pinf3306 ad2193   pinm2064 inpro5101   pre4314 ppro4571

he tarry till I come, what *is that* to thee?

depro3778 pin2076 art3588   nn3101   pr/art,pap3140   pre4012   depro5023   2532 pr/apta1125

24 This   is   the disciple which testifieth of   these things, and wrote

depro5023   2532   pin1492 3754 ppro846   art,nn3141   pin2076 pr/an,aj227

these things: and we know that his testimony is   true.

1161   pin2076 2532   an,aj4183   an,ajn243   an,ajn3745 art,nn2424 aina4160   repro3748 1437

25 And there are also many other things which Jesus did, the which, if

psmp1125   pre2596/nu,ajn1520   pin3633   art3588   nn2889   epn846

they should be written every one, I suppose that even the world itself could

3761   ainf5562 art3588   nn975   ppmp1125   281

not contain the books that should be written. Amen.

THE ACTS

of the Apostles

The Book of Acts was written by Luke, the physician, to Theophilus as a supplement to the Gospel of Luke (Acts 1:1, cf. Luke 1:1–3). The Book of Luke relates "all that Jesus began both to do and teach" (Acts 1:1). The Acts of the Apostles, on the other hand, begins with the Ascension of Jesus and tells the story of how the gospel was spread far beyond the confines of the Jewish community to the whole world. The statement of Jesus in Acts 1:8, ". . . and ye shall be witnesses unto me both in Jerusalem, and in all Judea, and in Samaria, and unto the uttermost part of the earth," provides an excellent outline for the book.

The Book of Acts concludes rather abruptly with Paul's imprisonment in Rome. It is assumed that the reason for this unexpected closing is that Luke had recorded all the significant events known to him at that time. Hence, the date for the writing of the book is generally agreed to be about A.D. 61. It is clear from certain passages within the Book of Acts that the author was with the Apostle Paul on several occasions (Acts 16:10–17; 20:5—21:18; 27:1—28:16). In fact, many believe that Paul was referring to Luke in 2 Corinthians 8:18 when he mentions "the brother" who was praised "throughout all the churches."

Luke's purpose in writing Acts was not to give a complete history of the growth of the church, but only to list those events with which he was familiar. He does not record how the gospel spread to the east and south of Palestine, or why there were already believers in Damascus before Paul arrived. Nevertheless, the lives and ministries of the prominent individuals that Luke does include sufficiently demonstrate the shift of the evangelical concerns of Christianity from Jews to Gentiles.

1
art3588 nu,aj4413 nn3056 (3303) aom4160 5599 an,nn2321 pre4012 an,ajn3956 repro3739 art,nn2424
The former treatise have I made, O Theophilus, of all that Jesus
aom756 5037 pinf4160 2532 pinf1321
began both to do and teach,

ad891 an,nn2250 repro3739 ainp353 pre1223 an,aj40
2 Until the day in which he was taken up, after that he through the Holy
an,nn4151 aptm1781 art3588 nn652 repro3739 aom1586
Ghost had given commandments unto the apostles whom he had chosen:

repro3739 2532 aina3933 rxpro1438 pr/pap2198 ppro846 aime3958 pre1722 an,aj4183
3 To whom also he showed himself alive after his passion by many
an,nn5039 ppmp3700 ppro846 (pre1223) nu5062 an,nn2250 2532 pap3004 art3588
infallible proofs, being seen of them forty days, and speaking of the things
pre4012 art3588 nn932 art,nn2316
pertaining to the kingdom of God:

2532 ppmp4871 aina3853 ppro846
4 And, being assembled*together*with *them*, commanded them that they

³³⁶¹   ^{pifm5563}   ^{pre575}   ^{an,nn2414}   ²³⁵   ^{pinf4037}   ^{art3588}   ⁿⁿ¹⁸⁶⁰   ^{art3588}   ⁿⁿ³⁹⁶²

should not depart from Jerusalem, but wait for the promise of the Father,

^{repro3739}   ^{aina191}   ^{ppro3450}

which, *saith he,* ye have heard of me.

³⁷⁵⁴   ^{an,nn2491}   ³³⁰³   ^{aina907}   ^{an,nn5204}   ¹¹⁶¹   ^{epn5210}   ^{fp907}   ^{pre1722}

☞ 5 For John truly baptized with water; but ye shall be baptized with the

^{an,aj40}   ^{an,nn4151}   ^{3756 (pre3326)}   ^{an,aj4183}   ^{an,nn2250}   ^{depro5025}

Holy Ghost not   many days hence.

The Holy Spirit Will Come

^{art3588 (3303)}   ³⁷⁶⁷   ^{apta4905}   ^{ipf1905}   ^{ppro846}   ^{pap3004}

6 When they   therefore were come together, they asked of him, saying,

^{an,nn2962}   ⁽¹⁴⁸⁷⁾   ^{pre1722}   ^{depro5129}   ^{art,nn5550}   ^{pin600}   ^{art3588}   ⁿⁿ⁹³²   ²⁴⁷⁴

Lord, wilt thou at   this   time restore again the kingdom to Israel?

¹¹⁶¹   ^{aina2036}   ^{pre4314}   ^{ppro846}   ^{pin2076}   ³⁷⁵⁶   ^{epn5216}   ^{ainf1097}   ^{an,nn5550}   ²²²⁸

7 And he said unto them, It   is   not for you to know the times or the

^{an,nn2540}   ^{repro3739}   ^{art3588}   ⁿⁿ³⁹⁶²   ^{aom5087}   ^{pre1722}   ^{art,aj2398}   ^{an,nn1849}

seasons, which the Father hath put   in   his own power.

²³⁵   ^{fm2983}   ^{an,nn1411}   ^{art3588}   ^{an,aj40}   ⁿⁿ⁴¹⁵¹   ^{apta1904}   ^{pre1909}

8 But ye shall receive power, after that the Holy Ghost is come upon

^{ppro5209}   ²⁵³²   ^{fm2071}   ^{pr/an,nn3144}   ^{ppro3427}   ⁵⁰³⁷   ^{pre1722}   ²⁴¹⁹   ²⁵³²   ^{pre1722}   ^{an,aj3956}

you: and ye shall be witnesses unto me both in Jerusalem, and in   all

^{art,nn2449}   ²⁵³²   ^{an,nn4540}   ²⁵³²   ^{ad*2193}   ^{an,ajn2078}   ^{art3588}   ⁿⁿ¹⁰⁹³

Judea, and in Samaria, and unto the uttermost part of the earth.

²⁵³²   ^{apta2036}   ^{depro5023}   ^{ppro846}   ^{pap991}

9 And when he had spoken these things, while they beheld, he was

^{ainp1869}   ²⁵³²   ^{an,nn3507}   ^{aina5274}   ^{ppro846}   ^{pre575}   ^{ppro846}   ^{art,nn3788}

taken up; and a cloud received him out of their sight.

²⁵³²   ^{ad5613}   ^{ipf2258/pap816}   ^{pre1519}   ^{art,nn3772}   ^{ppro846}   ^{ppmp4198}

10 And while they looked steadfastly toward heaven as he   went up,

²⁴⁰⁰   ^{nu1417 an,nn435 (2532)}   ^{plpf3936}   ^{ppro846 pre1722}   ^{an,aj3022}   ^{an,nn2066}

behold, two men   stood by them   in   white apparel;

^{repro3739}   ²⁵³²   ^{aina2036}   ^{an,nn435}   ^{art,aj1057}   ^{inpro5101}   ^{pfi2476}

☞ 11 Which also said, Ye   men   of   Galilee,   why   stand   ye

^{pap1689}   ^{pre1519}   ^{art,nn3772}   ^{depro3778}   ^{art,nn2424}   ^{art,aptp353}   ^{pre575}   ^{ppro5216}   ^{pre1519}

gazing up into heaven? this same Jesus, which*is*taken*up from you into

^{art,nn3772}   ^{ad3779}   ^{fm2064}   ^{repro3739/an,nn5158}   ^{aom2300}   ^{ppro846}   ^{ppmp4198}   ^{pre1519}

heaven, shall so   come in*like*manner as ye have seen him   go   into

^{art,nn3772}

heaven.

☞ **1:5** Many times this is interpreted to mean that the Holy Spirit did the baptizing. The correct understanding of this, however, is that the Holy Spirit is the element of the baptism just as water was the element of the baptism of John. This is the fifth time that the phrase, "baptized with the Holy Ghost," occurs in the NT (see Matt. 3:11; Mark 1:8; Luke 3:16; John 1:33). In each of the previous four instances Jesus Christ is said to be the One performing the baptism.

☞ **1:11** See notes on 1 Thessalonians 1:10; 2:19.

Matthias Replaces Judas

ad5119   aina5290   pre1519   2419   pre575   an,nn3735 art,ppmp2564 an,nn1638
12 Then returned they unto Jerusalem from the mount called Olivet,

repro,pin3603 ad1451   2419   (pap2192)   an,nn4521   an,nn3598
which is from Jerusalem   a   sabbath day's journey.

2532   ad3753   aina1525   aina305   pre1519   art,nn5253
13 And when they were come in, they went up into an upper room,

repro3757 ipf2258/pap2650 5037 (repro3739) art,nn4074 2532 an,nn2385 2532 an,nn2491 2532 an,nn406 an,nn5376 2532
where abode both   Peter, and James, and John, and Andrew, Philip, and

an,nn2381   an,nn918   2532   an,nn3156   an,nn2385   an,nn256   2532 an,nn4613
Thomas, Bartholomew, and Matthew, James *the son* of Alphaeus, and Simon

art,ajn2208   2532 an,nn2455   an,nn2385
Zelotes, and Judas *the brother* of James.

depro3778 an,aj3956   ipf2258/pap4342   ad3661   art,nn4335   2532   art,nn1162   pre4862
14 These all   continued with*one*accord in prayer and supplication, with

an,nn1135   2532 an,nn3137 art3588   nn3384   art,nn2424 2532 pre4862 ppro846   art,nn80
the women, and Mary the mother of Jesus, and with his brethren.

2532 pre1722 depro5025 art,nn2250 an,nn4074   apta450   pre1722   an,ajn3319   art3588   nn3101
15 And in those days Peter stood up in the midst of the disciples, and

aina2036   (5037) an,nn3793   an,nn3686 pre1909/art,ppro846 ipf2258 ad5613   pr/nu,ajn1540/nu1501
said, (the number of names together were about a*hundred*and*twenty,)

an,nn435   an,nn80   depro5026   art,nn1124   ipf1163   aifp4137
16 Men *and* brethren, this Scripture must needs have been fulfilled,

repro3739 art3588 aj40   art,nn4151 pre1223   an,nn4750   1138   aina4277   pre4012
which the Holy Ghost by the mouth of David spake before concerning

an,nn2455   art,aptm1096   pr/an,nn3595   art,apta4815   art,nn2424
Judas, which was guide to them*that*took Jesus.   *(Ps. 41:9)*

3754   ipf2258   pr/pfpp2674   pre4862 ppro2254 2532   aina2975   art,nn2819   depro5026
17 For he was numbered with us, and had obtained part of this

art,nn1248
ministry.

3767   depro3778 (3303)   aom2932   an,nn5564 pre1537 art3588   nn3408   art,nn93   2532 aptm1096
18 Now this man   purchased a field with the reward of iniquity; and falling

pr/an,aj4248   aina2997   an,aj3319 2532 an,aj3956 ppro846 art,nn4698   ainp1632
headlong, he burst asunder in the midst, and   all   his bowels gushed out.

2532   aom1096 pr/an,aj1110   an,aj3956 art3588   pap2730   2419   5620
19 And it was known unto all   the dwellers at Jerusalem; insomuch as

depro1565 art,nn5564   aifp2564   ppro846 art,aj2398   an,nn1258   184   depro,pin5123
that field is called in their proper tongue, Aceldama, that*is*to*say, The

an,nn5564   an,nn129
field of blood.

1063   pfip1125   pre1722   an,nn976   an,nn5568   ppro846   art,nn1886   aipp1096
20 For it is written in the book of Psalms, Let his habitation be

pr/an,aj2048   2532   3361 (aima2077) art,pap2730 pre1722/ppro846 2532 ppro846   art,nn1984   an,ajn2087   opt2983
desolate, and let no man dwell therein: and his bishopric let another take.

(Ps. 69:25; 109:8)

3767   (pin1163)   art,nn435   art,apta4905   ppro2254 (pre1722) an,aj3956
21 Wherefore of these men which*have*companied with us   all

an,nn5550 pre1722/repro3739 art3588 nn2962 an,nn2424 aina1525   2532 aina1831   pre1909 ppro2248
the time   that   the Lord Jesus went in and out among us,

aptm756   pre575 art3588   nn908   an,nn2491 ad*2193   art,nn2250 repro3739

22 Beginning from the baptism of John, unto that same day that he was

ainp353   pre575 ppro2257   nu,ajn1520 (repro5130) aifm1096   pr/an,nn3144 pre4862 ppro2254

taken up from us, must one   be ordained to be a witness with us of

ppro846   art,nn386

his resurrection.

2532   aina2476   nu,ajn1417 2501 art,ppmp2564 an,nn923   repro3739   ainp1941

23 And they appointed two, Joseph called Barsabas, who was surnamed

an,nn2459 2532   an,nn3159

Justus, and Matthias.

2532   aptm4336   aina2036   epn4771 an,nn2962   an,nn2589

24 And they prayed, and said, Thou, Lord, which*knowest*the*hearts of

an,ajn3956   aima322 repro3739/nu1520 pre1537 depro5130 art,nu,ajn1417   aom1586

all men, show whether of these two thou hast chosen,

ainf2983 art,nn2819   depro5026   art,nn1248   2532   an,nn651   pre1537 repro3739

25 That he may take part of this ministry and apostleship, from which

an,nn2455   aina3845   ainf4198 pre1519 art,aj2398 art,nn5117

Judas by*transgression*fell, that he might go to his own place.

2532   aina1325   ppro846 an,nn2819 2532 art3588 nn2819 aina4098 pre1909 an,nn3159   2532

26 And they gave forth their lots; and the lot fell upon Matthias; and he

ainp4785   pre3326 art3588 nu1733   nn652

was numbered with the eleven apostles.   *(Prov. 16:33)*

The Baptism of the Holy Spirit

2532   art3588 nn2250   art,ajn4005   aie4845   ipf2258 an,ajn537

2 ☞And when the day of Pentecost was fully come, they were all

ad3661   pre1909 art,ppro846

with*one*accord in one place.   *(Lev. 23:15-21; Deut. 16:9-11)*

2532   ad869   aom1096   an,nn2279 pre1537 art,nn3772 ad5618   ppmp5342   an,aj972

2 And suddenly there came a sound from heaven as of a rushing mighty

an,nn4157 2532   aina4137 an,aj3650 art3588   nn3624   repro3757   ipf2258 ppmp2521

wind, and it filled all   the house where they were sitting.

2532   ainp3700   ppro846 ppmp1266   an,nn1100   ad5616   an,nn4442 5037

3 And there appeared unto them cloven tongues like as of fire, and it

aina2523 pre1909 an,ajn1538/nu,ajn1520   ppro846

sat upon   each   of them.

☞ **2:1–13** This is the fulfillment of Jesus' promise to send the Holy Spirit. The purpose of the coming of the Holy Spirit was to glorify Jesus Christ (John 16:7–14).

The Holy Spirit came on the day of Pentecost and filled not just a selected few, but every believer that was present in the upper room (Acts 2:4). One result of this baptism was that these people spoke in languages that they did not previously understand. In Acts 2:6, 8, the writer uses the Greek word *dialéto* (1258), which referred to known and understood ethnic languages, or "dialects." The "other tongues," mentioned in verse four should not be confused with the "unknown tongue" spoken by the Corinthians (see 1 Cor. 14:2, 4, 13, 19, 27). This "unknown tongue" is always in the singular and is accompanied by a singular personal pronoun. The Apostle Paul demanded that this unknown tongue always be interpreted. The tongues that were spoken in this passage, however, needed no interpreter because each man heard the message of the Lord in his own language.

2532   an,ajn537 ainp4130   an,aj40 an,nn4151 2532 aom756   pinf2980
4 And they were   all filled with the Holy Ghost, and began to speak with
an,aj2087   an,nn1100 ad2531 art3588 nn4151 ipf1325 ppro846   pifm669
other tongues, as the Spirit gave them utterance.
1161   ipf2258   pap2730 pre1722 2419 an,nn2453 an,aj2126 an,nn435 pre575 an,aj3956
5 And there were dwelling at Jerusalem Jews, devout men, out of every
an,nn1484 art,pre5259 art,nn3772
nation under heaven.
1161   depro5026   aptm1096/art,nn5456 art3588   nn4128   aina4905   2532
6 Now when this was noised abroad, the multitude came together, and
ainp4797   3754   an,ajn1538/nu,ajn1520 ipf191 ppro846 pap2980   art,aj2398
were confounded, because that every man heard them speak in his own
an,nn1258
language.
1161   an,ajn3956   ipf1839   2532   ipf2296   pap3004   rcpro240/pre4314
7 And they were   all   amazed and marvelled, saying one*to*another,
2400   pin1526 3756 an,aj3956 depro3778 art,pap2980 pr/an,ajn1057
Behold, are not all these which speak Galilaeans?
2532 ad4459 pin191 epn2249 an,ajn1538 art,ppro2257 art,aj2398 art,nn1258 pre1722/repro3739
8 And how hear we every man in our own tongue, wherein we were
ainp1080
born?
an,nn3934   2532 an,nn3370   2532 an,ajn1639 2532 art3588   pap2730   art,nn3318
9 Parthians, and Medes, and Elamites, and the dwellers in Mesopotamia,
5037   an,nn2449 2532   an,nn2587   an,nn4195 2532 art,nn773
and in Judea, and Cappadocia, in Pontus, and Asia,
(5037) an,nn5435   2532 an,nn3828   an,nn125 2532 art3588   nn3313   art,nn3033 art,pre2596
10   Phrygia, and Pamphylia, in Egypt, and in the parts of Libya about
an,nn2957 2532 art,pap1927   an,nn4514 (5037) an,nn2453 2532   an,ajn4339
Cyrene, and strangers of Rome,   Jews and proselytes,
an,nn2912 2532 an,nn690   pin191 ppro846 pap2980   art,popro2251 an,nn1100 art3588
11 Cretes and Arabians, we do hear them speak in our tongues the
nn3167   art,nn2316
wonderful works of God.
1161   an,ajn3956 ipf1839   2532   ipf1280   pap3004
12 And they were all   amazed, and were*in*doubt, saying
an,ajn243/pre4314/an,ajn243 pr/inpro5101 opt2309/302/pinf1511 depro5124
one*to*another, What meaneth this?
(1161) an,ajn2087 pap5512 ipf3004   pin1526 pr/pfpp3325 an,nn1098
13   Others mocking said, These men are full of new wine.

Peter's Sermon

1161 an,nn4074   aptp2476   pre4862 art3588 nu,ajn1733 aina1869 ppro848 art,nn5456 2532 aom669
14 But Peter, standing up with the eleven, lifted up his voice, and said
ppro846   an,nn435   an,nn2453 2532 an,aj537   art,pap2730   2419 aima2077 depro5124
unto them, Ye men of Judea, and all *ye* that dwell at Jerusalem, be this
pr/an,aj1110   ppro5213 2532 aipm1801 ppro3450 art,nn4487
known unto you, and hearken to my words:

1063   depro3778   3756   pin3184 ad5613 epn5210   pin5274   1063   pin2076
15 For these are not drunken, as ye suppose, seeing it is *but* the

an,nu,aj5154 an,nn5610   art3588 nn2250
third hour of the day.

235   depro5124 pin2076   pr/art,pfpp2046   pre1223 art3588   nn4396   2493
16 But this is that*which*was*spoken by the prophet Joel;

2532   fm2071   pre1722 art3588 aj2078 an,nn2250 pin3004 art,nn2316   ft1632
17 And it shall come*to*pass in the last days, saith God, I will pour out

pre575 ppro3450 art,nn4151 pre1909 an,aj3956 an,nn4561 2532   ppro5216 art,nn5207 2532 ppro5216   art,nn2364
of my Spirit upon all flesh: and your sons and your daughters shall

ft4395   2532 ppro5216   art,ajn3495   fm3700   an,nn3706   2532 ppro5216   art,ajn4245
prophesy, and your young men shall see visions, and your old men shall

fp1797   an,nn1798
dream dreams:

2532 (1065) pre1909 ppro3450   art,ajn1401   2532 pre1909 ppro3450   art,ajn1399   ft1632
18 And   on my servants and on my handmaidens I will pour out

pre1722 depro1565 art,nn2250 pre575 ppro3450 art,nn4151 2532   ft4395
in those days of my Spirit; and they shall prophesy:

2532   ft1325   an,nn5059 pre1722 art,nn3772 ad507   2532 an,nn4592 pre1909 art3588 nn1093
19 And I will show wonders in heaven above, and signs in the earth

ad2736   an,nn129 2532 an,nn4442 2532 an,nn822   an,nn2586
beneath; blood, and fire, and vapor of smoke:

art3588   nn2246   fp3344   pre1519 an,nn4655   2532 art3588 nn4582 pre1519 an,nn129
20 The sun shall be turned into darkness, and the moon into blood,

ad4250   (2228) art,aj3173 2532 an,aj2016 art,nn2250   an,nn2962 ainf2064
before that great and notable day of the Lord come:

2532   fm2071   an,aj3956/repro3739/302   asbm1941 art3588   nn3686
21 And it shall come*to*pass, *that* whosoever shall call on the name of

an,nn2962   fp4982
the Lord shall be saved.   *(Joel 2:28-32)*

an,nn435   an,nn2475   aima191 depro5128 art,nn3056 an,nn2424   art,aj3480   an,nn435
22 Ye men of Israel, hear these words; Jesus of Nazareth, a man

pfpp584   pre575 art,nn2316 pre1519 ppro5209   an,nn1411   2532   an,nn5059   2532 an,nn4592 repro3739
approved of God among you by miracles and wonders and signs, which

art,nn2316 aina4160 pre1223 ppro846 pre1722   an,ajn3319   ppro5216 ad2531 epn846   2532 pin1492
God did by him in the midst of you, as ye yourselves also know:

depro5126   an,aj1560   art3588   pfpp3724   nn1012 2532   an,nn4268
☞ 23 Him, being delivered by the determinate counsel and foreknowledge of

art,nn2316   apta2983   pre1223 an,aj459 an,nn5495   apta4362   aina337
God, ye have taken, and by wicked hands have crucified and slain:

repro3739 art,nn2316   aina450   apta3089 art3588 nn5604   art,nn2288   2530
24 Whom God hath raised up, having loosed the pains of death: because it

ipf2258 3756 pr/an,ajn1415   ppro846   pifp2902 pre5259 ppro846
was not possible that he should be holden of it.   *(Ps. 18:4; 116:3)*

1063   1138   pin3004   pre1519   ppro846   ipf4308 art3588 nn2962 pre1223/an,ajn3956
25 For David speaketh concerning him, I foresaw the Lord always

ad*1799   ppro3450   3754 pin2076 pre1537 ppro3450 an,ajn1188   2443   3361   asbp4531
before my face, for he is on my right hand, that I should not be moved:

---

pre1223/depro5124   ppro3450 art,nn2588   aina2165   2532 ppro3450 art,nn1100   aom21   1161/ad2089

26 Therefore did my heart rejoice, and my tongue was glad; moreover

2532 ppro3450 art,nn4561   ft2681 pre1909 an,nn1680

also my flesh shall rest in hope:

3754   3756   ft1459 ppro3450 art,nn5590 pre1519 an,nn86   3761   ft1325

27 Because thou wilt not leave my soul in hell, neither wilt thou suffer

ppro4675   art,ajn3741   ainf1492   an,nn1312

thine Holy One to see corruption.

aina1107   ppro3427   an,nn3598   an,nn2222

28 Thou hast made known to me the ways of life; thou shalt

ft4137/ppro3165   an,nn2167 pre3326 ppro4675   art,nn4383

make*me*full of joy with thy countenance.   *(Ps. 16:8-11)*

an,nn435   an,nn80   pap1832   pre3326/an,nn3954   ainf2036   pre4314 ppro5209 pre4012 art3588

29 Men *and* brethren, let me freely speak unto you of the

nn3966   1138   3754   aina5053/2532   2532 ainp2290   2532 ppro846   art,nn3418   pin2076 pre1722

patriarch David, that he is*both*dead and buried, and his sepulcher is with

ppro2254 ad891 depro5026 art,nn2250

us unto this day.

3767   pap5225   pr/an,nn4396   2532   pfp1492   3754 art,nn2316   aina3660

30 Therefore being a prophet, and knowing that God had sworn with an

an,nn3727   ppro846   pre1537   an,nn2590   ppro846 art,nn3751   art,pre2596   an,nn4561

oath to him, that of the fruit of his loins, according to the flesh, he would

finf450   art,nn5547   ainf2523 pre1909 ppro846   art,nn2362

raise up Christ to sit on his throne;   *(Ps. 132:11)*

apta4275   aina2980 pre4012 art3588   nn386   art,nn5547   3754 ppro846

31 He seeing*this*before spake of the resurrection of Christ, that his

art,nn5590   3756 ainp2641 pre1519 an,nn86   3761   ppro846 art,nn4561   aina1492   an,nn1312

soul was not left in hell, neither his flesh did see corruption. *(Ps. 16:10)*

depro5126 art,nn2424   art,nn2316   aina450   repro3739 epn2249 an,aj3956 pin2070   pr/an,nn3144

32 This Jesus hath God raised up, whereof we all are witnesses.

3767   art3588   ajn1188   art,nn2316   aptp5312   5037

33 Therefore being by the right hand of God exalted, and having

apta2983   pre3844 art3588   nn3962   art3588   nn1860   art3588 an,aj40   nn4151   aina1632

received of the Father the promise of the Holy Ghost, he hath shed forth

depro5124 repro3739 epn5210 ad3568 pim991 2532   pin191

this, which ye now see and hear.

1063   1138   3756   aina305   pre1519 art3588   nn3772   1161 epn846 pin3004   art3588

34 For David is not ascended into the heavens: but he saith himself, The

nn2962 aina2036   ppro3450 art,nn2962 pim2521   pre1537 ppro3450   an,ajn1188

Lord said unto my Lord, Sit thou on my right hand,

ad2193   asba5087/302 ppro4675 art,ajn2190 an,nn5286/ppro4675/art,nn4228

35 Until I make thy foes thy footstool.   *(Ps. 110:1)*

3767   an,aj3956   an,nn3624   2474   pim1097   ad806   3754 art,nn2316

36 Therefore let all the house of Israel know assuredly, that God hath

aina4160 (ppro846)   depro5126   art,nn2424 repro3739 epn5210   aina4717   2532 pr/an,nn2962 2532 pr/an,nn5547

made that same Jesus, whom ye have crucified, both Lord and Christ.

1161   apta191   ainp2660   art,nn2588 5037 aina2036

37 Now when they heard *this,* they were pricked in their heart, and said

pre4314 art,nn4074 2532   art3588 aj3062   an,nn652   an,nn435   an,nn80   inpro5101

unto Peter and to the rest of the apostles, Men *and* brethren, what shall we

ft4160

do?   *(Zech. 12:10)*

1161   an,nn4074 aina5346 pre4314   ppro846   aima3340   2532   aipp907   an,aj1538   ppro5216

☞ 38 Then Peter said unto them, Repent, and be baptized every one of you

pre1909 art3588   nn3686   an,nn2424 an,nn5547 pre1519   an,nn859   an,nn266 2532   fm2983

in the name of Jesus Christ for the remission of sins, and ye shall receive

art3588 nn1431   art3588 an,aj40   nn4151

the gift of the Holy Ghost.

1063 art3588   nn1860   pin2076   epn5213 2532   ppro5216   art,nn5043   2532   an,aj3956 art3588

39 For the promise is unto you, and to your children, and to all that are

pre1519/ad3112   an,ajn3745/302   an,nn2962 ppro2257 art,nn2316   asbm4341

afar off, *even* as*many*as the Lord our God shall call.   *(Is. 57:19; Joel 2:32)*

5037   cd/an,aj4119 an,aj2087 an,nn3056   ipf1263   2532   ipf3870   pap3004 aipp4982

40 And with many other words did he testify and exhort, saying, Save your-

pre575 depro5026   art,aj4696   art,nn1074

selves from this untoward generation.   *(Deut. 32:5; Ps. 78:8)*

3767   art,aptm588/ad780   (3303) ppro846 art,nn3056   ainp907   2532   art3588

41 Then they*that*gladly*received   his word were baptized: and the

depro1565 nn2250   ainp4369   ad5616   nu5153   an,nn5590

same day there were added *unto them* about three thousand souls.

1161   ipf2258/pr/pap4342   art3588   nn652   art,nn1322 · 2532   art,nn2842

42 And they continued steadfastly in the apostles' doctrine and fellowship,

2532   art,nn2800   art,nn740   2532   art,nn4335

and in breaking of bread, and in prayers.

"All Things Common"

1161   an,nn5401 aom1096   an,aj3956 an,nn5590 5037 an,aj4183   an,nn5059   2532 an,nn4592

43 And fear came upon every soul: and many wonders and signs were

ipf1096 pre1223 art3588   nn652

done by the apostles.

1161 an,aj3956   art,pap4100   ipf2258 pre1909/art,ppro846 2532 ipf2192   an,ajn537   pr/an,aj2839

44 And all   that believed were together, and had all things common;

2532   ipf4097   art,nn2933   2532   art,nn5223 2532 ipf1266   ppro846   an,ajn3956

45 And sold their possessions and goods, and parted them to all   *men,*

2530   idpro5100/302   ipf2192 an,nn5532

as every man had need.

5037   pap4342   pre2596/an,nn2250   ad3661   pre1722 art3588   nn2411   5037

46 And they, continuing daily   with*one*accord in the temple, and

pap2806   an,nn740   pre2596/an,nn3624   ipf3335   an,nn5160 pre1722   an,nn20   2532

breaking bread from*house*to*house, did eat their meat with gladness and

an,nn858   an,nn2588

singleness of heart,

☞ **2:38** The main verb in this verse is *metanoésate* (3340), meaning "repent." This refers to that initial repentance of a sinner unto salvation. The verb translated "be baptized" is in the indirect passive imperative of *baptízo* (907) which means that it does not have the same force as the direct command of "repent." The preposition "for" in the phrase "for the remission of sins" in Greek is *eis* (1519), "unto." Literally, it means "for the purpose of identifying you with the remission of sins." This same preposition is used in 1 Corinthians 10:2 in the phrase "and were all baptized unto [*eis*] Moses." These people were identifying themselves with the work and ministry of Moses. Repentance is something that concerns an individual and God, while baptism is intended to be a testimony to other people. That is why *baptisthéto*, "to be baptized," is in the passive voice indicating that one does not baptize himself, but he is baptized by another usually in the presence of others.

pap134   art,nn2316   2532   pap2192   an,nn5485 pre4314 an,aj3650 art3588   nn2992   1161   art3588   nn2962

47 Praising God, and having favor with   all   the people. And the Lord

ipf4369   art3588   nn1577   pre2596/an,nn2250   art,ppmp4982

added to the church   daily   such*as*should*be*saved.

The Healing of the Lame Man

1161   an,nn4074   2532 an,nn2491   ipf305   pre1909/art,ppro846 pre1519 art3588   nn2411   pre1909 art3588 nn5610

3 Now Peter and John went up together into the temple at the hour of

art,nn4335   art3588 nu,ajn1766

prayer, *being* the ninth *hour.*

2532   idpro5100   an,nn435 (pap5225) pr/an,aj5560   pre1537 ppro848   an,nn3384   an,nn2836   ipf941

2 And a certain man   lame from his mother's womb was carried,

repro3739   ipf5087 pre2596/an,nn2250 pre4314 art3588 nn2374   art3588   nn2411   art,ppmp3004   an,aj5611

whom they laid   daily   at the gate of the temple which*is*called Beautiful,

infg154 an,nn1654 pre3844   art,ppmp1531   pre1519 art3588   nn2411

to ask alms of them*that*entered into the temple;

repro3739   apta1492   an,nn4074 2532 an,nn2491   pap3195   pinf1524 pre1519 art3588   nn2411   ipf2065   (pinf2983)

3 Who seeing Peter and John about to   go   into the temple asked   an

an,nn1654

alms.

1161   an,nn4074   apta816   pre1519 ppro846 pre4862 art,nn2491 aina2036   aima991   pre1519

4 And Peter, fastening*his*eyes upon him with John, said, Look   on

ppro2248

us.

1161   art3588   ipf1907   ppro846   pap4328   ainf2983   idpro5100   pre3844

5 And   he   gave heed unto them, expecting to receive something of

ppro846

them.

1161   an,nn4074 aina2036   an,nn694   2532   an,nn5553 pin5225 ppro3427   3756   1161 repro3739

6 Then Peter said, Silver and gold have   I   none; but such as I

pin2192 (depro5124)pin1325 ppro4671 pre1722 art3588   nn3686   an,nn2424 an,nn5547   art,aj3480   aipm1453   2532

have   give I thee: In the name of Jesus Christ of Nazareth rise up and

pim4043

walk.

2532   apta4084 ppro846   art3588 an,aj1188   nn5495   aina1453   1161   ad3916

7 And he took him by the right hand, and lifted*him*up: and immediately

ppro846 art,nn939 2532   art,nn4974   ainp4732

his feet and ankle bones received strength.

2532   ppmp1814   aina2476   2532   ipf4043   2532   aina1525   pre4862 ppro846 pre1519 art3588

8 And he leaping up stood, and walked, and entered with them into the

nn2411   pap4043   2532   ppmp242   2532   pap134 art,nn2316

temple, walking, and leaping, and praising God.   (Is. 35:6)

2532 an,aj3956 art3588   nn2992   aina1492 ppro846   pap4043   2532   pap134 art,nn2316

9 And all   the people saw him walking and praising God:

5037   ipf1921 (ppro846) 3754   ipf2258 depro3778 pr/art,ppmp2521 pre4314 art,nn1654 pre1909 art3588

10 And they knew   that it was   he   which sat for alms   at   the

an,aj5611   nn4439   art3588   nn2411   2532   ainp4130   an,nn2285   2532

Beautiful gate of the temple: and they were filled with wonder and

an,nn1611   pre1909   art,pfp4819   ppro846

amazement at that*which*had*happened unto him.

Peter Addresses the People

¹¹⁶¹ ^{art3588} ^{ajn5560}   ^{aptp2390} ^{pap2902} ^{art,nn4074} ²⁵³² ^{an,nn2491} ^{an,aj3956} ^{art3588}

11 And as the lame man which was healed held Peter and John, all the

ⁿⁿ²⁹⁹² ^{aina4936} ^{pre4314} ^{ppro846} ^{pre1909} ^{art3588} ⁿⁿ⁴⁷⁴⁵ ^{art,ppmp2564} ^{an,nn4672}

people ran together unto them in the porch that*is*called Solomon's,

^{an,aj1569}

greatly wondering.

¹¹⁶¹ ^{an,nn4074} ^{apta1492}   ^{aom611} ^{pre4314} ^{art3588} ⁿⁿ²⁹⁹² ^{an,nn435}

12 And when Peter saw *it,* he answered unto the people, Ye men of

^{an,nn2475} ^{inpro5101} ^{pin2296} ^{pre1909} ^{depro5129} ²²²⁸ ^{inpro5101} ^{pin816} ^{ppro2254}

Israel, why marvel ye at this? or why look*ye*so*earnestly on us,

^{ad5613} ^{an,aj2398} ^{an,nn1411} ²²²⁸ ^{an,nn2150} ^{pfp4160} ^{ppro846} ^{infg4043}

as though by our own power or holiness we had made this man to walk?

^{art3588} ⁿⁿ²³¹⁶ ¹¹ ²⁵³² ²⁴⁶⁴ ²⁵³² ²³⁸⁴ ^{art3588} ⁿⁿ²³¹⁶ ^{ppro2257}

13 The God of Abraham, and of Isaac, and of Jacob, the God of our

^{art,nn3962} ^{aina1392} ^{ppro848} ^{art,nn3816} ^{an,nn2424} ^{repro3739} ^{epn5210} ^{aina3860} ²⁵³² ^{aom720}

fathers, hath glorified his Son Jesus; whom ye delivered up, and denied

^{ppro846} ^{pre2596/an,nn4383} ^{an,nn4091} ^{depro1565} ^{apta2919} ^{pinf630}

him in*the*presence of Pilate, when he was determined to let*him*go.

(Ex. 3:6,15; Is. 52:13)

¹¹⁶¹ ^{epn5210} ^{aom720} ^{art3588} ^{ajn40} ²⁵³² ^{an,ajn1342} ²⁵³² ^{aom154} ^(an,nn435)

14 But ye denied the Holy One and the Just, and desired a

^{an,nn5406} ^{aifp5483} ^{ppro5213}

murderer to be granted unto you;

¹¹⁶¹ ^{aina615} ^{art3588} ⁿⁿ⁷⁴⁷ ^{art,nn2222} ^{repro3739} ^{art,nn2316} ^{aina1453} ^{pre1537} ^{an,ajn3498}

15 And killed the Prince of life, whom God hath raised from the dead;

^{repro3739} ^{epn2249} ^{pin2070} ^{pr/an,nn3144}

whereof we are witnesses.

²⁵³² ^{ppro846} ^{art,nn3686} ^{pre1909} ^{art,nn4102} ^{ppro846} ^{art,nn3686} ^{aina4732/depro5126}

16 And his name through faith in his name hath made*this*man*strong,

^{repro3739} ^{pin2334} ²⁵³² ^{pin1492} ²⁵³² ^{art3588} ⁿⁿ⁴¹⁰² ^{art3588} ^{pre1223} ^{ppro846} ^{aina1325} ^{ppro846} ^{depro5026}

whom ye see and know: yea, the faith which is by him hath given him this

^{art,nn3647} ^{ad*561} ^{ppro5216} ^{an,aj3956}

perfect soundness in*the*presence of you all.

²⁵³² ^{ad3568} ^{an,nn80} ^{pin1492} ³⁷⁵⁴ ^{pre2596} ^{an,nn52} ^{aina4238} ^{ad5618}

17 And now, brethren, I wot that through ignorance ye did *it,* as *did*

²⁵³² ^{ppro5216} ^{art,nn758}

also your rulers.

¹¹⁶¹ ^{repro3739} ^{art,nn2316} ^{aina4293} ^{pre1223} ^{an,nn4750}

18 But those things, which God before*had*showed by the mouth of

^{an,aj3956} ^{ppro846} ^{art,nn4396} ^{art,nn5547} ^{ainf3958} ^{ad3779} ^{aina4137}

all his prophets, that Christ should suffer, he hath so fulfilled.

^{aima3340} ³⁷⁶⁷ ²⁵³² ^{aima1994} ^{ppro5216} ^{art,nn266}

19 Repent ye therefore, and be converted, that your sins may be

^{aies1813} ³⁷⁰⁴ ^{an,nn2540} ^{an,nn403} ^{asba2064/302} ^{pre575} ^{an,nn4383}

blotted out, when the times of refreshing shall come from the presence of

^{art3588} ⁿⁿ²⁹⁶²

the Lord;

²⁵³² ^{asba649} ^{an,nn2424} ^{an,nn5547} ^{art,pfpp4296} ^{ppro5213}

20 And he shall send Jesus Christ, which*before*was*preached unto you:

repro3739   an,nn3772   pin1163 (3303) aifm1209   ad891   an,nn5550   an,nn605
21 Whom the heaven must receive until the times of restitution of
an,ajn3956   repro3739 art,nn2316   aina2980   pre1223   an,nn4750   an,aj3956 ppro848 an,aj40   an,nn4396
all things, which God hath spoken by the mouth of all his holy prophets
pre575/an,nn165
since*the*world*began.   *(Is. 49:6; Ezek. 36:26-28; Zech. 12:10)*
1063   an,nn3475   3303   aina2036 pre4314 art3588   nn3962   an,nn4396   an,nn2962 ppro5216
22 For Moses truly said unto the fathers, A prophet shall the Lord your
art,nn2316   ft450   ppro5213 pre1537 ppro5216   art,nn80   ad5613   ppro1691 epn846   fm191
God raise up unto you of your brethren, like unto me; him shall ye hear
pre2596   an,aj3956   an,ajn3745/302   asba2980 pre4314 ppro5209
in all things whatsoever he shall say unto you.   *(Deut. 18:15,16)*
1161   fm2071   an,aj3956 an,nn5590 repro3748   3361 asba191/302 depro1565
23 And it shall come*to*pass, *that* every soul, which will not hear that
art,nn4396   fp1842   pre1537   art3588   nn2992
prophet, shall be destroyed from among the people.   *(Deut. 18:19)*
1161   2532 an,aj3956 art3588   nn4396   pre575   4545   2532   art,ad2517
24 Yea, and all the prophets from Samuel and those*that*follow*after,
an,ajn3745   aina2980   2532   aina4293   depro5025 art,nn2250
as*many*as have spoken, have likewise foretold of these days.
epn5210 pin2075   pr/an,nn5207   art3588   nn4396   2532   art3588   nn1242   repro3739 art,nn2316
25 Ye are the children of the prophets, and of the covenant which God
aom1303   pre4314 ppro2257 art,nn3962 pap3004 pre4314   11   2532   ppro4675 art,nn4690   an,aj3956
made with our fathers, saying unto Abraham, And in thy seed shall all
art3588   nn3965   art3588   nn1093   fp1757
the kindreds of the earth be blessed.   *(Gen. 22:18; 26:4)*
epn5213 nu,aj4412 art,nn2316   apta450   ppro848 art,nn3816 an,nn2424 aina649 ppro846
26 Unto you first God, having raised up his Son Jesus, sent him to
pap2127 ppro5209   aie654   an,ajn1538   pre575 ppro5216   art,nn4189
bless you, in turning away every one of you from his iniquities.

Peter and John Are Brought Before the Jewish Leaders

1161   ppro846 pap2980 pre4314 art3588   nn2992   art3588   nn2409 2532 art3588   nn4755   art3588
4 And as they spake unto the people, the priests, and the captain of the
nn2411   2532 art3588   nn4523   aina2186   ppro846
temple, and the Sadducees, came upon them,
ppmp1278   ppro846 aid1321 art3588   nn2992 2532   aid2605   pre1722 art,nn2424
2 Being grieved that they taught the people, and preached through Jesus
art3588   nn386   art,pre1537 an,ajn3498
the resurrection from the dead.
2532   aina1911/art,nn5495   ppro846 2532 aom5087   pre1519 an,nn5084 pre1519 art3588
3 And they laid*hands*on them, and put *them* in hold unto the
ad839   1063   ipf2258 ad2235   an,nn2073
next day: for it was now eventide.
1161   an,ajn4183   art,apta191   art3588 nn3056   aina4100   2532 art3588   nn706
4 Howbeit many of them*which*heard the word believed; and the number
art3588   nn435 ainp1096 ad5616 nu4002   an,nn5505
of the men was about five thousand.

5 And it came*to*pass on the morrow, that their rulers, and elders, and scribes,

6 And Annas the high priest, and Caiaphas, and John, and Alexander, and as*many*as were of the kindred of the high priest, were gathered together at Jerusalem.

7 And when they had set them in the midst, they asked, By what power, or by what name, have ye done this?

8 Then Peter, filled with the Holy Ghost, said unto them, Ye rulers of the people, and elders of Israel,

9 If we this day be examined of the good*deed*done to the impotent man, by what means he is made whole;

10 Be it known unto you all, and to all the people of Israel, that by the name of Jesus Christ of Nazareth, whom ye crucified, whom God raised from the dead, *even* by him doth this man stand here before you whole.

11 This is the stone which*was*set*at*naught of you builders, which*is*become the head of the corner.   *(Ps. 118:22)*

12 Neither is there salvation in any other: for there is none other name under heaven given among men, whereby we must be saved.

13 Now when they saw the boldness of Peter and John, and perceived that they were unlearned and ignorant men, they marvelled; and they took knowledge of them, that they had been with Jesus.

14 And beholding the man which*was*healed standing with them, they could say*nothing*against it.

15 But when they had commanded them to go aside out of the council, they conferred among themselves,

16 Saying, What shall we do to these men? for that indeed a notable

an,nn4592   pfi1096 pre1223 ppro846   pr/an,aj5318   an,aj3956   art,pap2730
miracle hath been done by them *is* manifest to all them*that*dwell in
2419   2532   pinm1410/3756 aifm720
Jerusalem; and we cannot deny *it*.

235   2443   asbp1268 3361 pre1909/cd/an,ajn4119 pre1519 art3588 nn2992
17 But that it spread no further among the people, let us
aosi546/an,nn547 ppro846   pinf2980   ad3371   an,aj3367 an,nn444 pre1909 depro5127
straitly threaten them, that they speak henceforth to no man in this
art,nn3686
name.

2532   apta2564 ppro846   aina3853   ppro846 3361   pifm5350 art,ad2527 3366
18 And they called them, and commanded them not to speak at all nor
pinf1321 pre1909 art3588 nn3686   art,nn2424
teach in the name of Jesus.

1161 art,nn4074 2532 an,nn2491 aptp611   aina2036 pre4314 ppro846   1487   pin2076
19 But Peter and John answered and said unto them, Whether it be
pr/an,ajn1342   ad*1799   art,nn2316   pinf191   epn5216 ad3123 2228   art,nn2316
right in*the*sight of God to hearken unto you more than unto God,
aima2919
judge ye.

1063 epn2249 pinm1410/3756 3361   pinf2980   repro3739   aina1492 2532 aina191
20 For we cannot but speak the things which we have seen and heard.

1161   art3588   aptm4324   aina630/ppro846   pap2147
21 So when they had further threatened them, they let*them*go, finding
an,ajn3367 art,ad4459   asbm2849 ppro846 pre1223   art3588   nn2992   3754 an,ajn3956
nothing how they might punish them, because of the people: for all *men*
ipf1392 art,nn2316 pre1909   art,pfp1096
glorified God for that*which*was*done.

1063 art3588 nn444 ipf2258 cd/an,aj4119 pr/nu5062   an,nn2094   pre1909 repro3739 depro5124 art,nn4592
22 For the man was above forty years old, on whom this miracle of
art,nn2392   plpf1096
healing was showed.

The Apostles Pray for Courage

1161   aptp630   aina2064 pre4314   art,ajn2398   2532   aina518
23 And being let go, they went to their*own*company, and reported
an,ajn3745 art3588   nn749   2532 art,ajn4245   aina2036 pre4314 ppro846
all that the chief priests and elders had said unto them.

1161   art3588 apta191   aina142   an,nn5456 pre4314 art,nn2316
24 And when they heard that, they lifted up their voice to God
ad3661   2532 aina2036 an,nn1203 epn4771 art,nn2316   art,apta4160   art,nn3772 2532
with*one*accord, and said, Lord, thou *art* God, which*hast*made heaven, and
art,nn1093 2532 art3588 nn2281 2532 an,aj3956 art3588 pre1722 ppro846
earth, and the sea, and all that in them is: *(Ex. 20:11; Ps. 146:6)*
pre1223   an,nn4750   ppro4675 art,nn3816   1138   art,apta2036 inpro2444
25 Who by the mouth of thy servant David hast said, Why did
an,nn1484 aina5433 2532   an,nn2992 aina3191   an,ajn2756
the heathen rage, and the people imagine vain things?

art3588   nn935   art3588 nn1093   aina3936   2532   art3588   nn758   aina4863
26 The kings of the earth stood up, and the rulers were gathered

pre1909/art,ppro846 pre2596 art3588 nn2962 2532   pre2596 ppro846 art,nn5547
together against the Lord, and against his Christ.   *(Ps. 2:1,2)*

1063 pre1909   an,nn225   pre1909   ppro4675 art,aj40 an,nn3816 an,nn2424   repro3739   aina5548
27 For of a truth against thy holy child Jesus, whom thou hast anointed,

5037   an,nn2264   2532   an,nn4194   an,nn4091 pre4862   an,nn1484   2532   an,nn2992   2474
both Herod, and Pontius Pilate, with the Gentiles, and the people of Israel,

ainp4863
were gathered together,   *(Is. 61:1)*

ainf4160   an,ajn3745   ppro4675 art,nn5495 2532 ppro4675 art,nn1012   aina4309
☞ 28 For to do whatsoever thy hand and thy counsel determined before

aifm1096
to be done.

2532   art,ad3569 an,nn2962 aima1896(pre1909) ppro846   art,nn547   2532   aima1325   ppro4675
29 And now, Lord, behold their threatenings: and grant unto thy

art,ajn1401   pre3326 an,aj3956   an,nn3954   pinf2980 ppro4675 art,nn3056
servants, that with all boldness they may speak thy word,

(ppro4571)   aie1614   ppro4675 art,nn5495 pre1519 an,nn2392 2532   an,nn4592 2532   an,nn5059
30 By stretching forth thine hand to heal; and that signs and wonders

pifm1096 pre1223 art3588   nn3686   ppro4675 art,aj40 an,nn3816 an,nn2424
may be done by the name of thy holy child Jesus.

2532   ppro846   aptp1189 art3588 nn5117   ainp4531   pre1722/repro3739   ipf2258
31 And when they had prayed, the place was shaken where they were

pr/pfpp4863   2532   an,ajn537 ainp4130   an,aj40   an,nn4151   2532
assembled together; and they were all filled with the Holy Ghost, and they

ipf2980 art3588 nn3056   art,nn2316 pre3326   an,nn3954
spake the word of God with boldness.

The Believers Had All Things Common

1161 art3588   nn4128   art,apta4100   ipf2258   pr/nu3391 art,nn2588 2532
32 And the multitude of them*that*believed were of one heart and of one

art,nn5590   2532/3761 ipf3004 nu,ajn1520   idpro5100   art,pap5224/ppro846
soul: neither said any *of them* that aught of the*things*which*he*possessed

pinf1511 pr/an,ajn2398 235 ppro846 ipf2258 an,ajn537   pr/an,aj2839
was his own; but they had all things common.

2532   an,aj3173 an,nn1411 ipf591 art3588   nn652   art,nn3142   art3588   nn386
33 And with great power gave the apostles witness of the resurrection of

art3588 nn2962   an,nn2424 5037 an,aj3173 an,nn5485 ipf2258 pre1909 ppro846 an,aj3956
the Lord Jesus: and great grace was upon them all.

(1063)   3761   ipf5225   idpro5100   pre1722   ppro846   pr/an,ajn1729 1063   an,ajn3745
34 Neither was there any among them that lacked: for as*many*as

ipf5225   pr/an,nn2935   an,nn5564 2228 an,nn3614 pap4453   ipf5342 art3588   nn5092
were possessors of lands or houses sold them, and brought the prices of

art,ppmp4097
the*things*that*were*sold,

☞ **4:28** See note on Ephesians 1:4, 5.

35 And laid*them*down at the apostles' feet: and distribution*was*made
unto every man according as he had need.

36 And Joses, who by the apostles was surnamed Barnabas, (which is, being
interpreted, The son of consolation,) a Levite, *and* of*the*country*of*Cyprus,

37 Having land, sold *it,* and brought the money, and laid *it* at the
apostles' feet.

Ananias and Sapphira

5 ☞But a certain man named Ananias, with Sapphira his wife, sold a possession,

2 And kept back *part* of the price, his wife also being privy *to it,* and
brought a certain part, and laid *it* at the apostles' feet.

3 But Peter said, Ananias, why hath Satan filled thine heart to lie to
the Holy Ghost, and to keep back *part* of the price of the land?

4 While it remained, was*it*not*thine*own? and after it was sold, was it
not in thine own power? why hast thou conceived this thing in thine
heart? thou hast not lied unto men, but unto God. *(Deut. 23:21)*

5 And Ananias hearing these words fell down, and gave*up*the*ghost:
and great fear came on all them*that*heard these things.

6 And the young men arose, wound*him*up, and carried*him*out, and
buried *him.*

☞**5:1–16** Ananias and Sapphira were not only guilty of lying to the Holy Spirit (v. 3, 9), but of hypocrisy and coveteousness as well. They were obviously concerned with what the other believers would think of them once they gave their gift. Christ also noted this characteristic among the Pharisees when he contrasted them to the widow who gave all she had (Luke 21:2, 3).

1161   aom1096   ad5613   an,nn1292   nu5140   an,nn5610   2532   ppro846 art,nn1135 3361

7 And it was about the space of three hours after, when his wife, not

pfp1492   art,pfp1096   aina1525

knowing what*was*done, came in.

1161   art,nn4074   ainp611   ppro846 aima2036 ppro3427   1487   aom591 art3588 nn5564

8 And Peter answered unto her, Tell me whether ye sold the land for

an,ajn5118   1161 art3588 aina2036   3483   an,ajn5118

so much? And she said, Yea, for so much.

1161   art,nn4074 aina2036 pre4314 ppro846 inpro5101   3754 ppro5213   ainp4856

9 Then Peter said unto her, How is it that ye have agreed together to

ainf3985 art3588   nn4151   an,nn2962   2400   art3588 nn4228   art,apta2290   ppro4675

tempt the Spirit of the Lord? behold, the feet of them*which*have*buried thy

art,nn435   pre1909 art3588 nn2374   2532   ft1627/ppro4571

husband *are* at the door, and shall carry*thee*out.

1161   aina4098   ad3916   pre3844   ppro846   art,nn4228   2532

10 Then   fell*she*down   straightway   at   his   feet,   and

aina1634   1161 art3588   ajn3495   apta1525   aina2147 ppro846 pr/an,aj3498 2532

yielded*up*the*ghost: and the young men came in, and found her dead, and,

apta1627   aina2290   pre4314 ppro846   art,nn435

carrying*her*forth, buried *her* by her husband.

2532   an,aj3173   an,nn5401 aom1096   pre1909 an,aj3650 art3588   nn1577   2532   pre1909   an,ajn3956

11 And great fear came upon all the church, and upon as*many*as

art,pap191   depro5023

heard these things.

"Many Signs and Wonders"

1161   pre1223 art3588   nn5495   art3588   nn652   an,aj4183 an,nn4592 2532   an,nn5059

12 And by the hands of the apostles were many signs and wonders

ipf1096   pre1722   art3588   nn2992   2532   ipf2258 an,ajn537   ad3661   pre1722

wrought among the people; (and they were all with*one*accord in

an,nn4672   art,nn4745

Solomon's porch.

1161   art3588   ajn3062   ipf5111   an,ajn3762   pifm2853   ppro846   235   art3588   nn2992

13 And of the rest durst no man join himself to them: but the people

ipf3170   ppro846

magnified them.

1161   pap4100   ad3123   ipf4369   art3588   nn2962   an,nn4128   5037

14 And believers were the more added to the Lord, multitudes both of

an,nn435 2532   an,nn1135

men and women.)

5620   pinf1627   art3588 ajn772 pre2596 art3588   ajn4113   2532 pinf5087

15 Insomuch that they brought forth the sick into the streets, and laid

pre1909 an,nn2825 2532   an,nn2895   2443   2579   art3588   nn4639   an,nn4074 ppmp2064

them on beds and couches, that at*the*least the shadow of Peter passing by

asba1982   idpro5100   ppro846

might overshadow some of them.

(1161)   ipf4905   2532   art,nn4128   art3588   nn4172   ad4038   pre1519

16 There came also a multitude *out* of the cities round about unto

2419   pap5342   an,ajn772   2532   an,ppmp3791   pre5259   an,aj169

Jerusalem, bringing sick folks, and them*which*were*vexed with unclean
an,nn4151   repro3748   ipf2323   an,aj537

spirits: and they were healed every one.

The Apostles Are Arrested

1161   art3588   nn749   apta450   2532 an,aj3956 art3588   pre4862 ppro846

17 Then the high priest rose up, and all they that were with him,
art,pap5607   pr/an,nn139 art3588   nn4523   ainp4130   an,nn2205

(which is the sect of the Sadducees,) and were filled with indignation,
2532   aina1911 ppro846 art,nn5495 pre1909 art3588   nn652   2532 aom5087 ppro848 pre1722

18 And laid their hands on the apostles, and put them in the
an,aj1219   an,nn5084

common prison.
1161   an,nn32   an,nn2962 pre1223 art,nn3571   aina455   art3588   nn5438   art,nn2374   5037

19 But the angel of the Lord by night opened the prison doors, and
apta1806/ppro846   aina2036

brought*them*forth, and said,   (Ps. 34:7)
pim4198 (2532) aptp2476   pim2980 pre1722 art3588   nn2411   art3588   nn2992   an,aj3956 art3588   nn4487

20 Go,   stand and speak in the temple to the people all the words
depro5026 art,nn2222

of this life.
1161   apta191   aina1525 pre1519 art3588   nn2411

21 And when they heard *that,* they entered into the temple
pre5259/art,nn3722   2532 ipf1321   1161 art3588   nn749   aptm3854 2532 art3588

early*in*the*morning, and taught. But the high priest came, and they that were
pre4862 ppro846   aina4779/art3588/nn4892   2532 an,aj3956 art3588   nn1087   art3588

with him, and called*the*council*together, and all the senate of the
nn5207   2474   2532 aina649 pre1519 art3588   nn1201   ppro846   aifp71

children of Israel, and sent to the prison to have them brought.
1161   art3588   nn5257   aptm3854   aina2147   ppro846 3756 pre1722 art3588   nn5438   (1161)

22 But when the officers came, and found them not in the prison, they
apta390   aina518

returned, and told,
pap3004   art3588   nn1201   3303   aina2147   pfpp2808 pre1722 an,aj3956 an,nn803   2532 art3588

23 Saying, The prison truly found we shut with all safety, and the
nn5441   pfp2476   ad1854   pre4253 art3588   nn2374   1161   apta455

keepers standing without before the doors: but when we had opened, we
aina2147 an,ajn3762   ad2080

found no man within.
1161   ad5613   (5037 repro3739)   an,nn2409   2532 art3588   nn4755   art3588   nn2411   2532 art3588

24 Now when the high priest and the captain of the temple and the
nn749   aina191   depro5128 art,nn3056   ipf1280   pre4012 ppro846   inpro5101   pr/depro5124

chief priests heard these things, they doubted of them whereunto this would
opt1096/302

grow.
1161   aptm3854 idpro5100   aina518   ppro846   pap3004   2400   art3588   nn435   repro3739

25 Then came one and told them, saying, Behold, the men whom

ye put in prison are standing in the temple, and teaching the people.

26 Then went the captain with the officers, and brought them without violence: for they feared the people, lest they should have been stoned.

27 And when they had brought them, they set *them* before the council: and the high priest asked them,

28 Saying, Did not we straitly command you that ye should not teach in this name? and, behold, ye have filled Jerusalem with your doctrine, and intend to bring this man's blood upon us.

29 Then Peter and the *other* apostles answered and said, We ought to obey God rather than men.

30 The God of our fathers raised up Jesus, whom ye slew and hanged on a tree.

31 Him hath God exalted with his right hand *to be* a Prince and a Savior, for to give repentance to Israel, and forgiveness of sins.

32 And we are his witnesses of these things; and *so is* also the Holy Ghost, whom God hath given to them*that*obey him.

33 When they heard *that,* they were cut *to the heart,* and took counsel to slay them.

34 Then stood*there*up one in the council, a Pharisee, named Gamaliel, a doctor*of*the*law, had*in*reputation among all the people, and commanded to put the apostles forth a little space;

35 And said unto them, Ye men of Israel, take heed to yourselves what ye intend to do as touching these men.

36 For before these days rose up Theudas, boasting himself to be somebody; to whom a number of men, about four hundred, joined themselves:

repro3739   ainp339   2532   an,aj3956   an,ajn3745   ipf3982   ppro846   ainp1262   2532
who was slain; and all, as*many*as obeyed him, were scattered, and

aom1096   pre1519   an,ajn3762
brought to naught.

aina450   an,nn2455   art,aj1057   pre1722 art3588   nn2250   art3588   nn582   2532
☞ 37 After this man rose up Judas of Galilee in the days of the taxing, and

aina868   an,aj2425   an,nn2992   ad*3694   ppro848   depro2548   aom622   2532   an,aj3956
drew away much people after him: he also perished; and all, *even*

an,ajn3745   ipf3982   ppro846   ainp1287
as*many*as obeyed him, were dispersed.

2532   art,ad3569   pin3004   ppro5213   aima868   pre575   depro5130   art,nn444   2532
☞ 38 And now I say unto you, Refrain from these men, and

aima1439/ppro846   3754   1437   depro3778   art,nn1012   2228   depro5124   art,nn2041   psa5600   pre1537   an,nn444
let*them*alone: for if this counsel or this work be of men, it will

fp2647
come*to*nought:

1161   1487   pin2076   pre1537   an,nn2316   pinm1410/3756   ainf2647   ppro846   3379
39 But if it be of God, ye cannot overthrow it; lest haply ye be

asbp2147   2532   pr/an,nn2311
found even to fight*against*God.

1161   ppro846   ainp3982   2532   aptm4341   art3588   nn652
40 And to him they agreed: and when they had called the apostles, and

apta1194   aina3853   3361   pinf2980   pre1909 art3588   nn3686
beaten *them,* they commanded that they should not speak in the name of

art,nn2424   2532   aina630/ppro846
Jesus, and let*them*go.

3767   (3303) art3588   ipf4198   pre575   an,nn4383   art3588   nn4892   pap5463   3754
41 And they departed from the presence of the council, rejoicing that they

ainp2661   aifp818   pre5228 ppro846   art,nn3686
were counted worthy to suffer shame for his name.

5037   an,aj3956/an,nn2250 pre1722 art3588   nn2411   2532   pre2596/an,nn3624   ipf3973   3756
42 And daily in the temple, and in*every*house, they ceased not to

pap1321   2532   ppmp2097   an,nn2424   art,nn5547
teach and preach Jesus Christ.

Seven Are Chosen

1161   pre1722   depro5025   art,nn2250   art3588   nn3101   pap4129
6 And in those days, when the number of the disciples were multiplied,

aom1096   an,nn1112   art3588   nn1675   pre4314   art3588   nn1445   3754
there arose a murmuring of the Grecians against the Hebrews, because

ppro846   art,nn5503   ipf3865   pre1722 art3588   aj2522   art,nn1248
their widows were neglected in the daily ministration.

☞ **5:37, 38** See note on 2 Thessalonians 2:3.

☞ **5:38, 39** In the Greek NT there are two different words that begin the conditional clauses in these two verses. Each one gives a distinctly different meaning to the clause it begins, but in English both words are translated "if." As a result, much of the meaning is lost to the English reader. In verse thirty-eight, the clause, "for if this counsel or this work be of men," is introduced by the Greek word *eán* (1437), which signifies that Gamaliel thought that it was only a possibility that it was the work of the men. In verse thirty-nine, however, the word *ei* (1487) is used which indicates that he was assuming that it was of God.

¹¹⁶¹   ^{art3588}   ^{nu,ajn1427}   ^{aptm4341}   ^{art3588}   ⁿⁿ⁴¹²⁸   ^{art3588}   ⁿⁿ³¹⁰¹

2 Then the twelve called the multitude of the disciples *unto them,* and

^{aina2036}   ^{pin2076}   ³⁷⁵⁶   ^{an,ajn701}   ^{ppro2248}   ^{apta2641} ^{art3588} ⁿⁿ³⁰⁵⁶   ^{art,nn2316}   ^{pinf1247}

said, It is not reason that we should leave the word of God, and serve

^{an,nn5132}

tables.

³⁷⁶⁷   ^{an,nn80}   ^{aipm1980}   ^{pre1537}   ^{ppro5216}   ^{nu2033}   ^{an,nn435}

3 Wherefore, brethren, look*ye*out among you seven men

^{ppmp3140}   ^{an,aj4134}   ^{an,aj40} ^{an,nn4151} ²⁵³² ^{an,nn4678}   ^{repro3739}   ^{ft2525}

of*honest*report, full of the Holy Ghost and wisdom, whom we may appoint

^{pre1909} ^{depro5026} ^{art,nn5532}

over this business.

¹¹⁶¹ ^{epn2249}   ^{ft4342}   ^{art,nn4335} ²⁵³²   ^{art3588}   ⁿⁿ¹²⁴⁸

4 But we will give*ourselves*continually to prayer, and to the ministry of

^{art3588}   ⁿⁿ³⁰⁵⁶

the word.

²⁵³² ^{art3588}   ⁿⁿ³⁰⁵⁶   ^{aina700}   ^(ad*1799) ^{an,aj3956} ^{art,nn4128}   ²⁵³²   ^{aom1586}   ^{an,nn4736}

5 And the saying pleased the whole multitude: and they chose Stephen, a

^{an,nn435} ^{an,aj4134}   ^{an,nn4102} ²⁵³²   ^{an,aj40} ^{an,nn4151} ²⁵³² ^{an,nn5376} ²⁵³²   ^{an,nn4402}   ²⁵³²

man full of faith and of the Holy Ghost, and Philip, and Prochorus, and

^{an,nn3527}   ²⁵³² ^{an,nn5096}   ²⁵³²   ^{an,nn3937}   ²⁵³² ^{an,nn3532}   ^{an,ajn4339}   ^{an,nn491}

Nicanor, and Timon, and Parmenas, and Nicolas a proselyte of Antioch:

^{repro3739}   ^{aina2476} ^{ad*1799} ^{art3588}   ⁿⁿ⁶⁵²   ²⁵³²   ^{aptm4336}

6 Whom they set before the apostles: and when they had prayed, they

^{aina2007/art,nn5495}   ^{ppro846}

laid**their**hands*on them.

²⁵³²   ^{art3588}   ⁿⁿ³⁰⁵⁶   ^{art,nn2316}   ^{ipf837}   ²⁵³² ^{art3588}   ⁿⁿ⁷⁰⁶   ^{art3588}   ⁿⁿ³¹⁰¹

7 And the word of God increased; and the number of the disciples

^{ipf4129}   ^{pre1722}   ²⁴¹⁹   ^{ad4970}   ⁵⁰³⁷   ^{an,aj4183} ^{an,nn3793}   ^{art3588}   ⁿⁿ²⁴⁰⁹

multiplied in Jerusalem greatly; and a great company of the priests

^{ipf5219}   ^{art3588} ⁿⁿ⁴¹⁰²

were obedient to the faith.

Stephen Taken Prisoner

¹¹⁶¹   ^{an,nn4736}   ^{an,aj4134}   ^{an,nn4102} ²⁵³²   ^{an,nn1411} ^{ipf4160} ^{an,aj3173}   ^{an,nn5059}   ²⁵³² ^{an,nn4592}

8 And Stephen, full of faith and power, did great wonders and miracles

^{pre1722}   ^{art3588}   ⁿⁿ²⁹⁹²

among the people.

¹¹⁶¹   ^{aina450}   ^{idpro5100} ^{pre1537} ^{art3588}   ⁿⁿ⁴⁸⁶⁴   ^{art,ppmp3004}

9 Then there arose certain of the synagogue, which*is*called *the synagogue*

^{an,nn3032}   ²⁵³²   ^{an,nn2956}   ²⁵³²   ^{an,nn221}   ²⁵³²   ^{art3588} ^{pre575} ^{an,nn2791} ²⁵³²

of the Libertines, and Cyrenians, and Alexandrians, and of them of Cilicia and

^{an,nn773}   ^{pap4802}   ^{art,nn4736}

of Asia, disputing with Stephen.

²⁵³²   ^{ipf2480/3756}   ^{ainf436} ^{art3588}   ⁿⁿ⁴⁶⁷⁸   ²⁵³² ^{art3588} ⁿⁿ⁴¹⁵¹   ^{repro3739}

10 And they were*not*able to resist the wisdom and the spirit by which

^{ipf2980}

he spake.

ad5119 aina5260 an,nn435 pap3004 pfi191 ppro846 pap2980
11 Then they suborned men, which said, We have heard him speak

an,aj989 an,nn4487 pre1519 an,nn3475 2532 art,nn2316
blasphemous words against Moses, and *against* God.

5037 aina4787 art3588 nn2992 2532 art3588 ajn4245 2532 art3588 nn1122 2532
12 And they stirred up the people, and the elders, and the scribes, and

apta2186 aina4884 ppro846 2532 aina71 pre1519 art3588 nn4892
came upon *him,* and caught him, and brought *him* to the council,

5037 aina2476 an,aj5571 an,nn3144 pap3004 depro3778 art,nn444 pinm3973 3756
13 And set up false witnesses, which said, This man ceaseth not to

pap2980 an,aj989 an,nn4487 pre2596 depro5127 art,aj40 art,nn5117 2532 art3588 nn3551
speak blasphemous words against this holy place, and the law:

1063 pfi191 ppro846 pap3004 3754 depro3778 an,nn2424 art,aj3480 ft2647
14 For we have heard him say, that this Jesus of Nazareth shall destroy

depro5126 art,nn5117 2532 ft236 art3588 nn1485 repro3739 an,nn3475 aina3860 ppro2254
this place, and shall change the customs which Moses delivered us.

2532 an,aj537 art,ppmp2516 pre1722 art3588 nn4892 apta816 pre1519 ppro846 aina1492
15 And all that sat in the council, looking steadfastly on him, saw

ppro846 art,nn4383 ad5616 an,nn4383 an,nn32
his face as*it*had*been the face of an angel.

Stephen's Sermon

7

1161 aina2036 art3588 nn749 (1487 686) pin2192 depro5023 ad3779
Then said the high priest, Are these things so?

1161 art3588 aina5346 an,nn435 an,nn80 2532 an,nn3962 aima191 art3588 nn2316
☞ 2 And he said, Men, brethren, and fathers, hearken; The God of

art,nn1391 ainp3700 ppro2257 art,nn3962 11 pap5607 pre1722 art,nn3318
glory appeared unto our father Abraham, when he was in Mesopotamia,

ad4250 (2228) ppro846 ainf2730 pre1722 5488
before he dwelt in Haran, *(Ps. 29:3; Gen. 11:31—12:1)*

2532 aina2036 pre4314 ppro846 aima1831 pre1537 ppro4675 art,nn1093 2532 pre1537 ppro4675
3 And said unto him, Get thee out of thy country, and from thy

art,nn4772 2532 ad1204 pre1519 an,nn1093 repro3739/302 asba1166 ppro4671
kindred, and come into the land which I shall show thee. *(Gen. 12:1)*

ad5119 apta1831 pre1537 an,nn1093 an,nn5466 aina2730 pre1722 5488
4 Then came he out of the land of the Chaldeans, and dwelt in Haran:

☞ **7:2–4** Some have suggested that there is a contradiction between this passage and Genesis 11:26, 32; 12:4. In his sermon, Stephen states that Abraham dwelt in Haran until his father (Terah) died, and then moved to Canaan. The Genesis account states that Terah was seventy-five years old when he begat his sons (Gen. 11:26), and that Abraham left Haran when he was seventy-five years old (Gen. 12:4). However, it also states that Terah died when he was 205 years old (Gen. 11:32). Some explain this fifty-five year gap by saying that Stephen had only the Samaritan Pentateuch to refer to as a source for historical events. They propose that this document was corrupted and simply contained inaccurate figures. Others suggest that Terah reverted to his old life of idolatry (cf. Josh. 24:2), and Abraham declared him spiritually dead by leaving him at Haran. Still others point out that, Abraham was not necessarily the eldest son of Terah, but was listed first in Genesis 11:26 because of his prominence in Scripture. This could mean that many years separated the births of Terah's three sons, thus Stephen's statement is not in conflict.

^{ad2547} ^{ppro846 art,nn3962} ^{aime599} ^{aina3351 ppro846 pre1519 depro5026}
and*from*thence, when his father was dead, he removed him into this
^{art,nn1093 pre1519/repro3739 epn5210 ad3568 pin2730}
land, wherein ye now dwell.   *(Gen. 11:31—12:1,5)*

²⁵³² ^{aina1325 ppro846} ³⁷⁵⁶ ^{an,nn2817} ^{pre1722} ^{ppro846 3761}
5 And he gave him none inheritance in it, no, not *so much as* to
^{an,nn968/an,nn4228} ²⁵³² ^{aom1861} ^{ainf1325 ppro846} ^{ppro846 pre1519}
set*his*foot*on: yet he promised that he would give it to him for a
^{an,nn2697} ²⁵³² ^{ppro846 art,nn4690 pre3326 ppro846} ^{ppro846 pap5607 3756 an,nn5043}
possession, and to his seed after him, when *as yet* he had no child.

                              (Gen. 12:7; 13:15; 15:2,18; 16:1; 17:8; 24:7; 48:4)

¹¹⁶¹ ^{art,nn2316 aina2980} ^{ad3779} ^{3754 ppro846 art,nn4690 fm2071 pr/an,nn3941 pre1722 an,aj245}
6 And God spake on*this*wise, That his seed should sojourn in a strange
^{an,nn1093} ²⁵³² ^{ft1402/ppro846} ²⁵³² ^{ft2559}
land; and that they should bring*them*into*bondage, and entreat*them*evil
^{nu5071} ^{an,nn2094}
four hundred years.

²⁵³² ^{art3588} ⁿⁿ¹⁴⁸⁴ ^{repro3739} ⁽¹⁴³⁷⁾ ^{asba1398} ^{epn1473 ft2919 aina2036}
7 And the nation to whom they shall be*in*bondage will I judge, said
^{art,nn2316 2532 pre3326 depro5023} ^{fm1831} ^{2532 ft3000 ppro3427 pre1722 depro5129 art,nn5117}
God: and after that shall they come forth, and serve me in this place.

                              (Gen. 15:13,14; Ex. 3:12)

²⁵³² ^{aina1325 ppro846} ^{an,nn1242} ^{an,nn4061} ^{2532 ad3779} ^{aina1080}
8 And he gave him the covenant of circumcision: and so *Abraham* begat
²⁴⁶⁴ ²⁵³² ^{aina4059} ^{ppro846 art3588 nu,aj3590 art,nn2250 2532 2464} ^{2384 2532 2384}
Isaac, and circumcised him the eighth day; and Isaac *begat* Jacob; and Jacob
^{art3588} ^{nu1427} ⁿⁿ³⁹⁶⁶
begat the twelve patriarchs.   *(Gen. 17:10-14; 21:4)*

²⁵³² ^{art3588} ⁿⁿ³⁹⁶⁶ ^{apta2206} ^{aom591} ²⁵⁰¹ ^{pre1519} ^{an,nn125} ²⁵³²
9 And the patriarchs, moved*with*envy, sold Joseph into Egypt: but
^{art,nn2316 ipf2258 pre3326 ppro846}
God was with him,   *(Gen. 37:11,28; 39:2,3,21,23; 45:4)*

²⁵³² ^{aina1807} ^{ppro846 pre1537 an,aj3956 ppro846} ^{art,nn2347} ^{2532 aina1325 ppro846 an,nn5485 2532}
10 And delivered him out of all his afflictions, and gave him favor and
^{an,nn4678} ^{ad*1726} ⁵³²⁸ ^{an,nn935} ^{an,nn125 2532} ^{aina2525 ppro846 pr/ppmp2233}
wisdom in*the*sight of Pharaoh king of Egypt; and he made him governor
^{pre1909 an,nn125 2532 an,aj3650 ppro848 art,nn3624}
over Egypt and all his house.   *(Gen. 41:37-44; Ps. 105:21)*

¹¹⁶¹ ^{aina2064} ^{an,nn3042} ^{pre1909 an,aj3650 art3588 nn1093} ^{an,nn125 2532 5477}
11 Now there came a dearth over all the land of Egypt and Canaan,
^{2532 an,aj3173} ^{an,nn2347} ^{2532 ppro2257 art,nn3962 ipf2147 3756 an,nn5527}
and great affliction: and our fathers found no sustenance.   *(Gen. 41:54; 42:5)*

¹¹⁶¹ ²³⁸⁴ ^{apta191} ^{pap5607 an,nn4621 pre1722 an,nn125} ^{aina1821}
12 But when Jacob heard that there was corn in Egypt, he sent out
^{ppro2257 art,nn3962 nu,ajn4412}
our fathers first.   *(Gen. 42:1,2)*

²⁵³² ^{pre1722 art3588} ^{nu,ajn1208} ²⁵⁰¹ ^{ainp319} ^{ppro848 art,nn80}
13 And at the second *time* Joseph was made known to his brethren;
²⁵³² ²⁵⁰¹ ^{art,nn1085} ^{aom1096 pr/an,aj5318} ⁵³²⁸
and Joseph's kindred was made known unto Pharaoh.   *(Gen. 45:3,4,16)*

1161   apta649   2501   aom3333 ppro848 art,nn3962   2384   2532 an,aj3956 ppro848
☞ 14 Then sent Joseph, and called his father Jacob to *him,* and all his

art,nn4772   nu1440/nu4002   (pre1722) an,nn5590
kindred, threescore*and*fifteen   souls.

(Gen. 45:9-11;18,19; 46:27; Deut. 10:22)

1161   2384   aina2597   pre1519 an,nn125 2532 aina5053 epn846 2532 ppro2257 art,nn3962
15 So Jacob went down into Egypt, and died, he, and our fathers,

(Gen. 46:5,6; 49:33; Ex. 1:6)

2532   ainp3346   pre1519   4966   2532 ainp5087 pre1722 art3588   nn3418   repro3739
16 And were carried over into Shechem, and laid in the sepulcher that

11   aom5608   an,nn5092   an,nn694 pre3844 art3588 nn5207   1697
Abraham bought for a sum of money of the sons of Hamor *the father* of

4966
Shechem.   *(Gen. 23:2-20; 49:29,30; 50:7-13; Josh. 24:32)*

1161   ad2531 art3588 nn5550   art3588   nn1860   ipf1448   repro3739 art,nn2316 aina3660
17 But when the time of the promise drew nigh, which God had sworn to

11   art3588   nn2992   aina837 2532   ainp4129   pre1722 an,nn125
Abraham, the people grew and multiplied in Egypt,

ad891(repro3739) an,aj2087 an,nn935 aina450 repro3739 ipf1492 3756   2501
18 Till   another king arose, which knew not Joseph.   *(Ex. 1:7,8)*

depro3778   aptm2686   ppro2257   art,nn1085   aina2559   ppro2257
19 The same dealt*subtlely*with our kindred, and evil entreated our

art,nn3962   art,infg4160/an,nn1570 ppro846   art,nn1025
fathers, so that they cast out their young children, to the end they might

3361 aies2225
not live.   *(Ex. 1:10,11,22)*

pre1722 repro3739 an,nn2540 an,nn3475   ainp1080   2532 ipf2258   pr/an,aj791 (art,nn2316) 2532
20 In which time Moses was born, and was exceeding fair, and

(repro3739) ainp397   pre1722 ppro848 art,nn3962 art,nn3624 nu5140 an,nn3376
nourished up in his father's house three months: *(Ex. 2:2)*

1161   ppro846   aptp1620   5328   art,nn2364   aina337/ppro846   2532
21 And when he was cast out, Pharaoh's daughter took*him*up, and

aom397   ppro846 pre1519 rxpro1438   an,nn5207
nourished him for her own son.   *(Ex. 2:3-10)*

2532   an,nn3475   ainp3811   an,aj3956   an,nn4678   an,nn124   1161 ipf2258
22 And Moses was learned in all the wisdom of the Egyptians, and was

pr/an,aj1415 pre1722 an,nn3056 2532 pre1722 an,nn2041
mighty in words and in deeds.

1161   ad5613   ppro846   ipf4137 an,aj5063   an,nn5550   aina305 pre1909 ppro846 art,nnn2588   aifm1980
23 And when he was full forty years old, it came into his heart to visit

ppro848 art,nn80   art3588   nn5207   2474
his brethren the children of Israel.

2532   apta1492 idpro5100   ppmp91   aom292   2532 aina4160/an,nn1557
24 And seeing one *of them* suffer wrong, he defended *him,* and avenged

art,ppmp2669   apta3960 art3588   nn124
him*that*was*oppressed, and smote the Egyptian: *(Ex. 2:11,12)*

1161   ipf3543   ppro848   art,nn80   pinf4920   3754
25 For he supposed his brethren would have understood how that

art,nn2316 pre1223 ppro846 an,nn5495   pin1325/an,nn4991 ppro846 1161 art3588   aina4920   3756
God   by   his   hand   would   deliver   them: but   they   understood   not.

5037 art3588 pap1966 an,nn2250   ainp3700   ppro846   ppmp3164   2532
26 And the next day he showed himself unto them as they strove, and

aina4900/ppro846/pre1519/an,nn1515 apta2036 an,nn435 epn5210 pin2075 pr/an,nn80 inpro2444
would have set*them*at*one*again, saying, Sirs, ye are brethren; why

pin91   rcpro240
do*ye*wrong one*to*another?

1161   art,pap91/art,ad4139   aom683/ppro846   apta2036   inpro5101
27 But he*that*did*his*neighbor*wrong thrust*him*away, saying, Who

aina2525 ppro4571 pr/an,nn758 2532 pr/an,nn1348 pre1909 ppro2248
made thee a ruler and a judge over us?

pin2309 (3361) epn4771 ainf337 ppro3165 repro3739/an,nn5158/aina337 art3588   nn124   ad5504
28 Wilt   thou kill me, as*thou*didst the Egyptian yesterday?

(Ex. 2:13,14)

1161 aina5343 an,nn3475 pre1722 depro5129 art,nn3056 2532 aom1096 pr/an,ajn3941 pre1722 an,nn1093
29 Then fled Moses at this saying, and was a stranger in the land of

3099 repro3757 aina1080 nu1417 an,nn5207
Midian, where he begat two sons.   *(Ex. 2:15,21,22; 18:3,4)*

2532   nu5062 an,nn2094   aptp4137   ainp3700   ppro846 pre1722 art3588
30 And when forty years were expired, there appeared to him in the

ajn2048   art,nn3735 4614   an,nn32   an,nn2962 pre1722 an,nn5395 an,nn4442 an,nn942
wilderness of mount Sinai an angel of the Lord in a flame of fire in a bush.

1161 art,nn3475 apta1492   aina2296   art3588 nn3705 1161   ppro846 ppmp4334
31 When Moses saw *it,* he wondered at the sight: and as he drew near

ainf2657   an,nn5456   an,nn2962 aom1096 pre4314 ppro846
to behold *it,* the voice of the Lord came unto him,

epn1473   art3588 pr/nn2316   ppro4675 art,nn3962   art3588 pr/nn2316   11   2532
32 *Saying,* I *am* the God of thy fathers, the God of Abraham, and

art3588 pr/nn2316   2464 2532 art3588 pr/nn2316   2384   1161 an,nn3475 ppmp1096/pr/an,aj1790   ipf5111
the God of Isaac, and the God of Jacob. Then Moses trembled, and durst

3756 ainf2657
not behold.

1161 aina2036 art3588 nn2962   ppro846 aima3089   art,nn5266   ppro4675 art,nn4228 1063 art3588
33 Then said the Lord to him, Put off thy shoes from thy feet: for the

nn5117 pre1722/repro3739   pfi2476   pin2076 an,aj40 pr/an,nn1093
place where thou standest is holy ground.

apta1492   aina1492 art3588   nn2561   ppro3450 art,nn2992 art3588   pre1722
34 I have seen, I have seen the affliction of my people which is in

an,nn125 2532   aina191 ppro846 art,nn4725 2532   aina2597 aifm1807 ppro846
Egypt, and I have heard their groaning, and am come down to deliver them.

2532 ad3568 ad1204   ft649 ppro4571 pre1519 an,nn125
And now come, I will send thee into Egypt.   *(Ex. 3:2-10)*

depro5126 art,nn3475 repro3739   aom720 apta2036 inpro5101 aina2525 ppro4571 pr/an,nn758 2532
35 This Moses whom they refused, saying, Who made thee a ruler and a

pr/an,nn1348 depro5126   art,nn2316 aina649   pr/an,nn758 2532 pr/an,nn3086 pre1722 an,nn5495
judge? the same did God send *to be* a ruler and a deliverer by the hand of

an,nn32   art,aptp3700   ppro846 pre1722 art3588 nn942
the angel which appeared to him in the bush.   *(Ex. 2:14; 3:2)*

depro3778   aina1806/ppro846   apta4160 an,nn5059 2532 an,nn4592
36 He brought*them*out, after that he had showed wonders and signs

pre1722 an,nn1093 an,nn125 2532 pre1722 an,aj2063 an,nn2281 2532 pre1722 art3588 ajn2048 nu5062

in the land of Egypt, and in the Red sea, and in the wilderness forty

an,nn2094

years. *(Ex. 7:3; 14:21; Num. 14:33)*

depro3778 pin2076 pr/art,nn3475 art,apta2036 art3588 nn5207 2474 an,nn4396

37 This is that Moses, which said unto the children of Israel, A prophet

an,nn2962 ppro5216 art,nn2316 ft450 ppro5213 pre1537 ppro5216 art,nn80 ad5613

shall the Lord your God raise up unto you of your brethren, like unto

ppro1691 epn846 fm191

me; him shall ye hear. *(Deut. 18:15)*

depro3778 pin2076 pr/art,aptm1096 pre1722 art3588 nn1577 pre1722 art3588 ajn2048 pre3326 art3588

38 This is he, that was in the church in the wilderness with the

nn32 art,pap2980 ppro846 pre1722 art3588 nn3735 4614 2532 ppro2257 art,nn3962 repro3739

angel which spake to him in the mount Sinai, and *with* our fathers: who

aom1209 pap2198 an,nn3051 ainf1325 ppro2254

received the lively oracles to give unto us:

(Ex. 19:1-6; 20:1-17; Deut. 5:4-22; 9:10)

repro3739 ppro2257 art,nn3962 aina2309 3756 aifm1096/pr/an,nn5255 235 aom683

39 To whom our fathers would not obey, but thrust*him*from them,

2532 ppro848 art,nn2588 ainp4762 pre1519 an,nn125

and in their hearts turned*back*again into Egypt, *(Num. 14:3)*

apta2036 2 aima4160 ppro2254 an,nn2316 (repro3739) fm4313 ppro2257 1063

40 Saying unto Aaron, Make us gods to go before us: for *as for*

depro3778 art,nn3475 repro3739 aina1806 ppro2248 pre1537 an,nn1093 an,nn125 pin1492 3756 inpro5101

this Moses, which brought us out of the land of Egypt, we wot not what is

pfi1096 ppro846

become of him. *(Ex. 32:1,23)*

2532 aina3447 pre1722 depro1565 art,nn2250 2532 aina321 an,nn2378 art3588

41 And they made*a*calf in those days, and offered sacrifice unto the

nn1497 2532 ipf2165 pre1722 art3588 nn2041 ppro848 art,nn5495

idol, and rejoiced in the works of their own hands. *(Ex. 32:4-6)*

1161 art,nn2316 aina4762 2532 aina3860/ppro846 pinf3000 art3588 nn4756 art,nn3772

42 Then God turned, and gave*them*up to worship the host of heaven;

ad2531 pfip1125 pre1722 an,nn976 art3588 nn4396 an,nn3624 2474 (3361)

as it is written in the book of the prophets, O ye house of Israel, have ye

aina4374 ppro3427 an,nn4968 2532 an,nn2378 nu5062 an,nn2094 pre1722 art3588

offered to me slain beasts and sacrifices *by the space of* forty years in the

ajn2048

wilderness? *(Jer. 7:18)*

2532 aina353 art3588 nn4633 3434 2532 art3588 nn798 ppro5216 art,nn2316

43 Yea, ye took up the tabernacle of Moloch, and the star of your god

4481 art,nn5179 repro3739 aina4160 pinf4352 ppro846 2532 ft3351/ppro5209

Remphan, figures which ye made to worship them: and I will carry*you*away

ad1900 an,nn847

beyond Babylon. *(Amos 5:25-27)*

(pre1722) ppro2257 art,nn3962 ipf2258 art3588 nn4633 art,nn3142 pre1722 art3588 ajn2048

44 Our fathers had the tabernacle of witness in the wilderness, as

aom1299 art,pap2980 art,nn3475 ainf4160 ppro846 pre2596

he had appointed, speaking unto Moses, that he should make it according to

art3588 nn5179 repro3739 pipf3708

the fashion that he had seen. *(Ex. 27:21; Num. 1:50; Ex. 25:9,40)*

repro3739　2532　ppro2257　art,nn3962　　　　　　aptm1237　　　aina1521　　pre3326　an,nn2424　pre1722　art3588
45 Which also our fathers that came after brought in with Joshua into the

nn2697　　art3588　　nn1484　　repro3739　art,nn2316　　aina1856　　pre575　　an,nn4383　ppro2257
possession of the Gentiles, whom God drove out before the face of our

art,nn3962　ad2193　art3588　nn2250　　1138
fathers, unto the days of David;　　　*(Josh. 3:14-17; 18:1; 23:9; 24:18)*

repro3739　aina2147　an,nn5485　ad*1799　art,nn2315　2532　aom154　　ainf2147　　an,nn4638　　art3588
46 Who found favor before God, and desired to find a tabernacle for the

nn2316　　2384
God of Jacob.　　*(2 Sam. 7:2-16; 1 Kgs. 8:17,18; 1 Chr. 17:1-14; Ps. 132:1-5)*

1161　an,nn4672　aina3618　ppro846　an,nn3624
47 But Solomon built him a house.

(1 Kgs. 6:1,14; 8:19,20; 2 Chr. 3:1; 5:1; 6:2,10)

235　　art3588　ajn5310　　pin2730　3756　pre1722　an,nn3485　　　an,aj5499
48 Howbeit the most High dwelleth not in temples made*with*hands;

ad2531　pin3004　art3588　nn4396
as saith the prophet,

art,nn3772　　ppro3427　pr/an,nn2362　1161　art,nn1093　ppro3450　pr/an,nn5286/art,nn4228　an,aj4169　an,nn3624
49 Heaven *is* my throne, and earth *is* my footstool: what house will ye

ft3618　ppro3427　pin3004　an,nn2962　2228　inpro5101　pr/an,nn5117　ppro3450　art,nn2663
build me? saith the Lord: or what *is* the place of my rest?

3780　ppro3450　art,nn5495　aina4160　an,ajn3956　depro5023
50 Hath not my hand made all these things?　　　*(Is. 66:1,2)*

an,aj4644　2532　an,aj564　　art,nn2588　2532　art,nn3775　epn5210　ad104
51 Ye stiffnecked and uncircumcised in heart and ears, ye do always

pin496　art3588　aj40　art,nn4151　ad5613　ppro5216　art,nn3962　2532　epn5210
resist the Holy Ghost: as your fathers *did*, so do ye.

(Ex. 32:9; 33:3,5; Lev. 26:41; Jer. 6:10; 9:26; Is. 63:10)

inpro5101　art3588　nn4396　　3756　ppro5216　art,nn3962　aina1377　2532
52 Which of the prophets have not your fathers persecuted? and they have

aina615　　　　art,apta4293　　pre4012　art3588　nn1660　　art3588　ajn1342　　repro3739
slain them*which*showed*before of the coming of the Just One; of whom

epn5210　pfip1096　ad3568　pr/an,nn4273　2532　pr/an,nn5406
ye have been now the betrayers and murderers:　　*(2 Chr. 36:16)*

repro3748　aina2983　art3588　nn3551　pre1519　an,nn1296　an,nn32　2532　3756
53 Who have received the law by the disposition of angels, and have not

aina5442
kept *it.*

Stephen Is Put to Death

1161　pap191　depro5023　　　ipf1282 (ppro848) art3588　nn2588　2532
54 When they heard these things, they were cut to the heart, and they

ipf1031　pre1909　ppro846　art,nn3598
gnashed on him with *their* teeth.　　*(Ps. 35:16; 37:12; 112:10)*

1161　pap5225　pr/an,aj4134　an,aj40　an,nn4151　apta816　pre1519
55 But he, being full of the Holy Ghost, looked*up*steadfastly into

art,nn3772   aina1492   an,nn1391   an,nn2316   2532   an,nn2424   pfp2476   pre1537   an,ajn1188

heaven, and saw the glory of God, and Jesus standing on the right hand of

art,nn2316

God,

          2532   aina2036   2400   pin2334 art3588   nn3772   pfpp455   2532 art3588 nn5207   art,nn444

56 And said, Behold, I see the heavens opened, and the Son of man

pfp2476   pre1537   an,ajn1188   art,nn2316

standing on the right hand of God.

          1161   apta2896   an,aj3173 an,nn5466   aina4912   ppro848 art,nn3775   2532

57 Then they cried out with a loud voice, and stopped their ears, and

aina3729 pre1909 ppro846   ad3661

ran upon him with*one*accord,

          2532   apta1544   ad1854   art3588   nn4172   ipf3036   2532   art3588   nn3144

58 And cast *him* out of the city, and stoned *him:* and the witnesses

aom659   ppro848 art,nn2440 pre3844   an,nn3494   art,nn4228   ppmp2564   an,nn4569

laid down their clothes at a young man's feet, whose name was Saul.

          2532   ipf3036   art,nn4736   ppmp1941   2532   pap3004   an,nn2962 an,nn2424

59 And they stoned Stephen, calling upon *God,* and saying, Lord Jesus,

aipm1209   ppro3450 art,nn4151

receive my spirit.   *(Ps. 31:5)*

          1161   apta5087/art,nn1119   aina2896   an,aj3173 an,nn5456 an,nn2962 aosi2476   3361

60 And he kneeled down, and cried with a loud voice, Lord, lay not

depro5026 art,nn266   ppro846   2532   apta2036 depro5124   ainp2837

this sin to their charge. And when he had said this, he fell asleep.

The Congregation Is Persecuted

          1161   an,nn4569 ipf2258   pap4909   ppro846 art,nn336   1161 pre1722 depro1565 art,nn2250

8 And Saul was consenting unto his death. And at that time there

aom1096   an,aj3173   an,nn1375   pre1909 art3588   nn1577   art3588   pre1722   an,nn2414

was a great persecution against the church which was at Jerusalem;

5037   an,ajn3956   ainp1289   pre2596   art3588   nn5561   art,nn2449 2532

and they were all scattered abroad throughout the regions of Judea and

an,nn4540   4133   art3588   nn652

Samaria, except the apostles.

          1161   an,aj2126   an,nn435   aina4792   art,nn4736   2532   aom4160   an,aj3173

2 And devout men carried Stephen *to his burial,* and made great

an,nn2870   pre1909 ppro846

lamentation over him.

          (1161)   an,nn4569   ipf3075   art3588   nn1577   ppmp1531   pre2596/art,nn3624

3 As for Saul, he made havoc of the church, entering into every house,

5037   pap4951 an,nn435 2532   an,nn1135   ipf3860   pre1519 an,nn5438

and haling men and women committed *them* to prison.

The Gospel Proclaimed in Samaria

          3767   (3303)   art,aptp1289   aina1330

4 Therefore   they*that*were*scattered*abroad   went*every*where

ppmp2097   art3588   nn3056

preaching the word.

1161   an,nn5376   apta2718   pre1519   an,nn4172   art,nn4540   ipf2784   art,nn5547

5 Then Philip went down to the city of Samaria, and preached Christ

ppro846

unto them.

5037   art3588   nn3793   ad3661   ipf4337   (pre5259)

6 And the people with*one*accord gave heed unto those things which

art,nn5376 art,ppmp3004 (ppro846)   aie191   2532   aie991   art3588   nn4592   repro3739   ipf4160

Philip spake,   hearing and seeing the miracles which he did.

1063   an,aj169   an,nn4151   pap994   an,aj3173   an,nn5456   ipf1831   an,ajn4183

7 For unclean spirits, crying with loud voice, came out of many

art,pap2192   1161   an,aj4183   pfpp3886   2532

that*were*possessed *with* *them*: and many taken*with*palsies, and

an,ajn5560   aina2323

that*were*lame, were healed.

2532   aom1096 an,aj3173   pr/an,nn5479 pre1722 depro1565 art,nn4172

8 And there was great joy in that city.

1161   idpro5100   an,nn435   an,nn3686   an,nn4613   ipf4391   pre1722

9 But there was a certain man, called Simon, which beforetime in

art3588   nn4172   pap3096   2532   pap1839   art3588   nn1484   art,nn4540   pap3004

the same city used sorcery, and bewitched the people of Samaria, giving out

rxpro1438   pinf1511 idpro5100   pr/an,ajn3173

that himself was some great one:

repro3739   an,ajn3956   ipf4337   pre575   an,ajn3398 ad*2193   an,ajn3173

10 To whom they all gave heed, from the least to the greatest,

pap3004   depro3778   pin2076 art3588   aj3173   pr/art,nn1411   art,nn2316

saying, This man is the great power of God.

1161   ppro846   ipf4337   an,aj2425   an,nn5550

11 And to him they had regard, because that of long time he had

aid1839   ppro846   art,nn3095

bewitched them with sorceries.

1161   ad3753   aina4100   art,nn5376   ppmp2097   art3588   pre4012   art3588

12 But when they believed Philip preaching the things concerning the

nn932   art,nn2316 2532 art3588   nn3686   art,nn2424   an,nn5547   ipf907   5037   an,nn435

kingdom of God, and the name of Jesus Christ, they were baptized, both men

2532   an,nn1135

and women.

1161   art,nn4613   epn846   aina4100   2532   2532   aptp907

13 Then Simon himself believed also: and when he was baptized, he

ipf2258/pap4342   art,nn5376   5037   ipf1839   pap2334   (an,aj3173)   an,nn1411   2532 an,nn4592

continued with Philip, and wondered, beholding the miracles and signs which

ppmp1096

were done.

1161   art3588   nn652   art3588   pre1722   an,nn2414   apta191   3754

14 Now when the apostles which were at Jerusalem heard that

art,nn4540   pfi1209   art3588   nn3056   art,nn2316   aina649   pre4314   ppro846   art,nn4074   2532

Samaria had received the word of God, they sent unto them Peter and

an,nn2491

John:

repro3748   apta2597   aom4336   pre4012   ppro846   3704

15 Who, when they were come down, prayed for them, that they might

asba2983   an,aj40   an,nn4151

receive the Holy Ghost:

1063   ad3768   ipf2258   pfp1968   pre1909 an,ajn3762   ppro846   (1161) an,ajn3440   ipf5225

☞ 16 (For as yet he was fallen upon none of them: only they were

pfpp907   pre1519 art3588 nn3686   art3588 nn2962   an,nn2424

baptized in   the name of the Lord Jesus.)

ad5119   ipf2007   art,nn5495 pre1909 ppro846   2532   ipf2983   an,aj40

17 Then laid they *their* hands on   them, and they received the Holy

an,nn4151

Ghost.

1161   art,nn4613 aptm2300 3754   pre1223 art,nn1936   art3588   nn652   art,nn5495

18 And when Simon saw that through laying on of the apostles' hands

art3588 aj40 art,nn4151   pinp1325   aina4374   ppro846   an,nn5536

the Holy Ghost was given, he offered them money,

pap3004   aima1325   epn2504   depro5026 art,nn1849 2443   repro3739/302   asba2007 art,nn5495

19 Saying, Give me also this power, that on whomsoever I lay hands, he

psa2983   an,aj40   an,nn4151

may receive the Holy Ghost.

1161 an,nn4074 aina2036 pre4314 ppro846 ppro4675 art,nn694   opt1498/pre1519/an,nn684 pre4862 ppro4671   3754

20 But Peter said unto him, Thy money   perish   with thee, because

aina3543   art3588 nn1431   art,nn2316   pifm2932   pre1223   an,nn5536

thou hast thought that the gift of God may be purchased with money.

ppro4671 pin2076   3756   an,nn3310 3761 an,nn2819 pre1722 depro5129   art,nn3056   1063 ppro4675 art,nn2588 pin2076

21 Thou hast neither part nor lot   in   this matter: for thy heart is

3756   pr/an,aj2117   ad*1799   art,nn2316

not right in*the*sight of God.   *(Ps. 78:37)*

aima3340   3767   pre575 depro5026 ppro4675   art,nn2549   2532 aipp1189 art,nn2316 1487   686

22 Repent therefore of this   thy wickedness, and pray God, if perhaps

art3588   nn1963   ppro4675 art,nn2588   fp863   ppro4671

the thought of thine heart may be forgiven thee.

1063   pin3708   ppro4571 pap5607 pre1519   an,nn5521   an,nn4088   2532

23 For I perceive that thou art   in   the gall of bitterness, and *in* the

an,nn4886   an,nn93

bond of iniquity.   *(Deut. 29:18; Lam. 3:15[Sept.])*

1161   aptp611   art,nn4613   aina2036 aipp1189 epn5210 pre4314 art3588 nn2962 pre5228 ppro1700 3704

24 Then answered Simon, and said, Pray ye to the Lord for me, that

an,ajn3367   repro3739   pfi2046   asba1904 pre1909 ppro1691

none of these things which ye have spoken come upon me.

3767   art3588   (3303 3767)   aptm1263   2532   apta2980   art3588 nn3056   art3588   nn2962

25 And they, when they had testified and preached the word of the Lord,

aina5290   pre1519   2419   5037   aom2097   an,aj4183   an,nn2968   art3588

returned   to Jerusalem, and preached*the*gospel in many villages of the

nn4541

Samaritans.

Philip and the Ethiopian Eunuch

1161   an,nn32   an,nn2962 aina2980 pre4314 an,nn5376   pap3004   aipp450   2532 pim4198

26 And the angel of the Lord spake unto Philip, saying, Arise, and go

---

☞ **8:16** See note on 1 Corinthians 10:2.

pre2596   an,nn3314   pre1909 art3588 nn3598   art,pap2597   pre575   2419   pre1519   an,nn1048
toward the south unto the way that*goeth*down from Jerusalem unto Gaza,

depro3778 pin2076 pr/an,aj2048
which is desert.

2532   apta450   2532   ainp4198   2532   2400   an,nn435   an,nn128   an,nn2135
27 And he arose and went: and, behold, a man of Ethiopia, an eunuch of

an,nn1413   an,nn2582   art,nn938   an,nn128   repro3739   ipf2258/pre1909
great authority under Candace queen of the Ethiopians, who had*the*charge of

an,aj3956 ppro848 art,nn1047   2532 (repro3739) plpf2064 pre1519   2419   fpta4352
all her treasure, and had come to Jerusalem for to worship,

(5037) ipf2258 pap5290   2532   ppmp2521 pre1909 ppro848 art,nn716 (2532) ipf314 an,nn2268 art3588   nn4396
28   Was returning, and sitting in his chariot   read Isaiah the prophet.

1161 art3588   nn4151   aina2036   art,nn5376   aima4334   2532   aipp2853   depro5129
29 Then the Spirit said unto Philip, Go near, and join thyself to this

art,nn716
chariot.

1161 art3588   apta4370   aina191 ppro846 pap314 art3588   nn4396   an,nn2268
30 And Philip ran thither to *him,* and heard him read the prophet Isaiah,

2532 aina2036 (687 1065)   pin1097   repro3739   pin314
and said,   Understandest thou what thou readest?

1161 art3588 aina2036(1063) ad4459 opt1410/302   3362   idpro5100   asba3594 ppro3165
31 And he said, How can I, except some man should guide me?

5037   aina3870 art,nn5376   apta305   ainf2523 pre4862 ppro846
And he desired Philip that he would come up and sit with him.

(1161)art3588 nn4042   art3588   nn1124   repro3739   ipf314 ipf2258 pr/depro3778   ainp71 ad5613
32   The place of the Scripture which he read was this, He was led as

an,nn4263 pre1909   an,nn4967   2532 ad5613   an,nn286 an,aj880   ad*1726   ppro846 art,pap2751 ad3779
a sheep to the slaughter; and like a lamb dumb before his shearer, so

pin455   3756 ppro848 art,nn4750
opened he not his mouth:

pre1722 ppro846   art,nn5014   ppro846   art,nn2920   ainp142   1161 inpro5101
33 In   his humiliation his judgment was taken away: and who shall

fm1334   ppro846   art,nn1074   3754 ppro846 art,nn2222 pinp142 pre575 art3588   nn1093
declare his generation? for his life is taken from the earth.

(Is. 53:7,8[Sept.])

1161 art3588   nn2135   aptp611   art,nn5376   aina2036   pinm1189 ppro4675 pre4012 inpro5101
34 And the eunuch answered Philip, and said, I pray thee, of whom

pin3004   art3588   nn4396 depro5124 pre4012 rxpro1438 2228 pre4012 inpro5101/an,aj2087
speaketh the prophet this? of himself, or of some*other*man?

1161 art,nn5376   apta455 ppro848 art,nn4750   2532 aptm756 pre575 depro5026 art,nn1124
35 Then Philip opened his mouth, and began at the same Scripture, and

aom2097   ppro846 art,nn2424
preached unto him Jesus.

1161 ad5613   ipf4198 pre2596   art,nn3598   aina2064 pre1909   idpro5100 an,nn5204 2532
36 And as they went on *their* way, they came unto a certain water: and

art3588   nn2135 pin5346 2400   an,nn5204 inpro5101   pin2967 ppro3165   aifp907
the eunuch said, See, *here is* water; what doth hinder me to be baptized?

1161 art,nn5376 aina2036 1487   pin4100 pre1537 an,aj3650   art,nn2588   pin1832
37 And Philip said, If thou believest with all thine heart, thou mayest.

1161   aptp611   aina2036 pin4100   art,nn2424 an,nn5547 pinf1511 art3588 pr/nn5207 art,nn2316
And he answered and said, I believe that Jesus Christ is the Son of God.

2532   aina2753   art3588   nn716   ainf2476   2532   aina2597   an,ajn297
38 And he commanded the chariot to stand still: and they went down both

pre1519 art3588   nn5204   5037   art,nn5376 2532 art3588   nn2135   2532   aina907   ppro846
into the water, both Philip and the eunuch; and he baptized him.

1161   ad3753   aina305   pre1537 art3588   nn5204   an,nn4151   an,nn2962
☞ 39 And when they were come up out of the water, the Spirit of the Lord

aina726   art,nn5376   2532   art3588   nn2135   (3756) aina1492 ppro846   ad3765   (1063)   ipf4198
caught away Philip, that the eunuch   saw him no more: and he went on

ppro848 art,nn3598   pap5463
his way rejoicing.

1161   an,nn5376   ainp2147 pre1519 an,nn108   2532   ppmp1330   ipf2097
40 But Philip was found   at Azotus: and passing through he preached in

an,aj3956 art3588   nn4172   ad2193 ppro846 infg2064 pre1519   an,nn2542
all the cities, till he came to Caesarea.

Paul Conversion
(Acts 22:6-16; 26:12-18)

         1161   art,nn4569 ad2089   pap1709   an,nn547   2532 an,nn5408   pre1519 art3588   nn3101
9 And Saul, yet breathing out threatenings and slaughter against the disciples

art3588   nn2962 apta4334   art3588   nn749
of the Lord, went unto the high priest,

         aom154   pre3844 ppro846 an,nn1992 pre1519   an,nn1154   pre4314 art3588   nn4864   3704
2 And desired of him letters to Damascus to the synagogues, that

1437   asba2147 idpro5100 (pap5607) art,nn3598   5037   an,nn435 2532 an,nn1135
if he found any of this way, whether they were men or women, he might

asba71   pfpp1210   pre1519   2419
bring them bound unto Jerusalem.

1161   aie4198 (aom1096) ppro846   pinf1448   art,nn1154   2532   ad1810
3 And as he journeyed,   he came near Damascus: and suddenly

aina4015   ppro846 an,nn5457 pre575   art,nn3772
there shined*round*about him a light from heaven:

2532   apta4098 pre1909 art3588   nn1093   aina191   an,nn5456   pap3004   ppro848   4549
4 And he fell to the earth, and heard a voice saying unto him, Saul,

4549   inpro5101   pin1377   ppro3165
Saul, why persecutest thou me?

1161   aina2036 pr/inpro5101 pin1488   an,nn2962   1161 art3588 nn2962 aina2036 epn1473 pin1510 pr/an,nn2424
5 And he said, Who art thou, Lord? And the Lord said, I   am Jesus

repro3739 epn4771   pin1377   pr/an,ajn4642 ppro4671   pinf2979 pre4314   an,nn2759
whom thou persecutest: it is hard for thee to kick against the pricks.

5037   pap5141   2532   pap2284   alna2036 an,nn2962 inpro5101 pin2309   ppro3165
6 And he trembling and astonished said, Lord, what wilt thou have me to

ainf4160 2532 art3588 nn2962   pre4314 ppro846 aipp450   2532 aima1525 pre1519 art3588 nn4172 2532
do? And the Lord said unto him, Arise, and go into the city, and it shall be

fp2980 ppro4671 inpro5101   pin1163 pinf4160
told thee what thou must do.

☞ **8:39** See note on 1 Thessalonians 4:17.

1161 art3588 nn435 art,pap4922 ppro846 plpf2476 pr/an,aj1769 pap191 (3303)

7 And the men which*journeyed*with him stood speechless, hearing a

art,nn5456 1161 pap2334 an,ajn3367

voice, but seeing no man.

1161 art,nn4569 ainp1453 pre575 art3588 nn1093 1161 ppro848 art,nn3788 pfpp455

8 And Saul arose from the earth; and when his eyes were opened, he

ipf991 an,ajn3762 1161 pap5496/ppro846 aina1521 pre1519 an,nn1154

saw no man: but they led*him*by*the*hand, and brought him into Damascus.

2532 ipf2258 nu5140 an,nn2250 3361 pap991 2532 3756 aina5315 3761 aina4095

9 And he was three days without sight, and neither did eat nor drink.

1161 ipf2258 idprp5100 an,nn3101 pre1722 an,nn1154 an,nn3686 an,nn367 2532

10 And there was a certain disciple at Damascus named Ananias; and

pre4314 ppro846 aina2036 art3588 nn2962 pre1722 an,nn3705 an,nn367 1161 art3588 aina2036 2400 epn1473

to him said the Lord in a vision, Ananias. And he said, Behold, I am

an,nn2962

here, Lord.

1161 art3588 nn2962 pre4314 ppro846 apta450 aipp4198 pre1909 art3588 nn4505

11 And the Lord said unto him, Arise, and go into the street

art,ppmp2564 an,aj2117 2532 aima2212 pre1722 an,nn3614 an,nn2455 an,nn3686 an,nn4569

which*is*called Straight, and inquire in the house of Judas for one called Saul

an,nn5018 1063 2400 pinm4336

of Tarsus: for, behold, he prayeth,

2532 aina1492 pre1722 an,nn3705 an,nn435 an,nn3686 an,nn367 apta1525 2532

12 And hath seen in a vision a man named Ananias coming in, and

apta2007 an,nn5495 ppro846 3704 asba308

putting his hand on him, that he might receive*his*sight.

1161 art,nn367 ainp611 an,nn2962 pfi191 pre575 an,ajn4183 pre4012 depro5127 art,nn435

13 Then Ananias answered, Lord, I have heard by many of this man,

an,aj3745 an,ajn2556 aina4160 ppro4675 art,ajn40 pre1722 2419

how much evil he hath done to thy saints at Jerusalem:

2532 ad5602 pin2192 an,nn1849 pre3844 art3588 nn749 ainf1210 an,aj3956 art,ppmp1941

14 And here he hath authority from the chief priests to bind all that*call*on

ppro4675 art,nn3686

thy name.

1161 art3588 nn2962 aina2036 pre4314 ppro846 pim4198 3754 depro3778 pin2076 an,nn1589

15 But the Lord said unto him, Go*thy*way: for he is a chosen

pr/an,nn4632 ppro3427 infg941 ppro3450 art,nn3686 ad*1799 an,nn1484 2532 an,nn935 5037

vessel unto me, to bear my name before the Gentiles, and kings, and the

an,nn5207 2474

children of Israel:

1063 epn1473 ft5263 ppro846 an,ajn3745 ppro846 pin1163 ainf3958 pre5228

16 For I will show him how*great*things he must suffer for

ppro3450/art,nn3686

my*name's*sake.

1161 an,nn367 aina565 2532 aina1525 pre1519 art3588 nn3614 2532 apta2007

17 And Ananias went*his*way, and entered into the house; and putting his

art,nn5495 pre1909 ppro846 aina2036 an,nn80 4549 art3588 nn2962 an,nn2424 art,aptp3700

hands on him said, Brother Saul, the Lord, even Jesus, that appeared unto

ppro4671 pre1722 art3588 nn3598 repro3739 ipf2064 pfi649 ppro3165 3704

thee in the way as thou camest, hath sent me, that thou mightest

asba308 2532 asbp4130 an,aj40 an,nn4151

receive*thy*sight, and be filled with the Holy Ghost.

2532   ad2112   aina634 pre575 ppro846 art,nn3778   ad5616   an,nn3013 5037
18 And immediately there fell from his eyes as*it*had*been scales: and

aina308   ad3916   2532 apta450   ainp907
he received sight forthwith, and arose, and was baptized.

2532   apta2983 an,nn5160   aina1765   1161 aom1096
19 And when he had received meat, he was strengthened. Then was

art,nn4569 idpro5100 an,nn2250 pre3326 art3588   nn3101   pre1722 an,nn1154
Saul certain days with the disciples which were at Damascus.

Paul Preaches at Damacus

2532   ad2112   ipf2784   art,nn5547 pre1722 art3588   nn4864   3754 depro3778
20 And straightway he preached Christ in the synagogues, that he

pin2076 art3588 pr/nn5207   art,nn2316
is the Son of God.

1161   an,aj3956   art,pap191   ipf1839   2532   ipf3004 pin2076 3756 depro3778
21 But all that heard *him* were amazed, and said; Is not this

pr/art,apta4199   art,ppmp1941   depro5124 art,nn3686 pre1722   2419   2532 plpf2064
he*that*destroyed them*which*called*on this name in Jerusalem, and came

ad5602 pre1519   depro5124   2443   asba71 ppro846 pfpp1210 pre1909 art3588   nn749
hither for that intent, that he might bring them bound unto the chief priests?

1161   an,nn4569   ipf1743/ad3123   2532   ipf4797   art3588   nn2453
22 But Saul increased*the*more*in*strength, and confounded the Jews

art,pap2730   pre1722   an,nn1154   pap4822   3754 depro3778 pin2076   pr/art,nn5547
which dwelt at Damascus, proving that this is very Christ.

Paul's Escape (2 Cor. 11:32, 33)

1161   ad5613   an,aj2425 an,nn2250   4137   art3588 nn2453   aom4823   ainf337
23 And after that many days were fulfilled, the Jews took counsel to kill

ppro846
him:

1161   ppro846   art,nn1917   ainp1097   art,nn4569 5037   ipf3906   art3588
24 But their laying await was known of Saul. And they watched the

nn4439 (5037)an,nn2250 2532 an,nn3571 3704 asba337 ppro846
gates   day and night to kill him.

1161   art3588   nn3101   apta2983 ppro846   an,nn3571   aina2524   pre1223 art3588 nn5038
25 Then the disciples took him by night, and let*him*down by the wall

(apta5465) pre1722   an,nn4711
in a basket.

Paul Goes to Jerusalem (Gal. 1:18-24)

1161   art,nn4569   aptm3854 pre1519   2419   ipf3987   pifm2853
26 And when Saul was come to Jerusalem, he attempted to join himself

to

art3588   nn3101   2532   ipf5399/an,ajn3956   ppro846   pap4100   3361 3754   pin2076
the disciples: but they were*all*afraid of him, and believed not that he was a

pr/an,nn3101
disciple.

27 But Barnabas took him, and brought him to the apostles, and declared
unto them how he had seen the Lord in the way, and that he had spoken to
him, and how he had preached boldly at Damascus in the name of Jesus.

28 And he was with them coming in and going out at Jerusalem.

29 And he spake boldly in the name of the Lord Jesus, and disputed
against the Grecians: but they went about to slay him.

30 *Which* when the brethren knew, they brought*him*down to
Caesarea, and sent*him*forth to Tarsus.

31 Then had the churches rest throughout all Judea and Galilee and
Samaria, and were edified; and walking in the fear of the Lord, and in the
comfort of the Holy Ghost, were multiplied.

Aeneas Healed

32 And it came*to*pass, as Peter passed throughout all *quarters,* he
came down also to the saints which dwelt at Lydda.

33 And there he found a certain man named Aeneas, which had
kept*his*bed eight years, and was sick*of*the*palsy.

34 And Peter said unto him, Aeneas Jesus Christ maketh*thee*whole:
arise, and make*thy*bed. And he arose immediately.

35 And all that dwelt at Lydda and Saron saw him, and turned to
the Lord.

Peter Raises Dorcas

36 Now there was at Joppa a certain disciple named Tabitha, which
by interpretation is called Dorcas: this woman was full of good works and
almsdeeds which she did.

37 And it came*to*pass in those days, that she was sick, and died: whom when they had washed, they laid *her* in an upper chamber.

38 And forasmuch as Lydda was nigh to Joppa, and the disciples had heard that Peter was there, they sent unto him two men, desiring *him* that he would not delay to come to them.

39 Then Peter arose and went with them. When he was come, they brought him into the upper chamber: and all the widows stood by him weeping, and showing the coats and garments which Dorcas made, while she was with them.

40 But Peter put them all forth, and kneeled down, and prayed; and turning *him* to the body said, Tabitha, arise. And she opened her eyes: and when she saw Peter, she sat up.

41 And he gave her *his* hand, and lifted*her*up, and when he had called the saints and widows, presented her alive.

42 And it was known throughout all Joppa; and many believed in the Lord.

43 And it came*to*pass, that he tarried many days in Joppa with one Simon a tanner.

The Conversion of Cornelius

10 There was a certain man in Caesarea called Cornelius, a centurion of the band called the Italian *band,*

2 A devout *man,* and one*that*feared God with all his house, which gave much alms to the people, and prayed to God always.

3 He saw in a vision evidently about the ninth hour of the day an angel of God coming in to him, and saying unto him, Cornelius.

1161   art3588   apta816   ppro846 (2532) ppmp1096 pr/an,aj1719   aina2036 inpro5101 pin2076

4 And when he looked on him, he was afraid, and said, What is it,

an,nn2962 1161   aina2036   ppro846 ppro4675 art,nn4335 2532 ppro4675 art,nn1654   aina305   pre1519

Lord? And he said unto him, Thy prayers and thine alms are come up for a

an,nn3422   ad*1799 art,nn2316

memorial before God.

2532   ad3568   aima3992   an,nn435 pre1519   an,nn2445   2532   aipm3343   an,nn4613   repro3739

5 And now send men to Joppa, and call for *one* Simon, whose

pin1941 pr/an,nn4074

surname is Peter:

depro3778   pinp3579   pre3844 idpro5100   an,nn4613   an,nn1038   repro3739   an,nn3614 pin2076 pre3844

6 He lodgeth with one Simon a tanner, whose house is by the

an,nn2281   depro3778   ft2980 ppro4671 inpro5101 ppro4571   pin1163   pinf4160

sea side: he shall tell thee what thou oughtest to do.

1161   ad5613   art3588   nn32   art,pap2980   art,nn2883   aina565

7 And when the angel which spake unto Cornelius was departed,

apta5455 nu1417   ppro848   art,nn3610   2532   an,aj2152   an,nn4757

he called two of his household servants, and a devout soldier of

art,pap4342/ppro846

them*that*waited*on*him*continually;

2532   aptm1834   an,ajn537   ppro846   aina649 ppro846

8 And when he had declared all *these* things unto them, he sent them

pre1519 art,nn2445

to Joppa.

(1161) art3588   ad1887   depro1565   pap3596   2532   pap1448

9 On the morrow, as they went*on*their*journey, and drew nigh unto

art3588   nn4172   an,nn4074   aina305   pre1909 art3588   nn1430   aifm4336 pre4012   nu,aj1622 an,nn5610

the city, Peter went up upon the housetop to pray about the sixth hour:

1161   aom1096   pr/an,aj4361   2532   ipf2309   aifm1089   1161   depro1565

10 And he became very hungry, and would have eaten: but while they

pap3903   aina1968 pre1909 (ppro846) an,nn1611

made ready, he fell into a trance,

2532   pin2334 art,nn3772   pfpp455   2532   idpro5100   an,nn4632   pap2597   pre1909 ppro846

11 And saw heaven opened, and a certain vessel descending unto him,

ad5613   an,aj3173   an,nn3607 pfpp1210   an,nu5064   an,nn746   2532   ppmp2524   pre1909 art3588

as*it*had*been a great sheet knit at the four corners, and let down to the

nn1093

earth:

pre1722/repro3739 ipf5225   an,aj3956   art,ajn5074   art3588   nn1093   2532

12 Wherein were all manner of fourfooted beasts of the earth, and

art,nn2342   2532   art,nn2062   2532 art,nn4071   art3588 nn3772

wild beasts, and creeping things, and fowls of the air.

2532   aom1096   an,nn5456 pre4314 ppro846 apta450   an,nn4074 aima2380 2532 aima5315

13 And there came a voice to him, Rise, Peter; kill, and eat.

1161   art,nn4074 aina2036   ad3365   an,nn2962 3754   ad3762   aina5315   an,aj3956

14 But Peter said, Not so, Lord; for I have never eaten any thing that is

an,ajn2839 2228   an,ajn169

common or unclean.   *(Lev. 11:1-47; Deut. 14:3-21; Ezek. 4:14)*

2532   an,nn5456   pre4314 ppro846 ad3825 (pre1537)   nu,ajn1208   repro3739 art,nn2316

15 And the voice *spake* unto him again the second time, What God hath

aina2511   pim2840/3361/epn4771

cleansed, *that* call*not*thou*common.

(1161) depro5124 aom1096 (pre1909)   nu,ad5151   2532 art3588   nn4632   ainp353   ad3825   pre1519

16   This was done thrice: and the vessel was received up again into
art,nn3772

heaven.

1161   ad5613   art,nn4074   ipf1280   pre1722 rxpro1438   inpro5101   art,nn3705   repro3739

17 Now while Peter doubted in himself what this vision which he had
aina1492   opt1498/302 (2532)   2400   art3588   nn435   art,pfpp649   pre575   art,nn2883

seen should mean,   behold, the men which*were*sent from Cornelius had
apta1331   an,nn4613   art,nn3614   aina2186   pre1909 art3588   nn4440

made inquiry for Simon's house, and stood before the gate,
2532   apta5455   ipf4441   1487   an,nn4613   art,ppmp1941   an,nn4074

18 And called, and asked whether Simon, which*was*surnamed Peter, were
pinp3579   ad1759

lodged there.
1161   art,nn4074   ppmp1760   pre4012 art3588   nn3705   art3588   nn4151   aina2036   ppro846   2400

19 While Peter thought on the vision, the Spirit said unto him, Behold,
nu5140   an,nn435 pin2212 ppro4571

three men seek thee.
apta450   235   aipp2597   2532   pim4198   pre4862   ppro846   ppmp1252

20 Arise therefore, and get*thee*down, and go with them, doubting
an,ajn3367   1360 epn1473   pfi649   ppro846

nothing: for I have sent them.
1161   an,nn4074   apta2597   pre4314 art3588   nn435   art,pfpp649   pre4314 ppro846   pre575

21 Then Peter went down to the men which*were*sent unto him from
art,nn2883   aina2036   2400   epn1473 pin1510   pr/repro3739   pin2212   inpro5101   art3588   nn156

Cornelius; and said, Behold, I   am he whom ye seek: what is the cause
pre1223/repro3739   pin3918

wherefore ye are come?
1161   art3588   aina2036   an,nn2883   an,nn1543   an,aj1342   an,nn435   2532

22 And they said, Cornelius the centurion, a just man, and
an,ppmp5399   art,nn2316 5037   ppmp3140   pre5259   an,aj3650 art3588   nn1484   art3588

one*that*feareth God, and of*good*report among all the nation of the
nn2453   aipp5537   pre5259   an,aj40 an,nn32   aifm3343   ppro4571 pre1519 ppro848

Jews, was warned*from*God by a holy angel to send for thee into his
art,nn3624   2532   ainf191   an,nn4487 pre3844 ppro4675

house, and to hear words of thee.
3767   aptm1528/ppro846   aina3579   1161   art3588   ad1887

23 Then called*he*them*in, and lodged them. And on the morrow
art,nn4074   aina1831   pre4862   ppro846   2532   idpro5100   art,nn80   art,pre575 art,nn2445   aina4905

Peter went away with them, and certain brethren from Joppa accompanied
ppro846

him.
2532   art3588   ad1887   aina1525   pre1519   art,nn2542   1161   art,nn2883

24 And the morrow after they entered into Caesarea. And Cornelius
ipf2258/pap4328   ppro846   aptm4779   ppro848 art,ajn4773   2532 art,aj316   an,ajn5384

waited for them, and had called together his kinsmen and near friends.
1161   ad5613 art,nn4074 aom1096   ainf1525   art,nn2883   apta4876 ppro846   apta4098   pre1909

25 And as Peter was coming in, Cornelius met him, and fell down at his
art,nn4228   aina4352

feet, and worshipped him.
1161   art,nn4074   aina1453/ppro846   pap3004   aipp450   ppro2504/epn846   pin1510   pr/an,nn444

26 But Peter took*him*up, saying, Stand up; I*myself*also am a man.

2532 pap4926 ppro846 aina1525 2532 pin2147 an,ajn4183

27 And as he talked with him, he went in, and found many that were

pfp4905

come together.

5037 aina5346 pre4314 ppro846 epn5210 pinm1987 ad5613 pin2076 pr/an,ajn111

28 And he said unto them, Ye know how that it is an unlawful thing for

an,nn435 an,nn2453 pifm2853 2228 pifm4334 an,ajn246

a man that is a Jew to keep company, or come unto one*of*another*nation;

2532 art,nn2316 aina1166 epn1698 pinf3004 an,ajn3367 an,nn444 an,aj2839 2228

but God hath showed me that I should not call any man common or

an,aj169

unclean.

pre,repro1352 (2532) aina2064 ad369

29 Therefore came I *unto you* without gainsaying, as soon as I was

aptp3343 pinm4441 3767 inpro5101 an,nn3056 aom3343 ppro3165

sent for: I ask therefore for what intent ye have sent for me?

2532 art,nn2883 aina5346 nu5067 an,nn2250 pre575 ipf2252 pr/pap3522 ad3360 depro5026 art,nn5610 2532

30 And Cornelius said, Four days ago I was fasting until this hour; and at

art3588 nu,aj1766 an,nn5610 ppmp4336 pre1722 ppro3450 art,nn3624 2532 2400 an,nn435 aina2476 ad*1799

the ninth hour I prayed in my house, and, behold, a man stood before

ppro3450 pre1722 an,aj2986 an,nn2066

me in bright clothing,

2532 pin5346 an,nn2883 ppro4675 art,nn4335 ainp1522 2532 ppro4675 art,nn1654

31 And said, Cornelius, thy prayer is heard, and thine alms are

ainp3415 ad*1799 art,nn2316

had*in*remembrance in*the*sight of God.

aima3992 3767 pre1519 an,nn2445 2532 aipm3333 an,nn4613 repro3739 pinp1941

32 Send therefore to Joppa, and call hither Simon, whose surname is

an,nn4074 depro3778 pinp3579 pre1722 an,nn3614 an,nn4613 an,nn1038 pre3844 an,nn2281

Peter; he is lodged in the house of *one* Simon a tanner by the sea side:

repro3739 aptm3854 ft2980 ppro4671

who, when he cometh, shall speak unto thee.

ad1824 3767 aina3992 pre4314 ppro4571 5037 epn4771 ad2573 aina4160

33 Immediately therefore I sent to thee; and thou hast well done that

aptm3854 ad3568 3767 pin3918/epn2249/an,aj3956 ad*1799 art,nn2316 ainf191

thou art come. Now therefore are*we*all*here* present before God, to hear

an,aj3956 art,pfpp4367 ppro4671 pre5259 art,nn2316

all things that*are*commanded thee of God.

1161 an,nn4074 apta455 art,nn4750 aina2036 pre1909 an,nn225 pinm2638 3754

34 Then Peter opened *his* mouth, and said, Of a truth I perceive that

art,nn2316 pin2076 3756 pr/an,nn4381

God is no respecter*of*persons: *(Deut. 10:17; 2 Chr. 19:7)*

235 pre1722 an,aj3956 an,nn1484 art,ppmp5399 ppro846 2532 ppmp2038 an,nn1343

35 But in every nation he*that*feareth him, and worketh righteousness,

pin2076 pr/an,aj1184 ppro846

is accepted with him.

art3588 an,nn3056 repro3739 aina649 art3588 nn5207 2474 ppmp2097 an,nn1515

36 The word which *God* sent unto the children of Israel, preaching peace

pre1223 an,an2424 an,nn5547 depro3778 pin2076 pr/an,nn2962 an,ajn3956

by Jesus Christ: (he is Lord of all:) *(Ps. 107:20; 147:18; Is. 52:7)*

art,nn4487 epn5210 pin1492 aptm1096 pre2596

37 That word, *I say,* ye know, which was published throughout

an,aj3650 art,nn2449 aptm756 pre575 art,nn1056 pre3326 art3588 nn908 repro3739 an,nn2491 aina2784
all Judea, and began from Galilee, after the baptism which John preached;

ad5613 art,nn2316 aina5548 (ppro846) an,nn2424 art,pre575 3478 an,aj40 an,nn4151
38 How God anointed Jesus of Nazareth with the Holy Ghost

2532 an,nn1411 repro3739 aina1330 pap2109 2532 ppmp2390 an,aj3956
and with power: who went about doing good, and healing all

art,ppmp2616 pre5259 art3588 ajn1228 3754 art,nn2316 ipf2258 pre3326 ppro846
that*were*oppressed of the devil; for God was with him. *(Is. 61:1)*

2532 epn2249 pin2070 pr/an,nn3144 an,ajn3956 repro3739 aina4160 5037 pre1722 art3588 nn5561
39 And we are witnesses of all things which he did both in the land of

art3588 nn2453 2532 pre1722 2419 repro3739 aina337 apta2910 pre1909 an,nn3586
the Jews, and in Jerusalem; whom they slew and hanged on a tree:

(Deut. 21:22)

depro5126 art,nn2316 aina1453 art3588 nu,aj5154 an,nn2250 2532 aina1325/ppro846/aifm1096/pr/an,aj1717
40 Him God raised up the third day, and showed*him*openly;

3756 an,aj3956 art3588 nn2992 235 an,nn3144 art,pfpp4401 pre5259 art,nn2316
41 Not to all the people, but unto witnesses chosen before of God,

epn2254 repro3748 aina4906 2532 aina4844 ppro846 ppro846 aime450 pre1537 an,ajn3498
even to us, who did eat and drink with him after he rose from the dead.

2532 aina3853 ppro2254 ainf2784 art3588 nn2992 2532 aifm1263 3754
42 And he commanded us to preach unto the people, and to testify that

pin2076 epn846 pr/art,pfpp3724 pre5259 art,nn2316 pr/an,nn2923 an,pap2198 2532 an,ajn3498
it is he which*was*ordained of God *to be* the Judge of quick and dead.

depro5129 pin3140/an,aj3956/art3588/nn4396 pre1223 ppro846 art,nn3686
43 To him give*all*the*prophets*witness, that through his name

an,aj3956 art,pap4100 pre1519 ppro846 ainf2983 an,nn859 an,nn266
whosoever believeth in him shall receive remission of sins.

(Is. 33:24; 53:5,6; Jer. 31:34; Dan. 9:24)

The Gentiles Receive the Holy Spirit

art,nn4074 ad2089 pap2980 depro5023 art,nn4487 art3588 aj40 art,nn4151 aina1968 pre1909 an,aj3956
☞ 44 While Peter yet spake these words, the Holy Ghost fell on all

art,pap191 art3588 nn3056
them*which*heard the word.

2532 art,ajn4103/pre1537/an,nn4061 aina1839
45 And they*of*the*circumcision*which*believed were astonished,

---

☞ **10:44—48** This is similar to the circumstances at Jerusalem and Samaria in that each time, many believers were baptized in the Holy Spirit at the same time (cf. Acts 2:1–4; 8:14–17). It is interesting to note that apostles were present in each instance. The special manifestation of the Holy Spirit here which allowed these Gentiles to speak in tongues proved that God gave the Gentiles the same "gift" (v. 45) as the Jews. Notice that the baptism of the Holy Spirit took place prior to the water baptism. "Spiritual" baptism is what actually places believers into the body of Christ while water baptism only demonstrates to others that a person is in the body of Christ (1 Cor. 12:13). See notes on Acts 2:1–13 and 1 Corinthians 12:13; 14:1–3.

_{an,ajn3745} _{aina4905} _{art,nn4074} ₃₇₅₄ _{pre1909 art3588} _{nn1484} ₂₅₃₂

as*many*as came with Peter, because that on the Gentiles also was

_{pfip1632} _{art3588 nn1431} _{art3588 an,aj40} _{nn4151}

poured out the gift of the Holy Ghost.

₁₀₆₃ _{ipf191} _{ppro846} _{pap2980} _{an,nn1100} ₂₅₃₂ _{pap3170} _{art,nn2316} _{ad5119}

46 For they heard them speak with tongues, and magnify God. They

_{ainp611} _{art,nn4074}

answered Peter,

_{pinm1410} _{idpro5100} _{ainf2967 (3385) art,nn5204} _{depro5128} ₃₃₆₁ _{infg907} _{repro3748}

47 Can any man forbid   water, that these should not be baptized, which

_{aina2983} _{art3588 aj40} _{art,nn4151} _{ad2531/2532} _{epn2249}

have received the Holy Ghost as*well*as we?

₅₀₃₇ _{aina4367} _{ppro846} _{aifp907} _{pre1722 art3588} _{nn3686} _{art3588} _{nn2962}

☞ 48 And he commanded them to be baptized in the name of the Lord.

_{ad5119} _{aina2065} _{ppro846} _{ainf1961} _{idpro5100} _{an,nn2250}

Then prayed they him to tarry certain days.

Peter Reports to the Jerusalem Church

₁₁₆₁ _{art3588} _{nn652} ₂₅₃₂ _{art,nn80} _{art,pap5607} _{pre2596 art,nn2449} _{aina191} ₃₇₅₄ _{art3588}

11 And the apostles and brethren that were in Judea heard that the

_{nn1484} ₂₅₃₂ _{aom1209} _{art3588} _{nn3056} _{art,nn2316}

Gentiles had also received the word of God.

₂₅₃₂ _{ad3753} _{an,nn4074} _{aina305} _{pre1519} _{an,nn2414} _{art3588} _{pre1537}

2 And when Peter was come up to Jerusalem, they that were of the

_{an,nn4061} _{ipf1252} _{pre4314 ppro846}

circumcision contended with him,

_{pap3004} _{aina1525} _{pre4314 an,nn435 (pin2192)} _{an,nn203} ₂₅₃₂ _{aina4906}

3 Saying, Thou wentest in to men   uncircumcised, and didst eat with

_{ppro846}

them.

₁₁₆₁ _{art,nn4074} _{aptm756} _{ipf1620}

4 But Peter rehearsed*_the_*_matter_*from*the*beginning, and expounded _it_

_{ad2517} _{ppro846} _{pap3004}

by order unto them, saying,

_{epn1473} _{ipf2252 pre1722} _{an,nn4172} _{an,nn2445} _{ppmp4336} ₂₅₃₂ _{pre1722} _{an,nn1611} _{aina1492}

5 I was in the city of Joppa praying: and in a trance I saw a

_{an,nn3705} _{idpro5100} _{an,nn4632} _{pap2597} _{ad5613} _{an,aj3173} _{an,nn3607} _{ppmp2524} _{pre1537}

vision, A certain vessel descend, as*it*had*been a great sheet, let down from

_{art,nn3772} _{nu5064} _{an,nn746} ₂₅₃₂ _{aina2064} _{ad891} _{ppro1700}

heaven by four corners; and it came even to me:

_{pre1519} _{repro3739} _{apta816} _{ipf2657} ₂₅₃₂ _{aina1492}

6 Upon the which when I had fastened*mine*eyes, I considered, and saw

_{art,ajn5074} _{art3588} _{nn1093} ₂₅₃₂ _{art,nn2342} ₂₅₃₂ _{art,nn2062} _{2532 art,nn4071}

fourfooted beasts of the earth, and wild beasts, and creeping things, and fowls

_{art3588 nn3772}

of the air.

☞ **10:48** See notes on Mark 16:16 and 1 Corinthians 10:2.

7 And I heard a voice saying unto me, Arise, Peter; slay and eat.

8 But I said, Not so, Lord: for nothing common or unclean hath at*any*time entered into my mouth.

9 But the voice answered me again from heaven, What God hath cleansed, *that* call*not*thou*common.

10 And this was done three times: and all were drawn up again into heaven.

11 And, behold, immediately there were three men already come unto the house where I was, sent from Caesarea unto me.

12 And the Spirit bade me go with them, nothing doubting. Moreover these six brethren accompanied me, and we entered into the man's house:

13 And he showed us how he had seen an angel in his house, which stood and said unto him, Send men to Joppa, and call for Simon, whose surname is Peter;

14 Who shall tell thee words, whereby thou and all thy house shall be saved.

15 And as I began to speak, the Holy Ghost fell on them, as on us at the beginning.

16 Then remembered I the word of the Lord, how that he said, John indeed baptized with water; but ye shall be baptized with the Holy Ghost.

17 Forasmuch then as God gave them the like gift as *he did* unto us, who believed on the Lord Jesus Christ; what was I, that I could withstand God?

18 When they heard these things, they held*their*peace, and glorified God, saying, Then hath God also to the Gentiles granted repentance unto life.

The New Believers in Antioch

³⁷⁶⁷   ^{art,aptp1289}   ⁽³³⁰³⁾   ^{pre575}   ^{art3588}   ⁿⁿ²³⁴⁷
19 Now they*which*were*scattered*abroad   upon   the   persecution
^{art,aptm1096}   ^{pre1909}   ^{an,nn4736}   ^{aina1330}   ^{ad2193}   ^{an,nn5403}   ²⁵³²   ^{an,nn2954}   ²⁵³²   ^{an,nn490}
that arose about Stephen traveled as*far*as Phoenicia, and Cyprus, and Antioch,
^{pap2980}   ^{art3588} ⁿⁿ³⁰⁵⁶   ^{an,ajn3367} ¹⁵⁰⁸   ^{an,nn2453} ^{an,ajn3440}
preaching the word to none but unto the Jews only.
¹¹⁶¹   ^{idpro5100} ^{pre1537} ^{ppro846} ^{ipf2258} ^{pr/an,nn435}   ^{an,nn2953}   ²⁵³²   ^{an,nn2956}   ^{repro3748}
20 And some of them were men of Cyprus and Cyrene, which, when
^{apta1525} ^{pre1519} ^{an,nn490} ^{ipf2980} ^{pre4314} ^{art3588}   ⁿⁿ¹⁶⁷⁵   ^{ppmp2097}   ^{art3588} ⁿⁿ²⁹⁶²
they were come to Antioch, spake unto the Grecians, preaching the Lord
^{an,nn2424}
Jesus.
²⁵³²   ^{an,nn5495}   ^{an,nn2962} ^{ipf2258} ^{pre3326} ^{ppro846}   ⁵⁰³⁷   ^{an,aj4183}   ^{an,nn706}
21 And the hand of the Lord was with them: and a great number
^{apta4100}   ^{aina1994}   ^{pre1909} ^{art3588} ⁿⁿ²⁹⁶²
believed, and turned unto the Lord.
¹¹⁶¹   ^{art,nn3056/pre4012/ppro846/ainp191}   ^{pre1519} ^{art3588} ⁿⁿ³⁷⁷⁵   ^{art3588}   ⁿⁿ¹⁵⁷⁷   ^{art3588}
22 Then tidings*of*these*things*came unto the ears of the church which
^{pre1722}   ^{an,nn2414}   ²⁵³²   ^{aina1821}   ^{an,nn921}   ^{ainf1330}
was in Jerusalem: and they sent forth Barnabas, that he should go
^{ad2193}   ^{an,nn490}
as*far*as Antioch.
^{repro3739}   ^{aptm3854}   ²⁵³²   ^{apta1492} ^{art3588} ⁿⁿ⁵⁴⁸⁵   ^{art,nn2316}   ^{aina5463}   ²⁵³²
23 Who, when he came, and had seen the grace of God, was glad, and
^{ipf3870}   ^{an,ajn3956}   ^{art,nn4286}   ^{art,nn2588}   ^{pinf4357}   ^{art3588}
exhorted them all, that with purpose of heart they would cleave unto the
ⁿⁿ²⁹⁶²
Lord.
³⁷⁵⁴   ^{ipf2258}   ^{pr/an,aj18} ^{an,nn435} ²⁵³² ^{pr/an,aj4134}   ^{an,aj40}   ^{an,nn4151}   ²⁵³²   ^{an,nn4102} ²⁵³²
24 For he was a good man, and   full of the Holy Ghost and of faith: and
^{an,aj2425} ^{an,nn3793}   ^{ainp4369}   ^{art3588}   ⁿⁿ²⁹⁶²
much people was added unto the Lord.
¹¹⁶¹   ^{aina1831}   ^{art,nn921}   ^{pre1519}   ^{an,nn5019}   ^{ainf327} ^{an,nn4569}
25 Then departed Barnabas to Tarsus, for to seek Saul:
²⁵³²   ^{apta2147} ^{ppro846}   ^{aina71}   ^{ppro846} ^{pre1519}   ^{an,nn490}   ¹¹⁶¹
26 And when he had found him, he brought him unto Antioch. And it
^{aom1096}   ^{an,aj3650} ^{an,nn1763} ^{ppro846}   ^{aifp4863}   ^{pre1722} ^{art3588}
came*to*pass, that a whole year they assembled themselves with the
ⁿⁿ¹⁵⁷⁷   ²⁵³²   ^{ainf1321} ^{an,aj2425}   ^{an,nn3793}   ⁵⁰³⁷ ^{art3588}   ⁿⁿ³¹⁰¹   ^{ainf5537}   ^{an,nn5546}
church, and taught much people. And the disciples were called Christians
^{nu,ajn4412} ^{pre1722}   ^{an,nn490}
first in Antioch.
¹¹⁶¹   ^{pre1722} ^{depro5025} ^{art,nn2250} ^{aina2718}   ^{an,nn4396}   ^{pre575}   ^{an,nn2414}   ^{pre1519}   ^{an,nn490}
27 And in these days came prophets from Jerusalem unto Antioch.
¹¹⁶¹   ^{apta450}   ^{nu1520} ^{pre1537} ^{ppro846}   ^{an,nn3686}   ^{an,nn13}   ^{aina4591}   ^{pre1223}
28 And there stood up one of them named Agabus, and signified by
^{art3588}   ⁿⁿ⁴¹⁵¹   ^{pinf3195} ^{fifm1510} ^{an,aj3173} ^{an,nn3042}   ^{pre1909}   ^{an,aj3650} ^{art3588}   ⁿⁿ³⁶²⁵
the spirit that there should be great dearth throughout all   the world:
^{repro3748} ⁽²⁵³²⁾   ^{aom1096}   ^{pre1909}   ^{an,nn2804}   ^{an,nn2541}
which   came*to*pass in*the*days*of Claudius Caesar.

¹¹⁶¹ ^{art3588} ⁿⁿ³¹⁰¹   ^{an,ajn1538} ^(ppro846)   ^{ad2531}   ^{idpro5100/ipf2141}   ^{aina3724}
29 Then the disciples, every man   according to his ability, determined to
^{ainf3992} ^{pre1519/an,nn1248}   ^{art3588}   ⁿⁿ⁸⁰   ^{art,pap2730}   ^{pre1722 art,nn2449}
send   relief   unto the brethren which dwelt in Judea:
^{repro3739}   ²⁵³²   ^{aina4160}   ^{apta649}   ^{pre4314 art3588}   ^{ajn4245}   ^{pre1223}   ^{an,nn5495}
30 Which also they did, and sent it to   the elders by the hands of
^{an,nn921}   ²⁵³² ^{an,nn4569}
Barnabas and Saul.

Peter Is Put in Jail

¹¹⁶¹   ^{pre2596} ^{depro1565} ^{art,nn2540} ^{an,nn2264} ^{art3588} ⁿⁿ⁹³⁵   ^{aina1911}   ^{art,nn5495}

12
Now about that time Herod the king stretched forth *his* hands to
^{ainf2559} ^{idpro5100} ^{art,pre575/art3588}   ⁿⁿ¹⁵⁷⁷
vex certain of   the church.
¹¹⁶¹   ^{aina337} ^{an,nn2385} ^{art3588}   ⁿⁿ⁸⁰   ^{an,nn2491}   ^{an,nn3162}
2 And he killed James the brother of John with the sword.
²⁵³²   ^{apta1492} ⁽³⁷⁵⁴⁾ ^{pin2076/pr/an,ajn701} ^{art3588}   ⁿⁿ²⁴⁵³   ^{aom4369}
3 And because he saw it   pleased   the Jews, he proceeded further to
^{ainf4815} ^{an,nn4074} ²⁵³²   ¹¹⁶¹   ^{ipf2258}   ^{an,nn2250}   ^{art,ajn106}
take Peter also. (Then were the days of unleavened bread.)
²⁵³²   ^(repro3739)   ^{apta4084}   ^{aom5087}   ^{pre1519} ^{an,nn5438}
4 And when   he   had apprehended him, he put *him* in prison, and
^{apta3860}   ^{nu5064}   ^{an,nn5069}   ^{an,nn4757}   ^{pinf5442} ^{ppro846} ^{ppmp1014}   ^{pre3326}
delivered *him* to four quaternions of soldiers to keep him; intending after
^(art3588) ³⁹⁵⁷   ^{ainf321/ppro846}   ^{art3588}   ⁿⁿ²⁹⁹²
Easter to bring*him*forth to the people.
^{art,nn4074}   ³⁷⁶⁷   ⁽³³⁰³⁾   ^{ipf5083} ^{pre1722}   ^{art,nn5438}   ¹¹⁶¹   ^{an,nn4335} ^{ipf2258} ^{ppmp1096}
5 Peter therefore was kept in   prison: but prayer was made
^{an,aj1618}   ^{pre5259 art3588}   ⁿⁿ¹⁵⁷⁷   ^{pre4314 art,nn2316} ^{pre5228 ppro846}
without ceasing of the church unto God for him.

Peter Delivered From Prison

¹¹⁶¹   ^{ad3753}   ^{art,nn2264} ^{ipf3195}   ^{pinf4254/ppro846}   ^{art3588 depro1565} ⁿⁿ³⁵⁷¹ ^{art,nn4074}
6 And when Herod would have brought*him*forth, the same night Peter
^{ipf2258} ^{ppmp2837}   ^{ad*3342} ^{nu1417} ^{an,nn4757}   ^{pfpp1210}   ^{nu1417} ^{an,nn254} ⁵⁰³⁷   ^{an,nn5441}
was sleeping between two soldiers, bound with two chains: and the keepers
^{pre4253}   ^{art3588} ⁿⁿ²³⁷⁴ ^{ipf5083} ^{art3588}   ⁿⁿ⁵⁴³⁸
before the door kept the prison.
²⁵³²   ²⁴⁰⁰   ^{an,nn32}   ^{an,nn2962}   ^{aina2186}   ²⁵³² ^{an,nn5457} ^{aina2989}
7 And, behold, the angel of the Lord came upon *him,* and a light shined
^{pre1722 art3588} ⁿⁿ³⁶¹²   ¹¹⁶¹   ^{apta3960} ^{art,nn4074}   ^{art3588 nn4125}   ^{aina1453/ppro846}   ^{pap3004}
in   the prison: and he smote Peter on the side, and raised*him*up, saying,
^{aima450}   ^{pre1722/an,nn5034} ²⁵³² ^{ppro846} ^{art,nn254} ^{aina1601} ^{pre1537}   ^{art,nn5495}
Arise up quickly. And his chains fell off from *his* hands.

⁵⁰³⁷ ^{art3588} ⁿⁿ³² ^{aina2036} ^{pre4314} ^{ppro846} ^{aipm4024} ²⁵³² ^{aipm5265} ^{ppro4675} ^{art,nn4547}

8 And the angel said unto him, Gird thyself, and bind on thy sandals.

¹¹⁶¹ ^{ad3779} ^{aina4160} ²⁵³² ^{pin3004} ^{ppro846} ^{aipm4016/ppro4675/art,nn2440} ²⁵³²

And so he did. And he saith unto him, Cast*thy*garment*about thee, and

^{pim190} ^{ppro3427}

follow me.

²⁵³² ^{apta1831} ^{ipf190} ^{ppro846} ²⁵³² ^{ipf1492} ³⁷⁵⁶ ³⁷⁵⁴ ^{pin2076} ^{pr/an,aj227}

9 And he went out, and followed him; and wist not that it was true

^{art,ppmp1096} ^{pre1223 art3588} ⁿⁿ³² ¹¹⁶¹ ^{ipf1380} ^{pinf991} ^{an,nn3705}

which*was*done by the angel; but thought he saw a vision.

¹¹⁶¹ ^{apta1330} ^{nu,aj4413} ²⁵³² ^{nu,aj1208} ^{an,nn5438} ^{aina2064} ^{pre1909}

10 When they were past the first and the second ward, they came unto

^{art3588} ^{aj4603} ^{art,nn4439} ^{art,pap5342} ^{pre1519} ^{art3588} ⁿⁿ⁴¹⁷² ^{repro3748} ^{ainp455} ^{ppro846}

the iron gate that leadeth unto the city; which opened to them

^{an,ajn844} ²⁵³² ^{apta1831} ^{aina4281} ^{nu3391} ^{an,nn4505} ²⁵³²

of*his*own*accord: and they went out, and passed on through one street; and

^{ad2112} ^{art3588} ⁿⁿ³² ^{aina868} ^{pre575} ^{ppro846}

forthwith the angel departed from him.

²⁵³² ^{art,nn4074} ^{aptm1096} ^{pre1722} ^{rxpro1438} ^{aina2036} ^{ad3568} ^{pin1492}

11 And when Peter was come to himself, he said, Now I know

^{ad230} ³⁷⁵⁴ ^{an,nn2962} ^{aina1821} ^{ppro848} ^{art,nn32} ²⁵³² ^{aom1807} ^{ppro3165}

of*a*surety, that the Lord hath sent his angel, and hath delivered me

^{pre1537} ^{an,nn5495} ^{an,nn2264} ²⁵³² ^{an,aj3956} ^{art3588} ⁿⁿ⁴³²⁹ ^{art3588} ⁿⁿ²⁹⁹²

out of the hand of Herod, and *from* all the expectation of the people

^{art3588} ⁿⁿ²⁴⁵³

of the Jews.

⁵⁰³⁷ ^{apta4894} ^{aina2064} ^{pre1909} ^{art3588} ⁿⁿ³⁶¹⁴

12 And when he had considered *the thing,* he came to the house of

^{an,nn3137} ^{art3588} ⁿⁿ³³⁸⁴ ^{an,nn2491} ^{art,ppmp1941} ^{an,nn3138} ^{repro3757} ^{an,ajn2425} ^{ipf2258}

Mary the mother of John, whose surname was Mark; where many were

^{pr/pfpp4867} ⁽²⁵³²⁾ ^{pr/ppmp4336}

gathered together praying.

¹¹⁶¹ ^{art,nn4074} ^{apta2925} ^{art3588} ⁿⁿ²³⁷⁴ ^{art3588} ⁿⁿ⁴⁴⁴⁰ ^{an,nn3814} ^{aina4334}

13 And as Peter knocked at the door of the gate, a damsel came to

^{ainf5219} ^{an,nn3686} ^{an,nn4498}

hearken, named Rhoda.

²⁵³² ^{apta1921} ^{art,nn4074} ^{art,nn5456} ^{aina455} ³⁷⁵⁶ ^{art3588} ⁿⁿ⁴⁴⁴⁰ ^{pre575}

14 And when she knew Peter's voice, she opened not the gate for

^{art,nn5479} ¹¹⁶¹ ^{apta1532} ^{aina518} ^{art,nn4074} ^{pfin2476} ^{pre4253} ^{art3588} ⁿⁿ⁴⁴⁴⁰

gladness, but ran in, and told how Peter stood before the gate.

¹¹⁶¹ ^{art3588} ^{aina2036} ^{pre4314} ^{ppro846} ^{pinm3105} ¹¹⁶¹ ^{art3588} ^{ipf1340}

15 And they said unto her, Thou art mad. But she constantly affirmed that

^{pinf2192} ^{ad3779} ¹¹⁶¹ ^{ipf3004} ^{art3588} ^{pin2076} ^{ppro846} ^{pr/art,nn32}

it was even so. Then said they, It is his angel.

¹¹⁶¹ ^{art,nn4074} ^{ipf1961} ^{pap2925} ¹¹⁶¹ ^{apta455}

16 But Peter continued knocking: and when they had opened *the door,* and

^{aina1492} ^{ppro846} ⁽²⁵³²⁾ ^{aina1839}

saw him, they were astonished.

¹¹⁶¹ ^{apta2678} ^{ppro846} ^{art3588} ⁿⁿ⁵⁴⁹⁵ ^{pinf4601}

17 But he, beckoning unto them with the hand to hold*their*peace,

^{aom1334} ^{ppro846} ^{ad4459} ^{art3588} ⁿⁿ²⁹⁶² ^{aina1806} ^{ppro846} ^{pre1537} ^{art3588} ⁿⁿ⁵⁴³⁸ ¹¹⁶¹

declared unto them how the Lord had brought him out of the prison. And he

aina2036   aima518   depro5023   an,nn2385   2532   art3588   nn80   2532

said, Go show these things unto James, and to the brethren. And he

apta1831   ainp4198 pre1519   an,aj2087   an,nn5117

departed, and went into another place.

1161   aptm1096 an,nn2250   ipf2258 3756 an,aj3641 an,nn5017 pre1722 art3588

18 Now as soon as it was day, there was no small stir among the

nn4757   inpro5101 (686)   aom1096   art,nn4074

soldiers, what was become of Peter.

1161   an,nn2264   apta1934   ppro846   2532   apta2147   3361

19 And when Herod had sought for him, and found him not, he

apta350   art3588   nn5441   aina2753

examined the keepers, and commanded that *they* should be

aifp520   2532   apta2718   pre575 art,nn2449 pre1519   art,nn2542

put*to*death. And he went down from Judea to Caesarea, and *there*

ipf1304

abode.

Herod Dies

1161   art,nn2264   ipf2258   pr/pap2371   an,nn5183   2532

20 And Herod was highly displeased with them of Tyre and

an,nn4606   1161   ipf3918   ad3361   pre4314   ppro846   2532

Sidon: but they came with*one*accord to him, and, having

apta3982/an,nn986/art3588/nn935/art,pre1909/art,nn2846   ipf154   an,nn1515

made*Blastus*the*king's*chamberlain*their*friend, desired peace; because

ppro846   art,nn5561   aid5142   pre575 art3588   ajn937

their country was nourished by the king's *country.*

1161   an,aj5002 an,nn2250 art,nn2264   apta1746   an,aj937   an,nn2066   (2532) apta2523 pre1909

21 And upon a set day Herod, arrayed in royal apparel, sat upon

art,nn968   ipf1215   pre4314   ppro846

his throne, and made*an*oration unto them.

1161   art3588   nn1218   ipf2019   an,nn5456   an,nn2316 2532 3756

22 And the people gave*a*shout, *saying, It is* the voice of a god, and not

an,nn444

of a man.

1161   ad3916   an,nn32   an,nn2962   aina3960   ppro846   pre473/repro3739

23 And immediately the angel of the Lord smote him, because

aina1325   3756 art,nn2316   art3588   nn1391   2532   aptm1096   pr/an,aj4662

he gave not God the glory: and he was eaten*of*worms, and

aina1634

gave*up*the*ghost.

1161 art3588   nn3056   art,nn2316   ipf837   2532   ipf4129

24 But the word of God grew and multiplied.

1161   an,nn921   2532 an,nn4569   aina5290   pre1537   2419

25 And Barnabas and Saul returned from Jerusalem, when they

apta4137   art,nn1248   2532   apta4838   an,nn2491   art,apta1941

had fulfilled *their* ministry, and took with them John, whose*surname*was

an,nn3138

Mark.

Paul and Barnabas Are Chosen

13 ☞Now there were in the church that was at Antioch
₁₁₆₁ _{ipf2258} _{pre2596} _{art3588} _{nn1577} _{pap5607} _{pre1722} _{an,nn490}

certain prophets and teachers; as Barnabas, and Simeon
_{idpro5100} _{an,nn4396} ₂₅₃₂ _{an,nn1320} _(5037 repro3739) _{art,nn921} ₂₅₃₂ ₄₈₂₆

that*was*called Niger, and Lucius of Cyrene, and Manaen,
_{art,ppmp2564} ₃₅₂₆ ₂₅₃₂ _{an,nn3066} _{art,nn2956} ₅₀₃₇ ₃₁₂₇

which*had*been*brought*up*with Herod the tetrarch, and Saul.
_{an,ajn4939} _{an,nn2264} _{art3588} _{nn5076} _{2532 an,nn4569}

2 As they ministered to the Lord, and fasted, the Holy Ghost said,
₍₁₁₆₁₎ _{ppro846} _{pap3008} _{art3588} _{nn2962} ₂₅₃₂ _{pap3522} _{art3588} _{aj40} _{art,nn4151} _{aina2036}

Separate me Barnabas and Saul for the work whereunto I have called
_{aima873} _{(1211) ppro3427 (5037)} _{art,nn921} _{2532 art,nn4569} _{pre1519 art3588} _{nn2041} _{repro3739} _{pfip4341}

them.
_{ppro846}

3 And when they had fasted and prayed, and laid *their* hands on them,
_{ad5119} _{apta3522} ₂₅₃₂ _{aptm4336} ₂₅₃₂ _{apta2007} _{art,nn5495} _{ppro846}

they sent*them*away.
_{aina630}

Ministry On Cyprus

4 So they, being sent forth by the Holy Ghost, departed unto Seleucia;
₃₇₆₇ _{depro3778} ₍₃₃₀₃₎ _{aptp1599} _{pre5259 art3588} _{aj40} _{art,nn4151} _{aina2718} _{pre1519} _{art,nn4581}

and from thence they sailed to Cyprus.
₅₀₃₇ _{ad1564} _{aina636} _{pre1519} _{art,nn2954}

5 And when they were at Salamis, they preached the word of God in
₂₅₃₂ _{aptm1096 pre1722} _{an,nn4529} _{ipf2605} _{art3588 nn3056} _{art,nn2316 pre1722}

the synagogues of the Jews: and they had also John to *their* minister.
_{art3588} _{nn4864} _{art3588 nn2453} ₁₁₆₁ _{ipf2192 2532 an,nn2491} _{an,nn5257}

6 And when they had gone through the isle unto Paphos, they found a
₁₁₆₁ _{apta1330} _{art3588 nn3520} _{ad891} _{an,nn3974} _{aina2147}

certain sorcerer, a false prophet, a Jew, whose name *was* Barjesus:
_{idpro5100} _{an,nn3097} _{an,nn5578} _{an,nn2453} _{repro3739 an,nn3686} _{pr/an,nn919}

7 Which was with the deputy*of*the*country, Sergius Paulus, a prudent
_{repro3739} _{ipf2258} _{pre4862 art3588} _{nn446} _{an,nn4588} _{an,nn3972} _{an,aj4908}

man; who called for Barnabas and Saul, and desired to hear the word of
_{an,nn435} _{depro3778} _{aptm4341} _{an,nn921} ₂₅₃₂ _{an,nn4569} _{aina1934} _{ainf191} _{art3588} _{nn3056}

God.
_{art,nn2316}

8 But Elymas the sorcerer (for so is*his*name*by*interpretation)
₁₁₆₁ _{an,nn1681} _{art3588} _{nn3097} ₁₀₆₃ _{ad3779} _{pinp3177/ppro846/art,nn3696}

withstood them, seeking to turn away the deputy from the faith.
_{ipf436} _{ppro846} _{pap2212} _{ainf1294} _{art3588} _{nn446} _{pre575 art3588} _{nn4102}

☞ **13:1** The fact that Manaen "had been brought up with Herod the tetrarch" is also noted in Josephus' writings and the Talmud. According to these sources, Manaen was the son of a man named Essene who had gained favor and position with Herod the Great. As a result, Manaen was brought up in the king's court with Herod the Great's son Herod Antipas (the tetrarch).

<small>1161   an,nn4569   art3588   2532   an,nn3972   aptp4130   an,aj40   an,nn4151 (2532)</small>

9 Then Saul, (who also *is called* Paul,) filled with the Holy Ghost,

<small>apta816   pre1519 ppro846</small>

set*his*eyes on him,

<small>aina2036   5599 an,aj4134   an,aj3956   an,nn1388   2532 an,aj3956   an,nn4468   an,nn5207</small>

10 And said, O full of all subtlety and all mischief, *thou* child of the

<small>an,ajn1228   an,ajn2190   an,aj3956   an,nn1343   3756   fm3973   pap1294   art3588</small>

devil, *thou* enemy of all righteousness, wilt thou not cease to pervert the

<small>aj2117   art,nn3598   an,nn2962</small>

right ways of the Lord?   *(Prov. 10:9; Hos. 14:9)*

<small>2532   ad3568   2400   an,nn5495   art3588   nn2962   pre1909 ppro4571   2532</small>

11 And now, behold, the hand of the Lord *is* upon thee, and thou shalt

<small>fm2071 pr/an,aj5185   3361   pap991 art3588 nn2246 ad891   an,nn2540   1161   ad3916   aina1968 pre1909</small>

be blind, not seeing the sun for a season. And immediately there fell on

<small>ppro846   an,nn887   2532   an,nn4655   2532   pap4013   ipf2212</small>

him a mist and a darkness; and he went about seeking

<small>an,ajn5497</small>

some*to*lead*him*by*the*hand.

<small>ad5119   art3588   nn446   apta1492   art,pfp1096   aina4100</small>

12 Then the deputy, when he saw what*was*done, believed, being

<small>ppmp1605   pre1909 art3588   nn1322   art3588   nn2962</small>

astonished at the doctrine of the Lord.

In Antioch of Pisidia

<small>1161   art,nn3972   art,pre4012   aptp321   pre575   art,nn3974   aina2064   pre1519</small>

13 Now when Paul and his company loosed from Paphos, they came to

<small>art,nn4011   art,nn3828   1161 an,nn2491   apta672   pre575 ppro846   aina5290   pre1519   an,nn2414</small>

Perga in Pamphylia: and John departing from them returned to Jerusalem.

<small>1161   ppro846   apta1330   pre575 art,nn4011   aom3854 pre1519   an,nn490   art,nn4099</small>

14 But when they departed from Perga, they came to Antioch in Pisidia,

<small>2532 apta1525 pre1519 art3588   nn4864   art3588   nn4521   art,nn2250   aina2523</small>

and went into the synagogue on the sabbath day, and sat down.

<small>1161   pre3326   art3588   nn320   art3588   nn3551   2532   art3588   nn4396   art3588</small>

15 And after the reading of the law and the prophets the

<small>nn752   aina649   pre4314   ppro846   pap3004   an,nn435   an,nn80   1487</small>

rulers*of*the*synagogue sent unto them, saying, *Ye* men *and* brethren, if

<small>pin2076/pre1722/ppro5213   an,nn3056   an,nn3874   pre4314 art3588   nn2992   pim3004</small>

ye have any word of exhortation for the people, say on.

<small>1161   an,nn3972   apta450   2532   apta2678   art,nn5495 aina2036 an,nn435   an,nn2475</small>

16 Then Paul stood up, and beckoning with *his* hand said, Men of Israel,

<small>2532   art,ppmp5399   art,nn2316   aina191</small>

and ye*that*fear God, give audience.

<small>artr3588   nn2316   depro5127 art,nn2992   2474   aom1586 ppro2257 art,nn3962   2532   aina5312   art3588</small>

17 The God of this people of Israel chose our fathers, and exalted the

<small>nn2992   pre1722   art,nn3940   pre1722   an,nn1093   an,nn125   2532   pre3326</small>

people when they dwelt*as*strangers in the land of Egypt, and with a

<small>an,aj5308 an,nn1023   aina1806   ppro846   pre1537 ppro846</small>

high arm brought he them out of it.   *(Ex. 6:1,6; 12:51)*

2532 ad5613   an,nn5550   an,aj5063   aina5159/ppro846   pre1722 art3588
18 And about the time of forty years suffered*he*their*manners in the
ajn2048
wilderness.   *(Ex. 16:35; Num. 14:34)*
                    2532   apta2507   nu2033   an,nn1484 pre1722   an,nn1093   5477
19 And when he had destroyed seven nations in the land of Canaan, he
aina2624/ppro846/art,nn1093/ppro846
divided*their*land*to*them*by*lot.   *(Deut. 7:1; Josh. 14:1)*
        2532   pre3326 depro5023   aina1325   an,nn2923   ad5613
20 And after that he gave *unto them* judges about*the*space*of
nu5071   2532 nu4004 an,nn2094 ad2193   4545   art3588   nn4396
four hundred and fifty years, until Samuel the prophet.

                                            (Judg. 2:16; 1 Sam. 3:20)
        ad2547   aom154   an,nn935 2532 art,nn2316 aina1325   ppro846   4549
21 And afterward they desired a king: and God gave unto them Saul the
an,nn5207   2797   an,nn435 pre1537   an,nn5443   958   nu5062 an,nn2094
son of Kish, a man of the tribe of Benjamin, by the space of forty years.

                                        (1 Sam. 8:5,19; 10:20,21,24; 11:15)
        2532   apta3179   ppro846   aina1453   ppro846   1138
22 And when he had removed him, he raised up unto them David
pre1519/an,nn935   repro3739 2532   apta3140   aina2036
to*be*their*king; to whom also he gave testimony, and said, I have
aina2147 1138 art3588   2421   pr/an,nn435 pre2596   ppro3450   art,nn2588 repro3739
found David the *son* of Jesse, a man after mine own heart, which shall
ft4160 an,aj3956 ppro3450 art,nn2307
fulfil all my will.

                    (1 Sam. 13:14; Hos. 13:11; 1 Sam. 16:12,13; Ps. 89:20; Is. 44:28)
        pre575   depro5127   art,nn4690   art,nn2316   pre2596   an,nn1860   aina1453
23 Of this man's seed hath God according to *his* promise raised unto
2474   an,nn4990   an,nn2424
Israel a Savior, Jesus: *(Is. 11:1)*
                    an,nn2491   apta4296   pre4253 (an,nn4383) ppro846 art,nn1529   an,nn908
24 When John had first preached before   his coming the baptism of
an,nn3341   an,aj3956 art3588 nn2992   2474
repentance to all the people of Israel.
        1161   ad5613 art,nn2491 ipf4137   art,nn1408   ipf3004 pr/inpro5101 pin5282   ppro3165
25 And as John fulfilled his course, he said, Whom think ye that I
pinf1511 epn1473 pin1510 3756   235   2400   pinm2064   pre3326 ppro1691 repro3739 art,nn5266
am? I am not *he.* But, behold, there cometh one after me, whose shoes of
art,nn4228 pin1510 3756 pr/an,aj514   ainf3089
his feet I am not worthy to loose.
        an,nn435   an,nn80   an,nn5207   an,nn1085   11   2532
26 Men *and* brethren, children of the stock of Abraham, and
        pre1722   ppro5213 art,ppmp5399 art,nn2316   epn5213   art3588 nn3056   depro5026   art,nn4991
whosoever among you feareth God, to you is the word of this salvation
ainp649
sent.
        1063   art,pap2730   pre1722   2419   2532 ppro846   art,nn758
27 For they*that*dwell at Jerusalem, and their rulers, because they

apta50/depro5126   2532   art3588   nn5456   art3588   nn4396   art,ppmp314   pre2596/an,aj3956
knew*him*not, nor yet the voices of the prophets which*are*read   every

an,nn4521   aina4137   apta2919
sabbath day, they have fulfilled *them* in condemning *him.*

2532   apta2147 an,aj3367 an,nn156   an,nn2288   aom154
28 And though they found no   cause of death *in him,* yet desired they

an,nn4091   ppro846   aifp337
Pilate that he should be slain.

1161   ad5613   aina5055   an,aj537   art,pfpp1125   pre4012   ppro846
29 And when they had fulfilled all   that*was*written of   him,   they

apta2057   pre575 art3588 nn3586   aina5087   pre1519   an,nn3419
took*him*down from the tree, and laid *him* in a sepulcher.

1161 art,nn2316 aina1453 ppro846 pre1537   an,ajn3498
30 But God raised him from the dead:

repro3739   ainp3700 (pre1909) cd/an,aj4119 an,nn2250   apt,apta4872   ppro846
31 And he was seen   many days of them*which*came*up*with him

pre575   art,nn1056 pre1519   2419   repro3748 pin1526 ppro846 pr/an,nn3144   pre4314 art3588   nn2992
from Galilee to Jerusalem, who are his witnesses unto the people.

2532 epn2249   pinm2097/ppro5209   art3588   nn1860
32 And we declare*unto*you*glad*tidings, how that the promise which was

aptm1096 pre4314 art3588   nn3962
made unto the fathers,

(3754) art,nn2316   pfi1603   depro5026   ppro2254 ppro846   art,nn5043
33   God hath fulfilled the same unto us   their children, in that he hath

apta450/an,nn2424   ad5613   2532   pfip1125   pre1722 art3588 nu,aj1208   art,nn5568   epn4771 pin1488
raised*up*Jesus*again; as it is also written in   the second psalm, Thou art

ppro3450 pr/an,nn5207   ad4594   epn1473   pfi1080   ppro4571
my   Son, this day have I   begotten thee.   *(Ps. 2:7)*

1161   3754   aina450/ppro846   pre1537   an,ajn3498   ad3371
34 And as concerning that he raised*him*up from the dead, *now* no more

(pap3195)   pinf5290   pre1519   an,nn1312   pfi2046   ad3779   ft1325   ppro5213 art3588   aj4103
to return to   corruption, he said on*this*wise, I will give you the sure

art,ajn3741   1138
mercies of David.   *(Is. 55:3 [Sept.])*

pre,repro1352   pin3004 2532 pre1722 an,ajn2087   3756   ft1325   ppro4675
35 Wherefore he saith also in   another *psalm,* Thou shalt not suffer thine

art,ajn3741   ainf1492   an,nn1312
Holy One to see corruption.   *(Ps. 16:10 [Sept.])*

1063   1138   (3303)   apta5256   an,aj2398   an,nn1074   art3588 nn1012   art,nn2316
36 For David, after he had served his own generation by the will of God,

ainp2837   2532   ainp4369 pre4314 ppro848 art,nn3962 2532 aina1492   an,nn1312
fell*on*sleep, and was laid unto his fathers, and saw corruption:

                              (1 Kgs. 2:10; Judg. 2:10)

1161   repro3739 art,nn2316   aina1453   aina1492 3756   an,nn1312
37 But he, whom God raised again, saw no corruption.

pim2077   pr/an,ajn1110   ppro5213   3767   an,nn435   an,nn80   3754   pre1223
☞ 38 Be it known unto you therefore, men *and* brethren, that through

depro5127   pinp2605   ppro5213   an,nn859   an,nn266
this man is preached unto you the forgiveness of sins:

☞ **13:38, 39** See note on Romans 3:19, 20.

²⁵³² ^{pre1722} ^{depro5129} ^{an,aj3956} ^{art,pap4100} ^{pinp1344} ^{pre575} ^{an,ajn3956}

39 And by him all that believe are justified from all things, from

^{repro3739} ^{ainp1410} ³⁷⁵⁶ ^{aifp1344} ^{pre1722} ^{art3588} ⁿⁿ³⁵⁵¹ ^{an,nn3475}

which ye could not be justified by the law of Moses.

^{pim991} ³⁷⁶⁷ ³³⁶¹ ^{asbp1904} ^{pre1909} ^{ppro5209} ^{art,pfpp2046} ^{pre1722}

40 Beware therefore, lest that come upon you, which*is*spoken*of in

^{art3588} ⁿⁿ⁴³⁹⁶

the prophets;

^{aima1492} ^{art,nn2707} ²⁵³² ^{aima2296} ²⁵³² ^{aipp853} ³⁷⁵⁴ ^{epn1473} ^{pinm2038} ^{an,nn2041}

41 Behold, ye despisers, and wonder, and perish: for I work a work

^{pre1722} ^{ppro5216} ^{art,nn2250} ^{an,nn2041} ^{repro3739} ^{efn3364} ^{asba4100} ¹⁴³⁷ ^{idpro5100}

in your days, a work which ye shall in*no*wise believe, though a man

^{psmp1555} ^{ppro5213}

declare it unto you.   *(Hab. 1:5)*

¹¹⁶¹ ^{art3588} ⁿⁿ²⁴⁵³ ^{pap1826} ^{pre1537} ^{art3588} ⁿⁿ⁴⁸⁶⁴ ^{art3588} ⁿⁿ¹⁴⁸⁴

42 And when the Jews were gone out of the synagogue, the Gentiles

^{ipf3870} ^{depro5023} ^{art,nn4487} ^{aifp2980} ^{ppro848} ^(pre1519) ^{art3588} ^{ad3342} ⁿⁿ⁴⁵²¹

besought that these words might be preached to them   the next sabbath.

¹¹⁶¹ ^{art3588} ⁿⁿ⁴⁸⁶⁴ ^{aptp3089} ^{an,ajn4183} ^{art3588} ⁿⁿ²⁴⁵³ ²⁵³²

43 Now when the congregation was broken up, many of the Jews and

^{ppmp4576} ^{art,nn4339} ^{aina190} ^{art,nn3972} ²⁵³² ^{art,nn921} ^{repro3748} ^{pap4354} ^{ppro846}

religious proselytes followed Paul and Barnabas: who, speaking to them,

^{ipf3982} ^{ppro846} ^{pinf1961} ^{art3588} ⁿⁿ⁵⁴⁸⁵ ^{art,nn2316}

persuaded them to continue in the grace of God.

¹¹⁶¹ ^{art3588} ^{ppmp2064} ⁿⁿ⁴⁵²¹ ^{ainp4863/ad4975/art3588/an,aj3956/nn4172}

44 And the next sabbath day came*almost*the*whole*city*together

^{ainf191} ^{art3588} ⁿⁿ³⁰⁵⁶ ^{art,nn2316}

to hear the word of God.

¹¹⁶¹ ^{art3588} ⁿⁿ²⁴⁵³ ^{apta1492} ^{art3588} ⁿⁿ³⁷⁹³ ^{ainp4130} ^{an,nn2205}

45 But when the Jews saw the multitudes, they were filled with envy,

²⁵³² ^{ipf48} ^{art,ppmp3004} ^{pre5259} ^{art,nn3972} ^{pap483} ²⁵³²

and spake against those*things*which*were*spoken by Paul, contradicting and

^{pap987}

blaspheming.

¹¹⁶¹ ^{art,nn3972} ²⁵³² ^{art,nn921} ^{aptm3955} ^{aina2036} ^{ipf2258} ^{an,ajn316}

46 Then Paul and Barnabas waxed bold, and said, It was necessary that

^{art3588} ⁿⁿ³⁰⁵⁶ ^{art,nn2316} ^{nu,ajn4412} ^{aifp2980} ^{epn5213} ¹¹⁶¹ ¹⁸⁹⁴

the word of God should first have been spoken to you: but seeing ye

^{pinm683/ppro846} ²⁵³² ^{pin2919} ^{rxpro1438} ^{3756/pr/an,aj514} ^{art,aj166} ^{an,nn2222} ²⁴⁰⁰

put*it*from*you, and judge yourselves unworthy of everlasting life, lo, we

^{pinm4762} ^{pre1519} ^{art3588} ⁿⁿ¹⁴⁸⁴

turn to the Gentiles.

¹⁰⁶³ ^{ad3779} ^{art3588} ⁿⁿ²⁹⁶² ^{pfip1781} ^{ppro2254} ^{pfi5087} ^{ppro4571}

47 For so hath the Lord commanded us, *saying,* I have set thee

^{pre1519/an,nn5457} ^{an,nn1484} ^{ppro4571} ^{infg1511} ^{pre1519} ^{an,nn4991} ^{ad2193}

to*be*a*light of the Gentiles, that thou shouldest be for salvation unto the

^{an,ajn2078} ^{art3588} ⁿⁿ¹⁰⁹³

ends of the earth.   *(Is. 49:6)*

¹¹⁶¹ ^{art3588} ⁿⁿ¹⁴⁸⁴ ^{pap191} ^{ipf5463} ²⁵³² ^{ipf1392} ^{art3588}

48 And when the Gentiles heard this, they were glad, and glorified the

ⁿⁿ³⁰⁵⁶ ^{art3588} ⁿⁿ²⁹⁶² ²⁵³² ^{an,ajn3745} ^{ipf2258} ^{pr/pfpp5021} ^{pre1519} ^{an,aj166} ^{an,nn2222} ^{aina4100}

word of the Lord: and as*many*as were ordained to eternal life believed.

1161 art3588 nn3056   art3588 nn2962   ipf1308   pre1223   an,aj3650 art3588   nn5561

49 And the word of the Lord was published throughout all   the region.

1161   art3588   nn2453   aina3951   art3588 ppmp4576   2532   art,aj2158   an,nn1135   2532   art3588

50 But the Jews stirred up the devout and honorable women, and the

nu,ajn4413   art3588 nn4172   2532   aina1892   an,nn1375   pre1909 art,nn3972 2532   art,nn921   2532

chief men of the city, and raised persecution against Paul and Barnabas, and

aina1544   pre575   ppro848   art,nn3725

expelled them out of their coasts.

1161   art3588   aptm1621   art3588 nn2868   ppro846 art,nn4228 pre1909   ppro846   aina2064 pre1519

51 But they shook off the dust of their feet against them, and came unto

an,nn2430

Iconium.

1161   art3588   nn3101   ipf4137   an,nn5479 2532   an,aj40   an,nn4151

52 And the disciples were filled with joy, and with the Holy Ghost.

Paul and Barnabas in Iconium

1161   aom1096   pre1722   an,nn2430   ppro846 ainf1525   pre2596/art,ppro846

14 And it came*to*pass in Iconium, that they went both together

pre1519 art3588   nn4864   art3588   nn2453   2532   ad3779   ainf2980   5620   an,aj4183

into the   synagogue of the Jews, and so   spake, that a great

an,nn4128   5037   an,nn2453 2532   an,nn1672   ainf4100

multitude both of the Jews and also of the Greeks believed.

1161   art3588   pap544   an,nn2453   aina1892   art3588   nn1484   2532

2 But   the   unbelieving   Jews   stirred   up   the   Gentiles,   and

aina2559/art,nn5590   pre2596 art3588   nn80

made*their*minds*evil*affected against the brethren.

an,nn2425   an,nn5550   (3303) 3767   aina1304   aptm3955   pre1909 art3588   nn2962

☞ 3 Long time   therefore abode they speaking boldly   in   the Lord,

art3588   pap3140   art3588 nn3056   ppro848 art,nn5485   2532   pap1325   an,nn4592 2532

which gave testimony unto the word of his   grace, and granted signs and

an,nn5059   pifm1096 pre1223 ppro846 art,nn5495

wonders to be done by their hands.

1161   art3588   nn4128   art3588 nn4172   ainp4977   2532   art3588/3303 ipf2258 pre4862 art3588

4 But the multitude of the city was divided: and   part   held   with the

nn2453   1161   art3588 pre4862 art3588   nn652

Jews, and part with the apostles.

1161   ad5613   aom1096   an,nn3730   5037   art3588   nn1484   2532

5 And when there was an assault made both of the Gentiles, and also of

an,nn2453 pre4862 ppro846 art,pap758   ainf5195   2532   ainf3036   ppro846

the Jews with their rulers, to use*them*despitefully, and to stone them,

apta4894   aina2703 pre1519 an,nn3082   2532   an,nn1191   art,nn4172

6 They were*aware*of it, and fled unto Lystra and Derbe, cities of

art,nn3071   2532   art3588   nn4066

Lycaonia, and into the region*that*lieth*round*about:

ad2546   ipf2258/ppmp2097

7 And there they preached*the*gospel.

☞ **14:3, 10** See note on 2 Timothy 4:20.

In Lystra

8 And there sat a certain man at Lystra, impotent in his feet, being a cripple from his mother's womb, who never had walked:

9 The same heard Paul speak: who steadfastly beholding him, and perceiving that he had faith to be healed,

☞ 10 Said with a loud voice, Stand upright on thy feet. And he leaped and walked.

☞ 11 And when the people saw what Paul had done, they lifted up their voices, saying in*the*speech*of*Lycaonia, The gods are come down to us in*the*likeness of men.

12 And they called Barnabas, Jupiter; and Paul, Mercurius, because he was the chief speaker.

13 Then the priest of Jupiter, which was before their city, brought oxen and garlands unto the gates, and would have done sacrifice with the people.

14 *Which* when the apostles, Barnabas and Paul, heard *of,* they rent their clothes, and ran in among the people, crying out,

15 And saying, Sirs, why do ye these things? We also are men of like passions with you, and preach unto you that ye should turn from these vanities unto the living God, which made heaven, and earth, and the sea, and all things that are therein: *(Ex. 20:11; Ps. 146:6)*

16 Who in times past suffered all nations to walk in their own ways.

17 Nevertheless he left not himself without witness, in that he did good,

---

☞ **14:11, 12** The names given to Paul and Barnabas were significant because the people were referring to them as their own heathen gods in human form. The reason that Paul and Barnabas did not refuse the people's worship immediately was that in the people's excitement after witnessing the miracle, they reverted back to speaking their native language which Paul and Barnabas did not understand.

<small>pap1325 ppro2254 an,nn5205   ad3771   2532   an,aj2593   an,nn2540   pap1705 ppro2257 art,nn2588</small>
and gave us   rain from heaven, and fruitful seasons, filling our hearts with
<small>an,nn5160 532   an,nn2167</small>
food and gladness.   *(Ps. 147:8; Jer. 5:24)*

<small>2532   depro5023   pap3004   ad3433   aina2664   art3588   nn3793</small>
18 And with these sayings scarce restrained they the people, that they had
<small>3361   infg2380   ppro846</small>
not done sacrifice unto them.

<small>1161   aina1904   an,nn2453 pre575   an,nn490   2532   an,nn2430   (2532)</small>
19 And there came thither *certain* Jews from Antioch and Iconium, who
<small>apta3982   art3588   nn3793   2532   apta3034 art,nn3972 aina4951   ad1854   art3588   nn4172</small>
persuaded the people, and, having stoned Paul, drew *him* out of the city,
<small>apta3543   ppro846   pfin2348</small>
supposing he had been dead.

<small>1161   art3588   nn3101   apta2944   ppro846   apta450</small>
20 Howbeit, as the disciples stood*round*about him, he rose up, and
<small>aina1525 pre1519 art3588 nn4172 2532 art3588   ad1887   aina1831   pre4862   art,nn921   pre1519 an,nn1191</small>
came into the city: and the next day he departed with Barnabas to Derbe.

Returning to Antioch in Syria

<small>5037   aptm2097   depro1565 art,nn4172 2532   aina3100</small>
21 And when they had preached*the*gospel to that city, and had taught
<small>an,ajn2425   aina5290   pre1519 art,nn3082 2532   an,nn2430   2532   an,nn490</small>
many, they returned again to Lystra, and *to* Iconium, and Antioch,
<small>pap1991   art3588 nn5590   art3588   nn3101   pap3870   pinf1696</small>
22 Confirming the souls of the disciples, *and* exhorting them to continue in
<small>art3588   nn4102   2532 3754 ppro2248 pin1163   pre1223   an,aj4183   an,nn2347   ainf1525 pre1519 art3588   nn932</small>
the faith, and that we must through much tribulation enter into the kingdom
<small>art,nn2316</small>
of God.

<small>1161   apta5500   ppro846 an,ajn4245   pre2596/an,nn1577</small>
23 And when they had ordained them elders in every church, and had
<small>aptm4336   pre3326 an,nn3521   aom3908   ppro846   art3588   nn2962   pre1519 repro3739</small>
prayed with fasting, they commended them to the Lord, on whom they
<small>plpf4100</small>
believed.

<small>2532   apta1330   art,nn4099   aina2064   pre1519</small>
24 And after they had passed throughout Pisidia, they came to
<small>an,nn3828</small>
Pamphylia.

<small>2532   apta2980   art3588 nn3056 pre1722 an,nn4011   aina2597</small>
25 And when they had preached the word in Perga, they went down
<small>pre1519 an,nn825</small>
into Attalia:

<small>ad2547   aina636   pre1519   an,nn490   ad3606   ipf2258</small>
26 And thence sailed to Antioch, from whence they had been
<small>pr/pfpp3860   art3588 nn5485   art,nn2316 pre1519 art3588 nn2041   repro3739   aina4173</small>
recommended to the grace of God for the work which they fulfilled.
<small>1161   aptm3854 2532   apta4863/art3588/nn1577</small>
27 And when they were come, and had gathered*the*church*together, they

rehearsed all that God had done with them, and how he had opened the door
of faith unto the Gentiles.

28 And there they abode long time with the disciples.

Is Circumcision Required?

15 And certain men which came down from Judea taught the brethren, *and said,* Except ye be circumcised after the manner of Moses,
ye cannot be saved.   *(Lev. 12:3)*

2 When therefore Paul and Barnabas had no small dissension and
disputation with them, they determined that Paul and Barnabas, and certain
other of them, should go up to Jerusalem unto the apostles and elders
about this question.

3 And being brought*on*their*way by the church, they passed through
Phoenicia and Samaria, declaring the conversion of the Gentiles: and they
caused great joy unto all the brethren.

4 And when they were come to Jerusalem, they were received of the
church, and *of* the apostles and elders, and they declared all*things*that God
had done with them.

5 But there rose up certain of the sect of the Pharisees which
believed, saying, That it was needful to circumcise them, and to command *them*
to keep the law of Moses.

6 And the apostles and elders came together for to consider of this
matter.

7 And when there had been much disputing, Peter rose up, and said unto
them, Men *and* brethren, ye know how that a*good*while*ago God

aom1586   pre1722   pppro2254   art3588   nn1484   pre1223 pppro3450 art,nn4750   ainf191 art3588

made choice among us, that the Gentiles by my mouth should hear the

nn3056   art3588   nn2098   2532   ainf4100

word of the gospel, and believe.

2532   an,nn2316   art,aj2589   aina3140/ppro846   apta1325 ppro846

8 And God, which*knoweth*the*hearts, bare*them*witness, giving them

art3588 aj40   art,nn4151   ad2531   (2532)   pppro2254

the Holy Ghost, even as *he* did unto us;

2532   aina1252/an,ajn3762   ad*3342   (5037) ppro2257 2532   ppro846   apta2511   ppro846   art,nn2588

9 And put*no*difference between   us and them, purifying their hearts

art,nn4102

by faith.

ad3568   3767   inpro5101 pin3985   art,nn2316   ainf2007   an,nn2218 pre1909 art3588

10 Now therefore why tempt ye God, to put a yoke upon the

nn5137   art3588   nn3101   repro3739 3777 ppro2257 art,nn3962 3777 ppro2249   aina2480

neck of the disciples, which neither our fathers nor we were able to

ainf941

bear?

235   pin4100   pre1223 art3588 nn5485   art3588 nn2962 an,nn2424 an,nn5547

11 But we believe that through the grace of the Lord Jesus Christ we shall

aifp4982   pre2596/repro3739/an,nn5158/depro2548

be saved,   even*as*they.

1161   an,aj3956 art3588   nn4128   aina4601   2532   ipf191   an,nn921

12 Then all   the multitude kept silence, and gave audience to Barnabas

2532 an,nn3972 ppmp1834   an,aj3745 an,nn4592 2532 an,nn5059 art,nn2316   aina4160   pre1722 art3588

and Paul, declaring what miracles and wonders God had wrought among the

nn1484   pre1223   ppro846

Gentiles by them.

1161   ppro846   aime4601   an,nn2384   ainp611   pap3004 an,nn435

13 And after they had held*their*peace, James answered, saying, Men *and*

an,nn80   aima191   ppro3450

brethren, hearken unto me:

4826   aom1834   ad2531 art,nn2316   nu,ajn4412   aom1980   an,nn1484

14 Simeon hath declared how God at*the*first did visit the Gentiles, to

ainf2983 pre1537   an,nn2992 pre1909 ppro848 art,nn3686

take out of them a people for his name.

2532   depro5129 pin4856 art3588 nn3056   art3588   nn4396   ad2531   pfip1125

15 And to this agree the words of the prophets; as it is written,

pre3326 depro5023   ft390   2532   ft456   art3588   nn4633   1138

16 After this I will return, and will build again the tabernacle of David,

art,pfp4098   2532   ft456   art3588 pfpp2679   ppro846   2532

which*is*fallen*down; and I will build again the ruins thereof, and I will

ft461/ppro846

set*it*up:

3704   art3588 ajn2645   art,nn444   asba1567/302 art3588 nn2962   2532 an,aj3956 art3588

17 That the residue of men might seek after the Lord, and all   the

nn1484   pre1909 repro3739 ppro3450 art,nn3686   pfip1941 (pre1909) pin3004 (ppro846)   an,nn2962   art,pap4160

Gentiles, upon whom my name is called,   saith   the Lord, who doeth

an,ajn3956   depro5023

all   these things.   *(Amos 9:11,12)*

pr/an,aj1110   art,nn2316 pin2076 an,aj3956 ppro848 art,nn2041 pre575   an,nn165

18 Known unto God are all his works from the beginning*of*the*world.

pre,repro1352   epn1473   pin2919   pinf3926 3361   pre575
19 Wherefore my sentence is, that we trouble not them, which from among
art3588   nn1484   art,pap1994 pre1909 art,nn2316
the Gentiles are turned to   God:

235   ainf1989   ppro846   infg567   pre575   art,nn234   art,nn2497
20 But that we write unto them, that they abstain from pollutions of idols,
2532   art,nn4202   2532   art,ajn4156   2532   art,nn129
and *from* fornication, and *from* things strangled, and *from* blood.

(Gen. 9:4; Lev. 3:17; 17:10-14; Deut. 12:16)

1063   an,nn3475   pre1537/an,aj744/an,nn1074 pin2192   pre2596/an,nn4172   art,pap2784   ppro846
21 For Moses of*old*time hath in every city them*that*preach him, being
ppmp314 pre1722 art3588   nn4864   pre2596/an,aj3956   an,nn4521
read in   the synagogues   every   sabbath day.

The Letter to Antioch

ad5119   aina1380   art3588   nn652   2532   art,ajn4245   pre4862 art3588 an,nn3650   nn1577
22 Then pleased it the apostles and elders, with the whole church, to
ainf3992   aptm1586   an,nn435 pre1537   ppro846   pre1519   an,nn490   pre4862 art,nn3972   2532
send chosen men   of   their*own*company to   Antioch with Paul and
an,nn921   an,nn2455   art,ppmp1941   an,nn923   2532 an,nn4609 ppmp2233 an,nn435 pre1722 art3588
Barnabas: *namely,* Judas surnamed Barsabas, and Silas, chief men among the
nn80
brethren:

apta1125   pre1223 ppro848 (an,nn5495)   depro3592   art3588   nn652
23 And they wrote *letters* by them   after*this*manner; The apostles
art,ajn4245   2532   art,nn80   pinf5463   art3588   nn80   art3588   pre1537
and elders and brethren *send* greeting unto the brethren which are of   the
an,nn1484   art,pre2596 art,nn490   2532 an,nn4947 2532   an,nn2791
Gentiles in   Antioch and Syria and Cilicia.

1894   aina191   3754 idpro5100   apta1831   pre1537 ppro2257
24 Forasmuch as we have heard, that certain which went out from us
aina5015   ppro5209   an,nn3056   pap384   ppro5216 art,nn5590   pap3004
have troubled you with words, subverting your souls, saying, *Ye must* be
pifp4059   2532 pinf5083 art3588 nn3551   repro3739   aom1291/3756
circumcised, and keep the law: to whom we gave*no*such*commandment:

aina1380   ppro2254   aptm1096   ad3661   ainf3992
25 It seemed good unto us, being assembled with*one*accord, to send
aptm1586   an,nn435 pre4314 ppro5209 pre4862 ppro2257 art,aj27   an,nn921 2532 an,nn3972
chosen men unto you with our beloved Barnabas and Paul,

an,nn444   pfp3860   ppro848 art,nn5590 pre5228 art3588   nn3686   ppro2257 art,nn2962 an,nn2424
26 Men that have hazarded their lives for the name of our Lord Jesus
an,nn5547
Christ.

pfi649   3767   an,nn2455 2532 an,nn4609 epn846   2532 pap518   art3588
27 We have sent therefore Judas and Silas, who shall also tell *you* the
ppro846   pre1223/an,nn3056
same things by mouth.

28 For it seemed good to the Holy Ghost, and to us, to lay upon you no greater burden than these necessary things;

29 That ye abstain from meats*offered*to*idols, and from blood, and from things strangled, and from fornication: from which if ye keep yourselves, ye shall do well, Fare*ye*well.   *(Gen. 9:4; Lev. 3:17; 17:10-14; Deut. 12:16)*

30 So when they were dismissed, they came to Antioch: and when they had gathered*the*multitude*together, they delivered the epistle:

31 *Which* when they had read, they rejoiced for the consolation.

32 And Judas and Silas, being prophets also themselves, exhorted the brethren with many words, and confirmed *them.*

33 And after they had tarried *there* a space, they were let go in peace from the brethren unto the apostles.

34 Notwithstanding it pleased Silas to abide there still.

35 Paul also and Barnabas continued in Antioch, teaching and preaching the word of the Lord, with many others also.

Paul and Barnabas Separate

36 And some days after Paul said unto Barnabas, Let us go again and visit our brethren in every city where we have preached the word of the Lord, *and see* how they do.

37 And Barnabas determined to take with them John, whose*surname*was Mark.

38 But Paul thought*not*good to take*him*with them, who departed from them from Pamphylia, and went*not*with them to the work.

15:36 See introduction to 1 Timothy.

3767   an,nn3948/aom1096   5620   ppro846
39 And   the   contention*was*so*sharp*between   them,   that   they
aifp673   pre575/rcpro240   5037   art,nn921   apta3880 art,nn3138   ainf1602
departed asunder one*from*the*other: and so Barnabas took Mark, and sailed
pre1519 an,nn2954
unto Cyprus;

1161   an,nn3972 aptm1951 an,nn4609   aina1831   aptp3860   pre5259 art3588
40 And Paul chose Silas, and departed, being recommended by the
nn80   art3588   nn5485   art,nn2316
brethren unto the grace of God.

1161   ipf1330   art,nn4947 2532 an,nn2791   pap1991   art3588   nn1577
41 And he went through Syria and Cilicia, confirming the churches.

Timothy Joins Paul

1161   aina2658   pre1519 an,nn1191 2532 an,nn3082 2532   2400   idpro5100   an,nn3101
Then came he to Derbe and Lystra: and, behold, a certain disciple
ipf2258   ad1563   an,nn3686   an,nn5095   an,nn5207   idpro5100   an,nn1135
16 was there, named Timothy, the son of a certain woman, which
an,nn2453   an,aj4103   1161   an,nn2962   an,nn1672
was a Jewess, and believed; but his father *was* a Greek:

repro3739   ipf3140   pre5259 art3588   nn80   pre1722 an,nn3082 2532
2 Which was well*reported*of by the brethren that were at Lystra and
an,nn2430
Iconium.

depro5126 aina2309 art,nn3972   ainf1831   pre4862 ppro846 2532 apta2983   aina4059
3 Him would Paul have to go forth with him; and took and circumcised
ppro846   pre1223   art3588   nn2453   art,pap5607   pre1722 depro1565   art,nn5117   1063   ipf1492 an,ajn537
him because of the Jews which were in those quarters: for they knew all
3754 ppro848 art,nn3962 ipf5225   pr/an,nn1672
that his father was a Greek.

1161   ad5613   ipf1279   art3588   nn4172   ipf3860   ppro846 art3588   nn1378
4 And as they went through the cities, they delivered them the decrees
pinf5442   art,pfpp2919   pre5259 art3588   nn652   2532 art,ajn4245   art3588   pre1722
for to keep, that*were*ordained of the apostles and elders which were at
2419
Jerusalem.

Paul's Vision of the Man of Macedonia

3767   3303   art3588   nn1577   ipf4732   art3588   nn4102   2532   ipf4052
5 And so were the churches established in the faith, and increased in
art,nn706   pre2596/an,nn2250
number   daily.

1161   apta1330   art,nn5435   2532 art3588   nn5561   an,aj1054
6 Now when they had gone throughout Phrygia and the region of Galatia,
aptp2967   pre5259 art3588 an,aj40   nn4151   ainf2980   art3588   nn3056 pre1722 art,nn773
and were forbidden of the Holy Ghost to preach the word in Asia,

apta2064 pre2596 art,nn3465   ipf3985   pifm4198 pre2596 art,nn978

7 After they were come to Mysia, they attempted to go into Bithynia:

2532 art3588 nn4151 aina1439 ppro846 3756

but the Spirit suffered them not.

1161   apta3928 art,nn3465 aina2597 pre1519 an,nn5174

8 And they passing by Mysia came down to Troas.

2532 an,nn3705 ainp3700 art,nn3972 pre1223 art3588 nn3571   ipf2258/pfp2476 (idpro5100) an,nn435

9 And a vision appeared to Paul in the night; there stood a man

an,nn3110 2532 pap3870 ppro846 pap3004 apta1224 pre1519 an,nn3109 aima997

of Macedonia, and prayed him, saying, Come over into Macedonia, and help

ppro2254

us.

1161 ad5613 aina1492 art3588 nn3705 ad2112 aina2212 ainf1831

10 And after he had seen the vision, immediately we endeavored to go

pre1519 art,nn3109 pap4822 3754 art3588 nn2962 pfi4341 ppro2248

into Macedonia, assuredly gathering that the Lord had called us for to

aifm2097 ppro846

preach*the*gospel unto them.

In Philippi

3767 aptp321 pre575 art,nn5174 aina2113 pre1519

11 Therefore loosing from Troas, we came*with*a*straight*course to

an,nn4543 5037 art3588 pap1966 pre1519 an,nn3496

Samothracia, and the next *day* to Neapolis;

5037 ad1564 pre1519 an,nn5375 repro3748 pin2076 pr/nu,aj4413 an,nn4172 art,nn3310

☞ 12 And from thence to Philippi, which is the chief city of that part

art,nn3109 an,nn2862 1161 ipf2258 pre1722 depro5026 art,nn4172 pap1304 idpro5100 an,nn2250

of Macedonia, *and* a colony: and we were in that city abiding certain days.

5037 (art,nn2250) art3588 nn4521 aina1831 ad1854 art3588 nn4172 pre3844 an,nn4215

13 And on the sabbath we went out of the city by a river side,

repro3757 an,nn4335 ipf3543 pinf1511 2532 apta2523 ipf2980 art3588

where prayer was wont to be made; and we sat down, and spake unto the

nn1135 apta4905

women which resorted *thither.*

2532 idpro5100 an,nn1135 an,nn3686 an,nn3070 an,nn4211 an,nn4172

14 And a certain woman named Lydia, a seller*of*purple, of the city of

an,nn2363 ppmp4576 art,nn2316 ipf191 repro3739 art,nn2588 art3588 nn2962 aina1272

Thyatira, which worshipped God, heard *us*: whose heart the Lord opened, that

pinf4337 art,ppmp2980 pre5259 art,nn3972

she attended unto the*things*which*were*spoken of Paul.

1161 ad5613 ainp907 2532 ppro848 art,nn3624 aina3870

15 And when she was baptized, and her household, she besought *us,*

pap3004 1487 pfi2919 ppro3165 pinf1511 pr/an,aj4103 art3588 nn2962 apta1525 pre1519 ppro3450

saying, If ye have judged me to be faithful to the Lord, come into my

art,nn3624 aima3306 2532 aom3849 ppro2248

house, and abide *there.* And she constrained us.

☞ **16:12** See introduction to 1 Timothy.

Paul and Silas Imprisoned

1161   aom1096   ppro2257 ppmp4198 pre1519 an,nn4335 idpro5100 an,nn3814
16 And it came*to*pass, as we went to prayer, a certain damsel

pap2192 an,nn4151   an,nn4436 ainf528 ppro2254 repro3748 ipf3930 ppro848 art,nn2962
possessed with a spirit of divination met us, which brought her masters

an,aj4183 an,nn2039 ppmp3132
much gain by soothsaying:

depro3778 apta2628 art,nn3972 2532 ppro2254 ipf2896 pap3004 depro3778 art,nn444 pin1526
17 The same followed Paul and us, and cried, saying, These men are

pr/an,ajn1401 art3588 aj5310 art,nn2316 repro3748 pin2605 ppro2254 an,nn3598
the servants of the most high God, which show unto us the way of

an,nn4991
salvation.

1161 depro5124 ipf4160 (pre1909) an,aj4183 an,nn2250 1161 art,nn3972 aptp1278 apta1994 2532
18 And this did she many days. But Paul, being grieved, turned and

aina2036 art3588 nn4151 pin3853 ppro4671 pre1722 art3588 nn3686 an,nn2424 an,nn5547 ainf1831
said to the spirit, I command thee in the name of Jesus Christ to come

pre575 ppro846 2532 aina1831 art3588 epn846 nn5610
out of her. And he came out the same hour.

1161 ppro848 art,nn2962 apta1492 3754 art3588 nn1680 ppro848 art,nn2039 aina1831
19 And when her masters saw that the hope of their gains was gone, they

aptm1949 art,nn3972 2532 art,nn4609 aina1670 pre1519 art3588 nn58 pre1909 art3588 nn758
caught Paul and Silas, and drew *them* into the marketplace unto the rulers,

2532 apta4317 ppro846 art3588 nn4755 aina2036 depro3778 art,nn444 pap5225
20 And brought them to the magistrates, saying, These men, being

pr/an,nn2453 pin1613 ppro2257 art,nn4172
Jews, do exceedingly trouble our city,

2532 pin2605 an,nn1485 repro3739 pin1832/3756 ppro2254 pifm3858 3761
21 And teach customs, which are*not*lawful for us to receive, neither to

pinf4160 pap5607 pr/an,nn4514
observe, being Romans.

2532 art3588 nn3793 aina4911 pre2596 ppro846 2532 art3588 nn4755
22 And the multitude rose*up*together against them: and the magistrates

apta4048 ppro846 art,nn2440 ipf2753 pinf4463
rent off their clothes, and commanded to beat *them*.

5037   apta2007 an,aj4183 an,nn4127 ppro846 aina906 pre1519
23 And when they had laid many stripes upon them, they cast *them* into

an,nn5438 apta3853 art3588 nn1200 pinf5083 ppro846 ad806
prison, charging the jailer to keep them safely:

repro3739 pfp2983 an,aj5108 an,nn3852 aina906 ppro846 pre1519 art3588 cd/aj2082 an,nn5438
24 Who, having received such a charge, thrust them into the inner prison,

2532 aom805/ppro846/art,nn4228 pre1519 art3599 nn3586
and made*their*feet*fast in the stocks.

1161 pre2596 art,nn3317 an,nn3972 2532 an,nn4609 ppmp4336 2532 ipf5214 art,nn2316
25 And at midnight Paul and Silas prayed, and sang praises unto God:

1161 art3588 ajn1198 ipf1874 ppro846
and the prisoners heard them.

☞ **16:18** See note on 2 Timothy 4:20.

1161   ad869   aom1096   an,aj3173   an,nn4578   5620   art3588   nn2310
26 And suddenly there was a great earthquake, so that the foundations of
art3588   nn1201   aifp4531   5037   ad3916   an,aj3956 art3588   nn2374   ainp455   2532
the prison were shaken: and immediately all the doors were opened, and
an,ajn3956   art,nn1191   ainp447
every one's bands were loosed.

1161   art3588   nn1200   aptm1096/pr/an,aj1853   2532   apta1492
27 And the keeper*of*the*prison awaking*out*of*his*sleep, and seeing
art3588   nn5438   art,nn2374 pfpp455   aptm4685   an,nn3162   ipf3195   pinf337   rxpro1438
the prison doors open, he drew out his sword, and would have killed himself,
pap3543   art3588   ajn1198   pfin1628
supposing that the prisoners had been fled.

1161   art,nn3972 aina5455   an,aj3173 an,nn5456   pap3004   aosi4238   rxpro4572 an,aj3367 an,ajn2556 1063
28 But Paul cried with a loud voice, saying, Do thyself no harm: for
pin2070 an,ajn537 ad1759
we are all here.

1161   apta154   an,nn5457   aina1530   2532   aptm1096   pr/an,aj1790
29 Then he called for a light, and sprang in, and came trembling, and
aina4363   art,nn3972 2532 art,nn4609
fell*down*before Paul and Silas,

2532   apta4254   ppro846   ad1854   aina5346 an,nn2962 inpro5101 pin1163 ppro3165 pinf4160 2443
30 And brought them out, and said, Sirs, what must I do to be
asbp4982
saved?

1161   art3588   aina2036   aima4100   pre1909 art3588   nn2962   an,nn2424 an,nn5547   2532   epn4771
31 And they said, Believe on the Lord Jesus Christ, and thou shalt be
fp4982   2532   ppro4675 art,nn3624
saved, and thy house.

2532   aina2980   ppro846 art3588   nn3056   art3588   nn2962   2532   an,aj3956 art3588
32 And they spake unto him the word of the Lord, and to all that were
pre1722 ppro848 art,nn3614
in his house.

2532   apta3880 ppro846 (pre1722) art3588 depro1565   nn5610   art3588   nn3571   aina3068   (pre575)
33 And he took them the same hour of the night, and washed their
art,nn4127   2532   ainp907   epn846 2532 an,aj3956 art,ppro846   ad3916
stripes; and was baptized, he and all his, straightway.

5037   apta321   ppro846 pre1519 ppro848 art,nn3624   aina3908/an,nn5132
34 And when he had brought them into his house, he set*meat*before
2532   aom21   pfp4100   art,nn2316   ad3832
them, and rejoiced, believing in God with*all*his*house.

1161   aptm1096 an,nn2250 art3588   nn4755   aina649 art3588   nn4465   pap3004
35 And when it was day, the magistrates sent the sergeants, saying,
aina630/depro1565/art,nn444
Let*those*men*go.

1161   art3588   nn1200   aina518 depro5128 art,nn3056   pre4314 art,nn3972   art3588
36 And the keeper*of*the prison told this saying to Paul, The
nn4755   pfi649 2443   asbp630   ad3568   3767   apta4196   pim1831 pre1722
magistrates have sent to let*you*go: now therefore depart, and go in
an,nn1515
peace.

1161   art,nn3972 aina5346 pre4314 ppro846   apta1194 ppro2248 an,ajn1219
37 But Paul said unto them, They have beaten us openly

^{an,aj178}   ^{pap5225}   ^{pr/an,nn4514}   ^(an,nn444)   ^{aina906}   ^{pre1519}   ^{an,nn5438}   ²⁵³²   ^{ad3568}

uncondemned, being Romans, and have cast *us* into prison; and now do they
^{pin1544/ppro2248}   ^{ad2977}   ³⁷⁵⁶   ¹⁰⁶³   ²³⁵   ^{apta2064}   ^{epn848}

thrust*us*out privily? nay verily; but let them come themselves and
^{aima1806/ppro2248}

fetch*us*out.

    ¹¹⁶¹   ^{art3588}   ⁿⁿ⁴⁴⁶⁵   ^{aina312} ^{depro5023} ^{art,nn4487}   ^{art3588}   ⁿⁿ⁴⁷⁵⁵   ²⁵³²

38 And the sergeants told these words unto the magistrates: and they
^{ainp5399}   ^{apta191} ³⁷⁵⁴   ^{pin1526} ^{pr/an,nn4514}

feared, when they heard that they were Romans.

    ²⁵³²   ^{apta2064}   ^{aina3870}   ^{ppro846}   ²⁵³²   ^{apta1806}

39 And they came and besought them, and brought**them**out, and
^{ipf2065}   ^{ainf1831}   ^{art3588} ⁿⁿ⁴¹⁷²

desired *them* to depart out of the city.

    ¹¹⁶¹   ^{apta1831}   ^{pre1537} ^{art3588}   ⁿⁿ⁵⁴³⁸   ^{aina1525} ^{pre1519}   ^{art,nn3070}

40 And they went out of the prison, and entered into *the house of* Lydia:
²⁵³²   ^{apta1492 art3588}   ⁿⁿ⁸⁰   ^{aina3870}   ^{ppro846}   ²⁵³²   ^{aina1831}

and when they had seen the brethren, they comforted them, and departed.

In Thessalonica

17 ¹¹⁶¹   ^{apta1353}   ^{art,nn295}   ²⁵³²   ^{an,nn624}

      ☞ Now when they had passed through Amphipolis and Apollonia,
      ^{aina2064} ^{pre1519} ^{an,nn2332}   ^{ad3699} ^{ip 2258}   ^{art,nn4864}   ^{art3588} ⁿⁿ²⁴⁵³

      they came to Thessalonica, where was a synagogue of the Jews:
¹¹⁶¹   ^{art,nn3972}   ^{pre2596/art,nn1486}   ^{aina1525} ^{pre4314} ^{ppro846}   ²⁵³² ^(pre1909) ^{nu5140}

2 And Paul, as*his*manner*was, went in unto them, and   three
^{an,nn4521}   ^{ipf1256}   ^{ppro846} ^{pre575} ^{art3588}   ⁿⁿ¹¹²⁴

sabbath days reasoned with them out of the Scriptures,
    ^{pap1272}   ²⁵³²   ^{ppmp3908}   ³⁷⁵⁴   ^{art,nn5547}   ^{ipf1163}   ^{ainf3958}   ²⁵³²

3 Opening and alleging, that Christ must needs have suffered, and
^{ainf450}   ^{pre1537}   ^{an,ajn3498} ²⁵³² ³⁷⁵⁴ ^{depro3778} ^{an,nn2424} ^{repro3739} ^{epn1473} ^{pin2605}   ^{ppro5213}

risen again from the dead; and that this Jesus, whom I preach unto you,
^{pin2076} ^{pr/art,nn5547}

is Christ.

    ²⁵³²   ^{idpro5100} ^{pre1537} ^{ppro846}   ^{ainp3982}   ²⁵³²   ^{ainp4345}   ^{art,nn3972} ²⁵³² ^{art,nn4609} ⁵⁰³⁷

4 And some of them believed, and consorted with Paul and Silas; and of
^{art3588} ^{ppmp4576}   ^{an,nn1672}   ^{an,aj4183}   ^{an,nn4128}   ⁵⁰³⁷   ^{art3588} ^{nu,ajn4413} ^{an,nn1135} ³⁷⁵⁶   ^{an,aj3641}

the devout Greeks a great multitude, and of the chief women not a few.
    ¹¹⁶¹ ^{art3588} ⁿⁿ²⁴⁵³   ^{pap544}   ^{apta2206}   ⁽²⁵³²⁾   ^{aptm4355}

5 But the Jews which believed not, moved*with*envy,   took unto them
^{adpro5100} ^{an,ajn4190} ^{an,nn435}   ^{art3588}   ^{aj60}   ²⁵³²   ^{apta3792}

certain lewd fellows of the baser sort, and gathered*a*company, and
^{ipf2530/art3588/nn4172}   ⁵⁰³⁷   ^{apta2186}   ^{art3588} ⁿⁿ³⁶¹⁴   ^{an,nn2394}   ^{ipf2212}

set*all*the*city*on*an*uproar, and assaulted the house of Jason, and sought
^(ppro846)   ^{ainf71}   ^{pre1519 art3588}   ⁿⁿ¹²¹⁸

  to bring*them*out to the people.

☞ **17:1–10** See introduction to 1 Thessalonians.

1161   apta2147   ppro846   3361   ipf4951   art,nn2394   2532
6 And   when   they   found   them   not,   they   drew   Jason   and

idpro5100   an,nn80   pre1909   art3588   nn4173   pap994   depro3778
certain   brethren   unto   the   rulers*of*the*city,   crying,   These

art,apta387/art3588/nn3625   pin3918   ad1759   2532
that*have*turned*the*world*upside*down are come hither also;

repro3739   an,nn2394   pfip5264   2532 depro3778 an,aj3956 pin4238   ad561   art3588   nn1378
7 Whom Jason hath received: and these   all   do contrary to the decrees

an,nn2541   pap3004   pinf1511   an,aj2087   an,nn935   an,nn2424
of Caesar, saying that there   is   another king, *one* Jesus.

1161   aina5015   art3588   nn3793   2532   art3588   nn4173
8 And they troubled the people and the rulers*of*the*city, when they

pap191   depro5023
heard these things.

2532   apta2983   art,ajn2425   pre3844   art,nn2394   2532   art3588   pl/ajn3062
9 And when they had taken security   of   Jason, and of the other, they

aina630/ppro846
let*them*go.

In Berea

1161   art3588   nn80   ad2112   aina1599   (5037) art,nn3972   2532   art,nn4609 pre1223
10 And   the   brethren   immediately   sent   away   Paul   and   Silas   by

art,nn3571 pre1519 an,nn960   repro3748   aplm3854   ipf549   pre1519   art3588   nn4864   art3588
night   unto   Berea: who   coming   *thither*   went   into   the   synagogue   of   the

nn2453
Jews.

(1161) depro3778   ipf2258   pr/cd/an,aj2104   art3588   pre1722   an,nn2332   repro3748
11   These   were more noble than those   in   Thessalonica, in that they

aom1209   art3588   nn3056   pre3326 an,aj3956   an,nn4288   pap350   art3588   nn1124
received the word with   all   readiness*of*mind, and searched the Scriptures

pre2596/art,nn2250   1487   depro5023   opt2192 ad3779
daily,   whether those things were so.

3767   an,ajn4183 (3303) pre1537 ppro846   aina4100   2532   art,aj2158   an,nn1135
12 Therefore many   of   them believed; also of honorable women which

art,nn1674   2532   an,nn435   3756   an,aj3641
were Greeks, and of men, not a few.

1161   ad5613   art3588   nn2453   pre575   art,nn2332   aina1097   3754 art3588 nn3056
13 But when the Jews of Thessalonica had knowledge that the word of

art,nn2316   ainp2605   pre5259 art,nn3972 pre1722 art,nn960   aina2064   ad2546
God   was   preached   of   Paul   at   Berea,   they   came   thither   also,   and

pap4531   art3588   nn3793
stirred up the people.

1161   ad5119   ad2112   art3588   nn80   aina1821   art,nn3972   pifm4198   ad5613
14 And then immediately the brethren sent away Paul to   go   as*it*were

pre1909 art3588 nn2281 1161 (5037) an,nn4609 (repro3739) 2532 art,nn5095   ipf5278   ad1563
to the sea: but   Silas   and Timothy abode there still.

1161   art,pap2525   art,nn3972 aina71   ppro846 ad2193   an,nn116   2532   apta2983
15 And they*that*conducted Paul brought him unto Athens: and receiving

an,nn1785   pre4314 art,nn4609 2532   an,nn5095   asba2064 pre4314 ppro846   ad5613/ad5033

a commandment unto Silas and Timothy for to come to him with*all*speed,
ipf1826

they departed.

In Athens

1161   art,nn3972   ppmp1551   ppro846 pre1722 art,nn116   ppro848 art,nn4151   ipf3947

16 Now while Paul waited for them at Athens, his spirit was stirred
pre1722 ppro846   pap2334 art3588 nn4172 (pap5607)   pr/an,ajn2712

in him, when he saw the city   wholly*given*to*idolatry.
3767   ipf1256   (3303) pre1722 art3588   nn4864   art3588   nn2453   2532

17 Therefore disputed he in the synagogue with the Jews, and with
art3588   ppmp4576   2532   pre1722 art3588   nn58   pre2596/an,aj3956/an,nn2250   pre4313

the devout persons, and in the market daily   with
art,pap3909

them*that*met*with him.
1161   idpro5100   an,nn5386   art3588 aj1946   2532   art3588 aj4470

18 Then certain philosophers of the Epicureans, and of the Stoics,
ipf4820   ppro846 2532 idpro5100 ipf3004 inpro5101 opt2309/302 depro3778 art,nn4691 pinf3004(1161) art3588

encountered him. And some said, What will this babbler say? other some,
pin1380   pinf1511   pr/an,nn2604   an,aj3581   an,nn1140 3754   ipf2097

He seemeth to be a setter forth of strange gods: because he preached unto
ppro846 art,nn2424 2532 art3588   nn386

them Jesus, and the resurrection.
5037   aptm1949 ppro846   aina71   pre1909 art,aj,an,nn697 pap3004 pinm1410

19 And they took him, and brought him unto Areopagus, saying, May we
ainf1097 inpro5101 depro3778 art,aj2537 pr/an,nn1322   art3588 (pre5259) ppro4675 ppmp2980

know what this new doctrine, whereof   thou speakest, is?
1063   pin1533 idpro5100   pap3579   pre1519 ppro2257 art,nn189   pinm1014 ainf1097

20 For thou bringest certain strange things to our ears: we would know
3767   inpro5101   depro5023   opt2309/302 (pinf1511)

therefore what these things   mean.
(1161) an,aj3956   an,nn117   2532   art,ajn3581   pap1927

21 (For all the Athenians and strangers which were there
ipf2119   pre1519 an,aj3762 an,ajn2087 2228   pinf3004 2532   pinf191 idpro5100

spent*their*time in nothing else, but either to tell, or to hear some
cd/an,ajn2537

new thing.)
1161   art,nn3972 aptp2476 pre1722   an,ajn3319   art,aj,an,nn697 aina5346   an,nn435

22 Then Paul stood in the midst of Mars' hill, and said, Ye men of
an,nn117   pin2334   pre2596 an,ajn3956 ppro5209 (ad5613) pr/cd/an,aj1174

Athens, I perceive that in all things ye are too superstitious.
1063   ppmp1330   2532 pap333 ppro5216 art,nn4574   aina2147 (2532) an,nn1041

23 For as I passed by, and beheld your devotions, I found an altar
pre1722/repro3739/plpf1924   an,aj57   an,nn2316 repro3739   3767

with*this*inscription, TO THE UNKNOWN GOD. Whom therefore ye
pap50   pin2151 depro5126 pin2065 epn1473   ppro5213

ignorantly worship, him declare I unto you.
art,nn2316 art,apta4160 art3588 nn2889 2532   an,aj3956   art,pre1722/ppro846   depro3778

24 God that made the world and all things therein, seeing that he

pap5225 pr/an,nn2962   an,nn3772   2532   an,nn1093   pin2730   3756 pre1722   an,nn3485   an,aj5499

is   Lord of heaven and earth, dwelleth not in temples made*with*hands;

(Ps. 146:6; Is. 42:5)

3761   pinp2323   pre5259   an,nn444   an,nn5495   ppmp4326

25 Neither   is   worshiped with   men's   hands,   as*though*he*needed

idpro5100   epn846 pinf1325   an,ajn3956 an,nn2222 2532   an,nn4157   pre2596/art,ajn3956

any thing, seeing he giveth to   all   life, and breath, and all things;

(Ps. 50:12; Is. 42:5)

5037   aina4160   pre1537 nu1520 an,nn129 an,aj3956   an,nn1484   an,nn444   pinf2730 pre1909

26 And hath made of   one blood   all   nations of men for to dwell on

an,aj3956 art3588 nn4383   art3588   nn1093   apta3724   an,nn2540   pfpp4384

all   the face of the earth, and hath determined the times before appointed,

2532 art3588   nn3734   ppro848   art,nn2733

and the bounds of their habitation;   *(Deut. 32:8)*

pinf2212 art3588   nn2962   1487   686/1065   opt5584   ppro846

27 That they should seek the Lord, if haply they might feel after him,

2532 opt2147   2544   pap5225 3756 ad3112 pre575 an,ajn1538 nu1520   ppro2257

and find him, though he be not far from every one of us:

(Is. 55:6; Ps. 145:18; Jer. 23:23)

1063   pre1722 epn846   pin2198   2532 pinm2795   2532   pin2070   ad5613 idpro5100   2532

28 For in him we live, and move, and have*our*being; as certain also of

pre2596/ppro5209 art,nn4163   pfi2046 1063   pin2070 2532 art5120 pr/an,nn1085

your own poets have said, For we are also his offspring.

3767   pap5225   pr/an,nn1085   art,nn2316   pin3784   3756   pinf3543

29 Forasmuch then as we are the offspring of God, we ought not to think

art3588 ajn2304   pinf1511 pr/an,ajn3664 an,nn5557 2228 an,nn696 2228 an,nn3037   an,nn5480   an,nn5078 2532

that the Godhead is   like unto gold, or silver, or stone, graven by art and

an,nn444 an,nn1761

man's device.   *(Gen. 1:27; Is. 40:18-20; 44:10-17)*

(3767 3303)   art3588   nn5550   art,nn52   art,nn2316 apta5237   art,ad3569

30 And   the times of this ignorance God   winked at; but   now

pin3853   an,aj3956 art,nn444   ad3837   pinf3340

commandeth all   men every where to repent:

1360   aina2476   an,nn2250 pre1722   repro3739   pin3195 pinf2919 art3588

31 Because he hath appointed a day,   in   the which he will judge the

nn3625 pre1722   an,nn1343   pre1722   an,nn435 repro3739   aina3724

world in righteousness by *that* man whom he hath ordained; *whereof* he hath

apta3930   an,nn4102   an,ajn3956   apta450 ppro846 pre1537   an,ajn3498

given assurance unto   all   *men,* in that he hath raised him from the dead.

(Ps. 9:8; 96:13; 98:9)

1161   apta191   an,nn386   an,ajn3498 art3588/3303 ipf5512

32 And when they heard of the resurrection of the dead, some mocked:

1161   art3588 aina2036   fm191 ppro4675 ad3825 pre4012 depro5127

and others said, We will hear thee again of this *matter.*

(2532) ad3779 art,nn3972 aina1831   pre1537 an,ajn3319   ppro846

33   So Paul departed from among them.

1161   idpro5100 an,nn435 aptp2853   ppro846 2532   aina4100   pre1722   repro3739

34 Howbeit certain men cleaved unto him, and believed: among the which

an,nn1354 art3588 nn698 2532 an,nn1135 an,nn3686 an,nn1152 2532 an,ajn2087 pre4862
was Dionysius the Areopagite, and a woman named Damaris, and others with
ppro846
them.

In Corinth

(1161) pre3326 depro5023 art,nn3972 aptp5563 pre1537 art,nn116 aina2064 pre1519
18 After these things Paul departed from Athens and came to
an,nn2882
Corinth;

2532 apta2147 idpro5100 an,nn2453 an,nn3686 an,nn207 art,nn1085 an,nn4193 ad4373
2 And found a certain Jew named Aquila, born in Pontus, lately
pfp2064 pre575 art,nn2482 2532 ppro848 an,nn1135 an,nn4252 an,nn2804
come from Italy, with his wife Priscilla; (because that Claudius had
aid1299 an,aj3956 art,nn2453 pifmp5563 pre1537 art,nn4516 aina4334 ppro846
commanded all Jews to depart from Rome:) and came unto them.

2532 aid1511 art3588 pr/ajn3673 ipf3306 pre3844 ppro846 2532
3 And because he was of the same craft, he abode with them, and
ipf2038 1063 art,nn5078 ipf2258 pr/an,nn4635
wrought: for by their occupation they were tentmakers.

1161 ipf1256 pre1722 art3588 nn4864 pre2596/an,aj3956 an,nn4521 5037 ipf3982
4 And he reasoned in the synagogue every sabbath, and persuaded
an,nn2453 2532 an,nn1672
the Jews and the Greeks.

1161 ad5613 (5037) art,nn4609 2532 art,nn5095 aina2718 pre575 art,nn3109 art,nn3972
☞ 5 And when Silas and Timothy were come from Macedonia, Paul was
ipf4912 art3588 nn4151 ppmp1263 art3588 nn2453 pr/an,nn2424 art,nn5547
pressed in the spirit, and testified to the Jews *that* Jesus *was* Christ.

1161 ppro846 ppmp498 2532 pap987 aptm1621
6 And when they opposed themselves, and blasphemed, he shook *his*
art,nn2440 aina2036 pre4314 ppro846 ppro5216 art,nn129 pre1909 ppro5216 art,nn2776 epn1473
raiment, and said unto them, Your blood *be* upon your own heads; I *am*
pr/an,aj2513 pre575 art,ad3568 fm4198 pre1519 art3588 nn1484
clean: from henceforth I will go unto the Gentiles.

2532 apta3327 ad1564 aina2064 pre1519 idpro5100 an,nn3614
7 And he departed thence, and entered into a certain *man's* house,
an,nn3686 an,nn2459 ppmp4576 art,nn2316 repro3739 art,nn3614 ipf2258/pr/pap4927 art3588
named Justus, *one* that worshipped God, whose house joined hard to the
nn4864
synagogue.

1161 an,nn2921 art3588 nn752 aina4100 art3588 nn2962
8 And Crispus, the chief*ruler*of*the*synagogue, believed on the Lord
pre4862 an,aj3650 ppro848 art,nn3624 2532 an,ajn4183 art3588 nn2881 pap191 ipf4100 2532
with all his house; and many of the Corinthians hearing believed, and were
ipf907
baptized.

☞ **18:5** See introduction to 1 Thessalonians.

9 Then spake the Lord to Paul in the night by a vision,
Be*not*afraid, but speak, and hold*not*thy*peace:

10 For I am with thee, and no man shall set on thee to hurt thee: for
I have much people in this city.

11 And he continued *there* a year and six months, teaching the word of
God among them.

12 And when Gallio was*the*deputy of Achaia, the Jews
made*insurrection*with*one*accord*against Paul, and brought him to
the judgment seat,

13 Saying, This *fellow* persuadeth men to worship God contrary to the
law.

14 And when Paul was*now*about to open *his* mouth, Gallio said unto
the Jews, If it were a matter*of*wrong or wicked lewdness, O *ye*
Jews, reason would that I should bear with you:

15 But if it be a question of words and names, and of your law,
look ye *to it*; for I will be no judge of such *matters*.

16 And he drove them from the judgment seat.

17 Then all the Greeks took Sosthenes, the
chief*ruler*of*the*synagogue, and beat *him* before the judgment seat. And
Gallio cared for none of those things.

Paul Sails for Syria

18 And Paul *after this* tarried *there* yet a good while, and then
took*his*leave of the brethren, and sailed thence into Syria, and with him
Priscilla and Aquila; having shorn *his* head in Cenchrea: for he had a vow.

(Num. 6:18)

1161   aina2658   pre1519   an,nn2181   depro2548/aina2641   ad847   1161   epn848
19 And he came to Ephesus, and*left*them there: but he himself

apta1525   pre1519 art3588   nn4864   ainp1256   art3588   nn2453
entered into the synagogue, and reasoned with the Jews.

1161   ppro846   pap2065   aina3306 (pre1909) cd/an,aj4119 an,nn5550 pre3844 ppro846
20 When they desired *him* to tarry   longer time with them, he

aina1962   3756
consented not;

235   aom657/ppro846   apta2036   ppro3165 pin1163   ad3843   ainf4160   art,nn1859
21 But bade*them*farewell, saying,   I   must by*all*means keep this feast

art,ppmp2064   pre1519   an,nn2414   1161   ft344   ad3825   pre4314 ppro5209 art,nn2316 pap2309 2532
that cometh in Jerusalem: but I will return again unto you, if God will. And

ainp321   pre575   art,nn2181
he sailed from Ephesus.

2532   apta2178   pre1519   an,nn2542   apta305   2532   aptm782   art3588
22 And when he had landed at Caesarea, and gone up, and saluted the

nn1577   aina2597   pre1519 an,nn490
church, he went down to Antioch.

2532   apta4160 idpro5100 an,nn5550   aina1831   ppmp1330
23 And after he had spent some time *there,* he departed, and went over *all*

art3588   nn5561   an,aj1054   2532   an,nn5435   ad2517   pap1991   an,aj3956 art3588   nn3101
the country of Galatia and Phrygia in order, strengthening all the disciples.

Apollos Preaches at Ephesus

1161   idpro5100 an,nn2453   an,nn3686   an,nn625   art,nn1085   an,nn221   an,aj3052
24 And a certain Jew named Apollos, born at Alexandria, an eloquent

an,nn435 (pap5607) pr/an,aj1415 pre1722 art3588   nn1124   aina2658 pre1519   an,nn2181
man, and mighty in the Scriptures, came to Ephesus.

depro3778 ipf2258   pr/pfpp2727   art3588 nn3598   art3588 nn2962   2532   pap2204
25 This man was instructed in the way of the Lord; and being fervent in

art3588   nn4151   ipf2980   2532   ipf1321   ad199   art3588   pre4012 art3588   nn2962   ppmp1987
the spirit, he spake and taught diligently the things of the Lord, knowing

an,ajn3440 art3588   nn908   an,nn2491
only the baptism of John.

5037   depro3778   aom756   pifm3955   pre1722 art3588   nn4864   (1161) ppro846
26 And he began to speak boldly in the synagogue: whom when

an,nn207   2532   an,nn4252   apta191   aom4355/ppro846   2532   aom1620
Aquila and Priscilla had heard, they took*him*unto *them,* and expounded unto

ppro846 art3588 nn3598   art,nn2316   cd/an,ajn197
him the way of God more perfectly.

1161   ppro846   ppmp1014   ainf1330 pre1519   art,nn882   art3588   nn80   aina1125
27 And when he was disposed to pass into Achaia, the brethren wrote,

aptm4389   art3588   nn3101   aifm588   ppro846 repro3739   apta3854   aom4820
exhorting the disciples to receive him: who, when he was come, helped them

an,ajn4183   art,pfp4100   pre1223   art,nn5485
much which*had*believed through grace:

1063   ad2159   ipf1246   art3588   nn2453   an,nn1219   pap1925   pre1223
28 For he mightily convinced the Jews, *and that* publicly, showing by

art3588   nn1124   an,nn2424 pinf1511 pr/art,nn5547
the Scriptures that Jesus was Christ.

In Ephesus

19 ☞And it came*to*pass, that, while Apollos was at Corinth, Paul
having passed through the upper coasts came to Ephesus: and
finding certain disciples,

2 He said unto them, Have ye received the Holy Ghost since ye believed?
And they said unto him, We have not*so*much*as heard whether there be
any Holy Ghost.

☞3 And he said unto them, Unto what then were ye baptized? And they
said, Unto John's baptism.

4 Then said Paul, John verily baptized with the baptism of repentance,
saying unto the people, that they should believe on him*which*should*come
after him, that is, on Christ Jesus.

☞5 When they heard *this,* they were baptized in the name of the Lord
Jesus.

☞6 And when Paul had laid *his* hands upon them, the Holy Ghost came
on them; and they spake with tongues, and prophesied.

7 And all the men were about twelve.

8 And he went into the synagogue, and spake boldly for*the*space*of

---

☞ **19:1–7** This event took place in Ephesus, and it concerned the disciples of John the Baptist there. These people had received the baptism of John but not the baptism of the Holy Spirit, which would be consequent to their exercise of faith in the Lord. The statement that they made, "We have not so much as heard whether there be any Holy Ghost," reflects their lack of knowledge about the Holy Spirit's work or ministry, not their denial of His existence. Many have pointed out that Paul asked these people if they had received the Holy Ghost "since" they believed. Their purpose is to show that Paul accepted the idea that some do not receive the Spirit until after salvation. It should be understood, however, that the Greek text does not support this translation. A literal rendering of the Greek would be: "Did you receive the Holy Spirit, having believed?" It is plain in verses four and five that these people had not believed in Jesus Christ but in the repentance that John the Baptist had preached. Thus there is no conflict here with the belief that all believers receive the Holy Spirit at salvation.
☞ **19:3, 5** See note on 1 Corinthians 10:2.
☞ **19:6** See notes on Acts 2:1–13; 1 Corinthians 14:1–3.

nu5140   an,nn3376   ppmp1256   2532   pap3982   art3588   pre4012   art3588   nn932

three months, disputing and persuading the things concerning the kingdom of

art,nn2316

God.

1161   ad5613   idpro5100   ipf4645   2532   ipf544   pap2551

☞ 9 But when divers were hardened, and believed not, but spake evil of that

art,nn3598   ad*1799   art3588   nn4128   apta868   pre575   ppro846   aina873   art3588

way before the multitude, he departed from them, and separated the

nn3101   ppmp1256   pre2596/an,nn2250 pre1722 art3588   nn4981   idpro5100   an,nn5181

disciples, disputing   daily   in the school of one Tyrannus.

1161   depro5124   aom1096   pre1909   nu1417   an,nn2094   5620   an,aj3956

10 And this continued by*the*space*of two years; so that all

art,pap2730   art,nn773   ainf191   art3588   nn3056   art3588   nn2962   an,nn2424   5037   an,nn2453   2532

they*which*dwelt in Asia heard the word of the Lord Jesus, both Jews and

an,nn1672

Greeks.

5037   art,nn2316   ipf4160   3756/art,apta5177   an,nn1411   pre1223 art3588   nn5495   an,nn3972

☞ 11 And God wrought special miracles by the hands of Paul:

5620   (2532) pre575   ppro846 art,nn5559   pifp2018   pre1909 art3588 pap770   an,nn4676   2228

12 So that from his body were brought unto the sick handkerchiefs or

an,nn4612   2532 art3588   nn3554   pifp525   pre575   ppro846   5037 art3588 aj4190 art,nn4151 pifm1831   pre575

aprons, and the diseases departed from them, and the evil spirits went out of

ppro846

them.

1161   idpro5100   pre575 art3588   ppmp4022   an,nn2453   an,nn1845   aina2021   pinf3687

13 Then certain of the vagabond Jews, exorcists, took upon them to call

pre1909   art,pap2192   art,aj4190   art,nn4151 art3588   nn3686   art3588   nn2962   an,nn2424   pap3004

over them*which*had evil spirits the name of the Lord Jesus, saying, We

pin3726   ppro5209   art,nn2424 repro3739 art,nn3972   pin2784

adjure you by Jesus whom Paul preacheth.

1161   ipf2258   (idpro5100)   nu2033   an,nn5207   an,nn4630   an,nn2453

14 And there were   seven sons of one Sceva, a Jew, and

an,nn749   art,pap4160   depro5124

chief*of*the*priests, which did so.

1161   art3588   aj4190 art,nn4151   aptp611   aina2036 art,nn2424   pin1097   2532 art,nn3972 pinm1987

15 And the evil spirit answered and said, Jesus I know, and Paul I know;

1161   pr/inpro5101 pin2075 epn5210

but who are ye?

2532   art3588   nn444   pre1722   repro3739   art3588   aj4190   art,nn4151   ipf2258   ppmp2177   pre1909   ppro846   2532

16 And the man in whom the evil spirit was leaped on them, and

apta2634   ppro846   aina2480   pre2596   ppro846   5620   ainf1628   pre1537   depro1565

overcame them, and prevailed against them, so that they fled out of that

art,nn3624 an,aj1131   2532   pfpp5135

house naked and wounded.

1161   depro5124   aom1096   pr/an,aj1110   an,aj3956   an,nn2453   2532   an,nn1672   5037   art,pap2730

17 And this was known to all the Jews and Greeks also dwelling at

art,nn2181   2532   an,nn5401 aina1968 pre1909 ppro846 an,aj3956 2532 art3588   nn3686   art3588   nn2962 an,nn2424
Ephesus; and fear fell on them all, and the name of the Lord Jesus was
ipf3170
magnified.

5037   an,ajn4183   art,pfp4100   ipf2064   ppmp1843   2532   pap312   ppro848 art,nn4234
18 And many that believed came, and confessed, and showed their deeds.

(1161) an,ajn2425   art,apta4238   art,ajn4021
19   Many of them * also * which * used curious arts
apta4851/art,nn976   ipf2618   ad*1799 an,ajn3956   2532
brought*their*books*together, and burned them before all *men*: and they
aina4860   art3588 nn5092   ppro846 2532 aina2147   nu4002/pr/an,nn3461   an,nn694
counted the price of them, and found *it* fifty thousand *pieces* of silver.

ad3779 pre2596/an,nn2904 ipf537 art3588 nn3056   art,nn2962 2532   ipf2480
20 So mightily grew the word of God and prevailed.

(1161) ad5613   depro5023   ainp4137 art,nn3972 aom5087   pre1722 art3588 nn4151
21   After these things were ended, Paul purposed in the spirit, when
apta1330   art,nn3109   2532   art,nn882   pifm4198 pre1519   2419   ainf2036
he had passed through Macedonia and Achaia, to go to Jerusalem, saying,
ppro3165   aime1096 ad1563 ppro3165 pin1163 2532 ainf1492 an,nn4516
After I have been there, I must also see Rome.

1161   apta649 pre1519 art,nn3109   nu1417   art,pap1247   ppro846
22 So he sent into Macedonia two of them*that*ministered unto him,
an,nn5095   2532 an,nn2037   epn846   aina1907 pre1519 art,nn773   an,nn5550
Timothy and Erastus; but he himself stayed in Asia for a season.

The Riot at Ephesus

1161   pre2596/depro1565 art,nn2540   aom1096 3756 an,aj3641 an,nn5017 pre4012   art,nn3598
23 And the same time there arose no small stir about that way.
1063   idpro5100   an,nn3686   an,nn1216   an,nn695   pap4160 an,aj693
24 For a certain *man* named Demetrius, a silversmith, which made silver
an,nn3485   an,nn735   ipf3930   3756 an,aj3641 an,nn2039   art3588   nn5079
shrines for Diana, brought no small gain unto the craftsmen;
repro3739   apta4867   2532   art3588   nn2040   pre4012   art,ajn5108
25 Whom he called together with the workmen of like occupation, and
aina2036 an,nn435   pinm1987 3754 pre1537 depro5026 art,nn2039   pin2076 ppro2257   art,nn2142
said, Sirs, ye know that by this craft we have our wealth.
2532   pin2334 2532 pin191   3754 3756 an,ajn3440   an,nn2181   235   ad4975
26 Moreover ye see and hear, that not alone at Ephesus, but almost
an,aj3956 art,nn773 depro3778 art,nn3972   apta3982   aina3179   an,aj2425
throughout all Asia, this Paul hath persuaded and turned away much
an,nn3793 pap3004 3754   pin1526 3756 an,nn2316 art3588   pr/ppmp1096 pre1223 an,nn5495
people, saying that they be no gods, which are made with hands:
(1161)   3756 an,ajn3440 depro5124 ppro2254 art,nn3313   pin2793   ainf2064/pre1519/an,nn557 235
27 So that not only this our craft is*in*danger to be set*at*naught; but
2532   art3588   nn2411   art3588 an,aj3173   nn2299   an,nn735   pre1519/an,ajn3762/aifp3049   1161 ppro848
also that the temple of the great goddess Diana should*be*despised, and her
art,nn3168   pinf3195 (2532)   pifm2507   repro3739 an,aj3650 art,nn773 2532 art3588 nn3625   pinm4576
magnificence should be destroyed, whom all Asia and the world worshippeth.
1161   apta191   aptm1096 pr/an,aj4134
28 And when they heard *these* *sayings*, they were full of

an,nn2372　　2532　　ipf2896　　pap3004　　pr/an,aj3173　　art,nn735　　an,nn2180

wrath, and cried out, saying, Great *is* Diana of the Ephesians.

2532　art3588　an,aj3650　nn4172　　ainp4130　　art,nn4799　5037　　apta4884　an,nn1050

☞ 29 And the whole city was filled with confusion: and having caught Gaius

2532　an,nn708　　an,nn3110　　art,nn3972　an,ajn4989　　aina3729

and Aristarchus, men*of*Macedonia, Paul's companions*in*travel, they rushed

ad3661　　pre1519 art3588　nn2302

with*one*accord into the theater.

1161　　art,nn3972　ppmp1014　　ainf1525　pre1519 art3588　nn1218　art3588　nn3101

30 And when Paul would have entered in unto the people, the disciples

ipf1439　ppro846　3756

suffered him not.

1161　idpro5100　(2532) art3588　　nn775　　　pap5607 ppro846　pr/an,ajn5384 apta3992 pre4314

31 And certain of the chief*of*Asia, which were his friends, sent unto

ppro846　ipf3870　　　　3361　ainf1325　rxpro1438　pre1519 art3588　nn2302

him, desiring *him* that he would not adventure himself into the theater.

an,ajn243/3303/3767/ipf2896　　an,ajn243　idpro5100　1063　art3588　　nn1577

32 Some*therefore*cried*one*thing, and some another: for the assembly

ipf2258　pr/pfpp4797　2532　art3588　cd/ajn4119　ipf1492　3756　inpro5101/ad*1752

was confused; and the more part knew not wherefore they were

plpf4095

come together.

1161　　aina4264　an,nn223　pre1537 art3588　nn3793　art3588　nn2453

33 And they drew Alexander out of the multitude, the Jews

pap4261/ppro846　1161　art,nn223　apta2678　art3588 nn5495　ipf2309

putting*him*forward. And Alexander beckoned with the hand, and would have

pifm626　art3588　nn1218

made*his*defense unto the people.

1161　apta1921　3754　pin2076　pr/an,nn2453　aom1096/an,nn5456/nu3391/pre1537/an,ajn3956

34 But when they knew that he was a Jew, all*with*one*voice

ad5613/pre1909　nu1417 an,nn4610　pap2896　pr/an,aj3173　art,nn735　an,nn2180

about*the*space*of two hours cried out, Great *is* Diana of the Ephesians.

1161　art3588　nn1122　apta2687　art3588　nn3793　pin5346　an,nn435

35 And when the town clerk had appeased the people, he said, *Ye* men of

an,ajn2180 (1063) inpro5101 an,nn444 pin2076　repro3739　pin1097　3756　art3588 nn4172

Ephesus, what man is there that knoweth not how that the city of the

an,ajn2180　pap5607　pr/an,nn3511　art3588　an,aj3173　nn2299　an,nn735　2532

Ephesians is a worshiper of the great goddess Diana, and of

art,ajn1356

the*image*which*fell*down*from*Jupiter?

3767　　depro5130　　pap5607/pr/an,aj368　　ppro5209 (pin2076)

36 Seeing then that these things cannot*be*spoken*against, ye

pap1163　pinf5225 pr/pfpp2687 2532　pinf4238　an,ajn3367　an,ajn4312

ought to be quiet, and to do nothing rashly.

1063　aina71　depro5128　art,nn435　3777

37 For ye have brought hither these men, which are neither

an,ajn2417　3777　pap987　ppro5216　art,nn2299

robbers*of*churches, nor yet blasphemers of your goddess.

3767　1487 (3303)　an,nn1216　2532 art3588　nn5079　pre4862 ppro846

38 Wherefore if Demetrius, and the craftsmen which are with him,

---

☞ **19:29** See note on 3 John 1:1.

pin2192 an,nn3056 pre4314 idpro5100 an,ajn60/pinm71 2532 pin1526 an,nn446
have a matter against any man, the law*is*open, and there are deputies: let

pim1458 rcpro240
them implead one another.

1161 1487 pin1934 idpro5100 pre4012 an,ajn2087
39 But if ye inquire any thing concerning other matters, it shall be

fp1956 pre1722 art,aj1772 an,nn1577
determined in a lawful assembly.

1063 pin2793 (2532) pifm1458 pre4012 art,ad4594
40 For we are*in*danger to be called*in*question for this day's

an,nn4714 pap5225 an,nn3367 an,nn158 pre4012/repro3739 fm1410 ainf591 an,nn3056 depro5026
uproar, there being no cause whereby we may give an account of this

art,nn4963
concourse.

2532 depro5023 apta2036 aina630 art3588 nn1577
41 And when he had thus spoken, he dismissed the assembly.

Paul's Journey to Macedonia and Greece

1161 art3588 nn2351 aime3973 art,nn3972 aptm4341 art3588
20 ☞And after the uproar was ceased, Paul called unto *him* the

nn3101 2532 aptm782 aina1831 aifp4198 pre1519
disciples, and embraced *them,* and departed for to go into

art,nn3109
Macedonia.

1161 apta1330 depro1565 art,nn3313 2532 apta3870 ppro846 an,aj4183
2 And when he had gone over those parts, and had given them much

an,nn3056 aina2064 pre1519 art,nn1671
exhortation, he came into Greece,

5037 apta4160 nu5140 art,nn3376 (pre5259) art3588 nn2453 an,nn1917/aptm1096 ppro846
3 And *there* abode three months. And when the Jews laid*wait*for him, as

pap3195 pifm321 pre1519 art,nn4947 aom1096/an,nn1106 infg5290 pre1223 an,nn3109
he was about to sail into Syria, he purposed to return through Macedonia.

1161 ipf4902 ppro846 ad891 art,nn773 an,nn4986 an,nn961 1161
☞ 4 And there accompanied him into Asia Sopater of Berea; and of the

an,nn2331 an,nn708 2532 an,nn4580 2532 an,nn1050 an,nn1190 2532
Thessalonians, Aristarchus and Secundus; and Gaius of Derbe, and

an,nn5095 1161 an,nn774 an,nn5190 2532 an,nn5161
Timothy; and of Asia, Tychicus and Trophimus.

depro3778 apta4281 ipf3306 ppro2248 pre1722 an,nn5174
5 These going before tarried for us at Troas.

1161 epn2249 aina1602 pre575 an,nn5375 pre3326 art3588 nn2250
6 And we sailed away from Philippi after the days of

art,ajn106 2532 aina2064 pre4314 ppro846 pre1519 art,nn5174 ad891 nu4002 an,nn2250 repro3757
unleavened bread, and came unto them to Troas in five days; where we

aina1304 nu2033 an,nn2250
abode seven days.

☞ **20:1–5** See notes on 2 Timothy 4:20; 3 John 1:1.
☞ **20:4, 5** See introduction to 1 Timothy and also notes on Colossians 4:7, 10; 3 John 1:1.

Paul's Farewell Visit to Troas

¹¹⁶¹ ^{pre1722} ^{art3588} ^{nu,ajn3391}   ^{art3588} ⁿⁿ⁴⁵²¹   ^{art3588} ⁿⁿ³¹⁰¹   ^{pfpp4863}
7 And upon the first *day* of the week, when the disciples came together
^{infg2806} ^{an,nn740} ^{art,nn3972} ^{ipf1256}   ^{ppro846} ^{pap3195}   ^{pinf1826}   ^{art3588} ^{ad1887}
to break bread, Paul preached unto them, ready to depart on the morrow;
⁵⁰³⁷   ^{ipf3905}   ^{art,nn3056} ^{ad3360}   ^{an,ajn3317}
and continued his speech until midnight.

¹¹⁶¹   ^{ipf2258} ^{an,aj2425} ^{an,nn2985} ^{pre1722} ^{art3588}   ⁿⁿ⁵²⁵³   ^{repro3757}   ^{ipf2258}
8 And there were many lights in the upper chamber, where they were
^{pr/pfpp4863}
gathered together.

¹¹⁶¹   ^{ppmp2521} ^{pre1909}   ^{art,nn2376}   ^{idpro5100}   ^{an,nn3494}   ^{an,nn3686}   ^{an,nn2169}
9 And there sat in a window a certain young man named Eutychus, being
^{ppmp2702}   ^{an,aj901} ^{an,nn5258}   ^{art,nn3972} ^(pre1909) ^{cd/an,ajn4119} ^{ppmp1256}   ^{aptp2702}
fallen into a deep sleep: and as Paul was long preaching, he sunk down
^{pre575} ^{art,nn5258}   ^{aina4098} ^{ad2736}   ^{pre575} ^{art3588}   ^{ajn5152}   ²⁵³²   ^{ainp142} ^{an,aj3498}
with sleep, and fell down from the third loft, and was taken up dead.

¹¹⁶¹ ^{art,nn3972}   ^{apta2597}   ^{aina1968} ^{ppro846} ²⁵³²   ^{apta4843}   ^{aina2036}
10 And Paul went down, and fell on him, and embracing *him* said,
^{pin2350/3361}   ¹⁰⁶³ ^{ppro846} ^{art,nn5590} ^{pin2076} ^{pre1722} ^{ppro846}
Trouble*not*yourselves; for his life is in him.

¹¹⁶¹   ^{apta305}   ²⁵³²   ^{apta2806} ^{an,nn740} ²⁵³²
11 When he therefore was come*up*again, and had broken bread, and
^{aptm1089} ⁵⁰³⁷ ^{apta3656}   ^{pre1909/an,ajn2425}   ^{ad891}   ^{an,nn827}   ^{ad3779}   ^{aina1831}
eaten, and talked a long while, even till break*of*day, so he departed.

¹¹⁶¹   ^{aina71}   ^{art3588}   ⁿⁿ³⁸¹⁶   ^{pap2198}   ²⁵³²   ³⁷⁵⁶   ^{ad3357}
12 And they brought the young man alive, and were not a little
^{ainp3870}
comforted.

From Troas to Miletus

¹¹⁶¹ ^{epn2249}   ^{apta4281}   ^{pre1909} ^{art,nn4143}   ^{ainp321}   ^{pre1519} ^{art,nn789}   ^{ad1564}   ^{pap3195}
13 And we went before to ship, and sailed unto Assos, there intending
^{pinf353}   ^{art,nn3972} ¹⁰⁶³ ^{ad3779} ^{ipf2258}   ^{pr/pfpp1299}   ^{pap3195}   ^{epn846}   ^{pinf3978}
to take in Paul: for so had he appointed, minding himself to go afoot.

¹¹⁶¹ ^{ad5613}   ^{aina4820}   ^{ppro2254} ^{pre1519} ^{art,nn789}   ^{apta353/ppro846}   ^{aina2064}
14 And when he met with us at Assos, we took*him*in, and came
^{pre1519} ^{an,nn3412}
to Mitylene.

^{ad2547/apta636}   ^{aina2658} ^{art3588} ^{pap1966}   ^{ad*481}   ^{an,nn5508} ¹¹⁶¹
15 And*we*sailed*thence, and came the next *day* over against Chios; and
^{art3588} ^{an,ajn2087}   ^{aina3846}   ^{pre1519} ^{an,nn4544} ²⁵³² ^{apta3306} ^{pre1722} ^{an,nn5175}   ^{art3588}
the next *day* we arrived at Samos, and tarried at Trogyllium; and the
^{ppmp2192}   ^{aina2064} ^{pre1519} ^{an,nn3399}
next *day* we came to Miletus.

¹⁰⁶³ ^{art,nn3972}   ^{aina2919}   ^{ainf3896} ^{art,nn2181}   ³⁷⁰⁴   ^{ppro846} ^{asbm1096} ³³⁶¹
16 For Paul had determined to sail by Ephesus, because he would not

spend*the*time in Asia: for he hasted, if it were possible for him, to be

at Jerusalem the day of Pentecost.

Paul Meets With the Ephesian Elders

17 And from Miletus he sent to Ephesus, and called the elders of the church.

18 And when they were come to him, he said unto them, Ye know, from the first day that I came into Asia, after*what*manner I have been with you at all seasons,

19 Serving the Lord with all humility*of*mind, and with many tears, and temptations, which befell me by the lying*in*wait of the Jews:

20 *And* how I kept back nothing that*was*profitable *unto* you, but have showed you, and have taught you publicly, and from*house*to*house,

21 Testifying both to the Jews, and also to the Greeks, repentance toward God, and faith toward our Lord Jesus Christ.

22 And now, behold, I go bound in the spirit unto Jerusalem, not knowing the*things*that*shall*befall me there:

23 Save that the Holy Ghost witnesseth in every city, saying that bonds and afflictions abide me.

24 But none*of*these*things*move*me, neither count I my life dear unto myself, so that I might finish my course with joy, and the ministry, which I have received of the Lord Jesus, to testify the gospel of the grace of God.

25 And now, behold, I know that ye all, among whom I have gone preaching the kingdom of God, shall see my face no more.

^{pre,repro1352}   ^{pinm3143/ppro5213}   ^(pre1722) ^{art,ad4594} ^{an,nn2250} ³⁷⁵⁴ ^{epn1473}   ^{pr/an,aj2513}

26 Wherefore I take*you*to*record   this   day,   that   I   *am*   pure

^{pre575} ^{art3588} ⁿⁿ¹²⁹   ^{an,ajn3956}

from the blood of   all   *men.*

¹⁰⁶³   ³⁷⁵⁶   ^{aom5288}   ⁽³³⁶¹⁾ ^{infg312}   ^{ppro5213} ^{an,aj3956} ^{art3588}   ⁿⁿ¹⁰¹²

27 For I have not shunned to declare unto you   all   the counsel of

^{art,nn2316}

God.

^{pim4337}   ³⁷⁶⁷   ^{rxpro1438}   ²⁵³²   ^{an,aj3956} ^{art3588} ⁿⁿ⁴¹⁶⁸ ^{pre1722}

28 Take heed therefore unto yourselves, and to   all   the flock, over the

^{repro3739} ^{art3588} ^{aj40}   ^{art,nn4151}   ^{aom5087} ^{ppro5209}   ^{pr/an,nn1985}   ^{pinf4165} ^{art3588}   ⁿⁿ¹⁵⁷⁷   ^{art,nn2316}

which the Holy Ghost hath made you overseers, to feed the church of God,

^{repro3739}   ^{aom4046}   ^{pre1223}   ^{art,aj2398}   ^{an,nn129}

which he hath purchased with his own blood.

¹⁰⁶³ ^{epn1473} ^{pin1492} ^{depro5124} ³⁷⁵⁴   ^{pre3326}   ^{ppro3450}   ^{art,nn867}   ^{an,aj926}   ^{an,nn3074}

29 For   I   know this, that after my departing shall grievous wolves

^{fm1525}   ^{pre1519} ^{ppro5209} ³³⁶¹ ^{ppmp5339} ^{art3588} ⁿⁿ⁴¹⁶⁸

enter in among you, not sparing the flock.

²⁵³² ^{pre1537}   ^{ppro5216/epn846}   ^{an,nn435} ^{fm450}   ^{pap2980}   ^{pfpp1294}

30 Also of your*own*selves shall men arise, speaking perverse things, to

^{infg645}   ^{art,nn3101}   ^{ad*3694} ^{ppro846}

draw away disciples after them.

^{pre,repro1352}   ^{pim1127}   ^{pap3421}   ³⁷⁵⁴   ^{an,nn5148}

31 Therefore watch, and remember, that by the space of three years I

^{aom3973} ³⁷⁵⁶   ^{pap3560} ^{an,ajn1538} ^{nu1520} ^{an,nn3571} ²⁵³² ^{an,nn2250} ^{pre3326} ^{an,nn1144}

ceased not to warn every one night and day with tears.

²⁵³² ^{art,ad3569}   ^{an,nn80}   ^{pinm3908}   ^{ppro5209}   ^{art,nn2316} ²⁵³²   ^{art3588}   ⁿⁿ³⁰⁵⁶   ^{ppro846}

32 And now, brethren, I commend you to God, and to the word of his

^{art,nn5485}   ^{art,ppmp1410}   ^{ainf2026}   ²⁵³²   ^{ainf1325} ^{ppro5213}   ^{an,nn2817}   ^{pre1722}

grace, which*is*able to build*you*up, and to give you an inheritance among

^{an,aj3956}   ^{art,pfpp37}

all   them*which*are*sanctified.

^{aina1937}   ^{an,ajn3762} ^{an,nn694} ²²²⁸ ^{an,nn5553} ²²²⁸   ^{an,nn2441}

33 I have coveted no man's silver, or gold, or apparel.

¹¹⁶¹   ^{epn846}   ^{pin1097} ³⁷⁵⁴ ^{depro3778} ^{art,nn5495}   ^{aina5256}   ^{ppro3450}

34 Yea, ye yourselves know, that these hands have ministered unto my

^{art,nn5532}   ²⁵³²   ^{art,pap5607}   ^{pre3326} ^{ppro1700}

necessities, and to them*that*were with me.

^{aina5263}   ^{ppro5213} ^{an,ajn3956}   ³⁷⁵⁴ ^{ad3779}   ^{pap2872}   ^{pin1163}

35 I have showed you all things, how that so laboring ye ought to

^{pifm482}   ^{art3588} ^{pap770} ⁵⁰³⁷   ^{pinf3421}   ^{art3588} ⁿⁿ³⁰⁵⁶   ^{art3588} ⁿⁿ²⁹⁶² ^{an,nn2424} ³⁷⁵⁴ ^{epn848}

support the weak, and to remember the words of the Lord Jesus, how he

^{aina2036}   ^{pin2076} ^{ad3123} ^{pr/an,ajn3107}   ^{pinf1325} ²²²⁸   ^{pinf2983}

said, It is more blessed to give than to receive.

²⁵³²   ^{depro5023}   ^{apta2036}   ^{apta5087/ppro846/art,nn1119}   ^{aom4336}   ^{pre4862}

36 And when he had thus spoken, he kneeled down, and prayed with

^{ppro846} ^{an,aj3956}

them all.

¹¹⁶¹   ^{aom1096/an,aj2425/an,nn2805/an,ajn3956} ²⁵³² ^{apta1968} ^{pre1909} ^{art,nn3972} ^{art,nn5137}   ^{ipf2705}

37 And they all*wept*sore, and fell on Paul's neck, and kissed

^{ppro846}

him,

ppmp3600   ad3122   pre1909 art3588   nn3056 repro3739   plpf2046   3754   pin3195
38 Sorrowing most*of*all for the words which he spake, that they should

pinf2334 ppro848 art,nn4383   ad3765   1161   ipf4311   ppro846 pre1519 art3588 nn4143
see his face no more. And they accompanied him unto the ship.

Paul's Voyage to Jerusalem

        1161   (ad5613)   aom1096   ppro2248   aptp645 pre575 ppro846
2 1 And it came*to*pass, that after we were gotten from them,
        aifp321   aina2064   apta2113   pre1519 art,nn2972 1161
        and had launched, we came with a straight course unto Coos, and
art3588   ad1836   pre1519 art,nn4499   ad2547   pre1519 an,nn3959
the day following unto Rhodes, and*from*thence unto Patara:

        2532   apta2147   an,nn4143   pap1276   pre1519 an,nn5403   apta1910
2 And finding a ship sailing over unto Phenicia, we went aboard, and
ainp321
set forth.

        1161   apta398   art,nn2954 (2532) apta2641 ppro846   an,ajn2176
3 Now when we had discovered Cyprus, we left it on the left hand, and
ipf4126   pre1519 an,nn4947   2532   ainp2609 pre1519 an,nn5184 1063 ad1566 art3588 nn4143 ipf2258   ppmp670
sailed into Syria, and landed at Tyre: for there the ship was to unlade her
art,nn1117
burden.

        2532   apta429   art,nn3101   aina1961 ad847   nu2033 an,nn2250 repro3748 ipf3004   art,nn3972
4 And finding disciples we tarried there seven days: who said to Paul
pre1223 art3588 nn4151   3361 pinf305 pre1519   2419
through the Spirit, that he should not go up to Jerusalem.

        1161   ad3753   ppro2248   aom1096   ainf1822   art,nn2250   apta1831
5 And when we had accomplished those days, we departed and
ipf4198   an,ajn3956   pap4311/ppro2248   pre4862 an,nn1135 2532
went*our*way; and they all brought*us*on*our*way, with wives and
an,nn5043 ad2193   ad1854   art3588 nn4172 2532   apta5087/art,nn1119 pre1909 art3588   nn123
children, till we were out of the city: and we kneeled down on the shore, and
aom4336
prayed.

        2532   apta782   rcpro240   aina1910/pre1519/art,nn4143
6 And when we had taken*our*leave one*of*another, we took ship;
1161 depro1565   aina5290   pre1519/art,ajn2398
and they returned home again.

        1161   epn2249   apta1274   art,nn4144 pre575 an,nn5184   aina2658   pre1519
7 And when we had finished our course from Tyre, we came to
an,nn4424   2532 aptm782 art3588   nn80   aina3306 pre3844 ppro846 nu3391 an,nn2250
Ptolemais, and saluted the brethren, and abode with them one day.

        1161 art3588 ad1887   art,pre4012/art,nn3972   apta1831   aina2064
8 And the next day we*that*were*of*Paul's*company departed, and came
pre1519 an,nn2542   2532   apta1525 pre1519 art3588   nn3624   an,nn5376 art3588   nn2099
unto Caesarea: and we entered into the house of Philip the evangelist,
art,pap5607 pap5607   pre1537 art3588 nu,ajn2033   aina3306 pre3844 ppro846
which was was one of the seven; and abode with him.

9 And the same man had <u>four daughters, virgins, which did prophesy.</u>

(Joel 2:28)

10 And as we tarried *there* many days, there came down from Judea a certain prophet, named Agabus.

11 And when he was come unto us, he took Paul's girdle, and bound his own hands and feet, and said, Thus saith the Holy Ghost, So shall the Jews at Jerusalem bind the man that owneth this girdle, and shall deliver *him* into the hands of the Gentiles.

12 And when we heard these things, both we, and they*of*that*place, besought him not to go up to Jerusalem.

13 Then Paul answered, What mean ye to weep and to break mine heart? for I am ready not to be bound only, but also to die at Jerusalem for the name of the Lord Jesus.

14 And when he would not be persuaded, we ceased, saying, The will of the Lord be done.

15 And after those days we took*up*our*carriages, and went up to Jerusalem.

16 There went with us also *certain* of the disciples of Caesarea, and brought with them one Mnason of Cyprus, an old disciple, with whom we should lodge.

Paul Arrives In Jerusalem

17 And when we were come to Jerusalem, the brethren received us gladly.

1161 art3588 pap1966 art,nn3972 ipf1524 pre4862 ppro2254 pre4314 an,nn2385 5037 an,aj3956

18 And the *day* following Paul went in with us unto James; and all

art3588 ajn4245 aom3854

the elders were present.

2532 aptm782 ppro846 ipf1834 pre2596/nu1520/an,ajn1538 repro3739

19 And when he had saluted them, he declared particularly what things

art,nn2316 aina4160 pre1722 art3588 nn1484 pre1223 ppro848 art,nn1248

God had wrought among the Gentiles by his ministry.

1161 art3588 apta191 ipf1392 art3588 nn2962 5037 aina2036 ppro846

20 And when they heard *it,* they glorified the Lord, and said unto him,

pin2334 an,nn80 an,aj4214 an,nn3461 an,nn2453 pin1526 art,pfp4100

Thou seest, brother, how many thousands of Jews there are which believe;

2532 pin5225 an,ajn3956 pr/an,nn2207 art3588 nn3551

and they are all zealous of the law:

1161 ainp2727 pre4012 ppro675 3754 pin1321 art,aj3956 an,nn2453

21 And they are informed of thee, that thou teachest all the Jews

art3588 pre2596 art3588 nn1484 an,nn646 (pre575) an,nn3475 pap3004 ppro846 3361

which are among the Gentiles to forsake Moses, saying that they ought not

pinf4059 art,nn5043 3366 pinf4043 art3588 nn1485

to circumcise *their* children, neither to walk after the customs.

inpro5101 pin2076 3767 an,nn4128 pin1163 ad3843 ainf4095 1063

22 What is it therefore? the multitude must needs come together: for they

fm191 3754 pfi2064

will hear that thou art come.

aima4160 3767 depro5124 repro3739 pin3004 ppro4671 ppro2254 pin1526 nu5064 an,nn435

23 Do therefore this that we say to thee: We have four men which

pap2192 an,nn2171 pre1909 rxpro1438

have a vow on them;

depro5128 apta3880 aipp48 pre4862 ppro846 2532 aima1159 pre1909

24 Them take, and purify thyself with them, and be*at*charges with

ppro846 2443 asbm3587 art,nn2776 2532 an,ajn3956 asba1097 3754

them, that they may shave *their* heads: and all may know that those things,

repro3739 pfip2727 pre4012 ppro4675 pin2076 pr/an,aj3762 235 epn848

whereof they were informed concerning thee, are nothing; but *that* thou thyself

2532 pin4748 pap5442 art3588 nn3551

also walkest orderly, and keepest the law.   *(Num. 6:5,13-18,21)*

(1161) pre4012 art3588 nn1484 pfp4100 epn2249 aina1989

25 As touching the Gentiles which believe, we have written *and*

apta2919 ppro846 pinf5083 an,aj3367 an,ajn5108 1508 pifm5442

concluded that they observe no such thing, save only that they keep

ppro846 (5037) art,ajn1494 2532 art,nn129 2532 an,ajn4156

themselves from *things* offered*to*idols, and from blood, and from strangled,

2532 an,nn4202

and from fornication.

ad5119 art,nn3972 apta3880 art3588 nn435 art3588 ppmp2192 an,nn2250 aptp48 pre4862

26 Then Paul took the men, and the next day purifying himself with

ppro846 ipf1524 pre1519 art3588 nn2411 pap1229 art3588 nn1604 art3588 nn2250

them entered into the temple, to signify the accomplishment of the days of

art,nn49 ad2193 repro3739 art,nn4376 ainp4374 pre5228 an,ajn1538 nu1520 ppro846

purification, until that an offering should be offered for every one of them.

(Num. 6:2-5,13-21)

The Riot and Paul's Arrest In the Temple

₁₁₆₁ _{ad5613} _{art3588} _{nu2033} _{nn2250} _{ipf3195} _{pifm4931} _{art3588} _{nn2453}

☞ 27 And when the seven days were almost ended, the Jews which were

_{pre575} _{art,nn773} _{aptm2300} _{ppro846} _{pre1722} _{art3588} _{nn2411} _{ipf4797} _{an,aj3956} _{art3588} _{nn3793}

of Asia, when they saw him in the temple, stirred up all the people,

₂₅₃₂ _{aina1911} _{art,nn5495} _{pre1909} _{ppro846}

and laid hands on him,

_{pap2896} _{an,nn435} _{an,nn2475} _{pim997} _{pr/depro3778} _{pin2076} _{art3588} _{nn444} _{art,pap1321}

28 Crying out, Men of Israel, help: This is the man, that teacheth

_{an,ajn3956} _{ad3837} _{pre2596} _{art3588} _{nn2992} ₂₅₃₂ _{art3588} _{nn3551} ₂₅₃₂ _{depro5127} _{art,nn5117} ₅₀₃₇

all *men* every where against the people, and the law, and this place: and

_{ad2089} _{aina1521} _{an,nn1672} ₂₅₃₂ _{pre1519} _{art3588} _{nn2411} ₂₅₃₂ _{pfi2840} _{depro5126} _{art,aj40}

further brought Greeks also into the temple, and hath polluted this holy

_{an,nn5117}

place.   *(Ezek. 44:7)*

₁₀₆₃ _{ipf2258} _{pfp4308} _{pre4862} _{ppro846} _{pre1722} _{art3588} _{nn4172} _{an,nn5161}

29 (For they had seen before with him in the city Trophimus an

_{art,nn2180} _{repro3739} _{ipf3543} ₃₇₅₄ _{art,nn3972} _{aina1521} _{pre1519} _{art3588} _{nn2411}

Ephesian, whom they supposed that Paul had brought into the temple.)

₅₀₃₇ _{an,aj3650} _{art3588} _{nn4172} _{ainp2795} ₂₅₃₂ _{art3588} _{nn2992} _{aom1096/an,nn4890} ₂₅₃₂

30 And all the city was moved, and the people ran together: and they

_{aptm1949} _{art,nn3972} _{ipf1670} _{ppro846} _{ad1854} _{art3588} _{nn2411} ₂₅₃₂ _{ad2112} _{art3588} _{nn2374}

took Paul, and drew him out of the temple: and forthwith the doors were

_{ainp2808}

shut.

₁₁₆₁ _{pap2212} _{ainf615} _{ppro846} _{an,nn5334} _{aina305} _{art3588} _{nn5506}

31 And as they went about to kill him, tidings came unto the chief captain

_{art3588} _{nn4686} ₃₇₅₄ _{an,aj3650} ₂₄₁₉ _{pfip4797}

of the band, that all Jerusalem was*in*an*uproar.

_{repro3739} _{ad1824} _{apta3880} _{an,nn4757} ₂₅₃₂ _{an,nn1543} _{aina2701} _{pre1909}

32 Who immediately took soldiers and centurions, and ran down unto

_{ppro846} ₁₁₆₁ _{art3588} _{apta1492} _{art3588} _{nn5506} ₂₅₃₂ _{art3588} _{nn4757} _{aom3793}

them: and when they saw the chief captain and the soldiers, they left

_{pap5180} _{art,nn3972}

beating of Paul.

_{ad5119} _{art3588} _{nn5506} _{apta1448} _{aom1949} _{ppro846} ₂₅₃₂ _{aina2753}

33 Then the chief captain came near, and took him, and commanded *him* to

_{aifp1210} _{nu1417} _{an,nn254} ₂₅₃₂ _{ipf4441} _{pr/inpro5101} _{opt1498/302} ₂₅₃₂ _{inpro5101} _{pin2076}

be bound with two chains; and demanded who he was, and what he had

_{pfp4160}

done.

₁₁₆₁ _{an,ajn243/ipf994/an,ajn243/idpro5100} _{pre1722} _{art3588} _{nn3793} ₁₁₆₁

34 And some*cried*one*thing,*some*another, among the multitude: and

_{ppmp1410} ₃₃₆₁ _{ainf1097} _{art3588} _{ajn804} _{pre1223} _{art3588} _{nn2351} _{aina2753} _{ppro846}

when he could not know the certainty for the tumult, he commanded him to

_{pifm71} _{pre1519} _{art3588} _{nn3925}

be carried into the castle.

☞ **21:27–36** See note on 2 Timothy 4:20.

1161   ad3753   aom1096   pre1909 art3588   nn304   aina4819   ppro846   pifm941

35 And when he came upon the stairs, so*it*was, that he was borne

pre5259 art3588   nn4757   pre1223 art3588   nn970   art3588   nn3793

of the soldiers for the violence of the people.

1063   art3588   nn4128   art3588   nn2992   ipf190   pap2896   pim142

36 For the multitude of the people followed after, crying, Away with

ppro846

him.

Paul's Defense Before the Jews

5037   art,nn3972 (ipf3195)   pifm1521 pre1519 art3588   nn3925   pin3004   art3588   nn5506(1487)

37 And as Paul was to be led into the castle, he said unto the chief captain,

pin1832   ppro3427   ainf2036 (idpro5100) pre4314   ppro4571 (1161) art3588   aina5346   pin1097/ad1676

May I speak unto thee? Who said, Canst*thou*speak*Greek?

pin1488 3756 epn4771 (686)   pr/art,nn124   pre4253 depro5130 art,nn2250   art,apta387

38 Art not thou that Egyptian, which before these days madest*an*uproar,

2532   apta1806   pre1519   art3588   ajn2048   nu5070   art,nn435

and leddest out into the wilderness four thousand men that were

art,nn4607

murderers?

1161   art,nn3972 aina2036 epn1473 pin1510   an,nn444   (3303)   pr/an,nn2453   an,nn5018

39 But Paul said, I am a man *which am* a Jew of Tarsus, *a city* in

art,nn2791   an,nn4177   3756 an,aj767 an,nn4172 1161   pinm1189   ppro4675 aima2010 ppro3427   ainf2980

Cilicia, a citizen of no mean city: and, I beseech thee, suffer me to speak

pre4314 art3588   nn2992

unto the people.

1161   ppro846   apta2010   art,nn3972 pfp2476 pre1909 art3588   nn304

40 And when he had given*him*license, Paul stood on the stairs, and

aina2673   art3588   nn5495   art3588   nn2992   1161   aptm1096   an,aj4183

beckoned with the hand unto the people. And when there was made a great

an,nn4602   aina4377   art3588   aj1446   an,nn1258   pap3004

silence, he spake unto *them* in the Hebrew tongue, saying,

an,nn435   an,nn80   2532   an,nn3962   aima191   ppro3450   art,nn627

22

Men, brethren, and fathers, hear ye my defense *which I make*

ad3568   pre4314 ppro5209

now unto you.

1161   apta191   3754   ipf4377   art3588   aj1446   an,nn1258   ppro846

2 (And when they heard that he spake in the Hebrew tongue to them, they

aina3930   ad3123   an,nn2271   2532   pin5346

kept the more silence: and he saith,)

epn1473 pin1510   3303   pr/an,nn435   pr/an,nn2453 pfpp1080 pre1722   an,nn5019

3 I am verily a man *which am* a Jew, born in Tarsus, *a city* in

art,nn2791   1161   pfpp397   pre1722 depro5026 art,nn4172 pre3844 art3588   nn4228   1059   pfpp3811

Cilicia, yet brought up in this city at the feet of Gamaliel, *and* taught

pre2596　　　　　　an,nn195　　　　　　　　　an,nn3551　art3588　　aj3971　　　　pap5225　pr/an,nn2207
according to the perfect manner of the　law　of the fathers, and was zealous

art,nn2316　ad2531　epn5210　an,aj3956　pin2075　　ad4594
toward God,　as　ye　　all　are this day.

(repro3739)　　aina1377　　　depro5026　art,nn3598　ad891　　　an,nn2288　pap1195　2532　　pap3860　　pre1519
4 And I persecuted this　way　unto the death, binding and delivering into

an,nn5438　　5037　an,nn435　2532　　an,nn1135
prisons both men and women.

ad5613　　2532　　art3588　　　　　　nn749　　　　　　　　　pin3140/ppro3427　　　　　2532　　an,aj3956　　art3588
5 As　also　the　high　priest　doth　bear*me*witness,　and　　all　　the

nn4244　　　　　　pre3844　repro3739　2532　　aptm1209　　an,nn1992　pre4314　art3588　　　nn80
estate*of*the*elders: from whom also I received letters unto the brethren, and

ipf4198　pre1519　　an,nn1154　　　fpta71　(2532)　　art,pap5607　　ad1566　pfpp1210　pre1519　　　2419
went　to　Damascus, to bring　them*which*were there bound unto Jerusalem,

2443　　　　asbp5097
for to be punished.

Paul's Testimony of His Conversion

1161　　　　aom1096　　　　　　　ppro3427　　　　　ppmp4198　　　　　2532　　　　　　pap1448
6 And it came*to*pass, that, as　I　made*my*journey, and was come nigh

art,nn1154　　　pre4012　an,nn3314　　ad1810　　　　ainf4015　pre1537　art,nn3772　an,aj2425　an,nn5457
unto Damascus about noon, suddenly there shone from heaven a great light

pre4012　　ppro1691
round about me.

5037　　aina4098　pre1519　art3588　　nn1475　　2532　aina191　　an,nn5456　pap3004　　　ppro3427　4549
7 And I fell　unto　the　ground, and heard a voice saying unto me, Saul,

4549　inpro5101　　pin1377　　　　ppro3165
Saul, why persecutest thou me?

1161　epn1473　ainp611　　pr/inpro5101 pin1488　　an,nn2962　5037　　aina2036 pre4314 ppro3165 epn1473
8 And　I　answered, Who　art thou, Lord? And he said unto me,　I

pin1510 pr/an,nn2424　art,nn3480　repro3739　epn4771　pin1377
am Jesus of Nazareth, whom thou persecutest.

1161　　　art,pap5607　　pre4862 ppro1698 aom2300　3303　　art3588　nn5457　2532　aom1096　pr/an,aj1719
9 And they*that*were with　me　saw indeed the light, and were afraid;

1161　　　aina191　3756 art3588　nn5456　　art,pap2980　　ppro3427
but they heard not the voice of him*that*spake to me.

1161　　aina2036　inpro5101　　ft4160 an,nn2962　1161　art3588　nn2962 aina2036 pre4314 ppro3165 apta450
10 And I said, What shall I do, Lord? And the Lord said unto me, Arise,

pim4198 pre1519　an,nn1154　　ad2546　　　fp2980 ppro4671 pre4012　an,ajn3956　repro3739
and　go　into Damascus; and there it shall be told thee　of　all things which are

pfip5021　　ppro4671　ainf4160
appointed for thee to do.

1161　　　ad5613　　I　　　3756　ipf1689　pre575　art3588　nn1391　　depro1565　art,nn5457
11 And　when　I　could　not　see　for　the　glory　of　that　light,

ppmp5496　　pre5259　　art,pap4895　　ppro3427　aina2064　pre1519
being　led*by*the*hand　of　them*that*were*with　me,　I　came　into

an,nn1154
Damascus.

12 ¹¹⁶¹ And ^{idpro5100} one ^{an,nn367} Ananias, a devout ^{an,aj2152} man ^{an,nn435} according ^{pre2596} to the ^{art3588} law, ⁿⁿ³⁵⁵¹

having*a*good*report ^{ppmp3140} of all ^{pre5259 an,aj3956} the Jews ^{art3588 nn2453} which dwelt ^{pap2730} *there,*

13 Came ^{apta2064} unto ^{pre4314} me, ^{ppro3165} and ²⁵³² stood, ^{apta2186} and said ^{aina2036} unto me, ^{ppro3427} Brother ^{an,nn80} Saul, ⁴⁵⁴⁹

receive*thy*sight. ^{aima308} And the ^{art3588} same ^{epn846} hour ⁿⁿ⁵⁶¹⁰ I ^{epn2504} looked up ^{aina308} upon ^{pre1519} him. ^{ppro846}

14 And ¹¹⁶¹ he ^{art3588} said, ^{aina2036} The ^{art3588} God ⁿⁿ²³¹⁶ of our ^{ppro2257} fathers ^{art,nn3962} hath chosen ^{aom4400} thee, ^{ppro4571} that thou shouldest

know ^{ainf1097} his ^{ppro848} will, ^{art,nn2307} and ²⁵³² see ^{ainf1492} that Just ^{art,ajn1342} One, and ²⁵³² shouldest hear ^{ainf191} the voice ^{an,nn5456} of ^{pre1537} his ^{ppro848}

mouth. ^{art,nn4750}

15 For ³⁷⁵⁴ thou shalt be ^{fm2071} his ^{ppro846} witness ^{pr/an,nn3144} unto ^{pre4314} all ^{an,aj3956} men ^{an,nn444} of what ^{repro3739} thou hast seen ^{pfi3708}

and heard. ^{2532 aina191}

16 And ²⁵³² now ^{ad3568} why ^{inpro5101} tarriest thou? ^{pin3195} arise, ^{apta450} and be baptized, ^{aipm907} and ²⁵³² wash away ^{aipm628}

thy ^{ppro4675} sins, ^{art,nn266} calling on ^{aptm1941} the ^{art3588} name ⁿⁿ³⁶⁸⁶ of the ^{art3588} Lord. ⁿⁿ²⁹⁶²

Paul Sent to the Gentiles

17 And ¹¹⁶¹ it came*to*pass, ^{aom1096} that, when I ^{ppro3427} was come again ^{apta5290} to ^{pre1519} Jerusalem, ²⁴¹⁹

even while ²⁵³² I ^{ppro3450} prayed ^{ppmp4336} in ^{pre1722} the ^{art3588} temple, ⁿⁿ²⁴¹¹ I ^{ppro3165} was ^{aifm1096} in ^{pre1722} a trance; ^{an,nn1611}

18 And ²⁵³² saw ^{ainf1492} him ^{ppro846} saying ^{pap3004} unto me, ^{ppro3427} Make haste, ^{aima4692} and ²⁵³² get ^{aima1831} thee

quickly ^{pre1722/an,nn5034} out of ^{pre1537} Jerusalem: ²⁴¹⁹ for ¹³⁶⁰ they will not ³⁷⁵⁶ receive ^{fm3858} thy ^{ppro4675} testimony ^{art,nn3141} concerning ^{pre4012}

me. ^{ppro1700}

19 And I ^{epn2504} said, ^{aina2036} Lord, ^{an,nn2962} they ^{epn846} know ^{pinm1987} that ³⁷⁵⁴ I ^{epn1473} imprisoned ^{ipf2252/pap5439} and ²⁵³² beat ^{pap1194} in

every synagogue ^{pre2596/art,nn4864} them*that*believed ^{art,pap4100} on ^{pre1909} thee: ^{ppro4571}

20 And ²⁵³² when ^{ad3753} the ^{art3588} blood ⁿⁿ¹²⁹ of thy ^{ppro4675} martyr ^{art,nn3144} Stephen ^{an,nn4736} was shed, ^{ipf1632} I ^{epn848} also ²⁵³² was ^{ipf2252}

standing by, ^{pfp2186} and ²⁵³² consenting ^{pap4909} unto his ^{ppro848} death, ^{art,nn336} and ²⁵³² kept ^{pap5442} the ^{art3588} raiment ⁿⁿ²⁴⁴⁰ of

them*that*slew ^{art,pap337} him. ^{ppro846}

21 And ²⁵³² he said ^{aina2036} unto ^{pre4314} me, ^{ppro3165} Depart: ^{pim4198} for ³⁷⁵⁴ I ^{epn1473} will send ^{ft1821} thee ^{ppro4571} far hence ^{ad3112} unto ^{pre1519} the

Gentiles. ^{an,nn1484}

Paul Before the Roman Court

22 And they gave*him*audience unto this word, and *then* lifted up their voices, and said, Away with such a *fellow* from the earth: for it is*not*fit that he should live.

23 And as they cried out, and cast off *their* clothes, and threw dust into the air,

24 The chief captain commanded him to be brought into the castle, and bade that he should be examined by scourging; that he might know wherefore they cried*so*against him.

25 And as they bound him with thongs, Paul said unto the centurion that*stood*by, Is*it*lawful for you to scourge a man that is a Roman, and uncondemned?

26 When the centurion heard *that,* he went and told the chief captain, saying, Take heed what thou doest: for this man is a Roman.

27 Then the chief captain came, and said unto him, Tell me, art thou a Roman? He said, Yea.

28 And the chief captain answered, With a great sum obtained I this freedom. And Paul said, But I was *free* born.

29 Then straightway they departed from him which should have examined him: and the chief captain also was afraid, after he knew that he was a Roman, and because he had bound him.

30 On the morrow, because he would have known the certainty wherefore he was accused of the Jews, he loosed him from *his* bands, and commanded the chief priests and all their council to appear, and brought*Paul*down, and set him before them.

Paul Speaks to the Sanhedrin

23 1161 art,nn3972 apta816 art3588 nn4892 aina2036 an,nn435 an,nn80
And Paul, earnestly beholding the council, said, Men *and* brethren,

epn1473 pfip4176 an,aj3956 an,aj18 an,nn4893 art,nn2316 ad891 depro5026
I have lived in all good conscience before God unto this

art,nn2250
day.

1161 art3588 nn749 an,nn367 aina2004 art,pfp3936 ppro846
2 And the high priest Ananias commanded them*that*stood*by him to

pinf5180 ppro848 art3588 nn4750
smite him on the mouth.

ad5119 aina2036 art,nn3972 pre4314 ppro846 art,nn2316 pin3195 pinf5180 ppro4571 pfpp2867 an,nn5109 2532
3 Then said Paul unto him, God shall smite thee, *thou* whited wall: for

pinm2521 epn4771 pap2919 ppro3165 pre2596 art3588 nn3551 2532 pin2753 ppro3165 pip5180
sittest thou to judge me after the law, and commandest me to be smitten

pap3891
contrary*to*the*law?   (*Lev. 19:15*)

1161 art,pfp3936 aina2036 pin3058 art,nn2316 art,nn749
4 And they*that*stood*by said, Revilest thou God's high priest?

5037 aina5346 art,nn3972 ipf1492 3756 an,nn80 3754 pin2076 pr/an,nn749 1063
5 Then said Paul, I wist not, brethren, that he was the high priest: for it is

pfip1125 3756 ft2046 ad2560 an,nn758 ppro4675 art,nn2992
written, Thou shalt not speak evil of the ruler of thy people.   (*Ex. 22:28*)

1161 art,nn3972 apta1097 3754 art3588 nu1520 nn3313 pin2076 pr/an,nn4523 1161 art3588
6 But when Paul perceived that the one part were Sadducees, and the

aj2087 pr/an,nn5330 aina2896 pre1722 art3588 nn4892 an,nn435 an,nn80 epn1473 pin1510
other Pharisees, he cried out in the council, Men *and* brethren, I am a

pr/an,nn5330 pr/an,nn5207 an,nn5330 pre4012 an,nn1680 2532 an,nn386 an,ajn3498
Pharisee, the son of a Pharisee: of the hope and resurrection of the dead

epn1473 pinp2919
I am called*in*question.

1161 ppro846 depro5124 apta2980 aom1096 an,nn4714 art3588
7 And when he had so said, there arose a dissension between the

nn5330 2532 art3588 nn4523 2532 art3588 nn4128 ainp4977
Pharisees and the Sadducees: and the multitude was divided.

1063 (3303) an,nn4523 pin3004 pinf1511 3361 an,nn386 3366 an,nn32
8 For the Sadducees say that there is no resurrection, neither angel,

3383 an,nn4151 1161 an,nn5330 pin3670 art,ajn297
nor spirit: but the Pharisees confess both.

1161 aom1096 an,aj3173 an,nn2906 2532 art3588 nn1122
9 And there arose a great cry: and the scribes *that were*

art3588 nn5330 art,nn3313 apta450 ipf1264 pap3004 pin2147 an,aj3762 an,ajn2556
of the Pharisees' part arose, and strove, saying, We find no evil

pre1722 depro5129 art,nn444 1161 1487 an,nn4151 2228 an,nn32 aina2980 ppro846 3361
in this man: but if a spirit or an angel hath spoken to him, let us not

aosi2313
fight*against*God.

1161 aptm1096 an,aj4183 an,nn4714 art3588 nn5506 aptp2125
10 And when there arose a great dissension, the chief captain, fearing

3361 art,nn3972 asbp1288 pre5259 ppro846 aina2753 art3588
lest Paul should have been pulled*in*pieces of them, commanded the

<small>nn4753   apta2597   ainf726/ppro846   pre1537   an,ajn3319   ppro848   5037</small>
soldiers to go down, and to take*him*by* force from among them, and to
<small>pinf71   pre1519 art3588   nn3925</small>
bring *him* into the castle.

<small>1161   art3588   nn3571   pap1966   art3588   nn2962   apta2186   ppro846   aina2036</small>
11 And the night following the Lord stood by him, and said,
<small>pim2293   an,nn3972 1063 ad5613   aom1263 art,pre4012 ppro1700 pre1722   2419</small>
Be*of*good*cheer, Paul: for as thou hast testified of me in Jerusalem,
<small>ad3779 pin1163 ppro4571   ainf3140   2532 pre1519 an,nn4516</small>
so must thou bear witness also at Rome.

A Plot to Kill Paul

<small>1161   aptm1096 an,nn2250 idpro5100   art3588 nn2453   apta4160/an,nn4963</small>
12 And when it was day, certain of the Jews banded together, and bound*
<small>aina332/rxpro1438   pap3004   3383   ainf5315 3383 ainf4095 ad2193</small>
*themselves*under*a*curse, saying that they would neither eat nor drink till
<small>(repro3739)   asba615 art,nn3972</small>
they had killed Paul.
<small>1161   ipf2258 cd/an,aj4119   nu,ajn5062   art,pfp4160 depro5026 art,nn4945</small>
13 And they were more than forty which*had*made this conspiracy.
<small>repro3748 apta4334   art3588   nn749   2532 art,ajn4245   aina2036</small>
14 And they came to the chief priests and elders, and said, We have
<small>aina332/rxpro1438/an,nn331   aifm1089   an,ajn3367   ad2193</small>
bound*ourselves*under*a*great*curse, that we will eat nothing until
<small>(repro3739)   asba615 art,nn3972</small>
we have slain Paul.
<small>ad3568   3767   epn5210 pre4862 art3588   nn4892   aima1718   art3588   nn5506   3704</small>
15 Now therefore ye with the council signify to the chief captain that he
<small>asba2609/ppro846   pre4314 ppro5209   ad839   ad5613   pap3195   pinf1231</small>
bring*him*down unto you tomorrow, as though ye would inquire something
<small>cd/an,ajn197   art,pre4012 ppro846 1161 epn2249 pre4253 ppro846   infg1448   pin2070 pr/an,aj2092</small>
more perfectly concerning him: and we, or ever he come near, are ready to
<small>infg337 ppro846</small>
kill him.
<small>1161   an,nn3972 art,nn79 art,nn5207 apta191   art,nn1749   aptm3854</small>
16 And when Paul's sister's son heard of their lying*in*wait, he went
<small>2532   apta1525 pre1519 art3588 nn3925   aina518 art,nn3972</small>
and entered into the castle, and told Paul.
<small>1161   art,nn3972   aptm4341/nu1520/art3588/nn1543   aina5346   aima520</small>
17 Then Paul called*one*of*the*centurions*unto *him,* and said, Bring
<small>depro5126   art,nn3494   pre4314 art3588   nn5506   1063   pin2192   idpro5100   ainf518 ppro846</small>
this young man unto the chief captain: for he hath a certain thing to tell him.
<small>3767 art3588(3303) apta3880 ppro846   aina71   pre4314 art3588   nn5506   2532 pin5346</small>
18 So he took him, and brought *him* to the chief captain, and said,
<small>an,nn3972 art3588 ajn1198   aptm4341/ppro3165   aina2065   ainf71   depro5126</small>
Paul the prisoner called*me*unto *him,* and prayed me to bring this
<small>art,nn3494   pre4314 ppro4571   pap2192   idpro5100 ainf2980   ppro4671</small>
young man unto thee, who hath something to say unto thee.
<small>1161   art3588   nn5506   aptm1949 ppro848   art3588   nn5495   2532</small>
19 Then the chief captain took him by the hand, and

apta402   pre2596/an,ajn2398   ipf4441   inpro5101 pin2076 pr/repro3739   pin2192

went*with*him*aside privately, and asked him, What is that thou hast to

ainf518 ppro3427

tell me?

1161   aina2036 art3588 nn2453   aom4934   infg2065 ppro4571 3704

20 And he said, The Jews have agreed to desire thee that thou wouldest

asba2609   art,nn3972   ad839   pre1519 art3588   nn4892   ad5613   pap3195   pifm4441

bring down Paul tomorrow into the council, as though they would inquire

idpro5100   pre4012 ppro846   cd/an,ajn197

somewhat of him more perfectly.

3767   3361 epn4771 aosi3982   ppro846   1063   pin1748   ppro846 pre1537

21 But do not thou yield unto them: for there lie*in*wait for him of

ppro846 cd/an,aj4119   nu5062 an,nn435 repro3748   aina332/rxpro1438

them more than forty men, which have bound*themselves*with*an*oath, that

3383   ainf5315 3383   ainf4095 ad2193   (repro3739)   asba337   ppro846   2532   ad3568 pin1526

they will neither eat nor drink till they have killed him: and now are they

pr/an,aj2092   ppmp4327   art,nn1860   pre575   ppro4675

ready, looking for a promise from thee.

3767 art3588   nn5506   (3303)   aina630/art3588/nn3494   apta3853

22 So the chief captain then let*the*young*man* depart, and charged him,

ainf1583 an,ajn3367   3754   aina1718   depro5023   pre4314 ppro3165

See thou tell no man that thou hast showed these things to me.

2532   aptm4341   nu1417 (idpro5100)   art,nn1543   aina2036   aima2090

23 And he called unto him two centurions, saying, Make ready two

nu1250   an,nn4754   3704 asbp4198 ad*2193   an,nn2542   2532   an,nn2460   nu1440

hundred soldiers to go to Caesarea, and horsemen threescore*and*ten,

2532   an,nn1187   nu1250   pre575   an,nu,aj5154 an,nn5610   art3588   nn3571

and spearmen two hundred, at the third hour of the night;

5037   ainf3936   an,nn2934   2443   apta1913/art,nn3972

24 And provide them beasts, that they may set*Paul*on, and

asba1295   pre4314 an,nn5344 art3588   nn2232

bring*him*safe unto Felix the governor.

apta1125   an,nn1992 pap4023 depro5126   art,nn5179

25 And he wrote a letter after this manner:

an,nn2804   an,nn3079   art3588   cd/aj2903   an,nn2232   an,nn5344

26 Claudius Lysias unto the most excellent governor Felix sendeth

pinf5463

greeting.

depro5126 art,nn435   aptp4815 pre5259 art3588   nn2453   2532   pap3195   pifm337   pre5259

27 This man was taken of the Jews, and should have been killed of

ppro846   apta2186   pre4862   art,nn4753   aom1807   ppro846   apta3129   3754

them: then came I with an army, and rescued him, having understood that he

pin2076   pr/an,nn4514

was a Roman.

1161   ppmp1014   ainf1097 art3588   nn156   pre1223/repro3739   ipf1458   ppro846

28 And when I would have known the cause wherefore they accused him, I

aina2609/ppro846   pre1519 ppro848   art,nn4892

brought*him*forth into their council:

repro3739   aina2147   ppmp1458   pre4012   an,nn2213   ppro848 art,nn3551 1161

29 Whom I perceived to be accused of questions of their law, but to

pap2192 an,ajn3367   an,nn1462   pr/an,aj514   an,nn2288 2228   an,nn1199

have nothing laid*to*his*charge worthy of death or of bonds.

¹¹⁶¹ ^{aptp3377} ^{ppro3427} ^(pre5259) ^{art3588} ⁿⁿ²⁴⁵³ ^{an,nn1917/pifm3195/fifm1510} ^{pre1519} ^{art3588}

30 And when it was told me how that the Jews laid wait for the

ⁿⁿ⁴³⁵ ^{aina3992} ^{ad1824} ^{pre4314} ^{ppro4571} ^{apta3853} ^{art,nn2725}

man, I sent straightway to thee, and gave commandment to his accusers

²⁵³² ^{pinf3004} ^{pre1909} ^{ppro4675} ^{art3588} ^{pre4314} ^{ppro846} ^{pfimm4517}

also to say before thee what *they had* against him. Farewell.

³⁷⁶⁷ ⁽³³⁰³⁾ ^{art3588} ⁿⁿ⁴⁷⁵⁷ ^{pre2596} ^{art,pfpp1299} ^{ppro846} ^{apta353} ^{art,nn3972}

31 Then the soldiers, as it was commanded them, took Paul, and

^{aina71} ^{pre1223} ^{art,nn3571} ^{pre1519} ^{art,nn494}

brought *him* by night to Antipatris.

⁽¹¹⁶¹⁾ ^{art3588} ^{ad1887} ^{apta1439} ^{art3588} ⁿⁿ²⁴⁶⁰ ^{pifm4198} ^{pre4862} ^{ppro846} ^{aina5290}

32 On the morrow they left the horsemen to go with him, and returned

^{pre1519} ^{art3588} ⁿⁿ³⁹²⁵

to the castle:

^{repro3748} ^{apta1525} ^{pre1519} ^{art,nn2542} ²⁵³² ^{apta325} ^{art3588} ⁿⁿ¹⁹⁹² ^{art3588}

33 Who, when they came to Caesarea, and delivered the epistle to the

ⁿⁿ²²³² ^{aina3936} ^{art,nn3972} ²⁵³² ^{ppro846}

governor, presented Paul also before him.

¹¹⁶¹ ^{art3588} ⁿⁿ²²³² ^{apta314} ⁽²⁵³²⁾ ^{apta1905} ^{pre1537} ^{an,aj4169}

34 And when the governor had read *the letter,* he asked of what

^{an,nn1885} ^{pin2076} ²⁵³² ^{aptm4441} ³⁷⁵⁴ ^{pre575} ^{an,nn2791}

province he was. And when he understood that *he was* of Cilicia;

^{fm1251} ^{ppro4675} ^{aina5346} ^{ad3752} ^{ppro4675} ^{art,nn2725} ²⁵³² ^{asbm3854} ⁵⁰³⁷

35 I will hear thee, said he, when thine accusers are also come. And he

^{aina2753} ^{ppro846} ^{pifm5442} ^{pre1722} ^{art,nn2264} ^{art,nn4232}

commanded him to be kept in Herod's judgment hall.

In Caesarea

¹¹⁶¹ ^{pre3326} ^{nu4002} ^{an,nn2250} ^{an,nn367} ^{art3588} ⁿⁿ⁷⁴⁹ ^{aina2597} ^{pre3326} ^{art3588}

24 And after five days Ananias the high priest descended with the

^{ajn4245} ²⁵³² ^{idpro5100} ^{an,nn4489} ^{an,nn5061} ^{repro3748}

elders, and *with* a certain orator *named* Tertullus, who

^{aina1718} ^{art3588} ⁿⁿ²²³² ^{pre2596} ^{art,nn3972}

informed the governor against Paul.

¹¹⁶¹ ^{ppro846} ^{aptp2564} ^{art,nn5061} ^{aom756} ^{pinf2723} ^{pap3004}

2 And when he was called forth, Tertullus began to accuse *him,* saying,

^{pre1223} ^{ppro4675} ^{pap5177} ^{an,aj4183} ^{an,nn1515} ²⁵³² ^{an,nn2735}

Seeing that by thee we enjoy great quietness, and that very*worthy*deeds

^{ppmp1096} ^{depro5129} ^{art,nn1484} ^{pre1223} ^{art,popro4674} ^{an,nn4307}

are done unto this nation by thy providence,

^{pinm588} ⁽⁵⁰³⁷⁾ ^{ad3839} ²⁵³² ^{ad3837} ^{an,aj2903} ^{an,nn5344} ^{pre3326} ^{an,aj3956}

3 We accept *it* always, and in*all*places, most noble Felix, with all

^{an,nn2169}

thankfulness.

¹¹⁶¹ ²⁴⁴³ ^{psa1465/3361/pre1909/cd/an,ajn4119} ^{ppro4571} ^{pin3870}

4 Notwithstanding, that I be*not*further*tedious unto thee, I pray thee that

^{ppro4571} ^{ainf191} ^{ppro2257} ^{art,popro4674} ^{an,nn1932} ^{ad4935}

thou wouldest hear us of thy clemency a*few*words.

¹⁰⁶³ ^{apta2147} ^{depro5126} ^{art,nn435} ^{pr/an,nn3061} ²⁵³² ^{pap2795} ^{an,nn4714}

5 For we have found this man *a* pestilent *fellow,* and a mover of sedition

<small>an,aj3956 art3588 nn2453   art,pre2596   art3588   nn3625   5037   an,nn4414   art3588   nn139</small>
among   all   the Jews throughout the world, and a ringleader of the sect of
<small>art3588   nn3480</small>
the Nazarenes:

<small>repro3739 2532   aina3985   ainf953 art3588 nn2411 repro3739   aina2902 2532</small>
6 Who also hath gone about to profane the temple: whom we took, and
<small>aina2309   pinf2919   pre2596   art,popro2251 an,nn3551</small>
would have judged according to   our   law.

<small>1161   art3588   nn5506   an,nn3079   apta3928   pre3326 an,aj4183   an,nn970</small>
7 But the chief captain Lysias came *upon us,* and with great violence
<small>aina520   pre1537 ppro2257 art,nn5495</small>
took*him*away out of our hands,

<small>apta2753   ppro848   art,nn2725   pifm2064 pre1909 ppro4571   apta350   pre3844 repro3739</small>
8 Commanding his accusers to come unto thee: by examining   of whom
<small>epn846   fm1410   ainf1921   pre4012 an,aj3956   depro5130   repro3739 epn2249 pin2723   ppro846</small>
thyself mayest take knowledge of   all   these things, whereof we accuse him.

<small>1161 art3588 nn2453 2532   aom4934   pap5335   depro5023   pinf2192 ad3779</small>
9 And the Jews also assented, saying that these things were so.

<small>1161   art,nn3972   art3588   nn2232   apta3506   ppro846   pinf3004</small>
10 Then Paul, after that the governor had beckoned unto him to speak,
<small>pinp611   ppmp1987   ppro4571   pap5607 pre1537 an,aj4183 an,nn2094   pr/an,nn2923</small>
answered, Forasmuch as I know that thou hast been of many years a judge
<small>depro5129 art,nn1484   cd/an,ajn2115   pinm626 art,pre4012 rxpro1683</small>
unto this nation, I do the more cheerfully answer for myself:

<small>ppro4675   ppmp1410   ainf1097   3754   pin1526(ppro3427) 3756/cd/an,aj4119/2228</small>
11 Because that thou mayest understand, that there   are   yet but
<small>nu1177   an,nn2250 pre575/repro3739 aina305   pre1722   2419   fpta4352</small>
twelve days   since   I went up to Jerusalem for to worship.

<small>2532   3777   aina2147 ppro3165 pre1722 art3588   nn2411   ppmp1256   pre4314   idpro5100</small>
12 And they neither found me   in   the temple disputing with any man,
<small>2228   pap4160/an,nn1999   an,nn3793   3777   pre1722 art3588   nn4864   3777 pre2596 art3588 nn4172</small>
neither raising up the people, neither in   the synagogues, nor in   the city:

<small>3777   pinm1410   ainf3936   pre4012/repro3739   ad3568   pin2723   ppro3450</small>
13 Neither can they prove the things whereof they now accuse me.

<small>1161   depro5124   pin3670   ppro4571   3754   pre2596 art3588 nn3598   repro3739   pin3004</small>
14 But this I confess unto thee, that after the way which they call
<small>an,nn139   ad3779   pin3000   an,nn2316   art,aj3971   pap4100   an,aj3956</small>
heresy, so   worship I the God of my fathers, believing all things
<small>art,pfpp1125   pre2596 art3588 nn3551 2532   pret3588   nn4396</small>
which*are*written in the law and in the prophets:

<small>pap2192 an,nn1680   pre1519 art,nn2316 repro3739 depro3778   epn846   2532 pinm4327</small>
15 And have hope toward God, which they themselves also allow, that there
<small>pinf3195 fifm1510   an,nn386   an,ajn3498 5037   an,ajn1342 2532 an,ajn94</small>
shall be a resurrection of the dead, both of the just and unjust. *(Dan. 12:2)*

<small>1161   pre1722/depro5129   pin778   epn846   pinf2192 pre,an,ajn1275   an,nn4893</small>
16 And   herein   do I exercise myself, to have always a conscience
<small>an,aj677   pre4314 art,nn2316 2532   art,nn444</small>
void*of*offense toward God, and *toward* men.

<small>1161   pre1223 cd/an,aj4119 an,nn2094   aom3854   fpta4160 an,nn1654 pre1519 ppro3450 art,nn1484   2532</small>
17 Now after many years I came to bring alms to my nation, and
<small>an,nn4376</small>
offerings.

pre1722/repro3739 (1161) idpro5100   an,nn2453   pre575   art,nn773   aina2147   ppro3165   pfpp48   pre1722 art3588
18 Whereupon   certain Jews   from Asia found   me   purified   in   the
nn2411   3756   pre3326   an,nn3793   3761 pre3326   an,nn2351
temple, neither with multitude. nor with tumult.

repro3739   ipf1163   pinf3918   pre1909   ppro4675   2532   pinf2723
19 Who   ought   to   have   been   here   before   thee,   and   object,
idpro1536/opt2192   pre4314   ppro3165
if*they*had*aught against me.

2228   depro3778 ppro846   aima2036   idpro1536/aina2147   an,nn92
20 Or else let these same *here* say, if*they*have*found*any evil doing
pre1722 ppro1698   ppro3450 apta2476   pre1909 art3588   nn4892
in   me, while   I   stood before the council,

2228   pre4012 depro5026 nu3391 an,nn5456 repro3739   aina2896   pfp2476   pre1722 ppro846 (3754)
21 Except it be for   this one voice, that I cried standing among them,
pre4012   an,nn386   an,ajn3498 epn1473   pinp2919   pre5259 ppro5216
Touching the resurrection of the dead   I   am called*in*question by you
ad4594
this day.

1161   art,nn5344 apta191   depro5023   pfp1492/cd/an,ajn197
22 And when Felix heard these things, having*more*perfect*knowledge
art,pre4012   art,nn3598   aom306   ppro846   apta2036   ad3752 an,nn3079 art3588   nn5506
of *that* way, he deferred them, and said, When Lysias the chief captain
asba2597   fm1231   art,pre2596/ppro5209
shall come down, I will*know*the*uttmost of*your*matter.

5037   aptm1299   art,nn1543   pifm5083 art,nn3972   5037   pinf2192
23 And he commanded a centurion to keep Paul, and to let *him* have
an,nn425   2532   pinf2967 an,ajn3367   ppro846   art,ajn2398   pinf5256   2228
liberty, and that he should forbid none of his acquaintance to minister or
pifm4334   ppro846
come unto him.

Felix and Drusilla

1161   pre3326 idpro5100   an,nn2250   art,nn5344 aptm3854 pre4862 ppro848 art,nn1135   an,nn1409
24 And after certain days, when Felix came with his   wife Drusilla,
pap5607   pr/an,nn2453   aom3343   art,nn3972 2532 aina191 ppro846   pre4012   art3588 nn4102 pre1519
which was a Jewess, he sent for Paul, and heard him concerning the faith in
an,nn5547
Christ.

1161   ppro846   ppmp1256   pre4012   an,nn1343   (2532)   an,nn1466   2532   art,nn2917
25 And as he reasoned of righteousness,   temperance, and judgment
(art,pap3195)   fifm1510 art,nn5344 aptm1096/pr/an,aj1719   ainp611   pim4198   art,ad3568/pap2192
to come, Felix trembled, and answered, Go*thy*way for*this*time;
(1161)   apta3335   an,nn2540   fm3333   ppro4571
when I have a convenient season, I will call for thee.

(1161)   pap1679 (ad260) 2532   3754 an,nn5536   fp1325   ppro846 pre5259 art,nn3972 3704
26 He hoped   also that money should have been given him of Paul, that
asba3089 ppro846   pre,repro1352 (2532) ppmp3343 ppro846   cd/an,ajn4437   ipf3656
he might loose him: wherefore he sent for him the oftener, and communed
ppro846
with him.

1161   aptp4137/an,nn1333   an,nn4201   an,nn5347   aina2983/an,ajn1240/art,nn5344   5037
27 But   after*two*years   Porcius   Festus   came*into*Felix'*room: and

art,nn5344   pap2309   aifm2698 art3588 nn2453   an,nn5485   aina2641,art,nn3972 pfpp1210
Felix, willing to show the Jews a pleasure, left Paul bound.

Paul Appears Before Festus

            3767   an,nn5347   apta1910   art3588   nn1885   pre3326   nu5140 an,nn2250
25 Now when Festus was come into the province, after three days he

            aina305   pre575   an,nn2542   pre1519   an,nn2414
ascended from Caesarea to Jerusalem.

1161   art3588   nn749   2532 art3588 nu,ajn4413   art3588   nn2453   aina1718   ppro846   pre2596
2 Then the high priest and the chief of the Jews informed him against

art,nn3972 2532   ipf3870   ppro846
Paul, and besought him,

            ppmp154   an,nn5485   pre2596   ppro846   3704   asbm3343   ppro846 pre1519
3 And desired favor against him, that he would send for him to

2419   pap4160/an,nn1747 pre2596/art3588 nn3598   ainf337 ppro846
Jerusalem, laying wait in the way to kill him.

            3767 (3303) art,nn5437   ainp611   art,nn3972   pifm5083 pre1722 an,nn2542   1161
4 But   Festus answered, that Paul should be kept at Caesarea, and that

rxpro1438   pifm3195   pip1607   pre1722/an,nn5034
he himself would depart shortly *thither.*

            art3588   3767   pin5346   pre1722   ppro5213   pr/art,ajn1415
5 Let them therefore, said he, which among you are able,

apta4782   pim2723   depro5129 art,nn435   idpro1536/pin2076   an,ajn824   pre1722
go*down*with *me,* and accuse this man, if*there*be*any wickedness in

ppro846
him.

            1161   apta1304   pre1722   ppro846   cd/an,aj4119   2228   nu1176 an,nn2250
6 And when he had tarried among them more than ten days, he

apta2597   pre1519   an,nn2542   art3588   ad1887   apta2523 pre1909 art3588   nn968
went down unto Caesarea; and the next day sitting on the judgment seat

aina2753   art,nn3972   aifp71
commanded Paul to be brought.

            1161   ppro846   aptm3854 art3588 nn2453   pfp2597   pre575   an,nn2414
7 And when he was come, the Jews which came down from Jerusalem

aina4026   pap5342 an,aj4183   2532   an,aj926   an,nn157   pre2596   art,nn3972
stood*round*about, and laid many and grievous complaints against Paul,

repro3739   ipf2480   3756   ainf584
which they could not prove.

            ppro846   ppmp626   3777   pre1519   art3588 nn3551   art3588 nn2453
8 While he answered*for*himself, Neither against the law of the Jews,

3777   pre1519   art3588   nn2411   3777   pre1519   an,nn2541   aina264   idpro5100
neither against the temple, nor yet against Caesar, have I offended any thing

at all.

            1161   art,nn5347   pap2309   aifm2698 art3588 nn2453   an,nn5485   aptp611   art,nn3972
9 But Festus, willing to do   the Jews a pleasure, answered Paul, and

aina2036   pin2309   apta305   pre1519   an,nn2414   ad1563   pifm2919   pre4012   depro5130

said, Wilt thou go up to Jerusalem, and there be judged of these things

pre1909   ppro1700

before me?

1161   aina2036   art,nn3972   pin1510/pr/pfp2476   pre1909   an,nn2541   art,nn968   repro3757   ppro3165

10 Then said Paul, I stand at Caesar's judgment seat, where I

pin1163   pifm2919   an,nn2453   aina91/an,ajn3762   ad5613(2532)   epn4771   cd/an,ajn2573

ought to be judged: to the Jews have I done*no*wrong, as thou very well

pin1921

knowest.

1063   1437   (3303)   pin91   2532   pfi4238   idpro5100   an,ajn514

11 For if I be*an*offender, or have committed any thing worthy

an,nn2288   pinm3868   3756   art,ainf599   1161   1487   pin2076   an,ajn3762

of death, I refuse not to die: but if there be none of these things

repro3739   depro3778   pin2723   ppro3450   an,ajn3762   pinm1410   aifm5483   ppro3165   ppro846   pinm1941

whereof these accuse me, no man may deliver me unto them. I appeal

an,nn2541

unto Caesar.

(1161)   ad5119   art,nn5347   apta4814   pre3326 art3588   nn4824   ainp611

12 Then Festus, when he had conferred with the council, answered, Hast

pfip1941   an,nn2541   pre1909   an,nn2541   fm4198

thou appealed unto Caesar? unto Caesar shalt thou go.

Agrippa and Bernice

1161   aptm1230   idpro5100   an,nn2250 art,nn935   an,nn67   2532   an,nn959   aina2658 pre1519   an,nn2542

13 And after certain days king Agrippa and Bernice came unto Caesarea to

fptm782   art,nn5347

salute Festus.

1161   ad5613   ipf1304   ad1563   cd/an,aj4119   an,nn2250   art,nn5347   aom394

14 And when they had been there many days, Festus declared

art,pre2596/art,nn3972   art3588   nn935   pap3004   pin2076   idpro5100   an,nn435

Paul's cause unto the king, saying, There is a certain man

pr/pfpp2641/an,ajn1198   pre5259 an,nn5344

left*in*bonds by Felix:

pre4012   repro3739   ppro3450 aptm1096 pre1519   an,nn2414   art3588   nn749   2532 art3588

15 About whom, when I was at Jerusalem, the chief priests and the

ajn4245   art3588   nn2453   aina1718   ppmp154   an,nn1349   pre2596   ppro846

elders of the Jews informed me, desiring to have judgment against him.

pre4314   repro3739   ainp611   (3754)   pin2076   3756   an,nn1485   an,nn4514   pifm5483

16 To whom I answered, It is not the manner of the Romans to deliver

idpro5100   an,nn444   pre1519   an,nn684   ad4250   2228   ppmp2723   opt2192   art3588   nn2725

any man to die, before that he*which*is*accused have the accusers

pre2596/an,nn4383   5037   opt2983/an,nn5117   an,nn627   pre4012   art3588

face*to*face, and have license to answer*for*himself concerning the

nn1462

crime*laid*against*him.

3767   ppro846   apta4905   ad1759   (aptm4160)   an,aj3367   an,nn311   art3588

17 Therefore, when they were come hither, without any delay on the

ad1836   apta2523 pre1909 art3588   nn968   aina2753   art3588 nn435

morrow I sat on the judgment seat, and commanded the man to be

aifp71

brought forth.

pre4012   repro3739   art3588   nn2725   aptp2476   ipf2018   an,aj3762

18 Against whom when the accusers stood up, they brought none

an,nn156   repro3739   epn1473   ipf5282

accusation of such things as I supposed:

1161   ipf2192 idpro5100   an,nn2213   pre4314 ppro846 pre4012   art,aj2398   an,nn1175   2532

19 But had certain questions against him of their own superstition, and

pre4012 idpro5100 an,an2424   pfp2348   repro3739 art,nn3972   ipf5335   pinf2198

of one Jesus, which was dead, whom Paul affirmed to be alive.

1161   epn1473 ppmp639   pre1519   art,nn2214/pre4012/depro5127   ipf3004

20 And because I doubted of such*manner*of*questions, I asked *him*

1487   opt1014 pifm4198 pre1519   2419   ad2546   pifm2919   pre4012

whether he would go to Jerusalem, and there be judged of

depro5130

these matters.

1161   art,nn3972   aptm1941   (ppro846)   aifp5083   pre1519 art3588   nn1233

21 But when Paul had appealed to be reserved unto the hearing of

art,aj4575   aina2753   ppro846   pifm5083 ad2193   (repro3739) asba3992 ppro846 pre4314 an,nn2541

Augustus, I commanded him to be kept till I might send him to Caesar.

1161   an,nn67   aina5346 pre4314 art,nn5347   ipf1014   2532   ainf191 art3588 nn444 epn848 (1161)

22 Then Agrippa said unto Festus, I would also hear the man myself.

ad839   pin5346 art3588   fm191   ppro846

Tomorrow, said he, thou shalt hear him.

3767   art3588   ad1887   art,nn67   apta2064   2532   art,nn959   pre3326 an,aj4183

23 And on the morrow, when Agrippa was come, and Bernice, with great

an,nn5325   2532   apta1525 pre1519 art3588   nn201   pre4862(5037) art3588   nn5506

pomp, and was entered into the place*of*hearing, with the chief captains,

2532 art,pre2596/an,nn1851 an,nn435 (pap5607) art3588 nn4172 (2532) art,nn5347   apta2753   art,nn3972

and principal men of the city, at Festus' commandment Paul was

ainp71

brought forth.

2532   art,nn5347 pin5346 an,nn935   an,nn67   2532 an,aj3956 art,nn435   an,pap4840

24 And Festus said, King Agrippa, and all men which*are*here*present

ppro2254   pin2334   depro5126   pre4012 repro3739 an,aj3956 art3588   nn4128   art3588 nn2453

with us, ye see this man, about whom all the multitude of the Jews have

aina1793   ppro3427 5037 pre1722   an,nn2414   2532   ad1759 pap1916   ppro846 pinf1163

dealt with me, both at Jerusalem, and *also* here, crying that he ought

3361   pinf2198   ad3371

not to live any longer.

1161   epn1473 aptm2638   ppro846   pfin4238   an,ajn3367 pr/an,aj514   an,nn2288

25 But when I found that he had committed nothing worthy of death,

1161   depro5127 epn848   (2532) aptm1941   art,aj4575   aina2919   pinf3992

and that he himself hath appealed to Augustus, I have determined to send

ppro846

him.

pre4012 repro3739   pin2192 3756 an,ajn804/idpro5100   ainf1125   art,nn2962 pre,repro1352

26 Of whom I have no certain thing to write unto my lord. Wherefore I

aina4254/ppro846   pre1909 ppro5216   2532   ad3122   pre1909 epn4675   an,nn935

have brought*him*forth before you, and especially before thee, O king

an,nn67   3704   art,nn351   aptm1096   asba2192   idpro5100   ainf1125
Agrippa, that, after examination had, I might have somewhat to write.

1063   pin1380   ppro3427   pr/an,ajn249   pap3992   an,ajn1198   2532 3361 2532
27 For it seemeth to me unreasonable to send a prisoner, and not withal
ainf4591   art3588   nn156   pre2596   ppro846
to signify the crimes *laid* against him.

Paul Defends Himself Before Agrippa

1161   an,nn67   aina5346   pre4314   art,nn3972 ppro4671   pinp2010   pinf3004   pre5228
26 Then Agrippa said unto Paul, Thou art permitted to speak for
rxpro4572   ad5119   art,nn3972   apta1614   art3588   nn5495
thyself. Then Paul stretched forth the hand, and
ipf626
answered*for* himself:

pfip2233   rxpro1683 pr/an,aj3107 an,nn935   an,nn67   pap3195   pifm626
2 I think myself happy, king Agrippa, because I shall answer*for*myself
ad4594   pre1909   ppro4675   pre4012 an,aj3956   repro3739   pinp1458   pre5259
this day before thee touching all the things whereof I am accused of the
an,nn2453
Jews:

ad3122   (pfp1492) ppro4571   pap5607 pr/an,nn1109   an,aj3956   art,nn1485   5037(2532)
3 Especially *because I know* thee to be expert in all customs and
an,nn2213   pre2596   an,nn2453 pre,repro1352   pinm1189   ppro4675   ainf191   ppro3450
questions which are among the Jews: wherefore I beseech thee to hear me
ad3116
patiently.

ppro3450   art,nn981   (3303, 3767) art,pre1537   an,nn3503   art,aptm1096   pre575   an,nn746   pre1722
4 My manner*of*life   from my youth, which was at the first among
ppro3450   art,nn1484 pre1722   an,nn2414   pfi2467 an,aj3956 art3588 nn2453
mine own nation at Jerusalem, know all the Jews;

pap4267   ppro3165   ad509   1437   psa2309   pinf3140   3754 pre2596
5 Which knew me from*the*beginning, if they would testify, that after
art3588   cd/aj196   an,nn139   art,popro2251   an,nn2356   aina2198   an,nn5330
the most straitest sect of our religion I lived a Pharisee.

2532   ad3568   pfi2476   ppmp2919 pre1909   an,nn1680   art3588   nn1860   aptm1096 pre5259
6 And now I stand and am judged for the hope of the promise made of
art,nn2316 pre4314   art,nn3962
God unto our fathers:

pre1519   repro3739   ppro2257   art,nn1429   pre1722/an,nn1616   pap3000   an,nn2250 2532
7 Unto which *promise* our twelve tribes, instantly serving *God* day and
an,nn3571   pinp1679   ainf2658   pre4012 repro3739 an,nn1680   an,nn935   an,nn67   pinp1458   pre5259
night, hope to come. For which hope's sake, king Agrippa, I am accused of
art3588   nn2453
the Jews.

inpro5101   pinp2919   an,ajn571   pre3844 ppro5213 1487 art,nn2316
8 Why should it be thought a*thing*incredible with you, that God should
pin1453   an,ajn3498
raise the dead?

epn1473 3303(3767) aina1380 rxpro1683 pinf1163 ainf4238 an,ajn4183

9 I verily thought with myself, that I ought to do many things

an,ajn1727 pre4314 art3588 nn3686 an,nn2424 art,nn3480

contrary to the name of Jesus of Nazareth.

repro3739 2532 aina4160 pre1722 an,nn2414 2532 an,ajn4183 art3588 ajn40 epn1473

10 Which thing I also did in Jerusalem: and many of the saints did I

aina2623 an,nn5438 apta2983 art,nn1849 pre3844 art3588 nn749 5037

shut up in prison, having received authority from the chief priests; and when

ppro846 ppmp337 aina2702/an,nn5586

they were put*to*death, I gave*my*voice*against *them.*

2532 pap5097 ppro846 ad4178 pre2596/an,aj3956 art,nn4864 ipf315

11 And I punished them oft in every synagogue, and compelled *them* to

pinf987 5037 ppmp1693/ad4057 ppro846 ipf1377

blaspheme; and being*exceedingly*mad*against them, I persecuted *them*

ad2193 (2532) pre1519 art,ad1854 an,nn4172

even unto strange cities.

Paul Preaches to King Agrippa (Acts 9:1-19; 22:6-16)

pre1722/repro3739 (2532) ppmp4198 pre1519 art,nn1154 pre3326 an,nn1849 2532 an,nn2011

12 Whereupon as I went to Damascus with authority and commission

art,pre3844 art3588 nn749

from the chief priests,

an,aj3319/an,nn2250 an,nn935 aina1492 pre2596 art3588 nn3598 an,nn5457 ad3771

13 At midday, O king, I saw in the way a light from heaven,

pre5228 art3588 nn2987 art3588 nn2246 apta4034 ppro3165 2532

above the brightness of the sun, shining*round*about me and

art,ppmp4198 pre4862 ppro1698

them*which*journeyed with me.

1161 ppro2257 an,aj3956 apta2667 pre1519 art3588 nn1093 aina191

14 And when we were all fallen to the earth, I heard

an,nn5456 pap2980 pre4314 ppro3165 2532 pap3004 art3588 aj1446 an,nn1258 4549

a voice speaking unto me, and saying in the Hebrew tongue, Saul,

4549 inpro5101 pin1377 ppro3165 pr/an,ajn4642 ppro4671 pinf2979 pre4314

Saul, why persecutest thou me? *it is* hard for thee to kick against the

an,nn2759

pricks.

1161 epn1473 aina2036 pr/inpro5101 pin1488 an,nn2962 1161 art3588 aina2036 epn1473 pin1510 pr/an,nn2424

15 And I said, Who art thou, Lord? And he said, I am Jesus

repro3739 epn4771 pin1377

whom thou persecutest.

235 aima450 2532 aima2476 pre1909 ppro4675 art,nn4228 1063 ainp3700 ppro4671

16 But rise, and stand upon thy feet: for I have appeared unto thee

pre1519 depro5124 aifm4400 ppro4571 pr/an,nn5257 2532 pr/an,nn3144 5037

for this purpose, to make thee a minister and a witness both of these

repro3739 aina1492 5037 repro3739 fp3700

things which thou hast seen, and of those things in the which I will appear

ppro4671

unto thee;

ppmp1807 ppro4571 pre1537 art3588 nn2992 2532 art3588 nn1484 pre1519 repro3739

17 Delivering thee from the people, and *from* the Gentiles, unto whom

ad3568 pin649 ppro4571

now I send thee,

ainf455 ppro846 an,nn3788 infg1994 pre575 an,nn4655 pre1519 an,nn5457 2532

18 To open their eyes, *and* to turn *them* from darkness to light, and *from*

art3588 nn1849 art,nn4567 pre1909 art,nn2316 3588 ppro846 infg2983 an,nn859 an,nn266 2532

the power of Satan unto God, that they may receive forgiveness of sins, and

an,nn2819 pre1722 art3588 pfpp37 an,nn4102 art3588 pre1519 ppro1691

inheritance among them which are sanctified by faith that is in me.

(Is. 35:5; 42:7; 61:1 [Sept.])

ad3606 an,nn935 an,nn67 aom1096 3756 pr/an,aj545 art3588 aj3770

19 Whereupon, O king Agrippa, I was not disobedient unto the heavenly

an,nn3701

vision:

235 ipf518 nu,ajn4412 art3588 pre1722 an,nn1154 2532 an,nn2414 5037

20 But showed first unto them of Damascus, and at Jerusalem, and

pre1519 an,aj3956 art3588 nn5561 art,nn2449 2532 art3588 nn1484

throughout all the coasts of Judea, and *then* to the Gentiles, that they should

pinf3340 2532 pinf1994 pre1909 art,nn2316 pap4238 an,nn2041 an,aj514 art,nn3341

repent and turn to God, and do works meet for repentance.

ad*1752/depro5130 art3588 nn2453 aptm4815 ppro3165 pre1722 art3588 nn2411

21 For*these*causes the Jews caught me in the temple, and

ipf3987 aifm1315

went about to kill *me.*

3767 apta5177 an,nn1947 art,pre3844 art,nn2316 pfi2476 ad891 depro5026 art,nn2250

22 Having therefore obtained help of God, I continue unto this day,

ppmp3140 5037 an,ajn3398 2532 an,ajn3173 pap3004 an,ajn3762 ad1622

witnessing both to small and great, saying none other things than those

repro3739 (5037) art3588 nn4396 2532 an,nn3475 aina2980 pap3195 pifm1096

which the prophets and Moses did say should come:

(1487) art,nn5547 an,aj3805 (1487) an,nu,ajn4413 pre1537/an,nn386

23 That Christ should suffer, *and* that he should be the first that should rise

an,ajn3498 pin3195 pinf2605 an,nn5457 art3588 nn2992 2532 art3588 nn1484

from the dead, and should show light unto the people, and to the Gentiles.

(Is. 42:6; 49:6)

1161 ppro846 depro5023 ppmp626 art,nn5347 aina5346 an,aj3173 art,nn5456

24 And as he thus spake*for*himself, Festus said with a loud voice,

an,nn3972 pinm3105 art,aj4183 an,nn1121 pin4062 ppro4571 (pre1519) an,nn3130

Paul, thou art*beside*thyself; much learning doth make thee mad.

1161 art3588 pin5346 pinm3105/3756 an,aj2903 an,nn5347 235 pinm669

25 But he said, I am*not*mad, most noble Festus; but I speak forth the

an,nn4487 an,nn225 2532 an,nn4997

words of truth and soberness.

1063 art3588 nn935 pinm1987 pre4012 depro5130 pre4314 repro3739 2532 pin2980

26 For the king knoweth of these things, before whom also I speak

ppmp3955 1063 pinm3982 3756/idpro5100 depro5130 pinf2990

freely: for I am persuaded that none of these things are hidden from

ppro846(an,ajn3762)1063 depro5124 pin2076 3756 pr/pfpp4238 pre1722 an,nn1137

him; for this thing was not done in a corner.

an,nn935   an,nn67   pin4100   art3588   nn4396   pin1492   3754   pin4100

27 King Agrippa, believest thou the prophets? I know that thou believest.

1161   art,nn67   aina5346 pre4314 art,nn3972 pre1722/an,ajn3641   pin3982   ppro3165   aifm1096

28 Then Agrippa said unto Paul, Almost thou persuadest me to be a

pr/an,nn5546

Christian.

1161   art,nn3972 aina2036   opt2172/302   art,nn2316   3756 an,ajn3440 ppro4571   235   2532   an,aj3956

29 And Paul said, I would to God, that not only thou, but also all

art,pap191   ppro3450   ad4594   aifm1096   2532   pre1722/an,ajn3641 2532   pre1722/an,ajn4183 pr/an, aj5108 an,aj3697 epn2504

that hear me this day, were both almost, and altogether such as I

pin1510   ad3924   depro5130 art,nn1199

am, except these bonds.

2532   ppro846   depro5023   apta2036   art3588 nn935   aina450   2532   art3588   nn2232

30 And when he had thus spoken, the king rose up, and the governor,

5037 (repro3739)   an,nn959   2532   art,ppmp4775   ppro846

and   Bernice, and they*that*sat*with them:

2532   apta402   ipf2980   pre4314/rcpro240

31 And when they were gone aside, they talked between themselves,

pap3004   depro3778 art,nn444 pin4238   an,ajn3762   an,aj514   an,nn2288 2228   an,nn1199

saying, This man doeth nothing worthy of death or of bonds.

1161   aina5346   an,nn67   art,nn5347   depro3778   art,nn444   ipf1410

32 Then said Agrippa unto Festus, This man might have been

pfinp630   1487   3361   plpf1941   an,nn2541

set*at*liberty, if he had not appealed unto Caesar.

They Sail For Italy

27

1161   ad5613   ainp2912   ppro2248   infg636 pre1519 art,nn2482

And when it was determined that we should sail into Italy, they

ipf3860   (5037) art,nn3972 2532   idpro5100   an,aj2087   an,nn1202   an,nn3686

delivered   Paul and certain other prisoners unto one named

an,nn2457   an,nn1543   an,aj4575   an,nn4686

Julius, a centurion of Augustus' band.

1161   apta1910   an,nn4143   an,aj98   ainp321   pap3195   ainf4126

☞ 2 And entering into a ship of Adramyttium, we launched, meaning to sail

art3588   nn5117   pre2596 art,nn773   an,nn708   an,nn3110   an,nn2331   pap5607

by the coasts of Asia; one Aristarchus, a Macedonian of Thessalonica, being

pre4862 ppro2254

with us.

5037   art3588   ajn2087   ainp2609   pre1519   an,nn4605   5037   art,nn2457   ad5364

3 And the next day we touched at Sidon. And Julius courteously

aptm5530   art,nn3972   aina2010   aptp4198   pre4314   art,ajn5384

entreated Paul, and gave*him*liberty to go unto his friends to

ainf5177/an,nn1958

refresh himself.

☞ **27:2** See note on Colossians 4:10.

                                                          aina5284   art,nn2954
☞ 4 And*when*we*had*launched*from*thence, we sailed under Cyprus, be-
    art3588   nn417   aid1511   pr/an,aj1727
cause the winds were contrary.

        5037   apta1277   art3588 nn3989 art,pre2596 art,nn2791   2532   an,nn3828
    5 And when we had sailed over the sea   of   Cilicia and Pamphylia, we
aina2718 pre1519 an,nn3460   art,nn3073
came to Myra, *a city* of Lycia.

        ad2546   art3588   nn1543   apta2147   an,nn4143   an,aj222   pap4126 pre1519 art,nn2482
    6 And there the centurion found a ship of Alexandria sailing into Italy; and
aina1688 ppro2248 pre1519/ppro846
he put us therein.

        1161   pap1020   (pre1722) an,aj2425 an,nn2250 2532   ad3433   aptm1096
    7 And when we had sailed slowly   many days, and scarce were come
    pre2596   art,nn2834 art3588   nn417   3361   pap4330   ppro2248   aina5284   art,nn2914
over against Cnidus, the wind not suffering us, we sailed under Crete,
    pre2596   an,nn4534
over against Salmone;

        5037   ad3433   ppmp3881   ppro846 aina2064 pre1519 idpro5100 an,nn5117   ppmp2564   an,aj2570
    8 And, hardly passing it, came unto a   place which is called The fair
an,nn3040 ad1451 repro3739   ipf2258   an,nn4172   an,nn2996
havens; nigh whereunto was the city *of* Lasea.

        1161   an,aj2425   an,nn5550   aptm1230 2532   art,nn4144 pap5607 ad2235
    9 Now when much time was spent, and when sailing was now
pr/an,aj2000   (2532)   art3588 nn3521   aid3928/ad2235   art,nn3972   ipf3867
dangerous, because the fast was*now*already*past, Paul admonished *them,*

                                                              (Lev. 16:29)

        pap3004   ppro846 an,nn435   pin2334   3754   art,nn4144 pinf3195 fifm1510
    10 And said unto them, Sirs, I perceive that this voyage will be
pre3326 an,nn5196 2532 an,aj4183 an,nn2209 3756 an,ajn3440   art3588 nn5414 2532 art,nn4143 235   2532
with hurt and much damage, not only of the lading and ship, but also of
ppro2257 art,nn5590
our lives.

        1161   art3588   nn1543   ipf3982   art3588   nn2942   2532   art3588
    11 Nevertheless the centurion believed the master and the
                nn3490   ad3123 2228   art,ppmp3004   pre5259 art,nn3972
owner*of*the*ship, more than those*things*which*were*spoken by Paul.

        1161   art3588   nn3040   pap5225   pr/an,aj428   pre4314 an,nn3915   art3588
    12 And because the haven was not commodious to winter in, the
cd/ajn4119 aom5087/an,nn1012 aifp321   ad2547   ad1513   opt1410 apta2658
more part advised to depart thence also, if*by*any*means they might attain
pre1519 an,nn5045   ainf3914   an,nn3040 art,nn2914 pap991 pre2596
to Phenice, *and there* to winter; *which is* an haven of Crete, and lieth toward
    an,nn3047   2532 (pre2596)   an,nn5566
the southwest and   northwest.

☞ **27:4** The phrase, "the winds were contrary," refers to the unfavorable weather conditions that existed on the Mediterranean Sea during that time of year. The sailors brought the ship close to Cyprus in hopes that they might catch a good westerly headwind. This would have enabled them to get the ship into a harbor along the coast of Asia Minor before winter came.

The Storm

1161 an,nn3558 apta5285 apta1380 pfin2902
13 And when the south wind blew softly, supposing that they had obtained

art,nn4286 apta142/ad788 ipf3881 art,nn2914
their purpose, loosing *thence,* they sailed*close*by Crete.

1161 3756 an,ajn4183 pre3326 aina906 pre2596 ppro846 an,aj5189 an,nn417
☞ **14** But not long after there arose against it a tempestuous wind,

art,ppmp2564 an,nn2148
called Euroclydon.

1161 art3588 nn4143 aptp4884 2532 ppmp1410 3361 pinf503 art3588 nn417
15 And when the ship was caught, and could not bear up into the wind, we

apta1929/ipf5342
let*her*drive.

1161 apta5295 idpro5100 an,nn3519 ppmp2564 an,nn2802
16 And running under a certain island which is called Clauda, we

aina2480/ad3433 aifm1096/pr/an,aj4031 art3588 nn4627
had*much*work to come by the boat:

repro3739 apta142 ipf5330 an,nn996 pap5269 art3588
17 Which when they had taken up, they used helps, undergirding the

nn4143 5037 ppmp5399 3361 asba1601 pre1519 art3588 nn4950 apta5465/art,nn4632
ship; and, fearing lest they should fall into the quicksands, strake sail, and

ad3779 ipf5342
so were driven.

1161 ppro2257 ad4971 ppmp5492 art3588 ad1836
18 And we being exceedingly tossed*with*a*tempest, the next *day* they

ipf4160/an,nn1546
lightened*the*ship;

2532 art3588 nu,ajn5154 aina4496 an,nn849 art3588 nn4631 art3588
19 And the third *day* we cast out with our*own*hands the tackling of the

nn4143
ship.

1161 3383 an,nn2246 3383 an,nn798 pre1909 cd/an,aj4119 an,nn2250 pap2014 5037 3756
20 And when neither sun nor stars in many days appeared, and no

an,aj3641 an,nn5494 ppmp1945 an,aj3956 an,nn1680 ppro2248 infg4982 an,ajn3063
small tempest lay on *us,* all hope that we should be saved was then

ipf4014
taken away.

1161 (pap5225) an,aj4183 pr/an,nn776 (ad5119) art,nn3972 apta2476 pre1722 an,ajn3319 ppro848
21 But after long abstinence Paul stood forth in the midst of them,

aina2036(5599) an,nn435 ipf1163 (3303) apta3980 ppro3427 3361 pifm321
and said, Sirs, ye should have hearkened unto me, and not have loosed

pre575 art,nn2914 5037 ainf2770 depro5026 art,nn5196 2532 art,nn2209
from Crete, and to have gained this harm and loss.

2532 art,ad3569 pin3867 ppro5209 pinf2114 1063 fm2071 an,aj3762
22 And now I exhort you to be*of*good*cheer: for there shall be no

an,nn580 an,nn5590 pre1537 ppro5216 4133 art3588 nn4143
loss of *any man's* life among you, but of the ship.

☞ **27:14** The word "Euroclydon" is a half-Greek, half-Latin term that sailors used to describe the strong northeasterly wind that blew the ship off course.

23 For there stood by me this night the angel of God, whose I am, and whom I serve,

24 Saying, Fear not, Paul; thou must be brought before Caesar: and, lo, God hath given thee all them*that*sail with thee.

25 Wherefore, sirs, be*of*good*cheer: for I believe God, that it shall be   even as   it was told me.

26 Howbeit we must be cast upon a certain island.

27 But when the fourteenth night was come, as   we   were driven*up*and*down in Adria, about midnight the shipmen deemed that they drew near to some country;

28 And sounded, and found it twenty fathoms: and when they had gone*a*little*further, they sounded again, and found it fifteen fathoms.

29 Then fearing lest we should have fallen upon   rocks,   they cast four anchors out of the stern, and wished for the   day.

30 And as the shipmen were about to flee out of the ship, when they had let down the boat into the sea, under color as though they would have cast anchors out of the foreship,

31 Paul said to the centurion and to the soldiers, Except these abide in the ship, ye cannot be saved.

32 Then the soldiers cut off the ropes of the boat, and let her fall off.

33 And while the day was coming on, Paul besought *them* all to take meat, saying, This day is the fourteenth day that ye have tarried and continued fasting, having taken nothing.

34 Wherefore I pray you to take *some* meat: for this is for your health: for there shall not an hair fall from the head of any of you.

35 And when he had thus spoken, he took bread, and gave thanks to

art,nn2316   ad*1799   an,ajn3956 2532   apta2806   aom756   pinf2068

God in presence of them all: and when he had broken *it,* he began to eat.

    1161   aptm1096   an,aj3956 pr/an,aj2115   epn848 2532 aom4355   an,nn5160

36 Then were they all of*good*cheer, and they also took *some* meat.

   1161   ipf2258   art,aj3956 pre1722 art3588 nn4143   nu1250/nu1440/nu1803

37 And we were in all in the ship two*hundred*threescore*and*sixteen

an,nn5590

souls.

   1161   aptp2880/an,nn5160   ipf2893 art3588 nn4143

38 And when they had eaten enough, they lightened the ship, and

ppmp1544 art3588 nn4621 pre1519 art3588 nn2281

cast out the wheat into the sea.

Shipwreck

   1161   ad3753   aom1096 an,nn2250   ipf1921 3756 art3588 nn1093 1161   ipf2657

39 And when it was day, they knew not the land: but they discovered a

idpro5100 an,nn2859 (pap2192) an,nn123 pre1519 repro3739   ainm1011   1487

certain creek with a shore, into the which they were minded, if it

opt1410   ainf1856 art3588 nn4143

were possible, to thrust in the ship.

    2532   apta4104 art3588   nn45   ipf1439

40 And when they had taken up the anchors, they committed *themselves*

pre1519 art3588 nn2281 (ad260) apta447 art3588 nn4079 art,nn2202 2532   apta1869 art3588 nn736

unto the sea, and loosed the rudder bands, and hoisted up the mainsail to

art3588 pap4154   ipf2722 pre1519 art,nn123

the wind, and made toward shore.

   1161   apta4045   pre1519   an,nn5117   an,aj1337

41 And falling into a place where two*seas*met, they

aina2027/art3588/nn3491   2532 art3588   nn4408 (3303) apta2043   aina3306

ran*the*ship*aground; and the forepart stuck fast, and remained

pr/an,aj761   1161 art3588   nn4403   ipf3089 pre5259 art3588 nn970   art3588

unmovable, but the hinder part was broken with the violence of the

nn2949

waves.

   1161 art3588   nn4757 an,nn1012 aom1096 2443 asba615 art3588   nn1202   3361/idpro5100

42 And the soldiers' counsel was to kill the prisoners, lest*any*of*them

     apta1579   opt1309

should swim out, and escape.

   1161 art3588   nn1543 ppmp1014   ainf1295 art,nn3972 aina2967 ppro846   art,nn1013

43 But the centurion, willing to save Paul, kept them from *their* purpose;

5037   aina2753   art,ppmp1410   pinf2860   apta641   nu,ajn4413

and commanded that they*which*could swim should cast *themselves* first *into*

    pinf1826 pre1909 art,nn1093

the sea, and get to land:

    2532 art3588 ajn3062 repro3739 pre1909 an,nn4548   1161 repro3739 (3303) pre1909   (idpro5100)   art,pre575

44 And the rest, some on boards, and some on *broken pieces* of

art3588 nn4143 2532 ad3779   aom1096   aifp1295/an,ajn3956 pre1909 art,nn1093

the ship. And so it came*to*pass, that they escaped*all*safe to land.

On Malta

28 ²⁵³² And when they ^{aptp1295} were escaped, ^{ad5119} then they ^{aina1921} knew ³⁷⁵⁴ that ^{art3588} the island ⁿⁿ³⁵²⁰ was ^{pinp2564} called ^{an,nn3194} Melita.

¹¹⁶¹ And ^{art3588} the ^{ajn915} barbarous people ^{ipf3930} showed ^{ppro2254} us ³⁷⁵⁶ no ^{art,apta5177} little ^{an,nn5363} kindness: ¹⁰⁶³ for they ^{apta381} kindled ^{an,nn4443} a fire, and ^{aom4355} received ^{ppro2248} us ^{an,aj3956} every one, because ^{pre1223} of ^{art3588} the ^{pfp2186} present ^{art,nn5205} rain, ²⁵³² and because ^{pre1223} of ^{art3588} the ⁿⁿ⁵⁵⁹² cold.

3 ¹¹⁶¹ And when ^{art,nn3972} Paul ^{apta4962} had gathered ^{an,nn4128} a bundle ^{an,nn5434} of sticks, ²⁵³² and ^{apta2007} laid *them* ^{pre1909} on ^{art3588} the ⁿⁿ⁴⁴⁴³ fire, ^{apta1831} there came ^{an,nn2191} a viper ^{pre1537} out of ^{art3588} the ⁿⁿ²³²⁹ heat, ^{aina2510} and fastened ^{ppro848} on his ^{art,nn5495} hand.

4 ¹¹⁶¹ And ^{ad5613} when ^{art3588} the ^{ajn915} barbarians ^{aina1492} saw ^{art3588} the *venomous* ⁿⁿ²³⁴² beast ^{ppmp2910} hang ^{pre1537} on ^{ppro848} his ^{art,nn5495} hand, they ^{ipf3004} said ^{pre4314} among ^{rcpro240} themselves, ^{ad3843} No doubt ^{depro3778} this ^{art,nn444} man ^{pin2076} is ^{pr/an,nn5406} a murderer, ^{repro3739} whom, though ^{aptp1295} he hath escaped ^(pre1537) ^{art3588} the ⁿⁿ²²⁸¹ sea, yet ^{art,nn1349} vengeance ^{aina1439} suffereth ³⁷⁵⁶ not ^{pinf2198} to live.

☞ **5** ³⁷⁶⁷ And he ^{art3588} ⁽³³⁰³⁾ ^{apta660} shook off ^{art3588} the ⁿⁿ²³⁴² beast ^{pre1519} into ^{art3588} the ⁿⁿ⁴⁴⁴² fire, and ^{aina3958} felt ^{an,aj3762} no ^{an,ajn2556} harm.

6 ¹¹⁶¹ Howbeit they ^{art3588} ^{ipf4238} looked when ^{ppro846} he ^{pinf3195} should have ^{pifm4092} swollen, ²²²⁸ or ^{pinf2667} fallen down ^{an,aj3498} dead ^{ad869} suddenly: ¹¹⁶¹ but ^{ppro846} after they ^{pap4328} had looked a great while, ^{pre1909/an,aj4183} ²⁵³² and ^{pap2334} saw ^{an,aj3367/an,ajn824} no harm ^{ppmp1096} come ^{pre1519} to ^{ppro846} him, they ^{ppmp3328} changed*their*minds, and ^{ipf3004} said that ^{ppro846} he ^{pinf1511} was ^{pr/an,nn2316} a god.

7 ⁽¹¹⁶¹⁾ In ^{pre1722} the ^{art3588} same quarters ^{pre4012/depro1565/art,nn5117} were ^{ipf5225} possessions ^{an,nn5564} of ^{art3588} the chief man ^{nu,ajn4413} of ^{art3588} the island, ⁿⁿ³⁵²⁰ whose name ^{an,nn3686} was Publius; ^{an,nn4196} who ^{repro3739} received ^{aptm324} us, ^{ppro2248} and lodged ^{aina3579} us three ^{nu5140} days ^{an,nn2250} courteously. ^{ad5390}

8 ¹¹⁶¹ And it ^{aom1096} came*to*pass, that ^{art3588} the ⁿⁿ³⁹⁶² father ^{art,nn4196} of Publius ^{pifm2621} lay ^{ppmp4912} sick of a fever ^{an,nn4446} ²⁵³² and ^{an,nn1420} of a bloody flux: ^{pre4314} to whom ^{repro3739} ^{art,nn3972} Paul ^{apta1525} entered in, ²⁵³² and ^{aptm4336} prayed, and ^{apta2007} laid his ^{art,nn5495} hands on ^{ppro846} him, and ^{aom2390} healed ^{ppro846} him.

9 ³⁷⁶⁷ So when ^{depro5127} this ^{aptm1096} was done, ^{art,ajn3062} others ²⁵³² also, which ^{art,pap2192} had ^{an,nn769} diseases ^{pre1722} in ^{art3588} the island, ⁿⁿ³⁵²⁰ ^{ipf4334} came, ²⁵³² and were ^{ipf2323} healed:

10 Who ^{repro3739} ²⁵³² also ^{aina5092} honored ^{ppro2248} us ^{an,aj4183} with many ^{an,nn5091} honors; ²⁵³² and when we ^{ppmp321} departed, they ^{aom2007} laded *us* with ^{art,pre4314/art,nn5532} such*things*as*were*necessary.

☞ **28:5, 8** See note on 2 Timothy 4:20.

1161   pre3326   nu5140   an,nn3376   ainp321   pre1722   an,nn4143   an,aj222
11 And after three months we departed in a ship of Alexandria, which

pfp3914   pre1722 art3588 nn3520   an,ajn3902   an,nn1359
had wintered in the isle, whose sign was Castor*and*Pollux.

2532   aptp2609   pre1519   an,nn4946   aina1961   nu5140   an,nn2250
12 And landing at Syracuse, we tarried *there* three days.

ad3606   apta4022   aina2658 pre1519   an,nn4484   2532
13 And from thence we fetched*a*compass, and came to Rhegium: and

pre3326   nu3391 an,nn2250   an,nn3558   aptm1920   aina2064   an,ajn1206   pre1519   an,nn4223
after one day the south wind blew, and we came the next day to Puteoli:

repro3757   apta2147   an,nn80   ainp3870   ainf1961   pre1909   ppro846   nu2033
14 Where we found brethren, and were desired to tarry with them seven

an,nn2250 2532   ad3779   aina2064   pre1519   art,nn4516
days: and so we went toward Rome.

ad2547   art3588   nn80   apta191   art,pre4012 ppro2257   aina1831   pre1519
15 And from thence, when the brethren heard of us, they came to

an,nn529 ppro2254   ad891   an,nn675   an,nn5410   2532   an,nu5140   an,nn4999   repro3739   art,nn3972
meet us as*far*as Appii Forum, and The Three Taverns: whom when Paul

apta1492   apta2168   art,nn2316   aina2983   an,nn2294
saw, he thanked God, and took courage.

Arrival at Rome

1161   ad3753   aina2064 pre1519   an,nn4516 art3588   nn1543   aina3860   art3588   ajn1198
16 And when we came to Rome, the centurion delivered the prisoners to

art3588   nn4759   1161 art,nn3972   ainp2010   pinf3306   pre2596   rxpro1438   pre4862
the captain*of*the*guard: but Paul was suffered to dwell by himself with a

art,nn4757   pap5442 ppro846
soldier that kept him.

1161   aom1096   pre3326   nu5140   an,nn2250   art,nn3972
17 And it came*to*pass, that after three days Paul

aifm4779/art3588/pap5607/pr/nu,aj4413/art3588/nn2453   1161   ppro848   apta4905
called*the*chief*of*the*Jews*together: and when they were come together, he

ipf3004   pre4314   ppro846   an,nn435   an,nn80   epn1473   apta4160   an,ajn3762
said unto them, Men *and* brethren, though I have committed nothing

an,ajn1727   art3588   nn2992   2228   art,nn1485   art,aj3971   ainp3860   an,ajn1198
against the people, or customs of our fathers, yet twas I delivered prisoner

pre1537   an,nn2414   pre1519 art3588   nn5495   art3588   nn4514
from Jerusalem into the hands of the Romans.

repro3748   apta350   ppro3165   ipf1014   ainf630
18 Who, when they had examined me, would have let*me*go, because there

aid5225 an,aj3367   an,nn156   an,nn2288 pre1722 ppro1698
was no cause of death in me.

1161   art3588   nn2453   pap483   ainp315   aifm1941
19 But when the Jews spake against *it,* I was constrained to appeal unto

an,nn2541   3756 ad5613   pap2192 idpro5100   ainf2723   ppro3450 art,nn1484
Caesar; not that I had aught to accuse my nation of.

28:11 "Castor and Pollux" were twin brothers, the sons of the mythological god, Zeus. The "sign" mentioned in this verse was a figurehead of these two brothers on the front of the ship, which was believed to provide safety for those who traveled at sea.

^{pre1223 depro5026 art,nn156   3767}   ^{aina3870   ppro5209   ainf1492   2532}
20 For   this cause therefore have I called for you, to see *you*, and to

^{ainf4354}   ^{ad*1752}   ^{1063 art3588   nn1680   2474}   ^{pinm4029}   ^{depro5026}
speak with *you*: because that for the hope of Israel I am bound with this
^{art,nn254}
chain.

^{1161   art3588 aina2036 pre4314 ppro846 epn2249   3777}   ^{aom1209   an,nn1121   pre575   art,nn2449}
21 And they said unto him, We neither received letters out of Judea

^{pre4012}   ^{ppro4675}   ^{3777   idpro5100}   ^{art3588}   ⁿⁿ⁸⁰   ^{aptm3854 aina518 2228 aina2980}
concerning thee, neither any of the brethren that came showed or spake
^{idpro5100 an,ajn4190 pre4012 ppro4675}
any harm of thee.

¹¹⁶¹   ^{pin515}   ^{ainf191 pre3844 ppro4675 repro3739}   ^{pin5426}   ^{1063 (3303)}   ^{pre4012}
22 But we desire to hear of thee what thou thinkest: for as concerning

^{depro5026 art,nn139 ppro2254 pin2076/pr/an,ajn1110 ajn1110 3754}   ^{ad3837}   ^{pinp483}
this sect, we   know   that every where it is spoken against.

¹¹⁶¹   ^{aptm5021}   ^{ppro846}   ^{an,nn2250}   ^{aina2240 cd/an,ajn4119 pre4314 ppro846}
23 And when they had appointed him a day, there came many   to him

^{pre1519}   ^{art,nn3578}   ^{repro3739}   ^{ipf1620}   ^{ppmp1263 art3588   nn932}   ^{art,nn2316 (5037)}
into *his* lodging; to whom he expounded and testified the kingdom of God,

^{pap3982}   ^{ppro846} ^{art,pre4012} ^{art,nn2424} ⁵⁰³⁷ ^{pre575 art3588 nn3551}   ^{an,nn3475 2532}
persuading them concerning Jesus, both out of the law of Moses, and *out of*

^{art3588}   ⁿⁿ⁴³⁹⁶   ^{pre575} ^{ad4404}   ^{ad2193} ^{an,nn2073}
the prophets, from morning till evening.

²⁵³²   ^{art3588/3303}   ^{ipf3982}   ^{art,ppmp3004}   ¹¹⁶¹   ^{art3588}
24 And some   believed the* things*which*were*spoken, and some
^{ipf569}
believed not.

¹¹⁶¹   ^{pap5607/pr/an,ajn800}   ^{pre4314}   ^{rcpro240}   ^{ipf630}
25 And when they agreed not among themselves, they departed, after that
^{art,nn3972}   ^{apta2036}   ^{nu1520 an,nn4487} ^{ad2573} ^{aina2980 art3588 aj40}   ^{art,nn4151 pre1223 an,nn2268 art3588}
Paul had spoken one word, Well spake the Holy Ghost by Isaiah the
ⁿⁿ⁴³⁹⁶   ^{pre4314 ppro2257 art,nn3962}
prophet unto our fathers,

^{pap3004}   ^{aipp4198 pre4314 depro5126 art,nn2992 2532 aima2036 an,nn189}   ^{ft191 2532}
26 Saying, Go unto this people, and say, Hearing ye shall hear, and shall
^{efn3364 asba4920   2532 pap991}   ^{ft991 2532 efn3364 asba1492}
not understand; and seeing ye shall see, and not perceive:

^{1063 art3588 nn2588}   ^{depro5127 art,nn2992}   ^{ainp3975}   ²⁵³²   ^{art,nn3775}
27 For the heart of this people is waxed gross, and their ears
^{aina191/ad917}   ^{2532 ppro848 art,nn3788}   ^{aina2576 3379}   ^{asba1492}
are*dull*of*hearing, and their eyes have they closed; lest they should see with
^{art,nn3788 2532 asba191}   ^{art,nn3775 2532 asba4920}   ^{art,nn2588 2532}
their eyes, and hear with *their* ears, and understand with *their* heart, and should
^{asba1994   2532}   ^{fm2390 ppro846}
be converted, and I should heal them.   (*Is. 6:9,10*)

^{pim2077}   ^{pr/an,ajn1110}   ³⁷⁶⁷   ^{ppro5213   3754 art3588 ajn4992}   ^{art,nn2316}
28 Be it known therefore unto you, that the salvation of God is
^{ainp649}   ^{art3588 nn1484} ²⁵³²   ^{epn846}   ^{fm191}
sent unto the Gentiles, and *that* they will hear it.

(*Ps. 67:2; 98:3; Is. 40:5 [Sept.]*)

2532   ppro846   apta2036   depro5023   art3588   nn2453   aina565   pap2192
29 And when he had said these words, the Jews departed, and had

an,aj4183   an,nn4803   pre1722   rxpro1438
great reasoning among themselves.

1161   art,nn3972   aina3306   an,nn1333/an,aj3650   pre1722   an,aj2398   an,nn3410   2532
30 And Paul dwelt two*whole*years in his own hired house, and

ipf588   an,aj3956   art,ppmp1531   pre4314 ppro846
received all that*came*in unto him,

pap2784   art3588   nn932   art,nn2316 2532   pap1321   art3588   pre4012
31 Preaching the kingdom of God, and teaching those things which concern

art3588 nn2962   an,nn2424 an,nn5547   pre3326 an,aj3956   an,nn3954   ad209
the Lord Jesus Christ, with all confidence, no*man*forbidding*him.

The Epistle of Paul to the

ROMANS

The Book of Romans was written by the Apostle Paul from the city of Corinth shortly after he wrote 2 Corinthians. Since it is known that the date of his arrival in Jerusalem on his third missionary journey was A.D. 58 or 59, and that he was preparing to leave for Jerusalem (Rom. 15:25, cf. Acts 20:16), Romans is believed to have been written in the spring of A.D. 56.

Although it is commonly believed that Peter founded the church at Rome, there is very little evidence for this. In fact, the evidence does not even give us enough information to suggest who was responsible for leading the believers in Rome. It is true, however, that the dispersion of the Jews led to a multitude of synagogues being established in the midst of heathenism throughout the Roman Empire. The Apostles and many other converts to Christianity had ready access to these synagogues. During that period, the polytheistic religion of the Roman Empire was becoming increasingly unpopular, and there is a great deal of evidence that many became proselytes to Judiasm or began to worship the one true God. These were the most receptive to the message of the Gospel since they did not have the hostile predisposition of the Jews, yet were also convinced that polytheism was false.

Paul was writing to a predominently Gentile audience (Rom. 1:13). His main concerns in writing the Book of Romans were to educate the believers in the basic doctrines related to salvation (chaps. 1—8) and to help them understand the unbelief of the Jews and how they benifited from it (chaps. 9—11). He also explained general principles of the Christian life that he wanted them to be aware of and put into practice (Rom. 12:1—15:13).

Introduction

1 ^{an,nn3972   an,ajn1401   an,nn2424 an,nn5547   an,aj2822   an,nn652   pfpp873   pre1519}
Paul, a servant of Jesus Christ, called *to be* an apostle, separated unto
^{an,nn2098   an,nn2316}
the gospel of God,

^{repro3739   aom4279   pre1223 ppro848 art,nn4396   pre1722   an,aj40   an,nn1124}
2 (Which he had promised afore by his prophets in the Holy Scriptures,)

^{pre4012   ppro848 art,nn5207 an,nn2424 an,nn5547 ppro2257 art,nn2962   art3588   aptm1096 pre1537}
3 Concerning his Son Jesus Christ our Lord, which was made of the
^{an,nn4690   1138   pre2596   an,nn4561}
seed of David according to the flesh;

^{art,aptp3724   an,nn5207   an,nn2316 pre1722 an,nn1411   pre2596   an,nn4151}
4 And declared *to be* the Son of God with power, according to the spirit
^{an,nn42   pre1537   an,nn386   an,ajn3498}
of holiness, by the resurrection from the dead:

pre1223 repro3739   aina2983 an,nn5485 2532 an,nn651 pre1519 an,nn5219

5 By whom we have received grace and apostleship, for obedience to the

an,nn4102 pre1722 an,aj3956 art,nn1484 pre5228 ppro848 art,nn3686

faith among all nations, for his name;

pre1722 repro3739 pin2075 epn5210 2532 pr/an,aj2822 an,nn2424 an,nn5547

6 Among whom are ye also the called of Jesus Christ:

an,aj3956 art,pap5607 pre1722 an,nn4516 an,aj27 an,nn2316 an,aj2822 an,ajn40 an,nn5485

7 To all that be in Rome, beloved of God, called *to be* saints: Grace to

ppro5213 2532 an,nn1515 pre575 an,nn2316 ppro2257 an,nn3962 2532 an,nn2962 an,nn2424 an,nn5547

you and peace from God our Father, and the Lord Jesus Christ.

(Num. 6:25,26)

The Gentiles' Need of Righteousness

nu,ajn4412 (3303) pin2168 ppro3450 art,nn2316 pre1223 an,nn2424 an,nn5547 pre5228 ppro5216 an,aj3956 3754 ppro5216

8 First, I thank my God through Jesus Christ for you all, that your

art,nn4102 pinp2605/pre1722 art3588 an,aj3650 nn2889

faith is spoken of throughout the whole world.

1063 art,nn2316 pin2076 ppro3450 pr/art,nn3144 repro3739 pin3000 pre1722 ppro3450 art,nn4151 pre1722 art3588

9 For God is my witness, whom I serve with my spirit in the

nn2098 ppro848 art,nn5207 ad5613 ad89 pinm4160 an,nn3417 ppro5216 ad3842 pre1909

gospel of his Son, that without ceasing I make mention of you always in

ppro3450 art,nn4335

my prayers;

ppmp1189 ad1513 ad2235 ad4218

☞ 10 Making request, if*by*any*means now at length I might

fp2137 pre1722 art3588 nn2307 art,nn2316 ainf2064 pre4314 ppro5209

have*a*prosperous*journey by the will of God to come unto you.

1063 pin1971 ainf1492 ppro5209 2443 asba3330 ppro5213 idpro5100 an,aj4152 an,nn5486

11 For I long to see you, that I may impart unto you some spiritual gift,

ppro5209 aies4741

to the end ye may be established;

(1161) depro5124 pin2076 aifp4837 pre1722 ppro5213 pre1223 art3588

12 That is, that I may be comforted together with you by the

pre1722/rcpro240 nn4102 5037 epn5216 2532 epn1700

mutual faith both of you and me.

1161 pin2309 3756 pinf50/ppro5209 an,nn80 3754 ad4178

13 Now I would not have*you*ignorant, brethren, that oftentimes I

aom4388 ainf2064 pre4314 ppro5209 2532 ainp2967 ad891/art,ad1204 2443 asba2192 idpro5100

purposed to come unto you, (but was let hitherto,) that I might have some

an,nn2590 pre1722 ppro5213 2532 2532 ad2531 pre1722 art,aj3062 an,nn1484

fruit among you also, even as among other Gentiles.

pin1510 pr/an,nn3781 5037 an,nn1672 2532 an,ajn915 5037

14 I am debtor both to the Greeks, and to the Barbarians; both to the

an,ajn4680 2532 an,ajn453

wise, and to the unwise.

☞ **1:10** See note on 3 John 1:2.

^{ad3779} ^{art,pre2596/ppro1691}   ^{an,ajn4289}   ^{aifm2097}   ^{ppro5213}

15 So, as*much*as*in*me*is, I am ready to preach*the*gospel to you

^{art3588}   ^{pre1722 an,nn4516}   ²⁵³²

that are at Rome also.

¹⁰⁶³   ³⁷⁵⁶   ^{pinm1870}   ^{art3588}   ⁿⁿ²⁰⁹⁸   ^{art,nn5547} ¹⁰⁶³   ^{pin2076}   ^{pr/an,nn1411}

16 For I am not ashamed of the gospel of Christ: for it is the power of

^{an,nn2316} ^{pre1519}   ^{an,nn4991}   ^{an,aj3956}   ^{art,pap4100}   ^{an,nn2453} ^{nu,ajn4412} ²⁵³²   ⁵⁰³⁷

God unto salvation to every one that believeth; to the Jew first, and also to

^{an,nn1672}

the Greek.   *(Ps. 119:46)*

¹⁰⁶³   ^{pre1722/ppro846}   ^{an,nn1343}   ^{an,nn2316}   ^{pinm601}   ^{pre1537} ^{an,nn4102} ^{pre1519}

☞ 17 For therein is the righteousness of God revealed from faith to

^{an,nn4102 ad2531}   ^{pfip1125(1161)} ^{art3588 ajn1342}   ^{fm2198 pre1537 an,nn4102}

faith: as it is written. The just shall live by faith.   *(Hab. 2:4)*

Sin Will Be Punished

¹⁰⁶³   ^{an,nn3709}   ^{an,nn2316}   ^{pinm601}   ^{pre575}   ^{an,nn3772}   ^{pre1909}   ^{an,aj3956}

☞ 18 For the wrath of God is revealed from heaven against all

^{an,nn763}   ²⁵³²   ^{an,nn93}   ^{an,nn444}   ^{art,pap2722} ^{art3588}   ⁿⁿ²²⁵   ^{pre1722}

ungodliness and unrighteousness of men, who hold the truth in

^{an,nn93}

unrighteousness;

¹³⁶⁰   ^{art,ajn1110}   ^{art,nn2316} ^{pin2076} ^{pr/an,aj5318} ^{pre1722} ^{ppro846}

19 Because that*which*may*be*known of God is manifest in them;

^{1063 art,nn2316}   ^{aina5319}   ^{ppro846}

for God hath showed *it* unto them.

¹⁰⁶³   ^{art3588}   ^{ajn517}   ^{ppro846} ^{pre575}   ^{an,nn2937}   ^{an,nn2889}

☞ 20 For the invisible*things of him from the creation of the world are

^{pinm2529}   ^{ppmp3539}   ^{art3588}   ⁿⁿ⁴¹⁶¹   ^(5037 repro 3739)   ^{ppro848}

clearly seen, being understood by the things*that*are*made, *even* his

^{an,aj126}   ^{an,nn1411} ²⁵³² ^{an,nn2305}   ^{ppro846 aies1511}   ^{pr/an,aj379}

eternal power and Godhead; so that they are without excuse:

(Job 12:7-9; Ps. 19:1)

☞ **1:17** The expression "from faith to faith" is merely an intensive form meaning "faith alone." Remembering that Paul was a Hebrew, compare the Hebrew form for superlative adjectives, "holy of holies" and "vanity of vanities."

☞ **1:18** The expression "hold the truth in unrighteousness" does not mean that the men mentioned here actually possessed the truth but simply did not practice it. *Katechō* (2722), the verb translated "hold," is better translated in this context "hold back" or "restrain." This use of the word is also found in 2 Thessalonians 2:6, 7, where *katechō* is translated "withholdeth" and "letteth," respectively. These ungodly attempt to restrain the truth through unrighteousness.

☞ **1:20** The word translated "Godhead" is *theiótēs* (2305), which merely means "divinity," or the demonstrated power of the Godhead, not the essence and the character of the Godhead. By looking at nature, one can observe that God is indeed all-powerful, but creation does not necessarily reveal that He is an all-loving God of righteousness and justice. There is only so much of God that one can know from God's creation (Rom. 1:19). However, in order to know the essence of God as a triune Deity, one needs to receive His revelation by faith.

21 ¹³⁶⁰ Because that, when they ^{apta1097} knew ^{art,nn2316} God, they ^{aina1392} glorified *him* ³⁷⁵⁶ not ^{ad5613} as ^{an,nn2316} God,

²²²⁸ neither ^{aina2168} were thankful; ²³⁵ but ^{ainp3154} became vain ^{pre1722} in ^{ppro848} their ^{art,nn1261} imaginations, ²⁵³² and ^{ppro848} their

^{art,aj801} foolish ^{an,nn2588} heart was ^{ainp4654} darkened.

22 ^{pap5335} Professing themselves ^{pinf1511} to be ^{pr/an,aj4680} wise, they became ^{ainp3471} fools,   *(Jer. 10:14)*

23 ²⁵³² And ^{aina236} changed ^{art3588} the ⁿⁿ¹³⁹¹ glory of ^{art3588} the ^{aj862} incorruptible ^{an,nn2316} God ^{pre1722} into ^{an,nn1504} an image

^{an,nn3667} made*like*to ^{an,aj5349} corruptible ^{an,nn444} man, ²⁵³² and to ^{an,nn4071} birds, ²⁵³² and ^{an,ajn5074} fourfooted beasts, ²⁵³² and

^{an,nn2062} creeping things.   *(Deut. 4:15-19; Ps. 106:20)*

24 ^{pre,repro1352} Wherefore ^{art,nn2316} God ²⁵³² also ^{aina3860/ppro846} gave*them*up ^{pre1519} to ^{an,nn167} uncleanness ^{pre1722} through ^{art3588} the ⁿⁿ¹⁹³⁹ lusts

^{ppro848} of their own ^{art,nn2588} hearts, ^{infg818} to dishonor ^{ppro848} their own ^{art,nn4983} bodies ^{pre1722} between ^{rxpro1438} themselves:

25 ^{repro3748} Who ^{aina3337} changed ^{art3588} the ⁿⁿ²²⁵ truth ^{art,nn2316} of God ^{pre1722} into ^{art,nn5579} a lie, ²⁵³² and ^{ainp4573} worshiped ²⁵³² and

^{aina3000} served ^{art3588} the ⁿⁿ²⁹³⁷ creature ^{pre3844} more than ^{art3588} the ^{apta2936} Creator, ^{repro3739} who ^{pin2076} is ^{pr/an,aj2128} blessed ^{pre1519/art,nn165} forever.

²⁸¹ Amen.   *(Jer. 13:25; 16:19)*

26 ^{pre1223/depro5124} For*this*cause ^{art,nn2316} God ^{aina3860/ppro846} gave*them*up ^{pre1519} unto ^{an,nn819} vile ^{an,nn3806} affections: ¹⁰⁶³ for ^{5037(repro3739)} even

^{ppro848} their ^{an,nn2338} women ^{aina3337} did change ^{art3588} the ^{aj5446} natural ^{an,nn5540} use ^{pre1519} into ^{art3588} that which is ^{pre3844} against ^{an,nn5449} nature:

27 ⁵⁰³⁷ And ^{ad3668} likewise ²⁵³² also ^{art3588} the ⁿⁿ⁷³⁰ men, ^{apta863} leaving ^{art3588} the ^{aj5446} natural ^{an,nn5540} use ^{art3588} of the ^{ajn2338} woman,

^{ainp1572} burned ^{pre1722} in ^{ppro848} their ^{art,nn3715} lust ^{rcpro240/pre1519} one*toward*another; ^{an,nn730} men ^{pre1722} with ^{an,nn730} men ^{ppmp2716} working

^{art,nn808} that*which*is*unseemly, ²⁵³² and ^{pap618} receiving ^{pre1722} in ^{rxpro1438} themselves that ^{art,nn489} recompense of

^{ppro848} their ^{art,nn4106} error ^{repro3739} which was ^{ipf1163} meet.   *(Lev. 18:22; 20:13)*

28 ²⁵³² And ^{ad2531} even as they did ³⁷⁵⁶ not ^{aina1381} like ^{pinf2192} to retain ^{art,nn2316} God ^{pre1722} in *their*

^{an,nn1922} knowledge, ^{art,nn2316} God ^{aina3860/ppro846} gave*them*over ^{pre1519} to ^{an,aj96} a reprobate ^{an,nn3563} mind, ^{pinf4160} to do

^{art,pap2520/3361} those*things*which* are*not*convenient;

29 ^{pfpp4137} Being filled with ^{an,aj3956} all ^{an,nn93} unrighteousness, ^{an,nn4202} fornication, ^{an,nn4189} wickedness,

^{an,nn4124} covetousness, ^{an,nn2549} maliciousness; ^{an,aj3324} full of ^{an,nn5355} envy, ^{an,nn5408} murder, ^{an,nn2054} debate, ^{an,nn1388} deceit, ^{an,nn2550} malignity;

^{an,nn5588} whisperers,

30 ^{an,nn2637} Backbiters, ^{an,ajn2319} haters*of*God, ^{an,nn5197} despiteful, ^{an,ajn5244} proud, ^{an,ajn213} boasters, ^{an,nn2182} inventors of

^{an,ajn2556} evil things, ^{an,ajn545} disobedient to ^{an,nn1118} parents,

31 Without understanding, covenant breakers, without*natural*affection, implacable, unmerciful:

32 Who knowing the judgment of God, that they*which*commit such things are worthy of death, not only do the same, but have pleasure in them*that*do them.

God's Law

2 Therefore thou art inexcusable, O man, whosoever thou art that judgest: for wherein thou judgest another, thou condemnest thyself; for thou*that*judgest doest the same things.

2 But we are sure that the judgment of God is according to truth against them*which*commit such things.

3 And thinkest thou this, O man, that judgest them*which*do such things, and doest the same, that thou shalt escape the judgment of God?

4 Or despisest thou the riches of his goodness and forbearance and longsuffering; not knowing that the goodness of God leadeth thee to repentance?

5 But after thy hardness and impenitent heart treasurest up unto thyself wrath against the day of wrath and revelation of the righteous judgment of God;

6 Who will render to every man according to his deeds:

(Ps. 62:12; Prov. 24:12; Jer. 17:10)

7 To them who by patient continuance in well doing seek for glory and honor and immortality, eternal life:

8 But unto them that are contentious, and do*not*obey the truth, but obey unrighteousness, indignation and wrath,

an,nn2347   2532   an,nn4730   pre1909 an,aj3956 an,nn5590   an,nn444   art,ppmp2716   art,ajn2556   (5037)

9 Tribulation and anguish, upon every soul of man that doeth evil, of the

an,nn2453 nu,ajn4412 2532   an,nn1672

Jew first, and also of the Gentile;

1161   an,nn1391   an,nn5092   2532   an,nn1515   an,aj3956   art,ppmp2038   art,ajn18   (5037)

10 But glory, honor, and peace, to every man that worketh good, to the

an,nn2453 nu,ajn4412 2532   an,nn1672

Jew first, and also to the Gentile:

1063   pin2076 3756   an,nn4382   pre3844 art,nn2316

11 For there is no respect*of*persons with God.

(Deut. 10:17; 2 Chr. 19:7)

1063   an,ajn3745   aina264   ad460   2532   fm622   ad460

12 For as*many*as have sinned without law shall also perish without law:

2532   an,ajn3745   aina264 pre1722   an,nn3551   fp2919 pre1223   an,nn3551

and as*many*as have sinned in the law shall be judged by the law;

1063 3756 art3588   nn202   art3588 nn3551   pr/an,aj1342 pre3844 art,nn2316 235 art3588   nn4163

13 (For not the hearers of the law *are* just before God, but the doers of

art3588 nn3551   fp1344

the law shall be justified.

1063   ad3752   an,nn1484   art,pap2192 3361   an,nn3551 psa4160   an,nn5449   art3588

14 For when the Gentiles, which have not the law, do by nature the things

art3588 nn3551 depro3778 pap2192 3361   an,nn3551 pin1526 pr/an,nn3551   rxpro1438

contained in the law, these, having not the law, are a law unto themselves:

repro3748   pinm1731 art3588 nn2041   art3588 nn3551 an,aj1123 pre1722 ppro848 art,nn2588   ppro848

15 Which show the work of the law written in their hearts, their

art,nn4893   pap4828   2532   art,nn3053   pap2723

conscience also bearing witness, and *their* thoughts the mean while accusing

2228 2532   ppmp626   (ad*3342)   rcpro240

or else excusing   one another;)

pre1722   an,nn2250   ad3753 art,nn2316   ft2919 art3588   ajn2927   art,nn444 pre1223 an,nn2424

16 In the day when God shall judge the secrets of men by Jesus

an,nn5547   pre2596   pp ro3450 art,nn2098

Christ according to my gospel.

Obeying God's Law

aima2396   epn4771   pinm2028   pr/an,nn2453 2532   pinm1879 art3588 nn3551 2532

17 Behold, thou art called a Jew, and restest in the law, and

pinm2744   pre1722 an,nn2316

makest*thy*boast of God,

2532   pin1097   art,nn2307   2532   pin1381

18 And knowest *his* will, and approvest the*things*

art,pap1308   ppmp2727 pre1537 art3588 nn3551

that*are*more*excellent, being instructed out of the law;

5037   pfi3982   rxpro4572 pinf1511 pr/an,nn3595   an,ajn5185 pr/an,nn5457

19 And art confident that thou thyself art a guide of the blind, a light of

art3588   pre1722   an,nn4655

them which are in darkness,

pr/an,nn3810   an,ajn878   pr/an,nn1320   an,ajn3516   pap2192 art3588   nn3446

20 An instructor of the foolish, a teacher of babes, which hast the form of

art,nn1108   2532   art3588   nn225   pre1722 art3588 nn3551

knowledge and of the truth in the law.

art,pap1321/3767   an,ajn2087   pin1321   3756   rxpro4572

21 Thou*therefore*which*teachest another, teachest thou not thyself?

art,pap2784   3361   pinf2813   pin2813

thou*that*preachest a man should not steal, dost thou steal?

pap3004   3361   pinf3431

22 Thou that sayest a man should not commit adultery, dost thou

pin3431   art,ppmp948   art,nn1497   pin2416

commit adultery? thou*that*abhorrest idols, dost thou commit sacrilege?

repro3739   pinm2744   pre1722   an,nn3551   pre1223   art,nn3847   art3588 nn3551

23 Thou that makest*thy*boast of the law, through breaking the law

pin818   art,nn2316

dishonorest thou God?

1063 art3588   nn3686   art,nn2316   pinp987   pre1722   art3588   nn1484   pre1223   ppro5209

24 For the name of God is blasphemed among the Gentiles through you,

ad2531   pfip1125

as it is written.   *(Is. 52:5; Ezek. 36:20)*

1063   an,nn4061   3303   pin5623   1437   psa4238   an,nn3551   1161   1437

25 For circumcision verily profiteth, if thou keep the law: but if thou

psa5600   pr/an,nn3848   an,nn3551 ppro4675   art,nn4061   pfi1096   pr/an,nn203

be a breaker of the law, thy circumcision is made uncircumcision.

(Jer. 4:4; 9:25)

3767   1437 art3588   nn203   psa5442 art3588   nn1345   art3588 nn3551

26 Therefore if the uncircumcision keep the righteousness of the law, shall

3780 ppro848   art,nn203   fp3049   pre1519   an,nn4061

not his uncircumcision be counted for circumcision?

2532   art,nn203   pre1537   an,nn5449   pap5055 art3588   nn3551

27 And shall not uncircumcision which is by nature, if it fulfill the law,

ft2919   ppro4571   pre1223   an,nn1121 2532   an,nn4061   pr/art,nn3848   an,nn3551

judge thee, who by the letter and circumcision dost transgress the law?

1063   pin2076 3756   an,nn2453   pre1722/art,ajn5318   3761

28 For he is not a Jew, which is one outwardly; neither *is that*

art,nn4061   pre1722/art,ajn5318 pre1722   an,nn4561

circumcision, which is outward in the flesh:

235   art,nn2453   pre1722/art,ajn2927 2532   an,nn4061

29 But he *is* a Jew, which is one inwardly; and circumcision *is that* of the

an,nn2588 pre1722   an,nn4151   3756   an,nn1121 repro3739 art,nn1868   3756 pre1537 an,nn444   235

heart, in the spirit, *and* not in the letter; whose praise *is* not of men, but

pre1537 art,nn2316

of God.   *(Deut. 30:6)*

inpro5101   art,ajn4053   3767   art3588   nn2453   2228 inpro5101 art,nn5622

3 What advantage then hath the Jew? or what profit *is there* of

art,nn4061

circumcision?

an,ajn4183 (pre2596) an,aj3956   an,nn5158   nu,ajn4412 (3303)   1063   3754

2 Much   every way: chiefly, because that unto them were

ainp4100   art3588   nn3051   art,nn2316
committed the oracles of God.   *(Deut. 4:7,8; Ps. 103:7; 147:19,20)*

1063   inpro5101   1487   idpro5100   aina569   ppro848   art,nn570(3361)
3 For what if some did not believe? shall their unbelief

ft2673/art3588/nn4102/art,nn2316
make*the*faith*of*God*without*effect?

opt1096/3361   art,nn2316 pim1096 pr/an,aj227 1161 an,aj3956 an,nn444 pr/an,nn5583 ad2531
4 God forbid: yea, let God be true, but every man a liar; as it is

pfip1125   3704   asbp1344/302 pre1722 ppro4675 art,nn3056 2532
written, That thou mightest be justified in thy sayings, and mightest

asba3528   ppro4571   aies2919
overcome when thou art judged.   *(Ps. 116:11; 51:4)*

1161 1487 ppro2257   art,nn93   pin4921   an,nn1343   an,nn2316 inpro5101
5 But if our unrighteousness commend the righteousness of God, what

ft2046   art,nn2316 pr/an,aj94   art,pap2018   art,nn3709   pin3004 pre2596 an,nn444
shall we say? *Is* God unrighteous who taketh vengeance? (I speak as a man)

opt1096/3361   1893   ad4459   art,nn2316 ft2919 art3588 nn2889
6 God forbid: for then how shall God judge the world?

1063 1487 art3588 nn225   art,nn2316   aina4052   pre1722 art,popro1699 an,nn5582 pre1519
7 For if the truth of God hath more abounded through my   lie unto

ppro848 art,nn1391 inpro5101 ad2089   epn2504 pinp2919 ad5613 an,ajn268
his glory; why yet am I also judged as a sinner?

2532 3361   ad2531   pinp987   2532 ad2531 idpro5100 pin5346
8 And not *rather,* (as we be slanderously reported, and as some affirm

ppro2248 pinf3004   aosi4160 art,ajn2556 2443 art,ajn18   asba2064 repro3739 art,nn2917   pin2076
that we say,) Let us do evil, that good may come? whose damnation is

pr/an,aj1738
just.

"All Have Sinned"

inpro5101   3767   pinm4284   3756   ad3843   1063
9 What then? are*we*better *than they?* No, in*no*wise: for we have

aom4256   5037 an,nn2453 2532 an,nn1672   pinf1511 an,ain3956 pre5259 an,nn266
before proved both Jews and Gentiles, that they are   all   under sin;

ad2531   pfip1125   pin2076 3756 an,ajn1342   3761 nu,ajn1520
10 As it is written, There is none righteous, no, not one:

pin2076 3756   art,pap4920   pin2076 3756   art,pap1567
11 There is none that understandeth, there is none that*seeketh*after

art,nn2316
God.

an,ajn3956   aina1578   ad260
12 They are all gone*out*of*the*way, they are together

ainp889   pin2076 3756 pap4160 an,nn5544 (pin2076) 3756(ad2193) nu,ajn1520
become unprofitable; there is none that doeth good, no, not one.

(Ps. 14:1-3)

ppro848 art,nn2995   pfpp455 pr/an,nn5028   ppro848 art,nn1100   ipf1387
13 Their throat *is* an open sepulcher; with their tongues they have used deceit;

an,nn2447   an,nn785   pre5259 ppro848 art,nn5491
the poison of asps *is* under their lips: *(Ps. 5:9; 140:3)*

repro3739   art,nn4750   pin1073   an,nn685   2532   an,nn4088

14 Whose mouth *is* full of cursing and bitterness: *(Ps. 10:7)*

ppro848   art,nn4228   pr/an,aj3691   ainf1632   an,nn129

15 Their feet *are* swift to shed blood:

an,nn4938   2532   an,nn5004   pre1722 ppro848 art,nn3598

16 Destruction and misery *are* in their ways:

2532   an,nn3598   an,nn1515   3756   aina1097

17 And the way of peace have they not known: *(Prov. 1:16; Is. 59:7,8)*

pin2076 3756 an,nn5401   an,nn2316   ad*561   ppro848 art,nn3788

18 There is no fear of God before their eyes.   *(Ps. 36:1)*

1161   pin1492   3754   an,ajn3745   art3588 nn3551   pin3004   pin2980   art3588

☞ 19 Now we know that what*things*soever the law saith, it saith to them

pre1722 art3588 nn3551   2443   an,aj3956   an,nn4750   asbp5420   2532 an,aj3956 art3588   nn2889

who are under the law: that every mouth may be stopped, and all the world

asbm1096   pr/an,aj5267   art,nn2316

may become guilty before God.

1360   pre1537   an,nn2041   an,nn3551   3756/an,aj3956 an,nn4561

☞ 20 Therefore by the deeds of the law there shall no flesh be

fp1344   ad*1799/ppro846   1063 pre1223   an,nn3551   an,nn1922   an,nn266

justified in*his*sight: for by the law *is* the knowledge of sin.   *(Ps. 143:2)*

The Only Way of Salvation

1161   ad3570   an,nn1343   an,nn2316   ad*5565   an,nn3551   pfip5319

21 But now the righteousness of God without the law is manifested, being

ppmp3140   pre5259 art3588 nn3551 2532 art3588   nn4396

witnessed by the law and the prophets;

1161   an,nn1343   an,nn2316   pre1223 an,nn4102   an,nn2424 an,nn5547 pre1519

22 Even the righteousness of God *which is* by faith of Jesus Christ unto

an,aj3956 2532 pre1909 an,aj3956   art,pap4100   1063   pin2076 3756   an,nn1293

all and upon all them*that*believe: for there is no difference:

1063   an,ajn3956   aina264   2532   pinm5302   art3588   nn1391   art,nn2316

23 For all have sinned, and come short of the glory of God;

ppmp1344   an,nn1432   ppro848 art,nn5485   pre1223   art3588   nn629   art3588   pre1722

24 Being justified freely by his grace through the redemption that is in

an,nn5547   an,nn2424

Christ Jesus:

☞ **3:19, 20** These verses form a key conclusion in Paul's argument regarding sin and righteousness. In the previous verses, Paul has quoted the OT to demonstrate man's sinfulness (vv. 10–18). The "law" (v. 19), referring to the OT, was designed to silence all mankind under the conviction that they have nothing to say against the charge of sin. Likewise, the law was intended to convince all men of their guilt, or liability to punishment, before God.

Paul concludes that since all men are guilty, they cannot be "justified" by their own personal character or conduct (v. 20). Justification is a legal term meaning to remove the guilt (liability to punishment) of the sinner. It does not involve making one inwardly holy, but merely declares that the demands of justice have been satisfied. Hence, there is no grounds for condemnation (Rom. 8:1). Not even obedience to the law can justify one before God, Paul reasons, because the very nature of the law is to prove to man that he is sinful and deserves God's punishment. Thus, the purpose of the law is to lead man to renounce his own righteousness and trust in the imputation of Christ's righteousness as the only grounds for acceptance with God.

repro3739 art,nn2316   aom4388   pr/an,nn2435   pre1223   art,nn4102 pre1722 ppro848
25 Whom God hath set forth *to be* a propitiation through faith in his

art,nn129 pre1519/an,nn1732 ppro848   art,nn1343   pre1223 art3588   nn3929   art,nn265   pfp4266
blood, to declare his righteousness for the remission of sins that are past,

pre1722 art3588   nn463   art,nn2316
through the forbearance of God;

pre4314 an,nn1732   pre1722 art,ad3568 an,nn2540 ppro846   art,nn1343   ppro846
26 To declare, *I say,* at this time his righteousness: that he might

aies1511 pr/an,aj1342 2532   an,pap1344   art3588   pre1537/an,nn4102   an,nn2424
be just, and the justifier of him which believeth in Jesus.

ad4226   art,nn2746   3767   ainp1576   pre1223 an,aj4169 an,nn3551   art,nn2041   3780
27 Where *is* boasting then? It is excluded. By what law? of works? Nay:

235 pre1223   an,nn3551   an,nn4102
but by the law of faith.

3767   pinm3049   an,nn444   pifm1344   an,nn4102   ad*5565
28 Therefore we conclude that a man is justified by faith without the

an,nn2041   an,nn3551
deeds of the law.

(2228) art3588 nn2316   an,nn2453 an,ajn3440 (1161) 3780 2532   an,nn1484   3483
29 *Is he* the God of the Jews only? *is he* not also of the Gentiles? Yes, of

an,nn1484   2532
the Gentiles also:

1897   nu1520 art,nn2316 repro3739   ft1344   an,nn4061   pre1537 an,nn4102 2532
30 Seeing *it is* one God, which shall justify the circumcision by faith, and

an,nn203   pre1223   art,nn4102
uncircumcision through faith.   *(Deut. 6:4)*

3767   pin2673   an,nn3551   pre1223   art,nn4102   opt1096/3361   235
31 Do we then make void the law through faith? God forbid: yea, we

pin2476   an,nn3551
establish the law.

inpro5101   ft2046 3767   11   ppro2257 art,nn3962   pre2596
What shall we say then that Abraham our father, as pertaining to the

an,nn4561   pfin2147
flesh, hath found?

1063 1487   11   ainp1344 pre1537 an,nn2041   pin2192   an,nn2745 235
☞ 2 For if Abraham were justified by works, he hath *whereof* to glory; but

3756   pre4314 art,nn2316
not before God.

1063   inpro5101 pin3004 art3588   nn1124   (1161)   11   aina4100   art,nn2316 2532
3 For what saith the Scripture? Abraham believed God, and it was

ainp3049   ppro846 pre1519   an,nn1343
counted unto him for righteousness.   *(Gen. 15:6)*

1161   art,ppmp2038   art3588 nn3408   3756 pinp3049   pre2596 an,nn5485 235
4 Now to him*that*worketh is the reward not reckoned of grace, but

pre2596 art,nn3783
of debt.

☞ **4:2, 5, 8** See note on Romans 3:19, 20.

₁₁₆₁ _{art,ppmp2038} ₃₃₆₁ ₁₁₆₁ _{pap4100} _{pre1909} _{art,pap1344} _{art3588}

☞ 5 But to him*that*worketh not, but believeth on him*that*justifieth the

_{ajn765} _{ppro848 art,nn4102} _{pinp3049} _{pre1519} _{an,nn1343}

ungodly, his faith is counted for righteousness.

_{ad2509} ₁₁₃₈ ₂₅₃₂ _{pin3004} _{art3588} _{nn3108} _{art3588} _{nn444} _{repro3739}

6 Even as David also describeth the blessedness of the man, unto whom

_{art,nn2316} _{pinm3049} _{an,nn1343} _{ad*5565} _{an,nn2041}

God imputeth righteousness without works,

_{pr/an,aj3107} _{repro3739} _{art,nn458} _{ainp863} ₂₅₃₂ _{repro3739 art,nn266}

7 *Saying,* Blessed *are* they whose iniquities are forgiven, and whose sins

_{ainp1943}

are covered.

_{pr/an,aj3107} _{an,nn435} _{repro3739} _{an,nn2962} _{efn3364} _{fm3049} _{an,nn266}

☞ 8 Blessed *is* the man to whom the Lord will not impute sin.   *(Ps. 32:1,2)*

_{depro3778} _{art,nn3107} ₃₇₆₇ _{pre1909 art3588} _{nn4061} _{2228 pre1909 art3588}

9 *Cometh* this blessedness then upon the circumcision *only,* or upon the

_{nn203} ₂₅₃₂ ₁₀₆₃ _{pin3004} ₃₇₅₄ _{art,nn4102} _{ainp3049} ₁₁ _{pre1519}

uncircumcision also? for we say that faith was reckoned to Abraham for

_{an,nn1343}

righteousness.   *(Gen. 15:6)*

_{ad4459} ₃₇₆₇ _{ainp3049} _{pap5607 pre1722} _{an,nn4061} _{2228 pre1722}

10 How was it then reckoned? when he was in circumcision, or in

_{an,nn203} _{3756 pre1722} _{an,nn4061} _{235 pre1722} _{an,nn203}

uncircumcision? Not in circumcision, but in uncircumcision.

₂₅₃₂ _{aina2983} _{an,nn4592} _{an,nn4061} _{an,nn4973} _{art3588} _{nn1343}

11 And he received the sign of circumcision, a seal of the righteousness

_{art3588} _{nn4102} _{art3588} _{pre1722/art,nn203} _{ppro846} _{aies1511}

of the faith which *he had yet* being uncircumcised: that he might be the

_{pr/an,nn3962} _{an,aj3956} _{art,pap4100} _{pre1223/an,nn203}

father of all them*that*believe, though they be*not*circumcised; that

_{art,nn1343} _{aies3049} _{ppro846} ₂₅₃₂

righteousness might be imputed unto them also: *(Gen. 17:10,11)*

₂₅₃₂ _{an,nn3962} _{an,nn4061} _{art3588} ₃₇₅₆ _{pre1537}

12 And the father of circumcision to them who are not of the

_{an,nn4061} _{an,aj3440 235} _{art,pap4748/2532} _{art3588} _{nn2487} _{art,nn4102} _{ppro2257 art,nn3962}

circumcision only, but who*also*walk in the steps of that faith of our father

₁₁ _{pre1722/art,nn203}

Abraham, which *he had* being*yet*uncircumcised.

God's Promise to Abraham

₁₀₆₃ _{art3588} _{nn1860} _{ppro846} _{pinf1511 art3588 pr/nn2818} _{art3588} _{nn2889} ₃₇₅₆

13 For the promise, that he should be the heir of the world, *was* not

₁₁ ₂₂₂₈ _{ppro848 art,nn4690} _{pre1223} _{an,nn3551} ₂₃₅ _{pre1223} _{an,nn1343}

to Abraham, or to his seed, through the law, but through the righteousness

_{an,nn4102}

of faith.   *(Gen. 17:4-9)*

14 For if they which are of the law *be* heirs, faith is made void, and the promise made*of*none*effect:

15 Because the law worketh wrath: for where no law is, *there is* no transgression.

16 Therefore *it is* of faith, that *it might be* by grace; to the end the promise might be sure to all the seed; not to that only which is of the law, but to that also which is of the faith of Abraham; who is the father of us all,

17 (As it is written, I have made thee a father of many nations,) before him whom he believed, *even* God, who quickeneth the dead, and calleth those*things*which*be not as though they were. *(Gen. 17:5; Is. 48:13)*

18 Who against hope believed in hope, that he might become the father of many nations, according to that*which*was*spoken, So shall thy seed be. *(Gen. 15:5)*

19 And being*not*weak in faith, he considered not his own body now dead, when he was about a*hundred*years*old, neither yet the deadness of Sarah's womb: *(Gen. 17:17)*

20 He staggered not at the promise of God through unbelief; but was strong in faith, giving glory to God;

21 And being fully persuaded that, what he had promised, he was able also to perform.

22 And therefore it was imputed to him for righteousness. *(Gen. 15:6)*

23 Now it was not written for*his*sake alone, that it was imputed to him;

24 But for us also, to whom it shall be imputed, if we believe on him*that*raised*up Jesus our Lord from the dead;

repro3739   ainp3860   pre1223 ppro2257   art,nn3900   2532   ainp1453   pre1223 ppro2257

25 Who was delivered for our offences, and was raised again for our

art,nn1347

justification.

(Is. 53:4,5)

The Results of Justification

5 3767   aptp1344 pre1537 an,nn4102   pin2192 an,nn1515 pre4314 art,nn2316   pre1223

Therefore being justified by faith, we have peace with God through

ppro2257 art,nn2962 an,nn2424 an,nn5547

our Lord Jesus Christ:

pre1223 repro3739   2532   pfi2192   art,nn4318   art,nn4102 pre1519 depro5026 art,nn5485 pre1722/repro3739

2 By whom also we have access by faith into this grace wherein we

pfi2476   2532 pinm2744 pre1909 an,nn1680 art3588 nn1391 art,nn2316

stand, and rejoice in hope of the glory of God.

1161   3756 an,ajn3440   235   pinm2744 pre1722 art,nn2347   2532   pfp1492   3754

3 And not only so, but we glory in tribulations also: knowing that

art,nn2347   pinm2716 an,nn5281

tribulation worketh patience;

1161   art,nn5281   an,nn1382   1161   art,nn1382 an,nn1680

4 And patience, experience; and experience, hope:

1161 art,nn1680   pin2617/3756   3754 art3588   nn26   art,nn2316

5 And hope maketh*not*ashamed; because the love of God is

pfip1632   pre1722 ppro2257 art,nn2588 pre1223 an,aj40 an,nn4151 art,aptp1325   ppro2254

shed abroad in our hearts by the Holy Ghost which*is*given unto us.

(Ps. 25:20)

1063   ppro2257 pap5607 ad2089   pr/an,aj772   pre2596 an,nn2540 an,nn5547 aina599

6 For when we were yet without strength, in due time Christ died

pre5228   an,ajn765

for the ungodly.

1063   ad3433   pre5228   an,ajn1342   idpro5100 fm599 1063   ad5029   pre5228

7 For scarcely for a righteous man will one die: yet peradventure for a

art,ajn18 idpro5100   2532 pin5111 ainf599

good man some would even dare to die.

1161 art,nn2316   pin4921 rxpro1438 art,nn26 pre1519 ppro2248 3754   ppro2257 pap5607

8 But God commendeth his love toward us, in that, while we were

ad2089 pr/an,ajn268 an,nn5547 aina599 pre5228 ppro2257

yet sinners, Christ died for us.

an,aj4183 ad3123   3767   ad3568 aptp1344 pre1722 ppro848 art,nn129   fp4982

9 Much more then, being now justified by his blood, we shall be saved

pre575 art,nn3709 pre1223 ppro846

from wrath through him.

1063 1487   pap5607 pr/an,ajn2190   ainp2644 art,nn2316 pre1223 art3588

10 For if, when we were enemies, we were reconciled to God by the

nn2288 ppro848 art,nn5207 an,aj4183 ad3123   aptp2644   fp4982 pre1722 ppro848

death of his Son, much more, being reconciled, we shall be saved by his

art,nn2222

life.

1161   3756   an,ajn3440   235   2532   ppmp2744 pre1722 art,nn2316   pre1223   ppro2257 art,nn2962   an,nn2424
11 And not only *so,* but we also joy   in   God through our   Lord Jesus

an,nn5547   pre1223   repro3739   ad3568   aina2983   art3588   nn2643
Christ,   by   whom we have now received the atonement.

Christ and Adam Contrasted

pre1223/depro5124   ad5618   pre1223   nu1520 an,nn444 art,nn266   aina1525   pre1519 art3588   nn2889   2532   art,nn2288
12 Wherefore, as   by one man   sin entered into the world, and death

pre1223 art,nn266 2532 ad3779 art,nn2288   aina1330   pre1519 an,aj3956 an,nn444 pre1909 repro3739 an,ajn3956   aina264
by sin; and so death passed upon all   men, for   that   all have sinned:

(Gen. 3:6,19; 2:17)

1063   ad891   an,nn3551 an,nn266 ipf2258 pre1722   an,nn2889   1161 an,nn266   3756   pinp1677
13 (For until the law   sin was in   the world: but sin is not imputed

pap5607 3361 an,nn3551
when there is   no law.

235   art,nn2288   aina936   pre575   76   ad3360   an,nn3475   2532   pre1909
14 Nevertheless death reigned from Adam   to Moses, even   over

art,apta264/3361   pre1909 art3588   nn3667   76   art,nn3847   repro3739
them*that*had*not*sinned after the similitude of Adam's transgression, who

pin2076   pr/an,nn5179   art3588   pap3195
is the figure of him that was to come.

235   3756   ad5613 art3588   nn3900   ad3779 2532   art3588   nn5486   1063 1487   art3588
15 But not as   the offense, so also *is* the free gift. For if through the

nn3900   art,nu,ajn1520 art,ajn4183   aina599   an,aj4183   ad3123 art3588 nn5485   art,nn2316 2532 art3588 nn1431
offense of   one   many be dead, much more the grace of God, and the gift

pre1722 an,nn5485 (art3588)   art,nu1520 an,nn444 an,nn2424   an,nn5547   aina4052   pre1519 art,ajn4183
by grace, *which is* by one man, Jesus Christ, hath abounded unto many.

2532   3756   ad5613   pre1223 nu,ajn1520   apta264   art3588   1434 1063 art3588(3303)
16 And not as *it was* by   one   that sinned, *so is* the gift: for   the

nn2917   pre1537 nu,ajn1520 pre1519   an,nn2631   1161 art3588   nn5486   pre1537 an,aj4183
judgment *was* by   one   to condemnation, but the free gift *is* of many

an,nn3900   pre1519   an,nn1345
offenses unto justification.

1063   1487   art,nu,ajn1520 art,nn3900 art,nn2288   aina936   pre1223 art,nu,ajn1520 an,aj4183   ad3123
17 For if by one man's offense death reigned by   one; much more

art,pap2983   art,nn4050   art,nn5485 2532   art3588 nn1431   art,nn1343
they*which*receive abundance of grace and of the gift of righteousness shall

ft936   pre1722 an,nn2222 pre1223 art,nu,ajn1520 an,nn2424 an,nn5547
reign in   life by one, Jesus Christ.)

686/3767   ad5613 pre1223   an,nn3900 nu,ajn1520   pre1519 an,aj3956 an,nn444
18 Therefore as by the offense of one *judgment came* upon all men

pre1519   an,nn2631   2532 ad3779 pre1223   an,nn1345   nu,ajn1520
to condemnation; even so by the righteousness of one *the free gift came*

pre1519 an,aj3956 an,nn444 pre1519   an,nn1347   an,nn2222
upon all   men unto justification of life.

1063   ad5618 pre1223 art,nu1520 an,nn444   art,nn3876   art,ajn4183   ainp2525 pr/an,ajn268 ad3779(2532)
19 For as   by   one man's disobedience many were made sinners,   so

pre1223 art3588   nn5218   art,nu,ajn1520   art,ajn4183 fp2525 pr/an,aj1342
by the obedience of one   shall many be made righteous.   *(Is. 53:11)*

20 Moreover the ^{an,nn3551} law entered, that the offense might abound. But where
sin abounded, grace did much*more*abound:

21 That as sin hath reigned unto death, even so might grace reign
through righteousness unto eternal life by Jesus Christ our Lord.

Dead to Sin

6 What shall we say then? Shall we continue in sin, that grace may abound?
2 God forbid. How shall we, that are dead to sin, live any longer
therein?

3 Know*ye*not, that so*many*of*us*as were baptized into Jesus Christ
were baptized into his death?

4 Therefore we are buried with him by baptism into death: that like as
Christ was raised up from the dead by the glory of the Father, even so
we also should walk in newness of life.

5 For if we have been planted together in the likeness of his death, we
shall be also *in the likeness* of *his* resurrection:

6 Knowing this, that our old man is crucified with *him,* that the body of
sin might be destroyed, that henceforth we should not serve sin.

7 For he*that*is*dead is freed from sin.

8 Now if we be dead with Christ, we believe that we shall also live with
him:

9 Knowing that Christ being raised from the dead dieth no more; death
hath*no*more*dominion*over him.

10 For in that he died, he died unto sin once: but in that he liveth, he
liveth unto God.

6:3 See note on 1 Corinthians 10:2.

ad3779   pim3049   epn5210 2532   rxpro1438   pinf1511 pr/an,ajn3498   3303   art,nn266

11 Likewise reckon ye also yourselves to be dead indeed unto sin,

1161 pr/pap2198   art,nn2316   pre1722   an,nn2424 an,nn5547 ppro2257 art,nn2962

but alive unto God through Jesus Christ our Lord.

3361   art,nn266   3767   pim936   pre1722 ppro5216 art,aj2349   an,nn4983

12 Let not sin therefore reign in your mortal body, that ye should

aies5219 ppro846 pre1722 art3588 nn1939   ppro848

obey it in the lusts thereof.   *(Gen. 4:7)*

3366   pim3936   ppro5216   art,nn3196   an,nn3696   an,nn93

13 Neither yield ye your members *as* instruments of unrighteousness unto

art,nn266 235 aima3936   rxpro1438   art,nn2316 ad5613   an,pap2198   pre1537   an,ajn3498

sin: but yield yourselves unto God, as those*that*are*alive from the dead,

2532 ppro5216   art,nn3196   an,nn3696   an,nn1343   art,nn2316

and your members *as* instruments of righteousness unto God.

1063   an,nn266   3756   ft2961   ppro5216 1063   pin2075 3756   pre5259

14 For sin shall not have*dominion*over you: for ye are not under the

an,nn3551 235   pre5259 an,nn5485

law, but under grace.

Servants to God

inpro5101   3767   ft264   3754   pin2070 3756   pre5259   an,nn3551 235

15 What then? shall we sin, because we are not under the law, but

pre5259 an,nn5485   opt1096/3361

under grace? God forbid.

pin1492   3756   3754   repro3739   pin3936   rxpro1438   pr/an,ajn1401   pre1519 an,nn5218

16 Know ye not, that to whom ye yield yourselves servants to obey, his

pr/an,ajn1401   pin2075   repro3739   pin5219   2273   an,nn266   pre1519   an,nn2288   2228

servants ye are to whom ye obey; whether of sin unto death, or of

an,nn5218   pre1519   an,nn1343

obedience unto righteousness?

1161   art,nn2316/an,nn5485   3754   ipf2258   pr/an,ajn1401   art,nn266 1161

17 But God*be*thanked, that ye were the servants of sin, but ye have

aina5219   pre1537   an,nn2588   an,nn5179 an,nn1322 (pre1519) repro3739   ainp3860

obeyed from the heart that form of doctrine which was delivered you.

(1161)   aptp1659   pre575 art,nn266   ainp1402

18 Being then made free from sin, ye became*the*servants of

art,nn1343

righteousness.

pin3004   an,ajn442   pre1223   art3588   nn769   ppro5216

19 I speak after*the*manner*of*men because of the infirmity of your

art,nn4561 1063 ad5618   aina3936   ppro5216   art,nn3916   pr/an,ajn1400   art,nn167   2532

flesh: for as ye have yielded your members servants to uncleanness and to

art,nn458   pre1519   art,nn458   ad3779   ad3568 aim3936 ppro5216   art,nn3196   pr/an,ajn1400

iniquity unto iniquity; even so now yield your members servants to

art,nn1343   pre1519   an,nn38

righteousness unto holiness.

1063   ad3753   ipf2258   pr/an,ajn1401   art,nn266   ipf2258   pr/an,aj1658

20 For when ye were the servants of sin, ye were free from

art,nn1343

righteousness.

21 What fruit had ye then in those things whereof ye are*now*ashamed? for the end of those things *is* death.

22 But now being made free from sin, and become servants to God, ye have your fruit unto holiness, and the end everlasting life.

23 For the wages of sin *is* death; but the gift of God *is* eternal life through Jesus Christ our Lord.

Released From the Law

7 Know*ye*not, brethren, (for I speak to them*that*know the law,) how that the law hath*dominion*over a man as*long*as he liveth?

2 For the woman which*hath*an*husband is bound by the law to *her* husband so long as he liveth; but if the husband be dead, she is loosed from the law of *her* husband.

3 So then if, while *her* husband liveth, she be married to another man, she shall be called an adulteress: but if her husband be dead, she is free from that law; so that she is no adulteress, though she be married to another man.

4 Wherefore, my brethren, ye also are become dead to the law by the body of Christ; that ye should be married to another, *even* to him*who*is*raised from the dead, that we should bring*forth*fruit unto God.

5 For when we were in the flesh, the motions of sins, which were by the law, did work in our members to bring*forth*fruit unto death.

6 But now we are delivered from the law, that being dead wherein we were held; that we should serve in newness of spirit, and not *in* the oldness of the letter.

inpro5101   ft2046 3767   art3588 nn3551 pr/an,nn266   opt1096/3361   235   3756

7 What shall we say then? *Is* the law sin? God forbid. Nay, I had not

aina1097 art,nn266 1508 pre1223   an,nn3551 1063 (5037) 3756 ipf1492 art,nn1939 1508 art3588 nn3551

known sin, but by the law: for I had not known lust, except the law had

ipf3004   3756 ft1937

said, Thou shalt not covet.   *(Ex. 20:17; Deut. 5:21)*

1161 art,nn266 apta2983 an,nn874 pre1223 art3588   nn1785   aom2716 pre1722 ppro1698

8 But sin, taking occasion by the commandment, wrought in me

an,aj3956   an,nn1939 1063 ad*5565 an,nn3551 an,nn266 pr/an,aj3498

all manner of concupiscence. For without the law sin *was* dead.

1161 epn1473 ipf2198 ad*5565 an,nn3551 ad4218 1161 art3588   nn1785

9 For I was alive without the law once: but when the commandment

apta2064 art,nn266 aina326 1161 epn1473 aina599

came, sin revived, and I died.

2532 art3588   nn1785   art3588   pre1519 an,nn2222 ppro3427 ainp2147

10 And the commandment, which *was ordained* to life, I found

(depro3778) pre1519 an,nn2288

to be unto death.   *(Lev. 18:5)*

1063 art,nn266 apta2983 an,nn874 pre1223 art3588   nn1785   aina1818 ppro3165 2532

11 For sin, taking occasion by the commandment, deceived me, and

pre1223 ppro846 aina615

by it slew *me*.   *(Gen. 3:13)*

5620   art3588 nn3551 pr/an,aj40 2532 art3588   nn1785   pr/an,aj40 2532 pr/an,aj1342 2532

12 Wherefore the law *is* holy, and the commandment holy, and just, and

pr/an,aj18

good.

3767   art,ajn18   pfi1096 pr/an,nn2288   ppro1698   opt1096/3361

13 Was then that*which*is*good made death unto me? God forbid.

235 art,nn266 2443   asbp5316 an,nn266 ppmp2716 an,nn2288 ppro3427 pre1223

But sin, that it might appear sin, working death in me by

art,ajn18   2443 art,nn266 pre1223 art3588   nn1785   asbm1096 pre2596/an,nn5236

that*which*is*good; that sin by the commandment might become exceeding

pr/an,aj268

sinful.

The Sin Nature Still Remains

1063   pin1492 3754 art3588 nn3551 pin2076 pr/an,aj4152   1161 epn1473 pin1510 pr/an,aj4559 pr/pfpp4097

14 For we know that the law is spiritual: but I am carnal, sold

pre5259 art,nn266

under sin.   *(Ps. 51:5)*

1063   repro3739 pinm2716 pin1097 3756 1063 repro3739 pin2309 depro5124 pin4238   3756

15 For that which I do I allow not: for what I would, that do I not;

235 repro3739 pin3404 depro5124 pin4160

but what I hate, that do I.

1487 1161 pin4160 depro5124 repro3739 pin2309 3756 pin4852   art3588 nn3551 3754

16 If then I do that which I would not, I consent unto the law that *it is*

pr/an,aj2570

good.

☞ 17 Now then it is no more I that do it, but sin that dwelleth in
me.

18 For I know that in me (that is, in my flesh,) dwelleth no
good thing: for to will is present with me; but *how* to perform
that*which*is*good I find not.   *(Gen. 6:5; 8:21)*

19 For the good that I would I do not: but the evil which I would not,
that I do.

20 Now if I do that I would not, it is no more I that do
it, but sin that dwelleth in me.

21 I find then a law, that, when I would do good, evil is present
with me.

22 For I delight in the law of God after the inward man:

☞ 23 But I see another law in my members, warring against the law of
my mind, and bringing*me*into*captivity to the law of sin which is in
my members.

24 O wretched man that I am! who shall deliver me from the body of
this death?

25 I thank God through Jesus Christ our Lord. So then with the
mind I myself serve the law of God; but with the flesh the law of
sin.

☞ **7:17–19** Paul's statement "Now then it is no more I that do it, but sin that dwelleth in me" (v. 17) should not be taken as an abdication of his responsibility for his actions. Instead, he reveals the nature of the inner conflict between his two natures. To will (v. 15; *thélō* [2309]) was his attitude, but to perform (*katergázomai* [2716], "to accomplish") that which is good Paul could not realize (v. 18). Paul bemoans that the good he desired, he did not do (*poió* [4160], stressing the object of an act), but the evil he did not desire was what he practiced (*prássō* [4238], emphasizing the means by which an act is accomplished).
☞ **7:23** Paul further develops the concept of conflict between his new nature, in which he "rejoices with" (*sunédomai* [4913]) the law of God, and his old nature, by which he is captivated (*aichmalōtizontá* [163]).

No Condemnation Now

8 *There is* therefore now   no   condemnation to them which are   in   Christ Jesus, who walk not after the flesh, but after the Spirit.

2 For the law of the Spirit of   life   in   Christ Jesus hath made*me*free from the law of sin and death.

3 For what the law could*not*do,   in   that it was weak through the flesh, God sending his own Son in the likeness of sinful flesh, and for sin, condemned sin   in the flesh:

4 That the righteousness of the law might be fulfilled in   us, who walk not after the flesh, but after the Spirit.

5 For they*that*are after the flesh do mind the things of the flesh; but they that are after the Spirit the things of the Spirit.

6 For to be carnally minded *is* death; but to be spiritually minded *is*   life and peace.

☞ 7 Because the carnal mind *is* enmity against God: for it is*not*subject to the law of God, neither indeed can be.

8 So then they*that*are in the flesh cannot please God.

9 But ye are not in the flesh, but in the Spirit, if*so*be*that the Spirit of God dwell in you. Now if*any*man have not the Spirit of Christ, he is none of his.

10 And if Christ *be* in you, the body *is* dead because of sin; but the Spirit *is* life   because of righteousness.

11 But if the Spirit of him*that*raised*up Jesus from the dead dwell in you, he*that*raised*up Christ from the dead shall also quicken your mortal bodies by his Spirit that dwelleth in you.

☞ **8:7** See note on Romans 3:19, 20.

686/3767   an,nn80   pin2070   pr/an,nn3781   3756   art3588   nn4561   infg2198   pre2596

12 Therefore, brethren, we are debtors, not to the flesh, to live after

art3588   nn4561

the flesh.

1063   1487   psa2198   pre2596   an,nn4561   pin3195   pinf599   1161   1487   an,nn4151

13 For if ye live after the flesh, ye shall die: but if ye through the Spirit

pin2289   art3588   nn4234   art3588   nn4983   fm2198

do mortify the deeds of the body, ye shall live.

1063   an,ajn3745   pinp71   an,nn4151   an,nn2316   depro3778   pin1526   pr/an,nn5207

14 For as*many*as are led by the Spirit of God, they are the sons of

an,nn2316

God.

1063   3756   aina2983   an,nn4151   an,nn1397   ad3825   pre1519   an,nn5401   235

15 For ye have not received the spirit of bondage again to fear; but ye

aina2983   an,nn4151   an,nn5206   pre1722/repro3739   pin2896   5   art,nn3962

have received the Spirit of adoption, whereby we cry, Abba, Father.

art3588   nn4151   epn846   pin4828   ppro2257   art,nn4151   3754   pin2070

16 The Spirit itself beareth*witness*with our spirit, that we are the

pr/an,nn5043   an,nn2316

children of God:

1161   1487   an,nn5043   2532   an,nn2818   an,nn2818   (3303) an,nn2316   1161   an,nn4789   an,nn5547

17 And if children, then heirs; heirs of God, and joint-heirs with Christ;

1512   pin4841   2443   2532   asbp4888

if*so*be*that we suffer with *him,* that we may be also glorified together.

The Revelation of God's Glory Through Believers

1063   pinm3049   3754   art3588   nn3804   art,ad3568   an,nn2540   3756   pr/an,aj514

18 For I reckon that the sufferings of this present time *are* not worthy *to*

pre4314   art3588   nn1391   pap3195   aifp601   pre1519   ppro2248

be compared with the glory which shall be revealed in us.

1063   art3588   nn603   art3588   nn2937   pinm553   art3588

19 For the earnest expectation of the creature waiteth for the

nn602   art3588   nn5207   art,nn2316

manifestation of the sons of God.

1063   art3588   nn2937   ainp5293   art,nn3153   3756   pap1635   235

20 For the creature was made subject to vanity, not willingly, but

pre1223   art,apta5293   pre1909   an,nn1680

by*reason*of him*who*hath*subjected *the same* in hope,

(Gen. 3:17,18; 5:29; Eccl. 1:2)

3754   art3588   nn2937   epn848   2532   fp1659   pre575   art3588   nn1397

21 Because the creature itself also shall be delivered from the bondage of

art,nn5356   pre1519   art3588   nn1391   art,nn1657   art3588   nn5043   art,nn2316

corruption into the glorious liberty of the children of God.

1063   pin1492   3754   an,aj3956   art,nn2937   pin4959   2532

22 For we know that the whole creation groaneth and

pin4944   ad891   art,ad3568

travaileth*in*pain*together until now.

1161   3756   an,ajn3440   235   epn848   2532   pap2192   art3588   sg/nn536   art3588

23 And not only *they,* but ourselves also, which have the firstfruits of the

nn4151   2532   ppro2249   epn848   pin4727   pre1722   rxpro1438   ppmp553   an,nn5206
Spirit, even we ourselves groan within ourselves, waiting for the adoption, *to*
art3588   nn629   ppro2257   art,nn4983
wit, the redemption of our body.
1063   ainp4982   art,nn1680   1161   an,nn1680   ppmp991   pin2076   3756   pr/an,nn1680   1063
24 For we are saved by hope: but hope that is seen is not hope: for
repro3739   idpro5100   pin991   inpro5101   2532   pin1679
what a man seeth, why doth he yet hope for?
1161   1487   pin1679   repro3739   pin991   3756   pre1223   an,nn5281   pinm553
25 But if we hope for that we see not, *then* do we with patience wait for
it.
(1161)   ad5615   art3588   nn4151   2532   pinm4878   ppro2257   art,nn769   1063   pin1492   3756
26 Likewise the Spirit also helpeth our infirmities: for we know not
art,inpro5101   asba4336   ad2526   pin1163   235   art3588   nn4151   epn848
what we should pray for as we ought: but the Spirit itself
pin5241   pre5228 ppro2257   an,nn4726   an,aj215
maketh intercession for us with groanings which*cannot*be*uttered.
1161   art,pap2045   art3588   nn2588   pin1492   inpro5101   art3588   pr/nn5427   art3588
27 And he*that*searcheth the hearts knoweth what *is* the mind of the
nn4151   3754   pin1793   pre5228   an,ajn40   pre2596
Spirit, because he maketh intercession for the saints according to *the will of*
an,nn2316
God.   *(Ps. 139:1)*
1161   pin1492   3754   an,ajn3956   pin4903   pre1519 an,ajn18   art,pap25
28 And we know that all things work together for good to them*that*love
art,nn2316   an,pap5607   art3588 pr/ajn2822   pre2596   an,nn4286
God, to them*who*are the called according to *his* purpose.
3754   repro3739   aina4267   2532   aina4309   an,aj4832
29 For whom he did foreknow, he also did predestinate *to be* conformed to
art3588   nn1504   ppro848 art,nn5207   ppro846   aies1511   pr/an,aj4416   pre1722   an,aj4183   an,nn80
the image of his Son, that he might be the firstborn among many brethren.
1161   repro3739   aina4309   depro5128   2532   aina2564   2532   repro3739
30 Moreover whom he did predestinate, them he also called: and whom he
aina2564   depro5128   2532   aina1344   1161   repro3739   aina1344   depro5128   2532   aina1392
called, them he also justified: and whom he justified, them he also glorified.

Nothing Separates the Believer From God's Love

inpro5101   3767   ft2046 pre4314 depro5023   1487 art,nn2316   pre5228 ppro2257 inpro5101
31 What shall we then say to these things? If God *be* for us, who
pre2596   ppro2257
can be against us?   *(Ps. 118:6)*
repro3739(1065)   aom5339   3756   art,aj2398   an,nn5207   235   aina3860/ppro846   pre5228 ppro2257 an,aj3956
32 He that spared not his own Son, but delivered*him*up for us all,
ad4459   3780 pre4862 ppro846 2532   fm5483   ppro2254   art,ajn3956
how shall he not with him also freely give us all things?

☞ **8:28, 29, 33** See note on Ephesians 1:4, 5.
☞ **9:11-13** See notes on Psalm 5:5 and Ephesians 1:4, 5.

inpro5101   ft1458/pre2596   an,nn2316   an,ajn1588   an,nn2316

☞ 33 Who shall lay*any*thing*to*the*charge of God's elect? *It is* God

pr/art,pap1344

that justifieth.   *(Is. 50:8)*

inpro5101   pr/art,pap2632   an,nn5547   art,apta599   1161   ad3123   (2532)

34 Who *is* he*that*condemneth? *It is* Christ that died, yea rather, that is

aptp1453   repro3739   pin2076   2532   pre1722   an,ajn1188   art,nn2316 repro3739 2532

risen again, who is even at the right hand of God, who also

pin1793   pre5228 ppro2257

maketh intercession for us.   *(Ps. 110:1)*

inpro5101   ft5563   ppro2248 pre575 art3588   nn26   art,nn5547   an,nn2347   2228

35 Who shall separate us from the love of Christ? *shall* tribulation, or

an,nn4730 2228   an,nn1375   2228 an,nn3042 2228   an,nn1132   2228 an,nn2794 2228 an,nn3162

distress, or persecution, or famine, or nakedness, or peril, or sword?

ad2531   pfip1125   ad⁺1752/ppro4675   pinp2289 an,aj3650 art3588 nn2250

36 As it is written, For*thy*sake we are killed all the day long; we are

ainp3049   ad5613 an,nn4263   an,nn4967

accounted as sheep for the slaughter.   *(Ps. 44:22)*

235   pre1722 an,aj3956   depro5125   pin5245   pre1223

37 Nay, in all these things we are*more*than*conquerors through

art,apta25   ppro2248

him*that*loved us.

1063   pfip3982   3754   3777   an,nn2288   3777 an,nn2222 3777   an,nn32   3777

38 For I am persuaded, that neither death, nor life, nor angels, nor

an,nn746   3777 an,nn1411 3777   an,pfp1764   3777   an,pap3195

principalities, nor powers, nor things present, nor things*to*come,

3777   an,nn5313   3777   an,nn899   3777 idpro5100 an,aj2087   an,nn2937   fm1410

39 Nor height, nor depth, nor any other creature, shall be able to

ainf5563   ppro2248 pre575 art3588   nn26   art,nn2316 art3588   pre1722 an,nn5547 an,nn2424 ppro2257 art,nn2962

separate us from the love of God, which is in Christ Jesus our Lord.

The People of Israel

pin3004   an,nn225   pre1722   an,nn5547   pinm5574   3756   ppro3450   art,nn4983

9 I say the truth in Christ, I lie not, my conscience also

pap4828/ppro3427   pre1722   an,aj40   an,nn4151

bearing*me*witness in the Holy Ghost,

3754 ppro3427 pin2076 an,aj3173   an,nn3077   2532   an,aj88   an,nn3601   ppro3450 art,nn2588

2 That I have great heaviness and continual sorrow in my heart.

1063 epn1473   ipf2172   epn848   pinf1511 pr/an,nn331   pre575 art,nn5547 pre5228 ppro3450

3 For I could wish that myself were accursed from Christ for my

art,nn80   ppro3450 art,ajn4773   pre2596   an,nn4561

brethren, my kinsmen according to the flesh: *(Ex. 32:32)*

repro3748 pin1526 pr/an,nn2475   repro3739   art3588   nn5206   2532 art3588   nn1391

4 Who are Israelites; to whom *pertaineth* the adoption, and the glory,

2532 art3588   nn1242   2532 art3588   nn3548   2532 art3588   nn2999   2532

and the covenants, and the giving*of*the*law, and the service *of God*, and

art3588   nn1860

the promises;   *(Ex. 4:22; Deut. 7:6; 14:1,2)*

repro3739   art3588   nn3962   2532   pre1537   repro3739   art,pre2596   an,nn4561   art,nn5547

5 Whose *are* the fathers, and of whom as concerning the flesh Christ

art,pap5607   pre1909 an,ajn3956 an,nn2316   pr/an,aj2128   pre1519/art,nn165   281

came, who is over all, God blessed forever. Amen.   *(Ps. 41:13)*

(1161) 3756   3754(an,ajn3634) art3588   nn3056   art,nn2316   pfi1601   1063 depro3778

6   Not as though the word of God hath taken*none*effect. For they *are*

3756 an,ajn3956   2474   art3588   pre1537   2474

not all Israel, which are of Israel: *(Num. 23:19)*

3761   3754   pr/an,nn4690   11   an,ajn3956

7 Neither, because they are the seed of Abraham, *are they* all

pr/an,nn5043   235   pre1722 2464   ppro4671 an,nn4690   fp2564

children: but, In Isaac shall thy seed be called.   *(Gen. 21:12)*

depro,pin5123   art3588   nn5043   art3588   nn4561   depro5023   3756

8 That is, They which are the children of the flesh, these *are* not

pr/an,nn5043   art,nn2316   235   art3588   nn5043   art3588   nn1860   pinp3049   pre1519

the children of God: but the children of the promise are counted for the

an,nn4690

seed.

1063   depro3778   art3588   nn3056   an,nn1860   pre2596 depro5126 art,nn2540   fm2064   2532 art,nn4564

9 For this *is* the word of promise, At this time will I come, and Sarah

fm2071   an,nn5207

shall have a son.   *(Gen. 18:10,14)*

1161   3756 an,ajn3440   235   an,nn4479   2532 pap2192   an,nn2845   pre1537 nu,ajn1520

10 And not only *this*; but when Rebecca also had conceived by one,

ppro2257 art,nn3962   2464

even by our father Isaac;   *(Gen. 25:21)*

1063   ad3380   aptp1080   3366   apta4238 idpro5100 an,ajn18 2228

☞ 11 (For *the children* being not yet born, neither having done any good or

an,ajn2556   2443   art3588   nn4286   art,nn2316   pre2596   an,nn1589   psa3306   3756 pre1537

evil, that the purpose of God according to election might stand, not of

an,nn2041   235 pre1537   art,pap2564

works, but of him*that*calleth;)

ainp4483   ppro846 art3588 cd/ajn3187   ft1398   art3588   cd/ajn1640

12 It was said unto her, The elder shall serve the younger.   *(Gen. 25:23)*

ad2531   pfip1125   2384   aina25   1161   2269   aina3404

13 As it is written, Jacob have I loved, but Esau have I hated. *(Mal. 1:2,3)*

inpro5101   ft2046   3767   (3361)   an,nn93   pre3844 art,nn2316

14 What shall we say then? Is *there* unrighteousness with God?

opt1096/3361

God forbid.

1063   pin3004   art,nn3475   ft1653   repro3739/302   pin1653

15 For he saith to Moses, I will have mercy on whom I will have mercy,

2532   ft3627   repro3739/302   pin3627

and I will have compassion on whom I will have compassion.   *(Ex. 33:19)*

686   3767   3756   art,pap2309   3761   art,pap5143   235

16 So then *it is* not of him*that*willeth, nor of him*that*runneth, but of

an,nn2316   art,pap1653

God that*showeth*mercy.

☞ **9:17** God said of Pharaoh, in Exodus 4:21 and 7:13, "I will harden his heart, that he should not let
(continued on next page)

           1063 art3588   nn1124   pin3004   5328   pre1519   depro5124/ppro846

☞ 17 For the Scripture saith unto Pharaoh, Even for this* same*purpose have

aina1825/ppro4571   3704   asbm1731 ppro3450 art,nn1411 pre1722 ppro4671 2532   3704   ppro3450 art,nn3686

I raised*thee*up, that I might show my power in thee, and that my name

            asbp1229   pre1722   an,aj3956 art3588   nn1093

might be declared throughout all the earth.   *(Ex. 9:16)*

        686/3767   pin1653   repro3739   pin2309   1161   repro3739

  18 Therefore hath*he*mercy on whom he will *have mercy,* and whom he

pin2309   pin4645

will he hardeneth.   *(Ex. 4:21; 7:3; 9:12; 14:4,17)*

           ft2046   3767   ppro3427 inpro5101   ad2089   pinm3201   1063 inpro5101

  19 Thou wilt say then unto me, Why doth he yet find fault? For who hath

pfi436   ppro846 art,nn1013

resisted his will?

          3304   5599 an,nn444 inpro5101 pin1488 pr/epn4771   art,ppmp470   art,nn2316   (3361)

  20 Nay but, O man, who art thou that*repliest*against God? Shall

art3588   nn4110   ft2046   art,apta4111   inpro5101   aina4160   ppro3165

the thing formed say to him*that*formed *it,* Why hast thou made me

ad3779

thus?   *(Is. 29:16; 45:9)*

    (2228) pin2192   3756 art3588   nn2763   an,nn1849   art3588 nn4081   pre1537 art3588 ppro846   nn5445

  21 Hath not the potter power over the clay, of the same lump to

ainf4160 repro3739/3303 an,nn4632 pre1519 an,nn5092   1161   repro3739   pre1519   an,nn819

make one vessel unto honor, and another unto dishonor?   *(Jer. 18:6)*

    (1161) 1487 art,nn2316 pap2309   aifm1731   art,nn3709   2532   ainf1107/ppro848/art,ajn1415

  22 *What* if God, willing to show *his* wrath, and to make*his*power*known,

aina5342   pre1722 an,aj4183   an,nn3115   an,nn4632   an,nn3709   pfpp2675 pre1519   an,nn684

endured with much longsuffering the vessels of wrath fitted to destruction:

                                                    (Jer. 50:25)

     2532   2443   asba1107   art3588   nn4149   ppro848 art,nn1391 pre1909

  23 And that he might make known the riches of his glory on the

an,nn4632   an,nn1656 repro3739   aina4282   pre1519 an,nn1391

vessels of mercy, which he had afore prepared unto glory,

(continued from previous page)

the people go . . . And he hardened Pharaoh's heart, that he hearkened not unto him." The same phrase occurs in Exodus 9:12: "And the LORD hardened the heart of Pharaoh." However, the Scripture also declares that Pharaoh hardened his own heart (Ex. 8:15, 32; 9:34). Paul is here answering the objection in verse fourteen that some might bring against his doctrine, "Is there unrighteousness with God?" God claims and exercises His right, by reason of His sovereignty over men, to dispense His mercy as He sees fit (cf. Ex. 33:19). He did so in the case of Pharaoh. It is not that Pharaoh was "beyond" the help of God's mercy, nor that God made him wicked, but simply that God withheld His mercy and left him to his own wickedness.

In ancient Egypt, the Pharaohs themselves were frequently reverenced as gods. The Pharaoh that ruled during the time of Moses seemed to have regarded himself as a deity capable of resisting Jehovah Himself. His attitude toward God is expressed in Exodus 5:2, "Who is the LORD, that I should obey his voice to let Israel go?" God exalted Himself by His mighty judgments upon Egypt and His mighty deliverance of Israel. Even the Philistines in Canaan knew about these judgments and feared God as a result (1 Sam. 4:8).

2532   epn2248 repro3739   aina2564   3756 pre1537   an,nn2453 an,ajn3440   235   2532   pre1537

24 Even us, whom he hath called, not of the Jews only, but also of

an,nn1484

the Gentiles?

ad5613   pin3004   2532 pre1722   5617   ft2564   ppro3450 an,nn2992   art3588

25 As he saith also in Hosea, I will call them my people, which were

3756 ppro3450 an,nn2992 2532   pfpp25   art,pfpp25/3756

not my people; and her beloved, which*was*not*beloved.   *(Hos. 2:23)*

2532   fm2071   pre1722 art3588   nn5117   repro3757   ainp4483

26 And it shall come*to*pass, *that* in the place where it was said unto

ppro846 epn5210   3756 ppro3450 an,nn2992   ad1563   fp2564   an,nn5207

them, Ye *are* not my people; there shall they be called the children of the

an,pap2198 an,nn2316

living God.   *(Hos. 1:10)*

an,nn2268   1161   pin2896   pre5228   2474   1437   art3588   nn706   art3588

27 Isaiah also crieth concerning Israel, Though the number of the

nn5207   2474   psa5600 ad5613 art3588 pr/nn285   art3588 nn2281   art,nn2640   fp4982

children of Israel be as the sand of the sea, a remnant shall be saved:

1063   pap4931   an,nn3056   2532   pap4932   pre1722   an,nn1343

28 For he will finish the work, and cut*it*short in righteousness:

3754   pfpp4932 an,nn3056   an,nn2962 ft4160 pre1909 art3588 nn1093

because a short work will the Lord make upon the earth.

(Is. 10:22,23; Hos. 1:10)

2532 ad2531 an,nn2268   pfi4280   1508   an,nn2962   4519   aina1459 ppro2254

29 And as Isaiah said before, Except the Lord of Sabaoth had left us a

an,nn4690   ainp1096/302 ad5613 pr/an,nn4670 2532   ainp3666/302 ad5613   an,nn1116

seed, we had been as Sodom, and been made like unto Gomorrah.   *(Is. 1:9)*

The Gentiles Are Called

inpro5101   ft2046 3767 3754   an,nn1484   art3588   pap1377   3361

30 What shall we say then? That the Gentiles, which followed not after

an,nn1343   aina2638   an,nn1343   1161   an,nn1343   art3588

righteousness, have attained to righteousness, even the righteousness which is

pre1537 an,nn4102

of faith.

1161   2474   pap1377   an,nn3551   an,nn1343   3756

31 But Israel, which followed after the law of righteousness, hath not

aina5348   pre1519 an,nn3551   an,nn1343

attained to the law of righteousness.

pre,inpro1302   3754   3756 pre1537 an,nn4102 235   ad5613   pre1537

32 Wherefore? Because *they sought it* not by faith, but as*it*were by the

an,nn2041   an,nn3551 1063   aina4350   art,nn4348/art,nn3037

works of the law. For they stumbled at that stumblingstone;   *(Is. 8:14)*

ad2531   pfip1125   2400   pin5087 pre1722 4622   an,nn4348/an,nn3037   2532 an,nn4073

33 As it is written, Behold, I lay in Zion a stumblingstone and rock of

an,nn4625   2532   an,ajn3956   art,pap4100 pre1909 ppro846   3756   fp2617

offense: and whosoever believeth on him shall not be ashamed.   *(Is. 28:16)*

10 Brethren, my heart's desire and prayer to God for Israel is, that they*might*be*saved.

2 For I bear*them*record that they have a zeal of God, but not according to knowledge.

3 For they being ignorant of God's righteousness, and going about to establish their own righteousness, have not submitted themselves unto the righteousness of God.

4 For Christ *is* the end of the law for righteousness to every one that believeth.

The Method of Justification

5 For Moses describeth the righteousness which is of the law, That the man which doeth those things shall live by them. *(Lev. 18:5)*

6 But the righteousness which is of faith speaketh on*this*wise, Say not in thine heart, Who shall ascend into heaven? (that is, to bring*Christ*down *from above*:) *(Deut. 9:4; 30:12)*

7 Or, Who shall descend into the deep? (that is, to bring*up*Christ*again from the dead.) *(Deut. 30:13)*

8 But what saith it? The word is nigh thee, *even* in thy mouth, and in thy heart: that is, the word of faith, which we preach; *(Deut. 30:14)*

☞ 9 That if thou shalt confess with thy mouth the Lord Jesus, and shalt believe in thine heart that God hath raised him from the dead, thou shalt be saved.

☞ **10:9** See note on Mark 3:28, 29.

10 For with the heart man believeth unto righteousness; and with the mouth confession*is*made unto salvation.

11 For the Scripture saith, Whosoever believeth on him shall not be ashamed.

(Is. 28:16)

12 For there is no difference between the Jew and the Greek: for the same Lord over all is rich unto all that*call*upon him.

13 For whosoever shall call upon the name of the Lord shall be saved.

(Joel 2:32)

14 How then shall they call on him in whom they have not believed? and how shall they believe in him of whom they have not heard? and how shall they hear without a preacher?

15 And how shall they preach, except they be sent? as it is written, How beautiful are the feet of them*that*preach*the*gospel of peace, and bring*glad*tidings of good things!

(Is. 52:7; Nah. 1:15)

16 But they have not all obeyed the gospel. For Isaiah saith, Lord, who hath believed our report?

(Is. 53:1)

17 So then faith *cometh* by hearing, and hearing by the word of God.

18 But I say, Have they not heard? Yes verily, their sound went into all the earth, and their words unto the ends of the world.

(Ps. 19:4)

19 But I say, Did not Israel know? First Moses saith, I will provoke*you*to*jealousy by *them that are* no people, *and* by a foolish nation I will anger you.

(Deut. 32:21)

20 But Isaiah is*very*bold, and saith, I was found of them*that*sought me not; I was made manifest unto them*that*asked*not*after me.

(Is. 65:1)

21 But to Israel he saith, All day long I have stretched forth my hands unto a disobedient and gainsaying people.

(Is. 65:2)

God's Chosen People

11 I say then, Hath God cast away his people? God forbid. For I also am an Israelite, of the seed of Abraham, *of* the tribe of Benjamin.

2 God hath not cast away his people which he foreknew. Wot ye not what the Scripture saith of Elijah? how he maketh intercession to God against Israel, saying,

(1 Sam. 12:22; Ps. 94:14)

3 Lord, they have killed thy prophets, and digged down thine altars; and I am left alone, and they seek my life.

(1 Kgs. 19:10,14)

4 But what saith the answer*of*God unto him? I have reserved to myself seven thousand men, who have not bowed the knee to *the image of* Baal.

(1 Kgs. 19:18)

5 Even so then at this present time also there is a remnant according to the election of grace.

6 And if by grace, then *is it* no more of works: otherwise grace is no more grace. But if *it be* of works, then is it no more grace: otherwise work is no more work.

7 What then? Israel hath not obtained that which he seeketh for; but the election hath obtained it, and the rest were blinded.

8 (According as it is written, God hath given them the spirit of slumber, eyes that they should not see, and ears that they should not hear;) unto this day.

(Deut. 29:4; Is. 29:10)

2532   1138   pin3004   ppro848 art,nn5132   ainp1096 (pre1519) an,nn3803 2532 (pre1519) an,nn2339 2532
9 And David saith, Let their table be made a snare, and a trap, and
(pre1519)   an,nn4625   2532 (pre1519)   an,nn468   ppro846
a stumblingblock, and a recompense unto them:

ppro848 art,nn3788   aipp4654   3361 infg991 2532   aima4781
10 Let their eyes be darkened, that they may not see, and bow down
ppro848 art,nn3577 pre,an,ajn1275
their back always.   *(Ps. 35:8; 69:22,23)*

pin3004 3767   (3361)   aina4417   2443   asba4098 opt1096/3361   235
11 I say then, Have they stumbled that they should fall? God forbid: but
ppro848 art,nn3900 art,nn4991   art3588   nn1484
rather through their fall salvation *is come* unto the Gentiles, for to
aies3863/ppro846
provoke*them*to*jealousy.   *(Deut. 32:21)*

1161   1487 art3588 nn3900   ppro848   pr/an,nn4149   an,nn2889 2532 art3588
12 Now if the fall of them *be* the riches of the world, and the
nn2275   ppro848   pr/an,nn4149   an,nn1484 an,aj4214 ad3123 ppro848 art,nn4138
diminishing of them the riches of the Gentiles; how much more their fullness?

Two Kinds of Branches

1063   pin3004   epn5213 art,nn1484 pre1909/an,aj3745/3303 epn1473 pin1510   pr/an,nn652
13 For I speak to you Gentiles, inasmuch as I   am the apostle of the
an,nn1484   pin1392 ppro3450 art,nn1248
Gentiles, I magnify mine office:

ad1513   asba3863   ppro3450
14 If*by*any*means I may provoke*to*emulation *them which are* my
art,nn4561 2532   asba4982 idpro5100 pre1537 ppro846
flesh, and might save some of them.

1063 1487 art3588   nn580   ppro846   pr/an,nn2643   an,nn2889 inpro5101
15 For if the casting away of them *be* the reconciling of the world, what
art3588   pr/nn4356   1508 pr/an,nn2222 pre1537   an,ajn2498
shall the receiving *of them be,* but life from the dead?

1161 1487 art3588   nn536   pr/an,aj40 art3588 pr/nn5445 2532   2532 1487 art3588 nn4491
16 For if the firstfruit *be* holy, the lump *is* also *holy*: and if the root *be*
pr/an,aj40 2532   art3588   pr/nn2798
holy, so *are* the branches.   *(Num. 15:17-21; Neh. 10:37; Ezek. 44:30)*

1161 1487 idpro5100   art3588   nn2798   ainp1575 1161 epn4771 pap5607
17 And if some of the branches be broken off, and thou, being a
pr/an,nn65   ainp1461 pre1722 ppro846 2532 (aom1096) pr/an,ajn4791   art3588
wild*olive*tree, wert grafted in among them, and with them partakest of the
nn4491 2532 art,nn4096   art3588   nn1636
root and fatness of the olive tree;

pim2620/3361   art3588   nn2798   1161 1487   pinm2620 epn4771 pin941 3756
18 Boast*not*against the branches. But if thou boast, thou bearest not
art3588 nn4491   235 art3588 nn4491 ppro4571
the root, but the root thee.

ft2046 3767 art3588   nn2798   ainp1575 2443 epn1473
19 Thou wilt say then, The branches were broken off, that I   might be
asbp1461
grafted in.

^{ad2573} ^{art,nn570} ^{ainp1575} ¹¹⁶¹ ^{epn4771} ^{pfi2476}
20 Well; because of unbelief they were broken off, and thou standest by

^{art,nn4102} ^{pim5309/3361} ²³⁵ ^{pim5399}
faith. Be*not*highminded, but fear:

¹⁰⁶³ ¹⁴⁸⁷ ^{art,nn2316} ^{aom5339} ³⁷⁵⁶ ^{art3588} ^{pre2596/an,nn5449} ^{an,nn2798} ³³⁸¹
21 For if God spared not the natural branches, *take heed* lest he also

^{asbm5339} ³⁷⁶¹ ^{epn4675}
spare not thee.

^{aima1492} ³⁷⁶⁷ ^{an,nn5544} ²⁵³² ^{an,nn663} ^{an,nn2316} ^{pre1909} ⁽³³⁰³⁾
22 Behold therefore the goodness and severity of God: on

^{art,apta4098} ^{an,nn663} ¹¹⁶¹ ^{pre1909} ^{ppro4571} ^{an,nn5544} ¹⁴³⁷ ^{asba1961}
them*which*fell, severity; but toward thee, goodness, if thou continue in *his*

^{art,nn5544} ¹⁸⁹³ ^{epn4771} ²⁵³² ^{asbm1581}
goodness: otherwise thou also shalt be cut off.

¹¹⁶¹ ^{depro1565} ²⁵³² ^{3362/asba1961} ^{art,nn570} ^{fp1461}
23 And they also, if*they*abide*not still in unbelief, shall be grafted in:

¹⁰⁶³ ^{art,nn2316} ^{pin2076} ^{pr/an,aj1415} ^{ainf1461/ppro846} ^{ad3825}
for God is able to graft*them*in again.

¹⁰⁶³ ¹⁴⁸⁷ ^{epn4771} ^{ainp1581} ^{pre1537} ^{art3588} ⁿⁿ⁶⁵ ^{pre2596} ^{an,nn5449} ²⁵³²
24 For if thou wert cut out of the olive*tree*which*is*wild by nature, and

^{ainp1461} ^{pre3844} ^{an,nn5449} ^{pre1519} ^{an,nn2565} ^{an,aj4214} ^{ad3123}
wert grafted contrary to nature into a good*olive*tree: how much more shall

^{depro3778} ^{art3588} ^{pre2596/an,nn5449} ^{fp1461} ^{art,aj2398} ^{an,nn1636}
these, which be the natural *branches,* be grafted into their own olive tree?

"All Israel Shall Be Saved"

¹⁰⁶³ ^{pin2309} ³⁷⁵⁶ ^{an,nn80} ^{ppro5209} ^{pinf50} ^{depro5124}
25 For I would not, brethren, that ye should be ignorant of this

^{art,nn3466} ³³⁶³ ^{psa5600} ^{pr/an,aj5429} ^{pre3844} ^{rxpro1438} ³⁷⁵⁴ ^{an,nn4457} ^{pre575}
mystery, lest ye should be wise in your*own*conceits; that blindness in

^{an,nn3313} ^{pfi1096} ²⁴⁷⁴ ^{ad891 (repro3739)} ^{art3588} ⁿⁿ⁴¹³⁸ ^{art3588} ⁿⁿ¹⁴⁸⁴ ^{asba1525}
part is happened to Israel, until the fullness of the Gentiles be come in.

²⁵³² ^{ad3779} ^{an,aj3956} ²⁴⁷⁴ ^{fp4982} ^{ad2531} ^{pfip1125} ^{ft2240}
26 And so all Israel shall be saved: as it is written, There shall come

^{pre1537} ⁴⁶²² ^{art3588} ^{ppmp4506} ²⁵³² ^{ft654} ^{an,nn763} ^{pre575} ²³⁸⁴
out of Zion the Deliverer, and shall turn away ungodliness from Jacob:

²⁵³² ^{depro3778 (pre3844)} ^{ppro1700} ^{pr/art,nn1242} ^{ppro846} ^{ad3752} ^{asbm851} ^{ppro848}
27 For this *is* my covenant unto them, when I shall take away their

^{art,nn266}
sins. *(Is. 59:20,21; 27:9; Jer. 31:33,34)*

^{pre2596 (3303)} ^{art3588} ⁿⁿ²⁰⁹⁸ ^{pr/an,ajn2190} ^{pre1223/ppro5209} ¹¹⁶¹
28 As concerning the gospel, *they are* enemies for*your*sakes: but

^{pre2596} ^{art3588} ⁿⁿ¹⁵⁸⁹ ^{pr/an,aj27} ^{pre1223/art3588/nn3962}
as touching the election, *they are* beloved for*the*fathers'*sakes.

¹⁰⁶³ ^{art3588} ⁿⁿ⁵⁴⁸⁶ ²⁵³² ^{art,nn2821} ^{art,nn2316} ^{pr/an,aj278}
29 For the gifts and calling of God *are* without repentance.

¹⁰⁶³ ^{ad5618} ^{epn5210} ^{ad4218} ⁽²⁵³²⁾ ^{aina544} ^{art,nn2316} ¹¹⁶¹ ^{ad3568}
30 For as ye in*times*past have not believed God, yet have now

^{ainp1653} ^{depro5130} ^{art,nn543}
obtained mercy through their unbelief:

^{ad3779} ^{depro3778} ²⁵³² ^{ad3568} ^{aina544} ²⁴⁴³ ^{art,popro5212} ^{an,nn1656}
31 Even so have these also now not believed, that through your mercy
^{epn846} ²⁵³² ^{asbp1653}
they also may obtain mercy.

¹⁰⁶³ ^{art,nn2316} ^{aina4788} ^{art,ajn3956} ^{pre1519} ^{an,nn543} ²⁴⁴³
32 For God hath concluded them all in unbelief, that he might
^{asba1653} ^{art,ajn3956}
have mercy upon all.

⁵⁵⁹⁹ ^{an,nn899} ^{an,nn4149} ²⁵³² ^{an,nn4678} ²⁵³² ^{an,nn1108} ^{an,nn2316}
33 O the depth of the riches both of the wisdom and knowledge of God!
^{ad5613} ^{pr/an,aj419} ^{ppro848} ^{art,nn2917} ²⁵³² ^{ppro848} ^{art,nn3598} ^{pr/an,aj421}
how unsearchable *are* his judgments, and his ways past*finding*out!

(Is. 45:15; 55:8)

¹⁰⁶³ ^{inpro5101} ^{aina1097} ^{an,nn3563} ^{an,nn2962} ²²²⁸ ^{inpro5101} ^{aom1096} ^{ppro848}
34 For who hath known the mind of the Lord? or who hath been his
^{pr/an,nn4825}
counselor?   *(Job 15:8; Is. 40:13; Jer. 23:18)*

²²²⁸ ^{inpro5101} ^{aina2472} ^{ppro846} ²⁵³² ^{fp467} ^{ppro846}
35 Or who hath first given to him, and it shall be recompensed unto him
again?   *(Job 41:11)*

³⁷⁵⁴ ^{pre1537} ^{epn846} ²⁵³² ^{pre1223} ^{epn846} ²⁵³² ^{pre1519} ^{epn846} ^{art,ajn3956} ^{epn846}
36 For of him, and through him, and to him, *are* all things: to whom *be*
^{art,nn1391} ^{pre1519/art,nn165} ²⁸¹
glory forever. Amen.

Exhortation to Practical Living

^{pin3870} ^{ppro5209} ³⁷⁶⁷ ^{an,nn80} ^{pre1223} ^{art3588} ⁿⁿ³⁶²⁸ ^{art,nn2316}
12 I beseech you therefore, brethren, by the mercies of God, that
^{ainf3936} ^{ppro5216} ^{art,nn4983} ^{pap2198} ^{an,nn2378} ^{an,aj40} ^{an,ajn2101}
ye present your bodies a living sacrifice, holy, acceptable unto
^{art,nn2316} ^{ppro5216} ^{art,aj3050} ^{an,nn2999}
God, *which is* your reasonable service.

²⁵³² ³³⁶¹ ^{pim4964} ^{depro5129} ^{art,nn165} ²³⁵ ^{pim3339} ^{art3588}
2 And be not conformed to this world: but be ye transformed by the
ⁿⁿ³⁴² ^{ppro5216} ^{art,nn3563} ^{ppro5209} ^{aies1381} ^{inpro5101} ^{pr/art,ajn18} ²⁵³²
renewing of your mind, that ye may prove what *is* that good, and
^{pr/an,nn2101} ²⁵³² ^{pr/an,nn5046} ^{pr/art,nn2307} ^{art,nn2316}
acceptable, and perfect, will of God.

¹⁰⁶³ ^{pin3004} ^{pre1223} ^{art3588} ⁿⁿ⁵⁴⁸⁵ ^{art,aptp1325} ^{ppro3427} ^{an,aj3956} ^{art,pap5607}
☞ 3 For I say, through the grace given unto me, to every man that is
^{pre1722} ^{ppro5213} ³³⁶¹ ^{pinf5252/pre3844/repro3739} ^{pin1163} ^{pinf5426} ²³⁵
among you, not to think*of*himself*more*highly*than he ought to think; but
^{pinf5426} ^{aies4993} ^{ad5613} ^{art,nn2316} ^{aina3307} ^{an,ajn1538} ^{an,nn3358}
to think soberly, according as God hath dealt to every man the measure
^{an,nn4102}
of faith.

☞ **12:3** See note on 1 Corinthians 4:6, 7.

1063 ad2509   pin2192 an,aj4183 an,nn3196   pre1722 nu1520 an,nn4983   1161 an,aj3956   art,nn3196

4 For as we have many members in one body, and all members

pin2192 3756 art3588 ppro846   nn4234

have not the same office:

ad3779   art,aj4183 pin2070 nu1520 pr/an,nn4983 pre1722 an,nn5547   1161 art,pre2596 nu1520

5 So we, *being* many, are one body in Christ, and every one

an,nn3196   rcpro240

members one*of*another.

pap2192 1161 an,nn5486 an,aj1313   pre2596   art3588   nn5485   art,aptp1325   ppro2254

☞ 6 Having then gifts differing according to the grace that*is*given to us,

1535   an,nn4394   pre2596   art3588   nn356   art,nn4102

whether prophecy, *let us prophesy* according to the proportion of faith;

1535   an,nn1248   pre1722   art,nn1248   1535   art,pap1321   pre1722

7 Or ministry, *let us wait* on *our* ministering: or he*that*teacheth, on

art,nn1319

teaching;

1535   art,pap3870   pre1722   art,nn3874   art,pap3330

8 Or he*that*exhorteth, on exhortation: he*that*giveth, *let him do it*

pre1722   an,nn572   art,ppmp4291   pre1722   an,nn4710   art,pap1653   pre1722

with simplicity; he*that*ruleth, with diligence; he*that*showeth*mercy, with

an,nn2432

cheerfulness.

art,nn26   pr/an,aj505   pap655   art,ajn4190   ppmp2853

9 *Let* love be without dissimulation. Abhor that*which*is*evil; cleave

art,ajn18

to that*which*is*good.   *(Amos 5:15)*

pr/an,aj5387   rcpro240/pre1519   art,nn5360   art,nn5092

10 *Be* kindly affectioned one*to*another with brotherly love; in honor

pr/pmpp4285   rcpro240

preferring one another;

3361   pr/an,aj3636   art,nn4710   pr/pap2204   art,nn4151 pr/pap1398 art3588 nn2962

11 Not slothful in business; fervent in spirit; serving the Lord;

pr/pap5463   art,nn1680 pr/pap5278   art,nn2347   pr/pap4342   art,nn4335

12 Rejoicing in hope; patient in tribulation; continuing instant in prayer;

pr/pap2841   art3588   nn5532   art,ajn40   pr/pap1377   art,nn5381

13 Distributing to the necessity of saints; given to hospitality.

pim2127   art,pap1377   ppro5209 pim2127 2532 pim2672 3361

14 Bless them*which*persecute you: bless, and curse not.

pinf5463   pre3326   an,pap5463   2532 pinf2799 pre3326   an,pap2799

15 Rejoice with them*that*do*rejoice, and weep with them*that*weep.

(Ps. 35:13)

art3588 ppro846 pap5426   rcpro240/pre1519   pap5426 3361 art,ajn5308   235

16 *Be* of the same mind one*toward*another. Mind not high things, but

ppmp4879   art,ajn5011   pim1096 3361 pr/an,aj5429 pre3844   rxpro1438

condescend to men*of*low*estate. Be not wise in your*own*conceits.

(Prov. 3:7; Is. 5:21)

☞ **12:6–8** See note on 1 Corinthians 12:1–11.

pap591   an,ajn3367 an,ajn2556 pre473 an,ajn2556   ppmp4306   an,ajn2570

17 Recompense to no man evil for evil. Provide things honest

ad*1799   an,aj3956 an,nn444

in*the*sight of all men.   *(Prov. 3:4[Sept.])*

1487   an,ajn1415   art,pre1537/ppro5216   pap1514   pre3326 an,aj3956 an,nn444

18 If it be possible, as*much*as*lieth*in*you, live peaceably with all men.

an,ajn27   pap1556   3361   rxpro1438   235   aima1325 an,nn5117

19 Dearly beloved, avenge not yourselves, but *rather* give place unto

art,nn3709 1063   pfip1125   an,nn1557   epn1698 epn1473   ft467   pin3004   an,nn2962

wrath: for it is written, Vengeance *is* mine;   I   will repay, saith the Lord.

(Lev. 19:18; Deut. 32:35)

3767   1437   ppro4675 art,ajn2190   psa3983   ppro846 1437   psa1372

20 Therefore if   thine enemy hunger, feed him; if   he thirst,

pim4222/ppro846   1063   depro5124 pap4160   ft4987   an,nn440   an,nn4442 pre1909 ppro848 art,nn2776

give*him*drink: for in so doing thou shalt heap coals of fire on his head.

(Prov. 25:21,22)

3361   psa3528   pre5259 art,ajn2556 235   pim3528   art,ajn2556 pre1722 art,ajn18

21 Be not overcome of evil, but overcome evil with good.

"Subject Unto the Higher Powers"

an,aj3956 an,nn5590   pim5293   an,pap5242 an,nn1849 1063

13 ☞Let every soul be subject unto the higher powers. For there

pin2076 3756 an,nn1849 1508 pre575 an,nn2316(1161) art3588 nn1849   pap5607 pin1526 pr/pfpp5021

is no power but of   God: the powers that be are ordained

pre5259 art,nn2316

of God.   *(Prov. 8:15)*

art,ppmp498/5620   art3588 nn1849   pfi436   art3588   nn1296

2 Whosoever*therefore*resisteth the power, resisteth the ordinance of

art,nn2316 1161   art,pfp436   fm2983   rxpro1438   an,nn2917

God: and they*that*resist shall receive to themselves damnation.

1063   art,nn758 pin1526 3756 pr/an,nn5401 art,aj18 an,nn2041 235   art3588 an,ajn2556 pin2309

3 For rulers are not a terror to good works, but to the evil. Wilt thou

1161 3361   pifm5399   art3588   nn1849 pim4160   art,ajn18   2532   ft2192

then not be afraid of the power? do that*which*is*good, and thou shalt have

an,nn1868 pre1537   ppro846

praise of the same:

1063   pin2076   pr/an,nn1249   an,nn2316   ppro4671 pre1519 art,ajn18 1161 1437   psa4160

4 For he is   the minister of God to thee for good. But if thou do

art,ajn2556   pim5399   1063   pin5409   3756 art3588   nn3162   ad1500   1063   pin2076

that*which*is*evil, be afraid; for he beareth not the sword in vain: for he is

pr/an,nn1249   an,nn2316   pr/an,ajn1558 pre1519   an,nn3709   art,pap4238   art,ajn2556

the minister of God, a revenger to *execute* wrath upon him*that*doeth evil.

pre,repro1352   an,nn318   pip5293   3756 an,ajn3440 pre1223 art,nn3709 235 2532

5 Wherefore *ye* must needs be subject, not only for wrath, but also

pre1223/art,nn4983

for*conscience*sake.

☞ **13:1** See note on 1 Peter 2:17.

6 For for*this*cause pay ye tribute also: for they are God's ministers, attending continually upon this*very*thing.

7 Render therefore to all their dues: tribute to whom tribute *is due*; custom to whom custom; fear to whom fear; honor to whom honor.

8 Owe no man any thing, but to love one another: for he*that*loveth another hath fulfilled the law.

9 For this, Thou shalt not commit adultery, Thou shalt not kill, Thou shalt not steal, Thou shalt not bear*false*witness, Thou shalt not covet; and if*there*be*any other commandment, it is briefly comprehended in this saying, namely, Thou shalt love thy neighbor as thyself.

(Ex. 20:13-17; Deut. 5:17-21; Lev. 19:18)

10 Love worketh no ill to his neighbor: therefore love *is* the fulfilling of the law.

☞ 11 And that, knowing the time, that now *it is* high time to awake out of sleep: for now *is* our salvation nearer than when we believed.

12 The night is*far*spent, the day is*at*hand: let us therefore cast off the works of darkness, and let us put on the armor of light.

13 Let us walk honestly, as in the day; not in rioting and drunkenness, not in chambering and wantonness, not in strife and envying.

14 But put*ye*on the Lord Jesus Christ, and make not provision for the flesh, to *fulfill* the lusts *thereof*.

"Why Doest Thou Judge Thy Brother?"

14 Him*that*is*weak in the faith receive ye, *but* not to doubtful disputations.

☞ **13:11** See note on 1 Peter 1:5.

repro3739/3303   pin4100   ainf5315   an,ajn3956 (1161) art3588   pap770

2 For   one   believeth that he may eat all things: another, who is weak,

pin2068   an,nn3001

eateth herbs.

3361   art,pap2068   pim1848   art,pap2068/3361   2532   3361

3 Let not him*that*eateth despise him*that*eateth*not; and let not

art,pap2068/3361   pim2919   art,pap2068   1063 art,nn2316   aom4355

him*which*eateth*not   judge   him*that*eateth: for   God   hath   received

ppro846

him.

pr/inpro5101 pin1488 epn4771 art,pap2919   an,ajn245   an,nn3610   art,aj2398 an,nn2962

4 Who art thou that judgest another man's servant? to his own master he

pin4739   2228   pin4098   1161   fp2476   1063 art,nn2316 pin2076 pr/an,aj415

standeth or falleth. Yea, he shall be holden up: for God is able to

ainf2476/ppro846

make*him*stand.

repro3739/3303   pin2919   an,nn2250/pre3844/an,nn2250   (1161) repro3739   pin2919   an,aj3956

5 One man esteemeth one*day*above*another: another esteemeth every

an,nn2250   an,ajn1538   pim4135   pre1722 art,aj2398 an,nn3563

day alike. Let every man be fully persuaded in his own mind.

art,pap5426   art3588   nn2250   pin5426   an,nn2962   2532

6 He*that*regardeth   the   day,   regardeth it unto   the   Lord;   and

art,pap5426/3361   art3588 nn2250   an,nn2962   3756 pin5426   art,pap2068

he*that*regardeth*not the day, to the Lord he doth not regard it. He*that*eateth,

pin2068   an,nn2962 1063   pin2168/art,nn2316   2532   art,pap2068/3361

eateth to the Lord, for he giveth*God*thanks; and he*that*eateth*not to the

an,nn2962   pin2068 3756 2532   pin2168/art,nn2316

Lord he eateth not, and giveth*God*thanks.

1063 an,ajn3762   ppro2257 pin2198   rxpro1438   2532 an,ajn3762   pin599   rxpro1438

7 For none of us liveth to himself, and no man dieth to himself.

1063   1437   (5037) psa2198   pin2198   art3588   nn2962   5037   1437   psa599

8 For whether we live, we live unto the Lord; and whether we die,

pin599   art3588 nn2962 (5037)   1437   psa2198   3767   5037 (1437) psa599   pin2070 art3588

we die unto the Lord: whether we live therefore, or die, we are the

nn2962

Lord's.

1063 pre1519   depro5124 an,nn5547 2532 aina599 2532 aina450 2532   aina326   2443

9 For to this end Christ both died, and rose, and revived, that he might

asba2961   2532   an,ajn3498 2532 an,pap2198

be Lord both of the dead and living.

1161   inpro5101   epn4771 pin2919 ppro4675 art,nn80   2228 (2532) inpro5101   epn4771

10 But why dost thou judge thy brother? or why dost thou

pin1848   ppro4675 art,nn80 1063   an,ajn3956 fm3936   art3588   nn968

set*at*naught thy brother? for we shall all stand before the judgment seat

art,nn4457

of Christ.

1063   pfip1125   epn1473 pin2198 pin3004   an,nn2962 (3754) an,aj3956 an,nn1119   ft2578

11 For it is written, As I live, saith the Lord, every knee shall bow

epn1698 2532 an,aj3956 an,nn1100   fm1843   art,nn2316

to me, and every tongue shall confess to God.   (Is. 45:23)

686   3767   an,ajn1538   ppro2257   ft1325 an,nn3056 pre4012 rxpro1438   art,nn2316

12 So then every one of us shall give account of himself to God.

The Christian's Liberty

13 Let*us*not*therefore*judge one another any more: but judge this rather, that no man put a stumblingblock or an occasion*to*fall in *his* brother's way.

14 I know, and am persuaded by the Lord Jesus, that *there is* nothing unclean of itself: but to him*that*esteemeth any thing to be unclean, to him *it is* unclean.

15 But if thy brother be grieved with *thy* meat, now*walkest*thou*not charitably. Destroy not him with thy meat, for whom Christ died.

16 Let not then your good be evil*spoken*of:

17 For the kingdom of God is not meat and drink; but righteousness, and peace, and joy in the Holy Ghost.

18 For he that in these things serveth Christ *is* acceptable to God, and approved of men.

19 Let*us*therefore*follow*after the things which make for peace, and things wherewith one*may*edify another.

20 For meat destroy not the work of God. All things indeed *are* pure; but *it is* evil for that man who eateth with offense.

21 *It is* good neither to eat flesh, nor to drink wine, nor *any thing* whereby thy brother stumbleth, or is offended, or is made weak.

22 Hast thou faith? have *it* to thyself before God. Happy *is* he*that*condemneth not himself in that thing which he alloweth.

23 And he*that*doubteth is damned if he eat, because *he eateth* not of faith: for whatsoever *is* not of faith is sin.

Edify One Another

15

epn2249 1161   art,aj1415   pin3784   pinf941 art3588   nn771   art3588   ajn102
We then that*are*strong ought to bear the infirmities of the weak,
2532 3361   pinf700   rxpro1438
and not to please ourselves.

(1063)   an,ajn1538   ppro2257   pim700   art,ad4139   pre1519   art,ajn18   pre4314
2 Let every one of us please *his* neighbor for *his* good to
an,nn3619
edification.

1063   2532   art,nn5547   aina700   3756   rxpro1438   235   ad2531   pfip1125   art3588
3 For even Christ pleased not himself: but, as it is written, The
nn3680   art,pap3679   ppro4571 aina1968 pre1909 ppro1691
reproaches of them*that*reproached thee fell on me.   *(Ps. 69:9)*

1063   an,ajn3745   aina4270   aina4270   pre1519 art,popro2251
4 For whatsoever things were written aforetime were written for our
an,nn1319   2443   pre1223   art,nn5281   2532   art,nn3874   art3588   nn1124   psa2192
learning, that we through patience and comfort of the Scriptures might have
art,nn1680
hope.

1161   art3588   nn2316   art,nn5281   2532   art,nn3874   opt1325 ppro5213   pinf5426/art,ppro846
5 Now the God of patience and consolation grant you to be likeminded
rcpro240/pre1722   pre2596   an,nn5547 an,nn2424
one*toward*another according to Christ Jesus:

2443   ad3661   (pre1722) nu1520 an,nn4750   psa1392   art,nn2316   2532
6 That ye may with*one*mind *and* one mouth glorify God, even the
an,nn3962   ppro2257 art,nn2962 an,nn2424 an,nn5547
Father of our Lord Jesus Christ.

pre,repro1352   pim4355   rcpro240   ad2531 art,nn5547 2532   aom4355   ppro2248 pre1519
7 Wherefore receive ye one another, as Christ also received us to the
an,nn1391   an,nn2316
glory of God.

1161   pin3004   an,nn2424 an,nn5547 pfin1096   pr/an,nn1249   an,nn4061   pre5228
8 Now I say that Jesus Christ was a minister of the circumcision for the
an,nn225   an,nn2316   aies950 art3588   nn1860   art3588   nn3962
truth of God, to confirm the promises *made* unto the fathers: *(Mic. 7:20)*

1161   art3588   nn1484   ainf1392 art,nn2316 pre5228   an,nn1656   ad2531
9 And that the Gentiles might glorify God for *his* mercy; as it is
pfip1125   pre1223/depro5124   fm1843   ppro4671 pre1722   an,nn1484   2532   ft5567
written, For*this*cause I will confess to thee among the Gentiles, and sing unto
ppro4675 art,nn3686
thy name.   *(Ps. 18:49)*

2532   ad3825   pin3004   aipp2165   an,nn1484   pre3326 ppro848   art,nn2992
10 And again he saith, Rejoice, ye Gentiles, with his people.

                                                                  (Deut. 32:43)

2532   ad3825   pim134 art3588   nn2962 an,aj3956   art,nn1484   2532 aima1867 ppro846 an,aj3956
11 And again, Praise the Lord, all ye Gentiles; and laud him, all ye
art,nn2992
people.   *(Ps. 117:1)*

2532   ad3825   an,nn2268 pin3004   fm2071   art,nn4491   2421   2532
12 And again, Isaiah saith, There shall be a root of Jesse, and

art,ppmp450 pinf757 an,nn1484 pre1909 ppro846 an,nn1484 ft1679
he*that*shall*rise to reign over the Gentiles; in him shall the Gentiles trust.

(Is. 11:10)

1161 art3588 nn2316 an,nn1680 opt4137 ppro5209 an,aj3956 an,nn5479 2532 an,nn1515 aie4100
13 Now the God of hope fill you with all joy and peace in believing,

ppro5209 aies4052 pre1722 art,nn1680 pre1722 an,nn1411 an,aj40 an,nn4151
that ye may abound in hope, through the power of the Holy Ghost.

Paul's Diligence in Preaching the Gospel

1161 ppro1473 epn848 2532 pfip3982 pre4012 ppro5216 ppro3450 an,nn80 3754 epn848
14 And I myself also am persuaded of you, my brethren, that ye

2532 pin2075 pr/an,aj3324 an,nn19 pr/pfpp4137 an,aj3956 an,nn1108 pr/ppmp1410 2532
also are full of goodness, filled with all knowledge, able also to

pinf3560 rcpro240
admonish one another.

1161 an,nn80 aina1125 cd/an,ajn5112 ppro5213
15 Nevertheless, brethren, I have written the more boldly unto you

pre575/an,nn3313 ad5613 pap1878/ppro5209 pre1223 art3588 nn5485 art,aptp1325
in*some*sort, as putting*you*in*mind, because of the grace that*is*given

ppro3427 pre5259 art,nn2316
to me of God,

ppro3165 aies1511 pr/an,nn3011 an,nn2424 an,nn5547 pre1519 art3588 nn1484
16 That I should be the minister of Jesus Christ to the Gentiles,

pr/pap2418 art3588 nn2098 art,nn2316 2443 art3588 nn4376 art3588 nn1484 asbm1096
ministering the gospel of God, that the offering up of the Gentiles might be

pr/an,aj2144 pr/pfpp37 pre1722 an,aj40 an,nn4151
acceptable, being sanctified by the Holy Ghost.

pin2192 3767 an,nn2746 pre1722 an,nn2424 an,nn5547
17 I have therefore whereof*I*may*glory through Jesus Christ in

art,pre4314 an,nn2316
those*things*which*pertain to God.

1063 3756 ft5111 pinf2980 idpro5100 repro3739 an,nn5547
18 For I will not dare to speak of any of those things which Christ

3756 aom2716 pre1223 ppro1700 pre1519 an,nn5218/an,nn1484 an,nn3056 2532
hath not wrought by me, to make*the*Gentiles*obedient, by word and

an,nn2041
deed,

pre1722 an,nn1411 an,nn4592 2532 an,nn5059 pre1722 an,nn1411 an,nn4151
19 Through mighty signs and wonders, by the power of the Spirit of

an,nn2316 5620 pre575 2419 2532 an,ajn2945 ad3360 art,nn2437 ppro3165
God; so that from Jerusalem, and round about unto Illyricum, I have

pfin4137 art3588 nn2098 art,nn5547
fully preached the gospel of Christ.

1161 ad3779 ppmp5389 pifm2097 3756 ad3699 an,nn5547
20 Yea, so have I strived to preach*the*gospel, not where Christ was

ainp3687 3363 psa3618 pre1909 an,aj245 an,nn2310
named, lest I should build upon another man's foundation:

235   ad2531   pfip1125   repro3739   3756   ainp312   pre4012 (ppro846)   fm3700

21 But as it is written, To whom he was not spoken of, they shall see:

2532 repro3739   3756   pfi191   ft4920

and they that have not heard shall understand.   (Is. 52:15)

pre,repro1352   2532   art,ajn4183   ipf1465   infg2064   pre4314 ppro5209

22 For*which*cause also I have been much hindered from coming to you.

1161   ad3570   pap2192   ad3371   an,nn5117 pre1722 depro5125 art,nn2824   1161   pap2192

23 But now having no more place in these parts, and having a

an,nn1974   (pre575) an,aj4183 an,nn2094   infg2064   pre4314 ppro5209

great desire these many years to come unto you;

ad5613/1437   psmp4198   pre1519 art,nn4681   fm2064   pre4314 ppro5209 1063

24 Whensoever I take*my*journey into Spain, I will come to you: for I

pim1679   aifm2300 ppro5209   ppmp1279   2532   aifp4311   ad1563

trust to see you in*my*journey, and to be brought*on*my*way thitherward

pre5259 ppro5216 1437 nu,ajn4412   pre575/an,nn3313 asbp1705   ppro5216

by you, if first I be somewhat filled with your *company*.

1161   ad3570   pinm4198 pre1519   2419   pap1247   art3588 ajn40

25 But now I go unto Jerusalem to minister unto the saints.

1063   aina2106   an,nn3109   2532   an,nn882   aifm4160   idpro5100

26 For it hath pleased them of Macedonia and Achaia to make a certain

an,nn2842   pre1519 art3588 ajn4434 art,ajn40   art3588   pre1722   2419

contribution for the poor saints which are at Jerusalem.

aina2106   1063   2532 ppro848 pr/an,nn3781   pin1526 1063 1487 art3588

27 It hath pleased them verily; and their debtors they are. For if the

nn1484   aina2841   ppro848   art,ajn4152   pin3784   2532

Gentiles have been made partakers of their spiritual things, their duty is also to

ainf3008   ppro846   art,ajn4559

minister unto them in carnal things.

3767   apta2005   depro5124 2532   aptm4972   ppro846 depro5126

28 When therefore I have performed this, and have sealed to them this

art,nn2590   fm565   pre1223 ppro5216 pre1519 art,nn4681

fruit, I will come by you into Spain.

1161   pin1492   3754   ppmp2064 pre4314 ppro5209   fm2064 pre1722

29 And I am sure that, when I come unto you, I shall come in the

an,nn4138   an,nn2129   art3588 nn2098   art,nn5547

fullness of the blessing of the gospel of Christ.

1161   pin3870 ppro5209   an,nn80   pre1223/ppro2257/art,nn2962/an,nn2424/an,nn5547   2532

30 Now I beseech you, brethren, for*the*Lord*Jesus*Christ's*sake, and

pre1223 art3588   nn26   art3588   nn4151   aifm4865   ppro3427 pre1722

for the love of the Spirit, that ye strive*together*with me in your

art,nn4335   pre4314 art,nn2316 pre5228 ppro1700

prayers to God for me;

2443   asbp4506   pre575   art,pap544   pre1722 art,nn2449

31 That I may be delivered from them*that*do*not*believe in Judea;

2532 2443 ppro3450 art,nn1248 art3588   pre1519   2419   asbm1096 pr/an,aj2144 art3588

and that my service which *I have* for Jerusalem may be accepted of the

ajn40

saints;

2443   asba2064 pre4314 ppro5209 pre1722 an,nn5479 pre1223   an,nn2307   an,nn2316 2532

32 That I may come unto you with joy by the will of God, and may

ppro5213   asbm4875

with you be refreshed.

1161   art3588 nn2316   art,nn1515   pre3326 ppro5216 an,aj3956   281

33 Now the God of peace *be* with you all. Amen.

Greetings

16

(1161)   pin4921   ppro5213 an,nn5402 ppro2257 art,nn79   pap5607   pr/an,nn1249

☞ I commend unto you Phebe our sister, which is a servant

art3588   nn1577   art3588   pre1722   an,nn2747

of the church which is at Cenchrea:

2443   asbm4327 ppro846 pre1722   an,nn2962   ad516   art,ajn40   2532

2 That ye receive her in the Lord, as becometh saints, and that ye

asba3936 ppro846 pre1722 repro3739/302   an,nn4229   psa5535   ppro5216 1063 depro3778 (2532) ainp1096

assist her in whatsoever business she hath need of you: for she hath been

pr/an,nn4368   an,ajn4183 2532 (ppro1700) epn848

a succorer of many, and of myself also.

aipm782   an,nn4252   2532   an,nn207 ppro3450 art,ajn4904 pre1722 an,nn5547 an,nn2424

3 Greet Priscilla and Aquila my helpers in Christ Jesus:

repro3748   pre5228 ppro3450 art,nn5590   aina5294   art,rxpro1438 sg/an,nn5137   repro3739 3756

4 Who have for my life laid down their own necks: unto whom not

an,ajn3441 epn1473   pin2168   235 2532 an,aj3956 art3588 nn1577   art3588   nn1484

only I give thanks, but also all the churches of the Gentiles.

(2532)   art3588   nn1577   pre2596 ppro848   an,nn3624 aipm782   ppro3450

5 Likewise *greet* the church that is in their house. Salute my

art,aj27   an,nn1866   repro3739 pin2076   pr/an,nn536   art,nn882 pre1519 an,nn5547

well beloved Epaenetus, who is the firstfruits of Achaia unto Christ.

aipm782   3137   repro3748   aina2872/an,ajn4183   pre1519 ppro2248

6 Greet Mary, who bestowed*much*labor on us.

aipm782   an,nn408   2532 an,nn2458 ppro3450 art,ajn4773   2532 ppro3450   an,ajn4869

7 Salute Andronicus and Junia, my kinsmen, and my fellow prisoners,

repro3748 pin1526   pr/an,aj1978 pre1722 art3588   nn652   repro3739 2532   pfi1096 pre1722 an,nn5547 pre4253

who are of note among the apostles, who also were in Christ before

ppro1700

me.

aipm782   an,nn291   ppro3450 art,aj27 pre1722   an,nn2962

8 Greet Amplias my beloved in the Lord.

aipm782   an,nn3773   ppro2257 art,ajn4904 pre1722 an,nn5547 2532   an,nn4720 ppro3450   art,aj27

9 Salute Urbane, our helper in Christ, and Stachys my beloved.

aipm782   an,nn559   art,aj1384   pre1722 an,nn5547 aipm782   art3588   pre1537

10 Salute Apelles approved in Christ. Salute them which are of

art,nn711

Aristobulus' *household*.

aipm782   an,nn2267   ppro3450 art,ajn4773 aipm782 art3588   pre1537 art3588

11 Salute Herodion my kinsman. Greet them that be of the *household* of

nn3488   art,pap5607 pre1722   an,nn2962

Narcissus, which are in the Lord.

☞ **16:1–4** See note on 1 Timothy 2:9–15.

aipm782   an,nn5170   2532   an,nn5173   art3588   pap2872   pre1722   an,nn2962   aipm782   art3588

12 Salute Tryphena and Tryphosa, who labor in the Lord. Salute the

aj27   an,nn4069   repro3748   aina2872   an,ajn4183 pre1722   an,nn2962

beloved Persis, which labored much in the Lord.

aipm782   an,nn4504   art,aj1488   pre1722   an,nn2962   2532   ppro848   art,nn3384   2532   ppro1700

13 Salute Rufus chosen in the Lord, and his mother and mine.

aipm782   an,nn799   an,nn5393   an,nn2057   an,nn3969   an,nn2060   2532   art3588

14 Salute Asyncritus, Phlegon, Hermas, Patrobas, Hermes, and the

nn80   pre4862 ppro846

brethren which are with them.

aipm782   an,nn5378   2532 an,nn2456   an,nn3517   2532 ppro848 art,nn79   2532   an,nn3652   2532

15 Salute Philologus, and Julia, Nereus, and his sister, and Olympas, and

an,aj3956 art3588   ajn40   pre4862 ppro846

all the saints which are with them.

aipm782   rcpro240   pre1722 an,aj40 an,nn5370 art3588   nn1577   art,nn5547   pinm782 ppro5209

16 Salute one another with a holy kiss. The churches of Christ salute you.

Exhortation to Unity

1161   pin3870   ppro5209   an,nn80   pinf4648   art,pap4160   art,nn1370   2532

17 Now I beseech you, brethren, mark them*which*cause divisions and

art,nn4625   pre3844   art3588   nn1322   repro3739 epn5210   aina3129   2532 aima1578/pre575 ppro846

offenses contrary to the doctrine which ye have learned; and avoid them.

1063   art,ajn5108   pin1398   3756 ppro2257 art,nn2962 an,nn2424   an,nn5547   235

18 For they*that*are*such serve not our Lord Jesus Christ, but

rxpro1438   art,nn2836   2532 pre1223   art,nn5542   2532   an,nn2129   pin1818   art3588   nn2588

their own belly; and by good words and fair speeches deceive the hearts of

art3588   ajn172

the simple.

1063   ppro5216   art,nn5218   aina864   pre1519 an,ajn3956   pin5463

19 For your obedience is come abroad unto all *men*. I am glad

3767   art,pre1909/ppro5213   1161   pin2309   ppro5209   (pinf1511) pr/an,aj4680

therefore on*your*behalf: but yet I would have you wise

(3303) pre1519   art,ajn18   1161 pr/an,aj185   pre1519   art,ajn2556

unto that*which*is*good, and simple concerning evil.

1161   art3588   nn2316   art,nn1515   ft4937   art,nn4567   pre5259 ppro2257 art,nn4228 pre1722/an,nn5034

20 And the God of peace shall bruise Satan under your feet shortly.

art3588   nn5485   ppro2257 art,nn2962 an,nn2424 an,nn5547   pre3326 ppro5216   281

The grace of our Lord Jesus Christ *be* with you. Amen.   *(Gen. 3:15)*

an,nn5095   ppro3450   art,ajn4904   2532   an,nn3066 2532 an,nn2394 2532   an,nn4989   ppro3450

21 Timothy my workfellow, and Lucius, and Jason, and Sosipater, my

art,ajn4773   pinm782 ppro5209

kinsmen, salute you.

epn1473   an,nn5060   art,apta1125   art,nn1992   pinm782 ppro5209 pre1722   an,nn2962

22 I Tertius, who wrote *this* epistle, salute you in the Lord.

an,nn1053 ppro3450 art,aj3581 2532   art3588 an,aj3650   nn1577   pinm782 ppro5209 an,nn2037   art3588

☞ 23 Gaius mine host, and of the whole church, saluteth you. Erastus the

nn3623   art3588 nn4172   pinm782 ppro5209 2532   an,nn2890   art,nn80

chamberlain of the city saluteth you, and Quartus a brother.

☞ **16:23** See note on 3 John 1:1.

art3588 nn5485   ppro2257 art,nn2962 an,nn2424 an,nn5547   pre3326 ppro5216 an,aj3956   281

24 The grace of our Lord Jesus Christ *be* with you all. Amen.

1161   art,ppmp1410   ainf4741 ppro5209   pre2596   ppro3450 art,nn2098

25 Now to him*that*is*of*power to establish you according to my gospel,

2532 art3588   nn2782   an,nn2424 an,nn5547 pre2596   an,nn602   an,nn3466

and the preaching of Jesus Christ, according to the revelation of the mystery,

pfpp4601   an,nn5550/an,aj166

which was kept secret since*the*world*began,

1161   ad3568   aptp5319   5037 pre1223   an,nn1124   an,aj4397

26 But now is made manifest, and by the Scriptures of the prophets,

pre2596   an,nn2003   art3588   aj166   an,nn2316   aptp1107   pre1519 an,aj3956

according to the commandment of the everlasting God, made known to all

art,nn1484 pre1519   an,nn5218   an,nn4102

nations for the obedience of faith:

an,nn2316 an,aj3441 an,aj4680 (repro3739) art,nn1391   pre1223   an,nn2424 an,nn5547 pre1519/art,nn165   281

27 To God only wise, be glory through Jesus Christ forever. Amen.

The First Epistle of Paul the Apostle to the

CORINTHIANS

Corinth was an important cosmopolitan city located in the Roman province of Achaia (the southern part of modern-day Greece) on a large isthmus about fifty miles west of Athens. It was situated along a major trade route and had a thriving economy. For this reason, large numbers of sailors and merchants from every nation flocked to the city of Corinth. During the first century, it was one of the largest cities in the Roman Empire and by the end of the second century it had become one of richest cities in the world.

Corinth was a strategic center of influence for the gospel since those travelers who heard the gospel there could carry it to all parts of the world. The city of Corinth, however, was one of the wickedest cities of ancient times. Immorality, unscrupulous business dealings, and pagan practices abounded. Of the scores of heathen religions that were practiced in the city, the most well-known was the worship of Aphrodite, the goddess of love and beauty. The temple of Aphrodite stood on the most prominent point in the city, a hill called Acrocorinth, and housed one thousand "temple prostitutes."

Paul was able to establish a church in Corinth during his eighteen month residence there (about A.D. 52–53) on his second missionary journey (Acts 18:1–11; 1 Cor. 2:1, 2). Paul lived and worked as a tentmaker with two other Jewish converts, Aquila and Priscilla, who had recently come from Rome (Acts 18:1, 2). When Paul left Corinth, a man named Apollos ministered there after Aquila and Priscilla had more completely expounded the gospel to him (Acts 18:26, 27; 19:1; see 1 Cor. 1:12; 16:12). Three years after this, Paul wrote this letter from Ephesus to the Corinthian believers. Later, Paul received a report from the members of the household of Chloe concerning the bad conduct of some in the church (1 Cor. 1:11). Many of the members had recently been converted from paganism and were having difficulty breaking habits of their former lifestyles. There were such deep divisions among them that some of the believers were bringing lawsuits against one another and allowing unbelieving judges to settle the disputes (chap. 6).

Paul reprimanded the church for failing to discipline certain of its members who were guilty of gross immorality (chap. 5). He also gave them counsel regarding some of the common marriage problems, and instructed them in the proper conduct of those who were unmarried (chap. 7). In addition, Paul discussed the eating of meats offered to idols (1 Cor. 8; 10:18–31), abuses of the Lord's Supper (1 Cor. 11:17–34), spiritual gifts (chaps. 12; 13), conduct in the formal assemblies for worship (1 Cor. 11:2–16; 14:1–40), and the resurrection (chap. 15).

1
an,nn3972 an,aj2822   an,nn652   an,nn2424 an,nn5547   pre1223   an,nn2307   an,nn2316 2532
Paul called *to be* an apostle of Jesus Christ through the will of God, and
an,nn4988   art,nn80
Sosthenes *our* brother,

2 Unto the church of God which is at Corinth, to them that are sanctified in Christ Jesus, called *to be* saints, with all that in every place call upon the name of Jesus Christ our Lord, both theirs and ours:

3 Grace *be* unto you, and peace, from God our Father, and *from* the Lord Jesus Christ.

☞ 4 I thank my God always on*your*behalf, for the grace of God which*is*given you by Jesus Christ;

5 That in every thing ye are enriched by him, in all utterance, and *in* all knowledge;

6 Even as the testimony of Christ was confirmed in you:

7 So that ye come behind in no gift; waiting for the coming of our Lord Jesus Christ:

☞ 8 Who shall also confirm you unto the end, *that ye may be* blameless in the day of our Lord Jesus Christ.

9 God *is* faithful, by whom ye were called unto the fellowship of his Son Jesus Christ our Lord.   *(Deut. 7:9)*

Exhortation to Unity

☞ 10 Now I beseech you, brethren, by the name of our Lord Jesus Christ, that ye all speak the same thing, and *that* there be no divisions among you; but *that* ye be perfectly*joined*together in the same mind and in the same judgment.

☞ 1:4–7 See note on 1 Corinthians 12:1–11.

☞ 1:8 See note on 1 Thessalonians 5:2.

☞ 1:10–13 The Apostle Paul opens chapter one with a statement that believers are sanctified and secure in their position in Christ (vv. 2, 8). Then, in verse ten, Paul gives the occasion for his letter; that is, it had been reported to him that there were divisions in the church (v. 11). One such division concerned the leaders that the people followed. There were some who followed after Apollos, some after Peter, and some after Paul (cf. 1 Cor. 3:4, 5). Paul was exhorting these believers to be joined together in Christ, not to another man (see note on 1 Cor. 4:6, 7).

1063   ainp1213   pre4012 ppro5216 ppro3450   an,nn80   pre5259 art3588
11 For it hath been declared unto me of you, my brethren, by them

an,nn5514   3754   pin1526   an,nn2054   pre1722 ppro5213
which are of the house of Chloe, that there are contentions among you.

1161   depro5124   pin3004   3754   an,ajn1538   ppro5216   pin3004   epn1473 (3303) pin1510   an,nn3972   1161
12 Now this I say, that every one of you saith,   I   am of Paul; and

epn1473   an,nn625   1161 epn1473   an,nn2786   1161 epn1473   an,nn5547
I of Apollos; and I of Cephas; and I of Christ.

art,nn5547   pfip3307   (3361) an,nn3972   ainp4717   pre5228 ppro5216   2228   ainp907
☞ 13 Is Christ divided? was Paul crucified for you? or were ye baptized

pre1519 art3588   nn3686   an,nn3972
in the name of Paul?

pin2168 art,nn2316   3754   aina907   an,ajn3762   ppro5216 1508   an,nn2921   2532   an,nn1050
☞ 14 I thank God that I baptized none of you, but Crispus and Gaius;

3363   idpro5100   asba2036   3754   aina907   pre1519 art,popro1699   an,nn3686
15 Lest any should say that I had baptized in mine own name.

1161   aina907   2532   art3588   nn3624   an,nn4734   an,ajn3063   pin1492 3756
16 And I baptized also the household of Stephanas: besides, I know not

idpro1536/aina907   an,ajn243
whether*I*baptized*any other.

1063   an,nn5547   aina649 ppro3165   3756   pinf907   235   pifm2097   3756
17 For Christ sent me not to baptize, but to preach*the*gospel: not

pre1722   an,nn4678   an,nn3056   3363   art3588   nn4716   art,nn5547
with wisdom of words, lest the cross of Christ should be

asbp2758
made*of*none*effect.

True and False Wisdom

1063 art3588   nn3056   (art3588) art3588 nn4716 pin2076   art,ppmp622   (3303)   pr/an,nn3472
18 For the preaching of the cross is to them*that*perish   foolishness;

1161   ppro2254 art3588   ppmp4982   pin2076   pr/an,nn1411   an,nn2316
but unto us which are saved it is the power of God.

1063   pfip1125   ft622   art3588   nn4678   art3588   ajn4680   2532
19 For it is written, I will destroy the wisdom of the wise, and will

ft114   art3588   nn4907   art3588   ajn4908
bring*to*nothing the understanding of the prudent.   *(Is. 29:14)*

ad4226   an,ajn4680   ad4226   an,nn1122   ad4226   an,nn4804   depro5127
20 Where *is* the wise? where *is* the scribe? where *is* the disputer of this

art,nn165   3780 art,nn2316   aina3471   art3588   nn4678   depro5127 art,nn2889
world? hath not God made foolish the wisdom of this world?

(Is. 19:12; 33:18; 44:25)

1063   1894   pre1722 art3588   nn4678   art,nn2316 art3588   nn2889 pre1223 art,nn4678   aina1097
21 For after that in the wisdom of God the world by wisdom knew

---

☞ **1:13** See note on Mark 16:16 concerning baptism.
☞ **1:14** See note on 3 John 1:1 concerning Gaius.

_{3756   art,nn2316   aina2106   art,nn2316   pre1223   art3588   nn3472   art,nn2782   ainf4982}

not God, it pleased God by the foolishness of preaching to save

_{art,pap4100}

them*that*believe.

_{1894   (2532) an,nn2453   pin154   an,nn4592 2532   an,nn1672   pin2212   an,nn4678}

22 For the Jews require a sign, and the Greeks seek after wisdom:

_{1161   epn2249   pin2784   an,nn5547   pfpp4717   an,nn2453   (3303) pr/an,nn4625   1161}

23 But we preach Christ crucified, unto the Jews a stumblingblock, and

_{an,nn1672   pr/an,nn3472}

unto the Greeks foolishness;

_{1161   epn846   art,ajn2822   5037 an,nn2453 2532   an,nn1672   an,nn5547}

24 But unto them which*are*called, both Jews and Greeks, Christ the

_{pr/an,nn1411   an,nn2316 2532   pr/an,nn4678   an,nn2316}

power of God, and the wisdom of God.

_{3754   art3588   ajn3474   art,nn2316 pin2076 pr/cd/an,aj4680   art,nn444 2532 art3588}

25 Because the foolishness of God is wiser than men; and the

_{ajn772   art,nn2316 pin2076 pr/cd/an,aj2478   art,nn444}

weakness of God is stronger than men.

_{1063   pin991 ppro5216 art,nn2821   an,nn80   3754 3756 an,aj4183   an,ajn4680   pre2596}

26 For ye see your calling, brethren, how that not many wise men after

_{an,nn4561 3756 an,aj4183   an,ajn1415   3756 an,aj4183 an,ajn2104}

the flesh, not many mighty, not many noble, *are called*:

_{235   art,nn2316   aom1586   art3588   ajn3474   art3588   nn2889 2443 asba2617   art3588}

27 But God hath chosen the foolish things of the world to confound the

_{ajn4680 2532 art,nn2316   aom1586   art3588   ajn772   art3588   nn2889 2443 asba2617}

wise; and God hath chosen the weak things of the world to confound

_{art,ajn2478}

the*things*which*are*mighty;

_{2532   art,ajn36   art3588   nn2889   2532   art,pfpp1848}

28 And base things of the world, and things*which*are*despised, hath

_{art,nn2316   aom1586   2532   art3588   pap5607   3361   2554   asba2673}

God chosen, *yea,* and things which are not, to bring*to*naught

_{art,pap5607}

things*that*are:

_{3704   an,aj3956/3361 an,nn4561   asbm2744   ad*1799/ppro846}

29 That no flesh should glory in*his*presence.

_{1161   pre1537 epn846 pin2075 epn5210 pre1722 an,nn5547   an,nn2424 repro3739 pre575 an,nn2316   ainp1096}

30 But of him are ye in Christ Jesus, who of God is made unto

_{ppro2254 pr/an,nn4678 5037   pr/an,nn1343   2532   pr/an,nn38   2532   pr/an,nn629}

us wisdom, and righteousness, and sanctification, and redemption:

_{2443   ad2531   pfip1125   art3588   ppmp2744   pim2744 pre1722}

31 That, according as it is written, He that glorieth, let him glory in the

_{an,nn2962}

Lord.
                                                              (Jer. 9:24)

The Power of God

_{epn2504   an,nn80   apta2064 pre4314 ppro5209 aina2064 3756 pre2596   an,nn5247}

2 And I, brethren, when I came to you, came not with excellency of

_{an,nn3056 2228   an,nn4678 pap2605   ppro5213 art3588   nn3142   art,nn2316}

speech or of wisdom, declaring unto you the testimony of God.

1063   aina2919   3756   infg1492   idpro5100   pre1722 ppro5213 1508   an,nn2424   an,nn5547

2 For I determined not to know any thing among you, save Jesus Christ,

2532 depro5126 pfpp4717

and him crucified.

2532 epn1473 aom1096 pre4314 ppro5209 pre1722   an,nn769   2532 pre1722 an,nn5401 2532 pre1722 an,aj4183

3 And I was with you in weakness, and in fear, and in much

an,nn5156

trembling.

2532   ppro3450 art,nn3056   2532 ppro3450   art,nn2782   3756 pre1722   an,aj3981   an,nn3056

4 And my speech and my preaching *was* not with enticing words of

an,aj442   an,nn4678   235 pre1722   an,nn585   an,nn4151 2532   an,nn1411

man's wisdom, but in demonstration of the Spirit and of power:

2443   ppro5216 art,nn4102   3361 psa5600 pre1722   an,nn4678   an,nn444   235 pre1722

5 That your faith should not stand in the wisdom of men, but in the

an,nn1411   an,nn2316

power of God.

True Wisdom

1161   pin2980   an,nn4678   pre1722   art,ajn5046   1161   3756

6 Howbeit we speak wisdom among them*that*are*perfect: yet not the

an,nn4678   depro5127 art,nn165 3761   art3588 nn758   depro5127 art,nn165

wisdom of this world, nor of the princes of this world,

art,ppmp2673

that*come*to*naught:

235   pin2980   an,nn4678   an,nn2316 pre1722 an,nn3466   art3588 pfpp613

7 But we speak the wisdom of God in a mystery, *even* the hidden *wisdom,*

repro3739 art,nn2316   aina4309   pre4253 art3588   nn165   pre1519 ppro2257 an,nn1391

which God ordained before the world unto our glory:

repro3739 an,ajn3762   art3588   nn758   depro5127 art,nn165 pfi1097 1063 (1487)   aina1097

8 Which none of the princes of this world knew: for had they known *it,*

3756   (302)   aina4717   art3588 nn2962   art,nn1391

they would not have crucified the Lord of glory.

235   ad2531   pfip1125 (repro3739) an,nn3788   3756 aina1492 3756 an,nn3755 aina191   2532/3756

9 But as it is written, Eye hath not seen, nor ear heard, neither have

aina305   pre1909   an,nn2588   an,nn444   repro3739 art,nn2316   aina2090

entered into the heart of man, the things which God hath prepared for

art,pap25   ppro846

them*that*love him.   *(Is. 64:40)*

1161 art,nn2316   aina601   epn2254 pre1223 ppro848 art,nn4151 1063 art3588 nn4151

10 But God hath revealed *them* unto us by his Spirit: for the Spirit

pin2045   an,ajn3956   2532 art3588   nn899   art,nn2316

searcheth all things, yea, the deep things of God.

1063 inpro5101 an,nn444 pin1492   art3588   art,nn444 1508 art3588   nn4151   art,nn444

11 For what man knoweth the things of a man, save the spirit of man

art3588   pre1722 ppro846 253 ad3779   art3588   art,nn2316 pin1492   an,ajn3762 1508 art3588

which is in him? even so the things of God knoweth no man, but the

nn4151   art,nn2316

Spirit of God.   *(Prov. 20:27)*

1161 epn2249   aina2983   3756 art3588 nn4151   art3588 nn2889   235 art3588 nn4151

12 Now we have received, not the spirit of the world, but the Spirit

art3588   pre1537 art,nn2316 2443   asba1492   art3588   aptp5483
which is of God; that we might know the things that are freely given
pppro2254 pre5259 art,nn2316
to us   of God.

repro3739   2532   pin2980   3756 pre1722   an,nn3056   an,aj442   an,nn4678
13 Which things also we speak, not in the words which man's wisdom
an,aj1318   235   pre1722   an,aj40 an,nn4151   an,aj1318   pap4793   an,ajn4152
teacheth, but which the Holy Ghost teacheth; comparing spiritual things with
an,ajn4152
spiritual.

1161   an,nn5591   an,nn444   pinm1209   3756   art3588   art3588   nn4151   art,nn2316 1063
☞ 14 But the natural man receiveth not the things of the Spirit of God: for
pin2076   pr/an,nn3472   ppro846   2532/3756 pinm1410   ainf1097   3754
they are foolishness unto him: neither can he know *them,* because they are
ad4153   pinp350
spiritually discerned.

1161   art,ajn4152   (3303)   pin350   an,ajn3956   1161 epn846   pinp350
15 But he*that*is*spiritual   judgeth all things, yet he himself is judged
pre5259   an,ajn3762
of no man.

1063   inpro5101   aina1097   an,nn3563   an,nn2962 repro3739   ft4822   ppro846
16 For who hath known the mind of the Lord, that he may instruct him?
1161 epn2249 pin2192   an,nn3563   an,nn5547
But we have the mind of Christ.   *(Is. 40:13)*

Jesus Is the Foundation

2532 epn1473   an,nn80   ainp1410 3756 ainf2980   ppro5213 ad5613   an,ajn4152   235 ad5613
3 And I, brethren, could not speak unto you as unto spiritual, but as
an,ajn4559   ad5613   an,ajn3516 pre1722 an,nn5547
unto carnal, *even* as unto babes in Christ.

aina4222   ppro5209   an,nn1051   2532   3756   an,nn1033   1063
2 I   have   fed   you   with   milk,   and   not   with   meat: for
ad3768/ipf1410   (235)   3777   ad2089 ad3568   pinm1410
hitherto*ye*were*not*able *to bear* it, neither yet now are ye able.

1063   pin2075 ad2089 pr/an,aj4559 1063   ad3699   pre1722 ppro5213 an,nn2205   2532
3 For ye are yet carnal: for whereas *there is* among you envying, and
an,nn2054 2532   an,nn1370   pin2075   3780 pr/an,aj4559 2532 pin4043 pre2596 an,nn444
strife, and divisions, are ye not carnal, and walk as men?

1063   ad3752 idpro5100 psa3004 epn1473 (3303) pin1510   an,nn3972 1161 an,ajn2087 epn1473
4 For while one saith,   I   am of Paul; and another, I *am* of
an,nn625   pin2075   3780 pr/an,aj4559
Apollos; are ye not carnal?

☞ **2:14** The word translated "natural" from the Greek is *psuchikós* (5591) referring to the man who is governed only by his environment; namely, his natural or animal instincts, as a result of his fallen Adamic nature (Rom 5:12). This man is unable to understand spiritual truths because he does not possess the indwelling Spirit of God.

inpro5101   3767   pin2076 pr/an,nn3972 1161 inpro5101   pr/an,nn625   235 (2228)   pr/an,nn1249   pre1223 repro3739

5 Who then is Paul, and who *is* Apollos, but ministers by whom ye

aina4100   2532   ad5613 art3588 nn2962 aina1325   an,ajn1538

believed, even as the Lord gave to every man?

epn1473   aina5452   an,nn625   aina4222   235 art,nn2316   ipf837

6 I have planted, Apollos watered; but God gave*the*increase.

5620   3777   pin2076   art,pap5452   pr/idpro5100   3777

7 So then neither is he*that*planteth any thing, neither

art,pap4222   235 art,nn2316   pap837

he*that*watereth; but God that giveth*the*increase.

1161   art,pap5452   2532   art,pap4222   pin1526 pr/nu,ajn1520 1161   an,ajn1538

8 Now he*that*planteth and he*that*watereth are one: and every man

fm2983   art,aj2398   an,nn3408   pre2596   art,aj2398   an,nn2873

shall receive his own reward according to his own labor.

1063   pin2070   pr/an,aj4904   an,nn2316   pin2075 an,nn2316   pr/an,nn1091

9 For we are laborers*together*with God: ye are God's husbandry, *ye are*

an,nn2316   pr/an,nn3619

God's building.

pre2596   art3588   nn5485   art,nn2316   art,aptp1325   ppro3427 ad5613   an,aj4680

10 According to the grace of God which*is*given unto me, as a wise

an,nn753   pfi5087   an,nn2310   1161   an,ajn243   pin2026   1161

masterbuilder, I have laid the foundation, and another buildeth thereon. But let

an,ajn1538   pim991   ad4459   pin2026

every man take heed how he buildeth thereupon.

1063   an,aj243   an,nn2310   pinm1410 an,ajn3762 ainf5087 pre3844   art,ppmp2749   repro3739 pin2076

11 For other foundation can no man lay than that*is*laid, which is

pr/an,nn2424 pr/art,nn5547

Jesus Christ.   *(Is. 28:16)*

1161   idpro1536   pin2026   pre1909 depro5126   art,nn2310   an,nn5557   an,nn696   an,aj5093

12 Now if*any*man build upon this foundation gold, silver, precious

an,nn3037   an,nn3586 an,nn5528   an,nn2562

stones, wood, hay, stubble;

an,ajn1538   art,nn2041   fm1096   pr/an,aj5318   1063 art3588 nn2250   ft1213

13 Every man's work shall be made manifest: for the day shall declare it,

3754   pinp601   pre1722 an,nn4442 2532 art3588 nn4442   ft1381   an,ajn1538   art,nn2041

because it shall be revealed by fire; and the fire shall try every man's work

pr/an,aj3697   pin2076

of what sort it is.

idpro1536   art,nn2041   pin3306 repro3739   aina2026

14 If*any*man's work abide which he hath built thereupon, he shall

fm2983   an,nn3408

receive a reward.

idpro1536   art,nn2041   fm2618   ft2210   1161 epn848

15 If*any*man's work shall be burned, he shall suffer loss: but he himself

fp4982   1161 ad3779 ad5613 pre1223 an,nn4442

shall be saved; yet so as by fire.

pin1492   3756   3754   pin2075   pr/an,nn3485   an,nn2316 2532   art3588 nn4151

16 Know ye not that ye are the temple of God, and *that* the Spirit of

art,nn2316   pin3611   pre1722 ppro5213

God dwelleth in you?

17 If*any*man defile the temple of God, him shall God destroy; for the temple of God is holy, which *temple* ye are.

18 Let no man deceive himself. If*any*man among you seemeth to be wise in this world, let him become a fool, that he may be wise.

19 For the wisdom of this world is foolishness with God. For it is written, He taketh the wise in their own craftiness. *(Job 5:13)*

20 And again, The Lord knoweth the thoughts of the wise, that they are vain. *(Ps. 94:11)*

21 Therefore let no man glory in men. For all things are yours;

22 Whether Paul, or Apollos, or Cephas, or the world, or life, or death, or things present, or things*to*come; all are yours;

23 And ye are Christ's; and Christ *is* God's.

4 ☞ Let a man so account of us, as of the ministers of Christ, and stewards of the mysteries of God.

2 Moreover it is required in stewards, that a man be found faithful.

3 But with me it is a very*small*thing that I should be judged of you, or of man's judgment: yea, I judge not mine*own*self.

4 For I know nothing by myself; yet am I not hereby justified: but he*that*judgeth me is the Lord. *(Ps. 143:2)*

5 Therefore judge nothing before the time, until the Lord come, who both will bring*to*light the hidden things of darkness, and will make manifest the counsels of the hearts: and then shall every man have praise of God.

☞ **4:1** A steward (*oikonómos*, [3623]) is one who manages a house and is accountable to the owner. Christians are called "stewards" in that they have been entrusted with the "mysteries of God," which is the Gospel message. It is a responsibility for which believers are held accountable.

1161   depro5023   an,nn80   aina3345   pre1519   rxpro1683

☞ 6 And these things, brethren, I have in a figure transferred to myself

2532   an,nn625   pre1223/ppro5209   2443   asba3129 pre1722 ppro2254 3361   art,pinf5426

and *to* Apollos for*your*sakes; that ye might learn in us not to think *of*

pre5228   repro3739   pfip1125   2443 3361 nu,ajn1520   pinm5448   pre5228 art,nu,ajn1520

men above that which is written, that no one of you be puffed up for one

pre2596   art,ajn2087

against another.

1063   inpro5101   pin1252/ppro4571   1161   inpro5101   pin2192   repro3739

7 For who maketh*thee*to*differ *from another?* and what hast thou that

3756   aina2983   1161 1487   (2532)   aina2983   inpro5101   pinm2744 ad5613

thou didst not receive? now if thou didst receive *it,* why dost thou glory, as

1487   3361   apta2983

if thou hadst not received *it?*

ad2235   pin2075 pr/pfpp2880 ad2235   aina4147   aina936

8 Now ye are full, now ye are rich, ye have reigned*as*kings

ad*5565 ppro2257 2532   ipf3785/1065   aina936   2443 epn2249 2532   asba4821

without us: and I would*to*God ye did reign, that we also might reign with

ppro5213

you.

1063   pin1380 3754 art,nn2316   aina584   ppro2248 art3588   nn652   an,aj2078   ad5613

9 For I think that God hath set forth us the apostles last, as*it*were

an,aj1935   3754   ainp1096   pr/an,nn2302   art3588   nn2889   2532

appointed*to*death: for we are made a spectacle unto the world, and to

an,nn32   2532   an,nn444

angels, and to men.

epn2249   pr/an,ajn3474   pre1223 an,nn5547   1161 epn5210   pr/an,aj5429 pre1722

10 We *are* fools for*Christ's*sake, but ye *are* wise in

an,nn5547 epn2249   pr/an,aj772 1161 epn5210   pr/an,aj2478 epn5210   pr/an,aj1741   1161 epn2249

Christ; we *are* weak, but ye *are* strong; ye *are* honorable, but we *are*

pr/an,aj820

despised.

ad891   art,ad737   an,nn5610   2532   pin3983   2532   pin1372   2532

11 Even unto this present hour we both hunger, and thirst, and

pin1130   2532   pinp2852   2532   pin790

are naked, and are buffeted, and have*no*certain* dwellingplace;

2532   pin2872   ppmp2038   art,aj2398   an,nn5495   ppmp3058   pin2127

12 And labor, working with our own hands: being reviled, we bless; being

ppmp1377   pinm430

persecuted, we suffer it: *(Ps. 109:28)*

ppmp987   pin3870   ainp1096 ad5613   pr/an,nn4027   art3588   nn2889

13 Being defamed, we entreat: we are made as the filth of the world,

pr/an,nn4067   an,ajn3956   ad2193   ad737

and are the offscouring of all things unto this day.   *(Lam. 3:45)*

☞ **4:6, 7** This difficult verse can be better understood when it is examined in its context. In the phrase ". . . in a figure transferred to myself . . ." Paul was implying that he was working out the divisions within the Corinthian congregation with Apollos (1 Cor. 1:10–13). This relationship was intended to be an example for them to follow in settling their divisions. Paul used his own humility as an example by not allowing others to place him on a pedestal. In verse seven, Paul gives the primary reason for not acknowledging the Corinthians' accolades. He intimates that all believers are servants of Christ, not of themselves (cf. Rom. 12:3, 16).

pin1125 3756   depro5023   pap1788 ppro5209 235 ad5613 ppro3450 an,aj27   an,nn5043

14 I write not these things to shame you, but as my beloved sons I

pin3560

warn *you.*

1063   1437   psa2192   nu3463   an,nn3807   pre1722 an,nn5547   235

15 For though ye have ten thousand instructors in Christ, yet *have ye*

3756 an,aj4183 an,nn3962   1063 pre1722 an,nn5547 an,nn2424 epn1473   aina1080   ppro5209 pre1223 art3588

not many fathers: for in Christ Jesus I have begotten you through the

nn2098

gospel.

3767   pin3870 ppro5209 pim1096   pr/an,nn3402   ppro3450

16 Wherefore I beseech you, be ye followers of me.

pre1223/depro5124   aina3992   ppro5213   an,nn5095   repro3739 pin2076 ppro3450   an,aj27

☞ 17 For*this*cause have I sent unto you Timothy, who is my beloved

pr/an,nn5043 2532 pr/an,aj4103 pre1722   an,nn2962 repro3739   ft363/ppro5209

son, and faithful in the Lord, who shall bring*you*into*remembrance

ppro3450 art,nn3598 art3588   pre1722 an,nn5547   ad2531   pin1321   ad3837   pre1722 an,aj3956

of my ways which be in Christ, as I teach every where in every

an,nn1577

church.

1161 idpro5100   ainp5448   ad5613   ppro3450   3361 ppmp2064 pre4314 ppro5209

18 Now some are puffed up, as though I would not come to you.

1161   fm2064   pre4314 ppro5209   ad5030   1437 art3588 nn2962 asba2309 2532   fm1097   3756

19 But I will come to you shortly, if the Lord will, and will know, not

art3588   nn3056   art,pfpp5448   235 art3588   nn1411

the speech of them*which*are*puffed*up, but the power.

1063 art3588   nn932   art,nn2316   3756 pre1722 an,nn3056 235 pre1722 an,nn1411

20 For the kingdom of God *is* not in word, but in power.

inpro5101 pin2309   asba2064 pre4314 ppro5209 pre1722   an,nn4464 2228 pre1722 an,nn26 5037

21 What will ye? shall I come unto you with a rod, or in love, and *in*

an,nn4151   an,nn436

the spirit of meekness?

Concerning Church Discipline

pinp191   ad3654   an,nn4202   pre1722 ppro5213 2532 an,aj5108

5 It is reported commonly *that there is* fornication among you, and such

an,nn4202   repro3748   3761   pinp3687 pre1722 art3588   nn1484   5620

fornication as is not*so*much*as named among the Gentiles, that

idpro5100   pinf2192   art,nn3962 an,nn1135

one should have his father's wife.   (Lev. 18:7,8; Deut. 22:30; 27:20)

2532 epn5210 pin2075   pr/pfpp5448   2532   3780   ad3123   aina3996   2443

2 And ye are puffed up, and have not rather mourned, that

art,apta4160   depro5124 art,nn2041   asbp1808   pre1537 an,ajn3319 ppro5216

he*that*hath*done this deed might be taken away from among you.

1063 epn1473   3303 ad5613   pap548   art,nn4983 1161   pap3918   art,nn4151   pfi2919

3 For I verily, as absent in body, but present in spirit, have judged

---

☞ **4:17** See the introduction to 1 Timothy.

ad2235   ad5613   pap3918   art,aptm2716/ad3779

already, as though I were present, *concerning* him*that*hath*so*done

depro5124

this deed.

pre1722 art3588 nn3686   ppro2257 art,nn2962 an,nn2424 an,nn5547   ppro5216

4 In the name of our Lord Jesus Christ, when ye are

aptp4863   2532 art,popro1699 an,nn4151 pre4862 art3588   nn1411   ppro2257 art,nn2962 art,nn2424

gathered together, and my spirit, with the power of our Lord Jesus

an,nn5547

Christ,

ainf3860   art,ajn5108   art,nn4567 pre1519   an,nn3639 art3588 nn4561

5 To deliver such*a*one unto Satan for the destruction of the flesh,

2443 art3588 nn4151   asbp4982 pre1722 art3588 nn2250   art3588 nn2962 an,nn2424

that the spirit may be saved in the day of the Lord Jesus.

ppro5216   art,nn2745   3756 pr/an,aj2570 pin1492   3756 3754   an,aj3398 an,nn2219 pin2220

6 Your glorying *is* not good. Know ye not that a little leaven leaveneth

art3588 an,aj3650 nn5445

the whole lump?

aima1571   3767   art3588 aj3820 an,nn2219 2443   ps5600 an,aj3501 pr/an,nn5445 ad2531

7 Purge out therefore the old leaven, that ye may be a new lump, as

pin2075   pr/an,aj106   1063 2532 an,nn5547 ppro2257 (art3588) 3957   ainp2380   pre5228 ppro2257

ye are unleavened. For even Christ our passover is sacrificed for us:

(Ex. 13:7; 12:21; Is. 53:7)

5620   aosi1858   3361 pre1722 an,aj3820 an,nn2219   3366   pre1722

8 Therefore let us keep*the*feast, not with old leaven, neither with the

an,nn2219 an,nn2549 2532 an,nn4189   235 pre1722   an,ajn106   an,nn1505

leaven of malice and wickedness; but with the unleavened *bread* of sincerity

2532 an,nn225

and truth.   *(Ex. 12:3-20; 13:7; Deut. 16:3)*

aina1125   ppro5213 pre1722   art,nn1992 3361   pifm4874   an,nn4205

9 I wrote unto you in an epistle not to company with fornicators:

2532 3756   ad3843   art3588   nn4205   depro5127 art,nn22889 2228   art3588

10 Yet not altogether the fornicators of this world, or with the

nn4123   2228 an,nn727   2228   an,nn1496 1893 686   ipf3784   ainf1831

covetous, or extortioners, or with idolaters; for then must*ye*needs go

pre1537 art3588 nn2889

out of the world.

1161 ad3570   aina1125   ppro5213 3361   pifm4874   1437 idpro5100

11 But now I have written unto you not to keep company, if any man that

ppmp3687   an,nn80   psa5600 pr/an,nn4205 2228 pr/an,nn4123 2228 pr/an,nn1496 2228 pr/an,nn3060 2228

is called a brother be a fornicator, or covetous, or an idolater, or a railer, or

pr/an,nn3183 2228   pr/an,nn727   art,ajn5108   3366   pinf4906

a drunkard, or an extortioner; with such*a*one no not to eat.

1063   inpro5101/ppro3427   pinf2919   art,ad1854/2532   3780

12 For what*have*I*to*do to judge them*also*that*are*without? do not

epn5210 pin2919   art,ad2080

ye judge them*that*are*within?

1161   art,ad1854   art,nn2316 pin2919   2532   ft1808   pre1537

13 But them*that*are*without God judgeth. Therefore put away from among

ppro5216/epn848   art,ajn4190

yourselves that wicked person.   *(Deut. 12:7; 19:19; 22:21,23; 24:7)*

Concerning Believers and Legal Matters

pin5111 idpro5100   ppro5216 pap2192   an,nn4229   pre4314   art,ajn2087   pifm2919   pre1909   art3588

6 Dare any of you, having a matter against another, go*to*law before the

ajn94   2532 3780   pre1909 art3588   ajn40

unjust, and not before the saints?

3756   pin1492   3754 art3588   ajn40   ft2919 art3588   nn2889   2532 1487 art3588   nn2889

2 Do ye not know that the saints shall judge the world? and if the world

pinp2919   pre1722 ppro5213 pin2075   pr/an,aj370   an,nn2922/an,aj1646

shall be judged by you, are ye unworthy to judge*the*smallest*matters?

(Dan. 7:22)

pin1492   3756   3754   ft2919   an,nn32   3386

3 Know ye not that we shall judge angels? how*much*more

an,ajn982

things*that*pertain*to*this*life?

1437 3767 (3303) psa2192   an,nn2922   an,ajn982   pin2523 depro5128

4 If then ye have judgments of things*pertaining*to*this*life, set them to

art,pfpp1848   pre1722 art3588   nn1577

judge who*are*least*esteemed in the church.

pin3004   pre4314 ppro5213   an,nn1791   ad3779   pin2076 3756   an,ajn4680   pre1722

5 I speak to your shame. Is it so, that there is not a wise man among

ppro5213   3761 nu,ajn1520 repro3739   fm1410   ainf1252 pre303/an,ajn3319 ppro848   art,nn80

you? no, not one that shall be able to judge between his brethren?

235   an,nn80   pinp2919   pre3326   an,nn80   2532   depro5124   pre1909

6 But brother goeth*to*law with brother, and that before the

an,ajn571

unbelievers.

ad2235   3767 (3303)   pin2076   ad3654   an,nn2275 pre1722 ppro5213   3754

7 Now therefore there is utterly a fault among you, because ye

pin2192/an,nn2917   pre3326/rxpro1438   pre,inpro1302   3780   ad3123   pinp91   pre,inpro1302

go*to*law one*with*another. Why do ye not rather take wrong? why do

3780   ad3123   pinp650

ye not rather *suffer yourselves* to be defrauded?

235   epn5210   pin91   2532   pin650   2532 depro5023   an,nn80

8 Nay, ye do wrong, and defraud, and that *your* brethren.

(2228) pin1492   3756   3754   an,ajn94   3756   ft2816   an,nn932

9 Know ye not that the unrighteous shall not inherit the kingdom of

an,nn2316   3361   pim4105   3777   an,nn4205   3777   an,nn1496   3777   an,nn3432   3777

God? Be not deceived: neither fornicators, nor idolaters, nor adulterers, nor

an,ajn3120   3777   an,nn733

effeminate, nor abusers*of*themselves*with*mankind,

3777   an,nn2812   3777   an,nn4123   3777   an,nn3183   3756   an,nn3060   3756

10 Nor thieves, nor covetous, nor drunkards, nor revilers, nor

an,nn727   (3756)   ft2816   an,nn932   an,nn2316

extortioners, shall inherit the kingdom of God.

2532   pr/depro5023   ipf2258   idpro5100   235   aom628   235

11 And such were some of you: but ye are washed, but ye are

ainp37   235   ainp1344   pre1722 art3588   nn3686   art3588   nn2962   an,nn2424 2532 pre1722 art3588

sanctified, but ye are justified in the name of the Lord Jesus, and by the

nn4151   ppro2257 art,nn2316

Spirit of our God.

Abuses of Christian Liberty

12 All things are lawful unto me, but all things are*not*expedient: all things are lawful for me, but I will not be brought*under*the*power of any.

13 Meats for the belly, and the belly for meats: but God shall destroy both it and them. Now the body is not for fornication, but for the Lord; and the Lord for the body.

14 And God hath both raised up the Lord, and will also raise up us by his own power.

15 Know ye not that your bodies are the members of Christ? shall I then take the members of Christ, and make them the members of a harlot? God forbid.

16 What? know ye not that he*which*is*joined to a harlot is one body? for two, saith he, shall be one flesh. *(Gen. 2:24)*

17 But he*that*is*joined unto the Lord is one spirit.

18 Flee fornication. Every sin that a man doeth is without the body; but he*that*committeth*fornication sinneth against his own body.

19 What? know ye not that your body is the temple of the Holy Ghost which is in you, which ye have of God, and ye are not your own?

20 For ye are bought with a price: therefore glorify God in your body, and in your spirit, which are God's.

Concerning Marriage

7 Now concerning the things whereof ye wrote unto me: *It is* good for a man not to touch a woman.

2 Nevertheless, to avoid fornication, let every man have his own wife, and let every woman have her own husband.

3 Let the husband render unto the wife due benevolence: and likewise also the wife unto the husband.

4 The wife hath*not*power of her own body, but the husband: and likewise also the husband hath*not*power of his own body, but the wife.

5 Defraud ye not one*the*other, except *it be* with consent for a time, that ye may give yourselves to fasting and prayer; and come together again, that Satan tempt you not for your incontinency.

6 But I speak this by permission, *and* not of commandment.

7 For I would that all men were even as I myself. But every man hath his proper gift of God, one after*this*manner, and another after that.

8 I say therefore to the unmarried and widows, It is good for them if they abide even*as*I.

9 But if they cannot contain, let them marry: for it is better to marry than to burn.

10 And unto the married I command, *yet* not I, but the Lord, Let not the wife depart from *her* husband:

11 But and if she depart, let her remain unmarried, or be reconciled to *her* husband: and let not the husband put away *his* wife.

12 But to the rest speak I, not the Lord: If any brother hath a wife that believeth not, and she be pleased to dwell with him, let him not put*her*away.

2532   an,nn1135   repro3748   pin2192   an,nn435   an,aj571   2532   epn846
13 And the woman which hath a husband that believeth not, and if he

pin4909   pinf3611   pre3326 ppro846   3361   pim863   ppro846
be pleased to dwell with her, let her not leave him.

1063   art3588   aj571   art,nn435   pfip37   pre1722 art3588   nn1135   2532   art3588
14 For the unbelieving husband is sanctified by the wife, and the

aj571   art,nn1135   pfip37   pre1722 art3588   nn435   1893 (686)   pin2076 ppro5216 art,nn5043
unbelieving wife is sanctified by the husband: else were your children

pr/an,aj169   1161   ad3568 pin2076   pr/an,aj40
unclean; but now are they holy.

1161   1487   art3588   ajn571   pinm5563   pim5563   art,nn80   2228
15 But if the unbelieving depart, let him depart. A brother or a

art,nn79   3756   pfip1402   pre1722 art,ajn5108   1161 art,nn2316   pfi2564   ppro2248 pre1722
sister is not under bondage in such *cases*: but God hath called us to

an,nn1515
peace.

1063   inpro5101   pin1492   an,nn1135   1487   ft4982   art,nn435
16 For what knowest thou, O wife, whether thou shalt save *thy* husband?

2228 inpro5101   pin1492   an,nn435   1487   ft4982   art,mm135
or how knowest thou, O man, whether thou shalt save *thy* wife?

1508   ad5613 art,nn2316   aina3307   an,aj1538   ad5613 art3588 nn2962   pfi2564
17 But as God hath distributed to every man, as the Lord hath called

an,ajn1538   ad3779   pim4043 2532 ad3779 pinm1299   pre1722 an,aj3956 art,nn1577
every one, so let him walk. And so ordain I in all churches.

idpro5100   ainp2564   pfpp4059   3361
18 Is any man called being circumcised? let him not

pim1986   idpro5100   ainp2564 pre1722   an,nn203   3361
become uncircumcised. Is any called in uncircumcision? let him not be

pim4059
circumcised.

art,nn4061   pin2076 pr/an,ajn3762   2532   art,nn203   pin2076 pr/an,ajn3762   235
19 Circumcision is nothing, and uncircumcision is nothing, but the

an,nn5084   an,nn1785   an,nn2316
keeping of the commandments of God.

an,ajn1538 (pre1722 depro5026) pim3306 pre1722   art3588   nn2821   repro3739   ainp2564
20 Let every man abide in the same calling wherein he was called.

ainp2564   pr/an,ajn1401 pim3199 3361 (ppro4671)   235 1487   pinm1410
21 Art thou called *being* a servant? care not for it: but if thou mayest be

aifm1096 pr/an,aj1658 aima5530   ad3123
made free, use *it* rather.

1063   art,aptp2564   pre1722   an,nn2962   pr/an,ajn1401   pin2076
22 For he*that*is*called in the Lord, *being* a servant, is the

an,nn2962   pr/an,ajn558   ad3668   2532   art,aptp2564   pr/an,ajn1658 pin2076   an,nn5547
Lord's freeman: likewise also he*that*is*called, *being* free, is Christ's

pr/an,ajn1401
servant.

ainp59   an,nn5092 pim1096 3361   pr/an,ajn1401   an,nn444
23 Ye are bought with a price; be not ye the servants of men.

an,nn80   an,ajn1538   pre1722/repro3739   ainp2564 pre1722/depro5129 pim3306 pre3844
24 Brethren, let every man, wherein he is called, therein abide with

art,nn2316
God.

Concerning Virgins

25 Now concerning virgins I have no commandment of the Lord: yet I give my judgment, as one*that*hath*obtained*mercy of the Lord to be faithful.

26 I suppose therefore that this is good for the present distress, *I say,* that *it is* good for a man so to be.

27 Art thou bound unto a wife? seek not to*be*loosed. Art thou loosed from a wife? seek not a wife.

28 But and if thou marry, thou hast not sinned; and if a virgin marry, she hath not sinned. Nevertheless such shall have trouble in the flesh: but I spare you.

29 But this I say, brethren, the time *is* short: it remaineth, that both they*that*have wives be as though they had none;

30 And they*that*weep, as though they wept not; and they*that*rejoice, as though they rejoiced not; and they*that*buy, as though they possessed not;

31 And they*that*use this world, as not abusing *it:* for the fashion of this world passeth away.

32 But I would have you without carefulness. He*that*is*unmarried careth for the things that belong to the Lord, how he may please the Lord:

33 But he*that*is*married careth for the things that are of the world, how he may please *his* wife.

34 There is*difference*also*between a wife and a virgin. The unmarried woman careth for the things of the Lord, that she may be holy both in body and in spirit: but she*that*is*married careth for the things of the world, how she may please *her* husband.

35 And this I speak for your own profit; not that I may cast a snare upon

ppro5213 235 pre4314   art,ajn2158   2532   an,ajn2145 art3588 nn2962

you, but for that*which*is*comely, and that ye may attend upon the Lord

ad563

without distraction.

1161 1487 idpro5100 pin3543   pinf807   pre1909 ppro848

36 But if any man think that he behaveth*himself*uncomely toward his

art,nn3933 1437   psa5600/pr/an,aj5230   2532 pin3784 ad3779 pifm1096

virgin, if she pass*the*flower*of*her*age, and need so require, let him

pim4160 repro3739 pin2309   pin264   3756   pim1060

do what he will, he sinneth not: let them marry.

1161   repro3739   pfi2476   pr/an,ajn1476 pre1722   art,nn2588 pap2192 3361

37 Nevertheless he that standeth steadfast in his heart, having no

an,nn318 1161 pin2192 an,nn1849 pre4012 art,aj2398 an,nn2307 2532   depro5124 pfi2919 pre1722 ppro848

necessity, but hath power over his own will, and hath so decreed in his

art,nn2588   infg5083 rxpro1438 art,nn3933 pin4160 ad2573

heart that he will keep his virgin, doeth well.

5620 (2532)   art,pap1547   pin4160   ad2573   1161

38 So then he*that*giveth*her*in*marriage doeth well; but

art,pap1547/3361   pin4160 cd/an,ajn2908

he*that*giveth*her*not*in*marriage doeth better.

an,nn1135   pfip1210   an,nn3551 pre1909/an,aj3745/an,nn5550 ppro848 art,nn435 pin2198 1161

39 The wife is bound by the law as*long*as her husband liveth; but

1437 ppro848 art,nn435 asbp2837   pin2076 pr/an,aj1658   aifp1060   repro3739   pin2309

if her husband be dead, she is at liberty to be married to whom she will;

an,ajn3440 pre1722   an,nn2962

only in the Lord.

1161   pin2076 pr/cd/an,aj3107 1437   ad3779 asba3306   pre2596 art,popro1699   an,nn1106   1161

40 But she is happier if she so abide, after my judgment: and I

pin1380   epn2504 pinf2192   an,nn4151   an,nn2316

think also*that*I have the Spirit of God.

Things Offered to Idols

1161   pre4012   art,ajn1494   pin1492 3754   an,ajn3956 pin2192

8 Now as touching things*offered*unto*idols, we know that we all have

an,nn1108   an,nn1108   pin5448 1161 art,nn26   pin3618

knowledge. Knowledge puffeth up, but charity edifieth.

1161 1487 idpro5100   pin1380   pinf1492 idpro5100   pfi1097   an,ajn3762

2 And if any man think that he knoweth any thing, he knoweth nothing

ad3764 ad2531   pin1163   ainf1097

yet as he ought to know.

1161 1487 idpro5100   pin25 art,nn2316 depro3778   pfip1097 pre5259 ppro846

3 But if any man love God, the same is known of him.

pre4012   3767   art3588   nn1035

4 As concerning therefore the eating of

art,ajn1494   pin1492 3574   an,nn1497

those*things*that*are*offered*in*sacrifice*unto*idols, we know that an idol

pr/an,ajn3762 pre1722   an,nn2889 2532 3754   an,aj3762 an,aj2087 an,nn2316 1508 nu,ajn1520

is nothing in the world, and that *there is* none other God but one.

(Deut. 4:35,39; 6:4)

5 For though there be that*are*called gods, whether in heaven or in earth, (as there be gods many, and lords many,)

6 But to us *there is but* one God, the Father, of whom *are* all things, and we in him; and one Lord Jesus Christ, by whom *are* all things, and we by him.   *(Mal. 2:10)*

7 Howbeit *there is* not in every man that knowledge: for some with conscience of the idol unto this hour eat *it* as a thing*offered*unto*an*idol; and their conscience being weak is defiled.

8 But meat commendeth us not to God: for neither, if we eat, are*we*the*better; neither, if we eat not, are*we*the*worse.

9 But take heed lest*by*any*means this liberty of yours become a stumblingblock to them*that*are*weak.

10 For if any man see thee which hast knowledge sit*at*meat in the idol's temple, shall not the conscience of him which is weak be emboldened to eat those things*which*are*offered*to*idols;

11 And through thy knowledge shall the weak brother perish, for whom Christ died?

12 But when ye sin so against the brethren, and wound their weak conscience, ye sin against Christ.

13 Wherefore, if meat make*my*brother*to*offend, I will eat no flesh while*the*world*standeth, lest I make*my*brother*to*offend.

The Necessity of Self-denial

9 Am I not an apostle? am I not free? have I not seen Jesus Christ our Lord? are not ye my work in the Lord?

1487   pin1510 3756   pr/an,nn652   an,ajn243   235   1065   pin1510   epn4213 1063 art3588

2 If I be not an apostle unto others, yet doubtless I am to you: for the

pr/nn4973   art,popro1699   an,nn651   pin2075 epn5210 pre1722   an,nn2962

seal of mine apostleship are ye in the Lord.

art,popro1699   an,nn627   epn1691 pin2076 pr/depro3778

3 Mine answer to them*that*do*examine me is this,

pin2192   3378 an,nn1849   ainf5315 2532 ainf4095

4 Have we not power to eat and to drink?

pin2192   3378 an,nn1849   pinf4013   an,nn79   an,nn1135   ad5613/2532 art,aj3062

5 Have we not power to lead about a sister, a wife, as* well*as other

an nn652 2532 art3588   nn80   art3588 nn2962 2532 an,nn2786

apostles, and as the brethren of the Lord, and Cephas?

2228 ppro1473 an,aj3441 2532   an,nn921   pin2192 3756   an,nn1849   infg2038/3361

6 Or I only and Barnabas, have not we power to forbear working?

inpro5101   pinm4754   ad4218   an,aj2398   an,nn3800 inpro5101 pin5452

7 Who goeth*a*warfare any time at his own charges? who planteth a

an,nn290   2532   pin2068   3756 pre1537 art3588 nn2590 ppro848 2228 inpro5101 pin4165 an,nn4167 2532

vineyard, and eateth not of the fruit thereof? or who feedeth a flock, and

pin2068   3756 pre1537 art3588 nn1051   art3588 nn4167

eateth not of the milk of the flock?

pin2980   depro5023 (3361)   pre2596   an,nn444 2228 pin3004 3780 art3588 nn3551   depro5023

8 Say I these things as a man? or saith not the law the same

2532

also?

1063   pfip1125   pre1722 art3588 nn3551   an,nn3475   3756   ft5392

9 For it is written in the law of Moses, Thou shalt not muzzle the mouth

an,nn1016   pap248   (3361) art,nn2316 pin3199   art,nn1016

of the ox that treadeth*out*the*corn. Doth God take care for oxen?

(Deut. 25:4)

2228 pin3004   ad3843   pre1223/epn2248   pre1223/epn2248   1063

10 Or saith he *it* altogether for*our*sakes? For*our*sakes, no doubt, *this*

ainp1125   3754   art,pap722   pin3784   pinf722 pre1909 an,nn1680 2532

is written: that he*that*ploweth should plow in hope; and that

art,pap248   pre1909 an,nn1680   pinf3348   ppro848 art,nn1680

he*that*thresheth in hope should be partaker of his hope.

1487 epn2249   aina4687   ppro5213   art,ajn4152   pr/an,ajn3173 1487 epn2249

11 If we have sown unto you spiritual things, *is it* a great thing if we

ft2325 epn5216   art,ajn4559

shall reap your carnal things?

1487 an,ajn243   pin3348   art,nn1849   ppro5216   3756 epn2249 ad3123

12 If others be partakers of *this* power over you, *are* not we rather?

235   3756 aom5530 depro5026 art,nn1849 235 pin4722 an,ajn3956 3363

Nevertheless we have not used this power; but suffer all things, lest we should

asba1325/idpro5100/an,nn1464 art3588 nn2098   art,nn5547

hinder the gospel of Christ.

3756 pin1492 3754   art,ppmp2038   art,ajn2413   pin2068

13 Do ye not know that they*which*minister about holy things live *of the*

pre1537 art3588   nn2411   art,pap4332   art3588 nn2379   pinm4829

things of the temple? and they*which*wait at the altar are*partakers*with

art3588 nn2379

the altar?   *(Lev. 6:16,26; Num. 18:8,31; Deut. 18:1-3)*

2532   ad3779   art3588   nn2962   aina1299   art,pap2605   art3588   nn2098
14 Even so hath the Lord ordained that they*which*preach the gospel
pinf2198 pre1537 art3588   nn2098
should live of the gospel.

1161   epn1473   aom5530   an,ajn3762   depro5130   1161/3756   aina1125
15 But I have used none of these things: neither have I written
depro5023   2443   ad3779 asbm1096 pre1722 ppro1698 1063   an,ajn2570   ppro3427
these things, that it should be so done unto me: for *it were* better for me
(ad3123) ainf599 2228 2443   idpro5100   asba2758/ppro3450/art,nn2745
to die, than that any man should make*my*glorying*void.

1063   1437   psmp2097   ppro3427 pin2076   3756   an,nn2745   1063
16 For though I preach*the*gospel,   I   have nothing to*glory*of: for
an,nn318   pinm1945   ppro3427   1161   3759   pin2076   ppro3427 1437
necessity is laid upon me; yea, woe is unto me, if I
psmp2097/3361
preach*not*the gospel!   *(Jer. 20:9)*

1063   1487   pin4238   depro5124   an,aj1635   pin2192   an,nn3408   1161 1487
17 For if I do this thing willingly, I have a reward: but if
an,aj210   an,nn3622   pfip4100
against*my*will, a dispensation *of the gospel* is committed unto me.

pr/inpro5101 pin2076 ppro3427 art,nn3408   3767   2443   ppmp2097
18 What is my reward then? *Verily* that, when I preach*the*gospel, I
ft5087 art3588   nn2098   art,nn5547   pr/an,aj77   aies2710 3361 ppro3450 art,nn1849
may make the gospel of Christ without charge, that I abuse not my power
pre1722 art3588   nn2098
in the gospel.

1063   pap5607   pr/an,aj1658   pre1537   an,ajn3956
19 For though I be free from all *men,* yet have I
aina1402/rxpro1683   an,ajn3956 2443   asba2770 art3588 cd/ajn4119
made*myself*servant unto all, that I might gain the more.

2532   art3588 nn2453   aom1096   ad5613 pr/an,nn2453 2443   asba2770   an,nn2453
20 And unto the Jews I became as a Jew, that I might gain the Jews; to
art3588   pre5259   an,nn3551 ad5613 pre5259   an,nn3551 2443   asba2770 art3588
them that are under the law, as under the law, that I might gain them that
pre5259   an,nn3551
are under the law;

art,ajn459   ad5613   pr/an,aj459   pap5607   3361
21 To them*that*are*without*law,   as   without   law,   (being not
pr/an,ajn459   an,nn2316 235   pr/an,aj1772   an,nn5547 2443   asba2770
without law to God, but under*the*law to Christ,) that I might gain
art,ajn459
them*that*are*without*law.

art3588   ajn772   aom1096   ad5613 pr/an,aj772   2443   asba2770 art3588
22 To the weak became I as weak, that I might gain the
ajn772   pfi1096   pr/art,ajn3956   art,ajn3956   2443   ad3843   asba4982
weak: I am made all things to all *men,* that I might by*all*means save
idpro5100
some.

1161   depro5124   pin4160   pre1223/art3588/nn2098   2443   asbm1096
23 And this I do for*the*gospel's*sake, that I might be
pr/an,aj4791/ppro846
partaker*thereof*with *you.*

pin1492   3756   3754   art,pap5143   pre1722   an,nn4712 pin5143 an,ajn3956 (3303)   1161   nu,ajn1520
24 Know ye not that they*which*run in a race run all, but one
pin2983   art3588   nn1017   ad3779 pim5143 2443   asba2638
receiveth the prize? So run, that ye may obtain.

1161   an,aj3956   art,ppmp75   pinm1467
25 And every man that*striveth*for*the*mastery is temperate in
an,ajn3956   3767   depro1565 (3303) 2443 asba2983   an,aj5349   an,nn4735   1161 epn2249
all things. Now they *do it* to obtain a corruptible crown; but we an
an,ajn862
incorruptible.

epn1473   5106   ad3779 pin5143 3756 ad5613   ad84   ad3779 pin4438   3756 ad5613
26 I therefore so run, not as uncertainly; so fight I, not as
an,pap1194   an,nn109
one*that*beateth the air:

235   pin5299   ppro3450 art,nn4983   2532   pin1396
27 But I keep under my body, and bring*it*into*subjection:
3381   apta2784   an,ajn243   epn848
lest*that*by*any*means, when I have preached to others, I myself should
asbm1096   pr/an,aj96
be a castaway.

Admonitions From Israel's History

1161   an,nn80   pin2309 3756   ppro5209   pinf50
10 Moreover, brethren, I would not that ye should be ignorant, how
3754   an,aj3956 ppro2257 art,nn3962 ipf2258 pre5259 art3588 nn3507 2532 an,aj3956 aina1330
that all our fathers were under the cloud, and all passed
pre1223   art3588 nn2281
through the sea;   *(Ex. 13:21,22; 14:22-29)*

2532   an,aj3956   aom907   pre1519 art,nn3475 pre1722 art3588 nn3507 2532 pre1722 art3588 nn2281
☞ 2 And were all baptized unto Moses in the cloud and in the sea;
2532   an,aj3956 aina5315 art3588 ppro846   an,aj4152   an,nn1033
3 And did all eat the same spiritual meat;

(Ex. 16:4,35; Deut. 8:3, Ps. 78:24-29)

2532   an,aj3956   aina4095 art3588 ppro846   an,aj4152   an,nn4188 1063   ipf4095   pre1537
4 And did all drink the same spiritual drink: for they drank of that
an,aj4152   an,nn4073   pap190   1161   art,nn4073 ipf2258 pr/art,nn5547
spiritual Rock that followed them: and that Rock was Christ.

(Ex. 17:6; Num. 20:11; Ps. 78:15)

235   pre1722 cd/art,ajn4119   ppro846   art,nn2316   aina2106/3756   1063
5 But with many of them God was*not*well*pleased: for they were
ainp2693   pre1722 art3588   ajn2048
overthrown in the wilderness.   *(Num. 14:16,23,29,30; Ps. 78:31)*

☞ **10:2** In this verse, the word *baptízō* (907), means "to be identified with." In the exodus from Egypt, the Israelites identified with the work and purposes of their leader, Moses. See note on Mark 16:16.

6 Now these things were our examples, to the intent we should*not*lust*after evil things, as they also lusted.

(Num. 11:4,34; Ps. 106:14)

7 Neither be ye idolaters, as *were* some of them; as it is written, The people sat down to eat and drink, and rose up to play. *(Ex. 32:6)*

8 Neither let us commit fornication, as some of them committed, and fell in one day three*and*twenty*thousand. *(Num. 25:1,9)*

9 Neither let us tempt Christ, as some of them also tempted, and were destroyed of serpents. *(Num. 21:5,6)*

10 Neither murmur ye, as some of them also murmured, and were destroyed of the destroyer. *(Num. 14:2,36; 16:41-44; Ps. 106:25-27)*

11 Now all these things happened unto them for examples: and they are written for our admonition, upon whom the ends of the world are come.

12 Wherefore let him*that*thinketh he standeth take heed lest he fall.

13 There hath no temptation taken you but such*as*is*common*to*man: but God *is* faithful, who will not suffer you to be tempted above that ye are able; but will with the temptation also make a way*to*escape, that ye may be able to bear *it*. *(Deut. 7:9)*

14 Wherefore, my dearly beloved, flee from idolatry.

15 I speak as to wise men; judge ye what I say.

16 The cup of blessing which we bless, is it not the communion of the blood of Christ? The bread which we break, is it not the communion of the body of Christ?

17 For we *being* many are one bread, *and* one body: for we are*all*partakers of that one bread.

pim991   2474   pre2596   an,nn4561 pin1526 3780   art,pap2068   art3588   nn2378

18 Behold Israel after the flesh: are not they*which*eat of the sacrifices

pr/an,pn2844   art3588 nn2379

partakers of the altar?   *(Lev. 7:6,15)*

inpro5101   pin5346   3767   3754   an,nn1497 pin2076   pr/idpro5100   2228

19 What   say   I   then?   that   the   idol   is   any   thing,   or

(3754)   san,ajn1494   pin2076   pr/idpro5100

that*which*is*offered*in*sacrifice*to*idols is any thing?

235   3754   repro3739 art3588   nn1484   pin2380   pin2380

20 But *I say*, that the things which the Gentiles sacrifice, they sacrifice to

an,nn1140 2532 3756   an,nn2316 1161   pin2309 3756   ppro5209   pifm 1096   pr/an,aj2844

devils, and not to God: and I would not that ye should have fellowship with

art,nn1140

devils.   *(Deut. 32:17; Ps. 106:37)*

pinm1410/3756 pinf4095   an,nn4221   an,nn2962 2532   an,nn4221   an,nn1140

21 Ye cannot drink the cup of the Lord, and the cup of devils: ye

pinm1410/3756   pinf3348   an,nn2962 an,nn5132 2532   an,nn5132   an,nn140

cannot be partakers of the Lord's table, and of the table of devils.

(Mal. 1:7,12)

(2228)   pin3863/art3588/nn2962   pin2070 (3361) pr/cd/an,aj2478   ppro846

22 Do we provoke*the*Lord*to* jealousy? are we stronger than he?

(Deut. 32:21)

an,ajn3956   pin1832   ppro3427   235   an,ajn3956   pin4851/3756

23 All things are lawful for me, but all things are*not*expedient:

an,ajn3956   pin1832   ppro3427 235   an,ajn3956   pin3618   3756

all things are lawful for me, but all things edify not.

an,ajn3367   pim2212 art,rxpro1438   235   an,ajn1538   (art3588) art,ajn2087

24 Let no man seek his own, but every man another's *wealth.*

an,aj3956   art,ppmp4453   pre1722   an,nn3111   pim2068

25 Whatsoever   is   sold   in   the   meat   market,   *that*   eat,

pap350/an,ajn3367   pre1223/art,nn4983

asking*no*question for*conscience*sake:

1063 art3588   nn1093   art3588   nn2962   2532 art3588   nn4138   ppro848

26 For the earth *is* the Lord's, and the fullness thereof.

(Ps. 24:1; 50:12; 89:11)

(1161) 1487   idpro5100   art,ajn571   pin2564 ppro5209   2532

27   If   any of them*that*believe*not bid you *to a feast*, and ye

pin2309   pifm4198   an,aj3956   art,ppmp3908   ppro5213 pim2068   pap350/an,ajn3367

be disposed to go; whatsoever is set before you, eat, asking*no*question

pre1223/art,nn4983

for*conscience*sake.

1161   1437   idpro5100   asba2036   ppro5213   depro5124   pin2076

28 But   if   any   man   say   unto   you,   This   is

pr/an,ajn1494   pim2068 3361   pre1223/depro1565   art,apta3377   2532

offered*in*sacrifice*unto*idols, eat not for*his*sake that showed it, and for

art,nn4893   1063 art3588   nn1093   art3588   nn2962   2532 art3588   nn4138   ppro848

conscience sake: for the earth *is* the Lord's, and the fullness thereof:

(Ps. 24:1; 50:12; 89:11)

(1161)   an,nn4893   pin3004   3780   art,rxpro1438   235   (art3588)   art3588   ajn2087   1063   inpro2444

29   Conscience, I say, not thine own, but   of   the other: for why is

ppro3450   art,nn1657   pre5259   an,aj243   an,nn4893

my liberty judged of   another *man's* conscience?

           1161   1487   epn1473   an,nn5485   pin3348   inpro5101   pinp987   pre5228

30 For if   I   by grace be*a*partaker, why am I evil*spoken*of for

repro3739   epn1473   pin2168

that for which   I   give thanks?

        1535   3767   pin2068 1535 pin4095 1535   idpro5100   pin4160 pim4160 an,ajn3956

31 Whether therefore ye eat, or drink, or whatsoever ye do,   do   all   to

pre1519 an,nn1391   an,nn2316

the glory of God.

         pim1096/pr/an,aj677   2532   an,nn2453   2532   an,nn1672   2532

32 Give*none*offense, neither to the Jews, nor to the Gentiles, nor to

art3588   nn1577   art,nn2316

the church of God:

       epn2504/ad2531   pin700   an,ajn3956   an,ajn3956   3361   pap2212   art,rxpro1683

33 Even*as*I please   all   *men* in   all   *things,* not seeking mine own

an,nn4851   235   art3588   art,ajn4183 2433   asbp4982

profit, but the *profit* of many, that they may be saved.

11

pim1096   pr/an,nn3402   ppro3450   ad2531   epn2504   an,nn5547

Be ye followers of me, even as I also *am* of Christ.

God's Ordained Order

      1161   pin1867   ppro5209   an,nn80   3754   pfip3415   ppro3450   an,ajn3956   2532

☞ 2 Now I praise you, brethren, that ye remember   me   in all things, and

pin2722 art3588   nn3862   ad2531   aina3860   ppro5213

keep the ordinances, as I delivered *them* to you.

☞ **11:2–16** Paul is writing here to the Corinthian Christians who customarily consented to Greek traditions (e.g., men had their heads uncovered and the women covered their's, which was contrary to the Jewish tradition. Even to this day, Jewish men cover their heads at worship, while the women no longer do). The question which faced the Corinthians was what to do with the existing custom of their day. Paul's advice is to examine the symbolism of the custom and determine whether or not it is contrary to God's Word or His order in creation. Paul indicated that there is nothing wrong with this, for in creation God created man, and from man came the woman (see note on 1 Tim. 2:9–15). In spite of the fact that he prays without a covering, man still is accountable to Christ (v. 3). It is clear from verse eleven that man and woman are equal in the Lord (Gal. 3:28 and 1 Pet. 3:7). Although there is equality in Christ, the husband is still the head of the family. It was God who caused there to be differences in males and females. Since this custom of head coverings revealed what was evident in the creative order of things, the Greek custom was not to be looked down on by those upholding Jewish traditions. In the event of having to choose between the two, the decision was left entirely up to the Corinthian believers (v. 13). The goal was to give the believers an opportunity to evaluate the customs and determine whether or not they are in accordance to God's word. Scripture teaches that existing customs, as long as they are not contrary to morals and Scripture, are to be adhered to for the sake of unity among the believers and not to be flaunted. See note on 1 Corinthians 14:33–40.

<small>1161   pin2309   ppro5209 pinf1492   3754 art3588   nn2776   an,aj3956 an,nn435 pin2076 pr/art,nn5547</small>

3 But I would have you know, that the head of every man is Christ;

<small>1161   an,nn2776   an,nn1135   art3588 pr/nn435 1161   an,nn2776   an,nn5547   pr/art,nn2316</small>

and the head of the woman *is* the man; and the head of Christ *is* God.

(Gen. 3:16)

<small>   an,aj3956   an,nn435   ppmp4336   2228   pap4395   pap2192   pre2596/an,nn2776</small>

4 Every man praying or prophesying, having *his* head covered,

<small>pin2617   ppro848 art,nn2776</small>

dishonoreth his head.

<small>   1161   an,aj3956   an,nn1135   ppmp4336   2228   pap4395   art,nn2776</small>

5 But every woman that prayeth or prophesieth with *her* head

<small>an,aj177   pin2617   rxpro1438 art,nn2776   1063   pin2076   nu,ajn1520/2532/art,ppro848</small>

uncovered dishonoreth her head: for that is even*all*one as if

<small>art,pfpp3587</small>

she*were*shaven.

<small>1063 1487 art3588   nn1135   3756   pinm2619   2532   pim2751   1161 1487</small>

6 For if the woman be not covered, let her also be shorn: but if it be a

<small>an,aj149   an,nn1135   art,pinf2751 28 an,pinf3587   pim2619</small>

shame for a woman to be shorn or shaven, let her be covered.

<small>1063   an,nn435 3303 pin3784 3756   pifm2619   art,nn2776   pap5225</small>

7 For a man indeed ought not to cover *his* head, forasmuch as he is the

<small>pr/an,nn1504 2532 pr/an,nn1391   an,nn2316 1161   an,nn1135 pin2076   pr/an,nn1391   an,nn435</small>

image and glory of God: but the woman is the glory of the man.

(Gen. 1:27; 5:1; 9:6)

<small>1063   an,nn435 pin2076 3756 pre1537   an,nn1135 235   an,nn1135 pre1537   an,nn435</small>

8 For the man is not of the woman; but the woman of the man.

(Gen. 2:21-23)

<small> (1063)   2532/3756   an,nn435 ainp2936   pre1223 art3588   nn1135   235   an,nn1135 pre1223</small>

9   Neither was the man created for the woman; but the woman for

<small>art3588   nn435</small>

the man.

(Gen. 2:18)

<small>   pre1223/depro5124   pin3784 art3588   nn1135   pinf2192 an,nn1849 pre1909   art,nn2776   pre1223</small>

10 For*this*cause ought the woman to have power on *her* head because

<small>art3588   nn32</small>

of the angels.

<small>   4133   3777   an,nn435 ad*5565   an,nn1135   3777</small>

11 Nevertheless neither is the man without the woman, neither the

<small>an,nn1135   ad*5565   an,nn435 pre1722   an,nn2962</small>

woman without the man, in the Lord.

<small>1063   ad5618 art3588   nn1135   pre1537 art3588   nn435   ad3779   art3588 nn435   2532 pre1223 art3588</small>

12 For as the woman *is* of the man, even so *is* the man also by the

<small>nn1135   1161 art,ajn3956 pre1537 art,nn2316</small>

woman; but all things of God.

<small>   aima2919 pre1722 ppro5213/epn846 pin2076   pap4241   an,nn1135 pifm4336   art,nn2316</small>

13 Judge in yourselves: is it comely that a woman pray unto God

<small>an,aj177</small>

uncovered?

(2228)   3761   art,nn5449   ppro846 pin1321 ppro5209 3754 1437   an,nn435   (3303) psa2863

☞ 14 Doth not even nature itself teach you, that, if a man have*long*hair, it

pin2076   pr/an,nn819   ppro846

is a shame unto him?

1161   1437   an,nn1135   psa2863   pin2076   an,nn1391   ppro846 3754   art,nn2864

15 But if a woman have*long*hair, it is a glory to her: for *her* hair is

pifp1325 ppro846 pre473   an,nn4018

given her for a covering.

1161   1487   idpro5100   pin1380   pinf1511   pr/an,ajn5380   epn2249 pin2192 3756 an,aj5108   an,nn4914

16 But if any man seem to be contentious, we have no such custom,

3761   art3588   nn1577   art,nn2316

neither the churches of God.

The Lord's Supper

1161   depro5124   pap3853   pin1867   3756   3754

17 Now in this that I declare *unto you* I praise *you* not, that ye

pinm4905   3756 pre1519 art3588   cd/ajn2909   235 pre1519 art3588   cd/ajn2276

come together not for the better, but for the worse.

1063   nu,ajn4412   (3303) ppro5216   ppmp4905   pre1722 art3588   nn1577   pin191

18 For first*of*all, when ye come together in the church, I hear that

pinf5225   an,nn4978   pre1722 ppro5213 2532   an,nn3313/idpro5100   pin4100

there be divisions among you; and I partly believe it.

1063   pin1163   pinf1511   2532   pr/an,nn139   pre1722   ppro5213   2443

19 For there must be also heresies among you, that

art,ajn1384   asbm1096   pr/an,aj5318   pre1722   ppro5213

they*which*are*approved may be made manifest among you.   *(Deut. 13:3)*

ppro5216   ppmp4905   3767   pre1909   art,ppro846   pin2076 3756   ainf5315

20 When ye come together therefore into one place, *this* is not to eat

an,aj2960   an,nn1173

the Lord's supper.

1063   pre1722 art,ainf5315   an,ajn1538   pin4301   art,aj2398   an,nn1173   2532

21 For in eating every one taketh before *other* his own supper: and

repro3739/3303   pin3983   1161   repro3739   pin3184

one is hungry, and another is drunken.

(1063 3361) pin2192   3756   an,nn3614   aies2068 2532   aies4095   2228 pin2706   art3588

22 What? have ye not houses to eat and to drink in? or despise ye the

nn1577   art,nn2316 2532   pin2617   art,pap2192   3361   inpro5101   asba2036   ppro5213

church of God, and shame them*that*have not? What shall I say to you? shall I

asba1867   ppro5209 pre1722 depro5129   pin1867   3756

praise you in this? I praise *you* not.

1063   epn1473   aina3880   pre575 art3588   nn2962   repro3739 2532   aina3860

23 For I have received of the Lord that which also I delivered unto

ppro5213 3754 art3588   nn2962 an,nn2424 (pre1722) art3588   nn3571   repro3739   ipf3860   aina2983

you, That the Lord Jesus   the *same* night in which he was betrayed took

an,nn740

bread:

☞ **11:14, 15** The verb *komáō* (2863) means "to have long hair." The passage continues: "But if a woman have long hair, it is a glory to her." A woman wearing her hair longer than a man's identifies her distinctively as a woman. See notes on 1 Corinthians 14:33–40 and 1 Timothy 2:9–15.

24 And when he had given thanks, he broke *it,* and said, Take, eat: this is my body, which*is*broken for you: this do in remembrance of me.

25 After the*same*manner also *he took* the cup, when he had supped, saying, This cup is the new testament in my blood: this do ye, as*oft*as ye drink *it,* in remembrance of me.

(Ex. 24:6-8; Jer.31:31; 32:40; Zech. 9:11)

26 For as*often*as ye eat this bread, and drink this cup, ye do show the Lord's death till he come.

27 Wherefore whosoever shall eat this bread, and drink *this* cup of the Lord, unworthily, shall be guilty of the body and blood of the Lord.

28 But let a man examine himself, and so let him eat of *that* bread, and drink of *that* cup.

29 For he*that*eateth and drinketh unworthily, eateth and drinketh damnation to himself, not discerning the Lord's body.

30 For*this*cause many *are* weak and sickly among you, and many sleep.

31 For if we would judge ourselves, we should not be judged.

32 But when we are judged, we are chastened of the Lord, that we should not be condemned with the world.

33 Wherefore, my brethren, when ye come together to eat, tarry one*for*another.

34 And if any man hunger, let him eat at home; that ye come*not*together unto condemnation. And the rest will I set*in*order when I come.

Spiritual Gifts

12 ☞ 1161 ... pre4012 ... art,ajn4152 ... an,nn80 ... pin2309 ... 3756
Now concerning spiritual *gifts*, brethren, I would not have
ppro5209 ... pinf50
you ignorant.

pin1492 ... 3754 ... ipf2258 ... pr/an,nn1484 ... ppmp520 ... pre4314 ... art,aj880 ... art,nn1497
2 Ye know that ye were Gentiles, carried away unto these dumb idols,
ad5613 ... ipf71/302
even as ye were led.   *(Hab. 2:18,19)*

pre,repro1352 ... pin1107/ppro5213 ... 3754 ... an,ajn3762 ... pap2980 ... pre1722
3 Wherefore I give*you*to*understand, that no man speaking by the
an,nn4151 ... an,nn2316 ... pin3004 ... an,nn2424 ... pr/an,nn331 ... 2532 ... an,ajn3762 ... pinm1410 ... ainf2036 ... an,nn2424
Spirit of God calleth Jesus accursed: and *that* no man can say that Jesus is
pr/an,nn2962 ... 1508 ... pre1722 ... an,aj40 ... an,nn4151
the Lord, but by the Holy Ghost.

1161 ... pin1526 ... an,nn1243 ... an,nn5486 ... 1161 ... art3588 ... ppro846 ... an,nn4151
4 Now there are diversities of gifts, but the same Spirit.

2532 ... pin1526 ... an,nn1243 ... an,nn1248 ... 2532 ... art3588 ... ppro846 ... an,nn2962
5 And there are differences of administrations, but the same Lord.

2532 ... pin1526 ... an,nn1243 ... an,nn1755 ... 1161 ... pin2076 ... art3588 ... ppro846 ... an,nn2316
6 And there are diversities of operations, but it is the same God
art,pap1754 ... art,ain3956 ... pre1722 ... an,ajn3956
which worketh all in all.

1161 ... art3588 ... nn5321 ... art3588 ... nn4151 ... pinp1325 ... an,ajn1538 ... pre4314 ... art,pap4851
7 But the manifestation of the Spirit is given to every man to profit withal.

1063 ... repro3739/3303 ... pinp1325 ... pre1223 ... art3588 ... nn4151 ... an,nn3056 ... an,nn4678 ... (1161) ... an,ajn243
8 For to one is given by the Spirit the word of wisdom; to another
an,nn3056 ... an,nn1108 ... pre2596 ... art3588 ... ppro846 ... an,nn4151
the word of knowledge by the same Spirit;

(1161) ... an,ajn2087 ... an,nn4102 ... pre1722 ... art3588 ... ppro846 ... an,nn4151 ... (1161) ... an,ajn243 ... an,nn5456 ... pl/an,nn2386
9 To another faith by the same Spirit; to another the gifts of healing
pre1722 ... art3588 ... ppro846 ... an,nn4151
by the same Spirit;

(1161) ... an,ajn243 ... pl/an,nn1755 ... an,nn1411 ... (1161) ... an,ajn243 ... an,nn4394 ... (1161) ... an,ajn243
10 To another the working of miracles; to another prophecy; to another
pl/an,nn1253 ... an,nn4151 ... (1161) ... an,ajn2087 ... an,nn1085 ... an,nnl1100 ... (1161) ... an,ajn243
discerning of spirits; to another *divers* kinds of tongues; to another the
an,nn2058 ... an,nn1100
interpretation of tongues:

1161 ... an,ajn3956 ... depro5023 ... pin1754 ... art,nu1520 ... 2532 ... art3588 ... ppro846 ... an,nn4151 ... pap1244
11 But all these worketh that one and the selfsame Spirit, dividing to
an,ajn1538 ... an,ajn2398 ... ad2531 ... pinm1014
every man severally as he will.

☞ **12:1–11** This is not a complete list of the gifts of the Holy Spirit (cf. Rom. 12:6–8 and Eph. 4:11, 12). These may have been specifically mentioned because they constituted a portion of the questioning in the Corinthian's letter to Paul (1 Cor. 7:1). In 1 Corinthians 1:4–7, Paul is telling the Corinthians that the grace of God was given unto them in Christ Jesus, so that they would not be lacking in any spiritual gifts. Since every Christian has been given the Holy Spirit, he has the potential to demonstrate the particular gift which has been given to him. The intent of this passage is to first exhort the Corinthians to seek God's grace, then it will be revealed further through the manifestation of the gift that God will give to them.

One Body, Many Members

1063   ad2509   art3588   nn4983   pin2076   pr/nu,ajn1520   2532   pin2192   an,aj4183   an,nn3196   1161   an,aj3956   art3588

12 For   as   the   body   is   one,   and hath many members, and   all   the

nn3196   art,nu1520   art,nn4983   pap5607   pr/an,aj4183   pin2076   pr/hu1520   an,nn4983   ad3779   2532   art,nn5547

members of that   one   body, being many, are   one   body: so also *is* Christ.

1063   pre1722   nu1520   an,nn4151   epn2249 an,aj3956   ainp907   pre1519 nu1520 an,nn4983   1535

☞ 13 For   by   one Spirit are we   all   baptized into one body, whether *we be*

an,nn2453 1535   an,nn1672   1535   an,aj1401 1535 an,aj1658 2532   an,ajn3956

Jews or Gentiles, whether *we be* bond or free; and have been   all   made to

ainp4222 pre1519 nu1520 an,nn4151

drink into one Spirit.

1063   (2532)art3588   nn4983   pin2076 3756 nu1520   pr/an,nn3196   235   pr/an,ajn4183

14 For   the   body   is   not one member, but many.

1437 art3588 nn4228   asba2036   pin1510 3756   pr/an,nn5495   pin1510 3756 pre1537 art3588

15 If   the foot shall say, Because I am not the hand, I am not of   the

nn4983   pin2076 (3756) pre3844/depro5124 3756 pre1537 art3588   nn4983

body; is   it therefore not of   the body?

2532   1437 art3588 nn3775   asba2036   3754   pin1510 3756   pr/an,nn3788   pin1510 3756 pre1537

16 And if   the ear shall say, Because I am not the   eye,   I am not of

art3588   nn4983   pin2076 (3756) pre3844/depro5124 3756 pre1537 art3588   nn4983

the body; is   it therefore not of   the body?

1487   art3588 an,aj3650   nn4983   pr/an,nn3788   ad4226   art3588   nn189   1487

17 If   the whole body *were* an   eye,   where *were* the hearing? If the

an,aj3650   pr/an,nn189   ad4226   art3588   nn3750

whole *were* hearing, where *were* the smelling?

1161   ad3570   art,nn2316 aom5087 art3588   nn3196   an,aj1538   nu1520   ppro846   pre1722 art3588

18 But now hath   God   set   the members every one of them   in   the

nn4983   ad2531   aina2309

body,   as it hath pleased him.

1161   1487   ipf2258 art,ajn3956 pr/nu1520   an,nn3196   ad4226   art3588   nn4983

19 And if they were   all   one member, where *were* the body?

1161   ad3568   pr/an,aj4183   an,nn3196   1161   pr/hu1520 an,nn4983

20 But now *are they* many members, yet but   one   body.

1161   an,nn3788 pinm1410/3756 ainf2036   art3588   nn5495   pin2192 3756 an,nn5532   ppro4675   2228

21 And the   eye   cannot   say unto the hand, I have no need of thee: nor

ad3825 art3588 nn2776   art3588 nn4228   pin2192 3756 an,nn5532   ppro5216

again the head to the feet, I have no need of you.

235   an,aj4183   ad3123   art,nn3196   art3588   nn4983   pap1380   pinf5225

22 Nay, much more those members of the   body, which seem to   be

pr/cd/an,aj772   pin2076   pr/an,aj316

more feeble, are necessary:

2532   art3588   nn4983   repro3739   pin1380   pinf1511

23 And   those   *members*   of   the   body,   which   we   think   to   be

pr/cd/an,aj820   depro5125   pin4060   cd/an,aj4055   an,nn5092   2532   ppro2257

less honorable, upon these we bestow more abundant honor; and   our

art,ajn809   pin2192   cd/an,aj4055   an,nn2157

uncomely *parts* have more abundant comeliness.

☞ **12:13** This is the final time that the baptism of the Holy Spirit is used in the NT (see note on Acts 1:5).

1161   ppro2257   art,ajn2158   pin2192   3756   an,nn5532   235   art,nn2316
24 For   our   comely   *parts*   have   no   need: but   God   hath

aina4786/art3588/nn4983   apta1325   an,aj4055   an,nn5092
tempered*the*body*together,   having   given   more   abundant   honor   to

art,pap5302
that*part*which*lacked:

2443   psa5600   3361   an,nn4978   pre1722   art3588   nn4983   235   art3588   nn3196
25 That there should   be   no   schism   in   the   body;   but   *that*   the   members

psa3309/art3588/ppro846   rcpro240/pre5228
should have*the*same*care   one*for*another.

2532   1535   nu1520   an,nn3196   pin3958   an,aj3956   art3588   nn3196   pin4841   1535
26 And whether one   member   suffer,   all   the   members   suffer with it;   or

nu1520   an,nn3196   pinp1392   an,aj3956   art3588   nn3196   pin4796
one member be honored,   all   the   members   rejoice with it.

1161   epn5210 pin2075   pr/an,nn4983   an,nn5547   2532   pr/an,nn3196   pre1537   an,nn3313
27 Now   ye   are   the   body   of Christ,   and members   in   particular.

2532   art,nn2316   aom5087   repro3739/3303   pre1722   art3588   nn1577   nu,ajn4412   an,nn652
28 And   God   hath   set   some   in   the   church,   first   apostles,

nu,ajn1208   an,nn4396   nu,ajn5154   an,nn1320   ad1899   an,nn1411   ad1534   an,nn5486
secondarily   prophets,   thirdly   teachers,   after that   miracles,   then   gifts of

an,nn2386   an,nn484   an,nn2941   an,nn1085   an,nn1100
healings,   helps,   governments,   diversities of tongues.

(3361)   an,ajn3956   pr/an,nn652   (3361)   an,ajn3956   pr/an,nn4396   (3361)   an,ajn3956   pr/an,nn1320   (3361)   an,ajn3956
29 *Are*   all   apostles?   *are*   all   prophets?   *are*   all   teachers?   *are*   all

pr/an,nn1411
workers*of*miracles?

(3361)   pin2192   an,ajn3956   an,nn5486   pl/an,nn2386   (3361)   an,ajn3956   pin2980   an,nn1100   (3361)
30   Have   all   the   gifts of healing?   do   all   speak with tongues?   do

an,ajn3956   pin1329
all   interpret?

Love

1161   pim2206   art3588   cd/aj2909   art,nn5486   2532   ad2089   pin1166   ppro5213
☞ 31 But covet earnestly   the   best   gifts: and yet   show   I   unto   you   a

pre2596/an,nn5236   an,nn3598
more excellent way.

1437   psa2980   art3588   nn1100   art,nn444   2532   art,nn32   1161
13 Though I speak with   the   tongues   of men   and   of angels,   and

psa2192   3361   an,nn26   pfi1096   pap2278   pr/an,nn5475   2228   pap214
have   not charity,   I   am become   *as*   sounding   brass,   or a tinkling

pf/ an,nn2950
cymbal.

2532   1437   psa2192   an,nn4394   2532   psa1492   an,aj3956   art,nn3466
2 And though I have   *the gift of*   prophecy,   and   understand   all   mysteries,

---

☞ **12:31** The "best gifts" mentioned here refer to those which are most useful. The Corinthian believers were desiring the gifts that would bring them the most acclaim and prestige among their fellow brethren in Christ (e.g., the gifts of tongues, prophecies, and knowledge, cf. 1 Cor. 13:8). Instead, Paul urged them to "covet" (earnestly desire) the gifts that would best benefit the cause of Christ, not themselves. In chapter thirteen, Paul further explains that the gifts must be done in love for Christ, not for self.

2532 an,aj3956 art,nn1108 2532 1437 psa2192 an,aj3956 art,nn4102 5620 pinf3179

and all knowledge; and though I have all faith, so that I could remove

an,nn3735 1161 psa2192 3361 an,nn26 pin1510 pr/an,ajn3762

mountains, and have not charity, I am nothing.

2532 1437 asba5595/an,aj3956/ppro3450/art,pap5224 2532 1437 asba3860

3 And though I bestow*all*my*goods*to*feed *the poor,* and though I give

ppro3450 art,nn4983 2443 asbp2545 and psa2192 3361 an,nn26 pinm5623 an,ajn3762

my body to be burned, and have not charity, it profiteth me nothing.

art,nn26 pin3114 pinm5541 art,nn26 pin2206 3756 art,nn26

4 Charity suffereth long, *and* is kind; charity envieth not; charity

pinm4068/3756 3756 pinm5448

vaunteth*not*itself, is not puffed up,

3756 pin807 pin2212 3756 art,rxpro1438 3756

5 Doth not behave*itself*unseemly, seeketh not her own, is not

pinm3947 pinm3049 3756 art,ajn2556

easily provoked, thinketh no evil;   *(Zech. 8:17)*

pin5463 3756 pre1909 art,nn93 1161 pin4796 art3588 nn225

6 Rejoiceth not in iniquity, but rejoiceth in the truth;

pin4722 an,ajn3956 pin4100 an,ajn3956 pin1679 an,ajn3956 pin5278

7 Beareth all things, believeth all things, hopeth all things, endureth

an,ajn3956

all things.   *(Prov. 10:12)*

art,nn26 ad3762 pin1601 1161 1535 an,nn4394 fp2673

☞ 8 Charity never faileth: but whether *there be* prophecies, they shall fail;

1535 an,nn1100 fm3973 1535 an,nn1108

whether *there be* tongues, they shall cease; whether *there be* knowledge, it shall

fp2673

vanish away.

1063 pin1097 pre1537 an,nn3313 2532 pin4395 pre1537 an,nn3313

9 For we know in part, and we prophesy in part.

1161 ad3752 art,ajn5046 asba2064 ad5119 art3588 pre1537 an,nn3313

☞ 10 But when that*which*is*perfect is come, then that which is in part

fp2673

shall be done away.

ad3753 ipf2252 pr/an,ajn3516 ipf2980 ad5613 an,ajn3516 ipf5426 ad5613 an,ajn3516

11 When I was a child, I spake as a child, I understood as a child, I

ipf3049 ad5613 an,ajn3516 1161 ad3753 pfi1096 pr/an,nn435 pfi2673 art3588/art,ajn3516

thought as a child: but when I became a man, I put away childish things.

1063 ad737 pin991 pre1223 an,nn2072 pre1722/an,nn135 1161 ad5119 an,nn4383 pre4314 an,nn4383

12 For now we see through a glass, darkly; but then face to face:

ad737 pin1097 pre1537 an,nn3313 1161 ad5119 fm1921 ad2531 2532 ainp1921

now I know in part; but then shall I know even as also I am known.

1161 ad3570 pin3306 an,nn4102 an,nn1680 an,nn26 depro5023 art,nu5140 1161 pr/cd/an,aj3187

13 And now abideth faith, hope, charity, these three; but the greatest of

depro5130 art,nn26

these *is* charity.

☞ **13:8, 10** It is clear from these verses that tongues no longer continue today. The phrase "when that which is perfect is come" refers to the written revelation of Scripture. When this revelation was completed, there was no need for the temporary gifts (e.g., tongues, prophecies, and knowledge) which were given in order to substantiate the message that the apostles were preaching.

Concerning Speaking in Tongues

14 ☞ Follow after charity, and desire spiritual *gifts,* but rather that ye may prophesy.

2 For he*that*speaketh in an *unknown* tongue speaketh not unto men, but unto God: for no man understandeth *him*; howbeit in the spirit he speaketh mysteries.

3 But he*that*prophesieth speaketh unto men *to* edification, and exhortation, and comfort.

4 He*that*speaketh in an *unknown* tongue edifieth himself; but he*that*prophesieth edifieth the church.

5 I would that ye all spake with tongues, but rather that ye prophesied: for greater *is* he*that*prophesieth than he*that*speaketh, with tongues, except he interpret, that the church may receive edifying.

(Num. 11:29)

6 Now, brethren, if I come unto you speaking with tongues, what shall I profit you, except I shall speak to you either by revelation, or by knowledge, or by prophesying, or by doctrine?

7 And even things*without*life giving sound, whether pipe or harp, except they give a distinction in the sounds, how shall it be known what*is*piped or harped?

☞ **14:1–3** One observation needs to be made. In these three historical occurrences (Acts 2:4, 6, 8; 10:46; 19:6) speaking in tongues refers to dialects or languages (*héterai* [2087]) other than the ones known by the speakers. When the word "tongue" is used in the singular, *glóssa* ([1100] cf. 1 Cor. 14:2, 4, 13, 19, 26, 27), it refers to the Corinthian ecstatic utterance. In 1 Corinthians 14:9, it refers to the physical tongue of man, and in 1 Corinthians 14:23, being in the plural with a plural pronoun, it refers to the Corinthian ecstatic utterances. The whole thesis of the Apostle Paul is that no one should be speaking in the presence of other human beings unless the hearers can understand what is being said. See note on 1 Corinthians 14:33–40.

8 For if the trumpet give an uncertain sound, who shall prepare himself to the battle?

9 So likewise ye, except ye utter by the tongue words easy*to*be*understood, how shall it be known what*is*spoken? for ye shall speak into the air.

10 There are, it*may*be, so many kinds of voices in the world, and none of them is without signification.

11 Therefore if I know not the meaning of the voice, I shall be unto him*that*speaketh a barbarian, and he*that*speaketh shall be a barbarian unto me.

12 Even so ye, forasmuch as ye are zealous of spiritual gifts, seek that ye may excel to the edifying of the church.

13 Wherefore let him*that*speaketh in an unknown tongue pray that he may interpret.

14 For if I pray in an unknown tongue, my spirit prayeth, but my understanding is unfruitful.

15 What is it then? I will pray with the spirit, and I will pray with the understanding also: I will sing with the spirit, and I will sing with the understanding also.

16 Else when thou shalt bless with the spirit, how shall he*that*occupieth the room of the unlearned say Amen at thy giving*of*thanks, seeing he understandeth not what thou sayest?

17 For thou verily givest thanks well, but the other is not edified.

18 I thank my God, I speak with tongues more than ye all:

19 Yet in the church I had rather speak five words with my

^{art,nn3563} ²⁴⁴³ ^{asba2727} ^{an,ajn243} ²⁵³² ²²²⁸ ^{nu3463}
understanding, that *by my voice* I might teach others also, than ten thousand
^{an,nn3056} ^{pre1722} ^{an,nn1100}
words in an *unknown* tongue.

^{an,nn80} ^{pim1096} ³³⁶¹ ^{pr/an,nn3813} ^{art,nn5424} ²³⁵ ^{art,nn2549}
20 Brethren, be not children in understanding: howbeit in malice
^{pim3515} ¹¹⁶¹ ^{art,nn5424} ^{pim1096} ^{pr/an,aj5046}
be*ye*children, but in understanding be men.

^{pre1722} ^{art3588} ⁿⁿ³⁵⁵¹ ^{pfip1125} ^{pre1722} ^{an,ajn2084} ²⁵³² ^{(pre1722)an,aj2087}
21 In the law it is written, With *men of* other tongues and other
^{an,nn5491} ^{ft2980} ^{depro5129} ^{art,nn2992} ²⁵³² ^{ad3779} ³⁷⁶¹ ^{fm1522}
lips will I speak unto this people; and yet for*all*that will they not hear
^{ppro3450} ^{pin3004} ^{an,nn2962}
me, saith the Lord.   *(Deut. 28:49: Is. 28:11,12)*

⁵⁶²⁰ ^{art,nn1100} ^{pin1526} ^{pre1519} ^{an,nn4592} ³⁷⁵⁶ ^{art,pap4100} ²³⁵
22 Wherefore tongues are for a sign, not to them*that*believe, but to
^{art,ajn571} ¹¹⁶¹ ^{art,nn4394} ³⁷⁵⁶
them*that*believe*not: but   prophesying   *serveth*   not   for
^{art,ajn571} ²³⁵ ^{art,pap4100}
them*that*believe*not, but for them*which*believe.

¹⁴³⁷ ³⁷⁶⁷ ^{art3588} ^{an,aj3650} ⁿⁿ¹⁵⁷⁷ ^{asba4905} ^{pre1909} ^{art,ppro846} ²⁵³²
23 If therefore the whole church be come together into one place, and
^{an,ajn3956} ^{psa2980} ^{an,nn1100} ¹¹⁶¹ ^{asba1525} ^{an,nn2399} ²²²⁸
all speak with tongues, and there come in *those that are* unlearned, or
^{an,ajn571} ³⁷⁵⁶ ^{ft2046} ³⁷⁵⁴ ^{pinm3105}
unbelievers, will they not say that ye are mad?

¹¹⁶¹ ¹⁴³⁷ ^{an,ajn3956} ^{psa4395} ¹¹⁶¹ ^{asba1525} ^{idpro5100} ^{an,ajn571} ²²²⁸
24 But if all prophesy, and there come in one that believeth not, or
^{an,nn2399} ^{pinp1651} ^{pre5259} ^{an,ajn3956} ^{pinp350} ^{pre5259} ^{an,ajn3956}
one unlearned, he is convinced of all, he is judged of all:

²⁵³² ^{ad3779} ^{art3588} ^{ajn2927} ^{ppro848} ^{art,nn2588} ^{pinp1096} ^{pr/an,aj5318} ²⁵³² ^{ad3779}
25 And thus are the secrets of his heart made manifest; and so
^{apta4098} ^{pre1909} ^{an,nn4383} ^{ft4352} ^{art,nn2316} ^{pap518} ³⁷⁵⁴ ^{art,nn2316} ^{pin2076} ^{pre1722}
falling down on *his* face he will worship God, and report that God is in
^{ppro5213} ^{ad3689}
you of*a*truth.   *(Dan. 2:47; Is. 45:14)*

Do Things Properly and Orderly

^{inpro5101} ^{pin2076} ³⁷⁶⁷ ^{an,nn80} ^{ad3752} ^{psmp4905} ^{an,ajn1538} ^{ppro5216}
26 How is it then, brethren? when ye come together, every one of you
^{pin2192} ^{an,nn4468} ^{pin2192} ^{an,nn1322} ^{pin2192} ^{an,nn1100} ^{pin2192} ^{an,nn602} ^{pin2192}
hath a psalm, hath a doctrine, hath a tongue, hath a revelation, hath an
^{an,nn2058} ^{an,ajn3956} ^{aipm1096} ^{pre4314} ^{an,nn3619}
interpretation. Let all things be done unto edifying.

¹⁵³⁵ ^{idpro5100} ^{pin2980} ^{an,nn1100} ^{pre2596} ^{nu,ajn1417} ²²²⁸ ^{art3588}
27 If any man speak in an *unknown* tongue, *let it be* by two, or at the
^{ajn4118} ^{nu,ajn5140} ²⁵³² ^{pre303} ^{an,nn3313} ²⁵³² ^{nu,ajn1520} ^{pim1329}
most *by* three, and *that* by course; and let one interpret.

28 But if there be no interpreter, let him keep silence in the church; and let him speak to himself, and to God.

29 Let the prophets speak two or three, and let the other judge.

30 If *any thing* be revealed to another that sitteth by, let the first hold*his*peace.

31 For ye may all prophesy one*by*one, that all may learn, and all may be comforted.

32 And the spirits of the prophets are subject to the prophets.

☞ 33 For God is not *the author* of confusion, but of peace, as in all churches of the saints.

34 Let your women keep silence in the churches: for it is not permitted

---

☞ **14:33–40** The question frequently asked concerning this portion of Scripture is "Does the Apostle Paul forbid women to speak at all or to pray or prophesy in church?" The main verse that constitutes the foundation of all that Paul says in 1 Corinthians 14:33, "For God is not the author of confusion but of peace, as in all the churches of the saints." The instruction of Paul is found in verse thirty-nine: "Therefore, my brethren, desire earnestly to prophesy," meaning "be zealous about giving forth the word of God." In verse forty, Paul states, "But let all things be done decently and in order." This as a principle applies to all the churches (v. 34) although it was born out of a practice existing only in Corinth. When Paul says, "Your women in the churches, let them be silent" (v. 40), it was not an instruction to all the men in general not to permit any women to speak in church, but to husbands to guide and teach their own wives lest they produce confusion and disturbance in a meeting. This may have resulted from the exercising of a gift that they thought they had and were anxious to externalize. One cannot take Paul's indirect imperative in 1 Corinthians 14:34, "Let the women keep silent in the churches," as absolute. It must be taken in conjunction with what follows: "for they are not permitted to speak." The word "speak" should be taken to mean "uttering sounds that are incoherent and not understood by others." Paul says that instead it is better to have silence. Paul uses the same word "keep silent" to admonish a man who speaks in an unknown tongue without an interpreter (vv. 28, 30). What Paul is saying is that only one man must speak at a time, for if two speak at once, there will be confusion. The phrase, "let him keep silent" is then qualified to the woman (v. 34). Under no circumstances does the injunction of Paul indicate that women should not utter a word at any time during the church service. The issue is not men versus women, but it is confusion versus order. In God's sight, it makes no difference who causes the confusion. It is a shame for any woman to bring confusion into the local church (v. 35), even as it is for any man to do so. Furthermore, the word *gunaíkes* (1135) should not be translated as "women" in its generic sense, but as "wives" (v. 34). It is wives who should submit (*hupotássomai* [5293]) to their own husbands (v. 35, from *ándras* [435]). The whole argument is not the subjection of women to men in general, but of wives to their own husbands in the family unit that has been ordained by God (see note on 1 Tim. 2:9–15). Paul states the principle that the duty of the husbands is to restrain their own wives from outbursts during the worship service. Whenever Paul speaks of submissiveness by a woman, it is always on the part of a wife to her own husband. See note on Titus 2:1–5.

ppro846   pinf2980   235   pip5293   ad2531   2532

unto them to speak; but *they are commanded* to be*under*obedience, as also

pin3004 art3588 nn3551

saith the law.   *(Gen. 3:16)*

     1161   1487   pin2309   ainf3129   idpro5100   pim1905 art,aj2398   an,nn435   pre1722

36 And if they will learn any thing, let them ask their husbands at

an,nn3624 1063   pin2076   an,ajn149   an,nn1135   pinf2980 pre1722   an,nn1577

home: for it is a shame for women to speak in the church.

     2228   aina1831 art3588   nn3056   art,nn2316   pre575   ppro5216 2228   aina2658   pre1519 ppro5209

36 What? came the word of God out from you? or came it unto you

an,aj3441

only?

     idpro1536   pin1380   pinf1511   pr/an,nn4396   2228   pr/an,ajn4152

37 If*any*man think himself to be a prophet, or spiritual, let him

pim1921   3754   repro3739   pin1125   ppro5213 pin1526   pr/an,nn1785

acknowledge that the things that I write unto you are the commandments of

art3588   nn2962

the Lord.

     1161   1487   idpro5100   pin50   pim50

38 But if any man be ignorant, let him be ignorant.

     5620   an,nn80   pim2206   art,pinf4395   2532   pim2967   3361   art,pinf2980

39 Wherefore, brethren, covet to prophesy, and forbid not to speak with

an,nn1100

tongues.

     an,ajn3956   pim1096   ad2156   2532 pre2596 an,nn5010

40 Let all things be done decently and in order.

A Summary of the Gospel

             1161   an,nn80   pin1107   ppro5213 art3588   nn2098   repro3739

15 Moreover, brethren, I declare unto you the gospel which I

             aom2097   ppro5213 repro3739   2532   aina3880   2532   pre1722/repro3739

preached unto you, which also ye have received, and wherein

pfi2476

ye stand;

   pre1223   repro3739   2532   pinp4982   1487   pin2722   inpro5101   (an,nn3056)

2 By which also ye are saved, if ye keep*in*memory what I

aom2097   ppro5213 ad1622/1508   aina4100   ad1500

preached unto you, unless ye have believed in vain.

   1063   aina3860   ppro5213 pre1722/nu,ajn4413   repro3739   2532   aina3880

3 For I delivered unto you first*of*all that which I also received, how

3754   an,nn5547 aina599 pre5228 ppro2257 art,nn266   pre2596   art3588   nn1124

that Christ died for our sins according to the Scriptures;   *(Is. 53:8,9)*

   2532   3754   ainp2290   2532   3754   pfip1453   art3588 nu,aj5124 an,nn2250   pre2596

4 And that he was buried, and that he rose again the third day according

art3588   nn1124

to the Scriptures: *(Hos. 6:2)*

   2532   3754   ainp3700   an,nn2786   ad1534   art3588   nu,ajn1427

5 And that he was seen of Cephas, then of the twelve:

ad1899   ainp3700   ad1883   nu4001   an,nn80   nu,ad2178
6 After that, he was seen of above five hundred brethren at once;
pre1537 repro3739 art3588   cd/ajn4119   pin3306 ad2193   ad737   1161 idpro5100 (2532)
of whom the greater part remain unto this present, but some are
ainp2837
fallen asleep.

ad1899   ainp3700   an,nn2385 ad1534   an,aj3956 art3588   nn652
7 After that, he was seen of James; then of all the apostles.

1161   an,ajn2078   an,ajn3956   ainp3700   ppro2504   ad5619
8 And last of all he was seen of me also, as of
art,nn1626
one*born*out*of*due*time.

1063 epn1473 pin1510 art3588 pr/cd/aj1646   art3588   nn652   repro3739 pin1510 3756 pr/an,aj2425   pip2564
9 For I am the least of the apostles, that am not meet to be called
an,nn652   1360   aina1377   art3588   nn1577   art,nn2316
an apostle, because I persecuted the church of God.

1161   an,nn5485   an,nn2316   pin1510 pr/repro3739   pin1510 2532 ppro848 art,nn5485   art3588
10 But by the grace of God I am what I am: and his grace which
pre1519 ppro1691 ainp1096 3756   pr/an,aj2756   235   aina2872   cd/an,ajn4054
was bestowed upon me was not in vain; but I labored more abundantly
ppro846 an,aj3956 1161 3756 epn1473 235 art3588 nn5485   art,nn2316 art3588   pre4862
than they all: yet not I, but the grace of God which was with
ppro1698
me.

3767   1535   ppro1473   depro1565 ad3779   pin2784 2532 ad3779
11 Therefore whether it were I or they, so we preach, and so ye
aina4100
believed.

1161   1487 an,nn5547   pinp2784   3754   pfip1453 pre1537   an,ajn3498 ad4459 pin3004 idpro5100
12 Now if Christ be preached that he rose from the dead, how say some
pre1722 ppro5213 3754   pin2076 3756   an,nn386   an,ajn3498
among you that there is no resurrection of the dead?

1161   1487   pin2076 3756   an,nn386   an,ajn3498   an,nn5547   3761
13 But if there be no resurrection of the dead, then is Christ not
pfip1453
risen:

1161   1487 an,nn5547   3756 pfip1453   686   ppro2257 art,nn2782 pr/an,aj2756 1161 ppro5216
14 And if Christ be not risen, then is our preaching vain, and your
art,nn4102   2532 pr/an,aj2756
faith is also vain.

1161   2532   pinp2147   pr/an,nn5575   art,nn2316   3754
15 Yea, and we are found false witnesses of God; because we have
aina3140   pre2596 art,nn2316 3754   aina1453   art,nn5547 repro3739   aina1453/3756
testified of God that he raised up Christ: whom he raised*not*up,
1512/686   an,ajn3498 pinp1453 3756
if*so*be*that the dead rise not.

1063 1487   an,ajn3498 pinp1453 3756   3761 an,nn5547   pfip1453
16 For if the dead rise not, then is not Christ raised:

1161 1487 an,nn5547   3756 pfip1453 ppro5216 art,nn4102 pr/an,aj3152   pin2075 ad2089 pre1722 ppro5216
17 And if Christ be not raised, your faith is vain; ye are yet in your
art,nn266
sins.

686   art,aptp2837/2532   pre1722 an,nn5547   aom622

18 Then they*also*which*are*fallen*asleep in Christ are perished.

1487 pre1722 depro5026 art,nn2222 an,ajn3440   pr/pfp1679 pre1722 an,nn5547   pin2070   an,aj3956

19 If in this life only we have hope in Christ, we are of all

an,nn444   pr/cd/an,aj1652

men most miserable.

1161   ad3570   an,nn5547   pfi1453   pre1537   an,ajn3498   aom1096   pr/an,nn536

20 But now is Christ risen from the dead, *and* become the firstfruits of

art,pfp2837

them*that*slept.

1063   1894   pre1223 an,nn444   art,nn2288 pre1223 an,nn444   2532   an,nn386

21 For since by man *came* death, by man *came* also the resurrection of

an,ajn3498

the dead.   *(Gen. 3:17-19)*

1063   ad5618 pre1722   76   an,aj3956   pin599   2532   ad3779 pre1722 art,nn5547   an,aj3956

22 For as in Adam all die, even so in Christ shall all be

fp2227

made alive.

1161   an,ajn1538   pre1722 art,aj2398   an,nn5001 an,nn5547   an,nn536   ad1899   art3588

23 But every man in his own order: Christ the firstfruits; afterward they

an,nn5547   pre1722 ppro848   art,nn3952

that are Christ's at his coming.

ad1534   art3588 nn5056   ad3752   asba3860   art3588   nn932

24 Then *cometh* the end, when he shall have delivered up the kingdom to

art,nn2316 2532   an,nn3962   ad3752   asba2673   an,aj3956 an,nn746 2532 an,aj3956

God, even the Father; when he shall have put down all rule and all

an,nn1849   2532   an,nn1411

authority and power.   *(Dan. 2:44)*

1063 ppro846 pin1163   pinf936 ad891 repro3739/302   asba5087 an,aj3956   art,ajn2190   pre5259 ppro848

25 For he must reign, till he hath put all enemies under his

art,nn4228

feet.   *(Ps. 110:1)*

an,aj2078 pr/an,ajn2190   pinp2673   art,nn2288

26 The last enemy *that* shall be destroyed *is* death.

1063   aina5293   an,ajn3956   pre5259 ppro848 art,nn4228 1161 ad3752   asba2036 (3754) an,ajn3956

27 For he hath put all things under his feet. But when he saith all things

pfip5293   an,ajn1212   3754   ad1622

are put under *him,* *it* *is* manifest that he is accepted,

art,apta5293/art,ajn3956   ppro846

which*did*put*all*things*under him.   *(Ps. 8:6)*

1161   ad3752   art,ajn3956   asbp5293   ppro846 ad5119   art3588 nn5207 2532

28 And when all things shall be subdued unto him, then shall the Son also

epn848   fm5293   art,apta5293/art,aj3956   ppro846 2443 art,nn2316

himself be subject unto him*that*put*all*things*under him, that God may

psa5600 pr/art,aj3956 pre1722 an,aj3956

be all in all.

1893   inpro5101   ft4160   art,ppmp907   pre5228 art3588 ajn3498 1487   an,ajn3498

29 Else what shall they do which*are*baptized for the dead, if the dead

pinp1453 3756   ad3654 inpro5101   2532   pinp907   pre5228 art3588 ajn3498

rise not at all? why are they then baptized for the dead?

2532   inpro5101   pin2793/epn2249   an,aj3956 an,nn5610

30 And why stand*we*in*jeopardy every hour?

31 I protest by your rejoicing which I have in Christ Jesus our
Lord, I die daily.

32 If after*the*manner of men I have fought*with*beasts at Ephesus,
what advantageth it me, if the dead rise not? let us eat and drink; for
tomorrow we die. *(Is. 22:13)*

33 Be not deceived: evil communications corrupt good manners.

34 Awake to righteousness, and sin not; for some
have*not* the*knowledge of God: I speak *this* to your shame.

Resurrection Promised

35 But some *man* will say, How are the dead raised up? and with what
body do they come?

36 *Thou* fool, that which thou sowest is not quickened, except it die:

37 And that which thou sowest, thou sowest not that body that*shall*be,
but bare grain, it*may*chance of wheat, or of some other *grain*:

38 But God giveth it a body as it hath pleased him, and to every
seed his own body. *(Gen. 1:11)*

39 All flesh *is* not the same flesh: but *there is* one *kind of* flesh of
men, another flesh of beasts, another of fishes, *and* another of birds.

40 *There are* also celestial bodies, and bodies terrestrial: but the glory of
the celestial *is* one, and the *glory* of the terrestrial *is* another.

41 *There is* one glory of the sun, and another glory of the moon, and
another glory of the stars: for *one* star differeth from *another* star in glory.

42 So also *is* the resurrection of the dead. It is sown in corruption; it is
raised in incorruption:

43 It is sown in dishonor; it is raised in glory: it is sown in weakness; it is raised in power:

44 It is sown a natural body; it is raised a spiritual body. There is a natural body, and there is a spiritual body.

45 And so it is written, The first man Adam was made a living soul; the last Adam *was* made a quickening spirit.   *(Gen. 2:7)*

46 Howbeit that *was* not first which*is*spiritual, but that*which*is*natural; and afterward that*which*is*spiritual.

47 The first man *is* of the earth, earthy: the second man *is* the Lord from heaven.   *(Gen. 2:7)*

48 As *is* the earthy, such *are* they*also*that*are*earthy: and as *is* the heavenly, such *are* they*also*that*are*heavenly.

49 And as we have borne the image of the earthy, we shall also bear the image of the heavenly.   *(Gen. 5:2)*

50 Now this I say, brethren, that flesh and blood cannot inherit the kingdom of God; neither doth corruption inherit incorruption.

☞ 51 Behold, I show you a mystery; We shall not all sleep, but we shall all be changed,

52 In a moment, in the twinkling of an eye, at the last trump: for the trumpet*shall*sound, and the dead shall be raised incorruptible, and we shall be changed.

53 For this corruptible must put on incorruption, and this mortal *must* put on immortality.

54 So when this corruptible shall have put on incorruption, and this

---

☞ **15:51, 52** See note on 1 Thessalonians 4:17.

art,ajn2349   asbm1746   an,nn110   ad5119   fm1096   art3588   nn3056
mortal shall have put on immortality, then shall be brought*to*pass the saying

art,pfpp1125   art,nn2288   ainp2666   pre1519   an,nn3534
that*is*written, Death is swallowed up in victory.   *(Is. 25:8)*

an,nn2288   ad4226   ppro4675 art,nn2759   an,nn86   ad4226   ppro4675 art,nn3534
55 O death, where *is* thy sting? O grave, where *is* thy victory?

(Hos. 13:14)

(1161)art3588   nn2759   art,nn2288   pr/art,nn266   1161   art3588   nn1411   art,nn266   art3588
56 The sting of death *is* sin; and the strength of sin *is* the

pr/nn3551
law.

1161   an,nn5485   art,nn2316   art,pap1325   ppro2254 art3588   nn3534   pre1223   ppro2257
57 But thanks *be* to God, which giveth us the victory through our

art,nn2962 an,nn2424   an,nn5547
Lord Jesus Christ.

5620   ppro3450   an,aj27   an,nn80   pim1096   pr/an,aj1476   pr/an,nn277
58 Therefore, my beloved brethren, be ye steadfast, unmovable,

ad3842   pr/pap4052   pre1722 art3588   nn2041   art3588   nn2962   pfp1492   3754   ppro5216
always abounding in the work of the Lord, forasmuch as ye know that your

art,nn2873 pin2076   3756   pr/an,aj2756 pre1722   an,nn2962
labor is not in vain in the Lord.   *(2 Chr. 15:7)*

Concerning the Collection from the Churches

1161   pre4012   art3588   nn3048   art,pre1519 art3588   ajn40   ad5618
16 ☞ Now concerning the collection for the saints, as I have

aina1299   art3588   nn1577   art,nn1053   2532   ad3779 aima4160 epn5210
given order to the churches of Galatia, even so do ye.

pre2596/an,nu,ajn3391   an,nn4521   an,ajn1538   ppro5216 pim5087 pre3844 rxpro1438
2 Upon*the*first *day* of the week let every one of you lay by him

pap2343   repro3748/302   psmp2137   2443   psmp1096 3361   an,nn3048   (ad5119) ad3752
in store, as God hath prospered him, that there be no gatherings when

asba2064
I come.

1161   ad3752   asbm3854   repro3739/1437   asba1381   pre1223   an,nn1992   depro5128
3 And when I come, whomsoever ye shall approve by *your* letters, them

ft3992   ainf667   ppro5216   art,nn5485   pre1519   2419
will I send to bring your liberality unto Jerusalem.

1161   1437   psa5600 an,ajn514   ppro2504/infg4198   fm4198 pre4862 ppro1698
4 And if it be meet that I*go*also, they shall go with me.

1161   fm2064   pre4314 ppro5209   ad3752   asba1330   an,nn3109   1063
5 Now I will come unto you, when I shall pass through Macedonia: for I do

pinm1330   an,nn3109
pass through Macedonia.

☞ **16:1–4** See notes on Colossians 4:7 and 2 Timothy 4:20.

6 And it*may*be that I will abide, yea, and winter with you, that ye may bring*me*on*my*journey whithersoever I go.

7 For I will not see you now by*the*way; but I trust to tarry a while with you, if the Lord permit.

8 But I will tarry at Ephesus until Pentecost.

(Lev. 23:15-21; Deut. 16:9-11)

9 For a great door and effectual is opened unto me, and *there are* many adversaries.

☞ 10 Now if Timothy come, see that he may be with you without fear: for he worketh the work of the Lord, as I also *do.*

11 Let no man therefore despise him: but conduct*him*forth in peace, that he may come unto me: for I look for him with the brethren.

12 As touching *our* brother Apollos, I greatly desired him to come unto you with the brethren: but his will was not*at*all to come at*this*time; but he will come when he shall have*convenient*time.

13 Watch ye, stand fast in the faith, quit*you*like*men, be strong.

(Ps. 31:24)

14 Let all*your*things be done with charity.

15 I beseech you, brethren, (ye know the house of Stephanas, that it is the firstfruits of Achaia, and *that* they have addicted themselves to the ministry of the saints,)

16 That ye submit*yourselves*unto such, and to every one that*helpeth*with *us,* and laboreth.

17 I am glad of the coming of Stephanas and Fortunatus

☞ **16:10, 11** See the introduction to 1 Timothy.

2532   an,nn883   3754   art,nn5303   ppro5216   depro3778   aina378
and Achaicus: for that*which*was*lacking on your part they have supplied.

1063   aina373   art,popro1699 an,nn4151   2532   art,ppro5216   3767
18 For   they   have   refreshed   my   spirit   and   yours: therefore

pim1921   art,ajn5108
acknowledge ye them*that*are*such.

art3588   nn1577   art,nn773 pinm782 ppro5209 an,nn207   2532   an,nn4252   pinm782 ppro5209 an,ajn4183
19 The churches of Asia salute you. Aquila and Priscilla salute you much

pre1722   an,nn2962 pre4862 art3588   nn1577   pre2596 ppro848   an,nn3624
in the Lord, with the church that is in their house.

an,aj3956 art3588   nn80   pinm782 ppro5209 aipm782   rcpro240   pre1722 an,aj40 an,nn5370
20 All the brethren greet you. Greet ye one another with a holy kiss.

art3588   nn783   an,nn3972   art,popro1699 an,nn5495
21 The salutation of *me* Paul with mine own hand.

idpro1536   pin5368   3756 art3588 nn2962   an,nn2424 an,nn5547   pim2277   pr/an,nn331
22 If*any*man love not the Lord Jesus Christ, let him be Anathema

3134
Maranatha.

art3588   nn5485   art,nn2962 an,nn2424 an,nn5547   pre3326 ppro5216
23 The grace of our Lord Jesus Christ *be* with you.

ppro3450 art,nn26   pre3326 ppro5216 an,aj3956 pre1722 an,nn5547 an,nn2424   281
24 My love *be* with you   all   in Christ Jesus. Amen.

CORINTHIANS

Paul had established the church at Corinth during his first stay there and later wrote the first letter to them concerning the less-than-honorable behavior of some of its members. Apparently Paul paid them another visit, which was not very pleasant, between the first time he stayed there and the time that this letter was written (2 Cor 12:14; 13:1). As he traveled through Macedonia (northern Greece) on his way to Corinth (located in Achaia or southern Greece), he met with Titus and discovered that his first letter to the Corinthian church had been received and accomplished much good (2 Cor. 7:5–11). Nevertheless, there were still some serious problems in the church at Corinth, including a faction in the congregation who denied that Paul was truly an apostle of Jesus. As a result, Paul immediately wrote this letter, probably from Philippi, and sent it on ahead with Titus (see 2 Cor. 8:16, 17; 9:2–4). This is believed to have been written about A.D. 54 or 55 only eight months to a year after the writing of the Book of 1 Corinthians. Paul spent the next winter in Corinth as he had planned (Acts 20:2, 3; 1 Cor. 16:5, 6).

The Apostle Paul's intense emotions and fiery personality are more evident in this letter than in any other epistle. The Book of 2 Corinthians has only a vague systematic form, and except for Paul's letter to Philemon, has the least emphasis on doctrinal issues. He shared some of his personal experiences such as the vision in which he was "caught up into the third heaven" (2 Cor. 12:1–4) and his "thorn in the flesh" (2 Cor. 12:7–9)

Paul warned them about certain doctrinal errors, instructed them in matters of duty as Christians, and expressed joy that they had heeded his instructions in the first letter. He also defended his authority as an apostle against the attacks of legalistic teachers who sought to disrupt his work. The main theme of the Book of 2 Corinthians is that one should always be faithful to Christ.

1
an,nn3972   an,nn652   an,nn2424 an,nn5547 pre1223   an,nn2307   an,nn2316 2532   an,nn5095
Paul, an apostle of Jesus Christ by the will of God, and Timothy *our*

art,nn80   art3588   nn1577   art,nn2316 art,pap5607 pre1722   an,nn2882   pre4862 an,aj3956
brother, unto the church of God which is at Corinth, with all

art3588 ajn40   art,pap5607 pre1722 an,aj3650 art,nn882
the saints which are in all Achaia:

an,nn5485   ppro5213 2532 an,nn1515 pre575 an,nn2316 ppro2257 an,nn3962 2532   an,nn2962
2 Grace *be* to you and peace from God our Father, and *from* the Lord

an,nn2424 an,nn5547
Jesus Christ.

"The God of All Comfort"

^{pr/an,aj2128} ^{art,nn2316} ²⁵³² ^{an,nn3962} ^{ppro2257 art,nn2962 an,nn2424} ^{an,nn5547} ^{art3588} ⁿⁿ³⁹⁶²
3 Blessed *be* God, even the Father of our Lord Jesus Christ, the Father

^{art,nn3628} ²⁵³² ^{an,nn2316} ^{an,aj3956} ^{an,nn3874}
of mercies, and the God of all comfort;

^{art3588} ^{pap3870} ^{ppro2248 pre1909 an,aj3956 ppro2257} ^{art,nn2347} ^{ppro2248} ^{aies1410}
4 Who comforteth us in all our tribulation, that we may be able to

^{pinf3870} ^{art3588} ^{pre1722 an,aj3956} ^{an,nn2347} ^{pre1223 art3588} ⁿⁿ³⁸⁷⁴ ^{repro3739} ^{epn848}
comfort them which are in any trouble, by the comfort wherewith we our-

^{pinp3870} ^{pre5259 art,nn2316}
selves are comforted of God.

³⁷⁵⁴ ^{ad2531 art3588} ⁿⁿ³⁸⁰⁴ ^{art,nn5547} ^{pin4052} ^{pre1519 ppro2248 ad3779 ppro2257} ^{art,nn3874}
5 For as the sufferings of Christ abound in us, so our consolation

²⁵³² ^{pin4052} ^{pre1223 an,nn5547}
also aboundeth by Christ.   *(Ps. 34:19; 94:19)*

¹¹⁶¹ ¹⁵³⁵ ^{pinp2346} ^{pre5228 ppro5216} ^{art,nn3874} ²⁵³² ^{an,nn4991}
6 And whether we be afflicted, *it is* for your consolation and salvation,

^{art,ppmp1754} ^{pre1722} ^{an,nn5281} ^{art3588} ^{ppro846} ⁿⁿ³⁸⁰⁴ ^{repro3739} ^{epn2249} ²⁵³²
which*is*effectual in the enduring of the same sufferings which we also

^{pin3958} ¹⁵³⁵ ^{pinp3870} ^{pre5228 ppro5216} ^{art,nn3874} ²⁵³² ^{an,nn4991}
suffer: or whether we be comforted, *it is* for your consolation and salvation.

²⁵³² ^{ppro2257} ^{art,nn1680} ^{pre5228} ^{ppro5216} ^{pr/an,aj949} ^{pfp1492} ³⁷⁵⁴ ^{ad5618} ^{pin2075}
7 And our hope of you *is* steadfast, knowing, that as ye are

^{pr/an,ajn2844} ^{art3588} ⁿⁿ³⁸⁰⁴ ^{ad3779} ²⁵³² ^{art3588} ⁿⁿ³⁸⁷⁴
partakers of the sufferings, so *shall ye be* also of the consolation.

¹⁰⁶³ ^{pin2309} ³⁷⁵⁶ ^{an,nn80} ^{pinf50/ppro5209} ^{pre5228} ^{ppro2257} ^{art,nn2347}
8 For we would not, brethren, have*you*ignorant of our trouble

^{art,aptm1096} ^{ppro2254 pre1722 art,nn773} ³⁷⁵⁴ ^{ainp916} ^{pre2596/an,nn5236} ^{pre5228}
which came to us in Asia, that we were pressed out*of*measure, above

^{an,nn1411} ⁵⁶²⁰ ^{ppro2248} ^{aifp1820} ²⁵³² ^{art,pinf2198}
strength, insomuch that we despaired even of life:

²³⁵ ^{epn848} ^{pfp2192 art3588} ⁿⁿ⁶¹⁰ ^{art,nn2288} ^{pre1722} ^{rxpro1438} ²⁴⁴³ ^{psa5600} ³³⁶¹
9 But we had the sentence of death in ourselves, that we should not

^{pfp3982 pre1909} ^{rxpro1438} ²³⁵ ^{pre1909 art,nn2316} ^{art,pap1453} ^{art3588} ^{ajn3498}
trust in ourselves, but in God which raiseth the dead:

^{repro3739} ^{aom4506} ^{ppro2248} ^{pre1537} ^{an,aj5082} ^{an,nn2288} ²⁵³² ^{pinm4506} ^{pre1519}
10 Who delivered us from so great a death, and doth deliver: in

^{repro3739} ^{pfi1679} ³⁷⁵⁴ ⁽²⁵³²⁾ ^{ad2089} ^{fm4506}
whom we trust that he will yet deliver *us;*

^{ppro5216} ²⁵³² ^{pap4943} ^{art,nn1162} ^{pre5228 ppro2257} ²⁴⁴³ ^{art,nn5486}
11 Ye also helping together by prayer for us, that for the gift *bestowed*

^{pre1519} ^{ppro2248} ^{pre1537} ^{an,aj4183} ^{an,nn4383} ^{asbp2168} ^{pre1223 an,ajn4183}
upon us by*the*means*of many persons thanks* may*be*given by many

^{pre5228/ppro2257}
on*our*behalf.

Paul's Sincerity

¹⁰⁶³ ^{ppro2257} ^{art,nn2746} ^{pin2076} ^{pr/depro3778 art3588} ⁿⁿ³¹⁴² ^{ppro2257} ^{art,nn4893} ³⁷⁵⁴
12 For our rejoicing is this, the testimony of our conscience, that

pre1722   an,nn572   2532 an,nn2316   an,nn1505   3756 pre1722   an,aj4559   an,nn4678   235   pre1722   an,nn5485

in   simplicity and godly sincerity, not with fleshly wisdom, but by the grace

an,nn2316   ainp390   pre1722 art3588   nn2889   1161   ad4056

of God, we have had*our*conversation in   the world, and more abundantly

pre4314   ppro5209

to you-ward.

1063   pin1125   3756   an,ajn243   ppro5213 235/2228 repro3739   pin314   2228(2532)

13 For we write none other things unto you, than what ye read   or

pin1921   1161   pin1679   (3754)   fm1921   2532 ad2193   an,nn5056

acknowledge; and I trust ye shall acknowledge even to the end;

ad2531   2532   aina1921   ppro2248 pre575 an,nn3313 3754   pin2070 ppro5216

☞ 14 As also ye have acknowledged us   in part, that we are your

pr/an,nn2745   ad2509 epn5210 2532   ppro2257 pre1722 art3588 nn2250   art3588 an,nn2962 an,nn2424

rejoicing, even as ye also *are* ours in the day of the Lord Jesus.

2532   depro5026   art,nn4006   ipf1014   ainf2064 pre4314 ppro5209 an,ajn4386   2443

15 And in this confidence I was minded to come unto you before, that ye

psa2192   nu,aj1208   an,nn5485

might have a second benefit;

2532   ainf1330 pre1223 ppro5216 pre1519   an,nn3109   2532   ainf2064   ad3825

16 And to pass by   you into Macedonia, and to come again

pre575   an,nn3109   pre4314 ppro5209 2532 pre5259 ppro5216   aifp4311   pre1519

out of Macedonia unto you, and of   you to be brought*on*my*way toward

art,nn2449

Judea.

3767   ppmp1011/depro5124   (3385 686) aom5530 art,nn1644   2228

17 When I therefore was*thus*minded, did I use lightness? or the things

repro3739   pinm1011   pinm1011   pre2596   an,nn4561 2443 pre3844 ppro1698

that I purpose, do I purpose according to the flesh, that with me there should

psa5600 (art3588) 3483   3483   2532 (art3588) 3756   3756

be   yea yea, and   nay nay?

1161   art,nn2316   pr/an,aj4103(3754) ppro2257 art,nn3056 art,pre4314   ppro5209 aom1096 3756

18 But *as* God *is*   true,   our word toward you was not

pr/3483/2532/3756

yea*and*nay.

1063   art3588 nn5027   art,nn2316 an,nn2424 an,nn5547   art,aptp2784   pre1722 ppro5213 pre1223

☞ 19 For the Son of God, Jesus Christ, who*was*preached among you by

ppro2257   pre1223 ppro1700 2532 an,nn4610   2532   an,nn5095   aom1096 3756   pr/3483/2532/3756   235   pre1722

us, *even* by   me and Silvanus and Timothy, was not yea*and*nay, but in

ppro846 pfi1096   3483

him was yea.

1063   an,aj3745   an,nn1860   an,nn2316 pre1722 ppro846 (art3588) pr/3483   2532 pre1722 ppro846(art3588)

20 For all the promises of God in him *are* yea, and in   him

pr/281   pre4314   an,nn1391   art,nn2316 pre1223 ppro2257

Amen, unto the glory of God by us.

1161   art,pap950   ppro2248 pre4862 ppro5213 pre1519   an,nn5547   2532

21 Now he*which*establisheth   us   with you   in   Christ, and hath

apta5548   ppro2248   pr/an,nn2316

anointed us, *is* God;

☞ **1:14** See note on 1 Thessalonians 5:2.
☞ **1:19** See the introduction to 1 Timothy.

art,aptm4972/2532   ppro2248 2532 apta1325 art3588   nn728   art3588   nn4151 pre1722 ppro2257

22 Who*hath*also*sealed us, and given the earnest of the Spirit in   our

art,nn2588

hearts.

1161   epn1473 pinm1941 art,nn2316   an,nn3144 pre1909 art,popro1699 an,nn5590 3754   ppmp5339

23 Moreover I   call God for a record upon   my   soul, that to spare

ppro5216   aina2064   ad3765   pre1519   an,nn2882

you I came not*as*yet unto Corinth.

3756   3754   pin2961   ppro5216 art,nn4102 235 pin2070 pr/an,ajn4904

24 Not for that we have*dominion*over your faith, but are helpers of

ppro5216 art,nn5479 1063   art,nn4102   pfi2476

your joy: for by faith ye stand.

1161   aina2919 depro5124   rxpro1683   3361 art,ainf2064 ad3825 pre4314

2 But I determined this with myself, that I would not come again to

ppro5209 pre1722   an,nn3077

you   in heaviness.

1063 1487 epn1473   pin2076/ppro5209   inpro510 (2532) pin2076   pr/art,pap2165/ppro3165

2 For if I make*you*sorry, who   is he*then* that*maketh*me*glad,

1508   art,ppmp3076   pre1537 ppro1700

but the*same*which*is*made*sorry by me?

2532   aina1125 depro5124 ppro846   ppro5213 3363   apta2064   psa2192

3 And I wrote this same unto you, lest, when I came, I should have

an,nn3077   pre575   repro3739 ppro3165 ipf1163   pinf5463   pfp3982   pre1909 ppro5209

sorrow from them of whom   I   ought to rejoice; having confidence in   you

an,aj3956 3754 art,popro1699 an,nn5479 pin2076   ppro5216 an,aj3956

all, that my   joy   is *the joy* of you all.

1063   pre1537 an,aj4183   an,nn2347 2532 an,nn4928   an,nn2588 aina1125   ppro5213 pre1223

4 For out of much affliction and anguish of heart I wrote unto you with

an,aj4183 an,nn1144 3756 2443   asbp3076   235 2443   asba1097 art3588 nn26

many tears; not that ye should be grieved, but that ye might know the love

repro3739 pin2192   ad4056   pre1519 ppro5209

which I have more abundantly unto you.

Forgiveness for a Penitent Man

1161 1487 idpro5100   pfi3076   3756 pfi3076 epn1691 235 pre575/an,nn3313

5 But if any have caused grief, he hath not grieved me, but in part:

2443   3361   psa1912   ppro5209 an,aj3956

that I may not overcharge you all.

pr/an,ajn2425   art,ajn5108   depro3778   art,nn2009   art3588   pre5259

6 Sufficient to such*a*man *is* this punishment, which *was inflicted* of

cd/art,ajn4119

many.

5620   art,ajn5121   ppro5209   ad3123   aifm5483   2532 ainf3870

7 So that contrariwise ye *ought* rather to forgive *him,* and comfort *him,*

3381   art,ajn5108   asbp2666   cd/art,aj4055 an,nn3077

lest perhaps such*a*one should be swallowed up with overmuch sorrow.

pre,repro1352   pin3870 ppro5209   ainf2964   an,nn26 pre1519 ppro846

8 Wherefore I beseech you that ye would confirm *your* love toward him.

1063 pre1519 depro5124 2532 aina1125 2443 asba1097 art3588 nn1382 ppro5216
9 For to this end also did I write, that I might know the proof of you,
1487 pin2075 pr/an,aj5255 pre1519 an,ajn3956
whether ye be obedient in all things.

(1161) repro3739 pinm5483 idpro5100 epn1473 2532 1063
10 To whom ye forgive any thing, I *forgive* also: for
idpro1536/epn1473/pfip5483 (2532) repro3739 pfip5483 pre1223/ppro5209 pre1722
if*I*forgave*any*thing, to whom I forgave *it,* for*your*sakes *forgave I it* in
an,nn4383 an,nn5547
the person of Christ;

3363 (pre5259) art,nn4567 asbp4122 1063 pin50/3756
11 Lest Satan should get*an*advantage of us: for we are*not*ignorant
ppro846 art,nn3540
of his devices.

1161 apta2064 pre1519 art,nn5174 pre1519 art,nn5547 art,nn2098 2532
12 Furthermore, when I came to Troas to *preach* Christ's gospel, and a
an,nn2374 pfpp455 ppro3427 pre1722 an,nn2962
door was opened unto me of the Lord,
pfi2192 3756 an,nn425 ppro3450 art,nn4151 ppro3165 art,ainf2147 3361 an,nn5103 ppro3450 art,nn80
13 I had no rest in my spirit, because I found not Titus my brother:
235 aptm657 ppro846 aina1831 pre1519 an,nn3109
but taking*my*leave of them, I went*from*thence into Macedonia.

Victory In Christ

1161 an,nn5485 art,nn2316 art,pap2358/ad3842/ppro2248 pre1722
14 Now thanks *be* unto God, which*always*causeth*us*to*triumph in
art,nn5547 2532 pap5319 art3588 nn3744 ppro848 art,nn1108 pre1223 ppro2257 pre1722 an,aj3956
Christ, and maketh manifest the savor of his knowledge by us in every
an,nn5117
place.

3754 pin2070 art,nn2316 pr/an,nn2175 an,nn5547 pre1722
15 For we are unto God a sweet savor of Christ, in
art,ppmp4982 2532 pre1722 art,ppmp622
them*that*are*saved, and in them*that*perish:

repro3739/3303 an,nn3744 an,nn2288 pre1519 an,nn2288 1161 repro3739
16 To the one *we are* the savor of death unto death; and to the other
an,nn3744 an,nn2222 pre1519 an,nn2222 2532 inpro5101 pr/an,aj2425 pre4314 depro5023
the savor of life unto life. And who *is* sufficient for these things?
1063 pin2070 3756 ad5613 pr/art,ajn4183 pap2585 art3588 art3588 art,nn2316 235 ad5613
17 For we are not as many, which corrupt the word of God: but as
pre1537 an,nn1505 235 ad5613 pre1537 an,nn2316 ad*2714 art,nn2316 pin2980 pre1722 an,nn5547
of sincerity, but as of God, in*the*sight of God speak we in Christ.

A New Ministry

pinm756 ad3825 pinf4921 rxpro1438 1508 pin5535 ad5613 idpro5100
3 Do we begin again to commend ourselves? or need we, as some *others,*
an,nn1992 an,aj4956 pre4314 ppro5209 2228 an,ajn4956 pre1537 ppro5216
epistles of commendation to you, or *letters* of commendation from you?

pr/epn5210 pin2075 ppro2257 art,nn1992 pfpp1449 pre1722 ppro2257 art,nn2588 ppmp1097 2532 ppmp314 pre5259

2 Ye are our epistle written in our hearts, known and read of

an,aj3956 an,nn444

all men:

ppmp5319 (3754) pin2075 pr/an,nn1992 an,nn5547

3 *Forasmuch as ye are* manifestly declared to be the epistle of Christ

aptp1247 pre5259 ppro2257 pfpp1449 3756 an,nn3188 235 an,nn4151 an,pap2198

ministered by us, written not with ink, but with the Spirit of the living

an,nn2316 3756 pre1722 an,nn4109 an,aj3035 235 pre1722 an,aj4560 an,nn4109 an,nn2588

God; not in tables of stone, but in fleshy tables of the heart.

(Ex. 24:12; 31:18; Deut. 9:10,11; Prov. 3:3; Jer. 31:33)

1161 an,aj5108 an,nn4006 pin2192 pre1223 art,nn5547 pre4314 art,nn2316

4 And such trust have we through Christ to God-ward:

3756 3754 pin2070 pr/an,aj2425 pre575 rxpro1438 aifm3049 idpro5100 ad5613 pre1537

5 Not that we are sufficient of ourselves to think any thing as of

rxpro1438 235 ppro2257 art,nn2426 pre1537 art,nn2316

ourselves; but our sufficiency *is* of God;

repro3739 2532 aina2427/ppro2248 pr/an,nn1249 an,aj2537 an,nn1242 3756

6 Who also hath made*us*able ministers of the new testament; not of the

an,nn1121 235 an,nn4151 1063 art3588 nn1121 pin615 1161 art3588 nn4151 pin2226

letter, but of the spirit: for the letter killeth, but the spirit giveth life.

(Ex. 24:8; Jer. 31:31; 32:40)

1161 1487 art3588 nn1248 art,nn2288 pre1722/an,nn1121 pfpp1795 pre1722 an,nn3037

7 But if the ministration of death, written *and* engraven in stones,

ainp1096 pre1722/an,nn1391 5620 art3588 nn5207 2474 pifm1410 3361 ainf816 (pre1519)

was glorious, so that the children of Israel could not steadfastly behold

art3588 nn4383 an,nn3475 pre1223 art3588 nn1391 ppro846 art,nn4383

the face of Moses for the glory of his countenance;

art,ppmp2673

which*glory*was*to*be*done*away: *(Ex. 34:29,30)*

ad4459 3780 art3588 nn1248 art3588 nn4151 fm2071 ad3123 pre1722/an,nn1391

8 How shall not the ministration of the spirit be rather glorious?

1063 1487 art3588 nn1248 art,nn2633 pr/an,nn1391 an,ajn4183 ad3123 art3588

9 For if the ministration of condemnation *be* glory, much more doth the

nn1284 art,nn1343 pin4052 pre1722 an,nn1391

ministration of righteousness exceed in glory.   *(Deut. 27:26)*

1063 2532 art,pfpp1392 pfip1392/3761 pre1722 depro5129

10 For even that*which*was*made*glorious had*no*glory in this

art,nn3313 ad*1752 art3588 nn1391 pap5235

respect, by*reason*of the glory that excelleth.   *(Ex. 34:29,30)*

1063 1487 art,ppmp2673 pre1223/an,nn1391 an,ajn4183 ad3123

11 For if that*which*is*done*away *was* glorious, much more

art,pap3306 pre1722/an,nn1391

that*which*remaineth *is* glorious.

3767 pap2192 an,aj5108 an,nn1680 pinm5530 an,aj4183

12 Seeing then that we have such hope, we use great

an,nn3954

plainness*of*speech:

2532 3756 ad2509 an,nn3475 ipf5087 an,nn2571 pre1909 rxpro1438 art,nn4383 art3588

13 And not as Moses, *which* put a veil over his face, that the

nn5207   2474   3361   aipr816   pre1519   art3588   nn5056
children   of   Israel   could   not   steadfastly   look   to   the   end   of

art,ppmp2673
that*which*is*abolished: (Ex. 34:33,35)

         235   ppro846   art,nn3540   ainp4456   1063   ad891   art,ad4594   pin3306   art3588   ppro846
14 But   their   minds   were   blinded: for until this day remaineth the same

nn2571   ppmp343/3361   pre1909   art3588   nn320   art3588   an,aj3820   nn1242   repro3748
veil untaken away   in   the   reading   of the   old   testament; which veil is

pinp2673   pre1722   an,nn5547
done away   in   Christ.

         235   ad2193   ad4594   ad2259   an,nn3475   pinp314   an,nn2571 pinm2749 pre1909 ppro846
15 But even unto this day, when Moses is read, the   veil   is   upon their

art,nn2588
heart.

         1161   ad2259/302   asba1994   pre4314   an,nn2962   art3588   nn2571
16 Nevertheless   when   it   shall   turn   to   the   Lord,   the   veil   shall be

pinp4014
taken away.   (Ex. 34:34)

         1161   art3588   nn2962   pin2076   pr/art,nn4151   1161   repro3757   art3588   nn4151   an,nn2962
17 Now the Lord   is   that Spirit: and where the Spirit of the Lord is,

ad1563   an,nn1657
there is liberty.

         1161   pro2249 an,aj3956   pfpp343 an,nn4383   ppmp2734   art3588   nn1391
18 But we   all,   with open face beholding*as*in*a*glass the glory of the

an,nn2962   pinm3339   art3588 ppro846   nn1504   pre575   an,nn1391 pre1519 an,nn1391   ad2509 pre575
Lord, are changed into the same image from glory to   glory, even as   by the

an,nn4151   an,nn2962
Spirit of the Lord.   (Ex. 16:7; 24:17)

Never Give Up

pre1223/depro5124   pap2192 depro5026   art,nn1248   ad2531   ainp1653
4 Therefore seeing we have this   ministry,   as   we have received mercy,

pin1573   3756
we faint not;

         235   aom550   art3588   ajn2927   art,nn152   3361   pap4043   pre1722
2 But have renounced the hidden things of dishonesty, not walking   in

an,nn3834   3366   pap1389/art3588/nn3056/art,nn2316   235   art,nn5321
craftiness, nor handling*the*word*of*God*deceitfully; but by manifestation of

art3588   nn225   pap4921   rxpro1438   pre4314 an,aj3956   an,nn444   an,nn4893   ad*1799
the truth commending ourselves   to   every man's conscience in*the*sight of

art,nn2316
God.

         1161   1487(2532) ppro2257   art,nn2098   pin2076   pr/pfpp2572   pin2076 pr/pfpp2572 pre1722   art,ppmp622
3 But   if   our gospel be   hid, it   is   hid   to them*that*are*lost:

         pre1722   repro3739   art3588   nn2316   depro5127   art,nn165   aina5186   art3588   nn3540
4 In   whom   the   god   of   this   world hath blinded   the   minds of

         art,ajn571   3361 art3588 nn5462   art3588   nn1391   art,nn2098   art,nn5547 repro3739
them*which*believe*not, lest the light of the glorious gospel of Christ, who

pin2076   pr/an,nn1504   art,nn2316   aies826   ppro846
is the image of God, should shine unto them.

_{1063   pin2784   3756   rxpro1438   235   an,nn5547 an,nn2424   an,nn2962 1161   rxpro1438}
5 For we preach not ourselves, but Christ Jesus the Lord; and ourselves
_{ppro5216   an,ajn1401   pre1223/an,nn2424}
your servants for*Jesus'*sake.

_{3754   art,nn2316   art,apta2036   an,nn5457   ainf2989   pre1537   an,nn4655   (repro3739)}
6 For God, who commanded the light to shine out of darkness, hath
_{aina2989   pre1722 ppro2257 art,nn2588   pre4314   an,nn5462   art3588   nn1108   art3588   nn1391}
shined in   our hearts, to *give* the light of the knowledge of the glory of
_{art,nn2316 pre1722   an,nn4383   an,nn2424   an,nn5547}
God   in   the face of Jesus Christ.   *(Gen. 1:3; Is. 9:2)*

_{1161   pin2192 depro5126   art,nn2344   pre1722   an,aj3749   an,nn4632   2443   art3588   nn5236}
7 But we have this treasure in earthen vessels, that the excellency of
_{art3588   nn1411   psa5600   art,nn2316 2532 3361 pre1537 ppro2257}
the power may be of God, and not of   us.

_{ppmp2346   pre1722   an,ajn3956   235   3756   ppmp4729   ppmp639}
8 *We are* troubled on every side, yet not distressed; *we are* perplexed,
_{235   3756   ppmp1820}
but not in despair;

_{ppmp1377   235 3756   ppmp1459   ppmp2598   235 3756   ppmp622}
9 Persecuted, but not forsaken; cast down, but not destroyed;

_{ad3842   pap4064   pre1722 art3588   nn4983   art3588   nn3500   art3588   nn2962   an,nn2424   2443}
10 Always bearing about in   the body the dying of the Lord Jesus, that
_{art3588 nn2222 2532   art,nn2424   asbp5319   pre1722 ppro2257 art,nn4983}
the life also of Jesus might be made manifest in   our body.

_{1063   epn2249   art,pap2198   ad104   pinp3860   pre1519 an,nn2288   pre1223/an,nn2424}
☞ 11 For we   which live are always delivered unto death for*Jesus'*sake,
_{2443 art3588 nn2222 2532   art,nn2424   asbp5319   pre1722 ppro2257 art,aj2349 an,nn4561}
that the life also of Jesus might be made manifest in   our mortal flesh.

_{5620   (3303) art,nn2288   pinm1754   pre1722 ppro5213 1161 art,nn2222 pre1722 ppro2254}
12 So then   death worketh in   us, but life   in you.

_{(1161)   pap2192   art3588   ppro846   an,nn4151   art,nn4102   pre2596   art,pfpp1125}
13   We having the   same spirit of faith, according as it is written, I
_{aina4100   2532   pre,repro1352   aina2980   epn2249 2532   pin4100   2532 pre,repro1352   pin2980}
believed, and therefore have I spoken; we also believe, and therefore speak;

                                                                (Ps. 116:10)
_{pfp1492   3754   art,apta1453   art3588   nn2962 an,nn2424   ft1453   epn2248}
14 Knowing that he*which*raised*up the Lord Jesus shall raise up   us
_{2532 pre1223 an,nn2424 2532   ft3936   pre4862 ppro5213}
also by Jesus, and shall present *us* with you.

_{1063   art,ajn3956   pre1223/ppro5209   2443   art3588   apta4121   nn5485}
15 For all things *are* for*your*sakes, that the abundant grace might
_{pre1223   art3588   nn2169   cd/art,ajn4119   asba4052   pre1519 art3588 nn1391   art,nn2316}
through the thanksgiving of many redound to the glory of God.

_{pre,repro1352   pin1573   3756   235   1499   ppro2257 art,ad1854   an,nn444   pinm1311}
16 For*which*cause we faint not; but though our outward man perish,
_{235 art3588   ad2081   pinm341   an,nn2250/2532/an,nn2250}
yet the inward *man* is renewed day*by*day.

☞ **4:11** See note on 2 Timothy 1:12.

1063   ppro2257 art,ajn1645   art,nn2347   ad3910   pinm2716   ppro2254

17 For our light affliction, which is but*for*a*moment, worketh for us a

pre2596/an,nn5236/pre1519/an,nn5236   an,aj166   an,nn922   an,nn1391

far*more*exceeding *and* eternal weight of glory;

ppro2257   pap4648/3361   art,ppmp991   235

18 While we look*not*at the*things*which*are*seen, but at

art,ppmp991/3361   1063   art,ppmp991   pr/an,aj4340

the*things*which*are*not*seen: for the*things*which*are*seen *are* temporal;

1161   art,ppmp991/3361   pr/an,aj166

but the*things*which*are*not*seen *are* eternal.

1063   pin1492   3754   1437   ppro2257   art,aj1919   an,nn3614   art,nn4636

5 ☞ For we know that if our earthly house of *this* tabernacle were

asbp2647   pin2192   an,nn3619   pre1537 an,nn2316   an,nn3614   an,aj886

dissolved, we have a building of God, a house not*made*with*hands,

an,aj166   pre1722 art3588   nn3772

eternal in the heavens.   *(Job 4:19)*

☞ **5:1** The phrase "we know" is translated from the Greek word *oídamen* (1492), meaning "to know intuitively" as a result of being a child of God. It is the knowledge that accompanies the new birth in Christ Jesus.

Verse one continues: ". . . if our earthly house of this tabernacle [tent] . . . ." What Paul is saying here is the spirit is the real person found in the body. The body is represented by the Greek word *skénon* (4633) "tent," which refers to the material portion of a person. Paul continues on to explain that though this earthly body ("house") will be "dissolved," God has promised that there will be a "building of God." This is a description of death of the mortal body, yet it is intended to be encouragement for the believer as he looks at death. The word that is translated "building," is the Greek word *oikodomén* (3619), which means "the process of building something." The basic idea in this verse is that God is building a new house for the believer's spirit which will be disembodied at the point of death, leaving the body remaining on earth. This indicates that God will create something completely new. Then Paul uses the word *oikían* (3614), "dwelling place," which refers to the completion of the "eternal body." There are two qualities of this new body that must be understood. First, it will be similar to the present one and identifiable, yet not identical because it is not going to be made by human hands, but it will be produced by God. The word translated "not made with hands" is *acheiropoíēton* (886). This is the same word that the Lord used in Mark 14:58 when He spoke of destroying the temple, which was made by the hands of men, and in three days, building another, not made by man. Christ was speaking of His body following his resurrection. Although His own body was "made of a woman" (Gal. 4:4) at His birth, yet no human being was involved at the time of His resurrection. The believer's human body will have the same outcome. The first time, one is born into this world, the body is physically produced. However, at the resurrection by Christ of the righteous dead (1 Thess. 4:15–17), God will change them to new, glorified bodies (1 Cor. 15:50–57). The second quality is that it is going to be "eternal," translated from the Greek word *aiónion* (166). This idea of eternality focused on what characterizes God Himself. The life that is given at salvation to believers is the promise of eternal life, (*aiónios* [166], *zōé* [2222]), not denoting duration of a period time, but to the quality of the life. This life can never be lost or taken away once a person accepts Jesus Christ as Lord and Savior. The word, *aiónios*, however, is always related to time using the form *aión* (165), "age or generation." One must consider its usage in 2 Corinthians 4:17, 18 where contrast is made to "the things which are seen . . . are temporal," comparing the affliction the Corinthians were undergoing to the "more exceeding and eternal weight of glory." Therefore, *aiónios* means that which is not temporal, cannot be lost, nor destroyed. Paul gives the location of this "life to be" as "in the heavens" (see also 1 Cor. 8:5; 15:57; 2 Cor. 5:2; 12:2). Paul recognized this place to be where God is and where the believer will find his ultimate rest (1 Thess. 4:17, 18).

2 For in this we groan, earnestly desiring to be clothed upon with our house which is from heaven:

3 If*so*be that being clothed we shall not be found naked.

☞ 4 For we*that*are in *this* tabernacle do groan, being burdened: not for that we would be unclothed, but clothed upon, that mortality might be swallowed up of life.

5 Now he*that*hath*wrought us for the selfsame thing *is* God, who*also*hath*given unto us the earnest of the Spirit.

6 Therefore *we are* always confident, knowing that, whilst we are*at*home in the body, we are absent from the Lord:

7 (For we walk by faith, not by sight:)

8 We are confident, *I say,* and willing rather to be absent from the body, and to be present with the Lord.

9 Wherefore we labor, that, whether present or absent, we may be accepted of him.

10 For we must all appear before the judgment seat of Christ; that every one may receive the things *done* in *his* body, according to that he hath done, whether *it be* good or bad.

Paul Defends Himself

11 Knowing therefore the terror of the Lord, we persuade men; but we are made manifest unto God; and I trust also are made manifest in your consciences.

12 For we commend not ourselves again unto you, but give you occasion to glory on*our*behalf, that ye may have somewhat

---

☞ **5:4** See note on 2 Timothy 1:12.

pre4314   art,ppmp2744   pre1722   an,nn4383   2532   3756   an,nn2588

to *answer* them*which*glory in appearance, and not in heart.

1063   1535   aina1839   an,nn2316   1535

13 For whether we be*beside*ourselves, *it is* to God: or whether we

pin4993   ppro5213

be sober, *it is* for your cause.

1063   art3588   nn26   art,nn5547   pin4912   ppro2248   depro5124   apta2919   3754

14 For the love of Christ constraineth us; because we thus judge, that

1487 nu,ajn1520 aina599 pre5228 an,ajn3956   686   aina599/art,ajn3956

if one died for all, then were*all*dead:

2532   aina599 pre5228 an,ajn3956   2443   art,pap2198   ad3371

15 And *that* he died for all, that they*which*live should not henceforth

psa2198   rxpro1438   235   art,apta599   pre5228 ppro846 2532   aptp1453

live unto themselves, but unto him*which*died for them, and rose again.

5620   pre575/art,ad3568   pin1492 epn2249 an,ajn3762   pre2596   an,nn4561 1161   1499

16 Wherefore henceforth know we no man after the flesh: yea, though we

pfi1097   an,nn5547   pre2596   an,nn4561   235   ad3568   pin1097

have known Christ after the flesh, yet now henceforth know we *him*

ad3765

no more.

5620   idpro1536   pre1722   an,nn5547   pr/an,aj2537   an,nn2937   art,ajn744

17 Therefore if*any*man *be* in Christ, *he is* a new creature: old things

aina3928   2400   art,ajn3956   pfi1096   pr/an,aj2537

are passed away; behold, all things are become new.   *(Is. 43:18,19)*

1161   art,ajn3956   pre1537 art,nn2316   art,apta2644   ppro2248   rxpro1438   pre1223

18 And all things *are* of God, who*hath*reconciled us to himself by

an,nn2424 an,nn5547 2532   apta1325   ppro2254 art3588   nn1248   art,nn2643

Jesus Christ, and hath given to us the ministry of reconciliation;

ad5613   3754   an,nn2316 ipf2258 pre1722   an,nn5547   pap2644   an,nn2889   rxpro1438

19 To wit, that God was in Christ, reconciling the world unto himself,

3361   ppmp3049   ppro846   art,nn3900   ppro846   2532   aptm5087   pre1722 ppro2254 art3588

not imputing their trespasses unto them; and hath committed unto us the

nn3056   art,nn2643

word of reconciliation.

3767   pin4243   pre5228 an,nn5547   5613   art,nn2316   pap3870

20 Now then we are ambassadors for Christ, as though God did beseech

pre1223 ppro2257   pinm1189   pre5228/an,nn5547   aipp2644   art,nn2316

you by us; we pray *you* in*Christ's*stead, be ye reconciled to God.

1063   aina4160   pr/an,nn266 pre5228 ppro2257   art,apta1097   3361 an,nn266   2443

21 For he hath made him *to be* sin for us, who knew no sin; that

epn2249   psa1096   pr/an,nn1343   an,nn2316 pre1722 ppro846

we might be made the righteousness of God in him.

The Apostle's Fidelity and Love

       1161   pap4903   pin3870   2532   ppro5209 aifm1209

6 We then, as workers together *with him*, beseech *you* also that ye receive

3361 art3588   nn5485   art,nn2316 pre1519 an,ajn2756

not the grace of God in vain.

1063   pin3004   aina1873 ppro4675   an,nn2540   an,aj1184   2532 pre1722   an,nn2250

2 (For he saith, I have heard thee in a time accepted, and in the day of

salvation have I succored thee: behold, now *is* the accepted time; behold, now

is the day of salvation.)   *(Is. 49:8)*

3 Giving no offense in any thing, that the ministry be not blamed:

4 But in all *things* approving ourselves as the ministers of God, in

much patience, in afflictions, in necessities, in distresses,

5 In stripes, in imprisonments, in tumults, in labors, in

watchings, in fastings;

6 By pureness, by knowledge, by longsuffering, by kindness, by the

Holy Ghost, by love unfeigned,

7 By the word of truth, by the power of God, by the armor of

righteousness on the right hand and on the left,

8 By honor and dishonor, by evil report and good report: as deceivers,

and *yet* true;

9 As unknown, and *yet* well known; as dying, and, behold, we live; as

chastened, and not killed;   *(Ps. 118:18)*

10 As sorrowful, yet always rejoicing; as poor, yet making* many*rich;

as having nothing, and *yet* possessing all things.

11 O *ye* Corinthians, our mouth is open unto you, our heart is

enlarged.

12 Ye are not straitened in us, but ye are straitened in your own

bowels.

13 Now for a recompense in the same, (I speak as unto *my* children,) be

ye also enlarged.

14 Be ye not unequally*yoked*together with unbelievers: for what

fellowship hath righteousness with unrighteousness? and what communion hath

light with darkness?

15 And what concord hath Christ with Belial? or what part hath he*that*believeth with an infidel?

16 And what agreement hath the temple of God with idols? for ye are the temple of the living God; as God hath said, I will dwell in them, and walk in *them*; and I will be their God, and they shall be my people.

(Lev. 26:12; Jer. 32:38; Ezek. 37:27)

17 Wherefore come out from among them, and be*ye*separate, saith the Lord, and touch not the unclean *thing*; and I will receive you.

(Is. 52:11; Ezek. 20:34,41)

18 And will be a Father unto you, and ye shall be my sons and daughters, saith the Lord Almighty.

(2 Sam. 7:14; Is. 43:6, 7; Jer. 31:9; Amos 3:13 [Sept.]; 4:13 [Sept.]

7 Having therefore these promises, dearly beloved, let us cleanse ourselves from all filthiness of the flesh and spirit, perfecting holiness in the fear of God.

The Former Letter

2 Receive us; we have wronged no man, we have corrupted no man, we have defrauded no man.

3 I speak not *this* to condemn *you*: for I have said before, that ye are in our hearts to die and live with *you*.

4 Great *is* my boldness*of*speech toward you, great *is* my glorying of you: I am filled with comfort, I am exceeding joyful in all our tribulation.

1063   2532   ppro2257   apta2064   pre1519   an,nn3109   ppro2257 art,nn4561 aina2192 an,aj3762 an,nn425

5 For, when we were come into Macedonia, our flesh had no rest,

235   ppmp2346 pre1722   an,ajn3956   ad1855   an,nn3163   ad2081

but we were troubled on every side; without *were* fightings, within *were*

an,nn5401

fears.

235   art,nn2316   art,pap3870   art,ajn5011

6 Nevertheless God, that comforteth those*that*are*cast*down,

aina3870   ppro2248 pre1722 art3588   nn3952   an,nn5103

comforted us by the coming of Titus;   (*Is. 49:13*)

1161   3556 pre1722 ppro846 art,nn3952 an,ajn3440 235(2532) pre1722 art3588   nn3874   repro3739

7 And not by his coming only, but by the consolation wherewith

ainp3870   pre1909 ppro5213   pap312 ppro2254 ppro5216   art,nn1972

he was comforted in you, when he told us your earnest desire,

ppro5216   art,nn3602   ppro5216   art,nn2205   pre5228 ppro1700   5620   ppro3165   ainf5463

your mourning, your fervent mind toward me; so that I rejoiced

ad3123

the more.

3754   1499   aina3076/ppro5209   pre1722 art,nn1992   3756   pinm3338   1499

8 For though I made*you*sorry with a letter, I do not repent, though I did

ipf3338   1063   pin991   3754 art3588 depro1565 nn1992   aina3076/ppro5209   1499

repent: for I perceive that the same epistle hath made*you*sorry, though *it*

pre4314   an,nn5610

were but for a season.

ad3568   pin5463   3756 3754   ainp3076   235 3754   ainp3076   pre1519

9 Now I rejoice, not that ye were made sorry, but that ye sorrowed to

an,nn3341   1063   ainp3076   pre2596/an,nn2316   2443

repentance: for ye were made sorry after*a*godly*manner, that ye might

asbp2210   pre1537 ppro2257 pre1722   an,ajn3367

receive damage by us in nothing.

1063   pre2596/an,nn2316 art,nn3077   pinm2716   an,nn3341   pre1519   an,nn4991

10 For godly sorrow worketh repentance to salvation

an,aj278   1161 art3588 nn3077   art3588 nn2889 pinm2716 an,nn2288

not*to*be*repented*of: but the sorrow of the world worketh death.

1063   2400   depro5124   ppro846   ppro5209   aifp3076

11 For behold this selfsame thing, that ye sorrowed

art,pre2596/an,nn2316   an,aj4214   an,nn4710   aom2716   ppro5213   235

after*a*godly*sort, what carefulness it wrought in you, yea, *what*

an,nn627   235   an,nn24   235   an,nn5401   235

clearing*of*yourselves, yea, *what* indignation, yea, *what* fear, yea, *what*

an,nn1972   235   an,nn2205 235   an,nn1557 pre1722 an,ajn3956

vehement desire, yea, *what* zeal, yea, *what* revenge! In all *things* ye have

aina4921   rxpro1438   pinf1511 pr/an,aj53 pre1722   art,nn4229

approved yourselves to be clear in this matter.

686   1499   aina1125   ppro5213   3756   ad*1752

12 Wherefore, though I wrote unto you, I *did it* not for*his*cause

art,apta91   3761   ad*1752   art,aptp91   235   ppro2257

that*had*done*the*wrong, nor for*his*cause that*suffered*wrong, but that our

art,nn4710 art,pre5228 ppro5216   ad*1799   art,nn2316   infg5319 pre4314 ppro5209

care for you in*the*sight of God might appear unto you.

pre1223/depro5124   pfi3870   pre1909 ppro5216 art,nn3874   1161   ad4056

13 Therefore we were comforted in your comfort: yea, and exceedingly

ad3123   aina5463   pre1909 art3588 nn5479   an,nn5103   3754   ppro846 art,nn4151   pfip373

the more joyed we for the joy of Titus, because his spirit was refreshed

pre575 ppro5216 an,aj3956

by you all.

3754   idpro1536/pfip2744   ppro846 pre5228 ppro5216   ainp2617/3756

☞ 14 For if*I*have*boasted*any*thing to him of you, I am*not*ashamed;

235   ad5613   aina2980   an,ajn3956   ppro5213 pre1722 an,nn225   2532   ad3779 pro2257 art,nn2746   art3588

but as we spake all things to you in truth, even so our boasting, which *I*

pre1909   an,nn5103   ainp1096   pr/an,nn225

made before Titus, is found a truth.

2532   ppro846   art,nn4698   pin2076   ad4056   pre1519   ppro5209

15 And his inward affection is more abundant toward you, whilst he

ppmp363   art3588   nn5218   ppro5216 an,aj3956 ad5613 pre3326 an,nn5401 2532   an,nn5156

remembereth the obedience of you all, how with fear and trembling ye

aom1209   ppro846

received him.

pin5463   3767   3754   pin2292   pre1722 ppro5213 pre1722 an,ajn3956

16 I rejoice therefore that I have confidence in you in all *things*.

The Macedonian Saints

1161   an,nn80   pin1107/ppro5213   art3588 nn5485   art,nn2316 art,pfpp1325

8 Moreover, brethren, we do*you*to*wit of the grace of God bestowed

pre1722 art3588   nn1577   art,nn3109

on the churches of Macedonia;

3754   pre1722   an,aj4183 an,nn1382   an,nn2347 art3588   nn4050   ppro846 art,nn5479 2532

2 How that in a great trial of affliction the abundance of their joy and

ppro846 an,nn899 art,nn4432   aina4052   pre1519 art3588 nn4149   ppro846   art,nn572

their deep poverty abounded unto the riches of their liberality.

3754   pre2596   an,nn1411   pin3140   2532   pre5228   an,nn1411

3 For to *their* power, I bear record, yea, and beyond *their* power *they*

pr/an,aj830

were willing*of*themselves;

ppmp1189   ppro2257 pre3326 an,aj4183   an,nn3874   ppro2248   aifm1209   art3588 nn5485 2532

4 Praying us with much entreaty that we would receive the gift, and

art3588   nn2842   art3588   nn1248   art,pre1519 art3588   ajn40

take upon us the fellowship of the ministering to the saints.

2532   3756 ad2531   aina1679   235   nu,aj4412 aina1325   rxpro1438

5 And *this they did,* not as we hoped, but first gave their*own*selves to

art3588 nn2962 2532   ppro2254 pre1223   an,nn2307   an,nn2316

the Lord, and unto us by the will of God.

ppro2248   aies3870   an,nn5103 2443 ad2531   aom4278   ad3779

6 Insomuch that we desired Titus, that as he had begun, so he would

2532   asba2005 pre1519 ppro5209 art3588 depro5026   nn5485   2532

also finish in you the same grace also.

☞ **7:14, 15** See the introduction to Titus.

235   ad5618   pin4052   pre1722 an,ajn3956   an,nn4102 2532   an,nn3056   2532

7 Therefore, as ye abound in every *thing, in* faith, and utterance, and

an,nn1108   2532   an,aj3956   an,nn4710   2532 (art,pre1537) ppro5216 an,nn26 pre1722 ppro2254   2443

knowledge, and *in* all diligence, and *in* your love to us, *see* that ye

psa4052   pre1722 depro5026 at,nn5485   2532

abound in this grace also.

pin3004   3756   pre2596   an,nn2003   235   pre1223   ar13588   nn4710

8 I speak not by commandment, but by*occasion*of the forwardness of

an,ajn2087   2532   pap1381 art3588   ajn1103   art,popro5212 an,nn26

others, and to prove the sincerity of your love.

1063   pin1097 art3588   nn5485   ppro2257 art,nn2962 an,nn2424 an,nn5547   3574   pap5607

9 For ye know the grace of our Lord Jesus Christ, that, though he was

pr/an,aj4145   pre1223/ppro5209   aina4433   2443 epn5210   depro1565 art,nn4432

rich, yet for*your*sakes he became poor, that ye through his poverty might

asba4147

be rich.

2532   pre1722/depro5129   pin1325   an,nn1106 1063 depro5124   pin4851   ppro5213 repro3748

10 And herein I give *my* advice: for this is expedient for you, who have

aom 4278   3756 an,aj3440   art,ainf4160 235   2532   art,pinf 2309   pre575/ad4070

begun before, not only to do, but also to be forward a*year*ago.

(1161) ad3570   2532   aima2005   art3588 ainf4160   3704 ad2509   art,nn4288

11 Now therefore perform the doing *of it*; that as *there was* a readiness

art,pinf2309 ad3779   art,ainf2005   2532   pre1537   art,pinf2192

to will, so *there may be* a performance also out of that*which*ye*have.

1063   1487   pinm4295   art,nn4228   pr/an,aj2144   ad2526

12 For if there be first a willing mind, *it is* accepted according*to*that

idpro5100 psa2192/1437   3756   ad2526   pin2192 3756

a man hath, *and* not according*to*that he hath not.   *(Prov. 3:27,28)*

1063   3756 2443   an,ajn243   an,nn425 1161 ppro5213 an,nn2347

13 For *I mean* not that other men be eased, and ye burdened:

235   pre1537   an,nn2471   ad3568 pre1722   art,nn2540 ppro5216   art,nn4051

14 But by an equality, *that* now at this time your abundance *may be a*

pre1519 depro1565 art,nn5303   2443 depro1565   art,nn4051   2532   asbm1096   pre1519 ppro5216

supply for their want, that their abundance also may be *a supply* for your

art,nn5303 3704   asbm1096 pr/an,nn2471

want: that there may be equality:

ad2531   pfip1125   art3588   art,ajn4183   aina4121/3756   2532

15 As it is written, He that *had gathered* much had*nothing*over; and

art3588   art,ajn3641   aina1641/3756

he that *had gathered* little had*no*lack.   *(Ex. 16:18)*

Paul Receives a Report From Titus and Another Brother

1161   an,nn5485   art,nn2316   art,pap1325   art3588 ppro846   an,nn4710   pre1722 art3588   nn2588

☞ 16 But thanks *be* to God, which put the same earnest care into the heart

an,nn5103 pre5228 ppro5216

of Titus for you.

☞ **8:16–23** See the introduction to Titus.

³⁷⁵⁴ ³³⁰³ ^{aom1209} ^{art3588} ⁿⁿ³⁸⁷⁴ ¹¹⁶¹ ^{pap5225} ^{pr/cd/an,aj4707}

17 For indeed he accepted the exhortation; but being more forward,

^{an,aj830} ^{aina1831} ^{pre4314} ^{ppro5209}

of*his*own*accord he went unto you.

¹¹⁶¹ ^{aina4842} ^{pre3326} ^{ppro846} ^{art3588} ⁿⁿ⁸⁰ ^{repro3739} ^{art,nn1868} ^{pre1722} ^{art3588}

18 And we have sent with him the brother, whose praise is in the

ⁿⁿ²⁰⁹⁸ ^{pre1223} ^{an,aj3956} ^{art3588} ⁿⁿ¹⁵⁷⁷

gospel throughout all the churches;

¹¹⁶¹ ³⁷⁵⁶ ^{an,ajn3440} ²³⁵ ²⁵³² ^{aptp5500} ^{pre5259} ^{art3588} ⁿⁿ¹⁵⁷⁷

19 And not that only, but who was also chosen of the churches to

^{pr/an,ajn4898} ^{ppro2257} ^{pre4862} ^{depro5026} ^{art,nn5485} ^{art,ppmp1247} ^{pre5259} ^{ppro2257} ^{pre4314} ^{art3588}

travel with us with this grace, which*is*administered by us to the

ⁿⁿ¹³⁹¹ ^{art3588} ^{ppro846} ⁿⁿ²⁹⁶² ²⁵³² ^{ppro5216} ^{an,nn4288}

glory of the same Lord, and declaration of your ready mind:

^{ppmp4724} ^{depro5124} ³³⁶¹ ^{idpro5100} ^{asba3469} ^{ppro2248} ^{pre1722} ^{depro5026} ^{art,nn100}

20 Avoiding this, that no man should blame us in this abundance

^{art,ppmp1247} ^{pre5259} ^{ppro2257}

which*is*administered by us:

^{ppmp4306} ^{an,ajn2570} ³⁷⁵⁶ ^{an,ajn3440} ^{ad*1799} ^{an,nn2962} ²³⁵

21 Providing for honest things, not only in*the*sight of the Lord, but

²⁵³² ^{ad*1799} ^{an,nn444}

also in*the*sight of men.   *(Prov. 3:4 [Sept.])*

---

¹¹⁶¹ ^{aina4842} ^{ppro846} ^{ppro2257} ^{art,nn80} ^{repro3739} ^{ad4178}

22 And we have sent with them our brother, whom we have oftentimes

^{aina1381(pap5607)} ^{pr/an,aj4705} ^{pre1722} ^{an,ajn4183} ¹¹⁶¹ ^{ad3570} ^{an,ajn4183} ^{pr/cd/an,aj4707}

proved diligent in many things, but now much more diligent, upon the

^{an,aj4183} ^{an,nn4006} ^{art3588} ^{pre1519} ^{ppro5209}

great confidence which I have in you.

¹⁵³⁵ ^{pre5228} ^{an,nn5103} ^{popro1699} ^{pr/an,ajn2844} ²⁵³² ^{pr/an,ajn4904}

23 Whether any do inquire of Titus, he is my partner and fellowhelper

^{pre1519} ^{ppro5209} ¹⁵³⁵ ^{ppro2257} ^{an,nn80} ^{pr/an,nn652}

concerning you: or our brethren be inquired of, they are the messengers of the

^{an,nn1577} ^{an,nn1391} ^{an,nn5547}

churches, and the glory of Christ.

³⁷⁶⁷ ^{aipm1731} ^{pre1519} ^{ppro846} ²⁵³² ^{pre1519/an,nn4383} ^{art3588} ⁿⁿ¹⁵⁷⁷ ^{art3588} ⁿⁿ¹⁷³²

24 Wherefore show ye to them, and before the churches, the proof of

^{ppro5216} ^{art,nn26} ²⁵³² ^{ppro2257} ^{an,nn2746} ^{pre5228/ppro5216}

your love, and of our boasting on*your*behalf.

Free and Cheerful Giving

¹⁰⁶³ ^{pre4012} ⁽³³⁰³⁾ ^{art3588} ⁿⁿ¹²⁴⁸ ^{art,pre1519} ^{art3588} ^{ajn40} ^{pin2076} ^{pr/an,ajn4053}

9 For as touching the ministering to the saints, it is superfluous

^{ppro3427} ^{art,pinf1125} ^{ppro5213}

for me to write to you:

¹⁰⁶³ ^{pin1492} ^{art3588} ^{nn4288/ppro5216} ^{repro3739} ^{pinm2744} ^{pre5228} ^{ppro5216}

2 For I know the forwardness*of*your*mind, for which I boast of you to

^{an,nn3110} ³⁷⁵⁴ ^{an,nn882} ^{pfip3903} ^{pre575/ad4070} ^{2532(pre1537)} ^{ppro5216} ^{art,nn2205}

them*of*Macedonia, that Achaia was ready a*year*ago; and your zeal hath

^{aina2042} ^{cd/art,ajn4119}

provoked very many.

_{1161   aina3992 art3588   nn80   3363 ppro2257   art,nn2745   art,pre5228 ppro5216}
3 Yet have I sent the brethren, lest our boasting of you should

_{asbp2758   pre1722 depro5129 art,nn3313 2443 ad2531   ipf3004   psa5600 pr/pfpp3903}
be*in*vain in this behalf; that, as I said, ye may be ready:

_{3381   1437   an,nn3110   asba2064 pre4862 ppro1698 2532 asba2147 ppro5209}
4 Lest haply if they*of*Macedonia come with me, and find you

_{pr/an,aj532 epn2249   2443   psa3004 3361 epn5210   asbp2617   pre1722   depro5026}
unprepared, we (that we say not, ye) should be ashamed in this same

_{art,nn5287   art,nn2746}
confident boasting.

_{3767   aom2233   pr/an,ajn316 ainf3870 art3588   nn80   2443}
5 Therefore I thought it necessary to exhort the brethren, that they would

_{asba4281   pre1519 ppro5209 2532   asba4294   ppro5216 art,nn2129}
go before unto you, and make*up*beforehand your bounty, whereof ye

_{pfpp4293   depro5026   pinf1511 pr/an,aj2092(ad3779) ad5613}
had*notice*before, that the same might be ready,   as *a matter of*

_{an,nn2129   2532 3361 ad5618   an,nn4124}
bounty, and not as *of* covetousness.

_{1161 depro5124   art,pap4687   ad5340   ft2325 2532   ad5340}
6 But this *I say,* He*which*soweth sparingly shall reap also sparingly;

_{2532   art,pap4687   pre1909/an,nn2129   ft2325 2532 pre1909/an,nn2129}
and he*which*soweth bountifully shall reap also bountifully. *(Prov. 11:24; 22:9)*

_{an,ajn1538   ad2531   pinm4255   art,nn2588   3361}
7 Every man according as he purposeth in his heart, *so let him give*; not

_{pre1537/an,nn3077 2228 pre1537   an,nn318 1063 art,nn2316 pin25   an,aj2431   an,nn1395}
grudgingly, or of necessity: for God loveth a cheerful giver.

(Prov. 22:8 [Sept.]

_{1161   art,nn2316   pr/an,aj1415   ainf4052/an,aj3956/an,nn5485   pre1519   ppro5209 2443}
8 And God *is* able to make*all*grace*abound toward you; that ye,

_{ad3842   pap2192 an,aj3956   an,nn841   pre1722 an,ajn3956   psa4052   pre1519 an,aj3956   an,aj18}
always having all sufficiency in   all *things,* may abound to every good

_{an,nn2041}
work:

_{ad2531   pfip1125   aina4650   aina1325   art3588   nn3993}
9 (As it is written, He hath dispersed abroad; he hath given to the poor:

_{ppro846   art,nn1343   pin3306   pre1519/art,nn165}
his righteousness remaineth forever.   *(Ps. 112:9)*

_{1161   art,pap2023   an,nn4690 art3588 pap4687 2532   opt5524   an,nn740 pre1519}
10 Now he*that*ministereth seed to the sower both minister bread for

_{an,nn1035 2532   opt4129 ppro5216   art,nn4703 2532   opt837   art3588   nn1081   ppro5216}
your food, and multiply your seed sown, and increase the fruits of your

_{art,nn1343}
righteousness;)   *(Is. 55:10; Hos. 10:12 [Sept.]*

_{ppmp4148   pre1722 an,ajn3956   pre1519 an,aj3956   an,nn572   repro3748   pinm2716}
11 Being enriched in every thing to   all bountifulness, which causeth

_{pre1223 ppro2257 an,nn2169   art,nn2316}
through us thanksgiving to God.

_{3754 art3588   nn1248   depro5026 art,nn3009 3756 an,ajn3440 pin2076/pap4322 art3588 nn5303}
12 For the administration of this service not only supplieth the want of

_{art3588 ajn40   235   pap4052   2532 pre1223 an,aj4183   an,nn2169   art,nn2316}
the saints, but is abundant also by many thanksgivings unto God;

pre1223 art3588   nn1382   depro5026   art,nn1248   pap1392 art,nn2316
13 While   by   the experiment of this ministration they glorify God for

ppro5216   art,nn3671 (pre1909) art,nn5292   pre1519 art3588   nn2098   art,nn5547   2532   an,nn572
your professed   subjection unto the gospel of Christ, and for *your* liberal

art,nn2842   pre1519   ppro846   2532   pre1519 an,ajn3956
distribution unto them, and unto   all   *men*;

2532   ppro846 an,nn1162 pre5228 ppro5216   pap1971   ppro5209 pre1223 art3588   pap5235
14 And by their prayer for you, which long after you for the exceeding

an,nn5485   art,nn2316 pre1909 ppro5213
grace of God in you.

(1161)   an,nn5485   art,nn2316 pre1909 ppro846   art,aj411   an,nn1431
15   Thanks *be* unto God for his unspeakable gift.

Paul's Self-vindication

1161   ppro1473 an,nn3972 epn846   pin3870   ppro5209 pre1223 art3588   nn4236   2532   an,nn1932
10 Now I   Paul myself beseech you by the meekness and gentleness

art,nn5547 repro3739 pre2596   an,nn4383   (3303) pr/an,aj5011 pre1722 ppro5213 1161   pap548
of Christ, who   in presence *am* base among you, but being absent

pin2292   pre1519   ppro5209
am bold toward you:

1161   pinm1189   3361   ainf2292   art,pap3918
2 But I beseech *you,* that I may not be bold when I am present with that

art,nn4006   repro3739   pinm3049   ainf5111   pre1909 idpro5100   art,ppmp3049   ppro2248
confidence, wherewith I think to be bold against some, which think of us

ad5613   pap4043   pre2596   an,nn4561
as if we walked according to the flesh.

1063   pap4043 pre1722   an,nn4561   3756 pinm4754 pre2596   an,nn4561
3 For though we walk in the flesh, we do not war after the flesh:

1063 art3588   nn3696   ppro2257 art,nn4752   3756 pr/an,aj4559 235 pr/an,aj1415
4 (For the weapons of our   warfare *are* not carnal, but mighty through

art,nn2316 pre4314   an,nn2506   an,nn3794
God   to the pulling down of strongholds;)

pap2507   an,nn3053   2532   an,aj3956   an,nn5313   ppmp1869
5 Casting down imaginations, and every high thing that exalteth itself

ore2596 art3588   nn1108   art,nn2316 2532   pap163   an,aj3956 an,nn3540 pre1519
against the knowledge of God, and bringing*into*captivity every thought to

art3588   nn5218   art,nn5547
the obedience of Christ;

2532   pap2192   pre1722   an,ajn2092   ainf1556 an,aj3956   an,nn3876   ad3752   ppro5216
6 And having in a readiness to revenge   all   disobedience, when your

art,nn5218   asbp4137
obedience is fulfilled.

pin991   art3588   pre2596   an,nn4383   idpro1536   pfi3982
7 Do ye look on things after the outward appearance? If*any*man trust to

rxpro1438   pinf1511 an,nn5547   pre575 rxpro1438 pim3049 depro5124 ad3825   3754 ad2531
himself that he   is   Christ's, let him of himself think this again, that, as

ppro846   an,nn5547   2532   ad3779   epn2249   an,nn5547
he *is* Christ's, even so *are* we Christ's.

1063   1437/5037   asbm2744 (2532)   idpro5100   cd/an,ajn4055 pre4012 ppro2257   art,nn1849   repro3739
8 For though I should boast   somewhat more of   our authority, which

art3588 nn2962   aina1325 ppro2254 pre1519   an,nn3619   2532 2756 pre1519 ppro5216   an,nn2506

the Lord hath given us   for edification, and not for your destruction, I should

3756   fp153

not be ashamed:

         2443   3361 asba1380 ad5613/302   pinf1629 ppro5209 pre1223 art,nn1992

9 That I may not seem   as   if I would terrify you by letters.

      3754   art,nn1992(3303) pin5346   pr/an,aj926   2532   pr/an,aj2478   1161   art,nn4983

10 For *his* letters, say they, *are* weighty and powerful; but *his* bodily

art,nn3952   pr/an,aj772 2532   art,nn3056   pr/pfpp1848

presence *is* weak, and *his* speech contemptible.

          art,ajn5108   pim3049 depro5124   3754   pr/an,ajn3634   pin2070   art,nn3056   pre1223

11 Let such*a*one think this, that, such as we are in word by

an,nn1992   pap548   pr/an,ajn5108   2532   art,nn2041

letters when we are absent, such *will we be* also in deed when we

pap3918

are present.

      1063   pin5111   3756   ainf1469/rxpro1438   2228   ainf4973

12 For we dare not make*ourselves*of*the*number, or compare

rxpro1438   idpro5100   art,pap4921   rxpro1438   235   epn846   pap3354

ourselves with some that commend themselves: but they measuring

rxpro1438   pre1722   rxpro1438   2532   pap4793   rxpro1438   rxpro1438

themselves by themseves, and comparing themselves among themselves,

pin4920/3756

are*not*wise.

      1161 epn2249   3780   fm2744   pre1519   art,ajn280   235   pre2596

13 But we will not boast of things*without*our*measure, but according

art3588   nn3358   art3588 nn2583 repro3739 art,nn2316   aina3307   ppro2254   an,nn3358

to the measure of the rule which God hath distributed to us, a measure to

aifm2185   2532   ad891   ppro5216

reach even unto you.

      1063   pin5239/3756/rxpro1438   ad5613

14 For we stretch*not*ourselves*beyond *our measure,* as though we

ppmp2185   3361   pre1519 ppro5209 1063   aina5348   ad891   ppro5216 2532   pre1722

reached not unto you: for we are come as*far*as to you also in *preaching*

art3588   nn2098   art,nn5547

the gospel of Christ:

      3756   ppmp2744   pre1519   art,ajn280   pre1722

15 Not boasting of things*without*our*measure, *that is,* of

an,aj245   an,nn2873   1161   pap2192   an,nn1680   ppro5216 art,nn4102   ppmp837

other men's labors; but having hope, when your faith is increased, that we

      aifp3170   pre1722 ppro5213   pre2596   ppro2257 art,nn2583   pre1519/an,nn4050

shall be enlarged by you according to our rule abundantly,

          aifm2097   pre1519   art,ad5238   ppro5216   3756   aifm2744

16 To preach*the*gospel in the*regions*beyond you, *and* not to boast

pre1722   an,aj245   an,nn2583   pre1519/art,ajn2092

in another man's line*of*things made*ready*to*our*hand.

      1161   art,ppmp2744   pim2744 pre1722   an,nn2962

17 But he*that*glorieth, let him glory in the Lord.   (*Jer. 9:24*)

        1063   3756 depro1565   art,pap4921   rxpro1438 pin2076   pr/an,aj1384   235   repro3739 art3588

18 For not he that commendeth himself is approved, but whom the

nn2962   pin4921

Lord commendeth.

11

aina3785   ipf430   ppro3450   an,ajn3398   art,nn877   235
Would*to*God ye could bear with me a little in *my* folly: and
2532   pim430   ppro3450
indeed bear with me.

1063   pin2206   ppro5209   an,nn2316   an,nn2205   1063   aom718
2 For I am jealous over you with godly jealousy: for I have espoused
ppro5209   nu1520   an,nn435   ainf3936   an,aj53   an,nn3933   art,nn5547
you to one husband, that I may present *you as* a chaste virgin to Christ.

1161   pinm5399   3381   ad5613 art3588   nn3789   aina1818   an,nn2096   pre1722
3 But I fear, lest*by*any*means, as the serpent beguiled Eve through
ppro848   art,nn3834   ad3779 ppro5216 art,nn3540   asbp5351   pre575   art3588   nn572   art3588
his subtlety, so your minds should be corrupted from the simplicity that is
pre1519   art,nn5547
in Christ.

(Gen. 3:13)

1063   1487   art,ppmp2064   pin2784   an,aj243   an,nn2424   repro3739   3756
4 For if he*that*cometh preacheth another Jesus, whom we have not
aina2784   2228   pin2983   an,aj2087   an,nn4151   repro3739   3756   aina2983
preached, or *if* ye receive another spirit, which ye have not received,
2228   an,aj2087   an,nn2098   repro3739   3756   aom1209   ad2573   ipf430
or another gospel, which ye have not accepted, ye might well bear with
him.

1063   pinm3049   pfin5302/an,ajn3367   art3588   pre5228/ad3029   an,nn652
☞ 5 For I suppose I was*not*a*whit*behind the very chiefest apostles.

1161   1487/2532   pr/an,nn2399   art,nn3056   235   3756   art,nn1108   235
6 But though *I be* rude in speech, yet not in knowledge; but we have
pre1722/an,ajn3956   aptp5319   pre1519 ppro5209 pre1722   an,ajn3956
been throughly made manifest among you in all things.

(2228)   aina4160   an,nn266   pap5013   rxpro1683   2443   epn5210
7 Have I committed an offense in abasing myself that ye might be
asbp5312   3754   aom2097   ppro5213 art3588   nn2098   art,nn2316   an,nn1432
exalted, because I have preached to you the gospel of God freely?

aina4813   an,aj243   an,nn1577   apta2983   an,nn3800   pre4314   ppro5216   art,nn1248
8 I robbed other churches, taking wages *of them,* to do you service.

2532   pap3918   pre4314 ppro5209   2532   aptp5302   (3756)   aina2655
9 And when I was present with you, and wanted, I was chargable to
an,ajn3762   1063   art,nn5303   ppro3450 art3588   nn80   apta2064   pre575
no man: for that*which*was*lacking to me the brethren which came from
an,nn3109   aina4322   2532   pre1722   an,ajn3956   aina5083   rxpro1683
Macedonia supplied: and in all *things* I have kept myself
pr/an,aj4   ppro5213   2532   ft5083
from*being*burdensome unto you, and *so* will I keep *myself.*

☞ **11:5** The phrase "very chiefest" is a translation of the Greek word *hupérlian* (5244) meaning "exceed-ingly great." Some believe that this word should be understood as an indication that Paul was equal in authority and station to the Twelve Apostles. Hence, Paul declared in Galatians 2:6 that he was equal with Peter in every respect. Others suggest that Paul used this word to speak sarcastically of those people who wanted to be seen as outstanding apostles, whose words should be regarded as more valid than those of the Twelve Apostles of Jesus Christ (cf. 2 Cor. 12:11). The context indicates that there were those in Corinth who wanted to impose their views over Paul's teaching. It is to these "false apostles" that Paul makes reference (see also 2 Cor. 11:13–15).

10 As the truth of Christ is in me, no man shall stop me of this boasting in the regions of Achaia.

11 Wherefore? because I love you not? God knoweth.

12 But what I do, that I will do, that I may cut off occasion from them*which*desire occasion; that wherein they glory, they may be found even as we.

13 For such *are* false apostles, deceitful workers, transforming themselves into the apostles of Christ.

14 And no marvel; for Satan himself is transformed into an angel of light.

15 Therefore *it is* no great thing if his ministers also be transformed as the ministers of righteousness; whose end shall be according to their works.

Paul's Apostolic Labors and Sufferings

16 I say again, Let no man think me a fool; if otherwise, yet as a fool receive me, that I may boast myself a little.

17 That which I speak, I speak *it* not after the Lord, but as*it*were foolishly, in this confidence of boasting.

18 Seeing that many glory after the flesh, I*will*glory*also.

19 For ye suffer fools gladly, seeing ye *yourselves* are wise.

20 For ye suffer, if*a*man bring*you*into*bondage, if*a*man devour *you*, if*a*man take *of you*, if*a*man exalt himself, if*a*man smite you on the face.

21 I speak as concerning reproach, as though we had been weak. Howbeit wheresoever any is bold, (I speak foolishly,) I*am*bold*also.

pin1526 pr/an,nn1445 epn2504 pin1526 pr/an,nn2475 epn2504 pin1526

22 Are they Hebrews? so*am*I. Are they Israelites? so*am*I. Are they

pr/an,nn4690 11 epn2504

the seed of Abraham? so*am*I.

pin1526 pr/an,nn1249 an,nn5547 pin2980 pap3912 epn1473 pre5228 pre1722

23 Are they ministers of Christ? (I speak as*a*fool) I am more; in

an,nn2873 ad4056 pre1722 an,nn4127 ad5234 pre1722 an,nn5438

labors more abundant, in stripes above measure, in prisons

ad4056 pre1722 an,nn2288 ad4178

more frequent, in deaths oft.

pre5259 an,nn2453 nu,ad3999 aina2983 nu,ajn5062 pre3844 nu,ajn3391

24 Of the Jews five times received I forty *stripes* save one. *(Deut. 25:3)*

nu,ad5151 ainp4463 nu,ad530 ainp3034 nu,ad5151

25 Thrice was I beaten*with*rods, once was I stoned, thrice I

aina3489 an,nn3574 pfi4160 pre1722 art3588 nn1037

suffered shipwreck, a night*and*a*day I have been in the deep;

an,nn3597 ad4178 an,nn2794 an,nn4215 an,nn2794 an,nn3027 an,nn2794

☞ 26 *In* journeyings often, *in* perils of waters, *in* perils of robbers, *in* perils

pre1537 an,nn1085 an,nn2794 pre1537 an,nn1484 an,nn2794 pre1722 an,nn4172

by *mine own* countrymen, *in* perils by the heathen, *in* perils in the city, *in*

an,nn2794 pre1722 an,nn2047 an,nn2794 pre1722 an,nn2281 an,nn2794 pre1722

perils in the wilderness, *in* perils in the sea, *in* perils among

an,nn5569

false brethren;

pre1722 an,nn2873 2532 an,nn3449 pre1722 an,nn70 ad4178 pre1722 an,nn3042 2532

27 In weariness and painfulness, in watchings often, in hunger and

an,nn1372 pre1722 an,nn3521 ad4178 pre1722 an,nn5592 2532 an,nn1132

thirst, in fastings often, in cold and nakedness.

ad*5565 art,ad3924 art,nn1999 ppro3450

28 Beside those*things*that*are*without, that*which*cometh*upon me

art,pre2596/an,nn2250 art3588 nn3308 an,aj3956 art3588 nn1577

daily, the care of all the churches.

inpro5101 pin770 2532 pin770/3756 inpro5101 pinm4624 2532 epn1473 pinm4448

29 Who is weak, and I am*not*weak? who is offended, and I burn

3756

not?

1487 pin1163 pifm2744 fm2744 art3588 ppro3450

30 If I must needs glory, I will glory of the things which concern mine

art,nn769

infirmities.

art3588 nn2316 2532 an,nn3962 ppro2257 art,nn2962 an,nn2424 an,nn5547 art,pap5607 pr/an,aj2128

31 The God and Father of our Lord Jesus Christ, which is blessed

pre1519/art,nn165 pin1492 3754 pinm5574 3756

forevermore, knoweth that I lie not.

pre1722 an,nn1154 art3588 nn1481 an,nn702 art3588 nn935

32 In Damascus the governor under Aretas the king

ipf5432/art3588/nn4172/an,nn1153 pap2309 ainf4084

kept*the*city*of*the*Damascenes*with*a*garrison, desirous to apprehend

ppro3165

me:

☞ **11:26** See note on Galatians 2:4 concerning the "false brethren" that Paul had encountered.

₂₅₃₂ _{pre1223} _{an,nn2376} _{pre1722} _{an,nn4553} _{ainp5465} _{pre1223} _{art3588} _{nn5038} ₂₅₃₂

33 And through a window in a basket was I let down by the wall, and

_{aina1628} _{ppro846} _{art,nn5495}

escaped his hands.

Paul's Vision

_{pin4851/3756} _{ppro3427} ₁₂₁₁ _{pifm2744} ₍₁₀₆₃₎ _{fm2064}

12 ☞ It*is*not*expedient for me doubtless to glory. I will come

_{pre1519} _{an,nn3701} ₂₅₃₂ _{an,nn602} _{an,nn2962}

to visions and revelations of the Lord.

_{pin1492} _{an,nn444} _{pre1722} _{an,nn5547} _{pre4253} _{nu1180} _{an,nn2094} ₁₅₃₅ _{pre1722}

2 I knew a man in Christ above fourteen years ago, (whether in the

_{an,nn4983} _{pin1492/3756} ₁₅₃₅ _{ad*1622} _{art3588} _{nn4983} _{pin1492/3756} _{art,nn2316} _{pin1492}

body, I cannot tell; or whether out of the body, I cannot tell: God knoweth;)

_{art,ajn5108} _{aptp726} _{ad2193} _{an,nu,aj5154} _{an,nn3772}

such*a*one caught up to the third heaven.

₂₅₃₂ _{pin1492} _{art,aj5108} _{an,nn444} ₁₅₃₅ _{pre1722} _{an,nn4983} ₁₅₃₅ _{ad*1622} _{art3588} _{nn4983}

3 And I knew such a man, (whether in the body, or out of the body, I

_{pin1492/3756} _{art,nn2316} _{pin1492}

cannot tell: God knoweth;)

₃₇₅₄ _{ainp726} _{pre1519} _{art,nn3857} ₂₅₃₂ _{aina191} _{an,aj731} _{an,nn4487}

4 How that he was caught up into paradise, and heard unspeakable words,

_{repro3739} _{pap1832/3756} _{an,nn444} _{ainf2980}

which it is*not*lawful for a man to utter.

_{pre5228} _{art,ajn5108} _{fm2744} ₁₁₆₁ _{pre5228} _{rxpro1683} ₃₇₅₆ _{fm2744} ₁₅₀₈ _{pre1722}

5 Of such*a*one will I glory: yet of myself I will not glory, but in

_{ppro3450} _{art,nn769}

mine infirmities.

₁₀₆₃ ₁₄₃₇ _{asba2309} _{aifm2744} ₃₇₅₆ _{fm2071} _{pr/an,aj878} ₁₀₆₃ _{ft2046}

6 For though I would desire to glory, I shall not be a fool; for I will say

_{an,nn225} ₁₁₆₁ _{pinm5339} ₃₃₆₁ _{idpro5100} _{asbm3049} _{pre1519} _{ppro1691} _{pre5228} _{repro3739}

the truth: but *now* I forbear, lest any man should think of me above that

_{pin991} _{ppro3165} ₂₂₂₈ _{pin191(idpro5100)} _{pre1537} _{ppro1700}

which he seeth me *to be*, or *that* he heareth of me.

₂₅₃₂ ₃₃₆₃ _{psmp5229} _{art3588} _{nn5236}

7 And lest I should be exalted*above*measure through the abundance of

_{art3588} _{nn602} _{ainp1325} _{ppro3427} _{an,nn4647} _{art3588} _{nn4561} _{an,nn32}

the revelations, there was given to me a thorn in the flesh, the messenger of

₄₅₆₆ ₂₄₄₃ _{psa2852} _{ppro3165} ₃₃₆₃ _{psmp5229}

Satan to buffet me, lest I should be exalted*above*measure.   *(Job 2:6)*

☞ **12:1–10** The Apostle Paul reveals a unique experience of his own of being "caught up to the third heaven." Although the person mentioned in verse two is not named, it is obvious from verse seven that he is speaking about himself. Perhaps Paul mentioned this experience to the Corinthians because they were bragging about their own spiritual visions and gifts. Paul wanted to demonstrate to the Corinthians that he had a spiritual experience far superior to anything they had encountered. Yet, Paul was modest about his experience (seen in the use of the third person). This was to serve as an example to the Corinthians.

8 ^{pre5228} ^{depro5127} ^{aina3870} ^{art3588} ⁿⁿ²⁹⁶² ^{nu,ad5151} ²⁴⁴³ ^{asba868} ^{pre575}

For this thing I besought the Lord thrice, that it might depart from
^{ppro1700}
me.

9 ²⁵³² ^{pfi2046} ^{ppro3427} ^{ppro3450} ^{art,nn5485} ^{pin714} ^{ppro4671} ¹⁰⁶³ ^{ppro3450} ^{art,nn1411}

And he said unto me, My grace is sufficient for thee: for my strength
^{pinm5048} ^{pre1722} ^{an,nn769} ^{ad2236} ³⁷⁶⁷ ^{ad3123} ^{fm2744} ^{pre1722}
is made perfect in weakness. Most gladly therefore will I rather glory in
^{ppro3450} ^{art,nn769} ²⁴⁴³ ^{art3588} ⁿⁿ¹⁴¹¹ ^{art,nn5547} ^{asba1981} ^{pre1909} ^{ppro1691}
my infirmities, that the power of Christ may rest upon me.

10 ^{pre,repro1352} ^{pin2106} ^{pre1722} ^{an,nn769} ^{pre1722} ^{an,nn5196} ^{pre1722}

Therefore I take pleasure in infirmities, in reproaches, in
^{an,nn318} ^{pre1722} ^{an,nn1375} ^{pre1722} ^{an,nn4730} ^{pre5228/an,nn5547} ¹⁰⁶³ ^{ad3752}
necessities, in persecutions, in distresses for* Christ's*sake: for when I
^{psa770} ^{ad5119} ^{pin1510} ^{pr/an,aj1415}
am weak, then am I strong.

☞ 11 ^{pfi1096} ^{pr/an,aj878} ^{ppmp2744} ^{epn5210} ^{aina315} ^{ppro3165} ¹⁰⁶³ ^{epn1473}

I am become a fool in glorying; ye have compelled me: for I
^{ipf3784} ^{pifp4921} ^{pre5259} ^{ppro5216} ¹⁰⁶³ ^{an,ajn3762} ^{aina5302} ^{art3588}
ought to have been commended of you: for in nothing am*I*behind the
^{pre5228/ad3029} ^{an,nn652} ¹⁴⁹⁹ ^{pin1510} ^{pr/an,ajn3762}
very chiefest apostles, though I be nothing.

12 ³³⁰³ ^{art3588} ⁿⁿ⁴⁵⁹² ^{art,nn652} ^{ainp2716} ^{pre1722} ^{ppro5213} ^{pre1722} ^{an,aj3956}

Truly the signs of an apostle were wrought among you in all
^{an,nn5281} ^{pre1722} ^{an,nn4592} ²⁵³² ^{an,nn5059} ²⁵³² ^{an,nn1411}
patience, in signs, and wonders, and mighty deeds.

13 ¹⁰⁶³ ^{inpro5101} ^{pin2076} ^{repro3739} ^{ainp2274} ^{pre5228} ^{art,aj3062} ^{an,nn1577} ¹⁵⁰⁸

For what is it wherein ye were inferior to other churches, except *it*
³⁷⁵⁴ ^{ppro1473} ^{epn846} ^{aina2655/3756} ^{ppro5216} ^{aipm5483} ^{ppro3427} ^{depro5026} ^{art,nn93}
be that I myself was*not*burdensome to you? forgive me this wrong.

14 ²⁴⁰⁰ ^{an,nu,ajn5154} ^{pin2192} ^{ad2093} ^{ainf2064} ^{pre4314} ^{ppro5209} ²⁵³² ³⁷⁵⁶

Behold, the third time I am ready to come to you; and I will not
^{ft2655} ^{ppro5216} ¹⁰⁶³ ^{pin2212} ³⁷⁵⁶ ^{art,ppro5216} ²³⁵ ^{ppro5209} ¹⁰⁶³ ^{art3588} ⁿⁿ⁵⁰⁴³ ^{pin3784}
be burdensome to you: for I seek not yours, but you: for the children ought
³⁷⁵⁶ ^{pinf2343} ^{art3588} ⁿⁿ¹¹¹⁸ ²³⁵ ^{art3588} ⁿⁿ¹¹¹⁸ ^{art3588} ⁿⁿ⁵⁰⁴³
not to lay up for the parents, but the parents for the children.

15 ¹¹⁶¹ ^{epn1473} ^{ad2236} ^{ft1159} ²⁵³² ^{fp1550} ^{pre5228} ^{ppro5216 (art,nn5590)} ¹⁴⁹⁹

And I will very gladly spend and be spent for you; though
^{ad4056} ^{pap25} ^{ppro5209} ^{ad2276} ^{pinp25}
the*more*abundantly I love you, the less I be loved.

16 ¹¹⁶¹ ^{pim2077} ^{epn1473} ³⁷⁵⁶ ^{aina2599} ^{ppro5209} ²³⁵ ^{pap5225} ^{pr/an,aj3835}

But be it so, I did not burden you: nevertheless, being crafty, I
^{aina2983} ^{ppro5209} ^{an,nn1388}
caught you with guile.

17 ^(pre1223 ppro846) ^{aina4122} ^{ppro5209} ⁽³³⁶¹⁾ ^{idpro5100} ^{repro3739} ^{pfi649} ^{pre4314}

Did I make*a*gain of you by any of them whom I sent unto
^{ppro5209}
you?

☞ 12:11 See note on 2 Corinthians 11:5.

        aina3870   an,nn5103   2532   aina4882   art,nn80   (3387) an,nn5103   aina4122

☞ 18 I desired Titus, and with *him* I sent a brother. Did Titus make*a*gain of

ppro5209 aina4043   3756   art3588 ppro846 an,nn4151   3756   art3588 ppro846 an,nn2487

you? walked we not in the same spirit? *walked we* not in the same steps?

         ad3825   pin1380   3754   pinm626   ppro5213   pin2980

    19 Again, think ye that we excuse ourselves unto you? we speak

ad*2714   art,nn2316   pre1722   an,nn5547   1161   art,ajn3956   an,ajn27   pre5228 ppro5216

before God in Christ: but *we do* all things, dearly beloved, for your

art,nn3619

edifying.

        1063   pinm5399 3381   apta2064   3756 asba2147 ppro5209 pr/an,ajn3634   pin2309

    20 For I fear, lest when I come, I shall not find you such as I would,

        epn2504   asbp2147   ppro5213   pr/an,ajn3634   pin2309   3756   3381

and*that*I shall be found unto you such as ye would not: lest *there be*

an,nn2054   an,nn2205   an,nn2372   an,nn2052   an,nn2636   an,nn5587   an,nn5450

debates, envyings, wraths, strifes, backbitings, whisperings, swellings,

an,nn181

tumults:

        3361   apta2064   ad3825   ppro3450 art,nn2316   asba5013   ppro3165   pre4314   ppro5209

    21 *And* lest, when I come again, my God will humble me among you,

2532   asba3996 an,ajn4183   art,pfp4258   2532   3361   apta3340

and *that* I shall bewail many which*have*sinned*already, and have not repented

pre1909 art3588   nn167   2532   an,nn4202   2532   an,nn766   repro3739

of the uncleanness and fornication and lasciviousness which they have

aina4238

committed.

Paul's Desire to Visit Corinth Again

        depro5124   an,nu,ajn5154   pinm2064   pre4314 ppro5209 pre1909   an,nn4750   nu1417

13 This *is* the third *time* I am coming to you. In the mouth of two

        2532   nu5140   an,nn3144   an,aj3956 an,nn4487   fp2476

or three witnesses shall every word be established. *(Deut. 19:15)*

      pfi4280   2532   pin4302   ad5613   pap3918   art3588

   2 I told*you*before, and foretell you, as if I were present, the

nu,ajn1208   2532   pap548   ad3568   pin1125

second time; and being absent now I write to

       art,pfp4258   2532   art,aj3956   an,ajn3062   3754   1437

them*which*heretofore*have*sinned, and to all other, that, if I

asba2064 (pre1519) art,ad3825   3756   fm5339

come again, I will not spare:

     1893   pin2212   an,nn1382   art,nn5547   pap2980   pre1722 ppro1698 repro3739 pre1519   ppro5209

   3 Since ye seek a proof of Christ speaking in me, which to you-ward

pin770/3756   235   pin1414   pre1722 ppro5213

is*not*weak, but is mighty in you.

      1063   2532/1487   ainp4717   pre1537   an,nn769   235   pin2198   pre1537

   4 For though he was crucified through weakness, yet he liveth by the

---

☞ **12:18** See the introduction to Titus.

an,nn1411   an,nn2316 1063 epn2249 2532   pin770   pre1722 ppro846 235   fm2198 pre4862 ppro846 pre1537

power of God. For we also are weak in him, but we shall live with him by

an,nn1411   an,nn2316   pre1519 ppro5209

the power of God toward you.

pim3985   rxpro1438   1487   pin2075 pre1722 art3588   nn4012   pim1381

5 Examine yourselves, whether ye be in the faith; prove

rxpro1438   (2228) pin1921   3756   rxpro1438   (2228)   3754   an,nn2424 an,nn5547

your*own*selves.   Know ye not your*own*selves,   how that Jesus Christ

pin2076 pre1722 ppro5213 1509   pin2075   pr/an,aj96

is in you, except ye be reprobates?

1161   pin1679 3754   fm1097   3754 epn2249 pin2070 3756   pr/an,aj96

6 But I trust that ye shall know that we are not reprobates.

1161   pinm2172 pre4314 art,nn2316   ppro5209(3361) ainf4160 an,aj3367 an,ajn2556 3756 2443 epn2449

7 Now I pray to God that ye do no evil; not that we should

asbp5316   pr/an,aj1384 235 2443 epn5210   psa4160   art,ajn2570   1161 epn2249

appear approved, but that ye should do that*which*is*honest, though we

psa5600 ad5613   pr/an,aj96

be as reprobates.

1063   pinm1410 idpro5100/3756   pre2596 art3588 nn225   235 pre5228 art3588 nn225

8 For we can do nothing against the truth, but for the truth.

1063   pin5463   ad3752 epn2249   psa770   1161 epn5210 psa5600 pr/an,aj1415 1161 depro5124

9 For we are glad, when we are weak, and ye are strong: and this

2532   pinm2172   ppro5216   art,nn2676

also we wish, *even* your perfection.

pre1223/depro5124   pin1125   depro5023   pap548   3363   pap3918

10 Therefore I write these things being absent, lest being present I should

asbm5530   ad664   pre2596   art3588 nn1849 repro3739 art3588 nn2962   aina1325 ppro3427 pre1519

use sharpness, according to the power which the Lord hath given me to

an,nn3619   2532 3756 pre1519 an,nn2506

edification, and not to destruction.

an,ajn3063   an,nn80   pim5463   pim2675   pim3870

11 Finally, brethren, farewell. Be perfect, be*of*good*comfort,

pim5426/art,ppro846   pim1514   2532 art3588 nn2316 art,nn26 2532 an,nn1515   fm2071 pre3326

be*of*one*mind, live*in*peace; and the God of love and peace shall be with

ppro5216

you.

aipm782   rcpro240   pre1722 an,aj40 an,nn5370

12 Greet one another with a holy kiss.

an,aj3956 art3588 ajn40 pinm782 ppro5209

13 All the saints salute you.

art3588   nn5485   art3588 nn2962 an,nn2424 an,nn5547 2532 art3588 nn26   art,nn2316 2532 art3588

14 The grace of the Lord Jesus Christ, and the love of God, and the

nn2842   art3588 aj40 an,nn4151   pre3326 ppro5216 an,aj3956 281

communion of the Holy Ghost, *be* with you all. Amen.

The Epistle of Paul the Apostle to the

GALATIANS

There are two prominent theories, called the North Galatia Theory and the South Galatia Theory, which present differing views of the location and identification of these Galatian believers. The disagreement revolves around what Paul meant when he used the term "Galatian." Some say that he was referring to the people living in the Roman Province of Galatia while others believe he was addressing a group of believers who were mainly of Gallic descent. Both theories have their own set of suppositions with respect to when the book was written, the place from which it was written, and the time periods in which other details mentioned in the book took place.

The area of northern Galatia (which included the chief cities of Ancyra, Tavium, and Pessinus) was conquered by the Gauls in the third century B.C. and existed as an independent nation for about two hundred years. During this period, however, the Gallic people were absorbed into the native populace there. If Paul was using the term "Galatian" in the racial sense, he was referring to those who had descended from the Gauls. In accordance with this assumption, it is suggested that Paul visited this church on his second and third missionary journeys (Acts 16:6; 18:23), and wrote this epistle from either Ephesus or Corinth during his last journey.

Those who hold the South Galatia Theory suggest that Paul used the term "Galatian" to refer to those who lived in the Roman province of Galatia which was established in 25 B.C. In this year, King Amyntas, of the old kingdom of Galatia, bequeathed his kingdom to Rome. This province covered the southern part of central Asia Minor and encompassed the cities of Iconium, Lystra, Antioch of Pisidia, and Derbe. If this theory is true, it is probable that Paul visited these believers once on his first missionary journey (Acts 13; 14), and then again during his later travels. A reasonable date for the writing of the book then would be about A.D. 55 or 56 or sometime between his first and second missionary journeys. According to this theory, the cities of Corinth and Antioch in Syria are the most likely places for Paul to have written the book.

It is generally accepted that Paul visited these believers twice before he wrote this epistle. During his absence, teachers came from Palestine, called "Judaizers," and insisted that these Gentile believers could not be true Christians until they submitted to the Jewish ordinance of circumcision. Furthermore, they maintained that the Galatians must adhere to the Law of Moses. These naive Galatian Christians accepted their teachings just as enthusiastically as they had Paul's. The purpose of the Book of Galatians is to combat this vicious heresy in which the work of Christ was considered insufficient for salvation.

The first way Paul chose to do this was to disprove the Judaizers claim that Paul was not a true apostle. They maintained that since he was not one of the twelve original apostles, he must have received his teachings and doctrines second-hand from the other apostles. Paul showed that he was equal with the original apostles because he received his doctrine from a revelation straight from Jesus Christ (Gal. 1:11–19). He had even rebuked the Apostle Peter when there was a dispute over whether he, as a Jew, should be allowed to disregard the Mosaic Law (Gal. 2:11–14).

Once he had established his apostolic authority, he proved that men are justified by faith in Christ's atoning work rather than by the works of the Law (Gal. 2:15—4:15). This leads into his final topic of being led by the Spirit (Gal. 5:16—6:10). The threat of the Judaizers came to an end at the fall of Jerusalem in A.D. 70. Prior to that time, Jewish Christians were considered by many to be a sect (Acts 2:45), or a new branch of Judaism.

1
an,nn3972   an,nn652   3756 pre575 an,nn444   3761   pre1223 an,nn444 235 pre1223 an,nn2424 an,nn5547
Paul, an apostle, (not of men, neither by man, but by Jesus Christ,
2532 an,nn2316   an,nn3962   art,apta1453 ppro846 pre1537   an,ajn3498
and God the Father, who raised him from the dead;)

2532 art,aj3956 art3588   nn80   pre4862 ppro1698   art3588   nn1577
☞ 2 And all the brethren which are with me, unto the churches of
art,nn1053
Galatia:

an,nn5485   ppro5213 2532 an,nn1515 pre575 an,nn2316   an,nn3962 2532   ppro2257 an,nn2962
3 Grace *be* to you and peace from God the Father, and *from* our Lord
an,nn2424 an,nn5547
Jesus Christ,

art,apta1325   rxpro1438 pre5228 ppro2257 art,nn266 3704   asbm1807 ppro2248 pre1537
4 Who gave himself for our sins, that he might deliver us from this
art,pfp1764 an,aj4190 an,nn165   pre2596   art3588 nn2307 art,nn2316 2532 ppro2257 an,nn3962
present evil world, according to the will of God and our Father:
repro3739   art,nn1391   pre1519/art,nn165/art,nn165   281
5 To whom *be* glory forever*and*ever. Amen.

The One True Gospel

pin2296   3754   ad3779 ad5030 pinm3346   pre575   art,apta2564   ppro5209 pre1722
☞ 6 I marvel that ye are so soon removed from him*that*called you into
an,nn5485 an,nn5547 pre1519 an,aj2087   an,nn2098
the grace of Christ unto another gospel:

☞ **1:2** See the introduction to Titus.
☞ **1:6–8** The context of the Book of Galatians indicates that a different gospel from the one Paul preached had penetrated the church in Galatia. Paul calls this "another gospel," and the Greek word for "different" in verse six is *héteron* (2087), which means qualitatively different. However, in verse seven, Paul uses an entirely different word which is also translated "another." It is *állō* (243) which means "another of the same kind." The true Gospel of Christ can be declared in different ways by different people, but its truth can never be altered.

repro3739 pin2076 3756   pr/an,aj243   1508   pin1526 idpro5100   art,pap5015   ppro5209 2532   pap2309

7 Which is not another; but there be some that trouble you, and would

ainf3344 art3588 nn2098   art,nn5547

pervert the gospel of Christ.

235   2352/1437 epn2249 2228   an,nn32 pre1537 an,nn3772   psmp2097

8 But though we, or an angel from heaven, preach*any*other*gospel unto

ppro5213 pre3844 repro3739   aom2097   ppro5213   pim2077 pr/an,nn331

you than that which we have preached unto you, let him be accursed.

ad5613   pfi4280   2532 pim3004   ad737   ad3825   idpro1536

9 As   we   said before, so say I now again, if any *man*

pinm2097   ppro5209 pre3844 repro3739   aina3880   pim2077

preach*any*other*gospel unto you than that ye have received, let him be

pr/an,nn331

accursed.

1063   ad737   pin3982   an,nn444 2228 art,nn2316 2228   pin2212   pinf700 an,nn444 1063

10 For do I now persuade men, or God? or do I seek to please men? for

1487   ad2089 ipf700   an,nn444   3756 ipf2252/302   pr/an,ajn1401   an,nn5547

if I yet pleased men, I should not be   the servant of Christ.

Paul's Call to the Ministry

1161   pin1107 ppro5213   an,nn80   art3588   nn2098   art,aptp2097   pre5259

11 But I certify you, brethren, that the gospel which*was*preached of

ppro1700 pin2076 3756 pre2596 an,nn444

me is not after man.

1063   epn1473   3761   aina3880   ppro846 pre3844 an,nn444   3777   ainp1321   235

12 For I neither received it of man, neither was I taught *it*, but

pre1223   an,nn602   an,nn2424 an,nn5547

by the revelation of Jesus Christ.

1063   aina191   art,popro1699   an,nn391   ad4218   pre1722 art3588

13 For ye have heard of   my   conversation in*time*past in   the

nn2454   3754   pre2596/an,nn5236   ipf1377   art3588 nn1577   art,nn2316 2532

Jews' religion, how that beyond measure I persecuted the church of God, and

ipf4199   ppro846

wasted it:

2532   ipf4298 pre1722 art3588   nn2454   pre5228 an,aj4183   an,nn4915   pre1722

14 And profited in   the Jews' religion above many my equals in

ppro3450 art,nn1085 pap5225   ad4056   pr/an,nn2207   an,nn3862   ppro3450

mine own nation, being more exceedingly zealous of the traditions of my

art,aj3967

fathers.

1161   ad3753   aina2106   art,nn2316   art,apta873   ppro3165 pre1537 ppro3450   an,nn3384

15 But when it pleased God, who separated me from my mother's

an,nn2836 2532 apta2564   pre1223 ppro848 art,nn5485

womb, and called *me* by his grace,   *(Is. 49:1; Jer. 1:5)*

ainf601   ppro848 art,nn5207 pre1722 ppro1698 2443   psmp2097 ppro846 pre1722 art3588

16 To reveal his Son   in me, that I might preach him among the

nn1484   ad2112   aom4323   3756   an,nn4561 2532 an,nn129

heathen; immediately I conferred not with flesh and blood:

3761   aina424   pre1519 an,nn2414   pre4314   art,nn652

17 Neither went*I*up to Jerusalem to   them*which*were*apostles

pre4253   ppro1700   235   aina565 pre1519 an,nn688   2532   aina5290   ad3825   pre1519   an,nn1154
before me; but I went into Arabia, and returned again unto Damascus.

ad1899   pre3326 nu5140 an,nn2094   aina424   pre1519   an,nn2414   ainf2477 an,nn4074   2532
18 Then after three years I went up to Jerusalem to see Peter, and

aina1961 pre4314 ppro846 nu1178 an,nn2250
abode with him fifteen days.

1161   an,ajn2087   art3588   nn652   aina1492   3756   1508   an,nn2385 art3588   nn2962   art,nn80
19 But other of the apostles saw I none, save James the Lord's brother.

1161   repro3739   pin1125   ppro5213   2400   ad*1799   art,nn2316 (3754) pinm5574
20 Now the things which I write unto you, behold, before God, I lie

3756
not.

ad1899   aina2064 pre1519 art3588   nn2824   art,nn4947 2532 art,nn2791
21 Afterwards I came into the regions of Syria and Cilicia;

1161   ipf2252   pr/ppmp50   art,nn4383   art3588   nn1577   art,nn2449 art3588
22 And was unknown by face unto the churches of Judea which were

pre1722 an,nn5547
in Christ:

1161   ipf2258   pap191 an,ajn3440   3754   art,pap1377   ppro2248
23 But they had heard only, That he*which*persecuted us

ad4218   ad3568   pinm2097   art3588   nn4102 repro3739 ad4218   ipf4199
in*times*past now preacheth the faith which once he destroyed.

2532   ipf1392   art,nn2316 pre1722 ppro1698
24 And they glorified God in me.

In Jerusalem

ad1899   nu1180   an,nn2094 pre1223 aina305   ad3825 pre1519 an,nn2414   pre3326   an,nn921
2 Then fourteen years after I went up again to Jerusalem with Barnabas,

apta4838/an,nn5103   2532
and took*Titus*with *me* also.

1161   aina305   pre2596   an,nn602   2532   aom394   ppro846
2 And I went up by revelation, and communicated unto them that

art,nn2098   repro3739   pin2784   pre1722   art3588   nn1484   1161   pre2596/an,ajn2398
gospel which I preach among the Gentiles, but privately to

art,pap1380   3381   psa5143 2228   aina5143
them*which*were*of*reputation, lest*by*any*means I should run, or had run,

pre1519 an,ajn2756
in vain.

235   3761   an,nn5103 art3588   pre4862 ppro1698 pap5607   pr/an,nn1672   ainp314
☞ 3 But neither Titus, who was with me, being a Greek, was compelled to

aifp4059
be circumcised:

1161   pre1223   an,nn5569   art,aj3920   repro3748
☞ 4 And that because of false brethren unawares*brought*in, who

---

☞ **2:3** See the introduction to Titus.
☞ **2:4** In this verse, Paul is warning the church in Galatia that there were those endeavoring to bring the Christians under the Law of Moses. Although Paul circumcised Timothy, who was half Jew and half

(continued on next page)

came*in*privily to spy out our liberty which we have in Christ Jesus, that

they might bring*us*into*bondage:

5 To whom we gave place by subjection, no, not for an hour; that the

truth of the gospel might continue with you.

6 But of these who seemed to be somewhat, (whatsoever they were, it

maketh*no*matter to me: God accepteth no man's person:) for

they*who*seemed to be somewhat in*conference*added nothing to me:

(Deut. 10:17)

7 But contrariwise, when they saw that the gospel of the

uncircumcision was committed unto me, as *the gospel* of the circumcision *was*

unto Peter;

8 (For he*that*wrought*effectually in Peter to the apostleship of the

circumcision, the same was mighty in me toward the Gentiles:)

9 And when James, Cephas, and John, who seemed to be pillars,

perceived the grace that*was*given unto me, they gave to me and Barnabas

the right hands of fellowship; that we *should go* unto the heathen, and they

unto the circumcision.

(continued from previous page)
Gentile (Acts 16:3), he did not yield to pressure to circumcise Titus. Had he voluntarily chosen to be circumcised, it would have been acceptable.

Judaizers were teaching that Christians should still be under obligation to keep the law. Paul calls them *pareisáktous* (3920), which is translated "false brethren." These people had infiltrated the church secretly, without declaring from the start who they were or what they intended to do. This does not indicate that they were brought in by the church itself, but that they managed to deceive them and enter the fellowship. Paul calls these intruders "false brethren," *pseudadélphoi* (5569), the same term that Paul used in 2 Corinthians 11:26 speaking of himself being "in dangers among false brethren." In other words, these false brethren became violently opposed to Paul. God alone knows the true spiritual condition of these "false brethren," but the Scripture points to them as unbelievers. They insisted on certain petty doctrines designed to destroy the gospel and those who had preached it.

That which is translated "who came in privily," is from the Greek word *pareisélthon*, which indicates the deceitfulness of these people who joined the local church in Galatia in order to spread their own form of legalism. Their purpose is further demonstrated because they had come to spy out the freedom which these believers had in Jesus Christ. Enslaving one's self contradicts what Paul taught about believers being guided by Jesus Christ.

10 Only *they would* that we should remember the poor; the same which I also was forward to do.

Paul Confronts Peter

11 But when Peter was come to Antioch, I withstood him to the face, because he was to be blamed.

12 For before that certain came from James, he did eat with the Gentiles: but when they were come, he withdrew and separated himself, fearing them which were of the circumcision.

13 And the other Jews dissembled*likewise*with him; insomuch that Barnabas also was carried*away*with their dissimulation.

14 But when I saw that they walked*not*uprightly according to the truth of the gospel, I said unto Peter before *them* all, If thou, being a Jew, livest after*the*manner*of*Gentiles, and not as*do*the*Jews, why compellest thou the Gentiles to live*as*do*the*Jews?

15 We *who are* Jews by nature, and not sinners of the Gentiles,

☞ 16 Knowing that a man is not justified by the works of the law, but by the faith of Jesus Christ, even we have believed in Jesus Christ, that we might be justified by the faith of Christ, and not by the works of the law: for by the works of the law shall no flesh be justified.   *(Ps. 143:2)*

17 But if, while we seek to be justified by Christ, we ourselves also are found sinners, *is* therefore Christ the minister of sin? God forbid.

18 For if I build again the things which I destroyed, I make myself a transgressor.

☞ **2:16** See notes on Romans 3:19, 20 and James 2:14–19.

1063 epn1473 pre1223 an,nn3551 aina599 an,nn3551 2443 asba2198

19 For I through the law am dead to the law, that I might live unto

an,nn2316

God.

pfip4957 an,nn5547 1161 pin2198 ad3765 epn1473 1161 an,nn5547

20 I am crucified with Christ: nevertheless I live; yet not I, but Christ

pin2198 pre1722 ppro1698 1161 repro3739 ad3568 pin2198 pre1722 an,nn4561 pin2198 pre1722 an,nn4102

liveth in me: and the life which I now live in the flesh I live by the faith

(art3588) art3588 nn5207 art,nn2316 art,apta25 ppro3165 2532 apta3860 rxpro1438 pre5228 ppro1700

of the Son of God, who loved me, and gave himself for me.

3756 pin114 art3588 nn5485 art,nn2316 1063 1487 an,nn1343 pre1223

21 I do not frustrate the grace of God: for if righteousness *come* by the

an,nn3551 686 an,nn5547 aina599 an,nn1432

law, then Christ is dead in vain.

The Experience of the Galatians

5599 an,aj453 an,nn1052 inpro5101 aina940 ppro5209 3361 pifm3982

3 O foolish Galatians, who hath bewitched you, that ye should not obey

art3588 nn225 pre2596 repro3739 an,nn3788 an,nn2424 an,nn5547 ainp4270

the truth, before whose eyes Jesus Christ hath been evidently*set*forth,

pr/pfpp4717 pre1722 ppro5213

crucified among you?

depro5124 an,ajn3440 pin2309 ainf3129 pre575 ppro5216 aina2983 art3588 nn4151 pre1537 an,nn2041

2 This only would I learn of you, Received ye the Spirit by the works

an,nn3551 2228 pre1537 an,nn189 an,nn4102

of the law, or by the hearing of faith?

pin2075 ad3779 pr/an,aj453 aptm1728 an,nn4151 ad3568 pinm2005

3 Are ye so foolish? having begun in the Spirit, are ye now made perfect

an,nn4561

by the flesh?

ainp3958 an,ajn5118 ad1500 1489 2532 ad1500

4 Have ye suffered so*many*things in vain? if *it be* yet in vain.

art,pap2023/3767 ppro5213 art3588 nn4151 2532 pap1754 an,nn1411

5 He*therefore*that*ministereth to you the Spirit, and worketh miracles

pre1722 ppro5213 pre1537 an,nn2041 an,nn3551 2228 pre1537 an,nn189 an,nn4102

among you, *doeth he it* by the works of the law, or by the hearing of faith?

ad2531 11 aina4100 art,nn2316 2532 ainp3049 ppro846 pre1519

6 Even as Abraham believed God, and it was accounted to him for

an,nn1343

righteousness. *(Gen. 15:6)*

pim1097 686 3754 art3588 pre1537 an,nn4102 depro3778 pin1526

7 Know ye therefore that they which are of faith, the same are the

pr/an,nn5207 11

children of Abraham.

1161 art3588 nn1124 apta4275 3754 art,nn2316 pin1344 art3588 nn1484

8 And the Scripture, foreseeing that God would justify the heathen

pre1537 an,nn4102 aom4283 11 pre1722 ppro4671

through faith, preached*before*the*gospel unto Abraham, *saying,* In thee shall

an,aj3956 art,nn1484 fp1757

all nations be blessed. *(Gen. 12:3)*

9 So then they which be of faith are blessed with faithful Abraham.

10 For as*many*as are of the works of the law are under the curse: for it is written, Cursed *is* every one that continueth not in all things which*are*written in the book of the law to do them. *(Deut. 27:26)*

☞ 11 But that no man is justified by the law in*the*sight of God, *it is* evident: for, The just shall live by faith. *(Hab. 2:4)*

12 And the law is not of faith: but, The man that doeth them shall live in them. *(Lev. 18:5)*

13 Christ hath redeemed us from the curse of the law, being made a curse for us: for it is written, Cursed *is* every one that hangeth on a tree: *(Deut. 21:23)*

14 That the blessing of Abraham might come on the Gentiles through Jesus Christ; that we might receive the promise of the Spirit through faith.

15 Brethren, I speak after*the*manner of men; Though *it be* but a man's covenant, yet *if it be* confirmed, no man disannulleth, or addeth thereto.

16 Now to Abraham and his seed were the promises made. He saith not, And to seeds, as of many; but as of one, And to thy seed, which is Christ. *(Gen. 13:15; 17:7)*

17 And this I say, *that* the covenant, that was confirmed before of God in Christ, the law, which was four hundred and thirty years after, cannot disannul, that it should make*the*promise*of*none*effect. *(Ex. 12:40)*

18 For if the inheritance *be* of the law, *it is* no more of promise: but God gave *it* to Abraham by promise.

☞ **3:11, 12** See note on James 2:14–19.

The Purpose of the Law

19 Wherefore then *serveth* the law? It was added because of transgressions, till the seed should come to whom the promise*was*made; *and it was* ordained by angels in the hand of a mediator.

20 Now a mediator is not *a mediator* of one, but God is one.

21 *Is* the law then against the promises of God? God forbid: for if there had been a law given which could have given life, verily righteousness should have been by the law.

☞ 22 But the Scripture hath concluded all under sin, that the promise by faith of Jesus Christ might be given to them*that*believe.

23 But before faith came, we were kept under the law, shut up unto the faith which should afterwards be revealed.

24 Wherefore the law was our schoolmaster *to bring us* unto Christ, that we might be justified by faith.

25 But after that faith is come, we are no longer under a schoolmaster.

26 For ye are all the children of God by faith in Christ Jesus.

27 For as many of you as have been baptized into Christ have put on Christ.

☞ 28 There is neither Jew nor Greek, there is neither bond nor free, there is neither male nor female: for ye are all one in Christ Jesus.

29 And if ye *be* Christ's, then are ye Abraham's seed, and heirs according to the promise.

☞ **3:22** See notes on Luke 8:13; Hebrews 6:1–6; 10:26, 27; and 1 John 3:6–9.
☞ **3:28** See note on 1 Timothy 2:9–15 concerning a woman's conduct in the church.

The Believer's Inheritance

1161   pin3004   art3588 nn2818 (pre1909) an,ajn3745   (an,nn5550) pin2076 pr/an,ajn3516 pin1308
4 Now I say, *That* the heir,   as*long*as   he   is a child, differeth
an,ajn3762   an,ajn1401   pap5607 pr/an,nn2962 an,ajn3956
nothing from a servant, though he be   lord of all;

235   pin2076   pre5259 an,nn2012   2532   an,nn3623   ad891 art3588   nn4287   art3588
2 But is under tutors and governors until the time appointed of the
nn3962
father.

2532   ad3779 epn2249 ad3753   ipf2258   pr/an,ajn3516   ipf2258   pr/pfpp1402   pre5259 art3588
3 Even so   we, when we were children, were in bondage under the
nn4747   art3588 nn2889
elements of the world:

1161   ad3753 art3588 nn4138   art3588 nn5550   aina2064 art,nn2316 aina1821 ppro848 art,nn5207
4 But when the fullness of the time was come, God sent forth his Son,
aptm1096 pre1537   an,nn1135 aptm1096 pre5259   an,nn3551
made of a woman, made under the law,

2443   asba1805   art3588   pre5259   an,nn3551 2443   asba618 art3588
5 To redeem them that were under the law, that we might receive the
nn5206
adoption*of*sons.

1161   3754   pin2075 pr/an,nn5207 art,nn2316   aina1821   art3588 nn4151   ppro848 art,nn5207
6 And because ye are sons, God hath sent forth the Spirit of his Son
pre1519 ppro5216 art,nn2588 pap2896   5   art,nn3962
into your hearts, crying, Abba, Father.

5620   pin1488 ad3765   pr/an,ajn1401 235   pr/an,nn5207 1161 1487   pr/an,nn5207
7 Wherefore thou art no more a servant, but a   son; and if a son,
2532   pr/an,nn2818 an,nn2316 pre1223 an,nn5547
then an   heir   of God through Christ.

235   ad5119   (3303)   pfp1492 3756 an,nn2316   aina1398
8 Howbeit then, when ye knew not God, ye did service unto
art,nn5449   pap5607 3361 pr/an,nn2316
them*which*by*nature are no gods.   *(2 Chr. 13:9; Is. 37:19; Jer. 2:11)*

1161 ad3568   apta1097   an,nn2316 1161 ad3123   aptp1097   pre5259 an,nn2316
9 But now, after that ye have known God, or rather are known of God,
ad4459 pin1994   ad3825 pre1909 art3588 an,aj772   2532 an,aj4434   nn4747   repro3739 (ad3825)
how turn ye again to   the weak and beggarly elements, whereunto ye
pin2309 ad509   pinf1398
desire again to be*in*bondage?

pinm3906   an,nn2250 2532   an,nn3376   2532 an,nn2540 2532 an,nn1763
10 Ye observe days, and months, and times, and years.

(Ex. 20:8; 23:14; Lev. 16:29; 25:3,4; Ezra 3:5)
pinm5399   ppro5209   3381   pfi2872/pre1519/ppro5209
11 I am afraid of you, lest I have bestowed*upon*you*labor
ad1500
in vain.

an,nn80   pinm1189 ppro5216 pim1096 ad5613 ppro1473   3754 epn2504   ad5613 ppro5210
12 Brethren, I beseech you, be as I *am*; for I *am* as ye *are*:
an,ajn3762/aina91/ppro3165
ye have not*injured*me*at*all.

(1161)   pin1492   3754   pre1223   an,nn769   art3588   nn4561   aom2097
13 Ye know how through infirmity of the flesh I preached*the*gospel unto

ppro5213   cd/art/ajn4386
you at*the*first.

2532   ppro3450   art,nn3986   art3588   pre1722 ppro3450 art,nn4561   aina1848   3756   3761
14 And my temptation which was in my flesh ye despised not, nor

aina1609   235   aom1209   ppro3165 ad5613   an,nn32   an,nn2316   ad5613 an,nn5547   an,nn2424
rejected; but received me as an angel of God, *even* as Christ Jesus.

pr/inpro5101   ipf2258   3767 art3588   nn3107   ppro5216   1063   pin3140/ppro5213
15 Where is then the blessedness ye spake of? for I bear*you*record,

3754   1487   an,ajn1415   apta1846/302   ppro5216 art,nn3788
that, if *it had been* possible, ye would have plucked out your own eyes, and

aina1325   ppro3427
have given them to me.

5620   pfi1096   ppro5216 pr/an,ajn2190   pap226/ppro5213
16 Am I therefore become your enemy, because I tell*you*the*truth?

(Amos 5:10)

pin2206   ppro5209   3756 ad2573   235   pin2309   ainf1576   ppro5209
17 They zealously affect you, *but* not well; yea, they would exclude you,

2443   psa2206   ppro846
that ye might affect them.

1161   an,aj2570   art,pifm2206   ad3842   pre1722   an,ajn2570   2532
18 But *it is* good to be zealously affected always in *a* good *thing,* and

3361 an,ajn3440   ppro3165   aie3918   pre4314 ppro5209
not only when I am present with you.

ppro3450   an,nn5040   repro3739   pin5605   ad3825   ad891   (repro3739) an,nn5547
19 My little children, of whom I travail*in*birth again until Christ be

asbp3445   pre1722 ppro5213
formed in you,

(1161)   ipf2309   pinf3918   pre4314 ppro5209   ad737   2532   ainf236   ppro3450 art,nn5456 3754
20 I desire to be present with you now, and to change my voice; for I

pinm639   pre1722 ppro5213
stand*in*doubt of you.

Isaac and Ishmael

pim3004 ppro3427   art,pap2309   pinf1511   pre5259   an,nn3551   3756 pin191 art3588
21 Tell me, ye*that*desire to be under the law, do ye not hear the

nn3551
law?

1063   pfip1125   3754   11   aina2192 nu1417 an,nn5207   an,nu,ajn1520 pre1537
22 For it is written, that Abraham had two sons, the one by a

art,nn3814   (2532) an,nu,ajn1520 pre1537   art,ajn1658
bondmaid, the other by a freewoman.   *(Gen. 16:15; 21:2)*

235   art3588/3303   pre1537 art3588   nn3814   pfip1080 pre2596   an,nn4561 1161
23 But he *who was* of the bondwoman was born after the flesh; but

art3588 pre1537 art3588   ajn1658   pre1223   art,nn1860
he of the freewoman *was* by promise.

repro3748   pin2076   ppmp238   1063 depro3778 pin1526 art3588 nu1417   pr/nn1242
24 Which things are an allegory: for these are the two covenants; the

^{an,nu,ajn3391/3303} ^{pre575}   ^{an,nn3735} ⁴⁶¹⁴   ^{pap1080} ^{pre1519} ^{an,nn1397} ^{repro3748} ^{pin2076}

one   from the mount Sinai, which gendereth to bondage, which is

^{pr/28}

Hagar.

¹⁰⁶³   ²⁸   ^{pin2076} ^{pr/an,nn3735} ⁴⁶¹⁴ ^{pre1722} ^{art,nn688} ¹¹⁶¹   ^{pin4960}   ²⁴¹⁹

25 For this Hagar is mount Sinai in Arabia, and answereth to Jerusalem

^{art,ad3568} ¹¹⁶¹   ^{pin1398}   ^{pre3326} ^{ppro848} ^{art,nn5043}

which now is, and is*in*bondage with her children.

¹¹⁶¹   ²⁴¹⁹   ^{art,ad507}   ^{pin2076} ^{pr/an,aj1658} ^{repro3748} ^{pin2076}   ^{pr/an,nn3384}   ^{ppro2257}

26 But Jerusalem which*is*above is free, which is the mother of us

^{an,aj3956}

all.

¹⁰⁶³   ^{pfip1125}   ^{aipp2165}   ^{an,ajn4723}   ^{art,pap5088}   ³⁷⁵⁶   ^{aima4486}   ²⁵³²

27 For it is written, Rejoice, *thou* barren that bearest not; break forth and

^{aima994}   ^{art,pap5605}   ³⁷⁵⁶   ³⁷⁵⁴ ^{art3588}   ^{ajn2048}   ^{pin2192} ^{an,aj4183}   ^{ad2123}   ^{art,nn5043}   ²²²⁸

cry, thou*that*travailest not; for the desolate hath many more children than

^{art,pap2192}   ^{art,nn435}

she*which*hath a husband.   *(Is. 54:1)*

¹¹⁶¹   ^{epn2249}   ^{an,nn80}   ^{pre2596} ²⁴⁶⁴   ^{pin2070}   ^{pr/an,nn5043}   ^{an,nn1860}

28 Now we, brethren, as Isaac was, are the children of promise.

²³⁵   ^{ad5618} ^{ad5119}   ^{art,aptp1080}   ^{pre2596}   ^{an,nn4561}   ^{ipf1377}   ^{art3588}

29 But as then he*that*was*born after the flesh persecuted him *that was*

^{pre2596}   ^{an,nn4151}   ²⁵³²   ^{ad3779}   ^{ad3568}

born after the Spirit, even so *it is* now.   *(Gen. 21:9)*

²³⁵   ^{inpro5101} ^{pin3004} ^{art3588}   ⁿⁿ¹¹²⁴   ^{aima1544}   ^{art3588}   ⁿⁿ³⁸¹⁴   ²⁵³²

30 Nevertheless what saith the Scripture? Cast out the bondwoman and

^{ppro846} ^{art,nn5207} ¹⁰⁶³ ^{art3588} ⁿⁿ⁵²⁰⁷   ^{art3588}   ⁿⁿ³⁸¹⁴   ^{efn3364}   ^{asba2816}   ^{pre3325} ^{art3588} ⁿⁿ⁵²⁰⁷   ^{art3588}

her son: for the son of the bondwoman shall not be heir with the son of the

^{ajn1658}

freewoman.   *(Gen. 21:10)*

⁶⁸⁶   ^{an,nn80}   ^{pin2070} ³⁷⁵⁶   ^{pr/an,nn5043}   ^{an,nn3814}   ²³⁵   ^{art3588}

31 So then, brethren, we are not children of the bondwoman, but of the

^{ajn1658}

free.

The Privileges of Christian Liberty

^{pim4739}   ³⁷⁶⁷   ^{art3588}   ⁿⁿ¹⁶⁵⁷   ^{repro3739}   ^{an,nn5547}   ^{aina1659/ppro2248}

5 Stand fast therefore in the liberty wherewith Christ hath made*us*free,

²⁵³²   ³³⁶¹   ^{pim1758/ad3825}   ^{an,nn2218}   ^{an,nn1397}

and be not entangled*again*with the yoke of bondage.

^{aima2396}   ^{epn1473} ^{an,nn3972} ^{pin3004}   ^{ppro5213} ³⁷⁵⁴ ¹⁴³⁷   ^{psmp4059}   ^{an,nn5547}

2 Behold, I Paul say unto you, that if ye be circumcised, Christ shall

^{ft5623} ^{ppro5209} ^{an,ajn3762}

profit you nothing.

¹¹⁶¹   ^{pinm3143}   ^{ad3825}   ^{an,aj3956} ^{an,nn444}   ^{ppmp4059}   ³⁷⁵⁴   ^{pin2076}

3 For I testify again to every man that is circumcised, that he is a

^{pr/an,nn3781}   ^{ainf4160} ^{art3588} ^{an,aj3650} ⁿⁿ³⁵⁵¹

debtor to do the whole law.

(pre575) art,nn5547   ainp2673   repro3748

☞ 4   Christ is become*of*no*effect unto you, whosoever of you are

pinm1344   pre1722   an,nn3551   aina1601   art,nn5485

justified by the law; ye are fallen from grace.

1063   epn2249   an,nn4151   pinm553   an,nn1680   an,nn1343   pre1537 an,nn4102

5 For we through the Spirit wait for the hope of righteousness by faith.

1063   pre1722   an,nn2424   an,nn5547   3777   an,nn4061   pin2480   idpro5100   3777

6 For in Jesus Christ neither circumcision availeth any thing, nor

an,nn203   235 an,nn4102   ppmp1754   pre1223 an,nn26

uncircumcision; but faith which worketh by love.

ipf5143   ad2573 inpro5101   aina348   ppro5209   3361 pifm3982 art3588   nn225

7 Ye did run well; who did hinder you that ye should not obey the truth?

art,nn3988   3756 pre1537   art,pap2564   ppro5209

8 This persuasion *cometh* not of him*that*calleth you.

an,aj3398   an,nn2219   pin2220 art3588 an,aj3650   nn5445

9 A little leaven leaveneth the whole lump.

epn1473   pfi3982   pre1519 ppro5209   pre1722   an,nn2962   3754

10 I have confidence in you through the Lord, that ye will

ft5426/an,ajn3762/an,aj243   1161   art,pap5015   ppro5209   ft941

be*none*otherwise*minded: but he*that*troubleth you shall bear his

art,nn2917   repro3748/302   psa5600

judgment, whosoever he be.

1161   epn1473   an,nn80   1487   ad2089 pin2784   an,nn4061   inpro5101   ad2089

11 And I, brethren, if I yet preach circumcision, why do I yet

pinp1377   686   art3588   nn4625   art3588   nn4716   pfip2673

suffer persecution? then is the offense of the cross ceased.

aina3785   2532   fm609   art,pap387   ppro5209

12 I would they were even cut off which trouble you.

1063   an,nn80   epn5210   ainp2564 pre1909 an,nn1657   an,ajn3440   3361 art,nn1657

13 For, brethren, ye have been called unto liberty; only *use* not liberty

pre1519   an,nn874   art3588 nn4561   235 pre1223 art,nn26 pim1398   rcpro240

for an occasion to the flesh, but by love serve one another.

1063   art,aj3956   an,nn3551   pinp4137 pre1722 nu1520 an,nn3056   pre1722 art3588

14 For all the law is fulfilled in one word, *even* in this; Thou shalt

ft25   ppro4675   art,ad4139   ad5613 rxpro1438

love thy neighbor as thyself.

(Lev. 19:18)

1161   1487   pin1143   2532   pin2719   rcpro240   pim991   3361

15 But if ye bite and devourone another, take heed that ye be not

asbp355   (pre5259)   rcpro240

consumed   one*of*another.

☞ 5:4 This text is often misused to teach that the phrase "fall from grace" means that a person can lose his salvation. In the context of verses one through three, Paul is teaching how depending on the Law of Moses for salvation makes Christ work on the cross meaningless. Then in verse four, he speaks about those who justify themselves in or by means of the law or through the law. Because these individuals chose to obey the law for salvation, they have no room for Jesus Christ and His grace. The key to understanding the phrase "you are fallen from grace" is seen in the verb *exepésate* (1601) which is better translated "have fallen." It does not mean that the grace of God was evident at one time, and then was lost. Rather, this person deviates from the true path of grace by choosing justification by law instead of by grace. Grace has a law associated with it, but the law has no grace, only restrictions. See note on James 2:14–19.

16 *This* I say then, Walk in the Spirit, and ye shall not fulfill the lust of the flesh.

17 For the flesh lusteth against the Spirit, and the Spirit against the flesh: and these are contrary the*one*to*the*other: so that ye cannot do the things that ye would.

18 But if ye be led of the Spirit, ye are not under the law.

19 Now the works of the flesh are manifest, which are *these*; adultery, fornication, uncleanness, lasciviousness,

20 Idolatry, witchcraft, hatred, variance, emulations, wrath, strife, seditions, heresies,

21 Envyings, murders, drunkenness, revellings, and such like: of the which I tell*you*before, as I have also told* *you*in*time*past, that they*which*do such things shall not inherit the kingdom of God.

22 But the fruit of the Spirit is love, joy, peace, longsuffering, gentleness, goodness, faith,

23 Meekness, temperance: against such there is no law.

24 And they that are Christ's have crucified the flesh with the affections and lusts.

25 If we live in the Spirit, let us also walk in the Spirit.

26 Let us not be desirous*of*vain*glory, provoking one another, envying one another.

The Practice of Love

6 Brethren, if a man be overtaken in a fault, ye which are spiritual, restore such*a*one in the spirit of meekness; considering thyself, lest thou also be tempted.

pim941   rcpro240   art,nn922   2532 ad3779 aima378 art3588 nn3551   art,nn5547

2 Bear ye one another's burdens, and so fulfill the law of Christ.

1063   1487 idpro5100   pin1380   pinf1511 pr/idpro5100   pap5607   pr/an,ajn3367

3 For if a man think himself to be something, when he is nothing, he

pin5422   rxpro1438

deceiveth himself.

1161   an,ajn1538   pim1381   rxpro1438 art,nn2041 2532 ad5119   ft2192   art,nn2745

4 But let every man prove his own work, and then shall he have rejoicing

pre1519 rxpro1438 an,ajn3441 2532 3756 pre1519 art,ajn2087

in himself alone, and not in another.

1063   an,ajn1538   ft941   art,aj2398   an,nn5413

5 For every man shall bear his own burden.

(1161)   art,ppmp2727   art3588   nn3056   pim2841

6   Let   him*that*is*taught   in   the   word   communicate   unto

art,pap2727   pre1722 an,aj3956   an,ajn18

him*that*teacheth   in   all   good things.

The Law of Sowing and Reaping

3361   pim4105   an,nn2316   3756   pinp3456   1063 repro3739/1437   an,nn444   psa4687

7 Be not deceived; God is not mocked: for whatsoever a man soweth,

depro5124   2532   ft2325

that shall he also reap.

3734   art,pap4687   pre1519 rxpro1438 art,nn4561   pre1537 art3588 nn4561 ft2325   an,nn5356

8 For he*that*soweth to his flesh shall of the flesh reap corruption;

1161   art,pap4687   pre1519 art3588   nn4151   pre1537 art3588   nn4151   ft2325   an,nn2222

but he*that*soweth to the Spirit shall of the Spirit reap life

an,aj166

everlasting.

1161   3361   psa1573   art,ajn2570 pap4160   1063   an,aj2398   an,nn2540

9 And let us not be weary in well doing: for in due season we shall

ft2325   ppmp1590 3361

reap, if we faint not.

ad5613   pin2192   686/3767   an,nn2540   psi2038 art,ajn18 pre4314 an,ajn3956 (1161)

10 As we have therefore opportunity, let us do good unto all *men,*

ad3122   pre4314   art,ajn3609   art,nn4102

especially unto them*who*are*of*the*household of faith.

Paul's Closing Remarks

aima1492   an,aj4080   an,nn1121   aina1125   ppro5213   art,popro1699

11 Ye see how large a letter I have written unto you with mine own

an,nn5495

hand.

an,ajn3745   pin2309   ainf2146   pre1722   an,nn4561 depro3778   pin314

12 As*many*as desire to make*a*fair*show in the flesh, they constrain

ppro5209   pifm4059   an,ajn3440 3363   psmp1377   art3588 nn4716

you to be circumcised; only lest they should suffer persecution for the cross

art,nn5547

of Christ.

^{1063   3761   epn846} ^{art,ppmp4059} ^{pin5442} ^{an,nn3551   235}
13 For neither they themselves who*are*circumcised keep the law; but
^{pin2309} ^{ppro5209} ^{pifm4059} ²⁴⁴³ ^{asbm2744 pre1722 art,popro5212 an,nn4561}
desire to have you circumcised, that they may glory in   your flesh.

^{1161   opt1096/3361} ^{epn1698} ^{pifm2744   1508   pre1722 art3588 nn4716} ^{ppro2257 art,nn2962}
14 But God forbid that   I   should glory, save in   the cross of our Lord
^{an,nn2424   an,nn5547   pre1223   repro3739} ^{an,nn2889} ^{pfip4717} ^{ppro1698   ppro2504} ^{art3588}
Jesus Christ, by   whom the world is crucified unto me, and I unto the
ⁿⁿ²⁸⁸⁹
world.

^{1063   pre1722   an,nn5547   an,nn2424   3777} ^{an,nn4061} ^{pin2480} ^{idpro5100} ³⁷⁷⁷
15 For in   Christ Jesus neither circumcision availeth any thing, nor
^{an,nn203} ^{235   an,aj2537   an,nn2937}
uncircumcision, but a new creature.

^{2532   an,ajn3745   ft4748} ^{depro5129 art,nn2583 an,nn1515   pre1909 ppro846   2532}
16 And as*many*as walk according to this rule, peace be on them, and
^{an,nn1656   2532 pre1909 art3588   2474} ^{art,nn2316}
mercy, and upon the Israel of God.   *(Ps. 128:6)*

^{art,ajn3064} ^{an,ajn3367} ^{pim3930/an,nn2873 ppro3427 1063 epn1473 pin941   pre1722 ppro3450}
☞ 17 From henceforth let no man   trouble   me: for   I   bear in   my
^{art,nn4983 art3588   nn4742} ^{art3588 nn2962   an,nn2424}
body the marks of the Lord Jesus.

^{an,nn80} ^{art3588 nn5485} ^{ppro2257 art,nn2962 an,nn2424 an,nn5547} ^{pre3326 ppro5216 art,nn4151}
18 Brethren, the   grace of   our   Lord Jesus Christ be with your spirit.
²⁸¹
Amen.

☞ **6:17** See note on 2 Timothy 1:12.

The Epistle of Paul the Apostle to the

EPHESIANS

Ephesus was the capital of the chief province of Asia. It was located about one mile from the Aegean Sea. The temple of Diana (Artemis) was important to the commerce of the city because the Mediterranean world considered it to be such a sacred and impeccable institution, that it became the chief banking establishment in all of Asia Minor. The great number of pilgrims that came to worship at the temple also bolstered the economy in Ephesus. In fact, the population is believed to have exceeded a quarter million.

Paul came to Ephesus during his second missionary journey with Aquila and Priscilla but journeyed on to Jerusalem by himself not long afterward (Acts 18:18–21). On his next missionary journey, Paul spent three years in Ephesus (Acts 19). He had so much influence on the people there that the craftsman who manufactured silver shrines for Diana incited a riot against him, concerned that his trade would become obsolete (Acts 19:24–29). As a result, Paul left Ephesus, traveling to Macedonia (Acts 20:1). Upon a return trip to Jerusalem, he requested that the elders of the Ephesian congregation meet with him at Miletus, a city located thirty-five miles to the north, so that he could bid them his last farewell (Acts 20:16–38).

The words "at Ephesus" (Eph. 1:1) do not appear in several important Greek manuscripts. Consequently, many believe that this letter was not originally sent to the congregation at Ephesus but was meant to be a letter that would be circulated to the many Gentile churches in Asia. This would explain why he would completely omit any personal greetings to believers with whom he had spent three years (Acts 19). Scholars believe that it eventually became known as the Epistle to the Ephesians because the church in Ephesus would have been the mother church from which the letter would have been distributed to the other churches in Asia.

The Book of Ephesians was probably written by Paul during his imprisonment in Rome (ca. A.D. 60–64) about the same time that he wrote Colossians and Philemon. The content of the Book of Ephesians is very similar to that of Colossians; both stress doctrine and give instruction in practical Christian duties. One difference between them, however, is that Colossians portrays Christ as the head of the Church, while Ephesians goes on to display Jesus as the ascended, glorified Christ. Also, in Colossians Paul attacks the gnostic heresy; but in Ephesians, Paul examines the splendor of Christ in glory.

The major theme of this letter is that the Church (*ekklēsía* [1577]) is the body of Christ (Eph. 1:22, 23; 2:15, 16). Paul also metaphorically spoke of the Church as a building of which Christ is the chief cornerstone (Eph. 2:20–22) and compared the Church to a bride who will soon be united with Christ (Eph. 5:21–33). The key idea is that a body has individual parts that must operate as a unit. God's plan is to bring all believers together (Eph. 1:10) with Christ as the head (Eph. 1:22, 23).

1   an,nn3972   an,nn652   an,nn2424   an,nn5547   pre1223   an,nn2307   an,nn2316   art3588   ajn40
Paul, an apostle of Jesus Christ by the will of God, to the saints
art,pap5607   pre1722   an,nn2181   2532   an,ajn4103   pre1722   an,nn5547   an,nn2424
which are at Ephesus, and to the faithful in Christ Jesus:
   an,nn5485   ppro5213   2532   an,nn1515   pre575   an,nn2316 ppro2257   an,nn3962   2532   an,nn2962
2 Grace *be* to you, and peace, from God our Father, and *from* the Lord
an,nn2424   an,nn5547
Jesus Christ.

The Blessings of Redemption

   pr/an,aj2128   art3588   nn2316   2532   an,nn3962   ppro2257 art,nn2962   an,nn2424   an,nn5547
3 Blessed *be* the God and Father of our Lord Jesus Christ,
art,apta2127   ppro2248 pre1722 an,aj3956   an,aj4152   sg/an,nn2129   pre1722   pl/art,ajn2032   pre1722
who*hath*blessed us with all spiritual blessings in heavenly *places* in
an,nn5547
Christ:

  ☞   ad2531   aom1586   ppro2248 pre1722 ppro846   pre4253   an,nn2602
☞ 4 According as he hath chosen us in him before the foundation of the
an,nn2889   ppro2248   pinf1511 pr/an,aj40 2532   pr/an,aj299   ad*2714   ppro846 pre1722 an,nn26
world, that we should be holy and without blame before him in love:
        apta4309   ppro2248   pre1519   an,nn5206   pre1223   an,nn2424
5 Having predestinated us unto the adoption*of*children by Jesus
an,nn5547 pre1519   ppro848   pre2596   art3588   nn2107   ppro848 art,nn2307
Christ to himself, according to the good pleasure of his will,
     pre1519   an,nn1868   an,nn1391   ppro848   art,nn5485   pre1722/repro3739
6 To the praise of the glory of his grace, wherein he hath
aina5487/ppro2248   pre1722 art3588   pfpp25
made*us*accepted in the beloved.

☞ **1:4, 5** The real dilemma in this passage is determining how a person can know if he is one of the elect, or even if he can be given that kind of knowledge. There are two words in this passage that must be examined in order to explain the much debated subject of God's election and predestination. The first is found in verse four, "he has chosen," referring to the Greek word *exeléxato* (1586) meaning "chosen out of." In this context, this word means that at one particular time in the past, God chose individuals for salvation (Matt. 24:31; Luke 18:7; Rom. 8:33; 2 Tim. 2:10; James 2:5).

    The second verb in verse five is *proorísas* (4309), "to determine beforehand or predestinate" (cf. Acts 4:28; Rom. 8:29; 9:11; 1 Pet. 1:2, 20). It is interesting to note that Peter referred to the concept of predestination in his sermon on the day of Pentecost. He said (speaking of Christ), "Him, being delivered by the determinate counsel and foreknowledge of God, ye have taken, and by wicked hands have crucified and slain." In this verse, one can note the evidence of the concept of man's free choice coupled with the responsibility for his actions. God delivered up His Son, and man was given the choice of what they would do with Christ. They chose to crucify Him, leaving them with the responsiblity for their act.

    Furthermore, the teaching of Scripture is clear: Christ died for all. In 1 John 2:2 the writer states, "And he is the propitiation for our sins, (i.e., believers) and not for ours only, but also for the sins of the whole world." Therefore, the ministry of Christ that He did on the cross was intended for all. Repeatedly, God says that "whosoever believeth in Him" can obtain salvation (John 3:16–18, 36; Acts 10:43). To come to Christ is an invitation to all, and all who hear the gospel are responsible and without excuse to either accept or reject Christ. If one perishes in his sin, he is condemned as a result of his own choice (Titus 3:10, 11). As one reflects on the salvation experience of the believer, he should note that God alone knows the point at which a person receives Christ for salvation. It is also evident that the believer is fulfilling God's purposes for his life, resulting in him becoming one of God's elect.

pre1722   repro3739   pin2192   art,nn629   pre1223   ppro846   art,nn129   art3588   nn859

7 In whom we have redemption through his blood, the forgiveness of

art,nn3900   pre2596   art3588   nn4149   ppro846   art,nn5485

sins, according to the riches of his grace;

repro3739   aina4052   pre1519   ppro2248   pre1722   an,aj3956   an,nn4678   2532

8 Wherein he hath abounded toward us in all wisdom and

an,nn5428

prudence;

apta1107   ppro2254 art3588   nn3466   ppro848 art,nn2307   pre2596

9 Having made known unto us the mystery of his will, according to

ppro848   art,nn2107   repro3739   aom4388   pre1722   ppro848

his good pleasure which he hath purposed in himself:

pre1519   an,nn3622   art3588   nn4138   art,nn2540

10 That in the dispensation of the fullness of times he might

aifm346   art,aj3956   pre1722 art,nn5547   5037   art3588   pre1722   art,nn3772   2532

gather*together*in*one all things in Christ, both which are in heaven, and

art3588   pre1909 art,nn1093   pre1722 ppro846

which are on earth; *even* in him:

pre1722 repro3739   2532   ainp2820   aptp4309

☞ 11 In whom also we have obtained*an*inheritance, being predestinated

pre2596   an,nn4286   art,pap1754   art,aj3956   pre2596 art3588   nn1012

according to the purpose of him*who*worketh all things after the counsel of

ppro848   art,nn2307

his own will:

ppro2248   aies1511 pre1519   an,nn1868   ppro846 art,nn1391   art,pfp4276

12 That we should be to the praise of his glory, who*first*trusted

pre1722 art,nn5547

in Christ.

pre1722 repro3739 epn5210 2532   apta191 art3588   nn2056   art,nn225 art3588

☞ 13 In whom ye also *trusted,* after that ye heard the word of truth, the

nn2098   ppro5216   art,nn4991   pre1722 repro3739   2532   apta4100

gospel of your salvation: in whom also after that ye believed, ye were

ainp4972   art,aj40 art,nn4151   art,nn1860

sealed with that Holy Spirit of promise,

repro3739   pin2076   pr/an,nn728   ppro2257   art,nn2817   pre1519   an,nn629   art3588

14 Which is the earnest of our inheritance until the redemption of the

nn4047   pre1519   an,nn1868   ppro846 art,nn1391

purchased possession, unto the praise of his glory.

pre1223/depro5124   epn2504   apta191   pre2596 ppro5209 art,nn4102 pre1722 art3588   nn2962   an,nn2424

15 Wherefore I also, after I heard of your faith in the Lord Jesus,

2532   art,nn26 art,pre1519 an,aj3956 art3588   ajn40

and love unto all the saints,

pinm3973   3756   pap2168   pre5228 ppro5216   ppmp4160   an,nn3417   ppro5216 pre1909 ppro3450

16 Cease not to give thanks for you, making mention of you in my

art,nn4335

prayers,

☞ **1:11** See note on Ephesians 1:4, 5.

☞ **1:13, 14** The phrase "the earnest of our inheritance" refers to the act of the Holy Spirit whereby He makes a pledge, providing assurance for the believer of an eternal life in Christ, which he must accept by faith.

17 That the God of our Lord Jesus Christ, the Father of glory, may give unto you the spirit of wisdom and revelation in the knowledge of him:

(Is. 11:2)

18 The eyes of your understanding being enlightened; that ye may know what is the hope of his calling, and what the riches of the glory of his inheritance in the saints,

19 And what *is* the exceeding greatness of his power to us-ward who believe, according to the working of his mighty power,

20 Which he wrought in Christ, when he raised him from the dead, and set *him* at his own right hand in the heavenly *places*,   *(Ps. 110:1)*

21 Far above all principality, and power, and might, and dominion, and every name that is named, not only in this world, but also in that*which*is*to*come:

22 And hath put all *things* under his feet, and gave him *to be* the head over all *things* to the church,   *(Ps. 8:6)*

23 Which is his body, the fullness of him*that*filleth all in all.

Salvation From Sin

2 And you *hath he quickened,* who were dead in trespasses and sins;

2 Wherein in*time*past ye walked according to the course of this world, according to the prince of the power of the air, the spirit that*now*worketh in the children of disobedience:

3 Among whom also we all had*our*conversation in*times*past in the lusts of our flesh, fulfilling the desires of the flesh and of the mind; and were by nature the children of wrath, even as others.

1161 art,nn2316   pap5607 pr/an,aj4145 pre1722   an,nn1656   pre1223 ppro848 art,aj4183 an,nn26   repro3739

4 But God, who is rich in mercy, for his great love wherewith he

aina25 ppro2248

loved us,

2532   ppro2248 pap5607 pr/an,aj3498   art,nn3900   aina4806

5 Even when we were dead in sins, hath quickened*us*together with

art,nn5547   an,nn5485   pin2075 pr/pfpp4982

Christ, (by grace ye are saved;)

2532   aina4891   2532   aina4776   pre1722

6 And hath raised*us*up*together, and made*us*sit*together in

pl/art,ajn2032   pre1722 an,nn5547 an,nn2424

heavenly *places* in Christ Jesus:

2443   pre1722 art3588 nn165 art,ppmp1904   asbm1731 art3588   pap5235   sg/nn4149 ppro848

7 That in the ages to come he might show the exceeding riches of his

art,nn5485 pre1722   an,nn5544   pre1909 ppro2248 pre1722   an,nn5547 an,nn2424

grace in *his* kindness toward us through Christ Jesus.

1063   art,nn5485 pin2075   pr/pfpp4982   pre1223 art,nn4102 2532 depro5124 3756 pre1537   ppro5216

☞ 8 For by grace are ye saved through faith; and that not of yourselves: *it*

art3588 pr/nn1435   an,nn2316

is the gift of God:

3756 pre1537 an,nn2041   3363   idpro5100   asbm2744

9 Not of works, lest any man should boast.

1063   pin2070 epn846   pr/an,nn4161   aptp2936   pre1722 an,nn5547 an,nn2424 pre1909

10 For we are his workmanship, created in Christ Jesus unto

an,aj18   an,nn2041   repro3739 art,nn2316   aina4282   2443   asba4043 pre1722

good works, which God hath before ordained that we should walk in

ppro846

them.

No Longer Strangers

pre,repro1352   pim3421   3754 epn5210   ad4218   art,nn1484 pre1722

11 Wherefore remember, that ye *being* in*time*past Gentiles in the

an,nn4561 art3588 ppmp3004   an,nn203   pre5259 art,ppmp3004   an,nn4061

flesh, who are called Uncircumcision by that*which*is*called the Circumcision

pre1722   an,nn4561   an,aj5499

in the flesh made*by*hands;

3754 pre1722 depro1565 art,nn2540 ipf2258   ad*5565   an,nn5547   pr/pfpp526   art3588

12 That at that time ye were without Christ, being aliens from the

nn4174   2474   2532 pr/an,aj3581   art3588   nn1242   art,nn1860 pr/pap2192

commonwealth of Israel, and strangers from the covenants of promise, having

3361 an,nn1680 2532   pr/an,ajn112   pre1722 art3588   nn2889

no hope, and without God in the world:

1161 ad3570 pre1722 an,nn5547 an,nn2424 epn5210   art,pap5607/ad4218   ad3112   ainp1096

13 But now in Christ Jesus ye who*sometimes*were far off are made

pr/ad1451 pre1722 art3588   nn129   art,nn5547

nigh by the blood of Christ.   *(Is. 57:19)*

☞ **2:8** See note on Mark 16:16.

　　　　　1063　　epn846　pin2076　ppro2257　pr/art,nn1515　　　　art,apta4160　　　　art,ajn297　pr/nu,ajn1520　2532

14 For　he　is　our　peace,　who*hath*made　both　one,　and hath

　　apta3089　　art3588　　nn3320　　　art,nn5418

broken down the middle wall of partition *between us*;　　　　　　*(Is. 9:6)*

　　　　　apta2673　　　pre1722　ppro848　art,nn4561　art3588　　nn2189　　　art3588　　nn3551

15 Having　abolished　in　his　flesh　the　enmity,　*even*　the　law　of

art,nn1785　　　　　　　pre1722　　an,nn1378　　　2243　asba2936　pre1722　rxpro1438

commandments *contained* in　ordinances; for　to　make　in　himself　of

art,nu,ajn1417 (pre1519) nu1520 an,aj2537 an,nn444　　pap4160　　an,nn1515

twain　　one　new　man, *so* making peace;

　　　　　2532　　　　　　　　　asba604　　art,ajn297　　　　　art,nn2316　pre1722　nu1520　an,nn4983　pre1223　art3588

16 And that he might reconcile both unto God　in　one　body　by　the

nn4716　　　　apta615　art3588　　nn2189　　pre1722/ppro846

cross, having slain the enmity thereby:

　　　　　2532　apta2064　　　aom2097　　an,nn1515　　ppro5213　　　art,ad3112　　　2532

17 And came and preached peace to　you　which*were*afar*off, and to

　　art,ad1451

them*that*were*nigh.　　　　　　*(Is. 52:7; 57:19; Zech. 9:10)*

　　　　　3754　　pre1223　　ppro846　　art,ajn297 pin2192　art,nn4318　pre1722 nu1520 an,nn4151　pre4314　art3588

18 For through him we both have access by　one　Spirit　unto　the

nn3962

Father.

　　　　　686　　　3767　　　　pin2075　　ad3765　　pr/an,ajn3581　2532　pr/an,ajn3941　235

19 Now therefore ye　are　no　more　strangers　and　foreigners,　but

pr/an,nn4847　　　　art3588　ajn40　2532　pr/an,ajn3609　art,nn2316

fellowcitizens with the saints, and of*the*household of God;

　　　　　aptp2026　pre1909 art3588　nn2310　　art3588　　nn652　　2532　　an,nn4396　an,nn2424

20 And are built upon the foundation of the apostles and prophets, Jesus

an,nn5547　epn846　pap5607　　pr/an,ajn204

Christ himself being the chief corner *stone*;　　　　　　*(Is. 28:16)*

　　　　　pre1722　repro3739　an,aj3956 art3588　nn3619　　　　ppmp4883　　　　pim837　pre1519　an,aj40

21 In whom all　the building fitly*framed*together groweth unto a holy

an,nn3485　pre1722　　an,nn2962

temple　in　the Lord:

　　　　　pre1722　repro3739　epn5210　2532　　　　　pinp4925　　　pre1519　　an,nn2732　　art,nn2316

22 In whom ye also are builded together for a habitation of God

pre1722　　an,nn4151

through the Spirit.

God's Plan

　　　　　ad*5484/depro5127　　epn1473 an,nn3972 art3588　nn1198　　an,nn2424 art,nn5547 pre5228 ppro5216

3 For*this*cause　I　Paul,　the　prisoner of Jesus Christ for　you

　　art,nn1484

Gentiles,

　　1489　　aina191　art3588　　　nn3622　　art3588　nn5485　art,nn2316

2 If　ye have heard of　the　dispensation of　the　grace of God

art,aptp1325　　ppro3427 pre1519　ppro5209

which*is*given me　to you-ward:

3 How that by revelation he made known unto me the mystery; (as I
wrote afore in few words,

4 Whereby, when ye read, ye may understand my knowledge in the
mystery of Christ)

5 Which in other ages was not made known unto the sons of
men, as it is now revealed unto his holy apostles and prophets by the
Spirit;

6 That the Gentiles should be fellowheirs, and of*the*same*body, and
partakers of his promise in Christ by the gospel:

7 Whereof I was made a minister, according to the gift of the grace of
God given unto me by the effectual working of his power.

8 Unto me, who am less*than*the*least of all saints, is this grace
given, that I should preach among the Gentiles the unsearchable riches of
Christ;

9 And to make*all*men*see what is the fellowship of the mystery, which
from the beginning*of*the*world hath been hid in God, who created
all things by Jesus Christ:

10 To*the*intent*that now unto the principalities and powers in
heavenly places might be known by the church the manifold wisdom of
God,

11 According to the eternal purpose which he purposed in Christ Jesus
our Lord:

12 In whom we have boldness and access with confidence by the faith
of him.

13 Wherefore I desire that ye faint not at my tribulations for you,
which is your glory.

Paul's Prayer for the Ephesians

ad*548/depro5127   pin2578 ppro3450 art,nn1119 pre4314 art3588   nn3962   ppro2257 art,nn2962 an,nn2424

14 For*this*cause I bow my knees unto the Father of our Lord Jesus

an,nn5547

Christ,

pre1537 repro3739   an,aj3956 an,nn3965 pre1722 an,nn3772   2532 (pre1909) an,nn1093   pinm3687

15 Of whom the whole family in heaven and   earth is named,

2443   opt1325 ppro5213   pre2596   art3588   nn4149   ppro848 art,nn1391

16 That he would grant you, according to the riches of his glory, to be

aifp2901   an,nn1411 pre1223 ppro848 art,nn4151 pre1519 art3588 ad2080   an,nn444

strengthened with might by his Spirit in the inner man;

art,nn5547   ainf2730 pre1722 ppro5216 art,nn2588 pre1223 art,nn4102   2443   pfpp4492

17 That Christ may dwell in your hearts by faith; that ye, being rooted

2532   pfpp2311   pre1722 an,nn26

and grounded in love,

asba1840   aifm2638   pre4862 an,aj3956 art,ajn40 inpro5101   art3588   pr/nn4114   2532

18 May be able to comprehend with all   saints what *is* the breadth, and

pr/an,nn3372 2532   pr/an,nn899   2532   pr/an,nn5311

length, and depth, and height;

5037   ainf1097 art3588 nn26   art,nn5547   art,pap5235   art,nn1108   2443

19 And to know the love of Christ, which passeth knowledge, that ye might

asbp4137 pre1519 an,aj3956 art3588   nn4138   art,nn2316

be filled with all   the fullness of God.

1161   art,ppmp1410   ainf4160   pre5228/pre1537/an,ajn4053

20 Now   unto   him*that*is*able   to   do   exceeding   abundantly

pre5228 an,aj3956 repro3739   pinm154 2228 pin3539   pre2596   art3588   nn1411   art,ppmp1754   pre1722

above all   that we ask or think, according to the power that worketh in

ppro2254

us,

epn846   art,nn1391 pre1722 art3588   nn1577   pre1722 an,nn5547 an,nn2424   pre1519   an,aj3956

21 Unto him *be* glory in   the church by Christ Jesus throughout   all

art,nn1074   art,nn165/art,nn165   281

ages, world*without*end. Amen.

Oneness

epn1473   3767   art3588   nn1198   pre1722   an,nn2962   pin3870   ppro5209   ainf4043

4 I   therefore, the prisoner of the Lord, beseech you that ye walk

ad516   art3588   nn2821   repro3739   ainp2564

worthy of the vocation wherewith ye are called,

pre3326 an,aj3956   an,nn5012   2532   an,nn4236   pre3326   an,nn3115   ppmp430

2 With   all   lowliness and meekness, with longsuffering, forbearing

rcpro240   pre1722 an,nn26

one another in love;

pap4704   pinf5083 art3588   nn1775   art3588   nn4151   pre1722 art3588   nn4886

3 Endeavoring to keep the unity of the Spirit in   the bond of

an,nn1515

peace.

nu1520 an,nn4983 2532 nu1520 an,nn4151 ad2531   ainp2564 pre1722 nu3391 an,nn1680

☞ 4 *There is* one body, and one Spirit, even as ye are called in one hope of

ppro5216 art,nn2821

your calling;

nu1520 an,nn2962 nu3391 an,nn4102 nu1520 an,nn908

5 One Lord, one faith, one baptism,

nu1520 an,nn2316 2532 an,nn3962 an,ajn3956 art3588 pre1909 an,ajn3956 2532 pre1223 an,ajn3956 2532

6 One God and Father of all, who *is* above all, and through all, and

pre1722 ppro5213 an,aj3956

in you all.

1161 an,aj1538 nu1520 ppro2257 ainp1325 art,nn5485 pre2596 art3588 nn3358

7 But unto every one of us is given grace according to the measure of

art3588 nn1431 art,nn5547

the gift of Christ.

pre,repro1352 pin3004 apta305 pre1519 an,nn5311

☞ 8 Wherefore he saith, When he ascended up on high, he

aina162/an,nn161 2532 aina1325 an,nn1390 art,nn444

led*captivity*captive, and gave gifts unto men.   *(Ps. 68:18)*

1161 art3588 aina305 inpro5101 pin2076 1508 3754 2532 aina2597 nu,aj4412

9 (Now that he ascended, what is it but that he also descended first

pre1519 art3588 cd/aj2737 an,nn3313 art3588 nn1093

into the lower parts of the earth?

art,apta2597 pin2076 epn846 2532 pr/art,apta305 ad*5231 an,aj3956

10 He*that*descended is the same also that*ascended*up far above all

art,nn3772 2443 asba4137 art,ajn3956

heavens, that he might fill all things.)

☞ **4:4** This verse begins with the statement, "There is one body . . . ." Paul is emphasizing the unity of believers, specifically that Jews and Gentiles are equal in Christ. Gentiles could become Christians without having to conform to Jewish traditions. However, many Jewish Christians, who had always been prejudiced against the Gentiles, thought they were not true followers of the Messiah unless they were first circumcised, then obedient to the Law of Moses. The tendency for Jews was to see themselves as the center of God's plan of salvation instead of placing Christ there. Paul taught that they should view the Gentiles as their brothers in Christ, on an equal level. God is sovereign over all races, cultures, problems of humanity (e.g., social and family situations), and even the unseen beings (Eph. 3:10). God's chosen people having been set free from sin and made to be equals by Jesus' death and resurrection, must live in the unity of Christ.

☞ **4:8–10** This passage discusses in detail Christ's incarnation, resurrection and ascension. In verse nine, Paul uses the phrase, "Now that he ascended . . ." which is designed to state the fact that Christ ascended to heaven following his resurrection. The verse continues by making note that if Christ ascended, he obviously had to have come ("descended") to earth at a previous time. Therefore, the "descent" of Jesus "into the lower parts of the earth" is His incarnation, making it possible for Him to experience death. The "ascent" is His ascension from earth to heaven after His resurrection (John 8:23; 16:28).

In verse eight, there is some controversy to what Christ is actually "leading captive." However, the meaning of this passage is simple: Christ defeated sin and death by His resurrection, taking them captive and rendering them powerless as would a king after a victory over his enemies. The "gifts" (i.e., eternal life and forgiveness of sin) that are given to believers were consequent to Christ's defeat of sin and death. The analogy is that Christ is sharing the spoils of His ultimate victory over Satan with those who have received Him. In Psalm 68:18, David is expressing the same idea of God Almighty obtaining victory over His enemies and leading them away as captives. The gifts given by Christ (Eph. 4:8) are those things that are given to enable a Christian to live a more victorious life for Christ while on earth.

☞ 11 And he gave some, apostles; and some, prophets; and some, evangelists; and some, pastors and teachers;

12 For the perfecting of the saints, for the work of the ministry, for the edifying of the body of Christ:

13 Till we all come in the unity of the faith, and of the knowledge of the Son of God, unto a perfect man, unto the measure of the stature of the fullness of Christ:

14 That we *henceforth* be no more children, tossed*to*and*fro, and carried about with every wind of doctrine, by the sleight of men, *and* cunning craftiness, whereby they lie*in*wait*to*deceive;

15 But speaking*the*truth in love, may grow up into him in all things, which is the head, *even* Christ:

16 From whom the whole body fitly*joined*together and compacted by that which every joint supplieth, according to the effectual working in the measure of every part, maketh increase of the body unto the edifying of itself in love.

A New Way of Thinking

17 This I say therefore, and testify in the Lord, that ye henceforth*walk*not as other Gentiles walk, in the vanity of their mind,

18 Having the understanding darkened, being alienated from the life of God through the ignorance that is in them, because of the blindness of their heart:

☞ **4:11, 12** See note on 1 Corinthians 12:1–11.

19 Who being*past*feeling have given*themselves*over unto lasciviousness, to work all uncleanness with greediness.

20 But ye have not so learned Christ;

21 If*so*be that ye have heard him, and have been taught by him, as the truth is in Jesus:

22 That ye put off concerning the former conversation the old man, which*is*corrupt according to the deceitful lusts;

23 And be renewed in the spirit of your mind;

24 And that ye put on the new man, which after God is created in righteousness and true holiness. *(Gen. 1:26)*

25 Wherefore putting away lying, speak every man truth with his neighbor: for we are members one*of*another. *(Zech. 8:16)*

26 Be*ye*angry, and sin not: let not the sun go down upon your wrath:

(Ps. 4:4)

27 Neither give place to the devil.

28 Let him*that*stole steal no more: but rather let him labor, working with his hands the*thing*which*is*good, that he may have to give to him*that*needeth.

29 Let no corrupt communication proceed out of your mouth, but that which is good to the use of edifying, that it may minister grace unto the hearers.

30 And grieve not the Holy Spirit of God, whereby ye are sealed unto the day of redemption. *(Is. 63:10)*

31 Let all bitterness, and wrath, and anger, and clamor, and evil speaking, be put away from you, with all malice:

32 And be ye kind one*to*another, tenderhearted, forgiving one another, even as God for*Christ's*sake hath forgiven you.

Walk in Love

5 Be ye therefore followers of God as dear children:

2 And walk in love, as Christ also hath loved us, and hath given himself for us an offering and a sacrifice to God for a sweetsmelling savor.

(Ex. 29:18; Ezek. 20:41)

3 But fornication, and all uncleanness, or covetousness, let it not*be*once*named among you, as becometh saints;

4 Neither filthiness, nor foolish talking, nor jesting, which*are*not*convenient: but rather giving*of*thanks.

5 For this ye know, that no whoremonger, nor unclean person, nor covetous man, who is an idolater, hath any inheritance in the kingdom of Christ and of God.

6 Let no man deceive you with vain words: for because of these things cometh the wrath of God upon the children of disobedience.

7 Be not ye therefore partakers with them.

8 For ye were sometimes darkness, but now *are ye* light in the Lord: walk as children of light:

9 (For the fruit of the Spirit *is* in   all goodness and righteousness and truth;)

10 Proving what is acceptable unto the Lord.

11 And have*no*fellowship with the unfruitful works of darkness, but rather reprove *them*.

¹⁰⁶³ ^{pin2076} ^{pr/an,aj149} ²⁵³² ^{pinf3004} ^{art,ppmp1096} ^{pre5259}
12 For it is a shame even to speak of those*things*which*are*done of
^{ppro846} ^{ad2931}
them in secret.

¹¹⁶¹ ^{art,ajn3956} ^{ppmp1651} ^{pinp5319} ^{pre5259} ^{art3588} ⁿⁿ⁵⁴⁵⁷ ¹⁰⁶³
13 But all things that are reproved are made manifest by the light: for
^{an,aj3956} ^{art,ppmp5319} ^{pin2076} ^{pr/an,nn5547}
whatsoever doth make manifest is light.

^{pre,repro1352} ^{pin3004} ^{aipm1453} ^{art,pap2518} ²⁵³² ^{aima450} ^{pre1537} ^{art3588} ^{ajn3498}
14 Wherefore he saith, Awake thou*that*sleepest, and arise from the dead,
²⁵³² ^{art,nn5547} ^{ft2017/ppro4671}
and Christ shall give*thee*light.   *(Is. 26:19; 51:17; 52:1; 60:1)*

^{pim991} ³⁷⁶⁷ ^{ad4459} ^{pin4043} ^{ad199} ³³⁶¹ ^{ad5613} ^{an,ajn781} ²³⁵ ^{ad5613} ^{an,ajn4680}
15 See then that ye walk circumspectly, not as fools, but as wise,

^{ppmp1805} ^{art3588} ⁿⁿ²⁵⁴⁰ ³⁷⁵⁴ ^{art3588} ⁿⁿ²²⁵⁰ ^{pin1526} ^{pr/an,aj4190}
16 Redeeming the time, because the days are evil.   *(Amos 5:13)*

^{pre1223/depro5124} ^{pim1096} ³³⁶¹ ^{pr/an,aj878} ²³⁵ ^{pr/pap4920} ^{inpro5101} ^{art3588} ^{pr/nn2307} ^{art3588}
17 Wherefore be ye not unwise, but understanding what the will of the
ⁿⁿ²⁹⁶²
Lord *is.*

²⁵³² ^{pim3182/3361} ^{an,nn3631} ^{pre1722/repro3739} ^{pin2076} ^{pr/an,nn810} ²³⁵ ^{pim4137} ^{pre1722}
18 And be*not*drunk with wine, wherein is excess; but be filled with
^{an,nn4151}
the Spirit;   *(Prov. 23:31 [Sept.]*

^{pap2980} ^{rxpro1438} ^{an,nn5568} ²⁵³² ^{an,nn5215} ²⁵³² ^{an,aj4152} ^{an,nn5603}
19 Speaking to yourselves in psalms and hymns and spiritual songs,
^{pap103} ²⁵³² ^{pap5567} ^{pre1722} ^{ppro5216} ^{art,nn2588} ^{art3588} ⁿⁿ²⁹⁶²
singing and making melody in your heart to the Lord;   *(Ps. 33:2,3)*

^{pap2168} ^{ad3842} ^{pre5228} ^{an,ajn3956} ^{art,nn2316} ²⁵³² ^{an,nn3962} ^{pre1722}
20 Giving thanks always for all things unto God and the Father in the
^{an,nn3686} ^{ppro2257} ^{art,nn2962} ^{an,nn2424} ^{an,nn5547}
name of our Lord Jesus Christ;

^{ppmp5293} ^{rcpro240} ^{pre1722} ^{an,nn5401} ^{an,nn2316}
☞ 21 Submitting yourselves one*to*another in the fear of God.

Husbands and Wives

^{art,nn1135} ^{pim5293} ^{art,aj2398} ^{an,nn435} ^{ad5613} ^{art3588} ⁿⁿ²⁹⁶²
22 Wives, submit yourselves unto your own husbands, as unto the Lord.

(Gen. 3:16)

³⁷⁵⁴ ^{art3588} ⁿⁿ⁴³⁵ ^{pin2076} ^{pr/an,nn2776} ^{art3588} ⁿⁿ¹¹³⁵ ²⁵³² ^{ad5613} ^{art,nn5547}
23 For the husband is the head of the wife, even as Christ is the
^{pr/an,nn2776} ^{art3588} ⁿⁿ¹⁵⁷⁷ ²⁵³² ^{epn846} ^{pin2076} ^{pr/an,nn4990} ^{art3588} ⁿⁿ⁴⁹⁸³
head of the church: and he is the savior of the body.

²³⁵ ^{ad5613} ^{art3588} ⁿⁿ¹⁵⁷⁷ ^{pinm5293} ^{art,nn5547} ^{ad3779} ^{art3588} ⁿⁿ¹¹³⁵
24 Therefore as the church is subject unto Christ, so *let* the wives *be* to
^{art,aj2398} ^{an,nn435} ^{pre1722} ^{an,ajn3956}
their own husbands in every thing.

☞ **5:21, 22** See notes on 1 Corinthians 14:33–40 and 1 Timothy 2:9–15.

art,nn435   pim25   art,rxpro1438   an,nn1135   ad2531   art,nn5547   2532   aina25   art3588   nn1577

25 Husbands, love your wives, even as Christ also loved the church,

2532   aina3860   rxpro1438   pre5228   ppro846

and gave himself for it;

2443   asba37   apta2511   ppro846   art3588   nn3067   art,nn5204   pre1722

26 That he might sanctify and cleanse it with the washing of water by

an,nn4487

the word,

2443   asba3936   ppro846   rxpro1438   an,aj1741   art,nn1577   3361   pap2192

27 That he might present it to himself a glorious church, not having

an,nn4695   2228   an,nn4512   2228   idpro5100   art,ajn5108   235   2443   psa5600   pr/an,aj40   2532

spot, or wrinkle, or any such thing; but that it should be holy and

pr/an,aj299

without blemish.

ad3779   pin3784   art,nn435   pinf25   art,rxpro1438   an,nn1135   ad5613   art,rxpro1438   an,nn4983

28 So ought men to love their wives as their own bodies.

art,pap25   art,rxpro1438 an,nn1135   pin25   rxpro1438

He*that*loveth his wife loveth himself.

1063   an,ajn3762   ad4218   aina3404   art,rxpro1438   an,nn4561   235   pin1625   2532

29 For no man ever yet hated his own flesh; but nourisheth and

pin2282   ppro846   2532   ad2531   art3588   nn2962   art3588   nn1577

cherisheth it, even as the Lord the church:

3754   pin2070   pr/an,nn3196   ppro846   art,nn4983   pre1537   ppro846   art,nn4561   2532   pre1537   ppro846

30 For we are members of his body, of his flesh, and of his

art,nn3747

bones.

pre473/depro5127   art,nn444   ft2641   ppro848   art,nn3962   2532   art,nn3384   2532

31 For*this*cause shall a man leave his father and mother, and shall be

fp4347   pre4314   ppro848 art,nn1135   2532   art,nu,ajn1417   fm2071 (pre1519) nu3391 an,nn4561

joined unto his wife, and they two shall be one flesh. *(Gen. 2:24)*

depro5124 pin2076   pr/an,aj3173   art,nn3466   1161   epn1473   pin3004   pre1519   an,nn5547   2532

32 This is a great mystery: but I speak concerning Christ and

(pre1519) art3588   nn1577

the church.

4133   an,aj1538   epn5210 (2532) art,pre2596/nu1528   ad3779   pim25   art,rxpro1438

33 Nevertheless let every one of you in particular so love his

an,nn1135   ad5613   rxpro1438   1161   art3588   nn1135   2443   psmp5399   art,nn435

wife even as himself; and the wife *see* that she reverence *her* husband.

Children and Parents

art,nn5043   pim5219 ppro5216   art,nn1118   pre1722   an,nn2962   1063 depro5124 pin2076 pr/an,aj1342

6 Children, obey your parents in the Lord: for this is right.

pim5091   ppro4675   art,nn3962   2532   art,nn3384   repro3748   pin2076   nu,aj4413

2 Honor thy father and mother; which is the first

pr/an,nn1785   pre1722   an,nn1860

commandment with promise;

2443   asbm1096   ad2095   ppro4671   2532   (fm2071)   pr/an,ajn3118   pre1909 art3588

3 That it may be well with thee, and thou mayest live long on the

nn1093

earth.   *(Ex. 20:12; Deut. 15:16)*

2532　　　　　　　　art,nn3962　　　　　pim3949/3361/ppro5216/art,nn5043　　　　235
4 And,　　ye　　fathers,　　provoke*not*your*children*to*wrath:　　but
pim1625/ppro846　　pre1722　　an,nn3809　2532　an,nn3559　　　an,nn2962
bring*them*up　in　the nurture and admonition of the Lord.

(Deut. 6:7,20-25; Ps. 78:4; Prov. 19:18; 22:6)

Servants and Masters

art,ajn1401　　　pim5219　　　　　　art,nn2962　　　　　pre2596
5 Servants, be obedient to them*that*are*your*masters according to the
an,nn4561　pre3326　an,nn5401　2532　an,nn5156　pre1722　an,nn572　　ppro5216　art,nn2588　ad5613
flesh, with　fear　and trembling,　in　singleness of your heart,　as　unto
art,nn5547
Christ;
　　3361　pre2596　　an,nn3787　　ad5613　　　an,ajn441　　235　ad5613　　an,ajn1401　　art,nn5547
6 Not with eyeservice,　as　menpleasers; but　as　the servants of Christ,
pap4160 art3588 nn2307　art,nn2316 pre1537　an,nn5590
doing the will of God from the heart;
　　pre3326　an,nn2133　　pap1398　　ad5613　art3588　nn2962　2532　3756　　an,nn444
7 With good will doing service,　as　to the Lord, and not to men:
　　pfp1492　　3754　repro3739/idpro5100/1437　an,ajn18　　an,ajn1538　asba4160　　depro5124
8 Knowing that　whatsoever　good thing any man doeth, the same shall he
fm2865　pre3844 art3588　nn2962　　1535　　pr/an,aj1401 1535 pr/an,aj1658
receive of　the Lord, whether *he be* bond　or　free.
　　　2532　　　　art,nn2962　pim4160　art3588　　　ppro846　　　pre4314　ppro846　　　pap447
9 And,　ye　masters,　do　the　same　things　unto　them,　forbearing
art,nn547　　pfp1492　　3754　ppro5216 (epn846)　art,nn2962　2532 pin2076 pre1722　an,nn3772　2532/3756　pin2076
threatening: knowing that your　　Master also　is　in　heaven; neither is
　　　　an,nn4382　　　pre3844 ppro846
there respect*of*persons with him.　　　　*(Deut. 10:17; 2 Chr. 19:7)*

The Christian's Armor

art,ajn3063　ppro3450　an,nn80　　pim1743　pre1722　an,nn2962 2532 pre1722 art3588　nn2904
10 Finally,　my　brethren, be strong　in　the Lord, and　in　the power of
ppro846 art,nn2479
his might.
aipm1746 art3588　　nn3833　　art,nn2316　ppro5209　　aipr1410　　ainf2476　pre4314
11 Put on the whole armor of God, that　ye　may be able to stand against
art3588　nn3180　　art3588 ajn1228
the wiles of the devil.
　　3754　ppro2254 pin2076/art,nn3823　3756　pre4314　an,nn4561　2532　an,nn129　235　pre4314
12 For　we　wrestle　not against　flesh　and　blood,　but　against
art,nn746　　pre4314　art,nn1849　pre4314 art3588　nn2888　　art3588　nn4655　　depro5127
principalities, against powers, against the rulers of the darkness of this
art,nn165　pre4314　art,ajn4152　art,nn4189　pre1722 pl/art,ajn2032
world, against spiritual wickedness in　high *places.*

13 Wherefore take unto you the whole armor of God, that ye may be able to withstand in the evil day, and having done all, to stand.

14 Stand therefore, having your loins girt about with truth, and having on the breastplate of righteousness;   *(Is. 11:5; 59:17)*

15 And your feet shod with the preparation of the gospel of peace;

(Is. 52:7; Nah. 1:15)

16 Above all, taking the shield of faith, wherewith ye shall be able to quench all the fiery darts of the wicked.   *(Ps. 7:13)*

17 And take the helmet of salvation, and the sword of the Spirit, which is the word of God: *(Is. 59:17; 11:4; Hos. 6:5)*

18 Praying always with all prayer and supplication in the Spirit, and watching thereunto with all perseverance and supplication for all saints;

19 And for me, that utterance may be given unto me, that I may open my mouth boldly, to make known the mystery of the gospel,

20 For which I am*an*ambassador in bonds: that therein I may speak boldly, as I ought to speak.

Benediction

☞ 21 But that ye also may know my affairs, *and* how I do, Tychicus, a beloved brother and faithful minister in the Lord, shall make known to you all things:

22 Whom I have sent unto you for the*same*purpose, that ye might know our affairs, and *that* he might comfort your hearts.

☞ **6:21, 22** See note on Colossians 4:7.

an,nn1515   art3588   nn80   2532 an,nn26 pre3326 an,nn4102 pre575 an,nn2316   an,nn3962
23 Peace *be* to the brethren, and love with faith, from God the Father

2532   an,nn2962 an,nn2424 an,nn5547
and the Lord Jesus Christ.

art,nn5485   pre3326 an,aj3956   art,pap25   ppro2257 art,nn2962 an,nn2424 an,nn5547 pre1722
24 Grace *be* with   all   them*that*love   our   Lord   Jesus   Christ   in

an,nn861   281
sincerity. Amen.

The Epistle of Paul the Apostle to the

PHILIPPIANS

The city of Philippi was named for Philip of Macedon, the father of Alexander the Great, who seized the city in 358 B.C. from the Thracians. Later, Octavius (Augustus Caesar) made Philippi a Roman colony. It was a principal city on the great *Egnatia* highway in Macedonia (this highway extended from Rome to Byzantium), and traders from both eastern and western countries stopped there often. This made it a strategic place for the spreading of the gospel.

In the early portion of Paul's second missionary journey, the Lord indicated that He wanted Paul to preach the gospel in Macedonia (Acts 16:9, 10). Apparently there were no synagogues in the city because on the Sabbath, Paul went out of the city and down to the bank of the river where he found Lydia and a number of other women who accepted what Paul had to say (Acts 16:13, 14). After Lydia and her family had been baptized, she asked Paul and his companions to stay at her house (Acts 16:15). Later, Paul and Silas were imprisoned for casting the unclean spirit out of a slave-girl (Acts 16:16–25). This led to the salvation of the jailor and his family (Acts 16:26–34).

Paul may have visited them again when he journeyed from Ephesus to Macedonia, because he spent the spring with them (Acts 20:1, 6; 2 Cor. 2:12, 13). The church that Paul established there was probably the first in all of Europe. The Apostle Paul is thought to have written this letter to the Philippians during his first Roman imprisonment (ca. A.D. 60–62). Paul, who was a tentmaker by trade (Acts 18:3), ordinarily refused to receive any financial assistance from the churches (2 Cor. 11:7–9). However, he did accept gifts from the Philippian brethren when he was in Thessalonica (Phil. 4:16, 18). Epaphroditus brought another gift to Paul during his imprisonment in Rome (Phil. 4:18). While Epaphroditus was there, he became severely sick and nearly died. He did recover, however, and carried this letter back to Philippi (Phil. 2:25–30).

Although there is no development of one particular theme, the concept of the all-sufficiency of Christ is found throughout the book. Christ gives meaning to life and causes people to serve Him even to their death (Phil. 1:20, 21).

1
an,nn3972 2532 an,nn5095 an,ajn1401 an,nn5547 an,nn5547 an,aj3956 art3588 ajn40
Paul and Timothy, the servants of Jesus Christ, to all the saints
pre1722 an,nn5547 an,nn2424 art,pap5607 pre1722 an,nn5375 pre4862 an,nn1985 2532
in Christ Jesus which are at Philippi, with the bishops and
an,nn1249
deacons:

an,nn5485 ppro5213 2532 an,nn1515 pre575 an,nn2316 ppro2257 an,nn3962 2532
2 Grace *be* unto you, and peace, from God our Father, and *from* the
an,nn2962 an,nn2424 an,nn5547
Lord Jesus Christ.

pin2168 ppro3450 art,nn2316 pre1909 an,aj3956 art,nn3417 ppro5216
3 I thank my God upon every remembrance of you,

ad3842   pre1722   an,aj3956   an,nn,1162   ppro3450 pre5228 ppro5216 an,aj3956   ppmp4160   art,nn1162   pre3326

4 Always in every prayer of mine for you   all making request with

am,nn5479

joy,

pre1909 ppro5216   art,nn2842   pre1519 art3588   nn2098   pre575   an,nu,aj4413 an,nn2250 ad891   art,ad3568

5 For your fellowship in the gospel from the first   day until now;

pfp3982   depro5124/ppro848   3754   art,aptm1728   an,aj18

☞ 6 Being confident of this*very*thing, that he*which*hath*begun a good

an,nn2041 pre1722 ppro5213   ft2005   ad891   an,nn2250   an,nn2424   an,nn5547

work in   you will perform *it* until the day of Jesus Christ:

ad2531   pin2076   pr/an,ajn1342   ppro1698   pinf5426 depro5124 pre5228 ppro5216 an,aj3956

7 Even as it is   meet for me to think this   of   you   all, because

ppro3165 aid2192 ppro5209 pre1722   art,nn2588   5037   pre1722 ppro3450 art,nn1199   2532   art3588

I have you in my heart; inasmuch as both in   my bonds, and in the

nn627   2532   an,nn951   art3588   nn2098   ppro5209 an,aj3956 pap5607   pr/an,ajn4791   ppro3450

defense and confirmation of the gospel, ye   all   are partakers of my

art,nn5485

grace.

1063   art,nn2316 pin2076 ppro3450 pr/an,nn3144 ad5613   pin1971   ppro5209 an,aj3956 pre1722

8 For God is   my record, how greatly*I*long*after you   all   in the

an,nn4698   an,nn2424 an,nn5547

bowels of Jesus Christ.

2532   depro5124   pinm4336   if2443 ppro5216 art,nn26   psa4052   ad2089 ad3123   2532   ad3123   pre1722

9 And this I pray, that your love may abound yet more and more   in

an,nn1922   2532   an,aj3956   an,nn144

knowledge and *in* all judgment;

ppro5209   aies1381   art,pap1308   2443   psa5600

☞ 10 That ye may approve things*that*are*excellent; that ye may be

pr/an,an1506 2532   pr/an,aj677   pre1519   an,nn2250   an,nn5547

sincere and without offense till the day of Christ;

pfpp4137   an,nn2590   an,nn1343   art3588   pre1223 an,nn2424

11 Being filled with the fruits of righteousness, which are by Jesus

an,nn5547   pre1519   an,nn1391 2532 an,nn1868   an,nn2316

Christ, unto the glory and praise of God.

Paul Glories in His Affliction

1161   pinm1014 ppro5209   pinf1097   an,nn80   3754   art3588

12 But I would ye should understand, brethren, that the things *which hap-*

pre2596 ppro1691   pfi2064   ad3123   pre1519   an,nn4297   art3588   nn2098

pened unto me have fallen out rather unto the furtherance of the gospel;

5620   ppro3450 art,nn1199 pre1722 an,nn5547 aifm1096   pr/an,aj5318 pre1722 an,aj3650 art3588   nn4232   2532

13 So that my bonds in Christ are manifest in   all   the palace, and in

an,aj3956 art,ajn3062

all other *places*;

2532   cd/art,aj4119   art3588   nn80   pre1722   an,nn2962   pfp3982   ppro3450

14 And many of the brethren in the Lord, waxing confident by my

art,nn1199   pinf5111/ad4056   pinf2980 art3588 nn3056   ad870

bonds, are*much*more*bold to speak the word without fear.

☞ **1:6, 10** See note on 1 Thessalonians 5:2.

idpro5100   3303   pin2784   art,nn5547   2532   pre1223   an,nn5355   2532   an,nn2054   1161   idpro5100   2532

15 Some indeed preach Christ even of envy and strife; and some also

pre1223   an,nn2107

of good will:

art3588/3303   pin2605   art,nn5547   pre1537   an,nn2052   3756   ad55   ppmp3633   pinf2018

16 The one preach Christ of contention, not sincerely, supposing to add

an,nn2347   ppro3450   art,nn1199

affliction to my bonds:

1161   art3588   pre1537   an,nn26   pfp1492   3754   pinm2749   pre1519   an,nn627

17 But the other of love, knowing that I am set for the defense of

art3588   nn2098

the gospel.

inpro5101   1063   4133   an,aj3956   an,nn5158   1535   an,nn4392   1535

18 What then? notwithstanding, every way, whether in pretense, or in

an,nn225   an,nn5547   pinp2605   2532   pre1722/depro5129   pin5463   235   2532   fm5463

truth, Christ is preached; and I therein do rejoice, yea, and will rejoice.

1063   pin1492   3754   depro5124   fm576   pre1519   ppro3427   an,nn4991   pre1223   ppro5216

19 For I know that this shall turn to my salvation through your

art,nn1162   2532   an,nn2024   art3588   nn4151   an,nn2424   an,nn5547

prayer, and the supply of the Spirit of Jesus Christ,   *(Job 13:16)*

pre2596   ppro3450   art,nn603   2532   an,nn1680   3854   pre1722

20 According to my earnest expectation and *my* hope, that in

an,ajn3762   fp153   235   pre1722   an,aj3956   an,nn3954   ad5613   ad3842   ad3568

nothing I shall be ashamed, but *that* with all boldness, as always, *so* now

2532   an,nn5547   fp3170   pre1722   ppro3450   art,nn4983   1535   pre1223   an,nn2222   1535   pre1223

also Christ shall be magnified in my body, whether *it be* by life, or by

an,nn2288

death.

1063   epn1698   art,pinf2198   pr/an,nn5547   2532   art,ainf599   pr/an,nn2771

21 For to me to live *is* Christ, and to die *is* gain.

1161   1487   art,pinf2198   pre1722   an,nn4561   depro5124   an,nn2590   ppro3427   an,nn2041   2532   inpro5101

22 But if I live in the flesh, this *is* the fruit of my labor: yet what I

fm138   pin1107   3756

shall choose I wot not.

1063   pinm4912   pre1537   art,nu,ajn1417   pap2192   art,nn1939   aies360   2532

23 For I am*in*a*strait between two, having a desire to depart, and to

pinf1511   pre4862   an,nn5547   an,ajn4183/ad3123   cd/an,aj2909

be with Christ; which is far better:

1161   art,ainf1961   pre1722   art3588   nn4561   pr/cd/an,aj316   pre1223   ppro5209

24 Nevertheless to abide in the flesh *is* more needful for you.

2532   pfp3982/depro5124   pin1492   3754   ft3306   2532   ft4839

25 And having*this*confidence, I know that I shall abide and continue with

ppro5213 an,aj3956 pre1519 ppro5216   art,nn4297   2532   an,nn5479   art,nn4102

you all for your furtherance and joy of faith;

2443   ppro5216   art,nn2745   psa4052   pre1722   an,nn2424   an,nn5547   pre1722   ppro1698

26 That your rejoicing may be*more*abundant in Jesus Christ for me

pre1223 ppro1699   art,nn3952   pre4314   ppro5209   ad3825

by my coming to you again.

an,aj3440   pim4176   ad516   art3588   nn2098   art,nn5547

27 Only let*your*conversation*be as*it*becometh the gospel of Christ:

2443   1535   apta2064   2532   apta1492   ppro5209   1535   pap548   asba191

that whether I come and see you, or else be absent, I may hear of ppro5216/art,pre4012   3754   pin4739   pre1722 nut1520 an,nn4151   nu3391 an,nn5590   pap4866

your affairs, that ye stand fast in one spirit, with one mind striving together

art3588 nn4102   art3588   nn2098

for the faith of the gospel;

2532   pre1722   an,ajn3367   ppmp4426/3361 pre5259   art,ppmp480   repro3748 pin2076   epn846   (3303)

28 And in nothing terrified by your adversaries: which is to them an

pr/an,nn1732   an,nn684   1161   epn5213   an,nn4991   2532 depro5124 pre575 an,nn2316

evident token of perdition, but to you of salvation, and that of God.

3754   epn5213   ainp5483   art,pre5228   an,nn5547   3756 an,ajn3440   art,pinf4100

29 For unto you it is given in*the*behalf of Christ, not only to believe

pre1519 ppro846   235   2532   art,pinf3958   pre5228/ppro846

on him, but also to suffer for*his*sake;

pap2192   art3588   ppro846   an,nn73   an,aj3634   aina21492 pre1722 ppro1698   2532   ad3568   pin191

30 Having the same conflict which ye saw in me, and now hear *to be*

pre1722 ppro1698

in me.

Exhortation to Be Like Christ

idpro1536/3767   an,nn3874   pre1722 an,nn5547 idpro1536   an,nn3890   an,nn26

2 If*there*be*therefore*any consolation in Christ, if any comfort of love,

idpro1536   an,nn2842   an,nn4151 idpro1536 an,nn4698   2532   an,nn3628

if any fellowship of the Spirit, if any bowels and mercies,

aima4137   ppro3450 art,nn5479 2443   psa5426/art,ppro846   pap2192 art3588 ppro846 an,nn26

2 Fulfill ye my joy, that ye be likeminded, having the same love, *being* of

pr/an,aj4861   art,nu1520 pr/pap5426

one accord, of one mind.

an,ajn3367   pre2596   an,nn2052 2228   an,nn2754   235   art,nn5012

3 *Let* nothing *be done* through strife or vainglory; but in lowliness*of*mind

rcpro240/ppmp2233   pap5242   rxpro1438

let each*esteem*other better than themselves.

pin4648   3361   an,ajn1538   art,rxpro1438   235   an,ajn1538   2532

4 Look not every man on his*own*things, but every man also on

art,ajn2087

the*things*of*others.

(1063)   pim5426/depro5124   pre1722 ppro5213 repro3739   2532 pre1722 an,nn5547 an,nn2424

5 Let*this*mind*be in you, which was also in Christ Jesus:

repro3739 pap5225 pre1722   an,nn3444   an,nn2316   aom2233   3756   an,nn725   art,pinf1511 pr/an,ajn2470

6 Who, being in the form of God, thought it not robbery to be equal

an,nn2316

with God:

2:6–8 This passage deals with the deity of Jesus Christ which was evidenced prior to His incarnation and continued through His death on the cross.

In comparing verse six of this passage with John 10:30, one can note that Christ is equal to God. In addition to this fact, He proved in His incarnation and death that He was still deity. In other words, in becoming a human being, Christ did not become less than deity. In speaking to His disciples, Jesus said, "My Father, which gave them me, is greater than all; and no man is able to pluck them out of the Father's hand. I and my Father are one" (John 10:29, 30). Because Christ is equal with God, those who would seek to "snatch" His true followers out of His hand would also be to remove them out of God's hand as well.

(continued on next page)

²³⁵   aina2758/rxpro1438   apta2983   an,nn3444

7 But made*himself*of*no*reputation, and took upon him the form of a

an,ajn1401   aptm1096 pre1722   an.nn3667   an,nn444

servant, and was made in the likeness of men:

2532   aptp2147   an,nn4976 ad5613   an,nn444   aina5013   rxpro1438   aptm1096

8 And being found in fashion as a man, he humbled himself, and became

pr/an,aj5255   ad3360 an,nn2288   1161   an,nn2288   an,nn4716

obedient unto death, even the death of the cross.

pre,repro1352 art,nn2316   2532   aina5251   ppro846   2532   aom5483   ppro846   an,nn3686

9 Wherefore God also hath highly exalted him, and given him a name

art3588   pre5228   an,aj3956   an,nn3686

which is above every name:

2443   pre1722 art3588   nn3686   an,nn2424   an,aj3956   an,nn1119   asba2578

10 That at the name of Jesus every knee should bow, of *things*

an,ajn2032   2532   an,ajn1919   2532   an,ajn2709

in heaven, and *things* in earth, and *things* under*the*earth;

2532   an,aj3956   an,nn1100   asbm1843   3754   an,nn2424 an,nn5547   pr/an,nn2962 pre1519

11 And *that* every tongue should confess that Jesus Christ *is* Lord, to the

an,nn1391   an,nn2316   an,nn3962

glory of God the Father.   *(Is. 45:23)*

"Work Out Your Own Salvation"

5620   ppro3450   an,ajn27   ad2531   ad3842   aina5219   3361   ad5613   pre1722

12 Wherefore, my beloved, as ye have always obeyed, not as in

ppro3450   art,nn3952   an,ajn3440   235   ad3568   an,ajn4183   ad3123   pre1722   ppro3450   art,nn666   pim2716

my presence only, but now much more in my absence, work out

rxpro1438   art,nn4991   pre3326 an,nn5401 2532   an,nn5156

your own salvation with fear and trembling.   *(Ps. 2:11)*

(continued from previous page)

     Therefore, Paul states in Philippians 2:6, 7 that Christ ". . . thought it not robbery to be equal with God: but made himself of no reputation . . . ." What is to be understood here is that Christ merely relinquished His glory which He had due to the fact that He was deity. Prior to His death, He asked the Father to glorify Him in a position next to God with the glory which He had even before the world was created (John 17:5). If Christ had come to the earth with an emphasis on His equality with God and all that entailed, the world would have only wondered at Him, not received Him as Savior. The Lord lacked recognition and glory by men while He was on earth as the Incarnate God. However, as far as God was concerned, Christ never lost His position before God.

     The phrase in verse seven, "took upon him the form of a servant," should be understood as "having taken . . ." which denotes that He became as a servant in man's likeness at His incarnation, and that he did not possess that form before that time. His purpose in coming as a man in order to die for the sins of mankind. The key idea to consider is that Christ was and is who He claimed to be—God. He appeared in the form of man so that He could die in order to satisfy God's righteous indignation against man's sin (1 John 2:2). The fact that He came as a human being did not remove His position in heaven, but allowed Him to carry out His Father's will. Christ was still equal with God even while He was dying on the cross. In fact, Jesus experienced all the feelings that exist in the human body, yet He never allowed those things to block His mindset away from the cross or even lead to sin (Heb. 4:15).

     The last verse of this passage illustrates true humility in action. It is said of Christ that ". . . he humbled himself, and became obedient unto death . . . ." The obedience was a result of the humility that Christ displayed in willingly going to the cross. At that time He was fully God, yet He set aside that glory in order to accomplish God's will.

1063   pin2076 art,nn2316   pr/art,pap1754   pre1722 ppro5213   2532   art,pinf2309   2532   art,pinf1754

13 For it is God which worketh in you both to will and to do of

pre5228   art,nn2107

his good pleasure.

pim4160   an,ajn3956   ad*5565   an,nn1112   2532   an,nn1261

14 Do all things without murmurings and disputings:

2443   asbm1096   pr/an,nj273   2532   pr/an,aj185   pr/an,nn5043   an,nn2316

15 That ye may be blameless and harmless, the sons of God,

pr/an,aj298   pre1722   an,ajn3319   an,aj4646   2532   pfpp1294   an,nn1074   pre1722

without rebuke, in the midst of a crooked and perverse nation, among

repro3739   pim5316 ad5613 an,nn5458 pre1722   an,nn2889

whom ye shine as lights in the world;   *(Deut. 32:5; Dan. 12:3)*

       pap1907   an,nn3056   an,nn2222   3754   ppro1698   pre1519/an,nn2745 pre1519   an,nn2250

☞ 16 Holding forth the word of life; that I may rejoice in the day of

an,nn5547   3754   3756   aina5143 pre1519 an,ajn2756   3761   aina2872   pre1519 an,ajn2756

Christ, that I have not run in vain, neither labored in vain.

                                                  (Is. 49:4; 65:23)

235   1499   pinm4689   pre1909 art3588   nn2378   2532   an,nn3009   ppro5216 art,nn4102

17 Yea, and if I be offered upon the sacrifice and service of your faith, I

pin5463 2532   pin4796   ppro5213 an,aj3956

joy, and rejoice with you all.

(1611)   art3588   ppro846   2532   epn5210 pim5463 2532   pin4796   ppro3427

18 For the same cause also do ye joy, and rejoice with me.

1161   pin1679 pre1722   an,nn2962 an,nn2424   ainf3992   an,nn5095   ad5030   ppro5213 2443

19 But I trust in the Lord Jesus to send Timothy shortly unto you, that

epn2504   psa2174   apta1097 art,pre4012/ppro5216

I also may be*of*good*comfort, when I know your state.

1063   pin2192 an,ajn3762   pr/an,aj2473   repro3748   ad1104   ft3309   pre4012/art,ppro5216

20 For I have no man likeminded, who will naturally care for*your*state.

1063   art,ajn3956 pin2212   art,rxpro1438   3756   art3588   an,nn2424   art,nn5547

21 For all seek their own, not the things which are Jesus Christ's.

1161   pin1097 art3588   nn1382   ppro846   3754   ad5613   an,nn5043   an,nn3962

22 But ye know the proof of him, that, as a son with the father, he hath

aina1398   pre4862 ppro1698 pre1519 art3588   nn2098

served with me in the gospel.

depro5126   (3303) 3767   pin1679   ainf3992   ad1824   ad5613   asba872/302

23 Him therefore I hope to send presently, so*soon*as I shall see

art,pre4012   ppro1691

how*it*will*go*with me.

1161   pfi3982 pre1722   an,nn2962 3754   2532   epn846   fm2064   ad5030

24 But I trust in the Lord that I also myself shall come shortly.

1161   aom2233   an,ajn316   ainf3992 pre4314 ppro5209   an,nn1891   ppro3450

25 Yet I supposed it necessary to send to you Epaphroditus, my

art,nn80   2532   an,ajn4904   2532   an,nn4961   1161 epn5216   an,nn652   2532

brother, and companion*in*labor, and fellow soldier, but your messenger, and

an,nn3011   ppro3450 art,nn5532

he*that*ministered to my wants.

☞ **2:16** See note on 1 Thessalonians 5:2.

26 For he longed after you all, and was full*of*heaviness, because that ye had heard that he had been sick.

27 For indeed he was sick nigh unto death: but God had mercy on him; and not on him only, but on me also, lest I should have sorrow upon sorrow.

28 I sent him therefore the*more*carefully, that, when ye see him again, ye may rejoice, and that I may be the less sorrowful.

29 Receive him therefore in the Lord with all gladness; and hold such in reputation:

30 Because for the work of Christ he was nigh unto death, not regarding his life, to supply your lack of service toward me.

Count All Gain As Loss

3 Finally, my brethren, rejoice in the Lord. To write the same things to you, to me indeed is not grievous, but for you it is safe.

2 Beware of dogs, beware of evil workers, beware of the concision.

(Ps. 22:16,20)

3 For we are the circumcision, which worship God in the spirit, and rejoice in Christ Jesus, and have*no*confidence in the flesh.

4 Though I might also have confidence in the flesh. If any other man thinketh that he hath whereof he might trust in the flesh, I more:

5 Circumcised the eighth day, of the stock of Israel, of the tribe of Benjamin, a Hebrew of the Hebrews; as touching the law, a Pharisee;

(Gen. 17:12)

6 Concerning zeal, persecuting the church; touching the righteousness which is in the law, blameless.

235   repro3748   ipf2258   pr/an,nn2771   ppro3427   depro5023   pfip2233   pr/an,nn2209   pre1223

7 But what things were gain to me, those I counted loss for

art,nn5547

Christ.

235   3304   2532   pinm2233   an,ajn3956   (pinf1511)   pr/an,nn2209   pre1223   art3588   pap5242

8 Yea doubtless, and I count all things *but* loss for the excellency of

art3588   nn1108   an,nn5547   an,nn2424   ppro3450   art,nn2962   pre1223   repro3739   ainp2210

the knowledge of Christ Jesus my Lord: for whom I have suffered*the*loss

art,ajn3956   2532   pinm2233   (pinf1511)   pr/an,nn4657   2443   asba2770   an,nn5547

of all things, and do count them *but* dung, that I may win Christ,

2532   asbp2147   pre1722   ppro846   3361   pap2192   popro1699   an,nn1343   art3588

9 And be found in him, not having mine own righteousness, which is

pre1537   an,nn3551   235   art3588   pre1223   an,nn4102   an,nn5547   art3588   nn1343

of the law, but that which is through the faith of Christ, the righteousness

pre1537 an,nn2316 pre1909 art,nn4102

which is of God by faith:

infg1097   ppro846   2532   art3588   nn1411   ppro846   art,nn386   2532   art3588

10 That I may know him, and the power of his resurrection, and the

nn2842   ppro846   art,nn3804   ppmp4833   ppro846   art,nn2288

fellowship of his sufferings, being made conformable unto his death;

ad1513   asba2658   pre1519   art3588   nn1815   art3588   ajn3498

11 If*by*any*means I might attain unto the resurrection of the dead.

"The High Calling of God"

3756   3754   ad2235   aina2983   2228   pfip5048/ad2235   1161

12 Not as though I had already attained, either were*already*perfect: but

pin1377   1499   asba2638   pre1909 repro3739   2532   ainp2638

I follow after, if that I may apprehend that for which also I am apprehended

pre5259 art,nn5547 an,nn2424

of Christ Jesus.

an,nn80   epn1473   pinm3049   3756   rxpro1683   pfin2638   1161

13 Brethren, I count not myself to have apprehended: but *this*

nu,ajn1520   ppmp1950   art,ad*3694/3303   1161   ppmp1901

one thing *I do,* forgetting those*things*which*are*behind, and reaching forth

art,ad*1715

unto those*things*which*are*before,

pin1377   pre2596   an,nn4649 pre1909 art3588   nn1017   art3588   ad507   nn2821   art,nn2516 pre1722

14 I press toward the mark for the prize of the high calling of God in

an,nn5547 an,nn2424

Christ Jesus.

3767   an,ajn3745   pr/an,aj5046   psa5426/depro5124   2532

15 Let us therefore, as*many*as be perfect, be*thus*minded: and

idpro1536   pin5426/ad2088   art,nn2316   ft601   2532   depro5124

if*in*any*thing ye be*otherwise*minded, God shall reveal even this unto

ppro5213

you.

4133   pre1519/repro3739   aina5348   pinf4748   art3588

16 Nevertheless, whereto we have already attained, let us walk by the

ppro846 an,nn2583   pinf5426 art3588   ppro846

same rule, let us mind the same thing.

17 Brethren, be followers together of me, and mark them*which*walk so as ye have us for an example.

18 (For many walk, of whom I have told you often, and now tell you even weeping, *that they are* the enemies of the cross of Christ:

19 Whose end *is* destruction, whose God *is their* belly, and *whose* glory *is* in their shame, who mind earthly things.)

20 For our conversation is in heaven; from whence also we look for the Savior, the Lord Jesus Christ:

21 Who shall change our vile body, that it may be fashioned like unto his glorious body, according to the working whereby he is able even to subdue all things unto himself.

(*Ps. 8:6*)

"Rejoice in the Lord"

4 Therefore, my brethren dearly beloved and longed for, my joy and crown, so stand fast in the Lord, *my* dearly beloved.

2 I beseech Euodias, and beseech Syntyche, that they be*of*the*same*mind in the Lord.

3 And I entreat thee also, true yokefellow, help those women which labored with me in the gospel, with Clement also, and *with* other my fellowlaborers, whose names *are* in the book of life.

(*Ex. 32:32,33; Ps. 69:28; Dan. 12:1*)

4 Rejoice in the Lord always: *and* again I say, Rejoice.

5 Let your moderation be known unto all men. The Lord *is* at hand.

6 Be careful for nothing; but in every thing by prayer and supplication with thanksgiving let your requests be made known unto God.

²⁵³² ^{art3588} ⁿⁿ¹⁵¹⁵ ^{art,nn2316} ^{art,pap5242} ^{an,aj3956} ^{an,nn3563} ^{ft5432}
7 And the peace of God, which passeth all understanding, shall keep
^{ppro5216} ^{art,nn2588} ^{2532 (ppro5216)} ^{art,nn3540} ^{pre1722} ^{an,nn5547} ^{an,nn2424}
your hearts and   minds through Christ Jesus.   *(Is. 26:3)*

^{art,ajn3063} ^{an,nn80} ^{an,ajn3745} ^{pin2076} ^{pr/an,aj227} ^{an,ajn3745}
8 Finally, brethren, whatsoever things are true, whatsoever things *are*
^{pr/an,aj4586} ^{an,ajn3745} ^{pr/an,aj1342} ^{an,ajn3745} ^{pr/an,aj53}
honest, whatsoever things *are* just, whatsoever things *are* pure,
^{an,ajn3745} ^{pr/an,aj4375} ^{an,ajn3745} ^{pr/an,aj2163}
whatsoever things *are* lovely, whatsoever things *are* of good report;
^{idpro1536} ^{an,nn703} ²⁵³² ^{idpro1536} ^{an,nn1868} ^{pim3049} ^{depro5023}
if*there*be*any virtue, and if*there*be*any praise, think on these things.
^{depro5023} ^{repro3739} ²⁵³² ^{aina3129} ²⁵³² ^{aina3880} ²⁵³² ^{aina191} ²⁵³²
9 Those things, which ye have both learned, and received, and heard, and
^{aina1492} ^{pre1722} ^{ppro1698} ^{pim4238} ²⁵³² ^{art3588} ⁿⁿ²³¹⁶ ^{art,nn1515} ^{fm2071} ^{pre3326} ^{ppro5216}
seen in me, do: and the God of peace shall be with you.

Contentment

¹¹⁶¹ ^{aina5463} ^{pre1722} ^{an,nn2962} ^{ad3171} ³⁷⁵⁴ ^{ad2235} ^{ad4218} ^{art,pinf5426}
10 But I rejoiced in the Lord greatly, that now at*the*last your care
^{pre5228} ^{ppro1700} ^{aina330} ^{pre1909/repro3739} ²⁵³² ^{ipf5426} ¹¹⁶¹
of me hath flourished again; wherein ye were also careful, but ye
^{ipf170}
lacked opportunity.
³⁷⁵⁶ ³⁷⁵⁴ ^{pin3004} ^{pre2596} ^{an,nn5304} ¹⁰⁶³ ^{epn1473} ^{aina3129} ^{pre1722}
11 Not that I speak in*respect*of want: for I have learned, in
^{repro3739} ^{pin1510} ^{pinf1511} ^{pr/an,aj842}
whatsoever state I am, *therewith* to be content.
⁽¹¹⁶¹⁾ ^{pin1492} ^{pifm5013} ²⁵³² ^{pin1492} ^{pinf4052 (pre1722)}
12 I know both how to be abased, and I know how to abound:
^{an,ajn3956} ²⁵³² ^{pre1722} ^{an,ajn3956} ^{pfip3453} ²⁵³² ^{pifm5526} ²⁵³²
every where and in all things I am instructed both to be full and to
^{pinf3983} ²⁵³² ^{pinf4052} ²⁵³² ^{pifm5302}
be hungry, both to abound and to suffer need.
^{pin2480} ^{an,ajn3956} ^{pre1722} ^{an,nn5547} ^{art,pap1743} ^{ppro3165}
13 I can do all things through Christ which strengtheneth me.
⁴¹³³ ^{ad2573} ^{aina4160} ^{apta4790} ^{ppro3450}
14 Notwithstanding ye have well done, that ye did communicate with my
^{art,nn2347}
affliction.
¹¹⁶¹ ^{epn5210} ^{an,nn5374} ^{pin1492} ²⁵³² ³⁷⁵⁴ ^{pre1722} ^{an,nn746} ^{art3588} ⁿⁿ²⁰⁹⁸
15 Now ye Philippians know also, that in the beginning of the gospel,
^{ad3753} ^{aina1831} ^{pre575} ^{an,nn3109} ^{an,aj3762} ^{an,nn1577} ^{aina2841} ^{ppro3427}
when I departed from Macedonia, no church communicated with me
^{pre1519/an,nn3056} ^{an,nn1394} ²⁵³² ^{an,nn3028} ¹⁵⁰⁸ ^{ppro5210} ^{an,aj3441}
as concerning giving and receiving, but ye only.
³⁷⁵⁴ ²⁵³² ^{pre1722} ^{an,nn2332} ^{aina3992 (2532)} ^{nu,ad530/2532/nu,ad1364} ^{pre1519} ^{ppro3427}
16 For even in Thessalonica ye sent once*and*again unto my
^{art,nn5532}
necessity.

17 Not because I desire a gift: but I desire fruit that*may*abound to your account.

18 But I have all, and abound: I am full, having received of Epaphroditus the things *which were sent* from you, an odor of a sweet smell, a sacrifice acceptable, well-pleasing to God. *(Gen. 8:21; Ex. 29:18; Ezek. 20:41)*

19 But my God shall supply all your need according to his riches in glory by Christ Jesus.

20 Now unto God and our Father *be* glory forever*and*ever. Amen.

21 Salute every saint in Christ Jesus. The brethren which are with me greet you.

22 All the saints salute you, chiefly they that are of Caesar's household.

23 The grace of our Lord Jesus Christ *be* with you all. Amen.

The Epistle of Paul the Apostle to the
COLOSSIANS

The town of Colosse was located on a ridge overlooking the Lycus River valley in central Asia Minor. At the time of Paul's writing, its neighboring cities, Laodicea and Hierapolis, were becoming more important while Colosse was in a period of decline. Travelers were using a newer road that went through the other two cities but by-passed Colosse. Churches were established in all three of these cities by Epaphras (Col. 4:12, 13) and Timothy, but Paul never visited the believers there personally (Col. 2:1). However, he did tell Philemon, a native of Colosse, that he was hoping to visit him (Phile. 1:22).

Paul is believed to have written to the Colossians about A.D. 60 during his first imprisonment in Rome. While most agree that it was written about the same time as Philemon, Ephesians, and Philippians, it is not certain which was written first. Epaphras (also a native of Colosse) came to visit Paul in prison and gave him a report not only of the progress being made there but also of the problem with false teachers who had gained a foothold in the church. Paul sent the letter back with Onesimus (Philemon's slave) and Tychicus (Col. 4:7–9), but for some unknown reason Epaphras did not return at that time (Col. 4:12).

Paul's purpose in writing this letter was to refute the heretical teaching that was influencing the Colossian church. Paul's references to circumcision, food regulations, and feast days (Col. 2:11–16) indicate that this heresy involved Judaistic tendencies. It differed from the heresy in Galatia in that it integrated an early form of Gnostic philosophy which consisted of ascetic ideas (Col. 2:20–23), and the worship of angels as intermediaries between God and man (Col. 2:18, 19). Supposedly, one could achieve perfection by progressing through a number of initiations and levels of wisdom in spiritual mysteries.

Instead of refuting the false teaching point by point, Paul shows that all things are fulfilled in the person of Christ. He stresses that all wisdom and spiritual understanding can be found in the God-Man who redeemed them and now holds authority over all things (Col. 1:9—2:19). He then goes on to explain the relationship of "mortifying" the deeds of the flesh to being alive through the Spirit (Col. 2:20—3:17). Finally, he gives practical injunctions for Christian behavior (Col. 3:18—4:6).

1
an,nn3972　　　an,nn652　　　an,nn2424　an,nn5547　pre1223　　　an,nn2307　　　an,nn2316　2532　　an,nn5095
Paul, an apostle of Jesus Christ by the will of God, and Timothy *our*
art,nn80
brother,

art3588　　2532　　2532　　an,aj4103　　an,nn80　　pre1722　an,nn5547　　　　　　pre1722　an,nn2857
2 To the saints and faithful brethren in Christ which are at Colosse:

an,nn5485　　　　　ppro5213　2532　an,nn1515　pre575　an,nn2316　ppro2257　an,nn3962　2532　　　an,nn2962　an,nn2424

Grace *be* unto you, and peace, from God our Father and the Lord Jesus

an,nn5547

Christ.

The Progress of the Gospel

　　　　　　　　　pin2168　　　　　art,nn2316　2532　　　　an,nn3962　　ppro2257　art,nn2962　an,nn2424　an,nn5547

3 We give thanks to God and the Father of our Lord Jesus Christ,

ppmp4336　ad3842　pre4012　ppro5216

praying always for you,

　　　　　　　apta191　　ppro5216　art,nn4102　pre1722　an,nn5547　an,nn2424　2532　　art3588　nn26

☞ 4 Since we heard of your faith in Christ Jesus, and of the love *which*

(art3588)　　pre1519　an,aj3956　art3588　ajn40

ye have to all the saints.

　　　pre1223　art3588　nm1680　　　art,ppmp606　　　　ppro5213　pre1722　art,nn3772　repro3739

5 For the hope which*is*laid*up for you in heaven, whereof ye

　aina4257　　pre1722　art3588　nn3056　art3588　nn225　art3588　nn2098

heard before in the word of the truth of the gospel;

　　　　art,pap3918　　　pre1519　ppro5209　ad2531　(2532)　　　pre1722　an,aj3956　art3588　nn2889　2532　(pin2076)

6 Which*is*come unto you, as *it is* in all the world; and

　　　　　　　　pr/ppmp2592　　ad2531　　　2532　pre1722　ppro5213　pre575　(repro3739)　an,nn2250　aina191

bringeth*forth*fruit, as *it doth* also in you, since the day ye heard *of it,*

2532　aina1921　art3588　nn5485　art,nn2316　pre1722　an,nn225

and knew the grace of God in truth:

　　ad2531　　　2532　aina3129　pre575　an,nn1889　ppro2257　art,aj27　　an,nn4889　repro3739　pin2076　pre5228

☞ 7 As ye also learned of Epaphras our dear fellowservant, who is for

ppro5216　an,aj4103　pr/an,nn1249　art,nn5547

you a faithful minister of Christ;

　　art3588　2532　apta1213　　　ppro2254　ppro5216　art,nn26　pre1722　an,nn4151

8 Who also declared unto us your love in the Spirit.

pre1223　depro5124　epn2249　2532　pre575　(repro3739)　an,nn2250　aina191　　3756　pinm3793

☞ 9 For this cause we also, since the day we heard *it,* do not cease to

ppmp4336　pre5228　ppro5216　2532　ppmp154　2443　　　asbp4137　art3588　nn1922　ppro846

pray for you, and to desire that ye might be filled with the knowledge of his

art,nn2307　pre1722　an,aj3956　an,nn4678　2532　an,aj4152　an,nn4907

will in all wisdom and spiritual understanding;

　　　ppro5209　　ainf4043　ad516　art3588　nn2962　pre1519　an,aj3956　an,nn699

10 That ye might walk worthy of the Lord unto all pleasing,

pap2592　pre1722　an,aj3956　an,aj18　an,nn2041　2532　ppmp837　pre1519　art3588　nn1922　art,nn2316

being fruitful in every good work, and increasing in the knowledge of God;

☞ 1:4–8 See introduction to Colossians.

☞ 1:7 Epaphras (also mentioned in Col. 4:12 and Phile. 1:23) was one of Paul's friends and associates, called by him a "fellow bondservant" and "fellow prisoner." He may have been imprisoned with Paul. Epaphras evangelized the cities of the Lycus Valley in Phrygia under Paul's direction and founded the churches of Colosse, Hierapolis, and Laodicea. Later, he visited Paul in prison in Rome, and it was his news of the conditions in the churches of the Lycus Valley that caused Paul to write the Book of Colossians.

☞ 1:9 The heresy that prevailed in Colosse as well as in other contemporary churches was Gnosticism (see note on Col. 2:8–23).

_{ppmp1412   pre1722 an,aj3956   an,nn1411   pre2596   ppro846 art,an1391   art,nn2904   pre1519}

11 Strengthened with all might, according to his glorious power, unto

_{an,aj3956   an,nn5281   2532   an,nn3115   pre3326   an,nn5479}

all patience and longsuffering with joyfulness;

_{pap2168   art3588   nn3962   art,apta2427/ppro2248}

12 Giving thanks unto the Father, which*hath*made*us*meet to

_{pre1519/art,nn3310   art3588   nn2819   art3588   ajn40   pre1722 art,nn5457}

be partakers of the inheritance of the saints in light:

_{repro3739   aom4506   ppro2248 pre1537 art3588   nn1849   art,nn4655   2532}

13 Who hath delivered us from the power of darkness, and hath

_{aina3179   pre1519 art3588   nn932   ppro848 art,nn26 art,nn5207}

translated *us* into the kingdom of his dear Son:

_{pre1722   repro3739   pin2192   art,nn629   pre1223   ppro846   art,nn129   art3588}

14 In whom we have redemption through his blood, *even* the

_{nn859   art,nn266}

forgiveness of sins:

The Preeminence of Christ

_{repro3739 pin2076   pr/an,nn1504   art3588   aj517   art,nn2316   pr/an,aj4416   an,aj3956}

🔑 15 Who is the image of the invisible God, the firstborn of every

_{an,nn2937}

creature:

_{3754   pre1722 ppro846   art,ajn3956   ainp2936   art3588   pre1722 art,nn3772   2532 art3588}

16 For by him were all things created, that are in heaven, and that are

_{pre1909 art,nn1093 art,ajn3707   2532   art,ajn517   1535   an,nn2362   1535   an,nn2963   1535}

in earth, visible and invisible, whether *they be* thrones, or dominions, or

_{an,nn746   1535   an,nn1849   art,ajn3956   pfip2936   pre1223 ppro846 2532 pre1519 ppro846}

principalities, or powers: all things were created by him, and for him:

_{2532 epn846 pin2076   pre4253   an,ajn3956   2532 pre1722 ppro846   art,ajn3956   pfi4921}

17 And he is before all things, and by him all things consist.

_{2532   epn846 pin2076 art3588 pr/nn2776   art3588   nn4983   art3588   nn1577   repro3739 pin2076}

18 And he is the head of the body, the church: who is the

_{pr/an,nn746   pr/an,aj4416 pre1537 art3588 ajn3498 2443 pre1722 an,ajn3956   epn846}

beginning, the firstborn from the dead; that in all *things* he might

_{asbm1096   pr/pap4409}

have the preeminence.

_{3754   aina2106   pre1722 epn846   an,aj3956 art,nn4138   ainf2730}

19 For it pleased *the Father* that in him should all fullness dwell;

_{2532   apta1517   pre1223   art3588   nn129   ppro846 art,nn4716 pre1223 ppro846}

20 And, having made peace through the blood of his cross, by him to

---

🔑 **1:15–18** In the first verse of this passage, Jesus Christ is presented as the image of God, the invisible One (John 1:18). *Eikốn* (1504) "image," always assumes a prototype (the original form from which it is drawn), not merely a thing it resembles (e.g., the reflection of the sun in the water is an *eikốn*). Paul was telling the Colossians here that Jesus Christ has a "prototype," God the Father who is invisible. The relationship between Christ and the Father God is not coincidental (see the notes on John 1:18 and Phil. 2:6–8).

The other significant word is *prōtótokos* (4416), translated as "firstborn." What it means in this passage is that Christ holds the same relation to all creation as God the Father, because He is above all creation.

ainf604 · art,ajn3956 · pre1519 · ppro848 · pre1223 · ppro846 · 1535 · art3588 · pre1909

reconcile all things unto himself; by him, *I say,* whether *they be* things in

art,nn1093 1535 art3588 pre1722 art,nn3772

earth, or things in heaven.

2532 · ppro5209 · pap5607 · ad4218 · pr/pfpp526 · 2532 · pr/an,ajn2190 · art,nn1271 · pre1722

21 And you, that were sometime alienated and enemies in *your* mind by

art,aj4190 · art,nn2041 · 1161 · ad3570 · aina604

wicked works, yet now hath he reconciled

pre1722 · art3588 · nn4983 · ppro848 · art,nn4561 · pre1223 · art,nn2288 · ainf3936 · ppro5209 · pr/an,aj40 · 2532

22 In the body of his flesh through death, to present you holy and

pr/an,aj299 · 2532 · pr/an,aj410 · pre2714/ppro848

unblamable and unreprovable in*his*sight:

1489 · pin1961 · art3588 · nn4102 · pr/pfpp2311 · 2532 · pr/an,aj1476 · 2532 · 3361

23 If ye continue in the faith grounded and settled, and *be* not

pr/ppmp3334 · pre575 · art3588 · nn1680 · art3588 · nn2098 · repro3739 · aina191

moved away from the hope of the gospel, which ye have heard, *and*

art,aptp2784 · pre1722 · an,aj3956 · art,nn2937 · art3588 · pre5259 · art,nn3772 · repro3739 · epn1473

which*was*preached to every creature which is under heaven; whereof I

an,nn3972 · aom1096 · pr/an,nn1249

Paul am made a minister;

Exhortation to Steadfastness

repro3739 · ad3568 · pin5463 · pre1722 · ppro3450 · art,nn3804 · pre5228 · ppro5216 · 2532 · pin466

24 Who now rejoice in my sufferings for you, and fill up

art,nn5303 · art3588 · nn2347 · art,nn5547 · pre1722 · ppro3450 · art,nn4561

that*which*is*behind of the afflictions of Christ in my flesh

pre5228/ppro846/art,nn4983 · repro,pin3603 · art,3588 · pr/nn1577

for*his*body's*sake, which is the church:

repro3739 · epn1473 · aom1096 · pr/an,nn1249 · pre2596 · art3588 · nn3622

25 Whereof I am made a minister, according to the dispensation of

art,nn2316 · art,aptp1325 · ppro3427 · pre1519 · ppro5209 · ainf4137 · art3588 · nn3056 · art,nn2316

God which*is*given to me for you, to fulfill the word of God;

art3588 · nn3466 · art,pfpp613 · pre575 · art,nn165 · 2532 · pre575

26 *Even* the mystery which*hath*been*hid from ages and from

art,nn1074 · 1161 · ad3570 · ainp5319 · ppro846 · art,ajn40

generations, but now is made manifest to his saints:

repro3739 · art,nn2316 · aina2309 · ainf1107 · inpro5101 · art3588 · pr/nn4149 · art3588 · nn1391

27 To whom God would make known what *is* the riches of the glory of

depro5127 · art,nn3466 · pre1722 · art3588 · nn1484 · repro3739 · pin2076 · pr/an,nn5547 · pre1722 · ppro5213 · art3588 · pr/nn1680

this mystery among the Gentiles; which is Christ in you, the hope of

art,nn1391

glory:

repro3739 · epn2249 · pin2605 · pap3560 · an,aj3956 · an,nn444 · 2532 · pap1321 · an,aj3956 · an,nn444 · pre1722

28 Whom we preach, warning every man, and teaching every man in

an,aj3956 · an,nn4678 · 2443 · asba3936 · an,aj3956 · an,nn444 · pr/an,aj5046 · pre1722 · an,nn5547 · an,nn2424

all wisdom; that we may present every man perfect in Christ Jesus:

pre1519/repro3739 · 2532 · pin2872 · ppmp75 · pre2596 · ppro846 · art,nn1753

29 Whereunto I also labor, striving according to his working,

art,ppmp1754 · pre1722 · ppro1698 · pre1722/an,nn1411

which worketh in me mightily.

Warnings Against Errors

2 For I would that ye knew what great conflict I have for you, and *for*
them at Laodicea, and *for* as*many*as have not seen my face in
the flesh;

2 That their hearts might be comforted, being knit together in love, and
unto all riches of the full assurance of understanding, to the
acknowledgement of the mystery of God, and of the Father, and of
Christ;

3 In whom are hid all the treasures of wisdom and knowledge.

(Is. 45:3)

4 And this I say, lest any man should beguile you with enticing words.

5 For though I be absent in the flesh, yet am I with you in the spirit,
joying and beholding your order, and the steadfastness of your faith in
Christ.

6 As ye have therefore received Christ Jesus the Lord, *so* walk ye in
him:

7 Rooted and built up in him, and established in the faith, as ye have
been taught, abounding therein with thanksgiving.

☞ 8 Beware lest any man spoil you through philosophy and vain deceit,

---

☞ **2:8–23** Gnosticism is derived from the Greek word *gnósis* (1108) meaning "knowledge." This heresy was repudiated not only by the writers of the NT epistles, but also by the church fathers who lived in the period after the early church. It is from them that there is a knowledge of Gnosticism's general tenets.

The Gnostics separated matter from thought. They concluded that matter was evil, and formulated the idea that the possession of knowledge was the only requirement for salvation. This is why they did not want to attribute humanity to Jesus Christ because to them, material things were evil. Docetism resulted, which taught that the body of Christ was something that only appeared material, but in reality it was only spiritual. Such a belief led to an immoral life, for since the spirit was separate from the physical body, they ignored their responsibility for the actions done in the body. This is the reason why Paul stressed that ". . . in him [Jesus Christ, as He appeared on earth], dwelleth all the fullness of the Godhead bodily" (v. 9). Jesus *was* truly God in the flesh (John 1:14). As a result of the philosophical

(continued on next page)

^{pre2596 art3588} ⁿⁿ³⁸⁶² ^{art,nn444} ^{pre2596 art3588} ⁿⁿ⁴⁷⁴⁷ ^{art3588} ⁿⁿ²⁸⁸⁹ ²⁵³² ³⁷⁵⁶ ^{pre2596}

after the tradition of men, after the rudiments of the world, and not after

^{an,nn5547}

Christ.

³⁷⁵⁴ ^{pre1722 ppro846} ^{pin2730} ^{an,aj3956 art3588} ⁿⁿ⁴¹³⁸ ^{art3588} ⁿⁿ²³²⁰ ^{ad4985}

9 For in him dwelleth all the fullness of the Godhead bodily.

²⁵³² ^{pin2075} ^{pr/pfpp4137} ^{pre1722 ppro846} ^{repro3739 pin2076 art3588} ^{pr/nn2776} ^{an,aj3956} ^{an,nn746}

10 And ye are complete in him, which is the head of all principality

²⁵³² ^{an,nn1849}

and power:

^{pre1722} ^{repro3739} ²⁵³² ^{ainp4059} ^{an,nn4061}

11 In whom also ye are circumcised with the circumcision

^{an,aj886} ^{pre1722} ^{art,nn555} ^{art3588} ⁿⁿ⁴⁹⁸³ ^{art3588} ⁿⁿ²⁶⁶ ^{art3599} ⁿⁿ⁴⁵⁶¹ ^{pre1722}

made*without*hands, in putting off the body of the sins of the flesh by

^{art3588} ⁿⁿ⁴⁰⁶¹ ^{art,nn5547}

the circumcision of Christ: *(Deut. 10:16; Jer. 4:4)*

^{aptp4916} ^{ppro846 pre1722} ^{art,nn908} ^{pre1722/repro3739} ²⁵³² ^{ainp4891}

12 Buried with him in baptism, wherein also ye are risen with *him*

^{pre1223} ^{art3588} ⁿⁿ⁴¹⁰² ^{art3588} ⁿⁿ¹⁷⁵³ ^{art,nn2316} ^{art,apta1453} ^{ppro846} ^{pre1537} ^{art3588}

through the faith of the operation of God, who*hath*raised him from the

^{ajn3498}

dead.

²⁵³² ^{ppro5209} ^{pap5607} ^{pr/an,aj3498} ^{pre1722} ^{art,nn3900} ²⁵³² ^{art3588} ⁿⁿ²⁰³ ^{ppro5216}

13 And you, being dead in your sins and the uncircumcision of your

^{art,nn461} ^{aina4806} ^{pre4862} ^{ppro846} ^{aptm5483} ^{ppro5213} ^{an,aj3956}

flesh, hath he quickened together with him, having forgiven you all

^{art,nn3900}

trespasses;

^{apta1813} ^{art3588} ⁿⁿ⁵⁴⁹⁸ ^{art,nn1378} ^{pre2596} ^{ppro2257}

14 Blotting out the handwriting of ordinances that was against us,

^{repro3739} ^{ipf2258} ^{pr/an,aj5227} ^{ppro2254} ²⁵³² ^{pfi142} ^{ppro846} ^{pre1537} ^{art3588} ^{ajn3319} ^{apta4338} ^{ppro846}

which was contrary to us, and took it out of the way, nailing it to his

^{art,nn4716}

cross;

^{aptm554} ^{art,nn746} ²⁵³² ^{art,nn1849} ^{aina1165}

15 *And* having spoiled principalities and powers, he made*a*show of them

^{pre1722/an,nn3954} ^{apta2358} ^{ppro846} ^{pre1722 ppro848}

openly, triumphing over them in it.

³³⁶¹ ^{idpro5100} ³⁷⁶⁷ ^{pim2919} ^{ppro5209} ^{pre1722} ^{an,nn1035} ²²²⁸ ^{pre1722} ^{an,nn4213}

16 Let no man therefore judge you in meat, or in drink,

(continued from previous page)

concept of the evil of the body, the Gnostics ignored or diminished the significance of the historic facts of the ministry, death, and resurrection of Jesus Christ as not being real but simply apparent. To them, all the secrets of God were in the mind, or appearing in an immaterial identity. The result was a complete denial of sexual and other bodily appetites (i.e., one being virtual asceticism and the other a practice of unrestrained indulgence of the body [vv. 20–23]).

In this passage, Paul countered the teaching that stressed the way to holiness was through asceticism. He emphasized that spirituality is not achieved by self-centered efforts to control the passions, but by putting on Christ, "setting one's affections on Him," and in so doing, removing all that is contrary to His will (vv. 20–23; Col. 3:1–17). Furthermore, as far as immaterial knowledge are concerned, true wisdom is not a man-made philosophy (v. 8). See note on Colossians 1:15–18.

2228 pre1722   an,nn3313   an,nn1859   2228   an,nn3561   2228   an,nn4521
or in respect of a holy day, or of the new moon, or of the sabbath *days*:

     repro3739 pin2076   pr/an,nn4639   art,pap3195   1161 art3588   nn4983   art,nn5547
17 Which are a shadow of things*to*come; but the body *is* of Christ.

           an,ajn3367   pim2603/ppro5209   pap2309/pre1722/an,nn5012   2532
18 Let no man beguile*you*of*your*reward in a voluntary humility and

an,nn2356   art,nn32   pap1687   repro3739   3361   pfi3708
worshiping of angels, intruding into those things which he hath not seen,

ad1500   ppmp5448   pre5259 ppro848 art,nn4561 art,nn3563
vainly puffed up by his fleshly mind,

     2532   3756   pap2902 art3588   nn2776   pre1537 repro3739 an,aj3956 art3588 nn4983 pre1223 art,nn860 2532
19 And not holding the Head, from which all   the body by joints and

an,nn4886   ppmp2023   2532   ppmp4822   pin837   art3588
bands having nourishment ministered, and knit together, increaseth with the

nn838   art,nn2316
increase of God.

Legalism

           3767   1487   aina599   pre4862 art,nn5547 pre575 art3588   nn4747   art3588 nn2889
20 Wherefore if ye be dead with Christ from the rudiments of the world,

inpro5101   ad5613   pap2198 pre1722   an,nn2889   pinm1379
why, as though living in the world, are ye subject*to*ordinances,

           aosi680   3361 aosi1089 3366 aosi2345 3366
21 (Touch not; taste not; handle not;

repro3739 an,aj3956 pin2076   pre1519/an,nn5356   art3588   nn671   pre2596 art3588   nn1778
22 Which all   are to   perish with the using;) after the commandments

2532   an,nn1319   art,nn444
and doctrines of men?   *(Is. 29:13)*

           repro3748   pin2076/pap2192   3303   an,nn3056   an,nn4678 pre1722 an,nn1479   2532
23 Which things   have   indeed a show of wisdom in will-worship, and

an,nn5012   2532   an,nn857   an,nn4983 3756 pre1722 idpro5100 an,nn5092 pre4314   an,nn4140
humility, and neglecting of the body; not in   any honor to the satisfying of

art3588   nn4561
the flesh.

"Renewed in Knowledge"

     1487   3767   ainp4891   art,nn5547 pim2212   art,ad507
3 If ye then be risen with Christ, seek those*things*which*are*above,

repro3757   art,nn5547 pin2076/ppmp2521 pre1722   an,ajn1188   art,nn2316
where Christ   sitteth   on the right hand of God.   *(Ps. 110:1)*

     pim5426   art,ad507   3361   art3588 pre1909 art3588   nn1093
2 Set*your*affection*on things above, not on things on the earth.

     1063   aina599   2532 ppro5216 art,nn2222   pfip2928 pre4862 art,nn5547 pre1722 art,nn2316
3 For ye are dead, and your life is hid with Christ in God.

     ad3752   art,nn5547   ppro2257 pr/art,nn2222   asbp5319   ad5119   epn5210 2532   fp5319
4 When Christ, *who is* our   life, shall appear, then shall ye also appear

pre4862 ppro846 pre1722 an,nn1391
with him in glory.

aima3499　　3767　　　ppro5216　art,nn3196　art3588　　　　　pre1909　art3588　　nn1093　　　an,nn4202

☞ 5 Mortify therefore your members which are upon the earth; fornication,

an,nn167　　　　　　　an,nn3806　　　　　an,aj2556　　　an,nn1939　　　　2532　　　art,nn4124

uncleanness, inordinate affection, evil concupiscence, and covetousness,

repro3748 pin2076 pr/an,nn1495

which is idolatry:

pre1223/repro3739　　　art3588　　nn3709　　art,nn2316　　pinm2064　pre1909 art3588　　nn5207

6 For*which*things'*sake the wrath of God cometh on the children of

art,nn543

disobedience:

pre1722　　repro3739 enp5210　2532　　aina4043　　　ad4218　　　ad3753　　ipf2198 pre1722 ppro846

7 In the which ye also walked some time, when ye lived in them.

1161　　ad3570　epn5210　2532　aipm659　　art,ajn3956　an,nn3709　an,nn2372　an,nn2549　　an,nn988

8 But now ye also put off all these; anger, wrath, malice, blasphemy,

an,nn148　　　pre1537　ppro5216 art,nn4750

filthy communication out of your mouth.

pim5574　3361　　rcpro240/pre1519　　　　　　　aptm554　art3588 aj3820 an,nn444 pre4862

9 Lie not one*to*another, seeing that ye have put off the old man with

ppro846 art,nn4234

his deeds;

2532　　　aptm1746 art3588 ajn3501　　　　　art,ppmp341　　　pre1519　an,nn1922　pre2596

10 And have put on the new *man*, which*is*renewed in knowledge after

an,nn1504　　　　art,apta2936　　ppro846

the image of him*that*created him:　　　　　　　　　　*(Gen. 1:26,27)*

ad3699　　　　　pin1762　3756　an,nn1672　2532　an,nn2453　　an,nn4061　　　2532

11 Where there is neither Greek nor Jew, circumcision nor

an,nn203　　　　an,ajn915　　an,nn4658　an,ajn1401　　an,ajn1658　235　an,nn5547　pr/art,ajn3956　2532

uncircumcision, Barbarian, Scythian, bond *nor* free: but Christ *is* all, and

pre1722 an,ajn3956

in all.

aipm1746　　3767　　ad5613　an,aj1588　art,nn2316 an,aj40　2532　　pfpp25　　an,nn4698

12 Put on therefore, as the elect of God, holy and beloved, bowels of

an,nn3628　　　an,nn5544　　　　an,nn5012　　　　an,nn4236　　　an,nn3115

mercies, kindness, humbleness*of*mind, meekness, longsuffering;

ppmp430　　　rcpro240　　2532　ppmp5483　　rxpro1438　　1437　idpro5100　psa2192

13 Forbearing one another, and forgiving one another, if any man have a

an,nn3437　　pre4314 idpro5100　2532　ad2531 art,nn5547　aom5483　ppro5213 ad3779 2532　　epn5210

quarrel against any: even as Christ forgave you, so also *do* ye.

1161　pre1909　an,aj3956　depro5125　　　art,nn26　repro3748 pin2076　pr/an,nn4886

14 And above all these things *put on* charity, which is the bond of

art,nn5047

perfectness.

2532　　art3588　　nn1515　　art,nn2316 pin1018 pre1722 ppro5216　art,nn2588　pre1519　repro3739　2532

15 And let the peace of God rule in your hearts, to the which also ye

ainp2564　pre1722 nu1520 an,nn4983　2532 pim1096　　pr/an,aj2170

are called in one body; and be ye thankful.

☞ **3:5** This verse also combats the teachings of Gnosticism which state that the physical body is evil. Since it is evil in itself and cannot be redeemed from its evil ways, it might as well do whatever it wants. This is the reason why Paul says, "Mortify therefore your members which are upon the earth [meaning 'bring them under control and treat them as though they were dead']."

art3588 nn3056 art,nn5547 pim1774 pre1722 ppro5213 ad4146 pre1722 an,aj3956 an,nn4678

☞ 16 Let the word of Christ dwell in you richly in all wisdom;

pap1321 2532 pap3560 rxpro1438 an,nn5568 2532 an,nn5215 2532 an,aj4152

teaching and admonishing one another in psalms and hymns and spiritual

an,nn5603 pap103 pre1722 an,nn5485 pre1722 ppro5216 art,nn2588 art3588 nn2962

songs, singing with grace in your hearts to the Lord.

2532 repro3748/302 psa4160 pre1722 an,nn3056 2228 an,nn2041 an,aj3956 pre1722 an,nn3686

17 And whatsoever ye do in word or deed, *do* all in the name of

an,nn2962 an,nn2424 pap2168 art,nn2316 2532 an,nn3962 pre1223 ppro846

the Lord Jesus, giving thanks to God and the Father by him.

Domestic Duties

art,nn1135 pim5293 art,aj2398 an,nn435 ad5613 ipf433 pre1722

☞ 18 Wives, submit yourselves unto your own husbands, as it is fit in the

an,nn2962

Lord.

(Gen. 3:16)

art,nn435 pim25 art,nn1135 2532 pim4087/3361 pre4314 ppro846

19 Husbands, love *your* wives, and be*not*bitter against them.

art,nn5043 pim5219 art,nn1118 pre2596 an,ajn3956 1063 depro5124 pin2076 pr/an,aj2101

20 Children, obey *your* parents in all things: for this is well pleasing

art3588 nn2962

unto the Lord.

art,nn2962 pim2042 3361 ppro5216 art,nn5043 3363 psa120

21 Fathers, provoke not your children *to anger,* lest they be discouraged.

art,ajn1401 pim5219 pre2596 an,ajn3956 art,nn2962 pre2596 an,nn4561

22 Servants, obey in all things *your* masters according to the flesh;

3361 pre1722 an,nn3787 ad5613 an,ajn441 235 pre1722 an,nn572 an,nn2588 ppmp5399

not with eyeservice, as menpleasers; but in singleness of heart, fearing

art,nn2316

God:

2532 repro3748/1437 psa4160 pim2038 pre1537/an,nn5590 ad5613 art3588 nn2962 2532 3756

23 And whatsoever ye do, do *it* heartily, as to the Lord, and not unto

an,nn444

men;

pfp1492 3754 pre575 an,nn2962 fm618 art3588 nn469

24 Knowing that of the Lord ye shall receive the reward of the

nn2817 1063 pin1398 art3588 nn2962 an,nn5547

inheritance; for ye serve the Lord Christ.

1161 art,pap91 fm2865

25 But he*that*doeth*wrong shall receive for the

aina91/repro3739 2532 pin2076 3756 an,nn4382

wrong*which*he*hath*done; and there is no respect*of*persons.

(Deut. 10:17; 2 Chr. 19:7)

☞ **3:16** The expression "the word (*lógos* [3056]) of Christ" refers to the revelation which Jesus Christ brought into the world (see note on John 1:1–17).

☞ **3:18, 19** See note on 1 Timothy 2:9–15 concerning a woman's conduct in the home.

Sundry Admonitions

4 art,nn2962 pin3930   art,ajn1401   art,ajn1342   2532 art,nn2471 pfp1492
Masters, give unto *your* servants that*which*is*just and equal; knowing

3754 epn5210 2532 pin2192   an,nn2962 pre1722 an,nn3772
that ye also have a Master in heaven.   *(Lev. 25:43,53)*

pim4342   art,nn4335   ppmp1127 pre1722 ppro846   pre1722   an,nn2169
2 Continue in prayer, and watch in the same with thanksgiving;

ad260   ppmp4336   2352   pre4012 ppro2257 2443 art,nn2316   asba455   ppro2254 an,nn2374
3 Withal praying also for us, that God would open unto us a door of

art,nn3056   ainf2980 art3588   nn3466   art,nn5547 pre1223 repro3739   pfip1210/2532
utterance, to speak the mystery of Christ, for which I am*also*in*bonds:

2443   asba5319/ppro846   ad5613 ppro3165 pin1163   ainf2980
4 That I may make*it*manifest, as I ought to speak.

pim4043 pre1722 an,nn4678   pre4314   art,ad1854   ppmp1805 art3588 nn2540
5 Walk in wisdom toward them*that*are*without, redeeming the time.

ppro5216 art,nn3056   ad3842   pre1722 an,nn5485   pfpp741   an,nn217
6 Let your speech *be* always with grace, seasoned with salt, that ye may

pinf1492 ad4459 ppro5209 pin1163   pifm611   an,nu,aj1520/an,ajn1538
know how ye ought to answer every man.

art,ajn3956   pre2596/ppro1691   an,nn5190   ft1107   ppro5213   art,aj27
☞ 7 All my state shall Tychicus declare unto you, *who is* a beloved

an,nn80   2532   an,aj4103   an,nn1249   2532   an,nn4889   pre1722   an,nn2962
brother, and a faithful minister and fellowservant in the Lord:

repro3739   aina3992 pre4314 ppro5209 pre1519   ppro846/depro5124   2443
8 Whom I have sent unto you for the*same*purpose, that he might

asba1097 art,pre4012/ppro5216 2532   asba3870   ppro5216 art,nn2588
know your estate, and comfort your hearts;

pre4862   an,nn3682   art,aj4103 2532   an,aj27   an,nn80   repro3739 pin2076   pre1537 ppro5216
9 With Onesimus, a faithful and beloved brother, who is *one* of you.

ft1107   ppro5213 an,aj3956   art,ad5602
They shall make known unto you all things which*are*done*here.

an,nn708   ppro3450   art,nn4869   pinm782   ppro5209 2532 an,nn3138   art,nn431
☞ 10 Aristarchus my fellowprisoner saluteth you, and Mark, sister's son

an,nn921   pre4012   repro3739   aina2983   an,nn1785   1437   asba2064 pre4314
to Barnabas, (touching whom ye received commandments: if he come unto

ppro5209 aipm1209 ppro846
you, receive him;)

2532   an,nn2424   art,ppmp3004   an,nn2459   art,pap5607   pre1537   an,nn4061
11 And Jesus, which*is*called Justus, who are of the circumcision.

☞ **4:7** Tychicus was an Ephesian who accompanied Paul to Jerusalem, doubtless as a delegate of his church carrying the collection (Acts 20:4, cf. 1 Cor. 16:1–4), and was well trusted by Paul (Eph. 6:21). He was Paul's personal representative to the churches in Colosse and Ephesus (Eph. 6:21, 22). Paul sent him to Crete as a messenger to Titus (Titus 3:12), which was followed by a mission to the church at Ephesus (2 Tim. 4:12).

☞ **4:10** The first reference to Aristarchus in Acts 19:29 describes him as being Paul's fellow traveler when they were seized by the Ephesian mob. In Acts 20:4, he accompanied Paul to Jerusalem, probably as an Thessalonian church delegate with the collection. Acts 27:2 refers to him as one of Paul's companion when he sailed to Rome. He possibly rejoined Paul and became His fellow prisoner, alternating with Epaphras in voluntary imprisonment (Phile. 1:23, 24).

depro3778 an,aj3441 pr/an,ajn4904 pre1519 art3588 nn932 art,nn2316 repro3748 ainp1096

These only *are my* fellowworkers unto the kingdom of God, which have been a

pr/an,nn3931 ppro3427

comfort unto me.

an,nn1889 art3588 pre1537 ppro5216 an,ajn1401 an,nn5547 pinm782 ppro5209

12 Epaphras, who is *one* of you, a servant of Christ, saluteth you,

ad3842 ppmp75 pre5228 ppro5216 pre1722 art,nn4335 2443 asba2476 pr/an,aj5046 2532

always laboring fervently for you in prayers, that ye may stand perfect and

pr/pfpp4137 pre1722 an,aj3956 an,nn2307 art,nn2316

complete in all the will of God.

1063 pin3140/ppro846 3754 pin2192 an,aj4183 an,nn2205 pre5228 ppro5216 2532 art3588

13 For I bear*him*record, that he hath a great zeal for you, and them

pre1722 an,nn2993 2532 art3588 pre1722 an,nn2404

that are in Laodicea, and them in Hierapolis.

an,nn3065 art3588 aj27 art,nn2395 2532 an,nn1214 pinm782 ppro5209

14 Luke, the beloved physician, and Demas, greet you.

aipm782 art3588 nn80 pre1722 an,nn2993 2532 an,nn3564 2532 art3588

15 Salute the brethren which are in Laodicea, and Nymphas, and the

nn1577 pre2596 ppro846 an,nn3624

church which is in his house.

2532 ad3752 art,nn1992 asbp314 pre3844 ppro5213 aima4160 2443 asbp314 2532

16 And when this epistle is read among you, cause that it be read also

pre1722 art3588 nn1577 an,nn2993 2532 epn5210 2532 asba314 art3588 pre1537

in the church of the Laodiceans; and that ye likewise read the *epistle* from

an,nn2993

Laodicea.

2532 aima2036 an,nn751 pim991 art3588 nn1248 repro3739

17 And say to Archippus, Take heed to the ministry which thou hast

aina3380 pre1722 an,nn2962 2443 psa4137 ppro846

received in the Lord, that thou fulfill it.

art3588 nn783 an,nn5495 art,popro1699 an,nn3972 pim3421 ppro3450 art,nn1199

18 The salutation by the hand of me Paul. Remember my bonds.

art,nn5495 pre3326 ppro5216 281

Grace *be* with you. Amen.

The First Epistle of Paul the Apostle to the

THESSALONIANS

The city of Thessalonica was ideally situated along the Egnatian Way on the western side of Chalcidic peninsula. It was the chief seaport of ancient Macedonia and an important commercial and military center.

After Paul and Silas were forced to leave Philippi, they traveled along the Egnatian Way to Thessalonica (Acts 16:39—17:1) where Paul taught in the synagogue for three sabbaths. They were forced to leave the city when antagonistic Jews, after stirring up the people of Thessalonica, brought some of the believers before the city officials and accused them of promoting treasonous ideas (Acts 17:5–10). The believers there came under great persecution following this uproar. Paul, feeling that he had not had enough time to ground them in Christian doctrine, desired to return to Thessalonica, but was hindered by Satan (1 Thess. 2:17, 18). Consequently, he sent Timothy to complete the work he had begun (1 Thess. 3:1, 2).

The Book of 1 Thessalonians was probably written by the Apostle Paul between the years A.D. 50 and 51 when Timothy returned to him in Corinth (Acts 18:5). He brought good news of their steadfastness and zeal in propagating the gospel (1 Thess. 3:6). Nevertheless, he reported that there were some ethical problems (1 Thess. 3:4–7) as well as some eschatological misconceptions. The Thessalonian believers were concerned that those believers who had already died would miss Christ's coming. Paul assured them that those who had died would be caught up to meet the Lord just like those who are alive at His coming (1 Thess. 4:13–18). Despite these problems and the persecution that they had faced, the church at Thessalonica had faithfully spread the gospel (1 Thess. 1:8).

1
an,nn3972 2532   an,nn4610   2532   an,nn5095   art3588   nn1577   an,nn2331
Paul, and Silvanus, and Timothy, unto the church of the Thessalonians
           pre1722 an,nn2316   an,nn3962 2532   an,nn2962 an,nn2424 an,nn5547
which is in God the Father and *in* the Lord Jesus Christ:
an,nn5485   ppro5213 2532 an,nn1515 pre575 an,nn2316 ppro2257 an,nn3962 2532   an,nn2962 an,nn2424
Grace *be* unto you, and peace, from God our Father, and the Lord Jesus
an,nn5547
Christ.

The Power of the Gospel

        pin2168   art,nn2316   ad3842   pre4012 ppro5216 an,aj3956 ppmp4160   an,nn3417   ppro5216
2 We give thanks to God always for you all, making mention of you
pre1909 ppro2257   art,nn4335
in our prayers;

pap3421   ad89   ppro5216 art,nn2041   art,nn4102 2532 art,nn2873   art,nn26 2532

3 Remembering without ceasing your work of faith, and labor of love, and

art,nn5281   art,nn1680   ppro2257 art,nn2962 an,nn2424 an,nn5547   ad*1715   art,nn2316 2532 ppro2257

patience of hope in our Lord Jesus Christ, in*the*sight of God and our

an,nn3962

Father;

pfp1492   an,nn80   pfpp25   ppro5216 art,nn1589 pre5259 an,nn2316

4 Knowing, brethren beloved, your election of God.

3754 ppro2257 art,nn2098 ainp1096 3756 pre1519 ppro5209 pre1722 an,nn3056 an,ajn3440 235 2532 pre1722

5 For our gospel came not unto you in word only, but also in

an,nn1411 2532 pre1722   an,aj40 an,nn4151   2532 pre1722 an,aj4183   an,nn4136   ad2531   pin1492

power, and in the Holy Ghost, and in much assurance; as ye know

pr/an,aj3634   ainp1096 pre1722 ppro5213   pre1223/ppro5209

what*manner*of*men we were among you for*your*sake.

2532 epn5210 ainp1096 pr/an,nn3402 ppro2257 2532 art3588 nn2962   aptm1209 art3588

6 And ye became followers of us, and of the Lord, having received the

nn3056 pre1722 an,aj4183 an,nn2347 pre3326 an,nn5479   an,aj40 an,nn4151

word in much affliction, with joy of the Holy Ghost:

5620 ppro5209 aifm1096 pr/an,nn5179   an,aj3956 art,pap4100 pre1722 art,nn3109 2532

7 So that ye were examples to all that believe in Macedonia and

art,nn882

Achaia.

1063   pre575   ppro5216   pfip1837   art3588   nn3056   art3588   nn2962 3756

8 For from you sounded out the word of the Lord not

an,ajn3440 pre1722 art,nn3109 2532 an,nn882 235 2532 pre1722 an,aj3956 an,nn5117 ppro5216 art,nn4102

only in Macedonia and Achaia, but also in every place your faith

art,pre4314   art,nn2316   pfi1831   5620   ppro2248 pin2192/an,nn5532 3361   pinf2980

to God-ward is spread abroad; so that we need not to speak

idpro5100

any thing.

1063 epn846   pin518 pre4012 ppro2257   an,aj3697   an,nn1529   aina2192

9 For they themselves show of us what manner of entering in we had

pre4314 ppro5209 2532 ad4459   aina1994 pre4314 art,nn2316 pre575 art,nn1497 pinf1398   an,pap2198 2532 an,aj228

unto you, and how ye turned to God from idols to serve the living and true

an,nn2316

God;

2532   pinf362   ppro846 art,nn5207 pre1537 art,nn3772 repro3739   aina1453 pre1537   an,ajn3498

10 And to wait for his Son from heaven, whom he raised from the dead,

an,nn2424   art,ppmp4506   ppro2248 pre575 art3588 nn3709 art,ppmp2064

even Jesus, which delivered us from the wrath to come.

1063   epn846   an,nn80   pin1492 ppro2257   art,nn1529   art,pre4314 ppro5209 3754   pfi1096

2 For yourselves, brethren, know our entrance in unto you, that it was

3756 pr/an,aj2756

not in vain:

235   2532   apta4310   2532

2 But even after that we had suffered before, and were

aptp5195   ad2531   pin1492 pre1722 an,nn5375   aom3955   pre1722

shamefully entreated, as ye know, at Philippi, we were bold in

ppro2257 art,nn2316   ainf2980 pre4314 ppro5209 art3588   nn2098   art,nn2316 pre1722 an,aj4183   an,nn73

our God to speak unto you the gospel of God with much contention.

1063 ppro2257   art,nn3874   3756 pre1537 an,nn4106 3761 pre1537 an,nn167   3777 pre1722

3 For our exhortation *was* not of deceit, nor of uncleanness, nor in

an,nn1388

guile:

235 ad2531   pfip1381   pre5259 art,nn2316   aifp4100   art3588   nn2098

4 But as we were allowed of God to be put*in*trust with the gospel,

ad3779   pin2980 3756 ad5613 pap700 an,nn444 235 art,nn2316 art,pap1381 ppro2257 art,nn2588

even so we speak; not as pleasing men, but God, which trieth our hearts.

(Jer. 11:20)

1063   3777   ad4218   ainp1096/pre1722/sg/an,nn3056/an,nn2850   ad2531   pin1492

5 For neither at*any*time used*we*flattering*words, as ye know,

3777 (pre1722) an,nn4392   an,nn4124   an,nn2316 pr/an,nn3144

nor   a cloak of covetousness; God *is* witness:

3777 pre1537 an,nn444 pap2212   an,nn1391   3777 pre575 ppro5216 3777   pre575 an,ajn243

6 Nor of men sought we glory, neither of you, nor *yet* of others, when

ppmp1410   pinf1511 pre1722/an,nn922 ad5613   an,nn652 an,nn5547

we might have been burdensome, as the apostles of Christ.

235   ainp1096 pr/an,aj2261 pre1722/an,ajn3319 ppro5216   5613/302   an,nn5162   art,rxpro1438

7 But we were gentle   among you, even as a nurse cherisheth her

an,nn5043

children:

ad3779   ppmp2442   ppro5216   pin2106

8 So being*affectionately*desirous of you, we were willing to have

ainf3330   ppro5213 3756 art3588 nn2098 art,nn2316 an,ajn3440 235 2532   rxpro1438 art,nn5590

imparted unto you, not the gospel of God only, but also our own souls,

1360   pfip1096 pr/an,aj27 ppro2254

because ye were dear unto us.

1063   pin3421   an,nn80 ppro2257 art,nn2873 2532 art,nn3449 1063 ppmp2038 an,nn3571

9 For ye remember, brethren, our labor and travail: for laboring night

2532 an,nn2250   3361   aipr1912   idpro5100 ppro5216 aina2784

and day, because we would not be chargable unto any of you, we preached

pre1519 ppro5209 art3588   nn2098   art,nn2316

unto you the gospel of God.

ppro5210   pr/an,nn3144   2532 art,nn2316   ad5613 ad3743 2532 ad1346 2532

10 Ye *are* witnesses, and God *also,* how holily and justly and

ad274   ainp1096   ppro5213 art,pap4100

unblamably we behaved ourselves among you that believe:

ad2509   pin1492 ad5613 pap3870 (ppro5209) 2532 ppmp3888   2532 ppmp3140 an,aj1538 nu1520

11 As ye know how we exhorted and comforted and charged every one of

ppro5216 ad5613 an,nn3962 rxpro1438 an,nn5043

you, as a father *doth* his children,

ppro5209   aies4043 ad516   art,nn2316   art,pap2564 ppro5209 pre1519 rxpro1438

12 That ye would walk worthy of God, who*hath*called you unto his

art,nn932 2532 an,nn1391

kingdom and glory.

pre1223/depro5124   2532 pin2168 epn2249 art,nn2316   ad89   3754

13 For*this*cause also thank we God without ceasing, because, when ye

apta3880   an,nn3056 art,nn2316   an,nn182 pre3844 ppro2257 aom1209   3756

received the word of God which ye heard of us, ye received *it* not *as* the an,nn3056   an,nn444   235   ad2531   pin2076   ad230   an,nn3056   an,nn2316   repro3739

word of men, but as it is in truth, the word of God, which

pinm1754   2532   pre1722 ppro5213   art,pap4100

effectually worketh also in you that believe.

1063   epn5210   an,nn80   ainp1096   pr/an,nn3402   art3588   nn1577   art,nn2316

14 For ye, brethren, became followers of the churches of God which

pre1722 art,nn2449 art,pap5607 pre1722 an,nn5547   an,nn2424   3754 epn5210 2532   aina3958   depro5024   pre5259

in Judea are in Christ Jesus: for ye also have suffered like things of

art,aj2398   an,nn4853   ad2531   ppro846   (2532) pre5259 art3588   nn2453

your own countrymen, even as they *have* of the Jews:

art,apta615/2532   art3588   nn2962   an,nn2424   2532   art,aj2398   an,nn4396   2532

15 Who*both*killed the Lord Jesus, and their own prophets, and have

apta1559   ppro2248 2532   pap700   3361 an,nn2316 2532   pr/an,aj1727   an,aj3956 an,nn444

persecuted us; and they please not God, and are contrary to all men:

pap2967   ppro2248   ainf2980   art3588   nn1484   2443   asbp4982

16 Forbidding us to speak to the Gentiles that they might be saved, to

aies378   ppro848 art,nn266   ad3842   1161 art3588   nn3709   aina5348   pre1909   ppro846   pre1519   an,nn5056

fill up their sins always: for the wrath is come upon them to the uttermost.

(Gen. 15:16)

1161   epn2249   an,nn80   aptp642   pre575   ppro5216 pre4314   an,nn5610/an,nn2540   an,nn4383

17 But we, brethren, being taken from you for a short time in presence,

3756   an,nn2588   aina4704   ad4056   ainf1492 ppro5216 art,nn4383 pre1722 an,aj4183

not in heart, endeavored the*more*abundantly to see your face with great

an,nn1939

desire.

pre,repro1352   aina2309   ainf2064   pre4314   ppro5209   3303   epn1473   an,nn3972 (2532)

18 Wherefore we would have come unto you, even I Paul,

nu,ad530/2532/nu,ad1364   2532 art,nn4567   aina1465   ppro2248

once*and*again; but Satan hindered us.

1063   inpro5101   ppro2257 pr/an,nn1680 2228 pr/an,nn5479 2228 pr/an,nn4735   an,nn2746   (2228) 3780   2532

☞ 19 For what *is* our hope, or joy, or crown of rejoicing? *Are* not even

ppro5210   ad*1715   ppro2257 art,nn2962 an,nn2424 an,nn5547 pre1722 ppro846   art,nn3952

ye in*the*presence of our Lord Jesus Christ at his coming?

1063   epn5210 pin2075 ppro2257 pr/art,nn1391 2532 pr/art,nn5479

20 For ye are our glory and joy.

☞ **2:19** The word *parousía* (3952), translated "coming" in this verse, basically means "presence" or "arrival" (1 Cor. 16:17; 2 Cor. 7:7). Thus, the same Jesus who ascended to heaven will again visit the earth in a bodily presence (Acts 1:11) at the end of the age (Matt. 24:3). He will come in power and glory to destroy the Antichrist and evil (2 Thess. 2:8).

The return of Christ will also be a "revelation" or a "removing the cover" from something that is hidden, noted by the Greek word *apokálupsis* (602). or disclosure. The power and glory that Christ now possesses will be unveiled and disclosed to the world (1 Pet. 4:13). Christ is now reigning as Lord at God's right hand (Heb. 12:2), sharing God's throne (Rev. 3:21). Although His authority is not discernible to the world, it will be made visible by His *apokálupsis*, "revelation."

Another word that is related to the Second Coming of the Lord is *epipháneia* (2015) which means "a manifestation." In Ancient Greek, the word was used especially to refer to the appearance of gods and of the manifestation of divine power or providence. However, in the NT, it is used of the appearing of the manifestation of Jesus Christ on earth (2 Thess. 2:8; 2 Tim. 1:10; 4:1, 8; Titus 2:13).

"Stand Fast in the Lord"

pre,repro1352   ad3371   pap4722   aina2106
3 Wherefore when we could no longer forbear, we thought*it*good to
aifp2641   pre1722 an,nn116 an,aj3441
be left at Athens alone;

2532   aina3992   an,nn5095   ppro2257 art,nn80   2532   an,nn1249   art,nn2316 2532 ppro2257
2 And sent Timothy, our brother, and minister of God, and our

an,nn4904   pre1722 art3588 nn2098   art,nn5547   aies4741   ppro5209 2532   ainf3870   ppro5209
fellowlaborer in the gospel of Christ, to establish you, and to comfort you

pre4012   ppro5216 art,nn4102
concerning your faith:

art,ajn3367   pifm4525 pre1722 depro5025 art,nn2347 1063   epn846   pin1492
3 That no man should be moved by these afflictions: for yourselves know

3754   pinm2749   pre1519/depro5124
that we are appointed thereunto.

1063   2532   ad3753   ipf2258 pre4314 ppro5209   ipf4302/ppro5213   3754   pin3195
4 For verily, when we were with you, we told*you*before that we should

pifm2346   2532 ad2531   aom1096   2532   pin1492
suffer tribulation; even as it came*to*pass, and ye know.

pre1223/depro5124   epn2504   ad3771   pap4722   aina3992   aies1097 ppro5216
5 For*this*cause, when I could no longer forbear, I sent to know your
art,nn4102   3381   art3588   pap3985   aina3985   ppro5209 2532 ppro2257 art,nn2873
faith, lest*by*some*means the tempter have tempted you, and our labor
asbm1096 pre1519 an,ajn2756
be in vain.

1161   ad737   an,nn5095   apta2104 pre575 ppro5216 pre4314   ppro2248 2532
6 But now when Timothy came from you unto us, and
aptm2097/ppro2254   ppro5216 art,nn4102 2532 art,nn26 2532 3754   pin2192 an,aj18
brought*us*good*tidings of your faith and charity, and that ye have good
an,nn3417   ppro2257   ad3842   pap1971   ainf1492 ppro2248 ad2509 ppro2249 2532
remembrance of us always, desiring greatly to see us, as we also *to see*
ppro5209
you:

pre1223/depro5124   an,nn80   ainp3870   pre1909 ppro5213 pre1909 an,aj3956 ppro2257
7 Therefore, brethren, we were comforted over you in all our
art,nn2347   2532   an,nn318 pre1223 ppro5216 art,nn4102
affliction and distress by your faith:

3754   ad3568   pin2198 1437 epn5210 psa4739   pre1722   an,nn2962
8 For now we live, if ye stand fast in the Lord.

1063   inpro5101 an,nn2169 pinm1410   ainf467/art,nn2316   pre4012 ppro5216 pre1909 an,aj3956 art3588
9 For what thanks can we render*to*God*again for you, for all the
nn5479   repro3739   pin5463   pre1223/ppro5209   ad*1715 ppro2257 art,nn2316
joy wherewith we joy for*your*sakes before our God;

an,nn3571   2532 an,nn2250 ppmp1189 pre5228/pre1537/an,ajn4053   aies1492 ppro5216 art,nn4383
10 Night and day praying exceedingly that we might see your face,
2532   ainf2675   art,nn5303   ppro5216 art,nn4102
and might perfect that*which*is*lacking in your faith?

1161   art,nn2316 epn846 2532 ppro2257 an,nn3962 2532 ppro2257 art,nn2962 an,nn2424 an,nn5547 opt2720
11 Now God himself and our Father, and our Lord Jesus Christ, direct
ppro2257 art,nn3598 pre4314 ppro5209
our way unto you.

¹¹⁶¹   ^{art3588}   ⁿⁿ²⁹⁶²   ^{opt4121/ppro5209}   ²⁵³²   ^{opt4052}   ^{art,nn26}

12 And the Lord make*you*to*increase and abound in love

^{repro240/pre1519}   ²⁵³²   ^{pre1519}   ^{an,ajn3956}   ²⁵³²   ^{ad2509 ppro2249}   ^{pre1519}   ^{ppro5209}

one*toward*another, and toward all *men,* even as we *do* toward you:

^{aies4741}   ^{ppro5216 art,nn2588}   ^{pr/an,aj273}   ^{pre1722}   ^{an,nn42}   ^{ad*1715}

☞ 13 To the end he may establish your hearts unblamable in holiness before

^{art,nn2316}   ²⁵³²   ^{ppro2257}   ^{an,nn3962}   ^{pre1722 art3588}   ⁿⁿ³⁹⁵²   ^{ppro2257 art,nn2962 an,nn2424 an,nn5547}   ^{pre3326 an,aj3956}

God, even our Father, at the coming of our Lord Jesus Christ with all

^{ppro846}   ^{art,ajn40}

his saints.

Sanctification

^{art,ajn3063}   ³⁷⁶⁷   ^{pin2065}   ^{ppro5209}   ^{an,nn80}   ²⁵³²   ^{pin3870}   ^{pre1722}

4 Furthermore then we beseech you, brethren, and exhort *you* by the

^{an,nn2962}   ^{an,nn2424}   ^{ad2531}   ^{aina3880}   ^{pre3844 ppro2257 art,ad4459 ppro5209}   ^{pin1163}

Lord Jesus, that as ye have received of us how ye ought to

^{pinf4043}   ²⁵³²   ^{pinf700 an,nn2316}   ⁽²⁴⁴³⁾   ^{psa4052}   ^{ad3123}

walk and to please God, *so* ye would abound more*and*more.

¹⁰⁶³   ^{pin1492}   ^{inpro5101}   ^{an,nn3852}   ^{aina1325 ppro5213 pre1223 art3588 nn2962 an,nn2424}

2 For ye know what commandments we gave you by the Lord Jesus.

¹⁰⁶³   ^{depro5124 pin2076}   ^{pr/an,nn2307}   ^{art,nn2316}   ^{ppro5216}   ^{art,nn38}   ^{ppro5209}

3 For this is the will of God, *even* your sanctification, that ye should

^{pifm567}   ^{pre575}   ^{art,nn4202}

abstain from fornication:

^{an,ajn1538}   ^{ppro5216}   ^{pinf1492}   ^{pifm2932}   ^{rxpro1438 art,nn4632}   ^{pre1722}

☞ 4 That every one of you should know how to possess his vessel in

^{an,nn38}   ²⁵³²   ^{an,nn5092}

sanctification and honor;

³³⁶¹   ^{pre1722}   ^{an,nn3806}   ^{an,nn1939}   ²⁵³²   ^{ad2509 art3588}   ⁿⁿ¹⁴⁸⁴   ^{art,pfp1492}

5 Not in the lust of concupiscence, even as the Gentiles which know

^{3361 art,nn2316}

not God: *(Ps. 79:6; Jer. 10:25)*

³³⁶¹   ^{art,pinf5233}   ²⁵³²   ^{pinf4122}   ^{ppro848}   ^{art,nn80}   ^{pre1722}   ^{art,nn4229}

6 That no *man* go beyond and defraud his brother in *any* matter:

¹³⁶⁰   ^{art3588}   ⁿⁿ²⁹⁶²   ^{pr/an,aj1558}   ^{pre4012 an,aj3956}   ^{depro5130 ad2531}   ²⁵³²

because that the Lord *is* the avenger of all such, as we also have

^{aina4277}   ^{ppro5213 2532}   ^{aom1263}

forewarned you and testified.   *(Ps. 94:1)*

^{1063 art,nn2316}   ^{3756 aina2564 ppro2248 pre1909}   ^{an,nn167}   ^{235 pre1722 an,nn38}

7 For God hath not called us unto uncleanness, but unto holiness.

^{art,pap114/5105}   ^{pin114}   ³⁷⁵⁶   ^{an,nn444}   ²³⁵   ^{art,nn2316}

8 He*therefore*that*despiseth, despiseth not man, but God,

^{art,apta1325/2532}   ^{pre1519 ppro2248 ppro848 art,aj40 art,nn4151}

who*hath*also*given unto us his Holy Spirit.   *(Ezek. 36:27; 37:14)*

¹¹⁶¹   ^{pre4012}   ^{art,nn5360}   ^{pin2192/an,nn5532}   ³⁷⁵⁶   ^{pinf1125}   ^{ppro5213}

9 But as touching brotherly love ye need not that I write unto you:

☞ **3:13** See note on 1 Thessalonians 2:19.
☞ **4:4–7** See the introduction to 1 Thessalonians.

1063 ppro5210   epn846   pin2075   pr/an,aj2312   pre1519 art,pinf25   rcpro240
for ye yourselves are taught*of*God to love one another.   *(Jer. 31:33,34)*

　　　　　　1063   2532   pin4160 ppro846   pre1519   an,aj3956 art3588   nn80   art3588   pre1722 an,aj3650
10 And indeed ye do   it toward all the brethren which are in   all

art,nn3109   1161   pin3870 ppro5209   an,nn80   pinf4052   ad3123
Macedonia: but we beseech you, brethren, that ye increase more*and*more;

　　　　　　2532   pifm5389   pinf2270   2532   pinf4238/art,ajn2398   2532
11 And that ye study to be quiet, and to do*your*own*business, and to

pifm2038   ppro5216 art,aj2398 art,nn5495 ad2531   aina3853   ppro5213
work with your own hands, as we commanded you;

　　　　　　2443   psa4043   ad2156   pre4314   art,ad1854   2532
12 That ye may walk honestly toward them*that*are*without, and *that* ye

psa2192 an,nn5532   an,ajn3367
may have lack of nothing.

Christ's Return

　　　　1161   pin2309   3756   ppro5209   pinf50   an,nn80   pre4012
☞ 13 But I would not have you to be ignorant, brethren, concerning

art,pfpp2837   2443   psmp3076   3361   2532   ad2531 art,ajn3062   art,pap2192   3361
them*which*are*asleep, that ye sorrow not, even as others which have no

an,nn1680
hope.

　　　1063   1487   pin4100   3754   an,nn2424   aina599   2532   aina450   ad3779
14 For if we believe that Jesus died and rose again, even so

art,apta2837/2532   pre1223 art,nn2424   art,nn2316   ft71   pre4862 ppro846
them*also*which*sleep in Jesus will God bring with him.

　　　1063   depro5124   pin3004   ppro5213 pre1722   an,nn3056   an,nn2962   3754   ppro2249
☞ 15 For this we say unto you by the word of the Lord, that we

art,pap2198   art,ppmp4035 pre1519 art3588   nn3952   art3588   nn2962   efn3364   asba5348
which*are*alive *and* remain unto the coming of the Lord shall not prevent

art,aptp2837
them*which* are*asleep.

　　　3754 art3588   nn2962   epn846   fm2597   pre575   an,nn3772   pre1722   an,nn2752 pre1722
16 For the Lord himself shall descend from heaven with a shout, with the

an,nn5456   an,nn743   2532 pre1722   an,nn4536   an,nn2316 2532 art3588 ajn3498 pre1722 an,nn5547
voice of the archangel, and with the trump of God: and the dead in Christ

fm450   nu,aj4412
shall rise first:

　　　　ad1899   ppro2249   art,pap2198   art,ppmp4035   fp726   ad260   pre4862
☞ 17 Then we which*are*alive *and* remain shall be caught up together with

───────────────────────────

☞ **4:13–18** See the introduction to 1 Thessalonians and the note on 1 Thessalonians 2:19.

☞ **4:15** The word here that is translated "prevent" is derived from the Greek verb *phthánō* (5348) which means "to anticipate, to be before." Also in this verse, the dead are called, "them which are asleep." The Greek word used is *koimēthéntas* (2837), "to sleep or slumber." In this verse, it refers to the body being asleep, not the soul.

☞ **4:17** There are two important Greek words in this verse. The first is *harpagēsómetha*, translated "caught up." This refers to a specific moment in the future when believers will be caught up by Jesus

(continued on next page)

ppro846 pre1722   an,nn3507   pre1519/an,nn529 art3588 nn2962 pre1519   an,nn109 2532 ad3779   ad3842
them in the clouds to meet the Lord in the air: and so shall we ever
fm2071 pre4862   an,nn2962
be with the Lord.

5620   pim3870   rcpro240   pre1722 depro5125 art,nn3056
18 Wherefore comfort one another with these words.

"A Thief in the Night"

5
1161   pre4012 art3588   nn5550   2532   art3588   nn2540   an,nn80   pin2192 3756 an,nn5532
But of the times and the seasons, brethren, ye have no need that I
pifm1125   ppro5213
write unto you.

1063   epn846   pin1492   ad199   3754   art3588 nn2250   an,nn2962 ad3779   pinm2064   ad5613
2 For yourselves know perfectly that the day of the Lord so cometh as
an,nn2812 pre1722   an,nn3571
a thief in the night.

1063   ad3752   psa3004 an,nn1515   2532   an,nn803   ad5119   an,aj160   an,nn3639
3 For when they shall say, Peace and safety; then sudden destruction
pinm2186   ppro846   ad5618 art,nn5604   pap2192/art,pre1722/an,nn1064   2532   efn3364
cometh upon them, as travail upon a woman*with*child; and they shall not
asba1628
escape.   *(Jer. 6:14; 8:11; Ezek. 13:10)*

(continued from previous page)
Christ, as He descends from heaven. The other word is "meet" translated from the Greek phrase *eis apántēsin* (1519, 529) which means "to come into the presence of, to meet." This occurs after the dead have been raised (1 Thess. 4:14–16). Then the bodies of those who are alive will be transformed into new bodies (see note on 2 Cor. 5:1).

5:2 The "Day of the Lord" holds an important place in prophecy. Amos declared that the "Day" signified judgment for Israel (cf. Is. 2:12–24; Ezek. 13:5; Joel 1:15; 2:1, 11; Zeph. 1:7, 14; Zech. 13:1).

Several prophets refer to it as God's "day of judgment" upon individual nations such as Babylon (Is. 13:6–9), Egypt (Jer. 46:10), Edom (Obad. 1:8), and many other nations (Joel 2:31; 3:14; Obad. 1:15). Thus, the Day of the Lord represents the occasion when Jehovah will actively intervene to punish sin.

During the time period of the Day of the Lord, there will be those who truly repent and are saved, but those who remain enemies of the Lord, whether Jews or Gentiles, will be punished.

In the NT, the Day of the Lord is related to the Second Coming of Christ. So also is the phrase "the Day of our Lord Jesus Christ" (1 Cor. 1:8; 5:5; Phil. 1:6, 10; 2:16; 2 Thess. 2:2). Both expressions, the "Day of the Lord" and the "Day of Christ," refer to time periods of judgment by Christ. The Day of the Lord will include the time of the Great Tribulation (cf. Rev. 6—20). It also refers to the liberation by Christ of His Church. Zechariah 14:1–4 explains that the events of the Second Advent are included in the program of the Day of the Lord. Thus, the Day of the Lord and the Day of Christ occur simultaneously. For the Church, it is the rapture; and for the unbelieving world, it is the beginning of judgment and the Tribulation. If the Day of the Lord began after the Second Advent, it could not come as a "thief in the night," unexpected and unheralded, since that particular advent is preceded by signs (1 Thess. 5:2; 2 Pet. 3:10). Consequently, the only way these events could occur unexpectedly would be for them to begin immediately after the rapture of the Church. The Day of the Lord, therefore, is that extended period of time when God begins to deal with Israel after the rapture of the church. It also continues through the Second Advent and the millennial age preceding the creation of the new heaven and new earth.

¹¹⁶¹ ^{epn5210} ^{an,nn80} ^{pin2075} ³⁷⁵⁶ ^{pre1722} ^{an,nn4655} ²⁴⁴³ ^{art,nn2250}

4 But ye, brethren, are not in darkness, that that day should

^{asba2638} ^{ppro5209} ^{ad5613} ^{an,nn2812}

overtake you as a thief.

^{epn5210} ^{pin2075} ^{an,aj3956} ^{pr/an,nn5207} ^{an,nn5457} ²⁵³² ^{pr/an,nn5207} ^{an,nn2250} ^{pin2070}

5 Ye are all the children of light, and the children of the day: we are

³⁷⁵⁶ ^{pr/an,nn3571} ³⁷⁶¹ ^{pr/an,nn4655}

not of the night, nor of darkness.

^{686/3767} ³³⁶¹ ^{psa2518} ^{ad5613} ⁽²⁵³²⁾ ^{art,ajn3062} ²³⁵ ^{psa1127} ²⁵³²

6 Therefore let us not sleep, as do others; but let us watch and

^{psa3525}

be sober.

¹⁰⁶³ ^{art,pap2518} ^{pin2518} ^{an,nn3571} ²⁵³² ^{art,ppmp3182}

7 For they*that*sleep sleep in the night; and they*that*be*drunken

^{pin3184} ^{an,nn3571}

are drunken in the night.

¹¹⁶¹ ^{epn2249} ^{pap5607} ^{an,nn2250} ^{psa3525} ^{apton1746} ^{an,nn2382}

8 But let us, who are of the day, be sober, putting on the breastplate of

^{an,nn4102} ²⁵³² ^{an,nn26} ²⁵³² ^{an,nn4030} ^{an,nn1680} ^{an,nn4991}

faith and love; and for a helmet, the hope of salvation.   *(Is. 59:17)*

³⁷⁵⁴ ^{art,nn2316} ³⁷⁵⁶ ^{aom5087} ^{ppro2248} ^{pre1519} ^{an,nn3709} ²³⁵ ^{pre1519/an,nn4047} ^{an,nn4991}

9 For God hath not appointed us to wrath, but to obtain salvation

^{pre1223} ^{ppro2257} ^{art,nn2962} ^{an,nn2424} ^{an,nn5547}

by our Lord Jesus Christ,

^{art,apta599} ^{pre5228} ^{ppro2257} ²⁴⁴³ ¹⁵³⁵ ^{psa1127} ¹⁵³⁵ ^{psa2518} ^{asba2198}

10 Who died for us, that, whether we wake or sleep, we should live

^{ad260} ^{pre4862} ^{ppro846}

together with him.

^{pre,repro1352} ^{pim3870} ^{rcpro240} ²⁵³² ^{pim3618} ^{nu,ajn1520/art,nu,ajn1520}

11 Wherefore comfort yourselves together, and edify one another,

^{ad2531} ²⁵³² ^{pin4160}

even as also ye do.

Final Instructions

¹¹⁶¹ ^{pin2065} ^{ppro5209} ^{an,nn80} ^{pinf1492} ^{art,pap2872} ^{pre1722} ^{ppro5213}

12 And we beseech you, brethren, to know them*which*labor among you,

²⁵³² ^{ppmp4291} ^{ppro5216} ^{pre1722} ^{an,nn2962} ²⁵³² ^{pap3560} ^{ppro5209}

and are over you in the Lord, and admonish you;

²⁵³² ^{pifm2233} ^{ppro846} ^{pre5228/pre1537/an,ajn4053} ^{pre1722} ^{an,nn26} ^{pre1223/ppro846/art,nn2041}

13 And to esteem them very highly in love for*their*work's*sake. *And*

^{pim1514} ^{pre1722} ^{rxpro1438}

be*at*peace among yourselves.

¹¹⁶¹ ^{pin3870} ^{ppro5209} ^{an,nn80} ^{pim3560} ^{art,ajn813} ^{pim3888}

14 Now we exhort you, brethren, warn them*that*are*unruly, comfort

^{art3588} ^{ajn3642} ^{pim472} ^{art3588} ^{ajn772} ^{pim3114} ^{pre4314} ^{an,ajn3956}

the feebleminded, support the weak, be patient toward all *men.*

^{pim3708} ^{idpro5100/3361} ^{asba591} ^{an,ajn2556} ^{pre473} ^{ajn2556} ^{idpro5100} ²³⁵ ^{ad3842} ^{pim1377}

15 See that none render evil for evil unto any *man*; but ever follow

^{art,ajn18} ²⁵³² ^{pre1519} ^{rcpro240} ²⁵³² ^{pre1519} ^{an,ajn3956}

that*which*is*good, both among yourselves, and to all *men. (Prov. 20:22)*

pim5463   ad3842
16 Rejoice evermore.

pimm4336   ad89
17 Pray without ceasing.

pre1722   an,ajn3956   pim2168   1063 depro5124   pr/an,nn2307   an,nn2316 pre1722   an,nn5547
18 In every thing give thanks: for this is the will of God in Christ
an,nn2424   pre1519   ppro5209
Jesus concerning you.

pim4570   3361 art3588   nn4151
19 Quench not the Spirit.

pim1848   3361   an,nn4394
20 Despise not prophesyings.

pim1381   an,ajn3956   pim2722   art,ajn2570
21 Prove all things; hold fast that*which*is*good.

pim567   pre575 an,aj3956   an,nn1491   an,ajn4190
22 Abstain from all appearance of evil.   (Job 1:1,8; 2:3)

1161   art3588   epn846   nn2316   art,nn1515   opt37   ppro5209   an,aj3651   2532   ppro5216
☞ 23 And the very God of peace sanctify you wholly; and I pray God your
an,aj3648   art,nn4151   2532   art,nn5590   2532   art,nn4983   opt5083   ad274   pre1722 art3588   nn3952
whole spirit and soul and body be preserved blameless unto the coming of
ppro2257 art,nn2962 an,nn2424   an,nn5547
our Lord Jesus Christ.

pr/an,aj4103   art,pap2564   ppro5209 repro3739   2532   ft4160
24 Faithful is he*that*calleth you, who also will do it.

an,nn80   pim4336 pre4012 ppro2257
25 Brethren, pray for us.

aipm782 an,aj3956 art3588   nn80   pre1722   an,aj40 an,nn5370
26 Greet all the brethren with a holy kiss.

pin3726   ppro5209   art3588 nn2962   art,nn1992   aifp314   an,aj3956 art3588 an,aj40
27 I charge you by the Lord that this epistle be read unto all the holy
nn80
brethren.

art3588   nn5485   ppro2257 art,nn2962 an,nn2424 an,nn5547   pre3326 ppro5216   281
28 The grace of our Lord Jesus Christ be with you. Amen.

☞ 5:23 See the note on 1 Thessalonians 2:19 concerning the Second Coming of Christ.

The Second Epistle of Paul the Apostle to the

THESSALONIANS

This second letter of Paul to the Thessalonians was written about A.D. 51–52, and was sent from Corinth soon after his first letter. Some members of the congregation in Thessalonica did not have a clear understanding of Paul's teaching concerning the "Day of the Lord" in his first epistle to them (1 Thess. 5:1–11). There was also a misunderstanding among some of the people regarding the imminent return of the Lord Jesus. They apparently had misinterpreted the meaning of the phrase "as a thief in the night" (1 Thess. 5:2) and confused the concepts of the suddenness of the Lord's coming with its immediacy. They thought that since Christ would be coming soon, there was no point in continuing to work. When the people encountered increased persecution, they felt that the "Day of the Lord" had already come and they had somehow missed Christ's return.

Paul corrects them in this second epistle by explaining that certain events must take place before Christ will return. For example, he states that there will be a world-wide rebellion against God, led by one who will represent the epitome of lawlessness and anarchy (2 Thess. 2:3–9). Moreover, Paul tells the believers in Thessalonica not to live at the expense of others, but to return to the Lord's work (2 Thess. 3:10–12).

In summary, the Thessalonians were apprehensive about the persistent persecution that they were enduring (2 Thess. 1:4, 5). Paul wrote this letter to comfort and exhort these believers to continue serving the Lord in spite of the hardships.

1
an,nn3972 2532 an,nn4610 2532 an,nn5095 art3588 nn1577 an,nn2331
Paul, and Silvanus, and Timothy, unto the church of the Thessalonians
pre1722 an,nn2316 ppro2257 an,nn3962 2532 an,nn2962 an,nn2424 an,nn5547
in God our Father and the Lord Jesus Christ:

an,nn5485 ppro5213 2532 an,nn1515 pre575 an,nn2316 ppro2257 an,nn3962 2532 an,nn2962 an,nn2424
2 Grace unto you, and peace, from God our Father and the Lord Jesus
an,nn5547
Christ.

We Know You Are Suffering

pin3784 pinf2168 art,nn2316 ad3842 pre4012 ppro5216 an,nn80 ad2531 pin2076
3 We are bound to thank God always for you, brethren, as it is
pr/an,ajn514 3754 ppro5216 art,nn4102 pin5232 2532 art3588 nn26 an,ajn1538
meet, because that your faith groweth exceedingly, and the charity of every
nu1520 ppro5216 an,aj3956 pre1519 rcpro240 pin4121
one of you all toward each other aboundeth;

5620 ppro2248 epn846 pifm2744 pre1722 ppro5213 pre1722 art3588 nn1577 art,nn2316 pre5228

4 So that we ourselves glory in you in the churches of God for

ppro5216 art,nn5281 2532 an,nn4102 pre1722 an,aj3956 ppro5216 art,nn1375 2532 art,nn2347 repro3739

your patience and faith in all your persecutions and tribulations that ye

pinm430

endure:

an,nn1730 art3588 an,aj1342 nn2920 art,nn2316

5 *Which is* a manifest token of the righteous judgment of God, that

ppro5209 aies2661 art3588 nn932 art,nn2316 pre5228 repro3739 2532

ye may be counted worthy of the kingdom of God, for which ye also

pin3958

suffer:

1512 an,ajn1342 pre3844 an,nn2316 ainf467 an,nn2347

6 Seeing *it is* a righteous thing with God to recompense tribulation to

art,pap2346 ppro5209

them*that*trouble you;

2532 ppro5213 art,ppmp2346 an,nn425 pre3326 ppro2257 pre1722 art3588 nn2962 an,nn2424

☞ 7 And to you who*are*troubled rest with us, when the Lord Jesus shall

art,nn602 pre575 an,nn3772 pre3326 ppro848 an,nn1411 an,nn32

be revealed from heaven with his mighty angels, *(Zech. 14:5)*

pre1722 an,nn5395 an,nn4442 pap1325 an,nn1557 art,pap1492 3361 an,nn2316 2532

8 In flaming fire taking vengeance on them*that*know not God, and

art,pap5219 3361 art3588 nn2098 ppro2257 art,nn2962 an,nn2424 an,nn5547

that obey not the gospel of our Lord Jesus Christ:

(Ps. 79:6; Is. 66:15; Jer. 10:25)

repro3748 ft5099/an,nn1349 an,aj166 an,nn3639 pre575 an,nn4383

9 Who shall be punished with everlasting destruction from the presence of

art3588 nn2962 2532 pre575 art3588 nn1391 ppro846 art,nn2479

the Lord, and from the glory of his power; *(Is. 2:10,19,21)*

ad3752 asba2064 aifp1740 pre1722 ppro848 art,ajn40 2532 aifp2296

10 When he shall come to be glorified in his saints, and to be admired

pre1722 an,aj3956 art,pap4100 3754 ppro2257 art,nn3142 pre1909 ppro5209 ainp4100

in all them*that*believe (because our testimony among you was believed)

pre1722 depro1565 art,nn2250

in that day. *Ps. 88:8 [Sept.]; Ps. 67:36 [Sept.]*

pre1519/repro3739 2532 pinm4336 ad3842 pre4012 ppro5216 2443 ppro2257 art,nn2316

11 Wherefore also we pray always for you, that our God would

asba515/ppro5209 art,nn2821 2532 asba4137 an,aj3956 an,nn2107

count*you*worthy of *this* calling, and fulfill all the good pleasure of *his*

an,nn19 2532 an,nn2041 an,nn4102 pre1722 an,nn1411

goodness, and the work of faith with power:

3704 art3588 nn3686 ppro2257 art,nn2962 an,nn2424 an,nn5547 asbp1740 pre1722 ppro5213

12 That the name of our Lord Jesus Christ may be glorified in you,

2532 ppro5210 pre1722 ppro846 pre2596 art3588 nn5485 ppro2257 art,nn2316 2532 an,nn2962 an,nn2424

and ye in him, according to the grace of our God and the Lord Jesus

an,nn5547

Christ. *(Is. 24:15; 66:5; Mal. 1:11)*

☞ 1:7 See note on 1 Thessalonians 2:19.

The Day of the Lord

2 ☞ Now we beseech you, brethren, by the coming of our Lord
Jesus Christ, and *by* our gathering together unto him,

☞ 2 That ye be not soon shaken in mind, or be troubled, neither by
spirit, nor by word, nor by letter as from us, as that the day of Christ
is*at*hand.

☞ 3 Let no man deceive you by any means: for *that day shall not come,*
except there come a falling away first, and that man of sin be revealed, the
son of perdition;

4 Who opposeth and exalteth himself above all that is called God, or
that*is*worshiped; so that he as God sitteth in the temple of God,
showing himself that he is God.   *(Dan. 11:36; Ezek. 28:2)*

5 Remember ye not, that, when I was yet with you, I told you
these things?

☞ 6 And now ye know what withholdeth that he might be revealed in
his time.

☞ **2:1** See note on 1 Thessalonians 2:19.

☞ **2:2** See note on 1 Thessalonians 5:2.

☞ **2:3–12** See note on Revelation 13:1–18.

☞ **2:3–9** The "man of sin" is called the Antichrist in other Scripture passages (1 John 2:18; 4:3; 2 John 1:7). The preposition *antí* (473), "against," indicates this man's opposition to, not a replacement of Christ (Dan. 7:7, 8, 21; Matt. 24:15; Rev. 13:1–18). The characteristic of this individual is that he "opposeth and exalteth himself above all that is called God, or that is worshiped" (v. 4). He will be a miracle worker and even claim to be God. His coming will be "after the working of Satan" (v. 9), but it will not be Satan. It is clear that Paul thinks that Satan is not concerned with the past, but with the future. Paul does not see the world evolving gradually into a perfected state, but the fact of evil continuing right up until the end. At that time, evil will make its greatest challenge to good, and the forces of evil will be led by a mysterious figure. This person will be empowered by Satan and is the instrument of Satan's climactic challenge to the things of God. Paul predicts that Christ will consume the "man of sin . . . with the spirit of his mouth" (vv. 3, 8). At that time, Satan and all of his conspirators will be defeated.

☞ **2:6, 7** Paul refers here to the Holy Spirit as the restraining force in this world, restricting the many little "antichrists" existing today (1 John 2:18) as well as the final Antichrist. In verse six, the Holy Spirit is called *tó* katéchon (3588, 2722) or "that (which) withholdeth." This uses the neuter gender and corresponds to the phrase *tó* Pneúma (3588, 4151), "the Spirit," also in the neuter (John 14:26). In verse seven, it is *hó* katéchōn, "he who letteth," denoting that the Antichrist will never be able to do

(continued on next page)

1063   art3588   nn3466   art,nn458   ad2235   pinm1754   an,ajn3440

7 For the mystery of iniquity doth already work: only

art,pap2722/737   ad2193   asbm1096   pre1537   an,ajn3319

he*who*now*letteth *will let,* until he be taken out of the way.

2532   ad5119   art,ajn459   fp601   repro3739 art3588 nn2962   ft355

☞ 8 And then shall that Wicked be revealed, whom the Lord shall consume

art3588   nn4151   ppro848 art,nn4750   2532   ft2673   art3588   nn2015   ppro848

with the spirit of his mouth, and shall destroy with the brightness of his

art,nn3952

coming: *(Job 4:9; Is. 11:4)*

repro3739   art,nn3952   pin2076   pre2596   an,nn1753   art,nn4567 pre1722 an,aj3956

☞ 9 *Even him,* whose coming is after the working of Satan with all

an,nn1411   2532 an,nn4592   2532 an,nn5579   an,nn5059

power and signs and lying wonders,

2532   pre1722   an,aj3956   an,nn539   art,nn93   pre1722

☞ 10 And with all deceivableness of unrighteousness in

art,ppmp622   pre473/repro3739   aom1209   3756 art3588   nn26   art3588   nn225   ppro846

them*that*perish; because they received not the love of the truth, that they

aies4982

might be saved.

2532   pre1223/depro5124   art,nn2316   ft3992 ppro846   an,nn1753/an,nn4106   ppro846

11 And for*this*cause God shall send them strong delusion, that they should

aies4100   art,nn5579

believe a lie:

2443   an,ajn3956   asbp2919   art,apta4100   3361 art3588   nn225   235

12 That they all might be damned who believed not the truth, but

apta2106   pre1722   art,nn93

had pleasure in unrighteousness.

Stand Firm

1161 epn2249   pin3784   pinf2168   ad3842   art,nn2316 pre4012 ppro5216   an,nn80

13 But we are bound to give thanks always to God for you, brethren

pfpp25   pre5259   an,nn2962   3754   art,nn2316   pre575   an,nn746   aom138   ppro5209 pre1519

beloved of the Lord, because God hath from the beginning chosen you to

an,nn4991   pre1722   an,nn38   an,nn4151 2532 an,nn4102   an,nn225

salvation through sanctification of the Spirit and belief of the truth: *(Deut. 33:12)*

(continued from previous page)
anything without the specific permission of the Holy Spirit. Of course, verse seven does not refer to a departure of the Holy Spirit, but to the removal of His restraining power. This will allow Satan and the Antichrist to have free reign on the earth, but whatever happens will help to further God's plan according to His own timetable.

☞ **2:8** See note on 1 Thessalonians 2:19.

☞ **2:9** In this verse there are three words which explain supernatural manifestations or miracles: *dúnamis* (1411), *sēmeion* (4592), and *téras* (5059). Observe how the miracles mentioned in this verse are accomplished by the power of Satan. Miracle working is not necessarily evidence of God's power (Acts 19:13, cf. Ex. 7:22).

☞ **2:10–12** See note on Revelation 7:1–17.

pre1519/repro3739   aina2564   ppro5209   pre1223   ppro2257   art,nn2098   pre1519   an,nn4047

14 Whereunto he called you   by   our   gospel,   to   the obtaining of the

an,nn1391   ppro2257 art,nn2962 an,nn2424   an,nn5547

glory of our Lord Jesus Christ.

686/3767   an,nn80   pim4739   2532   pim2902 art3588   nn3862   repro3739

15 Therefore, brethren, stand fast, and hold the traditions which ye have

ainp1321   1535   pre1223 an,nn3056 1535 (pre1223) ppro2257   an,nn1992

been taught, whether by word,   or   our epistle.

1161   ppro2257 art,nn2962   an,nn2424   an,nn5547   epn846   2532   art,nn2316   2532   ppro2257   an,nn3962

16 Now our Lord Jesus Christ himself, and God, even our Father,

art,apta25   ppro2248   2532   apta1325   an,aj166   an,nn3874   2532   an,aj18

which*hath*loved us,   and hath given *us* everlasting consolation and good

an,nn1680   pre1722   an,nn5485

hope through grace,

opt3870   ppro5216   art,nn2588   2532   opt4741   ppro5209   pre1722   an,aj3956   an,aj18   an,nn3056   2532

17 Comfort your hearts, and establish you   in   every good word and

an,nn2041

work.

art,ajn3063   an,nn80   pim4336   pre4012 ppro2257   2443   art3588   nn3056   art3588   nn2962

3 Finally, brethren, pray for us, that the word of the Lord may

psa5143   2532   psmp1392   2532   ad2531   pre4314 ppro5209

have*free*course, and be glorified, even as *it is* with you:

2532   2443   asbp4506   pre575   art,aj824   2532   an,aj4190   an,nn444   1063

2 And that we may be delivered from unreasonable and wicked men: for

an,ajn3956   3756 art,nn4102

all   *men* have not faith.

1161   art3588   nn2962   pin2076   pr/an,aj4103   repro3739   ft4741   ppro5209   2532   ft5442   pre575

3 But the Lord is   faithful, who shall establish you, and keep *you* from

art,ajn4190

evil.

1161   pfi3982   pre1722   an,nn2962   pre1909   ppro5209   3754   2532   pin4160

4 And we have confidence in the Lord touching you, that ye both do

2532   ft4160   repro3739   pin3853   ppro5213

and will do the things which we command you.

1161   art3588   nn2962   opt2720   ppro5216   art,nn2588   pre1519 art3588   nn26   art,nn2316   2532   pre1519 art3588

5 And the Lord direct your hearts into the love of God, and into the

nn5281   art,nn5547

patient waiting for Christ.

"Be Not Weary in Well Doing"

1161   pin3853   ppro5213   an,nn80   pre1722   an,nn3686   ppro2257 art,nn2962 an,nn2424

6 Now we command you, brethren,   in   the name of our Lord Jesus

an,nn5547   ppro5209   pifm4724   pre575   an,aj3956   an,nn80   pap4043

Christ, that   ye   withdraw yourselves from every brother that walketh

ad814   2532   3361   pre2596 art3588   nn3862   repro3739   aina3880   pre3844 ppro2257

disorderly, and not after the tradition which he received of us.

7 For yourselves know how ye ought to follow us: for we behaved*not*ourselves*disorderly among you;

8 Neither did we eat any man's bread for naught; but wrought with labor and travail night and day, that we might not be chargable to any of you:

9 Not because we have not power, but to make ourselves an example unto you to follow us.

10 For even when we were with you, this we commanded you, that if any would not work, neither should he eat.

11 For we hear that there are some which walk among you disorderly, working not*at*all, but are busybodies.

12 Now them*that*are*such we command and exhort by our Lord Jesus Christ, that with quietness they work, and eat their own bread.

13 But ye, brethren, be*not*weary in well doing.

14 And if any man obey not our word by this epistle, note that man, and have*no*company with him, that he may be ashamed.

15 Yet count *him* not as an enemy, but admonish *him* as a brother.

16 Now the Lord of peace himself give you peace always by all means. The Lord *be* with you all.

17 The salutation of Paul with mine own hand, which is the token in every epistle: so I write.

18 The grace of our Lord Jesus Christ *be* with you all. Amen.

The First Epistle of Paul the Apostle to

TIMOTHY

The two epistles to Timothy and the one to Titus, because of their special instruction for church leaders, are commonly known as the Pastoral Epistles. It is generally believed that they were written just before Paul's martyrdom about A.D. 66. In these letters, Paul records his thoughts and feelings as he prepared to pass his ministry on to others.

Timothy's mother was a Jewess, and his father was a Greek (Acts. 16:1). By the time of Paul's second missionary journey, Timothy's mother had also become a Christian. His mother and grandmother had instructed him in the Scriptures (2 Tim. 1:5).

Timothy was a native of Lystra (Acts 16:1) and was highly esteemed by his Christian brethren both in Lystra and Iconium (Acts 16:2). He came to know the Lord through Paul's ministry in Lystra on his first missionary journey. During the second journey, Paul and Silas added Timothy to their party (Acts 15:36–41). To avoid criticism from the Jews, Timothy was circumcised by Paul before they set out on their journey. Paul sent Timothy back to Thessalonica as his repesentative (1 Thess. 3:1, 2) when he was hindered by Satan from going there himself (1 Thess. 2:17, 18). The next time he is mentioned, Paul is sending him away from Ephesus with Erastus on another important mission to Macedonia (Acts 19:22). From there, he was to proceed to Corinth (1 Cor. 4:17). Apparently, Timothy was of a timid nature because Paul encouraged the believers in Corinth to accept him (1 Cor. 16:10, 11, cf. 1 Tim. 4:12).

Timothy also accompanied Paul on the journey to Jerusalem (Acts 20:4, 5) and was with Paul in Rome when he wrote three of the Prison Epistles (Phil. 1:1; 2:19; Col. 1:1; Phile. 1:1). After his release from prison, Paul became engaged in further ministry in the East, and left Timothy at Ephesus (1 Tim. 1:3) to deal with the false teachers, supervise public worship, and aid the church in the appointment of officials. Paul hoped to eventually rejoin Timothy, but wrote this letter because he feared that he might be delayed. The second letter to Timothy was written after Paul was arrested again and put on trial for his life (see the introduction to 2 Timothy). There is no indication as to whether Timothy visited Paul as he had requested. In fact, nothing else is known about Timothy except that he himself became a prisoner (Heb. 13:23).

Paul was writing to Timothy to instruct him on how to deal with the growing problem of false teachers that was evident in the church at Ephesus. The fact that these false teachers had infiltrated the church in Ephesus was a sad fulfillment of Paul's prediction nearly five years earlier (Acts 20:28–30). Paul urged Timothy to boldly withstand these evil men by upholding the truth of the Scripture.

1 an,nn3972 an,nn652 an,nn2424 an,nn5547 pre2596 an,nn2003 an,nn2316 ppro2257
Paul, an apostle of Jesus Christ by the commandment of God our

an,nn4990 2532 an,nn2962 an,nn2424 an,nn5547 ppro2257 art,nn1680
Savior, and Lord Jesus Christ, *which is* our hope;

an,nn5095 an,aj1103 an,nn5043 pre1722 an,nn4102 an,nn5485 an,nn1656 an,nn1515
2 Unto Timothy, *my* own son in the faith: Grace, mercy, *and* peace,

pre575 an,nn2316 ppro2257 an,nn3962 2532 an,nn2424 an,nn5547 ppro2257 art,nn2962
from God our Father and Jesus Christ our Lord.

False Doctrine

ad2531 aina3870 ppro4571 ainf4537 pre1722 an,nn2181 ppmp4198 pre1519
☞ 3 As I besought thee to abide still at Ephesus, when I went into

an,nn3109 2443 asba3853 idpro5100 pinf2085/3361
Macedonia, that thou mightest charge some that they teach*no*other*doctrine,

3366 pinf4337 an,nn3454 2532 an,aj562 an,nn1076 repro3748 pin3930
4 Neither give heed to fables and endless genealogies, which minister

an,nn2214 ad3123 2228 an,nn2316 an,nn3618 art3588 pre1722 an,nn4102
questions, rather than godly edifying which is in faith: *so do.*

1161 art3588 nn5056 art3588 nn3852 pin2076 pr/an,nn26 pre1537 an,aj2513 an,nn2588 2532
5 Now the end of the commandment is charity out of a pure heart, and

an,aj18 an,nn4893 2532 an,nn4102 an,aj505
of a good conscience, and *of* faith unfeigned:

repro3739 idpro5100 apta795 aina1624 pre1519 an,nn3150
6 From which some having swerved have turned aside unto vain jangling;

pap2309 pinf1511 pr/an,nn3547 (3361) pap3539 3383 repro3739
7 Desiring to be teachers*of*the*law; understanding neither what they

pin3004 3383 pre4012/inpro5101 pinm1226
say, nor whereof they affirm.

1161 pin1492 3754 art3588 nn3551 pr/an,aj2570 1437 idpro5100 psmp5530 ppro846 ad3545
8 But we know that the law *is* good, if a man use it lawfully;

pfp1492 depro5124 3754 nn3551 3756 pinm2749 an,ajn1342 1161
9 Knowing this, that the law is not made for a righteous man, but for the

an,ajn459 2532 an,ajn506 an,ajn765 2532 an,ajn268 an,ajn462 2532
lawless and disobedient, for the ungodly and for sinners, for unholy and

an,ajn952 an,nn3964 2532 an,nn3389 an,nn409
profane, for murderers*of*fathers and murderers*of*mothers, for manslayers,

an,nn4205 an,nn733
10 For whoremongers, for them*that*defile*themselves*with*mankind, for

an,nn405 an,nn5583 an,ajn1965 2532 idpro1536 an,ajn2087
menstealers, for liars, for perjured persons, and if*there*be*any other thing

pinm480 art,pap5198 an,nn1319
that is contrary to sound doctrine;

pre2596 art3588 nn1391 art,nn2098 art3588 aj3107 an,nn2316 repro3739
11 According to the glorious gospel of the blessed God, which was

ainp4100 epn1473
committed to my trust.

☞ **1:3** See the introduction to 1 Timothy.

Paul's Personal Expression of Thanksgiving to God

2532   pin2192/an,nn5485   an,nn5547   an,nn2424   ppro2257   art,nn2962   art,apta1743   ppro3165   3754

12 And I   thank   Christ Jesus our Lord, who*hath*enabled me, for that

aom2233   ppro3165   pr/an,aj4103   aptm5087   pre1519   an,nn1248

he counted me   faithful, putting me into the ministry;

art,pap5607   cd/an,ajn4386   pr/an,ajn989   2532   pr/an,nn1376   2532   pr/an,nn5197   235

13 Who was before a blasphemer, and a persecutor, and injurious: but I

ainp1653   3754   aina4160   pap50   pre1722   an,nn570

obtained mercy, because I did *it* ignorantly in unbelief.

1161   art3588   nn5485   ppro2257 art,nn2962   aina5250   pre3326 an,nn4102   2532

14 And the grace of our   Lord was*exceeding*abundant with faith and

an,nn26   art3588   pre1722 an,nn5547   an,nn2424

love which is   in   Christ Jesus.

pr/an,aj4103   art,nn3056   2532   pr/an,aj514   an,aj3956   an,nn594   3754   an,nn5547

15 This *is* a faithful saying, and worthy of   all   acceptation, that Christ

an,nn2424 aina2064 pre1519 art3588   nn2889   ainf4982   an,ajn268   repro3739 epn1473 pin1510 pr/nu,aj4413

Jesus came into the world to save sinners; of whom   I   am chief.

235   pre1223/depro5124   ainp1653   2443   pre1722 ppro1698 nu,aj4413 an,nn2424

16 Howbeit for*this*cause I obtained mercy, that   in   me   first Jesus

an,nn5547   asba1731   art,aj3956   an,nn3115   pre4314   an,nn5296

Christ might show   forth   all   longsuffering,   for   a   pattern   to

art,pap3195   pinf4100   pre1909 ppro846 pre1519 an,nn2222   an,aj166

them*which*should*hereafter believe on him to   life everlasting.

1161   art3588   nn935   art,nn165   an,aj862   an,aj517   an,aj3441 an,aj4680 an,nn2316

17 Now unto the King eternal, immortal, invisible, the   only   wise God, *be*

an,nn5092   2532   an,nn1391   pre1519/art,nn165/art,nn165   281

honor and glory forever*and*ever. Amen.

depro5026   art,nn3852   pinm3908   ppro4671   an,nn5043   an,nn5095   pre2596   art3588

18 This   charge I commit unto thee,   son   Timothy, according to the

nn4394   pap4254   pre1909 ppro4571   2443   pre1722 ppro846   psmp4754

prophecies which went before on thee, that thou   by   them mightest   war   a

art,aj2570   an,nn4752

good warfare;

pap2192   an,nn4102   2532   an,aj18   an,nn4893   repro3739   idpro5100   aptm683

☞ 19 Holding faith, and a   good   conscience; which some having put away

pre4012   art,nn4102   aina3489

concerning faith have made shipwreck:

repro3739   pin2076   an,nn5211   2532   an,nn223   repro3739   aina3860

20 Of whom   is   Hymenaeus and Alexander; whom I have delivered unto

art,nn4567   2443   asbp3811 3361   pinf987

Satan, that they may learn not to blaspheme.

☞ **1:19, 20** In encouraging Timothy to be strengthened in the Christian warfare, Paul reminds him of the inseparable relation of faith and a good conscience. Those who are constantly doubting and questioning, have come to this point by thrusting away the pricks of their conscience. Such men were Hymenaeus and Alexander, whose doubt and immoral character had led them to blasphemy, to contradict and revile the doctrines of grace. Paul says that these men have been "delivered unto Satan." This is not merely some mental "giving up," convinced that his concern and prayers were to no end. Likewise, it does not indicate that Paul, through some supernatural power, delivered them over to be tormented by Satan, whether such torment be given in this life or the next. Instead, Paul has excluded them from the local fellowship of believers. Until they would repent of their wicked deeds, they would be left outside of the fellowship of God's people, so that Satan might buffet them.

Pray for Those in Authority

2 ☞ I exhort therefore, that, first of all, supplications, prayers,
intercessions, *and* giving*of*thanks, be made for all men;

2 For kings, and *for* all that are in authority; that we may lead a
quiet and peaceable life in all godliness and honesty.

3 For this *is* good and acceptable in*the*sight of God our Savior;

4 Who will have all men to be saved, and to come unto the knowledge
of the truth.   *(Ezek. 18:23)*

5 For *there is* one God, and one mediator between God and men, the
man Christ Jesus;

6 Who gave himself a ransom for all, to be testified in due time.

7 Whereunto I am ordained a preacher, and an apostle, (I speak the
truth in Christ, *and* lie not;) a teacher of the Gentiles in faith and
verity.

8 I will therefore that men pray every where, lifting up holy hands,
without wrath and doubting.

☞ 9 In*like*manner also, that women adorn themselves in modest apparel,
with shamefacedness and sobriety; not with braided hair, or gold, or pearls,
or costly array.

☞ **2:1, 2** These remarks are designed to encourage believers to pray for kings and all those in authority over them, whether such leaders are believers or unbelievers (see note on 1 Peter 2:17). The object of the prayer is explained, "That we may lead a tranquil and quiet life." Praying for a person does not necessarily involve approving of his personality or acts.

☞ **2:9–15** These verses indicate that women were full and active members in the early church (cf. 1 Cor. 11:4–5; Titus 2:1–10). From an examination of 1 Corinthians 11:2–16, it is also clear that both wives and husbands could pray and prophesy in the worship service (see note on 1 Cor. 14:33–40). In all this discussion, Paul's chief concern is that no woman would be of immoral character by having short hair or a shaven head, because in this manner she dishonors God, her husband's character, and herself. Peter also had something to say concerning the witness of women and their conduct at home (1 Pet. 3:1–7). In marital relationships, a woman is not presented as having any fewer rights over her

(continued on next page)

235   repro3739   pin4241   an,nn1135   ppmp1861   an,nn2317   pre1223 an,aj18   an,nn2041

10 But (which becometh women professing godliness) with good works.

an,nn1135   pim3129 pre1722   an,nn227   pre1722 an,aj3956   an,nn5292

11 Let the woman learn in silence with all subjection.

1161   pin2010   3756   an,nn1135   pinf1321   3761   pinf831

12 But I suffer not a woman to teach, nor to usurp*authority*over the

an,nn435 235   pinf1511 pre1722   an,nn2271

man, but to be in silence.

1063   76   nu,aj4413   ainp4111   ad1534 an,nn2096

13 For Adam was first formed, then Eve. *(Gen. 1:27; 2:7,22)*

(continued from previous page)

husband than he has over his wife. The key to understanding what the Apostle Paul is teaching is that women should not try to appear or act like men. In addition to this, they should not attempt to usurp the position of their husbands in the home and in the church. God has appointed specific tasks for both women and for men. Childbearing is reserved for women, just as the role of a husband is set aside for men. Paul emphatically states that these were differences created by God Himself.

Furthermore, in Galatians 3:28, Paul made it clear that there are no distinctions between male and female in Christ. He indicates that there are differences between the sexes, but no distinctions of believers in Christ. Moreover, Paul explains that the general attitude of Christians should not be to flaunt one's customs even if they are the proper ones. If the acceptable code of behavior indicates a definite distinction between the manner of dress of a man and a woman, adhere to that which will characterize one's own sex. In addition to this, differentiation should exist between women and men by the method of hair grooming or style, and it is necessary to maintain that accepted distinction. Paul's other concern is that a woman should not dress in a provocative manner, bringing the attention of men to herself. A Christian woman should be one man's wife, and in like manner, a husband should have only one wife (1 Cor. 7:2).

In 1 Timothy chapter two, the Apostle Paul is concerned about women appearing modest in their clothing. In verse nine, the Greek word *sōphrosúnē* (4997; cf. v. 15) provides the clue for the interpretation of this difficult passage. This Greek word, translated "sobriety," means "the voluntary limitation of one's freedom of thought and behavior," or "sober mindedness." The truth is that in Christianity women became free and equal to their husbands. Nevertheless, there was always a danger that they might take this freedom beyond the limitations that God had placed when He appointed man as head over woman in the marital relationship. No two people or things can be exactly the same. The inherent differences in people and things must be recognized by a *sōphrón*, or a "sober minded" person. This is one who recognizes his abilities and his limitations, and is mindful of his behavior in certain given circumstances.

There are numerous references in the Scripture where women are recognized as friends and co-workers in the gospel (Rom. 16:1–4). Peter refers to women as "heirs together of the grace of life" (1 Pet. 3:7). In one such instance, Paul does not differentiate between Priscilla and her husband Aquila, rather he refers to them both with the same word, *sunergoús* (4904), meaning "fellow workers" (Rom. 16:3). He does not distinguish between the work each can do because one is male and the other female (cf. Rom. 16:21; Phile. 1:24).

To function properly, everything needs a person in the position of leadership, especially a family. The marriage unit consists of two people that have two distinct personalities. These two require a "headship," that being the man according to God's creation and ordinance. In 1 Timothy 2:11, there are several key words that show how a wife should convey a proper relationship to her husband. The first of these terms is *gunḗ* (1135) which, depending on the context, may indicate a woman in general or a wife. The close relationship of this word with the word *andrós* (from *anḗr* [435]) meaning "husband," not simply "man," requires that the word be translated "wife." The subsequent term to consider is *hēsuchía* (2271), translated "silence." In the NT it occurs numerous times referring to tranquility or the state of being undisturbed. This should be the understanding in this verse. One must bear in mind here that during the era of time when Paul was writing, it was usually men who were the ones to

(continued on next page)

2532   76   3756   ainp538   1161 art3588   nn1135   aptp538   pfi1096 pre1722

14 And Adam was not deceived, but the woman being deceived was in

an,nn3847

the transgression.   *(Gen. 3:6,13)*

1161   fp4982   pre1223   art,nn5042   1437   asba3306

15 Notwithstanding she shall be saved in childbearing, if they continue

pre1722 an,nn4102 2532   an,nn26   2532   an,nn38   pre3326   an,nn4997

in faith and charity and holiness with sobriety.

Qualifications to Be an Overseer

pr/an,aj4103 art,nn3056   idpro1536   pinm3713   an,nn1984   pin1937

3 This *is* a true saying, If*a*man desire the office*of*a* bishop, he desireth

an,aj2570 an,nn2041

a good work.

art,nn1985   3767   pin1163   pinf1511   pr/an,aj423   pr/an,nn435   nu3391 an,nn1135   pr/an,aj3524

☞ 2 A bishop then must be blameless, the husband of one wife, vigilant,

pr/an,aj4998   pr/an,aj2887   pr/an,aj5382   pr/an,aj1317

sober, of*good*behavior, given*to*hospitality, apt*to*teach;

(continued from previous page)
receive an education. If this word meant "complete silence," women would never have the opportunity to ask questions or increase her knowledge of the Scriptures. Simply speaking, the wife ought to be displaying a tranquil spirit in her attempt to learn. The final word of key importance in understanding the "silence" mentioned in this verse is *hupotagé* (5292) meaning "to place in proper order," translated "subjection." Paul wanted to express the idea that in the wife's desire to learn, she should respect her husband's position over her in Christ (cf. 1 Cor. 11:3).

The phrase in 1 Timothy 1:12, "But I suffer not a woman to teach . . ." should be understood as "But I suffer not a *wife* to teach." The discussion continues drawing contrasts between the Greek words for wife and for husband. The usage of *guné* in this verse must be translated as "a wife" corresponding to the reference in verse eleven. However, *andrós* (435) is translated as "man" in verse twelve. However, it is better rendered "husband" when the usage of this Greek word occurs in relation to a discussion of wives. Furthermore, the word for "teach" in this verse is the Greek infinitive *didáskein* (1321). In this instance, it means "to teach continuously." The situation refers to the home, an assembly, or anywhere the husband and wife may be interacting together. If this were the case, the position of the husband as the head would be undermined, and would not be in accordance with God's ordained order in creation. A wife should place limitations on her speech. Paul does not want women to be lackluster or even mute, but to be careful lest they go beyond the bounds of accepted propriety (see discussion on v. 9).

Moreover, the word translated "to usurp authority over" is the Greek word *authentein* (831). Essentially, a wife's private or public life should be beyond reproach and never undermine the position that her husband has been given by God. Also, a wife should never encroach upon the role of her husband. In verse thirteen, Paul explains why this is so: "For Adam was first formed, then Eve." This is not because the husband is better, more intelligent, or more worthy than she; rather, it is the order originally ordained by God, for her to respect. See note on Titus 2:1–5.

☞ **3:2** The phrase "husband of one wife" does not mean that the bishop or the deacon was never married before else it would exclude a remarried widower (see 1 Tim. 3:12). Furthermore, it does not mean that in order to become a bishop or a deacon, one must be married. In Romans 7:1–3, the Apostle Paul placed no restrictions upon a widower to remarry. The meaning of this phrase is that the bishop or the deacon should not be married to more than one woman simultaneously. In the Greek, *miás gunaikós* (3391, 1135), meaning "of one woman," would have been better translated "a one-woman husband." The total context speaks of the moral conduct of the bishop and the deacon. He should be a man totally dedicated to his wife and not flirtatious (cf. Titus 1:6).

3361   pr/an,aj3943   3361   pr/an,nn4131   3361   pr/an,aj146   235   pr/an,aj1933

3 Not given*to*wine, no striker, not greedy*of*filthy*lucre; but patient,

pr/an,aj269   pr/an,aj866

not*a*brawler, not covetous;

pr/an,ppmp4291   ad2573   art,aj2398   an,nn3624   pr/pap2192   an,nn5043   pre1722   an,nn5292

4 One*that*ruleth well his own house, having his children in   subjection

pre3326 an,aj3956   an,nn4587

with   all   gravity;

1161   1487   idpro5100 pin1492 3756   ainf4291   art,aj2398   an,nn3624   ad4459

5 (For if a man know not how to rule his own house, how shall he

fm1959   an,nn1577   an,nn2316

take*care*of the church of God?)

3361   pr/an,ajn3504   3363   aptp5187   asba1706   pre1519

6 Not a novice, lest being lifted*up*with*pride he   fall   into   the

an,nn2917   art3588   ajn1228

condemnation of the devil.

1161   ppro846 pin1163(2532) pinf2192   an,aj2570 an,nn3141 pre575   art,ad1855

7 Moreover he   must have a good report of them*which*are*without;

3363   asba1706 pre1519   an,nn3680   2532   an,nn3803   art3588 ajn1228

lest he fall into reproach and the snare of the devil.

Qualifications for Servants

ad5615   an,nn1249   pr/an,aj4586 3361   pr/an,aj1351   3361 pr/pap4337

8 Likewise *must* the deacons *be* grave, not doubletongued, not given to

an,aj4183 an,nn3631 3361   pr/an,aj146

much wine, not greedy*of*filthy*lucre;

pr/pap2192 art3588   nn3466   art3588 nn4102 pre1722   an,aj2513   an,nn4983

9 Holding the mystery of the faith in   a pure conscience.

2532   depro3778   1161   nu,aj4412   pim1381   ad1534

10 And   let   these   also   first   be   proved;   then   let   them

pim1247   pap5607   pr/an,aj410

use*the*office*of*a*deacon, being *found* blameless.

ad5615   an,nn1135   pr/an,aj4586 3361   pr/an,ajn1228 pr/an,aj3524 pr/an,aj4103 pre1722

11 Even so *must* *their* wives *be* grave, not slanderers, sober, faithful in

an,ajn3956

all things.

an,nn1249   pim2077   pr/an,nn435   nu3391 an,nn1135 pr/ppmp4291   an,nn5043

12 Let the deacons be the husbands of one wife, ruling their children

2532   art,aj2398   an,nn3624   ad2573

and their own houses well.

1063   art,apta1247   ad2573   pinm4046

13 For   they*that*have*used*the*office*of*a*deacon   well   purchase to

rxpro1438   an,aj2570   an,nn898   2532 an,aj4183 an,nn3954 pre1722   an,nn4102 art3588   pre1722

themselves a good degree, and great boldness in   the faith which is in

an,nn5547 an,nn2424

Christ Jesus.

depro5023   pin1125   ppro4671 pap1679   ainf2064 pre4314 ppro4571 cd/an,ajn5032

14 These things write I unto thee, hoping to come unto thee shortly:

1161   1437   psa1019   2443   asba1492 ad4459   pin1163

15 But if I tarry long, that thou mayest know how thou oughtest to

pifm390   pre1722   an,nn3624   an,nn2316 repro3748 pin2076   pr/an,nn1577   an,pap2198 an,nn2316

behave thyself in the house of God, which is the church of the living God,

pr/an,nn4769 2532 pr/an,nn1477   art3588   nn225

the pillar and ground of the truth.

2532   ad3672   pr/an,aj3173 pin2076 art3588   nn3466   art,nn2150   an,nn2316

16 And without controversy great is the mystery of godliness: God was

ainp5319   pre1722   an,nn4561 ainp1344   pre1722   an,nn4151 ainp3700   an,nn32   ainp2784   pre1722

manifest in the flesh, justified in the Spirit, seen of angels, preached unto

an,nn1484   ainp4100   pre1722   an,nn2889   ainp353   pre1722 an,nn1391

the Gentiles, believed on in the world, received up into glory.

Apostasy

4

1161   art3588   nn4151   pin3004   ad4490   3754   pre1722   an,aj5306 an,nn2540 idpro5100

Now the Spirit speaketh expressly, that in the latter times some

fm868   art3588   nn4102   pap4337   an,aj4108   an,nn4151   2532

shall depart from the faith, giving heed to seducing spirits, and

an,nn1319   an,nn1140

doctrines of devils;

an,aj5573   pre1722   an,nn5272   art,aj2398   an,nn4893

2 Speaking lies in hypocrisy; having their conscience

pfpp2743

seared*with*a*hot*iron;

pap2967   pinf1060   pifm567   an,nn1033 repro3739

3 Forbidding to marry, *and commanding* to abstain from meats, which

art,nn2316   aina2936   pre1519/an,nn3336   pre3326   an,nn2169   art,ajn4103

God hath created to*be*received with thanksgiving of them*which*believe

2532   pfp1921 art3588   nn225

and know the truth.   *(Gen. 2:16; 9:3)*

3754   an,aj3956   an,nn2938   an,nn2316   pr/an,aj2570 2532 an,ajn3762   pr/an,aj579

4 For every creature of God *is* good, and nothing to be refused, if it be

ppmp2983   pre3326   an,nn2169

received with thanksgiving: *(Gen. 1:31)*

1063   pinp37   pre1223   an,nn3056   an,nn2316 2532   an,nn1783

5 For it is sanctified by the word of God and prayer.

Be an Example

ppmp5294/art3588/nn80   depro5023

6 If thou put*the*brethren*in*remembrance of these things, thou shalt

---

☞ **4:1–3** See note on 2 Thessalonians 2:3.

fm2071　an,aj2570　pr/an,nn1249　　an,nn2424　an,nn5547　　ppmp1789　　　art3588　　nn3056　　art,nn4102　2532
be a good minister of Jesus Christ, nourished up in the words of faith and of

art,aj2570　an,nn1319　repro3739　　　　　pfi3877
good doctrine, whereunto thou hast attained.

　　　　1161　pim3868　art,aj952　2532　　an,aj1126　　an,nn3454　1161　pim1128　rxpro4572
7 But refuse profane and old wives' fables, and exercise thyself *rather*

pre4314　an,nn2150
unto godliness.

　　　1063　art,aj4984　an,nn1129　pin2076/pr/an,aj5624　(pre4314) an,aj3641　1161　art,nn2150　pin2076　pr/an,aj5624
8 For bodily exercise profiteth   little: but godliness is profitable

pre4314　an,ajn3956　pap2192　an,nn1860　　　　an,nn2222　art,ad3568　2532
unto all things, having promise of the life that*now*is, and of

art,pap3195
that*which*is*to*come.

　　　　pr/an,aj4103　art,nn3056　2532　pr/an,aj514　an,aj3956　an,nn594
9 This *is* a faithful saying and worthy of all   acceptation.

1063　pre1519/depro5124　2532　pin2872　2532　　pinp3679　　　3754　　pfi1679 pre1909
10 For therefore we both labor and suffer reproach, because we trust in

an,pap2198　an,nn2316　repro3739　pin2076　　pr/an,nn4990　an,aj3956　an,nn444　ad3122
the living God, who is the Savior of all men, especially of

an,ajn4103
those*that*believe.

　　depro5023　pim3853　2532　pim1321
11 These things command and teach.

　　an,ajn3367　pim2706　ppro4675　art,nn3503　235　pim1096　　pr/an,nn5179　art3588
12 Let no man despise thy youth; but be thou an example of the

ajn4103　pre1722 an,nn3056 pre1722　an,nn391　pre1722　an,nn26　pre1722 an,nn4151 pre1722 an,nn4102 pre1722
believers, in word, in conversation, in charity, in spirit, in faith, in

an,nn47
purity.

ad2193　pinm2064　　pin4337　　　art,nn320　　　art,nn3874　　　art,nn1319
13 Till I come, give attendance to reading, to exhortation, to doctrine.

pim272　3361 art3588 nn5486　　　pre1722 ppro4671 repro3739　　ainp1325 ppro4671 pre1223
14 Neglect not the gift that is in thee, which was given thee by

an,nn4394　pre3326　an,nn1936　art3588　nn5495　art3588　nn4244
prophecy, with the laying on of the hands of the presbytery.

　　pim3191　　depro5023　　　pim2468　　pre1722 depro5125 2443 ppro4675
15 Meditate upon these things; give*thyself*wholly to them; that thy

art,nn4297　psa5600/pr/an,aj5318 pre1722 an,ajn3956
profiting may appear to all.

　　pim1907　rxpro4572　2532　art3588　nn1319　pim1961　ppro846　1063
16 Take heed unto thyself, and unto the doctrine; continue in them: for in

pap4160 depro5124　　2532　ft4982　rxpro4572　2532　art,pap191　ppro4675
doing this thou shalt both save thyself, and them*that*hear thee.

☞ **4:12** A comparison of this verse and Titus 2:15 suggests that Titus may have been older and more mature than Timothy, in that he had been the stronger of the two during the difficulties in Corinth (1 Cor. 16:10; 2 Cor. 7:13–15). Titus volunteered readily for the delicate task of leading a church (2 Cor. 8:17), and he was full of affection and enthusiasm for the Corinthian brethren (2 Cor. 7:15). He was one who shared in Paul's spirit and example (2 Cor. 12:18). In this case, Paul was exhorting Timothy to continue on and not allow men to undermine his abilities. Paul understood the difficulty in being a leader, and his advice to Timothy was for him to lead by example.
☞ **4:14** See note on 2 Timothy 1:6.

More Instructions

5 ^{aosi1969} ³³⁶¹ ^{cd/an,ajn4245} ²³⁵ ^{pim3870} ^{ad5613} ^{an,nn3962} ^{cd/an,ajn3501}
Rebuke not an elder, but entreat *him* as a father; *and* the younger men

^{ad5613} ^{an,nn80}
as brethren;   *(Lev. 19:32)*

^{cd/an,ajn4245} ^{ad5613} ^{an,nn3384} ^{cd/an,ajn3501} ^{ad5613} ^{an,nn79} ^{pre1722} ^{an,aj3956}
2 The elder women as mothers; the younger as sisters, with all

^{an,nn47}
purity.

^{pim5091} ^{an,nn5503} ^{an,nn5503} ^{art,ad3689}
3 Honor widows that are widows indeed.

¹¹⁶¹ ¹⁴⁸⁷ ^{idpro5100} ^{an,nn5503} ^{pin2192} ^{an,nn5043} ²²²⁸ ^{an,nn1549} ^{pim3129} ^{nu,aj4412}
4 But if any widow have children or nephews, let them learn first to

^{pinf2151} ^(art,aj2398) ^{an,nn3624} ²⁵³² ^{pinf591/an,nn287} ^{art,nn4269} ¹⁰⁶³ ^{depro5124} ^{pin2076} ^{pr/an,aj2570} ²⁵³²
show piety at home, and to requite their parents: for that is good and

^{pr/an,aj587} ^{ad*1799} ^{art,nn2316}
acceptable before God.

¹¹⁶¹ ^{art,nn5503} ^{ad3689} ²⁵³² ^{pfpp3443} ^{pfi1679} ^{pre1909} ^{art,nn2316} ²⁵³²
5 Now she*that*is*a*widow indeed, and desolate, trusteth in God, and

^{pin4357} ^{art,nn1162} ²⁵³² ^{art,nn4335} ^{an,nn3571} ²⁵³² ^{an,nn2250}
continueth in supplications and prayers night and day.   *(Jer. 49:11)*

¹¹⁶¹ ^{art,pap4684} ^{pfi2348} ^{pap2198}
6 But she*that*liveth*in*pleasure is dead while she liveth.

²⁵³² ^{depro5023} ^{pim3853} ²⁴⁴³ ^{psa5600} ^{pr/an,aj423}
7 And these things give*in*charge, that they may be blameless.

¹¹⁶¹ ¹⁴⁸⁷ ^{idpro5100} ^{pin4306/3756} ^{art,ajn2398} ²⁵³² ^{ad3122}
8 But if any provide*not*for his own, and especially for

^{art,ajn3609} ^{pfip720} ^{art3588} ⁿⁿ⁴¹⁰² ²⁵³² ^{pin2076} ^{pr/cd/an,aj5501}
those*of*his*own*house, he hath denied the faith, and is worse than an

^{an,ajn571}
infidel.

³³⁶¹ ^{an,nn5503} ^{pim2639} ^{cd/an,ajn1640} ^{nu1835}
☞ 9 Let not a widow be taken*into*the*number under threescore

^{an,nn2094} ^{pfp1096} ^{pr/an,nn1135} ^{nv1520} ^{an,nn435}
years old, having been the wife of one man,

^{ppmp3140} ^{pre1722} ^{an,aj2570} ^{an,nn2041} ¹⁴⁸⁷ ^{aina5044}
10 Well*reported*of for good works; if she have brought*up*children,

¹⁴⁸⁷ ^{aina3580} ¹⁴⁸⁷ ^{aina3538} ^{an,ajn40} ^{an,nn4228} ¹⁴⁹⁷
if she have lodged*strangers, if she have washed the saints' feet, if she

^{aina1884} ^{ppmp2346} ¹⁴⁸⁷ ^{aina1872} ^{an,aj3956} ^{an,aj18} ^{an,nn2041}
have relieved the afflicted, if she have diligently followed every good work.

¹¹⁶¹ ^{cd/an,aj3501} ^{an,nn5503} ^{pim3868} ¹⁰⁶³ ^{ad3752}
11 But the younger widows refuse: for when they have

^{asba2691} ^{art,nn5547} ^{pin2309} ^{pinf1060}
begun*to*wax*wanton*against Christ, they will marry;

^{pap2192} ^{an,nn2917} ³⁷⁵⁴ ^{aina114} ^{art,nu,aj4413} ^{an,nn4102}
12 Having damnation, because they have cast off their first faith.

¹¹⁶¹ ^{ad260} ^{pin3129} ^{pr/an,ajn692}
13 And withal they learn *to* *be* idle,

☞ **5:9** See note on 1 Timothy 3:2 concerning a woman having one husband.

wandering*about*from*house*to*house; and not only idle, but tattlers also and busybodies, speaking things*which*they*ought not.

14 I will therefore that the younger women marry, bear children, guide*the*house, give none occasion to the adversary to*speak*reproachfully.

15 For some are already turned aside after Satan.

16 If any man or woman*that*believeth have widows, let them relieve them, and let not the church be charged; that it may relieve them*that*are*widows indeed.

17 Let the elders that rule well be counted worthy of double honor, especially they*who*labor in the word and doctrine.

18 For the Scripture saith, Thou shalt not muzzle the ox that treadeth out the corn. And, The laborer *is* worthy of his reward. *(Deut. 25:4)*

19 Against an elder receive not an accusation, but before two or three witnesses. *(Deut. 17:6; 19:15)*

20 Them*that*sin rebuke before all, that others also may fear.

21 I charge *thee* before God, and the Lord Jesus Christ, and the elect angels, that thou observe these things without preferring*one*before*another, doing nothing by partiality.

22 Lay hands suddenly on no man, neither be partaker of other men's sins: keep thyself pure.

23 Drink*no*longer*water, but use a little wine for*thy*stomach's*sake and thine often infirmities.

24 Some men's sins are open beforehand, going before to judgment; and some *men* they follow after.

25 Likewise also the good works *of some* are manifest beforehand; and they*that*are otherwise cannot be hid.

6 ^{an,ajn3745} ^{an,ajn1401} ^{pin1526} ^{pre5259} ^{an,nn2218} ^{pim2233} ^{art,aj2398} ^{an,nn1203}
Let as many servants as are under the yoke count their own masters

^{pr/an,aj514} ^{an,aj3956} ^{an,nn5092} ²⁴⁴³ ^{art3588} ⁿⁿ³⁶⁸⁶ ^{art,nn2316} ²⁵³² ^{art,nn1319} ³³⁶¹
worthy of all honor, that the name of God and *his* doctrine be not

^{psmp987}
blasphemed.

¹¹⁶¹ ^{art,pap2192} ^{an,aj4103} ^{an,nn1203} ³³⁶¹ ^{pim2706}
2 And they*that*have believing masters, let them not despise *them,*

³⁷⁵⁴ ^{pin1526} ^{pr/an,nn80} ²³⁵ ^{ad3123} ^{pim1398} ³⁷⁵⁴ ^{pin1526}
because they are brethren; but rather do*them*service, because they are

^{pr/an,aj4103} ²⁵³² ^{pr/an,aj27} ^{art,ppmp482} ^{art3588} ⁿⁿ²¹⁰⁸ ^{depro5023} ^{pim1321} ²⁵³² ^{pim3870}
faithful and beloved, partakers of the benefit. These things teach and exhort.

Healthy Teaching

^{idpro1536} ^{pin2085} ²⁵³² ^{pinm4334} ³³⁶¹ ^{pap5198} ^{an,nn3056}
3 If*any*man teach otherwise, and consent not to wholesome words, *even*

^{art3588} ^{ppro2257} ^{art,nn2962} ^{an,nn2424} ^{an,nn5547} ²⁵³² ^{art3588} ⁿⁿ¹³¹⁹ ^{pre2596}
the words of our Lord Jesus Christ, and to the doctrine which is according to

^{an,nn2150}
godliness;

^{pfip5187} ^{ppmp1987} ^{an,ajn3367} ²³⁵ ^{pap3552} ^{pre4012} ^{an,nn2214} ²⁵³²
4 He is proud, knowing nothing, but doting about questions and

^{an,nn3055} ^{pre1537/repro3739} ^{pinm1096} ^{an,nn5355} ^{an,nn2054} ^{an,nn988} ^{an,aj4190} ^{an,nn5283}
strifes*of*words, whereof cometh envy, strife, railings, evil surmisings.

^{an,nn3859} ^{an,nn444} ^{pfpp1311} ^{art,nn3563} ²⁵³² ^{pfpp650} ^{art3588} ⁿⁿ²²⁵
5 Perverse disputings of men of corrupt minds, and destitute of the truth,

^{pap3543} ^{pr/an,nn4200} ^{pinf1511} ^{art,nn2150} ^{pre575} ^{art,ajn5108} ^{pim868}
supposing that gain is godliness: from such withdraw thyself.

¹¹⁶¹ ^{art,nn2150} ^{pre3326} ^{an,nn841} ^{pin2076} ^{an,aj3173} ^{pr/an,nn4200}
6 But godliness with contentment is great gain.

¹⁰⁶³ ^{aina1533} ^{an,ajn3762} ^{pre1519} ^{art,nn2889} ^{an,ajn1212} ⁽³⁷⁵⁴⁾ ⁽³⁷⁶¹⁾ ^{pinm1410}
7 For we brought nothing into *this* world, *and it is* certain we can

^{pinf1627/idpro5100}
carry*nothing*out.   *(Job 1:21; Eccl. 5:15)*

¹¹⁶¹ ^{pap2192} ^{an,nn1305} ²⁵³² ^{an,nn4629} ^{fp714/depro5125}
8 And having food and raiment let us be*therewith*content.   *(Prov. 30:8)*

¹¹⁶¹ ^{art,ppmp1014} ^{pinf4147} ^{pin1706} ^{pre1519} ^{an,nn3986} ²⁵³² ^{an,nn3803} ²⁵³²
9 But they*that*will be rich fall into temptation and a snare, and *into*

^{an,aj4183} ^{an,aj453} ²⁵³² ^{an,aj983} ^{an,nn1939} ^{repro3748} ^{pin1036} ^{art,nn444} ^{pre1519} ^{an,nn3639} ²⁵³² ^{an,nn684}
many foolish and hurtful lusts, which drown men in destruction and perdition.

(Prov. 23:4; 28:22)

¹⁰⁶³ ^{art3588} ⁿⁿ⁵³⁶⁵ ^{pin2076} ^{pr/an,nn4491} ^{an,aj3956} ^{art,nn2556} ^{repro3739}
10 For the love*of*money is the root of all evil: which while

^{idpro5100} ^{ppmp3713} ^{ainp635} ^{pre575} ^{art3588} ⁿⁿ⁴¹⁰² ²⁵³²
some coveted after, they have erred from the faith, and

^{aina4044/rxpro1438} ^{an,aj4183} ^{an,nn3601}
pierced*themselves*through with many sorrows.

"Fight the Good Fight"

1161 · epn4771 · 5599 · an,nn444 · art,nn2316 · pim5343 · depro5023 · 1161 · pim1377

11 But thou, O man of God, flee these things; and follow after

an,nn1343 · an,nn2150 · an,nn4102 · an,nn26 · an,nn5281 · an,nn4236

righteousness, godliness, faith, love, patience, meekness.

pim75 · art3588 · aj2570 · an,nn73 · art,nn4102 · aipm1949 · art,aj166 · an,nn2222 · pre1519/repro3739

12 Fight the good fight of faith, lay*hold*on eternal life, whereunto

2532 · ainp2564 · 2532 · aina3670 · art,aj2570 · an,nn3671 · ad*1799 · an,aj4183

thou art also called, and hast professed a good profession before many

an,nn3144

witnesses.

pin3853/ppro4671 · ad*1799 · art,nn2316 · art,pap2227 · art,ajn3956 · 2532

13 I give*thee*charge in*the*sight of God, who quickeneth all things, and

an,nn5547 · an,nn2424 · pre1909 · an,nn4194 · an,nn4091 · art,apta3140 · art,aj2570 · an,nn3671

before Christ Jesus, who before Pontius Pilate witnessed a good confession;

ppro4571 · ainf5083 · art,nn1785 · an,aj784 · an,aj423 · ad3360 · art3588

14 That thou keep *this* commandment without spot, rebukable, until the

nn2015 · ppro2257 · art,nn2962 · an,nn2424 · an,nn5547

appearing of our Lord Jesus Christ:

repro3739 · an,aj2398 · an,nn2540 · ft1166 · art3588 · aj3107 · 2532 · an,aj3441

15 Which in his times he shall show, *who is* the blessed and only

an,nn1413 · art3588 · nn935 · art,pap936 · 2532 · an,nn2962 · art,pap2961

Potentate, the King of kings, and Lord of lords;   *(Deut. 10:17)*

art3588 · art,aj3441 · pap2192 · an,nn110 · pap3611 · an,nn5457

16 Who only hath immortality, dwelling in the light

an,aj676 · repro3739 · an,ajn3762 · an,nn444 · aina1492 · 3761 · pinm1410 · ainf1492

which*no*man*can*approach*unto; whom no man hath seen, nor can see:

repro3739 · an,nn5092 · 2532 · an,nn2904 · an,aj166 · 281

to whom *be* honor and power everlasting. Amen.   *(Ps. 104:2; Ex. 33:20)*

pim3853 · art,ajn4145 · pre1722 · art,ad3568/an,nn165

17 Charge them*that*are*rich in this world, that they

pinf5309/3361 · 3366 · pfin1679 · pre1909 · an,nn83 · an,nn4149 · 235 · pre1722 · art3588 · pap2198 · art,nn2316

be*not*highminded; nor trust in uncertain riches, but in the living God,

art,pap3930 · ppro2254 · ad4146 · an,ajn3956 · pre1519 · an,nn619

who giveth us richly all things to enjoy;   *(Ps. 62:10)*

pinf14 · pinf4147 · pre1722 · an,aj2570 · an,nn2041(pinf1511)

18 That they do good, that they be rich in good works,

pr/an,aj2130 · pr/an,aj2843

ready*to*distribute, willing*to*communicate;

pr/pap597 · rxpro1438 · an,aj2570 · an,nn2310 · pre1519 · art3588

19 Laying*up*in*store for themselves a good foundation against the

pap3195 · 2443 · asbm1949 · art,aj166 · an,nn2222

time*to*come, that they may lay*hold*on eternal life.

5599 · an,nn5095 · aima5442 · art,nn3872 · ppmp1624

20 O Timothy, keep that*which*is*committed*to*thy*trust, avoiding

art,aj952 · an,nn2757 · 2532 · an,nn477 · an,nn1108 · art,aj5581

profane *and* vain babblings, and oppositions of science falsely*so*called:

repro3739 · idpro5100 · ppmp1861 · aina795 · pre4012 · art3588 · nn4102 · art,nn5485 · pre3326

21 Which some professing have erred concerning the faith. Grace *be* with

ppro4675 · 281

thee. Amen.

The Second Epistle of Paul the Apostle to

TIMOTHY

Paul wrote this second letter to Timothy (see introduction to 1 Timothy) from a prison in Rome toward the close of his life (2 Tim. 1:8). This would place the date of the writing of this letter toward the end of A.D. 66. The Book of Acts concludes with Paul being placed under house arrest (Acts 28:30–31), but there is evidence in the Book of 2 Timothy that Paul was imprisoned a second time (2 Tim. 4:16–18). Most scholars believe that Paul was acquitted in the first trial and subsequently returned to Greece and Asia Minor to continue his missionary work. It is suggested that he was arrested again, taken back to Rome, and imprisoned in what is known as the Mamertine prison. This is evident from the fact that John Mark, who was present during Paul's first imprisonment (Col. 4:10), was not with Paul at the time he wrote 2 Timothy. Some believe that the second time Paul was imprisoned, he was being held for a much more serious charge (2 Tim. 2:9) than the one he was imprisoned for the first time. Paul believed that his death was near, but he was satisfied that he had done his best (2 Tim. 4:6–8).

Paul wrote this letter to encourage Timothy in the work of the ministry. Timothy would encounter persecution and turmoil in dealing with false teachers in his congregation. Paul urged him to exercise his spiritual gifts (2 Tim. 1:6), to boldly face suffering "as a good soldier of Jesus Christ" (2 Tim. 2:3), to deal wisely with false teachers in his church (2 Tim. 2:14–26), and to continue to exhibit a strong testimony for Christ in the wake of the apostasy and wickedness in the world (2 Tim. 3:1–9).

Some suggest that Paul was writing a more personal letter to Timothy because of the fact that he was expecting to die soon. The style of the epistle is less didactic than Paul's first letter to Timothy. Paul talks to Timothy as a father who would soon be leaving his son. The references to Timothy's own spiritual heritage and call to the ministry (1 Tim. 1:3, 5, 6) reveal how Paul reflected on his own influence on Timothy's life.

1
an,nn3972   an,nn652   an,nn2424 an,nn5547 pre1223   an,nn2307   an,nn2316   pre2596
Paul, an apostle of Jesus Christ by the will of God, according to the
an,nn1860   an,nn2222 art3588   pre1722 an,nn5547 an,nn2424
promise of life which is in Christ Jesus,

an,nn5095   an,aj27   an,nn5043 an,nn5485   an,nn1656   an,nn1515 pre575
2 To Timothy, *my* dearly beloved son: Grace, mercy, *and* peace, from
an,nn2316   an,nn3962   2532 an,nn5547 an,nn2424 ppro2257 art,nn2962
God the Father and Christ Jesus our Lord.

"Stir Up the Gift of God"

<small>pin2192/an,nn5485　art,nn2316　repro3739　pin3000　pre575　an,nn4269　pre1722　an,aj2513</small>
3 I　thank　God, whom I　serve　from　*my*　forefathers　with　pure
<small>an,nn4893　ad5613　an,aj88　pin2192　art,nn3417　pre4012　ppro4675　pre1722　ppro3450</small>
conscience, that without ceasing I have remembrance　of　thee　in　my
<small>art,nn1162　an,nn3571　2532　an,nn2250</small>
prayers night and day;

<small>pap1971　ainf1492　ppro4571　pfpp3415　ppro4675　art,nn1144　2443</small>
4 Greatly desiring to see thee, being mindful of thy　tears, that I may be
<small>asbp4137　an,nn5479</small>
filled with joy;

<small>pap2983　an,nn5280　art3588　an,aj505　nn4102　art3588　pre1722　ppro4671</small>
5 When I　call　to　remembrance　the　unfeigned　faith　that　is　in　thee,
<small>repro3748　aina1774　nu,aj4412　pre1722　ppro4675　art,nn3125　an,nn3030　2532　ppro4675　art,nn3384　an,nn2131　1161</small>
which dwelt first　in　thy　grandmother Lois, and　thy　mother Eunice; and I
<small>pfip3982　3754　pre1722　ppro4671　2532</small>
am persuaded that　in　thee also.

<small>pre1223/repro3739/an,nn156　pin363/ppro4671　pinf329　art3588　nn5486</small>
☞ 6　Wherefore　I　put*thee*in*remembrance　that　thou　stir　up　the　gift of
<small>art,nn2316　repro3739　pin2076　pre1722　ppro4671　pre1223　art3588　nn1936　ppro3450　art,nn5495</small>
God, which is　in　thee by　the putting on of　my　hands.

<small>1063　art,nn2316　3756　aina1325　ppro2254　an,nn4151　an,nn1167　235　an,nn1411　2532</small>
7 For　God　hath　not　given　us　the　spirit　of fear; but　of power, and of
<small>an,nn26　2532　an,nn4995</small>
love, and of a sound mind.

<small>3361　3767　aosi1870　art3588　nn3142　ppro2257　art,nn2962　3366</small>
8 Be　not　thou　therefore　ashamed　of　the　testimony　of　our　Lord,　nor of
<small>ppro1691　ppro846　art,nn1198　235　aima4777　art3588　nn2098</small>
me　his　prisoner: but be*thou*partaker*of*the*afflictions　of　the　gospel
<small>pre2596　an,nn1411　an,nn2316</small>
according to the power of God;

<small>art,apta4982　ppro2248　2532　apta2564　an,aj40　an,nn2821　3756　pre2596</small>
☞ 9 Who*hath*saved　us,　and called　*us*　with　a　holy　calling, not according to
<small>ppro2257　art,nn2041　235　pre2596　an,aj2398　an,nn4286　2532　an,nn5485　art,aptp1325</small>
our　works,　but　according　to　his　own　purpose　and　grace,　which*was*given
<small>ppro2254　pre1722　an,nn5547　an,nn2424　pre4253　an,nn5550/an,aj166</small>
us　in　Christ Jesus before the world began,

<small>1161　ad3568　aptp5319　pre1223　art3588　nn2015　ppro2257　art,nn4990　an,nn2424　an,nn5547</small>
10 But is　now made manifest　by　the　appearing　of　our　Savior Jesus Christ,

---

☞ **1:6** Paul mentions a "gift" which Timothy possessed as a result of the "putting on" of his hands on him. It is identical to the word used by Paul to describe the gifts (*chárismata* [5486]) of the Spirit (1 Cor. 12:1–11). This gift mentioned in 2 Timothy 1:6 is not identified in any specific detail. Undoubtedly, this particular gift that came upon Timothy was the outcome of his ordination to the ministry of the gospel in 1 Timothy 4:14. In this verse, Paul speaks of "the presbytery" having participated in Timothy's ordination. This is an indication that in a local church in addition to the pastor acting as an elder, there should be "a presbytery," or better, a body of elders, known as presbyters.

☞ **1:9** In this verse, the Greek word *próthesin* (4286) is translated "purpose," but actually means "God's intention beforehand" (see note on Ephesians 1:4, 5 dealing with God's election of believers to salvation and grace).

apta2673   (3303) art,nn2288   1161   apta5461/an,nn2222/2532/an,nn861

who hath abolished   death, and hath brought*life*and*immortality*to*light

pre1223   art3588   nn2098

through the gospel:

pre1519/repro3739   epn1473   ainp5087   an,nn2783   2532   an,nn652   2532

11 Whereunto   I   am appointed a preacher, and an apostle, and a

an,nn1320   an,nn1484

teacher of the Gentiles.

pre1223   repro3739 an,nn156   2532   pin3958   depro5023   235   3756

12 For the which cause I also suffer these things: nevertheless I am not

pinm1870   1063   pin1492   repro3739   pfi4100   2532   pfip3982   3754   pin2076

ashamed: for I know whom I have believed, and am persuaded that he is

pr/an,aj1415   ainf5442   art,nn3866/ppro3450   pre1519   depro1565 art,nn2250

able to keep that*which*I*have*committed*unto*him against that day.

pim2192   an,nn5296   pap5198   an,nn3056   repro3739   aina191   pre3844 ppro1700

13 Hold fast the form of sound words, which thou hast heard of me,

pre1722 an,nn4102 2532 an,nn26 art3588   pre1722 an,nn5547 an,nn2424

in faith and love which is in Christ Jesus.

art,aj2570   an,nn3872   aima5442 pre1223   an,aj40

14 That good thing which*was*committed*unto*thee keep by the Holy

an,nn4151   art,pap1774   pre1722 ppro2254

Ghost which dwelleth in us.

depro5124   pin1492   3754 an,aj3956   art3588   pre1722 art,nn773

15 This   thou knowest, that all   they which are in Asia be

ainp654   ppro3165   repro3739 pin2076   an,nn5436   2532   an,nn2061

turned*away*from me; of whom are Phygellus and Hermogenes.

art3588   nn2962   opt1325 an,nn1656   art3588   nn3624   an,nn3683   3754   ad4178

16 The Lord give mercy unto the house of Onesiphorus; for he oft

aina404   ppro3165 2532   3756   ainp1870   ppro3450 art,nn254

refreshed me, and was not ashamed of my chain:

235   aptm1096 pre1722 an,nn4516   aina2212/ppro3165   cd/an,ajn4706   2532

17 But, when he was in Rome, he sought*me*out very diligently, and

aina2147

found me.

art3588   nn2962   opt1325   ppro846   ainf2147 an,nn1656 pre3844   an,nn2962 pre1722

18 The Lord grant unto him that he may find mercy of the Lord in

depro1565 art,nn2250 2532   an,ajn3745   aina1247   pre1722 an,nn2181   epn4771

that day: and in how*many*things he ministered unto me at Ephesus, thou

pin1097   cd/an,ajn957

knowest very well.

1:12 Paul states, ". . . I also suffer . . . ." This does not mean that he was suffering due to some sin in his own life. Rather, it is an inevitable part of the life of the Christian because he has the same mortal and corruptible body as unbelievers (Rom. 6:12; 8:11; 1 Cor. 15:53, 54; 2 Cor. 4:11; 5:4). The word thnētón (2349), "mortal," appearing in all previous verses referenced, deals only with believers. The word translated "corruptible," is the Greek word phthartón (5349) referring to the deterioration of the human body (Rom. 1:23; 1 Cor. 15:53, 54). The use of this word makes it clear that upon receiving Christ, the physical body of the believer does not become exempt from mortality or corruptibility. Suffering may also come as a result of persecution from the world because the Christian does not conform to its standards. However, Christ will ultimately overcome (John 16:33; Gal. 6:17; 2 Tim. 3:12). Therefore, Paul states, "I also suffer these things, nevertheless I am not ashamed."

The Christian Warfare

2 epn4771　3767　ppro3450 an,nn5043　pim1743　pre1722 art3588　nn5485　art3588　pre1722 an,nn5547
Thou therefore, my son, be strong in the grace that is in Christ
an,nn2424
Jesus.

2532　　　　　　　repro3739　　　　　aina191　pre3844 ppro1700　pre1223　an,aj4183　an,nn3144
2 And the things that thou hast heard of me among many witnesses,
depro5023　aima3908　　　　an,aj4103　an,nn444 repro3748　　fm2071 pr/an,aj2425　ainf1321 an,ajn2087
the same commit thou to faithful men, who shall be able to teach others
2532
also.

epn4771　3767　　　　aima2553　　ad5613　　an,aj2570　an,nn4757　　an,nn2424
3 Thou therefore endure hardness, as a good soldier of Jesus
an,nn5547
Christ.

an,aj3762　　pppmp4754　　　pinm1707　　　art3588　nn4230　　art,nn979 2443
4 No man that warreth entangleth*himself*with the affairs of *this* life; that
asba700　　art,apta4758
he may please him*who*hath*chosen*him*to*be*a*soldier.

1161 1437 idpro5100 2532　　psa118　　　　　3756　pinp4737　3362
5 And if a man also strive*for*masteries, *yet* is he not crowned, except he
asba118　ad3545
strive lawfully.

an,nn1092　　art,pap2872　pin1163　pinf3335/nu,aj4413　　art3588 nn2590
6 The husbandman that laboreth must be*first*partaker of the fruits.

pim3539　repro3739　pin3004 1063 art3588　nn2962　opt1325 ppro4671　an,nn4907　pre1722
7 Consider what I say; and the Lord give thee understanding in
an,ajn3956
all things.

pim3421　　　an,nn2424 an,nn5547 pre1537　an,nn4690　　1138　　pfpp1453　pre1537
8 Remember that Jesus Christ of the seed of David was raised from the
an,ajn3498　pre2596　ppro3450 art,nn2098
dead according to my gospel:

pre1722/repro3739　pin2553　ad5613　an,nn2557　　ad3360 an,nn1199　235 art3588
9 Wherein I suffer trouble, as an evil doer, *even* unto bonds; but the
nn3056　art,nn2316　3756　pfip1210
word of God is not bound.

pre1223/depro5124　pin5278　an,ajn3956　pre1223/art3588/ajn1588　2443 epn846　　2532
☞ 10 Therefore I endure all things for*the*elect's*sakes, that they may also
asba5177　an,nn4991　art3588　pre1722 an,nn5547 an,nn2424 pre3326 an,aj166 an,nn1391
obtain the salvation which is in Christ Jesus with eternal glory.

pr/an,aj4103　art,nn3056　1063 1487　　aina4880　　　　2532
11 *It is* a faithful saying: For if we be*dead*with *him*, we shall also
ft4800
live with *him*:

☞ **2:10** See note on Ephesians 1:4, 5 dealing with the subject of election.

1487   pin5278   2532   ft4821   1487   pinm720   depro2548
☞ 12 If we suffer, we shall also reign with *him*: if we deny *him,* he also will

fm720   ppro2248
deny us:

1487   pin569   depro1565   pin3306 pr/an,aj4103   pinm1410/3756 aifm720   rxpro1438
13 If we believe not, *yet* he abideth faithful: he cannot deny himself.

(Num. 23:19)

Be a Good Example

depro5023   pim5279   ppmp1263   ad*1799   art3588
14 Of these things put*them*in*remembrance, charging *them* before the

nn2962   pinf3054/3361   pre1519/an,ajn3762/an,aj5539 pre1909   an,nn2692
Lord that they strive*not*about*words to*no*profit, *but* to the subverting of

art3588   pap191
the hearers.

aima4704   ainf3936   rxpro4572   pr/an,aj1384   art,nn2316   an,nn2040
15 Study to show thyself approved unto God, a workman that

pr/an,aj422   pr/ppmp3718   art3588 nn3056   art,nn225
needeth*not*to*be*ashamed, rightly dividing the word of truth.

1161   pim4026 art,aj952   an,nn2757   1063   ft4298   pre1909 cd/an,ajn4119
16 But shun profane *and* vain babblings: for they will increase unto more

an,nn763
ungodliness.

2532   ppro846 art,nn3056   ft2192/an,nn3542 ad5613   an,nn1044   repro3739   pin2076
17 And their word will eat as doth a canker: of whom is

an,nn5211   2532   an,nn5372
Hymenaeus and Philetus;

repro3748   pre4012   art3588   nn225   aina795   pap3004   art3588   nn386
18 Who concerning the truth have erred, saying that the resurrection

pfin1096   ad2235   2532   pin396   art3588 nn4102   idpro5100
is past already; and overthrow the faith of some.

3305   an,nn2310   art,nn2316   pfi2476   pr/art,aj4731   pap2192 depro5026 art,nn4973
19 Nevertheless the foundation of God standeth sure, having this seal,

an,nn2962   aina1097   art,pap5607   ppro848   2532   an,aj3956   art,pap3687   art3588
The Lord knoweth them*that*are his. And, Let every one that nameth the

nn3686   an,nn5547   aima868   pre575   an,nn93
name of Christ depart from iniquity.   *(Num. 16:5)*

1161   pre1722   an,aj3173   an,nn3614   pin2076   3756 an,ajn3440   an,nn4632   an,aj5552   2532
20 But in a great house there are not only vessels of gold and of

---

☞ **2:12, 13** In this passage, Paul is encouraging Timothy that though he is suffering in this life, there
is the prospect of future blessing. The believer who continues trusting in Christ, remaining faithful to his
call, certainly will receive a blessed reward in heaven. On the other hand, those who are unfaithful to
the call of Christ (i.e., those who "deny" or "believe not") will receive his just reward as well, namely,
judgment from God. The phrase "yet he abideth faithful" means that Christ will be true to His promise
of judgment on those who are unfaithful to Him.

an,aj693 235 2532 an,aj3585 2532 an,aj3749 2532 repro3739/3303 pre1519 an,nn5092 1161 repro3739 pre1519

silver, but also of wood and of earth; and some to honor, and some to

an,nn819

dishonor.

1437 idpro5100 3767 asba1571 rxpro1438 pre575 depro5130 fm2071 pr/an,nn4632

21 If a man therefore purge himself from these, he shall be a vessel

pre1519 an,nn5092 pr/pfpp37 2532 pr/an,aj2173/art3588/nn1203 pr/pfpp2090 pre1519

unto honor, sanctified, and meet*for*the*master's*use, *and* prepared unto

an,aj3956 an,aj18 an,nn2041

every good work.

pim5343 1161 art,aj3512 an,nn1939 1161 pim1377 an,nn1343 an,nn4012 an,nn26 an,nn1515

22 Flee also youthful lusts: but follow righteousness, faith, charity, peace,

pre3326 art,ppmp1941 art3588 nn2962 pre1537 an,aj2513 an,nn2588

with them*that*call*on the Lord out of a pure heart.

1161 art,aj3474 2532 an,aj521 an,nn2214 pim3868 pfp1492 3754 pin1080

23 But foolish and unlearned questions avoid, knowing that they do gender

an,nn3163

strifes.

1161 an,ajn1401 an,nn2962 pin1163 3756 pifm3164 235 pinf1511 pr/an,aj2261 pre4314 an,ajn3956

24 And the servant of the Lord must not strive; but be gentle unto all

pr/an,aj1317 pr/an,aj420

men, apt*to*teach, patient,

pre1722 an,nn4236 pap3811 art,ppmp475

25 In meekness instructing those*that*oppose*themselves;

3379/art,nn2316 asba1325 ppro846 an,nn3341 pre1519 an,nn1922

if*God*peradventure will give them repentance to the acknowledging of the

an,nn225

truth;

2532 asba366 pre1537 art3588 nn3803 art3588 ajn1228

26 And *that* they may recover themselves out of the snare of the devil,

pfpp2221 pre5259 ppro846 pre1519 depro1565 art,nn2307

who are taken captive by him at his will.

The Last Times

depro5124 pim1097 1161 3754 pre1722 an,aj2078 an,nn2250 an,aj5467 an,nn2540 fm1764

3 This know also, that in the last days perilous times shall come.

1063 art,nn444 fm2071 pr/an,aj5367 pr/an,aj5366

2 For men shall be lovers*of*their*own*selves, covetous,

pr/an,aj213 pr/an,aj5244 pr/an,aj989 pr/an,aj545 an,nn1118 pr/an,aj884 pr/an,aj462

boasters, proud, blasphemers, disobedient to parents, unthankful, unholy,

pr/an,aj794 pr/an,aj786 pr/an,aj1228 pr/an,aj193

3 Without*natural*affection, trucebreakers, false accusers, incontinent,

pr/an,aj434 pr/an,aj865

fierce, despisers*of*those*that*are*good,

pr/an,nn4273 pr/an,aj4312 pr/pfpp5187 pr/an,aj5369 ad3123 2228

4 Traitors, heady, highminded, lovers*of*pleasures more than

pr/an,aj5377

lovers*of*God;

pap2192   an,nn3446   an,nn2150   1161   pfpp720 art3588   nn1411   ppro846
5 Having a form of godliness, but denying the power thereof:
pim665/depro5128
from*such*turn*away.

1063 pre1537 depro5130 pin1526   pr/art,pap1744   pre1519 art,nn3614   2532   pap162
6 For of this sort are they*which*creep into houses, and lead captive
art,nn1133   pfpp4987   an,nn266   ppmp71   an,aj4164 an,nn1939
silly women laden with sins, led away with divers lusts,

ad3842   pap3129   2532   ad3368   ppmp1410   ainf2064 pre1519   an,nn1922   an,nn225
7 Ever learning, and never able to come to the knowledge of the truth.

1161   repro3739/an,nn5158   2389   2532   2387   aina436   an,nn3475   ad3779   depro3778
8 Now as Jannes and Jambres withstood Moses, so do these
2532   pinm436 art3588   nn225 an,nn444   pfpp2704   art,nn3563 an,aj96   pre4012   art3588 nn4102
also resist the truth: men of corrupt minds, reprobate concerning the faith.

(Ex. 7:12,12)

235   ft4298   3756 pre1909/cd/an,ajn4119 1063 ppro846 art,nn454   fm2071   pr/an,aj1552
9 But they shall proceed no further: for their folly shall be manifest
an,ajn3956   ad5613 art,depro1565 2532 aom1096
unto all *men,* as theirs also was.

Live a Godly Life

1161   epn4771   pfi3877   ppro450 art,nn1319   art,nn72   art,nn4286   art,nn4102
10 But thou hast fully known my doctrine, manner*of*life, purpose, faith,
art,nn3115   art,nn26   art,nn5281
longsuffering, charity, patience,

art,nn1375   art,nn3804   an,ajn3634 aom1096   ppro3427 pre1722   an,nn490   pre1722
11 Persecutions, afflictions, which came unto me at Antioch, at
an,nn2430   pre1722   an,nn3082 an,aj3634   an,nn1375   aina5297   2532   pre1537   an,ajn3956 art3588
Iconium, at Lystra; what persecutions I endured: but out of *them* all the
nn2962   aom4506 ppro3165
Lord delivered me.   *(Ps. 34:19)*

1161   2532   an,aj3956   art,pap2309   pinf2198 ad2153   pre1722 an,nn5547   an,nn2424
☞ 12 Yea, and all that will live godly in Christ Jesus shall
fp1377
suffer persecution.

1161   an,aj4190   an,nn444   2532   an,nn1114   ft4298/pre1909/cd/art,ajn5501   pap4105
13 But evil men and seducers shall wax*worse*and*worse, deceiving,
2532   ppmp4105
and being deceived.

1161   pim3306   epn4771 pre1722   repro3739   aina3129   2532
14 But continue thou in the things which thou hast learned and hast been
ainp4104   pfp1492   pre3844 inpro5101   aina3129
assured of, knowing of whom thou hast learned *them;*

2532   3754   pre575   an,nn1025   pin1492 art3588 an,aj2413   nn1121
15 And that from a child thou hast known the holy Scriptures,

---

☞ **3:12** See note on 2 Timothy 1:12.

art,ppmp1410   ainf4679/ppro4571   pre1519   an,nn4991   pre1223   an,nn4102   art3588

which*are*able to make*thee*wise unto salvation through faith which is

pre1722 an,nn5547 an,nn2424

in Christ Jesus.

     an,aj3956   an,nn1124   pr/an,aj2315   2532   pr/an,aj5624

16 All Scripture *is* given*by*inspiration*of*God, and *is* profitable

pre4314   an,nn1319   pre4314   an,nn1650   pre4314   an,nn1882   pre4314   an,nn3809   art,pre1722

for doctrine, for reproof, for correction, for instruction in

an,nn1343

righteousness:

     2443   art3588   nn444   art,nn2316   psa5600   pr/an,aj739   pr/pfpp1822   pre4314

17 That the man of God may be perfect, thoroughly furnished unto

an,aj3956 an,aj18 an,nn2041

all good works.

epn1473   pinm1263   3767   ad*1799   art,nn2316   2532   art3588   nn2962   an,nn5547   an,nn5547

4 I charge *thee* therefore before God, and the Lord Jesus Christ,

art,pap3195   pinf2919   an,pap2198   2532   an,ajn3498 pre2596 ppro848   art,nn2015   2532   ppro848

who shall judge the quick and the dead at his appearing and his

art,nn932

kingdom;

     aima2784   art3588   nn3056   aima2186   ad2122   ad171   aima1651   aima2008

2 Preach the word; be instant in season, out*of*season; reprove, rebuke,

aima3870   pre1722 an,aj3956   an,nn3115   2532   an,nn1322

exhort with all longsuffering and doctrine.

     1063   an,nn2540   fm2071   ad3753   3756   fm430   art,pap5198   an,nn1319   235

3 For the time will come when they will not endure sound doctrine; but

pre2596   art,aj2398   art,nn1939   ft2002   rxpro1438   an,nn1320   ppmp2833

after their own lusts shall they heap to themselves teachers, having itching

art,nn189

ears;

     2532   ft654   art,nn189   pre575 (3303) art3588   nn225   1161

4 And they shall turn away *their* ears from the truth, and shall be

fm1624   pre1909   art,nn3454

turned unto fables.

     1161   pim3525   epn4771   pre1722   an,ajn3956   aima2553   aima4160   an,nn2041

5 But watch thou in all things, endure afflictions, do the work of an

an,nn2099   aima4135   ppro4675   art,nn1248

evangelist, make*full*proof of thy ministry.

     1063   epn1473   pinm4689/ad2235   2532   art3588   nn2540   art,popro1699

6 For I am*now*ready*to*be*offered, and the time of my

an,nn359   pfi2186

departure is*at*hand.

     pfip75   art,aj2570   art,nn73   pfi5055   art,nn1408   pfi5083   art3588

7 I have fought a good fight, I have finished *my* course, I have kept the

nn4102

faith:

     an,ajn3063   pinm606   ppro3427   art,nn4735   art,nn1343   repro3739 art3588

8 Henceforth there is laid up for me a crown of righteousness, which the

nn2962   art3588   an,aj1342   nn2923   ft591   ppro3427 pre1722 depro1565 art,nn2250 1161   3756   ppro1698

Lord, the righteous judge, shall give me at that day: and not to me

an,ajn3440 235   an,aj3956   art,pfp25/2532   ppro846   art,nn2015

only, but unto all them*also*that*love his appearing.

Paul's Personal Closing Words

aima4704   ainf2064   ad5030   pre4314 ppro3165

9 Do*thy*diligence to come shortly unto me:

1063   an,nn1214   aina1459   ppro3165   apta25   ort,ad3568   an,nn165   2532

☞ 10 For Demas hath forsaken me, having loved this present world, and is

ainp4198   pre1519   an,nn2332   an,nn2913 pre1519 an,nn1053 an,nn5103 pre1519   an,nn1149

departed unto Thessalonica; Crescens to Galatia, Titus unto Dalmatia.

pr/an,aj3441 an,nn3065 pin2076 pre3326 ppro1700 apta353   an,nn3138   pim71   pre3326 rxpro4572 1063

11 Only Luke is with me. Take Mark, and bring him with thee: for he

pin2076   pr/an,aj2173   ppro3427 pre1519   an,nn1248

is profitable to me for the ministry.

1161   an,nn5190   aina649 pre1519   an,nn2181

☞ 12 And Tychicus have I sent to Ephesus.

art3588   nn5341   repro3739 aina620 pre1722 an,nn5174 pre3844   an,nn2591   ppmp2064   pim5342

13 The cloak that I left at Troas with Carpus, when thou comest, bring

2532 art3588   nn975   ad3122   art3588   nn3200

with thee, and the books, but especially the parchments.

an,nn223   art3588   nn5471   aom1731 ppro3427 an,aj4183 an,ajn2556 art3588   nn2962   opt591   ppro846

14 Alexander the coppersmith did me much evil: the Lord reward him

pre2596   ppro846   art,nn2041

according to his works: (2 Sam. 3:39; Ps. 28:4; 62:12; Prov. 24:12)

repro3739   pim5442/epn4771   2532   1063   ad3029   pfi436   art,popro2251

15 Of whom be*thou*ware also; for he hath greatly withestood our

an,nn3056

words.

pre1722 ppro3450 art,nu,aj4413 an,nn627 an,ajn3762   aom4836   ppro3427 235 an,ajn3956   aina1459

16 At my first answer no man stood with me, but all men forsook

ppro3165   3361   opt3049/ppro846

me: I pray God that it may not be laid*to*their*charge.

1161   art3588   nn2962   aina3936   ppro3427 2532   aina1743   ppro3165 2443

17 Notwithstanding the Lord stood with me, and strengthened me; that

pre1223 ppro1700 art3588   nn2782   asbp4135   2532   an,aj3956 art3588   nn1484

by me the preaching might be*fully*known, and that all the Gentiles might

asba191   2532   ainp4506   pre1537   an,nn4750   an,nn3023

hear: and I was delivered out of the mouth of the lion.   (Ps. 22:21; Dan. 6:21)

2532   art3588   nn2962   fm4506   ppro3165   pre575   an,aj3956 an,aj4190 an,nn2041   2532

18 And the Lord shall deliver me from every evil work, and will

ft4982   pre1519   ppro848   art,aj2032   art,nn932   repro3739   art,nn1391

preserve me unto his heavenly kingdom: to whom be glory

pre1519/art,nn165/art,nn165   281

forever*and*ever. Amen.

☞ 4:10 See the introduction to Titus.
☞ 4:12 See note on Colossians 4:7.

aipm782 an,nn4251 2532 an,nn207 2532 art3588 nn3624 an,nn3683

19 Salute Prisca and Aquila, and the household of Onesiphorus.

an,nn2037 aina3306 pre1722 an,nn2882 1161 an,nn5161 aina620 pre1722 an,nn3399

☞ 20 Erastus abode at Corinth: but Trophimus have I left at Miletum

pap770

sick.

aima4704 ainf2064 pre4253 an,nn5494 an,nn2103 pinm782 ppro4571 2532

21 Do*thy*diligence to come before winter. Eubulus greeteth thee and

an,nn4227 2532 an,nn3044 2532 an,nn2803 2532 an,aj3956 art3588 nn80

Pudens, and Linus, and Claudia, and all the brethren.

art3588 nn2962 an,nn2424 an,nn5547 pre3326 ppro4675 art,nn4151 art,nn5485 pre3326 ppro5216 281

22 The Lord Jesus Christ *be* with thy spirit. Grace *be* with you. Amen.

☞ **4:20** Trophimus was an Ephesian Christian who accompanied Paul to Europe after the riot in Ephesus. He returned to Ephesus, but later left to wait for Paul at Troas. He continued with Paul on his journey to Jerusalem as one of the delegates of the Asian churches bringing the collection for the church leaders there (Acts 20:1–5, cf.1 Cor. 16:1–4). In Jerusalem, however, Jewish pilgrims from Asia recognized Trophimus in Paul's company. Then, finding Paul in the temple with four other men, they presumed that Paul had introduced Trophimus there (Acts 21:27–36). To take him beyond the court of the Gentiles would be to risk the penalty of death. The incident initiated a riot and was followed by Paul's arrest.

The Epistle of Paul to

TITUS

Titus was most likely a Gentile from Macedonia (Gal. 2:3) who was led to Christ by Paul (Titus 1:4). Titus was with Paul in Jerusalem (Gal. 2:1) when some dogmatic, Jewish brethren insisted that Titus should be circumcised. Paul would not allow it (Gal. 2:3–5) because this would have suggested that all non-Jewish Christians were second-class citizens in the church.

Titus remained as Paul's traveling companion and may have been with Paul when he wrote the letter to the Galatians. After Paul's release from his first imprisonment in Rome, Titus traveled with Paul to do mission work in the East. They landed at Crete and evangelized several towns (Titus 1:5). However, since Paul was unable to stay, he left Titus on Crete to complete the organization of congregations in that region. Titus met with considerable opposition and insubordination in the church, especially from the Jews (Titus 1:10). It is quite possible that Titus had written to Paul to report this problem and ask for spiritual advice. Paul responded with this short letter encouraging him to complete the process of organization, to ordain elders, to exercise his own authority firmly, and to teach sound doctrine while avoiding unnecessary strife.

Paul asked Titus to join him at Nicopolis (Titus 3:12), where he planned to spend the winter. It is probable that Titus was dispatched from there on a new mission to Dalmatia (2 Tim. 4:10).

The letter was probably delivered by Zenas and Apollos (Titus 3:13). It is believed, however, that Paul penned this sometime between his first and second imprisonments in Rome (ca. A.D. 64) when he was in the city of Nicopolis (Titus 3:12). This was about the same time that the Book of 1 Timothy was written. The instructive tone of this epistle to Titus is similar to that of Paul's first letter to Timothy. Both Titus and Timothy endured much criticism from false teachers during their ministries. Paul exhorts Titus to continue to preach sound doctrine (Titus 2:1) and to use wise judgment concerning the appointing of leaders in the church (Titus 1:5–9).

1
an,nn3972   an,ajn1401   an,nn2316 1161   an,nn652   an,nn2424 an,nn5547   pre2596
Paul, a servant of God, and an apostle of Jesus Christ, according to the
an,nn4102   an,nn2316 an,ajn1588 2532   an,nn1922   an,nn225 art3588   pre2596
faith of God's elect, and the acknowledging of the truth which is after
an,nn2150
godliness;

pre1909 an,nn1680   an,aj166   an,nn2222 repro3739 an,nn2316   art,aj893   aom1861   pre4253
2 In hope of eternal life, which God, that*cannot*lie, promised before
an,nn166/an,aj5550
the world*began;

¹¹⁶¹   ^{an,aj2398}   ^{an,nn2540}   ^{aina5319}   ^{ppro848}   ^{art,nn3056}   ^{pre1722}   ^{an,nn2782}   ^{repro3739}

3 But hath in due times manifested his word through preaching, which is

^{ainp4100}   ^{epn1473}   ^{pre2596}   ^{an,nn2003}   ^{an,nn2316} ^{ppro2257}   ^{art,nn4990}

committed unto me according to the commandment of God our Savior;

        ^{an,nn5103}   . ^{an,aj1103} ^{an,nn5043}   ^{pre2596}   ^{an,aj2839}   ^{an,nn4102}   ^{an,nn5485}   ^{an,nn1656}

4 To Titus, *mine* own son after the common faith: Grace, mercy, *and*

^{an,nn1515}   ^{pre575}   ^{an,nn2316}   ^{an,nn3962}   ²⁵³²   ^{an,nn2962} ^{an,nn2424} ^{an,nn5547} ^{ppro2257} ^{art,nn4990}

peace, from God the Father and the Lord Jesus Christ our Savior.

The Qualifications of an Elder

     ^{ad*5485/depro5127}   ^{aina2641}   ^{ppro4571} ^{pre1722}   ^{an,nn2914}   ²⁴⁴³   ^{asba1930}

☞ 5 For*this*cause left I thee in Crete, that thou shouldest set*in*order

     ^{art,pap3007}   ²⁵³²   ^{asba2525}   ^{cd/an,ajn4245}   ^{pre2596/an,nn4172}   ^{ad5613} ^{epn1473}

the*things*that*are*wanting, and ordain elders in*every*city, as I had

^{aom1299}   ^{ppro4671}

appointed thee:

     ^{idpro1536}   ^{pin2076}   ^{pr/an,aj410}   ^{pr/an,nn435}   ^{nu3391} ^{an,nn1135} ^{pap2192}   ^{an,aj4103}   ^{an,nn5043}

☞ 6 If any be blameless, the husband of one wife, having faithful children

³³⁶¹ ^{pre1722/an,nn2724}   ^{an,nn810} ²²²⁸   ^{an,aj506}

not accused of riot or unruly.

     ¹⁰⁶³   ^{art,nn1985}   ^{pin1163} ^{pinf1511}   ^{pr/an,aj410}   ^{ad5613}   ^{pr/an,nn3623}   ^{an,nn2316} ³³⁶¹   ^{pr/an,aj829}

7 For a bishop must be blameless, as the steward of God; not self-willed,

³³⁶¹   ^{pr/an,aj3711}   ³³⁶¹   ^{pr/an,aj3943}   ³³⁶¹   ^{pr/an,nn4131}   ³³⁶¹   ^{pr/an,aj146}

not soon angry, not given*to*wine, no striker, not given*to*filthy*lucre;

     ²³⁵   ^{pr/an,aj5382}   ^{pr/an,aj5358}   ^{pr/an,aj4998}   ^{pr/an,aj1342}   ^{pr/an,aj3741}

8 But a lover*of*hospitality, a lover*of*good*men, sober, just, holy,

^{pr/an,aj1468}

temperate;

     ^{ppmp472}   ^{art3588}   ^{an,aj4103}   ⁿⁿ³⁰⁵⁶   ^{pre2596/art,nn1322}   ²⁴⁴³   ^{psa5600}

9 Holding fast the faithful word as*he*hath*been*taught, that he may be

^{pr/an,aj1415} ^{pre1722} ^{art,pap5198}   ^{art,nn1319}   ²⁵³²   ^{pinf3870}   ²⁵³²   ^{pinf1651}   ^{art3588}   ^{pap483}

able by sound doctrine both to exhort and to convince the gainsayers.

     ¹⁰⁶³   ^{pin1526} ^{pr/an,aj4183} ⁽²⁵³²⁾ ^{pr/an,aj506}   ^{an,aj3151}   ²⁵³²   ^{pr/an,nn5423}   ^{ad3122}

10 For there are many unruly and vain talkers and deceivers, especially

^{art3588} ^{pre1537}   ^{an,nn4061}

they of the circumcision:

     ^{repro3739}   ^{pinf1993/pin1163}   ^{repro3748}   ^{pin396}   ^{an,aj3650}   ^{an,nn3624}

11 Whose mouths*must*be*stopped, who subvert whole houses,

^{pap1321}   ^{repro3739}   ^{pin1163}   ³³⁶¹   ^{ad*5484/an,aj150/an,nn2771}

teaching things which they ought not, for*filthy*lucre's*sake.

     ^{idpro5100} ^{pre1537}   ^{ppro846}   ^{an,nn4396}   ^{ppro846} ^{an,aj2398}   ^{aina2036}   ^{an,nn2912}

12 One of themselves, *even* a prophet of their own, said, The Cretians

     ^{ad104}   ^{pr/an,nn5583} ^{an,aj2556}   ^{pr/an,nn2342} ^{an,aj692}   ^{pr/an,nn1064}

are always liars, evil beasts, slow bellies.

☞ **1:5** See the introduction to Titus.
☞ **1:6** See note on 1 Timothy 3:2.

depro3778   art,nn3141   pin2076   pr/an,aj227   pre1223/repro3739/an,nn156   pim1651   ppro846   ad664   2443

13 This witness is true. Wherefore rebuke them sharply, that they

psa5198   pre1722 art3588   nn4102

may be sound in the faith;

3361   pap4337   an,aj2451   an,nn3454   2532   an,nn1785   an,nn444

14 Not giving heed to Jewish fables, and commandments of men, that

ppmp654   art3588   nn225

turn from the truth.

art3588 ajn2513   an,ajn3956   (3303)   pr/an,aj2513   1161   art3588   pfpp3392   2532

15 Unto the pure all things *are* pure: but unto them that are defiled and

an,ajn571   an,ajn3762   pr/an,aj2513   235   2532   ppro846 art,nn3563 2532   art,nn4983   pfip3392

unbelieving *is* nothing pure; but even their mind and conscience is defiled.

pin3670   pinf1492   an,nn2316   1161   art,nn2041   pinm720   pap5607

16 They profess that they know God; but in works they deny *him,* being

pr/an,aj947   2532   pr/an,aj545   2532   pre4314   an,aj3956   an,aj18   an,nn2041   pr/an,aj96

abominable, and disobedient, and unto every good work reprobate.

Teach Sound Doctrine

1161   pim2980   epn4771   repro3739   pin4241   art,pap5198   an,nn1319

2 ☞ But speak thou the things which become sound doctrine:

an,nn4246   pinf1511   pr/an,aj3524   pr/an,aj4586   pr/an,aj4998   pr/pap5198

2 That the aged men be sober, grave, temperate, sound in

art,nn4102   art,nn26   art,nn5281

faith, in charity, in patience.

an,nn4247   ad5615   pre1722   an,nn2688

3 The aged women likewise, that *they be* in behavior

pr/an,aj2412   3361   pr/an,aj1228   3361   pr/pfpp1402   an,aj4183   an,nn3631

as*becometh*holiness, not false accusers, not given to much wine,

pr/an,nn2567

teachers*of*good*things;

2443   psa4994/art3588/ajn3501   (pinf1511)

4 That they may teach*the*young*women*to*be*sober,   to

pr/an,ajn5362   pr/an,ajn5388

love*their*husbands, to love*their*children,

pr/an,aj4998   pr/an,aj53   pr/an,nn3626   pr/an,aj18   pr/ppmp5293   art,aj2398

5 *To be* discreet, chaste, keepers*at*home, good, obedient to their own

an,nn435   2443   art3588   nn3056   art,nn2316   3361   psmp987

husbands, that the word of God be not blasphemed.

cd/art,ajn3501   ad5615   pim3870   pinf4993

6 Young men likewise exhort to be*sober*minded.

☞ **2:1–5** In verse four, the word "sober" is the Greek verb *sōphronízō* (4994). It means "to be sober minded or to voluntarily place limitations on one's own freedom." Some have mistakenly thought that the Apostle Paul inferred that women should not teach at all in the church (1 Cor. 14:34–40; 1 Tim. 2:12). However, Paul instructs Titus to teach the older women (v. 3) as well as the older men (v. 2). In addition, he urges the aged women to be "teachers of good things" (v. 3). Those older women who evidence spiritual maturity are to teach the younger women, both in the church and at home, by counsel and by example.

7 In all things showing thyself a pattern of good works: in doctrine *showing*

uncorruptness, gravity, sincerity,

8 Sound speech, that cannot*be*condemned; that he that is of the

contrary part may be ashamed, having no evil thing to say of you.

9 *Exhort* servants to be obedient unto their own masters, *and* to

please*them*well in   all   *things*; not answering again;

10 Not purloining, but showing all good fidelity; that they may adorn

the doctrine of God our Savior in all things.

11 For the grace of God that*bringeth*salvation hath appeared to all

men,

12 Teaching us that, denying ungodliness and worldly lusts, we should

live soberly, righteously, and godly, in this present world;

13 Looking for that blessed hope, and the glorious appearing of the great

God and our Savior Jesus Christ;

14 Who gave himself for us, that he might redeem us from all

iniquity, and purify unto himself a peculiar people, zealous of good works.

(Ps. 130:8; Ex. 19:5; Deut. 4:20; 7:6; 14:2; Ezek. 37:23)

15 These things speak, and exhort, and rebuke with all   authority. Let

no man despise thee.

God's Mercy Remembered

3 ☞ Put*them*in*mind to be subject to principalities and powers, to

obey magistrates, to be ready to every good work,

☞ **3:1** See note on 1 Peter 2:17.

^{pinf987} ^{an,ajn3367} ^{pinf1511} ^{pr/an,aj269} ^{pr/an,aj1933} ^{ppmp1731} ^{an,aj3956}

2 To speak evil of no man, to be no brawlers, *but* gentle, showing all

^{an,nn4236} ^{pre4314} ^{an,aj3956} ^{an,nn444}

meekness unto all men.

¹⁰⁶³ ^{epn2249} ²⁵³² ^{ipf2258} ^{ad4218} ^{pr/an,aj453} ^{pr/an,aj545} ^{pr/ppmp4105}

3 For we ourselves also were sometimes foolish, disobedient, deceived,

^{pr/pap1398} ^{an,aj4164} ^{an,nn1939} ²⁵³² ^{an,nn2237} ^{pr/pap1236} ^{pre1722} ^{an,nn2549} ²⁵³² ^{an,nn5355} ^{pr/an,aj4767}

serving divers lusts and pleasures, living in malice and envy, hateful, *and*

^{pap3404} ^{rcpro240}

hating one another.

¹¹⁶¹ ^{ad3753} ^{art3588} ⁿⁿ⁵⁵⁴⁴ ²⁵³² ^{art,nn5363/an,nn2316/ppro2257/art,nn4990}

4 But after that the kindness and love*of*God*our*Savior*toward*man

^{ainp2014}

appeared,

³⁷⁵⁶ ^{pre1537} ^{an,nn2041} ^{art,pre1722} ^{an,nn1343} ^{repro3739} ^{epn2249} ^{aina4160} ²³⁵ ^{pre2596}

5 Not by works of righteousness which we have done, but according

^{ppro848} ^{art,nn1656} ^{aina4982} ^{ppro2248} ^{pre1223} ^{an,nn3067} ^{an,nn3824} ²⁵³² ^{an,nn342}

to his mercy he saved us, by the washing of regeneration, and renewing of

^{an,aj40} ^{an,nn4151}

the Holy Ghost;

^{repro3739} ^{aina1632} ^{pre1909} ^{ppro2248} ^{ad4146} ^{pre1223} ^{an,nn2424} ^{an,nn5547} ^{ppro2257} ^{art,nn4990}

6 Which he shed on us abundantly through Jesus Christ our Savior;

(Joel 2:28)

²⁴⁴³ ^{aptp1344} ^{depro1565} ^{art,nn5485} ^{asbm1096} ^{pr/an,nn2818} ^{pre2596}

☞ 7 That being justified by his grace, we should be made heirs according

^{an,nn1680} ^{an,aj166} ^{an,nn2222}

to the hope of eternal life.

^{pr/an,aj4103} ^{art,nn3056} ²⁵³² ^(pre4012) ^{depro5130} ^{pinm1014}

8 *This is* a faithful saying, and these things I will that

^{ppro4571} ^{pifm1226} ²⁴⁴³ ^{art,pfp4100} ^{art,nn2316}

thou affirm constantly, that they*which*have*believed in God might

^{psa5431} ^{psa4291} ^{an,aj2570} ^{an,nn2041} ^{depro5023} ^{pin2076} ^{pr/art,ajn2570} ²⁵³² ^{pr/an,ajn5624}

be careful to maintain good works. These things are good and profitable

^{art,nn444}

unto men.

¹¹⁶¹ ^{pim4026} ^{an,aj3474} ^{an,nn2214} ²⁵³² ^{an,nn1076} ²⁵³² ^{an,nn2054} ²⁵³²

9 But avoid foolish questions, and genealogies, and contentions, and

^{an,nn3163} ^{an,aj3544} ¹⁰⁶³ ^{pin1526} ^{pr/an,aj512} ²⁵³² ^{pr/an,aj3152}

strivings about*the*law; for they are unprofitable and vain.

^{an,nn444} ^{an,aj141} ^{pre3326} ^{an,nu,aj3391} ²⁵³² ^{an,nu,aj1208} ^{an,nn3559} ^{pim3868}

10 A man that is a heretic after the first and second admonition reject;

^{pfp1492} ³⁷⁵⁴ ^{art,ajn5108} ^{pfip1612} ²⁵³² ^{pin264} ^{pap5607}

11 Knowing that he*that*is*such is subverted, and sinneth, being

^{pr/an,aj843}

condemned*of*himself.

Conclusion

ad3752   asba3992   an,nn734   pre4314 ppro4571 2228   an,nn5190   aima4704   ainf2064

☞ 12 When I shall send Artemas unto thee, or Tychicus, be diligent to come
pre4314 ppro3165 pre1519   an,nn3533   1063   pfi2919   ad1563   ainf3914

unto me   to Nicopolis: for I have determined there to winter.
                                    aima4311/an,nn2211/art3588/ajn3544/2532/an,nn625   ad4709   2443

    13 Bring*Zenas*the*lawyer*and*Apollos*on*their*journey diligently,   that
an,ajn3367   psa3007   ppro846

nothing be wanting unto them.
            1161   art,popro2251 2532 pim3129   pifm4291   an,aj2570 an,nn2041 pre1519   art,aj316   an,nn5532

    14 And let   ours   also learn to maintain good works for necessary uses,
2443   psa5600 3361   pr/an,aj175

that they be not unfruitful.
         an,aj3956 art3588   pre3326 ppro1700 pinm782   ppro4571   aipm782   art,pap5368   ppro2248 pre1722

    15 All   that are with me salute thee. Greet them*that*love us   in the
an,nn4102 art,nn5485   pre3326 ppro5216 an,aj3956   281

faith. Grace *be* with you   all. Amen.

☞ **3:12, 13** See the introduction to Titus.

PHILEMON

The Epistle to Philemon was a private letter written by Paul during his first imprisonment in Rome (A.D. 62). The focus of the letter is to give a proper understanding of the Hebrew fugitive law found in Deuteronomy 23:15, 16. It reveals how Paul acted in strict accordance with the requirements of the law in dealing with Onesimus, a slave who had run away from Philemon. First, Paul gave him shelter in his own hired house. He did not betray him as a fugitive, nor did he send word to Philemon to come to Rome to take Onesimus back. Furthermore, Paul instructed Onesimus in the gospel, eventually leading him to a saving knowledge of Christ (Phile. 1:10). He then sent Onesimus back to Philemon as a trusted messenger and brother in Christ, bearing a request for Philemon to grant Onesimus his freedom (Phile. 1:12). Paul did not accuse Onesimus of wrongdoing by running away from Philemon. Instead, Paul stated that it was by the merciful providence of God that he had departed from Philemon. Paul desired for Philemon to receive Onesimus back no longer as a servant, but as a beloved brother and partner in Christ (Phile. 1:15–17).

Some suggest that Onesimus had stolen something from Philemon and had run away because he was afraid of the punishment he would receive. Paul graciously offered to repay this and any debts that Onesimus owed to Philemon (Phile. 1:18). It is commonly believed that Onesimus was received by Philemon and forgiven his debt, just as Paul had expected (Phile. 1:21).

1
an,nn3972　　　an,nn1198　　　　an,nn2424　an,nn5547　　2532　　an,nn5095　　　　　art,nn80　　　　　　an,nn5371
Paul, a prisoner of Jesus Christ, and Timothy *our* brother, unto Philemon
　　　　　　　art,aj27　　　　　2532 (ppro2257)　　　an,ajn4904
our dearly beloved, and　　　　　fellowlaborer,

2532　　　　　art,aj27　　an,nn682　　2532　　an,nn751　　ppro2257　　art,nn4961　　2532　　art3588
2 And to *our* beloved Apphia, and Archippus our fellowsoldier, and to the
nn1577　pre2596 ppro4675 an,nn3624
church in　thy house:
　　an,nn5485　　ppro5213　2532　　an,nn1515　　pre575　an,nn2316 ppro2257　an,nn3962　　2532　　　an,nn2962 an,nn2424
3 Grace to you, and peace, from God　our　Father and the Lord Jesus
an,nn5547
Christ.

Paul's Expression of Thanksgiving

pin2168　ppro3450 art,nn2316　ppmp4160　　an,nn3417　　　ppro4675　ad3842　pre1909 ppro3450　art,nn4335
4 I thank my God, making mention of thee always in　my prayers,

5 Hearing of thy love and faith, which thou hast toward the Lord Jesus, and toward all saints;

6 That the communication of thy faith may become effectual by the acknowledging of every good thing which is in you in Christ Jesus.

7 For we have great joy and consolation in thy love, because the bowels of the saints are refreshed by thee, brother.

Onesimus

8 Wherefore, though I might be much bold in Christ to enjoin thee that*which*is*convenient,

9 Yet for*love's*sake I rather beseech *thee,* being such*a*one as Paul the aged, and now also a prisoner of Jesus Christ.

10 I beseech thee for my son Onesimus, whom I have begotten in my bonds:

11 Which in*time*past was to thee unprofitable, but now profitable to thee and to me:

12 Whom I have sent again: thou therefore receive him, that is, mine own bowels:

13 Whom I would have retained with me, that in*thy*stead he might have ministered unto me in the bonds of the gospel:

14 But without thy mind would I do nothing; that thy benefit should not be as*it*were of necessity, but willingly.

15 For perhaps he therefore departed for a season, that thou shouldest receive him forever;

16 Not now as a servant, but above a servant, a brother beloved,

^{ad3122} ^{ppro1698 1161} ^{an,aj4214} ^{ad3123} ^{ppro4671} ²⁵³² ^{pre1722} ^{an,nn4561 2532 pre1722}
especially to me, but how much more unto thee, both in the flesh and in the
^{an,nn2962}
Lord?

¹⁴⁸⁷ ^{pin2192} ^{ppro1691} ³⁷⁶⁷ ^{pr/an,ajn2844} ^{aipm4355} ^{ppro846 ad5613} ^{ppro1691}
17 If thou count me therefore a partner, receive him as myself.

^{(1161) 1487} ^{aina91} ^{ppro4571} ²²²⁸ ^{pin3784} ^{idpro5100}
18 If he hath wronged thee, or oweth *thee* aught,
^{pim1677/depro5124/ppro1698}
put*that*on*mine*account;

^{epn1473 an,nn3972} ^{aina1125} ^{art,popro1699} ^{an,nn5495 epn1473} ^{ft661} ²⁴⁴³
19 I Paul have written *it* with mine own hand, I will repay *it*: albeit I
³³⁶¹ ^{psa3004} ^{ppro4671 3754} ^{pin4359} ^{ppro3427 2532} ^{rxpro4572}
do not say to thee how thou owest unto me even thine*own*self besides.

³⁴⁸³ ^{an,nn80} ^{epn1473} ^{opt3685} ^{ppro4675 pre1722} ^{an,nn2962} ^{aima373} ^{ppro3450}
20 Yea, brother, let me have joy of thee in the Lord: refresh my
^{art,nn4698} ^{pre1722} ^{an,nn2962}
bowels in the Lord.

^{pfp3982} ^{ppro4675} ^{art,nn5218} ^{aina1125} ^{ppro4671} ^{pfp1492} ³⁷⁵⁴
21 Having confidence in thy obedience I wrote unto thee, knowing that
²⁵³² ^{ft4160} ^{pre5228/repro3739} ^{pin3004}
thou wilt also do more than I say.

¹¹⁶¹ ^{ad260} ^{pim2090} ^{ppro3427} ²⁵³² ^{an,nn3578} ¹⁰⁶³ ^{pin1679} ³⁷⁵⁴ ^{pre1223} ^{ppro5216}
22 But withal prepare me also a lodging: for I trust that through your
^{art,nn4335} ^{fp5483} ^{ppro5213}
prayers I shall be given unto you.

^{pinm782} ^{ppro4571} ^{an,nn1889} ^{ppro3450} ^{art,nn4869} ^{pre1722 an,nn5547} ^{an,nn2424}
23 There salute thee Epaphras, my fellowprisoner in Christ Jesus;
^{an,nn3138} ^{an,nn708} ^{an,nn1214} ^{an,nn3065 ppro3450} ^{art,ajn4904}
24 Mark, Aristarchus, Demas, Luke, my fellowlaborers.
^{art3588} ⁿⁿ⁵⁴⁸⁵ ^{ppro2257 art,nn2962 an,nn2424} ^{an,nn5547} ^{pre3326 ppro5216 art,nn4151} ²⁸¹
25 The grace of our Lord Jesus Christ *be* with your spirit. Amen.

1:23 See notes on Colossians 1:7; 4:10.

The Epistle to the

HEBREWS

The author of the Book of Hebrews is unknown. Martin Luther suggested that Apollos was the author. This is based on Acts 18:24–28, where Apollos is referred to as a well-read, Hellenistic Jew from Alexandria in Egypt. Tertullian (writing in A.D. 150–230) said that Hebrews was a letter of Barnabas. Adolf Harnack and J. Rendel Harris speculated that it was written by Priscilla (or Prisca). William Ramsey suggested that it was done by Philip. However, the traditional position is that the Apostle Paul wrote Hebrews. From the very beginning, the eastern church attributed the letter to him, but the western church did not accept this until the fourth century. Eusebius (A.D. 263–339) believed that Paul wrote it, but Origen (ca. A.D. 185–254) was not positive of Pauline authorship. About the end of the second century, Clement of Alexandria thought that Paul had originally written the letter in the Hebrew language and that it was later translated by Luke or by someone else into Greek. Notwithstanding, the recipients of the letter knew who the author was and recognized his credibility in writing the work.

There is also uncertainty as to the exact date of the writing of Hebrews. Numerous references to the temple in Jerusalem seem to place the date of writing prior to the fall of Jerusalem in A.D. 70 (Heb. 10:11; 13:10–11).

The purpose of the epistle was to reassure Jewish believers that their faith in Jesus as the Messiah was secure and legitimate. Also, it was intended to prepare them for the impending disaster of the Roman destruction of Jerusalem. The temple, with its system of animal sacrifices, and the office of the priest, would soon be done away with, just as Jesus had predicted. The Book of Hebrews explains that there was no more need for a priest to intercede before God on an individual's behalf since Christ's death provided believers with direct access to God's throne (Heb. 4:14–16; 10:19–22). Furthermore, the blood of Christ now continually takes away sin (Heb. 9:18–26).

The Book of Hebrews is divided into two major sections: the first deals with doctrinal issues (Heb. 1:1—10:18), and the second focuses on practical living (Heb. 10:19—13:25). In addition to this, it contains several warnings to Jewish Christians not to revert back to Judaism and that system of worship (Heb. 10:39). It was evident that these believers were weak in their faith; when they should have been teaching others, they themselves still required teaching. The writer urges them to grow and not remain as "babes" in Christ (Heb. 5:12–14). A major them in the book, often expressed by the words "better" and "great," is the superiority and preeminence of Christ (Heb. 1:4; 2:3; 4:14; 7:19, 22; 8:6; 9:11, 23; 10:32, 34, 35; 11:16, 34, 40; 12:1; 13:20).

God Has Spoken Through His Son

1 God who at*sundry*times and in*divers*manners spake in*time*past unto the fathers by the prophets,

art,nn2316 · ad4181 · 2532 · ad4187 · apta2980 · ad3819
art3588 · nn3962 · pre1722 · art3588 · nn4396

2 Hath in these last days spoken unto us by *his* Son, whom he hath appointed heir of all things, by whom also he made the worlds; *(Ps. 2:8)*

pre1909 · depro5130 · an,aj2078 · art,nn2250 · aina2980 · ppro2254 · pre1722 · an,nn5207 · repro3739
aina5087 · pr/an,nn2818 · an,ajn3956 · pre1223 · repro3739 · 2532 · aina4160 · art3588 · nn165

3 Who being the brightness of *his* glory, and the express image of his person, and upholding all things by the word of his power, when he had by himself purged our sins, sat down on the right hand of the Majesty on high; *(Ps. 110:1)*

repro3739 · pap5607 · pr/an,nn541 · art,nn1391 · 2532 · pr/an,nn5481 · ppro848
art,nn5287 · 5037 · pap5342 · art,ajn3956 · art3588 · nn4487 · ppro846 · art,nn1411 · pre1223
rxpro1438 · aptm4160/an,nn2512 · ppro2257 · art,nn266 · aina2523 · pre1722 · an,ajn1188 · art3588 · nn3172 · pre1722
an,ajn5308

Christ's Superiority to Angels

4 Being made so much better than the angels, as he hath by*inheritance*obtained a more excellent name than they.

aptm1096 · an,ajn5118 · pr/cd/an,aj2909 · art3588 · nn32 · an,aj3745
pfi2816 · cd/an,aj1313 · an,nn3686 · pre3844 · ppro846

5 For unto which of the angels said he at*any*time, Thou art my son, this day have I begotten thee? And again, I will be to him a Father, and he shall be to me a Son?

1063 · inpro5101 · art3588 · nn32 · aina2036 · ad4218 · epn4771 · pin1488 · ppro3450
pr/an,nn5207 · ad4594 · epn1473 · pfi1080 · ppro471 · 2532 · ad3825 · epn1473 · fm2071 · ppro846 · (pre1519)
an,nn3962 · 2532 · epn846 · fm2071 · ppro3427 · (pre1519) · an,nn5207

(Ps. 2:7; 2 Sam. 7:14; 2 Chr. 17:13)

⚷ 6 And again, when he bringeth in the first begotten into the world, he saith, And let all the angels of God worship him. *(Deut. 32:43 [Sept.])*

1161 · ad3825 · ad3752 · asba1521 · art3588 · ajn4416 · pre1519 · art3588 · nn3625
pin3004 · 2532 · an,aj3956 · an,nn32 · an,nn2316 · aima4352 · ppro846

7 And of the angels he saith, Who maketh his angels spirits, and his ministers a flame of fire. *(Ps. 104:4)*

2532 · pre4314 · (3303) · art3588 · nn32 · pin3004 · art,pap4160 · ppro848 · art,nn32 · pr/an,nn4151 · 2532 · ppro848
art,nn3011 · pr/an,nn5395 · an,nn4442

8 But unto the Son *he saith,* Thy throne, O God, *is* forever*and*ever: a scepter of righteousness *is* the scepter of thy kingdom.

1161 · pre4314 · art3588 · nn5207 · ppro4675 · art,nn2262 · art,nn2316 · pre1519/art,nn165/art,nn165
pr/an,nn4464 · an,nn2118 · art3588 · nn4464 · ppro4675 · art,nn932

⚷ **1:6** See note on Colossians 1:15–18.

9 Thou hast loved righteousness, and hated iniquity; therefore God, *even*
thy God, hath anointed thee with the oil of gladness above thy fellows.

(Ps. 45:6, 7)

10 And, Thou, Lord, in the beginning hast laid*the*foundation of the
earth; and the heavens are the works of thine hands:

11 They shall perish; but thou remainest; and they all shall wax old as
doth a garment;

12 And as a vesture shalt thou fold*them*up, and they shall be changed:
but thou art the same, and thy years shall not fail. *(Ps. 102:25-27)*

13 But to which of the angels said he at*any*time, Sit on my
right hand, until I make thine enemies thy footstool? *(Ps. 110:1)*

14 Are they not all ministering spirits, sent forth to minister for
them*who*shall*be heirs of salvation? *(Ps. 91:11)*

2 Therefore we ought to give*the*more*earnest*heed to
the*things*which*we*have*heard, lest*at*any*time we should
let*them*slip.

2 For if the word spoken by angels was steadfast, and every
transgression and disobedience received a just recompense*of*reward;

3 How shall we escape, if we neglect so great salvation; which
at*the*first*began to be spoken by the Lord, and was confirmed unto us
by them*that*heard *him*;

4 God also bearing*them*witness, both with signs and wonders,
and with divers miracles, and gifts of the Holy Ghost, according to his own
will?

Christ is Preeminent

1063   an,nn32   3756   aina5293   art3588 nn3625   art,pap3195

5 For unto the angels hath he not put*in*subjection the world to come,

pre4012/repro3739   pin2980

whereof we speak.

1161 idpro5100   ad4225   aom1263   pap3004 pr/inpro5101 pin2076 an,nn444 3754

6 But one in a certain place testified, saying, What is man, that thou

pinm3403   ppro846 2228   an,nn5207 an,nn444 3754   pinm1980 ppro846

art mindful of him? or the son of man, that thou visitest him?

aina1642   ppro846   idpro5100/an,aj1024 pre3844   an,nn32   aina4737

7 Thou madest him a little lower than the angels; thou crownedst

ppro846   an,nn1391 2532 an,nn5092 2532   aina2525 ppro846 pre1909 art3588 nn2041   ppro4675

him with glory and honor, and didst set him over the works of thy

art,nn5495

hands:

aina5293/an,ajn3956   ad*5270 ppro846 art,nn4228 1063

8 Thou hast put*all*things*in*subjection under his feet. For in that he

aie5293/art,ajn3956   ppro846 aina863 an,ajn3762   pr/an,aj506   ppro846

put*all*in*subjection*under him, he left nothing *that is* not*put*under him.

1161 ad3568   ad3768 art,ajn3956 pfpp5293 ppro846

But now we see not yet all things put under him.   *(Ps. 8:5-7 [Sept.])*

1161   pin991 art,nn2424   art,pfpp1642/an,aj1023/idpro5100   pre3844   an,nn32   pre1223

9 But we see Jesus, who*was*made*a*little*lower than the angels for

art3588 nn3804   art,nn2288 pfpp4737   an,nn1391 2532 an,nn5092 3704   an,nn5485

the suffering of death, crowned with glory and honor; that he by the grace of

an,nn2316   asbm1089 an,nn2288 pre5228 an,ajn3956

God should taste death for every man.

1063   ipf4241   ppro846 pre1223 repro3739   art,ajn3956   2532 pre1223 repro3739

10 For it became him, for whom *are* all things, and by whom *are*

art,ajn3956   apta71   an,aj4183 an,nn5207 pre1519 an,nn1391

all things, in bringing many sons unto glory, to

ainf5048/art3588/nn747/ppro846/art,nn4991   pre1223   an,nn3804

make*the*captain*of*their*salvation*perfect through sufferings.

1063 5037 art,pap37   2532 art,ppmp37   an,aj3956 pre1537

11 For both he*that*sanctifieth and they*who*are*sanctified *are* all of

nu,ajn1520 pre1223 repro3739 an,nn156   3756 pinm1870   pinf2564 ppro846 an,nn80

one: for which cause he is not ashamed to call them brethren,

pap3004   ft518   ppro4675 art,nn3686   ppro3450 art,nn80 pre1722 an,ajn3319

12 Saying, I will declare thy name unto my brethren, in the midst of

an,nn1577   ft5214   ppro4571

the church will I sing praise unto thee.   *(Ps. 22:22)*

2532 ad3825 epn1473 fm2071/pfp3982 pre1909 ppro846 2532 ad3825   2400 ppro1473 2532

13 And again, I will put*my*trust in him. And again, Behold I and

art3588 nn3813 repro3739 art,nn2316 aina1325 ppro3427

the children which God hath given me.   *(Is. 8:17b [Sept.]; 8:18)*

1893   3767   art3588 nn3813   pfi2841   an,nn4561 2532 an,nn129 epn846

14 Forasmuch then as the children are partakers of flesh and blood, he

2532   ad3898   aina3348 art3588 ppro846 2443 pre1223 art,nn2288

also himself likewise took part of the same; that through death he might

asba2673   art,pap2192 art3588 nn2904 art,nn2288 depro,pin5123 art3588 ajn1228

destroy him*that*had the power of death, that is, the devil;

15 And deliver them who through fear of death were all their lifetime subject to bondage.

16 For verily he took*not*on *him the nature of* angels; but he took on *him the seed of Abraham.*   *Is. 41:8,9)*

17 Wherefore in all things it behooved him to be made*like*unto *his* brethren, that he might be a merciful and faithful high priest in things *pertaining* to God, to make*reconciliation*for the sins of the people.

18 For in that he himself hath suffered being tempted, he is able to succor them*that*are*tempted.

Superior to Moses

3 Wherefore, holy brethren, partakers of the heavenly calling, consider the Apostle and High Priest of our profession, Christ Jesus;

2 Who was faithful to him*that*appointed him, as also Moses *was faithful* in all his house.   *(Num. 12:7)*

3 For this *man* was counted worthy of more glory than Moses, inasmuch as he*who*hath*builded the house hath more honor than the house.

4 For every house is builded by some *man*; but he*that*built all things *is* God.

5 And Moses verily *was* faithful in all his house, as a servant, for a testimony of those*things*which*were*to*be*spoken*after;

6 But Christ as a son over his own house; whose house are we, if we hold fast the confidence and the rejoicing of the hope firm unto the end.

^{pre,repro1352} ^{ad2531} ^{art3588} ^{aj40} ^{art,nn4151} ^{pin3004} ^{ad4594} ¹⁴³⁷ ^{asba191} ^{ppro846} ^{art,nn5456}

7 Wherefore (as the Holy Ghost saith, Today if ye will hear his voice,

^{psi4645} ³³⁶¹ ^{ppro5216} ^{art,nn2588} ^{ad5613} ^{pre1722} ^{art3588} ⁿⁿ³⁸⁹⁴ ^{pre2596} ^{art3588} ⁿⁿ²²⁵⁰

8 Harden not your hearts, as in the provocation, in the day of

^{art,nn3986} ^{pre1722 art3588} ^{ajn2048}

temptation in the wilderness:

^{repro3757} ^{ppro5216} ^{art,nn3962} ^{aina3985} ^{ppro3165} ^{aina1381} ^{ppro3165} ²⁵³² ^{aina1492} ^{ppro3450} ^{art,nn2041} ^{nu5062}

9 When your fathers tempted me, proved me, and saw my works forty

^{an,nn2094}

years.

^{pre,repro1352} ^{aina4360} ^{depro1565} ^{art,nn1074} ²⁵³² ^{aina2036}

10 Wherefore I was grieved with that generation, and said, They do

^{ad104} ^{pinp4105} ^{art,nn2588} ¹¹⁶¹ ^{epn846} ³⁷⁵⁶ ^{aina1097} ^{ppro3450} ^{art,nn3598}

always err in *their* heart; and they have not known my ways.

^{ad5613} ^{aina3660} ^{pre1722} ^{ppro3450} ^{art,nn3709} ⁽¹⁴⁸⁷⁾ ^{fm1525} ^{pre1519} ^{ppro3450} ^{art,nn2663}

11 So I sware in my wrath, They shall not enter into my rest.

(Ex. 17:7; Num. 14:21-23; 20:2-5; Ps. 95:7-11)

^{pim991} ^{an,nn80} ³³⁷⁹ ^{fm2071} ^{pre1722} ^{idpro5100} ^{ppro5216} ^{an,aj4190} ^{an,nn2588}

☞ 12 Take heed, brethren, lest there be in any of you an evil heart of

^{an,nn570} ^{aie868} ^{pre575} ^{an,pap2198} ^{an,nn2316}

unbelief, in departing from the living God.

²³⁵ ^{pim3870} ^{rxpro1438} ^{pre2596/an,aj1538/an,nn2250} ^{ad891} ^(repro3739) ^{pinm2564} ^{art,ad4594}

13 But exhort one another daily, while it is called Today;

³³⁶³ ^{idpro5100} ^{pre1537} ^{ppro5216} ^{asbp4645} ^{an,nn539} ^{art,nn266}

lest any of you be hardened through the deceitfulness of sin.

¹⁰⁶³ ^{pfi1096} ^{pr/an,ajn3353} ^{art,nn5547} ^{1437/4007} ^{asba2722} ^{art3588} ⁿⁿ⁷⁴⁶

14 For we are made partakers of Christ, if we hold the beginning of

^{art,nn5287} ^{pr/an,aj949} ^{ad3360} ^{an,nn5056}

our confidence steadfast unto the end;

^{aie3004} ^{ad4594} ¹⁴³⁷ ^{asba191} ^{ppro846} ^{art,nn5456} ^{psa4645} ³³⁶¹ ^{ppro5216}

15 While it is said, Today if ye will hear his voice, harden not your

^{art,nn2588} ^{ad5613} ^{pre1722} ^{art3588} ⁿⁿ³⁸⁹⁴

hearts, as in the provocation. *(Ps. 95:7,8)*

¹⁰⁶³ ^{idpro5100} ^{apta191} ^{aina3893} ²³⁵ ³⁷⁵⁶ ^{an,aj3956}

16 For some, when they had heard, did provoke: howbeit not all

^{art,apta1831} ^{pre1537} ^{an,nn125} ^{pre1223} ^{an,nn3475}

that came out of Egypt by Moses. *(Num. 14:29)*

¹¹⁶¹ ^{inpro5101} ^{aina4360} ^{nu5062} ^{an,nn2094} ³⁷⁸⁰

17 But with whom was he grieved forty years? *was* *it* not with

^{art,apta264} ^{repro3739} ^{art,nn2966} ^{aina4098} ^{pre1722} ^{art3588} ^{ajn2048}

them*that*had*sinned, whose carcasses fell in the wilderness?

¹¹⁶¹ ^{inpro5101} ^{aina3660} ³³⁶¹ ^{finf1525} ^{pre1519} ^{ppro848} ^{art,nn2663} ¹⁵⁰⁸

18 And to whom sware he that they should not enter into his rest, but to

^{art,apta544}

them*that*believed*not? *(Num. 14:22,23,29; Ps. 95:11)*

²⁵³² ^{pin991} ³⁷⁵⁴ ^{ainp1410} ³⁷⁵⁶ ^{ainf1525} ^{pre1223} ^{an,nn570}

19 So we see that they could not enter in because of unbelief.

☞ **3:12** See note on 2 Thessalonians 2:3.

The Saints' Everlasting Rest

3767   aosi5399 3379   an,nn1860   ppmp2641   ainf1525 pre1519 ppro846

4 Let us therefore fear, lest, a promise being left *us* of entering into his

art,nn2663 idpro5100 pre1537 ppro5216   psa1380   pfin5302

rest, any of you should seem to come short of it.

1063   (2532)   pin2070/pfpp2097   ad2509   depro2548 235 art3588

2 For unto us was*the*gospel*preached, as*well*as unto them: but the

nn3056   art,nn189   3756 aina5623 depro1565 3361   pfpp4786 art,nn4102

word preached did not profit them, not being mixed with faith in

art,apta191

them*that*heard *it.*

1063   art,apta4100   pinm1525 pre1519 art,nn2663 ad2531 pfi2046 ad5613

3 For we*which*have*believed do enter into rest, as he said, As I have

aina3660 pre1722 ppro3450 art,nn3709 1487   fm1525 pre1519 ppro3450 art,nn2663 2543 art3588 nn2041

sworn in my wrath, if they shall enter into my rest: although the works

aptp1096 pre575   an,nn2602   an,nn2889

were finished from the foundation of the world.   *(Ps. 95:11)*

1063   pfi2046   ad4225   pre4012 art3588 nu,ajn1442   ad3779   2532

4 For he spake in*a*certain*place of the seventh *day* on*this*wise, And

art,nn2316   aina2664 (pre1722) art3588 nu,aj1442 art,nn2250 pre575 an,aj3956 ppro848 art,nn2041

God did rest the seventh day from all his works.   *(Gen. 2:2)*

2532 pre1722 depro5129   ad3825 1487   fm1525 pre1519 ppro3450 art,nn2663

5 And in this *place* again, If they shall enter into my rest.

(Ps. 95:11)

1893   3767   pinm620   idpro5100   ainf1525 pre1519/ppro846

6 Seeing therefore it remaineth that some must enter therein,

2532   art,aptp2097/art,ajn4386   aina1525/3756   pre1223

and they*to*whom*it*was*first*preached entered*not*in because of

an,nn543

unbelief:

ad3825   pin3724   idpro5100 an,nn2250 pap3004 pre1722 1138 ad4594   pre3326

7 Again, he limiteth a certain day, saying in David, Today, after

an,aj5118   an,nn5550 ad2531   pfip2046 ad4594 1437   asba191 ppro846 art,nn5456 psi4645 3361

so long a time; as it is said, Today if ye will hear his voice, harden not

ppro5216 art,nn2588

your hearts.   *(Ps. 95:7,8)*

1063 1487 an,nn2424   aina2664/ppro846   3756 (302) pre3326/depro5023

8 For if Joshua had given*them*rest, then would he not afterward have

ipf2980 pre4012 an,aj243 an,nn2250

spoken of another day.   *(Deut. 31:7; Josh. 22:4)*

pinm620   686   an,nn4520 art3588 nn2992 art,nn2316

9 There remaineth therefore a rest to the people of God.

1063   art,apta1525   pre1519 ppro846 art,nn2663 epn846 2532   aina2664 pre575

10 For he*that*is*entered into his rest, he also hath ceased from

ppro848 art,nn2041 ad5618 art,nn2316   pre575 art,ajn2398

his own works, as God *did* from his.   *(Gen. 2:2)*

aosi4704   3767   ainf1525 pre1519 depro1565 art,nn2663 3363 idpro5100 asba4098 pre1722

11 Let us labor therefore to enter into that rest, lest any man fall after

art3588 ppro846 an,nn5262   art,nn543

the same example of unbelief.

1063   art3588   nn3056   art,nn2316   pr/pap2198   2532   pr/an,aj1756   2532   pr/cd/an,aj5114   pre5228   an,aj3956

12 For the word of God *is* quick, and powerful, and sharper than any

an,aj1366   an,nn3162   pr/ppmp1338   2532   ad891   an,nn3311   (5037) an,nn5590   2532   an,nn4151

two-edged sword, piercing even to the dividing asunder of soul and spirit,

5037   an,nn719   2532   an,nn3452   2532   pr/an,aj2924   an,nn1761   2532   an,nn1771

and of the joints and marrow, and *is* a discerner of the thoughts and intents of

an,nn2588

the heart.   *(Is. 49:2)*

2532/3756   pin2076   an,nn2937   an,aj852   ad*1799/ppro846   1161

13 Neither is there any creature that is not manifest in*his*sight: but

an,ajn3956   pr/an,aj1131   2532   pr/ppmp5136   art3588   nn3788   ppro846   pre4314   repro3739

all things *are* naked and opened unto the eyes of him with whom

ppro2254/art,nn3056

we*have*to*do.

Jesus, the Great High Priest

3767   pap2192   an,aj3173   an,nn749   pfp1330   art3588

14 Seeing then that we have a great high priest, that is passed into the

nn3772   an,nn2424 art3588 nn5207   art,nn2316   psa2902   art,nn3671

heavens, Jesus the Son of God, let us hold fast *our* profession.

1063   pin2192   3756   an,nn749   ppmp1410/3361

15 For we have not a high priest which cannot

ainf4834   ppro2257   art,nn769   1161   pre2596   an,ajn3956

be*touched*with*the*feeling*of our infirmities; but was in all points

pfpp3985   pre2596/an,nn3665   ad*5565   an,nn266

tempted like as *we are, yet* without sin.

3767   psa4334   pre3326/an,nn3954   art3588   nn2362   art,nn5485   2443

16 Let us therefore come boldly unto the throne of grace, that we may

asba2983   an,nn1656   2532 asba2147 an,nn5485   pre1519/an,aj2121/an,nn996

obtain mercy, and find grace to*help*in*time*of*need.

           1063   an,aj3956   an,nn749   ppmp2983   pre1537   an,nn444   pinm2525   pre5228 an,nn444

5 For every high priest taken from among men is ordained for men in

       art3588   pre4314 art,nn2316   2443   psa4374   5037   an,nn1435   2532   an,nn2378

things *pertaining* to God, that he may offer both gifts and sacrifices

pre5228 an,nn266

for sins:

ppmp1410   pinf3356   art3588   pap50   2532

2 Who can have compassion on the ignorant, and on

an,ppmp4105   1893   epn846   2532   pinm4029

them*that*are*out*of*the*way; for that he himself also is compassed with

an,nn769

infirmity.

2532   pre1223/depro5026   pin3784   ad2531   pre4012 art3588   nn2992   ad3779   2532   pre4012

3 And by*reason*hereof he ought, as for the people, so also for

rxpro1438   pinf4374 pre5228 an,nn266

himself, to offer for sins.   *(Lev. 9:7; 16:6)*

4 And no man taketh this honor unto himself, but he*that*is*called

of God, as *was* Aaron.   (Ex. 28:1)

5 So also Christ glorified not himself to be made a high priest; but

he*that*said unto him, Thou art my Son, today have I begotten thee.

(Ps. 2:7)

6 As he saith also in another *place,* Thou *art* a priest forever after the

order of Melchizedek.   (Ps. 110:4)

7 Who in the days of his flesh, when he had offered up   prayers and

supplications with strong crying and tears unto him*that*was*able to save him

from death, and was heard in*that*he*feared;

8 Though he were a Son, yet learned he obedience by the things which

he suffered;

9 And being made perfect, he became the author of eternal salvation unto

all them*that*obey him;   (Is. 45:17)

10 Called of God a high priest after the order of Melchizedek.

(Ps. 110:4)

11 Of whom we have*many*things*to*say, and hard to be uttered,

seeing ye are dull of hearing.

12 For when for the time ye ought to be teachers, ye have need that

one teach you again which *be* the first principles of the oracles of God; and

are become such*as*have need of milk, and not of strong meat.

13 For every one that useth milk *is* unskillfull in the word of

righteousness: for he is a babe.

14 But strong meat belongeth to them*that*are*of*full*age, *even* those who

by*reason*of use have their senses exercised to discern both good and

evil.

pre,repro1352   apta863   art3588   nn746   art3588   nn3056   art,nn5547

6 ☞ Therefore leaving the principles of the doctrine of Christ, let us

psmp5342   pre1909   art,nn5047   3361   ppmp2598   ad3825   an,nn2310   an,nn3341

go on unto perfection; not laying again the foundation of repentance

pre575 an,aj3498 an,nn2041   2532   an,nn4102   pre1909   an,nn2316

from dead works, and of faith toward God,

an,nn1322   an,nn909   5037   an,nn1926   an,nn5495   5037

2 Of the doctrine of baptisms, and of laying on of hands, and of

an,nn386   an,ajn3498 2532   an,aj166   an,nn2917

resurrection of the dead, and of eternal judgment.

2532   depro5124   ft4160 1437/4007 art,nn2316   psa2010

3 And this will we do, if God permit.

☞ **6:1–6** The goal of the Christian is expressed fully by the Greek word *teleióteta* (5047) which is translated "perfection" (v. 1). The idea being explained here is that the believer is to pursue a state of maturity, instead of going back to the initial rudiments of Christianity and basic faith (v. 2). The phrase "laying again a foundation" refers to the idea if that a Christian could lose his salvation, he would need to be regenerated again and again.

In laying the groundwork for this passage, there needs to be a proper understanding of the controversial section consisting of verses four through six. The key idea to consider is that the whole passage is hypothetical. For the sake of argument, one must accept the supposition that one can undergo the process of salvation, and then "fall away" (v. 6), or lose his salvation. The explanation in the following verses is designed to show the oddity of this idea (v. 4). The nature of the impossibility is tied directly to the infinitive in verse six "to renew" (*anakaini zein* [340]). In the Greek text, between this phrase, there are five participles between which must be explained thoroughly in order to properly understand the Holy Spirit's intent in this passage.

The first of these participles, which appears in verse four, and is the Greek word *phōtisthéntas* (5461). This term is translated "those who were once enlightened." However, it should be rendered "having been enlightened," noting the usage of the passive voice. The latter meaning reveals that the salvation process is initiated by God giving "light" to every man (John 1:9).

The next phrase to consider in this salvation process, also found in verse four, is "and have tasted of the heavenly gift." This too could be better expressed "having tasted" (the Greek word is *geusaménous* [1089]). In this case, the middle voice is used to reveal that a person is responding to the light God has given. The focus changes to man's responsibility in initiating a reaction to his "enlightened state." In this verse, the person involved exercises his choice to "taste" of God's free gift of salvation. This fact is always clear in the salvation process: God offers the gift, but man must take the initiative to receive it (John 1:12; 3:16). The gift must be understood as nothing that a person earns, rather, it is God's free offer of salvation. This "gift" is specified as having a heavenly origin.

The third participle is *genēthéntas* (v. 4, from *gínomai* [1096]) translated "were made." This also should be rendered in the passive voice as "having been made," indicating a result of man's receiving the gift of God. Connected with the phrase "partakers of the Holy Ghost," this participle expresses that by virtue of the receiving, one is made a partaker. Therefore, the Holy Spirit is involved in the process by coming to indwell the believer. The Holy Spirit not only works in the indwelling, but it is indicated that the divine revelation and conviction processes previous to salvation are based on the activity and energy of the Holy Spirit.

In examining the fourth Greek participle (found in verse five), *geusaménous* (cf. v. 4) one should consider that the same interpretation is intended by the middle voice in the phrase "having tasted." It appears in this form to reveal to man his responsibility to God's word. The believer is not merely accountable to simply follow the "good word of God," he is also urged to understand God's future plan to exercise His "power" (v. 5, *dúnameis* [1411]) to benefit the believer as well. The word for "power" here refers to miracles which God will perform in believers, not of the impending judgment and destruction to come.

Now one must turn his attention back to the phrase in verse four, "it is impossible," and combine it with the Greek infinitive *anakainízein* (340), meaning "to renew again" (v. 6). Applied to verse six, this word refers to a repentance which is qualitatively new and different. If a different form of repen-

(continued on next page)

1063 an,ajn102 art,aptp5461/nu,ad5030 5037
4 For *it is* impossible for those*who*were*once*enlightened, and have

aptm1089 art3588 aj2032 art,nn1431 2532 aptp1096 pr/an,ajn3353 an,aj40 an,nn4151
tasted of the heavenly gift, and were made partakers of the Holy Ghost,

2532 aptm1089 an,aj2570 an,nn4487 an,nn2316 5037 an,nn1411 an,nn165
5 And have tasted the good word of God, and the powers of the world

pap3195
to come,

(2532) apta3895 pinf340 ad3825 pre1519 an,nn3341
6 If they shall fall away, to renew them again unto repentance;

pap388/rxpro1438/art3588/nn5207/art,nn2316 2532
seeing they crucify*to*themselves*the*Son*of*God*afresh, and

pap3856
put*him*to*an*open*shame.

1063 an,nn1093 art,pap4095 art3588 nn5205 ppmp2064 ad4178 pre1909 ppro846 2532
7 For the earth which*drinketh*in the rain that cometh oft upon it, and

pap5088 an,nn1008 an,aj2111 depro1565 pre1223 repro3739 (2532) pinp1090 pin3335
bringeth forth herbs meet for them by whom it is dressed, receiveth

an,nn2129 pre575 art,nn2316
blessing from God:

1161 an,pap1627 an,nn173 2532 an,nn5146 pr/an,aj96 2532 pr/ad1451
8 But that*which*beareth thorns and briars *is* rejected, and *is* nigh unto

an,nn2671 repro3739 art,nn5056 pre1519/an,nn2740
cursing; whose end *is* to*be*burned. *(Gen. 3:17,18)*

1161 an,ajn27 pfip3982 cd/art,ajn2909 pre4012 ppro5216 2532
9 But, beloved, we are persuaded better things of you, and

an,ppmp2192 an,nn4991 1499 ad3779 pin2980
things*that*accompany salvation, though we thus speak.

1063 art,nn2316 3756 pr/an,aj94 aifm1950 ppro5216 art,nn2041 2532 art,nn2873 art,nn26
10 For God *is* not unrighteous to forget your work and labor of love,

repro3739 aom1731 pre1519 ppro846 art,nn3686 apta1247 art3588
which ye have showed toward his name, in that ye have ministered to the

ajn40 2532 pap1247
saints, and do minister.

1161 pin1937 an,ajn1538 ppro5216 pifm1731 art3588 ppro846 nn4710 pre4314
11 And we desire that every one of you do show the same diligence to

art3588 nn4136 art,nn1680 ad891 an,nn5056
the full assurance of hope unto the end:

(continued from previous page)
tance was needed, Christ would also have to die on the cross a second time. This, however, is inconsistent with the context of the rest of Hebrews (cf. Heb. 9:28; 10:11, 12). The teaching is clear: Christ died once for man's sin. If His death was insufficient, there would be no security for believers. This is precisely why the writer of Hebrews uses this illustration. In philosophical language, this form of reasoning is called *reductio ad absurdum* (a reduction to an absurdity). From a false assumption one deduces absurd conclusions. It would be false to assume a believer could fall, because his repentance, based on Christ's death, would be invalidated. There would be no security, and Christ would need to be crucified again.

The difficulty in this controversy is in determining when the actual decision to follow Christ becomes true salvation. One is saved at the point of genuine acceptance of God's gift of "light," and then he is received by God (Eph. 1:6). God ultimately judges man's heart and knows those who are truly repentant. The decision for salvation is made ineffective when it is based on emotions and of his own abilities (2 Thess. 2:13). See note on 1 John 3:6–9.

2443   asbm1096   3361   pr/an,aj3576   1161   pr/an,nn3402   pre1223   an,nn4102   2532

12 That ye be not slothful, but followers of them who through faith and

an,nn3115   art,pap2816   art3588   nn1860

patience inherit the promises.

God Keeps His Promises

1063   art,nn2316   aptm1861   11   1893   ipf2192   ainf3660

13 For when God made promise to Abraham, because he could swear

pre2596 an,aj3762   cd/an,ajn3187   aina3660   pre2596   rxpro1438

by no greater, he sware by himself,　　　　　　　*(Gen. 22:16)*

pap3004   2229/3375   pap2127   ft2127   ppro4571   2532   pap4129   ft4129

14 Saying, Surely blessing I will bless thee, and multiplying I will multiply

ppro4571

thee.　　　　　　　　　　　　　　　　　　　*(Gen. 22:17)*

2532   ad3779   apta3114   aina2013   art3588   nn1860

15 And so, after he had patiently endured, he obtained the promise.

1063   art,nn444   3303   pin3660   pre2596 art3588   cd/ajn3187   2532   art,nn3727 pre1519   an,nn951

16 For men verily swear by the greater: and an oath for confirmation *is*

ppro846   pr/an,nn4009   an,aj3956   an,nn485

to them an end of all strife.　　　　　　*(Ex. 22:11)*

pre1722/repro3739   art,nn2316   ppmp1014   cd/an,ajn4054   ainf1925   art3588   nn2818

17 Wherein God, willing more abundantly to show unto the heirs of

art,nn1860   art3588   ajn276   ppro848   art,nn1012   aina3315   an,nn3727

promise the immutability of his counsel, confirmed *it* by an oath:

2443   pre1223   nu1417   an,aj276   an,nn4229   pre1722   repro3739   an,ajn102   an,nn2316

18 That by two immutable things, in which *it was* impossible for God to

aifm5574   psa2192   an,aj2478   an,nn3874   art,apta2703

lie, we might have a strong consolation, who*have*fled*for*refuge to

ainf2902   an,nn1680   art,ppmp4295

lay*hold*upon the hope set before us:　　*(Num. 23:19; 1 Sam. 15:29)*

repro3739   pin2192   ad5613   an,nn45   art3588   nn5590   5037   pr/an,aj804   2532

19 Which *hope* we have as an anchor of the soul, both sure and

pr/an,aj949   2532   pr/ppmp1525   pre1519   cd/art,ajn2082 art3588 nn2665

steadfast, and which entereth into that within the veil;　*(Lev. 16:2,3,12,15)*

ad3699   an,ajn4274   pre5228   ppro2257   aina1525   art,nn2424   aptm1096

20 Whither the forerunner is for us entered, *even* Jesus, made a

pr/an,nn749   pre1519/art,nn165 pre2596 art3588   nn5010   3198

high priest forever after the order of Melchizedek.　　*(Ps. 110:4)*

Superior to Melchizedek

1063   depro3778   3198   an,nn935   4532   an,nn2409   art3588   pr/aj5310   art,nn2316

7 ☞ For this Melchizedek, king of Salem, priest of the most high God,

art,apta4876   11   pap5290   pre575 art3588   nn2871   art3588   nn935   2532   apta2127

who met Abraham returning from the slaughter of the kings, and blessed

ppro846

him;

☞ **7:1–28** This chapter describes the similarities in priestly ministries of Melchizedek and Christ. This

(continued on next page)

2 <u>To</u> ^{repro3739} <u>whom</u> ²⁵³² also ¹¹ Abraham ^{aina3307} gave a ^{nu,aj1181} tenth ^{pre575} part of ^{an,ajn3956} all; ^{nu,aj4412/3303} first

^{ppmp2059} being*by*interpretation ^{an,nn935} King of ^{an,nn1343} righteousness, ¹¹⁶¹ and ^{ad1899} after that ²⁵³² also ^{an,nn935} King of

⁴⁵³² Salem, ^{repro,pin3603} which is, ^{pr/an,nn935} King of ^{an,nn1515} peace; *(Gen. 14:17-20)*

3 <u>Without</u> ^{an,ajn540} father, without ^{an,ajn282} mother, without ^{an,ajn35} descent, having ^{pap2192} neither ³³⁸³

^{an,nn746} beginning of days, ^{an,nn2250} nor ³³⁸³ end ^{an,nn5056} of life; ^{an,nn2222} but ¹¹⁶¹ <u>made*like*unto</u> ^{pfpp871} the ^{art3588} Son ⁿⁿ⁵²⁰⁷ of God; ^{art,nn2316}

abideth ^{pin3306} a priest ^{an,nn2409} continually. ^{pre1519/art,ajn1336} *(Ps. 110:4)*

4 Now ¹¹⁶¹ consider ^{pin2334} how great ^{pr/an,aj4080} this man ^{depro3778} *was,* unto whom ^{repro3739} even ²⁵³² the ^{art3588} patriarch ⁿⁿ³⁹⁶⁶

¹¹ Abraham gave ^{aina1325} the tenth ^{an,nu,ajn1181} of ^{pre1537} the ^{art3588} spoils. ⁿⁿ²⁰⁵

5 And ²⁵³² verily ³³⁰³ they ^{art3588} that are of ^{pre1537} the ^{art3588} sons ⁿⁿ⁵²⁰⁷ of Levi, ³⁰¹⁷ who receive ^{pap2983} the ^{art3588}

ⁿⁿ²⁴⁰⁵ office*of*the*priesthood, have ^{pin2192} a commandment ^{an,nn1785} to take tithes ^{pinf586} of the ^{art3588} people ⁿⁿ²⁹⁹²

<u>according</u> ^{pre2596} to the ^{art3588} law, ⁿⁿ³⁵⁵¹ that is, ^{depro,pin5123} of their ^{ppro848} brethren, ^{art,nn80} though ²⁵³⁹ they come out ^{pfp1831} of ^{pre1537} the ^{art3588}

ⁿⁿ³⁷⁵¹ loins of Abraham: ¹¹ *(Num. 18:21)*

6 But ¹¹⁶¹ <u>he*whose*descent*is*not*counted</u> ^{art,ppmp1075/3361} from ^{pre1537} them ^{ppro846} received tithes ^{pfi1183} of

¹¹ Abraham, and ²⁵³² blessed ^{pfi2127} him*that*had ^{art,pap2192} the ^{art3588} promises. ⁿⁿ¹⁸⁶⁰

7 And ¹¹⁶¹ without ^{ad*5565} all ^{an,aj3956} contradiction ^{an,nn485} the ^{art3588} less ^{cd/ajn1640} is blessed ^{pinp2127} of ^{pre5259} the ^{art3588} better. ^{cd/ajn2909}

8 And ²⁵³² here ^{ad5602/3303} men ^{an,nn444} that die ^{pap599} receive tithes ^{pin2983}; but ^{nu,ajn1181} ¹¹⁶¹ there ^{ad1563} he *receiveth them,* of

whom it is witnessed ^{ppmp3140} that ³⁷⁵⁴ he liveth. ^{pin2198}

9 And ²⁵³² as*I*may*so*say, ^{ad5613/an,nn2031/ainf2036} Levi ³⁰¹⁷ also, ²⁵³² who ^{art,pap2983} receiveth tithes, ^{nu,ajn1181} paid tithes ^{pfip1183} in ^{pre1223}

¹¹ Abraham.

10 For ¹⁰⁶³ he was ^{ipf2258} yet ^{ad2089} in ^{pre1722} the ^{art3588} loins ⁿⁿ³⁷⁵¹ of his father, ^{art,nn3962} when ^{ad3753} Melchizedek ³¹⁹⁸ met ^{aina4876}

^{ppro846} him.

11 If ¹⁴⁸⁷ (3303) therefore ³⁷⁶⁷ perfection ^{an,nn5050} were ^{ipf2258} by ^{pre1223} the ^{art3588} Levitical ^{aj3020} priesthood, ^{an,nn2420} (for ¹⁰⁶³

under ^{pre1909} it ^{ppro846} the ^{art3588} people ⁿⁿ²⁹⁹² received*the*law,) ^{plpf3549} what further ^{inpro5101} need ^{ad2089} *was there* ^{an,nn5532} that

---

(continued from previous page)
arises from an examination of verse eleven where the writer of Hebrews reveals that Christ, being after the priestly order of Melchizedek (v. 17), has a different ministry than those priests who followed the order of Aaron. Since the Law of Moses had not been established during Melchizedek's day, Christ's ministry, being separate from that of the Law, was in fact similar to Melchizedek's.

an,aj2087   an,nn2409   pifm450 pre2596 art3588   nn5010   3198   2532   3756   pifm3004
another priest should rise after the order of Melchizedek, and not be called

pre2596 art3588   nn5010   2
after the order of Aaron?

1063   art3588   nn2420   ppmp3346   pinm1096 pre1537   an,nn318
12 For the priesthood being changed, there is made of necessity a

an,nn3331   2532   an,nn3551
change also of the law.

1063   pre1909 repro3739   depro5023   pinm3004   pfi3348   an,aj2087   an,nn5443
13 For he of whom these things are spoken pertaineth to another tribe,

pre575 repro3739 an,ajn3762   pfi4337   art3588   2379
of which no man gave attendance at the altar.

1063   an,ajn4271   3754 ppro2257 art,nn2962 pfi393   pre1537   2455   pre1519 repro3739 an,nn5443
14 For *it is* evident that our Lord sprang out of Judah; of which tribe

an,nn3475   aina2980   an,ajn3762   pre4012   an,nn2420
Moses spake nothing concerning priesthood.   *(Gen. 49:10; Is. 11:1)*

2532   pin2076   ad2089   cd/an,ajn4054   an,ajn2612   1487   pre2596 art3588   nn3665
15 And it is yet far more evident: for that after the similitude of

3198   pinm450   an,aj2087   an,nn2409
Melchizedek there ariseth another priest,

repro3739   pfi1096   3756   pre2596   an,nn3551   an,aj4559   an,nn1785   235   pre2596
16 Who is made, not after the law of a carnal commandment, but after

an,nn1411   an,aj179 an,nn2222
the power of an endless life.

1063   pin3140   epn4771   pr/an,nn2409 pre1519/art,nn165 pre2596 art3588   nn5010
17 For he testifieth, Thou *art* a priest forever after the order of

3198
Melchizedek.   *(Ps. 110:4)*

1063   pinm1096   3303   an,nn115   an,nn1785   pap4254
18 For there is verily a disannulling of the commandment going before

pre1223 art3588   ajn772   2532   an,ajn512   ppro846
for the weakness and unprofitableness thereof.

1063   art3588 nn3551   aina5048/an,ajn3762   1161   an,nn1898   cd/an,aj2909 an,nn1680
19 For the law made*nothing*perfect, but the bringing in of a better hope

pre1223   repro3739   pin1448   art,nn2316
did; by the which we draw nigh unto God.

2532   pre2596/an,ajn3745   3756   ad*5565   an,nn3728
20 And inasmuch as not without an oath *he was made priest*:

1063   pr/art,nn2409 (3303) pin1526 pfp1096   ad*5565   an,nn3728 1161 art3588 pre3326   an,nn3728
21 (For those priests were made without an oath; but this with an oath

pre1223   art,pap3004   pre4314 ppro846   an,nn2962 aina3660 2532   3756   fp3338   epn4771
by him*that*said unto him, The Lord sware and will not repent, Thou *art* a

pr/an,nn2409 pre1519/art,nn165 pre2596 art3588   nn5010   3198
priest forever after the order of Melchizedek:)   *(Ps. 110:4)*

pre2596   an,ajn5117   an,nn2424   pfi1096   pr/an,ajn1450   cd/an,aj2909   an,nn1242
22 By so much was Jesus made a surety of a better testament.

2532   art3588   3303   pin1526 (pfp1096) cd/an,ajn4119 pr/an,nn2409   aid2967
23 And they truly were many priests, because they were not suffered

pinf3887   an,nn2288
to continue by reason of death:

^{1161 art3588}   ^{ppro846}   ^{aid3306}   ^{pre1519/art,nn165} ^{pin2192}   ^{pr/an,aj531}

24 But this *man,* because he continueth ever, hath an unchangeable

^{art,nn2420}

priesthood.

^{ad3606}   ^{pinm1410}   ²⁵³²   ^{pinf4982}   ^{pre1519 art3588}   ^{ajn3838}   ^{art,ppmp4334}

25 Wherefore he is able also to save them to the uttermost that come

^{art,nn2316 pre1223 ppro846}   ^{ad3842}   ^{pap2198}   ^{aies1793}   ^{pre5228}   ^{ppro846}

unto God by him, seeing he ever liveth to make intercession for them.

¹⁰⁶³   ^{an,aj5108}   ^{an,nn749}   ^{ipf4241}   ^{ppro2254}   ^{pr/an,aj3741}   ^{pr/an,aj172}   ^{pr/an,aj283}

26 For such a high priest became us, *who is* holy, harmless, undefiled,

^{pr/ppmp5563}   ^{pre575}   ^{art,ajn268}   ²⁵³²   ^{aptm1096} ^{pr/cd/an,aj5308}   ^{art3588}   ⁿⁿ³⁷⁷²

separate from sinners, and made higher than the heavens;

^{repro3739} ^{pin2192/an,nn318} ³⁷⁵⁶   ^{pre2596/an,nn2250} ^{ad5618}   ^{art,nn749}   ^{pinf399}   ^{an,nn2378}

27 Who needeth not daily, as those high priests, to offer up sacrifice,

^{an,ajn4386 pre5228} ^{art,aj2398} ^{an,nn266}   ^{ad1899} ^(art3588) ^{art3588}   ⁿⁿ²⁹⁹²   ¹⁰⁶³ ^{depro5124}   ^{aina4160}   ^{nu,ad2178}

first for his own sins, and then for the people's: for this he did once,

^{apta399}   ^{rxpro1438}

when he offered up himself.   *(Lev. 9:7; 16:6,15)*

¹⁰⁶³   ^{art3588 nn3551}   ^{pin2525}   ^{an,nn444}   ^{pr/an,nn749}   ^{pap2192}   ^{an,nn769}   ¹¹⁶¹ ^{art3588}

28 For the law maketh men high priests which have infirmity; but the

ⁿⁿ³⁰⁵⁶   ^{art3588}   ⁿⁿ³⁷²⁸   ^{art3588}   ^{pre3326}   ^{art3588}   ⁿⁿ³⁵⁵¹   ^{an,nn5207}

word of the oath, which was since the law, *maketh* the Son, who is

^{pfpp5048}   ^{pre1519/art,nn165}

consecrated forevermore.

Christ Supercedes the Levitical System

¹¹⁶¹   ^{pre1909}   ^{art,ppmp3004}   ^{an,nn2774}   ^{pin2192}

8 Now of the*things*which*we*have*spoken *this is* the sum: We have

^{an,aj5108}   ^{an,nn749}   ^{repro3739}   ^{aina2523} ^{pre1722}   ^{an,ajn1188}   ^{art3588}   ⁿⁿ²³⁶²

such a high priest, who is set on the right hand of the throne

^{art3588}   ⁿⁿ³¹⁷²   ^{pre1722 art3588}   ⁿⁿ³⁷⁷²

of the Majesty in the heavens;   *(Ps. 110:1)*

^{an,nn3011}   ^{art3588}   ^{ajn39}   ²⁵³²   ^{art3588} ^{aj228}   ^{art,nn4633}   ^{repro3739 art3588 nn2962}

2 A minister of the sanctuary, and of the true tabernacle, which the Lord

^{aina4078}   ²⁵³² ³⁷⁵⁶ ^{an,nn444}

pitched, and not man.   *(Num. 24:6 [Sept.])*

¹⁰⁶³   ^{an,aj3956}   ^{an,nn749}   ^{pinp2525}   ^{aies4374}   ⁽⁵⁰³⁷⁾   ^{an,nn1435}   ²⁵³²   ^{an,nn2378}

3 For every high priest is ordained to offer gifts and sacrifices:

^{ad3606}   ^{an,ajn316}   ^{depro5126}   ^{pinf2192} ^{idpro5100/repro3739} ²⁵³²   ^{asba4374}

wherefore *it is* of necessity that this man have somewhat also to offer.

¹⁰⁶³   ¹⁴⁸⁷   ⁽³³⁰³⁾   ^{ipf2258}   ^{pre1909} ^{an,nn1093}   ^{ad3761} ^{ipf2258/302}   ^{pr/an,nn2409}

4 For if he were on earth, he should not be a priest, seeing that

^{pap5607} ^{art,nn2409}   ^{art,pap4374} ^{art,nn1435}   ^{pre2596}   ^{art3588 nn3551}

there are priests that offer gifts according to the law:

^{repro3748}   ^{pin3000}   ^{an,nn5262}   ²⁵³²   ^{an,nn4639}   ^{art,ajn2032}   ^{ad2531} ^{an,nn3475}

5 Who serve unto the example and shadow of heavenly things, as Moses

^{pfip5537}   ^{pap3195}   ^{pinf2005} ^{art3588}   ⁿⁿ⁴⁶³³   ¹⁰⁶³

was admonished*of*God when he was about to make the tabernacle: for,

_{pim3708   pin5346   asba4160   an,ajn3956   pre2596   art3588   nn5179   art,aptp1166}

See, saith he, *that* thou make all things according to the pattern showed to

_{ppro4671 pre1722 art3588   nn3735}

thee in the mount.   *(Ex. 25:40)*

_{1161   ad3570   pfi5177   cd/an,aj1313   an,nn3009   repro3745   2532}

6 But now hath he obtained a more excellent ministry, by how much also

_{pin2076   pr/an,nn3316   cd/an,aj2909   an,nn1242   repro3748   pfip3549   pre1909 cd/an,aj2909}

he is the mediator of a better covenant, which was established upon better

_{an,nn1860}

promises.

Better Promises

_{1063   1487 depro1565 art,nu,ajn4413   ipf2258   pr/an,aj273   3756 (302) an,nn5117}

7 For if that   first   *covenant* had been faultless, then should no   place

_{ipf2212   an,nu,aj1208}

have been sought for the second.

_{1063   ppmp3201   ppro846   pin3004   2400   an,nn2250   pinm2064   pin3004}

8 For finding fault with them, he saith, Behold, the days come, saith the

_{2962   2532   ft4931   an,aj2537   an,nn1242   pre1909 art3588   nn3624   2474   2532   pre1909 art3588}

Lord, when I will make a new covenant with the house of Israel and with the

_{nn3624   an,nn2455}

house of Judah:

_{3756   pre2596   art3588   nn1242   repro3739   aina4160   ppro846   art,nn3962   pre1722}

9 Not according to the covenant that I made with their fathers in the

_{an,nn2250   ppro3450   aptm1949   ppro846   art3588   nn5495   ainf1806   ppro846   pre1537   an,nn1093}

day when I took them by the hand to lead them out of the land of

_{an,nn125   3754   epn846   aina1696   3756   pre1722   ppro3450   art,nn1242   epn2504}

Egypt; because they continued not in my covenant, and I

_{aina272/ppro846   pin3004   an,nn2962}

regarded*them*not, saith the Lord.

_{3754   pr/depro3778   art3588   nn1242   repro3739   fm1303   art3588   nn3624   2474}

10 For this *is* the covenant that I will make with the house of Israel

_{pre3326   depro1565 art,nn2250   pin3004   an,nn2962   pap1325 ppro3450 an,nn3551 pre1519 ppro846 art,nn1271   2532}

after those days, saith the Lord; I will put my laws into their mind, and

_{ft1924   ppro846   pre1909 ppro846   an,nn2588   2532   fm2071   ppro846   (pre1519) an,nn2316   2532   epn846}

write them in their hearts: and I will be to them a God, and they shall

_{fm2071   ppro3427   (pre1519)   an,nn2992}

be to me a people:

_{2532   efn3364   asba1321   an,ajn1538   ppro848   art,ad4139   2532   an,ajn1538   ppro848}

11 And they shall not teach every man his neighbor, and every man his

_{art,nn80   pap3004   aima1097 art3588   nn2962   3754 an,ajn3956   ft1492   ppro3165   pre575   an,ajn3398 (ppro846)}

brother, saying, Know the Lord: for all shall know me, from the least

_{ad2193   an,ajn3173 (ppro846)}

to the greatest.

_{3754   fm2071   pr/an,aj2436   ppro846   art,nn93   2532   ppro846 art,nn266   2532}

12 For I will be merciful to their unrighteousness, and their sins and

_{ppro846   art,nn458   asbp3415   efn3364/ad2089}

their iniquities will I remember no more.   *(Jer. 31:31-34)*

aie3004　　　an,ajn2537　　　　　　　　　　　　　pfi3822/art3588/nu,ajn4413　　　1161

13 In that he saith, A new *covenant,* he hath made*the*first*old. Now

art,ppmp3822　　　　2532　　pap1095　　　　　　　ad1451/an,nn854

that*which*decayeth and waxeth old *is* ready*to*vanish*away.　　*(Jer. 31:31-34)*

A New Covenant

3767　　3303　art3588 nu,ajn4413　　　　ipf2192 2532　　an,nn1345　　　　　an,nn2999　　5037

9 Then verily the first *covenant* had also ordinances of divine service, and

an,aj2886　　art,ajn39

a worldly sanctuary.

1063　　　　　　　　　an,nn4633　ainp2680　art3588　nu,aj4413　pre1722/repro3739　(5037/repro3739)

2 For there was a tabernacle made; the first, wherein *was* the

an,nn3087　　　2532 art3588　nn5132　2532 art3588　nn4286/art,nn740　repro3748　pinp3004　　an,ajn39

candlestick, and the table, and the showbread; which is called the sanctuary.

(Ex. 26:1-30; 25:23-40)

1161　　pre3326　art3588　　nu,aj1208　　an,nn2665　　　　an,nn4633　　　art,ppmp3004

3 And after the second veil, the tabernacle which*is*called the

an,ajn39/an,ajn39

holiest*of*all;　　　　　　　　　　　　　　　　　*(Ex. 26:31-33)*

pap2192　　　　an,aj5552　　an,nn2369　　2532 art3588　nn2787　　art3588　　nn1242　　pfpp4028

4 Which had the golden censer, and the ark of the covenant overlaid

ad3840　　　　　　an,nn5552　pre1722/repro3739　　　an,aj5553　an,nn4713　　pap2192　3131　2532

round about with gold, wherein *was* the golden pot that had manna, and

2　　art,nn4464　art,apta985　　2532 art3588　nn4109　　art3588　nn1242

Aaron's rod that budded, and the tables of the covenant;

(Ex. 30:1-6; 25:10-16; 16:33; Num. 17:8-10; Ex. 25:16; Deut. 10:3-5)

1161　ad*5231　ppro846　　　5502　　an,nn1391　pap2683　art3588　　nn2435　　pre4012

5 And over it the cherubim of glory shadowing the mercy seat; of

repro3739　　　pin2076/3756 ad3568　pinf3004　　pre2596/an,nn3313

which we cannot now speak particularly.　　　　　　*(Ex. 25:18-22)*

1161　　　　depro5130　　　　　ad3779　　pfpp2680　art3588　　nn2409　pin1524　pre,an,ajn1275

6 Now when these things were thus ordained, the priests went always

pre1519 (3303) art3588 nu,aj4413　　nn4633　　pap2005　　art3588　nn2999

into the first tabernacle, accomplishing the service *of God.* *(Num. 18:2-6)*

1161　　pre1519 art3588　nu,ajn1208　　art3588　　nn749　an,aj3441　nu,ad530　art,nn1763　3756

7 But into the second *went* the high priest alone once every year, not

ad*5565　an,nn129　repro3739　　pin4374　pre5228　rxpro1438　2532　art3588　nn51　art3588　nn2992

without blood, which he offered for himself, and *for* the errors of the people:

(Ex. 30:10; Lev. 16:2,14,15)

art3588　aj40　art,nn4151 depro5124　pap1213　　art3588 nn3598　　art3588　　ajn39

8 The Holy Ghost this signifying, that the way into the holiest*of*all was

ad3380　　　pfin5319　　　　art3588 nu,aj4413　an,nn4633　pap2192 ad2089　an,nn4714

not yet made manifest, while as the first tabernacle was yet standing:

repro3748　　pr/an,nn3850 pre1519 art3588　nn2540　　art,pfp1764　pre2596 repro3739

9 Which *was* a figure for the time then present, in which were

pinp4374   5037   an,nn1435   2532   an,nn2378   ppmp1410   3361
offered   both   gifts   and   sacrifices,   that   could   not

ainf5048/art3588/pap3000   pre2596   an,nn4893
make*him*that*did*the*service*perfect, as pertaining to the conscience;

                 an,ajn3440   pre1909 an,nn1033   2532   an,nn4188   2532   an,aj1313   an,nn909   2532
10 *Which stood* only   in   meats and drinks, and divers washings, and

an,nn4561   an,nn1345   ppmp1945   ad3360   an,nn2540   an,nn1357
carnal ordinances, imposed *on them* until the time of reformation.

(Lev. 11:2; 11:25; 15:18; Num. 19:13)

The Blood of Christ

     1161   an,nn5547   aptm3854   an,nn749   an,ajn18   art,pap3195   pre1223
11 But Christ being come a high priest of good things to come, by a

cd/art,aj3187 2532   cd/an,aj5046   an,nn4633   3756   pr/an,aj5499   depro,pin5123
greater and more perfect tabernacle, not made*with*hands, that*is*to*say,

3756   depro5026   art,nn2937
not of this building;

        3761   pre1223   an,nn129   an,nn5131 2532   an,nn3448   1161 pre1223 art,aj2398 an,nn129
12 Neither by the blood of goats and calves, but by his own blood he

aina1525   nu,ad2178 pre1519 art3588   ajn39   aptm2147   an,aj166   an,nn3085
entered in once into the holy place, having obtained eternal redemption *for us.*

        1063   1487 art3588   nn129   an,nn5022 2532   an,nn5131   2532   an,nn4700   an,nn1151
13 For if the blood of bulls and of goats, and the ashes of a heifer

pap4472   art3588   pfpp2840   pin37   pre4314 art3588   nn2514   art3588   nn4561
sprinkling the unclean, sanctifieth to the purifying of the flesh:

(Lev. 16:3,14,15; Num. 19:9,17-19)

         an,aj4124   ad3123   art3588   nn129   art,nn5547 repro3739   pre1223   an,aj166
14 How much more shall the blood of Christ, who through the eternal

an,nn4151   aina4374   rxpro1438   pr/an,aj299   art,nn2316 ft2511 ppro5216   art,nn4893   pre575 an,aj3498
Spirit offered himself without spot to God, purge your conscience from dead

an,nn2041   aies3000   an,pap2198 an,nn2316
works to serve the living God?

       2532   pre1223/depro5124   pin2076   pr/an,nn3316   an,aj2537   an,nn1242   3704
15 And for*this*cause he is the mediator of the new testament, that

an,nn2288/aptm1096   pre1519   an,nn629   art3588   nn3847   art,pre1909
by*means*of*death, for the redemption of the transgressions *that were* under

art3588   nu,aj4413   an,nn1242   art,pfpp2564   asba2983   art3588   nn1860
the first testament, they*which*are*called might receive the promise of

art,aj166   an,nn2817
eternal inheritance.

        1063   ad3699   an,nn1242   an,nn318   pifm5342   an,nn2288
16 For where a testament *is,* there must also of necessity be the death

art3588   aptm1303
of the testator.

        1063   an,nn1242   pr/an,aj949   pre1909/an,ajn3498   1893
17 For a testament *is* of force after*men*are*dead: otherwise

     pin2480/ad3379   ad3753 art3588   aptm1303   pin2198
it*is*of*no*strength*at*all while the testator liveth.

18 Whereupon neither the first *testament* was dedicated without blood.
19 For when Moses had spoken every precept to all the people according to the law, he took the blood of calves and of goats, with water, and scarlet wool, and hyssop, and sprinkled both the book, and all the people,

(Ex. 24:3,6-8; Lev. 14:4; Num. 19:6)

20 Saying, This *is* the blood of the testament which God hath enjoined unto you.

(Ex. 24:8)

21 Moreover he sprinkled with blood both the tabernacle, and all the vessels of the ministry.

(Lev. 8:15,19)

22 And almost all things are by the law purged with blood; and without shedding*of*blood is no remission.

(Lev. 17:11)

A Better Sacrifice

23 *It was* therefore necessary that the patterns of things in the heavens should be purified with these; but the heavenly things themselves with better sacrifices than these.

24 For Christ is not entered into the holy places made* with*hands, *which are* the figures of the true; but into heaven itself, now to appear in the presence of God for us:

25 Nor yet that he should offer himself often, as the high priest entereth into the holy place every year with blood of others;

26 For then must he often have suffered since the foundation of the world: but now once in the end of the world hath he appeared to*put*away sin by the sacrifice of himself.

27 And as it is appointed unto men once to die, but after this the judgment:

(Gen. 3:19)

☞ 28 So Christ was once offered to bear the sins of many; and unto them*that*look*for him shall he appear the second time without sin unto salvation.

(Is. 53:12)

Christ's Sacrifice Is Once for All

10 For the law having a shadow of good things to come, *and* not the very image of the things, can never with those sacrifices which they offered year*by*year continually make*the*comers*thereunto*perfect.

2 For then would they not have ceased to be offered? because that the worshipers once purged should have had no more conscience of sins.

3 But in those *sacrifices there* is a remembrance again *made* of sins every year.

4 For *it is* not possible that the blood of bulls and of goats should take away sins.

(Lev. 16:15,21)

5 Wherefore when he cometh into the world, he saith, Sacrifice and offering thou wouldest not, but a body hast thou prepared me:

6 In burnt offerings and *sacrifices* for sin thou hast had*no*pleasure.

7 Then said I, Lo, I come (in the volume of the book it is written of me,) to do thy will, O God.

(Ps. 40:6-8)

8 Above when he said, Sacrifice and offering and burnt offerings and *offering* for sin thou wouldest not, neither hadst pleasure *therein*; which are offered by the law;

(Ps. 40:6)

9 Then said he, Lo, I come to do thy will, O God. He taketh away the first, that he may establish the second.

(Ps. 40:7,8)

☞ 9:28 See note on Hebrews 6:1–6.

pre1722   repro3739 an,nn2307   pin2070 pr/pfpp37   pre1223 art3588   nn4376   art3588 nn4983

10 By the which will we are sanctified through the offering of the body

art,nn2424 an,nn5547 nu,ad2178

of Jesus Christ once *for all.*

2532   an,aj3956 (3303)   an,nn2409   pfi2476   pre2596/an,nn2250   pap3008   2532   pap4374

☞ 11 And every priest standeth daily ministering and offering

ad4178   art3588 ppro846   nn2378   repro3748 pinm1410 ad3762   ainf4014   an,nn266

oftentimes the same sacrifices, which can never take away sins: *(Ex. 29:38)*

1161   epn846   apta4374   nu3391 an,nn2378 pre5228 an,nn266pre1519/art,ajn1336

12 But this man, after he had offered one sacrifice for sins forever,

aina2523   pre1722   an,ajn1188   art,nn2316

sat down on the right hand of God; *(Ps. 110:1)*

art,ajn3063   ppmp1551   ad2193 ppro846 art,ajn2190   asbp5087 an,nn5286/ppro846/art,nn4228

13 From henceforth expecting till his enemies be made his footstool.

(Ps. 110:1)

1063   nu3391   an,nn4376   pfi5048   pre1519/art,ajn1336

14 For by one offering he hath perfected forever

art,ppmp37

them*that*are*sanctified.

(1161)   art3588 aj40   art,nn4151 2532   pin3140   ppro2554 1063 pre3326

15 *Whereof* the Holy Ghost also is*a*witness to us: for after

aime4280

that he had said before,

depro3778   art3588 pr/nn1242 repro3739   fm1303 pre4314 ppro846 pre3326 depro1565 art,nn2250

16 This *is* the covenant that I will make with them after those days,

pin3004   an,nn2962   pap1325 ppro3450 an,nn3551 pre1909 ppro846 an,nn2588 2532 pre1909 ppro846 art,nn1271

saith the Lord, I will put my laws into their hearts, and in their minds

ft1924   ppro846

will I write them;

2532 ppro846 art,nn266 2532 (ppro846) art,nn458   asbp3415   efn3364/ad2089

17 And their sins and iniquities will I remember no more. *(Jer. 31:33,34)*

1161   ad3699   an,nn859   depro5130   ad3765   an,nn4376 pre4012 an,nn266

18 Now where remission of these *is, there is* no more offering for sin.

The Believer's Access to God

pap2192   3767   an,nn80   an,nn3954   pre1519/art,nn1529 art3588 ajn39   pre1722 art3588

19 Having therefore, brethren, boldness to*enter*into the holiest by the

nn129   an,nn2424

blood of Jesus,

an,aj4372 2532 an,pap2198 an,nn3598 repro3739   aina1457   ppro2554   pre1223

20 By a new and living way, which he hath consecrated for us, through

art3588 nn2665   depro,pin5123   ppro848 pr/art,nn4561

the veil, that*is*to*say, his flesh;

2532   an,aj3173 an,nn2409 pre1909 art3588   nn3624   art,nn2316

21 And *having* a high priest over the house of God;

---

psa4334   pre3326   an,aj228   an,nn2588   pre1722   an,nn4136   an,nn4102

22 Let us draw near with a true heart in full assurance of faith, having

art,nn2588   pfpp4472   pre575   an,aj4190   an,nn4893   2532   art,nn4983   pfpp3068

our hearts sprinkled from an evil conscience, and our bodies washed with

an,aj2513   an,nn5204

pure water.   *(Ezek. 36:25)*

psa2722   art3588   nn3671   art,nn1680   an,aj186   1063

23 Let us hold fast the profession of *our* faith without wavering; (for he

pr/an,aj4103   art,aptm1861

is faithful that promised;)

2532   psa2657   rcpro240   pre1519/an,nn3948   an,nn26   2532   an,aj2570

24 And let us consider one another to*provoke*unto love and to good

an,nn2041

works:

3361   pap1459   art3588   nn1997/rxpro1438   ad2531   pr/an,nn1485

25 Not forsaking the assembling*of*ourselves*together, as the manner of

idpro5100   235   pap3870   2532   an,aj5118   ad3123   an,ajn3745   pin991   art3588

some *is*; but exhorting *one another*: and so much the more, as ye see the

nn2250   pap1448

day approaching.

1063   ppro2257   pap264   ad1596   aime2983   art3588   nn1922

☞ 26 For if we sin willfully after that we have received the knowledge of

art3588   nn225   pinm620   ad3765   an,nn2378   pre4012   an,nn266

the truth, there remaineth no more sacrifice for sins,

1161   idpro5100   an,aj5398   an,nn1561   an,nn2920   2532   an,nn4442   an,nn2205

27 But a certain fearful looking for of judgment and fiery indignation, which

pap3195   pinf2068   art3588   ajn5227

shall devour the adversaries.   *(Is. 26:11)*

idpro5100   apta114   an,nn3475   an,nn3551   pin599   ad*5565   an,nn3628   pre1909   nu1417   2228

28 He that despised Moses' law died without mercy under two or

nu5140   an,nn3144

three witnesses: *(Deut. 17:6; 19:15)*

an,aj4214   pr/an,aj5501   an,nn5098   pin1380

29 Of how much sorer punishment, suppose ye, shall he

fp515   art,apta2662   art3588   nn5207   art,nn2316   2532

be*thought*worthy, who*hath*trodden*under*foot the Son of God, and hath

aptm2233   art3588   nn129   art3588   nn1242   pre1722/repro3739   ainp37

counted the blood of the covenant, wherewith he was sanctified, an

pr/an,aj2839   2532   apta1796   art3588   nn4151   art,nn5485

unholy thing, and hath done despite unto the Spirit of grace?   *(Ex. 24:8)*

1063   pin1492   art,apta2036   an,nn1557   epn1698 epn1473

30 For we know him*that*hath*said, Vengeance *belongeth* unto me, I

☞ **10:26, 27** The key idea expressed in these verses is that there will be no restitution made for one who wilfully rejects Christ. The emphasis is seen in the Greek word *oukéti* (3765), which is translated "no more." Once Christ is rejected, there cannot be another sacrifice on the cross in order to forgive that individual (see notes on Mark 3:28, 29 and Heb. 6:1–6). The only consequence for such a person is "judgment and fiery indignation" reflection God's judgment for sin (v. 27).This refers to the ultimate punishment for the one who has received the knowledge of God's truth, but chose to forsake it (cf. Rom. 1:21, 25).

^{ft467}   ^{pin3004}   ^{an,nn2962}   ²⁵³²   ^{ad3825}   ^{an,nn2962}   ^{ft2919}   ^{ppro848}   ^{art,nn2992}

will recompense, saith the Lord. And again, The Lord shall judge his people.

(Deut. 32:35; 32:36; Ps. 135:14)

^{pr/an,aj5398}   ^{art,ainf1706} ^{pre1519}   ^{an,nn5495}   ^{an,pap2198} ^{an,nn2316}

31 *It is* a fearful thing to   fall   into the hands of the living God.

¹¹⁶¹   ^{pim363}   ^{art3588}   ^{ajn4386}   ^{an,nn2250} ^{pre1722}   ^{repro3739}

32 But call*to*remembrance the former days, in which, after ye were

^{aptp5461}   ^{aina5278}   ^{an,aj4183} ^{an,an119}   ^{an,nn3804}

illuminated, ye endured a great fight of afflictions;

^{depro5124/3303}   ^{ppmp2301}   ⁵⁰³⁷   ^{an,nn3680}   ²⁵³²

33 Partly, whilst ye were made*a*gazingstock both by reproaches and

^{an,nn2347}   ¹¹⁶¹   ^{depro5124}   ^{aptp1096}   ^{pr/an,ajn2844}

afflictions;   and   partly,   whilst   ye   became   companions   of

^{art,ppmp390/ad3779}

them*that*were*so*used.

¹⁰⁶³   ^{aina4834 (2532)}   ^{ppro3450} ^{art,nn1199}   ²⁵³²   ^{aom4327} ^{pre3326/an,nn5479} ^{art3588}

34 For ye had compassion of me in my bonds, and took joyfully the

ⁿⁿ⁷²⁴   ^{ppro5216} ^{art,pap5224}   ^{pap1097}   ^{pre1722}   ^{rxpro1438}   ^{pinf2192} ^{pre1722}   ^{an,nn3772}

spoiling of your goods, knowing in yourselves that ye have in heaven a

^{cd/an,aj2909} ²⁵³²   ^{pap3306}   ^{an,nn5223}

better and an enduring substance.

^{aosi577/3361}   ³⁷⁶⁷   ^{ppro5216}   ^{art,nn3954}   ^{repro3748}   ^{pin2192}   ^{an,aj3173}

35 Cast*not*away   therefore   your   confidence,   which   hath   great

^{an,nn3405}

recompense*of*reward.

¹⁰⁶³   ^{pin2192} ^{an,nn5532}   ^{an,nn5281}   ²⁴⁴³   ^{apta4160} ^{art3588}   ⁿⁿ²³⁰⁷

36 For ye have need of patience, that, after ye have done the will of

^{art,nn2316}   ^{asbm2865}   ^{art3588}   ⁿⁿ¹⁸⁶⁰

God, ye might receive the promise.

¹⁰⁶³   ^{ad2089}   ^{an,aj3398/an,aj3745/an,ajn3745}   ^{art,ppmp2064}   ^{ft2240}   ²⁵³²

37 For yet, a   little while,   and he*that*shall*come will come, and will

³⁷⁵⁶   ^{ft5549}

not tarry.   (Is. 26:20 [Sept.])

¹¹⁶¹   ^{art3588} ^{ajn1342}   ^{fm2198} ^{pre1537} ^{an,nn4102} ²⁵³² ¹⁴³⁷   ^{asbm5288}   ^{ppro3450}

38 Now the just shall live by faith: but if *any man* draw back, my

^{art,nn5590}   ^{pin2106/3756}   ^{pre1722} ^{ppro846}

soul shall have*no*pleasure in him.   (Hab. 2:3,4 [Sept.])

¹¹⁶¹   ^{epn2249} ^{pin2070} ³⁷⁵⁶   ^{pr/an,nn5289}   ^{pre1519}   ^{an,nn684}   ²³⁵

39 But we are not of them*who*draw*back unto perdition; but of

^{an,nn4102}   ^{pre1519/an,nn4047}   ^{an,nn5590}

them*that*believe to*the*saving of the soul.

"By Faith"

11

¹¹⁶¹   ^{an,nn4102} ^{pin2076}   ^{pr/an,nn5287}   ^{ppmp1679}   ^{pr/an,nn1650}

Now faith is the substance of things*hoped*for, the evidence of

^{an,nn4229} ³⁷⁵⁶ ^{ppmp991}

things not seen.

2 For by   it   the elders obtained*a*good*report.

3 Through faith we understand that the worlds were framed by the word

of   God,   so   that   things*which*are*seen   were   not   made   of

things*which*do*appear.   *(Gen. 1:1; Ps. 33:6,9).*

4 By faith Abel offered unto God a more excellent sacrifice than Cain,

by which he obtained witness that he was righteous, God testifying of his

gifts: and by   it he being dead yet speaketh.   *(Gen. 4:3-10)*

5 By faith Enoch was translated that he should not see death; and was

not found, because God had translated him: for before his translation he

had*this*testimony, that he pleased God.   *(Gen. 5:24)*

6 But without faith *it is* impossible to please *him*: for he*that*cometh to

God must believe that he is,   and *that* he   is   a   rewarder of

them*that*diligently*seek him.

7 By faith Noah, being warned*of*God   of   things*not*seen*as*yet,

moved*with*fear, prepared an ark to*the*saving of his house; by the which

he condemned the world, and became heir of the righteousness which is

by faith.   *(Gen. 6:13-22; 7:1)*

8 By faith Abraham, when he was called to go out into a place which he

should after receive for an inheritance, obeyed; and he went out, not

knowing whither he went.   *(Gen. 12:1-5)*

9 By faith he sojourned in the land of promise, as *in* a strange country,

dwelling in   tabernacles with Isaac and Jacob, the heirs*with*him of the

same promise: *(Gen. 23:4; 26:3; 35:12,17)*

10 For he looked for a city which hath foundations, whose builder and

maker *is* God.

11 Through faith also Sarah herself received strength to conceive seed,

2532   aina5088   pre3844/an,nn2244/an,nn2540   1893

and was delivered*of*a*child when she was   past age,   because she

aom2233   pr/an,aj103   art,aptm1861

judged him faithful who*had*promised.   *(Gen. 17:19; 18:11-14; 21:2)*

1352   aina1080   2532   pre575 nu,ajn1520 2532 depro5023   pfpp3499

12 Therefore sprang there even of one, and him as*good*as* dead, *so*

ad2531 art3588   nn798   art3588   nn3772   art,nn4128   2532 ad5616   an,nn285   art3588   pre3844

many as the stars of the sky in multitude, and as the sand which is by

art3588 nn5491/art,nn2281   art,aj382

the sea shore innumerable.

(Gen. 15:5,6; 22:17; 32:12; Ex. 32:13; Deut. 1:10; 10:22; Dan. 3:36 [Sept.])

depro3778 an,ajn3956 aina599 pre2596 an,nn4102 3361   apta2983   art3588   nn1860   235

13 These   all   died in faith, not having received the promises, but having

apta1492 ppro846   ad4207   2532   aptp3982   2532   aptm782   2532

seen them afar off, and were persuaded of *them,* and embraced *them,* and

apta3670   3754   pin1526   pr/an,ajn3581   2532   pr/an,ajn3927 pre1909 art3588   nn1093

confessed that they were strangers and pilgrims on the earth.

(Gen. 23:4; 47:9; 1 Chr. 29:15; Ps. 39:12)

1063   art,pap3004   an,ajn5108   pin1718   3754   pin1934

14 For they*that*say such things declare plainly that they seek a

an,nn3968

country.

2532   3303   1487   ipf3421   depro1565   pre575   repro3739

15 And truly, if they had been mindful of that *country* from whence they

aina1831   ipf2192/302   an,nn2540   ainf344

came out, they might have had opportunity to have returned.

1161   ad3570   pinm3713   cd/an,ajn2909   depro,pin5123   pr/an,aj2032   pre,repro1352

16 But now they desire a better *country,* that is, a heavenly: wherefore

art,nn2316   3756   pinm1870   pifm1941 ppro846 am.mm2316 1063   aina2090   ppro846

God is not ashamed to be called their God: for he hath prepared for them a

an,nn4172

city.   *(Ex. 3:6,15; 4:5)*

an,nn4102   11   ppmp3985   pfi4374   2464   2532

17 By   faith Abraham, when he was tried, offered up Isaac: and

art,aptm324   art3588   nn1860   aina4374   art,ajn3439

he*that*had*received the promises offered up his only begotten *son,*

(Gen. 22:1-10)

pre4314 repro3739   ainp2980   3754   pre1722   2464   ppro4671 an,nn4690   fp2564

18 Of whom it was said, That in Isaac shall thy seed be called:

(Gen. 21:12)

aptm3049   3754 art,nn2316   pr/an,aj1415   pinf1453   2532   pre1537   an,ajn3498

19 Accounting that God *was* able to raise*him*up, even from the dead;

ad3606   2532   aom2865   ppro846 pre1722   an,nn3850

from whence also he received him in a figure.

an,nn4102 2464   aina2127   2384   2532   2269   pre4012   pap3195

20 By faith Isaac blessed Jacob and Esau concerning things*to*come.

(Gen. 27:27-29,39,40)

an,nn4102   2384   pap599   aina2127 an,ajn1538 art3588 nn5207   2501

21 By faith Jacob, when he was a dying, blessed both the sons of Joseph;

2532   aina4352   pre1909 art3588 ajn206   ppro848 art,nn4464

and worshiped, *leaning* upon the top of his staff.

(Gen. 48:15,16; 47:31 [Sept.])

an,nn4102   2501   pap5053   aina3421   pre4012 art3588   nn1841

22 By faith Joseph, when he died, made mention of the departing of

art3588 nn5207   2474   2532   aom1781   pre4012   ppro848 art,nn3747

the children of Israel; and gave commandment concerning his bones.

(Gen. 50:24,25; Ex. 13:19)

an,nn4102   an,nn3475   aptp1080   ainp2928   an,ajn5150   pre5259 ppro848

23 By faith Moses, when he was born, was hid three months of his

art,nn3962   1360   aina1492   pr/an,aj791 art,nn3813 2532   ainp5399/3756

parents, because they saw *he was* a proper child; and they were*not*afraid of

art3588 nn935   art,nn1297

the king's commandment.   *(Ex. 1:22; 2:2)*

an,nn4102   an,nn3475   aptm1096/pr/an,aj3173   aina720   pifm3004

24 By faith Moses, when he was come*to*years, refused to be called the

an,nn5207   5328   an,nn2364

son of Pharaoh's daughter;   *(Ex. 2:10-12)*

aptm138   ad3123   pifm4778   art3588   nn2992   art,nn2316 2228

25 Choosing rather to suffer*affliction*with the people of God, than to

pinf2192/an,nn619   an,nn266   an,aj4340

enjoy*the*pleasures of sin for*a*season;

aptm2233   art3588   nn3680   art,nn5547   cd/an,aj3187 pr/an,nn4149   art3588   nn2344

26 Esteeming the reproach of Christ greater riches than the treasures

pre1722 an,nn125 1063   ipf578   pre1519 art3588   nn3405

in Egypt: for he had respect unto the recompense*of*the*reward.

an,nn4102   aina2641   an,nn125   3361 aptp5399 art3588   nn2372   art3588 nn935 1063

27 By faith he forsook Egypt, not fearing the wrath of the king: for he

aina2594   ad5613 pap3708   art,ajn517

endured, as seeing him*who*is*invisible.   *(Ex. 2:15; 12:51)*

an,nn4102   pfi4160 art3588   3957   2532 art3588   nn4378   art,nn129 3363

28 Through faith he kept the passover, and the sprinkling of blood, lest

art,pap3645   art3588   ajn4416   asba2345 ppro846

he*that*destroyed the firstborn should touch them.   *(Ex. 12:21-30)*

an,nn4102   aina1224   art3588 aj2063 an,nn2281 ad5613 pre1223 an,ajn3584   repro3739

29 By faith they passed through the Red sea as by dry *land*: which

art3588   nn124   apta2983/an,nn3984   ainp2666

the Egyptians attempting*to*do were drowned.   *(Ex. 14:21-31)*

an,nn4102   art3588   nn5038   2410   ainp4098

30 By faith the walls of Jericho fell down, after they were

aptp2944 (pre1909)   nu2033   an,nn2550

compassed about seven days.   *(Josh. 6:12-21)*

an,nn4102 3588   nn4204   4460   aom4881   3756   art,apta544

31 By faith the harlot Rahab perished not with them*that*believed*not, when

aptm1209   art3588 nn2685   pre3326 an,nn1515

she had received the spies with peace.   *(Josh. 2:11,12; 6:21-25)*

32 ²⁵³² ^{inpro5101} ^{ad2089} ^{pin3004} ¹⁰⁶³ ^{art3588} ⁿⁿ⁵⁵⁵⁰ ^{ft1952} ^{ppro3165} ^{ppmp1334} ^{pre4012}

32 And what shall I more say? for the time would fail me to tell of

¹⁰⁶⁶ ⁵⁰³⁷ ⁹¹³ ²⁵³² ⁴⁵⁴⁶ ²⁵³² ²⁴²² ¹¹³⁸ ⁵⁰³⁷ ²⁵³²

Gideon, and *of* Barak, and *of* Samson, and *of* Jephthah; *of* David also, and

⁴⁵⁴⁵ ²⁵³² ^{art3588} ⁿⁿ⁴³⁹⁶

Samuel, and *of* the prophets:

^{repro3739} ^{pre1223} ^{an,nn4102} ^{aom2610} ^{an,nn932} ^{aom2038} ^{an,nn1343}

33 Who through faith subdued kingdoms, wrought righteousness,

^{aina2013} ^{an,nn1860} ^{aina5420} ^{an,nn4750} ^{an,nn3023}

obtained promises, stopped the mouths of lions,

(Judg. 14:6,7; 1 Sam. 17:34-36; Dan. 6:1-27)

^{aina4570} ^{an,nn1411} ^{an,nn4442} ^{aina5343} ^{an,nn4750} ^{an,nn3162} ^{pre575}

34 Quenched the violence of fire, escaped the edge of the sword, out of

^{an,nn769} ^{ainp1743} ^{ainp1096} ^{pr/an,aj2478} ^{pre1722} ^{an,nn4171} ^{aina2827}

weakness were made strong, waxed valiant in fight, turned*to*flight the

^{an,nn3925} ^{an,ajn245}

armies of the aliens.

(Dan. 3:23-25)

^{an,nn1135} ^{aina2983} ^{ppro848} ^{art,ajn3498} ^{pre1537/an,nn386} ¹¹⁶¹ ^{an,ajn243}

35 Women received their dead raised*to*life*again: and others were

^{ainp5178} ³⁷⁵⁶ ^{aptm4327} ^{art,nn629} ²⁴⁴³ ^{asba5177} ^{cd/an,aj2909}

tortured, not accepting deliverance; that they might obtain a better

^{an,nn386}

resurrection:

(1 Kgs. 17:17-24; 2 Kgs. 4:25-37)

¹¹⁶¹ ^{an,ajn2087} ^{aina2983} ^{an,nn3984} ^{an,nn1701} ²⁵³² ^{an,nn3148} ¹¹⁶¹ ^{ad2089}

36 And others had trial of *cruel* mockings and scourgings, yea, moreover

^{an,nn1199} ²⁵³² ^{an,nn5438}

of bonds and imprisonment:

(1 Kgs. 22:26,27; 2 Chr. 18:25,26; Jer. 20:2; 37:15; 38:6)

^{ainp3034} ^{ainp4249} ^{ainp3985} ^{aina599}

37 They were stoned, they were sawn asunder, were tempted, were slain

^{pre1722} ^(an,nn5408) ^{an,nn3162} ^{aina4022} ^{pre1722} ^{an,nn3374} ²⁵³² ^{(pre1722) an,aj122/an,nn1192}

with the sword: they wandered about in sheepskins and goatskins;

^{ppmp5302} ^{ppmp2346} ^{ppmp2558}

being destitute, afflicted, tormented;

(2 Chr. 24:21)

^{repro3739} ^{art3588} ⁿⁿ²⁸⁸⁹ ^{ipf2258} ³⁷⁵⁶ ^{pr/an,aj514} ^{ppmp4105} ^{pre1722} ^{an,nn2047} ²⁵³²

38 (Of whom the world was not worthy:) they wandered in deserts, and

^{an,nn3735} ²⁵³² ^{an,nn4693} ^{2532 art,nn3692} ^{art3588} ⁿⁿ¹⁰⁹³

in mountains, and *in* dens and caves of the earth.

²⁵³² ^{depro3778} ^{an,aj3956} ^{aptp3140} ^{pre1223} ^{art,nn4102} ^{aom2865}

39 And these all, having obtained*a*good*report through faith, received

³⁷⁵⁶ ^{art3588} ⁿⁿ¹⁸⁶⁰

not the promise:

^{art,nn2316} ^{aptm4265} ^{idpro5100} ^{cd/an,aj2909} ^{pre4012} ^{ppro2257} ²⁴⁴³ ^{ad*5565}

40 God having provided some better thing for us, that they without

^{ppro2257} ³³⁶¹ ^{asbp5048}

us should not be made perfect.

Exhortations to Follow Christ

12 Wherefore seeing we also are compassed about with so great a cloud of witnesses, let us lay aside every weight, and the sin which*doth*so*easily*beset *us,* and let us run with patience the race that is set before us,

2 Looking unto Jesus the author and finisher of *our* faith; who for the joy that was set before him endured the cross, despising the shame, and is set down at the right hand of the throne of God.   *(Ps. 110:1)*

3 For consider him*that*endured such contradiction of sinners against himself, lest ye be wearied and faint in your minds.

4 Ye have not yet resisted unto blood, striving against sin.

5 And ye have forgotten the exhortation which speaketh unto you as unto children, My son, despise not thou the chastening of the Lord, nor faint when thou art rebuked of him:

6 For whom the Lord loveth he chasteneth, and scourgeth every son whom he receiveth.   *(Prov. 3:11,12)*

7 If ye endure chastening, God dealeth with you as with sons; for what son is he whom the father chasteneth not?   *(Deut. 8:5; 2 Sam. 7:14)*

8 But if ye be without chastisement, whereof all are partakers, then are ye bastards, and not sons.

9 Furthermore we have had fathers of our flesh which corrected *us,* and we gave*them*reverence: shall we not much rather be*in*subjection unto the Father of spirits, and live?   *(Num. 16:22; 27:16)*

10 For they verily for a few days chastened *us* after their own pleasure; but he for *our* profit, that *we* might be partakers of his holiness.

11 Now no chastening for the present seemeth to be joyous, but

^{pr/an,nn3077}   ¹¹⁶¹   ^{ad5305}   ^{pin591}   ^{an,aj1516}   ^{an,nn2590}

grievous: nevertheless afterward it yieldeth the peaceable fruit of

^{an,nn1343}   ^{art,pfpp1128}   ^{pre1223/ppro846}

righteousness unto them*which*are*exercised thereby.

Exhortations to Holiness

^{pre,repro1352}   ^{aima461}   ^{an,nn5495}   ^{art3588}   ^{pfpp3935}   ²⁵³²   ^{art3588}   ^{pfpp3886}   ⁿⁿ¹¹¹⁹

12 Wherefore lift up the hands which hang down, and the feeble knees;

(Is. 35:3)

²⁵³²   ^{aima4160}   ^{an,aj3717}   ^{an,nn5163}   ^{ppro5216}   ^{art,nn4228}   ³³⁶³   ^{art,ajn5560}

13 And make straight paths for your feet, lest that*which*is*lame be

^{asbp1624}   ¹¹⁶¹   ^{ad3123}   ^{asbp2390}

turned*out*of*the*way; but let it rather be healed.   *(Prov. 4:26 [Sept.])*

^{pim1377}   ^{an,nn1515}   ^{pre3326} ^{an,ajn3956}   ²⁵³²   ^{art,nn38}   ^{ad*5565}   ^{repro3739}   ^{an,ajn3762}

14 Follow peace with   all   *men,* and holiness, without which no man shall

^{fm3700} ^{art3588}   ⁿⁿ²⁹⁶²

see the Lord: *(Ps. 34:14)*

^{pap1983}   ³³⁶¹   ^{idpro5100}   ^{pap5302} ^{pre575} ^{art3588}   ⁿⁿ⁵⁴⁸⁵   ^{art,nn2316}   ³³⁶¹   ^{idpro5100}

15 Looking diligently lest any man fail   of   the grace of God; lest   any

^{an,nn4491}   ^{an,nn4088}   ^{pap5453}   ^{ad507}   ^{psa1776}   ²⁵³²   ^{pre1223/depro5026} ^{an,ajn4183}   ^{asbp3392}

root of bitterness springing up trouble *you,* and   thereby   many be defiled;

(Deut. 29:18 [Sept.])

³³⁶¹   ^{idpro5100}   ^{an,nn4205}   ²²²⁸   ^{an,ajn952}   ^{ad5613}   ²²⁶⁹   ^{repro3739} ^{pre473}

16 Lest there *be* any fornicator, or profane person, as   Esau, who for

^{nu3391}   ^{an,nn1035}   ^{aom591} ^{ppro848}   ^{art,nn4415}

one morsel*of*meat sold his birthright.   *(Gen. 25:33,34)*

¹⁰⁶³   ^{pin2467}   ³⁷⁵⁴   ^{ad3347}   ^{pap2309}   ^{ainf2816}   ^{art3588}

17 For ye know how that afterward, when he would have inherited the

ⁿⁿ²¹²⁹   ^{ainp593}   ¹⁰⁶³   ^{aina2147} ³⁷⁵⁶ ^{an,nn5117}   ^{an,nn3341}   ²⁵³⁹

blessing, he was rejected: for he found no place of repentance, though he

^{apta1567/ppro846}   ^{pre3326} ^{an,nn1144}

sought*it*carefully with tears.   *(Gen. 27:30-40)*

¹⁰⁶³   ³⁷⁵⁶   ^{pfi4334}   ^{an,nn3735}   ^{ppmp5584}   ²⁵³²

18 For ye are not come unto the mount that might be touched, and that

^{pfpp2545}   ^{an,nn4442} ²⁵³²   ^{an,nn1105}   ²⁵³²   ^{an,nn4655}   ²⁵³²   ^{an,nn2366}

burned with fire, nor unto blackness, and darkness, and tempest,

²⁵³²   ^{an,nn2279}   ^{an,nn4536}   ²⁵³²   ^{an,nn5456}   ^{an,nn4487}   ^{repro3739}

19 And the sound of a trumpet, and the voice of words; which *voice*

^{art,apta191}   ^{aom3868}   ^{an,nn3056}   ³³⁶¹

they*that*heard   entreated   that   the   word   should   not   be

^{pfin4369/ppro846}

spoken*to*them*any*more: *(Ex. 19:16-22; 20:18-21; Deut. 4:11,12; 5:22-27)*

¹⁰⁶³   ³⁷⁵⁶   ^{ipf5342}   ^{art,ppmp1291}

20 (For   they   could   not   endure   that*which*was*commanded,

²⁵⁷⁹   ^{an,nn2342}   ^{asba2345} ^{art3588}   ⁿⁿ³⁷³⁵   ^{fp3036}

And*if*so*much*as a beast touch the mountain, it shall be stoned, or

^{fp2700}   ^{an,nn1002}

thrust through with a dart: *(Ex. 19:13)*

2532   ad3779   pr/an,aj5398   ipf2258   art3588   ppmp5324   an,nn3475   aina2036   (pin1510) pr/an,aj1630   2532

21 And so terrible was the sight, *that* Moses said, I exceedingly fear and

pr/an,aj1790

quake:)   *(Deut. 9:19)*

235   pfi4334   an,nn3735   4622   2532   an,nn4172   an,pap2198

22 But ye are come unto mount Zion, and unto the city of the living

an,nn2316   an,aj2032   2419   2532   an,nn3461   an,nn32

God, the heavenly Jerusalem, and to an innumerable company of angels,

an,nn3831   2532   an,nn1577   an,ajn4416   pfpp583

23 To the general assembly and church of the firstborn, which are written

pre1722   an,nn3772   2532   an,nn2316   an,nn2923   an,ajn3956   2532   an,nn4151   an,ajn1342

in heaven, and to God the Judge of all, and to the spirits of just men

pfpp5048

made perfect,   *(Gen. 18:25; Ps. 50:6)*

2532   an,nn2424   an,nn3316   an,aj3501   an,nn1242   2532   an,nn129

24 And to Jesus the mediator of the new covenant, and to the blood of

an,nn4473   pap2980   cd/an,ajn2909   pre3844   6

sprinkling, that speaketh better things than *that of* Abel.   *(Gen. 4:10)*

pim991   asbm3868   3361   art,pap2980   1063   1487 depro1565   aina5343   3756

25 See that ye refuse not him*that*speaketh. For if they escaped not who

aptm3868   art,pap5537   pre1909   art,nn1093   cd/an,aj4183   ad3123   ppro2249

refused him*that*spake on earth, much more *shall not* we *escape,* if we

art,ppmp654   art3588   pre575   an,nn3772

turn*away*from him that *speaketh* from heaven:

repro3739   art,nn5456   ad5119   aina4531   art3588   nn1093   1161   ad3568   pfip1861   pap3004

26 Whose voice then shook the earth: but now he hath promised, saying,

ad2089   nu,ad530   epn1473   pin4579   3756   art3588   nn1093   an,ajn3440   235   2532   art,nn3772

Yet once more I shake not the earth only, but also heaven.

(Ex. 19:18; Judg. 5:4; Ps. 68:8; Hag. 2:6)

1161   art3588   ad2089   nu,ad530   pin1213   art3588   nn3331

27 And this *word,* Yet once more, signifieth the removing of

art,ppmp4531   ad5613   pfpp4160   2443

those*things*that*are*shaken, as of things*that*are*made, that

art,ppmp4531/3361   asba3306

those*things*which*cannot*be*shaken may remain.   *(Hag. 2:6)*

pre,repro1352   pap3880   an,nn932   an,aj761

28 Wherefore we receiving a kingdom which*cannot*be*moved, let us

psi2192   an,nn5485   pre1223/repro3739   psa3000   art,nn2316   ad2102   pre3326   an,nn127   2532

have grace, whereby we may serve God acceptably with reverence and

an,nn2124

godly fear:

1063   (2532) ppro2257 art,nn2316   pap2654   pr/an,nn4442

29 For our God *is* a consuming fire.   *(Deut. 4:24; 9:3; Is. 33:14)*

Social and Religious Duties

13

art,nn5360   pim3306

Let brotherly love continue.

pim1950/3361   art,nn5381   1063   pre1223/depro5026

2 Be*not*forgetful to entertain strangers: for thereby

^{idpro5100}   ^{apta3579}   ^{an,nn32}   ^{aina2990}

some have entertained angels unawares.   *(Gen. 18:1-8; 19:1-3)*

^{pim3403}   ^{art,nn1198}   ^{ad5613}   ^{pfpp4887}

3 Remember them*that*are*in*bonds,   as   bound with them; *and*

^{art,ppmp2558}   ^{ad5613} ^{pap5607}   ^{epn848}   ²⁵³² ^{pre1722}   ^{an,nn4983}

them*which*suffer*adversity, as being yourselves also in the body.

^{art,nn1062}   ^{pr/an,aj5093}   ^{pre1722} ^{an,ajn3956}   ²⁵³² ^{art3588} ⁿⁿ²⁸⁴⁵   ^{pr/an,aj283}   ¹¹⁶¹

4 Marriage *is* honorable in   all,   and the bed undefiled: but

^{an,nn4205}   ²⁵³²   ^{an,nn3432}   ^{art,nn2316}   ^{ft2919}

whoremongers and adulterers God will judge.

^{art,nn5158}   ^{pr/an,aj866}   ^{ppmp714}

5 *Let your* conversation *be* without covetousness; *and be* content with

^{art,pap3918}   ¹⁰⁶³ ^{epn846}   ^{pfi2046}   ^{efn3364} ^{asba447} ^{ppro4571} ³⁷⁶¹

such*things*as*ye*have: for he hath said, I will never leave thee, nor

^(efn3364) ^{asba1459} ^{ppro4571}

forsake thee.   *(Deut. 31:6-8; Josh 1:5)*

⁵⁶²⁰   ^{ppro2248}   ^{pap2292} ^{pinf3004}   ^{an,nn2962}   ^{ppro1698} ^{pr/an,nn998} ²⁵³²   ³⁷⁵⁶ ^{fp5399}

6 So that we may boldly say, The Lord *is* my helper, and I will not fear

^{inpro5101} ^{an,nn444}   ^{ft4160}   ^{ppro3427}

what man shall do unto me.   *(Ps. 118:6)*

^{pim3421}   ^{art,ppmp2233}   ^{ppro5216} ^{repro3748}   ^{aina2980}

7 Remember them*which*have*the*rule*over you, who have spoken unto

^{ppro5213} ^{art3588}   ⁿⁿ³⁰⁵⁶   ^{art,nn2316} ^{repro3739} ^{art,nn4102} ^{pim3401}   ^{pap333}   ^{art3588} ⁿⁿ¹⁵⁴⁵

you the word of God: whose faith follow, considering the end of *their*

^{art,nn391}

conversation.

^{an,nn2424} ^{an,nn5547} ^{art3588} ^{pr/ppro846}   ^{ad5504}   ²⁵³² ^{ad4594}   ²⁵³² ^{pre1519/art,nn165}

8 Jesus Christ the same yesterday, and today, and forever.

³³⁶¹   ^{pim4064}   ^{an,aj4164}   ²⁵³² ^{an,aj3581}   ^{an,nn1322}   ¹⁰⁶³

9 Be not carried about with divers and strange doctrines. For *it is* a

^{an,ajn2570}   ^{art3588} ⁿⁿ²⁵⁸⁸   ^{pifm950}   ^{an,nn5485} ³⁷⁵⁶   ^{an,nn1033} ^(pre1722) ^{repro3739}

good thing that the heart be established with grace; not with meats,   which

³⁷⁵⁶   ^{ainp5623}   ^{art,apta4043}

have not profited them*that*have*been*occupied*therein.

^{pin2192}   ^{an,nn2379} ^{pre1537/repro3739}   ^{pin2192} ³⁷⁵⁶ ^{an,nn1849}   ^{ainf5315}   ^{art,pap3000}   ^{art3588}

10 We have an altar, whereof they have no right to eat which serve the

ⁿⁿ⁴⁶³³

tabernacle.

¹⁰⁶³   ^{art3588}   ⁿⁿ⁴⁹⁸³   ^{depro5130}   ^{an,nn2226}   ^{repro3739} ^{art,nn129}   ^{pinp1533}   ^{pre1519} ^{art3588}

11 For the bodies of those beasts, whose blood is brought into the

^{ajn39}   ^{pre1223} ^{art3588}   ⁿⁿ⁷⁴⁹   ^{pre4012} ^{an,nn266}   ^{pinp2618}   ^{ad1854}   ^{art3588} ⁿⁿ³⁹²⁵

sanctuary by the high priest for sin, are burned without the camp.

(Lev. 16:27)

¹³⁵²   ^{an,nn2424} ²⁵³² ²⁴⁴³   ^{asba37}   ^{art3588}   ⁿⁿ²⁹⁹²   ^{pre1223} ^{art,aj2398}

12 Wherefore Jesus also, that he might sanctify the people with his own

^{an,nn129}   ^{aina3958}   ^{ad1854}   ^{art3588} ⁿⁿ⁴⁴³⁹

blood, suffered without the gate.

^{psi1831}   ⁵¹⁰⁶   ^{pre4314} ^{ppro846}   ^{ad1854}   ^{art3588} ⁿⁿ³⁹²⁵   ^{pap5342}   ^{ppro846}

13 Let us go forth therefore unto him without the camp, bearing his

^{art,nn3680}

reproach.

1063 ad5602 pin2192   3756 pap3306 an,nn4172 235 pin1934 art,pap3195

14 For here have we no continuing city, but we seek one*to*come.

pre1223 ppro846   3767   psa399 an,nn2378 an,nn133 art,nn2316

15 By him therefore let us offer the sacrifice of praise to God

pre,an,ajn1275 depro,pin5123 an,nn2590 an,nn5491 pap3670 ppro846 art,nn3686

continually, that is, the fruit of *our* lips giving thanks to his name.

(Ps. 50:14,23; Hos. 14:2)

1161 art,nn2140 2532 an,nn2842 pim1950 3361 1063 an,aj5108 an,nn2378

16 But to*do*good and to communicate forget not: for with such sacrifices

art,nn2316 pinm2100

God is*well*pleased.

pim3982 art,ppmp2233 ppro5216 2532 pim5226 1063

17 Obey them*that*have*the*rule*over you, and submit yourselves: for

epn846 pin69 pre5228 ppro5216 art,nn5590 ad5613 an,fpta591 an,nn3056 2443

they watch for your souls, as they*that*must*give account, that they may

psa4160 depro5124 pre3326 an,nn5479 2532 3361 pap4727 1063 depro5124 pr/an,ajn255 ppro5213

do it with joy, and not with grief: for that *is* unprofitable for you.

(Is. 62:6; Ezek. 3:17)

pim4336 pre4012 ppro2257 1063 pfi3982 (3754) pin2192 an,aj2570 an,nn4893 pre1722 an,ajn3956

18 Pray for us: for we trust we have a good conscience, in all things

pap2309 pifm390/ad2573

willing to live honestly.

1161 pin3870 ad4056 ainf4160 depro5124 2443 asbp600

19 But I beseech *you* the rather to do this, that I may be restored to

ppro5213 cd/an,ajn5032

you the sooner.

"Jesus, the Great Shepherd"

1161 art3588 nn2316 art,nn1515 art,apta321 pre1537 an,ajn3498 ppro2257 art,nn2962

20 Now the God of peace, that*brought*again from the dead our Lord

an,nn2424 art,aj3173 art,nn4166 art3588 nn4263 pre1722 an,nn129 an,nn166

Jesus, that great shepherd of the sheep, through the blood of the everlasting

an,nn1242

covenant,   *(Is. 55:3; Jer. 32:40; Zech. 9-11)*

opt2675/ppro5209 pre1722 an,aj3956 an,aj18 an,nn2041 aies4160 ppro848 art,nn2307 pap4160

21 Make*you*perfect in every good work to do his will, working

pre1722 ppro5213 art,ajn2101 ad*1799/ppro848 pre1223 an,nn2424 an,nn5547

in you that*which*is*wellpleasing in*his*sight, through Jesus Christ; to

repro3739 art,nn1391 pre1519/art,nn165/art,nn165 281

whom *be* glory forever*and*ever. Amen.

1161 pin3870 ppro5209 an,nn80 pin430 art3588 nn3056 art,nn3874 1063

22 And I beseech you, brethren, suffer the word of exhortation: for I

(2532) aina1989 ppro5213 pre1223 an,ajn1024

have written*a*letter unto you in few words.

^{pim1097}   ^{art,nn80}   ^{an,nn5095}   ^{pfpp630}   ^{pre3326} ^{repro3739} ¹⁴³⁷

23 Know ye that *our* brother Timothy is set*at*liberty; with whom, if he

^{psa2064} ^{cd/an,ajn5032}   ^{fm3700} ^{ppro5209}

come shortly, I will see you.

^{aipm782} ^{an,aj3956}   ^{art,ppmp2233}   ^{ppro5216} ²⁵³² ^{an,aj3956} ^{art3588}   ^{ajn40}

24 Salute all them*that*have*the*rule*over you, and all   the saints.

^{art3588} ^{pre575} ^{art,nn2482} ^{pinm782} ^{ppro5209}

They of Italy salute you.

^{art,nn5485}   ^{pre3326} ^{ppro5216} ^{an,aj3956}   ²⁸¹

25 Grace *be* with you   all. Amen.

The Epistle of
JAMES

James was the oldest half-brother of the Lord Jesus (Matt. 13:55). He witnessed Christ's appearance following His resurrection (1 Cor. 15:7), and he was among those who assembled together following the Ascension (Acts 1:14), to await the coming of the Holy Spirit. Later, James became a leader of the believers in Jerusalem (Acts 12:17; Gal. 1:18, 19). Even Paul took his advice on how to deal with the new Gentile converts (Acts 21:18–26). James kept the potentially explosive situation concerning Gentile evangelism under control. In addition, he helped draft a very tolerant letter to the Gentile Christians in Antioch regarding their status (Acts 15:13–19). James was cognizant of Paul's ministry to the Gentiles, but concentrated his own efforts on winning his Jewish brethren to Jesus.

The phrase "to the twelve tribes which are scattered abroad" (James 1:1) is a symbolic reference to the Jews in general (cf. James 1:2, 18). The phrase "scattered abroad" denotes those Jews who were living outside of Palestine due in great part to the intense persecution of Christians living in Jerusalem (Acts 8:1). Since the letter was written in the Greek language, it is logical to assume that these Jews had been scattered far enough north to have ended up in a locale chiefly populated by Greek speaking peoples (Acts 11:19).

Most scholars suggest that this book was written shortly before James' martyrdom in A.D. 62. There are some, however, who place the time of writing close to the time of the Jerusalem council in A.D. 46. Nevertheless, it seems likely that the Book of James was the first New Testament book that was written.

The Book of James is a simple yet organized and logical treatise on the ethical aspects of the Christian life. This fact, along with the realization that the book is largely composed of general exhortations and admonitions, has led some to call the Book of James the "New Testament Book of Proverbs." The major theme of the book is James' appeal to the believer that it is necessary to put outward actions with inward faith or else that kind of faith will accomplish nothing (James 1:22).

1
an,nn2385   an,ajn1401   an,nn2316   2532   an,nn2962 an,nn2424   an,nn5547   art3588   nu1427
James, a servant of God and of the Lord Jesus Christ, to the twelve
an,nn5443   art3588   pre1722/art,nn1290   pinf5463
tribes which are scattered abroad, greeting.

The Prayer of Faith

ppro3450   an,nn80   aipm2233   an,aj3956   pr/an,nn5479   ad3752   asba4045   an,aj4164
2 My brethren, count it all joy when ye fall into divers
an,nn3986
temptations;

pap1097   3754   art3588   nn1383   ppro5216 art,nn4102   pinm2716   an,nn5281

3 Knowing *this,* that the trying of your faith worketh patience.

1161   art,nn5281   pim2192   an,aj5046 an,nn2041 2443   psa5600 pr/an,aj5046 2532

4 But let patience have *her* perfect work, that ye may be perfect and

pr/an,aj3648 ppmp3007 (pre1722) an,ajn3367

entire, wanting   nothing.

(1161) 1487 idpro5100   ppro5216 pinm3007 an,nn4678   pim154 pre3844 an,nn2316 art,pap1325

5   If any of you lack wisdom, let him ask of God, that giveth to

an,ajn3956   ad574   2532   pap3679   3361 2532   fp1325 ppro846

all *men* liberally, and upbraideth not; and it shall be given him.   *(Prov. 2:3-6)*

1161   pim154 pre1722 an,nn4102 an,ajn3367 ppmp1252   1063   art,ppmp1252

6 But let him ask in faith, nothing wavering. For he*that*wavereth

pfi1503   an,nn2830   an,nn2281   ppmp416   2532 ppmp4494

is like a wave of the sea driven*with*the*wind and tossed.

1063   3361 depro1565 art,nn444 pim3633 3754   fm2983   idpro5100   pre3844 art3588

7 For let not that man think that he shall receive any thing of the

nn2962

Lord.

an,aj1374   pr/an,nn435 pr/an,aj182 pre1722 an,aj3956 ppro848 art,nn3598

8 A double minded man *is* unstable in   all his ways.

(1161)   art3588   nn80   art,aj5011   pim2744 pre1722   ppro848 art,nn5311

9   Let the brother of low degree rejoice in that he is exalted:

1161 art3588 ajn4145 pre1722 ppro848   art,nn5014   3754   ad5613   an,nn438

10 But the rich, in that he is*made*low: because as the flower of the

an,nn5528   fm3928

grass he shall pass away.

1063 art3588 nn2246   aina393 pre4862   art,nn2742   2532   aina3583

11 For the sun is no sooner risen with a burning heat, but it withereth

art3588   nn5528 2532 art3588   nn438   ppro846 aina1601 2532 art3588 nn2143   art3588   nn4383   ppro846

the grass, and the flower thereof falleth, and the grace of the fashion of it

aom622   ad3779 2532   art3588   ajn4145   fp3133   pre1722 ppro848 art,nn4197

perisheth: so also shall the rich man fade away in his ways.

(Ps. 102:4,11; Is. 40:6,7)

Enduring Tests

pr/an,aj3107   an,nn435 repro3739   pin5278   an,nn3986   3754   aptm1096 pr/an,aj1384

12 Blessed *is* the man that endureth temptation: for when he is   tried,

fm2983   art3588   nn4735   art,nn2222 repro3739 art3588 nn2962   aom1861

he shall receive the crown of life, which the Lord hath promised to

art,pap25   ppro846

them*that*love him.

an,ajn3367 pim3004   ppmp3985   ppmp3985   pre575 art,nn2316 1063 art,nn2316

13 Let no man say when he is tempted, I am tempted of God: for God

pin2076/pr/an,aj551   an,ajn2556 1161   pin3985   epn848   an,ajn3762

cannot*be*tempted with evil, neither tempteth he any man:

1161   an,ajn1538   pinp3985   ppmp1828   pre5259 art,aj2398 an,nn1939

14 But every man is tempted, when he is drawn away of his own lust,

2532   ppmp1185

and enticed.

ad1534   art,nn1939   apta4815   pin5088   pin616 1161 art,nn266

15 Then when lust hath conceived, it bringeth forth sin: and sin, when it

aptp658   pin616   an,nn2288

is finished, bringeth forth death.

3361 pim4105 ppro3450 an,aj27   an,nn80

16 Do not err, my beloved brethren.

an,aj3956   an,aj18   an,nn1394 2532   an,aj3956 an,aj5046   an,nn1434 pin2076   ad509

17 Every good gift and every perfect gift is from above, and

pap2597   pre575 art3588   nn3962   art,nn5457 pre3844 repro3739 pin1762 3756   an,nn3883

cometh down from the Father of lights, with whom is no variableness,

2228   an,nn644   an,nn5157

neither shadow of turning.

aptp1014   aina616   ppro2248   an,nn3056 an,nn225   ppro2248

18 Of*his*own*will begat he us with the word of truth, that we

aies1511 idpro5100 pr/an,nn536   ppro848   art,nn2938

should be a kind of firstfruits of his creatures.

Be a Doer of the Word

5620   ppro3450 an,aj27   an,nn80   an,aj3956 an,nn444 pim2077 pr/an,aj5036 aies191

19 Wherefore, my beloved brethren, let every man be swift to hear,

pr/an,aj1021   aies2980 pr/an,aj1021 pre1519 an,nn3709

slow to speak, slow to wrath: *(Eccl. 7:9)*

1063   an,nn3709   an,nn435 pnm2716 3756   an,nn1343   an,nn2316

20 For the wrath of man worketh not the righteousness of God.

pre,repro1352 aptm659 an,aj3956 an,nn4507 2532   an,nn4050   an,nn2549

21 Wherefore lay apart all filthiness and superfluity of naughtiness, and

aipm1209 pre1722 an,nn4240 art3588 an,aj1721   nn3056   art,ppmp1410 ainf4982 ppro5216 art,nn5590

receive with meekness the engrafted word, which*is*able to save your souls.

1161   pim1096   pr/an,nn4163   an,nn3056 2532 3361 pr/an,nn202 an,ajn3440 ppmp3884

22 But be ye doers of the word, and not hearers only, deceiving

rxpro1438

your*own*selves.

3754 idpro1536 pin2076   pr/an,nn202   an,nn3056 2532 3756   pr/an,nn4163 depro3778   pfi1503

23 For if any be a hearer of the word, and not a doer, he is*like*unto

an,nn435   pap2657   ppro846 art,nn1078 art,nn4383 pre1722   an,nn2072

a man beholding his natural face in a glass:

1063   aina2657   rxpro1438   2532   pfi565   2532   ad2112

24 For he beholdeth himself, and goeth*his*way, and straightway

aom1950   pr/an,aj3697   ipf2258

forgetteth what*manner*of*man he was.

1161 art,apta3879 pre1519   an,aj5046 an,nn3551 (art3588) art,nn1657 2532 apta3887

25 But whoso looketh into the perfect law of liberty, and continueth

depro3778 aptm1096 3756   an,nn1953 pr/an,nn202 235   pr/an,nn4163   an,nn2041 depro3778

therein, he being not a forgetful hearer, but a doer of the work, this man

fm2071 pr/an,aj3107 pre1722 ppro848 art,nn4162

shall be blessed in his deed.

idpro1536   pre1722 ppro5213 pin1380 pinf1511 pr/an,nn2357   pap5468 3361 ppro848

26 If*any*man among you seem to be religious, and bridleth not his an,nn1100   235   pap538   ppro848   an,nn2588   depro5127   art,nn2356   pr/an,aj3152

tongue, but deceiveth his own heart, this man's religion *is* vain.

(Ps. 34:13; 39:1; 141:3)

an,an2513   an,nn2356   2532   an,aj283   pre3844   art,nn2316   2532   an,nn3962   pin2076   pr/depro3778

27 Pure religion and undefiled before God and the Father is this, To

pifm1980   an,aj3737   2532   an,nn5503   pre1722   ppro846   art,nn2347   pinf5083   rxpro1438

visit the fatherless and widows in their affliction, *and* to keep himself

pr/an,aj784   pre575   art3588   nn2889

unspotted from the world.

Respect for Others

2 ppro3450   an,nn80   pin2192   3361   art3588   nn4102   ppro2257   art,nn2962   an,nn2424   an,nn5547

My brethren, have not the faith of our Lord Jesus Christ, *the Lord* of

art,nn1391   pre1722   an,nn4382

glory, with respect*of*persons.   *(Job 34:19)*

1063   1437   asba1525   pre1519   ppro5216   art,nn4864   an,nn435   pl/an,aj5554   pre1722

2 For if there come unto your assembly a man with a gold ring, in

an,aj2986   an,nn2066   1161   asba1525   2532   an,ajn4434   pre1722 an,aj4508   an,nn2066

goodly apparel, and there come in also a poor man in   vile raiment;

2532   asba1914   pre1909   art,pap5409   art3588 aj2986   art,nn2066   2532   asba2036

3 And ye have respect   to him*that*weareth the gay clothing, and say

ppro846   pim2521   epn4771   ad5602   ad2573   2532   asba2036   art3588   ajn4434   pim2476   epn4771

unto him, Sit thou here in*a*good*place; and say to the poor, Stand thou

ad1563   2228   pim2521   ad5602   pre5259   ppro3450   art,nn5286

there, or sit here under my footstool:

ainp1252/3756/2532   pre1722   rxpro1438   2532   aom1096   pr/an,nn2923   an,aj4190

4 Are*ye*not*then*partial in yourselves, and are become judges of evil

an,nn1261

thoughts?

aima191   ppro3450   an,aj27   an,nn80   3756   art,nn2316   aom1586   art3588   ajn4434

☞ 5 Hearken, my beloved brethren, Hath not God chosen the poor of

depro5127   art,nn2889   pr/an,aj4145   pre1722   an,nn4102   2532   pr/an,nn2818   art3588   nn932   repro3739

this world rich in faith, and heirs of the kingdom which he hath

aom1861   art,pap25   ppro846

promised to them*that*love him?

1161   epn5210   aina818   art3588   ajn4434   3756   art,ajn4145   pin2616   ppro5216   2532

6 But ye have despised the poor. Do not rich men oppress you, and

pin1670   ppro5209   pre1519   an,nn2922

draw you before the judgment seats?

3756   epn846   pin987   art,aj2570   an,nn3686   art3588 (pre1909) ppro5209   aptp1941

7 Do not they blaspheme that worthy name by the which ye are called?

1487 (3305) pin5055   an,aj937   an,nn3551   pre2596   art3588   nn1124   ft25

8 If ye fulfill the royal law according to the Scripture, Thou shalt love

ppro4675   art,ad4139   ad5613   rxpro4572   pin4160   ad2573

thy neighbor as thyself, ye do well: *(Lev. 19:18)*

☞ **2:5** See note on Ephesians 1:4, 5.

1161   1487   pin4380   pinm2038   an,nn266   ppmp1651

9 But if ye have*respect*to*persons, ye commit sin, and are convinced

pre5259 art3588 nn3551 ad5613   an,nn3848

of the law as transgressors.

1063   repro3748   ft5038 art3588 an,aj3650 nn3551 1161   ft4417   pre1722 nu,ajn1520

10 For whosoever shall keep the whole law, and yet offend in   one *point,*

pfi1096 pr/an,aj1777   an,ajn3956

he is guilty of all.

1063   art,apta2036   3361   aosi3431   aina2036 2532   3361 aosi5407 1161

11 For he*that*said, Do not commit adultery, said also, Do not kill. Now

1487   ft3431/3756   1161   ft5407   pfi1096   pr/an,nn3848

if thou commit*no*adultery, yet if thou kill, thou art become a transgressor of

an,nn3551

the law.   *(Ex. 20:14; Deut. 5:18; Ex. 20:13; Deut. 5:17)*

ad3779 pim2980   2532 ad3779 pim4160 ad5613   art,pap3195   pip2919   pre1223   an,nn3551

☞ 12 So speak ye, and so do, as they*that*shall*be judged by the law

an,nn1657

of liberty.

1063   art,nn2920   pr/an,aj448   art,apta4160   3361

13 For he shall have judgment without mercy, that*hath*showed no

an,nn1656   2532   an,nn1656   pinm2620   an,nn2920

mercy; and mercy rejoiceth against judgment.

"Faith Without Works Is Dead"

inpro5101   art,nn3786   ppro3450   an,nn80   1437   idpro5100 psa3004   pinf2192 an,nn4102

☞ 14 What *doth it* profit, my brethren, though a man say he hath faith,

1161 psa2192 3361 an,nn2041 (3361) pinm1410 art,nn4102 ainf4982 ppro846

and have not works? can faith save him?

☞ **2:12, 13** The more correct literal translation of these two verses is "Thus speak and thus do, as if you are going to be judged by a law of freedom or liberality." James tells us here that the believer is going to be judged (2 Cor. 5:10). The Judge, of course, is Jesus Christ. However, He is not going to be absolutely rigid, but He is going to exercise liberality or generosity in many cases toward those who are judged. In verse thirteen, James explains how this judgment is going to be determined: "For judgment will be merciless to one who has shown no mercy." This explains the fifth Beatitude in Matthew 5:7, "Blessed are the merciful, for they shall receive mercy." The Judge's generosity toward the believer will be in proportion to the amount of mercy that the believer showed while on earth. If he showed no mercy, he will receive no mercy. The entrance into heaven is a result of the work which Christ alone did, yet one's enjoyment of heaven and its rewards will be reflected in what the believer did for Christ in his life of faith on earth. Then follows the last part of James 2:13 which literally translated says, "Mercy or mercifulness boasts against judgment." This means that the believer whose life has been full of mercifulness will face the Judge unafraid because the Judge in His liberality will take into account the mercy that the believer demonstrated on earth.

☞ **2:14–19** In Romans 3:20, Paul says, "By the works of the law no flesh will be justified." On the other hand, James 2:21–24 apparently states that man is not justified by faith only but also by works. The difficulty of the seeming contradiction is accentuated by the statement of Paul himself in Romans 2:13, "The doers of the law will be justified." How can these two statements be reconciled?

James 2:14 does not say, "What doth it profit . . . though a man have faith?" rather, "What use is it, my brethren, if a man says he has faith." A mere profession of faith does not mean the possession of faith or the natural accompaniments of faith. Faith that is not accompanied by its inevitable and expectant fruits of faith is no faith at all. It is a mockery, and James calls such a faith "dead."

(continued on next page)

15 ^{(1161) 1437} ^{an,nn80} ²²²⁸ ^{an,nn79} ^{psa5225} ^{pr/an,aj1131} ²⁵³² ^{psa5600/ppmp3007} ^{art,aj2184} ^{an,nn5160}
If a brother or sister be naked, and destitute of daily food,

16 ¹¹⁶¹ ^{idpro5100} ^{pre1537} ^{ppro5216} ^{asba2036} ^{ppro846} ^{pim5217} ^{pre1722} ^{an,nn1515}
And one of you say unto them, Depart in peace, be

^{pim2328} ²⁵³² ^{pim5526} ¹¹⁶¹ ^{asba1325} ^{ppro846} ³³⁶¹
ye warmed and filled; notwithstanding ye give them not

^{art,ajn2006} ^{art3588} ⁿⁿ⁴⁹⁸³ ^{inpro5101} ^{art,nn3786}
those*things*which*are*needful to the body; what doth it profit?

17 ²⁵³² ^{ad3779} ^{art,nn4102} ¹⁴³⁷ ^{psa2192} ³³⁶¹ ^{an,nn2041} ^{pin2076} ^{pr/an,aj3498} ^{pre1596/ rxpro1438}
Even so faith, if it hath not works, is dead, being alone.

18 ²³⁵ ^{idpro5100} ^{ft2046} ^{epn4771} ^{pin2192} ^{an,nn4102} ^{epn2504} ^{pin2192} ^{an,nn2041} ^{aima1166}
Yea, a man may say, Thou hast faith, and I have works: show

^{ppro3427} ^{ppro4675} ^{art,nn4102} ^{ad*5565} ^{ppro4675} ^{art,nn2041} ^{epn2504} ^{ft1166} ^{ppro4671} ^{ppro3450} ^{art,nn4102} ^{pre1537} ^{ppro3450}
me thy faith without thy works, and I will show thee my faith by my

^{art,nn2041}
works.

19 ^{epn4771} ^{pin4100} ³⁷⁵⁴ ^{pin2076} ^{pr/nu,ajn1520} ^{art,nn2316} ^{pin4160} ^{ad2573} ^{art3588} ⁿⁿ¹¹⁴⁰
Thou believest that there is one God; thou doest well: the devils

²⁵³² ^{pin4100} ²⁵³² ^{pin5425}
also believe, and tremble.

20 ¹¹⁶¹ ^{pin2309} ^{ainf1097} ⁵⁵⁹⁹ ^{an,aj2756} ^{an,nn444} ³⁷⁵⁴ ^{art,nn4102} ^{ad*5565} ^{art,nn2041} ^{pin2076}
But wilt thou know, O vain man, that faith without works is

^{pr/ an,aj3498}
dead?

21 ³⁷⁵⁶ ¹¹ ^{ppro2257} ^{art,nn3962} ^{ainp1344} ^{pre1537} ^{an,nn2041} ^{apta399}
Was not Abraham our father justified by works, when he had offered

²⁴⁶⁴ ^{ppro848} ^{art,nn5207} ^{pre1909} ^{art3588} ⁿⁿ²³⁷⁹
Isaac his son upon the altar? *(Gen. 22:9,12)*

22 ^{pin991} ³⁷⁵⁴ ^{art,nn4102} ^{ipf4903} ^{ppro846} ^{art,nn2041} ²⁵³² ^{pre1537} ^{art,nn2041}
Seest thou how faith wrought with his works, and by works

^{art,nn4102} ^{ainp5048}
was faith made perfect?

23 ²⁵³² ^{art3588} ⁿⁿ¹¹²⁴ ^{ainp4137} ^{art,pap3004} ⁽¹¹⁶¹⁾ ¹¹ ^{aina4100}
And the Scripture was fulfilled which saith, Abraham believed

---

(continued from previous page)

Moreover, Paul speaks of a true, living faith which purifies the heart and works by love (Gal. 5:6). James in this instance speaks of a profession or presumption of faith, barren and destitute of good fruit. Such a faith is dead (v. 17); it is a "faith" like the devils may have (v. 19). It consists only of an intellectual belief of God's being or existence, not consenting to His offer of salvation through repentance and turning from sin nor a reliance on His promises. When Paul speaks of faith, he speaks of it as including the works of faith. When James speaks of faith in this instance, he speaks of false faith that does not result in the works of faith. When any Apostle speaks of works resulting from faith as saving any one, inherent in those works is included the faith that is the only way whereby those works can be produced. When they speak of fruit, the whole process of the development of the fruit is included. When works, however, are spoken about as the works not resulting from faith, they are meant to be false works or fruits, fruits of a nonexistent faith. One cannot have the fruits of faith that are true and real without true and real faith, no more than oranges can come from pine trees.

This sort of reasoning would shed light upon a statement concerning baptism which results from the exercise of living faith in Jesus Christ (see 1 Pet. 3:21). It is not actually the baptism that saves, because the act of physical baptism without the antecedent of living, spiritual faith in Christ is nothing but an empty and ineffective act (see note on Mark 16:16).

art,nn2316 2532   ainp3049   ppro846 pre1519   an,nn1343   2532   ainp2564

God, and it was imputed unto him for righteousness: and he was called the

an,ajn5384   an,nn2316

Friend of God.   *(Gen. 15:6; 2 Chr. 20:7; Is. 41:8)*

pin3708 5106 3754   pre1537 an,nn2041   an,nn444   pinp1344   2532 3756 pre1537 an,nn4102

24 Ye see then how that by works a man is justified, and not by faith

an,ajn3440

only.

ad3668   2532   3756   4460   art3588   nn4204   ainp1344 pre1537 an,nn2041

25 Likewise also was not Rahab the harlot justified by works, when she

aptm5264   art3588   nn32   2532   apta1544   an,aj2087   an,nn3598

had received the messengers, and had sent*them*out another way?

(Josh. 2:4,15; 6:7)

1063 ad5618 art3588 nn4983   ad*5565   an,nn4151 pin2076 pr/an,aj3498 ad3779 art,nn4102   ad*5565   art,nn2041

26 For as the body without the spirit is dead, so faith without works

pin2076 pr/an,aj3498 2532

is dead also.

Control the Tongue

ppro3450   an,nn80   pim1096 3361 an,aj4183   pr/an,nn1320   pfp1492   3754   fm2983

3 My brethren, be not many masters, knowing that we shall receive the

cd/an,aj3187   an,nn2917

greater condemnation.

1063   an,aj4183   pin4417   an,aj537   idpro1536   pin4417   3756 pre1722 an,nn3056

2 For in many things we offend all. If*any*man offend not in word,

depro3778   pr/an,aj5046 an,nn435   pr/an,aj1415 2532   ainf5468 art3588 an,aj3650   nn4983

the same *is* a perfect man, *and* able also to bridle the whole body.

2400   pin906 art,nn5469 pre1519 art3588   nn2462   art,nn4750   ppro846   aipr3982 ppro2254

3 Behold, we put bits in the horses' mouths, that they may obey us;

2532   pin3329   ppro846 an,aj3650 art,nn4983

and we turn about their whole body.

2400   2532 art3588   nn4143   (pap5607) pr/an,aj5082 2532   ppmp1643

4 Behold also the ships, which though *they be* so great, and *are* driven

pre5259 an,aj4642   an,nn417   pinp3329   pre5259   cd/an,aj1646   an,nn4079

of fierce winds, yet are they turned about with a very small helm,

ad3699/302   art3588 nn3730/art,pap2116 psmp1014

whithersoever the governor listeth.

2532   ad3779 art3588   nn1100   pin2076   an,aj3398 pr/an,nn3196   2532   pin3166

5 Even so the tongue is a little member, and boasteth*great*things.

2400   an,aj2245   an,nn5208   an,aj3641 an,nn4442 pin381

Behold, how great a matter a little fire kindleth!

2532 art3588   nn1100   pr/an,nn4442   pr/art,nn2889   art,nn93   ad3779 pinm2525 art3588   nn1100

6 And the tongue *is* a fire, a world of iniquity; so is the tongue

pre1722 ppro2257   art,nn3196   art,pap4696 art3588 an,aj3650 nn4983 2532   pap5394

among our members, that it defileth the whole body, and setteth*on*fire

art3588   nn5164   art,nn1078 2532   pap5394   pre5259 art,nn1067

the course of nature; and it is set* on*fire of hell.

7 For every kind of beasts, and of birds, and of serpents, and of things*in*the*sea, is tamed, and hath been tamed of mankind: 8 But the tongue can no man tame; *it is* an unruly evil, full of deadly poison. *(Ps. 140:3)*

9 Therewith bless we God, even the Father; and therewith curse we men, which*are*made after the similitude of God. *(Gen. 1:26,27)*

10 Out of the same mouth proceedeth blessing and cursing. My brethren, these things ought not so to be. 11 Doth a fountain send forth at the same place sweet *water* and bitter? 12 Can the fig tree, my brethren, bear olive berries? either a vine, figs? so *can* no fountain both yield salt water and fresh.

True Wisdom Comes from God

13 Who *is* a wise man and endued*with*knowledge among you? let him show out of a good conversation his works with meekness of wisdom. 14 But if ye have bitter envying and strife in your hearts, glory not, and lie not against the truth. 15 This wisdom descendeth not from above, but *is* earthly, sensual, devilish. 16 For where envying and strife *is*, there *is* confusion and every evil work. 17 But the wisdom that is from above is first pure, then peaceable, gentle, *and* easy*to*be*entreated, full of mercy and good fruits, without partiality, and without hypocrisy.

```
      1161        an,nn2590         art,nn1343           pinp4687  pre1722 an,nn1515      art3588            pap4160
```
18 And the fruit of righteousness is sown in peace of them that make
```
an,nn1515
```
peace.   *(Is. 32:7)*

Warnings Against Loving the World

```
              ad4159                 an,nn4171  2532   an,nn3163   pre1722  ppro5213                3756    ad1782
```
4 From whence *come* wars and fightings among you? *come they* not hence,
```
     pre1537·ppro5216 art,nn2237  art,ppmp4754  pre1722 ppro5216   art,nn3196
```
even of your lusts that war in your members?
```
          pin1937  2532   pin2192  3756       pin5407 2532          pin2206           2532 pinm1410/3756   ainf2013
```
2 Ye lust, and have not: ye kill, and desire*to*have, and cannot obtain: ye
```
pinm3164 2532  pin4170 1161    pin2192  3756              ppro5209 aid154  3361
```
fight and war, yet ye have not, because ye ask not.
```
          pin154  2532   pin2983  3756   1360       pinm154  ad2560   2443            asba1159
```
3 Ye ask, and receive not, because ye ask amiss, that ye may consume *it*
```
pre1722 ppro5216 art,nn2237
```
upon your lusts.
```
            an,nn3432     2532      an,nn3428    pin1492   3756  3754 art3588      nn5373        art3588
```
4 Ye adulterers and adulteresses, know ye not that the friendship of the
```
nn2889  pin2076 pr/an,nn2189      art,nn2316   repro3739/302     3767    asbp1014 pinf1511  pr/an,ajn5384   art3588
```
world is enmity with God? whosoever therefore will be a friend of the
```
nn2889   pinm2525    pr/an,ajn2190  art,nn2316
```
world is the enemy of God.
```
        (2228)     pin1380  3754 art3588     nn1124    pin3004    ad2761    art3588   nn4151   repro3739   aina2730
```
☞ 5 Do ye think that the Scripture saith in vain, The spirit that dwelleth
```
pre1722 ppro2554   pin1971  pre4314 an,nn5355
```
in us lusteth to envy?   *(Ex. 20:5)*
```
        1161      pin1325  cd/an,aj3187  an,nn5485    pre,repro1352      pin3004  art,nn2316   pinm498
```
6 But he giveth more grace. Wherefore he saith, God resisteth the
```
an,ajn5244  1161  pin1325 an,nn5485        an,ajn5011
```
proud, but giveth grace unto the humble.   *(Prov. 3:34 [Sept.])*
```
     aipp5293             3767      art,nn2316  aima436   art3588  ajn1228  2532          fm5343
```
7 Submit yourselves therefore to God. Resist the devil, and he will flee
```
pre575  ppro5216
```
from you.
```
          aima1448       art,nn2316 2532         ft1448      ppro5213  aima2511       art,nn5495
```
8 Draw nigh to God, and he will draw nigh to you. Cleanse *your* hands, *ye*
```
an,nn268     2532  aima48        an,nn2588      an,ajn1374
```
sinners; and purify *your* hearts, *ye* double minded.   *(Zech. 1:3; Is. 1:16)*

☞ **4:5** The best solution to this difficult verse is to interpret the word "spirit" not as referring to the Holy Spirit, but to the fallen spirit of man (that which is responsible for man's propensity to sin; cf. Rom 5:12). The fallen spirit in man "lusteth" (*epipothei* [1971]) toward envy. This envy manifests itself in selfishness and malice.

aima5003   2532   aina3996   2532   aima2799   ppro5216   art,nn1071   aipp3344   pre1519

9 Be afflicted, and mourn, and weep: let your laughter be turned to

an,nn3997   2532   art,nn5479 pre1519   an,nn2726

mourning, and *your* joy   to heaviness.

aipp5013   ad*1799   art3588   nn2962   2532   ft5312/ppro5209

10 Humble yourselves in*the*sight of the Lord, and he shall lift*you*up.

(Job 5:11)

Cautions Concerning Criticism

pim2635/3361   rcpro240   an,nn80   art,pap2635

11 Speak*not*evil one*of*another, brethren. He*that*speaketh*evil of *his*

an,nn80   2532   pap2919   ppro848   art,nn80   pin2635   an,nn3551   2532   pin2919

brother, and judgeth his brother, speaketh evil of the law, and judgeth the

an,nn3551   1161   1487   pin2919   an,nn3551   pin1488   3756   pr/an,nn4163   an,nn3551   235

law: but if thou judge the law, thou art not a doer of the law, but a

pr/an,nn2923

judge.

pin2076   pr/nu,ajn1520   art,nn3550   art,ppmp1410   ainf4982   2532   ainf622   pr/inpro5101

12 There is   one   lawgiver, who*is*able to save and to destroy: who

pin1488   epn4771   repro3739   pin2919   art,ajn2087

art thou that judgest another?

"If the Lord Will"

pim33   ad3568   art,pap3004   ad4594   2532   ad839   fm4198   pre1519   depro3592

13 Go to now, ye*that*say, Today or tomorrow we will   go   into   such a

art,nn4172   2532   ft4160   ad1563   nu1520 an,nn1763   2532   fm1710   2532   ft2770

city, and continue there   a   year, and buy*and*sell, and get gain:

repro3748   pinm1987   3756   art3588   art3588   ad839   1063   an,aj4169   ppro5216

14 Whereas ye know not what *shall be* on the morrow. For what *is* your

art,nn2222   pin2076   1063   pr/an,nn822   art,ppmp5316   pre4314   an,ajn3641   1161   ad1899

life? It   is   even a vapor, that appeareth for a little time, and then

ppmp853

vanisheth away.   *(Prov. 27:1)*

pre473   ppro5209   infg3004   1437 art3588   nn2962   asba2309   (2532)   ft2198   2532   ft4160

15 For that   ye   *ought* to say, If the Lord will, we shall live, and do

depro5124 2228 depro1565

this, or that.

1611   ad3568   pinm2744   pre1722 ppro5216   art,nn212   an,aj3956 an,aj5108   an,nn2746   pin2076 pr/an,aj4190

16 But now ye rejoice in   your boastings: all   such rejoicing is   evil.

3767   art,pfp1492   pinf4160 an,ajn2570   2532   pap4160   3361   epn846

☞ 17 Therefore to him*that*knoweth to   do   good, and doeth *it* not, to him it

pin2076 an,nn266

is sin.

☞ **4:17** See note on 1 John 3:6–9.

Warnings to the Rich

5 Go to now, *ye* rich men, weep and howl for your miseries
<small>pin33   ad3568   art,ajn4145   aima2799   pap3649   pre1909   pro5216   art,nn5004</small>

<small>art,ppmp1904</small>
that*shall*come*upon *you*.

<small>ppro5216 art,nn4149   pfi4595   2532 ppro5216   art,nn2440   pfi1096   pr/an,aj4598</small>
2 Your riches are corrupted, and your garments are motheaten.

<small>ppro5216 art,nn5557 2532 art,nn696   pfip2728   2532   art3588   nn2447   ppro846   fm2071</small>
3 Your gold and silver is cankered; and the rust of them shall be
<small>(pre1519)   an,nn3142   ppro5213 2532   ft5315 ppro5216 art,nn4561   ad5613   an,nn4442</small>
a witness against you, and shall eat your flesh as*it*were fire. Ye
<small>aina2343   pre1722   an,aj2078 an,nn2250</small>
have heaped*treasure*together for the last days.   *(Ps. 21:9)*

<small>2400   art3588   nn3408   art3588   nn2040   art,apta270   ppro5216 art,nn5561</small>
4 Behold, the hire of the laborers who*have*reaped*down your fields,
<small>pre575   ppro5216   art,aptp650   pin2896   2532   art3588   nn994</small>
which is of you kept*back*by*fraud, crieth: and the cries of
<small>art,apta2325   pfi1525   pre1519 art3588 nn3775   an,nn2962   4519</small>
them*which*have*reaped are entered into the ears of the Lord of Sabaoth.

(Lev. 19:13; Deut. 24:14,15; Mal. 3:5; Gen. 4:10; Ps. 18:6; Is. 5:9)

<small>aina5171   pre1909 art3588   nn1093   2532   aina4684</small>
5 Ye have lived*in*pleasure on the earth, and been wanton; ye have
<small>aina5142   ppro5216 art,nn2588   pre1722   an,nn2250   an,nn4967</small>
nourished your hearts, as in a day of slaughter.   *(Jer. 12:3; 25:34)*
<small>aina2613   aina5407 art3588 ajn1342   3756   pinm498 ppro5213</small>
6 Ye have condemned *and* killed the just; *and* he doth not resist you.

Patience Exhorted

<small>aima3114   3767   an,nn80   ad2193 art3588   nn3952   art3588   nn2962   2400</small>
☞ 7 Be patient therefore, brethren, unto the coming of the Lord. Behold,
<small>art3588   nn1092   pinm1551   art3588   an,aj5093   nn2590   art3588   nn1093   2532</small>
the husbandman waiteth for the precious fruit of the earth, and
<small>pap3114   pre1909 ppro846 ad2193/302   asba2983   an,aj4406 2532 an,aj3797 an,nn5205</small>
hath*long*patience for it, until he receive the early and latter rain.

(Deut. 11:14; Jer. 2:23)

<small>aima3114/epn5210/2532   aima4741   ppro5216 art,nn2588   3754 art3588   nn3952   art3588   nn2962</small>
8 Be*ye*also*patient; establish your hearts: for the coming of the Lord
<small>pfi1448</small>
draweth nigh.

☞ **5:7, 8** The phrase "the early and latter rain" in some important texts exclude the noun "rain," while most Greek manuscripts include it. Since numerous references to rain in the OT are accompanied by the expression "early" or "latter" (Deut. 11:14; Job 29:23; Prov. 16:15; Jer. 3:3; Hos. 6:3; Joel 2:23), it stands to reason that the analogy James is making in this passage relates to the severe weather patterns that existed in early Palestine.

^{pim4727} ³³⁶¹ ^{rcpro240/pre2596} ^{an,nn80} ³³⁶³ ^{asbp2632}
9 Grudge not one*against*another, brethren, lest ye be condemned:
²⁴⁰⁰ ^{art3588} ⁿⁿ²⁹²³ ^{pfi2476} ^{pre4253} ^{art3588} ⁿⁿ²³⁷⁴
behold, the judge standeth before the door.

^{aima2983} ^{ppro3450} ^{an,nn80} ^{art3588} ⁿⁿ⁴³⁹⁶ ^{repro3739} ^{aina2980} ^{art3588} ⁿⁿ³⁶⁸⁶
10 Take, my brethren, the prophets, who have spoken in the name of
^{an,nn2962} ^{an,nn5262} ^{art,nn2552} ²⁵³² ^{art,nn3115}
the Lord, for an example of suffering affliction, and of patience.

²⁴⁰⁰ ^{pin3106} ^{art,pap5278} ^{aina191} ^{art3588}
11 Behold, we count*them*happy which endure. Ye have heard of the
ⁿⁿ⁵²⁸¹ ²⁴⁹² ²⁵³² ^{aina1492} ^{art3588} ⁿⁿ⁵⁰⁵⁶ ^{an,nn2962} ³⁷⁵⁴ ^{art3588} ⁿⁿ²⁹⁶² ^{pin2076}
patience of Job, and have seen the end of the Lord; that the Lord is
^{pr/an,aj4184} ²⁵³² ^{pr/an,aj3629}
very pitiful, and of*tender*mercy.　　　　　　*(Ex. 34:6; Ps. 103:8; 111:4)*

¹¹⁶¹ ^{pre4253} ^{an,ajn3956} ^{ppro3450} ^{an,nn80} ^{pim3660} ³³⁶¹ ³³⁸³ ^{art,nn3772}
12 But above all things, my brethren, swear not, neither by heaven,
³³⁸³ ^{art3588} ⁿⁿ¹⁰⁹³ ³³⁸³ ^{an,aj243} ^{idpro5100} ^{an,nn3727} ¹¹⁶¹ ^{ppro5216} ^(art3588) ³⁴⁸³ ^{pim2277}
neither by the earth, neither by any other oath: but let your　　yea be
³⁴⁸³ ²⁵³² ^(art3588) ³⁷⁵⁶ ³⁷⁵⁶ ³³⁶³ ^{asba4098} ^{pre1519} ^{an,nn5272}
yea; and *your* nay, nay; lest ye fall into condemnation.

^{pin2553/idpro5100/pre1722/ppro5213} ^{pim4336} ^{pin2114/idpro5100}
13 Is*any*among*you*afflicted? let him pray. Is*any*merry? let him
^{pim5567}
sing psalms.

^{pin770/idpro5100} ^{pre1722} ^{ppro5213} ^{aipm4341} ^{art3588} ^{ajn4245} ^{art3588} ⁿⁿ¹⁵⁷⁷ ²⁵³²
☞ 14 Is*any*sick among you? let him call for the elders of the church; and let
^{aipm4336} ^{pre1909} ^{ppro846} ^{apta218} ^{ppro846} ^{an,nn1637} ^{pre1722} ^{art3588} ⁿⁿ³⁶⁸⁶ ^{art3588} ⁿⁿ²⁹⁶²
them pray over him, anointing him with　oil　in　the name of the Lord:

☞ **5:14, 15** The key question that arises from this passage is to determine whether Christianity prohibits the use of medicine. In the original Greek text, verse fourteen began with a statement rather than a question, and should be rendered "Someone among you is sick." James begins the discussion with the fact that there is sickness in the world and the Christian is not exempt. In the examination of this verse, one can conclude that the initiative to call the elders of the church to the sick believer's bedside must come from the believer himself. At the time of the apostolic church, its elders performed many duties. One such task was treating sick people in whatever manner possible. This verse reads: ". . . let them pray over him, anointing him with oil in the name of the Lord . . . ." There are qualifying statements to be understood in regard to the application of medicine as opposed to offering of prayer for a sick believer. Before prayer is to be offered, the elders were to provide any medical assistance necessary. The specific order these two things were to be performed is clarified in the Greek text. The word translated "anointing him" is the aorist participle, *aleí psantes* (from *aleíphō* [218]). This term describes an act which preceded the prayer and should be translated "having anointed." Therefore, this instance denotes the application of medicine first, then the elders are commanded to pray for the sick person.

In addition to this, prayer is to be made "in the name of the Lord," not necessarily the anointing act. This is explained by the aorist imperative verb, *proseuxásthōsan* (from *proseúchomai* [4336]) translated "let them pray." Also the verb *proskalesásthō* (from *proskaléomai* [4341]), meaning "let him call," denotes the aorist tense. In both cases reference is made to one action at one point in the past, not a repetitive connotation. The participle, *aleípsantes*, does not refer back to the main verb or the main action in the clause. The application of medicine can be rendered by both believers and unbelievers, but prayer as an exercise of faith is the key to seeking God's will in regard to healing. Furthermore, the phrase "in the name of the Lord" does not refer to a matter of habit by which one must close his prayers. Rather, it indicates a willingness to place prayer into the sovereign will and purpose of God. In John 14:13, the

(continued on next page)

2532   art3588   nn2171   art,nn4102   ft4982   art3588   pap2577   2532   art3588   nn2962

15 And the prayer of faith shall save the sick, and the Lord shall

ft1453/ppro846   2579   psa5600   pfp4160   an,nn266   fp863   ppro846

raise*him*up; and if he have committed sins, they shall be forgiven him.

pim1843   art,nn3900   rcpro240   2532   pim2172   rcpro240/pre5228   3704

16 Confess *your* faults one*to*another, and pray one*for*another, that ye

asbp2390   ppmp1754   an,nn1162   an,ajn1342   pin2480   an,ajn4183

may be healed. The effectual fervent prayer of a righteous man availeth much.

an,nn2243   ipf2258   pr/an,nn444   an,ajn3663   ppro2254   2532

17 Elijah was a man subject*to*like*passions as we are, and he

aom4336/an,nn4335   3361   infg1026   2532   aina1026   3756   pre1909   art3588   nn1093

prayed earnestly that it might not rain: and it rained not on the earth by the

nu5140   an,nn1763   2532   nu1803   an,nn3376

space of three years and six months.   *(1 Kgs. 17:1)*

2532   aom4336   ad3825   2532   art3588   nn3772   aina1325   an,nn5205   2532   art3588   nn1093

18 And he prayed again, and the heaven gave rain, and the earth

aina985   ppro848 art,nn2590

brought forth her fruit.   *(1 Kgs. 18:42-45)*

an,nn80   1437   idpro5100   pre1722   ppro5213   asbp4105   pre575   art3588   nn225   2532   idpro5100   asba1994

19 Brethren, if any of you do err from the truth, and one convert

ppro846

him;

pim1097   3754   art,apta1994   an,ajn268   pre1537   an,nn4106

20 Let him know, that he*which*converteth the sinner from the error of

ppro846 an,nn3598   ft4982   an,nn5590 pre1537 an,nn2288   2532   ft2572   an,nn4128   an,nn266

his way shall save a soul from death, and shall hide a multitude of sins.

(Prov. 10:12)

(continued from previous page)
Lord said, "And whatsoever ye shall ask in my name, that will I do, that the Father may be glorified in the Son." It is true that believers do not always receive the things for which they ask, even perfect health. However, there is coming a time when the bodies of Christians are going to be redeemed (Rom. 8:23), and they will be given glorified, resurrected ones (1 Cor. 15:51–54). Also, the "name of the Lord" indicates His character and purpose. For instance, if a parent were to say to a child, "Respect my name," he is requiring obedience to do what he commands. In the same way, the Lord gives His children the freedom to pray for all that they would wish the Heavenly Father to grant to them. However, He knows and gives the best according to His will. God's best may be sickness and privation, instead of health and wealth, but it is designed to bring the believer into a closer walk with Him (Rom. 8:28).

    Ultimately, it is God that does the healing for both believers and unbelievers, with or without the use of medicine. Often times, God heals even when prayer is not offered. In the case of the believer there must be the realization that the prayer of faith to God has power. While He is a sovereign God, He is also a prayer-hearing and prayer-answering God. In verse fifteen, James explains the believer's assurance: "And the prayer of faith save the sick, and the Lord shall raise him up."

The First Epistle of

PETER

The Apostle Peter was the most prominent disciple during the ministry of Jesus and had a tremendous impact on the early church. The first twelve chapters of Acts are devoted to his ministry and to the development of the church in the East where he was the dominant figure. Paul mentioned him in 1 Corinthians (1 Cor. 1:12; 3:22; 9:5; 15:5) and Galatians (Gal. 1:18; 2:7–9, 11, 14), and he wrote two New Testament books. This first letter is addressed to the five Roman provinces in Asia Minor (modern-day Turkey) north of the Taurus Mountains (1 Pet. 1:1).

This letter was written to encourage the believers to endure the intense persecution that was prevalent in the area and to prepare the readers for the difficult times ahead them. The first empire-wide persecution of Christians did not come until A.D. 249 under the brutal emperor Decius, but local persecutions many times were quite severe. One in particular took place early in the second century in Bithynia, one of the provinces to which Peter wrote (1 Pet. 1:1). A letter was sent from Pliny, governor of Bithynia, to the Roman emperor Trajan, in A.D. 112. He explained that he had been executing people who confessed that they were Christians. Trajan's reply expressed his approval of Pliny's policy but instructed him to set free those Christians who would renounce their faith and worship the Roman gods. Since 1 Peter was most likely written in the A.D. 60's, persecution of the severest kind was yet to come. Peter used Jesus' own suffering as the cornerstone of his exhortation. Likewise, Peter admonished believers to suffer as "Christians," not as lawbreakers.

1

an,nn4074   an,nn652   an,nn2424 an,nn5547   an,ajn3927   an,nn1290
Peter, an apostle of Jesus Christ, to the strangers scattered throughout
an,nn4195   an,nn1053   an,nn2587   an,nn773   2532   an,nn978
Pontus, Galatia, Cappadocia, Asia, and Bithynia,
an,aj1588   pre2596   an,nn4268   an,nn2316   an,nn3962   pre1722
☞ 2 Elect according to the foreknowledge of God the Father, through
an,nn38   an,nn4151   pre1519   an,nn5218   2532   an,nn4473   an,nn129   an,nn2424
sanctification of the Spirit, unto obedience and sprinkling of the blood of Jesus
an,nn5547   an,nn5485   ppro5213 2532   an,nn1515   opt4129
Christ: Grace unto you, and peace, be multiplied.

Heaven Is Worth Suffering For

pr/an,aj2128   art3588 nn2316   2532   an,nn3962   ppro2257 art,nn2962 an,nn2424 an,nn5547
3 Blessed *be* the God and Father of our Lord Jesus Christ, which

---

☞ 1:2 See note on Ephesians 1:4, 5.

pre2596   ppro848   art,aj4183   an,nn1656   art,apta313/ppro2248   pre1519   pap2198   an,nn1680

according to his abundant mercy hath begotten*us*again unto a lively hope

pre1223   an,nn386   an,nn2424 an,nn5547 pre1537   an,ajn3498

by the resurrection of Jesus Christ from the dead,

pre1519   an,nn2817   an,aj862   2532   an,aj283   2532

4 To   an   inheritance   incorruptible,   and   undefiled,   and

an,aj263   pfpp5083   pre1722 an,nn3772 pre1519 ppro2248

that*fadeth*not*away, reserved in heaven for you,

art,ppmp5432   pre1722   an,nn1411   an,nn2316   pre1223   an,nn4102 pre1519 an,nn4991   an,aj2092

☞ 5 Who*are*kept by the power of God through faith unto salvation ready

aifp601   pre1722   an,aj2078 an,nn2540

to be revealed in the last time.

pre1722/repro3739   pinm21   ad737   an,ajn3641   1487   pap1163/pin2076

6 Wherein ye greatly rejoice, though now for a season, if need be, ye

aptp3076   pre1722   an,aj4164   an,nn3986

are*in*heaviness through manifold temptations:

2443   art3588   nn1383   ppro5216 art,nn4102   an,ajn4183   pr/cd/an,aj5093   an,nn5553

☞ 7 That the trial of your faith, being much more precious than of gold

art,ppmp622   1161   ppmp1381 pre1223 an,nn4442   asbp2147 pre1519 an,nn1868 2532

that perisheth, though it be tried with fire, might be found unto praise and

an,nn5092 2532 an,nn1391 pre1722   an,nn602   an,nn2424 an,nn5547

honor and glory at the appearing of Jesus Christ:

(Job 23:10; Ps. 66:10; Prov. 17:3; Is. 48:10; Zech. 13:9; Mal. 3:3)

repro3739   3756   apta1492   pin25 pre1519 repro3739   ad737   pap3708

8 Whom having not seen, ye love; in whom, though now ye see *him*

3361   1161   pap4100   pinm21   an,nn5479   an,aj412   2532   pfpp1392

not, yet believing, ye rejoice with joy unspeakable and full*of*glory:

ppmp2865   art3588 nn5056   ppro5216 art,nn4102   an,nn4991   an,nn5590

9 Receiving the end of your faith, *even* the salvation of *your* souls.

pre4012 repro3739   an,nn4991   an,nn4396   aina1567   2532   aina1830

10 Of which salvation the prophets have inquired and searched diligently,

art,apta4395   pre4012 art3588   nn5485   pre1519 ppro5209

who prophesied of the grace *that should come* unto you:

pap2045   (pre1519) inpro5101   2228   an,aj4169   an,nn2540 art3588   nn4151   an,nn5547

11 Searching   what, or what manner of time the Spirit of Christ

pre1722 ppro846   ipf1213   ppmp4303   art3588   nn3804   pre1519

which was in them did signify, when it testified beforehand the sufferings of

an,nn5547 2532 art3588 nn1391   pre3326/depro5023

Christ, and the glory that*should* follow.   *(Ps. 22:1-31; Is. 53:1-12)*

repro3739   ainp601   3754   3756   rxpro1438   1161   ppro2254

12 Unto whom it was revealed, that not unto themselves, but unto us

---

☞ **1:5** The phrase "who are kept by the power of God" refers to believers (1 Pet. 1:3). These also have become heirs of a resurrection body (1 Pet. 1:4), and their inheritance is reserved in heaven. The sense in which the perfect participle, *tetērēménēn* (meaning "reserved," and derived from *teréō* [5083]), is used denotes that the act was made possible by Christ sometime in the past and is now being kept by Him until the proper time of delivery. Also, the purpose of the protection indicated in verse five is related to the believer's future liberation noted in the phrase, "kept by the power of God . . . unto salvation" (Rom. 8:23; 13:11).

☞ **1:7, 13** See note on 1 Thessalonians 2:19.

they did minister the things, which are now reported unto you by them*that* have*preached*the*gospel unto you with the Holy Ghost sent down from heaven; which things the angels desire to look into.

Exhortation to Holiness

☞ 13 Wherefore gird up the loins of your mind, be sober, and hope to*the*end for the grace that is to be brought unto you at the revelation of Jesus Christ;

14 As obedient children, not fashioning yourselves according to the former lusts in your ignorance:

15 But as he*which*hath*called you is holy, so be ye holy in all manner of conversation;

16 Because it is written, Be ye holy; for I am holy.

(Lev. 11:44,45; 19:2; 20:7)

17 And if ye call on the Father, who*without*respect*of*persons*judgeth according to every man's work, pass the time of your sojourning *here* in fear: (Ps. 89:26; Is. 64:8; Jer. 3:19; Ps. 28:4; 62:12; Prov. 24:12; Is. 59:18;

Jer. 17:10)

18 Forasmuch as ye know that ye were not redeemed with corruptible things, *as* silver and gold, from your vain conversation *received* by tradition*from*your*fathers;

19 But with the precious blood of Christ, as of a lamb without blemish and without spot:

(Ex. 12:5)

☞ 20 Who verily was foreordained before the foundation of the world, but was manifest in these last times for you,

---

☞ **1:20** See note on Ephesians 1:4, 5.

pre1223 ppro846   art,pap4100   pre1519 an,nn2316   art,apta1453/ppro846   pre1537   an,ajn3498

21 Who by him do believe in God, that*raised*him*up from the dead,

2532 apta1325 ppro846 an,nn1391   5620 ppro5216 art,nn4102 2532 an,nn1680   pinf1511 pre1519 an,nn2316

and gave him glory; that your faith and hope might be in God.

pfp48   ppro5216 art,nn5590 pre1722 art,nn5218 art3588   nn225   pre1223

22 Seeing ye have purified your souls in obeying the truth through the

an,nn4151 pre1519   an,aj505   an,nn5360   aima25   rcpro240   pre1537

Spirit unto unfeigned love*of*the*brethren, *see that ye* love one another with a

an,aj2513 an,nn2588   ad1619

pure heart fervently:

pfpp313   3756 pre1537   an,aj5349   an,nn4701   235   an,aj862   pre1223

23 Being*born*again, not of corruptible seed, but of incorruptible, by

an,nn3056   an,nn2316   pap2198 2532 pap3306   pre1519/art,nn165

the word of God, which liveth and abideth forever.

1360   an,aj3956   an,nn4561   ad5613   pr/an,nn5528   2532   an,aj3956   an,nn1391   an,nn444   ad5613

24 For all flesh *is* as grass, and all the glory of man as

pr/an,nn438   an,nn5528   art3588   nn5528   ainp3583   2532   art3588   nn438   ppro846

the flower of grass. The grass withereth, and the flower thereof

aina1601

falleth away:

1611   art3588   nn4487   an,nn2962   pin3306   pre1519/art,nn165 1161 pr/depro5124 pin2076 art3588   nn4487

25 But the word of the Lord endureth forever. And this is the word

art,aptp2097   pre1519 ppro5209

which*by*the*gospel*is*preached unto you.   *(Is. 40:6-8)*

The People of God

3767   aptm659   an,aj3956 an,nn2549   2532 an,aj3956 an,nn1388 2532   an,nn5272   2532

2 Wherefore laying aside all malice, and all guile, and hypocrisies, and

an,nn5355 2532 an,aj3956   an,nn2636

envies, and all evil speakings,

ad5613   an,aj738   an,nn1025 aima1971 art3588 an,aj97   nn1051   an,aj3050   2443

2 As newborn babes, desire the sincere milk of the word, that ye may

asbp837   pre1722/ppro846

grow thereby:

1512   aom1089 3754 art3588 nn2962   pr/an,aj5543

3 If*so*be ye have tasted that the Lord *is* gracious.   *(Ps. 34:8)*

pre4314 repro3739 ppmp4334   pap2198 an,nn3037   pfpp593   3303 pre5259 an,nn444

4 To whom coming, *as unto* a living stone, disallowed indeed of men,

1161   an,aj1588   pre3844 an,nn2316   an,aj1784

but chosen of God, *and* precious,   *(Ps. 118:22; Is. 28:16)*

epn846   2532   ad5613 pap2198   an,nn3037   pinm3618   an,aj4152   an,nn3624   an,aj40

5 Ye also, as lively stones, are built up a spiritual house, an holy

an,nn2406   aifm399   an,aj4152   an,nn2378   an,aj2144   art,nn2316 pre1223 an,nn2424

priesthood, to offer up spiritual sacrifices, acceptable to God by Jesus

an,nn5547

Christ.   *(Ex. 19:6; Is. 61:6)*

pre,repro1352   2532   pin4023   pre1722 art3588   nn1124   2400   pin5087 pre1722

6 Wherefore also it is contained in the scripture, Behold, I lay in

4622   an,aj204/an,nn3037   an,aj1588   an,aj1784   2532   art,pap4100   pre1909

Zion a chief corner stone, elect, precious: and he*that*believeth on

ppro846 efn3364 asbp2617
him shall not be confounded. *(Is. 28:16)*

epn5213 3767 art,pap4100 art,nn5092 1161
7 Unto you therefore which believe *he is* precious: but unto

an,pap544 an,nn3037 repro3739 art3588 pap3618 aina593
them*which*be*disobedient, the stone which the builders disallowed,

depro3778 ainp1096 (pre1519) an,nn2776 an,nn1137
the same is made the head of the corner, *(Ps. 118:22)*

2532 pr/an,nn3037 an,nn4348 2532 pr/an,nn4073 an,nn4625 repro3739
8 And a stone of stumbling, and a rock of offense, *even to them* which

pin4350 art3588 nn3056 pap544 pre1519/repro3739 2532 ainp5087
stumble at the word, being disobedient: whereunto also they were appointed.

(Is. 8:14)

1161 epn5210 an,aj40 pr/an,nn1085 an,aj934 pr/an,nn2406 an,aj40 pr/an,nn1484
9 But ye *are* a chosen generation, a royal priesthood, a holy nation, a

pre1519/an,nn4047 pr/an,nn2992 3704 asbp1804 art3588 nn703 art3588 apta2564
peculiar people; that ye should show forth the praises of him who hath called

ppro5209 pre1537 an,nn4655 pre1519 art,aj2298 an,nn5457
you out of darkness into marvelous light: *(Deut. 7:6; 10:15; Is. 43:20;*

Ex. 19:6; 23:22 [Sept.]; Is. 61:6; Ex. 19:6; 23:22 [Sept.]; Deut. 4:20; 7:6; 14:2;

Ex. 19:5; 23:22 [Sept.] Is. 9:2; 42:12; 43:21)

art3588 ad4218 3756 pr/an,nn2992 1161 ad3568 pr/an,nn2992 an,nn2316
10 Which in*time*past *were* not a people, but *are* now the people of God:

art,pfpp1653/3756 1161 ad3568 aptp1653
which*had*not*obtained*mercy, but now have obtained mercy.

(Hos. 1:6,9; 2:1,23)

an,ajn27 pin3870 ad5613 an,ajn3941 2532 an,ajn3927 pifm567
11 Dearly beloved, I beseech *you* as strangers and pilgrims, abstain from

art,aj4559 an,nn1939 repro3748 pinm4754 pre2596 art3588 nn5590
fleshly lusts, which war against the soul; *(Ps. 39:12)*

pap2192 ppro5216 art,nn391 pr/an,aj2570 pre1722 art3588 nn1484 2443 pre1722/repro3739
12 Having your conversation honest among the Gentiles: that, whereas they

pin2635 ppro5216 ad5613 an,ajn2555 pre1537 art,aj2570 an,nn2041
speak against you as evildoers, they may by *your* good works, which they

apta2029 asba1392 art,nn2316 pre1722 an,nn2250 an,nn1984
shall behold, glorify God in the day of visitation. *(Is. 10:3)*

aipp5293 (3767) an,aj3956 an,nn2937 an,aj442 pre1223/art3588/nn2962
13 Submit yourselves to every ordinance of man for*the*Lord's*sake:

1535 an,nn935 ad5613 pap5242
whether it be to the king, as supreme;

1535 an,nn2232 ad5613 an,ppmp3992 pre1223 ppro846 pre1519
14 Or unto governors, as unto them*that*are*sent by him for the

an,nn1557 (3303) an,ajn2555 1161 an,nn1868 an,ajn17
punishment of evildoers, and for the praise of them*that*do*well.

3754 ad3779 pin2076 art3588 nn2307 art,nn2316 pap15
15 For so is the will of God, that with well doing ye may

pinf5392 art3588 nn56 art,aj878 an,nn444
put*to*silence the ignorance of foolish men:

ad5613 an,aj1658 2532 3361   pap2192   art,nn1657 ad5613   an,nn1942   art,nn2549   235
16 As free, and not using *your* liberty for a cloak of maliciousness, but

ad5613   an,ajn1401   an,nn2316
as the servants of God.

aima5091   an,ajn3956   pim25 art3588   nn81   pin5399 art,nn2316 pim5091 art3588
☞ **17** Honor   all   *men.* Love   the   brotherhood.   Fear   God.   Honor   the

nn935
king.   *(Prov. 24:21)*

Subjection to Authority

art,nn3610   ppmp5293   art,nn1203   pre1722 an,aj3956 an,nn5401 3756 an,ajn3440   art3588
18 Servants, *be* subject to *your* masters with all   fear; not only to the

ajn18 2532 an,ajn1933   235   2532   art3588   ajn4646
good and gentle, but also to the froward.

1063   depro5124   pr/an,nn5485   1487   idpro5100 pre1223   an,nn4893   an,nn2316
19 For   this   *is* thankworthy, if a man for conscience toward God

pin5297 an,nn3077   pap3958   ad95
endure grief, suffering wrongfully.

1063   an,aj4169 an,nn2811   1487   ppmp2852 (2532)   pap264
20 For what glory *is it,* if, when ye be buffeted   for*your*faults, ye shall

ft5278   235   1487   pap15   2532   pap3958
take*it*patiently? but if, when ye do well, and suffer *for it,* ye

ft5278   depro5124   pr/an,nn5485 pre3844 an,nn2316
take*it*patiently, this *is* acceptable with God.

1063   pre1519/depro5124   ainp2564   3754   an,nn5547 2532   ainp3958 pre5228
21 For even hereunto were ye called: because Christ also suffered for

ppro2257 pap5277   ppro2254   an,nn5261   2443   asba1872 ppro846 art,nn2487
us, leaving us an example, that ye should follow his steps:

repro3739 aina4160 3756 an,nn266   3761   an,nn1388 ainp2147 pre1722 ppro846 art,nn4750
22 Who did no sin, neither was guile found in his mouth: *(Is. 53:9)*

repro3739   ppmp3058   ipf486/3756   pap3958
23 Who, when he was reviled, reviled*not*again; when he suffered, he

ipf546   3756 1161   ipf3860   art,pap2919   ad1346
threatened not; but committed *himself* to him*that*judgeth righteously:

repro3739   epn848   aina399 ppro2257 art,nn266 pre1722   ppro848   art,nn4983 pre1909 art3588 nn3586 2443
24 Who his*own*self bare our sins in his own body on the tree, that

---

☞ **2:17** The Christian's submission to higher powers is the theme of this verse. People normally object to those whose rule is tyrannical, oppressive, and ungodly. While the Bible does not condone tyranny or oppression, it is taught, as evidenced by this verse, that believers should respect the established authorities.

At the time Peter was writing these words, there was not one king that professed Christianity. Hence, the recipients of Peter's first epistle were governed by a pagan king. No doubt Peter had fully explained to them that Christ had abolished forever the ideas of kingship and lordship among His followers. Peter's advice to them was not to be rebellious with regard to the governing powers under which they lived. Rather, they were to submit quietly to their rulers, giving due honor and respect to them. The result would be that they would not have the reputation of being rebels, whereby shame might be brought on Christ's name. Furthermore, they would be able to receive the protection and privileges of the kingdom if they needed them. See note on Titus 3:1.

aptm581　　　art,nn266　　　asba2198　　　art,nn1343　　　repro3739　(ppro848)　art,nn3468
we, being dead to sins, should live unto righteousness: by whose   stripes

ainp2390
ye were healed.   *(Is. 53:5)*

1063　　　ipf2258　ad5613　pr/an,nn4263　　ppmp4105　　　235　　　ad3568　　ainp1994　　pre1909　art3588
25 For ye were as sheep going astray; but are now returned unto the

nn4166　　　2532　　an,nn1985　　ppro5216　art,nn5590
Shepherd and Bishop of your souls.   *(Is. 53:6; Ezek. 34:5,6)*

Advice to Wives and Husbands

ad3668　　　　art,nn1135　　　ppmp5293　　　　art,aj2398　　　an,nn435　　　2443　idpro1536
3 ☞ Likewise, ye wives, *be* in subjection to your own husbands; that, if any

pin544　art3588　nn3056　　　2532　　ad*427　　　an,nn3056　　fp2770　pre1223　art3588
obey not the word, they also may without the word be won by the

nn391　　　　art3588　nn1135
conversation of the wives;

apta2029　ppro5216　art,aj53　　　an,nn391　　　　　　pre1722　an,nn5401
2 While they behold your chaste conversation *coupled* with fear.

repro3739　an,nn2889　　　3756　pim2077　art3588　ad1855　　　　　　an,nn1708
3 Whose adorning let it not be that outward *adorning* of plaiting the

an,nn2359　2532　an,nn4025　an,nn5553　2228　an,nn1745　　an,nn2440
hair, and of wearing of gold, or of putting on of apparel;

235　　　　　　　　　　　art3588　　aj2927　　　an,nn444　　　art3588　　nn2588　　pre1722
4 But *let it be* the hidden man of the heart, in

art,ajn862　　　　　　　　　　　　　　art,aj4239　2532　an,aj2272　an,nn4151
that*which*is*not*corruptible, *even the ornament* of a meek and quiet spirit,

repro3739　pin2076　ad*1799　　art,nn2316　　pr/an,aj4185
which is in*the*sight of God of*great*price.

1063　　　　ad3779　　　　　　ad4218　　art3588　aj40　　an,nn1135　　2532
5 For after*this*manner in*the*old*time the holy women also,

art,pap1679　　pre1909　art,nn2316　　ipf2885　　rxpro1438　　　ppmp5293　　　　art,aj2398
who trusted in God, adorned themselves, being*in*subjection unto their own

an,nn435
husbands:

ad5613　　　an,nn4564　aina5219　　　11　　pap2564　ppro846　an,nn2962　repro3739　pr/an,nn5043
6 Even as Sarah obeyed Abraham, calling him lord: whose daughters ye

ainp1096　　　　　pap15　　2532　　ppmp5399/3361　　　an,aj3367　　an,nn4423
are, as long as ye do well, and are*not*afraid with any amazement.

(Gen. 18:12)

ad3668　　　art,nn435　　pap4924　　　　pre2596　　　an,nn1108　　pap632
7 Likewise, ye husbands, dwell with *them* according to knowledge, giving

an,nn5092　　art3588　ajn1134　ad5613　　cd/an,aj772　　an,nn4632　　2532　　ad5613
honor unto the wife, as unto the weaker vessel, and as being

pr/an,nn4789　　an,nn5485　an,nn2222　ppro5216　art,nn4335　　3361　aies1581
heirs together of the grace of life; that your prayers be not hindered.

☞ **3:1-4** See note on 1 Timothy 2:9-15 concerning the conduct of women.

The Blessedness of Suffering for Righteousness' Sake

(1161) art,nn5056   an,ajn3956   pr/an,aj3675   pr/an,aj4835

8   Finally, *be ye* all of*one*mind, having*compassion*one*of*another,

pr/an,aj5361   pr/an,aj2155   pr/an,aj5391

love*as*brethren, *be* pitiful, *be* courteous:

3361   pap591   an,ajn2556   pre473   an,ajn2556   2228   an,nn3059   pre473   an,nn3059   1161   art,ajn5121

9 Not rendering evil   for   evil,   or railing for railing: but contrariwise

pap2127   pfp1492   3754   pre1519/depro5124   ainp2564   2443   asba2816

blessing; knowing that ye are thereunto called, that ye should inherit a

an,nn2129

blessing.

1063   art,pap2309   pinf25   an,nn2222   2532   ainf1492   an,aj18   an,nn2250   aima3973   ppro848

10 For he*that*will love   life,   and see good days, let him refrain his

art,nn1100   pre575   an,ajn2556   2532   ppro848   an,nn5491   infg2980   3361   an,nn1388

tongue from evil, and his   lips that they speak no guile:

           aima1578   (pre575)   an,ajn2556   2532   aima4160   an,ajn18   aima2212   an,nn1515

11 Let him eschew   evil,   and   do   good; let him seek peace,

2532   aima1377   ppro846

and ensue it.

3754   art3588   nn3788   an,nn2962   pre1909   an,ajn1342   2532   ppro846 an,nn3775

12 For the eyes of the Lord *are* over the righteous, and his   ears *are*

pre1519 ppro846   an,nn1162   1161   an,nn4383   an,nn2962   pre1909   an,pap4160   an,ajn2556

open unto their prayers: but the face of the Lord *is* against them*that*do evil.

(Ps. 34:12-16)

2532   pr/inpro5101   art,fpta2559   ppro5209   1437   asbm1096   pr/an,nn3402

13 And   who   *is* he*that*will*harm   you,   if   ye   be   followers of

art,ajn18

that*which*is*good?

235   2532   1487   opt3958   pre1223/an,nn1343   pr/an,aj3107   1161

14 But and if   ye suffer for*righteousness'*sake, happy *are ye:* and

aosi5399/3361   ppro846   art,nn5401   3366   aosi5015

be*not*afraid of their terror, neither be troubled;

1161   aima37   an,nn2962 art,nn2316 pre1722 ppro5216   art,nn2588   1161   pr/an,ajn2092   ad104

15 But sanctify the Lord God   in   your hearts: and *be* ready always

pre4314/an,nn627   an,aj3956   art,pap154   ppro5209   an,nn3056   pre4012 art3588   nn1680

to*give*an*answer to every man that asketh you a reason of   the hope that

pre1722 ppro5213 pre3326   an,nn4240   2532 an,nn5401

is   in   you with meekness and fear: *(Is. 8:12,13)*

pap2192   an,aj18   an,nn4893   2443   pre1722/repro3739   psa2635   ppro5216 ad5613

16 Having a good conscience; that, whereas they speak*evil*of you, as of

an,ajn2555   asbp2617   art,pap1908   ppro5216   art,aj18   an,nn391

evildoers, they may be ashamed that*falsely*accuse your good conversation

pre1722   an,nn5547

in   Christ.

1063   pr/cd/an,ajn2909   1487 art3588   nn2307   art,nn2316 pin2309   pinf3958

17 For *it is* better, if   the   will of   God   be   so, that ye suffer for

pap15   2228   pap2554

well doing, than for evil doing.

3754   an,nn5547   2532   nu,ad530   aina3958   pre4012 an,nn266   an,ajn1342 pre5228   an,ajn94

18 For Christ also hath once suffered for   sins, the   just   for the unjust,

2443   asba4317 ppro2248   art,nn2316   aptp2289   (3303)   an,nn4561   1161

that he might bring us to God, being put*to*death in the flesh, but

aptp2227   art3588 nn4151

quickened by the Spirit:

pre1722 repro3739   2532   aptp4198   aina2784   art3588   nn4151   pre1722

☞ 19 By which also he went and preached unto the spirits in

an,nn5438

prison;

ad4218   apta544   ad3753   nu,ad530 art3588   nn3115

20 Which sometime were disobedient, when once the longsuffering of

art,nn2316 ipf1551   pre1722 an,nn2250 3575   an,nn2787   ppmp2680   pre1519/repro3739

God waited in the days of Noah, while the ark was a preparing, wherein

an,aj3641 depro,pin5123 nu3638 an,nn5590   ainp1295 pre1223 an,nn5204

few, that is, eight souls were saved by water.   *(Gen. 6:1-7:24)*

an,nn499   repro3739   an,nn908   2532 ad3568 pin4982 epn2248 3756

☞ 21 The like figure whereunto *even* baptism doth also now save us (not the

an,nn595   an,nn4509   an,nn4561 235   an,nn1906   an,aj18   an,nn4893

putting away of the filth of the flesh, but the answer of a good conscience

pre1519 an,nn2316 pre1223   an,nn386   an,nn2424 an,nn5547

toward God,) by the resurrection of Jesus Christ:

repro3739 aptp4198 pre1519 an,nn3772 pin2076 pre1722   an,ajn1188 art,nn2316 an,nn32

22 Who is gone into heaven, and is on the right hand of God; angels

2532 an,nn1849   2532 an,nn1411   aptp5293   ppro846

and authorities and powers being made*subject*unto him.

☞ **3:19** One common interpretation of this passage is that subsequent to Christ's death, possibly before His resurrection, His disembodied spirit went to the unseen world and there preached to the disobedient dead. This interpretation is based on the reference to the dead during the days of Noah. However, there is no justification at all that such a small number of people who lived during the span of about 120 years should be singled out from the great mass of mankind for so singular and great a blessing. Those who hold such a theory of interpretation extend it to include the theory of the doctrine of probation after death, meaning that the impenitent dead have a second chance. Nowhere in Scripture is there any indication that those who die unrepentant have a second chance.

In this verse, it is simply stated that Christ preached. It does not describe what message He might have preached. Every time the word *kērússō* (2784) "preach," occurs it does not necessarily mean "to preach the Gospel." Even the word *euaggelízō* (2097), "to proclaim good news," does not always refer to preaching salvation. The same verb is used in Ephesians 2:17, but the object of the verb is peace, "He came and preached [*euēggelísato*] peace to you." The glorious result of Christ being put to death, "the just for the unjust," was not merely the attainment of a resurrection body; for Peter goes on to say, "By which also he went and preached unto spirits in prison." Whatever the nature of this preaching may have been, it had to take place between His death and resurrection. There is certainly no need to put an arbitrary interpretation on the words "spirits in prison," as referring simply to those who had passed to the unseen world, because the ungodly are constantly spoken of in Scripture as being in a state of imprisonment, bondage or captivity. If, therefore, this passage does not refer to certain individuals but to the declaration of Christ's victory over death and hell, then the meaning of the phrase "preached unto spirits in prison" is clarified. See note on Ephesians 4:8–10.

☞ **3:21** The expression "baptism doth also now save" should be understood in light of verse twenty: "eight souls were saved by water." Noah and his family, being in the ark, were able to pass safely "through" the waters (seen in the Greek word *diá* [1223]). In the same way, the term "baptism" (v. 21) should be understood as the visible representation of deliverance through Christ, just as the ark represented deliverance from the waters of the Flood. When a person accepts Christ, he is saved; when the believer is baptized, he is identified with the One who has delivered him (i.e., Jesus Christ). See note on Mark 16:16.

                        3767   an,nn5547   aptp3958   pre5228 ppro2257   an,nn4561 aipm3695
4 Forasmuch then as Christ hath suffered for us in the flesh, arm
        epn5210   2532   art3588 ppro846 nn1771 3754   art,aptp3958   pre1722
yourselves likewise with the same mind: for he*that*hath*suffered in
an,nn4561   pfip3973   an,nn266
the flesh hath ceased from sin;

                    ad3371   aies980 art3588 aj1954   an,nn5550 pre1722   an,nn4561
2 That he no longer should live the rest of *his* time in the flesh to the
an,nn1939   an,nn444 235   an,nn2307 an,nn2316
lusts of men, but to the will of God.

      1063   an,nn5550 art,pfp3928   art,nn979   pr/an,aj713 ppro2254   aifm2716
3 For the time past of *our* life may suffice us to have wrought
art3588   nn2307   art3588   nn1484   pfpp4198 pre1722   pl/an,nn766
the will of the Gentiles, when we walked in lasciviousness,
an,nn1939   pl/an,nn3632   an,nn2970   an,nn4224   2532   an,aj111
lusts, excess*of*wine, revellings, banquetings, and abominable
an,nn1495
idolatries:

      pre1722/repro3739   pinm3579   ppro5216 pap4936/3361   pre1519 art3588
4 Wherein they think*it*strange that ye run*not*with *them* to the
ppro846   nn401   art,nn810 pap987
same excess of riot, speaking*evil*of *you*:

      repro3739   ft591   an,nn3056   art,pap2192 pr/ad2093 ainf2919   an,pap2198 2532
5 Who shall give account to him*that*is ready to judge the quick and the
an,ajn3498
dead.

      1063   pre1519   depro5124   ainp2097   2532
6 For for this cause was*the*gospel*preached also to
an,ajn3498   2443   asbp2919 (3303) pre2596   an,nn444
them*that*are*dead, that they might be judged according to men in the
an,nn4561 1161 psa2198 pre2596 an,nn2316   an,nn4151
flesh, but live according to God in the spirit.

      1161 art3588 nn5056   an,ajn3956 pfi1448   aima4993/3767   2532 aima3525
7 But the end of all things is*at*hand: be*ye*therefore*sober, and watch
pre1519 art,nn4335
unto prayer.

      1161   pre4253   an,ajn3956 pap2192 an,aj1618 art,nn26 pre1519   rxpro1438 3754 art,nn26
8 And above all things have fervent charity among yourselves: for charity
      ft2572   an,nn4128   an,nn266
shall cover the multitude of sins.   (*Prov.* 20:12)

          an,ajn5382   rcpro240/pre1519   ad*427   an,nn1112
9 Use hospitality one*to*another without grudging.
      ad2531   an,ajn1538   aina2983   an,nn5486   pap1247
10 As every man hath received the gift, *even so* minister
ppro846   pre1519/rxpro1438   ad5613 an,aj2570 an,nn3623   an,aj4164 an,nn5485
the same one*to*another, as good stewards of the manifold grace of
an,nn2316
God.

      idpro1536   pin2980   ad5613   an,nn3051 an,nn2316 idpro1536
11 If*any*man speak, *let him speak* as the oracles of God; if*any*man
pin1247   ad5613 pre1537 an,nn2479 repro3739 art,nn2316 pin5524 2443 art,nn2316 pre1722
minister, *let him do it* as of the ability which God giveth: that God in

an,ajn3956   psmp1392   pre1223   an,nn2424   an,nn5547   repro3739   pin2076   art,nn1391   2532

all things may be glorified through Jesus Christ, to whom be praise and

art,nn2904   pre1519/art,nn165/art,nn165   281

dominion forever*and*ever. Amen.

Believers Should Not Be Ashamed

an,ajn27   pim3579/3361   art3588   nn4451   (pre1722 ppro5213) ppmp1096

12 Beloved, think*it*not*strange concerning the fiery trial   which   is

pre4314/an,nn3986 ppro5213 ad5613   an,ajn3581   pap4819   ppro5213

to try   you, as though some*strange*thing happened unto you:

235   pin5463   ad2526   pin2841   art,nn5547   art,nn3804

☞ 13 But rejoice, inasmuch as ye are partakers of Christ's sufferings;

2443   pre1722   ppro846   art,nn1391   art,nn602   asba5463   2532

that, when his glory shall be revealed, ye may be glad also with

ppmp21

exceeding joy.

1487   pinp3679   pre1722   an,nn3686   an,nn5547   pr/an,aj3107   3754 art3588

14 If ye be reproached for the name of Christ, happy *are ye*; for the

nn4151   art,nn1391   2532   art,nn2316   pinm373   pre1909   ppro5209   pre2596/ppro846   (3303)

Spirit of glory and of God resteth upon you: on*their*part he is

pinp987   1161   pre2596/ppro5209   pinp1392

evil*spoken*of, but on*your*part he is glorified.   (Is. 11:2)

1063   idpro5100/3361   ppro5216 pim3958 ad5613   an,nn5406   2228   an,nn2812 2228

15 But let none of you suffer as a murderer, or *as* a thief, or *as* an

an,ajn2555   2228 ad5613   an,nn244

evildoer, or as a busybody*in*other*men's*matters.

1161 1487   ad5613   an,nn5546   3361   pim153   1161

16 Yet if *any man suffer* as a Christian, let him not be ashamed; but let

pim1392   art,nn2316 pre1722 depro5129 art,nn3313

him glorify God on this behalf.

3754 art3588 nn2540   art,nn2917   art,aifm756 pre575 art3588   nn3624   art,nn2316

17 For the time *is come* that judgment must begin at the house of God:

1161 1487   nu,ajn4412   pre575 ppro2257 inpro5101   art3588 nn5056   art,pap544   art3588

and if *it* first *begin* at us, what shall the end *be* of them*that*obey*not the

nn2098   art,nn2316

gospel of God?   (Jer. 25:29; Ezek. 9:6)

2532   1487 art3588   ajn1342   ad3433   pinp4982   ad4226   art3588 ajn765   2532

18 And if the righteous scarcely be saved, where shall the ungodly and

an,ajn268   fm5316

the sinner appear?   (Prov. 11:31 [Sept.])

5620   (2532)   art,pap3958   pre2596   art3588 nn2307   art,nn2316

19 Wherefore let them*that*suffer according to the will of God

pim3908   rxpro1438 art,nn5590   pre1722   an,nn16   ad5613   an,aj4103

commit*the*keeping*of their souls *to him* in well doing, as unto a faithful

an,nn2939

Creator.   (Ps. 31:5)

☞ **4:13** See note on 1 Thessalonians 2:19.

Exhortations to Elders

^{an,ajn4245} ^{art3588}   ^{pre1722}   ^{ppro5213}   ^{pin3870}   ^{art,nn4850}   ²⁵³²

5 The elders which are among you I exhort, who*am*also*an*elder, and a
^{an,nn3144}   ^{art3588}   ⁿⁿ³⁸⁰⁴   ^{art,nn5547} ²⁵³²   ^{art,nn2844}   ^{an,nn1391}
witness of the sufferings of Christ, and also a partaker of the glory
^{art,pap3195}   ^{pifm601}
that shall be revealed:

^{aima4165} ^{art3588} ⁿⁿ⁴¹⁶⁸   ^{art,nn2316}   ^{pre1722} ^{ppro5213}   ^{pap1983}
2 Feed the flock of God which is among you, taking*the*oversight *thereof,*
³³⁶¹   ^{ad317}   ²³⁵   ^{ad1596}   ³³⁶⁶   ^{ad147}   ²³⁵   ^{ad4290}
not by constraint, but willingly; not for*filthy*lucre, but of*a*ready*mind;
³³⁶⁶   ^{ad5613}   ^{pap2634}   ^{art,nn2819} ²³⁵ ^{ppmp1096} ^{pr/an,nn5179}   ^{art3588}
3 Neither as being*lords*over *God's* heritage, but being examples to the
ⁿⁿ⁴¹⁶⁸
flock.

²⁵³²   ^{art3588}   ⁿⁿ⁷⁵⁰   ^{aptp5319}   ^{fm2865}   ^{an,nn4735}
4 And when the chief Shepherd shall appear, ye shall receive a crown of
^{art,nn1391}   ^{art,aj262}
glory that*fadeth*not*away.

Concluding Injunctions

^{ad3668}   ^{an,ajn3501}   ^{aima5293}   ^{an,ajn4245} ¹¹⁶¹ ^{an,ajn3956}

5 Likewise, ye younger, submit yourselves unto the elder. Yea, all *of*
^{ppmp5293}   ^{rcpro240}   ²⁵³²   ^{aipm1463}   ^{art,nn5012} ³⁷⁵⁴ ^{art,nn2316}
you be subject one*to*another, and be*clothed*with humility: for God
^{pinm498}   ^{an,ajn5244} ¹¹⁶¹ ^{pin1325} ^{an,nn5485}   ^{an,ajn5011}
resisteth the proud, and giveth grace to the humble.   *(Prov. 3:34 [Sept.])*
^{aipp5013}   ³⁷⁶⁷   ^{pre5259} ^{art3588} ^{an,aj2900}   ⁿⁿ⁵⁴⁹⁵   ^{art,nn2316} ²⁴⁴³
6 Humble yourselves therefore under the mighty hand of God, that he may
^{asba5312} ^{ppro5209} ^{pre1722}   ^{an,nn2540}
exalt you in due time:
^{apta1977}   ^{an,aj3956} ^{ppro5216} ^{art,nn3308} ^{pre1909} ^{ppro846} ³⁷⁵⁴ ^{ppro846}   ^{pin3199}   ^{pre4012} ^{ppro5216}
7 Casting all your care upon him; for he careth for you.   *(Ps. 55:22)*
^{aima3525}   ^{aima1127}   ³⁷⁵⁴   ^{ppro5216}   ^{art,ajn476}   ^{an,ajn1228} ^{ad5613}   ^{ppmp5612}
8 Be sober, be vigilant; because your adversary the devil, as a roaring
^{an,nn3023}   ^{pin4043}   ^{pap2212}   ^{inpro5101}   ^{asba2666}
lion, walketh about, seeking whom he may devour:
^{repro3739}   ^{aima436}   ^{an,ajn4731}   ^{art3588} ⁿⁿ⁴¹⁰²   ^{pfp1492}   ^{art3588} ^{ppro846}   ^{art,nn3804}
9 Whom resist steadfast in the faith, knowing that the same afflictions are
^{pifm2005}   ^{ppro5216}   ^{art,nn81}   ^{pre1722} ^{an,nn2889}
accomplished in your brethren that are in the world.
¹¹⁶¹   ^{art3588} ⁿⁿ²³¹⁶   ^{an,aj3956} ^{an,nn5485}   ^{art,apta2564}   ^{ppro2248} ^{pre1519} ^{ppro848} ^{art,aj166}
10 But the God of all grace, who*hath*called us unto his eternal
^{an,nn1391}   ^{pre1722} ^{an,nn5547} ^{an,nn2424}   ^{apta3958}   ^{an,ajn3641 (epn846)}
glory by Christ Jesus, after that ye have suffered a while,
^{opt2675/ppro5209}   ^{opt4741}   ^{opt4599}   ^{opt2311}
make*you*perfect, establish, strengthen, settle *you.*

epn846   art,nn1391   2532   art,nn2904   pre1519/art,nn165/art,nn165   281

11 To him *be* glory and dominion forever*and*ever. Amen.

pre1223   an,nn4610   art,aj4103   an,nn80   ppro5213 ad5613   pinm3049   aina1125

12 By Silvanus, a faithful brother unto you, as I suppose, I have written

pre1223/an,ajn3641   pap3870   2532   pap1957   depro5026 pinf1511   an,aj227 pr/an,nn5485   art,nn2316

briefly,   exhorting, and testifying that   this   is   the true grace of God

pre1519/repro3739   pfi2476

wherein ye stand.

art3588   pre1722   an,nn897   an,ajn4899   pinm782

13 The *church that is* at Babylon, elected*together*with *you,* saluteth

ppro5209 2532   an,nn3138 ppro3450 art,nn5207

you; and *so doth* Mark my   son.

aipm782   rcpro240   pre1722   an,nn5370   an,nn26   an,nn1515   ppro5213 an,aj3956

14 Greet ye one another with a kiss of charity. Peace *be* with you   all

art3588   pre1722 an,nn5547 an,nn2424   281

that are   in   Christ Jesus. Amen.

The Second Epistle of

PETER

The Book of 2 Peter is similar in both order and content to the Book of
Jude (2 Pet. 2:1—3:3, cf. Jude 1:3–18). Peter, however, issues a warning concerning the false teachers that eventually would come, while Jude states that they
were already present. It is reasonable to conclude from the phrase, "to them
that have obtained like precious faith with us" (2 Pet. 1:1), that Peter was writing
to Gentile believers. Though it is possible that Peter was addressing the same
group of believers to whom the Book of 1 Peter (1 Pet. 3:1), some believe that
it was addressed to an entirely different group. This second letter of Peter was
particularly directed against the gnostic and antinomian philosophies. Gnostics
taught that in addition to believing in Christ, one must also receive the *"gnôsis"*
or esoteric knowledge (see note on Col. 2:8–23). Peter refuted this idea by
stressing the fact that they had already received the true knowledge (2 Pet.
1:16–21).

Antinomians believe that since salvation was by grace alone, the requirements
of the moral law were irrelevant. Peter devotes the second chapter to attacking
the licentious lifestyle that naturally resulted among those who held this belief.
Paul also addressed this philosophy (Rom. 6) and denied the accusation that he
himself held this view (Rom. 3:8). In the third chapter, Peter reproves them
for their skepticism about Christ's return. Included within the discussion in which
he corrects of their faulty perception of this event, he gives one of the most
detailed descriptions of end-time events in all of Scripture. The delay of Jesus'
return is only apparent, he explains, because God does not exist within the
concept of time (2 Pet. 3:8). Peter also tells them that when the Day of the
Lord comes, it will be accompanied by the total destruction of the physical universe
(2 Pet. 3:10–12).

1 Simon Peter, a servant and an apostle of Jesus Christ, to
them*that*have*obtained like precious faith with us through the
righteousness of God and our Savior Jesus Christ:

2 Grace and peace be multiplied unto you through the knowledge of God,
and of Jesus our Lord,

"Great and Precious Promises"

ad5613   pppro846 art,aj2304 an,nn1411   pfpp1433   ppro2254   an,ajn3956 art3588
3 According as his divine power hath given unto us all things that *pertain*

pre4314 an,nn2222 2532   an,nn2150   pre1223   art3588   nn1922   art,apta2564   ppro2248
unto life and godliness, through the knowledge of him*that*hath*called us

pre1223 an,nn1391 2532   an,nn703
to glory and virtue:

pre1223/repro3739   pfip1433   ppro2254   cd/art,aj3176   2532   an,aj5093   an,nn1862
4 Whereby are given unto us exceeding great and precious promises:

2443 pre1223 depro5130   asbm1096   pr/an,ajn2844   an,aj2304   an,nn5449   apta668
that by these ye might be partakers of the divine nature, having escaped

art3588   nn5356   pre1722   an,nn2889   pre1722   an,nn1939
the corruption that is in the world through lust.

1161   pppro846/depro5124 (2532) apta3923 an,aj3956   an,nn4710 aima2023 pre1722 ppro5216 art,nn4102 art,nn703   1161
5 And beside this, giving all diligence, add to your faith virtue; and

pre1722 art,nn703   art,nn1108
to virtue knowledge;

1161   pre1722   art,nn1108   art,nn1466   1161 pre1722   art,nn1466   art,nn5281   1161 pre1722
6 And to knowledge temperance; and to temperance patience; and to

art,nn5281   art,nn2150
patience godliness;

1161   pre1722   art,nn2150   art,nn5360   1161   pre1722   art,nn5360
7 And to godliness brotherly kindness; and to brotherly kindness

art,nn26
charity.

1063   depro5023   pap5225   ppro5213 2532   pap4121   pin2525
8 For if these things be in you, and abound, they make *you that ye shall*

3756   pr/an,aj692   3761   pr/an,aj175   pre1519 art3588   nn1922   ppro2257 art,nn2962 an,nn2424
neither *be* barren nor unfruitful in the knowledge of our Lord Jesus

an,nn5547
Christ.

1063   repro3739   pin3918/3361   depro5023   pin2076 pr/an,aj5185   pr/pap3467
9 But he that lacketh these things is blind, and cannot*see*afar*off,

apta2983/an,nn3024   art,nn2512   ppro848 art,ad3819 art,nn266
and hath forgotten that he was purged from his old sins.

pre,repro1352   ad3123   an,nn80   aima4704   pifm4160   ppro5216
10 Wherefore the rather, brethren, give diligence to make your

art,nn2821   2532   an,nn1589   an,aj949 1063   pap4160   depro5023   efn3364/ad4218
calling and election sure: for if ye do these things, ye shall never

asba4417
fall:

1063   ad3779   art,nn1529   ainp2023   ppro5213   ad4146   pre1519 art3588
11 For so an entrance shall be ministered unto you abundantly into the

an,aj166   nn932   ppro2257 art,nn2962 2532 an,nn4990 an,nn2424 an,nn5547
everlasting kingdom of our Lord and Savior Jesus Christ.

pre,repro1352   3756   ft272   pinf5279/ppro5209/ad104
12 Wherefore I will not be negligent to put*you*always*in*remembrance

pre4012   depro5130   2539   pfp1492   2532   pfpp4741   pre1722 art3588 pap3918
of these things, though ye know *them,* and be established in the present

nn225
truth.

1161   pinm2233   pr/an,ajn1342   pre1909/an,ajn3745   pin1510 pre1722 depro5129   art,nn4638
13 Yea, I think it meet, as*long*as I am in this tabernacle, to

pinf1326/ppro5209   pre1722/an,nn5280
stir*you*up by*putting*you*in*remembrance;

pfp1492   3754   pr/an,aj5031   pin2076 art,nn595   ppro3450   art,nn4638   2532   ad2531 ppro2257
14 Knowing that shortly I must put off *this* my tabernacle, even as our

art,nn2962 an,nn2424 an,nn5547   aina1213 ppro3427
Lord Jesus Christ hath showed me.

1161   ft4704   (2532) ppro5209   pre3326 art,popro1699   an,nn1841
15 Moreover I will endeavor that ye may be able after my decease to

pinf2192   art,depro5130   ad1539   pifm4160/an,nn3420
have these things always in remembrance.

A More Sure Word of Prophecy

1063   3756   apta1811   pfpp4679   an,nn3454
☞ 16 For we have not followed cunningly devised fables, when we

aina1107   ppro5213 art3588   nn1411   2532 an,nn3952   ppro2257 art,nn2962 an,nn2424 an,nn5547 235
made known unto you the power and coming of our Lord Jesus Christ, but

aptp1096   pr/an,nn2030   depro1565   art,nn3168
were eyewitnesses of his majesty.

1063   apta2983   pre3844 an,nn2316   an,nn3962 an,nn5092 2532 an,nn1391
17 For he received from God the Father honor and glory, when there

aptp5342 an,aj5107   an,nn5456   ppro846 pre5259 art3588   an,aj3169   nn1391 depro3778 pin2076 ppro3450   art,aj27
came such a voice to him from the excellent glory, This is my beloved

pr/art,nn5207 pre1519 repro3739 epn1473   aina2106
Son, in whom I am*well*pleased.

2532   depro5026 art,nn5456   aptp5342 pre1537 an,nn3772 epn2249 aina191   pap5607
18 And this voice which came from heaven we heard, when we were

pre4862 ppro846 pre1722 art3588 aj40   art,nn3735
with him in the holy mount.

pin2192   2532   cd/an,aj949   an,nn3056   art,aj4397   repro3739   pin4160 ad2573
19 We have also a more sure word of prophecy; whereunto ye do well

pap4337   ad5613   an,nn3088   pap5316 pre1722 an,aj850 an,nn5117 ad2193 (repro3739)
that ye take heed, as unto a light that shineth in a dark place, until the

an,nn2250 asba1306 2532   an,ajn5459 asba393 pre1722 ppro5216 art,nn2588
day dawn, and the day star arise in your hearts:

pap1097   depro5124 nu,ajn4412 3754 an,aj3956/3756 an,nn4394   an,nn1124   pinm1096
20 Knowing this first, that no prophecy of the Scripture is of any

an,aj2398   an,nn1955
private interpretation.

1063   an,nn4394   ainp5342 3756   ad4218   an,nn2307 an,nn444 235 an,aj40
21 For the prophecy came not in*old*time by the will of man: but holy

an,nn444   an,nn2316 aina2980   ppmp5342 pre5259   an,aj40 an,nn4151
men of God spake *as they were* moved by the Holy Ghost.

☞ **1:16** See note on 1 Thessalonians 2:19.

Warnings Against False Teachers

2 But there were false prophets also among the people, even as there
¹¹⁶¹ ^{aom1096} ^{an,nn5578} ²⁵³² ^{pre1722} ^{art3588} ⁿⁿ²⁹⁹² ²⁵³² ^{ad5613}

^{fm2071} ^{an,nn5572} ^{pre1722} ^{epn5213} ^{repro3748} ^{ft3919} ^{an,nn684}
shall be false teachers among you, who privily*shall* bring*in damnable

^{an,nn139} ²⁵³² ^{ppmp720} ^{art3588} ⁿⁿ¹²⁰³ ^{apta59} ^{ppro846} ^{pap1863}
heresies, even denying the Lord that bought them, and bring upon

^{rxpro1438} ^{an,aj5031} ^{an,nn684}
themselves swift destruction.

²⁵³² ^{an,ajn4183} ^{ft1811} ^{ppro846} ^{art,nn684} ^{pre1223} ^{repro3739} ^{art3588}
2 And many shall follow their pernicious ways; by*reason*of whom the

ⁿⁿ³⁵⁹⁸ ^{art,nn225} ^{fp987}
way of truth shall be evil*spoken*of. *(Is. 52:5)*

²⁵³² ^{pre1722} ^{an,nn4124} ^{an,aj4112} ^{an,nn3056}
3 And through covetousness shall they with feigned words

^{fm1710} ^{ppro5209} ^{repro3739} ^{art,nn2917} ^{ad1597} ^{pin691} ³⁷⁵⁶
make merchandise of you: whose judgment now*of*a*long*time lingereth not,

²⁵³² ^{ppro846} ^{art,nn684} ^{pin3573} ³⁷⁵⁶
and their damnation slumbereth not.

¹⁰⁶³ ¹⁴⁸⁷ ^{art,nn2316} ^{aom5339} ³⁷⁵⁶ ^{an,nn32} ^{apta264} ²³⁵
4 For if God spared not the angels that sinned, but

^{apta5020} ^{aina3860} ^{an,nn4577} ^{an,nn2217}
cast*them*down*to*hell, and delivered *them* into chains of darkness, to be

^{pfpp5083} ^{pre1519} ^{an,nn2920}
reserved unto judgment;

²⁵³² ^{aom5339} ³⁷⁵⁶ ^{an,aj744} ^{an,nn2889} ²³⁵ ^{aina5442} ³⁵⁷⁵ ^{an,nu,ajn3590}
5 And spared not the old world, but saved Noah the eighth *person,* a

^{an,nn2783} ^{an,nn1343} ^{apta1863} ^{an,nn2627} ^{an,nn2889}
preacher of righteousness, bringing in the flood upon the world of the

^{an,ajn765}
ungodly; *(Gen. 8:18)*

²⁵³² ^{apta5077/an,nn4172/an,nn4670/2532/an,nn1116} ^{aina2632}
6 And turning*the*cities*of*Sodom*and*Gomorrah*into*ashes condemned

^{an,nn2692} ^{pfp5087} ^{an,nn5262}
them with an overthrow, making *them* an example unto

^{an,pap3195} ^{pinf764}
those*that*after*should live ungodly; *(Gen. 19:24)*

²⁵³² ^{aom4506} ^{an,aj1342} ³⁰⁹¹ ^{ppmp2669} ^{pre5259} ^{art3588} ^{pre1722/an,nn766/nn391} ^{art3588}
7 And delivered just Lot, vexed with the filthy conversation of the

^{ajn113}
wicked: *(Gen. 19:1-16)*

¹⁰⁶³ ^{art,ajn1342} ^{pap1460} ^{pre1722} ^{ppro846} ^{an,nn990} ²⁵³² ^{an,nn189}
8 (For that righteous man dwelling among them, in seeing and hearing,

^{ipf928} ^{an,aj1342} ^{an,nn5590} ^{an,nn2250 pre1537 an,nn2250} ^{an,aj459} ^{an,nn2041}
vexed *his* righteous soul from day to day with *their* unlawful deeds);

^{an,nn2962} ^{pin1492} ^{pifm4506} ^{an,ajn2152} ^{pre1537} ^{an,nn3986} ¹¹⁶¹
9 The Lord knoweth how to deliver the godly out of temptations, and to

^{pinf5083} ^{an,ajn94} ^{pre1519} ^{an,nn2250} ^{an,nn2920} ^{ppmp2849}
reserve the unjust unto the day of judgment to be punished:

¹¹⁶¹ ^{ad3122} ^{art,ppmp4198} ^{ad*3694} ^{an,nn4561} ^{pre1722} ^{an,nn1939}
10 But chiefly them*that*walk after the flesh in the lust of

an,nn3394   2532   pap2706   an,nn2963   an,nn5113   an,ajn829

uncleanness, and despise government. Presumptuous *are they*, self-willed, they

3756   pin5141   ppmp987   an,nn1391

are not afraid to speak evil of dignities.

ad3699   an,nn32   pap5607   pr/cd/an,aj3187   an,nn2479   2532   an,nn1411   pin5342   3756

11 Whereas angels, which are greater in power and might, bring not

an,aj989   an,nn2920   pre2596   ppro846   pre3844   an,nn2962

railing accusation against them before the Lord.

1161   depro3778   ad5613   an,aj5446   an,aj249   an,nn2226   ppmp1080   pre1519/an,nn259   2532   an,nn5336

12 But these, as natural brute beasts, made to*be*taken and destroyed,

pap987   pre1722   repro3739   pin50   fp2704

speak evil of the things that they understand not; and shall utterly perish

pre1722   ppro848   art,nn5356

in their own corruption;

ppmp2865   an,nn3408   an,nn93   an,ppmp2233

13 And shall receive the reward of unrighteousness, *as* they*that*count it

pr/an,nn2237   art,nn5172   pre1722   an,nn2250   an,nn4695   2532   an,nn3470

pleasure to riot in the day time. Spots *they are* and blemishes,

pap1792   pre1722   ppro848   art,nn539   ppmp4190   ppro5213

sporting themselves with their own deceivings while they feast with you;

pap2192   an,nn3788   an,aj3324   an,nn3428   2532   an,aj180   an,nn266

14 Having eyes full of adultery, and that cannot cease from sin;

pap1185   an,aj793   an,nn5590   an,nn2588   pap2192   pfpp1128   an,nn4124

beguiling unstable souls: a heart they have exercised with covetous practices;

an,nn2671   an,nn5043

cursed children:

apta2641   art3588 an,aj2117   nn3598   ainp4105   apta1811   art3588

15 Which have forsaken the right way, and are gone astray, following the

nn3598   903   1007   repro3739   aina25   an,nn3408   an,nn93

way of Balaam *the son* of Bosor, who loved the wages of unrighteousness;

1161   aina2192/an,nn1649   an,aj2398   an,nn3892   an,aj880   an,nn5268   aptm5350   pre1722   an,nn444

16 But was rebuked for his iniquity: the dumb ass speaking with man's

an,nn5456   aina2967   art3588   nn3913   art3588   nn4396

voice forbade the madness of the prophet.   *(Num. 22:28-35)*

depro3778   pin1526   pr/an,nn4077   an,aj504   pr/an,nn3507   ppmp1643   pre5259

17 These are wells without water, clouds that are carried with a

an,nn2978   repro3739 art3588 nn2217   art,nn4655   pfip5083   pre1519/an,nn165

tempest: to whom the mist of darkness is reserved forever.

1063   ppmp5350   an,ajn5246   an,nn3153   pin1185

18 For when they speak great swelling *words* of vanity, they allure

pre1722   an,nn1939   an,nn4561   an,nn766

through the lusts of the flesh, *through   much* wantonness,

art,apta668/ad3689   art,ppmp390   pre1722 an,nn4106

those*that*were*clean*escaped from them*who*live in error.

ppmp1861   ppro846   an,nn1657   epn846   pap5225   pr/an,ajn1401

19 While they promise them liberty, they themselves are the servants of

art,nn5356   1063   repro3739   idpro5100   pfip2274   depro5129   (2532)

corruption: for of whom a man is overcome, of the same is he

pfip1402

brought*in*bondage.

1063   1487   apta668   art3588   nn3393   art3588   nn2889   pre1722

20 For if after they have escaped the pollutions of the world through the

an,nn1922   art3588   nn2962   2532   an,nn4990   an,nn2424   an,nn5547   (1161)   ad3825   aptp1707
knowledge of the Lord and Savior Jesus Christ, they are again entangled

depro5125   2532   pinp2274   art3588   ajn2078   pfi1096   pr/an,aj5501   ppro846   art3588
therein, and overcome, the latter end is worse with them than the

nu,ajn4413
beginning.

        1063   ipf2258   cd/an,ajn2909   ppro846   3361   pfin1921   art3588   nn3598
21 For it had been better for them not to have known the way of

art,nn1343   2228   apta1921   ainf1994   pre1537   art3588   an,aj40
righteousness, than, after they have known *it,* to turn from the holy

nn1785   aptp3860   ppro846
commandment delivered unto them.

        1161   pfi4819   ppro846   (art3588)   art3588 an,aj227   nn3942   an,nn2965
☞ 22 But it is happened unto them according to the true proverb, The dog

apta1994/pre1909/art,aj2398/an,nn1829   2532   an,nn5300   aptm3068   pre1519
is turned*to*his*own*vomit*again; and the sow that was washed to her

an,nn2946   an,nn1004
wallowing in the mire.   *(Prov. 26:11)*

Exhortations to Steadfastness

depro5026   nu,aj1208   an,nn1992   an,ajn27   ad2235   pin1125   ppro5213 pre1722   repro3739
3 This second epistle, beloved, I now write unto you; in *both* which I

pin1326   ppro5216 art,aj1506   an,nn1271   pre1722   an,nn5280
stir up your pure minds by*way*of remembrance:

            aifp3415   art3588   nn4487   pfpp4280   pre5259
2 That ye may be mindful of the words which were spoken before by

art3588 an,aj40   nn4396   2532   art3588   nn1785   ppro2257 art3588   nn652   art3588 nn2962
the holy prophets, and of the commandment of us the apostles of the Lord

2532   an,nn4990
and Savior:

        pap1097   depro5124 nu,aj4412   3754   fm2064   pre1909   an,ajn2078 art,nn2250   an,nn1703
3 Knowing this first, that there shall come in the last days scoffers,

ppmp4198   pre2596   ppro848 art,aj2398   an,nn1939
walking after their own lusts,

        2532   pap3004   ad4226   pin2076 art3588   nn1860   ppro846   art,nn3952   1063   pre575/repro3739 art3588
4 And saying, Where is the promise of his coming? for since the

nn3962   ainp2837   an,ajn3956   pin1265   ad3779   pre575   an,nn746
fathers fell asleep, all things continue as *they were* from the beginning of the

an,nn2937
creation.

        1063   depro5124 ppro846   pap2309   pin2990   3754   art3588   nn3056   art,nn2316
5 For this they willingly are*ignorant*of, that by the word of God the

---

☞ **2:22** The dog and pig mentioned in this verse may symbolize temporary external changes resulting from conformity to a false profession of faith. Contrastly, a sheep is designated as the one representing a true believer with a living faith in Jesus Christ (John 10:1–21). This faith is indicated by the fruits of his faith. See note on James 2:14–19.

an,nn3772   ipf2258   ad1597   2532   an,nn1093   pfp4921   pre1537   an,nn5204   2532   pre1223

heavens were of old, and the earth standing out of the water and in the

an,nn5204

water: *(Gen. 1:6-9)*

pre1223/repro3739   art3588   nn2889   ad5119   aptp2626   an,nn5204

☞ 6 Whereby the world that then was, being overflowed with water,

aom622

perished.   *(Gen. 7:11-21)*

1161   art3588   nn3772   2532   art3588   nn1093   ad3568   art3588   ppro846   nn3056   pin1526

7 But the heavens and the earth, which are now, by the same word are

pr/pfpp2343   ppmp5083   an,nn4442   pre1519   an,nn2250   an,nn2920   2532   an,nn684

kept*in*store, reserved unto fire against the day of judgment and perdition

art,aj765   an,nn444

of ungodly men.

1161   an,ajn27   pim2990/3361   (ppro5209)   depro5124   nu,ajn1520   3754   nu3391   an,nn2250

8 But, beloved, be*not*ignorant   of this one thing, that one day *is*

pre3844   an,nn2962   ad5613   nu5507   an,nn2094   2532   nu5507   an,nn2094   ad5613   nu3391   an,nn2250

with the Lord as a thousand years, and a thousand years as one day.

(Ps. 90:4)

art3588   nn2962   pin1019/3756   art,nn1860   ad5613   idpro5100   pinm2233

9 The Lord is*not*slack concerning his promise, as some men count

an,nn1022   235   pin3114   pre1519   ppro2248   3361   ppmp1014   idpro5100

slackness; but is longsuffering to us-ward, not willing that any should

aifm622   235   an,ajn3956   ainf5562   pre1519   an,nn3341

perish, but that all should come to repentance.   *(Hab. 2:3)*

1161   art3588   nn2250   an,nn2962   ft2240   ad5613   an,nn2812   pre1722   an,nn3571   pre1722

☞ 10 But the day of the Lord will come as a thief in the night; in the

repro3739   art3588   nn3772   fm3928   ad4500   1161   an,nn4747

which the heavens shall pass away with*a*great*noise, and the elements shall

fp3089   fptp2741   an,nn1093   2532   2532   art3588   nn2041   pre1722/ppro846

melt with*fervent*heat, the earth also and the works that are therein shall be

fm2618

burned up.

3767   an,aj3956   depro5130   ppmp3089   pr/an,aj4217

11 *Seeing* then *that* all these things shall be dissolved, what manner *of*

pin1163   ppro5209   pinf5225   pre1722   an,aj40   an,nn391   2532   an,nn2150

persons ought ye to be in *all* holy conversation and godliness,

pap4328   2532   pap4692   art3588   nn3952   art3588   nn2250   art,nn2316   pre1223/repro3739

12 Looking for and hasting unto the coming of the day of God, wherein

an,nn3772   ppmp4448   fp3089   2532   an,nn4747   pinp2741

the heavens being*on*fire shall be dissolved, and the elements shall melt

fptm5080

with*fervent*heat?

1161   pre2596   ppro846   art,nn1862   pin4328   an,aj2537   an,nn3772   2532

13 Nevertheless we, according to his promise, look for new heavens and

an,aj2537   an,nn1093   pre1722/repro3739   pin2730   an,nn1343

a new earth, wherein dwelleth righteousness.   *(Is. 65:17; 66:22)*

☞ **3:6, 7** See note on 1 Peter 3:21.
☞ **3:10** See note on 1 Thessalonians 5:2.

14 Wherefore, beloved, seeing that ye look for such things, be diligent that ye may be found of him in peace, without spot, and blameless.

15 And account *that* the longsuffering of our Lord *is* salvation; even as our beloved brother Paul also according to the wisdom given unto him hath written unto you;

16 As also in all *his* epistles, speaking in them of these things; in which are some things hard*to*be*understood, which they*that*are*unlearned and unstable wrest, as *they do* also the other Scriptures, unto their own destruction.

17 Ye therefore, beloved, seeing ye know*these*things*before, beware lest ye also, being*led*away*with the error of the wicked, fall from your own steadfastness.

18 But grow in grace, and *in* the knowledge of our Lord and Savior Jesus Christ. To him *be* glory both now and forever. Amen.

JOHN

The similarities between this epistle and the Gospel of John provide conclusive evidence that the author of 1 John was the Apostle John (see introduction to the Gospel of John). The usage of words like "truth," "light," and phrases like "in the light," and "born of God" in 1 John reveal the significant resemblances in structure, style, and vocabulary to John's Gospel. It is also significant that John's anonymity is evident in his epistles as it was in his gospel (see introduction to John). He never uses his authority as an apostle in substantiating his message, but begins this first epistle much the same way as with the Gospel of John (1 John 1:1, 2, cf. John 1:1, 2, 14). This differs from both Paul's and Peter's writings where they use their authority as apostles of Christ to give weight to their message.

John was writing this epistle to believers, namely to those who were members of the churches of Asia Minor. Because the letter addresses such broad moral topics, it is clear that John's goal was to provide direction for those Christians who faced new challenges to their faith. At this time, there was an emergence of various groups whose teachings opposed Christianity. These people infiltrated the church, and there were many who gave in to their denial of the key fundamentals of Christianity (e.g., Christ's deity and resurrection). As opposition to the believers' faith arose, they were encouraged to continue walking in fellowship with Christ so as to not be drawn into false beliefs (1 John 1:5—2:2).

The Book of 1 John is believed to have been written in approximately A.D. 90. There are several ways that this date can be substantiated. First, there are no references by John to any persecutions of believers. From an examination of church history during the first century A.D., one may observe that there were no significant persecutions on Christians until the reign of the Roman emperor Trajan (A.D. 98–117). Secondly, if the date were closer to A.D. 70, John would certainly had reason to refer to the catastrophic events surrounding the destruction of the city of Jerusalem and the temple. However, an examination of the focus of John's epistle makes it obvious that he is instructing believers concerning the heresies that were being spread among them, not concerning some disaster that had come as a result of political events. Hence, the infiltration of these corrupt ideas that the church was experiencing was most likely from Gentile influences, not Jewish opposition. Thus, this would most certainly place the date of writing much later than A.D. 70.

It has been suggested that this Book of 1 John is divided into four major sections. John seeks first to warn believers concerning indifference to morality and sin (1 John 1:1—2:11). Next, he admonishes concerning a love for the things of the world as opposed to a love for the things of Christ (1 John 2:12–28). A third section deals with importance of the believer exhibiting a pure and righteous love, especially when relating to another brother in Christ (1 John 2:29—3:22). Finally, John reveals that a true faith in Christ as the Son of God is the foundation on which all of Christianity is based (1 John 3:23—4:21).

1
repro3739 ipf2258 pre575   an,nn746   repro3739   pfi191   repro3739
That which was from the beginning, which we have heard, which we
pfi3708   ppro2257 art,nn3788 repro3739   aom2300   2532   ppro2257
have seen with our eyes, which we have looked upon, and our
art,nn5495   aina5584   pre4012 art3588   nn3056   art,nn2222
hands have handled, of the Word of life;

2532   art3588 nn2222   ainp5319   2532   pfi3708   2532   pin3140
2 (For the life was manifested, and we have seen *it,* and bear witness,
2532   pin518   ppro5213   art,aj166   art,nn2222 repro3748 ipf2258 pre4314 art3588   nn3962   2532
and show unto you that eternal life, which was with the Father, and was
ainp5319   ppro2254
manifested unto us;)

repro3739   pfi3708   2532   pfi191   pin518   ppro5213   2443   epn5210   2532
3 That which we have seen and heard declare we unto you, that ye also
psa2192   an,nn2842   pre3326 ppro2257   2532   1161   art,popro2251   art,nn2842   pre3326 art3588   nn3962
may have fellowship with us: and truly our fellowship *is* with the Father,
2532   pre3326 ppro848 art,nn5207 an,nn2424   an,nn5547
and with his Son Jesus Christ.
2532   depro5023   pin1125   ppro5213   2443   ppro5216 art,nn5479   psa5600 pr/pfpp4137
4 And these things write we unto you, that your joy may be full.

"Walk in the Light"

pr/depro3778   2532   pin2076 art3588   nn1860   repro3739   pfi191   pre575   ppro846   2532
☞ 5 This then is the message which we have heard of him, and

☞ **1:5–10** This passage describes God's nature and the relation that man has to God. "God is light" is depicting the essence of His character in holiness and purity (v. 5). To understand this concept, man must examine who God is in relation to who man is. Man is the creation of God and must acknowledge His superiority over him. However, man was created in God's image (Gen. 1:27), a reflection of God Himself. As a result of man's fall into sin, his relationship with God was broken (Rom. 3:10–12, 23; 5:12). In order to restore mankind into fellowship with God, He sent His Son, Jesus Christ, who is also in God's image (though He was not created), to give His life so man could come back into a right relationship with God (see note on Col. 1:15–18). To walk in darkness (v. 6; cf. John 3:19), would be to continue in sin. On the other hand, to walk in light is to have continuous fellowship with God (v. 7; cf. John 8:12).

In this passage, there are three false appeals that man makes against God. First, man claims that he has fellowship with God, but in reality, he is living apart from God in his sin (v. 6). This reveals man's indifference to morality with regards to his relationship to God. John states that in fact, this man does not possess the truth because he has not been cleansed from his sin (v. 7). Secondly, man suggests that he does not even have sin (v. 8). In this attitude is the denial of any consequence for wrong actions by an individual. This is a rejection that there is a sin nature within man at all. On the other hand, if a person will acknowledge his sinfulness, confessing his sin before God (i.e., saying the same thing as God says about sin), then he can receive forgiveness and be brought back to a proper relationship to God. The final plea that man makes is an actual denial that sin is even present in his life. Man essentially says that he is not in any way practicing sin. Even though by His death Christ

(continued on next page)

pin312   ppro5213 3754 art,nn2316 pin2076 pr/an,nn5457 2532 pre1722 ppro846 pin2076 3756   nn4653   an,aj3762

declare unto you, that God is light, and in him is no darkness at all.

1437   asba2036   3754   pin2192   an,nn2842   pre3326 ppro846 2532 pin4043 pre1722   art,nn4655

6 If we say that we have fellowship with him, and walk in darkness, we

pinm5574 2532 pin4160 3756 art3588   nn225

lie, and do not the truth:

1161   1437   psa4043 pre1722 art3588   nn5457   ad5613 epn846 pin2076 pre1722 art3588   nn5457   pin2192

7 But if we walk in the light, as he is in the light, we have

an,nn2842   rcpro240/pre3326   2532 art3588   nn129   an,nn2424 an,nn5547 ppro846 art,nn5207

fellowship one*with*another, and the blood of Jesus Christ his Son

pin2511   ppro2248 pre575 an,aj3956 an,nn266

cleanseth us from all sin.   *(Is. 2:3,5)*

1437   asba2036 3754   pin2192 3756 an,nn266   pin4105   rxpro1438   2532 art3588 nn225

8 If we say that we have no sin, we deceive ourselves, and the truth

pin2076 3756 pre1722 ppro2254

is not in us.

1437   psa3670   ppro2257 art,nn266   pin2076 pr/an,aj4103 2532 pr/an,aj1342 2443   asba863   ppro2254

9 If we confess our sins, he is faithful and just to forgive us *our*

art,nn266 2532   asba2511   ppro2248 pre575 an,aj3956   an,nn93

sins, and to cleanse us from all unrighteousness.   *(Ps. 32:5; Prov. 28:13)*

1437   asba2036 3754   3756   pfi264   pin4160 ppro846 pr/an,nn5583 2532 ppro848

10 If we say that we have not sinned, we make him a liar, and his

art,nn3056 pin2076 3756 pre1722 ppro2254

word is not in us.

ppro3450   an,nn5040   depro5023   pin1125   ppro5213 2443   asba264 3361

2 ☞ My little children, these things write I unto you, that ye sin not.

2532   1437   idpro5100   asba264   pin2192   an,nn3875   pre4314 art3588   nn3962   an,nn2424

And if any man sin, we have an advocate with the Father, Jesus

an,nn5547   an,aj1342

Christ the righteous:

2532 epn846 pin2076   pr/an,nn2434   pre4012 ppro2257 art,nn266 1161 3756 pre4012 art,popro2251 an,ajn3440

2 And he is the propitiation for our sins: and not for ours only,

235 2532 pre4012   art3588 an,aj3650   nn2889

but also for *the sins of* the whole world.

The Believer's Assurance

2532   pre1722/depro5129   pin1097 3754   pfi1097 ppro846 1437   psa5083 ppro848

3 And hereby we do know that we know him, if we keep his

art,nn1785

commandments.

(continued from previous page)
satisfied God's wrath on the believer's sin (1 John 2:1, 2), the sin nature still remains within man.
Therefore, he must realize that there must be a desire to continue in a right relationship with God by
confession of sin.

It is obvious that John is speaking of believers in this passage. He is urging them to seek proper
fellowship with God, realizing that he has been purchased by God through Christ's death on the cross
(1 Cor. 6:20).

☞ 2:1 See note on 1 John 3:6–9.

art,pap3004   pfi1097 ppro846 2532 pap5083 3361 ppro848 art,nn1785 pin2076

4 He*that*saith, I know him, and keepeth not his commandments, is a

pr/an,nn5583 2532 art3588 nn225 pin2076 3756 pre1722 depro5129

liar, and the truth is not in him.

1161 repro3739/302 psa5083 ppro848 art,nn3056 pre1722 depro5129 ad230 art3588 nn26 art,nn2316

5 But whoso keepeth his word, in him verily is the love of God

pfip5048 pre1722/depro5129 pin1097 3754 pin2070 pre1722 ppro846

perfected: hereby know we that we are in him.

art,pap3004 pinf3306 pre1722 ppro846 pin3784 epn848 2532 ad3779 pinf4043

6 He*that*saith he abideth in him ought himself also so to walk,

ad2531 depro1565 aina4043

even as he walked.

Exhortations to Brotherly Love

an,nn80 pin1125 3756 an,aj2537 an,nn1785 ppro5213 235 an,aj3820

7 Brethren, I write no new commandment unto you, but an old

an,nn1785 repro3739 ipf2192 pre575 an,nn746 art3588 aj3820 art,nn1785 pin2076

commandment which ye had from the beginning. The old commandment is

art3588 pr/nn3056 repro3739 aina191 pre575 an,nn746

the word which ye have heard from the beginning.

ad3825 an,aj2537 an,nn1785 pin1125 ppro5213 repro3739 pin2076 pr/an,aj227

8 Again, a new commandment I write unto you, which thing is true

pre1722 ppro846 2532 pre1722 ppro5213 3754 art3588 nn4653 pinm3855 2532 art3588 aj228 art,nn5457 ad2235

in him and in you: because the darkness is past, and the true light now

pin5316

shineth.

art,pap3004 pinf1511 pre1722 art3588 nn5457 2532 pap3404 ppro846 art,nn80 pin2076 pre1722

9 He*that*saith he is in the light, and hateth his brother, is in

art,nn4653 ad2193 ad737

darkness even until now.

art,pap25 ppro848 art,nn80 pin3306 pre1722 art3588 nn5457 2532 pin2076 3756

10 He*that*loveth his brother abideth in the light, and there is none

an,nn4625 pre1722 ppro846

occasion*of*stumbling in him.   *(Ps. 119:165)*

1161 art,pap3404 ppro848 art,nn80 pin2076 pre1722 art,nn4653 2532 pin4043 pre1722

11 But he*that*hateth his brother is in darkness, and walketh in

art,nn4653 2532 pin1492 3756 ad4226 pin5217 3754 art,nn4653

darkness, and knoweth not whither he goeth, because that darkness hath

aina5186 ppro848 art,nn3788

blinded his eyes.

pin1125 ppro5213 an,nn5040 3754 art,nn266 pfip863 ppro5213

12 I write unto you, little children, because your sins are forgiven you

pre1223/ppro848/art,nn3686

for*his*name's*sake.   *(Ps. 25:11)*

pin1125 ppro5213 an,nn3962 3754 pfi1097 art3588 pre575

13 I write unto you, fathers, because ye have known him *that is* from the

an,nn746 pin1125 ppro5213 an,nn3495 3754 pfi3528 art3588

beginning. I write unto you, young men, because ye have overcome the wicked one. I write unto you, little children, because ye have known the Father.

14 I have written unto you, fathers, because ye have known him *that is* from the beginning. I have written unto you, young men, because ye are strong, and the word of God abideth in you, and ye have overcome the wicked one.

"Love Not the World"

15 Love not the world, neither the things *that are* in the world. If any man love the world, the love of the Father is not in him.

16 For all that *is* in the world, the lust of the flesh, and the lust of the eyes, and the pride of life, is not of the Father, but is of the world.   (Prov. 27:20)

17 And the world passeth away, and the lust thereof: but he*that*doeth the will of God abideth forever.   (Is. 24:4)

The Promise of Eternal Life

18 Little children, it is the last time: and as ye have heard that antichrist shall come, even now are there many antichrists; whereby we know that it is the last time.

19 They went out from us, but they were not of us: for if they had been of us, they would *no doubt* have continued with us: but *they went out,* that they might be made manifest that they were not all of us.

20 But ye have an unction from the Holy One, and ye know all things.

21 I have not written unto you because ye know not the truth, but because ye know it, and that no lie is of the truth.

22 ^{inpro5101} Who ^{pin2076} is a ^{pr/art,nn5583} liar ¹⁵⁰⁸ but he*that*denieth ^{art,ppmp720} that Jesus ^{3754 an,nn2424} is ^{pin2076 (3756)} the ^{art3588} Christ? ^{pr/nn5547}

He ^{depro3778} is ^{pin2076} antichrist, ^{pr/art,nn500} that denieth ^{art,ppmp720} the ^{art3588} Father ⁿⁿ³⁹⁶² and ²⁵³² the ^{art3588} Son. ⁿⁿ⁵²⁰⁷

23 Whosoever ^{an,aj3956} denieth ^{art,ppmp720} the ^{art3588} Son, ⁿⁿ⁵²⁰⁷ the same hath ^{pin2192} not ³⁷⁶¹ the ^{art3588} Father: ⁿⁿ³⁹⁶² [but]
he*that*acknowledgeth ^{art,pap3670} the ^{art3588} Son ⁿⁿ⁵²⁰⁷ hath ^{pin2192} the ^{art3588} Father ⁿⁿ³⁹⁶² also. ²⁵³²

24 Let that therefore ³⁷⁶⁷ abide ^{pim3306} in ^{pre1722} you, ^{ppro5213} which ye have heard ^{epn5210} ^{aina191} from the ^{pre575}
beginning. ^{an,nn746} If ¹⁴³⁷ that which ^{repro3739} ye have heard ^{aina191} from ^{pre575} the beginning ^{an,nn746} shall remain ^{asba3306} in ^{pre1722}
you, ^{ppro5213} ye ^{epn5210} also ²⁵³² shall continue ^{ft3306} in ^{pre1722} the ^{art3588} Son, ⁿⁿ⁵²⁰⁷ and ²⁵³² in ^{pre1722} the ^{art3588} Father. ⁿⁿ³⁹⁶²

25 And ²⁵³² this ^{pr/depro3778} is ^{pin2076} the ^{art3588} promise ⁿⁿ¹⁸⁶⁰ that ^{repro3739} he ^{epn846} hath promised ^{aom1861} us, ^{ppro2254} even eternal ^{art,aj166}
life, ^{art,nn2222}

26 These things ^{depro5023} have I written ^{aina1125} unto you ^{ppro5213} concerning ^{pre4012} them*that*seduce ^{art,pap4105}
you. ^{ppro5209}

27 But ²⁵³² the ^{art3588} anointing ⁿⁿ⁵⁵⁴⁵ which ^{repro3739} ye ^{epn5210} have received ^{aina2983} of ^{pre575} him ^{ppro846} abideth ^{pin3306} in ^{pre1722} you, ^{ppro5213}
and ²⁵³² ye need ^{pin2192/an,nn5532} not ³⁷⁵⁶ that ²⁴⁴³ any man ^{idpro5100} teach ^{psa1321} you: ^{ppro5209} but ²³⁵ as ^{ad5613} the ^{art3588} same ^{ppro846} anointing ⁿⁿ⁵⁵⁴⁵
teacheth ^{pin1321} you ^{ppro5209} of ^{pre4012} all things, ^{an,ajn3956} and ²⁵³² is ^{pin2076} truth, ^{pr/an,aj227} and ²⁵³² is ^{pin2076} no ³⁷⁵⁶ lie, ^{pr/an,nn5579} and even as ²⁵³² it ^{ad2531}
hath taught ^{aina1321} you, ^{ppro5209} ye shall abide ^{ft3306} in ^{pre1722} him. ^{ppro846}

28 And ²⁵³² now, ^{ad3568} little children, ^{an,nn5040} abide ^{pim3306} in ^{pre1722} him; ^{ppro846} that, ²⁴⁴³ when ^{ad3752} he shall appear, ^{asbp5319} we
may have ^{psa2192} confidence, ^{an,nn3954} and ²⁵³² not ³³⁶¹ be ashamed ^{asbp153} before ^{pre575} him ^{ppro846} at ^{pre1722} his ^{ppro848} coming. ^{art,nn3952}

29 If ¹⁴³⁷ ye know ^{asba1492} that ³⁷⁵⁴ he is ^{pin2076} righteous, ^{pr/an,aj1342} ye know ^{pin1097} that ³⁷⁵⁴ every one ^{an,aj3956} that doeth ^{art,pap4160}
righteousness ^{art,nn1343} is born ^{pfip1080} of ^{pre1537} him. ^{ppro846}

Evidences of a True Believer

3 Behold, ^{aima1492} what manner ^{an,aj4217} of love ^{an,nn26} the ^{art3588} Father ⁿⁿ³⁹⁶² hath bestowed ^{pfi1325} upon us, ^{ppro2254} that ²⁴⁴³
we should be called ^{asbp2564} the sons ^{pr/an,nn5043} of God: ^{an,nn2316} therefore ^{pre1223/depro5124} the ^{art3588} world ⁿⁿ²⁸⁸⁹ knoweth ^{pin1097}
us ^{ppro2248} not, ³⁷⁵⁶ because ³⁷⁵⁴ it knew ^{aina1097} him ^{ppro846} not. ³⁷⁵⁶

2 Beloved, ^{an,ajn27} now ^{ad3568} are we ^{pin2070} the sons ^{pr/an,nn5043} of God, ^{an,nn2316} and ²⁵³² it doth ^{ad3768} not yet appear ^{ainp5319}

inpro5101   fm2071   1161   pin1492   3754   1437   asba5319   fm2071

what we shall be: but we know that, when he shall appear, we shall be

pr/an,aj3664   ppro846 3754   fm3700 ppro846 ad2531   pin2076

like him; for we shall see him as he is.

2532   an,aj3956   art,pap2192   depro5026 art,nn1680 pre1909 ppro846   pin48   rxpro1438   ad2531

3 And every man that hath this hope in him purifieth himself, even as

depro1565 pin2076 pr/an,aj53

he is pure.

an,aj3956   art,pap4160   art,nn266   pin4160/2532/art,nn458   2532 art,nn266 pin2076

4 Whosoever committeth sin transgresseth*also*the*law. for sin is

art3588   pr/nn458

the transgression*of*the*law.

2532   pin1492   3754   depro1565   ainp5319   2443   asba142   ppro2257 art,nn266 2532 pre1722

5 And ye know that he was manifested to take away our sins; and in

ppro846 pin2076 3756 an,nn266

him is no sin.   *(Is. 53:9)*

an,aj2956   art,pap3306   pre1722   ppro846   pin264   3756   an,aj3956   art,pap264   3756

☞ 6 Whosoever abideth in him sinneth not: whosoever sinneth hath not

pfi3708 ppro846   3761   pfi1097   ppro846

seen him, neither known him.

☞ **3:6–9** In this passage, John examines the question of whether the person "born of God" can commit sin. In verse six, The Apostle writes, "Whosoever abideth in him sinneth not . . . ," and in verse eight, "He that committeth sin is of the devil . . . ." Furthermore, in verse nine there is an emphatic declaration: "Whosoever is of God doth not commit sin . . . and he cannot sin . . . ." If it were possible for a Christian to sin, there would appear to be a contradiction in these portions of Scripture. In this instance, John says if it is not possible for those who are really born again to sin, there must be very few genuine Christians. Man still possesses a fallen, sin nature, as well as the indwelling Holy Spirit. Also, the doctrine of eternal security is evident in Scripture (John 1:12; 10:28; Rom. 8:38, 39). Though they may fall into sin, the believer's sonship is not affected, nor his eternal salvation (see note on 1 Thess. 2:3).

These verse expose two erroneous doctrines: antinomianism and perfectionism. Antinomians (derived from the Greek words *antí* [473], "against," and *nómos* [3551], "law") contend that the covenant of grace was not established based on conditions. The result is man cannot be held accountable to any moral law. It is only required of him that he believe, then he can then live as he pleases. The perfectionists go as far as to say that the sin nature in man has been eradicated as though surgically removed as a cancer. John was warning believers against this form of thinking, that they not continue in sin, but abide in righteousness (vv. 8, 9). Moreover, the Apostle exposes these doctrines in the command, "My little children, these things write I unto you, that ye sin not. And if any man sin, we have an advocate with the Father, Jesus Christ the righteous" (1 John 2:1). This is not the proper rendering of this verse. It should denote the mere action of a sin, not the idea of habitually sinning. John explains that even he was capable of committing sin, not in a habitual sense, but as one particular action. The phrase, used in verse nine, "does not commit sin" is in the present tense denoting continuous action. On the other hand, in chapter two, verse one, John uses the aorist sense, speaking of one point in the past when a sin was committed.

Furthermore, there were those who taught that mere intellectual knowledge was enough to make men acceptable to God, even though they lived impure lives (Perfectionism). Therefore, John reiterates in verse seven that only those who continued in righteousness (*ho poión*, [4160], a participle phrase meaning "the one habitually doing"), were considered righteous. They were not only making the righteousness and holy life of Christ the object of their trust, but also the pattern of their walk and practice.

John's idea of committing sin on a permanent basis is further explained in 3 John 1:11: ". . . He that doeth good is of God: But he that doeth evil hath not seen God." There are two participial nouns in this verse, *ho agathopoión* (215), meaning "the one being a doer of good, a benevolent person,"

(continued on next page)

7 Little children, let no man deceive you: he*that*doeth righteousness is righteous, even as he is righteous.

8 He*that*committeth sin is of the devil; for the devil sinneth from the beginning. For this purpose the Son of God was manifested, that he might destroy the works of the devil.

9 Whosoever is born of God doth not commit sin; for his seed remaineth in him: and he cannot sin, because he is born of God.

10 In this the children of God are manifest, and the children of the devil: whosoever doeth not righteousness is not of God, neither he*that*loveth not his brother.

Love in Deed and Truth

11 For this is the message that ye heard from the beginning, that we should love one another.

12 Not as Cain, *who* was of that wicked one, and slew his brother. And wherefore slew he him? Because his own works were evil, and his brother's righteous.

(Gen. 4:8)

13 Marvel not, my brethren, if the world hate you.

(continued from previous page)
and *ho kakopoión* (2554), referring to "the one doing evil, a malicious person." This is the same usage found in 1 John 3:7: ". . . he that doeth righteousness is righteous . . . ." John does not imply that merely acting good will make one righteous. A man is an artisan who has acquired a skill and works at that trade as his calling or occupation. Hence, the correct translation of 1 John. 3:8 should be, "The one who practices sin." The expression, "he cannot sin," (1 John 3:9) simply means the true believer cannot sin habitually, deliberately, easily and maliciously (e.g., Cain sinned out of hatred of goodness, 1 John 3:12). There is a distinct contrast drawn between divine and human natures of man. John speaks of the divine nature in this abstract way, however, he does not ignore the existence of the sinful nature in the believer, which exists as a mortal in a corrupt world. Consequently, John states in 1 John. 1:8: "If we say that we have no sin, we deceive ourselves, and the truth is not in us."

epn2249 pin1492 3754   pfi3327 pre1537 art,nn2288 pre1519 art,nn2222 3754   pin25

14 We know that we have passed from death unto life, because we love

art3588 nn80 art,pap25 3361 art,nn80 pin3306 pre1722 art,nn2288

the brethren. He*that*loveth not *his* brother abideth in death.

an,aj3956 art,pap3404 ppro848 art,nn80 pin2076 pr/an,ajn443 2532 pin1492 3754

15 Whosoever hateth his brother is a murderer: and ye know that

an,aj3956/3756 an,ajn443 pin2192 an,aj166 an,nn2222 pap3306 pre1722 ppro846

no murderer hath eternal life abiding in him.

pre1722/depro5129 pfi1097 art3588 nn26 (art,nn2316) 3754 depro1565 aina5087

16 Hereby perceive we the love *of God,* because he laid down

ppro848 art,nn5590 pre5228 ppro2257 2532 epn2249 pin3784 pinf5087 art,nn5590 pre5228 art3588

his life for us: and we ought to lay down *our* lives for the

nn80

brethren.

1161 repro3739/302 psa2192 art,nn2889 art,nn979 2532 psa2334 ppro848 art,nn80 pap2192 an,nn5532

17 But whoso hath this world's good, and seeth his brother have need,

2532 asba2808 ppro848 art,nn4698 pre575 ppro846 ad4459 pin3306 art3588 nn26

and shutteth up his bowels *of compassion* from him, how dwelleth the love of

art,nn2316 pre1722 ppro846

God in him?   *(Deut. 15:7,8)*

ppro3450 an,nn5040 3361 psa25 an,nn3056 3366 an,nn1100 235

18 My little children, let us not love in word, neither in tongue; but in

an,nn2041 2532 an,nn225

deed and in truth.

2532 pre1722/depro5129 pin1097 3754 pin2070 pre1537 art3588 nn225 2532 ft3982

19 And hereby we know that we are of the truth, and shall assure

ppro2257 art,nn2588 ad*1715 ppro846

our hearts before him.

3754 1437 ppro2257 art,nn2588 psa2607 (3754) art,nn2316 pin2076 pr/cd/an,aj3187 ppro2257 art,nn2588 2532

20 For if our heart condemn us, God is greater than our heart, and

pin1097 an,ajn3956

knoweth all things.

an,ajn27 1437 ppro2257 art,nn2588 psa2607 ppro2257 3361 pin2192 an,nn3954

21 Beloved, if our heart condemn us not, *then* have we confidence

pre4314 art,nn2316

toward God.

2532 repro3739/1437 psa154 pin2983 pre3844 ppro846 3754 pin5083 ppro848

22 And whatsoever we ask, we receive of him, because we keep his

art,nn1785 2532 pin4160 art,ajn701 ad*1799/ppro846

commandments, and do those*things*that*are*pleasing in* his*sight.

2532 pr/depro3778 pin2076 ppro848 art,nn1785 2443 asba4100 art3588

23 And this is his commandment, That we should believe on the

nn3686 ppro848 art,nn5207 an,nn2424 an,nn5547 2532 psa25 rcpro240 ad2531 aina1325 ppro2254

name of his Son Jesus Christ, and love one another, as he gave us

an,nn1785

commandment.

2532 art,pap5083 ppro848 art,nn1785 pin3306 pre1722 ppro846 2532 ppro846

24 And he*that*keepeth his commandments dwelleth in him, and he

pre1722 ppro846 2532 pre1722/depro5129 pin1097 3754 pin3306 pre1722 ppro2254 pre1537 art3588 nn4151

in him. And hereby we know that he abideth in us, by the Spirit

repro3739 aina1325 ppro2254

which he hath given us.

"Try the Spirits"

4 an,ajn27 pim4100 3361 an,aj3956 an,nn4151 235 pim1381 art3588 nn4151 1487
Beloved, believe not every spirit, but try the spirits whether they
pin2076 pre1537 art,nn2316 3754 an,aj4183 an,nn5578 pfi1831 pre1519 art3588
are of God: because many false prophets are gone out into the
nn2889
world.

pre1722/depro5129 pin1097 art3588 nn4151 art,nn2316 an,aj3956 an,nn4151 repro3739 pin3670
2 Hereby know ye the Spirit of God: Every spirit that confesseth that
an,nn2424 an,nn5547 pfp2064 pre1722 an,nn4561 pin2076 pre1537 art,nn2316
Jesus Christ is come in the flesh is of God:

2532 an,aj3956 an,nn4151 repro3739 pin3670 3361 art,nn2424 an,nn5547 pfp2064 pre1722
☞ 3 And every spirit that confesseth not that Jesus Christ is come in the
an,nn4561 pin2076 3756 pre1537 art,nn2316 2532 depro5124 pin2076 art3588 art,nn500 repro3739
flesh is not of God: and this is that *spirit* of antichrist, whereof ye have
pfi191 3754 pinm2064 2532 ad3568 ad2235 pin2076 pre1722 art3588 nn2889
heard that it should come; and even now already is it in the world.

epn5210 pin2075 pre1537 art,nn2316 an,nn5040 2532 pfi3528 ppro846 3754
4 Ye are of God, little children, and have overcome them: because
pr/cd/an,aj3187 pin2076 art3588 pre1722 ppro5213 2228 art3588 pre1722 art3588 nn2889
greater is he that is in you, than he that is in the world.

epn846 pin1526 pre1537 art3588 nn2889 pre1223/depro5124 pin2980 pre1537 art3588 nn2889 2532 art3588
5 They are of the world: therefore speak they of the world, and the
nn2889 pin191 ppro846
world heareth them.

epn2249 pin2070 pre1537 art,nn2316 art,pap1097 art,nn2316 pin191 ppro2257 repro3739 pin2076
6 We are of God: he*that*knoweth God heareth us; he that is
3756 pre1537 art,nn2316 pin191 3756 ppro2257 pre1537/depro5127 pin1097 art3588 nn4151 art,nn225 2532 art3588
not of God heareth not us. Hereby know we the spirit of truth, and the
nn4151 art,nn4106
spirit of error.

"God is Love"

an,ajn27 psa25 rcpro240 3754 art,nn26 pin2076 pre1537 art,nn2316 2532 an,aj3956
7 Beloved, let us love one another: for love is of God; and every one
art,pap25 pfip1080 pre1537 art,nn2316 2532 pin1097 art,nn2316
that loveth is born of God, and knoweth God.

art,pap25 3361 aina1097 3756 art,nn2316 3754 art,nn2316 pin2076 pr/an,nn26
8 He*that*loveth not knoweth not God; for God is love.

pre1722 depro5129 ainp5319 art3588 nn26 art,nn2316 pre1722 ppro2254 3754
9 In this was manifested the love of God toward us, because that
art,nn2316 pfi649 ppro848 art,aj3439 art,nn5207 pre1519 art3588 nn2889 2443 asba2198 pre1223
God sent his only begotten Son into the world, that we might live through
ppro846
him.

☞ **4:3** See notes on 2 Thessalonians 2:3–9.

pre1722/depro5129 pin2076 art,nn26 3756 3754 epn2249 aina25 art,nn2316 235 3754 epn846 aina25 ppro2248
10 Herein is love, not that we loved God, but that he loved us,

2532 aina649 ppro848 art,nn5207   pr/an,nn2434   pre4012 ppro2257 art,nn266
and sent his Son *to be* the propitiation for our sins.

an,ajn27   1487 art,nn2316 ad3779 aina25 ppro2248 epn2249 pin3784 2532   pinf25   rcpro240
11 Beloved, if God so loved us, we ought also to love one another.

an,ajn3762   pfip2300 an,nn2316   ad4455   1437   psa25   rcpro240   art,nn2316
12 No man hath seen God at*any*time. If we love one another, God

pin3306 pre1722 ppro2254 2532 ppro848 art,nn26 pin2076 pr/pfpp5048 pre1722 ppro2254
dwelleth in us, and his love is perfected in us.

pre1722/depro5129 pin1097   3754   pin3306 pre1722 ppro846 2532 ppro846 pre1722 ppro2254 3754
13 Hereby know we that we dwell in him, and he in us, because he

pfi1325 ppro2254 pre1537 ppro848 art,nn4151
hath given us of his Spirit.

2532 epn2249   pfip2300 2532   pin3140 3754 art3588 nn3962 pfi649 art3588 nn5207
14 And we have seen and do testify that the Father sent the Son *to be*

pr/an,nn4990 art3588 nn2889
the Savior of the world.

repro3739/302   asba2670 3754 an,nn2424 pin2076 art3588 pr/nn5207 art,nn2316 art,nn2316
15 Whosoever shall confess that Jesus is the Son of God, God

pin3306 pre1722 ppro846 2532 ppro846 pre1722 art,nn2316
dwelleth in him, and he in God.

2532 epn2249   pfi1097 2532   pfi4100 art3588 nn26 repro3739 art,nn2316 pin2192 pre1722 ppro2254
16 And we have known and believed the love that God hath to us.

art,nn2316 pin2076 pr/an,nn26 2532   art,pap3306   pre1722 art,nn26 pin3306 pre1722 art,nn2316 2532 art,nn2316
God is love; and he*that*dwelleth in love dwelleth in God, and God

pre1722 ppro846
in him.

pre1722/depro5129 (pre3326) ppro2257 art,nn26 pfip5048   2443   psa2192 an,nn3954
17 Herein is our love made perfect, that we may have boldness

pre1722 art3588 nn2250   art,nn2920   3754   ad2531 depro1565 pin2076 2532 pin2070 epn2249 pre1722 depro5129
in the day of judgment: because as he is, so are we in this

art,nn2889
world.

pin2076 3756 an,nn5401 pre1722 art,nn26 235 art,aj5046 an,nn26 pin906 ad1854
18 There is no fear in love; but perfect love casteth out

art,nn5401 3754 art,nn5401 pin2192 an,nn2851 (1161) art,ppmp5399   3756 pfip5048 pre1722
fear: because fear hath torment. He*that*feareth is not made perfect in

art,nn26
love.

epn2249 pin25 ppro846 3754   epn846 nu,aj4413 aina25 ppro2248
19 We love him, because he first loved us.

1437 idpro5100 asba2036   pin25 art,nn2316 2532 psa3404 ppro848 art,nn80   pin2076 pr/an,nn5583 1063
20 If a man say, I love God, and hateth his brother, he is a liar: for

art,pap25   3361 ppro848 art,nn80 repro3739   pfi3708 ad4459 pinm1410   pinf25 art,nn2316
he*that*loveth not his brother whom he hath seen, how can he love God

repro3739   3756 pfi3708
whom he hath not seen?

2532 depro5026   art,nn1785   pin2192   pre575 ppro846 2443   art,pap25   art,nn2316
21 And this commandment have we from him, That he*who*loveth God

psa25 ppro848 art,nn80 2532
love his brother also.

The Believer's Victory

5 Whosoever believeth that Jesus is the Christ is born of God: and every one that loveth him*that*begat loveth him*also*that*is*begotten of him.

2 By this we know that we love the children of God, when we love God, and keep his commandments.

3 For this is the love of God, that we keep his commandments: and his commandments are not grievous.   *(Ex. 20:6; Deut. 5:10)*

4 For whatsoever is born of God overcometh the world: and this is the victory that overcometh the world, *even* our faith.

5 Who is he*that*overcometh the world, but he*that*believeth that Jesus is the Son of God?

6 This is he*that*came by water and blood, *even* Jesus Christ; not by water only, but by water and blood. And it is the Spirit that*beareth*witness, because the Spirit is truth.

7 For there are three that*bear*record in heaven, the Father, the Word, and the Holy Ghost: and these three are one.

8 And there are three that*bear*witness in earth, the spirit, and the water, and the blood: and these three agree in one.

9 If we receive the witness of men, the witness of God is greater: for this is the witness of God which he hath testified of his Son.

10 He*that*believeth on the Son of God hath the witness in himself: he*that*believeth not God hath made him a liar; because he believeth not the record that God gave of his Son.

2532 pr/depro3778 pin2076 art3588　nn3141　3754 art,nn2316　aina1325　pppro2254 an,aj166　an,nn2222
11 And this is the record, that God hath given to us eternal life,

2532 depro3778 art,nn2222 pin2076 pre1722 ppro848 art,nn5207
and this life is in his Son.

art,pap2192　art3588　nn5207 pin2192　art,nn2222　art,pap2192　3361 art3588　nn5207
12 He*that*hath the Son hath life: *and* he*that*hath not the Son of

art,nn2316 pin2192 3756 art,nn2222
God hath not life.

God Answers Prayer

depro5023　aina1125　ppro5213 art,pap4100　pre1519 art3588　nn3686
13 These things have I written unto you that believe on the name of

art3588 nn5207　art,nn2316 2443　psa1492　3754　pin2192 an,aj166　an,nn2222 2532 2443
the Son of God; that ye may know that ye have eternal life, and that ye may

psa4100　pre1519 art3588　nn3686　art3588 nn5207 art,nn2316
believe on the name of the Son of God.

2532 pr/depro3778 pin2076 art3588　nn3954　repro3739 pin2192 pre4314 ppro846　3754 1437 psa154
14 And this is the confidence that we have in him, that, if we ask

idpro5100　pre2596　ppro848 art,nn2307　pin191 ppro2257
any thing according to his will, he heareth us:

2532 1437　psa1492　3754　pin191 ppro2257　repro3739/302　psa154　pin1492 3754
15 And if we know that he hear us, whatsoever we ask, we know that

pin2192 art3588　nn155　repro3739　pfi154　pre3844 ppro846
we have the petitions that we desired of him.

1437　idpro5100　asba1492 ppro848　art,nn80　pap264　an,nn266　3361 pre4314
16 If any man see his brother sin a sin *which is* not unto

an,nn2288　ft154　2532　ft1325 ppro846 an,nn2222　art,pap264　3361
death, he shall ask, and he shall give him life for them*that*sin not

pre4314 an,nn2288　pin2076　an,nn266 pre4314 an,nn2288　3756 pin3004 2443　asba2065 pre4012
unto death. There is a sin unto death: I do not say that he shall pray for

depro1565
it.

an,aj3956　an,nn93　pin2076 pr/an,nn266 2532　pin2076　an,nn266 3756 pre4314
17 All unrighteousness is sin: and there is a sin not unto

an,nn2288
death.

pin1492　3754　an,aj3956　art,pfpp1080 pre1537 art,nn2316　pin264　3756 235
18 We know that whosoever is born of God sinneth not; but

art,aptp1080　pre1537 art,nn2316　pin5083　rxpro1438 2532　art,ajn4190　pinm680
he*that*is*begotten of God keepeth himself, and that wicked one toucheth

ppro846 3756
him not.

pin1492　3754　pin2070 pre1537 art,nn2316 2532 art3588　an,aj3650　nn2889 pinm2749 pre1722
19 *And* we know that we are of God, and the whole world lieth in

art,ajn4190
wickedness.

1161　pin1492　3754 art3588 nn5207　art,nn2316　pin2240 2532　pfi1325 ppro2254
20 And we know that the Son of God is come, and hath given us an

^{an,nn1271} ²⁴⁴³ ^{psa1097} ^{art,ajn228} ²⁵³² ^{pin2070} ^{pre1722}

understanding, that we may know him*that*is*true, and we are in

^{art,ajn228} ^{pre1722} ^{ppro848} ^{art,nn5207} ^{an,nn2424} ^{an,nn5547} ^{pr/depro3778} ^{pin2076} ^{art3588} ^{aj228} ^{an,nn2316}

him*that*is*true, *even* in his Son Jesus Christ. This is the true God,

²⁵³² ^{an,aj166} ^{art,nn2222}

and eternal life.

^{an,nn5040} ^{aima5442} ^{rxpro1438} ^{pre575} ^{art,nn1497} ²⁸¹

21 Little children, keep yourselves from idols. Amen.

The Second Epistle of

JOHN

The Apostle John is unmistakably the author of this book (see introduction to 1 John). It was probably written about the same time as the Book of 1 John (A.D. 85–90) and may have been addressed to some of the same people. The "elect lady and her children" (2 John 1:1) may be a reference to an actual lady and her children, but many scholars contend that this is a cryptic way of addressing a church to safeguard against the letter falling into the hands of those who were hostile to the Church.

The purpose of the book was to warn against false teachers who commonly traveled from church to church spreading heresy. John instructed that these people should not even receive ordinary hospitality from those in the church (2 John 1:10, 11). Another objective of the Book of 2 John was to inform the recipients of his plans to visit them soon. This is also given as the reason for the brevity of the letter (2 John 1:12).

1
art3588 ajn4245   an,aj1588 an,nn2959 2532 ppro848   art,nn5043   repro3739 epn1473 pin25 pre1722
The elder unto the elect lady and her children, whom I love in the
an,nn225   2532   3756   epn1473 an,aj3441   235   2532   an,aj3956   art,pfp1097   art3588
truth; and not I only, but also all they*that*have*known the
nn225
truth;

pre1223/art3588/nn225   art,pap3306   pre1722 ppro2254 2532   fm2071 pre3326 ppro2257
2 For*the*truth's*sake, which dwelleth in us, and shall be with us
pre1519/art,nn165
forever.

an,nn5485 fm2071 pre3326 ppro5216 an,nn1656   an,nn1515   pre3844 an,nn2316   an,nn3962   2532 pre3844
3 Grace be with you, mercy, *and* peace, from God the Father, and from
an,nn2962 an,nn2424 an,nn5547 art3588 nn5207   art3588   nn3962   pre1722 an,nn225 2532 an,nn26
the Lord Jesus Christ, the Son of the Father, in truth and love.

"Love One Another"

aina5463   ad3029   3754   pfi2147   pre1537 ppro4675 art,nn5043   pap4043   pre1722 an,nn225 ad2531
4 I rejoiced greatly that I found of thy children walking in truth, as
aina2983   an,nn1785   pre3844 art3588   nn3962
we have received a commandment from the Father.
2532   ad3568   pin2065   ppro4571 an,nn2959 3756   ad5613   pap1125   an,aj2537
5 And now I beseech thee, lady, not as though I wrote a new
an,nn1785   ppro4671 235   repro3739   ipf2192 pre575   an,nn746   2443
commandment unto thee, but that which we had from the beginning, that we
psa25   rcpro240
love one another.
2532 pr/depro3778 pin2076 art,nn26 2443   psa4043 pre2596 ppro848   art,nn1785   pr/depro3778
6 And this is love, that we walk after his commandments. This

pin2076 art3588   nn1785   (2443)   ad2531   aina191   pre575   an,nn746

is the commandment, That, as ye have heard from the beginning, ye should

psa4043 pre1722 ppro846

walk in it.

Exhortation to Steadfastness

3754   an,aj4183   an,nn4108   aina1525   pre1519 art3588   nn2889   art,pap3670   3361

☞ 7 For many deceivers are entered into the world, who confess not that

an,nn2424 an,nn5547   ppmp2064 pre1722   an,nn4561   pr/depro3778 pin2076   art,nn4108   2532   art,nn500

Jesus Christ is come in the flesh. This is a deceiver and an antichrist.

pim991   rxpro1438   2443   asba622 3361   repro3739

8 Look to yourselves, that we lose not those things which we have

aom2038   235   asba618   an,aj4134   an,nn3408

wrought, but that we receive a full reward.

an,aj3956   art,pap3845   2532   pap3306   3361 pre1722 art3588   nn1322   art,nn5547

9 Whosoever transgresseth, and abideth not in the doctrine of Christ,

pin2192 3756 an,nn2316   art,pap3306   pre1722 art3588   nn1322   art,nn5547 depro3778 pin2192 2532 art3588

hath not God. He*that*abideth in the doctrine of Christ, he hath both the

nn3962   2532 art3588 nn5207

Father and the Son.

idpro1536/pinm2064   pre4314 ppro5209 2532   pin5342 3756 depro5026   art,nn1322   pim2983   ppro846

10 If*there*come*any unto you, and bring not this doctrine, receive him

3361 pre1519   an,nn3614   2532/3361 pim3004 ppro846   pinf5463

not into *your* house, neither bid him God speed:

1063   art,pap3004   ppro846   pinf5463   pin2841   ppro848 art,aj4190 art,nn2041

11 For he*that*biddeth him God speed is partaker of his evil deeds.

pap2192   an,ajn4183   pinf1125   ppro5213   ainp1014 3756   pre1223 an,nn5489

12 Having many things to write unto you, I would not *write* with paper

2532   an,nn3188 235   pin1679   ainf2064   pre4314 ppro5209 2532   ainf2980 an,nn4750/pre4314/an,nn4750 2532 ppro2257

and ink: but I trust to come unto you, and speak face*to*face, that our

art,nn5479   psa5600 pr/pfpp4137

joy may be full.   *(Num. 12:7)*

art3588   nn5043   ppro4675 art,aj1588 art,nn79 pinm782 ppro4571   281

13 The children of thy elect sister greet thee. Amen.

☞ 1:7 See note on 2 Thessalonians 2:3–9.

The Third Epistle of

JOHN

The Book of 3 John was written by the Apostle John who calls himself "the elder." It is closely related to the books of 1 and 2 John (see introductions to these books) in that they deal with similar subjects and were all written about the same time (ca. A.D. 85–90). John addressed this letter to Gaius who was a leader in the congregation of a church that John had most likely helped to establish. The purpose of this epistle was to encourage Gaius to continue to help those who were spreading the gospel and teaching the truth (3 John 1:5–8). John also wanted to express his displeasure about the offensive behavior of Diotrephes who refused to accept John and was mistreating other believers (3 John 1:9). Furthermore, he revealed his intention to visit the church there himself and reprove this proud, selfish, and indifferent man (3 John 1:10).

1
⚷ The elder unto the wellbeloved Gaius, whom I love in the
art3588 ajn4245 art3588 aj27 an,nn1050 repro3739 epn1473 pin25 pre1722

truth.
an,nn225

⚷ 2 Beloved, I wish above all things that thou mayest prosper and
an,ajn27 pinm2172 pre4012 an,ajn3956 ppro4571 pifm2137 2532

be*in*health, even as thy soul prospereth.
pinf5198 ad2531 ppro4675 art,nn5590 pinm2137

3 For I rejoiced greatly, when the brethren came and testified
1063 aina5463 ad3029 an,nn80 ppmp2064 2532 pap3140

⚷ **1:1** Originally from Macedonia, Gaius was one of Paul's companions who was caught during a riot in Ephesus (Acts 19:29). He was also among those who accompanied Paul to Jerusalem, perhaps as an official delegate of his church in Derbe, and was a member of the party which awaited the Apostle at Troas (Acts 20:4, 5). He was baptized by Paul in Corinth (1 Cor. 1:14). His house was used as a regular meeting place for the congregation; in fact, Paul stayed with him during one of his visits to Corinth (Rom. 16:23). John is commending Gaius for his good hospitality, as well as expressing his desire to see him shortly (3 John 1:14).

⚷ **1:2** There are some who misapply this verse to mean that God's will for His children is to always prosper and be in good health, which would give credence to the belief in a "health and wealth gospel." However, the writer is conveying nothing more than a wish to Gaius that this letter might find him well and in good health.

There are several words in this verse mistranslated in the KJV. For instance, the preposition *perí* (4012) should be rendered "concerning" or "about," rather than "above." John states that prosperity and wealth should not be considered the important priorities of one's life. The idea of mere wishing is expressed by the verb *eúchomai* (2172), not of a promise given by an Apostle to a fellow believer. The word translated "prosper" is *euodoústhai* (a present infinitive from *euodóō* [2137]). Essentially, this word means to have a good and safe journey throughout one's life (cf. Rom. 1:10). In 1 Corinthians 16:2, Paul used it in regard to the giving benevolence to the church. Although it is translated ". . . that thou mayest prosper . . . ," one should accept the idea that prospering necessarily means to gain riches. Rather, one should understand that the Lord will make sufficient provision for the believer, and the idea of wealth should not be interpreted here. The third word of importance in this verse is *hugiaínein* (5198), "to be healthy." Likewise, this is not a guarantee that Gaius is going to be healthy, but simply expresses a wish.

art3588   nn225   ppro4675   ad2531   epn4771   pin4043   pre1722   an,nn225
of   the   truth   that   is   in   thee,   even   as   thou   walkest   in   the   truth.

pin2192 3756 cd/an,aj3186 an,nn5479 (depro5130) 2443 psa191   art,popro1699 an,nn5043 pap4043 pre1722
4 I   have   no   greater   joy   than   to   hear   that   my   children   walk   in

an,nn225
truth.

Concerning Helping Others

an,ajn27   pin4160   an,ajn4103   repro3739/1437   asbm2038 pre1519 art3588   nn80
5 Beloved, thou doest faithfully whatsoever thou doest   to   the brethren,

2532 pre1519   art,ajn3581
and   to   strangers;

repro3739   aina3140   ppro4675   art,nn26   ad*1799   an,nn1577   repro3739
6 Which have borne witness of   thy   charity before the church: whom

apta4311   ad1516/art,nn2316   ft4160
if   thou   bring*forward*on*their*journey   after*a*godly*sort,   thou   shalt   do

ad2573
well:

1063   pre5228/ppro846/art,nn3686   aina1831   pap2983   an,ajn3367   pre575
7 Because that for*his*name's*sake they went forth, taking nothing of

art3588   nn1484
the Gentiles.

epn2249   3767   pin3784   pinf618   art,ajn5108 2443   psmp1096   pr/an,ajn4904
8 We therefore ought to receive such, that we might   be   fellowhelpers to

art3588   nn225
the truth.

aina1125   art3588   nn1577   235   an,nn1361
☞ 9 I   wrote   unto   the   church: but   Diotrephes,

art,pap5383   ppro848   pinm1926   ppro2248 3756
who*loveth*to*have*the*preeminence among them, receiveth   us   not.

pre1223/depro5124   1437   asba2064   ft5279   ppro846 art,nn2041 repro3739   pin4160
10 Wherefore,   if   I   come,   I   will   remember   his   deeds   which he doeth,

pap5396   ppro2248   an,aj4190   an,nn3056   2532 3361   ppmp714   pre1909/depro5125   3777
prating against   us   with malicious words: and not content therewith, neither

epn848   pinm1926 art3588   nn80   2532   pin2967   art,ppmp1014   2532
doeth   he   himself receive the brethren, and forbiddeth them*that*would, and

pin1544   pre1537 art3588   nn1577
casteth   *them*   out of the church.

an,ajn27   pim3401   3361   art,ajn2556   235   art,ajn18
11 Beloved,   follow   not   that*which*is*evil,   but   that*which*is*good.

art,pap15   pin2076 pre1537 art,nn2316   1161   art,pap2554   3756   pfi3708
He*that*doeth*good   is   of   God: but he*that*doeth*evil hath not seen

art,nn2316
God.

☞ **1:9** Diotrephes was an ambitious person who resisted the authority of the elders in the church. He attacked them publicly, and forbade the reception of John and his adherents. Also, whether by formal excommunication or physical violence, he excluded those who received them.

an,nn1216   pfip3140   pre5259 an,aj3956   2532   pre5259 art3588   nn225   ppro846

12 Demetrius hath*good*report of all *men*, and of the truth itself:

1161   2532   epn2249   pin3140   2532   pin1492   3754   ppro2257   art,nn3141   pin2076 pr/an,aj227

yea, and we *also* bear record; and ye know that our record is true.

Benediction

ipf2192   an,ajn4183   pinf1125   235   pin2309 3756   pre1223 an,nn3188 2532 an,nn2563 ainf1125

13 I had many things to write, but I will not with ink and pen write unto

ppro4671

thee:

1161   pin1679   ad2112   ainf1492 ppro4571 2532   ft2980   an,nn4750/pre4314/an,nn4750

14 But I trust I shall shortly see thee, and we shall speak face*to*face.

an,nn1515   ppro4671   art,ajn5384   pinm782 ppro4571 pim782   art3588   ajn5384   pre2596 an,nn3686

Peace *be* to thee. *Our* friends salute thee. Greet the friends by name.

(Num. 12:8)

The Epistle of
JUDE

The author of this letter is identified as "Jude, the servant of Jesus Christ, and brother of James" (Jude 1:1). In the early church, there was only one James who could be referred to in this way without further specification; namely, "James, the Lord's brother" (Gal. 1:19, see introduction to James). This Jude was most likely the same one who is listed as one of the half-brothers of the Lord Jesus (Matt. 13:55; Mark 6:3; Acts 1:13).

There are differing views concerning the recipients of the Book of Jude. Some scholars feel that he wrote to believers in the churches of Asia Minor, to whom also the Book of 2 Peter was directed. Others support the view that Jude wrote to believers in Palestine who would have been familiar with the references to Jewish history (Jude 1:7–11).

Little is known of the circumstances of those to whom Jude addresses this letter, and no one knows the precise time when the book was written. It has been suggested that the Book of 2 Peter sparked the ideas that Jude wrote in his epistle (2 Pet. 2:1—3:3, cf. Jude 1:3–18). Consequently, Jude is thought to have written this book after Peter's death, but before the destruction of Jerusalem (A.D. 70).

Both Peter and Jude were alarmed at the great number of false teachers that were being accepted in the churches (see introduction to 2 Peter). Serious apostasy, similar to the one of which Paul had spoken (cf. Acts 20:29–31), seems to have been prevalent in Jude's day (Jude 1:4). Therefore, Jude urged these believers to "earnestly contend for the faith which was once delivered unto the saints" (Jude 1:3).

1
an,nn2455 · an,ajn1401 · an,nn2424 · an,nn5547 · 1151 · an,nn80 · an,nn2385
Jude, the servant of Jesus Christ, and brother of James, to
art,pfpp37 · pre1722 an,nn2316 · an,nn3962 · 2532 · pfpp5083 · an,nn2424
them*that*are*sanctified by God the Father, and preserved in Jesus
an,nn5547 · an,ajn2822
Christ, *and* called.

an,nn1656 · ppro5213 2532 · an,nn1515 · 2532 · an,nn26 · opt4129
2 Mercy unto you, and peace, and love, be multiplied.

Warnings from History to the Ungodly

an,ajn27 · ppmp4160 an,aj3956 · an,nn4710 · pinf1125 · ppro5213 pre4012 art3588
3 Beloved, when I gave all diligence to write unto you of the
aj2839 · an,nn4991 · aina2192/an,nn318 · ainf1125 · ppro5213 · pap3870
common salvation, it was needful for me to write unto you, and exhort *you* that
pifm1864 · art3588 nn4102 · nu,ad530 aptp3860 · art3588
ye should earnestly*contend*for the faith which was once delivered unto the
ajn40
saints.

1063
4 For   there   are   idpro5100   an,nn444   aina3921
4 For   there   are   certain   men   crept*in*unawares,

pr/art,pfpp4270/ad3819   pre1519 depro5124   art,nn2917   pr/an,ajn765   pr/pap3346
who*were*before*of*old*ordained to   this   condemnation, ungodly men, turning

art3588   nn5485   ppro2257 art,nn2316 pre1519   an,nn766   2532   pr/ppmp720 art3588 an,aj3441 nn1203 an,nn2316
the grace of our   God into lasciviousness, and denying the   only   Lord God,

2532   ppro2257 an,nn2962 an,nn2424   an,nn5547
and our   Lord Jesus Christ.

(1161)   pinm1014   ainf5279/ppro5209   ppro5209   nu,ad530   pfp1492
5 I   will   therefore   put*you*in*remembrance,   though   ye   once   knew

depro5124   3754   art3588   nn2962   apta4982   an,nn2992   pre1537   an,nn1093   an,nn125
this, how that the Lord, having saved the people out of the   land   of Egypt,

art,nu,ajn1208   aina622   art,apta4100   3361
afterward destroyed them*that*believed not.   *(Ex. 12:51; Num. 14:29,30,35)*

5037   an,nn32   art,apta5083   3361   rxpro1438   art,nn746   235   apta620   art,aj2398
6 And the angels which kept not their first estate, but   left   their   own

an,nn3613   pfi5083   an,aj126   an,nn1199   pre5259   an,nn2217   pre1519
habitation, he hath reserved in everlasting chains under darkness unto the

an,nn2920   an,aj3173 an,nn2250
judgment of the great day.

ad5613   an,nn4670   2532   an,nn1116   2532   art3588   nn4172   pre4012   ppro846
7 Even   as   Sodom   and   Gomorrah,   and   the   cities   about   them

art,aj3664/an,nn5158   (depro5125)   apta1608   2532   apta565   ad3694
in*like*manner,   giving*themselves*over*to*fornication,   and   going   after

an,aj2087   an,nn4561   pinm4295   an,nn1164   pap5254   an,nn1349   an,aj166
strange flesh, are set forth for an example, suffering the vengeance of eternal

an,nn4442
fire.   *(Gen. 19:4-25)*

ad3668   2532   depro3778   ppmp1797   pin3392   an,nn4561 (3303)   pin114   an,nn2963
8 Likewise also these *filthy* dreamers defile the flesh,   despise dominion,

1161   pin987   an,nn1391
and speak*evil*of dignities.

1161   3413   art3588   nn743   ad3753   ppmp1252   art3588   ajn1228   ipf1256
☞ **9** Yet Michael the archangel, when contending with the   devil he disputed

pre4012   art3588   nn4983   an,nn3475   aina5111   3756   ainf2018   an,nn988   an,nn2920   235
about the body of Moses, durst not bring against him a railing accusation, but

aina2036   an,nn2962   opt2008   ppro4671
said, The Lord rebuke thee.   *(Dan. 10:13,21; 12:1; Zech. 3:2)*

1161   depro3778   pin987   an,ajn3745   (3303)   pin1492   3756   1161   an,ajn3745
10 But these speak*evil*of those things which they know not: but what

pinm1987   ad5447   ad5613   art,aj249   an,nn2226   pre1722   depro5125
they   know   naturally,   as   brute   beasts,   in   those   things   they

pinm5351
corrupt themselves.

☞ **1:9** This records an otherwise unknown incident of a dispute between Michael the archangel and the devil concerning the burial of Moses' body. Jude related this incident to tell us that the archangel Michael did not bring a railing accusation against the devil, but said, "The Lord rebuke you." He wanted to show that neither believers nor angels will be able to put the devil out of commission, but that the time of his demise will soon come. It is said of him in Revelation 20:2 that he will be bound for a thousand years during Christ's millennial kingdom, and that finally, he is going to be cast into the lake of fire and brimstone (Rev. 20:10).

11 Woe unto them! for they have gone in the way of Cain, and ran*greedily*after the error of Balaam for reward, and perished in the gainsaying of Korah.   *(Gen. 4:3-8; Num. 22:7; 31:16; 16:19-35)*

12 These are spots in your feasts*of*charity, when they feast with you, feeding themselves without fear: clouds *they are* without water, carried about of winds; trees whose*fruit*withereth, without fruit, twice dead, plucked*up*by*the*roots;   *(Ezek. 34:8)*

13 Raging waves of the sea, foaming out their own shame; wandering stars, to whom is reserved the blackness of darkness forever.

(Is. 57:20)

☞ 14 And Enoch also, the seventh from Adam, prophesied of these, saying, Behold, the Lord cometh with ten thousands of his saints,

(Deut. 33:2; Zech. 14:5)

15 To execute judgment upon all, and to convince all that*are*ungodly among them of all their ungodly deeds which they have ungodly committed, and of all their hard *speeches* which ungodly sinners have spoken against him.

16 These are murmurers, complainers, walking after their own lusts; and their mouth speaketh great swelling *words,* having*men's*persons*in*admiration because of advantage.

☞ **1:14–16** In this passage, Jude quotes from the apocryphal Book of Enoch. Although this book was not included in the canon of Scripture, early church historians wrote that the church accepted it as a valid source of information. Therefore, it is plausible to conclude that Jude, writing under the inspiration of the Holy Spirit, used this prophecy of Enoch as a means of describing those false teachers who sought to lead astray believers from the true faith in Christ.

For some time this passage was the chief reason for the Book of Jude's rejection into the canon of Scripture. However, by the fourth century A.D., Jude's letter had been fully accepted by the entire church.

"Keep Yourselves in the Love of God"

¹¹⁶¹   ^{an,ajn27}   ^{aipp3415}   ^{epn5210} ^{art3588}   ⁿⁿ⁴⁴⁸⁷   ^{art,pfpp4280}

17 But, beloved, remember ye the words which*were*spoken*before
^{pre5259} ^{art3588}   ⁿⁿ⁶⁵²   ^{ppro2257} ^{art,nn2962} ^{an,nn2424}   ^{an,nn5547}

of the apostles of our Lord Jesus Christ;

³⁷⁵⁴   ^{ipf3004} ^{ppro5213}   ⁽³⁷⁵⁴⁾   ^{fm2071}   ^{an,nn1703}   ^{pre1722}   ^{cd/an,aj2078} ^{an,nn5550}

18 How that they told you there should be mockers in the last time,
^{ppmp4198} ^{pre2596}   ^{art,rxpro438}   ^{an,nn763}   ^{an,nn1939}

who should walk after their own ungodly lusts.

^{depro3778}   ^{pin1526}   ^{pr/art,pap592}   ^{rxpro1438}   ^{pr/an,aj5591}   ^{pr/pap2192}   ³³⁶¹

19 These be they*who*separate themselves, sensual, having not the
^{an,nn4151}

Spirit.

¹¹⁶¹   ^{epn5210}   ^{an,ajn27}   ^{pap2026}   ^{rxpro1438}   ^{ppro5216}   ^{cd/art,aj40}   ^{an,nn4102}

20 But ye, beloved, building up yourselves on your most holy faith,
^{ppmp4336}   ^{pre1722}   ^{an,aj40}   ^{an,nn4151}

praying in the Holy Ghost,

^{aima5083}   ^{rxpro1438}   ^{pre1722}   ^{an,nn26}   ^{an,nn2316}   ^{ppmp4327}   ^{art3588}   ⁿⁿ¹⁶⁵⁶   ^{ppro2257}

21 Keep yourselves in the love of God, looking for the mercy of our
^{art,nn2962} ^{an,nn2424} ^{an,nn5547} ^{pre1519}   ^{an,aj166}   ^{an,nn2222}

Lord Jesus Christ unto eternal life.

²⁵³²   ^{repro3739/3303}   ^{pim1653}   ^{ppmp1252}

22 And of some have compassion, making*a*difference:

¹¹⁶¹   ^{repro3739}   ^{pim4982}   ^{pre1722}   ^{an,nn5401}   ^{pap726}   ^{pre1537}   ^{art3588}   ⁿⁿ⁴⁴⁴²   ^{pap3404}   ²⁵³²

23 And others save with fear, pulling *them* out of the fire; hating even
^{art3588}   ⁿⁿ⁵⁵⁰⁹   ^{pfpp4696}   ^{pre575} ^{art3588}   ⁿⁿ⁴⁵⁶¹

the garment spotted by the flesh.   *(Amos 4:11; Zech. 3:2)*

¹¹⁶¹   ^{art,ppmp1410}   ^{ainf5442} ^{ppro5209}   ^{an,aj679}   ²⁵³²   ^{ainf2476}

24 Now unto him*that*is*able to keep you from falling, and to present *you*
^{pr/an,aj299}   ^{ad*2714}   ^{ppro848} ^{art,nn1391} ^{pre1722}   ^{an,nn20}

faultless before*the*presence of his glory with exceeding joy,
^{an,aj3441} ^{an,aj4680} ^{an,nn2316} ^{ppro2257}   ^{an,nn4990}   ^{an,nn1391}   ²⁵³²   ^{an,nn3172}   ^{an,nn2904}   ²⁵³²

25 To the only wise God our Savior, *be* glory and majesty, dominion and
^{an,nn1849}   ²⁵³²   ^{ad3568}   ²⁵³²   ^{pre1519/an,aj3956/art,nn165}   ²⁸¹

power, both now and ever. Amen.   *(Job 36:5)*

THE REVELATION
to John

The author of the Book of Revelation is the Apostle John (Rev. 1:1, 9; 21:2; 22:8; see the introductions to John's Gospel and 1 John). The title of the book describes the content and purpose of John's writing. The word "Revelation" means "to take the cover off," from the Greek word *apokálupsis* (602). It is the uncovering or unveiling of the glory of Christ and of future events (1 Thess. 1:19).

Revelation was addressed to the churches of Asia Minor (Rev. 1:4) mentioned in chapters two and three. This book was written at a time when these churches were undergoing persecution and difficulty. The two most important such periods were during the reigns of Nero in A.D. 37–68 and Domitian in A.D. 51–96.

There are four views on the interpretation of the Book of Revelation. The first is the preterist view. It places the events and visions described as belonging to the past, particularly to the Roman Empire of the first century A.D. The proponents of this view explain the highly symbolic nature of the book as John's endeavor to hide the real meaning of what he was saying from the general populace, making it relative to the believers who lived at that time. They also consider the main purpose of this writing was encouragement for believers regarding God's ultimate intervention in the affairs of men. It is very unlikely that this view is correct in light of the prophetic nature of the book (Rev. 1:3). Some of the descriptions are of future events and cannot possibly be identified as historical ones.

The second view is the historical view, maintaining that Revelation is a panoramic view of history from the first century A.D. to the Second Coming of Christ. However, this position is unsubstantiated because historians have been unable to identify precise events in history which would answer particular visions that are symbolized.

The third view is the symbolic (allegorical) view which contends that Revelation portrays the continuing conflict between the forces of good and evil throughout the span of human history. According to this view, the book was designed to give encouragement because good will triumph in the end.

The fourth view is the futuristic view, maintaining that from chapter four to the end of the book, Revelation deals with end-time events. According to this view, Revelation is not concerned with the events of John's own day as much as later historical events, particularly those things that will take place in connection with the Second Coming of Christ. The proponents of this view would outline Revelation as follows (cf. Rev. 1:19): chapter one deals with the past; chapters two and three discuss things that were present at that time and throughout the church age; chapters four through twenty-two speak of things that are yet to come, which things include the "Day of the Lord" as well as the Second Coming of Christ (cf. Rev. 4:1).

1

an,nn602 an,nn2424 an,nn5547 repro3739 art,nn2316 aina1325 ppro846 ainf1166

☞ The Revelation of Jesus Christ, which God gave unto him, to show

ppro848 art,ajn1401 repro3739 pin1163 pre1722/an,nn5034 aifm1096

unto his servants things which must shortly come*to*pass;

2532 apta649 aina4591 pre1223 ppro848 art,nn32 ppro848 art,ajn1401 an,nn2491

and he sent and signified *it* by his angel unto his servant John:

(Dan. 2:28,29,45)

repro3739 aina3140 art3588 nn3056 art,nn2316 2532 art3588 nn3141 an,nn2424

2 Who bare record of the word of God, and of the testimony of Jesus

an,nn5547 5037 an,ajn3745 aina1492

Christ, and of all*things*that he saw.

pr/an,aj3107 art,pap314 2532 art,pap191 art3588 nn3056

3 Blessed *is* he*that*readeth, and they*that*hear the words of this

art,nn4394 2532 pap5083 art,pfpp1125 pre1722/ppro846 1063 art3588 nn2540

prophecy, and keep those*things*which*are*written therein: for the time *is*

pr/ad1451

at hand.

"To The Seven Churches"

an,nn2491 art3588 nu2033 nn1577 art3588 pre1722 art,nn773 an,nn5485 ppro5213 2532

4 John to the seven churches which are in Asia: Grace *be* unto you, and

an,nn1515 pre575 3801 [art,pap5607/2532/art,ipf2258/2532/art,ppmp2064] 2532 pre575

peace, from him*which*is,*and*which*was,*and*which*is*to*come; and from

art3588 nu2033 an,nn4151 repro3739 pin2076 ad*1799 ppro848 art,nn2362

the seven Spirits which are before his throne; *(Ex. 3:14)*

2532 pre575 an,nn2424 an,nn5547 art3588 aj4103 art,nn3144 art3588

☞ 5 And from Jesus Christ, *who is* the faithful witness, *and* the

aj4416 pre1537 art3588 ajn3498 2532 art3588 nn758 art3588 nn935 art3588 nn1093

first begotten of the dead, and the prince of the kings of the earth. Unto

art,apta25 ppro2248 2532 apta3068 ppro2248 pre575 ppro2257 art,nn266 pre1722 ppro848 art,nn129

him*that*loved us, and washed us from our sins in his own blood,

(Ps. 89:27; 130:8)

2532 aina4160 ppro2248 an,nn935 2532 an,nn2409 art,nn2316 2532 ppro848 an,nn3962 epn846

6 And hath made us kings and priests unto God and his Father; to him

---

☞ **1:1** There are some who interpret the phrase, "must shortly come to pass," to mean that the events of the Book of Revelation have already taken place. They suggest that John wrote about things that happened either in his lifetime or the lifetime of those in the churches to which he was writing. The problem with this view is that in Revelation 22:7, Jesus said He Himself was coming "quickly." This is the same Greek word that is translated "shortly" here in chapter one. Therefore, if these things have already taken place, Christ has already come and there is no hope for believers.

This verse should be understood to mean that the events in the book will occur "soon" in God's view of time. He is relating these events to infinite time frames. The human mind is only able to relate to those things which he can see and understand. Hence, the proper way to interpret this verse is to realize that when these events do happen (though the specific time is unknown to believers but known to God), they will occur suddenly and quickly.

☞ **1:5** See note on Colossians 1:15–18.

art,nn1391 2532 art,nn2904   pre1519/art,nn165/art,nn165   281

be glory and dominion forever*and*ever. Amen.   *(Ex. 19:6; Is. 61:6)*

2400   pinm2064   pre3326 art,nn3507   2532   an,aj3956 an,nn3788   fm3700 ppro846 2532

7 Behold, he cometh with clouds; and every eye shall see him, and they

repro3748   aina1574   ppro846 2532 an,aj3956 art,nn5443   art3588 nn1093   fm2875   pre1909

also which pierced him: and . all   kindreds of the earth shall wail because of

ppro846   3483   281

him. Even so, Amen.   *(Dan. 7:13; Zech. 12:10,12,14)*

epn1473 pin1510 (art3588) pr/1   2532 (art3588)   pr/5598   pr/an,nn746   2532   pr/an,nn5056 pin3004

8   I   am   Alpha   and   Omega, the beginning and the ending, saith

art3588   nn2962   [art,pap5607/2532/art,ipf2258/2532/art,ppmp2064]**3801   art3588   nn3841

the Lord, which*is,*and*which*was,*and*which*is*to*come, the Almighty.

(Ex. 3:14; Is. 4:14; Amos 3:13; 4:13 [Sept.])

John on the Isle of Patmos

epn1473 an,nn2491   2532   ppro5216 art,nn80   2532   an,ajn4791 pre1722 art,nn2347   2532

9   I   John, who also am your brother, and companion in   tribulation, and

pre1722 art3588   nn932   2532 an,nn5281   an,nn2424 an,nn5547 aom1096 pre1722 art3588 nn3520   art,ppmp2564

in   the kingdom and patience of Jesus Christ, was   in   the isle that*is*called

an,nn3963   pre1223 art3588 nn3056   art,nn2316 2532 pre1223 art3588   nn3141   an,nn2424 an,nn5547

Patmos, for the word of God, and for the testimony of Jesus Christ.

aom1096 pre1722   an,nn4151 pre4151 art3588 ajn2960 an,nn2250 2532 aina191   ad*3694 ppro3450

10 I was   in   the Spirit on   the Lord's day, and heard behind me a

an,aj3173 an,nn5456 ad5613   an,nn4536

great voice, as of a trumpet,

pap3004   epn1473 pin1510 (art3588)   pr/1   2532 (art3588)   pr/5598   art3588 pr/nu,ajn4413 2532 art3588 pr/ajn2078

11 Saying, I   am   Alpha and   Omega, the first and the last:

2532 repro3739   pin991   aima1125 pre1519 an,nn975 2532 aima3992   art3588 nu2033   nn1577

and, What thou seest, write in a book, and send *it* unto the seven churches

art3588   pre1722 an,nn773 pre1519   an,nn2181   2532 pre1519   an,nn4667   2532 pre1519   an,nn4010   2532

which are in Asia; unto Ephesus, and unto Smyrna, and unto Pergamos, and

pre1519   an,nn2363   2532 pre1519 an,nn4554 2532 pre1519   an,nn5359   2532 pre1519 an,nn2993

unto Thyatira, and unto Sardis, and unto Philadelphia, and unto Laodicea.

2532   aina1994   pinf991 art3588 nn5456 repro3748 aina2980 pre3326 ppro1700 2532   apta1994

12 And I turned to see the voice that spake with me. And being turned, I

aina1492   nu2033   an,aj5552   an,nn3087

saw seven golden candlesticks;

2532   pre1722   an,ajn3319   art3588 nu2033   nn3087   an,ajn3664   an,nn5207

13 And in the midst of the seven candlesticks *one* like unto the Son of

an,nn444   pfpp1746   an,ajn4158   2532 pfpp4024 (pre4314) art3588 nn3149

man, clothed with a garment*down*to*the*foot, and girt about the paps with a

an,aj5552 an,nn2223

golden girdle.   *(Dan. 7:9; Ezek. 9:2,11 [Sept.]; Dan. 10:5)*

(1161) ppro848 art,nn2776 2532   art,nn2359   pr/an,aj3022 ad5616 an,nn2053   an,aj3022 ad5613 pr/an,nn5510

14 His head and *his* hairs *were* white like wool, as white as snow;

2532 ppro848 art,nn3788   ad5613 pr/an,nn5395 an,nn4442

and his eyes *were* as a flame of fire;   *(Dan. 7:9; 10:6)*

2532   ppro848 art,nn4228   pr/an,aj3664   an,nn5474   ad5613   pr/pfpp4448 pre1722   an,nn2575
15 And his feet like unto fine brass, as if they burned in a furnace;
2532 ppro848 art,nn5456 ad5613   pr/an,nn5456   an,aj4183   an,nn5204
and his voice as the sound of many waters.

(Ezek. 1:7; Dan. 10:6; Ezek. 1:24; 43:2)

2532   pap2192 pre1722 ppro848 art,aj1188 an,nn5495 nu2033 an,nn792 2532   pre1537 ppro848 art,nn4750
16 And he had in his right hand seven stars: and out of his mouth
ppmp1607   an,aj3691   an,aj1366   an,nn4501 2532 ppro848   art,nn3799   ad5613 art3588 pr/nn2246 pin5316
went a sharp two-edged sword and his countenance *was* as the sun shineth
pre1722 ppro848   art,nn1411
in his strength.   *(Is. 49:2)*

2532   ad3753   aina1492 ppro846   aina4098 pre4314 ppro848 art,nn4228 ad5613 an,ajn3498 2532   aina2007 ppro848
17 And when I saw him, I fell at his feet as dead. And he laid his
art,aj1188 an,nn5495 pre1909 ppro1691 pap3004   ppro3427 pim5399 3361 epn1473 pin1510 art3588 pr/nu,ajn4413 2532 art3588
right hand upon me, saying unto me, Fear not; I am the first and the
pr/ajn2078
last: *(Is. 44:6; 48:12)*

(2532)   pr/art,pap2198   2532   aom1096 pr/an,aj3498 2532   2400   pin1510 pr/pap2198
☞ 18 I am he*that*liveth, and was dead; and, behold, I am alive
pre1519/art,nn165/art,165   281   2532 pin2192 art3588 nn2807   art,nn86 2532   art,nn2288
for evermore, Amen; and have the keys of hell and of death.

aima1125   repro3739   aina1492 2532   repro3739 pin1526 2532
19 Write the things which thou hast seen, and the things which are, and
repro3739 pin3195 pifm1096 pre3326/depro5023
the things which shall be hereafter;   *(Is. 48:6 [Sept.]; Dan. 2:28,29,45)*

art3588   nn3466   art3588 nu2033   nn792 repro3739   aina1492 pre1909 ppro3450
20 The mystery of the seven stars which thou sawest in my
art,ajn1188   2532 art3588 nu2033 art,aj5552   nn3087   art3588 nu2033   nn792 pin1526 pr/an,nn32
right hand, and the seven golden candlesticks. The seven stars are the angels
art3588   nu2033   nn1577   2532 art3588 nu2033   nn3087   repro3739   aina1492 pin1526
of the seven churches: and the seven candlesticks which thou sawest are the
nu2033   pr/an,nn1577
seven churches.

Ephesus

art3588   nn32   art3588 an,nn1577   an,aj2179 aima1125   depro3592   pin3004
2 ☞Unto the angel of the church of Ephesus write; These things saith
art,pap2902   art3588 nu2033   nn792 pre1722 ppro848   art,ajn1188   art,pap4043   pre1722
he*that*holdeth the seven stars in his right hand who walketh in
an,ajn3319   art3588 nu2033 art,aj5552   nn3087
the midst of the seven golden candlesticks;

☞ **1:18** See note on Ephesians 4:8–10.
☞ **2:1—3:22** These chapters contain letters to the seven churches. These were local churches in Asia Minor. Each one also represents a particular time period in church history. See the introduction.
☞ **2:1–7** Ephesus was sixty miles northeast of the Isle of Patmos, where the Apostle John was writing, and thirty-five miles South of modern Izmir.
The church of Ephesus represents the apostolic period of the church (A.D. 30–100).

2 I know thy works, and thy labor, and thy patience, and how thou canst not bear them*which*are*evil: and thou hast tried them*which*say they are apostles, and are not, and hast found them liars:

3 And hast borne, and hast patience, and for*my*name's*sake hast labored, and hast not fainted.

4 Nevertheless I have *somewhat* against thee, because thou hast left thy first love.

5 Remember therefore from whence thou art fallen, and repent, and do the first works; or else I will come unto thee quickly, and will remove thy candlestick out of his place, except thou repent.

6 But this thou hast, that thou hatest the deeds of the Nicolaitanes, which I also hate.

7 He*that*hath an ear, let him hear what the Spirit saith unto the churches; To him that overcometh will I give to eat of the tree of life, which is in the midst of the paradise of God.

(Gen. 2:9; 3:22,24; Gen. 2:8 [Sept.]; Ezek. 28:13 [Sept.]; 31:8,9 [Sept.])

Smyrna

8 And unto the angel of the church in Smyrna write; These things saith the first and the last, which was dead, and is alive;   (Is. 44:6; 48:12)

9 I know thy works, and tribulation, and poverty, (but thou art rich)

☞ **2:8–11** Smyrna (modern-day Izmir) was thirty-five miles north of Ephesus. It was the most splendid of the seven cities and was the pride of Asia. Emperor worship developed in this city and the Christians there suffered greatly because they would not worship Caesar. Polycarp, the bishop of the church in Smyrna, was martyred here in A.D. 156 because he refused to call Caesar "Lord."

The church in Smyrna finds its counterpart in the age of martyrs of the church in the second and third centuries.

2532   art3588   nn988   art,pap3004   rxpro1438 pinf1511 pr/an,nn2453 2532 pin1526 3756

and *I know* the blasphemy of them*which*say they are Jews, and are not,

235   an,nn4864   art,nn4567

but *are* the synagogue of Satan.

           pim5399 an,ajn3367   repro3739   pin3195 pinf3958   2400   art3588 ajn1228

    10 Fear none of those things which thou shalt suffer: behold, the devil

pin3195 ainf906   pre1537 ppro5216 pre1519 an,nn5438   2443   asbp3985 2532   fm2192

shall cast *some* of you into prison, that ye may be tried; and ye shall have

an,nn2347 nu1176 an,nn2250 pim1096   pr/an,aj4103 ad891   an,nn2288   2532   ft1325 ppro4671 art,nn4735

tribulation ten days; be thou faithful unto death, and I will give thee a crown

art,nn2222

of life.   *(Dan. 1:12,14)*

       art,pap2192   an,nn3775   aima191 inpro5101 art3588 nn4151   pin3004   art3588

    11 He*that*hath an ear, let him hear what the Spirit saith unto the

nn1577   art,pap3528   efn3364 asbp91   pre1537 art3588 nu,aj1208   art,nn2288

churches; He*that*overcometh shall not be hurt of the second death.

Pergamos

         2532   art3588   nn32   art3588   nn1577   pre1722   an,nn4010   aima1125   depro3592

☞ 12 And to the angel of the church in Pergamos write; These things

pin3004   art,pap2192   art3588 aj3691 art,nn4501   1366

saith he*which*hath the sharp sword with two edges;   *(Is. 49:2)*

          pin1492 ppro4675 art,nn2041   2532   ad4226   pin2730   ad3699 art,nn4567

    13 I know thy works, and where thou dwellest, *even* where Satan's

art,nn2362   2532   pin2902   ppro3450 art,nn3686 2532   3756 aom720 ppro3450 art,nn4102 2532

seat *is:* and thou holdest fast my name, and hast not denied my faith, even

pre1722   art,nn2250 pre1722/repro3739 an,nn493   ppro3450   art,aj4103   art,nn3144 repro3739   ainp615

in those days wherein Antipas *was* my faithful martyr, who was slain

pre3844 ppro5213 ad3699 art,nn4567 pin2730

among you, where Satan dwelleth.

       235   pin2192   an,ajn3641   pre2596   ppro4675   3754   pin2192   ad1563

    14 But I have a few things against thee, because thou hast there

an,pap2902   art3588   nn1322   903   repro3739 ipf1321 904   ainf906

them*that*hold the doctrine of Balaam, who taught Balac to cast a

an,nn4625   ad˙1799 art3588 nn5207   2474   ainf5315   an,ajn1494

stumblingblock before the children of Israel, to eat things*sacrificed*unto*idols,

2532   ainf4203

and to commit fornication.   *(Num. 25:1,2; 31:16)*

       ad3779 pin2192 epn4771 2532   an,pap2902   art3588   nn1322   art3588   nn3531

    15 So hast thou also them*that*hold the doctrine of the Nicolaitanes,

repro3739   pin3404

which thing I hate.

☞ **2:12–17** The city of Pergamus (or Pergamos) was fifteen miles from the Aegean Coast and seventy miles north of Smyrna. An immense altar to Zeus, the chief of the Greek mythological gods, stood on the Acropolis (the upper or higher part of the city) one thousand feet above the plain. This may be what is being referred to as "Satan's seat" (v. 13).

    The church in Pergamum represents the age of the state church, which began with Constantine and continued until the first pope was recognized to have authority over the catholic church (A.D. 313–590).

16 Repent; or else I will come unto thee quickly, and will fight against them with the sword of my mouth.

17 He*that*hath an ear, let him hear what the Spirit saith unto the churches; To him that overcometh will I give to eat of the hidden manna, and will give him a white stone, and in the stone a new name written, which no man knoweth saving he*that*receiveth *it.* (*Ex. 16:33; Is. 62:2; 65:15*)

Thyatira

18 And unto the angel of the church in Thyatira write; These things saith the Son of God, who hath his eyes like unto a flame of fire, and his feet *are* like fine brass; (*Dan. 10:6*)

19 I know thy works, and charity, and service, and faith, and thy patience, and thy works; and the last *to be* more than the first.

20 Notwithstanding I have a few things against thee, because thou sufferest that woman Jezebel, which calleth herself a prophetess, to teach and to seduce my servants to commit fornication, and to eat things*sacrificed*unto*idols. (*1 Kgs. 16:31; 2 Kgs. 9:22*)

21 And I gave her space to repent of her fornication; and she repented not.

22 Behold, I will cast her into a bed, and them*that*commit*adultery with her into great tribulation, except they repent of their deeds.

23 And I will kill her children with death; and all the churches shall

---

2:18–29 Thyatira was the least important of the seven cities that are mentioned and was about halfway between Pergamum and Sardis. It was more important commercially than politically.

The church in Thyatira corresponds to the time period when the church was firmly established not only as a church, but also as a state (A.D. 590–1517). It begins with the first pope, Gregory the Great, and continues to the time of the Protestant Reformation.

fm1097   3754 epn1473 pin1510   pr/art,pap2045   an,nn3510 2532 an,nn2588 2532   ft1325

know that   I   am he*which*searcheth the reins and hearts: and I will give

       an,ajn1538   pppro5213   pre2596   pppro5216   art,nn2041

unto every one of you according to your works.

(Ps. 7:9; Jer. 11:20; 17:10; Ps. 62:12; Prov. 24:12; Is. 59:18; Jer. 17:10)

        1161   epn5213   pin3004 2532   an,ajn3062 art,pre1722   an,nn2363   an,ajn3745

24   But unto you I say, and unto the rest   in   Thyatira, as*many*as

pin2192 3756 depro5026 art,nn1322   2532 repro3748   3756 aina1097 art3588   nn899   art,nn4567 ad5613

have not this doctrine, and which have not known the depths of Satan, as

     pin3004   ft906 pre1909 pppro5209 3756 an,aj243   an,nn922

they speak; I will put upon you none other burden.

       4133   repro3739   pin2192   aima2902 ad891 (repro3739) asba2240/302

25   But that which ye have *already* hold fast till   I   come.

      2532   art,pap3528   2532 art,pap5083 pppro3450 art,nn2041   ad891   an,nn5056

26   And he*that*overcometh, and keepeth my works unto the end, to

pppro846   ft1325 an,nn1849 pre1909 art3588   nn1484

him will I give power over the nations:

       2532   ft4165 pppro846 pre1722   an,nn4464   an,aj4603 ad5613 art3588   nn4632

27   And he shall rule them with a rod of iron; as the vessels of a

art,aj2764   pinp4937   ad5613   epn2504   pfi2983   pre3844 pppro3450

potter shall they be broken*to*shivers: even as   I   received of   my

art,nn3962

Father.   (Ps. 2:8,9)

      2532   ft1325 pppro846 art3588 aj4407   art,nn792

28   And I will give him the morning star.

       art,pap2192   an,nn3775   aima191 inpro5101 art3588 nn4151   pin3004   art3588

29   He*that*hath an   ear, let him hear what the Spirit saith unto the

nn1577

churches.

Sardis

         2532   art3588   nn32   art3588   nn1577   pre1722 an,nn4554 animal1125   depro3592

3 ☞ And unto the angel of the church in   Sardis write; These things

     pin3004   art,pap2192   art3588 nu2033   nn4151   art,nn2316 2532 art3588 nu2033   nn792   pin1492

saith he*that*hath the seven Spirits of God, and the seven stars; I know

pppro4675 art,nn2041 3754   pin2192 art,nn3686 3754   pin2198 2532 pin1488 pr/an,ajn3498

thy works, that thou hast a name that thou livest, and art dead.

      pim1096   pr/pap1127   2532   aima4741   art,ajn3062   repro3739   pin3195

2   Be watchful, and strengthen the*things*which*remain that are ready

ainf599 1063   3756 pfi2147 pppro4675 art,nn2041 pr/pfpp4137 ad*1799 art,nn2316

to die: for I have not found thy works perfect before God.

      pim3421   3767   ad4459   pfi2983   2532 aina191 2532 pim5083

3   Remember therefore how thou hast received and heard, and hold fast,

---

☞ **3:1–6** Sardis was fifty miles due east of Smyrna and thirty miles southeast of Thyatira. The richest man living, Croesus, reigned here. The city was devastated by an earthquake in A.D. 17, but was later rebuilt.

The church in Sardis pictures the Reformation era of the church (A.D. 1517–1790).

2532   aima3340   1437   3767   3361   asba1127   ft2240   pre1909   ppro4571   ad5613

and repent. If therefore thou shalt not watch, I will come on thee as a

an,nn2812 2532   efn3364 asba1097 an,aj4169 an,nn5610   ft2240   pre1909   ppro4571

thief, and thou shalt not know what hour I will come upon thee.

pin2192   an,aj3641   an,nn3686   2532   pre1722   an,nn4554   repro3739   3756   aina3435   ppro848

4 Thou hast a few names even in Sardis which have not defiled their

art,nn2440   2532   ft4043   pre3326 ppro1700 pre1722 an,ajn3022   3754   pin1526   pr/an,aj514

garments; and they shall walk with me in white: for they are worthy.

art,pap3528   depro3778   fm4016   pre1722 an,aj3022   an,nn2440   2532

5 He*that*overcometh, the same shall be clothed in white raiment; and I

efn3364   asba1813   ppro848 art,nn3686 pre1537   art3588   nn976   art,nn2222 2532   fm1843   ppro848

will not blot out his name out of the book of life, but I will confess his

art,nn3686   ad*1799   ppro3450   art,nn3962   2532   ad*1799   ppro848   art,nn32

name before my Father, and before his angels.

(Ex. 32:32,33; Ps. 69:28; Dan. 12:1)

art,pap2192   an,nn3775   aima191   inpro5101 art3588   nn4151   pin3004   art3588

6 He*that*hath an ear, let him hear what the Spirit saith unto the

nn1577

churches.

Philadelphia

2532   art3588   nn32   art3588   nn1577   pre1722   an,nn5359   aima1125   depro3592

☞ 7 And to the angel of the church in Philadelphia write; These things

pin3004   art,ajn40   art,ajn228   art,pap2192   art3588   nn2807   1138

saith he*that*is*holy, he*that*is*true, he*that*hath the key of David,

art,pap455   2532   an,ajn3762   pin2808   2532   pin2808   2532   an,ajn3762   pin455

he*that*openeth, and no man shutteth; and shutteth, and no man openeth;

(Is. 22:22)

pin1492   ppro4675   art,nn2041   2400   pfi1325   ad*1799   ppro4675   pfpp455 an,nn2374   2532

8 I know thy works: behold, I have set before thee an open door, and

an,ajn3762   pinm1410 ainf2808 ppro846 3754   pin2192   an,aj3398   an,nn1411   2532   aina5083 ppro3450 art,nn3056

no man can shut it: for thou hast a little strength, and hast kept my word,

2532   3756   aom720   ppro3450 art,nn3686

and hast not denied my name.

2400   pin1325   art3588 pre1537 art3588   nn4864   art,nn4567   art,pap3004   rxpro1438

9 Behold, I will make them of the synagogue of Satan, which say they

pinf1511 pr/an,nn2453 2532 pin1526 3756   235   pinm5574   2400   ft4160   ppro846 2443 asba2240 2532

are Jews, and are not, but do lie; behold, I will make them to come and

asba4352   ad*1799   ppro4675 art,nn4228 2532   asba1097   3754   epn1473   aina25   ppro4571

worship before thy feet, and to know that I have loved thee.

(Is. 45:14; 49:23; 60:14; 43:4)

☞ **3:7–13** The city of Philadelphia was built in a dangerous volcanic area located about twenty-eight miles southeast of Sardis. It was completely destroyed by an earthquake in A.D. 17, but was completely rebuilt.

The church in Philadelphia represents the age of the missionary church which began with the rise of modern missions under William Carey (A.D. 1730–1900).

3754   aina5083 art3588   nn3056   ppro3450   art,nn5281   epn2504   ft5083
10 Because thou hast kept the word of my patience, I also will keep

ppro4571 pre1537 art3588 nn5610   art,nn3986   art,pap3195   pifm2064 pre1909 an,aj3650 art3588 ainf3985
thee from the hour of temptation, which shall come upon all   the world, to

ainf3985 art3588   pap2730 pre1909 art3588   nn1093
try them that dwell upon the earth.

2400   pinm2064   an,ajn5035   pim2902   repro3739   pin2192   2443   an,ajn3367
11 Behold, I come quickly: hold*that*fast which thou hast, that no man

asba2983 ppro4675 art,nn4735
take thy crown.

ppro846   art,pap3528   ft4160   pr/an,nn4769 pre1722 art3588   nn3485   ppro3450
12 Him that overcometh will I make a pillar   in   the temple of my

art,nn2316 2532   asba1831 efn3364 ad2089 ad1854 2532   ft1125 pre1909 ppro846 art3588 nn3686
God, and he shall go   no more out: and I will write upon him the name of

ppro3450 art,nn2316 2532 art3588   nn3686   art3588 nn4172   ppro3450 art,nn2316   art,aj2537   2419
my God, and the name of the city of my God, *which is* new Jerusalem,

repro3739   pin2597   pre1537 art,nn3772   pre575 ppro3450 art,nn2316 2532
which cometh down out of heaven from my God: and *I will write upon him*

ppro3450 art,aj2537 art,nn3686
my new name.

(1 Kgs. 7:15-22; 2 Chr. 3:15-17; Ezek. 48:35; Is. 62:2; 65:15)

art,pap2192   an,nn3775   aima191 inpro5101 art3588   nn4151   pin3004   art3588
13 He*that*hath an ear, let him hear what the Spirit saith unto the

nn1577
churches.

Laodicea

2532   art3588   nn32   art3588   nn1577   an,nn2994   aima1125
14 And unto the angel of the church of the Laodiceans write;

depro3592   pin3004 art3588   281   art3588 aj4103   2532 art,aj228   art,nn3144   art3588   nn746
These things saith the Amen, the faithful and true witness, the beginning of

art3588   nn2937   art,nn2316
the creation of God;   *(Prov. 8:22)*

pin1492 ppro4675 art,nn2041 3754   pin1488   3777 pr/an,aj5593 3777 pr/an,aj2200 aina3785
15 I know thy works, that thou art neither cold nor hot: I would

opt1498 pr/an,aj5593 2228 pr/an,aj2200
thou wert cold or hot.

ad3779   3754   pin1488   pr/an,aj5513   2532   3777   pr/an,aj5593 3777 pr/an,aj2200
16 So then because thou art lukewarm, and neither cold nor hot, I

pin3195 ainf1692 ppro4571 pre1537 ppro3450 art,nn4750
will spew thee out of my mouth.

☞ **3:14–22** Laodicea was located about forty miles southeast of Philadelphia and one hundred miles east of Ephesus. It was known as a banking center and had a famous medical school. The city is in complete ruins today.

The church in Laodicea portrays the apostate church of the last days (A.D. 1900–present).

☞ **3:14** In this verse, the Lord Jesus Christ is called "the beginning of the creation of God." In this instance, the Greek word *arché* (746), translated "beginning," literally refers to the originator or cause of creation.

17 Because thou sayest, I am rich, and increased*with*goods, and have need of nothing; and knowest not that thou art wretched, and miserable, and poor, and blind, and naked: *(Hos. 12:8)*

18 I counsel thee to buy of me gold tried in the fire, that thou mayest be rich; and white raiment, that thou mayest be clothed, and *that* the shame of thy nakedness do not appear; and anoint thine eyes with eye salve, that thou mayest see.

19 As*many*as I love, I rebuke and chasten: be zealous therefore, and repent. *(Prov. 3:12)*

20 Behold, I stand at the door, and knock: if any man hear my voice, and open the door, I will come in to him, and will sup with him, and he with me.

21 To him that overcometh will I grant to sit with me in my throne, even as I also overcame, and am set down with my Father in his throne.

22 He*that*hath an ear, let him hear what the Spirit saith unto the churches.

The Throne in Heaven

4 After this I looked, and, behold, a door *was* opened in heaven: and the first voice which I heard *was* as*it*were of a trumpet talking with me; which said, Come up hither, and I will show thee things which must be hereafter. *(Is. 48:6 [Sept.]; Dan. 2:28,29,45)*

2 And immediately I was in the spirit: and, behold, a throne was set in heaven, and *one* sat on the throne.

(1 Kgs. 22:19; 2 Chr. 18:18; Ps. 47:8; Is. 6:1; Ezek. 1:26)

    2532   art,ppmp2521   ipf2258   an,nn3706   pr/an,ajn3664   an,nn2393   2532   an,nn4555
3 And he*that*sat was to look upon like a jasper and a sardine

an,nn3037   2532   an,nn2463   ad*2943   art3588   nn2362   an,nn3706   an,aj3664
stone: and *there was* a rainbow round about the throne, in sight like unto an

an,aj4664
emerald.

    2532   ad*2943   art3588   nn2362   nu5064/2532/nu1501   an,nn2362   2532   pre1909 art3588
4 And round about the throne *were* four*and*twenty seats: and upon the

nn2362   aina1492   nu5064/2532/nu1501   art,ajn4245   ppmp2521   pfpp4016   pre1722 an,aj3022   an,nn2440   2532
seats I saw four*and*twenty elders sitting, clothed in white raiment; and they

aina2192 pre1909 ppro848 art,nn2776   an,nn4735   an,aj5552
had on their heads crowns of gold.   *(Is. 24:23)*

      2532   pre1537   art3588   nn2362   pim1607   an,nn796   2532   an,nn1027   2532   an,nn5456
5 And out of the throne proceeded lightnings and thunderings and voices:

2532   nu2033   an,nn2985   an,nn4442   ppmp2545   ad*1799 art3588   nn2362   repro3739 pin1526 art3588
and *there were* seven lamps of fire burning before the throne, which are the

nu2033   pr/nn4151   art,nn2316
seven Spirits of God.   *(Ex. 19:16; Esth. 1:1 [Sept.]; Zech. 4:2)*

     2532   ad*1799   art3588   nn2362   an,nn2281   an,aj5193 pr/an,aj3664   an,nn2930 2532
6 And before the throne *there was* a sea of glass like unto crystal: and

pre1722   an,ajn3319   art3588   nn2362   2532   an,ajn2945   art3588   nn2362   nu5064 an,nn2226
in the midst of the throne, and round about the throne, *were* four beasts

pap1073   an,nn3778   ad1715   2532   ad3693
full of eyes before and behind.

      2532   art3588 nu,aj4413 art,nn2226   pr/an,ajn3664   an,nn3023 2532 art3588 nu,aj1208 an,nn2226 pr/an,ajn3664
7 And the first beast *was* like a lion, and the second beast like a

an,nn3448   2532 art3588 nu,aj5154 an,nn2226 pap2192   art,nn4383 ad5613   an,nn444   2532 art3588 nu,aj5067 an,nn2226
calf, and the third beast had a face as a man, and the fourth beast *was*

pr/an,ajn3664   ppmp4072 an,nn105
like a flying eagle.   *(Ezek. 1:5-10; 10:14)*

     2532   nu5064   an,nn2226 ipf2192 pre303/nu1520/pre2596/rxpro1438 nu1803 an,nn4420 ad*2943   2532
8 And the four beasts had each*of*them six wings about *him*; and *they*

pap1073   an,nn3788   ad2081   2532   pin2192/an,nn372 3756 an,nn2250 2532 an,nn3571 pap3004   pr/an,aj40
were full of eyes within: and they rest not day and night, saying, Holy,

pr/an,aj40 pr/an,aj40 an,nn2962 art,nn2316   art,nn3841   3801 [art,pap5607/2532/art,ipf2258/2532/art,ppmp2064]
holy, holy, Lord God Almighty, which*was,*and*is,*and*is*to*come.

                              (Is. 6:2; Ezek. 1:8; 10:12; Is. 6:3;

                              Amos 3:13 [Sept.]; 4:13 [Sept.]; Ex. 3:14; Is. 41:4)

     2532   ad3752   art,nn2226   ft1325   an,nn1391   2532   an,nn5092   2532   an,nn2169
9 And when those beasts give glory and honor and thanks to

art,ppmp2521   pre1909 art3588   nn2362   art,pap2198   pre1519/art,nn165/art,nn165
him*that*sat on the throne, who liveth forever*and*ever,

                              (1 Kgs. 22:19; 2 Chr. 18:18; Ps. 47:8;

                              Is. 6:1; Ezek. 1:26; Dan. 4:34; 6:26; 12:7)

art3588   nu5064/2523/nu1501   ajn4245   fm4098   ad*1799   art,ppmp2521   pre1909 art3588
10 The four*and*twenty elders fall down before him*that*sat on the

nn2362   2532   pin4352   art,pap2198   pre1519/art,nn165/art,nn165   2532   pin906   ppro848   art,nn4735

throne, and worship him*that*liveth forever*and*ever, and cast their crowns

ad*1799   art3588   nn2362   pap3004

before the throne, saying,

(1 Kgs. 22:19; 2 Chr. 18:18; Ps. 47:8;

Is. 6;1; Ezek. 1:26; Dan. 4:34; 6:26; 12:7)

pin1488   pr/an,aj514   an,nn2962   ainf2983 art,nn1391 2532 art,nn5092 2532 art,nn1411   3754

11 Thou art worthy, O Lord, to receive glory and honor and power: for

epn4771   aina2936   art,ajn3956   2532   pre1223 ppro4675   art,nn2307   pin1526   2532

thou hast created all things, and for thy pleasure they are and were

ainp2936

created.   (Gen. 1:1-31; Ps. 148:5; Is. 42:5; 45:12,18; Amos 4:13; Mal. 2:10)

The Seven-sealed Book

2532   aina1492 pre1909 art3588   ajn1188   art,ppmp2521   pre1909 art3588   nn2362   an,nn975

5 And I saw in the right hand of him*that*sat on the throne a book

pfpp1125   ad2081   2532   ad3693   pfpp2696   nu2033 an,nn4973

written within and on*the*backside, sealed with seven seals.

(1 Kgs. 22:19; 2 Chr. 18:18; Ps. 47:8; Is. 6:1; Ezek. 1:26; 2:9,10)

2532   aina1492   an,aj2478   an,nn32   pap2784   an,aj3173 an,nn5456 inpro5101 pin2076

2 And I saw a strong angel proclaiming with a loud voice, Who is

pr/an,aj514   ainf455 art3588 nn975   2532   ainf3089 art3588 nn4973   ppro848

worthy to open the book, and to loose the seals thereof?

2532   an,ajn3762   pre1722 art,nn3772   3761 pre1909 art,nn1093   3761   ad*5270 art3588   nn1093

3 And no man in heaven, nor in earth, neither under the earth,

ipf1410   ainf455 art3588   nn975   3761   pinf991   ppro846

was able to open the book, neither to look thereon.

2532 epn1473 ipf2799 an,ajn4183   3754   an,ajn3762   ainp2147 pr/an,aj514   ainf455   2532

4 And I wept much, because no man was found worthy to open and to

ainf314 art3588   nn975   3777   pinf991   ppro846

read the book, neither to look thereon.

2532   nu1520 pre1537 art3588   ajn4245   pin3004   ppro3427 pim2799   3361   2400   art3588

5 And one of the elders saith unto me, Weep not: behold, the

nn3023 (art,pap5607) pre1537 art3588 nn5443   an,nn2455 art3588 nn4491   1138   aina3528   ainf455

Lion   of the tribe of Judah, the Root of David, hath prevailed to open

art3588   nn975   2532   ainf3089 art3588 nu2033   nn4973   ppro848

the book, and to loose the seven seals thereof.   (Gen. 49:9,10; Is. 11:1,10)

2532   aina1492   2532   2400 pre1722   an,ajn3319   art3588   nn2362   2532   art3588 nu5064

6 And I beheld, and, lo, in the midst of the throne and of the four

nn2226   2532 pre1722   an,ajn3319   art3588 ajn4245   pfp2476   an,nn721 ad5613   pfpp4969

beasts, and in the midst of the elders, stood a Lamb as it had been slain,

pap2192 nu2033 an,nn2768   2532   nu2033   an,nn3788   repro3739 pin1526 art3588 nu2033 pr/nn4151   art,nn2316

having seven horns and seven eyes, which are the seven Spirits of God

art,pfpp649   pre1519 an,aj3956 art3588   nn1093

sent forth into all the earth.   (Is. 53:7)

7 And he came and took the book out of the right hand of
him*that*sat upon the throne.

(1 Kgs. 22:19; 2 Chr. 18:18; Ps. 47:8; Is. 6:1; Ezek. 1:26)

8 And when he had taken the book, the four beasts and four*and*twenty
elders fell down before the Lamb, having every*one*of*them harps, and
golden vials full of odors, which are the prayers of saints. *(Ps. 141:2)*

9 And they sung a new song, saying, Thou art worthy to take the book,
and to open the seals thereof: for thou wast slain, and hast redeemed us to
God by thy blood out of every kindred, and tongue, and people, and
nation; *(Ps. 33:3; 40:3; 96:1; 98:1; 144:9; 149:1; Is. 42:10)*

10 And hast made us unto our God kings and priests: and we shall
reign on the earth. *(Ex. 19:6; Is. 61:6)*

11 And I beheld, and I heard the voice of many angels round about
the throne and the beasts and the elders: and the number of
them was ten*thousand*times*ten*thousand, and thousands*of*thousands;

(Dan. 7:10)

12 Saying with a loud voice, Worthy is the Lamb that*was*slain to
receive power, and riches, and wisdom, and strength, and honor, and glory,
and blessing. *(Is. 53:7; 1 Chr. 29:11)*

13 And every creature which is in heaven, and on the earth, and
under the earth, and such as are in the sea, and all that are in them,
heard I saying, Blessing, and honor, and glory, and power, *be* unto
him*that*sitteth upon the throne, and unto the Lamb forever*and*ever.

(1 Kgs. 22:19; 2 Chr. 18:18; Ps. 47:8; Is. 6:1; Ezek. 1:26)

14 And the four beasts said, Amen. And the four*and*twenty elders
fell down and worshipped him*that*liveth forever*and*ever.

The Seven Seals Opened

6   And I saw when the Lamb opened one of the seals, and I heard,
as*it*were the noise of thunder, one of the four beasts saying, Come
and see.

2 And I saw, and behold a white horse: and he*that*sat on him had a
bow; and a crown was given unto him: and he went forth conquering, and to
conquer.   *(Zech. 1:8; 6:3,6)*

3 And when he had opened the second seal, I heard the second beast
say, Come and see.

4 And there went out another horse *that was* red: and *power* was
given to him that sat thereon to take peace from the earth, and that
they should kill one another: and there was given unto him a great sword.

                    (Zech. 1:8; 6:2)

5 And when he had opened the third seal, I heard the third beast say,
Come and see. And I beheld, and lo a black horse; and he*that*sat on
him had a pair*of*balances in his hand.   *(Zech. 6:2,6)*

6 And I heard a voice in the midst of the four beasts say, A measure of
wheat for a penny, and three measures of barley for a penny; and *see* thou
hurt not the oil and the wine.

7 And when he had opened the fourth seal, I heard the voice of the
fourth beast say, Come and see.

8 And I looked, and behold a pale horse: and his name that sat on
him was Death, and Hell followed with him. And power was given unto them

---

 6:1–17 This chapter tells of the beginning of the time known as the "Day of the Lord" in which
God's judgment will be poured out on the earth (see note on 1 Thess. 5:2).

pre1909 art3588   nu,ajn5067   art3588   nn1093   ainf615 pre1722 an,nn4501 2532 pre1722 an,nn3042 2532
over the fourth part of the earth, to kill with sword, and with hunger, and

pre1722 an,nn2288 2532 pre5259 art3588   nn2342   art3588   nn1093
with death, and with the beasts of the earth.

(Jer. 14:12; 15:3; Ezek. 5:12,17; 14:21; 33:27)

2532   ad3753   aina455 art3588 nu,aj3991 an,nn4973   aina1492 ad*5270 art3588 nn2379 art3588
9 And when he had opened the fifth seal, I saw under the altar the

nn5590   art,pfpp4969   pre1223 art3588 nn3056   art,nn2316 2532 pre1223 art3588   nn3141
souls of them*that*were*slain for the word of God, and for the testimony

repro3739   ipf2192
which they held:

2532   ipf2896   an,aj3173 an,nn5456 pap3004 ad2193/ad4219 art,nn1203 art,aj40 2532
10 And they cried with a loud voice, saying, How long, O Lord, holy and

art,aj2228   3756 pin2919 2532 pin1556 ppro2257 art,nn129 pre575   art,pap1730   pre1909 art3588
true, dost thou not judge and avenge our blood on them*that*dwell on the

nn1093
earth?   *(Deut. 32:43; 2 Kgs. 9:7; Ps. 79:10)*

2532 an,aj3022 an,nn4749   ainp1325   an,ajn1538   2532   ainp4483
11 And white robes were given unto every*one*of*them; and it was said

ppro846 24433   asbm373 ad2089   an,aj3398 an,nn5550 ad2193 (repro3739) ppro848
unto them, that they should rest yet for a little season,   until   their

art,nn4889   2532 2532 ppro848 art,nn80   art,pap3195   pip615 ad5613   (2532)ppro848
fellowservants also and their brethren, that should be killed as they *were,*

fm4137
should be fulfilled.

2532 aina1492 ad3753   aina455 art3588 nu,aj1622 art,nn4973 2532 2400   aom1096
12 And I beheld when he had opened the sixth seal, and, lo, there was a

an,aj3173   an,nn4578   2532 art3588 nn2246 aom1096 pr/an,aj3189 ad5613 an,nn4526   an,aj5155 2532 art3588
great earthquake; and the sun became black as sackcloth of hair, and the

nn4582 aom1096 ad5613 pr/an,nn129
moon became as blood;   *(Is. 13:10; Ezek. 32:7,8; Joel 2:10,31; 3:15)*

2532 art3588 nn792   art,nn3772 aina4098 pre1519 art3588 nn1093 ad5613 an,nn4808 pin906
13 And the stars of heaven fell unto the earth, even as a fig tree casteth

ppro848 art,nn3653   ppmp4579 pre5259 an,aj3173 an,nn417
her untimely figs, when she is shaken of a mighty wind.

(Is. 13:10; 34:4; Ezek. 32:7,8; Joel 2:10; 3:15)

2532   an,nn3772 ainp673 ad5613 an,nn975   ppmp1507   2532
14 And the heaven departed as a scroll when it is rolled together; and

an,aj3956 an,nn3735 2532 an,nn3520   ainp2795 pre1537 ppro848 art,nn5117
every mountain and island were moved out of their places.   *(Is. 34:4)*

2532 art3588 nn935   art3588 nn1093 2532 art3588   nn3175   2532 art3588 ajn4145
15 And the kings of the earth, and the great men, and the rich men,

2532 art3588   nn5506   2532 art3588   ajn1415   2532 an,aj3956 an,ajn1401 2532
and the chief captains, and the mighty men, and every bondman, and

an,aj3956 an,ajn1658 aina2928 rxpro1438 pre1519 art3588 nn4693 2532 pre1519 art3588 nn4073   art3588
every free man, hid themselves in the dens and in the rocks of the

nn3735
mountains;   *(Is. 2:10,19,21; Jer. 4:29)*

2532 pin3004 art3588   nn3735   2532 art,nn4073 aima4098 pre1909 ppro2248 2532 aima2928 ppro2248 pre575
16 And said to the mountains and rocks, Fall on us, and hide us from

an,nn4383　　　art,ppmp2521　　　pre1909 art3588　　nn2362　　2532　pre575　art3588　nn3709　　art3588　nn721

the face of him*that*sitteth on the throne, and from the wrath of the Lamb:

(Hos. 10:8; 1 Kgs. 22:19; 2 Chr. 18:18; Ps. 47:8; Is. 6:1; Ezek. 1:26)

3754　art3588　aj3173　art,nn2250　　pp ro848 art,nn3709　　aina2064　2532　inpro5101　　　pinm1410

17 For the great day of his wrath is come; and who shall be able to

aifp2476

stand?　　　　　　　　　　　　　　　　　　　*(Joel 2:11; Nah. 1:6; Mal. 3:2)*

The 144,000

2532　pre3326　　depro5023　　aina1492 nu5064　an,nn32　　pfp2476　　pre1909 art3588 nu5064　　nn1137

7 ☞ And after these things I saw four angels standing on the four corners

art3588　nn1093　　pap2902　art3588 nu5064　nn417　　　art3588　nn1093　2443　　an,nn417

of the earth, holding the four winds of the earth, that the wind should

3361　psa4154 pre1909 art3588　nn1093　3383　pre1909 art3588 nn2281　3383　pre1909 an,aj3956 an,nn1186

not blow on the earth, nor on the sea, nor on any tree.

(Jer. 49:36; Ezek. 37:9; Dan. 7:2; Zech. 6:5)

2532　aina1492　an,aj243　an,nn32　　pap305　　pre575　　an,nn395/an,nn2246　pap2192　　an,nn4973

2 And I saw another angel ascending from the　　east,　　having the seal

an,pap2198 an,nn2316 2532　aina2896　　an,aj3173 an,nn5456　art3588 nu5064　nn32　　repro3739

of the living God: and he cried with a loud voice to the four angels, to whom it

ainp1325　(ppro846) ainf91　art3588　nn1093　2532　art3588　nn2281

was given　to　hurt the earth and the sea,

pap3004　aosi91　3361 art3588　nn1093　3383　art3588 nn2281　3383　art3588　nn1186　ad891　(repro3739)

3 Saying, Hurt not the earth, neither the sea, nor the trees, till we have

asba4972　art3588　ajn1401　　ppro2257 art,nn2316 pre1909 ppro848　art,nn3359

sealed the servants of our　God　in　their foreheads.　　　　*(Ezek. 9:4)*

2532　　aina191　art3588　nu706　　　　　art,pfpp4972

4 And I heard the number of them*which*were*sealed: *and there were*

pfpp4972　　　　nu1540/nu5062/nu5064/an,nn5055　　　　　pre1537　an,aj3956　　an,nn5543

sealed a*hundred*and*forty*and*four*thousand of　all　the tribes of the

an,nn5207　　2474

children of Israel.

pre1537　an,nn5443　　an,nn2455　pfpp4972　nu1427　an,nn5505　pre1537　an,nn5543

5 Of the tribe of Judah *were* sealed twelve thousand. Of the tribe of

4502　pfpp4972　nu1427　an,nn5505　pre1537　an,nn5543　1045　pfpp4972　nu1427

Reuben *were* sealed twelve thousand. Of the tribe of Gad *were* sealed twelve

an,nn5505

thousand.

☞ **7:1–17** This chapter contains a parenthetical portion between the opening of the sixth and seventh seals. In this period there are two distinct groups mentioned: (1) The 144,000 servants of God that are sealed are representative of the twelve tribes of Israel. This does not mean that only 144,000 Israelites will be saved, but that 12,000 chosen in each tribe will be protected from the wrath of Satan and the Antichrist. (2) The great multitude that will be saved. These are described as "they which come out of the great tribulation, and have washed their robes, and made them white in the blood of the Lamb" (Rev. 7:14). It is clear from 2 Thessalonians 2:10–12, that those who hear the Gospel before the Tribulation and reject it, will be doomed to spend an eternity without Christ. The only ones who can possibly be saved during the Tribulation are those who do not hear the Gospel previous to that time.

pre1537   an,nn5443   768   pfpp4972   nu1427   an,nn5505   pre1537   an,nn5443

6 Of the tribe of Aser *were* sealed twelve thousand. Of the tribe of

3508   pfpp4972   nu1427   an,nn5505   pre1537   an,nn5543   3128

Naphtali *were* sealed twelve thousand. Of the tribe of Manasses *were*

pfpp4972   nu1427   an,nn5505

sealed twelve thousand.

pre1537   an,nn5543   4826   pfpp4972   nu1427   an,nn5505   pre1537   an,nn5443

7 Of the tribe of Simeon *were* sealed twelve thousand. Of the tribe of

3017   pfpp4972   nu1427   an,nn5505   pre1537   an,nn5543   2466   pfpp4972

Levi *were* sealed twelve thousand. Of the tribe of Issachar *were* sealed

nu1427   an,nn5505

twelve thousand.

pre1537   an,nn5543   2194   pfpp4972   nu1427   an,nn5505   pre1537   an,nn5543

8 Of the tribe of Zebulun *were* sealed twelve thousand. Of the tribe of

2501   pfpp4972   nu1427   an,nn5505   pre1537   an,nn5543   958   pfpp4972

Joseph *were* sealed twelve thousand. Of the tribe of Benjamin *were* sealed

nu1427   an,nn5505

twelve thousand.

The Congregation in Heaven

pre3326   depro5023   aina1492   2532   2400   an,aj4183   an,nn3793   repro3739   an,ajn3762   ipf1410

9 After this I beheld, and, lo, a great multitude, which no man could

ainf705(ppro846) pre1537 an,aj3956 an,nn1484   2532   an,nn5443   2532   an,nn2992   2532   an,nn1100   pfp2476

number,   of   all   nations, and kindreds, and people, and tongues, stood

ad*1799   art3588   nn2362   2532   ad*1799   art3588   nn721   pfpp4016   an,aj3022   an,nn4749   2532   an,nn5404

before the throne, and before the Lamb, clothed with white robes, and palms

pre1722 ppro848   art,nn5495

in   their hands;

2532   pap2896   an,aj3173   an,nn5456   pap3004   art,nn4991   ppro2257   art,nn2316

10 And cried with a loud voice, saying, Salvation to our   God

art,ppmp2521   pre1909 art3588   nn2362   2532   art3588   nn721

which sitteth upon the throne, and unto the Lamb.

(1 Kgs. 22:19; 2 Chr. 18:18; Ps. 47:8; Is. 6:1; Ezek. 1:26)

2532   an,aj3956 art3588   nn32   plpf2476   an,ajn2945   art3588   nn2362   2532   art3588

11 And   all   the angels stood round about the throne, and *about* the

ajn4245   2532   art3588 nu5064   nn2226   2532   aina4098   ad*1799   art3588   nn2362   pre1909 ppro848   an,nn4383   2532

elders and the four beasts, and fell before the throne on   their faces, and

aina4352   art,nn2316

worshiped God,

pap3004   281   art,nn2129   2532   art,nn1391   2532   art,nn4678   2532   art,nn2169   2532

12 Saying, Amen: Blessing, and glory, and wisdom, and thanksgiving, and

art,nn5092   2532   art,nn1411   2532   art,nn2749   ppro2257 art,nn2316   pre1519/art,nn165/art,nn165   281

honor, and power, and might, *be* unto our   God forever*and*ever. Amen.

2532   nu1520 pre1537 art3588   ajn4245   ainp611   pap3004   ppro3427 inpro5101 pin1526 depro3778

13 And one of   the elders answered, saying unto me, What are these

pr/art,pfpp4016   art,aj3022   art,nn4749   2532   ad4159   aina2064

which*are*arrayed in white robes? and whence came they?

2532   pfi2046   ppro846 an,nn2962 epn4771   pin1492   2532   aina2036   ppro3427 depro3778

14 And I said unto him, Sir, thou knowest. And he said to me, These

pin1526   pr/art,ppmp2064   pre1537 art,aj3173   art,nn2347   2532   aina4150   ppro848 art,nn4749

are they*which*came out of great tribulation, and have washed their robes,

2532   aina3021/ppro848/   pre1722 art3588 nn129   art3588   nn721

and made*them*white in the blood of the Lamb.   *(Dan. 12:1)*

pre1223/depro5124 pin1526   ad*1799 art3588 nn2362   art,nn2316 2532 pin3000 ppro846 an,nn2250 2532

15 Therefore are they before the throne of God, and serve him day and

an,nn3571 pre1722 ppro848 art,nn3485   2532   art,ppmp2521   pre1909 art3588   nn2362   ft4637   pre1909

night in his temple: and he*that*sitteth on the throne shall dwell among

ppro846

them.   *(1 Kgs. 22:19; 2 Chr. 18:18; Ps. 47:8; Is. 6:1; Ezek. 1:26)*

fr3983 3756 ad2089   3761   ft1372   ad2089 efn3761,3361 art3588

16 They shall hunger no more, neither thirst any more; neither shall the

nn2246 asba4098 pre1909 ppro846 3761 an,aj3956 an,nn2738

sun light on them, nor any heat.   *(Is. 49:10)*

3754 art3588   nn721   art3588   pre303   an,ajn3319 art3588 nn23622   ft4165 ppro846

17 For the Lamb which is in the midst of the throne shall feed them,

2532   ft3594 ppro846 pre1909 pap2198   an,nn4077   an,nn5204 2532 art,nn2316   ft1813

and shall lead them unto living fountains of waters: and God shall wipe away

an,aj3956 an,nn1144 pre575 ppro848 art,nn3788

all tears from their eyes.

(Ps. 23:1; Ezek. 34:23; Ps. 23:2; Is. 49:10; Jer. 2:13; Is. 25:8)

Silence in Heaven

2532   ad3753   aina455 art3588 nu,aj1442 art,nn4973   aom1096 an,nn4602 pre1722

8 ☞And when he had opened the seventh seal, there was silence in

art,nn3772 ad5613   an,nn2256

heaven about the*space*of*half*an*hour.

2532 aina1492 art3588 nu2033   nn32   repro3739 pfi2476 ad*1799 art,nn2316 2532   ppro846

2 And I saw the seven angels which stood before God; and to them were

ainp1325 nu2033 an,nn4536

given seven trumpets.

2532 an,aj243   an,nn32   aina2064 2532   ainp2476 pre1909 art3588   nn2379   pap2192   an,aj5552

3 And another angel came and stood at the altar, having a golden

an,nn3031 2532   ainp1325   ppro846 an,aj4183 an,nn2368   2443   asba1325

censer; and there was given unto him much incense, that he should offer *it*

art3588   nn4335   an,aj3956 art,ajn40 pre1909 art3588 aj5552 art,nn2379 art3588   ad*1799 art3588

with the prayers of all saints upon the golden altar which was before the

nn2362

throne.   *(Ps. 141:2; Ex. 30:1-3)*

2532 art3588 nn2586   art3588   nn2368   art3588   nn4335   art3588

4 And the smoke of the incense, *which came* with the prayers of the

ajn40   aina305   ad*1799 art,nn2316 pre1537 art3588   nn32 an,nn5495

saints, ascended up before God out of the angel's hand.   *(Ps. 141:2)*

2532 art3588 nn32   pfi2983 art3588   nn3031   2532 aina1072 ppro846 pre1537 art,nn4442   art3588 nn2379

5 And the angel took the censer, and filled it with fire of the altar,

---

☞ **8:1–7** The silence in heaven that accompanies the opening of the seventh seal (v. 1) is in anticipation of the sounding of the seven trumpet judgments (v. 6).

2532   aina906   pre1519 art3588   nn1093   2532   aom1096   an,nn5456   2532   an,nn1027   2532

and cast *it* into the earth: and there were voices, and thunderings, and

an,nn796   2532   an,nn4578

lightnings, and an earthquake.   *(Lev. 16:12; Ex. 19:16; Esth. 1:1 [Sept.])*

The Seven Trumpets

2532   art3588   nu2033   nn32   art,pap2192   art3588   nu2033   nn4536   aina2090

6 And the seven angels which had the seven trumpets prepared

rxpro1438   2443   asba4537

themselves to sound.

(2532)art3588 nu,aj4413 an,nn32   aina4537   2532   aom1096 an,nn5464 2532 an,nn4442   pfpp3396

7 The first angel sounded, and there followed hail and fire mingled

an,nn129   2532   ainp906 pre1519 art3588 nn1093 2532 art3588   nu,ajn5154   art,nn1186

with blood, and they were cast upon the earth: and the third part of trees was

ainp2618   2532 an,aj3956 an,aj5515 an,nn5528   ainp2618

burnt up, and all green grass was burnt up.   *(Ex. 9:23-25; Ezek. 38:22)*

2532   art3588   nu,aj1208   an,nn32   aina4537   2532   ad5613   an,aj3173   an,nn3735

8 And the second angel sounded, and as*it*were a great mountain

ppmp2545   an,nn4442   ainp906 pre1519 art3588 nn2281 2532   art3588   nu,ajn5154   art3588 nn2281

burning with fire was cast into the sea: and the third part of the sea

aom1096   pr/an,nn129

became blood;   *(Ex. 7:20,21)*

2532   art3588   nu,ajn5154   art3588   nn2938   art3588   pre1722 art3588 nn2281 2532 art,pap2192

9 And the third part of the creatures which were in the sea, and had

an,nn5590 aina599 2532 art3588   nu,ajn5154   art3588 nn4143   ainp1311

life, died; and the third part of the ships were destroyed.

2532 art3588 nu,aj5154 an,nn32   aina4537   2532   aina4098 an,aj3173 an,nn792 pre1537   art,nn3772

10 And the third angel sounded, and there fell a great star from heaven,

ppmp2545   ad5613   an,nn2985   2532   aina4098 pre1909 art3588 nu,ajn5154   art3588 nn4215   2532

burning as*it*were a lamp, and it fell upon the third part of the rivers, and

pre1909 art3588   nn4077   an,nn5024

upon the fountains of waters;

2532   art3588   nn3686   art3588 nn792   pinp3004   pr/an,nn894   2532 art3588   nu,ajn5154

11 And the name of the star is called Wormwood: and the third part of

art3588   nn5204   pinm1096   (pre1519) an,nn894 2532 an,aj4183 an,nn444 aina599 pre1537 art3588   nn5204   3754

the waters became wormwood; and many men died of the waters, because

ainp4087

they were made bitter.

2532   art3588   nu,aj5067   an,nn32   aina4537   22532 art3588   nu,ajn5154   art3588 nn2246

12 And the fourth angel sounded, and the third part of the sun was

ainp4141   2532 art3588   nu,ajn5154   art3588 nn4582 2532 art3588   nu,ajn5154   art3588 nn792   2443

smitten, and the third part of the moon, and the third part of the stars; so as

art3588   nu,ajn5154   ppro846   asbp4654   2532 art3588 nn2250 psa5316 3361   art,nu,ajn5154

the third part of them was darkened, and the day shone not for a third part of

ppro848 2532 art3588 nn3571   ad3668

it, and the night likewise.   *(Is. 13:10; Ezek. 32:7,8; Joel 2:10; 3:15)*

2532   aina1492   2532   aina191 nu1520 an,nn32 ppmp4072   pre1722   an,nn3321

13 And I beheld, and heard an angel flying through the midst*of*heaven,

pap3004   an,aj3173 an,nn5456   3759   3759   3759   art3588   pap2730 pre1909 art3588 nn1093

saying with a loud voice, Woe, woe, woe, to the inhabiters of the earth

pre1537　　art3588　　an,aj3062　　nn5456　　　　art3588　　　nn4536　　　　art3588　　nu5140　　　nn32
by*reason*of the other voices of the trumpet of the three angels,
art,pap3195　　　pinf4537
which*are*yet to sound!

2532　　art3588　nu,aj3991　an,nn32　　aina4537　　2532　　aina1492　　an,nn792　pfp4098　pre1537　art,nn37721　pre1519
9 And the fifth angel sounded, and I saw a star fall from heaven unto
art3588　nn1093　　2532　　ppro846　　ainp1325　art3588　nn2807　　art3588　　nn12　　art,nn5421
the earth: and to him was given the key of the bottomless pit.

2532　　aina455　art3588　　nn12　　art,nn5421　2532　　　aina305　an,nn2586　pre1537
2 And he opened the bottomless pit; and there arose a smoke out of
art3588 nn5421 ad5613　　an,nn2586　　an,aj3173　an,nn2575　　2532　art3588 nn2246 2532 art3588 nn109
the pit, as the smoke of a great furnace; and the sun and the air were
ainp4654　pre1537　　art3588　nn2586　　art3588 nn5421
darkened by*reason*of the smoke of the pit.　　　　　*(Gen. 19:28; Ex. 19:18)*

2532　　　aina1831　pre1537 art3588　nn2586　　an,nn200　pre1519　art3588　nn1093　2532
3 And there came out of the smoke locusts upon the earth: and unto
ppro846　　ainp1325　an,nn1849　ad5613 art3588　nn4651　　art3588 nn1093 pin2192 an,nn1849
them was given power, as the scorpions of the earth have power.

2532　　　ainp4483　ppro846　2443　　　　3361 asba91 art3588　nn5528　　art3588
4 And it was commanded them that they should not hurt the grass of the
nn1093　3761　an,aj3956　an,ajn5515　　3761　an,aj3956 an,nn1186 1508 an,aj3441　art,nn444 repro3748
earth, neither any green thing, neither any tree; but only those men which
pin2192 3756 art3588 nn4973　art,nn2316 pre1909 ppro848　art,nn3359
have not the seal of God in their foreheads.　　　　　*(Ezek. 9:4)*

2532　　ppro846　　ainp1325　2443　　　　　3361 asba615 ppro846　235　2443
5 And to them it was given that they should not kill them, but that they
asbp928　nu4002　an,nn3376　2532　ppro848　art,nn929　　　an,nn929
should be tormented five months: and their torment *was* the torment of a
an,nn4651　ad3752　asba3817　an,nn444
scorpion, when he striketh a man.

2532　pre1722 depro1565 art,nn2250　art,nn444　ft2212　art,nn2288　2532　　　3756 ft2147 ppro846 2532
6 And in those days shall men seek death, and shall not find it; and
ft1937　　ainf599 2532 art,nn2288　fm5343 pre575　ppro846
shall desire to die, and death shall flee from them.　　　*(Job 3:21; Jer. 8:3)*

2532 art3588　nn3667　art3588　nn200　　pr/an,ajn3664　an,nn2462　pfpp2090　pre1519
7 And the shapes of the locusts *were* like unto horses prepared unto
an,nn4171　2532　pre1909 ppro848　art,nn2776　　ad5613　　an,nn4735　pr/an,aj3664 an,nn5557　2532　ppro848
battle; and on their heads *were* as*it*were crowns like gold, and their
art,nn4383　　ad5613　pr/an,nn4383　an,nn444
faces *were* as the faces of men.　　　　　*(Joel 2:4,5)*

2532　　ipf2192 an,nn2359 ad5613　an,nn2359　　an,nn1135　2532　ppro848 art,nn3599 ipf2258 ad5613
8 And they had hair as the hair of women, and their teeth were as *the*
an,nn3023
teeth of lions.　　　　　*(Joel 1:6)*

2532　　　ipf2192　　an,nn2382　　ad5613　　an,nn2382　　an,aj4603 2532 art3588
9 And they had breastplates, as*it*were breastplates of iron; and the
nn5456　ppro848 art,nn4420　ad5613　pr/an,nn5456　an,nn716　an,aj4183 an,nn2462 pap5143
sound of their wings *was* as the sound of chariots of many horses running
pre1519 an,nn4171
to battle.　　　　　*(Joel 2:5)*

2532   pin2192 an,nn3769   pr/an,ajn3664   an,nn4651   2532   ipf2258 an,nn2759 pre1722
10 And they had tails like unto scorpions, and there were stings in

ppro848 art,nn3769 2532 ppro848 art,nn1849   ainf91 art,nn444 nu4002 an,nn3376
their tails: and their power *was* to hurt men five months.

2532   pin2192   an,nn935 pre1909 ppro846   art3588   nn32   art3588
11 And they had a king over them, *which is* the angel of the

nn12   ppro846 an,nn3686   ad1447   pr/3   2532 pre1722 art3588
bottomless pit, whose name in*the*Hebrew*tongue *is* Abaddon, but in the

ajn1673   pin2192   an,nn3686   pr/an,nn623
Greek tongue hath *his* name Apollyon.

art,nu3391 (art3588) 3759   aina565   2400   pinm2064 nu1417 3759   ad2089 pre3326/depro5023
12 One   woe is past; *and,* behold, there come two woes more hereafter.

2532 art3588 nu,aj1622 an,nn32   aina4537   2532   aina191 nu3391 an,nn5456 pre1537 art3588 nu5064
13 And the sixth angel sounded, and I heard a voice from the four

nn2768   art3588 aj5552 art,nn2379 art3588   ad·1799 art,nn2316
horns of the golden altar which is before God,   *(Ex. 30:1-3)*

pap3004   art3588 nu,aj1622   an,nn32 repro3739 ipf2192 art3588   nn4536   aima3089 art3588 nu5064
14 Saying to the sixth angel which had the trumpet, Loose the four

nn32   art,pfpp1210   pre1909 art3588 aj3173 art,nn4215   an,nn2166
angels which*are*bound in the great river Euphrates.

2532 art3588 nu5064   nn32   ainp3089   art,pfpp2090   pre1519   art,nn5610
15 And the four angels were loosed, which*were*prepared for an hour,

2532 an,nn2250 2532 an,nn3376   2532   an,nn1763 2443 asba615 art3588 nu,ajn5154   art,nn444
and a day, and a month, and a year, for to slay the third part of men.

2532   art3588   nn706   an,nn4753   art3588   ajn2461
16 And the number of the army of the horsemen *were*

pr/nu1417/an,nn3461/an,nn3461   2532   aina191 art3588 nn706   ppro846
two*hundred*thousand*thousand: and I heard the number of them.

2532   ad3779   aina1492 art3588   nn2462 pre1722 art3588 nn3706   2532   art,ppmp2521   pre1909
17 And thus I saw the horses in the vision, and them*that*sat on

ppro846   pap2192   an,nn2382   an,aj4447 2532 an,aj5191 2532   an,aj2306   2532 art3588
them, having breastplates of fire, and of jacinth, and brimstone: and the

nn2776   art3588   nn2462   ad5613   pr/an,nn2776   an,nn3023 2532 pre1537 ppro848 art,nn4750
heads of the horses *were* as the heads of lions; and out of their mouths

pinm1607 an,nn4442 22532 an,nn2586 2532   an,nn2303
issued fire and smoke and brimstone.

pre5259 depro5130 art,nu,ajn5140   art3588   nu,ajn5154   art,nn444 ainp615 pre1537 art3588 nn4442 2532
18 By these three was the third part of men killed, by the fire, and

pre1537 art3588   nn2586   2532 pre1537 art3588   nn2303   art,ppmp1607   pre1537 ppro848 art,nn4750
by the smoke, and by the brimstone, which issued out of their mouths.

1063 ppro848 art,nn1849 pin1526 pre1722 ppro848 art,nn4750   2532 pre1722 ppro848 art,nn3769 1063 ppro848
19 For their power is in their mouth, and in their tails: for their

art,nn3769   pr/an,ajn3664   an,nn3789   pap2192 an,nn2776 2532 pre1722 ppro846   pin91
tails *were* like unto serpents, and had heads, and with them they do hurt.

2532 art3588 ajn3062   art3588 nn444 repro3739   3756 ainp615 pre1722 depro5025 art,nn4127
20 And the rest of the men which were not killed by these plagues

3777/aina3340   pre1537 art3588 nn2041   ppro848 art,nn5495   2443   3361 asba4352
yet*repented*not of the works of their hands, that they should not worship

art,nn1140   2532 an,nn1497   art,aj5552 2532 art,aj693   2532 art,aj5470 2532 art,aj3035 2532   art,aj3585 repro3739
devils, and idols of gold, and silver, and brass, and stone, and of wood: which

3777   pinm1410 pinf991   3777 pinf191   3777 pinf4043
neither can see, nor hear, nor walk: *(Ps. 115:4-7; 135:15-17; Dan. 5:23)*

21 Neither repented they of their murders, nor of their sorceries, nor of their fornication, nor of their thefts.

A Strong Angel

10 ☞And I saw another mighty angel come down from heaven, clothed with a cloud: and a rainbow *was* upon his head, and his face *was* as*it*were the sun, and his feet as pillars of fire:

2 And he had in his hand a little book open: and he set his right foot upon the sea, and his left *foot* on the earth,

3 And cried with a loud voice, as *when* a lion roareth: and when he had cried, seven thunders uttered their voices.

4 And when the seven thunders had uttered their voices, I was about to write: and I heard a voice from heaven saying unto me, Seal up those things which the seven thunders uttered, and write them not.   *(Dan. 8:26; 12:4,9)*

5 And the angel which I saw stand upon the sea and upon the earth lifted up his hand to heaven,   *(Deut. 32:40; Dan. 12:7)*

6 And sware by him*that*liveth forever*and*ever, who created heaven, and the things that therein are, and the earth, and the things that therein are, and the sea, and the things which are therein, that there should be time no longer: *(Dan. 12:7; Gen. 14:19,22; Ex. 20:11; Neh. 9:6; Ps. 146:6)*

7 But in the days of the voice of the seventh angel, when he shall begin to sound, the mystery of God should be finished, as he hath declared to his servants the prophets.   *(Dan. 9:6,10; Amos 3:7; Zech. 1:6)*

☞ **10:1–11** This chapter is a parenthetical portion between the sixth and the seventh trumpets. The words of the seven thunders were the only thing that John was not permitted to reveal.

2532 art3588 nn5456 repro3739 aina191 pre1537 art,nn3772 pap2980 pre3326 ppro1700 ad3825 2532
8 And the voice which I heard from heaven spake unto me again, and

pap3004 aima5217 aima2983 art3588 nn974 art,pfpp455 pre1722 art3588 nn5495 an,nn32
said, Go *and* take the little book which*is*open in the hand of the angel

art,pfp2476 pre1909 art3588 nn2281 2532 pre1909 art3588 nn1093
which standeth upon the sea and upon the earth.

2532 aina565 pre4314 art3588 nn32 pap3004 ppro846 aima1325 ppro3427 art3588
9 And I went unto the angel, and said unto him, Give me the

nn974 2532 pin3004 ppro3427 aima2983 2532 aima2719/ppro846 2532
little book. And he said unto me, Take *it,* and eat*it*up; and it

ft4087/ppro4675/art,nn2836 235 fm2071 pre1722 ppro4675 art,nn4750 pr/an,aj1099 ad5613
shall make*thy*belly*bitter, but it shall be in thy mouth sweet as

an,nn3192
honey.

2532 aina2983 art3588 nn974 pre1537 art3588 nn32 art,nn5495 2532 aina2719/ppro846 2532
10 And I took the little book out of the angel's hand, and ate*it*up; and it

ipf2258 pre1722 ppro3450 art,nn4750 pr/an,aj1099 ad5613 an,nn3192 2532 ad3753 aina5315 ppro846 ppro3450
was in my mouth sweet as honey: and as*soon*as I had eaten it, my

art,nn2836 ainf4087
belly was bitter.   *(Ezek. 2:8; 3:1-3)*

2532 pin3004 ppro3427 ppro4571 pin1163 ainf4395 ad3825 pre1909 an,aj4183 an,nn2992
11 And he said unto me, Thou must prophesy again before many peoples,

2532 an,nn1484 2532 an,nn1100 2532 an,nn935
and nations, and tongues, and kings.   *(Jer. 1:10; Dan. 3:4; 7:14)*

The Two Prophets of God

2532 ainp1325 ppro3427 an,nn2563 an,aj3664 an,nn4464 2532 art3588
11 And there was given me a reed like unto a rod: and the

nn32 pipf2476 pap3004 aipm1453 2532 aima3354 art3588 nn3485 art,nn2316
angel stood, saying, Rise, and measure the temple of God,

2532 art3588 nn2379 2532 art,pap4352 pre1722/ppro846
and the altar, and them*that*worship therein.   *(Ezek. 40:3; Zech. 2:1,2)*

2532 art3588 nn833 art,ad1855 art3588 nn3485 aima1544 ad1854 2532 aosi3354 ppro846
2 But the court which*is*without the temple leave out, and measure it

3361 3754 ainp1325 art3588 nn1484 2532 art3588 aj40 art,nn4172
not; for it is given unto the Gentiles: and the holy city shall they

ft3961 nu5062/nu1417 an,nn3376
tread*under*foot forty*and*two months.

(Ps. 79:1; Is. 63:18; Zech. 12:3 [Sept.])

2532 ft1325 ppro3450 nu1417 art,nn3144 2532 ft4395
3 And I will give *power* unto my two witnesses, and they shall prophesy

nu5507/nu1250/nu1835 an,nn2250 pfpp4016 an,nn4526
a*thousand*two*hundred*and*threescore days, clothed in sackcloth.

11:1–12 The exact identity of these two witnesses is unknown. There is speculation that they will be either Moses and Elijah, or Enoch and Elijah.

4 These are the two olive trees, and the two candlesticks standing before the God of the earth. *(Zech. 4:3; 11-14)*

5 And if*any*man will hurt them, fire proceedeth out of their mouth, and devoureth their enemies: and if*any*man will hurt them, he must in*this*manner be killed.

(2 Sam. 22:9; 2 Kgs. 1:10; Ps. 97:3; Jer. 5:14)

6 These have power to shut heaven, that it*rain*not in the days of their prophecy: and have power over waters to turn them to blood, and to smite the earth with all plagues, as*often*as they will.

(1 Kgs. 17:1; Ex. 7:17,19,20; 1 Sam. 4:8)

7 And when they shall have finished their testimony, the beast that ascendeth out of the bottomless pit shall make war against them, and shall overcome them, and kill them. *(Dan. 7:3,7,21)*

8 And their dead bodies *shall lie* in the street of the great city, which spiritually is called Sodom and Egypt, where also our Lord was crucified.

(Is. 1:10)

9 And they of the people and kindreds and tongues and nations shall see their dead bodies three days and a half, and shall not suffer their dead bodies to be put in graves.

10 And they*that*dwell upon the earth shall rejoice over them, and make merry, and shall send gifts one*to*another; because these two prophets tormented them*that*dwelt on the earth.

11 And after three days and a half the Spirit of life from God entered into them, and they stood upon their feet; and great fear fell upon them*which*saw them. *(Ezek. 37:5,10)*

12 And they heard a great voice from heaven saying unto them, Come up

ad5602   2532   aina305   pre1519 art,nn3772 pre1722   art,nn3507 2532 ppro848 art,ajn2190

hither. And they ascended up to heaven in a cloud; and their enemies

aina2334   ppro846

beheld them.   *(2 Kgs. 2:11)*

2532   depro1565   art,nn5610 aom1096   an,aj3173   an,nn4578   2532 art3588   nu,ajn1182

13 And the same hour was there a great earthquake, and the tenth part of

art3588 nn4172 aina4098 2532 pre1722 art3588   nn4578   ainp615 (an,nn3686) an,nn444 nu2033   an,nn5505

the city fell, and in the earthquake were slain of men seven thousand:

2532 art3588   ajn3062   aom1096   pr/an,aj1719   2532 aina1325 an,nn1391   art3588 nn2316   art,nn3772

and the remnant were affrighted, and gave glory to the God of heaven.

(Ezek. 38:19,20)

art3588   nu,aj1208   (art3588) 3759   aina565   2400   art3588 nu,aj5154 (art3588) 3759 pinm2064

14 The second woe is past; *and,* behold, the third woe cometh

an,ajn5035

quickly.

Christ Will Rule Forever

2532   art3588   nu,aj1442   an,nn32   aina4537   2532   aom1096 an,aj3173 an,nn5456 pre1722

15 And the seventh angel sounded; and there were great voices in

art,nn3772   pap3004   art3588   nn932   art,nn2889   aom1096   ppro2257

heaven, saying, The kingdoms of this world are become *the kingdoms* of our

art,nn2962 2532   ppro848 art,nn5547 2532   ft936   pre1519/art,nn165/art,nn165

Lord, and of his Christ; and he shall reign forever*and*ever.

(Ex. 15:18; Ps. 10:16; 22:28; Dan. 2:44; 7:14; Obad. 21; Zech. 14:9)

2532 art3588   nu5064/2532/nu1501   ajn4245   art,ppmp2521   ad*1799   art,nn2316 pre1909 ppro848

16 And the four*and*twenty elders, which sat before God on their

art,nn2362 aina4098 pre1909 ppro848 art,nn483   2532   aoma4352   art,nn2316

seats, fell upon their faces, and worshiped God,

pap3004   pin2168/ppro4671   an,nn2962   art,nn2316   art,nn3841

17 Saying, We give*thee*thanks, O Lord God Almighty,

3801 [art,pap5607/2532/art,ipf2258/2532/art,ppmp2064]   3754   pfi2983   ppro4675

which*art,*and*wast,*and*art*to*come; because thou hast taken to thee thy

art,aj3173   art,nn1411   2532   aina936

great power, and hast reigned.

(Amos 3:13 [Sept.]; 4:13 [Sept.]; Ex. 3:14; Is. 41:4)

2532 art3588   nn1484   ainp3710   2532 ppro4675 art,nn3709   aina2064 2532 art3588 nn2540

18 And the nations were angry, and thy wrath is come, and the time of

art3588 ajn3498   aifp2919   2532   ainf1325 art,nn3408

the dead, that they should be judged, and that thou shouldest give reward unto

ppro4675 art,ajn1401 art3588 nn4396 2532 art3588 ajn40 2532   art,ppmp5399 ppro4675 art,nn3686

thy servants the prophets, and to the saints, and them*that*fear thy name,

art,ajn3398 2532 art,ajn3173 2532   ainf1311   art,pap1311   art3588 nn1093

small and great; and shouldest destroy them*which*destroy the earth.

(Ps. 2:1; 46:6; Dan. 9:6,10; Amos 3:7; Zech. 1:6; Ps. 115:3)

2532 art3588   nn3485   art,nn2316   ainp455   pre1722   art,nn3772   2532   ainp3700

19 And the temple of God was opened in heaven, and there was seen

pre1722 ppro848 art,nn3485 art3588 nn2787   ppro848   art,nn1242   2532   aom1096   an,nn796   2532

in his temple the ark of his testament: and there were lightnings, and

an,nn5456   2532   an,nn1027   2532   an,nn4578   2532 an,aj3173 an,nn5464

voices, and thunderings, and an earthquake, and great hail.

(1 Kgs. 8:1,6; 2 Chr. 5:7; Ex. 19:16; Esth. 1:1 [Sept.]; Ex. 9:24)

A Woman Gives Birth to a Son

2532   ainp3700   an,aj3173   an,nn4592   pre1722   art,nn3772   an,nn1135   pfpp4016

12 And there appeared a great wonder in heaven; a woman clothed with

art3588 nn2246   2532 art3588   nn4582   ad*5270   ppro848 art,nn4228   2532   pre1909 ppro848 art,nn2776

the sun, and the moon under her feet, and upon her head a

an,nn4735   nu1427   an,nn792

crown of twelve stars:

2532   pap2192/pre1722/an,nn1064   pin2896   pap5605   2532   ppmp928

2 And she being*with*child cried, travailing*in*birth, and pained to be

ainf5088

delivered.   *(Is. 66:7; Mic. 4:10)*

2532   ainp3700   an,aj243   an,nn4592   pre1722   art,nn3772   2532   2400   an,aj3173

3 And there appeared another wonder in heaven; and behold a great

an,aj4450   an,nn1404   pap2192   nu2033   an,nn2776   2532 nu1176   an,nn2768   2532   nu2033   an,nn1238   pre1909 ppro848

red dragon, having seven heads and ten horns, and seven crowns upon his

art,nn2776

heads.   *(Dan. 7:7)*

2532   ppro848 art,nn3769 pin4951 art3588   nu,ajn5154   art3588   nn792   art,nn3772   2532   aina906

4 And his tail drew the third part of the stars of heaven, and did cast

ppro846   pre1519   art3588   nn1093   2532   art3588   nn1404   pfi2476   ad*1799   art3588   nn1135

them to the earth: and the dragon stood before the woman

art,pap3195   ainf5088   2443   asba2719   ppro848 art,nn5043   ad3752

which*was*ready to be delivered, for to devour her child as*soon*as it was

asba5088

born.   *(Dan. 8:10)*

2532   aina5088   an,nn730 an,nn5207 repro3739 pin3195   pinf4165 an,aj3956 art,nn1484   pre1722

5 And she brought forth a man child, who was to rule all nations with a

an,nn4464   an,aj4603 2532 ppro848 art,nn5043   ainp726   pre4314 art,nn2316 2532   ppro848 art,nn2362

rod of iron: and her child was caught up unto God, and *to* his throne.

(Is. 7:14; Ps. 2:9; Is. 9:6)

2532   art3588   nn1135   aina5343 pre1519 art3588   ajn2048   ad3699   pin2192   an,nn5117

6 And the woman fled into the wilderness, where she hath a place

pfpp2090   pre575   art,nn2316   2443   psa5142   ppro846   ad1563

prepared of God, that they should feed her there

nu5507/nu1250/nu1835   an,nn2250

a*thousand*two*hundred**and*threescore days.

2532   aom1096 an,nn4171 pre1722   art,nn3772   3413   2532 ppro848 art,nn32   aina4170   pre2596

7 And there was war in heaven: Michael and his angels fought against

art3588　nn1404　　2532　art3588　nn1404　　aina4170　2532　ppro848　art,nn32
the dragon; and the dragon fought and his angels,　　　　*(Dan. 10:13,21; 12:1)*

2532　　aina2480　　3756　　3777　　　　ppro848　an,nn5117　ainp2147　　ad2089　　pre1722
8 And prevailed not; neither was their place found any more in

art,nn3772
heaven.

2532　art3588　aj3173　art,nn1404　　　ainp906　　art,aj744　art,nn3789　art,ppmp2564　an,ajn1228
9 And the great dragon was cast out, that old serpent, called the Devil,

2532　art,nn4567　art,pap4105　　art3588　an,aj3650　nn3625　　　　　ainp906　pre1519 art3588　nn1093
and Satan, which deceiveth the whole world: he was cast out into the earth,

2532　ppro848　art,nn32　　　ainp906　pre3326 ppro846
and his angels were cast out with him.　　　　　　　*(Is. 14:12)*

2532　　aina191　　an,aj3173 an,nn5456　pap3004　pre1722　art,nn3772　ad737　aom1096　art,nn4991
10 And I heard a loud voice saying in heaven, Now is come salvation,

2532　art,nn1411　　2532 art3588　　nn932　　ppro2257 art,nn2316　2532 art3588　nn1849　ppro848　art,nn5547　3754
and strength, and the kingdom of our God, and the power of his Christ: for

art3588　nn2725　　ppro2257　art,nn80　　　ainp2598　　art,pap2723　　ppro846　ad*1799　ppro2257
the accuser of our brethren is cast down, which accused them before our

art,nn2316 an,nn2250　2532　an,nn3571
God day and night.　　　　　　　*(Job 1:9-11; Zech. 3:1)*

2532　epn846　aina3528　　ppro846 pre1223 art3588　nn129　　art3588　nn721　　2532　pre1223 art3588
11 And they overcame him by the blood of the Lamb, and by the

nn3056　ppro848　art,nn3141　2532　aina25　3756　ppro848 art,nn5590　ad891　an,nn2288
word of their testimony; and they loved not their lives unto the death.

pre1223/depro5124　pim2165　art,nn3772　2532　art,pap4637　pre1722　ppro846　3759
12 Therefore rejoice, *ye* heavens, and ye*that*dwell in them. Woe to

art3588　pap3730　　art3588　nn1093　2532　　art3588　nn2281　3754 art3588　ajn1228　　aina2597
the inhabitants of the earth and of the sea! for the devil is come down

pre4314 ppro5209　pap2192　an,aj3173　an,nn2372　　　　pfp1492　3754　　pin2192　　an,aj3641
unto you, having great wrath, because he knoweth that he hath but a short

an,nn2540
time.

2532　ad3753　art3588　nn1404　aina1492　3754　　　ainp906　pre1519 art3588　nn1093
13 And when the dragon saw that he was cast unto the earth, he

aina1377　art3588　nn1135　repro3748　aina5088　　art3588　nn730
persecuted the woman which brought forth the man *child.*

2532　art3588　nn1135　　ainp1325　nu1417 an,nn4420　　art,aj3173　art,nn105　2443
14 And to the woman were given two wings of a great eagle, that she

psmp4072 pre1519 art3588　ajn2048　pre1519 ppro848 art,nn5117　ad3699　　　pinp5142　(ad1563)
might fly into the wilderness, into her place, where she is nourished for a

an,nn2540　2532　an,nn2540　2532　nu2255　an,nn2540　pre575　an,nn4383　art3588　nn3789
time, and times, and half a time, from the face of the serpent.

(Dan. 7:25; 12:7)

2532　art3588　nn3789　aina906　pre1537　ppro848　art,nn4750　an,nn5204　ad5613　an,nn4215　ad*3694 art3588
15 And the serpent cast out of his mouth water as a flood after the

nn1135　2443　　asba4160 depro5026　　an,aj4216
woman, that he might cause her to be carried*away*of*the*flood.

2532　art3588　nn1093　aina997　art3588　nn1135　2532　art3588　nn1093　aina455　ppro848　art,nn4750
16 And the earth helped the woman, and the earth opened her mouth,

2532　aina2666　art3588　nn4215　repro3739 art3588　nn1404　aina906　pre1537 ppro848 art,nn4750
and swallowed up the flood which the dragon cast out of his mouth.

2532   art3588   nn1404   ainp3710   pre1909 art3588   nn1135   2532   aina565   ainf4160   an,nn4171

17 And the dragon was wroth with the woman, and went to make war

pre3326 art3588   ajn3062   ppro848 art,nn4690   art,pap5083   art3588   nn1785   art,nn2316   2532

with the remnant of her seed, which keep the commandments of God, and

pap2192 art3588   nn3141   art,nn2424 an,nn5547

have the testimony of Jesus Christ.   *(Dan. 7:7,21)*

The Beast

13   2532   ainp2476   pre1909 art3588   nn285   art3588 nn2281   2532   aina1492   an,nn2342   pap305

☞ **And I stood upon the sand of the sea, and saw a beast rise up**

pre1537   art3588   nn2281   pap2192   nn2033   an,nn2776   2532   nu1176   an,nn2768   2532   pre1909

out of the sea, having seven heads and ten horns, and upon

ppro848 art,nn2768 nu1176   an,nn1238   2532   pre1909 ppro848 art,nn2776   an,nn3686   an,nn988

his horns ten crowns, and upon his heads the name of blasphemy.

(Dan. 7:3)

2532   art3588   nn2342   repro3739   aina1492   ipf2258   pr/an,ajn3664   an,nn3917   2532   ppro848 art,nn4228

2 And the beast which I saw was like unto a leopard, and his feet were

ad5613   an,nn715   2532   ppro848 art,nn4750 ad5613   pr/an,nn4750   an,nn3023   2532   art3588   nn1404

as *the feet* of a bear, and his mouth as the mouth of a lion: and the dragon

aina1325 ppro846 ppro848   art,nn1411   2532   ppro848 art,nn2362   2532   an,aj3173   an,nn1849

gave him his power, and his seat, and great authority.   *(Dan. 7:4-6)*

2532   aina1492   nu3391   ppro848 art,nn2776   ad5613   pfpp4969   pre1519   an,nn2288   2532   ppro848

3 And I saw one of his heads as*it*were wounded to death; and his

art,nn2288   art,nn4127   ainp2323   2532   an,aj3650 art3588   nn1093   aina2296   ad*3694 art3588   nn2342

deadly wound was healed: and all the world wondered after the beast.

2532   aina4352   art3588   nn1404   repro3739 aina1325   an,nn1849   art3588   nn2342   2532

4 And they worshiped the dragon which gave power unto the beast: and

aina4352   art3588   nn2342   pap3004   inpro5101   pr/an,ajn3664 art3588   nn2342   inpro5101   pinm1410

they worshiped the beast, saying, Who *is* like unto the beast? who is able to

ainf4170   pre3326 ppro846

make war with him?

2532   ainp1325   ppro846   an,nn4750   pap2980   an,ajn3173   2532

5 And there was given unto him a mouth speaking great things and

an,nn988   2532   an,nn1849   ainp1325   ppro846   ainf4160   nu5062/nu1417

blasphemies; and power was given unto him to continue forty*and*two

an,nn3376

months.   *(Dan. 7:8,20,25; 11:26)*

2532   aina455   ppro848 art,nn4750 pre1519   an,nn988   pre4314 art,nn2316   ainf987

6 And he opened his mouth in blasphemy against God, to blaspheme

---

☞ **13:1–18** There are two personalities mentioned in this chapter. The first is the Antichrist (vv. 1–10). He will be the political ruler of the world at that time, bringing a false sense of peace (Rev. 6:2). Jesus warned his disciples of this deceiver. In John 5:43, the Lord said, "I am come in my Father's name, and ye receive me not: if another shall come in his own name, him ye will receive." See note on 2 Thessalonians 2:3–9 which deals with the Antichrist.

The second beast (vv. 11–18) will become the religious leader of the day and will be worshiped. Those people that receive the mark of the beast on their right hand or on their forehead will be cast into the lake of fire (Rev. 14:9–11).

pqurepro848   art,nn3686   2532   pquepro848   art,nn4633   2532   art,pap4637   pre1722   art,nn3772

his name, and his tabernacle, and them*that*dwell in heaven.

2532   ainp1325   ppro846   ainf4160   an,nn4171   pre3326   art3588   ajn40   2532

7 And it was given unto him to make war with the saints, and to

ainf3528   ppro846   2532   an,nn1849   ainp1325   ppro846   pre1909   an,aj3956   an,nn5443   2532   an,nn1100

overcome them: and power was given him over all kindreds, and tongues,

2532   an,nn1484

and nations.   *(Dan. 7:7,21)*

2532   an,aj3956   art,pap2730   pre1909   art3588   nn1093   ft4352   ppro846   repro3739   art,nn3686

8 And all that dwell upon the earth shall worship him, whose names are

3756   pfip1125   pre1722   art3588   nn976   art,nn2222   art3588   nn721   pfpp4969   pre575   an,nn2602

not written in the book of life of the Lamb slain from the foundation of the

an,nn2889

world.   *(Ex. 32:32,33; Ps. 69:28; Dan. 12:1; Is. 53:7)*

idpro1536   pin2192   an,nn3775   aima191

9 If*any*man have an ear, let him hear.

idpro1536   pin4863   an,nn161   pin5217   pre1519   an,nn161   idpro1536   ft615

10 He that leadeth into captivity shall go into captivity: he that killeth

pre1722   an,nn3162   pin1163   (ppro846)   aifp615   pre1722   an,nn3162   ad5602   pin2076   art3588   nn5281   2532

with the sword must be killed with the sword. Here is the patience and

art3588   nn4102   art3588   ajn40

the faith of the saints.   *(Jer. 15:2; 43:11)*

2532   aina1492   an,aj243   an,nn2342   pap305   pre1537   art3588   nn1093   2532   ipf2192

11 And I beheld another beast coming up out of the earth; and he had

nu1417   an,nn2768   an,ajn3664   an,nn721   2532   ipf2980   ad5613   an,nn1404

two horns like a lamb, and he spake as a dragon.

2532   pin4160   an,aj3956   art3588   nn1849   art3588   nu,aj4413   nn2342   ad*1799   ppro846   2532

12 And he exerciseth all the power of the first beast before him, and

pin4160   art3588   nn1093   2532   art,pap2730   pre1722/ppro846   2443   asba4532   art3588   nu,aj4413   an,nn2342

causeth the earth and them*which*dwell therein to worship the first beast,

repro3739   ppro848/art,nn2288/art,nn4127   ainp2323

whose deadly wound was healed.

2532   pin4160   an,aj3173   an,nn4592   2443   (2532)   psa4160   an,nn4442   pinf2597

13 And he doeth great wonders, so that he maketh fire come down

pre1537   art,nn3772   pre1519   art3588   nn1093   ad*1799   art,nn444

from heaven on the earth in*the*sight of men,

2532   pin4105   art,pap3720   pre1909   art3588   nn1093   pre1223

14 And deceiveth them*that*dwell on the earth by *the means of* those

art,nn4592   repro3739   ainp1325/ppro846   ainf4160   ad*1799   art3588   nn2342   pap3004

miracles which he had power to do in*the*sight of the beast; saying to

art,pap2730   pre1909   art3588   nn1093   ainf4160   an,nn1504   art3588   nn2342

them* that*dwell on the earth, that they should make an image to the beast,

repro3739   pin2192   art3588   nn4127   art,nn3162   2532   aina2198

which had the wound by a sword, and did live.

2532   ainp1325/ppro846   ainf1325   an,nn4151   art3588   nn1504   art3588   nn2342   2443   art3588

15 And he had power to give life unto the image of the beast, that the

nn1504   art3588   nn2342   2532   asba2980   2532   asba4160   an,ajn3745/302   3361

image of the beast should both speak, and cause that as*many*as would not

asba4352   art3588   nn1504   art3588   nn2342   (2443)   asbp615

worship the image of the beast should be killed.   *(Dan. 3:5,6)*

2532   pin4160   an,ajn3956   art,ajn3398   2532   art,ajn3173(2532)   art,ajn4145   2532   art,ajn4434(2532)   art,ajn1658

16 And he causeth all, both small and great, rich and poor, free

2532 art,ajn1401 2443 asba1325/ppro846   an,nn5480 pre1909 ppro848 art,aj1188 art,nn5495 2228 pre1909 ppro848   art,nn3359

and bond, to receive a mark in their right hand, or in their foreheads:

2532   2443   3361 idpro5100 psmp1410 ainf59 2228 ainf4453 1508   art,pap2192   art3588 nn5480 2228

17 And that no man might buy or sell, save he*that*had the mark, or

art3588 nn3686   art3588 nn2342 2228 art3588   nn706   ppro848 art,nn3686

the name of the beast, or the number of his name.

ad5602 pin2076 art,nn4678   art,pap2192   art,nn3563   aima5585 art3588   nn706

18 Here is wisdom. Let him*that*hath understanding count the number

art3588   nn2342 1063   pin2076   pr/an,nn706   an,nn444 2532 ppro848 art,nn706

of the beast: for it is the number of a man; and his number *is*

pr/nu1812/nu1835/nu1803

Six*hundred*threescore*and*six.

Jesus and His People

2532   aina1492 2532 2400   an,nn721 pfp2476 pre1909 art3588   nn3735   4622   2532 pre3326

14 And I looked, and, lo, a Lamb stood on the mount Zion, and with

ppro846   nu1540/nu5062/nu5064/nu5505   pap2192 ppro848 art,nn3962

him a*hundred*forty*and*four*thousand, having his Father's

art,nn3686 pfpp1125 pre1909 ppro848   art,nn3359

name written in their foreheads.   *(Ezek. 9:4)*

2532   aina191   an,nn5456 pre1537 art,nn3772 ad5613   an,nn5456   an,aj4183 an,nn5204 2532

2 And I heard a voice from heaven, as the voice of many waters, and

ad5613   an,nn5456   an,aj3173 an,nn1027 2532 aina191   an,nn5456   an,nn2790 pap2789 pre1722

as the voice of a great thunder: and I heard the voice of harpers harping with

ppro848 art,nn2788

their harps: *(Ezek. 1:24; 43:2)*

2532   pin103   ad5613   an,aj2537 an,nn5603 ad*1799 art3588   nn2362   2532 ad*1799

3 And they sung as*it*were a new song before the throne, and before

art3588 nu5064   nn2226   2532 art3588 ajn4245   2532 an,ajn3762 ipf1410 ainf3129   art,nn5603 1508 art3588

the four beasts, and the elders: and no man could learn that song but the

nu1540/nu5062/nu5064/an,nn5505   art,pfpp59   pre575 art3588 nn1093

hundred*and*forty*and*four*thousand, which*were*redeemed from the earth.

(Ps. 33:3; 40:3; 96:1; 98:1; 144:9; 149:1; Is. 42:10)

depro3778 pin1526   pr/repro3739   3756 ainp3435 pre3326 an,nn1135 1063   pin1526

4 These are they which were not defiled with women; for they are

pr/an,ajn3933 depro3778 pin1526   pr/art,pap190   art3588   nn721   ad3699/302   psa5217

virgins. These are they*which*follow the Lamb whithersoever he goeth.

depro3778   ainp59   pre575   art,nn444   pr/an,nn536   art,nn2316 2532

These were redeemed from among men, *being* the firstfruits unto God and to

art3588   nn721

the Lamb.

2532 pre1722 ppro848 art,nn4750   ainp2147 3756 an,nn1388 1063   pin1526   pr/an,aj299

5 And in their mouth was found no guile: for they are without fault

ad*1799 art3588   nn2362   art,nn2316

before the throne of God.   *(Ps. 32:2; Is. 53:9; Zeph. 3:13)*

6 And I saw another angel fly in the midst*of*heaven, having the everlasting gospel to preach unto them*that*dwell on the earth, and to every nation, and kindred, and tongue, and people,

7 Saying with a loud voice, Fear God, and give glory to him; for the hour of his judgment is come: and worship him*that*made heaven, and earth, and the sea, and the fountains of waters. *(Ex. 20:11; Ps. 146:6)*

8 And there followed another angel, saying, Babylon is fallen, is fallen, that great city, because she made*all*nations*drink of the wine of the wrath of her fornication. *(Is. 21:9; Jer. 51:8; 51:7)*

9 And the third angel followed them, saying with a loud voice, If*any*man worship the beast and his image, and receive *his* mark in his forehead, or in his hand,

10 The same shall drink of the wine of the wrath of God, which*is*poured*out without mixture into the cup of his indignation; and he shall be tormented with fire and brimstone in*the*presence of the holy angels, and in*the*presence of the Lamb:

(Ps. 75:8; Is. 51:17,22; Jer. 25:15; Gen. 19:24; Ps. 11:6; Ezek. 38:22)

11 And the smoke of their torment ascendeth up forever*and*ever: and they have no rest day nor night, who worship the beast and his image, and whosoever receiveth the mark of his name. *(Is. 34:10)*

12 Here is the patience of the saints: here *are* they*that*keep the commandments of God, and the faith of Jesus.

13 And I heard a voice from heaven saying unto me, Write, Blessed *are* the dead which die in the Lord from henceforth: Yea, saith the Spirit, that they may rest from their labors; and their works do follow them.

The Time for Judgment

2532   aina1492 2532 2400   an,aj3022 an,nn3507 2532 pre1909 art3588 nn3507   ppmp2521

14 And I looked, and behold a white cloud, and upon the cloud *one* sat

an,ajn3664   an,nn5207 an,nn444 pap2192 pre1909 ppro848 art,nn2776   an,aj5552 an,nn4735 2532 pre1722 ppro848

like unto the Son of man, having on his head a golden crown, and in his

art,nn5495 an,aj3691 an,nn1407

hand a sharp sickle.   *(Dan. 7:13)*

2532 an,aj243 an,nn32 aima1831 pre1537 art3588   nn3485   pap2896 pre1722   an,aj3173 an,nn5456

15 And another angel came out of the temple, crying with a loud voice to

art,ppmp2521   pre1909 art3588 nn3507   aima3992   ppro4675 art,nn1407 2532 aima2325 3754 art3588 nn5610

him*that*sat on the cloud, Thrust in thy sickle, and reap: for the time is

aina2064 ppro4671   infg2325 3754 art3588 nn2326   art3588 nn1093   ainp3583

come for thee to reap; for the harvest of the earth is ripe.   *(Joel 3:13)*

2532   art,ppmp2521   pre1909 art3588 nn3507   aina906   ppro848 art,nn1407 pre1909 art3588   nn1093

16 And he*that*sat on the cloud thrust in his sickle on the earth;

2532 art3588 nn1093   ainp2325

and the earth was reaped.

2532 an,aj243 an,nn32 aina1831 pre1537 art3588 nn3485   art3588   pre1722 art,nn3772 epn846

17 And another angel came out of the temple which is in heaven, he

2532 pap2192 an,aj3691 an,nn1407

also having a sharp sickle.

2532 an,aj243 an,nn32 aina1831 pre1537 art3588 nn2379   pap2192 an,nn1849 pre1909

18 And another angel came out from the altar, which had power over

art,nn4442 2532 aina5455   an,aj3173 an,nn2906   art,pap2192 art3588 aj3691 art,nn1407 pap3004

fire; and cried with a loud cry to him*that*had the sharp sickle, saying,

aina3992   ppro4675 art,aj3691 art,nn1407 2532 aima5166 art3588   nn1009   art3588 nn288   art3588 nn1093

Thrust in thy sharp sickle, and gather the clusters of the vine of the earth;

3754 ppro848 art,nn4718   aina187

for her grapes are*fully*ripe.   *(Joel 3:13)*

2532 art3588 nn32   aina906   ppro848 art,nn1407 pre1519 art3588 nn1093 2532 aina5166

19 And the angel thrust in his sickle into the earth, and gathered

art3588 nn288   art3588 nn1093 2532 aina906   pre1519 art3588 aj3173 art,nn3025   art3588 nn2372

the vine of the earth, and cast *it* into the great winepress of the wrath of

art,nn2316

God.

2532 art3588   nn3025   ainp3961   ad1854 art3588 nn4172 2532 an,nn129 aina1831

20 And the winepress was trodden without the city, and blood came

pre1537 art3588   nn3025   ad891   art3588 nn2462 art,nn5469   pre575

out of the winepress, even unto the horse bridles, by*the*space*of

nu5507/nu1812   an,nn4712

a*thousand*and*six*hundred furlongs.   *(Is. 63:3; Lam. 1:15)*

14:14—20 In this passage, the record is given of the Lord Jesus Christ's ultimate triumph over evil at the Battle of Armageddon. Although man has desperately tried to abolish war, the word of God clearly teaches that he will never be successful. In Matthew 24:6, the Lord said that there would be "wars and rumors of wars" until the Second Coming of Christ. At this time, the war to end all wars will take place, the Battle of Armageddon (cf. Is. 34:1—8; 63:1—6; Joel 2:1—11; 3:9—13; Zeph. 1:14—18; 3:8; Zech. 12:9—11; 14:1—3).

The Seven Plagues

15 2532 aina1492 an,aj243 an,nn4592 pre1722 art,nn3772 an,aj3173 2532 an,aj2298
And I saw another sign in heaven, great and marvelous,
nu2033 an,nn32 pap2192 art3588 nu2033 aj2078 an,nn4127 3754 pre1722 ppro846
seven angels having the seven last plagues; for in them is
ainp5055 art,nn2372 art,nn2316
filled up the wrath of God.   *(Lev. 26:21)*

2532 aina1492 ad5613 an,nn2281 an,aj5193 pfpp3396 an,nn4442 2532
2 And I saw as*it*were a sea of glass mingled with fire: and
art,pap3528 pre1537 art3588 nn2342 2532 pre1537 ppro848 art,nn1504 2532
them*that*had*gotten*the*victory over the beast, and over his image, and
pre1537 ppro848 art,nn5480 pre1537 art3588 nn706 ppro848 art,nn3686 pfp2476 pre1909 art3588 nn2281
over his mark, *and* over the number of his name, stand on the sea of
art,aj5193 pap2192 an,nn2788 art,nn2316
glass, having the harps of God.

2532 pin103 art3588 nn5603 an,nn3475 art3588 ajn1401 art,nn2316 2532 art3588 nn5603
3 And they sing the song of Moses the servant of God, and the song of
art3588 nn721 pap3004 pr/an,aj3173 2532 pr/an,aj2298 ppro4675 art,nn2041 an,nn2962 art,nn2316
the Lamb, saying, Great and marvellous *are* thy works, Lord God
art,nn3841 pr/an,aj1342 2532 pr/an,aj228 ppro4675 art,nn3598 art,nn935 art,ajn40
Almighty; just and true *are* thy ways, thou King of saints.

(Ex. 15:1; 15:11; Ps. 92:5; 111:2; 139:14;

Amos 3:13; 4:13 [Sept.]; Deut. 32:4; Ps. 145:17)

inpro5101 efn3364 asbp5399 ppro4571 an,nn2962 2532 asba1392 ppro4675 art,nn3686 3754 an,aj3440
4 Who shall not fear thee, O Lord, and glorify thy name? for *thou* only
pr/an,aj3741 3754 an,aj3956 art,nn1484 ft2240 2532 ft4352 ad*1799 ppro4675 3754 ppro4675
art holy: for all nations shall come and worship before thee; for thy
art,nn1345 ainp5319
judgments are made manifest.   *(Jer. 10:6,7; Ps. 86:9; Mal. 1:11)*

2532 pre3326 depro5023 aina1492 2532 2400 art3588 nn3485 art3588 nn4633
5 And after that I looked, and, behold, the temple of the tabernacle of
art3588 nn3142 pre1722 art,nn3772 ainp455
the testimony in heaven was opened: *(Ex. 38:21; 40:34)*

2532 art3588 nu2033 nn32 aina1831 pre1537 art3588 nn3485 pap2192 art3588 nu2033
6 And the seven angels came out of the temple, having the seven
nn4127 pfpp1746 an,aj2513 2532 an,aj2986 an,nn3043 2532 (pre4012) art,nn4738 pfpp4024
plagues, clothed in pure and white linen, and having their breasts girded with
an,aj5552 an,nn2223
golden girdles.   *(Lev. 26:21)*

2532 nu1520 pre1537 art3588 nu5064 nn2226 aina1325 art3588 nu2033 nn32 nu2033 an,aj5552
7 And one of the four beasts gave unto the seven angels seven golden

---

15:1–8 This chapter describes the preparation for the pouring out of the seven vials (bowls) which will constitute the final expression of the wrath of God during the Tribulation.

The first expression of God's wrath is seen in the seven seals (Rev. 6:1–17). The seventh seal contains the seven trumpet judgments (Rev. 8:1–13; 9:1–21; 11:15–19). Then out of the seventh trumpet judgment comes the seven vials of God's wrath (Rev. 15:1; 16:1–21).

an,nn5357 pap1073   art3588   nn2372   art,nn2316   art,pap2198   pre1519/art,nn165/art,nn165

vials full of the wrath of God, who liveth forever*and*ever.

(Ps. 75:8; Is. 51:17,22; Jer. 25:15)

   2532   art3588   nn3485   ainp1072   an,nn2586   pre1537 art3588   nn1391   art,nn2316   2532   pre1537

8 And the temple was filled with smoke from the glory of God, and from

ppro848   art,nn1411   2532   an,ajn3762   ipf1410   ainf1525   pre1519 art3588   nn3485   ad891   art3588   nu2033

his power; and no man was able to enter into the temple, till the seven

nn4127   art3588   nu2033   nn32   asbp5055

plagues of the seven angels were fulfilled.

(Ex. 40:34; 1 Kgs. 8:10,11; Is. 6:4; Ezek. 44:4)

The Seven Vials of Wrath

        2532   aina191   an,aj3173 an,nn5456   pre1537 art3588   nn3485   pap3004   art3588   nu2033

16 And I heard a great voice out of the temple saying to the seven

        nn32   aima5217   2532   aima1632   art3588   nn5357   art3588   nn2372

angels, Go*your*ways, and pour out the vials of the wrath of

art,nn2316 pre1519 art3588   nn1093

God upon the earth.

(Is. 66:6; Ps. 69:24; Jer. 10:25; Ezek. 22:31; Zeph. 3:8)

    2532   art3588   nu,ajn4413   aina565   2532   aina1632   ppro848 art,nn5357 pre1909 art3588   nn1093   2532

2 And the first went, and poured out his vial upon the earth; and

aom1096   an,aj2556   2532   an,aj4190   an,nn1668   pre1519   art3588   nn444   art,pap2192   art3588

there fell a noisome and grievous sore upon the men which had the

nn5480   art3588   nn2342   2532   art,pap4352   ppro848 art,nn1504

mark of the beast, and *upon* them*which*worshiped his image.

(Ex. 9:10; Deut. 28:35)

    2532   art3588   nu,aj1208   an,nn32   aina1632   ppro848 art,nn5357 pre1519 art3588   nn2281   2532

3 And the second angel poured out his vial upon the sea; and it

aom1096   ad5613   pr/an,nn129   an,ajn3498   2532   an,aj3956   pap2198 an,nn5590 aina599 pre1722 art3588

became as the blood of a dead *man*: and every living soul died in the

nn2281

sea.   *(Ex. 7:17-21)*

    2532   art3588   nu,aj5154   an,nn32   aina1632   ppro848 art,nn5357 pre1519 art3588   nn4215   2532(pre1519)

4 And the third angel poured out his vial upon the rivers and

art,nn4077   art,nn5204   2532   aom1096   pr/an,nn129

fountains of waters; and they became blood.   *(Ex. 7:19-24; Ps. 78:44)*

    2532   aina191   art3588   nn32   art3588   nn5204   pap3004   pin1488   pr/an,aj1342   an,nn2962

5 And I heard the angel of the waters say, Thou art righteous, O Lord,

art,pap5607   2532 art,ipf2258 2532   art,fptm2071   3754   aina2919   depro5023

which art, and wast, and shalt be, because thou hast judged thus.

(Ps. 119:137; 145:17; Ex. 3:14)

    3754   aina1632   an,nn129   an,ajn40   2532   an,nn4396   2532

6 For they have shed the blood of saints and prophets, and thou hast

aina1325   ppro846   an,nn129   ainf4095   1063   pin1526   pr/an,aj514
given them blood to drink; for they are worthy.

(Ps. 79:3; Is. 49:26)

2532   aina191   an,ajn243   pre1537 art3588 nn2379 pap3004   3483   an,nn2962 art,nn2316   art,nn3841
7 And I heard another out of the altar say, Even so, Lord God Almighty,

pr/an,aj228 2532   pr/an,aj1342   ppro4675   art,nn2920
true and righteous *are* thy judgments.

(Amos 3:13; 4:13 [Sept.]; Ps. 19:9; 119:137)

2532 art3588 nu,aj5067 an,nn32   aina1632   ppro848 art,nn5357 pre1909 art3588 nn2246   2532
8 And the fourth angel poured out his vial upon the sun; and power was

ainp1325   ppro846   ainf2739 art,nn444 pre1722 an,nn4442
given unto him to scorch men with fire.

2532 art,nn444   ainp2739   an,aj3173 an,nn2738 2532   aina987   art3588 nn3686
9 And men were scorched with great heat, and blasphemed the name of

art,nn2316   art,pap2192   an,nn1849 pre1909 depro5025 art,nn4127   2532   aina3340   3756   ainf1325
God, which hath power over these plagues: and they repented not to give

ppro846 an,nn1391
him glory.

2532 art3588 nu,aj3991 an,nn32   aina1632   ppro848 art,nn5357 pre1909 art3588 nn2362   art3588 nn2342
10 And the fifth angel poured out his vial upon the seat of the beast;

2532 ppro848   art,nn932   aom1096   pfpp4656   2532   ipf3145 ppro848 art,nn1100 pre1537
and his kingdom was full*of*darkness; and they gnawed their tongues for

art,nn4192
pain,

(Ex. 10:21; Is. 8:22)

2532   aina987   art3588 nn2316   art,nn3772   pre1537   ppro848 art,nn4192 2532(pre1537) ppro848
11 And blasphemed the God of heaven because of their pains   and   their

art,nn1668 2532   aina3440   3756 pre1537 ppro848 art,nn2041
sores, and repented not of their deeds.

2532 art3588 nu,aj1622 an,nn32   aina1632   ppro848 art,nn5357 pre1909 art3588   aj3173
12 And the   sixth angel poured out his   vial upon the great

art,nn4215   art,nn2166   2532 art3588   nn5204   ppro848   ainp3583   2443 art3588 nn3598
river Euphrates; and the water thereof was dried up, that the way of

art3588   nn935 art,pre575   an,nn395/an,nn2246   asbp2090
the kings of the   east   might be prepared.

(Is. 11:15; 44:27; Jer. 50:38; 51:36)

2532   aina1492 nu5140   an,aj169   an,nn4151 an,aj3664 an,nn944   pre1537 art3588   nn4750
13 And I saw three unclean spirits like frogs *come* out of the mouth of

art3588   nn1404   2532 pre1537 art3588 nn4750   art3588 nn2342 2532 pre1537 art3588 nn4750   art3588
the dragon, and out of the mouth of the beast, and out of the mouth of the

nn5578
false prophet.

1063   pin1526   pr/an,nn4151   an,nn1142   pap4160   an,nn4592 (repro3739)   pinm1607
14 For they are the spirits of devils, working miracles, *which* go forth

pre1909 art3588 nn935   art3588 nn1093 2532   art3588 an,aj3650   nn3625   ainf4863 ppro846 pre1519 art3588
unto the kings of the earth and of the whole world, to gather them to the

nn4171   depro1565 art,aj3173 art,nn2250   art,nn2316   art,nn3841
battle of that great day of God Almighty.

(Amos 3:13; 4:13 [Sept.])

2400   pinm2064 ad5613   an,nn2812 pr/an,aj3107   art,pap1127   2532   pap5083
15 Behold, I come as a thief. Blessed *is* he*that*watcheth, and keepeth

ppro848   art,nn2440   3363   psa4043 an,aj1131 2532   psa991 ppro848 art,nn808
his garments, lest he walk naked, and they see his shame.

16 And he gathered*them*together into a place called in*the*Hebrew*tongue Armageddon.

(Judg. 5:19; 2 Kgs. 9:27; 23:29; Zech. 12:11)

17 And the seventh angel poured out his vial into the air; and there came a great voice out of the temple of heaven, from the throne, saying, It is done.

(Is. 66:6)

18 And there were voices, and thunders, and lightnings; and there was a great earthquake, such as was not since men were upon the earth, so mighty an earthquake, *and* so great.

(Ex. 19:16; Esth. 1:1 [Sept.])

19 And the great city was divided into three parts, and the cities of the nations fell: and great Babylon came*in*remembrance before God, to give unto her the cup of the wine of the fierceness of his wrath.

(Ps. 75:8; Is. 51:17,22; Jer. 25:15)

20 And every island fled away, and the mountains were not found.

21 And there fell upon men a great hail out of heaven, *every stone* about the weight*of*a*talent: and men blasphemed God because of the plague of the hail; for the plague thereof was exceeding great.

(Ex. 9:24)

The Great Mystery

17 And there came one of the seven angels which had the seven vials, and talked with me, saying unto me, Come hither; I will show unto thee the judgment of the great whore that sitteth upon many waters:

(Jer. 51:13)

2 With whom the kings of the earth have committed fornication, and the inhabitants of the earth have been made drunk with the wine of her fornication.

(Jer. 51:7)

2532   aina667/ppro3165   pre1722   an,nn4151 pre1519   an,ajn2048   2532   aina1492

3 So he carried*me*away in the spirit into the wilderness: and I saw a

an,nn1135 ppmp2521 pre1909   an,aj2847   an,nn2342 pap1073   an,nn3686   an,nn988   pap2192

woman sit upon a scarlet colored beast, full of names of blasphemy, having

nu2033 an,nn2776 2532 nu1176 an,nn2768

seven heads and ten horns.

2532   art3588   nn1135   ipf2258   pfpp4016   an,ajn4209   2532   an,ajn28467   2532

4 And the woman was arrayed in purple and scarlet color, and

pfpp5558   an,nn5557   2532   an,aj5093   an,nn3037   2532   an,nn3135   pap2192   an,aj5552

decked with gold and precious stones and pearls, having a golden

an,nn4221 pre1722 ppro848 art,nn5495 pap1073   an,nn946   2532   an,nn168   ppro848   an,nn4202

cup in her hand full of abominations and filthiness of her fornication:

(Ezek. 28:13)

2532   pre1909 ppro848   art,nn3359   an,nn3686 pfpp1125   an,nn3466   an,nn897

5 And upon her forehead *was* a name written, MYSTERY, BABYLON

art3588   aj3173   art3588   nn3384   art,nn4204   2532   art,nn946

THE GREAT, THE MOTHER OF HARLOTS AND ABOMINATIONS

art3588   nn1093

OF THE EARTH.

2532   aina1492 art3588   nn1135   pap3184   pre1537 art3588   nn129   art3588   ajn40   2532 pre1537

6 And I saw the woman drunken with the blood of the saints, and with

art3588   nn129   art3588   nn3144   an,nn2424   2532   apta1492 ppro846   aina2296

the blood of the martyrs of Jesus: and when I saw her, I wondered

an,aj3173   an,nn2295

with great admiration.

2532   art3588   nn32   aina2036   ppro3427   pre,inpro1302   aina2296   epn1473   ft2046

7 And the angel said unto me, Wherefore didst thou marvel? I will tell

ppro4671   art3588   nn3466   art3588   nn1135   nn2532   art3588   nn2342   art,pap941   ppro846

thee the mystery of the woman, and of the beast that carrieth her,

art,pap2192   art3588   nu2033   nu2776   2532 nu1176 art,nn2768

which hath the seven heads and ten horns.

art3588   nn2342   repro3739   aina1492 ipf2258   2532 pin2076   3756   2532 pin3195   pinf305   pre1537

8 The beast that thou sawest was, and is not; and shall ascend out of

art3588   nn12   2532 pinf5217 pre1519 an,nn684   2532   art,pap2730   pre1909 art3588

the bottomless pit, and go into perdition: and they*that*dwell on the

nn1093   fm2296   repro3739 art,nn3686   3756   pfip1125   pre1909 art3588   nn975   art,nn2222 pre575

earth shall wonder, whose names were not written in the book of life from

an,nn2602   an,nn2889   pap991   art3588   nn2342   repro3748 ipf2258 2532 pin2076

the foundation of the world, when they behold the beast that was, and is

3756   2539   pin2076

not, and yet is.   *(Dan. 7:3; Ex. 32:32,33; Ps. 69:28; Dan. 12:1)*

ad5602   art3588   nn3563   art,pap2192   an,nn4678   art3588   nu2033   nu2776 pin1526   nu2033

9 And here *is* the mind which hath wisdom. The seven heads are seven

pr/an,nn3735 (ad 3699) pre1909 ppro846 art3588   nn1135   pinm2521

mountains, on which the woman sitteth.

2532   pin1526   nu2033   an,nn935   art,nu,ajn4002   aina4098   2532 art,nu,ajn1520 pin2076

10 And there are seven kings: five are fallen, and one is,

art3588   ajn243   ad3768   aina2064   2532   ad3752   asba2064   ppro846 pin1163   ainf3306

and the other is not yet come; and when he cometh, he must continue a

an,ajn3641

short space.

²⁵³² ^{art3588} ⁿⁿ²³⁴² ^{repro3739} ^{ipf2258} ²⁵³² ^{pin2076} ³⁷⁵⁶ ²⁵³² ^{epn846} ^{pin2076} ^{pr/an,nu,ajn3590} ²⁵³²

11 And the beast that was, and is not, even he is the eighth, and

^{pin2076} ^{pre1537} ^{art3588} ^{nu,ajn2033} ²⁵³² ^{pin5217} ^{pre1519} ^{an,nn684}

is of the seven, and goeth into perdition.

²⁵³² ^{art3588} ^{nu1176} ⁿⁿ²⁷⁶⁸ ^{repro3739} ^{aina1492} ^{pinf1526} ^{nu1176} ^{pr/an,nn935} ^{repro3748}

12 And the ten horns which thou sawest are ten kings, which have

^{aina2983} ^{ad3768/an,nn932} ²³⁵ ^{pin2983} ^{an,nn1849} ^{ad5613} ^{an,nn935} ^{nu3391} ^{an,nn5610} ^{pre3326} ^{art3588}

received no*kingdom*as*yet; but receive power as kings one hour with the

ⁿⁿ²³⁴²

beast.   *(Dan. 7:24)*

^{depro3778} ^{pin2192} ^{nu3391} ^{an,nn1106} ²⁵³² ^{ft1239} ^{rxpro1438} ^{art,nn1411} ²⁵³² ^{art,nn1849} ^{art3588}

13 These have one mind, and shall give their power and strength unto the

ⁿⁿ²³⁴²

beast.

^{depro3778} ^{ft4170} ^{pre3326} ^{art3588} ⁿⁿ⁷²¹ ²⁵³² ^{art3588} ⁿⁿ⁷²¹ ^{ft3528}

14 These shall make war with the Lamb, and the Lamb shall overcome

^{ppro846} ³⁷⁵⁴ ^{pin2076} ^{pr/an,nn2962} ^{an,nn2962} ²⁵³² ^{pr/an,nn935} ^{an,nn935} ²⁵³² ^{art3588} ^{pre3326}

them: for he is Lord of lords, and King of kings: and they that are with

^{ppro846} ^{pr/an,aj2822} ²⁵³² ^{pr/an,aj1588} ²⁵³² ^{pr/an,aj4103}

him *are* called, and chosen, and faithful.   *(Deut. 10:17; Dan. 2:47)*

²⁵³² ^{pin3004} ^{ppro3427} ^{art3588} ⁿⁿ⁵²⁰⁴ ^{repro3739} ^{aina1492} ^{repro3757} ^{art3588}

15 And he saith unto me, The waters which thou sawest, where the

ⁿⁿ⁴²⁰⁴ ^{pinm2521} ^{pin1526} ^{pr/an,nn2992} ²⁵³² ^{pr/an,nn3793} ²⁵³² ^{pr/an,nn1484} ²⁵³² ^{pr/an,nn1100}

whore sitteth, are peoples, and multitudes, and nations, and tongues.

²⁵³² ^{art3588} ^{nu1176} ⁿⁿ²⁷⁶⁸ ^{repro3739} ^{aina1492} ^{pre1909} ^{art3588} ⁿⁿ²³⁴² ^{depro3778} ^{ft3404}

16 And the ten horns which thou sawest upon the beast, these shall hate

^{art3588} ⁿⁿ⁴²⁰⁴ ²⁵³² ^{ft4160} ^{ppro846} ^{pr/pfpp2049} ²⁵³² ^{pr/an,nn1131} ²⁵³² ^{fm5315} ^{ppro848} ^{art,nn4561}

the whore, and shall make her desolate and naked, and shall eat her flesh,

²⁵³² ^{ft2618} ^{ppro846} ^{pre1722} ^{an,nn4442}

and burn her with fire.   *(Lev. 21:9)*

¹⁰⁶³ ^{art,nn2316} ^{aina1325} ^{pre1519} ^{ppro848} ^{art,nn2588} ^{ainf4160} ^{ppro848} ^{art,nn1106} ²⁵³²

17 For God hath put in their hearts to fulfill his will, and to

^{ainf4160/nu3391/an,nn1106} ²⁵³² ^{ainf1325} ^{ppro848} ^{art,nn932} ^{art3588} ⁿⁿ²³⁴² ^{ad891} ^{art3588} ⁿⁿ⁴⁴⁸⁷ ^{art,nn2316}

agree,   and give their kingdom unto the beast, until the words of God

^{asbp5055}

shall be fulfilled.

²⁵³² ^{art3588} ⁿⁿ¹¹³⁵ ^{repro3739} ^{aina1492} ^{pin2076} ^{art,aj3173} ^{pr/art,nn4172}

18 And the woman which thou sawest is that great city,

^{art,pap2192/an,nn932} ^{pre1909} ^{art3588} ⁿⁿ⁹³⁵ ^{art3588} ⁿⁿ¹⁰⁹³

which reigneth over the kings of the earth.

The Fall of Babylon

²⁵³² ^{pre3326} ^{depro5023} ^{aina1492} ^{an,aj243} ^{an,nn32} ^{pap2597} ^{pre1537} ^{art,nn3772}

18 And after these things I saw another angel come down from heaven,

^{pap2192} ^{an,aj3173} ^{an,nn1849} ²⁵³² ^{art3588} ⁿⁿ¹⁰⁹³ ^{ainp5461} ^{pre1537} ^{ppro848}

having great power; and the earth was lightened with his

^{art,nn1391}

glory.

2532   aina2896   pre1722/an,nn2479   an,aj3173   an,nn5456   pap3004   an,nn897   art3588   aj3173
2 And he cried mightily with a strong voice, saying, Babylon the great is

aina4098   aina4098   2532   aom1096   pr/an,nn2732   an,nn1142   2532   an,nn5438   an,aj3956
fallen, is fallen, and is become the habitation of devils, and the hold of every

an,aj169 an,nn4151   2532   an,nn5438   an,aj3956   an,aj169   2532   pfpp3404   an,nn3732
foul spirit, and a cage of every unclean and hateful bird.

(Is. 21:9; Jer. 51:8; Is. 13:21; 34:11; Jer. 50:39)

3754   an,aj3956   art,nn1484   pfi4095   pre1537 art3588   nn3631   art3588   nn2372   ppro848
3 For   all   nations have drunk   of   the wine of the wrath of her

art,nn4202   2532 art3588   nn935   art3588   nn1093   aina4203   pre3326 ppro846
fornication, and the kings of the earth have committed fornication with her,

2532 art3588   nn1713   art3588   nn1093   aina4147   pre1537   art3588   nn1411   ppro846
and the merchants of the earth are waxed rich through the abundance of her

art,nn4764
delicacies.   *(Is. 23:17; Jer. 51:7)*

2532   aina191   an,aj243   an,nn5456   pre1537   art,nn3772   pap3004   aima1831   pre1537 ppro846 ppro3450
4 And I heard another voice from heaven, saying, Come out of her, my

art,nn2992   2443   asba4790/3361   ppro848 art,nn266 2532   2443   asba2983   3361 pre1537 ppro848
people, that ye be*not*partakers of her sins, and that ye receive not of her

art,nn4127
plagues.   *(Is. 48:20; 52:11; Jer. 50:8; 51:6,9,45)*

3754   ppro848 art,nn266   ainp190   ad891   art,nn3772 2532   art,nn2316   aina3421
5 For her sins have reached unto heaven, and God hath remembered

ppro848   art,nn92
her iniquities.   *(Gen. 18:19,20; Jer. 51:9)*

aima591   ppro846   2532   ad5613 epn846   aina591   ppro5213 2532   aima1363   ppro846 an,ajn1362
6 Reward her even as she rewarded you, and double unto her double

pre2596   ppro848   art,nn2041   pre1722 art3588 nn4221   repro3739   aina2767 aima2767   ppro846
according to her works: in the cup which she hath filled fill to her

an,ajn1362
double.   *(Ps. 137:8; Jer. 50:15,29)*

an,ajn3745   aina1392   rxpro1438   2532   aina4763   an,aj5118
7 How much she hath glorified herself, and lived deliciously, so much

an,nn929   2532   an,nn3997   aima1325 ppro846 3754   pin3004 pre1722 ppro848 art,nn2588   pin2521   pr/an,nn938 2532
torment and sorrow give her: for she saith in her heart, I sit a queen, and

pin1510 3756 pr/an,nn5503 2532   asba1492 efn3364   an,nn3997
am no widow, and shall see no sorrow.   *(Is. 47:7,8)*

pre1223/depro5124   ppro848 art,nn4127   ft2240   pre1722 nu3391 an,nn2250 an,nn2288   2532   an,nn3997
8 Therefore shall her plagues come in one day, death, and mourning,

2532 an,nn3042   2532   fp2618   pre1722 an,nn4442 3754 pr/an,aj2478   an,nn2962
and famine; and she shall be utterly burned with fire: for strong *is* the Lord

art,nn2316   art,pap2919   ppro846
God who judgeth her.   *(Is. 47:9; Lev. 21:9; Jer. 50:34)*

2532 art3588   nn935   art3588   nn1093   art,apta4763   2532
9 And the kings of the earth, who*have*committed*fornication and

apta4763   pre3326 ppro846   fm2799   ppro846 2532   fm2875   pre1909 ppro846 ad3752
lived deliciously with her, shall bewail her, and lament for her, when they shall

psa991 art3588   nn2586   ppro848   art,nn4451
see the smoke of her burning,

pfp2476   pre575/ad3113 pre1223 art3588 nn5401   ppro848   art,nn929   pap3004   3759   3759
10 Standing afar off for the fear of her torment, saying, Alas, alas that

art,aj3173 art,nn4172 an,nn897   art,aj2478 art,nn4172 3754 pre1722 nu3391 an,nn5610   ppro4675 art,nn2920

great city Babylon, that mighty city! for in one hour is thy judgment

aina2064

come.   *(Ezek. 26:17; Dan. 4:30)*

2532 art3588   nn1713   art3588 nn1093   pin2799 2532 pin3996 pre1909 ppro846 3754

11 And the merchants of the earth shall weep and mourn over her; for

an,ajn3762 pin59 ppro848 art,nn1117   ad3765

no man buyeth their merchandise any more: *(Ezek. 27:32)*

an,nn1117   an,nn5557 2532 an,nn696   2532 an,aj5093 an,nn3037 2532

12 The merchandise of gold, and silver, and precious stones, and of

an,nn3135 2532   an,nn1040 2532 an,nn4209 2532 an,ajn4596 2532 an,ajn2847 2532 an,aj3956 an,aj2367

pearls, and fine linen, and purple, and silk, and scarlet, and all thyine

an,nn3586 2532   an,aj3956   an,nn4632   an,aj1661 2532   an,aj3956   an,nn4632 pre1537

wood, and all manner vessels of ivory, and all manner vessels of

an,aj5093   an,nn3586 2532   an,nn5475 2532 an,nn4604 2532   an,nn3139

most precious wood, and of brass, and iron, and marble,

2532 an,nn2792   2532 an,nn2368 2532   an,nn3464   2532   an,nn3030   2532 an,nn3631

13 And cinnamon, and odors, and ointments, and frankincense, and wine,

2532 an,nn1637 2532   an,nn4585   2532 an,nn4621 2532   an,nn2934 2532 an,nn4263 2532 an,nn2462 2532

and oil, and fine flour, and wheat, and beasts, and sheep, and horses, and

an,nn4480 2532 an,nn4983 2532 an,nn5590   an,nn444

chariots, and slaves, and souls of men.   *(Ezek. 27:12-24)*

2532 art3588   nn3703   ppro4675 art,nn5590   art,nn1939   aina565   pre575 ppro4675 2532

14 And the fruits that thy soul lusted after are departed from thee, and

an,aj3956   art,ajn3045   2532 art,ajn2986   aina565   pre575 ppro4675 2532

all things which*were*dainty and goodly are departed from thee, and thou shalt

asba2147 ppro846   ad3765/efn3364

find them no*more*at*all.

art3588   nn1713   depro5130   art,apta4147   pre575 ppro846

15 The merchants of these things, which*were*made*rich by her, shall

fm2476 pre575/ad3113 pre1223 art3588 nn5401 ppro848 art,nn929 pap2799 2532 pap3996

stand afar off for the fear of her torment, weeping and wailing,

2532 pap3004 3759 3759 art,aj3173 art,nn4172   art,pfpp4016   an,ajn1039

16 And saying, Alas, alas that great city, that*was*clothed in fine linen,

2532 an,ajn4210 2532 an,ajn2847 2532   pfpp5558 pre1722 an,nn5557 2532 an,aj5093 an,nn3037 2532

and purple, and scarlet, and decked with gold, and precious stones, and

an,nn3135

pearls!   *(Ezek. 28:13)*

3754   nu3391 an,nn5610 art,aj5118   an,nn4149   ainp2049   2532 an,aj3956

17 For in one hour so great riches is come*to*naught. And every

an,nn2942 2532 an,aj3956 art3588   nn3658 pre1909 art,nn4143 2532 an,nn3492 2532 an,ajn3745

shipmaster, and all the company in ships, and sailors, and as*many*as

pinm2038 art,nn2281 aina2476 pre575/ad3113

trade by sea, stood afar off,   *(Ezek. 27:27-29)*

2532 ipf2896   pap3708 art3588 nn2586   ppro848 art,nn4451 pap3004 inpro5101

18 And cried when they saw the smoke of her burning, saying, What *city*

pr/an,aj3664   art,aj3173 art,nn4172

is like unto this great city!   *(Ezek. 27:32)*

2532   aina906 an,nn5522 pre1909 ppro848 art,nn2776 2532 ipf2896 pap2799 2532 pap3996

19 And they cast dust on their heads, and cried, weeping and wailing,

pap3004 3759 3759   art,aj3173 art,nn4172 pre1722/repro3739   aina4147 an,aj3956 art,pap2192

saying, Alas, alas, that great city, wherein were made rich all that had

an,nn4143 pre1722 art3588 nn2281   pre1537   pppro848   art,nn5094   3754   nu3391 an,nn5610
ships   in   the   sea by*reason*of her   costliness! for in one hour is she
pinp2049
made desolate.   *(Ezek. 27:30–34)*

pim2165   pre1909 pppro846   an,nn3772   2532   art,aj40   an,nn652   2532   art,nn4396   3754
20 Rejoice over her, *thou* heaven, and *ye* holy apostles and prophets; for
art,nn2316   aina2919/art,nn2917 pppro5216 pre1537 pppro846
God hath avenged you on her.

(Deut. 32:43 [Sept.]; Ps. 96:11; Is. 44:23; 49:13; Jer. 51:48)

2532   nu1520 an,aj2478   an,nn32   aina142   an,nn3037 ad5613   an,aj3173   an,nn3458   2532   aina906
21 And a mighty angel took up a stone like a great millstone, and cast *it*
pre1519 art3588   nn2281   pap3004   ad3779   an,nn3731   art,aj3173 an,nn4172 an,nn897
into the sea, saying, Thus with violence shall that great city Babylon be
fp906   2532   asbp2147   ad2089/efn3364
thrown down, and shall be found no*more*at*all.   *(Jer. 51:63,64; Ezek. 26:21)*

2532   an,nn5456   an,nn2790   2532   an,nn3451   2532   an,nn834   2532
22 And the voice of harpers, and musicians, and of pipers, and
an,nn4538   asbp191   ad2089/efn3364   pre1722 pppro4671   an,aj3956   an,nn5079
trumpeters, shall be heard no*more*at*all in thee; and no craftsman, of
an,aj3956   an,nn5078   asbp2147   ad2089/efn3364 pre1722 pppro4671 2532   an,nn5456
whatsoever craft *he be,* shall be found any more in thee; and the sound of
an,nn3458   asbp191   ad2089/efn3364   pre1722 pppro4671
a millstone shall be heard no* more*at*all in thee;   *(Is. 24:8; Ezek. 26:13)*

2532   an,nn5457   an,nn3088   asbp5316   ad2089/efn3364   pre1722 pppro4671 2532
23 And the light of a candle shall shine no*more*at*all in thee; and the
an,nn5456   an,nn3566   2532   an,nn3565   asbp191   ad2089/efn3364   pre1722
voice of the bridegroom and of the bride shall be heard no*more*at*all in
pppro4671 3754 pppro4675 art,nn1713   ipf2258 art3588 pr/an,nn3175   art3588   nn1093   3754 pre1722 pppro4675
thee: for thy merchants were the great men of the earth; for by thy
art,nn5331   an,aj3956 art,nn1484   ainp4105
sorceries were all nations deceived.   *(Jer. 7:34; 16:9; 25:10; Is. 23:8; 47:9)*

2532 pre1722 pppro846   ainp2147   an,nn129   an,nn4396   2532   an,ajn40   2532
24 And in her was found the blood of prophets, and of saints, and of
an,aj3956   art,pfpp4969   pre1909 art3588 nn1093
all that*were*slain upon the earth.   *(Jer. 51:49; Ezek. 24:7)*

"The Testimony of Jesus"

2532   pre3326   depro5023   aina191   an,aj3173 an,nn5456   an,aj4183 an,nn3793 pre1722
19 ☞ And after these things I heard a great voice of much people in
art,nn3772 pap3004   239   art,nn4991   2532 art,nn1391 2532 art,nn5092 2532 art,nn1411
heaven, saying, Alleluia; Salvation, and glory, and honor, and power,
an,nn2962 pppro2257 art,nn2316
unto the Lord our God:

☞ **19:1–21** This passage which is the climax to the whole Book of Revelation, begins with the Second Coming of Christ to the earth. Heaven is opened and a white horse appears, and the rider on its back, Jesus Christ, is called "Faithful and True" (v. 11). At this time, He will introduce true peace and righteousness, a stark contrast to the false peace brought by the first white horse and its rider, the Antichrist (Rev. 6:1–17).

2 For true and righteous *are* his judgments: for he hath judged the great whore, which did corrupt the earth with her fornication, and hath avenged the blood of his servants at her hand.

(Ps. 19:9; 119:37; Deut. 32:43; 2 Kgs. 9:7; Ps. 79:10)

3 And again they said, Alleluia. And her smoke rose up forever*and*ever.

(Is. 34:10)

4 And the four*and*twenty elders and the four beasts fell down and worshiped God that sat on the throne, saying, Amen; Alleluia.

(1 Kgs. 22:19; 2 Chr. 18:18; Ps. 47:8; Is. 6:1; Ezek. 1:26)

5 And a voice came out of the throne, saying, Praise our God, all ye his servants, and ye*that*fear him, both small and great.

(Ps. 22:23; 115:13; 134:1; 135:1)

6 And I heard as*it*were the voice of a great multitude, and as the voice of many waters, and as the voice of mighty thunderings, saying, Alleluia: for the Lord God omnipotent reigneth.

(Ezek. 1:24; 43:2; Ex. 15:18;

Ps. 22:28; 93:1; 97:1; 99:1; Dan. 7:14; Zech. 14:9)

7 Let us be glad and rejoice, and give honor to him: for the marriage of the Lamb is come, and his wife hath made*herself*ready.

8 And to her was granted that she should be arrayed in fine linen, clean and white: for the fine linen is the righteousness of saints.

9 And he saith unto me, Write, Blessed *are* they*which*are*called unto the marriage supper of the Lamb. And he saith unto me, These are the true sayings of God.

10 And I fell at his feet to worship him. And he said unto me, See *thou do it* not: I am thy fellowservant, and of thy brethren that have the

nn3141   art,nn2424   aima4352   art,nn2316 1063 art3588   nn3141   art,nn2424   art3588 pr/nn4151

testimony of Jesus: worship God: for the testimony of Jesus is the spirit of

art,nn4394

prophecy.

The Righteous Judge

        2532   aina1492   art,nn3772   pr/pfpp455   2532   2400   an,aj3022   an,nn2462   2532

11 And I saw heaven opened, and behold a white horse; and

art,ppmp2521   pre1909 ppro846   ppmp2564   pr/an,ajn4103 2532 pr/an,ajn228 2532 pre1722   an,nn1343

he*that*sat upon him *was* called Faithful and True, and in righteousness

pin2919 2532   pin4170

he doth judge and make war.   *(Ezek. 1:1; Zech. 1:8; 6:3,6; Ps. 96:13; Is. 11:4)*

   (1161) ppro848 art,nn3788   ad5613   pr/an,nn5395   an,nn4442 2532 pre1909 ppro848 art,nn2776   an,aj4183

12   His eyes *were* as a flame of fire, and on his head *were* many

an,nn1238   pap2192   an,nn3686   pfpp1125   repro3739 an,ajn3762   pin1492   1508   epn848

crowns; and he had a name written, that no man knew, but he himself.

(Dan. 10:6)

      2532   pfpp4016   an,nn2440   pfpp911   an,nn129   2532   ppro848 art,nn3686

13 And he *was* clothed with a vesture dipped in blood: and his name is

pinp2564 art3588   nn3056   art,nn2316

called The Word of God.   *(Is. 63:1–3)*

      2532   art3588   nn4753   art,pre1722   art,nn3772   ipf190   ppro846 pre1909 an,aj3022

14 And the armies *which were* in heaven followed him upon white

an,nn2462   pfpp1746   an,ajn1039   an,aj3022 2532 an,aj2513

horses, clothed in fine linen, white and clean.

      2532   pre1537   ppro848 art,nn4750   pinm1607   an,aj3691   an,nn4501   2443   pre1722 ppro846

15 And out of his mouth goeth a sharp sword, that with it he should

psa3960   art3588   nn1484   2532   epn846   ft4165   ppro846 pre1722   an,nn4464   an,aj4603 2532 epn846

smite the nations: and he shall rule them with a rod of iron: and he

pin3961   art3588 nn3025/art,nn3631   art3588   nn2372   2532 art,nn3709   art,nn3841   art,nn2316

treadeth the winepress of the fierceness and wrath of Almighty God.

(Is. 49:2; Ps. 2:9; Is. 63:3; Lam. 1:15; Amos 3:13; 4:13 [Sept.])

      2532   pin2192 pre1909   art,nn2440   2532 pre1909 ppro848 art,nn3382   an,nn3686   pfpp1125   an,nn935

16 And he hath on *his* vesture and on his thigh a name written, KING

an,nn935   2532   an,nn2962   an,nn2962

OF KINGS, AND LORD OF LORDS.   *(Deut. 10:17; Dan. 2:47)*

      2532   aina1492 nu1520   an,nn32   pfp2476   pre1722 art3588   nn2246   2532   aina2896

17 And I saw an angel standing in the sun; and he cried with a

an,aj3173 an,nn5456   pap3004   an,aj3956 art3588   nn3732   art,ppmp4072 pre1722   an,nn3321

loud voice, saying to all the fowls that fly in the midst*of*heaven,

ad1205   2532   pim4863   pre1519 art3588 nn1173   art3588   aj3173

Come and gather*yourselves*together unto the supper of the great

an,nn2316

God;

      2443   asba5315   an,nn4561   an,nn935 2532   an,nn4561   an,nn5506   2532

18 That ye may eat the flesh of kings, and the flesh of captains, and the

an,nn4561　　　an,ajn2478　　2532　　an,nn4561　　an,nn2462　　2532　　art,ppmp2521　　pre1909

flesh of mighty men, and the flesh of horses, and of them*that*sit on

ppro846　2532　　an,nn4561　　an,ajn3956　　　　an,ajn1658　2532　an,ajn1401　2532　an,ajn3398　2532　an,ajn3173

them, and the flesh of all *men, both* free and bond, both small and great.

(Ezek. 39:17-20)

2532　aina1492　art3588　nn2342　　2532　art3588　nn935　　art3588　nn1093　　2532　ppro848　art,nn4753

☞ 19 And I saw the beast, and the kings of the earth, and their armies,

pfpp4863　　　　ainf4160　an,nn4171　pre3326　art,ppmp2521　pre1909 art3588　nn2462　　2532

gathered together to make war against him*that*sat on the horse, and

pre3326　ppro848 art,nn4753

against his army.

2532　art3588　nn2342　　ainp4084　　2532　pre3326　depro5127　art3588　　nn5578

20 And the beast was taken, and with him the false prophet

art,apta4160　art,nn4592　　ad*1799　ppro846　pre1722　repro3739　　aina4105

that wrought miracles before him, with which he deceived

art,apta2983　art3588　nn5480　art3588　nn2342　2532　　art,pap4352

them*that*had*received the mark of the beast, and them*that*worshiped

ppro848　art,nn1504　art,nu,ajn1417　ainp906 pap2198 pre1519　art,nn3041　art,nn4442 art,ppmp2545 pre1722

his image. These both were cast alive into a lake of fire burning with

art,nn2303

brimstone.　　　　　　　　　　　　　　　　　　　　*(Is. 30:33)*

2532　art3588　ajn3062　　ainp615 pre1722 art3588　nn4501　　art,ppmp2521　pre1909 art3588

21 And the remnant were slain with the sword of him*that*sat upon the

nn2462　　art,ppmp1607　　pre1537　ppro848　art,nn4750　2532　an,aj3956 art3588　nn3732

horse, which*sword*proceeded out of his mouth: and all the fowls were

ainp5526 pre1537 ppro848 art,nn4561

filled with their flesh.　　　　　　　　　　　　　*(Ezek. 39:17,20)*

The Millennial Kingdom

2532　　aina1492　　an,nn32　　pap2597　　pre1537　art,nn3772　pap2192 art3588 nn2807

20 ☞ And I saw an angel come down from heaven, having the key of

art3588　　nn12　　2532　an,aj3173 an,nn254 pre1909 ppro848 art,nn5495

the bottomless pit and a great chain in his hand.

2532　　aina2902　art3588　nn1404　　art,aj744　　art,nn3789　repro3739　pin2076

☞ 2 And he laid*hold*on the dragon, that old serpent, which is the

pr/an,ajn1228 2532 pr/an,nn4567 2532　aina1210 ppro846　nu5507　　an,nn2094

Devil, and Satan, and bound him a thousand years,

2532　aina906 ppro846 pre1519 art3588　　nn12　　2532　aina2808/ppro846　2532　aina4972

3 And cast him into the bottomless pit, and shut*him*up, and set*a*seal

---

☞ **19:19, 20** See note on Revelation 13:1–18.

☞ **20:1–15** In this chapter, Jesus Christ comes back to set up His millennial (one thousand year) reign on the earth (vv. 1–6). There are a number of prophetic references which describe a particular time when Christ will establish a kingdom on the earth (2 Sam. 7:14–17; Ps. 24:1–10; Is. 2:1–4; 11:5–12; 35:1–10; Dan. 2:44). At this time, the unrighteous dead will be judged (v. 12).

☞ **20:2–10** See note on Jude 1:9.

ad*1883　ppro846　2443　　　　　asba4105　art3588　nn1484　3361　ad2089　ad891　art3588　nu5507
upon him, that he should deceive the nations no more, till the thousand

nn2094　　　　　　asbp5055　2532　pre3326　depro5023　ppro846　pin1163　　aifp3089　an,aj3398
years should be fulfilled: and after that he must be loosed a little

an,nn5550
season.

2532　aina1492　an,nn2362　2532　aina2523　pre1909　ppro846　2532　an,nn2917　ainp1325
4 And I saw thrones, and they sat upon them, and judgment was given

ppro846　2532　art3588　nn5590　　art,pfpp3990　　pre1223　art3588　nn3141
unto them: and *I saw* the souls of them*that*were*beheaded for the witness

an,nn2424　2532　pre1223　art3588　nn3056　art,nn2316　2532　repro3748　3756　aina4352　art3588　nn2342
of Jesus, and for the word of God, and which had not worshiped the beast,

3777　ppro846　art,nn1504　2532/3756　aina2983　art,nn5480　pre1909　ppro848　art,nn3359　2532　pre1909
neither his image, neither had received *his* mark upon their foreheads, or in

ppro848　art,nn5495　2532　aina2198　2532　aina936　pre3326　an,nn5547　nu5507　art,nn2094
their hands; and they lived and reigned with Christ a thousand years.

(Dan. 7:9,22,27)

1161　art3588　ajn3062　art3588　ajn3498　aina326/3756　ad2193　art3588　nu5507　nn2094
5 But the rest of the dead lived*not*again until the thousand years were

asbp5055　depro3778　art3588　nu,aj4413　pr/art,nn386
finished. This *is* the first resurrection.

pr/an,aj3107　2532　pr/an,aj40　art,pap2192　an,nn3313　pre1722　art3588　nu,aj4413　art,nn386　pre1909
6 Blessed and holy *is* he*that*hath part in the first resurrection: on

sepro5130　art3588　nu,aj1208　art,nn2288　pin2192　3756　an,nn1849　235　　fm2071　pr/an,nn2409　art,nn2316　2532
such the second death hath no power, but they shall be priests of God and

art,nn5547　2532　ft936　pre3326　ppro846　nu5507　an,nn2094
of Christ, and shall reign with him a thousand years.　　*(Ex. 19:6; Is. 61:6)*

2532　ad3752　art3588　nu5507　nn2094　asbp5055　art,nn4567　fp3089　pre1537
7 And when the thousand years are expired, Satan shall be loosed out of

ppro846　art,nn5438
his prison,

2532　fm1831　ainf4105　art3588　nn1484　art3588　pre1722　art3588　nu5064　nn1137
8 And shall go out to deceive the nations which are in the four quarters

art3588　nn1093　(art3588) nn1136　2532 (art3588)　3098　ainf4863/ppro846　pre1519　an,nn4171
of the earth, Gog and Magog, to gather*them*together to battle:

art3588　nn706　repro3739　ad5613　art3588　nn285　art3588　nn2281
the number of whom *is* as the sand of the sea.　　*(Ezek. 7:2; 38:2)*

2532　aina305　pre1909　art3588　nn4114　art3588　nn1093　2532
9 And they went up on the breadth of the earth, and

aina2944/art3588/nn3925/art3588/ajn40　2532　art3588　pip25　art,nn4172　2532　an,nn4442
compassed*the*camp*of*the*saints*about, and the beloved city: and fire

ainp2597　pre575　art,nn2316　pre1537　art,nn3772　2532　aina2719　ppro846
came down from God out of heaven, and devoured them.

(2 Kgs. 1:10; Ezek. 38:22; 39:6)

2532　art3588　ajn1228　art,pap4105　ppro846　ainp906　pre1519　art3588　nn3041　art,nn4442　2532
10 And the devil that deceived them was cast into the lake of fire and

an,nn2303　ad3699　art3588　nn2342　2532　art3588　nn5578　2532　fp928
brimstone, where the beast and the false prophet *are*, and shall be tormented

an,nn2250　2532　an,nn3571　pre1519/art,nn165/art,nn165
day and night forever*and*ever　　*(Ps. 11:6; Is. 30:33; Ezek. 38:25)*

The Final Judgment Day

11 And I saw a great white throne, and him*that*sat on it, from whose face the earth and the heaven fled away; and there was found no place for them.

12 And I saw the dead, small and great, stand before God; and the books were opened: and another book was opened, which is *the book* of life: and the dead were judged out of those*things*which*were*written in the books, according to their works.   *(Dan. 7:9,10; Ex. 32:32,33; Ps. 69:28;*

Dan. 12:1 Ps. 62:12; Prov. 24:12; Is. 59:18; Jer. 17:10)

13 And the sea gave up the dead which were in it; and death and hell delivered up the dead which were in them: and they were judged every man according to their works.

14 And death and hell were cast into the lake of fire. This is the second death.

15 And whosoever was not found written in the book of life was cast into the lake of fire.   *(Ex. 32:32,33; Ps. 69:28; Dan. 12:1)*

The New Jerusalem

21 And I saw a new heaven and a new earth: for the first heaven and the first earth were passed away; and there was no more sea.   *(Is. 65:17; 66:22)*

2 And I John saw the holy city, new Jerusalem, coming down from God out of heaven, prepared as a bride adorned for her husband.

(Is. 52:1; 61:10)

☞ 21:1—22:5 In these final two chapters, the new heaven and new earth are described in detail. The word "new" is a translation of the Greek word *kainón* (2537) which means "qualitatively new." The new heaven and the new earth are not duplicates of the heaven and earth that now exist. Some have suggested that the new heaven and earth will be as this heaven and earth were at their creation.

3 And I heard a great voice out of heaven saying, Behold, the tabernacle of God *is* with men, and he will dwell with them, and they shall be his people, and God himself shall be with them, *and be* their God.

(Lev. 26:11,12; 2 Chr. 6:18; Ezek. 37:27; Zech. 2:10)

4 And God shall wipe away all tears from their eyes; and there shall be no more death, neither sorrow, nor crying, neither shall there be any more pain: for the former things are passed away. *(Is. 25:8; 35:10; 65:19)*

5 And he*that*sat upon the throne said, Behold, I make all things new. And he said unto me, Write: for these words are true and faithful.

(1 Kgs. 22:19; 2 Chr. 18:18; Ps. 47:8; Is. 6:1; Ezek. 1:26)

6 And he said unto me, It is done. I am Alpha and Omega, the beginning and the end. I will give unto him*that*is*athirst of the fountain of the water of life freely.

(Is. 44:6; 48:12; Ps. 36:9; Is. 55:1; Jer. 2:13)

7 He*that*overcometh shall inherit all things; and I will be his God, and he shall be my son.

8 But the fearful, and unbelieving, and abominable, and murderers, and whoremongers, and sorcerers, and idolaters, and all liars, shall have their part in the lake which burneth with fire and brimstone: which is the second death.

(Gen. 19:24; Ps. 1:6; Ezek. 38:22)

The City Walls

9 And there came unto me one of the seven angels which had the seven vials full of the seven last plagues, and talked with me, saying, Come hither, I will show thee the bride, the Lamb's wife.

10 And he carried*me*away in the spirit to a great and high mountain, and showed me that great city, the holy Jerusalem, descending out of heaven from God,   *(Ezek. 40:2)*

11 Having the glory of God: and her light *was* like unto a stone most precious, even like a jasper stone, clear*as*crystal;   *(Is. 60:1,2,19)*

12 And had a wall great and high, *and* had twelve gates, and at the gates twelve angels, and names written thereon, which are *the names* of the twelve tribes of the children of Israel:

13 On the east three gates; on the north three gates; on the south three gates; and on the west three gates.

14 And the wall of the city had twelve foundations, and in them the names of the twelve apostles of the Lamb.

15 And he*that*talked with me had a golden reed to measure the city, and the gates thereof, and the wall thereof.   *(Ezek. 40:3,5)*

16 And the city lieth foursquare, and the length is as large as the breadth: and he measured the city with the reed, twelve thousand furlongs. The length and the breadth and the height of it are equal.

17 And he measured the wall thereof, a*hundred*and*forty*and*four cubits, *according to* the measure of a man, that is, of the angel.

(Ezek. 48:16,17)

18 And the building of the wall of it was *of* jasper: and the city *was* pure gold, like unto clear glass.

19 And the foundations of the wall of the city *were* garnished with all manner of precious stones. The first foundation was jasper; the second, sapphire; the third, a chalcedony; the fourth, an emerald;   *(Is. 54:11,12)*

20 The fifth, sardonyx; the sixth, sardius; the seventh, chrysolyte; the

nu,ajn3590   pr/an,nn969 art3588 nu,ajn1766   pr/an,nn5116 art3588 nu,ajn1182   pr/an,nn5556   art3588   nu,ajn1734

eighth, beryl; the ninth, a topaz; the tenth, a chrysoprasus; the eleventh, a

pr/an,nn5192 art3588 nu,ajn1428   pr/an,nn271

jacinth; the twelfth, an amethyst.

2532   art3588   nu1427   nn4440   nu1427   pr/an,nn3135 pre303/an,ajn1538/nu1520 art,nn4440 ipf2258 pre1537

21 And the twelve gates *were* twelve pearls; every several gate was of

nu1520 an,nn3135   2532 art3588   ajn4113   art3588 nn4172   an,aj2513 pr/an,nn5553   ad5613   an,aj1307

one pearl: and the street of the city *was* pure gold, as*it*were transparent

pr/an,nn5194

glass.

2532   aina1492 3756 an,nn3485   pre1722/ppro846   1063 art3588   nn2962   art,nn2316   art,nn3841   2532   art3588

22 And I saw no temple therein: for the Lord God Almighty and the

nn721   pin2076   pr/an,nn3485   ppro846

Lamb are the temple of it.   *(Amos 3:13; 4:13 [Sept.])*

2532   art3588   nn4172 pin2192 3756 an,nn5532   art3588 nn2246   3761   art3588   nn4582   2443 psa5316

23 And the city had no need of the sun, neither of the moon, to shine

pre1722 ppro846   1063 art3588   nn1391   art,nn2316   aina5461   ppro846   2532 art3588   pr/nn721   art3588   nn3088

in it: for the glory of God did lighten it, and the Lamb *is* the light

ppro846

thereof.   *(Is. 60:19,20)*

2532   art3588   nn1484   art,ppmp4982   ft4043   pre1722 art3588 nn5457

24 And the nations of them*which*are*saved shall walk in the light of

ppro846 2532 art3588   nn935   art3588   nn1093   pin5342   ppro848 art,nn1391 2532 art,nn5092 pre1519 ppro846

it: and the kings of the earth do bring their glory and honor into it.

(Is. 60:3,5)

2532   art3588   nn4440   ppro846   efn3364/asbp2808   an,nn2250 1063

25 And the gates of it shall not*be*shut*at*all by day: for there shall

fm2071 3756 an,nn3571   ad1563

be no night there.

2532   ft5342   art3588   nn1391 2532 art,nn5092   art3588   nn1484   pre1519 ppro846

26 And they shall bring the glory and honor of the nations into it.

(Ps. 72:10,11)

2532   efn3364   asba1525   pre1519 ppro846   an,ajn3956   pap2840

27 And there shall in*no*wise enter into it any thing that defileth,

2532   pap4160   an,nn946   2532   an,nn5579

neither *whatsoever* worketh abomination, or *maketh* a lie:

art,pfpp1125 pre1722 art3588   nn721   art,nn975   art,nn2222

but they*which*are*written in the Lamb's book of life.

(Is. 52:1; Ex. 32:32,33; Ps. 69:28; Dan. 12:1)

2532   aina1166   ppro3427 an,aj2513 an,nn4215   an,nn5204   an,nn2222 an,aj2986 ad5613   an,nn2930

22

And he showed me a pure river of water of life, clear as crystal,

ppmp1607   pre1537 art3588   nn2362   art,nn2316 2532   art3588 nn721

proceeding out of the throne of God and of the Lamb.

(Ezek. 47:1; Joel 3:18; Zech. 14:8)

pre1722   an,ajn3319   art3588   ajn4113   ppro846 2532   ad1782/2532/ad1782   art3588 nn4215

2 In the midst of the street of it, and on*either*side of the river, *was*

an,nn3586 an,nn2222   pap4160   nu1427   an,nn2590   pap591 ppro848

there the tree of life, which bare twelve *manner of* fruits, *and* yielded her

art,nn2590 pre2596/an,aj1538/nu1520 an,nn3376 2532 art3588   nn5444   art3588 nn3586   pre1519   an,nn2322

fruit   every   month: and the leaves of the tree *were* for the healing of

art3588   nn1484

the nations.   *(Gen. 2:9; 3:22; Ezek. 47:12)*

2532   fm2071 3756/an,aj3956/ad2089 an,nn2652 2532 art3588   nn2362   art,nn2316 2532

3 And there shall be   no more   curse: but the throne of God and of

art3588 nn721   fm2071 pre1722 ppro846 2532 ppro848   art,ajn1401   ft3000   ppro846

the Lamb shall be in   it; and his servants shall serve him: *(Zech. 14:11)*

2532   fm3700 ppro846 art,nn4383 2532 ppro846 art,nn3686   pre1909 ppro848

4 And they shall see his face; and his name *shall be* in   their

art,nn3359

foreheads.   *(Ps. 17:15; 42:2)*

2532   fm2071 3756 an,nn3571 ad1563   2532   pin2192/an,nn5532 3756 an,nn3088 2532

5 And there shall be no night there; and they   need   no candle, neither

an,nn5457   an,nn2246   an,nn2962 art,nn2316   pin5461/ppro846   2532   ft936

light of the sun; for the Lord God giveth*them*light: and they shall reign

pre1519/art,nn165/art,nn165

forever*and*ever.   *(Zech. 14:7; Is. 60:19,20; Dan. 7:18,27)*

Christ Is Coming Quickly

2532   aina2036   ppro3427 depro3778 art,nn3056   pr/an,aj4103 2532 pr/an,aj228 2532   an,nn2962

6 And he said unto me, These sayings *are* faithful and true: and the Lord

art,nn2316   art3588 aj40   an,nn4396   aina649 ppro848 art,nn32   ainf1166   ppro848 art,ajn1401

God of the holy prophets sent his angel to show unto his servants the things

repro3739 pin1163 pre1722/an,nn5034   aifm1096

which must   shortly be done.   *(Dan. 2:28,29,45)*

2400   pinm2064 an,ajn5035   pr/an,aj3107   art,pap5083   art3588 nn3056   art3588

7 Behold, I come quickly: blessed *is* he*that*keepeth the saying of the

nn4394   depro5127 art,nn975

prophecy of this book.

2532   epn1473 an,nn2491 pr/art,pap991   depro5023   2532 pr/pap191   2532 ad3753

8 And   I   John   saw   these things, and heard *them.* And when I had

aina191 2532   aina991   aina4098   ainf4352   ad*1715 art3588 nn4228   art3588   nn32

heard and seen, I fell down to worship before the feet of the angel

art,pap1166 ppro3427   depro5023

which showed me these things.

2532   pin3004   ppro3427 pim3708   3361 1063   pin1510 ppro4675

9 Then saith he unto me, See *thou do it* not: for I am   thy

pr/an,nn4889   2532 ppro4675 art,nn80 art3588   nn4396   2532   art,pap5083   art3588

fellowservant, and of thy brethren the prophets, and of them*which*keep the

nn3056   depro5127 art,nn975   aima4352   art,nn2316

sayings of this book: worship God.

2532   pin3004   ppro3427 aosi4972 3361 art3588   nn3056   art3588   nn4394   depro5127
10 And he saith unto me, Seal not the sayings of the prophecy of this

art,nn975 3754 art3588 nn2540 pin2076 pr/ad1451
book: for the time is at hand.   *(Dan. 12:4)*

                    art,pap91   aima91   ad2089 2532   art,pap4510
11 He*that*is*unjust, let him be unjust still: and he*which*is*filthy, let him

aima4510   ad2089   2532   art,ajn1342   aipp1344   ad2089   2532
be filthy still: and and he*that*is*righteous, let him be righteous still: and

      art,ajn40   aipp37   ad2089
he*that*is*holy, let him be holy still.

            2532   2400   pinm2064   an,ajn5035   2532 ppro3450 art,nn3408   pre3326 ppro1700   ainf591
12 And, behold, I come quickly; and my reward *is* with me, to give

an,ajn1538   ad5613 ppro848 art,nn2041   fm2071
every man according as his work shall be.

               (Is. 40:10; 62:11; Ps. 28:4; 62:12; Prov. 24:12; Is. 59:18; Jer. 17:10)
       epn1473 pin1510 (art3588) pr/1   2532 (art3588)   pr/5598   pr/an,nn746   2532   pr/an,nn5056 art3588
13   I   am   Alpha   and   Omega, the beginning and the end,   the

pr/nu,ajn4413 2532 art3588 pr/ajn2078
first and the last.   *(Is. 44:6; 48:12)*

         pr/an,aj3107   art,pap4160   ppro848   art,nn1785   2443   ppro846   fm2071
14 Blessed *are* they*that*do his commandments, that they may have

art,nn1849 pre1909 art3588 nn3586   art,nn2222 2532   asba1525   art3588 nn4440 pre1519 art3588 nn4172
right to the tree of life, and may enter in through the gates into the city.

                                                       (Gen. 2:9; 3:22; Ezek. 47:12)
      1161   ad1854   art,nn2965 2532   art,nn5333   2532   art,nn4205   2532
15 For without *are* dogs, and sorcerers, and whoremongers, and

art,nn5406   2532   art,nn1496   2532   an,aj3956   art,pap5368 2532   pap4160   an,nn5579
murderers, and idolaters, and whosoever loveth and maketh a lie.

       epn1473 an,nn2424   aina3992 ppro3450 art,nn32   ainf3140   ppro5213   depro5023   pre1909
16   I   Jesus have sent mine angel to testify unto you these things in

art3588   nn1577   epn1473 pin1510 art3588 pr/nn4491 2532 art3588 pr/nn1085   1138   art3588   aj2986
the churches. I   am the root and the offspring of David, *and* the bright

2532   an,aj3720   pr/art,nn792
and morning star.   *(Num. 24:17; Is. 11:1,10)*

       2532 art3588   nn4151   2532 art3588 nn3565   pin3004 aima2064   2532   art,pap191   aima2036
17 And the Spirit and the bride say, Come. And let him*that*heareth say,

aima2064   2532   art,pap1372   aima2064 2532   art3588 pap2309   pim2983 art3588
Come. And let him*that*is*athirst come. And whosoever will, let him take the

nn5204   art,nn2222 an,nn1432
water of life freely.   *(Is. 55:1)*

        1063   pinm4828   an,aj3956   pap191 art3588   nn3056   art3588   nn4394
18 For I testify unto every man that heareth the words of the prophecy of

depro5127 art,nn975 1437 idpro5100   psa2007 pre4314   depro5023   art,nn2316   ft2007 pre1909 ppro846
this book, If any man shall add unto these things, God shall add unto him

art3588   nn4127   art,pfpp1125   pre1722 depro5129 art,nn975
the plagues that*are*written in this book:

         2532   1437 idpro5100   psa851   pre575 art3588 nn3056   an,nn976   depro5026
19 And if any man shall take away from the words of the book of this

art,nn4394   art,nn2316   ft851   ppro846 art,nn3313 pre575   an,nn976   art,nn2222 2532
prophecy, God shall take away his part out of the book of life, and

^{pre1537} ^{art3588} ^{aj40} ^{art,nn4172} ²⁵³²   ^{art,pfpp1125}   ^{pre1722} ^{depro5129} ^{an,nn975}
out of the holy city, and *from* the*things*which*are*written in this book.

(Deut. 4:2; 12:32; Ex. 32:32,33; Ps. 79:28; Dan. 12:1)

^{art,pap3140}   ^{depro5023}   ^{pin3004}   ³⁴⁸³   ^{pinm2064} ^{an,ajn5035}   ²⁸¹
20 He*which*testifieth these things saith, Surely I come quickly. Amen.
³⁴⁸³   ^{pim2064} ^{an,nn2962} ^{an,nn2424}
Even so, come, Lord Jesus.

^{art3588}   ⁿⁿ⁵⁴⁸⁵   ^{ppro2257} ^{art,nn2962} ^{an,nn2424} ^{an,nn5547}   ^{pre3326} ^{ppro5216} ^{an,aj3956}   ²⁸¹
21 The grace of our Lord Jesus Christ *be* with you all. Amen.

STUDY HELPS

Grammatical Codes
Grammatical Notations
List of Irregular Adverbs
Guide to Transliteration
Lexical Aids to the New Testament
Greek Concordance
Translational Reference Index
Scripture Index to Footnotes and Introductions
Strong's Dictionary

GRAMMATICAL CODES TO THE GRAMMATICAL NOTATIONS

The grammatical codes, the small codes in the line above the text of this New Testament, are listed alphabetically below. These codes represent grammatical constructions found in the Greek New Testament. The number(s) in parentheses after each of the codes refer to the particular grammatical notations, found in the Study Helps section, that will explain the construction. For example, the future middle, **fm**, is explained by its own notation **36** (in bold type) with cross references to notations 35 (future tense) and 50 (middle voice).

ad . . . . . .adverb **(4)**

aid . . . . . .articular infinitive with *dia*
(**25**: *see* 24, 46, 78)

aie . . . . . .articular infinitive with *en*
(**27**: *see* 24, 46, 78)

aies . . . . .articular infinitive with *eis*
(**26**: *see* 24, 46, 78)

aifm . . . . .aorist infinitive middle
(**14**: *see* 6, 46, 50)

aifp . . . . .aorist infinitive passive
(**15**: *see* 6, 46, 60)

aima . . . .aorist imperative active
(**7**: *see* 1, 6, 43)

aime . . . .articular infinitive with *metá*
(**28**: *see* 24, 46, 78)

aina . . . . .aorist indicative active
(**10**: *see* 1, 6, 45)

ainf . . . . .aorist infinitive active
(**13**: *see* 1, 6, 46)

ainm . . . .aorist indicative middle
(**11**: *see* 6, 45, 50)

ainp . . . . .aorist indicative passive
(**12**: *see* 6, 45, 60)

aip . . . . . .articular infinitive with *pro*
(**29**: *see* 24, 46, 78)

aipm . . . .aorist imperative middle
(**8**: *see* 6, 43, 50)

aipp . . . . .aorist imperative passive
(**9** *see:* 6,43, 60)

aipr . . . . .articular infinitive with *pros*
(**30**: *see* 24, 46, 78)

aj . . . . . . .adjective **(2)**

ajn . . . . . .adjectival noun (**3**: *see* 2, 51)

an . . . . . .anarthrous (**5**: *see* 24).

aom . . . . .aorist middle
(**16**: *see* 6, 50)

aop . . . . .aorist passive (**12**: *see* 6, 50)

aosi . . . . .aorist subjunctive used as an
imperative (**20**: *see* 6, 7, 43, 94)

apta . . . . .aorist participle active
(**17**: *see* 1, 6, 57)

aptm . . . .aorist participle middle
(**18**: *see* 6, 50, 57)

aptp . . . .aorist participle passive
(**19**: *see* 6, 57, 60)

art . . . . . .definite article (**24**: *see* 5)

asba . . . .aorist subjunctive active
(**21**: *see* 1, 6, 94)

asbm . . .aorist subjunctive middle
(**22**: *see* 6, 50, 94)

asbp . . . .aorist subjunctive passive
(**23**: *see* 6, 60, 94)

cd . . . . . .comparative degree **(31)**

depro . . .demonstrative pronoun
(**32**: *see* 72)

efn . . . . . .emphatic future negative **(33)**

epn . . . . .emphatic personal pronoun
(**34**: *see* 72)

fifm . . . . .future infinitive middle
(**39**: *see* 35, 46, 50)

finf . . . . . .future infinitive active
(**38**: *see* 1, 35, 46)

fm . . . . . .future middle (**36**: *see* 35, 50)

fp . . . . . . .future passive (**37**: *see* 35, 60)

fpta . . . . .future participle active
(**40**: *see* 1, 35, 57)

fptm . . . .future participle middle
(**41**: *see* 35, 50, 57)

fptp . . . . .future participle passive
(**42:** *see* 35, 57, 60)

ft . . . . . . .future tense **(35)**

idpro . . . .indefinite pronoun (**48:** *see* 72)

infg . . . . .infinitive with genitive article
(**47:** *see* 24, 46)

inpro . . . .interrogative pronoun
(**49:** *see* 72)

ipf . . . . . .imperfect tense **(44)**

nn . . . . . .noun **(51)**

nu . . . . . .cardinal number **(52)**

nu,ad . . .cardinal number used as an adverb **(54:** *see* 4)

nu,aj . . . .ordinal number used as an adjective (**53:** *see* 2)

nu,ajn . . .ordinal number used as an adjectival noun (**55:** *see* 2, 51)

opt . . . . . .optative mood **(56)**

pap . . . . .present active participle
(**58:** *see* 1, 57)

pfi . . . . . .perfect indicative active
(**63:** *see* 1, 45, 61)

pfim . . . .perfect indicative middle
(**64:** *see* 45, 50, 61)

pfimm . . .perfect imperative middle
(**62:** *see* 43, 50, 61)

pfin . . . . .perfect infinitive active
(**66:** *see* 1, 46, 61)

pfinm . . .perfect infinitive middle
(**67:** *see* 46, 50, 61)

pfinp . . . .perfect infinitive passive
(**68:** *see* 46, 60, 61)

pfip . . . . .perfect indicative passive
(**65:** *see* 45, 60, 61)

pfmp . . . .perfect participle middle
(**70:** *see* 50, 57, 61)

pfp . . . . . .perfect participle active
(**69:** *see* 1, 57, 61)

pfpp . . . .perfect participle passive
(**71:** *see* 57, 60, 61)

pifm . . . .present infinitive middle
(**86:** *see* 46, 50, 79)

pifp . . . . .present infinitive passive
(**87:** *see* 46, 60, 79)

pim . . . . .present imperative active
(**80:** *see* 1, 43, 79)

pimm . . .present imperative middle
(**81:** *see* 43, 50, 79)

pin . . . . . .present indicative active
(**82:** *see* 1, 45, 79)

pinf . . . . .present infinitive active
(**85:** *see* 1, 46, 79)

pinm . . . .present indicative middle
(**83:** *see* 45, 50, 79)

pinp . . . .present indicative passive
(**84:** *see* 45, 60, 79)

pl . . . . . . .plural **(75)**

plpf . . . . .pluperfect tense **(74)**

popro . . .possessive pronoun (**76:** *see* 72)

ppmp . . .present passive/middle participle
(**59:** *see* 50, 57, 60, 79)

ppro . . . .personal pronoun (**73:** *see* 72)

pr . . . . . . .predicate **(77)**

pre . . . . . .preposition **(78)**

psa . . . . .present subjunctive active
(**88:** *see* 1, 79, 94)

psmp . . .present subjunctive middle/pas-
sive (**89:** *see* 50, 60, 79, 94)

rcpro . . . .reciprocal pronoun (**90:** *see* 72)

repro . . . .relative pronoun (**92:** *see* 72)

rxpro . . . .reflexive pronoun (**91:** *see* 72)

sg . . . . . .singular **(93)**

GRAMMATICAL NOTATIONS

DEFINITIONS OF THE GRAMMATICAL CATEGORIES

1. The **Active Voice** represents the action as being accomplished by the subject of the verb: *árti ginōskō ek mérous, tóte de epignōsomai, kathōs kai epegnōsthēn,* "now I know in part; but then shall I know even as also I am known" (1 Cor. 13:12). In Greek it is to be distinguished from the **Middle Voice (50)** and **Passive Voice (60)**. See also **95**.

2. The **Adjective (aj)** is a word which modifies a noun by describing certain properties or qualities of the noun. An adjective can be attributive: *pan déndron agathón karpoús kaloús poieí,* "every good tree bringeth forth good fruit" (Matt. 7:17). It can also be predicative, following an explicit or implied verb of being: *di' hēs emarturēthē eínai díkaios,* "by which he obtained witness that he was righteous" (Heb. 11:4). See also **77**.

3. The **Adjectival Noun (ajn)** is an adjective used as a noun: *ton hélion autoú anatéllei epí ponēroús kai agathoús,* "he maketh his sun to rise on the evil and the good" (Matt. 5:45). See also **2, 51**.

4. The **Adverb (ad)** is a word which qualifies the meaning of a verb by indicating the time, place, or manner in which its action is accomplished: *ekeí estaúrōsan autón,* "there they crucified him" (Luke 23:33). An adverb can also be used to qualify the meaning of an adjective or another adverb: *echárēsan charán megálēn sphódra,* "they rejoiced with exceeding great joy". (Matt. 2:10).

5. **Anarthrous (an)** refers to a word or group of words which appear without a definite article (*ho, he, to* [3588], the). Greek has no indefinite article, "a" or "an" in English. Sometimes it is best to translate an anarthrous word by supplying "a" or "an" before it. In fact, due to reasons of English style or Greek idiom, the word "the" is even an appropriate translation in some cases. However, there are many times when supplying an article would be incorrect. Anarthrous constructions are most often intended to point out the quality of something: *Toigaroún kai hēmeís, tosoúton échontes perikeímenon hemín néphos martúrōn,* "Wherefore, seeing we also are compassed about with so great a cloud of witnesses" (Heb. 12:1). See also **24**.

6. The **Aorist Tense** is used for simple, undefined action. In the indicative mood, the aorist tense can indicate punctiliar action (action that happens at a specific point in time) in the past. It must be distinguished from the **Imperfect Tense (44)** which denotes continuous action in the past. With few exceptions, whenever the aorist tense is used in any mood other than the indicative, the verb does not have any temporal significance. In other words, it refers only to the reality of an event or action, not to the time when it took place. See also **95**.

AORIST IMPERATIVE The aorist imperative denotes a command, request, or entreaty. Unlike the **Present Imperative (80, 81)**, it does not involve a command or entreaty for continuous or repetitive action. Instead, it is often used for general exhortations and for things that must be begun at that very moment. See also **6, 43**.

7. The **Aorist Imperative Active (aima):** *népsate, grēgorésate,* "Be sober, be vigilant" (1 Pet. 5:8). See also **1**.

8. The **Aorist Imperative Middle (aipm):** *eípé te ho ággelos prós autón, Perízōsai kai hupódēsai ta sandáliá sou.* "And the angel said unto him, Gird thyself, and bind on thy sandals" (Acts 12:8). See Also **50**.

9. The **Aorist Imperative Passive (aipp):** *genēthētō to thélēmá sou,* "Thy will be done" (Matt. 6:10). See also **60**.

AORIST INDICATIVE The aorist indicative expresses action that is not continuous. It does not specify the relative time of the action to the time of speaking. See also **6, 45**.

10. The **Aorist Indicative Active (aina):** *to chrísma ho elábete ap' autoú,* "the anointing which ye have received of him" (1 John 2:27). See also **1**.

11. The **Aorist Indicative Middle (ainm/aom):** *eis hon ebouleúsanto,* "into the which they were minded" (Acts 27:39). See also **50.**

12. The **Aorist Indicative Passive (ainp/aop):** *kai parachrḗma anōrthṓthē,* "and immediately she was made straight" (Luke 13:13). See also **60.**

AORIST INFINITIVE The aorist infinitive refers to punctiliar action, and not continuous action (as with the **Present Infinitive**). Furthermore, it does not signify the time of action. See also **6, 46.**

13. The **Aorist Infinitive Active (ainf):** *éxesti tois sábbasin, agathopoiḗsai ē̄ kakopoiḗsai,* "Is it lawful on the sabbath days to do good or to do evil" (Luke 6:9). See also **1.**

14. The **Aorist Infinitive Middle (aifm):** *apóthesthai humás . . . ton palaión ánthrōpon,* "That ye put off . . . the old man" (Eph. 4:22). See also **50.**

15. The **Aorist Infinitive Passive (aifp):** *kai apenechthḗnai autón hupó tōn aggélōn,* "and was carried by the angels" (Luke 16:22). See also **60.**

16. The **Aorist Middle (aom/ainm)** represents non-continuous action by the subject as acting upon himself or concerning himself: *anechṓrēse, kai apelthṓn apégxato,* "and departed, and went and hanged himself" (Matt. 27:5). See also **6, 50.**

AORIST PARTICIPLE The aorist participle expresses simple action, as opposed to continuous action which would be expressed by the **Present Active Participle (58)**. It does not in itself indicate the time of the action. However, when its relationship to the main verb is temporal, it usually signifies action prior to that of the main verb. See also **6, 57.**

17. The **Aorist Participle Active (apta):** *eipón de taúta, kai labṓn árton, eucharístēse tō theō̄ enṓpion pántōn,* "And when he had thus spoken, he took bread, and gave thanks to God in presence of them all" (Acts 27:35). See also **1.**

18. The **Aorist Participle Middle (aptm):** *allá apotaxámenos autoís exélthon eis Makedonían,* "but taking my leave of them, I went from thence into Macedonia" (2 Cor. 2:13). See also **50.**

19. The **Aorist Participle Passive (aptp):** *oudé eíneken tou adikēthéntos,* "nor for his cause that suffered wrong" (2 Cor. 7:12). See also **60.**

20. The **Aorist Subjunctive used as an Imperative (aosi)** usually forbids an action which is not in progress, and thus commands that it not be started: *kai mē eisenégkēs hēmás eis peirasmón,* "And lead us not into temptation" (Luke 11:4). For the command to stop something already in progress, see the **Present Imperative (80).** See also **1, 6, 94.**

AORIST SUBJUNCTIVE This tense in the three voices differs from the **Present Subjunctive (psa)** and the **Present Subjunctive Middle/Passive (psmp)** by referring to simple, undefined action, as opposed to continuous or repeated action. See also **6, 94.**

21. The **Aorist Subjunctive Active (asba):** *hína agnísōsin heautoús,* "to purify themselves" (John 11:55). See also **1.**

22. The **Aorist Subjunctive Middle (asbm):** *eán mē pugmē̄ nípsōntai tas cheíras,* "except they wash their hands oft" (Mark 7:3). See also **50.**

23. The **Aorist Subjunctive Passive (asbp):** *ho nikṓn ou mē adikēthē̄ ek tou thanátou tou deutérou,* "He that overcometh shall not be hurt of the second death" (Rev. 2:11). See also **60.**

24. The **Definite Article (art)** in Greek is sometimes translated with the English definite article "the." However, the function of the two is quite different. In English, the definite article serves merely to particularize, to refer to a particular object. In Greek, however, it serves to emphasize, in some way, the person or thing it modifies. Hence, in most cases, the definite article in Greek serves to identify: *di' hupomonés trechómen ton prokeímenon hémin agōna,* "and let us run with patience the race that is set before us." The term "articular" refers to a word or group of words which appear with a defi-

nite article (*ho, he, to* [3588], the). There is perhaps no other part of Greek grammar where the Greek idiom differs so greatly from the English. For instance, an English grammarian would never place the definite article before a proper noun (e.g., the "Thomas"), though in Greek it is very common. Recognizing the significance of the presence or absence of the definite article requires the most intimate knowledge of the Greek language. Contrast the use of articular constructions with anarthous constructions which refers to quality. See also **5**.

25. The **Articular Infinitive with the Preposition** *diá* **(aid)** is used with the accusative article to denote cause: *diá to eínai autoú phílon*, "because he is his friend" (Luke 11:8). See also **24, 46, 78**.

26. The **Articular Infinitive with the Preposition** *eis* **(aies)** is used with the accusative article and usually denotes purpose: *eis to thanatôsai autón* "[in order] to put him to death" (Mark 14:55). See also **24, 46, 78**.

27. The **Articular Infinitive with the Preposition** *en* **(aie)** is used with the dative article and usually expresses the time at which something occurs. It is usually translated with the English words "while" or "when": *en de tô hupágein autón*, "But as [while] he went the people thronged him" (Luke 8:42). See also **24, 46, 78**.

28. The **Articular Infinitive with the Preposition** *metá* **(aime)** is used with the accusative article and indicates subsequent action. It is often translated with the English word "after": *metá de to paradothênai ton Iōánnēn*, "Now after that John was put in prison" (Mark 1:14). See also **24, 46, 78**.

29. The **Articular Infinitive with the Preposition** *pro* **(aip)** is used with the genitive article and indicates antecedent action. It is translated with the English word "before": *tê dóxē hē eíchon pro tou ton kósmon eínai pará soi*, "the glory which I had with thee before the world was" (John 17:5). See also **24, 46, 47, 78**.

30. The **Articular Infinitive with the Preposition** *pros* **(aipr)** is used with the accusative article and usually denotes purpose: *pros to dúnasthai humás*, "[in order] that ye may be able" (Eph. 6:11). See also **24, 46, 78**.

31. The **Comparative Degree (cd)** is used, with adjectives and adverbs, only when two items are being compared. There are four different degrees: positive (e.g., good); comparative (e.g., better); superlative (e.g., best); and emphatic superlative (e.g., very best). The positive degree is used of one thing without relation to any other. The superlative degree is used when three or more things are being compared. There is no Greek form for the superlative degree with relative meaning. However, in the Greek New Testament there is a tendency for each degree to be used in the place of the next higher degree. Hence, the positive degree can be used with the comparative meaning, the comparative with the superlative meaning, and the superlative with the emphatic superlative meaning. Thus, in 1 Corinthians 13:13, the construction *meízōn de toútōn hē agápē*, should be translated "the greatest of these is charity," since three items are being compared.

32. The **Demonstrative Pronoun (depro)** is used to distinguish one object or person from other objects or persons. There are two demonstrative pronouns used in the New Testament. The first of these pronouns, most often translated "this, this one" (*hoútos, auté, toúto*), is used to point out objects or persons nearby in space or time: *hoútos estín ho huiós mou ho agapētós*, "This is my beloved son" (Matt. 17:5). The other pronoun, most often translated "that, that one" (*ekeínos, ekeíne, ekeíno*), is used in connection with more remote objects or persons: *kai en ekeínē tē nuktí epíasan oudén*, "and that night they caught nothing" (John 21:3). See also **72**.

33. The **Emphatic Future Negative (efn)** is indicated by the negative particles *ou*, "not," and *mē*, "not," which are used together to emphasize the negation. It is normally used with the aorist subjunctive, but sometimes it accompanies a future indicative to indicate strong future negation: *kaí ou mē eisélthē eis autḗn pan koinoún*, "And there shall in no wise enter into it anything that defileth" (Rev. 21:27).

34. The **Emphatic Personal Pronoun (epn)** is used when emphasis is being placed on a person, and is especially useful when the subject of a verb is being emphasized. Since the verb endings in Greek indicate person and number, a personal pronoun is usually not expressed as a separate word. Hence, when a pronoun is used, it calls special attention to the subject: *egó de légō humín*, "But, I [myself] say to you" (Matthew 5:22). See also **72**.

FUTURE TENSE Though on occasion the future tense may refer to linear action, it almost always refers to punctiliar action. However, the emphasis is always on the fact that the action will take place in the future, not what kind of action is represented. See also **95**.

35. The **Future Active (ft)**: *tóte hoi díkaioi eklámpsousin hōs ho hélios*, "Then shall the righteous shine forth as the sun" (Matt. 13:43). See also **1**.

36. The **Future Middle (fm)**: *kai ti airésomai ou gnōrízō*, "what I shall choose I wot not" (Phil. 1:22). See also **50**.

37. The **Future Passive (fp)**: *ho de agapōn me, agapēthésetai hupó tou patrós mou*, "he that loveth me shall be loved of my Father" (John 14:21). See also **60**.

FUTURE INFINITIVE The future infinitive refers to a simple, undefined action expected to occur in the future. See also **35, 46**.

38. The **Future Infinitive Active (finf)**: *me eiseleúsesthai eis tēn katápausin*, "they should not enter into his rest" (Heb. 3:18). See also **1**.

39. The **Future Infinitive Middle (fifm)**: *theōrō hóti metá húbreōs . . . méllein ésesthai ton ploún*, "I perceive that this voyage will be with hurt . . ." (Acts 27:10). See also **50**.

FUTURE PARTICIPLE The participial mood does not in itself indicate the time of action. The future participle is used to denote an action that is subsequent to that of the main verb in the sentence. See also **35, 57**.

40. The **Future Participle Active (fpta)**: *ídōmen ei érchetai Elías sósōn autón*, "let us see whether Elijah will come to save him" (Matt. 27:49). See also **1**.

41. The **Future Participle Middle (fptm)**: *ou to sōma to genēsómenon speíreis*, "thou sowest not that body that shall be" (1 Cor. 15:37). See also **50**.

42. The **Future Participle Passive (fptp)**: *eis martúrion tōn lalēthēsoménōn*, "for a testimony of those things which were to be spoken after" (Heb. 3:5). See also **60**.

43. The **Imperative Mood** is used to give a command: *húpage, seautón deíxon tō hiereí*, "go thy way, show thyself to the priest" (Mark 1:44); an exhortation *poiésate oun karpoús axíous tēs metanoías*, "Bring forth therefore fruits meet for repentance" (Matt. 3:8); or an entreaty *ton árton hēmón ton epioúsion dídou hēmín to kath' hēméran*, "Give us day by day our daily bread" (Luke 11:3). See also **7–9, 20, 62, 80, 81, 95**.

44. The **Imperfect Tense (ipf)** is only used in the indicative mood and refers to continuous or linear action in past time. It is distinguished from the aorist indicative which conceives of an action in past time as simply having taken place, without further defining it: *kai hoi óchloi ezétoun autón*, "and the people sought [i.e., were continuously seeking] him" (Luke 4:42). See also **45, 95**.

45. The **Indicative Mood** makes an assertion of fact and is used with all six Greek tenses. It is the only mood in which distinctions can regularly be made about the time when an action occurs: *all' egenéthēmen épioi en mésō humón*, "But we were gentle among you" (1 Thess. 2:7). See also **95**.

46. The **Infinitive (inf)** is a verbal noun. In Greek it has many more uses than it does in English, most of which are idiomatic and difficult to translate properly. In many instances, the infinitive is translated using the English word "to": *kai élthomen proskunésai autó*, "and are come to worship him" (Matt. 2:2). See also **13–15, 25–30, 38, 39, 47, 66–68, 85–87**.

47. The **Infinitive with a Genitive Article (infg)** frequently denotes purpose. Hence, it is

translated like the **Articular Infinitive with the Preposition** *eis* (26) and the **Articular Infinitive with the Preposition** *pros* (30), but unlike them does not have a preceding preposition: *zēteín to paidíon tou apolésai autó*, "will seek the young child [in order] to destroy him" (Matt. 2:13). See also **24, 46**.

48. The **Indefinite Pronoun (idpro)** is simply a pronoun that does not refer to any specific person or persons. It corresponds to the English indefinite pronoun: *pōs légousi tinés en humín hóti anástasis nekrōn ouk éstín*, "how say some among you that there is no resurrection of the dead?" (1 Cor. 15:12). See also **72**.

49. The **Interrogative Pronoun (inpro)**, translated by English interrogative pronouns "who" or "which": *tis ára meízōn estín en tē basileía tōn ouranōn*, "Who is the greatest in the kingdom of heaven?" (Matt. 18:1). See also **72**.

50. The **Middle Voice** represents the subject as acting in some way upon himself or concerning himself. Since English does not have a middle voice, it is usually difficult to translate the middle voice into English: *árti ginōskō ek mérous tóte de epignōsomai, kathōs kai epegnōsthēn*, "now I know in part; but then shall I know even as also I am known" (1 Cor. 13:12). See also **95**.

51. A **noun (nn)** is the name of a person, place, or thing. Greek nouns have cases and declensions which indicate their function in a sentence. A noun in the nominative case is the subject or subject complement of the verb: *Ouk ep' ártō mónō zēsetai ánthrōpos*, "Man shall not live by bread alone" (Matt. 4:4); the genitive case primarily indicates possession, source, or separation and often includes the English word "of" in its translation: *ou gar thelēmati anthrōpou ēnéchthē poté prophēteía*, "For the prophecy came not in old time by the will of man" (2 Peter 1:21); the dative case is primarily the case of the indirect object: *tóte légei tō anthrōpō*, Then saith he to the man (Matt. 12:13); A noun in the accusative case is usually the direct object of the verb: *hōs basanismós skorpíou, hótan paísē ánthrōpon*, "as the torment of a scorpion, when he striketh a man" (Rev. 9:5); the vocative case is the case of direct address: *eípen autō Ánthrōpe, aphéōntai soi hai hamartíai sou*, "he said unto him, Man, thy sins are forgiven thee" (Luke 5:20). While these are the normal functions of each case, there are exceptions and other uses for each. For instance, the meaning of some prepositions is greatly affected by the case of the noun or pronoun that is their object (see **78**).

52. A **Cardinal Number (nu)** is a number used to express quantity, not order, and may serve as a noun, pronoun, adjective, or, in Greek, an adverb **(54)**: *kai su en trisín hemérais egereís autón*, "and wilt thou rear it up in three days" (John 2:20).

53. An **Ordinal Number used as an Adjective (nu,aj)** is a number used to express order rather than quantity: *en tē prōtē mou apología oudeís moi sumparegéneto*, "At my first answer no man stood with me" (2 Tim. 4:16). See also **2**.

54. A **Cardinal Number used as an adverb (nu,ad)** denotes frequency. Whereas English has separate forms for numbers that serve as adverbs, Greek uses the cardinal number: *prin ē dis aléktora phōnēsai, tris aparnēsē me*, "before the cock crow twice, thou shalt deny me thrice" (Mark 14:30). See also **4**.

55. An **Ordinal Number used as an Adjectival Noun (nu,ajn)** is a number used to express order rather than quantity, used as a noun or pronoun: *kai éstēsan dúo*, "And they appointed two" (Acts 1:23). See also **2, 51**.

56. The **Optative Mood (opt)** is rare in the Greek New Testament. This mood is used in two ways. It may be used to express a wish: *ho theós . . . dōē humín pneúma sophías kai apokalúpseōs*, "God . . . may give unto you the spirit of wisdom and revelation." (Eph. 1:17). It can also introduce an indirect question: *kai dielogízeto potapós eíē ho aspasmós hoútos*, "and cast in her mind what manner of salutation this should be" (Luke 1:29). See also **95**.

57. The **Participle** is a verbal adjective. As such, the participle may function as a verb, noun, or adjective in the sentence. It has a wide range of possible meanings, some of

which can only be inferred from the context: *ho agathopoiṓn ek tou theoú estín*, "He that doeth good is of God" (3 John 1:11).

PRESENT PARTICIPLE The present participle expresses continuous or repeated action. Since in Greek the time of the action represented by participles is relative to the main verb, the present participle is used to signify action that is contemporaneous with the leading verb, whether that action occurs in the past, present, or future. See also **57, 79.**

58. The **Present Active Participle (pap):** *spoudázontes tēreín tēn henótēta tou Pneúmatos*, "Endeavoring to keep the unity of the Spirit" (Eph. 4:3). See also **1, 57.**

59. The **Present Passive/Middle Participle (ppmp):** *auxanómenoi eis tēn epígnōsin tou Theoú*, "increasing in the knowledge of God" (Col. 1:10). See also **50, 57, 60.**

60. The **Passive Voice** represents the subject as receiving the action of the verb. In English, it usually takes a form of the verb "to be" to express the passive: *árti ginṓskō ek mérous tóte de epignṓsomai, kathṓs kai epegnṓsthēn*, "now I know in part; but then shall I know even as also I am known" (1 Cor. 13:12). See also **1, 50, 95.**

61. The **Perfect Tense** describes an action, or more correctly a process, that took place in the past, the results of which have continued to the present. It has no exact equivalent in English, but is usually translated by using the auxiliary verbs "has" or "have": *Thúgater, hē pístis sou sesōké se*, "Daughter, thy faith hath made thee whole" (Mark 5:34). See also **95.**

62. The **Perfect Imperative Middle (pfimm)** is used to express a strong command or exhortation, representing the action as already completed, and as remaining in the state of completion: *kai eípe tē thalássē, Siṓra, pephímōso*, "And said unto the sea, Peace, be still" (Mark 4:39). See also **43, 50, 61.**

PERFECT INDICATIVE It is in the indicative mood that the special meaning and temporal significance of the perfect tense is at its height. However, the context of the Greek may emphasize either the completeness of the action or the finished results. See also **1, 45, 61.**

63. The **Perfect Indicative Active (pfi):** *kai hoi ouk akēkóasi, sunḗsousi*, "and they that have not heard shall understand" (Rom. 15:21). See also **1, 45, 61.**

64. The **Perfect Indicative Middle (pfim):** *kai béblētai eis tén thálassan*, "and he were cast [lit. "cast himself"] into the sea" (Mark 9:42). See also **45, 50, 61.**

65. The **Perfect Indicative Passive (pfip):** *Gúnai, apolélusai tēs astheneías sou*, "Woman, thou art loosed from thine infirmity" (Luke 13:12). See also **45, 60, 61.**

PERFECT INFINITIVE The Perfect infinitive is used almost exclusively in the New Testament in indirect discourse. See also **46, 61.**

66. The **Perfect Infinitive Active (pfin):** *kreítton gar ēn autoís mē epegnōkénai tēn hodón tēs dikaiosúnēs*, "For it had been better for them not to have known the way of righteousness" (2 Pet. 2:21). See also **1, 46, 61.**

67. The **Perfect Infinitive Middle (pfinm):** *tó boúlēma tōn ethnōn kateirásthai* (UBS), "to have carried out the desire of the Gentiles," (1 Pet. 4:3, NASB). To the best of our knowledge this is the only place the perfect infinitive middle occurs. See also **46, 60, 61.**

68. The **Perfect Infinitive Passive (pfinp):** *apolelústhai edúnato ho ánthrōpos hoútos*, "This man might have been set at liberty" (Acts 26:32). See also **46, 60, 61.**

PERFECT PARTICIPLE The perfect participle stresses the state brought about by the finished results of the action. See also **57, 61.**

69. The **Perfect Participle Active (pfp):** *pánta heōrakótes ha epoíēsen*, "having seen all the things that he did" (John 4:45). See also **1, 6, 57, 61.**

70. The **Perfect Participle Middle (pfmp):** *all' hupodedeménous sandália; kaí mē endúsesthe dúo chitónas*. "but be shod with sandals; and not put on two coats" (Mark 6:9). See also **50, 57, 61.**

71. The **Perfect Participle Passive (pfpp):** *hína kai autoí ōsin hēgiasménoi en alētheía,* "that they also might be <u>santicified</u> through the truth" (John 17:19). See also **57, 60, 61.**

72. The **Pronoun** is used in place of a noun. In Greek, there are eight categories of pronouns: the **Demonstrative Pronoun (32)**, the **Emphatic Personal Pronoun (34)**, the **Indefinite Pronoun (48)**, the **Interrogative Pronoun (49)**, the **Personal Pronoun (73)**, the **Possessive Pronoun (76)**, the **Reciprocal Pronoun (90)**, the **Reflexive Pronoun (91)**, and the **Relative Pronoun (92)**.

73. The **Personal Pronoun (ppro)** is found in three persons: *egṓ eími tó phṓs tou kósmou,* "<u>I</u> am the light of the world" (John 8:12); *su ei ho huiós tou theoú,* "<u>Thou</u> art the Son of God" (Mark 3:11); *autós gár egínōsken ti ēn en tō anthrōpṓ;* "For <u>he</u> knew what was in man." (John 2:25). The third person is found in three genders, exactly as in English *autós, autḗ, aúto;* he, she, it. See also **72.**

74. The **Pluperfect Tense (plpf)** is like the **Perfect Tense (61)**, except that the result of the action is also in the past. Usually the English auxiliary verb "had" is used to translate a Greek word in the pluperfect tense. However, the auxiliary verb "had" is also used to translate the aorist tense: *hos elēlúthei proskunḗsōn eis Ierousalḗm,* "(who) <u>had come</u> to Jerusalem for to worship" (Acts 8:27). See also **95.**

75. The **Plural (pl)** number in the Greek New Testament, as in English, refers to two or more persons or objects: *állō de energḗmata dunámeōn,* "to another the <u>working</u> of miracles" (1 Cor. 12:10). See also **93.**

76. The **Possessive Pronoun (popro)**, in English is not a separate class of pronouns, but simply one of the three cases of a pronoun (nominative and objective being the other two). A similar sense of possession can be obtained in Greek by using the personal pronoun in the genitive case. However, in Greek there are also separate possessive pronoun forms, which are used for greater emphasis. These possessive pronouns occur only in the first and second persons. *Hē basileía hē emḗ ouk éstín ek tou kósmou toútou,* "<u>My</u> kingdom is not of this world" (John 18:36). See also **72.**

77. The **Predicate Nominative and Adjective (pr)** are those parts of a sentence that makes an assertion about the subject: *Humeís este to phōs tou kósmou,* "Ye are the <u>light</u> of the world" (Matt. 5:14, which uses the predicate nominative). In these cases, the predicate is usually that part of the sentence which follows a form of the verb "to be" Greek *eimí,* which is often omitted in the Greek: *Pneúma ho Theós* "God <u>is</u> a Spirit" (John 4:24). Likewise the predicate adjective omits the verb, *makárioi hoi katharoí tñ kardía,* "Blessed <u>are</u> the pure in heart" (Matt. 5:8).

78. The **Preposition (pre)** is a word used to relate a noun or pronoun with some other word in the sentence: *Christós hupér hēmṓn apéthane,* "Christ died <u>for</u> us" (Romans 5:8); *Ho . . . pisteúōn tō pémpsantí me . . . metabébēken ek tou thanátou eis tēn zōén,* "He that . . . believeth on him that sent me . . . is passed <u>from</u> death <u>unto</u> life" (John 5:24).

There are several special uses of the preposition, such as the various types of the articular infinitives (see **25–30**). Prepositions are also used in the formation of compound words: *tóte de epignósomai* (from *epí* and *ginóskō) kathós kai epignósthēn,* "then shall I know even as also I am known" (1 Cor. 13:12). In this particular case the addition of the preposition *epí* to the original verb serves to intensify its meaning.

There are some prepositions that occur only with nouns of one case: *mēdení kakón antí kakoú* [genitive] *apodidóntes,* "Recompense to no man evil for evil" (Rom. 12:17). Other prepositions can have objects in two or more cases, with each case encompassing different meanings of the preposition: *kai en metá tōn thēríōn* [genitive], "and was <u>with</u> the wild beasts" (Mark 1:13); *metá dúo hēméras* [accusative] *to páscha gínetai,* "<u>after</u> two days is the feast of the passover" (Matt. 26:2).

79. The **Present Tense in the Indicative Mood (45)** represents contemporaneous action,

as opposed to action in the past or the future. In moods other than in the indicative mood, it refers only to continuous or repeated action. See also **95**.

PRESENT IMPERATIVE The present imperative occurs only in the active and middle voices in the New Testament. In the active voice, it may indicate a command to do something in the future which involves continuous or repeated action or, when it is negated, a command to stop doing something. See also **43, 79**.

80. The **Present Imperative Active (pim):** *tē eleuthería oun hē Christós hēmás ēleuthérōse*, *stékete*, "Stand fast therefore in the liberty wherewith Christ hath made us free" (Gal. 5:1); *kai eis ek tōn presbutérōn légei moi*, *Mḗ klaíe*, "And one of the elders saith unto me, Weep not" (Rev. 5:5), indicating that the subject had been weeping see verse four. See also **1, 43**.

81. The **Present Imperative Middle (pimm):** In the middle voice, the present imperative is used to give a command for something which concerns particularly the recipient of the command: *adialeíptōs proseúchesthe*, "Pray without ceasing" (1 Thess. 5:17). See also **43, 50, 79**.

PRESENT INDICATIVE The present indicative asserts something which is occurring while the speaker is making the statement. See also **45, 79**.

82. The **Present Indicative Active (pin):** *pan déndron agathón karpoús kaloús poieí*, "every good tree bringeth forth good fruit" (Matt. 7:17). See also **1**.

83. The **Present Indicative Middle (pinm):** *kai en kairō peirasmoú aphístantai*, "and in time of temptation fall away" (Luke 8:13). See also **45, 50, 79**.

84. The **Present Indicative Passive (pinp):** *hétton agapōmai*, "the less I be loved" (2 Cor. 12:15). See also **45, 60, 79**.

PRESENT INFINITIVE The present infinitive pertains to continuous or repeated action, without any implications as to when the action takes place. See also **46**.

85. The **Present Infinitive Active (pinf):** *hōste ton tuphlón kai kōphón kai laleín kai blépein*, "insomuch that the blind and dumb both spake and saw" (Matt. 12:22). See also **1**.

86. The **Present Infinitive Middle (pifm):** *kai ḗrxanto dialogízesthai hoi grammateís kai hoi Pharisaíoi*, "And the scribes and the Pharisees began to reason" (Luke 5:21). See also **46, 50**.

87. The **Present Infinitive Passive (pifp):** *hḗtis, archḗn laboúsa laleísthai diá tou Kuríou*, "which at the first began to be spoken by the Lord" (Heb. 2:3). See also **46, 60**.

PRESENT SUBJUNCTIVE This tense refers to continuous or repeated action, regardless of when the action took place. The subjunctive mood suggests that the action is subject to some condition. The present subjunctive can be used to give exhortation: *chaírōmen kai* *agalliōmetha*, "Let us be glad and rejoice" (Rev. 19:7). See also **79, 94**.

88. The **Present Subjunctive Active (psa):** *hótan de diōkōsin humás*, "But when they persecute you" (Matt. 10:23). See also **1**.

89. The **Present Subjunctive Middle/Passive (psmp):** *hō eán boúlētai ho huiós apokalúpsai*, "to whomsoever the Son will reveal him" (Matt. 11:27). See also **50, 60**.

90. The **Reciprocal Pronoun (rçpro)** is used in reciprocal constructions, constructions where a plural subject is represented as being influenced by an interchange of the action or idea conveyed by the verb: *hóti esmén allḗlōn mélē*, "for we are members one of another" (Eph. 4:25). It is declined only in the genitive plural, and is found in the New Testament only in the masculine gender. See also **72**.

91. The **Reflexive Pronoun (rxpro)** is used when the action indicated by the verb reflects back upon the subject. Thus the subject of the verb and the pronoun refer to the same person or thing: *kai emphanísō autō emautón*, "and will manifest myself to him" (John 14:21). See also **72**.

92. The **Relative Pronoun (repro)** replaces a substantive mentioned in a previous main

clause (known as the antecedent). The relative pronoun agrees with its antecedent in gender and number, but not necessarily in case; the latter depends on the particular function assigned to the relative pronoun: *hos estín eikón tou theoú tou aorátou*, "<u>Who</u> is the image of the invisible God" (Col. 1:15). See also **72**.

93. The **Singular (sg)** number in Greek, as in English, denotes that there is one of something. Though there is no indefinite article in Greek, an English translation of a singular noun often requires that one be added: *échōn zugón en tē cheirí autoú*, "had <u>a pair of balances</u> in his hand" (Rev. 6:5). See also **75**.

94. The **Subjunctive Mood** makes an assertion about which there is some doubt, uncertainty, or indefiniteness: *eán eípōmen hóti hamartían ouk échomen, heautoús planómen*, "If <u>we say</u> that we have no sin, we deceive ourselves" (1 John 1:8). It is closely related to the future tense, which helps to explain the fact that often the uncertainty arises only because the action has not yet occurred: *hína lutrósētai hēmás apó pásēs anomías*, "that <u>he might redeem</u> us from all iniquity" (Titus 2:14). Compare the **Emphatic Future Negative (33)**. See also **95**.

95. The **Verb** in Greek has at least five distinct features: **Tense, Voice, Mood, Person,** and **Number**.

Tense: There are six tenses in Greek—the **Aorist Tense (6)**, the **Future Tense (35)**, the **Imperfect Tense (44)**, the **Perfect Tense (61)**, the **Pluperfect Tense (74)**, and the **Present Tense (79)**.

Voice: There are three voices in Greek—the **Active Voice (1)**, the **Middle Voice (50)**, and the **Passive Voice (60)**. In English, there are only two voices: active and passive.

Mood: There are four moods in Greek—The **Indicative Mood (45)** is used with a statement of fact or a question; the **Subjunctive Mood (94)** is connected with some supposed or desired action; the **Imperative Mood (43)** indicates a command, request, or entreaty; and the **Optative Mood (56)**, rare in the New Testament, usually expresses a wish or introduces an indirect quotation.

Person and **Number** are the same as in English.

LIST OF IRREGULAR ADVERBS
(Encoded as *AD**)

This is a list of certain adverbs, that in special instances function as adjectives. Each verse where this irregular use of an adverb is found is listed below, followed by the adverb that occurs in that passage and the Strong's number for that particular word.

MATTHEW

Matt. 2:9	ἐπάνω	1883
Matt. 3:11	ὀπίσω	3694
Matt. 4:19	ὀπίσω	3694
Matt. 5:10,11	ἕνεκα	1752
Matt. 5:14	ἐπάνω	1883
Matt. 5:16,24	ἔμπροσθεν	1715
Matt. 5:24	παρεκτός	3924
Matt. 6:1,2	ἔμπροσθεν	1715
Matt. 7:6	ἔμπροσθεν	1715
Matt. 10:18	ἕνεκα	1752
Matt. 10:29	ἄνευ	427
Matt. 10:32,33	ἔμπροσθεν	1715
Matt. 10:38	ὀπίσω	3694
Matt. 10:39	ἕνεκα	1752
Matt. 11:10,26	ἔμπροσθεν	1715
Matt. 13:29	ἅμα	260
Matt. 13:34	χωρίς	5565
Matt. 14:21	χωρίς	5565
Matt. 15:23	ὄπισθεν	3693
Matt. 15:38	χωρίς	5565
Matt. 16:23,24	ὀπίσω	3694
Matt. 16:25	ἕνεκα	1752
Matt. 17:2	ἔμπροσθεν	1715
Matt. 18:14	ἔμπροσθεν	1715
Matt. 18:15	μεταξύ	3342
Matt. 19:5,29	ἕνεκα	1752
Matt. 21:2	ἀπέναντι	561
Matt. 21:7	ἐπάνω	1883
Matt. 23:13	ἔμπροσθεν	1715
Matt. 23:18,20,22	ἐπάνω	1883
Matt. 23:35	μεταξύ	3342
Matt. 25:32	ἔμπροσθεν	1715
Matt. 26:70	ἔμπροσθεν	1715
Matt. 27:37	ἐπάνω	1883
Matt. 27:61	ἀπέναντι	561
Matt. 28:1	ὀψέ	3796
Matt. 28:2	ἐπάνω	1883

MARK

Mark 1:2	ἔμπροσθεν	1715
Mark 1:7,17,20	ὀπίσω	3694
Mark 2:1	ἐναντίον	1726
Mark 4:34	χωρίς	5565
Mark 6:11	ὑποκάτω	5270
Mark 7:28	ὑποκάτω	5270
Mark 8:33,34	ὀπίσω	3694
Mark 8:35	ἕνεκα	1752
Mark 9:2	ἔμπροσθεν	1715
Mark 10:7,29	ἕνεκα	1752
Mark 11:2	κατέναντι	2713
Mark 12:41	κατέναντι	2713
Mark 13:3	κατέναντι	2713
Mark 13:9	ἕνεκα	1752
Mark 14:5	ἐπάνω	1883
Mark 14:54	ἔσω	2090
Mark 15:16	ἔσω	2090

LUKE

Luke 1:6	ἐνώπιον	1799
Luke 1:8	ἔναντι	1725
Luke 1:15,17	ἐνώπιον	1799
Luke 1:19,75	ἐνώπιον	1799
Luke 4:7	ἐνώπιον	1799
Luke 4:8	ὀπίσω	3694
Luke 4:13	ἄχρι	891
Luke 4:18	ἕνεκα	1752
Luke 4:29	ἔξω	1854
Luke 4:39	ἐπάνω	1883
Luke 4:42	ἕως	2193
Luke 5:18	ἐνώπιον	1799
Luke 5:19	ἔμπροσθεν	1715
Luke 5:25	ἐνώπιον	1799
Luke 6:22	ἕνεκα	1752
Luke 6:49	χωρίς	5565
Luke 7:27	ἔμπροσθεν	1715
Luke 7:47	χάριν	5484
Luke 8:16	ὑποκάτω	5270
Luke 8:26	ἀντιπέραν	495
Luke 8:47	ἐνώπιον	1799
Luke 9:23	ὀπίσω	3694
Luke 9:24	ἕνεκα	1752
Luke 10:19	ἐπάνω	1883
Luke 10:21	ἔμπροσθεν	1715

Luke 11:44	ἐπάνω	1883
Luke 11:51	ἕως	2193
Luke 11:51	μεταξύ	3342
Luke 12:6	ἐνώπιον	1799
Luke 12:8	ἔμπροσθεν	1715
Luke 12:9	ἐνώπιον	1799
Luke 12:59	ἕως	2193
Luke 13:26	ἐνώπιον	1799
Luke 13:33	ἔξω	1854
Luke 14:2	ἔμπροσθεν	1715
Luke 14:10	ἐνώπιον	1799
Luke 14:27	ὀπίσω	3694
Luke 15:10,18,21	ἐνώπιον	1799
Luke 16:15	ἐνώπιον	1799
Luke 16:16	ἕως	2193
Luke 16:26	μεταξύ	3342
Luke 17:21	ἐντός	1787
Luke 18:29	ἕνεκα	1752
Luke 19:11	ἐγγύς	1451
Luke 19:14	ὀπίσω	3694
Luke 19:17,19	ἐπάνω	1883
Luke 19:27	ἔμπροσθεν	1715
Luke 20:26	ἐναντίον	1726
Luke 21:8	ὀπίσω	3694
Luke 21:12	ἕνεκα	1752
Luke 21:36	ἔμπροσθεν	1715
Luke 22:6,35	ἄτερ	817
Luke 22:51	ἕως	2193
Luke 23:5	ἕως	2193
Luke 23:14	ἐνώπιον	1799
Luke 23:26	ὄπισθεν	3693
Luke 24:11	ἐνώπιον	1799
Luke 24:19	ἐναντίον	1726
Luke 24:43	ἐνώπιον	1799

JOHN

John 1:3	χωρίς	5565
John 1:15,27,30	ἔμπροσθεν	1715
John 1:15,27,30	ὀπίσω	3694
John 1:50	ὑποκάτω	5270
John 3:31	ἐπάνω	1883
John 6:66	ὀπίσω	3694
John 8:9	ἕως	2193
John 10:4	ἔμπροσθεν	1715
John 12:19	ὀπίσω	3694
John 12:37	ἔμπροσθεν	1715
John 15:5	χωρίς	5565
John 18:6	ὀπίσω	3694
John 20:14	ὀπίσω	3694
John 20:30	ἐνώπιον	1799

ACTS

Acts 1:8,22	ἕως	2193
Acts 2:25	ἐνώπιον	1799
Acts 3:16	ἀπέναντι	561
Acts 4:10,19	ἐνώπιον	1799
Acts 5:37	ὀπίσω	3694
Acts 6:5,6	ἐνώπιον	1799
Acts 7:10	ἐναντίον	1726
Acts 7:46	ἐνώπιον	1799
Acts 8:10	ἕως	2193
Acts 8:21	ἐνώπιον	1799
Acts 8:32	ἐναντίον	1726
Acts 9:15	ἐνώπιον	1799
Acts 9:38	ἕως	2193
Acts 10:4,30	ἐνώπιον	1799
Acts 10:31,33	ἐνώπιον	1799
Acts 12:6	μεταξύ	3342
Acts 15:9	μεταξύ	3342
Acts 17:7	ἀπέναντι	561
Acts 18:17	ἔμπροσθεν	1715
Acts 19:9,19	ἐνώπιον	1799
Acts 19:32	ἕνεκα	1752
Acts 20:15	ἀντικρύ	481
Acts 20:30	ὀπίσω	3694
Acts 23:23	ἕως	2193
Acts 26:21	ἕνεκα	1752
Acts 26:22	ἐκτός	1622
Acts 27:35	ἐνώπιον	1799
Acts 28:20	ἕνεκα	1752

ROMANS

Rom. 2:15	μεταξύ	3342
Rom. 3:18	ἀπέναντι	561
Rom. 3:20	ἐνώπιον	1799
Rom. 3:21,28	χωρίς	5565
Rom. 4:6	χωρίς	5565
Rom. 4:17	κατέναντι	2713
Rom. 7:8,9	χωρίς	5565
Rom. 8:36	ἕνεκα	1752
Rom. 10:14	χωρίς	5565
Rom. 12:17	ἐνώπιον	1799
Rom. 14:20	ἕνεκα	1752
Rom. 14:22	ἐνώπιον	1799

1 CORINTHIANS

1 Cor. 1:29	ἐνώπιον	1799
1 Cor. 4:8	χωρίς	5565
1 Cor. 11:1	χωρίς	5565
1 Cor. 16:18	ἐκτός	1622

2 CORINTHIANS

2 Cor. 2:7	κατενώπιον	2714
2 Cor. 3:10	ἕνεκα	1752
2 Cor. 4:2	ἐνώπιον	1799
2 Cor. 5:10	ἔμπροσθεν	1715
2 Cor. 7:12	ἕνεκα	1752
2 Cor. 7:12	ἐνώπιον	1799
2 Cor. 8:21	ἐνώπιον	1799
2 Cor. 10:16	ὑπερέκεινα	5238
2 Cor. 11:28	χωρίς	5565
2 Cor. 12:2,3	ἐκτός	1622
2 Cor. 12:19	κατενώπιον	2714

GALATIANS

Gal. 1:20	ἐνώπιον	1799
Gal. 2:14	ἔμπροσθεν	1715
Gal. 3:19	χάριν	5484

EPHESIANS

Eph. 1:4	κατενώπιον	2714
Eph. 1:21	ὑπεράνω	5231
Eph. 2:12	χωρίς	5565
Eph. 3:1,14	χάριν	5484
Eph. 4:10	ὑπεράνω	5231

PHILIPPIANS

Phil. 2:14	χωρίς	5565
Phil. 2:27	παραπλήσιον	3897
Phil. 3:13	ἔμπροσθεν	1715
Phil. 3:13	ὀπίσω	3694

COLOSSIANS

Col. 1:22	κατενώπιον	2714

1 THESSALONIANS

1 Thess. 1:3	ἔμπροσθεν	1715
1 Thess. 2:9	ἔμπροσθεν	1715
1 Thess. 3:9,13	ἔμπροσθεν	1715

1 TIMOTHY

1 Tim. 2:3	ἐνώπιον	1799
1 Tim. 2:8	χωρίς	5565
1 Tim. 5:4	ἐνώπιον	1799
1 Tim. 5:14	χάριν	5484
1 Tim. 5:15	ὀπίσω	3694
1 Tim. 5:20,21	ἐνώπιον	1799
1 Tim. 5:21	χωρίς	5565
1 Tim. 6:12,13	ἐνώπιον	1799

2 TIMOTHY

2 Tim. 2:14	ἐνώπιον	1799
2 Tim. 4:1	ἐνώπιον	1799

TITUS

Titus 1:5,11	χάριν	5484

PHILEMON

Phile. 1:14	χωρίς	5565

HEBREWS

Heb. 2:8	ὑποκάτω	5270
Heb. 4:13	ἐνώπιον	1799
Heb. 4:15	χωρίς	5565
Heb. 7:12,20,21	χωρίς	5565
Heb. 9:5	ὑπεράνω	5231
Heb. 9:7,18	χωρίς	5565
Heb. 9:22,28	χωρίς	5565
Heb. 10:28	χωρίς	5565
Heb. 11:6,40	χωρίς	5565
Heb. 12:8,14	χωρίς	5565
Heb. 13:21	ἐνώπιον	1799

JAMES

James 2:18,20,26	χωρίς	5565
James 4:10	ἐνώπιον	1799

1 PETER

1 Pet. 3:1	ἄνευ	427
1 Pet. 3:4	ἐνώπιον	1799
1 Pet. 4:9	ἄνευ	427

2 PETER

2 Pet. 2:10	ὀπίσω	3694

1 JOHN

1 John 3:12	χάριν	5484
1 John 3:19	ἔμπροσθεν	1715
1 John 3:22	ἐνώπιον	1799

3 JOHN

| 3 John 1:6 | ἐνώπιον | 1799 |

JUDE

| Jude 1:16 | χάριν | 5484 |
| Jude 1:24 | κατενώπιον | 2714 |

REVELATION

Rev. 1:4	ἐνώπιον	1799
Rev. 1:10	ὀπίσω	3694
Rev. 2:14	ἐνώπιον	1799
Rev. 3:2,5,8,9	ἐνώπιον	1799
Rev. 4:3,4	κυκλόθεν	2943
Rev. 4:5,6	ἐνώπιον	1799
Rev. 4:8	κυκλόθεν	2943
Rev. 4:10	ἐνώπιον	1799
Rev. 5:3	ὑποκάτω	5270
Rev. 5:8	ἐνώπιον	1799

Rev. 5:11	κυκλόθεν	2943
Rev. 5:13	ὑποκάτω	5270
Rev. 6:8	ἐπάνω	1883
Rev. 6:9	ὑποκάτω	5270
Rev. 7:9,11,15	ἐνώπιον	1799
Rev. 8:2,3,4	ἐνώπιον	1799
Rev. 9:13	ἐνώπιον	1799
Rev. 11:4,16	ἐνώπιον	1799
Rev. 12:1	ὑποκάτω	5270
Rev. 12:4,10	ἐνώπιον	1799
Rev. 12:15	ὀπίσω	3694
Rev. 13:3	ὀπίσω	3694
Rev. 13:12,13,14	ἐνώπιον	1799
Rev. 14:3,5,10	ἐνώπιον	1799
Rev. 15:4	ἐνώπιον	1799
Rev. 16:19	ἐνώπιον	1799
Rev. 19:10	ἔμπροσθεν	1715
Rev. 19:20	ἐνώπιον	1799
Rev. 20:3	ἐπάνω	1883
Rev. 20:12	ἐνώπιον	1799
Rev. 22:8	ἔμπροσθεν	1715

LEXICAL AIDS TO THE NEW TESTAMENT

BY

SPIROS ZODHIATES, TH.D.

The following Lexical Aids provide more extended definitions of key words than Strong's *Dictionary of the Greek Testament,* found at the back of this Bible. Hence, the reader has in the same volume with the text of the Bible, information that is normally found only in Greek lexicons, word studies and commentaries. Dr. Spiros Zodhiates, whose native tongue is Greek, has devoted over forty years to the study of Koine Greek, the language in which the New Testament was written.

LEXICAL AIDS TO THE NEW TESTAMENT

14. Agathoergéō; to do good, from *agathós* (18), benevolent, and *ergéō*, from *érgon* (2041), work. To work good, that is, to act for someones advantage. Only in 1 Timothy 6:18. See *agathopoiéō* (15).

15. Agathopoléō; from *agathos;* (18), benevolent, and *poiéō* (4160), to do. To do the good as opposite to *hamartánō* (264), to miss the mark, sin (1 Pet. 2:20; 3 John 1:11). To do good so that someone derives advantage from it; contrast *agathoergéō* (14). Opposite: *kakopoiéō* (2554), to do evil (Mark 3:4; Luke 6:9; 1 Pet. 3:17; 3 John 1:11) The subst.: *agathopoiía* (16), well doing (1 Pet. 4:19), the practice of good.

18. Agathós; good and benevolent, profitable, useful; contrast *kalós* (2570), constitutionally good but not necessarily benefiting others (Matt. 5:45; Rom. 2:7; James 1:7). Related words: *agathōsúnē* (19), goodness; *agathoergéō* (14), to do good to benefit others (1 Tim. 6:18); *agathopoiía* (16), well-doing; *agathopoiós* (17), doer of good (1 Pet. 4:19); *philágathos* (5358), from *philos* (5384) friend, and *agathós*, friend or lover of good men (Titus 1:8); *aphilágathos* (865), from the negative *a* (1) and *philágathos*, not a lover or a friend of good men or of goodness. See *chrēstótēs* (5544) and *agathopoiéō* (15).

19. Agathōsúnē; active goodness. In Galatians 5:22, referred to as goodness; but the Eng. word is inclusive of particular graces whereas Paul must refer to a particular grace. It is more than *chrēstótēs* (5544), a mellowing of character. It is character energized expressing itself in *agathón* (18), active good. Thus *chrēstótēs* in action is *agathōsúnē*. A person may display his *agathōsúnē*, his zeal for goodness and truth in rebuking, correcting, chastising. Christ's righteous indignation in the temple (Matt. 21:13) showed His *agathōsúnē*, but not His *chrēstótēs*, mellowness. *Agathōsúnē* does not spare sharpness and rebuke to cause good, *agathón* in others whereas *chrēstótēs* demonstrates only its softness and benignity.

20. Agallíasis; exultation, exuberant joy (Luke 6:27; Gal. 2:20; Heb. 1:9). See verb *agalliáō* (21). Syn.: *chará*; (5479) joy, delight; *euphrosúnē* (2167), good cheer, joy, mirth, gladness of heart.

21. Agalliáō; used in the pass. and mid. voice from *ágan*, very much, and *állomai*, to leap. To exult, leap for joy, to show one's joy by leaping and skipping denoting excessive or ecstatic joy and delight (John 5:35; Acts 16:34); hence it is sometimes put after *chaírō* (5463), to rejoice, which is of less intense signification (Matt. 5:12; 1 Pet. 4:13; Rev. 19:7). Noun: *agallíasis* (20). Syn.: *euphraínō* (2165), to cheer, gladden.

25. Agapáō; to love, indicates a direction of the will and finding one's joy in something. Contrast with *philéō* (5368), to be contented with, denoting common interests, hence befriending. *Agapáō* is used of God's love toward man and vice versa. The range of *philéō* in that it may or may not include a choice of the will.

26. Agápē; love, a word not found in Class. Gr. but only in revealed religion. Translated charity meaning benevolent love. Its benevolence, however, is not shown by doing what the person loved desires but what the one who loves deems as needed by the one loved; (e.g., For God so loved [*ēgápēsen*] the world that He gave . . . John 3:16). He gave not what man wanted, but what man needed as God perceived his need, namely His Son who brought forgiveness to man. God's love for man is His doing what He thinks best for man and not what man desires. It is God's willful direction toward man. But for man to show love to God, he must first appropriate God's *agápē*, for only God has such an unselfish love. Contrast *philía* (5373), friendship, based on having common interests. Deriv.: *agapáō* (25); *agapētós* (27).

27. Agapētós; beloved, dear. In the NT, it is used with the force of the perfect part. pass., *ēgapēménos*, beloved, dear. NT meanings: (1) as an adj., My son, the beloved (Matt. 3:17; 17:5; Mark 1:11; 9:7; Luke 3:22; 2 Pet. 1:17). One must not, however, connect this use with the designation in Matthew 3:17 (etc.), as the latter is traceable to Luke 9:35 and expresses the relation of the Son to the Father in the history of redemption (Rom. 11:28) and also the addition in whom I am well pleased (Matt. 3:17; 17:5; Mark 1:11; 2 Pet. 1:17). (2) As a subst. in Rom. 11:28 it is used also in address as in 3 John 1:2, 5, 11, or in the pl. in Romans 12:19; 2 Corinthians 7:1; 12:19. The importance of the expression is in agreement with the meaning of the verb *agapáō* (25), to love.

29. Aggareúō; to press into service; to send off an *ággaros* or public courier. This word is of Persian origin, and after being received into the Gr. language, passed also into use among the Jews and Romans. The *ággaroi* couriers had authority to press into their service men, horses, ships or anything which came in their way and which might serve to hasten their journey. Afterwards *aggareúō* came to mean to press into service for a journey in the manner of *ággaros*. In the NT, used as a trans. verb, to compel, to press, to accompany one (Matt. 5:41; 27:32; Mark 15:21). Contrast *anagkázō* (315), to constrain.

31. Aggelía; message, related to *ággelos* (32), messenger, occurs only in 1 John 3:11. Some mss. have *epaggelía* (1860) from *epí* (1909), upon, and *aggelía* (31), a promise.

32. Ággelos; messenger, from *aggéllō*, to bring a message, announce, proclaim. As a simple verb it does not occur in the NT but it does occur in its comp. forms: *apaggéllō* (518), to announce; *anaggéllō* (312), to report, announce. These two comp. verbs are variously employed to designate the proclamation of salvation. *Ággelos* is a name not of nature but of office, or human messenger (Matt. 11:10), a bishop or presiding elder of a particular church (Rev. 1:20); or created spiritual angel, whether good (Matt. 24:36; Mark 13:32) or evil (Matt. 25:41; 1 Cor. 6:3). Angels are always spoken of in the masc. gender. Other deriv.: *aggelía* (31), message; *diaggéllō* (1229), to divulge (Luke 9:60; Rom. 9:17) or to declare; *exaggéllō* (1804), to declare abroad (1 Pet. 2:9); *kataggéllō* (2605), to proclaim, preach, publish (Acts 4:2; Rom. 1:8); *kataggeleús* (2604), a proclaimer, publisher; *prokataggéllō* (4293), to declare or speak beforehand (Acts 3:18) or signify plainly.

35. Agenealógētos; from the neg. *a*, and *genealogéō*, to trace a genealogy. Without a genealogy or pedigree, having no genealogy, that is, from any sacerdotal family as the Levitical priests had from Aaron (Heb. 7:3) which might prove the right of Melchizedek to the priesthood (Heb. 7:14).

37. Hagiázō; to hallow, sanctify. *Hágios* (40) stands in contrast with *koinós* (2839), defiled or common, thus the verb *hagiázō*, to sanctify, when its object is something that is filthy or common, cannot be accomplished without someone separating himself (*aphorízō* [873]) or withdrawing from fellowship with the world. *Hagiázō* means to withdraw from fellowship with the world by first gaining fellowship with God. Related words: *hagiasmós* (38), sanctification; *hágion* (39), sacred thing; *hagiótēs* (41) and *hagiōsúnē* (42), holiness. In this passage some MSS have *haplótēs* (572), sincerity without duplicity related to *haploús* (573). *Hagiótēs* is to be distinguished from *hosiótēs* (3742), sanctity related to *hósios* (3741) as contrast with *hágios*. *Hagiótēs* is to be distinguished from *hagiasmós*, sanctification which is active sanctification as effected by God and passed on to the character of man. *Hagiótēs* is syn. with *hagiōsúnē* as the attribute of holiness.

38. Hagiasmós; sanctification, translated holiness (Rom. 6:19, 22; 1 Thess. 4:7; 1 Tim. 2:15; Heb. 12:14). It is separation unto God (1 Cor. 1:30; 2 Thess. 2:13; 1 Pet. 1:2). The resultant state, the behavior befitting those so separated (1 Thess. 4:3, 4, 7), the sanctification resulting in the abstaining from fornication. There are two other Gr. words which are translated as holiness but they must be distinguished from *hagiasmós*. *Hagiasmós*, sanctification, is not like *hagiótēs* or *hagiōsúnē*, the attribute of holiness, but is the state of being sanctified, not a process, but the result of a process. It is similar to *dikaíōsis* (1347), not only denoting the activity of God's justification in Christ for the sinner, but also the result of that justification upon the sinner in making him just, recognizing the rights of God on his life. Therefore, *hagiasmós* (2 Thess. 2:13) means not only the activity of the Holy Spirit to set man apart unto salvation but also enabling him to be holy even as God is holy. See *hagiótēs* (41); *hagiōsúnē* (42); and *hagiázō* (37).

39. Hágion; neut. of the adj. *hágios* (40), holy. Used of those structures set apart for God. (1) Of the Tabernacle in the wilderness (Heb. 9:1, 2). In verse two, *hágia*, pl. without the art. as *hágia hagíōn*, holies of holies. The term *hágia* is probably intended to fix attention on the character of the sanctuary as being holy. The pl. suggests the idea of the sanctuary with all its parts. The *hágia hagíōn*, holies of holies in Hebrews 9:3 as well as the phrase with the definite art. in the pl., *tōn hagíōn* of Hebrews 9:8, may very well refer to the inner part the holy of holies, the holiest of all. In Hebrews 9:24, *hágia*, pl. without the art., and Hebrews 9:25, *ta hágia*, the holies with the art. In Matthew 24:15, *en*, in, *tópō*, place, dat. without the art., *hagíō*, the dat. holy, in a holy place. (2) *Hagíon* (Heb. 8:2) in the pl. gen. *tōn hagíōn* refers to heaven itself, the immediate presence of God and His throne (v. 1), Hebrews 9:24, 25 refers to heaven as *ta hágia*, the holies, also Hebrews 13:11. Heaven is designated as the true Tabernacle (Heb. 8:2; 9:12; 10:19).

40. Hágios; holy, set apart, sanctified, consecrated. It has a common root, *hag-*, with *hagnós* (53), chaste, pure. Its fundamental ideas are separation, consecration, devotion to God, and sharing in God's purity and abstaining from earths defilement (Luke 9:26; 2 Pet. 1:18). Contrast to *hierós* (2413), *hágios* has moral significance while *hierós* has only ritual significance. Thus *hiereús* (2409), priest, may not be *hágios*, as long as he only performs priestly duties or ordinances and is *hósios* (3741). Deriv.: verb, *hagiázō* (37), to render holy, separate from sin in general and in particular as abstaining from fornication, and the noun, *hagiasmós* (38) the act of sanctification as completed; *hagiótēs* (41), sanctification, the result of sanctification; *hagiōsúnē* (42), holiness, the quality of sanctification. See *to hágion* (39), sacred thing; *hágios* (40), saint, separated not only ceremonially but also morally. Contrast with *hagnós* (53), pure, sometimes only externally or ceremonially pure.

41. Hagiótēs; holiness. Like all deriv. of *hágios* (40), holy, sanctity, the word is unknown in Class. Gr. In the NT it occurs only in Hebrews 12:10. Syn.: *hagiōsúnē* (42), a quality that can be perceived by others, while *hagiótēs* speaks of the essence of the character of God.

42. Hagiōsúnē; sanctity or holiness. Derived not from *hagiázō* (37), but from *hágios* (40), holy. Denotes sanctity, not sanctification. *Hagiōsúnē* with *hagiótēs* (41) are qualities of character for which there need not be any proof; but for *hagiasmós*, the process of sanctification and the result of that process upon the individual, proof has to be at each stage of its progressive achievement. *Hagiōsúnē* occurs in only three places in the NT (1) Romans 1:4, of the holiness of God developing the plan of redemption and manifested in Christ. Here we do not have Holy Spirit (*pneúma hágion*) but *pneúma hagiōsúnēs*, spirit of sanctity or holiness which is not what Christ achieved but what Christ was in Himself, that is, holy. (2) 2 Corinthians 7:1, perfecting holiness in the fear of God. (3) 1 Thessalonians 3:13 speaks of the holiness of man. Also see Ephesians 1:4; 5:27; Colossians 1:22.

47. Hagneía; from *hagnós* (53). Purity. Refers to chastity.

Used only in 1 Timothy 4:12; 5:2. In this verse, it refers to one's moral attitude toward younger sisters in Christ and denotes the chastity which shuts out whatever impurity of spirit or manner might be mixed up with a Christian benevolent task of comforting. When a male comforts young women, he must be especially careful lest he mix his divine task with any impure thoughts.

48. Hagnízo; to consecrate, to purify, from *hagnós* (53), dedicated by sacrifice. Such purification was required for priests in the divine service (Num. 8:21), and indeed for all who belong to the chosen people (Ex. 19:10, 11; Josh. 3:5; 2 Chr. 30:17). Opposite: *miaínō* (3392), to contaminate, defile. In the NT used in the same sense as in the OT on the same basis as the Israelites relation to God (John 11:55; Acts 21:24, 26; 24:18).

49. Hagnismós; act of consecration, purification, from *hagnós* (53), dedicated by sacrifice. To expiate, referring to the purification and consecration of the Levites (Num. 8:7; 31:23). In the NT only in Acts 21:26.

50. Agnoéō; from the neg. *a* and *noéō* (3539), not to recognize, not to know, to be unacquainted with, usually followed by the acc. (Acts 17:23; Rom. 10:3; 11:25; 2 Cor. 2:11). Followed by the prep. *perí* (4012), concerning, meaning to be in ignorance concerning something (1 Cor. 12:1; 1 Thess. 4:13). Followed by *hóti* (3748), that (Rom. 1:13; 2:4; 6:3; 7:1; 11:25; 1 Cor. 10:1; 2 Cor. 1:8). In the pass. form, to be unknown, unrecognized. In antithesis to *epiginóskō* (1921), to know clearly, it means to be mistaken, misunderstood (1 Cor. 14:38; 2 Cor. 6:9; Gal. 1:22). It came to mean to be ignorant, to have no discernment of, not to understand (Mark 9:32; Luke 9:45; Acts 13:27; 1 Cor. 2:8; 14:38). To err, to commit a fault arising from the want of discernment, denoting conduct, the result and import of which is not perceived by the agent (Heb. 5:2, cf. Rom. 7:7, 8, 13) in which case the conduct cannot be regarded as deliberate. In consequence of the interposition of the law it has become *parábasis* (3847), transgression, that is, it involves guilt (Rom. 7:7, 8). Ignorant ones, *agnooúsi*, are those who are under the power of sin but not necessarily actively pursuing it (Heb. 5:2). Deriv.: *agnóēma* (51), mistake, oversight; *ágnoia* (52), want of knowledge, ignorance.

51. Agnóēma; error, only in Hebrews 9:7. Derived from *agnoía* (52), ignorance, and designates a sin of ignorance or thoughtlessness. Such a sin is considered as mitigated sinfulness. Its forgiveness cannot be demanded merely because of ignorance although it can be requested (Luke 23:34; 1 Tim. 1:13). The *agnoémata*, errors of the people for which the high priest offered sacrifice on the great day of atonement, were not willful transgressions, presumptuous sins (Ps. 19:13). Verb: *agnoéō* (50), to be ignorant. Deriv.: *noéō* (3539), to think.

52. Ágnoia; want of knowledge, ignorance, which leads to wrong conduct and forbids the imputation of the guilt to the ignorant individual (Acts 3:17; 1 Pet. 1:14, cf. Luke 23:34; 1 Cor. 2:8). This *ágnoia*, ignorance, according to Paul is the characteristic of heathendom (Acts 17:30; Eph. 4:18, cf. v. 17) and is a state which renders repentance necessary (Acts 17:30) and eventually furnishes ground for blame (Eph. 4:18). Deriv.: *agnoéō* (50), not to know.

53. Hagnós; chaste, pure. An adj. predominantly used to express freedom from defilements or impurities. In a more restricted sense, not only chastity but also virginity. Deriv.: verb, *hagnízō* (48), to purify (James 4:8; 1 Pet. 1:22; 1 John 3:3); *hagnismós* (49), purification (Acts 21:26); *hagnótēs* (54), the quality of purity (2 Cor. 6:6); adv., *hagnós* (55), purely. Joseph (Gen. 39:7–12 in the Sept.) was *hósios* (3741), unpolluted, in that he reverenced the everlasting sanctities of marriage, the defilement of which he considered sinning against God, the Originator of marriage; he was *hágios* (40), holy, in that he separated himself from any unholy fellowship with his temptress; he proved himself *hagnós*, pure, in that he kept his body pure and undefiled.

54. Hagnótēs; purity, sincerity (2 Cor. 6:6). In 2 Corinthians 11:3, the TR has haplótēs (572), singleness, the opposite of duplicity, instead of hagnótēs, the two words coinciding in meaning. Refers to sincerity as part of the character of a person and not necessarily its influence on others.

55. Hagnós; adv. of hagnós (53), chaste. Purely, sincerely. In Philippians 1:16, it refers to the simplicity of the spirit with the absence of other motives that could be selfish. Therefore, hagnós can really mean without duplicity.

56. Agnōsía; ignorance, from the neg. a (1) and gnōsis (1108), knowledge. In Class. Gr., not being acquainted with something. In the NT, it corresponds to the use of ginōskō (1097), to know, to be influenced by ones knowledge of an object. Agnōsía means not merely an intellectual, but a moral defect or fault (1 Cor. 15:34; Eph. 2:12). In 1 Peter 2:15 there is a demonstration of something that is more than an intellectual defect and the gnōsis supposed is that of moral discernment.

57. Ágnōstos; from the neg a (1), and gnōstós (1110), known. Unknown. In the Class. Gr., not knowable, withdrawing itself from being known, unrecognizable. In the NT, it is used with a pass. meaning (Acts 17:23), to the unknown god, to the god who did not make himself known to man, as were those gods in the pantheon of Athenian gods. This unknown god did not refer to the true God revealed to them by the Apostle Paul.

58. Agorá; from the verb ágō (71), to lead. A place in which the people assemble, assembly. A market place, serving also as a court of justice (Matt. 20:3; 23:7; Mark 7:4; Acts 16:19; 17:17).

59. Agorázō; from agóra; (58), market place. To buy. With the acc., to buy a thing (Matt. 13:44, 46; 14:15). With the gen., it indicates value (Mark 6:37). In the pass. (1 Cor. 6:20; 7:23). In these passages: you were bought with a price or for a price, indicates the opposite of acquisition free of charge. Thus the one who buys something has the full right of possession. Used of the redemptive work of Christ (1 Cor. 6:20; 7:23; 2 Pet. 2:1; Rev. 5:9, 14:3, 4). The idea is that Christ paid the price required (Gal. 3:13), and thus removed the sinner's responsibility to pay it.

71. Ágō; to lead, to lead along, to bring, carry, remove. Trans., to bring, to lead gently and without violence (Acts 5:26; 9:27; 21:16; 2 Tim. 4:11). To bring, carry, drag, or hurry away by force and violence (Mark 13:11; Luke 4:29; Acts 6:12; 17:5, 19); to lead, rule, govern (Rom. 8:14; Gal. 5:18; 2 Tim. 3:6); to entice (Rom. 2:4); to spend, hold or celebrate a particular day or time (Matt. 14:6; Luke 24:21). Intrans., to carry or convey oneself. To go, go away (Matt. 26:46; Mark 1:38; 14:42; John 11:15, 16). Deriv.: agōgḗ (72), course of life, manner of leading or spending it; anágō (321) (aná; [303], up, again, or away) to bring, lead, carry, or take up, to bring or offer up as a sacrifice. In the pass. voice anágomai (321), literally to be carried up as a term of navigation, to put out to sea, to set sail (Luke 8:22; Acts 13:13), to bring back (Rom. 10:7). Apágō (520) (apó [575], from), to lead, carry or take away. In the pass., to be led or carried away to execution or death; to lead or tend, as a way. Eiságō (1521) (eis [1519], into, in), to bring in, introduce; exágō (1806) (ex [1537], out), to lead forth or bring out; epágō (1863) (epí [1909], upon), to bring upon; katágnumi (2608) (katá (2596), down, as an intens.), to break in pieces; katágō (2609), to bring down; as a term of navigation (Luke 5:11; Acts 21:3; 27:3; 28:12); pareiságō (3919) (pará [3844], denoting ill, and eiságō, to bring in) to introduce craftily or secretly (2 Pet. 2:1). Derived from pareisaktos (3920), an adj. used as a noun, something brought in secretly, introduced by craftiness, those that have crept in (Gal. 2:4); proágō (4254) (pro [4253], before or forth), of place it means to go before, or lead properly when others follow (Matt. 14:22), less properly when others do not follow, to go before, to proceed in time (1 Tim. 1:18); to bring out or forth (Acts 16:30) particularly to condemnation or punishment; proságō (4317) (pros [4314], to or towards), to bring to, to bring (Luke

9:41; Acts 16:20); to come to or towards, to approach (Acts 27:27). The noun of proságō is prosagōgḗ (4318), approach, access or introduction (Rom. 5:2; Eph. 2:18). Sunágō (4863) (sun [4862], together), to bring together (Matt. 2:4); to take in or receive with hospitality and kindness (Matt. 25:35, 43). Also the corresponding noun sunagōgḗ (4864), a public or large assembly of men, a synagogue, a building where the Jews met for the purpose of public prayer and hearing the Scriptures read and expounded. Episunágō (1996) (epi [1909], to, and sunágō, to gather, collect), to gather together in one place (Mark 1:33), to gather together as a hen does her chicks under her wings (Matt. 23:37), to assemble the elect into the Christian Church (Matt. 24:31); episunagōgḗ (1997), a being gathered together (2 Thess. 2:1); an assembling together at one place (Heb. 10:25); epeisagōgḗ (1898), from epeiságō, to superinduce from epi (1909), upon, and eiságō (1521), to introduce, bring in, a superinduction, bringing in one thing after or upon another, an introduction of something more.

73. Agōn; from the verb ágō (71), implying force or violence. Strife, contention, contest for victory or mastery such as pertained to the Greek games of running, boxing, wrestling. Paul plainly uses the word in this fashion (1 Tim. 6:12; 2 Tim. 4:7) and applies the word to the struggles in the Christian life (cf. 1 Cor. 9:24). A race (Heb. 12:1). A struggle, contest, contention (Phil. 1:29; Col. 2:1; 1 Thess. 2:2).

74. Agōnía; combat, more abstract and eclectic than agōn (73), a contest, giving prominence to the pain and labor of the conflict. It is used to refer to the trembling excitement and anxiety produced by fear or tension before a wrestling match or a fight. It occurs in Luke 22:44 (cf. Matt. 26:37, 38; John 12:27), denoting not the fear which makes one shrink and flee, but the fear which trembles in the face of the issue, yet allows one to remain and face it.

75. Agōnízomai; to contend for victory in the public games (1 Cor. 9:25). Generally it meant to fight or wrestle (John 18:36); the task of faith in persevering amid temptation and opposition (1 Tim. 6:12; 2 Tim. 4:7). It came also to mean to take pains, to wrestle as in a prize contest, making every effort to achieve the goal (Luke 13:24, cf. 1 Cor. 9:25; Phil. 3:12ff.; Heb. 4:1). Special pains and toil (Col. 1:29; 4:12; 1 Tim. 4:10). It implies hindrances in the development of the Christian life.

80. Adelphós; a brother, from the coll. a (1) and délphus, a womb; a brother, and the fem. adelphḗ, a sister. The equivalent Hebr. word was used of more distant relatives (Gen. 14:16; 29:12, 15) and, because of that, some think that this circumstance ought to be taken into consideration where brothers and sisters of the Lord Jesus are referred to (Matt. 12:46, 47; 13:55; Mark 3:31, 32; Luke 8:19, 20; John 2:12; 7:3, 5, 10; Acts 1:14). Further, adelphós denotes in general a commaraderie based on common origin, (e.g., see Acts 3:22; 7:23; Rom. 9:3). A neighbor is regarded as a brother (Matt. 5:22–24, 47). Adelphós also came to designate a community of love based on the commonality of believers due to Christ's work (Matt. 12:50; Mark 10:29, 30; Acts 12:17). In this manner Jesus speaks of His brethren (Matt. 25:40; 28:10; John 20:17; Rom. 8:29; Heb. 2:11, 17). The members of the same Christian community are called brothers (John 21:23; Acts 9:30; Rom. 16:14; 1 Cor. 7:12).

81. Adelphótēs; brotherhood, a brotherly or sisterly relation. Occurs only in 1 Peter 2:17; 5:9. Equivalent to philadelphía (5360), brotherly love and philádelphos (5361), fond of brethren, the adj. in 1 Peter 3:8. While adelphótēs is used in a special sense in the NT and ecclesiastical Gr., it is not used by Class. Gr. writers who used philadelphía to denote only the love of natural brothers and sisters for each other. In Christianity it is adelphótēs, a brotherhood or sisterhood which has been made possible by Jesus Christ, and since all believers are given the new birth, it is truly indeed by spiritual birth that men and women are brothers and sisters.

86. Hádēs; the region of departed spirits of the lost but including departed believers (Luke 16:23). Most probable derivation is from *hádō*, all-receding. It corresponds to *sheól* in the OT. Both words have been inadequately translated in the KJV as hell (Ps. 16:10), or the grave (Gen. 37:35), or the pit (Num. 16:30, 33). *Hádēs* never denotes the physical grave nor is it the permanent region of the lost. Some feel it is the intermediate state between death and the ultimate hell, Gehenna. *Hádēs* is used four times in the Gospels and always by the Lord (Matt. 11:23; 16:18; Luke 10:15; 16:23). Used with reference to the soul of Christ (Acts 2:27, 31). Christ declares that He has the keys of *hádēs* (Rev. 1:18). In Revelation 6:8 it is personified as accompanying the rider of the pale horse. It is to give up those who are in it (Rev. 20:13) and is to be cast into the lake of fire (Rev. 20:14). See *géenna* (1067); *tartaróō* and *tártaros* (5020).

87. Adiákritos; from the neg. *a* (1), without, and *diákrisis* (1253), separation, discrimination. Indistinguishable, free from partial regards, impartial (James 3:17).

91. Adikéō; to do wrong, hurt, damage; from the neg. *a*, without, and *díkē* (1349), right, justice. Intrans., to act unjustly, do wrong (Acts 25:11; 2 Cor. 7:12; Col. 3:25; Rev. 22:11). Trans., to act unjustly, to do wrong to or injure someone (Matt. 20:13, Acts 7:24, 26, 27; 25:10; Phile. 1:18); to hurt, damage, harm (Luke 10:19; Rev. 2:11; 6:6; 7:2, 3). Deriv.: *adíkēma* (92); *adikía* (93); *ádikos* (94).

92. Adíkēma; from *adikéō* (91), to injure, to act unjustly. That which results from an injustice, a crime, a criminal act (Acts 18:14; 24:20; Rev. 18:5).

93. Adikía; from *a* (1), neg., *díkē* (1349), justice. What is not conformable to justice, what ought not to be, that which is wrong. Related to *ádikos* (94), unjust, hence, injustice, unrighteousness. There is *adikía* only because there is *alḗtheia* (225), truth, which occupies the place of *díkē* (1349), justice. In 1 John 5:17, all unrighteousness (*adikía*) is sin (*hamartía* [266]). It is not meeting God's justice or His goal for us. The result of *adikía*, unrighteousness, is *adíkēma* (92), evil doing (Acts 18:14). In the context of Luke 16:8, *adikía* is used to symbolize money that is acquired dishonestly. In Acts 1:18 the reward of iniquity is the pay of *adikía*, the pay of unrighteousness.

94. Ádikos; from *a* (1) neg., and *díkē* (1349), justice. Unjust, unrighteous, falling short of the righteousness required by divine laws (1 Pet. 3:18). A lack of the imputed righteousness of faith (Matt. 5:45; Acts 24:15; 1 Cor. 6:9). Opposite *dikaíos* (1342), fair, just. Not in conformity with *díkē*, justice, also the opposite of *éndikos* (1738), meaning not as it should and ought to be, unjust, unrighteous. In Luke 16:10 it stands as the opposite of *pistós* (4103), faithful or dependable. In this sense *ádikos* is one who disappoints expectations or neglects claims. Used as an adj. in Luke 16:11 referring to mammon. *Ádikos* (2 Pet. 2:9) may stand in contrast with *eusebēs* (2152), devout, godly. It could, therefore, be taken as syn. with *asebēs* (765), impious, ungodly.

96. Adókimos; unapproved, unworthy, from the neg. *a* and *dókimos* (1384), acceptable. Spurious, worthless. In a pass. sense, disapproved, rejected, cast away (1 Cor. 9:27; Heb. 6:8, cf. 2 Cor. 13:5–7; 2 Tim. 3:8; Titus 1:16). In the act. sense, undiscerning, not distinguishing, void of judgment (Rom. 1:28); also in this text it may be understood in the pass. to be a reprobate, abominable mind, or a mind to be abhorred by God and man.

97. Ádolos; sincere. Only in 1 Peter 2:2, from the priv. *a* (1) and *dólos* (1388), guile. Indicates the absence of fraud and deceit as in Nathanael's case, in whom there was no guile (John 1:47). See *haploús* (573), single, without duplicity; *ákakos* (172), constitutionally harmless; and *akéraios* (185), without admixture.

100. Hadrótēs; bounty (2 Cor. 8:20), derived from *hadrós*, thick, fat, full-grown, rich. Bountiful giving or fat offering and not just mere abundance. See *perisseía* (4050), overflowing, and *perísseuma* (4051), abundance in a slightly more concrete form, of substance as in 2 Corinthians 8:13, 14 where it stands for the gifts sup-

plied by the saints.

106. Ázumos; unleavened. In the NT used of the Feast of the Passover (Matt. 26:17; Mark 14:1, 12; Luke 22:1, 7; Acts 12:3; 20:6). Figuratively meaning unpenetrated by evil (1 Cor. 5:7, 8). Deriv.: see *zúmē* (2219).

110. Athanasía; from the priv. *a* (1), without, and *thánatos* (2288), death. Rendered immortality in 1 Corinthians 15:53, 54 of the glorified body of the believer. In 1 Timothy 6:16 used of the nature of God. In the NT it expresses the nature not of life itself, but strictly speaking, only a quality of life such as the quality of the life of God and the resurrection body of the believer. See *thnētós* (2349), mortal, from *thánatos*, death.

111. Athémitos; from the neg. *a* (1) and *themitós*, an adj. from *thémis*, law. Unlawful (Acts 10:28; 1 Pet. 4:3). Also *áthesmos* (113), wicked (2 Pet. 2:7; 3:17), stems from *a* (1) and *thémis* meaning lawless.

112. Átheos; from the neg. *a* (1), without, and *Theós* (2316), God. In Class. Gr., it primarily and actively meant godless, destitute of God, without God and consequently *álogos* (249), devoid of reason, denoting a person who was forgetful of God and did not care about the existence of the gods and consequently did not honor them. In the NT it occurs only in Ephesians 2:12 in the pass., meaning without divine help, forsaken by God, excluded from communion with God. See also 1 Thessalonians. 4:5.

126. Aídios; from *aeí* (104), ever, always. Eternal, absolutely, without beginning or end (Rom. 1:20). Perpetual, without end (Jude 1:6).

127. Aidós; modesty, an innate moral repugnance to a dishonorable act, which repugnance scarcely or not at all exists in *aischúnē* (152), shame. The grief which a man conceives from his own imperfections considered with relation to the world taking notice of them; grief upon the sense of disesteem. *Aidós* finds its motive in itself, implies reverence for the good as good, not merely as that to which honor and reputation are attached. Only in 1 Timothy 2:9; Hebrews 12:28.

129. Haíma; the blood of the human or animal body (Mark 5:25, 29; Luke 8:43, 44; 13:1). Meanings: (1) Blood as the substantial basis of the individual life (John 1:13; Acts 17:26). The concept corresponds to the idea contained in Leviticus 17:11, For the life of the flesh is in the blood. There is a joining of the word blood with flesh in Hebrews 2:14. Flesh and blood designate mankind, insofar as men owe their distinctive character to the material aspect of their being (Eph. 6:12). The expression means the physical origin of man in Matthew 16:17; 1 Corinthians 15:50; and Galatians 1:16. The physical and the spiritual natures of man are contrasted in Ephesians 6:12 (cf. Hebrews 2:14). (2) *Haíma* by itself may denote life passing away in bloodshed, and generally life taken away by force (Matt. 23:30, 35; 27:4; Luke 11:50, 51; Acts 1:19). The expression "to shed blood," *háima ekchéō* (1632), emphasizes not so much the manner of slaying, but rather the fact of the forcible taking away of life, whether produced by or only accompanied with the shedding of blood (Matt. 26:28; Mark 14:24; Luke 22:20; Acts 22:20). (3) (Related to [2]) *Haíma* is used to denote life given up or offered as an atonement, since, in the ritual of sacrifice, special emphasis is laid upon it as the material basis of the individual life. The blood of the animal was separated form the flesh when it was sacrificed, resulting in appeasement for the sins of the offerers (Heb. 9:13, 18, 19, 21, 22, 25; 10:4; 13:11). The blood was then taken and presented to God and applied to man through sprinkling (Heb. 9:7, 19, 20). This blood becomes the representation of the covenant which God commanded to us (Heb. 9:20). The same is true of the blood of Christ (Heb. 10:29); the blood of the covenant (Matt. 26:28; Mark 14:24; Luke 22:20; Heb. 13:20), the New Testament in Christ's blood (1 Cor. 11:25). Designates the life of Christ offered for an atonement contrasted with the blood of beasts slain in sacrifice (Heb. 9:12, cf. vv. 14, 25). The blood of Christ, therefore, represents the life that He gave for our atonement (Matt. 26:28; Heb. 9:12, 25; 1 John 1:7).

130. Haímatekchusia; shedding of blood, from *haíma*, blood, and *ekchúō* or *ekchéō* (1632) to pour out. Strictly speaking, the bringing of the blood to the altar, the application of the blood for objective expiation (Ex. 29:16; Lev. 8:15; 9:9; Deut. 12:27; 2 Kgs. 16:15), whose correlative meaning is *rhantismós* (4473), sprinkling, the application of the atonement to its object. *Haímatekchusia* does not include the shedding of blood or the slaying of a victim, or the sprinkling of that blood on the object to be expiated. The question dealt with in Hebrews 9:22 is not the manner, but the means of atonement, *haíma*, blood (see Heb. 9:18, 19, 22a, 23, 25) denoting only a part of the act of atonement, and as such would exclude the sprinkling of the people (v. 19); it could not include this, and at the same time, the sprinkling of the holy vessels (v. 21). Thus the shedding of blood denotes not only the act of killing, but the ritualistic act which requires bringing the blood unto or toward the altar (Lev. 8:15; 9:9) or on the altar (2 Kgs. 16:15). The verb *proschéō* and the noun *próschusis* (4378) are commonly used and should not be translated as sprinkling but as shedding forth, toward. Therefore, *haímatekchusia* means blood shedding and not the actual pouring out of the blood, the expression employed concerning the blood of Christ (Luke 22:20) which for our sakes was poured out.

133. Aínesis; from *ainéō* (134), the act of praise (Heb. 13:15).

134. Ainéō; from *aínos* (136). To sing alternately praises to God (Ex. 15:21; 1 Sam. 21:11). In the NT it only refers to praising God (Luke 2:13, 20).

136. Aínos; praise returned for benefits received or expected (Matt. 21:16; Luke 18:43). See *aínesis* (133) and *ainéō* (134).

138. Hairéomai; from *hairō* (142), to take up, to choose, (cf. *eklégomai* [1586], to choose out, elect). *Epilégomai* (1951), to be called or named; *hairetízō* (140), to choose, akin to *hairetós*, a verbal adj. signifying that which may be taken.

139. Haíresis; heresy, from *hairéō* or *hairéomai* (138) to choose, select. A form of religious worship, discipline or opinion (Acts 5:17; 24:14; Gal. 5:20). In contrast to *schisma* (4978), schism, it is only theoretical. One can hold different views than the majority and remain in the same body but he is a heretic. But when he tears himself away, *schízō* (4977) then he is schismatic. Heresy is theoretically schismatic; schismaticalness is practical heresy.

140. Hairetízō; choose, only in Matthew 12:18, related to the verbal adj. *hairetós*, that which may be taken. To take with the implication that what is taken is eligible or suitable; to choose by reason of its suitability. Contrast *eklégomai* (1586), meaning to choose because of love and desirability of attaching the object to oneself. See also *epilégomai* (1951); *hairéomai* (138).

141. Hairetikós; heretic, pertaining to choice, capable of choice. In Titus 3:10, heretic. See Romans 16:17 where clearly one still belongs to the fellowship, but whom the fellowship eventually had to exclude.

142. Aírō; to lift, raise, take up; to lift up the hands (Rev. 10:5); the eyes (John 11:41); to lift or take up (Matt. 17:27; Mark 6:29, 43; Acts 20:9); as applied to the mind, keep in suspense (John 10:24); take up as a yoke (Matt. 11:29); a cross (Matt. 16:24); bear or carry as a burden (Matt. 4:6; 27:32; Mark 15:21; John 5:8, 9); remove (Matt. 22:13; John 11:39, 41), take away (John 1:29; 1 John 3:5); receive, take (Matt. 20:14; Mark 6:8); to loose a ship, namely from shore (Acts 27:13); lift up or raise the voice (Acts 4:24). Deriv.: *epairō* (1869) (with prefix *epí* [1909], upon), to lift up, as the eyes (Matt. 17:8); the head (Luke 21:28); the hands (Luke 24:50; 1 Tim. 2:8), the heel (John 13:18). In the pass. voice *epaíromai*, to be lifted up from the ground as our Lord at His ascension; to hoist or sail (Acts 27:40); in the middle or pass., to lift up or exalt oneself, to be lifted up or exalted in pride (2 Cor. 11:20), lift up, exalt, raise the voice.

143. Aisthánomai; to perceive, primarily with the senses.

Figuratively of spiritual perception, to become conscious of, observe, understand, used more of immediate knowledge than that arrived at by reasoning (Luke 9:45).

144. Aísthēsis; perception, sensational as well as mental. Pass., to become cognizant of, to make oneself observed by anyone. Involves knowledge based upon experience, experimental knowledge. In Philippians 1:9 it is contrasted with *epígnōsis* (1922), the insight obtained by knowledge. *Aísthēsis*, however, is experimental knowledge which is or becomes naturally manifold, and therefore has the addition of *pása* (3956), all (Phil. 1:9).

145. Aisthētērion; organ of sense, seldom applied to the spiritual life, but when it is, it is used in a figurative manner (Heb. 5:14).

152. Aischúnē; shame, that feeling which leads to shunning what is unworthy, out of an anticipation of dishonor (Luke 14:9; 2 Cor. 4:2; Phil. 3:19; Heb. 12:2; Jude 1:13; Rev. 3:18).

154. Altéō; ask, request, beg; from which is derived *epaitéō* (1871), to beg for alms. The seeking by the inferior from the superior (Acts 12:20); by a beggar from the giver (Acts 3:2); by the child from the parent (Matt. 7:9); by man from God (Matt. 7:7; James 1:5; 1 John 3:22). Contrast *erōtáō* (2065), ask, when it is not used as a mere interrogatory which implies that he who asks stands on a footing of equality with the giver (Luke 14:32). The Lord never uses *aitéō*, to beg, but *erōtáō*, to ask as an equal of the Father on behalf of Himself or His disciples. Martha reveals her false concept of Christ when she tells Him He should *aitein* of the Father (John 11:22).

155. Aítēma; occurs twice in the NT (Phil. 4:6; 1 John 5:15) in the sense of a petition of men to God, both times in the pl. They are particular requests of which prayer, *proseuché* (4335), may consist; for example, in the Lord's Prayer there are seven *aitḗmata*, petitions, although some have regarded the first three as *euché* (2171), wishes. *Aítēma* is used in Luke 23:24 in the sense of petition by the Jews for releasing Barabbas. Related words: *déēsis* (1162), supplication or prayer for particular benefits; *énteuxis* (1783), intercession; *eucharistía* (2169), thanksgiving; *hiketēría* (2428), entreaty, supplication.

156. Aitía; accusation, true or false (Matt. 27:37; Mark 15:26; John 18:38). Derived from *aitéō* (154), to ask, require, because an accusation or crime is that for which one is required to appear before a judge to be questioned. A cause, reason, incitement (Matt. 19:3; Luke 8:47; Acts 10:21). Deriv.: *aitíōma*, charge, sometimes *aitíama* (157).

165. Aiṓn; age, refers to an age or time, in contrast to *kósmos* (2889), referring to people or space. Derived from *aei* (104), always, and *ōn*, being. Denotes duration or continuance of time, but with great variety. (1) Both in the sing. and pl. it signifies eternity whether past or to come (Matt. 6:13; Mark 3:29; Luke 1:55; John 4:14; 6:51; Acts 15:18; Eph. 3:11); for ages, of ages (Rev. 1:6, 18; 5:14; 10:6; 14:11; 15:7; 20:10). (2) The duration of this world (Matt. 28:20; John 9:32; Acts 3:21); since the beginning of the world (Matt. 13:39). (3) Pl., *hoi aiṓnes*, the ages of the world (1 Cor. 2:7; Eph. 3:9; Col. 1:26). (4) *Ho aiṓn hoútos*, this age, generation (Luke 16:8; 20:34, cf. Matt. 13:22; 1 Cor. 1:20; 2:6; Gal. 1:4; Eph. 2:2; 1 Tim. 6:17; 2 Tim. 4:10; Titus 2:12). (5) *Ho aiṓn ho erchómenos*, the age, the coming one, meaning the next life (Mark 10:30, Luke 18:30, cf. 20:35). (6) An age or dispensation of providence (Matt. 24:3, cf. 12:32; 1 Cor. 10:11; Heb. 1:2; 6:5; 9:26). (7) *Aiṓnes*, ages, in Hebrews 11:3 refers to the great occurrences which took place in the universe. *Aiṓn* also has an ethical meaning. It can refer to the present world with its cares, temptations, and desires. It includes, both moral and physical, implied (Matt. 13:22; Luke 16:8; 20:34; Rom. 2:2; I Cor. 1:20; 2:6; 8:2; 2 Cor. 4:10; Tit. 2:12). Hence it is called *aiṓn ponērós*, evil world (Gal. 1:4), and Satan is called "the god of this world" (2 Cor. 4:4).

166. Aiṓnios; eternal, belonging to the *aiṓn* (165), time in its duration, that is, constant, abiding, eternal. Used when referring to eternal life, the life which is God's and hence not affected by the limitations of time. *Aiōnios* is specially predicated of the saving blessings of divine revelation, denoting not belonging to what is transitory. Meanings: (1) Having neither beginning nor end (Rom. 16:26; Heb. 9:14). (2) Without end (Matt. 25:41, 46; 2 Thess. 1:9). In Philemon 1:15, meaning forever, not only during the term of ones natural life, but through endless ages of eternal life and blessedness. (3) In Jude 1:7, eternal fire refers to the miraculous fire from heaven which destroyed the cities of Sodom and Gomorrha. This is evidenced not only because the effect thereof shall be of equal duration with the world, but also because the burning of those cities is a dreadful emblem of that everlasting fire (Matt. 25:41) which awaits the ungodly and unclean (cf. 2 Pet. 2:6). (4) *Chrónoi*, times, *aiōnioi*, eternal, means the ages of the world, the times since the beginning of the world's existence (Rom. 16:25; 2 Tim. 1:9; Titus 1:2, cf. Eph. 1:4; 1 Pet. 1:20).

167. Akatharsía; from the neg. *a* (1), and *kathairō* (2508), to cleanse. Uncleanness, filth, in a natural or physical sense (Matt. 23:27); moral uncleanness, lewdness, incontinence in general (Rom. 6:19; Eph. 4:19; 1 Thess. 2:3; 4:7); any kind of uncleanness different from whoredom (2 Cor. 12:21); any unnatural pollution, whether acted out by oneself (Gal. 5:19; Col. 3:5), or with another (Rom. 1:24, cf. vv. 26, 27). Deriv.: *katharízō* (2511), to cleanse.

168. Akáthartēs; an abbreviation of *akatharótēs*, from the neg. *a*, and *katharótēs*, cleanness; uncleanness, filthiness (Rev. 17:4). Deriv.: *katharízō* (2511) to cleanse.

169. Akáthartos; from the neg. *a* (1), and *kathairō* (2508), to cleanse. Meanings: (1) Unclean, by legal or ceremonial uncleanness (Acts 10:14, 28; 11:8, cf. Lev. 5:2; 11:25; 13:45) whereas in the Sept. compares it with 2 Corinthians 6:17 where *akáthartos* seems to refer to all idolatrous worship and heathen impurity. (2) Unclean, unfit to be admitted to the peculiar rights and privileges of the church and particularly to baptism (1 Cor. 7:14). (3) Unclean by unnatural pollution (Eph. 5:5). (4) Unclean as applied to the devils (who are frequently called unclean spirits in the NT) because, having lost their original purity, they are become unclean themselves. Furthermore, through their solicitations, they have filled mankind with all uncleanness and every abomination which the Lord hates (Mark 5:2, 8, 13). Deriv.: *katharízō* (2511), to cleanse.

172. Ákakos; harmless (Rom. 16:18; Heb. 7:26) from the neg. *a*, without, and *kakós* (2556), constitutionally bad. Contrast *haploús* (573), single or without duplicity; *ádolos* (97), without guile; *akéraios* (185), without any foreign matter or without admixture.

176. Akatágnōstos; from the neg. *a* (1), without, and *katágnōstos*, blamed, from *kataginōskō* (2607), condemn. Irreprehensible, not to be condemned or blamed (Titus 2:8).

181. Akatastasía; from the neg. *a* (1), not, and *katástasis*, a setting in its place, from *kathístēmi* (2525), to place, set in its place. Commotion, tumult (Luke 21:9; 1 Cor. 14:33; 2 Cor. 6:5; 12:20; James 3:16). Related to *akatástatos* (182), unsettled. See *hístēmi* (2476), to hold, to stand, to place.

182. Akatástatos; from the neg. *a* (1), not, and *kathístēmi* (2525), to settle. Unsettled, unsteady, unstable (James 1:8). See *akatastasía* (181); *hístēmi* (2476).

185. Akéraios; from the neg. *a* (1), and *keráō*, to mix (Matt. 10:16; Rom. 16:19; Phil. 2:15). Without any mixture of deceit, without any foreign material in him. Distinguished from *ákakos* (172), without being constitutionally bad; *ádolos* (97), without any guile; and *haploús* (573), without wrinkles or duplicity, single or simple.

189. Akoé; hearing, from *akoúō* (191). The act of hearing (Rom. 10:17, cf. Matt. 13:14; Acts 28:26; 3:2, 5); the sense of hearing (1 Cor. 12:17; Heb. 5:11); the organ or instrument of hearing, the ear (Mark 7:35; Acts 17:20; 2 Tim. 4:4); something which is or may be heard, a rumor, report (Matt. 4:24; 14:1; John 12:38; Rom. 10:16).

190. Akolouthéō; from the coll. *a*, together, and *kéleu-*

thos, a way; from *kellō*, to move quickly and *euthús*, straight. Related to *akólouthos*, attendant. To be an attendant, to accompany, to go with or follow (Matt. 4:20, 22, 25; 27:55; John 12:26). Contrast *proágō* (4254), to go before (Mark 11:9). With reference to time, *akoloutheō* means to follow thereupon (Rev. 14:8, 9). It may refer to spiritual or moral relations. Syn.: *hupakoúō* (5219), to obey, to serve the time or to act according to circumstances. Distinguished from the occasional and temporary following of Jesus by the crowds (Matt. 4:25; 8:1) and the following to which Jesus calls individuals (Matt. 9:9; 19:21) or people generally (Matt. 10:38; 16:24; John 8:12; 12:26), or which was undertaken by individuals (Matt. 8:19; Luke 9:57, 61). The individual calling to follow Jesus involved abiding fellowship with Him, not only for the sake of learning as a scholar from his teacher (Matt. 8:19), but also for the sake of the salvation known or looked for, which presented itself in this fellowship (Matt. 19:21; Luke 9:61). The first thing involved in following Jesus is a cleaving to Him in believing trust and obedience, those cleaving to Him, also following His leading, acting according to His example (John 8:12; 10:4, 5, 27). Hence the constant stress laid by the Lord Jesus upon the need of self-denial and fellowship with Himself in the cross (Matt. 8:19, 20; 10:38; Mark 8:34; John 8:12; 12:26). Thus following Jesus denotes a fellowship of faith as well as a fellowship of life, sharing in His sufferings not only inwardly, but outwardly if necessary (Matt. 9:9; 19:21). Such outward fellowship with Jesus, however, could not continue without inner moral and spiritual fellowship. The expression following Jesus occurs only in Revelation 14:4. In John 8:12; 10:4, 5, 27; 12:26, to follow Jesus appears as an independent concept apart from any outward act or momentary circumstances of time and place which union with Jesus might involve.

191. Akoúō; to hear. It governs a gen. either of the person or thing, to hear someone or something, or more usually an acc. of the thing. To hear in general (Matt. 2:3, 18; 11:5; 12:19; Mark 14:64); to hear, hearken, or listen to (Mark 12:37; Luke 5:1; 10:39; 11:31; Acts 15:12); to understand, hear with the ear of the mind (Matt. 11:15; John 8:43, 47; 1 Cor. 14:2); to hear effectually or so as to perform or grant what is spoken (Matt. 18:16; John 9:31; 11:41; 1 John 5:14, 15); to obey (Luke 10:16; 16:29, 31, cf. John 8:47; 1 John 4:6).

203. Akrobustía; from *ákros*, the extreme, and *buō*, to fill up, plug, stop up, cover. Uncircumcision (Rom. 4:10; 1 Cor. 7:18). In the NT, and especially the Pauline writings, the word is never applied to moral and spiritual things. Colossians 2:13 and 3:11 seem to hint of the aforementioned figurative application. A state of being uncircumcised means to designate somebody as outside of the promises pertaining to Israel (Rom. 2:26, 27; 3:30; Eph. 2:11).

210. Ákon; unwillingly, against ones will, forced. Occurs only in 1 Corinthians 9:17. Opposite of *hekōn* (1635), willing. Syn.: *akoúsiōs*, unwillingly, often used in the Sept., but not in the NT.

213. Alazōn; boaster in words (Rom. 1:30; 2 Tim. 3:2). Noun: *alazoneía* (212), vaunting in those things one does not possess. Contrast: *pérperos* and the verb *perpereúomai* (4068), boasting about things one has with contempt for others; *huperéphanos* (5244), proud, one who shows himself above his fellows, *tuphóō* (5187), from *turphós*, smoke, or *tuphóomai*, to be drunk with pride with a heart lifted up not only against man but against God; *hubristés* (5197), insolent wrongdoer to others for the pleasure which the affliction imparts.

218. Aleíphō; to rub, to cover over, from *liparós* (3045), greasy. Contrast *chríō* (5548), anoint, pertaining to the sacred and religious. *Aleíphō* is used indiscriminately in all actual anointings, whether with oil or ointment (*aleiphé* in Mod. Gr.). See Matthew 6:17 and James 5:14.

225. Alétheia; truth, as the unveiled reality lying at the basis of and agreeing with an appearance; the manifested, or the veritable essence of matter. The reality pertaining to an appearance. The adj: *aléthés* also means the same thing (Rom. 1:18, 25). Therefore, *alétheia* denotes the reality clearly lying before our eyes as opposite to a mere appearance, without reality (Mark 5:33; John 5:33; 16:7; Acts 26:25; Rom. 9:1; 2 Cor. 12:6; Eph. 4:25; 2 Tim. 3:7). Used with three distinctive meanings: (1) Truth as opposite to falsehood, error or insincerity (Matt. 22:16; Mark 5:33; 12:14, 32; Gal. 2:5, 14; Eph. 4:25; Phil. 1:18; Col. 1:5; 1 John 3:18). (2) Truth as opposite to types, emblems or shadows (John 1:14, 17, cf. Col. 2:17; John 4:23, 24, cf. John 14:6). (3) Integrity, rectitude of nature (John 8:44).

226. Alêtheúō; to be *aléthés* (227), real, actual, not counterfeit, and to act as such. Answering to the truth, to make it ones study. Thus in Ephesians 4:15 the expression speaking the truth in love is *alétheúontes* which means to make it ones business to express the reality of love and not to feign it. In Galatians 4:16, it refers not only to speaking the truth, but to presenting an action as the truth and not counterfeit.

227. Alêthês; a true one who cannot lie (John 8:13; 3 John 1:12). Distinguished from *aléthinós* (228), real, genuine. The one true God as distinguished from idols and all other false gods.

228. Alêthinós; real, genuine, as distinguished from *aléthés* (227), true, one who cannot lie (John 17:3; 1 Thess. 1:9).

236. Allássō; or *alláttō*, to change (Acts 6:14; Gal. 4:20); transform (1 Cor. 15:51, 52; Heb. 1:12); exchange (Rom. 1:23). Deriv.: *antállagma* (465); *apallássō* (525); *diallássō* (1259); *katallagé* (2643); *katallássō* (2644); *metallássō* (3337).

238. Allêgoréō; to speak differently from what one thinks or actually means, to speak allegorically where the thing spoken of is an emblem or representative (Gal. 4:24). See *túpos* (5179), type.

240. Allélōn; genitive of the reciprocal pron. *allélous*, one another. This pron. is used only in the acc., gen. and dat. cases: *allélous*, one another; *allélōn*, of one another; *allélois*, for, in, to one another (Matt. 23:10; Eph. 4:2; Titus 3:3).

241. Allogenês; from *állos* (243), other, and *génos* (1085), a nation, race. One of another nation, a stranger, foreigner (Luke 17:18).

243. Állos; another numerically, but of the same kind. Contrast *héteros* (2087), another qualitatively. In the pl. *álloi*, others, in an inclusive sense (Matt. 4:21; Mark 7:4) or an exclusive one (Matt. 2:12; 10:23). With the def. art., *ho*, *hē*, *to* (3588), the, (masc., fem., neut.) prefixed, the other of two, the two being of the same kind (Matt. 5:39; 12:13; John 19:32). *Hoi álloi*, the others, the rest (John 20:25; 21:8; 1 Cor. 14:29). *Állos* and *állos* repeated, one and another (Mark 6:15; John 4:37). Belonging to another (1 Cor. 10:29). Deriv.: *allótrios* (245), anothers; *apallotrióō* (526), to alienate; *allogenês* (241), one of another nation; *allóphulos* (246), one of another race or nation; *állōs* (247), adv. meaning otherwise.

244. Allotriepískopos; from *allótrios* (245), anothers, and *episkopéō* (1983), to inspect, observe. See *állos* (243) for the basic meaning as an adj. A curious inspector and meddler in other peoples affairs, a busybody in other peoples matters (1 Pet. 4:15).

245. Allótrios; from *állos* (243), other, the opposite of *idios* (2398) and *oikeíos* (3609), the same, a relative. Meanings: (1) Belonging to another, not ones own; when used in the pl. *ta allótria*, it means others goods (Luke 16:12; Rom. 14:4; Heb. 9:25). (2) Spoken of a country, strange, foreign, belonging to other people; opposite *oikeíos*, relative (Acts 7:6; Heb. 11:9). (3) Spoken of men or nations, a stranger, foreigner, alien (Heb. 11:34). Distinguished from *allóphulos* (246), which means one of another race, combining *állos* (243), other, different, and *phúnē* (5443), a tribe or race. Distinguish *allogenês* (241) from *állos*, which means other, and *génos*, a nation, race, one of another nation, not a Jew, a stranger, or a foreigner

246. Allóphulos; from *állos* (243), other, and *phulé* (5443), a tribe or race. One of another race or nation (Acts 10:28).

247. Állōs; adv. of *állos* (243), other. Otherwise (1 Tim. 5:25).

262. Amarántinos; made of *amárantos*, a fabled flower that did not fade away. Hence it symbolizes perpetuity and immortality and is translated as "fadeth not away" in 1 Peter 5:4. See also *amárantos* (263); *áphthartos* (862); *amíantos* (283).

263. Amárantos; unfading, only in 1 Peter 1:4. Our heavenly inheritance is exempt from that swift withering *maraínomai*, from *maraínō* (3133) which is the portion of all the loveliness springing out of an earthly root. The flower is said to fade away, and yet for the time of its life is something of great beauty. It is beautiful, yet short-lived, falls away, fades, and dies quickly (Job 14:2; Ps. 37:2; 103:15; Is. 40:6, 7; Matt. 6:30; James 1:11; 1 Pet. 1:24). Our heavenly inheritance is not something beautiful which lasts only for a while and then fades away. It is of unfailing loveliness, reserved for the faithful in heaven. The heavenly inheritance of the believer does not decay; corruption cannot touch it or ever wear out its freshness, brightness, and beauty. See also *amíantos* (283), undefiled.

264. Hamartánō; to sin, to miss; one who keeps missing the mark in his relationship to God (Matt. 27:4; 1 Tim. 5:20). Opposite: *sophós* (4680), wise, one who knows how to regulate his relationship with God. See *hamartía* (266); *hamártēma* (265).

265. Hamártēma; deed of disobedience to a divine law, nouns ending in *-ma* indicate the result of a certain action, in this case *hamartía* (266), sin. *Hamártēma* is sin as an individual act (Mark 3:28; 4:12; Rom. 3:25; 1 Cor. 6:18). See *hamartánō* (264), to sin.

266. Hamartía; sin, missing the true goal and scope of life. Offense in relation to God with emphasis on the resulting guilt. See *hamártēma* (265), sin as an individual act. Individual sins do not annul the general character of the regenerate. There is a sin, *hamartía* (266), unto death (1 John 5:16) which refers to the willful and intentional sin (Heb. 10:26, 29), death being physical death (Acts 5:1–11; 1 Cor. 11:30). Perfection in this life for the regenerate is unattainable in view of our present unredeemed body (Rom. 8:23) and the environment in which we live (1 John 2:2). See *hamartánō*, to sin (264).

268. Hamartōlós; from *hamartéō*, to deviate, sin. A sinner (Matt. 9:13; 1 Tim. 1:15; Heb. 7:26). Frequently denotes a heinous and habitual sinner (Matt. 11:19; Mark 2:15; Luke 7:37). Used also as an adj. (Mark 8:38; Luke 5:8; Rom. 7:13). Opposite *díkaios* (1342), just, one who has received Christ as Savior and has acknowledged God's possession of his life. And because of the enablement of the indwelling Christ, he has performed his duty to God in this regard. Syn.: *asebês* (765), ungodly; *ápistos* (571), an unbeliever (Rev. 21:8). *Hamartōlós* is often used in connection with *telōnēs* (5057), publicans or tax collectors (Matt. 9:10, 11; 11:19; Mark 2:15, 16; Luke 7:34; 15:1) or those who were in bad repute among Jews and Greeks.

273. Ámemptos; unblamed, from the neg. *a* and *memptós*, blameable, and the verb *mémphomai* (3201), to find fault. Distinguished from *ámōmos* (299) unblemished, unspoiled. Christ was never said to be *ámemptos*. This is because He took upon Himself man's sin and consequently became blamed. Believers, however, should strive to be unblamed, that is, that fault, will not be found in them. The *ámōmos*, the unblemished, may be *ámemptos*, unblamed (Luke 1:6; Phil. 2:15), although not always proving themselves so (1 Pet. 2:12, 15). Related words: *áspilos* (784), without spot; *anégklētos* (410), legally irreproachable; *anepíleptos* (423), irreprehensible, one who cannot be caught and accused.

279. Ametanóētos; from the priv. *a* (1) and *metanoéō* (3340), to repent or change ones mind. Unrepenting, impenitent (Rom. 2:5). See *noéō* (3539); *nous* (3563). Contrast *ametamélētos* (278), not to be concerned after an act has been committed.

283. Amíantos; from the neg. *a* (1) and *miaínō* (3392), to defile. That which has nothing in it which defiles, unpolluted (Heb. 7:26; 13:4; James 1:27; 1 Pet. 1:4). See also *míasma* (3393), pollution; *amarántinos* (262), not capable of fading; *amárantos* (263), unfading; *ápthartos* (862), incorruptible.

286. Amnós; lamb. After John 1:29, 36, "Behold the Lamb of God" (*amnós* and not *arníon*, [721]) it became normal to designate Christ as *amnós* of God." The term *arnos* or *arníon* was adopted throughout Revelation where it is used exclusively. *Amnós* does not appear there *arníon*. In fact, *amnós* is found only in John 1:29, 36; Acts 8:32; 1 Peter 1:19. In the Sept. in Exodus 12:5 *arnós* is used for the Paschal Lamb. However, in Exodus 29:38ff., Leviticus 14:10ff.; Numbers 6:12, the expression *ho amnós, tou Théou*, of God, means the lamb provided by God (see Gen. 22:8). The Lord Jesus is called the *amnós* of God because He offered Himself as a sacrifice at the time of the Passover (see John 2:13; 1 Cor. 5:7). His deliverance of sinners would be similar to the deliverance of Israel out of Egypt. Thus John the Baptist recognized Jesus Christ as the One who was to bring in the awaited day of deliverance. The application of the lamb's blood during the Exodus was the means of sparing the people, and on account of it, destruction passed them by. In like manner Jesus is now the means of sparing those who are willing to apply His blood in order to escape the judgment of God. *Amnós* is used more to designate the sacrifice of the Lamb (1 Pet. 1:19), referring to the Paschal Lamb or a lamb given up to death in the service of God.

293. Amphíblēstron; a casting net which, when skillfully cast from over the shoulder by one standing on the shore or in a boat, spreads out into a circle (*amphibál-letai*) as it falls upon the water. Then it sinks swiftly because of the weights attached to it and encloses whatever is below it (Matt. 4:18; Mark 1:16). See *diktuon* (1350); *sagēnē* (4522).

299. Ámōmos; from the neg. *a* (1) and *mōmos* (3470), spot, blemish; (inaccurately rendered in the KJV as without blame [Eph. 1:4] or unblameable, [Col. 1:22]). In Class. Gr. used as a technical word to designate the absence of anything amiss in a sacrifice or anything which would render it unworthy to be offered (Ex. 29:1; Num. 6:14; Ezek. 43:22). Occurs in Ephesians 1:4; 5:27; Colossians 1:22; Hebrews 9:14; 1 Peter 1:19; Jude 1:24; Revelation 14:5. Used in conjunction with *áspilos* (784), without spot, unspotted. In this case, *ámōmos* would indicate the absence of internal blemish, and *áspilos* (784) that of external spot. Used in Colossians 1:22 with *anégklētos* (410), legally unaccused, and Ephesians 1:4; 5:27 with *hágios* (40), holy. Therefore, *ámōmos* is the unblemished. (Cf. *ámemptos* [273], unblamed.) Christ was *ámōmos* in that He was no spot or blemish in Him, and He could say, Which of you convinceth me of sin? (John 8:46). But strictly He was not *ámemptos*, unblamed. This adjective is never attributed to Him in the NT seeing that He endured the contradiction of sinners against Himself who slandered Him and laid to His charge things that He did not do, *anégklē-tos*. See also *anepíleptos* (423), irreprehensible.

302. Án; a part. used with the opt., subst., and indic. moods, sometimes properly rendered by perhaps, not commonly expressed in English by any corresponding particle, but only giving to a prep. or sentence an element of uncertainty and mere possibility, and indicating a dependence on circumstances. In this way it serves to modify or strengthen the force of the opt. and subst. and it may also affect the meaning of the indic. (the pres. and perf. excepted) and other verbal forms. Uses: (1) A conditional conj., if (John 20:23; 1 Thess. 2:7). (2) Indefiniteness, translated "soever" (Matt. 10:33; Mark 3:28; Rev. 14:4). (3) Potentiality. It is added to verbs of the indic. and sometimes of the opt. moods, giving the meaning of may, might, would, could, or should (Matt. 11:21, 23; 23:30; 25:27; John 11:21; 18:30; Acts 2:12). (4) *Héōs an*, until (Matt. 2:13; 5:18; 16:28). (5) *Hópōs an*, that, to the end that (Matt. 6:5; Rom. 3:4, cf. Acts 3:19). (6) *Hōs án*, even as (1 Thess. 2:7).

303. Aná; a prep. meaning on, upon, in. Found only in

the acc., it forms a periphrase for an adv. (e.g., *aná méros*, by turns, alternatively [1 Cor. 14:27]); followed by the gen, *aná méson*, in the midst of, through the midst of, between; spoken of place (Matt. 13:25; Mark 7:31; Rev. 7:17); spoken of persons (1 Cor. 6:5). With numerical words it marks distribution (Mark 6:40; Luke 9:3, 14; 10:1; John 2:6; Rev. 4:8). In composition with other words forming a comp., *aná* denotes: up, upward, as *anabaínō* (305), I go up, back, again (equal to the English return, implying repetition, increase, intensity), as *anakainízō* (340), to renew.

305. Anabaínō; from *aná*, up, and *baínō*, to go. The simple *baínō* verb does not occur in the NT. To go or come up, to ascend in whatever manner (Matt. 3:16; 5:1); to spring or grow up, as vegetables (Matt. 13:7); to arise, of thoughts (Acts 7:23; 1 Cor. 2:9).

312. Anaggéllō; to announce, from *aná*, back, and *ag-géllō*, to announce (in its basic form in the UBS Gr. text in John 20:18). Possibly the *ana* carries the significance of upward, that is, heavenly, as characteristic of the nature of the tidings. To tell in return, bring word back (John 5:15; Acts 14:27; 16:38; 2 Cor. 7:7); to tell or declare freely, openly or eminently (Mark 5:14, 19; John 4:25; 16:13–15; Acts 20:20, 27). See *apaggéllō* (518) (*apó* [575], from, and *aggéllō*, announce, declare), to tell from someone; *exaggéllō* (1804) (*ex*, out, and *aggéllō*), to tell out, abroad.

313. Anagennáō; to beget again, to regenerate (1 Pet. 1:3). In the pass. *anagennáomai*, to be begotten again, to be regenerated (1 Pet. 1:23). The subst. *anagénnēsis*, new birth, never occurs in the NT. However, *paliggenesía* (3824), restoration, becoming something new, is the closest to *anagénnēsis*, new birth. *Paliggenesía* comes from *pálin* (3825), once more, again, and *ginomai*, to become, whereas *anagennáō* comes from *aná*, again, and *gennáō*, to beget.

314. Anaginóskō; from the emphatic *aná* (303) and *ginōskō* (1097), to know, take knowledge of. To perceive accurately. Later it came to mean to recognize. In Attic Gr. it usually meant to read and so always in the NT and the Sept. The consequential meaning is to know by reading (Matt. 12:3; John 19:20; Col. 4:16).

315. Anagkázō; from *anágkē*, necessity. To force, compel by external violence (Acts 26:11). To force, compel in a moral sense as by authoritative command (Matt. 14:22; Mark 6:45); by importunate persuasion (Luke 14:23); by prevalent example (Gal. 2:14); by injustice (Acts 28:19). See also *aggareuō*, to press into service (29). Noun: *anágkē* (318), need. Adj.: *anagkaíos* (316), needful.

316. Anagkaíos; an adj. from the noun *anágkē* (318), necessity. Necessary by a physical need (1 Cor. 12:22, cf. Titus 3:14); necessary by a moral or spiritual need (Acts 13:46; 2 Cor. 9:5; Phil. 2:25; Heb. 8:3); near, intimate, closely connected (Acts 10:24). Verb: *anagkázō* (315).

318. Anágkē; from *aná*, an emphatic, and *ágchō*, to constrict, bind hard, compress. Necessity, compelling force, as opposite to willingness (2 Cor. 9:7; Phile. 1:14); moral necessity (Matt. 18:7), which means that as a result of the depravity and wickedness of men, there is a moral necessity that offenses should come (also Luke 14:18; 23:17, etc.); spiritual or religious necessity (Rom. 13:5; 1 Cor. 9:16; Jude 1:3); distress, affliction (Luke 21:23; 1 Cor. 7:26; 2 Cor. 6:4; 12:10; 1 Thess. 3:7). Deriv.: *anagkázō* (315), to force; the adj. *anagkaíos* (316), necessary; syn. *chreiá* (5532), a need.

319. Anagnōrízō; from *ana,*, again, and *gnōrízō* (1107), to know. To know again. Pass.: *anagnōrízomai*, to be made known again (Acts 7:13).

320. Anágnōsis; reading (Acts 13:15; 2 Cor. 3:14) and especially the public reading of Holy Scriptures. In 1 Timothy 4:13 it refers to the public reading of the OT Scriptures or of the portion of Scripture appointed to be read in public which is called *anágnōsma*. The readers in the church whose duty was reading and expounding or appying the Scripture were called *an-ágnōstai*, the public readers.

324. Anadéchomai; from the emphatic *aná* (303), and *déchomai* (1209), to receive. To undertake, to take up, to take upon oneself. Used in Hebrews 11:17, He who had taken up, undertaken, not merely received. The verb implies the seizing or laying hold upon that which is presented. In Acts 28:7, to receive hospitably.

331. Anáthema; from the same root verb *anatíthemai* or *anatíthēmi* (394), to separate as *anáthema*, a consecrated gift. A gift given by vow or in fulfillment of a promise, and devoted to destruction for God's sake (Sept.: Num. 21:1–3; Deut. 13:16–18); therefore, given up to a curse and destruction, accursed (Gal. 1:8, 9; 1 Cor. 12:3; 16:22). In Romans 9:3, estrangement from Christ and His salvation. The word does not denote punishment intended as discipline, but a being given over, or devotion to divine condemnation (Ex. 32:32; Gal. 3:13). It denotes an indissoluble vow.

332. Anathematízō; from *anáthema* (331), a curse. To bind by a curse (Acts 23:12, 14, 21) or simply to curse (Mark 14:71).

334. Anáthēma; a consecrated gift hung up or laid up in a temple (Luke 21:5), from *anatíthemai* (394) or *anatíthēmi*, to separate, lay up. Such a gift was dedicated to God. Contrast *anáthema* (331).

335. Anaídeia; recklessness, audacity, shamelessness. Recklessness or disregard for someone making a request (Luke 11:8). The adj. *anaidēs*, one who knows no restraint, no deference, who is reckless, imprudent in his relationship with others.

340. Anakainízō; to renew, from *aná* (303), again, and *kainízō*, to renew, from *kainós* (2537), qualitatively new. Occurs only in Hebrews 6:6 meaning to have a new kind or qualitatively different repentance which would see the person who had it through to the very end. Syn. to *anakainóō* (341), a different form used only in the pass. by the Apostle Paul.

341. Anakainóō; used only in the pass., to be renewed completely by God (2 Cor. 4:16; Col. 3:10). Refers to the redemptive activity of God corresponding to the creation of man, which, by putting an end to mans existing corrupt state, establishes a new beginning, qualitatively different than the past in agreement with the meaning of the word *kainós* (2537), qualitatively new as contrasted to *néos* (3501), numerically another or a new one. Used in the act. voice in Hebrews 6:6 in the form of *anakainízō* (340) which means that man himself must have a new and qualitatively different kind of repentance if the first repentance did not see him through to its desired purpose of eternal redemption. Deriv.: *anakaínōsis* (342) qualitative renewal; *kainótēs* (2538), newness; *egkainízō* (1457), to dedicate. Contrast *ananeóō* (365), to reform, to renew with the same kind of experience as in the past; *neótēs* (3503), youth with reference simply to age and not quality of life.

342. Anakaínōsis; from *aná*, again, and *kaínōsis*, related to *kainós* (2537), qualitatively new. Therefore, a renewing or·a renovation which makes a person different than in the past. Occurs in Romans 12:2; Titus 3:5. Deriv.: see *anakainóō* (341), to renew qualitatively.

346. Anakephalaíomai; to be reduced to a *kephálaion*, a head or sum total. In the mid. voice, to gather together again in one, to reunite under one head (Eph. 1:10). In the pass., to be summed up, to be comprised (Rom. 13:9).

356. Analogía; from *aná* (303), denoting distribution, and *lógos* (3056), account, proportion. Analogy, the right relation, the coincidence or agreement existing or demanded according to the standard of the several relations, not agreement as equality. In Aristotle it meant arithmetical or geometric proportion. It is unfortunate that the word is translated as proportion of . . . faith in Romans 12:6. The faith spoken of here is not that of the individual, but that which is made available by God Himself. One should not allow his presumed faith to guide him in what he says, but that faith is assured in God's revelation to man. What Paul means here is that prophecy is to stand in a right relation to the faith, the established doctrine, and is to correspond thereto. Prophesying is to build itself

up upon the foundation of a rightly acting faith, which in turn is to build up and promote (cf. 1 Cor. 14:1ff.). The imminent danger is that a pretended prophecy should affect the faith of the individual and the church. What one preaches ought not to stand in opposition or in disproportion to the doctrine, but in analogy to it. The faith should be preserved and cherished by the exercise of this gift, prophecy.

361. Anamártētos; from the neg. *a* (1) and *hamartánō* (264), to sin. Without sin, sinless, but not absolutely, only in a particular case. Occurs only in John 8:7, referring to one who was not guilty of the particular sin of which they were accusing the woman whom they had brought to Jesus; not to be confused with *téleios* (5046), perfect, reaching ones goal.

364. Anámnēsis; remembrance. A commemoration (Heb. 10:3). A memorial (Luke 22:19; 1 Cor. 11:24, 25), as applied to the Lord's Supper. In remembrance of Me means that the participant may remember Christ and the expiatory sacrifice of His death. The memory of the greatness of the sacrifice should cause the believer to abstain from sin. Deriv. *anamimnéskō* (363), to call to mind.

365. Ananeóō; to renew, to make young. Used in Ephesians 4:23, *ananeóomai*, and is to be taken in the pass. made up of *aná* (303), again, and *néos* (3501), new. To be renewed insofar as spiritual vitality is concerned. Contrast *anakainízō* (340); *anakainóō* (341), with *kainós* (2537), qualitatively new.

372. Anápausis; pause or cessation from labor, from *aná* (303), again, and *paúō* (3973), to cease. To give rest (Matt. 11:29; 12:43; Luke 11:24; Rev. 14:11). Verb: *anapaúō* (373), act., and *anapaúomai*, mid. On the other hand, *ánesis* (425) implies the relaxing or letting down of chords or strings which have been strained or drawn tight. In Matthew 11:28, 29 the Lord promises *anápausin* (cessation from their toils) to the weary and heavy laden who come to Him.

378. Anaplēróō; from *aná* (303), up, or as an emphatic, and *plēróō* (4137), to fill. To fill, as a seat or place (1 Cor. 14:16); to fill up or supply a deficiency (1 Cor. 16:17; Phil. 2:30); to fulfill a prophecy (Matt. 13:14), a law (Gal. 6:2); in 1 Thessalonians 2:16, to make the measure of sin quite full, distinguishing it from *plēróō* meaning just to make it full. The word is stronger than *plēróō* and means very full, to perfection, to the very end. Thus *plēróō* emphasizes the act while *anaplēróō* emphasizes the measure.

386. Anástasis; from *anístēmi*, to rise (450); a standing on the feet again or rising as opposed to falling; used figuratively in Luke 2:34. A rising or resurrection of the body from the grave (John 5:29; Acts 1:22; 2:31; 24:15). See *hístēmi* (2476), to stand.

387. Anastatóō; from *anástatos*, disturbed; in turn from *anístēmi* (450), to stand up. To disturb, disquiet, unsettle (Acts 17:6; Gal. 5:12); to excite, stir up to sedition (Acts 21:38). See *hístēmi* (2476), to stand.

388. Anastauróō; from *aná* (303), again or up, and *stauróō*, to crucify. To crucify again or afresh (Heb. 6:6).

392. Anatássomai; to compose in an orderly manner, from *aná* (303), an intens., and *tássō* (5021) to place in ones proper category (Luke 1:1).

404. Anapsuchō; from *aná* (303), again, and *psúchos* (5592), cold. To make cool, to refresh. Cooling again, refrigerating or refreshing with cool air as the body when overheated. Not used in the NT in this sense, but used figuratively meaning to refresh, to relieve when under distress (2 Tim. 1:15). Deriv.: subst., *anápsuxis* (403), recreation, refreshment.

410. Anégklētos; from the neg. *a* (1), without, and *egkaléō* (1458), to accuse in court. Not merely unaccusable but unaccused, free from any legal charge at all. Occurs in 1 Corinthians 1:8; Colossians 1:22; 1 Timothy 3:10; Titus 1:6, 7. Related words: *ámemptos* (273), unblamable; *ámōmos* (299), unblemished; *anepílēptos* (423), irreproachable; *áspilos* (784), unspotted.

415. Aneleḗmōn; from the neg. *a* (1), without, and *eleḗmōn* (1655), merciful. Unmerciful, not compassionate (Rom. 1:31).

417. Ánemos; violent wind; from *áēmi*, to blow, or *aneímai*, perf. pass. of *aniēmi* (447), to loose, let loose.

Wind (Matt. 7:25; 11:7; John 6:18; Acts 27:14, 15, cf. Eph. 4:14). The four winds are used for the four cardinal points, or the East, West, North and South (Matt. 24:31; Mark 13:27). See *pnoé* (4157), breath.

420. Anexíkakos; from *anéchomai* (430), to bear, and *kakós* (2556), bad. Occurs only in 2 Timothy 2:24, translated patient. One who bears evil, sorrow, ill.

423. Anepíleptos; from the neg. *a* (1), without, and *epilambánomai* (1949) to seize; one who has nothing which an adversary could seize on which to base a charge. Rendered in 1 Timothy 3:2; 5:7 as blameless and in 6:14 as irreprovable. Irreprehensible is a closer translation giving the true meaning of the word.

425. Anesis; rest, relaxation (2 Cor. 8:13) from strain (*éntasis*), tribulation or affliction (*thlípsis* [2347]). Paul promises to the troubled, tense Thessalonians that they would find *ánesin* in the Day of Christ (2 Thess. 1:7) as he anticipates for them not so much cessation from labor (*anápausis* [372]), as relaxation of the chords of affliction, now so tightly drawn, strained, and stretched to the uttermost (Acts 24:23; 2 Cor. 2:13; 7:5).

430. Anéchomai; from *aná*, up, and *échomai*, the mid. voice of *échō* (2192), to have, to hold. Used only in the mid. voice. To hold up against a thing; to bear with (1 Cor. 4:12; 2 Cor. 11:19, 20; Heb. 13:22); to bear with, endure (Matt. 17:17; 2 Cor. 11:1, 4; Eph. 4:2; Col. 3:13; 2 Thess. 1:4; 2 Tim. 4:3). Related words: *anochē* (463), forbearance, a delay of punishment; *anektós*, tolerable, used in the NT in the comparative form *anektóteros* (414). Contrast *epieíkeia* (1932), clemency; *makrothumía* (3115), longsuffering; *hupomonē* (5281), patience.

435. Anér; man, male, as contrasted with the generic *ánthrōpos* (444) which may refer to either sex. A man as distinguished from a woman or child (Matt. 14:21; 15:38; 1 Cor. 13:11). A man as related to a woman, a husband (Matt. 1:16; Mark 10:2; John 1:13; 4:16–18).

441. Anthrōpáreskos; from *ánthrōpos*, man, and *aréskō* (700), to try to please men and not God. Denotes one who endeavors to please all (Eph. 6:6; Col. 3:22).

443. Anthrōpoktónos; manslayer or one who commits homicide (John 8:44; 1 John 3:15). Contrast with the more general word *phoneús* (5406), murderer, and *sikários* (4607), used in Acts 21:38 and involving an assassin hired to kill someone.

444. Anthrōpos; man, a generic name in distinction from gods and the animals. In the NT used to make the distinction between sinful man; whose conduct or way or nature is opposed to God, and *anér* (435), male or husband. Derived from *ánō* (507), upwards, and *trépō óra*, turning ones view upward. NT meanings: A name of the species without respect to sex (Matt. 5:13, 16; 6:1); a man as distinguished from a woman (Matt. 19:3, 5, 10); every man, every one, any one (1 Cor. 4:1; 11:28; Gal. 3:12).

448. Anileō; or *anileōs* unmerciful. The Class. Gr. form would be *anēleēs*, without mercy. Occurs only in James 2:13 where it means that in the day of the judgment of the believers works, he will not be shown mercy if he did not perform works of mercifulness on earth. A leniency of the judge is expressed in proportion to ones mercifulness on earth.

450. Anístēmi; from *aná* (303), again, and *hístēmi* (2476), to stand. Meanings: (1) In the second aor. act. intrans., to stand again, to rise from a sitting or reclining posture (Matt. 9:9; Mark 1:35; 2:14; 14:60). In Acts 12:7, an-*ásta*, rise up, the second aor. imper., second person act. for *anástēthi* (Eph. 5:14). (2) In the second aor. act. and first fut. mid. used intrans., to rise or arise from the dead. It is applied to Christ in Matthew 17:9; 20:19, referring to the fact that He was going to rise in His own strength and will. It also applies to men in general (Mark 12:23, 25, Luke 16:31; John 11:23, 24; 1 Thess. 4:16). Yet to show the equality of the Father, He also is presented as raising Jesus from the dead (Acts 2:24, 32). In this case, however, the verb is used trans. in the fut. and aor. act. meaning to raise, cause to rise from the dead. Jesus is also said to be the One who will raise the dead (John

6:39, 40). Thus we have both the Lord Jesus raising Himself and being raised by the Father. (3) To rise from the spiritual death of sin (Eph. 5:14, cf. John 5:25; Eph. 2:5, 6; Col. 3:1). (4) In the second aor. act. intrans., to rise, arise, appear, begin to act (Acts 5:36, 37; 7:18); *anístamai* in the pass. meaning the same (Rom. 15:12; Heb. 7:11, 15). In the first fut. act. used trans., to raise up, cause to appear (Matt. 22:24; Acts 2:30; 3:22). (5) In the second aor. act. used intrans., it emphasizes hostility or opposition; to rise up, to begin hostilities or opposition (Mark 3:26; Acts 6:9). The noun *anástasis* (386), rising up or resurrection.

453. Anóētos; lacking intelligence but demonstrating moral fault; one who does not govern his lusts, one without *nous* (3563), mind, the highest knowing power in man, the organ by which divine things are comprehended and known, being the ultimate seat of the error (Luke 24:25; Rom. 1:14; Gal. 3:1, 3; 1 Tim. 6:9; Titus 3:3).

454. Anoía; from *ánous*, mad, foolish, from the priv. *a* (1), without, and *nous* (3563), mind, understanding. Madness, folly, want of understanding (Luke 6:11; 2 Tim. 3:9). See *noéō* (3539), to understand.

458. Anomía; transgression of the law, iniquity (Matt. 7:23; Rom. 4:7; 1 John 3:7). Adj.: *ánomos* (459), lawless, not having, knowing, or acknowledging the law. Adv.: *anómōs* (460), without having the law.

459. Ánomos; from the neg. *a* (1) and *nómos* (3551), law. Without law, lawless. Not having, knowing or acknowledging the law (1 Cor. 9:21); lawless in the sense of transgressing the law, a transgressor, wicked (Mark 15:28; Acts 2:23; 2 Pet. 2:8). Syn.: *ádikos* (94), unjust; *anósios* (462), wicked, unholy, is the strongest term denoting presumptuous and wicked self-assertion. In the NT, *ánomos* and the subst. *anomía* (458) are predicated of the sinner in order to describe his sin as opposition to or contempt for the will of God.

461. Anorthóō; from *aná* (303), again or up, and *orthóō*, to erect. To make straight or upright again (Luke 13:13, cf. Heb. 12:12); to erect again (Acts 15:16).

463. Anoché; forbearance, from *anéchomai* (430), to bear with, suffer, from *aná* (303), up, and *échō* (2192), to hold, bear. Indulgence, temporary toleration as in Romans 3:25. The temporary character of God's attitude toward sin is demonstrated in Romans 3:25 where the word *páresis* (3929), bypassing, is used which does not mean remission of sins. *Páresis* was temporary. God winked at the sins of the people because of their animal sacrifices. That was the *páresis* of v. 25, the overlooking, which in this verse is also called *anoché*, forbearance. The sacrifice of Christ provides *áphesis* (859), remission, the forgiveness of sins which is once and for all, taking them away, and is more than *páresis*, bypassing, or skirting their sins. Before Christ's sacrifice for the punishment of sin, God provided *páresis* through His *anoché*, temporary suspension of His wrath. Redemption through Christ's blood, however, provided permanent satisfaction of His justice.

464. Antagōnízomai; from *anti* (473), against, and *agōnízomai* (75), to fight against a person. To be in conflict with someone (Heb. 12:4).

465. Antállagma; that which is given in exchange, from *antallássō*, to exchange barter (Matt. 16:26; Mark 8:37). In the NT equivalent to *lútron* (3083), ransom.

470. Antapokrínomai; from *anti* (473), against, and *apokrínomai* (611), to answer; to answer against (Luke 14:6). To reply to something, make a declaratory and argumentative reply, dispute (see Rom. 9:20).

472. Antéchomai; from *anti* (473), against or to, and *échō* (2192), have; in the mid. voice *antéchomai*, to hold firmly, to cleave to (Matt. 6:24; Luke 16:13); of holding to the faithful word (Titus 1:9); to support (1 Thess. 5:14).

473. Antí; prep. meaning both equivalence and exchange, in our stead. Christ died *anti*, in our stead. He was sufficient for the need and was accepted in exchange for our dying. Syn.: prep. *hupér* (5228), for, also embraces both meanings. He died on behalf of us and for our good. *Antí*, in our stead, is used to provide absolute and definitive proof of the death of Christ being vicarious. Christ died *antí*, on behalf of many (Matt. 20:28) and gave Himself as an *antílutron* (487), ransom on behalf (1 Tim. 2:6).

476. Antídikos; from *antí* (473), against, and *díkē* (1349), a cause or fault at law. An adversary or opponent in a lawsuit (Matt. 5:25; Luke 12:58; 18:3) and also applied to the devil, the great adversary of man and the accuser of our brethren (1 Pet. 5:8, cf. Job. 1:9; 2:5; Zech. 3:1).

482. Antilambánō; used in the pass. form *antilambánomai*, from *antí* (473), mutually or against, and *lambánō* (2983), to take, to hold. To mutually take hold of one another with the hand. Figuratively to support, keep from falling, help, assist (Luke 1:54; Acts 20:35); to take part in turn in order to help (1 Tim. 6:2). *Antilambánomai* often means in Class. Gr. writings to partake of, receive, enjoy, and would explain 1 Timothy 6:2 as but rather let them do service, because they who receive the benefit of their service are believers, and beloved (cf. Eph. 6:8; Phile. 1:16).

484. Antílēpsis; literally the receiving of remuneration. It came to mean a laying hold of anything, the hold which one has, perception, apprehension. In NT Gr. used like the verb *antilambánomai* (482), to receive in return for something, to denote a rendering of assistance, help. It is in this way that we must understand the meaning of the word helps as one of the gifts of the Spirit (1 Cor. 12:28), implying the duties toward the poor and sick even as the deacons were appointed to attend to. If we take it as manual services or helps associated with the office of the deacon, then the *kubernēsis* (2941), translated government, must be attributed to the elders (1 Cor. 12:28).

487. Antílutron; from *antí* (473), in return, or correspondency, and *lútron* (3083), a ransom (1 Tim. 2:6). The phrase ransom for many used in Matthew 20:28; Mark 10:45 is *lútron* in order to lay stress upon the fact of Christ's coming and suffering in the place of all and for their advantage (*hupér*, [5228]). Compare Galatians 1:4; Titus 2:14.

499. Antítupon; neut. of *antítupos*; from *antí* (473), denoting correspondency, and *túpos* (5179), a form or figure. Antitype, a form or figure corresponding to or representing a reality (Heb. 9:24), as an impression in wax corresponds to the likeness on the seal or mold, or vice versa. The ancient Christians called the bread and wine of the communion the *antítupa* (pl.) of Christ's body and blood. An antitype, somewhat answering to and represented by a type (1 Pet. 3:21). See also *hupotúpōsis* (5296).

500. Antíchristos; antichrist, from *antí* (473), instead of or against. It may mean substitution or opposition. The term *antíchristos* is peculiar to Johns Epistles (1 John 2:18, 22; 4:3; 2 John 1:7). It occurs nowhere else in the NT. Pauls references to the same person include the man of sin, son of perdition, wicked one (*ánomos* [459]) as in 2 Thessalonians 2:3, 8. He is the one opposing (*antikeímenos* [480]) as in 2 Thessalonians 2:4. He will attempt to assert the fulfillment of God's Word in himself and will seek to establish his own throne. See *pseudóchristos* (5580), false Christ.

505. Anupókritos; from the neg. *a* (1), and *hupokrínomai* (5271), to pretend, simulate. Originally it meant inexperienced in the art of acting. In the NT it came to mean unfeigned, genuine (Rom. 12:9; 2 Cor. 6:6; 1 Tim. 1:5; 2 Tim. 1:5; 1 Pet. 1:22; James 3:17).

506. Anupótaktos; from the neg. *a* (1) and *hupotássō* (5293), to subject. Not subject (Heb. 2:8); disobedient to authority, disorderly (1 Tim. 1:9; Titus 1:6, 10).

507. Anō; above, in a higher place (Acts 2:19). Opposite *kátō* (2736), below. With the neut. pl. art., *ta*, the things above (John 8:23; Col. 3:1, 2); with the sing. neut. art. *to*, that which is above (Gal. 4:26; Phil. 3:14). With *héōs* (2193), as far as, up to the brim (John 2:7); upwards (John 11:41; Heb. 12:15). Deriv.: *anōteros* (511), the comparative degree meaning higher; neut., used of motion to a higher place (Luke 14:10); of location in a higher place meaning in the preceding part of a passage (Heb. 10:8); *epánō*

(1883), from *epí*, over, and *ánō*, above, used verbally of number (Mark 14:5; 1 Cor. 15:6) *ánōthen* (509), the suffix -*then* denotes source used of a place meaning from the top (Matt. 27:51; John 19:23); of things which come from heaven or from God in heaven (John 3:15, 17; 19:11).

509. Ánōthen; an adv. of place or time, from *ánō*, above, and the suffix -*then* denoting from. From above (John 3:31; James 1:17), from the beginning (Luke 1:3; Acts 26:5); again, anew, as before (John 3:3, 7; Gal. 4:9) In these two passages it is plain that it means again, and not the literal meaning of from above. Nicodemus understood the Lord to mean again because in John 3:4 he mentions being born for the second time. With a prep. as in Matthew 27:51; Mark 15:38, it is used in the sense of a noun meaning the top or upper part. See *ánō* (507), up.

518. Apaggéllō; from *apó* (575), from, and *aggéllō*, to tell, declare, tell from someone else (Matt. 12:18; Heb. 2:12; 1 John 1:2, 3). To bring or carry word back (Matt. 2:8; 11:4; Luke 7:22), to tell (Luke 8:34, 47; 13:1).

521. Apaídeutos; from the neg *a*, without, and *paideúō* (3811), to instruct, chastise, correct. Unlearned. Used only in 2 Timothy 2:23.

523. Apaitéō; from *apó* (575), again, and *aitéō* (154), to ask. To recall, demand back, legal exaction of a demand or legitimate claim (Sept.: Deut. 15:2, 3). To require, ask again (Luke 6:30); demand again (Luke 12:20 in the third person plural, *apaitoúsin*, they require thy soul of thee). The they require must be understood as the three Persons of the Triune God (Sept.: Deut. 32:39; 1 Sam. 2:6; 2 Kgs. 5:7; Luke 6:38; 12:48).

525. Apallássō; to transfer from one state to another, a stronger form of *allássō* (236). Strictly to change by separating, therefore, to break up an existing connection and set one part into a different state, a different relation; to set free, make loose. In the mid. voice, *apallássomai*, to escape (Acts 19:12) In the act., to set free (Heb. 2:15). In the pass., to be freed, get loose (Luke 12:58). *Apallássō* is also a technical term to denote the satisfaction of the plaintiff by the defendant, especially of the creditor by the debtor.

526. Apallotrióō; from *apó* (575), from, *allotrióō*, to alienate, and from *allótrios* (245), alien, strange, foreign. To estrange, alienate entirely (Eph. 2:12; 4:18; Col. 1:21).

531. Aparábatos; from the neg. *a* (1) and *parabaínō* (3845), to go beyond, transgress. That which does not pass from one to another as the Jewish high priesthood did from father to son and successor (Heb. 7:24). This word speaks of an unchangeable, eternal priesthood.

533. Aparnéomai; from the prep. *apó* (575), from, denoting a putting away on the part of the speaker, a recoiling, and *arnéomai* (720), to deny. To remove from oneself, refuse, deny, disown. In the NT usage the reflexive reference to the subj. is very plain. Occurs only with a personal obj. which means to decline or withdraw from fellowship with anyone. The NT use of this comp. verb is related to the simple verb *arnéomai* (720), to deny something or someone. To deny Christ or to remove oneself from Him (Matt. 26:34, 35; Mark 14:30, 31, 72; Luke 22:61; John 13:38). To deny oneself (Matt. 16:24; Mark 8:34; Luke 9:23), to refuse oneself, to give up oneself. See also John 12:25; Galatians 5:24. The fut. *aparnēthēsomai*, to deny oneself, occurs once in Luke 12:9.

536. Aparchē; from *apó* (575), from, and *archē* (746), beginning. The first of the ripe fruits, firstfruits always in the sing. Applied to Christ as the firstfruits of the resurrection with believers to follow later (1 Cor. 15:20, 23); to the gifts of the Holy Spirit as a foretaste of their eternal inheritance (Rom. 8:23, cf. Eph. 1:14; Heb. 6:5); to the first believers converted in any particular place or country (Rom. 16:5; 1 Cor. 16:15); to believers in general consecrated to God from among the rest of mankind (James 1:18; Rev. 14:4); to the patriarchs and ancestors of the Jewish people (Rom. 11:16).

541. Apaúgasma; from *apaugázō*, to emit light or splendor, which is from *apó* (575), from, and *augázō* (826), to shine. Occurs only in Hebrews 1:3 in reference to the person of Jesus Christ, meaning effulgence, light, or splendor emitted or issuing from a luminous body. Jesus as the Son is called the effulgence or shining forth of God's glory, being the likeness of the Father. The Lord Jesus is the radiance of the eternal light, and must also be eternal (John 1:4, 5). The all-glorious divinity of the Son of God is essentially one, but not personally one with the Father. (To distinguish the meaning of *apaúgasma* from the word *charaktḗr* found in Hebrews 1:3 and translated as the express image, see the discussion under [5481] and *eikṓn* [1504], image.) Contrast *homoíōma* (3667), similitude; *homoíōsis* (3669), likeness.

543. Apeítheia; from the neg. *a* (1) and *peíthō* (3982), to persuade. Disobedience (Heb. 4:6). In the NT it corresponds with the verb unbelief which opposes the gracious word and purpose of God. It is a stronger term than the syn. *apistía* (570), unbelief. Hence we have the syn. of *apeítheias*, disobedience (Rom. 11:30; Eph. 2:2; 5:6; Col. 3:6).

544. Apeithéō; from the neg. *a* (1), without, and *peíthō* (3982), to persuade. Not to believe, to disbelieve implying disobedience also (John 3:36; Acts 14:2; Rom. 10:21; Heb. 3:18); to disobey as through unbelief (Rom. 2:8; 1 Pet. 3:20). The above two meanings seem to coincide, but *apeithéo* sometimes refers more to inward attitude which is sometimes outwardly expressed. Ant.: *peíthomai*, verb, in the mid. and pass., to allow oneself to be persuaded, to obey; *pisteúō* (4100), to believe (John 3:36; Acts 14:1).

545. Apeithḗs; from the neg. *a* (1), without, and *peíthō* (3982), to persuade. Unbelieving (Luke 1:17); disobedient (Acts 26:19; Rom. 1:30; 2 Tim. 3:2; Titus 1:16); not letting oneself be persuaded, hard, stubborn (Titus 3:3). Deriv. verb: *apeithéō* (544), to be disobedient.

548. Ápeimi; to be absent, from *apó* (575), from, and *eimí* (1510) to be (1 Cor. 5:3; 2 Cor. 10:1, 11; 13:2, 10; Phil. 1:27; Col. 2:5). Deriv.: *apousía* (666), absence (Phil. 2:12). Contrast *parousía* (3952), presence.

551. Apeírastos; a verbal adj. from the neg. *a* (1) without, and *peirázō* (3985), to tempt or to test. Used only in James 1:13 where it means incapable of being tempted to do evil.

553. Apekdéchomai; from *apó* (575), an intens., and *ekdéchomai* (1551), to expect, look for. To wait for, used as a suitable expression for Christian hope including the two elements of hope and patience (Rom. 8:25). In Romans 8:23 the obj. of this fut. expectation is the *huiothesía* (5206), the adoption, as will be realized in the redemption of the body (Rom. 8:19; 1 Cor. 1:7; Gal. 5:5; Phil. 3:20; Heb. 9:28, cf. 1 Pet. 3:20).

558. Apeleútheros; from *apó* (575), from, and *eleútheros* (1658), free. Freed from, emancipated. Occurs only in 1 Corinthians 7:22 where it indicates that the slavery which the earthly relation may involve does not really exist in the new sphere into which the divine calling introduces one.

560. Apelpízō; from *apó* (575), from, and *elpízō* (1679), to hope. To cease to hope, renounce or give up a thing or a person, to despair. With the acc., to give up what one does not expect to keep. Used only in Luke 6:35 in the phrase lend *mēdén apelpízones*, hoping for nothing, meaning not expecting something for oneself.

564. Aperítmētos; from the neg *a* (1), without, and *peritémnō* (4059), to circumcise, which in turn is derived from *perí* (4012), around, and *témnō*, to cut, circumcise. Uncircumcised (Acts 7:51, cf. Lev. 26:41; Jer. 6:10; 9:25; Ezek. 44:7, 9).

566. Apéchei; used impersonally, it is enough, sufficient (Mark 14:41), implying that no further directions are needed on the subject. See *apéchō* (568).

567. Apéchomai; the mid. voice of *apéchō* (568), to keep oneself from, to abstain or refrain from (Acts 15:20, 29).

568. Apéchō; from *apó* (575), from, and *échō* (2192), to have, be. To receive or obtain from another (Matt.

6:2, 5; Phil. 4:18; Phile. 1:15); to be distant or at a distance (Luke 7:6; 15:20; 24:13). Applied figuratively to the heart (Matt. 15:8; Mark 7:6). Receiving in full without expectation of any more coming (Matt. 6:2, 5, 16; Luke 6:24). See *apéchei* (566); *apéchomai* (567).

569. Apistéō; from *ápistos* (571), untrustworthy, which is from the neg. *a* (1) and *pístis* (4102). faith, belief. To put no confidence in, not to believe or to disbelieve (Mark 16:11; Luke 24:11, 41; Acts 28:24; Rom. 3:3). To be unfaithful as in 2 Timothy 2:13 where it is opposite to *pistós* (4103), faithful; to doubt or not to acknowledge.

570. Apistía; faithlessness or uncertainty, distrust, unbelief. In the NT, the lack of acknowledgment of Christ (Matt. 13:58; Mark 6:6); want of confidence in Christs power (Matt. 17:20; Mark 9:24). In general, a want of trust in the God of promise (Rom. 4:20; Heb. 3:12, 19).

571. Ápistos; not worthy of confidence, untrustworthy, unbeliever. In the NT in a pass. sense, a thing not to be believed, incredible (Acts 26:8); in an act. sense, not believing (Matt. 17:17; Luke 12:46; John 20:27). Denotes one who disbelieves the Gospel of Christ, an unbeliever, an infidel (1 Cor. 6:6; 7:12–15; 2 Cor. 6:15). Contrast: *pistós* (4103), a believer.

572. Haplótēs; simplicity, purity, sincerity, faithfulness, plenitude. In the NT used only in a moral sense as the opposite of duplicity meaning sincerity, faithfulness toward others, manifest in helpfulness and giving assistance to others. Equivalent to being faithful and benevolent. Although in some portions (2 Cor. 8:2; 9:11, 13) translated liberality, it is not exactly so; it is rather faithful benevolence out of proper motivation.

573. Haploús; occurs only in Matthew 6:22; Luke 11:34 translated single. Singleness, simplicity, absence of folds. This, however, does not involve stupidity on the part of the Christian, but rather *phrónēsis* (5428), prudence, knowing how to deal with fellow humans and the circumstances of life. Thus the Christian is supposed to be not only *haploús*, single, without duplicity, but also *phrónimos* (5429), prudent (Matt. 10:16; Rom. 16:19). See also *ákakos* (172), harmless, without willingness to hurt which willingness is innate in the corrupted nature of man; *akéraios* (185), harmless; *ádolos* (97), without guile.

581. Apogínomai; second aor. part. *apogenómenos*, from *apó* (575), from, and *gínomai* (1096), to become. To be afar off, separated, take no part in, and later it came to mean to cease to be, to die. It is used in this sense in 1 Peter 2:24 corresponding with Romans 6:11. Denotes not a legal, but a moral relation to sin, which is here represented according to its individual manifestations (Rom. 6:2; 7:6; Col. 2:20), and indeed a relation of such a kind that the molding of the character of the person by sin ceases.

587. Apodektós; from *apodéchomai* (588), to welcome, from the intens. *apó* (575) and *déchomai* (1209), to receive. Acceptable (1 Tim. 2:3; 5:4), pleasing, grateful.

588. Apodéchomai; from *apó* (575), an intens., and *déchomai* (1209), to receive. Used only by Luke, of persons, to receive kindly or hospitably (Luke 8:40; Acts 15:4; 18:27); of God's Word, to receive or embrace heartily (Acts 2:41), of benefits, to receive or accept gratefully (Acts 24:3).

592. Apodiorízō; from *apó* (575), from, and *diorízō*, to divide, separate, derived from *día* (1223), denoting separation, and *horízō* (3724), to limit. Occurs only in Jude 1:19, to separate from other Christians.

593. Apodokimázō; from *apó* (575), from, and *dokimázō* (1381), prove. To reject as the result of examination, answering to the Attic use of *dokimázō* (1381), to denote testing or qualification of one nominated to an office. Later it came to mean to put out of office or place, to reject, to disapprove, to refuse. Used of the rejection of Christ (Matt. 21:42; Mark 8:31; 12:10; Luke 9:22; 17:25; 20:17; 1 Pet. 2:4, 7); of the refusal of Esau (Hebrews 12:17).

594. Apodochḗ; the subst. of *apodéchomai* (588), to receive from. Recognition, acknowledgment, approval, or more exactly, ready or willing acknowledgment. Used only in 1 Timothy 1:15; 4:9.

599. Apothnḗskō; from *apó* (575), as an intens., and *thnḗskō* (2348), to die. Literally, to die off, but used with the simple meaning of to die. To die a natural death applied to both men and animals (Matt. 8:32; 22:24, 27; 26:35); to be dead to sin, as the truly regenerate are, by having renounced and abandoned it in consequence of their conformity with Christ in His death (Rom. 6:2, cf. Col. 3:3); when applied to Christ, to die for or on account of sin, that is, to make an atonement and satisfaction for it (Rom. 6:10, cf. Heb. 9:26–28); to be dead to the law, that is, to have no more dependence upon mere legal righteousness for justification and salvation than a dead man would have; as being one self-crucified and dead together with Christ (Gal. 2:19, cf. Rom. 6:4; Col. 2:20).

600. Apokathístēmi; or *apokathistánō*, from *apo;* (575), back again, and *kathístēmi* or *kathistánō* (2525), to constitute. To restore, as to health or soundness (Matt. 12:13; Mark 3:5; 8:25; Luke 6:10). To restore, reform, applied to the reformation brought about by the preaching and ministry of John the Baptist (Matt. 17:11; Mark 9:12, cf. Mal. 4:6; Luke 1:16, 17). To restore lost dominion or authority (Acts 1:6). In the pass., to be restored, brought or sent back again (Heb. 13:19). The noun, *apokatástasis* (605), restitution of a thing to its former condition.

601. Apokalúptō; from *apó* (575), from, and *kalúptō* (2572), to cover, conceal. Literally, to remove a veil or covering exposing to open view what was before hidden. To make manifest or reveal a thing previously secret or unknown (Luke 2:35; 1 Cor. 3:13). Particularly applied to supernatural revelation (Matt. 11:25, 27; 16:17; 1 Cor. 2:10). Opposite of *kalúptō* (Matt. 10:26); *sugkalúptō* (4780), to cover or conceal closely (Luke 12:2); *krúptō* (2928), to hide (Matt. 11:25); *apokrúptō* (613), to hide from someone (Luke 10:21).

602. Apokálupsis; revelation, uncovering, unveiling, disclosure. One of three words referring to the Second Coming of Christ (1 Cor. 1:7; 2 Thess. 1:7; 1 Pet. 1:7, 13). The other two words are *epipháneia* (2015), appearing (2 Tim. 6:14), and *parousía* (3952), presence, coming (2 Thess. 2:1). *Apokálupsis*, a grander and more comprehensive word, includes not merely the thing shown and seen but the interpretation, the unveiling of the same. The *epipháneiai* (pl.), appearings, are contained in the *apokálupsis*, revelation, being separate points or moments therein. Christ's first coming was an *epipháneia* (2 Tim. 1:10); the *apokálupsis* will be far more glorious.

603. Apokaradokía; from *apó* (575), from, and *kará*, the head, and *dokáō*, to expect. Attentive or earnest expectation or looking for, as with the neck stretched out and the head thrust forward (Rom. 8:19; Phil. 1:20, where it is *karadokía* in some MSS).

604. Apokatallássō; the stronger term for reconcile with the prep. *apó* (575), from, indicating the state to be left, and *katá* (2596), an intens. or toward the state to be sought after. It differs from *katallássō* (2644) the setting up of a relationship of peace not existing before, while *apokatallássō* is the restoration of a relationship of peace which has been disturbed (Eph. 2:16; Col. 1:20, 21).

605. Apokatástasis; from the verb *apokathístēmi* (600), to restore, which in turn is derived from *apó* (575), back again, and *kathístēmi* (2525), or *kathistáno*, to constitute. A restitution of a thing to its former condition. Occurs only in Acts 3:21 where the restitution of all things is to be understood as the day of judgment and of the consummation of the age when the Lord will return. It is at that time that life will be restored to the bodies of the dead, and the image of God in man, defaced by Adams fall, will be perfectly renewed in righteousness. This restoration affects not only man as he has been depraved of the character of God his Creator, but also it affects God's glory. At this time, God is not recognized in nature and among men for all that He really is, a wise God who governs the affairs of men. God's power and justice will be recognized once again. He will then render to each

person according to his works (2 Cor. 5:10). At that time the veracity of God's predictions will be proven (2 Pet. 3:3, 4). In Acts 3:21 the relative pron. *hōn*, translated which in the phrase Whom the heaven must receive until the times of restitution of all things, which God hath spoken by the mouth of all his holy prophets since the world began, does not refer to *pántōn*, of all things, because then it would limit *pántōn*, namely, this restoration would concern not all things, but only those things spoken by God through the mouth of His saints. The relative pron *hōn* in the masc. gen. pl. must, therefore, refer to the times of restoration and be taken as its attribute. An understandable translation then would be Whom (the ascended Christ; see Acts 1:11) heaven must receive until the period of restoration of all things, of which (period of restoration) God spoke by the mouth of all His holy prophets. See also 1 Corinthians 14:2, 3; Colossians 4:3; Hebrews 2:3. *Apokatástasis* may be taken as syn. with *paliggenesía* (3824), regeneration, in its application in Matthew 19:28. See also Romans 8:19ff.; Revelation 21:5. Although the believer enjoys Christ's salvation on this earth, it is not complete in view of the fact that man is still in his mortal body and the environment in which he lives has been tainted by sin. Both the body and the environment will one day be changed completely when this restoration takes place (Rom. 8:23; Rev. 21:1 where a qualitatively new [*kainé* (2537), new] heaven and earth are going to be created).

610. Apókrima; answer, not the act of answering (*apókrisis*, [612]) but the answer itself Used in 2 Corinthians 1:9 as syn. with *katákrima* (2631), condemnation, in the sense of those who have been rejected, who have been given a verdict against, sentenced to death in the opinions and minds of others.

611. Apokrínomai; from *apó* (575), from, and *krínō* (2919), to separate, discern, judge. In the pass. meaning to be separated, selected. In the mid. voice, to answer, to return answer which ought to be done with discretion (Matt. 3:15; 4:4; 26:23; 27:12) and also to take occasion to speak or say, not strictly in answering but in relation or reference to preceding circumstances (Matt. 11:4; 12:38; 17:4; 22:1; 26:25, 63; Mark 9:5, 17; Luke 7:40).

612. Apókrisis; from *apokrínomai* (611), answer. Decision or answer (Luke 2:47; 20:26; John 1:22; 19:9).

616. Apokuéō; from *apó* (575), from, and *kuō*, to be pregnant. To beget (James 1:15, 18, cf. 1 Cor. 4:15; 1 Pet. 1:3, 23). To bring forth, as sin brings death (James 1:15). Related to *tíktō* (5088) which properly denotes bringing forth as by a female, but is often spoken of the male. Paul applies it to himself as being in labor in Galatians 4:19.

622. Apóllumi; or *apollúō*, from the intens. *apó* (575), and *ollúō*, to destroy. In the NT to kill, destroy, whether temporally (Matt. 2:13; 27:20; Mark 11:18; John 10:10) or eternally (Matt. 10:28; 18:14); in the mid. and pass., to be destroyed, perish, whether temporally (Matt. 26:52, cf. 9:17; Heb. 1:11; Mark 4:38; Luke 11:51; 15:17), or eternally (John 3:15, 16; 10:28; Rom. 2:12; 1 Cor. 1:18); to lose (Matt. 10:39; 16:25; Luke 15:4); in the pass. and mid., to be lost (Matt. 15:24, 18:11, Luke 15:6, 24). Deriv.: *apóleia* (684), lost; *Apollúōn* (623), the Destroyer; *sunapóllumi* (4881), to destroy with.

623. Apollúōn; from *apóllumi* (622), to destroy, corrupt. The Destroyer (Rev. 9:11). A Gr. name for the angel of the abyss, *ábussos* (12). The corresponding Heb. name is *Abaddōn* (3).

628. Apoloúō; from *apó* (575), from, and *loúō* (3068), to wash, bathe. The comp. verb means to wash away. In Acts 22:16 it gives prominence to the cleansing from sin connected with salvation. In 1 Corinthians 6:11, a failure to distinguish between the outward and the inward cleansing is guarded against by the use of *apeloúsasthe* instead of *ebaptísthēte*, you were washed, instead of you were baptized. In the mid. voice, to have oneself washed or to wash oneself.

629. Apolútrōsis; from *apolutróō*, to release on payment of ransom, redeem, which is from the prep. *apó* (575), from, and *lutróō* (3084), to redeem. Redemption. A *lútron* (3083), ransom, or *antállagma* (465), a price paid. The recalling of captives (sinners) from captivity (sin) through the payment of a ransom for them, that is, Christ's death (Rom. 3:24; Col. 1:14). Sin is presented as slavery and sinners as slaves (John 8:34; Rom. 6:17, 20; 2 Pet. 2:19). Deliverance from sin is freedom (John 8:33, 36; Rom. 8:21; Gal. 5:1).

630. Apolúō; from *apó* (575), from, and *lúō* (3089), to loose. To loose, set loose, release as from bond; a disease (Luke 13:12, cf. v. 16); bonds or imprisonment (Matt. 27:15, 17, 21, 26; Heb. 13:23); obligation to punishment (Matt. 18:27; Luke 6:37). To dismiss, allow to depart (Matt. 14:15; 15:23, 39; Luke 2:29), in the mid. and pass. *apolúomai*, to depart (Acts 28:25). To dismiss from life, let depart, die (Luke 2:29). To dismiss a wife by loosing her from the bond of marriage (Matt. 1:19; 5:31, 32; 19:3); to put away a husband (Mark 10:12).

646. Apostasía; from *aphístēmi* (868), which is from *apó* (575), from, and *hístēmi* (2476), to place, stand. Occurs in Acts 21:21 translated forsake and in 2 Thessalonians 2:3 falling away. In the majority of occasions the verb is intrans. meaning that person does not depart from where he is to go somewhere else, but stays away, having chosen from the beginning to stay away, not to believe instead of believing, in which case the basic verb *hístēmi* (2476) is to be interpreted not as departing, but as standing away, placing oneself away; with the prep. *apó* (575), to stay away from. In Acts 21:21 the new Christian believers among the Jews decided to stand apart from the Jewish practices of Moses for they were in a new dispensation. They were not Judaizing Christians, but Christians standing apart from Moses. Having departed from Moses and coming to Jesus Christ, they decided that they should stay apart from Moses, that is, his Judaistic practices. In 2 Thessalonians 2:3 the word *apostasía* does not refer to the Christians who would depart from the faith, but those who would reject Christ.

649. Apostéllō; from *apo* (575), from, and *stéllō* (4724), to send. Distinguished from *pémpō* (3992), to send, in that *apostéllō* is to send forth on a certain mission such as to preach (Mark 3:14; Luke 9:2); speak (Luke 1:19); bless (Acts 3:26; 7:35); rule, redeem, propitiate (1 John 4:10); save (1 John 4:14). The expression that Jesus was sent by God (John 3:34) denotes the mission which He had to fulfill and the authority which backed Him. The importance of this mission is denoted by the fact that it is His Son whom God sent. In the NT, to send forth from one place to another, to send upon some business or employment (Matt. 2:16; 10:5; 20:2); to send away, dismiss (Mark 12:3, 4); to send or thrust forth as a sickle among corn (Mark 4:29) Deriv.: *apóstolos* (652), one sent, apostle, ambassador; *apostolé* (651), dispatching or sending forth.

651. Apostolé; dispatching or sending forth; also that which is sent, that is, a present. In the NT, apostleship (Acts 1:25; Rom. 1:5; 1 Cor. 9:2; Gal. 2:8).

652. Apóstolos; primarily an adj., sent forth. Used as a subst. meaning one sent, apostle, ambassador. From the verb *apostéllō* (649), to send forth. Sometimes used syn. with *présbus*, ambassador, related to *presbeúō* (4243), to act as an ambassador (2 Cor. 5:20; Eph. 6:20). An ambassador is not greater than the one who sends him (John 13:16). The Lord chose the term *apóstoloi* to indicate the distinctive relation of the Twelve whom He chose to be His witnesses because the word was seldom used in the Class. Gr. (Luke 6:13; Acts 1:2, 26); therefore, it designates the office as instituted by Christ (John 17:18). It also designates the authority which those called to this office possess. See the verb *apostéllō* in Romans 10:15. Paul combines both these meanings (Rom. 1:1; 1 Cor. 1:1; 9:1, 2; 15:9; 2 Cor. 1:1; 12:12; Gal. 1:1). The distinctive name of the Twelve (or eleven) with whom Paul himself was reckoned, as he says in 1 Corinthians 15:7, 9, justifying his being counted as an apostle by the fact that he had been called to

the office by Christ Himself. And yet the name seems from the very beginning to have been applied, in a much wider sense, to all who bore witness of Christ (Acts 14:4, 14; 15:2); and even by Paul (2 Cor. 11:13; 1 Thess. 2:6). This general meaning of the word held its place side by side with the special and distinctive application. There is no continuity of the office of an apostle as in no place were the churches instructed to ordain apostles. The term is applied to Christ (Hebrews 3:1) who was sent by the Father into the world, not to condemn but to save it (John 3:17; 17:3, 8, 21, 23; 20:21).

654. Apostréphō; from *apó* (575), from or back again, and *stréphō* (4762), to turn. To turn away from (Acts 3:26; Rom. 11:26; 2 Tim. 4:4); to return, put back (Matt. 26:52); to return, bring back (Matt. 27:3); in the pass., *apostréphomai*, with an acc., to turn or be turned away from, to reject (Matt. 5:42; 2 Tim. 1:15; Titus 1:14; Heb. 12:25).

655. Apostugéō; from *apó* (575), from or an intens. and *stugéō*, to shudder with horror. To abhor, detest with horror (Rom. 12:9).

656. Aposunágōgos; separated from the synagogue, excommunicated. Only in John 9:22; 12:42; 16:2. There were three degrees of excommunication or banishment among the Jews. The first step was only a rebuke pronounced upon the offender for up to thirty days. This did not necessarily mean exclusion from attendance to and participation in the synagogue worship, but exclusion from the fellowship of the congregation and their blessings and privileges. The second step was an exclusion from the assembly and from communication with others for another thirty days. This degree was accompnanied by curses and severe restrictions. The final degree was a ban of indefinite duration. This ban was an exclusion from all the rights and privileges of the Jewish peole, both civil and religious. The offended was considered as dead. The first two degrees were primarily disciplinary, the third was a cutting off from the congregation. John 16:2, in particular, hardly allows for a mere temporary exclusion such as the first step involved, which might be proposed and even decreed for the injured person, without consultation with the Sanhedrin. Thus *aposunágōgos* denotes one who has been excommunicated from the commonwealth of the people of God and is given over to the curse (Ezra 10:8). See Luke 6:22 where it uses the term *aphorízō* (873), to put out of bounds or to excommunicate.

657. Apotássomai; from *apó* (575), from, and *tássō* (5021), to place in order. Translated forsaketh in Luke 14:33 but has the meaning of our belongings being placed away from us into their proper category and not being permitted to become part of us. In Luke 9:61 the man who expressed the desire to follow Jesus wanted first to see that his own family was properly cared for. Jesus knew that by the time the man did that he would have forgotten his promise to Him. In other references it means separating oneself from others, places, or things (Mark 6:46; Acts 18:18, 21; 2 Cor. 2:13).

674. Apopsuchō; from *apó* (575), denoting priv., and *psuché*, breath, life, soul. To expire, die (Luke 21:26).

677. Apróskopos; from the neg. *a*, and *proskóptō* (4350), to strike, to stumble. Intrans., not stumbling or falling, figuratively speaking, in the path of duty and religion (Phil. 1:10). Applied to the conscience, not stumbling or impinging against anything for which our heart condemns us (Acts 24:16, cf. Acts 23:1; 1 Cor. 4:4; 2 Cor. 1:12; 2 Tim. 1:3) Trans., causing others to stumble, giving occasion to fall into sin (1 Cor. 10:32, cf. 2 Cor. 6:3).

680. Háptomai; from *háptō* (681), touch. Refers to such handling of an object as to exert a modifying influence upon it or upon oneself. The same effect may be conveyed by the verb *thiggánō* (2345). These words sometimes may be exchanged one for the other as they are in the Sept. (Ex. 19:12). They are used together in Colossians 2:21. *Háptomai* is usually stronger than *thiggánō* (1 John 5:18; Sept.: Ps. 104:15). *Thiggánō* is correctly translated in Colossians

2:21 in the KJV as handle not, but the basic meaning is touching for the purpose of manipulating. Distinguished from *psēlapháō* (5584), which actually only means to touch the surface of something (Luke 24:39; 1 John 1:1).

681. Háptō; handle an object so as to exert a modifying influence upon it (Luke 8:16; 11:33; 15:8; 22:55). Syn.: *thigganō* (2345), to touch, stronger than *thigō*, to finger. *Háptō* (1 John 5:18) sometimes involves a self-conscious effort which is is always absent from *thigō*.

684. Apóleia; from *apóllumi* (622), to destroy, ruin, lose. Trans., the losing or loss (Matt. 26:8); intrans., perdition, ruin. In the NT *apóleia* refers to the state of perdition after death, exclusion from salvation. Destruction, either temporal (Acts 25:16, cf. Acts 8:20), or eternal (Matt. 7:13; Phil. 1:28; 3:19; 2 Pet. 2:1). Destruction or waste (Matt. 26:8; Mark 14:4).

685. Ará; originally it meant prayer, but more often the imprecation of something evil, a curse which the deity is to execute. Opposite *euchē* (2171), wish, vow. *Ará* is the basic word from which *katára* (2671), curse, is derived. Finally the word came to mean the evil imprecated, the mischief itself, the realized curse. Used only in Romans 3:14 while the comp. *katára* (2671) is used more frequently (Gal. 3:10, 13; Heb. 6:8; James 3:10; 2 Pet. 2:14).

691. Argéō; to be an *argós* (692), idle, to do nothing. Only in 2 Peter 2:3, to be inactive, to rest. Deriv.: *katargéō* (2673), to render inactive.

692. Argós; contracted from *áergos*, which is from the neg. *a* (1), and *érgon* (2041), work. Not at work, idle, not employed, inactive (Matt. 20:3, 6; 1 Tim. 5:13; Titus 1:12; 2 Pet. 1:8). Idle, unprofitable (Matt. 12:36, cf. 2 Pet. 1:9).

699. Aréskeia; from *aréskō* (700), to please. An endeavor to please, sometimes referring to an excessive desire to please in a bad sense. In a good sense, to please God. Only in Colossians 1:10.

700. Aréskō; fut. *arésō*, aor. *éresa*. To please, to make one inclined to, to be content with, soften one's heart towards another. In the NT the meaning evolved from the active to please into to be pleasing, that is, passing from a relationship to behavior (1 Thess. 2:15). The pres. and imperf. tenses denote intentional, deliberate and continuous conduct and have nothing to do with verbs denoting states or relationships; yet the word involves a relationship prior to behavior. It is actually satisfying or behaving properly toward one with whom one is related. Deriv.: *arestós* (701), dear, pleasant, well-pleasing; *aréskeia* (699), the endeavor to please; *anthrōpáreskos* (441), one who endeavors to please men; *euárestos* (2101), pleasing, agreeable; *euárestōs* (2102), well-pleasing as an adverb; *euarestéō* (2100), to be well-pleasing. Syn.: *dektós* (1184), approved, indicates only relationship. *Arestós* presupposes mans relationship with God, but it also relates God's judgment on mans conduct. In 1 Corinthians 10:33 the expression *pánta* (all things), *pásin* (to anyone), *aréskō* (I am pleasing to), means to do something to please someone.

701. Arestós; from *aréskō* (700), to please one or to be content with. To be dear, pleasant, to do that which pleases somebody (Acts 12:3); elsewhere used only of God's will (John 8:29). It is in this sense that it is used in 1 John 3:22, distinguishing between claim or requirement and satisfaction, the claim being the commandments and the satisfaction being those things that are done out of the love that one has for God. In Acts 6:2 reference is made to that which is pleasing to God and not to what is pleasing to the apostles.

703. Areté; excellency, being pleasing to God, the excellence of God revealed in the work of salvation. *Areté* denotes in a moral sense what gives man his worth, his efficiency. In the NT: virtue, excellency, perfection (1 Pet. 2:9); the virtue as a force or energy of the Holy Spirit accompanying the preaching of the glorious Gospel, called glory in 2 Peter 1:3; human virtue in general (Phil. 4:8); courage, fortitude, resolution (2 Pet. 1:5), moral excellence.

720. Arnéomai; To deny, refuse (Heb. 11:24). With the acc. of person, meaning to refuse anyone, not to know or recognize him, to reject him either in the face of former relationship or better knowledge. To deny, decline, reject, give up, it can include the idea of contradiction, not only of the subject against the object, but on the part of the subject against himself (Matt. 10:33; Luke 12:9; 22:57; Acts 3:13, 14; 7:35; 2 Tim. 2:12, 13; 2 Pet. 2:1; 1 John 2:22, 23; Jude 1:4; Rev. 3:8). Used with a thing as its object; to reject anything, retract, renounce, deny, disown, depending on the context (1 Tim. 5:8; 2 Tim. 3:5; Titus 1:16; 2:12; Rev. 2:13). To gainsay, without further specification of the object (Luke 8:45, Acts 4:16). Falsely, to deny, disown (Matt. 26:70, 72; Mark 14:68, 70; John 18:25, 27). Opposite, *homologéō* (3670), to confess or say together with (Matt. 10:32; John 1:20; Titus 1:16).

721. Arníon; the diminutive of *árēn*, later *arnós*, lamb (John 21:15). Designation of the exalted Christ in Revelation 5:6, where the little Lamb is contrasted to the Lion of the tribe of Judah in verse five (see Acts 8:32). The words *hōs esphagménon*, as slaughtered, point to His death. *Spházō* (4969) is the usual expression in the Class. Gr. and the Sept. for sacrifice. *Arníon* denotes sacrificial death as demonstrated in Revelation 7:14; 12:11; 14:4. See also Hebrews 9:26; 1 Peter 1:19, 20; 1 John 1:7; Revelation 13:8. Later the term *arníon* became syn. with *amnós* (286), the sacrificial lamb.

724. Harpagé; from *harpázō* (726), to seize upon with force. In the act. sense, the act of plundering, robbery (Heb. 10:34). In the pass. sense, the thing seized, plunder. Metaphorically, a disposition to plunder, ravening (Matt. 23:25; Luke 11:39). Although the reference to the contents of the cup in Matthew 23:25 may make *harpagé* pass., its use with *akrasía* (192), incontinency, denotes an attribute.

725. Harpagmós; from *harpázō* (726), to seize upon with force. Robbery. The word occurs only in Philippians 2:6, "Who [Christ], being in the form of God thought it not robbery (*harpagmón*) to be equal with God," meaning the Lord did not esteem being equal with God as identical with the coming forth or action of a robber (*hárpax*). Christ was in the *morphē* (3444), form or inward identifiable existence of God. The participle *hupárchōn* means that Jesus continued to be in the flesh what He was before He became man. He has always been God. In *schéma* (4976), outer appearance, Jesus was man; in *morphē* He was God.

726. Harpázō; to strip, spoil, snatch. Literally, to seize upon with force, to rob; differing from *kléptō* (2813), to steal secretly. An open act of violence in contrast to cunning and secret thieving. Though generally *harpázō* denotes robbery of anothers property, it is not exclusively used thus, but sometimes generally meaning forcibly to seize upon, to snatch away, or take to oneself (Matt. 13:19; John 6:15; 10:12, 28, 29; Acts 23:10; Jude 1:23). Especially used of a rapture (Acts 8:39; 2 Cor. 12:2, 4; 1 Thess. 4:17; Rev. 12:5); to use force against one (Matt. 11:12). Deriv.: *harpagé* (724), robbery, plundering; *harpagmós* (725), robbery, usurpation.

728. Arrabón; a word adopted by the Greeks, Romans, and Egyptians from the Phoenicians meaning earnest money, pledge. Something which stands for part of the price and paid beforehand to confirm the bargain. Used in the NT only in a figurative sense and spoken of the Holy Spirit which God has given to believers in this present life to assure them of their future and eternal inheritance (2 Cor. 1:22; 5:5; Eph. 1:14). Syn.: *aparchē* (536), translated as firstfruits.

732. Árrōstos; from *a* (1), without, and *rhónnumi* (4517), to strengthen. Infirm, sick, invalid (Matt. 14:14; Mark 6:5, 13; 16:18; 1 Cor. 11:30). Used in ancient Greece to indicate moral weakness or slackness. Noun: *arróstia*, weakness, sickness, a lingering ailment, bad state of health; not occurring in the NT.

738. Artigénnētos; from *árti* (737), now, just now, lately, and *gennētós* (1084), born, which in turn is derived from *gennáō* (1080), to bring forth. Lately born, newborn; occurs only in 1 Peter 2:2.

739. Ártios; from *árō*, to fit. Complete, sufficient, completely qualified (2 Tim. 3:17). Closely syn. with *holóklēros* (3648), one, all the parts of which are complete, whole, what they are supposed to be so that they might serve their destined purpose.

743. Archággelos; from *árchō* (757), to rule, and *ággelos* (32), angel or messenger. Denotes the first or highest angel, archangel, leader of the angels. Denotes a definite rank by virtue of which one is qualified for special work and service. The prefix *archi-* always expresses a gradation in the sphere spoken of as in the NT *archiereús* (749), chief priest; *archipoimén* (750), chief shepherd; *architelónēs* (754), chief tax collector. It always expresses a distinction of rank and not only of the special work and service for which one is sent. The archangel, head or ruler of the angels, sometimes denotes Christ being the God-Man (1 Thess. 4:16, cf. John 5:25–27; Jude 1:9, cf. Zech. 3:2).

744. Archaíos; old, but expressing that which was from the beginning, *arché* (746) Contrast to *palaiós* (3820), old, as having existed a long period of time (*pálai*). Since there may be many later beginnings, it is quite possible to conceive the *palaiós* as older than *archaíos*. *Archaíos* reaches back to a beginning, whatever that beginning may have been. *Archaíos* disciple (Acts 21:16), not necessarily an old disciple but one who had been such from the beginning of the faith, from the day of Pentecost (Acts 2). See also Matt. 5:21; Luke 9:8, 19, Acts 15:7, 21; 2 Corinthians 5:17; 2 Peter 2:5; Revelation 12:9, 20:2.

746. Arché; beginning. *Arché* means a pass. beginning or an act. cause (Col. 1:18; Rev. 3:14, cf. Rev. 1:8; 21:6; 22:13). Christ is called the beginning because He is the efficient cause of the creation; the head because He is before all things and all things were created by Him and for Him (John 1:1–3, Col. 1:16–17; Heb. 1:10). *Arché* also means extremity or outermost point (Acts 10:11; 11:5); rule, authority, dominion, power (Luke 20:20; 1 Cor. 15:24). The verb *árchō* (757), to be first or to rule (Mark 10:42; Rom. 15:12). The noun *árchon* (758) denotes a ruler; *archaíos* (744), of old time; *archēgós* (747), leader.

747. Archēgós; from *arché* (746), beginning or rule. Beginning, originating, as a subst. it means originator, founder, leader, chief, prince. Jesus Christ is called the *archēgós* of life (Acts 3:15); of faith (Heb. 12:2); of salvation (Heb. 2:10). He is also called the *aparché* (536), firstfruits, of them that sleep, the originator of the resurrection of those who are going to be raised from the dead. *Archēgós* occurs also in Acts 5:31.

749. Archiereús; from *arché* (746), a head or chief, and *hiereús* (2409), a priest. The high or chief priest, having to do with eminence. The Jewish high or chief priest has great spiritual import to Christ (Heb. 2:17; 3:1; 5:10; 6:20; 9:11). The Jewish high priest was a type of Christ. The high priest offered gifts and sacrifices for sins, and entering the Holy of Holies, appeared in the presence of God to make intercession for the people (Lev. 16). In like manner, Christ is the believer's high priest (Mt. 26:57, 58, 62, 63, 65; Heb. 9:7, 11, 25). In the pl., chief priests means not only the current high priest, and his deputy, with those who had formerly borne the high priests office, but also the chiefs or heads of the twenty-four Sacerdotal families which David distributed into as many courses. These are called chiefs of the priests (2 Chr. 36:11; Ezra 8:24; 10:5) and heads of the priests (Neh. 12:7; see Matt. 2:4; 27:1, 3, 41; Mark 11:27; Luke 22:52); used in the sing. in this sense for a chief of the priests in Acts 19:14.

750. Archipoimén; from *arché* (746), chief, and *poimēn* (4166), a shepherd. Used in 1 Peter 5:4 with the meaning of a chief shepherd, applying the word spiritually to Christ (cf. Heb. 13:20).

757. Árchō; To rule, govern (Mark 10:42; Rom. 15:12). In the Class. Gr. *árchō*, the act. voice, and *árchomai* (756), the mid. voice, meant to begin. But in the NT, only *árchomai* (756) is used only in this sense (Matt. 4:17; 11:7, 12:1). In Luke 24:47, *arxámenon* is an impersonal part. and may be rendered beginning, making a beginning.

758. Árchōn; a ruler, chief, prince magistrate (Matt. 9:34; 20:25; Luke 12:58; John 14:30; Acts 4:8; 7:27; Rev. 1:5). It would seem from a comparison of John 3:1 and John 7:50 that *árchōn* of the Jews in the former passage means a member of the Jewish Sanhedrin, but it is plain from comparing Matthew 9:18, 23 with Mark 5:22 and Luke 8:41 that *árchōn* in those texts means only a ruler of a synagogue.

763. Asébeia; from the neg. *a* (1) and *sébomai* (4576), to worship. Impiety towards God, ungodliness, lack of reverence (Rom. 1:18); wickedness in general; neglect or violation of duty towards God, our neighbor or ourselves, joined with and springing from impiety towards God (Rom. 11:26; 2 Tim. 2:16; Titus 2:12; Jude 1:15, 18). See *sebázomai* (4573), to venerate. Subst.: *sébasma* (4574), the object of holy respectful reverence; *asebéō*(764), to act impiously; *asebés* (765), impious.

764. Asebéō; from the neg. *a* (1), without, and *sébomai* (4576), to worship, venerate. To act impiously, to sin against anything which we should consider sacred. Without an obj. to trespass, commit an offense. In the NT it occurs in a very strong reference to sinfulness in 2 Peter 2:6; Jude 1:15. See *asébeia* (763), ungodliness; *asebés* (765), impious.

765. Asebés; from the neg. *a*, without, and *sébomai* (4576), to worship, venerate. Basically it means godless, without fear and reverence of God. It does not mean irreligious, but one who actively practices the opposite of what the fear of God demands. *Asebés* is the one characterized by immoral and impious behavior. *Asebés* also occurs in 2 Peter 2:5; 3:7; Jude 1:4, 15. Often opposite of *díkaios* (1342), just (Rom. 4:5; 5:6). Syn.: *hamartōlós* (268), sinful, sinner (Rom. 5:6, 8), and joined with it in 1 Timothy 1:9; 1 Peter 4:18; Jude 1:15. See *asébeia* (763), ungodliness; *asebéō* (764), to act impiously.

766. Asélgeia; lasciviousness (Mark 7:22; 2 Cor. 12:21; Gal. 5:19; Eph. 4:19; 1 Pet. 4:3; Jude 1:4); wantonness (Rom. 13:13; 2 Pet. 2:18), readiness for all pleasure. *Aselgés*, adj., is one who acknowledges no restraints, who does whatever his caprice and unmanageable frowardness dictates. Syn.: *asōtía* (810), wastefulness and riotous excess.

769. Asthéneia; from *a*, without, and *sthenós*, strength. Weakness, sickness (John 5:5; Gal. 4:13). In the NT this word and related words, *asthenés* (772), weak, sick, and *asthenéō* (770), to be of sickness or weakness, are the most common expressions for sickness and are used in the comprehensive sense of the whole man; but it can also refer to a special form of bodily weakness or sickness.

770. Asthenéō; from *asthenés* (772), without strength, powerless, sick. To be weak, infirm, sick (Matt. 10:8; 25:36; Luke 4:40); weak spiritually as in faith (Rom. 4:19; 14:1, 2; 1 Cor. 8:9); weak in riches, poor, indigent (Acts 20:35); weak; destitute of authority, dignity, or power; contemptible (2 Cor. 11:21). Related words: *asthéneia* (769), weakness, sickness; *asthénēma*, the result of weakness.

771. Asthénēma; from *asthenéō* (770), to be weak or powerless. The suffix *-ma* indicates the result of being weak (Rom. 15:1, cf. 2 Cor. 11:29).

772. Asthenés; from the neg. *a*, and *sthenóō* (4599), to strengthen. Basically it means without strength, powerless. In Class. Gr. never used with the meaning of moral weakness, but only in a physical sense, weak, powerless, without ability; so also in 1 Corinthians 12:22, 2 Corinthians 10:10; in 1 Peter 3:7 of the wife as the weaker vessel; in 1 Corinthians 1:25, 27; 4:10 with reference to Christ crucified. Infirm, sick, sickly (Matt. 25:39; Acts 4:9; 5:15, 16), without strength or weak in a spiritual sense, weak with regard to spiritual things (Matt. 26:41; Mark 14:38; Rom. 5:6; 1 Cor. 9:22). Related words: *asthéneia* (769), lack of strength, powerlessness, weakness; *asthenéō* (770), to be weak or powerless, sick, *asthénēma* (771), infirmity.

784. Áspilos; from the neg. *a*, without, and *spílos*, spot. Without spot, free from spot. In 1 Peter 1:19 the *ámōmos* (299) indicates the absence of internal blemish, and *áspilos* that of external spot. See 1 Timothy 6:14;

James 1:27; 2 Peter 3:14. Related words: *ámemptos* (273), blameless; *anégklētos* (410), unaccused; *anepílēptos* (423), unindictable.

786. Áspondos; the absolutely irreconcilable who, being at war, refuses to lay aside his enmity or to listen to terms of reconciliation, implacable, in a state of war (Rom. 1:31; 2 Tim. 3:3). See *asúnthetos* (802), covenant breaker.

790. Astatéō; from the neg. *a*, not, and *státos*, fixed, settled. Derived from *hístēmi* (2476), to stand, be fixed. To be unsettled, have no certain or fixed abode (1 Cor. 4:11).

791. Asteíos; translated lovely; beautiful (Acts 7:20; Heb. 11:23). Derived from *astu*, a city, and came to mean one who dwells in a city and by consequence is well-bred, polite, eloquent, as the inhabitants of cities frequently are in comparison with those of the country. Used only of Moses. The Greeks used to call the opposite of *asteíos*, the urban person, the *agroíkos*, the one who comes from *agrós*, field or countryside. Therefore, *asteíos* came to be assumed as one who is fair to look on and comely, a suggestion of beauty but not generally of a high character. Syn.: *hōraíos* (5611), beautiful. Derived from *hōra*, which basically means hour, indicating the turning point of ones existence, the time when one is at its loveliest and best. The first meaning, however, of *hōraíos* is timely. Thus, *asteíos* and *hōraíos* may mean the same thing, fair or beautiful but they reach that beauty by paths which are entirely different, resting as they do on different images. *Asteíos* belongs to art and to it are attributed the notions of neatness, symmetry, and elegance. *Hōraíos* receives its hour of beauty by nature which may be brief but which constitutes the season of highest perfection. Another syn.: *kalós* (2570), occurs many times in the NT and is usually translated good. It may be used, however, to mean beautiful, but its beauty is contemplated from a point of view which is especially dear to the Greek mind, namely as the harmonious completeness, the balance, proportion and measure of all the parts with one another.

794. Ástorgos; from the priv. *a* (1) without, and the noun *storgē*, family love. Without family love (Rom. 1:31; 2 Tim. 3:3).

801. Asúnetos; without insight, unintelligent (Matt. 15:16; Mark 7:18; Rom. 1:21, 31; 10:19), without *súnesis* (4907), knowledge, understanding. Opposite *sunetós* (4908), prudent.

802. Asúnthetos; Paul uses this word to refer to those who, being in covenant and treaty with others, refuse to abide by these covenants and treaties, faithless (Rom. 1:31). Contrast *áspondos* (786), implacable.

810. Asōtía; extravagant squandering (Eph. 5:18; Titus 1:6; 1 Pet. 4:4) as opposed to *aneleuthería*, stinginess. In the middle stands *eleuthería* (1657), freedom to do as one ought to. An *asōtos*, a prodigal (Luke 15:13), is one who slides easily under the fatal influence of flatterers and the temptations with which he has surrounded himself and spends freely on his own lusts and appetites. *Asōtía* is a dissolute, debauched, profligate manner of living. Contrast *asélgeia* (766), lawless insolence and unmanageable caprice.

812. Ataktéō; from *átaktos* (813), one out of order. To behave irregularly or disorderly (2 Thess. 3:7).

813. Átaktos; from the neg. *a*, and *tétaktai*, perf. pass. of *tássō* (5021), to set in order. Disorderly, irregular. Verb: *ataktéō* (812), to behave irregularly; adv. *átaktōs* (814), irregularly in a disorderly fashion (2 Thess. 3:6, 11).

816. Atenízō; from *atenés*, strained intent. To look fixedly, gaze (Luke 4:20; 22:56; Acts 1:10; 3:4, 12; 6:15; 7:55; 10:4; 11:6; 13:9; 23:1; 2 Cor. 3:7).

819. Atimía; fem. noun from the adj. *átimos* (820), without honor, from the priv. *a* and *timē* (5092), honor. It refers to dishonor, disgrace (Rom. 1:26, shameful passions; 9:21; 1 Cor. 11:14, something improper; 15:43, vileness, dishonor; 2 Cor. 6:8; 11:21; 2 Tim. 2:20, for a dishonorable use; Sept.: Job 12:21; Prov. 11:2; 12:9; 13:18; Jer. 20:11; 23:40). Syn.: *aischúnē* (152), shame; *entropéa* (1791), shame; *aschēmosúnē* (808), unseemliness; *oneidismós* (3680), reproach; *óneidos*

(3681), disgrace; *húbris* (5196), insolence, injury, reproach; *loidoréō* (3058), to heap abuse upon; *blasphēméō* (987), to revile, blaspheme. Ant.: *timē* (5092), value, honor; *dóxa* (1391), glory, honor (John 5:41, 44; 8:54; 2 Cor. 6:8; Rev. 19:7); *kaúchēma* (2745), boasting, glorying; *kaúchēsis* (2746), the act of boasting.

826. Augázō; trans.: to illuminate; intrans.: to shine, appear. In 2 Corinthians 4:4 it means to irradiate, shine forth.

827. Augé; brightness, light, splendor, as used by the Class. Gr. In the NT, the dayspring, daybreak, first appearance of daylight (Acts 20:11). Verb: *augázō* (826), to shine.

829. Authádēs; from *autós* (846), himself, and *hadéō*, to please. One who is pleased with himself and despises others, insolent, surly, the opposite of courteous or affable. A person who obstinately maintains his own opinion or asserts his own rights but is reckless in regard to the rights, feelings, and interests of others. He regulates his life with no respect to others (Titus 1:7; 2 Pet. 2:10). See *philautos* (5367), selfish.

840. Austērós; austere as related to the taste (Luke 19:21, 22). Contrast *sklērós* (4642), related to the touch. Often associated with honor meaning earnest and severe, but not so with *sklērós* which always conveys a harsh, inhuman character (John 6:60).

843. Autokatákritos; from *autós* (846), himself, and *katakrínō* (2632), to condemn. Self-condemned, condemned by his own sentence (Titus 3:11), meaning passing sentence upon himself. This is done either as a voluntarily cutting off of himself from the church by an open revolt, or as rendering himself incapable of the privileges and blessings that belong to the church by renouncing his faith. The result becomes judging or declaring himself unworthy of the blessings tendered by the church.

859. Áphesis; forgiveness, remission, from the verb *aphíēmi* (863), to cause to stand away, to release sins from the sinner. This required Christ's sacrifice as punishment of sin, hence the putting away of sin and the deliverance of the sinner from the power of sin although not from the presence of sin. That will come later after the resurrection when our very bodies will be redeemed (Rom. 8:23). See Matthew 26:28; Mark 3:29; Luke 1:77; 3:3, 4:18; 24:47, Acts 10:43, 13:38 26:18; Ephesians 1:7; Colossians 1:14; Hebrews 9:22; 10:18. Distinguished from *páresis* (3929), the temporary bypassing of sin.

862. Áphthartos; from the priv. *a*, not, and *phthartós* (5349), corruptible. Incorruptible, not capable of corruption. See 1 Corinthians 9:25; 15:52; 1 Peter 1:23. The word is not found in the Sept. In Romans 1:23 Paul calls God *áphthartos*, incorruptible, an attribute of deity that even the heathen recognize. 1 Timothy 1:17 incorrectly renders *áphthartos* as immortal. It should be rendered as incorruptible. Distinguished from *athánatos*, immortal, and as the one having *athanasían* (110), immortality. When predicated of God, *áphthartos* means that He is exempt from the wear, waste and final perishing which characterize the present body of man. Therefore, *phthorá* (5356), corruptibility, is the characteristic of the perishableness of the body of man as presently constituted. This body which is now corruptible will receive God's *aphtharsía* (861), incorruptibility, on the day of the resurrection (Is. 51:6; 1 Cor. 15:52; Heb. 1:10–12). Therefore, the two words *athanasía* (110), immortality, and *aphtharsía*, incorruption (*áphthartos*, incorruptible), are not referring to the body that is going to be done away with. It is something that the believer will receive at the resurrection, and it is not subject to the same kind of deterioration as the present body in which the believer suffers. See *amiantos* (283), undefiled, and *amárantos* (263), unfading.

863. Aphíēmi; from *apó* (575), from, and *híēmi*, to send. To send away, dismiss (Matt. 13:36; Mark 4:36); to emit, send forth as a voice (Mark 15:37); to yield, give up a spirit (Matt. 27:50 referring to Christ's voluntarily giving up of His spirit); to dismiss, put away a wife (1 Cor. 7:11–13); to forsake, leave, (Matt. 4:20,

22; 5:24, 40; 26:56; John 14:18; 16:28, 32): to leave behind after one (Matt. 24:2; Mark 12:19, 20; Luke 19:44) to leave or let alone (Mark 14:6; Luke 13:8); to omit or neglect (Matt. 23:23; Luke 11:42); to permit, suffer, let (Matt. 3:15; 7:4; 8:22; 13:30; 19:14); to remit, forgive debts, sins, or offenses (Matt. 6:12, 14, 15; 9:2, 5). The expression to forgive sins means to remove the sins from another. Only God is said to be able to do this (Mark 2:10). To forgive sins is not to disregard them and do nothing about them, but to liberate a person from their guilt, and their power. We are to ask God to forgive us our sins, remove them away from us so that we do not stand guilty of them or under their power. We are never expected to forgive the sins of others because we have no power to do so, but we are expected to forgive others (Forgive us our debts, as we forgive those who trespass against us or those who are our debtors [Matt. 6:12]). This means that we should do everything in our power to see that the sins of others are removed from them through the grace and power of Jesus Christ.

865. Aphilágathos; from the neg *a*, and *philágathos* (5358), a lover of goodness. A person who despises goodness or good men. Occurs only in 2 Timothy 3:3.

868. Aphístēmi; from *apó* (575), from, and *hístēmi* (2476). to stand, to place. Trans.: to put away, remove, as in Acts 5:37 where the word means to seduce, make disloyal. Intrans.: to withdraw, remove oneself, retire, cease from something (Luke 4:13; 13:27; Acts 5:38; 12:10; 15:38; 19:9; 22:29; 2 Cor. 12:8; 1 Tim. 6:5). In all of the above, the verb is followed by the phrase *apó, tinós*, from someone or something; in Luke 2:37 it is followed by the simple gen. Transferred to moral conduct in 2 Timothy 2:19, it is followed by *apó adikías*, from unrighteousness, and in Hebrews 3:12, from the living God. This latter expression does not mean that they once belonged to God and now they no longer belong to Him, but rather that they stood away from God, never having belonged to Him. The same is true with 1 Timothy 4:1 in which the word is translated as fall away. The word expresses standing alone in contrast to *pisteúō* (4100), to believe. This does not refer to those who had at one time been believers, but to those who refuse to believe, who stand aloof, alone (Heb. 3:12). The word *aphístēmi* is also used in Luke 8:13 in connection with the interpretation of the seed that falls on stony ground. The seed finds a little soil on top of the stone, but it is not enough to take root and so the growth is short lived. When harsh weather comes, there is no root to hold it down. The word *aphistantai* here does not indicate a destruction of the root because there was never one to begin with; rather, the temporary plant existed on the surface. The union with the soil was only an apparent union, never a true foundation with roots capable of holding up the plant.

873. Aphorízō; from *apó* (575), from, and *horízō* (3724), to define. To separate locally (Matt. 13:49; 25:32, cf. Acts 19:9; 2 Cor. 6:17; Gal. 2:12), to separate from or cast out of society as wicked and abominable (Luke 6:22); to separate, select to some office or work (Acts 13:2; Rom. 1:1 Gal. 1:15). The Pharisees, the sect to which Paul belonged before his conversion (Acts 23:6; 26:5; Phil. 3:5), had their name from this word which meant to separate, *aphōrisménoi*, separated ones. This is probably what Paul alludes to in Romans 1:1 where he who was before separated unto the law, or to the study of it, now says of himself that he was separated to the Gospel.

887. Achlús; a thick mist, found only in Acts 13:11. Denotes a collection of heavy vapors which diverts the rays of light by turning them out of their direct course. Hence a certain disorder of the eye is called *achlús* and those who are afflicted with it seem to see through a thick mist or fog. Elymas the Sorcerer was miraculously punished by Paul with a disorder of this kind, previous to his total blindness. Syn.: *skótos* (4655), darkness; *gnóphos* (1105), a thick dark cloud; and *zóphos* (2217), thick darkness resulting from foggy

weather or smoke.

888. Achreíos; from the neg. *a*, and *chreía*, utility, usefulness. One who has been set aside and is no more useful (Matt. 25:30; Luke 17:10).

890. Áchrēstos; from the neg. *a*, and *chrēstós* (5543), profitable. Unprofitable, useless (Phile. 1:11). See also *chrēstótēs* (5544), profitableness.

895. Ápsuchos; from the neg. *a*, without, and *psuché*, soul or the breathing of life. Lifeless (1 Cor. 14:7). In Class. Gr. it means without character, spiritless, cowardly. Ant. *émpsuchos*, possessing a soul, does not occur in the NT.

906. Bállo; to cast off or to bring, to carry. The verb in all its applications retains the idea of impulse. To cast, throw (Matt. 3:10; 4:6, 18; 5:13, 25, 30; John 8:7, 59); to put (Matt. 9:17; Mark 2:22; 7:33; John 5:7; 13:2); to thrust (Rev. 14:16, 19); to strike (Mark 14:65) in an intrans. sense to rush (Acts 27:14); in the pass. perf., to be cast down, lie as upon a bed or the ground (Matt. 8:6, 14; 9:2; Luke 16:20).

907. Baptízō; to immerse, submerge for a religious purpose, baptize (John 1:25). Washing or ablution was frequently by immersion, hence the pass. or mid., *baptízomai*, to wash oneself, be washed, wash, that is, the hands (Mark 7:4; Luke 11:38, cf. Mark 7:3); to baptize or immerse in or wash with water in token of purification from sin and from spiritual pollution (Matt. 3:6, 11; Mark 1:8; Luke 3:16; Acts 2:38; 22:16). In 1 Corinthians 15:29 the expression *hoi baptizómenoi hupér tōn nekrōn*, those who are being baptized for or over the dead. Baptism in those days was a public declaration that the Christian thus giving his testimony for Christ was willing to die for Christ following those who indeed became victims of persecution unto death. Without the resurrection of Christ and the Christian hope being a reality, such a baptism even unto death would be mockery. Therefore, the expression means to succeed into the place of those who are fallen martyrs in the cause of Christ. To baptize in its general signification means to be identified with, as the Israelites were identified with the work and purpose of Moses (1 Cor. 10:2). The baptism in or with the Holy Ghost means the work of Christ through the miraculous effusion of the Holy Spirit upon the apostles and other believers at Pentecost (Acts 1:5), at Caesarea (Acts 10:47; 11:15, 16) at Ephesus (Acts 19:1–7). This is the baptism with the Holy Spirit that John the Baptist spoke of (Matt. 3:11; Mark 1:8; Luke 3:16; John 1:33). Believers are baptized or identified spiritually into the body of Christ, the Church, by one Spirit (1 Cor. 12:13). Figuratively, it also means to be immersed or plunged into a flood or sea, as it were of grievous afflictions and sufferings (Matt. 20:22, 23; Mark 10:38, 39; Luke 12:50).

908. Báptisma; baptism, derived from *báptō*, to dip. The suffix *-ma* indicates the result of the act of dipping (Luke.3:3; 1 Pet. 3:21). Contrast to *baptisis*, the suffix *-is* indicates the act of baptism while *baptismós* (909) with the suffix *-os*, indicates the completed act.

909. Baptismós; washing, from *baptízō* (907), to baptize. In Hebrews 9:10 the word translated various washings is not *baptísmata*, pl. of *báptisma* (baptism), but the pl. of *baptismós*, that is, *baptismoí*, washings, as constituents of the rites of OT law. *Baptismós* denotes the act as a fact, *báptisma* (908) the result of the act; hence the former word is suitable as a designation of the institution (Mark 7:4, 8; Heb. 6:2).

910. Baptistēs; from *baptízō* (907), a baptizer or baptist (Matt. 3:1; 11:11). A name given to John, suggested by the function committed to and exercised by him (Matt. 21:25; Mark 11:30; Luke 20:4; John 1:33).

911. Báptō; to immerse (Luke 16:24; John 13:26). Dye by dipping (Rev. 19:13). As a comp. with the prep., in, *embáptō* (1686), to dip in (Matt. 26:23; Mark 14:20). Deriv.: *baptízō* (907), to baptize.

932. Basileía; from *basileús* (935), king. Royal dominion, kingdom (Matt. 4:8). The kingdom of heaven or of the heavens, a phrase peculiar to Matthew for which the other evangelists use *basileía toú Theoú*, the kingdom of God (Matt. 4:17, cf. Mark 1:15; Matt. 11:11, cf. Matt. 13:11; Matt. 19:14, cf. Mark 10:14). Essentially the two terms mean the same and are interchangeable (Matt. 19:23f.). Spiritually the kingdom of God is within the human heart (Luke 17:21). Both expressions also refer to the prophecies of Daniel 2:44; 7:13f. and denote the everlasting kingdom which God would set up and give to Christ, or the spiritual and eternal kingdom which was to subsist first in more imperfect circumstances on earth, but afterwards to appear complete in the world of glory. In some verses the kingdom of heaven more particularly signifies God's rule within believers while on this earth (Matt. 13:41, 47; 20:1); at other times it indicates only the state of glory (1 Cor. 6:9, 10; 15:50; Gal. 5:21).

934. Basíleios; royal, belonging to, appointed, suitable for the king. Royal priesthood, *basíleion*, neut. (1 Pet. 2:9) suggests a priesthood called to royal dominion or clothed with royal dignity (Rev. 1:6).

935. Basileús; from *básis*, the support, *tou laoú*, of the people: A king, monarch. Applies to God and Christ (Matt. 5:35; 25:34, 40; John 18:37; 1 Tim. 1:17), to men (Matt. 1:6; 2:1; 10:18; 14:9; 1 Pet. 2:13, 17).

936. Basileúō; to be king, to rule (Matt. 2:22; Luke 1:33; 1 Tim. 6:15). Applies to God (Rev. 11:15, 17; 19:6); to Christ (1 Cor. 15:25); those who belong to Christ (Rev. 5:10; 20:4, 6; 22:5). Pauls usage; to reign or have predominance (Rom. 5:14, 17, 21; 6:12).

937. Basilikós; from *basileús* (935), king. Kingly, belonging to a king (John 4:46, 49; Acts 12:20). Befitting a king, of kingly dignity (Acts 12:21; James 2:8).

945. Battologéō; to speak foolishly. Not to be confused with *battarízō*, to stutter. Characterizes *polulogía*, wordiness, much talking (Matt. 6:7) as contrasted to succinct knowledgeable speech, thus foolish speaking or indiscreet vowing in prayer. Much useless speaking without distinct expression of the purpose.

946. Bdélugma; from *bdelússō* or *bdelússomai* (948), to turn away through loathing or disgust, to abhor. An abomination, an abominable thing (Matt. 24:15; Luke 16:15). By a comparison of Matthew 24:15f.; Mark 13:14 and Luke 21:20f., it is plain that the expression the abomination of desolation or that which makes desolate, refers to the desecration of the Jewish places of worship by the Antichrist (Dan. 11:31; 12:11).

947. Bdeluktós; abominable (Titus 1:16). That which is an abomination to God. Does not occur in Class. Gr. and not to be confused with *bdelurós*, shameless disgusting.

948. Bdelússō; or *bdelússomai*, to render foul, from *bdéō*, to stink. To cause to be abhorred, turn oneself away from a stench, detest (Rom. 2:22; Rev. 21:8). Noun: *bdélugma* (946), an abomination (Rev. 17:4, 5). Adj.: *bdeluktós* (947), abominable.

949. Bébaios; firm, from *baínō*, to go. Fixed, sure, certain. Figuratively, that upon which one may build, rely or trust. In the NT not used of persons but objects (Heb. 6:19), that which does not fail or waver, immovable, and on which one may rely. See Romans 4:16; Galatians 3:15; Hebrews 2:2; 9:17. Used as a subj. in 2 Corinthians. 1:7; Hebrews 3:6, 14. Syn.: *alēthés* (227), true; *asphalḗs* (804), safe, sure; *pistós* (4103), faithful, trustworthy. Equivalent to *stereós* (4731), fast, firm, hard.

950. Bebaióō; to make firm or reliable so as to warrant security and inspire confidence, to strengthen, make true, fulfill (Mark 16:20; Rom. 15:8; 1 Cor. 1:6; Heb. 2:3). In the NT used with the personal obj. and signifies confirming a persons salvation, preservation in a state of grace. Syn.: *stērízō* (4741), to steadfastly set (1 Thess. 3:13; 1 Pet. 5:10).

951. Bebaíōsis; ratification, confirmation, corroboration (Phil. 1:7; Heb. 6:16). See *bebaióō* (950), to make firm or reliable.

952. Bébēlos; profane, void of religion, piety. Applied to persons (1 Tim. 1:9; Heb. 12:16). From *baínō*, to go, and *bēlós*, a threshold. Unhallowed, opposite of *hierós* (2413), sacred. *Bébēlos* lacks all relationship or affinity to God.

953. Bebēlóō; to profane, to cross the threshold (Matt. 12:5; Acts 24:6). See *bébēlos* (952), profane.

971. Biázō; or *biázomai*, to overpower, compel. In the NT only in Matthew 11:12; Luke 16:16. In Matthew

used in the pass., meaning the kingdom of God is overpowered. In the mid. voice, meaning presses himself in with energy (Luke 16:16).

976. Bíblos; the Egyptian papyrus from which paper was made. A book, roll, volume, as of the prophet Isaiah, of Johns Gospel, of the law (Mark 12:26; Luke 3:4); a scroll, a bill as of divorcement, which according to the Talmudists was always to consist of twelve lines, no more, no less. A catalog, an account (Matt. 1:1). The Book of Life is designated as the book in which the names of the redeemed are written (Phil. 4:3; Rev. 13:8; 20:15; 22:19). In Revelation 3:5 the blotting out of a name from the Book of Life is presented as an utter impossibility with a double negative *ou* (3756) and *mē* (3361). If it were possible then the Lord Jesus would admit He was wrong in recording the name in the first place. See *biblíon* (975), a diminutive of *bíblos*.

979. Bíos; life, but not as in *zōḗ* (2222), life, in which is meant the element or principle of the spirit and soul. *Bíos*, from which biography is derived, refers to duration, means, and manner of life. See Mark 12:44; Luke 8:14, 43; 15:12, 30; 21:4; 1 Timothy 2:2; 2 Timothy 2:4; 1 Peter 4:3; 1 John 2:16; 3:17.

987. Blasphēméō; to blaspheme, revile; derived either from *bláptō* (984), to hurt, and *phḗmē* (5345), reputation, fame, or from *bállō* (906). to cast and *phḗmai*, pl. dat. of *phḗmē*. To hurt the reputation or smite with reports or words, speak evil of, rail (Rom. 3:8; 1 Cor. 4:13; 10:30; Titus 3:2). To speak with impious irreverence concerning God Himself, or what stands in some peculiar relation to Him, to blaspheme, a transliteration of the Gr. word (Matt. 9:3; 26:65; 27:39; Mark 3:29; Luke 22:65; Acts 13:45; Titus 2:5). In the NT generally syn. with *oneidízō* (3679), revile, and *loidoréō* (3058), to reproach (Matt. 27:39; Mark 15:29; Luke 22:65; 23:39; Rom. 3:8; 14:16; 1 Cor. 4:13; Titus 3:2; 2 Pet. 2:10; Jude 1:8); especially to revile God and divine things (Rev. 13:6). Reviling against the Holy Spirit (Mark 3:29; Luke 12:10), means to resist the convicting power of the Holy Spirit unto repentance. Deriv.: *blasphēmía* (988), blasphemy; *blásphēmos* (989), a blasphemer.

988. Blasphēmía; blasphemy, abuse against someone. Denotes the very worst type of slander, mentioned in Matthew 15:19 with false witness; wounding ones reputation by evil reports, evil speaking. See Mark 7:22; Ephesians 4:31; Colossians 3:8; 1 Timothy 6:4; 2 Peter 2:11; Jude 1:9, *blásphēmos* (989), a blasphemer. Used especially in a religious sense; blasphemy toward or against God (Rev. 13:6); against the Holy Spirit (Luke 12:10 the verb *blasphēméō*, [987]) including the resistance against the convincing power of the Holy Spirit.

989. Blásphēmos; derived probably from *bláx*, sluggish, slow, stupid. To be abusive, reviling, destroying ones good name (2 Tim. 3:2); blasphemous, a blasphemer (Acts 6:11, 13; 1 Tim. 1:13). See the subst. *blasphēmía* (988), blaspheming abuse against someone.

991. Blépō; to see, of bodily vision (Matt. 11:4); of mental vision (Matt. 13:13, 14). Stresses the perception of the seeing one. To perceive (Matt. 13:13); to take heed (Matt. 24:4; Mark 13:23, where it indicates greater vividness than *horáō* [3708], expressing a more intent, earnest contemplation); to beware as a warning (Mark 8:15; 12:38; Acts 13:40; Phil. 3:2; Col. 2:8). Deriv.: *emblépō* (1689), earnest looking (Matt. 6:26; 19:26; Mark 8:25; Luke 20:17; John 1:36; Acts 1:11); *anablépō* (308), to look up (Matt. 14:19; Mark 8:24), to recover sight (Matt. 11:5; 20:34; John 9:11); *anáblepsis* (309), recovering sight (Luke 4:18); *periblépō* (4017) with *peri*, around, to look around (Mark 3:5; Luke 6:10); *apoblépō* (578), to look away from all else to one object, to look steadfastly (Heb. 11:26); *epiblépō* (1914), used of favorable regard (Luke 1:48).

1006. Bóskō; to feed the sheep, swine (Matt. 8:30, 33; Mark 5:11, 14; Luke 8:32, 34; 15:15; John 21:15, 17). Contrast *poimaínō* (4165), to shepherd, tend; involving much more than feeding (Matt. 2:6; Luke 17:7; John 21:16; Acts 20:28; 1 Cor. 9:7; 1 Pet. 5:2; Jude 1:12; Rev. 2:27; 7:17; 12:5; 19:15).

1012. Boulḗ; will, project, intention, as the result of reflections; counsel, decree, aim, or estimation, as it denotes deliberation and reflection; the assembly of the council. In Mod. Gr., parliament is called *boulḗ*. The will (*boulḗ*) of God refers only to God's own act, His saving purpose. Distinguished from *thélēma* (2307) which stands also for the commanding and executing will of God. *Thélēma* signifies the will which urges on to action, while *boulḗ*, the counsel preceding the resolve, the decision. Therefore, Ephesians 1:11 should be translated according to the decision or plan of His will. The Apostle not only gives prominence to the absolute freedom of the decision of the divine will, but calls attention to the saving plan lying at the basis of the saving will as it manifests itself. In some instances *boulḗ* and *thélēma* are perfectly syn. *Boulḗ* is also used to denote the divine decree lying at the basis of the history of redemption (Luke 7:30; Acts 2:23; 4:28; 13:36; 20:27; Heb. 6:17). Occurs also in Luke 23:51; Acts 5:38; 27:12, 42; 1 Cor. 4:5.

1013. Boúlēma; the thing willed, the intention. Contrast *thélēma* (2307), which is not only a will or a wish, but also the execution of it or the desire to execute it. *Thélēma* gives prominence to the element of wish or inclination (Acts 27:43; Rom. 9:19).

1014. Boúlomai; to will, designating an inner decision or thinking (Matt. 1; 19; Phile. 1:13; Jude 1:15), while *thélō* (2309) denotes a more active resolution urging on to action.

1021. Bradús; slow in time as opposite of *tachús* (5036), swift or quick. Implies no moral fault or blame. In the three occasions used, it has a good meaning (Luke 24:25; James 1:19 twice). The subst. *bradútēs* (1022), slackness, is found in 2 Peter 3:9. Syn.: *nōthrós* (3576), sluggish, found only in Hebrews 6:12; *argós* (692), inactive.

1025. Bréphos; babe, from *phérbos* by transposition from *phérbō*, to feed, nourish, for babes are nourished in the womb and when born require frequent nourishment; an unborn child (Luke 1:41, 44); a newborn child, an older infant (Luke 2:12, 16; 18:15); .

1041. Bōmós; an idol altar (Acts 17:23). Contrast *thusiastḗrion* (2379), an altar of the true God.

1051. Gála; milk (1 Cor. 9:7). Figuratively, the sincere and sweet word of Christ by which believers grow in grace and are nourished to life eternal (1 Pet. 2:2). The rudiments of Christianity are to nourish the babes in Christ (1 Cor. 3:2; Heb. 5:12, 13).

1062. Gámos; marriage, marriage feast (Luke 14:8; John 2:1, 2); the actual joining of a husband and wife (Heb. 13:4). Used also in the pl., *gámoi* (Luke 12:36; Matt. 22:2–4, 9, alternatively with the sing., vv. 8, 10–12; 25:10). The expression The wedding feast of the Lamb (Rev. 19:7, 9), like the parables (Matt. 22:2ff.; 25:1–10), rests upon the relation of God to Israel and points back thereto as it is presented in Isaiah 54:4ff.; Ezekial 16:7ff.; Hosea 2:19. This relationship of Jehovah to Israel was accomplished in the Messianic time, to which the expression in John 3:29, and perhaps Matthew 9:15, points. This relationship of God to His people in the NT is Christ's relation to His redeemed Church (2 Cor. 11:2; Eph. 5:26, 27; Rev. 21:2; 22:17). The marriage of the Lamb is the consummation of salvation to be ushered in by the *parousía* (3952), the appearing of the Lord.

1067. Géenna; hell, the place or state of the lost and condemned (Matt. 5:29, 30; 10:28, cf. Matt. 23:15; James 3:6). Represents the Hebr. *gē hinnōm*, the valley of Hinnom (also called *gē ben-hinnôm*, the valley of the son of Hinnom, see Josh. 15:8; 18:16) and the corresponding Aramaic word, *gēhinnam*. Many times the word *hádēs* (86) is wrongly translated as hell or grave. Terms descriptive of hell are found in Matthew 13:42; 25:46; Philippians 3:19; 2 Thessalonians 1:9; Hebrews 10:39; 2 Peter 2:17; Jude 1:13; Revelation 2:11; 19:20; 20:6, 10, 14; 21:8. See also *tartaróō* and *tártaros* (5020), to cast down to hell.

1074. Geneá; a coll. noun whose original meaning was generation, that is, a multitude of contemporaries. In NT Gr. *genea;* literally means space of time, circle of time, which only in a derived sense signifies the meaning of a time, a race; then generally in the sense of affinity of communion based upon the sameness of stock. Race or posterity (Acts 8:33). Generation (Matt. 1:17), occurs with special reference to the physical or moral circumstances, speaking of an age or time referring to the spiritual state of society at that time (Heb. 3:10, cf. Luke 7:31; 11:31; Acts 13:36). The connection alone must decide whether the sense is limited to the state of society at a certain time or to race or stock. The word *geneá* in Matthew 24:34 meant the type of Jew with whom Jesus was conversing during that particular time (Matt. 21:23; 23:29). He was telling them that this generation or type, such as the Sadducees and Pharisees of that day, would not pass away until all these things occurred and until His coming again in His *parousía* (3952), Second Coming. He was prophesying the destruction of their nation (Matt. 24:15–28).

1075. Genealogéō; or *genealogéomai*, to make a genealogical register. To trace ones descent (Heb. 7:6).

1076. Genealogía; genealogy. The expression in 1 Timothy 1:4 and Titus 3:9 denotes busying oneself about traditions of the past, based upon the slightest historical hints. This diverted the heart from God's truth and, as it appears to imply in Titus 1:10, was especially the practice of Jewish false teachers. These Jews were turning the entire historical substance into mere myth, claiming that whether something occurred or not was unimportant, but what one felt about it was important, thus resorting to a subjectivism without objective reality. The Jews studied genealogies while the Greeks studied mythology (fables). Since Timothy was partly Greek and partly Jewish, Paul referred to both myths and genealogies. One was the Greek manipulation and the other was the Jewish manipulation of truth in Scripture. Since these did not represent belief based on fact, they were useless.

1078. Génesis; in the act., origin, rise. From the verb *gínomai* (1096), to form. Contrast *génnēsis* (1083), birth (Matthew 1:18, the becoming of Christ as a human being) with *génesis*, origination, the beginning of existence. In John 1:14 And the Word became (*egéneto* from *gínomai*, to become) flesh. He began His life in the body at Bethlehem, but this was not His origination as a personality. He had been as *Lógos* (3056), Word, spiritual, immaterial (John 4:24) prior to His becoming flesh (man). In the pass., *génesis* means race, lineage, equivalent to *geneá*, meaning genealogy, book of genealogy (Matt. 1:1). It also means generation, kind, species, as well as being, existence, in which latter sense used in James 1:23; 3:6, meaning the aspect, the form of His being.

1080. Gennáō; to beget, pass. voice, to be born, mainly used of men begetting children (Matt. 1:2–16); more rarely of women begetting children (Luke 1:13, 57; 23:29; John 16:21) Syn.: *tíktō* (5088), deliver. Used allegorically (Gal. 4:24); of conception (Matt. 1:20); of the act of God in the birth of Jesus (Acts 13:33; Heb. 1:5; 5:5; all quoting Ps. 2:7, none of which indicate that Christ became the Son of God at His birth). Metaphorically, of God's divine nature imparted in the believer (John 3:3, 5, 7; 1 John 2:29; 3:9; 4:7; 5:1, 4, 18); of a Gospel preacher used as a means in the impartation of spiritual life (1 Cor. 4:15; Phile. 1:10); of the animal nature of the unregenerate (2 Pet. 2:12); of engendering strife (2 Tim. 2:23). Deriv.: *anagennáō* (313), to beget again, and the composite *gennáō ánōthen* (509), to beget from above.

1089. Geúō; or *geúomai*, to give or receive a taste. Usually used in the mid. voice, to taste, to try or perceive the taste (Matt. 27:34; Luke 14:24; John 2:9; Acts 23:14; Col. 2:21). In later writings it meant to get or take food (Acts 10:10; 20:11). Metaphorically, to have or receive a sensation or impression of anything, to experience anything (Heb. 6:4, 51; Pet. 2:3). Used in combination with death, to taste or to experience death (Matt. 16:28; Mark 9:1; Luke 9:27; John 8:52; Heb. 2:9). When used in this connection, it gives prominence to what is really involved in dying.

1093. Gḗ; earth. The earth, land, or ground considered

as fit or unfit for producing fruit (Matt. 13:5, 8, 23; Mark 4:28, cf. Heb. 6:7); the dry land or ground, as distinguished from the waters (Luke 5:11; John 21:8, 9, 11); a particular land, tract, or country (Matt. 2:5, 20f.; 4:15; 9:26); the globe of earth and water as distinguished either from the material or from the holy heavens (Matt. 5:18, 35; 6:10; 16:19; 24:35; 28:18; Mark 13:31; Luke 21:33; Acts 17:24; 1 Cor. 8:5; Eph. 1:10; Col. 1:16, 20; Heb. 12:26); the earth or ground in general (Matt. 10:29; 25:18). The earth which is given to man stands in a relation of dependence to heaven, which is the dwelling place of God (Ps. 2:4; Matt. 5:35), for which reason the question always is How will that· which occurs on earth be estimated in heaven"? (See Matt. 9:6; 16:19; 18:18f.; 23:9; Mark 2:10; Luke 5:24). Since earth stands in antithesis to heaven, it is associated with the idea of emptiness, weakness, sinfulness, and does not correspond with the wisdom and power of God (Matt. 6:10; Mark 9:3; John 3:31; 1 Cor. 15:47; Rev. 14:3; 17:5). Thus the earth is the sphere of the *kósmos* (2889), world, designating the people dwelling on earth; *aiṓn* (165), age, *hoútos*, this age, generation or group of people holding on to earthly principles (see Matt. 6:19; Phil. 2:10; 1 Tim. 6:17, 19; Heb. 11:13; Rev. 5:3, 13).

1096. Gínomai; or *gígnomai*, to become, from *geinṓ* or *genṓ*, to form. To be made or formed (Matt. 4:3; John 1:12, 14; 2:9; Acts 26:28); to be made or created from nothing (John 1:3, 10; Heb. 11:3); to occur, come to pass (Matt. 1:22; 21:4; 24:6); to be or become in general (Matt. 5:45; 6:16; 8:26; Luke 12:40); to be done, performed (Matt. 6:10; Acts 4:16); to be fulfilled, accomplished (Matt. 5:18; 6:10; 1 Cor. 15:45); of a place followed by *en* or *eis*, in, to be in or at (Matt. 26:6; Mark 9:33; 2 Tim. 1:17); to come to oneself, to have recovered ones senses or understanding (Acts 12:11). *Mḗ*, not, *génoito*, to be, may it not be (Luke 20:16; Rom. 3:4, 6, 31).

1097. Ginṓskō; or *gignṓskō*, usually to know experientially as contrasted to *oída* or *eídō* (1492), usually to know intuitively. Formed from the obsolete verb *gnóō*, to know, by adding the reduplication *gi-* as a prefix. It means to know (Mark 7:24; 9:30; Luke 2:43); to perceive (Mark 5:29; Luke 8:46); to know, be acquainted with a person (Matt. 25:24; Acts 19:15; 2 Cor. 5:16, cf. John 1:10); to know, understand (Matt. 12:7; 13:11; 16:3; Mark 4:13; Acts 8:30); to know, be conscious of (2 Cor. 5:21); discern, distinguish (Matt. 12:33; Luke 6:44; John 13:35); approve, acknowledge with approbation (Matt. 7:23; Rom. 7:15; 2 Tim. 2:19); to have sexual relations (Matt. 1:25; Luke 1:34); to think, be aware of (Matt. 24:50; Luke 12:46); as a part., *ginṓskōn*, thinking, reflecting upon, being mindful of (Rom. 6:6; 2 Pet. 1:20).

1098. Gleúkos; from *glukús* (1099), sweet. Musk, sweet wine (Acts 2:13). Some believe that it is what distills of its own accord in the grapes. It was mentioned at Pentecost (Acts 2:13) indicating that the ancients probably had a method of preserving the sweetness, and by consequence the strongly inebriating quality of the *gleúkos*, for a long time. In instituting the Lord's Supper, the Lord speaks of the contents of the cup as neither wine, *oínos* (3631), nor *gleúkos*, but as the *génnēma* (1081), fruit, *tēs ampélou* (288), of the vine (Matt. 26:29; Mark 14:25; Luke 22:18). The word *génnēma* also means offspring (Matt. 3:7; 12:34). But in connection with *ámpelos*, vine, it means fruit or produce.

1100. Glóssa; tongue, the tongue of a man (Mark 7:33, 35; Luke 16:24; 1 Pet. 3:10); used for the fiery tongues appearing upon the apostles on the day of Pentecost (Acts 2:3); a tongue, language (Acts 2:4, 11; 10:46); people of different languages (Rev. 5:9; 7:9; 14:6); a foreign or strange language which one has not learned but yet is enabled to speak as a result of the supernatural intervention of the Holy Spirit, particularly in what the NT calls the baptism in the Holy Spirit by Jesus Christ. See *baptízō* (907); *báptisma* (908). The historic events of speaking in foreign tongues or dialects came with the Jews at Pentecost in Acts 2:4, 11, the Gentiles at Caesarea in Acts 10:46,

and the disciples of John the Baptist at Ephesus in Acts 19:6. These were all languages unknown to the speakers, spoken at that particular time in demonstration of their being baptized into the body of Jesus Christ (1 Cor. 12:13). These are the same languages demonstrated as *charísmata* (the results of the grace of God in the human heart) spoken of by Paul in 1 Corinthians 12:10, 30; 14:5, 6, 18, 22, 39. In 1 Corinthians 14:6, 18, Paul refers to speaking in *glóssais*, languages or tongues. He meant the languages which he already knew or the ones that he was enabled to speak by the Holy Spirit when and if so needed. The pl. *glóssai* with a sing. pron. or subj. refers to known, understandable languages (Acts 2:3, 8, 11) and not to an unknown tongue as practiced in Corinth. But even when utilizing these, one must make sure he is understood by those who hear him otherwise he will be taken as a maniac, *maínomai* (3105), be beside oneself, mad (1 Cor. 14:23). Whenever the word *glóssa* in the sing. with a sing. subj. or pron. is used, translated in the KJV as unknown tongue (1 Cor. 14:2, 4, 13, 14, 19, 26, 27), it refers to the Corinthian practice of speaking in ecstatic utterances not comprehended by anyone and therefore, not an ordinarily spoken language. In 1 Corinthians 14:26 it may refer to a language foreign to the hearers and uninterpreted.

1105. Gnóphos; from *néphos* (3509), a cloud. A thick dark cloud (Heb. 12:18). Syn.: *skótos* (4655), darkness; *zóphos* (2217), darkness, foggy weather, smoke which is used to imply infernal darkness and occurs only in 2 Peter 2:4, 17; Jude 1:6, 13; *achlús* (887), a thick mist or a fog.

1106. Gnṓmē; the subst. of the verb *gnṓnai* and *ginṓskō* (1097), to discern, to know. Generally meaning capacity of judgment, faculty of discernment as far as conduct is determined. In 1 Corinthians 1:10 used in conj. with *noús*; (3563), mind. These two, although connected, must be distinguished. The distinction cannot be that of the organ being *noús*, mind, and *gnṓmē*, its function. *Gnṓmē* is discernment which determines conduct. *Noús*, mind, refers only to thinking without direction; signifies consciousness, mind, opinion, thought. *Gnṓmē* can be syn. with will (Rev. 17:13 which must be taken in conj. with v. 17, meaning God's direction, inclination). *Gnṓmē*, when referring to pleasure or purpose means decision (Acts 20:3); judgment, conviction, opinion in the sense of *dokéō* (1380), to think, to recognize, indicating purely subjective opinion (1 Cor. 7:25, 40; 2 Corinthians 8:10 where Paul gives an entirely subjective view of the matter. By using this word, Paul indicates that he expects the counsel he gives will be recognized without a command on his part.).

1107. Gnōrízō; to know, from *ginóskō* (1097), to know or perceive. Except for 2 Cor. 8:1; Eph. 6:21; Col. 4:7, 9, used mainly in the NT of the revelation of God's saving purpose; also of apostolic activity (1 Cor. 12:3; 15:1; Gal. 1:11; 2 Pet. 1:16); of divinely communicated things (Rom. 16:26; Eph. 3:3, 5, 10; 6:19; Col. 1:27); of God making His power known (Rom. 9:22, 23); of Christ's work in revealing (John 15:15; 17:26); used in the pass. in Romans 16:26 and Philippians 4:6 of communications made to God.

1108. Gnṓsis; knowledge, from *ginóskō* (1097), to know experientially. Present and fragmentary knowledge as contrast with *epígnōsis* (1922), clear and exact knowledge which expresses a more thorough participation on the part of the subject. Present intuitive knowledge is expressed by the verb *oída* or *eídō* (1492) (Luke 1:77; 11:52; Rom. 11:33; 1 Cor. 13:2; Col. 2:3; 2 Pet. 1:5, 6).

1109. Gnṓstēs; one who knows (Acts 26:3). Deriv.: *kardiognṓstēs* (2589), knower of the heart.

1110. Gnōstós; from *ginóskō* (1097), to know, perceive, learn, recognize. Known (Acts 1:19; 2:14; 15:18); pl., known to one, acquaintances (Luke 2:44; 23:49, cf. John 18:15, 16); knowable, which may be known (Rom. 1:19). The Greeks used it as a syn. of *noētós*, from *noéō* (3539), to know with ones mind, hence that which could be known, capable of being known. The question is whether to take the phrase in Romans

1:19, *to gnōstón*, that which is known of God and manifest in them with the same sense. The gen. *tou Theoú*, of God. is not gen. partitive here, but gen. poss. It is not what is knowable or known of God, but rather God, as He is knowable or known. Thus it refers to the fact that God is knowable or known by man because of the demonstration of His power in His creation. Here reference is made not to the knowledge possessed by God, but to our knowledge of God. Ant.: *ágnōstos* (57), unknown (Acts 17:23).

1121. Grámma; that which is written, a letter of the alphabet, a book, letter, bond. A letter or character of literal writing (Luke 23:38, cf. 2 Cor. 3:7; Gal. 6:11); a writing (John 5:47); a bill, an account (Luke 16:6, 7); the letter of the law, that is, the literal sense and outward ordinances of the law (Rom. 2:27, 29; 7:6; 2 Cor. 3:6, 7); a letter, an epistle (Acts 28:21); pl.: *grámmata* with the definite art. *ta*, letters, learning, erudition gained from books (John 7:15; Acts 26:24); *hierá* (holy), *grámmata*, letters, the Holy Scriptures (2 Tim. 3:15, cf. John 5:47). *Ta hierá grámmata*, an expression distinct from *hē graphḗ* (the writing), describing them as the object of study or knowledge; whereas *graphḗ* (1124) describes them as an authority (2 Tim. 3:15). It cannot be proved that *ta grámmata*, the writings, without the qualifying word *hierá*, holy, means Holy Scriptures; there is no sufficient reason for taking it thus in John 7:15 where it occurs without the article: How knoweth this man letters, having never learned? The expression means knowledge contained in writings, learning, or usually the elements of knowledge. At a later period it meant science. The Jews simply asked, How has this man attained knowledge which he has not acquired by pursuing the usual course of study? The word in Acts 26:24 means, Thou hast studied too much. In the letters of Paul we have the antithesis between *grámma*, letter, and *pneúma* (4151), spirit (Rom. 2:29; 7:6; 2 Cor. 3:6). *Grámma* denotes the law in its written form whereby the relation of the law to the man is the more inviolably established (Rom. 2:27; 2 Cor. 3:7). Thus the antithesis is between the external, fixed, and governing law, and the *pneúma*, the spirit, meaning the inner, effective, energizing and divine principle of life (Rom. 7:6).

1122. Grammateús; from *grámma* (1121), a writing, letter. A scribe or writer. Such was in public service among the Greeks and acted as the reader of legal and state papers. In the Septuagint *grammateús* is frequently used for a political officer who assisted kings or magistrates by keeping written accounts of public acts and occurrences or royal revenues (2 Kgs. 12:10). Used for one skilled in the Mosaic law (Jer. 36:26; Ezra 7:6, 11, 12, 21), and commonly used in the same sense in the NT (Matt. 2:4; 13:52; 23:34; 1 Cor. 1:20); especially for those who sat in Moses seat (Matt. 23:2, 3) explaining the law in the schools and synagogues. Thus it became syn. with public instructors (Matt. 2:4, cf. Neh. 8:4). In the NT, scribes are frequently joined with Pharisees and probably many were of that sect (Acts 23:9). The civil magistrate of Ephesus, a town clerk, a recorder or chancellor (Acts 19:35). Scribes were well versed in the law, that is, in the Holy Scriptures, and expounded them (Matt. 7:29; 17:10; 23:2, 13; Mark 1:22). They were supposed to be acquainted with and the interpreters of God's saving purpose (Matt. 13:52; 23:34), but in the time of Jesus they opposed His saving purpose. Where they appear clothed with special authority or side by side with those in authority (Matt. 2:4; 20:18; 23:2; 26:57; Mark 14:1; Luke 22:2, 66; 23:10), they can hardly be regarded as in legal possession of such authority. Their authority seems to have been granted to them in a general way only by virtue of their occupation (Matt. 13:52; John 7:15) and did not have decisive power. Authorities allied themselves with them for the sake of the respect attached to them due to their knowledge of the law. Syn.: *nomikós* (3544), lawyer (Matt. 22:35) *nomodidáskalos* (3547), teacher of the law (Luke 5:17).

1124. Graphḗ; used in the pl. in the NT for the Holy Scriptures, or in the sing. for a part of it (Matt. 21:42; 22:29;

Mark 12:10; 15:28; Rom. 1:2); in 2 Timothy 3:16 called God-breathed or inspired. Matthew 26:56 and Romans 16:26 have reference to the prophetic Scriptures within the totality of Scriptures. The Holy Scriptures are everywhere termed as *hē*, the, *graphḗ*, Scripture, giving it authoritativeness. The Scripture may refer to a single text (Mark 12:10; Luke 4:21: John 19:37; Acts 1:16; 8:35) or to the whole (John 2:22; 10:35).

1125. Gráphō; primarily to engrave, write (Mark 10:4; Luke 1:63; John 21:25; Gal. 6:11; 2 Thess. 3:17). The ancient Greeks equated *gráphō* with *xéō*, to carve. They carved figures with meaning on wooden tablets and later replaced these when letters were developed. The engraved tablet was covered with another, and being tied together and sealed, constituted the form of an ancient letter. The Sept. several times applies the word in this sense of engraving, carving, or cutting out (1 Kgs. 6:29; Is. 22:16, cf. Job. 19:23, 24). From Exodus 31:18; 32:16; 2 Corinthians 3:7 we deduce that the first literal writing was of this kind. Thus originally the word meant to cut in, make an incision. Later, with the invention of the parchment and paper, it came to mean to write, to delineate literal characters on a tablet, parchment or paper (Luke 1:63; 16:6, 7; John 8:6; 19:19; Acts 23:25; 3 John 13). It also came to mean to describe in writing (John 1:45; Rom. 10:5); write a law, command in writing, as a legislator (Mark 12:19). The writing of names in heaven emphasizes that God remembers and will not forget, since by writing, the name of a person is fixed The use of *gégraptai*, it is written, in the perf. tense refers absolutely to what is found written in Holy Scripture and denotes legislative act or enactment. In the sphere of revelation the written records hold this authoritative position, and *gégraptai* always implies an appeal to the indisputable and legal authority of the passage quoted (Matt. 4:4, 6, 7, 10; 11:10). It is completed by additions such as in the law (Luke 2:23; 10:26); in the book of the words of Isaiah (Luke 3:4); in the prophets (John 6:45).

1127. Grēgoreúō; from *egeírō*, to rouse. To watch, to refrain from sleep. It was finally transferred in meaning from the physical to the moral religious sphere (Matt. 26:38, 40, 41). It denotes attention to God's revelation or to the knowledge of salvation (Mark 13:34; 1 Thess. 5:6); a mindfulness of threatening dangers which, with conscious earnestness and an alert mind , keeps one from all drowsiness and all slackening in the energy of faith and conduct (Matt. 26:40; Mark 14:38; 1 Thess. 5:6; 1 Pet. 5:8). It denotes the caution needed against the anxiety resulting from the fear of the loss of ones salvation (1 Cor. 16:13; Col. 4:2; Rev. 16:15); the care for the salvation and preservation of others (Acts 20:31; Rev. 3:2, 3). In His eschatological discourses, the Lord demands constant watching and preparation for the decisive day of His appearing, *parousía* (Matt. 24:42, 43; 25:13; Mark 13:34, 35, 37; Luke 12:37, 39). It is equivalent to be ready of Luke 12:40. It is used only once of life as the opposite of sleeping, *katheúdō* (2518), to die (1 Thess. 5:10) Syn.: *agrupnéō* (69), keep awake.

1131. Gumnós; naked, stark naked (Mark 14:51, 52, cf. Rev. 17:16); comparatively naked or ill-dressed (Matt. 25:36, 38, 43, 44; James 2:15, cf. 2 Cor. 5:3); naked or stripped of the upper garment (John 21:7; Acts 19:16); naked, open, uncovered, manifest (Heb. 4:13, cf. Job 26:6); naked, bare, mere (1 Cor. 15:37); naked of spiritual clothing, that is, the imputed righteousness of faith (Rev. 3:17; 16:15).

1132. Gumnótēs; from *gumnós* (1131), naked. Nakedness, destitute of convenient or decent clothing (Rom. 8:35; 2 Cor. 11:27); spiritual nakedness, being destitute of the spiritual clothing of the righteousness which is by faith (Rev. 3:18).

1139. Daimonízomai; (pass.) from *daimónion* (1140), little demon, and *daímōn* (1142), demon. The Class. Gr. form: *daimonáō*, to be violently possessed by or be in the power of a demon. NT meanings: possessed by a demon or a devil (Matt. 8:28, 33), having a demon (John 10:21). The *daimonizómenoi*, those violently possessed by demons, are distinguished from other sick folk in Matthew 4:24; Mark 1:32.

1142. Daímōn; demon (Matt. 8:31; Mark 5:12; Luke 8:29; Rev. 16:14 TR; 18:2 TR). Elsewhere in the NT instead of *ho daímon,* we have the diminutive *to daimónion* (1140), in the neut. but with the same sense. The Greeks gave the word *daímōn* the same meaning as god. What they meant, however, by the word is still a conjecture. They may have related a demon with *daémon* as knowing or being experienced in a thing, or they may have derived the word from *daíomai,* to assign or award ones lot in life (*diaítētai kai dioikḗtai tōn ánthrōpōn*), the arbitrators or umpires and governors of men. They conceived of them as those who rule and direct human affairs, not as a personality, but primarily as a destructive power. Thus they called the happy or lucky person *eudaímōn,* one who is favored by this divine power. The adj. *daimónios* was used for one who demonstrated power irrespective of whether it was saving or destructive. The Tragic Poets use *daímōn* to denote fortune or fate, frequently bad fortune, but also good fortune if the context represents it as such. Thus, *daímōn* is associated with the idea of gloomy and sad destiny independent of man, coming upon and prevailing over him. Consequently, *daímōn* and *túchē,* luck, are often combined, and the doctrine of demons developed into signifying either a beneficent or evil power in the lives of people. The diminutive *to daimónion,* being abstract and generally less used than *daímōn,* fell into disuse as a belief in or doctrine of demons became more defined and concrete. On the contrary, n NT Gr. the use of *daimónion* prevailed. Strange gods, on account of their remote relations in dark mysterious essence, were called *daimonia* (not *daimones*) instead of *theoí,* gods. The nature of the evil Spirits thus designated being obscure to human knowledge and alien to human life. The Sept. does not use *daímōn.* In Plutarch and Xenophon, the verb *daimonáō* (in the NT *daimonízomai* [1139]) meant to be deranged, a syn. of *paraphronéō* (3912), to act insanely. *Daímōn* or *daimónion* was applied especially to evil spirits (Ps. 78:49; Prov. 16:14) They were considered unclean spirits (Mark 5:12; 3:22, 30; Luke 4:33; 8:2, 29; Rev. 16:13, 14; 18:2) wicked or evil spirits. They make their appearance in connection with Satan (Matt. 12:24ff.; Mark 3:22ff.; Luke 10:17, 18; 11:18, cf. Matt. 9:34; 12:24, 26; Mark 3:22; Luke 11:15). These are put into opposition with God (1 Cor. 10:20, 21; as also in Deut. 32:17, cf. 1 Tim. 4:1; James 2:19; Rev. 9:20). While in some parts of the NT, *daimónia* (1140), demons, are viewed in their morally destructive influence (1 Cor. 10:20f.; 1 Tim. 4:1; Rev. 9:20; 16:14), they appear in the Gospel as special powers of evil, as spirits (Luke 10:17, 20) in the service of Satan (Matt. 12:26–28), influencing the life, both spiritual and physical, of individuals, so that the man is no longer master of himself (Luke 13:11, 16). Demoniacal possession never seems to occur without some outward signs of derangement (Matt. 11:18; Luke 7:33; John 7:20; 8:48–52; 10:20, 21). This demoniacal, violent overpowering of a man (Mark 9:20) essentially differs from satanic influence (John 13:2, 27), wherein the man becomes, like the demons, the instrument of Satan. The kingdom of God, including all divine influences obtained by Christ's mediation, testifies effectually against demoniacal violence as the worst form of human suffering produced by Satans agency (1 John 3:8; see also Matt. 12:28; 7:22; 9:33, 34; 10:8; Mark 1:34, 39; 3:15; 6:13; 7:26; 9:38; 16:9, 17, Luke 9:49; 11:14, 15, 18–20; 13:32).

1162. Déēsis; supplication or prayer for particular benefits (Luke 1:13; 1 Tim. 2:1). *Proseuchḗ* (4335) is a more general request directed to God in particular. *Déēsis* can be a request for specific benefits from God or anyone else. Therefore, *proseuchḗ* is a more sacred word.

1163. Deí; must, necessary by the nature of things. Contrast to *opheílō* (3784), obliged to, morally or by virtue of personal obligation. An unavoidable, urgent compulsory necessity (Mark 8:31; Titus 1:7).

1167. Deilía; cowardice, timidity, fearfulness (2 Tim. 1:7).

Used always in a bad sense as contrasted with *phóbos* (5401), fear, from *péphoba* (perf. mid. of *phebómai*), to flee or run away from, which is also capable of a good interpretation such as reverence (Acts 9:31; Rom. 3:18). *Phóbos* lies in between *deilía,* cowardice, and *eulábeia* (2124), religious reverence (Heb. 5:7; 12:28). Deriv.: *deiliáō* (1168), to shrink for fear (John 14:27); *deilós* (1169), adj., fearful, timid.

1174. Deisidaimonésteros; is the comparative form of *deisidaímōn* in Acts 17:22. It is *deilía* (1167), fear of the demon-gods (*daimónia,* [1140]); superstitious but not in a bad sense; the recognition of God or the gods showing more fear than trust. Related words: *eusebḗs* (2152), godly; *theosebḗs* (2318), devout, godly; *eulabḗs* (2126), pious; *thrēskos* (2357), religious.

1175. Deisidaimonía; commonly translated superstition from *deisidaímōn,* superstitious. Actually the word had a milder meaning than superstition, that is, reverence towards the deity or fear of God in which sense it may be used in Acts 25:19. Ii indicates a dread of the gods, usually in a condemnatory or contemptuous sense.

1184. Dektós; a verbal adj. with the meaning of the perf. part. pass. of *déchomai* (1209), to accept, decide favorably. Elected, acceptable, one of whom there is or has been a favorable decision of the will. Particularly used of the sacrifice; not to distinguish it from unacceptable sacrifices, but to specify it as the object of the divine approval (Phil. 4:18). Used with elements of time such as *kairós* (2540), season, and *eniautós* (1763), year, meaning a time which God has pleasure in, which He Himself has chosen (Luke 4:19; 2 Cor. 6:2). When spoken of men (Luke 4:24), it means liked or valued men (Acts 10:35).

1188. Dexiós; from *déxasthai,* first aor. inf. of the deponent verb *déchomai* (1209), to receive, take, on account of the aptitude of the right hand for this action. Right side. When giving or receiving is spoken of, preference is given to the right hand (Matt. 6:3; Luke 6:6; Rev. 5:7). In the case of division and apportionment, the right hand is chosen as that which comes first (Matt. 5:29, 30, 39; Rev. 10:2), both when the division is indifferent (Matt. 20:21, 23; Mark 10:37, 40; 2 Cor. 6:7, cf. 2 Sam. 16:6; 1 Kgs. 22:19; 2 Chr. 18:18), and when preference is clearly given to one side (Matt. 25:33, 34). In all-important transactions when definiteness must be given to the action, in full participation of the actor made prominent and when energy and emphasis are intended, the right hand is employed (Rev. 1:16, 17, 20; 2:1; 5:1, 7). Not only in the case of the actor, but also in that of the person acted upon, the right hand or side is preferred (Acts 3:7), hence God is said to be at the right hand of the person whom He helps as the enemy is to the right of him whom He seeks to overcome and the accuser to the right of the accused. By the right hand the whole man is claimed, whether in action or in suffering (Acts 2:25, quoted from Ps. 16:8; Ps. 73:23; Ps. 109:6, 31; 110:5; 121:5; Is. 41:13; Zech. 3:1). A person of high rank who puts anyone on his right hand gives him equal honor with himself and recognizes him as of equal dignity (1 Kgs. 2:19; Ps. 45:9; Matt. 20:21, 23; 22:44; 26:64; 27:38; Mark 14:62; Luke 22:69; Acts 2:33, 34; 5:31; 7:55, 56; Rom. 8:34; Eph. 1:20; Col. 3:1 where Christ is said to sit on the right hand of God the Father; Heb. 1:13; 1 Pet. 3:22).

1189. Déomai; act. *déō,* to be deprived of, want, need; used chiefly in the impersonal form *dei* (1163), it is necessary, it ought or must be, for which Homer always uses *chrḗ* (5534), it needs, ought. *Déomai,* by some construed as pass. and meaning to be reduced to want, is perhaps more correctly to be regarded as mid. voice, meaning to be in want of for oneself, to need. Hence, *déēsis* (1162) is prayer for a particular need, supplication. Used with the gen. of the person (Luke 8:38; 9:40, cf. Acts 26:3; 2 Cor. 10:2). With the acc. (2 Cor. 8:4). Followed by *hópōs* (3704), so that (Matt. 9:38; Luke 10:2, cf. Acts 8:24). Followed by *hina* (2443), in order (Luke 9:40, cf. 21:36; 22:32). Followed by *mḗ* (3378), an interrogative neg. meaning never, not (Luke 8:28). While *proseuché* (4335) refers to prayer in general, *déēsis* refers to a particular need for which one prays. Thus *déomai* is related to *aitéō* (154), to make a request, ask as an inferior of a superior.

1203. Despótēs; despot (Luke 2:29; Rev. 6:10), more commonly as a comp. noun with *oíkos* (3621), house, household, *oikodespótēs* (3617), master in respect to his slaves. Contrast *kúrios* (2962), lord, master in regard to his wife and children. A *despótēs* wields unlimited authority, not always for the good, while a *kúrios* exercises morally restricted authority for good. Jesus is predominantly called *Kúrios*, Lord, because of His omnipotent concern.

1209. Déchomai; to accept an offer deliberately and readily (Matt. 10:44; Gal. 4:14). Distinguished from *lambánō* (2983) which sometimes means to receive as merely a self-prompted action without necessarily signifying a favorable reception. Deriv.: *apodéchomai* (588), from *apó* (575), from, an intens., and *déchomai* meaning to receive heartily, welcome. (See *prosdokáō* [4328], to anticipate.) *Ekdéchomai* (1551), from *ek* (1537), from, and *déchomai*, literally to take or receive from, hence to await, expect, suggesting a reaching out eagerly to receive something. *Ekdoché* (1561), the noun of *ekdéchomai* (1551), meaning a looking for, expectation (Heb. 10:27) contrasted to *prosdokía* (4329), expectation of evil. *Doché* (1403), a noun meaning an entertainment, a feast. Related words: *apodoché* (594), from *apodéchomai* (588), acceptance, reception; *apekdéchomai* (553), from *apó*, an intens., and *ekdéchomai* (1551), to expect, wait for with earnest expectation and desire; *eisdéchomai* (1523), from *eis* (1519), in, and *déchomai* to receive into, namely, favor or communion; *prosdéchomai* (4327), from *pros* (4314), receive or take, (e.g., as the spoiling of ones goods with joy), accept as deliverance, receive kindly as a friend; entertain; receive, admit as a hope; expect, look or wait for; *dektós* (1184), accepted, acceptable, agreeable; *apodektós* (587), from *apodéchomai* (588), acceptable, pleasing, grateful; *euprósdektos* (2144), from *eu* (2095), well, and *prosdektós*, from *pros* (4314), unto, and *dektós* (1184), accepted, acceptable.

1210. Déō; to fasten or tie. NT meanings: to bind, tie, as with a chain or cord (Matt. 22:13; 27:2; Mark 5:3, 4); bind up, swathe (John 19:40); bind or oblige by a moral or religious obligation (Rom. 7:2; 1 Cor. 7:27, 39); pronounce or determine to be binding or obligatory, that is, of duties for performance, transgressions for punishment (Matt. 16:19; 18:18).

1217. Dēmiourgós; from *démios*, public, which in turn is from *démos*, a people, and *érgon*, work. One who works for the public or performs public works such as an architect. Applied to God, the Architect of that continuing and glorious city which Abraham looked for (Heb. 11:10). It brings out the power of the divine creator in contrast to *technítēs* (5079), from *téchnē*, trade and *teúchō*, to fabricate, meaning an artificer, craftsman, workman. *Technítēs* expresses rather God's manifold wisdom, the infinite variety and beauty of the works of His hand (Acts 19:24, 38; Heb. 11:10; Rev. 18:22).

1218. Dêmos; from *déō*, to bind. A people, so called because they are united by laws and ties of society (Acts 12:22; 17:5; 19:30, 33). Deriv.: *dēmósios* (1219), public, common (Acts 5:18); *dēmósia*, adv., publicly. From this word is derived democracy where the people or the public rules.

1225. Diabállō or diabállomai; (mid. voice) from the prep. *diá* (1223), through, and *bállō* (906), to cast, throw. To accuse. The verb from which is derived the noun *diábolos* (1228), the devil or false accuser. Used in the pass. voice only in Luke 16:1 and should be translated he was falsely accused if this difficult parable is to be understood.

1226. Diabebaióomai; a deponent verb. To firmly assure, from *diá* (1223), an intens., and *bebaióō* (950), make firm (1 Tim. 1:7; Titus 3:8).

1228. Diábolos; from the prep. *diá* (1223), through, and the verb *bállō* (906), to cast. The devil, one who falsely

accuses and divides people without any reason. He is an accuser, a slanderer (1 Tim. 3:11; 2 Tim. 3:3; Titus 2:3). The devil is called by that name because originally he accused or slandered God in paradise, averse to the increase of mans knowledge and happiness (Gen. 3:5; John 8:44). The devil still slanders God by false and blasphemous suggestions, and because he is also the accuser of the brethren before God (Rev. 12:9, 10, cf. Job 1:2). He is called our adversary, *antídikos* (476), or opponent. *Diábolos* is used either for the prince of devils (Matt. 4:1; Rev. 12:9; 20:2) or for evil spirits in general (Acts 10:38; Eph. 4:27; 6:11). The Lord Jesus calls Judas *diábolos* (John 6:70), because under the influence of an evil spirit he would be Christ's accuser and betrayer (cf. Matt. 16:23 where the Lord calls Peter *Satanás*, [4567], Satan, and not *diábolos*, devil).

1229. Diaggéllō; to announce, declare fully or far and wide (Luke 9:60; Rom. 9:17), to declare plainly (Acts 21:26).

1231. Diaginóskō; from the prep. *diá* (1223), denoting separation or emphasis, and *ginóskō* (1097), to know. To discuss, examine thoroughly (Acts 23:15; 24:22). Generally it means to perceive clearly, discriminatingly, discern, distinguish, decide. Deriv.: *diágnōsis* (1233), discernment, (Eng., diagnosis).

1232. Diagnōrízō; from *diá* (1223), denoting separation, and *gnōrízō* (1107), to know. To know by distinguishing. In Luke 2:17, to make known throughout a district, spread abroad the tidings.

1233. Diágnōsis; from the verb *diaginóskō*, to discern. Discernment or distinguishing (Eng., diagnosis); only in Acts 25:21.

1237. Diadéchomai; from *diá* (1223), denoting transition, and *déchomai* (1209), receive. To receive by succession from another or former possessor (Acts 7:45).

1238. Diádēma; diadem, not a crown, but a filament of silk, linen or some related thing. Used in Revelation 12:3; 13:1; 19:12. Contrast *stéphanos* (4735), crown, referring to the conquerors crown, and not a royal crown.

1240. Diádochos; from the verb *diadéchomai*. A successor (Acts 24:27).

1242. Diathḗkē; testament, covenant. In Class. Gr. it always meant the disposition which a person makes of his property in prospect of death, that is, his testament. This is the meaning when used either in the sing. or pl. The pl. also means the testamentary arrangements of a person. It should be understood that the disposition of God becomes an institution of God. In the NT it means a solemn disposition, institution or appointment of God to man (Heb. 9:16–18), to which our word dispensation answers adequately; for the religious dispensation or institution which God appointed to Abraham and the patriarchs (Acts 3:25); for the dispensation begun at Sinai (Heb. 8:9); for the dispensation of faith and free justification of which Christ is the mediator (Heb. 7:22; 8:6) and which is called new (*kainḗ* [2537], qualitatively new), in that it is a dispensation of faith in respect of the old, the old being the Sinaitical one (2 Cor. 3:6; Heb. 9:15). On the other hand, the old dispensation is called *palaiá* (3820) *diathḗkē* and should be distinguished from *archaía* (744) which is related to *arché* (746) referring to the beginning. *Palaiá*, which relates to the OT, is not the original testament and dispensation of God but is simply the old contrasted to the new and refers to the dispensation contained in the books of Moses (2 Cor. 3:14). *Diathḗkē*, translated covenant, gives the misleading idea that God came to an agreement with fallen man as if signing a contract. Rather, it involves only the declaration of God's unconditional disposition as given to Abraham in regard to Israel as a nation (Gen. 13:14–17; 15:18; 17:7, 8; 17:19–21; 21:12; 22:2, 12). God is bringing about His prearranged disposition in regard to Israel in spite of the fact that Israel has not yet believed in the Messiah. The Sinaitic *diathḗkē* to Moses, however, was a conditional dispensation or series of promises (Ex. 19:58; 20–23; Heb. 12:18–21) which God made for the Jews only if they obeyed. In the NT God provided His Son in the execution of His plan and dispensation, but not as a result of the obedience to any rule that He preset. However, the giving of eternal life to individuals is presupposed on the acceptance of that sacrifice of the Son of God. It also means a solemn disposition or appointment of man (Gal. 3:15). Deriv.: *títhēmi* (5087), to set, place, lay. The term the covenant of the new testament may be understood as personally referring to Christ (Matt. 26:28; Mark 14:24). The same meaning would pertain to the blood of His covenant which would be the blood of His promise, the blood of His own body (Heb. 9:20; 10:29).

1243. Diairesis; from *diá* (1223), involving separation, and *hairéō* or *hairéomai* (138), to take, grasp, seize. Dividing, distribution, classification or separation. Used only in 1 Corinthians 12:4–6 in regard to the gifts, services and results of energies or operations. Apportionments or distributions in a pass. sense. Here the Apostle does not merely mean the Spirit bestows different gifts, but bestows certain gifts to certain people, not the same to all. The possessors of these gifts are exhorted to a mutual communication and fellowship.

1244. Diairéō; from *diá* (1223), through, or with the meaning of separation, and *hairéō* or *hairéomai* (138), to take, grasp, seize. To take one from another, divide, part, apportion, assign. In the NT it means to take one thing from another (Luke 15:12; 1 Cor. 12:11).

1247. Diakonéō; to serve, wait upon, with emphasis on the work to be done and not on the relationship between lord and servant. In *doúlos* (1401), slave, the work is involuntary, as with *hupērétēs* (5257), servant, in contrast to the voluntary service of *thérapōn* (2324) attendant. In its narrowest sense, *diakonéō* means to wait on a table, serve at dinner (Matt. 8:15; Mark 1:31; Luke 4:39; 10:40; 12:37; 17:8; John 12:2). Generally it means to do someone a service, care for someones needs (Matt. 4:11; 25:44). There is an inferred service rendered, bringing advantage to others; to help. One may work, *douleúō*, and not help anybody, but when *diakonéō* is used, helping someone directly is involved (John 12:26; Acts 19:22; 1 Tim. 3:10, 13).

1248. Diakonía; serviceable labor, service (Luke 10:40; Heb. 1:14), assistance (2 Cor. 11:8; 2 Tim. 4:11). *Diakonía* involves compassionate love toward the needy within the Christian community (Acts 6:1, 4; 2 Cor. 8:4; 9:12, 13; Rev. 2:19). Every business, every calling, so far as its labor benefits others is a *diakonía*. In this sense Paul and Luke in the Acts use the word to designate the vocation of those who preach the Gospel and have the care of the churches (Acts 20:24; Rom. 11:13; 1 Cor. 12:5; Col. 4:17; 1 Tim. 1:12; 2 Tim. 4:5) Therefore, *diakonía* is an office or ministration in the Christian community viewed with reference to the labor needed for others both in the case of individuals (1 Cor. 12:5), and generally as a total concept including all branches of service (Rom. 12:7; 2 Cor. 4:1; 6:3; Eph. 4:12; 1 Tim. 1:12). See *diakonéō* (1247), to minister; *diákonos* (1249) deacon, minister.

1249. Diákonos; a minister, servant, deacon. Its derivation is uncertain. According to some it comes from *diakonís*, laboring in the dust, or running through dust. Others believe it is from *diákō*, the same as *diékō*, to hasten, related to *diōkō*, to pursue. Verb: *diakonéō* (1247), from the emphatic prep. *diá* (1223), and *konéō*, to minister, adjust, regulate, set in order. It is not servile as a *doúlos* (1401), slave, but voluntary as a *thérapōn* (2324), attendant. Those who serve at a feast are *doúloi*, but those who execute the kings sentence are *diákonoi* (Matt. 22:13, 14). In *doúlos* the relationship of having dependence upon the master is prominent and a state of servitude is the main thought, while in *diákonos* the main reference is to the service or advantage rendered to another (serviceableness). In *hupērétēs* (5257), servant, the predominant reference is to the labor done for a lord. In *thérapōn* the idea originally was of voluntary subjection and honorable rendering of service, the opposite of *doúlos*, a slave. *Diákonos* thus represents the servant in this activity for the work, not in his relation, either servile as that of the *doúlos*, or more voluntary as in the case of the *therápōn*, to a person. The emphasis with *diákonos* is the service rendered. It also means the servant of an employer, as is said of the magistrate that he is God's deacon (Rom. 13:4). He acts in the employ of God (1 Tim. 4:6) being a good deacon of Jesus Christ (John 12:26; 2 Cor. 6:4; 11:15, 23; Col. 1:7; 1 Thess. 3:2). Also used in the NT as a technical term side by side with *epískopos* (1985), bishop or overseer (Phil. 1:1; 1 Tim. 3:8, 12). The deacons in this sense were helpers or were serving the bishops or elders, and this is why they were probably called deacons. Tychicus was called a deacon in his relation to Paul (Eph. 6:21; Col. 4:7, cf. Acts 19:22). The origin of this relationship is found in Acts 6:1–4. Stephen and Philip were deacons and were first chosen as distributors of alms but soon appeared side by side with the Apostles as their helpers and also as evangelists (Acts 6:8–10; 8:5–8). The care of the churches came to rest upon the deacons as the helpers of the elders who held distinct offices. In Romans 16:1 a woman, Phoebe, is named as a *diákonos*, deacon, of the church (1 Tim. 5:10, cf. Rom. 16:2; 1 Tim. 3:11), but many believe this carries with it only the idea of service, not the idea of an established office since the requirements in 1 Timothy 3:8–13 are addressed to men. Deriv.: *diakonéō* (1247), to serve; *diakonía* (1248), ministry.

1252. Diakrínō; from *diá* (1223), denoting separation, and *krínō* (2919), to distinguish, decide, judge. To discern, distinguish (Matt. 16:3); to make a distinction or difference (Acts 15:9); to make to differ (1 Cor. 4:7; 11:29); to judge, determine (1 Cor. 6:5, cf. 1 Cor. 14:29); in the pass. *diakrínomai*, to contend, dispute with another person; that is, to be distinguished or divided from him when speaking (Acts 11:2; Jude 1:9); also in the pass., to doubt, to be distinguished or divided in ones mind (Matt. 21:21; Mark 11:23; Acts 10:20; Rom. 4:20; James 1:6). In the mid. or pass. (James 2:4; Jude 1:22).

1253. Diákrisis; from *diakrínō* (1252), to separate one from another, divide, part. Discerning, distinguishing (1 Cor. 12:10; Heb. 5:14); a difference, dispute, controversy (Rom. 14:1).

1257. Dialeípō; from *diá* (1223), between, and *leípō* (3007), to leave. To intermit, desist, cease, leave an interval whether of space or time (Luke 7:45). Related words: *adiáleiptos* (88), from the neg. *a*, *diá* (1223), through, and *leípō* (3007), to leave, meaning unceasing, continual (Rom. 9:2; 2 Tim. 1:3). The meaning is not that of unbroken continuity but indicates being without the omission of any occasion. *Adialeíptōs* (89), adv., unceasingly, that which is constantly reoccurring (1 Thess. 5:17).

1259. Diallássō; in the mid. voice, *diallássomai* or *dialátomai*. To be reconciled; only occurs in Matthew 5:24. Applies to a quarrel in which the fault may be twosided or one-sided. The context must show on which side the active enmity is. *Katallássō* (2644) is more frequent in later Gr. and differs from *diallássō* (act.) only in that in the same construction the acc. may denote either of the parties.

1260. Dialogízomai; from the emphatic *diá* (1223), denoting separation, and *logízomai* (3049), to reckon, reason. To reason, discourse, whether in silence with oneself (Mark 2:6; Luke 1:29; 3:15; 5:22; 12:17), or by speaking with others (Matt. 16:7, 8; Luke 20:14); to consider (John 11:50); to dispute (Mark 9:33). Deriv.: *logízomai* (3049), to reason, reckon.

1261. Dialogismós; from *dialogízomai* (1260). In the NT only with a negative meaning and referring to objectionable thoughts and directions. Reasoning, rationalization (Matt. 15:19; Mark 7:21, Luke 2:35; 1 Cor. 3:20; James 2:4); doubtful reasoning, doubt (Luke 24:38; 1 Tim. 2:8); discourse, dispute, disputation (Luke 9:46, 47; Rom. 14:1; Phil. 2:14). Deriv.: *logízomai* (3049), to reckon.

1263. Diamartúromai; from the emphatic *diá* (1223) and *martúromai* (3143), to witness, bear witness, or from *diá* (1223), meaning in the presence of, and *mártur* or *mártus* (3144), a witness. To bear witness, testify earnestly or repeatedly, or to charge before witnesses

(Acts 20:23, Heb. 2:6). Attesting to the truths of redemption (Acts 8:25; 10:42; 18:5; 20:21, 24; 23:11; 28:23; 1 Thess. 4:6). To charge anyone, exhort earnestly (2 Tim. 2:14; 4:1). With *hína* (2443), so that (Luke 16:28; 1 Tim. 5:21).

1270. Dianóēma; from *dianoéō*, to agitate in mind, from the prep. *diá* (1223), denoting separation, and *noéō* (3539), think. A thought, reflection (Luke 11:17). See *noús* (3563), mind.

1271. Diánoia; understanding, intellect, intellectual faculty, mind (Matt. 22:37; Eph. 1:18; 4:18; Heb. 8:10); an operation of the understanding, thought, imagination (Luke 1:51). See *noéō* (3539), to think; *noús* (3563), mind.

1295. Diasōzō; from *diá* (1223), through, an emphatic, and *sōzō* (4982), to save. To save or preserve (Acts 27:43; 1 Pet. 3:20); carry or convey safely (Acts 23:24). Pass.: *diasózomai*, to be carried safely, escape safely (Acts 27:44; 28:1, 4); heal, save, deliver from some present bodily disorder (Matt. 14:36; Luke 7:3).

1296. Diatagē; from *diatássō* (1299), to appoint, order. A disposition, ordinance, appointment, order (Acts 7:53; Rom. 13:2). The expression received the law as ordained by angels, *eis diatagás aggélōn*, means by or through the dispositions of angels. Deriv.: *diátagma* (1297), an order, commandment (Heb. 11:23).

1297. Diátagma; an order, commandment, or edict. Only in Hebrews 11:23.

1299. Diatássō; from *diá* (1223), through, an intens., and *tássō* (5021), to appoint, order. To command, used in connection with the amount appointed for tax officials to collect (Luke 3:13); of the tabernacle as appointed by God for Moses to make (Acts 7:44); of travel arrangements made by Paul (Acts 20:13); of what the Apostle ordained in the churches in regard to marital conditions (1 Cor. 7:17); of what the Lord ordained in regard to the support of those who proclaimed the Gospel (1 Cor. 9:14); of the law as administered through angels, by Moses (Gal. 3:19). In Titus 1:5 the meaning is to command rather than to appoint. Deriv.: *anatássomai* (392); *epitássō* (2004); *apotássomai* (657); *hupotássō* (5293); *prostássō* (4367); *diatagē* (1296), an ordinance; *diátagma* (1297), what is imposed by decree or law (Heb. 11:23) stressing the concrete character of the commandment more then *epitagē* (2003), which stresses the action of commanding.

1301. Diatēréō; from *diá* (1223), an intens., and *tēréō* (5083), to keep. To keep carefully, as the mother of Jesus in keeping His sayings in her heart (Luke 2:51); in keeping the command of the Apostles (Acts 15:29).

1303. Diatíthemai; from *diá* (1223), an emphatic, and *títhēmi* (5087), to place. To place separately, distribute, arrange, appoint anyone to a place. In biblical Gr. used usually in the mid. voice, to dispose or arrange for oneself (Acts 3:25; Heb. 8:10; 9:16, 17; 10:16). Commonly it means to arrange and dispose of ones goods by will and testament. Followed by the dat. of person, to bequeath a thing to anyone, (Luke 22:29), allow or assign.

1317. Didaktikós; apt to teach. A quality named as a requirement for a bishop (1 Tim. 3:2; 2 Tim. 2:24); also with reference to Christian teaching (Acts 18:24, 25).

1319. Didaskalía; that which belongs to a *didáskalos* (1320), teacher. That which is taught, teaching, instruction. In the NT commonly used obj. in a pass. sense meaning that which is taught, doctrine (Matt. 15:9; Mark 7:7; Col. 2:22, cf. Eph. 4:14; 1 Tim. 4:1 in antithesis to Titus 2:10). Distinguished from *didaché* (1322), the act of teaching, instructing, tutoring. *Didaskalía* refers not only to that which is taught but also to the authority of the teacher, thus not simply the subject taught but also the act of teaching or instructing. Used absolutely as *hē didaskalía*, the teaching (Rom. 12:7; 1 Tim. 1:10; 4:6, 16; 6:1, 3; 2 Tim. 4:3; Titus 1:9; 2:1, 7, 10); used with reference to the authority of the teacher behind the teaching (Rom. 15:4; 2 Tim. 3:10, 16).

1320. Didáskalos; a teacher (Rom. 2:20; Heb. 5:12), from *didáskō* (1321), to teach. It correlates with *mathētés*

(3101), a learner, pupil, disciple (Matt. 10:24, 25; Luke 6:40). When used in addressing Jesus (Matt. 22:16; John 1:38), it is meant as a name of respect which was given to Jewish scribes (Luke 2:46). The Pharisees opposed the usage of the title of father, *patér* (3962), and *kathēgētēs* (2519), a guide, leader, hence a teacher or master, or *kúrios* (2962), lord (John 13:13, 14). Acts 13:1 refers to *didáskaloi*, teachers, with *prophētai* (4396), prophets. From this passage it can be concluded that in the Christian Church the *didáskaloi*, teachers, appear as having a distinct function (Acts 13:1; 1 Cor. 12:28, 29; Eph. 4:11; James 3:1). These *didáskaloi* correlate to the Jewish *grammateís*, pl., (1122), scribes, and are to be viewed like them, as being acquainted in a special sense with and interpreters of God's salvation (Matt. 13:52). Upon them rested the duty of giving progressive instruction concerning God's redeeming purposes. It was a function which, with that of *poimēn* (4166), pastor, seems to have been united in one person (Eph. 4:11). See *hēgoúmenoi*, leaders, from *hēgéomai* (2233), in Hebrews 13:7, 17. The *poiménes*, pastors or shepherds, and the *didáskaloi*, teachers, seem to have been members of the presbytery (Acts 20:28; 1 Tim. 3:2; 2 Tim. 2:24). The *didáskalos* was distinct from the *kērux* (2783), preacher, and *euaggelistés* (2099), evangelist (Eph. 4:11; 1 Tim. 2:7). False teachers appeared with them side by side, not only outside, but probably within the presbytery (1 Tim. 1:3; 2 Tim. 4:3) and were called *pseudodidáskaloi* (5572), false teachers (2 Pet. 2:1); *heterodidaskaleín* (2085), teaching qualitatively different doctrine (1 Tim. 1:3; 6:3). Paul called himself, besides *kērux* (2783), preacher, an *apóstolos* (652), apostle in a restrictive sense as with the same authority as the Twelve, and with special emphasis, *didáskalos ethnōn*, teacher of nations or the Gentiles (1 Tim. 2:7; 2 Tim. 1:11; see also John 3:10; Gal. 2:7ff.; Eph. 3:8, 9).

1321. Didáskō; either from *daíō* or *dáō*. To know or teach, and the Ionic *dáskō* with the reduplicate syllable *di*. Teach, instruct by word of mouth (Matt. 28:15, 20; Luke 11:1; 12:12; Acts 15:1; Rev. 2:14). *Didáskō* has inherent in it the calculation of the increase in understanding of the pupil. Its counterparts are *akoúō* (191), to hear for the purpose of understanding, and *manthánō* (3129), to learn, from which *mathētés* (3101), learner, pupil, disciple, is derived. The one teaches (*didáskei*) and the other learns or assimilates as part of himself (*mathēteúei* [3100]) (Matt. 10:24, 25; Luke 6:40; 19:39). *Kērússō* (2784), to preach, proclaim, does not inherently have the same expectation of learning and assimilation as *didáskō* does (Matt. 4:23; 9:35; 11:1; 13:54; Luke 20:1; Acts 5:42; 15:35). The thing aimed at when teaching (*didáskō*) is the shaping of the will of the pupil (Matt. 5:19; Acts 21:21; Col. 1:28). *Didáskō* is used absolutely of Christ's teaching (Mark 9:31; 10:1; John 18:20; Col. 1:28); as instruction in the Christian faith and Christian teaching (Acts 11:26; Rom. 12:7; Col. 1:28; Heb. 5:12).

1322. Didaché; in an act. sense it means the art of teaching, instructing, tutoring (Mark 4:2; 12:38; 2 Tim. 4:2); in a pass. sense, teaching which is given, that which anyone teaches (Matt. 7:28). In an absolute sense, it denotes the teaching of Jesus (2 John 9, 10), the Lord (Acts 13:12); and the Apostles (Acts 2:42; Titus 1:9).

1334. Diēgéomai; from *diá* (1223), through, an intens., and *hēgéomai* (2233), to lead. To conduct a narration through to the end. To recount, relate in full (Mark 5:16; 9:9; Luke 8:39; 9:10; Acts 8:33; 9:27; 12:17; Heb. 11:32). Noun: *diégēsis* (1335), a narrative and not a declaration. Deriv.: *ekdiēgéomai* (1555), from *ek* (1537) out, and *diēgéomai*, to recount, meaning to rehearse or relate particularly (Acts 15:3).

1341. Dikaiokrisía; from *díkaios* (1342), just, and *krísis* (2920), judgment. A judgment which renders justice or produces right. Righteous judgment (Rom. 2:5).

1342. Díkaios; adj. or adj. noun from *díkē* (1349), right, justice. Used in the neut. *to díkaion*, that which is right, conformable to right, pertaining to right, that which is just, which is expected by the one who sets the rules and regulations whereby man must live, whether that be society or God. Therefore, it is that which is expected as duty or is claimed as a right because of ones conformity to the rules of God or society. When used in the masc. or fem. as an adj. or an adj. noun and used of persons, it refers to the one who acts conformably to justice and right without any deficiency or failure. Thus it is applied to God (John 17:25; Rom. 3:26); Christ as God-Man (Acts 3:14; 7:52; 22:14; 1 Pet. 3:18; 1 John 2:1). Being *díkaios*, just, means that one conforms in his actions to his constitutionally just character. The rules for these actions are self-imposed. When this absolute justice is applied to man, it is stated that there is no man who in his behavior can fully meet the expectations of God in his life (Rom. 3:10). *Díkaios* may also apply to the person who establishes his own rules of life. Such was a Pharisee whom the Lord exposed as righteous in himself (Matt. 9:13; Luke 18:9). Having set up and kept, or pretended to keep, certain standards, the Pharisees called themselves righteous or just in the sight of God. Most of these rules and regulations, however, were not those of inner holiness and conformity to God, but mere performance of external ceremonial ordinances (Rom. 10:3). In the NT those are called righteous (*díkaioi*) who have conditioned their lives by the standard which is not theirs, but God's. They are the people related to God, who, as a result of this relationship, walk with God (Rom. 1:17; 3:21, 22; Eph. 4:24). A righteous person is one justified by faith and showing forth his faith by his works. The nonbelievers, referred to as heathen, call others righteous or just, as they compare them with their own standards. *Díkaios* has more of a social than a divine reference. In the heathen mind a *díkaios*, a righteous person, is one who does not selfishly nor forgetfully transgress the bounds fixed for him and gives to everyone from his own means, yet still desires what is his, and does not in the least withdraw an assertion of his own claims. Christianity must continually combat such a view. The heathen say, My right is my duty, whereas the Christian says, My duty is my right. Plato designated *dikaiosúnē* (1343), righteousness, as inseparably linked with *sōphrosúnē* (4997), soberness or sobriety, the expression of a sound mind, the ability to place restrictions on ones freedom in action. *Díkaios* is equivalent to *eusebés* (2152), pious (Acts 10:2) and fearing God (v. 22). Peter spoke of Cornelius as having fear of God and of his righteousness as being accepted by God (Acts 10:35). This coincides with the Pauline doctrine of justification. A person is just or righteous because of the righteousness which is through the faith of Christ, the righteousness which is of God by faith (Phil. 3:9). He is justified through faith (Rom. 5:19), and brings forth the fruits of righteousness or justification (Phil. 1:11; see also Matt. 13:43; 25:46; Luke 14:14; Heb. 11:4). The OT righteous were those whose conduct was made conformable to God and whose justification was made possible through their faith in the promised Redeemer (Hab. 2:4; Gal. 3:11, cf. Gen. 6:9; Heb. 11:7). The word *díkaios* is also used of things to indicate their just or right or conformable relation to justice or righteousness (John 7:24; Rom. 7:12). Syn.: *agathós* (18), good, whose goodness and works of goodness are transferred to others. Yet *díkaios* is a concept of a relation and presupposes a norm, whereas the subject of *agathós*, good and doing good, is its own norm. Therefore, *agathós* includes the pred. of *díkaios*. In the NT *díkaios* stands in opposition to *paránomos*, unlawful (related to *paranomía* [3892]), transgression. In 1 Peter 3:12 the righteous stand as opposite to those who do evil; in 1 Peter 4:18 as contrary to the ungodly and the sinner; in 2 Peter 2:7 as opposite to *áthesmoi* (113), translated wicked (KJV) but actually meaning without an acceptable standard, which is from the neg. *a*, and *thesmós*, that which is laid down and established, an ordinance; and in 1 Peter 2:8 contrasted to *ánomos* (459), lawless. See also 1 Timothy 1:9. In most instances *díkaios* stands in opposition to *ádikos* (94), unrighteous. Deriv.: *díkē* (1349). Syn.:

hágios (40), holy in the sense of blameless; *hósios* (3741), the performer of the ordinances.

1343. Dikaiosúnē; from *díkaios* (1342), righteous, and *díkē* (1349), justice or righteousness. It is the essence of *to díkaion*, that which is just, or *díkaios*, of him who is just or righteous. Righteousness fulfills the claims of *díkē*, which in the case of the believer is a fulfillment of God's claims. *Dikaiosúnē*, righteousness, is thus conformity with the claims of higher authority and stands as an opposite to *anomía* (458), lawlessness. In both the OT and NT, righteousness is the state commanded by God and standing the test of His judgment (2 Cor. 3:9; 6:14; Eph. 4:24). It is conformity to all that He commands or appoints. Since God Himself is the standard for the believer, the righteousness of God means the righteousness which belongs to God or God-like righteousness (Matt. 6:33; James 1:20). The righteousness of God is the right which God has upon man. In order for man to recognize and fully submit to the right of God upon his life, he must receive God who offers Himself or His righteousness to man as a gift (Rom. 5:17). The recognition and acceptance of God's right upon man, realized through faith, stands in opposition to the righteousness which is of the law (Rom. 10:5; Gal. 3:21), which is man's acceptance of the claims of the law upon his life. Man in his natural, fallen condition tends rather to accept his own set of standards, creating his own righteousness (Rom. 10:3; Phil. 3:6). Such behavior, however, is not really righteousness (Rom. 10:5; Gal. 3:21) and does not satisfy God. God's righteousness is imputed and imparted as a gift to man but can not be earned. It results in God's act of justification of man by his faith through Christ. Man only needs to accept the claims of God upon his life and repent of his sin, receiving Christ as his Savior by faith, thus becoming a child of God. The result is the realization of God's claims upon him by the miraculous regenerating action of the Holy Spirit (John 1:12; Rom. 4:11–13; 5:21; 6:16; 8:10; 9:30; 10:6; 2 Cor. 6:7, 14; Eph. 4:24; 6:14; 2 Pet. 1:1).

1344. Dikaióō; verbs that end in -oō generally mean to bring out that which a person is or that which is desired. They do not have reference to the mode in which the action takes place. In the case of *dikaióō*, it means either to bring out the fact that a person is righteous, or if he is not, to make him righteous. To justify someone, therefore, means to bring out the fact that he is just or to make him just without necessarily referring to how he is made just. In Class. Gr. *dikaióō* could also mean to make anyone righteous by permitting such a one to bear his own condemnation, judgment, punishment, or chastisement. Such judgment of guilt upon the one being tried in court would have been better expressed by the verb *dikázō* which does not occur in the NT although the subst. *dikastés* (1348), a judge, does occur. The more common word referring to the condemning of a guilty person examined in court is *katadikázō* (2613), to condemn. The noun *katadíkē* does not occur in the NT, but it does in Class. Gr. and means a judgment given against someone, a sentence. It must be clearly understood that in the NT the verb *dikaióō*, to justify, never means to make someone righteous by doing away with his violation of law by himself bearing the condemnation of the imposed sentence. In the NT man in his fallen condition can never do anything in order to pay for his own sinfulness and thus be liberated from the sentence of guilt that is upon him, as may be done in a legal system (i.e., when a guilty person has paid the penalty of a crime, he is free from condemnation). In the NT, *dikaióō* in the act. tense means to recognize, to set forth as righteous, to justify, first of all as a judicial act. This is clear from Luke 10:29 in which a lawyer who came to Jesus asked Him how he could inherit eternal life. Wishing to justify himself means that the lawyer wanted to make himself righteous. The same was the case with the Pharisees to whom the Lord said in Luke 16:15, "You are those who justify yourselves in the sight of men"; that is, you have set yourselves forth as righteous, as if there is nothing wrong with you if you were to stand in a court of justice. The word is used in the same sense in Luke 7:29 in stating that the people recognized that God acted justly in sending John the Baptist to preach repentance. This was an indirect recognition that indeed man needed to repent. In the OT in some instances such as Psalms 73:13, the Sept. translation of *edikaiōsa*, I justified my heart, really means I cleansed my heart. Elsewhere the verb used in regard to a thing or a person means to find anything as right, to recognize or acknowledge anyone as just, to set forth as right or just. Noteworthy is Exodus 23:7 (Sept.), Keep thee far from a false matter; and the innocent (*athóon*, [121]) and righteous (*díkaion* [1342]) slay thou not: for I will not justify (thou shall not justify) because of receiving gifts. In other words, no man can declare someone righteous because of the gifts he receives from him or from anybody else. *Dikaióō* is one aspect of judicial activity as demonstrated in the Sept. by the expression *díkaion*, just, and the verb *krínō* (2919), which in the Bible is the main verb referring to judicial activity, deciding whether a person is guilty or not; He who justifies the wicked, and he who condemns the just, both of them alike are an abomination to the Lord (Prov. 17:15). In this verse *díkaion* is translated just, and *ádikon* (94) is translated the wicked which really means unjust. Everywhere in the OT the root meaning of *dikaióō* is to set forth as righteous, to justify in a legal sense (Ezek. 16:51, 52). In the NT it means to recognize, set forth as righteous, justify as a judicial act (Luke 10:29; 16:15). It has the same meaning in the pass., to be recognized, found, set forth as righteous, justified (Matt. 12:37; Rom. 2:13; 3:20). A comment is necessary on Romans 2:13: For not the hearers of the Law are just before God, but the doers of the Law will be justified. Here there is a contrast between the hearers, *akroatai* (202), and the doers, *poiētai* (4163). The verb used here is *dikaiōthḗsontai*, fut. pass. punctiliar, which indicates that at a particular time in the future they will be judicially declared as righteous. The first part of the verse could be better translated: For the hearers of the law not just by the side or before God. There is no verb at all which makes the statement true without any time limitation. What it declares was, is, and will be true. It declares that the ones who merely hear the law have never been and never will be considered by God as just. If, however, they change from being merely hearers to being doers of the law, then God will pronounce them as just. This verse declares a standard or norm that it is not he who knows the law but he who does the law that can be declared just before the Judge. See Romans 3:20 where a seemingly contradictory statement is given because by the works of the Law no flesh will be justified in His sight; for through the Law comes the knowledge of sin. The explanation is that whereas Romans 2:13 declares the norm that the doer will be declared just, in Romans 3:20 a matter-of-fact declaration is made that by the deeds of the law no man can be justified. Even if man is able to do the works of the law, he still cannot be justified since a person can be legally correct but morally wrong. He may conform to a certain law in spite of the fact that he may hate it, and if he did not fear the consequences of transgression, he might never obey it. No law can make a person morally right, though he can be proven legally conforming to the law. Therefore, *dikaiōthḗsontai*, shall be justified, in Romans 2:13 must be interpreted not as to be made or found righteous in character, but simply to appear as righteous because of having conformed to the directions of the law. This is made clear in Romans 4:2: For if Abraham was justified by works, he has something to boast about; but not before God. Here the verb *edikaiōthē*, was justified, does not have the meaning of being declared righteous in reality, but only in appearance. No law could condemn a person who keeps it, but that does not mean that God will declare the individual to be morally right before Him, as recognizing His (God's) rightful ownership of the

man. Abraham, even though he obeyed the law, could not stand before God as righteous and boast about it. His declaration of his righteousness by the law was not equal to God's declaration of righteousness. Paul says in 1 Timothy 3:16 that Jesus Christ was not declared righteous by the law, but in the Spirit. This means that His high claims of being the Son of God, the Messiah, the Redeemer, were justified or proved true by the descent of the Holy Spirit upon Him at His baptism, by the miracles that He performed, the life that He lived, and finally through His resurrection from the dead (Rom. 1:4; 1 Pet. 3:18). The NT tells how being justified by God and declared just before Him are achieved in the lives of men. We are justified before God by Christ through grace (Gal. 2:16; 3:11; Titus 3:6, 7). When one receives Christ, he recognizes God's right over him. His justification simultaneously performs a miracle in him and changes his character. He does not then obey God because he is afraid of the consequences of his disobedience, but because of His grace in Christ which has changed his character and made him just. When one becomes a child of God, he exercises rights toward God and acts as His child. He is thus liberated from the guilt and power of sin, but not from the presence of it. That will come later (Rom. 8:23). In 1 Timothy 3:16 it is said of Jesus Christ, God incarnate, that He was justified in (*en* [1722]) the Spirit, or by means of the Spirit. In the appearance of the Spirit upon Jesus, there was the acknowledgment of the claims of the Son of God that He was the Messiah, the King of Israel, the Redeemer of mankind. This refers to the descent of the Holy Spirit upon Him at His baptism and through the miracles which He performed in full agreement with the Spirit and with God the Father. The ultimate justification of His claims, however, was through His resurrection (Rom. 1:4; 1 Pet. 3:18). The phrase "the righteousness of God" (*dikaiosúnē Theoú*), constantly referred to, especially in Romans, must never be taken as meaning the righteousness which God acquired as if He needed such righteousness, but the righteousness which characterizes Him and which He dispenses. It refers to what God wants to achieve in the lives of men since their recognition of His rights upon them is naturally missing because of man's fall in Adam (Rom. 5:12). His standard of integrity should characterize the life of man when he acknowledges God's rights upon him and what God in Christ can do in him. *Dikaiosúnē* should be clearly distinguished from *dikaíōsis* (1347), the first being the state of having the right to demand duties from people, inherent righteousness, and the other an action which establishes righteousness or which makes a person righteous (*díkaion*). Hence, the first should be translated as righteousness and the second as justification. Deriv.: *díkē* (1349).

1345. Dikaíōma; the product or result of being justified by God. The rights or claims which one has before God when he becomes His child by faith through Christ. In Revelation 19:8 where the translation is the righteousness of saints, it is actually the legal rights of saints (*dikaiṓmata*). In Hebrews 9:1, what is translated as ordinances of divine service actually are *dikaiṓmata*, legal rights. See also Luke 1:6; Romans 1:32; 2:26; 5:16, 18; 8:4; Hebrews 9:10; Revelation 15:4.

1346. Dikaíōs; an adv. from *díkaios* (1342), just. Justly, conformable to justice (1 Pet. 2:23); honestly, without injuring anyone (1 Thess. 2:10; Titus 2:12), deservedly (Luke 23:41); as it is fit, proper, right (1 Cor. 15:34). Deriv: *díkē* (1349).

1347. Dikaíōsis; the act which establishes a right or a just person as such; justification (Rom. 4:25; 5:18), but as an act and not as the essence or character of justice which is *dikaiosúnē* (1343). Opposite *katákrima* (2631), condemnation.

1348. Dikastḗs; judge (Luke 12:14; Acts 7:27, 35). One who executes *díkē* (1349), justice, one who maintains law and equity. Because he arrives at a conclusion and gives final judgment, the judge is also called *kritḗs* (2923), which is a more general term for judge. In contrast, *dikastḗs* is a judge who is nominated or elected to become part of a tribunal and arrive at a conclusion concerning a case.

1349. Díkē; a fem. noun connected with the verb *deíknumi* or *deiknúō* (1166), to show. Originally *díkē* meant manner, tendency. Gradually it became the designation for the right of established custom or usage and was personified as the daughter of the mythological Gr. god Zeus and goddess Themis (see Acts 28:4). The basic meaning of the word involves the assertion by human society of a certain standard expected by its people and, if not kept, can bring judgment. Thus it can be said that *díkē* is expected behavior or conformity, not according to ones own standard, but according to an imposed standard with prescribed punishment for non-conformity. It refers to a legitimate custom. When *díkē* as expected conformity becomes judgment for violation, it becomes in Gr. *katadíkē*, used in the NT only in a verbal form, *katadikázō* (2613), to condemn. In all instances when *díkē* occurs in the NT (Acts 25:15; 28:4; 2 Thess. 1:9; Jude 1:7) it is used with the sense of *katadíkē*, judgment, to render justice, and refers to those who suffer punishment in order that the acceptable behavior or custom violated by them might be reestablished. From the basic word comes *dikaíōma* (1345), legitimate claim. The person adhering to the expectations of his society has certain legitimate claims (*dikaiṓmata*) of which a stranger or one violating the standard of expectation is deprived. The enjoyment of ones right in a society presupposes the acceptance of duties by that citizen. In the Scriptures God is presented as the One who expects a certain conformity of man to His principles. When they are accepted and conformed to, then God gives man certain rights which do not belong to those who do not recognize His authority or their duties to him. Other important deriv.: *díkaios* (1342), just; *díkaiōs* (1346), an adv. meaning justly or righteously; *dikaiosúnē* (1343), righteousness or justice; *dikaióō* (1344), to declare innocent or just or to justify; *dikaíōsis* (1347), justification; *dikastḗs* (1348), judge; *ádikos* (94), unjust or unrighteous; *adikía* (93) injustice or unrighteousness; *adikéō* (91), to act unjustly toward or to do wrong; *ékdikos* (1558), a punisher or one who carries out the right of an issue, an avenger; *ekdikéō* (1556), to take revenge or avenge; *ekdíkēsis* (1557), the fem. noun, revenge; *éndikos* (1738), one who acts within his rights, fair, just, a syn. of *díkaios*; *hupódikos* (5267), under sentence, guilty, or one who comes under *díkē*, the standard by God or by society.

1350. Díktuon; from *díkō*, to cast, cast down. Net, a general name for all nets including the hunting net, the net with which birds are taken; also the fishing net (Matt. 4:20, 21; Mark 1:18, 19; Luke 5:2, 4–6; John 21:6, 8, 11). Other names for nets: *amphíblēstron* (293), a casting net which, when skillfully cast from over the shoulder by one standing on the shore or in a boat, spreads out into a circle (*amphibálettai*) as it falls upon the water and then sinks swiftly by the weight of the lead attached to it enclosing whatever is below it; *sagḗnē* (4522), a sweep-net, the ends of which are carried out in separate boats so as to include a large extent of open sea, and are then drawn together. All which is enclosed is taken.

1357. Diórthōsis; from *diorthóō*, to correct, amend, which in turn is made up of *diá* (1223), an emphatic, and *orthóō*, to make right, which is derived from *órthos*, right (3717). Amendment, reformation, only in Hebrews 9:10.

1370. Dichostasía; from *dícha*, separately, and *stásis*, faction, sedition. A separate faction, division, separation (Rom. 16:17; 1 Cor. 3:3; Gal. 5:20). See *histḗmi* (2476), to stand.

1374. Dípsuchos; from *dis* (1364), twice, and *psuchḗ* (5590), soul, mind. Double-minded, which can mean doubting. Only in James 1:8 referring to the doubter or waverer which corresponds to *diakrínō* (1252); also in James 4:8 where it is used in a general sense to indicate an unstable person.

1378. Dógma; from the verb *dokéō* (1380), to think. Con-

clusion, ordinance, opinion, proposition, dogma. It has the meaning of conclusion (Acts 16:4) as decree or command (Luke 2:1; Acts 17:7; Eph. 2:15; Col. 2:14). It is used in reference to dogmas of Christianity; it means views, doctrinal statements, principles.

1379. Dogmatízō; to conclude, ordain, establish as a dogma, conclusion or ordinance (1378). In the mid. voice, *dogmatizomai*, to let oneself fall into a certain order, subject oneself to ordinances (Col. 2:20).

1380. Dokéō; to think, imagine, consider, appear. Expresses the subjective mental estimate or opinion which men form about a matter. Such recognition may be correct (Acts 15:28; 1 Cor. 4:9; 7:40), or incorrect, involving error (Matt. 6:7; Mark 6:49; John 16:2; Acts 27:13) Contrast *phaínō* or *phaínomai* (5316), to appear, be conspicuous, shine, be seen. Deriv.: *doxázō* (1392), to glorify, make glorious or honorable or cause to appear as one really is, to admit to the eternal state of glory; *sundoxázō* (4888) (*sun* [4862], together), to glorify together; *éndoxos* (1741) (*en* [1722], in), glorious, honorable, splendid of dress; *endoxázō* or *endoxázomai* (1740) (*en* [1722], in) in the pass., to be glorified or exhibit ones glory. Noun: *dóxa* (1391), glory, estimate recognition of what one or something is.

1381. Dokimázō; to try, prove, discern, distinguish, approve. It has the notion of proving a thing whether it be worthy to be received or not. Something good is expected of every *dokimei* (1382), trial, proof. *Dokimázō* is to prove or bring forth the good in us or to make us good (Rom. 2:18; 12:2; 1 Cor. 11:28) as contrasted with *peirázō* (3985), to tempt, which purposes to discover what good or evil is in us. *Dokimázō* could not be used of Satan since he never wants us to experience God's approval. He always tempts us, *peirázei*, with the intent to make us fall. Deriv: *dokímion* (1383), test; *dókimos* (1384), that which endures the test, worthy (*áxios*, [514]). The opposite of *dókimos* is *adókimos* (96), unapproved, reprobate.

1382. Dokimḗ; proof of genuineness, trustworthiness. It has a reflexive sense, hence, it must be either the experience itself, or the fact that one has proved oneself true, or the act of proving oneself true. For example, 2 Corinthians 13:3 has the meaning: You desire that Christ speaking in me shall prove itself true. In 2 Corinthians 2:9 it means: Whether you prove yourselves true (also Rom. 5:4). The meaning in Philippians 2:22 is: How he has proved himself true (see also 2 Cor. 8:2; 9:13).

1383. Dokímion; the means of proving, a criterion, test by which anything is proved or tried; for example, as faith is tested by afflictions (James 1:3; 1 Pet. 1:7).

1384. Dókimos; from *dokéō* (1380), to appear, form an opinion, to recognize. To be proved, to be tried as metals are tried by fire and thus are purified. Hence it refers to being approved as acceptable men in the furnace of adversity (James 1:12, cf. Rom. 16:10); to be approved or accepted (Rom. 14:18; 2 Cor. 10:18; 13:7; 2 Tim. 2:15, cf. 1 Cor. 11:19). Ant.: *adókimos* (96), unapproved.

1389. Dolóō; to adulterate (2 Cor. 4:2), as being part of *kapēleúō* (2585), to adulterate for the sake of unworthy personal gain. Mixing human traditions with the pure word of the Gospel. *Kapēleúō* always includes *dólos* (1388), deceit, but *dolóō* never extends to *kapēleúō* which in addition to adulterating has a notion of unjust lucre, gain, profit, advantage.

1390. Dóma; gift (Matt. 7:11; Luke 11:13; Eph. 4:8; Phil. 4:17); lends greater emphasis to the character of the gift rather than its beneficent nature.

1391. Dóxa; glory. The meanings of this word can be divided conformably with the use of the verb *dokéō* (1380), to think, recognize a person or thing for what it is. Thus, *dóxa* can mean appearance, reputation, glory. It basically refers to the recognition belonging to a person, honor, renown. Opposite *atimía* (819), dishonor, shame (1 Cor. 11:14, 15; 2 Cor. 6:8). Romans 3:23 speaks of coming short of or lacking the glory of God, meaning man is not what God intended him to be. He lacks God's image and character. *Dóxa* may denote appearance, form, aspect, that appearance of a person or thing which catches the eye or attracts attention, commanding recognition, looking like something; thus equivalent to splendor, brilliance, glory attracting the gaze which makes it a strong syn. of *eikṓn* (1504), image (Rom. 1:23). *Dóxa* embraces the excellence and perfection of the divine nature (Rom. 6:4; Eph. 1:7). It comprises all that God will appear to be in His final revelation to us (Rom. 5:2; Rev. 21:23). God's glory made itself manifest in and through Jesus Christ (John 1:14; 2 Cor. 4:6; Heb. 1:3). His Second Coming is spoken of as the blessed hope and the appearing of His glory. It is not the glorious appearing as the KJV translation has it, but *epiphaneia* (2015), *tēs dóxēs*, the appearance of the glory of the great God and our Savior Jesus Christ (Titus 2:13). At Christ's Second Coming He will be truly recognized for all that He is. The glory of the Son of Man in Matthew 19:28; 25:31; Mark 10:37, cf. Luke 9:32; 24:26 is to be understood in contrast with His earthly manifestation (John 17:22, 24; Phil. 3:21) and is brought by Christ Himself into connection with the *dóxa*, glory, which He had before His humiliation in the incarnation (John 17:5, cf. 12:41; Phil. 2:11). Hebrews 1:3 equates the glory of Jesus to God's glory, being the revelation of God in the economy of redemption. In this sense, future glory is the hope of Christians. More specifically, *dóxa* means not the outward glorious appearance, attracting attention to the person or thing itself, but that glory shown from within reflecting in the appearance which attracts attention, namely, splendor, glory, brightness, adornment (Matt. 4:8; Luke 4:6). *Dóxa* may stand in opposition to *alḗtheia* (225), truth, denoting seeming appearance, from *dokéō*, to appear, in opposition to *eínai* (1511), to be.

1392. Doxázō; from *dóxa* (1391), glory, To glorify, to recognize, honor, praise (Matt. 6:2; Luke 4:15; Rom. 11:13); to bring to honor, (strictly, to give anyone importance), make glorious, glorify (1 Cor. 12:26; Heb. 5:5; 1 Pet. 1:8). In the writings of John, the *dóxa* of God is the revelation and manifestation of all that He has and is. It is His revelation in which He manifests all the goodness that He is (John 12:28). Since Christ made this manifest, He is said to glorify the Father (John 17:1, 4); or the Father is glorified in Him (John 13:31; 14:13). When Christ is said to be glorified, it means simply that His innate glory is brought to light, made manifest (John 7:39; 11:4; 12:16, 23; 13:31; 17:1, 5). Christ glorified in His disciples (John 17:10, cf. 14:13). The revelation of the Holy Spirit in the glorification of Christ (John 16:14).

1394. Dósis; the act of giving (Phil. 4:15; James 1:17). Contrast *dórēma* (1434), the result of giving or the thing given.

1396. Doulagōgéō; from *doúlos* (1401), servant, and *ágō* (71), to lead, bring. To bring into servitude or subjection (1 Cor. 9:27).

1397. Douleía; servitude, dependence; the stale of a *doúlos* (1401), slave. That state of man in which he is prevented from freely possessing and enjoying his life; a state opposed to liberty. In NT used only figuratively (Rom. 8:15, 21; Gal. 4:24; 5:1; Heb. 2:15).

1398. Douleúō; from *doúlos* (1401), servant. To be in the position of a servant and act accordingly; to be subject and serve in subjection, bondage; used of actions which are directed by others. NT meanings: subjugated, reduced to bondage under someone (John 8:33; Acts 7:7; Rom. 9:12); used in the absolute sense, it means to be deprived of freedom (Gal. 4:25); to be under the law; serve in bondage, put ones dependence into effect, that is to obey (Matt. 6:24; Luke 15:29; 16:13; Gal. 5:13; Eph. 6:7; 1 Tim. 6:2); metaphorically, to be a slave to, such as to pleasures (Rom. 7:25; Titus 3:3).

1401. Doúlos; slave, one who is in a permanent relation of servitude to another, his will altogether consumed in the will of the other (Matt. 8:9; 20:27; 24:45, 46) Verb: *doulóō* (1402), reduce to servitude; in the pass, to be enslaved.

1402. Doulóō; from *doúlos* (1401), slave. To make a servant, subject, subjugate (Acts 7:6; 1 Cor. 9:19); in

the pass., to be subjugated, subdued (Rom. 6:18, 22). In the perf. tense, to be dependent (Gal. 4:3). Denotes not so much a relation of service, as primarily a relation of dependence upon, bondage to anyone (i.e., in the case of subjugated nations, etc.; see Titus 2:3; 2 Pet. 2:19). In 1 Corinthians 7:15 the verb refers to a brother or sister being bound by law.

1403. Doché; from *déchomai* (1209), to receive. A reception, entertainment, banquet Only in Luke 5:29; 14:13.

1410. Dúnamai; to be able, have power, by virtue of ones own ability and resources (Rom. 15:14); through a state of mind or favorable circumstances (1 Thess. 2:6); by permission of law or custom (Acts 24:8, 11), or simply to be able, powerful (Matt. 3:9; 2 Tim. 3:15).

1411. Dúnamis; power, especially inherent power (Mark 5:30; Eph. 1:19). All the words derived from the stem *dúna-* have the basic meaning of being able, capable. Contrast *ischús* (2479) which stresses the factuality of the ability. It may even mean to will. *Dunatós* (1415), the adj. noun means one who has an ability, the opposite of which is *adúnatos* (102), not able, incapable or incompetent, impossible. Verbs: *dúnamai* (1410), to be able; *dunatéō* (1414) to have great ability (2 Cor. 13:3); *dunamóō* (1412) and *endunamóō* (1743), to strengthen (Col. 1:11). Nouns: *dunástēs* (1413), one who exercises dominion authority; *dunámeis* (pl). powers, miracles coming out of that mighty power of God inherent in Christ and which power was lent to His witnesses and ambassadors. See *sēmeía* (4592), signs; *megaleía* (3167), great works; *éndoxa* (1741), glorious works; *parádoxa* (3861), strange works; *thaumásia* (2297), marvelous works, *térata* (5059), terrifying works.

1412. Dunamóō; to strengthen. In the NT used in the pass., to be strengthened, grow strong (Col. 1:11), of moral strengthening (cf. Eph. 3:16). Related to *dúnamis* (1411), power.

1413. Dunástēs; possessor of power or authority, one who occupies high position (Acts 8:27), especially of independent rulers of territories (Luke 1:52). Referring to the Lord as the absolute ruler (1 Tim. 6:15).

1425. Dusnóētos; from *dus-* (1418), hardly, and *noētós*, understood. Hardly understood, hard to be understood (2 Pet. 3:16). See *noéō* (3539), to understand; *nous* (3563) mind.

1431. Dōreá; a free gift with emphasis on its gratuitous character. Used in the NT of a spiritual or supernatural gift (John 4:10; Acts 2:38; 8:20; 10:45; 11:17; Rom. 5:15, 17; 2 Cor. 9:15; Eph. 3:7; 4:7; Heb. 6:4) Adv.: *dōreán* (1432), freely (Rom. 3:24).

1434. Dórēma; the thing given (Rom. 5:16; James 1:17). The suffix *-ma* makes it the result of *dósis* (1394), the act of giving.

1435. Dóron; gift, related to *dídōmi* (1325), to give. This word is used of gifts given as an expression of honor (Matt. 2:11); for support of the temple (Matt. 15:5; Mark 7:11; Luke 21:1, 4); for God (Matt. 5:23, 24; 8:4; 23:18, 19; Heb. 5:1; 8:3, 4; 9:9; 11:4); as the gift of salvation (Eph. 2:8), for celebrating (Rev. 11:10).

1448. Eggízō; to bring near and come near used in a trans. and intrans. sense, as is often the case with verbs of motion such as *ágō* (71), lead. Usually in the NT used intrans. meaning to come near, approach (Luke 7:12; 15:1, 25; 22:47; Acts 10:9); in the expression *éggiken*, is near, referring to the kingdom of God or heaven (Matt. 3:2; 4:17; 10:7; Mark 1:15; Luke 10:11). The verb has reference to space, meaning that something is here. When used in speaking of approaching God or coming near to God (Heb. 7:19; James 4:8), it means communion with God in prayer and the desired and cherished fellowship with Him. Deriv.: *proseggízō* (4331), approaching, coming close to.

1450. Égguos; bail, security. In the NT, occurs only in Hebrews 7:22 which is not to be used in reference to the death of Christ by which He has answered for us, but to His eternal priesthood through which (not with which) He is surety for the better covenant (cf. vv. 21, 24, 25).

1451. Eggús; close, near. Used in an absolute sense of both space and time (Matt. 24:32, 33; 26:18; Phil.

4:5). Figuratively used of spiritual relations (Eph. 2:13, 17).

1453. Egeírō; to awaken, wake up. Primarily used of waking those who sleep. In the pass., to be awakened (Matt. 1:24; Rom. 13:11). Used figuratively meaning to become attentive to ones dangerous position and to the salvation of God (Rom. 13:11; Eph. 5:14); also used of those who are sick and need help to raise themselves up (Mark 1:31; 9:27, cf. Matt. 12:11). In the pass. sense, to recover, rise up from bed (Matt. 8:15; 9:5–7). Especially, however, used of the dead recalled to life or who rise to new life (Matt. 10:8; Acts 3:15; 1 Cor. 6:14). The pass. to rise again, with or without from the dead, always refers to the resurrection of the body (Matt. 11:5; 14:2). To erect, build up (John 2:19). With a personal obj., to call forth, cause to appear; in the pass, to appear, come forth (Matt. 24:7, 11, 24; Mark 13:8, 22; Acts 13:22). The pass. generally denotes to quit ones previous position, rise, get up (John 14:31; Rev. 11:1). Syn: *anístēmi* (450), to stand up or arise.

1454. Égersis; from *egeírō* (1453), to wake up. Resurrection, resuscitation of the dead (Matt. 27:53).

1456. Egkaínia; from *en* (1722), in or at, and *kainós* (2537), qualitatively new. Occurs only in John 10:22 in the neut. pl. referring to the Feast of Dedication which commemorated the dedication of the Temple at Jerusalem, or of its purification and making it qualitatively new, as it were, after it had been polluted by heathen idolatries and impurities. See *egkainízō* (1457), dedicate. For deriv. of *kainós*, qualitatively new, see *anakainóō* (341), to renew.

1457. Egkainízō; from *en* (1722), in or at, and *kainós* (2537), qualitatively new. To dedicate, consecrate (Heb. 9:18; 10:20). Deriv.: *egkaínia* (1456), dedication; *anakainóō* (341), to renew.

1458. Egkaléō; from *en* (1722) in, and *kaléō* (2564), to call, to bring a charge against. Call to account, accuse (Acts 19:38, 40; 23:28, 29; 26:2, 7; Rom. 8:33).

1462. Égklēma; an accusation made in public but not necessarily before a tribunal (Acts 23:29), complaint, charge (Acts 25:16).

1469. Egkrínō; from *en* (1722), in or among, and *krínō* (2919), to judge, to reckon. In 2 Corinthians 10:12 it is joined with *heautoús* (1438), ourselves, and the dat. *tisí* (5100), to someone; to ajudge ourselves to the number or rank of. In later Gr. it came to mean to approve, esteem as being up to the standard and therefore admissible.

1482. Ethnikós; from *éthnos* (1484), nation. In the NT this word answers to the biblical idea of *éthnē*, nations, and means heathenish, that which pertains to those who are unconnected with the people and the God of salvation (only in Matt. 6:7; 18:17).

1483. Ethnikôs; an adv. from *ethnikós* (1482) a heathen, Gentile. Heathenishly, after the manner of the heathen of the Gentiles. Used only in Galatians 2:14 meaning to live in a non-Israelitish manner, not bound to the Israelitish mode of life.

1484. Éthnos; a nation, people (Matt. 24:7; 25:32; Luke 7:5; John 11:48; Acts 7:7; 8:9). Used by Paul for the whole race of mankind considered in a noble or enlarged view as one nation (Acts 17:26). *Éthnē*, pl., frequently signifies the heathen or Gentiles as distinguished from the Jews or believers. The Jews usually are called *Laós* (2992), the people of God or the Israel of God. Syn.: *dêmos* (1218), a popular assembly or organized crowd from which is derived the English word democracy, the rule of organized people; *óchlos* (3793), unorganized multitude.

1491. Eídos; from *eidō* (1492), to see, the act of seeing. Sight (2 Cor. 5:7); the object of sight, form, appearance (Luke 3:22; 9:29; John 5:37; 1 Thess. 5:22). In 2 Corinthians 5:7 it refers to the visible appearance of things, in contrast to invisible things which are the objects of faith, meaning that the believer is guided not only by what he beholds, but by what he knows to be true though he cannot see it. In 1 Thessalonians 5:22, it signifies the appearance of evil.

1492. Eídō; or *eidéō, oída*; to perceive with the outward

senses, particularly with physical sight (Matt. 2:2, 9, 10); perceive with the mind, understand (John 21:15, 16; Rom. 8:28; 1 Cor. 2:11; 2 Cor. 11:31; Heb. 10:30); to experience, such as death, corruption, grief (Luke 2:26; Acts 2:27; Heb. 11:5); be acquainted with, as a person (Matt. 26:72, 74; Mark 14:71); esteem, regard (2 Cor. 5:16; 1 Thess. 5:12); acknowledge, own (Matt. 25:12); to know how, implying both knowledge and inclination (Matt. 7:11; Luke 11:13; 2 Pet. 2:9, cf. Matt. 27:65); consider (Acts 15:6); converse with (Luke 8:20); to perceive, know intuitively as contrasted with *ginōskō* (1097), to know experientially.

1492a. Oída; or *eídō, eidéō* (see 1492).

1494. Eidólóthuton; from *eídōlon* (1497), idol, and *thúō* (2380), to sacrifice. Whatever is sacrificed or offered to an idol, such as flesh or heathen sacrifices (Acts 15:29; 1 Cor. 8:1, 4).

1495. Eidōlolatreía; from *eídōlon* (1497), idol, and *latreía* (2999), worship. Idolatry (1 Cor. 10:14; Gal. 5:20; Col. 3:5; 1 Pet. 4:3). Worship of idols or false gods. An idolater is *eidōlolátrēs* (1496).

1496. Eidōlolátrēs; from *eídōlon* (1497), idol, and *látris*, a servant, worshiper. Idolater. A servant or worshipper of idols (1 Cor. 5:10, 11; 6:9; 10:7; Eph. 5:5; Rev. 21:8; 22:15).

1497. Eídōlon; from *eídos* (1491), a form, appearance. An image or representation whether corporeal or mental. In Class. Gr. used for a statue of man or even for a concept of the mind. In the NT it stands for an idol or image set up to be worshiped as a god (Acts 7:41; 15:20; 1 Cor. 12:2; Rev. 9:20). Also stands for a false god, usually worshiped in the form of an image (2 Cor. 6:16; 1 Thess. 1:9; 1 John 5:21). Paul in 1 Corinthians 8:4 says that an idol is nothing in the world yet it held significance to its worshipers as an object of worship. Paul meant that an idol is not a representation of the true God. Idols may be material as they may be the works of mens hands, such as statues of gold, or the moon. But as to their being of any excellency which might deserve divine worship, they are nothing. See Isaiah 41:24; Habakkuk 2:18, 19.

1504. Eikốn; from *eíkō*, to be like, resemble. A bodily representation, an image as of a man made of gold, silver, etc. (Rom. 1:23); a monarchs likeness impressed on a coin (Matt. 22:20; Mark 12:16, Luke 20:24); image, resemblance, likeness (Rom. 8:29; 1 Cor. 11:7; 15:49; Col. 1:15; 3:10). *Eikốn* sometimes may be used synonymously with *homoíōma* (3667), and both may refer to the earthly copies and resemblances of the archetypal things in the heavens. However, there is a distinction: *eikốn*, image, always assumes a prototype, that which it not merely resembles, but from which it is drawn. Thus, the reflection of the sun on the water is *eikốn*; and more importantly, the child is *émpsuchos* (possessed of a soul) *eikốn*, image of his parents. *Homoíōma* is the result, the likeness or resemblance. *Homoíōsis* (3669), is the process or act of producing a likeness or resemblance. However, while with the terms *homoíōma* and *homoíōsis* there is resemblance, it by no means follows that the item under discussion is derived from what it resembles. For example, there may be a resemblance between two men in no way related to each other. The *eikốn*, image, includes and involves the resemblance of similitude (*homoíōsis*), but the *homoíōsis* does not involve the image. The Son is an *homoíōma* of God in that both are God, but He is also the *eikốn*, the image of God, humanly indicating His relation to the Father (2 Cor. 4:4; Col. 1:15). There are two other Gr. words that stand in contrast to *eikốn* and *homoíōma*. They are *charaktếr* (5481), character, and *apaúgasma* (541), brightness (used only in Heb. 1:3). *Charaktếr* signifies the image impressed as corresponding with the original or pattern. On account of this idea of close resemblance it has for its syn. *mímēma*, imitation, anything imitated, a copy; *apeikónisma*, representation. On the other hand, *apaúgasma* means radiation, not merely reflection. Furthermore, Hebrews 1:3 uses *charaktếr*, not *cháragma* (5480), because the latter word was used in a narrower sense and rarely denoted the peculiar characteristics of an individual or a people and always prominently suggests the pass. bearing of the subject spoken of. *Cháragma* occurs in Acts 17:29; Revelation 13:16, 17; 14:9, 11; 15:2 TR; 16:2; 19:20; 20:4 meaning impression, mark, symbol.

1505. Eilikríneia; purity, sincerity (1 Cor. 5:8; 2 Cor. 1:12; 2:17). Adj.: *eilikrinḗs* (1506), sincere.

1506. Eilikrinḗs; from *heílē* or *hélē*, the shining or splendor of the sun and *krínō* (2919), judge, discern. Sincere, pure, unsullied, free from spot or blemish to such a degree as to bear examination in the full splendor of the sun. In the NT generally understood to relate to the lives or wills of Christians, since in Paul it seems to refer to *dokimázō* (1381), to discern. Peter joins it with *diánoia* (1271), understanding, and thus meaning clearness or perspicuity of mind or understanding by which one is able to see all things intelligibly, clearly, and proceed without mistake. Therefore, *eilikrinḗs* may be rendered,clear, clearly discerning, of clear spiritual judgment or discernment, in all things both of Christian faith and practice (Phil. 1:10; 2 Pet. 3:1). Another Gr. word with which *eilikrinḗs* is continually found is *katharós* (2513), pure, clean, free from soil or stain. Some relate *eilikrinḗs* to the verb *elíō*, that which is cleansed by much rolling and shaking to and fro in the sieve. According to one element of etymology, therefore, *eilikrinḗs* is the clear and transparent, and, according to another, the purged, winnowed, unmingled. See *katharós* (2513); *koinós* (2839), unclean; *achreíos* (888), useless.

1510. Eimí; to be, exist, have existence or being (John 1:1, 2, 10; 8:58; Heb. 11:6); denoting the quality, state, condition or situation of a person or thing (Matt. 1:18, 19; 2:9, 13, 15; 3:11; Mark 1:6; 9:7); to happen (Matt. 13:40, 49; 16:22; Mark 13:4); to be reckoned or reputed (Matt. 18:17; 1 Cor. 3:19; 1 Tim. 1:7); to represent figuratively (Matt. 13:37–39); to mean, to count important (Matt. 9:13; 12:7; Mark 9:10; Acts 10:17); with a gen. case it denotes possession or property (Matt. 6:13 TR), also with a dat. (Luke 8:42); with the neg. *ouk* (not), not to be alive (Matt. 2:18); *eimí eis* ([1519] in), to be for, become (Matt. 19:5).

1514. Eirēneúō; to live in peace, keep peace toward someone or with someone (Mark 9:50; Rom. 12:18; 2 Cor. 13:11; 1 Thess. 5:13). Syn.: *to autó* ([846], same) *phronéō* ([5426], to think). thinking the same (2 Cor. 13:11).

1515. Eirḗnē; peace, rest. In contrast with strife; denoting the absence or end of strife. *Eirḗnē* denotes a state of untroubled, undisturbed, well-being (James 3:18). This is its meaning when used as a form of salutation in greeting (Luke 24:36; John 20:19, 21, 26) and when taking leave (Mark 5:34; Luke 8:48; Acts 15:33; 16:36; 1 Cor. 16:11; James 2:16). It may also when contrasted with strife, such a state of peace is the object of divine promise and is brought about by God's mercy, granting deliverance and freedom from all the distresses that are experienced as a result of sin. Used together with *éleos* (1656), it refers to mercy for the consequences of sin, and also with *cháris* (5485), grace, which affects the character of the person. Peace as a Messianic blessing is that state brought about by the grace and loving mind of God wherein the derangement and distress of life caused by sin are removed. Hence the message of salvation is called the Gospel of peace (Acts 10:36; Rom. 10:15 TR; Eph. 6:15). It is called the peace of God, not that God needs it, but God gives it (Phil. 4:7), the peace of Christ. It can be the result only of accomplished reconciliation (Rom. 5:1; Eph. 2:16, 17), referring to the new relationship between man and God brought about by the atonement (Rom. 5:9, 10). Syn.: *asphaleia* (803), security. Ant.: *machaira* (3162), sword (Matt. 10:34); *diamerismós* (1267), division (Luke 12:51); *laléō* (2980), to speak; *dólos* (1388), guile (1 Pet. 3:10); *akatastasía* (181), commotion or confusion (1 Cor. 14:33).

1516. Eirēnikós; adj. pertaining to peace, peaceable or peaceful (Heb. 12:11; James 3:17). The reference is to *eirḗnē* (1515), peace, as the blessing of salvation.

1517. Eirēnopoiéō; to make peace, put an end to strife (only in Col. 1:20).

1518. Eirēnopoiós; The one who makes peace in others having first received the peace of God in his own heart (only in Matt. 5:9); not simply one who makes peace between two parties.

1519. Eis; A prep. which usually governs the acc. with the primary idea of motion into any place or thing; also of motion or direction to, towards, upon any place or thing. The opposite idea is expressed by *ek* (1537), out (of a place). As to time, *eis* implies when, referring to a term or limit, up to, towards, until (Acts 4:3, until tomorrow). Many times in the NT it is used to indicate intention, purpose, identity, aim, such as baptism of repentance unto the remission of sins (Mark 1:4); baptized into Moses, that is, identified with Moses in what he was doing (1 Cor. 10:2). In composition with verbs, *eis* implies motion into, as *eisdéchomai* (1523), to receive into; also motion or direction to, towards, as *eisakoúō* (1522), to let words sink into ones ear.

1520. Heis; one; *mía* (fem.); *hen* (neut.) In the mas. *heis* must be distinguished from the neut. *hen*. *Heis* means one numerically while *hen* means one in essence, as in John 10:30; "I and my Father are one (*hen*)" (i.e., one in essence although two different personalities). Had it said *heis*, it would have meant one person.

1523. Eisdéchomai; from the prep. *eis* (1519), into, and *déchomai* (1209), to receive. To receive into favor or communion (only in 2 Cor. 6:17).

1537. Ek; before a vowel, *ex*; a prep. governing the gen. with the primary meaning out of, from, of; spoken of such objects which before were in another object but are now separated from it, either in respect of place, time, source, or origin. The direct opposite of *eis* (1519), unto, which means "to become part of" or "to be identified with." Metaphorically, after verbs of motion or direction, *ek* speaks of a state or condition, out of which one comes, is brought, or tends toward. After verbs implying motion of any kind, out of or from any place or object; used for example, with verbs of going, coming, sending, throwing, falling, gathering, separating, or removing. After verbs implying direction out of or from any place, it is used to mark the point from which the direction sets off or tends toward. Related meanings: (1) Of time, the beginning of a period of time, a point after which something takes place. (2) Of the origin or source of anything, that is, the primary, direct, immediate source, in distinction from *apó* (575). (3) When used of persons, it refers to the place, stock, family, or condition, out of which one is derived or to which one belongs. (4) Referring to the source, namely the person or thing, out of or from which anything proceeds, is derived, to which it pertains. (5) Of the motive, ground, occasion, from which anything proceeds, the incidental, translated from, out of; that is, by reason of, because of, in consequence of. (6) It also may speak of the efficient cause, or agent from which any action or thing proceeds, is produced, or effected, from, or by. (7) To the manner or mode in which anything is done, translated out of, from, in, with. (8) To the means, instrument, instrumental cause, translated from; that is, by means of, by, through, with (e.g., Luke 16:9, ". . . by means of the mammon of unrighteousness"). (9) When referring to the material, translated out of, from, as in Matthew 27:29, a crown of thorns, refers to one made out of thorns. (10) Referring to a whole in relation to a part, a whole from which a part is spoken, such as in 1 Corinthians 12:15, 16.

1538. Hékastos; from *hékas*, separate, each, everyone, of any number separately. In construction with pl. verbs, it means distributively, where it is in opposition to an implied pl. noun (Matthew 18:35 where *hékastos* should not be rendered everyone [KJV] but rather each one).

1551. Ekdéchomai; from *ek* (1537), out, and *déchomai* (1209), to receive, to watch for, expect (John 5:3; 1 Cor. 16:11; Heb. 11:10). Expect, wait for (Acts 17:16; 1 Cor. 11:33; 1 Pet. 3:20).

1553. Ekdēméō; from *ek* (1537), from, or out of, and *démos* (1218), people. To go abroad, to part , as the parting from the body as the earthly abode of the spirit (2 Cor. 5:8); to be away or absent from the body and present with the Lord.

1556. Ekdikéō; to revenge (Luke 18:3, 5; Rom. 12:19; Rev. 6:10; 19:2); to avenge, punish (2 Cor. 10:6).

1557. Ekdíkēsis; revenge, or vengeance (Luke 18:7, 8; 21:22; Rom. 12:19; 2 Cor. 7:11); punishment (1 Pet. 2:14).

1558. Ékdikos; the one outside of that which is lawful; lawless, mischievous. In later Gr. it came to mean he who brings to pass what he believes to be his right, an avenger. Only, in Romans 13:4 and 1 Thessalonians 4:6, translated avenger, in referring to the magistracy. Ant. : hosios (3741), holy.

1561. Ekdoché; from the verb ekdéchomai (1551), to expect the verb. A looking for, expectation (Heb. 10:27).

1573. Ekkakéō; or egkakéō. Denotes cowardice, faintheartedness. To be unfortunate, desperate (2 Cor. 4:1). Usually translated to lose heart (Luke 18:1; 2 Cor. 4:1, 16; Gal. 6:9; Eph. 3:13; 2 Thess. 3:13).

1577. Ekklēsía; originally seems to have been derived from ekkaléō, to call out. It was a common term for a congregation of the ekklētoí, those called out or assembled in the public affairs of a free state; a body of free citizens called together by a herald (kérux, [2783]). The ekklētoí, the called people, constituted the ekklēsía. In the NT the word is applied to the congregation of the people of Israel (Acts 7:38). On the other hand, sunagōgḗ (4864) seems to have been used to designate the people from Israel in distinction from all other nations (Acts 13:43, cf. Matt. 4:23; 6:2; James 2:2; Rev. 2:9; 3:9). But when in Hebrews 10:25 the gathering of the Christians is referred to, it is not called sunagōgḗ but episunagōgḗ (1997), with the prep. epí (1909), upon, translated the assembling together. The Christian community was designated for the first time as ekklēsía to differentiate it from the Jewish community, sunagōgḗ (Acts 2:47 TR). The term ekklēsía denotes the NT community of the redeemed in its twofold aspect; all who were called by and to Christ in the fellowship of His salvation, the Church worldwide of all times, and only secondarily to an individual church (Matt. 16:18; Acts 2:47; 9:31; 1 Cor. 6:4; 10:32; 11:22; 12:28; 14:4, 5, 12; 15:9; Gal. 1:13; Phil. 3:6; Col. 1:18, 24). Designated Church of God (1 Cor. 10:32; 11:22; 15:9; Gal. 1:13; 1 Tim. 3:5, 15); the body of Christ (Eph. 5:23, 24); the entire Church exclusively (Eph. 1:22; 3:10, 21; 5:23–25, 27, 29, 32; Heb. 12:23). The NT churches, however, are also confined to particular places (Rom. 16:5; 1 Cor. 1:2; 16:19; 2 Cor. 1:1; Col. 4:15; 1 Thess. 2:14; Phile. 1:2); to single local churches (Acts 8:1; 11:22; Rom. 16:1; 1 Thess. 1:1; 2 Thess. 1:1).

1586. Eklégomai; mid. voice of eklégō, from ek (1537), out, and légō (3004). To speak intelligently. To choose, select, choose for oneself, not necessarily implying the rejection of what is not chosen but giving favor to the chosen subject, keeping in view a relation to be established between him and the object (Mark 13:20; Acts 1:2). It involves preference and choice from among many. (Cf. epilégomai [1951], to select; hairéomai [138], to prefer; hairetízō [140], to choose.)

1588. Eklektós; chosen, elected (Matt. 20:16; Luke 18:7); related to eklégomai (1586), to choose.

1589. Eklogé; choice, election (Acts 9:15; 1 Thess. 1:4); related to eklégomai (1586), to choose.

1595. Hekoúsion; adj. voluntary; related to hekón (1635) willingly. Only in Philemon 1:14 where it refers to the idea of willingly, uncompelled, gladly.

1596. Hekousíōs; adv., voluntarily, intentionally. Refers to the sins committed willingly, deliberately (only in Heb. 10:26; 1 Pet. 5:2).

1598. Ekpeirázō; from the intens. ek (1537), out, and peirázō (3985), to tempt. To try, prove, tempt, put to the test. Sinners are said to tempt God (Matt. 4:7); putting Him to the test, refusing to believe Him or His Word until He has manifested His power. When God is said to tempt (peirázō) man (Heb. 11:17, cf. Gen. 22:1; Ex. 15:25; Deut. 12:3, 4), in no other sense can He do this (James 1:13) but to train him in order to elevate him as a result of the knowledge which may be won

through these temptations (peirasmoí, [3986]). That man may emerge from his testings holier, humbler, stronger than when he entered in (James 1:2, 12). Peirázō is used predominantly of testing someone in order to show whether he is approved of God or reprobate. Used of Satans solicitations (Matt. 4:1; 1 Cor. 7:5; Rev. 2:10).

1603. Ekplēróō; from the intens. ek (1537), and plēróō (4137), to fulfill. To fulfill entirely (Acts 13:33).

1604. Ekplérōsis; from ekplēróō (1603), to fulfill. A fulfillment, an accomplishment (only in Acts 21:26).

1611. Ékstasis; from exístēmi (1839), to remove out of its place or state. An ecstasy in which the mind is for a time carried out of its normal state. Great astonishment, amazement (Mark 5:42; 16:8; Luke 5:26; Acts 3:10). It may mean sacred ecstasy or rapture of the mind when the use of the external senses are suspended and God reveals something in an unusual manner (Acts 10:10; 11:5; 22:17). See hístēmi (2476), to stand.

1618. Ektenés; adj ,meaning stretched out, continual, intense (Acts 12:5 TR; 1 Pet. 4:8). Verb: ekteinō (1614), to stretch out, extend, as the hand (Matt. 8:3; 12:13); to cast out, let down, as an anchor from a ship (Acts 27:30). Deriv: ektenōs (1619), intensely, earnestly (1 Pet. 1:22); ekteneía (1616), intenseness or continuance (Acts 26:7); ektenésteron (1617), the comparative neut. of ektenés used adverbially, meaning more intensely, earnestly (Luke 22:44 TR).

1634. Ekpsuchō; from ek (1537), out, and psuchō (5594), to breathe. To expire (Acts 5:5, 10; 12:23).

1635. Hekón; willing, unconstrained, gladly. Usually stands opposite to violence or compulsion (only in Rom. 8:20; 1 Cor. 9:17).

1637. Elaión; oil, originally the express use of the oil of the olive (Luke 7:46; 10:34). Élaion agalliáseōs (20), the oil of gladness, denotes the exhilarating influence of the Holy Spirit typified by oil (Heb. 1:9). As oil is used to give light, so the Holy Spirit enlightens mens hearts concerning their need of God in Jesus Christ. Élaion should be distinguished from múron (3464), ointment. Ointment has oil as its base, to which spice or scent or other aromatic ingredients are added. There is evidence that in ancient times oil was applied to men while ointment was applied to women. This distinction clarifies Luke 7:46 in which the Lord is found in the house of the Pharisee telling him, You did not anoint my head with oil (élaion) but she anointed my feet with perfume (múron). Oil represented the common courtesy that would be expressed to a man. It was as if our Lord said to the Pharisee, You withheld from me a cheap and ordinary courtesy (represented by oil) while this woman bestowed upon me costly and rare homage (represented by múron) which she did not put on my head, but on my feet (meaning that the least honored part, the feet, received the highest honor, múron.)

1650. Élegchos; conviction, only in 2 Timothy 3:16 and Hebrews 11:1. It implies not merely the charge on the basis of which one is convicted, but also the manifestation of the truth of that charge. The results to be reaped from that charge and the acknowledgement, (if not outwardly, yet inwardly) of its truth on the part of the accused are referred to as well. See the verb elégchō (1651), to convict, reprove. Contrast aitía (156), an accusation, true or false.

1651. Elégchō; to reprove with conviction upon the offender (Luke 3:19; Eph. 5:11, 13). Contrast epitimáō (2008), to rebuke without conviction on the part of the offender.

1652. Eleeinós; from éleos (1656); mercy. Worthy of pity, pitiable, full of misery. In the NT used only in 1 Corinthians 15:19; Revelation 3:17.

1653. Eleeō; sometimes eleáō, to have pity, be compassionate (Matt. 5:7; Rom. 9:15). To show mercy (éleos, [1656]); to show compassion, extend help for the consequence of sin. Opposite to sklērúnomai (4645), to be hardened. Contrast with cháris (5485), grace.

1654. Eleēmosúnē; mercifulness. The result of éleos (1656), mercy, which becomes part and parcel of a person's character (Acts 3:2; 10:2, 4, 31). Eleēmosúnē is the expression of mercy, to be contrasted with *oiktir-mós* (3628), which means more the expression of inner pity and compassion rather than the outward manifestation of character. *Oiktos*, from *oikteírō* (3627) and the subst. *oiktirmós*, only mentally express pity for a situation or a person, while *éleos*, mercy, *eleéō*, to be merciful, and the subst. *eleēmosúnē* refer to the actual helpful action resulting from the pity. Therefore, *oiktirmós* (3628) refers only to the mental and emotional agony of a situation. This is the reason why *eleēmosúnē* is consistently translated alms" or "alms-giving although it is derived from *éleos*, mercy, while *oiktirmós* is consistently translated mercy (Rom. 12:1; 2 Cor. 1:3; Phil. 2:1; Col. 3:12; Heb. 10:28).

1655. Eleêmōn; from *éleos* (1656), mercy. Compassionate, benevolently merciful, involving thought and action (Matt. 5:7; Heb. 2:17), while *oiktirmon* (3629), involves compassion from sensation (Luke 6:36; James 5:11). Both expressions are used of God in the manifestation of His pardoning and saving grace. *Oiktirmon* (3629) denotes one tenderly compassionate, one who grieves within for the condition and need of another. *Éleos*, from which *eleêmōn* is derived, gives expression to the love which is inherent in an individual and which finds its emphasis in the expression and the power of that love, not merely being inspired by a need. The adj. *eleêmōn* occurs in Matthew 5:7, blessed are the merciful ones', not merely those who express acts of mercifulness, but who have this attribute as a result of the indwelling of God within them, being *makárioi* (3107) blessed, because of Christ.

1656. Éleos; mercy. A special and immediate regard to the misery which is the consequence of sins (Luke 1:50; Eph. 2:4). Contrast *cháris* (5485), which is God's free grace and gift displayed in the forgiveness of sins as extended to men in their guilt. God's mercy, *éleos*, is extended for the alleviation of the consequences of sin. The lower creation is the object of God's mercy inasmuch as the burden of mans curse has redounded also upon it (Rom. 8:20–23). The guilt and power of sin must be removed through God's grace before the alleviation of the misery of sin can be experienced. The believer is to exercise mercifulness, for he can feel compassion for the misery of sin upon others, but he has no power to exercise grace since that is exclusively God's work. Blessed are the merciful for they shall obtain mercy (Matt. 5:7; KJV). See James 2:12, 13; 1 John 4:17.

1657. Eleuthería; freedom, generosity, independence. Freedom is presented as a distinctive blessing of the economy of grace which, in contrast with the OT economy, is represented as including independence from legal restrictions and rules of life (1 Cor. 10:29; Gal. 2:4; 5:1, 13). In contrast to the present subjection of the creature to the bondage of corruption, freedom represents the future state of the children of God (Rom. 8:21; see also vv. 20, 23). The perfect law of freedom (referred to in James 1:25) is the freedom of generosity, seen exclusively in James 2:12, 13, when the Judge shows his generosity in proportion to the mercifulness of the believers on earth. Ant.: *douleía* (1397), slavery.

1658. Eleútheros; connected with *eleúsomai*, the fut. of *érchomai* (2064), I come. One capable of movement, the free one. In the absolute sense: free, unconstrained, unfettered, independent. One who is not dependent upon another, for the most part in a social and political sense. In a relative sense: free, separate from or independent of (John 8:32, 33; 1 Cor. 9:19). Ant: *doúlos* (1401), slave, whose will and power is directed by another (John 8:32, 33; 1 Cor. 7:21, 22; 12:13; Gal. 3:28; Eph. 6:8; Col. 3:11).

1659. Eleutheróō; to make free, liberate, the result of redemption (John 8:32, 36; Rom. 6:18, 22; 8:2, 21; Gal. 5:1).

1670. Helkúō; or *hélkō*, to draw, without necessarily connoting the notion of force as in *súrō* (4951). See Acts 8:3; 14:19; 17:6; Revelation 21:6; James 2:6). To drag, although it may be implied (Acts 16:19; 21:30; James 2:6). *Helkúō* is used of Jesus on the cross drawing men

unto Himself by His love, not force (John 6:44; 12:32). It is drawing to a certain point as in John 21:6, 11 indicating the drawing of the net while *súrō* (4951) is merely dragging something after one. In John 21:8 *helkúō* gives place to *súrō* (4951) for nothing is intended there but the dragging of the net.

1677. Ellogéō; from *en*, (1722)in or into, and *lógos* (3056) an account, to charge, impute, take into account or consideration. (Rom. 5:13; Phile. 1:18).

1679. Elpízō; from *elpís* (1680), hope. To hope, expect with desire (Luke 6:34; 23:8; 24:21); hope in the manner of trust, to confide; used with prep. *en* (1722), in or with; *eis* (1519), unto; *epí* (1909), on (John 5:45; 1 Cor. 15:19; 2 Cor. 1:10; Phil. 2:19). To set ones hope upon something, that is, the hope of future good fortune (1 Tim. 6:17).

1680. Elpís; hope, desire of some good with expectation of obtaining it (Acts 16:19; Rom. 5:4; Titus 1:2; 1 John 3:3). The object of hope, the thing hoped for (Rom. 8:24; Heb. 6:18, cf. Gal. 5:5; Col. 1:5; Titus 2:13; Heb. 7:19). The foundation or ground of hope (Col. 1:27; 1 Tim. 1:1). Trust, confidence in someone, when used with *eis* (1519), in or unto, following (1 Pet. 1:21). Confidence, security (Acts 2:26).

1696. Emménō; from *en* (1722), in, and *ménō* (3306), to remain. To remain, persevere in (Acts 14:22; Gal. 3:10; Heb. 8:9); with topographical reference (Acts 28:30).

1722. En; in. The prep. *en* usually governs the dat. with a primary idea of rest in any place or thing, and may be translated as on, at, by. *En*, When contrasted with *eis* (1519), unto, and *ek* (1537), from, stands between the two, *eis* implying motion into, *en*, in or remaining in, and *ek*, indicating motion out of. Commonly used of place, *en* means remaining, taking place within some definite place or limits, in, on, at, or by. If spoken of elevated objects or a surface, it may mean in, that is, on, upon, as on a fig tree, literally, in it (Mark 11:13), on the mountain (*en tō orei*) (Luke 8:32). In a somewhat wider sense, implying simply contact, it means close proximity (Matt. 6:5), on the corners of the streets, near the corners of the streets, so that the Pharisees could be seen by people who passed through the intersection. Used of a number or multitude, as indicating place, it means in, among, with, equivalent to *en mésō*, in the midst (Matt. 2:6; 11:11, 21). When used of persons, by implication it means before, in the presence of (Mark 8:38). When spoken of that by which one is surrounded or in which one is enveloped, in, with (Matt. 16:27). When used of time, it means when, such as a definite point or period, in, during, on, at which time anything takes place (Matt. 2:1; 3:1; 8:13). When used of time it may also mean how long, namely a space or period within which anything takes place, in, within, as in three days (Matt. 27:40).

1735. Endéchomai; from the prep. *en* (1722), in, upon, and *déchomai* (1209), to receive. As an impersonal verb *endéchetai* means it is possible, it may be (Luke 13:33).

1738. Éndikos; fair, just. *Díkaios* characterizes the subject so far as it is one with *díkē* (1349), justice, while *éndikos* characterizes the subject so far as it occupies the due relation to *díkē*, justice, or is within the confines of the law. Thus, in Hebrews 2:2 it means a just or fair recompense. In Romans 3:8, *éndikon* presupposes that which has been decided justly. *Dikaíōs* is that which leads to the just sentence. Syn. *díkaios* (1342), just.

1740. Endoxázō; used only in 2 Thessalonians 1:10, 12 in the mid. voice, *endoxázomai*, from *en* (1722), in, and *doxázō* (1392), to glorify. In the aor. pass., to appear glorious (e.g., for Christ to appear and be recognized for all that He is).

1741. Éndoxos; glorious, splendid (Luke 13:17; Eph. 5:27). Neut. pl. *éndoxa*, as in Luke 13:17, works, miracles in which the *dóxa* (1391), glory of God and of the Son of God, shone forth manifestly (John 2:11; 11:40, cf. Luke 7:25). See *sēmeía* (4592), signs; *dunámeis* (1411), mighty works; *megaleía* (3167), great works; *parádoxa* (3861), strange works; *thaumásia*

(2297), admirable works.

1743. Endunamóō; to strengthen, only in biblical and ecclesiastical Gr., from *en* (1722), in, and *dunamóō* (1412), to strengthen. To make strong, vigorous. Used in the pass., to be strengthened, become strong. In connection with Hebrews 11:34 (TR), reference is appropriately made to Samson and Hezekiah. Elsewhere only metaphorically or spiritually and in the moral sphere (1 Tim. 1:12; 2 Tim. 4:17, where it is used of the equipment with the power necessary for executing the office of an apostle). Used also in Acts 9:22; Romans 4:20; Philippians 4:13; 2 Timothy 2:1.

1754. Energéō; to be active and energetic, to effect, prove oneself strong (Matt. 14:2; Mark 6:14; 1 Cor. 12:6, 11; Eph. 1:11, 20; 2:2). In the pass. and mid., *energéomai*, to be effected, accomplished (2 Cor. 1:6, cf. 2 Cor. 4:12). In James 5:16 it seems to denote the inspired prayer or the prayer of a righteous man wrought by the operation of the Holy Spirit (cf. Rom. 8:26, 27). To be in action, to be acting (2 Thess. 2:7), in the mid. voice the meaning to prove oneself strong or to make oneself felt by energetic working is, except in Philippians 2:13, used of the Apostle Paul when he predicates it to other subjects (Rom. 7:5; 2 Cor. 1:6; 4:12; Gal. 5:6; Eph. 3:20; Col. 1:29; 1 Thess. 2:13; 2 Thess. 2:7).

1755. Enérgēma; the suffix *-ma* makes it the result or effect of *enérgeia* (1753), energy. In the NT used only in 1 Corinthians 12:6, 10 of the results of the energy of God in the believer, translated effects, but actually it is the results energized by God's grace.

1756. Energés; from *enérgeia* (1753), energy. Refers to energy, engaged in work, capable of doing, active, powerful (1 Cor. 16:9; Phile. 1:6; Heb. 4:12). In Class. Gr. *energés*, *enérgeia* (energy), and the verb *energéō* (1754), to be at work, seem to have been used almost exclusively as medical terms referring to medical treatment and the influence of medicine.

1758. Enéchō; from *en* (1722), in or upon, and *échō* (2192), to have. To hold in, endure. To urge, press upon (Luke 11:53), to have a quarrel, to spite or have resentment (Mark 6:19). Deriv: *énochos* (1777), to be held fast, bound, obliged; with a gen. following: bound, subject to, subject of (Heb. 2:15), guilty, deserving of and subject to punishment (Matt. 14:64; 26:66); bound by sin or guilt, guilty of sin and deserving of punishment (1 Cor. 11:27; James 2:10).

1764. Enístēmi; from *en* (1722), in, with, and *hístēmi* (2476), to stand. Be present, instant, or at hand (Rom. 8:38; 1 Cor. 7:26; 2 Thess. 2:2; 2 Tim. 3:1).

1771. Énnoia; from *en* (1722), in, and *noús* (3563), mind. Intention, purpose, mind (Heb. 4:12; 1 Pet. 4:1). See *noéō* (3539), to think; *nous* (3563), mind.

1772. Énnomos; from *en* (1722), in, and *nómos* (3551), law. What is within range of law, based upon law, and governed or determined by law. *Énnomos* applies to the church (1 Cor. 9:21, cf. Gal. 6:2). Ant.: *paránomos*, not in accordance with the law, which word does not occur in the NT; the verb *paranoméō (3891), to act contrary to the law (Acts 23:3);*. the subst. *paranomía* (3892), wrongdoing, (2 Pet. 2:16).

1778. Éntalma; commandment, but emphasizing the thing commanded, a commission (Matt. 15:9; Mark 7:7; Col. 2:22). Deriv.: *entéllomai* (1781), from *en* (1722), in, and *téllō*, to charge, command, emphasizing the thing commanded; *entolé* (1785), commandment, which stresses the authority of the one commanding.

1783. Énteuxis; from the verb *entugchánō* (1793), to interrupt another in speaking. Intercession, prayer, address to God for oneself or others (1 Tim. 2:1; 4:5) Coming to God with boldness (*parrhēsía*, [3954]).

1785. Entolé; commandment, whether from God or man (Matt. 15:3; 1 John 2:3). Related to *entéllomai* (1781), from *en* (1722), in, upon, and *téllō*, to charge, command (Matt. 4:6; Mark 13:34; John 15:17; Acts 13:47). *Entolé* is the most common of the words meaning commandment. See *diátagma*, (1297), edict, decree; *diatagé* (1296), ordinance, disposition; *éntalma* (1778), a religious commandment; *epitagé* (2003), commanding authority, order, command; *paraggelía*

(3852), charge. Entole stresses the authority of the one commanding, while *entálma* (1778) stresses the thing commanded. Syn: *prostássō* (4367), to charge.

1791. Entropé; from the verb *entrépō* (1788), which is from *en* (1722), in, upon, and *trépō*, to turn, to cause to return upon oneself through shame (Matt. 21:37; Mark 12:6; Luke 18:2, 4; 20:13; 1 Cor. 4:14; 2 Thess. 3:14; Titus 2:8; Heb. 12:9). Shame (1 Cor. 6:5; 15:34). Entrope differs from aischune in that e is a shame in an individual resulting from a public address, to an audience in general concerning their sins collectively, while a is shame resulting from exposure of a specific individual's actions to be known by all.

1804. Exaggéllō; from *ex* (*ek* [1537]), out, and *aggéllō*, to tell, declare. To tell, declare abroad (1 Pet. 2:9).

1805. Exagorázō; from *ex* (see *ek* [1537]), out or from, and *agorázō* (59), to buy. To buy or redeem from, as applied to our redemption by Christ from the curse and yoke of the law (Gal. 3:13; 4:5). To redeem, as spoken of time (Eph. 5:16; Col. 4:5). The same phrase is used in the Gr. version of Daniel 2:8 meaning, Ye are gaining or protracting time. Similarly to be understood in Ephesians 5:16, because the days are evil, or afflicting, abounding in troubles and persecutions. This sense of the expression is still more evident in Colossians 4:5 as redeeming the time (KJV) by prudent and blameless conduct, gaining as much time and opportunity as possible in view of persecution and death. The word generally means to buy up, to buy all that can be bought, not allowing a suitable moment to pass by unheeded.

1809. Exaitéō; from *ex* (see *ek* [1537]), out, and *aitéō* (154), to require or demand. To claim back, require something to be delivered up. In the mid. voice, *exaitéomai*, to claim back for oneself (Luke 22:31).

1815. Exanástasis; from *ex* (see *ek* [1537]), from, and *anástasis* (386), arising again. The resurrection from the dead (Phil. 3:11). See *hístēmi* (2476), to stand.

1817. Exanístēmi; related to *exanástasis* (1815), from *ex* (see *ek* [1537]), out or from, and *anístēmi* (450), to rise up. To rise up from among others (Acts 15:5); trans., to raise up seed from the woman (Mark 12:19; Luke 20:28). See *hístēmi* (2476), to stand.

1822. Exartízō; from the intens. *ex* (see *ek*, [1537]), from, and *ártios* (739), complete. The verb *artízō*, to put in appropriate condition. To complete entirely, spoken of time (Acts 21:5), to furnish, or fit completely (2 Tim. 3:17). Deriv.: *katartízō* (2675), to put a thing in its appropriate position, establish, set up.

1825. Exegeírō; from *ex* (see *ek*, [1537]), out, and *egeírō* (1453), to raise. To raise up (Rom. 9:17; 1 Cor. 6:14).

1834. Exēgéomai; from *ex* (see *ek* [1537]), out, used emphatically, and *hēgéomai* (2233), to tell, lead forward. To bring out, declare thoroughly and particularly (Luke 24:35; John 1:18; Acts 10:8; 15:12, 14; 21:19). From this verb comes the English word "exegesis" the unfolding through teaching.

1839. Exístēmi; or *exístamai*, from *ex* (see *ek* [1537]), out, and *hístēmi* (2476), to stand. To remove out of its place or state. In the NT applied only to the mind, meaning to be out of ones mind, to be beside oneself (2 Cor. 5:13); in a general sense, to be transported beyond oneself with astonishment, to be amazed, astounded (Matt. 12:23; Mark 2:12; 5:42) in an act. or trans. sense, to astonish (Luke 24:22; Acts 8:9).

1843. Exomologéō; verb made up of three distinct words: *ex* (see *ek* [1537]), out of, or *éxō* (1854), out; *homoú* (3674), together; and *logéō* or *légō* (3004), to reason, speak intelligently. To agree together with God or with ones conscience, and to externalize that which is inside oneself; to profess, express in agreement with, confess, to promise (Luke 22:6). In the mid. voice, *exomologéomai*, to confess as ones own sins (Matt. 3:6; Mark 1:5; Acts 19:18; James 5:16). To profess, confess, as the truth (Phil. 2:11). To confess, acknowledge as belonging to one (Rev. 3:5). With a dat. following, to give praise or glory to, glorify (Matt. 11:25; Luke 10:21; Rom. 14:11; 15:9).

1849. Exousía; from *éxesti* (1832), it is permissible, allowed. Permission, authority, right, liberty, power to do anything (Acts 26:12). As *éxesti* denies the presence of a hindrance, it may be used either of the capability or the right to do a certain action. The words *éxesti* and *exousía* combine the two ideas of right and might. As far as right, authority, or capability is concerned it involves ability, power, strength (*dúnamis* [1411]), (Matt. 9:8; 28:18). *Exousía* denotes executive power while *arché* (746), rule, represents the authority granting that power (Luke 20:20). The combined meaning of right and might is indicated in John 5:27; 17:2; 19:10, 11. *Exousía* also means justified, having the right to exercise power (Matt. 8:9; Rev. 18:1). In 1 Corinthians 11:10, it is clear from the connection in vv. 6, 7 that authority on the head is the same as the covering of the head (cf. *kálumma* [2571], and the verb *katakalúptō* [2619], to cover wholly, and *akatakáluptos* [177], uncovered). In Romans 13:1–3; Titus 3:1, *exousía* in the pl. denotes not so much the magistracy of a court, but the powers which govern and is syn. with *arché* (746), authority; *thrónos* (2362), throne; and *kuriótēs* (2963), dominion or government (1 Cor. 15:24; Eph. 1:21; 3:10; 6:12; Col. 2:10, 15; 1 Pet. 3:22). In the Pauline passages it probably refers to evil powers who oppose Christ (1 Cor. 15:24; Eph. 6:12; Col. 2:15).Syn.: *krátos* (2904), dominion (Jude 1:25); *dúnamis* (Luke 4:36)

1860. Epaggelía; from *epí* (1909), upon, and *aggéllō* (32), to report, declare. It is primarily a legal term denoting a summons or promise undertaking to do or give something. Used only of the promises of God, except in Acts 23:21. The thing promised, a gift graciously given, not a pledge secured by negotiation (Luke 24:49 Acts 2:33; Gal. 3:14; Eph. 1:13; Heb. 9:15). Deriv.: *epággelma* (1862), a promise made with emphasis on the promise fulfilled, the result of the promise.

1861. Epaggéllō; from the intens. *epí* (1909), upon, and *aggéllō* (32), to tell, declare. To proclaim as public announcements or decrees; hence to announce a message, summons, or promise. In Class. Gr. used more in the sense of announcing a summons, or issuing a command for something. In the NT used only in the mid. voice, *epaggéllomai*, as a deponent verb basically meaning to announce oneself, offer ones services. Used primarily as to promise in Mark 14:11; Acts 7:5; Romans 4:21; 2 Peter 2:19, and to profess in 1 Timothy 2:10; 6:21 with the meaning of pretending. When used with this special meaning, the word and its deriv. refers to God's divine promise of spontaneous salvation. To render a service. (See Acts 1:4, *epaggelían* [1860], the promise; also Acts 7:5; Romans 4:21; Titus 1:2; Hebrews 12:26; James 1:12; 2:5) Used absolutely, meaning to give a promise (Gal. 3:19; Heb. 6:13; 10:23; 11:11). Deriv.: *proepaggéllō*, in the NT only in the pass. form, *proepaggéllomai* (4279), to proclaim beforehand, promise beforehand; *epaggelía* (1860), proclamation; *epággelma* (1862), promise or assurance.

1862. Epággelma; promise, assurance. The suffix *-ma* makes it the result of *epaggéllō* (1861), to proclaim. Occurs only in 2 Peter 1:4; 3:13. Deriv.: *epaggéllō* (1861), to proclaim.

1864. Epagōnízomai; from *epí* (1909), for, and *agōnízomai* (75), to strive, contend earnestly. To fight for or in reference to something, with the dat. of that which gives the occasion (Jude 1:3).

1871. Epaitéō; from *epí* (1909), an intens., and *aitéō* (154), to ask, implore, claim. To beg, ask for alms (Luke 16:3). It is the literal word for beg. *Ptōchós* (4434), helplessly poor and depending upon others for survival (Luke 16:20) is translated poor man only by inference. A helplessly poor person can survive only by begging. *Epaitēs* (the noun derived from *epaitéō*).is one who realizes his inferior position and need and begs.

1876. Epanagkés; from *epí* (1909), upon, on account of, and *anágkē* (318), necessity. An adv. meaning necessity or necessarily. With the art. it assumes the meaning of the adj., *ta epanagkés*, things of necessity (Acts 15:28).

1879. Epanapaúō; or in the pass. form, *epanapaúomai*, from *epí* (1909), upon, and *anapaúomai* (373), to rest.

To rely, to rest, repose oneself upon (Rom. 2:17); to rest, with the sense of remaining upon (Luke 10:6).

1882. Epanórthōsis; from *epanorthóō*, to set right again, correct, from *epí* (1909), upon, used as an intens., and *anorthóō* (461), to make right. Correction or amendment of what is wrong in a mans life. Occurs only in 2 Timothy 3:16. See *nouthesía* (3559), admonition; *paideía* (3809), instruction.

1896. Epeídon; from *epí* (1909), upon, and eldon, the second aor. imper. of *horáō* (3708), to see. To look upon favorably (Luke 1:25) or unfavorably (Acts 4:29).

1905. Eperōtáō; from the intens. prep. *epí* (1909), and *erōtáō* (2065), to ask, inquire of, beg of. In the NT, to interrogate, inquire of, with the acc. *tína* (Matt. 12:10; 17:10; 27:11); used in the sense of to ask for, demand (Matt. 16:1). Deriv.: *eperótēma* (1906), inquiry.

1910. Epibaínō; from *epí* (1909), upon, to, and *baínō*, to go. To go upon, mount, as upon a donkey (Matt. 21:5); to go on shipboard (Acts 21:2, 6 TR; 27:2); to come to, enter into (Acts 20:18).

1919. Epígeios; from *epí* (1909), upon, and *gē* (1093), the earth. Earthly, being upon the earth (Phil. 2:10; 3:19). Earthly, belonging to the earth or wrought in men upon the earth (John 3:12). Earthly, terrestrial, made of earth (1 Cor. 15:40; 2 Cor. 5:1, cf. Job 4:19). Earthly, arising from the earth and attached to it (James 3:15). In the NT always opposite *epouránios* (2032), that which pertains to heaven (1 Cor. 15:40). In 2 Corinthians 5:1 *epígeios* is contrasted as an earthly house, to the house not made by hands, eternal in the heavens (see also John 3:12; Phil. 2:10). Occurs with a moral import, answering to the moral contrast between earth and heaven (Phil. 3:19, cf. v. 14; Col. 3:2; James 3:15, cf. v. 14, 16, 17).

1922. Epígnōsis; from *epí* (1909), an intens., and *gnósis* (1108), knowledge, meaning clear and exact knowledge. Epignosis is more intens. than *gnósis*, because it expresses a more thorough participation in the object of knowledge on the part of the subject. In the NT it appears in the Pauline writings and in Hebrews 10:26; 2 Peter 1:2, 3, 8; 2:20, and always refers to knowledge which very powerfully influences the form of the religious life, a knowledge laying claim to personal sympathy and exerting an influence upon the person. When used as an obj. (Eph. 1:17; 4:13; Col. 1:9, 10; 2:2; 1 Tim. 2:4; 2 Tim. 2:25; 3:7; Titus 1:1; Heb. 10:26; 2 Pet. 1:2, 3), it evinces the relation of the person knowing to the object of his knowledge (2 Pet. 1:8). It affects the religious blessings possessed by the subject (Eph. 1:17; 2 Pet. 1:2, 3) and determines the manifestations of the religious life (2 Pet. 2:20). When used without an obj. in a formal sense (Rom. 1:28; Col. 3:10), it is more precisely defined as knowledge which is determined by, or which regulates itself according to, so that the difference mentioned in Colossians 3:10 disappears. In Colossians 2:2, 23 it means discernment in connection with the knowledge of possession of salvation which determines the moral conduct (see Phil. 1:9, the knowledge which enables one to avoid error, cf. Rom. 10:2; 11:33; 2 Pet. 1:5).

1930. Epidiorthóō; from *epí* (1909), besides, above, and *diorthóō*, to correct. See *diórthōsis* (1357), an amendment, restoration. Occurs only in Titus 1:5, meaning to proceed in correcting or setting in order.

1932. Epieíkeia; clemency or gentleness (Acts 24:4; 2 Cor. 10:1). The virtue that rectifies and redresses the requisites of justice. The adj. *epieikḗs* (1933) occurs in Philippians 4:5; 1 Timothy 3:3; Titus 3:2; James 3:17; 1 Peter 2:18. Contrast *épios* (2261), mild. See *anochḗ* (463), forbearance; *makrothumía* (3115), longsuffering; *hupomonḗ* (5281), patience.

1937. Epithuméō; from *epí* (1909), in, and *thumós* (2372), the mind. To have the affections directed toward anything; to desire, long after. To desire in a good sense (Matt. 13:17; Luke 22:15; 1 Tim. 3:1; Heb. 6:11; 1 Pet. 1:12). To desire or long for as a matter of natural course (Luke 15:16; 16:21; 17:22; Gal. 5:17). To desire in a bad sense as coveting and lusting after (Matt. 5:28; Rom. 7:7; 13:9; 1 Cor. 10:6, cf. James 4:2).

1939. Epithumía; the active and individual desire resulting from *páthos* (3806), the diseased condition of the soul (Mark 4:19; Jude 1:16). See *hormé* (3730), an impulse; *órexis* (3715), lust.

1941. Epikaléomai; from *epí* (1909), upon, and *kaléō* (2564), to call. To be called by a persons name, declared to be dedicated to a person as to the Lord (Acts 15:17; James 2:7); to call a person by a name by charging him with an offense (Matt. 10:25 UBS); to call upon or invoke; in the mid. voice, to call upon a person as a witness (2 Cor. 1:23) or to appeal to an authority (Acts 25:25); to call upon by way of adoration; making use of the name of the Lord (Acts 2:21; Rom. 10:12–14; 2 Tim. 2:22).

1944. Epikátaratos; from *epí* (1909), upon, and *katáratos*, cursed. Used as a verbal adj. from *epikataráomai*, to lay a curse on, or to connect it with anything. One on whom a curse rests or in whom it is realized. See Galatians 3:10 which corresponds with being under the curse (also Gal. 3:13).

1949. Epilambánomai; from *epí* (1909), upon, and the mid. form of *lambánō* (2983), to take. With a gen. or more rarely with an acc., to lay hold of, take, catch hold of (Matt. 14:31; Mark 8:23; Luke 9:47; 23:26; Acts 9:27; 16:19, cf. 1 Tim. 6:12, 19). Figuratively, to lay hold of ones words (Luke 20:20, 26). With a gen., the meaning would be to take upon oneself,to assume (Heb. 2:16). The text means that Christ came to redeem us, and that He took upon Himself human nature of the seed of Abraham (Gal. 3:16). "For even though He was in the form of God, (He) . . . did not regard equality with God a thing to be grasped, but emptied Himself, taking the form of a bond-servant, and being made in the likeness of men" (Phil. 2:6, 7 NASB).

1951. Epilégomai; from *epí* (1909), to, moreover, and *légō* (3004), to say. To choose either in addition to or in succession to another (John 5:2; Acts 15:40). See *eklégomai* (1586), to select out of; *hairéomai* (138), to choose in preference; *hairetízō* (140), to select in preference.

1957. Epimarturéō; from *epí* (1909), intens., and *marturéō* (3140), to witness. To testify emphatically, appear as a witness. Used in 1 Peter 5:12; also with the prep. *sun* (4862), together, as *sunepimarturéō* (4901), to give additional testimony (Heb. 2:4).

1963. Epínoia; from *epinoéō*, to think upon, from *epí* (1909), upon, and *noéō* (3539), to think. A thought, a device (Acts 8:22). See *nous* (3563), mind.

1967. Epioúsios; from *epí* (1909), for, into, and *ousía*, being, substance. Occurs only in the Lord's Prayer in Matthew 6:11; Luke 11:3. It was coined by the evangelist analogous to *perioúsios* (4041), from *perí* (4012), beyond, and *ousía*, being or substance meaning special or peculiar. The Gr. church father Chrysostom explained the *epioúsion árton* ([740], bread) as that bread which is needed for our daily support of life. It is that bread which is needful to the *ousía*, substance, of our being, that will sustain us.

1980. Episképtomai; a deponent verb meaning that it has a mid. or pass. form but it is used in an act. sense. Basically it signifies to look at something, examine closely, inspect, observe. To look upon with mercy, favor; to regard (Luke 1:68; 7:16; Acts 15:14; Heb. 2:6); to look after, take care of, tend. Frequently used in Class. Gr. for taking care or nursing the sick (Matt. 25:36, 43); to look accurately or diligently (Acts 6:3); to visit, go, or come to see (Luke 1:78; Acts 7:23; 15:36).

1983. Episkopéō; from *epí* (1909), upon, and *skopéō* (4648), to regard, give attention to. The comp. verb means to look upon, observe, examine, look after. In the NT used in Hebrews 12:15; 1 Peter 5:2 as to the work of shepherding the flock, in an exhortation to elders. See *epískopos* (1985), a bishop, overseer; *episkopé* (1984), the office of a bishop; *allotriepískopos* (244), a bishop who looks inquisitively into other peoples affairs; busybody.

1984. Episkopé; fem., a purely biblical and patristic word. The office of an overseer or bishop in Christ's Church (Acts 1:20; 1 Tim. 3:1). The word may be derived

from *episkéō*, to visit, consider, examine, and provide covering for (Luke 19:44; 1 Pet. 2:12). Deriv.: *episkopéō* (1983), to look after.

1985. Epískopos; watcher, overseer. In the NT the elders are called *epískopoi* (Acts 20:28), knowing the watchful care which those holding this office are to exercise (cf. 1 Pet. 5:2). In Philippians 1:1 the *epískopoi*, elsewhere called elders (*presbúteroi*, [4245]), are mentioned along with the deacons (*diákonoi*, [1249]). They are also mentioned in 1Timothy 3:2 (cf. v. 8; see also Titus 1:7, cf. v. 5). An elder denotes the dignity of the office, and *epískopos*, (bishop or overseer,) denotes its duties (cf. 1 Pet. 5:1, 2; see 1 Pet. 2:25; 5:4). Deriv.: episkopeō (1983), to look after.

1994. Epistréphō; from *epí* (1909), to, and *stréphō* (4762), to turn. To turn, turn to or towards (Matt. 9:22 TR; Mark 5:30; 8:33; Acts 16:18). To return (Matt. 10:13; 12:44; 24:18; Luke 2:20 TR). Trans., to convert, turn to God and holiness (Luke 1:16, 17; James 5:19, 20). Intrans., to turn, to be thus converted or turned (Matt. 13:15; Luke 22:32; Acts 3:19; 9:35; 14:15; 26:18, 20). Deriv.: *stréphō* (4762), to turn.

1995. Epistrophé; from *epistréphō* (1994), to turn about. Ant.: apostrepho (654), to turn away from, a turning oneself around. Conversion; occurs only in Acts 15:3.

1997. Episunagōgé; from *episunágō* (1996), to gather together, from *epí* (1909), to, and *sunágō* (4863), to gether, collect. A gathering together (2 Thess. 2:1, cf. 1 Thess. 4:17). An assembling together at one place. In Hebrews 10:25 it does not merely denote the worshiping assembly of the church from which some were likely to absent themselves, but the assembling for corporate worship, not as a solitary or occasional act, but as customary conduct. The verb *egkataleípō* (1459), to desert or leave stranded, to leave neglected, give up or abandon, which term is used of betrayers, is too strong an expression for the mere avoidance of assembling for religious worship (see 2 Cor. 4:9; 2 Tim. 4:10, 16; Heb. 10:25). It refers rather to the separating of oneself from the local Christian community because of the dread of persecution. The prep. *epí* (1909), to, must refer to Christ Himself as the One to which this assembly was attached. Therefore, it would have the meaning of not betraying ones attachment to Jesus Christ and other believers, not avoiding ones own personal responsibility as part of the body of Christ.

1999. Epistasis; from *episunístēmi*, which does not occur in the NT and which is made up of the intens. *epi* (1909), and *sunístēmi* (4921), from the prep. *sun* (4862), together, and *histēmi* (2476), to stand. As an intrans. verb, to stand together against, in a hostile sense, rebel; and in a friendly sense, to stand by or together with, unite together. The subst. *epistasis*, uprising, disturbance, occurs only in Acts 24:12 (TR) and in 2 Corinthians 11:28 referring to all that the Apostle Paul had to encounter in opposition to him.

2003. Epitagé; authority, command imposed upon someone or something (Rom.16:26). Verb: *epitássō* (2004), to command.

2004. Epitássō; from *epí* (1909), over, and *tássō* (5021), to appoint or place appropriately. To appoint over, put in charge; put upon one as a duty, enjoin (Mark 1:27; 6:27, 39).

2005. Epiteléō; from *epí* (1909), intens., and *teléō* (5055), to finish, complete, perfect (Rom. 15:28; 2 Cor. 7:1; 8:6, 11; Gal. 3:3; Phil. 1:6; Heb. 8:5); to perform, accomplish (Luke 13:32 TR; Heb. 9:6; 1 Pet. 5:9). Deriv.: see *télos* (5056), end, goal.

2008. Epitimáō; from *epí* (1909), upon, and *timáō* (5091), to evaluate. To rebuke, but not effectually so as to bring the offender to conviction, To punish, rebuke. One, however, may rebuke another without bringing the rebuke to a conviction of any fault on the offenders part, perhaps because there may not have been any fault or because there was fault but the rebuke was insufficient and ineffectual to bring the offender to acknowledge it. Therefore, *epitimáō* is merely the rebuke without any result on the part of the person who is being rebuked. For instance, Peter began to rebuke (*epitimáō*) his Lord (Matt. 16:2), but without any effect upon the Lord. The same was true when the penitent robber rebuked (epitimōn) his fellow malefactor (Luke 23:40). Contrast with the verb elégchō (1651), to reprove with conviction, which refers to effectual rebuke leading, if not to a confession, at least to a conviction of sin (John 8:46).

2014. Epiphaínō; from epí (1909), over, upon, and phaínō (5316), to shine. Trans. to show forth, shine light upon: for example, upon the surface. Usually used in the pass., to show oneself openly or before others, to come forward, appear, with the idea of sudden or unexpected appearing. Often used of the gods and hence the significance of the NT epipháneia (2015), appearing, the subst. of epiphaínō (Titus 2:11; 3:4). The word is often used in patristic Gr. of the incarnation of Christ. Intrans., to show oneself, used of the break of day (Acts 27:20); to appear, shine (Luke 1:79).

2015. Epipháneia; from epiphaínō (2014), to appear, which is from epí (1909), over, upon, to, and phaínō (5316), to shine, shine over or upon, give light to. Appearing. Epipháneia is used only by Paul (2 Thess. 2:8; 1 Tim. 6:14; 2 Tim. 1:10; 4:1, 8; Titus 2:13). Deriv.: adj., epíphanēs (2016), glorious, illustrious.

2026. Epoikodoméō; from epí (1909), upon, and oikodoméō (3618), to build. To build upon (1 Cor. 3:10, 12, 14; Eph. 2:20); figuratively, to build up, edify (Acts 20:32 TR; Col. 2:7; Jude 1:20).

2032. Epouránios; from epí (1909), upon, in, and ouranós (3772), heaven. What pertains to or is in heaven, chiefly of the gods. In Matthew 18:35 the Father, the heavenly One (epouránios). The meaning of this word is determined according to the various meanings of heaven. Deriv.: ouranós (3772), heaven.

2038. Ergázomai; from érgon (2041), work, labor (Matt. 21:28; Luke 13:14; Acts 18:3; 1 Cor. 4:12; 1 Thess. 2:9). To perform (Matt. 26:10; John 3:21; 6:28; 9:4); practice (in a good sense as in Acts 10:35; Rom. 2:10; or evil as in Matt. 7:23; Rom. 13:10; James 2:9); be employed in or about (1 Cor. 9:13; Rev. 18:17); procure, acquire by labor, as the word is frequently applied in Class. Gr. (John 6:27); trade with the idea of gaining (Matt. 25:16).

2041. Érgon; (neut.) work, performance, the result or object of employment, making or working. Sometimes it means work as a single performance (Matt. 26:10; Mark 14:6; John 7:21; 10:32, 33; 1 Cor. 5:2). Denotes any matter or thing, any object which one may have to do or attain (1 Tim. 3:1; 2 Tim. 4:18); the general object or result of doing and working, an object or result whose attainment or realization is not accomplished by a single act but by accumulated labor and continued work (Rom. 14:20; 1 Cor. 3:14, 15; 9:1); calling or occupation (Acts 14:26; Eph. 4:12; 1 Thess. 5:13; 2 Tim. 4:5); labor enjoined by and done for Christ as the spreading of His Gospel and the furthering of His Church; moral conduct (Rom. 2:6; 1 Cor. 3:13; 1 Pet. 1:7). It is especially used in the pl., ta érga (Matt. 11:2). In John used of Christ's miracles (John 5:20, 36; 7:3). In John 6:28, the works of God must be understood as works such as those which God does. On the other hand, John 6:29, the work of God must be understood as what God requires to be done. The question in John 6:28 implies a misapprehension of Christ's words which He corrects in John 6:29. In the Pauline Epistles those works to which Christians are called are designated not simply as érga, but érga agathá (18), which refers to benevolent works. In James, however, érga generally denotes acts by which the man proves his genuineness and his faith (James 2:14). Faith is proven by its works (James 2:22, 25). Elsewhere in the NT ta érga, the works, usually denotes comprehensively what a man is and how he acts (Rom. 2:6; 2 Cor. 11:15; 2 Tim. 4:14; 3 John 1:10; Rev. 2:2, 5, 6, 22, 23; 3:1, 2, 8, 15; 14:13; 16:11; 18:6; 20:12, 13). The sum total of created things (Heb. 13:21).

2046. Ereō; sometimes rhéō (4483) or érō (2036), to say, declare (Matt. 26:75; Luke 2:24; 22:13; John 4:13). To promise (Heb. 13:5); to call (John 15:15). The verbal adj. rhētós, spoken, expressly named, and the adv. rhētōs (4490), expressly occur especially in later

writers denoting the literalness of the quotation (1 Tim. 4:1, in which case reference is made to the clearness of the statement cited, indicating that there is no mystery about it). Contrast árrētos (731), that which cannot or dare not be uttered, unknown, full of mystery (2 Cor. 12:4).

2052. Eritheía; or erithía, derived from érithos, one who works for hire. Eritheúō has an identical meaning, usually in the mid. voice, used in a bad sense of those who seek only their own, namely those who take bribes. Eritheía is not bribery (seeking after situations of honor), but susceptibility of being bribed or corrupted, selfishness, a self-willed positiveness. Generally speaking, the word means selfishness, self-willed (Phil. 1:16; 2:3). See Romans 2:8; 2 Corinthians 12:20; Galatians 5:20; James 3:14, 16.

2064. Érchomai; to come; opposite hupágō (5217), to go. It primarily and properly denotes motion from one place to another. NT meanings: (1) To come (Matt. 2:2, 8; 8:2 TR; Mark 4:22; Luke 19:18; Acts 19:6). To come to Christ is to believe on Him (John 6:35; 7:37). (2) To go (Matt. 12:9; Luke 2:44; John 6:17; Acts 13:51; 28:14). (3) To come, referring to time (Luke 22:7; Gal. 4:4). (4) Yet to come, the future (Mark 10:30; Luke 18:30; John 16:13; 1 Thess. 1:10). Ho erchómenos, the coming One or He who is coming is a title of the Messiah (Matt. 11:3; Luke 7:19). (5) To be coming, following, next, or instant (Acts 13:44; 18:21). (6) To happen (John 18:4; Phil. 1:12; 2 Thess. 2:3; Rev. 3:10). (7) To be brought (Mark 4:21). (8) To come back, return (John 14:18, 28). (9) To come to oneself, meaning to recover ones senses or understanding (Luke 15:17).

2065. Erōtáō; to ask, with the acc. of a person, to ask someone (John 9:21; 16:30); to ask for something, in the acc. (Matt. 21:24; Mark 4:10; Luke 20:3; John 16:23); with perí (4012) following, about, concerning (Luke 9:45; John 18:19); or with a direct question following (Luke 19:31; John 1:19, 21; 5:12; 16:5); introduced by légōn (3004), saying, or the like (Matt. 16:13; John 1:25; 9:2, 19); with an indirect question following (John 9:15). A very distinct meaning of erōtáō is to pray, but in distinction from the verb aitéō (154). The first provides the most delicate and tender expression for prayer or request with the one asking and the one being asked on an equal level, such as the Lord Jesus asking of the Father. This is made very clear in John 14:13, 14 where the word aitéō is used in the case of us asking God as an inferior ask something of a superior, leaving it up to Him to do that which pleases Him. In v. 16 when the Lord Jesus is praying to the Father or asking the Father, the verb erōtáō is used, also used in John 17:9, 15, 20. Deriv.: eperōtáō (1905), to interrogate, to inquire of; eperótēma (1906), inquiry.

2078. Éschatos; probably connected with échō (2192), primarily with reference to place; The extreme, most remote (Acts 1:8; 13:47). With reference to time, the last, generally that which concludes anything (Matt. 12:45; Luke 11:26; 2 Pet. 2:20; Rev. 15:1). Denotes the time when the development of God's plan of salvation shall come to a close, the time of the final and decisive judgment (Heb. 1:2; 1 Pet. 1:20; 2 Pet. 3:3). Thus we have the eschátē hēméra, the last day (John 6:39, 40, 44, 54; 11:24; 12:48) which refers to the conclusive character of the final time. In the pl. the éschatai hēmérai, the last days (Acts 2:17), denote the time and era referred to in the context rather than the time previous to Christ's second advent in 2 Timothy 3:1; James 5:3, 7. With reference to rank or order, generally in a bad sense (Luke 14:9). Of persons, referring to the lowest (Mark 9:35; John 8:9; 1 Cor. 4:9). Sometimes denoting a moral lowness (Matt. 19:30; 20:16; Mark 10:31; Luke 13:30).

2084. Heteróglōssos; from héteros (2087), another, but different, and glōssa (1100), a tongue, language. One of another tongue or language (1 Cor. 14:21). See heterodidaskaléō (2085), to teach a different doctrine; heterozugéō (2086), to be yoked differently, unequally; héterōs (2088), differently, otherwise.

2085. Heterodidaskaléō; from héteros (2087), other but

different, and *didaskalía* (1319), doctrine or teaching. To teach a doctrine different from ones own (1 Tim. 1:3; 6:3). See *heteróglōssos* (2084), of a different language. Contrast: *állos* (243), numerically another or one coming after.

2086. Heterozugéō; from *héteros* (2087), another, different, and *zugós* (2218), a yoke. To draw the other side of a different yoke. To be yoked unequally, particularly in marriage (2 Cor. 6:14). See *heteróglōssos* (2084), of a different language. Contrast: *állos* (243), numerically another or one coming after.

2087. Héteros; another, in a qualitative sense (Matt. 6:24; 8:21; 11:3; 12:45; Luke. 7:41; 17:34, 35). Contrast *állos* (243), another, numerically. *Héteros* and *héteros* repeated, one and another, different from each other (1 Cor. 15:40). Different, altered (Luke. 9:29); other, foreign, strange (Acts 2:4). Deriv.: *héterōs* (2088). adv., otherwise differently; *heteróglōssos* (2084), one of another (different) tongue; *heterodidaskaléō* (2085), to teach a different doctrine than ones own; *heterozugéō* (2086), to be unequally yoked.

2088. Héterōs; adv. of *héteros* (2087), a different one, another of a different quality. Otherwise, differently (Phil. 3:15). See *heteróglōssos* (2084), of a different language. Contrast: *állos* (243), another, numerically but not qualitatively different.

2095. Eu; an adv. meaning well, good. In commendations, Well done! as in Matthew 25:21; followed by a noun and an adj. as in verse twenty-three, "Well done, good . . . servant." Used extensively as a prefix to comp. verbs with the meaning of well, good, and hence often used as an intens., for example *eulogéō* (2127), to eulogize, bless; *eukairía* (2120), good or appropriate opportunity.

2097. Euaggelízō; to evangelize, proclaim the good news, almost always concerning the Son of God as declared in the Gospel (exceptions: Luke 1:19; Gal. 1:8; 1 Thess. 3:6). Used in the act. voice, to declare, proclaim (Rev. 10:7; 14:6); in the pass. voice, *euaggelízomai*, of matters to be proclaimed as glad tidings (Luke 16:16; Gal. 1:11; 1 Pet. 1:25), of persons to whom the proclamation is made (Matt. 11:5; Luke. 7:22; Heb. 4:2, 6; 1 Pet. 4:6); in the mid. voice, especially of the message of salvation, with a personal obj., either of the person preached (Acts 5:42; 11:20; Gal. 1:16), or with a prep., of the persons evangelized (Acts 8:4, 12; 13:32: 15:35; 1 Cor. 15:1; 2 Cor. 11:7; Gal. 1:23; Eph. 2:17; 3:8). Deriv.: *euaggélion* (2098), Gospel; *euaggelistés* (2099), evangelist; *proeuaggelízomai* (4283), to announce good news beforehand (Gal. 3:8).

2098. Euaggélion; gospel. Originally a reward for good news, later becoming the good news itself. The good news of the kingdom of God and salvation through Christ (Matt 4:23; 9:35; 24:14; 26:13; Mark 1:1, 14; 8:35; 10:29; 13:10; 14:9; 16:15; Acts 15:7; 20:24; 1 Pet. 4:17); in Pauls epistles used of the basic facts of the death, burial, and resurrection of Christ (1 Cor. 15:1–3) and of the interpretation of these facts (Rom. 2:16; Gal. 1:7, 11; 2:2).

2099. Euaggelistés; evangelist, one who declares the good news. Used of Philip (Acts 21:8; see also 8:4, 5, 12, 35, 40); of evangelists along with apostles, prophets, pastors, and teachers (Eph. 4:11); of Timothy (2 Tim. 4:5). The number of evangelists must have been greater than the number suggested by NT references (2 Cor. 8:18; Phil. 4:3; Col. 1:7; 4:12). Originally *euaggelistés* denoted a function rather than an office, and there could have been little difference between an apostle and an evangelist, all the apostles being evangelists, but not all evangelists being apostles. Evangelists were subordinate to the apostles. In Ephesians 4:11 the evangelists are mentioned only after the apostles. Evangelists were not just missionaries. A distinction must be made between the office of an evangelist and the work of one. An evangelist is also an author of the Gospel.

2100. Euarestéō; to be well pleasing (Heb. 11:5, 6). Pass., to give satisfaction, make content, satisfy (Heb. 13:16). Syn.: *aréskō* (700), to make one inclined to, content with.

2101. Euárestos; from *eu* (2095), well, and *arestós* (701), pleasing, agreeable. Well-pleasing, acceptable. Used with reference to God, that which God wills and recognizes (Rom. 12:1, 2; Eph. 5:10; Phil. 4:18; Col. 3:20; Heb. 13:21); to persons (Rom. 14:18; 2 Cor. 5:9); to men and of slaves (Titus 2:9).

2102. Euaréstōs; the adv. of *euárestos* (2101), pleasing, well-pleasing (Heb. 12:28).

2106. Eudokéō; from *eu* (2095), well, good, and *dokéō* (1380), to think. To be well-pleased or to think something good; not merely an understanding of what is right and good (as in *dokéō*), but stressing the willingness and freedom of an intention or resolve regarding what is good (Luke 12:32; Rom. 15:26, 27; 1 Cor. 1:21; Gal. 1:15; Col. 1:19; 1 Thess. 2:8). To take pleasure in (Matt. 3:17; 12:18; 17:5; 1 Cor. 10:5; 2 Cor. 12:10; 2 Thess. 2:12; Heb. 10:6, 8, 38; 2 Pet. 1:17). The noun *eudokía* (2107), good pleasure, implying a gracious purpose, a good object with the idea of a resolution showing the willingness with which it is made.

2107. Eudokía; from *eudokéō* (2106) which is from *eu* (2095), well, good, and *dokéō* (1380), to think, appear. Good will, good pleasure (Matt. 11:26; Luke 10:21), a free will (willingness, pleasure) whose intent is something good; benevolence, gracious purpose. In this sense it is parallel to *eulogía* (2129), blessed. *Eudokía* never denotes good will in the moral sense, not even in 2 Thessalonians 1:11 where it is used in the phrase, "good pleasure of his goodness." It must be an outcome of *agathōsúnē* (19), goodness, the virtue of beneficence, even as works are the product of faith. Therefore, the *eudokía*, the good will of *agathōsúnē*, denotes that which pleases, goodness, the tendency to good.

2120. Eukairía; from *eu* (2095), well, good, and *kairós* (2540), time, with the meaning of season or a suitable or convenient time. Contrast *chrónos* (5550) which relates only to time as a measurement. The right and suitable time or convenient opportunity (Matt. 26:16; Luke 22:6). Deriv.: *kairós* (2540), time or season; *eúkairos* (2121), a convenient, seasonable time, suitable to the time, well-timed; *eukaírōs* (2122), an adv., conveniently as far as time is concerned; *eukairéō* (2119), verb, to have convenient time or opportunity.

2124. Eulábeia; godly fear, (Heb. 5:7; 12:28); predominantly used in a good sense, though like *phóbos* (5401), fear, it has not altogether escaped being employed in an evil sense. *Eulábeia* relates to the good and *deilía* (1167), cowardice, relates to the bad, with *phóbos*, fear or reverence, as the mid. term. Verb: *eulabéomia* (2125), fearing; adj.: *eulabḗs* (2126), devout.

2125. Eulabéomai; from *eulabḗs* (2126). To be cautious, thoughtful, circumspect. To be afraid, to be moved or impressed with a natural or religious fear (Acts 23:10 TR; Heb. 11:7).

2126. Eulabḗs; devout, from *eu* (2095), well, carefully, and *élabon*, second aor. of *lambánō* (2983), to take (Luke 2:25; Acts 2:5; 8:2). One who takes anything carefully which is held out to him, cautious, circumspect, careful in the worship of God and in his duties toward God. On all three occasions where *eulabḗs* occurs it expresses Jewish piety: Luke 2:25, with Simeon; Acts 2:5, those Jews who came from distant places to keep the commanded feasts at Jerusalem; Acts 8:2, those who carry Stephen to his burial, devout Jews who had separated themselves in spirit from the murder of Stephen. *Eulabḗs* is the scrupulous worshiper who is careful about changing or writing anything lest he offend.

2127. Eulogéō; from *eu* (2095), good, well, and *légō* (3004), to speak. To bless, or more accurately, to speak well of. When the subject is God, His speaking is His action, for God's speaking and acting are the same thing. When God is said to bless us, eulogize us, speak well of us, He acts for our good as He sees what we need most and not what we desire. When we bless (eulogize) God we speak well of Him, we laud or praise Him because He deserves it (Luke 1:64; 2:28; 24:53). When we bless (eulogize) one another, we express good wishes. When we bless, as Christ did the loaves and fishes when He miraculously multiplied them (Matt. 14:19; Mark 6:41; 8:7; Luke 9:16), and as He did the memorial bread (Matt. 26:26; 1 Cor. 10:16), and the infants (Mark 10:16 TR), we consecrate them to divine use. Distinguished from *makarízō* (3106), to pronounce blessed, and *makários* (3107), blessed, indwelt by God. Part: *eulogēménos;* blessed, but more accurately one well spoken of and acted upon. One upon whom God has acted or who has experienced the blessing (*eulogían* [2129]) of God (Matt. 21:9; 23:39; 25:34; Mark 11:9, 10; Luke 1:28, 42; 13:35; 19:38; John 12:13). The *eulogía* of God is Gods action in mans life to bring him to the desired relationship with Himself. Distinguished from *eulogētós* (2128), spoken only of God as inherently worthy to be well-spoken of by man, and from *makários* (3107) which refers to a permanent state of being and not the particular effect of a certain cause such as *eulogēménos* would imply. Related to *eulogētós*, worthy to be well-spoken of.

2128. Eulogētós; derived from *eulogéō* (2127) which is from *eu* (2095), good or well, and *légō* (3004), to speak; to bless or to speak well of, to eulogize. Therefore, *eulogētós* means one to be well spoken of, worthy of praise (Mark 14:61; Luke 1:68; Rom. 1:25; 9:5; 2 Cor. 1:3; 11:31; Eph. 1:3; 1 Pet. 1:3). This adj. ending in *-tos*, has the meaning of worthy to be praised, and is in all instances ascribed to God. No one is inherently worthy of praise except God. On the other hand, the part. adj. *eulogēménos* (fem.: *eulogēménē*) refers to humans who have been well spoken of and acted upon by God. Distinguished from *makários* (3107), the blessed one possessing God's nature because of Christ and hence fully satisfied, as compared to the happy person favored by circumstances. The non-permanent state of happiness is not referred to in the NT. In Mod. Gr. a happy person is called *eutuchḗs*, from *eu* (2095), good or well, and *túchē*, luck, meaning one who has good luck. The verb *tug-chánō* (5177), to happen, to come upon or to be found in a certain state, related to *eutuchía*, happiness, occurs in Luke 10:30 TR; 20:35; Acts 19:11; 24:2; 26:22; 27:3; 28:2; 1 Corinthians 14:10; 15:37; 2 Timothy 2:10; Hebrews 8:6; 11:35.

2129. Eulogía; from *eulogéō* (2127), to bless, as distinguished from *makarízō* (3106), to declare as indwelt by God and thereby fully satisfied. Expressing good wishes, blessing, praise, eulogy to God (Rev. 5:12, 13; 7:12); commendation to man (Rom. 16:18); the blessing, good word, or action of God (Rom. 15:29; Eph. 1:3; Gal. 3:14; Heb. 6:7); consecration, beneficence (2 Cor. 9:5, 6). Contrast *makarismós*, blessedness or the action of becoming blessed (Rom. 4:6, 9; Gal. 4:15).

2132. Eunoéō; from *eu* (2095), well and *nous* (3563), mind. To favor, be well affected or well-minded toward another, to be friends (Matt. 5:25). Noun: *eúnoia* (2133), benevolence. See *noéō* (3539), to think.

2133. Eúnoia; the noun of *eunoéō* (2132), to favor. Benevolence, good will (1 Cor. 7:3 TR; Eph. 6:7). See *noéō* (3539) to think; *nous* (3563), mind.

2141. Euporéō; from *eu* (2095), well, *poréō*, to journey. To prosper (Acts 11:29).

2144. Euprósdektos; from *eu* (2095), well, and *prósdektos*, accepted, acceptable, which is from *prosdéchomai* (4327), to receive, accept. Well-accepted, acceptable (Rom. 15:16; 2 Cor. 6:2; 1 Pet. 2:5). A strong affirmation of acceptability, favorably accepted, predicated as *dektós* (1184), of the time of grace (Rom. 15:31; 2 Cor. 8:12).

2146. Euprosōpéō; from *eu* (2095), well, and *prósōpon* (4383), a face, appearance. Occurs only in Galatians 6:12, to make a fair appearance or show. It presents the contrast between appearance and reality.

2147. Heurískō; to find, either with a search (Matt. 7:7, 8) or without (Matt. 27:32). In the pass. voice, of Enoch's disappearance (Heb. 11:5), of mountains (Rev. 16:20), of Babylon and its occupants (Rev. 18:21, 22). Metaphorically, to find out by inquiry, to learn, discover (Luke 19:48; John 18:38; 19:4, 6; Acts 4:21;

13:28; Rom. 7:10; Gal. 2:17; 1 Pet. 1:7; Rev. 5:4). In the mid. voice, to find for oneself, gain, procure, obtain (Matt. 10:39; 11:29; Luke 1:30; Acts 7:46; 2 Tim. 1:18). Deriv.: *aneurískō* (429), to find out by search, discover, from *aná* (303), up, and *heurísko*, as in Luke 2:16 of the shepherds in searching for and finding Mary and Joseph and the Child; also in Acts 21:4 of Paul searching for and finding the disciples at Tyre.

2150. Eusébeia; from *eu* (2095), well, and *sébomai* (4576), to worship. Devotion, piety toward God (Acts 3:12; 1 Tim. 2:2; 2 Pet. 1:6, 7). Godliness or the whole of true religion, so named because piety toward God is the foundation and principal part of it (Matt. 22:37, 38; 1 Tim. 4:7, 8; 6:6; Heb. 11:6). Related words: *eusebéō* (2151), verb, to exercise piety or true religion, to worship; *eusebḗs* (2152), adj., devout, pious, religious, godly; *eusebṓs* (2153), adv., piously, religiously, godly (2 Tim. 3:12; Titus 2:12). All these words originally were often provided with more precise definitions to show to whom the worship was directed. It has the general sense of a pious life or a life which is morally good.

2151. Eusebéō; from *eu* (2095), well, and *sébomai* (4576), to worship, venerate. To be pious, to act as in the fear of God (Acts 17:23; 1 Tim. 5:4), in which instance it means to fulfill ones duty in reference to God, in the fear of God.

2152. Eusebḗs; one who reverences aright, shows piety toward God, parents, or others (Acts 10:2, 7; 22:12; 2 Pet. 2:9). Noun: *eusébeia* (2150), godliness, well-directed piety or worship, formerly called worthship (Acts 3:12; 1 Tim. 2:2; 3:16; 4:7, 8; 6:3, 5, 6, 11; 2 Tim 3:5; Titus 1:1; 2 Pet. 1:3, 6, 7; 3:11). Adv.: *eusebṓs* (2153), in a godly manner (2 Tim. 3:12; Titus 2:12).

2160. Eutrapélia; from *eutrápelos*, which is from *eu* (2095), easily, and *étrapon*, second aor. of *trépō*, to turn. One who can easily or readily turn his speech for the purpose of exciting mirth or laughter. A wit, but since such persons are very apt to deviate into mischief-making and clownishness, *eutrápelos* is sometimes used in a bad sense as a scoffer, a sneerer. In a bad sense it means obscene jesting, to which Paul probably refers in Ephesians 5:4, the only usage in the NT.

2165. Euphraínō; from *eu* (2095), well, and *phrén* (5424), mind. To rejoice, make joyful in mind. In a good and spiritual sense, to rejoice, make joyful (2 Cor. 2:2); in the pass., *euphraínomai*, to be glad, joyful (Acts 2:26; Rom. 15:10; Gal. 4:27). To be joyful, merry, in a natural sense (Luke 15:23, 24, 29, 32) or in a bad sense (Luke 12:19; Acts 7:41). In Luke 16:19, it refers to the rich mans luxurious and sumptuous living. Noun: *euphrosúnē* (2167), gladness.

2167. Euphrosúnē; from the verb *euphraínō* (2165), to rejoice. Joy, joyfulness, gladness (Acts 2:28; 14:17).

2168. Eucharistéō; from *eu* (2095), good or well, and *cháris* (5485), grace. The good response or reception by that which does not deserve grace. Such a response expresses itself in thanksgiving and praise, to be thankful, to thank. It does not occur in the Sept. where instead we find *eulogéō* (2127), to speak well of or eulogize. In the NT, except in Romans 16:4, used in a religious sense with or without reference to God. In Lukes and Pauls writings, it is followed by God in the dat., *tō Theō*. There is, however, a difference between *eucharistéō* with the dat. and *eucharistéō* by itself. With the dat. it always stands where there is inferred a kindness done, a favor, a *cháris* (5485), grace, for an undeserved gift received. The reason for thanks is designated by *húper* (5228), for the sake or on the part of (Rom. 1:8; 1 Cor. 10:30; Eph. 1:16; 5:20); by *perí* (4012), with respect to, with the gen. (1 Cor. 1:4; 1 Thess. 1:2; 2 Thess. 1:3; 2:13; Phile. 4); by *epí* (1909), upon, with the dat. (1 Cor. 1:4; Phil. 1:3); by *diá* (1223), through, with the acc. (Col. 1:3). Sometimes it is added on with *hóti* (3754), that (Luke 18:11; John 11:41; Rom. 1:8; 1 Cor. 1:14; 1 Thess. 2:13; Rev. 11:17).Deriv.: *eucharistía* (2169), thankfulness, giving of thanks; *eucháristos* (2170), thankful, grateful, well-pleasing. Syn.: *eulogéō* (2127), to bless, praise, eulogize, meaning praising and glorifying God which is prompted only by God Himself and His revealed glory.

2169. Eucharistía; from *eu* (2095), well, and *cháris* (5485), grace, thanksgiving To receive something as an expression of grace by someone and accept it as if one does not deserve it (Acts 24:3; Rev. 7:12). From this is derived the verb *eucharistéō* (2168), to be thankful or to give thanks. *Eucharistía*, Eucharist, which is also the word used for Holy Communion, embodies the highest act of thanksgiving for the greatest benefit received from God, the sacrifice of Jesus. It is the grateful acknowledgement of past mercies as distinguished from the earnest seeking of the future.

2170. Eucháristos; from *eu* (2095), well, and *cháris* (5485), grace or thanks. Thankful, grateful (Col. 3:15).

2173. Eúchrēstos; from *eu* (2095), well, and *chrēstós* (5543), useful. Useful or very useful (2 Tim. 2:21; 4:11; Phile. 1:11). See *chreía* (5532), need, and *chrēstótēs* (5544), kindness.

2192. Échō; to have, to hold, hold on, to count, consider, regard, wear (Matt. 3:4; 22:12; John 18:10); used idiomatically, to be with child (Mark 13:17; Rom. 9:10); to possess. Deriv.: *apéchō* (568), to receive; *paréchō* (3930), to grant; *antéchomai* (472), to hold firmly to; *enéchō* (1758), to have a grudge against; *katéchō* (2722), to hold fast; *metéchō* (3348), to share; *nounechēs* (3562), wisely; *anéchomai* (430), to bear with; *schēma* (4976), fashion.

2198. Záō; or *zō*, from *zéō* (2204), to be warm. To have life, be alive, used of natural living (Matt. 27:63; Luke 2:36; Acts 17:28; 22:22, cf. Mark 16:11; Luke 24:23; Acts 1:3; Rev. 2:8); spiritual living (Gal. 2:20); eternal living (Luke 10:28; John 6:58) spiritual and eternal living (John 6:57; Rom. 1:172; Gal. 3:12). The part. *zōn* is used in a trans. sense and means not only living, but causing to live, vivifying, quickening (John 6:51, cf. vv. 33, 50, 54, 58; Acts 7:38; 1 Pet. 1:3, cf. John 4:10). The inf. *zēn*, with the neut. art. to is used as a noun for life (Heb. 2:15). It is applied to God who has life independently from anyone and from whom all living beings derive their life and existence (Matt. 16:16; 26:63; John 6:57, 69 TR; 1 Thess. 1:9; 1 Tim. 4:10; 6:17 TR; Heb. 10:31). It is joined with other words to denote a particular manner of living (Rom. 6:10, 11; Gal. 2:19; 1 Pet. 4:6). In 1 Peter 2:24, to "live unto righteousness" means to live in all righteousness and holiness as persons justified by the death of Christ (Rom. 6:2, 4, 6, 7, 11). To live in the Spirit (Gal. 5:25) is to live under His constant guidance and influence (cf. Rom. 8:15). To live to oneself (2 Cor. 5:15) means to live according to ones own evil and corrupt inclinations. To live, as recovering from an illness (John 4:50, 51, 53). The subst. *zōē* (2222), life, is animal life, bare existence as compared to *bíos* (979), mental life with consciousness, from which our word biography is derived.

2200. Zestós; from *zéō* (2204), to be hot; Hot, used figuratively in Revelation 3; 15, 16.

2204. Zéō; to seethe, bubble, connected with *zélos* (2205), zeal. Onomatopoeic of the sound of boiling water. In the NT only applied spiritually (Acts 18:25; Rom. 12:11).

2205. Zēlos; zeal, used in a good sense (John 2:17; Rom. 10:2; 2 Cor. 9:2) but more often in an evil sense (Acts 5:17; Rom. 13:13; Gal. 5:20; James 3:14). Unlike *phthónos* (5355), envy, when used in a good sense. *Zélos* signifies honorable emulation with the consequent imitation of that which seems excellent. According to Aristotle, *zélos* grieves, not because another has the good, but that one does not have it, and seeks to supply such deficiencies in himself. However, *zélos* may degenerate into a desire to make war upon the good which it beholds in another, and thus to trouble that good and diminish it. This is why we find *zélos* joined together with *éris* (2054), contention (Rom. 13:13; 2 Cor. 12:20; Gal. 5:20).

2219. Zúmē; most probably from *zéō* (2204), to heat. Leaven, fermenting matter, so called from heating, fermentation, the mass of dough (*phúrama* [5445]) with which it is mixed (Matt. 13:33; Rom. 11:16;1 Cor.

5:6, 7). Everywhere in Scripture the word *zúmē* represents evil, including Matthew 13:33; Luke 13:21, if properly understood. The real significance of leaven is shown in 1 Corinthians 5:7 as being destructive and typifies what does not belong originally and essentially to life, that by which it is disturbed and penetrated, namely, sin. It is sin penetrating daily life. *Zúme* first appears in the institution of the Passover (Ex. 12:15, 19, 20, 34, 39; 13:3, 7) and in the ritual of sacrifices (Ex. 23:18; 34:25; Lev. 2:11; 6:17; 7:13; Deut. 16:3, 4; Amos 4:5). All that disgraces the Christian and detracts from his holy newness of life is after the manner of leaven (1 Cor. 5:6; Gal. 5:9). It represents false doctrine as opposed to that which has been received (Gal. 5:9). In Luke 12:1, hypocrisy is named in the same connection with leaven, which finds its embodiment in the doctrine covering such conduct. Deriv.: *zúmoō* (2220), to leaven, mix with leaven; *ázumos* (106), unleavened.

2220. Zumóō; to leaven, mix with leaven (*zúmē* [2219]). In the act. voice, to permeate with leaven (1 Cor. 5:6; Gal 5:9). In the pass. voice, used intrans., to be leavened or mixed with leaven, and thus to ferment (Matt. 13:33; Luke 13:21). Deriv.: *zúmē* (2219), leaven.

2222. Zōé; life, referring to the principle of life in the spirit and soul. Distinguished from *bíos* (979), physical life, livelihood, of which *zōé* is the nobler word, expressing all of the highest and best which Christ is (John 14:6; 1 John 1:2) and which He gives to the saints. The highest blessedness of the creature.

2225. Zōogonéō; from *zóos*, alive, and *gégona*, the perf. mid. of the obsolete *genō*, to form, make. To give birth to living creatures. To vivify, make alive. In the NT, occurs only in Luke 17:33; Acts 7:19; 1 Timothy 6:13 (UBS) to retain life.

2226. Zōon; derived from *záō* (2198), to live. A living creature, an animal (Heb. 13:11; 2 Pet. 2:12; Rev. 4:6, 7). Sometimes used syn. with *thēríon* (2342), a wild beast. However, there is a distinction between the two. Although in the Class. Gr. *zōon* is designated as a thinking animal to indicate that man also is such, this is not so in the NT. The fact that man lives does not make him a *zōon*, an animal. He is a living creature but not an animal in the sense of a nonthinking animal. Similarly, in spite of the fact that God is alive, He is never called a *zōon*, but He is called life itself, as is also Jesus Christ (John 1:4; 1 John 1:2, *zōé* [2222]), the source of life. *Thēríon* gives predominance to the lower animal life and is associated with a hellish symbolism.

2227. Zōopoiéō; from *zōos*, alive, and *poiéō* (4160), to make. Make alive, vivify (John 6:63; 1 Cor. 15:45; 2 Cor. 3:6). Used primarily in the NT of raising the dead to life (John 5:21; Rom. 4:17; 8:11; 1 Cor. 15:22, 36; 1 Pet. 3:18). Generally used in reference to salvation, answering to the Pauline connection between righteousness and life (Gal. 3:21).

2233. Hēgéomai; from *ágō* (71); to bring, lead;. It primarily signifies to lead on or forward, to be the chief or principal participant (Acts 14:12); to preside, govern, rule, whether in a temporal sense (Acts 7:10) or in a spiritual one (Heb. 13:7, 17, 24, cf. Matt. 2:6; Luke 22:26). To think, esteem, reckon (Acts 26:2; 2 Cor. 9:5; Phil. 2:3; 1 Thess. 5:13). Deriv.: *exēgéomai* (1834), to bring forth, thoroughly explain; *proēgéomai* (4285), from *pro* (4253), before, and *hēgéomai*, to think, meaning to esteem another before oneself, to prefer or go before another (Rom. 12:10).

2250. Hēmera; the day as distinguished from night, quantitatively as a division of time. Sometimes used, however, of a longer space of time. Daytime as distinguished from nighttime (Matt. 20:6, 12; John 11:9; Acts 12:18; 26:13; 27:29, 33, 39). A day in the Eastern way of thinking may be any part of a twenty-four-hour period or the entire twenty-four-hour period. Thus the day in the Eastern calculation of time is considered as a night and a day (*nuchthēmeron* [3574] a unit consisting of a night and a day). Therefore, the three days and three nights of Matthew 12:40 in which Jesus was in the grave should be considered as Friday (being part of the first day), all of Saturday (being the second day), and part of Sunday (being the third day). Figuratively, time for work or labor (John 9:4, cf. Matt 20:6, 12). The day of eternal life, as opposite to the spiritual darkness of our present state (Rom. 13:12). A day including both the day and night, *nuchthēmerón* (Matt. 15:32; 17:1; Acts 28:7, 12, 14; 2 Cor. 4:16). In the pl., days means time measured by periods of time, as in those days (Matt. 3:1, meaning at that time, Luke 5:35; 17:22; 23:29). In the pl., days may mean time of life or office (Matt. 2:1; 23:30; Luke 1:5; 4:25; 17:28).That day *Ekeinē*, that; *hē*, the; *hēméra*, day, means that great Day of the Lord, the day of judgment (Matt. 7:22; Luke 10:12; 2 Thess. 1:10; 2 Tim. 1:18; 4:8), also the expressions that day, the last day, the Day of the Lord, the day of judgment all refer to the same thing. In 1 Corinthians 4:3 mans day speaks of the opposition to the coming of the Lord. The Day of Christ or. Day of our Lord Jesus (1 Cor. 5:5; 2 Cor. 1:14; Phil. 1:6, 10; 2:16; 2 Thess. 2:2) refers to the day when the Lord Jesus Christ will appear and take His Church unto Himself as described in 1 Thessalonians 4:14–17.

2261. Épios; from *hepó*, to follow, as denoting one who readily follows the will of another and is ready to do what he desires or wants (1 Thess. 2:7; 2 Tim. 2:24). Placid, mild, easy, compliant. Contrast *práos* (4235), meek, and *epieikēs* (1933), gentle, tolerant.

2270. Hēsucházō; to rest from labor (Luke 23:56); to be quiet, live quietly (1 Thess. 4:11); to be silent, quiet from speaking (Luke 14:4); to acquiesce (Acts 11:18; 21:14). Deriv.: *hēsuchía* (2271), quietness, quiet (2 Thess. 3:12), silence, quietness from speaking (1 Tim. 2:11, 12); *hēsúchios* (2272), quiet, peaceable (1 Tim. 2:2; 1 Pet. 3:4).

2281. Thálassa; from *tarássō* (5015), to agitate. Some consider it as the sea as contrasted with the land (Matt. 23:15; Acts 4:24) or perhaps more strictly in contrast with the shore. Another Gr. word, *pélagos* (3989), is also translated as sea, but there is a difference. The latter word, occurring in Matthew 18:6 and Acts 27:5, represents the vast uninterrupted level and expanse of open water.

2288. Thánatos; death. Natural or temporal death (Matt. 10:21; 16:28; Luke 2:26). In 1 John 5:16, a sin leading to death is a sin which, should a believer continue to engage in it, may lead him to premature physical death (Eccl. 7:17; Jer. 14:11, 12; 34:18–20; Acts 5:1–11; 1 Cor. 11:30). Spiritual death (John 5:24; 1 John 3:14). As spiritual life consists in constant communication with God who is life, so spiritual death is the separation from His blessed influence. Eternal death (Rom. 6:21, 23; James 5:20; 1 John 5:16, 17), which, in respect to the natural and temporal, is called the second death (Rev. 2:11; 20:6, 14) and implies everlasting punishment (Rev. 21:8). Plague or pestilence. *Thánatos* is joined with *limós* (3042), famine (Rev. 6:8, cf. Ezek. 14:21).

2297. Thaumásios; wonderful things, miracles, as provoking admiration and astonishment (Matt 21:15). See *thaumázō* (2296) (Matt. 8:27; 9:8; 15:31; Mark 5:20; Acts 3:12). To the Gr. church fathers and in Mod. Gr. miracles are known as *thaúmata* (pl.), a word not used with such meaning in the NT, although it occurs as *thaúma* (2295), astonishment (sing.) in Revelation 17:6, This word was used prior to this period by magicians and impostors of various kinds. See *sēmeíon* (4592), sign; *dúnamis* (1411), power, mighty work; *megaleíos* (3167), great work; *éndoxos* (1741), glorious, glorious work; *parádoxos* (3861), strange, astonishing work; *téras* (5059), frightful, terrifying work.

2300. Theáomai; to behold, view attentively, contemplate, indicating the sense of wondering regard involving a careful and deliberate vision which interprets its object. It involves more than merely seeing (Matt. 6:1; 11:7; 22:11; 23:5; Mark 16:11, 14; Luke 5:27; 7:24; 23:55; John 1:14, 32, 38; 4:35; 6:5; 8:10; 11:45; Acts 1:11; 8:18; 21:27; 22:9; Rom. 15:24; 1 John 1:1; 4:12, 14).

2304. Theíos; an adj. meaning divine, what is God's especially and what proceeds from Him. Distinguished

from *Theós* (2316), God, as indeed *Theiótēs* (2305), divinity, is distinguished from *Theótēs* (2320), Godhead. *Theíos* denotes an attribute of God and not the character of God in its totality. See Acts 17:29; 2 Peter 1:3, 4. In Class. Gr. the adj. denoted the power of God as the noun *Theiótēs* definitely does in Romans 1:20.

2305. Thelótēs; divinity, only in Rom. 1:20. Syn: *theíos* (2304), divine; *dúnamis* (1411), power, in 2 Peter 1:3, a concept derived from His works. Distinguished from *theótēs* (2320), deity, the personality of God or Godhead, a concept not logically arrived at by observing His might, but directly revealed (Col. 2:9).

2307. Thélēma; from the verb *thélō* (2309), to will. The suffix *-ma* indicates that it is the result of the will. The will, not to be conceived as demand, but as an expression or inclination of pleasure towards that which is liked, that which pleases and creates joy. When it denotes God's will, it signifies His gracious disposition toward something. Used to designate what God Himself does of His own good pleasure. As a rule, NT usage refers to the will of God. Used in Luke 23:25; John 1:13; 1 Corinthians 7:37; Ephesians 2:3; 2 Timothy 2:26; 2 Peter 1:21. Nowhere, however, is it a name for the commands of God as such, whether in any particular case or in general. However, it does designate what occurs or what should be done by others as the object of God's good pleasure in the carrying out of the divine purpose or the accomplishment of what He would have (i.e., that which He purposes or has purposed, what He regards or does as good [Matt. 18:14; 26:42; Luke 22:42; Acts 21:14; 1 Pet. 3:17; 4:19]). Paul uses it especially with reference to God's saving purpose (Eph. 1:5, 9, 11), and in particular to the tracing back of his apostleship to the will of God (1 Cor. 1:1; 2 Cor. 1:1; Gal. 1:4; Col. 1:1; 2 Tim. 1:1); as bestowed upon him not only by the sovereign, but by the gracious will of God (Gal. 1:15; Eph. 3:7, 8; Titus 1:3). Also used of the execution of God's will by others with reference to what God has ordained (Acts 13:22), of the Fathers will in redemption as carried out by Christ (John 4:34; 5:30; 6:38–40; 9:31, cf. Heb. 10:7, 9, 10), and God's will or good pleasure to be carried out by us (Rom. 12:2), with an implied reference to God's judgment (Rom. 2:18; Eph. 5:17; 6:6; Col. 1:9; 4:12). The pl. form occurs only in Acts 13:22; Ephesians 2:3.

2309. Thélō; to will. There is a distinction between *thélō* and *boúlomai* (1014), to design, to decree. *Thélō* indicates not only willing something, but also pressing on to action. *Boúlomai* is deciding, but not pressing on to execute that which is decided. When the subst. *boúlēma* (1013) is used, it denotes the substance of the law and also the intention underlying the law but not the execution thereof. Thus *boulē* (1012) is counsel, decision, conclusion. In Mod. Gr. this is the name given to a parliament which makes the laws and provides the intent of the law, but not the execution of it. *Thélēma* (2307), on the other hand is resolve and denotes the will of God which must be done. However, *boulē Theoú*, the will of God, refers only to God's self-affirmation in His own acting. *Boúlomai* (1014), therefore, is not in agreement with the meaning *eudokéō* (2106), to be possessed of good will. *Boúlomai* and *thélō* differ as to degree and resolve. *Thélō* in the NT denotes elective inclination, love. It occurs frequently in biblical Gr. with the acc. of the obj., which is rare with *boúlomai*. The refusal is usually rendered by *ou*, not, *thélō*, and rarely by *ou boúlomai*. *Thélō* may mean to be about to, but never *boúlomai*. This latter word demonstrates resolve, but not necessarily action. Nevertheless, *boúlomai* may be used for *thélō*, and *thélō*, though far more rarely, for *boúlomai*. *Thélō*, therefore, means to will as the equivalent of to purpose, to be decided upon seeing ones desire to its execution. It may stand side-by-side with *poiéō* (4160), to do, to make (John 8:44; Rom. 7:21; 2 Cor. 8:11); with *energéō* (1754), to effect. The neg. *ou*, not, and *thélō* means not to will, to refuse, oppose (Matt. 18:30; 21:29; 23:37). *Thélō* also means to be inclined (Acts 26:5); to have a mind to, to wish or desire (John 3:8); and with the neg. *ou*, not to be inclined, often not intend to (Matt. 1:19). Used with the inf. of the subject matter following (Matt. 14:5; 26:15). Used in the sense of to endeavor, desire; rarely by itself as in Matthew 5:42; 12:38; 15:28; 19:17; 20:26, 27. It may stand for what one chooses, likes, is inclined toward (Matt. 9:13; 12:7; 27:43; Heb. 10:5, 8). Deriv.: *thélēma* (2307), will as an expression or inclination of pleasure, passion (John 1:13; 1 Cor. 7:37; Eph. 2:3); *thélēsis* (2308), the act of the will, pleasure, desire.

2315. Theópneustos; from Theos (2316), God, and *pépneustai*, from *pnéō* (4154), to breathe. Prompted by God, divinely inspired, occurs only in 2 Timothy 3:16 in the NT. In Class. Gr. opposite to *phusikós*, natural, as opposite to divine. In reality the formation of the word should be traced rather to *empnéō* (1709), to inspire (Acts 9:1), urged by the *pneúma* (4151), spirit, whether ones own, or God's or the spirit world, instead of *pnéō*, the root word meaning to breathe or to blow. The simple verb *pnéō* (4154) is never used of divine action. Neither *empnéō* nor *pnéō* is used in 2 Peter 1:21 but the expression by the Spirit, the Holy one, being driven or carried (*pherómenoi* [5342]), referring to those who wrote God's utterances or prophecies.

2316. Theós; God. Originally used by the heathen and adopted in the NT as the name of the true God. The most probable deriv. is from the verb *théō*, to place (see *títhēmi*, [5087]) The heathen thought the gods were disposers (*thetéres*, placers) and formers of all things. In using the pl. form, the Greeks intimated their belief that elements such as the heavens had their own disposer or placer, namely the god of money called mammon (Matt. 6:24; Luke 16:9, 13). The heavens were the grand objects of divine worship throughout the heathen world as is apparent from the names attributed to the gods by the ancient Greeks. The Scriptures also attest to this (Deut. 4:19; 17:3; 2 Kgs. 17:16; 23:4, 5; Job 31:26, 27; Jer. 8:2; 19:13; Zeph. 1:5; Acts 7:42, 43). The only gods the Greeks worshiped were the various aspects of created nature and especially the heavens, or some demons or intelligences which they supposed resided in them. For instance, Orpheus, a legendary poet and musician of ancient Thrace, had the power of charming animate and inanimate objects with his lyre, and calls almost all the gods of the Greeks demons. The Sept. constantly translated the Hebr. pl. name *Elohím*, when used for the true God by the sing. *Theós*, God, never by the pl. *theoí*, gods. The reason for this was that at the time the Sept. translation was made, Greek idolatry was the prevailing superstition, especially in Egypt under the Ptolemies. Their gods were regarded as demons, that is, intelligent beings totally separate and distinct from each other. If the translators rendered the name of the true God by the pl. *theoí*, they would have given the heathen under Greek culture an idea of God which was inconsistent with the unity of the divine essence and conformable to their own polytheistic notions. However, by translating the Hebrew *gods* as God, they inculcated the unity of God and at the same time did not deny a plurality of persons in the divine nature. In the NT and the Sept. *Theós*, God, generally answers to the OT pl. name *Elohím* and so denotes the Triune God (see Matt. 4:7, cf. Deut. 6:16 in the Hebr. and the Sept.; Matt. 4:10, cf. Deut. 6:3; Matt. 22:32, cf. Ex. 3:6; Matt. 22:37, cf. Deut. 6:5; Mark 1:14, 15, cf. Dan. 2:44; Mark 12:29, cf. Deut. 6:4, 5; John 1:12, cf. Gen. 6:2; Acts 4:24, cf. Gen. 1:1; Eccl. 12:1 in the Hebr.; Acts 10:34, cf. Deut. 10:17). It is applied personally, but very rarely to the Father (John 5:18; 13:3; 16:27, 30, cf. vv. 28, 29; 2 Cor. 13:14; Phil. 2:6); to the Son (Matt. 1:23; John 1:1; 20:28; Rom. 9:5; 1 Tim. 3:16 TR; Titus 2:13; 2 Pet. 1:1; 1 John 5:20); to the Holy Spirit (Luke 1:35; Acts 5:3, 4, cf. 1 Cor. 3:16, 17; 6:19; 2 Cor. 6:16; also cf. Acts 4:24, 25 with Acts 1:16; 2 Pet. 1:21) Also denotes the heathen gods or idols (Acts 14:11; 1 Cor. 8:5), magistrates (John 10:34, 35); by false application to Satan (2 Cor. 4:4); to the belly which some people make their god or in which

they place their supreme happiness (Phil. 3:19). Many times *Théos* occurs with the def. art. *ho*, but it is not so rendered in the translation because in English we never refer to God as *the God* except if He is designated as belonging to someone specifically such as the God of Abraham (Matt. 22:32). In many instances when the def. art. *ho* occurs before *Theós*, God, particular reference is made to God the Father, making the distinction in the personalities of the Trinity evident, for example in John 1:1b, And the Word was (*ēn*) with (*pros* [4314]) God (*ton Theón*.) The def. art. here designates the Father. The Word (*Lógos* [3056]) is Jesus Christ in His pre-incarnate existence as one personality of the Trinity and the God was God the Father. In the third statement of John 1:1, and the Word was God, the word God, *Theós,* is without the art. and is used as a predicate, stating the Word was God equal in meaning to the adj. divine. Therefore, *Theós*, not having the def. art. before it cannot be the subj. Only if it did have the definite art. before it, could it be interchangeable with the subj. *ho Lógos*, the Word. Furthermore, the indef. art. a could not be added in the English making it and the Word was a God. This translation would make the verse declare that the Bible teaches polytheism. If so, then the statement in John 1:18 which in Gr. begins with *Theón*, God, without the art., should also be translated, A God, no man hath seen at any time. Then the question would be; which of the many gods? In John 1:18 the word *Theós* is used without the art. not to indicate God as He appeared in a limited spatial environment as in the various theophanies to Moses and others, and finally to mankind in the physical person of the Lord Jesus, but God, in His eternity, infinity, totality, and in His essence, remaining as Spirit. The Creator being larger than any of His creatures cannot possibly be seen in His totality (see 1 Tim. 6:16). In the grammatical notations the designation *an* meaning anarthrous, or without the art. shows when a certain word, and particularly *Theós*, occurs in Gr. without the def. article.

2318. Theosebḗs; from the noun *Theós* (2316), God, and *sébomai* (4576), worship, venerate. Godly, devout, translated God-fearing (John 9:31). The noun *theosébeia* (2317) in 1 Timothy 2:10 is translated godliness.

2319. Theostugḗs; from *Theós* (2316), God, and *stugéō*, to hate, abhor. Occurs only in Romans 1:30, translated haters of God and could be held syn. with *átheos* (112), destitute of God. The ancient Greeks used to call *theostugḗs* someone who turned against God, accusing Him and His providence when any heavy calamity befell that person.

2320. Theótēs; deity, Godhead as directly revealed; God's personality (Col. 2:9), as distinguished from *theiótēs* (2305) in Romans 1:20, divinity or divine power and majesty, a concept arrived at by observing God's mighty works.

2323. Therapeúō; heal. *Therapeúō* means to heal miraculously (Matt. 4:23, 24; 10:1, 8; Acts 4:14), not effectively healed (Luke 8:43). Distinguished from other verbs: *iáomai* (2390), to cure diseases mainly of the body, also used metaphorically; *sṓzō* (4982), to save, mostly spiritually but sometimes physically, to rescue; *diasṓzō* (1295), to bring safely through, to preserve, maintain. The subst.: *íama* (2386), cure, and *íasis* (2392), the process of curing (Luke 13:32; Acts 4:30). Deriv.: noun *therapeía* (2322), caring, attention (Luke 12:42), medical service or therapy (Luke 9:11; Rev. 22:2), also household servants (Matt. 24:45 TR; Luke 12:42)

2324. Therápōn; servant. Denotes a faithful friend to one who is superior, who solicitously regards his interest or looks after his affairs, not a common or domestic servant (*oikétēs* [3610]). One who serves regardless of whether he is a free man (*eleútheros* [1658]) or a slave (*doúlos* [1401]), bound by duty or impelled by love (Heb. 3:5). Thus the services of a *therápōn* are higher than those of a *doúlos*, slave. *Therapeúō* (2323) may be used both of the physicians watchful attendance of the sick and of mans service to God. *Therá-*

pōn approaches more closely the position of *oikonómos* (3623), manager, in God's house. Verb: *therapeúō* (2323), to heal, cure, serve.

2334. Theōréō; from *theōros*, a spectator. To gaze, to look with interest and for a purpose, usually indicating the careful observation of details. Distinguished from *blépō* (991), to look, see, to look to someone from whom help is expected, to take care, beware (Mark 15:47; Luke 10:18; 23:35; John 20:6, 12, 14). Used of experience in the sense of partaking of (John 8:51; 17:24). Noun: *theōría* (2335), sight (Luke 23:48), from which our English word theory is derived. Deriv.: *anatheōréō* (333), from *ana* (303), up again, (intens.), and *theōréō*, to view with interest, meaning to consider contemplatively (Acts 17:23; Heb. 13:7).

2338. Thēlus; from *thēlē*, the nipple of a woman's breast, which Plato deduced from *thállō*, to thrive, because it has this effect on the child. The verb *thēlázō* (2337), therefore, means to give the breast, give suck, suck the breast. The adj. *thēlus*, female or woman, is used in the fem. in Romans 1:26 and in the neut. in Matthew 19:4; Mark 10:6; Galatians 3:28.

2342. Thēríon; the same as *thēr*, to run, or a wild beast (Mark 1:13; Acts 10:12 TR; 11:6; Rev. 6:8, cf. Rev. 15:1, 2). Denotes particularly a venomous animal and is applied to a viper (Acts 28:4, 5). May also refer to any kind of beast including the tame species (Heb. 12:20), the same as *zōon* (2226), animal. Paul applies to the Cretans the character of *kaká* (2556), evil, *thēría*, wild beasts (Titus 1:12). In the Sept. where sacrifices of beasts are mentioned, they are never mentioned as *thēría*, but as *zóa*, because the bestial element is brought out in *thēríon*, which is regrettable. Throughout the NT both *zōon* and *thēríon* are rendered by the word beast. Yet these animals represented by the two words are far removed from one another. The *zóa* or living creatures stand before the throne and in them dwells the fullness of all creaturely life, as it gives praise and glory to God (Rev. 4:6–9; 5:6; 6:1). They constitute a part of the heavenly symbolism. The *thēría*, the first and second beast which rise up, one from the bottomless pit (Rev. 11:7) and the other from the sea (Rev. 13:1), one making war upon the two witnesses and the other opening his mouth in blasphemies, form parts of the hellish symbolism. Therefore, *thēríon* brings out the predominance of the lower animal life and can never be the name applied to glorious creatures in the very court and presence of heaven. Consequently, *zóa* should always be rendered as living creatures and *thēría* as beasts in Scripture.

2345. Thiggánō; to touch so that one can exert a modifying influence on something (Col. 2:21; Heb. 11:28; 12:20). Syn.: *háptomai* (680), like thiggano, but stronger; to hurt, as in Hebrews 11:28. See *psēlapháō* (5584), to touch lightly.

2347. Thlípsis; from *thlíbō* (2346), which in turn is derived from *thláō*, to break. *Thlíbō* means to crush, press, compress, squeeze. *Thlipsis* symbolically means grievous affliction or distress (Mattt. 13:21; 24:21; John 16:21; Acts 7:10; 11:19; 14:22; 1 Cor. 7:28; James 1:27), pressure or a burden upon the spirit. Related to *stenochōría* (4730), distress, narrowness, occurring only four times with the connotation of narrowness, from *stenós* (4728), narrow of room, confined space. In three of the four occurrences in the NT *stenochōría* is associated with *thlipsis* (Rom. 2:9; 8:35; 2 Cor. 6:4). *Thlipsis* refers more to being crushed while *stenochōría* refers more to narrowness of room or discomfort.

2348. Thnēskō; to die a natural death (Matt. 2:20; Mark 15:44; Luke 8:49). To die a spiritual death (1 Tim. 5:6). See *thánatos*, (2288), death.

2349. Thnētós; from the verb *thnēskō* (2348), to die, mortal. In Class. Gr. contrast *athánatos*, immortal, which does not occur in the NT and which denoted that essential distinction between men and gods which lies at the foundation of all other differences. However, the subst. *athanasía* (110), immortality, occurs in the NT in 1 Corinthians 15:53, 54; 1 Timothy 6:16, referring always to the immortality of the body. *Thnētós*, accord-

ing to the NT, is a condition of changeability or mortality of the body which is indirect punitive suffering as a result of mans sin. There is no indication whatsoever in the NT that this condition of the mortality of the body does not also belong to the Christian who receives Jesus Christ. Matthew 8:17, speaking of Isaiah 53:5, refers to the fact that the Lord Jesus on the cross bore upon His body both spiritual iniquities and physical sicknesses which resulted from our sin in Adam. When one exercises repentant faith, he is instantly redeemed from his spiritual iniquities and he remains so until he meets the Lord face to face. The redeemed soul remains in an unredeemed body. The body is unredeemed because, as presently constituted, it is incapable of avoiding suffering, sickness, and death. Whenever the body is referred to, even if it is a body that belongs to a Christian (Rom. 6:12; 8:11; 1 Cor. 15:53, 54; 2 Cor. 4:11; 5:4), it is referred to as a mortal body. Man's present body, though now mortal, will be redeemed after the resurrection, as indicated by Paul in Romans 8:23. This redemption of the mortal body was accomplished by Christ on the cross, but its effective realization takes place at the resurrection. An equivalent term of *thnētós* is *phthartós* (5349), corruptible.

2354. Thrēnéō; from *thrénos* (2355), lamentation. To audibly lament (Matt. 11:17; Luke 7:32; 23:27; John 16:20). The subst. *thrénos* occurs together with *klauthmós* (2805), weeping, in Matthew 2:18 TR. This demonstration of grief may take the form of a poem, such as the beautiful lamentation which David composed over Saul and Jonathan (Sept.: 2 Sam. 1:17). The sublime dirge over Tyre is called a *thrénos* (Sept.: Ezek. 26:17, cf. 2 Chr. 35:25; Amos 8:10; Rev. 18:11). It is an outward demonstration of an inner grief. *Lúpē* (3077) is a stronger and more expressive outward demonstration of grief than what is involved in *penthéō* (3996), to mourn, but not as strong as *kóptō* (2875), to strike ones breast in demonstration of grief.

2357. Thrēskos; religious, devout, only in James 1:26, describing the diligent performer of the divinely ascribed duties of the outward service of God. The subst. *thrēskeía* (2356), religion, (Acts 26:5; Col. 2:18; James 1:26, 27) is predominantly the ceremonial service of religion. It is the external framework whereas *eusébeia* (2150), godliness, is the inward piety of soul. According to James, *thrēskeía*, religion, is not mere ceremonial formality, but involves acts of mercy, love, and holiness.

2372. Thumós; from *thúō*, to move impetuously, particularly as the air or wind; a violent motion, or passion of the mind; as ascribed to God (Rev. 14:10, 19; 15:1, 7; 19:15); to man (Luke 4:28; Acts 19:28); to the devil (Rev. 12:12). Found together with *orgé* (3709) (see Rom. 2:8, indignation; Eph. 4:31, wrath; Col. 3:8, wrath; Rev. 19:15, fierce wrath), which means the more abiding and settled habit of mind, whereas thumos is the more passionate and, at the same time, more temporary character of anger and wrath. *Thumós* is an outburst of *orgé* (3709), anger.

2378. Thusía; from *thúō* (2380), to sacrifice. A sacrifice (Luke 2:24; 13:1; Acts 7:41; Heb. 5:1; 7:27, cf. Eph. 5:2; Heb. 9:26; 10:12). Spoken of the bodies of Christians (Rom. 12:1); of their religious services (1 Pet. 2:5); of their praises of God and works of charity to men (Heb. 13:15, 16) and to the preachers of the Gospel (Phil. 4:18).

2379. Thysiastérion; an altar of the true God (Matt. 5:23, 24; James 2:21). Contrast *bōmós* (1041), an idol's altar.

2380. Thúō; to offer, sacrifice. In a ritualistic sense, primarily to smoke or burn incense. Generally, to offer bloody or unbloody offerings, and only in a derived sense, to slay (Matt. 22:4; Luke 15:23, 27, 30; Acts 10:13; 11:7); to kill (John 10:10).

2390. Iáomai; mid. voice of *iáō*. To heal, cure, restore to bodily health (Luke 5:17; 6:19; 22:51); to heal spiritually (Matt. 13:15; Luke 4:18; TR; John 12:40). Pass. voice, to be bodily healed (Matt 8:8, 13; 15:28; Mark 5:29); to be spiritually healed (1 Pet. 2:24). Noun: *iatrós* (2395), physician (Matt. 9:12; Mark 2:17; 5:26;

Luke 4:23; 5:31; 8:43; Col 4:14) used even in Mod. Gr. Deriv.; *íasis* (2392), the act or process of healing; *íama* (2386), the result of healing; used in the pl. in 1 Corinthians 12:9, 28, 30. Although there are a number of verbs used for healing, there is a distinction in their meaning: *therapeúō* (2323), to heal; *sōzō* (4982), to save, restore (Mark 5:23; Luke 8:36); *diasōzō* (1295), to bring safely through (Luke 7:3).

2396. Íde; from *horáō* (3708), to see; act. voice, *idoú* (2400). Behold, an exclamation calling attention to what may be seen or heard or mentally apprehended in any way (Matt. 25:20; John 1:29).

2397. Idéa; or *eíde;*. from *eídō* (1492), to see, equivalent to *eídos* (1491), appearance. Appearance, only in Matthew 28:3. Something conceived in the mind without an objective reality. Contrast *morphḗ* (3444) and *schḗma* (4976), form and fashion which have an objective reality. *Idéa* implies someone in whose mind an appearance is formed; there must be one forming the idea before the object can become visible. The Eng. word idea is derived from the Gr. *idéa*.

2398. Idios; property, ones own. Denotes property or special relationship (Mark 15:20; Luke 2:3 TR; 6:41, 44; John 1:11, 41; 5:43; Acts 1:19; 4:32; Rom. 8:32; 14:4). The phrase *eis ta ídia* (neut. pl. of *ídios*) occurring in John 1:11 means to those he was familiar with. This form may be used with *oikḗmata* (pl. of *oíkēma* [3612], houses or house) implied (John 16:32; 19:27). The expression *kat idían*, with the prep. *katá* (2596), and with the word *chṓran* (5561), place, understood, means in a private place, privately, apart (Matt. 14:13, 23; 17:1, 19; Mark 4:34); joined with *kairós* (2540) time, proper or convenient time (Gal. 6:9; 1 Tim. 2:6; 6:15). Deriv.: *Idiṓtēs* (2399), a common man or a private man. Adv.: *idía*, (dat. of *ídios*), separately.

2399. Idiṓtēs; from *ídios* (2398), one's own. A common man, as opposite to either a man of power or a man of education and learning (1 Cor. 14:16); a person in a private station, a private or common man (Acts 4:13); uninstructed, unskilled (1 Cor. 14:23, 24); plain in speech (2 Cor. 11:6, in this context, refers both to speech and knowledge). The Eng. word idiot is derived from *idiṓtēs*, but it has a very different meaning. The Gr. word never signifies, either in the sacred or secular writers, a person deficient in natural capacity for understanding.

2409. Hiereús; priest, a sacred person, as serving at God's altar but not implying that he also is holy (*hágios* [40]). See Matthew 8:4; Acts 4:1. Adj.: *hierós* (2413), performing the ordinances, sacred.

2411. Hierón; from *hierós* (2413), sacred. A temple, whether of the true God (Matt. 12:5; 6) or of an idol (Acts 19:27). Often includes not only the building but the courts and all the sacred ground or enclosure. See *naos* (3485), temple.

2412. Hieroprepés; from *hierós* (2413), sacred, and *prépō* (4241), to suit, become. Such as becomes sacred persons, venerable. Only in Titus 2:3, to act like a sacred person.

2413. Hierós; sacred, not used of persons but of things (1 Cor. 9:13) and of the Scriptures (2 Tim. 3:15); that which may not be violated, externally related to God but not necessarily having a holy (*hágios* [40]) character. Thus, *hiereús* (2409), priest, is a sacred person as serving at God's altar, but it is not in the least implied that he is a holy person as far as his character is concerned. The true antithesis of *hierós* is *bébēlos* (952), profane.

2416. Hierosuléō; from *hierósulos* (2417), a sacrilegious person. To commit sacrilege, take to ones own private use what is consecrated to God as in Romans 2:22.

2417. Hierósulos; from *hierosuléō*, which is from *hierón* (2413), sacred, and *suláō* (4813), to rob, spoil. A robber of a temple, a sacrilegious person; Only in Acts 19:37.

2418. Hierourgéō; from *hierón* (2413), sacred, and *érgon* (2041), work. To perform or be employed in a sacred office. Only in Romans 15:16, referring to the sacred business of preaching or administering the Gospel.

2425. Hikanós; from *hikanō*, to reach, attain the desired end. Sufficient, fit (2 Cor. 2:16; 3:5); worthy (Matt.

3:11); adequate, enough (Luke 22:38; 2 Cor. 2:6); sufficiently many, great, a considerable number or quantity (Matt. 28:12; Mark 10:46). Deriv.: *hikanótēs* (2426), sufficiency, fitness (2 Cor 3:5). Verb: *hikanóō* (2427), to make sufficient or fit, qualify (Col. 1:12). Syn: *arketós* (713), enough; *perissós* (4053), abundant; *korénnumi* (2880), to satisfy.

2428. Hiketēría; from *hikétēs*, a suppliant, which is from *hikómai*, to come, approach, particularly as suppliant, from the act. *híkō*, to come. Supplication, equivalent to a supplication or humble and earnest prayer (Heb. 5:7). Related words: *euchḗ* (2171), wish; *proseuchḗ* (4335), prayer; *déēsis* (1162), supplication for a particular need; *enteuxís* (1783), intercession; *eucharistía* (2169), thanksgiving; *aítēma* (155), petition.

2433. Hiláskomai; to make reconciliation (Luke 18:13; Heb. 2:17). It provides the satisfaction demanded by God's justice whereby the removal of sins is attained. *Katallássō* (2644), however, signifies not only the removal of the demands of justice but God taking upon Himself the expiation (*hilasmós* [2434]) and establishing a relationship of peace between God and man. While God *katallássei*, reconciles particularly, Christ *hilásketai*, expiates.

2434. Hilasmós; propitiation, only in 1 John 2:2; 4:10. The noun *hilasmós* (2434), propitiation may have a personal object, the sinner, or an impersonal object, our sins. The benefit of Christ's death for man, *katallagḗ* (2643), reconciliation, sets forth the benefit of the death of Christ for the sinner, but *hilasmós* indicates not only the benefit of reconciliation, but the manner whereby sinners are made friends of God. *Hilasmós* refers to Christ as the One who propitiates and offers Himself as the propitiation. He is both the sacrifice and the High Priest sacrificing Himself (John 1:29, 36; 1 Cor. 5:7; Eph. 5:2; Heb. 10:14; 1 Pet 1:19; Rev. 5:6, 8). Deriv.: *hiláskomai* (2433), to propitiate, appease because of Christ's sacrifice.

2435. Hilastḗrion; mercy seat, viewed as a subst. The lid or covering of the Ark of the Covenant made of pure gold, on and before which the high priest was to sprinkle the blood of the expiatory sacrifices on the great day of atonement, was where the Lord promised to meet His people (Ex. 25:17, 22; 29:42; 30:36; Lev. 16:2, 14, 15). Paul, by applying this name to Christ in Romans 3:25, asserts that Christ was the true mercy seat, the antitype of the cover of the Ark of the Covenant (Heb. 9:5). Therefore *hilastḗrion* means a place of conciliation, expiation, what the ancients called *thusiastḗrion* (2379), altar or place of sacrifice. It does not refer to the expiatory sacrifices themselves. Jesus Christ is designated as *hilastḗrion* in Romans 3:25 and Hebrews 9:5 because He is designated not only as the place where the sinner deposits his sin, but He Himself is the means of expiation. He is not like the high priest of the OT whose expiation of the people was accomplished through the blood of another and not his own (Heb. 9:25). What the Jews called the Capporeth (3727 [in OT Lexical Aids]), *hilastḗrion*, was the principal part of the Holy of Holies. Later it was even termed as the house of the Capporeth (1 Chr. 28:11). Philo calls the Capporeth the symbol of the mercy of the power of God.

2436. Híleōs; Attic Gr. for *hiláō*, to be propitious (Matt. 16:22; Heb. 8:12). Propitious, favorable, merciful. In Matthew 16:22, what is translated "God forbid it, Lord" in Gr. is *híleōs soi*, unto you, *Kúrie*, Lord. Literally it is "Be merciful to thyself, Lord." In such phrases the word *híleōs* implies an invocation of mercy for the overturning of evil, that is to say for the cancellation of the consequence of the evil that others are contemplating to do. See *éleos* (1656), mercy. In modern vernacular we would say. God forbid. In Hebrews 8:12 what is meant is I will be merciful to their iniquities or I will alleviate the results of their iniquities. Anti.: *aníleos* (448), without mercy.

2440. Himátion; a large outer garment. In a more restricted sense, it refers to a loose upper garment so large that a man would sometimes sleep in it (Luke 5:36; 1 Pet. 3:3).

2441. Himatismós; garments which are stately and costly

(Luke 7:25; 9:29; John 19:24; Acts 20:33; 1 Tim. 2:9).

2465. Isággelos; from *ísos* (2470), similar or equal, and *ággelos* (32) angel. Angel-like (Luke 20:36, which, if taken in connection with Mark 12:25, should be translated as like instead of equal; see also Matt. 22:30. According to this passage, neither mortality nor sexual union pertains either to the sons of the resurrection or to the angels [1 Cor. 6:3]. Therefore, the meaning of 2 Peter 2:4; Jude 1:6, 7 is that sexual union must not be attributed to the angels).

2473. Isópsuchos; from *ísos* (2470), equal and *psuché* (5590), soul, mind. To be activated by the same motives, of like character, like-minded (Phil. 2:20).

2476. Hístēmi; trans., to set, place (Matt. 4:5; 18:2; Mark 9:36; Luke 9:47); intrans., to stand (Matt 12:46, 47; 13:2; 16:28). To remain, abide, continue (John 8:44), to stand still, stop (Acts 8:38); to make to stand, establish, confirm (Rom. 14:4). In the pass., to be established, stand firm, stand (Matt. 12:25, 26; Mark 3:25, 26) to be confirmed (Matt. 18:16; 2 Cor. 13:1); to appoint (Acts 17:31); to agree, covenant (Matt. 26:15, cf. *epéggeilantō* [1861] in Mark 14:11; Luke 22:5); impute, lay to ones charge (Acts 7:60). Deriv.: *akatástasis* (181); *akatástatos* (182); *anástasis* (386), *anastatóō* (387); *anístēmi* (450); *apokathístēmi* (600); *apokatástasis* (605); *apostasía* (646); *apostásiō* (647); *astatéō* (790); *aphístēmi* (868); *dichostasía* (1370); *ékstasis* (1611); *enístēmi* (1764); *exanástasis* (1815); *exanístēmi* (1817); *exístēmi* (1839); *kathístēmi* (2525); *methístēmi* (3179); *stásis* (4714); *sunistáō* (4921), *hupóstasis* (5287).

2479. Ischús; strength, especially physical power as an endowment (Mark 12:30, 33; 2 Thess. 1:9). In *dúnamis* (1411), there is implied ability or capacity. The stem of *ischús* is linked with *isch-*, strength, and *échō* (2192), I have. *Ischúō*, therefore, may mean to have health, syn. with *hugiaínō* (5198), to be healthy, as opposite to *asthénēō* (770), to be weak, sick. Deriv.: *enischúō* (1765), from *en* (1722), in, and *ischúō*, to strengthen, to gain strength (Luke 22:43; Acts 9:19), *katischúō* (2729), from *katá* (2596), against; to prevail against. The adj. *ischurós* (2478), strong.

2480. Ischúō; from *ischús* (2479), strength. To be strong; to avail, to be of use, or force; to be able, can (Matt. 8:28; 26:40; Mark 5:4; 9:18; Luke 6:48); to be strong in body (Matt. 9:12; Mark 2:17); to have power as of the Gospel (Acts 19:20); to prevail against (Acts 19:16; Rev. 12:8); to be effective, capable of producing results (Matt. 5:13; Gal. 5:6; Heb. 9:17; James 5:16); to be whole, healthy, strong (Matt. 9:12; Mark 2:17). Contrast *dúnamai* (1410), denoting a more forceful strength or ability. Still stronger forms are *exischúō* (1840), to be thoroughly strong (Eph. 3:18); *katischúō* (2729), used negatively, of the powerlessness of the gates of Hades to prevail against the Church.

2508. Kathaírō; related to *katharós* (2513), pure, clean, without stain, without spot. To cleanse, purify. Occurs twice in John 15:2 referring to the vine in that the vine dresser cuts off certain branches in order that other branches may bear more fruit. In Hebrews 10:2, expiate, redeem, referring to the once-and-for-all initial redemption by Jesus Christ, cleansing the sinner and positioning him in Christ.

2511. Katharízō; in Attic Gr. *katharíō* (Heb. 9:14), from *katharós* (2513), pure. To cleanse, free from filth (Matt 23:25; Luke 11:39, cf. Mark 7:19). To cleanse or make clean from leprosy (Matt. 8:2, 3; 10:8), often used in the Sept. for legal cleansing from leprosy (Lev. 14). To cleanse in the sense of purification, legal or ceremonial (Heb. 9:22, 23, cf. Acts 10:15; 11:9), frequently so used in the Sept. In a spiritual sense, to purify from the pollution and guilt of sin (Acts 15:9; 2 Cor. 7:1; Eph. 5:26; Titus 2:14; Heb. 9:14; James 4:8; 1 John 1:7, 9). Deriv.: *katharismós* (2512), purification; *katharótēs* (2514), purity; *perikátharma* (4027), offscouring, refuse; *akáthartos* (169), unpurified; *akatharsía* (167), uncleanness; *kathaírō* (2508), to cleanse, to purify.

2512. Katharismós; purification. In Class. Gr. *katharmós*. Actually refers to the process of purification, the sacrifice of purification. In Luke 2:22, it is the purification

of women. In Mark 1:44; Luke 5:14; and John 2:6 it is ritual purification. The baptism both of John and the Lord Jesus is designated as *katharismós* in John 3:25, not that the ritual of physical baptism brought about spiritual results or spiritual purification, but only as a parallel in its results. As water cleanses the body, so baptism symbolizes the work of repentance and forgiveness of sin. Its designation as a baptism of repentance unto forgiveness of sins (Mark 1:4; Luke 3:3; Acts 2:38) means an identification of the forgiveness of sins. In Hebrews 1:3 the word denotes the objective removal of our sins by Jesus Christ (see also Heb. 9:22, 23). In 2 Peter 1:9 it refers to the actual purification accomplished in man; while in Hebrews 1:3, it refers to the propitiation provided by the Lord Jesus.

2513. Katharós; clean, pure, clear, in a natural sense (Matt. 27:59; John 13:10; Heb. 10:22; Rev. 15:6; 22:1). Clean in the sense that something is lawful to be eaten or used (Luke 11:41; Rom. 14:20; Titus 1:15). In all these passages there is a plain reference to a legal or ceremonial cleanness. Clean or pure, in a spiritual sense, from the pollution and guilt of sin (Matt. 5:8; John 13:10, 11; 15:3; 1 Tim. 1:5; 3:9; James 1:27). Sometimes applied to purity or cleanness from blood or blood guiltiness (Acts 18:6; 20:26). In the physical or nonethical sense, the opposite of *rhuparós* (4508), dirty (Matt. 27:59; Heb. 10:22; Rev. 15:6). Sometimes the meaning of *katharós* is very close to the meaning of *eilikrinḗs* (1506), sincere, something that has been cleansed by shaking to and fro as in a sieve or in winnowing. *Katharós* describes the purity contemplated under the aspect of that which is free from soil or stain (James 1:27). Sometimes seen as the opposite of *koinós* (2839), common as well as *akáthartos* (169) unpurified (Rom. 14:14, 20; Heb. 9:13).

2514. Katharótēs; purity, referring to the result of cleansing or purification. *Katharismós* (2512) refers to the process of purification instead of the result. In Hebrews 9:13, *katharótēs* is freedom from the guilt of filthiness of the flesh.

2525. Kathístēmi; from the intens. prep. *katá* (2596), down, and *hístēmi* (2476), to set, place. Trans. to set down, bring to (Acts 17:15); to place anywhere in an office, in a condition (Matt. 24:45, 47; 25:21, 23; Luke 12:42, 44; Acts 6:3); with double acc., to make somebody something, to put in a situation or position (Luke 12:14; Acts 7:10, 27, 35; Titus 1:5; Heb. 5:1; 7:28; 8:3). In Romans 5:19: "For as by one mans disobedience many were made (*katestáthēsan*) sinners, so by the obedience of one shall many be made (*katastathḗtasontai*) righteous." Another Gr. word that could have been used is *gínomai* (1096), to become, or in this case, to make. To have used this latter word would have actually meant that God is responsible for making transgressors. As a judge does not make lawbreakers or bear moral responsibility for what they do, so it is with the Lord. God does not make sinners, but He declares them to be sinners. He set the consequence of the disobedience of man, but He was not responsible for that disobedience. The verb *kathístēmi* used in this regard means that God has set or placed man in a definite place or position, that of the transgressor, but He did not make him a transgressor. The responsibility is entirely mans. Intrans., existing as inactive and unfruitful (2 Pet. 1:8). In the pres. mid. voice, to take a position, come forward, appear (James 3:6; 4:4). See *hístēmi* (2476), to stand.

2537. Kainós; qualitatively new as contrasted with *néos* (3501), numerically new or the last one numerically (Matt. 9:17; Eph. 2:15). Deriv.: *kainótēs* (2538), newness; *anakainízō* (340), to renew qualitatively; *anakainóō* (341), to renew; *anakaínōsis* (342), the act of renewing; *egkainízō* (1457), to dedicate, consecrate into a qualitatively new use; hence the NT is *kainḗ diathḗkē*, qualitatively new, not merely numerically new (*néa* [3501]).

2538. Kainótēs; renewal, not simply an experience similar to the past, but a qualitatively different one (Rom.

6:4; 7:6). Related to *kainós* (2537), new, but qualitatively different. Contrast *néos* (3501), numerically new; and also the verb *ananéóō* (365), to renew, to have a new experience, the same as in the past. See *neótēs* (3503), newness, youthfulness; *anakainízō* (340); *anakainóō* (341); *anakaínōsis* (342); *ananéōo* (365); *egkainízō* (1457); *kainós* (2537).

2540. Kairós; season, time, but not merely as a succession of moments which is *chrónos* (5550). *Kairós* implies that which time gives an opportunity to do. Related to *eukairía* (2120), from *eu* (2095), good, and *kairós*, opportune time, opportunity. *Kairós*, however, implies not the convenience of the season, but the necessity of the task at hand whether the time provides a good, convenient opportunity or not (Mark 1:15; Col. 4:5). When used in the pl. with *chrónoi* (times), it is translated as seasons, times at which certain foreordained events take place or necessary accomplishments need to take place.

2549. Kakía; wickedness (Acts 8:22; Titus 3:3), as an evil habit of the mind, while *ponēría* (4189) is the act. outcoming of the same. *Ponēría* is, therefore, malevolence, the doing of evil and not only of being evil. Contrast *kakós* (2556) with *ponērós* (4190). Deriv.: *kakoétheia* (2550), evil manners or morals (Rom. 1:29), ill-nature, depravity.

2550. Kakoétheia; from *kakós* (2556), bad, evil, and *éthos*, (2239), custom. Occurs only in Romans 1:29, translated malice. It actually means ill-nature, taking everything with an evil connotation and giving a malicious interpretation of the actions of others. That nature which is evil and makes one suspect evil in others. On the other hand *kakía* (2549), wickedness, is the name not of one vice but of the viciousness out of which all vices spring as the ancients saw it. In the NT, however, *kakía* is not so much viciousness as a special form of vice. It is more the evil habit of the mind. Contrast *ponēría* (4189), malevolence, the acting out, or externalization of the evil habit of the mind; attributing to others and their actions the worst imaginable motives (Rom. 1:29).

2552. Kakopátheia; from *kakopathéō* (2553), to suffer misfortune, hardship. Suffering evil, a bearing of affliction (James 5:10, cf. 2 Tim. 1:8).

2553. Kakopathéō; from *kakós* (2556), evil, and *páschō* (3958), to suffer. To suffer evil or affliction, to be afflicted (2 Tim. 2:9; James 5:13, cf. 2 Tim. 1:8). To endure, to sustain affliction (2 Tim. 2:3; 4:5).

2554. Kakopoiéō; from *kakós* (2556), bad, and *poiéō* (4160), to do. To do evil, in the moral sense (3 John 1:11, cf. 1 Pet. 3:17). Equivalent to doing mischief, doing evil, with a reference to being morally offensive to another (Mark 3:4; Luke 6:9). Ant.: *agathopoiéō* (15), to do good.

2555. Kakopoiós; from *kakopoiéō*, to do evil. Evil-doer. Used as an adj. noun, meaning pernicious, injurious; an evil-doer or a malefactor, behaving in a bad way. Used in John 18:30 and 1 Peter 2:12, 14; 3:16 in a moral sense corresponding to behaving in an evil way or doing evil. Only in 1 Peter 4:15 does it appear in the sense of generally injurious, denoting one who is injurious to the community.

2556. Kakós; from the verb *cházō* or *cházomai*, to give back, recede, retire, retreat in battle. Evil, wicked. One that is evil and as such gets others into trouble (Mark 7:21; Rom. 1:30). From this is derived *kakía* (2549), wickedness, iniquity, evil, affliction. Syn.: *ponērós* (4190), malicious, indicating willful harm to others, an element not necessarily found in *kakós*. The *kakós* may be content to perish in his own corruption, but the *ponērós* (a name also attributed to Satan, Matt. 6:13; Eph. 6:16) is not content unless he is corrupting others as well and drawing them into the same destruction with himself.

2557. Kakoúrgos; from *kakoergós*, which is derived from *kakós* (2556), bad, and *érgon* (2041), work. An evil-doer, malefactor (Luke 23:32, 33, 39; 2 Tim. 2:9). In the Gr. writers the word is joined with "thieves," as also in Luke 23:32. There are some who suggest the derivation of the word is from *kakós*, bad, and *orgé* (3709), anger. In this sense it would stress the mali-

cious, cunning, and treacherous character of an evildoer.

2559. Kakóō; to harm or do evil to anyone, to ill-treat, plague, injure (Acts 7:6, 19; 12:1; 18:10; 1 Pet. 3:13); to put one into a bad mood against someone (Acts 14:2). Subst.: *kákōsis* (2561), distress (Acts 7:34).

2560. Kakós; badly; with *échō* (2192), to have, literally meaning to have it badly, that is, to be ill (Matt. 14:35; Mark 1:32; Luke 7:2). See *árrhōstos* (732); *asthéneia* (769); *asthenēs* (772).

2564. Kaléō; call; with a personal obj., to call anyone, invite (Matt. 20:8; 25:14); of the divine invitation to participate in the blessings of redemption (Rom. 8:30; 1 Cor. 1:9; Heb. 9:15); to name; in the pass. voice, to be called by name. It suggests either vocation or destination. Noun: *klēsis* (2821), a calling; *klētós* (2822), called. Deriv.: *eiskaléō* (1528), to call in (Acts 10:23); *epikaléomai* (1941), to be called; *metakaléō* (3333), to recall; *proskaléomai* (4341), to invite; *sugkaléō* (4779), to call together; *parakaléō* (3870), to call near, to comfort.

2570. Kalós; constitutionally good without necessarily being benevolent; expresses beauty as a harmonious completeness, balance, proportion (John 2:10; James 2:7).

2572. Kalúptō; to wrap around, as bark, skin, shell or plaster; to cover up (Matt. 8:24; 10:26; Luke 8:16; 23:30; 2 Cor. 4:3; James 5:20; 1 Pet. 4:8). Deriv.: *apokalúptō* (601), to unveil, discover, make visible, reveal; *apokálupsis* (602), uncovering, unveiling, disclosure, revelation. Syn.: *krúptō* (2928), to hide.

2577. Kámnō; to work, to be weary from constant work (Heb. 12:3). When used in connection with *asthenéō* (770), to be sick, it suggests the common accompaniment of sickness, weariness of mind which may hinder physical recovery. In some mss. it occurs also in Revelation 2:3.

2585. Kapēleúō; to treat as if for personal profit, profiteer. Used only in 2 Corinthians 2:17, translated "corrupt." To adulterate wine and make it thick like *pēlós* (4081), mud, mire; to make a gain of anything. The *kápēlos* may also be derived from *kápē*, food, victuals, from *káptō*, to eat; a huckster or petty retail trader, contrast *émporos* (1713), merchant (Matt. 13:45; Rev. 18:3, 11, 15, 23) who sells his wares wholesale. *Kápēlos* is especially used of the retailer of wine who is exposed to the strong temptation to tamper with it or sell it in short measure in order to make a greater profit. *Kapēleúō* includes *dolóō* (1389), to falsify (2 Cor. 4:2); committing adultery not simply for the sake of personal gain. Profiteering from God's Word, preaching for money, or professing faith for personal gain.

2588. Kardía; heart (Acts 2:26). The Scriptures attributed to the heart: thoughts, reasonings, understanding, will, judgment; designs, affections, love, hatred, fear, joy, sorrow, and anger; these things can actually affect a man's physical heart. Therefore, "heart" is used as a metonym for the mind in general (Matt. 12:34; John 13:2; Rom. 2:15; 10:9, 10; 1 Pet. 3:4); the understanding (Luke 3:15; 9:47; Acts 28:27; Rom. 1:21; 2 Cor. 4:6); the will (Acts 11:23; 13:22; Rom. 10:1); the memory (Luke 1:66; 2:51); the intention, affection, or desire (Matt. 6:21; 18:35; Mark 7:6; Luke 1:17; 8:15; Acts 8:21; 1 Thess. 2:4); the conscience (1 John 3:20, 21). It can also mean the middle or inner part, as the heart is in relation to the breast (Matt. 12:40), as the heart of the earth is the inner part of the earth, the grave. Deriv.: *kardiognóstēs* (2589), heart-knower, heart-searcher; *sklērokardía* (4641), hardening of the heart, stubbornness.

2589. Kardiognóstēs; from *kardía* (2588), heart, and *gnóstēs* (1109), a knower (which in turn is derived from *gnóō* or *ginóskō* [1097], to know). A knower of hearts; one who knows the hearts, that is, the most secret thoughts, desires, and intentions (Acts 1:24; 15:8).

2594. Karteréō; to be strong, steadfast, firm, to endure, hold out, bear the burden. In Hebrews 11:27, it means that Moses endured exile with strength and courage.

2596. Katá; a prep. governing the gen. and acc., with

the primary meaning of down, that is, down from, down upon, or down in. With the gen., used of place indicating motion down from a higher to a lower place (Matt. 8:32; Mark 5:13; Luke 8:33). Generally used of motion or direction, upon, towards, or through any place or object, in the sense of against (Acts 27:14), of, through, throughout (Luke 4:14; 23:5); with *hólou*, the whole, in the adv. phrase *kath' hólou* (or as one word *kathólou*). After verbs of swearing it has the meaning of upon or by something (Matt. 26:63; Heb. 6:13,16). Metaphorically, used of the obj. toward or upon which anything tends or aims, upon, in respect to (1 Cor. 15:15). With the acc., used of place with verbs of motion either expressed or implied. Used of extension: out, over, through, throughout a place (Luke 8:39). Used of motion or situation: upon, at, near to, adjacent to (Luke 10:32); sometimes as *en* ([1722] within), might be employed, though not strictly syn., as in the Eng. phrase "at a house" or "in a house," used interchangeably. Used of time: of a period or point of time upon which, that is, in, at, during which anything takes place (Acts 14:1, at the same time). In a distributive sense, derived strictly from the idea of pervading all the parts of a whole; also of place (Heb. 9:5); *katá méros*, that is, part for part; particularly of number, *kath' héna*, one by one (1 Cor. 14:31); *katá; dúo*, two and two (1 Cor. 14:27). It may also express the relation in which one thing stands toward another thus everywhere implying manner (Matt. 9:29; 23:3; Mark 7:5; Luke 2:22). Used of an occasion: by virtue of, because of, for, by, through, where the idea of accordance or adaptedness still lies at its basis (Matt. 19:3; Acts 3:17). Used of any general reference or allusion: in respect to, as to (Rom. 1:3; 9:5; 11:28; Phil. 3:6); of likeness, similitude in which case it is equivalent to like, after the manner of (2 Cor. 1:17; Heb. 5:6, 10). It may also refer to the end, aim, purpose, in which case it means towards, for, by way of (2 Cor. 11:21; 1 Tim. 6:3). In composition *katá* used as a prefix usually implies motion downward (as *katabaínō* [2597], to go down); against, in a hostile sense (as *katēgoréō* [2723], to speak against); distribution (as *kataklērodotéō* [2624], to distribute an inheritance); in a general sense, down, down upon, and also throughout, but it often cannot be expressed in Eng. and is then simply intens. in effect. Sometimes it gives a trans. sense to an intrans. verb (as *katargéō* [2673], to render inoperative).

2597. Katabaínō; from *katá* (2596), down, and *baínō*, to go or come. To come down, descend (Matt. 3:16; 7:25).

2602. Katabolé; from *katabállō* (2598), to throw down. A casting or laying down. *Katabolé kósmou*, the foundation of the world (Matt. 13:35; 25:34).

2604. Kataggeleús; from *kataggéllō* (2605), to proclaim. A proclaimer, publisher (only in Acts 17:18).

2605. Kataggéllō; from *katá* (2596). intens., and *aggéllō* (32), to tell, declare. To declare plainly, openly, or aloud (Acts 4:2; 13:5, 38; 16:21; 17:23; Rom. 1:8). Deriv.: *kataggeleús* (2604), a proclaimer, publisher.

2607. Kataginóskō; from *katá* (2596), against, and *ginóskō* (1097), to know. To perceive something, observe; usually to discern in a bad sense and therefore to discern something against another, to incriminate, condemn (1 John 3:20, 21), to blame (Gal. 2:11). In the perf. pass., to be blamed, worthy of blame, reprehensible.

2610. Katagōnízomai; from *katá* (2596), against, and *agōnízomai* (75), to contend for victory in the public games. To throw down, subdue (only in Heb. 11:33).

2613. Katadikázō; from *katá* (2596), against, and *dikázō*, to judge, pronounce sentence, which in turn is from *díkē* (1349), judgment. To give judgment against a person, recognize the right against him, pass sentence, condemn (Matt. 12:7, 37; Luke 6:37; James 5:6). Ant.: *apolúō* (630), to dismiss as innocent; *dikaióō* (1344), to justify.

2615. Katadoulóō; from the intens. prep. *katá* (2596), and *doulóō* (1402), to enslave. To enslave entirely, reduce to absolute slavery (2 Cor. 11:20; Gal. 2:4).

2624. Kataklērodotéō; to distribute by or according to

lot or for an inheritance (Acts 13:19). The verb *kataklērō*, which in Class. Gr. is equivalent to *kataklērodotéō* or *kataklēronoméō*, embraces the two meanings, to distribute or receive by lot.

2631. Katákrima; related to *krínō* (2919), to divide, separate, judge, with the suffix *-ma* (which makes it the result of judgment). Something to be decided against anyone, a condemnatory judgment. Only in Romans 5:16, 18; 8:1. In Romans 5:16 contrast *dikaíōma* (1345), the right given to the believer as a result of his acknowledgment of the right of God in his life. In Romans 5:18 *katákrima* is contrasted with the more definite *dikaíōsis* (1347), the act of making life righteous, therefore, a judgment of condemnation in the sense of the economy of redemption.

2632. Katakrínō; from *katá* (2596), against, and *krínō* (2919), to judge. To pronounce sentence against, condemn, adjudge to punishment, whether temporal (Matt. 20:18; 27:3; John 8:10, 11) or eternal (Mark 16:16); to furnish matter or occasion for condemnation, to prove or show worthy of condemnation (Matt. 12:41, 42; Luke 11:31, 32; Heb. 11:7); to punish (2 Pet. 2:6); to weaken, enervate, repress; spoken of sin, to take away condemning power (Rom. 8:3). Deriv.: *krínō* (2919), to judge.

2633. Katákrisis; from *katakrínō* (2632), which is in turn from *kata;* (2596), against, and *krínō* (2919) to judge. Condemnation against anyone; the act of condemning or the performance of it. Distinguished from *katákrima* (2631), which is the actual condemnation or judgment itself (2 Cor. 3:9; 7:3).

2635. Katalaléō; from *katá* (2596), against, and *laléō* (2980), to speak. To speak against, allowing thoughtless words to be spoken (James 4:11; 1 Pet. 2:12; 3:16). Contrast *katalégō*, from *katá*, against, and *légō* (3004), to say. *Légō* does not only mean to speak what is in one's mind but to mentally consider what is spoken. *Katálogos*, from the verb *katalégō*, used as the Eng. "catalogue." Contrast *diabállō* (1225), to falsely accuse.

2637. Katálalos; from the verb *katalaléō* (2635) which is from *katá* (2596), against, and *laléō* (2980), to speak. To speak evil of someone, slander with whatever words come to one's mouth without giving thought to them (Rom. 1:30), evil-speaking, slander, insult.

2638. Katalambánō; from *katé* (2596), an intens. prep., and *lambánō* (2983), to take. To seize (Mark 9:18), to lay hold of, apprehend, in a figurative sense (Phil. 3:12); to receive, admit (John 1:5, meaning the darkness did not admit or receive the light, cf. vv. 10–12; 3:19); to take, catch unawares (John 8:3f.); to come upon, overtake (John 12:35; 1 Thess. 5:4); to attain, obtain (Rom. 9:30; 1 Cor. 9:24); to comprehend mentally (Eph. 3:18). In the mid. voice, *katalambánomai*, to perceive, understand, find (Acts 4:13; 25:25).

2643. Katallagé; from *katallássō* (2644) which is from the intens. *katá* (2596), and *allássō* (236), to change. A change or reconciliation from a state of enmity to one of friendship (Rom. 5:8; 11:15; 2 Cor. 5:18, 19). It is the result of the *apolútrōsis* (629), redemption, the divine act of salvation, the ceasing of God's wrath.

2644. Katallássō; reconcile. Used of the divine work of redemption, denoting that act of redemption insofar as God Himself, by taking upon Himself our sin and becoming an atonement, establishes that relationship of peace with mankind which the demands of His justice have hitherto prevented (Rom. 5:10; 1 Cor. 7:11). In this usage of *katallássō*, God is the subject, man the object. While *hilasmós* (2434), propitiation (1 John 2:2; 4:10) and *hiláskomai* (2433), to make reconciliation (Luke 18:13; Heb. 2:17), aim at the avenging of God's wrath, *katallássō* implies that God has laid aside or withdrawn wrath.

2647. Katalúō; from the intens. prep. *katá* (2596), and *lúō* (3089), to loose. To loose, unloose what had been bound or fastened, as used in Class. Gr. To refresh oneself, to lodge or be a guest (Luke 9:12; 19:7). It properly refers to travelers loosening their own burdens or those of their animals when they stayed at a house on a journey (Luke 9:12). To dissolve, demolish, destroy, or throw down, as a building or its materials (Matt. 24:2; 26:61; 27:40); as the law and the prophets (Matt. 5:17); as a work (Acts 5:38, 39; Rom. 14:20).

2657. Katanoéō; from the intens. prep. *katá* (2596), and *noéō* (3539), to mind. To observe, remark, consider, contemplate (Matt. 7:3; Luke 12:24, 27; 20:23; Acts 7:31; 11:6; 27:39; Heb. 3:1; 10:24). See *noéō* (3539), to understand, and *noús* (3563), mind.

2663. Katápausis; from *katapaúō* (2664), to make to cease. As a noun, it means a rest (Heb. 3:11, 18; 4:1, 3, 10, 11). Used as a dwelling in Acts 7:49.

2664. Katapaúō; from the intens. prep. *katá* (2596), and *paúō* (3973), to make to cease. Trans., to cause to rest, give rest (Heb. 4:8); to restrain (Acts 14:18). Intrans., to rest entirely (Heb. 4:4, 10).

2671. Katára; from *kata* (2596), against, and *ará* (685), a curse. Contrasted with *eulogía* (2129), blessing (James 3:10). The same antithesis occurs in Galatians 3:10, 13; Hebrews 6:8; 2 Peter 2:14, meaning the curse proceeding from God, the rejection and surrender to punishment, the destruction caused by judgment. It is equivalent to judgment without mercy in James 2:13. The word involves both the sentence of the divine judgment and the ruin therein inflicted, the manifested curse. In Galatians 3:13, the expression, "being made a curse [*katára*] for us," means that the Lord Himself and the curse He bore are not to be separated from each other. See 2 Corinthians 5:21.

2672. Kataráomai; from *katára* (2671), a curse. Used only in the mid. voice, to wish anyone evil or ruin, to curse. In the pass. perf., to be cursed (Matt. 25:41). In the NT, with the acc., to give one over to ruin (Matt. 5:44 TR; Mark 11:21; Luke 6:28; James 3:9).

2673. Katargéō; from *katá* (2596), an intens. prep., and *argéō* (691), to be idle. *Katá* gives to the intrans. *argéō*, a trans. meaning, that is, to make to cease (Luke 13:7; Heb. 2:14). Paul uses it often to signify more than hindrance or cessation from outward activity. With Paul it always denotes a complete, not a temporary or partial ceasing (1 Cor. 1:28; 6:13). To rest, as in Luke 13:7, where the idle earth does not denote unused or untilled land, but land which is unfruitful or lying fallow; opposite of *energés* (1756), active. To abrogate, make void, do away with or put an end to the Law (Rom. 3:3, 31; 1 Cor. 13:11; 15:24; Gal. 3:17; Eph. 2:15; 2 Tim. 1:10).

2675. Katartízō; from the intens. prep. *katá* (2596), with, and *artízō* to adjust, fit, finish, derived in turn from *ártios* (739), fit, complete. The fundamental meaning is to put a thing in its appropriate position, to establish, set up, equip, arrange. NT meanings: to adjust, adapt, dispose of, perhaps with great wisdom and propriety (Heb. 10:5; 11:3); to fit (Rom. 9:22); to perfect, finish, complete (Matt. 21:16; 1 Thess. 3:10; Heb. 13:21; 1 Pet. 5:10); to instruct fully or perfectly (Luke 6:40); to refit, repair, mend, applied to nets which have been broken (Matt. 4:21; Mark 1:19); to reunite in mind and sentiment, to reconcile, as opposed to having schisms, ruptures (1 Cor. 1:10); to reduce, restore as it were a disjointed limb (Gal. 6:1). Deriv.: *katártisis* (2676), completion; *prokatartízō* (4294), to perfect beforehand, make right, equip beforehand.

2676. Katártisis; completing, perfecting (2 Cor. 13:9). Denotes a process in its progress while *katartismós* (2677) denotes a process as completed.

2677. Katartismós; perfection or completion. Differs from *katártisis* (2676) in that the latter denotes a process in progress while *katartismós* denotes a process as completed (Eph. 4:12).

2699. Katatomē; from the intens. prep. *katá* (2596), and *témnō*, to cut. A cutting away, mangling, concision (only in Phil. 3:2). Paul here uses sarcasm. *Katatomē* and *peritomē* (4061), circumcision, sound alike. *Peritomē*, ordained by the law of Moses, has a spiritual meaning, that is, to distinguish the Jews from the Gentiles. If the spiritual meaning is forgotten, then *peritomē*, circumcision, becomes *katatomē*, butchering up, merely cutting away flesh which in itself is of no value. Paul thus calls the Jewish teachers "butchers," because after the coming of Christ they taught that the outward circumcision of the flesh was necessary for salvation while at the same time they were

destitute of the circumcision of the heart. This word of the Apostle not only depreciates the carnal circumcision, but seems also to allude to the superstitious cuttings and manglings of the flesh practiced among the heathen (Lev. 21:5).

2710. Katachráomai; from *katá* (2596), denoting ill, and *chráomai* (5530), to use. To use immoderately, abuse (1 Cor. 7:31; 9:18).

2711. Katapsúchō; from the intens. prep. *katá* (2596), and *psuchō* (5594), to cool. To cool, to refresh (Luke 16:24).

2712. Kateídōlos; from the intens. prep. *katá* (2596), and *eídōlon* (1497), idol. Full of idols (Acts 17:16). It is a peculiar word describing the *deisidaimōn* (1174), superstitious, those wholly given up to the worship of false gods.

2722. Katéchō; from the intens. prep. *katá* (2596), and *échō* (2192), to have, hold, hold fast in a spiritual sense (Luke 8:15; 1 Cor. 11:2; 15:2; 1 Thess. 5:21; Heb. 3:6, 14; 10:23, cf. Rom. 7:6); to possess (1 Cor. 7:30; 2 Cor. 6:10), to take possession, seize (Matt. 21:38 TR, cf. John 5:4, a disease); to take as a place (Luke 14:9); detain (Luke 4:42; Phile. 1:13); restrain, withhold (2 Thess. 2:6, 7, cf. Rom. 1:18); with prep. *eis* (1519), to bring a ship toward the shore (Acts 27:40).

2723. Katēgoréō; from *katá* (2596), against, and *agoréō* or *agoreúō*, to speak. To speak openly against, to impeach, accuse mainly in a legal sense (Matt. 12:10; John 5:45; Rom. 2:15; Rev. 12:10). Deriv.: *katēgoros* (2725), accuser; *katēgoría* (2724), accusation, incrimination; *katēgōr* is used instead of *katēgoros* in Revelation 12:10 UBS.

2724. Katēgoría; accusation, incrimination against a person (Luke 6:7 TR; John 18:29; 1 Tim. 5:19). With the gen. (Titus 1:6) it does not refer to judicial punishment, but public condemnation.

2725. Katēgoros; accuser (John 8:10 TR; Acts 23:30, 35; 24:8; 25:16,. 18). In the Sept., it refers to one who brought his own complaint, he who accused in his own behalf (Prov. 18:17). In Revelation 12:10 TR, it is used of the devil instead of *katēgōr*.

2730. Katoikéō; from *katá* (2596), an intens. prep., and *oikéō* (3611), to dwell. Refers to a certain fixed and durable dwelling (Matt. 2:23; 4:13; Luke 13:4; Acts 1:19). In Acts 2:5 it means to sojourn or to dwell in a place for a time, as *paroikéō*; to dwell, as God in the temple at Jerusalem (Matt. 23:21); to dwell, as the fullness of the Godhead in Christ (Col. 1:19); as Christ (Eph. 3:17); and the Holy Ghost (James 4:5) in the faithful; as devils possessing a man (Matt. 12:45; Luke 11:26); as righteousness in the new heavens and the new earth (2 Pet. 3:13). Deriv.: *katoikēsis* (2731), a dwelling, habitation (Mark 5:3); *katoikētērion* (2732), a place of dwelling, a habitation (Eph. 2:22; Rev. 18:2); *katoikia* (2733), a dwelling (Acts 17:26). Ant.: *paroikéō* (3939), to sojourn, dwell in a place for a time only, to dwell in, inhabit a house or place.

2736. Kátō; from *katá* (2596), down; an adv. of place; downwards (Matt. 4:6; Luke 4:9); beneath, below (Mark 14:66; Acts 2:19); *katōtérō* an adv. of the comparative degree from *kátō*, under, time and age (Matt. 2:16). Deriv.: *katōteros* (2737), comparative adj. from *kátō*, below, lower (Eph. 4:9).

2749. Keímai; the mid. form of the obsolete *keō* or *keíō*, to cause to lie. To lay, be laid down (Luke 2:12, 16; 24:12 TR; John 11:41 TR); to be placed or set (Matt. 5:14; John 2:6; 19:29; Rev. 4:2); to be laid, as a foundation (1 Cor. 3:11); to be stored (Luke 12:19); to be set, appointed (Luke 11:34; Phil. 1:17; 1 Thess. 3:3); to be made or promulgated, as a law (1 Tim. 1:9); to be in the power of someone (1 John 5:19). In Matthew 3:10 and Luke 3:9, in regard to the axe that lies at the root of the trees, it does not simply mean that it is laid there, but it speaks also of the necessity of its being taken up and used. Deriv.: *antikeimai* (480), to lie over against or to oppose.

2756. Kenós; empty, indicating the hollowness of something or somebody. Contrast *mátaios* (3152), a sense of vanity and aimlessness. In 1 Thessalonians 2:1 it means unaccompanied by the demonstration of the

Spirit and of power. When used not of things but of persons, it predicates not merely an absence and emptiness of good, but (since the moral nature of man endures no vacuum) it indicates the presence of evil (James 2:20).

2757. Kenophōnía; from *kenós* (2756), vain, and *phōnḗ* (5456), a voice. Empty, fruitless speaking. In 1 Timothy 6:20; 2 Timothy 2:16 Paul designates the *bébēloi* ([952], godless) babblings as *kenophōnía*, destitute or wicked discourses, speeches that are devoid of any divine or spiritual character, fruitless as far as the satisfaction of man's need of salvation and the molding of the Christian life and character are concerned. It is equivalent to the "vain" words (*kenoí* [2756]; *lógoi* [3056]) in Ephesians 5:6.

2758. Kenóō; from *kenós* (2756), empty, void. The antithesis of *plēróō* (4137), to fill. To empty (Rom. 4:14; 1 Cor. 1:17; 9:15; 2 Cor. 9:3; Phil. 2:7). It is used metaphorically, meaning to bring to naught in the sense of not accomplishing what one set out to accomplish (e. g., Rom. 4:14, the faith not accomplishing its purpose). Used in reference to the working of faith and its fruitfulness and to the cross of Christ, meaning the cross not accomplishing its purpose, salvation for man (1 Cor. 1:17, 18). In the same manner, life can be vain or empty, not accomplishing its purpose (1 Cor. 9:15; 2 Cor. 9:3). The use of *kenóō* in Philippians 2:7 is of extreme theological importance. It refers to Jesus Christ as emptying Himself at the time of His incarnation, denoting the beginning of his self-humiliation in Philippians 2:8. In order to understand what is meant by Jesus' emptying Himself, the whole passage of Philippians 2:6–8 must be examined. The two states of the Lord Jesus are spoken of here. In Philippians 2:7 the state of His humiliation is referred to as His having taken "the form of a servant" (*morphḗn* [3444]); *doúlou* [1401]); having become "in the likeness of men" (*homoiōmati* [3667]; *ánthrōpōn* [444]). In contrast to this, we have His preincarnate, eternal state of being in v. 6 as "being in the form of God" (*morphḗ* [3444]), and "equal with God" (*ísa* [2470]). The truth expressed here concerning His preincarnate state is that He had to be equal with God to have the form of God. He could not be God the Son without being God. He who revealed the *morphḗ*, the form of God, the essence of God, had to be equal with God. The fact that He showed us God in the form in which He appeared was not something that He merely claimed to be without really being that in His essence. If He appeared to be something that He was not in His essence, then that would have been robbery. As to the use of the subst. *harpagmós* (725), robbery or plunder, see the verb *harpázō* (726), to seize, catch, pluck or pull (2 Cor. 12:2, 4; 1 Thess. 4:17; Jude 1:23; Rev. 12:5). As a subst., *harpagmós* is only used in Philippians 2:6. It refers to the form of God in which Christ appeared as not being considered something taken upon Himself that did not belong to Him. His whole life was characterized by being *huparchón* (5225), continuing to be that which He always was. Prior to His incarnation, He was in the "form" or the "essence" of God, and after His incarnation, in spite of His voluntary humiliation, He was still in the form of God. But in spite of His essence of deity, He took upon Himself the true essence of a servant. However, in order to be a servant, He had to become a man and appear "in the likeness of men" (signified by the phrase, *en homoiōmati ánthrēpōn*). When He became man, He emptied Himself of the proper recognition that He had with the Father and entered into the world of men who failed to properly recognize Him as God. The part. *labṓn* (from *lambánō* [2983]), having taken, "the form of a servant" does not mean that deity was displaced from His personality. Rather it means that He took upon Himself voluntarily something in addition to what He was which caused His improper recognition by men. Proper recognition in Gr. is called *dóxa* (1391), glory, praise (from the verb *dokéō* [1380], to recognize). Among men, in the form of a man and a servant, He lacked the recognition that He had

with the Father (John 17:5).

2776. Kephalḗ; the head (Matt. 6:17; 8:20; 10:30); the head as the top (Matt. 21:42; Luke 20:17); the head as the superior (Eph. 5:23); as the husband of the wife (1 Cor. 11:3); Christ as head of the Church (Eph. 4:15, 16; Col. 2:19), and of all principality and power (Col. 2:10, cf. Eph. 1:22); so God the Father is designated as the head of Christ in His manifestation as man, or as the divinity is superior to the humanity (1 Cor. 11:3).

2782. Kḗrugma; from *kērússō* (2784), to discharge a herald's office, to cry out, proclaim, preach. With the suffix -*ma*, *kḗrugma* means the result of preaching, that which is cried by the herald; the command, the communication, the proclamation of the redeeming purpose of God in Christ (Rom. 16:25); the proclamation of Jesus Christ (1 Cor. 1:21; 2:4; 15:14; 2 Tim. 4:17; Titus 1:3); the message of God to the Ninevites through Jonah (Matt. 12:41; Luke 11:32).

2783. Kḗrux; herald, crier. In Class. Gr., a public servant of supreme power both in peace and in war, the one who summoned the *ekklēsía* (1577), the town gathering. *Ekklēsía* later was used to refer to the Church. A *kḗrux*, messenger, was the public crier and reader of state messages such as the conveyor of a declaration of war. In the NT, except in 2 Peter 2:5, where it speaks of Noah as the herald of righteousness, the word denotes one who is employed by God in the work of proclaiming salvation (1 Tim. 2:7, cf. vv. 5, 6; 2 Tim. 1:11, where it is enjoined with *apóstolos* [652], apostle). When both designations are used, *kḗrux* designates the herald according to his commission and work as a proclaimer, while *apóstolos*, apostle, points more to the relation to the one who sent him. The authority of the herald or preacher lies in the message he has to bring (2 Pet. 2:5), but the apostle is protected by the authority of his Lord who sends him. In 1 Timothy 2:7 and 2 Timothy 1:11, *kḗrux* is conjoined with *didáskalos* (1320), teacher.

2784. Kērússō; to preach, herald, proclaim (Matt. 3:1; Mark 1:45; Luke 4:18, 19; 12:3; Acts 10:37; Rom. 2:21; Rev. 5:2). In 1 Peter 3:19 there is no reference to evangelizing, but to the act of Christ, after His resurrection, in proclaiming His victory to fallen spirits. To preach the gospel as a herald (Matt. 24:14; Mark 13:10; 14:9; 16:15, 20; Luke 8:1; 9:2; 24:47; Acts 8:5; 19:13; 28:31; Rom. 10:14); to preach the Word (2 Tim. 4:2). Deriv.: *prokērússō* (4296), from *pro* (4253), before, and *kērússō*, to proclaim before or ahead (Acts 3:20 TR; 13:24); *kḗrugma* (2782), a proclamation by a herald, denotes preaching, the substance of which is distinct from the act of preaching; *kḗrux* (2783), a herald, used of the preacher of the gospel (1 Tim. 2:7; 2 Tim. 1:11), and of Noah as a preacher of righteousness (2 Pet. 2:5).

2800. Klásis; from *kláō* (2806), to break. The breaking, particularly of the bread in the Lord's Supper (Luke 24:35; Acts 2:42).

2801. Klásma; in the neut., that which is broken off, a fragment, crumb; used only of pieces of bread (Matt. 14:20; 15:37; Mark 6:43; 8:8, 19, 20; Luke 9:17; John 6:12, 13). Deriv.: see *kláō* (2806), to break.

2806. Kláō; to break. In later Gr. it especially came to mean the breaking off of leaves, sprouts, tendrils. In the NT used only of the breaking of bread which was made in thin cakes, not in loaves (Matt. 14:19; 15:36). Applied to the body of Christ broken on the cross (1 Cor. 11:24). Denotes the celebration of the Lord's Supper (Acts 20:7, 11; 1 Cor. 10:16). The fellowship of the Lord with His people is described as a table fellowship (Luke 24:30, cf. John 13:18). Deriv.: *klásis* (2800), the breaking; *klásma* (2801), that which is broken off, a fragment, crumb; *kládos* (2798), branch (Rom. 11:21).

2812. Kléptēs; thief, along with *lēstḗs* (3027), robber, occurring together in John 10:1, 8. Both appropriate what is not theirs, but the *kléptēs* steals by fraud and in secret (Matt. 24:43; John 12:6) while the *lēstḗs* by violence and openly. *Lēstḗs*, as the case may be with the penitent one on a cross near Jesus, may have been a noble person who turned insurgent for some presumed righteous cause, thus seeking by the wrath of man to work out God's righteousness.

2814. Kléma; from *kláō* (2806), to break. A shoot, young twig, as the shoots of the vine or the branches (John 15:5).

2816. Klēronoméō; from *klēronómos* (2818), an heir. To inherit, obtain for an inheritance properly by lot, as the children of Israel did the Promised Land (Num. 26:55; 33:54; Josh. 14:1, 2). See also Matthew 5:5; 19:29; Hebrews 1:4, 14; 6:12. Deriv.: *klḗros* (2819), lot.

2817. Klēronomía; from *klēronómos* (2818), an heir. Inheritance, that which constitutes one as a *klēronómos*, heir. An inheritance by lot. See *klēronoméō* (2816), to inherit. As the inheritance of the earthly Canaan typified that of the heavenly Canaan, so the latter is often called *klēronomía*, inheritance (Acts 20:32; Eph. 1:14; 5:5; Heb. 9:15), heritage (Acts 7:5). Divine salvation, considered both as promised and as already bestowed, is designated an inheritance in the NT so far as man, the heir, obtains possession of it. Deriv.: *klḗros* (2819), lot.

2818. Klēronómos; from *klḗros* (2819), lot, and the verb *némō*, to hold, have in one's power. *Klēronómos* does not mean one to whom a *klḗros*, a lot, is allotted, because it is derived from the act (like *oikonómos* [3623], steward). It probably means an heir or inheritor, or an inheritance divided by lot (Matt. 21:38; Mark 12:7; Luke 20:14). It applies to the heirs of the heavenly Canaan (Rom. 8:17; Gal. 4:7; Titus 3:7; Heb. 6:17; James 2:5) and to Christ who is appointed heir and possessor, the Lord of all things (Matt. 21:38; Heb. 1:2).

2819. Klḗros; this has several different meanings: (1) A lot, the object that is used in casting lots (Matt. 27:35; Acts 1:26). The Gr. method of casting lots was in this way: The lots of the several parties were properly marked or distinguished and put into a vessel which was violently shaken by one who turned away his face. The lot which first fell upon the ground indicated the man chosen or preferred for the occasion. It seems that the Romans followed the same method. They attributed divine choice to this method. (2) A lot, allotment, part, or share (Acts 1:17 TR; 8:21). (3) An inheritance cf. the noun *klēronomía* [2817], inheritance (Acts 26:18, cf. 20:32; Col. 1:12). *Klḗroi*, in the pl. (1 Pet. 5:3) seems to denote those distinct congregations of Christians (cf. Deut. 4:20; 9:29) which fell to the lot of different pastors. Deriv.: *klēróō* (2820) to cast lots, determine by lot; *holóklēros* (3648), an entire portion, intact; *klēronómos* (2818), one who has a *klḗros*, inheritance or a lot; *klēronomía* (2817), that which constitutes one as heir, an inheritance; *klēronoméō* (2816), to be an heir (*klēronómos*); *sugklēronómos* (4789), one who participates in the same inheritance or lot with another, joint-heir; *kataklērodotéō* (2624), to divide by lot.

2820. Klēróō; to cast lots, determine by lot, that is, to determine something. In Ephesians 1:11 it means, "in whom the lot has fallen upon us also, as foreordained." This refers to the completion of one's election to salvation.

2821. Klḗsis; from *kaléō* (2564), to call. A calling (Rom. 11:29; 1 Cor. 1:26; Eph. 4:1). A calling, vocation, employment (1 Cor. 7:20).

2822. Klētós; from *kaléō* (2564), to call. Called, invited, welcomed, appointed. One who is called to an office (Rom. 1:1; 1 Cor. 1:1). The called ones (*klḗti*) are those who have received the divine call (*klḗsis* [2821]), having conformed to God's saving purpose (Rom. 1:6, 7; 8:28; 1 Cor. 1:2, 24), without implying immediate obedience to the call (Matt. 20:16; 22:14, cf. Rev. 17:14). See *eklektós* (1588), elect.

2839. Koinós; defiled, common, unclean; to lie common or open to all; common or belonging to several or of which several are partakers (Acts 2:44; 4:32; Titus 1:4; Jude 1:3); unclean hands (Mark 7:2), of unclean meats (Acts 10:14; 11:8; Rom. 14:14); such as were common to other nations but were avoided by the Jews as polluted and unclean (Mark 7:2). Verb: *koinóō* (2840), to make common, unclean.

2840. Koinóō; from *koinós* (2839), common. To make common, unclean, pollute or defile (Matt. 15:11; Acts 21:28; Heb. 9:13; Rev. 21:27 TR); to pronounce or call common or unclean (Acts 10:15; 11:9). Related to *miaínō* (3392), to defile.

2841. Koinōnéō; from *koinós* (2839), lying open to all, common. With a dat. of the thing, to communicate, partake, participate, be a partaker in or of something (Rom. 15:27; 1 Tim. 5:22; 1 Pet. 4:13; 2 John 1:11), as it is also with the gen. in Hebrews 2:14. With a dat. of the person, to communicate, distribute, impart (Rom. 12:13; Gal. 6:6; Phil. 4:15).

2842. Koinōnía; fellowship with or participation in anything (1 Cor. 10:16); a communion, fellowship, society (Acts 2:42; 1 Cor. 1:9; 2 Cor. 6:14; Phile. 1:6, cf. 2 Cor. 8:4); communication, distribution, alms-giving (Rom. 15:26; 2 Cor. 9:13; Heb. 13:16).

2844. Koinōnós; from *koinóō* (2840), to make anything common (*koinón* [2839]). A partaker (Matt. 23:30; 1 Cor. 10:18; 2 Cor. 1:7; 1 Pet. 5:1; 2 Pet. 1:4; see Phile. 1:17). Partner, companion (Luke 5:10; 1 Cor. 10:20; Heb. 10:33). Deriv.: *koinós* (2839), common; *koinóō* (2840), to make anything common; *koinōnéō* (2841), to share; *koinōnía* (2842), fellowship with, participation in anything; *koinōnikós* (2843), communicative or cultivating a loving fellowship; *sugkoinōnéō* (4790), to participate in something with someone; *sugkoinōnós* (4791), partaker.

2851. Kólasis; from *kolázō* (2849), to punish; punishment (Matt. 25:46); torment (1 John 4:18). In Class. Gr. *timōría* (5098) is the vindictive character of the punishment as the predominant thought which satisfies the inflicter's sense of outraged justice, as defending his own honor or that of the violated law. *Kólasis*, on the other hand, conveys the notion of punishment for the correction and bettering of the offender. It does not always, however, have the same meaning in the NT. For instance, in Matthew 25:46 *kólasis aiṓnios* ([166], eternal), does not refer to temporary corrective punishment and discipline; rather it has more the meaning of *timōría*, punishment, because of the violation of the eternal law of God. It is the punishment with finality with which our Lord threatens the offenders (Mark 9:43–48). In this sense it does not imply the bettering of one who endures such punishment. In *kólasis* we have the relation of the punishment to the punished while in *timōría* the relationship is to the punisher himself.

2869. Kopázō; from *kópos* (2873), labor, fatigue. To cease through extreme fatigue or being worn out with labor; to cease, as the wind (Matt. 14:32; Mark 4:39; 6:51). Deriv.: *kopiáō* (2872), to toil, labor even to exhaustion and weariness (Matt. 6:28; Luke 5:5); *kópos* (2873), labor, travail (2 Cor. 11:23, 27), trouble, disturbance, uneasiness (Matt. 26:10).

2873. Kópos; from *kékopa*, the perf. mid. voice of *kóptō* (2875), to strike. Labor, travail (2 Cor. 11:23, 27; 1 Thess. 2:9; 3:5) trouble, disturbance, uneasiness. Used to denote not so much the actual exertion which a man makes, but the weariness which he experiences from that exertion. It designates that which we as Christians ought to render to the Lord as labor in the Christian ministry. *Kópos* is to be distinguished from *móchthos* (3449), the everyday word for human labor, and *pónos* (4192), the labor which demands that the whole strength of a man be exerted to the uttermost if he is to accomplish the task which is before him. Verb: *kopiáō* (2872), labor, toil.

2875. Kóptō; to cut off or down (Matt. 21:8; Mark 11:8); in the mid. voice *kóptomai*, to strike or beat one's body, particularly ones breast's, with the hands in lamentation, to lament, wail. Used trans. in Luke 8:52 and intrans. in Luke 23:27. Used with the intens. prep. *epí* (1909) in Revelation 1:7; 18:9. It is strongest form used describe the outward expression of inner grief. The words *lúpē* [3077] and *lupéō* (3076), refer to inner grief without necessarily an outward expression. The two milder words expressing outward grief are *penthéō* (3996), to mourn, and *thrēnéō* (2354), to wail.

2880. Korénnumi; to have enough, abundance (Acts 27:38; 1 Cor. 4:8). Deriv.: *kóros* (2884), a measure equal to ten baths (Gr. *bátoi* [943]) or seventy-five gallons (Luke 16:6).

2886. Kosmikós; worldly, what belongs to the world. In the NT it corresponds to the idea of *kósmos* (2889) world (Heb. 9:1) and is opposite that which is heavenly and spiritual (9:11). In Titus 2:12, worldly desires pertain to those desires of the world which estrange a person from God (Eph. 2:1, 2).

2887. Kósmios; from *kósmos* (2889), order. Orderly, decent (1 Tim. 2:9; 3:2). Plato presented a *kósmios* as the citizen who is quiet in the land, who fulfills the duties which are incumbent on him as such and is not disorderly. He, as well as Paul, associated such persons with *sōphrōn* (4998), sensible, self-controlled, one who voluntarily places limitations on his freedom. The virtue of the *kósmios*, however, is not only the propriety of his dress and demeanor, but of his inner life, unerring and expressing itself in the outward conversation. Contrast with *semnós* (4586), venerable, one who has a grace and dignity not obtained from earth only. While one who is *kósmios* behaves himself well in his earthly citizenship and is an asset, the *semnós* owes his quality to that higher citizenship which is also his. *Semnós* inspires not only respect but reverence and worship. Syn.: *hieroprepés* (2412), one who acts like a sacred person.

2888. Kosmokrátōr; from *kósmos* (2889), order or world, and *krátos* (2904), power, authority. A ruler of this world (Eph. 6:12, spoken of evil spirits, cf. John 12:31; 14:30). Contrast *pantokrátōr* (3841), the ruler of everything, from *pánta* (*pas* [3956]), all, and *krátōr*, one holding authority (2 Cor. 6:18; Rev. 1:8).

2889. Kósmos; from *kosméō* (2885), to set in order, adorn. That which pertains to space and not time (*aiōn* [165], age) The sum total of the material universe, the beauty in it; the sum total of persons living in the world (Matt. 4:8; 1 John 2:15–17).

2897. Kraipálē; from *kra*, the head, an abbreviation of *karēnon* or *kranión* (2898), and *pállō*, to agitate. A headache, a shooting pain in the head arising from intemperance in drinking wine or strong liquors. Translated in Luke 21:34 as "surfeiting," the sense of disgust and loathing from being full of wine. Related words: *méthē* (3178), drunkenness in the abstract; *potós* (4224), a drinking bout possibly leading to excess; *oinophlugía* (3632), excess of wine; *kōmos* (2970), pl., revellings and rioting.

2902. Kratéō; from *krátos* (2904), strength. To hold fast (Matt. 26:48, 50; Mark 14:44, 46; Acts 3:11); to detain (Acts 2:24), to maintain, retain (Mark 7:3, 4, 8; 2 Thess. 2:15; Heb. 4:14; Rev. 2:13–15, 25); to lay hold of or take. In this sense, either with a gen. (Matt. 9:25; Mark 1:31; Luke 8:54), or with an acc. (Matt. 12:11; 14:3; 22:6; 26:4); to hold, as in the hands (Rev. 2:1); to obtain (Acts 27:13); to hold, restrain (Luke 24:16); to retain, not to remit, as sins (John 20:23).

2904. Krátos; from *kratéō* (2902) to hold fast. Force, strength, might, more especially manifested power, dominion. More closely related to *ischús* (2479), strength, than *dúnamis* (1411), power. *Krátos* denotes the presence and significance of force or strength rather than its exercise (Luke 1:51; Col. 1:11). Deriv.: *krataiós* (2900), adj. describing God's power manifested in the blows and severe punishments which He sends and which man cannot escape (1 Pet. 5:6); *krataióō* (2901), to make strong, in the pass., to become strong (Luke 1:80; 2:40; 1 Cor. 16:13; Eph. 3:16); *kosmokrátōr* (2888), indicating the terrifying power of the rulers of the world (Eph. 6:12); *pantokrátōr* (3841), the Almighty, from *pánta* (3956), all, and *krátōr*, the ruler, the One who holds everything together (2 Cor. 6:18; Rev. 1:8; 4:8; 11:17; 15:3; 16:7, 14; 19:6, 15; 21:22).

2908. Kreísson; the neut. of *kreissōn or kreittōn* (2909), occurs as an adv. in Hebrews 12:24 meaning more emphatically, in 1 Corinthians 7:38, more advantageously, more appropriately (cf. 1 Cor. 7:35).

2909. Kreissōn; or *kreittōn*, comparative of *agathós* (18), benevolently good. Others make it the comparative from *krátus*, strong, the adj from *krátos* (2904), power, strength, dominion. Stronger, more powerful, superior

or better in strength (Heb. 1:4) better, more excellent (1 Cor. 11:17; 12:31 TR) better, more profitable (2 Pet. 2:21), better, more favorable (Heb. 12:24).

2917. Kríma; the suffix *-ma* indicates the result of *krínō* (2919), to judge, or *krísis* (2920), the act of judging. A solemn judgment, judicial trial (Acts 24:25; Heb. 6:2) or judicial sentence (Rom. 2:2, 3, cf. Rom. 5:16) a private judgment, pronouncement of a private sentence or opinion (Matt. 7:2); being adjudged or sentenced to punishment, condemnation, damnation (Matt. 23:14 TR; Luke 23:40; 24:20; Rom. 3:8; 13:2); the execution or judgment, punishment (Mark 12:40; James 3:1); judicial or legal contest, a lawsuit (1 Cor. 6:7); judicial authority, power of judging (Rev. 20:4). Deriv.: *krínō* (2919), to judge.

2919. Krínō; to divide, separate, make a distinction, come to a decision. To judge, try in a solemn judicial manner. Spoken of men (John 18:31; Acts 24:6); of God (Acts 17:31; Rom. 3:6); of Christ as the God-Man (2 Tim. 4:1, cf. Luke 19:22). To judge, pass sentence or give one's opinion in a private manner (Matt. 7:1, 2; Luke 6:37; John 8:15). To judge, discern, form a mental judgment or opinion (Luke 12:57; John 7:24; Acts 4:19; 1 Cor. 10:15; 11:13). To judge, think, esteem (Acts 16:15; 26:8, cf. Acts 13:46; Rom. 14:5; 1 Cor. 4:5). In the last two passages the verb seems to denote preferring one to another. To judge properly, determine (Acts 15:19; 16:4; 20:16; 21:25; 25:25; 1 Cor. 5:3). To adjudge to punishment, condemn (John 3:17, 18; 7:51; Acts 13:27). To furnish matter or occasion for condemnation, to condemn in this sense (Rom. 2:27, cf. *katakrínō* (2632), to condemn. In the pass.: *krínomai*, to be judged, to be brought or called into judgment, to be called in question (Acts 23:6; 24:21; 26:6); also *krínomai*, to be judged, that is, to enter into a judicial contest with, to go to law with (Matt. 5:40; 1 Cor. 6:1, 6). With the inf., followed by the prep. *en* (1722), in, *krínetai en* (1 Cor. 6:2), to be judged by. Deriv.: *krísis* (2920), separation, judgment; *kríma* (2917), the result or issue of judging the decision arrived at or judgment; *kritēs* (2923), the one who decides, a judge; *kritērion* (2922), an instrument of judging, a court of justice; *kritikós* (2924), one whose business and special gift is to judge; *apokrínomai* (611), the mid. or pass. of *apokrínō*, to be separated, selected to answer, to take occasion to speak; *apókrisis* (612), a decision, answer; *apókrima* (610), an answer against, condemnation; *diakrínō* (1252), separate one from another, divide, part; *diákrisis* (1253), separation, discrimination; *adiákritos* (87), indistinguishable; *egkrínō* (1469), to divide up, place in a series, to rank with; *katakrínō* (2632), decide, judge, condemn anyone; *katákrima* (2631), that which is decided against anyone, a condemnatory judgment; *katákrisis* (2633), the act of condemnation; *eilikrinēs* (1506), tested or judged by the sun, by the light as spotless, pure, clear, sincere; *eilikríneia* (1505), purity, sincerity; *prókrima* (4299), that which is decided ahead of time; *sugkrínō* (4793) to separate and arrange together, combine, unite, compare, measure or estimate; *hupokrínō* (5271), to act out what one is not, act like a hypocrite; *hupókrisis* (5272), pretense, hyprocrisy; *hupokritēs* (5273), a hypocrite; *anupókritos* (505), inexperienced in the art of acting, unhypocritical, genuine.

2920. Krísis; a separation, sundering, judgment, sentence, from *krínō* (2919), to judge. Judgment (John 5:22, 30; 7:24; 8:16, cf. John 16:11). The final judgment (Matt. 10:15; 12:36, 41, 42). Used with the verb *poiéō* (4160), to make; to pass judgment or sentence (John 5:27; Jude 1:15). In judgment, justice (Matt. 12:20, cf. 23:23). Judgment of condemnation, damnation (Mark 3:29 TR; John 5:24, 29); the punishment consequent to condemnation (Matt. 23:33). The cause or ground of condemnation or punishment (John 3:19). A particular court of justice among the Jews consisting of twenty-three men, which, before the Roman government was established in Judea, had the power of life and death so far as its jurisdiction extended and punished criminals by strangling or beheading (Matt. 5:21, 22). Deriv.: *krínō* (2919), to judge.

2922. Kritḗrion; from *krínō* (2919), to judge. Judgment, the art, act or authority of judging or determining (1 Cor. 6:2); judicial contest or controversy, a lawsuit (1 Cor. 6:4); judgment seat, tribunal, court of justice (James 2:6).

2923. Kritḗs; he who decides, a judge (Matt. 5:25; 12:27; Luke 18:2; Acts 10:42; 13:20). Deriv.: *krínō* (2919), to judge.

2924. Kritikós; one whose business and special gift is to judge. Used only in Hebrews 4:12.

2936. Ktízō; from *ktáō*, or *ktáomai* (2932), in the pass. or mid., to possess. In Homer the word meant to found a city or a habitable place. To create, produce from nothing (Mark 13:19; Col. 1:16; Rev. 4:11); to form out of preexistent matter (1 Cor. 11:9); to make, compose (Eph. 2:15); to create and form in a spiritual sense, regeneration or renewal (Eph. 2:10; 4:24). Deriv.: *ktísis* (2937), the founding, creation; *ktísma* (2938), a place founded, built, or colonized; *ktístēs* (2939), a settler, founder, inventor.

2937. Ktísis; a founding, that is, of a city, colonization of a habitable place. Creation in a pass. sense, what is created, the sum total of what is created (Mark 10:6; 13:19; 1 Pet. 2:13). Denotes particularly the individual creature or what is created (Rom. 1:25; 8:39; Col. 1:15; Heb. 4:13). The sum total of what God has created, the creation (Mark 10:6; 13:19; Rom. 1:20; Heb. 9:11; 2 Pet. 3:4; Rev. 3:14). Refers specifically to mankind as God's creation (Mark 16:15; Col. 1:23). See also *kainḗ* (2537), qualitatively new, with *ktísis*, creation or creature. Deriv.: *ktízō* (2936), to create, make.

2938. Ktísma; from the verb *ktízō* (2936), to build, plant a colony, with the suffix *-ma* the result of building. That which is created. In the NT, creature, created thing (1 Tim. 4:4; James 1:18; Rev. 5:13; 8:9).

2939. Ktístēs; settler, founder, inventor. Only in 1 Peter 4:19. A creator.

2955. Kúptō; to bow the head, stoop down (Mark 1:7, John 8:6, 8). Deriv.: *parakúptō* (3879) from *pará* (3844), aside, and *kúptō*, and it denotes bending forward, stooping down to look into something (Luke 24:12; John 20:5, 11); *anakúptō* (352), from *aná* (303), up, and *kúptō*, to lift up (Luke 21:28).

2960. Kuriakós; belonging to a lord or ruler. Only in 1 Corinthians 11:20 and Revelation 1:10, as belonging to Christ; to the Lord, having special reference to Him. Hence, *kuriakḗ* came to mean *kuriakḗ hēméra* (2250), the day of the Lord, what we call Sunday. It was the day kept in commemoration of Christ's resurrection (John 20:1, 24–29; Acts 20:7; 1 Cor. 16:2). See Rev. 1:5, 18.

2962. Kúrios; masc. proper noun from *kúros*, might, power. Lord, master, owner, as the possessor, owner, master, e. g., of property (Matt. 20:8; 21:40; Gal. 4:1); master or head of a house (Matt. 15:27; Mark 13:35). Spoken of a husband (1 Pet. 3:6). Followed by the gen. of thing and without the art., lord, master of something and having absolute authority over it, for example, master of the harvest (Matt. 9:38; Luke 10:2); master of the Sabbath (Matt. 12:8; Mark 2:28). As an honorary title of address, especially to superiors, equivalent to mister, sir, as a servant to his master (Matt. 13:27; Luke 13:8); a son to his father (Matt. 21:30); to a teacher, master (Matt. 8:25; Luke 9:54); equal to *epistátes* (1988), superintendent, commander; to a person of dignity and authority (Mark 7:28; John 4:11, 15, 19, 49); to a Roman procurator (Matt. 27:63). Spoken of God and Christ: of God as the supreme Lord and Sovereign of the universe, usually corresponding to Jehovah. Of the Lord Jesus Christ: in reference to His abode on earth as a master and teacher, where it is equivalent to rabbi (4461), rabbi, and *epistátes*, master, superintendent (Matt. 17:4, cf. Mark 9:5; Luke 9:33. See John 13:13, 14). *En Kúrio* means: in the Lord, after verbs of rejoicing, trusting (1 Cor. 1:31; Phil. 2:19; 3:1); in or by the Lord, meaning by His authority (Eph. 4:17; 1 Thess. 4:1). In or through the Lord, meaning through His aid and influence, by His help (1 Cor. 15:58; 2 Cor. 2:12; Gal. 5:10; Eph. 2:21; Col. 4:17). In the work of

the Lord, in the gospel work (Rom. 16:8, 13; 1 Cor. 4:17; 9:2; Eph. 6:21; 1 Thess. 5:12). As marking condition meaning one of the Lord's, united with Him, His follower, a Christian (Rom. 16:11; Phil. 4:1; Phile. 1:16). As denoting manner, meaning in the Lord, as becomes those who are in the Lord, Christians (Rom. 16:2, 22; 1 Cor. 7:39; Eph. 6:1; Phil. 2:29; Col. 3:18). Deriv.: *kúria* (2959), lady; *kuriakós* (2960), the Lord's; *kuriótēs* (2963), lordship, dominion; *kurieúō* (2961), to be lord; *katakurieúō* (2634), to dominate, lord it over. Syn.: *archṓn* (758), ruler; *despótēs* (1203), despot; *pantokrátōr* (3841), almighty; *hēgemṓn* (2232), governor ruler; *Kaísar* (2541), Caesar; *ethnárchēs* (1481), leader of a nation; *archēgós* (747), leader; *kosmokrátōr* (2888), world ruler. Ant.: *idiṓtēs* (2399), private person; *hupērétēs* (5257), lower servant; *doúlos* (1401), slave; *therápōn* (2324), attendant; *diákonos* (1249), minister; *polítēs* (4177), citizen.

2963. Kuriótēs; from *kúrios* (2962), lord, mighty one. Dominion, civil power, authority or magistracy (2 Pet. 2:10; Jude 1:8); a certain order of angels, an abstract term being used for a concrete form (Eph. 1:21; Col. 1:16). Reference is made to evil angelic powers as indicated in 2 Peter 2:11, although not in Jude 1:9. The word is peculiar to NT and Patristic Gr. and denotes the kingly glory of Christ.

2970. Kṓmos; derived from *Cómus*, the god of feasting and reveling. His sacred rights consisted in feasting and drunkenness with impurity and obscenity of the grossest kind. Actually there were lascivious feastings with songs, music, and drinking wine. Therefore, it always presupposes a festal company and drunken revelers. Used only in the pl. in the NT, riotings (Rom. 13:13); revelings (Gal. 5:21; 1 Pet. 4:3). Related words: *méthē* (3178), drunkenness in the abstract sense; *potós* (4224), a drinking bout or banquet giving opportunity for excessive drinking but not necessarily realizing it; *oinophlugía* (3632), excess of wine; *kraipálē* (2897), the sense of overfullness of wine.

2980. Laléō; to talk at random. The dumb man is *álalos* (216), mute (Mark 7:37; 9:17, 25); when there is restoration of speech, *elálēse*, aor. of *laléō* is used (Matt. 9:33; Luke 11:14), emphasizing the fact of speech versus speechlessness. When reference is made to those who spoke in tongues, whether foreign languages or the Corinthian unknown tongue, it is always referred to as *laléō glṓssais* (Mark 16:17; Acts 2:4; 1 Cor. 12:30), emphasizing not the content of the speech, but merely that they uttered sounds as far as the hearers were concerned. *Laléō* is ascribed to God (Heb. 1:1, 2), indicating not that the content of His speech was meaningless, but that He spoke at all instead of keeping silent. Contrast *légō* (3004), to speak expressing thoughts. Subst.: *laliá* (2981), articulated words, as contrasted with silence, mere sounds, or animal cries (Mark 14:70).

2983. Lambánō; to take in whatever manner. Almost syn. with *déchomai* (1209), to take or receive, and yet distinct from it in that *lambánō* sometimes means to receive as merely a self-prompted action without necessarily signifying a favorable reception (Gal. 2:6). Deriv.: *analambánō* (353); from *aná* (303), up, and *lambánō* (2983), meaning to take up (Mark 16:19; Acts 1:2; 20:13, 14; Eph. 6:13, 16); *lēpsis* (3028), or *lēmpsis*, a receiving, related to *lambánō; análēpsis* (354), from *aná* (303), up, and *lambánō*, meaning a taking up as in reference to Christ's ascension (Luke 9:51); *metalambánō* (3335), from *metá* (3326), with, and *lambánō*, meaning to have or get a share of, partake of (Heb. 6:7); *metálē(m)psis* (3336), a participation (1 Tim. 4:3) in connection with food; *paralambánō* (3880), from *pará* (3844) beside, and *lambánō*, meaning not only to receive, but denoting taking to or with oneself, as taking a wife (Matt. 1:20, 24), or taking a person or persons with oneself (Matt. 2:13, 14, 20, 21; 4:5, 8); of the removal of persons from earth in judgment (Matt. 24:40, 41; Luke 17:34, 35); of the taking of Christ by the soldiers for scourging (Matt. 27:27) and to crucifixion (John 19:16); *proslambánō* (4355) from *prós* (4314), to, and *lambánō*, always in the mid. voice signifying a special interest on the part of the receiver, suggesting a welcome (Acts 27:33–36), of persons (Matt. 16:22; Mark 8:32), for evil purposes (Acts 17:5), for good purposes (Acts 18:26), *próslē(m)psis* (4356), receiving (Rom. 11:15); *apolambánō* (618), from *apó* (575), from, and *lambánō*, meaning to receive from another as one's due (Luke 18:30; 23:41; Rom. 1:27; Col. 3:24; 2 John 1:8), without the indication of what is due (Luke 16:25; Gal 4:5), to receive back (Luke 6:34; 15:27), to take apart (Mark 7:33); *epilambánō* (1919), from *epí* (1909), upon, and *lambánō*, in the mid voice *epilambánomai*, with a gen. or more rarely with an acc. to lay, take, or catch hold of (Matt. 14:31; Mark 8:23, Luke 9:47; 23:26; Acts 9:27; 16:19); to lay hold of one's words in order to accuse him (Luke 20:20, 26); with a gen., to assume, to take upon one (Heb. 2:16), which means that when Christ came to redeem us, He did not assume a glorious appearance that He had before the time of His incarnation (John 17:5), but He took upon Himself human nature (Gal 3:16; Phil 2:6, 7). The adj. derived from *epilambánomai* is *anepílēptos* (423), from the priv. *a* and *epílēptos*, meaning blamable, which is derived. from *epilambánomai*, to reprehend, blame. Therefore, the adj. *anepílēptos* means unblamable, blameless, irreprehensible (1 Tim 3:2; 5:7; 6:14). Further deriv.: *katalambánō* (2638), from *katá* (2596), and *lambánō*, meaning to seize; *prolambánō* (4301), from *pro* (4253), before, and *lambánō*, to take before another (1 Cor. 11:21), to anticipate, do somewhat beforehand (Mark 14:8), in the mid. voice, to be taken before one is aware, to be overtaken, surprised as in a fault (Gal. 6:1); *hupolambánō* (5274), from *hupó* (5259), under, and *lambánō*, meaning to take under (Acts 1:9), to answer, to take up (Luke 10:30), to suppose, apprehend, think (Luke 7:43; Acts 2:15; see Matt. 25:1, 3, 4, 7, 8).

2985. Lampás; a torch. Contrast *lúchnos* (3088), lamp. In the East a torch, as well as a lamp, that is fed with oil.

2992. Laós; a people, nation, a number of men joined together by the common bands of society (Luke 2:10, 31, 32). The common people, the multitude (Matt. 26:5; 27:64; Luke 1:10). The society of Christians or of the Christian church (Matt. 1:21; 1 Pet. 2:9, 10). In the Sept., it is a title almost totally reserved for the elect people, the Israel of God. Contrast *éthnos* (1484), nation, which signifies the heathen, or Gentiles, as distinguished from the Jews or believers (Matt. 8:32; 10:5, 18; 20:19, 25; Luke 2:32; 1 Cor. 5:1; 12:2; Eph. 2:11; 3:6). Syn.: *dêmos* (1218), from the verb *déō* (1210), to bind, a people commonly bound together from which comes the word democracy; *óchlos* (3793), a disorganized crowd or multitude.

2999. Latreía; from *latreúō* (3000), to worship. Service or divine service. Occurs only in John 16:2; Romans 9:4; 12:1; and Hebrews 9:1, 6. It is clear from Romans 9:4; 12:1 and Hebrews 9:1, 6 that sacrifice seems especially to be the service denoted.

3000. Latreúō; to serve; in a religious sense to worship, God (Matt. 4:10; Luke 1:74; 2:37) or creatures (Acts 7:42; Rom. 1:25). It refers particularly to the performance of the Levitical service (Heb. 8:5; 9:9; 10:2; 13:10). Allied to *látris*, a hired servant, as opposed to *doúlos* (1401), a slave. Therefore, to serve or worship but not out of compulsion.

3004. Légō; to speak by linking and knitting together in connected discourse the inward thoughts and feelings of the mind (Matt. 2:2; Acts 1:3). Subst.: *lógos* (3056), thought, intelligence, and also that which expresses it, speech. Contrast *laléō* (2980), to speak, and *lalía* (2981), speech.

3008. Leitourgéō; derived from *leitós*, public, and *érgon* (2041), work. To minister publicly in sacred office (Acts 13:2; Heb 10:11); in works of charity (Rom. 15:27). It came to mean performing of priestly or ministerial functions, leading in public worship (*latreía* [2999]). To serve God (*latreúō* [3000]) is the duty of all, but to serve Him in special offices and ministries can be the duty and privilege of only a few who are set apart to the same. Deriv.: *leitourgía* (3009), public

ministry whether in sacred offices (Luke 1:23; Phil. 2:17; Heb. 8:6; 9:21) or in works of charity (2 Cor. 9:12; Phil. 2:30) from which are derived the English words "liturgy" and "liturgical"; *leitourgós* (3011), a public officer or minister (Rom. 13:6; 15:16; Phil. 2:25; Heb. 1:7; 8:2); *leitourgikós* (3010), performing public service (Heb 1:14).

3027. Lēstḗs; one who deprives another of his property openly and by violence (Matt. 27:38, 44; 2 Cor. 11:26). This does not devote whether the cause or reason for doing this is right or wrong. Contrast *kléptēs* (2812), thief.

3049. Logízomai; derived from *lógos* (3056), reason, word, account. Actually, the verb *légō* (3004) means to put together with one's mind, to count, to occupy oneself with reckonings or calculations. In the NT, the pres. in a pass. sense (as in Rom. 4:4, 5, 24; 9:8) also means to reckon, count (1 Cor. 13:5). To reckon anything to a person is to put something to his account, either in his favor or what he must be answerable for (Rom. 4:4, 6, 11; 2 Cor. 5:19; 2 Tim. 4:16). In Romans 4:11, the expression is used as a technical term to apply to God's act of justification which is more fully explained in v. 6. It is that imputation of righteousness whose correlative is freedom from guilt, and the emphasis clearly rests upon "it was reckoned" (Rom. 4:10, 23, 24). In Acts 19:27, it means to esteem or reckon as of no account. Such a rendering is common with Paul (Rom. 2:26; 9:8). When something is accounted to somebody for something, it is imputed to the person in a substitutionary manner. The expression "to count someone with somebody" means to number anyone with someone else (Mark 15:28; Luke 22:37). *Logízomai* also means to reckon, to value or esteem (Rom. 8:36; 1 Cor. 4:1, 2 Cor. 10:2; 12:6), followed by the acc. with the inf. (Rom. 14:14; 2 Cor. 11:5; Phil. 3:13); followed by *hóti* (3754), that (Heb. 11:19); followed by two acc. (Rom. 6:11). To account, to conclude or infer, to believe (Rom. 3:28); to consider (John 11:50). Deriv.: *logismós* (3053), reckoning; *dialogízomai* (1260), to reckon distributively, to settle with one, to ponder, consider; *dialogismós* (1261), calculation, consideration.

3050. Logikós; pertaining to reason and therefore reasonable, or pertaining to speech as reasonable expression. In Romans 12:1 the reasonable service or worship is to be understood as that service to God which implies intelligent meditation or reflection, without heathen practices as intimated in 1 Corinthians 12:2, and without the OT cultic worship which had become mere thoughtless habit (Is. 1:12–15). On the other hand, in 1 Peter 2:2, *logikón gála* ([1051], milk) cannot possibly mean reasonable milk. *Lógos*, from which *logikós* is derived, means God's reason or intelligence expressed in human speech in John 1:1, 14. Understanding *lógos* as the Word of God, *logikón gála* becomes the milk of the Word, milk to be found in the Word. The Word of God is spiritual nourishment as milk is physical nourishment The second adj. *ádolos* (97), unadulterated, agrees with this, meaning that the Word of God when not mixed with human error is nourishing. See *ádolons*, in 2 Corinthians 4:2, not beguiling the Word of God.

3051. Lógion; sentence, declaration, especially the utterance of the oracles of the gods, equivalent to *chrēsmós*. In Acts 7:38, Romans 3:2, Hebrews 5:12, and 1 Peter 4:11 the expression *ta logía* (in the neut. pl.) means the declaration of God and differs from *ho lógos*, the Word of God, that which God has to say. The neut. pl., *ta logía*, denotes rather the historical manifestations of this Word of God. In 1 Peter 4:11 it does not say the Word (*lógon*) of God, the object being to give prominence to the contrast between the word and the mere subjectivity of the speaker.

3053. Logismós; from *logízomai* (3049), to reckon. A reckoning, calculation, consideration, reflection. In the Class. writers used of the consideration and reflection preceding and determining conduct, the same meaning as in John 11:50. In this sense the subst. is used in 2 Corinthians 10:5, translated "imaginations." Actually it is considerations and intentions which are hostile to the gospel. On the other hand, in Romans 2:15 used of considerations and reflections following upon conduct. Syn.: *boulḗ* (1012), purpose or thought still in the mind, not executed.

3056. Lógos; from *légō* (3004), to speak. Intelligence, a word as the expression of that intelligence. Contrast *laliá* (2981), unintelligent sound, noise, or utterance, and *laléō* (2980), to speak without necessarily saying anything intelligent or understanding it as such. *Lógos* is the articulate utterance of human language. It can be unspoken as formulation of thought in the mind which in that case stands in contrast to *phōnḗ* (5456), voice. When the differentiation is between intelligent speech by man and unintelligent sounds by animals the two contrasted words are *lógos* and *laliá*. *Lógos*, when it refers to discourse, is regarded as the orderly linking and knitting together in connected arrangement of words of the inward thoughts and feelings of the mind. The animals produce sounds, *laloún*, while God and human beings produce thoughtful expressions, *légoun*. In Mark 2:2; 4:33; 8:32 we have the two words used together. *Laléō* (2980) expresses the opening of the mouth to speak, as opposed to remaining silent (Acts 18:9). A problematic passage is John 8:43 in which we have both *laliá* and *lógos* spoken by our Lord. The context referred to was when Jesus was debating with the Pharisees. They were listening to what He had to say, but they were not capable of understanding because they did not want to understand. The Lord said to them, "Why do ye not understand my speech (*lalián*)?" In other words, "What I am saying to you is as if it had no meaning whatsoever." And why did it have no meaning? The reason is explained in the balance of the paragraph, "Even because ye cannot hear my word (*lógon*)," or better still, "Because you cannot understand and obey (*akoúō* [191]) my *lógon* (speech with its intended meaning). Hence, those who will not give room in their hearts to His truth will not understand His speech or utterance, the outward form of His language which His Word (*lógos*) assumes. Those who are of God hear God's words (*rhḗma, rhḗmata* [4487]; John 3:34; 8:47). *Rhḗma* here is equivalent to *laliá*. John 3:34 says that Jesus Christ, being sent of God, speaks exactly God's utterances, which those who are of God understand and those who are not do not understand. The *lógos* not being accepted as the intelligent utterance of God, even His speech (*laliá* and *rhḗma*) is not known or recognized. In the first chapter of the Gospel of John, Jesus Christ in His preincarnate state is called *ho Lógos*, the Word, meaning first immaterial intelligence and then the expression of that intelligence in speech that humans could understand. Additional meanings of *lógos*: (1) A word (Matt. 8:8, 16; Luke 7:7). (2) A saying, discourse, conversation (Matt. 12:37; 15:12; 19:22; 22:15; 26:1; John 4:39; Acts 5:24). (3) A report, rumor (Matt. 28:15; Luke 5:15; 7:17). (4) A common saying, a proverb (John 4:37). (5) The Word of God, whether of the law (Mark 7:13) or of the gospel (Matt. 13:19–23; Mark 2:2; 16:20; Acts 8:4; 2 Tim. 4:2). In this regard it sometimes implies the profession and practice of the gospel (Matt. 13:21; Mark 4:17; John 8:31; Rev. 1:9; 20:4). (6) Speech, eloquence (1 Cor. 2:1; 2 Cor. 11:6). (7) Ability to speak, utterance (Eph. 6:19). (8) Reason, the faculty of reasoning. *Katá lógon*, according to reason, reasonably (Acts 18:14). This use was very common among the heathen writers. See *álogos* (249), irrational, without intelligence, unreasonable; and its opposite *logikós* (3050), reasonable. See also *phēmí* (5346), to speak with a prophetic tinge to one's message.

3058. Loidoréō; to revile, reproach (John 9:28; Acts 23:4; 1 Cor. 4:12; 1 Pet. 2:23). Syn.: *blasphēméō* (987), to revile, to blaspheme; *oneidízō* (3679), to reproach.

3067. Loutrón; bath, answering to the biblical use of *loúō* (3068), to bathe, wash. In Ephesians 5:26, it is used metaphorically of the Word of God as the instrument of spiritual cleansing. In Titus 3:5, "the washing of regeneration," brings to mind the close connection between cleansing from sin and regeneration (cf. John 3:8; Rom. 6:4; 2 Cor. 5:17).

3068. Loúō; to bathe oneself (John 13:10; Rev. 1:5), used of washing the whole body and not part of it, as indicated by *níptō* (3538). Both of these verbs refer to the washing of living persons while *plúnō* (4150) refers to the washing of inanimate things.

3076. Lupéomai; or *lupéō*, from *lúpē* (3077), sorrow. Used trans., to grieve, to cause to grieve, make sorrowful (2 Cor. 2:2, 5; 7:8, 9; Eph. 4:30); the mid. or pass. *lupéomai*, to be grieved, sorrowful (Matt. 14:9; 17:23; 26:37; Rom. 14:15). This is the most common word used to express grief and is the opposite of *chaírō* (5463), to rejoice. However, this grief is inward, unlike the other words, *penthéō* (3996), mourn; *thrēnéō* (2354), bewail; and *kóptō* (2875), to strike the bosom or beat the breast as an outward sign of an inward grief. Paul expressed the outwardness of the inner grief (*lupéō* [3077]); therefore, in *lupéō* and the subst. *lúpē* (3077), there is not necessarily outward manifestation of the inner grief. It depends on whether or not the individual chooses to outwardly reveal his inner grief (Rom. 9:2).

3083. Lútron; from *lúō* (3089), to loose, from which is derived *lutróō* (3084), to ransom. Ransom or a price paid for redeeming captives, loosing them from their bonds and setting them at liberty. In Matt. 20:28; Mark 10:45 it applies spiritually to the ransom paid by Christ for the delivering of men from the bondage of sin and death. Deriv.: *lútrōsis* (3085), the act of redemption or deliverance; *lutrōtḗs* (3086), redeemer; *antílutron* (487), ransom; *apolútrōsis* (629), ransoming, redemption as the result of expiation.

3084. Lutróō; literally to bring forward a ransom (*lútron* [3083]). The act. verb is used not of him who gives, but of him who receives; hence to release on receipt of a ransom. In the mid. voice, to release by payment of a ransom to redeem; in the pass., to be redeemed or ransomed. Therefore, *lutróō* means to receive a ransom. In the NT it is used in the mid. voice in Luke 24:21; Titus 2:14; in the pass. in 1 Pet. 1:18. Denotes that aspect of the Savior's work wherein He appears as the redeemer of mankind from bondage. This bondage was still regarded quite generally as oppression in Luke 24:21 because of the deficient understanding of Christ's death on the part of the Emmaus disciples (see Titus 2:14; 1 Pet 1:18). *Lútrōsis* (3085) or *apolútrōsis* (629), denotes redemption and deliverance from suffering, redemption as the result of expiation, which is the view of salvation in the NT. This was foreshadowed in the connection between the sins of Israel and their oppression (see Eph. 1:7; 1 Pet. 1:18; Titus 2:14).

3085. Lútrōsis; derived from the act. meaning of *lutróō* (3084), to release on receipt of a ransom. The act of freeing or releasing, deliverance. In NT Gr., redemption, deliverance, used not with reference to the person delivering, but to the person delivered, and, therefore, in a pass. sense like most subst. ending in *-sis* (Luke 1:68; 2:38). Used of redemption from guilt and punishment of sin brought about by expiation (Heb. 9:12).

3086. Lutrōtḗs; from *lutróō* (3084), to redeem. Redeemer, liberator; in the NT used only in Acts 7:35 of Moses.

3088. Lúchnos; a hand lamp fed with oil, not a candle as commonly translated (Matt. 5:15; John 5:35). Contrast *lámpas* (2985), torch.

3089. Lúō; to loose as opposed to *déō* (1210), to bind. To loose something tied or bound (Matt. 21:2; Mark 1:7; 11:2, 4, 5; Luke 13:15; 1 Cor. 7:27). Spoken of seals (Rev. 5:2, 5 TR); to loose; to pronounce or determine not to be bound (Matt. 16:19; 18:18); to break or violate a commandment or law (Matt. 5:19; John 7:23), the Sabbath (John 5:18); the Scripture (John 10:35); to dissolve, destroy (John 2:19; Eph. 2:14; 2 Pet. 3:10, 11, cf. 1 John 3:8); to break or beat to pieces, as a ship (Acts 27:41). Deriv.: *analúō* (360), to return; *análusis* (359), departure or return; *epilúō* (1956), to loose, dissolve; *epílusis* (1955), exposition, interpretation; *katalúō* (2647), to loose, unloose; *katáluma* (2646), an inn; *akatálutos* (179), not to be dissolved, indissoluble; *apolúō* (630), dismiss.

3100. Mathēteúō; from *mathētḗs* (3101), disciple. Governing a dat., to be a disciple or follower of another's doctrine (Matt. 27:57); governing an acc., to make a disciple (Matt. 28:19; Acts 14:21); to instruct (Matt. 13:52) with the purpose of making a disciple. *Mathēteúō* must be distinguished from the verb *mathéō* (which is not found in the NT), which simply means to learn without any attachment to the teacher who teaches. *Mathēteúō* means not only to learn but to become attached to one's teacher and to become his follower in doctrine and conduct. It is really not sufficient to translate this verb as "learn" but as "making a disciple" in its trans. meaning, in the NT sense of *mathētḗs*. Deriv.: *manthánō* (3129), to cause oneself to know.

3101. Mathētḗs; from *mathéō*, to learn, not used in the NT. A learner, pupil. Contrast *didáskalos* (1320), an instructor, a teacher; for example, in Matt. 10:24 where the learner cannot be higher than the instructor (See Luke 6:40). The term is used only in the Gospels and Acts. *Mathētḗs* means more in the NT than a mere pupil or learner. It means an adherent who accepts the instruction given to him and makes it his rule of conduct; for example, the disciples of John (Matt. 11:2; Mark 2:18; Luke 5:33; 7:18; John 3:25); the disciples of the Pharisees (Mark 2:18). In John 9:28 the Pharisees told the healed blind man, "Thou art his disciple, but we are Moses' disciples." Jesus had disciples in the sense that they were His adherents who made His teaching the basis of their conduct. In this sense He had many disciples and He invited all those who believed to become His disciples in this manner (Matt. 5:1; 9:19; 14:22; Luke 14:26, 27, 33; John 9:27; 15:8). Besides these believers, however, there was a smaller select group of twelve apostles whom Jesus chose to be with Him. They were to teach and exercise power in performing miracles in substantiation of His authority transferred to them. These were not ordinary disciples, but they were those who were with Him and followed Him (Matt. 5:1; 8:23, 25 TR; 9:10; 11:1; 14:22). Sometimes they are called the disciples (Matt. 12:1; 14:19; Mark 2:18; 9:14; John 15:8). These original twelve were chosen out of the general group of those who were called the followers of Jesus (Matt. 8:21; Luke 6:13, 17; 7:11; John 6:60, 66). The general designation was given as a name to those who believed on Christ (John 8:31). They were disciples but not the Twelve disciples (Matt. 10:42; John 8:31; Acts 6:2; 19:9). The name *mathētaí* (pl. of *mathētḗs*; Acts 19:1) was applied to John's disciples at Ephesus due to the relationship of John the Baptist to the Messiah. These disciples were ignorant of the fact that Jesus was the Messiah (Acts 19:4). Generally speaking, however, the term *mathētaí*, disciples, denoted just the followers of Christ, the Messiah. Deriv.: *manthánō* (3129), to learn by putting what one learns into experience.

3106. Makarízō; to pronounce blessed, as indwelt by God, and thus fully satisfied. Used only of the virgin Mary (Luke 1:48) and of the persecuted prophets (James 5:11). Contrast *eulogéō* (2127), to speak well of, the more common verb in the NT. The adj. *makários* (3107), blessed, which occurs many times in the NT, means to have the kingdom of God within one's heart because of Christ (Matt. 5:2, 11) and as a result to be fully satisfied (Luke 17:21).

3107. Makários; blessed, to be fully satisfied, *makariótēs*. In the NT, it indicates the state of the believer in Christ (Matt. 5:3–11, "Blessed . . . for my sake"; Luke 6:20–22, "Blessed . . . for the Son of man's sake"). He is indwelt by God because of Christ and as a result is fully satisfied. Contrast *eulogētós* (2128), worthy to be well-spoken of; eulogized from *eulogéō* (2127), to speak well of. *Makários* differs from "happy" because "happy" describes the person who has good luck (from the Eng. root "hap," favorable circumstances). In the biblical sense, a blessed person is one whom God makes fully satisfied, not because of favorable circumstances, but because He indwells the believer through Christ. Aristotle contrasts *makár-*

ios to *endeés* (1729), the needy one. *Makários* is the one who is in the world yet independent of the world; his satisfaction comes from God and not from favorable circumstances.

3114. Makrothuméō; to suffer long, be longsuffering, as opposed to being given to hasty anger or punishment (1 Cor. 13:4; 1 Thess. 5:14; 2 Pet. 3:9); to forbear (Matt. 18:26, 29); to endure patiently as opposed to despondency (Heb. 6:15; James 5:7, 8); to tarry, delay (Luke 18:7). In Hebrews 6:15, *makrothuméō* (3114) is used of Abraham's longsuffering toward God under the pressure of trying circumstances (James 5:7, 8). *Makrothuméō* involves exercising understanding and patience toward persons while *hupoménō* (5278) involves being patient toward things or circumstances. See *hupomonḗ* (5281), patience, and *makrothumía* (3115), longsuffering.

3115. Makrothumía; from the adj. *makróthumos*, which does not occur in the NT. Patience; a self-restraint of the mind before it gives room to action or passion; forbearance, long-suffering. The person who has power to avenge himself, yet refrains from the exercise of this power. It is patience with respect to persons while *hupomonḗ* (5281), endurance, is patience toward things or circumstances. *Makrothumía* and *hupomonḗ* are often found together (2 Cor. 6:4, 6; 2 Tim. 3:10). *Makrothumía* is associated with mercy (*éleos* [1656]) and is used of God (Rom. 2:4; 1 Pet. 3:20). See *anochḗ* (463), tolerance.

3116. Makrothúmōs; adv. from the adj. *makróthumos*, longsuffering. Verb: *makrothuméō* (3114), to be longsuffering. It is wrong to translate *makrothúmōs* as "patiently," because patience is exercised toward things and circumstances, while *makrothumía* is exercised toward God or people. When exercised toward another, one suffers long and extends himself to the life of that person, wishing to win such a one to a godly life in spite of his sinfulness. This adv. occurs only in Acts 26:3. The basic word *makrothumía* stands in contrast to *hupomonḗ* (5281), patience or ability to stand under pressure of circumstances and things.

3119. Malakía; from *malakós* (3120) soft, which is from *malássō*, to soften. An indisposition, infirmity (Matt. 4:23; 9:35; 10:1). Literally, softness; referring to men, meaning delicacy, effeminacy. In Aristotelian ethics, the opposite of *kartería*, patient endurance, weakness. The verb *karteréō* (2594), to endure, is used in Hebrews 11:27.

3126. Mamōnás; or *mammonás*, mammon, the comprehensive word for all kinds of possessions, earnings, and gains, a designation of material value. In Luke 16:9, 11 it denotes riches. In Matthew 6:24 and Luke 16:13, the Lord personifies mammon.

3129. Manthánō; from the obsolete *mathéō*, to learn, from which we have the 2 aor. *émathon* and the inf. *mathein*, as well as the aor. part. of *mathōn*. Probably related to *máomai*, to endeavor, to desire, to seek; thus meaning to learn, experience, bring into experience (Acts 23:27; Gal. 3:2). In the aor., to have learned anything, to understand it (Phil. 4:11). Answers to the verb *didáskō* (1321), to teach (1 Tim. 2:11, 12), which denotes instruction concerning the facts and plan of salvation. In this sense it means to cause oneself to know with a moral bearing and responsibility (John 6:45; Phil. 4:9). In Colossians 1:7 *manthánō* is equivalent to *epiginṓskō* (1921), to know more fully. The syn. use is also indicated in 2 Timothy 3:7 where the two words *manthánō* and *epignōsis* (1922), a full knowledge, are used. In Ephesians 4:20 the verb *manthánō* has Christ as the direct obj. He is presented as the subject matter and the sum and substance of the gospel. To become related to Him is to know Him and knowing Him is to know His teaching and abide by it. Deriv.: *mathētḗs* (3101), disciple; *mathḗtria* (3102), a female disciple (Acts 9:36); *mathēteúō* (3100), to make anyone a disciple.

3132. Manteúomai; from *mántis*, a soothsayer, diviner, which is deduced from *maínomai* (3105), to be mad, beside oneself, from the mad extravagant behavior of such persons among the heathen. Such soothsayers raged, foamed, and yelled, making strange and terrible noises, sometimes gnashing with their teeth, shaking and trembling, with many strange motions. Plato calls such people possessed of madness from Muses, which excited the mind and inspired enthusiastic songs and poems. They were caught up in such ecstasy that they were beside themselves. No one in his right senses was seized with the true spirit of divination. In many instances there was a real possession by the devil, namely, in the case of the prophetic damsel (Acts 16:16, 18). The *mánteis* (pl.) were possessed of a mantic fury which displayed itself by the eyes rolling, the mouth foaming, the hair flying, and so forth. It is quite possible that these symptoms were sometimes produced by the inhalation of vapors or other artificial stimulants. The Word of God knows nothing of this mantic fury except to condemn it. Paul says in 1 Corinthians 14:32: "The spirits of the prophets are subject to the prophets," not to any devilish powers. Such prophets speak not in an unknown tongue, as the soothsayers, but in understandable languages. The true prophet indeed speaks not of himself, but he is possessed by the Spirit of God (Rev. 1:10); his ecstasy is of God (Acts 11:5), being led of the Holy Spirit (2 Pet. 1:21), which is much more than being 'Omoved by the Holy Spirit,' as Eng. translations have it. Man is not beside himself when he is led by the Spirit, but is wise and discreet when he is filled with the presence of God. However, in the *mántis*, the sorcerer, as Plato testifies, we have one in whom all sense of reason is suspended. Thus the line is drawn broadly and distinctly between a *mántis* and a *prophétēs* (4396), prophet.

3140. Marturéō; from *mártur* or *mártus* (3144), witness. To witness, bear witness, testify (John 1:7, 8; 3:26, 28; 5:32; 10:25; 15:26, 27; Acts 22:5; 23:11; 26:22; 1 John 5:7); with a dat., to bear witness to, or concern (Matt. 23:31); implying praise or commendation (Luke 4:22). In the pass., *marturéomai*, to be of good report, having good character (Acts 6:3; 10:22; 22:12; Heb. 11:2, 39, cf. vv. 4, 5). It also means to bear witness to, denoting accent or confirmation (Acts 14:3; Heb. 10:15); the pass. *marturéomai*, to implore, beseech, to charge (1 Thess. 2:11).

3141. Marturía; bearing witness, certifying, (John 1:7); witnessing to (Mark 14:55, 56, 59; Luke 22:71); that which anyone witnesses or states concerning a person or thing (Acts 22:18; 1 Tim. 3:7; Titus 1:13). Also used of the testimony of John the Baptist concerning Jesus (John 1:19; 5:36); of the declarations of Jesus concerning Himself (John 5:31; 8:13, 14). It is a declaration which not only informs but corroborates a testimony borne by a witness who speaks with the authority of one who knows (John 5:34). In 1 John 5:9, 10, the apostle designates the eternal life possessed by believers as God's gift as they witness, testifying of Him (v. 11). In John 3:11, 32, 33, the testimony of Jesus is that which He declares with the authority of a witness, of one who knows (v. 11). But in Revelation 1:9 the testimony of Jesus is the announcement of the gospel, the apostolic preaching of Christ as it is determined by the apostle's testimony (v. 2, those things that he saw). This testimony, which especially concerns Christ and which is based upon a knowledge of Him specifically vouchsafed, is also spoken of as the testimony of Jesus (Rev. 12:17; 19:10; 20:4). That *marturía* is used in the NT to denote martyrdom is an untenable inference from Revelation 11:7; 12:11. See *mártus* (3144), witness.

3142. Martúrion; a neut. noun meaning witness; ordinarily, the declaration which confirms or makes known anything (2 Cor. 1:12). That which testifies to anything (James 5:3). In Class. Gr. *martúrion* was also used to denote proof. In the NT usage it is the witness or the testimony of Christ (1 Cor. 1:6, cf. 2 Tim. 1:8). The meaning is that the preacher bases what he says on his own direct knowledge coincident with reality. The Gospel is preached as a narrative of actual and practical truth, a declaration of facts. This form of expression distinguishes *martúrion* from the work of Christian doctrinal teaching (Acts 4:33; 5:32; 2 Thess.

1:10; 1 Tim. 2:6). The preaching of the Gospel in 1 Corinthians 2:1 is called a *martúrion*, the witness of God (Acts 7:44; Rev. 15:5). Deriv.: *mártus* (3144), witness.

3143. Martúromai; to cause to witness for oneself, to call to witness. To attest, to announce and ratify as truth, to affirm (Acts 20:26; 26:22; Gal. 5:3; Eph. 4:17; 1 Thess. 2:12).

3144. Mártus; witness. Literally, one who remembers, one who has information or knowledge or joint-knowledge of anything; hence, one who can give information, bring to light, or confirm anything (Matt. 18:16; 26:65; Mark 14:63; Acts 7:58; 2 Cor. 13:1; 1 Tim. 5:19; Heb. 10:28). It usually denotes simply that the witness confirms something, though in many cases it also implies that he avoids something and supports his statement on the strength of his own authority (Acts 6:13). In the sense of a simple confirmation (2 Cor. 1:23). Of the knowledge or cognizance which the witness possesses (Rom. 1:9; Phil. 1:8; 1 Thess. 2:5, 10; 1 Tim. 6:12; 2 Tim. 2:2). In Hebrews 12:1 they are described as witnesses who have an experimental knowledge of that which is required of us, faith (Heb. 10:35–37; 11:6ff.; 12:2). Peculiar to the NT is the designation as *mártures* (pl., witnesses) of those who announce the facts of the Gospel and tell its tidings (Acts 1:8; 2:32; 3:15; 10:39; 13:31). Also *mártus* is used as a designation of those who have suffered death in consequence of confessing Christ (of Stephen, Acts 22:20; of Antipas, Rev. 2:13; see Rev. 17:6). This verse and the previous ones, however, should not be understood as if their witness consisted in their suffering death but rather that their witnessing of Jesus became the cause of their death. The Lord Jesus in Rev. 1:5 is called the Witness, the Faithful One (see also Rev. 3:14; 22:20). Deriv.: *martúrion* (3142), the declaration which confirms or makes known anything; *marturía* (3141), certifying, witnessing; *martúromai* (3143), to cause to witness for oneself, to call to witness; *diamartúromai* (1263), to call to witness, to protest, to assert or attest anything; *marturéō* (3140), to be witness, to bear witness; *epimarturéō* (1957), to testify emphatically.

3151. Mataiológos; from *mátaios* (3152), vain, and *légō* (3004), to speak. A vain talker, one idly speaking what is useless (Titus 1:10). The subst. *mataiología* (3150), used in 1 Timothy 1:6 denotes speech which lacks reason, worth, and the fruit of divine and eternal life.

3152. Mátaios; vain, characterized by aimlessness, leading to no object or end, especially that end being God. It is building houses on sand, chasing the wind, shooting at stars, pursuing one's own shadow. Contrast *kenós* (2756), empty, indicating the hollowness of something or somebody. Subst.: *mataiótēs* (3153), vanity; *mataiología* ([3150], from *mátaios*, and *légō* [3004], to speak), vain talking (1 Tim. 1:6); *mataiológos* (3151), one who talks vainly (Titus 1:10). Verb: *mataioómai* (3154), become vain (Rom. 1:21), *mátēn* (3155), used in the acc. with the prep. *eís* (1519), in (Matt. 15:9; Mark 7:7), in vain.

3153. Mataiótēs; vanity, nothingness, worthlessness; used in Romans 8:20 to show the emptiness of the present in contrast with the living fullness of the future (Eph. 4:17; 2 Pet. 2:18).

3154. Mataióō; to make vain or worthless. In the pass., *mataíoomai*, to become vain, destitute of real wisdom (Rom. 1:21), to be perverse, foolish, or act perversely, foolishly. In reality, to get off the right path, to follow foolish or bad courses.

3155. Mátēn; an adv., strictly the acc. of *mátē*, folly, fault, with the prep. *eís* (1519) in front of it. In vain. In a causal sense, groundless, invalid; and in a final sense, objectless, useless, futile, and according to circumstances may combine both "idle" and "vain." Untrue, false (Matt. 15:9; Mark 7:7). Deriv.: *mátaios* (3152) vain, idle; *mataiótēs* (3153), vanity, nothingness, worthlessness; *mataióō* (3154), to make vain or worthless; *mataiológos* (3151), one who speaks emptiness or vanity.

3163. Máchē; fighting, battle (2 Cor. 7:5; James 4:1). The actual battle of hostile armies, as differentiated from *pólemos* (4171), war, which embraces the whole course of hostilities. The noun *máchē* and the verb *máchomai* (3164), to fight, may fall short of denoting actual battle, although the word may mean that. There are battles of all kinds such as legal battles (as in Titus 3:9) and battles of words (as in 1 Tim. 6:4). Another related word is *stásis* (4714), insurrection or sedition, distinguished from *pólemos* (4171), war, with *stásis* being a civil war and *pólemos* a foreign one.

3167. Megaleíos; from *mégas* (3173), great; indicating great works or miracles (Luke 1:49 TR; Acts 2:11) contemplated as outcomings of the greatness (*megaleíon*) of God's power and glory. See *sēmeía* (4592), signs; *dunámeis* (1411), mighty works; *éndoxa* (1741) glorious things; *parádoxa* (3861), strange or extraordinary things; *thaumásia* (2297), astonishing things; *térata* (5059), wonders.

3178. Méthē; drunkenness (Luke 21:34; Rom. 13:13; Gal. 5:21). Used in an abstract sense; contrast *pótos* (4224), used in a concrete sense, a drinking bout, a banquet, a symposium, not necessarily excessive but giving opportunity for excess. *Méthē* is stronger and expresses a greater excess than *oínōsis*, the influence of wine. The excess of wine in the NT is expressed as *oinophlugía* (3632).

3179. Methístēmi; from *metá* (3326), denoting change of place, and *hístēmi* (2476), to place, stand. To remove from an office (Luke 16:4; Acts 13:22); to remove, to translate into the kingdom of the Son of God (Col. 1:13); to turn away, pervert (Acts 19:26); to transfer (1 Cor. 13:2).

3180. Methodeía; from *méthodos*, method; the following or pursuing of orderly and technical procedure in the handling of a subject. In the NT connected with evildoing, a device, artifice, art, artificial method, or wile (Eph. 4:14; 6:11). Verb: *methodeúō*, to go systematically to work, to do or pursue something methodically and according to the rules.

3195. Méllō; signifying intention, being about to do something (Acts 3:3; 18:14); certainty, compulsion or necessity; to be certain to act (John 6:71); almost (Acts 21:27, cf. 26:28); to be about to (Rev. 10:7), to be about to do something often implying the necessity and, therefore, the certainty of what is to take place (Matt. 3:7; 11:14; Eph. 1:21; 1 Tim. 4:8; 6:19; Heb. 2:5) to be about to do a thing, indicating simply the formation of a design (Acts 5:35; 20:7, 13); used of purpose, certainty, compulsion, or necessity (2 Pet. 1:12 UBS *mellēsō*). Expressed by "shall" or "should," which elsewhere frequently represents part of the fut. tense of the verb as expressed by the Gr. verbal suffix.

3306. Ménō; to remain, dwell. ntrans. to remain, abide, dwell (Matt. 10:11; Mark 14:34; Luke 1:56; John 1:39; 2:12, cf. John 14:10, 16; 15:4, 7; 1 John 4:12, 15, 16); to remain, endure, last (Matt. 11:23; 1 Cor 13:13; 2 Cor. 9:9, cf. Heb. 7:3, 24; 10:34); to persevere (1 Tim. 2:15, cf. John 15:9, 10; 1 John 4:16), to stand firm or steadfast (Rom. 9:11); to remain alive (John 21:22, 23; 1 Cor. 15:6); trans. with an acc., to wait for (Acts 20:5). Deriv.: *hupoménō* (5278), to remain under, be patient; *hupomonē* (5281), patience toward things and circumstances as distinguished from *makrothumía* (3115), longsuffering or patience toward people.

3311. Merismós; from *merízō* (3307), to divide. Distribution, translated "gifts" in Hebrews 2:4 and "dividing asunder" in Hebrews 4:12.

3315. Mesiteúō; from *mesítēs* (3316), mediator. To be a mediator between two contending parties (Heb. 6:17ff.)

3316. Mesítēs; from *mésos* (3319), the middle. A mediator, one who mediates between two parties (Gal. 3:20). Ascribed to Christ (1 Tim. 2:5; Heb 8:6; 9:15; 12:24); to Moses (Gal. 3:19). In Paul's language, *mesítēs* is one who unites parties, one who mediates for peace (1 Tim. 2:5). Christ is thus called a mediator because, in man's behalf, He satisfies the claims of God upon man. In Hebrews He is called mediator clearly in the sense of a surety, one who becomes security for some-

thing (Heb. 8:6, cf. 7:22; 9:15; 12:24). It is He who (with reference to mankind) mediates or guarantees for them a new and better covenant, and (with reference to God) appears as High Priest (Heb. 7:20–22). What the Epistle to the Hebrews divides into these two elements, the High Priesthood and the Mediatorship of Christ, Paul represents as blended in His Mediatorship (1 Tim. 2:5).

3319. Mésos; middle, in the midst. Used of time or place (Matt. 14:24; 25:6; John 1:26; Acts 1:18). With the neut. art., *to méson*, the middle part, the midst (Acts 27:27). Used with different prep.: *ek* ([1537], from) *mésou*, from the midst, from among, away (Matt. 13:49; 1 Cor. 5:2; 2 Cor. 6:17; Col. 2:14); *aná* ([303], up) *méson*, in or through the midst, between (Matt. 13:25; Mark 7:31; 1 Cor. 6:5); *diá* ([1223], through) *mésou*, through the midst (Luke 4:30; 17:11); *eis* ([1519], into) *to méson*, in or into the midst (Mark 14:60; Luke 5:19; 6:8); *en* ([1722], in) *mésō*, in the midst, among (Matt. 18:20; Luke 2:46; 8:7).

3326. Metá; a prep. governing the gen. and acc. with the primary significance of amid, in the midst, with, among, implying accompaniment; differing from *sun* (4862), together, which expresses conjunction, union. With the gen., *metá* implies companionship, fellowship, meaning amid, among, as where one is said to sit, stand, and so forth, with or in the midst of others (Matt. 26:58); when followed with a gen. of persons, with, that is, together with (Luke 22:28; 24:29; John 6:66); where one is said to do or suffer anything with another, implying joint or mutual action, influence, suffering (Matt. 2:3; 5:41); nearness or contiguity (Matt. 21:2); indicates the state or emotion of mind which accompanies the doing of anything, with which one acts (Matt. 28:8); designates an external action, circumstance, or condition with which another action or event is accompanied (Matt. 14:7; 24:31); implies accord or discord denoting common agreement or disagreement (Luke 23:12); signifies participation, fellowship (2 Cor. 6:15, 16). With the acc., *metá* strictly implies motion towards the middle or into the midst of anything, but also motion after any person or thing; that is, either so as to follow and be with a person or to bring a person or thing. After, as spoken of succession either in place or time (Matt. 1:12; John 2:12). In composition *metá* implies fellowship, partnership, as *metadídōmi* (3330), to impart; also proximity, contiguity, as *methórion* (3181), border, boundary (from *metá* and *horíon* [3725], limit, border); motion or direction after, as *methodeía* (3180), a device, method (from *metá* and *hodeúō* [3593], to travel, to contrive); transition, transposition, changeover, as *metabaínō* (3327), to go over.

3327. Metabaínō; from *metá* (3326), denoting change of place or condition, and *baínō*, to go or come. To pass or go from one place or state to another (Matt. 17:20; Luke 10:7; John 5:24); to go away, depart (Matt. 8:34; John 13:1; Acts 18:7).

3333. Metakaléō; from *metá* (3326), implying change, and *kaléō* (2564), to call from one place to another, summon. As used in the mid. voice, to call for oneself, to send for, to call here (Acts 7:14; 10:32; 20:17; 24:25).

3337. Metallássō; from *metá* (3326), denoting change of condition, and *allássō* (236), to change. To exchange, to convert from one state to another (Rom. 1:25, 26).

3338. Metaméllomai; to regret (Matt. 21:29, 32; 27:3; 2 Cor. 7:8; Heb. 7:21). Contrast *metanoéō* (3340), to repent. To express the mere desire that what is done may be undone, accompanied with regrets or even remorse, but with no effective change of heart. An ineffective repentance, *metaméleia* (which nowhere occurs in the NT), to which forgiveness of sins is not promised as it is for *metánoia* (3341), repentance. *Metaméllomai* means little or nothing more than a selfish dread of the consequence of what one has done whereas *metanoéō* means regret and turning away by a change of heart brought about by God's Spirit.

3339. Metamorphóō; and *metamorphóomai* (mid.), from *metá* (3326), denoting change of condition, and *morphóō* (3445), to form. Used of Jesus' transfiguration on the Mount (Matt. 17:2; Mark 9:2) involving the miracle of transformation from an earthly form into a supernatural which is denoted by the radiance of the garments, also the countenance, suggesting what the bodies of the righteous may be like in the age to come (1 Cor. 15:51f.). In Romans 12:2 and 2 Corinthians 3:18, the idea of transformation refers to an invisible process in Christians which takes place or begins to take place already during their life in this age. See *metaschēmatízo* (3345), to change one's outward form; *metastréphō* (3344), to turn from; *schēma* (4976), external condition, fashion.

3340. Metanoéō; to repent with regret accompanied by a true change of heart toward God. *Metánoia* (3341), repentance, is retrospection as *prónoia* (4307), is foreknowledge. It signifies a change of mind consequent to retrospection, indicating regret for the course pursued and resulting in a wiser view of the past and future. Most importantly, it is distinguished from *metaméllomai* (3338), to regret because of the consequences of one's actions. Deriv.: *noéō* (3539), to comprehend; *noús* (3563), mind.

3341. Metánoia; from *metanoéō* (3340), to repent. A change or alteration of mind (Heb. 12:17). Repentance, change of mind from evil to good or from worse to better (Matt. 3:11; 9:13 TR; Acts 20:21). In the NT used with reference to *noús* (3563), mind, as the faculty of moral reflection (Acts 11:18; 20:21; 2 Cor. 7:9, 10; 2 Tim. 2:25; Heb. 6:1). It is combined with *áphesis* (859), remission of sins (Luke 24:47). Compare baptism of repentance (Matt. 3:11; Mark 1:4; Luke 3:3; Acts 13:24; 19:4), baptism which identifies one as having repented. For deriv., see *noéō* (3539), to perceive. For a distinction from *metaméleia* and *metaméllomai* (3338), to change one's mind because of the consequences of one's sin, see *metanoéō* (3340).

3345. Metaschēmatízō; from *metá* (3326), denoting change of condition, and *schēma* (4976), form, fashion. To transfigure. Occurs only in 1 Corinthians 4:6; 2 Corinthians 11:13–15; Philippians 3:21. The difference between *metaschēmatízo* and *metamorphóō* is best illustrated in this way. If one were to change a Dutch garden into an Italian one, this would be *metaschēmatízo*. But if one were to transform a garden into something wholly different, as into a ballfield, it is *metamorphóō* (3339), from *morphé* (3444). It is possible for Satan to *metaschēmatízo*, transform himself into an angel of light (i.e., he can change his whole outward semblance), but to any such change it would be impossible to apply the word *metamorphóō*, for this would imply an internal change, a change not of appearance but of essence, which lies beyond his power. In the *metaschēmatismós*, a transformation of the bodies (1 Cor. 15:53; Phil. 3:21) there is to be seen a transition but no absolute dissolution of continuity. The outer physical transformation of believers at the end of the days (1 Cor. 15:44ff., 51f.) is called *metaschēmatízo* by Paul in Philippians 3:21, but such transformation has already begun in this life from within.

3348. Metéchō; from *metá* (3326), with, and *échō* (2192), have. To have together with others, to partake (1 Cor. 10:21, 30; Heb. 5:13; 7:13). Deriv.: *metochḗ* (3352), a partaking, participation, fellowship (2 Cor. 6:14); *métochos* (3353), a partaker (Heb. 3:1, 14; 6:4; 12:8), an associate, a partner (Luke 5:7); *summétochos* (4830), from *sun* (4862), together, and *métochos* (3353), partaker; co-partaker (Eph. 3:6; 5:7).

3356. Metriopathéō; to act with moderation; from *metriopathḗs*, one moderate in his passions (which in its turn is derived from *métrios*, moderate, and *páthos* [3806], passion). In Plutarch, *metriopátheia*, moderation, is the same as *praótēs* or *praútēs* (4240), meekness. With a dat. following, to moderate one's anger towards, to pardon, treat with mildness or meekness (Heb. 5:2).

3367. Mēdeís; not even one, no one, that is, no one no matter who he may be. Used with moods other than the indic., namely, the imper., the subjunctive, and

the inf. When the indic. is used, then *oudeís* (3762) is utilized instead of *mēdeís*. After verbs of profit or loss, deficiency (Luke 4:35; 2 Cor. 11:5; Phil. 4:6). Neut.: *mēdén*, nothing (used with an adv.: not at all, in no respect). Metaphorically, *mēdén ōn*, being nothing, that is, of no account, no weight of character (Gal. 6:3).

3392. Miaínō; to stain with color, as the staining of glass. Contrast *molúnō* (3435), to besmear or besmirch as with mud or filth, to defile. *Molúnō* is not used in a ritual or ceremonial sense as is *miaíno*.

3393. Míasma; from the verb *miaíno* (3392), to defile. Pollution (2 Pet. 2:20); the contaminating effect of the world upon the godly as a result of their living in it; the result of *miasmós* (3394), the act of polluting.

3394. Miasmós; the act of defiling resulting in *miasma* (3393), as in 2 Peter 2:10.

3405. Misthapodosía; from *misthós* (3408), reward, recompense, and *apodídōmi* (591), to render. A recompense, whether a reward (Heb. 10:35; 11:26) or a punishment (Heb. 2:2).

3406. Misthapodótēs; from *misthós* (3408), a reward, and *apodídōmi* (591), to render. A recompenser, a rewarder (Heb. 11:6).

3407. Místhios; hired servant, an adj. related to *misthōtós* (3411), a hireling (Luke 15:17, 19).

3408. Misthós; wages, hire, reward received in this life (Matt. 5:46; 6:2, 5, 16; Rom. 4:4; 1 Cor. 9:17, 18); of evil rewards (Acts 1:18) to be received hereafter (Matt. 5:12; 10:41; Mark 9:41; Luke 6:23, 35).

3411. Misthōtós; an adj. meaning hired. Used as an adj. noun, one who is hired, sometimes indicating one who is not showing real interest in his duty and who is unfaithful; a hireling (Mark 1:20; John 10:12, 13). Related words: *místhios* (3107); hired servant; *misthós* (3408), wages.

3435. Molúnō; to defile, besmear or besmirch as with mud or filth (1 Cor. 8:7; Rev. 3:4; 14:4). Contrast *miaínō* (3392), to stain; *spilóō* (4695), to spot, pollute.

3436. Molusmós; from the verb *molúnō* (3435), the act of defilement produced by the body. Filthiness (2 Cor. 7:1). See *miasmós* (3394), the act of defiling.

3438. Monḗ; from *ménō* (3306), to remain, dwell. A mansion, habitation, abode (John 14:2, 23). Also related to *mónos* (3441), alone, only, single.

3439. Monogenḗs; from *mónos* (3441), only, and *genő*, to form, to make, and *gínomai* (1096). To be differentiated from *gennáō* (1080), to beget, generate. *Gínomai* is related to *génos* (1085) as in genealogy, species, family, kindred. *Monogenḗs* means the only one of the family, as in Luke 7:12 referring to the only son of his mother; in Luke 8:42, the daughter of Jairus; in Luke 9:38, the demoniac boy. Only John uses *monogenḗs* to describe the relation of Jesus to God the Father, presenting Him as the unique One, the only One (*mónos*) of the family (*génos*), in the discussion of the relationship of the Son to the Father (John 1:14, 18; 3:16, 18; 1 John 4:9). Jesus is never called *téknon* ([5043], child) *Theoú* (2316), of God, as the believers are (John 1:12; 11:52; 1 John 3:1, 2, 10; 5:2). John 5:18 reveals that Jesus called God His very own Father (*idion* [2398]). He was not a Father to Him as He is to us. See John 20:17. He never spoke of God as the common Father of Himself and of believers. The term *monogenḗs* also occurs in Hebrews 11:17. The *génos* from which *genḗs* in *monogenḗs* is derived means race, stock, family, and *genő* comes from *gínomai*, become, as in John 1:14, ". . . and the Word became (*egéneto*) flesh," in distinction from *gennáō*, to beget, engender, create. The noun from *gennáō* is *génnēma* (1081), the result of birth. But in *monogenḗs* we have *génos*, Jesus Christ designated as the only One of the same stock in the relationship of the Son to the Father. He is not to be understood as eternally born of the Father, but only in His humanity was He born. Therefore, *monogenḗs* can be held as syn. with the God-Man.

3444. Morphé; form. *Morphé* appears together with *schēma* (4976), fashion, whole outward appearance, in Philippians 2:6–8. These two words are obj., for the form and the fashion of a thing would exist if it were alone in the universe, whether or not anyone was there to behold it. They cannot represent subj. ideas of non-existing entities. The word *idéa* ([2397], from *idéō, eidō* [1492], to see, which in turn is from *eídos* [1491], appearance, visible form), idea, concept of the mind, is subj. (Matt. 28:3). The appearance of *morphḗ* or *schḗma* implies someone to whom this appearance is made. There needs to be a seer before something can be seen. It becomes obj. real by its subj. realization. *Morphḗ* in Philippians 2:6–8 presumes an obj. reality. None could be in the form (*morphḗ*) of God who was not God. *Morphḗ* is the reality which can be externalized, not some shape that is the result of pure thought. It is the utterance of the inner life, a life which bespeaks the existence of God. He who had been from eternity *en morphḗ Theoú*, in the form of God (John 17:5), took at His incarnation *morphḗn doúlou* (1401), the form of a servant. Nothing appeared that was not in obj. reality from the beginning. The fact that He continued to be God in His humanity is demonstrated by the pres. part., *hupárchōn*, "being" in the form of God. *Hupárchō* (5225) involves continuing to be that which one was before. In His incarnation He took upon Himself the form (*morphḗ*) of a servant, which is an inner attitude by taking upon Himself the shape (*schḗma*) of man. That was the only way He could die for man's salvation. The *schḗma*, shape, fashion, is the outward form having to do not with its essential being, but with His appearance. In Mark 16:12 the expression *en* (1722), in, *hétera* (2087), qualitatively another, *morphḗ*, form, Christ was transformed (*metemorphōthē*, aor. pass. of *metamorphóō* [3339]) as in Matthew 17:2; Mark 9:2. The transformation upon the Mount was a prophetic anticipation of that which we shall all experience. This form in which the risen Lord also appeared to two disciples on the road to Emmaus (Luke 24:13ff.) is a human form, but different from that which Jesus bore during His life on earth.

3445. Morphóō; to form, fashion, originally used of artists who shape their material into an image. Used only in Galatians 4:19, where the Christian is described as a little child who needs to mature. See *morphḗ* (3444), form; *schḗma* (4976), outward appearance; *metamorphóō* (3339), transform.

3446. Mórphōsis; the activity of forming, shaping. In Romans 2:20 it refers to a sketch, summary, corresponding to the high sense of pride with which a Jew who feels himself to be a teacher regards a book of the Law as a physical representation of absolute knowledge, and truth as the actual depiction and representation of the idea of a divine form. In 2 Timothy 3:5 it refers to the external form of the Christian life with no inner power, the mere appearance or mask of pious conduct.

3449. Móchthos; from *mógos*, labor, toil (cf. *mogís* [3425], with difficulty). Toil, travail, afflicting and wearisome labor. It is the everyday word for that labor which, in one shape or another, is the lot of all of the sinful children of Adam. It is more than *kópos* (2873), labor, and it therefore follows *kópos* in all the three passages wherein it occurs, namely 2 Corinthians 11:27; 1 Thessalonians 2:9; 2 Thessalonians 3:8. Related words: *pónos* (4192), pain; *zḗlos* (2205), zeal; *agṓn* (73), conflict.

3454. Múthos; from *muéō*, to instruct. It is the word from which "mythology" is derived. Commonly rendered as a tale or a fable. There is nothing necessarily false in a myth. It is that which is fabricated by the mind set over against the real and actually true. There may be much logic and reasoning in a myth. In the NT, however, the word "myth" does not have the meaning of its being a vehicle of some lofty truth as the early use of the word did. Mostly used in the NT as a lying fable with all its falsehood and all its pretenses to be what it is not. Thus in 1 Timothy 4:7, fables are described as *bébēloi* (952), profane, and *graṓdeis* (1126), belonging to old women. In Titus 1:14, Jewish fables; in 2 Peter 1:16, *múthoi sesophisménoi* (perf. part. of *sophízō* [4679], to make wise), the result of sophistry or cunning fables for the purpose of deceiv-

ing. In 1 Timothy 1:4 and 2 Timothy 4:4, the use of the word is equally degrading and contemptuous. Although *lógos* (3056) and *múthos* begin together with the thought, intelligence, mind, they part ranks since the first ends in the kingdom of light and truth and the second in the kingdom of darkness and lies.

3464. Múron; ointment, the base of which is *élaion* (1637), oil. It is mixed, however, with aromatic substances and thus is fit for finer uses as by women, men preferring oil. Contrast *élaion* for the distinction between the two and the explanation of Luke 7:46.

3466. Mustḗrion; from *mústēs*, a person initiated in sacred mysteries (which in turn is derived from *múō*, to close or shut; namely, the lips or eyes). It is referred to as a locking up or that which serves for locking up. In Class. Gr. usually in the pl., *ta mustḗria*, the mysteries, as denoting secret politico-religious doctrines, especially of the Eleusinian Mysteries wherein some secret information communicated to the initiated was in turn to be kept secret. It denotes in general something hidden or not fully manifest. 2 Thessalonians 2:7 speaks of "the mystery of lawlessness" which began to work in secret but was not then completely disclosed or manifested. Some sacred thing hidden or secret which is naturally unknown to human reason and is only known by the revelation of God (1 Tim. 3:16; see 1 Cor. 2:7). When Paul speaks of the mystery of the incarnation as being great, he seems to allude plainly to the famous Eleusinian Mysteries (which were distinguished as being small and great, the latter of which were held in the highest reverence among the Greeks and Romans [cf. Eph. 5:32]). The term *mustḗrion* (Rom. 11:25; 1 Cor. 15:51), denotes what was hidden or unknown until revealed, and thus he speaks of a man understanding all mysteries (1 Cor. 13:2), i. e., all the revealed truths of the Christian religion which is elsewhere called the mystery of faith (1 Tim. 3:9). In Matthew 13:11, "because to them it was not given to know the mysteries of the kingdom of God," it means those things which are not revealed to them by virtue of their not being related to King Jesus. In the writings of Paul the word *mustḗrion* is sometimes applied in a peculiar sense to the calling of the Gentiles. In Ephesians 3:3–6, he styles as a mystery and the mystery of Christ, the fact that the Gentiles should be fellow-heirs, be of the same body and partakers of Christ by the gospel. In other generations, such a thing was not made known to the sons of man as it is now revealed by His holy apostles and prophets by the Spirit (cf. Rom. 16:25; Eph. 1:9; 3:9; 6:19; Col. 1:26, 27; 4:3). It denotes a spiritual truth couched in an external representation or similitude, and concealed or hidden thereby unless some explanation be given (Matt. 13:11; Mark 4:11; Luke 8:10; Eph. 5:32; Rev. 1:20; 17:5, 7, and their respective contexts).

3470. Mṓmos; blame, fault; used only in 2 Peter 2:13, blemish, disgrace. See *ámōmos* (299), without blame, without fault.

3473. Mōrología; from *mōrós* (3474), foolish, and *lógos* (3056), a word, speech. Foolish talking (Eph. 5:4). It is that type of speech that shows how foolish a person is. Besides this word there are two others that show the sins of the tongue, namely *aischrología* (148), foul speech, and *eutrápella* (2160), the ability to extricate oneself from difficult situations with witty or clever words.

3474. Mōrós; silly, stupid, foolish, from which the Eng. word "moron" is derived. Used of persons (Matt. 5:22), morally worthless, a more serious reproach than "*racá*," as the latter scorns a man's mind and calls him stupid. One who is *mōrós* scorns his heart and character. Used of things (2 Tim. 2:23); foolish and ignorant questionings (Titus 3:9). Noun: *mōría* (3472), foolishness as a personal quality (1 Cor. 1:21, 23; 2:14; 3:19). *Mōrología* (3473), foolish talking, denoting more than mere idle talk, talk of tools which is foolishness and sin together. Verb: *mōraínō* (3471) as used in the causal sense, to make foolish (1 Cor. 1:20); in the pass. sense to become foolish (Rom. 1:22).

3485. Naós; from *naíō*, to dwell (Acts 7:48 TR; 17:24; 1 Cor. 6:19). The temple itself is the heart and center of the whole sacred enclosure called *hierón* (2411). The *naós* was the Holy of Holies. The Lord never entered the *naós* during His ministry on earth, the right of such entry being reserved for the Jewish priests alone.

3498. Nekrós; dead. Natural death (Matt. 10:8; 11:5); spiritual death, dead in sin, separated from the vivifying grace of God, or more distinctly, having one's soul separated from the enlivening influences of the divine light and spirit, as a dead body is separated from the material light and air, and consequently having no hope of life eternal (Matt. 8:22; Eph. 2:1, 5; 5:14; Col. 2:13). Thus, sinful practices are called dead works, such as those performed by those who are dead in sin (Heb. 6:1; 9:14). Also, dead unto sin, meaning inactive with regard to sin, as a dead man is in respect to bodily functions (Rom. 6:11); a dead faith (James 2:17, 20 TR, 26), which means a faith unaccompanied by good works and therefore unprofitable (James 2:16, 17); a faith unable to justify (James 2:20, 21) and save (James 2:14); sin is said to have been dead without the law (Rom. 7:8), that is, apparently dead and inoperative. Deriv.: *nékrōsis* (3500), a killing, deadness.

3500. Nékrōsis; from *nekróō* (3499), to mortify. The act of putting to death (2 Cor. 4:10). Always carrying about in the body the putting to death of the Lord Jesus, that is, being exposed to cruelties resembling those which He sustained in His last sufferings (1 Cor. 15:31). It also means deadness (Rom. 4:19).

3501. Néos; new in relation to time, as that which has recently come into existence. New under the aspect of quality is *kainós* (2537), which also may indicate the novel and strange. The *kainón* is the *héteron* (2087), the qualitatively new. The *néon* is the *állon* (243), the numerically distinct. *Néos* may be derived from *néō*, to move, agitate, hence one who moves briskly; a young man, so named either because of the activity and vigor, or of the unsettled attitude of that age of life. Referring to young women (Titus 2:4); referring to new wine, but the same as was had before (Matt. 9:17; Mark 2:22); the new man (Col. 3:10). Here both *néos* and *anakainoúmenos* (part. of *anakainóō* [341]), to renew, are used. Paul refers to the new nature the believer puts on, but this new nature becomes qualitatively new by the activity of God Himself through His renewing (*anakainoúmenon*). Man on his own can only reform (become *néos*), but by God's activity, he becomes *kainós*, qualitatively new. This is God's impartation of His divine nature as it is spoken of in 2 Corinthians 5:17; 2 Peter 1:4. See *ananeóō* (365), to renew, having an experience of the same kind as previously; *neótēs* (3503), newness.

3502. Neossós; or *nossós*, from *néos* (3501), young. A young bird, a chicken (Luke 2:24). Deriv.: *neótēs* (3503), youth; *neóphutos* (3504), newly planted, a novice.

3503. Neótēs; from *néos* (3501), young; youth, age or time of youth (Matt. 19:20 TR; Mark 10:20; Luke 18:21; Acts 26:4; 1 Tim. 4:12). Deriv.: *ananeóō* (365), to renew *neossós* (3502), a fledgling, a young bird; *neóphutos* (3504), newly planted or a novice.

3504. Neóphutos; from *néos* (3501), new, and *phútos*, planted. Newly planted, or (figuratively) one who is but lately converted from Judaism or heathenism to Christianity and newly implanted in the Church; newly instructed or a novice (1 Tim. 3:6).

3516. Népios; from *né* (3513), not, and *épō* (2036), to speak. An infant, a child not yet able to speak plainly (Matt. 21:16, cf. 1 Cor. 13:11); a young person under age (Gal. 4:1, cf. v. 3); a child, a babe in ignorance and simplicity (Matt. 11:25, Luke 10:21; Rom. 2:20); a babe in Christ, a person weak in faith, a beginner (1 Cor. 3:1; Eph. 4:14; Heb. 5:13). Verb: *népiázō* (3515), to be an infant (1 Cor. 14:20).

3538. Níptō; to wash; compare with *louō* (3068), to bathe, especially the washing of living objects or persons; contrast *plúnō* (4150), to wash inanimate things. *Níptō*, however, usually expresses the washing of a part of the body, the hands (Mark 7:3), the feet (John 13:5), the face (Matt. 6:17), the eyes (John 9:7); *louō*, to bathe oneself, always implies not the washing of a part of the body, but of the whole. The lesson in John 13:9, 10 symbolizes justification as the bathing of the whole body (*louō*) while sanctification is the constant need of *níptō*, washing the feet.

3539. Noéō; from *noús* (3563), the mind. To perceive with thought coming into consciousness as distinct from the perception of senses. To mark, understand, apprehend, discern. Distinguished from *ginōskō* (1097), the relation to the object known instead of merely the act of knowing (Matt. 15:17; 16:9, 11; Mark 7:18; Eph. 3:4, 20; 1 Tim. 1:7; 2 Tim. 2:7). *Noéō* denotes the independent action of the mind or the heart. If the latter is used referring to the mind, it means to understand, think, reflect (John 12:40). Thus *noús*, mind, is the organ of the spirit and at the same time a function of the heart. Deriv.: *nóēma* (3540), the product of the action of the mind; *anóētos* (453), unthought of, inconceivable; *diánoia* (1271), the faculty of thought; *énnoia* (1771), what lies in thought, meaning; *metanoéō* (3340), to repent; *metánoia* (3341), a change of mind, repentance; *nouthetéō* (3560), to put in mind, work upon the mind of one, put the mind in its right course, admonish; *nouthesía* (3559), admonition. Syn.: *suniēmi* (4920), to put something all together and make out its meaning (Mark 7:18; 8:17; 2 Tim. 2:7).

3540. Nóēma; from *noéō* (3539), to perceive. A thought, concept of the mind (2 Cor. 10:5); a device, contrivance (2 Cor. 2:11); the understanding, the mind (2 Cor. 3:14; 4:4; 11:3; Phil. 4:7). See *noús* (3563), mind.

3544. Nomikós; a person who is learned in the law or legal practice, a lawyer. The *nomikoí* appear together with the Pharisees (Luke 7:30; 14:3). Apparently they were from among the Pharisees (Matt. 22:35; Mark 12:28) and with the scribes. In all places where the word is employed and legal questions come into consideration, the scribes appear as authorities in questions concerning prophecy (Matt. 2:4; 13:52). It may be inferred that "scribes" is the generic name, and *nomikoí*, the lawyers, are the specialists in law and jurisprudence. *Nomodidáskalos* (3547), teacher of the law (Luke 5:17; Acts 5:34), is apparently another name. Probably the members of the Sanhedrin and the Council were learned in the law.

3551. Nómos; from *nénoma*, perf. mid. voice of *némō*, to parcel out, either of distributing or assigning, because the law assigns to everyone his own, or of administering, because it administers all things either by commanding or forbidding. A law in general (Rom. 4:15; 5:13). Most frequently the divine Law given by Moses, whether moral, ceremonial, or judicial (Matt. 5:17, 18; 7:12; 23:23; Luke 2:22; John 7:51; 8:5). Sometimes it means the books of Moses or the Pentateuch containing the Law (Luke 24:44; Acts 13:15, cf. Gal. 4:21), or the OT in general (John 10:34; 12:34; 15:25; Rom. 3:19; 1 Cor. 14:21). The gospel or gospel method of justification is called the "law of faith," opposite the "law of works" (Rom. 3:27); "the law of the Spirit of life," opposite the law, that is, the power, dominion of sin and death (Rom. 8:2); "the royal law" (James 2:8), because it is the law of Christ, our King; "the perfect law, the law of liberty" (James 1:25, cf. 2:12) freeing believers from the yoke of ceremonial observances and slavery of sin, opposite to the Mosaic Law, which made nothing perfect (Heb. 7:19; 10:1). A force or principle of action equivalent to a law (Rom. 7:21, 23, 25; 8:2). Deriv.: *ánomos* (459), without law, lawless; *anomía* (458), lawlessness; *énnomos* (1772), what is within the range of law.

3554. Nosós; the regular word for disease, sickness. It is a disease of a grievous kind. It is joined to *malakía* (Matt. 4:23, 24) denoting a slighter infirmity. From *nosós* comes the English "nosology," the classification of diseases. Deriv.: *noséō* (3552), to be sick in body, but also to rave like a person in the delirium of a fever (1 Tim. 6:4); *nósēma* (3553), the result of *nósos*, disease (John 5:4 TR). Syn.: *asthéneia* (769), sickness, weakness; *malakía* (3119) ailment, softness; *arrhōstía*, although only the adj. or adj. noun, *árrhōstos* ([732], sick, ill) is found in the NT.

3557. Nosphízomai; from *nósphi*, apart, separated. Mid. voice to embezzle, keep back (Acts 5:2, 3; Titus 2:10). Applied by Gr. writers to public treasures.

3559. Nouthesía; from *noús* (3563), mind, and *thésis*, a placing which is from *títhēmi* (5087), to put. To put into the mind. An admonition (1 Cor. 10:11; Eph. 6:4; Titus 3:10). *Nouthesía* is the training by a word of encouragement when it proves sufficient, but also by a word of remonstrance, reproof, blame, as required. *Paideía* (3809) is instruction, training by act and discipline. *Nouthesía* is the milder term without which *paideía* would be incomplete. *Nouthesía* involves correction by deed as needed. In both words there is the appeal to the reasonable faculties See *epanórthōsis* (1882), correction.

3560. Nouthetéō; from *noús* (3563), mind, and *títhēmi* (5087), to put. To put into the mind, instruct, warn, admonish (Acts 20:31; 1 Cor. 4:14; Col. 1:28; 3:16; 1 Thess. 5:12). To admonish with reproof (Rom. 15:14; 1 Thess. 5:14; 2 Thess. 3:15). See *noéō* (3539), to perceive.

3562. Nounechôs; an adv. from *nounechés*, wise, discreet, which is from *noús* (3563), mind, and *échō* (2192), to have. Wisely, discreetly, sensibly (Mark 12:34). See *phrónimos* (5430), prudently; *sophrónōs* (4996), with sound mind.

3563. Noús; mind; the organ of mental perception and apprehension; the organ of conscious life; the organ of the consciousness preceding actions or recognizing and judging them; the understanding of word, concept, sense (Luke 24:45; Titus 1:15). Deriv.: verb *noéō* (3539), to perceive with the mind, as distinct from perception by feeling; *diánoia* (1271), the faculty of thought, from *dianoéō*, to agitate in the mind. Intellectual faculty, understanding or moral reflection. With an evil significance, a consciousness characterized by a perverted moral impulse, or with a good significance, the faculty renewed by the Holy Spirit. *Diánoia* also means a sentiment, disposition, not as a function but as a product in an evil sense or in a good sense. *Dianóēma* (1270), reflection with machinations; *énnoia* (1771), from *en* (1722), in, and *noús*, mind, meaning an idea, consideration which denotes purpose, intention, design; *nóēma* (3540), thought, a purpose, device of the mind; *epínoia* (1963), a thought by way of evil design; *anóētos* (453), not applying the mind sometimes with moral reproach, contrast *sóphrōn* (4998), self-controlled, one who governs his lusts; *katanoéō* (2657), from the intens. prep. *katá* (2596) and *noéō*, meaning to perceive making it the action of the mind in apprehending certain facts about a thing; *pronoéō* (4306), from *pro* (4253), before, and *noéō*, meaning to perceive, thus to take thought of before, provide; *prónoia* (4307), forethought, providence, provision; *huponoéō* (5282) from *hupo*; (5259), under, and *noéō*, denoting diminution, thus lack of proper knowledge and therefore to suspect, suppose; the noun *hupónoia* (5283), suspicion, surmising; *anoía* (454), without understanding, folly, senselessness (2 Tim. 3:9), violent, mad rage or madness resulting from it.

3576. Nōthrós; slothful, sluggish. It involves inborn sluggishness which makes a person unfit for activities of the mind or spirit (Heb. 5:11; 6:12). Syn: *bradús* (1021), slow; *argós* (692), idle.

3598. Hodós; way, path. A way, a road in which one travels (Matt. 2:12, 8:28; cf. 4:15; 10:5), a journey (Luke 2:44; Acts 1:12; 1 Thess. 3:11); a way, manner of life or action, custom (Acts 14:16; Rom. 3:16; James 1:8; Jude 1:11); particularly with a gen. following, a way leading to, a method or manner of obtaining (Acts 2:28; 16:17; Rom. 3:17, cf. Matt. 21:32; 2 Pet. 2:21); a way or manner of religion (Acts 24:14; cf. 9:2; 19:9, 23; 24:22); the way of the Lord or of God, sometimes denoting the revealed will of God as being shown by God and leading to Him (Matt. 22:16; Acts 13:10; 18:25, 26). The ways of the Lord (in the pl.) signify the directions of His providence in removing impedi-

ments for His reception (Matt. 3:3; Mark 1:2, 3; Luke 1:76); Christ calls Himself "the Way" (John 14:6) because no one comes to the Father in an established state of blessedness but only through Christ. Deriv.: *methodeía* (3180), from *méthodos*, method, the following or pursuing of orderly and technical procedures in the handling of a subject.

3609. Oikeíos; from *oíkos* (3624), a house or household. A person belonging to a certain household (1 Tim. 5:8); a believer, one belonging to the Church, which is the household of God (Gal. 6:10; Eph. 2:19). See *oikétēs* (3610), a household servant.

3610. Oikétēs; from *oikéō* (3611), to dwell in a house. A domestic servant, one of the household or of the family, but not one necessarily born in the house (*oikogenés*); *oiketeía*, a household of servants (Matt. 24:45 UBS). *Oikétēs* does not bring out the servile relation as strongly as does *doúlos* (1401), slave.

3611. Oikéō; from *oíkos* (3624), a dwelling. To dwell, inhabit (Rom. 7:17, 18, 20; 8:9, 11; 1 Cor. 3:16; 1 Tim. 6:16). Deriv.: *sunoikéō* (4924), from *sun* (4862), together with, and *oikéō*, meaning to dwell or cohabit with.

3612. Oíkēma; from *oikéō* (3611), to dwell. A house, a prison (Acts 12:7).

3614. Oikía; a building, house; originally distinguished from *oíkos* (3624), a dwelling. *Oíkos* had a broader range than *oikía*, being the whole of a deceased person's possessions (what he leaves behind), whereas *oikía* is simply his residence. In the NT *oikía* is used literally for house (Matt. 5:15; 7:24ff.; 10:12). Then it came to figuratively mean family, household (Matt. 10:13; 12:25; Mark 6:4). In Mark 10:29 *oikía* denotes the whole family. The word can also mean possessions, one's belongings, for example, in Mark 12:40 the expression "who devour widows' houses (*oikías*)," means appropriating widows' possessions. In Mark 13:35 the expression "the master of the house (*oikías*)" is equivalent to *ho oikodespótēs* (3617) which is commonly translated "the head of the house" (Matt. 24:43). The word *oikía* can also be used figuratively as in John 8:35, referring to the kingdom of God. It does not refer to a ruling house, but simply to a family. In John 14:2 "In my Father's house are many mansions" (or resting places *monaí*, pl. of *monē* [3438]). In 2 Corinthians 5:1–10 the metaphorical *oikía tou skḗnous*, the house of our tabernacle, denotes first the corruptible body which we have on earth. Its counterpart is *oikodomḗ* (3619), a building in process of preparation by God, incorruptible, eternal, a house "from heaven," not "in the heavens," as the KJV has it. In Philippians 4:22, those of the household of Caesar might mean the ruling family with all its members, but more likely the staff of the imperial household, both slaves and freedmen.

3617. Oikodespótēs; from *oíkos* (3624), house, and *despótēs* (1203), lord, despot, master. The master of the house (Matt. 10:25; 20:1, 11; Mark 14:14). Verb: *oikodespotéō* (3616), to govern or manage a household or the domestic affairs of a family (1 Tim. 5:14).

3618. Oikodoméō; from *oíkos* (3624), a house, and *doméō*, to build. To build a house, tower, town, and so forth (Matt. 7:24, 26); to build in a spiritual sense, as the Church (Matt. 16:18), to profit spiritually, to edify (1 Cor. 8:1; 14:4, 17); in the pass. voice, in a bad sense, to be built up, emboldened, encouraged (1 Cor. 8:10). Deriv.: *oikodomḗ* (3619), the act of building, but not used in this sense in the NT, rather used as a building, edifice, edification, spiritual profit or advancement (Eph. 2:22).

3619. Oikodomḗ; from *oikodoméō* (3618), to build. Literally the act of building, building as a process and, hence, also that which is built, the building edifice (Matt. 24:1; Mark 13:1, 2, cf. 1 Cor. 3:9; 2 Cor. 5:1; Eph. 2:21); edification, spiritual profit or advancement (Rom. 14:19; 15:2; 1 Cor. 14:3, 5; 2 Cor. 13:10). Deriv.: *oíkos* (3624), a house, a dwelling; *oikeíos* (3609), belonging to the house, relative; *oikéō* (3611), to dwell; *pároikos* (3941), sojourner; *oikodómos* (3623), one who builds a house or building; *epoikodoméō* (2026), to build upon.

3622. Oikonomía; administration of a house or of property, whether one's own or another's (Luke 16:2–4); a spiritual dispensation, management, or economy (1 Cor. 9:17; Eph. 1:10; 3:2; Col. 1:25). The "dispensation of God" (Col. 1:25 KJV) means the administration of divine grace. Act., the administrative activity of the owner or of the steward; pass., that which is administered, the administration or ordering of the house, the arrangement. "With a view to an administration suitable to the fullness of the times" (Eph. 1:10 NASB), the obj. of *oikonomía*, dispensation, is the relative phrase *hēn proétheto* of translated "which he purposed" (Eph. 1:9 NASB). It is the divine purpose which is said to be administered. The meaning is the administration of God's saving purpose pertaining to the fullness of the times. Therefore, *oikonomía* here is to be taken as pass.

3623. Oikonómos; from *oíkos* (3624), house, and *néomai* or *némō*, to administer. A steward, a person who manages the domestic affairs of a family or a minor, a treasurer, a chamberlain of a city; applies to apostles and ministers of the gospel (1 Cor. 4:1; Titus 1:7), but also to private believers (1 Pet. 4:10). Deriv.: *oikonoméō* (3621), verb, to be a steward; *oikonomía* (3622), stewardship, a spiritual dispensation, management.

3624. Oíkos; a house (Matt. 9:6, 7; 11:8); a household, a family dwelling in a house (Luke 19:9; Acts 10:2; 1 Cor. 1:16); a family, lineage (Luke 1:27; 2:4); the house (of God) denotes either the material temple at Jerusalem (Matt. 21:13; John 2:17) or the household of God's people, all who belong to Him (Heb. 3:2, 3, 5). See *oikia* (3614), a dwelling.

3625. Oikouménē; from *oikéō* (3611), to inhabit, the inhabited or habitable earth or world (Matt. 24:14; Rom. 10:18); the inhabitants of the world; the Roman Empire (Acts 11:28); a particular inhabited country (Luke 2:1; Acts 11:28); that area where the seven churches of Asia Minor were situated (Rev. 3:10); the world (Heb. 2:5); the state of the world under the Messiah or the kingdom of the Messiah. This is the word from which the Eng. word "ecumenical" is derived.

3626. Oikourós; from *oíkos* (3624), a house, and *ourós*, a keeper. A keeper at home, one who looks after domestic affairs with prudence and care (Titus 2:5).

3631. Oínos; wine derived from grapes. The mention of the bursting of the wine skins in Matthew 9:17; Mark 2:22; Luke 5:37 implies fermentation. (See Eph. 5:18, cf. John 2:10; 1 Tim. 3:8; Titus 2:3.) From the intoxicating effects of wine and the idolatrous use of it among the heathen, wine signifies communion in the intoxicating idolatries of the mystic Babylon (Rev. 14:8, cf. Jer. 51:7). From the Jewish custom of giving a cup of medicated wine to condemned criminals just before their execution to dull their senses, it figuratively denotes the dreadful judgments of God upon sinners (Rev. 14:10; 16:19, cf. Is. 51:17, 21, 23; Jer. 25:15). The drinking of wine could be a stumblingblock and Paul enjoins abstinence in this respect, as in others, so as to avoid giving an occasion of stumbling to a brother (Rom. 14:21). Contrast 1 Timothy 5:23 which has an entirely different connection. (Cf. the word *gleúkos* [1098], sweet, new wine, and *síkera* [4608], strong drink.)

3639. Ólethros; from *óllumi*, to ruin. Ruin, destruction (1 Cor. 5:5; 1 Thess. 5:3; 2 Thess. 1:9; 1 Tim. 6:9). The verb as such does not occur, but the comp. *apóllumi* (622), to destroy, does. The fundamental thought is not by any means annihilation, but perhaps corruption, an injurious force, which the subj. exerts or cannot hinder.

3640. Oligópistos; from *olígos* (3641), little, and *pístis* (4102), faith. Of little faith, having but little faith (Matt. 6:30; 8:26; 14:31; 16:8; Luke 12:28). Deriv.: *pistós* (4103), a believer.

3642. Oligópsuchos; from *olígos* (3641), small or little, and *psuchē* (5590), soul, mind. Feebleminded or weak-headed. Only in 1 Thessalonians 5:14.

3648. Holóklēros; from *hólos* (3650), all, the whole, and *klēros* (2819), a part, share. Whole, having all its parts, sound, perfect. That which retains all which was allotted to it at the first, wanting nothing for its completeness; bodily, mental and moral entireness. It expresses the perfection of man before the Fall (1 Thess. 5:23; James 1:4). The subst. *holoklēría* (3647), soundness (Acts 3:16). Related to *téleios* (5049), perfect, and *ártios* (739), with all its needed parts. The *holóklēros* is one who has preserved, or who, having once lost has now regained his completeness. In the *holóklēros*, no grace which ought to be in a Christian man is deficient.

3650. Hólos; whole, used as a demonstrative pron. (Matt. 5:29; James 2:10). To say "the whole," the noun must have the def. art., and *hólos* is to be placed in the position of predicate. It is declined as a mas. noun such as *ánthrōpos* (444), man; for example, *hólon to thérōs*, the whole summer. It can also be expressed with *hólon* at the end, as *to theros hólon*, the summer, all of it.

3651. Holotelés; from *hólos* (3650), all, the whole, and *teléō* (5055), to complete. All or the whole, completely or entirely (1 Thess. 5:23). Deriv.: see *télos* (5056).

3664. Hómoios; like, similar. It denotes coincidence in kind or quality, while *ísos* (2470), equal, refers primarily to quantity. In the NT, it means of the same kind, like. The two commandments which form the sum of the law, as on a par with each other (Matt. 22:38, 39; Mark 12:31). In Galatians 5:21, after a list of the works of the flesh, it denotes the rest that are of the same kind.

3667. Homoíōma; or *homoíōsis* (3669), likeness, resemblance (Rom. 1:23; 5:14; 6:5; 8:3; Phil. 2:7; Rev. 9:7). While there is resemblance, it by no means follows that one thing has been derived from the other. Therefore a resemblance may exist between two men who are in no way related to one another. See *eikōn* (1504), image.

3668. Hómoiōs; adv., in like manner, likewise (Matt. 22:26; Mark 4:16; Luke 3:11; 10:37; John 6:11; 1 Cor. 7:3, 4).

3669. Homoíōsis; likeness (only in James 3:9). In its distinction from *eikōn* (1504), image.

3670. Homoiogéō; from *homoú*, together with, or *hómoios* (3664), like, and *lógos* (3056). thoughtful word, speech. To accent, consent, as used commonly in Class. Gr.; to promise, that is, to speak the same with or consent to the desire of another (Matt. 14:7); to confess, that is, to speak agreeable to fact and truth (John 1:20; 9:22; 12:42; Acts 23:8; Heb. 11:13; 1 John 1:9); to confess, celebrate with public praises (Heb. 13:15); to confess, profess (Matt. 7:23; Titus 1:16); *homologéō en* (in or with), meaning to confess or publicly acknowledge anyone (Matt. 10:32; Luke 12:8). Deriv.: *ellogéō* (1677), to charge, impute; *homologfa* (3671), agreement, understanding, confession; *homologoúmenōs* (3672), adv., confessedly or in reality.

3671. Homología; from *homologéō* (3670), to say the same thing. A confession, profession or recognition. In Hebrews 3:1 Christ is called the chief priest of our confession. Used also in 2 Corinthians 9:13; Hebrews 10:23. Used absolutely, meaning confession of Christ and to Christ (1 Tim. 6:12, 13; Heb. 4:14, cf. Rom. 10:10), also as a vow, especially in the Sept.

3672. Homologoúmenōs; from *homologéō* (3670), to say the same thing. Confessedly (1 Tim. 3:16).

3686. Ónoma; from *ónēmi*, to help, or from *némō*, to attribute. A name (Matt. 1:21, 23; 10:2; Mark 14:32; Luke 1:26); character described by the name (Matt. 10:41, 42, cf. Matt. 24:5; Mark 13:6; Luke 21:8); fame, reputation (Mark 6:14); implying authority, dignity (Eph. 1:21; Phil. 2:9); name as the substitute or representative of a person, hence *ónoma* is used for the person himself, whether divine (Matt. 6:9; John 1:12; 2:23; 3:18; Rom. 15:9; Heb. 13:15) or human (Acts 1:15; Rev. 3:4; 11:13). It gives importance to the confession of a name, or for the sake of the person so confessed (Matt. 10:22; 19:29; 24:9, cf. 18:5; Mark 9:37; Acts

4:17), so to be baptized into (*eis* [1519]) someone's name means to be baptized into the faith or confession of that person and to be identified with his character and purpose (Matt. 28:19; Acts 2:38; 8:16; 10:48). It also refers to delegated power and authority (Matt. 7:22; Mark 16:17; Luke 10:17; Acts 3:6, cf. 3:16; 4:7, 10, 12, cf. Eph. 1:21; Phil. 2:9). The promise in John 14:13, "Whatsoever ye shall ask in my name, that will I do," means He will do, not simply what we ask, but whatever is conformable to His character and to His purpose.

3708. Horáō; to see, behold; of bodily vision (John 1:18); of mental perception (Col. 2:18); of taking heed (Matt. 8:4; 1 Thess. 5:15) but not with as great attention as *blépō* (991). Noun: *hórasis* (3706), the act of seeing, vision (Acts 2:17; Rev. 4:3; 9:17); *hórama* (3705), that which is seen (Acts 7:31). Deriv.: *aphoráō* (872), from *apo;* (575), from, and *horáō*, to look away from one thing so as to see another (Phil. 2:23; Heb. 12:2); *epopteúō* (2029), to observe, from *epí* (1909), upon, and a form of *horáō* (1 Pet. 2:12; 3:2); *epóptēs* (2030), noun, one who looks on (2 Pet. 1:16), used of one witnessing as a spectator, or overseer.

3709. Orgé; from *orégomai* (3713), to desire eagerly or earnestly. Wrath, anger as a state of mind. Contrast *thumós* (2372), indignation, wrath as an outburst of that state of mind with the purpose of revenge. Aristotle says *orgē* is desire with grief, cf. Mark 3:5. The Stoics considered it as a desire to punish one who seems to have hurt them in a manner he ought not. The anger, wrath of man (Eph. 4:31; Col. 3:8; James 1:19, 20), or of God (Heb. 3:11; 4:3); the effect of anger or wrath, that is, punishment, from man (Rom. 13:4, 5) or from God (Rom. 2:5; 3:5; Eph. 5:6; 1 Thess. 1:10; 5:9). Deriv.: *orgízō* (3710), to provoke to anger, irritate, *orgilos* (3711), prone to anger, passionate.

3715. Órexis; appetite, lust, concupiscence (Rom. 1:27). It always involves reaching out after and toward an object with the purpose of drawing it to oneself and appropriating it.

3717. Orthos; from *oró*, to excite. Straight, erect, upright. To stand straight up from a prostrate position (Acts 14:10). In Hebrews 12:13, in a moral sense, straight (as opposed to crooked), meaning upright, true, right, good. Syn.: *alēthinós* (228), truthful; *díkaios* (1342), just.

3718. Orthotoméō; from *órthos* (3717), right, and *témnō*, to cut or divide. Only in 2 Timothy 2:15, meaning rightly dividing.

3724. Horízō; from *hóros* (3735), boundary. To set a boundary, put limits to. Transferred from relations of space to those of time, it means to determine the time (Acts 17:26; Heb. 4:7). To establish, determine (Acts 11:29), to resolve, to decree (Luke 22:22; Acts 2:23). Determining that one is something or that one is to be something (Acts 10:42; 17:31).

3730. Hormé; from *hormáō* (3729), to rush violently or impetuously. Purpose and intention of assault or onset, only in Acts 14:5; James 3:4. *Hormé* oftentimes is the whole style of motion and springing toward an object with the purpose of propelling it still farther from itself. Contrast *órexis* (3715), translated as lust or concupiscence, from *orégomai* (3713), to covet after, desire, which is always the reaching out after and toward an object with the purpose of appropriation.

3741. Hósios; holy, righteous, unpolluted with wickedness. Often grouped with *díkaios* (1342), righteous, just (Titus 1:8) or its corresponding derivative. It cannot be ascertained that *ho;sios* (Acts 2:27; Heb. 7:26) refers to the one who is holy unto God and *díkaios* (Luke 1:6; Rom. 1:17; 1 John 2:1) to the one who is righteous toward his fellow men. The Scriptures recognize that all righteousness has one root, that is, one's relationship to God. Our righteousness toward men is rooted in our relationship to God. *Hierós* (2413), holy, is related to *hósios*, both referring to the ordinances of right which no law or custom of men has constituted. They rest on the divine constitution of the moral universe and man's relation to this. *Hósios* is one who reveres these everlasting sanctities and

recognizes the duty for such reverence. *Hósios* is the performer of the ordinances, but not necessarily *hágios* (40), holy in character. Deriv.: *hosíōs* (3743), adv., piously; *díkaiōs* (1346), righteously (1 Thess. 2:10); *hosiótēs* (3742), subst., holiness (Luke 1:75; Eph. 4:24); *dikaiosúnē* (1343), righteousness. Ant.: *anósios* (462), one who misses the ordinances of right (1 Tim. 1:9; 2 Tim. 3:2).

3742. Hosiótēs; related to *hósios* (3741), holy. Holiness manifesting itself in the discharge of pious duties in religious and social life. Twice in the NT joined with *dikaiosúnē* (1343), righteousness (Luke 1:75; Eph. 4:24). *Hosiótēs* is related more to the keeping of ordinances than to the character of life (*hagiótēs* [41]) which denotes the spirit and conduct of one who is joined in fellowship with God. Later *hosiótēs* was used as an ecclesiastical title or term of respect.

3748. Hóstis; *hētis* fem., *hóti* neut., derived from *hos* (3739), he who, and *tis* (5101), anyone, someone (Acts 3:23; Heb. 8:5, 6). The meaning of *hóstis* is virtually the same as the basic relative pron., *hos*, or the indef. pron., *tis.*

3754. Hóti; a conj. meaning that, for, because. When used to introduce a quotation, it is usually not translated. This is called *hóti* recitative and is equivalent (in Eng.) to quotation marks. For example, *humeís légete hóti* (introducing a direct quotation) *blasphēmeís hóti eipon Huiós tou; Theou; eimí* (John 10:36). The translation of these words is, "Say ye . . ., 'Thou blasphemest,' because I said 'I am the Son of God?'" Observe that, in the translation, in each instance of the introduction by *hóti* of a direct statement, that direct statement begins with a capital letter. *Hóti*, when introducing dependent clauses or indirect statements, will be translated "that." For example, *ginōskō* (1097) *hóti prophḗtēs* (4396) *estí* (2076) is translated "I know that he is a prophet." The *hóti* in that clause introduces an indirect statement. *Hóti* is used causally corresponding to the English word "because" (cf., the second *hóti* in John 10:36 above).

3762. Oudeís; made up of *ou* (3756), not, and *heís* (1520), one. Not even one, not the least, not a one (Mark 2:21; Luke 22:35). When it is used in the neut., *oudén*, it means "nothing" or "not a thing." *Oudeís* is used with the indic., but with the other moods (the imper., the subjunctive, and the inf.), *mēdeís* (3367) is used.

3770. Ouránios; from *ouranós* (3772), heaven, especially of the gods, heavenly. In the NT a heavenly host of angels (Luke 2:13); a heavenly vision (Acts 26:19). The expression "heavenly Father" occurs only in Matthew 6:14, 26, 32; 15:13; 18:35; 23:9.

3772. Ouranós; heaven. The sing. and pl. are used similarly and interchangeably. There is no difference in meaning between them. In the NT it means, in a physical sense, the whole expanse of the sky beneath which is the earth and all that is therein. In this not only do the fowls of the air fly (Matt. 6:26; 8:20; 13:32), but the clouds are supported (Matt. 24:30; 26:64; Luke 12:56), the rain is formed (James 5:18); the sun, moon and stars are placed in the same celestial expanse (Mark 13:25; Heb. 11:12). *Ouranós* also is used for that heaven where the residence of God is called by the Psalmist "the holy heaven," or "heaven of holiness," of separation (Ps. 20:6). It is God's dwelling or resting place (Matt. 5:34, 45, 48), where the blessed angels are (Mark 13:32), whence Christ descended (John 3:13, 31; 6:32, 33, 38), where after His resurrection and ascension "He sitteth at the right hand of the majesty on high" (Heb. 8:1) and appears in the presence of God for us (Heb. 9:24), and where a reward is reserved for the righteous (Matt. 5:12; 1 Pet. 1:4). The term "the heavens" is used as a name of God in the OT (2 Chr. 32:20, cf. 2 Kgs. 19:15; Is. 37:15, 16; Dan. 4:23, 26). *Ouranós*, heaven, is used with the same sense in the NT (Matt. 21:25; Mark 11:30, 31; Luke 15:18, 21; 20:4, 5; John 3:27). Thus the kingdom of the heavens, or heaven, is syn. with the kingdom of God (Matt. 19:23, 24). In 2 Corinthians 12:2 Paul was raptured to the third heaven and returned. This third heaven is called "paradise" (v. 4), which is applied to the state of the faithful souls between death and the resurrection, where they are admitted to immediate communion with God in Christ or to a participation in the true Tree of Life which is in the midst of the paradise of God (Luke 23:43; Rev. 2:7). There is a final heaven which, in Hebrews 11:16, is referred to as a better country; in Hebrews 13:14, as a continuing city; in Revelation 21:2, as the holy city, the new Jerusalem. This eternal heaven is also called a country that is heavenly (Heb. 11:16). It is the place where the believers are going to receive their incorruptible inheritance (1 Pet. 3:5). See also Matthew 6:19, 20; 1 Corinthians 2:9; Colossians 3:2; Revelation 21:1–5. Deriv.: *ouránios* (3770), heavenly; *epouránios* (2032), heavenly, what pertains to or is in heaven.

3781. Opheilétēs; from *opheílō* (3784), to owe. A debtor, one who is indebted to another (Matt. 18:24); a debtor, one who is obliged to do something (Rom. 1:14; 8:12; Gal. 5:3); an offender, a trespasser, one who is a debtor or obliged either to render reparation or suffer punishment (Matt. 6:12; Luke 13:4). Deriv.: *opheílēma* (3783), debt.

3782. Opheilē; a debt which must be paid (Matt. 18:32); obligation, a service which one owes another (Rom. 13:7; 1 Cor. 7:3). Only in NT. Gr. Deriv.: *opheilétē* (3781), debtor.

3783. Opheílēma; debt, that which is owed, which is strictly due (Rom. 4:4). Also an offense, a trespass which makes reparation obligatory (Matt. 6:12) The suffix *-ma* makes *opheílēma* that which is owed and makes it syn. with *opheilē* (3782), a debt. Deriv.: *opheílō* (3784), to owe; *opheilétēs* (3781), debtor.

3784. Opheílō; ought to, must; to owe out of moral or personal obligation (John 13:14; Eph. 5:28). Contrast *deí* (1163), must, to owe out of intrinsic necessity.

3787. Ophthalmodouleía; from *ophthalmós*, eye, and *douleía* (1397), service. Eyeservice, implying a mere outward service only, to falsify the eye of man (Eph. 6:6; Col. 3:22).

3793. Óchlos; a multitude, disorganized or unorganized mob (Matt. 21:8; Luke 9:38; Acts 14:14). Related words: *laós* (2992), people, usually referring to Israel; *éthnos* (1484), a heathen nation; *dēmos* (1218), an organized assembly of people.

3800. Opsónion; from *ópson*, meat, and *ōnéomai*, to buy. Primarily signifying whatever is bought to be eaten with bread, provisions, supplies for a soldier's pay (1 Cor. 9:7). See Luke 3:14; Romans 6:23; 2 Corinthians 11:8.

3804. Páthēma; from *páschō* (3958), to suffer. The suffix *-ma* makes it that which is suffered. Suffering, affliction (Rom. 8:18; 2 Cor. 1:5; Col. 1:24; Heb. 2:9). In this last verse, the sufferings of saints are called the sufferings of Christ because they are endured for Christ's sake and in conformity to His suffering (cf. 2 Cor. 4:10; Phil. 3:10; 1 Pet. 4:13). A passion, an affection (Rom. 7:5; Gal. 5:24). In this latter passage, *pathēmata* (pl.), passions or affections, denotes bad passions as equivalent to *epithumíai* (1939), desires.

3805. Pathētós; from *patheō* or *pēthō*, to bruise, wound, hurt, suffer; or from *páschō* (3958), to suffer, to undergo pain, inconvenience or punishment. One who can suffer, who should suffer, or one having suffered, as in Acts 26:23 where it must be understood in this sense (cf. Luke 24:26, 27). See *páthēma* (3804), suffering.

3806. Páthos; from *pēthō*, to wound, hurt, to suffer. *Páthos* is the soul's diseased condition out of which the various lusts spring. *Epithumía* is the active lust or desire springing from the diseased soul while *páthos* is the condition. *Páthos* occurs three times in the NT; once coordinated with *epithumía* (1939), desire (Col. 3:5), once subordinated to it, *páthos epithumías*, the lust of desire (1 Thess. 4:5), and in the third reference vile affections (Rom. 1:26). These are lusts that dishonor those who indulge in them.

3807. Paidagōgós; from *país* (3816), a child, and *agogós*, a leader (which in turn is derived from *ágō* [71], to lead). An instructor or teacher of children, a schoolmaster, a pedagogue (1 Cor. 4:15; Gal. 3:24, 25). Originally referred to the slave who conducted the

boys from home to the school. Then it came to denote a teacher or an educator. The ancient Greeks regarded a philosopher as a teacher, but not necessarily as *paidagōgós*.

3809. Paideía; from *país* (3816), a child, originally instruction of children. It evolved to mean chastening because all effectual instruction for the sinful children of men includes and implies chastening, correction. *Paideía* occurs with *epanórthōsis* (1882), rectification, in 2 Timothy 3:16. In *paideía* there is discipline. See *nouthesía* (3559), instruction mainly by word, while *paideía* is by deed.

3810. Paideutés; from *paideúō* (3811), to instruct, correct, chastise. An instructor (Rom. 2:20); a corrector, a chastiser (Heb. 12:9).

3811. Paideúō; derived from *país* (3816), a child. Originally to bring up a child, to educate. Used of activity directed toward the moral and spiritual nurture and training of the child, to influence conscious will and action. To instruct, particularly a child or youth (Acts 7:22; 22:3; 2 Tim. 2:25, cf. Titus 2:12); to instruct by chastisement (1 Tim. 1:20); to correct, chastise (Luke 23:16, 22; 1 Cor. 11:32; 2 Cor. 6:9). In a religious sense, to chastise in order to educate someone to conform to divine truth.

3816. País; a child, in relation to descent; a boy or girl, in relation to age; a manservant, attendant, maid, in relation to condition. Contrast *paidískē* (3814), a maidservant. Used of spiritual service to the God of Israel (Luke 1:54); of David (Luke 1:69; Acts 4:25); of Christ, so declared by God the Father (Matt. 12:18).

3819. Pálai; an adv. of time signifying the past in contrast with the present. Meaning in the past, long ago, of olden times, formerly, also much longer ago in contrast with what has just occurred or just appeared. Note the distinction between what is over and gone, passed away, and what has existed for a long time. *Pálai* in reality means old, what lies behind (Heb. 1:1). In 2 Peter 1:9 what is designated as old sins (*pálai*) does not mean as having taken place in the past but as belonging to a past which, in consequence of the cleansing, is over and gone. This differs from Romans 3:25, where the sins are called previous, *progegonótōn* (4266), and refer to what is past, not indeed long ago, but nevertheless already past for some time (Mark 15:44). *Pálai* may also mean a great while, now for a long while (Matt. 11:21; Luke 10:13).

3820. Palaiós; old, both of what had been formerly, and of what is of long standing. The OT (*hē palaiá diathēkē*) referred to in 2 Corinthians 3:14 means, "the covenant which was for a long time." In the Pauline Epistles, *ho palaiós ánthrōpos*, the old man, is the antithesis of *kainós* (2537), qualitatively new (Eph. 4:22, 24). Here a reference to the past cannot be directly denied. The expression "our old man" in Romans 6:6, denotes what we formerly were. See *archaíos* (744), one who has been from the beginning. *Palaiós* is not necessarily from the beginning but merely old.

3821. Palaiótēs; age, antiquity, length of time, existing a long time. Used only in Romans 7:6, referring to the oldness of the letter of the law as compared to the newness of the Spirit. As the Spirit comes in the place of the letter, the letter (in relation to the Spirit) is something belonging to the past. The letter therefore has no longer any right to prominence because it belongs to a time now past and gone (cf. Heb. 8:13).

3822. Palaióō; from *palaiós* (3820), old. In the act., to make old (Heb. 8:13). In the pass., to grow old, *palaioómai* or *palaioumai* (Luke 12:33; Heb. 1:11).

3824. Paliggenesía; from *pálin* (3825), again, and *gínomai* (1096), to become. Recovery, renovation, a new birth. Occurs in Matthew 19:28 which refers to the coming state of the whole creation, equivalent to the restoration of all things (Acts 3:21), which will occur when the Son of Man shall come in His glory. The washing of *paliggenesía* (Titus 3:5) refers to the regeneration of the individual soul. See *anagennáō* (313), to beget again.

3831. Panéguris; from *pan*, the neut. of *pas* (3956) any, all, and *águris*, an assembly (derived from *ageírō*, to assemble). A solemn assembly for purposes of festal rejoicing, and on this account it is found joined continually with *heortḗ* (1859), feast. Occurs only in Hebrews 12:23. Distinguished from *ekklēsía* (1577), church, and *sunagōgḗ* (4864), synagogue.

3838. Pantelḗs; from *pan*, the neut. of *pas* (3956), any, all, and *télos* (5056), end. Complete; in the expression *eis* ([1519], unto) *to pantelés* (neut.), unto the completion, completely (Heb. 7:25); at all, in any wise (Luke 13:11). Deriv.: see *télos* (5056).

3844. Pará; a prep. governing the gen., dat., and acc., with the primary meaning of near, nearby; expressing thus the relation of immediate vicinity or proximity, which is differently modified according to the force of the different cases. After verbs of motion, as of coming, sending, it has the meaning of "from" or "out from" (Luke 6:19; John 6:46). With the gen. of persons it denotes the source, author, director, from whom anything proceeds or is derived (Matt. 21:42). With the dat. both of person and thing, it expresses rest or position, near, hard by, with; with a dat. pl. it means among. With the acc. it expresses motion, nearby, or near to a place. It means by the side of anything or alongside when it is used after verbs of motion. Sometimes it expresses movement to a place, near to, to, at, after verbs of motion, and so it is equivalent to *pros* (4314) or *eis* (1519) with the acc. (Matt. 15:29, "he came near to the sea"). Sometimes it also expresses the idea of rest or remaining near a place, nearby, at, with the dat. Here, however, the idea of previous motion or coming to the place is strictly implied. Contrast *eis* (1519) where it is not implied. Metaphorically, *pará* is used of the ground or reason by or along with which a conclusion follows, by reason of, because of (1 Cor. 12:15, 16). Related meanings: (1) Motion by or past a place, that is, a passing by, going beyond. Aside from or contrary to, against (Acts 18:13). (2) Besides, in the sense of except, save, or falling short (2 Cor. 11:24, where it means forty stripes except one, or falling short of one). (3) Past, in the sense of beyond, besides, more than (Heb. 11:11) past the proper age. In composition *pará-* used as a prefix implies nearness, proximity, nearby, as *para-kathízō* (3869), to sit down near, motion or direction near to, to, or by, as *parabállō* (3846), to throw alongside, to compare, motion by or past any place, a going beyond, as *parérchomai* (3928), I go beyond. It also refers to whatever swerves from the true point, comes short of it, goes beyond it, like the Eng. prefix "mis-" meaning wrongly, falsely (*parakoúō* [3878], to disobey), or like the prefix "trans-" in transgress (*parabaínō* [3845]).

3845. Parabaínō; from *pará* (3844), beyond, and *baínō*, to go. To step on one side, and translated "to transgress, violate." In the NT it always has a moral sense (Matt. 15:2, 3; 2 John 1:9). To fall from or lose one's station or office by transgression (Acts 1:25). *Parabaínō*, transgress, has more of the guilt of willful stepping out of line than *parapíptō* (3895), which is not stepping out of line but falling off.

3846. Parabállō; from *pará* (3844), near, and *bállō* (906), to cast, put. To cast or put near. As a term of navigation to arrive or touch at, properly, to bring a ship or ships near or close (Acts 20:15). To compare (Mark 4:30). Deriv.: *bállō* (906), to cast, place, throw; *parabolḗ* (3850), parable.

3847. Parábasis; transgression, an act which is excessive. The *parábasis* as the transgression of a commandment distinctly given is more serious than *hamartía* (266), sin (Rom. 2:23; 1 Tim. 2:14).

3848. Parabátēs; transgressor of the law; used with reference to the imputation of sin so far as it is transgression of known law, deviation from recognized truth (Rom. 2:25, 27; Gal. 2:18; James 2:9, 11). Syn.: *parábasis* (3847), transgression, trespassing; *paráptōma* (3900), fault, mistake, neglect.

3850. Parabolḗ; from *parabállō*. The following meanings are to be distinguished: (1) A comparison, similitude, or simile in which one thing is compared with another (Mark 4:10); particularly spiritual things with natural,

by which means such spiritual things are better understood and make the deeper impression on the honest and attentive hearer while simultaneously they are concealed from the gross, carnal, and inattentive. See Matthew 13:3 (cf. vv. 9, 11, 15; 24:32). (2) Because these comparisons have an obscurity in their very nature, the word is used to denote a speech or maxim which is obscure to the person who hears it even though it contains no comparison (Matt. 15:15; Mark 7:17). (3) Since short parables or comparisons often grow into proverbs, or proverbs often imply a simile or comparison, the word denotes a proverb or by-word (Luke 4:23). (4) It is by some interpreted to mean merely a special doctrine or a weighty, memorable speech (Matt. 22:1; Luke 14:7; 19:11). (5) A visible type of emblem representing something different from and beyond itself (Heb. 9:9). The Mosaic tabernacle with its services was a parable, a type, emblem, or figurative representation of the good things of Christianity.

3852. Paraggelía; from *pará* (3844) an intens. prep., and *aggelía* (31), message. A proclamation, command (Acts 5:28; 16:24). The noun corresponds to the verb *paraggéllō* (3853), to command, charge, as by the apostles (1 Thess. 4:2; 1 Tim. 1:5, 18).

3853. Paraggéllō; from *pará* (3844), beside, and *aggéllō* (31), to announce. To pass on an announcement, hence to give a word, an order, a charge, a command (Mark 6:8; Luke 8:29; 9:21; Acts 5:28; 2 Thess. 3:4, 6, 10, 12). Deriv.: *paraggelía* (3852), a proclamation, strictly used of commands received from a superior and transmitted to others .

3858. Paradéchomai; from *pará* (3844), at or to, and *déchomai* (1209), to receive. In the NT, to receive, admit (Acts 16:21; 1 Tim. 5:19), to receive, embrace with assent and obedience (Mark 4:20; Acts 22:18); to receive or embrace with peculiar favor (Heb. 12:6, which is a citation from the Sept. version of Prov. 3:12).

3861. Parádoxos; from *pará* (3844), beyond, and *dóxa* (1391), opinion, expectation. Something beyond one's expectation, a miracle. In Luke 5:26, used to express new things, miracles not hitherto seen, and thus beside and beyond all opinion and expectation of men. Related words: *sēmeía* (4592), signs; *dunámeis* (1411), miracles; *megaleía* (3167), magnificent things; *éndoxa* (1741), glorious things *thaumásia* (2297), wonderful things; *térata* (5059), terrifying things.

3868. Paraitéomai; from *pará* (3844), an intens. prep., and *aitéō* (154), to ask or beg. Never used in the act. sense, but only in the mid. voice, to try to obtain by asking, to beg a person's release (the person addressed being regarded as reluctant to agree or the thing asked for difficult to obtain). It then came to mean to beg to be excused, to decline, or refuse the thing spoken of. In the NT, to decline, refuse, avoid, with acc. following (Acts 25:11; 1 Tim. 4:7; 5:11; 2 Tim. 2:23; Titus 3:10; Heb. 12:25). With *mē* (3361), not, following with the inf. (Heb. 12:19), to excuse oneself (see also Luke 14:18, 19, used as an inf. and followed by a part. adj.).

3870. Parakaléō; from *pará* (3844), by the side, and *kaléō*, to call (2564); to call to one's side, hence aid (Mark 1:40; 1 Pet. 2:11). Used for every kind of calling to a person which is intended to produce a particular effect; comfort, exhort, desire, call for, beseech, with a stronger force than *aitéō* (154). Deriv.: *paráklēsis* (3874), a calling to one's side and aid, hence, an appeal (2 Cor. 8:4), an encouragement, exhortation (Acts 4:36; Rom. 12:8), consolation, comfort (Rom. 15:4); *paráklētos* (3875), one called to one's side and aid, counsel for the defense, an advocate, comforter; *sumparakaléō* (4837), with, *sun* (4862), together, to comfort together (Rom. 1:12).

3874. Paráklēsis; from *parakaléō* (3870). The act of calling toward or hither to help, begging, and also of exhortation, encouragement toward virtue. The entire Scripture is actually a *paráklēsis*, an exhortation, admonition or encouragement for the purpose of strengthening and establishing the believer's possession of redemption (see Rom. 15:4; also Phil. 2:1;

Heb. 12:5; 13:22, the purpose of which is to strengthen faith). Paul speaks of his preaching of the gospel as *paráklēsis* in 2 Corinthians 8:4, 17; also 1 Thessalonians 2:2. The contents of the letter addressed to the church at Antioch from the apostolic council in Jerusalem is described as *paráklēsis* in Acts 15:31. Comforting words, consolation (Acts 9:31; 2 Thess. 2:16; Phile. 1:7). Opposite of tribulation and sufferings in 2 Corinthians 7:4 and joined with joy in 2 Corinthians 7:7, 13 (see also 2 Cor. 1:3–7). In Luke 6:24, used to designate the comfort in heaven to be denied the selfish, rich Christians who preferred to have their physical comfort on earth to the detriment of Christ's work. See the Beatitudes and woes in Luke 6:20–26. In Luke 2:25 the Messiah is described as the consolation of Israel, which refers to the proclamation of salvation belonging to the department of prophesying (1 Cor. 14:3) and appearing as a special gift (*chárisma* [5486]) in Rom. 12:8. In Acts 4:36 Barnabas is called "son of consolation," referring to his prophetic gift manifested especially in the exercise of comforting others. In connection with Acts 13:15; 1 Timothy 4:13, *paráklēsis* was regarded as based on the reading of a portion of Scripture (Luke 4:20, 21, an expository application of the prophetic word), although this was by no means the whole.

3875. Paráklētos; from *parakaléō* (3870), to call hither, toward, or to speak to, to speak cheerfully to, encourage. It is properly a verbal adj., that is, he who has been or may be called to help, a helper. Used in the Gr. writers of a legal advisor, pleader, proxy, or advocate, one who comes forward on behalf of and as the representative of another. Thus in 1 John 2:1, Christ is termed our substitutionary, intercessory advocate. Christ designates the Holy Spirit as "Paraclete" (John 14:16), and He calls Him *állos* (243), another, which means another of equal quality (and not *héteros* [2087], another of a different quality). Therefore, the Holy Spirit is designated by Jesus Christ as equal with Himself, God (1 John 2:1). This new Paraclete, the Holy Spirit, was to witness concerning Jesus Christ (John 14:26; 16:7, 14) and to glorify Him. The Holy Spirit is called a Paraclete because He undertakes Christ's office in the world while Christ is away from the world as the God-Man. He is also called the Paraclete because He acts as Christ's substitute on earth. When Christ, in John 14:16, designates Himself at the same time as the Paraclete, the word must not be understood as applying to Christ in the same sense as in 1 John 2:1, where it is used with the meaning of our substitutionary Advocate, but rather as He who pleads God's cause with us (see John 14:7–9). The verb *parakaléō* (3870) and the noun *paráklēsis* (3874) do not occur at all in the writings of John.

3876. Parakoé; in its strictest sense a failing to hear (*akoúo* [191]), or hearing amiss; with the notion of active disobedience which follows this inattentive or careless hearing (cf. Rom. 5:19; 2 Cor. 10:6; Heb. 2:2).

3887. Paraménō; from *pará* (3844), with, and *ménō* (3306), to remain. To stay, abide (1 Cor. 16:6; James 1:25), to remain alive (Heb. 7:23).

3892. Paranomía; from *paranoméō* (3891), which in turn is from *pará* (3844), beyond, and *nómos* (3551), a law. A transgression or an offense of the law, occurring only in 2 Peter 2:16. The verb *paranoméō* occurs in Acts 23:3. Syn.: *anomía* (458), lawlessness, without conformity to the law. It follows that where there is no law (Rom. 5:13), there may be *hamartía* (266), sin or missing the mark or standard which God has set up, and *adikía* (93), what God expects as a right from us, but not *anomía*, lawlessness, or *paranomía*, transgression or going beyond the law. Paul means in Romans 5:13 that *hamartía* as *anomía*, sin as lawlessness, cannot be if there exists no law to transgress. Thus, the Gentiles, not having a law (Rom. 2:14), could be charged with sin; but they, sinning without law (Rom. 2:12; 3:21), could not be charged with *anomía*, lawlessness, or *paranomía*, transgression. It is true that behind the Law of Moses which the Gentiles did

not have, there is another law, the original law and revelation of the righteousness of God written on the hearts of all (Rom. 2:14, 15). Since in no human heart is this original law totally obliterated, all sin, even that of the most ignorant savage, must still in a secondary sense remain as *anomía* or *paranomía*, a violation of this older, though partially obscured, law.

3895. Parapíptō; from *pará* (3844), either an intens. prep. or meaning by the side of, and *píptō* (4098), to fall. To fall beside, to fall down inadvertently. Used only in Hebrews 6:6 denoting a falling and not conscious and deceitful faithless action, blameworthy and willful carelessness and falling into sin (as would be expressed by *parabainō* [3845], to willfully transgress). Deriv.: *paráptōma* (3900), transgression.

3900. Paráptōma; fault. Sometimes used in profane Gr. when it is intended to designate a sin not of the deepest nature nor of the worst enormity. In the NT it means purposely stepping over. *Paráptōma* occurs only in Paul's writings, except for Matthew 6:14, 15; 18:35; Mark 11:25f.; James 5:16, and is often used where pardon is spoken of in Galatians 6:1. It is here translated "fault," indicating a sin involving guilt, a missing of the mark rather than a transgression of the law. Refers to a particular form of sin. Therefore, *paráptōma* has come to be used both of great and serious guilt and generally of all sin, unknown and unintentional (Ps. 19:13; Gal. 6:1). This is simply a missing of that which is right, involving little guilt; therefore, it is a missing or failure including the activity and passivity of the acting subj. In Romans 5:16, it is given as the antithesis of *dikaíōma* (1345), righteousness or justification, or an acquittal from past offences and ability to exercise the right of a child toward God as the legitimate Father (Rom. 5:18). *Paráptōma*, therefore, may be equated to defeat. Like its verb, *parapíptō* (3895), it is used syn. with *hamartía* (266) as the generic word for sin. In Romans 5:20 *paráptōma* is used as the missing of the mark (*hamartía*) and includes both *hamartía* and *parábasis* (3847), transgression. Occurs also in Romans 5:15, 17, 18. In Romans 11:11, 12 it means defeat. See Romans 4:25; 5:16, 20; 2 Corinthians 5:19; Ephesians 1:7; 2:1; Colossians 2:13. Syn.: *parábasis* (3847), which designates sin as the transgression of a known rule of life and as involving guilt (Rom. 5:14, 15). Still *paráptōma* is not quite as strong as *parábasis* (which is used in connection with salvation only in Hebrews 9:15, and elsewhere only when imputation and punishment are referred to e. g., Heb. 2:2). *Parábasis* denotes sin objectively viewed as a violation of a known rule of life; in *paráptōma*, reference is specially made to the subj. passivity and suffering of him who misses or falls short of the enjoined command.

3906. Paratēréō; from *pará* (3844), intens. prep. denoting ill, and *tēréō* (5083), keep, observe, especially with sinister intent. To watch narrowly, to observe, as the gates of a city (Acts 9:24); to observe a person insidiously (Mark 3:2; Luke 6:7; 14:1; 20:20); to observe days scrupulously (Gal. 4:10).

3907. Paratérēsis; from *paratereó* (3906), attentive watching (Luke 17:20), such as can be observed with the eyes.

3927. Parepídēmos; from *pará* (3844), to, at; *epí* (1909), in, among; and *dḗmos* (1218), a people. A stranger, sojourner (Heb. 11:13; 1 Pet. 1:1; 2:11).

3929. Páresis; from the verb *pariēmai* (3935), which is from *para;* (3844), by, and *hiēmi*, to send, place, stand. To put on the side. Putting our sins by (i. e., on the side), without punishment, as in Romans 3:25, where it is translated in the KJV as "remission" (which is the Eng. equivalent to *áphesis* [859], forgiveness, deliverance, remission). *Áphesis* presupposes Christ's sacrifice as punishment for sin, which *páresis* does not.

3930. Paréchō; from *pará* (3844), beside or near, and *échō* (2192), to have, hold. To present, as the cheek for smiting (Luke 6:29); to offer, hold near; to show oneself (Titus 2:7); to afford, furnish (Acts 16:16; 19:24; 1 Tim. 1:4; 6:17); to confer a favor (Luke 7:4); to afford or show kindness (Acts 28:2) or equity (Col. 4:1). In

Matthew 26:10; Mark 14:6, with *kópous* (2873), trouble, to give anyone trouble. In Acts 22:2, with silence, to be still that another may be heard better in speaking. In Acts 17:31 with faith to anyone, to give proof or demonstration to anyone.

3939. Paroikéō; from *pará* (3844), at, and *oikéō* (3611), to dwell. To be a stranger, dwell or sojourn as a stranger, to dwell at a place only for a short time (Luke 24:18; Heb. 11:9). Deriv.: *paroikía* (3940), sojourning, temporary dwelling in a strange or foreign country (Acts 13:17). *Pároikos* (3941), a sojourner, one who dwells in a foreign country, a temporary dweller, not having a settled habitat, the place where he is now. Contrast: *katoikéō* (2730), to dwell in a certain fixed and durable dwelling.

3941. Pároikos; from *paroikéō* (3939). A sojourner, one who dwells in a foreign country, a temporary dweller not having a settled habitation in the place where he is now (Acts 7:6, 29). Applied spiritually (Eph. 2:19; 1 Pet. 2:11). Deriv.: *paroikéō* (3939), to dwell near; *paroikía* (3940), foreign residence.

3950. Parorgismós; from the verb *parorgízō* (3949), which is from the intens. prep. *pará* (3844) and *orgízō* (3710), to anger, irritate, to provoke to violent or bitter anger. The irritation, exasperation, embitterment that may spring from *orgé*, wrath, anger as a state of mind; only in Ephesians 4:26. *Parorgismós* is not *orgé* (3709) although both are translated "wrath." *Parorgismós* is to be so angry that one is beside (*pará*) himself, out of his sound mind; hence it is strictly forbidden in Scripture. Contrast *orgé* (3709) which, under certain conditions, is to entertain a righteous passion which sometimes involves moderate anger for good which is not only permitted but demanded.

3952. Parousía; from *parōn*, present, presence, being present, coming to a place, from the verb *páreimi* (3918) which is from *pará;* (3844), near, with, and *eimí* (1510), to be. To be present, to be at hand. *Parousía* is connected with the Second Coming of Christ, as *apokálupsis* (602) and *epipháneia* (2015). See 1 Thessalonians 4:15–17; James 5:8; 2 Pet. 3:4; 1 John 2:28. The *parousía* corresponds with the *apokálupsis* of the Son of Man (Matt. 24:27, 37, 39); of Christ (1 Cor. 15:23); of our Lord (1 Thess. 3:13; 5:23). See 1 Thessalonians 2:19; 2 Thessalonians 1:7; and 1 Peter 1:7. The two expressions are used interchangeably in 2 Thessalonians 2:1, 2. Ant.: *apousía* (666), absence.

3954. Parrēsía; freedom or frankness in speaking; freely saying all that one thinks, all that he pleases (John 7:13, 26; Acts 4:13, 29); confidence or boldness, particularly in speaking (Eph. 3:12; 6:19, cf. 1 John 2:28; 3:21; 4:17; 5:14); plainness, perspicuity of speech (John 10:24; 11:14; 16:25, 29; 2 Cor. 3:12); openness, making speech public (John 18:20); freedom, liberty (Heb. 10:19); denotes being public or publicly known, in opposition to being concealed (John 7:4, cf. v. 10; John 11:54, cf. Col. 2:15). Especially in Hebrews and 1 John, the word particularly denotes the unwavering, fearless, and unhesitating confidence of faith in communion with God, in fulfilling the duties of the evangelist and holding fast our hope, and in every act which implies a special exercise of faith. *Parrēsía* removes the fear and anxiety which characterize man's relation to God. It comes as the result of the ground of guilt being set aside (Heb. 10:19, cf, vv. 17, 18; 1 John 3:21; 4:17) and manifests itself in undoubting confidence in prayer (Heb. 4:16; 1 John 5:14).

3955. Parrēsiázomai; from *parrēsía* (3954), freedom or frankness in speaking. To speak openly, boldly, and without constraint (Acts 9:27, 28; 13:46; Eph. 6:20; 1 Thess. 2:2).

3956. Pás; mas., *pása* fem., *pán* neut.; every, all. It can mean the individual within the totality and the totality of the individuals. It can stand alone as in the case of *pás*, anyone and everyone; 'Therefore, anyone and everyone who hears' (Matt. 7:24). It can refer to all things individually and in their totality as in the case of *pánta*, 'All things (all things in their totality but also each thing within that totality) came into existence

through Him' (John 1:3). *Pas* can also stand with a noun that does not have an art. as in the case of *pan déndron* (1186); meaning every good tree and all the good trees (Matt. 7:17).

3958. Páschō; the opposite of free action, to bar oneself passively from some influence from without; hence, to experience something evil, to suffer (Gal. 3:4). In all other places, to suffer something; experience evil, with the acc. of the obj. (Matt. 16:21; Acts 28:5; 2 Cor. 1:6; 1 Pet. 5:10). However, it occurs usually without an obj., to suffer (Matt. 17:15). In the NT it is mostly suffering on behalf of someone (Acts 9:16; Phil. 1:29; 2 Thess. 1:5).

3961. Patéō; from *pátos*, a path, a beaten way. To tread, trample (Luke 10:19); to tread as a winepress (Rev. 14:20; 19:15); to trample upon or have in subjection (Luke 21:24 Rev. 11:2).

3962. Patér; father (Matt. 2:22; 4:22); in the pl. *patéres*, for both parents (Heb. 11:23); a remote progenitor (Matt. 3:9; 23:30, 32; Luke 1:32; 11:47); a person respectable on account of his age or dignity (Acts 7:2; 22:1); a spiritual father, that is, one who converts another to the Christian faith (1 Cor. 4:15). When Christ forbids His disciples in Matt. 23:9 to call any man their father upon earth, the meaning seems to be that they should not, with regard to spiritual things, have that implicit faith in any mere man which young children are apt to have in their parents. It also means one who resembles another in disposition and actions, as children usually do their parents (John 8:44); an author or initiator of anything (John 8:44, where the devil is called the "father of lies"). It is spoken of God, essentially denoting the divine essence, or Jehovah, as the Creator of the lights of heaven (James 1:17) and as the Father of man by creation (Luke 3:8). He is thus called the Father of spirits or souls (Heb. 12:9), and by redemption (Matt. 6:9; 7:11; 10:29; Luke 11:13). God is also spoken of as a Father in His divine essence as the Father of Christ's human nature (Matt. 16:17; 24:36; 26:39, 42, 53; John 6:27, 46; 10:30; 14:6–13, 16, 20, 21, 23, 24, 26, 28, 31; 1 Cor. 15:24). As the first person of the Trinity, the Father is so designated to distinguish Him from the Son and the Holy Spirit (Matt. 28:19; John 15:26; 16:28; 1 John 2:1; 5:7).

3965. Patriá; from *pátēr* (3962), father. What is called after the father, belongs to or springs from him, family, descendants. In this manner used in Luke 2:4, "Of the lineage (i. e., of the descendants) of David." Used in a wider sense as a people, nationality, or race (Acts 3:25). In Ephesians 3:14, 15 the Father is represented as having only one *patriá*, family. This indicates the oneness of God's family, both Jews and Gentiles, both those saints of the OT as well as of the NT, who were all baptized into the body of Christ (as is so clearly indicated in Acts 2, 10, 11, 19, and explained in 1 Cor. 12:13).

3973. Paúō; to stop, make an end. Used chiefly in the mid. voice, meaning to come to an end, take one's rest, a willing cessation (contrast the pass. voice which denotes a forced cessation), Luke 5:4. Used in the act. voice in 1 Peter 3:10, to cause to cease. Deriv. *katapaúō* (2664), to rest, from *katá* (2596), down, intens., and *paúō* (3973), to cause to rest, to give rest; also intrans., to rest entirely; trans., to restrain; *katápausis* (2663), a rest, a dwelling; *akatápaustos* (180), incessant, not to be set at rest, from the priv. *a* (1), *katá* (2596), down, and *paúō* (2 Pet. 2:14).

3982. Peíthō; to entice or persuade; followed by an acc. (Acts 13:43; 18:4; 28:23); to seek to persuade or solicit the favor of (Gal. 1:10); to prevail by persuasion (Matt. 28:14; Acts 12:20; 14:19); in the pass., *peíthomai*, to be persuaded, assent, believe (Luke 16:31; 20:6; Acts 17:4; 21:14; 27:11); in the pass., accompanied by a dat., to obey, comply with (Acts 5:36, 37, 40; 23:21; 28:24; Gal. 3:1); to assure, make confident, to free from fear or doubt (1 John 3:19); in the perf. mid. voice, *pépoitha*, to be persuaded, trust (Heb. 13:18); with an acc. following, to be persuaded or confident of (Phil. 1:6, 25); with a dat. following, to depend upon, trust in, have confidence in (2 Cor.

10:7). Deriv.: *pepoíthēsis* (4006), confidence, trust; *apeithḗs* (545), disobedient; *apeithéō* (544), to be disobedient; *apeítheia* (543), disobedience.

3984. Peíra; connected with *peráō*, to penetrate, or from *peiró*, to perforate, pierce through by trying the durability of things or simply pass through. Therefore, it has come to mean experience, trial, attempt, especially when it is used actively (Heb. 11:29), to make an attempt. When used pass., to experience (Heb. 11:36). These are the only places the word occurs. It is from this word that *peirasmós* (3986), temptation, is derived. However, when *peirasmós* is brought by God, it is that the object of temptation may acquire *peíra*, experience. See *peirázō* (3985), tempt or test, and *peirasmós* (3986), temptation or testing.

3985. Peirázō; to try, to prove in a good sense (John 6:6; 2 Cor. 13:5; Heb. 11:17) or in a bad one (Matt. 16:1; 22:18, 35; 1 Cor. 10:9); to tempt, to prove by solicitation to sin (Matt. 4:1; 1 Thess. 3:5; James 1:13, 14). *Ho peirázōn*, the tempter (Matt. 4:3; 1 Thess. 3:5). The difference between *dokimázō* (1381) and *peirázō* is that the latter has the intention of proving that one has been evil or to make him evil, whereas the intent of *dokimázō* is to prove someone good and acceptable. *Peirázō* is connected with *peíra* (3984), experience. *Peirázō* involves entangling a person in sin or discovering what good or evil, weakness or strength, was in a person (Matt. 16:1; 19:3; 22:18); or, knowing it, making it manifest to the one tempted (2 Cor. 13:5, examine). Satan tempts (Matt. 4:1; 1 Cor. 7:5; Rev. 2:10) to show someone unapproved.

3986. Peirasmós; from the Attic *peírasis*, trial. Temptation, testing (Matt. 6:13; 1 Cor. 10:13). The meaning depends on who tempts. If it is God, it is for the purpose of proving someone and never for the purpose of causing him to fall. If it is the devil who tempts, then it is for the purpose of causing one to fall. See *peirázō* (3985).

3987. Peiráō; related to *peirázō* (3985), to tempt or test. Only in Acts 9:26; 26:21; used in the mid. voice, to try to take pains. In Class. Gr., when used with the gen. of the person, it meant to try anyone, put him to the test. It has to do primarily with the knowledge to be obtained concerning anyone. In the perf. pass. voice, to have tested, to have tried, to know from experience, to be experienced. Syn.: *epístamai* (1987), to comprehend, be acquainted with.

3989. Pélagos; closely related to *plax* (4109), *platús* (4116), flat. The vast uninterrupted lull and expanse of open water. Occurs only in Matthew 18:6; Acts 27:5 and translated "sea." Distinguished from *thálassa* (2281), which suggests depth; *pélagos* suggests breadth. It may refer to the open sea rather than to the shore or portions of the sea broken by islands and shut in by coasts and headlands. *Pélagos* and *thálassa* are used together in Matthew 18:6: "it were better for him that a millstone were hanged around his neck, and that he were drowned in the depth (*pelágei*, the dat. sing. of *pélagos*) of the sea (*thalássēs*, the gen. of *thálassa*)." Here, however, the depth is implied not by the word *pélagos*, but by the verb *katapontisthē̂*, drowned (derived from *póntos* [not used in the NT], but which is connected with the word *báthos* [899], depth, *buthós* [1037], deep, depth, implying the sea in its perpendicular depth, as *pélagos* implies the same in its horizontal dimensions and extent). In Class. Gr. *pélagos* also referred to the seemingly illimitable sands of the desert.

3993. Pénēs; poor but able to help himself through his own labor (*pónos* [4192], pain; 2 Cor. 9:9). Contrast *ptōchós* (4434), poor but helpless, one dependent on alms, a beggar (Luke 16:20).

3996. Penthéō; from *pénthos* (3997), mourning. To mourn, grieve, upon the death of a friend (Mark 16:10). Trans., with an acc., to mourn over or for (2 Cor. 12:21). This verb mildly expresses the inner grief which in Gr. is designated as *lúpē* (3077) or *lupéō* (3076), which in themselves do not necessarily denote outward expression of inner grief. The other two words related to grief are *thrēnéō* (2354), to bewail, and *kóptō* (2875), literally to cut or to strike the bosom

or beat the breast as an outward sign of inward grief (Luke 18:13).

4006. Pepoíthēsis; from the verb *peíthō* (3982), to persuade. Used as trust, confidence (2 Cor. 1:15; 3:4; 8:22; 10:2; Eph. 3:12). The object of trust or confidence, that upon which one trusts (Phil. 3:4).

4014. Periairéō; from *perí* (4012), around, and *hairéomai* (138), to lift up and take away. To take away from around (cf. 2 Cor. 3:16). Used of the taking away of sin by sacrifice (Heb. 10:11).

4027. Perikátharma; the defilement swept away by cleansing, *katharismós* (2512), the process of purification. Denotes the sacrificial victim laden with guilt, and therefore defiled. The dross discarded in cleaning metal; figuratively, the offscouring of mankind and is thus employed in 1 Corinthians 4:13.

4037. Periménō; from *perí* (4012), for, and *ménō* (3306), to remain, wait. Trans. with an acc., to wait for (as in Acts 1:4, where it means waiting for the fulfillment of the promise of the end).

4041. Perioúsios; from *periousía*, abundance (from *perí* [4012], beyond, and *ousía* [3776], being). Used only in Titus 2:14 and translated "peculiar people"; rather, it should be considered as people in whom God had a superlative propriety and interest above and besides His common interest in all the nations of the world. It should rather be "treasured people."

4050. Perisseía; an exceeding measure, overflowing, something above the ordinary (Rom. 5:17; 2 Cor. 8:2; 10:15; James 1:21).

4051. Perísseuma; denotes abundance in a slightly more concrete form (2 Cor. 8:13, 14) where it stands for the gifts in kind supplied by the saints. Of the abundance of the heart (Matt. 12:34; Luke 6:45); of the pieces left over (Mark 8:8). Deriv.: *perisseúō* (4052).

4053. Perissós; abundant (John 10:10). With the neut. art., *to perissón*, used adv. with *katá* ([2596], according to) being understood, abundantly. With the prep. *ek* (1537), from, *perissoú* (gen.), abundantly, of abundance (Mark 6:51; Eph. 3:20; 1 Thess. 3:10; 5:13). In the last three passages the prep. *húper* (5228), over, is prefixed, making it very emphatic (that is, exceedingly, above the greatest abundance, superabundantly, over and above, more exceeding [Matt. 5:37]); *ek* (1537), out of, *perissoú*, moreover (Mark 14:31); excellent, extraordinary (Matt. 5:47); superfluous (2 Cor. 9:1); with the neut. art., *to perissón*, advantage, prerogative, privilege (Rom. 3:1). The comparative form is *perissóteros* (4055), more, more abundant, greater (Matt. 23:14; Luke 12:4, 48; 20:47; 1 Cor. 12:23, 24; 2 Cor. 2:7); more excellent, greater (Matt. 11:9; Luke 7:26). The adv. as a comparative, *perissóterōs* (4056), more abundantly (Mark 15:14; 2 Cor. 1:12); used in a superlative sense (as comparatives are often used), very much, especially (1 Thess. 2:17, Heb. 2:1; 13:19). From *perissós* as an adv., *perissōs* (4057), abundantly, exceedingly (Mark 10:26; Acts 26:11), more, the more (Matt. 27:23). Deriv.: *huperperissōs* (5249), adv. (from *húper*, above, exceedingly, and *perissōs*, abundantly), more exceedingly, superabundantly, above measure (Mark 7:37); *huperperisseúō* (5248), to abound more, super abound (Rom. 5:20); in the mid. voice *huperperisseúomai* (5248), to abound exceedingly, to overflow (2 Cor. 7:4); *huperekperissoú* (5240), a further strengthened form meaning exceedingly abundant.

4059. Peritémnō; from *perí* (4012), around, about, and *témnō*, to cut off. To cut off around, to circumcise (Luke 1:59; 2:21; John 7:22). Spiritually, denotes the mortification of the sins of the flesh (Col. 2:11).

4061. Peritomé; from *peritémnō* (4059), to cut around, circumcise. Refers to circumcision or cutting off the foreskin (John 7:22, 23). It also refers to persons circumcised, namely the Jews, as opposed to the uncircumcised Gentiles (Rom. 3:30; 4:12; Gal. 2:7–9; Eph. 2:11). Denotes also spiritual circumcision of the heart and affections (see Deut. 10:16; 30:6; Jer. 4:4) by putting off the body of the sins of the flesh (Rom. 2:29; Col. 2:11); persons who were spiritually circumcised (Phil. 3:3).

4068. Perpereúomai; from *pérperos*, braggart. To exult in things one has (1 Cor. 13:4). Related words: *alazōn* (213), one who boasts of things which he has not; *huperêphanos* (5244), proud, one who shows himself above his fellows; *hubristês* (5197), one who takes revenge on others for pleasure; *tuphóō* (5187), to be drunk with pride and set against men and God; *hubristés* (5197), insolent wrongdoer.

4077. Pēgé; a fountain which either springs up or flows. Fountains of water (Rev. 8:10; 14:7; 16:4). Metaphorically of life-giving doctrine (John 4:14). An emblem of the highest enjoyment (Rev. 7:17; 21:6). *Pēgé* also means an issue, flux of blood (Mark 5:29) which is equivalent to *rhúsis* (4511), an issue of blood (Luke 8:44). See *phréar* (5421), a well or a pit in which water is stored.

4098. Píptō; to fall (Matt. 13:4; 15:14, 27); to fall down (Matt. 2:11; 4:9; 26:39; Mark 9:20; John 18:6; Acts 5:10); as a house (Matt. 7:25, 27), a tower (Luke 13:4), or walls (Heb. 11:30); with *epí* (1909), upon, following, to fall upon (Luke 23:30; Rev. 6:16), as a lot (Acts 1:26); to fall, perish, be destroyed (Matt. 10:29; Luke 21:24; 1 Cor. 10:8; Heb. 3:17); to fail (Luke 16:17); to fall into sin and a state of disfavor with God (Rom. 11:22; 1 Cor. 10:12); to fall in judgment, to be condemned and punished (Rom. 14:4). Deriv.: *parapíptō* (3895), to fall beside, to fall down; *paráptōma* (3900), fault, mistake.

4100. Pisteúō; from *pístis* (4102), faith, belief. Trans. with a dat. following, to believe, give credit to (Matt. 21:25, 32; 27:42; John 5:46; 12:38). Intrans., to believe, have a mental persuasion (Matt. 8:13; 9:28; James 2:19). To believe, be of an opinion (Rom. 14:2). *Pisteúomai* in the pass. with an acc., to be entrusted with (Rom. 3:2; 1 Cor. 9:17; Gal. 2:7; 1 Thess. 2:4). Followed by the prep. *eis* (1519), unto, to believe in or on Christ, implying knowledge or assent to and confidence in Him (John 3:15, 16, 18; 12:11; 14:1). Also followed by *epí* (1909), on, to believe on, either with an acc. (Rom. 4:5, 24) or dat. following (Rom. 9:33; 10:11); followed by the prep. *en* (1722), to, to believe in, give credit to. Since believing in Christ or in the gospel is the distinguishing characteristic of a Christian, believing is often used absolutely for believing in Christ (Mark 16:16, 17; Acts 2:44; 4:32; 8:13; 13:12; 19:2). Deriv.: see *pistós* (4103), faithful.

4102. Pístis; from *peíthō* (3982), to persuade. Being persuaded, faith, belief. In general it implies such a knowledge of, assent to, and confidence in certain divine truths, especially those of the gospel, as produces good works (Matt. 8:10; 15:28; Acts 3:16; Rom. 1:17; 3:22, 25, 28; Gal. 5:6; Heb. 11:1ff.). Sometimes, however, simply a knowledge and assent to religious truths without good works and, therefore, false faith (James 2:14, 17, 18, 24, 26). Miraculous faith or that faith in Christ to which, when the gospel was first propagated, was annexed the gift of working miracles (Matt. 17:20; 21:21, Mark 11:22; Luke 17:6; 1 Cor. 13:2). The doctrine of faith or of the gospel promising justification and salvation to a lively faith in Christ (Acts 6:7; 14:27; Rom. 1:5; Gal. 1:23; Eph. 4:5). The Christian religion (Gal. 6:10; Col. 2:7; 1 Tim. 4:1; Jude 1:3). Fidelity, faithfulness (Rom. 3:3; Titus 2:10). Assurance, proof (Acts 17:31). Deriv.: *pistós* (4103), faithful.

4103. Pistós; faithful, with the following meanings: certain, worthy to be believed (1 Tim. 1:15; 3:1; 4:9); true, just, trustworthy, observant of and steadfast to one's trust, word, or promises (Matt. 25:21, 23; Luke 12:42; 16:10; 1 Cor. 1:9; 4:2; 2 Cor. 1:18; Eph. 6:21; Rev. 1:5); believing or giving credit to another (John 20:27); one believing in the gospel of Christ, a believer, a Christian (Acts 10:45; 16:1; 2 Cor. 6:15; 1 Tim. 6:2; Titus 1:6). Deriv.: *pistóō* (4104), to make faithful; *pístis* (4102), faith; *pisteúō* (4100), to believe; *ápistos* (571), an unbeliever, untrustworthy; *apistía* (570), faithlessness, uncertainty; *apistéō* (569), to put no confidence in; *oligópistos* (3640), of little faith.

4104. Pistóō; from *pistós* (4103), faithful. As a verb: to confirm, establish, ascertain, make faithful or certain. In the pass.: *pistóomai* or *pistoúmai*, spoken of a person, meaning to be confirmed in or assured

of (2 Tim. 3:14).

4124. Pleonexía; derived from *pléōn*, more, and *échō* (2192), to have. Covetousness, the desire for having more or for what he has not. Contrast *philarguría* (5365), avarice. *Pleonexía* is a larger term which includes *philarguría*. It is connected with extortioners; with thefts (Mark 7:22); with sins of the flesh (Eph. 5:3; Col. 3:5). *Pleonexía* may be said to be the root from which these sins grow, the longing of the creature which has forsaken God to fill itself with the lower objects of nature.

4134. Plêrēs; from *pláō* or *plēmi*, to fill, compounded perhaps with *rhéō* (4482), to flow. Full, in a pass. sense, filled (Matt. 14:20; 15:37), abounding or abundant (John 1:14; Acts 9:36), ample (2 John 1:8); full, complete, perfect (Mark 4:28). Deriv.: *plēróō* (4137), to make full, to fulfill or complete; *plérōma* (4138), fullness; *plērophoréō* (4135), to fulfill, thoroughly accomplish; *plērophoría* (4136), fullness, completion.

4135. Plērophoréō; from *plêrēs* (4134), full, and *phoréō* (5409), to fill. Found for the most part only in biblical and Patristic Gr. To fulfill, thoroughly accomplish (2 Tim. 4:5), equivalent to *plēróō* (4137), to fill up. In the pass.: *plērophoréomai*, to be fulfilled (2 Tim. 4:17), being established or being brought to an end and completed, reaching its goal; to be proved fully, to be confirmed with the fullest evidence (Luke 1:1); to be fully persuaded (Rom. 4:21; 14:5).

4136. Plērophoría, from *plērophoréō* (4135), to fulfill. Perfect certitude, full conviction (1 Thess. 1:5), equivalent to *bebaíōsis* (951), confirmation. Fullness, completion of understanding (Col. 2:2).

4137. Plēróō; from *plêrēs* (4134), full. To fill, as a net with fish (Matt. 13:48), as a house with a perfumed smell (John 12:3); to fill up, as a valley (Luke 3:5), or measure (Matt. 23:32); fill up, supply (Phil. 4:19); to fulfill, complete, used of time (Matt. 2:15; Luke 21:24; John 7:8; Acts 24:27), of number (Rev. 6:11); to perfect (John 15:11; Phil. 2:2); to finish, end (Luke 7:1); to accomplish, perform fully (Matt. 3:15; Luke 9:31; Acts 12:25; Rom. 13:8; Col. 4:17); to preach or explain fully (Rom. 15:19; Col. 1:25); to accomplish or perform what was foretold or prefigured in the OT (Matt. 1:22; 21:4; John 19:24, 36); to fully satisfy (Matt. 5:17). When Jesus said that He came not to destroy the law or the prophets but to fulfill, meaning that He came not only to fulfill the types and prophecies by His actions and sufferings, but also to perform perfect obedience to the law of God in His own person and to enforce and explain it fully by His doctrine. Thus He has fully satisfied the requirements of the law.

4138. Plérōma; from *plēróō* (4137), to fill. A filling or filling up, a fullness, of being full (Mark 8:20); something put in to fill up (Matt. 9:16; Mark 2:21); a fullness, complete number (Rom. 11:12, 25); the expression "the fullness of the earth" means all the good things with which the earth is filled or plentifully stored (1 Cor. 10:26, 28); 'the fullness of time' denotes the completion of a particular period of time before ordained and appointed (Gal. 4:4; Eph. 1:10); completion. The Church is called the *plérōma* of Christ, who fills all in all (Eph. 1:23). It indicates that Christ has filled it with all kinds of gifts and dwells in it and walks in it. Also it denotes a fullness of the Godhead in Christ (Col. 1:19; 2:9) meaning that in the body of Christ as it was constituted, God was in His fullness and not simply in His manifestation. Jesus was fully God and fully man. Deriv.: *plêrēs* (4134), full.

4139. Plēsíon; adv. neut. of *plēsíos*, near, near to (John 4:5). With the art., it means neighbor, fellow man or fellow creature, indicating primarily an outward nearness or proximity. Occurs in Luke 10:29, the parable of the Good Samaritan, which teaches that he who is outwardly near us should be the object of our concern in spite of the fact that there are no ties of kindred or nation between us (Matt. 5:43; 19:19; 22:39; Mark 12:31, 33; Rom. 13:9; James 2:8).

4147. Ploutéō; to be rich, to become rich (Luke 12:21; 1 Tim. 6:9). Contrast *ploutízō* (4148), to make rich, to enrich. Deriv.: *ploútos* (4149), riches, abundance;

ploúsios (4145), rich, abounding; *ploúsiōs* (4146), richly, abundantly.

4150. Plúnō; to wash inanimate things (Rev. 7:14). Deriv.: *apoplúnō* (637), washing nets (Luke 5:2). See *niptō* (3538) to wash part of the body, and *loúō* (3068), bathe.

4151. Pneúma; related to *pnéō* (4154), to breathe, blow; primarily denotes the wind. Breath; the spirit which, like the wind, is invisible, immaterial, and powerful. The wind (John 3:8); breath (2 Thess. 2:8; Rev. 11:11; 13:15); the immaterial, invisible part of man (Luke 8:55; 24:37, 39; Acts 7:59; 1 Cor. 5:3–5; Heb. 12:23; James 2:26; 1 Pet. 3:19); man, the resurrection body (1 Cor. 15:45; 1 Pet. 3:18) the element in man by which he perceives, reflects, feels, desires (Matt. 5:3; 26:41; Mark 2:8); purpose, aim (2 Cor. 12:18; Phil. 1:27; Eph. 4:23); the character (Luke 1:17; Rom. 1:4); moral qualities and activities (Rom. 8:15; 11:8; 2 Tim. 1:7); the Holy Spirit (Matt. 4:1; Luke 4:18); the inward man, an expression used only of the believer (Rom. 7:6; 2 Cor. 4:13); the new life (Rom. 8:4–6, 10, 16; Heb. 12:9); unclean spirits, demons (Matt. 8:16; Luke 4:33; 1 Pet. 3:19); angels (Heb. 1:14); divine gifts for service (1 Cor. 14:12, 32). Sometimes *pneúma* is used without the def. art. and sometimes with it. Any meaning pertaining to the presence or absence of the def. art. must be sought through the context in which it is used. With the def. art. it refers to Jesus' spirit (John 11:33; 13:21), as contrasted with the Holy Spirit as the Third Person of the Triune Godhead. In 1 Corinthians 5:3 Paul refers to his spirit and in verse five to man's spirit. If not with the art., *pneúma* may still refer to the Holy Spirit, but it also may refer to the spirit of anyone or to the spirit as contrasted with the body. When the expression is *to Pneúma to ágion* (the Spirit, the Holy One), it stresses the character of the person of the Holy Spirit (Matt. 12:32; Mark 3:29; 12:36). Spirit is the element in man which gives him the ability to think of God. It is man's vertical window, while *psuchē* ([5590] soul) is man's horizontal window making him conscious of his environment. The animals do not have a spirit, but they do have a soul. A soul is the element of life whereas the spirit is the element of faith. Whenever the word "spirit" is used, it refers to the immaterial part of man including his spirit and soul. When just "soul" is used in regard to man, it may also refer to his immaterial part, including his spirit. Sometimes, however, the word "soul" refers to man's sinful propensities, as in Luke 14:26. In this verse and other similar ones, the translators have rendered *psuché* (5590), as "life," but in reality it refers to man's fallen nature and his sinfulness.

4152. Pneumatikós; from *pneúma* (4151), spirit. Spiritual (Rom. 7:14; 1 Cor. 10:3). Deriv.: *pneumatikōs* (4153), spiritually. Ant.: *psuchikós* (5591), an animalistic man, man with his sinful propensities ruling him; *sarkikós* (4559), carnal man.

4153. Pneumatikós; an adv. from the adj. *pneumatikós* (4152), spiritual. Spiritually, by the assistance of the Holy Spirit (1 Cor. 2:14); spiritually, emblematically, mystically (Rev. 11:8, cf. 17:5, 7).

4154. Pnéō; to blow, breathe, as the wind or air (Matt. 7:25, 27; Luke 12:55; John 3:8; 6:18; Acts 27:40; Rev. 7:1).

4157. Pnoé; derived from *pépnoa*, perf. mid. of *pnéō* (4154), to breathe, blow. In Acts 2:2 translated wind. In Acts 17:25 it is breath, the air considered as proper for breathing. Syn.: *pneúma* (4151) from *pépneumai*, perf. pass. of *pnéō* (4154), which in its earthly and natural sense means wind or air in motion. In Acts 2:2 the material blast of wind is differentiated from the spiritual *pneúma* used throughout the chapter to indicate the Holy Spirit. Thus, *pneúma* (4151) may mean something material or something purely spiritual such as a spiritual gift or the spirit of man which is the immaterial element in man enabling him to communicate with the Spirit of God. *Pnoé* conveys the impression of a lighter, gentler motion of the air than *pneúma*, spirit. See also *ánemos* (417), violent wind; *lailaps* (2978), storm, tempest, its deriv. probably from *lian*

(3029), very much, and *láptō*, to lick or lap up Therefore, *lailaps* actually means a whirlwind, a tornado, a violent storm. *Thúella* (2366), from *thúō* (2380), to move or rush impetuously, a hurricane, cyclone. Found only in Hebrews 12:18. *Thúella* is often a natural phenomenon wilder and fiercer than the *lailaps* itself. In it there is often the mingling in conflict of many opposing winds which makes it a turbulent cyclone. In Matthew 8:24, the word is *seismós* (4578), translated "tempest," though its real meaning is earthquake, as translated in all the other occurrences in the NT.

4158. Podérēs; a garment reaching down to the feet (Rev. 1:13). Almost the same as *stolé* (4749), long robe.

4160. Poiéō; from *poíos* (4169), quality. To make; to endow a person or thing with a certain quality; to qualify (Matt. 3:3; 4:19; 5:36; 23:15; Luke 15:19; John 5:11, 15); to appoint, constitute (Mark 3:14; Acts 2:36). Contrast *prássō* (4238), to do, perform. *Poiéō* brings out more the object and end of an act while *prássō* brings out more the means by which this object is attained. *Poiéō* may well refer to the doing once and for all, the producing and bringing forth something which, when produced, has an independent existence of its own.

4165. Poimaínō; to shepherd, tend. It involves much more than *bóskō* (1006), to feed. It implies the whole office of the shepherd, guiding, guarding, folding of the flock as well as leading it to nourishment (Matt. 2:6; Luke 17:7; John 21:16; Acts 20:28; 1 Cor. 9:7; 1 Pet. 5:2; Jude 1:12; Rev. 2:27).

4166. Poimén; shepherd (Matt. 9:36; 25:32; Mark 6:34; Luke 2:8, 15, 18, 20). Applied spiritually to Christ (Matt. 26:31; John 10:11, 12, 14, 16; Heb. 13:20; 1 Pet. 2:25) and also given as a designation for a spiritual pastor of the flock (Eph. 4:11).

4167. Poímnē; a flock of sheep (Luke 2:8; 1 Cor. 9:7). A spiritual flock of men (Matt. 26:31; John 10:16).

4168. Poímnion; a diminutive of *poímnē*. A flock, properly a little flock. In the NT it is applied only spiritually (Luke 12:32; Acts 20:28, 29; 1 Pet. 5:2, 3).

4171. Pólemos; from *pólus*, much, or many, and *oleó*, to destroy; or, according to others, from *palámē*, the hand, which is derived from *pállō* (3823), to shake, move. A war (Matt. 24:6; Mark 13:7). *Pólemos* embraces the whole course of hostilities while *máchē* (3163) is the actual stock of arms of hostile armies. Another related word is *stásis* (4714), insurrection, sedition.

4189. Ponēría; from *ponērós* (4190), which means a malicious person who is not only evil (*kakós* [2556]), but expresses his malice and thus affects others. Therefore, it is malevolence (Mark 7:22; Eph. 6:12). Contrast *kakía* (2549), which is simply the evil habit of mind without necessarily being expressed in affecting others. Contrast both words with *kakoḗtheia* (2550), nature attributing evil to the actions and speech of others.

4190. Ponērós; from the noun *pónos* (4192), labor, sorrow, pain. Evil in a moral or spiritual sense: wicked, malicious, mischievous. Distinguished from *kakós* (2556), being evil in oneself but not necessarily malicious. Satan is the author of all the mischief (*Ponērós*) in the world (Matt. 6:13; Eph. 6:16). From it is derived *ponēría* (4189), aptness to do shrewd turns, delight in mischief and tragedy, perverseness.

4192. Pónos; from *pépona*, the perf. mid. voice of *penómai*, to labor (Rev. 21:4); pain, misery (Rev. 16:10, 11). It is labor which does not stop short of demanding the whole strength of man. Contrast *móchthos* (3449), which is the everyday word for labor, and *kópos* (2873), which means not so much the actual exertion which a man makes as the weariness resulting from labor.

4224. Potós; from *pépotai*, perf. pass. of *póō*, to drink. A drinking match, drunken bout (1 Pet. 4:3). Contrast *méthē* (3178), drunkenness. It is abstract in meaning, it is the opportunity of drinking, the banquet, not necessarily excessive drinking but giving opportunity for excess. Syn.: *oinophlugía* (3632), excess of wine, which marks a step in advance of *méthē*, drunkenness. In strict definition, it is an insatiate desire for wine, alcoholism. Commonly used for debauchery. No single word rendering is better than *oinophlugía* since it is an extravagant indulgence in long, drawn-out drinking bouts which may induce permanent damage on the body. *Oinophlugía* is ascribed as the cause of death of Alexander the Great. See *kṓmos* (2970), rioting or reveling, and *kraipálē* (2897), the sense of being full of wine.

4238. Prássō; to make, perform in general (Acts 26:26; 1 Thess. 4:11); do good (Acts 26:20; Rom. 2:25) or more commonly do evil (Luke 22:23; 23:41; John 3:20; Rom. 13:4, cf. 9:11; 2 Cor. 5:10). Whenever the words *prássō* and *poiéō* (4160) assume an ethical connotation; *poiéō* is used in a good sense and *prássō* in an evil sense, the latter tendency appearing in a more marked way in the uses of *práxis* (4234), work, action, deed (Luke 23:51; Rom. 8:13; Col. 3:9), practice, behavior (Matt. 16:27), of office (Rom. 12:4). Except for Matthew 16:27 and Philippians 4:9, all the NT uses of *prássō* have an evil connotation.

4239. Praús; meek (Matt. 5:5; 21:5; 1 Pet. 3:4), or *práos* (4235), meek, lowly (Matt. 11:29). See *praútēs* (4240), meekness.

4240. Praútēs; meekness, expressed not in a man's outward behavior only nor in his relations to his fellow man or his mere natural disposition, but expressed rather as an inwrought grace of the soul, first and chiefly directed toward God (James 1:21). That attitude of spirit in which we accept God's dealings with us as good and do not dispute or resist. *Praútēs*, according to Aristotle, is the middle course in being angry, standing between two extremes, getting angry without reason (*orgulótēs*), and not getting angry at all (*aorgēsía*). Therefore, *praútēs* is getting angry at the right time, in the right measure, and for the right reason. *Praútēs* is not readily expressed in Eng. since the term "meekness" suggests weakness, but *praútēs* is a condition of mind and heart which demonstrates gentleness not in weakness but power. It is a virtue born in strength of character.

4244. Presbutérion; presbytery, referring to a group of elders (*présbus* [4245]), and also the Jewish people (Luke 22:66; Acts 22:5; 1 Tim. 4:14).

4245. Presbúteros; ambassador. The word, however, more commonly used in the comparative is *présbus*, a person who is older, commonly translated "elder" (Luke 15:25; John 8:9; Acts 2:17; 1 Tim. 5:1, 2; 1 Pet. 5:5). *Presbúteroi*, pl., ancestors, predecessors (Matt. 15:2; Mark 7:3, 5; Heb. 11:2). In the Sept. we read of the elders of the Egyptians (Gen. 50:7). These enjoyed the natural dignity of age. We find elders in Israel as the representatives of the people whose decisions held good for the whole people (Ex. 3:16, 18; 4:29; 19:7), who were apparently the foremost members of the tribes and families according to the rite of the firstborn (1 Kgs. 8:1, 3). From among them Moses, chose a college of seventy men who should bear with him the burden of the people (Num. 11:17), and who, therefore, were no longer the representatives of the people (Ex. 19:7; Deut. 27:1; Josh. 8:10). Later we have the institution of the Sanhedrin, made up of seventy members (Matt. 26:59; Luke 7:3; 22:52). In every city there were also elders who had no connection with the members of the Sanhedrin but who were perhaps men chosen from among the people. In the NT they are mentioned together with the chief priests and scribes, and served as assistants (Matt. 16:21; 26:3; 27:41; Mark 8:31; 11:27; 14:43, 53; 15:1; Luke 9:22; 20:1; Acts 6:12). Related to this institution (at least at first), the name *presbúteroi*, elders, was used to designate the *proestótes* (from the verb *proístēmi* [4291], to stand before or maintain rule over) within the Christian churches (1 Tim. 5:17). These were appointed and ordained everywhere in each church and each town (Acts 14:23; Titus 1:5). The first notice of them is in Acts 11:30 where the disciples at Antioch sent their contributions for their brethren in Judea to the presbyters in Jerusalem (Acts 12:25). In Acts 6, the appointment of the seven deacons as assistants to the apostles leads us to suppose that the Twelve were the beginning of the presbytery. See 1 Peter 5:1 which reveals the fellowship between the apostles and elders (Acts 15:2, 6; 16:4, cf. Acts 15:4, 22, 23). In the absence of the apostles, they entered upon their work (Acts 20:17, 28–30); and the deacons in like manner, though with a narrower sphere of work, were appointed to their side, just as they had been to the apostles. As to the range of their work, hints of it are given in Acts 20:28ff.; 1 Timothy 5:17, James 5:14; 1 Peter 5:1. The word *presbúteros* also occurs in Acts 21:18; 2 John 1:1; and 3 John 1:1. John called himself simply *presbúteros*, whether on account of his age (Phile. 1:9) or his office (1 Pet. 5:1), we are not sure. Priority of office usually implies that of age also. In the Book of Revelation, twenty-four elders appear with the four beasts around God's throne (Rev. 4:4, 10; 5:5, 6, 8, 11, 14; 7:11, 13; 11:16; 14:3; 19:4) as representatives of Israel and the nations, or of NT churches. Syn.: *archaíoi* (744), the original ones (Matt. 5:21, 27, 33), also used as a name of dignity, an official position in the senate or as an ambassador. See *epískopos* (1985), bishop.

4254. Proágō; from *pro* (4253), before, and *ágō* (71), to go. Lead, bring. Used of place, to go before, lead when others follow (Matt. 14:22; 21:9; 26:32; 28:7); figuratively, in relation to the kingdom of heaven (Matt. 21:31); to go before, precede in time (1 Tim. 1:18; 5:24; Heb. 7:18); to bring out or forth (Acts 16:30; 25:26), particularly to condemnation or punishment.

4267. Proginóskō; from *pro* (4253), before, and *ginóskō* (1097), to know. To perceive or recognize beforehand, to know previously, foreknow the correlative of time being given in the context; to know before, whether a person (Acts 26:5), or a thing (2 Pet. 3:17); to foreknow with approbation, to approve beforehand or make a previous choice of as a peculiar people (1 Pet. 1:20, cf. Rom. 8:29; 11:2). (3) To ordain before, foreordain (1 Pet. 1:20). In Romans 8:29, it occurs with the verb *prooorise* (4309), did predestinate. This foreknowledge and foreordination in the Scripture is always unto salvation and not unto perdition. Therefore, it could be said that the Lord never foreordains anyone to be lost, but those who are saved as a result of their exercise of faith in the Lord Jesus Christ were known ahead of time and thus chosen unto God (see Hosea 13:5; Amos 3:2; Matt. 7:23; John 10:14; Rom. 11:2; 1 Cor. 8:3; Gal. 4:9; 2 Tim. 2:19). The word "knowing" here denotes a previous uniting of oneself with someone. This divine knowledge and divine predestination in Romans 8:29 is coincident and present in the mind and will of God prior to its manifestation in history, resulting in salvation but not in condemnation. The salvation of every believer is known and determined in the mind of God before its actual accomplishment in a historical setting. Thus, *proginóskō*, to foreknow, corresponds with having been chosen before the foundation of the world (Eph. 1:4) and always precedes *prooorízō* (4309), which means foreordain. *Proginóskō* essentially includes a determining on God's part to fellowship with believers (Rom. 8:29), with whom God had beforehand entered into fellowship. However, *eklégomai* (1586), to choose, found in Ephesians 1:4, merely expresses a determination directed to the objects of the fellowship (1 Pet. 1:2).

4268. Prógnōsis; from *pro* (4253), before, and *ginóskō* or *gnósis* (1108), to know. Foreknowledge. Only in Acts 2:23; 1 Peter 1:2. Denotes the foreordained relation of the fellowship of God with the objects of His saving counsel; God's determination to fellowship with the objects of His sovereign counsel precedes the realization of such a relationship. It involves a resolution formed beforehand, though this meaning is foreign to Class. Gr.

4279. Proepaggéllō; in the NT only in the mid. form, *proepaggéllomai*. To proclaim beforehand or promise beforehand (Rom. 1:2). Deriv.: *epaggéllō* (1861), to promise or proclaim.

4283. Proeuaggelízomai; from *pro* (4253), before, and *euaggelízomai* (2097), to preach the gospel or the good news. Only in Galatians 3:8. To proclaim beforehand a joyful message.

4286. Próthesis; from *protíthēmi* (4388). A setting forth, setting up, an exposition. It involves purpose, resolve, and design. The motion of time is not in the prep. *pro* (4253), before, but the meaning is derived from its literal and local import, a putting forth to view or to openly display. A thought or purpose (Acts 11:23; 27:13). When used of the purpose of God, it refers exclusively to salvation (2 Tim. 1:9). Therefore, in Romans 8:28, "them who are the called according to His purpose," *katá próthesin* must be taken as syn. with *eudokéō* (2107), indicating that "them who are the called" are called because of God's good pleasure and not because they deserve it (Eph. 1:8, 9). The reference of time is not contained in the word itself, but is expressed by additional words; for example, Ephesians 1:11, "being predestinated" (*prooristhéntes* [4309]); Ephesians 3:11, "according to the eternal purpose" (*aiṓn* [165], eternal). NT meanings: (1) A setting before (Matt. 12:4; Mark 2:26; Luke 6:4; Heb. 9:2). The Sept. applies this word only to the showbread (2 Chr. 13:11; Heb. 9:2), referring not to time but to the position of the loaves set before the Lord on the holy tables. See Exodus 25:30; 40:23. Since part of the frankincense put upon the bread was to be burned on the altar for a memorial of the bread, even an offering made by fire unto the Lord, and since Aaron and his sons were to eat it in the holy place (see Lev. 24:5–9), it is evident that this bread typified Christ, first presented as a sacrifice to Jehovah and then becoming the spiritual priest to God the Father (Rev. 1:6; 5:10; 20:6, cf. 1 Pet. 2:5). (2) A predetermination, purpose, intent, design of God in calling men in general, Gentiles as well as Jews, to salvation (Rom. 8:28); of gathering together all things in Christ (Eph. 1:9–11); of making the Gentiles fellow-heirs with the Jews of the same body and partakers of His promise in Christ by the gospel (Eph. 3:6, 11, cf. 2 Tim. 1:9); in choosing one nation rather than another to enjoy certain privileges and blessings (Rom. 9:11). All these passages are applied to the purpose of God in the NT. (3) Predetermination, purpose, resolution of man (Acts 11:23; 2 Tim. 3:10). (4) Purpose, intent, design, (Acts 27:13).

4287. Prothésmios; and *prothesmía* (fem.), from *pro* (4253), before, and *títhēmi* (5087), to set, place, lay. A pre-appointed day or time, the day or time being understood (Gal. 4:2).

4293. Prokataggéllō; from *pro* (4253), before, and *kataggéllō* (2605), declare, publish. To speak beforehand (Acts 3:18, 24; 7:52; 2 Cor. 9:5).

4294. Prokatartízō; from the prep. *pro* (4253), before, and *katartízō* (2675), to establish, to set up. To perfect or equip beforehand, make right. Used in 2 Corinthians 9:5 of the offerings for the church in Jerusalem which Paul wished to find already made up.

4299. Prókrima; from *prokrínō*, to prefer, which is from *pro* (4253), before, and *krínō* (2919), to judge. In Class. Gr., with reference to place and time, to decide beforehand, prefer before, another being put aside. Used in 1 Timothy 5:21. *Prókrima* involves a partial, unfavorable prejudgment against one, partiality being included in the attitude of this prejudgment.

4306. Pronoéō; from the prep. *pro* (4253), before, and *noéō* (3539), to think, to comprehend. With a gen. of the person following, meaning to provide for (1 Tim. 5:8). In the mid. voice, *pronoéomai*, with an acc. of the thing to provide, to take thought, to care beforehand for (Rom. 12:17; 2 Cor. 8:21). See *nous* (3563); mind; the noun *prónoia* (4307), providence.

4307. Prónoia; from *pronoéō* (4306), to know ahead of time. Providence, care, prudence (Acts 24:2); provision (Rom. 13:14). See *noéō* (3539), to know; *nous* (3563), mind.

4309. Proorízō; from *pro* (4253), before. and *horízō* (3724), to determine. To determine or decree beforehand (Acts 4:28; Rom. 8:29, 30; 1 Cor. 2:7; Eph. 1:5, 11). It is a word that has caused a great deal of division within the Christian Church, as if it attributed to God absolute and capricious determination of who would be saved and who would not. A careful examination of each instance of its occurrence is important.

(1) In 1 Corinthians 2:7 it has a thing as its object; namely, the wisdom of God. (2) In Acts 4:28, the verb is followed by the inf. *genésthai* (1096), to be done. Here reference is made to the actions of Herod and Pontius Pilate in regard to the crucifixion of Jesus Christ as doing only what God knew and permitted them to do. This concerns Jesus Christ and His position in history in that it was not of man but of God. (3) In Romans 8:29 it is used with a personal object, the relative pron. *hous* (3739), whom, in the pl. This personal pron. applies also to the previous verb *proégnō* (4267), foreknew. The translation is, "For whom he did foreknow, he also did predestinate." The purpose of this foreordination is expressed in the phrase, "to be conformed to the image of his Son." (4) In Ephesians 1:5 the purpose of the foreordination is the adoption, which means the placing of those who were born of God into their proper position (*huiothesía* [5206], which is from *huiós* [5207], son, and the verb *títhēmi* [5087], to place). This is not condemnatory but rather beneficial for the believer. (5) In Ephesians 1:11, it is used again and the purpose of it is explained in verse twelve by the inf., "That we should be to the praise of his glory" (*eis to eínai*), that is, "For the purpose of being . . . ." This purpose is benevolent. (6) The occurrence in Romans 8:30 is to be explained by verse twenty-nine, in which it is clearly stated that this foreordination was neither capricious nor an independent concept that was complete in itself. It was joined with the verb "foreknew." The important thing for us to consider when the word is used is not who are the objects of this predestination, but what they are predestined to. They are always predestined to salvation, to adoption, or to glory.

4314. Pros; a prep. governing the gen., dat., and acc.; and corresponding in its basic meaning to the primary force of these cases themselves. With the gen., implying motion or direction, that is, from a place, hither; with a dat., rest or remaining by, at, near a place; with the acc., motion or direction towards or to a place. In the NT used once with the meaning of pertaining to, that is, for, for the benefit of (Acts 27:34). With a dat., *pros* marks a place or object by the side of which a person or thing is, that is, by, at, near, as if in answer to the question, "Where?" (Luke 19:37; John 18:16; 20:12; Rev. 1:13). With the acc., *pros* marks the object towards or to which anything moves or is directed. When used of time, it means towards, near, as in Luke 24:29, near the evening. Denotes the direction, reference, relation, which one object has towards another, that is, in reference to, in respect to, as to, implying the direction or remote object of an action (Mark 12:12; Acts 24:16). When spoken of a rule, norm, standard, it means according to, in conformity with, and so forth (Luke 12:47; 2 Cor. 5:10). When it is used of the motive, reason, occasion of an action, it means on account of, because of, for (Matt. 19:8). When it marks the end or result, the aim or purpose of an action, it may be translated for what, why, that is, to what end, for what purpose (John 13:28). Sometimes *pros* with the acc. is used after verbs which express simply rest: at, by, in a place; equivalent to *pros*, with a dat. But in such instances for the most part, the idea of a previous coming to or direction toward that place is either actually expressed or is implied in the context. Mark 11:4 expresses that the donkey was tied at or by the door. In composition, *pros* implies: motion, direction, reference, meaning towards, to, at, as *proságō* (4317), to lead towards or to bring toward; accession, addition, thereto, meaning over and above, more, further, as *prosaitéō* (4319), to request further; used as an intens., as in *prosphilḗs* (4375), very beloved; also implies nearness, a being or remaining near, at, by, as *prosménō* (4357), to abide near.

4316. Prosagoreúō; from *pros* (4314), to, and *agoreúō*, to speak. To address, to greet. In some instances, to designate, give a name to (Heb. 5:10). Used only in the mid. voice in the NT.

4317. Proságō; from *pros* (4314), to or towards, and *ágō* (71), to bring, come. To bring to (Luke 9:41; Acts

16:20; 1 Pet. 3:18); intrans., to come to or toward, to approach (Acts 27:27). Basically to make oneself inclined to one, to surrender oneself to another. Subst.: *prosagōgḗ* (4318), access, approach.

4318. Prosagōgḗ; from *pros* (4314), to or toward, and *ágō* (71), to bring or come. Used intrans., meaning access, approach (Rom. 5:2; Eph. 2:18; 3:12). Syn.: *parrēsía* (3954), boldness or confidence.

4319. Prosaitéō; from *pros* (4314), an intens. prep., and *aitéō* (154), to ask, beg. To ask earnestly, to beg (Mark 10:46; Luke 18:35; John 9:8). Syn.: *epaitéō* (1871), to beg.

4322. Prosanaplēróō; from the intens. prep. *pros* (4314), and *anaplēróō* (378), to supply. Used in 2 Corinthians 9:12; 11:9, meaning to supply abundantly.

4327. Prosdéchomai; from *pros* (4314), to, and *déchomai* (1209), to receive or accept. To receive or take the spoiling of one's goods with joy (Heb. 10:34); accept as deliverance (Heb. 11:35); receive kindly as a friend (Luke 15:2); receive, entertain (Rom. 16:2; Phil. 2:29); receive, admit, as a hope (Acts 24:15); expect, look or wait for (Mark 15:43; Luke 2:25, 38; 12:36; 23:51; Acts 23:21; Titus 2:13).

4328. Prosdokáō; from *pros* (4314), toward, and *dokáō*, to look for. Expect, wait for (Matt. 11:3; 24:50; Acts 3:5). Deriv.: *prosdokía* (4329), from *prosdéchomai* (4327), a looking for, expectation.

4329. Prosdokía; from *prosdéchomai* (4327), to accept, receive, or *prosdokáō* (4328), to wait, expect. A looking for, an expectation (Luke 21:26; Acts 12:11).

4331. Proseggízō; from *pros* (4314), to, and *eggízō* (1448), to approach. To approach or come near to (Mark 2:4).

4334. Prosérchomai; from *pros* (4314), to, and *érchomai* (2064), to come. To come to, approach, as to location (Matt. 5:1; 9:14, 20, 28); to come to, approach, draw near spiritually (Heb. 4:16; 7:25; 10:22; 11:6; 12:22); to accede, assent to (1 Tim. 6:3). In that verse, the clause, "If any man teach otherwise, and consent not to wholesome words, even the words of our Lord Jesus Christ," relates to those who, after admonition (cf. 1 Tim. 1:3), persisted in teaching otherwise and did not then accede to sound words.

4335. Proseuchḗ; from the prep. *pros* (4314), to, and *euchḗ* (2171), a prayer, a vow. Prayer to God (James 5:17). Contrast *déēsis* (1162), supplication to anyone, not necessarily to God, for particular benefits.

4336. Proseúchomai; from the prep. *pros* (4314), to, and *eúchomai* (2172), to wish, pray. To pray, vow. A deponent verb, that is, a verb that has a mid. or pass. form (ending in -*omai*), but used in an act. sense. In the NT this comp. verb almost totally supplants *eúchomai* in designating the act of praying. The combination with a dat., although constant in Class. Gr., occurs only in Matthew 6:6; 1 Corinthians 11:13 in the NT. The prep. *pros* implies praying to God, whether for the obtaining of good or the averting of evil (Matt. 6:9; 24:20; 26:36, 39, 44; Luke 1:10). *Proseúchomai* embraces all that is included in the idea of prayer, thanks, asking, requesting special things; however, the distinctive word for worshiping is not *proseúchomai*, but *proskunéō* (4352), which literally means to crouch, crawl, prostrate oneself before another. *Proseúchomai* appears in combination with *aitéomai* (154), to ask (Mark 11:24; Col. 1:9); with *eucharistéō* (2168), to thank (Col. 1:3; 1 Thess. 5:17). Deriv.: *proseuchḗ* (4335), prayer.

4339. Prosḗlutos; from the obsolete *proseleuthō̃*, to come to. A stranger, foreigner, one who comes from his own people to another. Used in this sense in the Sept. (Ex. 22:21; 23:9). The Sept. also applies it to a stranger or foreigner who came to dwell among the Jews and embraced their religion (Ex. 12:48, 49; Lev. 17:8, 10, 12, 15; Num. 9:14). In the NT it is used for a proselyte, or convert from heathenism to Judaism (Matt. 23:15; Acts 2:10; 6:5; 13:43). The words of Jesus in Matthew 23:15 refer to the zeal of the Jews in making proselytes, even at Rome, such zeal being so remarkable about this time that it became proverbial among the Romans. Thus at Pentecost we have those who came from Rome who were both Jews and proselytes (Acts

2:10). There were also a number of Jewish proselytes at Antioch in Syria (Acts 6:5; 11:20).

4341. Proskaléō; pass. *proskaléomai*, from *pros* (4314), to, and *kaléō* (2564), to call. Call to oneself, bid to come. Used only in the mid. voice (Matt. 10:1; Acts 5:40; James 5:14); of God's call to Gentiles through the gospel (Acts 2:39), and the Divine call in entrusting men with the preaching of the gospel (Acts 13:2; 16:10).

4342. Proskarteréō; from *pros* (4314), to, and *karteréō* (2594), to endure. To tarry, remain somewhere (Mark 3:9); to continue with someone (Acts 8:13); to cleave faithfully to someone (Acts 10:7); referring to those who insist on something or stay close to someone (Acts 2:46; Rom. 13:6); used metaphorically of steadfastness and faithfulness in the outgoings of the Christian life, especially in prayer (Acts 1:14; 2:42; 6:4; Rom. 12:12; Col. 4:2).

4350. Proskóptō; from *pros* (4314), to, against, and *kóptō* (2875), to cut, strike. Trans., to strike or dash against, as the foot against stone (Matt. 4:6; Luke 4:11). In these passages it is well worth our observation to note that the devil frames his temptation not only by quoting a detached sentence of Scripture without regard to the context, but by applying in a natural sense what was originally spoken in a spiritual sense. In the neut., with a dat. following, to dash or beat against, as winds and waters (Matt. 7:27). With a dat., to stumble at or against, but in a spiritual sense (Rom. 9:32; 1 Pet. 2:8). Used in an absolute sense, to stumble (John 11:9, 10; Rom. 14:21). Deriv.: *kóptō* (2875), to strike, hew, thrust; *apokóptō* (609), to hew off; *proskopḗ* (4349), stumblingblock, offense; *próskomma* (4348), the stumble or offense, hindrance.

4357. Prosménō; from *pros* (4314), to, with, and *ménō* (3306), to remain. To stay at a place (Acts 18:18; 1 Tim. 1:3); followed by a dat. of the person, meaning to remain or continue with (Matt. 15:32; Mark 8:2). In a spiritual sense, to adhere to (Acts 11:23). With a dat. of the thing, to continue or persevere (1 Tim. 5:5).

4382. Prosōpolēpsía; respect of persons, partiality (Rom. 2:11; Eph. 6:9; Col. 3:25; James 2:1). Deriv.: the subst. *prosōpolḗptēs* (4381), respecter of persons; the verb *prosōpolēptéō* (4380), to act with respect to persons (Acts 10:34; James 2:9); the adv. *aprosōpolḗptōs* (678), without respect of persons or impartially (1 Pet. 1:17).

4383. Prósōpon; from *pros* (4314), to, and *ōps*, the eye. In general, that part of anything which is turned or presented to the eye of another. The face, the countenance (Matt. 6:16, 17; 17:2, 6; Mark 14:65); face, surface, as of the earth (Luke 21:35; Acts 17:26); face, external or outward appearance (Matt. 16:3; Luke 12:56; 2 Cor. 5:12; 10:7; James 1:11); person, personal appearance (Matt. 22:16; Mark 12:14); *en* [1722], in, *prosōpō*, in person, meaning in the name of as the representative of and by the authority of (2 Cor. 2:10, cf. 1 Cor. 5:4); a human being (2 Cor. 1:11); with the prep. *apó* (575), from, *prosōpou*, from the face or presence of (Acts 3:19; 5:41), from before (Acts 7:45); *eis* (1519), unto, *prósōpon*, in the presence of or sight, before (2 Cor. 8:24); *katá* (2596), against or before, *prósōpon*, before the face or presence, before (Luke 2:31; Acts 3:13; 25:16; Gal. 2:11); *pro* ([4253], before) *prósōpon*, before the face, before, whether of place or time (Matt. 11:10; Luke 1:76; 9:52; Acts 13:24). Deriv.: *prosōpolēpsía* (4382), respect of persons, partiality.

4384. Protássō; to put a specific command forward for a specific purpose (Acts 17:26). See *tássō* (5021), to place something in its category.

4388. Protíthēmi; from *pro* (4253), before, forth, and *títhēmi* (5087), to place. To propose, to set forth or before the eyes (Rom. 3:25); to propose, purpose, design beforehand (Rom. 1:13; Eph. 1:9).

4394. Prophēteía; the prophetic rank or work, the office or gift of a prophet. In Romans 12:6 it is classed with *diakonía* (1248), ministry or serving, and *didaskalía* (1319), teaching as a *chárisma* (5486), the result of God's grace or divine enablement to be exercised within the church (1 Cor. 12:10; 13:2; 1 Thess. 5:20; 1 Tim. 4:14; Rev. 11:6; 19:10). Elsewhere it means prophecy, that which is prophesied, foretold (Matt. 13:14; 1 Cor. 13:8; 14:6, 22; 1 Tim. 1:18; 2 Pet. 1:20, 21; Rev. 1:3; 22:7, 10, 18, 19). A prophecy is something that any believer may proclaim as telling forth God's Word. This, however, does not make him a prophet (*prophḗtēs* [4396], which is used in the NT in a very restrictive sense). Prophets are placed side by side with the apostles as the foundation of the NT Church (Eph. 2:20; 3:5), and also with the evangelists who were the successors of the prophets (1 Cor. 12:28; Eph. 4:11). A prophet prophesies, but one who prophesies is not necessarily a prophet. Deriv.: see *prophḗtēs* (4396), prophet.

4395. Prophēteúō; from *prophḗtēs* (4396), prophet. To prophesy, to foretell things to come (Matt. 11:13; 15:7; Mark 7:6; 1 Pet. 1:10); to declare truths through the inspiration of God's Holy Spirit, whether by prediction or not (Luke 1:67; Acts 2:17; 19:6; 21:9; 1 Cor. 14:1, 3–5). The art of heathen divination, however, is described by the word *manteúomai* (3132).

4396. Prophḗtēs; from the prep. *pro* (4253), before or forth, and *phēmí* (5346), to speak. The word was used of soothsayers who announced beforehand the will of the gods with reference to the future, but this is only a secondary and derived sense, for *pro* must be regarded not as having reference to time meaning before, but rather as local, in the context of space (as in *próphasis* (4392), pretext, what one states or puts forth before another). *Prophḗtēs* means one who speaks openly before anyone, and is the technical name for an interpreter of the oracle, of a divine message. This meaning was never lost in Class. Gr. because the gods were thought of as knowing the future. This technical term came also to mean the interpreters of the future. In the OT, it indicates one to whom and through whom God spoke (Num. 12:2, cf. v. 6), also one to whom God made known His mysteries (Amos 3:7, 8). Hence, generally, one to whom God revealed His purposes, one to whom God spoke (Gen. 20:7, 8, 17, 18). Prediction of the future, while belonging to the subject matter of prophecy, did not form part of the true concept and is especially plain from the promise given in Deuteronomy 18:15, 18–20, cf. Numbers 12:8. The earlier name of a prophet indicating foretelling in Hebr. meant "seer" (1 Sam. 9:9). It is clear that what really characterized the prophet was immediate communion with God, a divine communication of what the prophet had to declare. This is confirmed by the two terms, "reveal myself" (*apokalúptomai* [601]) and "prophesy" in 1 Corinthians 14:29, 30. See Ephesians 3:5; 1 Peter 1:12. That the special element of prophesying was not merely predictions but a showing forth of God's will, especially of His saving purpose, is confirmed by 1 Corinthians 14:37. Two things are necessary for a prophet, an insight granted by God into the divine secrets or mysteries, and a communication to others of these secrets. It includes God's concept of grace, but with the warnings, announcements of judgment, and so forth, pertaining thereto. In the case of the OT, their preaching was a foretelling of the salvation yet to be accomplished. In the NT, prophecy was a publication of the salvation already accomplished, so far at least as it did not concern itself with realities still future. Accordingly, in Ephesians 2:20; 3:5, the prophets, named side by side with the Apostles (meaning the Twelve and those who were so commissioned by Jesus directly) as the foundation of the NT Church, are to be understood as exclusively NT prophets, named again in Ephesians 4:11 between apostles and evangelists (see 1 Cor. 12:28). NT prophets were for the Christian Church what OT prophets were for Israel. They maintained intact the immediate connection between the Church and the God of their salvation. They were messengers or communicators. Such prophets were not ordained in local churches nor do they have successors. The office of a prophet should not be confused with prophecy or the gift of prophecy, which pertains to all believers (1 Cor. 13:8; 14:3; 1 Tim.

1:18; 4:14; Rev. 11:6). Hence, the significant admonition in 1 Thessalonians 5:20, do not despise prophecies. One thing must be remembered—he who prophesies is not necessarily a prophet in the OT or NT sense of a restricted office. In the NT generally in the pl., *hoi prophḗtai*, the prophets, denotes the prophets of the OT. In the sing. *ho prophḗtēs*, the prophet, is applied to Christ with obvious reference to Deuteronomy 18; John 1:21; 6:14; 7:40; Acts 3:22; 7:37. *Prophḗtēs* is used of Christ (see Matt. 13:57; 14:5; 21:11; Mark 6:4, 15; Luke 4:24; 7:16, 39; 13:33; 24:19; John 4:19, 44; 9:17). We read of NT prophets in Acts 11:27; 13:1; 15:32; 21:10; 1 Corinthians 12:28, 29; 14:29, 32, 37; Ephesians 2:20; 3:5; 4:11; Revelation 11:10; 22:9. The word "prophet" is used in the general sense of the Cretan poet Epimenides (Titus 1:12). The fem. *prophḗtis* (4398) is used in Luke 2:36; Revelation 2:20. Deriv.: *phēmí* (5346), to say with the element of manifestation or enlightening; *prophēteúō* (4395), to prophesy; *prophēteía* (4394), the prophetic rank or work, the office or gift of a prophet; *blásphēmos* (989), blasphemer; *blasphēmía* (988), blasphemy or abuse; *blasphēméō* (987), to blaspheme, revile, calumniate.

4412. Próton; the neut. of *prótos* (4413), used adv. and signifying first. Of time, whether in a superlative sense (Matt. 6:33; Mark 16:9) or more commonly in a comparative sense (Matt. 5:24; 7:5; 8:21), *prótôn humốn*, before you (John 15:18). Of order, dignity (Rom. 3:2; 1 Cor. 12:28; 1 Tim. 2:1; 2 Pet. 1:20; 3:3).

4413. Prótos; the superlative degree of *pro* (4253), before. First; used of time (John 5:4; 1 Cor. 15:45, 47; 2 Tim. 4:16; Rev. 1:11, 17; 2:8); former, before, in a comparative sense, as first is often used in Eng. (Luke 2:2; John 1:15, 30, 42; 8:58; 20:4, 8; 1 Cor. 14:30); of order or situation (Acts 16:12); of dignity, first, chief, principal.

4416. Prōtótokos; from *prótos* (4413), first, and *tíktō* (5088), to bear, bring forth. The firstborn of man or beast (Heb. 11:28). As applied to Christ: (1) In respect of His being the firstborn of the virgin without excluding, however, the following higher sense in which He was eminently the firstborn (Matt. 1:25; Luke 2:7). (2) He is called the first-begotten or the firstborn of the whole creation (Col. 1:15), in that He existed before all things, and everything both in heaven and earth were created by Him. Furthermore, He was foreordained to inherit all things and to have the preeminence in all things, because all things were created unto Him or for Him (*eis autón*), as well as by Him (*di' autoú*). See Colossians 1:16–18. With the same meaning He is spoken of absolutely as the firstborn (*ton prōtótokon*) in Hebrews 1:6. (3) Christ is also called *prōtótokos ek tōn nekrōn*, the firstborn or first-begotten from the dead in regard to His being the first who rose from the dead, no more to die; being the first to arise to an immortal and incorruptible life. All those who were raised from the dead later died again, having had only a sample of the resurrection that is yet to come. The Lord Jesus, however, rose and did not become subject to death again (Col. 1:18; Rev. 1:5, cf. Acts 26:23; Rom. 6:9; 1 Cor. 15:20, 23). (4) This title is applied to Christ in respect of His being the firstborn among His brethren, both in holiness and glory (Rom. 8:29). The above are all the references where *prōtótokos* speaks of Christ. *Prōtótokos* also refers to saints. Saints are called the firstborn because under the law the firstborn were peculiarly appropriated to God and were heirs of a double honor and inheritance (Heb. 12:23, cf. Ex. 4:22). As an adj., *prōtótokos* is joined to *huiós* (5207), son, in Matthew 1:25; Luke 2:7: "and she gave birth to her firstborn son." The firstborn here adds prominence to the virginity of the mother of the Lord Jesus until that particular time (Ex. 13:2, 15; 34:19) where a child is spoken of as opening the womb. According to the laws of the OT, the firstborn male was holy to Jehovah and had to be redeemed (Num. 18:15; Luke 2:23, 24). The firstborn son also has special rights as the head of the family and heir (Gen. 25:31; 49:3; 2 Chr. 21:3, cf. Luke 1:32). As a subst., the firstborn, *ho prōtótokos* as above, is a name given to Christ with various attributes. In Colossians 1:15 Christ holds the same relation to all creation not that He is included as part of the creation, but that the relation of the whole creation to Him is determined by the fact that He is *prōtótokos*, the firstborn, *pásēs* (3956), of all, *ktíseōs* (2937), creation, so that without Him creation could not be (see v. 16). It is not said of Christ that He was *ktistheís*, created, and not of the creation that it was *techtheísa*, born or brought forth. Christ is spoken of in His relationship to creation as to time. He was before there was any creation whatsoever and was not part of the creation. Such relationship is quite a different and far more general one than that of the precedence of a firstborn. This difference in Christ's relationship to the creation is made clear by Colossians 1:17, a verse which has no meaning if *prōtótokos* does not denote Christ's superiority in dignity as well as in time. What is said of Him in Colossians 1:17, And He is before all things, shows that *prōtótokos* does not merely imply precedence in point of time, as if Christ were the beginning of a series of creations. In Hebrews 1:6 Christ is called *ho prōtótokos*, the firstborn, without any further qualification, and here (as in v. 5) a distinction between *huiós* (5207), son, and *ággelos* (32), angel, is referred to. In v. 6 this distinction is recognized. With reference to the angels, we are led to conclude that *prōtótokos* is here used instead of *huiós*, son, on account of this superiority, so that we have here before us a mode of expression analogous to that of Colossians 1:15, for the relationship of *gegénnēka* (1080), of being born of God, can no more be applied to the angels than to the *ktísis* (2937), creation, generally. In Hebrews 12:23, the Christian Church is called the "church of the firstborn, which are written in heaven," as holding a relationship to God analogous to that of Israel (Ex. 4:22) where Israel is presented as God's firstborn son, and perhaps as also holding a special relationship to all other creatures (James 1:18, cf. Heb. 12:16).

4434. Ptōchós; poor and helpless; one who in his abjectness (*ptōssō*) needs lifting. One who had fallen from a better estate. The *pénēs* (3993) may be poor but he earns his bread by daily labor. The *ptōchós* is so poor that he can only obtain his living by begging. The *pénēs* has nothing superfluous, while the *ptōchós* has nothing at all.

4456. Pōróō; from *pōros*, a small piece of stone broken off from a larger one. The verb means to harden, make hard like a stone, or to make callous and insensible to the touch. In the NT applied only in a spiritual sense to the hearts or minds of men (Mark 6:52; 8:17; John 12:40; Rom. 11:7; 2 Cor. 3:14). Deriv.: *pōrōsis* (4457), hardening.

4457. Pōrōsis; from *pōróō* (4456), to harden. Used figuratively, hardness, callousness, or blindness (Mark 3:5; Rom. 11:25; Eph. 4:18).

4472. Rantízō; from Class. Gr. *rainō*, to sprinkle. Sprinkling was the form of transfer of sacrificial blood in order to secure its atoning efficacy, the form of purifying connected with expiation. Sprinkling of persons took place only upon the ratifying of the covenant (Ex. 24:8); upon the consecration of the family of Aaron to the priesthood (Ex. 29:21); in cleansing from leprosy and pollution from a dead body (Lev. 14:7, 16; Num. 19:11). The first two cases dealt with the establishment of a covenant between God and His people and, accordingly, the application of the atoning blood by the mediator. In the last two we have the removal of fellowship with that which is of the nature of judgment against sin. But it is in keeping with the character of the provisional expiation that an operation (the sprinkling) took place only on God's side; on man's side once only at the outset and never afterward except when leprosy and contact with death (as anticipations of judgment) had actually annulled the covenant relation. It is thus that the sprinkling with the blood of Christ in Hebrews 12:24 is to be taken in the NT. It can properly be connected only with Exodus 24 and Numbers 19 and is to be understood of sprinkling on both sides (Heb. 9:13, 19, 21; 10:22), though no

mention is made of sprinkling corresponding with that of the holy place or the altar, as once done in the regular OT ritual (Heb. 9:12). Deriv.: *rantismós* (4473), sprinkling.

4473. Rantismós; from *rantízō* (4472), to sprinkle. Sprinkling. In the NT the blood of Christ corresponds to the blood of sprinkling (Heb. 12:24, cf. Heb. 9:13, 14; 1 Pet. 2). Denotes the application of the expiation made by Christ. In the OT it is the form of that purification which is accomplished by expiation.

4487. Rēma; from *réō*, to speak. A word spoken or uttered (Matt. 12:36; 27:14); a speech or sentence consisting of several words (Matt. 26:75; Mark 14:72; Luke 1:38; 2:50, cf. Rom. 10:8; Heb. 6:5; 1 Pet. 1:25); a word, command (Luke 5:5); denoting the operative or all-powerful word or command of God (Matt. 4:4; Heb. 1:3; 11:3, cf. 12:19); a report, account (Matt. 5:11). *Rēma* stands for the subject matter of the word, the thing which is spoken about (Luke 1:37; 2:15; Acts 10:37; 2 Cor. 13:1).

4506. Rúomai; or *rúō*. Properly denotes to draw with force and violence, to drag, pull, meaning to deliver or to draw out of danger or calamity and to liberate (Matt. 6:13; Luke 1:74; Rom. 7:24; 11:26; 2 Tim. 4:17).

4522. Sagénē; a long-drawn net or sweep-net, the ends of which were spread out by boats so as to cover a large portion of open sea. They were then drawn together, and all they contained was enclosed and taken (Matt. 13:47). Contrast *díktuon* (1350), net in a general sense; and *amphíblēstron* (293), casting net.

4559. Sarkikós; from *sárx* (4561), flesh. Carnal (Rom. 7:14; 1 Pet. 2:11). *Sárx* (4561) covers that entire domain of our fallen nature made subject to vanity in which sin springs up and moves (Rom. 7:18; 8:5). Syn.: *psuchikós* (5591), soulish, with affinity to natural sinful propensities. The person in whom the *sárx* (4561), the flesh, is more the ruling principle, even as *psuchikós* and *psuchē* (5590) is for the animalistic instincts. Ant.: *pneumatikós* (4152), spiritual.

4560. Sarkinos; fleshly material, made or consisting of flesh. Occurs only in 2 Corinthians 3:3. Characterized by the suffix *-inos* versus *-ikos* which carries an ethical meaning as in *sarkikós* (4559), with propensities of the flesh unto sin.

4561. Sárx; flesh, whether of men, beasts, fish, or birds (1 Cor. 15:39); the human body (Acts 2:26, 31; 2 Cor. 7:1; Eph. 2:15; 5:29; Col. 2:5). The expression in Jude 1:7, "going after strange flesh," denotes unnatural homosexual abominations (Rom. 1:27); man (Matt. 24:22; Luke 3:6; Acts 2:17; Rom. 3:20; 1 Cor. 1:29; Gal. 2:20; 1 Pet. 1:24). In John 1:14 when it speaks of the Word becoming flesh, it means He became man (or took human nature upon Himself) and became subject to suffering and mortality (1 Tim. 3:16; 1 John 4:2, 3). Also, the infirmity of human nature (Heb. 5:7); the corrupt nature of man subject to the filthy appetites and passions (John 3:6; Rom. 7:18; 8:6; Gal. 5:13, 16, 17, 19, 24; 6:9); natural relation or descent (Rom. 1:3; 9:3, 5; 11:14); fleshly and temporal advantages (2 Cor. 11:18); refers to the outward and carnal ordinances of the Mosaic Law (Gal. 3:3); the expression "flesh and blood" means either such infirm bodies as we now have (1 Cor. 15:50) in regard to our present weak and corruptible state (Matt. 16:17; Gal. 1:16; Eph. 6:12), or the corruptibility of our present body which will be replaced with incorruptibility (1 Cor. 15:50). Deriv.: *sarkikós* (4559), fleshly, carnal; *sarkinos* (4560), made or consisting of flesh, without any moral implication of following after fleshly lusts.

4567. Satanás; a Gr. form derived from the Aramaic (Hebr., *Satán*). An adversary. This is the second name given to the prince of the devils. The other name is *diábolos* (1228), devil (one who casts either himself or something else between two in order to separate them), the false accuser. In his name as Satan, he is the opposer, the adversary. *Satanás* is the prince of the fallen angels (Matt. 4:10; Mark 1:13) and also used as a collective word for evil spirits or devils (Matt. 12:26; Mark 3:23, 26; Luke 11:18). Applied by the Lord to Peter, who was considered as opposing the divine plan of man's redemption by Christ's sufferings and death, and thus as joining with Satan (Matt. 16:23; Mark 8:33).

4573. Sebázomai; from *sébō* or *sébomai* (4576), to worship religiously (Rom. 1:25). Occurs with *latreúō* (3000), to worship as in a cult. *Sebázomai* denotes not merely the act of pious reverence but the act or acts of worship. Applied to Nero (Acts 25:21, 25); Augustus (Acts 27:1). See *sébomai*, (4576), adore, worship. Deriv.: *sebastós* (4575), venerable, august.

4574. Sébasma; from *sebázomai* (4573), to worship religiously. The object of worship or veneration (Acts 17:23; 2 Thess. 2:4). See *sébomai* (4576), to worship religiously.

4576. Sébomai; worship, from the root *seb*, which originally meant to fall back, before. Such a bodily movement expressed an attitude of respect, being impressed by something great and lofty. Used only in the mid. voice in the NT, to worship, adore (Matt. 15:9; Mark 7:7; Acts 16:14; 18:7, 13; 19:27). The part. noun *sebómenos*, a worshiper of the true God (Acts 13:43, 50; 16:14; 17:4, 17). These were Gentile proselytes as expressed in Acts 13:43. See *sebázomai* (4573), to worship religiously.

4578. Seismós; earthquake (Matt. 24:7; Acts 16:26; Rev. 16:18); see *pnoē* (4157), breath, wind.

4586. Semnós; from *sebnós* (which in turn is from *sébomai* [4576], to worship, venerate). Venerable. *Semnós* does not merely indicate the earthly dignity (*kósmios* [2887]) lent to a person, but one who also owes his modesty to that higher citizenship which is also his, being one who inspires not only respect but reverence and worship. There lies something of majestic and awe-inspiring qualities in *semnós* which does not repel but rather invites and attracts (Phil. 4:8; 1 Tim. 3:8, 11; Titus 2:2). Syn.: *hieroprepés* (2412), acting like a sacred person.

4587. Semnótēs; from *semnós* (4586). Decency. Aristotle defined *semnótēs* as the average or the virtue that lies between two extremes of *authádeia* (related to *authádēs* [829], arrogance) and *aréskeia* (699), the subst. of *aréskō* [700], to please, or the ignoble seeking to please everybody. The endeavoring at all costs of dignity and truth to stand well with all the world. Therefore, *semnótēs* stands between caring to please nobody and endeavoring at all costs to please everybody. It is the ability to perform well one's duties as a citizen, but in addition showing that the dignity is not from this earth but from heaven, thus drawing respect and reverence. See 1 Timothy 2:2; 3:4; Titus 2:7.

4592. Sēmeíon; sign, miracle with an ethical end and purpose. They are valuable not so much for what they are as for what they indicate of the grace and power of the doer or of his immediate connection with a higher spiritual world (Mark 16:20; Acts 14:3; Heb. 2:4). See *dunámeis* (1411), mighty works; *megaleía* (3167), great works; *éndoxa* (1741), glorious works; *parádoxa* (3861), strange works; *thaumásia* (2297), admirable works; *térata* (5059), terrifying works.

4599. Sthenóō; or *stenóō*; from *sthenós*, strength; to strengthen. Only found in 1 Peter 5:10. Far more common with the priv. *a*, without, as in *asthenéō* (770), to lack in strength or to be sick; *asthéneia* (769), disease, infirmity, sickness, weakness; *asthenḗs* (772), sick, without strength, weak.

4607. Sikários; derived from the Latin *sica*, a short dagger. An assassin, robber. It is found only in Acts 21:38. Contrast the general term *phoneús* (5406), murderer, and *anthrōpoktónos* (443), man-slayer.

4608. Síkera; strong drink, an intoxicating liquor, whether wine (Num. 28:7), or more usually, that which is prepared from grain, fruit, honey, dates, as in Luke 1:15 where it occurs together with *oínos* (3631), wine. See Leviticus 10:9; Deuteronomy 29:6; Judges 13:4, 7, 14.

4624. Skandalízō; to commit that which leads to the fall or ruin of someone. Without reference to the element of deceit, it means to throw someone unawares into ruin; to give occasion for ungodly conduct resulting in the mischief incurred thereby (Matt. 5:29; 18:8, 9;

Mark 9:43, 45, 47; 1 Cor. 8:13, cf. Matt. 17:27; John 16:1; 1 Cor. 8:13); to craftily entice or lead to ruin, allowing someone to adopt a course in which he will unknowingly come to mischief and ruin (Matt. 18:6; Mark 9:42, 43; Luke 17:2). In the pass., to fall into ruin unawares; to be offended or to be caught or affected by a *skándalon* (4625), trap, or to regard something as a *skándalon*.

4625. Skándalon; the trigger in the trap on which the bait is placed and that springs the trap when it is touched by the animal, causing the trap to close. The word and its deriv. belong only to biblical and ecclesiastical Gr. Its counterpart in the Sept. is the word *pagís* (3803), trap. However, *pagís* simply implies a reference simply to the injury lurking or hidden in the ambush and not so much to the suffering; whereas, *skándalon* involves the conduct of the person who is thus injured. *Skándalon* always denotes the enticement or occasion leading to conduct which brings with it the ruin of the person in question. In the NT the concept of *skándalon* is concerned mainly with the fact that it incites certain behavior which leads to ruin and rarely denotes merely a hidden, unexpected cause of ruin (Rom. 9:33; 1 Pet. 2:8). In most cases, however, the *skándalon* is something which gives occasion to conduct leading to ruin; the course of sin leading to ruin or to a fall (Rom. 14:13; 1 Cor. 1:23; Gal. 5:11; Rev. 2:14). *Ta skándala* are things which lead others to turn away from God's salvation and thus to come to ruin (Matt. 18:7; Luke 17:1).

4641. Sklērokardía; from *sklērós* (4642), hard, and *kardía* (2588), heart. Hardness of heart, that is, stubbornness, obstinacy, perverseness (Matt. 19:8; Mark 10:5; 16:14). It indicates man's condition in his bearing toward God and the revelation of His grace for which He ought to have a willing and receptive place in his heart.

4642. Sklērós; hard (Matt. 25:24), related to touch. An adj. applied to that which, due to a lack of moisture, is hard and dry. In an ethical sense, it means rough, harsh. Contrast *austērós* (840), austere, related to the taste. Applies to things that draw together and contract the tongue, which are harsh and stringent to the palate (e. g., a new wine not yet mellowed by age, unripe fruit, etc.). *Sklērós* always conveys a grave reproach indicating a harsh, inhuman character, which is not the case with *austērós*.

4643. Sklērótēs; from *sklērós* (4642), dry, hard. Hardness, obstinacy, stubbornness (Rom. 2:5).

4645. Sklērúnō; to make hard or stiff, to harden, make obdurate. In the NT, applied only figuratively to the heart or mind (Acts 19:9; Rom. 9:18; Heb. 3:13). Joined with the pl. *kardiás* (2588), hearts (Heb. 3:8, 15; 4:7).

4648. Skopéō; used only in the pres. and imperfect. To look towards an object, to contemplate, give attention to; literally, to spy out (Luke 11:35; Rom. 16:17; 2 Cor. 4:18; Gal. 6:1; Phil. 2:4; 3:17). *Skopós* (4649), a scout or spy, also goal, aim, end (Phil. 3:14).

4649. Skopós; from *skopéō* (4648), to look toward a goal, give heed. Used as a mark at the goal or end of a race (Phil. 3:14, cf. 2 Cor. 4:18).

4653. Skotía; darkness (Matt. 10:27; Luke 12:3; John 6:17; 20:1). Figuratively, like *skótos* (4655), darkness, and with the prevailing associated idea of unhappiness or ruin (John 8:12; 12:35, 46). As light is not only the emblem of happiness but also of beneficence, darkness represents unhappiness (John 12:35; 1 John 2:11). Thus, *skotía* is not a figurative term for sin, but refers to the consequences of sin.

4655. Skótos; from *ischō*, to restrain, stop (for when one is overcome by the night he is forced to stop). Physical darkness (Matt. 27:45; Mark 15:33; Luke 23:44; 2 Cor. 4:6, cf. Acts 13:11); spiritual darkness, implying ignorance or error (John 3:19; Rom. 2:19); sin and misery (Matt. 4:16; Luke 1:79; Acts 26:18; 1 Thess. 5:4; 1 Pet. 2:9), also persons in such a state (Eph. 5:8); the works of darkness (Rom. 13:12; Eph. 5:11); such works as are usually practiced by men in darkness or secretly (cf. 1 Cor. 4:5; 1 John 1:6). Denotes the infernal spirits as opposite to Christ, the sun or light of righteousness (Luke 22:53). Eternal misery and damnation (Matt. 8:12; 2 Pet. 2:17; Jude 1:13). Syn.: *gnóphos* (1105), a thick dark cloud; *zóphos* (2217), infernal darkness; *achlús* (887), a thick mist, fog. Ant.: *phós* (5457), light.

4678. Sophía; wisdom, the knowledge of how to regulate one's relationship with God, wisdom which is related to goodness (Matt. 12:42; Eph. 1:8). When one is wise unto God, he is *phrónimos* (5429), prudent with others, and knows how to regulate circumstances. Adj. or adj. noun: *sophós* (4680), wise, applied to God and man, both in respect of true spiritual and heavenly wisdom; and also of false or worldly wisdom; skillful, expert; sensible, judicious although this is more frequently expressed by *phrónimos*, prudent. Related words: *sophízō* (4679), to make wise, instruct (2 Tim. 3:15); *sophízomai*, pass. voice, to devise cunningly or deceitfully (2 Pet. 1:16).

4680. Sophós; derived probably from the Hebr. *sophím*, signifying watchmen. In the OT these watchmen used to ascend to the mountains so that they might see all around (Num. 23:14). The Greeks observed the course and motions of the heavens and called themselves *sophoí*. Therefore, in its basic meaning *sophós* is one who knows how to regulate his course in view of movements of the heavens or of God. NT meanings: (1) Wise, as applied to God (Rom. 16:27; 1 Tim. 1:17); to man both in respect of truth (1 Cor. 3:18; Eph. 5:15) and also of false or worldly wisdom (Matt. 11:25; Rom. 1:22; 1 Cor. 1:19, 20, 26). (2) Skillful, expert (1 Cor. 3:10). In Class. Gr. used of workmen to show their expertise. (3) Prudent, sensible, judicious. To vindicate this quality the Greeks used to speak of a person as *phrónimos* (5429) rather than *sophós*. However, it is used in this manner in 1 Corinthians 6:5, and in the comparative degree, wiser, in 1 Corinthians 1:25. See *sophía* (4678), wisdom.

4684. Spataláō; to live in luxury; the same characteristics as *strēniáō* (4763), to live luxuriously, and *trupháō* (5171), to live in pleasure, but with the further notion of wastefulness and prodigality (1 Tim. 5:6; James 5:5). *Spataláō* applied to the prodigal son (Luke 15:13); *trupháō* to the rich man faring sumptuously every day (Luke 16:19); *strēniáō* to Jeshurun, when, waxing fat, he kicked (Sept.: Deut. 32:15).

4690. Spérma; seed for sowing and growing seed (i.e., both what is sown as containing the germ of new fruit and the seed which is growing out of the seed sown. Originally used of plants as seed (Matt. 13:24, 27, 32, 37, 38; 2 Cor. 9:10); as seed sown and growing, produce. In 1 John 3:9 the *spérma* of God denotes God's power at work, the Holy Spirit working in the hearts of believers (John 1:13). Also figuratively used of living beings, as of the seed of the man; of posterity or descendants. In Class. Gr. terminology it does not strictly signify descendants collectively, nor posterity as a whole, but primarily only the individual, the child, offspring, son or daughter. In the Bible, however, *spérma* has mostly a coll. meaning (Rev. 12:17). Thus, it denotes the immediate descendants, children (Matt. 22:24, 25; Mark 12:19–22; Luke 20:28). For this reason, especially in the Sept. (Psalms 37:28; 69:36; Proverbs 11:21; Isaiah 1:4; 57:4; 65:23), it is similar in meaning to *génnēma* (1081), offspring, and signifies a spiritual fellowship without reference to relationship of race. The expression "the seed of David" (John 7:42; Rom. 1:3; 2 Tim. 2:8) means progeny, posterity of David (see 2 Sam. 7:12; Ps. 89:4; Acts 13:23). Similarly with the term the *spérma* of Abraham (Luke 1:55; John 8:33, 37; Acts 3:25; 7:5, 6; Rom. 4:13, 16, 18). Where Christ is designated as the progeny or offspring of Abraham, He is referred to as the Messiah. There are, indeed, *spérmata*, seeds, of Abraham, lines of descent, those namely of Ishmael or Esau besides Isaac or Israel; yet the promise does not apply to all the lines of descent, but to one line which alone is always meant by the seed of Abraham. To take *spérmata* (pl.) as a coll. term, and *spérma* (sing.) of an individual person, is foreign to Pauline phraseology; the pl. is never used of a coll. concept. In Galatians 3:16, one line of progeny must be distinguished

from more than one, *spérma*, seed, coll. *spérmata*, seeds, lines of descendants, taking into account Genesis 21:12, 13 and Galatians 3:29. That Paul has in mind the several lines of descendants from Abraham is evident in Galatians 4:22.

4695. Spilóō; to defile, spot; found only in James 3:6; Jude 1:23. Close to the meaning of *miaínō* (3392), to defile.

4696. Spílos; a spot, moral blemish (Eph. 5:27; 1 Pet. 2:13). Related words: *áspilos* (784), without spot; *spílas* (4694), spot (Jude 1:12); equivalent to *spílos*.

4714. Stásis; from *hístēmi* (2476), to stand. A standing, stability, continuance (Heb. 9:8). An insurrection, sedition or a standing up (Mark 15:7; Luke 23:19, 25; Acts 19:40; 24:5) referring to a civil insurrection, while *pólemos* (4171), war, refers to a foreign strife. A contention, dissension, dispute (Acts 15:2; 23:7, 10).

4716. Staurós; from *hístēmi* (2476), to stand. A cross, a stake for execution, an instrument of torture. It was not abolished until the time of Constantine, who put an end to it out of regard to Christianity. Crucifixion was the same time an execution, a pillory, and an instrument of torture. In the NT it means: (1) A Roman cross consisting of a straight piece of wood fixed in the earth with a transverse beam fastened across its top to which the person's hands were nailed, and a small piece of wood projecting from the vertical piece, to which the crucified person's feet were nailed. This is the type of cross on which the Lord Jesus suffered (Matt. 27:32, 40, 42). (2) It refers to the whole passion of Christ and the merit of His sufferings and death (Gal. 6:14; Eph. 2:16) and also to the doctrine concerning these (1 Cor. 1:17; Gal. 6:12). (3) It denotes that portion of affliction which is endured by pious and good men as a trial of their faith, to conform them to the example of their crucified Master (Matt. 10:38; 16:24; Mark 8:34; 10:21; Luke 9:23; 14:27). The expressions of taking up or carrying the cross allude to the Roman custom of making the criminal carry the cross on which he was to suffer (John 19:17). When we read of the antagonism to the cross of Christ, we must understand it as antagonism to a redemption which was accomplished through the deepest humiliation, not through a display of power and glory (Gal. 6:14; Phil. 2:5–8). It is often not the sacrifice of Christ that is emphasized in the NT, but the blood of Christ (Col. 1:20) as the means of redemption. This is because the blood refers to the sacrifice, while the cross refers more to the shame. Deriv.: *stauróō* (4717), to crucify.

4717. Stauróō; from *staurós* (4716), cross. To crucify, spoken of the punishment of crucifixion (Matt. 20:19; 23:34; 26:2); to crucify the flesh along with its affections and lusts so as to mortify them through the faith and love of the crucified Christ (Gal. 5:24; 6:14). When Paul says in Galatians 6:14, "The world has been crucified unto me, and I to the world," he means that so great was his regard for his crucified Savior that the world no longer had any more charm for him than the corpse of a crucified malefactor would have, nor did he take any more delight in worldly things than a person expiring on a cross would take delight in the objects around him. Deriv.: *staurós* (4716), cross; *anastauróō* (388), to crucify again; *sunstauróō* (4957), to crucify with.

4724. Stéllō; related to *hístēmi* (2476), to set, place, or stand. To send, as such it does not occur in the NT, but it does occur in many deriv. with a prep., especially *apostéllō* (649), send, from *apóstolos* (652), an apostle or one sent from. In its mid. form, *stéllomai* with an acc. of the prep. *apó* (575) following, meaning to avoid or withdraw oneself from, to send oneself away from (2 Cor. 8:20; 2 Thess. 3:6).

4730. Stenochōría; from *stenós* (4728), narrow, and *chōréō* (5562), to be in or to fit in a space. A narrow place (Rom. 2:9). Symbolically, great distress, straights (Rom. 8:35; 2 Cor. 6:4; 12:10). Distinguished from *thlípsis* (2347), tribulation. In the four occurrences of stenochōría in the NT these two words are used together (Rom. 2:9; 8:35; 2 Cor. 6:4). *Thlípsis* has more the meaning of crushing or affliction and is more serious than *stenochōría* which may refer more to the narrowness of room or being pressed from the sides rather than from the top. *Stenochōría* may be the opposite of *ánesis* (425), which figuratively speaking means plenty of room for relaxation. Deriv.: *stenochōréomai* (4729), to be distressed, straitened.

4735. Stéphanos; crown. In Class. Gr. not used of the kingly crown but of the crown of victory in games, of civic worth, military valor, nuptial joy, festal gladness. Woven of oak, ivy, myrtle, olive leaves or flowers. Used as a wreath or the garland. Contrast *diádēma* (1238), diadem, a white linen band encircling the brow to indicate the assumption of royal dignity.

4747. Stoicheíon; from *stoíchos*, row, and *stoichéō* (4748), to put or go in a row, one of a series. In the pl. *ta stoicheía*, the elements or first principles of matter from which other things proceed in order or of which they are composed (2 Pet. 3:10, 12). Figuratively refers to the elements of first principles of the Christian doctrine (Heb. 5:12). Paul calls the ceremonial ordinances of the Mosaic Law the elements of the world or worldly elements (Gal. 4:3; Col. 2:8, 20). In Galatians 4:9, he calls them weak and poor elements when considered merely in themselves and in opposition to the great realities to which they were designed to lead. These elements contain the rudiments of the knowledge of Christ. The Law, as a schoolmaster, was to bring the Jews to this knowledge (Gal. 3:24). They are called worldly as consisting in outward worldly institutions (Heb. 9:1).

4749. Stolé; from *stéllō* (4724), to send. A stately robe reaching to the feet or a train sweeping the ground. More often worn by women (Mark 12:38; 16:5; Luke 15:22; 20:46; Rev. 6:11; 7:9, 13, 14).

4762. Stréphō; to turn. Intrans., to turn oneself (Acts 7:42); mid., to turn oneself (Acts 13:46); in a moral sense, to change, alter, adopt another course (Matt. 18:3). Deriv.: *epistréphō* (1994), to turn toward, turn about to; *apostréphō* (654), to turn away or back; *epistrophé* (1995), to return.

4763. Strēniáō; to be insolent because of wealth. To act with wantonness and petulance from abundance. It has the connotation of strength and vigor (not effeminacy and self-indulgence) like *trupháō* (5171), to live in pleasure. Occurs only in Revelation 18:7, 9. Deriv.: the noun, *strēnos* (4764), luxury (Rev. 18:3); the comp. verb *katastrēniáō* (2691), to become lascivious against.

4774. Suggnómē; from *sun* (4862), with, and *gnómē* (1106), opinion, sentiment, will. Concession, permission, leave (1 Cor. 7:6).

4777. Sugkakopathéō; from *sun* (4862), together with, and *kakopathéō* (2553), to suffer evil or affliction. Only in 2 Timothy 1:8. To suffer evil or affliction together with another.

4779. Sugkaléō; from *sun* (4862), together, and *kaléō* (2564), to call. To call together (Mark 15:16; Luke 9:1; 15:6, 9; 23:13; Acts 5:21; 10:24; 28:17).

4789. Sugklēronómos; from *sun* (4862), together, and *klēronómos* (2818), an heir, one who has a lot or who is allotted something. One who participates in the same lot, a joint heir (Rom. 8:17). Refers to a personal equality based on an equality of possession. In Hebrews 11:9 it speaks of Isaac and Jacob in their relation to Abraham; in 1 Peter 3:7 of women in relation to their husbands being joint heirs of the grace of life; in Ephesians 3:6 of the Gentiles being joint heirs with Israel (see also Eph. 1:11).

4790. Sugkoinōnéō; from *sun* (4862), together with, and *koinōnéō* (2841), to partake. To participate in something with someone. In the NT only, with a dat. of thing, as a strengthened form of *koinōnéō* (2841), to be common (Eph. 5:11; Phil. 4:14; Rev. 18:4; noun form *sugkoinōnós*).

4793. Sugkrínō; from *sun* (4862), together, and *krínō* (2919), to judge. Literally, to separate and arrange together, combine, unite. To compare (2 Cor. 10:12); comparing spiritual things with spiritual (1 Cor. 2:13). Ant.: *diakrínō* (1252), to separate one from another, divide, part.

4832. Súmmorphos; from *sun* (4862), together with, and *morphḗ* (3444), form. In Romans 8:29, it refers to the conformity of children of God "to the image of his Son" and in Philippians 3:21 of their physical conformity to His body of glory. Deriv.: *summorphóō* (4833), becoming conformed (Phil. 3:10).

4834. Sumpathéō; from *sun* (4862), together with, and *páschō* (3958), to suffer. With a dat., to sympathize with, to be compassionate, have compassion upon (Heb. 4:15; 10:34).

4835. Sumpathḗs; from *sumpathéō* (4834), to feel together with. Compassionate, sympathizing, adj. (1 Pet. 3:8).

4841. Sumpáschō; from *sun* (4862), together with, and *páschō* (3958), to suffer. To suffer together with (Rom. 8:17; 1 Cor. 12:26).

4845. Sumplēróō; from *sun* (4862), an intens. prep., and *plēróō* (4137), to fill. Fulfill. The comp. verb, to fill to the brim. Used in the pass., to be filled completely, as with water (Luke 8:23, cf. Mark 4:37). In the pass., used of time, to be fulfilled or fully come (Luke 9:51; Acts 2:1, cf. John 7:8).

4850. Sumpresbúteros; from *sun* (4862), together with, and *presbúteros* (4245), an elder. A fellow elder (1 Pet. 5:1). Peter reminds the elders of the dignity of their office that they might not forget its duties (vv. 2, 3).

4851. Sumphérō; from *sun* (4862), together, and *pherō* (5342), to bring. To bring together (Acts 19:19); absolutely or with a dat. following, to be profitable, advantageous, to conduce or bring together for the benefit of another. Used either personally (1 Cor. 6:12; 10:23; 2 Cor. 8:10) or impersonally, meaning that it is advantageous (Matt. 5:29; 19:10). The neut. part. *to* (neut. def. art.), the *sumphéron*, advantage, profit, benefit (1 Cor. 7:35; 10:33; 12:7; Heb. 12:10). See *phérō* (5342), to bring.

4854. Súmphutos; from *sun* (4862), together, and *phúō* (5453), to become, to increase. Growing at the same time, growing together, growing over (Rom. 6:5). It means not merely homogeneousness, but being united one with another.

4861. Súmpsuchos; from *sun* (4862) together, and *psuché* (5590), soul. Joined together in soul or sentiment, unanimous (Phil. 2:2). It signifies community of life and love. Deriv.: *psuché* (5590), soul; *psuchikós* (5591), soulish or driven by one's natural instinct; *ápsuchos* (895), without a soul, lifeless; *isópsuchos* (2473), equal-souled or like-minded; *dípsuchos* (1374), double-souled or double-minded.

4862. Sun; together, as a prep. governing only the dat., with, implying a nearer and closer connection than *metá* (3326), with. When *sun* demonstrates connection, consort, as arising from likeness of doing or suffering from a common lot or event, it means "in like manner with" (Rom. 6:8). When used, however, of connection arising from possession, it means being entrusted with anything (1 Cor. 15:10). Implies a joint working, cooperation, and when it does, it speaks of a means, instrument, with, through, by virtue of (1 Cor. 5:4); also addition, accession, like the Eng. "with," equivalent to besides, over and above (Luke 24:21). In composition, *sun* implies society, companionship, consort, with, together, as the English prefix con-; also therewith, withal, as in *sunágō* (4863), to gather together. Denotes completeness, all together, round about, on every side, wholly, and in this way it becomes an intens. as in *sugkalúptō* (4780), to cover altogether.

4863. Sunágō; from *sun* (4862), and *ágō* (71), to lead, from which comes *sunagōgḗ* (4864), synagogue. To take in, lodge, entertain (Matt. 25:35). It has a much gentler meaning than *sullégō* (4816), to gather together. The difference between the two words is demonstrated in Matthew 13:28, when the verb *sullégō* is used for collecting the tares and the word *sunágō* is used for gathering together the wheat in the barn (in v. 30).

4864. Sunagōgḗ; from *sunágō* (4863), to lead together, assemble. A gathering, congregation, synagogue. The congregation of Israel was designated by the term *sunagōgḗ* or *ekklēsía* (1577), church. As the word was used, it did not imply the natural unity of the people, but a community established in a special way and for a special object. In the NT, where *ekklēsía*, is adopted as the name for God's Church (that is, the congregation of the saved), *sunagōgḗ* is used to designate the fellowship only in Revelation 2:9; 3:9, where the unbelieving Jews as a body are called the "synagogue of Satan." See also Acts 14:1; 17:1; 18:7. The synagogue of Satan is set as opposite to the church of God. A synagogue was finally designated as the Sabbath assembly of the Jews (Acts 13:43). In James 2:2 a synagogue is used to designate the worshiping assembly of the Jewish Christians. In other places in the NT it is used as the assembly place of the Jews.

4865. Sunagōnízomai; from *sun* (4862), together, and *agōnízomai* (75), to contend for victory in the public games. To fight in company with, assist someone in a fight, help (Rom. 15:30). The word is chosen with reference to the opposers from whom the Apostle Paul desired to be delivered (v. 31), not like *agōnízomai* (Col. 4:12).

4888. Sundoxázō; from *sun* (4862), together, and *doxázō* (1392), to glorify. To glorify together (Rom. 8:17).

4889. Sundoulos; from *sun* (4862), together, and *doúlos* (1401), slave. A fellow slave found in the same natural conditions (Matt. 18:28, 29, 31, 33; 24:49); a servant of the same Lord (Col. 1:7; 4:7; Rev. 6:11); of angels (Rev. 19:10; 22:9).

4891. Sunegeírō; from *sun* (4862), together, and *egeírō* (1453), to raise. To awaken together, both with cooperation and common activity. In the NT it occurs first in Ephesians 2:6 where our being "raised up together" with Christ is referred to. The revivification of Christ, His assuming a new life (Rom. 6:10), involves at the same time revivifying those that are His. It refers to the delivery from the state into which they have been brought by sin and which brought death to them (Rom. 6:4, 10). Therefore, the *sun*, together, in *sunegeírō*, expresses not merely the similarity of the deliverance from the death of sin to new life in Christ, but it affirms that it is connected with Christ's resurrection. It also refers to an effect brought about on God's part through His death and resurrection and our appropriation of that and the symbolism of it in baptism (Rom. 6:4). It has a similar meaning in Colossians 2:12; 3:1. Practically, the meaning coincides with being justified (Rom. 4:25; 5:1; Col. 2:12, 13).

4893. Suneídēsis; conscience. A fem. noun from *suneídō* (4894), to know together with, from *sún* (4862), together with, and *eídō* (1492), to know intuitively (which see for deriv.). Conscience, to be one's own witness, one's own consciousness coming forward as witness. It denotes an abiding consciousness whose nature it is to bear witness to the subject regarding his own conduct in a moral sense (Tit. 1:15). It is self-consciousness. Particularly, a knowing with oneself, consciousness; and hence conscience, that faculty of the soul which distinguishes between right and wrong, and prompts to choose the former and avoid the latter (Jn. 8:9; Rom. 2:15; 9:1; 13:5; 1 Cor. 10:25, 27-29; 2 Cor. 1:12; 1 Tim. 4:2; Tit. 1:15; Heb. 9:9,14; 10:2, 22). Syn.: *súnesis* (4907), mentally putting it together, refers to the presentiment of an obligation bearing witness to itself in the consciousness. *Súnesis* is that which generally precedes action, therefore *súnesis* is moral obligation. However, in the NT *suneídēsis* is not merely the testimony of one's own conduct borne by consciousness (Rom. 9:1), but at the same time also the testimony concerning duty (Rom. 1:19, 21, 32; 2:15; 2 Cor. 1:12).

4894. Súnoida; from *sun* (4862), and *oída*, or *eídō* (1492), to know intuitively. (The form suneídō found in Strong's Dictionary is what the present form would be if it existed, but there is no such form in the Gr.) To know together with, to know what others know or do, intend to do, or have done. A precise definition would be to be conscious of oneself or to be one's own witness. The word is used by Paul in 1 Corinthians 4:4 in the sense of being compelled to testify against oneself. The verb suneídéō is used also in Acts 5:2; 12:12;

14:6. From this verb is derived the noun *suneídēsis* (4893), translated "conscience," the subject's own consciousness in which he bears witness to himself and appears as his own witness.

4895. Súneimi; fut. *sunésomai*, from *sun* (4862), together and *eimí* (1510), to be, to come. With the dat. (Luke 9:18; Acts 22:11). Syn.: *sunérchomai* (4905), to come together; *paragínomai* (3854), to come or be near; *sumparagínomai* (4836), to come together, to stand at one's side; *sunanabaín* (4872), to come up with; *suntugchánō* (4940), to chance upon with. Ant.: *sunporeúomai* (4848), to go together with; *ápeimi* (548), to go away; *sugkatabínō* (4782), to go down with; *éxeimi* (1826), to go out; *sunérchomai* (4905), to go with.

4896. Súneimi; only in the part. *suniṓn*, to go or come or gather together, convene, bring it together, understand, deliberate, from *sun* (4862), together, and *eimí*, to go, come, bring (see *ápeimi* [549] for other comp.). Equal to *suniēmi* (4920), to bring together, perceive, understand, from which is derived the noun *súnesis* (4907), understanding, perception; *sunetós* (4908), prudent, one who puts things together; *asúnetos* (801), one without understanding, discernment. Used absolutely (Luke 8:4). Syn.: *sunágō* (4863), to gather or bring together and the more inten. *episunágō* (1996), to gather together, emphasizing the place where they are gathered; *sullégō* (4816), to collect or gather up or out; *sunathroízō* (4867), to gather together. In a figurative sense of perceiving, understanding: *noéō* (3539), to perceive with the mind; *ginṓskō* (1097), to know experientially; *epístamai* (1987), to know well; *punthánomai* (4441), to understand by searching, inquiring; *gnōrízō* (1107), to make known, to come to know; *manthánō* (3129), understand, learn. Ant.: *agnoéō* (50), to be ignorant, not understand; *apistéō* (569), to disbelieve, not to allow one to be persuaded; *apeithéō* (544), to disbelieve, not to allow one to be persuaded by exercising his mental capacities.

4907. Súnesis; insight, the critical faculty of how to evaluate people, things, circumstances (Mark 12:33; Luke 2:47; 1 Cor. 1:19; Eph. 3:4; Col. 1:9; 2:2; 2 Tim. 2:7).

4908. Sunetós; intelligent, sagacious, penetrating. It refers to having *súnesis* (4907), the critical faculty of discernment (Matt. 11:25; Luke 10:21; Acts 13:7; 1 Cor. 1:19).

4912. Sunéchō; from *sun* (4862), an intens. prep., and *échō* (2192), to have. To hold fast (Luke 22:63); to straighten, confine (Luke 8:45; 19:43). Mid. voice, *sunéchomai*, to be in a moral strait (Luke 12:50; Acts 18:5; Phil. 1:23); to constrain, bind (2 Cor. 5:14); to stop the ears (Acts 7:57). Pass. voice, *sunéchomai*, to be detained, afflicted with, to be sick of (Matt. 4:24; Luke 4:38; Acts 28:8); to be under the influence of (Luke 8:37).

4920. Suniēmi; from *sun* (4862), together or together with, and *hiēmi*, to send or put. To bring together. When the word is confined to the sphere of mental perception, it means to hear, notice, perceive, recognize, understand, put something together and make sense out of it. Thus, it strictly denotes the collecting together of the individual features of an object into a whole, as collecting the pieces of a puzzle and putting them together. According to Aristotle it is a syn. of *manthánō* (3129), to learn, to understand, and differs from *noéō* (3539), to merely perceive. *Manthánō* involves the capability of knowing and *suniēmi* involves the activity of knowing (Matt. 15:16; Mark 8:17; Luke 24:45). The difference between *suniēmi* and *ginṓskō* (1097), to know, knowledge acquired by reflection and consideration, is that *suniēmi* involves immediate knowledge (Luke 8:9, 10; 18:34) even as the verb *oída*, derived from *eídō* (1492). It is a moral reflection, pondering, or laying to heart (Eph. 5:17) as opposed to merely reflecting on the meaning of something. It involves moral or religious conduct and is attributed to the heart (Mark 6:52; 8:17; Acts 28:27). The adj. *sunetós* (4908), judicious, and *asúnetos* (801), non-judicious, are also used with the same moral significance. The verb is seldom used with an obj. In a weakened sense, the verb means to notice, heed, hear, or listen to.

4921. Sunístēmi; or *sunistáō;* from *sun* (4862), together with, and *hístēmi* (2476) or *histáō,* to set, place. To set or place together with. In the perf. act. joined with a dat., to stand together with (Luke 9:32); to stand together, stand (2 Pet. 3:5), referring to the earth standing out of the water and in the water in its first formation (Sept.: Gen. 1:6) and at the height of the flood (Gen. 8:2); to consist, subsist (Col. 1:17); to commend, recommend or make acceptable or illustrious (Rom. 3:5; 5:8; 2 Cor. 4:2; 10:18; 12:11); to commend, recommend, commit to the care or kindness of another (Rom. 16:1); to show, prove, approve, manifest (2 Cor. 6:4; 7:11; Gal. 2:18).

4930. Suntéleia; from *suntéléō* (4931). A termination, completion. In the NT used only in the expressions *suntéleia tou aiốnos,* "the end of the world" (Matt. 13:39, 40, 49; 24:3; 28:20) and *tōn aiốnốn,* "of the world" (Heb. 9:26).

4931. Suntéléō; from *sun* (4862), an intens. prep., and *teléō* (5055), to finish. To finish entirely, make an end of (Matt. 7:28; Luke 4:13); of time (Luke 4:2; Acts 21:27); to accomplish, perform (Mark 13:4; Rom. 9:28); to complete (Heb. 8:8). Deriv.: *suntéleia* (4930), a finishing, consummation, end; not the termination but the heading up of events to the appointed climax.

4933. Suntēréō; from *sún* (4862), an intens. prep., and *tēréō* (5083), to guard, keep. To preserve, keep safe, close. In Luke 2:19, contrast *diatēréō* (1301) in v. 51 with the words of the shepherds. In Mark 6:20, used of the preservation of John the Baptist from Herodias. In Matthew 9:17 (in some MSS Luke 5:38), used of the preservation of wineskins.

4951. Súrō; to draw, drag, whether of things (John 21:8) or persons (Acts 8:3; 14:19; 17:6). It involves the notion of violence which is not necessarily expressed in *helkúō* (1670), to attract. Súrō has the sense of dragging something or someone which is unable to resist, like pulling in a fish already hooked or dragging a dead body.

4954. Sússōmos; from *sun* (4862), together, and *sốma* (4983), body. United in one body, that is, members of the body of Christ (Eph. 3:6). *Sốma* is used elsewhere of the preservation of the Church, meaning incorporated with the Church.

4957. Sustauróō; from *sun* (4862), together with, and *stauróō* (4717), to crucify. To crucify together with, whether bodily (Matt. 27:44; Mark 15:32; John 19:32), or spiritually by mortifying our worldly and fleshly lusts by the cross of Christ (Rom. 6:6; Gal. 2:20).

4964. Suschēmatízō; from *sun* (4862), together with, and *schēmatízō,* to fashion, which is from *schéma* (4976), fashion. With a dat. following, to conform to (Rom. 12:2; 1 Pet. 1:14). In Romans 12:2 is *mē* (3361), not, and *suschēmatízesthe,* with this age, that is, do not fall in with the external and fleeting fashions of this age nor be fashioned to them, but undergo a deep inner change (*metamorphoústhe* [3339]) by the qualitative renewing (*anakainốsei* [341]) of your mind as the Spirit of God alone can work in you (2 Cor. 3:18).

4976. Schéma; from *éschēmai,* perf. pass. of *échō* (2192), have. Fashion, external form, appearance (1 Cor. 7:31), possibly from *skéma* from the scene of the theater. The *schéma* of Philippians 2:8 is Jesus' whole outward appearance in which there was no difference between the Incarnate Son and the other children of men. It was the mode of His manifestation. The phrase in Philippians 2:8, "and being found in fashion (*schémati*) as a man," brings forward the distinction of *schéma* with *morphé* (3444), essence. The verity of the incarnation that He was God and continued to be God is expressed with *morphé.* The verb for this is *labốn* (*lambánō* [2983]) "took upon him," aor. act. part., having taken on His own initiative and power the form of a servant (*doúlou* [1401]). The words that follow, *kai schémati euretheís* (*heurískō* [2147]), "and being found in fashion as a man," declare the outward facts which came under the knowledge of His fellow men with an emphasis on the verb *euretheís,* "being found." The *schéma* here signifies the whole outward appearance. In no physical way was He found differ-

ent from other children of men in contrast to His *morphé* (3444) which was the externalization of His inner character which was without sin. Deriv.: *metaschēmatízō* (3345), to change the external shape. Contrast *metamorphóō* (3339), change, both internal and external. See *morphóō* (3445), to fashion.

4978. Schísma; from *schízō* (4977), to split, tear. Schism; division in mind, sentiment, and so into factions (Matt. 9:16; Mark 2:21; John 7:43; 9:16; 10:19; 1 Cor. 1:10; 11:18; 12:25). Contrast *haíresis* (139), heresy, which indicates a tendency opposite the accepted doctrine or practice.

4982. Sốzō; to save. Salvation in regard to: (1) Material and temporal deliverance from danger, suffering, and so forth. (Matt. 8:25; Mark 13:20; Luke 23:35; John 12:27; 1 Tim. 2:15; 2 Tim. 4:18); sickness (Matt. 9:22; Mark 5:34; Luke 8:48; James 5:15); preservation (Jude 1:5). (2) The spiritual and eternal salvation granted immediately by God to those who believe on Christ (Acts 2:47; 16:31; Rom. 8:24; Eph. 2:5, 8; 1 Tim. 2:4; 2 Tim. 1:9; Titus 3:5); human agency in this (Rom. 11:14; 1 Cor. 7:16; 9:22). (3) The present experience of God's power to deliver from the bondage of sin (Matt. 1:21; Rom. 5:10; 1 Cor. 15:2; Heb. 7:25; James 1:21); human agency in this (1 Tim. 4:16). (4) The future deliverance of believers at the Second Coming (Rom. 5:9). (5) The deliverance of Israel (Rom. 11:26). (6) All the blessings inclusively bestowed by God on men in Christ (Luke 19:10; John 10:9; 1 Cor. 10:33; 1 Tim. 1:15). (7) Those who endure to the end, the time of the Great Tribulation (Matt. 10:22; Mark 13:13). (8) The individual believer who, though losing his reward at the Judgment Seat of Christ, will not lose his salvation (1 Cor. 3:15). (9) The deliverance of the nations at the millenium (Rev. 21:24). Deriv.: *diasốzō* (1295), to rescue; *sōtēría* (4991), salvation; *sōtér* (4990), Savior; *sōtérion* (4992), salvation; *sōtérios* (4992), saving.

4983. Sốma; body. Various meanings: (1) A corporeal body, whether of a man (Matt. 6:25; 10:28) or of some other creature (James 3:3); either living or dead (Matt. 14:12; 27:58; Heb. 13:11). (2) In the pl., often used in the Gr. writers for the bodies of men taken in war and reduced to slavery, thus meaning slaves, as applied in Rev. 18:13. (3) The Church, in respect of Christ who is the head of this body and supplies its spiritual life and motion (Eph. 1:23; 4:16; Col. 1:18; 2:19); in respect of believers, who are mystical members of one body (Rom. 12:5; 1 Cor. 12:12 ff.). (4) An organized group, as of plants (1 Cor. 15:37, 38). (5) A body, material substance (1 Cor. 15:40). (6) Substance or reality as opposed to shadows or types (Col. 2:17). The body is the vessel of the spiritual part of man which is called *psuché,* distinguished from *pneúma* (4151) which only man possesses (1 Thess. 5:23). A separation of the physical from the spiritual is possible (Luke 12:4; 2 Cor. 12:2, 3) and is accomplished at death. With reference to this separation, the body may be regarded as the covering, the dwelling place (2 Cor. 5:1–4, 6, 8). The *sốma psuchikón* (5591), soulish body, means that body which is driven and directed by the natural sinful instincts of man while the *sốma pneumatikón* (4152) is our new resurrection body which will be governed only by our God-given spirit which enables us to communicate with God (1 Cor. 15:35–44). Deriv.: *sōmatikós* (4984), bodily or corporeal; *sússōmos* (4954), united in one body.

4984. Sōmatikós; from *sốma* (4983), body. An adj. meaning bodily, corporeal (1 Tim. 4:8). As an adv., *sōmatikốs* (4985), bodily, occurs in Colossians 2:9 (where the reference is to *sốma* [4983], body, denoting the manifestation of human nature, as in all the texts where the body of Christ is spoken about).

4990. Sōtér; from *sốzō* (4982), to save. A savior, deliverer, preserver. Used of God (Luke 1:47; 1 Tim. 1:1; 2:3; 4:10; Titus 1:3; 2:10; 3:4; Jude 1:25); of Christ (Luke 2:11; John 4:42; Acts 5:31; 13:23); and of His return to receive the Church to Himself (Titus 1:4; 2:13; 3:6; 2 Pet. 1:1).

4991. Sōtēría; from *sốzō* (4982), to save. Deliverance, preservation, salvation. Used of material and temporal deliverance (Luke 1:69; Acts 7:25; 27:34; Phil. 1:19; Heb. 11:7); of spiritual and eternal deliverance (Acts 4:12; Rom. 1:16; 10:10; Eph. 1:13); of the present experience of God's power to deliver (Phil. 2:12; 1 Pet. 1:9); of the future deliverance at the *parousía* (3952), the Second Coming of Christ (Luke 1:71; 2 Thess. 2:13; Rev. 12:10); inclusively of all the blessing of God (2 Cor. 6:2; Heb. 5:9; 1 Pet. 1:9, 10; Jude 1:3); occasionally standing for the Savior (Luke 19:9; John 4:22); ascriptions of praise to God (Rev. 7:10) and as to what He bestows (Rev. 19:1).

4992. Sōtḗrion; always with the neut. art. *to* while *sōtēría* (4991), salvation, is fem. Used as an adj. noun in Luke 2:30; 3:6, where it stands for the Savior (*sōtḗr* [4990]), as with *sōtēría* (4991) in Acts 28:28; in Ephesians 6:17, meaning the hope of salvation as in *sōtēría* and is metaphorically described as a helmet. *Sōtḗrios,* adj., related to *sṓzō* (4982), saving, bringing salvation, and describing God's grace (Titus 2:11).

4998. Sṓphrōn; from *sṓas,* sound, amd *phrḗn* [5424], cognitive faculties. Discreet, one who has a sound mind (1 Tim. 3:2; Titus 2:2, 5); a person who limits his own freedom and ability with proper thinking, demonstrating self-control with the proper restraints on all the passions and desires; one who voluntarily places limitations on his freedom. Deriv.: *sōphronéō* (4993), to be sober-minded, to prudently restrict one's freedom, to be discreet (Mark 5:15; Luke 8:35; Rom. 12:3; 2 Cor. 5:13; Titus 2:6; 1 Pet. 4:7); *sōphronízō* (4994), to teach to be discreet (Titus 2:4); *sōphronismós* (4995) a spimd, collected mind; accomplishing discreetness in someone (2 Tim. 1:7); *sōphrosúnē* (4997), the virtue of discreetness (Acts 26:25; 1 Tim. 2:9, 15); *sōphrónōs* (4996), adv., discreetly (Titus 2:12). *Sṓphrōn* is the exact antithesis of *hubristḗs* (5197), one whose insolence and contempt of others breaks forth in acts of wantonness and outrage.

5001. Tágma; an order, regular method. See *tássō* (5021), to categorize, place in one's proper order (only in 1 Cor. 15:23).

5010. Táxis; an arrangement, order, regularity (Luke 1:18; 1 Cor. 14:40; Col. 2:5; Heb. 5:6, 10). See *tássō* (5021), to place in one's proper order.

5011. Tapeinós; humble, lowly (Matt. 11:29; Luke 1:52; Rom. 12:16; 2 Cor. 7:6; 10:1; James 1:9; 4:6; 1 Pet. 5:5). The sinner is *tapeinós* when he recognizes the sinfulness which is his true condition; the unfallen creature, when merely recognizing that he is a creature; Jesus in His incarnate state, in recognizing His absolute dependence on the Father. Thus, the grace of *tapeinophrosúnē* (5012), humility, is a necessity for mankind, but also belongs to the highest angel before the throne since he is a creature. In His incarnation and humanity Jesus becomes the pattern of all humility. Only as a man does Jesus claim to be *tapeinós,* humble.

5012. Tapeinophrosúnē; humility, lowliness of mind, the esteeming of ourselves small inasmuch as we are so; the real estimate of ourselves (Acts 20:19; Eph. 4:2; Phil. 2:3; Col. 2:18, 23; 3:12; 1 Pet. 5:5). For the sinner *tapeinophrosúnē* involves the confession of sin as his true condition. For the unfallen creature it is the acknowledgment, not of sinfulness, but of creatureliness, of absolute dependence, having nothing, but receiving all things of God. Related to *tapeinós* (5011), humble, lowly; *tapeinóō* (5013), to humble; *tapeinōsis* (5014), the act of humiliation. See also *praútēs* (4240), meekness.

5013. Tapeinóō; to humble, bring about a recognition of one's sinfulness, to be recognized as a mere creature (Matt. 18:4; 2 Cor. 12:21; James 4:10; 1 Pet. 5:6); to abase (Matt. 23:12; Luke 14:11; 18:14; Phil. 4:12); to bring low (Luke 3:5). In the case of Jesus' incarnation (Phil. 2:8), He brought about the recognition of His humanity by demonstrating His absolute dependence on His Father.

5014. Tapeinōsis; the act of humiliation. In Luke 1:48 the virgin Mary is stated as possessed of *tapeinōsin,* the recognition of her sinfulness and therefore humility. In Philippians 3:21 *tapeinōsis* is translated "vile," refer-

ring to our present body being a sinful one. In James 1:10 the rich is made low (*tapeinōsis*) in his recognition that his riches should not be considered as a coverup for his sinfulness.

5020. Tartaróō; *tártaros,* found only in its verbal form in 2 Peter 2:4, meaning to consign to Tartarus (which is neither Sheol of the OT, nor Hades of the NT, nor Gehenna, nor hell, but the place where certain angels are confined, reserved unto judgment). This punishment for these angels is because of their special sin.

5021. Tássō; to place, set, appoint, order (Matt. 28:16; Acts 22:10; 28:23); to set in order or in its proper category (Luke 7:8; Rom. 13:1); to dispose, adapt (Acts 13:48). Deriv.: *táxis* (5010), an arrangement; *tágma* (5001), an order, regular method. *Anatássomai* (392), to compose in an orderly manner; *apotássō* or *apotássomai* (657), to set in its proper category away from oneself (*apó* [575]); *diatássō* (1299), from *diá* (1223]) emphatic, and *tássō,* to order, meaning to regulate, set in order, issue orderly and detailed instructions. The noun is *diatagḗ* (1296), an order, disposition, appointment, *diátagma* (1297), commandment; *epitagḗ* (2003), authority, command a commandment imposed on one, from *epitássō* (2004), which is from *epí* (1909), upon, and *tássō* to order; *prostássō* (4367), from *prós* (4314), to, and *tássō,* meaning a specific command for a specific person (Matt. 1:24; 8:4; 21:6; Mark 1:44; Luke 5:14; Acts 10:33, 48); *hupotássō* (5293), from *hupó* (5259), under, and *tássō,* meaning to place under; *hupotagḗ* (5292) submission; *protássō* and *protássomai* (4384), from *pró* (4253), before, and *tássō,* meaning to preordain (Acts 17:26); *taktós* (5002), appointed (Acts 12:21); *átaktos* (813), unruly (1 Thess. 5:14); *ataktéō* (812), to behave in a disorderly manner (2 Thess. 3:6, 11). All the deriv. have inherent in them order and categorization, classification.

5040. Téknion; diminutive of *téknon* (5043). A little child. Used only figuratively and always in the pl. A term of affection by a teacher to his disciples (John 13:33; Gal. 4:19; 1 John 2:1, 12, 28; 3:7, 18; 4:4; 5:21).

5043. Téknon; related to *tíktō* (5088), to beget, bear. Child; used both in the natural and the figurative senses, giving prominence to the fact of birth, whereas *huiós* (5207), son in a generic sense, stresses the dignity and character of the relationship. In the narrative of His human birth, Jesus Christ is never designated as *téknon,* or *téknon Theoú,* a child of God, but always *ho Huiós,* the Son or the Son of God or the Son of Man (Matt. 1:21, 23, 25; Luke 1:31; 2:7). Only His mother called Him *téknon* (Luke 2:48) as she viewed Him in His humanity. Jesus never presents Himself in His God-Man consciousness as a *téknon* of man or of God. He was only *huiós* (5207), denoting relationship of character with the Father God, not giving the idea He was a mere child of the Father. He was Mary's *téknon* but God's Son, *huiós* (5207). When speaking of Elizabeth and Zachariah, it was said of them that they had no child, *téknon* (Luke 1:7).

5046. Téleios; from *télos* (5056), goal, purpose. Adult, full-grown, of full age, as opposite to little children. This image of fully completed growth, as contrasted with infancy and childhood, underlies the ethical use of *téleioi* as being set over against the babes in Christ (1 Cor. 2:6; 14:20; Eph. 4:13; Phil. 3:15; Heb. 5:14). Can be used in a relative or absolute sense (Matt. 5:48; 19:21), that is, God's perfection is absolute; man's is relative, reaching the goal set for him by God with each individual differing according to his God-given ability. The *téleios* is one who has attained his moral end, the goal for which he was intended, namely, to be a man obedient in Christ. It may be true, though, that having reached this attainment, other and higher ends will open up before him in order to have Christ formed in him more and more. When one is *téleios,* it does not mean that he has had all of the grace available bestowed upon him. *Teleiótēs* (5047), perfection, is not a static state. In a physical or literal sense, used of spotless sacrifices, involving animals or objects wherein nothing is deficient; also as a full year, perfect work, or something done as it ought to be (1 Cor. 13:10; James 1:4). *To*, the, *téleion*, complete one, in contrast with *to ek mérous* (3313), that which in part indicates the ultimate goal in heaven as contrasted with something that can have only partial fulfillment on earth. In 1 John 4:18 *he*, the, *teleía agápē*, perfect love, means the love that is not wanting, the love which accomplishes its goal. Frequently it means full growth, either of men or beasts. Also generally, *téleios* means what is highest and preeminent (Heb. 9:11; James 1:25). When used in a moral sense, referring to God's expectation of us, completely blameless. A perfect gift in James 1:17 means that which meets the need of a person. In James 1:4, "that ye may be perfect" means that you may not be morally lacking. It has a similar meaning in Matthew 5:48; 19:21; Romans 12:2; Colossians 1:28; 4:12; James 3:2. *Holotelés* (3651), complete to the end (1 Thess. 5:23) holding a connecting link between *hólos* (3650) whole, and *holóklēros* (3648). complete in every part, and *téleios*, to the end. *Téleios* is not to be confused with *anámartētos* (361), without sin or sinless.

5047. Teleiótēs; from *téleios* (5046), perfect. Perfection or perfectness, stressing the actual accomplishment of the end in view (Col. 3:14; Heb. 6:1); not sinlessness, which would have been *anamartēsía* (which is never used in the NT, although the adj. *anamártētos* [361] is used in John 8:7 TR). Deriv.: *télos* (5056), end, goal.

5048. Teleióō; from *téleios* (5046), perfect. To complete, finish (John 4:34; 5:36; 17:4; Acts 20:24; Heb. 7:19; 9:9; 10:1, 14). To complete, accomplish, of time (Luke 2:43); of prophecy (John 19:28). In the pass., *teleíōmai* (5048), to be made perfect or complete only in the sense of reaching one's prescribed goal (2 Cor. 12:9; Phil. 3:12; Heb. 11:40; 12:23; James 2:22); *teleiōsai*, to make Christ perfect (Heb. 2:10); to consecrate Him by sufferings to His office (Heb. 5:9; 7:28, cf. Ex. 29:34; Lev. 8:22, 28, 33; 21:10) and fully to qualify and enable Him to discharge it (cf. Heb. 2:17, 18; 4:15; 5:1, 2). See also Luke 13:32 referring to Christ's death. Deriv.: *télos* (5056), end, goal.

5049. Téleiōs; from *télos* (5056), end, goal. Perfectly, entirely, to the end, in the sense of accomplishment of the hope (1 Pet. 1:13).

5050. Teleíōsis; fem., completion, successful issue, the attainment of a perfect whole, a *téleion* (5046) which needs nothing further to complete it (Heb. 7:11, 19). Also the fulfillment of a promise (Luke 1:45). Contrast *teleiótēs* (5047), completeness which refers to the attainment to be reached while *teleiōsis* refers to the completeness as an attainment already reached. Deriv.: *télos* (5056), end, goal.

5051. Teleiótēs; from *téleios* (5046), what achieves its goal. A completer, perfecter, one who brings something through to the goal so as to win and receive the prize (Heb. 12:2).

5052. Telesphoréō; from *télos* (5056), end, goal, perfection, and *phoréō* (5409), to bring, bear. To bring to its intended perfection or goal as the seed does the fruit (Luke 8:14).

5053. Teleutáō; from *teleutḗ* (5054), an end, accomplishment. To end, finish, accomplish (not used in this manner in the NT). In Matthew 2:19; 9:18 to end one's life, to die. Deriv.: *télos* (5056), end, goal.

5054. Teleutḗ; from *teléō* (5055), to end, finish. An end, accomplishment (not used in this manner in the NT). In Matthew 2:15 the end of life, death, decease.

5055. Teléō; from *télos* (5056), end, goal. To make an end or accomplishment, to complete anything, not merely to end it, but to bring it to perfection or to its destined goal, to carry it through. Generally it means to carry out something (Matt. 11:1; 13:53); to accomplish (Luke 2:39; 18:31; 22:37), to go over (Matt. 10:23); to end, finish, fulfill time (Rev. 20:3, 5, 7), to pay tribute (Matt. 17:24; Rom. 13:6). Frequently it speaks of fulfilling or answering promises and prayers. When it speaks of definite periods of time, it means to pass, spend, fulfill. In the pass., to be completed or fulfilled (John 19:28, 30; Rev. 15:1, 8; 17:17; 20:3, 5, 7), with the meaning of the perfect accomplishment

of that work whereby the Scripture is fulfilled, not merely to fulfill (Luke 18:31; 22:37; Acts 13:29; Rev. 10:7). When the word does not refer to the production or attainment of the object, it means to perform, execute, carry out (Luke 12:50; Rom. 2:27; Gal. 5:16; James 2:8). See *teleutḗ* (5054); *teleutáō* (5053); *telesphoréō* (5052); *teleiótēs* (5051); *teleíōsis* (5050); *téleiōs* (5049); *teleióō* (5048); *teleiótēs* (5047), and *téleios* (5046).

5056. Télos; neut., usually with *to* (the def. art.), end, goal. The limit, either at which a person or thing ceases to be what he or it was up to that point or at which previous activities ceased (2 Cor. 3:13; 1 Pet. 4:7). It does not, as is commonly supposed, mean the extinction, end, termination with reference to time, but the goal reached, the completion or conclusion at which anything arrives, either as issue or ending and including the termination of what went before; or as a result, acme, consummation; for example, when we speak of the end of a war, we speak of victory. When we speak of *télos andrós*, the end of man, we speak of the full age of man; also used of the ripening of the seed. It never denotes merely an end as to time, a termination in and for itself, for which another word, *teleutḗ* (5054), death, is always used. The issue, end, conclusion (Matt. 24:14; 26:58; Mark 13:7; Luke 21:9; 1 Cor. 10:11; James 5:11; 1 Pet. 4:7, 17) in which case *télos* means the termination of the present course and condition of the world. In 1 Corinthians 15:24; Hebrews 7:3 it means the goal reached, the beginning of a new order of things. The adv. phrase *eis télos* means "to the last" or to the conclusion of that spoken of, as in John 13:1 where reference is made to Christ's work of love (see also Matt. 10:22; 24:13; Mark 13:13); or it may mean at last or in the end, finally (Luke 18:5). In the gen., meaning until, with *héōs* (2193) *áchri* (891), *méchri* (3360) and the gen. *télous*, until the end (1 Cor. 1:8; Heb. 3:6 TR, 14; 6:11; Rev. 2:26). *To*, the, *télos*, finally (1 Pet. 3:8). Refers to the goal reached, the end (Rom. 6:21, 22; 13:10; 2 Cor. 11:15; Phil. 3:16; 1 Tim. 1:5; Heb. 6:8; 1 Pet. 1:9). In Romans 10:4 (see also vv. 3, 5; Acts 13:39) *télos* denotes the final end, the conclusion which the dominion of the law has found in Christ. Adv. phrases, *eis télos*, in 1 Thessalonians 2:16, means completely; *héōs télous*, in 2 Corinthians 1:13, means completely, as contrasted with *apo*; (575) *mérous* (3313), in part (2 Corinthians 1:14). *Télos*, also means toll or tax (Matt. 17:25; Rom. 13:7). Deriv.: *telṓnes* (5057), a collector of *télē* (5056), taxes; *telṓnion* (5058); a custom house (Matt. 9:9; Mark 2:14; Luke 5:27); *teléō* (5055); *epiteléō* (2005); *sunteléō* (4931); *suntéleia* (4930); *pantelḗs* (3838); *téleios* (5046); *teleiótēs* (5047); *teleióō* (5048); *teleíōsis* (5050); *teleiótēs* (5051); *teleutáō* (5053); *telesphoréō* (5052).

5059. Téras; derived from *tēréō* (5083), to watch, as being that which for its extraordinary character is apt to be observed and kept in the memory. It is often associated with *sēmeíon* (4592), sign, and usually translated as "wonder" (Matt. 24:24; Acts 4:30). These two words do not refer to different classes of miracles, but to different qualities of the same miracle. *Téras* is a miracle regarded as startling, imposing, amazing, frequently used elsewhere for strange appearances in the heavens. Related words: *dúnamis* (1411); *megaleíos* (3167); *éndoxos* (1741); *parádoxos* (3861); *thaumásios* (2297).

5083. Tēréō; to keep, watch (Matt. 27:36, 54; 28:4; Acts 12:6; 16:23; 24:23; 25:4, 21); to reserve, with unhappy results (2 Pet. 2:4, 9, 17; 3:7; Jude 1:6, 13) or with the possibility of either deliverance or execution (Acts 25:21); to maintain as opposed to leaving (Jude 1:6); to observe, as commands, ordinances, traditions, a law, and so forth (Matt. 19:17; 23:3). Deriv.: *tḗrēsis* (5084); *paratēréō* (3906); *paratḗrēsis* (3907); *diatēréō* (1301); *diatḗrēsis*.

5084. Tḗrēsis; from *tēréō* (5083), to keep. A prison, (Acts 4:3), of the imprisonment of the apostles (Acts 5:18). A keeping or observance of commandments (1 Cor. 7:19).

5087. Títhēmi; to set, place, lay put, lay (Matt. 5:15; 14:3; Mark 6:29, 56; 10:16; Luke 6:48); to put or lay down (Luke 19:21, 22); to put or set on, as food upon a table (John 2:10); to lay by, reserve (1 Cor. 16:2); to put off, lay aside (John 13:4); to appoint, assign (Matt. 24:51; Luke 12:46); to appoint, constitute, ordain (John 15:16; Acts 13:47; 20:28; Rom. 4:17; 1 Tim. 2:7; 2 Tim. 1:11; Heb. 1:2); to make, render (1 Cor. 9:18); in the 2 aor. mid., to purpose, propose, design (Acts 19:21); to give advice or counsel, advise (Acts 27:12). Deriv.: *anatíthēmi* (394), to lay upon, attribute something to someone; *anáthema* (331), a thing devoted to destruction, ruin, a consecrated gift; *diatíthēmi* (1303), to place separately, appoint anyone to a place, arrange and dispose of one's effects by will and testament; *diathḗkē* (1242), testament; *protíthēmi* (4388), to set or lay before; *próthesis* (4286), a setting forth, setting up, an exposition, purpose, resolve, design; *prothésmios* (4287), before appointed.

5088. Tíktō; to bring forth (Luke 1:57; John 16:21; Heb. 11:11 TR; Rev. 12:2, 4) or be born, as said of the child Jesus (Matt. 2:2; Luke 2:11); used metaphorically, of lust as bringing forth sin (James 1:15). See *apokuéō* (616), to bring forth; *gennáō* (1080), to give birth. Deriv.: *téknon* (5043), child.

5098. Timōría; from *timōréō* (5097), to punish, which is from *timḗ* (5092), revenge, punishment, and *horáō* (3708), to see, inspect. Punishment, only in Heb. 10:29. The verb *timōréō* is used only twice (Acts 22:5; 26:11). In *timōría,* in Class. Gr. the vindictiveness of the punishment is the predominant thought, a punishment satisfying the inflicter's sense of outraged justice, as defending his own honor or that of a violated law. From its etymology, the guardianship or protection of honor. Contrast *kólasis* (2851), to torment, which has more the notion of punishment rather than the correction and rehabilitation of the offender.

5100. Tis; (without an accent) used as an indef. pron., meaning someone, anyone, a certain one; and in the neut. *ti,* something (Matt. 5:23; Titus 1:12).

5101. Tís; or *tí,* (with the accent) can be used as an interrogative pron. meaning "who" or "what."

5171. Trupháō; to live in luxury, pleasure. As in *strēniáō* (4763) and *spataláō* (4684), *trupháō* and the intens. *entrupháō* have the notion of excess, wantonness, dissolute attitude, self-indulgence, prodigal living, but with special emphasis on self-indulgence (James 5:5). Includes the notion of insolence only as a secondary and rarer meaning. Deriv. verb: *entrupháō* (1792), to revel (2 Pet. 2:13); noun *truphḗ* (5172), luxury (Luke 7:25; 2 Pet. 2:13).

5179. Túpos; type, as a constituent element of a parable or model of some reality which was yet to appear, a prototype or that which was yet to be developed and evolved. For example, the ordinances and institutions in the OT were, in their inward essence, types of the NT. The first era serves as a type of the second. See *súmbolon,* a symbol, which does not occur in the NT. Whereas the outline, archetype, and model of some reality (which was yet to appear was called *túpos, súmbolon* was an equivalent, a visible sign of what is invisible, e. g., the tares in the parable of the wheat and the tares [Matt. 13:24–30, 36–43]) are symbols of the activity of the devil and his agents in one's spiritual life. A symbol is an outward manifestation of something inward, an emblem of what is higher. These two constituent elements of the parables are to be joined with the noun *allēgoría,* allegory, from the verb *allēgoréō* (238), which is from *állos* (243), another, and *agoréō,* to speak, and is found only in Galatians 4:24. Therefore, to allegorize is to speak symbolically about one thing whereas something somewhat different is meant, of which the thing spoken is the emblem or representative. An allegory is the mark, the indication of outward similarity, and also the internal relationship and connection of things. It is a counterpart and reappearance of what has the same shape, either in the world of matter or of mind. Thus, the enemy was an allegory of Satan; the book of the Revelation is full of allegories, and when our Lord spoke of Herod, "Tell that fox," (Luke 13:32)

He was using an allegory. Distinct meanings of *túpos:* a mark, impression made by striking, and used with this meaning to indicate the print of the nails on Jesus' hands and feet (John 20:25); a form, figure, image (Acts 7:43); a pattern or model of a building (Acts 7:44; Heb. 8:5, referring to Ex. 25:40); a pattern, example (Phil. 3:17; 1 Thess. 1:7, Titus 2:7); a figure, emblem, representative, type (Rom. 5:14, cf. 1 Cor. 10:6, 11) a form of a writing (Acts 23:25), a form of doctrine (Rom. 6:17). Deriv.: *hupotúpōsis* (5296), pattern; *antítupos* (499), an antitype, counterpart.

5180. Túptō; to strike, smite with the hand, stick, or other instrument (Matt. 27:30; Mark 15:19; Luke 6:29; 18:13; 22:64 TR; 23:48; Acts 23:2, 3); to beat (Matt. 24:49; Luke 12:45; Acts 18:17; 21:32); to smite, strike, punish (Acts 23:3); to hurt, wound spiritually (1 Cor. 8:12). Deriv.: *túpos* (5179), stroke, the impression left by striking, a trace or print; *antítupos* (499), that which gives a counterstroke, similar, like, antitype; *hupotúpōsis* (5296), a design or outline of a representation, pattern.

5187. Tuphóō; from *túphos,* smoke, symbolizing pride, insolence; in the pass. *tuphóomai,* to be drunk with pride, with a heart lifted up not only against man but against God (1 Tim. 3:6; 6:4; 2 Tim. 3:4).

5197. Hubristḗs; insolent wrongdoer to others for the pleasure which the affliction of the wrong imparts (Rom. 1:30; 1 Tim. 1:13). Deriv.: *húbris* (5196), injury, injurious treatment (Acts 27:10, 21; 2 Cor. 12:10); *hubrízō* (5195), to treat injuriously, reproach (Matt. 22:6; Luke 11:45; 18:32; Acts 14:5; 1 Thess. 2:2).

5198. Hugiaínō; to be healthy, sound, physically well (Eng., hygiene). See Mark 3:5 and Acts 4:10. *Hugeía,* health, does not occur in the NT. *Hugiḗs* (5199), healthy, is translated "whole." In Acts 27:34 what is translated "health" is *sōtēría* (4991), salvation, meaning safety.

5199. Hugiḗs; perhaps from *hugrós,* moist, as sound, healthy bodies are. NT meanings: sound, whole, in health (Matt. 12:13; 15:31; Mark 5:34; John 5:9 Acts 4:10); of sound speech or doctrine, wholesome, right (Titus 2:8).

5206. Huiothesía; from *huiós* (5207), son, and *títhēmi* (5087), to place. Adoption; receiving another into the relationship of a child of someone. Used by Paul in Romans 9:4 with reference to the filial relationship into which Israel was admitted by election to God (Deut. 14:1). In Romans 8:15; Galatians 4:5; Ephesians 1:5, used with reference to the NT adoption, answering to the Pauline *tékna Theoú,* children of God, in the sense of belonging to God. See *téknon* (5043), child, and also *huiós.* In Romans 8:23, *huiothesía* denotes adoption as it regards the future (see Rev. 21:7) and in contrast with the present slavery of corruption (v. 21). It is questionable whether *huiothesía,* the receiving into the relationship of children, denotes also the relationship itself as based upon adoption. In no case is it ever equivalent to *huiótēs* sonship. (Cf. Eph. 1:5 where it is precisely "adoption" which illustrates the greatness of divine love in making a stranger, such as a sinner to be a real son.) Whereas *huiothesía* places a person in the position of a son, *huiótēs* is the quality or character of a son. The expression here, *proorísas eis huiothesían,* means to appoint beforehand to adoption.

5207. Huiós; son, distinguished from *téknon* (5043), child. In 1 John 1:3, 7; 2:22–24; 3:8, 23; 4:9, 10, 14, 15; 5:5, 9–13, 20 *huiós* is reserved for the Son of God. *Huiós* primarily signifies the relation of offspring to parent and not simply the birth as indicated by *téknon* (5043) (John 9:18–20; Gal. 4:30). Used metaphorically of prominent moral characteristics (Matt. 5:9, 45; 8:12; 13:38; Mark 2:19; 3:17; Luke 6:35; 10:6; 16:8; 20:36; John 12:36; 17:12; Acts 10:36; 2 Cor. 6:18; Eph. 2:2). In the NT use of male offspring (Gal. 4:30); legitimate offspring (Heb. 12:8); descendants, irrespective of their gender (Rom. 9:27); generally demonstrating behavior or character (Matt. 23:15, 31; Luke 6:35; 20:36; John 17:12; Acts 4:36; 13:10; Rom. 8:14, 19; Gal. 3:26; Eph. 2:2). The difference between believers as children (*tékna*) of God and as sons (*huioí*) is brought out in Romans 8:14–21. *Tékna* refers to those who were born of God and *huioí* refers to those who show maturity acting as sons. When just the basic relationship as a born-again child of God is referred to, it is expressed as *tékna* (Rom. 8:16). *Huiós* gives evidence of the dignity of one's relationship and likeness to God's character. In John 1:12 *tékna* is used of new believers, not *huioí*. The expression "Son of God" (*huiòs Theoú*), is used of Jesus as a manifestation of His relationship with the Father or the expression of His character. The Lord Jesus is never called *téknon* (5043) *Theoú* (2316), a child of God, as believers are. Jesus used either the full title (John 5:25; 11:4) or more frequently "the Son" *ho Huiós*, which is to be understood as an abbreviation of "the Son of God," not "the Son of Man," which He always expressed in full (Luke 10:22; John 5:19), thus stressing the characteristic of humanity apart from sin. In Acts 13:33 (see also Ps. 2:7), the birth of Christ in His humanity and His sinless conformity to the Father's character is expressed not with *téknon*, but with *huiós*.

5215. Húmnos; a song in honor of God. It also came to mean praise to men. Whereas a psalm is the story of man's deliverance or a commemoration of mercies received, a hymn is a magnificent proclaiming how great someone or something is (Luke 1:46–55, 66–79; Acts 4:24; 16:25). It is a direct address of praise and glory to God. According to Augustine a hymn has three characteristics: it must be sung; it must be praise; it must be to God. The word "hymn" nowhere occurs in the writings of the Apostolic Fathers because it was used as a praise to heathen deities and thus the early Christians instinctively shrank from it. In Ephesians 5:19; Colossians 3:16 it occurs with *psalmós* (5568), psalm, and *hōdḗ* (5603) spiritual song, any kind of song (Eph. 5:19; Col. 3:16; Rev. 5:9; 14:3; 15:3).

5218. Hupakoé; from *hupakoúō* (5219), to obey, listen to something, hearken. Obedience, though this usage is unknown in Class. Gr. Generally in the NT it refers to obedience (Rom. 6:16). Elsewhere it always refers to obedience to God's will in a special sense, of willing subjection to that which, in the sphere of divine revelation, is right (Rom. 6:16; see also Rom. 5:19; Heb. 5:8). More especially, it refers to subjection to the saving will of God revealed in Christ and referred to as obedience to the truth (1 Pet. 1:22); obedience of faith (Rom. 1:5; 16:26) or obedience unto faith or by faith; the obedience that is demanded by Christ (2 Cor. 10:5). The word also stands alone as a mode of the manifestation of Christian faith (Rom. 15:18; 16:19; 2 Cor. 7:15; 10:6; Phile. 1:21; 1 Pet. 1:2, 14).

5219. Hupakoúō; from *húpo* (5259), under, and *akoúō* (191), to hear. To listen to something, hearken (Acts 12:13). Mostly it means to obey, give heed, follow, yield, of servants, soldiers, pupils (Matt. 8:27; Mark 1:27; 4:41; Luke 8:25; 17:6; Rom. 6:16, 17; Eph. 6:1, 5; Col. 3:20, 22; 1 Pet. 3:6). It refers to the manifestation of faith as revealed in the humble acceptance of the Gospel message (Acts 6:7; Rom. 6:17; 10:16; 2 Thess. 1:8; 3:14; Heb. 5:9; 11:8). It also denotes the continuous subjection of faith under the preached Word, the keeping of the Word in believing obedience (Phil. 2:12).

5225. Hupárchō; from *húpo* (5259), under, and *árchō* (757), to begin. To be, to subsist, to rule (Luke 7:25; 8:41; 16:23; Acts 21:20; 27:34). In Philippians 2:6 *hupárchōn* (pres. part.), refers to Christ continuing to be what He was before, God or in the form of God, in contrast to *hōn* (pres. part. of *eimí* [1510]) in John 1:18, "who is in the bosom of the Father (NASB)," referring to the same state of being as the immaterial *Lógos* (Word, John 1:1) before becoming (*gínomai* [1096]) something new, that is, flesh, which He was not before. In Philippians 2:6 it denotes an existence or condition both previous to the circumstances mentioned and continuing after, referring to the deity of Christ prior to His incarnation and its continuance at and after His birth. With a dat. following, it denotes property or possession (Acts 3:6, cf. Acts 4:37; 28:7; 2 Pet. 1:8); *ta hupárchonta* (5224), the belongings,

possessions, things one had before and continues to have (Matt. 19:21; 24:47; Luke 8:3; Acts 4:32).

5228. Hupér; a prep. governing the gen. and acc. With the gen. it means for the benefit of, for the sake of (Col. 1:7); in order to (John 11:4; Gal. 1:4); in the place of (Phile. 1:13); concerning (John 1:30); in behalf of (Matt. 5:44; 1 Tim. 2:6). With the acc. it means over, more than, beyond (Matt. 10:24; Eph. 1:22). It includes both equivalence and exchange. Hence, the death of Christ was equal to our need and in our behalf, showing His acceptance by the Father (Rom. 5:6, 8; 2 Cor. 5:14, 15). Syn.: *antí* (473), instead of, in behalf of, in the place of.

5233. Huperbaínō; from *hupér* (5228), beyond, and *baínō*, to go; used only in 1 Thessalonians 4:6 with the meaning of inconsiderate overreaching.

5244. Huperḗphanos; from *húper* (5228), over, and *phaínomai*, appear. Proud; one who shows himself above his fellow men, in honor preferring himself (Luke 1:51; 1 Pet. 5:5).

5255. Hupékoos; from *hupakoúō* (5219), to obey. Obedient to the will of God (Acts 7:39). Like *hupakoúō* it means the obedience required in believing (2 Cor. 2:9); of Christ in that He was obedient to the law (Phil. 2:8), and as man (Gal. 4:4; Heb. 5:8) shed His blood for our sins. This *hupékoos* has only a remote reference to John 10:18 as having received the commandment from the Father.

5257. Hupērétēs; from *hupó* (5259), under, and *erétēs*, literally meaning a rower. A subordinate, servant, attendant, or officer in general. This refers to the subordinate official who waits to accomplish the commands of his superior; applied to John Mark (Acts 12:25) as an inferior minister who performed certain defined functions for Paul and Barnabas (Acts 13:5). Allied to the meaning of *diákonos* (1249), deacon, and contrasted to *doúlos* (1401), slave; *therápōn* (2324), servant, healer, and *oikétēs* (3610), domestic servant.

5259. Hupó; a prep. governing the gen. and acc.; in Class. Gr., also the dat.; with a primary meaning of "under." When used with the gen. it refers to "from," "under," from which anything comes forth (Luke 1:26; 1 Cor. 1:11). With pass. verbs and the gen. of persons it means "by" (1 Cor. 1:4; 2 Thess. 2:13). Used of time it means "at," "during." In composition in comp. words *hupó* implies: (1) place, that is, beneath, as *hupobállō* (5260), to throw under or cast under; (2) subjection, dependence, the being under any person or thing, as *húpandros* (5220), under a husband, *hupotássō* (5293), to place under; (3) succession, being behind, after, as *hupoleípō* (5275), one or something left behind, as *hupoménō* (5278), to remain under; (4) *hupó* in composition also implies something done or happening underhand, covertly, unperceived, without noise or notice; also a little, somewhat by degrees, as *huponoéō* (5282), to let be understood little by little.

5261. Hupogrammós; from *hupó* (5259), before, and *gráphō* (1125), to write; used only in biblical and late Class. Gr., meaning a writing copy, pattern (1 Pet. 2:21). This subst. is related to the verb *hupográphō*, to write under, meaning writing a copy, to teach to write, since the writing copy of the teacher was to be followed by the scholars.

5264. Hupodéchomai; from *hupó* (5259), under, and *déchomai* (1209), to receive. To receive hospitably and kindly (Luke 10:38; 19:6; Acts 17:7; James 2:25).

5267. Hupódikos; from *hupó* (5259), under, and *díkē* (1349), judgment, justice. One who comes under *díkē*, justice, and is thus guilty. Opposite *éndikos*, the one who occupies the due relation to justice. *Hupódikos* denotes one who is bound to do or suffer what is imposed for the sake of justice because he has neglected to do what is right. Therefore, it denotes one who is under obligation to make compensation (Rom. 3:19).

5271. Hupokrínomai; from the prep. *hupó* (5259), under, indicating secrecy, and *krínō* (2919), to judge. To divide, separate. In its original, literal sense to divide secretly. Originally syn. to *apokrínomai* (611), to devise a proper answer. In its primary meaning to inquire, distinguish, get under the meaning of dreams, and then expound and interpret them. Later, it came to mean to represent, act, or simulate anything as an actor. It arose from the application of the word in Attic Gr. to persons in a play, and then to men generally who act a part or pretend to be what they are not, to present oneself, to simulate, to distinguish oneself. Used in Luke 20:20 See *hupókrisis* (5272). hypocrisy; *hupokritḗs* (5273), hypocrite; *anupókritos* (505), one without hypocrisy.

5273. Hupokritḗs; from *hupokrínomai* (5271), to act as a hypocrite. An expounder or interpreter of dreams, then an actor, and consequently a hypocrite. That is what the Greeks used to call a stage player who acted under a mask impersonating a character. A counterfeit, a man who assumes and speaks or acts under a feigned character (Matt. 6:2, 5, 16). A conjecturer, guesser, diviner (Matt. 16:3 TR; Luke 12:56). The Greeks used to call an expounder of dreams a hypocrite. Deriv.: *krínō* (2919), to judge.

5278. Hupoménō; from *hupó* (5259), under, and *ménō* (3306), to remain. To remain under, that is, to endure or sustain a load of miseries, adversities, persecutions or provocations in faith and patience (Matt. 10:22; 24:13; Rom. 12:12; 1 Cor. 13:7; 2 Tim. 2:10, 12; Heb. 12:2); to remain privately, stay behind (Luke 2:43; Acts 17:14). Deriv: *hupomonḗ* (5281), patience toward things or circumstances, contrast to *makrothumía* (3115), long-suffering (which is patience toward people).

5280. Hupómnēsis; from *hupó* (5259), under, and *mimnḗskō* (3403), to remind, recall someone. To call to remebrance (2 Tim. 1:5; 2 Pet. 1:13; 3:1). Contrast *anámnēsis* (364), recollection, remembering again, vanished impressions by a definite act of will in the consciousness; an act of the recollection of the death of Christ in the celebration of the Eucharist in the early church (Luke 22:19; 1 Cor. 11:24, 25; Heb. 10:3).

5281. Hupomonḗ; from *hupó* (5259), under, and *ménō* (3306), to abide. Patience, endurance as to things or circumstances, as contrasted to *makrothumía* (3115), long-suffering, endurance toward people. *Hupomonḗ* is associated with hope (1 Thess. 1:3) and refers to the quality that does not surrender to circumstances or succumb under trial.

5282. Huponoéō; from the prep. *hupó* (5259), under, denoting diminution, and *noéō* (3539), to think. To suppose, suspect (Acts 13:25; 25:18; 27:27). See also *nous* (3563), mind. Deriv.: noun *hupónoia* (5283), suspicion.

5283. Hupónoia; from the verb *huponoéō* (5282), to suppose, suspect. A suspicion, surmise (1 Tim. 6:4). See *noéō* (3539), to think; *noûs* (3563), mind.

5287. Hupóstasis; from *huphístamai*, to be placed or stand under. In general, something which has been put under; therefore, used for a basis or foundation, subsistence, existence; frequently applied by the church fathers as a distinct person in the Godhead (Heb. 1:3); applied to the mind, firm confidence, constancy (2 Cor. 9:4; 11:17; Heb. 3:14); confidence or confident expectation (Heb. 11:1). See *hístēmi* (2476), to stand.

5293. Hupotássō; from *hupó* (5259), under, and *tássō* (5021), to order. To place in an orderly fashion under something. Originally, it showed one's relation to superiors, either compulsory or voluntary subordination. If compulsory, the main idea may be that of either power or conquest on the one side or lack of freedom on the other. In the NT the verb does not immediately carry with it the thought of obedience. In the act., the verb occurs in Romans 8:20: "was made subject to vanity" (see Rom. 5:12). All the other act. statements are Christological, with Christ having supreme rule. The mid. voice used in the aor. pass. occurs once in the sense of compulsion and means to have one submit (Luke 10:17, 20). Deriv.: noun *hupotagé* (5292), submission, dependent position (2 Cor. 9:13; Gal. 2:5; 1 Tim. 2:11; 3:4).

5296. Hupotúpōsis; from *hupotupóō*, to draw a sketch or first draft as painters when they begin a picture. A delineation, sketch concise representation or form

(2 Tim. 1:13); a pattern, example (1 Tim. 1:16). See *túpos* (5179), type; *antítupos* (499), antitype.

5316. Phaínō; to shine (John 1:5; 5:35; 2 Pet. 1:19; 1 John 2:8; Rev. 1:16; 8:12; 21:23). In the pass., *phaínomai*, to appear, be conspicuous, shine (Matt. 24:27, cf. Phil. 2:15); to appear, be seen (Matt. 1:20; 2:13, 19); to appear, seem (Matt. 6:5, 16; 23:28, cf. Luke 24:11); to seem, appear, be thought (Mark 14:64). In the mid., to appear in judgment (1 Pet. 4:18) It indicates how a matter phenomenally shows and presents itself with no necessary assumption of any beholder at all. This suggests that something may shine without anybody necessarily seeing it, contrasted to something that exists but does not shine. *Nooúmenon* is that which is conceived in the mind but does not have any objective existence and does not necessarily manifest itself. *Phainómenon* is that which manifests itself, appears or shines (*phaínetai*), and must have a reality behind it. It cannot be just the figment of the imagination. Therefore, *phaínomai* is often syn. with *eimí* (1510), to be, and *gínomai* (1096), to become (Matt. 2:7; 13:26). It may also have no substance, yet presupposes one. *Dokéō* (1380), think, has in contrast the subj. estimate which may be formed of a thing, not the obj. showing and seeming which it may actually possess. One may *dokeí* (think) something which may not have an objective reality. The Docetic heresy owes its name to this verb. It taught that Christ's body was not real but imaginary. However, something that shines, *phaínei*, must exist objectively.

5318. Phanerós; from *phaínomai* or *phaínō* (5316), to shine, to make to shine or cause to appear. *Phanerós* means apparent, manifest, plain (Gal. 5:19; 1 Tim. 4:15; 1 John 3:10); apparent, manifest with the idea of being known (Matt. 12:16; Mark 3:12; Luke 8:17; Acts 4:16; 7:13; Phil. 1:13); apparent in the sense of being public, open (Matt. 6:4, 6, 18 TR), publicly famous or eminent (Mark 6:14); apparent in the sense of seeming in the expression *en tō*, in the, *phanerō̧*, appearance or outward show (Rom. 2:28). Deriv.: *phōs* (5457), light; *phaneróō* (5319), to make manifest, make known, show; *phanérōsis* (5321), manifestation, making known; *epiphaínō* (2014), to make visible, celebrated, distinguished, renowned; *epipháneia* (2015), manifestation.

5319. Phaneróō; to make manifest, make known, show. In the NT, syn. with *apokalúptō* (601), to reveal, remove a lid. Therefore, in this sense it means to denote the act of divine revelation (John 17:6; Rom. 1:19; 3:21; 16:26; Col. 1:26; 2 Tim. 1:10; Titus 1:3; Heb. 9:8; 1 John 1:2; 4:9). It differs from *apokalúptō* as "to exhibit" differs from "to disclose," so that in relation to each other *apokalúptō* must precede *phaneróō* (1 Cor. 3:13). *Apokalúptō* refers only to the obj. revealed, but *phaneróō* refers to those to whom the revelation is made (cf. Eph. 3:5; Col. 1:26; 3:4; 4:4; Titus 1:3). Note the combination in Ephesians 3:3, "by revelation was made known unto me the mystery." *Phaneróō* also signifies to make visible, to show (John 2:11; 21:1); to make known (John 7:4; 17:6; Rom. 1:19; 2 Cor. 2:14); to make public (1 Cor. 4:5; Col. 4:4). The pass. means to become or be made visible or manifest (Mark 4:22; John 3:21; 9:3; 2 Cor. 4:10, 11; Eph. 5:13; Heb. 9:8; 1 John 2:19; Rev. 3:18; 15:4); to appear (Mark 16:12, 14; John 21:14; 2 Cor. 5:10; 2 Tim. 1:10; Heb. 9:26; 1 Pet. 1:20; 5:4; 1 John 1:2; 2:28; 3:2, 5, 8; 4:9); to be made known, or to be known (John 1:31; Rom. 3:21; 16:26; 2 Cor. 3:3; 5:11; 7:12; Col. 1:26; 4:4; Titus 1:3).

5321. Phanérōsis; manifestation, only in 1 Corinthians 12:7; 2 Corinthians 4:2. The verb *phaneróō* (5319), to make manifest, is continuously employed of *apokálupsis* (602, revelation) and *epipháneia* (2015, appearing) of the first coming of Christ (1 Tim. 3:16; Heb. 9:26; 1 Pet. 1:20; 1 John 1:2); and of the Second Coming (Col. 3:4; 1 Pet. 5:4; 1 John 3:2); other uses (John 2:11; 21:1). *Phanérōsis*, however, does not attain to the meaning of either *apokálupsis*, revelation, or *epipháneia*, appearing, as to the Second Coming.

5337. Phaûlos; vile, refuse, evil, wicked, foul. Someone or something good-for-nothing from which nothing good can come; worthless, mediocre, unimportant. Distinguished from *kakós* (2556), bad, and *ponērós* (4190), malevolent (John 3:20; 5:29; Titus 2:8; James 3:16).

5338. Phéggos; the light of the moon or the other luminaries of the night (Matt. 24:29; Mark 13:24; Luke 11:33 TR). Contrast *phós* (5457), light *phōstḗr* (5458), luminary.

5342. Phérō; to bear, bring; sustain, uphold (Heb. 1:3); endure (Heb. 12:20); permit (Heb. 13:13); bear with (Rom. 9:22); cause to come (Matt. 17:17; Mark 1:32; 7:32); bring, as an accusation (John 18:29; Acts 25:7 TR); lead toward a certain direction (Acts 12:10); to bear fruit (Mark 4:8; John 12:24). Pass.: *phéromai*, to be carried, brought (Acts 2:2); to be driven, as persons in a storm (Acts 27:15, 17), to be borne away or actuated by the Holy Spirit (2 Pet. 1:21); to be carried, proceed (Heb. 6:1); to be produced, proved, or made apparent in a forensic sense as in a court of justice (Heb. 9:16). Related words: *prosphorá* (4376), an offering, the act of offering to God (Heb. 10:10), an oblation, the thing offered (Acts 21:26; 24:17; Eph. 5:2; Heb. 10:5, 8, 14, 18). See *sumphérō* (4851), to be profitable for; *phóros* (5411), tribute; *phortíon* (5413), burden. Deriv.: *anaphérō* (399), (*ana;*, [303], up), to carry or bring up (Matt. 17:1; Mark 9:2; Luke 24:51); to bring up sacrifices on the altar (Heb. 7:27); to bear sins by imputation, in reality or as the ancient sacrifices did typically (Heb. 9:28; 1 Pet. 2:24), *apophérō* (667) (apó [575], from), to carry away (Mark 15:1; Luke 16:22; 1 Cor. 16:3; Rev. 17:3; 21:10); *eisphérō* (1533) (*eis* [1519], in or to), to bring to or into (Heb. 13:11); *ekphérō* (1627) (*ek* [1537], out), to bring or carry out (Acts 5:15; 1 Tim. 6:7), to carry out to burial, bring forth, produce as the earth (Heb. 6:8); *epiphérō* (2018), (*epí* [1909], upon, besides, or against), to bring, carry to (Acts 19:12), inflict wrath or vengeance (Rom. 3:5), add or superadd; bring against as an accusation (Jude 1:9); *prophérō* (4393), (*pro* [4253], forth), bring forth or out, produce (Luke 6:45); *prosphérō* (4374), (*pros* [4314], to), to bring to (Matt. 4:24; 5:23), to bring to or before as a magistrate (Luke 12:11; 23:14), to offer, tender, proffer, as money for a benefit to be received, to offer to God as oblations or sacrifices (Matt. 5:24; 8:4). In the mid. voice inf. *prosphéresthai tiní* (dat., to someone) literally to offer oneself to anyone, that is, to behave towards, deal with or treat him (Heb. 12:7); *diaphérō* (1308) (*diá* [1223], denoting transition or separation), to carry through, to carry abroad or to publish throughout (Acts 13:49). In the pass.: *diaphéromai*, to be carried, driven, or tossed different ways, hither and thither or up and down (Acts 27:27). Governing a gen., to differ (1 Cor. 15:41; Gal. 4:1); to excel, be more important or valuable than (Matt. 6:26; 10:31; 12:12; Luke 12:7, 24). Impersonally, *diaphérei*, makes a difference, is of consequence, is important (Gal. 2:6).

5346. Phēmí; related to *pháō*, to speak, say or shine. To say, to speak. It has the sense of affirmation (Matt. 4:7; Rom. 3:8). See *laléō* (2980), to speak; *légō* (3004), to say.

5349. Phthartós; from *phtheírō* (5351), to corrupt. Corruptible, the essential quality of the body of man, equivalent to *thnētós* (2349), mortal, used in 1 Corinthians 15:53, 54 with a clear indication that this characteristic will be changed to incorruptibility, the characteristic of the believer's resurrection body. Used as an adj. to indicate degenerating mankind (Rom. 1:23), the temporal character of a crown won on this earth (1 Cor. 9:25), and the physical means which cannot bring spiritual salvation (1 Pet. 1:18, 23).

5351. Phtheírō; to corrupt, destroy. Related to *phthínō* or *phthíō*, which does not occur in the NT but from which *phthinópōron*, autumn, is derived (see *phthinopōrinós* [5352], pertaining to the fall season). In the NT used in general to denote corruption, destruction. To destroy, punish with destruction (1 Cor. 3:17); to corrupt, spoil, vitiate, in a moral or spiritual sense (1 Cor. 15:33); to corrupt, that is, to seduce to evil company or corrupt opinions (2 Cor. 7:2; 11:3).

5355. Phthónos; may be derived from *phthínō*, to decay, wither, pine away (Sept.: Prov. 14:30). Envy or pain felt and malignity conceived at the sight of excellence or happiness; malice. *Phthónos*, unlike *zélos* (2205), zeal, is incapable of good and is used always with an evil meaning (Mark 15:10; James 4:5).

5358. Philágathos; from *philos* (5384), friend, and *agathós* (18), benevolently good. One who loves and practices what is good (Titus 1:8). It combines not only the affinity to be kind but also the inclination to do good. The word stands in contradistinction to *philoiktírmōn* which means one who has or likes to have sympathetic feelings without necessarily externalizing those in good actions. Deriv.: *aphilágathos* (865), the opposite of *philágathos*.

5360. Philadelphía; from *philos* (5384), friend, and *adelphós* (80), brother. In the NT used of the love of Christians for one another, brotherly love out of a common spiritual life (Rom. 12:10; 1 Thess. 4:9; Heb. 13:1; 1 Pet. 1:22; 2 Pet. 1:7).

5361. Philádelphos; from *philos* (5384), friend, and *adelphós* (80), brother. In a wider sense it meant to love one's fellow countrymen. In the strictly Christian sense of "brother" (1 Pet. 3:8), used as a more comprehensive word in line with the meaning of the other adj. distinguishing the Christians from other people. *Philádelphoi* (pl.) sums up the bearing of Christians to each other, and the adj. which follows describes what their behavior should be to those who are outside the Christian fellowship (see 1 Pet. 3:8).

5363. Philanthrōpía; from *philos* (5384), friend, and *ánthrōpos* (444), man. Human friendship. Denotes that apparent and ready good will usually manifest in a friendly, considerate demeanor, and especially in the practice of hospitality, readiness to help, tenderheartedness, cherishing and maintaining fellowship. *Philanthrōpía*, which is used in English as "philanthrophy," is that disposition which does not always think of self, but takes thought for others, their needs and wishes. The philanthropist serves his fellow citizens, protects the oppressed, is mindful of the erring, gentle to the conquered, and self-renouncing in reference to his rights. The word does not occur in the Sept. In the NT it occurs as a subst. in Acts 28:2, referring to the hospitable reception of the shipwrecked. Philanthropy does not occur in the list of Israelitish or Christian virtues. This social virtue in the NT is expressed with the words *agápē* (26), love, and *philadelphía* (5360), brotherly love, which occupy the place of social righteousness. It is actually one further step to nobleness to be possessed of *philadelphía* because one considers man as his brother while *philanthrōpía* considers him only as a fellow human being. In Acts 27:3 the word is used as an adv., *philánthrōpōs* (5364), of the human treatment of Paul. Titus 3:4 is denoting the philanthropy of God as a Savior which means His manifestation in the salvation of man.

5365. Philarguría; from *philos* (5384), friend or loving, and *argurós* (696), silver, money. Love of money. To retain that which one has, and by accumulating, to multiply it (1 Tim. 6:10). *Philarguría* may be regarded as a type of *pleonexía* (4124), covetousness.

5367. Philautos; from *philos* (5384), loving, and *autós* (846), himself. In reality it is not the one who simply loves himself but one who loves himself more than he ought to, involving self-conceit and selfishness (2 Tim. 3:2). A person who is characterized by an undue sparing of self and whose primary concern is that things be easy and pleasant for himself. Contrast *authádēs* (829), insolent, one who is harsh and rigorous towards others. The *philautos* is one who loves his life so much that he seeks ignobly to save it.

5368. Philéō; to love, with the meaning of having common interests with another (Matt. 10:37; John 5:20). To befriend. Contrast *agapáō* (25), taking interest in somebody.

5373. Philía; friendship, from *philéō*, having common interests with another. Only in James 4:4.

5399. Phobéō; from *phóbos* (5401), in Class. Gr. to cause to run away, terrify, frighten. In the NT used in the pass. form *phobéomai*, to be terrified, afraid, whether intrans. (Matt. 14:27, 30), or trans., with an acc., to be afraid of, fear (Matt. 14:5; 21:26, 46; Luke 12:5; Heb. 11:23, 27), or joined with an inf. (Matt. 1:20; 2:22). Trans., with an acc., to fear, reverence (Mark 6:20; Luke 1:50; Acts 10:2; Eph. 5:33).

5401. Phóbos; Terror, fear (Matt. 14:26). Capable of a good connotation (Eph. 5:21), in which case it is syn. with *eulábeia* (2124, godly fear, reverence), or a bad connotation, syn. to *deilía* (1167), fearfulness, timidity, shrinking for fear (2 Tim. 1:7). Verb: *phobéomai* (5399), to flee, run away from. Adj.: *phoberós* (5398), dreadful, terrible, horrid.

5406. Phoneús; from *phónos* (5408), murder. A murderer (Matt. 22:7; 1 Pet. 4:15; Rev. 21:8). Two other words translated also as "murderer" have distinctive features: (1) *anthrōpoktónos* (443), from *ánthrōpos* (444), a man, and *éktona*, the perf. mid. of *kteínō*, to slay. "Manslayer" corresponds to the exact meaning. (2) *sikários* (4607), an assassin hired to kill somebody. *Phoneús* has the vaguest use of all three words.

5411. Phóros; from *péphora*, perf. mid. of *phérō* (5342), to bring. Tribute brought into a prince's treasury (Luke 20:22; 23:2; Rom. 13:6, 7). Related words: *phoréō* (5409), to bear, carry (1 Cor. 15:49); to wear (Matt. 11:8; John 19:5; James 2:3); *antilambánomai* (482), to help; *antílēpsis* (484), help, relief.

5413. Phortíon; the diminutive of *phórtos* (5414), a burden, load, from *phérō* (5342), to bear; the goods or merchandise carried by a ship (Acts 27:10). Used in the NT only figuratively as the burden of Christ's commandments (Matt. 11:30); the burden of ceremonial observances rigorously exacted and increased by human traditions (Matt. 23:4; Luke 11:46); sin and the punishment of it (Gal. 6:5). See also *phortízō* (5412), to load, burden (Matt. 11:28; Luke 11:46).

5421. Phréar; a well or pit for water dug in the earth and thus strictly distinguished from *pēgé* (4077), fountain (though a well may also be called a fountain). In Luke 14:5; John 4:11, 12, the depth of the well; in Revelation 9:1, 2, *Hádēs* (86), the bottomless pit.

5424. Phrḗn; pl., *phrénes*; only in 1 Corinthians 14:20, translated "understanding," as *noús* (3563), mind; *súnesis* (4907), putting it together; and *diánoia* (1271), penetrating mind. *Phrénes* is used in connection with Paul's discussion regarding speaking without being understood. *Phrénes* was regarded early as the seat of intellectual and spiritual activity. It was the diaphragm which determined the strength of the breath and hence also the human spirit and its emotions. *Phrénes* precisely refers to the ability not only to think, but also to control one's thoughts or one's inner attitude of mind. It is the heart as the seat of passions as well as the mind as the seat of mental faculties.

5426. Phronéō; to think, implying not only thought but also the affections, will, or moral consideration. Related to *phrénes* (5424) as contrasted with *noús* (3563), mind. In the Scripture it is most commonly applied to the actions of the will and affections. Trans., with an acc., to mind, set the affections on (Matt. 16:23; Rom. 8:5; 12:16; Phil. 3:19; Col. 3:2). Intrans., to be affected (2 Cor. 13:11). To think, be of opinion (Acts 28:22; Rom. 12:3; 1 Cor. 4:6 TR). Deriv.: *phrónēma* (5427), the result of *phrónēsis* (5428), a minding; *phrónimos* (5429), prudently.

5428. Phrónēsis; prudence, the knowledge of how to regulate one's relationships and dealings with other people. It skillfully adapts its means to the attainment of the ends which it desires without consideration to whether the ends themselves are good or not (Luke 1:17; Eph. 1:8). Adj.: *phrónimos* (5429), prudent. Deriv.: *aphrosúnē* (877), senselessness, related to *áphrōn* (878), imprudent, without reason, from *a* (1), without, and *phrénes* (5424), mind and heart; one who lacks mental sanity and sobriety, reckless and lacking the common sense perception of the reality of things natural and spiritual.

5429. Phrónimos; prudent, sensible, using practical wisdom in relationships with others (Matt. 7:24; 10:16; 24:45; 25:2, 4, 8, 9; Luke 12:42; 16:8; 1 Cor. 10:15). In an evil sense, thinking oneself to be prudent judging

by one's self-complacency (Rom. 11:25; 12:16; used ironically in 1 Cor. 4:10; 2 Cor. 11:19).

5438. Phulaké; from *phulássō* (5442), to keep. A keeping, guarding or watching (Luke 2:8); a guard, a number of sentinels (Acts 12:10); a prison (Matt. 14:3, 10); a hold, a dwelling (Rev. 18:2); a cage of birds (Rev. 18:2); as a division of time, a watch, the night being divided into four watches (*phulakai*; 6–9 p. m.; 9–12 midnight; 12–3 a. m.; 3–6 a. m.; then began the first hour of the day at 6 a. m. and so on [see Matt. 20:1–16]). Deriv.: *phulakízō* (5439), to imprison (Acts 22:19); *phúlax* (5441), a keeper, sentinel (Acts 5:23; 12:6, 19).

5442. Phulássō; or *phulátto*, to keep or preserve from danger of harm (John 12:25; 17:12). To guard, watch (Luke 2:8; 11:21); to observe a commandment or law (Matt. 19:20; Luke 11:28). In the mid. voice, to beware (2 Pet. 3:17). Deriv.: *phulaké* (5438), a prison, hold.

5453. Phúō; intrans., to become, increase (Heb. 12:15). Trans., to produce; pass., to become, to grow (Luke 8:6, 8).

5456. Phōné; from the obsolete *pháō* or *phṓ*, to speak. Plutarch calls it "that which brings light upon that which is thought of in the mind." The voice explains that which one has in his own mind for others. It is variably translated in John 3:8 as "sound"; Matthew 2:18 as "voice"; in Revelation 6:1 as "noise." *Phōné* is the cry of the living creature. Sometimes ascribed to God (Matt. 3:17); to men (Matt. 3:3); to animals, inanimate objects (1 Cor. 14:7); to the trumpet (Matt. 24:31 TR); to the wind (John 3:8); to the thunder (Rev. 6:1). *Phōné* is something that definitely can be heard by others. Contrast *lógos* (3056), saying or a rational utterance of the mind, whether spoken (*prophorikós*, with utterance, as in Dan. 7:11), or unspoken (*endiáthetos*, remaining with oneself), of which the latter meaning is equivalent to reason and which can only be predicated of men who can think. Therefore, *lógos*, thought or expressed thought, is something that only intelligent beings can exercise and it can be either spoken or unspoken. Thus Jesus Christ in His preincarnate state is called *Lógos* (3056), intelligence, but also the expression of that intelligence in terms that could make us understand what was in the mind of God eternally.

5457. Phṓs; light of the sun or of the day (Acts 9:3; Rev. 18:23). Contrast *phéggos* (5338), the light of the moon or the other luminaries of the night (Matt. 24:29; Mark 13:24; Luke 11:33). *Phṓs* is never kindled and therefore never quenched, but *lúchnos* (3088) is kindled by the hands of another.

5458. Phōstḗr; a heavenly body, a luminary, mainly the sun and moon (Phil. 2:15; Rev. 21:11).

5461. Phōtízō; related to *phōs* (5457), light. To enlighten, give light to (Luke 11:36; Rev. 18:1, cf. Rev. 21:23; 22:5); to enlighten, give light to, in a spiritual sense (John 1:9; Eph. 1:18; Heb. 6:4; 10:32); to instruct, to make to see or understand (Eph. 3:9); to bring to light (1 Cor. 4:5; 2 Tim. 1:10).

5462. Phōtismós; from *phōtízō* (5461), to enlighten. Enlightening, the illumination going forth from something, the light proceeding therefrom. As a subst., light, luster, illumination (2 Cor. 4:4, 6 where it is applied spiritually).

5463. Chaírō; related to *cháris* (5485), grace, as joy is a direct result of God's grace. To rejoice, be glad (Matt. 5:12; 18:13); with the same meaning in the 2 aor. pass. *echárēn*, and fut. pass., *charḗsomai* (Matt. 2:10; Mark 14:11; Luke 1:14; John 16:20). The imper. *chaire*, and (in the pl.) *chairete* are applied even in Mod. Gr. as terms of salutation or of wishing happiness to another corresponding to our hello (Matt. 28:9; Luke 1:28); used deceitfully (Matt. 26:49); ironically (Matt. 27:29; Mark 15:18; John 19:3). In 2 John 1:10, 11, the author forbids that such a salutation should be given to heretical teachers. In the pl., *chairete* is also applied as a form of salutation equal to "farewell," "adieu," "goodbye" (2 Cor. 13:11). The inf. *chairein* is used as a form of salutation at the beginning of a letter indicating the wish of health, happiness (Acts 15:23; 23:26; James 1:1). Deriv.: *chará* (5479), joy, delight, gladness. Syn.: *euphraínō* (2165), to cheer, gladden; *agalliáō* (21), to exult, rejoice greatly.

5479. Chará; from *chaírō* (5463), to rejoice. Joy (Matt. 2:10; 13:20; 25:21, 23; Luke 15:7, 10; 2 Cor. 7:4; Heb. 13:17; James 4:9; 1 Pet. 1:8). Cause or matter of joy or rejoicing (Luke 2:10; Phil. 4:1; 1 Thess. 2:19, 20). Syn.: *agallíasis* (20), exultation, exuberant joy; *euphrosúnē* (2167), good cheer, mirth, gladness of heart.

5480. Cháragma; engraving, impression, mark, symbol (Acts 17:29; Rev. 13:16, 17). Distinguished from *charaktḗr* (5481), the representation of a person. The difference between *charaktḗr* and *apaúgasma* (541), effulgence (both occurring in Hebrews 1:3), is discussed fully under *eikṓn* (1504), image (in its contrast with *homoíōsis* [3669], resemblance, and *homoíōma* [3667], likeness).

5481. Charaktḗr; representation, express image (English, character). Occurs only in Hebrews 1:3, where it is translated "express image," referring to the person of Jesus Christ. Distinguished from *cháragma* (5480), graven mark. See *eikṓn* (1504, image) for the distinction between these two and also the contrast between *charaktḗr* and *apaúgasma* (541), brightness, appearing in Hebrews 1:3.

5483. Charízomai; as a deponent verb, a pass. form which is used act.; to do a person a favor, be kind to. With the dat. (Gal. 3:18), in the NT sense of *cháris* (5485), grace, meaning to be gracious to. With the acc. of the thing, to give or bestow a thing willingly as a gift. With the dat. of a person (Luke 7:21; Acts 27:24; Rom. 8:32; Phil. 2:9); for an end proposed by the receiver, to yield to his will (Acts 25:11, 16). The end in view must be inferred from the context (Acts 3:14). The most common meaning peculiar to the NT is to pardon, that is, to graciously remit a person's sin (Col. 2:13) in which *cháris*, grace, must be viewed as the opposite of *hamartía* (266), sin. *Charízomai* means to forgive something (2 Cor. 2:10; Col. 2:13); with the dat only, to forgive someone, to be gracious to someone (Eph. 4:32; Col. 3:13). 2 Corinthians 2:7 uses it without any obj., with the meaning "to offer." In Luke 7:42, 43 it means simply "to give." In the pass., especially in the aor. *echarísthen*, and the fut., *charisthḗsomai*, to be kindly treated, to be pleasingly dealt with (Acts 3:14; 1 Cor. 2:12; Phil. 1:29; Phile. 1:22).

5485. Cháris; from *chaírō* (5463), to rejoice, or *chará* (5479), joy, favor, acceptance, a kindness granted or desired, a benefit, thanks, gratitude, grace. A favor done without expectation of return; absolute freeness of the loving-kindness of God to men, finding its only motive in the bounty and freeheartedness of the Giver; unearned and unmerited favor. *Cháris* stands in direct antithesis to *érga* (2041), works, the two being mutually exclusive. God's grace affects man's sinfulness and not only forgives the repentant sinner, but brings joy and thankfulness to him. In contrast to *cháris* stands *éleos* (1656), mercy, which is concerned not with sin itself, as does *cháris*, but with the misery brought upon the sinner as a consequence of that sin.

5486. Chárisma; derived from *cháris*, grace, and the suffix *-ma*, indicating the result of grace. A gift of grace; an undeserved benefit from God (Rom. 1:11; 1 Tim. 4:14).

5487. Charitóō; from the basic Gr. word *cháris* (5485), grace. Found only in Scripture and in later post-Christian Gr. Trans., with an acc., to make accepted or acceptable, make lovely or deserving of love, amiable (Eph. 1:6). To be acceptable, favored, highly favored as in Luke 1:28 meaning to bestow grace upon, as distinct from *charizomai*, to confer grace. It really does not mean to show favor to, but to give grace to, since Mary was to bear Jesus Christ, the whole treasure of God's grace, in her womb.

5500. Cheirotonéō; from *cheir* (5495), hand, and *tétona*, perf. mid. of *teínō*, to extend, stretch out. To elect or choose to an office by lifting up the hand; to choose to vote (2 Cor. 8:19), to appoint to an office without votes (Acts 14:23).

5509. Chitṓn; a close-fitting inner vest, an inner garment (Matt. 5:40). Used with *himátion* (2440), an outer cloak in Luke 6:29. In the pl., used generally for garments or clothes (Mark 14:63) and equivalent to *himátia* in Matt. 26:65. Contrast *himatismós* (2441); *chlamús* (5511); *stolḗ* (4749), and *podḗrēs* (4158).

5511. Chlamús; a garment of dignity and office. The purple robe with which our Lord was arrayed in scorn by the mockers in Pilate's Judgment Hall (Matt. 27:28, 31). A *chlamús* was constantly used as a garment of dignity and office and, when put over the shoulders of someone, was an indication that he was assuming a magistracy. Perhaps it was the cast-off cloak of some high Roman officer which was put over the body of Jesus to mock Him as if He were an official person. Contrast *himátion* (2440); *chitṓn* (5509); *himatismós* (2441); *stolḗ* (4749); *podḗrēs* (4158).

5517. Choikós; from *choós*, earth, dust. Earthly, made of earth or dust (1 Cor. 15:47–49). Contrast *gḗ* (1093).

5530. Chráomai; the mid. voice of *chráō* (5531), to lend. To borrow, receive for use. With a dat., to use, make use of, and, more literally, to hand (Acts 27:17; 1 Cor. 7:31); to behave toward, (Acts 27:3). See *chreía* (5532) and *chrēstótēs* (5544). Deriv.: *chrēsis* (5540), noun, use, manner of using; *apóchrēsis* (671), from *apochráomai*, to abuse, consume by use, from *apo* (575), from, or used as intens., and *chráomai*, to use, using or use (Col. 2:22) bearing the meaning of *chrēsis*, referring to the things that could not be used without rendering them unfit for further use. See *katachráomai* (2710), to abuse, misuse.

5531. Chráō; perhaps from *cheir* (5495), hand. To lend, furnish as a loan or to put into another's hands (Luke 11:5); the mid. voice, *chráomai* (5530), to borrow, receive for use.

5532. Chreía; from *chráomai* (5530), to use. Occasion, use, need, necessity (Acts 20:34; Rom. 12:13; Phil. 2:25); a necessary business or affair (Acts 6:3). Deriv.: *eúchrēstos* (2173), from *eu* (2095), well, or as an intens., and *chrēstós*, useful, very useful (2 Tim. 2:21; 4:11; Phile. 1:11). Contrast *áchrēstos* (890), of no use, unprofitable (Phile. 1:11); *chrḗ* (5534), impersonal verb, there is need or occasion; *chrḗzō* (5535), to need; *chrḗma* (5536), something useful, riches or money; *chrēmatízō* (5537), to give divine directions or information, the same as to utter oracles; *chrēmatismós* (5538), a divine answer or oracle; *chrḗsimos* (5539), useful, profitable; *chrḗsis* (5540), use; *chrēstótēs* (5544), benignity, kindness.

5534. Chrḗ; an impersonal verb, used by shortening it for *chrḗsis*, from *chreía* (5532), need, necessity. It is becoming, it is appropriate, it ought (James 3:10). See *chrēstótēs* (5544), benignity.

5535. Chrḗzō; from *chreía* (5532), need, necessity. Governing a gen., to have need of, want (Matt. 6:32; Rom. 16:2). See *chrēstótēs* (5544), benignity.

5536. Chrḗma; from *kéchrēmai*, the perf. of *chráomai* (5530), to handle. Something useful or capable of being used. In the pl., riches, wealth (Mark 10:23, 24 TR; Luke 18:24). In both the sing. and pl. it means money (Acts 4:37; 8:18, 20; 24:26). Contrast *chreía* (5532), need; *chrēstótēs* (5544), usefulness, gentleness.

5537. Chrēmatízō; from *chrḗma* (5536). To have business dealings, manage a business. To be called or named (Acts 11:26; Rom. 7:3). Particularly in the NT it means to utter oracles, give divine directions or information (Heb. 12:25) To be directed or warned by God or as by a divine oracle (Matt. 2:12, 22; Acts 10:22, Heb. 8:5; 11:7), or things revealed by divine oracle (Luke 2:26). Related to *kéchrēmai*, the perf. pass of *chráō*, uttering a divine oracle. See *chreía* (5532), need; *chrēstótēs* (5544) usefulness, gentleness.

5538. Chrēmatismós; the perf. pass. of *chrēmatízō* (5537), to utter an oracle. A divine answer or oracle (Rom. 11:4).

5539. Chrḗsimos; from *chrḗsis* (5540), use. Useful, profitable (2 Tim. 2:14). See *chreía* (5532); *chrēstótēs* (5544).

5540. Chrḗsis; from *chráomai* (5530), to use. Use, manner of using (Rom. 1:26, 27). See *chreía* (5532), need; *chrēstótēs* (5544).

5543. Chrēstós; from *chráomai* (5530), to furnish what is needed. Useful, profitable, good as opposed to bad (1 Cor. 15:33), good, kind, obliging, gracious (Luke 6:35; Eph. 4:32; 1 Pet. 2:3); of a yoke, gentle, easy (Matt. 11:30) See *chrēstótēs* (5544), and deriv. under *chreía* (5532).

5544. Chrēstótēs; benignity, kindness. It is joined to *philanthrōpía* (5363), philanthropy; *anochḗ* (463), forbearance (Rom. 2:4), and opposite *apotomía* (663), severity or cutting something short and quickly (Rom. 11:22). *Chrēstótēs* is translated as "good" (Rom. 3:12), "kindness" (2 Cor. 6:6; Eph. 2:7; Col. 3:12; Titus 3:4); "gentleness" (Gal. 5:22). It is the grace which pervades the whole nature, mellowing all which would have been harsh and austere. Thus, wine is *chrēstós* (5543), mellowed with age (Luke 5:39); Christ's yoke is *chrēstós*, as having nothing harsh or galling about it (Matt. 11:30). Contrast *agathōsúnē* (19), it pertains to character without the necessary altruistic externalization found in *agathōsúnē*, active benignity. *Chrēstótēs* has only the harmlessness of the dove, not the wisdom of the serpent, which *agathōsúnē* may have indicated in sharpness and rebuke. Related words: *chrēstós*, kind or good in oneself, mellow.

5545. Chrísma; the anointing (Ex. 30:25; 40:9; Lev. 21:10). The specially-prepared anointing oil was called *chrísma*, anointing, *hágion* (39), holy. See *chríō* (5548), to rub over, anoint. Only in 1 John 2:20, 27 where it signifies an anointing which had been experienced, a communication and reception of the Spirit (cf. John 16:13) *Chrísma* is not merely a figurative name for the Spirit as seen from the expression *chrísma échete* ("ye have an unction," v. 20) and *elábete* ("ye have received," v. 27). The word seems chosen in order to give prominence, on the one hand, to what the readers had experienced, and on the other hand, by referring to the OT practice, and especially to Christ, to remind them of their calling and mark (1 Pet. 2 5, 9).

5546. Christianós; Christian, a name given to the disciples or followers of Christ (see *mathētēs*, [3101], disciple of Jesus Christ), and first adopted at Antioch. It does not occur in the NT as a name commonly used by Christians themselves (Acts 11:26; 26:28; 1 Pet. 4:16). In Acts 11:26 the verb used for "were called" is *chrēmatísai*, the inf. of *chrēmatízō* (5537), which means to be directed by God as if by divine oracle. (The Bambas translation erroneously uses the word *ōnomásthēsan* here, from *onomázō* [3687]) This same verb was used by the magi from the East, who were divinely informed not to return to tell Herod where the baby Jesus was (Matt. 2:12, 22). See also Acts 10:22; Hebrews 8:5; 11:7 where the same verb is used. Thus the believers first became known as Christians not as an appellation of ridicule (as commonly taught) but by divine direction. See *chríō* (5548), to anoint.

5547. Christós; from *chríō* (5548), to anoint. Anointed; a term used in the OT applied to everyone anointed with the holy oil, primarily to the high priesthood (Lev. 4:3, 5, 16; 6:22). Also a name applied to others acting as redeemers. As an appellative and with the art. *ho*, the, *Christós*, Christ, occurs chiefly in the Gospels. Without the art. and as a proper noun alone, in the Gospels only in Mark 9:41 (cf. Acts 24:24); elsewhere only in the connection of Jesus Christ (Matt. 1:16), "Jesus who is called Christ." In the Pauline Epistles and in 1 Peter, "Christ" is used as a proper name (Rom. 5:8; 6:4, 8; 8:10, 34; 9:1; 1 Pet. 1:11, 19; 2:21; 3:16, 18). As to the different uses in the NT besides the name of our Lord, it denotes the Christian Church or that society of which Christ is the head (1 Cor. 12:12). The body of Christ means the Church because Christ is the head of the body (1 Cor. 12:27; Gal. 3:24, 28; Col. 1:24). It also means the doctrine of Christ (Eph. 4:20); the benefits (Heb. 3:14); and the Christian temper or disposition arising from a sound Christian faith (Gal. 4:19, cf. 2 Cor. 3:14; Eph. 3:17; Phil. 2:5) Deriv.: *antíchristos* (500), an opponent of

Christ or the one who takes the place of Christ; *christianós* (5546). Christian.

5548. Chríō; to anoint, with a sacred or religious meaning. From this is derived *Christós*, the Anointed One, Christ (Luke 4:18; Acts 4:27; 10:38; 2 Cor. 1:21; Heb. 1:9). Contrast *aleíphō* (218), to cover over, rub, used with mundane significance involving oil or ointment (Matt. 6:17; Mark 6:13; 16:1; Luke 7:38, 46; John 11:2; 12:3; James 5:14).

5550. Chrónos; time as succession or measurement of moments (as in chronometer, a meter of *chronos*); of the passing moments without any moral impact as to the opportunity and accomplishment in that time, as indicated by *kairós* (2540), the time of opportunities. *Chrónos* has only length, not challenge of accomplishment, as *kairós*. *Chrónos* embraces all possible *kairós*, and is often used as the larger and more inclusive term, but not the converse. In the NT used only in the pl., *chrónoi*, together with *kairoí*, times and opportunities or seasons (Acts 1:7; 1 Thess. 5:1).

5568. Psalmós; from *psáō*, actually a touching, and then a touching of the harp or other stringed instruments with the finger or with the plectrum; later known as the instrument itself, and finally it became known as the song sung with the musical accompaniment. This latest stage of its meaning, "psalm," was adopted in the Sept. In all probability the psalms of Ephesians 5:19; Colossians 3:16 are the inspired psalms of the Hebr. Canon. The word certainly designates these on all other occasions when it occurs in the NT, with the one possible exception of 1 Corinthians 14:26. These are the old songs to which new hymns and praises are added (Rev. 5:9) See *hymn* (5215); *ōdḗ* (5603) song of praise.

5569. Pseudadelphós; from *pseudḗs* (5571), false, and *adelphós* (80), brother; a false brother. In Galatians 2:4 it denotes those who had become members of the Christian church, sharers in its fellowship of life and love, but in reality were not so inwardly, and therefore had no right to be counted as brothers. They had the companionship of the brothers but the real kinship of spiritual life was missing (see 2 Cor. 11:26).

5572. Pseudodidáskalos; from *pseúdō*, to deceive, or the mid. or pass. voice *pseúdomai* (5574), to lie, and *didáskalos* (1320), a teacher. A false teacher, one who pretends to have the character of a Christian teacher and teaches false doctrine (2 Pet. 2:1).

5580. Pseudóchristos; from *pseudḗs* (5571), false, and *Christós* (5547), Christ (Matt. 24:24; Mark 13:22). The false Christ does not deny the being of Christ. On the contrary, he builds on the world's expectations of such a person, but he blasphemously appropriates these to himself and affirms that he is the foretold One in whom God's promises and men's expectations are fulfilled. While the *antíchristos* (500), antichrist, denies that there is a Christ, the *pseudóchristos* affirms himself to be the Christ. Both are against the Christ of God. The final antichrist will be a pseudochrist as well. He will usurp to himself Christ's offices, presenting himself to the world as the true center of its hopes, the satisfier of all its needs and the healer of all its ills. He will be a pseudochrist and antichrist in one.

5584. Psēlapháō; feel on the surface, feeling for or after an object without any actual coming in contact with it at all (Luke 24:39; Acts 17:27; Heb. 12:18; 1 John 1:1). See *háptomai* (680); *háptō* (681); *thiggánō* (2345).

5588. Psithuristés; from *psithurízō*, to whisper; a whisperer, a secret slanderer, versus *katálalos* (2637), a backbiter who does his slandering openly (Rom. 1:29, 30). Deriv.: *psithurismós* (5587), a whispering, slanderer (2 Cor. 12:20).

5590. Psuchḗ; soul, that immaterial part of man held in common with animals (Matt. 10:28; Rom. 2:9). Contrast *sṓma* (4983), body, and *pneúma* (4151), spirit (1 Thess. 5:23). The *psuchḗ*, no less than the *sárx* (4561), flesh, belongs to the lower region of man's being. Sometimes *psuchḗ* stands for the immaterial part of man made up of the soul, *psuchḗ* in the restrictive sense of the animus, the life element, and the *pneúma* (4151), spirit. But animals are not said to possess a spirit; only man has a spirit, giving him the ability to communicate with God.

5591. Psuchikós; from *psuché* (5590), soul, the part of the immaterial life held in common with the animals, as contrasted with spirit, *pneúma* (4151), only in man, enabling him to communicate with God. Pertaining to the natural, animal, as distinguished from spiritual or glorified nature of man. 1 Corinthians 15:44 refers to a body *psuchikón*, an animalistic or physical body governed by the soul or animal or fallen instinct of man, and a body *pneumatikón* (4152). spiritual, governed by the divine quality in man, the spirit. Rendered as "natural" in 1 Corinthians 2:14; 15:44, 46 and "sensual" in James 3:15; Jude 1:19. The term *psuchikós* is not a word of honor, even as *sarkikós* (4559), carnal.

5594. Psúchō; from *psúchos* (5592), cold. Derived from a word meaning to compress, condense, concrete, which is the property of coldness. Therefore, *psúchō* means to cool or refrigerate as with cool air. It is from this verb that *psuché* (5590), which has come to mean "soul," is derived. It is to refresh with cool air and naturally to breathe. Hence *psuché* is the breath of a living creature, animal life, and the verb *psúchō*, in the pass. *psúchomai*, means to be cool, to grow cool or cold in a spiritual sense, as in Christian love (Matt. 24:12).

5603. Ōdé; song, contracted from *aoidé*, which in turn comes from *aeidō* or *ádō* (103), to sing, confess, praise. The original use of singing among both believers and idolaters was in the confessions and praises of the respective gods. Paul qualifies it in Ephesians 5:19; Colossians 3:16 as spiritual songs in association with psalms and hymns, because *ōdé* by itself might mean any kind of song, as of battle, harvest, festal, whereas *psalmós* (5568), psalm, from its Hebr. use, and *húmnos* (5215), hymn, from its Gr. use, did not require any such qualifying adj. *Ōdé* is a harmonious song (Rev. 5:9; 14:3; 15:3).

5604. Ōdín; from *odúnē*, grief, sorrow. Used usually in the pl. and meaning pains of labor, distress, woe; compared to the pain which a woman experiences

in childbirth (Matt. 24:8; Mark 13:8). In Acts 2:24 the *ōdínas thanátou*, the cords or snares of death. Deriv.: *ōdínō* (5605), to be in pain.

5605. Ōdínō; from *ōdín* (5604). Intrans., to be in pain, as when a woman is in travail (Gal. 4:27; Rev. 12:2, in both cases applied spiritually to the Church); trans., with an acc., to travail in birth of, to be in labor with (Gal. 4:19 where Paul applies it in a spiritual sense to himself with respect to the Galatian converts).

5610. Hōra; hour. NT meanings: (1) Time, season. particular time (Mark 11:11; John 4:23; 5:35; 12:23; 17:1; 1 John 2:18, cf. Mark 14:35; Rev. 3:10; 14:7, 15). (2) A short time (John 5 35; 1 Thess. 2:17; Phile. 1:15). (3) Denotes the day or time of day (Matt. 14:15). The *hōra pollé* (much hour or much time) in Mark 6:35 means either a great part of the day already past or yet remaining. The *édē* (2235), "already," in this verse forces us to adopt the first meaning, a great part of the day already past. (4) An hour, the twelfth part of daylight, or the time the sun is above the horizon; for example, the third hour means 9:00 a. m., and the eleventh hour means 5 p.m. (Matt. 20:3, 5, 6 TR 9, 12; John 19:14) (5) The right time, the time fixed, the time determined upon or demanded, the fit time such as the time of judgment (Rev. 14:7), the time for harvest (Rev. 14:15), of temptation (Rev. 3:10). Also used in this manner in Matthew 26:45; John 4:21, 23. Often Christ's hour is spoken of as the time of His sufferings and death (Matt. 26:18; John 7:30; 8:20; 13:1).

5611. Hōraios; from *hōra* (5610), hour. Hence, indicating timely, fair, proper, good timing Used in the NT only in the figurative sense, beautiful (only in Matt. 23:27; Acts 3:2, 10; Rom. 10:15).

5613. Hōs; "as," used with numerals, it means "about" (Mark 5:13; 8:9; John 1:39; 6:19; 11:18; Acts 1:15; Rev. 8:1). Distinguished from *hōsei* (5616), which indicates greater indefiniteness.

5616. Hōsei; "as if," used before numerals and denotes "about," "nearly," "something like," with somewhat of an indication of greater indefiniteness than *hōs* (5613) (Matt. 14:21; Luke 3:23).

GREEK CONCORDANCE

This concordance, keyed to the numbers of Strong's *Dictionary of the Greek Testament,* lists the verses where a particular Greek word is used in the New Testament. However, certain words, such as proper nouns that denote the inhabitants of a specific city which occur only in the spurious subscriptions to the books, have been left out, even though Strong may have numbered them. Those words which occur numerous times in the Greek New Testament have also been omitted.

The active form has been given, even if the mid. or pass. forms are all that occur in the New Testament. Hence, any entry that ends in -ομαι is deponent in form or meaning.

Roman Numerals under an entry indicate words that are either different forms of one root or different words entirely. The letters A, B, etc., under an entry represents different uses, meanings, or applications of the exact same word. When more than one word is listed for a single entry, and they are separated by commas, the additional words for the entry represent variant spellings, variant readings, or contracted forms of a particular word.

At all points where it seemed especially critical, WH has been used to denote the primary texts of the Westcott and Hort theory, and TR has been used to refer to the Textus Receptus. In other places, it was deemed necessary to identify various forms or uses as to their part of speech or their grammatical relation to another word (for example, when a special form of a noun or adjective is used as an adverb). The abbreviations used in these identifications are listed below.

2 aor.	second aorist	masc.	masculine
adv.	adverb	mid.	middle voice
compar.	comparative	neut.	neuter
dat.	dative	obs.	obsolete
fem.	feminine	perf.	perfect
fut.	future	pl.	plural
gen.	genitive	prep.	preposition
impers.	impersonal	pres.	present
imperf.	imperfect	sing.	singular
imper.	imperative	subj.	subjunctive
indic.	indicative	subst.	substantive(ly)
infer.	inferential	TR	Textus Receptus
inter.	interrogative	WH	Westcott and Hort

A

1. A alpha
REV. 1:8,11; 21:6; 22:13

2. Ἀαρών Aarōn
LUKE 1:5; ACTS 7:40; HEB. 5:4; 7:11; 9:4

3. Ἀβαδδών Abaddōn
REV. 9:11

4. ἀβαρής abarēs
2 COR. 11:9

5. ἀββᾶ abba
MARK 14:36; ROM. 8:15; GAL. 4:6

6. Ἄβελ Abel
MATT. 23:35; LUKE 11:51; HEB. 11:4; 12:24

7. Ἀβιά Abia
MATT. 1:7; LUKE 1:5

8. Ἀβιάθαρ Abiathar
MARK 2:26

9. Ἀβιληνή Abilēnē
LUKE 3:1

10. Ἀβιούδ Abioud
MATT. 1:13

11. Ἀβραάμ Abraam
MATT. 1:1,2,17; 3:9; 8:11; 22:32; MARK 12:26; LUKE 1:55,73; 3:8,34; 13:16,28; 16:22-25,29,30; 19:9; 20:37; JOHN 8:33,37,39,40,52,53,56-58; ACTS 3:13,25; 7:2,16,17,32; 13:26; ROM. 4:1-3,9,12,13,16; 9:7; 11:1; 2 COR. 11:22; GAL. 3:6-9,14,16,18,29; 4:22; HEB. 2:16; 6:13; 7:1,2,4-6,9; 11:8,17; JAMES 2:21,23; 1 PET. 3:6

12. ἄβυσσος abussos
LUKE 8:31; ROM. 10:7; REV. 9:1,2,11; 11:7; 17:8; 20:1,3

13. Ἄγαβος Agabos
ACTS 11:28; 21:10

14. ἀγαθοεργέω agathoergeō
1 TIM. 6:18

15. ἀγαθοποιέω agathopoieō
MARK 3:4; LUKE 6:9,33,35; ACTS 14:17; 1 PET. 2:15,20; 3:6,17; 3 JOHN 1:11

16. ἀγαθοποιΐα agathopoiia
1 PET. 4:19

17. ἀγαθοποιός agathopoios
1 PET. 2:14

18. ἀγαθός agathos
MATT. 5:45; 7:11,17,18; 12:34,35; 19:16,17; 20:15; 22:10; 25:21,23; MARK 10:17,18; LUKE 1:53; 6:45; 8:8,15; 10:42; 11:13; 12:18,19; 16:25; 18:18,19; 19:17; 23:50; JOHN 1:46; 5:29; 7:12; ACTS 9:36; 11:24; 23:1; ROM. 2:7,10; 3:8; 5:7; 7:12,13,18,19; 8:28; 9:11; 10:15; 12:2,9,21; 13:3,4; 14:16; 15:2; 16:19; 2 COR. 5:10; 9:8; GAL. 6:6,10; EPH. 2:10; 4:28,29; 6:8; PHIL. 1:6; COL. 1:10; 1 THESS. 3:6; 5:15; 2 THESS. 2:16,17; 1 TIM. 1:5,19; 2:10; 5:10; 2 TIM. 2:21; 3:17; TITUS 1:16; 2:5,10; 3:1; PHILE. 1:6,14; HEB. 9:11; 10:1; 13:21; JAMES 1:17; 3:17; 1 PET. 2:18; 3:10,11,13,16,21; 3 JOHN 1:11

19. ἀγαθωσύνη agathōsunē
ROM. 15:14; GAL. 5:22; EPH. 5:9; 2 THESS. 1:11

20. ἀγαλλίασις agalliasis
LUKE 1:14,44; ACTS 2:46; HEB. 1:9; JUDE 1:24

21. ἀγαλλιάω agalliaō
MATT. 5:12; LUKE 1:47; 10:21; JOHN 5:35; 8:56; ACTS 2:26; 16:34; 1 PET. 1:6,8; 4:13; REV. 19:7

22. ἄγαμος agamos
1 COR. 7:8,11,32,34

23. ἀγανακτέω aganakteō
MATT. 20:24; 21:15; 26:8; MARK 10:14,41; 14:4; LUKE 13:14

24. ἀγανάκτησις *aganaktēsis*
2 COR. 7:11

25. ἀγαπάω *agapaō*
MATT. 5:43,44,46; 6:24; 19:19; 22:37,39;
MARK 10:21; 12:30,31,33; LUKE 6:27,32,35;
7:5,42,47; 10:27; 11:43; 16:13; JOHN
3:16,19,35; 8:42; 10:17; 11:5; 12:43; 13:1,23;
13:34; 14:15,21,23,24,28,31; 15:9,12,17;
17:23,24,26; 19:26; 21:7,15,16,20; ROM.
8:28,37; 9:13,25; 13:8,9; 1 COR. 2:9; 8:3;
2 COR. 9:7; 11:11; 12:15; GAL. 2:20; 5:14;
EPH. 1:6; 2:4; 5:2,25,28,33; 6:24; COL.
3:12,19; 1 THESS. 1:4; 4:9; 2 THESS. 2:13,16;
2 TIM. 4:8,10; HEB. 1:9; 12:6; JAMES 1:12;
2:5,8; 1 PET. 1:8,22; 2:17; 3:10; 2 PET. 2:15;
1 JOHN 2:10,15; 3:10,11,14,18,23; 4:7,8,10-
12,19-21; 5:1,2; 2 JOHN 1:1,5; 3 JOHN 1:1;
REV. 1:5; 3:9; 12:11; 20:9

26. ἀγάπη *agapē*
MATT. 24:12; LUKE 11:42; JOHN 5:42;
13:35; 15:9,10,13; 17:26; ROM. 5:5,8; 8:35,39;
12:9; 13:10; 14:15; 15:30; 1 COR. 4:21; 8:1;
13:1-4,8,13; 14:1; 16:14,24; 2 COR. 2:4,8; 5:14;
6:6; 8:7,8,24; 13:11,14; GAL. 5:6,13,22; EPH.
1:4,15; 2:4; 3:17,19; 4:2,15,16; 5:2; 6:23;
PHIL. 1:9,17; 2:1,2; COL. 1:4,8,13; 2:2; 3:14;
1 THESS. 1:3; 3:6,12; 5:8,13; 2 THESS. 1:3;
2:10; 3:5; 1 TIM. 1:5,14; 2:15; 4:12; 6:11;
2 TIM. 1:7,13; 2:22; 3:10; TITUS 2:2; PHILE.
1:5,7,9; HEB. 6:10; 10:24; 1 PET. 4:8; 5:14;
2 PET. 1:7; 1 JOHN 2:5,15; 3:1,16,17; 4:7,8-
10,12,16-18; 5:3; 2 JOHN 1:3,6; 3 JOHN 1:6;
JUDE 1:2,12,21; REV. 2:4,19

27. ἀγαπητός *agapētos*
MATT. 3:17; 12:18; 17:5; MARK 1:11; 9:7;
12:6; LUKE 3:22; 9:35; 20:13; ACTS 15:25;
ROM. 1:7; 11:28; 12:19; 16:5,8,9,12; 1 COR.
4:14,17; 10:14; 15:58; 2 COR. 7:1; 12:19; EPH.
5:1; 6:21; PHIL. 2:12; 4:1; COL. 1:7; 4:7,9,14;
1 THESS. 2:8; 1 TIM. 6:2; 2 TIM. 1:2; PHILE.
1:1,2,16; HEB. 6:9; JAMES 1:16,19; 2:5;
1 PET. 2:11; 4:12; 2 PET. 1:17; 3:1,8,14,15,17;
1 JOHN 3:2,21; 4:1,7,11; 3 JOHN 1:1,2,5,11;
JUDE 1:3,17,20

28. Ἄγαρ *Agar*
GAL. 4:24,25

29. ἀγγαρεύω *aggareuō*
MATT. 5:41; 27:32; MARK 15:21

30. ἀγγεῖον *aggeion*
MATT. 13:48; 25:4

31. ἀγγελία *aggelia*
1 JOHN 3:11

32. ἄγγελος *aggelos*
MATT. 1:20,24; 2:13,19; 4:6,11; 11:10;
13:39,41,49; 16:27; 18:10; 22:30; 24:31,36;
25:31,41; 26:53; 28:2,5; MARK 1:2,13; 8:38;
12:25; 13:27,32; LUKE 1:11,13,18,19,26,28,
30,34,35,38; 2:9,10,13,15,21; 4:10; 7:24,27;
9:26,52; 12:8,9; 15:10; 16:22; 22:43; 24:23;
JOHN 1:51; 5:4; 12:29; 20:12; ACTS 5:19;
6:15; 7:30,35,38,53; 8:26; 10:3,7,22; 11:13;
12:7-11,15,23; 23:8,9; 27:23; ROM. 8:38;
1 COR. 4:9; 6:3; 11:10; 13:1; 2 COR. 11:14;
12:7; GAL. 1:8; 3:19; 4:14; COL. 2:18;
2 THESS. 1:7; 1 TIM. 3:16; 5:21; HEB. 1:4-
7,13; 2:2,5,7,9,16; 12:22; 13:2; JAMES 2:25;
1 PET. 1:12; 3:22; 2 PET. 2:4,11; JUDE 1:6;
REV. 1:1,20; 2:1,8,12,18; 3:1,5,7,14; 5:2,11;
7:1,2,11; 8:2-8,10,12,13; 9:1,11,13-15; 10:1,5,7-
10; 11:1,15; 12:7,9; 14:6,8-10,15,17-19; 15:1,6-
8; 16:1,3-5,8,10,12,17; 17:1,7; 18:1,21; 19:17;
20:1; 21:9,12,17; 22:6,8,16

33. ἄγε *age*
JAMES 4:13; 5:1

34. ἀγέλη *agelē*
MATT. 8:30-32; MARK 5:11,13; LUKE
8:32,33

35. ἀγενεαλόγητος *agenealogētos*
HEB. 7:3

36. ἀγενής *agenēs*
1 COR. 1:28

37. ἁγιάζω *hagiazō*
MATT. 6:9; 23:17,19; LUKE 11:2; JOHN
10:36; 17:17,19; ACTS 20:32; 26:18; ROM.
15:16; 1 COR. 1:2; 6:11; 7:14; EPH. 5:26;
1 THESS. 5:23; 1 TIM. 4:5; 2 TIM. 2:21; HEB.
2:11; 9:13; 10:10,14,29; 13:12; 1 PET. 3:15;
JUDE 1:1; REV. 22:11

38. ἁγιασμός *hagiasmos*
ROM. 6:19,22; **1 COR.** 1:30; **1 THESS.**
4:3,4,7; **2 THESS.** 2:13; **1 TIM.** 2:15; **HEB.**
12:14; **1 PET.** 1:2

39. ἅγιον *hagion* subst.
  (Neut. of ἅγιος)
HEB. 8:2; 9:1-3,8,12,24,25; 10:19; 13:11

40. ἅγιος *hagios*
MATT. 1:18,20; 3:11; 4:5; 7:6; 12:32; 24:15;
25:31; 27:52,53; 28:19; **MARK** 1:8,24; 3:29;
6:20; 8:38; 12:36; 13:11; **LUKE** 1:15,35,41,
49,67,70,72; 2:23,25,26; 3:16,22; 4:1,34; 9:26;
11:13; 12:10,12; **JOHN** 1:33; 7:39; 14:26;
17:11; 20:22; **ACTS** 1:2,5,8,16; 2:4,33,38;
3:14,21; 4:8,27,30,31; 5:3,32; 6:3,5,13;
7:33,51,55; 8:15,17-19; 9:13,17,31,32,41;
10:22,38,44,45,47; 11:15,16,24; 13:2,4,9,52;
15:8,28; 16:6; 19:2,6; 20:23,28; 21:11,28; 26:10;
28:25; **ROM.** 1:2,7; 5:5; 7:12; 8:27; 9:1; 11:16;
12:1,13; 14:17; 15:13,16,25,26,31; 16:2,15,16;
1 COR. 1:2; 2:13; 3:17; 6:1,2,19; 7:14,34; 12:3;
14:33; 16:1,15,20; **2 COR.** 1:1; 6:6; 8:4; 9:1,12;
13:12-14; **EPH.** 1:1,4,13,15,18; 2:19,21;
3:5,8,18; 4:12,30; 5:3,27; 6:18; **PHIL.** 1:1;
4:21,22; **COL.** 1:2,4,12,22,26; 3:12; **1 THESS.**
1:5,6; 3:13; 4:8; 5:26,27; **2 THESS.** 1:10;
1 TIM. 5:10; **2 TIM.** 1:9,14; **TITUS** 3:5;
PHILE. 1:5,7; **HEB.** 2:4; 3:1,7; 6:4,10; 9:8;
10:15; 13:24; **1 PET.** 1:12,15,16; 2:5,9; 3:5;
2 PET. 1:18,21; 2:21; 3:2,11; **1 JOHN** 2:20; 5:7;
JUDE 1:3,14,20; **REV.** 3:7; 4:8; 5:8; 6:10;
8:3,4; 11:2,18; 13:7,10; 14:10,12; 15:3; 16:6;
17:6; 18:20,24; 19:8; 20:6,9; 21:2,10; 22:6,11,19

41. ἁγιότης *hagiotēs*
HEB. 12:10

42. ἁγιωσύνη *hagiōsunē*
ROM. 1:4; **2 COR.** 7:1; **1 THESS.** 3:13

43. ἀγκάλη *agkalē*
LUKE 2:28

44. ἄγκιστρον *agkistron*
MATT. 17:27

45. ἄγκυρα *agkura*
ACTS 27:29,30,40; **HEB.** 6:19

46. ἄγναφος *agnaphos*
MATT. 9:16; **MARK** 2:21

47. ἁγνεία *hagneia*
1 TIM. 4:12; 5:2

48. ἁγνίζω *hagnizō*
JOHN 11:55; **ACTS** 21:24,26; 24:18; **JAMES**
4:8; **1 PET.** 1:22; **1 JOHN** 3:3

49. ἁγνισμός *hagnismos*
ACTS 21:26

50. ἀγνοέω *agnoeō*
MARK 9:32; **LUKE** 9:45; **ACTS** 13:27; 17:23;
ROM. 1:13; 2:4; 6:3; 7:1; 10:3; 11:25; **1 COR.**
10:1; 12:1; 14:38; **2 COR.** 1:8; 2:11; 6:9; **GAL.**
1:22; **1 THESS.** 4:13; **1 TIM.** 1:13; **HEB.** 5:2;
2 PET. 2:12

51. ἀγνόημα *agnoēma*
HEB. 9:7

52. ἄγνοια *agnoia*
ACTS 3:17; 17:30; **EPH.** 4:18; **1 PET.** 1:14

53. ἁγνός *hagnos*
2 COR. 7:11; 11:2; **PHIL.** 4:8; **1 TIM.** 5:22;
TITUS 2:5; **JAMES** 3:17; **1 PET.** 3:2; **1 JOHN**
3:3

54. ἁγνότης *hagnotēs*
2 COR. 6:6

55. ἁγνῶς *hagnōs*
PHIL. 1:16

56. ἀγνωσία *agnōsia*
1 COR. 15:34; **1 PET.** 2:15

57. ἄγνωστος *agnōstos*
ACTS 17:23

58. ἀγορά *agora*
MATT. 11:16; 20:3; 23:7; **MARK** 6:56; 7:4;
12:38; **LUKE** 7:32; 11:43; 20:46; **ACTS** 16:19;
17:17

59. ἀγοράζω *agorazō*
MATT. 13:44,46; 14:15; 21:12; 25:9,10; 27:7;
MARK 6:36,37; 11:15; 15:46; 16:1; LUKE
9:13; 14:18,19; 17:28; 19:45; 22:36; JOHN 4:8;
6:5; 13:29; 1 COR. 6:20; 7:23,30; 2 PET. 2:1;
REV. 3:18; 5:9; 13:17; 14:3,4; 18:11

60. ἀγοραῖος *agoraios*
ACTS 17:5; 19:38

61. ἄγρα *agra*
LUKE 5:4,9

62. ἀγράμματος *agrammatos*
ACTS 4:13

63. ἀγραυλέω *agrauleō*
LUKE 2:8

64. ἀγρεύω *agreuō*
MARK 12:13

65. ἀγριέλαιος *agrielaios*
ROM. 11:17,24

66. ἄγριος *agrios*
MATT. 3:4; MARK 1:6; JUDE 1:13

67. Ἀγρίππας *Agrippas*
ACTS 25:13,22-24,26; 26:1,2,7,19,27,28,32

68. ἀγρός *agros*
MATT. 6:28,30; 13:24,27,31,36,38,44; 19:29;
22:5; 24:18,40; 27:7,8,10; MARK 5:14; 6:36,56;
10:29,30; 13:16; 15:21; 16:12; LUKE 8:34;
9:12; 12:28; 14:18; 15:15,25; 17:7,31,36; 23:26;
ACTS 4:37

69. ἀγρυπνέω *agrupneō*
MARK 13:33; LUKE 21:36; EPH. 6:18; HEB.
13:17

70. ἀγρυπνία *agrupnia*
2 COR. 6:5; 11:27

71. ἄγω *agō*
MATT. 10:18; 14:6; 21:2,7; 26:46; MARK

1:38; 11:2,7; 13:11; 14:42; LUKE 4:1,9,29,40;
10:34; 18:40; 19:27,30,35; 21:12; 22:54;
23:1,32; 24:21; JOHN 1:42; 7:45; 8:3; 9:13;
10:16; 11:7,15,16; 14:31; 18:28; 19:4,13; ACTS
5:21,26,27; 6:12; 8:32; 9:2,21,27; 11:26;
17:5,15,19; 18:12; 19:37,38; 20:12; 21:16,34;
22:5,24; 23:10,18,31; 25:6,17,23; ROM. 2:4;
8:14; 1 COR. 12:2; GAL. 5:18; 1 THESS. 4:14;
2 TIM. 3:6; 4:11; HEB. 2:10

72. ἀγωγή *agōgē*
2 TIM. 3:10

73. ἀγών *agōn*
PHIL. 1:30; COL. 2:1; 1 THESS. 2:2; 1 TIM.
6:12; 2 TIM. 4:7; HEB. 12:1

74. ἀγωνία *agōnia*
LUKE 22:44

75. ἀγωνίζομαι *agōnizomai*
LUKE 13:24; JOHN 18:36; 1 COR. 9:25;
COL. 1:29; 4:12; 1 TIM. 6:12; 2 TIM. 4:7

76. Ἀδάμ *Adam*
LUKE 3:38; ROM. 5:14; 1 COR. 15:22,45;
1 TIM. 2:13,14; JUDE 1:14

77. ἀδάπανος *adapanos*
1 COR. 9:18

78. Ἀδδί *Addi*
LUKE 3:28

79. ἀδελφή *adelphē*
MATT. 12:50; 13:56; 19:29; MARK 3:35; 6:3;
10:29,30; LUKE 10:39,40; 14:26; JOHN
11:1,3,5,28,39; 19:25; ACTS 23:16; ROM.
16:1,15; 1 COR. 7:15; 9:5; 1 TIM. 5:2; JAMES
2:15; 2 JOHN 1:13

80. ἀδελφός *adelphos*
MATT. 1:2,11; 4:18,21; 5:22-24,47; 7:3-5;
10:2,21; 12:46-50; 13:55; 14:3; 17:1;
18:15,21,35; 19:29; 20:24; 22:24,25; 23:8;
25:40; 28:10; MARK 1:16,19; 3:17,31-35; 5:37;
6:3,17,18; 10:29,30; 12:19,20; 13:12; LUKE
3:1,19; 6:14,41,42; 8:19-21; 12:13; 14:12,26;
15:27,32; 16:28; 17:3; 18:29; 20:28,29; 21:16;

22:32; **JOHN** 1:40,41; 2:12; 6:8; 7:3,5,10;
11:2,19,21,23,32; 20:17; 21:23; **ACTS** 1:14,16;
2:29,37; 3:17,22; 6:3; 7:2,13,23,25,26,37;
9:17,30; 10:23; 11:1,12,29; 12:2,17; 13:15,26,38;
14:2; 15:1,3,7,13,22,23,32,33,36,40; 16:2,40;
17:6,10,14; 18:18,27; 20:32; 21:7,17,20;
22:1,5,13; 23:1,5,6; 28:14,15,17,21; **ROM.** 1:13;
7:1,4; 8:12,29; 9:3; 10:1; 11:25; 12:1;
14:10,13,15,21; 15:14,15,30; 16:14,17,23;
1 COR. 1:1,10,11,26; 2:1; 3:1; 4:6; 5:11;
6:5,6,8; 7:12,15,24,29; 8:11-13; 9:5; 10:1;
11:2,33; 12:1; 14:6,20,26,39; 15:1,6,50,58;
16:11,12,15,20; **2 COR.** 1:1,8; 2:13;
8:1,18,22,23; 9:3,5; 11:9; 12:18; 13:11; **GAL.**
1:2,11,19; 3:15; 4:12,28,31; 5:11,13; 6:1,18;
EPH. 6:10,21,33; **PHIL.** 1:12,14; 2:25;
3:1,13,17; 4:1,8,21; **COL.** 1:1,2; 4:7,9,15;
1 THESS. 1:4; 2:1,9,14,17; 3:2,7; 4:1,6,10,13;
5:1,4,12,14,25-27; **2 THESS.** 1:3; 2:1,13,15;
3:1,6,13,15; **1 TIM.** 4:6; 5:1; 6:2; **2 TIM.** 4:21;
PHILE. 1:1,7,16,20; **HEB.** 2:11,12,17; 3:1,12;
7:5; 8:11; 10:19; 13:22,23; **JAMES** 1:2,9,16,19;
2:1,5,14,15; 3:1,10,12; 4:11; 5:7,9,10,12,19;
1 PET. 5:12; **2 PET.** 1:10; 3:15; **1 JOHN** 2:7,9-
11; 3:10,12-17; 4:20,21; 5:16; **3 JOHN** 1:3,5,10;
JUDE 1:1; **REV.** 1:9; 6:11; 12:10; 19:10; 22:9

81. ἀδελφότης *adelphotēs*
1 PET. 2:17; 5:9

82. ἄδηλος *adēlos*
LUKE 11:44; **1 COR.** 14:8

83. ἀδηλότης *adēlotēs*
1 TIM. 6:17

84. ἀδήλως *adēlōs*
1 COR. 9:26

85. ἀδημονέω *adēmoneō*
MATT. 26:37; **MARK** 14:33; **PHIL.** 2:26

86. ᾅδης *hadēs*
MATT. 11:23; 16:18; **LUKE** 10:15; 16:23;
ACTS 2:27,31; **1 COR.** 15:55; **REV.** 1:18; 6:8;
20:13,14

87. ἀδιάκριτος *adiakritos*
JAMES 3:17

88. ἀδιάλειπτος *adialeiptos*
ROM. 9:2; **2 TIM.** 1:3

89. ἀδιαλείπτως *adialeiptōs*
ROM. 1:9; **1 THESS.** 1:3; 2:13; 5:17

90. ἀδιαφθορία *adiaphthoria*
TITUS 2:7

91. ἀδικέω *adikeō*
MATT. 20:13; **LUKE** 10:19; **ACTS** 7:24,26,27;
25:10,11; **1 COR.** 6:7,8; **2 COR.** 7:2,12; **GAL.**
4:12; **COL.** 3:25; **PHILE.** 1:18; **REV.** 2:11; 6:6;
7:2,3; 9:4,10,19; 11:5; 22:11

92. ἀδίκημα *adikēma*
ACTS 18:14; 24:20; **REV.** 18:5

93. ἀδικία *adikia*
LUKE 13:27; 16:8,9; 18:6; **JOHN** 17:8; **ACTS**
1:18; 8:23; **ROM.** 1:18,29; 2:8; 3:5; 6:13; 9:14;
1 COR. 13:6; **2 COR.** 12:13; **2 THESS.**
2:10,12; **2 TIM.** 2:19; **HEB.** 8:12; **JAMES** 3:6;
2 PET. 2:13,15; **1 JOHN** 1:9; 5:17

94. ἄδικος *adikos*
MATT. 5:45; **LUKE** 16:10,11; 18:11; **ACTS**
24:15; **ROM.** 3:5; **1 COR.** 6:1,9; **HEB.** 6:10;
1 PET. 3:18; **2 PET.** 2:9

95. ἀδίκως *adikōs*
1 PET. 2:19

96. ἀδόκιμος *adokimos*
ROM. 1:28; **1 COR.** 9:27; **2 COR.** 13:5-7;
2 TIM. 3:8; **TITUS** 1:16; **HEB.** 6:8

97. ἄδολος *adolos*
1 PET. 2:2

98. Ἀδραμυττηνός *Adramuttēnos*
ACTS 27:2

99. Ἀδρίας *Adrias*
ACTS 27:27

100. ἁδρότης *hadrotēs*
2 COR. 8:20

101. ἀδυνατέω *adunateō*
MATT. 17:20; LUKE 1:37

102. ἀδύνατος *adunatos*
MATT. 19:26; MARK 10:27; LUKE 18:27;
ACTS 14:8; ROM. 8:3; 15:1; HEB. 6:4,18;
10:4; 11:6

103. ᾄδω *adō*
EPH. 5:19; COL. 3:16; REV. 5:9; 14:3; 15:3

104. ἀεί *aei*
MARK 15:8; ACTS 7:51; 2 COR. 4:11; 6:10;
TITUS 1:12; HEB. 3:10; 1 PET. 3:15; 2 PET.
1:12

105. ἀετός *aetos*
MATT. 24:28; LUKE 17:37; REV. 4:7; 12:14

106. ἄζυμος *azumos*
MATT. 26:17; MARK 14:1,12; LUKE 22:1,7;
ACTS 12:3; 20:6; 1 COR. 5:7,8

107. Ἀζώρ *Azōr*
MATT. 1:13,14

108. Ἄζωτος *Azōtos*
ACTS 8:40

109. ἀήρ *aēr*
ACTS 22:23; 1 COR. 9:26; 14:9; EPH. 2:2;
1 THESS. 4:17; REV. 9:2; 16:17

110. ἀθανασία *athanasia*
1 COR. 15:53,54; 1 TIM. 6:16

111. ἀθέμιτος *athemitos*
ACTS 10:28; 1 PET. 4:3

112. ἄθεος *atheos*
EPH. 2:12

113. ἄθεσμος *athesmos*
2 PET. 2:7; 3:17

114. ἀθετέω *atheteō*
MARK 6:26; 7:9; LUKE 7:30; 10:16; JOHN

12:48; 1 COR. 1:19; GAL. 2:21; 3:15;
1 THESS. 4:8; 1 TIM. 5:12; HEB. 10:28;
JUDE 1:8

115. ἀθέτησις *athetēsis*
HEB. 7:18; 9:26

116. Ἀθῆναι *Athēnai*
ACTS 17:15,16; 18:1; 1 THESS. 3:1

117. Ἀθηναῖος *Athēnaios*
ACTS 17:21,22

118. ἀθλέω *athleō*
2 TIM. 2:5

119. ἄθλησις *athlēsis*
HEB. 10:32

120. ἀθυμέω *athumeō*
COL. 3:21

121. ἀθῷος *athōos*
MATT. 27:4,24

122. αἴγειος *aigeios*
HEB. 11:37

123. αἰγιαλός *aigialos*
MATT. 13:2,48; JOHN 21:4; ACTS 21:5;
27:39,40

124. Αἰγύπτιος *Aiguptios*
ACTS 7:22,24,28; 21:38; HEB. 11:29

125. Αἴγυπτος *Aiguptos*
MATT. 2:13,14,15,19; ACTS 2:10; 7:9-12,
15,17,34,36,39,40; 13:17; HEB. 3:16; 8:9;
11:26,27; JUDE 1:5; REV. 11:8

126. ἀΐδιος *aidios*
ROM. 1:20; JUDE 1:6

127. αἰδώς *aidōs*
1 TIM. 2:9; HEB. 12:28

128. Αἰθίοψ *Aithiops*
ACTS 8:27

129. αἷμα haima
MATT. 16:17; 23:30,35; 26:28; 27:4,6,8,24,25;
MARK 5:25,29; 14:24; LUKE 8:43,44;
11:50,51; 13:1; 22:20,44; JOHN 1:13; 6:53-56;
19:34; ACTS 1:19; 2:19,20; 5:28; 15:20,29;
17:26; 18:6; 20:26,28; 21:25; 22:20; ROM.
3:15,25; 5:9; 1 COR. 10:16; 11:25,27; 15:50;
GAL. 1:16; EPH. 1:7; 2:13; 6:12; COL.
1:14,20; HEB. 2:14; 9:7,12-14,18-22,25;
10:4,19,29; 11:28; 12:4,24; 13:11,12,20; 1 PET.
1:2,19; 1 JOHN 1:7; 5:6,8; REV. 1:5; 5:9;
6:10,12; 7:14; 8:7,8; 11:6; 12:11; 14:20;
16:3,4,6; 17:6; 18:24; 19:2,13

130. αἱματεκχυσία haimatekchusia
HEB. 9:22

131. αἱμορροέω haimorroeō
MATT. 9:20

132. Αἰνέας Aineas
ACTS 9:33,34

133. αἴνεσις ainesis
HEB. 13:15

134. αἰνέω aineō
LUKE 2:13,20; 19:37; 24:53; ACTS 2:47; 3:8,9;
ROM. 15:11; REV. 19:5

135. αἴνιγμα ainigma
1 COR. 13:12

136. αἶνος ainos
MATT. 21:16; LUKE 18:43

137. Αἰνών Ainōn
JOHN 3:23

138. αἱρέω haireō
PHIL. 1:22; 2 THESS. 2:13; HEB. 11:25

139. αἵρεσις hairesis
ACTS 5:17; 15:5; 24:5,14; 26:5; 28:22; 1 COR.
11:19; GAL. 5:20; 2 PET. 2:1

140. αἱρετίζω hairetizō
MATT. 12:18

141. αἱρετικός hairetikos
TITUS 3:10

142. αἴρω airō
MATT. 4:6; 9:6,16; 11:29; 13:12; 14:12,20;
15:37; 16:24; 17:27; 20:14; 21:21,43; 22:13;
24:17,18,39; 25:28,29; 27:32; MARK 2:3,9,
11,12,21; 4:15,25; 6:8,29,43; 8:8,19,20,34;
10:21; 11:23; 13:15,16; 15:21,24; 16:18; LUKE
4:11; 5:24,25; 6:29,30; 8:12,18; 9:3,17,23;
11:22,52; 17:13,31; 19:21,22,24,26; 22:36;
23:18; JOHN 1:29; 2:16; 5:8-12; 8:59; 10:18,24;
11:39,41,48; 15:2; 16:22; 17:15; 19:15,31,38;
20:1,2,13,15; ACTS 4:24; 8:33; 20:9; 21:11,36;
22:22; 27:13,17; 1 COR. 6:15; EPH. 4:31;
COL. 2:14; 1 JOHN 3:5; REV. 10:5; 18:21

143. αἰσθάνομαι aisthanomai
LUKE 9:45

144. αἴσθησις aisthēsis
PHIL. 1:9

145. αἰσθητήριον aisthētērion
HEB. 5:14

146. αἰσχροκερδής aischrokerdēs
1 TIM. 3:3,8; TITUS 1:7

147. αἰσχροκερδῶς aischrokerdōs
1 PET. 5:2

148. αἰσχρολογία aischrologia
COL. 3:8

149. αἰσχρόν aischron subst.
(Neut. of αἰσχρός)
1 COR. 11:6; 14:35; EPH. 5:12

150. αἰσχρός aischros
TITUS 1:11

151. αἰσχρότης aischrotēs
EPH. 5:4

152. αἰσχύνη aischunē
LUKE 14:9; 2 COR. 4:2; PHIL. 3:19; HEB.
12:2; JUDE 1:13; REV. 3:18

153. αἰσχύνω aischunō
LUKE 16:3; **2 COR.** 10:8; **PHIL.** 1:20; **1 PET.**
4:16; **1 JOHN** 2:28

154. αἰτέω aiteō
MATT. 5:42; 6:8; 7:7-11; 14:7; 18:19; 20:20,22;
21:22; 27:20,58; **MARK** 6:22-25; 10:35,38;
11:24; 15:6,8,43; **LUKE** 1:63; 6:30; 11:9-13;
12:48; 23:23,25,52; **JOHN** 4:9,10; 11:22;
14:13,14; 15:7,16; 16:23,24,26; **ACTS** 3:2,14;
7:46; 9:2; 12:20; 13:21,28; 16:29; 25:3,15;
1 COR. 1:22; **EPH.** 3:13,20; **COL.** 1:9; **JAMES**
1:5,6; 4:2,3; **1 PET.** 3:15; **1 JOHN** 3:22; 5:14-
16

155. αἴτημα aitēma
LUKE 23:24; **PHIL.** 4:6; **1 JOHN** 5:15

156. αἰτία aitia
MATT. 19:3,10; 27:37; **MARK** 15:26; **LUKE**
8:47; **JOHN** 18:38; 19:4,6; **ACTS** 10:21; 13:28;
22:24; 23:28; 25:18,27; 28:18,20; **2 TIM.** 1:6,12;
TITUS 1:13; **HEB.** 2:11

157. αἰτίαμα aitiama
ACTS 25:7

158. αἴτιον aition subst.
(Neut. of αἴτιος)
LUKE 23:4,14,22; **ACTS** 19:40

159. αἴτιος aitios
HEB. 5:9

160. αἰφνίδιος aiphnidios
LUKE 21:34; **1 THESS.** 5:3

161. αἰχμαλωσία aichmalōsia
EPH. 4:8; **REV.** 13:10

162. αἰχμαλωτεύω aichmalōteuō
EPH. 4:8; **2 TIM.** 3:6

163. αἰχμαλωτίζω aichmalōtizō
LUKE 21:24; **ROM.** 7:23; **2 COR.** 10:5

164. αἰχμάλωτος aichmalōtos
LUKE 4:18

165. αἰών aiōn
MATT. 6:13; 12:32; 13:22,39,40,49; 21:19;
24:3; 28:20; **MARK** 3:29; 4:19; 10:30; 11:14;
LUKE 1:33,55,70; 16:8; 18:30; 20:34,35;
JOHN 4:14; 6:51,58; 8:35,51,52; 9:32; 10:28;
11:26; 12:34; 13:8; 14:16; **ACTS** 3:21; 15:18;
ROM. 1:25; 9:5; 11:36; 12:2; 16:27; **1 COR.**
1:20; 2:6-8; 3:18; 8:13; 10:11; **2 COR.** 4:4; 9:9;
11:31; **GAL.** 1:4,5; **EPH.** 1:21; 2:2,7; 3:9,11,21;
6:12; **PHIL.** 4:20; **COL.** 1:26; **1 TIM.** 1:17;
6:17; **2 TIM.** 4:10,18; **TITUS** 2:12; **HEB.** 1:2,8;
5:6; 6:5,20; 7:17,21,24,28; 9:26; 11:3; 13:8,21;
1 PET. 1:23,25; 4:11; 5:11; **2 PET.** 2:17; 3:18;
1 JOHN 2:17; **2 JOHN** 1:2; **JUDE** 1:13,25;
REV. 1:6,18; 4:9,10; 5:13,14; 7:12; 10:6; 11:15;
14:11; 15:7; 19:3; 20:10; 22:5

166. αἰώνιος aiōnios
MATT. 18:8; 19:16,29; 25:41,46; **MARK**
3:29; 10:17,30; **LUKE** 10:25; 16:9; 18:18,30;
JOHN 3:15,16,36; 4:14,36; 5:24,39; 5:24,39;
6:27,40,47,54,68; 10:28; 12:25,50; 17:2,3;
ACTS 13:46,48; **ROM.** 2:7; 5:21; 6:22,23;
16:25,26; **2 COR.** 4:17,18; 5:1; **GAL.** 6:8;
2 THESS. 1:9; 2:16; **1 TIM.** 1:16; 6:12,16,19;
2 TIM. 1:9; 2:10; **TITUS** 1:2; 3:7; **PHILE.**
1:15; **HEB.** 5:9; 6:2; 9:12,14,15; 13:20; **1 PET.**
5:10; **2 PET.** 1:11; **1 JOHN** 1:2; 2:25; 3:15;
5:11,13,20; **JUDE** 1:7,21; **REV.** 14:6

167. ἀκαθαρσία akatharsia
MATT. 23:27; **ROM.** 1:24; 6:19; **2 COR.**
12:21; **GAL.** 5:19; **EPH.** 4:19; 5:3; **COL.** 3:5;
1 THESS. 2:3; 4:7

168. ἀκαθάρτης akathartēs
REV. 17:4

169. ἀκάθαρτος akathartos
MATT. 10:1; 12:43; **MARK** 1:23,26,27;
3:11,30; 5:2,8,13; 6:7; 7:25; 9:25; **LUKE**
4:33,36; 6:18; 8:29; 9:42; 11:24; **ACTS** 5:16;
8:7; 10:14,28; 11:8; **1 COR.** 7:14; **2 COR.** 6:17;
EPH. 5:5; **REV.** 16:13; 18:2

170. ἀκαιρέομαι akaireomai
PHIL. 4:10

171. ἀκαίρως akairōs
2 TIM. 4:2

172. ἄκακος *akakos*
ROM. 16:18; HEB. 7:26

173. ἄκανθα *akantha*
MATT. 7:16; 13:7,22; 27:29; MARK 4:7,18;
LUKE 6:44; 8:7,14; JOHN 19:2; HEB. 6:8

174. ἀκάνθινος *akanthinos*
MARK 15:17; JOHN 19:5

175. ἄκαρπος *akarpos*
MATT. 13:22; MARK 4:19; 1 COR. 4:14;
EPH. 5:11; TITUS 3:14; 2 PET. 1:8; JUDE
1:12

176. ἀκατάγνωστος *akatagnōstos*
TITUS 2:8

177. ἀκατακάλυπτος *akatakaluptos*
1 COR. 11:5,13

178. ἀκατάκριτος *akatakritos*
ACTS 16:37; 22:25

179. ἀκατάλυτος *akatalutos*
HEB. 7:16

180. ἀκατάπαυστος *akatapaustos*
2 PET. 2:14

181. ἀκαταστασία *akatastasia*
LUKE 21:9; 1 COR. 14:33; 2 COR. 6:5; 12:20;
JAMES 3:16

182. ἀκατάστατος *akatastatos*
JAMES 1:8

183. ἀκατάσχετος *akataschetos*
JAMES 3:8

184. Ἀκελδαμά *Akeldama*
ACTS 1:19

185. ἀκέραιος *akeraios*
MATT. 10:16; ROM. 16:19; PHIL. 2:15

186. ἀκλινής *aklinēs*
HEB. 10:23

187. ἀκμάζω *akmazō*
REV. 14:18

188. ἀκμήν *akmēn*
MATT. 15:16

189. ἀκοή *akoē*
MATT. 4:24; 13:14; 14:1; 24:6; MARK 1:28;
7:35; 13:7; LUKE 7:1; JOHN 12:38; ACTS
17:20; 28:26; ROM. 10:16,17; 1 COR. 12:17;
GAL. 3:2,5; 1 THESS. 2:13; 2 TIM. 4:3,4;
HEB. 4:2; 5:11; 2 PET. 2:8

190. ἀκολουθέω *akoloutheō*
MATT. 4:20,22,25; 8:1,10,19,22,23; 9:9,19,27;
10:38; 12:15; 14:13; 16:24; 19:2,21,27,28;
20:29,34; 21:9; 26:58; 27:55; MARK 1:18;
2:14,15; 3:7; 5:24; 6:1; 8:34; 9:38;
10:21,28,32,52; 11:9; 14:13,51,54; 15:41;
LUKE 5:11,27,28; 7:9; 9:11,23,49,57,59,61;
18:22,28,43; 22:10,39,54; 23:27; JOHN
1:37,38,40,43; 6:2; 8:12; 10:4,5,27; 11:31;
12:26; 13:36,37; 18:15; 20:6; 21:19,20,22;
ACTS 12:8,9; 13:43; 21:36; 1 COR. 10:4; REV.
6:8; 14:4,8,9,13; 18:5; 19:14

191. ἀκούω *akouō*
MATT. 2:3,9,18,22; 4:12; 5:21,27,33,38,43;
7:24,26; 8:10; 9:12; 10:14,27; 11:2,4,5,15;
12:19,24,42; 13:9,13-20,22,23,43; 14:1,13;
15:10,12; 17:5,6; 18:15,16; 19:22,25; 20:24,
30; 21:16,33,45; 22:7,22,33,34; 24:6; 26:65;
27:13,47; 28:14; MARK 2:1,17; 3:8,21; 4:3,
9,12,15,16,18,20,23,24,33; 5:27,36; 6:2,11,
14,16,20,29,55; 7:14,16,25,37; 8:18; 9:7;
10:41,47; 11:14,18; 12:28,29,37; 13:7; 14:11,
58,64; 15:35; 16:11; LUKE 1:41,58,66; 2:18,
20,46,47; 4:23,28; 5:1,15; 6:17,27,47,49;
7:3,9,22,29; 8:8,10,12-15,18,21,50; 9:7,9,35;
10:16,24,39; 11:28,31; 12:3; 14:15,35; 15:1,25;
16:2,14,29,31; 18:6,22,23,26,36; 19:11,48;
20:16,45; 21:9,38; 22:71; 23:6,8; JOHN 1:37,
40; 3:8,29,32; 4:1,42,47; 5:24,25,28,30,37;
6:45,60; 7:32,40,51; 8:9,26,40,43,47; 9:27,31,
32,35,40; 10:3,8,16,20,27; 11:4,6,20,29,41,42;
12:12,18,29,34,47; 14:24,28; 15:15; 16:13;
18:21,37; 19:8,13; 21:7; ACTS 1:4; 2:6,8,11,
22,33,37; 3:22,23; 4:4,19,20,24; 5:5,11,21,24,33;
6:11,14; 7:2,12,34,37,54; 8:6,14,30; 9:4,7,13,
21,38; 10:22,33,44,46; 11:1,7,18,22; 13:7,16,
44,48; 14:9,14; 15:7,12,13,24; 16:14,38; 17:8,

21,32; 18:8,26; 19:2,5,10,26,28; 21:12,20,22;
22:1, 2,7,9,14,15,22,26; 23:16; 24:4,22,24;
25:22; 26:3,14,29; 28:15,22,26-28; **ROM.** 10:14,
18; 11:8; 15:21; **1 COR.** 2:9; 5:1; 11:18; 14:2;
2 COR. 12:4,6; **GAL.** 1:13,23; 4:21; **EPH.**
1:13,15; 3:2; 4:21,29; **PHIL.** 1:27,30; 2:26; 4:9;
COL. 1:4,6,9,23; **2 THESS.** 3:11; **1 TIM.** 4:16;
2 TIM. 1:13; 2:2,14; 4:17; **PHILE.** 1:5; **HEB.**
2:1,3; 3:7,15,16; 4:2,7; 12:19; **JAMES** 1:19; 2:5;
5:11; **2 PET.** 1:18; **1 JOHN** 1:1,3,5; 2:7,18,24;
3:11; 4:3,5,6; 5:14,15; **2 JOHN** 1:6; **3 JOHN**
1:4; **REV.** 1:3,10; 2:7,11,17,29; 3:3,6,13,20,22;
4:1; 5:11,13; 6:1,3,5-7; 7:4; 8:13; 9:13,16,20;
10:4,8; 11:12; 12:10; 13:9; 14:2,13; 16:1,5,7;
18:4,22,23; 19:1,6; 21:3; 22:8,17,18

192. *ἀκρασία akrasia*
MATT. 23:25; **1 COR.** 7:5

193. *ἀκρατής akratēs*
2 TIM. 3:3

194. *ἄκρατος akratos*
REV. 14:10

195. *ἀκρίβεια akribeia*
ACTS 22:3

196. *ἀκριβέστατος akribestatos*
ACTS 26:5

197. *ἀκριβέστερον akribesteron* **adv.**
ACTS 18:26; 23:15,20; 24:22

198. *ἀκριβόω akriboō*
MATT. 2:7,16

199. *ἀκριβῶς akribōs*
MATT. 2:8; **LUKE** 1:3; **ACTS** 18:25; **EPH.**
5:15; **1 THESS.** 5:2

200. *ἀκρίς akris*
MATT. 3:4; **MARK** 1:6; **REV.** 9:3,7

201. *ἀκροατήριον akroatērion*
ACTS 25:23

202. *ἀκροατής akroatēs*
ROM. 2:13; **JAMES** 1:22,23,25

203. *ἀκροβυστία akrobustia*
ACTS 11:3; **ROM.** 2:25-27; 3:30; 4:9-12;
1 COR. 7:18,19; **GAL.** 2:7; 5:6; 6:15; **EPH.**
2:11; **COL.** 2:13; 3:11

204. *ἀκρογωνιαῖος akrogōniaios*
EPH. 2:20; **1 PET.** 2:6

205. *ἀκροθίνιον akrothinion*
HEB. 7:4

206. *ἄκρον akron*
MATT. 24:31; **MARK** 13:27; **LUKE** 16:24;
HEB. 11:21

207. *Ἀκύλας Akulas*
ACTS 18:2,18,26; **ROM.** 16:3; **1 COR.** 16:19;
2 TIM. 4:19

208. *ἀκυρόω akuroō*
MATT. 15:6; **MARK** 7:13; **GAL.** 3:17

209. *ἀκωλύτως akōlutōs*
ACTS 28:31

210. *ἄκων akōn*
1 COR. 9:17

211. *ἀλάβαστρον alabastron*
MATT. 26:7; **MARK** 14:3; **LUKE** 7:37

212. *ἀλαζονεία alazoneia*
JAMES 4:16; **1 JOHN** 2:16

213. *ἀλαζών alazōn*
ROM. 1:30; **2 TIM.** 3:2

214. *ἀλαλάζω alalazō*
MARK 5:38; **1 COR.** 13:1

215. *ἀλάλητος alalētos*
ROM. 8:26

216. *ἄλαλος alalos*
MARK 7:37; 9:17,25

217. ἅλας halas
MATT. 5:13; MARK 9:50; LUKE 14:34;
COL. 4:6

218. ἀλείφω aleiphō
MATT. 6:17; MARK 6:13; 16:1; LUKE
7:38,46; JOHN 11:2; 12:3; JAMES 5:14

219. ἀλεκτοροφωνία alektorophōnia
MARK 13:35

220. ἀλέκτωρ alektōr
MATT. 26:34,74,75; MARK 14:30,68,72;
LUKE 22:34,60,61; JOHN 13:38; 18:27

221. Ἀλεξανδρεύς Alexandreus
ACTS 6:9; 18:24

222. Ἀλεξανδρῖνος Alexandrinos
ACTS 27:6; 28:11

223. Ἀλέξανδρος Alexandros
MARK 15:21; ACTS 4:6; 19:33; 1 TIM. 1:20;
2 TIM. 4:14

224. ἄλευρον aleuron
MATT. 13:33; LUKE 13:21

225. ἀλήθεια alētheia
MATT. 22:16; MARK 5:33; 12:14,32; LUKE
4:25; 20:21; 22:59; JOHN 1:14,17; 3:21;
4:23,24; 5:33; 8:32,40,44-46; 14:6,17; 15:26;
16:7,13; 17:17,19; 18:37,38; ACTS 4:27; 10:34;
26:25; ROM. 1:18,25; 2:2,8,20; 3:7; 9:1; 15:8;
1 COR. 5:8; 13:6; 2 COR. 4:2; 6:7; 7:14; 11:10;
12:6; 13:8; GAL. 2:5,14; 3:1; 5:7; EPH. 1:13;
4:21,24,25; 5:9; 6:14; PHIL. 1:18; COL. 1:5,6;
2 THESS. 2:10,12,13; 1 TIM. 2:4,7; 3:15; 4:3;
6:5; 2 TIM. 2:15,18,25; 3:7,8; 4:4; TITUS
1:1,14; HEB. 10:26; JAMES 1:18; 3:14; 5:19;
1 PET. 1:22; 2 PET. 1:12; 2:2; 1 JOHN 1:6,8;
2:4,21; 3:18,19; 4:6; 5:6; 2 JOHN 1:1-4;
3 JOHN 1:1,3,4,8,12

226. ἀληθεύω alētheuō
GAL. 4:16; EPH. 4:15

227. ἀληθής alēthēs
MATT. 22:16; MARK 12:14; JOHN 3:33;

4:18; 5:31,32; 7:18; 8:13,14,16,17,26; 10:41;
19:35; 21:24; ACTS 12:9; ROM. 3:4; 2 COR.
6:8; PHIL. 4:8; TITUS 1:13; 1 PET. 5:12;
2 PET. 2:22; 1 JOHN 2:8,27; 3 JOHN 1:12

228. ἀληθινός alēthinos
LUKE 16:11; JOHN 1:9; 4:23,37; 6:32; 7:28;
15:1; 17:3; 19:35; 1 THESS. 1:9; HEB. 8:2;
9:24; 10:22; 1 JOHN 2:8; 5:20; REV. 3:7,14;
6:10; 15:3; 16:7; 19:2,9,11; 21:5; 22:6

229. ἀλήθω alēthō
MATT. 24:41; LUKE 17:35

230. ἀληθῶς alēthōs
MATT. 14:33; 26:73; 27:54; MARK 14:70;
15:39; LUKE 9:27; 12:44; 21:3; JOHN 1:47;
4:42; 6:14,55; 7:26,40; 8:31; 17:8; ACTS 12:11;
1 THESS. 2:13; 1 JOHN 2:5

231. ἁλιεύς halieus
MATT. 4:18,19; MARK 1:16,17; LUKE 5:2

232. ἁλιεύω halieuō
JOHN 21:3

233. ἁλίζω halizō
MATT. 5:13; MARK 9:49

234. ἀλίσγημα alisgēma
ACTS 15:20

**236. ἀλλάσσω, ἀλλάττω
       allassō, allattō**
ACTS 6:14; ROM. 1:23; 1 COR. 15:51,52;
GAL. 4:20; HEB. 1:12

237. ἀλλαχόθεν allachothen
JOHN 10:1

238. ἀλληγορέω allēgoreō
GAL. 4:24

**239. ἀλληλούϊα, ἀλληλοϊά
       allēlouia, hallēloia**
REV. 19:1,3,4,6

240. ἀλλήλων allēlōn
MATT. 24:10; 25:32; MARK 4:41; 8:16;
9:34,50; 15:31; LUKE 2:15; 4:36; 6:11; 7:32;
8:25; 12:1; 23:12; 24:14,17,32; JOHN 4:43;
5:44; 6:43,52; 11:56; 13:14,22,34,35; 15:12,17;
16:17,19; 19:24; ACTS 2:7; 4:15; 7:26; 15:39;
19:38; 21:6; 26:31; 28:4,25; ROM. 1:12,27;
2:15; 12:5,10,16; 13:8; 14:13,19; 15:5,7,14;
16:16; 1 COR. 7:5; 11:33; 12:25; 16:20; 2 COR.
13:12; GAL. 5:13,15,17,26; 6:2; EPH. 4:2,25,
32; 5:21; PHIL. 2:3; COL. 3:9,13; 1 THESS.
3:12; 4:9,18; 5:11,15; 2 THESS. 1:3; TITUS
3:3; HEB. 10:24; JAMES 4:11; 5:9,16; 1 PET.
1:22; 4:9; 5:5,14; 1 JOHN 1:7; 3:11,23; 4:7,11,
12; 2 JOHN 1:5; REV. 6:4; 11:10

241. ἀλλογενής allogenēs
LUKE 17:18

242. ἅλλομαι hallomai
JOHN 4:14; ACTS 3:8; 14:10

243. ἄλλος allos
MATT. 2:12; 4:21; 5:39; 8:9; 10:23; 12:13;
13:5,7,8,24,31,33; 16:14; 19:9; 20:3,6;
21:8,33,36,41; 22:4; 25:16,17,20,22; 26:71;
27:42,61; 28:1; MARK 3:5; 4:5,7,8,36; 6:15;
7:4,8; 8:28; 10:11,12; 11:8; 12:4,5,9,31,32;
14:19,58; 15:31,41; LUKE 5:29; 6:10,29;
7:8,19,20; 9:8,19; 20:16; 22:59; 23:35; JOHN
4:37,38; 5:7,32,43; 6:22,23; 7:12,41; 9:9,16;
10:16,21; 12:29; 14:16; 15:24; 18:15,16,34;
19:18,32; 20:2-4,8,25,30; 21:2,8,18,25; ACTS
2:12; 4:12; 15:2; 19:32; 21:34; 1 COR. 1:16;
3:10,11; 9:2,12,27; 10:29; 12:8-10; 14:19,29,30;
15:39,41; 2 COR. 1:13; 8:13; 11:4,8; GAL. 1:7;
5:10; PHIL. 3:4; 1 THESS. 2:6; HEB. 4:8;
11:35; JAMES 5:12; REV. 2:24; 6:4; 7:2; 8:3;
10:1; 12:3; 13:11; 14:6,8,15,17,18; 15:1; 16:7;
17:10; 18:1,4; 20:12

244. ἀλλοτριοεπίσκοπος allotrioepiskopos
1 PET. 4:15

245. ἀλλότριος allotrios
MATT. 17:25,26; LUKE 16:12; JOHN 10:5;
ACTS 7:6; ROM. 14:4; 15:20; 2 COR.
10:15,16; 1 TIM. 5:22; HEB. 9:25; 11:9,34

246. ἀλλόφυλος allophulos
ACTS 10:28

247. ἄλλως allōs
1 TIM. 5:25

248. ἀλοάω aloaō
1 COR. 9:9,10; 1 TIM. 5:18

249. ἄλογος alogos
ACTS 25:27; 2 PET. 2:12; JUDE 1:10

250. ἀλόη aloē
JOHN 19:39

251. ἅλς hals
MARK 9:49

252. ἁλυκός halukos
JAMES 3:12

253. ἀλυπότερος alupoteros
PHIL. 2:28

254. ἅλυσις halusis
MARK 5:3,4; LUKE 8:29; ACTS 12:6,7;
21:33; 28:20; EPH. 6:20; 2 TIM. 1:16; REV.
20:1

255. ἀλυσιτελής alusitelēs
HEB. 13:17

256. Ἀλφαῖος Alphaios
MATT. 10:13; MARK 2:14; 3:18; LUKE 6:15;
ACTS 1:13

257. ἅλων halōn
MATT. 3:12; LUKE 3:17

258. ἀλώπηξ alōpēx
MATT. 8:20; LUKE 9:58; 13:32

259. ἅλωσις halōsis
2 PET. 2:12

260. ἅμα *hama*
MATT. 13:29; 20:1; ACTS 24:26; 27:40;
ROM. 3:12; COL. 4:3; 1 THESS. 4:17; 5:10;
1 TIM. 5:13; PHILE. 1:22

261. ἀμαθής *amathēs*
2 PET. 3:16

262. ἀμαράντινος *amarantinos*
1 PET. 5:4

263. ἀμάραντος *amarantos*
1 PET. 1:4

264. ἁμαρτάνω *hamartanō*
MATT. 18:15,21; 27:4; LUKE 15:18,21;
17:3,4; JOHN 5:14; 8:11; 9:2,3; ACTS 25:8;
ROM. 2:12; 3:23; 5:12,14,16; 6:15; 1 COR.
6:18; 7:28,36; 8:12; 15:34; EPH. 4:26; 1 TIM.
5:20; TITUS 3:11; HEB. 3:17; 10:26; 1 PET.
2:20; 2 PET. 2:4; 1 JOHN 1:10; 2:1; 3:6,8,9;
5:16,18

265. ἁμάρτημα *hamartēma*
MARK 3:28; 4:12; ROM. 3:25; 1 COR. 6:18

266. ἁμαρτία *hamartia*
MATT. 1:21; 3:6; 9:2,5,6; 12:31; 26:28; MARK
1:4,5; 2:5,7,9,10; LUKE 1:77; 3:3; 5:20,21,
23,24; 7:47-49; 11:4; 24:47; JOHN 1:29; 8:21,
24,34,46; 9:34,41; 15:22,24; 16:8,9; 19:11;
20:23; ACTS 2:38; 3:19; 5:31; 7:60; 10:43;
13:38; 22:16; 26:18; ROM. 3:9,20; 4:7,8;
5:12,13,20,21; 6:1,2,6,7,10-14,16-18,20,22,23;
7:5,7-9,11,13,14,17,20,23,25; 8:2,3,10; 11:27;
14:23; 1 COR. 15:3,17,56; 2 COR. 5:21; 11:7;
GAL. 1:4; 2:17; 3:22; EPH. 2:1; COL. 1:14;
2:11; 1 THESS. 2:16; 2 THESS. 2:3; 1 TIM.
5:22,24; 2 TIM. 3:6; HEB. 1:3; 2:17; 3:13; 4:15;
5:1,3; 7:27; 8:12; 9:26,28; 10:2-4,6,8,11,12,17,
18,26; 11:25; 12:1,4; 13:11; JAMES 1:15; 2:9;
4:17; 5:15,20; 1 PET. 2:22,24; 3:18; 4:1,8;
2 PET. 1:9; 2:14; 1 JOHN 1:7-9; 2:2,12;
3:4,5,8,9; 4:10; 5:16,17; REV. 1:5; 18:4,5

267. ἀμάρτυρος *amarturos*
ACTS 14:17

268. ἁμαρτωλός *hamartōlos*
MATT. 9:10,11,13; 11:19; 26:45; MARK 2:15-
17; 8:38; 14:41; LUKE 5:8,30,32; 6:32-34;

7:34,37,39; 13:2; 15:1,2,7,10; 18:13; 19:7; 24:7;
JOHN 9:16,24,25,31; ROM. 3:7; 5:8,19; 7:13;
GAL. 2:15,17; 1 TIM. 1:9,15; HEB. 7:26;
12:3; JAMES 4:8; 5:20; 1 PET. 4:18; JUDE
1:15

269. ἄμαχος *amachos*
1 TIM. 3:3; TITUS 3:2

270. ἀμάω *amaō*
JAMES 5:4

271. ἀμέθυστος *amethustos*
REV. 21:20

272. ἀμελέω *ameleō*
MATT. 22:5; 1 TIM. 4:14; HEB. 2:3; 8:9; 2
PET. 1:12

273. ἄμεμπτος *amemptos*
LUKE 1:6; PHIL. 2:15; 3:6; 1 THESS. 3:13;
HEB. 8:7

274. ἀμέμπτως *amemptōs*
1 THESS. 2:10; 5:23

275. ἀμέριμνος *amerimnos*
MATT. 28:14; 1 COR. 7:32

276. ἀμετάθετος *ametathetos*
HEB. 6:17,18

277. ἀμετακίνητος *ametakinētos*
1 COR. 15:58

278. ἀμεταμέλητος *ametamelētos*
ROM. 11:29; 2 COR. 7:10

279. ἀμετανόητος *ametanoētos*
ROM. 2:5

280. ἄμετρος *ametros*
2 COR. 10:13,15

281. ἀμήν *amēn*
MATT. 5:18,26; 6:2,5,13,16; 8:10; 10:15,
23,42; 11:11; 13:17; 16:28; 17:20; 18:3,13,18;
19:23,28; 21:21,31; 23:36; 24:2,34,47; 25:12,

40,45; 26:13,21,34; 28:20; **MARK** 3:28; 6:11;
8:12; 9:1,41; 10:15,29; 11:23; 12:43; 13:30;
14:9,18,25,30; 16:20; **LUKE** 4:24; 12:37; 13:35;
18:17,29; 21:32; 23:43; 24:53; **JOHN** 1:51;
3:3,5,11; 5:19,24,25; 6:26,32,47,53; 8:34,51,58;
10:1,7; 12:24; 13:16,20,21,38; 14:12; 16:20,23;
21:18,25; **ROM.** 1:25; 9:5; 11:36; 15:33; 16:24,
27; **1 COR.** 14:16; 16:24; **2 COR.** 1:20; 13:14;
GAL. 1:5; 6:18; **EPH.** 3:21; 6:24; **PHIL.** 4:20,
23; **COL.** 4:18; **1 THESS.** 5:28; **2 THESS.**
3:18; **1 TIM.** 1:17; 6:16,21; **2 TIM.** 4:18,22;
TITUS 3:15; **PHILE.** 1:25; **HEB.** 13:21,25;
1 PET. 4:11; 5:11,14; **2 PET.** 3:18; **1 JOHN**
5:21; **2 JOHN** 1:13; **JUDE** 1:25; **REV.** 1:6,7,18;
3:14; 5:14; 7:12; 19:4; 22:20,21

282. ἀμήτωρ *amētōr*
HEB. 7:3

283. ἀμίαντος *amiantos*
HEB. 7:26; 13:4; **JAMES** 1:27; **1 PET.** 1:4

284. Ἀμιναδάβ *Aminadab*
MATT. 1:4; **LUKE** 3:33

285. ἄμμος *ammos*
MATT. 7:26; **ROM.** 9:27; **HEB.** 11:12; **REV.**
13:1; 20:8

286. ἀμνός *amnos*
JOHN 1:29,36; **ACTS** 8:32; **1 PET.** 1:19

287. ἀμοιβή *amoibē*
1 TIM. 5:4

288. ἄμπελος *ampelos*
MATT. 26:29; **MARK** 14:25; **LUKE** 22:18;
JOHN 15:1,4,5; **JAMES** 3:12; **REV.** 14:19

289. ἀμπελουργός *ampelourgos*
LUKE 13:7

290. ἀμπελών *ampelōn*
MATT. 20:1,2,4,7,8; 21:28,33,39-41; **MARK**
12:1,2,8,9; **LUKE** 13:6; 20:9,10,13,15,16;
1 COR. 9:7

291. Ἀμπλίας *Amplias*
ROM. 16:8

292. ἀμύνω *amunō*
ACTS 7:24

293. ἀμφίβληστρον *amphiblēstron*
MATT. 4:18; **MARK** 1:16

294. ἀμφιέννυμι *amphiennumi*
MARK 6:30; 11:8; **LUKE** 7:25; 12:28

295. Ἀμφίπολις *Amphipolis*
ACTS 17:1

296. ἄμφοδον *amphodon*
MARK 11:4

297. ἀμφότερος *amphoteros*
MATT. 9:17; 13:30; 15:14; **LUKE** 1:6,7;
5:7,38; 6:39; 7:42; **ACTS** 8:38; 23:8; **EPH.**
2:14,16,18

298. ἀμώμητος *amōmētos*
PHIL. 2:15; **2 PET.** 3:14

299. ἄμωμος *amōmos*
EPH. 1:4; 5:27; **COL.** 1:22; **HEB.** 9:14; **1 PET.**
1:19; **JUDE** 1:24; **REV.** 14:5

300. Ἀμών *Amōn*
MATT. 1:10

301. Ἀμώς *Amōs*
LUKE 3:25

302. ἄν *an*
MATT. 2:13; 5:18,19,21,22,26,31,32; 6:5; 7:12;
10:11,23,33; 11:21,23; 12:7,20,32,50; 15:5;
16:25,28; 18:6; 19:9; 21:22,44; 22:9,44; 23:3,
16,18,30,39; 24:22,34,43; 25:27; 26:48; **MARK**
3:28,29,35; 4:25; 6:10,11,56; 8:35,38; 9:1,18,41,
42; 10:44; 11:23,24; 12:36; 13:20; 14:9,44;
LUKE 1:62; 2:35; 6:11; 7:39; 8:18; 9:4,5,24,
26,27,46,57; 10:5,8,10,13,35; 12:8,39; 13:25,35;
17:6; 19:23; 20:18,43; 21:32; **JOHN** 1:33; 2:5;
4:10,14; 5:19,46; 8:19,39,42; 9:41; 11:21,22,32;
13:24; 14:2,7,13,28; 15:16,19; 16:13,23; 18:30,
36; 20:23; **ACTS** 2:12,21,35,39,45; 3:19,22,23;
4:35; 5:24; 7:3; 8:19,31; 10:17; 15:17; 17:18,20;
18:14; 21:33; 26:29; **ROM.** 3:4; 9:15,29; 10:13;

16:2; **1 COR.** 2:8; 4:5; 7:5; 11:25-27,31,34;
12:2; 15:25; 16:2; **2 COR.** 3:16; 10:9; 11:21;
GAL. 1:10; 3:21; 4:15; 5:10,17; **PHIL.** 2:23;
COL. 3:17; **1 THESS.** 2:7; **HEB.** 1:13; 4:8;
8:4,7; 10:2; 11:15; **JAMES** 3:4; 4:4; 5:7;
1 JOHN 2:5,19; 3:17; 4:15; 5:15; **REV.** 2:25;
13:15; 14:4

303. A. ἀνά ana adv.
MATT. 20:9,10; **MARK** 6:40;
LUKE 9:3,14; 10:1; **JOHN** 2:6; **REV.**
4:8; 21:21

B. ἀνά ana prep.
MATT. 13:25; **MARK** 7:31;
1 COR. 6:5; 14:27; **REV.** 7:17

304. ἀναβαθμός anabathmos
ACTS 21:35,40

305. ἀναβαίνω anabainō
MATT. 3:16; 5:1; 13:7; 14:23; 15:29; 17:27;
20:17,18; **MARK** 1:10; 3:13; 4:7,8,32; 6:51;
10:32,33; **LUKE** 2:4,42; 5:19; 9:28; 18:10,31;
19:4,28; 24:38; **JOHN** 1:51; 2:13; 3:13; 5:1;
6:62; 7:8,10,14; 10:1; 11:55; 12:20; 20:17;
21:3,11; **ACTS** 1:13; 2:34; 3:1; 7:23; 8:31,39;
10:4,9; 11:2; 15:2; 18:22; 20:11; 21:4,12,15,31;
24:11; 25:1,9; **ROM.** 10:6; **1 COR.** 2:9; **GAL.**
2:1,2; **EPH.** 4:8-10; **REV.** 4:1; 7:2; 8:4; 9:2;
11:7,12; 13:1,11; 14:11; 17:8; 19:3; 20:9

306. ἀναβάλλω anaballō
ACTS 24:22

307. ἀναβιβάζω anabibazō
MATT. 13:48

308. ἀναβλέπω anablepō
MATT. 11:5; 14:19; 20:34; **MARK** 6:41; 7:34;
8:24,25; 10:51,52; 16:4; **LUKE** 7:22; 9:16;
18:41-43; 19:5; 21:1; **JOHN** 9:11,15,18; **ACTS**
9:12,17,18; 22:13

309. ἀνάβλεψις anablepsis
LUKE 4:18

310. ἀναβοάω anaboaō
MATT. 27:46; **MARK** 15:8; **LUKE** 9:38

311. ἀναβολή anabolē
ACTS 25:17

312. ἀναγγέλλω anaggellō
MARK 5:14,19; **JOHN** 4:25; 5:15; 16:13-15;
16:25; **ACTS** 14:27; 15:4; 16:38; 19:18;
20:20,27; **ROM.** 15:21; **2 COR.** 7:7; **1 PET.**
1:12; **1 JOHN** 1:5

313. ἀναγεννάω anagennaō
1 PET. 1:3,23

314. ἀναγινώσκω anaginoskō
MATT. 12:3,5; 19:4; 21:16,42; 22:31; 24:15;
MARK 2:25; 12:10,26; 13:14; **LUKE** 4:16; 6:3;
10:26; **JOHN** 19:20; **ACTS** 8:28,30,32; 13:27;
15:21,31; 23:34; **2 COR.** 1:23; 3:2,15; **EPH.**
3:4; **COL.** 4:16; **1 THESS.** 5:27; **REV.** 1:3; 5:4

315. ἀναγκάζω anagkazō
MATT. 14:22; **MARK** 6:45; **LUKE** 14:23;
ACTS 26:11; 28:19; **2 COR.** 12:11; **GAL.**
2:3,14; 6:12

316. ἀναγκαῖος anagkaios
ACTS 10:24; 13:46; **1 COR.** 12:22; **2 COR.**
9:5; **PHIL.** 1:24; 2:25; **TITUS** 3:14; **HEB.** 8:3

317. ἀναγκαστῶς anagkastōs
1 PET. 5:2

318. ἀνάγκη anagkē
MATT. 18:7; **LUKE** 14:18; 21:23; 23:17;
ROM. 13:5; **1 COR.** 7:26,37; 9:16; **2 COR.** 6:4;
9:7; 12:10; **1 THESS.** 3:7; **PHILE.** 1:14; **HEB.**
7:12,27; 9:16,23; **JUDE** 1:3

319. ἀναγνωρίζω anagnōrizō
ACTS 7:13

320. ἀνάγνωσις anagnōsis
ACTS 13:15; **2 COR.** 3:14; **1 TIM.** 4:13

321. ἀνάγω anagō
MATT. 4:1; **LUKE** 2:22; 4:5; 8:22; 22:66;
ACTS 7:41; 9:39; 12:4; 13:13; 16:11,34; 18:21;
20:3,13; 21:1,2; 27:2,4,12,21; 28:10,11; **ROM.**
10:7; **HEB.** 13:20

322. ἀναδείκνυμι *anaadeiknumi*
LUKE 10:1; ACTS 1:24

323. ἀνάδειξις *anadeixis*
LUKE 1:80

324. ἀναδέχομαι *anadechomai*
ACTS 28:7; HEB. 11:17

325. ἀναδίδωμι *anadidōmi*
ACTS 23:33

326. ἀναζάω *anazaō*
LUKE 15:24,32; ROM. 7:9; 14:9; REV. 20:9

327. ἀναζητέω *anazēteō*
LUKE 2:44; ACTS 11:25

328. ἀναζώννυμι *anazōnnumi*
1 PET. 1:13

329. ἀναζωπυρέω *anazōpureō*
2 TIM. 1:6

330. ἀναθάλλω *anathallō*
PHIL. 4:10

331. ἀνάθεμα *anathema*
ACTS 23:14; ROM. 9:3; 1 COR. 12:3; 16:22;
GAL. 1:8,9

332. ἀναθεματίζω *anathematizō*
MARK 14:71; ACTS 23:12,14,21

333. ἀναθεωρέω *anatheōreō*
ACTS 17:23; HEB. 13:7

334. ἀνάθημα *anathēma*
LUKE 21:5

335. ἀναίδεια *anaideia*
LUKE 11:8

336. ἀναίρεσις *anairesis*
ACTS 8:1; 22:20

337. ἀναιρέω *anaireō*
MATT. 2:16; LUKE 22:2; 23:32; ACTS 2:23;
5:33,36; 7:21,28; 9:23,24,29; 10:39; 12:2; 13:28;
16:27; 22:20; 23:15,21,27; 25:3; 26:10; HEB.
10:9

338. ἀναίτιος *anaitios*
MATT. 12:5,7

339. ἀνακαθίζω *anakathizō*
LUKE 7:15; ACTS 9:40

340. ἀνακαινίζω *anakainizō*
HEB. 6:6

341. ἀνακαινόω *anakainoō*
2 COR. 4:16; COL. 3:10

342. ἀνακαίνωσις *anakainōsis*
ROM. 12:2; TITUS 3:5

343. ἀνακαλύπτω *anakaluptō*
2 COR. 3:14,18

344. ἀνακάμπτω *anakamptō*
MATT. 2:12; LUKE 10:6; ACTS 18:21; HEB.
11:15

345. ἀνάκειμαι *anakeimai*
MATT. 9:10; 22:10,11; 26:7,20; MARK 5:40;
14:18; 16:14; LUKE 7:37; 22:27; JOHN 6:11;
13:23,28

346. ἀνακεφαλαιόω *anakephalaioō*
ROM. 13:9; EPH. 1:10

347. ἀνακλινῶ *anaklinō*
MATT. 8:11; 14:19; MARK 6:39; LUKE 2:7;
7:30; 9:15; 12:37; 13:29

348. ἀνακόπτω *anakoptō*
GAL. 5:7

349. ἀνακράζω *anakrazō*
MARK 1:23; 6:49; LUKE 4:33; 8:28; 23:18

350. ἀνακρίνω anakrinō
LUKE 23:14; ACTS 4:9; 12:19; 17:11; 24:8;
28:18; 1 COR. 2:14,15; 4:3,4; 9:3; 10:25,27;
14:24

351. ἀνάκρισις anakrisis
ACTS 25:26

352. ἀνακύπτω anakuptō
LUKE 13:11; 21:28; JOHN 8:7,10

353. ἀναλαμβάνω analambanō
MARK 16:19; ACTS 1:2,11,22; 7:43; 10:16;
20:13,14; 23:31; EPH. 6:13,16; 1 TIM. 3:16;
2 TIM. 4:11

354. ἀνάληψις analēpsis
LUKE 9:51

355. ἀναλίσκω analiskō
LUKE 9:54; GAL. 5:15; 2 THESS. 2:8

356. ἀναλογία analogia
ROM. 12:6

357. ἀναλογίζομαι analogizomai
HEB. 12:3

358. ἄναλος analos
MARK 9:50

359. ἀνάλυσις analusis
2 TIM. 4:6

360. ἀναλύω analuō
LUKE 12:36; PHIL. 1:23

361. ἀναμάρτητος anamartētos
JOHN 8:7

362. ἀναμένω anamenō
1 THESS. 1:10

363. ἀναμιμνήσκω anamimnēskō
MARK 11:21; 14:72; 1 COR. 4:17; 2 COR.
7:15; 2 TIM. 1:6; HEB. 10:32

364. ἀνάμνησις anamnēsis
LUKE 22:19; 1 COR. 11:24,25; HEB. 10:3

365. ἀνανεόω ananeoō
EPH. 4:23

366. ἀνανήφω ananēphō
2 TIM. 2:26

367. Ἀνανίας Ananias
ACTS 5:1,3,5; 9:10,12,13,17; 22:12; 23:2;
24:1

368. ἀναντίρρητος anantirrētos
ACTS 19:36

369. ἀναντιρρήτως anantirrētōs
ACTS 10:29

370. ἀνάξιος anaxios
1 COR. 6:2

371. ἀναξίως anaxiōs
1 COR. 11:27,29

372. ἀνάπαυσις anapausis
MATT. 11:29; 12:43; LUKE 11:24; REV. 4:8;
14:11

373. ἀναπαύω anapauō
MATT. 11:28; 26:45; MARK 6:31; 14:41;
LUKE 12:19; 1 COR. 16:18; 2 COR. 7:13;
PHILE. 1:7,20; 1 PET. 4:14; REV. 6:11;
14:13

374. ἀναπείθω anapeithō
ACTS 18:13

375. ἀναπέμπω anapempō
LUKE 23:7,11,15; PHILE. 1:12

376. ἀνάπηρος anapēros
LUKE 14:13,21

377. ἀναπίπτω anapiptō
MATT. 15:35; MARK 6:40; 8:6; LUKE 11:37;
14:10; 17:7; 22:14; JOHN 6:10; 13:12; 21:20

378. ἀναπληρόω *anaplēroō*
MATT. 13:14; **1 COR.** 14:16; 16:17; **GAL.** 6:2;
PHIL. 2:30; **1 THESS.** 2:16

379. ἀναπολόγητος *anapologētos*
ROM. 1:20; 2:1

380. ἀναπτύσσω *anaptussō*
LUKE 4:17

381. ἀνάπτω *anaptō*
LUKE 12:49; **ACTS** 28:2; **JAMES** 3:5

382. ἀναρίθμητος *anarithmētos*
HEB. 11:12

383. ἀνασείω *anaseiō*
MARK 15:11; **LUKE** 23:5

384. ἀνασκευάζω *anaskeuazō*
ACTS 15:24

385. ἀνασπάω *anaspaō*
LUKE 14:5; **ACTS** 11:10

386. ἀνάστασις *anastasis*
MATT. 22:23,28,30,31; **MARK** 12:18,23;
LUKE 2:34; 14:14; 20:27,33,35,36; **JOHN**
5:29; 11:24,25; **ACTS** 1:22; 2:31; 4:2,33;
17:18,32; 23:6,8; 24:15,21; 26:23; **ROM.** 1:4;
6:5; **1 COR.** 15:12,13,21,42; **PHIL.** 3:10;
2 TIM. 2:18; **HEB.** 6:2; 11:35; **1 PET.** 1:3;
3:21; **REV.** 20:5,6

387. ἀναστατόω *anastatoō*
ACTS 17:6; 21:38; **GAL.** 5:12

388. ἀνασταυρόω *anastauroō*
HEB. 6:6

389. ἀναστενάζω *anastenazō*
MARK 8:12

390. ἀναστρέφω *anastrephō*
MATT. 17:22; **JOHN** 2:15; **ACTS** 5:22,15:16;
2 COR. 1:12; **EPH.** 2:3; **1 TIM.** 3:5; **HEB.**
10:13,13:18; **1 PET.** 1:7; **2 PET.** 2:18

391. ἀναστροφή *anastrophē*
GAL. 1:13; **EPH.** 4:22; **1 TIM.** 4:12; **HEB.**
13:7; **JAMES** 3:13; **1 PET.** 1:15; 18; 2:12;
3:1,2,16; **2 PET.** 2:7; 3:11

392. ἀνατάσσομαι *anatassomai*
LUKE 1:1

393. ἀνατέλλω *anatellō*
MATT. 4:16; 5:45; 13:6; **MARK** 4:6; 16:2;
LUKE 12:54; **HEB.** 7:14; **JAMES** 1:11; **2 PET.**
1:19

394. ἀνατίθημι *anatithēmi*
ACTS 25:14; **GAL.** 2:2

395. ἀνατολή *anatolē*
MATT. 2:1,2,9; 8:11; 24:27 **LUKE** 1:78; 13:29;
REV. 7:2; 16:12; 21:13

396. ἀνατρέπω *anatrepō*
2 TIM. 2:18; **TITUS** 1:11

397. ἀνατρέφω *anatrephō*
ACTS 7:20,21; 22:3

398. ἀναφαίνω *anaphainō*
LUKE 19:11; **ACTS** 21:3

399. ἀναφέρω *anapherō*
MATT. 17:1; **MARK** 9:2; **LUKE** 24:51;
HEB. 7:27; 9:28; 13:15; **JAMES** 2:21;
1 PET. 2:5,24

400. ἀναφωνέω *anaphōneō*
LUKE 1:42

401. ἀνάχυσις *anachusis*
1 PET. 4:4

402. ἀναχωρέω *anachōreō*
MATT. 2:12,13,14,22; 4:12; 9:24; 12:15; 14:13;
15:21; 27:5; **MARK** 3:7; **JOHN** 6:15; **ACTS**
23:19; 26:31

403. ἀνάψυξις *anapsuxis*
ACTS 3:19

404. ἀναψύχω *anapsuchō*
2 TIM. 1:16

405. ἀνδραποδιστής *andrapodistēs*
1 TIM. 1:10

406. Ἀνδρέας *Andreas*
MATT. 4:18; 10:2; MARK 1:16,29; 3:18; 13:3;
LUKE 6:14; JOHN 1:40,44; 6:8; 12:22; ACTS
1:13

407. ἀνδρίζω *andrizō*
1 COR. 16:13

408. Ἀνδρόνικος *Andronikos*
ROM. 16:7

409. ἀνδροφόνος *androphonos*
1 TIM. 1:9

410. ἀνέγκλητος *anegklētos*
1 COR. 1:8; COL. 1:22; 1 TIM. 3:10; TITUS
1:6,7

411. ἀνεκδιήγητος *anekdiēgētos*
2 COR. 9:15

412. ἀνεκλάλητος *aneklalētos*
1 PET. 1:8

413. ἀνέκλειπτος *anekleiptos*
LUKE 12:33

414. ἀνεκτότερος *anektoteros*
MATT. 10:15; 11:22,24; MARK 6:11; LUKE
10:12,14

415. ἀνελεήμων *aneleēmōn*
ROM. 1:31

416. ἀνεμίζω *anemizō*
JAMES 1:6

417. ἄνεμος *anemos*
MATT. 7:5,27; 8:26,27; 11:7; 14:24,30,32;
24:31; MARK 4:37,39,41; 6:48,51; 13:27;

LUKE 7:24; 8:23-25; JOHN 6:18; ACTS
27:4,7,14,15; EPH. 4:14; JAMES 3:4; JUDE
1:12; REV. 6:13; 7:1

418. ἀνένδεκτος *anendektos*
LUKE 17:1

419. ἀνεξερεύνητος *anexereunētos*
ROM. 11:33

420. ἀνεξίκακος *anexikakos*
2 TIM. 2:24

421. ἀνεξιχνίαστος *anexichniastos*
ROM. 11:33; EPH. 3:8

422. ἀνεπαίσχυντος *anepaischuntos*
2 TIM. 2:15

423. ἀνεπίληπτος *anepilēptos*
1 TIM. 3:2; 5:7; 6:14

424. ἀνέρχομαι *anerchomai*
JOHN 6:3; GAL. 1:17,18

425. ἄνεσις *anesis*
ACTS 24:23; 2 COR. 2:13; 7:5; 8:13;
2 THESS. 1:7

426. ἀνετάζω *anetazō*
ACTS 22:24,29

427. ἄνευ *aneu*
MATT. 10:29; 1 PET. 3:1; 4:9

428. ἀνεύθετος *aneuthetos*
ACTS 27:12

429. ἀνευρίσκω *aneuriskō*
LUKE 2:16; ACTS 21:4

430. ἀνέχω *anechō*
MATT. 17:17; MARK 9:19; LUKE 9:41;
ACTS 18:14; 1 COR. 4:12; 2 COR. 11:1,4,
19,20; EPH. 4:2; COL. 3:13; 2 THESS. 1:4;
2 TIM. 4:3; HEB. 13:22

431. ἀνεψιός *anepsios*
COL. 4:10

432. ἄνηθον *anēthon*
MATT. 23:23

433. ἀνήκω *anēkō*
EPH. 5:4; COL. 3:18; PHILE. 1:8

434. ἀνήμερος *anēmeros*
2 TIM. 3:3

435. ἀνήρ *anēr*
MATT. 1:16,19; 7:24,26; 12:41; 14:21,35;
15:38; **MARK** 6:20,44; 10:2,12; **LUKE** 1:27,34;
2:36; 5:8,12,18; 7:20; 8:27,38,41; 9:14,30,32,38;
11:31,32; 14:24; 16:18; 17:12; 19:2,7; 22:63;
23:50; 24:4,19; **JOHN** 1:13,30; 4:16-18; 6:10;
ACTS 1:10,11,16,21; 2:5,14,22,29,37; 3:2,
12,14; 4:4; 5:1,9,10,14,25,35,36; 6:3,5,11;
7:2,26; 8:2,3,9,12,27; 9:2,7,12,13,38; 10:1,5,
17,19,21,22,28,30; 11:3,11-13,20,24; 13:7,15,
16,21,22,26,38; 14:8,15; 15:7,13,22,25; 16:9;
17:5,12,22,31,34; 18:24; 19:7,25,35,37; 20:30;
21:11,23,26,28,38; 22:1,3,4,12; 23:1,6,21,27,30;
24:5; 25:5,14,17,23,24; 27:10,21,25; 28:17;
ROM. 4:8; 7:2,3; 11:4; **1 COR.** 7:2-4,10,11,
13,14,16,34,39; 11:3,4,7-9,11,12,14; 13:11;
14:35; **2 COR.** 11:2; **GAL.** 4:27; **EPH.** 4:13;
5:22-25,28,33; **COL.** 3:18,19; **1 TIM.** 2:8,12;
3:2,12; 5:9; **TITUS** 1:6; 2:5; **JAMES**
1:8,12,20,23; 2:2; 3:2; **1 PET.** 3:1,5,7; **REV.**
21:2

436. ἀνθίστημι *anthistēmi*
MATT. 5:39; **LUKE** 21:15; **ACTS** 6:10; 13:8;
ROM. 9:19; 13:2; **GAL.** 2:11; **EPH.** 6:13;
2 TIM. 3:8; 4:15; **JAMES** 4:7; **1 PET.** 5:9

437. ἀνθομολογέομαι
anthomologeomai
LUKE 2:38

438. ἄνθος *anthos*
JAMES 1:10,11; **1 PET.** 1:24

439. ἀνθρακιά *anthrakia*
JOHN 18:18; 21:9

440. ἄνθραξ *anthrax*
ROM. 12:20

441. ἀνθρωπάρεσκος *anthrōpareskos*
EPH. 6:6; COL. 3:22

442. ἀνθρώπινος *anthrōpinos*
ROM. 6:19; **1 COR.** 2:4,13; 4:3; 10:13; **JAMES**
3:7; **1 PET.** 2:13

443. ἀνθροποκτόνος *anthropoktonos*
JOHN 8:44; **1 JOHN** 3:15

444. ἄνθρωπος *anthrōpos*
MATT. 4:4,19; 5:13,16,19; 6:1,2,5,14-16,18;
7:9,12; 8:9,20,27; 9:6,8,9,32; 10:17,23,
32,33,35,36; 11:8,19; 12:8,10-13,31,32,35,
36,40,43,45; 13:24,25,28,31,37,41,44,45,52;
15:9,11,18,20; 16:13,23,26-28; 17:9,12,14,22;
18:7,11,12,22; 19:3,5,6,10,12,26,28; 20:1,18,28;
21:25,26,28,33; 22:2,11,16; 23:4,5,7,13,28;
24:27,30,37,39,44; 25:13,14,24,31; 26:2,24,
45,64,72,74; 27:32,57; **MARK** 1:17,23; 2:10,
27,28; 3:1,3,5,28; 4:26; 5:2,8; 7:7,8,11,15,
18,20,21,23; 8:24,27,31,33,36,37,38; 9:9,12,
31; 10:7,9,27,33,45; 11:2,30,32; 12:1,14;
13:26,34; 14:13,21,41,62,71; 15:39; **LUKE**
1:25; 2:14,15,25,52; 4:4,33; 5:10,18,20,24;
6:5,6,8,10,22,26,31,45,48,49; 7:8,25,31,34;
8:29,33,35; 9:22,25,26,44,56,58; 10:30; 11:24,
26,30,44,46; 12:8-10,14,16,36,40; 13:4,19;
14:2,16,30; 15:4,11; 16:1,15,19; 17:22,24,26,30;
18:2,4,8,10,11,27,31; 19:10,12,21,22,30; 20:4,
6,9; 21:26,27,36; 22:10,22,48,58,60,69; 23:4,
6,14,47; 24:7; **JOHN** 1:4,6,9,51; 2:10,25;
3:1,4,13,14,19,27; 4:28,29,50; 5:5,7,9,12,15,
27,34,41; 6:10,14,27,53,62; 7:22,23,46,51;
8:17,28,40; 9:1,11,16,24,30; 10:33; 11:47,50;
12:23,34,43; 13:31; 16:1; 17:6; 18:14,17,29;
19:5; **ACTS** 4:9,12-14,16,17,22; 5:4,28,29,
35,38; 6:13; 7:56; 9:33; 10:26,28; 12:22;
14:11,15; 15:17,26; 16:17,20,35,37; 17:25,
26,29,30; 18:13; 19:16,35; 21:28,39; 22:15,
25,26; 23:9,24:16; 25:16,22; 26:31,32; 28:4;
ROM. 1:18,23; 2:1,3,9,16,29; 3:4,5,28; 4:6;
5:12,15,18,19; 6:6; 7:1,22,24; 9:20; 10:5;
12:17,18; 14:18,20; **1 COR.** 1:25; 2:5,9,11,14;
3:3,21; 4:1,9; 6:18; 7:1,7,23,26; 9:8; 11:28; 13:1;
14:2,3; 15:19,21,32,39,45,47; **2 COR.** 3:2;
4:2,16; 5:11; 8:21; 12:2-4; **GAL.** 1:1,10-12;
2:6,16; 3:12,15; 5:3; 6:1,7; **EPH.** 2:15; 3:5,16;

4:8,14,22,24; 5:31; 6:7; **PHIL.** 2:7,8; 4:5; **COL.**
1:28; 2:8,22; 3:9,23; **1 THESS.** 2:4,6,13,15; 4:8;
2 THESS. 2:3; 3:2; **1 TIM.** 2:1,4,5; 4:10; 5:24;
6:5,9,11,16; **2 TIM.** 2:2; 3:2,8,13,17; **TITUS**
1:14; 2:11; 3:2,8,10; **HEB.** 2:6; 5:1; 6:16; 7:8,28;
8:2; 9:27; 13:6; **JAMES** 1:7,19; 2:20,24; 3:8,9;
5:17; **1 PET.** 1:24; 2:4,15; 3:4; 4:2,6; **2 PET.**
1:21; 2:16; 3:7; **1 JOHN** 5:9; **JUDE** 1:4; **REV.**
1:13; 4:7; 8:11; 9:4-7,10,15,18,20; 11:13;
13:13, 18; 14:4,14; 16:2,8,9,18,21; 18:13;
21:3,17

445. ἀνθυπατεύω anthupateuō
ACTS 18:12

446. ἀνθύπατος anthupatos
ACTS 13:7,8,12; 19:38

447. ἀνίημι aniēmi
ACTS 16:26; 27:40; **EPH.** 6:9; **HEB.** 13:5

448. ἀνίλεως anileōs
JAMES 2:13

449. ἄνιπτος aniptos
MATT. 15:20; **MARK** 7:2,5

450. ἀνίστημι anistēmi
MATT. 9:9; 12:41; 17:9; 20:19; 22:24; 26:62;
MARK 1:35; 2:14; 3:26; 5:42; 7:24; 8:31;
9:9,10,27,31; 10; 1,34,50; 12:23,25; 14:57,60;
16:9; **LUKE** 1:39; 4:16,29,38,39; 5:25,28; 6:8;
8:55; 9:8,19; 10:25; 11:7,8,32; 15:18,20; 16:31;
17:19; 18:33; 22:45,46; 23:1; 24:7,12,33,46;
JOHN 6:39,40,44,54; 11:23,24,31; 20:9;
ACTS 1:15; 2:24,30,32; 3:22,26; 5:6,17,34,36,
37; 6:9; 7:18,37; 8:26,27; 9:6,11,18,34,39-41;
10:13,20,26,41; 11:7,28; 12:7; 13:16,33,34;
14:10,20; 15:7; 17:3,31; 20:30; 22:10,16; 23:9;
26:16,30; **ROM.** 14:9; 15:12; **ICOR.** 10:7; **EPH.**
5:14; **1 THESS.** 4:14,16; **HEB.** 7:11,15

451. ῎Αννα Anna
LUKE 2:36

452. ῎Αννας Annas
LUKE 3:2; **JOHN** 18:13,24; **ACTS** 4:6

453. ἀνόητος anoētos
LUKE 24:25; **ROM.** 1:14; **GAL.** 3:1,3; **1 TIM.**
6:9; **TITUS** 3:3

454. ἄνοια anoia
LUKE 6:11; **2 TIM.** 3:9

455. ἀνοίγω anoigō
MATT. 2:11; 3:16; 5:2; 7:7,8; 9:30; 13:35;
17:27; 20:33; 25:11; 27:52; **LUKE** 1:64; 3:21;
11:9,10; 12:36; 13:25; **JOHN** 1:51; 9:10,
14,17,21,26,30,32; 10:3,21; 11:37; **ACTS**
5:19,23; 7:56; 8:32,35; 9:8,40; 10:11,34;
12:10,14,16; 14:27; 16:26,27; 18:14; 26:18;
ROM. 3:13; **1 COR.** 16:9; **2 COR.** 2:12; 6:11;
COL. 4:3; **REV.** 3:7,8,20; 4:1; 5:2-5,9;
6:1,3,5,7,9,12; 8:1; 9:2; 10:2,8; 11:19; 12:16;
13:6; 15:5; 20:12

456. ἀνοικοδομέω anoikodomeō
ACTS 15:16

457. ἄνοιξις anoixis
EPH. 6:19

458. ἀνομία anomia
MATT. 7:23; 13:41; 23:28; 24:12; **ROM.** 4:7;
6:19; **2 COR.** 6:14; **2 THESS.** 2:7; **TITUS** 2:14;
HEB. 1:9; 8:12; 10:17; **1 JOHN** 3:4

459. ἄνομος anomos
MARK 15:28; **LUKE** 22:37; **ACTS** 2:23;
1 COR. 9:21; **2 THESS.** 2:8; **1 TIM.** 1:9;
2 PET. 2:8

460. ἀνόμως anomōs
ROM. 2:12

461. ἀνορθόω anorthoō
LUKE 13:13; **ACTS** 15:16; **HEB.** 12:12

462. ἀνόσιος anosios
1 TIM. 1:9; **2 TIM.** 3:2

463. ἀνοχή anochē
ROM. 2:4; 3:25

464. ἀνταγωνίζομαι antagōnizomai
HEB. 12:4

465. ἀντάλλαγμα *antallagma*
MATT. 16:26; MARK 8:37

466. ἀνταναπληρόω *antanaplēroō*
COL. 1:24

467. ἀνταποδίδωμι *antapodidōmi*
LUKE 14:14; ROM. 11:35; 12:19; 1 THESS.
3:9; 2 THESS. 1:6; HEB. 10:30

468. ἀνταπόδομα *antapodoma*
LUKE 14:12; ROM. 11:9

469. ἀνταπόδοσις *antapodosis*
COL. 3:24

470. ἀνταποκρίνομαι *antapokrinomai*
LUKE 14:6; ROM. 9:20

471. ἀντέπω *antepō*
LUKE 21:15; ACTS 4:14

472. ἀντέχω *antechō*
MATT. 6:24; LUKE 16:13; 1 THESS. 5:14;
TITUS 1:9

473. ἀντί *anti*
MATT. 2:22,5:38; 17:27; 20:28; MARK 10:45;
LUKE 1:20; 11:11; 12:3; 19:44; JOHN 1:16;
ACTS 12:23; ROM. 12:17; 1 COR. 11:15;
EPH. 5:31; 1 THESS. 5:15; 2 THESS. 2:10;
HEB. 12:2; JAMES 4:15; 1 PET. 3:9

474. ἀντιβάλλω *antiballō*
LUKE 24:17

475. ἀντιδιατίθημι *antidiatithēmi*
2 TIM. 2:25

476. ἀντίδικος *antidikos*
MATT. 5:25; LUKE 12:58; 18:3; 1 PET. 5:8

477. ἀντίθεσις *antithesis*
1 TIM. 6:20

478. ἀντικαθίστημι *antikathistēmi*
HEB. 12:4

479. ἀντικαλέω *antikaleō*
LUKE 14:12

480. ἀντίκειμαι *antikeimai*
LUKE 13:17,21:15; 1 COR. 16:9; GAL. 5:17;
PHIL. 1:28; 2 THESS. 2:4; 1 TIM. 1:10; 5:14

481. ἀντικρύ *antikru*
ACTS 20:15

482. ἀντιλαμβάνω *antilambanō*
LUKE 1:54; ACTS 20:35; 1 TIM. 6:2

483. ἀντιλέγω *antilegō*
LUKE 2:34,20:27; JOHN 19:12; ACTS 13:45;
28:19,22; ROM. 10:21; TITUS 1:9; 2:9

484. ἀντίληψις *antilēpsis*
1 COR. 12:28

485. ἀντιλογία *antilogia*
HEB. 6:16; 7:7; 12:3; JUDE 1:11

486. ἀντιλοιδορέω *antiloidoreō*
1 PET. 2:23

487. ἀντίλυτρον *antilutron*
1 TIM. 2:6

488. ἀντιμετρέω *antimetreō*
MATT. 7:2; LUKE 6:38

489. ἀντιμισθία *antimisthia*
ROM. 1:27; 2 COR. 6:13

490. Ἀντιόχεια *Antiocheia*
ACTS 11:19,20,22,26,27; 13:1,14; 14:19,21,26;
15:22,23,30,35; 18:22; GAL. 2:11; 2 TIM. 3:11

491. Ἀντιοχεύς *Antiocheus*
ACTS 6:5

492. ἀντιπαρέρχομαι
    antiparerchomai
LUKE 10:31,32

493. Ἀντίπας Antipas
REV. 2:13

494. Ἀντιπατρίς Antipatris
ACTS 23:31

495. ἀντιπέραν antiperan
LUKE 8:26

496. ἀντιπίπτω antipiptō
ACTS 7:51

497. ἀντιστρατεύομαι
antistrateuomai
ROM. 7:23

498. ἀντιτάσσω antitassō
ACTS 18:6; ROM. 13:2; JAMES 4:6; 5:6;
1 PET. 5:5

499. ἀντίτυπον antitupon
HEB. 9:24; 1 PET. 3:21

500. ἀντίχριστος antichristos
1 JOHN 2:18,22; 4:3; 2 JOHN 1:7

501. ἀντλέω antleō
JOHN 2:8,9; 4:7,15

502. ἄντλημα antlēma
JOHN 4:11

503. ἀντοφθαλμέω antophthalmeō
ACTS 27:15

504. ἄνυδρος anudros
MATT. 12:43; LUKE 11:24; 2 PET. 2:17;
JUDE 1:12

505. ἀνυπόκριτος anupokritos
ROM. 12:9; 2 COR. 6:6; 1 TIM. 1:5; 2 TIM.
1:5; 1 PET. 1:22; JAMES 3:17

506. ἀνυπότακτος anupotaktos
1 TIM. 1:9; TITUS 1:6,10; HEB. 2:8

507. ἄνω anō
JOHN 2:7; 8:23; 11:41; ACTS 2:19; GAL.
4:26; PHIL. 3:14; COL. 3:1,2; HEB. 12:15

508. ἀνώγεον anōgeon
MARK 14:15; LUKE 22:12

509. ἄνωθεν anōthen
MATT. 27:51; MARK 15:38; LUKE 1:3;
JOHN 3:3,7,31; 19:11,23; ACTS 26:5; GAL.
4:9; JAMES 1:17; 3:15,17

510. ἀνωτερικός anōterikos
ACTS 19:1

511. ἀνώτερος anōteros
LUKE 14:10; HEB. 10:8

512. ανωφελής anōphelēs
TITUS 6:9; HEB. 7:18

513. ἀξίνη axinē
MATT. 3:10; LUKE 3:9

514. ἄξιος axios
MATT. 3:8; 10:10,11,13,37,38; 22:8; LUKE
3:8; 7:4; 10:7; 12:48; 15:19,21; 23:15,41; JOHN
1:27; ACTS 13:25,46; 23:29; 25:11,25; 26:20,
31; ROM. 1:32; 8:18; 1 COR. 16:4; 2 THESS.
1:3; 1 TIM. 1:15; 4:9; 5:18; 6:1; HEB. 11:38;
REV. 3:4; 4:11; 5:2,4,9,12; 16:6

515. ἀξιόω axioō
LUKE 7:7; ACTS 15:38; 28:22; 2 THESS.
1:11; 1 TIM. 5:17; HEB. 3:3; 10:29

516. ἀξίως axiōs
ROM. 16:2; EPH. 4:1; PHIL. 1:27; COL. 1:10;
1 THESS. 2:12; 3 JOHN 1:6

517. ἀόρατος aoratos
ROM. 1:20; COL. 1:15,16; 1 TIM. 1:17; HEB.
11:27

518. ἀπαγγέλλω apaggellō
MATT. 2:8; 8:33; 11:4; 12:18; 14:12; 28:8-11;
MARK 6:30; 16:10,13; LUKE 7:18,22; 8:20,
34,36,47; 9:36; 13:1; 14:21; 18:37; 24:9; JOHN

4:51; 20:18; **ACTS** 4:23; 5:22,25; 11:13; 12:14,
17; 15:27; 16:36; 22:26; 23:16,17,19; 26:20;
28:21; **1 COR.** 14:25; **1 THESS.** 1:9; **HEB.**
2:12; **1 JOHN** 1:2,3

519. ἀπάγχω *apagchō*
MATT. 27:5

520. ἀπάγω *apagō*
MATT. 7:13,14; 26:57; 27:2,31; **MARK**
14:44,53; 15:16; **LUKE** 13:15; 23:26; **JOHN**
18:13; 19:16; **ACTS** 12:19; 23:17; 24:7; **1 COR.**
12:2

521. ἀπαίδευτος *apaideutos*
2 TIM. 2:23

522. ἀπαίρω *apairō*
MATT. 9:15; **MARK** 2:20; **LUKE** 5:35

523. ἀπαιτέω *apaiteō*
LUKE 6:30; 12:20

524. ἀπαλγέω *apalgeō*
EPH. 4:19

525. ἀπαλλάσσω, ἀπαλλάττω
apallassō, apallattō
LUKE 12:58; **ACTS** 19:12; **HEB.** 2:15

526. ἀπαλλοτριόω *apallotrioō*
EPH. 2:12; 4:18; **COL.** 1:21

527. ἀπαλός *hapalos*
MATT. 24:32; **MARK** 13:28

528. ἀπαντάω *apantaō*
MATT. 28:9; **MARK** 5:2; 14:13; **LUKE** 14:31;
17:12; **JOHN** 4:51; **ACTS** 16:16

529. ἀπάντησις *apantēsis*
MATT. 25:1,6; **ACTS** 28:15; **1 THESS.** 4:17

530. ἅπαξ *hapax*
2 COR. 11:25; **PHIL.** 4:16; **1 THESS.** 2:18;
HEB. 6:4; 9:7,26-28; 10:2; 12:26,27; **1 PET.**
3:18,20; **JUDE** 1:3,5

531. ἀπαράβατος *aparabatos*
HEB. 7:24

532. ἀπαρασκεύαστος
aparaskeuastos
2 COR. 9:4

533. ἀπαρνέομαι *aparneomai*
MATT. 16:24; 26:34,35,75; **MARK** 8:34;
14:30,31,72; **LUKE** 9:23; 12:9; 22:34,61;
JOHN 13:38

534. ἀπάρτι *aparti*
REV. 14:13

535. ἀπαρτισμός *apartismos*
LUKE 14:28

536. ἀπαρχή *aparchē*
ROM. 8:23; 11:16; 16:5; **1 COR.** 15:20,23;
16:15; **JAMES** 1:18; **REV.** 14:4

537. ἅπας *hapas*
MATT. 6:32; 24:39; 28:11; **MARK** 5:40; 8:25;
11:32; 16:15; **LUKE** 2:39; 3:16,21; 4:6;
5:11,26,28; 7:16; 8:37; 9:15; 15:13; 17:27,29;
19:7,37,48; 21:4,12; 23:1; **ACTS** 2:1,4,14,44;
4:31,32; 5:12,16; 6:15; 10:8; 11:10; 13:29;
16:3,28; 27:33; **EPH.** 6:13; **JAMES** 3:2

538. ἀπατάω *apataō*
EPH. 5:6; **1 TIM.** 2:14; **JAMES** 1:26

539. ἀπάτη *apatē*
MATT. 13:22; **MARK** 4:19; **EPH.** 4:22; **COL.**
2:8; **2 THESS.** 2:10; **HEB.** 3:13; **2 PET.** 2:13

540. ἀπάτωρ *apatōr*
HEB. 1:3

541. ἀπαύγασμα *apaugasma*
HEB. 1:3

542. ἀπείδον *apeidon*
     (2 aor. of ἀφοράω)
PHIL. 2:23

543. ἀπείθεια *apeitheia*
ROM. 11:30,32; EPH. 2:2; 5:6; COL. 3:6;
HEB. 4:6,11

544. ἀπειθέω *apeitheō*
JOHN 3:36; ACTS 14:2; 17:5; 19:9; ROM. 2:8;
10:21; 11:30,31; 15:31; HEB. 3:18; 11:31;
1 PET. 2:7,8; 3:1,20; 4:17

545. ἀπειθής *apeithēs*
LUKE 1:17; ACTS 26:19; ROM. 1:30; 2 TIM.
3:2; TITUS 1:16; 3:3

546. ἀπειλέω *apeileō*
ACTS 4:17; 1 PET. 2:23

547. ἀπειλή *apeilē*
ACTS 4:17,29; 9:1; EPH. 6:9

548. ἄπειμι *apeimi*
1 COR. 5:3; 2 COR. 10:1,11; 13:2,10; PHIL.
1:27; COL. 2:5

549. ἄπειμι *apeimi*
ACTS 17:10

550. ἀπεῖπον *apeipon*
2 COR. 4:2

551. ἀπείραστος *apeirastos*
JAMES 1:13

552. ἄπειρος *apeiros*
HEB. 5:13

553. ἀπεκδέχομαι *apekdechomai*
ROM. 8:19,23,25; 1 COR. 1:7; GAL. 5:5;
PHIL. 3:20; HEB. 9:28

554. ἀπεκδύομαι *apekduomai*
COL. 2:15; 3:9

555. ἀπέκδυσις *apekdusis*
COL. 2:11

556. ἀπελαύνω *apelaunō*
ACTS 18:16

557. ἀπελεγμός *apelegmos*
ACTS 19:27

558. ἀπελεύθερος *apeleutheros*
1 COR. 7:22

559. Ἀπελλῆς *Apellēs*
ROM. 16:10

560. ἀπελπίζω *apelpizō*
LUKE 6:35

561. ἀπέναντι *apenanti*
MATT. 21:2; 27:24,61; ACTS 3:16; 17:7;
ROM. 3:18

562. ἀπέραντος *aperantos*
1 TIM. 1:4

563. ἀπερισπάστως *aperispastōs*
1 COR. 7:35

564. ἀπερίτμητος *aperitmētos*
ACTS 7:51

565. ἀπέρχομαι *aperchomai*
MATT. 2:22; 4:24; 8:18,19,21,31-33; 9:7; 10:5;
13:25,28,46; 14:15,16,25; 16:4,21; 18:30; 19:22;
20:4; 21:29,30; 22:5,22; 25:10,18,25,46; 26:36,
42,44; 27:5,60; 28:10; MARK 1:20,35,42; 3:13;
5:17,20,24; 6:27,32,36,37,46; 7:24,30; 8:13;
9:43; 10:22; 11:4; 12:12; 14:10,12,39; 16:13;
LUKE 1:23,38; 2:15; 5:13,14,25; 7:24; 8:31,
34,37,39; 9:12,57,59,60; 10:30; 17:23; 19:32;
22:4,13; 23:33; 24:12,24; JOHN 4:3,8,28,43,47;
5:15; 6:1,22,66,68; 9:7,11; 10:40; 11:28,46,54;
12:19,36; 16:7; 18:6; 20:10; ACTS 4:15; 5:26;
9:17; 10:7; 28:29; ROM. 15:28; GAL. 1:17;
JAMES 1:24; JUDE 1:7; REV. 9:12; 10:9;
11:14; 12:17; 16:2 18:14; 21:4

566. ἀπέχει *apechei*
MARK 14:41

567. ἀπέχομαι *apechomai*
    (Mid. of ἀπέχω)
ACTS 15:20,29; 1 THESS. 4:3; 5:22; 1 TIM.
4:3; 1 PET. 2:11

568. ἀπέχω apechō
MATT. 6:2,5,16; 15:8; **MARK** 7:6; **LUKE**
6:24; 7:6; 15:20; 24:13; **PHIL.** 4:18; **PHILE.**
1:15

569. ἀπιστέω apisteō
MARK 16:11,16; **LUKE** 24:11,41; **ACTS**
28:24; **ROM.** 3:3; **2 TIM.** 2:13

570. ἀπιστία apistia
MATT. 13:58; 17:20; **MARK** 6:6; 9:24; 16:14;
ROM. 3:3; 4:20; 11:20,23; **1 TIM.** 1:13; **HEB.**
3:12,19

571. ἄπιστος apistos
MATT. 17:17; **MARK** 9:19; **LUKE** 9:41;
12:46; **JOHN** 20:27; **ACTS** 26:8; **1 COR.** 6:6;
7:12-15; 10:27; 14:22-24; **2 COR.** 4:4; 6:14,15;
1 TIM. 5:8; **TITUS** 1:15; **REV.** 21:8

572. ἁπλότης haplotēs
ROM. 12:8; **2 COR.** 1:12; 8:2; 9:11,13; 11:3;
EPH. 6:5; **COL.** 3:22

573. ἁπλόος, ἁπλοῦς haploos, haplous
MATT. 6:22; **LUKE** 11:34

574. ἁπλῶς haplōs
JAMES 1:5

576. ἀποβαίνω apobainō
LUKE 5:2; 21:13; **JOHN** 21:9; **PHIL.** 1:19

577. ἀποβάλλω apoballō
MARK 10:50; **HEB.** 10:35

578. ἀποβλέπω apoblepō
HEB. 11:26

579. ἀπόβλητος apoblētos
1 TIM. 4:4

580. ἀποβολή apobolē
ACTS 27:22; **ROM.** 11:15

581. ἀπογενόμενος apogenomenos
1 PET. 2:24

582. ἀπογραφή apographē
LUKE 2:2; **ACTS** 5:37

583. ἀπογράφω apographō
LUKE 2:1,3,5; **HEB.** 12:23

584. ἀποδείκνυμι apodeiknumi
ACTS 2:22; 25:7; **1 COR.** 4:9; **2 THESS.** 2:4

585. ἀπόδειξις apodeixis
1 COR. 2:4

586. ἀποδεκατόω apodekatoō
MATT. 23:23; **LUKE** 11:42; 18:12; **HEB.** 7:5

587. ἀπόδεκτος apodektos
1 TIM. 2:3; 5:4

588. ἀποδέχομαι apodechomai
LUKE 8:40; **ACTS** 2:41; 15:4; 18:27; 24:3;
28:30

589. ἀποδημέω apodēmeō
MATT. 21:31; 25:14,15; **MARK** 12:1; **LUKE**
15:13; 20:9

590. ἀπόδημος apodēmos
MARK 13:34

591. ἀποδίδωμι apodidōmi
MATT. 5:26,33; 6:4,6,18; 12:36; 16:27;
18:25,26,28-30,34; 20:8; 21:41; 22:21; 27:58;
MARK 12:17; **LUKE** 4:20; 7:42; 9:42; 10:35;
12:59; 16:2; 19:8; 20:25; **ACTS** 4:33; 5:8; 7:9;
19:40; **ROM.** 2:6; 12:17; 13:7; **1 COR.** 7:3;
1 THESS. 5:15; **1 TIM.** 5:4; **2 TIM.** 4:8,14;
HEB. 12:11,16; 13:17; **1 PET.** 3:9; 4:5; **REV.**
18:6; 22:2,12

592. ἀποδιορίζω apodirizō
JUDE 1:19

593. ἀποδοκιμάζω apodokimazō
MATT. 21:42; **MARK** 8:31; 12:10; **LUKE**
9:22; 17:25; 20:17; 12:17; **1 PET.** 2:4,7

594. ἀποδοχή apodochē
1 TIM. 1:15; 4:9

595. ἀπόθεσις *apothesis*
1 PET. 3:21; **2 PET.** 1:14

596. ἀποθήκη *apothēkē*
MATT. 3:12; 6:26; 13:30; **LUKE** 3:17;
12:18,24

597. ἀποθησαυρίζω *apothēsaurizo*
1 TIM. 6:19

598. ἀποθλίβω *apothlibō*
LUKE 8:45

599. ἀποθνήσκω *apothnēskō*
MATT. 8:32; 9:24; 22:24,27; 26:35; **MARK**
5:35,39; 9:26; 12:19-22; 15:44; **LUKE** 8:42,
52,53; 16:22; 20:28-32,36; **JOHN** 4:47,49;
6:49,50,58; 8:21,24,52,53; 11:14,16,25,
32,37,50,51; 12:24,33; 18:32; 19:7; 21:23;
ACTS 7:4; 9:37; 21:13; 25:11; **ROM.** 5:6-8,
15; 6:2, 7,8,9,10; 7:2,3,6,9; 8:13,34; 14:7,8,
9,15; **1 COR.** 8:11; 9:15; 15:3,22,31,32,
36; **2 COR.** 5:14,15; 6:9; **GAL.** 2:19,21;
PHIL. 1:21; **COL.** 2:20; 3:3; **1 THESS.** 4:14;
5:10; **HEB.** 7:8; 9:27; 10:28; 11:4,13,21,37;
JUDE 1:12; **REV.** 3:2; 8:9,11; 9:6; 14:13;
16:3

600. ἀποκαθίστημι *apokathistēmi*
MATT. 12:13; 17:11; **MARK** 3:5; 8:25; 9:12;
LUKE 6:10; **ACTS** 1:6; **HEB.** 13:19

601. ἀποκαλύπτω *apokaluptō*
MATT. 10:26; 11:25,27; 16:17; **LUKE** 2:35;
10:21,22; 12:2; 17:30; **JOHN** 12:38; **ROM.**
1:17,18; 8:18; **1 COR.** 2:10; 3:13; 14:30; **GAL.**
1:16; 3:23; **EPH.** 3:5; **PHIL.** 3:15; **2 THESS.**
2:3,6,8; **1 PET.** 1:5,12; 5:1

602. ἀποκάλυψις *apokalupsis*
LUKE 2:32; **ROM.** 2:5; 8:19; 16:25; **1 COR.**
1:7; 14:6,26; **2 COR.** 12:1,7; **GAL.** 1:12; 2:2;
EPH. 1:17; 3:3; **2 THESS.** 1:7; **1 PET.** 1:7,13;
4:13; **REV.** 1:1

603. ἀποκαραδοκία *apokaradokia*
ROM. 8:19; **PHIL.** 1:20

604. ἀποκαταλλάσσω,
ἀποκαταλλάττω
apokatallassō, apokatallattō
EPH. 2:16; **COL.** 1:20,21

605. ἀπόκατάστασις *apokatastasis*
ACTS 3:21

606. ἀπόκειμαι *apokeimai*
LUKE 19:20; **COL.** 1:5; **2 TIM.** 4:8; **HEB.**
9:27

607. ἀποκεφαλίζω *apokephalizo*
MATT. 14:10; **MARK** 6:16,27; **LUKE** 9:9

608. ἀποκλείω *apokleiō*
LUKE 13:25

609. ἀποκόπτω *apokoptō*
MARK 9:43,45; **JOHN** 18:10,26; **ACTS** 27:32;
GAL. 5:12

610. ἀπόκριμα *apokrima*
2 COR. 1:9

611. ἀποκρίνομαι *apokrinomai*
MATT. 3:15; 4:4; 8:8; 11:4,25; 12:38,39,48;
13:11,37; 14:28; 15:3,13,15,23,24,26,28;
16:2,16,17; 17:4,11,17; 19:4,27; 20:13,22;
21:21,24,27,29,30; 22:1,29,46; 24:4; 25:9,
12,26,37,40,44,45; 26:23,25,33,62,63,66;
27:12,14,21,25; 28:5; **MARK** 3:33; 5:9; 6:37;
7:6,28; 8:4,28,29; 9:5,12,17,19,38; 10:3,5,20,
24,29,51; 11:14,22,29,30,33; 12:17,24,28,
29,34,35; 13:2,5; 14:20,40,48,60,61; 15:2,4,
5,9,12; **LUKE** 1:19,35,60; 3:11,16; 4:4,8,12;
5:5,22,31; 6:3; 7:22,40,43; 8:21,50; 9:19,20,
41,49; 10:27,28,41; 11:7,45; 13:2,8,14,15,25;
14:3,5; 15:29; 17:17,20,37; 19:40; 20:3,7,
24,34,39; 22:51,68; 23:3,9,40; 24:18; **JOHN**
1:21,26,48-50; 2:18,19; 3:3,5,9 10,27; 4:10,
13,17; 5:7,11,17,19; 6:7,26,29,43,68,70; 7:16,
20,21,46,47,52; 8:14,19,33,34,39,48,49,54; 9:3,
11,20,25,27,30,34,36; 10:25,32-34; 11:9; 12:23,
30,34; 13:7,8,26,36,38; 14:23; 16:31; 18:5,8,20,
22,23,30,34-37; 19:7,11,15,22; 20:28; 21:5;
ACTS 3:12; 4:19; 5:8,29; 8:24,34,37; 9:13;
10:46; 11:9; 15:13; 19:15; 21:13; 22:8,28;

24:10, 25; 25:4,9,12,16; COL. 4:6; REV.
7:13

612. ἀπόκρισις apokrisis
LUKE 2:47; 20:26; JOHN 1:22; 19:9

613. ἀποκρύπτω apokruptō
MATT. 11:25; 25:18; LUKE 10:21; 1 COR.
2:7; EPH. 3:9; COL. 1:26

614. ἀπόκρυφος apokruphos
MARK 4:22; LUKE 8:17; COL. 2:3

615. ἀποκτείνω apokteinō
MATT. 10:28; 14:5; 16:21; 17:23; 21:35,38,39;
22:6; 23:34,37; 24:9; 26:4; MARK 3:4; 6:19;
8:31; 9:31; 10:34; 12:5,7,8; 14:1; LUKE 9:22;
11:47-49; 12:4,5; 13:4,31,34; 18:33; 20:14,15;
JOHN 5:16,18; 7:1,19,20,25; 8:22,37,40; 11:53;
12:10; 16:2; 18:31; ACTS 3:15; 7:52; 21:31;
23:12,14; 27:42; ROM. 7:11; 11:3; 2 COR. 3:6;
EPH. 2:16; 1 THESS. 2:15; REV. 2:13,23;
6:8,11; 9:5,15,18,20; 11:5,7,13; 13:10,15; 19:21

616. ἀποκυέω apokueō
JAMES 1:15,18

**617. ἀποκυλίνδω, ἀποκυλίω
apokulindō, apokuliō**
MATT. 28:2; MARK 16:3,4; LUKE 24:2

618. ἀπολαμβάνω apolambanō
MARK 7:33; LUKE 6:34; 15:27; 16:25; 18:30;
23:41; ROM. 1:27; GAL. 4:5; COL. 3:24;
2 JOHN 1:8; 3 JOHN 1:8

619. ἀπόλαυσις apolausis
1 TIM. 6:17; HEB. 11:25

620. ἀπολείπω apoleipō
2 TIM. 4:13,20; HEB. 4:6,9; 10:26; JUDE 1:6

621. ἀπολείχω apoleichō
LUKE 16:21

622. ἀπόλλυμι apollumi
MATT. 2:13; 5:29,30; 8:25; 9:17; 10:6,28,39,42;
12:14; 15:24; 16:25; 18:11,14; 21:41; 22:7;

26:52; 27:20; MARK 1:24; 2:22; 3:6; 4:38;
8:35; 9:22,41; 11:18; 12:9; LUKE 4:34; 5:37;
6:9; 8:24; 9:24,25,56; 11:51; 13:3,5,33;
15:4,6,8,9,17,24,32; 17:27,29,33; 19:10,47;
20:16; 21:18; JOHN 3:15,16; 6:12,27,39;
10:10,28; 11:50; 12:25; 17:12; 18:9,14; ACTS
5:37; ROM. 2:12; 14:15; 1 COR. 1:18,19; 8:11;
10:9,10; 15:18; 2 COR. 2:15; 4:3,9; 2 THESS.
2:10; HEB. 1:11; JAMES 1:11; 4:12; 1 PET.
1:7; 2 PET. 3:6,9; 2 JOHN 1:8; JUDE 1:5,11

623. Ἀπολλύων Apolluōn
REV. 9:11

624. Ἀπολλωνία Apollōnia
ACTS 17:1

625. Ἀπολλώς Apollōs
ACTS 18:24; 19:1; 1 COR. 1:12; 3:4-6,22; 4:6;
16:12; TITUS 3:13

626. ἀπολογέομαι apologeomai
LUKE 12:11; 21:14; ACTS 19:33; 24:10; 25:8;
26:1,2,24; ROM. 2:15; 2 COR. 12:19

627. ἀπολογία apologia
ACTS 22:1; 25:16; 1 COR. 9:3; 2 COR. 7:11;
PHIL. 1:7,17; 2 TIM. 4:16; 1 PET. 3:15

628. ἀπολούω apolouō
ACTS 22:16; 1 COR. 6:11

629. ἀπολύτρωσις apolutrōsis
LUKE 21:28; ROM. 3:24; 8:23; 1 COR. 1:30;
EPH. 1:7,14; 4:30; COL. 1:14; HEB. 9:15;
11:35

630. ἀπολύω apoluō
MATT. 1:19; 5:31,32; 14:15,22,23; 15:23,32,39;
18:27; 19:3,7-9; 27:15,17,21,26; MARK
6:36,45; 8:3,9; 10:2,4,11,12; 15:6,9,11,15;
LUKE 2:29; 6:37; 8:38; 9:12; 13:12; 14:4;
16:18; 22:68; 23:16-18,20,22,25; JOHN 18:39;
19:10,12; ACTS 3:13; 4:21,23; 5:40; 13:3;
15:30,33; 16:35,36; 17:9; 19:41; 23:22; 26:32;
28:18,25; HEB. 13:23

631. ἀπομάσσω apomassō
LUKE 10:11

632. ἀπονέμω *aponemō*
1 PET. 3:7

633. ἀπονίπτω *aponiptō*
MATT. 27:24

634. ἀποπίπτω *apopiptō*
ACTS 9:18

635. ἀποπλανάω *apoplanaō*
MARK 13:22; 1 TIM. 6:10

636. ἀποπλέω *apopleō*
ACTS 13:4; 14:26; 20:15; 27:1

637. ἀποπλύνω *apoplunō*
LUKE 5:2

638. ἀποπνίγω *apopnigō*
MATT. 13:7; LUKE 8:33

639. ἀπορέω *aporeō*
JOHN 13:22; ACTS 25:20; 2 COR. 4:8;
GAL. 4:20

640. ἀπορία *aporia*
LUKE 21:25

641. ἀπορρίπτω *aporriptō*
ACTS 27:43

642. ἀπορφανίζω *aporphanizō*
1 THESS. 2:17

643. ἀποσκευάζω *aposkeuazō*
ACTS 21:15

644. ἀποσκίασμα *aposkiasma*
JAMES 1:17

645. ἀποσπάω *apospaō*
MATT. 26:51; LUKE 22:41; ACTS 20:30; 21:1

646. ἀποστασία *apostasia*
ACTS 21:21; 2 THESS. 2:3

647. ἀποστάσιον *apostasion*
MATT. 5:31; 19:7; MARK 10:4

648. ἀποστεγάζω *apostegazō*
MARK 2:4

649. ἀποστέλλω *apostellō*
MATT. 2:16; 10:5,16,40; 11:10; 13:41; 14:35;
15:24; 20:2; 21:1,3,34,36,37; 22:3,4,16;
23:34,37; 24:31; 27:19; MARK 1:2; 3:14,31;
4:29; 5:10; 6:7,17,27; 8:26; 9:37; 11:1,3; 12:2-
6,13; 13:27; 14:13; LUKE 1:19,26; 4:18,43;
7:3,20,27; 9:2,48,52; 10:1,3,16; 11:49; 13:34;
14:17,32; 19:14,29,32; 20:10,20; 22:8,35; 24:49;
JOHN 1:6,19,24; 3:17,28,34; 4:38; 5:33,36,38;
6:29,57; 7:29,32; 8:42; 9:7; 10:36; 11:3,42;
17:3,8,18,21,23,25; 18:24; 20:21; ACTS 3:20,
26; 5:21; 7:14,34,35; 8:14; 9:17,38; 10:8,17,
20,21,36; 11:11,13,30; 13:15,26; 15:27; 16:35,
36; 19:22; 26:17; 28:28; ROM. 10:15; 1 COR.
1:17; 2 COR. 12:17; 2 TIM. 4:12; HEB. 1:14;
1 PET. 1:12; 1 JOHN 4:9,10,14; REV. 1:1; 5:6;
22:6

650. ἀποστερέω *apostereō*
MARK 10:19; 1 COR. 6:7,8; 7:5; 1 TIM. 6:5;
JAMES 5:4

651. ἀποστολή *apostolē*
ACTS 1:25; ROM. 1:5; 1 COR. 9:2; GAL. 2:8

652. ἀπόστολος *apostolos*
MATT. 10:2; MARK 6:30; LUKE 6:13; 9:10;
11:49; 17:5; 22:14; 24:10; JOHN 13:16;
ACTS 1:2,26; 2:37,42,43; 4:33,35-37; 5:2,
12,18,29,34,40; 6:6; 8:1,14,18; 9:27; 11:1;
14:4,14; 15:2,4,6,22,23,33; 16:4; ROM. 1:1;
11:13; 16:7; 1 COR. 1:1; 4:9; 9:1,2,5; 12:28,29;
15:7,9; 2 COR. 1:1; 8:23; 11:5,13; 12:11,12;
GAL. 1:1,17,19; EPH. 1:1; 2:20; 3:5; 4:11;
PHIL. 2:25; COL. 1:1; 1 THESS. 2:6; 1 TIM.
1:1; 2:7; 2 TIM. 1:1,11; TITUS 1:1; HEB. 3:1;
1 PET. 1:1; 2 PET. 1:1; 3:2; JUDE 1:17; REV.
2:2; 18:20; 21:14

653. ἀποστοματίζω *apostomatizō*
LUKE 11:53

654. ἀποστρέφω *apostrephō*
MATT. 5:42; 26:52; 27:3; LUKE 23:14; ACTS
3:26; ROM. 11:26; 2 TIM. 1:15; 4:4; TITUS
1:14; HEB. 12:25

655. ἀποστυγέω *apostugeō*
ROM. 12:9

656. ἀποσυνάγωγος *aposunagōgos*
JOHN 9:22; 12:42; 16:2

657. ἀποτάσσω, ἀποτάττω
    apotassō, apotattō
MARK 6:46; LUKE 9:61; 14:33; ACTS
18:18,21; 2 COR. 2:13

658. ἀποτελέω *apoteleō*
JAMES 1:15

659. ἀποτίθημι *apotithēmi*
ACTS 7:58; ROM. 13:12; EPH. 4:22,25; COL.
3:8; HEB. 12:1; JAMES 1:21; 1 PET. 2:1

660. ἀποτινάσσω *apotinassō*
LUKE 9:5; ACTS 28:5

661. ἀποτίνω, ἀποτίω *apotinō, apotiō*
PHILE. 1:19

662. ἀποτολμάω *apotolmaō*
ROM. 10:20

663. ἀποτομία *apotomia*
ROM. 11:22

664. ἀποτόμως *apotomōs*
2 COR. 13:10; TITUS 1:13

665. ἀποτρέπω *apotrepō*
2 TIM. 3:5

666. ἀπουσία *apousia*
PHIL. 2:12

667. ἀποφέρω *apopherō*
MARK 15:1; LUKE 16:22; 1 COR. 16:3;
REV. 17:3; 21:10

668. ἀποφεύγω *apopheugō*
2 PET. 1:4; 2:18,20

669. ἀποφθέγγομαι *apophtheggomai*
ACTS 2:4,14; 26:25

670. ἀποφορτίζομαι *apophortizomai*
ACTS 21:3

671. ἀπόχρησις *apochrēsis*
COL. 2:22

672. ἀποχωρέω *apochōreō*
MATT. 7:23; LUKE 9:39; ACTS 13:13

673. ἀποχωρίζω *apochōrizō*
ACTS 15:39; REV. 6:14

674. ἀποψύχω *apopsuchō*
LUKE 21:26

675. Ἀππίος *Appios*
    (only in Appii Forum)
ACTS 28:15

676. ἀπρόσιτος *aprositos*
1 TIM. 6:16

677. ἀπρόσκοπος *aproskopos*
ACTS 24:16; 1 COR. 10:32; PHIL. 1:10

678. ἀπροσωπολήπτως
    aprosōpolēptōs
1 PET. 1:17

679. ἄπταιστος *aptaistos*
JUDE 1:24

680. ἅπτομαι *haptomai*
MATT. 8:3,15; 9:20,21,29; 14:36; 17:7; 20:34;
MARK 1:41; 3:10; 5:27,28,30,31; 6:56; 7:33;
8:22; 10:13; LUKE 5:13; 6:19; 7:14,39; 8:44-47;
JOHN 20:17; 1 COR. 7:1; 2 COR. 6:17; COL.
2:21; 1 JOHN 5:18

681. ἅπτω *haptō*
LUKE 8:16; 11:33; 15:8; 22:55

682. Ἀπφία *Apphia*
PHILE. 1:2

683. ἀπωθέω *apōtheō*
ACTS 7:27,39; 13:46; **ROM.** 11:1,2; **1 TIM.**
1:19

684. ἀπώλεια *apōleia*
MATT. 7:13; 26:8; **MARK** 14:4; **JOHN** 17:12;
ACTS 8:20; 25:16; **ROM.** 9:22; **PHIL.** 1:28;
3:19; **2 THESS.** 2:3; **1 TIM.** 6:9; **HEB.** 10:39
2 PET. 2:1-3; 3:7,16; **REV.** 17:8,11

685. ἀρά *ara*   noun
ROM. 3:14

686. ἄρα *ara*   infer. particle
MATT. 7:20; 12:28; 17:16; 18:1; 19:25,27;
24:45; **MARK** 4:41; 11:13; **LUKE** 1:66; 8:25;
11:20,48; 12:42; 22:23; **ACTS** 7:1; 8:22; 11:18;
12:18; 17:27; 21:38; **ROM.** 5:18; 7:3,21,25;
8:1,12; 9:16,18; 10:17; 14:12,19; **1 COR.** 5:10;
7:14; 15:14,15,18; **2 COR.** 1:17; 5:14; 7:12;
GAL. 2:21; 3:7,29; 4:31; 5:11; 6:10; **EPH.** 2:19;
1 THESS. 5:6; **2 THESS.** 2:15; **HEB.** 4:9; 12:8

687. ἄρα *ara*   inter. particle
LUKE 18:8; ACTS 8:30; GAL. 2:17

688. Ἀραβια *Arabia*
GAL. 1:17; 4:25

689. Ἀράμ *Aram*
MATT. 1:3,4; LUKE 3:33

690. Ἄραψ *Araps*
ACTS 2:11

691. ἀργέω *argeō*
2 PET. 2:3

692. ἀργός *argos*
MATT. 12:36; 20:3,6; **1 TIM.** 5:13; **TITUS**
1:12; **2 PET.** 1:8

693. ἀργύρεος *argureos*
ACTS 19:24; 2 TIM. 2:20; REV. 9:20

694. ἀργύριον *argurion*
MATT. 25:18,27; 26:15; 27:3,5,6,9; 28:12,15;
MARK 14:11; **LUKE** 9:3; 19:15,23; 22:5;

ACTS 3:6; 7:16; 8:20; 19:19; 20:33; **1 PET.**
1:18

695. ἀργυροκόπος *argurokopos*
ACTS 19:24

696. ἄργυρος *arguros*
MATT. 10:9; **ACTS** 17:29; **1 COR.** 3:12;
JAMES 5:3; **REV.** 18:12

697. Ἄρειος Πάγος *Areios Pagos*
ACTS 17:19,22

698. Ἀρεοπαγίτης *Areopagitēs*
ACTS 17:34

699. ἀπέσκεια *areskeia*
COL. 1:10

700. ἀρέσκω *areskō*
MATT. 14:6; **MARK** 6:22; **ACTS** 6:5; **ROM.**
8:8; 15:1-3; **1 COR.** 7:32-34; 10:33; **GAL.** 1:10;
1 THESS. 2:4,15; 4:1; **2 TIM.** 2:4

701. ἀρεστός *arestos*
JOHN 8:29; ACTS 6:2; 12:3; 1 JOHN 3:22

702. Ἀρέτας *Aretas*
2 COR. 11:32

703. ἀρετή *aretē*
PHIL. 4:8; 1 PET. 2:9; 2 PET. 1:3,5

704. ἀρήν *arēn*
LUKE 10:3

705. ἀριθμέω *arithmeō*
MATT. 10:30; LUKE 12:7; REV. 7:9

706. ἀριθμός *arithmos*
LUKE 22:3; **JOHN** 6:10; **ACTS** 4:4; 5:36; 6:7;
11:21; 16:5; **ROM.** 9:27; **REV.** 5:11; 7:4; 9:16;
13:17,18; 15:2; 20:8

707. Ἀριμαθαία *Arimathaia*
MATT. 27:57; **MARK** 15:43; **LUKE** 23:51;
JOHN 19:38

708. Ἀρίσταρχος *Aristarchos*
ACTS 19:29; 20:4; 27:2; COL. 4:10; PHILE.
1:24

709. ἀριστάω *aristaō*
LUKE 11:37; JOHN 21:12,15

710. ἀριστερός *aristeros*
MATT. 6:13; LUKE 23:33; 2 COR. 6:7

711. Ἀριστόβουλος *Aristoboulos*
ROM. 16:10

712. ἄριστον *ariston*
MATT. 22:4; LUKE 11:38; 14:12

713. ἀρκετός *arketos*
MATT. 6:34; 10:25; 1 PET. 4:3

714. ἀρκέω *arkeō*
MATT. 25:9; LUKE 3:14; JOHN 6:7; 14:8;
2 COR. 12:9; 1 TIM. 6:8; HEB. 13:5; 3 JOHN
1:10

715. ἄρκτος *arktos*
REV. 13:2

716. ἅρμα *harma*
ACTS 8:28,29,38; REV. 9:9

717. Ἀρμαγεδδών *Armageddōn*
REV. 16:16

718. ἁρμόζω *harmozō*
2 COR. 11:2

719. ἁρμός *harmos*
HEB. 4:12

720. ἀρνέομαι *arneomai*
MATT. 10:33; 26:70,72; MARK 14:68,70;
LUKE 8:45; 12:9; 22:57; JOHN 1:20; 18:25,27;
ACTS 3:13,14; 4:16; 7:35; 1 TIM. 5:8; 2 TIM.
2:12,13; 3:5; TITUS 1:16; 2:12; HEB. 11:24;
2 PET. 2:1; 1 JOHN 2:22,23; JUDE 1:4; REV.
2:13; 3:8

721. ἀρνίον *arnion*
JOHN 21:15; REV. 5:6,8,12,13; 6:1,16;
7:9,10,14,17; 12:11; 13:8,11; 14:1,4,10; 15:3;
17:14; 19:7,9; 21:9,14,22,23,27; 22:1,3

722. ἀροτριάω *arotriaō*
LUKE 17:7; 1 COR. 9:10

723. ἄροτρον *arotron*
LUKE 9:62

724. ἁρπαγή *harpagē*
MATT. 23:25; LUKE 11:39; HEB. 10:34

725. ἁρπαγμός *harpagmos*
PHIL. 2:6

726. ἁρπάζω *harpazō*
MATT. 11:12; 13:19; JOHN 6:15; 10:12,28,29;
ACTS 8:39; 23:10; 2 COR. 12:2,4; 1 THESS.
4:17; JUDE 1:23; REV. 12:5

727. ἅρπαξ *harpax*
MATT. 7:15; LUKE 18:11; 1 COR. 5:10,11;
6:10

728. ἀρραβών *arrabōn*
2 COR. 1:22; 5:5; EPH. 1:14

729. ἄρραφος *arraphos*
JOHN 19:23

730. ἄρρην *arrēn*
MATT. 19:4; MARK 10:6; LUKE 2:23; ROM.
1:27; GAL. 3:28; REV. 12:5,13

731. ἄρρητος *arrētos*
2 COR. 12:4

732. ἄρρωστος *arrōstos*
MATT. 14:14; MARK 6:5,13; 16:18; 1 COR.
11:30

733. ἀρσενοκοίτης *arsenokoitēs*
1 COR. 6:9; 1 TIM. 1:10

734. Ἀρτεμᾶς *Artemas*
TITUS 3:12

735. Ἄρτεμις Artemis
ACTS 19:24,27,28,34,35

736. ἀρτέμων artemōn
ACTS 27:40

737. ἄρτι arti
MATT. 3:15; 9:18; 11:12; 23:39; 26:29,53,64;
JOHN 1:51; 2:10; 5:17; 9:19,25; 13:7,19,33,37;
14:7; 16:12,24,31; 1 COR. 4:11,13; 8:7; 13:12;
15:6; 16:7; GAL. 1:9,10; 4:20; 1 THESS. 3:6;
2 THESS. 2:7; 1 PET. 1:6,8; 1 JOHN 2:9;
REV. 12:10

738. ἀρτιγέννητος artigennētos
1 PET. 2:2

739. ἄρτιος artios
2 TIM. 3:17

740. ἄρτος artos
MATT. 4:3,4; 6:11; 7:9; 12:4; 14:17,19;
15:2,26,33,34,36; 16:5,7-12; 26:26; MARK
2:26; 3:20; 6:8,36-38,41,44,52; 7:2,5,27; 8:4-
6,14,16,17,19; 14:22; LUKE 4:3,4; 6:4; 7:33;
9:3,13,16; 11:3,5,11; 14:1,15; 15:17; 22:19;
24:30,35; JOHN 6:5,7,9,11,13,23,26,31-
35,41,48,50,51,58; 13:18; 21:9,13; ACTS
2:42,46; 20:7,11; 27:35; 1 COR. 10:16,17;
11:23,26-28; 2 COR. 9:10; 2 THESS. 3:8,12;
HEB. 9:2

741. ἀρτύω artuō
MARK 9:50; LUKE 14:34; COL. 4:6

742. Ἀρφαξάδ Arphaxad
LUKE 3:36

743. ἀρχάγγελος archaggelos
1 THESS. 4:16; JUDE 1:9

744. ἀρχαῖος archaios
MARK 5:21,27,33; LUKE 9:8,19; ACTS
15:7,21; 21:16; 2 COR. 5:17; 2 PET. 2:5; REV.
12:9; 20:2

745. Ἀρχέλαος Archelaos
MATT. 2:22

746. ἀρχή archē
MATT. 19:4,8; 24:8,21; MARK 1:1; 10:6;
13:8,19; LUKE 1:2; 12:11; 20:20; JOHN 1:1,2;
2:11; 6:64; 8:25,44; 15:27; 16:4; ACTS 10:11;
11:5,15; 26:4; ROM. 8:38; 1 COR. 15:24; EPH.
1:21; 3:10; 6:12; PHIL. 4:15; COL. 1:16,18;
2:10,15; 2 THESS. 2:13; TITUS 3:1; HEB.
1:10; 2:3; 3:14; 5:12; 6:1; 7:3; 2 PET. 3:4;
1 JOHN 1:1; 2:7,13,14,24; 3:8,11; 2 JOHN
1:5,6; JUDE 1:6; REV. 1:8; 3:14; 21:6; 22:13

747. ἀρχηγός archēgos
ACTS 5:31; 13:15; HEB. 2:10; 12:2

748. ἀρχιερατικός archieratikos
ACTS 4:6

749. ἀρχιερεύς archiereus
MATT. 2:4; 16:21; 20:18; 21:15,23,45;
26:3,14,47,51,57-59,62,63,65; 27:1,3,6,
12,20,41,62; 28:11; MARK 2:26; 8:31; 10:33;
11:18,27; 14:1,10,43,47,53-55,60,61,63,66;
15:1,3,10,11,31; LUKE 3:2; 9:22; 19:47;
20:1,19; 22:2,4,50,52,54,66; 23:4,10,13,23;
24:20; JOHN 7:32,45; 11:47,49,51,57; 12:10;
18:3,10,13,15,16,19,22,24,26,35; 19:6,15,21;
ACTS 4:6,23; 5:17,21,24,27; 7:1; 9:1,14,21;
19:14; 22:5,30; 23:2,4,5,14; 24:1; 25:2,15;
26:10,12; HEB. 2:17; 3:1; 4:14,15; 5:1,5,10;
6:20; 7:26-28; 8:1,3; 9:7,11,25; 13:11

750. ἀρχιποίμην archipoimēn
1 PET. 5:4

751. Ἄρχιππος Archippos
COL. 4:17; PHILE. 1:2

752. ἀρχισυνάγωγος archisunagōgos
MARK 5:22,35,36,38; LUKE 8:49; 13:14;
ACTS 13:15; 18:8,17

753. ἀρχιτέκτων architektōn
1 COR. 3:10

754. ἀρχιτελώνης architelōnēs
LUKE 19:2

755. ἀρχιτρίκλινος architriklinos
JOHN 2:8,9

756. ἄρχομαι archomai
(Mid. of ἄρχω)
MATT. 4:17; 11:7,20; 12:1; 14:30; 16:21,22;
18:24; 20:8; 24:49; 26:22,37,74; MARK 1:45;
2:23; 4:1; 5:17,20; 6:2,7,34,55; 8:11,31,32;
10:28,32,41,47; 11:15; 12:1; 13:5; 14:19,33,
65,69,71; 15:8,18; LUKE 3:8,23; 4:21; 5:21;
7:15,24,38,49; 9:12; 11:29,53; 12:1,45; 13:25,26;
14:9,18,29,30; 15:14,24; 19:37,45; 20:9; 21:28;
22:23; 23:2,5,30; 24:27,47; JOHN 8:9; 13:5;
ACTS 1:1,22; 2:4; 8:35; 10:37; 11:4,15; 18:26;
24:2; 27:35; 2 COR. 3:1; 1 PET. 4:17

757. ἄρχω archō
MARK 10:42; ROM. 15:12

758. ἄρχων archōn
MATT. 9:18,23,34; 12:24; 20:25; MARK 3:22;
LUKE 8:41; 11:15; 12:58; 14:1; 18:18;
23:13,35; 24:20; JOHN 3:1; 7:26,48; 12:31,42;
14:30; 16:11; ACTS 3:17; 4:5,8,26; 7:27,35;
13:27; 14:5; 16:19; 23:5; ROM. 13:3; 1 COR.
2:6,8; EPH. 2:2; REV. 1:5

759. ἄρωμα arōma
MARK 16:1; LUKE 23:56; 24:1; JOHN
19:40

760. Ἀσά Asa
MATT. 1:7,8

761. ἀσάλευτος asaleutos
ACTS 27:41; HEB. 12:28

762. ἄσβεστος asbestos
MATT. 3:12; MARK 9:43,45; LUKE 3:17

763. ἀσέβεια asebeia
ROM. 1:18; 11:26; 2 TIM. 2:16; TITUS 2:12;
JUDE 1:15,18

764. ἀσεβέω asebeō
2 PET. 2:6; JUDE 1:15

765. ἀσεβής asebēs
ROM. 4:5; 5:6; 1 TIM. 1:9; 1 PET. 4:18;
2 PET. 2:5; 3:7; JUDE 1:4,15

766. ἀσέλγεια aselgeia
MARK 7:22; ROM. 13:13; 2 COR. 12:21;
GAL. 5:19; EPH. 4:19; 1 PET. 4:3; 2 PET.
2:7,18; JUDE 1:4

767. ἄσημος asēmos
ACTS 21:39

768. Ἀσήρ Asēr
LUKE 2:36; REV. 7:6

769. ἀσθένεια astheneia
MATT. 8:17; LUKE 5:15; 8:2; 13:11,12;
JOHN 5:5; 11:4; ACTS 28:9; ROM. 6:19; 8:26;
1 COR. 2:3; 15:43; 2 COR. 11:30; 12:5,9,10;
13:4; GAL. 4:13; 1 TIM. 5:23; HEB. 4:15; 5:2;
7:28; 11:34

770. ἀσθενέω astheneō
MATT. 10:8; 25:36; MARK 6:56; LUKE 4:40;
7:10; 9:2; JOHN 4:46; 5:3,7; 6:2; 11:1-3,6;
ACTS 9:37; 19:12; 20:35; ROM. 4:19; 8:3;
14:1,2,21; 1 COR. 8:9,11,12; 2 COR. 11:21,29;
12:10; 13:3,4,9; PHIL. 2:26,27; 2 TIM. 4:20;
JAMES 5:14

771. ἀσθένημα asthenēma
ROM. 15:1

772. ἀσθενής asthenēs
MATT. 25:39,43,44; 26:41; MARK 14:38;
LUKE 10:9; ACTS 4:9; 5:15,16; ROM. 5:6;
1 COR. 1:25,27; 4:10; 8:7,10; 9:22; 11:30;
12:22; 2 COR. 10:10; GAL. 4:9; 1 THESS.
5:14; HEB. 7:18; 1 PET. 3:7

773. Ἀσία Asia
ACTS 2:9; 6:9; 16:6; 19:10,22,26,27;
20:4,16,18; 21:27; 24:18; 27:2; 1 COR. 16:19;
2 COR. 1:8; 2 TIM. 1:15; 1 PET. 1:1; REV.
1:4,11

774. Ἀσιανός Asianos
ACTS 20:4

775. Ἀσιάρχης Asiarchēs
ACTS 19:31

776. ἀσιτία *asitia*
ACTS 27:21

777. ἄσιτος *asitos*
ACTS 27:33

778. ἀσκέω *askeō*
ACTS 24:16

779. ἀσκός *askos*
MATT. 9:17; MARK 2:22; LUKE 5:37,38

780. ἀσμένως *asmenōs*
ACTS 2:41; 21:17

781. ἄσοφος *asophos*
EPH. 5:15

782. ἀσπάζομαι *aspazomai*
MATT. 5:47; 10:12; MARK 9:15; 15:18;
LUKE 1:40; 10:4; ACTS 18:22; 20:1; 21:6,7,19;
25:13; ROM. 16:3,5-16,21-23; 1 COR.
16:19,20; 2 COR. 13:12,13; PHIL. 4:21,22;
COL. 4:10,12,14,15; 1 THESS. 5:26; 2 TIM.
4:19,21; TITUS 3:15; PHILE. 1:23; HEB.
11:13; 13:24; 1 PET. 5:13,14; 2 JOHN 1:13;
3 JOHN 1:14

783. ἀσπασμός *aspasmos*
MATT. 23:7; MARK 12:38; LUKE 1:29,41,44;
11:43; 20:46; 1 COR. 16:21; COL. 4:18;
2 THESS. 3:17

784. ἄσπιλος *aspilos*
1 TIM. 6:14; JAMES 1:27; 1 PET. 1:19;
2 PET. 3:14

785. ἀσπίς *aspis*
ROM. 3:13

786. ἄσπονδος *aspondos*
ROM. 1:31; 2 TIM. 3:3

787. ἀσσάριον *assarion*
MATT. 10:29; LUKE 12:6

788. ἆσσον *asson*
ACTS 27:13

789. Ἄσσος *Assos*
ACTS 20:13,14

790. ἀστατέω *astateō*
1 COR. 4:11

791. ἀστεῖος *asteios*
ACTS 7:20; HEB. 11:23

792. ἀστήρ *astēr*
MATT. 2:2,7,9,10; 24:29; MARK 13:25;
1 COR. 15:41; JUDE 1:13; REV. 1:16,20;
2:1,28; 3:1; 6:13; 8:10-12; 9:1; 12:1,4; 22:16

793. ἀστήρικτος *astēriktos*
2 PET. 2:14; 3:16

794. ἄστοργος *astorgos*
ROM. 1:31; 2 TIM. 3:3

795. ἀστοχέω *astocheō*
1 TIM. 1:6; 6:21; 2 TIM. 2:18

796. ἀστραπή *astrapē*
MATT. 24:27; 28:3; LUKE 10:18; 11:36;
17:24; REV. 4:5; 8:5; 11:19; 16:18

797. ἀστράπτω *astraptō*
LUKE 17:24; 24:4

798. ἄστρον *astron*
LUKE 21:25; ACTS 7:43; 27:20; HEB. 11:12

799. Ἀσύγκριτος *Asugkritos*
ROM. 16:14

800. ἀσύμφωνος *asumphōnos*
ACTS 28:25

801. ἀσύνετος *asunetos*
MATT. 15:16; MARK 7:18; ROM. 1:21,31;
10:19

802. ἀσύνθετος *asunthetos*
ROM. 1:31

803. ἀσφάλεια *asphaleia*
LUKE 1:4; ACTS 5:23; 1 THESS. 5:3

804. ἀσφαλής *asphalēs*
ACTS 21:34; 22:30; 25:26; PHIL. 3:1; HEB.
6:19

805. ἀσφαλίζω *asphalizō*
MATT. 27:64-66; ACTS 16:24

806. ἀσφαλῶς *asphalōs*
MARK 14:44; ACTS 2:36; 16:23

807. ἀσχημονέω *aschēmoneō*
1 COR. 7:36; 13:5

808. ἀσχημοσύνη *aschēmosunē*
ROM. 1:27; REV. 16:15

809. ἀσχήμων *aschēmōn*
1 COR. 12:23

810. ἀσωτία *asōtia*
EPH. 5:18; TITUS 1:6; 1 PET. 4:4

811. ἀσώτως *asōtōs*
LUKE 15:13

812. ἀτακτέω *atakteō*
2 THESS. 3:7

813. ἄτακτος *ataktos*
1 THESS. 5:14

814. ἀτάκτως *ataktōs*
2 THESS. 3:6,11

815. ἄτεκνος *ateknos*
LUKE 20:28-30

816. ἀτενίζω *atenizō*
LUKE 4:20; 22:56; ACTS 1:10; 3:4,12; 6:15;
7:55; 10:4; 13:9; 14:9 23:1; 2 COR. 3:7,13

817. ἄτερ *ater*
LUKE 22:6,35

818. ἀτιμάζω *atimazō*
LUKE 20:11; JOHN 8:49; ACTS 5:41; ROM.
1:24; 2:23; JAMES 2:6

819. ἀτιμία *atimia*
ROM. 1:26; 9:21; 1 COR. 11:14; 15:43;
2 COR. 6:8; 11:21; 2 TIM. 2:20

820. ἄτιμος *atimos*
MATT. 13:57; MARK 6:4; 1 COR. 4:10; 12:23

821. ἀτιμόω *atimoō*
MARK 12:4

822. ἀτμίς *atmis*
ACTS 2:19; JAMES 4:14

823. ἄτομος *atomos*
1 COR. 15:52

824. ἄτοπος *atopos*
LUKE 23:41; ACTS 28:6; 2 THESS. 3:2

825. Ἀττάλεια *Attaleia*
ACTS 14:25

826. αὐγάζω *augazō*
2 COR. 4:4

827. αὐγή *augē*
ACTS 20:11

828. Αὔγουστος *Augoustos*
LUKE 2:1

829. αὐθάδης *authadēs*
TITUS 1:7; 2 PET. 2:10

830. αὐθαίρετος *authairetos*
2 COR. 8:3,17

831. αὐθεντέω *authenteō*
1 TIM. 2:12

832. αὐλέω *auleō*
MATT. 11:17; LUKE 7:32; 1 COR. 14:7

833. αὐλή aulē
MATT. 26:3,58,69; MARK 14:54,66; 15:16;
LUKE 11:21; 22:55; JOHN 10:1,16; 18:15;
REV. 11:2

834. αὐλητής aulētēs
MATT. 9:23; REV. 18:22

835. αὐλίζομαι aulizomai
MATT. 21:17; LUKE 21:37

836. αὐλός aulos
1 COR. 14:7

837. αὔξω, αὐξάνω auxō, auxanō
MATT. 6:28; 13:32; MARK 4:8; LUKE 1:80;
2:40; 12:27; 13:19; JOHN 3:30; ACTS 6:7;
7:17; 12:24; 19:20; 1 COR. 3:6,7; 2 COR. 9:10;
10:15; EPH. 2:21; 4:15; COL. 1:10; 2:19;
1 PET. 2:2; 2 PET. 3:18

838. αὔξησις auxēsis
EPH. 4:16; COL. 2:19

839. αὔριον aurion
MATT. 6:30,34; LUKE 10:35; 12:28; 13:32,33;
ACTS 4:3,5; 23:15,20; 25:22; 1 COR. 15:32;
JAMES 4:13,14

840. αὐστηρός austēros
LUKE 19:21,22

841. αὐτάρκεια autarkeia
2 COR. 9:8; 1 TIM. 6:6

842. αὐτάρκης autarkēs
PHIL. 4:11

843. αὐτοκατάκριτος autokatakritos
TITUS 3:11

844. αὐτόματος automatos
MARK 4:28; ACTS 12:10

845. αὐτόπτης autoptēs
LUKE 1:2

846. αὐτός autos
MATT. 1:20; 2:16; 3:5,7; 5:3,4,10; 7:13; 10:11;
13:2,4; 16:21; 17:18; 21:19,41; 22:34; 24:32;
25:16; MARK 1:19; 2:15; 6:22,31; 7:25;
12:37,44; 13:28; 16:14; LUKE 1:57; 2:22,35,38;
6:42; 7:12,21; 10:9,10; 11:4; 14:32; 17:35;
19:23; 21:21; 24:18,39; JOHN 11:4; 12:7;
14:17; 15:2; 17:11; 18:28; ACTS 3:12; 9:37;
11:22; 14:1; ROM. 8:16; 9:17; 13:6; 2 COR.
2:3; 5:5; 13:11; 1 THESS. 5:23; HEB. 3:3; 9:19;
10:1; JAMES 3:9; 1 PET. 1:12; 2:24; 4:14;
2 PET. 1:5; 3 JOHN 1:12; REV. 17:9

847. αὐτοῦ autou
MATT. 26:36; ACTS 15:34; 18:19; 21:4

849. αὐτόχειρ autocheir
ACTS 27:19

850. αὐχμηρός auchmēros
2 PET. 1:19

851. ἀφαιρέω aphaireō
MATT. 26:51; MARK 14:47; LUKE 1:25;
10:42; 16:3; 22:50; ROM. 11:27; HEB. 10:4;
REV. 22:19

852. ἀφανής aphanēs
HEB. 4:13

853. ἀφανίζω aphanizō
MATT. 6:16,19,20; ACTS 13:41; JAMES 4:14

854. ἀφανισμός aphanismos
HEB. 8:13

855. ἄφαντος aphantos
LUKE 24:31

856. ἀφεδρών aphedrōn
MATT. 15:17; MARK 7:19

857. ἀφειδία apheidia
COL. 2:23

858. ἀφελότης aphelotēs
ACTS 2:46

859. ἄφεσις aphesis
MATT. 26:28; MARK 1:4; 3:29; LUKE
1:77,3:3; 4:18; 24:47; ACTS 2:38; 5:31; 10:43;
13:38; 26:18; EPH. 1:7; COL. 1:14; HEB. 9:22;
10:18

860. ἁφή haphē
EPH. 4:16; COL. 2:19

861. ἀφθαρσία aphtharsia
ROM. 2:7; 1 COR. 15:42,50,53,54; EPH. 6:24;
2 TIM. 1:10; TITUS 2:7

862. ἄφθαρτος aphthartos
ROM. 1:23; 1 COR. 9:25; 15:52; 1 TIM. 1:17;
1 PET. 1:4,23; 3:4

863. ἀφίημι aphiēmi
MATT. 3:15; 4:11,20,22; 5:24,40; 6:12,14,15;
7:4; 8:15,22; 9:2,5,6; 12:31,32; 13:30,36; 15:14;
18:12,21,27,32,35; 19:14,27,29; 22:22,25;
23:13,23,38; 24:2,40,41; 26:44,56; 27:49,50;
MARK 1:18,20,31,34; 2:5,7,9,10; 3:28; 4:12,36;
5:19,37; 7:8,12,27; 8:13; 10:14,28,29; 11:6,
16,25,26; 12:12,19-22; 13:2,34; 14:6,50;
15:36,37; LUKE 4:39; 5:11,20,21,23,24; 6:42;
7:47-49; 8:51; 9:60; 10:30; 11:4,42; 12:10,39;
13:8,35; 17:3,4,34-36; 18:16,28,29; 19:44; 21:6;
23:34; JOHN 4:3,28,52; 8:29; 10:12; 11:44,48;
12:7; 14:18,27; 16:28,32; 18:8; 20:23; ACTS
8:22; 14:17; ROM. 1:27; 4:7; 1 COR. 7:11-13;
HEB. 2:8; 6:1; JAMES 5:15; 1 JOHN 1:9;
2:12; REV. 2:4; 11:9

864. ἀφικνέομαι aphikneomai
ROM. 16:19

865. ἀφιλάγαθος aphilagathos
2 TIM. 3:3

866. ἀφιλάργυρος aphilarguros
1 TIM. 3:3; HEB. 13:5

867. ἄφιξις aphixis
ACTS 20:29

868. ἀφίστημι aphistēmi
LUKE 2:37; 4:13; 8:13; 13:27; ACTS 5:37,38;
12:10; 15:38; 19:9; 22:29; 2 COR. 12:8; 1 TIM.
4:1; 6:5; 2 TIM. 2:19; HEB. 3:12

869. ἄφνω aphnō
ACTS 2:2; 16:26; 28:6

870. ἀφόβως aphobōs
LUKE 1:74; 1 COR. 16:10; PHIL. 1:14; JUDE
1:12

871. ἀφομοιόω aphomoioō
HEB. 7:3

872. ἀφοράω aphoraō
PHIL. 2:23; HEB. 12:2

873. ἀφορίζω aphorizō
MATT. 13:49; 25:32; LUKE 6:22; ACTS
13:2,19:9; ROM. 1:1; 2 COR. 6:17; GAL. 1:15;
2:12

874. ἀφορμή aphormē
ROM. 7:8,11; 2 COR. 5:12; 11:12; GAL. 5:13;
1 TIM. 5:14

875. ἀφρίζω aphrizō
MARK 9:18,20

876. ἀφρός aphros
LUKE 9:39

877. ἀφροσύνη aphrosunē
MARK 7:22; 2 COR. 11:1,17,21

878. ἄφρων aphrōn
LUKE 11:40; 12:20; ROM. 2:20; 1 COR.
15:36; 2 COR. 11:16,19; 12:6,11; EPH. 5:17;
1 PET. 2:15

879. ἀφυπνόω aphupnoō
LUKE 8:23

880. ἄφωνος aphōnos
ACTS 8:32; 1 COR. 12:2; 14:10; 2 PET. 2:16

881. Ἄχαζ Achaz
MATT. 1:9

882. Ἀχαΐα Achaia
ACTS 18:12,27; 19:21; ROM. 15:26; 16:5;

1 COR. 16:15; **2 COR.** 1:1; 9:2; 11:10;
1 THESS. 1:7,8

883. Ἀχαϊκός *Achaikos*
1 COR. 16:17

884. ἀχάριστος *acharistos*
LUKE 6:35; **2 TIM.** 3:2

885. Ἀχείμ *Acheim*
MATT. 1:14

886. ἀχειροποίητος *acheiropoiētos*
MARK 14:58; **2 COR.** 5:1; **COL.** 2:11

887. ἀχλύς *achlus*
ACTS 13:11

888. ἀχρεῖος *achreios*
MATT. 25:30; **LUKE** 17:10

889. ἀχρειόω *achreioō*
ROM. 3:12

890. ἄχρηστος *achrēstos*
PHILE. 1:11

891. ἄχρι *achri*
MATT. 24:38; **LUKE** 1:20; 4:13; 17:27; 21:24;
ACTS 1:2; 2:29; 3:21; 7:18; 11:5; 13:6,11;
20:4,6,11; 22:4,22; 23:1; 26:22; 27:33; 28:15;
ROM. 1:13; 5:13; 8:22; 11:25; **1 COR.** 4:11;
11:26; 15:25; **2 COR.** 3:14; 10:13,14; **GAL.**
3:19; 4:2,19; **PHIL.** 1:5,6; **HEB.** 3:13; 4:12;
6:11; **REV.** 2:10,25,26; 7:3; 12:11; 14:20; 15:8;
17:47; 18:5; 20:3

892. ἄχυρον *achuron*
MATT. 3:12; **LUKE** 3:17

893. ἀψευδής *apseudēs*
TITUS 1:2

894. ἄψινθος *apsinthos*
REV. 8:11

895. ἄψυχος *apsuchos*
1 COR. 14:7

B

896. Βάαλ *Baal*
ROM. 11:4

897. Βαβυλών *Babulōn*
MATT. 1:11,12,17; **ACTS** 7:43; **1 PET.** 5:13;
REV. 14:8; 16:19; 17:5; 18:2,10,21

898. βαθμός *bathmos*
1 TIM. 3:13

899. βάθος *bathos*
MATT. 13:5; **MARK** 4:5; **LUKE** 5:4; **ROM.**
8:39; 11:33; **1 COR.** 2:10; **2 COR.** 8:2; **EPH.**
3:18; **REV.** 2:24

900. βαθύνω *bathunō*
LUKE 6:48

901. βαθύς *bathus*
LUKE 24:1; **JOHN** 4:11; **ACTS** 20:9

902. βαΐον *baion*
JOHN 12:13

903. Βαλαάμ *Balaam*
2 PET. 2:15; **JUDE** 1:11; **REV.** 2:14

904. Βαλάκ *Balak*
REV. 2:14

905. βαλάντιον *balantion*
LUKE 10:4; 12:33; 22:35,36

906. βάλλω *ballō*
MATT. 3:10; 4:6,18; 5:13,25,29,30; 6:30;
7:6,19; 8:6,14; 9:2,17; 10:34; 13:42,47,48,50;
15:26; 17:27; 18:8,9,30; 21:21; 25:27; 26:12;
27:6,35; **MARK** 1:16; 2:22; 4:26; 7:27,30,33;
9:22,42,45,47; 11:23; 12:41-44; 14:65; 15:24;
LUKE 3:9; 4:9; 5:37; 12:28,49,58; 13:8,19;
14:35; 16:20; 21:1-4; 23:19,25,34; **JOHN**
3:24; 5:7; 8:7,59; 12:6; 13:2,5; 15:6; 18:11;
19:24; 20:25,27; 21:6,7; **ACTS** 16:23,24,37;
22:23; 27:14; **JAMES** 3:3; **1 JOHN** 4:18;
REV. 2:10,14,22,24; 4:10; 6:13; 8:5,7,8;
12:4,9,13,15,16; 14:16,19; 18:19,21; 19:20;
20:3,10,14,15

907. *βαπτίζω baptizō*
MATT. 3:6,11,13,14,16; 20:22,23; 28:19;
MARK 1:4,5,8,9; 6:14; 7:4; 10:38,39; 16:16;
LUKE 3:7,12,16,21; 7:29,30; 11:38; 12:50;
JOHN 1:25,26,28,31,33; 3:22,23,26; 4:1,2;
10:40; ACTS 1:5; 2:38,41; 8:12,13,16,36,38;
9:18; 10:47,48; 11:16; 16:15,33; 18:8; 19:3-5;
22:16; ROM. 6:3; 1 COR. 1:13-17; 10:2; 12:13;
15:29; GAL. 3:27

908. *βάπτισμα baptisma*
MATT. 3:7; 20:22,23; 21:25; MARK 1:4;
10:38,39; 11:30; LUKE 3:3; 7:29; 12:50; 20:4;
ACTS 1:22; 10:37; 13:24; 18:25; 19:3,4; ROM.
6:4; EPH. 4:5; COL. 2:12; 1 PET. 3:21

909. *βαπτισμός baptismos*
MARK 7:4,8; HEB. 6:2; 9:10

910. *βαπτιστής baptistēs*
MATT. 3:1; 11:11,12; 14:2,8; 16:14; 17:13;
MARK 6:24,25; 8:28; LUKE 7:20,28,33; 9:19

911. *βάπτω baptō*
LUKE 16:24; JOHN 13:26; REV. 19:13

912. *Βαραββᾶς Barabbas*
MATT. 27:16,17,20,21,26; MARK 15:7,11,15;
LUKE 23:18; JOHN 18:40

913. *Βαράκ Barak*
HEB. 11:32

914. *Βαραχίας Barachias*
MATT. 23:35

915. *βάρβαρος barbaros*
ACTS 28:2,4; ROM. 1:14; 1 COR. 14:11;
COL. 3:11

916. *βαρέω bareō*
MATT. 26:43; MARK 14:40; LUKE 9:32;
1 COR. 1:8; 5:4; 1 TIM. 5:16

917. *βαρέως bareōs*
MATT. 13:15; ACTS 28:27

918. *Βαρθολομαῖος Bartholomaios*
MATT. 10:3; MARK 3:18; LUKE 6:14; ACTS
1:13

919. *Βάρ-ἰησοῦς, Βαριησοῦς*
Bar-iēsous, Bariēsous
ACTS 13:6

920. *Βάρ-ἰωνᾶς, Βαριωνᾶ*
Bar-iōnas, Bariōna
MATT. 16:17

921. *Βαρνάβας Barnabas*
ACTS 4:36; 9:27; 11:22,25,30; 12:25;
13:1,2,7,43,46,50; 14:12,14,20; 15:2,12,
22,25,35-37,39; 1 COR. 9:6; GAL. 2:1,9,13;
COL. 4:10

922. *βάρος baros*
MATT. 20:12; ACTS 15:28; 2 COR. 4:17;
GAL. 6:2; 1 THESS. 2:6; REV. 2:24

923. *Βαρσαβᾶς Barsabas*
ACTS 1:23; 15:22

924. *Βαρτίμαιος Bartimaios*
MARK 10:46

925. *βαρύνω barunō*
LUKE 21:34

926. *βαρύς barus*
MATT. 23:4,23; ACTS 20:29; 25:7; 2 COR.
10:10; 1 JOHN 5:3

927. *βαρύτιμος barutimos*
MATT. 26:7

928. *βασανίζω basanizō*
MATT. 8:6,29; 14:24; MARK 5:7; 6:48; LUKE
8:28; 2 PET. 2:8; REV. 9:5; 11:10; 12:2; 14:10;
20:10

929. *βασανισμός basanismos*
REV. 9:5; 14:11; 18:7,10,15

930. βασανιστής basanistēs
MATT. 18:34

931. βάσανος basanos
MATT. 4:24; LUKE 16:23,28

932. βασιλεία basileia
MATT. 3:2; 4:8,17,23; 5:3,10,19,20; 6:10,
13,33; 7:21; 8:11,12; 9:35; 10:7; 11:11,12,
25,26,28; 13:11,19,24,31,33,38,41,43-45,47,52;
16:19,28; 18:1,3,4,23; 19:12,14,23,24; 20:1,21;
21:31,43; 22:2; 23:13; 24:7,14; 25:1,34; 26:29;
MARK 1:14,15; 3:24; 4:11,26,30; 6:23; 9:1,47;
10:14,15,23-25; 11:10; 12:34; 13:8; 14:25;
15:43; LUKE 1:33; 4:5,43; 6:20; 7:28; 8:1,10;
9:2,11,27,60,62; 10:9,11; 11:2,17,18,20; 12:31,
32; 13:18,20,28,29; 14:15;16:16; 17:20,21;
18:16,17,24,25,29; 19:11, 12,15; 21:10,31;
22:16,18,29,30; 23:42,51; JOHN 3:3,5; 18:36;
ACTS 1:3,6; 8:12; 14:22; 19:8; 20:25; 28:23,
31; ROM. 14:17; 1 COR. 4:20; 6:9,10;
15:24,50; GAL. 5:21; EPH. 5:5; COL. 1:13;
4:11; 1 THESS. 2:12; 2 THESS. 1:5; 2 TIM.
4:1,18; HEB. 1:8; 11:33; 12:28; JAMES 2:5;
2 PET. 1:11; REV. 1:9; 11:15; 12:10; 16:10;
17:12,17,18

933. βασίλειον basileion   subst.
LUKE 7:25

934. βασίλειος basileios
1 PET. 2:9

935. βασιλεύς basileus
MATT. 1:6; 2:1-3,9; 5:35; 10:18; 11:8; 14:9;
17:25; 18:23; 21:5; 22:2,7,11,13; 25:34,40;
27:11,29,37,42; MARK 6:14,22,25-27; 13:9;
15:2,9,12,18,26,32; LUKE 1:5; 10:24; 14:31;
19:38; 21:12; 22:25; 23:2,3,37,38; JOHN 1:49;
6:15; 12:13,15; 18:33,37,39; 19:3,12,14,15,
19,21; ACTS 4:26; 7:10,18; 9:15; 12:1,20;
13:21,22; 17:7; 25:13,14,24,26; 26:2,7,
13,19,26,27,30; 2 COR. 11:32; 1 TIM. 1:17;
2:2; 6:15; HEB. 7:1,2; 11:23,27; 1 PET. 2:13,
17; REV. 1:5,6; 5:10; 6:15; 9:11; 10:11; 15:3;
16:12,14; 17:2,10,12,14,18; 18:3,9; 19:16,18,19;
21:24

936. βασιλεύω basileuō
MATT. 2:22; LUKE 1:33; 19:14,27;
ROM. 5:14,17,21; 6:12; 1 COR. 4:8; 15:25;

1 TIM. 6:15; REV. 5:10; 11:15,17; 19:6; 20:4,6;
22:5

937. βασιλικός basilikos
JOHN 4:46,49; ACTS 12:20,21; JAMES 2:8

938. βασίλισσα basilissa
MATT. 12:42; LUKE 11:31; ACTS 8:27; REV.
18:7

939. βάσις basis
ACTS 3:7

940. βασκαίνω baskainō
GAL. 3:1

941. βαστάζω bastazō
MATT. 3:11; 8:17; 20:12; MARK 14:13;
LUKE 7:14; 10:4; 11:27; 14:27; 22:10; JOHN
10:31; 12:6; 16:12; 19:17; 20:15; ACTS 3:2;
9:15; 15:10; 21:35; ROM. 11:18; 15:1; GAL.
5:10; 6:2,5; 6:17; REV. 2:2,3; 17:7

942. ἡ βάτος batos   fem.
MARK 12:26; LUKE 6:44; 20:37; ACTS
7:30,35

943. ὁ βάτος batos   masc.
LUKE 16:6

944. βάτραχος batrachos
REV. 16:13

945. βαττολογέω battologeō
MATT. 6:7

946. βδέλυγμα bdelugma
MATT. 24:15; MARK 13:14; LUKE 16:15;
REV. 17:4,5; 21:27

947. βδελυκτός bdeluktos
TITUS 1:16

948. βδελύσσω bdelussō
ROM. 2:22; REV. 21:8

949. βέβαιος bebaios
ROM. 4:16; 2 COR. 1:7; HEB. 2:2; 3:6,14;
6:19; 9:17; 2 PET. 1:10,19

950. βεβαιόω *bebaioō*
MARK 16:20; ROM. 15:8; 1 COR. 1:6,8;
II COR. 1:21; COL. 2:7; HEB. 2:3; 13:9

951. βεβαίωσις *bebaiōsis*
PHIL. 1:7; HEB. 6:16

952. βέβηλος *bebēlos*
1 TIM. 1:9; 4:7; 6:20; 2 TIM. 2:16; HEB. 12:16

953. βεβηλόω *bebēloō*
MATT. 12:5; ACTS 24:6

954. Βεελζεβούλ *Beelzeboul*
MATT. 10:25; 12:24,27; MARK 3:22; LUKE
11:15,18,19

955. Βελίαλ *Belial*
2 COR. 6:15

956. βέλος *belos*
EPH. 6:16

957. βελτίων *beltiōn*
2 TIM. 1:18

958. Βενιαμίν *Beniamin*
ACTS 13:21; ROM. 11:1; PHIL. 3:5; REV. 7:8

959. Βερνίκη *Bernikē*
ACTS 25:13,23; 26:30

960. Βέροια *Beroia*
ACTS 17:10,13

961. Βεροιαῖος *Beroiaios*
ACTS 20:4

962. Βηθαβαρά *Bēthabara*
JOHN 1:28

963. Βηθανία *Bēthania*
MATT. 21:17; 26:6; MARK 11:1,11,12; 14:3;
LUKE 19:29; 24:50; JOHN 11:1,18; 12:1

964. Βηθεσδά *Bēthesda*
JOHN 5:2

965. Βηθλεέμ *Bēthleem*
MATT. 2:1,5,6,8,16; LUKE 2:4,15; JOHN 7:42

966. Βηθσαϊδά, Βηθσαϊδάν
Bēthsaida, Bēthsaidan
MATT. 11:21; MARK 6:45; 8:22; LUKE 9:10;
10:13; JOHN 1:44; 12:21

967. Βηθφαγή *Bēthphagē*
MATT. 21:1; MARK 11:1; LUKE 19:29

968. βῆμα *bēma*
MATT. 27:19; JOHN 19:13; ACTS 7:5; 12:21;
18:12,16,17; 25:6,10,17; ROM. 14:10; 2 COR.
5:10

969. βήρυλλος *bērullos*
REV. 21:20

970. βία *bia*
ACTS 5:26; 21:35; 24:7; 27:41

971. βιάζω *biazō*
MATT. 11:12; LUKE 16:16

972. βίαιος *biaios*
ACTS 2:2

973. βιαστής *biastēs*
MATT. 11:12

974. βιβλαρίδιον *biblaridion*
REV. 10:2,8-10

975. βιβλίον *biblion*
MATT. 19:7; MARK 10:4; LUKE 4:17,20;
JOHN 20:30; 21:25; GAL. 3:10; 2 TIM. 4:13;
HEB. 9:19; 10:7; REV. 1:11; 5:1-5,7-9; 6:14;
17:8; 20:12; 21:27; 22:7,9,10,18,19

976. βίβλος *biblos*
MATT. 1:1; MARK 12:26; LUKE 3:4; 20:42;
ACTS 1:20; 7:42; 19:19; PHIL. 4:3; REV. 3:5;
13:8; 20:15; 22:19

977. βιβρώσκω *bibrōskō*
JOHN 6:13

978. *Βιθυνία Bithunia*
ACTS 16:7; **1 PET.** 1:1

979. *βίος bios*
MARK 12:44; **LUKE** 8:14,43; 15:12,30;
21:4; **1 TIM.** 2:2; **2 TIM.** 2:4; **1 PET.** 4:3;
1 JOHN 2:16; 3:17

980. *βιόω bioō*
1 PET. 4:2

981. *βίωσις biōsis*
ACTS 26:4

982. *βιωτικός biōtikos*
LUKE 21:34; **1 COR.** 6:3,4

983. *βλαβερός blaberos*
1 TIM. 6:9

984. *βλάπτω blaptō*
MARK 16:18; **LUKE** 4:35

985. *βλαστάνω blastanō*
MATT. 13:26; **MARK** 4:27; **HEB.** 9:4;
JAMES 5:18

986. *Βλάστος Blastos*
ACTS 12:20

987. *βλασφημέω blasphēmeō*
MATT. 9:3; 26:65; 27:39; **MARK** 3:28,29;
15:29; **LUKE** 12:10; 22:65; 23:39; **JOHN**
10:36; **ACTS** 13:45; 18:6; 19:37; 26:11;
ROM. 2:24; 3:8; 14:16; **1 COR.** 4:13; 10:30;
1 TIM. 1:20; 6:1; **TITUS** 2:5; 3:2; **JAMES** 2:7;
1 PET. 4:4,14; **2 PET.** 2:2,10,12; **JUDE** 1:8,10;
REV. 13:6; 16:9,11,21

988. *βλασφημία blasphēmia*
MATT. 12:31; 15:19; 26:65; **MARK** 2:7;
3:28; 7:22; 14:64; **LUKE** 5:21; **JOHN** 10:33;
EPH. 4:31; **COL.** 3:8; **1 TIM.** 6:4; **JUDE** 1:9;
REV. 2:9; 13:1,5,6; 17:3

989. *βλάσφημος blasphēmos*
ACTS 6:11,13; **1 TIM.** 1:13; **2 TIM.** 3:2;
2 PET. 2:11

990. *βλέμμα blemma*
2 PET. 2:8

991. *βλέπω blepō*
MATT. 5:28; 6:4,6,18; 7:3; 11:4; 12:22;
13:13,14,16,17; 14:30; 15:31; 18:10,22:16;
24:2,4; **MARK** 4:12,24; 5:31; 8:15,18,23,24;
12:14,38; 13:2,5,9,23,33; **LUKE** 6:41,42;
7:21,44; 8:10,16,18; 9:62; 10:23,24; 11:33;
21:8,30; 24:12; **JOHN** 1:29; 5:19; 9:7,15,
19,21,25,39,41; 11:9; 13:22; 20:1,5; 21:9,20;
ACTS 1:9; 2:33; 3:4; 4:14; 8:6; 9:8,9; 12:9;
13:11,40; 27:12; 28:26; **ROM.** 7:23; 8:24,25;
11:8,10; **1 COR.** 1:26; 3:10; 8:9; 10:12,18;
13:12; 16:10; **2 COR.** 4:18; 7:8; 10:7; 12:6;
GAL. 5:15; **EPH.** 5:15; **PHIL.** 3:2; **COL.** 2:5,8;
4:17; **HEB.** 2:9; 3:12,19; 10:25; 11:1,3,7; 12:25;
JAMES 2:22; **2 JOHN** 1:8; **REV.** 1:11,12; 3:18;
5:3,4; 6:1,3,5,7; 9:20; 11:9; 16:15; 17:8; 18:9;
22:8

992. *βλητέος blēteos*
MARK 2:22; **LUKE** 5:38

993. *Βοανεργές Boanerges*
MARK 3:17

994. *βοάω boaō*
MATT. 3:3; **MARK** 1:3; 15:34; **LUKE** 3:4;
18:7,38; **JOHN** 1:23; **ACTS** 8:7; 17:6; 21:34;
GAL. 4:27

995. *βοή boē*
JAMES 5:4

996. *βοήθεια boētheia*
ACTS 27:17; **HEB.** 4:16

997. *βοηθέω boētheō*
MATT. 15:25; **MARK** 9:22,24; **ACTS** 16:9;
21:28; **2 COR.** 6:2; **HEB.** 2:18; **REV.** 12:16

998. *βοηθός boēthos*
HEB. 13:6

999. *βόθυνος bothunos*
MATT. 12:11; 15:14; **LUKE** 6:39

1000. *βολή bolē*
LUKE 22:41

1001. βολίζω bolizō
ACTS 27:28

1002. βολίς bolis
HEB. 12:20

1003. Βοόζ Booz
MATT. 1:5; LUKE 3:32

1004. βόρβορος borboras
2 PET. 2:22

1005. βορρᾶς borras
LUKE 13:29; REV. 21:13

1006. βόσκω boskō
MATT. 8:30,33; MARK 5:11,14; LUKE 8:32,
34; 15:15; JOHN 21:15,17

1007. Βοσόρ Bosor
2 PET. 2:15

1008. βοτάνη botanē
HEB. 6:7

1009. βότρυς botrus
REV. 14:18

1010. βουλευτής bouleutēs
MARK 15:43; LUKE 23:50

1011. βουλεύω bouleuō
LUKE 14:31; JOHN 12:10; ACTS 5:33; 15:37;
27:39; 2 COR. 1:7

1012. βουλή boulē
LUKE 7:30; 23:51; ACTS 2:23; 4:28; 5:38;
13:36; 20:27; 27:12,42; 1 COR. 4:5; EPH. 1:11;
HEB. 6:17

1013. βούλημα boulēma
ACTS 27:43; ROM. 9:19

1014. βούλομαι boulomai
MATT. 1:19; 11:27; MARK 15:15;
LUKE 10:22; 22:42; JOHN 18:39; ACTS 5:28;
12:4; 17:20; 18:15,27; 19:30; 22:30; 23:28;
25:20,22; 27:43; 28:18; 1 COR. 12:11 2 COR.

1:15; PHIL. 1:12; 1 TIM. 2:8; 5:14; 6:9; TITUS
3:8; PHILE. 1:13; HEB. 6:17; JAMES 1:18;
3:4; 4:4; 2 PET. 3:9; 2 JOHN 1:12; 3 JOHN
1:10; JUDE 1:5

1015. βουνός bounos
LUKE 3:5; 23:30

1016. βοῦς bous
LUKE 13:15; 14:5,19; JOHN 2:14,15; 1 COR.
9:9; 1 TIM. 5:18

1017. βραβεῖον brabeion
1 COR. 9:24; PHIL. 3:14

1018. βραβεύω brabeuō
COL. 3:15

1019. βραδύνω bradunō
1 TIM. 3:15; 2 PET. 3:9

1020. βραδυπλοέω braduploeō
ACTS 27:7

1021. βραδύς bradus
LUKE 24:25; JAMES 1:19

1022. βραδύτης bradutēs
2 PET. 3:9

1023. βραχίων brachiōn
LUKE 1:51; JOHN 12:38; ACTS 13:17

1024. βραχύς brachus
LUKE 22:58; JOHN 6:7; ACTS 5:34; 27:28;
HEB. 2:7,9; 13:22

1025. βρέφος brephos
LUKE 1:41,44; 2:12,16; 18:15; ACTS 7:19;
2 TIM. 3:15; 1 PET. 2:2

1026. βρέχω brechō
MATT. 5:45; LUKE 7:38,44; 17:29; JAMES
5:17; REV. 11:6

1027. βροντή brontē
MARK 3:17; JOHN 12:29; REV. 4:5; 6:1; 8:5;
10:3,4; 11:19; 14:2; 16:18; 19:6

1028. βροχή *brochē*
MATT. 7:25,27

1029. βρόχος *brochos*
1 COR. 7:35

1030. βρυγμός *brugmos*
MATT. 8:12; 13:42,50; 22:13; 24:51; 25:30;
LUKE 13:28

1031. βρύχω *bruchō*
ACTS 7:54

1032. βρύω *bruō*
JAMES 3:11

1033. βρῶμα *brōma*
MATT. 14:15; MARK 7:19; LUKE 3:11; 9:13;
JOHN 4:34; ROM. 14:15,20; 1 COR. 3:2;
6:13; 8:8,13; 10:3; 1 TIM. 4:3; HEB. 9:10;
13:9

1034. βρώσιμος *brōsimos*
LUKE 24:41

1035. βρῶσις *brōsis*
MATT. 6:19,20; JOHN 4:32; 6:27,55; ROM.
14:17; 1 COR. 8:4; 2 COR. 9:10; COL. 2:16;
HEB. 12:16

1036. βυθίζω *buthizō*
LUKE 5:7; 1 TIM. 6:9

1037. βυθός *buthos*
2 COR. 11:25

1038. βυρσεύς *burseus*
ACTS 9:43; 10:6,32

1039. βύσσινος *bussinos*
REV. 18:16; 19:8,14

1040. βύσσος *bussos*
LUKE 16:19; REV. 18:12

1041. βωμός *bōmos*
ACTS 17:23

Γ

1042. Γαββαθᾶ *Gabbatha*
JOHN 19:13

1043. Γαβριήλ *Gabriēl*
LUKE 1:19,26

1044. γάγγραινα *gaggraina*
2 TIM. 2:17

1045. Γάδ *Gad*
REV. 7:5

1046. Γαδαρηνός *Gadarēnos*
MARK 5:1; LUKE 8:26,37

1047. γάζα *gaza*
ACTS 8:27

1048. Γάζα *Gaza*
ACTS 8:26

1049. γαζοφυλάκιον *gazophulakion*
MARK 12:41,43; LUKE 21:1; JOHN 8:20

1050. Γάϊος *Gaios*
ACTS 19:29; 20:4; ROM. 16:23; 1 COR. 1:14;
3 JOHN 1:1

1051. γάλα *gala*
1 COR. 3:2; 9:7; HEB. 5:12,13; 1 PET. 2:2

1052. Γαλάτης *Galatēs*
GAL. 3:1

1053. Γαλατία *Galatia*
1 COR. 16:1; GAL. 1:2; 2 TIM. 4:10; 1 PET.
1:1

1054. Γαλατικός *Galatikos*
ACTS 16:6; 18:23

1055. γαλήνη *galēnē*
MATT. 8:26; MARK 4:39; LUKE 8:24

1056. Γαλιλαία Galilaia
MATT. 2:22; 3:13; 4:12,15,18,23,25; 15:29;
17:22; 19:1; 21:11; 26:32; 27:55; 28:7,10,16;
MARK 1:9,14,16,28,39; 3:7; 6:21; 7:31; 9:30;
14:28; 15:41; 16:7; **LUKE** 1:26; 2:4,39; 3:1;
4:14,31,44; 5:17; 8:26; 17:11; 23:5,6,49,55; 24:6;
JOHN 1:43; 2:1,11; 4:3,43,45-47,54; 6:1;
7:1,9,41,52; 12:21; 21:2; **ACTS** 9:31; 10:37;
13:31

1057. Γαλιλαῖος Galilaios
MATT. 26:69; **MARK** 14:70; **LUKE** 13:1,2;
22:59; 23:6; **JOHN** 4:45; **ACTS** 1:11; 2:7; 5:37

1058. Γαλλίων Galliōn
ACTS 18:12,14,17

1059. Γαμαλιήλ Gamaliēl
ACTS 5:34; 22:3

1060. γαμέω gameō
MATT. 5:32; 19:9,10; 22:25,30; 24:38; **MARK**
6:17; 10:11,12; 12:25; **LUKE** 14:20; 16:18;
17:27; 20:34,35; **1 COR.** 7:9,10,28,33,34,36,39;
1 TIM. 4:3; 5:11,14

1061. γαμίσκω gamiskō
MARK 12:25

1062. γάμος gamos
MATT. 22:2-4,8-12; 25:10; **LUKE** 12:36; 14:8;
JOHN 2:1,2; **HEB.** 13:4; **REV.** 19:7,9

1063. γάρ gar
MATT. 1:20; 1:18; 15:27; 27:23; **MARK** 7:28;
8:38; 15:14; **LUKE** 12:58; 20:36; 23:22; **JOHN**
3:19; 4:37; 7:41; 8:42; 9:30; 10:26; **ACTS** 2:15;
4:34; 8:31,39; 16:37; 19:35; 28:20; **ROM.** 3:2;
4:15; 5:7; 8:7; 15:2,27; **1 COR.** 9:10; 11:9,22;
2 COR. 12:1; **PHIL.** 1:18; 2:5; **1 THESS.** 4:10;
2 TIM. 2:7; **JAMES** 4:14; **1 PET.** 4:15; **2 PET.**
1:9; **3 JOHN** 1:7

1064. γαστήρ gastēr
MATT. 1:18,23; 24:19; **MARK** 13:17; **LUKE**
1:31; 21:23; **1 THESS.** 5:3; **TITUS** 1:12; **REV.**
12:2

1065. γέ ge
LUKE 11:8; 18:5; 19:42; 24:21; **ACTS** 2:18;
8:30; 11:18; **ROM.** 8:32; **1 COR.** 4:8; 6:3; 9:2

1066. Γεδεών Gedeōn
HEB. 11:32

1067. γέεννα geenna
MATT. 5:22,29,30; 10:28; 18:9; 23:15,33;
MARK 9:43,45,47; **LUKE** 12:5; **JAMES** 3:6

1068. Γεθσημανῆ Gethsēmanē
MATT. 26:36; **MARK** 14:32

1069. γείτων geitōn
LUKE 14:12; 15:6,9; **JOHN** 9:8

1070. γελάω gelaō
LUKE 6:21,25

1071. γέλως gelōs
JAMES 4:9

1072. γεμίζω gemizō
MARK 4:37,15:36; **LUKE** 14:23; 15:16; **JOHN**
2:7; 6:13; **REV.** 8:5; 15:8

1073. γέμω gemō
MATT. 23:25,27; **LUKE** 11:39; **ROM.** 3:14;
REV. 4:6,8; 5:8; 15:7; 17:3,4; 21:9

1074. γενεά genea
MATT. 1:17; 11:16; 12:39,41,42,45; 16:4;
17:17; 23:36; 24:34; **MARK** 8:12,38; 9:19;
13:30; **LUKE** 1:48,50; 7:31; 9:41; 11:29-
32,50,51; 16:8; 17:25; 21:32; **ACTS** 2:40; 8:33;
13:36; 14:16; 15:21; **EPH.** 3:5,21; **PHIL.** 2:15;
COL. 1:26; **HEB.** 3:10

1075. γενεαλογέω genealogeō
HEB. 7:6

1076. γενεαλογία genealogia
1 TIM. 1:4; **TITUS** 3:9

1077. γενέσια genesia
MATT. 14:6; **MARK** 6:21

1078. γένεσις *genesis*
MATT. 1:1; JAMES 1:23; 3:6

1079. γενετή *genetē*
JOHN 9:1

1080. γεννάω *gennaō*
MATT. 1:2-16,20; 2:1,4; 19:12; 26:24; MARK
14:21; LUKE 1:13,35,57; 23:29; JOHN 1:13;
3:3-8; 8:41; 9:2,19,20,32,34; 16:21; 18:37;
ACTS 2:8; 7:8,20,29; 13:33; 22:3,28; ROM.
9:11; 1 COR. 4:15; GAL. 4:23,24,29; 2 TIM.
2:23; PHILE. 1:10; HEB. 1:5; 5:5; 11:12,23;
2 PET. 2:12; 1 JOHN 2:29; 3:9; 4:7; 5:1,4,18

1081. γέννημα *gennēma*
MATT. 3:7; 12:34; 23:33; 26:29; MARK 14:25;
LUKE 3:7; 12:18; 22:18; 2 COR. 9:10

1082. Γεννησαρέτ *Gennēsaret*
MATT. 14:34; MARK 6:53; LUKE 5:1

1083. γέννησις *gennēsis*
MATT. 1:18; LUKE 1:14

1084. γεννητός *gennētos*
MATT. 11:11; LUKE 7:28

1085. γένος *genos*
MATT. 13:47; 17:21; MARK 7:26; 9:29; ACTS
4:6,36; 7:13,19; 13:26; 17:28,29; 18:2,24;
1 COR. 12:10,28; 14:10; 2 COR. 11:26; GAL.
1:14; PHIL. 3:5; 1 PET. 2:9; REV. 22:16

1086. Γεργεσηνός *Gergesēnos*
MATT. 8:28

1087. γερουσία *gerousia*
ACTS 5:21

1088. γέρων *gerōn*
JOHN 3:4

1089. γεύω *geuō*
MATT. 16:28; 27:34; MARK 9:1; LUKE 9:27;
14:24; JOHN 2:9; 8:52; ACTS 10:10; 20:11;
23:14; COL. 2:21; HEB. 2:9; 6:4,5; 1 PET. 2:3

1090. γεωργέω *geōrgeō*
HEB. 6:7

1091. γεώργιον *geōrgion*
1 COR. 3:9

1092. γεωργός *geōrgos*
MATT. 21:33-35,38,40,41; MARK 12:1,2,7,9;
LUKE 20:9,10,14,16; JOHN 15:1; 2 TIM. 2:6;
JAMES 5:7

1093. γῆ *gē*
MATT. 2:6,20,21; 4:15; 5:5,13,18,35; 6:10,19;
9:6,26,31; 10:15,29,34; 11:24,25; 12:40,42;
13:5,8,23; 14:34; 15:35; 16:19; 17:25; 18:18,19;
23:9,35; 24:30,35; 25:18,25; 27:45,51; 28:18;
MARK 2:10; 4:1,5,8,20,26,28,31; 6:47,53; 8:6;
9:3,20; 13:27,31; 14:35; 15:33; LUKE 2:14;
4:25; 5:3,11,24; 6:49; 8:8,15,27; 10:21; 11:2,31;
12:49,51,56; 13:7; 14:35; 16:17; 18:8; 21:23,
25,33,35; 22:44; 23:44; 24:5; JOHN 3:22,31;
6:21; 8:6,8; 12:24,32; 17:4; 21:8,9,11; ACTS
1:8; 2:19; 3:25; 4:24,26; 7:3,4,6,11,29,33,
36,40,49; 8:33; 9:4,8; 10:11,12; 11:6; 13:17,
19,47; 14:15; 17:24,26; 22:22; 26:14; 27:39,
43,44; ROM. 9:17,28; 10:18; 1 COR. 8:5;
10:26,28; 15:47; EPH. 1:10; 3:15; 4:9; 6:3;
COL. 1:16,20; 3:2,5; HEB. 1:10; 6:7; 8:4,9;
11:9,13,38; 12:25,26; JAMES 5:5,7,12,17,18;
2 PET. 3:5,7,10,13; 1 JOHN 5:8; JUDE 1:5;
REV. 1:5,7; 3:10; 5:3,6,10,13; 6:4,8,10,13,15;
7:1-3; 8:5,7,13; 9:1,3,4; 10:2,5,6,8; 11:4,6,10,18;
12:4,9,12,13,16; 13:3,8,11-14; 14:3,6,7,
15,16,18,19; 16:1,2,14,18; 17:2,5,8,18; 18:1,3,
9,11,23,24; 19:2,19; 20:8,9,11; 21:1,24

1094. γῆρας *gēras*
LUKE 1:36

1095. γηράσκω *gēraskō*
JOHN 21:18; HEB. 8:13

1096. γίνομαι *ginomai*
MATT. 1:22; 4:3; 5:18,45; 6:10,16; 7:28;
8:13,16,24,26; 9:10,16,29; 10:16,25;
11:1,20,21,23,26; 12:45; 13:21,22,32,53;
14:15,23; 15:28; 16:2; 17:2; 18:3,12,13,19,31;
19:1,8; 20:8,26; 21:4,19,21,42; 23:15,26;

24:6,20,21,32,34,44; 25:6; 26:1,2,5,6,
20,42,54,56; 27:1,24,45,54,57; 28:2,4,11;
MARK 1:4,9,11,17,32; 2:15,21,23,27;
4:4,10,11,17,19,22,32,35,37,39; 5:14,16,33;
6:2,14,21,26,35,47; 9:3,7,21,26,33,50; 10:43,44;
11:19,23; 12:10,11; 13:7,18,19,28-30; 14:4,17;
15:33,42; 16:10; **LUKE** 1:2,5,8,20,23,38,
41,44,59,65; 2:1,2,6,13,15,42,46; 3:2,21,22;
4:3,23,25,36,42; 5:1,12,17; 6:1,6,12,13,16,
36,48,49; 7:11; 8:1,17,22,24,34,35,40,56;
9:7,18,28,29,33-37,51,57; 10:13,21,32,36,38;
11:1,2,14,26,27,30; 12:40,54,55; 13:2,4,17,19;
14:1,12,22; 15:10,14; 16:11,12,22; 17:11,14,
26,28; 18:23,24,35; 19:9,15,17,19,29; 20:1,14,
16,17,33; 21:7,9,28,31,32,36; 22:14,24,26,
40,42,44,66; 23:8,12,19,24,31,44,47,48;
24:4,5,12,15,18,19,21,22,30,31,37,51; **JOHN**
1:3,6,10,12,14,15,17,27,28,30; 2:1,9; 3:9,25;
4:14; 5:4,6,9,14; 6:16,17,19,21,25; 7:43; 8:33,58;
9:22,27,39; 10:16,19,22,35; 12:29,30,36,42;
13:2,19; 14:22,29; 15:7,8; 16:20; 19:36; 20:27;
21:4; **ACTS** 1:16,18-20,22; 2:2,6,43; 4:4,5,
11,16,21,22,28,30; 5:5,7,11,12,24,36; 6:1;
7:13,29,31,32,38-40,52; 8:1,8,13; 9:3,19,
32,37,42,43; 10:4,10,13,16,25,37,40; 11:10,19,
26,28; 12:5,9,11,18,23; 13:5,12,32; 14:1,3,5;
15:2,7,25,39; 16:16,26,27,29,35; 19:1,10,
17,21,23,26,28,34; 20:3,16,18,37; 21:1,5,14,
17,30,35,40; 22:6,9,17; 23:7,9,10,12; 24:2,25;
25:15,26; 26:4,6,19,22,28,29; 27:7,16,27,29,
33,36,39,42,44; 28:6,8,9,17; **ROM.** 1:3; 2:25;
3:4,6,19,31; 4:18; 6:2,5,15; 7:3,4,7,13; 9:14,29;
10:20; 11:1,5,6,9,11,17,25,34; 12:16; 15:8,16,31;
16:2,7; **1 COR.** 1:30; 2:3; 3:13,18; 4:5,9,13,16;
6:15; 7:21,23,36; 8:9; 9:15,20,22,23,27;
10:6,7,20,32; 11:1,19; 13:1,11; 14:20,25,26,40;
15:10,20,37,45,54,58; 16:2,10,14; **2 COR.**
1:8,18,19; 3:7; 4:32; 5:17,21; 6:14; 7:14; 8:14;
12:11; **GAL.** 2:17; 3:13,14,17,21,24; 4:4,12,16;
5:26; 6:14; **EPH.** 2:13; 3:7; 5:1,7,12,17; 6:3;
PHIL. 1:13; 2:7,8,15; 3:6,17,21; **COL.** 1:18,
23,25; 3:15; 4:11; **1 THESS.** 1:5-7; 2:1,5,7,
8,10,14; 3:4,5; **2 THESS.** 2:7; **1 TIM.** 2:14;
4:12; 5:9; 6:4; **2 TIM.** 1:17; 2:18; 3:9,11; **TITUS**
3:7; **PHILE.** 1:6; **HEB.** 1:4; 2:2,17; 3:14; 4:3;
5:5,9,11,12; 6:4,12,20; 7:12,16,18,21-23,26;
9:15,22; 10:33; 11:3,6,7,24,34; 12:8; **JAMES**
1:12,22,25; 2:4,10,11; 3:1,9,10; 5:2; **1 PET.**
1:15,16; 2:7; 3:6; 13; 4:12; 5:3; **2 PET.** 1:4,
16,20; 2:1,20; **1 JOHN** 2:18; **3 JOHN** 1:8; **REV.**
1:1,9,10,18,19; 2:8,10; 3:2; 4:1,2; 6:12; 8:1,5,7,
8,11; 11:13,15,19; 12:7,10; 16:2-4,10,17-19;
18:2; 21:6; 22:6

1097. γινώσκω ginōskō

MATT. 1:25; 6:3; 7:23; 9:30; 10:26; 12:7,15,33;
13:11; 16:3,8; 21:45; 22:18; 24:32,33,39,43,50;
25:24; 26:10; **MARK** 4:11,13; 5:29,43; 6:38;
7:24; 8:17; 9:30; 12:12; 13:28,29; 15:10,45;
LUKE 1:18,34; 2:43; 6:44; 7:39; 8:10,17,46;
9:11,10:11,22; 12:2,39,46-48; 16:4,15; 18:34;
19:15,42,44; 20:19; 21:20,30,31; 24:18,35;
JOHN 1:10,48; 2:24,25; 3:10; 4:1,53; 5:6,42;
6:15,69; 7:17,26,27,49,51; 8:27,28,32,43,52,55;
10:6,14,15,27,38; 11:57; 12:9,16; 13:7,12,28,35;
14:7,9,17,20,31; 15:18; 16:3,19; 17:3,7,8,23,25;
19:4; 21:17; **ACTS** 1:7; 2:36; 8:30; 9:24;
17:13,19,20; 19:15,35; 20:34; 21:24,34,37;
22:14,30; 23:6,28; 24:11; **ROM.** 1:21; 2:18;
3:17; 6:6; 7:1,7,15; 10:19; 11:34; **1 COR.** 1:21;
2:8,14,16; 3:20; 4:19; 8:2,3; 13:9,12; 14:7,9;
2 COR. 2:4,9; 3:2; 5:16,21; 8:9; 13:6; **GAL.** 2:9;
3:7; 4:9; **EPH.** 3:19; 5:5; 6:22; **PHIL.** 1:12;
2:19,22; 3:10; 4:5; **COL.** 4:8; **1 THESS.** 3:5;
2 TIM. 1:18; 2:19; 3:1; **HEB.** 3:10; 8:11; 10:34;
13:23; **JAMES** 1:3; 2:20; 5:20; **2 PET.** 1:20;
3:3; **1 JOHN** 2:3-5,13,14,18,29; 3:1,6,16,
19,20,24; 4:2,6-8,13,16; 5:2,20; **2 JOHN** 1:1;
REV. 2:17,23,24; 3:3,9

1098. γλεῦκος gleukos
ACTS 2:13

1099. γλυκύς glukus
JAMES 3:11,12; **REV.** 10:9,10

1100. γλῶσσα glōssa
MARK 7:33,35; 16:17; **LUKE** 1:64; 16:24;
ACTS 2:3,4,11,26; 10:46; 19:6; **ROM.** 3:13;
14:11; **1 COR.** 12:10,28,30; 13:1,8; 14:2,4-
6,9,13,14,18,19,22,23,26,27,39; **PHIL.** 2:11;
JAMES 1:26; 3:5,6,8; **1 PET.** 3:10; **1 JOHN**
3:18; **REV.** 5:9; 7:9; 10:11; 11:9; 13:7; 14:6;
16:10; 17:15

1101. γλωσσόκομον glōssokomon
JOHN 12:6; 13:29

1102. γναφεύς gnapheus
MARK 9:3

1103. γνήσιος gnēsios
2 COR. 8:8; **PHIL.** 4:3; **1 TIM.** 1:2; **TITUS** 1:4

1104. *γνησίως* **gnēsiōs**
PHIL. 2:20

1105. *γνόφος* **gnophos**
HEB. 12:18

1106. *γνώμη* **gnōmē**
ACTS 20:3; **1 COR.** 1:10; 7:25,40; **2 COR.**
8:10; **PHILE.** 1:14; **REV.** 17:13,17

1107. *γνωρίζω* **gnōrizō**
LUKE 2:15; **JOHN** 15:15; 17:26; **ACTS** 2:28;
ROM. 9:22,23; 16:26; **1 COR.** 12:3; 15:1;
2 COR. 8:1; **GAL.** 1:11; **EPH.** 1:9; 3:3,5,10;
6:19,21; **PHIL.** 1:22; 4:6; **COL.** 1:27; 4:7,9;
2 PET. 1:16

1108. *γνῶσις* **gnōsis**
LUKE 1:77; 11:52; **ROM.** 2:20; 11:33; 15:14;
1 COR. 1:5; 8:1,7,10,11; 12:8; 13:2,8; 14:6;
2 COR. 2:14; 4:6; 6:6; 8:7; 10:5; 11:6; **EPH.**
3:19; **PHIL.** 3:8; **COL.** 2:3; **1 TIM.** 6:20;
1 PET. 3:7; **2 PET.** 1:5,6; 3:18

1109. *γνώστης* **gnōstēs**
ACTS 26:3

1110. *γνωστός* **gnōstos**
LUKE 2:44; 23:49; **JOHN** 18:15,16; **ACTS**
1:19; 2:14; 4:10,16; 9:42; 13:38; 15:18; 19:17;
28:22,28; **ROM.** 1:19

1111. *γογγύζω* **gogguzō**
MATT. 20:11; **LUKE** 5:30; **JOHN** 6:41,43,61;
7:32; **1 COR.** 10:10

1112. *γογγυσμός* **goggusmos**
JOHN 7:12; **ACTS** 6:1; **PHIL.** 2:14; **1 PET.** 4:9

1113. *γογγυστής* **goggustēs**
JUDE 1:16

1114. *γόης* **goēs**
2 TIM. 3:13

1115. *Γολγοθᾶ* **Golgotha**
MATT. 27:33; **MARK** 15:22; **JOHN** 19:17

1116. *Γόμορρα* **Gomorra**
MATT. 10:15; **MARK** 6:11; **ROM.** 9:29;
2 PET. 2:6; **JUDE** 1:7

1117. *γόμος* **gomos**
ACTS 21:3; **REV.** 18:11,12

1118. *γονεύς* **goneus**
MATT. 10:21; **MARK** 13:12; **LUKE** 2:27,41;
8:56; 18:29; 21:16; **JOHN** 9:2,3,18,20,22,23;
ROM. 1:30; **2 COR.** 12:14; **EPH.** 6:1; **COL.**
3:20; **2 TIM.** 3:2

1119. *γόνυ* **gonu**
MARK 15:19; **LUKE** 5:8; 22:41; **ACTS** 7:60;
9:40; 20:36; 21:5; **ROM.** 11:4; 14:11; **EPH.**
3:14; **PHIL.** 2:10; **HEB.** 12:12

1120. *γονυπετέω* **gonupeteō**
MATT. 17:14; 27:29; **MARK** 1:40; 10:17

1121. *γράμμα* **gramma**
LUKE 16:6,7; 23:38; **JOHN** 5:47; 7:15; **ACTS**
26:24; 28:21; **ROM.** 2:27,29; 7:6; **2 COR.** 3:6,7;
GAL. 6:11; **2 TIM.** 3:15

1122. *γραμματεύς* **grammateus**
MATT. 2:4; 5:20; 7:29; 8:19; 9:3; 12:38; 13:52;
15:1; 16:21; 17:10; 20:18; 21:15; 23:2,13-
15,23,25,27,29,34; 26:3,57; 27:41; **MARK** 1:22;
2:6,16; 3:22; 7:1,5; 8:31; 9:11,14,16; 10:33;
11:18,27; 12:28,32,35,38; 14:1,43,53; 15:1,31;
LUKE 5:21,30; 6:7; 9:22; 11:44,53; 15:2; 19:47;
20:1,19,39,46; 22:2,66; 23:10; **JOHN** 8:3;
ACTS 4:5; 6:12; 19:35; 23:9; **1 COR.** 1:20

1123. *γραπτός* **graptos**
ROM. 2:15

1124. *γραφή* **graphē**
MATT. 21:42; 22:29; 26:54,56; **MARK**
12:10,24; 14:49; 15:28; **LUKE** 4:21;
24:27,32,45; **JOHN** 2:22; 5:39; 7:38,42; 10:35;
13:18; 17:12; 19:24,28,36,37; 20:9; **ACTS** 1:16;
8:32,35; 17:2,11; 18:24,28; **ROM.** 1:2; 4:3; 9:17;
10:11; 11:2; 15:4; 16:26; **1 COR.** 15:3,4; **GAL.**
3:8,22; 4:30; **1 TIM.** 5:18; **2 TIM.** 3:16; **JAMES**
2:8,23; 4:5; **1 PET.** 2:6; **2 PET.** 1:20; 3:16

1125. γράφω graphō
MATT. 2:5; 4:4,6,7,10; 11:10; 21:13; 26:24,31;
27:37; MARK 1:2; 7:6; 9:12,13; 10:4,5; 11:17;
12:19; 14:21,27; LUKE 1:3,63; 2:23; 3:4;
4:4,8,10,17; 7:27; 10:20,26; 16:6,7; 18:31; 19:46;
20:17,28; 21:22; 22:37; 23:38; 24:44,46; JOHN
1:45; 2:17; 5:46; 6:31,45; 8:6,8,17; 10:34;
12:14,16; 15:25; 19:19-22; 20:30,31; 21:24,25;
ACTS 1:20; 7:42; 13:29,33; 15:15,23; 18:27;
23:5,25; 24:14; 25:26; ROM. 1:17; 2:24; 3:4,10;
4:17,23; 8:36; 9:13,33; 10:5,15; 11:8,26; 12:19;
14:11; 15:3,9,15,21; 16:22; 1 COR. 1:19,31; 2:9;
3:19; 4:6,14; 5:9,11; 7:1; 9:9,10,15; 10:7,11;
14:21,37; 15:45,54; 2 COR. 1:13; 2:3,4,9; 4:13;
7:12; 8:15; 9:1,9; 13:2,10; GAL. 1:20; 3:10,13;
4:22,27; 6:11; PHIL. 3:1; 1 THESS. 4:9; 5:1;
2 THESS. 3:17; 1 TIM. 3:14; PHILE. 1:19,21;
HEB. 10:7; 1 PET. 1:16; 5:12; 2 PET. 3:1,15;
1 JOHN 1:4; 2:1,7,8,12-14,21,26; 5:13; 2 JOHN
1:5,12; 3 JOHN 1:9,13; JUDE 1:3; REV.
1:3,11,19; 2:1,8,12,17,18; 3:1,7,12,14; 5:1; 10:4;
13:8; 14:1,13; 17:5,8; 19:9,12,16; 20:12,15;
21:5,27; 22:18,19

1126. γραώδης graōdēs
1 TIM. 4:7

1127. γρηγορέω grēgoreō
MATT. 24:42,43; 25:13; 26:38,40,41; MARK
13:34,35,37; 14:34,37,38; LUKE 12:37,39;
ACTS 20:31; 1 COR. 16:13; COL. 4:2;
1 THESS. 5:6,10; 1 PET. 5:8; REV. 3:2,3; 16:15

1128. γυμνάζω gumnazō
1 TIM. 4:7; HEB. 5:14; 12:11; 2 PET. 2:14

1129. γυμνασία gumnasia
1 TIM. 4:8

1130. γυμνητεύω gumnēteuō
1 COR. 4:11

1131. γυμνός gumnos
MATT. 25:36,38,43,44; MARK 14:51,52;
JOHN 21:7; ACTS 19:16; 1 COR. 15:37;
2 COR. 5:3; HEB. 4:13; JAMES 2:15; REV.
3:17; 16:15; 17:16

1132. γυμνότης gumnotēs
ROM. 8:35; 2 COR. 11:27; REV. 3:18

1133. γυναικάριον gunaikarion
2 TIM. 3:6

1134. γυναικεῖος gunaikeios
1 PET. 3:7

1135. γυνή gunē
MATT. 1:20,24; 5:28,31,32; 9:20,22; 11:11;
13:33; 14:3,21; 15:22,28,38; 18:25; 19:3,5,8-
10,29; 22:24,25,27,28; 26:7,10; 27:19,55; 28:5;
MARK 5:25,33; 6:17,18; 7:25,26; 10:2,7,11,
12,29; 12:19,20,22,23; 14:3; 15:40; LUKE
1:5,13,18,24,28,42; 2:5; 3:19; 4:26; 7:28,37,
39,44,50; 8:2,3,43,47; 10:38; 11:27; 13:11,12,21;
14:20,26; 15:8; 16:18; 17:32; 18:29; 20:28-
30,32,33; 22:57; 23:27,49,55; 24:22,24; JOHN
2:4; 4:7,9,11,15,17,19,21,25,27,28,39,42;
8:3,4,9,10; 16:21; 19:26; 20:13,15; ACTS 1:14;
5:1,2,7,14; 8:3,12; 9:2; 13:50; 16:1,13,14;
17:4,12,34; 18:2; 21:5; 22:4; 24:24; ROM. 7:2;
1 COR. 5:1; 7:1-4,10-14,16,27,29,33,34,39; 9:5;
11:3,5-13,15; 14:34,35; GAL. 4:4; EPH. 5:22-
25,28,31,33; COL. 3:18,19; 1 TIM. 2:9-12,14;
3:2,11,12; 5:9; TITUS 1:6; HEB. 11:35; 1 PET.
3:1,5; REV. 2:20; 9:8; 12:1,4,6,13-17; 14:4;
17:3,4,6,7,9,18; 19:7; 21:9

1136. Γώγ Gōg
REV. 20:8

1137. γωνία gōnia
MATT. 6:5; 21:42; MARK 12:10; LUKE
20:17; ACTS 4:11; 26:26; 1 PET. 2:7; REV.
7:1; 20:8

Δ

1138. Δαβίδ Dabid
MATT. 1:1,6,17,20; 9:27; 12:3,23; 15:22;
20:30,31; 21:9,15; 22:42,43,45; MARK 2:25;
10:47,48; 11:10; 12:35-37; LUKE 1:27,32,69;
2:4,11; 3:31; 6:3; 18:38,39; 20:41,42,44; JOHN
7:42; ACTS 1:16; 2:25,29,34; 4:25; 7:45;
13:22,34,36; 15:16; ROM. 1:3; 4:6; 11:9;
2 TIM. 2:8; HEB. 4:7; 11:32; REV. 3:7; 5:5;
22:16

1139. δαιμονίζομαι daimonizomai
MATT. 4:24; 8:16,28,33; 9:32; 12:22; 15:22;

MARK 1:32; 5:15,16,18; LUKE 8:36; JOHN 10:21

1140. δαιμόνιον daimonion
MATT. 7:22; 9:33,34; 10:8; 11:18; 12:24,27,28; 17:18; MARK 1:34,39; 3:15,22; 6:13; 7:26, 29,30; 9:38; 16:9,17; LUKE 4:33,35,41; 7:33; 8:2,27,30,33,35,38; 9:1,42,49; 10:17; 11:14, 15,18-20; 13:32; JOHN 7:20; 8:48,49,52; 10:20,21; ACTS 17:18; 1 COR. 10:20,21; 1 TIM. 4:1; JAMES 2:19; REV. 9:20

1141. δαιμονιώδης daimoniōdēs
JAMES 3:15

1142. δαίμων daimōn
MATT. 8:31; MARK 5:12; LUKE 8:29; REV. 16:14; 18:2

1143. δάκνω daknō
GAL. 5:15

**1144. δάκρυ, δάκρύον
dakru, dakruon**
MARK 9:24; LUKE 7:38,44; ACTS 20:19,31; 2 COR. 2:4; 2 TIM. 1:4; HEB. 5:7; 12:17; REV. 7:17; 21:4

1145. δακρύω dakruō
JOHN 11:35

1146. δακτύλιος daktulios
LUKE 15:22

1147. δάκτυλος daktulos
MATT. 23:4; MARK 7:33; LUKE 11:20,46; 16:24; JOHN 8:6; 20:25,27

1148. Δαλμανουθά Dalmanoutha
MARK 8:10

1149. Δαλματία Dalmatia
2 TIM. 4:10

1150. δαμάζω damazō
MARK 5:4; JAMES 3:7,8

1151. δάμαλις damalis
HEB. 9:13

1152. Δάμαρις Damaris
ACTS 17:34

1153. Δαμασκηνός Damaskēnos
2 COR. 11:32

1154. Δαμασκός Damaskos
ACTS 9:2,3,8,10,19,22,27; 22:5,6,10,11; 26:12,20; 2 COR. 11:32; GAL. 1:17

1155. δανείζω daneizō
MATT. 5:42; LUKE 6:34,35

1156. δάνειον daneion
MATT. 18:27

1157. δανειστής daneistēs
LUKE 7:41

1158. Δανιήλ Daniēl
MATT. 24:15; MARK 13:14

1159. δαπανάω dapanaō
MARK 5:26; LUKE 15:14; ACTS 21:24; 2 COR. 12:15; JAMES 4:3

1160. δαπάνη dapanē
LUKE 14:28

1162. δέησις deēsis
LUKE 1:13; 2:37; 5:33; ACTS 1:14; ROM. 10:1; 2 COR. 1:11; 9:14; EPH. 6:18; PHIL. 1:4,19; 4:6; 1 TIM. 2:1; 5:5; 2 TIM. 1:3; HEB. 5:7; JAMES 5:16; 1 PET. 3:12

1163. δεῖ dei
MATT. 16:21; 17:10; 18:33; 23:23; 24:6; 25:27; 26:35,54; MARK 8:31; 9:11; 13:7,10,14; 14:31; LUKE 2:49; 4:43; 9:22; 11:42; 12:12; 13:14, 16,33; 15:32; 17:25; 18:1; 19:5; 21:9; 22:7,37; 24:7,26,44,46; JOHN 3:7,14,30; 4:4,20,24; 9:4; 10:16; 12:34; 20:9; ACTS 1:16,22; 3:21; 4:12; 5:29; 9:6,16; 10:6; 14:22; 15:5; 16:30; 17:3; 18:21; 19:21,36; 20:35; 21:22; 23:11; 24:19; 25:10,24; 26:9; 27:21,24,26; ROM. 1:27; 8:26; 12:3; 1 COR. 8:2; 11:19; 15:25,53; 2 COR. 2:3; 5:10; 11:30; EPH. 6:20; COL. 4:4,6; 1 THESS. 4:1; 2 THESS. 3:7; 1 TIM. 3:2,7,15; 5:13;

2 TIM. 2:6,24; **TITUS** 1:7,11; **HEB.** 2:1; 9:26; 11:6; **1 PET.** 1:6; **2 PET.** 3:11; **REV.** 1:1; 4:1; 10:11; 11:5; 13:10; 17:10; 20:3; 22:6

1164. δεῖγμα deigma
JUDE 1:7

1165. δειγματίζω deigmatizō
COL. 2:15

1166. I. δεικνύω deiknuō
MATT. 16:21; **JOHN** 2:18; **REV.** 22:8

II. δείκνυμι deiknumi
MATT. 4:8; 8:4; **MARK** 1:44; 14:15; **LUKE** 4:5; 5:14; 22:12; **JOHN** 5:20; 10:32; 14:8,9; 20:20; **ACTS** 7:3; 10:28; **1 COR.** 12:31; **1 TIM.** 6:15; **HEB.** 8:5; **JAMES** 2:18; 3:13; **REV.** 1:1; 4:1; 17:1; 21:9,10; 22:1,6

1167. δειλία deilia
2 TIM. 1:7

1168. δειλιάω deiliaō
JOHN 14:27

1169. δειλός deilos
MATT. 8:26; **MARK** 4:40; **REV.** 21:8

1170. δεῖνα deina
MATT. 26:18

1171. δεινῶς deinōs
MATT. 8:6; **LUKE** 11:53

1172. δειπνέω deipneō
LUKE 17:8; 22:20; **1 COR.** 11:25; **REV.** 3:20

1173. δεῖπνον deipnon
MATT. 23:6; **MARK** 6:21; 12:39; **LUKE** 14:12,16,17,24; 20:46; **JOHN** 12:2; 13:2,4; 21:20; **1 COR.** 11:20,21; **REV.** 19:9,17

1174. δεισιδαιμονέστερος deisidaimonesteros
ACTS 17:22

1175. δεισιδαιμονία deisidaimonia
ACTS 25:19

1176. δέκα deka
MATT. 20:24; 25:1,28; **MARK** 10:41; **LUKE** 13:4,11,16; 14:31; 15:8; 17:12,17; 19:13,16, 17,24,25; **ACTS** 25:6; **REV.** 2:10; 12:3; 13:1; 17:3,7,12,16

1177. δεκαδύο dekaduo
ACTS 19:7; 24:11

1178. δεκαπέντε dekapente
JOHN 11:18; **ACTS** 27:28; **GAL.** 1:18

1179. Δεκάπολις Dekapolis
MATT. 4:25; **MARK** 5:20; 7:31

1180. δεκατέσσαρες dekatessares
MATT. 1:17; **2 COR.** 12:2; **GAL.** 2:1

1181. δεκάτη dekatē
HEB. 7:2,4,8,9

1182. δέκατος dekatos
JOHN 1:39; **REV.** 11:13; 21:20

1183. δεκατόω dekatoō
HEB. 7:6,9

1184. δεκτός dektos
LUKE 4:19,24; **ACTS** 10:35; **2 COR.** 6:2; **PHIL.** 4:18

1185. δελεάζω deleazō
JAMES 1:14; **2 PET.** 2:14,18

1186. δένδρον dendron
MATT. 3:10; 7:17-19; 12:33; 13:32; 21:8; **MARK** 8:24; 11:8; **LUKE** 3:9; 6:43,44; 13:19; 21:29; **JUDE** 1:12; **REV.** 7:1,3; 8:7; 9:4

1187. δεξιολάβος dexiolabos
ACTS 23:23

1188. δεξιός dexios
MATT. 5:29,30,39; 6:3; 20:21,23; 22:44; 25:33,34; 26:64; 27:29,38; **MARK** 10:37,40; 12:36; 14:62; 15:27; 16:5,19; **LUKE** 1:11; 6:6; 20:42; 22:50,69; 23:33; **JOHN** 18:10; 21:6;

ACTS 2:25,33,34; 3:7; 5:31; 7:55,56; **ROM.**
8:34; **2 COR.** 6:7; **GAL.** 2:9; **EPH.** 1:20; **COL.**
3:1; **HEB.** 1:3,13; 8:1; 10:12; 12:2; **1 PET.** 3:22;
REV. 1:16,17,20; 2:1; 5:1,7; 10:2; 13:16

1189. δέομαι deomai
MATT. 9:38; **LUKE** 5:12; 8:28,38; 9:38,40;
10:2; 21:36; 22:32; **ACTS** 4:31; 8:22,24,34;
10:2; 21:39; 26:3; **ROM.** 1:10; **2 COR.** 5:20;
8:4; 10:2; **GAL.** 4:12; **1 THESS.** 3:10

1190. Δερβαῖος Derbaios
ACTS 20:4

1191. Δέρβη Derbē
ACTS 14:6,20; 16:1

1192. δέρμα derma
HEB. 11:37

1193. δερμάτινος dermatinos
MATT. 3:4; **MARK** 1:6

1194. δέρω derō
MATT. 21:35; **MARK** 12:3,5; 13:9; **LUKE**
12:47,48; 20:10,11; 22:63; **JOHN** 18:23; **ACTS**
5:40; 16:37; 22:19; **1 COR.** 9:26; **2 COR.** 11:20

1195. δεσμεύω desmeuō
MATT. 23:4; **ACTS** 22:4

1196. δεσμέω desmeō
LUKE 8:29

1197. δέσμη desmē
MATT. 13:30

1198. δέσμιος desmios
MATT. 27:15,16; **MARK** 15:6; **ACTS**
16:25,27; 23:18; 25:14,27; 28:16,17; **EPH.** 3:1;
4:1; **2 TIM.** 1:8; **PHILE.** 1:1,9; **HEB.** 13:3

1199. δεσμός desmos
MARK 7:35; **LUKE** 8:29; 13:16; **ACTS** 16:26;
20:23; 22:30; 23:29; 26:29,31; **PHIL.** 1:7,13,
14,16; **COL.** 4:18; **2 TIM.** 2:9; **PHILE.** 1:10,13;
HEB. 10:34; 11:36; **JUDE** 1:6

1200. δεσμοφύλαξ desmophulax
ACTS 16:23,27,36

1201. δεσμωτήριον desmōtērion
MATT. 11:2; **ACTS** 5:21,23; 16:26

1202. δεσμώτης desmōtēs
ACTS 27:1,42

1203. δεσπότης despotēs
LUKE 2:29; **ACTS** 4:24; **1 TIM.** 6:1,2; **2 TIM.**
2:21; **TITUS** 2:9; **1 PET.** 2:18; **2 PET.** 2:1;
JUDE 1:4; **REV.** 6:10

1204. δεῦρο deuro
MATT. 19:21; **MARK** 10:21; **LUKE** 18:22;
JOHN 11:43; **ACTS** 7:3,34; **ROM.** 1:13; **REV.**
17:1; 21:9

1205. δεῦτε deute
MATT. 4:19; 11:28; 21:38; 22:4; 25:34; 28:6;
MARK 1:17; 6:31; 12:7; **LUKE** 20:14; **JOHN**
4:29; 21:12; **REV.** 19:17

1206. δευτεραῖος deuteraios
ACTS 28:13

1207. δευτερόπρωτος deuteroprōtos
LUKE 6:1

1208. δεύτερος deuteros
MATT. 21:30; 22:26,39; 26:42; **MARK** 12:21,
31; 14:72; **LUKE** 12:38; 19:18; 20:30; **JOHN**
3:4; 4:54; 9:24; 21:16; **ACTS** 7:13; 10:15; 11:9;
12:10; 13:33; **1 COR.** 12:28; 15:47; **2 COR.**
1:15; 13:2; **TITUS** 3:10; **HEB.** 8:7; 9:3,7,28;
10:9; **2 PET.** 3:1; **JUDE** 1:5; **REV.** 2:11; 4:7;
6:3; 8:8; 11:14; 16:3; 19:3; 20:6,14; 21:8,19

1209. δέχομαι dechomai
MATT. 10:14,40,41; 11:14; 18:5; **MARK** 6:11;
9:37; 10:15; **LUKE** 2:28; 8:13; 9:5,11,48,53;
10:8,10; 16:4,6,7,9; 18:17; 22:17; **JOHN** 4:45;
ACTS 3:21; 7:38,59; 8:14; 11:1; 17:11; 21:17;
22:5; 28:21; **1 COR.** 2:14; **2 COR.** 6:1; 7:15;
8:4,17; 11:4,16; **GAL.** 4:14; **EPH.** 6:17;
PHIL. 4:18; **COL.** 4:10; **1 THESS.** 1:6; 2:13;
2 THESS. 2:10; **HEB.** 11:31; **JAMES** 1:21

1210. δέω deō
MATT. 12:29; 13:30; 14:3; 16:19; 18:18; 21:2;
22:13; 27:2; **MARK** 3:27; 5:3,4; 6:17; 11:2,4;

15:1,7; **LUKE** 13:16; 19:30; **JOHN** 11:44;
18:12,24; 19:40; **ACTS** 9:2,14,21; 10:11; 12:6;
20:22; 21:11,13,33; 22:5,29; 24:27; **ROM.** 7:2;
1 COR. 7:27,39; **COL.** 4:3; **2 TIM.** 2:9; **REV.**
9:14; 20:2

1211. δή dē
MATT. 13:23; **LUKE** 2:15; **ACTS** 13:2; 15:36;
1 COR. 6:20; **2 COR.** 12:1

1212. δῆλος dēlos
MATT. 26:73; **1 COR.** 15:27; **GAL.** 3:11;
1 TIM. 6:7

1213. δηλόω dēloō
1 COR. 1:11; 3:13; **COL.** 1:8; **HEB.** 9:8; 12:27;
1 PET. 1:11; **2 PET.** 1:14

1214. Δημᾶς Dēmas
COL. 4:14; **2 TIM.** 4:10; **PHILE.** 1:24

1215. δημηγορέω dēmēgoreō
ACTS 12:21

1216. Δημήτριος Dēmētrios
ACTS 19:24,38; **3 JOHN** 1:12

1217. δημιουργός dēmiourgos
HEB. 11:10

1218. δῆμος dēmos
ACTS 12:22; 17:5; 19:30,33

1219. δημόσιος dēmosios
ACTS 5:18; 16:37; 18:28; 20:20

1220. δηνάριον dēnarion
MATT. 18:28; 20:2,9,10,13; 22:19; **MARK**
6:37; 12:15; 14:5; **LUKE** 7:41; 10:35; 20:24;
JOHN 6:7; 12:5; **REV.** 6:6

1221. δήποτε dēpote
JOHN 5:4

1222. δήπου dēpou
HEB. 2:16

1224. διαβαίνω diabainō
LUKE 16:26; **ACTS** 16:9; **HEB.** 11:29

1225. διαβάλλω diaballō
LUKE 16:1

1226. διαβεβαιόομαι daibebaioomai
1 TIM. 1:7; **TITUS** 3:8

1227. διαβλέπω diablepō
MATT. 7:5; **LUKE** 6:42

1228. διάβολος diabolos
MATT. 4:1,5,8,11; 13:39; 25:41; **LUKE** 4:2,3,
5,6,13; 8:12; **JOHN** 6:70; 8:44; 13:2; **ACTS**
10:38; 13:10; **EPH.** 4:27; 6:11; **1 TIM.** 3:6,7,11;
2 TIM. 2:26; 3:3; **TITUS** 2:3; **HEB.** 2:14;
JAMES 4:7; **1 PET.** 5:8; **1 JOHN** 3:8,10;
JUDE 1:9; **REV.** 2:10; 12:9,12; 20:2,10

1229. διαγγέλλω diaggellō
LUKE 9:60; **ACTS** 21:26; **ROM.** 9:17

1230. διαγίνομαι diaginomai
MARK 16:1; **ACTS** 25:13; 27:9

1231. διαγινώσκω diaginōskō
ACTS 23:15; 24:22

1232. διαγνωρίζω diagnōrizō
LUKE 2:17

1233. διάγνωσις diagnōsis
ACTS 25:21

1234. διαγογγύζω diagogguzō
LUKE 15:2; 19:7

1235. διαγρηγορέω diagrēgoreō
LUKE 9:32

1236. διάγω diagō
1 TIM. 2:2; **TITUS** 3:3

1237. διαδέχομαι diadechomai
ACTS 7:45

1238. διάδημα diadēma
REV. 12:3; 13:1; 19:12

1239. διαδίδωμι diadidōmi
LUKE 11:22; 18:22; JOHN 6:11; ACTS 4:35;
REV. 17:13

1240. διάδοχος diadochos
ACTS 24:27

1241. διαζώννυμι diazōnnumi
JOHN 13:4,5; 21:7

1242. διαθήκη diathēkē
MATT. 26:28; MARK 14:24; LUKE 1:72;
22:20; ACTS 3:25; 7:8; ROM. 9:4; 11:27;
1 COR. 11:25; 2 COR. 3:6,14; GAL. 3:15,17;
4:24; EPH. 2:12; HEB. 7:22; 8:6,8-10; 9:4,15-
17,20; 10:16,29; 12:24; 13:20; REV. 11:19

1243. διαίρεσις diairesis
1 COR. 12:4-6

1244. διαιρέω diaireō
LUKE 15:12; 1 COR. 12:11

1245. διακαθαρίζω diakatharizō
MATT. 3:12; LUKE 3:17

**1246. διακατελέγχομαι
diakatelegchomai**
ACTS 18:28

1247. διακονέω diakoneō
MATT. 4:11; 8:15; 20:28; 25:44; 27:55; MARK
1:13,31; 10:45; 15:41; LUKE 4:39; 8:3; 10:40;
12:37; 17:8; 22:26,27; JOHN 12:2,26; ACTS
6:2; 19:22; ROM. 15:25; 2 COR. 3:3; 8:19,20;
1 TIM. 3:10,13; 2 TIM. 1:18; PHILE. 1:13;
HEB. 6:10; 1 PET. 1:12; 4:10,11

1248. διακονία diakonia
LUKE 10:40; ACTS 1:17,25; 6:1,4; 11:29;
12:25; 20:24; 21:19; ROM. 11:13; 12:7; 15:31;
1 COR. 12:5; 16:15; 2 COR. 3:7-9; 4:1; 5:18;
6:3; 8:4; 9:1,12,13; 11:8; EPH. 4:12; COL. 4:17;
1 TIM. 1:12; 2 TIM. 4:5,11; HEB. 1:14; REV.
2:19

1249. διάκονος diakonos
MATT. 20:26; 22:13; 23:11; MARK 9:35;
10:43; JOHN 2:5,9; 12:26; ROM. 13:4; 15:8;

16:1; 1 COR. 3:5; 2 COR. 3:6; 6:4; 11:15,23;
GAL. 2:17; EPH. 3:7; 6:21; PHIL. 1:1; COL.
1:7,23,25; 4:7; 1 THESS. 3:2; 1 TIM. 3:8,12;
4:6

1250. διακόσιοι diakosioi
MARK 6:37; JOHN 6:7; 21:8; ACTS 23:23;
27:37; REV. 11:3; 12:6

1251. διακούω diakouō
ACTS 23:35

1252. διακρίνω diakrinō
MATT. 16:3; 21:21; MARK 11:23; ACTS
10:20; 11:2,12; 15:9; ROM. 4:20; 14:23;
1 COR. 4:7; 6:5; 11:29,31; 14:29; JAMES 1:6;
2:4; JUDE 1:9,22

1253. διάκρισις diakrisis
ROM. 14:1; 1 COR. 12:10; HEB. 5:14

1254. διακωλύω diakōluō
MATT. 3:14

1255. διαλαλέω dialaleō
LUKE 1:65; 6:11

1256. διαλέγομαι dialegomai
MARK 9:34; ACTS 17:2,17; 18:4,19; 19:8,9;
20:7,9; 24:12,25; HEB. 12:5; JUDE 1:9

1257. διαλείπω dialeipō
LUKE 7:45

1258. διάλεκτος dialektos
ACTS 1:19; 2:6,8; 21:40; 22:2; 26:14

**1259. διαλλάσσομαι, διαλλάττομαι
diallassomai, diallattomai**
MATT. 5:24

1260. διαλογίζομαι dialogizomai
MATT. 16:7,8; 21:25; MARK 2:6,8; 8:16,17;
9:33; LUKE 1:29; 3:15; 5:21,22; 12:17; 20:14;
JOHN 11:50

1261. διαλογισμός dialogismos
MATT. 15:19; MARK 7:21; LUKE 2:35; 5:22;

6:8; 9:46,47; 24:38; **ROM.** 1:21; 14:1; **1 COR.**
3:20; **PHIL.** 2:14; **1 TIM.** 2:8; **JAMES** 2:4

1262. *διαλύω dialuō*
ACTS 5:36

1263. *διαμαρτύρομαι diamarturomai*
LUKE 16:28; **ACTS** 2:40; 8:25; 10:42; 18:5;
20:21,23,24; 23:11; 28:23; **1 THESS.** 4:6;
1 TIM. 5:21; **2 TIM.** 2:14; 4:1; **HEB.** 2:6

1264. *διαμάχομαι diamachomai*
ACTS 23:9

1265. *διαμένω diamenō*
LUKE 1:22; 22:28; **GAL.** 2:5; **HEB.** 1:11;
2 PET. 3:4

1266. *διαμερίζω diamerizō*
MATT. 27:35; **MARK** 15:24; **LUKE** 11:17,18;
12:52,53; 22:17; 23:34; **JOHN** 19:24; **ACTS**
2:3,45

1267. *διαμερισμός diamerismos*
LUKE 12:51

1268. *διανέμω dianemō*
ACTS 4:17

1269. *διανεύω dianeuō*
LUKE 1:22

1270. *διανόημα dianoēma*
LUKE 11:17

1271. *διάνοια dianoia*
MATT. 22:37; **MARK** 12:30; **LUKE** 1:51;
10:27; **EPH.** 1:18; 2:3; 4:18; **COL.** 1:21; **HEB.**
8:10; 10:16; **1 PET.** 1:13; **2 PET.** 3:1; **1 JOHN**
5:20

1272. *διανοίγω dianoigō*
MARK 7:34,35; **LUKE** 2:23; 24:31,32,45;
ACTS 16:14; 17:3

1273. *διανυκτερεύω dianuktereuō*
LUKE 6:12

1274. *διανύω dianuō*
ACTS 21:7

1275. *διαπαντός diapantos*
MARK 5:5; **LUKE** 24:53; **ACTS** 10:2; 24:16;
ROM. 11:10; **HEB.** 9:6; 13:15

1276. *διαπεράω diaperaō*
MATT. 9:1; 14:34; **MARK** 5:21; 6:53; **LUKE**
16:26; **ACTS** 21:2

1277. *διαπλέω diapleō*
ACTS 27:5

1278. *διαπονέω diaponeō*
ACTS 4:2; 16:18

1279. *διαπορεύομαι diaporeuomai*
LUKE 6:1; 13:22; 18:36; **ACTS** 16:4; **ROM.**
15:24

1280. *διαπορέω diaporeō*
LUKE 9:7; 24:4; **ACTS** 2:12; 5:24; 10:17

1281. *διαπραγματεύομαι*
diapragmateuomai
LUKE 19:15

1282. *διαπρίω diapriō*
ACTS 5:33; 7:54

1283. *διαρπάζω diarpazō*
MATT. 12:29; **MARK** 3:27

1284. I. *διαρρήσσω diarrēssō*
    MATT. 26:65; **MARK** 14:63; **LUKE**
    8:29; **ACTS** 14:14

    II. *διαρρήγνυμι diarrēgnumi*
    LUKE 5:6

1285. *διασαφέω diasapheō*
MATT. 18:31

1286. *διασείω diaseiō*
LUKE 3:14

1287. διασκορπίζω *diaskorpizō*
MATT. 25:24,26; 26:31; MARK 14:27; LUKE
1:51; 15:13; 16:1; JOHN 11:52; ACTS 5:37

1288. διασπάω *diaspaō*
MARK 5:4; ACTS 23:10

1289. διασπείρω *diaspeirō*
ACTS 8:1,4; 11:19

1290. διασπορά *diaspora*
JOHN 7:35; JAMES 1:1; 1 PET. 1:1

1291. διαστέλλω *diastellō*
MATT. 16:20; MARK 5:43; 7:36; 8:15; 9:9;
ACTS 15:24; HEB. 12:20

1292. διάστημα *diastēma*
ACTS 5:7

1293. διαστολή *diastolē*
ROM. 3:22; 10:12; 1 COR. 14:7

1294. διαστρέφω *diastrephō*
MATT. 17:17; LUKE 9:41; 23:2; ACTS
13:8,10; 20:30; PHIL. 2:15

1295. διασώζω *diasōzō*
MATT. 14:36; LUKE 7:3; ACTS 23:24;
27:43,44; 28:1,4; 1 PET. 3:20

1296. διαταγή *diatagē*
ACTS 7:53; ROM. 13:2

1297. διάταγμα *diatagma*
HEB. 11:23

1298. διαταράσσω, διαταράττω
diatarassō, diatarattō
LUKE 1:29

1299. διατάσσω *diatassō*
MATT. 11:1; LUKE 3:13; 8:55; 17:9,10; ACTS
7:44; 18:2; 20:13; 23:31; 24:23; 1 COR. 7:17;
9:14; 11:34; 16:1; GAL. 3:19; TITUS 1:5

1300. διατελέω *diateleō*
ACTS 27:33

1301. διατηρέω *diatēreō*
LUKE 2:51; ACTS 15:29

1302. διατί *diati*
MATT. 9:11,14; 13:10; 15:2,3; 17:19; 21:25;
MARK 2:18; 7:5; 11:31; LUKE 5:30,33;
19:23,31; 20:5; 24:38; JOHN 7:45; 8:43,46;
12:5; 13:37; ACTS 5:3; ROM. 9:32; 1 COR.
6:7; 2 COR. 11:11; REV. 17:7

1303. διατίθεμαι *diatithemai*
LUKE 22:29; ACTS 3:25; HEB. 8:10; 9:16,17;
10:16

1304. διατρίβω *diatribō*
JOHN 3:22; 11:54; ACTS 12:19; 14:3,28;
15:35; 16:12; 20:6; 25:6,14

1305. διατροφή *diatrophē*
1 TIM. 6:8

1306. διαυγάζω *diaugazō*
2 PET. 1:19

1307. διαφανής *diaphanēs*
REV. 21:21

1308. διαφέρω *diapherō*
MATT. 6:26; 10:31; 12:12; MARK 11:16;
LUKE 12:7,24; ACTS 13:49; 27:27; ROM.
2:18; 1 COR. 15:41; GAL. 2:6; 4:1; PHIL. 1:10

1309. διαφεύγω *diapheugō*
ACTS 27:42

1310. διαφημίζω *diaphēmizō*
MATT. 9:31; 28:15; MARK 1:45

1311. διαφθείρω *diaphtheirō*
LUKE 12:33; 2 COR. 4:16; 1 TIM. 6:5; REV.
8:9; 11:18

1312. διαφθορά *diaphthora*
ACTS 2:27,31; 13:34-37

1313. διάφορος *diaphoros*
ROM. 12:6; HEB. 1:4; 8:6; 9:10

1314. διαφυλάσσω, διαφυλάττω
diaphulassō, diaphulattō
LUKE 4:10

1315. διαχειρίζω *diacheirizō*
ACTS 5:30; 26:21

1316. διαχωρίζω *diachōrizō*
LUKE 9:33

1317. διδακτικός *didaktikos*
1 TIM. 3:2; **2 TIM.** 2:24

1318. διδακτός *didaktos*
JOHN 6:45; **1 COR.** 2:13

1319. διδασκαλία *didaskalia*
MATT. 15:9; **MARK** 7:7; **ROM.** 12:7; 15:4;
EPH. 4:14; **COL.** 2:22; **1 TIM.** 1:10; 4:1,6,13,
16; 5:17; 6:1,3; **2 TIM.** 3:10,16; 4:3; **TITUS** 1:9;
2:1,7,10

1320. διδάσκαλος *didaskalos*
MATT. 8:19; 9:11; 10:24,25; 12:38; 17:24;
19:16; 22:16,24,36; 26:18; **MARK** 4:38; 5:35;
9:17,38; 10:17; 20:35; 12:14,19,32; 13:1; 14:14;
LUKE 2:46; 3:12; 6:40; 7:40; 8:49; 9:38; 10:25;
11:45; 12:13; 18:18; 19:39; 20:21,28,39; 21:7;
22:11; **JOHN** 1:38; 3:2,10; 8:4; 11:28; 13:13,14;
20:16; **ACTS** 13:1; **ROM.** 2:20; **1 COR.** 12:28,
29; **EPH.** 4:11; **1 TIM.** 2:7; **2 TIM.** 1:11; 4:3;
HEB. 5:12; **JAMES** 3:1

1321. διδάσκω *didaskō*
MATT. 4:23; 5:2,19; 7:29; 9:35; 11:1; 13:54;
15:9; 21:23; 22:16; 26:55; 28:15,20; **MARK**
1:21,22; 2:13; 4:1,2; 6:2,6,30,34; 7:7; 8:31; 9:31;
10:1; 11:17; 12:14,35; 14:49; **LUKE** 4:15,31;
5:3,17; 6:6; 11:1; 12:12; 13:10,22,26; 19:47;
20:1,21; 21:37; 23:5; **JOHN** 6:59; 7:14,28,35;
8:2,20,28; 9:34; 14:26; 18:20; **ACTS** 1:1; 4:2,18;
5:21,25,28,42; 11:26; 15:1,35; 18:11,25; 20:20;
21:21,28; 28:31; **ROM.** 2:21; 12:7; **1 COR.**
4:17; 11:14; **GAL.** 1:12; **EPH.** 4:21; **COL.** 1:28;
2:7; 3:16; **2 THESS.** 2:15; **1 TIM.** 2:12; 4:11;
6:2; **2 TIM.** 2:2; **TITUS** 1:11; **HEB.** 5:12; 8:11;
1 JOHN 2:27; **REV.** 2:14,20

1322. διδαχή *didachē*
MATT. 7:28; 16:12; 22:33; **MARK** 1:22,27;

4:2; 11:18; 12:38; **LUKE** 4:32; **JOHN** 7:16,17;
18:19; **ACTS** 2:42; 5:28; 13:12; 17:19; **ROM.**
6:17; 16:17; **1 COR.** 14:6,26; **2 TIM.** 4:2;
TITUS 1:9; **HEB.** 6:2; 13:9; **2 JOHN** 1:9,10;
REV. 2:14,15,24

1323. δίδραχμον *didrachmon*
MATT. 17:24

1324. Δίδυμος *Didumos*
JOHN 11:16; 20:24; 21:2

1325. δίδωμι *didōmi*
MATT. 4:9; 5:31,42; 6:11; 7:6,7,11; 9:8;
10:1,8,19; 12:39; 13:8,11,12; 14:7-9,11,16,19;
15:36; 16:4,19,26; 17:27; 19:7,11,21; 20:4,14,
23,28; 21:23,43; 22:17; 24:24,29,45; 25:8,15,
28,29,35,42; 26:9,15,26,27,48; 27:10,34; 28:12,
18; **MARK** 2:26; 4:7,8,11,25; 5:43; 6:2,7,22,
23,25,28,37,41; 8:6,12,37; 10:21,37,40,45;
11:28; 12:9,14,15; 13:11,22,24,34; 14:5,11,
22,23,44; 15:23; **LUKE** 1:32,74,77; 2:24; 4:6;
6:4,30,38; 7:15,44,45; 8:10,18,55; 9:1,13,16;
10:19,35; 11:3,7-9,13,29,41; 12:32,33,42,
48,51,58; 14:9; 15:12,16,22,29; 16:12; 17:18;
18:43; 19:8,13,15,23,24,26; 20:2,10,16,22;
21:15; 22:5,19; 23:2; **JOHN** 1:12,17,22;
3:16,27,34,35; 4:5,7,10,12,14,15; 5:22,26,27,36;
6:27,31-34,37,39,51,52,65; 7:19,22; 9:24;
10:28,29; 11:22,57; 12:5,49; 13:3,15,26,29,34;
14:16,27; 15:16; 16:23; 17:2,4,6-9,11,12,14,
22,24; 18:9,11,22; 19:3,9,11; 21:13; **ACTS** 1:26;
2:4,19,27; 3:6,16; 4:12,29; 5:31,32; 7:5,8,10,
25,38; 8:18,19; 9:41; 10:40; 11:17,18; 12:23;
13:20,21,34,35; 14:3,17; 15:8; 17:25; 19:31;
20:32,35; 24:26; **ROM.** 4:20; 5:5; 11:8; 12:3,6,
19; 14:12; 15:5,15; **1 COR.** 1:4; 3:5,10; 7:25;
9:12; 11:15; 12:7,8,24; 14:7-9; 15:38,57; **2 COR.**
1:22; 5:5,12,18; 6:3; 8:1,5,10,16; 9:9; 10:8; 12:7;
13:10; **GAL.** 1:4; 2:9; 3:21,22; 4:15; **EPH.**
1:17,22; 3:2,7,8,16; 4:7,8,11,27,29; 6:19; **COL.**
1:25; **1 THESS.** 4:2,8; **2 THESS.** 1:8; 2:16;
3:9,16; **1 TIM.** 2:6; 4:14; 5:14; **2 TIM.** 1:7,9,16,
18; 2:7,25; **TITUS** 2:14; **HEB.** 2:13; 7:4; 8:10;
10:16; **JAMES** 1:5; 2:16; 4:6; 5:18; **1 PET.**
1:21; 5:5; **2 PET.** 3:15; **1 JOHN** 3:1,23, 24;
4:13; 5:11,16,20; **REV.** 1:1; 2:7,10,17,21,23,
26,28; 3:8,9,21; 4:9; 6:2,4,8,11; 7:2; 8:2,3;
9:1,3,5; 10:9; 11:1-3,13,18; 12:14; 13:2,4,5,7,14-
16; 14:7; 15:7; 16:6,8,9,19; 17:17; 18:7; 19:7,8;
20:4,13; 21:6

1326. διεγείρω *diegeirō*
MATT. 1:24; MARK 4:38,39; LUKE 8:24;
JOHN 6:18; 2 PET. 1:13; 3:1

1327. διέξοδος *diexodos*
MATT. 22:9

1328. διερμηνευτής *diermēneutēs*
1 COR. 14:28

1329. διερμηνεύω *diermēneuō*
LUKE 24:27; ACTS 9:36; 1 COR. 12:30;
14:5,13,27

1330. διέρχομαι *dierchomai*
MATT. 12:43; 19:24; MARK 4:35; LUKE
2:15,35; 4:30; 5:15; 8:22; 9:6; 11:24; 17:11;
19:1,4; JOHN 4:4; 8:59; ACTS 8:4,40; 9:32,38;
10:38; 11:19,22; 12:10; 13:6,14; 14:24; 15:3,41;
16:6; 17:23; 18:23,27; 19:1,21; 20:2,25; ROM.
5:12; 1 COR. 10:1; 16:5; 2 COR. 1:16; HEB.
4:14

1331. διερωτάω *dierōtaō*
ACTS 10:17

1332. διετής *dietēs*
MATT. 2:16

1333. διετία *dietia*
ACTS 24:27; 28:30

1334. διηγέομαι *diēgeomai*
MARK 5:16; 9:9; LUKE 8:39; 9:10; ACTS
8:33; 9:27; 12:17; HEB. 11:32

1335. διήγησις *diēgēsis*
LUKE 1:1

1336. διηνεκές *diēnekes*
HEB. 7:3; 10:1,12,14

1337. διθάλασσος *dithalassos*
ACTS 27:41

1338. διϊκνέομαι *diikneomai*
HEB. 4:12

1339. διΐστημι *diistēmi*
LUKE 22:59; 24:51; ACTS 27:28

1340. διϊσχυρίζομαι *diischurizomai*
LUKE 22:59; ACTS 12:15

1341. δικαιοκρισία *dikaiokrisia*
ROM. 2:5

1342. δίκαιος *dikaios*
MATT. 1:19; 5:45; 9:13; 10:41; 13:17,43,49;
20:4,7; 23:28,29,35; 25:37,46; 27:19,24; MARK
2:17; 6:20; LUKE 1:6,17; 2:25; 5:32; 12:57;
14:14; 15:7; 18:9; 20:20; 23:47,50; JOHN 5:30;
7:24; 17:25; ACTS 3:14; 4:19; 7:52; 10:22;
22:14; 24:15; ROM. 1:17; 2:13; 3:10,26; 5:7,19;
7:12; GAL. 3:11; EPH. 6:1; PHIL. 1:7; 4:8;
COL. 4:1; 2 THESS. 1:5,6; 1 TIM. 1:9; 2 TIM.
4:8; TITUS 1:8; HEB. 10:38; 11:4; 12:23;
JAMES 5:6,16; 1 PET. 3:12,18; 4:18; 2 PET.
1:13; 2:7,8; 1 JOHN 1:9; 2:1,29; 3:7,12; REV.
15:3; 16:5,7; 19:2; 22:11

1343. δικαιοσύνη *dikaiosunē*
MATT. 3:15; 5:6,10,20; 6:33; 21:32; LUKE
1:75; JOHN 16:8,10; ACTS 10:35; 13:10;
17:31; 24:25; ROM. 1:17; 3:5,21,22,25,26;
4:3,5,6,9,11,13,22; 5:17,21; 6:13,16,18-20; 8:10;
9:28,30,31; 10:3-6,10; 14:17; 1 COR. 1:30;
2 COR. 3:9; 5:21; 6:7,14; 9:9,10; 11:15; GAL.
2:21; 3:6,21; 5:5; EPH. 4:24; 5:9; 6:14; PHIL.
1:11; 3:6,9; 1 TIM. 6:11; 2 TIM. 2:22; 3:16; 4:8;
TITUS 3:5; HEB. 1:9; 5:13; 7:2; 11:7,33; 12:11;
JAMES 1:20; 2:23; 3:18; 1 PET. 2:24; 3:14;
2 PET. 1:1; 2:5,21; 3:13; 1 JOHN 2:29; 3:7,10;
REV. 19:11

1344. δικαιόω *dikaioō*
MATT. 11:19; 12:37; LUKE 7:29,35; 10:29;
16:15; 18:14; ACTS 13:39; ROM. 2:13; 3:4,20,
24,26,28,30; 4:2,5; 5:1,9; 6:7; 8:30,33; 1 COR.
4:4; 6:11; GAL. 2:16,17; 3:8,11,24; 5:4; 1 TIM.
3:16; TITUS 3:7; JAMES 2:21,24,25; REV.
22:11

1345. δικαίωμα *dikaiōma*
LUKE 1:6; ROM. 1:32; 2:26; 5:16,18; 8:4;
HEB. 9:1,10; REV. 15:4; 19:8

1346. δικαίως *dikaiōs*
LUKE 23:41; 1 COR. 15:34; 1 THESS. 2:10;
TITUS 2:12; 1 PET. 2:23

1347. δικαίωσις *dikaiōsis*
ROM. 4:25; 5:18

1348. δικαστής *dikastēs*
LUKE 12:14; ACTS 7:27,35

1349. δίκη *dikē*
ACTS 25:15; 28:4; 2 THESS. 1:9; JUDE 1:7

1350. δίκτυον *diktuon*
MATT. 4:20,21; MARK 1:18,19; LUKE 5:2,4-6; JOHN 21:6,8,11

1351. δίλογος *dilogos*
1 TIM. 3:8

1352. διὸ *dio*
MATT. 27:8; LUKE 1:35; 7:7; ACTS 10:29; 13:35; 15:19; 20:26,31; 24:26; 25:26; 26:3; 27:25,34; ROM. 1:24; 2:1; 4:22; 13:5; 15:7,22; 1 COR. 12:3; 2 COR. 2:8; 4:13,16; 5:9; 6:17; 12:10; EPH. 2:11; 3:13; 4:8,25; 5:14; PHIL. 2:9; 1 THESS. 2:18; 3:1; 5:11; PHILE. 1:8; HEB. 3:7,10; 6:1; 10:5; 11:12,16; 12:12,28; 13:12; JAMES 1:21; 4:6; 1 PET. 1:13; 2:6; 2 PET. 1:10,12; 3:14

1353. διοδεύω *diodeuō*
LUKE 8:1; ACTS 17:1

1354. Διονύσιος *Dionusios*
ACTS 17:34

1355. διόπερ *dioper*
1 COR. 8:13; 10:14; 14:13

1356. διοπετής *diopetēs*
ACTS 19:35

1357. διόρθωσις *diorthōsis*
HEB. 9:10

1358. διορύσσω, διορύττω
diorussō, dioruttō
MATT. 6:19,20; 24:43; LUKE 12:39

1359. Διόσκουροι *Dioskouroi*
ACTS 28:11

1360. διότι *dioti*
LUKE 1:13; 2:7; 21:28; ACTS 10:20; 17:31; 18:10; 22:18; ROM. 1:19,21; 3:20; 8:7; 1 COR. 15:9; GAL. 2:16; PHIL. 2:26; 1 THESS. 2:8; 4:6; HEB. 11:5,23; JAMES 4:3; 1 PET. 1:16,24

1361. Διοτρεφής *Diotrephēs*
3 JOHN 1:9

1362. διπλοῦς *diplous*
MATT. 23:15; 1 TIM. 5:17; REV. 18:6

1363. διπλόω *diploō*
REV. 18:6

1364. δίς *dis*
MARK 14:30,72; LUKE 18:12; PHIL. 4:16; 1 THESS. 2:18; JUDE 1:12

1365. διστάζω *distazō*
MATT. 14:31; 28:17

1366. δίστομος *distomos*
HEB. 4:12; REV. 1:16; 2:12

1367. δισχίλιοι *dischilioi*
MARK 5:13

1368. διϋλίζω *diulizō*
MATT. 23:24

1369. διχάζω *dichazō*
MATT. 10:35

1370. διχοστασία *dichostasia*
ROM. 16:17; 1 COR. 3:3; GAL. 5:20

1371. διχοτομέω *dichotomeō*
MATT. 24:51; LUKE 12:46

1372. διψάω *dipsaō*
MATT. 5:6; 25:35,37,42,44; JOHN 4:13-15; 6:35; 7:37; 19:28; ROM. 12:20; 1 COR. 4:11; REV. 7:16; 21:6; 22:17

1373. δίψος *dipsos*
2 COR. 11:27

1374. δίψυχος dipsuchos
JAMES 1:8; 4:8

1375. διωγμός diōgmos
MATT. 13:21; MARK 4:17; 10:30; ACTS 8:1;
13:50; ROM. 8:35; 2 COR. 12:10; 2 THESS.
1:4; 2 TIM. 3:11

1376. διώκτης diōktēs
1 TIM. 1:13

1377. διώκω diōkō
MATT. 5:10-12,44; 10:23; 23:34; LUKE 17:23;
21:12; JOHN 5:16; 15:20; ACTS 7:52; 9:4,5;
22:4,7,8; 26:11,14,15; ROM. 9:30,31; 12:13,14;
14:19; 1 COR. 4:12; 14:1; 15:9; 2 COR. 4:9;
GAL. 1:13,23; 4:29; 5:11; 6:12; PHIL. 3:6,12,
14; 1 THESS. 5:15; 1 TIM. 6:11; 2 TIM. 2:22;
3:12; HEB. 12:14; 1 PET. 3:11; REV. 12:13

1378. δόγμα dogma
LUKE 2:1; ACTS 16:4; 17:7; EPH. 2:15; COL.
2:14

1379. δογματίζω dogmatizō
COL. 2:20

1380. δοκέω dokeō
MATT. 3:9; 6:7; 17:25; 18:12; 21:28; 22:17,42;
24:44; 26:53,66; MARK 6:49; 10:42; LUKE
1:3; 8:18; 10:36; 12:40,51; 13:2,4; 17:9; 19:11;
22:24; 24:37; JOHN 5:39,45; 11:13,56; 13:29;
16:2; 20:15; ACTS 12:9; 15:22,25,28,34; 17:18;
25:27; 26:9; 27:13; 1 COR. 3:18; 4:9; 7:40; 8:2;
10:12; 11:16; 12:22,23; 14:37; 2 COR. 10:9;
11:16; 12:19; GAL. 2:2,6,9; 6:3; PHIL. 3:4;
HEB. 4:1; 10:29; 12:10,11; JAMES 1:26;
4:5

1381. δοκιμάζω dokimazō
LUKE 12:56; 14:19; ROM. 1:28; 2:18; 12:2;
14:22; 1 COR. 3:13; 11:28; 16:3; 2 COR. 8:8,
22; 13:5; GAL. 6:4; EPH. 5:10; PHIL. 1:10;
1 THESS. 2:4; 5:21; 1 TIM. 3:10; HEB. 3:9;
1 PET. 1:7; 1 JOHN 4:1

1382. δοκιμή dokimē
ROM. 5:4; 2 COR. 2:9; 8:2; 9:13; 13:3; PHIL.
2:22

1383. δοκίμιον dokimion
JAMES 1:3; 1 PET. 1:7

1384. δόκιμος dokimos
ROM. 14:18; 16:10; 1 COR. 11:19; 2 COR.
10:18; 13:7; 2 TIM. 2:15; JAMES 1:12

1385. δοκός dokos
MATT. 7:3-5; LUKE 6:41,42

1386. δόλιος dolios
2 COR. 11:13

1387. δολιόω dolioō
ROM. 3:13

1388. δόλος dolos
MATT. 26:4; MARK 7:22; 14:1; JOHN 1:47;
ACTS 13:10; ROM. 1:29; 2 COR. 12:16;
1 THESS. 2:3; 1 PET. 2:1,22; 3:10; REV.
14:5

1389. δολόω doloō
2 COR. 4:2

1390. δόμα doma
MATT. 7:11; LUKE 11:13; EPH. 4:8; PHIL.
4:17

1391. δόξα doxa
MATT. 4:8; 6:13,29; 16:27; 19:28; 24:30; 25:31;
MARK 8:38; 10:37; 13:26; LUKE 2:9,14,32;
4:6; 9:26,31,32; 12:27; 14:10; 17:18; 19:38;
21:27; 24:26; JOHN 1:14; 2:11; 5:41,44; 7:18;
8:50,54; 9:24; 11:4,40; 12:41,43; 17:5,22,24;
ACTS 7:2,55; 12:23; 22:11; ROM. 1:23; 2:7,10;
3:7,23; 4:20; 5:2; 6:4; 8:18,21; 9:4,23; 11:36;
15:7; 16:27; 1 COR. 2:7,8; 10:31; 11:7,15;
15:40,41,43; 2 COR. 1:20; 3:7-11,18; 4:4,6,15,
17; 6:8; 8:19,23; GAL. 1:5; EPH. 1:6,12,14,17,
18; 3:13,16,21; PHIL. 1:11; 2:11; 3:19,21;
4:19,20; COL. 1:11,27; 3:4; 1 THESS. 2:6,12,
20; 2 THESS. 1:9; 2:14; 1 TIM. 1:11,17; 3:16;
2 TIM. 2:10; 4:18; TITUS 2:13; HEB. 1:3;
2:7,9,10; 3:3; 9:5; 13:21; JAMES 2:1; 1 PET.
1:7,11,21,24; 4:11,13,14; 5:1,4,10,11; 2 PET.
1:3,17; 2:10; 3:18; JUDE 1:8,24,25; REV. 1:6;
4:9,11; 5:12,13; 7:12; 11:13; 14:7; 15:8; 16:9;
18:1; 19:1,7; 21:11,23,24,26

1392. δοξάζω *doxazō*
MATT. 5:16; 6:2; 9:8; 15:31; MARK 2:12;
LUKE 2:20; 4:15; 5:25,26; 7:16; 13:13; 17:15;
18:43; 23:47; JOHN 7:39; 8:54; 11:4; 12:16,
23,28; 13:31,32; 14:13; 15:8; 16:14; 17:1,4,5,
10; 21:19; ACTS 3:13; 4:21; 11:18; 13:48;
21:20; ROM. 1:21; 8:30; 11:13; 15:6,9; 1 COR.
6:20; 12:26; 2 COR. 3:10; 9:13; GAL. 1:24;
2 THESS. 3:1; HEB. 5:5; 1 PET. 1:8; 2:12;
4:11,14,16; REV. 15:4; 18:7

1393. Δορκάς *Dorkas*
ACTS 9:36,39

1394. δόσις *dosis*
PHIL. 4:15; JAMES 1:17

1395. δότης *dotēs*
2 COR. 9:7

1396. δουλαγωγέω *doulagōgeō*
1 COR. 9:27

1397. δουλεία *douleia*
ROM. 8:15,21; GAL. 4:24; 5:1; HEB. 2:15

1398. δουλεύω *douleuō*
MATT. 6:24; LUKE 15:29; 16:13; JOHN 8:33;
ACTS 7:7; 20:19; ROM. 6:6; 7:6,25; 9:12;
12:11; 14:18; 16:18; GAL. 4:8,9,25; 5:13; EPH.
6:7; PHIL. 2:22; COL. 3:24; 1 THESS. 1:9;
1 TIM. 6:2; TITUS 3:3

1399. δούλη *doulē*
LUKE 1:38,48; ACTS 2:18

1400. δοῦλον *doulon*
ROM. 6:19

1401. δοῦλος *doulos* subst.
MATT. 8:9; 10:24,25; 13:27,28; 18:23,26-28,32;
20:27; 21:34-36; 22:3,4,6,8,10; 24:45,46,48,50;
25:14,19,21,23,26,30; 26:51; MARK 10:44;
12:2,4; 13:34; 14:47; LUKE 2:29; 7:2,3,8,10;
12:37,38,43,45-47; 14:17,21-23; 15:22; 17:7,9,
10; 19:13,15,17,22; 20:10,11; 22:50; JOHN
4:51; 8:34,35; 13:16; 15:15,20; 18:10,18,26;
ACTS 2:18; 4:29; 16:17; ROM. 1:1; 6:16,17,20;
1 COR. 7:21-23; 12:13; 2 COR. 4:5; GAL.

1:10; 3:28; 4:1,7; EPH. 6:5,6,8; PHIL. 1:1; 2:7;
COL. 3:11,22; 4:1,12; 1 TIM. 6:1; 2 TIM. 2:24;
TITUS 1:1; 2:9; PHILE. 1:16; JAMES 1:1;
1 PET. 2:16; 2 PET. 1:1; 2:19; JUDE 1:1; REV.
1:1; 2:20; 6:15; 7:3; 10:7; 11:18; 13:16; 15:3;
19:2,5,18; 22:3,6

1402. δουλόω *douloō*
ACTS 7:6; ROM. 6:18,22; 1 COR. 7:15; 9:19;
GAL. 4:3; TITUS 2:3; 2 PET. 2:19

1403. δοχή *dochē*
LUKE 5:29; 14:13

1404. δράκων *drakōn*
REV. 12:3,4,7,9,13,16,17; 13:2,4,11; 16:13; 20:2

1405. δράσσομαι, δράττομαι
      drassomai, drattomai
1 COR. 3:19

1406. δραχμή *drachmē*
LUKE 15:8,9

1407. δρέπανον *drepanon*
MARK 4:29; REV. 14:14-19

1408. δρόμος *dromos*
ACTS 13:25; 20:24; 2 TIM. 4:7

1409. Δρούσιλλα *Drousilla*
ACTS 24:24

1410. δύναμαι *dunamai*
MATT. 3:9; 5:14,36; 6:24,27; 7:18; 8:2; 9:15,28;
10:28; 12:29,34; 16:3; 17:16,19; 19:12,25; 20:22;
22:46; 26:9,42,53,61; 27:42; MARK 1:40,45;
2:4,7,19; 3:20,23-27; 4:32,33; 5:3; 6:5,19; 7:15,
18,24; 8:4; 9:3,22,23,28,29,39; 10:26,38,39;
14:5,7; 15:31; LUKE 1:20,22; 3:8; 5:12,21,34;
6:39,42; 8:19; 9:40; 11:7; 12:25,26; 13:11;
14:20,26,27,33; 16:2,13,26; 18:26; 19:3; 20:36;
21:15; JOHN 1:46; 3:2-5,9,27; 5:19,30,44;
6:44,52,60,65; 7:7,34,36; 8:21,22,43; 9:4,16,33;
10:21,29,35; 11:37; 12:39; 13:33,36,37; 14:5,17;
15:4,5; 16:12; ACTS 4:16,20; 5:39; 8:31; 10:47;
13:39; 15:1; 17:19; 19:40; 20:32; 21:34; 24:8,
11,13; 25:11; 26:32; 27:12,15,31,39,43; ROM.
8:7,8,39; 15:14; 16:25; 1 COR. 2:14; 3:1,2,11;

6:5; 7:21; 10:13,21; 12:3,21; 14:31; 15:50;
2 COR. 1:4; 3:7; 13:8; **GAL.** 3:21; **EPH.** 3:4,
20; 6:11,13,16; **PHIL.** 3:21; **1 THESS.** 2:6; 3:9;
1 TIM. 5:25; 6:7,16; **2 TIM.** 2:13; 3:7,15;
HEB. 2:18; 3:19; 4:15; 5:2,7; 7:25; 9:9; 10:1,11;
JAMES 1:21; 2:14; 3:8,12; 4:2,12; **1 JOHN** 3:9;
4:20; **JUDE** 1:24; **REV.** 2:2; 3:8; 5:3; 6:17; 7:9;
9:20; 13:4,17; 14:3; 15:8

1411. δύναμις dunamis
MATT. 6:13; 7:22; 11:20,21,23; 13:54,58; 14:2;
22:29; 24:29,30; 25:15; 26:64; **MARK** 5:30;
6:2,5,14; 9:1,39; 12:24; 13:25,26; 14:62; **LUKE**
1:17,35; 4:14,36; 5:17; 6:19; 8:46; 9:1; 10:13,19;
19:37; 21:26,27; 22:69; 24:49; **ACTS** 1:8; 2:22;
3:12; 4:7,33; 6:8; 8:10,13; 10:38; 19:11; **ROM.**
1:4,16,20; 8:38; 9:17; 15:13,19; **1 COR.** 1:18,24;
2:4,5; 4:19,20; 5:4; 6:14; 12:10,28,29; 14:11;
15:24,43,56; **2 COR.** 1:8; 4:7; 6:7; 8:3; 12:9,
12; 13:4; **GAL.** 3:5; **EPH.** 1:19,21; 3:7,16,20;
PHIL. 3:10; **COL.** 1:11,29; **1 THESS.** 1:5;
2 THESS. 1:7,11; 2:9; **2 TIM.** 1:7,8; 3:5; **HEB.**
1:3; 2:4; 6:5; 7:16; 11:11,34; **1 PET.** 1:5; 3:22;
2 PET. 1:3,16; 2:11; **REV.** 1:16; 3:8; 4:11; 5:12;
7:12; 11:17; 12:10; 13:2; 15:8; 17:13; 18:3; 19:1

1412. δυναμόω dynamoō
COL. 1:11

1413. δυνάστης dunastēs
LUKE 1:52; **ACTS** 8:27; **1 TIM.** 6:15

1414. δυνατέω dunateō
2 COR. 13:3

1415. δυνατός dunatos
MATT. 19:26; 24:24; 26:39; **MARK** 9:23;
10:27; 13:22; 14:35,36; **LUKE** 1:49; 14:31;
18:27; 24:19; **ACTS** 2:24; 7:22; 11:17; 18:24;
20:16; 25:5; **ROM.** 4:21; 9:22; 11:23; 12:18;
14:4; 15:1; **1 COR.** 1:26; **2 COR.** 9:8; 10:4;
12:10; 13:9; **GAL.** 4:15; **2 TIM.** 1:12; **TITUS**
1:9; **HEB.** 11:19; **JAMES** 3:2; **REV.** 6:15

1416. δύνω dunō
MARK 1:32; **LUKE** 4:40

1417. δύο duo
MATT. 4:18,21; 5:41; 6:24; 8:28; 9:27;
10:10,29; 11:2; 14:17,19; 18:8,9,16,19,20;

19:5,6; 20:21,24,30; 21:1,28,31; 22:40; 24:40,41;
25:15,17,22; 26:2,37,60; 27:21,38,51; **MARK**
6:7,9,38,41; 9:43,45,47; 10:8; 11:1; 12:42; 14:1,
13; 15:27,38; 16:12; **LUKE** 2:24; 3:11; 5:2;
7:19,41; 9:3,13,16,30,32; 10:1,35; 12:6,52;
15:11; 16:13; 17:34-36; 18:10; 19:29; 21:2;
22:38; 23:32; 24:4,13; **JOHN** 1:35,37,40; 2:6;
4:40,43; 6:9; 8:17; 11:6; 19:18; 20:4,12; 21:2;
ACTS 1:10,23,24; 7:29; 9:38; 10:7; 12:6;
19:10,22,34; 21:33; 23:23; **1 COR.** 6:16;
14:27,29; **2 COR.** 13:1; **GAL.** 4:22,24; **EPH.**
2:15; 5:31; **PHIL.** 1:23; **1 TIM.** 5:19; **HEB.**
6:18; 10:28; **REV.** 9:12,16; 11:2-4,10; 12:14;
13:5,11; 19:20

1419. δυσβάστακτος dusbastaktos
MATT. 23:4; **LUKE** 11:46

1420. δυσεντερία dusenteria
ACTS 28:8

1421. δυσερμήνευτος dusermēneutos
HEB. 5:11

1422. δύσκολος duskolos
MARK 10:24

1423. δυσκόλως duskolōs
MATT. 19:23; **MARK** 10:23; **LUKE** 18:24

1424. δυσμή dusmē
MATT. 8:11; 24:27; **LUKE** 12:54; 13:29; **REV.**
21:13

1425. δυσνόητος dusnoētos
2 PET. 3:16

1426. δυσφημία dusphēmia
2 COR. 6:8

1427. δώδεκα dōdeka
MATT. 9:20; 10:1,2,5; 11:1; 14:20; 19:28;
20:17; 26:14,20,47,53; **MARK** 3:14; 4:10;
5:25,42; 6:7,43; 8:19; 9:35; 10:32; 11:11; 14:10,
17,20,43; **LUKE** 2:42; 6:13; 8:1,42,43; 9:1,12,
17; 18:31; 22:3,14,30,47; **JOHN** 6:13,67,70,71;
11:9; 20:24; **ACTS** 6:2; 7:8; **1 COR.** 15:5;
JAMES 1:1; **REV.** 7:5-8; 12:1; 21:12,14,16,21;
22:2

1428. δωδέκατος *dōdekatos*
REV. 21:20

1429. δωδεκάφυλον *dōdekaphulon*
ACTS 26:7

1430. δῶμα *dōma*
MATT. 10:27; 24:17; MARK 13:15; LUKE
5:19; 12:3; 17:31; ACTS 10:9

1431. δωρεά *dōrea*
JOHN 4:10; ACTS 2:38; 8:20; 10:45; 11:17;
ROM. 5:15,17; 2 COR. 9:15; EPH. 3:7; 4:7;
HEB. 6:4

1432. δωρεάν *dōrean*
MATT. 10:8; JOHN 15:25; ROM. 3:24;
2 COR. 11:7; GAL. 2:21; 2 THESS. 3:8; REV.
21:6; 22:17

1433. δωρέομαι *dōreomai*
MARK 15:45; 2 PET. 1:3,4

1434. δώρημα *dōrēma*
ROM. 5:16; JAMES 1:17

1435. δῶρον *dōron*
MATT. 2:11; 5:23,24; 8:4; 15:5; 23:18,19;
MARK 7:11; LUKE 21:1,4; EPH. 2:8; HEB.
5:1; 8:3,4; 9:9; 11:4; REV. 11:10

E

1436. ἔα *ea*
MARK 1:24; LUKE 4:34

1439. ἐάω *eaō*
MATT. 24:43; LUKE 4:41; 22:51; ACTS 5:38;
14:16; 16:7; 19:30; 23:32; 27:32,40; 28:4;
1 COR. 10:13; REV. 2:20

1440. ἑβδομήκοντα *hebdomēkonta*
LUKE 10:1,17; ACTS 7:14; 23:23; 27:37

1441. ἑβδομηκοντάκις
  hebdomēkontakis
MATT. 18:22

1442. ἕβδομος *hebdomos*
JOHN 4:52; HEB. 4:4; JUDE 1:14; REV. 8:1;
10:7; 11:15; 16:17; 21:20

1443. Ἐβέρ *Eber*
LUKE 3:35

1444. Ἑβραϊκός *Hebraikos*
LUKE 23:38

1445. Ἑβραῖος *Hebraios*
ACTS 6:1; 2 COR. 11:22; PHIL. 3:5

1446. Ἑβραΐς *Hebrais*
ACTS 21:40; 22:2; 26:14

1447. Ἑβραϊστί *Hebraisti*
JOHN 5:2; 19:13,17,20; REV. 9:11; 16:16

1448. ἐγγίζω *eggizō*
MATT. 3:2; 4:17; 10:7; 15:8; 21:1,34; 26:45,46;
MARK 1:15; 11:1; 14:42; LUKE 7:12; 10:9,11;
12:33; 15:1,25; 18:35,40; 19:29,37,41; 21:8,20,
28; 22:1,47; 24:15,28; ACTS 7:17; 9:3; 10:9;
21:33; 22:6; 23:15; ROM. 13:12; PHIL. 2:30;
HEB. 7:19; 10:25; JAMES 4:8; 5:8; 1 PET. 4:7

1449. ἐγγράφω *eggraphō*
2 COR. 3:2,3

1450. ἔγγυος *egguos*
HEB. 7:22

1451. ἐγγύς *eggus*
MATT. 24:32,33; 26:18; MARK 13:28,29;
LUKE 19:11; 21:30,31; JOHN 2:13; 3:23;
6:4,19,23; 7:2; 11:18,54,55; 19:20,42; ACTS
1:12; 9:38; 27:8; ROM. 10:8; EPH. 2:13,17;
PHIL. 4:5; HEB. 6:8; 8:13; REV. 1:3; 22:10

1452. ἐγγύτερον *egguteron*
ROM. 13:11

1453. ἐγείρω *egeirō*
MATT. 2:13,14,20,21; 3:9; 8:15,25,26; 9:5-
7,19,25; 10:8; 11:5,11; 12:11,42; 14:2; 16:21;
17:7,23; 24:7,11,24; 25:7; 26:32,46; 27:52,63,64;
28:6,7; MARK 1:31; 2:9,11,12; 3:3; 4:27; 5:41;

6:14,16; 9:27; 10:49; 12:26; 13:8,22; 14:28,42;
16:6,14; **LUKE** 1:69; 3:8; 5:23,24; 6:8; 7:14,
16,22; 8:24,54; 9:7,22; 11:8,31; 13:25; 20:37;
21:10; 24:6,34; **JOHN** 2:19,20,22; 5:8,21; 7:52;
11:29; 12:1,9,17; 13:4; 14:31; 21:14; **ACTS**
3:6,7,15; 4:10; 5:30; 9:8; 10:26,40; 12:7; 13:22,
23,30,37; 26:8; **ROM.** 4:24,25; 6:4,9; 7:4; 8:11,
34; 10:9; 13:11; **1 COR.** 6:14; 15:4,12-17,20,29,
32,35,42-44,52; **2 COR.** 1:9; 4:14; 5:15; **GAL.**
1:1; **EPH.** 1:20; 5:14; **COL.** 2:12; **1 THESS.**
1:10; **2 TIM.** 2:8; **HEB.** 11:19; **JAMES** 5:15;
1 PET. 1:21; **REV.** 11:1

1454. ἔγερσις *egersis*
MATT. 27:53

1455. ἐγκάθετος *egkathetos*
LUKE 20:20

1456. ἐγκαίνια *egkainia*
JOHN 10:22

1457. ἐγκαινίζω *egkainizō*
HEB. 9:18; 10:20

1458. ἐγκαλέω *egkaleō*
ACTS 19:38,40; 23:28,29; 26:2,7; **ROM.**
8:33

1459. ἐγκαταλείπω *egkataleipō*
MATT. 27:46; **MARK** 15:34; **ACTS** 2:27;
ROM. 9:29; **2 COR.** 4:9; **2 TIM.** 4:10,16; **HEB.**
10:25; 13:5

1460. ἐγκατοικέω *egkatoikeō*
2 PET. 2:8

1461. ἐγκεντρίζω *egkentrizō*
ROM. 11:17,19,23,24

1462. ἔγκλημα *egklēma*
ACTS 23:29; 25:16

1463. ἐγκομβόομαι *egkomboomai*
1 PET. 5:5

1464. ἐγκοπή *egkopē*
1 COR. 9:12

1465. ἐγκόπτω *egkoptō*
ACTS 24:4; **ROM.** 15:22; **GAL.** 5:7; **1 THESS.**
2:18; **1 PET.** 3:7

1466. ἐγκράτεια *egkrateia*
ACTS 24:25; **GAL.** 5:23; **2 PET.** 1:6

1467. ἐγκρατεύομαι *egkrateuomai*
1 COR. 7:9; 9:25

1468. ἐγκρατής *egkratēs*
TITUS 1:8

1469. ἐγκρίνω *egkrinō*
2 COR. 10:12

1470. ἐγκρύπτω *egkruptō*
MATT. 13:33; **LUKE** 13:21

1471. ἔγκυος *egkuos*
LUKE 2:5

1472. ἐγχρίω *egchriō*
REV. 3:18

1474. ἐδαφίζω *edaphizō*
LUKE 19:44

1475. ἔδαφος *edaphos*
ACTS 22:7

1476. ἑδραῖος *hedraios*
1 COR. 7:37; 15:58; **COL.** 1:23

1477. ἑδραίωμα *hedraiōma*
1 TIM. 3:15

1478. Ἐζεκίας *Ezekias*
MATT. 1:9,10

1479. ἐθελοθρησκεία *ethelothrēskeia*
COL. 2:23

1480. ἐθίζω *ethizō*
LUKE 2:27

1481. ἐθνάρχης *ethnarchēs*
2 COR. 11:32

1482. ἐθνικός *ethnikos*
MATT. 6:7; 18:17

1483. ἐθνικῶς *ethnikōs*
GAL. 2:14

1484. ἔθνος *ethnos*
MATT. 4:15; 6:32; 10:5,18; 12:18,21; 20:19,25;
21:43; 24:7,9,14; 25:32; 28:19; MARK 10:33,
42; 11:17; 13:8,10; LUKE 2:32; 7:5; 12:30;
18:32; 21:10,24,25; 22:25; 23:2; 24:47; JOHN
11:48,50-52; 18:35; ACTS 2:5; 4:25,27; 7:7,45;
8:9; 9:15; 10:22,35,45; 11:1,18; 13:19,42,46-48;
14:2,5,16,27; 15:3,7,12,14,17,19,23; 17:26; 18:6;
21:11,19,21,25; 22:21; 24:2,10,17; 26:4,17,20,
23; 28:19,28; ROM. 1:5,13; 2:14,24; 3:29; 4:17,
18; 9:24,30; 10:19; 11:11-13,25; 15:9-12,16,18,
27; 16:4,26; 1 COR. 5:1; 10:20; 12:2; 2 COR.
11:26; GAL. 1:16; 2:2,8,9,12,14,15; 3:8,14;
EPH. 2:11; 3:1,6,8; 4:17; COL. 1:27; 1 THESS.
2:16; 4:5; 1 TIM. 2:7; 3:16; 2 TIM. 1:11; 4:17;
1 PET. 2:9,12; 4:3; 3 JOHN 1:7; REV. 2:26;
5:9; 7:9; 10:11; 11:2,9,18; 12:5; 13:7; 14:6,8;
15:4; 16:19; 17:15; 18:3,23; 19:15; 20:3,8; 21:24,
26; 22:2

1485. ἔθος *ethos*
LUKE 1:9; 2:42; 22:39; JOHN 19:40; ACTS
6:14; 15:1; 16:21; 21:21; 25:16; 26:3; 28:17;
HEB. 10:25

1486. ἔθω *ethō*
MATT. 27:15; MARK 10:1; LUKE 4:16;
ACTS 17:2

1488. εἶ *ei*
MATT. 2:6; 4:3,6; 5:25; 11:3; 14:28,33; 16:16-
18,23; 22:16; 25:24; 26:63,73; 27:11,40; MARK
1:11,24; 3:11; 8:29; 12:14,34; 14:61,70; 15:2;
LUKE 3:22; 4:3,9,34,41; 7:19,20; 15:31; 19:21;
22:58,67,70; 23:3,37,39,40; JOHN 1:19,21,22,
25,42,49; 3:10; 4:12,19; 6:69; 7:52; 8:25,48,53;
9:28; 10:24; 11:27; 18:17,25,33,37; 19:9,12;
21:12; ACTS 9:5; 13:33; 21:38; 22:8,27; 26:15;
ROM. 2:1; 9:20; 14:4; GAL. 4:7; HEB. 1:5,12;
5:5; JAMES 4:11,12; REV. 2:9; 3:1,15-17; 4:11;
5:9; 16:5

1489. εἴγε *eige*
2 COR. 5:3; GAL. 3:4; EPH. 3:2; 4:21; COL.
1:23

1490. I. εἰ δέ μή *ei de mē*
MARK 2:21,22; JOHN 14:2,11; REV.
2:5,16

II. εἰ δέ μή γε *ei de mē ge*
MATT. 6:1; 9:17; LUKE 5:36,37; 10:6;
13:9; 14:32; 2 COR. 11:16

1491. εἶδος *eidos*
LUKE 3:22; 9:29; JOHN 5:37; 2 COR. 5:7;
1 THESS. 5:22

1493. εἰδωλεῖον *eidōleion*
1 COR. 8:10

1494. εἰδωλόθυτον *eidōlothuton*
ACTS 15:29; 21:25; 1 COR. 8:1,4,7,10;
10:19,28; REV. 2:14,20

1495. εἰδωλολατρεία *eidōlolatreia*
1 COR. 10:14; GAL. 5:20; COL. 3:5; 1 PET.
4:3

1496. εἰδωλολάτρης *eidōlolatrēs*
I COR 5:10,11; 6:9; 10:7; EPH. 5:5; REV. 21:8;
22:15

1497. εἴδωλον *eidōlon*
ACTS 7:41; 15:20; ROM. 2:22; 1 COR. 8:4,7;
10:19; 12:2; 2 COR. 6:16; 1 THESS. 1:9;
1 JOHN 5:21; REV. 9:20

1498. εἴην *eiēn*
(All opt. forms of εἰμί)
LUKE 1:29; 3:15; 8:9; 9:46; 15:26; 18:36;
22:23; JOHN 13:24; ACTS 8:20; 10:17; 21:33;
REV. 3:15

1499. εἰ καί *ei kai*
MATT. 26:33; LUKE 11:8; 18:4; 2 COR. 4:3,
16; 5:16; 7:8,12; 11:15; 12:11,15; PHIL. 2:17;
3:12; HEB. 6:9

1500. εἰκῆ *eikē*
MATT. 5:22; ROM. 13:4; 1 COR. 15:2; GAL.
3:4; 4:11; COL. 2:18

1501. εἴκοσι *eikosi*
LUKE 14:31; JOHN 6:19; ACTS 1:15; 27:28;
1 COR. 10:8; REV. 4:4,10; 5:8,14; 11:16; 19:4

1502. εἴκω *eikō*
GAL. 2:5

1503. εἴκω *eikō*
JAMES 1:6,23

1504. εἰκών *eikōn*
MATT. 22:20; MARK 12:16; LUKE 20:24;
ROM. 1:23; 8:29; 1 COR. 11:7; 15:49; 2 COR.
3:18; 4:4; COL. 1:15; 3:10; HEB. 10:1; REV.
13:14,15; 14:9,11; 15:2; 16:2; 19:20; 20:4

1505. εἰλικρίνεια *eilikrineia*
1 COR. 5:8; 2 COR. 1:12; 2:17

1506. εἰλικρινής *eilikrinēs*
PHIL. 1:10; 2 PET. 3:1

1507. εἰλίσσω *heilissō*
REV. 6:14

1508. εἰ μή *ei mē*
MATT. 5:13; 11:27; 12:4,24,39; 13:57; 14:17;
15:24; 16:4; 17:8,21; 19:9,17; 21:19; 24:22,36;
MARK 2:7,26; 5:37; 6:4,5,8; 8:14; 9:9,29;
10:18; 11:13; 13:20,32; LUKE 4:26,27; 5:21;
6:4; 8:51; 10:22; 11:29; 17:18; 18:19; JOHN
3:13; 6:22,46; 9:33; 10:10; 14:6; 15:22,24;
17:12; 18:30; 19:11,15; ACTS 11:19; 21:25;
26:32; ROM. 7:7; 9:29; 11:15; 13:1,8; 14:14;
1 COR. 1:14; 2:2,11; 7:17; 8:4; 10:13; 12:3;
14:5; 15:2; 2 COR. 2:2; 3:1; 12:5,13; GAL.
1:7,19; 6:14; EPH. 4:9; PHIL. 4:15; 1 TIM.
5:19; HEB. 3:18; 1 JOHN 2:22; 5:5; REV. 2:17;
9:4; 13:17; 14:3; 19:12; 21:27

1509. εἰ μή τι *ei mē ti*
LUKE 9:13; 1 COR. 7:5; 2 COR. 13:5

1512. εἴ περ *ei per*
ROM. 8:9,17; 1 COR. 8:5; 15:15; 2 THESS.
1:6; 1 PET. 2:3

1513. εἴ πως *ei pōs*
ACTS 27:12; ROM. 1:10; 11:14; PHIL. 3:11

1514. εἰρηνεύω *eirēneuō*
MARK 9:50; ROM. 12:18; 2 COR. 13:11;
1 THESS. 5:13

1515. εἰρήνη *eirēnē*
MATT. 10:13,34; MARK 5:34; LUKE 1:79;
2:14,29; 7:50; 8:48; 10:5,6; 11:21; 12:51; 14:32;
19:38,42; 24:36; JOHN 14:27; 16:33; 20:19,21,
26; ACTS 7:96; 9:31; 10:36; 12:20; 15:33;
16:36; 24:2; ROM. 1:7; 2:10; 3:17; 5:1; 8:6;
10:15; 14:17,19; 15:13,33; 16:20; 1 COR. 1:3;
7:15; 14:33; 16:11; 2 COR. 1:2; 13:11; GAL.
1:3; 5:22; 6:16; EPH. 1:2; 2:14,15,17; 4:3;
6:15,23; PHIL. 1:2; 4:7,9; COL. 1:2; 3:15;
1 THESS. 1:1; 5:3,23; 2 THESS. 1:2; 3:16;
1 TIM. 1:2; 2 TIM. 1:2; 2:22; TITUS 1:4;
PHILE. 1:3; HEB. 7:2; 11:31; 12:14; 13:20;
JAMES 2:16; 3:18; 1 PET. 1:2; 3:11; 5:14;
2 PET. 1:2; 3:14; 2 JOHN 1:3; 3 JOHN 1:14;
JUDE 1:2; REV. 1:4; 6:4

1516. εἰρηνικός *eirēnikos*
HEB. 12:11; JAMES 3:17

1517. εἰρηνοποιέω *eirēnopoieō*
COL. 1:20

1518. εἰρηνοποιός *eirēnopoios*
MATT. 5:9

1520. εἷς, ἕν *heis, hen*
MATT. 5:18,29,30,41; 6:24,27,29; 8:19;
10:29,42; 12:11; 13:46; 16:14; 18:5,6,10,
12,14,16,24,28; 19:16,17; 20:13,21; 21:24;
22:35; 23:8-10,15; 24:40; 25:15,18,24,40,45;
26:14,21,47,51; 27:14,15,38,48; MARK 2:7;
4:8,20; 5:22; 6:15; 8:14,28; 9:17,37,42; 10:17,
18,21,37; 11:29; 12:6,28,29,32; 13:1; 14:10,18,
20,43,47,51; 15:6,27,36; LUKE 4:40; 5:3; 7:41;
9:8; 10:42; 11:46; 12:6,25,27,52; 15:4,7,10,15,
19,26; 16:5,13; 17:2,15,34; 18:10,19,22; 20:3;
22:47,50; 23:17,39; 24:18; JOHN 1:3,40;
6:8,9,22,70,71; 7:21,50; 8:41; 9:25; 10:16,30;
11:49,50,52; 12:2,4; 13:21,23; 17:11,21-23;
18:14,22,26,39; 19:34; 20:7,12,24; 21:25; ACTS
1:22,24; 2:3,6; 4:32; 11:28; 17:26,27; 20:31;
21:19,26; 23:6,17; 28:25; ROM. 3:10,12,30;
5:12,15-19; 9:10; 12:4,5; 15:6; 1 COR. 3:8; 4:6;
6:5,16,17; 8:4,6; 9:24; 10:17; 11:5; 12:11-14,18-
20,26; 14:27,31; 2 COR. 5:14; 11:2; GAL.
3:16,20,28; 4:22; 5:14; EPH. 2:14-16,18; 4:4-
7,16; 5:33; PHIL. 1:27; 2:2; 3:13; COL. 3:15;

4:6; **1 THESS.** 2:11; 5:11; **2 THESS.** 1:3;
1 TIM. 2:5; 5:9; **HEB.** 2:11; 11:12; **JAMES**
2:10,19; 4:12,13; **2 PET.** 3:8; **1 JOHN** 5:7,8;
REV. 4:8; 5:5; 6:1; 7:13; 8:13; 15:7; 17:1,10;
18:21; 19:17; 21:9,21; 22:2

1521. εἰσάγω eisagō
LUKE 2:27; 14:21; 22:54; **JOHN** 18:16; **ACTS**
7:45; 9:8; 21:28,29,37; **HEB.** 1:6

1522. εἰσακούω eisakouō
MATT. 6:7; **LUKE** 1:13; **ACTS** 10:31; **1 COR.**
14:21; **HEB.** 5:7

1523. εἰσδέχομαι eisdechomai
2 COR. 6:17

1524. εἴσειμι eiseimi
ACTS 3:3; 21:18,26; **HEB.** 9:6

1525. εἰσέρχομαι eiserchomai
MATT. 5:20; 6:6; 7:13,21; 8:5,8; 9:25; 10:5,11,
12; 12:4,29,45; 15:11; 17:25; 18:3,8,9; 19:17,23,
24; 21:10,12; 22:11,12; 23:13; 24:38; 25:10,21,
23; 26:41,58; 27:53; **MARK** 1:21,45; 2:1,26;
3:1,27; 5:12,13,39; 6:10,22,25; 7:17,24; 8:26;
9:25,28,43,45,47; 10:15,23-25; 11:11,15; 13:15;
14:14,38; 15:43; 16:5; **LUKE** 1:9,28,40; 4:16,38;
6:4,6; 7:1,6,36,44,45; 8:30,32,33,41,51; 9:4,34,
46,52; 10:5,8,10,38; 11:26,37,52; 13:24; 14:23;
15:28; 17:7,12,27; 18:17,24,25; 19:1,7,45; 21:21;
22:3,10,40,46; 24:3,26,29; **JOHN** 3:4,5; 4:38;
10:1,2,9; 13:27; 18:1,28,33; 19:9; 20:5,6,8;
ACTS 1:13,21; 3:8; 5:7,10,21; 9:6,12,17; 10:3,
24,25,27; 11:3,8,12,20; 13:14; 14:1,20,22; 16:15,
40; 17:2; 18:19; 19:8,30; 20:29; 21:8; 23:16,33;
25:23; 28:8; **ROM.** 5:12; 11:25; **1 COR.** 14:23,
24; **HEB.** 3:11,18,19; 4:1,3,5,6,10,11; 6:19,20;
9:12,24,25; 10:5; **JAMES** 2:2; 5:4; **2 JOHN** 1:7;
REV. 3:20; 11:11; 15:8; 21:27; 22:14

1527. εἷς καθ' εἷς heis kath heis
MARK 14:19; **JOHN** 8:9

1528. εἰσκαλέω eiskaleō
ACTS 10:23

1529. εἴσοδος eisodos
ACTS 13:24; **1 THESS.** 1:9; 2:1; **HEB.** 10:19;
2 PET. 1:11

1530. εἰσπηδάω eispēdaō
ACTS 14:14; 16:29

1531. εἰσπορεύομαι eisporeuomai
MATT. 15:17; **MARK** 1:21; 4:19; 5:40; 6:56;
7:15,18,19; 11:2; **LUKE** 8:16; 11:33; 19:30;
22:10; **ACTS** 3:2; 8:3; 9:28; 28:30

1532. εἰστρέχω eistrechō
ACTS 12:14

1533. εἰσφέρω eispherō
MATT. 6:13; **LUKE** 5:18,19; 11:4; **ACTS**
17:20; **1 TIM.** 6:7; **HEB.** 13:11

1534. εἶτα eita
MARK 4:17,28; 8:25; **LUKE** 8:12; **JOHN** 13:5;
19:27; 20:27; **1 COR.** 12:28; 15:5,7,24; **1 TIM.**
2:13; 3:10; **HEB.** 12:9; **JAMES** 1:15

1535. εἴτε eite
ROM. 12:6-8; **1 COR.** 3:22; 8:5; 10:31; 12:13,
26; 13:8; 14:7,27; 15:11; **2 COR.** 1:6; 5:9,10,13;
8:23; 12:2,3; **EPH.** 6:8; **PHIL.** 1:18,20,27;
COL. 1:16,20; **1 THESS.** 5:10; **2 THESS.** 2:15;
1 PET. 2:13,14

1536. εἴ τις ei tis
MATT. 16:24; **MARK** 4:23; 7:16; 8:23;
9:22,35; **LUKE** 14:26; 19:8; **ACTS** 24:19,20;
25:5; **ROM.** 13:9; **1 COR.** 1:16; 3:14,15,17,18;
7:12; 14:37; 16:22; **2 COR.** 2:10; 5:17; 7:14;
10:7; 11:20; **GAL.** 1:9; **EPH.** 4:29; **PHIL.** 2:1;
3:4,15; 4:8; **2 THESS.** 3:10; **1 TIM.** 1:10; 3:1;
5:16; 6:3; **TITUS** 1:6; **JAMES** 1:23; 3:2; **1 PET.**
3:1; 4:11; **2 JOHN** 1:10; **REV.** 11:5; 13:9,10;
14:9,11; 20:15

1538. ἕκαστος hekastos
MATT. 16:27; 18:35; 25:15; 26:22; **MARK**
13:34; **LUKE** 2:3; 4:40; 6:44; 13:15; 16:5;
JOHN 6:7; 7:53; 16:32; 19:23; **ACTS** 2:3,6,
8,38; 3:26; 4:35; 11:29; 17:27; 20:31; 21:19,26;
ROM. 2:6; 12:3; 14:5,12; 15:2; **1 COR.** 1:12;
3:5,8,10,13; 4:5; 7:2,7,17,20,24; 10:24; 11:21;
12:7,11,18; 14:26; 15:23,38; 16:2; **2 COR.** 5:10;
9:7; **GAL.** 6:4,5; **EPH.** 4:7,16,25; 5:33; 6:8;
PHIL. 2:4; **COL.** 4:6; **1 THESS.** 2:11; 4:4;
2 THESS. 1:3; **HEB.** 3:13; 6:11; 8:11; 11:21;

JAMES 1:14; **1 PET.** 1:17; 4:10; **REV.** 2:23; 5:8; 6:11; 20:13; 21:21; 22:2,12

1539. *ἐκάστοτε* **hekastote**
2 PET. 1:15

1540. *ἑκατόν* **hekaton**
MATT. 13:8,23; 18:12,28; **MARK** 4:8,20; 6:40; **LUKE** 15:4; 16:6,7; **JOHN** 19:39; 21:11; **ACTS** 1:15; **REV.** 7:4; 14:1,3; 21:17

1541. *ἑκατονταέτης* **hekatontaetēs**
ROM. 4:19

1542. *ἑκατονταπλασίων*
  hekatontaplasiōn
MATT. 19:29; **MARK** 10:30; **LUKE** 8:8

1543. I. *ἑκατοντάρχης* **hekatontarchēs**
  ACTS 10:1,22; 24:23; 27:1,31

  II. *ἑκατόνταρχος*
    hekatontarchos
  MATT. 8:5,8,13; 27:54; **LUKE** 7:2,6; 23:47; **ACTS** 21:32; 22:25,26; 23:17,23; 27:6,11,43; 28:16

1544. *ἐκβάλλω* **ekballō**
MATT. 7:4,5,22; 8:12,16,31; 9:25,33,34,38; 10:1,8; 12:20,24,26-28,35; 13:52; 15:17; 17:19; 21:12,39; 22:13; 25:30; **MARK** 1:12,34,39,43; 3:15,22,23; 5:40; 6:13; 7:26; 9:18,28,38,47; 11:15; 12:8; 16:9,17; **LUKE** 4:29; 6:22,42; 8:54; 9:40,49; 10:2,35; 11:14,15,18-20; 13:28,32; 19:45; 20:12,15; **JOHN** 2:15; 6:37; 9:34,35; 10:4; 12:31; **ACTS** 7:58; 9:40; 13:50; 16:37; 27:38; **GAL.** 4:30; **JAMES** 2:25; **3 JOHN** 1:10; **REV.** 11:2

1545. *ἔκβασις* **ekbasis**
1 COR. 10:13; **HEB.** 13:7

1546. *ἐκβολή* **ekbolē**
ACTS 27:18

1547. *ἐκγαμίζω* **ekgamizō**
MATT. 22:30; 24:38; **LUKE** 17:27; **1 COR.** 7:38

1548. *ἐκγαμίσκω* **ekgamiskō**
LUKE 20:34,35

1549. *ἔκγονος* **ekgonos**
1 TIM. 5:4

1550. *ἐκδαπανάω* **ekdapanaō**
2 COR. 12:15

1551. *ἐκδέχομαι* **ekdechomai**
JOHN 5:3; **ACTS** 17:16; **1 COR.** 11:33; 16:11; **HEB.** 10:13; 11:10; **JAMES** 5:7; **1 PET.** 3:20

1552. *ἔκδηλος* **ekdēlos**
2 TIM. 3:9

1553. *ἐκδημέω* **ekdēmeō**
2 COR. 5:6,8,9

1554. *ἐκδίδωμι* **ekdidōmi**
MATT. 21:33,41; **MARK** 12:1; **LUKE** 20:9

1555. *ἐκδιηγέομαι* **ekdiēgeomai**
ACTS 13:41; 15:3

1556. *ἐκδικέω* **ekdikeō**
LUKE 18:3,5; **ROM.** 12:19; **2 COR.** 10:6; **REV.** 6:10; 19:2

1557. *ἐκδίκησις* **ekdikēsis**
LUKE 18:7,8; 21:22; **ACTS** 7:24; **ROM.** 12:19; **2 COR.** 7:11; **2 THESS.** 1:8; **HEB.** 10:30; **1 PET.** 2:14

1558. *ἔκδικος* **ekdikos**
ROM. 13:4; **1 THESS.** 4:6

1559. *ἐκδιώκω* **ekdiōkō**
LUKE 11:49; **1 THESS.** 2:15

1560. *ἔκδοτος* **ekdotos**
ACTS 2:23

1561. *ἐκδοχή* **ekdochē**
HEB. 10:27

1562. *ἐκδύω* **ekduō**
MATT. 27:28,31; **MARK** 15:20; **LUKE** 10:30; **2 COR.** 5:4

1563. ἐκεῖ ekei
MATT. 2:13,15,22; 5:24; 6:21; 8:12; 12:45;
13:42,50,58; 14:23; 15:29; 17:20; 18:20; 19:2;
21:17; 22:11,13; 24:28,51; 25:30; 26:36,71;
27:36,47,55,61; 28:7; MARK 1:13; 2:6; 3:1;
5:11; 6:5,10,33,55; 11:5; 13:21; 14:15; 16:7;
LUKE 2:6; 6:6; 8:32; 9:4; 10:6; 11:26; 12:18,34;
13:28; 15:13; 17:21,23,37; 21:2; 22:12; 23:33;
JOHN 2:1,6,12; 3:22,23; 4:6,40; 5:5; 6:3,22,24;
10:40,42; 11:8,15,31; 12:2,9,26; 18:2,3; 19:42;
ACTS 9:33; 14:28; 16:1; 17:14; 19:21; 25:9,14;
ROM. 9:26; 15:24; 2 COR. 3:17; TITUS 3:12;
HEB. 7:8; JAMES 2:3; 3:16; 4:13; REV. 2:14;
12:6,14; 21:25; 22:5

1564. ἐκεῖθεν ekeithen
MATT. 4:21; 5:26; 9:9,27; 11:1; 12:9,15; 13:53;
14:13; 15:21,29; 19:15; MARK 1:19; 6:1,10,11;
7:24; 9:30; LUKE 9:4; 12:59; 16:26; JOHN
4:43; 11:54; ACTS 13:4; 16:12; 18:7; 20:13

1566. ἐκεῖσε ekeise
ACTS 21:3; 22:5

1567. ἐκζητέω ekzēteō
LUKE 11:50,51; ACTS 15:17; ROM. 3:11;
HEB. 11:6; 12:17; 1 PET. 1:10

1568. ἐκθαμβέω ekthambeō
MARK 9:15; 14:33; 16:5,6

1569. ἔκθαμβος ekthambos
ACTS 3:11

1570. ἔκθετος ekthetos
ACTS 7:19

1571. ἐκκαθαίρω ekkathairō
1 COR. 5:7; 2 TIM. 2:21

1572. ἐκκαίω ekkaiō
ROM. 1:27

1573. ἐκκακέω ekkakeō
LUKE 18:1; 2 COR. 4:1,16; GAL. 6:9; EPH.
3:13; 2 THESS. 3:13

1574. ἐκκεντέω ekkenteō
JOHN 19:37; REV. 1:7

1575. ἐκκλάω ekklaō
ROM. 11:17,19,20

1576. ἐκκλείω ekkleiō
ROM. 3:27; GAL. 4:17

1577. ἐκκλησία ekklēsia
MATT. 16:18; 18:17; ACTS 2:47; 5:11; 7:38;
8:1,3; 9:31; 11:22,26; 12:1,5; 13:1; 14:23,27;
15:3,4,22,41; 16:5; 18:22; 19:32,39,41; 20:17,28;
ROM. 16:1,4,5,16,23; 1 COR. 1:2; 4:17; 6:4;
7:17; 10:32; 11:16,18,22; 12:28; 14:4,5,12,
19,23,28,33-35; 15:9; 16:1,19; 2 COR. 1:1;
8:1,18,19,23,24; 11:8,28; 12:13; GAL. 1:2,13,
22; EPH. 1:22; 3:10,21; 5:23-25,27,29,32;
PHIL. 3:6; 4:15; COL. 1:18,24; 4:15,16;
1 THESS. 1:1; 2:14; 2 THESS. 1:1,4; 1 TIM.
3:5,15; 5:16; PHILE. 1:2; HEB. 2:12; 12:23;
JAMES 5:14; 3 JOHN 1:6,9,10; REV. 1:4,11,
20; 2:1,7,8,11,12,17,18,23,29; 3:1,6,7,13,14,22;
22:16

1578. ἐκκλίνω ekklinō
ROM. 3:12; 16:17; 1 PET. 3:11

1579. ἐκκολυμβάω ekkolumbaō
ACTS 27:42

1580. ἐκκομίζω ekkomizō
LUKE 7:12

1581. ἐκκόπτω ekkoptō
MATT. 3:10; 5:30; 7:19; 18:8; LUKE 3:9;
13:7,9; ROM. 11:22,24; 2 COR. 11:12; 1 PET.
3:7

1582. ἐκκρέμαμαι ekkremamai
LUKE 19:48

1583. ἐκλαλέω eklaleō
ACTS 23:22

1584. ἐκλάμπω eklampō
MATT. 13:43

1585. ἐκλανθάνω eklanthanō
HEB. 12:5

1586. ἐκλέγω *eklegō*
MARK 13:20; LUKE 6:13; 10:42; 14:7; JOHN 6:70; 13:18; 15:16,19; ACTS 1:2,24; 6:5; 13:17; 15:7,22,25; 1 COR. 1:27,28; EPH. 1:4; JAMES 2:5

1587. ἐκλείπω *ekleipō*
LUKE 16:9; 22:32; HEB. 1:12

1588. ἐκλεκτός *eklektos*
MATT. 20:16; 22:14; 24:22,24,31; MARK 13:20,22,27; LUKE 18:7; 23:35; ROM. 8:33; 16:13; COL. 3:12; 1 TIM. 5:21; 2 TIM. 2:10; TITUS 1:1; 1 PET. 1:2; 2:4,6,9; 2 JOHN 1:1,13; REV. 17:14

1589. ἐκλογή *eklogē*
ACTS 9:15; ROM. 9:11; 11:5,7,28; 1 THESS. 1:4; 2 PET. 1:10

1590. ἐκλύω *ekluō*
MATT. 9:36; 15:32; MARK 8:3; GAL. 6:9; HEB. 12:3,5

1591. ἐκμάσσω, ἐκμάττω
ekmassō, ekmattō
LUKE 7:38,44; JOHN 11:2; 12:3; 13:5

1592. ἐκμυκτηρίζω *ekmuktērizō*
LUKE 16:14; 23:35

1593. ἐκνεύω *ekneuō*
JOHN 5:13

1594. ἐκνήφω *eknēphō*
1 COR. 15:34

1595. ἑκούσιος *hekousios*
PHILE. 1:14

1596. ἑκουσίως *hekousiōs*
HEB. 10:26; 1 PET. 5:2

1597. ἔκπαλαι *ekpalai*
2 PET. 2:3; 3:5

1598. ἐκπειράζω *ekpeirazō*
MATT. 4:7; LUKE 4:12; 10:25; 1 COR. 10:9

1599. ἐκπέμπω *ekpempō*
ACTS 13:4; 17:10

1600. ἐκπετάννυμι *ekpetannumi*
ROM. 10:21

1601. ἐκπίπτω *ekpiptō*
MARK 13:25; ACTS 12:7; 27:17,26,29,32; ROM. 9:6; 1 COR. 13:8; GAL. 5:4; JAMES 1:11; 1 PET. 1:24; 2 PET. 3:17; REV. 2:5

1602. ἐκπλέω *ekpleō*
ACTS 15:39; 18:18; 20:6

1603. ἐκπληρόω *ekplēroō*
ACTS 13:33

1604. ἐκπλήρωσις *ekplērōsis*
ACTS 21:26

1605. ἐκπλήσσω, ἐκπλήττω
ekplēssō, ekplēttō
MATT. 7:28; 13:54; 19:25; 22:33; MARK 1:22; 6:2; 7:37; 10:26; 11:18; LUKE 2:48; 4:32; 9:43; ACTS 13:12

1606. ἐκπνέω *ekpneō*
MARK 15:37,39; LUKE 23:46

1607. ἐκπορεύομαι *ekporeuomai*
MATT. 3:5; 4:4; 15:11,18; 17:21; 20:29; MARK 1:5; 6:11; 7:15,19-21,23; 10:17,46; 11:19; 13:1; LUKE 3:7; 4:22,37; JOHN 5:29; 15:26; ACTS 9:28; 25:4; EPH. 4:29; REV. 1:16; 4:5; 9:17,18; 11:5; 16:14; 19:15,21; 22:1

1608. ἐκπορνεύω *ekporneuō*
JUDE 1:7

1609. ἐκπτύω *ekptuō*
GAL. 4:14

1610. ἐκριζόω *ekrizoō*
MATT. 13:29; 15:13; LUKE 17:6; JUDE 1:12

1611. ἔκστασις *ekstasis*
MARK 5:42; 16:8; LUKE 5:26; ACTS 3:10;
10:10; 11:5; 22:17

1612. ἐκστρέφω *ekstrephō*
TITUS 3:11

1613. ἐκταράσσω, ἐκταράττω
ektarassō, ektarattō
ACTS 16:20

1614. ἐκτείνω *ekteinō*
MATT. 8:3; 12:13,49; 14:31; 26:51; MARK
1:41; 3:5; LUKE 5:13; 6:10; 22:53; JOHN
21:18; ACTS 4:30; 26:1; 27:30

1615. ἐκτελέω *ekteleō*
LUKE 14:29,30

1616. ἐκτένεια *ekteneia*
ACTS 26:7

1617. ἐκτενέστερον
ektenesteron adv.
LUKE 22:44

1618. ἐκτενής *ektenēs*
ACTS 12:5; 1 PET. 4:8

1619. ἐκτενῶς *ektenōs*
1 PET. 1:22

1620. ἐκτίθημι *ektithēmi*
ACTS 7:21; 11:4; 18:26; 28:23

1621. ἐκτινάσσω, ἐκτινάττω
ektinassō, ektinattō
MATT. 10:14; MARK 6:11; ACTS 13:51; 18:6

1622. ἐκτός *ektos*
MATT. 23:26; ACTS 26:22; 1 COR. 6:18; 14:5;
15:2,27; 2 COR. 12:2,3; 1 TIM. 5:19

1623. ἕκτος *hektos*
MATT. 20:5; 27:45; MARK 15:33; LUKE
1:26,36; 23:44; JOHN 4:6; 19:14; ACTS 10:9;
REV. 6:12; 9:13,14; 16:12; 21:20

1624. ἐκτρέπω *ektrepō*
1 TIM. 1:6; 5:15; 6:20; 2 TIM. 4:4; HEB.
12:13

1625. ἐκτρέφω *ektrephō*
EPH. 5:29; 6:4

1626. ἔκτρωμα *ektrōma*
1 COR. 15:8

1627. ἐκφέρω *ekpherō*
LUKE 15:22; ACTS 5:6,9,10,15; 1 TIM. 6:7;
HEB. 6:8

1628. ἐκφεύγω *ekpheugō*
LUKE 21:36; ACTS 16:27; 19:16; ROM. 2:3;
2 COR. 11:33; 1 THESS. 5:3; HEB. 2:3

1629. ἐκφοβέω *ekphobeō*
2 COR. 10:9

1630. ἔκφοβος *ekphobos*
MARK 9:6; HEB. 12:21

1631. ἐκφύω *ekphuō*
MATT. 24:32; MARK 13:28

1632. I. ἐκχέω *ekcheō*
MATT. 9:17; MARK 2:22; JOHN 2:15;
ACTS 2:17,18,33; 22:20; ROM. 3:15;
TITUS 3:6; REV. 16:1-4,6,8,10,12,17

II. ἐκχύνω *ekchunō*
MATT. 23:35; 26:28; MARK 14:24;
LUKE 5:37; 11:50; 22:20; ACTS 1:18;
10:45; ROM. 5:5; JUDE 1:11

1633. ἐκχωρέω *ekchōreō*
LUKE 21:21

1634. ἐκψύχω *ekpsuchō*
ACTS 5:5,10; 12:23

1635. ἑκών *hekōn*
ROM. 8:20; 1 COR. 9:17

1636. ἐλαία elaia
MATT. 21:1; 24:3; 26:30; MARK 11:1; 13:3;
14:26; LUKE 19:29,37; 21:37; 22:39; JOHN
8:1; ROM. 11:17,24; JAMES 3:12; REV. 11:4

1637. ἔλαιον elaion
MATT. 25:3,4,8; MARK 6:13; LUKE 7:46;
10:34; 16:6; HEB. 1:9; JAMES 5:14; REV. 6:6;
18:13

1638. ἐλαιών elaiōn
ACTS 1:12

1639. Ἐλαμίτης Elamitēs
ACTS 2:9

1640. ἐλάσσων, ἐλάττων
    elassōn, elattōn
JOHN 2:10; ROM. 9:12; 1 TIM. 5:9; HEB. 7:7

1641. ἐλαττονέω elattoneō
2 COR. 8:15

1642. ἐλαττόω elattoō
JOHN 3:30; HEB. 2:7,9

1643. ἐλαύνω elaunō
MARK 6:48; LUKE 8:29; JOHN 6:19; JAMES
3:4; 2 PET. 2:17

1644. ἐλαφρία elaphria
2 COR. 1:17

1645. ἐλαφρός elaphros
MATT. 11:30; 2 COR. 4:17

1646. ἐλάχιστος elachistos
MATT. 2:6; 5:19; 25:40,45; LUKE 12:26;
16:10; 19:17; 1 COR. 4:3; 6:2; 15:9; JAMES
3:4

1647. ἐλαχιστότερος elakistoteros
EPH. 3:8

1648. Ἐλεάζαρ Eleazar
MATT. 1:15

1649. ἔλεγξις elegxis
2 PET. 2:16

1650. ἔλεγχος elegchos
2 TIM. 3:16; HEB. 11:1

1651. ἐλέγχω elegchō
MATT. 18:15; LUKE 3:19; JOHN 3:20; 8:9,46;
16:8; 1 COR. 14:24; EPH. 5:11,13; 1 TIM.
5:20; 2 TIM. 4:2; TITUS 1:9,13; 2:15; HEB.
12:5; JAMES 2:9; REV. 3:19

1652. ἐλεεινός eleeinos
1 COR. 15:19; REV. 3:17

1653. ἐλεέω eleeō
MATT. 5:7; 9:27; 15:22; 17:15; 18:33; 20:30,31;
MARK 5:19; 10:47,48; LUKE 16:24; 17:13;
18:38,39; ROM. 9:15,16,18; 11:30-32; 12:8;
1 COR. 7:25; 2 COR. 4:1; PHIL. 2:27; 1 TIM.
1:13,16; 1 PET. 2:10; JUDE 1:22

1654. ἐλεημοσύνη eleēmosunē
MATT. 6:1-4; LUKE 11:41; 12:33; ACTS
3:2,3,10; 9:36; 10:2,4,31; 24:17

1655. ἐλεήμων eleēmōn
MATT. 5:7; HEB. 2:17

1656. ἔλεος eleos
MATT. 9:13; 12:7; 23:23; LUKE
1:50,54,58,72,78; 10:37; ROM. 9:23; 11:31;
15:9; GAL. 6:16; EPH. 2:4; 1 TIM. 1:2; 2 TIM.
1:2,16,18; TITUS 1:4; 3:5; HEB. 4:16; JAMES
2:13; 3:17; 1 PET. 1:3; 2 JOHN 1:3; JUDE
1:2,21

1657. ἐλευθερία eleutheria
ROM. 8:21; 1 COR. 10:29; 2 COR. 3:17; GAL.
2:4; 5:1,13; JAMES 1:25; 2:12; 1 PET. 2:16;
2 PET. 2:19

1658. ἐλεύθερος eleutheros
MATT. 17:26; JOHN 8:33,36; ROM. 6:20; 7:3;
1 COR. 7:21,22,39; 9:1,19; 12:13; GAL. 3:28;
4:22,23,26,30,31; EPH. 6:8; COL. 3:11; 1 PET.
2:16; REV. 6:15; 13:16; 19:18

1659. ἐλευθερόω *eleutheroō*
JOHN 8:32,36; ROM. 6:18,22; 8:2,21; GAL.
5:1

1660. ἔλευσις *eleusis*
ACTS 7:52

1661. ἐλεφάντινος *elephantinos*
REV. 18:12

1662. Ἐλιακείμ *Eliakeim*
MATT. 1:13; LUKE 3:30

1663. Ἐλιέζερ *Eliezer*
LUKE 3:29

1664. Ἐλιούδ *Elioud*
MATT. 1:14,15

1665. Ἐλισάβετ *Elisabet*
LUKE 1:5,7,13,24,36,40,41,57

1666. Ἐλισσαῖος *Elissaios*
LUKE 4:27

1667. ἑλίσσω, ἑλίττω *helissō, helittō*
HEB. 1:12

1668. ἕλκος *helkos*
LUKE 16:21; REV. 16:2,11

1669. ἑλκόω *helkoō*
LUKE 16:20

1670. I. ἕλκω *helkō*
ACTS 21:30; JAMES 2:6

II. ἑλκύω *helkuō*
JOHN 6:44; 12:32; 18:10; 21:6,11;
ACTS 16:19

1671. Ἑλλάς *Hellas*
ACTS 20:2

1672. Ἕλλην *Hellēn*
JOHN 7:35; 12:20; ACTS 14:1; 16:1,3; 17:4;
18:4,17; 19:10,17; 20:21; 21:28; ROM. 1:14,16;
2:9,10; 3:9; 10:12; **1 COR.** 1:22-24; 10:32;
12:13; GAL. 2:3; 3:28; COL. 3:11

1673. Ἑλληνικός *Hellēnikos*
LUKE 23:38; REV. 9:11

1674. Ἑλληνίς *Hellēnis*
MARK 7:26; ACTS 17:12

1675. Ἑλληνιστής *Hellēnistēs*
ACTS 6:1; 9:29; 11:20

1676. Ἑλληνιστί *Hellēnisti*
JOHN 19:20; ACTS 21:37

1677. ἐλλογέω *ellogeō*
ROM. 5:13; PHILE. 1:18

1678. Ἐλμωδάμ *Elmōdam*
LUKE 3:28

1679. ἐλπίζω *elpizō*
MATT. 12:21; LUKE 6:34; 23:8; 24:21; JOHN
5:45; ACTS 24:26; 26:7; ROM. 8:24,25; 15:12,
24; **1 COR.** 13:7; 15:19; 16:7; **2 COR.** 1:10,13;
5:11; 8:5; 13:6; PHIL. 2:19,23; **1 TIM.** 3:14;
4:10; 5:5; 6:17; PHILE. 1:22; HEB. 11:1;
1 PET. 1:13; 3:5; **2 JOHN** 1:12; **3 JOHN** 1:14

1680. ἐλπίς *elpis*
ACTS 2:26; 16:19; 23:6; 24:15; 26:6,7; 27:20;
28:20; ROM. 4:18; 5:2,4,5; 8:20,24; 12:12;
15:4,13; **1 COR.** 9:10; 13:13; **2 COR.** 1:7; 3:12;
10:15; GAL. 5:5; EPH. 1:18; 2:12; 4:4; PHIL.
1:20; COL. 1:5,23,27; **1 THESS.** 1:3; 2:19;
4:13; 5:8; **2 THESS.** 2:16; **1 TIM.** 1:1; TITUS
1:2; 2:13; 3:7; HEB. 3:6; 6:11,18; 7:19; 10:23;
1 PET. 1:3,21; 3:15; **1 JOHN** 3:3

1681. Ἐλύμας *Elumas*
ACTS 13:8

1682. Ἐλωΐ *Elōi*
MARK 15:34

1683. ἐμαυτοῦ *emautou*
MATT. 8:9; LUKE 7:7,8; JOHN 5:30,31;
7:17,28; 8:14,18,28,42,54; 10:18; 12:32,49;
14:3,10,21; 17:19; ACTS 20:24; 24:10; 26:2,9;
ROM. 11:4; **1 COR.** 4:3,4,6; 7:7; 9:19; 10:33;
2 COR. 2:1; 11:7,9; 12:5; GAL. 2:18; PHIL.
3:13; PHILE. 1:13

1684. ἐμβαίνω embainō
MATT. 8:23; 9:1; 13:2; 14:22,32; 15:39;
MARK 4:1; 5:18; 6:45; 8:10,13; LUKE 5:3;
8:22,37; JOHN 5:4; 6:17,22,24

1685. ἐμβάλλω emballō
LUKE 12:5

1686. ἐμβάπτω embaptō
MATT. 26:23; MARK 14:20; JOHN 13:26

1687. ἐμβατεύω embateuō
COL. 2:18

1688. ἐμβιβάζω embibazō
ACTS 27:6

1689. ἐμβλέπω emblepō
MATT. 6:26; 19:26; MARK 8:25; 10:21,27;
14:67; LUKE 20:17; 22:61; JOHN 1:36,42;
ACTS 1:11; 22:11

1690. ἐμβριμάομαι embrimaomai
MATT. 9:30; MARK 1:43; 14:5; JOHN
11:33,38

1692. ἐμέω emeō
REV. 3:16

1693. ἐμμαίνομαι emmainomai
ACTS 26:11

1694. Ἐμμανουήλ Emmanouēl
MATT. 1:23

1695. Ἐμμαούς Emmaous
LUKE 24:13

1696. ἐμμένω emmenō
ACTS 14:22; GAL. 3:10; HEB. 8:9

1697. Ἐμμόρ Emmor
ACTS 7:16

1699. ἐμός emos
MATT. 18:20; 20:15,23; 25:27; MARK 8:38;
10:40; LUKE 9:26; 15:31; 22:19; JOHN 3:29;

4:34; 5:30,47; 6:38; 7:6,8,16; 8:16,31,37,43,51,
56; 10:14,26,27; 12:26; 13:35; 14:15,24,27;
15:8,9,11,12; 16:14,15; 17:10,13,24; 18:36;
ROM. 3:7; 10:1; 1 COR. 1:15; 5:4; 7:40; 9:2,3;
11:24,25; 16:18,21; 2 COR. 1:23; 2:3; 8:23;
GAL. 1:13; 6:11; PHIL. 1:26; 3:9; COL. 4:18;
2 THESS. 3:17; 2 TIM. 4:6; PHILE. 1:10,
12,19; 2 PET. 1:15; 3 JOHN 1:4; REV.
2:20

1701. ἐμπαιγμός empaigmos
HEB. 11:36

1702. ἐμπαίζω empaizō
MATT. 2:16; 20:19; 27:29,31,41; MARK
10:34; 15:20,31; LUKE 14:29; 18:32; 22:63;
23:11,36

1703. ἐμπαῖκτης empaiktēs
2 PET. 3:3; JUDE 1:18

1704. ἐμπεριπατέω emperipateō
2 COR. 6:16

1705. ἐμπίπλημι empiplēmi
LUKE 1:53; 6:25; JOHN 6:12; ACTS 14:17;
ROM. 15:24

1706. ἐμπίπτω empiptō
MATT. 12:11; LUKE 10:36; 14:5; 1 TIM.
3:6,7; 6:9; HEB. 10:31

1707. ἐμπλέκω emplekō
2 TIM. 2:4; 2 PET. 2:20

1708. ἐμπλοκή emplokē
1 PET. 3:3

1709. ἐμπνέω empneō
ACTS 9:1

1710. ἐμπορεύομαι emporeuomai
JAMES 4:13; 2 PET. 2:3

1711. ἐμπορία emporia
MATT. 22:5

1712. ἐμπόριον *emporion*
JOHN 2:16

1713. ἔμπορος *emporos*
MATT. 13:45; REV. 18:3,11,15,23

1714. ἐμπρήθω *emprēthō*
MATT. 22:7

1715. ἔμπροσθεν *emprosthen*
MATT. 5:16,24; 6:1,2; 7:6; 10:32,33; 11:10,26;
17:2; 18:14; 23:13; 25:32; 26:70; 27:11,29;
MARK 1:2; 9:2; LUKE 5:19; 7:27; 10:21; 12:8;
14:2; 19:4,27,28; 21:36; JOHN 1:15,27,30; 3:28;
10:4; 12:37; ACTS 18:17; 2 COR. 5:10; GAL.
2:14; PHIL. 3:13; 1 THESS. 1:3; 2:19; 3:9,13;
1 JOHN 3:19; REV. 4:6; 19:10; 22:8

1716. ἐμπτύω *emptuō*
MATT. 26:67; 27:30; MARK 10:34; 14:65;
15:19; LUKE 18:32

1717. ἐμφανής *emphanēs*
ACTS 10:40; ROM. 10:20

1718. ἐμφανίζω *emphanizō*
MATT. 27:53; JOHN 14:21,22; ACTS
23:15,22; 24:1; 25:2,15; HEB. 9:24; 11:14

1719. ἔμφοβος *emphobos*
LUKE 24:5,37; ACTS 10:4; 22:9; 24:25; REV.
11:13

1720. ἐμφυσάω *emphusaō*
JOHN 20:22

1721. ἔμφυτος *emphutos*
JAMES 1:21

1723. ἐναγκαλίζομαι *enagkalizomai*
MARK 9:36; 10:16

1724. ἐνάλιος *enalios*
JAMES 3:7

1725. ἔναντι *enanti*
LUKE 1:8

1726. ἐναντίον *enantion*
MARK 2:12; LUKE 20:26; 24:19; ACTS 7:10;
8:32

1727. ἐναντίος *enantios*
MATT. 14:24; MARK 6:48; 15:39; ACTS 26:9;
27:4; 28:17; 1 THESS. 2:15; TITUS 2:8

1728. ἐνάρχομαι *enarchomai*
GAL. 3:3; PHIL. 1:6

1729. ἐνδεής *endeēs*
ACTS 4:34

1730. ἔνδειγμα *endeigma*
2 THESS. 1:5

1731. ἐνδείκνυμι *endeiknumi*
ROM. 2:15; 9:17,22; 2 COR. 8:24; EPH. 2:7;
1 TIM. 1:16; 2 TIM. 4:14; TITUS 2:10; 3:2;
HEB. 6:10,11

1732. ἔνδειξις *endeixis*
ROM. 3:25,26; 2 COR. 8:24; PHIL. 1:28

1733. ἔνδεκα *hendeka*
MATT. 28:16; MARK 16:14; LUKE 24:9,33;
ACTS 1:26; 2:14

1734. ἐνδέκατος *hendekatos*
MATT. 20:6,9; REV. 21:20

1735. ἐνδέχομαι *endechomai*
LUKE 13:33

1736. ἐνδημέω *endēmeō*
2 COR. 5:6,8,9

1737. ἐνδιδύσκω *endiduskō*
LUKE 8:27; 16:19

1738. ἔνδικος *endikos*
ROM. 3:8; HEB. 2:2

1739. ἐνδόμησις *endomēsis*
REV. 21:18

1740. ἐνδοξάζω endoxazō
2 THESS. 1:10,12

1741. ἔνδοξος endoxos
LUKE 7:25; 13:17; 1 COR. 4:10; EPH. 5:27

1742. ἔνδυμα enduma
MATT. 3:4; 6:25,28; 7:15; 22:11,12; 28:3;
LUKE 12:23

1743. ἐνδυναμόω endunamoō
ACTS 9:22; ROM. 4:20; EPH. 6:10; PHIL.
4:13; 1 TIM. 1:12; 2 TIM. 2:1; 4:17; HEB.
11:34

1744. ἐνδύνω endunō
2 TIM. 3:6

1745. ἔνδυσις endusis
1 PET. 3:3

1746. ἐνδύω enduō
MATT. 6:25; 22:11; 27:31; MARK 1:6; 6:9;
15:17,20; LUKE 12:22; 15:22; 24:49; ACTS
12:21; ROM. 13:12,14; 1 COR. 15:53,54;
2 COR. 5:3; GAL. 3:27; EPH. 4:24; 6:11,14;
COL. 3:10,12; 1 THESS. 5:8; REV. 1:13; 15:6;
19:14

1747. ἐνέδρα enedra
ACTS 25:3

1748. ἐνεδρεύω enedreuō
LUKE 11:54; ACTS 23:21

1749. ἔνεδρον enedron
ACTS 23:16 TR

1750. ἐνειλέω eneileō
MARK 15:46

1751. ἔνειμι eneimi
LUKE 11:41

1752. ἕνεκα, ἕνεκεν heneka, heneken
MATT. 5:10,11; 10:18,39; 16:25; 19:5,29;
MARK 8:35; 10:7,29; 13:9; LUKE 4:18; 6:22;

9:24; 18:29; 21:12; ACTS 19:32; 26:21; 28:20;
ROM. 8:36; 14:20; 2 COR. 3:10; 7:12

1753. ἐνέργεια energeia
EPH. 1:19; 3:7; 4:16; PHIL. 3:21; COL. 1:29;
2:12; 2 THESS. 2:9,11

1754. ἐνεργέω energeō
MATT. 14:2; MARK 6:14; ROM. 7:5; 1 COR.
12:6,11; 2 COR. 1:6; 4:12; GAL. 2:8; 3:5; 5:6;
EPH. 1:11,20; 2:2; 3:20; PHIL. 2:13; COL.
1:29; 1 THESS. 2:13; 2 THESS. 2:7; JAMES
5:16

1755. ἐνέργημα energēma
1 COR. 12:6,10

1756. ἐνεργής energēs
1 COR. 16:9; PHILE. 1:6; HEB. 4:12

1757. ἐνευλογέω eneulogeō
ACTS 3:25; GAL. 3:8

1758. ἐνέχω enechō
MARK 6:19; LUKE 11:53; GAL. 5:1

1759. ἐνθάδε enthade
LUKE 24:41; JOHN 4:15,16; ACTS 10:18;
16:28; 17:6; 25:17,24

1760. ἐνθυμέομαι enthumeomai
MATT. 1:20; 9:4; ACTS 10:19

1761. ἐνθύμησις enthumēsis
MATT. 9:4; 12:25; ACTS 17:29; HEB. 4:12

1762. ἔνι eni
(For ἔνεστι)
GAL. 3:28; COL. 3:11; JAMES 1:17

1763. ἐνιαυτός eniautos
LUKE 4:19; JOHN 11:49,51; 18:13; ACTS
11:26; 18:11; GAL. 4:10; HEB. 9:7,25; 10:1,3;
JAMES 4:13; 5:17; REV. 9:15

1764. ἐνίστημι enistēmi
ROM. 8:38; 1 COR. 3:22; 7:26; GAL. 1:4;
2 THESS. 2:2; 2 TIM. 3:1; HEB. 9:9

1765. ἐνισχύω *enischuō*
LUKE 22:43; ACTS 9:19

1766. ἔννατος *ennatos*
MATT. 20:5; 27:45,46; MARK 15:33,34;
LUKE 23:44; ACTS 3:1; 10:3,30; REV. 21:20

1767. ἐννέα *ennea*
LUKE 17:17

1768. ἐννενηκονταεννέα
ennenēkontaennea
MATT. 18:12,13; LUKE 15:4,7

1769. ἐννεός *enneos*
ACTS 9:7

1770. ἐννεύω *enneuō*
LUKE 1:62

1771. ἔννοια *ennoia*
HEB. 4:12; 1 PET. 4:1

1772. ἔννομος *ennomos*
ACTS 19:39; 1 COR. 9:21

1773. ἔννυχον *ennuchon*   adv.
MARK 1:35

1774. ἐνοικέω *enoikeō*
ROM. 8:11; 2 COR. 6:16; COL. 3:16; 2 TIM.
1:5,14

1775. ἑνότης *henotēs*
EPH. 4:3,13

1776. ἐνοχλέω *enochleō*
HEB. 12:15

1777. ἔνοχος *enochos*
MATT. 5:21,22; 26:66; MARK 3:29; 14:64;
1 COR. 11:27; HEB. 2:15; JAMES 2:10

1778. ἔνταλμα *entalma*
MATT. 15:9; MARK 7:7; COL. 2:22

1779. ἐνταφιάζω *entaphiazō*
MATT. 26:12; JOHN 19:40

1780. ἐνταφιασμός *entaphiasmos*
MARK 14:8; JOHN 12:7

1781. ἐντέλλομαι *entellomai*
MATT. 4:6; 15:4; 17:9; 19:7; 28:20; MARK
10:3; 11:6; 13:34; LUKE 4:10; JOHN 8:5;
14:31; 15:14,17; ACTS 1:2; 13:47; HEB. 9:20;
11:22

1782. ἐντεῦθεν *enteuthen*
MATT. 17:20; LUKE 4:9; 13:31; 16:26; JOHN
2:16; 7:3; 14:31; 18:36; 19:18; JAMES 4:1;
REV. 22:2

1783. ἔντευξις *enteuxis*
1 TIM. 2:1; 4:5

1784. ἔντιμος *entimos*
LUKE 7:2; 14:8; PHIL. 2:29; 1 PET. 2:4,6

1785. ἐντολή *entolē*
MATT. 5:19; 15:3,6; 19:17; 22:36,38,40;
MARK 7:8,9; 10:5,19; 12:28-31; LUKE 1:6;
15:29; 18:20; 23:56; JOHN 10:18; 11:57;
12:49,50; 13:34; 14:15,21; 15:10,12; ACTS
17:15; ROM. 7:8-13; 13:9; 1 COR. 7:19; 14:37;
EPH. 2:15; 6:2; COL. 4:10; 1 TIM. 6:14;
TITUS 1:14; HEB. 7:5,16,18; 9:19; 2 PET.
2:21; 3:2; 1 JOHN 2:3,4,7,8; 3:22-24; 4:21;
5:2,3; 2 JOHN 1:4-6; REV. 12:17; 14:12; 22:14

1786. ἐντόπιος *entopios*
ACTS 21:12

1787. ἐντός *entos*
MATT. 23:26; LUKE 17:21

1788. ἐντρέπω *entrepō*
MATT. 21:37; MARK 12:6; LUKE 18:2,4;
20:13; 1 COR. 4:14; 2 THESS. 3:14; TITUS
2:8; HEB. 12:9

1789. ἐντρέφω *entrephō*
1 TIM. 4:6

1790. ἔντρομος *entromos*
ACTS 7:32; 16:29; HEB. 12:21

1791. ἐντροπή *entropē*
1 COR. 6:5; 15:34

1792. ἐντρυφάω *entruphaō*
2 PET. 2:13

1793. ἐντυγχάνω *entugchanō*
ACTS 25:24; ROM. 8:27,34; 11:2; HEB. 7:25

1794. ἐντυλίσσω, ἐντυλίττω
　　entulissō, entulittō
MATT. 27:59; LUKE 23:53; JOHN 20:7

1795. ἐντυπόω *entupoō*
2 COR. 3:7

1796. ἐνυβρίζω *enubrizō*
HEB. 10:29

1797. ἐνυπνιάζω *enupniazō*
ACTS 2:17; JUDE 1:8

1798. ἐνύπνιον *enupnion*
ACTS 2:17

1799. ἐνώπιον *enōpion*
LUKE 1:6,15,17,19,75; 4:7; 5:18,25; 8:47;
12:6,9; 13:26; 14:10; 15:10,18,21; 16:15; 23:14;
24:11,43; JOHN 20:30; ACTS 2:25; 4:10,19;
6:5,6; 7:46; 8:21; 9:15; 10:4,30,31,33; 19:9,19;
27:35; ROM. 3:20; 12:17; 14:22; 1 COR. 1:29;
2 COR. 4:2; 7:12; 8:21; GAL. 1:20; 1 TIM. 2:3;
5:4,20,21; 6:12,13; 2 TIM. 2:14; 4:1; HEB.
4:13; 13:21; JAMES 4:10; 1 PET. 3:4; 1 JOHN
3:22; 3 JOHN 1:6; REV. 1:4; 2:14; 3:2,5,8,9;
4:5,6,10; 5:8; 7:9,11,15; 8:2-4; 9:13; 11:4,16;
12:4,10; 13:12-14; 14:3,5,10; 15:4; 16:19; 19:20;
20:12

1800. Ἐνώς *Enōs*
LUKE 3:38

1801. ἐνωτίζομαι *enōtizomai*
ACTS 2:14

1802. Ἐνώχ *Enōch*
LUKE 3:37; HEB. 11:5; JUDE 1:14

1803. ἕξ *hex*
MATT. 17:1; MARK 9:2; LUKE 4:25; 13:14;
JOHN 2:6,20; 12:1; ACTS 11:12; 18:11; 27:37;
JAMES 5:17; REV. 4:8; 13:18

1804. ἐξαγγέλλω *exaggellō*
1 PET. 2:9

1805. ἐξαγοράζω *exagorazō*
GAL. 3:13; 4:5; EPH. 5:16; COL. 4:5

1806. ἐξάγω *exagō*
MARK 8:23; 15:20; LUKE 24:50; JOHN 10:3;
ACTS 5:19; 7:36,40; 12:17; 13:17; 16:37,39;
21:38; HEB. 8:9

1807. ἐξαιρέω *exaireō*
MATT. 5:29; 18:9; ACTS 7:10,34; 12:11;
23:27; 26:17; GAL. 1:4

1808. ἐξαίρω *exairō*
1 COR. 5:2,13

1809. ἐξαιτέω *exaiteō*
LUKE 22:31

1810. ἐξαίφνης *exaiphnēs*
MARK 13:36; LUKE 2:13; 9:39; ACTS 9:3;
22:6

1811. ἐξακολουθέω *exakoloutheō*
2 PET. 1:16; 2:2,15

1812. ἐξακόσιοι *hexakosioi*
REV. 13:18; 14:20

1813. ἐξαλείφω *exaleiphō*
ACTS 3:19; COL. 2:14; REV. 3:5; 7:17; 21:4

1814. ἐξάλλομαι *exallomai*
ACTS 3:8

1815. ἐξανάστασις *exanastasis*
PHIL. 3:11

1816. ἐξανατέλλω *exanatellō*
MATT. 13:5; MARK 4:5

1817. ἐξανίστημι *exanistēmi*
MARK 12:19; LUKE 20:28; ACTS 15:5

1818. ἐξαπατάω *exapataō*
ROM. 7:11; 16:18; **1 COR.** 3:18; **2 COR.** 11:3;
2 THESS. 2:3

1819. ἐξάπινα *exapina*
MARK 9:8

1820. ἐξαπορέομαι *exaporeomai*
2 COR. 1:8; 4:8

1821. ἐξαποστέλλω *exapostellō*
LUKE 1:53; 20:10,11; ACTS 7:12; 9:30; 11:22;
12:11; 17:14; 22:21; GAL. 4:4,6

1822. ἐξαρτίζω *exartizō*
ACTS 21:5; **2 TIM.** 3:17

1823. ἐξαστράπτω *exastraptō*
LUKE 9:29

1824. ἐξαυτῆς *exautēs*
MARK 6:25; ACTS 10:33; 11:11; 21:32; 23:30;
PHIL. 2:23

1825. ἐξεγείρω *exegeirō*
ROM. 9:17; **1 COR.** 6:14

1826. ἔξειμι *exeimi*
ACTS 13:42; 17:15; 20:7; 27:43

1827. ἐξελέγχω *exelegchō*
JUDE 1:15

1828. ἐξέλκω *exelkō*
JAMES 1:14

1829. ἐξέραμα *exerama*
2 PET. 2:22

1830. ἐξερευνάω *exereunaō*
1 PET. 1:10

1831. ἐξέρχομαι *exerchomai*
MATT. 2:6; 5:26; 8:28,32,34; 9:26,31,32;
10:11,14; 11:7-9; 12:14,43,44; 13:1,3,49; 14:14;
15:18,19,21,22; 17:18; 18:28; 20:1,3,5,6; 21:17;
22:10; 24:1,26,27; 25:1,6; 26:30,55,71,75;
27:32,53; 28:8; MARK 1:25,26,28,29,35,38,45;
2:12,13; 3:6,21; 4:3; 5:2,8,13,14,30; 6:1,10,12,
24,34,54; 7:29-31; 8:11,27; 9:25,26,29,30;
11:11,12; 14:16,26,48,68; 16:8,20; LUKE 1:22;
2:1; 4:14,35,36,41,42; 5:8,27; 6:12,19; 7:17,24-
26; 8:2,5,27,29,33,35,38,46; 9:4-6; 10:10,35;
11:14,24; 12:59; 13:31; 14:18,21,23; 15:28;
17:29; 21:37; 22:39,52,62; JOHN 1:43; 4:30,43;
8:9,42,59; 10:9,39; 11:31,44; 12:13; 13:3,30,31;
16:27,28,30; 17:8; 18:1,4,16,29,38; 19:4,5,17,34;
20:3; 21:3,23; ACTS 1:21; 7:3,4,7; 8:7; 10:23;
11:25; 12:9,10,17; 14:20; 15:24,40; 16:3,10,
13,18,19,36,39,40; 17:33; 18:23; 19:12;
20:1,11; 21:5,8; 22:18; 28:3,15; ROM. 10:18;
1 COR. 5:10; 14:36; **2 COR.** 2:13; 6:17; 8:17;
PHIL. 4:15; **1 THESS.** 1:8; HEB. 3:16; 7:5;
11:8,15; 13:13; JAMES 3:10; **1 JOHN** 2:19;
4:1; **3 JOHN** 1:7; REV. 3:12; 6:2,4; 9:3;
14:15,17, 18,20; 15:6; 16:17; 18:4; 19:5;
20:8

1832. ἔξεστι *exesti*
MATT. 12:2,4,10,12; 14:4; 19:3; 20:15; 22:17;
27:6; MARK 2:24,26; 3:4; 6:18; 10:2; 12:14;
LUKE 6:2,4,9; 14:3; 20:22; JOHN 5:10; 18:31;
ACTS 2:29; 8:37; 16:21; 21:37; 22:25; **1 COR.**
6:12; 10:23; **2 COR.** 12:4

1833. ἐξετάζω *exetazō*
MATT. 2:8; 10:11; JOHN 21:12

1834. ἐξηγέομαι *exēgeomai*
LUKE 24:35; JOHN 1:18; ACTS 10:8;
15:12,14; 21:19

1835. ἑξήκοντα *hexēkonta*
MATT. 13:8,23; MARK 4:8,20; LUKE 24:13;
1 TIM. 5:9; REV. 11:3; 12:6; 13:18

1836. ἑξῆς *hexēs*
LUKE 7:11; 9:37; ACTS 21:1; 25:17; 27:18

1837. ἐξηχέω *exēcheō*
1 THESS. 1:8

1838. ἕξις *hexis*
HEB. 5:14

1839. ἐξίστημι *existēmi*
MATT. 12:23; MARK 2:12; 3:21; 5:42; 6:51;
LUKE 2:47; 8:56; 24:22; ACTS 2:7,12;
8:9,11,13; 9:21; 10:45; 12:16; 2 COR. 5:13

1840. ἐξισχύω *exischuō*
EPH. 3:18

1841. ἔξοδος *exodos*
LUKE 9:31; HEB. 11:22; 2 PET. 1:15

1842. ἐξολοθρεύω *exolothreuō*
ACTS 3:23

1843. ἐξομολογέω *exomologeō*
MATT. 3:6; 11:25; MARK 1:5; LUKE 10:21;
22:6; ACTS 19:18; ROM. 14:11; 15:9; PHIL.
2:11; JAMES 5:16; REV. 3:5

1844. ἐξορκίζω *exorkizō*
MATT. 26:63

1845. ἐξορκιστής *exorkistēs*
ACTS 19:13

1846. ἐξορύσσω, ἐξορύττω
exorussō, exoruttō
MARK 2:4; GAL. 4:15

1847. ἐξουδενόω *exoudenoō*
MARK 9:12

1848. ἐξουθενέω *exoutheneō*
LUKE 18:9; 23:11; ACTS 4:11; ROM. 14:3,10;
1 COR. 1:28; 6:4; 16:11; 2 COR. 10:10; GAL.
4:14; 1 THESS. 5:20

1849. ἐξουσία *exousia*
MATT. 7:29; 8:9; 9:6,8; 10:1; 21:23,24,27;
28:18; MARK 1:22,27; 2:10; 3:15; 6:7;
11:28,29,33; 13:34; LUKE 4:6,32,36; 5:24; 7:8;
9:1; 10:19; 12:5,11; 19:17; 20:2,8,20; 22:53;
23:7; JOHN 1:12; 5:27; 10:18; 17:2; 19:10,11;
ACTS 1:7; 5:4; 8:19; 9:14; 26:10,12,18; ROM.
9:21; 13:1-3; 1 COR. 7:37; 8:9; 9:4-6,12,18;

11:10; 15:24; 2 COR. 10:8; 13:10; EPH. 1:21;
2:2; 3:10; 6:12; COL. 1:13,16; 2:10,15;
2 THESS. 3:9; TITUS 3:1; HEB. 13:10; 1 PET.
3:22; JUDE 1:25; REV. 2:26; 6:8; 9:3,10,19;
11:6; 12:10; 13:2,4,5,7,12; 14:18; 16:9; 17:12,13;
18:1; 20:6; 22:14

1850. ἐξουσιάζω *exousiazō*
LUKE 22:25; 1 COR. 6:12; 7:4

1851. ἐξοχή *exochē*
ACTS 25:23

1852. ἐξυπνίζω *exupnizō*
JOHN 11:11

1853. ἔξυπνος *exupnos*
ACTS 16:27

1854. ἔξω *exō*
MATT. 5:13; 12:46,47; 13:48; 21:17,39;
26:69,75; MARK 1:45; 3:31,32; 4:11; 5:10;
8:23; 11:4,19; 12:8; 14:68; LUKE 1:10; 4:29;
8:20,54; 13:25,28,33; 14:35; 20:15; 22:62; 24:50;
JOHN 6:37; 9:34,35; 11:43; 12:31; 15:6; 18:16;
19:4,5,13; 20:11; ACTS 4:15; 5:23,34; 7:58;
9:40; 14:19; 16:13,30; 21:5,30; 26:11; 1 COR.
5:12,13; 2 COR. 4:16; COL. 4:5; 1 THESS.
4:12; HEB. 13:11-13; 1 JOHN 4:18; REV. 3:12;
11:2; 14:20; 22:15

1855. ἔξωθεν *exōthen*
MATT. 23:25,27,28; MARK 7:15,18; LUKE
11:39,40; 2 COR. 7:5; 1 TIM. 3:7; 1 PET. 3:3;
REV. 11:2

1856. ἐξωθέω *exōtheō*
ACTS 7:45; 27:39

1857. ἐξώτερος *exōteros*
MATT. 8:12; 22:13; 25:30

1858. ἑορτάζω *heortazō*
1 COR. 5:8

1859. ἑορτή *heortē*
MATT. 26:5; 27:15; MARK 14:2; 15:6; LUKE
2:41,42; 22:1; 23:17; JOHN 2:23; 4:45; 5:1; 6:4;
7:2,8,10,11,14,37; 11:56; 12:12,20; 13:1,29;
ACTS 18:21; COL. 2:16

1860. ἐπαγγελία *epaggelia*
LUKE 24:49; **ACTS** 1:4; 2:33,39; 7:17;
13:23,32; 23:21; 26:6; **ROM.** 4:13,14,16,20;
9:4,8,9; 15:8; **2 COR.** 1:20; 7:1; **GAL.** 3:14,16-
18,21,22,29; 4:23,28; **EPH.** 1:13; 2:12; 3:6; 6:2;
1 TIM. 4:8; **2 TIM.** 1:1; **HEB.** 4:1; 6:12,15,17;
7:6; 8:6; 9:15; 10:36; 11:9,13,17,33,39; **2 PET.**
3:4,9; **1 JOHN** 1:5; 2:25

1861. ἐπαγγέλλω *epaggellō*
MARK 14:11; **ACTS** 7:5; **ROM.** 4:21; **GAL.**
3:19; **1 TIM.** 2:10; 6:21; **TITUS** 1:2; **HEB.**
6:13; 10:23; 11:11; 12:26; **JAMES** 1:12; 2:5;
2 PET. 2:19; **1 JOHN** 2:25

1862. ἐπάγγελμα *epaggelma*
2 PET. 1:4; 3:13

1863. ἐπάγω *epagō*
ACTS 5:28; **2 PET.** 2:1,5

1864. ἐπαγωνίζομαι *epagōnizomai*
JUDE 1:3

1865. ἐπαθροίζω *epathroizō*
LUKE 11:29

1866. Ἐπαίνετος *Epainetos*
ROM. 16:5

1867. ἐπαινέω *epaineō*
LUKE 16:8; **ROM.** 15:11; **1 COR.** 11:2,17,22

1868. ἔπαινος *epainos*
ROM. 2:29; 13:3; **1 COR.** 4:5; **2 COR.** 8:18;
EPH. 1:6,12,14; **PHIL.** 1:11; 4:8; **1 PET.** 1:7;
2:14

1869. ἐπαίρω *epairō*
MATT. 17:8; **LUKE** 6:20; 11:27; 16:23; 18:13;
21:28; 24:50; **JOHN** 4:35; 6:5; 13:18; 17:1;
ACTS 1:9; 2:14; 14:11; 22:22; 27:40; **2 COR.**
10:5; 11:20; **1 TIM.** 2:8

1870. ἐπαισχύνομαι *epaischunomai*
MARK 8:38; **LUKE** 9:26; **ROM.** 1:16; 6:21;
2 TIM. 1:8,12,16; **HEB.** 2:11; 11:16

1871. ἐπαιτέω *epaiteō*
LUKE 16:3

1872. ἐπακολουθέω *epakoloutheō*
MARK 16:20; **1 TIM.** 5:10,24; **1 PET.** 2:21

1873. ἐπακούω *epakouō*
2 COR. 6:2

1874. ἐπακροάομαι *epakroaomai*
ACTS 16:25

1875. ἐπάν *epan*
MATT. 2:8; **LUKE** 11:22,34

1876. ἐπάναγκες *epanagkes*
ACTS 15:28

1877. ἐπανάγω *epanagō*
MATT. 21:18; **LUKE** 5:3,4

1878. ἐπαναμιμνήσκω
epanamimnēskō
ROM. 15:15

1879. ἐπαναπαύω *epanapauō*
LUKE 10:6; **ROM.** 2:17

1880. ἐπανέρχομαι *epanerchomai*
LUKE 10:35; 19:15

1881. ἐπανίστημι *epanistēmi*
MATT. 10:21; **MARK** 13:12

1882. ἐπανόρθωσις *epanorthōsis*
2 TIM. 3:16

1883. ἐπάνω *epanō*
MATT. 2:9; 5:14; 21:7; 23:18,20,22; 27:37;
28:2; **MARK** 14:5; **LUKE** 4:39; 10:19; 11:44;
19:17,19; **JOHN** 3:31; **1 COR.** 15:6; **REV.** 6:8;
20:3

1884. ἐπαρκέω *eparkeō*
1 TIM. 5:10,16

1885. ἐπαρχία *eparchia*
ACTS 23:34; 25:1

1886. ἔπαυλις *epaulis*
ACTS 1:20

1887. ἐπαύριον *epaurion*
MATT. 27:62; MARK 11:12; JOHN
1:29,35,43; 6:22; 12:12; ACTS 10:9,23,24;
14:20; 20:7; 21:8; 22:30; 23:32; 25:6,23

1888. ἐπαυτοφώρῳ *epautophōrō*
JOHN 8:4

1889. Ἐπαφρᾶς *Epaphras*
COL. 1:7; 4:12; PHILE. 1:23

1890. ἐπαφρίζω *epaphrizō*
JUDE 1:13

1891. Ἐπαφρόδιτος *Epaphroditos*
PHIL. 2:25; 4:18

1892. ἐπεγείρω *epegeirō*
ACTS 13:50; 14:2

1893. ἐπεί *epei*
MATT. 18:32; 27:6; MARK 15:42; LUKE
1:34; 7:1; JOHN 13:29; 19:31; ROM. 3:6;
11:6,22; 1 COR. 5:10; 7:14; 14:12,16; 15:29;
2 COR. 11:18; 13:3; HEB. 2:14; 4:6; 5:2,11;
6:13; 9:17,26; 10:2; 11:11

1894. ἐπειδή *epeidē*
MATT. 21:46; LUKE 11:6; ACTS 13:46;
14:12; 15:24; 1 COR. 1:21,22; 14:16; 15:21;
2 COR. 5:4; PHIL. 2:26

1895. ἐπειδήπερ *epeidēper*
LUKE 1:1

1896. ἐπεῖδον *epeidon*
(All 2 aor. forms of ἐφοράω)
LUKE 1:25; ACTS 4:29

1897. ἐπείπερ *epeiper*
ROM. 3:30

1898. ἐπεισαγωγή *epeisagōgē*
HEB. 7:19

1899. ἔπειτα *epeita*
MARK 7:5; LUKE 16:7; JOHN 11:7; 1 COR.
12:28; 15:6,7,23,46; GAL. 1:18,21; 2:1;
1 THESS. 4:17; HEB. 7:2,27; JAMES 3:17; 4:14

1900. ἐπέκεινα *epekeina*
ACTS 7:43

1901. ἐπεκτείνω *epekteinō*
PHIL. 3:13

1902. ἐπενδύω *ependuō*
2 COR. 5:2,4

1903. ἐπενδύτης *ependutēs*
JOHN 21:7

1904. ἐπέρχομαι *eperchomai*
LUKE 1:35; 11:22; 21:26,35; ACTS 1:8; 8:24;
13:40; 14:19; EPH. 2:7; JAMES 5:1

1905. ἐπερωτάω *eperōtaō*
MATT. 12:10; 16:1; 17:10; 22:23,35,41,46;
27:11; MARK 5:9; 7:5,17; 8:5,23,27;
9:11,16,21,28,32,33; 10:2,10,17; 11:29;
12:18,28,34; 13:3; 14:60,61; 15:2,4,44; LUKE
2:46; 3:10,14; 6:9; 8:9,30; 9:18; 17:20; 18:18,40;
20:21,27,40; 21:7; 22:64; 23:3,6,9; JOHN
18:7,21; ACTS 1:6; 5:27; 23:34; ROM. 10:20;
1 COR. 14:35

1906. ἐπερώτημα *eperotēma*
1 PET. 3:21

1907. ἐπέχω *epechō*
LUKE 14:7; ACTS 3:5; 19:22; PHIL. 2:16;
1 TIM. 4:16

1908. ἐπηρεάζω *epēreazō*
MATT. 5:44; LUKE 6:28; 1 PET. 3:16

1910. ἐπιβαίνω *epibainō*
MATT. 21:5; ACTS 20:18; 21:2,6; 25:1; 27:2

1911. ἐπιβάλλω epiballō
MATT. 9:16; 26:50; MARK 4:37; 11:7;
14:46,72; LUKE 5:36; 9:62; 15:12; 20:19;
21:12; JOHN 7:30,44; ACTS 4:3; 5:18; 12:1;
21:27; 1 COR. 7:35

1912. ἐπιβαρέω epibareō
2 COR. 2:5; 1 THESS. 2:9; 2 THESS. 3:8

1913. ἐπιβιβάζω epibibazō
LUKE 10:34; 19:35; ACTS 23:24

1914. ἐπιβλέπω epiblepō
LUKE 1:48; 9:38; JAMES 2:3

1915. ἐπίβλημα epiblēma
MATT. 9:16; MARK 2:21; LUKE 5:36

1916. ἐπιβοάω epiboaō
ACTS 25:24

1917. ἐπιβουλή epiboulē
ACTS 9:24; 20:3,19; 23:30

1918. ἐπιγαμβρεύω epigambreuō
MATT. 22:24

1919. ἐπίγειος epigeios
JOHN 3:12; 1 COR. 15:40; 2 COR. 5:1; PHIL.
2:10; 3:19; JAMES 3:15

1920. ἐπιγίνομαι epiginomai
ACTS 28:13

1921. ἐπιγινώσκω epiginōskō
MATT. 7:16,20; 11:27; 14:35; 17:12; MARK
2:8; 5:30; 6:33,54; LUKE 1:4,22; 5:22; 7:37;
23:7; 24:16,31; ACTS 3:10; 4:13; 9:30; 12:14;
19:34; 22:24,29; 24:8; 25:10; 27:39; 28:1; ROM.
1:32; 1 COR. 13:12; 14:37; 16:18; 2 COR.
1:13,14; 6:9; 13:5; COL. 1:6; 1 TIM. 4:3;
2 PET. 2:21

1922. ἐπίγνωσις epignōsis
ROM. 1:28; 3:20; 10:2; EPH. 1:17; 4:13; PHIL.
1:9; COL. 1:9,10; 2:2; 3:10; 1 TIM. 2:4; 2 TIM.
2:25; 3:7; TITUS 1:1; PHILE. 1:6; HEB. 10:26;
2 PET. 1:2,3,8; 2:20

1923. ἐπιγραφή epigraphē
MATT. 22:20; MARK 12:16; 15:26; LUKE
20:24; 23:38

1924. ἐπιγράφω epigraphō
MARK 15:26; ACTS 17:23; HEB. 8:10; 10:16;
REV. 21:12

1925. ἐπιδείκνυμι epideiknumi
MATT. 16:1; 22:19; 24:1; LUKE 17:14; 20:24;
24:40; ACTS 9:39; 18:28; HEB. 6:17

1926. ἐπιδέχομαι epidechomai
3 JOHN 1:9,10

1927. ἐπιδημέω epidēmeō
ACTS 2:10; 17:21

**1928. ἐπιδιατάσσομαι,
    ἐπιδιατάττομαι
    epidiatassomai, epidiatattomai**
GAL. 3:15

1929. ἐπιδίδωμι epididōmi
MATT. 7:9,10; LUKE 4:17; 11:11,12; 24:30,42;
JOHN 13:26; ACTS 15:30; 27:15

1930. ἐπιδιορθόω epidiorthoō
TITUS 1:5

1931. ἐπιδύω epiduō
EPH. 4:26

1932. ἐπιείκεια epieikeia
ACTS 24:4; 2 COR. 10:1

1933. ἐπιεικής epieikēs
PHIL. 4:5; 1 TIM. 3:3; TITUS 3:2; JAMES
3:17; 1 PET. 2:18

1934. ἐπιζητέω epizēteō
MATT. 6:32; 12:39; 16:4; MARK 8:12; LUKE
11:29; 12:30; ACTS 12:19; 13:7; 19:39; ROM.
11:7; PHIL. 4:17; HEB. 11:14; 13:14

1935. ἐπιθανάτιος epithanatios
1 COR. 4:9

1936. ἐπίθεσις epithesis
ACTS 8:18; **1 TIM.** 4:14; **2 TIM.** 1:6; **HEB.** 6:2

1937. ἐπιθυμέω epithumeō
MATT. 5:28; 13:17; **LUKE** 15:16; 16:21; 17:22;
22:15; **ACTS** 20:33; **ROM.** 7:7; 13:9; **1 COR.**
10:6; **GAL.** 5:17; **1 TIM.** 3:1; **HEB.** 6:11;
JAMES 4:2; **1 PET.** 1:12; **REV.** 9:6

1938. ἐπιθυμητής epithumētēs
1 COR. 10:6

1939. ἐπιθυμία epithumia
MARK 4:19; **LUKE** 22:15; **JOHN** 8:44; **ROM.**
1:24; 6:12; 7:7,8; 13:14; **GAL.** 5:16,24; **EPH.**
2:3; 4:22; **PHIL.** 1:23; **COL.** 3:5; **1 THESS.**
2:17; 4:5; **1 TIM.** 6:9; **2 TIM.** 2:22; 3:6; 4:3;
TITUS 2:12; 3:3; **JAMES** 1:14,15; **1 PET.** 1:14;
2:11; 4:2,3; **2 PET.** 1:4; 2:10,18; 3:3; **1 JOHN**
2:16,17; **JUDE** 1:16,18; **REV.** 18:14

1940. ἐπικαθίζω epikathizō
MATT. 21:7

1941. ἐπικαλέω epikaleō
MATT. 10:3; **LUKE** 22:3; **ACTS** 1:23; 2:21;
4:36; 7:59; 9:14,21; 10:5,18,32; 11:13; 12:12,25;
15:17,22; 22:16; 25:11,12,21,25; 26:32; 28:19;
ROM. 10:12-14; **1 COR.** 1:2; **2 COR.** 1:23;
2 TIM. 2:22; **HEB.** 11:16; **JAMES** 2:7; **1 PET.**
1:17

1942. ἐπικάλυμμα epikalumma
1 PET. 2:16

1943. ἐπικαλύπτω epikaluptō
ROM. 4:7

1944. ἐπικατάρατος epikataratos
JOHN 7:49; **GAL.** 3:10,13

1945. ἐπίκειμαι epikeimai
LUKE 5:1; 23:23; **JOHN** 11:38; 21:9; **ACTS**
27:20; **1 COR.** 9:16; **HEB.** 9:10

1946. Ἐπικούρειος Epikoureios
ACTS 17:18

1947. ἐπικουρία epikouria
ACTS 26:22

1948. ἐπικρίνω epikrinō
LUKE 23:24

1949. ἐπιλαμβάνω epilambanō
MATT. 14:31; **MARK** 8:23; **LUKE** 9:47; 14:4;
20:20,26; 23:26; **ACTS** 9:27; 16:19; 17:19;
18:17; 21:30,33; 23:19; **1 TIM.** 6:12,19; **HEB.**
2:16; 8:9

1950. ἐπιλανθάνω epilanthanō
MATT. 16:5; **MARK** 8:14; **LUKE** 12:6; **PHIL.**
3:13; **HEB.** 6:10; 13:2,16; **JAMES** 1:24

1951. ἐπιλέγω epilegō
JOHN 5:2; **ACTS** 15:40

1952. ἐπιλείπω epileipō
HEB. 11:32

1953. ἐπιλησμονή epilēsmonē
JAMES 1:25

1954. ἐπίλοιπος epiloipos
1 PET. 4:2

1955. ἐπίλυσις epilusis
2 PET. 1:20

1956. ἐπιλύω epiluō
MARK 4:34; **ACTS** 19:39

1957. ἐπιμαρτυρέω epimartureō
1 PET. 5:12

1958. ἐπιμέλεια epimeleia
ACTS 27:3

1959. ἐπιμελέομαι epimeleomai
LUKE 10:34,35; **1 TIM.** 3:5

1960. ἐπιμελῶς epimelōs
LUKE 15:8

1961. ἐπιμένω epimenō
JOHN 8:7; **ACTS** 10:48; 12:16; 13:43; 15:34;

21:4,10; 28:12,14; **ROM.** 6:1; 11:22,23; **1 COR.** 16:7,8; **GAL.** 1:18; **PHIL.** 1:24; **COL.** 1:23; **1 TIM.** 4:16

1962. ἐπινεύω *epineuō*
ACTS 18:20

1963. ἐπίνοια *epinoia*
ACTS 8:22

1964. ἐπιορκέω *epiorkeō*
MATT. 5:33

1965. ἐπίορκος *epiorkos*
1 TIM. 1:10

1966. ἐπιοῦσα *epiousa*
ACTS 7:26; 16:11; 20:15; 21:18; 23:11

1967. ἐπιούσιος *epiousios*
MATT. 6:11; **LUKE** 11:3

1968. ἐπιπίπτω *epipiptō*
MARK 3:10; **LUKE** 1:12; 15:20; **JOHN** 13:25; **ACTS** 8:16; 10:10,44; 11:15; 13:11; 19:17; 20:10,37; **ROM.** 15:3

1969. ἐπιπλήσσω, ἐπιπλήττω
  epiplēssō, epiplēttō
1 TIM. 5:1

1970. ἐπιπνίγω *epipnigō*
LUKE 8:7

1971. ἐπιποθέω *epipotheō*
ROM. 1:11; **2 COR.** 5:2; 9:14; **PHIL.** 1:8; 2:26; **1 THESS.** 3:6; **2 TIM.** 1:4; **JAMES** 4:5; **1 PET.** 2:2

1972. ἐπιπόθησις *epipothēsis*
2 COR. 7:7,11

1973. ἐπιπόθητος *epipothētos*
PHIL. 4:1

1974. ἐπιποθία *epipothia*
ROM. 15:23

1975. ἐπιπορεύομαι *epiporeuomai*
LUKE 8:4

1976. ἐπιρράπτω *epirraptō*
MARK 2:21

1977. ἐπιρρίπτω *epirriptō*
LUKE 19:35; **1 PET.** 5:7

1978. ἐπίσημος *episēmos*
MATT. 27:16; **ROM.** 16:7

1979. ἐπισιτισμός *episitismos*
LUKE 9:12

1980. ἐπισκέπτομαι *episkeptomai*
MATT. 25:36,43; **LUKE** 1:68,78; 7:16; **ACTS** 6:3; 7:23; 15:14,36; **HEB.** 2:6; **JAMES** 1:27

1981. ἐπισκηνόω *episkēnoō*
2 COR. 12:9

1982. ἐπισκιάζω *episkiazō*
MATT. 17:5; **MARK** 9:7; **LUKE** 1:35; 9:34; **ACTS** 5:15

1983. ἐπισκοπέω *episkopeō*
HEB. 12:15; **1 PET.** 5:2

1984. ἐπισκοπή *episkopē*
LUKE 19:44; **ACTS** 1:20; **1 TIM.** 3:1; **1 PET.** 2:12

1985. ἐπίσκοπος *episkopos*
ACTS 20:28; **PHIL.** 1:1; **1 TIM.** 3:2; **TITUS** 1:7; **1 PET.** 2:25

1986. ἐπισπάω *epispaō*
1 COR. 7:18

1987. ἐπίσταμαι *epistamai*
MARK 14:68; **ACTS** 10:28; 15:7; 18:25; 19:15,25; 20:18; 22:19; 24:10; 26:26; **1 TIM.** 6:4; **HEB.** 11:8; **JAMES** 4:14; **JUDE** 1:10

1988. ἐπιστάτης *epistatēs*
LUKE 5:5; 8:24,45; 9:33,49; 17:13

1989. ἐπιστέλλω *epistellō*
ACTS 15:20; 21:25; HEB. 13:22

1990. ἐπιστήμων *epistēmōn*
JAMES 3:13

1991. ἐπιστηρίζω *epistērizō*
ACTS 14:22; 15:32,41; 18:23

1992. ἐπιστολή *epistolē*
ACTS 9:2; 15:30; 22:5; 23:25,33; ROM. 16:22;
1 COR. 5:9; 16:3; 2 COR. 3:1-3; 7:8; 10:9-11;
COL. 4:16; 1 THESS. 5:27; 2 THESS. 2:2,15;
3:14,17; 2 PET. 3:1,16

1993. ἐπιστομίζω *epistomizō*
TITUS 1:11

1994. ἐπιστρέφω *epistrephō*
MATT. 9:22; 10:13; 12:44; 13:15; 24:18;
MARK 4:12; 5:30; 8:33; 13:16; LUKE 1:16,17;
2:20; 8:55; 17:4,31; 22:32; JOHN 12:40; 21:20;
ACTS 3:19; 9:35,40; 11:21; 14:15; 15:19,36;
16:18; 26:18,20; 28:27; 2 COR. 3:16; GAL. 4:9;
1 THESS. 1:9; JAMES 5:19,20; 1 PET. 2:25;
2 PET. 2:21,22; REV. 1:12

1995. ἐπιστροφή *epistrophē*
ACTS 15:3

1996. ἐπισυνάγω *episunagō*
MATT. 23:37; 24:31; MARK 1:33; 13:27;
LUKE 12:1; 13:34

1997. ἐπισυναγωγή *episunagōgē*
2 THESS. 2:1; HEB. 10:25

1998. ἐπισυντρέχω *episuntrechō*
MARK 9:25

1999. ἐπισύστασις *episustasis*
ACTS 24:12; 2 COR. 11:28

2000. ἐπισφαλής *episphalēs*
ACTS 27:9

2001. ἐπισχύω *epischuō*
LUKE 23:5

2002. ἐπισωρεύω *episōreuō*
2 TIM. 4:3

2003. ἐπιταγή *epitagē*
ROM. 16:26; 1 COR. 7:6,25; 2 COR. 8:8;
1 TIM. 1:1; TITUS 1:3; 2:15

2004. ἐπιτάσσω, ἐπιτάττω
epitassō, epitattō
MARK 1:27; 6:27,39; 9:25; LUKE 4:36;
8:25,31; 14:22; ACTS 23:2; PHILE. 1:8

2005. ἐπιτελέω *epiteleō*
LUKE 13:32; ROM. 15:28; 2 COR. 7:1; 8:6,11;
GAL. 3:3; PHIL. 1:6; HEB. 8:5; 9:6; 1 PET.
5:9

2006. ἐπιτήδειος *epitēdeios*
JAMES 2:16

2007. ἐπιτίθημι *epitithēmi*
MATT. 9:18; 19:13,15; 21:7; 23:4; 27:29,37;
MARK 3:16,17; 4:21; 5:23; 6:5; 7:32; 8:23,25;
16:18; LUKE 4:40; 8:16; 10:30; 13:13; 15:5;
23:26; JOHN 9:15; 19:2; ACTS 6:6; 8:17,19;
9:12,17; 13:3; 15:10,28; 16:23; 18:10; 19:6;
28:3,8,10; 1 TIM. 5:22; REV. 1:17; 22:18

2008. ἐπιτιμάω *epitimaō*
MATT. 8:26; 12:16; 16:22; 17:18; 19:13; 20:31;
MARK 1:25; 3:12; 4:39; 8:30,32,33; 9:25;
10:13,48; LUKE 4:35,39,41; 8:24; 9:21,42,55;
17:3; 18:15,39; 19:39; 23:40; 2 TIM. 4:2; JUDE
1:9

2009. ἐπιτιμία *epitimia*
2 COR. 2:6

2010. ἐπιτρέπω *epitrepō*
MATT. 8:21,31; 19:8; MARK 5:13; 10:4;
LUKE 8:32; 9:59,61; JOHN 19:38; ACTS
21:39,40; 26:1; 27:3; 28:16; 1 COR. 14:34; 16:7;
1 TIM. 2:12; HEB. 6:3

2011. ἐπιτροπή *epitropē*
ACTS 26:12

2012. ἐπίτροπος *epitropos*
MATT. 20:8; LUKE 8:3; GAL. 4:2

2013. ἐπιτυγχάνω *epitugchanō*
ROM. 11:7; HEB. 6:15; 11:33; JAMES 4:2

2014. ἐπιφαίνω *epiphainō*
LUKE 1:79; ACTS 27:20; TITUS 2:11; 3:4

2015. ἐπιφάνεια *epiphaneia*
2 THESS. 2:8; 1 TIM. 6:14; 2 TIM. 1:10; 4:1,8;
TITUS 2:13

2016. ἐπιφανής *epiphanēs*
ACTS 2:20

2017. ἐπιφαύω *epiphauō*
EPH. 5:14

2018. ἐπιφέρω *epipherō*
ACTS 19:12; 25:18; ROM. 3:5; PHIL. 1:16;
JUDE 1:9

2019. ἐπιφωνέω *epiphōneō*
LUKE 23:21; ACTS 12:22; 22:24

2020. ἐπιφώσκω *epiphōskō*
MATT. 28:1; LUKE 23:54

2021. ἐπιχειρέω *epicheireō*
LUKE 1:1; ACTS 9:29; 19:13

2022. ἐπιχέω *epicheō*
LUKE 10:34

2023. ἐπιχορηγέω *epichorēgeō*
2 COR. 9:10; GAL. 3:5; COL. 2:19; 2 PET.
1:5,11

2024. ἐπιχορηγία *epichorēgia*
EPH. 4:16; PHIL. 1:19

2025. ἐπιχρίω *epichriō*
JOHN 9:6,11

2026. ἐποικοδομέω *epoikodomeō*
ACTS 20:32; 1 COR. 3:10,12,14; EPH. 2:20;
COL. 2:7; JUDE 1:20

2027. ἐποκέλλω *epokellō*
ACTS 27:41

2028. ἐπονομάζω *eponomazō*
ROM. 2:17

2029. ἐποπτεύω *epopteuō*
1 PET. 2:12; 3:2

2030. ἐπόπτης *epoptēs*
2 PET. 1:16

2031. ἔπος *epos*
HEB. 7:9

2032. ἐπουράνιος *epouranios*
MATT. 18:35; JOHN 3:12; 1 COR.
15:40,48,49; EPH. 1:3,20; 2:6; 3:10; 6:12;
PHIL. 2:10; 2 TIM. 4:18; HEB. 3:1; 6:4; 8:5;
9:23; 11:16; 12:22

2033. ἑπτά *hepta*
MATT. 12:45; 15:34,36,37; 16:10; 18:22;
22:25,26,28; MARK 8:5,6,8,20; 12:20,22,23;
16:9; LUKE 2:36; 8:2; 11:26; 20:29,31,33;
ACTS 6:3; 13:19; 19:14; 20:6; 21:4,8,27; 28:14;
HEB. 11:30; REV. 1:4,12,13,16,20; 2:1; 3:1;
4:5; 5:1,5,6; 8:2,6; 10:3,4; 11:13; 12:3; 13:1;
15:1,6-8; 16:1; 17:1,3,7,9-11; 21:9

2034. ἑπτάκις *heptakis*
MATT. 18:21,22; LUKE 17:4

2035. ἑπτακισχίλιοι *heptakischilioi*
ROM. 11:4

2037. Ἔραστος *Erastos*
ACTS 19:22; ROM. 16:23; 2 TIM. 4:20

2038. ἐργάζομαι *ergazomai*
MATT. 7:23; 21:28; 25:16; 26:10; MARK 14:6;
LUKE 13:14; JOHN 3:21; 5:17; 6:27,28,30;
9:4; ACTS 10:35; 13:41; 18:3; ROM. 2:10;
4:4,5; 13:10; 1 COR. 4:12; 9:6,13; 16:10; GAL.
6:10; EPH. 4:28; COL. 3:23; 1 THESS. 2:9;
4:11; 2 THESS. 3:8,10-12; HEB. 11:33;
JAMES 2:9; 2 JOHN 1:8; 3 JOHN 1:5; REV.
18:17

2039. ἐργασία *ergasia*
LUKE 12:58; ACTS 16:16,19; 19:24,25; EPH.
4:19

2040. ἐργάτης ergatēs
MATT. 9:37,38; 10:10; 20:1,2,8; LUKE 10:2,7;
13:27; ACTS 19:25; 2 COR. 11:13; PHIL. 3:2;
1 TIM. 5:18; 2 TIM. 2:15; JAMES 5:4

2041. ἔργον ergon
MATT. 5:16; 11:2; 23:3,5; 26:10; MARK
13:34; 14:6; LUKE 11:48; 24:19; JOHN 3:19-
21; 4:34; 5:20,36; 6:28,29; 7:3,7,21; 8:39,41;
9:3,4; 10:25,32,33,37,38; 14:10-12; 15:24; 17:4;
ACTS 5:38; 7:22,41; 9:36; 13:2,41; 14:26;
15:18,38; 26:20; ROM. 2:6,7,15; 3:20,27,28;
4:2,6; 9:11,32; 11:6; 13:3,12; 14:20; 15:18;
1 COR. 3:13-15; 5:2; 9:1; 15:58; 16:10; 2 COR.
9:8; 10:11; 11:15; GAL. 2:16; 3:2,5,10; 5:19;
6:4; EPH. 2:9,10; 4:12; 5:11; PHIL. 1:6,22;
2:30; COL. 1:10,21; 3:17; 1 THESS. 1:3; 5:13;
2 THESS. 1:11; 2:17; 1 TIM. 2:10; 3:1; 5:10,25;
6:18; 2 TIM. 1:9; 2:21; 3:17; 4:5,14,18; TITUS
1:16; 2:7,14; 3:1,5,8,14; HEB. 1:10; 2:7; 3:9;
4:3,4,10; 6:1,10; 9:14; 10:24; 13:21; JAMES
1:4,25; 2:14,17,18,20-22,24-26; 3:13; 1 PET.
1:17; 2:12; 2 PET. 2:8; 3:10; 1 JOHN 3:8,12,18;
2 JOHN 1:11; 3 JOHN 1:10; JUDE 1:15; REV.
2:2,5,6,9,13,19,22,23,26; 3:1,2,8,15; 9:20; 14:13;
15:3; 16:11; 18:6; 20:12,13; 22:12

2042. ἐρεθίζω erethizō
2 COR. 9:2; COL. 3:21

2043. ἐρείδω ereidō
ACTS 27:41

2044. ἐρεύγομαι ereugomai
MATT. 13:35

2045. ἐρευνάω ereunaō
JOHN 5:39; 7:52; ROM. 8:27; 1 COR. 2:10;
1 PET. 1:11; REV. 2:23

2046. ἐρέω ereō
MATT. 7:4,22; 13:30; 17:20; 21:3,24,25;
25:34,40,41; 26:75; MARK 11:29,31; LUKE
2:24; 4:12,23; 12:10,19; 13:25,27; 14:9; 15:18;
17:7,8,21,23; 19:31; 20:5; 22:11,13; 23:29;
JOHN 4:18; 6:65; 11:13; 12:50; 14:29; 15:15;
ACTS 2:16; 8:24; 13:34,40; 17:28; 20:38; 23:5;
ROM. 3:5; 4:1,18; 6:1; 7:7; 8:31; 9:14,19,20,30;
11:19; 1 COR. 14:16,23; 15:35; 2 COR. 12:6,9;
PHIL. 4:4; HEB. 1:13; 4:3,4,7; 10:9; 13:5;
JAMES 2:18; REV. 7:14; 17:7; 19:3

2047. ἐρημία erēmia
MATT. 15:33; MARK 8:4; 2 COR. 11:26;
HEB. 11:38

2048. A. ἔρημος erēmos
MATT. 14:13,15; 23:38; MARK
1:35,45; 6:31,32,35; LUKE 4:42;
9:10,12; 13:35; ACTS 1:20; 8:26; GAL.
4:27

B. ἔρημος erēmos subst.
MATT. 3:1,3; 4:1; 11:7; 24:26; MARK
1:3,4,12,13; LUKE 1:80; 3:2,4; 4:1;
5:16; 7:24; 8:29; 15:4; JOHN 1:23; 3:14;
6:31,49; 11:54; ACTS 7:30,36,38,42,44;
13:18; 21:38; 1 COR. 10:5; HEB.
3:8,17; REV. 12:6,14; 17:3

2049. ἐρημόω erēmoō
MATT. 12:25; LUKE 11:17; REV. 17:16;
18:17,19

2050. ἐρήμωσις erēmōsis
MATT. 24:15; MARK 13:14; LUKE 21:20

2051. ἐρίζω erizō
MATT. 12:19

2052. ἐριθεία eritheia
ROM. 2:8; 2 COR. 12:20; GAL. 5:20; PHIL.
1:16; 2:3; JAMES 3:14,16

2053. ἔριον erion
HEB. 9:19; REV. 1:14

2054. ἔρις eris
ROM. 1:29; 13:13; 1 COR. 1:11; 3:3; 2 COR.
12:20; GAL. 5:20; PHIL. 1:15; 1 TIM. 6:4;
TITUS 3:9

2055. ἐρίφιον eriphion
MATT. 25:33

2056. ἔριφος eriphos
MATT. 25:32; LUKE 15:29

2057. Ἑρμᾶς Hermas
ROM. 16:14

2058. ἑρμηνεία hermēneia
1 COR. 12:10; 14:26

2059. ἑρμηνεύω *hermēneuō*
JOHN 1:38,42; 9:7; **HEB.** 7:2

2060. Ἑρμῆς *Hermēs*
ACTS 14:12; **ROM.** 16:14

2061. Ἑρμογένης *Hermogenēs*
2 TIM. 1:15

2062. ἑρπετόν *herpeton*
ACTS 10:12; 11:6; **ROM.** 1:23; **JAMES** 3:7

2063. Ἐρυθρά Θάλασσα
Eruthra Thalassa
ACTS 7:36; **HEB.** 11:29

2066. ἐσθής *esthēs*
LUKE 23:11; **ACTS** 1:10; 10:30; 12:21;
JAMES 2:2,3

2067. ἔσθησις *esthēsis*
LUKE 24:4

2068. ἐσθίω *esthiō*
MATT. 9:11; 11:18,19; 12:1; 14:21; 15:2,27,38;
24:49; 26:21,26; **MARK** 1:6; 2:16; 7:2-5,28;
14:18,22; **LUKE** 5:30,33; 6:1; 7:33,34; 10:7,8;
12:45; 15:16; 17:27,28; 22:30; **ACTS** 27:35;
ROM. 14:2,3,6,20; **1 COR.** 8:7,10; 9:7,13;
10:18,25,27,28,31; 11:22,26-29,34; **2 THESS.**
3:10,12; **HEB.** 10:27

2069. Ἐσλί *Esli*
LUKE 3:25

2072. ἔσοπτρον *esoptron*
1 COR. 13:12; **JAMES** 1:23

2073. ἑσπέρα *hespera*
LUKE 24:29; **ACTS** 4:3; 28:23

2074. Ἐσρώμ *Esrōm*
MATT. 1:3; **LUKE** 3:33

2077. I. ἔστω *estō*
       (3rd. sing. pres. imper. of εἰμί)
       MATT. 5:37; 18:17; 20:26,27; **ACTS**

1:20; 2:14; 4:10; 13:38; 28:28; **2 COR.**
12:16; **GAL.** 1:8,9

II. ἔστωσαν *estōsan*
       (3rd pl. pres. imper. of εἰμί)
       LUKE 12:35; **1 TIM.** 3:12; **JAMES**
       1:19; **1 PET.** 3:3

2078. ἔσχατος *eschatos*
MATT. 5:26; 12:45; 19:30; 20:8,12,14,16;
27:64; **MARK** 9:35; 10:31; 12:6,22; **LUKE**
11:26; 12:59; 13:30; 14:9,10; **JOHN** 6:39,40,
44,54; 7:37; 8:9; 11:24; 12:48; **ACTS** 1:8; 2:17;
13:47; **1 COR.** 4:9; 15:8,26,45; 52; **2 TIM.** 3:1;
HEB. 1:2; **JAMES** 5:3; **1 PET.** 1:5,20; **2 PET.**
2:20; 3:3; **1 JOHN** 2:18; **JUDE** 1:18; **REV.**
1:11,17; 2:8,19; 15:1; 21:9; 22:13

2079. ἐσχάτως *eschatōs*
MARK 5:23

2080. ἔσω *esō*
MATT. 26:58; **MARK** 14:54; 15:16; **JOHN**
20:26; **ACTS** 5:23; **ROM.** 7:22; **1 COR.** 5:12;
EPH. 3:16

2081. ἔσωθεν *esōthen*
MATT. 7:15; 23:25,27,28; **MARK** 7:21,23;
LUKE 11:7,39,40; **2 COR.** 4:16; 7:5; **REV.** 4:8;
5:1; 11:2

2082. ἐσώτερος *esōteros*
ACTS 16:24; **HEB.** 6:19

2083. ἑταῖρος *hetairos*
MATT. 11:16; 20:13; 22:12; 26:50

2084. ἑτερόγλωσσος *heteroglōssos*
1 COR. 14:21

2085. ἑτεροδιδασκαλέω
       heterodidaskaleō
1 TIM. 1:3; 6:3

2086. ἑτεροζυγέω *heterozugeō*
2 COR. 6:14

2087. ἕτερος *heteros*
MATT. 6:24; 8:21; 11:3; 12:45; 15:30; 16:14;
MARK 16:12; **LUKE** 3:18; 4:43; 5:7; 6:6; 7:41;

8:3,6-8; 9:29,56,59,61; 10:1; 11:16,26; 14:19,
20,31; 16:7,13,18; 17:34,35; 18:10; 19:20; 20:11;
22:58,65; 23:32,40; **JOHN** 19:37; **ACTS** 1:20;
2:4,13,40; 4:12; 7:18; 8:34; 12:17; 13:35; 15:35;
17:7,21,34; 19:39; 20:15; 23:6; 27:1,3; **ROM.**
2:1,21; 7:3,4,23; 8:39; 13:8,9; **1 COR.** 3:4; 4:6;
6:1; 8:4; 10:24,29; 12:9,10; 14:17,21; 15:40;
2 COR. 8:8; 11:4; **GAL.** 1:6,19; 6:4; **EPH.** 3:5;
PHIL. 2:4; **1 TIM.** 1:10; **2 TIM.** 2:2; **HEB.** 5:6;
7:11,13,15; 11:36; **JAMES** 2:25; 4:12; **JUDE**
1:7

2088. ἑτέρως heterōs
PHIL. 3:15

2090. ἑτοιμάζω hetoimazō
MATT. 3:3; 20:23; 22:4; 25:34,41; 26:17,19;
MARK 1:3; 10:40; 14:12,15,16; **LUKE** 1:17,76;
2:31; 3:4; 9:52; 12:20,47; 17:8; 22:8,9,12,13;
23:56; 24:1; **JOHN** 14:2,3; **ACTS** 23:23;
1 COR. 2:9; **2 TIM.** 2:21; **PHILE.** 1:22; **HEB.**
11:16; **REV.** 8:6; 9:7,15; 12:6; 16:12; 19:7; 21:2

2091. ἑτοιμασία hetoimasia
EPH. 6:15

2092. ἕτοιμος hetoimos
MATT. 22:4,8; 24:44; 25:10; **MARK** 14:15;
LUKE 12:40; 14:17; 22:33; **JOHN** 7:6; **ACTS**
23:15,21; **2 COR.** 9:5; 10:6,16; **TITUS** 3:1;
1 PET. 1:5; 3:15

2093. ἑτοίμως hetoimōs
ACTS 21:13; **2 COR.** 12:14; **1 PET.** 4:5

2094. ἔτος etos
MATT. 9:20; **MARK** 5:25,42; **LUKE**
2:36,37,41,42; 3:1,23; 4:25; 8:42,43; 12:19;
13:7,8,11,16; 15:29; **JOHN** 2:20; 5:5; 8:57;
ACTS 4:22; 7:6,30,36,42; 9:33; 13:20,21; 19:10;
24:10,17; **ROM.** 15:23; **2 COR.** 12:2; **GAL.**
1:18; 2:1; 3:17; **1 TIM.** 5:9; **HEB.** 1:12; 3:9,17;
2 PET. 3:8; **REV.** 20:2-7

2095. εὖ eu
MATT. 25:21,23; **MARK** 14:7; **LUKE** 19:17;
ACTS 15:29; **EPH.** 6:3

2096. Εὖα Eua
2 COR. 11:3; **1 TIM.** 2:13

2097. εὐαγγελίζω euaggelizō
MATT. 11:5; **LUKE** 1:19; 2:10; 3:18; 4:18,43;
7:22; 8:1; 9:6; 16:16; 20:1; **ACTS** 5:42;
8:4,12,25,35,40; 10:36; 11:20; 13:32; 14:7,15,21;
15:35; 16:10; 17:18; **ROM.** 1:15; 10:15; 15:20;
1 COR. 1:17; 9:16,18; 15:1,2; **2 COR.** 10:16;
11:7; **GAL.** 1:8,9,11,16,23; 4:13; **EPH.** 2:17;
3:8; **1 THESS.** 3:6; **HEB.** 4:2,6; **1 PET.** 1:12,25;
4:6; **REV.** 10:7; 14:6

2098. εὐαγγέλιον euaggelion
MATT. 4:23; 9:35; 24:14; 26:13; **MARK**
1:1,14,15; 8:35; 10:29; 13:10; 14:9; 16:15;
ACTS 15:7; 20:24; **ROM.** 1:1,9,16; 2:16; 10:16;
11:28; 15:16,19,29; 16:25; **1 COR.** 4:15;
9:12,14,18,23; 15:1; **2 COR.** 2:12; 4:3,4; 8:18;
9:13; 10:14; 11:4,7; **GAL.** 1:6,7,11; 2:2,5,7,14;
EPH. 1:13; 3:6; 6:15,19; **PHIL.** 1:5,7,12,17,27;
2:22; 4:3,15; **COL.** 1:5,23; **1 THESS.** 1:5;
2:2,4,8,9; 3:2; **2 THESS.** 1:8; 2:14; **1 TIM.** 1:11;
2 TIM. 1:8,10; 2:8; **PHILE.** 1:13; **1 PET.** 4:17;
REV. 14:6

2099. εὐαγγελιστής euaggelistēs
ACTS 21:8; **EPH.** 4:11; **2 TIM.** 4:5

2100. εὐαρεστέω euaresteō
HEB. 11:5,6; 13:16

2101. εὐάρεστος euarestos
ROM. 12:1,2; 14:18; **2 COR.** 5:9; **EPH.** 5:10;
PHIL. 4:18; **COL.** 3:20; **TITUS** 2:9; **HEB.**
13:21

2102. εὐαρέστως euarestōs
HEB. 12:28

2103. Εὔβουλος Euboulos
2 TIM. 4:21

2104. εὐγενής eugenēs
LUKE 19:12; **ACTS** 17:11; **1 COR.** 1:26

2105. εὐδία eudia
MATT. 16:2

2106. εὐδοκέω eudokeō
MATT. 3:17; 12:18; 17:5; **MARK** 1:11; **LUKE**
3:22; 12:32; **ROM.** 15:26,27; **1 COR.** 1:21;

10:5; **2 COR.** 5:8; 12:10; **GAL.** 1:15; **COL.**
1:19; **1 THESS.** 2:8; 3:1; **2 THESS.** 2:12; **HEB.**
10:6,8,38; **2 PET.** 1:17

2107. εὐδοκία eudokia
MATT. 11:26; **LUKE** 2:14; 10:21; **ROM.** 10:1;
EPH. 1:5,9; **PHIL.** 1:15; 2:13; **2 THESS.** 1:11

2108. εὐεργεσία euergesia
ACTS 4:9; **1 TIM.** 6:2

2109. εὐεργετέω euergeteō
ACTS 10:38

2110. εὐεργέτης euergetēs
LUKE 22:25

2111. εὔθετος euthetos
LUKE 9:62; 14:35; **HEB.** 6:7

2112. εὐθέως eutheōs
MATT. 4:20,22; 8:3; 13:5; 14:22,27,31; 20:34;
21:2,3; 24:29; 25:15; 26:49,74; 27:48; **MARK**
1:10,18,20,21,29-31,42,43; 2:2,8,12; 3:6; 4:5,15-
17,29; 5:2,13,29,30,36,42; 6:25,27,45,50,54;
7:35; 8:10; 9:15,20,24; 10:52; 11:2,3; 14:43,45;
15:1; **LUKE** 5:13,39; 6:49; 12:36,54; 14:5; 17:7;
21:9; **JOHN** 5:9; 6:21; 13:30; 18:27; **ACTS**
9:18,20,34; 12:10; 16:10; 17:10,14; 21:30; 22:29;
GAL. 1:16; **JAMES** 1:24; **3 JOHN** 1:14; **REV.**
4:2

2113. εὐθυδρομέω euthudromeō
ACTS 16:11; 21:1

2114. εὐθυμέω euthumeō
ACTS 27:22,25; **JAMES** 5:13

2115. I. εὔθυμος euthumos
ACTS 27:36

     II. εὐθυμότερον euthumoteron
ACTS 24:10

2116. εὐθύνω euthunō
JOHN 1:23; **JAMES** 3:4

2117. A. εὐθύς euthus
MATT. 3:3; **MARK** 1:3; **LUKE** 3:4,5;
ACTS 8:21; 9:11; 13:10; **2 PET.** 2:15

     B. εὐθύς euthus   adv.
MATT. 3:16; 13:20,21; **MARK** 1:12,28;
JOHN 13:32; 19:34; 21:3

2118. εὐθύτης euthutēs
HEB. 1:8

2119. εὐκαιρέω eukaireō
MARK 6:31; **ACTS** 17:21; **1 COR.** 16:12

2120. εὐκαιρία eukairia
MATT. 26:16; **LUKE** 22:6

2121. εὔκαιρος eukairos
MARK 6:21; **HEB.** 4:16

2122. εὐκαίρως eukairōs
MARK 14:11; **2 TIM.** 4:2

2123. εὔκοπος eukopos
MATT. 9:5; 19:24; **MARK** 2:9; 10:25; **LUKE**
5:23; 16:17; 18:25

2124. εὐλάβεια eulabeia
HEB. 5:7; 12:28

2125. εὐλαβέομαι eulabeomai
ACTS 23:10; **HEB.** 11:7

2126. εὐλαβής eulabēs
LUKE 2:25; **ACTS** 2:5; 8:2

2127. εὐλογέω eulogeō
MATT. 5:44; 14:19; 21:9; 23:39; 25:34; 26:26;
MARK 6:41; 8:7; 10:16; 11:9,10; 14:22; **LUKE**
1:28,42,64; 2:28,34; 6:28; 9:16; 13:35; 19:38;
24:30,50,51,53; **JOHN** 12:13; **ACTS** 3:26;
ROM. 12:14; **1 COR.** 4:12; 10:16; 14:16; **GAL.**
3:9; **EPH.** 1:3; **HEB.** 6:14; 7:1,6,7; 11:20,21;
JAMES 3:9; **1 PET.** 3:9

2128. εὐλογητός eulogētos
MARK 14:61; **LUKE** 1:68; **ROM.** 1:25; 9:5;
2 COR. 1:3; 11:31; **EPH.** 1:3; **1 PET.** 1:3

2129. εὐλογία eulogia
ROM. 15:29; 16:18; **1 COR.** 10:16; **2 COR.**
9:5,6; GAL. 3:14; EPH. 1:3; HEB. 6:7; 12:17;
JAMES 3:10; **1 PET.** 3:9; REV. 5:12,13; 7:12

2130. εὐμετάδοτος eumetadotos
1 TIM. 6:18

2131. Εὐνίκη Eunikē
2 TIM. 1:5

2132. εὐνόεω eunoeō
MATT. 5:25

2133. εὔνοια eunoia
1 COR. 7:3; EPH. 6:7

2134. εὐνουχίζω eunouchizō
MATT. 19:12

2135. εὐνοῦχος eunouchos
MATT. 19:12; ACTS 8:27,34,36,38,39

2136. Εὐοδία Euodia
PHIL. 4:2

2137. εὐοδόω euodoō
ROM. 1:10; **1 COR.** 16:2; 3 JOHN 1:2

2138. εὐπειθής eupeithēs
JAMES 3:17

2139. εὐπερίστατος euperistatos
HEB. 12:1

2140. εὐποιΐα eupoiia
HEB. 13:16

2141. εὐπορέω euporeō
ACTS 11:29

2142. εὐπορία euporia
ACTS 19:25

2143. εὐπρέπεια euprepeia
JAMES 1:11

2144. εὐπρόσδεκτος euprosdektos
ROM. 15:16,31; **2 COR.** 6:2; 8:12; **1 PET.** 2:5

2145. εὐπρόσεδρος euprosedros
1 COR. 7:35

2146. εὐπροσωπέω euprosōpeō
GAL. 6:12

2147. εὑρίσκω heuriskō
MATT. 1:18; 2:8,11; 7:7,8,14; 8:10; 10:39;
11:29; 12:43,44; 13:44,46; 16:25; 17:27;
18:13,28; 20:6; 21:2,19; 22:9,10; 24:46;
26:40,43,60; 27:32; **MARK** 1:37; 7:30;
11:2,4,13; 13:36; 14:16,37,40,55; **LUKE** 1:30;
2:12,45,46; 4:17; 5:19; 6:7; 7:9,10; 8:35;
9:12,36; 11:9,10,24,25; 12:37,38,43; 13:6,7;
15:4-6,8,9,24,32; 17:18; 18:8; 19:30,32,48;
22:13,45; 23:2,4,14,22; 24:2,3,23,24,33; **JOHN**
1:41,43,45; 2:14; 5:14; 6:25; 7:34-36; 9:35; 10:9;
11:17; 12:14; 18:38; 19:4,6; 21:6; **ACTS** 4:21;
5:10,22,23,39; 7:11,46; 8:40; 9:2,33; 10:27;
11:26; 12:19; 13:6,22,28; 17:6,23,27; 18:2;
19:1,19; 21:2; 23:9,29; 24:5,12,18,20; 27:6,28;
28:14; **ROM.** 4:1; 7:10,18,21; 10:20; **1 COR.**
4:2; 15:15; **2 COR.** 2:13; 5:3; 9:4; 11:12; 12:20;
GAL. 2:17; PHIL. 2:8; 3:9; **2 TIM.** 1:17,18;
HEB. 4:16; 9:12; 11:5; 12:17; **1 PET.** 1:7; 2:22;
2 PET. 3:14; 2 JOHN 1:4; REV. 2:2; 3:2; 5:4;
9:6; 12:8; 14:5; 16:20; 18:14,21,22,24; 20:11,15

2148. Εὐροκλύδων Eurokludōn
ACTS 27:14

2149. εὐρύχωρος euruchōros
MATT. 7:13

2150. εὐσέβεια eusebeia
ACTS 3:12; **1 TIM.** 2:2; 3:16; 4:7,8; 6:3,5,6,11;
2 TIM. 3:5; TITUS 1:1; **2 PET.** 1:3,6,7; 3:11

2151. εὐσεβέω eusebeō
ACTS 17:23; 1 TIM. 5:4

2152. εὐσεβής eusebēs
ACTS 10:2,7; 22:12; **2 PET.** 2:9

2153. εὐσεβῶς eusebōs
2 TIM. 3:12; TITUS 2:12

2154. εὔσημος *eusēmos*
1 COR. 14:9

2155. εὔσπλαγχνος *eusplagchnos*
EPH. 4:32; **1 PET.** 3:8

2156. εὐσχημόνως *euschēmonōs*
ROM. 13:13; **1 COR.** 14:40; **1 THESS.** 4:12

2157. εὐσχημοσύνη *euschēmosunē*
1 COR. 12:23

2158. εὐσχήμων *euschēmōn*
MARK 15:43; ACTS 13:50; 17:12; **1 COR.**
7:35; 12:24

2159. εὐτόνως *eutonōs*
LUKE 23:10; ACTS 18:28

2160. εὐτραπελία *eutrapelia*
EPH. 5:4

2161. Εὔτυχος *Eutuchos*
ACTS 20:9

2162. εὐφημία *euphēmia*
2 COR. 6:8

2163. εὔφημος *euphēmos*
PHIL. 4:8

2164. εὐφορέω *euphoreō*
LUKE 12:16

2165. εὐφραίνω *euphrainō*
LUKE 12:19; 15:23,24,29,32; 16:19; ACTS
2:26; 7:41; **ROM.** 15:10; **2 COR.** 2:2; **GAL.**
4:27; **REV.** 11:10; 12:12; 18:20

2166. Εὐφράτης *Euphratēs*
REV. 9:14; 16:12

2167. εὐφροσύνη *euphrosunē*
ACTS 2:28; 14:17

2168. εὐχαριστέω *eucharisteō*
MATT. 15:36; 26:27; MARK 8:6; 14:23;

LUKE 17:16; 18:11; 22:17,19; **JOHN** 6:11,23;
11:41; ACTS 27:35; 28:15; **ROM.** 1:8,21; 7:25;
14:6; 16:4; **1 COR.** 1:4,14; 10:30; 11:24; 14:17,
18; **2 COR.** 1:11; **EPH.** 1:16; 5:20; **PHIL.** 1:3;
COL. 1:3,12; 3:17; **1 THESS.** 1:2; 2:13; 5:18;
2 THESS. 1:3; 2:13; **PHILE.** 1:4; **REV.** 11:17

2169. εὐχαριστία *eucharistia*
ACTS 24:3; **1 COR.** 14:16; **2 COR.** 4:15;
9:11,12; **EPH.** 5:4; **PHIL.** 4:6; **COL.** 2:7; 4:2;
1 THESS. 3:9; **1 TIM.** 2:1; 4:3,4; **REV.** 4:9;
7:12

2170. εὐχάριστος *eucharistos*
COL. 3:15

2171. εὐχή *euchē*
ACTS 18:18; 21:23; **JAMES** 5:15

2172. εὔχομαι *euchomai*
ACTS 26:29; 27:29; **ROM.** 9:3; **2 COR.** 13:7,9;
JAMES 5:16; **3 JOHN** 1:2

2173. εὔχρηστος *euchrēstos*
2 TIM. 2:21; 4:11; **PHILE.** 1:11

2174. εὐψυχέω *eupsucheō*
PHIL. 2:19

2175. εὐωδία *euōdia*
2 COR. 2:15; **EPH.** 5:2; **PHIL.** 4:18

2176. εὐώνυμος *euōnumos*
MATT. 20:21,23; 25:33,41; 27:38; **MARK**
10:37,40; 15:27; ACTS 21:3; **REV.** 10:2

2177. ἐφάλλομαι *ephallomai*
ACTS 19:16

2178. ἐφάπαξ *ephapax*
ROM. 6:10; **1 COR.** 15:6; **HEB.** 7:27; 9:12;
10:10

2179. Ἐφεσῖνος *Ephesinos*
REV. 2:1

2180. Ἐφέσιος *Ephesios*
ACTS 19:28,34,35; 21:29

2181. Ἔφεσος Ephesos
ACTS 18:19,21,24; 19:1,17,26; 20:16,17;
1 COR. 15:32; 16:8; EPH. 1:1; 1 TIM. 1:3;
2 TIM. 1:18; 4:12; REV. 1:11

2182. ἐφευρετής epheuretēs
ROM. 1:30

2183. ἐφημερία ephēmeria
LUKE 1:5,8

2184. ἐφήμερος ephēmeros
JAMES 2:15

2185. ἐφικνέομαι ephikneomai
2 COR. 10:13,14

2186. ἐφίστημι ephistēmi
LUKE 2:9,38; 4:39; 10:40; 20:1; 21:34; 24:4;
ACTS 4:1; 6:12; 10:17; 11:11; 12:7; 17:5;
22:13,20; 23:11,27; 28:2; 1 THESS. 5:3; 2 TIM.
4:2,6

2187. Ἐφραΐμ Ephraim
JOHN 11:54

2188. ἐφφαθά ephphatha
MARK 7:34

2189. ἔχθρα echthra
LUKE 23:12; ROM. 8:7; GAL. 5:20; EPH.
2:15,16; JAMES 4:4

2190. ἐχθρός echthros
MATT. 5:43,44; 10:36; 13:25,28,39; 22:44;
MARK 12:36; LUKE 1:71,74; 6:27,35; 10:19;
19:27,43; 20:43; ACTS 2:35; 13:10; ROM.
5:10; 11:28; 12:20; 1 COR. 15:25,26; GAL.
4:16; PHIL. 3:18; COL. 1:21; 2 THESS. 3:15;
HEB. 1:13; 10:13; JAMES 4:4; REV. 11:5,12

2191. ἔχιδνα echidna
MATT. 3:7; 12:34; 23:33; LUKE 3:7; ACTS
28:3

Z

2194. Ζαβουλών Zaboulōn
MATT. 4:13,15; REV. 7:8

2195. Ζακχαῖος Zakchaios
LUKE 19:2,5,8

2196. Ζαρά Zara
MATT. 1:3

2197. Ζαχαρίας Zacharias
MATT. 23:35; LUKE 1:5,12,13,18,21,40,59,67;
3:2; 11:51

2198. ζάω zaō
MATT. 4:4; 9:18; 16:16; 22:32; 26:63; 27:63;
MARK 5:23; 12:27; 16:11; LUKE 2:36; 4:4;
10:28; 15:13; 20:38; 24:5,23; JOHN 4:10,11,
50,51,53; 5:25; 6:51,57,58,69; 7:38; 11:25,26;
14:19; ACTS 1:3; 7:38; 9:41; 10:42; 14:15;
17:28; 20:12; 22:22; 25:19,24; 26:5; 28:4; ROM.
1:17; 6:2,10,11,13; 7:1-3,9; 8:12,13; 9:26; 10:5;
12:1; 14:7-9,11; 1 COR. 7:39; 9:14; 15:45;
2 COR. 1:8; 3:3; 4:11; 5:15; 6:9,16; 13:4; GAL.
2:14,19,20; 3:11,12; 5:25; PHIL. 1:21,22; COL.
2:20; 3:7; 1 THESS. 1:9; 3:8; 4:15,17; 5:10;
1 TIM. 3:15; 4:10; 5:6; 6:17; 2 TIM. 3:12; 4:1;
TITUS 2:12; HEB. 2:15; 3:12; 4:12; 7:8,25;
9:14,17; 10:20,31,38; 12:9,22; JAMES 4:15;
1 PET. 1:3,23; 2:4,5,24; 4:5,6; 1 JOHN 4:9;
REV. 1:18; 2:8; 3:1; 4:9,10; 5:14; 7:2,17; 10:6;
13:14; 15:7; 16:3; 19:20; 20:4

2199. Ζεβεδαῖος Zebedaios
MATT. 4:21; 10:2; 20:20; 26:37; 27:56; MARK
1:19,20; 3:17; 10:35; LUKE 5:10; JOHN 21:2

2200. ζεστός zestos
REV. 3:15,16

2201. ζεῦγος zeugos
LUKE 2:24; 14:19

2202. ζευκτηρία zeuktēria
ACTS 27:40

2203. Ζεύς Zeus
ACTS 14:12,13

2204. ζέω zeō
ACTS 18:25; ROM. 12:11

2205. ζῆλος zēlos
JOHN 2:17; ACTS 5:17; 13:45; ROM. 10:2;

13:13; **1 COR.** 3:3; **2 COR.** 7:7,11; 9:2; 11:2; 12:20; **GAL.** 5:20; **PHIL.** 3:6; **COL.** 4:13; **HEB.** 10:27; **JAMES** 3:14,16

2206. ζηλόω *zēloō*
ACTS 7:9; 17:5; **1 COR.** 12:31; 13:4; 14:1,39; **2 COR.** 11:2; **GAL.** 4:17,18; **JAMES** 4:2; **REV.** 3:19

2207. ζηλωτής *zēlōtēs*
ACTS 21:20; 22:3; **1 COR.** 14:12; **GAL.** 1:14; **TITUS** 2:14

2208. Ζηλωτής *Zēlōtēs*
LUKE 6:15; **ACTS** 1:13

2209. ζημία *zēmia*
ACTS 27:10,21; **PHIL.** 3:7,8

2210. ζημιόω *zēmioō*
MATT. 16:26; **MARK** 8:36; **LUKE** 9:25; **1 COR.** 3:15; **2 COR.** 7:9; **PHIL.** 3:8

2211. Ζηνᾶς *Zēnas*
TITUS 3:13

2212. ζητέω *zēteō*
MATT. 2:13,20; 6:33; 7:7,8; 12:43,46,47; 13:45; 18:12; 21:46; 26:16,59; 28:5; **MARK** 1:37; 3:32; 8:11; 11:18; 12:12; 14:1,11,55; 16:6; **LUKE** 2:45,48,49; 4:42; 5:18; 6:19; 9:9; 11:9,10,16, 24,54; 12:29,31,48; 13:6,7,24; 15:8; 17:33; 19:3,10,47; 20:19; 22:2,6; 24:5; **JOHN** 1:38; 4:23,27; 5:16,18,30,44; 6:24,26; 7:1,4,11,18-20,25,30,34,36; 8:21,37,40,50; 10:39; 11:8,56; 13:33; 16:19; 18:4,7,8; 19:12; 20:15; **ACTS** 9:11; 10:19,21; 13:8,11; 16:10; 17:5,27; 21:31; 27:30; **ROM.** 2:7; 10:3,20; 11:3; **1 COR.** 1:22; 4:2; 7:27; 10:24,33; 13:5; 14:12; **2 COR.** 12:14; 13:3; **GAL.** 1:10; 2:17; **PHIL.** 2:21; **COL.** 3:1; **1 THESS.** 2:6; **2 TIM.** 1:17; **HEB.** 8:7; **1 PET.** 3:11; 5:8; **REV.** 9:6

2213. ζήτημα *zētēma*
ACTS 15:2; 18:15; 23:29; 25:19; 26:3

2214. ζήτησις *zētēsis*
JOHN 3:25; **ACTS** 25:20; **1 TIM.** 1:4; 6:4; **2 TIM.** 2:23; **TITUS** 3:9

2215. ζιζάνιον *zizanion*
MATT. 13:25-27,29,30,36,38,40

2216. Ζοροβάβελ *Zorobabel*
MATT. 1:12,13; **LUKE** 3:27

2217. ζόφος *zophos*
2 PET. 2:4,17; **JUDE** 1:6,13

2218. ζυγός *zugos*
MATT. 11:29,30; **ACTS** 15:10; **GAL.** 5:1; **1 TIM.** 6:1; **REV.** 6:5

2219. ζύμη *zumē*
MATT. 13:33; 16:6,11,12; **MARK** 8:15; **LUKE** 12:1; 13:21; **1 COR.** 5:6-8; **GAL.** 5:9

2220. ζυμόω *zumoō*
MATT. 13:33; **LUKE** 13:21; **1 COR.** 5:6; **GAL.** 5:9

2221. ζωγρέω *zōgreō*
LUKE 5:10; **2 TIM.** 2:26

2222. ζωή *zōē*
MATT. 7:14; 18:8,9; 19:16,17,29; 25:46; **MARK** 9:43,45; 10:17,30; **LUKE** 1:75; 10:25; 12:15; 16:25; 18:18,30; **JOHN** 1:4; 3:15,16,36; 4:14,36; 5:24,26,29,39,40; 6:27,33,35,40,47, 48,51,53,54,63,68; 8:12; 10:10,28; 11:25; 12:25,50; 14:6; 17:2,3; 20:31; **ACTS** 2:28; 3:15; 5:20; 8:33; 11:18; 13:46,48; 17:25; **ROM.** 2:7; 5:10,17,18,21; 6:4,22,23; 7:10; 8:2,6,10,38; 11:15; **1 COR.** 3:22; 15:19; **2 COR.** 2:16; 4:10-12; 5:4; **GAL.** 6:8; **EPH.** 4:18; **PHIL.** 1:20; 2:16; 4:3; **COL.** 3:3,4; **1 TIM.** 1:16; 4:8; 6:12,19; **2 TIM.** 1:1,10; **TITUS** 1:2; 3:7; **HEB.** 7:3,16; **JAMES** 1:12; 4:14; **1 PET.** 3:7,10; **2 PET.** 1:3; **1 JOHN** 1:1,2; 2:25; 3:14,15; 5:11-13,16,20; **JUDE** 1:21; **REV.** 2:7,10; 3:5; 11:11; 13:8; 17:8; 20:12,15; 21:6,27; 22:1,2,14,17,19

2223. ζώνη *zōnē*
MATT. 3:4; 10:9; **MARK** 1:6; 6:8; **ACTS** 21:11; **REV.** 1:13; 15:6

2224. ζώννυμι, ζωννύω
zōnnumi, zōnnuō
JOHN 21:18

2225. ζωογονέω *zōogoneō*
LUKE 17:33; ACTS 7:19

2226. ζῷον *zōon*
HEB. 13:11; **2 PET.** 2:12; **JUDE** 1:10; **REV.**
4:6-9; 5:6,8,11,14; 6:1,3,5-7; 7:11; 14:3; 15:7;
19:4

2227. ζωοποιέω *zōopoieō*
JOHN 5:21; 6:63; **ROM.** 4:17; 8:11; **1 COR.**
15:22,36,45; **2 COR.** 3:6; **GAL.** 3:21; **1 TIM.**
6:13; **1 PET.** 3:18

H

2229. ἦ μήν *ē mēn*
HEB. 6:14

2230. ἡγεμονεύω *hēgemoneuō*
LUKE 2:2; 3:1

2231. ἡγεμονία *hēgemonia*
LUKE 3:1

2232. ἡγεμών *hēgemōn*
MATT. 2:6; 10:18; 27:2,11,14,15,21,23,27;
28:14; **MARK** 13:9; **LUKE** 20:20; 21:12;
ACTS 23:24,26,33,34; 24:1,10; 26:30; **1 PET.**
2:14

2233. ἡγέομαι *hēgeomai*
MATT. 2:6; **LUKE** 22:26; **ACTS** 7:10; 14:12;
15:22; 26:2; **2 COR.** 9:5; **PHIL.** 2:3,6,25; 3:7,8;
1 THESS. 5:13; **2 THESS.** 3:15; **1 TIM.** 1:12;
6:1; **HEB.** 10:29; 11:11,26; 13:7,17,24; **JAMES**
1:2; **2 PET.** 1:13; 2:13; 3:9,15

2234. ἡδέως *hēdeōs*
MARK 6:20; 12:37; **2 COR.** 11:19

2235. ἤδη *ēdē*
MATT. 3:10; 5:28; 14:15,24; 15:32; 17:12;
24:32; **MARK** 4:37; 6:35; 8:2; 11:11; 13:28;
15:42,44; **LUKE** 3:9; 7:6; 11:7; 12:49; 14:17;
19:37; 21:30; **JOHN** 3:18; 4:35,51; 5:6; 6:17;
7:14; 9:22,27; 11:17,39; 13:2; 15:3; 19:28,33;
21:4,14; **ACTS** 4:3; 27:9; **ROM.** 1:10; 4:19;
13:11; **1 COR.** 4:8; 5:3; 6:7; **PHIL.** 3:12; 4:10;

2 THESS. 2:7; **1 TIM.** 5:15; **2 TIM.** 2:18; 4:6;
2 PET. 3:1; **1 JOHN** 2:8; 4:3

2236. ἥδιστα *hēdista*
2 COR. 12:9,15

2237. ἡδονή *hēdonē*
LUKE 8:14; **TITUS** 3:3; **JAMES** 4:1,3; **2 PET.**
2:13

2238. ἡδύοσμον *hēduosmon*
MATT. 23:23; **LUKE** 11:42

2239. ἦθος *ēthos*
1 COR. 15:33

2240. ἥκω *hēkō*
MATT. 8:11; 23:36; 24:14,50; **MARK** 8:3;
LUKE 12:46; 13:29,35; 15:27; 19:43; **JOHN**
2:4; 4:47; 6:37; 8:42; **ACTS** 28:23; **ROM.**
11:26; **HEB.** 10:7,9,37; **2 PET.** 3:10; **1 JOHN**
5:20; **REV.** 2:25; 3:3,9; 15:4; 18:8

2241. ἠλί *ēli*
MATT. 27:46

2242. Ἡλί *Hēli*
LUKE 3:23

2243. Ἡλίας *Ēlias*
MATT. 11:14; 16:14; 17:3,4,10-12; 27:47,49;
MARK 6:15; 8:28; 9:4,5,11-13; 15:35,36;
LUKE 1:17; 4:25,26; 9:8,19,30,33,54; **JOHN**
1:21,25; **ROM.** 11:2; **JAMES** 5:17

2244. ἡλικία *hēlikia*
MATT. 6:27; **LUKE** 2:52; 12:25; 19:3; **JOHN**
9:21,23; **EPH.** 4:13; **HEB.** 11:11

2245. ἡλίκος *hēlikos*
COL. 2:1; **JAMES** 3:5

2246. ἥλιος *hēlios*
MATT. 5:45; 13:6,43; 17:2; 24:29; **MARK**
1:32; 4:6; 13:24; 16:2; **LUKE** 4:40; 21:25;
23:45; **ACTS** 2:20; 13:11; 26:13; 27:20; **1 COR.**
15:41; **EPH.** 4:26; **JAMES** 1:11; **REV.** 1:16;
6:12; 7:2,16; 8:12; 9:2; 10:1; 12:1; 16:8,12;
19:17; 21:23; 22:5

2247. ἧλος hēlos
JOHN 20:25

2250. ἡμέρα hēmera
MATT. 2:1; 3:1; 4:2; 6:34; 7:22; 9:15; 10:15;
11:12,22,24; 12:36,40; 13:1; 15:32; 16:21;
17:1,23; 20:2,6,12,19; 22:23,46; 23:30;
24:19,22,29,36-38,50; 25:13; 26:2,29,55,61;
27:40,63,64; 28:20; MARK 1:9,13; 2:1,20;
4:27,35; 5:5; 6:11,21; 8:1,2,31; 9:2,31; 10:34;
13:17,19,20,24,32; 14:1,12,25,49,58; 15:29;
LUKE 1:5,7,18,20,23-25,39,59,75,80;
2:1,6,21,22,36,37,43,44,46; 4:2,16,25,42;
5:17,35; 6:12,13,23; 8:22; 9:12,22,23,28,
36,37,51; 10:12; 11:3; 12:46; 13:14,16,31; 14:5;
15:13; 16:19; 17:4,22,24,26-31; 18:7,33;
19:42,43,47; 20:1; 21:6,22,23,34,37; 22:7,53,66;
23:7,12,29,54; 24:7,13,18,21,29,46; JOHN 1:39;
2:1,12,19,20; 4:40,43; 5:9; 6:39,40,44,54; 7:37;
8:56; 9:4; 11:6,9,17,24,53; 12:1,7,48; 14:20;
16:23,26; 19:31; 20:19,26; ACTS 1:2,3,5,15,22;
2:1,15,17,18,20,29,41,46,47; 3:2,24; 5:36,37,42;
6:1; 7:8,26,41,45; 8:1; 9:9,19,23,24,37,43;
10:3,30,40,48; 11:27; 12:3,18,21; 13:14,31,41;
15:7,36; 16:5,12,13,18,35; 17:11,17,31; 18:18;
19:9; 20:6,16,18,26,31; 21:4,5,7,10,15,26,27,38;
23:1,12; 24:1,11,24; 25:1,6,13,14; 26:7,13,22;
27:7,20,29,33,39; 28:7,12-14,17,23; ROM.
2:5,16; 8:36; 10:21; 11:8; 13:12,13; 14:5,6;
1 COR. 1:8; 3:13; 4:3; 5:5; 10:8; 15:4,31;
2 COR. 1:14; 4:16; 6:2; 11:28; GAL. 1:18; 4:10;
EPH. 4:30; 5:16; 6:13; PHIL. 1:5,6,10; 2:16;
COL. 1:6,9; 1 THESS. 2:9; 3:10; 5:2,4,5,8;
2 THESS. 1:10; 2:2; 3:8; 1 TIM. 5:5; 2 TIM.
1:3,12,18; 3:1; 4:8; HEB. 1:2; 3:8,13; 4:4,7,8;
5:7; 7:3,27; 8:8-10; 10:11,16,25,32; 11:30;
12:10; JAMES 5:3,5; 1 PET. 2:12; 3:10,20;
2 PET. 1:19; 2:8,9,13; 3:3,7,8,10,12,18;
1 JOHN 4:17; JUDE 1:6; REV. 1:10; 2:10,13;
4:8; 6:17; 7:15; 8:12; 9:6,15; 10:7; 11:3,6,9,11;
12:6,10; 14:11; 16:14; 18:8; 20:10; 21:25

2251. ἡμέτερος hēmeteros
ACTS 2:11; 24:6; 26:5; ROM. 15:4; 1 COR.
15:31; 2 TIM. 4:15; TITUS 3:14; 1 JOHN 1:3;
2:2

2252. ἤμην ēmēn
          (1st sing. imperf. indic. of εἰμί)
MATT. 25:35,36,43; MARK 14:49; JOHN
11:15; 16:4; 17:12; ACTS 10:30; 11:5,11,17;
22:19,20; 1 COR. 13:11; GAL. 1:10,22

2253. ἡμιθανής hēmithanēs
LUKE 10:30

2255. ἥμισυ hēmisu   subst.
MARK 6:23; LUKE 19:8; REV. 11:9,11; 12:14

2256. ἡμιώριον hēmiōrion
REV. 8:1

2259. ἡνίκα hēnika
2 COR. 3:15,16

2260. ἤπερ ēper
JOHN 12:43

2261. ἤπιος ēpios
1 THESS. 2:7; 2 TIM. 2:24

2262. Ἤρ Ēr
LUKE 3:28

2263. ἤρεμος ēremos
1 TIM. 2:2

2264. Ἡρῴδης Hērōdēs
MATT. 2:1,3,7,12,13,15,16,19,22; 14:1,3,6;
MARK 6:14,16-18,20-22; 8:15; LUKE 1:5;
3:1,19; 8:3; 9:7,9; 13:31; 23:7,8,11,12,15; ACTS
4:27; 12:1,6,11,19-21; 13:1; 23:35

2265. Ἡρῳδιανοί Hērōdianoi
MATT. 22:16; MARK 3:6; 12:13

2266. Ἡρῳδιάς Hērōdias
MATT. 14:3,6; MARK 6:17,19,22; LUKE 3:19

2267. Ἡρῳδίων Hērōdiōn
ROM. 16:11

2268. Ἡσαΐας Hēsaias
MATT. 3:3; 4:14; 8:17; 12:17; 13:14; 15:7;
MARK 7:6; LUKE 3:4; 4:17; JOHN 1:23;
12:38,39,41; ACTS 8:28,30; 28:25; ROM.
9:27,29; 10:16,20; 15:12

2269. Ἠσαῦ *Ēsau*
ROM. 9:13; HEB. 11:20; 12:16

2270. ἡσυχάζω *hēsuchazō*
LUKE 14:4; 23:56; ACTS 11:18; 21:14;
1 THESS. 4:11

2271. ἡσυχία *hēsuchia*
ACTS 22:2; 2 THESS. 3:12; 1 TIM. 2:11,12

2272. ἡσύχιος *hēsuchios*
1 TIM. 2:2; 1 PET. 3:4

2273. ἤτοι *ētoi*
ROM. 6:16

2274. ἡττάομαι *hēttaomai*
2 COR. 12:13; 2 PET. 2:19,20

2275. ἥττημα *hēttēma*
ROM. 11:12; 1 COR. 6:7

2276. ἥσσων, ἥττων *hēssōn, hēttōn*
1 COR. 11:17; 2 COR. 12:15

2277. ἤτω *ētō*
(3rd sing. pres. imper. of εἰμί)
1 COR. 16:22; JAMES 5:12

2278. ἠχέω *ēcheō*
LUKE 21:25; 1 COR. 13:1

2279. ἦχος *ēchos*
LUKE 4:37; ACTS 2:2; HEB. 12:19

Θ

2280. Θαδδαῖος *Thaddaios*
MATT. 10:3; MARK 3:18

2281. θάλασσα *thalassa*
MATT. 4:15,18; 8:24,26,27,32; 13:1,47; 14:24-
26; 15:29; 17:27; 18:6; 21:21; 23:15; MARK
1:16; 2:13; 3:7; 4:1,39,41; 5:1,13,21; 6:47-49;
7:31; 9:42; 11:23; LUKE 17:2,6; 21:25; JOHN
6:1,16-19,22,25; 21:1,7; ACTS 4:24; 7:36;
10:6,32; 14:15; 17:14; 27:30,38,40; 28:4; ROM.

9:27; 1 COR. 10:1,2; 2 COR. 11:26; HEB.
11:12,29; JAMES 1:6; JUDE 1:13; REV. 4:6;
5:13; 7:1-3; 8:8,9; 10:2,5,6,8; 12:12; 13:1; 14:7;
15:2; 16:3; 18:17,19,21; 20:8,13; 21:1

2282. θάλπω *thalpō*
EPH. 5:29; 1 THESS. 2:7

2283. Θάμαρ *Thamar*
MATT. 1:3

2284. θαμβέω *thambeō*
MARK 1:27; 10:24,32; ACTS 9:6

2285. θάμβος *thambos*
LUKE 4:36; 5:9; ACTS 3:10

2286. θανάσιμος *thanasimos*
MARK 16:18

2287. θανατηφόρος *thanatēphoros*
JAMES 3:8

2288. θάνατος *thanatos*
MATT. 4:16; 10:21; 15:4; 16:28; 20:18;
26:38,66; MARK 7:10; 9:1; 10:33; 13:12;
14:34,64; LUKE 1:79; 2:26; 9:27; 22:33;
23:15,22; 24:20; JOHN 5:24; 8:51,52; 11:4,13;
12:33; 18:32; 21:19; ACTS 2:24; 13:28; 22:4;
23:29; 25:11,25; 26:31; 28:18; ROM. 1:32;
5:10,12,14,17,21; 6:3-5,9,16,21,23; 7:5,10,13,24;
8:2,6,38; 1 COR. 3:22; 11:26; 15:21,26,54-56;
2 COR. 1:9,10; 2:16; 3:7; 4:11,12; 7:10; 11:23;
PHIL. 1:20; 2:8,27,30; 3:10; COL. 1:22; 2 TIM.
1:10; HEB. 2:9,14,15; 5:7; 7:23; 9:15,16; 11:5;
JAMES 1:15; 5:20; 1 JOHN 3:14; 5:16,17;
REV. 1:18; 2:10,11,23; 6:8; 9:6; 12:11; 13:3,12;
18:8; 20:6,13,14; 21:4,8

2289. θανατόω *thanatoō*
MATT. 10:21; 26:59; 27:1; MARK 13:12;
14:55; LUKE 21:16; ROM. 7:4; 8:13,36;
2 COR. 6:9; 1 PET. 3:18

2290. θάπτω *thaptō*
MATT. 8:21,22; 14:12; LUKE 9:59,60; 16:22;
ACTS 2:29; 5:6,9,10; 1 COR. 15:4

2291. Θάρα *Thara*
LUKE 3:34

2292. θαρρέω tharreō
2 COR. 5:6,8; 7:16; 10:1,2; HEB. 13:6

2293. θαρσέω tharseō
MATT. 9:2,22; 14:27; MARK 6:50; 10:49;
LUKE 8:48; JOHN 16:33; ACTS 23:11

2294. θάρσος tharsos
ACTS 28:15

2295. θαῦμα thauma
REV. 17:6

2296. θαυμάζω thaumazō
MATT. 8:10,27; 9:8,33; 15:31; 21:20; 22:22;
27:14; MARK 5:20; 6:6,51; 12:17; 15:5,44;
LUKE 1:21,63; 2:18,33; 4:22; 7:9; 8:25; 9:43;
11:14,38; 20:26; 24:12,41; JOHN 3:7; 4:27;
5:20,28; 7:15,21; ACTS 2:7; 3:12; 4:13; 7:31;
13:41; GAL. 1:6; 2 THESS. 1:10; 1 JOHN
3:13; JUDE 1:16; REV. 13:3; 17:6-8

2297. θαυμάσιος thaumasios
MATT. 21:15

2298. θαυμαστός thaumastos
MATT. 21:42; MARK 12:11; JOHN 9:30;
2 COR. 11:14; 1 PET. 2:9; REV. 15:1,3

2299. θεά thea
ACTS 19:27,35,37

2300. θεάομαι theaomai
MATT. 6:1; 11:7; 22:11; 23:5; MARK
16:11,14; LUKE 5:27; 7:24; 23:55; JOHN
1:14,32,38; 4:35; 6:5; 8:10; 11:45; ACTS 1:11;
8:18; 21:27; 22:9; ROM. 15:24; 1 JOHN 1:1;
4:12,14

2301. θεατρίζω theatrizō
HEB. 10:33

2302. θέατρον theatron
ACTS 19:29,31; 1 COR. 4:9

2303. θεῖον theion
LUKE 17:29; REV. 9:17,18; 14:10; 19:20;
20:10; 21:8

2304. θεῖος theios
ACTS 17:29; 2 PET. 1:3,4

2305. θειότης theiotēs
ROM. 1:20

2306. θειώδης theiōdēs
REV. 9:17

2307. θέλημα thelēma
MATT. 6:10; 7:21; 12:50; 18:14; 21:31; 26:42;
MARK 3:35; LUKE 11:2; 12:47; 22:42; 23:25;
JOHN 1:13; 4:34; 5:30; 6:38-40; 7:17; 9:31;
ACTS 13:22; 21:14; 22:14; ROM. 1:10; 2:18;
12:2; 15:32; 1 COR. 1:1; 7:37; 16:12; 2 COR.
1:1; 8:5; GAL. 1:4; EPH. 1:1,5,9,11; 2:3; 5:17;
6:6; COL. 1:1,9; 4:12; 1 THESS. 4:3; 5:18;
2 TIM. 1:1; 2:26; HEB. 10:7,9,10,36; 13:21;
1 PET. 2:15; 3:17; 4:2,3,19; 2 PET. 1:21;
1 JOHN 2:17; 5:14; REV. 4:11

2308. θέλησις thelēsis
HEB. 2:4

2309. θέλω thelō
MATT. 1:19; 2:18; 5:40,42; 7:12; 8:2,3; 9:13;
11:14; 12:7,38; 13:28; 14:5; 15:28,32; 16:24,25;
17:4,12; 18:23,30; 19:17,21; 20:14,15,21,
26,27,32; 21:29; 22:3; 23:4,37; 26:15,17,39;
27:15,17,21,34,43; MARK 1:40,41; 3:13;
6:19,22,25,26,48; 7:24; 8:34,35; 9:13,30,35;
10:35,36,43,44,51; 12:38; 14:7,12,36; 15:9,12;
LUKE 1:62; 4:6; 5:12,13,39; 6:31; 8:20;
9:23,24,54; 10:24,29; 12:49; 13:31,34; 14:28;
15:28; 16:26; 18:4,13,41; 19:14,27; 20:46; 22:9;
23:8,20; JOHN 1:43; 3:8; 5:6,21,35,40; 6:11,
21,67; 7:1,17,44; 8:44; 9:27; 12:21; 15:7; 16:19;
17:24; 21:18,22,23; ACTS 2:12; 7:28,39; 9:6;
10:10; 14:13; 16:3; 17:18,20; 18:21; 19:33;
24:6,27; 25:9; 26:5; ROM. 1:13; 7:15,16,18-21;
9:16,18,22; 11:25; 13:3; 16:19; 1 COR. 4:19,21;
7:7,32,36,39; 10:1,20,27; 11:3; 12:1,18; 14:5,
19,35; 15:38; 16:7; 2 COR. 1:8; 5:4; 8:10,11;
11:12,32; 12:6,20; GAL. 1:7; 3:2; 4:9,17,20,21;
5:17; 6:12,13; PHIL. 2:13; COL. 1:27; 2:1,18;
1 THESS. 2:18; 4:13; 2 THESS. 3:10; 1 TIM.
1:7; 2:4; 5:11; 2 TIM. 3:12; PHILE. 1:14; HEB.
10:5,8; 12:17; 13:18; JAMES 2:20; 4:15; 1 PET.
3:10; 2 PET. 3:5; 3 JOHN 1:13; REV. 11:5,6;
22:17

2310. θεμέλιος themelios

LUKE 6:48,49; 14:29; **ACTS** 16:26; **ROM.**
15:20; **1 COR.** 3:10-12; **EPH.** 2:20; **1 TIM.**
6:19; **2 TIM.** 2:19; **HEB.** 6:1; 11:10; **REV.**
21:14,19

2311. θεμελιόω themelioō

MATT. 7:25; **LUKE** 6:48; **EPH.** 3:17; **COL.**
1:23; **HEB.** 1:10; **1 PET.** 5:10

2312. θεοδίδακτος theodidaktos

1 THESS. 4:9

2313. θεομαχέω theomacheō

ACTS 23:9

2314. θεομάχος theomachos

ACTS 5:39

2315. θεόπνευστος theopneustos

2 TIM. 3:16

2316. Θεός Theos

MATT. 1:23; 3:9,16; 4:3,4,6,7,10; 5:8,9,34;
6:24,30,33; 8:29; 9:8; 12:4,28; 14:33; 15:3,4,
6,31; 16:16,23; 19:6,17,24,26; 21:12,31,43;
22:16,21,29-32,37; 23:22; 26:61,63; 27:40,43,
46,54; **MARK** 1:1,14,15,24; 2:7,12,26; 3:11,35;
4:11,26,30; 5:7; 7:8,9,13; 8:33; 9:1,47; 10:6,9,
14,15,18,23-25,27; 11:22; 12:14,17,24,26,
27,29,30,32,34; 13:19; 14:25; 15:34,39,43;
16:19; **LUKE** 1:6,8,16,19,26,30,32,35,37,
47,64,68,78; 2:13,14,20,28,40,52; 3:2,6,8,38;
4:3,4,8,9,12,34,41,43; 5:1,21,25,26; 6:4,12,20;
7:16,28-30; 8:1,10,11,21,28,39; 9:2,11,20,27,
43,60,62; 10:9,11,27; 11:20,28,42,49; 12:6,8,
9,20,21,24,28,31; 13:13,18,20,28,29; 14:15;
15:10; 16:13,15,16; 17:15,18,20,21; 18:2,4,
7,11,13,16,17,19,24,25,27,29,43; 19:11,37;
20:21,25,36-38; 21:4,31; 22:16,18,69,70;
23:35,40,47,51; 24:19,53; **JOHN** 1:1,2,6,12,13,
18,29,34,36,49,51; 3:2,3,5,16-18,21,33,34,36;
4:10,24; 5:18,25,42,44; 6:27-29,33,45,46,69;
7:17; 8:40-42,47,54; 9:3,16,24,29,31,33,35;
10:33-36; 11:4,22,27,40,52; 12:43; 13:3,31,32;
14:1; 16:2,27,30; 17:3; 19:7; 20:17,28,31; 21:19;
ACTS 1:3; 2:11,17,22-24,30,32,33,36,39,47;
3:8,9,13,15,18,21,22,25,26; 4:10,19,21,24,31;

5:4,29-32,39; 6:2,7,11; 7:2,6,7,9,17,20,25,
32,35,37,40,42,43,45,46,55,56; 8:10,12,14,20-
22,37; 9:20; 10:2-4,15,22,28,31,33,34,38,40-
42,46; 11:1,9,17,18,23; 12:5,22-24; 13:5,7,16,
17,21,23,26,30,33,36,37,43,44,46; 14:11,15,
22,26,27; 15:4,7,8,10,12,14,18,19,40; 16:14,17,
25,34; 17:13,23,24,29,30; 18:7,11,13,21,26;
19:8,11,26; 20:21,24,25,27,28,32; 21:19;
22:3,14; 23:1,3,4; 24:14-16; 26:6,8,18,20,22,29;
27:23-25,35; 28:6,15,23,28,31; **ROM.** 1:1,4,7-
10,16-19,21,23-26,28,32; 2:2-5,11,13,16,17,
23,24,29; 3:2-7,11,18,19,21-23,25,29,30;
4:2,3,6,17,20; 5:1,2,5,8,10,11,15; 6:10,11,13,
17,22,23; 7:4,22,25; 8:3,7-9,14,16,17,19,
21,27,28,31,33,34,39; 9:5,6,8,11,14,16,20,22,26;
10:1-3,9,17; 11:1,2,8,21-23,29,30,32,33; 12:1-3;
13:1,2,4,6; 14:3,4,6,11,12,17,18,20,22; 15:5-
9,13,15-17,19,30,32,33; 16:20,26,27; **1 COR.**
1:1-4,9,14,18,20,21,24,25,27,28,30; 2:1,5,7,9-
12,14; 3:6,7,9,10,16,17,19,23; 4:1,5,9,20; 5:13;
6:9-11,13,14,19,20; 7:7,15,17,19,24,40; 8:3-6,8;
9:9,21; 10:5,13,20,31,32; 11:3,7,12,13,16,22;
12:3,6,18,24,28; 14:2,18,25,28,33,36; 15:9,
10,15,24,28,34,38,50,57; **2 COR.** 1:1-4,9,12,
18-21,23; 2:14,15,17; 3:3-5; 4:2,4,6,7,15;
5:1,5,11,13,18-21; 6:1,4,7,16; 7:1,6,9-12;
8:1,5,16; 9:7,8,11-15; 10:4,5,13; 11:2,7,11,31;
12:2,3,19,21; 13:4,7,11,14; **GAL.** 1:1,3,4,10,
13,15,20,24; 2:6,19-21; 3:6,8,11,17,18,20,
21,26; 4:4,6-9,14; 5:21; 6:7,16; **EPH.** 1:1-3,
17,2:4,8,10,16,19,22; 3:2,7,9,10,19; 4:6,13,
18,24,30,32; 5:1,2,5,6,20,21; 6:6,11,13,17,23;
PHIL. 1:2,3,8,11,28; 2:6,9,11,13,15,27; 3:3,
9,14,15,19; 4:6,7,9,18-20; **COL.** 1:1-3,6,10,
15,25,27; 2:2,12,19; 3:1,3,6,12,15,17,22;
4:3,11,12; **1 THESS.** 1:1-4,8,9; 2:2,4,5,8-10,
12-15; 3:2,9,11,13; 4:1,3,5,7,8,14,16; 5:9,18,23;
2 THESS. 1:1-6,8,11,12; 2:4,11,13,16; 3:5;
1 TIM. 1:1,2,4,11,17; 2:3,5; 3:5,15,16; 4:3-5,10;
5:4,5,21; 6:1,11,13,17; **2 TIM.** 1:1-3,6-8;
2:9,15,19,25; 3:17; 4:1; **TITUS** 1:1-3,4,7,16;
2:5,10,11,13; 3:4,8; **PHILE.** 1:3,4; **HEB.**
1:1,6,8,9; 2:4,9,13,17; 8:4,12; 4:4,9,10,12,14;
5:1,4,10,12; 6:1,3,5-7,10,13,17,18; 7:1,3,19,25;
8:10; 9:14,20,24; 10:7,9,12,21,29,31,36; 11:3-
6,10,16,19,25,40; 12:2,7,15,22,23,28,29; 13:4,
7,15,16,20; **JAMES** 1:1,5,13,20,27; 2:5,19,23;
3:9; 4:4,6-8; **1 PET.** 1:2,3,5,21,23; 2:4,5,10,
12,15-17,19,20; 3:4,5,15,17,18,20-22; 4:2,6,
10,11,14,16,17,19; 5:2,5,6,10,12; **2 PET.** 1:1,2,
17,21; 2:4; 3:5,12; **1 JOHN** 1:5; 2:5,14,17;
3:1,2,8-10,17,20,21; 4:1-4,6-12,15,16,20,21; 5:1-
5,9-13,18-20; **2 JOHN** 1:3,9; **3 JOHN** 1:6,11;

JUDE 1:1,4,21,25; **REV.** 1:1,2,6,9; 2:7,18;
3:1,2,12,14; 4:5,8; 5:6,9,10; 6:9; 7:2,3,10-12,
15,17; 8:2,4; 9:4,13; 10:7; 11:1,4,11,13,16,17,19;
12:5,6,10,17; 13:6; 14:4,5,7,10,12,19; 15:1-3,7,8;
16:1,7,9,11,14,19,21; 17:17; 18:5,8,20; 19:1,4-
6,9,10,13,15,17; 20:4,6,9,12; 21:2-4,7,10,11,
22,23; 22:1,3,5,6,9,18,19

2317. θεοσέβεια *theosebeia*
1 TIM. 2:10

2318. θεοσεβής *theosebēs*
JOHN 9:31

2319. θεοστυγής *theostugēs*
ROM. 1:30

2320. θεότης *theotēs*
COL. 2:9

2321. Θεόφιλος *Theophilos*
LUKE 1:3; **ACTS** 1:1

2322. θεραπεία *therapeia*
MAT 24:45; **LUKE** 9:11; 12:42; **REV.** 22:2

2323. θεραπεύω *therapeuō*
MATT. 4:23,24; 8:7,16; 9:35; 10:1,8;
12:10,15,22; 14:14; 15:30; 17:16,18; 19:2; 21:14;
MARK 1:34; 3:2,10,15; 6:5,13; **LUKE** 4:23,40;
5:15; 6:7,18; 7:21; 8:2,43; 9:1,6; 10:9; 13:14;
14:3; **JOHN** 5:10; **ACTS** 4:14; 5:16; 8:7; 17:25;
28:9; **REV.** 13:3,12

2324. θεράπων *therapōn*
HEB. 3:5

2325. θερίζω *therizō*
MATT. 6:26; 25:24,26; **LUKE** 12:24; 19:21,22;
JOHN 4:36-38; **1 COR.** 9:11; **2 COR.** 9:6;
GAL. 6:7-9; **JAMES** 5:4; **REV.** 14:15,16

2326. θερισμός *therismos*
MATT. 9:37,38; 13:30,39; **MARK** 4:29; **LUKE**
10:2; **JOHN** 4:35; **REV.** 14:15

2327. θεριστής *theristēs*
MATT. 13:30,39

2328. θερμαίνω *thermainō*
MARK 14:54,67; **JOHN** 18:18,25; **JAMES**
2:16

2329. θέρμη *thermē*
ACTS 28:3

2330. θέρος *theros*
MATT. 24:32; **MARK** 13:28; **LUKE** 21:30

2331. Θεσσαλονικεύς *Thessalonikeus*
ACTS 20:4; 27:2; **1 THESS.** 1:1; **2 THESS.** 1:1

2332. Θεσσαλονίκη *Thessalonikē*
ACTS 17:1,11,13; **PHIL.** 4:16; **2 TIM.** 4:10

2333. Θευδᾶς *Theudas*
ACTS 5:36

2334. θεωρέω *theōreō*
MATT. 27:55; 28:1; **MARK** 3:11; 5:15,38;
12:41; 15:40,47; 16:4; **LUKE** 10:18; 14:29;
21:6; 23:35,48; 24:37,39; **JOHN** 2:23; 4:19;
6:19,40,62; 7:3; 8:51; 9:8; 10:12; 12:19,45;
14:17,19; 16:10,16,17,19; 17:24; 20:6,12,14;
ACTS 3:16; 4:13; 7:56; 8:13; 9:7; 10:11;
17:16,22; 19:26; 20:38; 21:20; 25:24; 27:10;
28:6; **HEB.** 7:4; **1 JOHN** 3:17; **REV.** 11:11,12

2335. θεωρία *theōria*
LUKE 23:48

2336. θήκη *thēkē*
JOHN 18:11

2337. θηλάζω *thēlazō*
MATT. 21:16; 24:19; **MARK** 13:17; **LUKE**
11:27; 21:23; 23:29

2338. I. θῆλυς *thēlus*
MATT. 19:4; **MARK** 10:6; **GAL.** 3:28

II. θήλεια thēleia   subst.
ROM. 1:26,27

2339. θήρα thēra
ROM. 11:9

2340. θηρεύω thēreuō
LUKE 11:54

2341. θηριομαχέω thēriomacheō
1 COR. 15:32

2342. θηρίον thērion
MARK 1:13; ACTS 10:12; 11:6; 28:4,5; TITUS
1:12; HEB. 12:20; JAMES 3:7; REV. 6:8; 11:7;
13:1-4,11,12,14,15,17,18; 14:9,11; 15:2;
16:2,10,13; 17:3,7,8,11-13,16,17; 19:19,20;
20:4,10

2343. θησαυρίζω thēsaurizō
MATT. 6:19,20; LUKE 12:21; ROM. 2:5;
1 COR. 16:2; 2 COR. 12:14; JAMES 5:3;
2 PET. 3:7

2344. θησαυρός thēsauros
MATT. 2:11; 6:19-21; 12:35; 13:44,52; 19:21;
MARK 10:21; LUKE 6:45; 12:33,34; 18:22;
2 COR. 4:7; COL. 2:3; HEB. 11:26

2345. θιγγάνω thigganō
COL. 2:21; HEB. 11:28; 12:20

2346. θλίβω thlibō
MATT. 7:14; MARK 3:9; 2 COR. 1:6; 4:8; 7:5;
1 THESS. 3:4; 2 THESS. 1:6,7; 1 TIM. 5:10;
HEB. 11:37

2347. θλίψις thlipsis
MATT. 13:21; 24:9,21,29; MARK 4:17;
13:19,24; JOHN 16:21,33; ACTS 7:10,11;
11:19; 14:22; 20:23; ROM. 2:9; 5:3; 8:35; 12:12;
1 COR. 7:28; 2 COR. 1:4,8; 2:4; 4:17; 6:4; 7:4;
8:2,13; EPH. 3:13; PHIL. 1:16; 4:14; COL.
1:24; 1 THESS. 1:6; 3:3,7; 2 THESS. 1:4,6;
HEB. 10:33; JAMES 1:27; REV. 1:9; 2:9,10,22;
7:14

2348. θνήσκω thnēskō
MATT. 2:20; MARK 15:44; LUKE 7:12; 8:49;

JOHN 11:21,39,41,44; 12:1; 19:33; ACTS
14:19; 25:19; 1 TIM. 5:6

2349. θνητός thnētos
ROM. 6:12; 8:11; 1 COR. 15:53,54; 2 COR.
4:11; 5:4

2350. θορυβέω thorubeō
MATT. 9:23; MARK 5:39; ACTS 17:5; 20:10

2351. θόρυβος thorubos
MATT. 26:5; 27:24; MARK 5:38; 14:2; ACTS
20:1; 21:34; 24:18

2352. θραύω thrauō
LUKE 4:18

2353. θρέμμα thremma
JOHN 4:12

2354. θρηνέω thrēneō
MATT. 11:17; LUKE 7:32; 23:27; JOHN 16:20

2355. θρῆνος thrēnos
MATT. 2:18

2356. θρησκεία thrēskeia
ACTS 26:5; COL. 2:18; JAMES 1:26,27

2357. θρῆσκος thrēskos
JAMES 1:26

2358. θριαμβεύω thriambeuō
2 COR. 2:14; COL. 2:15

2359. θρίξ thrix
MATT. 3:4; 5:36; 10:30; MARK 1:6; LUKE
7:38,44; 12:7; 21:18; JOHN 11:2; 12:3; ACTS
27:34; 1 PET. 3:3; REV. 1:14; 9:8

2360. θροέω throeō
MATT. 24:6; MARK 13:7; 2 THESS. 2:2

2361. θρόμβος thrombos
LUKE 22:44

2362. θρόνος thronos
MATT. 5:34; 19:28; 23:22; 25:31; LUKE

1:32,52; 22:30; **ACTS** 2:30; 7:49; **COL.** 1:16;
HEB. 1:8; 4:16; 8:1; 12:2; **REV.** 1:4; 2:13; 3:21;
4:2-6,9,10; 5:1,6,7,11,13; 6:16; 7:9-11,15,17;
8:3; 11:16; 12:5; 13:2; 14:3,5; 16:10,17; 19:4,5;
20:4,11; 21:5; 22:1,3

2363. Θυάτειρα Thuateira
ACTS 16:14; **REV.** 1:11; 2:18,24

2364. θυγάτηρ thugatēr
MATT. 9:18,22; 10:35,37; 14:6; 15:22,28; 21:5;
MARK 5:34,35; 6:22; 7:26,29,30; **LUKE** 1:5;
2:36; 8:42,48,49; 12:53; 13:16; 23:28; **JOHN**
12:15; **ACTS** 2:17; 7:21; 21:9; **2 COR.** 6:18;
HEB. 11:24

2365. θυγάτριον thugatrion
MARK 5:23; 7:25

2366. θύελλα thuella
HEB. 12:18

2367. θύϊνος thuinos
REV. 18:12

2368. θυμίαμα thumiama
LUKE 1:10,11; **REV.** 5:8; 8:3,4; 18:13

2369. θυμιατήριον thumiatērion
HEB. 9:4

2370. θυμιάω thumiaō
LUKE 1:9

2371. θυμομαχέω thumomacheō
ACTS 12:20

2372. θυμός thumos
LUKE 4:28; **ACTS** 19:28; **ROM.** 2:8; **2 COR.**
12:20; **GAL.** 5:20; **EPH.** 4:31; **COL.** 3:8; **HEB.**
11:27; **REV.** 12:12; 14:8,10,19; 15:1,7; 16:1,19;
18:3; 19:15

2373. θυμόω thumoō
MATT. 2:16

2374. θύρα thura
MATT. 6:6; 24:33; 25:10; 27:60; 28:2; **MARK**

1:33; 2:2; 11:4; 13:29; 15:46; 16:3; **LUKE** 11:7;
13:25; **JOHN** 10:1,2,7,9; 18:16; 20:19,26;
ACTS 3:2; 5:9,19,23; 12:6,13; 14:27; 16:26,27;
21:30; **1 COR.** 16:9; **2 COR.** 2:12; **COL.** 4:3;
JAMES 5:9; **REV.** 3:8,20; 4:1

2375. θυρεός thureos
EPH. 6:16

2376. θυρίς thuris
ACTS 20:9; **2 COR.** 11:33

2377. θυρωρός thurōros
MARK 13:34; **JOHN** 10:3; 18:16,17

2378. θυσία thusia
MATT. 9:13; 12:7; **MARK** 9:49; 12:33; **LUKE**
2:24; 13:1; **ACTS** 7:41,42; **ROM.** 12:1; **1 COR.**
10:18; **EPH.** 5:2; **PHIL.** 2:17; 4:18; **HEB.** 5:1;
7:27; 8:3; 9:9,23,26; 10:1,5,8,11,12,26; 11:4;
13:15,16; **1 PET.** 2:5

2379. θυσιαστήριον thusiastērion
MATT. 5:23,24; 23:18-20,35; **LUKE** 1:11;
11:51; **ROM.** 11:3; **1 COR.** 9:13; 10:18; **HEB.**
7:13; 13:10; **JAMES** 2:21; **REV.** 6:9; 8:3,5;
9:13; 11:1; 14:18; 16:7

2380. θύω thuō
MATT. 22:4; **MARK** 14:12; **LUKE**
15:23,27,30; 22:7; **JOHN** 10:10; **ACTS** 10:13;
11:7; 14:13,18; **1 COR.** 5:7; 10:20

2381. Θωμᾶς Thōmas
MATT. 10:3; **MARK** 3:18; **LUKE** 6:15; **JOHN**
11:16; 14:5; 20:24,26-29; 21:2; **ACTS** 1:13

2382. θώραξ thōrax
EPH. 6:14; **1 THESS.** 5:8; **REV.** 9:9,17

I

2383. Ἰάειρος Iaeiros
MARK 5:22; **LUKE** 8:41

2384. Ἰακώβ Iakōb
MATT. 1:2,15,16; 8:11; 22:32; **MARK** 12:26;
LUKE 1:33; 3:34; 13:28; 20:37; **JOHN**

4:5,6,12; **ACTS** 3:13; 7:8,12,14,15,32,46; **ROM.** 9:13; 11:26; **HEB.** 11:9,20,21

2385. Ἰάκωβος Iakōbos
MATT. 4:21; 10:2,3; 13:55; 17:1; 27:56;
MARK 1:19,29; 3:17,18; 5:37; 6:3; 9:2;
10:35,41; 13:3; 14:33; 15:40; 16:1; **LUKE** 5:10;
6:14-16; 8:51; 9:28,54; 24:10; **ACTS** 1:13;
12:2,17; 15:13; 21:18; **1 COR.** 15:7; **GAL.** 1:19;
2:9,12; **JAMES** 1:1; **JUDE** 1:1

2386. ἴαμα iama
1 COR. 12:9,28,30

2387. Ἰαμβρῆς Iambrēs
2 TIM. 3:8

2388. Ἰαννά Ianna
LUKE 3:24

2389. Ἰαννῆς Iannēs
2 TIM. 3:8

2390. ἰάομαι iaomai
MATT. 8:8,13; 13:15; 15:28; **MARK** 5:29;
LUKE 4:18; 5:17; 6:17,19; 7:7; 8:47; 9:2,11,42;
14:4; 17:15; 22:51; **JOHN** 4:47; 5:13; 12:40;
ACTS 3:11; 9:34; 10:38; 28:8,27; **HEB.** 12:13;
JAMES 5:16; **1 PET.** 2:24

2391. Ἰάρεδ Iared
LUKE 3:37

2392. ἴασις iasis
LUKE 13:32; **ACTS** 4:22,30

2393. ἴασπις iaspis
REV. 4:3; 21:11,18,19

2394. Ἰάσων Iasōn
ACTS 17:5-7,9; **ROM.** 16:21

2395. ἰατρός iatros
MATT. 9:12; **MARK** 2:17; 5:26; **LUKE** 4:23;
5:31; 8:43; **COL.** 4:14

2396. ἴδε ide
MATT. 25:20,22,25; 26:65; **MARK** 2:24; 3:34;

11:21; 13:1; 15:4; 16:6; **JOHN** 1:29,36,47; 3:26;
5:14; 7:26; 11:3,36; 12:19; 16:29; 18:21;
19:4,5,14; **ROM.** 2:17; **GAL.** 5:2

2397. ἰδέα idea
MATT. 28:3

2398. ἴδιος idios
MATT. 9:1; 14:13,23; 17:1,19; 20:17; 22:5;
24:3; 25:14,15; **MARK** 4:34; 6:31,32; 7:33;
9:2,28; 13:3; 15:20; **LUKE** 2:3; 6:41,44; 9:10;
10:23,34; **JOHN** 1:11,41; 4:44; 5:18,43; 7:18;
8:44; 10:3,4,12; 13:1; 15:19; 16:32; 19:27;
ACTS 1:7,19,25; 2:6,8; 3:12; 4:23,32; 13:36;
20:28; 21:6; 23:19; 24:23; 25:19; 28:30; **ROM.**
8:32; 10:3; 11:24; 14:4,5; **1 COR.** 3:8; 4:12;
6:18; 7:2,4,7,37; 9:7; 11:21; 12:11; 14:35;
15:23,38; **GAL.** 2:2; 6:5,9; **EPH.** 5:22,24; **COL.**
3:18; **1 THESS.** 2:14,15; 4:11; **1 TIM.** 2:6;
3:4,5,12; 4:2; 5:4,8; 6:1,15; **2 TIM.** 1:9; 4:3;
TITUS 1:3,12; 2:5,9; **HEB.** 4:10; 7:27; 9:12;
13:12; **JAMES** 1:14; **1 PET.** 3:1,5; **2 PET.** 1:20;
2:16,22; 3:3,16,17; **JUDE** 1:6

2399. ἰδιώτης idiōtēs
ACTS 4:13; **1 COR.** 14:16,23,24; **2 COR.** 11:6

2400. ἰδού idou
MATT. 1:20,23; 2:1,9,13,19; 3:16,17; 4:11; 7:4;
8:2,24,29,32,34; 9:2,3,10,18,20,32; 10:16;
11:8,10,19; 12:2,10,18,41,42,46,47,49; 13:3;
15:22; 17:3,5; 19:16,27; 20:18,30; 21:5; 22:4;
23:34,38; 24:23,25,26; 25:6; 26:45-47,51; 27:51;
28:2,7,9,11,20; **MARK** 1:2; 3:32; 4:3; 5:22;
10:28,33; 13:21,23; 14:41,42; 15:35; **LUKE**
1:20,31,36,38,44,48; 2:9,10,25,34,48; 5:12,18;
6:23; 7:12,25,27,34,37; 8:41; 9:30,38,39;
10:3,19,25; 11:31,32,41; 13:7,11,16,30,32,35;
14:2; 15:29; 17:21,23; 18:28,31; 19:2,8,20;
22:10,21,31,38,47; 23:14,15,29,50; 24:4,13,49;
JOHN 4:35; 12:15; 16:32; 19:26,27; **ACTS**
1:10; 2:7; 5:9,25,28; 7:56; 8:27,36; 9:10,11;
10:17,19,21,30; 11:11; 12:7; 13:11,25,46; 16:1;
20:22,25; 27:24; **ROM.** 9:33; **1 COR.** 15:51;
2 COR. 5:17; 6:2,9; 7:11; 12:14; **GAL.** 1:20;
HEB. 2:13; 8:8; 10:7,9; **JAMES** 3:3-5;
5:4,7,9,11; **1 PET.** 2:6; **JUDE** 1:14; **REV.**
1:7,18; 2:10,22; 3:8,9,11,20; 4:1,2; 5:5,6;
6:2,5,8,12; 7:9; 9:12; 11:14; 12:3; 14:1,14; 15:5;
16:15; 19:11; 21:3,5; 22:7,12

2401. Ἰδουμαία *Idoumaia*
MARK 3:8

2402. ἱδρώς *hidrōs*
LUKE 22:44

2403. Ἰεζαβήλ *Iezabēl*
REV. 2:20

2404. Ἱεράπολις *Hierapolis*
COL. 4:13

2405. ἱερατεία *hierateia*
LUKE 1:9; HEB. 7:5

2406. ἱεράτευμα *hierateuma*
1 PET. 2:5,9

2407. ἱερατεύω *hierateuō*
LUKE 1:8

2408. Ἱερεμίας *Hieremias*
MATT. 2:17; 16:14; 27:9

2409. ἱερεύς *hiereus*
MATT. 8:4; 12:4,5; MARK 1:44; 2:26; LUKE 1:5; 5:14; 6:4; 10:31; 17:14; JOHN 1:19; ACTS 4:1; 5:24; 6:7; 14:13; HEB. 5:6; 7:1,3,11,15, 17,21,23; 8:4; 9:6; 10:11,21; REV. 1:6; 5:10; 20:6

2410. Ἱεριχώ *Hierichō*
MATT. 20:29; MARK 10:46; LUKE 10:30; 18:35; 19:1; HEB. 11:30

2411. ἱερόν *hieron*
MATT. 4:5; 12:5,6; 21:12,14,15,23; 24:1; 26:55; MARK 11:11,15,16,27; 12:35; 13:1,3; 14:49; LUKE 2:27,37,46; 4:9; 18:10; 19:45,47; 20:1; 21:5,37,38; 22:52,53; 24:53; JOHN 2:14,15; 5:14; 7:14,28; 8:2,20,59; 10:23; 11:56; 18:20; ACTS 2:46; 3:1-3,8,10; 4:1; 5:20,21,24,25,42; 19:27; 21:26-30; 22:17; 24:6,12,18; 25:8; 26:21; 1 COR. 9:13

2412. ἱεροπρεπής *hieroprepēs*
TITUS 2:3

2413. ἱερός *hieros*
1 COR. 9:13; 2 TIM. 3:15

2414. Ἱεροσόλυμα *Hierosoluma*
MATT. 2:1,3; 3:5; 4:25; 5:35; 15:1; 16:21; 20:17,18; 21:1,10; MARK 3:8,22; 7:1; 10:32,33; 11:11,15,27; 15:41; LUKE 2:22,42; 18:31; 19:28; 23:7; JOHN 1:19; 2:13,23; 4:20,21,45; 5:1,2; 10:22; 11:18,55; 12:12; ACTS 1:4; 8:1,14; 11:2,22,27; 13:13; 18:21; 20:16; 21:17; 25:1,7,9,15,24; 26:4,10,20; 28:17; GAL. 1:17,18; 2:1

2415. Ἱεροσολυμίτης *Hierosolumitēs*
MARK 1:5; JOHN 7:25

2416. ἱεροσυλέω *hierosuleō*
ROM. 2:22

2417. ἱερόσυλος *hierosulos*
ACTS 19:37

2418. ἱερουργέω *hierourgeō*
ROM. 15:16

2419. Ἱερουσαλήμ *Hierousalēm*
MATT. 23:37; MARK 11:1; LUKE 2:25,38,41,43,45; 4:9; 5:17; 6:17; 9:31,51,53; 10:30; 13:4,22,33,34; 17:11; 19:11; 21:20,24; 23:28; 24:13,18,33,47,49,52; ACTS 1:8,12,19; 2:5,14; 4:6,16; 5:16,28; 6:7; 8:25-27; 9:2,13,21,26,28; 10:39; 12:25; 13:27,31; 15:2,4; 16:4; 19:21; 20:22; 21:4,11-13,15,31; 22:5,17,18; 23:11; 24:11; 25:3,20; ROM. 15:19,25,26,31; 1 COR. 16:3; GAL. 4:25,26; HEB. 12:22; REV. 3:12; 21:2,10

2420. ἱερωσύνη *hierōsunē*
HEB. 7:11,12,14,24

2421. Ἰεσσαί *Iessai*
MATT. 1:5,6; LUKE 3:32; ACTS 13:22; ROM. 15:12

2422. Ἰεφθάε *Iephthae*
HEB. 11:32

2423. Ἰεχονίας *Iechonias*
MATT. 1:11,12

2424. Ἰησοῦς Iēsous

MATT. 1:1,16,18,21,25; 2:1; 3:13,15,16,
4:1,7,10,12,17,18,23; 7:28; 8:3-5,7,10,13,14,
18,20,22,29,34; 9:2,4,9,10,12,15,19,22,23,
27,28,30,35; 10:5; 11:1,4,7,25; 12:1,15,25;
13:1,34,36,51,53,57; 14:1,12-14,16,22,25,27,
29,31; 15:1,16,21,28-30,32,34; 16:6,8,13,
17,20,21,24; 17:1,4,7-9,11,17-20,22,25,26;
18:1,2,22; 19:1,14,18,21,23,26,28; 20:17,22,
25,30,32,34; 21:1,6,11,12,16,21,24,27,31,42;
22:1,18,29,37,41; 23:1; 24:1,2,4; 26:1,4,6,10,
17,19,26,31,34,36,49-52,55,57,59,63,64,
69,71,75; 27:1,11,17,20,22,26,27,37,46,50,54,
55,57,58; 28:5,9,10,16,18; **MARK** 1:1,9,14,
17,24,25,41; 2:5,8,15,17,19; 3:7; 5:6,7,13,15,19-
21,27,30,36; 6:4,30,34; 7:27; 8:1,17,27; 9:2,4
,5,8,23,25,27,39; 10:5,14,18,21,23,24,27,29,32,
38,39,42,47,49,50,51,52; 11:6,7,11,14,15,
22,29,33; 12:17,24,29,34,35,41; 13:2,5; 14:6,
18,22,27,30,48,53,55,60,62,67,72; 15:1,5,15,
34,37,43; 16:6; **LUKE** 1:31; 2:21,27,43,52;
3:21,23; 4:1,4,8,12,14,34,35; 5:8,10,12,19,22,31;
6:3,9,11; 7:3,4,6,9,19,22,40; 8:28,30,35,38-41,
45,46,50; 9:33,36,41-43,47,50,58,60,62; 10:21,
29,30,37,39,41; 13:2,12,14; 14:3; 17:13,17;
18:16,19,22,24,37,38,40,42; 19:3,5,9,35; 20:8,
34; 22:47,48,51,52,63; 23:8,20,25,26,28,34,42,
43,46,52; 24:3,15,19,36; **JOHN** 1:17,29,36-
38,42,43,45,47,48,50; 2:1-4,7,11,13,19,22,24;
3:2,3,5,10,22; 4:1,2,6,7,10,13,16,17,21
,26,34,44,46-48,50,53,54; 5:1,6,8,13-17,19;
6:1,3,5,10,11,14,15,17,19,22,24,26,29,32,35,42,4
3,53,61,64,67,70; 7:1,6,14,16,21,28,33,37,39;
8:1,6,9-12,14,19-21,25,28,31,34,39,42,49,
54,58,59; 9:3,11,14,35,37,39,41; 10:6,7,23,25,
32,34; 11:4,5,9,13,14,17,20,21,23,25,30,32,33,
35,38-41,44-46,51,54,56; 12:1,3,7,9,11,12,
14,16,21-23,30,35,36,44; 13:1,3,7,8,10,21,23,25-
27,29,31,36,38; 14:6,9,23; 16:19,31; 17:1,3;
18:1,2,4,5,7,8,11,12,15,19,20,22,23,28,32-
34,36,37; 19:1,5,9,11,13,16,18-20,23,25,
26,28,30,33,38-40,42; 20:2,12,14-17,19,21,24,
26,29-31; 21:1,4,5,7,10,12-15,17,20-23,25;
ACTS 1:1,11,14,16,21; 2:22,32,36,38; 3:6,13,
20,26; 4:2,10,13,18,27,30,33; 5:30,40,42; 6:14;
7:45,55,59; 8:12,16,35,37; 9:5,17,27,29,34;
10:36,38; 11:17,20; 13:23,33; 15:11,26; 16:18,
31; 17:3,7,18; 18:5,28; 19:4,5,10,13,15,17;
20:21,24,35; 21:13; 22:8; 25:19; 26:9,15;
28:23,31; **ROM.** 1:1,3,6-8; 2:16; 3:22,24,26;
4:24; 5:1,11,15,17,21; 6:3,11,23; 7:25;
8:1,2,11,39; 10:9; 13:14; 14:14; 15:5,6,8,16,
17,30; 16:3,18,20,24,25,27; **1 COR.** 1:1-4,7-

10,30; 2:2; 3:11; 4:15; 5:4,5; 6:11; 8:6; 9:1;
11:23; 12:3; 15:31,57; 16:22-24; **2 COR.** 1:1-
3,14,19; 4:5,6,10,11,14; 5:18; 8:9; 11:4,31;
13:5,14; **GAL.** 1:1,3,12; 2:4,16; 3:1,14,22,26,28;
4:14; 5:6; 6:14,15,17,18; **EPH.** 1:1-3,5,15,17;
2:6,7,10,13,20; 3:1,9,11,14,21; 4:21; 5:20;
6:23,24; **PHIL.** 1:1,2,6,8,11,19,26; 2:5,10,11,
19,21; 3:3,8,12,14,20; 4:7,19,21,23; **COL.** 1:1-
4,28; 2:6; 3:17; **1 THESS.** 1:1,3,10; 2:14,15,19;
3:11,13; 4:1,2,14; 5:9,18,23,28; **2 THESS.**
1:1,2,7,8,12; 2:1,14,16; 3:6,12,18; **1 TIM.**
1:1,2,12,14-16; 2:5; 3:13; 4:6; 5:21; 6:3,13,14;
2 TIM. 1:1,2,9,10,13; 2:1,3,8,10; 3:12,15;
4:1,22; **TITUS** 1:1,4; 2:13; 3:6; **PHILE.**
1:1,3,5,6,9,23,25; **HEB.** 2:9; 3:1; 4:14; 6:20;
7:22; 10:10,19; 12:2,24; 13:8,12,20,21; **JAMES**
1:1; 2:1; **1 PET.** 1:1-3,7,13; 2:5; 3:21; 4:11;
5:10,14; **2 PET.** 1:1,2,8,11,14,16; 2:20; 3:18;
1 JOHN 1:3,7; 2:1,22; 3:23; 4:2,3,15; 5:1,5,6,20;
2 JOHN 1:3,7; **JUDE** 1:1,4,17,21; **REV.**
1:1,2,5,9; 12:17; 14:12; 17:6; 19:10; 20:4; 22:16,
20,21

2425. ἱκανός hikanos

MATT. 3:11; 8:8; 28:12; **MARK** 1:7; 10:46;
15:15; **LUKE** 3:16; 7:6,11,12; 8:27,32; 20:9;
22:38; 23:8,9; **ACTS** 5:37; 8:11; 9:23,43;
11:24,26; 12:12; 14:3,21; 17:9; 18:18; 19:19,26;
20:8,11,37; 22:6; 27:7,9; **1 COR.** 11:30; 15:9;
2 COR. 2:6,16; 3:5; **2 TIM.** 2:2

2426. ἱκανότης hikanotēs
2 COR. 3:5

2427. ἱκανόω hikanoō
2 COR. 3:6; **COL.** 1:12

2428. ἱκετηρία hiketēria
HEB. 5:7

2429. ἱκμάς hikmas
LUKE 8:6

2430. Ἰκόνιον Ikonion
ACTS 13:51; 14:1,19,21; 16:2; **2 TIM.** 3:11

2431. ἱλαρός hilaros
2 COR. 9:7

2432. *ἱλαρότης hilarotēs*
ROM. 12:8

2433. *ἱλάσκομαι hilaskomai*
LUKE 18:13; HEB. 2:17

2434. *ἱλασμός hilasmos*
1 JOHN 2:2; 4:10

2435. *ἱλαστήριος hilastērios*
ROM. 3:25; HEB. 9:5

2436. *ἵλεως hileōs*
MATT. 16:22; HEB. 8:12

2437. *Ἰλλυρικόν Illurikon*
ROM. 15:19

2438. *ἱμάς himas*
MARK 1:7; LUKE 3:16; JOHN 1:27; ACTS 22:25

2439. *ἱματίζω himatizō*
MARK 5:15; LUKE 8:35

2440. *ἱμάτιον himation*
MATT. 5:40; 9:16,20,21; 11:8; 14:36; 17:2; 21:7,8; 23:5; 24:18; 26:65; 27:31,35; MARK 2:21; 5:27,28,30; 6:56; 9:3; 10:50; 11:7,8; 13:16; 15:20,24; LUKE 5:36; 6:29; 7:25; 8:27,44; 19:35,36; 22:36; 23:34; JOHN 13:4,12; 19:2,5, 23,24; ACTS 7:58; 9:39; 12:8; 14:14; 16:22; 18:6; 22:20,23; HEB. 1:11; JAMES 5:2; 1 PET. 3:3; REV. 3:4,5,18; 4:4; 16:15; 19:13,16

2441. *ἱματισμός himatismos*
MATT. 27:35; LUKE 7:25; 9:29; JOHN 19:24; ACTS 20:33; 1 TIM. 2:9

2442. *ἱμείρομαι himeiromai*
1 THESS. 2:8

2444. *ἱνατί, ἵνα τί hinati, hina ti*
MATT. 9:4; 27:46; LUKE 13:7; ACTS 4:25; 7:26; 1 COR. 10:29

2445. *Ἰόππη Ioppē*
ACTS 9:36,38,42,43; 10:5,8,23,32; 11:5,13

2446. *Ἰορδάνης Iordanēs*
MATT. 3:5,6,13; 4:15,25; 19:1; MARK 1:5,9; 3:8; 10:1; LUKE 3:3; 4:1; JOHN 1:28; 3:26; 10:40

2447. *ἰός ios*
ROM. 3:13; JAMES 3:8; 5:3

2448. *Ἰούδα Iouda*
LUKE 1:39

2449. *Ἰουδαία Ioudaia*
MATT. 2:1,5,22; 3:1,5; 4:25; 19:1; 24:16; MARK 1:5; 3:7; 10:1; 13:14; LUKE 1:5,65; 2:4; 3:1; 5:17; 6:17; 7:17; 21:21; 23:5; JOHN 3:22; 4:3,47,54; 7:1,3; 11:7; ACTS 1:8; 2:9; 8:1; 9:31; 10:37; 11:1,29; 12:19; 15:1; 21:10; 26:20; 28:21; ROM. 15:31; 2 COR. 1:16; GAL. 1:22; 1 THESS. 2:14

2450. *ἰουδαΐζω ioudaizō*
GAL. 2:14

2451. *Ἰουδαϊκός Ioudaikos*
TITUS 1:14

2452. *Ἰουδαϊκῶς Ioudaikōs*
GAL. 2:14

2453. *Ἰουδαῖος Ioudaios*
MATT. 2:2; 27:11,29,37; 28:15; MARK 1:5; 7:3; 15:2,9,12,18,26; LUKE 7:3; 23:3,37,38,51; JOHN 1:19; 2:6,13,18,20; 3:1,22,25; 4:9,22; 5:1,10,15,16,18; 6:4,41,52; 7:1,2,11,13,15,35; 8:22,31,48,52,57; 9:18,22; 10:19,24,31,33; 11:8,19,31,33,36,45,54,55; 12:9,11; 13:33; 18:12,14,20,31,33,35,36,38,39; 19:3,7,12,14,19-21,31,38,40,42; 20:19; ACTS 2:5,10,14; 9:22,23; 10:22,28,39; 11:19; 12:3,11; 13:5,6,42,43,45,50; 14:1,2,4,5,19; 16:1,3,20; 17:1,5,10,13,17; 18:2,4,5,12,14,19,24,28; 19:10,13,14,17,33,34; 20:3,19,21; 21:11,20,21,27,39; 22:3,12,30; 23:12,20,27,30; 24:5,9,18,24,27; 25:2,7-10,15,24; 26:2-4,7,21; 28:17,19,29; ROM. 1:16; 2:9,10,17,28,29; 3:1,9,29; 9:24; 10:12; 1 COR. 1:22-24; 9:20; 10:32; 12:13; 2 COR. 11:24;

GAL. 2:13-15; 3:28; COL. 3:11; 1 THESS.
2:14; REV. 2:9; 3:9

2454. ιουδαϊσμός ioudaismos
GAL. 1:13,14

2455. Ἰούδας Ioudas
MATT. 1:2,3; 2:6; 10:4; 13:55; 26:14,25,47;
27:3; MARK 3:19; 6:3; 14:10,43; LUKE
3:26,30,33; 6:16; 22:3,47,48; JOHN 6:71; 12:4;
13:2,26,29; 14:22; 18:2,3,5; ACTS 1:13,16,25;
5:37; 9:11; 15:22,27,32; HEB. 7:14; 8:8; JUDE
1:1; REV. 5:5; 7:5

2456. Ἰουλία Ioulia
ROM. 16:15

2457. Ἰούλιος Ioulios
ACTS 27:1,3

2458. Ἰουνίας Iounias
ROM. 16:7

2459. Ἰοῦστος Ioustos
ACTS 1:23; 18:7; COL. 4:11

2460. ἱππεύς hippeus
ACTS 23:23,32

2461. ἱππικόν hippikon subst.
REV. 9:16

2462. ἵππος hippos
JAMES 3:3; REV. 6:2,4,5,8; 9:7,9,17; 14:20;
18:13; 19:11,14,18,19,21

2463. ἶρις iris
REV. 4:3; 10:1

2464. Ἰσαάκ Isaak
MATT. 1:2; 8:11; 22:32; MARK 12:26; LUKE
3:34; 13:28; 20:37; ACTS 3:13; 7:8,32; ROM.
9:7,10; GAL. 4:28; HEB. 11:9,17,18,20;
JAMES 2:21

2465. ἰσάγγελος isaggelos
LUKE 20:36

2466. Ἰσαχάρ Isachar
REV. 7:7

2467. ἴσημι isēmi
ACTS 26:4; HEB. 12:17

2468. ἴσθι isthi
(2nd sing. pres. imperf. of εἰμί)
MATT. 2:13; 5:25; MARK 5:34; LUKE 19:17;
1 TIM. 4:15

2469. Ἰσκαριώτης Iskariōtēs
MATT. 10:4; 26:14; MARK 3:19; 14:10;
LUKE 6:16; 22:3; JOHN 6:71; 12:4; 13:2,26;
14:22

2470. ἴσος isos
MATT. 20:12; MARK 14:56,59; LUKE 6:34;
JOHN 5:18; ACTS 11:17; PHIL. 2:6; REV.
21:16

2471. ἰσότης isotēs
2 COR. 8:14; COL. 4:1

2472. ἰσότιμος isotimos
2 PET. 1:1

2473. ἰσόψυχος isopsuchos
PHIL. 2:20

2474. Ἰσραήλ Israēl
MATT. 2:6,20,21; 8:10; 9:33; 10:6,23; 15:24,31;
19:28; 27:9,42; MARK 12:29; 15:32; LUKE
1:16,54,68,80; 2:25,32,34; 4:25,27; 7:9; 22:30;
24:21; JOHN 1:31,49; 3:10; 12:13; ACTS 1:6;
2:36; 4:8,10,27; 5:21,31; 7:23,37,42; 9:15; 10:36;
13:17,23,24; 28:20; ROM. 9:6,27,31; 10:1,19,
21; 11:2,7,25,26; 1 COR. 10:18; 2 COR. 3:7,13;
GAL. 6:16; EPH. 2:12; PHIL. 3:5; HEB.
8:8,10; 11:22; REV. 2:14; 7:4; 21:12

2475. Ἰσραηλίτης Israēlitēs
JOHN 1:47; ACTS 2:22; 3:12; 5:35; 13:16;
21:28; ROM. 9:4; 11:1; 2 COR. 11:22

2476. ἵστημι histēmi
MATT. 2:9; 4:5; 6:5; 12:25,26,46,47; 13:2;
16:28; 18:2,16; 20:3,6,32; 24:15; 25:33;

26:15,73; 27:11,47; **MARK** 3:24-26,31; 9:1,36;
10:49; 11:5; 13:9,14; **LUKE** 1:11; 4:9; 5:1,2;
6:8,17; 7:14,38; 8:20,44; 9:27,47; 11:18; 13:25;
17:12; 18:11,13,40; 19:8; 21:36; 23:10,35,49;
24:36; **JOHN** 1:26,35; 3:29; 6:22; 7:37; 8:3,9,44;
11:56; 12:29; 18:5,16,18,25; 19:25; 20:11,14,
19,26; 21:4; **ACTS** 1:11,23; 2:14; 3:8; 4:7,14;
5:20,23,25,27; 6:6,13; 7:33,55,56,60; 8:38; 9:7;
10:30; 11:13; 12:14; 16:9; 17:22,31; 21:40;
22:25,30; 24:20,21; 25:10,18; 26:6,16,22; 27:21;
ROM. 3:31; 5:2; 10:3; 11:20; 14:4; **1 COR.**
7:37; 10:12; 15:1; **2 COR.** 1:24; 13:1; **EPH.**
6:11,13,14; **COL.** 4:12; **2 TIM.** 2:19; **HEB.**
10:9,11; **JAMES** 2:3; 5:9; **1 PET.** 5:12; **JUDE**
1:24; **REV.** 3:20; 5:6; 6:17; 7:1,9,11; 8:2,3;
10:5,8; 11:4,11; 12:4; 13:1; 14:1; 15:2;
18:10,15,17; 19:17; 20:12

2477. ἱστορέω historeō
GAL. 1:18

2478. ἰσχυρός iskuros
MATT. 3:11; 12:29; 14:30; **MARK** 1:7; 3:27;
LUKE 3:16; 11:21,22; 15:14; **1 COR.** 1:25,27;
4:10; 10:22; **2 COR.** 10:10; **HEB.** 5:7; 6:18;
11:34; **1 JOHN** 2:14; **REV.** 5:2; 10:1;
18:8,10,21; 19:6,18

2479. ἰσχύς ischus
MARK 12:30,33; **LUKE** 10:27; **EPH.** 1:19;
6:10; **2 THESS.** 1:9; **1 PET.** 4:11; **2 PET.** 2:11;
REV. 5:12; 7:12 18:2

2480. ἰσχύω ischuō
MATT. 5:13; 8:28; 9:12; 26:40; **MARK** 2:17;
5:4; 9:18; 14:37; **LUKE** 6:48; 8:43; 13:24;
14:6,29,30; 16:3; 20:26; **JOHN** 21:6; **ACTS**
6:10; 15:10; 19:16,20; 25:7; 27:16; **GAL.** 5:6;
6:15; **PHIL.** 4:13; **HEB.** 9:17; **JAMES** 5:16;
REV. 12:8

2481. ἴσως isōs
LUKE 20:13

2482. Ἰταλία Italia
ACTS 18:2; 27:1,6; **HEB.** 13:24

2483. Ἰταλικός Italikos
ACTS 10:1

2484. Ἰτουραῖος Itouraios
LUKE 3:1

2485. ἰχθύδιον ichthudion
MATT. 15:34; **MARK** 8:7

2486. ἰχθύς ichthus
MATT. 7:10; 14:17,19; 15:36; 17:27; **MARK**
6:38,41,43; **LUKE** 5:6,9; 9:13,16; 11:11; 24:42;
JOHN 21:6,8,11; **1 COR.** 15:39

2487. ἴχνος ichnos
ROM. 4:12; **2 COR.** 12:18; **1 PET.** 2:21

2488. Ἰωάθαμ Iōatham
MATT. 1:9

2489. Ἰωάννα Iōanna
LUKE 8:3; 24:10

2490. Ἰωαννᾶς Iōannas
LUKE 3:27

2491. A. Ἰωάννης Iōannēs
(The Apostle)

MATT. 4:21; 10:2; 17:1; **MARK**
1:19,29; 3:17; 5:37; 9:2,38; 10:35,41;
13:3; 14:33; **LUKE** 5:10; 6:14; 8:51;
9:28,49,54; 22:8; **ACTS** 1:13; 3:1,3,4,11;
4:13,19; 8:14; 12:2,12; **GAL.** 2:9; **REV.**
1:1,4,9; 21:2; 22:8

B. Ἰωάννης Iōannēs
(The Baptist)

MATT. 3:1,4,13,14; 4:12; 9:14; 11:2,4,7,
11-13,18; 14:2-4,8,10; 16:14; 17:13
21:25,26,32; **MARK** 1:4,6,9,14; 2:18;
6:14,16-18,20,24,25; 8:28; 11:30,32;
LUKE 1:13,60,63; 3:2,15,16,20; 5:33;
7:18-20,22,24,28,29,33; 9:7,9,19; 11:1;
16:16; 20:4,6 **JOHN** 1:6,15,19,26,28,29,
32,35, 40; 3:23-27; 4:1; 5:33,36; 10:40,
41; **ACTS** 1:5,22; 10:37; 11:16; 13:24,
25; 18:25; 19:3,4

C. Ἰωάννης Iōannēs
(The Chief Priest)

ACTS 4:6

D. Ἰωάννης Iōannēs
   (John Mark)
   ACTS 12:25; 13:5,13; 15:37

2492. Ἰώβ Iōb
JAMES 5:11

2493. Ἰωήλ Iōēl
ACTS 2:16

2494. Ἰωνάν Iōnan
LUKE 3:30

2495. A. Ἰωνᾶς Iōnas
   (The Prophet)
   MATT. 12:39-41; 16:4; LUKE
   11:29,30,32

   B. Ἰωνᾶς Iōnas
   JOHN 1:42; 21:15-17

2496. Ἰωράμ Iōram
MATT. 1:8

2497. Ἰωρείμ Iōreim
LUKE 3:29

2498. Ἰωσαφάτ Iōsaphat
MATT. 1:8

2499. Ἰωσή Iōsē
LUKE 3:29

2500. Ἰωσῆς Iōsēs
MATT. 13:55; 27:56; MARK 6:3; 15:40,47;
ACTS 4:36

2501. A. Ἰωσήφ Iōsēph
   (Of Arimathaea)
   MATT. 27:57,59; MARK 15:43,45
   LUKE 23:50; JOHN 19:38

   B. Ἰωσήφ Iōsēph
   (Barsabas)
   ACTS 1:23

   C. Ἰωσήφ Iōsēph
   (Son of Jacob)

JOHN 4:5; ACTS 7:9,13,14,18; HEB.
11:21,22; REV. 7:8

D. Ἰωσήφ Iōsēph
   (Son of Judas)
   LUKE 3:26

E. Ἰωσήφ Iōsēph
   (Son of Jonan)
   LUKE 3:30

F. Ἰωσήφ Iōsēph
   (Husband of Mary)
   MATT. 1:16,18-20,24; 2:13,19; LUKE
   1:27; 2:4,16,33,43; 3:23; 4:22; JOHN
   1:45; 6:42

G. Ἰωσήφ Iōsēph
   (Son of Mattathias)
   LUKE 3:24

2502. Ἰωσίας Iōsias
MATT. 1:10,11

2503. ἰῶτα iōta
MATT. 5:18

K

2504. κἀγώ kagō
MATT. 2:8; 10:32,33; 11:28; 16:18; 21:24;
26:15; MARK 11:29; LUKE 1:3; 2:48; 11:9;
16:9; 20:3; 22:29; JOHN 1:31,33,34; 5:17; 6:56,
57; 7:28; 8:26; 10:15,27,28,38; 12:32; 14:20;
15:4,5,9; 17:18,21,26; 20:15,21; ACTS 8:19;
10:26; 22:13,19; 26:29; ROM. 3:7; 11:3;
1 COR. 2:1; 7:8,40; 10:33; 11:1; 15:8; 16:4;
2 COR. 6:17; 11:16,18,21,22; 12:20; GAL.
4:12; 6:14; EPH. 1:15; PHIL. 2:19,28;
1 THESS. 3:5; HEB. 8:9; JAMES 2:18;
REV. 2:6,27; 3:10,21

2505. καθά katha
MATT. 27:10

2506. καθαίρεσις kathairesis
2 COR. 10:4,8; 13:10

2507. καθαιρέω kathaireō
MARK 15:36,46; LUKE 1:52; 12:18; 23:53;
ACTS 13:19,29; 19:27; **2 COR.** 10:5

2508. καθαίρω kathairō
JOHN 15:2; HEB. 10:2

2509. καθάπερ kathaper
ROM. 4:6; 12:4; **1 COR.** 12:12; **2 COR.** 1:14;
3:13,18; 8:11; **1 THESS.** 2:11; 3:6,12; 4:5; **HEB.**
4:2; 5:4

2510. καθάπτω kathaptō
ACTS 28:3

2511. καθαρίζω katharizō
MATT. 8:2,3; 10:8; 11:5; 23:25,26; **MARK**
1:40-42; 7:19; LUKE 4:27; 5:12,13; 7:22; 11:39;
17:14,17; ACTS 10:15; 11:9; 15:9; **2 COR.** 7:1;
EPH. 5:26; TITUS 2:14; HEB. 9:14,22,23;
JAMES 4:8; **1 JOHN** 1:7,9

2512. καθαρισμός katharismos
MARK 1:44; LUKE 2:22; 5:14; JOHN 2:6;
3:25; HEB. 1:3; **2 PET.** 1:9

2513. καθαρός katharos
MATT. 5:8; 23:26; 27:59; LUKE 11:41; JOHN
13:10,11; 15:3; ACTS 18:6; 20:26; ROM.
14:20; **1 TIM.** 1:5; 3:9; **2 TIM.** 1:3; 2:22;
TITUS 1:15; HEB. 10:22; JAMES 1:27; **1 PET.**
1:22; REV. 15:6; 19:8,14; 21:18,21; 22:1

2514. καθαρότης katharotēs
HEB. 9:13

2515. καθέδρα kathedra
MATT. 21:12; 23:2; MARK 11:15

2516. καθέζομαι kathezomai
MATT. 26:55; LUKE 2:46; JOHN 4:6; 11:20;
20:12; ACTS 6:15

2517. καθεξῆς kathexēs
LUKE 1:3; 8:1; ACTS 3:24; 11:4; 18:23

2518. καθεύδω katheudō
MATT. 8:24; 9:24; 13:25; 25:5; 26:40,43,45;

MARK 4:27,38; 5:39; 13:36; 14:37,40,41;
LUKE 8:52; 22:46; EPH. 5:14; **1 THESS.**
5:6,7,10

2519. καθηγητής kathēgētēs
MATT. 23:8,10

2520. καθήκω kathēkō
ACTS 22:22; ROM. 1:28

2521. κάθημαι kathēmai
MATT. 4:16; 9:9; 11:16; 13:1,2; 15:29; 20:30;
22:44; 23:22; 24:3; 26:58,64,69; 27:19,36,61;
28:2; MARK 2:6,14; 3:32,34; 4:1; 5:15; 10:46;
12:36; 13:3; 14:62; 16:5; LUKE 1:79; 5:17,27;
7:32; 8:35; 10:13; 18:35; 20:42; 21:35; 22:55,
56,69; JOHN 2:14; 6:3; 9:8; 12:15; **ACTS**
2:2,34; 3:10; 8:28; 14:8; 20:9; 23:3; **1 COR.**
14:30; COL. 3:1; HEB. 1:13; JAMES 2:3;
REV. 4:2-4,9,10; 5:1,7,13; 6:2,4,5,8,16; 7:10,15;
9:17; 11:16; 14:14-16; 17:1,3,9,15; 18:7; 19:4,
11,18,19,21; 20:11; 21:5

2522. καθημερινός kathēmerinos
ACTS 6:1

2523. καθίζω kathizō
MATT. 5:1; 13:48; 19:28; 20:21,23; 23:2; 25:31;
26:36; MARK 9:35; 10:37,40; 11:2,7; 12:41;
14:32; 16:19; LUKE 4:20; 5:3; 14:28,31; 16:6;
19:30; 22:30; 24:49; JOHN 8:2; 12:14; 19:13;
ACTS 2:3,30; 8:31; 12:21; 13:14; 16:13; 18:11;
25:6,17; **1 COR.** 6:4; 10:7; EPH. 1:20;
2 THESS. 2:4; HEB. 1:3; 8:1; 10:12; 12:2;
REV. 3:21; 20:4

2524. καθίημι kathiēmi
LUKE 5:19; ACTS 9:25; 10:11; 11:5

2525. καθίστημι kathistēmi
MATT. 24:45,47; 25:21,23; LUKE 12:14,42,44;
ACTS 6:3; 7:10,27,35; 17:15; ROM. 5:19;
TITUS 1:5; HEB. 2:7; 5:1; 7:28; 8:3; JAMES
3:6; 4:4; **2 PET.** 1:8

2526. καθό katho
ROM. 8:26; **2 COR.** 8:12; **1 PET.** 4:13

2527. καθόλου katholou
ACTS 4:18

2528. καθοπλίζω kathoplizō
LUKE 11:21

2529. καθοράω kathoraō
ROM. 1:20

2530. καθότι kathoti
LUKE 1:7; 19:9; ACTS 2:24,45; 4:35

2533. Καϊάφας Kaiaphas
MATT. 26:3,57; LUKE 3:2; JOHN 11:49;
18:13,14,24,28; ACTS 4:6

2535. Κάϊν Kain
HEB. 11:4; 1 JOHN 3:12; JUDE 1:11

2536. Καϊνάν Kainan
LUKE 3:36,37

2537. καινός kainos
MATT. 9:17; 13:52; 26:28,29; 27:60; MARK
1:27; 2:21,22; 14:24,25; 16:17; LUKE 5:36,38;
22:20; JOHN 13:34; 19:41; ACTS 17:19,21;
1 COR. 11:25; 2 COR. 3:6; 5:17; GAL. 6:15;
EPH. 2:15; 4:24; HEB. 8:8,13; 9:15; 2 PET.
3:13; 1 JOHN 2:7,8; 2 JOHN 1:5; REV. 2:17;
3:12; 5:9; 14:3; 21:1,2,5

2538. καινότης kainotēs
ROM. 6:4; 7:6

2539. καίπερ kaiper
PHIL. 3:4; HEB. 5:8; 7:5; 12:17; 2 PET. 1:12;
REV. 17:8

2540. καιρός kairos
MATT. 8:29; 11:25; 12:1; 13:30; 14:1; 16:3;
21:34,41; 24:45; 26:18; MARK 1:15; 10:30;
11:13; 12:2; 13:33; LUKE 1:20; 4:13; 8:13;
12:42,56; 13:1; 18:30; 19:44; 20:10; 21:8,24,36;
JOHN 5:4; 7:6,8; ACTS 1:7; 3:19; 7:20; 12:1;
13:11; 14:17; 17:26; 19:23; 24:25; ROM. 3:26;
5:6; 8:18; 9:9; 11:5; 12:11; 13:11; 1 COR. 4:5;
7:5,29; 2 COR. 6:2; 8:14; GAL. 4:10; 6:9,10;
EPH. 1:10; 2:12; 5:16; 6:18; COL. 4:5;
1 THESS. 2:17; 5:1; 2 THESS. 2:6; 1 TIM. 2:6;
4:1; 6:15; 2 TIM. 3:1; 4:3,6; TITUS 1:3; HEB.
9:9,10; 11:11,15; 1 PET. 1:5,11; 4:17; 5:6; REV.
1:3; 11:18; 12:12,14; 22:10

2541. Καῖσαρ Kaisar
MATT. 22:17,21; MARK 12:14,16,17; LUKE
2:1; 3:1; 20:22,24,25; 23:2; JOHN 19:12,15;
ACTS 11:28; 17:7; 25:8,10-12,21; 26:32; 27:24;
28:19; PHIL. 4:22

2542. A. Καισάρεια Kaisareia
  (Caesarea Philippi)
  MATT. 16:13; MARK 8:27

  B. Καισάρεια Kaisareia
  (On the East Coast of the
  Mediterranean)
  ACTS 8:40; 9:30; 10:1,24; 11:11; 12:19;
  18:22; 21:8,16; 23:23,33; 25:1,4,6,13

2543. καίτοι kaitoi
HEB. 4:3

2544. καίτοιγε kaitoige
JOHN 4:2; ACTS 14:17; 17:27

2545. καίω kaiō
MATT. 5:15; LUKE 12:35; 24:32; JOHN 5:35;
15:6; 1 COR. 13:3; HEB. 12:18; REV. 4:5;
8:8,10; 19:20; 21:8

2546. κἀκεῖ kakei
MATT. 5:23; 10:11; 28:10; MARK 1:35,38;
JOHN 11:54; ACTS 14:7; 17:13; 22:10; 25:20;
27:6

2547. κἀκεῖθεν kakeithen
MARK 10:1; ACTS 7:4; 13:21; 14:26; 20:15;
21:1; 27:4,12; 28:15

2548. κἀκεῖνος kakeinos
MATT. 15:18; 20:4; 23:23; MARK 12:4,5;
16:11,13; LUKE 11:7,42; 20:11; 22:12; JOHN
6:57; 7:29; 10:16; 14:12; 17:24; 19:35; ACTS
5:37; 15:11; 18:19; 1 COR. 10:6; 2 TIM. 2:12;
HEB. 4:2

2549. κακία kakia
MATT. 6:34; ACTS 8:22; ROM. 1:29; 1 COR.
5:8; 14:20; EPH. 4:31; COL. 3:8; TITUS 3:3;
JAMES 1:21; 1 PET. 2:1,16

2550. κακοήθεια kakoētheia
ROM. 1:29

2551. κακολογέω *kakologeō*
MATT. 15:4; **MARK** 7:10; 9:39; **ACTS** 19:9

2552. κακοπάθεια *kakopatheia*
JAMES 5:10

2553. κακοπαθέω *kakopatheō*
2 TIM. 2:3,9; 4:5; JAMES 5:13

2554. κακοποιέω *kakopoieō*
MARK 3:4; **LUKE** 6:9; **1 PET.** 3:17; **3 JOHN**
1:11

2555. κακοποιός *kakopoios*
JOHN 18:30; **1 PET.** 2:12,14; 3:16; 4:15

2556. κακός *kakos*
MATT. 21:41; 24:48; 27:23; **MARK** 7:21;
15:14; **LUKE** 16:25; 23:22; **JOHN** 18:23;
ACTS 9:13; 16:28; 23:9; 28:5; **ROM.** 1:30; 2:9;
3:8; 7:19,21; 9:11; 12:17,21; 13:3,4,10; 14:20;
16:19; **1 COR.** 10:6; 13:5; 15:33; **2 COR.** 5:10;
13:7; **PHIL.** 3:2; **COL.** 3:5; **1 THESS.** 5:15;
1 TIM. 6:10; **2 TIM.** 4:14; **TITUS** 1:12; **HEB.**
5:14; **JAMES** 1:13; 3:8; **1 PET.** 3:9-12;
3 JOHN 1:11; **REV.** 2:2; 16:2

2557. κακοῦργος *kakourgos*
LUKE 23:32,33,39; **2 TIM.** 2:9

2558. κακουχέω *kakoucheō*
HEB. 11:37; 13:3

2559. κακόω *kakoō*
ACTS 7:6,19; 12:1; 14:2; 18:10; **1 PET.** 3:13

2560. κακῶς *kakōs*
MATT. 4:24; 8:16; 9:12; 14:35; 15:22; 17:15;
21:41; **MARK** 1:32,34; 2:17; 6:55; **LUKE** 5:31;
7:2; **JOHN** 18:23; **ACTS** 23:5; **JAMES** 4:3

2561. κάκωσις *kakōsis*
ACTS 7:34

2562. καλάμη *kalamē*
1 COR. 3:12

2563. κάλαμος *kalamos*
MATT. 11:7; 12:20; 27:29,30,48; **MARK**
15:19,36; **LUKE** 7:24; **3 JOHN** 1:13; **REV.**
11:1; 21:15,16

2564. καλέω *kaleō*
MATT. 1:21,23,25; 2:7,15,23; 4:21; 5:9,19;
9:13; 10:25; 20:8; 21:13; 22:3,4,8,9,43,45; 23:7-
10; 25:14; 27:8; **MARK** 1:20; 2:17; 11:17;
LUKE 1:13,31,32,35,36,59-62,76; 2:4,21,23;
5:32; 6:15,46; 7:11,39; 8:2; 9:10; 10:39; 14:7-
10,12,13,16,17,24; 15:19,21; 19:2,13,29; 20:44;
21:37; 22:25; 23:33; **JOHN** 1:42; 2:2; 10:3;
ACTS 1:12,19,23; 3:11; 4:18; 7:58; 9:11; 10:1;
13:1; 14:12; 15:37; 24:2; 27:8,14,16; 28:1;
ROM. 4:17; 8:30; 9:7,11,24-26; **1 COR.** 1:9;
7:15,17,18,20-22,24; 10:27; 15:9; **GAL.** 1:6,15;
5:8,13; **EPH.** 4:1,4; **COL.** 3:15; **1 THESS.** 2:12;
4:7; 5:24; **2 THESS.** 2:14; **1 TIM.** 6:12; **2 TIM.**
1:9; **HEB.** 2:11; 3:13; 5:4; 9:15; 11:8,18;
JAMES 2:23; **1 PET.** 1:15; 2:9,21; 3:6,9; 5:10;
2 PET. 1:3; **1 JOHN** 3:1; **REV.** 1:9; 11:8; 12:9;
16:16; 19:9,11,13

2565. καλλιέλαιος *kallielaios*
ROM. 11:24

2566. κάλλιων *kalliōn*
ACTS 25:10

2567. καλοδιδάσκαλος *kalodidaskalos*
TITUS 2:3

2568. Καλοὶ Λιμένες *Kaloi Limenes*
ACTS 27:8

2569. καλοποιέω *kalopoieō*
2 THESS. 3:13

2570. καλός *kalos*
MATT. 3:10; 5:16; 7:17-19; 12:33; 13:8,23,
24,27,37,38,45,48; 15:26; 17:4; 18:8,9; 26:10,24;
MARK 4:8,20; 7:27; 9:5,42,43,45,47,50;
14:6,21; **LUKE** 3:9; 6:38,43; 8:15; 9:33; 14:34;
21:5; **JOHN** 2:10; 10:11,14,32,33; **ACTS** 27:8;
ROM. 7:16,18,21; 12:17; 14:21; **1 COR.** 5:6;
7:1,8,26; 9:15; **2 COR.** 8:21; 13:7; **GAL.** 4:18;
6:9; **1 THESS.** 5:21; **1 TIM.** 1:8,18; 2:3;
3:1,7,13; 4:4,6; 5:4,10,25; 6:12,13,18,19; **2 TIM.**

1:14; 2:3; 4:7; **TITUS** 2:7,14; 3:8,14; **HEB.** 5:14; 6:5; 10:24; 13:9,18; **JAMES** 2:7; 3:13; 4:17; **1 PET.** 2:12; 4:10

2571. κάλυμμα kalumma
2 COR. 3:13-16

2572. καλύπτω kaluptō
MATT. 8:24; 10:26; **LUKE** 8:16; 23:30; **2 COR.** 4:3; **JAMES** 5:20; **1 PET.** 4:8

2573. καλῶς kalōs
MATT. 5:44; 12:12; 15:7; **MARK** 7:6,9,37; 12:28,32; 16:18; **LUKE** 6:26,27; 20:39; **JOHN** 4:17; 8:48; 13:13; 18:23; **ACTS** 10:33; 25:10; 28:25; **ROM.** 11:20; **1 COR.** 7:37,38; 14:17; **2 COR.** 11:4; **GAL.** 4:17; 5:7; **PHIL.** 4:14; **1 TIM.** 3:4,12,13; 5:17; **HEB.** 13:18; **JAMES** 2:3,8,19; **2 PET.** 1:19; **3 JOHN** 1:6

2574. κάμηλος kamēlos
MATT. 3:4; 19:24; 23:24; **MARK** 1:6; 10:25; **LUKE** 18:25

2575. κάμινος kaminos
MATT. 13:42,50; **REV.** 1:15; 9:2

2576. καμμύω kammuō
MATT. 13:15; **ACTS** 28:27

2577. κάμνω kamnō
HEB. 12:3; **JAMES** 5:15; **REV.** 2:3

2578. κάμπτω kamptō
ROM. 11:4; 14:11; **EPH.** 3:14; **PHIL.** 2:10

2579. κἄν kan
MATT. 21:21; 26:35; **MARK** 5:28; 6:56; 16:18; **LUKE** 13:9; **JOHN** 8:14; 10:38; 11:25; **ACTS** 5:15; **2 COR.** 11:16; **HEB.** 12:20; **JAMES** 5:15

2580. Κανᾶ Kana
JOHN 2:1,11; 4:46; 21:2

2581. Κανανίτης Kananitēs
MATT. 10:4; **MARK** 3:18

2582. Κανδάκη Kandakē
ACTS 8:27

2583. κανών kanōn
2 COR. 10:13,15,16; **GAL.** 6:16; **PHIL.** 3:16

2584. Καπερναούμ Kapernaoum
MATT. 4:13; 8:5; 11:23; 17:24; **MARK** 1:21; 2:1; 9:33; **LUKE** 4:23,31; 7:1; 10:15; **JOHN** 2:12; 4:46; 6:17,24,59

2585. καπηλεύω kapēleuō
2 COR. 2:17

2586. καπνός kapnos
ACTS 2:19; **REV.** 8:4; 9:2,3,17,18; 14:11; 15:8; 18:9,18; 19:3

2587. Καππαδοκία Kappadokia
ACTS 2:9; **1 PET.** 1:1

2588. καρδία kardia
MATT. 5:8,28; 6:21; 9:4; 11:29; 12:34,35,40; 13:15,19; 15:8,18,19; 18:35; 22:37; 24:48; **MARK** 2:6,8; 3:5; 4:15; 6:52; 7:6,19,21; 8:17; 11:23; 12:30,33; **LUKE** 1:17,51,66; 2:19,35,51; 3:15; 4:18; 5:22; 6:45; 8:12,15; 9:47; 10:27; 12:34,45; 16:15; 21:14,34; 24:25,32,38; **JOHN** 12:40; 13:2; 14:1,27; 16:6,22; **ACTS** 2:26,37,46; 4:32; 5:3,4; 7:23,39,51,54; 8:21,22,37; 11:23; 13:22; 14:17; 15:9; 16:14; 21:13; 28:27; **ROM.** 1:21,24; 2:5,15,29; 5:5; 6:17; 8:27; 9:2; 10:1,6,8-10; 16:18; **1 COR.** 2:9; 4:5; 7:37; 14:25; **2 COR.** 1:22; 2:4; 3:2,3,15; 4:6; 5:12; 6:11; 7:3; 8:16; 9:7; **GAL.** 4:6; **EPH.** 3:17; 4:18; 5:19; 6:5,22; **PHIL.** 1:7; 4:7; **COL.** 2:2; 3:15,16,22; 4:8; **1 THESS.** 2:4,17; 3:13; **2 THESS.** 2:17; 3:5; **1 TIM.** 1:5; **2 TIM.** 2:22; **HEB.** 3:8,10,12,15; 4:7,12; 8:10; 10:16,22; 13:9; **JAMES** 1:26; 3:14; 4:8; 5:5,8; **1 PET.** 1:22; 3:4,15; **2 PET.** 1:19; 2:14; **1 JOHN** 3:19-21; **REV.** 2:23; 17:17; 18:7

2589. καρδιογνώστης kardiognōstēs
ACTS 1:24; 15:8

2590. καρπός karpos
MATT. 3:8,10; 7:16-20; 12:33; 13:8,26; 21:19; 34,41,43; **MARK** 4:7,8,29; 11:14; 12:2; **LUKE** 1:42; 3:8,9; 6:43,44; 8:8; 12:17; 13:6,7,9; 20:10;

JOHN 4:36; 12:24; 15:2,4,5,8,16; ACTS 2:30;
ROM. 1:13; 6:21,22; 15:28; 1 COR. 9:7; GAL.
5:22; EPH. 5:9; PHIL. 1:11,22; 4:17; 2 TIM.
2:6; HEB. 12:11; 13:15; JAMES 3:17,18;
5:7,18; REV. 22:2

2591. Κάρπος Karpos
2 TIM. 4:13

2592. καρποφορέω karpophoreō
MATT. 13:23; MARK 4:20,28; LUKE 8:15;
ROM. 7:4,5; COL. 1:6,10

2593. καρποφόρος karpophoros
ACTS 14:17

2594. καρτερέω kartereō
HEB. 11:27

2595. κάρφος karphos
MATT. 7:3-5; LUKE 6:41,42

2597. καταβαίνω katabainō
MATT. 3:16; 7:25,27; 8:1; 14:29; 17:9; 24:17;
27:40,42; 28:2; MARK 1:10; 3:22; 9:9; 13:15;
15:30,32; LUKE 2:51; 3:22; 6:17; 8:23; 9:54;
10:30,31; 17:31; 18:14; 19:5,6; 22:44; JOHN
1:32,33,51; 2:12; 3:13; 4:47,49,51; 5:4,7;
6:16,33,38,41,42,50,51,58; ACTS 7:15,34;
8:15,26,38; 10:11,20,21; 11:5; 14:11,25; 16:8;
18:22; 20:10; 23:10; 24:1,22; 25:6,7; ROM.
10:7; EPH. 4:9,10; 1 THESS. 4:16; JAMES
1:17; REV. 3:12; 10:1; 12:12; 13:13; 16:21;
18:1; 20:1,9; 21:2,10

2598. καταβάλλω kataballō
2 COR. 4:9; HEB. 6:1; REV. 12:10

2599. καταβαρέω katabareō
2 COR. 12:16

2600. κατάβασις katabasis
LUKE 19:37

2601. καταβιβάζω katabibazō
MATT. 11:23; LUKE 10:15

2602. καταβολή katabolē
MATT. 13:35; 25:34; LUKE 11:50; JOHN
17:24; EPH. 1:4; HEB. 4:3; 9:26; 11:11; 1 PET.
1:20; REV. 13:8; 17:8

2603. καταβραβεύω katabrabeuō
COL. 2:18

2604. καταγγελεύς kataggeleus
ACTS 17:18

2605. καταγγέλλω kataggellō
ACTS 4:2; 13:5,38; 15:36; 16:17,21; 17:3,13,23;
26:23; ROM. 1:8; 1 COR. 2:1; 9:14; 11:26;
PHIL. 1:16,18; COL. 1:28

2606. καταγελάω katagelaō
MATT. 9:24; MARK 5:40; LUKE 8:53

2607. καταγινώσκω kataginōskō
GAL. 2:11; 1 JOHN 3:20,21

2608. κατάγνυμι katagnumi
MATT. 12:20; JOHN 19:31-33

2609. κατάγω katagō
LUKE 5:11; ACTS 9:30; 21:3; 22:30;
23:15,20,28; 27:3; 28:12; ROM. 10:6

2610. καταγωνίζομαι katagōnizomai
HEB. 11:33

2611. καταδέω katadeō
LUKE 10:34

2612. κατάδηλος katadēlos
HEB. 7:15

2613. καταδικάζω katadikazō
MATT. 12:7,37; LUKE 6:37; JAMES 5:6

2614. καταδιώκω katadiōkō
MARK 1:36

2615. καταδουλόω katadouloō
2 COR. 11:20; GAL. 2:4

2616. καταδυναστεύω *katadunasteuō*
ACTS 10:38; JAMES 2:6

2617. καταισχύνω *kataischunō*
LUKE 13:17; ROM. 5:5; 9:33; 10:11; 1 COR.
1:27; 11:4,5,22; 2 COR. 7:14; 9:4; 1 PET. 2:6;
3:16

2618. κατακαίω *katakaiō*
MATT. 3:12; 13:30,40; LUKE 3:17; ACTS
19:19; 1 COR. 3:15; HEB. 13:11; 2 PET. 3:10;
REV. 8:7; 17:16; 18:8

2619. κατακαλύπτω *katakaluptō*
1 COR. 11:6,7

2620. κατακαυχάομαι
katakauchaomai
ROM. 11:18; JAMES 2:13; 3:14

2621. κατάκειμαι *katakeimai*
MARK 1:30; 2:4,15; 14:3; LUKE 5:25,29;
JOHN 5:3,6; ACTS 9:33; 28:8; 1 COR. 8:10

2622. κατακλάω *kataklaō*
MARK 6:41; LUKE 9:16

2623. κατακλείω *katakleiō*
LUKE 3:20; ACTS 26:10

2624. κατακληροδοτέω
kataklērodoteō
ACTS 13:19

2625. κατακλίνω *kataklinō*
LUKE 9:14; 14:8; 24:30

2626. κατακλύζω *katakluzō*
2 PET. 3:6

2627. κατακλυσμός *kataklusmos*
MATT. 24:38,39; LUKE 17:27; 2 PET. 2:5

2628. κατακολουθέω *katakoloutheō*
LUKE 23:55; ACTS 16:17

2629. κατακόπτω *katakoptō*
MARK 5:5

2630. κατακρημνίζω *katakrēmnizō*
LUKE 4:29

2631. κατάκριμα *katakrima*
ROM. 5:16,18; 8:1

2632. κατακρίνω *katakrinō*
MATT. 12:41,42; 20:18; 27:3; MARK 10:33;
14:64; 16:16; LUKE 11:31,32; JOHN 8:10,11;
ROM. 2:1; 8:3,34; 14:23; 1 COR. 11:32; HEB.
11:7; JAMES 5:9; 2 PET. 2:6

2633. κατάκρισις *katakrisis*
2 COR. 3:9; 7:3

2634. κατακυριεύω *katakurieuō*
MATT. 20:25; MARK 10:42; ACTS 19:16;
1 PET. 5:3

2635. καταλαλέω *katalaleō*
JAMES 4:11; 1 PET. 2:12; 3:16

2636. καταλαλιά *katalalia*
2 COR. 12:20; 1 PET. 2:1

2637. κατάλαλος *katalalos*
ROM. 1:30

2638. καταλαμβάνω *katalambanō*
MARK 9:18; JOHN 1:5; 8:3,4; 12:35; ACTS
4:13; 10:34; 25:25; ROM. 9:30; 1 COR. 9:24;
EPH. 3:18; PHIL. 3:12,13; 1 THESS. 5:4

2639. καταλέγω *katalegō*
1 TIM. 5:9

2640. κατάλειμμα *kataleimma*
ROM. 9:27

2641. καταλείπω *kataleipō*
MATT. 4:13; 16:4; 19:5; 21:17; MARK 10:7;
12:19; 14:52; LUKE 5:28; 10:40; 15:4; 20:31;
JOHN 8:9; ACTS 2:31; 6:2; 18:19; 21:3; 24:27;
25:14; ROM. 11:4; EPH. 5:31; 1 THESS. 3:1;
TITUS 1:5; HEB. 4:1; 11:27; 2 PET. 2:15

2642. καταλιθάζω *katalithazō*
LUKE 20:6

2643. καταλλαγή *katallagē*
ROM. 5:11; 11:15; **2 COR.** 5:18,19

2644. καταλλάσσω, καταλλάττω
katallassō, katallattō
ROM. 5:10; **1 COR.** 7:11; **2 COR.** 5:18-20

2645. κατάλοιπος *kataloipos*
ACTS 15:17

2646. κατάλυμα *kataluma*
MARK 14:14; **LUKE** 2:7; 22:11

2647. καταλύω *kataluō*
MATT. 5:17; 24:2; 26:61; 27:40; **MARK** 13:2;
14:58; 15:29; **LUKE** 9:12; 19:7; 21:6; **ACTS**
5:38,39; 6:14; **ROM.** 14:20; **2 COR.** 5:1; **GAL.**
2:18

2648. καταμανθάνω *katamanthanō*
MATT. 6:28

2649. καταμαρτυρέω *katamartureō*
MATT. 26:62; 27:13; **MARK** 14:60; 15:4

2650. καταμένω *katamenō*
ACTS 1:13

2651. καταμόνας *katamonas*
MARK 4:10; **LUKE** 9:18

2652. κατανάθεμα *katanathema*
REV. 22:3

2653. καταναθεματίζω
katanathematizō
MATT. 26:74

2654. καταναλίσκω *katanaliskō*
HEB. 12:29

2655. καταναρκάω *katanarkaō*
2 COR. 11:9; 12:13,14

2656. κατανεύω *kataneuō*
LUKE 5:7

2657. κατανοέω *katanoeō*
MATT. 7:3; **LUKE** 6:41; 12:24,27; 20:23;
ACTS 7:31,32; 11:6; 27:39; **ROM.** 4:19; **HEB.**
3:1; 10:24; **JAMES** 1:23,24

2658. καταντάω *katantaō*
ACTS 16:1; 18:19,24; 20:15; 21:7; 25:13; 26:7;
27:12; 28:13; **1 COR.** 10:11; 14:36; **EPH.** 4:13;
PHIL. 3:11

2659. κατάνυξις *katanuxis*
ROM. 11:8

2660. κατανύσσω, κατανύττω
katanussō, katanuttō
ACTS 2:37

2661. καταξιόω *kataxioō*
LUKE 20:35; 21:36; **ACTS** 5:41; **2 THESS.** 1:5

2662. καταπατέω *katapateō*
MATT. 5:13; 7:6; **LUKE** 8:5; 12:1; **HEB.** 10:29

2663. κατάπαυσις *katapausis*
ACTS 7:49; **HEB.** 3:11,18; 4:1,3,5,10,11

2664. καταπαύω *katapauō*
ACTS 14:18; **HEB.** 4:4,8,10

2665. καταπέτασμα *katapetasma*
MATT. 27:51; **MARK** 15:38; **LUKE** 23:45;
HEB. 6:19; 9:3; 10:20

2666. καταπίνω *katapinō*
MATT. 23:24; **1 COR.** 15:54; **2 COR.** 2:7; 5:4;
HEB. 11:29; **1 PET.** 5:8; **REV.** 12:16

2667. καταπίπτω *katapiptō*
ACTS 26:14; 28:6

2668. καταπλέω *katapleō*
LUKE 8:26

2669. καταπονέω *kataponeō*
ACTS 7:24; **2 PET.** 2:7

2670. καταποντίζω *katapontizō*
MATT. 14:30; 18:6

2671. κατάρα katara
GAL. 3:10,13; HEB. 6:8; JAMES 3:10; 2 PET. 2:14

2672. καταράομαι kataraomai
MATT. 5:44; 25:41; MARK 11:21; LUKE 6:28; ROM. 12:14; JAMES 3:9

2673. καταργέω katargeō
LUKE 13:7; ROM. 3:3,31; 4:14; 6:6; 7:2,6; 1 COR. 1:28; 2:6; 6:13; 13:8,10,11; 15:24,26; 2 COR. 3:7,11,13,14; GAL. 3:17; 5:4,11; EPH. 2:15; 2 THESS. 2:8; 2 TIM. 1:10; HEB. 2:14

2674. καταριθμέω katarithmeō
ACTS 1:17

2675. καταρτίζω katartizō
MATT. 4:21; 21:16; MARK 1:19; LUKE 6:40; ROM. 9:22; 1 COR. 1:10; 2 COR. 13:11; GAL. 6:1; 1 THESS. 3:10; HEB. 10:5; 11:3; 13:21; 1 PET. 5:10

2676. κατάρτισις katartisis
2 COR. 13:9

2677. καταρτισμός katartismos
EPH. 4:12

2678. κατασείω kataseiō
ACTS 12:17; 13:16; 19:33; 21:40

2679. κατασκάπτω kataskaptō
ACTS 15:16; ROM. 11:3

2680. κατασκευάζω kataskeuazō
MATT. 11:10; MARK 1:2; LUKE 1:17; 7:27; HEB. 3:3,4; 9:2,6; 11:7; 1 PET. 3:20

2681. κατασκηνόω kataskēnoō
MATT. 13:32; MARK 4:32; LUKE 13:19; ACTS 2:26

2682. κατασκήνωσις kataskēnōsis
MATT. 8:20; LUKE 9:58

2683. κατασκιάζω kataskiazō
HEB. 9:5

2684. κατασκοπέω kataskopeō
GAL. 2:4

2685. κατάσκοπος kataskopos
HEB. 11:31

2686. κατασοφίζομαι katasophizomai
ACTS 7:19

2687. καταστέλλω katastellō
ACTS 19:35,36

2688. κατάστημα katastēma
TITUS 2:3

2689. καταστολή katastolē
1 TIM. 2:9

2690. καταστρέφω katastrephō
MATT. 21:12; MARK 11:15

2691. καταστρηνιάω katastrēniaō
1 TIM. 5:11

2692. καταστροφή katastrophē
2 TIM. 2:14; 2 PET. 2:6

2693. καταστρώννυμι katastrōnnumi
1 COR. 10:5

2694. κατασύρω katasurō
LUKE 12:58

2695. κατασφάζω, κατασφάττω katasphazō, katasphattō
LUKE 19:27

2696. κατασφραγίζω katasphragizō
REV. 5:1

2697. κατάσχεσις kataschesis
ACTS 7:5,45

2698. κατατίθημι katatithēmi
MARK 15:46; ACTS 24:27; 25:9

2699. κατατομή *katatomē*
PHIL. 3:2

2700. κατατοξεύω *katatoxeuō*
HEB. 12:20

2701. κατατρέχω *katatrechō*
ACTS 21:32

2702. καταφέρω *katapherō*
ACTS 20:9; 26:10

2703. καταφεύγω *katapheugō*
ACTS 14:6; HEB. 6:18

2704. καταφθείρω *kataphtheirō*
2 TIM. 3:8; 2 PET. 2:12

2705. καταφιλέω *kataphileō*
MATT. 26:49; MARK 14:45; LUKE 7:38,45;
15:20; ACTS 20:37

2706. καταφρονέω *kataphroneō*
MATT. 6:24; 18:10; LUKE 16:13; ROM. 2:4;
1 COR. 11:22; 1 TIM. 4:12; 6:2; HEB. 12:2;
2 PET. 2:10

2707. καταφρονητής *kataphronētēs*
ACTS 13:41

2708. καταχέω *katacheō*
MATT. 26:7; MARK 14:3

2709. καταχθόνιος *katachthonios*
PHIL. 2:10

2710. καταχράομαι *katachraomai*
1 COR. 7:31; 9:18

2711. καταψύχω *katapsuchō*
LUKE 16:24

2712. κατείδωλος *kateidōlos*
ACTS 17:16

2713. κατέναντι *katenanti*
MARK 11:2; 12:41; 13:3; LUKE 19:30; ROM.
4:17

2714. κατενώπιον *katenōpion*
2 COR. 2:17; 12:19; EPH. 1:4; COL. 1:22;
JUDE 1:24

2715. κατεξουσιάζω *katexousiazō*
MATT. 20:25; MARK 10:42

2716. κατεργάζομαι *katergazomai*
ROM. 1:27; 2:9; 4:15; 5:3; 7:8,13,15,17,18,20;
15:18; 1 COR. 5:3; 2 COR. 4:17; 5:5; 7:10,11;
9:11; 12:12; EPH. 6:13; PHIL. 2:12; JAMES
1:3,20; 1 PET. 4:3

2718. κατέρχομαι *katerchomai*
LUKE 4:31; 9:37; ACTS 8:5; 9:32; 11:27;
12:19; 13:4; 15:1; 18:5,22; 21:10; 27:5; JAMES
3:15

2719. A. κατεσθίω *katesthiō*
        MATT. 23:14; MARK 12:40; LUKE
        20:47;   2 COR. 11:20; GAL. 5:15;
        REV. 11:5

        B. καταφάγω *kataphagō*
        (2nd aor. of κατεσθίω)
        MATT. 13:4; MARK 4:4; LUKE 8:5;
        15:30; JOHN 2:17; REV. 10:9,10; 12:4;
        20:9

2720. κατευθύνω *kateuthunō*
LUKE 1:79; 1 THESS. 3:11; 2 THESS. 3:5

2721. κατεφίστημι *katephistēmi*
ACTS 18:12

2722. κατέχω *katechō*
MATT. 21:38; LUKE 4:42; 8:15; 14:9; JOHN
5:4; ACTS 27:40; ROM. 1:18; 7:6; 1 COR.
7:30; 11:2; 15:2; 2 COR. 6:10; 1 THESS. 5:21;
2 THESS. 2:6,7; PHILE. 1:13; HEB. 3:6,14;
10:23

2723. κατηγορέω *katēgoreō*
MATT. 12:10; 27:12; MARK 3:2; 15:3; LUKE
11:54; 23:2,10,14; JOHN 5:45; 8:6; ACTS
22:30; 24:2,8,13,19; 25:5,11,16; 28:19; ROM.
2:15; REV. 12:10

2724. κατηγορία *katēgoria*
LUKE 6:7; JOHN 18:29; 1 TIM. 5:19; TITUS
1:6

2725. κατήγορος katēgoros
JOHN 8:10; ACTS 23:30,35; 24:8; 25:16,18;
REV. 12:10

2726. κατήφεια katēpheia
JAMES 4:9

2727. κατηχέω katēcheō
LUKE 1:4; ACTS 18:25; 21:21,24; ROM. 2:18;
1 COR. 14:19; GAL. 6:6

2728. κατιόω katioō
JAMES 5:3

2729. κατισχύω katischuō
MATT. 16:18; LUKE 23:23

2730. κατοικέω katoikeō
MATT. 2:23; 4:13; 12:45; 23:21; LUKE 11:26;
13:4; ACTS 1:19,20; 2:5,9,14; 4:16; 7:2,4,48;
9:22,32,35; 11:29; 13:27; 17:24,26; 19:10,17;
22:12; EPH. 3:17; COL. 1:19; 2:9; HEB. 11:9;
JAMES 4:5; 2 PET. 3:13; REV. 2:13; 3:10;
6:10; 8:13; 11:10; 12:12; 13:8,12,14; 14:6; 17:2,8

2731. κατοίκησις katoikēsis
MARK 5:3

2732. κατοικητήριον katoikētērion
EPH. 2:22; REV. 18:2

2733. κατοικία katoikia
ACTS 17:26

2734. κατοπτρίζω katoptrizō
2 COR. 3:18

2735. κατόρθωμα katorthōma
ACTS 24:2

2736. A. κάτω katō
MATT. 4:6; 27:51; MARK 14:66;
15:38; LUKE 4:9; JOHN 8:6,8,23;
ACTS 2:19; 20:9

B. κατωτέρω katōterō
compar.
MATT. 2:16

2737. κατώτερος katōteros
EPH. 4:9

2738. καῦμα kauma
REV. 7:16; 16:9

2739. καυματίζω kaumatizō
MATT. 13:6; MARK 4:6; REV. 16:8,9

2740. καῦσις kausis
HEB. 6:8

2741. καυσόομαι kausoomai
2 PET. 3:10,12

2742. καύσων kausōn
MATT. 20:12; LUKE 12:55; JAMES 1:11

2743. καυτηριάζω kautēriazō
1 TIM. 4:2

2744. καυχάομαι kauchaomai
ROM. 2:17,23; 5:2,3,11; 1 COR. 1:29,31; 3:21;
4:7; 2 COR. 5:12; 7:14; 9:2; 10:8,13,15-17;
11:12,16,18,30; 12:1,5,6,9,11; GAL. 6:13,14;
EPH. 2:9; PHIL. 3:3; 2 THESS. 1:4; JAMES
1:9; 4:16

2745. καύχημα kauchēma
ROM. 4:2; 1 COR. 5:6; 9:15,16; 2 COR. 1:14;
5:12; 9:3; GAL. 6:4; PHIL. 1:26; 2:16; HEB.
3:6

2746. καύχησις kauchēsis
ROM. 3:27; 15:17; 1 COR. 15:31; 2 COR. 1:12;
7:4,14; 8:24; 9:4; 11:10,17; 1 THESS. 2:19;
JAMES 4:16

2747. Κεγχρεαί Kegchreai
ACTS 18:18; ROM. 16:1

2748. Κεδρών, κέδρος Kedrōn, kedros
JOHN 18:1

2749. κεῖμαι keimai
MATT. 3:10; 5:14; 28:6; LUKE 2:12,16,34; 3:9;
12:19; 23:53; 24:12; JOHN 2:6; 11:41; 19:29;

20:5-7,12; 21:9; **1 COR.** 3:11; **2 COR.** 3:15;
PHIL. 1:17; **1 THESS.** 3:3; **1 TIM.** 1:9;
1 JOHN 5:19; **REV.** 4:2; 21:16

2750. κειρία keiria
JOHN 11:44

2751. κείρω keirō
ACTS 8:32; 18:18; **1 COR.** 11:6

2752. κέλευσμα keleusma
1 THESS. 4:16

2753. κελεύω keleuō
MATT. 8:18; 14:9,19,28; 15:35; 18:25;
27:58,64; **LUKE** 18:40; **ACTS** 4:15; 5:34; 8:38;
12:19; 16:22; 21:33,34; 22:24,30; 23:3,10,35;
24:8; 25:6,17,21,23; 27:43

2754. κενοδοξία kenodoxia
PHIL. 2:3

2755. κενόδοξος kenodoxos
GAL. 5:26

2756. κενός kenos
MARK 12:3; **LUKE** 1:53; 20:10,11; **ACTS**
4:25; **1 COR.** 15:10,14,58; **2 COR.** 6:1; **GAL.**
2:2; **EPH.** 5:6; **PHIL.** 2:16; **COL.** 2:8;
1 THESS. 2:1; 3:5; **JAMES** 2:20

2757. κενοφωνία kenophōnia
1 TIM. 6:20; **2 TIM.** 2:16

2758. κενόω kenoō
ROM. 4:14; **1 COR.** 1:17; 9:15; **2 COR.** 9:3;
PHIL. 2:7

2759. κέντρον kentron
ACTS 9:5; 26:14; **1 COR.** 15:55,56; **REV.** 9:10

2760. κεντυρίων kenturiōn
MARK 15:39,44,45

2761. κενῶς kenōs
JAMES 4:5

2762. κεραία keraia
MATT. 5:18; **LUKE** 16:17

2763. κεραμεύς kerameus
MATT. 27:7,10; **ROM.** 9:21

2764. κεραμικός keramikos
REV. 2:27

2765. κεράμιον keramion
MARK 14:13; **LUKE** 22:10

2766. κέραμος keramos
LUKE 5:19

2767. κεράννυμι kerannumi
REV. 14:10; 18:6

2768. κέρας keras
LUKE 1:69; **REV.** 5:6; 9:13; 12:3; 13:1,11;
17:3,7,12,16

2769. κεράτιον keration
LUKE 15:16

2770. κερδαίνω kerdainō
MATT. 16:26; 18:15; 25:17,20,22; **MARK**
8:36; **LUKE** 9:25; **ACTS** 27:21; **1 COR.** 9:19-
22; **PHIL.** 3:8; **JAMES** 4:13; **1 PET.** 3:1

2771. κέρδος kerdos
PHIL. 1:21; 3:7; **TITUS** 1:11

2772. κέρμα kerma
JOHN 2:15

2773. κερματιστής kermatistēs
JOHN 2:14

2774. κεφάλαιον kephalaion
ACTS 22:28; **HEB.** 8:1

2775. κεφαλαιόω kephalaioō
MARK 12:4

2776. κεφαλή kephalē
MATT. 5:36; 6:17; 8:20; 10:30; 14:8,11; 21:42;
26:7; 27:29,30,37,39; **MARK** 6:24,25,27,28;
12:10; 14:3; 15:19,29; **LUKE** 7:38,44,46; 9:58;
12:7; 20:17; 21:18,28; **JOHN** 13:9; 19:2,30;

20:7,12; **ACTS** 4:11; 18:6,18; 21:24; 27:34;
ROM. 12:20; **1 COR.** 11:3-5,7,10; 12:21; **EPH.**
1:22; 4:15; 5:23; **COL.** 1:18; 2:10,19; **1 PET.**
2:7; **REV.** 1:14; 4:4; 9:7,17,19; 10:1; 12:1,3;
13:1,3; 14:14; 17:3,7,9; 18:19; 19:12

2777. κεφαλίς *kephalis*
HEB. 10:7

2778. κῆνσος *kēnsos*
MATT. 17:25; 22:17,19; **MARK** 12:14

2779. κῆπος *kēpos*
LUKE 13:19; **JOHN** 18:1,26; 19:41

2780. κηπουρός *kēpouros*
JOHN 20:15

2781. κηρίον *kērion*
LUKE 24:42

2782. κήρυγμα *kērugma*
MATT. 12:41; **LUKE** 11:32; **ROM.** 16:25;
1 COR. 1:21; 2:4; 15:14; **2 TIM.** 4:17; **TITUS**
1:3

2783. κῆρυξ *kērux*
1 TIM. 2:7; **2 TIM.** 1:11; **2 PET.** 2:5

2784. κηρύσσω, κηρύττω
kērussō, kēruttō
MATT. 3:1; 4:17,23; 9:35; 10:7,27; 11:1; 24:14;
26:13; **MARK** 1:4,7,14,38,39,45; 3:14; 5:20;
6:12; 7:36; 13:10; 14:9; 16:15,20; **LUKE** 3:3;
4:18,19,44; 8:1,39; 9:2; 12:3; 24:47; **ACTS** 8:5;
9:20; 10:37,42; 15:21; 19:13; 20:25; 28:31;
ROM. 2:21; 10:8,14,15; **1 COR.** 1:23; 9:27;
15:11,12; **2 COR.** 1:19; 4:5; 11:4; **GAL.** 2:2;
5:11; **PHIL.** 1:15; **COL.** 1:23; **1 THESS.** 2:9;
1 TIM. 3:16; **2 TIM.** 4:2; **1 PET.** 3:19; **REV.**
5:2

2785. κῆτος *kētos*
MATT. 12:40

2786. Κηφᾶς *Kēphas*
JOHN 1:42; **1 COR.** 1:12; 3:22; 9:5; 15:5;
GAL. 2:9

2787. κιβωτός *kibōtos*
MATT. 24:38; **LUKE** 17:27; **HEB.** 9:4; 11:7;
1 PET. 3:20; **REV.** 11:19

2788. κιθάρα *kithara*
1 COR. 14:7; **REV.** 5:8; 14:2; 15:2

2789. κιθαρίζω *kitharizō*
1 COR. 14:7; **REV.** 14:2

2790. κιθαρῳδός *kitharōdos*
REV. 14:2; 18:22

2791. Κιλικία *Kilikia*
ACTS 6:9; 15:23,41; 21:39; 22:3; 23:34; 27:5;
GAL. 1:21

2792. κινάμωμον *kinamōmon*
REV. 18:13

2793. κινδυνεύω *kinduneuō*
LUKE 8:23; **ACTS** 19:27,40; **1 COR.** 15:30

2794. κίνδυνος *kindunos*
ROM. 8:35; **2 COR.** 11:26

2795. κινέω *kineō*
MATT. 23:4; 27:39; **MARK** 15:29; **ACTS**
17:28; 21:30; 24:5; **REV.** 2:5; 6:14

2796. κίνησις *kinēsis*
JOHN 5:3

2797. Κίς *Kis*
ACTS 13:21

2798. κλάδος *klados*
MATT. 13:32; 21:8; 24:32; **MARK** 4:32; 13:28;
LUKE 13:19; **ROM.** 11:16-19,21

2799. κλαίω *klaiō*
MATT. 2:18; 26:75; **MARK** 5:38,39; 14:72;
16:10; **LUKE** 6:21,25; 7:13,32,38; 8:52; 19:41;
22:62; 23:28; **JOHN** 11:31,33; 16:20; 20:11,
13,15; **ACTS** 9:39; 21:13; **ROM.** 12:15; **1 COR.**
7:30; **PHIL.** 3:18; **JAMES** 4:9; 5:1; **REV.** 5:4,5;
18:9,11,15,19

2800. κλάσις klasis
LUKE 24:35; ACTS 2:42

2801. κλάσμα klasma
MATT. 14:20; 15:37; MARK 6:43; 8:8,19,20;
LUKE 9:17; JOHN 6:12,13

2802. Κλαύδη Klaudē
ACTS 27:16

2803. Κλαυδία Klaudia
2 TIM. 4:21

2804. Κλαύδιος Klaudios
ACTS 11:28; 18:2; 23:26

2805. κλαυθμός klauthmos
MATT. 2:18; 8:12; 13:42,50; 22:13; 24:51;
25:30; LUKE 13:28; ACTS 20:37

2806. κλάω klaō
MATT. 14:19; 15:36; 26:26; MARK 8:6,19;
14:22; LUKE 22:19; 24:30; ACTS 2:46;
20:7,11; 27:35; 1 COR. 10:16; 11:24

2807. κλείς kleis
MATT. 16:19; LUKE 11:52; REV. 1:18; 3:7;
9:1; 20:1

2808. κλείω kleiō
MATT. 6:6; 23:13; 25:10; LUKE 4:25; 11:7;
JOHN 20:19,26; ACTS 5:23; 21:30; 1 JOHN
3:17; REV. 3:7,8; 11:6; 20:3; 21:25

2809. κλέμμα klemma
REV. 9:21

2810. Κλεόπας Kleopas
LUKE 24:18

2811. κλέος kleos
1 PET. 2:20

2812. κλέπτης kleptēs
MATT. 6:19,20; 24:43; LUKE 12:33,39; JOHN
10:1,8,10; 12:6; 1 COR. 6:10; 1 THESS. 5:2,4;
1 PET. 4:15; 2 PET. 3:10; REV. 3:3; 16:15

2813. κλέπτω kleptō
MATT. 6:19,20; 19:18; 27:64; 28:13; MARK
10:19; LUKE 18:20; JOHN 10:10; ROM. 2:21;
13:9; EPH. 4:28

2814. κλῆμα klēma
JOHN 15:2,4-6

2815. Κλήμης Klēmēs
PHIL. 4:3

2816. κληρονομέω klēronomeō
MATT. 5:5; 19:29; 25:34; MARK 10:17;
LUKE 10:25; 18:18; 1 COR. 6:9,10; 15:50;
GAL. 4:30; 5:21; HEB. 1:4,14; 6:12; 12:17;
1 PET. 3:9; REV. 21:7

2817. κληρονομία klēronomia
MATT. 21:38; MARK 12:7; LUKE 12:13;
20:14; ACTS 7:5; 20:32; GAL. 3:18; EPH.
1:14,18; 5:5; COL. 3:24; HEB. 9:15; 11:8;
1 PET. 1:4

2818. κληρονόμος klēronomos
MATT. 21:38; MARK 12:7; LUKE 20:14;
ROM. 4:13,14; 8:17; GAL. 3:29; 4:1,7; TITUS
3:7; HEB. 1:2; 6:17; 11:7; JAMES 2:5

2819. κλῆρος klēros
MATT. 27:35; MARK 15:24; LUKE 23:34;
JOHN 19:24; ACTS 1:17,25,26; 8:21; 26:18;
COL. 1:12; 1 PET. 5:3

2820. κληρόω klēroō
EPH. 1:11

2821. κλῆσις klēsis
ROM. 11:29; 1 COR. 1:26; 7:20; EPH. 1:18;
4:1,4; PHIL. 3:14; 2 THESS. 1:11; 2 TIM. 1:9;
HEB. 3:1; 2 PET. 1:10

2822. κλητός klētos
MATT. 20:16; 22:14; ROM. 1:1,6,7; 8:28;
1 COR. 1:1,2,24; JUDE 1:1; REV. 17:14

2823. κλίβανος klibanos
MATT. 6:30; LUKE 12:28

2824. κλίμα klima
ROM. 15:23; **2 COR.** 11:10; **GAL.** 1:21

2825. κλίνη klinē
MATT. 9:2,6; **MARK** 4:21; 7:4,30; **LUKE** 5:18; 8:16; 17:34; **ACTS** 5:15; **REV.** 2:22

2826. κλινίδιον klinidion
LUKE 5:19,24

2827. κλίνω klinō
MATT. 8:20; **LUKE** 9:12,58; 24:5,29; **JOHN** 19:30; **HEB.** 11:34

2828. κλισία klisia
LUKE 9:14

2829. κλοπή klopē
MATT. 15:19; **MARK** 7:22

2830. κλύδων kludōn
LUKE 8:24; **JAMES** 1:6

2831. κλυδωνίζομαι kludōnizomai
EPH. 4:14

2832. Κλωπᾶς Klōpas
JOHN 19:25

2833. κνήθω knēthō
2 TIM. 4:3

2834. Κνίδος Knidos
ACTS 27:7

2835. κοδράντης kodrantēs
MATT. 5:26; **MARK** 12:42

2836. κοιλία koilia
MATT. 12:40; 15:17; 19:12; **MARK** 7:19; **LUKE** 1:15,41,42,44; 2:21; 11:27; 15:16; 23:29; **JOHN** 3:4; 7:38; **ACTS** 3:2; 14:8; **ROM.** 16:18; **1 COR.** 6:13; **GAL.** 1:15; **PHIL.** 3:19; **REV.** 10:9,10

2837. κοιμάω koimaō
MATT. 27:52; 28:13; **LUKE** 22:45; **JOHN** 11:11,12; **ACTS** 7:60; 12:6; 13:36; **1 COR.** 7:39; 11:30; 15:6,18,20,51; **1 THESS.** 4:13-15; **2 PET.** 3:4

2838. κοίμησις koimēsis
JOHN 11:13

2839. κοινός koinos
MARK 7:2; **ACTS** 2:44; 4:32; 10:14,28; 11:8; **ROM.** 14:14; **TITUS** 1:4; **HEB.** 10:29; **JUDE** 1:3

2840. κοινόω koinoō
MATT. 15:11,18,20; **MARK** 7:15,18,20,23; **ACTS** 10:15; 11:9; 21:28; **HEB.** 9:13; **REV.** 21:27

2841. κοινωνέω koinōneō
ROM. 12:13; 15:27; **GAL.** 6:6; **PHIL.** 4:15; **1 TIM.** 5:22; **HEB.** 2:14; **1 PET.** 4:13; **2 JOHN** 1:11

2842. κοινωνία koinōnia
ACTS 2:42; **ROM.** 15:26; **1 COR.** 1:9; 10:16; **2 COR.** 6:14; 8:4; 9:13; 13:14; **GAL.** 2:9; **EPH.** 3:9; **PHIL.** 1:5; 2:1; 3:10; **PHILE.** 1:6; **HEB.** 13:16; **1 JOHN** 1:3,6,7

2843. κοινωνικός koinōnikos
1 TIM. 6:18

2844. κοινωνός koinōnos
MATT. 23:30; **LUKE** 5:10; **1 COR.** 10:18,20; **2 COR.** 1:7; 8:23; **PHILE.** 1:17; **HEB.** 10:33; **1 PET.** 5:1; **2 PET.** 1:4

2845. κοίτη koitē
LUKE 11:7; **ROM.** 9:10; 13:13; **HEB.** 13:4

2846. κοιτών koitōn
ACTS 12:20

2847. κόκκινος kokkinos
MATT. 27:28; **HEB.** 9:19; **REV.** 17:3,4; 18:12,16

2848. κόκκος kokkos
MATT. 13:31; 17:20; **MARK** 4:31; **LUKE** 13:19; 17:6; **JOHN** 12:24; **1 COR.** 15:37

2849. κολάζω *kolazō*
ACTS 4:21; **2 PET.** 2:9

2850. κολακεία *kolakeia*
1 THESS. 2:5

2851. κόλασις *kolasis*
MATT. 25:46; **1 JOHN** 4:18

2852. κολαφίζω *kolaphizō*
MATT. 26:67; **MARK** 14:65; **1 COR.** 4:11;
2 COR. 12:7; **1 PET.** 2:20

2853. κολλάω *kollaō*
LUKE 10:11; 15:15; **ACTS** 5:13; 8:29; 9:26;
10:28; 17:34; **ROM.** 12:9; **1 COR.** 6:16,17

2854. κολλούριον, κολλύριον
kollourion, kollurion
REV. 3:18

2855. κολλυβιστής *kollubistēs*
MATT. 21:12; **MARK** 11:15; **JOHN** 2:15

2856. κολοβόω *koloboō*
MATT. 24:22; **MARK** 13:20

2857. Κολασσαί, Κολοσσαί
Kolassai, Kolossai
COL. 1:2

2859. κόλπος *kolpos*
LUKE 6:38; 16:22,23; **JOHN** 1:18; 13:23;
ACTS 27:39

2860. κολυμβάω *kolumbaō*
ACTS 27:43

2861. κολυμβήθρα *kolumbēthra*
JOHN 5:2,4,7; 9:7,11

2862. κολωνία *kolōnia*
ACTS 16:12

2863. κομάω *komaō*
1 COR. 11:14,15

2864. κόμη *komē*
1 COR. 11:15

2865. κομίζω *komizō*
MATT. 25:27; **LUKE** 7:37; **2 COR.** 5:10; **EPH.**
6:8; **COL.** 3:25; **HEB.** 10:36; 11:19,39; **1 PET.**
1:9; 5:4; **2 PET.** 2:13

2866. κομψότερον *kompsoteron*
JOHN 4:52

2867. κονιάω *koniaō*
MATT. 23:27; **ACTS** 23:3

2868. κονιορτός *koniortos*
MATT. 10:14; **LUKE** 9:5; 10:11; **ACTS** 13:51;
22:23

2869. κοπάζω *kopazō*
MATT. 14:32; **MARK** 4:39; 6:51

2870. κοπετός *kopetos*
ACTS 8:2

2871. κοπή *kopē*
HEB. 7:1

2872. κοπιάω *kopiaō*
MATT. 6:28; 11:28; **LUKE** 5:5; 12:27; **JOHN**
4:6,38; **ACTS** 20:35; **ROM.** 16:6,12; **1 COR.**
4:12; 15:10; 16:16; **GAL.** 4:11; **EPH.** 4:28;
PHIL. 2:16; **COL.** 1:29; **1 THESS.** 5:12;
1 TIM. 4:10; 5:17; **2 TIM.** 2:6; **REV.** 2:3

2873. κόπος *kopos*
MATT. 26:10; **MARK** 14:6; **LUKE** 11:7; 18:5;
JOHN 4:38; **1 COR.** 3:8; 15:58; **2 COR.** 6:5;
10:15; 11:23,27; **GAL.** 6:17; **1 THESS.** 1:3; 2:9;
3:5; **2 THESS.** 3:8; **HEB.** 6:10; **REV.** 2:2; 14:13

2874. κοπρία *kopria*
LUKE 13:8; 14:35

2875. κόπτω *koptō*
MATT. 11:17; 21:8; 24:30; **MARK** 11:8;
LUKE 8:52; 23:27; **REV.** 1:7; 18:9

2876. κόραξ *korax*
LUKE 12:24

2877. κοράσιον *korasion*
MATT. 9:24,25; 14:11; MARK 5:41,42; 6:22,28

2878. I. Κορβᾶν *Korban*
MARK 7:11

II. κορβανᾶς *korbanas*
MATT. 27:6

2879. Κορέ *Kore*
JUDE 1:11

2880. κορέννυμι *korennumi*
ACTS 27:38; 1 COR. 4:8

2881. Κορίνθιος *Korinthios*
ACTS 18:8; 2 COR. 6:11

2882. Κόρινθος *Korinthos*
ACTS 18:1; 19:1; 1 COR. 1:2; 2 COR. 1:1,23;
2 TIM. 4:20

2883. Κορνήλιος *Kornēlios*
ACTS 10:1,3,7,17,21,22,24,25,30,31

2884. κόρος *koros*
LUKE 16:7

2885. κοσμέω *kosmeō*
MATT. 12:44; 23:29; 25:7; LUKE 11:25; 21:5;
1 TIM. 2:9; TITUS 2:10; 1 PET. 3:5; REV.
21:2,19

2886. κοσμικός *kosmikos*
TITUS 2:12; HEB. 9:1

2887. κόσμιος *kosmios*
1 TIM. 2:9; 3:2

2888. κοσμοκράτωρ *kosmokratōr*
EPH. 6:12

2889. κόσμος *kosmos*
MATT. 4:8; 5:14; 13:35,38; 16:26; 18:7; 24:21;
25:34; 26:13; MARK 8:36; 14:9; 16:15; LUKE
9:25; 11:50; 12:30; JOHN 1:9,10,29; 3:16,17,19;
4:42; 6:14,33,51; 7:4,7; 8:12,23,26; 9:5,39;
10:36; 11:9,27; 12:19,25,31,46,47; 13:1; 14:17,
19,22,27,30,31; 15:18,19; 16:8,11,20,21,28,33;
17:5,6,9,11-16,18,21,23-25; 18:20,36,37; 21:25;
ACTS 17:24; ROM. 1:8,20; 3:6,19; 4:13; 5:12,
13; 11:12,15; 1 COR. 1:20,21,27,28; 2:12; 3:19,
22; 4:9,13; 5:10; 6:2; 7:31,33,34; 8:4; 11:32;
14:10; 2 COR. 1:12; 5:19; 7:10; GAL. 4:3; 6:14;
EPH. 1:4; 2:2,12; PHIL. 2:15; COL. 1:6; 2:8,
20; 1 TIM. 1:15; 3:16; 6:7; HEB. 4:3; 9:26;
10:5; 11:7,38; JAMES 1:27; 2:5; 3:6; 4:4;
1 PET. 1:20; 3:3; 5:9; 2 PET. 1:4; 2:5,20; 3:6;
1 JOHN 2:2,15-17; 3:1,13,17; 4:1,3-5,9,14,17;
5:4,5,19; 2 JOHN 1:7; REV. 11:15; 13:8; 17:8

2890. Κούαρτος *Kouartos*
ROM. 16:23

2891. κοῦμι *koumi*
MARK 5:41

2892. κουστωδία *koustōdia*
MATT. 27:65,66; 28:11

2893. κουφίζω *kouphizō*
ACTS 27:38

2894. κόφινος *kophinos*
MATT. 14:20; 16:9; MARK 6:43; 8:19; LUKE
9:17; JOHN 6:13

2895. κράββατος *krabbatos*
MARK 2:4,9,11,12; 6:55; JOHN 5:8-12; ACTS
5:15; 9:33

2896. κράζω *krazō*
MATT. 8:29; 9:27; 14:26,30; 15:23; 20:30,31;
21:9,15; 27:23,50; MARK 1:26; 3:11; 5:5,7;
9:24,26; 10:47,48; 11:9; 15:13,14,39; LUKE
4:41; 9:39; 18:39; 19:40; JOHN 1:15; 7:28,37;
12:13,44; 19:12; ACTS 7:57,60; 14:14; 16:17;
19:28,32,34; 21:28,36; 23:6; 24:21; ROM. 8:15;
9:27; GAL. 4:6; JAMES 5:4; REV. 6:10; 7:2,
10; 10:3; 12:2; 14:15; 18:2,18,19; 19:17

2897. κραιπάλη *kraipalē*
LUKE 21:34

2898. κρανίον *kranion*
MATT. 27:33; MARK 15:22; LUKE 23:33;
JOHN 19:17

2899. *κράσπεδον kraspedon*
MATT. 9:20; 14:36; 23:5; MARK 6:56; LUKE 8:44

2900. *κραταιός krataios*
1 PET. 5:6

2901. *κραταιόω krataioō*
LUKE 1:80; 2:40; 1 COR. 16:13; EPH. 3:16

2902. *κρατέω krateō*
MATT. 9:25; 12:11; 14:3; 18:28; 21:46; 22:6; 26:4,48,50,55,57; 28:9; MARK 1:31; 3:21; 5:41; 6:17; 7:3,4,8; 9:10,27; 12:12; 14:1,44,46,49,51; LUKE 8:54; 24:16; JOHN 20:23; ACTS 2:24; 3:11; 24:6; 27:13; COL. 2:19; 2 THESS. 2:15; HEB. 4:14; 6:18; REV. 2:1,13-15,25; 3:11; 7:1; 20:2

2903. *κράτιστος kratistos*
LUKE 1:3; ACTS 23:26; 24:3; 26:25

2904. *κράτος kratos*
LUKE 1:51; ACTS 19:20; EPH. 1:19; 6:10; COL. 1:11; 1 TIM. 6:16; HEB. 2:14; 1 PET. 4:11; 5:11; JUDE 1:25; REV. 1:6; 5:13

2905. *κραυγάζω kraugazō*
MATT. 12:19; 15:22; JOHN 11:43; 18:40; 19:6, 15; ACTS 22:23

2906. *κραυγή kraugē*
MATT. 25:6; ACTS 23:9; EPH. 4:31; HEB. 5:7; REV. 14:18; 21:4

2907. *κρέας kreas*
ROM. 14:21; 1 COR. 8:13

2908. *κρεῖσσον kreisson* neut.
1 COR. 7:9,38; 11:17; 12:31; PHIL. 1:23; HEB. 11:40; 12:24; 2 PET. 2:21

2909. *κρείσσων, κρείττων*
kreissōn, kreittōn
HEB. 1:4; 6:9; 7:7,19,22; 8:6; 9:23; 10:34; 11:16,35; 1 PET. 3:17

2910. *κρέμαννυμι kremannumi*
MATT. 18:6; 22:40; LUKE 23:39; ACTS 5:30; 10:39; 28:4; GAL. 3:13

2911. *κρημνός krēmnos*
MATT. 8:32; MARK 5:13; LUKE 8:33

2912. *Κρής Krēs*
ACTS 2:11; TITUS 1:12

2913. *Κρήσκης Krēskēs*
2 TIM. 4:10

2914. *Κρήτη Krētē*
ACTS 27:7,12,13,21; TITUS 1:5

2915. *κριθή krithē*
REV. 6:6

2916. *κρίθινος krithinos*
JOHN 6:9,13

2917. *κρίμα krima*
MATT. 7:2; 23:14; MARK 12:40; LUKE 20:47; 23:40; 24:20; JOHN 9:39; ACTS 24:25; ROM. 2:2,3; 3:8; 5:16; 11:33; 13:2; 1 COR. 6:7; 11:29,34; GAL. 5:10; 1 TIM. 3:6; 5:12; HEB. 6:2; JAMES 3:1; 1 PET. 4:17; 2 PET. 2:3; JUDE 1:4; REV. 17:1; 18:20; 20:4

2918. *κρίνον krinon*
MATT. 6:28; LUKE 12:27

2919. *κρίνω krinō*
MATT. 5:40; 7:1,2; 19:28; LUKE 6:37; 7:43; 12:57; 19:22; 22:30; JOHN 3:17,18; 5:22,30; 7:24,51; 8:15,16,26,50; 12:47,48; 16:11; 18:31; ACTS 3:13; 4:19; 7:7; 13:27,46; 15:19; 16:4,15; 17:31; 20:16; 21:25; 23:3,6; 24:6,21; 25:9,10,20, 25; 26:6,8; 27:1; ROM. 2:1,3,12,16,27; 3:4,6,7; 14:3-5,10,13,22; 1 COR. 2:2; 4:5; 5:3,12,13; 6:1-3,6; 7:37; 10:15,29; 11:13,31,32; 2 COR. 2:1; 5:14; COL. 2:16; 2 THESS. 2:12; 2 TIM. 4:1; TITUS 3:12; HEB. 10:30; 13:4; JAMES 2:12; 4:11,12; 1 PET. 1:17; 2:23; 4:5,6; REV. 6:10; 11:18; 16:5; 18:8,20; 19:2,11; 20:12,13

2920. *κρίσις krisis*
MATT. 5:21,22; 10:15; 11:22,24; 12:18,20, 36,41,42; 23:23,33; MARK 3:29; 6:11; LUKE 10:14; 11:31,32,42; JOHN 3:19; 5:22, 24,27,29,30; 7:24; 8:16; 12:31; 16:8,11; ACTS 8:33; 2 THESS. 1:5; 1 TIM. 5:24; HEB. 9:27;

10:27; **JAMES** 2:13; **2 PET.** 2:4,9,11; 3:7;
1 JOHN 4:17; **JUDE** 1:6,9,15; **REV.** 14:7; 16:7;
18:10; 19:2

2921. *Κρίσπος Krispos*
ACTS 18:8; **1 COR.** 1:14

2922. *κριτήριον kritērion*
1 COR. 6:2,4; **JAMES** 2:6

2923. *κριτής kritēs*
MATT. 5:25; 12:27; **LUKE** 11:19; 12:58; 18:2,
6; **ACTS** 10:42; 13:20; 18:15; 24:10; **2 TIM.**
4:8; **HEB.** 12:23; **JAMES** 2:4; 4:11; 5:9

2924. *κριτικός kritikos*
HEB. 4:12

2925. *κρούω krouō*
MATT. 7:7,8; **LUKE** 11:9,10; 12:36; 13:25;
ACTS 12:13,16; **REV.** 3:20

2926. *κρυπτή kruptē*
LUKE 11:33

2927. *κρυπτός kruptos*
MATT. 6:4,6,18; 10:26; **MARK** 4:22; **LUKE**
8:17; 12:2; **JOHN** 7:4,10; 18:20; **ROM.** 2:16,29;
1 COR. 4:5; 14:25; **2 COR.** 4:2; **1 PET.** 3:4

2928. *κρύπτω kruptō*
MATT. 5:14; 13:35,44; 25:25; **LUKE** 18:34;
19:42; **JOHN** 8:59; 12:36; 19:38; **COL.** 3:3;
1 TIM. 5:25; **HEB.** 11:23; **REV.** 2:17; 6:15,16

2929. *κρυσταλλίζω krustallizō*
REV. 21:11

2930. *κρύσταλλος krustallos*
REV. 4:6; 22:1

2931. *κρυφῇ kruphē*
EPH. 5:12

2932. *κτάομαι ktaomai*
MATT. 10:9; **LUKE** 18:12; 21:19; **ACTS** 1:18;
8:20; 22:28; **1 THESS.** 4:4

2933. *κτῆμα ktēma*
MATT. 19:22; **MARK** 10:22; **ACTS** 2:45; 5:1

2934. *κτῆνος ktēnos*
LUKE 10:34; **ACTS** 23:24; **1 COR.** 15:39;
REV. 18:13

2935. *κτήτωρ ktētōr*
ACTS 4:34

2936. *κτίζω ktizō*
MARK 13:19; **ROM.** 1:25; **1 COR.** 11:9; **EPH.**
2:10,15; 3:9; 4:24; **COL.** 1:16; 3:10; **1 TIM.** 4:3;
REV. 4:11; 10:6

2937. *κτίσις ktisis*
MARK 10:6; 13:19; 16:15; **ROM.** 1:20,25;
8:19-22,39; **2 COR.** 5:17; **GAL.** 6:15; **COL.**
1:15,23; **HEB.** 4:13; 9:11; **1 PET.** 2:13; **2 PET.**
3:4; **REV.** 3:14

2938. *κτίσμα ktisma*
1 TIM. 4:4; **JAMES** 1:18; **REV.** 5:13; 8:9

2939. *κτιστής ktistēs*
1 PET. 4:19

2940. *κυβεία kubeia*
EPH. 4:14

2941. *κυβέρνησις kubernēsis*
1 COR. 12:28

2942. *κυβερνήτης kubernētēs*
ACTS 27:11; **REV.** 18:17

2943. *κυκλόθεν kuklothen*
REV. 4:3,4,8; 5:11

2944. *κυκλόω kukloō*
LUKE 21:20; **JOHN** 10:24; **ACTS** 14:20; **HEB.**
11:30; **REV.** 20:9

2945. *κύκλῳ kuklō* adv.
(Dat. sing. of κύκλος)
MARK 3:34; 6:6,36; **LUKE** 9:12; **ROM.** 15:19;
REV. 4:6; 7:11

2946. κύλισμα *kulisma*
2 PET. 2:22

2947. κυλίω *kuliō*
MARK 9:20

2948. κυλλός *kullos*
MATT. 15:30,31; 18:8; MARK 9:43

2949. κῦμα *kuma*
MATT. 8:24; 14:24; MARK 4:37; ACTS 27:41;
JUDE 1:13

2950. κύμβαλον *kumbalon*
1 COR. 13:1

2951. κύμινον *kuminon*
MATT. 23:23

2952. κυνάριον *kunarion*
MATT. 15:26,27; MARK 7:27,28

2953. Κύπριος *Kuprios*
ACTS 4:36; 11:20; 21:16

2954. Κύπρος *Kupros*
ACTS 11:19; 13:4; 15:39; 21:3; 27:4

2955. κύπτω *kuptō*
MARK 1:7; JOHN 8:6,8

2956. Κυρηναῖος *Kurēnaios*
MATT. 27:32; MARK 15:21; LUKE 23:26;
ACTS 6:9; 11:20; 13:1

2957. Κυρήνη *Kurēnē*
ACTS 2:10

2958. Κυρήνιος *Kurēnios*
LUKE 2:2

2959. κυρία *kuria*
2 JOHN 1:1,5

2960. κυριακός *kuriakos*
1 COR. 11:20; REV. 1:10

2961. κυριεύω *kurieuō*
LUKE 22:25; ROM. 6:9,14; 7:1; 14:9; 2 COR.
1:24; 1 TIM. 6:15

2962. κύριος *kurios*
MATT. 1:20,22,24; 2:13,15,19; 3:3; 4:7,10;
5:33; 6:24; 7:21,22; 8:2,6,8,21,25; 9:28,38;
10:24,25; 11:25; 12:8; 13:27,51; 14:28,30;
15:22,25,27; 16:22; 17:4,15; 18:21,25-27,31,
32,34; 20:8,30,31,33; 21:3,9,30,40,42; 22:37,43-
45; 23:39; 24:42,45,46,48,50; 25:11,18-24,26,
37,44; 26:22; 27:10,63; 28:2,6; MARK 1:3;
2:28; 5:19; 7:28; 9:24; 11:3,9,10; 12:9,11,29,
30,36,37; 13:20,35; 16:19,20; LUKE 1:6,9,11,
15-17,25,28,32,38,43,45,46,58,66,68,76;
2:9,11,15,22-24,26,38,39; 3:4; 4:8,12,18,19;
5:8,12,17; 6:5,46; 7:6,13,31; 9:54,57,59,61;
10:1,2,17,21,27,40; 11:1,39; 12:36,37,41-43,45-
47; 13:8,15,23,25,35; 14:21-23; 16:3,5,8,13;
17:5,6,37; 18:6,41; 19:8,16,18,20,25,31,33,
34,38; 20:13,15,37,42,44; 22:31,33,38,49,61;
23:42; 24:3,24; JOHN 1:23; 4:1,11,15,19,49;
5:7; 6:23,34,68; 8:11; 9:36,38; 11:2,3,12,21,27,
32,34,39; 12:13,21,38; 13:6,9,13,14,16,25,36,37;
14:5,8,22; 15:15,20; 20:2,13,15,18,20,25,28;
21:7,12,15-17,20,21; ACTS 1:6,21,24; 2:20,21,
25,34,36,39,47; 3:19,22; 4:26,29,33; 5:9,14,19;
7:30,31,33,37,49,59,60; 8:16,24-26,39; 9:1,5,6,
10,11,13,15,17,27,29,31,35,42; 10:4,14,36,48;
11:8,16,17,20,21,23,24; 12:7,11,17,23; 13:2,10-
12,47-49; 14:3,23; 15:11,17,26,35,36; 16:10,14-
16,19,30-32; 17:24,27; 18:8,9,25; 19:5,10,13,
17,20; 20:19,21,24,35; 21:13,14,20; 22:8,10,
16,19; 23:11; 25:26; 26:15; 28:31; ROM. 1:3,7;
4:8,24; 5:1,11,21; 6:11,23; 7:25; 8:39; 9:28,29;
10:9,12,13,16; 11:3,34; 12:19; 13:14; 14:4,6,8,
11,14; 15:6,11,30; 16:2,8,11-13,18,20,22,24;
1 COR. 1:2,3,7-10,31; 2:8,16; 3:5,20; 4:4,5,17,
19; 5:4,5; 6:11,13,14,17; 7:10,12,17,22,25,32,34,
35,39; 8:5,6; 9:1,2,5,14; 10:21,22,26,28; 11:11,
23,26,27,29,32; 12:3,5; 14:21,37; 15:31,47,
57,58; 16:7,10,19,22,23; 2 COR. 1:2,3,14; 2:12;
3:16-18; 4:5,10,14; 5:6,8,11; 6:17,18; 8:5,9,19,
21; 10:8,17,18; 11:17,31; 12:1,8; 13:10,14;
GAL. 1:3,19; 4:1; 5:10; 6:14,17,18; EPH.
1:2,3,15,17; 2:21; 3:11,14; 4:1,5,17; 5:8,10,
17,19,20,22,29; 6:1,4,5,7-10,21,23,24; PHIL.
1:2,14; 2:11,19,24,29; 3:1,8,20; 4:1,2,4,5,10,23;
COL. 1:2,3,10; 2:6; 3:16-18,20,22-24; 4:1,7,17;
1 THESS. 1:1,3,6,8; 2:15,19; 3:8,11-13; 4:1,2,
6,15-17; 5:2,9,12,23,27,28; 2 THESS. 1:1,2,7-
9,12; 2:1,8,13,14,16; 3:1,3-6,12,16,18; 1 TIM.

1:1,2,12,14; 5:21; 6:3,14,15; **2 TIM.** 1:2,8,16,18; 2:7,14,19,22,24; 3:11; 4:1,8,14,17,18,22; **TITUS** 1:4; **PHILE.** 1:3,5,16,20,25; **HEB.** 1:10; 2:3; 7:14,21; 8:2,8-11; 10:16,30; 12:5,6,14; 13:6,20; **JAMES** 1:1,7,12; 2:1; 4:10,15; 5:4,7,8,10,11, 14,15; **1 PET.** 1:3,25; 2:3,13; 3:6,12,15; **2 PET.** 1:2,8,11,14,16; 2:9,11,20; 3:2,8-10,15,18; **2 JOHN** 1:3; **JUDE** 1:4,5,9,14,17,21; **REV.** 1:8; 4:8,11; 7:14; 11:8,15,17; 14:13; 15:3,4; 16:5,7; 17:14; 18:8; 19:1,6,16; 21:22; 22:5,6,20,21

2963. κυριότης kuriotēs
EPH. 1:21; **COL.** 1:16; **2 PET.** 2:10; **JUDE** 1:8

2964. κυρόω kuroō
2 COR. 2:8; **GAL.** 3:15

2965. κύων kuōn
MATT. 7:6; **LUKE** 16:21; **PHIL.** 3:2; **2 PET.** 2:22; **REV.** 22:15

2966. κῶλον kōlon
HEB. 3:17

2967. κωλύω kōluō
MATT. 19:14; **MARK** 9:38,39; 10:14; **LUKE** 6:29; 9:49,50; 11:52; 18:16; 23:2; **ACTS** 8:36; 10:47; 11:17; 16:6; 24:23; 27:43; **ROM.** 1:13; **1 COR.** 14:39; **1 THESS.** 2:16; **1 TIM.** 4:3; **HEB.** 7:23; **2 PET.** 2:16; **3 JOHN** 1:10

2968. κώμη kōmē
MATT. 9:35; 10:11; 14:15; 21:2; **MARK** 6:6,36,56; 8:23,26,27; 11:2; **LUKE** 5:17; 8:1; 9:6,12,52,56; 10:38; 13:22; 17:12; 19:30; 24:13, 28; **JOHN** 7:42; 11:1,30; **ACTS** 8:25

2969. κωμόπολις kōmopolis
MARK 1:38

2970. κῶμος kōmos
ROM. 13:13; **GAL.** 5:21; **1 PET.** 4:3

2971. κώνωψ kōnōps
MATT. 23:24

2972. Κῶς Kōs
ACTS 21:1

2973. Κωσάμ Kōsam
LUKE 3:28

2974. κωφός kōphos
MATT. 9:32,33; 11:5; 12:22; 15:30,31; **MARK** 7:32,37; 9:25; **LUKE** 1:22; 7:22; 11:14

Λ

2975. λαγχάνω lagchanō
LUKE 1:9; **JOHN** 19:24; **ACTS** 1:17; **2 PET.** 1:1

2976. Λάζαρος Lazaros
LUKE 16:20,23-25; **JOHN** 11:1,2,5,11,14,43; 12:1,2,9,10,17

2977. λάθρα lathra
MATT. 1:19; 2:7; **JOHN** 11:28; **ACTS** 16:37

2978. λαῖλαψ lailaps
MARK 4:37; **LUKE** 8:23; **2 PET.** 2:17

2979. λακτίζω laktizō
ACTS 9:5; 26:14

2980. λαλέω laleō
MATT. 9:18,33; 10:19,20; 12:22,34,36,46,47; 13:3,10,13,33,34; 14:27; 15:31; 17:5; 23:1; 26:13,47; 28:18; **MARK** 1:34; 2:2,7; 4:33,34; 5:35,36; 6:50; 7:35,37; 8:32; 9:6; 13:11; 14:9,43; 16:17,19; **LUKE** 1:19,20,22,45,55,64,70; 2:17, 18,20,33,38,50; 4:41; 5:4,21; 6:45; 7:15; 8:49; 9:11; 11:14,37; 12:3; 22:47,60; 24:6,25,32,36,44; **JOHN** 1:37; 3:11,31,34; 4:26,27; 6:63; 7:13,17, 18,26,46; 8:12,20,25,26,28,30,38,40,44; 9:21,29, 37; 10:6; 12:29,36,41,48,49,50; 14:10,25,30; 15:3,11,22; 16:1,4,6,13,18,25,29,33; 17:1,13; 18:20,21,23; 19:10; **ACTS** 2:4,6,7,11,31; 3:21, 22,24; 4:1,17,20,29,31; 5:20,40; 6:10,11,13; 7:6,38,44; 8:25,26; 9:6,27,29; 10:6,7,32,44,46; 11:14,15,19,20; 13:42,46; 14:1,9,25; 16:6,13, 14,32; 17:19; 18:9,25; 19:6; 20:30; 21:39; 22:9, 10; 23:7,9,18; 26:14,22,26,31; 27:25; 28:21,25; **ROM.** 3:19; 7:1; 15:18; **1 COR.** 2:6,7,13; 3:1; 9:8; 12:3,30; 13:1,11; 14:2-6,9,11,13,18,19, 21,23,27-29,34,35,39; **2 COR.** 2:17; 4:13; 7:14; 11:17,23; 12:4,19; 13:3; **EPH.** 4:25; 5:19; 6:20; **PHIL.** 1:14; **COL.** 4:3,4; **1 THESS.** 1:8; 2:2,

4,16; **1 TIM.** 5:13; **TITUS** 2:1,15; **HEB.** 1:1,2; 2:2,3,5; 3:5; 4:8; 5:5; 6:9; 7:14; 9:19; 11:4,18; 12:24,25; 13:7; **JAMES** 1:19; 2:12; 5:10; **1 PET.** 3:10; 4:11; **2 PET.** 1:21; 3:16; **1 JOHN** 4:5; **2 JOHN** 1:12; **3 JOHN** 1:14; **JUDE** 1:15,16; **REV.** 1:12; 4:1; 10:3,4,8; 13:5,11,15; 17:1; 21:9,15

2981. λαλιά *lalia*
MATT. 26:73; **MARK** 14:70; **JOHN** 4:42; 8:43

2982. λαμά, λαμμᾶ *lama, lamma*
MATT. 27:46; **MARK** 15:34

2983. λαμβάνω *lambanō*
MATT. 5:40; 7:8; 8:17; 10:8,38,41; 12:14; 13:20,31,33; 14:19; 15:26,36; 16:5,7-10; 17:24, 25,27; 19:29; 20:7,9-11; 21:22,34,35,39; 22:15; 23:14; 25:1,3,4,16,18,20,22,24; 26:26,27,52; 27:1,6,7,9,24,30,48,59; 28:12,15; **MARK** 4:16; 6:41; 7:27; 8:6,14; 9:36; 10:30; 11:24; 12:2,3, 8,19-22,40; 14:22,23; 15:23; **LUKE** 5:5,26; 6:4; 7:16; 9:16,39; 11:10; 13:19,21; 19:12,15; 20:21, 28-31,47; 22:17,19; 24:30,43; **JOHN** 1:12,16; 3:11,27,32,33; 4:36; 5:34,41,43,44; 6:7,11,21; 7:23,39; 10:17,18; 12:3,13,48; 13:4,12,20,30; 14:17; 16:14,15,24; 17:8; 18:3,31; 19:1,6,23, 27,30,40; 20:22; 21:13; **ACTS** 1:8,20,25; 2:23,33,38; 3:3,5; 7:53; 8:15,17,19; 9:19,25; 10:43,47; 15:14; 16:3,24; 17:9,15; 19:2; 20:24, 35; 24:27; 25:16; 26:10,18; 27:35; 28:15; **ROM.** 1:5; 4:11; 5:11,17; 7:8,11; 8:15; 13:2; **1 COR.** 2:12; 3:8,14; 4:7; 9:24,25; 10:13; 11:23,24; 14:5; **2 COR.** 11:4,8,20,24; 12:16; **GAL.** 2:6; 3:2,14; **PHIL.** 2:7; 3:12; **COL.** 4:10; **1 TIM.** 4:4; **2 TIM.** 1:5; **HEB.** 2:2,3; 4:16; 5:1,4; 7:5,8,9; 9:15,19; 10:26; 11:8,11,13,29,35,36; **JAMES** 1:7,12; 3:1; 4:3; 5:7,10; **1 PET.** 4:10; **2 PET.** 1:9,17; **1 JOHN** 2:27; 3:22; 5:9; **2 JOHN** 1:4,10; **3 JOHN** 1:7; **REV.** 2:17,27; 3:3,11; 4:11; 5:7-9, 12; 6:4; 8:5; 10:8-10; 11:17; 14:9,11; 17:12; 18:4; 19:20; 20:4; 22:17

2984. Λάμεχ *Lamech*
LUKE 3:36

2985. λαμπάς *lampas*
MATT. 25:1,3,4,7,8; **JOHN** 18:3; **ACTS** 20:8; **REV.** 4:5; 8:10

2986. λαμπρός *lampros*
LUKE 23:11; **ACTS** 10:30; **JAMES** 2:2,3; **REV.** 15:6; 18:14; 19:8; 22:1,16

2987. λαμπρότης *lamprotēs*
ACTS 26:13

2988. λαμπρῶς *lamprōs*
LUKE 16:19

2989. λάμπω *lampō*
MATT. 5:15,16; 17:2; **LUKE** 17:24; **ACTS** 12:7; **2 COR.** 4:6

2990. λανθάνω *lanthanō*
MARK 7:24; **LUKE** 8:47; **ACTS** 26:26; **HEB.** 13:2; **2 PET.** 3:5,8

2991. λαξευτός *laxeutos*
LUKE 23:53

2992. λαός *laos*
MATT. 1:21; 2:4,6; 4:16,23; 9:35; 13:15; 15:8; 21:23; 26:3,5,47; 27:1,25,64; **MARK** 7:6; 11:32; 14:2; **LUKE** 1:10,17,21,68,77; 2:10,31,32; 3:15, 18,21; 6:17; 7:1,16,29; 8:47; 9:13; 18:43; 19:47, 48; 20:1,6,9,19,26,45; 21:23,38; 22:2,66; 23:5, 13,14,27,35; 24:19; **JOHN** 8:2; 11:50; 18:14; **ACTS** 2:47; 3:9,11,12,23; 4:1,2,8,10,17,21,25, 27; 5:12,13,20,25,26,34,37; 6:8,12; 7:17,34; 10:2,41,42; 12:4,11; 13:15,17,24,31; 15:14; 18:10; 19:4; 21:28,30,36,39,40; 23:5; 26:17,23; 28:17,26,27; **ROM.** 9:25,26; 10:21; 11:1,2; 15:10,11; **1 COR.** 10:7; 14:21; **2 COR.** 6:16; **TITUS** 2:14; **HEB.** 2:17; 4:9; 5:3; 7:5,11,27; 8:10; 9:7,19; 10:30; 11:25; 13:12; **1 PET.** 2:9,10; **2 PET.** 2:1; **JUDE** 1:5; **REV.** 5:9; 7:9; 10:11; 11:9; 14:6; 17:15; 18:4; 21:3

2993. Λαοδίκεια *Laodikeia*
COL. 2:1; 4:13,15,16; **REV.** 1:11

2994. Λαοδικεύς *Laodikeus*
COL. 4:16; **REV.** 3:14

2995. λάρυγξ *larugx*
ROM. 3:13

2996. Λασαία *Lasaia*
ACTS 27:8

2997. λάσχω laschō
ACTS 1:18

2998. λατομέω latomeō
MATT. 27:60; MARK 15:46

2999. λατρεία latreia
JOHN 16:2; ROM. 9:4; 12:1; HEB. 9:1,6

3000. λατρεύω latreuō
MATT. 4:10; LUKE 1:74; 2:37; 4:8; ACTS
7:7,42; 24:14; 26:7; 27:23; ROM. 1:9,25; PHIL.
3:3; 2 TIM. 1:3; HEB. 8:5; 9:9,14; 10:2; 12:28;
13:10; REV. 7:15; 22:3

3001. λάχανον lachanon
MATT. 13:32; MARK 4:32; LUKE 11:42;
ROM. 14:2

3002. Λεββαῖος Lebbaios
MATT. 10:3

3003. λεγεών legeōn
MATT. 26:53; MARK 5:9,15; LUKE 8:30

3005. λεῖμμα leimma
ROM. 11:5

3006. λεῖος leios
LUKE 3:5

3007. λείπω leipō
LUKE 18:22; TITUS 1:5; 3:13; JAMES 1:4,5;
2:15

3008. λειτουργέω leitourgeō
ACTS 13:2; ROM. 15:27; HEB. 10:11

3009. λειτουργία leitourgia
LUKE 1:23; 2 COR. 9:12; PHIL. 2:17,30;
HEB. 8:6; 9:21

3010. λειτουργικός leitourgikos
HEB. 1:14

3011. λειτουργός leitourgos
ROM. 13:6; 15:16; PHIL. 2:25; HEB. 1:7; 8:2

3012. λέντιον lention
JOHN 13:4,5

3013. λεπίς lepis
ACTS 9:18

3014. λέπρα lepra
MATT. 8:3; MARK 1:42; LUKE 5:12,13

3015. λεπρός lepros
MATT. 8:2; 10:8; 11:5; 26:6; MARK 1:40;
14:3; LUKE 4:27; 7:22; 17:12

3016. λεπτόν lepton
MARK 12:42; LUKE 12:59; 21:2

3017. A. Λευΐ Leui
(Son of Jacob)
HEB. 7:5,9; REV. 7:7

B. Λευΐ Leui
(Son of Melchi)
LUKE 3:24

C. Λευΐ Leui
(Son of Simeon)
LUKE 3:29

3018. Λευΐς Leuis
MARK 2:14; LUKE 5:27,29

3019. Λευΐτης Leuitēs
LUKE 10:32; JOHN 1:19; ACTS 4:36

3020. Λευϊτικός Leuitikos
HEB. 7:11

3021. λευκαίνω leukainō
MARK 9:3; REV. 7:14

3022. λευκός leukos
MATT. 5:36; 17:2; 28:3; MARK 9:3; 16:5;
LUKE 9:29; JOHN 4:35; 20:12; ACTS 1:10;
REV. 1:14; 2:17; 3:4,5,18; 4:4; 6:2,11; 7:9,13;
14:14; 19:11,14; 20:11

3023. λέων *leōn*
2 TIM. 4:17; HEB. 11:33; 1 PET. 5:8; REV.
4:7; 5:5; 9:8,17; 10:3; 13:2

3024. λήθη *lēthē*
2 PET. 1:9

3025. ληνός *lēnos*
MATT. 21:33; REV. 14:19,20; 19:15

3026. λῆρος *lēros*
LUKE 24:11

3027. ληστής *lēstēs*
MATT. 21:13; 26:55; 27:38,44; MARK 11:17;
14:48; 15:27; LUKE 10:30,36; 19:46; 22:52;
JOHN 10:1,8; 18:40; 2 COR. 11:26

3028. λῆψις *lēpsis*
PHIL. 4:15

3029. λίαν *lian*
MATT. 2:16; 4:8; 8:28; 27:14; MARK 1:35;
6:51; 9:3; 16:2; LUKE 23:8; 2 COR. 11:5;
12:11; 2 TIM. 4:15; 2 JOHN 1:4; 3 JOHN 1:3

3030. λίβανος *libanos*
MATT. 2:11; REV. 18:13

3031. λιβανωτός *libanōtos*
REV. 8:3,5

3032. Λιβερτῖνος *Libertinos*
ACTS 6:9

3033. Λιβύη *Libuē*
ACTS 2:10

3034. λιθάζω *lithazō*
JOHN 10:31-33; 11:8; ACTS 5:26; 14:19;
2 COR. 11:25; HEB. 11:37

3035. λίθινος *lithinos*
JOHN 2:6; 2 COR. 3:3; REV. 9:20

3036. λιθοβολέω *lithoboleō*
MATT. 21:35; 23:37; MARK 12:4; LUKE
13:34; JOHN 8:5; ACTS 7:58,59; 14:5; HEB.
12:20

3037. λίθος *lithos*
MATT. 3:9; 4:3,6; 7:9; 21:42,44; 24:2; 27:60,66;
28:2; MARK 5:5; 9:42; 12:10; 13:1,2; 15:46;
16:3,4; LUKE 3:8; 4:3,11; 11:11; 19:40,44;
20:17,18; 21:5,6; 22:41; 24:2; JOHN 8:7,59;
10:31; 11:38,39,41; 20:1; ACTS 4:11; 17:29;
ROM. 9:32,33; 1 COR. 3:12; 2 COR. 3:7;
1 PET. 2:4,5-8; REV. 4:3; 17:4; 18:12,16,21;
21:11,19

3038. Λιθόστρωτος *Lithostrōtos*
JOHN 19:13

3039. λικμάω *likmaō*
MATT. 21:44; LUKE 20:18

3040. λιμήν *limēn*
ACTS 27:8,12

3041. λίμνη *limnē*
LUKE 5:1,2; 8:22,23,33; REV. 19:20;
20:10,14,15; 21:8

3042. λιμός *limos*
MATT. 24:7; MARK 13:8; LUKE 4:25;
15:14,17; 21:11; ACTS 7:11; 11:28; ROM.
8:35; 2 COR. 11:27; REV. 6:8; 18:8

3043. λίνον *linon*
MATT. 12:20; REV. 15:6

3044. Λῖνος *Linos*
2 TIM. 4:21

3045. λιπαρός *liparos*
REV. 18:14

3046. λίτρα *litra*
JOHN 12:3; 19:39

3047. λίψ *lips*
ACTS 27:12

3048. λογία *logia*
1 COR. 16:1,2

3049. λογίζομαι *logizomai*
MARK 11:31; 15:28; LUKE 22:37; ACTS
19:27; ROM. 2:3,26; 3:28; 4:3-6,8-11,22-24;
6:11; 8:18,36; 9:8; 14:14; 1 COR. 4:1; 13:5,11;

2 COR. 3:5; 5:19; 10:2,7,11; 11:5; 12:6; **GAL.** 3:6; **PHIL.** 3:13; 4:8; **2 TIM.** 4:16; **HEB.** 11:19; **JAMES** 2:23; **1 PET.** 5:12

3050. λογικός logikos
ROM. 12:1; **1 PET.** 2:2

3051. λόγιον logion
ACTS 7:38; **ROM.** 3:2; **HEB.** 5:12; **1 PET.** 4:11

3052. λόγιος logios
ACTS 18:24

3053. λογισμός logismos
ROM. 2:15; **2 COR.** 10:5

3054. λογομαχέω logomacheō
2 TIM. 2:14

3055. λογομαχία logomachia
1 TIM. 6:4

3056. λόγος logos
MATT. 5:32,37; 7:24,26,28; 8:8,16; 10:14; 12:32,36,37; 13:19-23; 15:12,23; 18:23; 19:1,11, 22; 21:24; 22:15,46; 24:35; 25:19; 26:1,44; 28:15; **MARK** 1:45; 2:2; 4:14-20,33; 5:36; 7:13, 29; 8:32,38; 9:10; 10:22,24; 11:29; 12:13; 13:31; 14:39; 16:20; **LUKE** 1:2,4,20,29; 3:4; 4:22,32, 36; 5:1,15; 6:47; 7:7,17; 8:11-13,15,21; 9:26,28, 44; 10:39; 11:28; 12:10; 16:2; 20:3,20; 21:33; 22:61; 23:9; 24:17,19,44; **JOHN** 1:1,14; 2:22; 4:37,39,41,50; 5:24,38; 6:60; 7:36,40; 8:31,37, 43,51,52,55; 10:19,35; 12:38,48; 14:23,24; 15:3, 20,25; 17:6,14,17,20; 18:9,32; 19:8,13; 21:23; **ACTS** 1:1; 2:22,40,41; 4:4,29,31; 5:5,24; 6:2,4, 5,7; 7:22,29; 8:4,14,21,25; 10:29,36,44; 11:1,19, 22; 12:24; 13:5,7,15,26,44,46,48,49; 14:3,12,25; 15:6,7,15,24,27,32,35,36; 16:6,32,36; 17:11,13; 18:11,14,15; 19:10,20,38,40; 20:2,7,24,32,35,38; 22:22; **ROM.** 3:4; 9:6,9,28; 13:9; 14:12; 15:18; **1 COR.** 1:5,17,18; 2:1,4,13; 4:19,20; 12:8; 14:9, 19,36; 15:2,54; **2 COR.** 1:18; 2:17; 4:2; 5:19; 6:7; 8:7; 10:10,11; 11:6; **GAL.** 5:14; 6:6; **EPH.** 1:13; 4:29; 5:6; 6:19; **PHIL.** 1:14; 2:16; 4:15,17; **COL.** 1:5,25; 2:23; 3:16,17; 4:3,6; **1 THESS.** 1:5,6,8; 2:5,13; 4:15,18; **2 THESS.** 2:2,15,17; 3:1,14; **1 TIM.** 1:15; 3:1; 4:5,6,9,12; 5:17; 6:8; **2 TIM.** 1:13; 2:9,11,15,17; 4:2,15; **TITUS** 1:3,9; 2:5,8; 3:8; **HEB.** 2:2; 4:2,12,13; 5:11,13; 6:1;

7:28; 12:19; 13:7,17,22; **JAMES** 1:18,21-23; 3:2; **1 PET.** 1:23; 2:8; 3:1,15; 4:5; **2 PET.** 1:19; 2:3; 3:5,7; **1 JOHN** 1:1,10; 2:5,7,14; 3:18; 5:7; **3 JOHN** 1:10; **REV.** 1:2,3,9; 3:8,10; 6:9; 12:11; 19:9,13; 20:4; 21:5; 22:6,7,9,10,18,19

3057. λόγχη logchē
JOHN 19:34

3058. λοιδορέω loidoreō
JOHN 9:28; **ACTS** 23:4; **1 COR.** 4:12; **1 PET.** 2:23

3059. λοιδορία loidoria
1 TIM. 5:14; **1 PET.** 3:9

3060. λοίδορος loidoros
1 COR. 5:11; 6:10

3061. λοιμός loimos
MATT. 24:7; **LUKE** 21:11; **ACTS** 24:5

3062. λοιπός loipos
MATT. 22:6; 25:11; 27:49; **MARK** 4:19; 16:13; **LUKE** 8:10; 12:26; 18:9,11; 24:9,10; **ACTS** 2:37; 5:13; 17:9; 27:44; 28:9; **ROM.** 1:13; 11:7; **1 COR.** 7:12; 9:5; 11:34; 15:37; **2 COR.** 12:13; 13:2; **GAL.** 2:13; **EPH.** 2:3; 4:17; **PHIL.** 1:13; 4:3; **1 THESS.** 4:13; 5:6; **1 TIM.** 5:20; **2 PET.** 3:16; **REV.** 2:24; 3:2; 8:13; 9:20; 11:13; 12:17; 19:21; 20:5

3063. λοιπόν loipon   adv.
    (Neut. sing. of λοιπός)
MATT. 26:45; **MARK** 14:41; **ACTS** 27:20; **1 COR.** 1:16; 4:2; 7:29; **2 COR.** 13:11; **EPH.** 6:10; **PHIL.** 3:1; 4:8; **1 THESS.** 4:1; **2 THESS.** 3:1; **2 TIM.** 4:8; **HEB.** 10:13

3064. λοιποῦ loipou   adv.
    (Gen. sing. of λοιπός)
GAL. 6:17

3065. Λουκᾶς Loukas
COL. 4:14; **2 TIM.** 4:11; **PHILE.** 1:24

3066. Λούκιος Loukios
ACTS 13:1; **ROM.** 16:21

3067. λουτρόν *loutron*
EPH. 5:26; TITUS 3:5

3068. λούω *louō*
JOHN 13:10; ACTS 9:37; 16:33; HEB. 10:22;
2 PET. 2:22; REV. 1:5

3069. Λύδδα *Ludda*
ACTS 9:32,35,38

3070. Λυδία *Ludia*
ACTS 16:14,40

3071. Λυκαονία *Lukaonia*
ACTS 14:6

3072. Λυκαονιστί *Lukaonisti*
ACTS 14:11

3073. Λυκία *Lukia*
ACTS 27:5

3074. λύκος *lukos*
MATT. 7:15; 10:16; LUKE 10:3; JOHN 10:12;
ACTS 20:29

3075. λυμαίνομαι *lumainomai*
ACTS 8:3

3076. λυπέω *lupeō*
MATT. 14:9; 17:23; 18:31; 19:22; 26:22,37;
MARK 10:22; 14:19; JOHN 16:20; 21:17;
ROM. 14:15; 2 COR. 2:2,4,5; 6:10; 7:8,9,11;
EPH. 4:30; 1 THESS. 4:13; 1 PET. 1:6

3077. λύπη *lupē*
LUKE 22:45; JOHN 16:6,20-22; ROM. 9:2;
2 COR. 2:1,3,7; 7:10; 9:7; PHIL. 2:27; HEB.
12:11; 1 PET. 2:19

3078. Λυσανίας *Lusanias*
LUKE 3:1

3079. Λυσίας *Lusias*
ACTS 23:26; 24:7,22

3080. λύσις *lusis*
1 COR. 7:27

3081. λυσιτελέω *lusiteleō*
LUKE 17:2

3082. A. Λύστρα (ἡ) *Lustra*
ACTS 14:6,21; 16:1

B. Λύστρα (τά) *Lustra*
ACTS 14:8; 16:2; 2 TIM. 3:11

3083. λύτρον *lutron*
MATT. 20:28; MARK 10:45

3084. λυτρόω *lutroō*
LUKE 24:21; TITUS 2:14; 1 PET. 1:18

3085. λύτρωσις *lutrōsis*
LUKE 1:68; 2:38; HEB. 9:12

3086. λυτρωτής *lutrōtēs*
ACTS 7:35

3087. λυχνία *luchnia*
MATT. 5:15; MARK 4:21; LUKE 8:16; 11:33;
HEB. 9:2; REV. 1:12,13,20; 2:1,5; 11:4

3088. λύχνος *luchnos*
MATT. 5:15; 6:22; MARK 4:21; LUKE 8:16;
11:33,34,36; 12:35; 15:8; JOHN 5:35; 2 PET.
1:19; REV. 18:23; 21:23; 22:5

3089. λύω *luō*
MATT. 5:19; 16:19; 18:18; 21:2; MARK 1:7;
7:35; 11:2,4,5; LUKE 3:16; 13:15,16; 19:30,
31,33; JOHN 1:27; 2:19; 5:18; 7:23; 10:35;
11:44; ACTS 2:24; 7:33; 13:25,43; 22:30;
24:26; 27:41; 1 COR. 7:27; EPH. 2:14; 2 PET.
3:10-12; 1 JOHN 3:8; REV. 5:2,5; 9:14,15;
20:3,7

3090. Λωΐς *Lōis*
2 TIM. 1:5

3091. Λώτ *Lōt*
LUKE 17:28,29,32; 2 PET. 2:7

M

3092. Μαάθ Maath
LUKE 3:26

3093. Μαγδαλά Magdala
MATT. 15:39

3094. Μαγδαληνή Magdalēnē
MATT. 27:56,61; 28:1; MARK 15:40,47;
16:1,9; LUKE 8:2; 24:10; JOHN 19:25; 20:1,18

3095. μαγεία mageia
ACTS 8:11

3096. μαγεύω mageuō
ACTS 8:9

3097. μάγος magos
MATT. 2:1,7,16; ACTS 13:6,8

3098. Μαγώγ Magōg
REV. 20:8

**3099. Μαδιάν, Μαδιάμ
Madian, Madiam**
ACTS 7:29

3100. μαθητεύω mathēteuō
MATT. 13:52; 27:57; 28:19; ACTS 14:21

3101. μαθητής mathētēs
MATT. 5:1; 8:21,23,25; 9:10,11,14,19,37; 10:1,
24,25,42; 11:1,2; 12:1,2,49; 13:10,36; 14:12,15,
19,22,26; 15:2,12,23,32,33,36; 16:5,13,20,21,24;
17:6,10,13,16,19; 18:1; 19:10,13,23,25; 20:17;
21:1,6,20; 22:16; 23:1; 24:1,3; 26:1,8,17-19,26,
35,36,40,45,56; 27:64; 28:7-9,13,16; MARK
2:15,16,18,23; 3:7,9; 4:34; 5:31; 6:1,29,35,41,45;
7:2,5,17; 8:1,4,6,10,27,33,34; 9:14,18,28,31;
10:10,13,23,24,46; 11:1,14; 12:43; 13:1; 14:12-
14,16,32; 16:7; LUKE 5:30,33; 6:1,13,17,20,40;
7:11,18,19; 8:9,22; 9:1,14,16,18,40,43,54; 10:23;
11:1; 12:1,22; 14:26,27,33; 16:1; 17:1,22; 18:15;
19:29,37,39; 20:45; 22:11,39,45; JOHN 1:35,37;
2:2,11,12,17,22; 3:22,25; 4:1,2,8,27,31,33; 6:3,8,
11,12,16,22,24,60,61,66; 7:3; 8:31; 9:2,27,28;
11:7,8,12,54; 12:4,16; 13:5,22,23,35; 15:8;
16:17,29; 18:1,2,15-17,19,25; 19:26,27,38; 20:2-

4,8,10,18-20,25,26,30; 21:1,2,4,7,8,12,14,20,23,
24; ACTS 1:15; 6:1,2,7; 9:1,10,19,25,26,38;
11:26,29; 13:52; 14:20,22,28; 15:10; 16:1; 18:23,
27; 19:1,9,30; 20:1,7,30; 21:4,16

3102. μαθήτρια mathētria
ACTS 9:36

3103. Μαθουσάλα Mathousala
LUKE 3:37

3104. Μαϊνάν Mainan
LUKE 3:31

3105. μαίνομαι mainomai
JOHN 10:20; ACTS 12:15; 26:24,25; 1 COR.
14:23

3106. μακαρίζω makarizō
LUKE 1:48; JAMES 5:11

3107. μακάριος makarios
MATT. 5:3-11; 11:6; 13:16; 16:17; 24:46;
LUKE 1:45; 6:20-22; 7:23; 10:23; 11:27,28;
12:37,38,43; 14:14,15; 23:29; JOHN 13:17;
20:29; ACTS 20:35; 26:2; ROM. 4:7,8; 14:22;
1 COR. 7:40; 1 TIM. 1:11; 6:15; TITUS 2:13;
JAMES 1:12,25; 1 PET. 3:14; 4:14; REV. 1:3;
14:13; 16:15; 19:9; 20:6; 22:7,14

3108. μακαρισμός makarismos
ROM. 4:6,9; GAL. 4:15

3109. Μακεδονία Makedonia
ACTS 16:9,10,12; 18:5; 19:21,22; 20:1,3; ROM.
15:26; 1 COR. 16:5; 2 COR. 1:16; 2:13; 7:5;
8:1; 11:9; PHIL. 4:15; 1 THESS. 1:7,8; 4:10;
1 TIM. 1:3

3110. Μακεδών Makedōn
ACTS 16:9; 19:29; 27:2; 2 COR. 9:2,4

3111. μάκελλον makellon
1 COR. 10:25

3112. μακράν makran
MATT. 8:30; MARK 12:34; LUKE 7:6; 15:20;
JOHN 21:8; ACTS 2:39; 17:27; 22:21; EPH.
2:13,17

3113. μακρόθεν makrothen
MATT. 26:58; 27:55; MARK 5:6; 8:3; 11:13;
14:54; 15:40; LUKE 16:23; 18:13; 22:54; 23:49;
REV. 18:10,15,17

3114. μακροθυμέω makrothumeō
MATT. 18:26,29; LUKE 18:7; 1 COR. 13:4;
1 THESS. 5:14; HEB. 6:15; JAMES 5:7,8;
2 PET. 3:9

3115. μακροθυμία makrothumia
ROM. 2:4; 9:22; 2 COR. 6:6; GAL. 5:22; EPH.
4:2; COL. 1:11; 3:12; 1 TIM. 1:16; 2 TIM.
3:10; 4:2; HEB. 6:12; JAMES 5:10; 1 PET.
3:20; 2 PET. 3:15

3116. μακροθύμως makrothumōs
ACTS 26:3

3117. μακρός makros
MATT. 23:14; MARK 12:40; LUKE 15:13;
19:12; 20:47

3118. μακροχρόνιος makrochronios
EPH. 6:3

3119. μαλακία malakia
MATT. 4:23; 9:35; 10:1

3120. μαλακός malakos
MATT. 11:8; LUKE 7:25; 1 COR. 6:9

3121. Μαλελεήλ Maleleēl
LUKE 3:37

3122. μάλιστα malista
ACTS 20:38; 25:26; 26:3; GAL. 6:10; PHIL.
4:22; 1 TIM. 4:10; 5:8,17; 2 TIM. 4:13; TITUS
1:10; PHILE. 1:16; 2 PET. 2:10

3123. μᾶλλον mallon
MATT. 6:26,30; 7:11; 10:6,25,28; 18:13; 25:9;
27:24; MARK 5:26; 7:36; 9:42; 10:48; 14:31;
15:11; LUKE 5:15; 10:20; 11:13; 12:24,28;
18:39; JOHN 3:19; 5:18; 12:43; 19:8; ACTS
4:19; 5:14,29; 9:22; 20:35; 22:2; 27:11; ROM.
5:9,10,15,17; 8:34; 11:12,24; 14:13; 1 COR. 5:2;
6:7; 7:21; 9:12,15; 12:22; 14:1,5,18; 2 COR.
2:7; 3:8,9,11; 5:8; 7:7,13; 12:9; GAL. 4:9,27;

EPH. 4:28; 5:4,11; PHIL. 1:9,12,23; 2:12; 3:4;
1 THESS. 4:1,10; 1 TIM. 1:4; 6:2; 2 TIM. 3:4;
PHILE. 1:9,16; HEB. 9:14; 10:25; 11:25;
12:9,13,25; 2 PET. 1:10

3124. Μάλχος Malchos
JOHN 18:10

3125. μάμμη mammē
2 TIM. 1:5

**3126. μαμμωνᾶς, μαμωνᾶς
mammōnas, mamōnas**
MATT. 6:24; LUKE 16:9,11,13

3127. Μαναήν Manaēn
ACTS 13:1

3128. Μανασσῆς Manassēs
MATT. 1:10; REV. 7:6

3129. μανθάνω manthanō
MATT. 9:13; 11:29; 24:32; MARK 13:28;
JOHN 6:45; 7:15; ACTS 23:27; ROM. 16:17;
1 COR. 4:6; 14:31,35; GAL. 3:2; EPH. 4:20;
PHIL. 4:9,11; COL. 1:7; 1 TIM. 2:11; 5:4,13;
2 TIM. 3:7,14; TITUS 3:14; HEB. 5:8; REV.
14:3

3130. μανία mania
ACTS 26:24

3131. μάννα manna
JOHN 6:31,49,58; HEB. 9:4; REV. 2:17

3132. μαντεύομαι manteuomai
ACTS 16:16

3133. μαραίνω marainō
JAMES 1:11

3134. μαράν ἀθά maran atha
1 COR. 16:22

3135. μαργαρίτης margaritēs
MATT. 7:6; 13:45,46; 1 TIM. 2:9; REV. 17:4;
18:12,16; 21:21

3136. Μάρθα Martha
LUKE 10:38,40,41; JOHN 11:1,5,19-21,24,30,39; 12:2

3137. A. Μαρία, Μαριάμ
Maria, Mariam
(Mother of Jesus)
MATT. 1:16,18,20; 2:11; 13:55; MARK 6:3; LUKE 1:27,30,34,38,39,41,46,56; 2:5,16,19,34; ACTS 1:14

B. Μαρία, Μαριάμ
Maria, Mariam
(Magdalene)
MATT. 27:56,61; 28:1; MARK 15:40, 47; 16:1,9; LUKE 8:2; 24:10; JOHN 19:25; 20:1,11,16,18

C. Μαρία Maria
(Wife of Clopas [Alpheus] and mother of James the Less and Joses)
MATT. 27:56,61; 28:1; MARK 15:40,47; 16:1; LUKE 24:10; JOHN 19:25

D. Μαρία, Μαριάμ
Maria, Mariam
(Sister of Lazarus)
LUKE 10:39,42; JOHN 11:1,2,19,20,28,31,32,45; 12:3

E. Μαρία Maria
(Mother of John Mark)
ACTS 12:12

F. Μαρία Maria
(Christian woman at Rome)
ROM. 16:6

3138. Μάρκος Markos
ACTS 12:12,25; 15:37,39; COL. 4:10; 2 TIM. 4:11; PHILE. 1:24; 1 PET. 5:13

3139. μάρμαρος marmaros
REV. 18:12

3140. μαρτυρέω martureō
MATT. 23:31; LUKE 4:22; 11:48; JOHN 1:7,8,15,32,34; 2:25; 3:11,26,28,32; 4:39,44; 5:31-33,36,37,39; 7:7; 8:13,14,18; 10:25; 12:17; 13:21; 15:26,27; 18:23,37; 19:35; 21:24; ACTS 6:3; 10:22,43; 13:22; 14:3; 15:8; 16:2; 22:5,12; 23:11; 26:5,22; ROM. 3:21; 10:2; 1 COR. 15:15; 2 COR. 8:3; GAL. 4:15; COL. 4:13; 1 THESS. 2:11; 1 TIM. 5:10; 6:13; HEB. 7:8,17; 10:15; 11:2,4,5,39; 1 JOHN 1:2; 4:14; 5:6-10; 3 JOHN 1:3,6,12; REV. 1:2; 22:16,20

3141. μαρτυρία marturia
MARK 14:55,56,59; LUKE 22:71; JOHN 1:7,19; 3:11,32,33; 5:31,32,34,36; 8:13,14,17; 19:35; 21:24; ACTS 22:18; 1 TIM. 3:7; TITUS 1:13; 1 JOHN 5:9-11; 3 JOHN 1:12; REV. 1:2,9; 6:9; 11:7; 12:11,17; 19:10; 20:4

3142. μαρτύριον marturion
MATT. 8:4; 10:18; 24:14; MARK 1:44; 6:11; 13:9; LUKE 5:14; 9:5; 21:13; ACTS 4:33; 7:44; 1 COR. 1:6; 2:1; 2 COR. 1:12; 2 THESS. 1:10; 1 TIM. 2:6; 2 TIM. 1:8; HEB. 3:5; JAMES 5:3; REV. 15:5

3143. μαρτύρομαι marturomai
ACTS 20:26; GAL. 5:3; EPH. 4:17

3144. μάρτυς martus
MATT. 18:16; 26:65; MARK 14:63; LUKE 24:48; ACTS 1:8,22; 2:32; 3:15; 5:32; 6:13; 7:58; 10:39,41; 13:31; 22:15,20; 26:16; ROM. 1:9; 2 COR. 1:23; 13:1; PHIL. 1:8; 1 THESS. 2:5,10; 1 TIM. 5:19; 6:12; 2 TIM. 2:2; HEB. 10:28; 12:1; 1 PET. 5:1; REV. 1:5; 2:13; 3:14; 11:3; 17:6

3145. μασσάομαι massaomai
REV. 16:10

3146. μαστιγόω mastigoō
MATT. 10:17; 20:19; 23:34; MARK 10:34; LUKE 18:33; JOHN 19:1; HEB. 12:6

3147. μαστίζω mastizō
ACTS 22:25

3148. μάστιξ mastix
MARK 3:10; 5:29,34; LUKE 7:21; ACTS 22:24; HEB. 11:36

3149. μαστός mastos
LUKE 11:27; 23:29; REV. 1:13

3150. ματαιολογία *mataiologia*
1 TIM. 1:6

3151. ματαιολόγος *mataiologos*
TITUS 1:10

3152. μάταιος *mataios*
ACTS 14:15; **1 COR.** 3:20; 15:17; **TITUS** 3:9;
JAMES 1:26; **1 PET.** 1:18

3153. ματαιότης *mataiotēs*
ROM. 8:20; **EPH.** 4:17; **2 PET.** 2:18

3154. ματαιόω *mataioō*
ROM. 1:21

3155. μάτην *matēn*
MATT. 15:9; **MARK** 7:7

3156. Ματθαῖος *Matthaios*
MATT. 9:9; 10:3; **MARK** 3:18; **LUKE** 6:15;
ACTS 1:13

3157. Ματθάν *Matthan*
MATT. 1:15

3158. Ματθάτ *Matthat*
LUKE 3:24,29

3159. Ματθίας *Matthias*
ACTS 1:23,26

3160. Ματταθά *Mattatha*
LUKE 3:31

3161. Ματταθίας *Mattathias*
LUKE 3:25,26

3162. μάχαιρα *machaira*
MATT. 10:34; 26:47,51,52,55; **MARK**
14:43,47,48; **LUKE** 21:24; 22:36,38,49,52;
JOHN 18:10,11; **ACTS** 12:2; 16:27; **ROM.**
8:35; 13:4; **EPH.** 6:17; **HEB.** 4:12; 11:34,37;
REV. 6:4; 13:10,14

3163. μάχη *machē*
2 COR. 7:5; **2 TIM.** 2:23; **TITUS** 3:9; **JAMES**
4:1

3164. μάχομαι *machomai*
JOHN 6:52; **ACTS** 7:26; **2 TIM.** 2:24; **JAMES**
4:2

3166. μεγαλαυχέω *megalaucheō*
JAMES 3:5

3167. μεγαλεῖος *megaleios*
LUKE 1:49; **ACTS** 2:11

3168. μεγαλειότης *megaleiotēs*
LUKE 9:43; **ACTS** 19:27; **2 PET.** 1:16

3169. μεγαλοπρεπής *megaloprepēs*
2 PET. 1:17

3170. μεγαλύνω *megalunō*
MATT. 23:5; **LUKE** 1:46,58; **ACTS** 5:13;
10:46; 19:17; **2 COR.** 10:15; **PHIL.** 1:20

3171. μεγάλως *megalōs*
PHIL. 4:10

3172. μεγαλωσύνη *megalōsunē*
HEB. 1:3; 8:1; **JUDE** 1:25

3173. μέγας *megas*
MATT. 2:10; 4:16; 5:19,35; 7:27; 8:24,26;
15:28; 20:25,26; 22:36,38; 24:21,24,31; 27:46,
50,60; 28:2,8; **MARK** 1:26; 4:32,37,39,41; 5:7,
11,42; 10:42,43; 13:2; 14:15; 15:34,37; 16:4;
LUKE 1:15,32,42; 2:9,10; 4:25,33,38; 5:29;
6:49; 7:16; 8:28,37; 9:48; 13:19; 14:16; 16:26;
17:15; 19:37; 21:11,23; 22:12; 23:23,46; 24:52;
JOHN 6:18; 7:37; 11:43; 19:31; 21:11; **ACTS**
2:20; 4:33; 5:5,11; 6:8; 7:11,57,60; 8:1,2,7-10,
13; 10:11; 11:5,28; 14:10; 15:3; 16:26,28; 19:27,
28,34,35; 23:9; 26:22,24; **ROM.** 9:2; **1 COR.**
9:11; 16:9; **2 COR.** 11:15; **EPH.** 5:32; **1 TIM.**
3:16; 6:6; **2 TIM.** 2:20; **TITUS** 2:13; **HEB.**
4:14; 8:11; 10:21,35; 11:24; 13:20; **JUDE** 1:6;
REV. 1:10; 2:22; 5:2,12; 6:4,10,12,13,17; 7:2,
10,14; 8:8,10,13; 9:2,14; 10:3; 11:8,11-13,15,17-
19; 12:1,3,9,10,12,14; 13:2,5,13,16; 14:2,7-9,15,
18,19; 15:1,3; 16:1,9,12,14,17-19,21; 17:1,5,6,
18; 18:1,2,10,16,18,19,21; 19:1,2,5,17,18; 20:1,
11,12; 21:3,10,12

3174. μέγεθος *megethos*
EPH. 1:19

3175. μεγιστᾶνες *megistanes*
MARK 6:21; REV. 6:15; 18:23

3176. μέγιστος *megistos*
2 PET. 1:4

3177. μεθερμηνεύω *methermēneuō*
MATT. 1:23; MARK 5:41; 15:22,34; JOHN 1:41; ACTS 4:36; 13:8

3178. μέθη *methē*
LUKE 21:34; ROM. 13:13; GAL. 5:21

3179. I. μεθιστάνω *methistanō*
1 COR. 13:2

　　II. μεθίστημι *methistēmi*
LUKE 16:4; ACTS 13:22; 19:26; COL. 1:13

3180. μεθοδεία *methodeia*
EPH. 4:14; 6:11

3181. μεθόριος *methorios*
MARK 7:24

3182. μεθύσκω *methuskō*
LUKE 12:45; EPH. 5:18; 1 THESS. 5:7

3183. μέθυσος *methusos*
1 COR. 5:11; 6:10

3184. μεθύω *methuō*
MATT. 24:49; JOHN 2:10; ACTS 2:15; 1 COR. 11:21; 1 THESS. 5:7; REV. 17:2,6

3185. μεῖζον *meizon*　adv.
MATT. 20:31

3186. μειζότερος *meizoteros*
3 JOHN 1:4

3187. μείζων *meizōn*
MATT. 11:11; 12:6; 13:32; 18:1,4; 23:11,17,19; MARK 4:32; 9:34; 12:31; LUKE 7:28; 9:46; 12:18; 22:24,26,27; JOHN 1:50; 4:12; 5:20,36; 8:53; 10:29; 13:16; 14:12,28; 15:13,20; 19:11;

ROM. 9:12; 1 COR. 13:13; 14:5; HEB. 6:13,16; 9:11; 11:26; JAMES 3:1; 4:6; 2 PET. 2:11; 1 JOHN 3:20; 4:4; 5:9

3188. μέλαν *melan*
2 COR. 3:3; 2 JOHN 1:12; 3 JOHN 1:13

3189. μέλας *melas*
MATT. 5:36; REV. 6:5,12

3190. Μελεᾶς *Meleas*
LUKE 3:31

3191. μελετάω *meletaō*
MARK 13:11; ACTS 4:25; 1 TIM. 4:15

3192. μέλι *meli*
MATT. 3:4; MARK 1:6; REV. 10:9,10

3193. μελίσσιος *melissios*
LUKE 24:42

3194. Μελίτη *Melitē*
ACTS 28:1

3195. μέλλω *mellō*
MATT. 2:13; 3:7; 11:14; 12:32; 16:27; 17:12,22; 20:22; 24:6; MARK 10:32; 13:4; LUKE 3:7; 7:2; 9:31,44; 10:1; 13:9; 19:4,11; 21:7,36; 22:23; 24:21; JOHN 4:47; 6:6,15,71; 7:35,39; 11:51; 12:4,33; 14:22; 18:32; ACTS 3:3; 5:35; 11:28; 12:6; 13:34; 16:27; 17:31; 18:14; 19:27; 20:3,7, 13,38; 21:27,37; 22:16,26,29; 23:3,15,20,27,30; 24:15,25; 25:4; 26:2,22,23; 27:2,10,30,33; 28:6; ROM. 4:24; 5:14; 8:13,18,38; 1 COR. 3:22; GAL. 3:23; EPH. 1:21; COL. 2:17; 1 THESS. 3:4; 1 TIM. 1:16; 4:8; 6:19; 2 TIM. 4:1; HEB. 1:14; 2:5; 6:5; 8:5; 9:11; 10:1,27; 11:8,20; 13:14; JAMES 2:12; 1 PET. 5:1; 2 PET. 2:6; REV. 1:19; 2:10; 3:2,10,16; 6:11; 8:13; 10:4,7; 12:4,5; 17:8

3196. μέλος *melos*
MATT. 5:29,30; ROM. 6:13,19; 7:5,23; 12:4,5; 1 COR. 6:15; 12:12,14,18-20,22,25-27; EPH. 4:25; 5:30; COL. 3:5; JAMES 3:5,6; 4:1

3197. Μελχί *Melchi*
LUKE 3:24,28

3198. Μελχισεδέκ Melchisedek
HEB. 5:6,10; 6:20; 7:1,10,11,15,17,21

3199. μέλει melei
(All impers. forms of μέλω)
MATT. 22:16; MARK 4:38; 12:14; LUKE
10:40; JOHN 10:13; 12:6; ACTS 18:17;
1 COR. 7:21; 9:9; 1 PET. 5:7

3200. μεμβράνα membrana
2 TIM. 4:13

3201. μέμφομαι memphomai
MARK 7:2; ROM. 9:19; HEB. 8:8

3202. μεμψίμοιρος mempsimoiros
JUDE 1:16

3203 - 3302 omitted in Strong's
Dictionary of the Greek Testament

3304. μενοῦνγε menounge
LUKE 11:28; ROM. 9:20; 10:18; PHIL. 3:8

3305. μέντοι mentoi
JOHN 4:27; 7:13; 12:42; 20:5; 21:4; 2 TIM.
2:19; JAMES 2:8; JUDE 1:8

3306. μένω menō
MATT. 10:11; 11:23; 26:38; MARK 6:10;
14:34; LUKE 1:56; 8:27; 9:4; 10:7; 19:5; 24:29;
JOHN 1:32,33,38,39; 2:12; 3:36; 4:40; 5:38;
6:27,56; 7:9; 8:31,35; 9:41; 10:40; 11:6; 12:24,
34,46; 14:10,16,17,25; 15:4,5-7,9-11,16; 19:31;
21:22,23; ACTS 5:4; 9:43; 16:15; 18:3,20; 20:5,
15,23; 21:7,8; 27:31,41; 28:16,30; ROM. 9:11;
1 COR. 3:14; 7:8,11,20,24,40; 13:13; 15:6;
2 COR. 3:11,14; 9:9; PHIL. 1:25; 1 TIM. 2:15;
2 TIM. 2:13; 3:14; 4:20; HEB. 7:3,24; 10:34;
12:27; 13:1,14; 1 PET. 1:23,25; 1 JOHN
2:6,10,14,17,19,24,27,28; 3:6,9,14,15,17,24;
4:12,13,15,16; 2 JOHN 1:2,9; REV. 17:10

3307. μερίζω merizō
MATT. 12:25,26; MARK 3:24-26; 6:41; LUKE
12:13; ROM. 12:3; 1 COR. 1:13; 7:17,34;
2 COR. 10:13; HEB. 7:2

3308. μέριμνα merimna
MATT. 13:22; MARK 4:19; LUKE 8:14;
21:34; 2 COR. 11:28; 1 PET. 5:7

3309. μεριμνάω merimnaō
MATT. 6:25,27,28,31,34; 10:19; LUKE 10:41;
12:11,22,25,26; 1 COR. 7:32-34; 12:25; PHIL.
2:20; 4:6

3310. μερίς meris
LUKE 10:42; ACTS 8:21; 16:12; 2 COR. 6:15;
COL. 1:12

3311. μερισμός merismos
HEB. 2:4; 4:12

3312. μεριστής meristēs
LUKE 12:14

3313. μέρος meros
MATT. 2:22; 15:21; 16:13; 24:51; MARK 8:10;
LUKE 11:36; 12:46; 15:12; 24:42; JOHN 13:8;
19:23; 21:6; ACTS 2:10; 5:2; 19:1,27; 20:2;
23:6,9; ROM. 11:25; 15:15,24; 1 COR. 11:18;
12:27; 13:9,10,12; 14:27; 2 COR. 1:14; 2:5;
3:10; 9:3; EPH. 4:9,16; COL. 2:16; HEB. 9:5;
1 PET. 4:16; REV. 16:19; 20:6; 21:8; 22:19

3314. μεσημβρία mesēmbria
ACTS 8:26; 22:6

3315. μεσιτεύω mesiteuō
HEB. 6:17

3316. μεσίτης mesitēs
GAL. 3:19,20; 1 TIM. 2:5; HEB. 8:6; 9:15;
12:24

3317. μεσονύκτιον mesonuktion
MARK 13:35; LUKE 11:5; ACTS 16:25; 20:7

3318. Μεσοποταμία Mesopotamia
ACTS 2:9; 7:2

3319. μέσος mesos
MATT. 10:16; 13:25,49; 14:6,24; 18:2,20; 25:6;
MARK 3:3; 6:47; 7:31; 9:36; 14:60; LUKE
2:46; 4:30,35; 5:19; 6:8; 8:7; 10:3; 17:11; 21:21;
22:27,55; 23:45; 24:36; JOHN 1:26; 8:3,9,59;
19:18; 20:19,26; ACTS 1:15,18; 2:22; 4:7;
17:22,33; 23:10; 26:13; 27:21,27; 1 COR. 5:2;
6:5; 2 COR. 6:17; PHIL. 2:15; COL. 2:14;

1 THESS. 2:7; 2 THESS. 2:7; HEB. 2:12; REV. 1:13; 2:1,7; 4:6; 5:6; 6:6; 7:17; 22:2

3320. μεσότοιχον *mesotoichon*
EPH. 2:14

3321. μεσουράνημα *mesouranēma*
REV. 8:13; 14:6; 19:17

3322. μεσόω *mesoō*
JOHN 7:14

3323. Μεσσίας *Messias*
JOHN 1:41; 4:25

3324. μεστός *mestos*
MATT. 23:28; JOHN 19:29; 21:11; ROM. 1:29; 15:14; JAMES 3:8,17; 2 PET. 2:14

3325. μεστόω *mestoō*
ACTS 2:13

3327. μεταβαίνω *metabainō*
MATT. 8:34; 11:1; 12:9; 15:29; 17:20; LUKE 10:7; JOHN 5:24; 7:3; 13:1; ACTS 18:7; 1 JOHN 3:14

3328. μεταβάλλω *metaballō*
ACTS 28:6

3329. μετάγω *metagō*
JAMES 3:3,4

3330. μεταδίδωμι *metadidōmi*
LUKE 3:11; ROM. 1:11; 12:8; EPH. 4:28; 1 THESS. 2:8

3331. μετάθεσις *metathesis*
HEB. 7:12; 11:5; 12:27

3332. μεταίρω *metairō*
MATT. 13:53; 19:1

3333. μετακαλέω *metakaleō*
ACTS 7:14; 10:32; 20:17; 24:25

3334. μετακινέω *metakineō*
COL. 1:23

3335. μεταλαμβάνω *metalambanō*
ACTS 2:46; 24:25; 27:33; 2 TIM. 2:6; HEB. 6:7; 12:10

3336. μετάληψις *metalēpsis*
1 TIM. 4:3

3337. μεταλλάσσω, μεταλλάττω
metallassō, metallattō
ROM. 1:25,26

3338. μεταμέλομαι *metamelomai*
MATT. 21:29,32; 27:3; 2 COR. 7:8; HEB. 7:21

3339. μεταμορφόω *metamorphoō*
MATT. 17:2; MARK 9:2; ROM. 12:2; 2 COR. 3:18

3340. μετανοέω *metanoeō*
MATT. 3:2; 4:17; 11:20,21; 12:41; MARK 1:15; 6:12; LUKE 10:13; 11:32; 13:3,5; 15:7,10; 16:30; 17:3,4; ACTS 2:38; 3:19; 8:22; 17:30; 26:20; 2 COR. 12:21; REV. 2:5,16,21,22; 3:3,19; 9:20,21; 16:9,11

3341. μετάνοια *metanoia*
MATT. 3:8,11; 9:13; MARK 1:4; 2:17; LUKE 3:3,8; 5:32; 15:7; 24:47; ACTS 5:31; 11:18; 13:24; 19:4; 20:21; 26:20; ROM. 2:4; 2 COR. 7:9,10; 2 TIM. 2:25; HEB. 6:1,6; 12:17; 2 PET. 3:9

3342. μεταξύ *metaxu*
MATT. 18:15; 23:35; LUKE 11:51; 16:26; JOHN 4:31; ACTS 12:6; 13:42; 15:9; ROM. 2:15

3343. μεταπέμπω *metapempō*
ACTS 10:5,22,29; 11:13; 24:24,26; 25:3

3344. μεταστρέφω *metastrephō*
ACTS 2:20; GAL. 1:7; JAMES 4:9

3345. μετασχηματίζω
metaschēmatizō
1 COR. 4:6; 2 COR. 11:13-15; PHIL. 3:21

3346. μετατίθημι *metatithēmi*
ACTS 7:16; GAL. 1:6; HEB. 7:12; 11:5; JUDE 1:4

3347. μετέπειτα *metepeita*
HEB. 12:17

3348. μετέχω *metechō*
1 COR. 9:10,12; 10:17,21,30; HEB. 2:14; 5:13; 7:13

3349. μετεωρίζω *meteōrizō*
LUKE 12:29

3350. μετοικεσία *metoikesia*
MATT. 1:11,12,17

3351. μετοικίζω *metoikizō*
ACTS 7:4,43

3352. μετοχή *metochē*
2 COR. 6:14

3353. μέτοχος *metochos*
LUKE 5:7; HEB. 1:9; 3:1,14; 6:4; 12:8

3354. μετρέω *metreō*
MATT. 7:2; MARK 4:24; LUKE 6:38; 2 COR. 10:12; REV. 11:1,2; 21:15-17

3355. μετρητής *metrētēs*
JOHN 2:6

3356. μετριοπαθέω *metriopatheō*
HEB. 5:2

3357. μετρίως *metriōs*
ACTS 20:12

3358. μέτρον *metron*
MATT. 7:2; 23:32; MARK 4:24; LUKE 6:38; JOHN 3:34; ROM. 12:3; 2 COR. 10:13; EPH. 4:7,13,16; REV. 21:17

3359. μέτωπον *metōpon*
REV. 7:3; 9:4; 13:16; 14:1,9; 17:5; 20:4; 22:4

3360. μέχρι, μέχρις *mechri, mechris*
MATT. 11:23; 13:30; 28:15; MARK 13:30; ACTS 10:30; 20:7; ROM. 5:14; 15:19; EPH. 4:13; PHIL. 2:8,30; 1 TIM. 6:14; 2 TIM. 2:9; HEB. 3:6,14; 9:10; 12:4

3362. ἐάν μή *ean mē*
MATT. 5:20; 6:15; 10:13,14; 11:6; 12:29; 18:3, 16,35; 26:42; MARK 3:27; 4:22; 7:3,4; 10:15, 30; LUKE 7:23; 13:3,5; 18:17; JOHN 3:2,3,5, 27; 4:48; 5:19; 6:44,53,65; 7:51; 8:24; 12:24,47; 13:8; 15:4,6; 16:7; 20:25; ACTS 8:31; 15:1; 27:31; ROM. 10:15; 11:23; 1 COR. 8:8; 9:16; 14:6,7,9,11,28; 15:36; GAL. 2:16; 2 THESS. 2:3; 2 TIM. 2:5; JAMES 2:17; 1 JOHN 3:21; REV. 2:5,22; 3:3

3363. ἵνα μή *hina mē*
MATT. 7:1; 12:16; 17:27; 24:20; 26:5,41; MARK 3:9,12; 5:10; 13:18; 14:38; LUKE 8:12,31; 9:45; 16:28; 18:5; 22:32,46; JOHN 3:15,20; 4:15; 5:14; 6:12,50; 7:23; 12:35,40,42, 46; 16:1; 18:28,36; 19:31; ACTS 2:25; 4:17; 5:26; 24:4; ROM. 11:25; 15:20; 1 COR. 1:15, 17; 4:6; 7:5; 8:13; 9:12; 11:32,34; 12:25; 16:2; 2 COR. 1:9; 2:3,5,11; 6:3; 9:3,4; 10:9; 12:7; GAL. 5:17; 6:12; EPH. 2:9; PHIL. 2:27; COL. 2:4; 3:21; 1 THESS. 4:13; 1 TIM. 3:6,7; 6:1; TITUS 2:5; 3:14; PHILE. 1:14,19; HEB. 3:13; 4:11; 6:12; 11:28,40; 12:3,13; JAMES 5:9,12; 2 PET. 3:17; 1 JOHN 2:1; 2 JOHN 1:8; REV. 7:1; 9:4,5,20; 11:6; 13:17; 16:15; 18:4; 20:3

3364. οὐ μή *ou mē*
MATT. 5:18,20,26; 10:23,42; 13:14; 15:6; 16:22,28; 18:3; 23:39; 24:2,21,34,35; 26:29,35; MARK 9:1,41; 10:15; 13:2,19,30,31; 14:25,31; 16:18; LUKE 1:15; 6:37; 9:27; 10:19; 12:59; 13:35; 18:7,17,30; 21:18,32,33; 22:16,18,34,67, 68; JOHN 4:14,48; 6:35,37; 8:12,51,52; 10:5,28; 11:26,56; 13:8,38; 18:11; 20:25; ACTS 13:41; 28:26; ROM. 4:8; 1 COR. 8:13; GAL. 4:30; 5:16; 1 THESS. 4:15; 5:3; HEB. 8:11,12; 10:17; 1 PET. 2:6; 2 PET. 1:10; REV. 2:11; 3:3,5,12; 15:4; 18:7,14,21-23; 21:25,27

3365. μηδαμῶς *mēdamōs*
ACTS 10:14; 11:8

3366. μηδέ *mēde*
MATT. 6:25; 7:6; 10:9,10,14; 22:29; 23:10;

24:20; **MARK** 2:2; 6:11; 8:26; 12:24; 13:11,15;
LUKE 3:14; 10:4; 12:22,47; 14:12; 16:26;
17:23; **JOHN** 4:15; 14:27; **ACTS** 4:18; 21:21;
23:8; **ROM.** 6:13; 9:11; 14:21; **1 COR.** 5:8,11;
10:7-10; **2 COR.** 4:2; **EPH.** 5:3; **COL.** 2:21;
2 THESS. 3:10; **1 TIM.** 1:4; 5:22; 6:17; **2 TIM.**
1:8; **HEB.** 12:5; **1 PET.** 3:14; 5:2,3; **1 JOHN**
2:15; 3:18

3367. μηδείς *mēdeis*
MATT. 8:4; 9:30; 16:20; 17:9; 27:19; **MARK**
1:44; 5:26,43; 6:8; 7:36; 8:30; 9:9; 11:14; **LUKE**
3:13,14; 4:35; 5:14; 6:35; 8:56; 9:3,21; 10:4;
JOHN 8:10; **ACTS** 4:17,21; 8:24; 9:7; 10:20,28;
11:12,19; 13:28; 15:28; 16:28; 19:36,40; 21:25;
23:14,22,29; 24:23; 25:17,25; 27:33; 28:6,18;
ROM. 12:17; 13:8; **1 COR.** 1:7; 3:18,21; 10:24,
25,27; **2 COR.** 6:3,10; 7:9; 11:5; 13:7; **GAL.**
6:3,17; **EPH.** 5:6; **PHIL.** 1:28; 2:3; 4:6; **COL.**
2:18; **1 THESS.** 3:3; 4:12; **2 THESS.** 2:3; 3:11;
1 TIM. 4:12; 5:14,21,22; 6:4; **TITUS** 2:8,15;
3:2,13; **HEB.** 10:2; **JAMES** 1:4,6,13; **1 PET.**
3:6; **1 JOHN** 3:7; **3 JOHN** 1:7; **REV.** 2:10; 3:11

3368. μηδέποτε *mēdepote*
2 TIM. 3:7

3369. μηδέπω *mēdepō*
HEB. 11:7

3370. Μῆδος *Mēdos*
ACTS 2:9

3371. μηκέτι *mēketi*
MATT. 21:19; **MARK** 1:45; 2:2; 9:25; 11:14;
JOHN 5:14; 8:11; **ACTS** 4:17; 13:34; 25:24;
ROM. 6:6; 14:13; 15:23; **2 COR.** 5:15; **EPH.**
4:14,17,28; **1 THESS.** 3:1,5; **1 TIM.** 5:23;
1 PET. 4:2

3372. μῆκος *mēkos*
EPH. 3:18; **REV.** 21:16

3373. μηκύνω *mēkunō*
MARK 4:27

3374. μηλωτή *mēlotē*
HEB. 11:37

3375. μήν *mēn*   particle
HEB. 6:14

3376. μήν *mēn*
LUKE 1:24,26,36,56; 4:25; **ACTS** 7:20; 18:11;
19:8; 20:3; 28:11; **GAL.** 4:10; **JAMES** 5:17;
REV. 9:5,10,15; 11:2; 13:5; 22:2

3377. μηνύω *mēnuō*
LUKE 20:37; **JOHN** 11:57; **ACTS** 23:30;
1 COR. 10:28

3378. μὴ οὐ *mē ou*
ROM. 10:18,19; **1 COR.** 9:4,5; 11:22

3379. μήποτε, μή ποτε
mēpote, mē pote
MATT. 4:6; 5:25; 7:6; 13:15,29; 15:32; 25:9;
27:64; **MARK** 4:12; 14:2; **LUKE** 3:15; 4:11;
12:58; 14:8,12,29; 21:34; **JOHN** 7:26; **ACTS**
5:39; 28:27; **2 TIM.** 2:25; **HEB.** 2:1; 3:12; 4:1;
9:17

3380. μήπω *mēpō*
ROM. 9:11; **HEB.** 9:8

3381. μήπως, μή πως *mēpōs, mē pōs*
ACTS 27:29; **ROM.** 11:21; **1 COR.** 8:9; 9:27;
2 COR. 2:7; 9:4; 11:3; 12:20; **GAL.** 2:2; 4:11;
1 THESS. 3:5

3382. μηρός *mēros*
REV. 19:16

3383. μήτε *mēte*
MATT. 5:34-36; 11:18; **MARK** 3:20; **LUKE**
7:33; 9:3; **ACTS** 23:8,12,21; 27:20; **EPH.** 4:27;
2 THESS. 2:2; **1 TIM.** 1:7; **HEB.** 7:3; **JAMES**
5:12; **REV.** 7:1,3

3384. μήτηρ *mētēr*
MATT. 1:18; 2:11,13,14,20,21; 10:35,37; 12:46-
50; 13:55; 14:8,11; 15:4-6; 19:5,12,19,29; 20:20;
27:56; **MARK** 3:31-35; 5:40; 6:24,28; 7:10-12;
10:7,19,29,30; 15:40; **LUKE** 1:15,43,60; 2:33,
34,43,48,51; 7:12,15; 8:19-21,51; 12:53; 14:26;
18:20; **JOHN** 2:1,3,5,12; 3:4; 6:42; 19:25-27;
ACTS 1:14; 3:2; 12:12; 14:8; **ROM.** 16:13;
GAL. 1:15; 4:26; **EPH.** 5:31; 6:2; **1 TIM.** 5:2;
2 TIM. 1:5; **REV.** 17:5

3385. μήτι *mēti*
MATT. 7:16; 12:23; 26:22,25; MARK 4:21;
14:19; LUKE 6:39; JOHN 4:29; 7:31; 8:22;
18:35; ACTS 10:47; 2 COR. 1:17; JAMES 3:11

3386. μήτι γε *mēti ge*
1 COR. 6:3

3387. μήτις, μή τις *mētis, mē tis*
JOHN 4:33; 7:48; 21:5; 2 COR. 12:18

3388. μήτρα *mētra*
LUKE 2:23; ROM. 4:19

3389. μητραλώας *mētralōas*
1 TIM. 1:9

3391. μία *mia*
MATT. 5:18,19,36; 17:4; 19:5,6; 20:12; 21:19;
24:41; 26:40,69; 28:1; MARK 9:5; 10:8; 12:42;
14:37,66; 16:2; LUKE 5:12,17; 8:22; 9:33;
13:10; 14:18; 15:8; 16:17; 17:22,34,35; 20:1;
22:59; 24:1; JOHN 10:16; 20:1,19; ACTS 4:32;
12:10; 19:34; 20:7; 21:7; 24:21; 28:13; 1 COR.
6:16; 10:8; 16:2; 2 COR. 11:24; GAL. 4:24;
EPH. 4:4,5; 5:31; PHIL. 1:27; 1 TIM. 3:2,12;
TITUS 1:6; 3:10; HEB. 10:12,14; 12:16; 2 PET.
3:8; REV. 6:1; 9:12,13; 13:3; 17:12,13,17;
18:8,10,17,19

3392. μιαίνω *miainō*
JOHN 18:28; TITUS 1:15; HEB. 12:15; JUDE
1:8

3393. μίασμα *miasma*
2 PET. 2:20

3394. μιασμός *miasmos*
2 PET. 2:10

3395. μίγμα *migma*
JOHN 19:39

3396. μίγνυμι *mignumi*
MATT. 27:34; LUKE 13:1; REV. 8:7; 15:2

3397. μικρόν *mikron*   subst.
MATT. 26:39,73; MARK 14:35,70; JOHN
13:33; 14:19; 16:16-19

3398. I. μικρός *mikros*
MATT. 10:42; 18:6,10,14; MARK 9:42;
15:40; LUKE 12:32; 17:2; 19:3; JOHN
7:33; 12:35; ACTS 8:10; 26:22; 1 COR.
5:6; 2 COR. 11:1, 16; GAL. 5:9; HEB.
8:11; 10:37; JAMES 3:5; REV. 3:8;
6:11; 11:18; 13:16; 19:5,18; 20:3,12

   II. μικρότερος *mikroteros*
MATT. 11:11; 13:32; MARK 4:31;
LUKE 7:28; 9:48

3399. Μίλητος *Milētos*
ACTS 20:15,17; 2 TIM. 4:20

3400. μίλιον *milion*
MATT. 5:41

3401. μιμέομαι *mimeomai*
2 THESS. 3:7,9; HEB. 13:7; 3 JOHN 1:11

3402. μιμητής *mimētēs*
1 COR. 4:16; 11:1; EPH. 5:1; 1 THESS. 1:6;
2:14; HEB. 6:12; 1 PET. 3:13

3403. μιμνήσκω *mimnēskō*
HEB. 2:6; 13:3

3404. μισέω *miseō*
MATT. 5:43,44; 6:24; 10:22; 24:9,10; MARK
13:13; LUKE 1:71; 6:22,27; 14:26; 16:13;
19:14; 21:17; JOHN 3:20; 7:7; 12:25; 15:18,19,
23-25; 17:14; ROM. 7:15; 9:13; EPH. 5:29;
TITUS 3:3; HEB. 1:9; 1 JOHN 2:9,11; 3:13,15;
4:20; JUDE 1:23; REV. 2:6,15; 17:16; 18:2

3405. μισθαποδοσία *misthapodosia*
HEB. 2:2; 10:35; 11:26

3406. μισθαποδότης *misthapodotēs*
HEB. 11:6

3407. μίσθιος *misthios*
LUKE 15:17,19

3408. μισθός *misthos*
MATT. 5:12,46; 6:1,2,5,16; 10:41,42; 20:8;
MARK 9:41; LUKE 6:23,35; 10:7; JOHN 4:36;
ACTS 1:18; ROM. 4:4; 1 COR. 3:8,14; 9:17,18;

1 TIM. 5:18; **JAMES** 5:4; **2 PET.** 2:13,15;
2 JOHN 1:8; **JUDE** 1:11; **REV.** 11:18; 22:12

3409. μισθόω misthoō
MATT. 20:1,7

3410. μίσθωμα misthōma
ACTS 28:30

3411. μισθωτός misthōtos
MARK 1:20; **JOHN** 10:12,13

3412. Μιτυλήνη Mitulēnē
ACTS 20:14

3413. Μιχαήλ Michaēl
JUDE 1:9; **REV.** 12:7

3414. μνᾶ mna
LUKE 19:13,16,18,20,24,25

3415. μνάομαι mnaomai
MATT. 5:23; 26:75; 27:63; **LUKE** 1:54,72;
16:25; 23:42; 24:6,8; **JOHN** 2:17,22; 12:16;
ACTS 10:31; 11:16; **1 COR.** 11:2; **2 TIM.** 1:4;
HEB. 8:12; 10:17; **2 PET.** 3:2; **JUDE** 1:17;
REV. 16:19

3416. Μνάσων Mnasōn
ACTS 21:16

3417. μνεία mneia
ROM. 1:9; **EPH.** 1:16; **PHIL.** 1:3; **1 THESS.**
1:2; 3:6; **2 TIM.** 1:3; **PHILE.** 1:4

3418. μνῆμα mnēma
MARK 5:5; **LUKE** 8:27; 23:53; 24:1; **ACTS**
2:29; 7:16; **REV.** 11:9

3419. μνημεῖον mnēmeion
MATT. 8:28; 23:29; 27:52,53,60; 28:8; **MARK**
5:2,3; 6:29; 15:46; 16:2,3,5,8; **LUKE** 11:44,47,
48; 23:55; 24:2,9,12,22,24; **JOHN** 5:28; 11:17,
31,38; 12:17; 19:41,42; 20:1-4,6,8,11; **ACTS**
13:29

3420. μνήμη mnēmē
2 PET. 1:15

3421. μνημονεύω mnēmoneuō
MATT. 16:9; **MARK** 8:18; **LUKE** 17:32;
JOHN 15:20; 16:4,21; **ACTS** 20:31,35; **GAL.**
2:10; **EPH.** 2:11; **COL.** 4:18; **1 THESS.** 1:3;
2:9; **2 THESS.** 2:5; **2 TIM.** 2:8; **HEB.** 11:15,22;
13:7; **REV.** 2:5; 3:3; 18:5

3422. μνημόσυνον mnēmosunon
MATT. 26:13; **MARK** 14:9; **ACTS** 10:4

3423. μνηστεύω mnēsteuō
MATT. 1:18; **LUKE** 1:27; 2:5

3424. μογιλάλος mogilalos
MARK 7:32

3425. μόγις mogis
LUKE 9:39

3426. μόδιος modios
MATT. 5:15; 4:21; **LUKE** 11:33

3428. μοιχαλίς moichalis
MATT. 12:39; 16:4; **MARK** 8:38; **ROM.** 7:3;
JAMES 4:4; **2 PET.** 2:14

3429. μοιχάω moichaō
MATT. 5:32; 19:9; **MARK** 10:11,12

3430. μοιχεία moicheia
MATT. 15:19; **MARK** 7:21; **JOHN** 8:3; **GAL.**
5:19

3431. μοιχεύω moicheuō
MATT. 5:27,28; 19:18; **MARK** 10:19; **LUKE**
16:18; 18:20; **JOHN** 8:4; **ROM.** 2:22; 13:9;
JAMES 2:11; **REV.** 2:22

3432. μοιχός moichos
LUKE 18:11; **1 COR.** 6:9; **HEB.** 13:4; **JAMES**
4:4

3433. μόλις molis
ACTS 14:18; 27:7,8,16; **ROM.** 5:7; **1 PET.** 4:18

3434. Μολόχ Moloch
ACTS 7:43

3435. μολύνω *molunō*
1 COR. 8:7; REV. 3:4; 14:4

3436. μολυσμός *molusmos*
2 COR. 7:1

3437. μομφή *momphē*
COL. 3:13

3438. μονή *monē*
JOHN 14:2,23

3439. μονογενής *monogenēs*
LUKE 7:12; 8:42; 9:38; JOHN 1:14,18; 3:16,
18; HEB. 11:17; 1 JOHN 4:9

3440. μόνον *monon* adv.
MATT. 5:47; 8:8; 9:21; 10:42; 14:36; 21:19,21;
MARK 5:36; 6:8; LUKE 8:50; JOHN 5:18;
11:52; 12:9; 13:9; 17:20; ACTS 8:16; 11:19;
18:25; 19:26,27; 21:13; 26:29; 27:10; ROM.
1:32; 3:29; 4:12,16,23; 5:3,11; 8:23; 9:10,24;
13:5; 1 COR. 7:39; 15:19; 2 COR. 7:7; 8:10,19,
21; 9:12; GAL. 1:23; 2:10; 3:2; 4:18; 5:13; 6:12;
EPH. 1:21; PHIL. 1:27,29; 2:12,27; 1 THESS.
1:5,8; 2:8; 2 THESS. 2:7; 1 TIM. 5:13; 2 TIM.
2:20; 4:8; HEB. 9:10; 12:26; JAMES 1:22; 2:24;
1 PET. 2:18; 1 JOHN 2:2; 5:6

3441. μόνος *monos*
MATT. 4:4,10; 12:4; 14:23; 17:8; 18:15; 24:36;
MARK 6:47; 9:2,8; LUKE 4:4,8; 5:21; 6:4;
9:36; 10:40; 24:12,18; JOHN 5:44; 6:15,22; 8:9,
16,29; 12:24; 16:32; 17:3; ROM. 11:3; 16:4,27;
1 COR. 9:6; 14:36; GAL. 6:4; PHIL. 4:15;
COL. 4:11; 1 THESS. 3:1; 1 TIM. 1:17; 6:15,
16; 2 TIM. 4:11; HEB. 9:7; 2 JOHN 1:1; JUDE
1:4,25; REV. 9:4; 15:4

3442. μονόφθαλμος *monophthalmos*
MATT. 18:9; MARK 9:47

3443. μονόω *monoō*
1 TIM. 5:5

3444. μορφή *morphē*
MARK 16:12; PHIL. 2:6,7

3445. μορφόω *morphoō*
GAL. 4:19

3446. μόρφωσις *morphōsis*
ROM. 2:20; II TIM 3:5

3447. μοσχοποιέω *moschopoieō*
ACTS 7:41

3448. μόσχος *moschos*
LUKE 15:23,27,30; HEB. 9:12,19; REV. 4:7

3449. μόχθος *mochthos*
2 COR. 11:27; 1 THESS. 2:9; 2 THESS. 3:8

3451. μουσικός *mousikos*
REV. 18:22

3452. μυελός *muelos*
HEB. 4:12

3453. μυέω *mueō*
PHIL. 4:12

3454. μῦθος *muthos*
1 TIM. 1:4; 4:7; 2 TIM. 4:4; TITUS 1:14;
2 PET. 1:16

3455. μυκάομαι *mukaomai*
REV. 10:3

3456. μυκτηρίζω *muktērizō*
GAL. 6:7

3457. μυλικός *mulikos*
MARK 9:42

3458. μύλος *mulos*
MATT. 18:6; LUKE 17:2; REV. 18:21,22

3459. μύλων *mulōn*
MATT. 24:41

3460. Μύρα *Mura*
ACTS 27:5

3461. μυριάς *murias*
LUKE 12:1; ACTS 19:19; 21:20; HEB. 12:22;
JUDE 1:14; REV. 5:11; 9:16

3462. μυρίζω *murizō*
MARK 14:8

3463. μυρίος *murios*
MATT. 18:24; 1 COR. 4:15; 14:19

3464. μύρον *muron*
MATT. 26:7,9,12; MARK 14:3,4; LUKE
7:37,38,46; 23:56; JOHN 11:2; 12:3,5; REV.
18:13

3465. Μυσία *Musia*
ACTS 16:7,8

3466. μυστήριον *mustērion*
MATT. 13:11; MARK 4:11; LUKE 8:10;
ROM. 11:25; 16:25; 1 COR. 2:7; 4:1; 13:2;
14:2; 15:51; EPH. 1:9; 3:3,4,9; 5:32; 6:19; COL.
1:26,27; 2:2; 4:3; 2 THESS. 2:7; 1 TIM. 3:9,16;
REV. 1:20; 10:7; 17:5,7

3467. μυωπάζω *muōpazō*
2 PET. 1:9

3468. μώλωψ *mōlōps*
1 PET. 2:24

3469. μωμάομαι *mōmaomai*
2 COR. 6:3; 8:20

3470. μῶμος *mōmos*
2 PET. 2:13

3471. μωραίνω *mōrainō*
MATT. 5:13; LUKE 14:34; ROM. 1:22;
1 COR. 1:20

3472. μωρία *mōria*
1 COR. 1:18,21,23; 2:14; 3:19

3473. μωρολογία *mōrologia*
EPH. 5:4

3474. μωρός *mōros*
MATT. 5:22; 7:26; 23:17,19; 25:2,3,8; 1 COR.
1:25,27; 3:18; 4:10; 2 TIM. 2:23; TITUS 3:9

3475. I. Μωσεύς *Mōseus*
MATT. 23:2; MARK 9:4,5; 12:26;
LUKE 2:22; 9:33; 16:29,31; 24:27,44;
JOHN 1:17; 7:22,23; 9:28; ACTS 13:39;
21:21; 28:23; ROM. 5:14; 1 COR. 9:9;
2 COR. 3:7; HEB. 3:16; 10:28; JUDE
1:9; REV. 15:3

II. Μωσῆς *Mōsēs*
MATT. 8:4; 17:3,4; 19:7,8; 22:24;
MARK 1:44; 7:10; 10:3,4; 12:19; LUKE
5:14; 9:30; 20:28,37; JOHN 1:45; 3:14;
5:45,46; 6:32; 7:19,22; 8:5; 9:29; ACTS
3:22; 6:11; 7:20,22,29,31,32,40,44;
15:21; 26:22; ROM. 9:15; 10:5,19; 1
COR. 10:2; 2 COR. 3:13,15; HEB. 3:2,
3,5; 7:14; 8:5; 11:23,24; 12:21

III. Μωϋσεύς *Mōuseus*
ACTS 15:1,5; 2 TIM. 3:8; HEB. 9:19

IV. Μωϋσῆς *Mōusēs*
ACTS 6:14; 7:35,37

N

3476. Ναασσών *Naassōn*
MATT. 1:4; LUKE 3:32

3477. Ναγγαί *Naggai*
LUKE 3:25

3478. Ναζαρέτ, Ναζαρέθ
   Nazaret, Nazareth
MATT. 2:23; 4:13; 21:11; MARK 1:9; LUKE
1:26; 2:4,39,51; 4:16; JOHN 1:45,46; ACTS
10:38

3479. Ναζαρηνός *Nazarēnos*
MARK 1:24; 14:67; 16:6; LUKE 4:34

3480. Ναζωραῖος *Nazōraios*
MATT. 2:23; 26:71; MARK 10:47; LUKE
18:37; 24:19; JOHN 18:5,7; 19:19; ACTS 2:22;
3:6; 4:10; 6:14; 22:8; 24:5; 26:9

3481. Ναθάν *Nathan*
LUKE 3:31

3482. Ναθαναήλ *Nathanaēl*
JOHN 1:45-49; 21:2

3483. ναί nai
MATT. 5:37; 9:28; 11:9,26; 13:51; 15:27; 17:25;
21:16; MARK 7:28; LUKE 7:26; 10:21; 11:51;
12:5; JOHN 11:27; 21:15,16; ACTS 5:8; 22:27;
ROM. 3:29; 2 COR. 1:17-20; PHILE. 1:20;
JAMES 5:12; REV. 1:7; 14:13; 16:7; 22:20

3484. Ναΐν Nain
LUKE 7:11

3485. ναός naos
MATT. 23:16,17,21,35; 26:61; 27:5,40,51;
MARK 14:58; 15:29,38; LUKE 1:9,21,22;
23:45; JOHN 2:19-21; ACTS 7:48; 17:24;
19:24; 1 COR. 3:16,17; 6:19; 2 COR. 6:16;
EPH. 2:21; 2 THESS. 2:4; REV. 3:12; 7:15;
11:1,2,19; 14:15,17; 15:5,6,8; 16:1,17; 21:22

3486. Ναούμ Naoum
LUKE 3:25

3487. νάρδος nardos
MARK 14:3; JOHN 12:3

3488. Νάρκισσος Narkissos
ROM. 16:11

3489. ναυαγέω nauageō
2 COR. 11:25; 1 TIM. 1:19

3490. ναύκληρος nauklēros
ACTS 27:11

3491. ναῦς naus
ACTS 27:41

3492. ναύτης nautēs
ACTS 27:27,30; REV. 18:17

3493. Ναχώρ Nachōr
LUKE 3:34

3494. νεανίας neanias
ACTS 7:58; 20:9; 23:17,18,22

3495. νεανίσκος neaniskos
MATT. 19:20,22; MARK 14:51; 16:5; LUKE
7:14; ACTS 2:17; 5:10; 1 JOHN 2:13,14

3496. Νεάπολις neapolis
ACTS 16:11

3497. Νεεμάν Neeman
LUKE 4:27

3498. νεκρός nekros
MATT. 8:22; 10:8; 11:5; 14:2; 17:9; 22:31,32;
23:27; 27:64; 28:4,7; MARK 6:14,16; 9:9,10,26;
12:25-27; LUKE 7:15,22; 9:7,60; 15:24,32;
16:30,31; 20:35,37,38; 24:5,46; JOHN 2:22;
5:21,25; 12:1,9,17; 20:9; 21:14; ACTS 3:15;
4:2,10; 5:10; 10:41,42; 13:30,34; 17:3,31,32;
20:9; 23:6; 24:15,21; 26:8,23; 28:6; ROM. 1:4;
4:17,24; 6:4,9,11,13; 7:4,8; 8:10,11; 10:7,9;
11:15; 14:9; 1 COR. 15:12,13,15, 16,20,21,
29,32,35,42,52; 2 COR. 1:9; GAL. 1:1; EPH.
1:20; 2:1,5; 5:14; PHIL. 3:11; COL. 1:18;
2:12,13; 1 THESS. 1:10; 4:16; 2 TIM. 2:8; 4:1;
HEB. 6:1,2; 9:14,17; 11:19,35; 13:20; JAMES
2:17,20,26; 1 PET. 1:3,21; 4:5,6; REV.
1:5,17,18; 2:8; 3:1; 11:18; 14:13; 16:3; 20:5,
12,13

3499. νεκρόω nekroō
ROM. 4:19; COL. 3:5; HEB. 11:12

3500. νέκρωσις nekrōsis
ROM. 4:19; 2 COR. 4:10

3501. I. νέος neos
MATT. 9:17; MARK 2:22; LUKE 5:37-
39; 1 COR. 5:7; COL. 3:10; TITUS 2:4;
HEB. 12:24

II. νεώτερος neōteros
(Compar. of νέος)
LUKE 15:12,13; 22:26; JOHN 21:18;
ACTS 5:6; 1 TIM. 5:1,2,11,14; TITUS
2:6; 1 PET. 5:5

3502. νεοσσός neossos
LUKE 2:24

3503. νεότης neotēs
MATT. 19:20; MARK 10:20; LUKE 18:21;
ACTS 26:4; 1 TIM. 4:12

3504. νεόφυτος neophutos
1 TIM. 3:6

3506. νεύω neuō
JOHN 13:24; ACTS 24:10

3507. νεφέλη nephelē
MATT. 17:5; 24:30; 26:64; MARK 9:7; 13:26;
14:62; LUKE 9:34,35; 12:54; 21:27; ACTS 1:9;
1 COR. 10:1,2; 1 THESS. 4:17; 2 PET. 2:17;
JUDE 1:12; REV. 1:7; 10:1; 11:12; 14:14-16

3508. Νεφθαλείμ Nephthaleim
MATT. 4:13,15; REV. 7:6

3509. νέφος nephos
HEB. 12:1

3510. νεφρός nephros
REV. 2:23

3511. νεωκόρος neōkoros
ACTS 19:35

3512. νεωτερικός neōterikos
2 TIM. 2:22

3513. νή nē
1 COR. 15:31

3514. νήθω nēthō
MATT. 6:28; LUKE 12:27

3515. νηπιάζω nēpiazō
1 COR. 14:20

3516. νήπιος nēpios
MATT. 11:25; 21:16; LUKE 10:21; ROM.
2:20; 1 COR. 3:1; 13:11; GAL. 4:1,3; EPH.
4:14; HEB. 5:13

3517. Νηρεύς Nēreus
ROM. 16:15

3518. Νηρί Nēri
LUKE 3:27

3519. νησίον nēsion
ACTS 27:16

3520. νῆσος nēsos
ACTS 13:6; 27:26; 28:1,7,9,11; REV. 1:9; 6:14;
16:20

3521. νηστεία nēsteia
MATT. 17:21; MARK 9:29; LUKE 2:37;
ACTS 14:23; 27:9; 1 COR. 7:5; 2 COR. 6:5;
11:27

3522. νηστεύω nēsteuō
MATT. 4:2; 6:16-18; 9:14,15; MARK 2:18-20;
LUKE 5:33-35; 18:12; ACTS 10:30; 13:2,3

3523. νῆστις nēstis
MATT. 15:32; MARK 8:3

3524. νηφάλεος, νηφάλιος
nēphaleos, nēphalios
1 TIM. 3:2,11; TITUS 2:2

3525. νήφω nēphō
1 THESS. 5:6,8; 2 TIM. 4:5; 1 PET. 1:13; 4:7;
5:8

3526. Νίγερ Niger
ACTS 13:1

3527. Νικάνωρ Nikanōr
ACTS 6:5

3528. νικάω nikaō
LUKE 11:22; JOHN 16:33; ROM. 3:4; 12:21;
1 JOHN 2:13,14; 4:4; 5:4,5; REV. 2:7,11,17,26;
3:5,12,21; 5:5; 6:2; 11:7; 12:11; 13:7; 15:2;
17:14; 21:7

3529. νίκη nikē
1 JOHN 5:4

3530. Νικόδημος Nikodēmos
JOHN 3:1,4,9; 7:50; 19:39

3531. Νικολαΐτης Nikolaitēs
REV. 2:6,15

3532. Νικόλαος Nikolaos
ACTS 6:5

3533. Νικόπολις *Nikopolis*
TITUS 3:12

3534. νῖκος *nikos*
MATT. 12:20; **1 COR.** 15:54,55,57

3535. Νινευΐ *Nineui*
LUKE 11:32

3536. Νινευΐτης *Nineuitēs*
MATT. 12:41; LUKE 11:30

3537. νιπτήρ *niptēr*
JOHN 13:5

3538. νίπτω *niptō*
MATT. 6:17; 15:2; **MARK** 7:3; **JOHN**
9:7,11,15; 13:5,6,8,10,12,14; **1 TIM.** 5:10

3539. νοέω *noeō*
MATT. 15:17; 16:9,11; 24:15; **MARK** 7:18;
8:17; 13:14; **JOHN** 12:40; **ROM.** 1:20; **EPH.**
3:4,20; **1 TIM.** 1:7; **2 TIM.** 2:7; **HEB.** 11:3

3540. νόημα *noēma*
2 COR. 2:11; 3:14; 4:4; 10:5; 11:3; **PHIL.** 4:7

3541. νόθος *nothos*
HEB. 12:8

3542. νομή *nomē*
JOHN 10:9; **2 TIM.** 2:17

3543. νομίζω *nomizō*
MATT. 5:17; 10:34; 20:10; **LUKE** 2:44; 3:23;
ACTS 7:25; 8:20; 14:19; 16:13,27; 17:29; 21:29;
1 COR. 7:26,36; **1 TIM.** 6:5

3544. νομικός *nomikos*
MATT. 22:35; **LUKE** 7:30; 10:25; 11:45,46,52;
14:3; **TITUS** 3:9,13

3545. νομίμως *nomimōs*
1 TIM. 1:8; **2 TIM.** 2:5

3546. νόμισμα *nomisma*
MATT. 22:19

3547. νομοδιδάσκαλος
nomodidaskalos
LUKE 5:17; **ACTS** 5:34; **1 TIM.** 1:7

3548. νομοθεσία *nomothesia*
ROM. 9:4

3549. νομοθετέω *nomotheteō*
HEB. 7:11; 8:6

3550. νομοθέτης *nomothetēs*
JAMES 4:12

3551. νόμος *nomos*
MATT. 5:17,18; 7:12; 11:13; 12:5; 22:36,40;
23:23; **LUKE** 2:22-24,27,39; 10:26; 16:16,17;
24:44; **JOHN** 1:17,45; 7:19,23,49,51; 8:5,17;
10:34; 12:34; 15:25; 18:31; 19:7; **ACTS** 6:13;
7:53; 13:15,39; 15:5,24; 18:13,15; 21:20,24,28;
22:3,12; 23:3,29; 24:6,14; 25:8; 28:23; **ROM.**
2:12-15,17,18,20,23,25-27; 3:19-21,27,28,31;
4:13-16; 5:13,20; 6:14,15; 7:1-9,12,14,16,21-
23,25; 8:2-4,7; 9:31,32; 10:4,5; 13:8,10; **1 COR.**
7:39; 9:8,9,20; 14:21,34; 15:56; **GAL.** 2:16,19,
21; 3:2,5,10-13,17-19,21,23,24; 4:4,5,21;
5:3,4,14,18,23; 6:2,13; **EPH.** 2:15; **PHIL.**
3:5,6,9; **1 TIM.** 1:8,9; **HEB.** 7:5,12,16,19,28;
8:4,10; 9:19,22; 10:1,8,16,28; **JAMES** 1:25; 2:8-
12; 4:11

3552. νοσέω *noseō*
1 TIM. 6:4

3553. νόσημα *nosēma*
JOHN 5:4

3554. νόσος *nosos*
MATT. 4:23,24; 8:17; 9:35; 10:1; **MARK** 1:34;
3:15; **LUKE** 4:40; 6:17; 7:21; 9:1; **ACTS** 19:12

3555. νοσσιά *nossia*
LUKE 13:34

3556. νοσσίον *nossion*
MATT. 23:37

3557. νοσφίζω *nosphizō*
ACTS 5:2,3; **TITUS** 2:10

3558. νότος notos
MATT. 12:42; LUKE 11:31; 12:55; 13:29;
ACTS 27:13; 28:13; REV. 21:13

3559. νουθεσία nouthesia
1 COR. 10:11; EPH. 6:4; TITUS 3:10

3560. νουθετέω noutheteō
ACTS 20:31; ROM. 15:14; 1 COR. 4:14; COL.
1:28; 3:16; 1 THESS. 5:12,14; 2 THESS. 3:15

3561. νουμηνία noumēnia
COL. 2:16

3562. νουνεχῶς nounechōs
MARK 12:34

3563. νοῦς nous
LUKE 24:45; ROM. 1:28; 7:23,25; 11:34; 12:2;
14:5; 1 COR. 1:10; 2:16; 14:14,15,19; EPH.
4:17,23; PHIL. 4:7; COL. 2:18; 2 THESS. 2:2;
1 TIM. 6:5; 2 TIM. 3:8; TITUS 1:15; REV.
13:18; 17:9

3564. Νυμφᾶς Numphas
COL. 4:15

3565. νύμφη numphē
MATT. 10:35; LUKE 12:53; JOHN 3:29;
REV. 18:23; 21:2,9; 22:17

3566. νυμφίος numphios
MATT. 9:15; 25:1,5,6,10; MARK 2:19,20;
LUKE 5:34,35; JOHN 2:9; 3:29; REV. 18:23

3567. νυμφών numphōn
MATT. 9:15; MARK 2:19; LUKE 5:34

3568. νῦν nun
MATT. 24:21; 26:65; 27:42,43; MARK 10:30;
13:19; 15:32; LUKE 1:48; 2:29; 5:10; 6:21,25;
11:39; 12:52; 16:25; 19:42; 22:36,69; JOHN 2:8;
4:18,23; 5:25; 8:40,52; 9:21,41; 11:8,22; 12:27,
31; 13:31,36; 14:29; 15:22,24; 16:5,22,29,30,32;
17:5,7,13; 18:36; 21:10; ACTS 2:33; 3:17;
7:4,34,52; 10:5,33; 12:11; 13:11; 15:10; 16:36,
37; 18:6; 20:22,25; 22:1,16; 23:15,21; 24:13,25;
26:6,17; ROM. 3:21,26; 5:9,11; 6:19,21; 8:1,18,
22; 11:5,30,31; 13:11; 16:26; 1 COR. 3:2; 7:14;

12:20; 16:12; 2 COR. 5:16; 6:2; 7:9; 8:14; 13:2;
GAL. 1:23; 2:20; 3:3; 4:9,25,29; EPH. 2:2;
3:5,10; 5:8; PHIL. 1:5,20,30; 2:12; 3:18; COL.
1:24; 1 THESS. 3:8; 2 THESS. 2:6; 1 TIM. 4:8;
6:17; 2 TIM. 1:10; 4:10; TITUS 2:12; HEB.
2:8; 9:5,24,26; 12:26; JAMES 4:13,16; 5:1;
1 PET. 1:12; 2:10,25; 3:21; 2 PET. 3:7,18;
1 JOHN 2:18,28; 3:2; 4:3; 2 JOHN 1:5; JUDE
1:25

3569. τανῦν, τά νῦν tanun, ta nun
ACTS 4:29; 5:38; 17:30; 20:32; 27:22

3570. νυνί nuni
ROM. 6:22; 7:6,17; 15:23,25; 1 COR. 5:11;
12:18; 13:13; 14:6; 15:20; 2 COR. 8:11,22;
EPH. 2:13; COL. 1:21,26; 3:8; PHILE. 1:9,11;
HEB. 8:6; 11:16

3571. νύξ nux
MATT. 2:14; 4:2; 12:40; 14:25; 25:6; 26:31,34;
27:64; 28:13; MARK 4:27; 5:5; 6:48; 14:27,30;
LUKE 2:8,37; 5:5; 12:20; 17:34; 18:7; 21:37;
JOHN 3:2; 7:50; 9:4; 11:10; 13:30; 19:39; 21:3;
ACTS 5:19; 9:24,25; 12:6; 16:9,33; 17:10; 18:9;
20:31; 23:11,23,31; 26:7; 27:23,27; ROM.
13:12; 1 COR. 11:23; 1 THESS. 2:9; 3:10;
5:2,5,7; 2 THESS. 3:8; 1 TIM. 5:5; 2 TIM. 1:3;
2 PET. 3:10; REV. 4:8; 7:15; 8:12; 12:10;
14:11; 20:10; 21:25; 22:5

3572. νύσσω, νύττω nussō, nuttō
JOHN 19:34

3573. νυστάζω nustazō
MATT. 25:5; 2 PET. 2:3

3574. νυχθήμερον nuchthēmeron
2 COR. 11:25

3575. Νῶε Nōe
MATT. 24:37,38; LUKE 3:36; 17:26,27; HEB.
11:7; 1 PET. 3:20; 2 PET. 2:5

3576. νωθρός nōthros
HEB. 5:11; 6:12

3577. νῶτος nōtos
ROM. 11:10

Ξ

3578. ξενία xenia
ACTS 28:23; PHILE. 1:22

3579. ξενίζω xenizō
ACTS 10:6,18,23,32; 17:20; 21:16; 28:7; HEB.
13:2; 1 PET. 4:4,12

3580. ξενοδοχέω xenodocheō
1 TIM. 5:10

3581. ξένος xenos
MATT. 25:35,38,43,44; 27:7; ACTS 17:18,21;
ROM. 16:23; EPH. 2:12,19; HEB. 11:13; 13:9;
1 PET. 4:12; 3 JOHN 1:5

3582. ξέστης xestēs
MARK 7:4,8

3583. ξηραίνω xērainō
MATT. 13:6; 21:19,20; MARK 3:1,3; 4:6; 5:29;
9:18; 11:20,21; LUKE 8:6; JOHN 15:6;
JAMES 1:11; 1 PET. 1:24; REV. 14:15; 16:12

3584. ξηρός xēros
MATT. 12:10; 23:15; LUKE 6:6,8; 23:31;
JOHN 5:3; HEB. 11:29

3585. ξύλινος xulinos
2 TIM. 2:20; REV. 9:20

3586. ξύλον xulon
MATT. 26:47,55; MARK 14:43,48; LUKE
22:52; 23:31; ACTS 5:30; 10:39; 13:29; 16:24;
1 COR. 3:12; GAL. 3:13; 1 PET. 2:24; REV.
2:7; 18:12; 22:2,14

3587. ξυράω xuraō
ACTS 21:24; 1 COR. 11:5,6

Ο

3589. ὀγδοήκοντα ogdoēkonta
LUKE 2:37; 16:7

3590. ὄγδοος ogdoos
LUKE 1:59; ACTS 7:8; 2 PET. 2:5; REV.
17:11; 21:20

3591. ὄγκος ogkos
HEB. 12:1

3592. ὅδε hode
LUKE 10:39; 16:25; ACTS 15:23; 21:11;
JAMES 4:13; REV. 2:1,8,12,18; 3:1,7,14

3593. ὁδεύω hodeuō
LUKE 10:33

3594. ὁδηγέω hodēgeō
MATT. 15:14; LUKE 6:39; JOHN 16:13;
ACTS 8:31; REV. 7:17

3595. ὁδηγός hodēgos
MATT. 15:14; 23:16,24; ACTS 1:16; ROM.
2:19

3596. ὁδοιπορέω hodoiporeō
ACTS 10:9

3597. ὁδοιπορία hodoiporia
JOHN 4:6; 2 COR. 11:26

3598. ὁδός hodos
MATT. 2:12; 3:3; 4:15; 5:25; 7:13,14; 8:28;
10:5,10; 11:10; 13:4,19; 15:32; 20:17,30;
21:8,19,32; 22:9,10,16; MARK 1:2,3; 2:23;
4:4,15; 6:8; 8:3,27; 9:33,34; 10:17,32,46,52;
11:8; 12:14; LUKE 1:76,79; 2:44; 3:4,5; 7:27;
8:5,12; 9:3,57; 10:4,31; 11:6; 12:58; 14:23;
18:35; 19:36; 20:21; 24:32,35; JOHN 1:23;
14:4-6; ACTS 1:12; 2:28; 8:26,36,39; 9:2,17,27;
13:10; 14:16; 16:17; 18:25,26; 19:9,23; 22:4;
24:14,22; 25:3; 26:13; ROM. 3:16,17; 11:33;
1 COR. 4:17; 12:31; 1 THESS. 3:11; HEB.
3:10; 9:8; 10:20; JAMES 1:8; 2:25; 5:20;
2 PET. 2:2,15,21; JUDE 1:11; REV. 15:3; 16:12

3599. ὀδούς odous
MATT. 5:38; 8:12; 13:42,50; 22:13; 24:51;
25:30; MARK 9:18; LUKE 13:28; ACTS 7:54;
REV. 9:8

3600. ὀδυνάω odunaō
LUKE 2:48; 16:24,25; ACTS 20:38

3601. ὀδύνη odunē
ROM. 9:2; 1 TIM. 6:10

3602. ὀδυρμός odurmos
MATT. 2:18; **2 COR.** 7:7

3603. ὅ ἐστι ho esti
MARK 3:17; 7:11,34; 12:42; 15:16,42; **EPH.**
6:17; **COL.** 1:24; **HEB.** 7:2; **REV.** 21:8,17

3604. Ὀζίας Ozias
MATT. 1:8,9

3605. ὄζω ozō
JOHN 11:39

3606. ὅθεν hothen
MATT. 12:44; 14:7; 25:24,26; **LUKE** 11:24;
ACTS 14:26; 26:19; 28:13; **HEB.** 2:17; 3:1;
7:25; 8:3; 9:18; 11:19; **1 JOHN** 2:18

3607. ὀθόνη othonē
ACTS 10:11; 11:5

3608. ὀθόνιον othonion
LUKE 24:12; **JOHN** 19:40; 20:5-7

3609. οἰκεῖος oikeios
GAL. 6:10; **EPH.** 2:19; **1 TIM.** 5:8

3610. οἰκέτης oiketēs
LUKE 16:13; **ACTS** 10:7; **ROM.** 14:4; **1 PET.**
2:18

3611. οἰκέω oikeō
ROM. 7:17,18,20; 8:9,11; **1 COR.** 3:16;
7:12,13; **1 TIM.** 6:16

3612. οἴκημα oikēma
ACTS 12:7

3613. οἰκητήριον oikētērion
2 COR. 5:2; **JUDE** 1:6

3614. οἰκία oikia
MATT. 2:11; 5:15; 7:24-27; 8:6,14; 9:10,23,28;
10:12-14; 12:25,29; 13:1,36,57; 17:25; 19:29;
23:14; 24:17,43; 26:6; **MARK** 1:29; 2:15;
3:25,27; 6:4,10; 7:24; 9:33; 10:10,29,30; 12:40;
13:15,34,35; 14:3; **LUKE** 4:38; 5:29; 6:48,49;

7:6,36,37,44; 8:27,51; 9:4; 10:5,7; 15:8,25;
17:31; 18:29; 20:47; 22:10,11; **JOHN** 4:53; 8:35;
11:31; 12:3; 14:2; **ACTS** 4:34; 9:11,17; 10:6,
17,32; 11:11; 12:12; 16:32; 17:5; 18:7; **1 COR.**
11:22; 16:15; **2 COR.** 5:1; **PHIL.** 4:22; **1 TIM.**
5:13; **2 TIM.** 2:20; 3:6; **2 JOHN** 1:10

3615. οἰκιακός oikiakos
MATT. 10:25,36

3616. οἰκοδεσποτέω oikodespoteō
1 TIM. 5:14

3617. οἰκοδεσπότης oikodespotēs
MATT. 10:25; 13:27,52; 20:1,11; 21:33; 24:43;
MARK 14:14; **LUKE** 12:39; 13:25; 14:21;
22:11

3618. οἰκοδομέω oikodomeō
MATT. 7:24,26; 16:18; 21:33,42; 23:29; 26:61;
27:40; **MARK** 12:1,10; 14:58; 15:29; **LUKE**
4:29; 6:48,49; 7:5; 11:47,48; 12:18; 14:28,30;
17:28; 20:17; **JOHN** 2:20; **ACTS** 4:11; 7:47,49;
9:31; **ROM.** 15:20; **1 COR.** 8:1,10; 10:23;
14:4,17; **GAL.** 2:18; **1 THESS.** 5:11; **1 PET.**
2:5,7

3619. οἰκοδομή oikodomē
MATT. 24:1; **MARK** 13:1,2; **ROM.** 14:19;
15:2; **1 COR.** 3:9; 14:3,5,12,26; **2 COR.** 5:1;
10:8; 12:19; 13:10; **EPH.** 2:21; 4:12,16,29

3620. οἰκοδομία oikodomia
1 TIM. 1:4 TR

3621. οἰκονομέω oikonomeō
LUKE 16:2

3622. οἰκονομία oikonomia
LUKE 16:2-4; **1 COR.** 9:17; **EPH.** 1:10; 3:2;
COL. 1:25; **1 TIM.** 1:4

3623. οἰκονόμος oikonomos
LUKE 12:42; 16:1,3,8; **ROM.** 16:23; **1 COR.**
4:1,2; **GAL.** 4:2; **TITUS** 1:7; **1 PET.** 4:10

3624. οἶκος oikos
MATT. 9:6,7; 10:6; 11:8; 12:4,44; 15:24; 21:13;
23:38; **MARK** 2:1,11,26; 3:19; 5:19,38; 7:17,30;

8:3,26; 9:28; 11:17; **LUKE** 1:23,27,33,40,56,69;
2:4; 5:24,25; 6:4; 7:10; 8:39,41; 9:61; 10:5,38;
11:17,24,51; 12:39,52; 13:35; 14:1,23; 15:6;
16:4,27; 18:14; 19:5,9,46; 22:54; **JOHN** 2:16,17;
7:53; 11:20; **ACTS** 2:2,36,46; 5:42; 7:10,20,
42,47,49; 8:3; 10:2,22,30; 11:12-14; 16:15,31,34;
18:8; 19:16; 20:20; 21:8; **ROM.** 16:5; **1 COR.**
1:16; 11:34; 14:35; 16:19; **COL.** 4:15; **1 TIM.**
3:4,5,12,15; 5:4; **2 TIM.** 1:16; 4:19; **TITUS**
1:11; **PHILE.** 1:2; **HEB.** 3:2-6; 8:8,10; 10:21;
11:7; **1 PET.** 2:5; 4:17

3625. οἰκουμένη oikoumenē
MATT. 24:14; **LUKE** 2:1; 4:5; 21:26; **ACTS**
11:28; 17:6,31; 19:27; 24:5; **ROM.** 10:18; **HEB.**
1:6; 2:5; **REV.** 3:10; 12:9; 16:14

3626. οἰκουρός oikouros
TITUS 2:5

3627. οἰκτείρω, οἰκτίρω
oikteirō, oiktirō
ROM. 9:15

3628. οἰκτιρμός oiktirmos
ROM. 12:1; **2 COR.** 1:3; **PHIL.** 2:1; **COL.**
3:12; **HEB.** 10:28

3629. οἰκτίρμων oiktirmōn
LUKE 6:36; **JAMES** 5:11

3630. οἰνοπότης oinopotēs
MATT. 11:19; **LUKE** 7:34

3631. οἶνος oinos
MATT. 9:17; **MARK** 2:22; 15:23; **LUKE** 1:15;
5:37,38; 7:33; 10:34; **JOHN** 2:3,9,10; 4:46;
ROM. 14:21; **EPH.** 5:18; **1 TIM.** 3:8; 5:23;
TITUS 2:3; **REV.** 6:6; 14:8,10; 16:19; 17:2;
18:3,13; 19:15

3632. οἰνοφλυγία oinophlugia
1 PET. 4:3

3633. οἴομαι oiomai
JOHN 21:25; **PHIL.** 1:16; **JAMES** 1:7

3634. οἷος hoios
MATT. 24:21; **MARK** 9:3; 13:19; **LUKE** 9:55;

ROM. 9:6; **1 COR.** 15:48; **2 COR.** 10:11; 12:20;
PHIL. 1:30; **1 THESS.** 1:5; **2 TIM.** 3:11; **REV.**
16:18

3635. ὀκνέω okneō
ACTS 9:38

3636. ὀκνηρός oknēros
MATT. 25:26; **ROM.** 12:11; **PHIL.** 3:1

3637. ὀκταήμερος oktaēmeros
PHIL. 3:5

3638. ὀκτώ oktō
LUKE 2:21; 9:28; 13:4,11,16; **JOHN** 5:5;
20:26; **ACTS** 9:33; **1 PET.** 3:20

3639. ὄλεθρος olethros
1 COR. 5:5; **1 THESS.** 5:3; **2 THESS.** 1:9;
1 TIM. 6:9

3640. ὀλιγόπιστος oligopistos
MATT. 6:30; 8:26; 14:31; 16:8; **LUKE** 12:28

3641. ὀλίγος oligos
MATT. 7:14; 9:37; 15:34; 20:16; 22:14;
25:21,23; **MARK** 1:19; 6:5,31; 8:7; **LUKE** 5:3;
7:47; 10:2; 12:48; 13:23; **ACTS** 12:18; 14:28;
15:2; 17:4,12; 19:23,24; 26:28,29; 27:20;
2 COR. 8:15; **EPH.** 3:3; **1 TIM.** 4:8; 5:23; **HEB.**
12:10; **JAMES** 3:5; 4:14; **1 PET.** 1:6; 3:20;
5:10,12; **REV.** 2:14,20; 3:4; 12:12; 17:10

3642. ὀλιγόψυχος oligopsuchos
1 THESS. 5:14

3643. ὀλιγωρέω oligōreō
HEB. 12:5

3644. ὀλοθρευτής olothreutēs
1 COR. 10:10

3645. ὀλοθρεύω olothreuō
HEB. 11:28

3646. ὀλοκαύτωμα holokautōma
MARK 12:33; **HEB.** 10:6,8

3647. ὁλοκληρία *holoklēria*
ACTS 3:16

3648. ὁλόκληρος *holoklēros*
1 THESS. 5:23; JAMES 1:4

3649. ὀλολύζω *ololuzō*
JAMES 5:1

3650. ὅλος *holos*
MATT. 1:22; 4:23,24; 5:29,30; 6:22,23; 9:26,31;
13:33; 14:35; 16:26; 20:6; 21:4; 22:37,40; 24:14;
26:13,56,59; 27:27; MARK 1:28,33,39; 6:55;
8:36; 12:30,33,44; 14:9,55; 15:1,16,33; LUKE
1:65; 4:14; 5:5; 7:17; 8:39,43; 9:25; 10:27;
11:34,36; 13:21; 23:5,44; JOHN 4:53; 7:23;
9:34; 11:50; 13:10; 19:23; ACTS 2:2,47; 5:11;
7:10,11; 8:37; 9:31,42; 10:22,37; 11:26,28;
13:49; 15:22; 18:8; 19:27,29; 21:30,31; 22:30;
28:30; ROM. 1:8; 8:36; 10:21; 16:23; 1 COR.
5:6; 12:17; 14:23; 2 COR. 1:1; GAL. 5:3,9;
PHIL. 1:13; 1 THESS. 4:10; TITUS 1:11;
HEB. 3:2,5; JAMES 2:10; 3:2,3,6; 1 JOHN 2:2;
5:19; REV. 3:10; 12:9; 13:3; 16:14

3651. ὁλοτελής *holotelēs*
1 THESS. 5:23

3652. Ὀλυμπᾶς *Olumpas*
ROM. 16:15

3653. ὄλυνθος *olunthos*
REV. 6:13

3654. ὅλως *holōs*
MATT. 5:34; 1 COR. 5:1; 6:7; 15:29

3655. ὄμβρος *ombros*
LUKE 12:54

3656. ὁμιλέω *homileō*
LUKE 24:14,15; ACTS 20:11; 24:26

3657. ὁμιλία *homilia*
1 COR. 15:33

3658. ὅμιλος *homilos*
REV. 18:17

3659. ὄμμα *omma*
MARK 8:23

3660. I. ὀμνύω *omnuō*
MATT. 5:34,36; 23:16,18,20-22; 26:74;
MARK 6:23; LUKE 1:73; ACTS 2:30;
7:17; HEB. 3:11,18; 4:3; 6:13,16; 7:21;
JAMES 5:12; REV. 10:6

II. ὄμνυμι *omnumi*
MARK 14:71

3661. ὁμοθυμαδόν *homothumadon*
ACTS 1:14; 2:1,46; 4:24; 5:12; 7:57; 8:6; 12:20;
15:25; 18:12; 19:29; ROM. 15:6

3662. ὁμοιάζω *homoiazō*
MARK 14:70

3663. ὁμοιοπαθής *homoiopathēs*
ACTS 14:15; JAMES 5:17

3664. ὅμοιος *homoios*
MATT. 11:16; 13:31,33,44,45,47,52; 20:1;
22:39; MARK 12:31; LUKE 6:47-49; 7:31,32;
12:36; 13:18,19,21; JOHN 8:55; 9:9; ACTS
17:29; GAL. 5:21; 1 JOHN 3:2; JUDE 1:7;
REV. 1:13,15; 2:18; 4:3,6,7; 9:7,10,19; 11:1;
13:2,4,11; 14:14; 16:13; 18:18; 21:11,18

3665. ὁμοιότης *homoiotēs*
HEB. 4:15; 7:15

3666. ὁμοιόω *homoioō*
MATT. 6:8; 7:24,26; 11:16; 13:24; 18:23; 22:2;
25:1; MARK 4:30; LUKE 7:31; 13:18,20;
ACTS 14:11; ROM. 9:29; HEB. 2:17

3667. ὁμοίωμα *homoiōma*
ROM. 1:23; 5:14; 6:5; 8:3; PHIL. 2:7; REV. 9:7

3668. ὁμοίως *homoiōs*
MATT. 22:26; 26:35; 27:41; MARK 4:16;
15:31; LUKE 3:11; 5:10,33; 6:31; 10:32,37;
13:5; 16:25; 17:28,31; 22:36; JOHN 5:19; 6:11;
21:13; ROM. 1:27; 1 COR. 7:3,4,22; HEB.
9:21; JAMES 2:25; 1 PET. 3:1,7; 5:5; JUDE
1:8; REV. 8:12

3669. ὁμοίωσις *homoiōsis*
JAMES 3:9

3670. ὁμολογέω *homologeō*
MATT. 7:23; 10:32; 14:7; LUKE 12:8; JOHN
1:20; 9:22; 12:42; ACTS 23:8; 24:14; ROM.
10:9,10; 1 TIM. 6:12; TITUS 1:16; HEB. 11:13;
13:15; 1 JOHN 1:9; 4:2,3,15; 2 JOHN 1:7

3671. ὁμολογία *homologia*
2 COR. 9:13; 1 TIM. 6:12,13; HEB. 3:1; 4:14;
10:23

3672. ὁμολογουμένως
    homologoumenōs
1 TIM. 3:16

3673. ὁμότεχνος *homotechnos*
ACTS 18:3

3674. ὁμοῦ *homou*
JOHN 4:36; 20:4; 21:2

3675. ὁμόφρων *homophrōn*
1 PET. 3:8

3676. ὅμως *homōs*
JOHN 12:42; 1 COR. 14:7; GAL. 3:15

3677. ὄναρ *onar*
MATT. 1:20; 2:12,13,19,22; 27:19

3678. ὀνάριον *onarion*
JOHN 12:14

3679. ὀνειδίζω *oneidizō*
MATT. 5:11; 11:20; 27:44; MARK 15:32;
16:14; LUKE 6:22; ROM. 15:3; 1 TIM. 4:10;
JAMES 1:5; 1 PET. 4:14

3680. ὀνειδισμός *oneidismos*
ROM. 15:3; 1 TIM. 3:7; HEB. 10:33; 11:26;
13:13

3681. ὄνειδος *oneidos*
LUKE 1:25

3682. Ὀνήσιμος *Onēsimos*
COL. 4:9; PHILE. 1:10

3683. Ὀνησίφορος *Onēsiphoros*
2 TIM. 1:16; 4:19

3684. ὀνικός *onikos*
MATT. 18:6; LUKE 17:2

3685. ὀνίνημι *oninēmi*
PHILE. 1:20

3686. ὄνομα *onoma*
MATT. 1:21,23,25; 6:9; 7:22; 10:2,22,41,42;
12:21; 18:5,20; 19:29; 21:9; 23:39; 24:5,9;
27:32,57; 28:19; MARK 3:16,17; 5:9,22; 6:14;
9:37-39,41; 11:9,10; 13:6,13; 14:32; 16:17;
LUKE 1:5,13,26,27,31,49,59,61,63; 2:21,25;
5:27; 6:22; 8:30,41; 9:48,49; 10:17,20,38; 11:2;
13:35; 16:20; 19:2,38; 21:8,12,17; 23:50;
24:13,18,47; JOHN 1:6,12; 2:23; 3:1,18; 5:43;
10:3,25; 12:13,28; 14:13,14,26; 15:16,21;
16:23,24,26; 17:6,11,12,26; 18:10; 20:31; ACTS
1:15; 2:21,38; 3:6,16; 4:7,10,12,17,18,30;
5:1,28,34,40,41; 8:9,12,16; 9:10-12,14-16,
21,27,29,33,36; 10:1,43,48; 11:28; 12:13; 13:6,8;
15:14,17,26; 16:1,14,18; 17:34; 18:2,7,15,24;
19:5,13,17,24; 20:9; 21:10,13; 22:16; 26:9; 27:1;
28:7; ROM. 1:5; 2:24; 9:17; 10:13; 15:9;
1 COR. 1:2,10,13,15; 5:4; 6:11; EPH. 1:21;
5:20; PHIL. 2:9,10; 4:3; COL. 3:17; 2 THESS.
1:12; 3:6; 1 TIM. 6:1; 2 TIM. 2:19; HEB. 1:4;
2:12; 6:10; 13:15; JAMES 2:7; 5:10,14; 1 PET.
4:14; 1 JOHN 2:12; 3:23; 5:13; 3 JOHN 1:7,14;
REV. 2:3,13,17; 3:1,4,5,8,12; 6:8; 8:11; 9:11;
11:13,18; 13:1,6,8,17; 14:1,11; 15:2,4; 16:9;
17:3,5,8; 19:12,13,16; 21:12,14; 22:4

3687. ὀνομάζω *onomazō*
LUKE 6:13,14; ACTS 19:13; ROM. 15:20;
1 COR. 5:1,11; EPH. 1:21; 3:15; 5:3; 2 TIM.
2:19

3688. ὄνος *onos*
MATT. 21:2,5,7; LUKE 13:15; 14:5; JOHN
12:15

3689. ὄντως *ontōs*
MARK 11:32; LUKE 23:47; 24:34; JOHN
8:36; 1 COR. 14:25; GAL. 3:21; 1 TIM.
5:3,5,16; 2 PET. 2:18

3690. ὄξος oxos
MATT. 27:34,48; MARK 15:36; LUKE 23:36; JOHN 19:29,30

3691. ὀξύς oxus
ROM. 3:15; REV. 1:16; 2:12; 14:14,17,18; 19:15

3692. ὀπή opē
HEB. 11:38; JAMES 3:11

3693. ὄπισθεν opisthen
MATT. 9:20; 15:23; MARK 5:27; LUKE 8:44; 23:26; REV. 4:6; 5:1

3694. ὀπίσω opisō
MATT. 3:11; 4:19; 10:38; 16:23,24; 24:18; MARK 1:7,17,20; 8:33,34; 13:16; LUKE 4:8; 7:38; 9:23,62; 14:27; 17:31; 19:14; 21:8; JOHN 1:15,27,30; 6:66; 12:19; 18:6; 20:14; ACTS 5:37; 20:30; PHIL. 3:13; 1 TIM. 5:15; 2 PET. 2:10; JUDE 1:7; REV. 1:10; 12:15; 13:3

3695. ὀπλίζω hoplizō
1 PET. 4:1

3696. ὅπλον hoplon
JOHN 18:3; ROM. 6:13; 13:12; 2 COR. 6:7; 10:4

3697. ὁποῖος hopoios
ACTS 26:29; 1 COR. 3:13; GAL. 2:6; 1 THESS. 1:9; JAMES 1:24

3698. ὁπότε hopote
LUKE 6:3

3699. ὅπου hopou
MATT. 6:19-21; 8:19; 13:5; 24:28; 25:24,26; 26:13,57; 28:6; MARK 2:4; 4:5,15; 5:40; 6:10,55,56; 9:18,44,46,48; 13:14; 14:9,14; 16:6; LUKE 9:57; 12:33,34; 17:37; 22:11; JOHN 1:28; 3:8; 4:20,46; 6:23,62; 7:34,36,42; 8:21,22; 10:40; 11:30,32; 12:1,26; 13:33,36; 14:3,4; 17:24; 18:1,20; 19:18,20,41; 20:12,19; 21:18; ACTS 17:1; ROM. 15:20; 1 COR. 3:3; COL. 3:11; HEB. 6:20; 9:16; 10:18; JAMES 3:4,16; 2 PET. 2:11; REV. 2:13; 11:8; 12:6,14; 14:4; 17:9; 20:10

3700. I. ὀπτάνομαι optanomai
ACTS 1:3

II. ὄπτομαι optomai
(Obs. theme to fut. of ὁράω)
MATT. 5:8; 17:3; 24:30; 26:64; 27:4,24; 28:7, 10; MARK 9:4; 13:26; 14:62; 16:7; LUKE 1:11; 3:6; 9:31; 13:28; 17:22; 21:27; 22:43; 24:34; JOHN 1:50,51; 3:36; 11:40; 16:16,17,19,22; 19:37; ACTS 2:3,17; 7:2,26,30,35; 9:17; 13:31; 16:9; 18:15; 20:25; 26:16; ROM. 15:21; 1 COR. 15:5-8; 1 TIM. 3:16; HEB. 9:28; 12:14; 13:23; 1 JOHN 3:2; REV. 1:7; 11:19; 12:1,3; 22:4

3701. ὀπτασία optasia
LUKE 1:22; 24:23; ACTS 26:19; 2 COR. 12:1

3702. ὀπτός optos
LUKE 24:42

3703. ὀπώρα opōra
REV. 18:14

3704. ὅπως hopōs
MATT. 2:8,23; 5:16,45; 6:2,4,5,16,18; 8:17,34; 9:38; 12:14,17; 13:35; 22:15; 23:35; 26:59; MARK 3:6; 5:23; LUKE 2:35; 7:3; 10:2; 11:37; 16:26,28; 24:20; JOHN 11:57; ACTS 3:19; 8:15,24; 9:2,12,17,24; 15:17; 20:16; 23:15,20,23; 24:26; 25:3,26; ROM. 3:4; 9:17; 1 COR. 1:29; 2 COR. 8:11,14; GAL. 1:4; 2 THESS. 1:12; PHILE. 1:6; HEB. 2:9; 9:15; JAMES 5:16; 1 PET. 2:9

3705. ὅραμα horama
MATT. 17:9; ACTS 7:31; 9:10,12; 10:3,17,19; 11:5; 12:9; 16:9,10; 18:9

3706. ὅρασις horasis
ACTS 2:17; REV. 4:3; 9:17

3707. ὁρατός horatos
COL. 1:16

3708. ὁράω horaō
MATT. 8:4; 9:30; 16:6; 18:10; 24:6; MARK 1:44; 8:15,24; LUKE 1:22; 9:36; 12:15; 16:23;

23:49; 24:23; **JOHN** 1:18,34; 3:11,32; 4:45;
5:37; 6:2,36,46; 8:38,57; 9:37; 14:7,9; 15:24;
19:35; 20:18,25,29; **ACTS** 7:44; 8:23; 22:15,26;
1 COR. 9:1; **COL.** 2:1,18; **1 THESS.** 5:15;
HEB. 2:8; 8:5; 11:27; **JAMES** 2:24; **1 PET.** 1:8;
1 JOHN 1:1-3; 3:6; 4:20; **3 JOHN** 1:11; **REV.**
18:18; 19:10; 22:9

3709. ὀργή orgē
MATT. 3:7; **MARK** 3:5; **LUKE** 3:7; 21:23;
JOHN 3:36; **ROM.** 1:18; 2:5,8; 3:5; 4:15; 5:9;
9:22; 12:19; 13:4,5; **EPH.** 2:3; 4:31; 5:6; **COL.**
3:6,8; **1 THESS.** 1:10; 2:16; 5:9; **1 TIM.** 2:8;
HEB. 3:11; 4:3; **JAMES** 1:19,20; **REV.** 6:16,17;
11:18; 14:10; 16:19; 19:15

3710. ὀργίζω orgizō
MATT. 5:22; 18:34; 22:7; **LUKE** 14:21; 15:28;
EPH. 4:26; **REV.** 11:38; 12:17

3711. ὀργίλος orgilos
TITUS 1:7

3712. ὀργυία orguia
ACTS 27:28

3713. ὀρέγω oregō
1 TIM. 3:1; 6:10; **HEB.** 11:16

3714. ὀρεινός oreinos
LUKE 1:39,65

3715. ὄρεξις orexis
ROM. 1:27

3716. ὀρθοποδέω orthopodeō
GAL. 2:14

3717. ὀρθός orthos
ACTS 14:10; **HEB.** 12:13

3718. ὀρθοτομέω orthotomeō
2 TIM. 2:15

3719. ὀρθρίζω orthrizō
LUKE 21:38

3720. ὀρθρινός orthrinos
REV. 22:16

3721. ὄρθριος orthrios
LUKE 24:22

3722. ὄρθρος orthros
LUKE 24:1; **JOHN** 8:2; **ACTS** 5:21

3723. ὀρθῶς orthōs
MARK 7:35; **LUKE** 7:43; 10:28; 20:21

3724. ὀρίζω horizō
LUKE 22:22; **ACTS** 2:23; 10:42; 11:29;
17:26,31; **ROM.** 1:4; **HEB.** 4:7

3725. ὅριον horion
MATT. 2:16; 4:13; 8:34; 15:22,39; 19:1;
MARK 5:17; 7:31; 10:1; **ACTS** 13:50

3726. ὁρκίζω horkizō
MARK 5:7; **ACTS** 19:13; **1 THESS.** 5:27

3727. ὅρκος horkos
MATT. 5:33; 14:7,9; 26:72; **MARK** 6:26;
LUKE 1:73; **ACTS** 2:30; **HEB.** 6:16,17;
JAMES 5:12

3728. ὁρκωμοσία horkōmosia
HEB. 7:20,21,28

3729. ὁρμάω hormaō
MATT. 8:32; **MARK** 5:13; **LUKE** 8:33; **ACTS**
7:57; 19:29

3730. ὁρμή hormē
ACTS 14:5; **JAMES** 3:4

3731. ὅρμημα hormēma
REV. 18:21

3732. ὄρνεον orneon
REV. 18:2; 19:17,21

3733. ὄρνις ornis
MATT. 23:37; **LUKE** 13:34

3734. ὁροθεσία horothesia
ACTS 17:26

3735. ὄρος oros
MATT. 4:8; 5:1,14; 8:1; 14:23; 15:29; 17:1,9,20; 18:12; 21:1,21; 24:3,16; 26:30; 28:16; MARK 3:13; 5:5,11; 6:46; 9:2,9; 11:1,23; 13:3,14; 14:26; LUKE 3:5; 4:5,29; 6:12; 8:32; 9:28,37; 19:29,37; 21:21,37; 22:39; 23:30; JOHN 4:20,21; 6:3,15; 8:1; ACTS 1:12; 7:30,38; 1 COR. 13:2; GAL. 4:24,25; HEB. 8:5; 11:38; 12:18,20,22; 2 PET. 1:18; REV. 6:14-16; 8:8; 14:1; 16:20; 17:9; 21:10

3736. ὀρύσσω, ὀρύττω orussō, oruttō
MATT. 21:33; 25:18; MARK 12:1

3737. ὀρφανός orphanos
JOHN 14:18; JAMES 1:27

3738. ὀρχέομαι orcheomai
MATT. 11:17; 14:6; MARK 6:22; LUKE 7:32

3740. ὀσάκις hosakis
1 COR. 11:25,26; REV. 11:6

3741. ὅσιος hosios
ACTS 2:27; 13:34,35; 1 TIM. 2:8; TITUS 1:8; HEB. 7:26; REV. 15:4; 16:5

3742. ὁσιότης hosiotēs
LUKE 1:75; EPH. 4:24

3743. ὁσίως hosiōs
1 THESS. 2:10

3744. ὀσμή osmē
JOHN 12:3; 2 COR. 2:14,16; EPH. 5:2; PHIL. 4:18

3746. ὅσπερ hosper
MARK 15:6

3747. ὀστέον osteon
MATT. 23:27; LUKE 24:39; JOHN 19:36; EPH. 5:30; HEB. 11:22

3749. ὀστράκινος ostrakinos
2 COR. 4:7; 2 TIM. 2:20

3750. ὄσφρησις osphrēsis
1 COR. 12:17

3751. ὀσφύς osphus
MATT. 3:4; MARK 1:6; LUKE 12:35; ACTS 2:30; EPH. 6:14; HEB. 7:5,10; 1 PET. 1:13

3755. ὅτου hotou
    (Gen. of ὅστις)
MATT. 5:25; LUKE 13:8; 15:8; 22:16,18; JOHN 9:18

3757. οὗ hou adv.
MATT. 2:9; 18:20; 28:16; LUKE 4:16,17; 10:1; 22:10; 23:53; 24:28; JOHN 11:41; ACTS 1:13; 2:2; 7:29; 12:12; 16:13; 20:6,8; 25:10; 28:14; ROM. 4:15; 5:20; 9:26; 1 COR. 16:6; 2 COR. 3:17; COL. 3:1; HEB. 3:9; REV. 17:15

3758. οὐά oua
MARK 15:29

3759. οὐαί ouai
MATT. 11:21; 18:7; 23:13-16,23,25,27,29; 24:19; 26:24; MARK 13:17; 14:21; LUKE 6:24-26; 10:13; 11:42-44,46,47,52; 17:1; 21:23; 22:22; 1 COR. 9:16; JUDE 1:11; REV. 8:13; 9:12; 11:14; 12:12; 18:10,16,19

3760. οὐδαμῶς oudamōs
MATT. 2:6

3762. οὐδείς oudeis
MATT. 5:13; 6:24; 9:16; 10:26; 11:27; 17:8,20; 19:17; 20:7; 21:19; 22:16,46; 23:16,18; 24:36; 26:62; 27:12,24; MARK 2:21,22; 3:27; 5:3,4,37; 6:5; 7:12,15,24; 9:8,29,39; 10:18,29; 11:2,13; 12:14,34; 13:32; 14:60,61; 15:4,5; 16:8; LUKE 1:61; 4:2,24,26,27; 5:5,36,37,39; 7:28; 8:16, 43,51; 9:36,62; 10:19,22; 11:33; 12:2; 14:24; 15:16; 16:13; 18:19,29,34; 19:30; 20:40; 22:35; 23:4,9,14,15,22,41,53; JOHN 1:18; 3:2,13, 27,32; 4:27; 5:19,22,30; 6:44,63,65; 7:4,13, 19,26,27,30,44; 8:10,11,15,20,28,33,54; 9:4,33; 10:18,29,41; 11:49; 12:19; 13:28; 14:6,30; 15:5,13,24; 16:5,22-24,29; 17:12; 18:9,20,31,38; 19:4,11,41; 21:3,12; ACTS 4:12,14; 5:13,23,36; 8:16; 9:8; 15:9; 17:21; 18:10,17; 19:27; 20:20, 24,33; 21:24; 23:9; 25:10,11,18; 26:22,26,31;

27:22,34; 28:5,17; **ROM.** 8:1; 14:7,14; **1 COR.**
1:14; 2:8,11,15; 3:11; 4:4; 7:19; 8:2,4; 9:15;
12:3; 13:2,3; 14:2,10; **2 COR.** 5:16; 7:2,5; 11:9;
12:11; **GAL.** 2:6; 3:11,15; 4:1,12; 5:2,10; **EPH.**
5:29; **PHIL.** 1:20; 2:20; 4:15; **1 TIM.** 4:4; 6:7,
16; **2 TIM.** 2:4,14; 4:16; **TITUS** 1:15; **PHILE.**
1:14; **HEB.** 2:8; 6:13; 7:13,14,19; 12:14;
JAMES 1:13; 3:8,12; **1 JOHN** 1:5; 4:12; **REV.**
2:17; 3:7,8,17; 5:3,4; 7:9; 14:3; 15:8; 18:11;
19:12

3763. οὐδέποτε oudepote
MATT. 7:23; 9:33; 21:16,42; 26:33; **MARK**
2:12,25; **LUKE** 15:29; **JOHN** 7:46; **ACTS**
10:14; 11:8; 14:8; **1 COR.** 13:8; **HEB.** 10:1,11

3764. οὐδέπω oudepō
LUKE 23:53; **JOHN** 7:39; 19:41; 20:9; **1 COR.**
8:2

3765. οὐκέτι, οὐκ ἔτι ouketi, ouk eti
MATT. 19:6; 22:46; **MARK** 7:12; 9:8; 10:8;
12:34; 14:25; 15:5; **LUKE** 15:19,21; 20:40;
22:16; **JOHN** 4:42; 6:66; 11:54; 14:19,30; 15:15;
16:10,21,25; 17:11; 21:6; **ACTS** 8:39; 20:25,38;
ROM. 6:9; 7:17,20; 11:6; 14:15; **2 COR.** 1:23;
5:16; **GAL.** 2:20; 3:18,25; 4:7; **EPH.** 2:19;
PHILE. 1:16; **HEB.** 10:18,26; **REV.** 18:11,14

3766. οὐκοῦν oukoun
JOHN 18:37

3768. οὔπω oupō
MATT. 15:17; 16:9; 24:6; **MARK** 8:17; 13:7;
JOHN 2:4; 3:24; 7:6,8,30,39; 8:20,57; 11:30;
20:17; **ACTS** 8:16; **1 COR.** 3:2; **HEB.** 2:8; 12:4;
1 JOHN 3:2; **REV.** 17:10,12

3769. οὐρά oura
REV. 9:10,19; 12:4

3770. οὐράνιος ouranios
MATT. 6:14,26,32; 15:13; **LUKE** 2:13; **ACTS**
26:19

3771. οὐρανόθεν ouranothen
ACTS 14:17; 26:13

3772. οὐρανός ouranos
MATT. 3:2,16,17; 4:17; 5:3,10,12,16,18-

20,34,45,48; 6:1,9,10,20,26; 7:11,21; 8:11,20;
10:7,32,33; 11:11,12,23,25; 12:50; 13:11,24,31-
33,44,45,47,52; 14:19; 16:1-3,17,19; 18:1,3,
4,10,14,18,19,23; 19:12,14,21,23; 20:1; 21:25;
22:2,30; 23:9,13,22; 24:29-31,35,36; 25:1; 26:64;
28:2,18; **MARK** 1:10,11; 4:4,32; 6:41; 7:34;
8:11; 10:21; 11:25,26,30,31; 12:25; 13:25,27,
31,32; 14:62; 16:19; **LUKE** 2:15; 3:21,22; 4:25;
6:23; 8:5; 9:16,54,58; 10:15,18,20,21; 11:2,13,
16; 12:33,56; 13:19; 15:7,18,21; 16:17; 17:24,29;
18:13,22; 19:38; 20:4,5; 21:11,26,33; 22:43;
24:51; **JOHN** 1:32,51; 3:13,27,31; 6:31-33,
38,41,42,50,51,58; 12:28; 17:1; **ACTS** 1:10,11;
2:2,5,19,34; 3:21; 4:12,24; 7:42,49,55,56; 9:3;
10:11,12,16; 11:5,6,9,10; 14:15; 17:24; 22:6;
ROM. 1:18; 10:6; **1 COR.** 8:5; 15:47; **2 COR.**
5:1,2; 12:2; **GAL.** 1:8; **EPH.** 1:10; 3:15; 4:10;
6:9; **PHIL.** 3:20; **COL.** 1:5,16,20,23; 4:1;
1 THESS. 1:10; 4:16; **2 THESS.** 1:7; **HEB.**
1:10; 4:14; 7:26; 8:1; 9:23,24; 10:34; 11:12;
12:23,25,26; **JAMES** 5:12,18; **1 PET.** 1:4,12;
3:22; **2 PET.** 1:18; 3:5,7,10,12,13; **1 JOHN**
5:7; **REV.** 3:12; 4:1,2; 5:3,13; 6:13,14; 8:1,10;
9:1; 10:1,4-6,8; 11:6,12,13,15,19; 12:1,3,4,7,8,
10,12; 13:6,13; 14:2,7,13,17; 15:1,5; 16:11,
17,21; 18:1,4,5,20; 19:1,11,14; 20:1,9,11; 21:1-
3,10

3773. Οὐρβανός Ourbanos
ROM. 16:9

3774. Οὐρίας Ourias
MATT. 1:6

3775. οὖς ous
MATT. 10:27; 11:15; 13:9,15,16,43; **MARK**
4:9,23; 7:16,33; 8:18; **LUKE** 1:44; 4:21; 8:8;
9:44; 12:3; 14:35; 22:50; **ACTS** 7:51,57; 11:22;
28:27; **ROM.** 11:8; **1 COR.** 2:9; 12:16; **JAMES**
5:4; **1 PET.** 3:12; **REV.** 2:7,11,17,29; 3:6,13,22;
13:9

3776. οὐσία ousia
LUKE 15:12,13

3777. οὔτε oute
MATT. 6:20; 12:32; 22:30; **MARK** 5:3; 12:25;
LUKE 12:26; 14:35; 20:35,36; **JOHN** 1:25;
4:11,21; 5:37; 8:19; 9:3; **ACTS** 4:12; 15:10;
19:37; 24:12,13; 25:8; 28:21; **ROM.** 8:38,39;
1 COR. 3:2,7; 6:9,10; 8:8; 11:11; **GAL.** 1:12;

5:6; 6:15; **1 THESS.** 2:3,5,6; **3 JOHN** 1:10;
REV. 3:15,16; 5:4; 9:20,21; 12:8; 20:4; 21:4

3781. ὀφειλέτης *opheiletēs*
MATT. 6:12; 18:24; **LUKE** 13:4; **ROM.** 1:14;
8:12; 15:27; **GAL.** 5:3

3782. ὀφειλή *opheilē*
MATT. 18:32; **ROM.** 13:7

3783. ὀφείλημα *opheilēma*
MATT. 6:12; **ROM.** 4:4

3784. ὀφείλω *opheilō*
MATT. 18:28,30,34; 23:16,18; **LUKE** 7:41;
11:4; 16:5,7; 17:10; **JOHN** 13:14; 19:7; **ACTS**
17:29; **ROM.** 13:8; 15:1,27; **1 COR.** 5:10;
7:3,36; 9:10; 11:7,10; **2 COR.** 12:11,14; **EPH.**
5:28; **2 THESS.** 1:3; 2:13; **PHILE.** 1:18; **HEB.**
2:17; 5:3,12; **1 JOHN** 2:6; 3:16; 4:11; **3 JOHN**
1:8

3785. ὄφελον *ophelon*
1 COR. 4:8; **2 COR.** 11:1; **GAL.** 5:12; **REV.**
3:15

3786. ὄφελος *ophelos*
1 COR. 15:32; **JAMES** 2:14,16

3787. ὀφθαλμοδουλεία
ophthalmodouleia
EPH. 6:6; **COL.** 3:22

3788. ὀφθαλμός *ophthalmos*
MATT. 5:29,38; 6:22,23; 7:3-5; 9:29,30;
13:15,16; 17:8; 18:9; 20:15,33,34; 21:42; 26:43;
MARK 7:22; 8:18,25; 9:47; 12:11; 14:40;
LUKE 2:30; 4:20; 6:20,41,42; 10:23; 11:34;
16:23; 18:13; 19:42; 24:16,31; **JOHN** 4:35; 6:5;
9:6,10,11,14,15,17,21,26,30,32; 10:21; 11:37,41;
12:40; 17:1; **ACTS** 1:9; 9:8,18,40; 26:18; 28:27;
ROM. 3:18; 11:8,10; **1 COR.** 2:9; 12:16,17,21;
15:52; **GAL.** 3:1; 4:15; **EPH.** 1:18; **HEB.** 4:13;
1 PET. 3:12; **2 PET.** 2:14; **1 JOHN** 1:1; 2;11,
16; **REV.** 1:7,14; 2:18; 3:18; 4:6,8; 5:6; 7:17;
19:12; 21:4

3789. ὄφις *ophis*
MATT. 7:10; 10:16; 23:33; **MARK** 16:18;

LUKE 10:19; 11:11; **JOHN** 3:14; **1 COR.** 10:9;
2 COR. 11;3; **REV.** 9:19; 12:9,14,15; 20:2

3790. ὀφρύς *ophrus*
LUKE 4:29

3791. ὀχλέω *ochleō*
LUKE 6:18; **ACTS** 5:16

3792. ὀχλοποιέω *ochlopoieō*
ACTS 17:5

3793. ὄχλος *ochlos*
MATT. 4:25; 5:1; 7:28; 8:1,18; 9:8,23,25,33,36;
11:7; 12:15,23,46; 13:2,34,36; 14:5,13-15,19,
22,23; 15:10,30-33,35,36,39; 17:14; 19:2;
20:29,31; 21:8,9,11,26,46; 22:33; 23:1; 26:47,55;
27:15,20,24; **MARK** 2:4,13; 3:9,20,32; 4:1,36;
5:21,24,27,30,31; 6:33,34,45; 7:14,17,33; 8:1,
2,6,34; 9:14,15,17,25; 10:1,46; 11:18; 12:12,
37,41; 14:43; 15:8,11,15; **LUKE** 3:7,10; 4:42;
5:1,3,15,19,29; 6:17,19; 7:9,11,12,24; 8:4,
19,40,42,45; 9:11,12,16,18,37,38; 11:14,27,29;
12:1,13,54; 13:14,17; 14:25; 18:36; 19:3,39;
22:6,47; 23:4,48; **JOHN** 5:13; 6:2,5,22,24;
7:12,20,31,32,40,43,49; 11:42; 12:9,12,
17,18,29,34; **ACTS** 1:15; 6:7; 8:6; 11:24,26;
13:45; 14:11,13,14,18,19; 16:22; 17:8,13;
19:26,33,35; 21:27,34,35; 24:12,18; **REV.** 7:9;
17:15; 19:1,6

3794. ὀχύρωμα *ochurōma*
2 COR. 10:4

3795. ὀψάριον *opsarion*
JOHN 6:9,11; 21:9,10,13

3796. ὀψέ *opse*
MATT. 28:1; **MARK** 11:19; 13:35

3797. ὄψιμος *opsimos*
JAMES 5:7

3798. ὀψία *opsia* subst.
MATT. 8:16; 14:15,23; 16:2; 20:8; 26:20; 27:57;
MARK 1:32; 4:35; 6:47; 11:11; 14:17; 15:42;
JOHN 6:16; 20:19

3799. ὄψις *opsis*
JOHN 7:24; 11:44; **REV.** 1:16

3800. ὀψώνιον *opsōnion*
LUKE 3:14; **ROM.** 6:23; **1 COR.** 9:7; **2 COR.** 11:8

3801. ὁ ὢν καὶ ὁ ἦν
καὶ ὁ ἐρχόμενος
ho ōn kai ho ēn kai ho erchomenos
REV. 1:4,8; 4:8; 11:17 TR

Π

3802. παγιδεύω *pagideuō*
MATT. 22:15

3803. παγίς *pagis*
LUKE 21:35; **ROM.** 11:9; **1 TIM.** 3:7; 6:9;
2 TIM. 2:26

3804. πάθημα *pathēma*
ROM. 7:5; 8:18; **2 COR.** 1:5-7; **GAL.** 5:24;
PHIL. 3:10; **COL.** 1:24; **2 TIM.** 3:11; **HEB.**
2:9,10; 10:32; **1 PET.** 1:11; 4:13; 5:1,9

3805. παθητός *pathētos*
ACTS 26:23

3806. πάθος *pathos*
ROM. 1:26; **COL.** 3:5; **1 THESS.** 4:5

3807. παιδαγωγός *paidagōgos*
1 COR. 4:15; **GAL.** 3:24,25

3808. παιδάριον *paidarion*
MATT. 11:16; **JOHN** 6:9

3809. παιδεία *paideia*
EPH. 6:4; **2 TIM.** 3:16; **HEB.** 12:5,7,8,11

3810. παιδευτής *paideutēs*
ROM. 2:20; **HEB.** 12:9

3811. παιδεύω *paideuō*
LUKE 23:16,22; **ACTS** 7:22; 22:3; **1 COR.**
11:32; **2 COR.** 6:9; **1 TIM.** 1:20; **2 TIM.** 2:25;
TITUS 2:12; **HEB.** 12:6,7,10; **REV.** 3:19

3812. παιδιόθεν *paidiothen*
MARK 9:21

3813. παιδίον *paidion*
MATT. 2:8,9,11,13,14,20,21; 14:21; 15:38;
18:2-5; 19:13,14; **MARK** 5:39-41; 7:28;
9:24,36,37; 10:13-15; **LUKE** 1:59,66,76,80;
2:17,21,27,40; 7:32; 9:47,48; 11:7; 18:16,17;
JOHN 4:49; 16:21; 21:5; **1 COR.** 14:20; **HEB.**
2:13,14; 11:23; **1 JOHN** 2:13,18

3814. παιδίσκη *paidiskē*
MATT. 26:69; **MARK** 14:66,69; **LUKE** 12:45;
22:56; **JOHN** 18:17; **ACTS** 12:13; 16:16; **GAL.**
4:22,23,30,31

3815. παίζω *paizō*
1 COR. 10:7

3816. παῖς *pais*
MATT. 2:16; 8:6,8,13; 12:18; 14:2; 17:18;
21:15; **LUKE** 1:54,69; 2:43; 7:7; 8:51,54; 9:42;
12:45; 15:26; **JOHN** 4:51; **ACTS** 3:13,26;
4:25,27,30; 20:12

3817. παίω *paiō*
MATT. 26:68; **MARK** 14:47; **LUKE** 22:64;
JOHN 18:10; **REV.** 9:5

3819. πάλαι *palai*
MATT. 11:21; **MARK** 15:44; **LUKE** 10:13;
HEB. 1:1; **2 PET.** 1:9; **JUDE** 1:4

3820. παλαιός *palaios*
MATT. 9:16,17; 13:52; **MARK** 2:21,22; **LUKE**
5:36,37,39; **ROM.** 6:6; **1 COR.** 5:7,8; **2 COR.**
3:14; **EPH.** 4:22; **COL.** 3:9; **1 JOHN** 2:7

3821. παλαιότης *palaiotēs*
ROM. 7:6

3822. παλαιόω *palaioō*
LUKE 12:33; **HEB.** 1:11; 8:13

3823. πάλη *palē*
EPH. 6:12

3824. παλιγγενεσία *paliggenesia*
MATT. 19:28; **TITUS** 3:5

3826. παμπληθεί *pamplēthei*
LUKE 23:18

3827. πάμπολυς pampolus
MARK 8:1

3828. Παμφυλία Pamphulia
ACTS 2:10; 13:13; 14:24; 15:38; 27:5

3829. πανδοχεῖον pandocheion
LUKE 10:34

3830. πανδοχεύς pandocheus
LUKE 10:35

3831. πανήγυρις panēguris
HEB. 12:23

3832. πανοικί panoiki
ACTS 16:34

3833. πανοπλία panoplia
LUKE 11:22; EPH. 6:11,13

3834. πανουργία panourgia
LUKE 20:23; 1 COR. 3:19; 2 COR. 4:2; 11:3;
EPH. 4:14

3835. πανοῦργος panourgos
2 COR. 12:16

3836. πανταχόθεν pantachothen
MARK 1:45

3837. πανταχοῦ pantachou
MARK 16:20; LUKE 9:6; ACTS 17:30; 21:28;
24:3; 28:22; 1 COR. 4:17

3838. παντελής pantelēs
(εἰς τὸ παντελές as adv.)
LUKE 13:11; HEB. 7:25

3839. πάντη pantē
ACTS 24:3

3840. πάντοθεν pantothen
LUKE 19:43; HEB. 9:4

3841. παντοκράτωρ pantokratōr
2 COR. 6:18; REV. 1:8; 4:8; 11:17; 15:3;
16:7,14; 19:6,15; 21:22

3842. πάντοτε pantote
MATT. 26:11; MARK 14:7; LUKE 15:31;
18:1; JOHN 6:34; 7:6; 8:29; 11:42; 12:8; 18:20;
ROM. 1:9; 1 COR. 1:4; 15:58; 2 COR. 2:14;
4:10; 5:6; 9:8; GAL. 4:18; EPH. 5:20; PHIL.
1:4,20; 2:12; 4:4; COL. 1:3; 4:6,12; 1 THESS.
1:2; 2:16; 3:6; 4:17; 5:15,16; 2 THESS. 1:3,11;
2:13; 2 TIM. 3:7; PHILE. 1:4; HEB. 7:25

3843. πάντως pantōs
LUKE 4:23; ACTS 18:21; 21:22; 28:4; ROM.
3:9; 1 COR. 5:10; 9:10,22; 16:12

3845. παραβαίνω parabainō
MATT. 15:2,3; ACTS 1:25; 2 JOHN 1:9

3846. παραβάλλω paraballō
MARK 4:30; ACTS 20:15

3847. παράβασις parabasis
ROM. 2:23; 4:15; 5:14; GAL. 3:19; 1 TIM.
2:14; HEB. 2:2; 9:15

3848. παραβάτης parabatēs
ROM. 2:25,27; GAL. 2:18; JAMES 2:9,11

3849. παραβιάζομαι parabiazomai
LUKE 24:29; ACTS 16:15

3850. παραβολή parabolē
MATT. 13:3,10,13,18,24,31,33-36,53; 15:15;
21:33,45; 22:1; 24:32; MARK 3:23; 4:2,10,
11,13,30,33,34; 7:17; 12:1,12; 13:28; LUKE
4:23; 5:36; 6:39; 8:4,9-11; 12:16,41; 13:6; 14:7;
15:3; 18:1,9; 19:11; 20:9,19; 21:29; HEB. 9:9;
11:19

**3851. παραβολεύομαι,
παραβουλεύομαι
paraboleuomai, parabouleuomai**
PHIL. 2:30

3852. παραγγελία paraggelia
ACTS 5:28; 16:24; 1 THESS. 4:2; 1 TIM.
1:5,18

3853. παραγγέλλω paraggellō
MATT. 10:5; MARK 6:8; 8:6; LUKE 5:14;

8:29,56; 9:21; **ACTS** 1:4; 4:18; 5:28,40; 10:42;
15:5; 16:18,23; 17:30; 23:22,30; **1 COR.** 7:10;
11:17; **1 THESS.** 4:11; **2 THESS.** 3:4,6,10,12;
1 TIM. 1:3; 4:11; 5:7; 6:13,17

3854. παραγίνομαι paraginomai
MATT. 2:1; 3:1,13; **MARK** 14:43; **LUKE**
7:4,20; 8:19; 11:6; 12:51; 14:21; 19:16; 22:52;
JOHN 3:23; 8:2; **ACTS** 5:21,22,25; 9:26,39;
10:32,33; 11:23; 13:14; 14:27; 15:4; 17:10;
18:27; 20:18; 21:18; 23:16,35; 24:17,24; 25:7;
28:21; **1 COR.** 16:3; **HEB.** 9:11

3855. παράγω paragō
MATT. 9:9,27; 20:30; **MARK** 2:14; 15:21;
JOHN 8:59; 9:1; **1 COR.** 7:31; **1 JOHN** 2:8,17

3856. παραδειγματίζω
paradeigmatizō
MATT. 1:19; **HEB.** 6:6

3857. παράδεισος paradeisos
LUKE 23:43; **2 COR.** 12:4; **REV.** 2:7

3858. παραδέχομαι paradechomai
MARK 4:20; **ACTS** 16:21; 22:18; **1 TIM.** 5:19;
HEB. 12:6

3859. παραδιατριβή paradiatribē
1 TIM. 6:5

3860. παραδίδωμι paradidōmi
MATT. 4:12; 5:25; 10:4,17,19,21; 11:27; 17:22;
18:34; 20:18,19; 24:9,10; 25:14,20,22; 26:2,15,
16,21,23-25,45,46,48; 27:2-4,18,26; **MARK**
1:14; 3:19; 4:29; 7:13; 9:31; 10:33; 13:9,11,12;
14:10,11,18,21,41,42,44; 15:1,10,15; **LUKE** 1:2;
4:6; 9:44; 10:22; 12:58; 18:32; 20:20; 21:12,16;
22:4,6,21,22,48; 23:25; 24:7,20; **JOHN** 6:64,71;
12:4; 13:2,11,21; 18:2,5,30,35,36; 19:11,16,30;
21:20; **ACTS** 3:13; 6:14; 7:42; 8:3; 12:4; 14:26;
15:26,40; 16:4; 21:11; 22:4; 27:1; 28:16,17;
ROM. 1:24,26,28; 4:25; 6:17; 8:32; **1 COR.** 5:5;
11:2,23; 13:3; 15:3,24; **2 COR.** 4:11; **GAL.**
2:20; **EPH.** 4:19; 5:2,25; **1 TIM.** 1:20; **1 PET.**
2:23; **2 PET.** 2:4,21; **JUDE** 1:3

3861. παράδοξος paradoxos
LUKE 5:26

3862. παράδοσις paradosis
MATT. 15:2,3,6; **MARK** 7:3,5,8,9,13; **1 COR.**
11:2; **GAL.** 1:14; **COL.** 2:8; **2 THESS.** 2:15; 3:6

3863. παραζηλόω parazēloō
ROM. 10:19; 11:11,14; **1 COR.** 10:22

3864. παραθαλάσσιος parathalassios
MATT. 4:13

3865. παραθεωρέω paratheōreō
ACTS 6:1

3866. παραθήκη parathēkē
2 TIM. 1:12

3867. παραινέω paraineō
ACTS 27:9,22

3868. παραιτέομαι paraiteomai
LUKE 14:18,19; **ACTS** 25:11; **1 TIM.** 4:7;
5:11; **2 TIM.** 2:23; **TITUS** 3:10; **HEB.** 12:19,25

3869. παρακαθίζω parakathizō
LUKE 10:39

3870. παρακαλέω parakaleō
MATT. 2:18; 5:4; 8:5,31,34; 14:36; 18:29,32;
26:53; **MARK** 1:40; 5:10,12,17,18,23; 6:56;
7:32; 8:22; **LUKE** 3:18; 7:4; 8:31,32,41; 15:28;
16:25; **ACTS** 2:40; 8:31; 9:38; 11:23; 13:42;
14:22; 15:32; 16:9,15,39,40; 19:31; 20:2,12;
21:12; 24:4; 25:2; 27:33,34; 28:14,20; **ROM.**
12:1,8; 15:30; 16:17; **1 COR.** 1:10; 4:13,16;
14:31; 16:12,15; **2 COR.** 1:4,6; 2:7,8; 5:20; 6:1;
7:6,7,13; 8:6; 9:5; 10:1; 12:8,18; 13:11; **EPH.**
4:1; 6:22; **PHIL.** 4:2; **COL.** 2:2; 4:8; **1 THESS.**
2:11; 3:2,7; 4:1,10,18; 5:11,14; **2 THESS.** 2:17;
3:12; **1 TIM.** 1:3; 2:1; 5:1; 6:2; **2 TIM.** 4:2;
TITUS 1:9; 2:6,15; **PHILE.** 1:9,10; **HEB.** 3:13;
10:25; 13:19,22; **1 PET.** 2:11; 5:1,12; **JUDE** 1:3

3871. παρακαλύπτω parakaluptō
LUKE 9:45

3872. παρακαταθήκη parakatathēkē
1 TIM. 6:20; **2 TIM.** 1:14

3873. παράκειμαι parakeimai
ROM. 7:18,21

3874. παράκλησις paraklēsis
LUKE 2:25; 6:24; ACTS 4:36; 9:31; 13:15;
15:31; ROM. 12:8; 15:4,5; 1 COR. 14:3;
2 COR. 1:3-7; 7:4,7,13; 8:4,17; PHIL. 2:1;
1 THESS. 2:3; 2 THESS. 2:16; 1 TIM. 4:13;
PHILE. 1:7; HEB. 6:18; 12:5; 13:22

3875. παράκλητος paraklētos
JOHN 14:16,26; 15:26; 16:7; 1 JOHN 2:1

3876. παρακοή parakoē
ROM. 5:19; 2 COR. 10:6; HEB. 2:2

3877. παρακολουθέω parakoloutheō
MARK 16:17; LUKE 1:3; 1 TIM. 4:6; 2 TIM.
3:10

3878. παρακούω parakouō
MATT. 18:17

3879. παρακύπτω parakuptō
LUKE 24:12; JOHN 20:5,11; JAMES 1:25;
1 PET. 1:12

3880. παραλαμβάνω paralambanō
MATT. 1:20,24; 2:13,14,20,21; 4:5,8; 12:45;
17:1; 18:16; 20:17; 24:40,41; 26:37; 27:27;
MARK 4:36; 5:40; 7:4; 9:2; 10:32; 14:33;
LUKE 9:10,28; 11:26; 17:34,35; 18:31; JOHN
1:11; 14:3; 19:16; ACTS 15:39; 16:33; 21:24,
26,32; 23:18; 1 COR. 11:23; 15:1,3; GAL.
1:9,12; PHIL. 4:9; COL. 2:6; 4:17; 1 THESS.
2:13; 4:1; 2 THESS. 3:6; HEB. 12:28

3881. παραλέγω paralegō
ACTS 27:8,13

3882. παράλιος paralios
LUKE 6:17

3883. παραλλαγή parallagē
JAMES 1:17

3884. παραλογίζομαι paralogizomai
COL. 2:4; JAMES 1:22

3885. παραλυτικός paralutikos
MATT. 4:24; 8:6; 9:2,6; MARK 2:3-5,9,10

3886. παραλύω paraluō
LUKE 5:18,24; ACTS 8:7; 9:33; HEB. 12:12

3887. παραμένω paramenō
1 COR. 16:6; HEB. 7:23; JAMES 1:25

3888. παραμυθέομαι paramutheomai
JOHN 11:19,31; 1 THESS. 2:11; 5:14

3889. παραμυθία paramuthia
1 COR. 14:3

3890. παραμύθιον paramuthion
PHIL. 2:1

3891. παρανομέω paranomeō
ACTS 23:3

3892. παρανομία paranomia
2 PET. 2:16

3893. παραπικραίνω parapikrainō
HEB. 3:16

3894. παραπικρασμός parapikrasmos
HEB. 3:8,15

3895. παραπίπτω parapiptō
HEB. 6:6

3896. παραπλέω parapleō
ACTS 20:16

3897. παραπλήσιον paraplēsion
PHIL. 2:27

3898. παραπλησίως paraplēsiōs
HEB. 2:14

3899. παραπορεύομαι paraporeuomai
MATT. 27:39; MARK 2:23; 9:30; 11:20; 15:29

3900. παράπτωμα paraptōma
MATT. 6:14,15; 18:3; MARK 11:25,26; ROM.

4:25; 5:15-18,20; 11:11,12; **2 COR.** 5:19; **GAL.** 6:1; **EPH.** 1:7; 2:1,5; **COL.** 2:13; **JAMES** 5:16

3901. παρарρέω pararreō
HEB. 2:1

3902. παράσημος parasēmos
ACTS 28:11

3903. παρασκευάζω paraskeuazō
ACTS 10:10; **1 COR.** 14:8; **2 COR.** 9:2,3

3904. παρασκευή paraskeuē
MATT. 27:62; **MARK** 15:42; **LUKE** 23:54; **JOHN** 19:14,31,42

3905. παρατείνω parateinō
ACTS 20:7

3906. παρατηρέω paratēreō
MARK 3:2; **LUKE** 6:7; 14:1; 20:20; **ACTS** 9:24; **GAL.** 4:10

3907. παρατήρησις paratērēsis
LUKE 17:20

3908. παρατίθημι paratithēmi
MATT. 13:24,31; **MARK** 6:41; 8:6,7; **LUKE** 9:16; 10:8; 11:6; 12:48; 23:46; **ACTS** 14:23; 16:34; 17:3; 20:32; **1 COR.** 10:27; **1 TIM.** 1:18; **2 TIM.** 2:2; **1 PET.** 4:19

3909. παρατυγχάνω paratugchanō
ACTS 17:17

3910. παραυτίκα parautika
2 COR. 4:17

3911. παραφέρω parapherō
MARK 14:36; **LUKE** 22:42

3912. παραφρονέω paraphroneō
2 COR. 11:23

3913. παραφρονία paraphronia
2 PET. 2:16

3914. παραχειμάζω paracheimazō
ACTS 27:12; 28:11; **1 COR.** 16:6; **TITUS** 3:12

3915. παραχειμασία paracheimasia
ACTS 27:12

3916. παραχρῆμα parachrēma
MATT. 21:19,20; **LUKE** 1:64; 4:39; 5:25; 8:44,47,55; 13:13; 18:43; 19:11; 22:60; **ACTS** 3:7; 5:10; 9:18; 12:23; 13:11; 16:26,33

3917. πάρδαλις pardalis
REV. 13:2

3918. πάρειμι pareimi
MATT. 26:50; **LUKE** 13:1; **JOHN** 7:6; 11:28; **ACTS** 10:21,33; 12:20; 17:6; 24:19; **1 COR.** 5:3; **2 COR.** 10:2,11; 11:9; 13:2,10; **GAL.** 4:18,20; **COL.** 1:6; **HEB.** 12:11; 13:5; **2 PET.** 1:9,12

3919. παρεισάγω pareisagō
2 PET. 2:1

3920. παρείσακτος pareisaktos
GAL. 2:4

3921. παρεισδύω pareisduō
JUDE 1:4

3922. παρεισέρχομαι pareiserchomai
ROM. 5:20; **GAL.** 2:4

3923. παρεισφέρω pareispherō
2 PET. 1:5

3924. παρεκτός parektos
MATT. 5:32; **ACTS** 26:29; **2 COR.** 11:28

3925. παρεμβολή parembolē
ACTS 21:34,37; 22:24; 23:10,16,32; **HEB.** 11:34; 13:11,13; **REV.** 20:9

3926. παρενοχλέω parenochleō
ACTS 15:19

3927. παρεπίδημος parepidēmos
HEB. 11:13; **1 PET.** 1:1; 2:11

3928. παρέρχομαι parerchomai
MATT. 5:18; 8:28; 14:15; 24:34,35; 26:39,42;
MARK 6:48; 13:30,31; 14:35; LUKE 11:42;
12:37; 15:29; 16:17; 17:7; 18:37; 21:32,33;
ACTS 16:8; 24:7; 27:9; 2 COR. 5:17; JAMES
1:10; 1 PET. 4:3; 2 PET. 3:10; REV. 21:1

3929. πάρεσις paresis
ROM. 3:25

3930. παρέχω parechō
MATT. 26:10; MARK 14:6; LUKE 6:29; 7:4;
11:7; 18:5; ACTS 16:16; 17:31; 19:24; 22:2;
28:2; GAL. 6:17; COL. 4:1; 1 TIM. 1:4; 6:17;
TITUS 2:7

3931. παρηγορία parēgoria
COL. 4:11

3932. παρθενία parthenia
LUKE 2:36

3933. παρθένος parthenos
MATT. 1:23; 25:1,7,11; LUKE 1:27; ACTS
21:9; 1 COR. 7:25,28,34,36,37; 2 COR. 11:2;
REV. 14:4

3934. Πάρθος Parthos
ACTS 2:9

3935. παρίημι pariēmi
HEB. 12:12

3936. I. παριστάνω paristanō
    (Later form of παρίστημι)
    ROM. 6:13,16

    II. παρίστημι paristēmi
    MATT. 26:53; MARK 4:29; 14:47,69,
    70; 15:35,39; LUKE 1:19; 2:22; 19:24;
    JOHN 18:22; 19:26; ACTS 1:3,10; 4:10,
    26; 9:39,41; 23:2,4,24,33; 24:13; 27:23,
    24; ROM. 6:13,19; 12:1; 14:10; 16:2;
    1 COR. 8:8; 2 COR. 4:14; 11:2; EPH.
    5:27; COL. 1:22,28; 2 TIM. 2:15; 4:17

3937. Παρμενᾶς Parmenas
ACTS 6:5

3938. πάροδος parodos
1 COR. 16:7

3939. παροικέω paroikeō
LUKE 24:18; HEB. 11:9

3940. παροικία paroikia
ACTS 13:17; 1 PET. 1:17

3941. πάροικος paroikos
ACTS 7:6,29; EPH. 2:19; 1 PET. 2:11

3942. παροιμία paroimia
JOHN 10:6; 16:25,29; 2 PET. 2:22

3943. πάροινος paroinos
1 TIM. 3:3; TITUS 1:7

3944. παροίχεω paroicheō
ACTS 14:16

3945. παρομοιάζω paromoiazō
MATT. 23:27

3946. παρόμοιος paromoios
MARK 7:8,13

3947. παροξύνω paroxunō
ACTS 17:16; 1 COR. 13:5

3948. παροξυσμός paroxusmos
ACTS 15:39; HEB. 10:24

3949. παροργίζω parorgizō
ROM. 10:19; EPH. 6:4

3950. παροργισμός parorgismos
EPH. 4:26

3951. παροτρύνω parotrunō
ACTS 13:50

3952. παρουσία parousia
MATT. 24:3,27,37,39; 1 COR. 15:23; 16:17;
2 COR. 7:6,7; 10:10; PHIL. 1:26; 2:12;
1 THESS. 2:19; 3:13; 4:15; 5:23; 2 THESS.
2:1,8,9; JAMES 5:7,8; 2 PET. 1:16; 3:4,12;
1 JOHN 2:28

3953. παροψίς *paropsis*
MATT. 23:25,26

3954. παρρησία *parrēsia*
MARK 8:52; JOHN 7:4,13,26; 10:24; 11:14,54;
16:25,29; 18:20; ACTS 2:29; 4:13,29,31; 28:31;
2 COR. 3:12; 7:4; EPH. 3:12; 6:19; PHIL. 1:20;
COL. 2:15; 1 TIM. 3:13; PHILE. 1:8; HEB.
3:6; 4:16; 10:19,35; 1 JOHN 2:28; 3:21; 4:17;
5:14

3955. παρρησιάζομαι *parrēsiazomai*
ACTS 9:27,29; 13:46; 14:3; 18:26; 19:8; 26:26;
EPH. 6:20; 1 THESS. 2:2

3957. πάσχα *pascha*
MATT. 26:2,17-19; MARK 14:1,12,14,16;
LUKE 2:41; 22:1,7,8,11,13,15; JOHN 2:13,23;
6:4; 11:55; 12:1; 13:1; 18:28,39; 19:14; ACTS
12:4; 1 COR. 5:7; HEB. 11:28

3958. πάσχω *paschō*
MATT. 16:21; 17:12,15; 27:19; MARK 5:26;
8:31; 9:12; LUKE 9:22; 13:2; 17:25; 22:15;
24:26,46; ACTS 1:3; 3:18; 9:16; 17:3; 28:5;
1 COR. 12:26; 2 COR. 1:6; GAL. 3:4; PHIL.
1:29; 1 THESS. 2:14; 2 THESS. 1:5; 2 TIM.
1:12; HEB. 2:18; 5:8; 9:26; 13:12; 1 PET. 2:19-
21,23; 3:14,17,18; 4:1,15,19; 5:10; REV. 2:10

3959. Πάταρα *Patara*
ACTS 21:1

3960. πατάσσω *patassō*
MATT. 26:31,51; MARK 14:27; LUKE
22:49,50; ACTS 7:24; 12:7,23; REV. 11:6;
19:15

3961. πατέω *pateō*
LUKE 10:19; 21:24; REV. 11:2; 14:20; 19:15

3962. πατήρ *patēr*
MATT. 2:22; 3:9; 4:21,22; 5:16,45,48; 6:1,4,
6,8,9,14,15,18,26,32; 7:11,21; 8:21; 10:20,21,
29,32,33,35,37; 11:25-27; 12:50; 13:43; 15:4-
6,13; 16:17,27; 18:10,14,19,35; 19:5,19,29;
20:23; 21:31; 23:9,30,32; 24:36; 25:34; 26:29,

39,42,53; 28:19; MARK 1:20; 5:40; 7:10-12;
8:38; 9:21,24; 10:7,19,29; 11:10,25,26; 13:12,32;
14:36; 15:21; LUKE 1:17,32,55,59,62,67,72,73;
2:48,49; 3:8; 6:23,26,36; 8:51; 9:26,42,59;
10:21,22; 11:2,11,13,47,48; 12:30,32,53; 14:26;
15:12,17,18,20-22,27-29; 16:24,27,30; 18:20;
22:29,42; 23:34,46; 24:49; JOHN 1:14,18; 2:16;
3:35; 4:12,20,21,23,53; 5:17-23,26,30,36,
37,43,45; 6:27,31,32,37,39,42,44-46,49,57,
58,65; 7:22; 8:16,18,19,27-29,38,39,41,42,
44,49,53,54,56; 10:15,17,18,25, 29,30,32,36-38;
11:41; 12:26-28,49,50; 13:1,3; 14:2,6-13,16,
20,21,23,24,26,28,31; 15:1,8-10,15,16,23,24,26;
16:3,10,15-17,23,25-28,32; 17:1,5,11,21,24,25;
18:11; 20:17,21; ACTS 1:4,7; 2:33; 3:13,22,25;
5:30; 7:2,4,11,12,14,15,19,20,32,38,39,44,45,
51,52; 13:17,32,36; 15:10; 16:1,3; 22:1,14; 26:6;
28:8,25; ROM. 1:7; 4:1,11,12,16-18; 6:4; 8:15;
9:5,10; 11:28; 15:6,8; 1 COR. 1:3; 4:15; 5:1; 8:6;
10:1; 15:24; 2 COR. 1:2,3; 6:18; 11:31; GAL.
1:1,3,4; 4:2,6; EPH. 1:2,3,17; 2:18; 3:14; 4:6;
5:20,31; 6:2,4,23; PHIL. 1:2; 2:11,22; 4:20;
COL. 1:2,3,12; 2:2; 3:17,21; 1 THESS. 1:1,3;
2:11; 3:11,13; 2 THESS. 1:1,2; 2:16; 1 TIM.
1:2; 5:1; 2 TIM. 1:2; TITUS 1:4; PHILE. 1:3;
HEB. 1:1,5; 3:9; 7:10; 8:9; 11:23; 12:7,9;
JAMES 1:17,27; 2:21; 3:9; 1 PET. 1:2,3,17;
2 PET. 1:17; 3:4; 1 JOHN 1:2,3; 2:1,13-16,22-
24; 3:1; 4:14; 5:7; 2 JOHN 1:3,4,9; JUDE 1:1;
REV. 1:6; 2:27; 3:5,21; 14:1

3963. Πάτμος *Patmos*
REV. 1:9

3964. πατραλῴας *patralōas*
1 TIM. 1:9

3965. πατριά *patria*
LUKE 2:4; ACTS 3:25; EPH. 3:15

3966. πατριάρχης *patriarchēs*
ACTS 2:29; 7:8,9; HEB. 7:4

3967. πατρικός *patrikos*
GAL. 1:14

3968. πατρίς *patris*
MATT. 13:54,57; MARK 6:1,4; LUKE
4:23,24; JOHN 4:44; HEB. 11:14

3969. Πατρόβας *Patrobas*
ROM. 16:14

3970. πατροπαράδοτος
patroparadotos
1 PET. 1:18

3971. πατρῷος *patrōos*
ACTS 22:3; 24:14; 28:17

3972. A. Παῦλος *Paulos*
(The deputy)
ACTS 13:7

B. Παῦλος *Paulos*
ACTS 13:9,13,16,43,45,46,50; 14:9,11,
12,14,19; 15:2,12,22,25,35,36,38,40;
16:3,9,14,17-19,25, 28,29,36,37; 17:2,4,
10,13-16,22,33; 18:1,5,9, 12,14,18; 19:1,
4,6,11,13,15,21,26,29,30; 20:1,7,9,10,13,
16,37; 21:4,8,11,13,18,26, 29,30,32,37,
39,40; 22:25,28,30; 23:1,3,5,6,10-12,14,
16-18,20,24,31,33; 24:1,10,23,24,26,27;
25:2,4,6,7,9,10,14,19,21,23; 26:1,24,28,
29; 27:1,3,9,11,21,24,31,33,43; 28:3,8,
15-17,25,30; ROM. 1:1; 1 COR. 1:1,12,
13; 3:4,5,22; 16:21; 2 COR. 1:1; 10:1;
GAL. 1:1; 5:2; EPH. 1:1; 3:1; PHIL.
1:1; COL. 1:1,23; 4:18; 1 THESS. 1:1;
2:18; 2 THESS. 1:1; 3:17; 1 TIM. 1:1;
2 TIM. 1:1; TITUS 1:1; PHILE. 1:1,9,
19; 2 PET. 3:15

3973. παύω *pauō*
LUKE 5:4; 8:24; 11:1; ACTS 5:42; 6:13; 13:10;
20:1,31; 21:32; 1 COR. 13:8; EPH. 1:16; COL.
1:9; HEB. 10:2; 1 PET. 3:10; 4:1

3974. Πάφος *Paphos*
ACTS 13:6,13

3975. παχύνω *pachunō*
MATT. 13:15; ACTS 28:27

3976. πέδη *pedē*
MARK 5:4; LUKE 8:29

3977. πεδινός *pedinos*
LUKE 6:17

3978. πεζεύω *pezeuō*
ACTS 20:13

3979. πεζῇ *pezē*
MATT. 14:13; MARK 6:33

3980. πειθαρχέω *peitharcheō*
ACTS 5:29,32; 27:21; TITUS 3:1

3981. πειθός *peithos*
1 COR. 2:4

3982. πείθω *peithō*
MATT. 27:20,43; 28:14; MARK 10:24; LUKE
11:22; 16:31; 18:9; 20:6; ACTS 5:36,37,40;
12:20; 13:43; 14:19; 17:4; 18:4; 19:8,26; 21:14;
23:21; 26:26,28; 27:11; 28:23,24; ROM. 2:8,19;
8:38; 14:14; 15:14; 2 COR. 1:9; 2:3; 5:11; 10:7;
GAL. 1:10; 3:1; 5:7,10; PHIL. 1:6,14,25; 2:24;
3:3,4; 2 THESS. 3:4; 2 TIM. 1:5,12; PHILE.
1:21; HEB. 2:13; 6:9; 11:13; 13:17,18; JAMES
3:3; 1 JOHN 3:19

3983. πεινάω *peinaō*
MATT. 4:2; 5:6; 12:1,3; 21:18; 25:35,37,42,44;
MARK 2:25; 11:12; LUKE 1:53; 4:2; 6:3,21,25;
JOHN 6:35; ROM. 12:20; 1 COR. 4:11;
11:21,34; PHIL. 4:12; REV. 7:16

3984. πεῖρα *peira*
HEB. 11:29,36

3985. πειράζω *peirazō*
MATT. 4:1,3; 16:1; 19:3; 22:18,35; MARK
1:13; 8:11; 10:2; 12:15; LUKE 4:2; 11:16;
20:23; JOHN 6:6; 8:6; ACTS 5:9; 15:10; 16:7;
24:6; 1 COR. 7:5; 10:9,13; 2 COR. 13:5; GAL.
6:1; 1 THESS. 3:5; HEB. 2:18; 3:9; 4:15;
11:17,37; JAMES 1:13,14; REV. 2:2,10; 3:10

3986. πειρασμός *peirasmos*
MATT. 6:13; 26:41; MARK 14:38; LUKE
4:13; 8:13; 11:4; 22:28,40,46; ACTS 20:19;
1 COR. 10:13; GAL. 4:14; 1 TIM. 6:9; HEB.
3:8; JAMES 1:2,12; 1 PET. 1:6; 4:12; 2 PET.
2:9; REV. 3:10

3987. πειράω *peiraō*
ACTS 9:26; 26:21

3988. πεισμονή *peismonē*
GAL. 5:8

3989. πέλαγος *pelagos*
MATT. 18:6; ACTS 27:5

3990. πελεκίζω *pelekizō*
REV. 20:4

3991. πέμπτος *pemptos*
REV. 6:9; 9:1; 16;10; 21:20

3992. πέμπω *pempō*
MATT. 2:8; 11:2; 14:10; 22:7; MARK 5:12;
LUKE 4:26; 7:6,10,19; 15:15; 16:24,27; 20:11-
13; JOHN 1:22,33; 4:34; 5:23,24,30,37; 6:38-
40,44; 7:16,18,28,33; 8:16,18,26,29; 9:4;
12:44,45,49; 13:16,20; 14:24,26; 15:21,26;
16:5,7; 20:21; ACTS 10:5,32,33; 11:29;
15:22,25; 19:31; 20:17; 23:30; 25:21,25,27;
ROM. 8:3; 1 COR. 4:17; 16:3; 2 COR. 9:3;
EPH. 6:22; PHIL. 2:19,23,25,28; 4:16; COL.
4:8; 1 THESS. 3:2,5; 2 THESS. 2:11; TITUS
3:12; 1 PET. 2:14; REV. 1:11; 11:10; 14:15,18;
22:16

3993. πένης *penēs*
2 COR. 9:9

3994. πενθερά *penthera*
MATT. 8:14; 10:35; MARK 1:30; LUKE 4:38;
12:53

3995. πενθερός *pentheros*
JOHN 18:13

3996. πενθέω *pentheō*
MATT. 5:4; 9:15; MARK 16:10; LUKE 6:25;
1 COR. 5:2; 2 COR. 12:21; JAMES 4:9; REV.
18:11,15,19

3997. πένθος *penthos*
JAMES 4:9; REV. 18:7,8; 21:4

3998. πενιχρός *penichros*
LUKE 21:2

3999. πεντάκις *pentakis*
2 COR. 11:24

4000. πεντακισχίλιοι *pentakischilioi*
MATT. 14:21; 16:9; MARK 6:44; 8:19; LUKE
9:14; JOHN 6:10

4001. πεντακόσιοι *pentakosioi*
LUKE 7:41; 1 COR. 15:6

4002. πέντε *pente*
MATT. 14:17,19; 16:9; 25:2,15,16,20; MARK
6:38,41; 8:19; LUKE 1:24; 9:13,16; 12:6,52;
14:19; 16:28; 19:18,19; JOHN 4:18; 5:2;
6:9,13,19; ACTS 4:4; 7:14; 19:19; 20:6; 24:1;
1 COR. 14:19; REV. 9:5,10; 17:10

4003. πεντεκαιδέκατος
      pentekaidekatos
LUKE 3:1

4004. πεντήκοντα *pentēkonta*
MARK 6:40; LUKE 7:41; 9:14; 16:6; JOHN
8:57; 21:11; ACTS 13:20

4005. πεντηκοστή *pentēkostē*
ACTS 2:1; 20:16; 1 COR. 16:8

4006. πεποίθησις *pepoithēsis*
2 COR. 1:15; 3:4; 8:22; 10:2; EPH. 3:12; PHIL.
3:4

4007. πέρ *per*   enclitic particle
MARK 15:6; HEB. 3:6,14; 6:3

4008. πέραν *peran*
MATT. 4:15,25; 8:18,28; 14:22; 16:5; 19:1;
MARK 3:8; 4:35; 5:1,21; 6:45; 8:13; 10:1;
LUKE 8:22; JOHN 1:28; 3:26; 6:1,17,22,25;
10:40; 18:1

4009. πέρας *peras*
MATT. 12:42; LUKE 11:31; ROM. 10:18;
HEB. 6:16

4010. Πέργαμος *Pergamos*
REV. 1:11; 2:12

4011. Πέργη *Pergē*
ACTS 13:13,14; 14:25

4013. περιάγω *periagō*
MATT. 4:23; 9:35; 23:15; MARK 6:6; ACTS 13:11; 1 COR. 9:5

4014. περιαιρέω *periaireō*
ACTS 27:20,40; 2 COR. 3:16; HEB. 10:11

4015. περιαστράπτω *periastraptō*
ACTS 9:3; 22:6

4016. περιβάλλω *periballō*
MATT. 6:29,31; 25:36,38,43; MARK 14:51; 16:5; LUKE 12:27; 19:43; 23:11; JOHN 19:2; ACTS 12:8; REV. 3:5,18; 4:4; 7:9,13; 10:1; 11:3; 12:1; 17:4; 18:16; 19:8,13

4017. περιβλέπω *periblepō*
MARK 3:5,34; 5:32; 9:8; 10:23; 11:11; LUKE 6:10

4018. περιβόλαιον *peribolaion*
1 COR. 11:15; HEB. 1:12

4019. περιδέω *perideō*
JOHN 11:44

4020. περιεργάζομαι *periergazomai*
2 THESS. 3:11

4021. περίεργος *periergos*
ACTS 19:19; 1 TIM. 5:13

4022. περιέρχομαι *perierchomai*
ACTS 19:13; 28:13; 1 TIM. 5:13; HEB. 11:37

4023. περιέχω *periechō*
LUKE 5:9; ACTS 23:25; 1 PET. 2:6

4024. περιζώννυμι *perizōnnumi*
LUKE 12:35,37; 17:8; ACTS 12:8; EPH. 6:14; REV. 1:13; 15:6

4025. περίθεσις *perithesis*
1 PET. 3:3

4026. περιΐστημι *periistēmi*
JOHN 11:42; ACTS 25:7; 2 TIM. 2:16; TITUS 3:9

4027. περικάθαρμα *perikatharma*
1 COR. 4:13

4028. περικαλύπτω *perikaluptō*
MARK 14:65; LUKE 22:64; HEB. 9:4

4029. περίκειμαι *perikeimai*
MARK 9:42; LUKE 17:2; ACTS 28:20; HEB. 5:2; 12:1

4030. περικεφαλαία *perikephalaia*
EPH. 6:17; 1 THESS. 5:8

4031. περικρατής *perikratēs*
ACTS 27:16

4032. περικρύπτω *perikruptō*
LUKE 1:24

4033. περικυκλόω *perikukloō*
LUKE 19:43

4034. περιλάμπω *perilampō*
LUKE 2:9; ACTS 26:13

4035. περιλείπω *perileipō*
1 THESS. 4:15,17

4036. περίλυπος *perilupos*
MATT. 26:38; MARK 6:26; 14:34; LUKE 18:23,24

4037. περιμένω *perimenō*
ACTS 1:4

4038. πέριξ *perix*
ACTS 5:16

4039. περιοικέω *perioikeō*
LUKE 1:65

4040. περίοικος *perioikos*
LUKE 1:58

4041. περιούσιος *periousios*
TITUS 2:14

4042. περιοχή *periochē*
ACTS 8:32

4043. περιπατέω *peripateō*
MATT. 4:18; 9:5; 11:5; 14:25,26,29; 15:31;
MARK 1:16; 2:9; 5:42; 6:48,49; 7:5; 8:24;
11:27; 12:38; 16:12; LUKE 5:23; 7:22; 11:44;
20:46; 24:17; JOHN 1:36; 5:8,9,11,12; 6:19,66;
7:1; 8:12; 10:23; 11:9,10,54; 12:35; 21:18;
ACTS 3:6,8,9,12; 14:8,10; 21:21; ROM. 6:4;
8:1,4; 13:13; 14:15; 1 COR. 3:3; 7:17; 2 COR.
4:2; 5:7; 10:2,3; 12:18; GAL. 5:16; EPH. 2:2,10;
4:1,17; 5:2,8,15; PHIL. 3:17,18; COL. 1:10;
2:6; 3:7; 4:5; 1 THESS. 2:12; 4:1,12; 2 THESS.
3:6,11; HEB. 13:9; 1 PET. 5:8; 1 JOHN 1:6,7;
2:6,11; 2 JOHN 1:4,6; 3 JOHN 1:3,4; REV.
2:1; 3:4; 9:20; 16:15; 21:24

4044. περιπείρω *peripeirō*
1 TIM. 6:10

4045. περιπίπτω *peripiptō*
LUKE 10:30; ACTS 27:41; JAMES 1:2

4046. περιποιέω *peripoieō*
ACTS 20:28; 1 TIM. 3:13

4047. περιποίησις *peripoiēsis*
EPH. 1:14; 1 THESS. 5:9; 2 THESS. 2:14;
HEB. 10:39; 1 PET. 2:9

4048. περιρρήγνυμι *perirrēgnumi*
ACTS 16:22

4049. περισπάω *perispaō*
LUKE 10:40

4050. περισσεία *perisseia*
ROM. 5:17; 2 COR. 8:2; 10:15; JAMES 1:21

4051. περίσσευμα *perisseuma*
MATT. 12:34; MARK 8:8; LUKE 6:45; 2
COR. 8:14

4052. περισσεύω *perisseuō*
MATT. 5:20; 13:12; 14:20; 15:37; 25:29;
MARK 12:44; LUKE 9:17; 12:15; 15:17; 21:4;
JOHN 6:12,13; ACTS 16:5; ROM. 3:7; 5:15;

15:13; 1 COR. 8:8; 14:12; 15:58; 2 COR. 1:5;
3:9; 4:15; 8:2,7; 9:8,12; EPH. 1:8; PHIL. 1:9,26;
4:12,18; COL. 2:7; 1 THESS. 3:12; 4:1,10

4053. I. περισσός *perissos*
MATT. 5:37,47; MARK 6:51; 14:31;
JOHN 10:10; ROM. 3:1; 2 COR. 9:1

II. ἐκ περισσός *ek perissos*
EPH. 3:20; 1 THESS. 3:10; 5:13

4054. περισσότερον
perissoteron adv.
MARK 7:36; 1 COR. 15:10; HEB. 6:17; 7:15

4055. περισσότερος *perissoteros*
MATT. 11:9; 23:14; MARK 12:33 WH; 12:40;
LUKE 7:26; 12:4,48; 20:47; 1 COR. 12:23,24;
2 COR. 2:7; 10:8

4056. περισσοτέρως *perissoterōs*
MARK 15:14; 2 COR. 1:12; 2:4; 7:13,15;
11:23; 12:15; GAL. 1:14; PHIL. 1:14;
1 THESS. 2:17; HEB. 2:1; 13:19

4057. περισσῶς *perissōs*
MATT. 27:23; MARK 10:26; ACTS 26:11

4058. περιστερά *peristera*
MATT. 3:16; 10:16; 21:12; MARK 1:10; 11:15;
LUKE 2:24; 3:22; JOHN 1:32; 2:14,16

4059. περιτέμνω *peritemnō*
LUKE 1:59; 2:21; JOHN 7:22; ACTS 7:8;
15:1,5,24; 16:3; 21:21; 1 COR. 7:18; GAL. 2:3;
5:2,3; 6:12,13; COL. 2:11

4060. περιτίθημι *peritithēmi*
MATT. 21:33; 27:28,48; MARK 12:1;
15:17,36; JOHN 19:29; 1 COR. 12:23

4061. περιτομή *peritomē*
JOHN 7:22,23; ACTS 7:8; 10:45; 11:2; ROM.
2:25-29; 3:1,30; 4:9-12; 15:8; 1 COR. 7:19;
GAL. 2:7-9,12; 5:6,11; 6:15; EPH. 2:11; PHIL.
3:3,5; COL. 2:11; 3:11; 4:11; TITUS 1:10

4062. περιτρέπω *peritrepō*
ACTS 26:24

4063. *περιτρέχω peritrechō*
MARK 6:55

4064. *περιφέρω peripherō*
MARK 6:55; **2 COR.** 4:10; **EPH.** 4:14; **HEB.**
13:9; **JUDE** 1:12

4065. *περιφρονέω periphroneō*
TITUS 2:15

4066. *περίχωρος perichōros*
MATT. 3:5; 14:35; MARK 1:28; 6:55; LUKE
3:3; 4:14,37; 7:17; 8:37; ACTS 14:6

4067. *περίψημα peripsēma*
1 COR. 4:13

4068. *περπερεύομαι perpereuomai*
1 COR. 13:4

4069. *Περσίς Persis*
ROM. 16:12

4070. *πέρυσι perusi*
2 COR. 8:10; 9:2

4071. *πετεινόν peteinon*
MATT. 6:26; 8:20; 13:4,32; MARK 4:4,32;
LUKE 8:5; 9:58; 12:24; 13:19; ACTS 10:12;
11:6; ROM. 1:23; JAMES 3:7

4072. I. *πέτομαι petomai*
    REV. 4:7; 8:13; 12:14; 14:6; 19:17

    II. *πετάομαι petaomai*
    (Later form in TR)
    REV. 4:7; 8:13; 14:6; 19:17

4073. *πέτρα petra*
MATT. 7:24,25; 16:18; 27:51,60; MARK
15:46; LUKE 6:48; 8:6,13; ROM. 9:33; 1 COR.
10:4; 1 PET. 2:8; REV. 6:15,16

4074. A. *πέτρος petros*
    JOHN 1:42

    B. *Πέτρος Petros*
    MATT. 4:18; 8:14; 10:2; 14:28,29;

15:15; 16:16,18,22,23; 17:1,4,24,26;
18:21; 19:27; 26:33,35,37,40,58,69,73,
75; **MARK** 3:16; 5:37; 8:29,32,33; 9:2,5;
10:28; 11:21; 13:3; 14:29,33,37,54,66,67,
70,72; 16:7; **LUKE** 5:8; 6:14; 8:45,51;
9:20,28,32,33; 12:41; 18:28; 22:8,34,54,
55,58,60-62; 24:12; **JOHN** 1:40,44;
6:8,68; 13:6,8,9,24,36,37; 18:10,11,15-
18,25-27; 20:2-4,6; 21:2,3,7,11,15,17,
20,21; **ACTS** 1:13,15; 2:14,37,38; 3:1,3,
4,6,11,12; 4:8,13,19; 5:3,8,9,15,29; 8:14,
20; 9:32,34,38-40; 10:5, 9,13,14,17-19,
21,23,25,26,32,34,44-46; 11:2, 4,7,13;
12:3,5-7,11,13,14,16,18; 15:7; **GAL.**
1:18; 2:7,8,11,14; **1 PET.** 1:1; **2 PET.** 1:1

4075. *πετρώδης petrōdēs*
MATT. 13:5,20; MARK 4:5,16

4076. *πήγανον pēganon*
LUKE 11:42

4077. *πηγή pēgē*
MARK 5:29; JOHN 4:6,14; JAMES 3:11,12;
2 PET. 2:17; REV. 7:17; 8:10; 14:7; 16:4; 21:6

4078. *πήγνυμι pēgnumi*
HEB. 8:2

4079. *πηδάλιον pēdalion*
ACTS 27:40; JAMES 3:4

4080. *πηλίκος pēlikos*
GAL. 6:11; HEB. 7:4

4081. *πηλός pēlos*
JOHN 9:6,11,14,15; ROM. 9:21

4082. *πήρα pēra*
MATT. 10:10; MARK 6:8; LUKE 9:3; 10:4;
22:35,36

4083. *πῆχυς pēchus*
MATT. 6:27; LUKE 12:25; JOHN 21:8; REV.
21:17

4084. *πιάζω piazō*
JOHN 7:30,32,44; 8:20; 10:39; 11:57; 21:3,10;
ACTS 3:7; 12:4; **2 COR.** 11:32; REV. 19:20

4085. *πιέζω piezō*
LUKE 6:38

4086. *πιθανολογία pithanologia*
COL. 2:4

4087. *πικραίνω pikrainō*
COL. 3:19; REV. 8:11; 10:9,10

4088. *πικρία pikria*
ACTS 8:23; ROM. 3:14; EPH. 4:31; HEB.
12:15

4089. *πικρός pikros*
JAMES 3:11,14

4090. *πικρῶς pikrōs*
MATT. 26:75; LUKE 22:62

4091. *Πιλάτος Pilatos*
MATT. 27:2,13,17,22,24,58,62,65; MARK
15:1,2,4,5,9,12,14,15,43,44; LUKE 3:1; 13:1;
23:1,3,4,6,11-13,20,24,52; JOHN 18:29,31,
33,35,37,38; 19:1,4,6,8,10,12,13,15,19,21,22,
31,38; ACTS 3:13; 4:27; 13:28; 1 TIM. 6:13

4092. *πίμπρημι pimprēmi*
ACTS 28:6

4093. *πινακίδιον pinakidion*
LUKE 1:63

4094. *πίναξ pinax*
MATT. 14:8,11; MARK 6:25,28; LUKE
11:39

4095. *πίνω pinō*
MATT. 6:25,31; 11:18,19; 20:22,23; 24:38,49;
26:27,29,42; 27:34; MARK 2:16; 10:38,39;
14:23,25; 15:23; 16:18; LUKE 1:15; 5:30,33,39;
7:33,34; 10:7; 12:19,29,45; 13:26; 17:8,27,28;
22:18,30; JOHN 4:7,9,10,12-14; 6:53,54,56;
7:37; 18:11; ACTS 9:9; 23:12,21; ROM. 14:21;
1 COR. 9:4; 10:4,7,21,31; 11:22,25-29; 15:32;
HEB. 6:7; REV. 14:10; 16:6; 18:3

4096. *πιότης piotēs*
ROM. 11:17

4097. *πιπράσκω pipraskō*
MATT. 13:46; 18:25; 26:9; MARK 14:5;
JOHN 12:5; ACTS 2:45; 4:34; 5:4; ROM. 7:14

4098. *πίπτω piptō*
MATT. 2:11; 4:9; 7:25,27; 10:29; 13:4,5,7,8;
15:14,27; 17:6,15; 18:26,29; 21:44; 24:29; 26:39;
MARK 4:4,5,7,8; 5:22; 9:20; 14:35; LUKE
5:12; 6:39,49; 8:5-8,14,41; 10:18; 11:17; 13:4;
16:17,21; 17:16; 20:18; 21:24; 23:30; JOHN
11:32; 12:24; 18:6; ACTS 1:26; 5:5,10; 9:4;
10:25; 15:16; 20:9; 22:7; 27:34; ROM. 11:11,22;
14:4; 1 COR. 10:8,12; 14:25; HEB. 3:17; 4:11;
11:30; JAMES 5:12; REV. 1:17; 4:10; 5:8,14;
6:13,16; 7:11,16; 8:10; 9:1; 11:11,13,16; 14:8;
16:19; 17:10; 18:2; 19:4,10; 22:8

4099. *Πισιδία Pisidia*
ACTS 13:14; 14:24

4100. *πιστεύω pisteuō*
MATT. 8:13; 9:28; 18:6; 21:22,25,32; 24:23,26;
27:42; MARK 1:15; 5:36; 9:23,24,42; 11:23,
24,31; 13:21; 15:32; 16:13,14,16,17; LUKE
1:20,45; 8:12,13,50; 16:11; 20:5; 22:67; 24:25;
JOHN 1:7,12,50; 2:11,22-24; 3:12,15,16,18,36;
4:21,39,41,42,48,50,53; 5:24,38,44,46,47;
6:29,30,35,36,40,47,64,69; 7:5,31,38,39,48;
8:24,30,31,45,46; 9:18,35,36,38; 10:25,26,37,
38,42; 11:15,25-27,40,42,45,48; 12:11,36-
39,42,44,46,47; 13:19; 14:1,10-12,29; 16:9,
27,30,31; 17:8,20,21; 19:35; 20:8,25,29,31;
ACTS 2:44; 4:4,32; 5:14; 8:12,13,37; 9:26,42;
10:43; 11:17,21; 13:12,39,41,48; 14:1,23;
15:5,7,11; 16:31,34; 17:12,34; 18:8,27; 19:2,4,
18; 21:20,25; 22:19; 24:14; 26:27; 27:25; ROM.
1:16; 3:2,22; 4:3,5,11,17,18,24; 6:8; 9:33;
10:4,9-11,14,16; 13:11; 14:2; 15:13; 1 COR.
1:21; 3:5; 9:17; 11:18; 13:7; 14:22; 15:2,11;
2 COR. 4:13; GAL. 2:7,16; 3:6,22; EPH.
1:13,19; PHIL. 1:29; 1 THESS. 1:7; 2:4,10,
13; 4:14; 2 THESS. 1:10; 2:11,12; 1 TIM.
1:11,16; 3:16; 2 TIM. 1:12; TITUS 1:3; 3:8;
HEB. 4:3; 11:6; JAMES 2:19,23; 1 PET.
1:8,21; 2:6,7; 1 JOHN 3:23; 4:1,16; 5:1,5,10,13;
JUDE 1:5

4101. *πιστικός pistikos*
MARK 14:3; JOHN 12:3

4102. *πίστις pistis*
MATT. 8:10; 9:2,22,29; 15:28; 17:20; 21:21;

23:23; **MARK** 2:5; 4:40; 5:34; 10:52; 11:22;
LUKE 5:20; 7:9,50; 8:25,48; 17:5,6,19; 18:8,42;
22:32; **ACTS** 3:16; 6:5,7,8; 11:24; 13:8;
14:9,22,27; 15:9; 16:5; 17:31; 20:21; 24:24;
26:18; **ROM.** 1:5,8,12,17; 3:3,22,25-28,30,31;
4:5,9,11-14,16,19,20; 5:1,2; 9:30,32; 10:6,8,17;
11:20; 12:3,6; 14:1,22,23; 16:26; **1 COR.** 2:5;
12:9; 13:2,13; 15:14,17; 16:13; **2 COR.** 1:24;
4:13; 5:7; 8:7; 10:15; 13:5; **GAL.** 1:23; 2:16,20;
3:2,5,7-9,11,12,14,22-26; 5:5,6,22; 6:10; **EPH.**
1:15; 2:8; 3:12,17; 4:5,13; 6:16,23; **PHIL.**
1:25,27; 2:17; 3:9; **COL.** 1:4,23; 2:5,7,12;
1 THESS. 1:3,8; 3:2,5-7,10; 5:8; **2 THESS.**
1:3,4,11; 2:13; 3:2; **1 TIM.** 1:2,4,5,14,19; 2:7,15;
3:9,13; 4:1,6,12; 5:8,12; 6:10-12,21; **2 TIM.**
1:5,13; 2:18,22; 3:8,10,15; 4:7; **TITUS** 1:1,4,13;
2:2,10; 3:15; **PHILE.** 1:5,6; **HEB.** 4:2; 6:1,12;
10:22,38,39; 11:1,3-9,11,13,17,20-24,27-31,33,
39; 12:2; 13:7; **JAMES** 1:3,6; 2:1,5,14,17,
18,20,22,24,26; 5:15; **1 PET.** 1:5,7,9,21; 5:9;
2 PET. 1:1,5; **1 JOHN** 5:4; **JUDE** 1:3,20; **REV.**
2:13,19; 13:10; 14:12

4103. πιστός pistos
MATT. 24:45; 25:21,23; **LUKE** 12:42; 16:10-
12; 19:17; **JOHN** 20:27; **ACTS** 10:45; 13:34;
16:1,15; **1 COR.** 1:9; 4:2,17; 7:25; 10:13;
2 COR. 1:18; 6:15; **GAL.** 3:9; **EPH.** 1:1; 6:21;
COL. 1:2,7; 4:7,9; **1 THESS.** 5:24; **2 THESS.**
3:3; **1 TIM.** 1:12,15; 3:1,11; 4:3,9,10,12; 5:16;
6:2; **2 TIM.** 2:2,11,13; **TITUS** 1:6,9; 3:8; **HEB.**
2:17; 3:2,5; 10:23; 11:11; **1 PET.** 4:19; 5:12;
1 JOHN 1:9; **3 JOHN** 1:5; **REV.** 1:5; 2:10,13;
3:14; 17:14; 19:11; 21:5; 22:6

4104. πιστόω pistoō
2 TIM. 3:14

4105. πλανάω planaō
MATT. 18:12,13; 22:29; 24:4,5,11,24; **MARK**
12:24,27; 13:5,6; **LUKE** 21:8; **JOHN** 7:12,47;
1 COR. 6:9; 15:33; **GAL.** 6:7; **2 TIM.** 3:13;
TITUS 3:3; **HEB.** 3:10; 5:2; 11:38; **JAMES**
1:16; 5:19; **1 PET.** 2:25; **2 PET.** 2:15; **1 JOHN**
1:8; 2:26; 3:7; **REV.** 2:20; 12:9; 13:14; 18:23;
19:20; 20:3,8,10

4106. πλάνη planē
MATT. 27:64; **ROM.** 1:27; **EPH.** 4:14;
1 THESS. 2:3; **2 THESS.** 2:11; **JAMES** 5:20;
2 PET. 2:18; 3:17; **1 JOHN** 4:6; **JUDE** 1:11

4107. πλανήτης planētēs
JUDE 1:13

4108. πλάνος planos
MATT. 27:63; **2 COR.** 6:8; **1 TIM.** 4:1;
2 JOHN 1:7

4109. πλάξ plax
2 COR. 3:3; **HEB.** 9:4

4110. πλάσμα plasma
ROM. 9:20

4111. πλάσσω plassō
ROM. 9:20; **1 TIM.** 2:13

4112. πλαστός plastos
2 PET. 2:3

4113. πλατεῖα plateia   subst.
MATT. 6:5; 12:19; **LUKE** 10:10; 13:26; 14:21;
ACTS 5:15; **REV.** 11:8; 21:21; 22:2

4114. πλάτος platos
EPH. 3:18; **REV.** 20:9; 21:16

4115. πλατύνω platunō
MATT. 23:5; **2 COR.** 6:11,13

4116. πλατύς platus
MATT. 7:13

4117. πλέγμα plegma
1 TIM. 2:9

4118. πλεῖστος pleistos
MATT. 11:20; 21:8; **1 COR.** 14:27

4119. I. πλείων pleiōn
MATT. 5:20; 6:25; 12:41,42; 20:10;
21:36; 26:53; **MARK** 12:33,43; **LUKE**
3:13; 7:43; 9:13; 11:31,32,53; 12:23;
21:3; **JOHN** 4:1,41; 7:31; 15:2; **ACTS**
2:40; 4:17,22; 13:31; 15:28; 18:20; 19:32;
21:10; 23:13,21; 24:11,17; 25:6,14;
27:12,20; 28:23; **1 COR.** 9:19; 10:5;
15:6; **2 COR.** 2:6; 4:15; 9:2; **PHIL.** 1:14;
HEB. 3:3; 7:23; 11:4; **REV.** 2:19

II. πλεῖον, πλέον
   pleion, pleon   adv.
   LUKE 7:42; JOHN 21:15; ACTS 20:9;
   24:4; 2 TIM. 2:16; 3:9

4120. πλέκω plekō
MATT. 27:29; MARK 15:17; JOHN 19:2

4121. πλεονάζω pleonazō
ROM. 5:20; 6:1; 2 COR. 4:15; 8:15; PHIL.
4:17; 1 THESS. 3:12; 2 THESS. 1:3; 2 PET. 1:8

4122. πλεονεκτέω pleonekteō
2 COR. 2:11; 7:2; 12:17,18; 1 THESS. 4:6

4123. πλεονέκτης pleonektēs
1 COR. 5:10,11; 6:10; EPH. 5:5

4124. πλεονεξία pleonexia
MARK 7:22; LUKE 12:15; ROM. 1:29;
2 COR. 9:5; EPH. 4:19; 5:3; COL. 3:5;
1 THESS. 2:5; 2 PET. 2:3,14

4125. πλευρά pleura
JOHN 19:34; 20:20,25,27; ACTS 12:7

4126. πλέω pleō
LUKE 8:23; ACTS 21:3; 27:2,6,24

4127. πληγή plēgē
LUKE 10:30; 12:48; ACTS 16:23,33; 2 COR.
6:5; 11:23; REV. 9:20; 11:6; 13:3,12,14;
15:1,6,8; 16:9,21; 18:4,8; 21:9; 22:18

4128. πλῆθος plēthos
MARK 3:7,8; LUKE 1:10; 2:13; 5:6; 6:17; 8:37;
19:37; 23:1,27; JOHN 5:3; 21:6; ACTS 2:6;
4:32; 5:14,16; 6:2,5; 14:1,4; 15:12,30; 17:4;
19:9; 21:22,36; 23:7; 25:24; 28:3; HEB. 11:12;
JAMES 5:20; 1 PET. 4:8

4129. πληθύνω plēthunō
MATT. 24:12; ACTS 6:1,7; 7:17; 9:31; 12:24;
2 COR. 9:10; HEB. 6:14; 1 PET. 1:2; 2 PET.
1:2; JUDE 1:2

4130. πίμπλημι, πλήθω
   pimplēmi, plēthō
MATT. 22:10; 27:48; LUKE 1:15,23,41,57,67;

2:6,21,22; 4:28; 5:7,26; 6:11; JOHN 19:29;
ACTS 2:4; 3:10; 4:8,31; 5:17; 9:17; 13:9,45;
19:29

4131. πλήκτης plēktēs
1 TIM. 3:3; TITUS 1:7

4132. πλημμύρα plēmmura
LUKE 6:48

4133. πλήν plēn
MATT. 11:22,24; 18:7; 26:39,64; MARK
12:32; LUKE 6:24,35; 10:11,14,20; 11:41;
12:31; 13:33; 18:8; 19:27; 22:21,22,42; 23:28;
JOHN 8:10; ACTS 8:1; 15:28; 20:23; 27:22;
1 COR. 11:11; EPH. 5:33; PHIL. 1:18; 3:16;
4:14; REV. 2:25

4134. πλήρης plērēs
MATT. 14:20; 15:37; MARK 4:28; 6:43; 8:19;
LUKE 4:1; 5:12; JOHN 1:14; ACTS 6:3,5,8;
7:55; 9:36; 11:24; 13:10; 19:28; 2 JOHN 1:8

4135. πληροφορέω plērophoreō
LUKE 1:1; ROM. 4:21; 14:5; 2 TIM. 4:5,17

4136. πληροφορία plērophoria
COL. 2:2; 1 THESS. 1:5; HEB. 6:11; 10:22

4137. πληρόω plēroō
MATT. 1:22; 2:15,17,23; 3:15; 4:14; 5:17; 8:17;
12:17; 13:35,48; 21:4; 23:32; 26:54,56; 27:9,35;
MARK 1:15; 14:49; 15:28; LUKE 1:20; 2:40;
3:5; 4:21; 7:1; 9:31; 21:22,24; 22:16; 24:44;
JOHN 3:29; 7:8; 12:3,38; 13:18; 15:11,25;
16:6,24; 17:12,13; 18:9,32; 19:24,36; ACTS
1:16; 2:2,28; 3:18; 5:3,28; 7:23,30; 9:23; 12:25;
13:25,27,52; 14:26; 19:21; 24:27; ROM. 1:29;
8:4; 13:8; 15:13,14,19; 2 COR. 7:4; 10:6; GAL.
5:14; EPH. 1:23; 3:19; 4:10; 5:18; PHIL. 1:11;
2:2; 4:18,19; COL. 1:9,25; 2:10; 4:12,17;
2 THESS. 1:11; 2 TIM. 1:4; JAMES 2:23;
1 JOHN 1:4; 2 JOHN 1:12; REV. 3:2; 6:11

4138. πλήρωμα plērōma
MATT. 9:16; MARK 2:21; 8:20; JOHN 1:16;
ROM. 11:12,25; 13:10; 15:29; 1 COR.
10:26,28; GAL. 4:4; EPH. 1:10,23; 3:19; 4:13;
COL. 1:19; 2:9

4139. A. πλησίον plēsion adv.
LUKE 10:29,36; JOHN 4:5

B. πλησίον plēsion subst.
MATT. 5:43; 19:19; 22:39; MARK
12:31,33; LUKE 10:27; ACTS 7:27;
ROM. 13:9,10; 15:2; GAL. 5:14; EPH.
4:25; HEB. 8:11; JAMES 2:8

4140. πλησμονή plēsmonē
COL. 2:23

4141. πλήσσω, πλήττω plēssō, plēttō
REV. 8:12

4142. πλοιάριον ploiarion
MARK 3:9; 4:36; JOHN 6:22,23; 21:8

4143. πλοῖον ploion
MATT. 4:21,22; 8:23,24; 9:1; 13:2;
14:13,22,24,29,32,33; 15:39; MARK 1:19,20;
4:1,36,37; 5:2,18,21; 6:32,45,47,51,54;
8:10,13,14; LUKE 5:2,3,7,11; 8:22,37; JOHN
6:17,19,21,24; 21:3,6; ACTS 20:13,38; 21:2,3,6;
27:2,6,10,15,17,19,22,30,31,37-39,44; 28:11;
JAMES 3:4; REV. 8:9; 18:17,19

4144. πλόος ploos
ACTS 21:7; 27:9,10

4145. πλούσιος plousios
MATT. 19:23,24; 27:57; MARK 10:25; 12:41;
LUKE 6:24; 12:16; 14:12; 16:1,19,21,22;
18:23,25; 19:2; 21:1; 2 COR. 8:9; EPH. 2:4;
1 TIM. 6:17; JAMES 1:10,11; 2:5,6; 5:1; REV.
2:9; 3:17; 6:15; 13:16

4146. πλουσίως plousiōs
COL. 3:16; 1 TIM. 6:17; TITUS 3:6; 2 PET.
1:11

4147. πλουτέω plouteō
LUKE 1:53; 12:21; ROM. 10:12; 1 COR. 4:8;
2 COR. 8:9; 1 TIM. 6:9,18; REV. 3:17,18;
18:3,15,19

4148. πλουτίζω ploutizō
1 COR. 1:5; 2 COR. 6:10; 9:11

4149. πλοῦτος ploutos
MATT. 13:22; MARK 4:19; LUKE 8:14;
ROM. 2:4; 9:23; 11:12,33; 2 COR. 8:2; EPH.
1:7,18; 2:7; 3:8,16; PHIL. 4:19; COL. 1:27; 2:2;
1 TIM. 6:17; HEB. 11:26; JAMES 5:2; REV.
5:12; 18:17

4150. πλύνω plunō
REV. 7:14

4151. πνεῦμα pneuma
MATT. 1:18,20; 3:11,16; 4:1; 5:3; 8:16; 10:1,20;
12:18,28,31,32,43,45; 22:43; 26:41; 27:50;
28:19; MARK 1:8,10,12,23,26,27; 2:8; 3:11,29,
30; 5:2,8,13; 6:7; 7:25; 8:12; 9:17,20,25; 12:36;
13:11; 14:38; LUKE 1:15,17,35,41,47,67,80;
2:25-27,40; 3:16,22; 4:1,14,18,33,36; 6:18; 7:21;
8:2,29,55; 9:39,42,55; 10:20,21; 11:13,24,26;
12:10,12; 13:11; 23:46; 24:37,39; JOHN
1:32,33; 3:5,6,8,34; 4:23,24; 6:63; 7:39; 11:33;
13:21; 14:17,26; 15:26; 16:13; 19:30; 20:22;
ACTS 1:2,5,8,16; 2:4,17,18,33,38; 4:8,31;
5:3,9,16,32; 6:3,5,10; 7:51,55,59; 8:7,15,17-
19,29,39; 9:17,31; 10:19,38,44,45,47; 11:12,
15,16,24,28; 13:2,4,9,52; 15:8,28; 16:6,7,16,18;
17:16; 18:5,25; 19:2,6,12, 13,15,16,21; 20:22,
23,28; 21:4,11; 23:8,9; 28:25; ROM. 1:4,9; 2:29;
5:5; 7:6; 8:1,2,4-6,9-11,13-16,23,26,27; 9:1;
11:8; 12:11; 14:17; 15:13, 16,19,30; 1 COR.
2:4,10-14; 3:16; 4:21; 5:3-5; 6:11,17,19,20;
7:34,40; 12:3,4,7-11,13; 14:2, 12,14-16,32;
15:45; 16:18; 2 COR. 1:22; 2:13; 3:3,6,8,17,18;
4:13; 5:5; 6:6; 7:1,13; 11:4; 12:18; 13:14; GAL.
3:2,3,5,14; 4:6,29; 5:5,16-18,22,25; 6:1,8,18;
EPH. 1:13,17; 2:2,18,22; 3:5,16; 4:3,4,23,30;
5:9,18; 6:17,18; PHIL. 1:19,27; 2:1; 3:3;
COL. 1:8; 2:5; 1 THESS. 1:5,6; 4:8; 5:19,23;
2 THESS. 2:2,8,13; 1 TIM. 3:16; 4:1,12;
2 TIM. 1:7,14; 4:22; TITUS 3:5; PHILE.
1:25; HEB. 1:7,14; 2:4; 3:7; 4:12; 6:4; 9:8,14;
10:15,29; 12:9,23; JAMES 2:26; 4:5;
1 PET. 1:2,11,12,22; 3:4,18,19; 4:6,14;
2 PET. 1:21; 1 JOHN 3:24; 4:1-3,6,13; 5:
6-8; JUDE 1:19,20; REV. 1:4,10; 2:7,11,17,
29; 3:1,6,13,22; 4:2,5; 5:6; 11:11; 13:15;
14:13; 16:13,14; 17:3; 18:2; 19:10; 21:10;
22:17

4152. πνευματικός pneumatikos
ROM. 1:11; 7:14; 15:27; 1 COR. 2:13,15; 3:1;
9:11; 10:3,4; 12:1; 14:1,37; 15:44,46; GAL. 6:1;

EPH. 1:3; 5:19; 6:12; **COL.** 1:9; 3:16; **1 PET.** 2:5

4153. πνευματικῶς pneumatikōs
1 COR. 2:14; **REV.** 11:8

4154. πνέω pneō
MATT. 7:25,27; **LUKE** 12:55; **JOHN** 3:8; 6:18; **ACTS** 27:40; **REV.** 7:1

4155. πνίγω pnigō
MATT. 18:28; **MARK** 5:13

4156. πνικτός pniktos
ACTS 15:20,29; 21:25

4157. πνοή pnoē
ACTS 2:2; 17:25

4158. ποδήρης podērēs
REV. 1:13

4159. πόθεν pothen
MATT. 13:27,54,56; 15:33; 21:25; **MARK** 6:2; 8:4; 12:37; **LUKE** 1:43; 13:25,27; 20:7; **JOHN** 1:48; 2:9; 3:8; 4:11; 6:5; 7:27,28; 8:14; 9:29,30; 19:9; **JAMES** 4:1; **REV.** 2:5; 7:13

4160. ποιέω poieō
MATT. 1:24; 3:3,8,10; 4:19; 5:19,32,36,44, 46,47; 6:1-3; 7:12,17-19,21,22,24,26; 8:9; 9:28; 12:2,3,12,16,33,50; 13:23,26,28,41,58; 17:4,12; 18:35; 19:4,16; 20:5,12,15,32; 21:6,13,15,21, 23,24,27,31,36,40,43; 22:2; 23:3,5,15,23; 24:46; 25:16,40,45; 26:12,13,18,19,73; 27:22,23; 28:14,15; **MARK** 1:3,17; 2:23-25; 3:6,8,12, 14,35; 4:32; 5:19,20,32; 6:5,20,21,30; 7:8,12, 13,37; 8:25; 9:5,13,39; 10:6,17,35,36,51; 11:3,5,17,28,29,33; 12:9; 14:7-9; 15:1,7,8, 12,14,15; **LUKE** 1:25,49,51,68,72; 2:27,48; 3:4,8-12,14,19; 4:23; 5:6,29,33,34; 6:2,3,10, 11,23,26,27,31,33,43,46,47,49; 7:8; 8:8,21,39; 9:10,15,33,43,54; 10:25,28,37; 11:40,42; 12:4,17,18,33,43,47,48; 13:9,22; 14:12,13,16; 15:19; 16:3,4,8,9; 17:9,10; 18:7,8,18,41; 19:18,46,48; 20:2,8,13,15; 22:19; 23:22,31,34; **JOHN** 2:5,11,15,16,18,23; 3:2,21; 4:1,29,34, 39,45,46,54; 5:11,15,16,18-20,27,29,30,36; 6:2,6,10,14,15,28,30,38; 7:3,4,17,19,21,23,31,51;

8:28,29,34,38-41,44,53; 9:6,11,14,16,26,31,33; 10:25,33,37,38,41; 11:37,45-47; 12:2,16,18,37; 13:7,12,15,17,27; 14:10,12-14,23,31; 15:5,14, 15,21,24; 16:2,3; 17:4; 18:18,35; 19:7,12,23,24; 20:30; 21:25; **ACTS** 1:1; 2:22,36,37; 3:12; 4:7,16,24,28; 5:34; 6:8; 7:19,24,36,40,43,44,50; 8:2,6; 9:6,13,36,39; 10:2,6,33,39; 11:30; 12:8; 13:22; 14:11,15,27; 15:3,4,12,17,33; 16:18,21, 30; 17:24,26; 18:21,23; 19:11,14,24; 20:3,24; 21:13,19,23,33; 22:10,26; 23:12,13; 24:12,17; 25:3,17; 26:10; 27:18; 28:17; **ROM.** 1:9,28,32; 2:3,14; 3:8,12; 4:21; 7:15,16,19-21; 9:20,21,28; 10:5; 12:20; 13:3,4,14; 15:26; 16:17; **1 COR.** 5:2; 6:15,18; 7:36-38; 9:23; 10:13,31; 11:24,25; 15:29; 16:1; **2 COR.** 5:21; 8:10,11; 11:7,12,25; 13:7; **GAL.** 2:10; 3:10,12; 5:3,17; 6:9; **EPH.** 1:16; 2:3,14,15; 3:11,20; 4:16; 6:6,8,9; **PHIL.** 1:4; 2:14; 4:14; **COL.** 3:17,23; 4:16; **1 THESS.** 1:2; 4:10; 5:11,24; **2 THESS.** 3:4; **1 TIM.** 1:13; 2:1; 4:16; 5:21; **2 TIM.** 4:5; **TITUS** 3:5; **PHILE.** 1:4,14,21; **HEB.** 1:2,3,7; 3:2; 6:3; 7:27; 8:5,9; 10:7,9,36; 11:28; 12:13,27; 13:6,17,19,21; **JAMES** 2:8,12,13,19; 3:12,18; 4:13,15,17; 5:15; **1 PET.** 2:22; 3:11,12; **2 PET.** 1:10,15,19; **1 JOHN** 1:6,10; 2:17,29; 3:4,7-10,22; 5:10; **3 JOHN** 1:5,6,10; **JUDE** 1:3,15; **REV.** 1:6; 2:5; 3:9,12; 5:10; 11:7; 12:15,17; 13:5,7,12-16; 14:7; 16:14; 17:16,17; 19:19,20; 21:5,27; 22:2, 14,15

4161. ποίημα poiēma
ROM. 1:20; **EPH.** 2:10

4162. ποίησις poiēsis
JAMES 1:25

4163. ποιητής poiētēs
ACTS 17:28; **ROM.** 2:13; **JAMES** 1:22,23,25; 4:11

4164. ποικίλος poikilos
MATT. 4:24; **MARK** 1:34; **LUKE** 4:40; **2 TIM.** 3:6; **TITUS** 3:3; **HEB.** 2:4; 13:9; **JAMES** 1:2; **1 PET.** 1:6; 4:10

4165. ποιμαίνω poimainō
MATT. 2:6; **LUKE** 17:7; **JOHN** 21:16; **ACTS** 20:28; **1 COR.** 9:7; **1 PET.** 5:2; **JUDE** 1:12; **REV.** 2:27; 7:17; 12:5; 19:15

4166. ποιμήν poimēn
MATT. 9:36; 25:32; 26:31; MARK 6:34; 14:27;
LUKE 2:8,15,18,20; JOHN 10:2,11,12,14,16;
EPH. 4:11; HEB. 13:20; 1 PET. 2:25

4167. ποίμνη poimnē
MATT. 26:31; LUKE 2:8; JOHN 10:16;
1 COR. 9:7

4168. ποίμνιον poimnion
LUKE 12:32; ACTS 20:28,29; 1 PET. 5:2,3

4169. ποῖος poios
MATT. 19:18; 21:23,24,27; 22:36; 24:42,43;
MARK 4:30; 11:28,29,33; 12:28; LUKE 5:19;
6:32-34; 12:39; 20:2,8; 24:19; JOHN 10:32;
12:33; 18:32; 21:19; ACTS 4:7; 7:49; 23:34;
ROM. 3:27; 1 COR. 15:35; JAMES 4:14;
1 PET. 1:11; 2:20; REV. 3:3

4170. πολεμέω polemeō
JAMES 4:2; REV. 2:16; 12:7; 13:4; 17:14;
19:11

4171. πόλεμος polemos
MATT. 24:6; MARK 13:7; LUKE 14:31; 21:9;
1 COR. 14:8; HEB. 11:34; JAMES 4:1; REV.
9:7,9; 11:7; 12:7,17; 13:7; 16:14; 19:19; 20:8

4172. πόλις polis
MATT. 2:23; 4:5; 5:14,35; 8:33,34; 9:1,35;
10:5,11,14,15,23; 11:1,20; 12:25; 14:13; 21:10,
17,18; 22:7; 23:34; 26:18; 27:53; 28:11; MARK
1:33,45; 5:14; 6:11,33,56; 11:19; 14:13,16;
LUKE 1:26,39; 2:3,4,11,39; 4:29,31,43; 5:12;
7:11,12,37; 8:1,4,27,34,39; 9:5,10; 10:1,8,10-12;
13:22; 14:21; 18:2,3; 19:17,19,41; 22:10; 23:19,
51; 24:49; JOHN 1:44; 4:5,8,28,30,39; 11:54;
19:20; ACTS 5:16; 7:58; 8:5,8,9,40; 9:6; 10:9;
11:5; 12:10; 13:44,50; 14:4,6,13,19-21; 15:21,36;
16:4,12-14,20,39; 17:5,16; 18:10; 19:29,35;
20:23; 21:5,29,30,39; 22:3; 24:12; 25:23; 26:11;
27:8; ROM. 16:23; 2 COR. 11:26,32; TITUS
1:5; HEB. 11:10,16; 12:22; 13:14; JAMES 4:13;
2 PET. 2:6; JUDE 1:7; REV. 3:12; 11:2,8,13;
14:8,20; 16:19; 17:18; 18:10,16,18,19,21; 20:9;
21:2,10,14-16,18,19,21,23; 22:14,19

4173. πολιτάρχης politarchēs
ACTS 17:6,8

4174. πολιτεία politeia
ACTS 22:28; EPH. 2:12

4175. πολίτευμα politeuma
PHIL. 3:20

4176. πολιτεύω politeuō
ACTS 23:1; PHIL. 1:27

4177. πολίτης politēs
LUKE 15:15; 19:14; ACTS 21:39

4178. πολλάκις pollakis
MATT. 17:15; MARK 5:4; 9:22; JOHN 18:2;
ACTS 26:11; ROM. 1:13; 2 COR. 8:22;
11:23,26,27; PHIL. 3:18; 2 TIM. 1:16; HEB.
6:7; 9:25,26; 10:11

4179. πολλαπλασίων pollaplasiōn
LUKE 18:30

4180. πολυλογία polulogia
MATT. 6:7

4181. πολυμερῶς polumerōs
HEB. 1:1

4182. πολυποίκιλος polupoikilos
EPH. 3:10

4183. πολύς polus
MATT. 2:18; 3:7; 4:25; 5:12; 6:30; 7:13,22;
8:1,11,16,18,30; 9:10,14,37; 10:31; 12:15;
13:2,3,5,17,58; 14:14; 15:30; 16:21; 19:2,22,30;
20:16,28,29; 22:14; 24:5,10-12,30; 25:19,21,23;
26:9,28,47,60; 27:19,52,53,55; MARK 1:34,45;
2:2,15; 3:7,8,10,12; 4:1,2,5,33; 5:9,10,21,23,
24,26,38,43; 6:2,13,20,31,33-35; 7:4,8,13; 8:31;
9:12,14,26; 10:22,31,45,48; 11:8; 12:5,27,37,41;
13:6,26; 14:24,43,56; 15:3,41; LUKE 1:1,14,16;
2:34-36; 3:18; 4:25,27,41; 5:6,15,29; 6:17,23,35;
7:11,21,47; 8:3,4,29,30; 9:22,37; 10:2,24,40,41;
12:7,19,47,48; 13:24; 14:16,25; 15:13; 16:10;
17:25; 18:39; 21:8,27; 22:65; 23:8,27; JOHN
2:12,23; 3:23; 4:39,41; 5:3,6; 6:2,5,10,60,66;
7:12,31,40; 8:26,30; 10:20,32,41,42; 11:19,45,
47,55; 12:9,11,12,24,42; 14:2,30; 15:5,8; 16:12;
19:20; 20:30; 21:25; ACTS 1:3,5; 2:43; 4:4;
5:12; 6:7; 8:7,25; 9:13,42; 10:2,27; 11:21; 13:43;

14:1,22; 15:7,32,35; 16:16,18,23; 17:4,12; 18:8,
10,27; 19:18; 20:2,19; 21:40; 22:28; 23:10; 24:2,
7,10; 25:7,23; 26:9,10,24,29; 27:10,14,21; 28:6,
10,29; **ROM.** 3:2; 4:17,18; 5:9,10,15-17,19;
8:29; 9:22; 12:4,5; 15:22,23; 16:2,6,12; **1 COR.**
1:26; 2:3; 4:15; 8:5; 10:17,33; 11:30; 12:12,14,
20,22; 16:9,12,19; **2 COR.** 1:11; 2:4,17; 3:9,11,
12; 6:4,10; 7:4; 8:2,4,15,22; 9:12; 11:18; 12:21;
GAL. 1:14; 3:16; 4:27; **EPH.** 2:4; **PHIL.** 1:23;
2:12; 3:18; **COL.** 4:13; **1 THESS.** 1:5,6; 2:2,17;
1 TIM. 3:8,13; 6:9,10,12; **2 TIM.** 2:2; 4:14;
TITUS 1:10; 2:3; **PHILE.** 1:7,8; **HEB.** 2:10;
5:11; 9:28; 10:32; 12:9,15,25; **JAMES** 3:1,2;
5:16; **1 PET.** 1:3,7; **2 PET.** 2:2; **1 JOHN** 2:18;
4:1; **2 JOHN** 1:7,12; **3 JOHN** 1:13; **REV.** 1:15;
5:4,11; 7:9; 8:3,11; 9:9; 10:11; 14:2; 17;1;
19;1,6,12

4184. πολύσπλαγχνος polusplagchnos
JAMES 5:11

4185. πολυτελής polutelēs
MARK 14:3; **1 TIM.** 2:9; **1 PET.** 3:4

4186. πολύτιμος polutimos
MATT. 13:46; **JOHN** 12:3

4187. πολυτρόπως polutropōs
HEB. 1:1

4188. πόμα poma
1 COR. 10:4; **HEB.** 9:10

4189. πονηρία ponēria
MATT. 22:18; **MARK** 7:22; **LUKE** 11:39;
ACTS 3:26; **ROM.** 1:29; **1 COR.** 5:8; **EPH.**
6:12

4190. πονηρός ponēros
MATT. 5:11,37,39,45; 6:13,23; 7:11,17,18; 9:4;
12:34,35,39,45; 13:19,38,49; 15:19; 16:4; 18:32;
20:15; 22:10; 25:26; **MARK** 7:22,23; **LUKE**
3:19; 6:22,35,45; 7:21; 8:2; 11:4,13,29,34; 19:22;
JOHN 3:19; 7:7; 17:15; **ACTS** 17:5; 18:14;
19:12,13,15,16; 28:21; **ROM.** 12:9; **1 COR.**
5:13; **GAL.** 1:4; **EPH.** 5:16; 6:13,16; **COL.**
1:21; **1 THESS.** 5:22; **2 THESS.** 3:2,3; **1 TIM.**
6:4; **2 TIM.** 3:13; 4:18; **HEB.** 3:12; 10:22;
JAMES 2:4; 4:16; **1 JOHN** 2:13,14; 3:12;
5:18,19; **2 JOHN** 1:11; **3 JOHN** 1:10; **REV.**
16:2

4191. πονηρότερος ponēroteros
MATT. 12:45; **LUKE** 11:26

4192. πόνος ponos
REV. 16:10,11; 21:4

4193. Ποντικός Pontikos
ACTS 18:2

4194. Πόντιος Pontios
MATT. 27:2; **LUKE** 3:1; **ACTS** 4:27; **1 TIM.**
6:13

4195. Πόντος Pontos
ACTS 2:9; **1 PET.** 1:1

4196. Πόπλιος Poplios
ACTS 28:7,8

4197. πορεία poreia
LUKE 13:22; **JAMES** 1:11

4198. πορεύομαι poreuomai
MATT. 2:8,9,20; 8:9; 9:13; 10:6,7; 11:4,7; 12:1,
45; 17:27; 18:12; 19:15; 21:2,6; 22:9,15; 24:1;
25:9,16,41; 26:14; 27:66; 28:7,9,11,16,19;
MARK 16:10,12,15; **LUKE** 1:6,39; 2:3,41;
4:30,42; 5:24; 7:6,8,11,22,50; 8:14,48; 9:13,51-
53,56,57; 10:37,38; 11:5,26; 13:31-33; 14;10,
19,31; 15:4,15,18; 16:30; 17:11,14,19; 19:12,
28,36; 21:8; 22:8,22,33,39; 24:13,28; **JOHN**
4:50; 7:35,53; 8:1,11; 10:4; 11:11; 14:2,3,12,28;
16:7,28; 20:17; **ACTS** 1:10,11,25; 5:20,41; 8:26,
27,36,39; 9:3,11,15,31; 10:20; 12:17; 14:16;
16:7,16,36; 17:14; 18:6; 19:21; 20:1,22; 21:5;
22:5,6,10,21; 23:23,32; 24:25; 25:12,20; 26:12,
13; 27:3; 28:26; **ROM.** 15:24,25; **1 COR.** 10:27;
16:4,6; **1 TIM.** 1:3; **2 TIM.** 4:10; **JAMES** 4:13;
1 PET. 3:19,22; 4:3; **2 PET.** 2:10; 3:3; **JUDE**
1:11,16,18

4199. πορθέω portheō
ACTS 9:21; **GAL.** 1:13,23

4200. πορισμός porismos
1 TIM. 6:5,6

4201. Πόρκιος Porkios
ACTS 24:27

4202. *πορνεία porneia*
MATT. 5:32; 15:19; 19:9; **MARK** 7:21; **JOHN**
8:41; **ACTS** 15:20,29; 21:25; **ROM.** 1:29;
1 COR. 5:1; 6:13,18; 7:2; **2 COR.** 12:21; **GAL.**
5:19; **EPH.** 5:3; **COL.** 3:5; **1 THESS.** 4:3; **REV.**
2:21; 9:21; 14:8; 17:2,4; 18:3; 19:2

4203. *πορνεύω porneuō*
1 COR. 6:18; 10:8; **REV.** 2:14,20; 17:2; 18:3,9

4204. *πόρνη pornē*
MATT. 21:31,32; **LUKE** 15:30; **1 COR.**
6:15,16; **HEB.** 11:31; **JAMES** 2:25; **REV.**
17:1,5,15,16; 19:2

4205. *πόρνος pornos*
1 COR. 5:9-11; 6:9; **EPH.** 5:5; **1 TIM.** 1:10;
HEB. 12:16; 13:4; **REV.** 21:8; 22:15

4206. *πόρρω porro*
MATT. 15:8; **MARK** 7:6; **LUKE** 14:32

4207. *πόρρωθεν porrōthen*
LUKE 17:12; **HEB.** 11:13

4208. *πορρωτέρω porrōterō*
LUKE 24:28

4209. *πορφύρα porphura* adv.
MARK 15:17,20; **LUKE** 16:19; **REV.** 17:4;
18:12

4210. *πορφύρεος porphureos*
JOHN 19:2,5; **REV.** 18:16

4211. *πορφυρόπωλις porphuropōlis*
ACTS 16:14

4212. *ποσάκις posakis*
MATT. 18:21; 23:37; **LUKE** 13:34

4213. *πόσις posis*
JOHN 6:55; **ROM.** 14:17; **COL.** 2:16

4214. *πόσος posos*
MATT. 6:23; 7:11; 10:25; 12:12; 15:34; 16:9,10;
27:13; **MARK** 6:38; 8:5,19,20; 9:21; 15:4;
LUKE 11:13; 12:24,28; 15:17; 16:5,7; **ACTS**

21:20; **ROM.** 11:12,24; **2 COR.** 7:1; **PHILE.**
1:16; **HEB.** 9:14; 10:29

4215. *ποταμός potamos*
MATT. 7:25,27; **MARK** 1:5; **LUKE** 6:48,49;
JOHN 7:38; **ACTS** 16:13; **2 COR.** 11:26; **REV.**
8:10; 9:14; 12:15,16; 16:4,12; 22:1,2

4216. *ποταμοφόρητος*
          potamophorētos
REV. 12:15

4217. *ποταπός potapos*
MATT. 8:27; **MARK** 13:1; **LUKE** 1:29; 7:39;
2 PET. 3:11; **1 JOHN** 3:1

4218. *ποτέ pote*
LUKE 22:32; **JOHN** 9:13; **ACTS** 28:27; **ROM.**
1:10; 7:9; 11:30; **1 COR.** 9:7; **GAL.** 1:13,23;
2:6; **EPH.** 2:2,3,11,13; 5:8,29; **PHIL.** 4:10;
COL. 1:21; 3:7; **1 THESS.** 2:5; **TITUS** 3:3;
PHILE. 1:11; **HEB.** 1:5,13; 2:1; 4:1; **1 PET.**
2:10; 3:5,20; **2 PET.** 1:10,21

4219. *πότε pote*
MATT. 17:17; 24:3; 25:37-39,44; **MARK** 9:19;
13:4,33,35; **LUKE** 9:41; 12:36; 17:20; 21:7;
JOHN 6:25; 10:24; **REV.** 6:10

4220. *πότερον poteron* adv.
JOHN 7:17

4221. *ποτήριον potērion*
MATT. 10:42; 20:22,23; 23:25,26; 26:27,39,42;
MARK 7:4,8; 9:41; 10:38,39; 14:23,36; **LUKE**
11:39; 22:17,20,42; **JOHN** 18:11; **1 COR.**
10:16,21; 11:25-28; **REV.** 14:10; 16:19; 17:4;
18:6

4222. *ποτίζω potizō*
MATT. 10:42; 25:35,37,42; 27:48; **MARK**
9:41; 15:36; **LUKE** 13:15; **ROM.** 12:20;
1 COR. 3:2,6-8; 12:13; **REV.** 14:8

4223. *Ποτίολοι Potioloi*
ACTS 28:13

4224. *πότος potos*
1 PET. 4:3

4225. πού pou
ROM. 4:19; HEB. 2:6; 4:4

4226. ποῦ pou
MATT. 2:2,4; 8:20; 26:17; MARK 14:12,14;
15:47; LUKE 8:25; 9:58; 12:17; 17:17,37;
22:9,11; JOHN 1:38,39; 3:8; 7:11,35; 8:10,14,
19; 9:12; 11:34,57; 12:35; 13:36; 14:5; 16:5;
20:2,13,15; ROM. 3:27; 1 COR. 1:20; 12:17,19;
15:55; HEB. 11:8; 1 PET. 4:18; 2 PET. 3:4;
1 JOHN 2:11; REV. 2:13

4227. Πούδης Poudēs
2 TIM. 4:21

4228. πούς pous
MATT. 4:6; 5:35; 7:6; 10:14; 15:30; 18:8,29;
22:13,44; 28:9; MARK 5:22; 6:11; 7:25; 9:45;
12:36; LUKE 1:79; 4:11; 7:38,44-46; 8:35,41;
9:5; 10:39; 15:22; 17:16; 20:43; 24:39,40; JOHN
11:2,32,44; 12:3; 13:5,6,8-10,12,14; 20:12;
ACTS 2:35; 4:35,37; 5:2,9,10; 7:5,33,49,58;
10:25; 13:25,51; 14:8,10; 16:24; 21:11; 22:3;
26:16; ROM. 3:15; 10:15; 16:20; 1 COR.
12:15,21; 15:25,27; EPH. 1:22; 6:15; 1 TIM.
5:10; HEB. 1:13; 2:8; 10:13; 12:13; REV.
1:15,17; 2:18; 3:9; 10:1,2; 11:11; 12:1; 13:2;
19:10; 22:8

4229. πρᾶγμα pragma
MATT. 18:19; LUKE 1:1; ACTS 5:4; ROM.
16:2; 1 COR. 6:1; 2 COR. 7:11; 1 THESS. 4:6;
HEB. 6:18; 10:1; 11:1; JAMES 3:16

4230. πραγματεία pragmateia
2 TIM. 2:4

4231. πραγματεύομαι pragmateuomai
LUKE 19:13

4232. πραιτώριον praitōrion
MATT. 27:27; MARK 15:16; JOHN 18:28,33;
19:9; ACTS 23:35; PHIL. 1:13

4233. πράκτωρ praktōr
LUKE 12:58

4234. πρᾶξις praxis
MATT. 16:27; LUKE 23:51; ACTS 19:18;
ROM. 8:13; 12:4; COL. 3:9

4235. πρᾶος praos
MATT. 11:29

4236. πραότης praotēs
1 COR. 4:21; 2 COR. 10:1; GAL. 5:23; 6:1;
EPH. 4:2; COL. 3:12; 1 TIM. 6:11; 2 TIM.
2:25; TITUS 3:2

4237. πρασιά prasia
MARK 6:40

4238. πράσσω, πράττω prassō, prattō
LUKE 3:13; 19:23; 22:23; 23:15,41; JOHN
3:20; 5:29; ACTS 3:17; 5:35; 15:29; 16:28; 17:7;
19:19,36; 25:11,25; 26:9,20,26,31; ROM. 1:32;
2:1-3,25; 7:15,19; 9:11; 13:4; 1 COR. 9:17;
2 COR. 5:10; 12:21; GAL. 5:21; EPH. 6:21;
PHIL. 4:9; 1 THESS. 4:11

4239. πραΰς praus
MATT. 5:5; 21:5; 1 PET. 3:4

4240. πραΰτης prautēs
JAMES 1:21; 3:13; 1 PET. 3:15

4241. πρέπω prepō
MATT. 3:15; 1 COR. 11:13; EPH. 5:3; 1 TIM.
2:10; TITUS 2:1; HEB. 2:10; 7:26

4242. πρεσβεία presbeia
LUKE 14:32; 19:14

4243. πρεσβεύω presbeuō
2 COR. 5:20; EPH. 6:20

4244. πρεσβυτέριον presbuterion
LUKE 22:66; ACTS 22:5; 1 TIM. 4:14

4245. πρεσβύτερος presbuteros
MATT. 15:2; 16:21; 21:23; 26:3,47,57,59; 27:1,
3,12,20,41; 28:12; MARK 7:3,5; 8:31; 11:27;
14:43,53; 15:1; LUKE 7:3; 9:22; 15:25; 20:1;
22:52; JOHN 8:9; ACTS 2:17; 4:5,8,23; 6:12;
11:30; 14:23; 15:2,4,6,22,23; 16:4; 20:17; 21:18;
23:14; 24:1; 25:15; 1 TIM. 5:1,2,17,19; TITUS
1:5; HEB. 11:2; JAMES 5:14; 1 PET. 5:1,5;
2 JOHN 1:1; 3 JOHN 1:1; REV. 4:4,10;
5:5,6,8,11,14; 7:11,13; 11:16; 14:3; 19:4

4246. πρεσβύτης *presbutēs*
LUKE 1:18; TITUS 2:2; PHILE. 1:9

4247. πρεσβῦτις *presbutis*
TITUS 2:3

4248. πρηνής *prēnēs*
ACTS 1:18

4249. πρίζω, πρίω *prizō, priō*
HEB. 11:37

4250. πρίν *prin*
MATT. 1:18; 26:34,75; MARK 14:30,72;
LUKE 2:26; 22:34,61; JOHN 4:49; 8:58; 14:29;
ACTS 2:20; 7:2; 25:16

4251. Πρίσκα *Priska*
2 TIM. 4:19

4252. Πρίσκιλλα *Priskilla*
ACTS 18:2,18,26; ROM. 16:3; 1 COR. 16:19

4254. προάγω *proagō*
MATT. 2:9; 14:22; 21:9,31; 26:32; 28:7;
MARK 6:45; 10:32; 11:9; 14:28; 16:7; LUKE
18:39; ACTS 12:6; 16:30; 25:26; 1 TIM. 1:18;
5:24; HEB. 7:18

4255. προαιρέω *proaireō*
2 COR. 9:7

4256. προαιτιάομαι *proaitiaomai*
ROM. 3:9

4257. προακούω *proakouō*
COL. 1:5

4258. προαμαρτάνω *proamartanō*
2 COR. 12:21; 13:2

4259. προαύλιον *proaulion*
MARK 14:68

4260. προβαίνω *probainō*
MATT. 4:21; MARK 1:19; LUKE 1:7,18; 2:36

4261. προβάλλω *proballō*
LUKE 21:30; ACTS 19:33

4262. προβατικός *probatikos*
JOHN 5:2

4263. πρόβατον *probaton*
MATT. 7:15; 9:36; 10:6,16; 12:11,12; 15:24;
18:12; 25:32,33; 26:31; MARK 6:34; 14:27;
LUKE 15:4,6; JOHN 2:14,15; 10:1-4,7,8,11-
13,15,16,26,27; 21:16,17; ACTS 8:32; ROM.
8:36; HEB. 13:20; 1 PET. 2:25; REV. 18:13

4264. προβιβάζω *probibazō*
MATT. 14:8; ACTS 19:33

4265. προβλέπω *problepō*
HEB. 11:40

4266. προγίνομαι *proginomai*
ROM. 3:25

4267. προγινώσκω *proginōskō*
ACTS 26:5; ROM. 8:29; 11:2; 1 PET. 1:20;
2 PET. 3:17

4268. πρόγνωσις *prognōsis*
ACTS 2:23; 1 PET. 1:2

4269. πρόγονος *progonos*
1 TIM. 5:4; 2 TIM. 1:3

4270. προγράφω *prographō*
ROM. 15:4; GAL. 3:1; EPH. 3:3; JUDE 1:4

4271. πρόδηλος *prodēlos*
1 TIM. 5:24,25; HEB. 7:14

4272. προδίδωμι *prodidōmi*
ROM. 11:35

4273. προδότης *prodotēs*
LUKE 6:16; ACTS 7:52; 2 TIM. 3:4

4274. πρόδρομος *prodromos*
HEB. 6:20

4275. προεῖδον *proeidon*
ACTS 2:31; GAL. 3:8

4276. προελπίζω *proelpizō*
EPH. 1:12

4277. προεῖπον *proeipon*
(2 aor. of προέπω)
ACTS 1:16; GAL. 5:21; 1 THESS. 4:6

4278. προενάρχομαι *proenarchomai*
2 COR. 8:6,10

4279. προεπαγγέλλω *proepaggellō*
ROM. 1:2

4280. προερέω *proereō*
(Perf. of προεῖπον)
MATT. 24:25; MARK 13:23; ROM. 9:29;
2 COR. 7:3; 13:2; GAL. 1:9; HEB. 10:15;
2 PET. 3:2; JUDE 1:17

4281. προέρχομαι *proerchomai*
MATT. 26:39; MARK 6:33; 14:35; LUKE
1:17; 22:47; ACTS 12:10; 20:5,13; 2 COR. 9:5

4282. προετοιμάζω *proetoimazō*
ROM. 9:23; EPH. 2:10

4283. προευαγγελίζομαι
proeuaggelizomai
GAL. 3:8

4284. προέχω *proechō*
ROM. 3:9

4285. προηγέομαι *proēgeomai*
ROM. 12:10

4286. πρόθεσις *prothesis*
MATT. 12:4; MARK 2:26; LUKE 6:4; ACTS
11:23; 27:13; ROM. 8:28; 9:11; EPH. 1:11;
3:11; 2 TIM. 1:9; 3:10; HEB. 9:2

4287. προθέσμιος *prothesmios*
GAL. 4:2

4288. προθυμία *prothumia*
ACTS 17:11; 2 COR. 8:11,12,19; 9:2

4289. πρόθυμος *prothumos*
MATT. 26:41; MARK 14:38; ROM. 1:15

4290. προθύμως *prothumōs*
1 PET. 5:2

4291. προΐστημι *proistēmi*
ROM. 12:8; 1 THESS. 5:12; 1 TIM. 3:4,5,12;
5:17; TITUS 3:8,14

4292. προκαλέω *prokaleō*
GAL. 5:26

4293. προκαταγγέλλω *prokataggellō*
ACTS 3:18,24; 7:52; 2 COR. 9:5

4294. προκαταρτίζω *prokatartizō*
2 COR. 9:5

4295. πρόκειμαι *prokeimai*
2 COR. 8:12; HEB. 6:18; 12:1,2; JUDE 1:7

4296. προκηρύσσω, προκηρύττω
prokērussō, prokēruttō
ACTS 3:20; 13:24

4297. προκοπή *prokopē*
PHIL. 1:12,25; 1 TIM. 4:15

4298. προκόπτω *prokoptō*
LUKE 2:52; ROM. 13:12; GAL. 1:14; 2 TIM.
2:16; 3:9,13

4299. πρόκριμα *prokrima*
1 TIM. 5:21

4300. προκυρόω *prokuroō*
GAL. 3:17

4301. προλαμβάνω *prolambanō*
MARK 14:8; 1 COR. 11:21; GAL. 6:1

4302. προλέγω *prolegō*
2 COR. 13:2; GAL. 5:21; 1 THESS. 3:4

4303. προμαρτύρομαι *promarturomai*
1 PET. 1:11

4304. προμελετάω *promeletaō*
LUKE 21:14

4305. προμεριμνάω *promerimnaō*
MARK 13:11

4306. προνοέω *pronoeō*
ROM. 12:17; **2 COR.** 8:21; **1 TIM.** 5:8

4307. πρόνοια *pronoia*
ACTS 24:2; **ROM.** 13:14

4308. προοράω *prooraō*
ACTS 2:25; 21:29

4309. προορίζω *proorizō*
ACTS 4:28; **ROM.** 8:29,30; **1 COR.** 2:7; **EPH.** 1:5,11

4310. προπάσχω *propaschō*
1 THESS. 2:2

4311. προπέμπω *propempō*
ACTS 15:3; 20:38; 21:5; **ROM.** 15:24; **1 COR.** 16:6,11; **2 COR.** 1:16; **TITUS** 3:13; **3 JOHN** 1:6

4312. προπετής *propetēs*
ACTS 19:36; **2 TIM.** 3:4

4313. προπορεύομαι *proporeuomai*
LUKE 1:76; **ACTS** 7:40

4315. προσάββατον *prosabbaton*
MARK 15:42

4316. προσαγορεύω *prosagoreuō*
HEB. 5:10

4317. προσάγω *prosagō*
LUKE 9:41; **ACTS** 16:20; 27:27; **1 PET.** 3:18

4318. προσαγωγή *prosagōgē*
ROM. 5:2; **EPH.** 2:18; 3:12

4319. προσαιτέω *prosaiteō*
MARK 10:46; **LUKE** 18:35; **JOHN** 9:8

4320. προσαναβαίνω *prosanabainō*
LUKE 14:10

4321. προσαναλίσκω *prosanaliskō*
LUKE 8:42

4322. προσαναπληρόω *prosanaplēroō*
2 COR. 9:12; 11:9

4323. προσανατίθημι *prosanatithēmi*
GAL. 1:16; 2:6

4324. προσαπειλέω *prosapeileō*
ACTS 4:21

4325. προσδαπανάω *prosdapanaō*
LUKE 10:35

4326. προσδέομαι *prosdeomai*
ACTS 17:25

4327. προσδέχομαι *prosdechomai*
MARK 15:43; **LUKE** 2:25,38; 12:36; 15:2; 23:51; **ACTS** 23:21; 24:15; **ROM.** 16:2; **PHIL.** 2:29; **TITUS** 2:13; **HEB.** 10:34; 11:35; **JUDE** 1:21

4328. προσδοκάω *prosdokaō*
MATT. 11:3; 24:50; **LUKE** 1:21; 3:15; 7:19,20; 8:40; 12:46; **ACTS** 3:5; 10:24; 27:33; 28:6; **2 PET.** 3:12-14

4329. προσδοκία *prosdokia*
LUKE 21:26; **ACTS** 12:11

4330. προσεάω *proseaō*
ACTS 27:7

4331. προσεγγίζω *proseggizō*
MARK 2:4

4332. προσεδρεύω *prosedreuō*
1 COR. 9:13

4333. *προσεργάζομαι prosergazomai*
LUKE 19:16

4334. *προσέρχομαι proserchomai*
MATT. 4:3,11; 5:1; 8:5,19,25; 9:14,20,28;
13:10,27,36; 14:12,15; 15:1,12,23,30; 16:1;
17:7,14,19,24; 18:1,21; 19:3,16; 20:20; 21:14,
23,28,30; 22:23; 24:1,3; 25:20,22,24; 26:7,17,
49,50,60,69,73; 27:58; 28:2,9,18; MARK 1:31;
6:35; 10:2; 12:28; 14:45; LUKE 7:14; 8:24,44;
9:12,42; 10:34; 13:31; 20:27; 23:36,52; JOHN
12:21; ACTS 7:31; 8:29; 9:1; 10:28; 12:13; 18:2;
22:26,27; 23:14; 24:23; 28:9; 1 TIM. 6:3; HEB.
4:16; 7:25; 10:1,22; 11:6; 12:18,22; 1 PET. 2:4

4335. *προσευχή proseuchē*
MATT. 17:21; 21:13,22; MARK 9:29; 11:17;
LUKE 6:12; 19:46; 22:45; ACTS 1:14; 2:42;
3:1; 6:4; 10:4,31; 12:5; 16:13,16; ROM. 1:9;
12:12; 15:30; 1 COR. 7:5; EPH. 1:16; 6:18;
PHIL. 4:6; COL. 4:2,12; 1 THESS. 1:2; 1 TIM.
2:1; 5:5; PHILE. 1:4,22; JAMES 5:17; 1 PET.
3:7; 4:7; REV. 5:8; 8:3,4

4336. *προσεύχομαι proseuchomai*
MATT. 5:44; 6:5-7,9; 14:23; 19:13; 23:14;
24:20; 26:36,39,41,42,44; MARK 1:35; 6:46;
11:24,25; 12:40; 13:18,33; 14:32,35,38,39;
LUKE 1:10; 3:21; 5:16; 6:12,28; 9:18,28,29;
11:1,2; 18:1,10,11; 20:47; 22:40,41,44,46;
ACTS 1:24; 6:6; 8:15; 9:11,40; 10:9,30; 11:5;
12:12; 13:3; 14:23; 16:25; 20:36; 21:5; 22:17;
28:8; ROM. 8:26; 1 COR. 11:4,5,13; 14:13-15;
EPH. 6:18; PHIL. 1:9; COL. 1:3,9; 4:3;
1 THESS. 5:17,25; 2 THESS. 1:11; 3:1; 1 TIM.
2:8; HEB. 13:18; JAMES 5:13,14,17,18; JUDE
1:20

4337. *προσέχω prosechō*
MATT. 6:1; 7:15; 10:17; 16:6,11,12; LUKE
12:1; 17:3; 20:46; 21:34; ACTS 5:35; 8:6,10,11;
16:14; 20:28; 1 TIM. 1:4; 3:8; 4:1,13; TITUS
1:14; HEB. 2:1; 7:13; 2 PET. 1:19

4338. *προσηλόω prosēloō*
COL. 2:14

4339. *προσήλυτος prosēlutos*
MATT. 23:15; ACTS 2:10; 6:5; 13:43

4340. *πρόσκαιρος proskairos*
MATT. 13:21; MARK 4:17; 2 COR. 4:18;
HEB. 11:25

4341. *προσκαλέω proskaleō*
MATT. 10:1; 15:10,32; 18:2,32; 20:25; MARK
3:13,23; 6:7; 7:14; 8:1,34; 10:42; 12:43; 15:44;
LUKE 7:19; 15:26; 16:5; 18:16; ACTS 2:39;
5:40; 6:2; 13:2,7; 16:10; 20:1; 23:17,18,23;
JAMES 5:14

4342. *προσκαρτερέω proskartereō*
MARK 3:9; ACTS 1:14; 2:42,46; 6:4; 8:13;
10:7; ROM. 12:12; 13:6; COL. 4:2

4343. *προσκαρτέρησις proskarterēsis*
EPH. 6:18

4344. *προσκεφάλαιον proskephalaion*
MARK 4:38

4345. *προσκληρόω prosklēroō*
ACTS 17:4

4346. *πρόσκλισις prosklisis*
1 TIM. 5:21

4347. *προσκολλάω proskollaō*
MATT. 19:5; MARK 10:7; ACTS 5:36; EPH.
5:31

4348. *πρόσκομμα proskomma*
ROM. 9:32,33; 14:13,20; 1 COR. 8:9; 1 PET.
2:8

4349. *προσκοπή proskopē*
2 COR. 6:3

4350. *προσκόπτω proskoptō*
MATT. 4:6; 7:27; LUKE 4:11; JOHN 11:9,10;
ROM. 9:32; 14:21; 1 PET. 2:8

4351. *προσκυλίω proskuliō*
MATT. 27:60; MARK 15:46

4352. *προσκυνέω proskuneō*
MATT. 2:2,8,11; 4:9,10; 8:2; 9:18; 14:33; 15:25;
18:26; 20:20; 28:9,17; MARK 5:6; 15:19;

LUKE 4:7,8; 24:52; **JOHN** 4:20-24; 9:38; 12:20; **ACTS** 7:43; 8:27; 10:25; 24:11; **1 COR.** 14:25; **HEB.** 1:6; 11:21; **REV.** 3:9; 4:10; 5:14; 7:11; 9:20; 11:1,16; 13:4,8,12,15; 14:7,9,11; 15:4; 16:2; 19:4,10,20; 20:4; 22:8,9

4353. προσκυνητής proskunētēs
JOHN 4:23

4354. προσλαλέω proslaleō
ACTS 13:43; 28:20

4355. προσλαμβάνω proslambanō
MATT. 16:22; **MARK** 8:32; **ACTS** 17:5; 18:26; 27:33,34,36; 28:2; **ROM.** 14:1,3; 15:7; **PHILE.** 1:12,17

4356. πρόσληψις proslēpsis
ROM. 11:15

4357. προσμένω prosmenō
MATT. 15:32; **MARK** 8:2; **ACTS** 11:23; 18:18; **1 TIM.** 1:3; 5:5

4358. προσορμίζω prosormizō
MARK 6:53

4359. προσοφείλω prosopheilō
PHILE. 1:19

4360. προσοχθίζω prosochthizō
HEB. 3:10,17

4361. πρόσπεινος prospeinos
ACTS 10:10

4362. προσπήγνυμι prospēgnumi
ACTS 2:23

4363. προσπίπτω prospiptō
MATT. 7:25; **MARK** 3:11; 5:33; 7:25; **LUKE** 5:8; 8:28,47; **ACTS** 16:29

4364. προσποιέομαι prospoieomai
LUKE 24:28

4365. προσπορεύομαι prosporeuomai
MARK 10:35

4366. προσρήγνυμι prosrēgnumi
LUKE 6:48,49

4367. προστάσσω, προστάττω prostassō, prostattō
MATT. 1:24; 8:4; 21:6; **MARK** 1:44; **LUKE** 5:14; **ACTS** 10:33,48

4368. προστάτις prostatis
ROM. 16:2

4369. προστίθημι prostithēmi
MATT. 6:27,33; **MARK** 4:24; **LUKE** 3:20; 12:25,31; 17:5; 19:11; 20:11,12; **ACTS** 2:41,47; 5:14; 11:24; 12:3; 13:36; **GAL.** 3:19; **HEB.** 12:19

4370. προστρέχω prostrechō
MARK 9:15; 10:17; **ACTS** 8:30

4371. προσφάγιον prosphagion
JOHN 21:5

4372. πρόσφατος prosphatos
HEB. 10:20

4373. προσφάτως prosphatōs
ACTS 18:2

4374. προσφέρω prospherō
MATT. 2:11; 4:24; 5:23,24; 8:4,16; 9:2,32; 12:22; 14:35; 17:16; 18:24; 19:13; 22:19; 25:20; **MARK** 1:44; 10:13; **LUKE** 5:14; 12:11; 18:15; 23:14,36; **JOHN** 16:2; 19:29; **ACTS** 7:42; 8:18; 21:26; **HEB.** 5:1,3,7; 8:3,4; 9:7,9,14,25,28; 10:1,2,8,11,12; 11:4,17; 12:7

4375. προσφιλής prosphilēs
PHIL. 4:8

4376. προσφορά prosphora
ACTS 21:26; 24:17; **ROM.** 15:16; **EPH.** 5:2; **HEB.** 10:5,8,10,14,18

4377. προσφωνέω prosphōneō
MATT. 11:16; **LUKE** 6:13; 7:32; 13:12; 23:20; **ACTS** 21:40; 22:2

4378. πρόσχυσις *proschusis*
HEB. 11:28

4379. προσψαύω *prospsauō*
LUKE 11:46

4380. προσωπολήπτεω *prosōpolēpteō*
JAMES 2:9

4381. προσωπολήπτης *prosōpolēptēs*
ACTS 10:34

4382. προσωποληψία *prosōpolēpsia*
ROM. 2:11; EPH. 6:9; COL. 3:25; JAMES 2:1

4383. πρόσωπον *prosōpon*
MATT. 6:16,17; 11:10; 16:3; 17:2,6; 18:10;
22:16; 26:39,67; MARK 1:2; 12:14; 14:65;
LUKE 1:76; 2:31; 5:12; 7:27; 9:29,51-53; 10:1;
12:56; 17:16; 20:21; 21:35; 22:64; 24:5; ACTS
2:28; 3:13,19; 5:41; 6:15; 7:45; 13:24; 17:26;
20:25,38; 25:16; 1 COR. 13:12; 14:25; 2 COR.
1:11; 2:10; 3:7,13,18; 4:6; 5:12; 8:24; 10:1,7;
11:20; GAL. 1:22; 2:6,11; COL. 2:1; 1 THESS.
2:17; 3:10; 2 THESS. 1:9; HEB. 9:24; JAMES
1:11,23; 1 PET. 3:12; JUDE 1:16; REV. 4:7;
6:16; 7:11; 9:7; 10:1; 11:16; 12:14; 20:11; 22:4

4384. προτάσσω, προτάττω
protassō, protattō
ACTS 17:26

4385. προτείνω *proteinō*
ACTS 22:25

4386. πρότερον *proteron* adv.
JOHN 6:62; 7:51; 9:8; 2 COR. 1:15; GAL.
4:13; 1 TIM. 1:13; HEB. 4:6; 7:27; 10:32;
1 PET. 1:14

4387. πρότερος *proteros*
EPH. 4:22

4388. προτίθημι *protithēmi*
ROM. 1:13; 3:25; EPH. 1:9

4389. προτρέπω *protrepō*
ACTS 18:27

4390. προτρέχω *protrechō*
LUKE 19:4; JOHN 20:4

4391. προϋπάρχω *prouparchō*
LUKE 23:12; ACTS 8:9

4392. πρόφασις *prophasis*
MATT. 23:14; MARK 12:40; LUKE 20:47;
JOHN 15:22; ACTS 27:30; PHIL. 1:18;
1 THESS. 2:5

4393. προφέρω *propherō*
LUKE 6:45

4394. προφητεία *prophēteia*
MATT. 13:14; ROM. 12:6; 1 COR. 12:10;
13:2,8; 14:6,22; 1 THESS. 5:20; 1 TIM. 1:18;
4:14; 2 PET. 1:20,21; REV. 1:3; 11:6; 19:10;
22:7,10,18,19

4395. προφητεύω *prophēteuō*
MATT. 7:22; 11:13; 15:7; 26:68; MARK 7:6;
14:65; LUKE 1:67; 22:64; JOHN 11:51; ACTS
2:17,18; 19:6; 21:9; 1 COR. 11:4,5; 13:9; 14:1,3-
5,24,31,39; 1 PET. 1:10; JUDE 1:14; REV.
10:11; 11:3

4396. προφήτης *prophētēs*
MATT. 1:22; 2:5,15,17,23; 3:3; 4:14; 5:12,17;
7:12; 8:17; 10:41; 11:9,13; 12:17,39; 13:17,35,
57; 14:5; 16:4,14; 21:4,11,26,46; 22:40; 23:29-
31,34,37; 24:15; 26:56; 27:9,35; MARK 1:2;
6:4,15; 8:28; 11:32; 13:14; LUKE 1:70,76; 3:4;
4:17,24,27; 6:23; 7:16,26,28,39; 9:8,19; 10:24;
11:29,47,49,50; 13:28,33,34; 16:16,29,31; 18:31;
20:6; 24:19,25,27,44; JOHN 1:21,23,25,45;
4:19,44; 6:14,45; 7:40,52; 8:52,53; 9:17; 12:38;
ACTS 2:16,30; 3:18,21-25; 7:37,42,48,52; 8:28,
30,34; 10:43; 11:27; 13:1,15,20,27,40; 15:15,32;
21:10; 24:14; 26:22,27; 28:23,25; ROM. 1:2;
3:21; 11:3; 1 COR. 12:28,29; 14:29,32,37; EPH.
2:20; 3:5; 4:11; 1 THESS. 2:15; TITUS 1:12;
HEB. 1:1; 11:32; JAMES 5:10; 1 PET. 1:10;
2 PET. 2:16; 3:2; REV. 10:7; 11:10,18; 16:6;
18:20,24; 22:6,9

4397. προφητικός *prophētikos*
ROM. 16:26; 2 PET. 1:19

4398. προφῆτις *prophētis*
LUKE 2:36; REV. 2:20

4399. προφθάνω *prophthanō*
MATT. 17:25

4400. προχειρίζομαι *procheirizomai*
ACTS 22:14; 26:16

4401. προχειροτονέω *procheirotoneō*
ACTS 10:41

4402. Πρόχορος *Prochoros*
ACTS 6:5

4403. πρύμνα *prumna*
MARK 4:38; ACTS 27:29,41

4404. πρωΐ *prōi*
MATT. 16:3; 20:1; MARK 1:35; 11:20; 13:35;
15:1; 16:2,9; JOHN 20:1; ACTS 28:23

4405. πρωΐα *prōia*
MATT. 21:18; 27:1; JOHN 18:28; 21:4

4406. πρώϊμος *prōimos*
JAMES 5:7

4407. πρωϊνός *prōinos*
REV. 2:28

4408. πρώρα *prōra*
ACTS 27:30,41

4409. πρωτεύω *prōteuō*
COL. 1:18

4410. πρωτοκαθεδρία *prōtokathedria*
MATT. 23:6; MARK 12:39; LUKE 11:43;
20:46

4411. πρωτοκλισία *prōtoklisia*
MATT. 23:6; MARK 12:39; LUKE 14:7,8;
20:46

4412. πρῶτον *prōton* adv.
MATT. 5:24; 6:33; 7:5; 8:21; 12:29; 13:30;
17:10,11; 23:26; MARK 3:27; 4:28; 7:27;
9:11,12; 13:10; 16:9; LUKE 6:42; 9:59,61; 10:5;
11:38; 12:1; 14:28,31; 17:25; 21:9; JOHN 2:10;
10:40; 12:16; 15:18; 18:13; 19:39; ACTS 3:26;
7:12; 11:26; 13:46; 15:14; 26:20; ROM. 1:8,

16; 2:9,10; 3:2; 15:24; 1 COR. 11:18; 12:28;
15:46; 2 COR. 8:5; EPH. 4:9; 1 THESS. 4:16;
2 THESS. 2:3; 1 TIM. 2:1; 3:10; 5:4; 2 TIM.
1:5; HEB. 7:2; JAMES 3:17; 1 PET. 4:17;
2 PET. 1:20; 3:3

4413. πρῶτος *prōtos*
MATT. 10:2; 12:45; 17:27; 19:30;
20:8,10,16,27; 21:28,31,36; 22:25,38; 26:17;
27:64; MARK 6:21; 9:35; 10:31,44; 12:20,28-
30; 14:12; 16:9; LUKE 2:2; 11:26; 13:30; 14:18;
15:22; 16:5; 19:16,47; 20:29; JOHN 1:15,30,41;
5:4; 8:7; 19:32; 20:4,8; ACTS 1:1; 12:10; 13:50;
16:12; 17:4; 20:18; 25:2; 26:23; 27:43; 28:7,17;
ROM. 10:19; 1 COR. 14:30; 15:3,45,47; EPH.
6:2; PHIL. 1:5; 1 TIM. 1:15,16; 2:13; 5:12;
2 TIM. 2:6; 4:16; HEB. 8:7,13; 9:1,2,6,8,15,18;
10:9; 2 PET. 2:20; 1 JOHN 4:19; REV. 1:11,17;
2:4,5,8,19; 4:1,7; 8:7; 13:12; 16:2; 20:5,6;
21:1,4,19; 22:13

4414. πρωτοστάτης *prōtostatēs*
ACTS 24:5

4415. πρωτοτόκια *prōtotokia*
HEB. 12:16

4416. πρωτοτόκος *prōtotokos*
MATT. 1:25; LUKE 2:7; ROM. 8:29; COL.
1:15,18; HEB. 1:6; 11:28; 12:23; REV. 1:5

4417. πταίω *ptaiō*
ROM. 11:11; JAMES 2:10; 3:2; 2 PET. 1:10

4418. πτέρνα *pterna*
JOHN 13:18

4419. πτερύγιον *pterugion*
MATT. 4:5; LUKE 4:9

4420. πτέρυξ *pterux*
MATT. 23:37; LUKE 13:34; REV. 4:8; 9:9;
12:14

4421. πτηνόν *ptēnon* subst.
1 COR. 15:39

4422. πτοέω *ptoeō*
LUKE 21:9; 24:37

4423. πτόησις *ptoēsis*
1 PET. 3:6

4424. Πτολεμαΐς *Ptolemais*
ACTS 21:7

4425. πτύον *ptuon*
MATT. 3:12; LUKE 3:17

4426. πτύρω *pturō*
PHIL. 1:28

4427. πτύσμα *ptusma*
JOHN 9:6

4428. πτύσσω *ptussō*
LUKE 4:20

4429. πτύω *ptuō*
MARK 7:33; 8:23; JOHN 9:6

4430. πτῶμα *ptōma*
MATT. 24:28; MARK 6:29; REV. 11:8,9

4431. πτῶσις *ptōsis*
MATT. 7:27; LUKE 2:34

4432. πτωχεία *ptōcheia*
2 COR. 8:2,9; REV. 2:9

4433. πτωχεύω *ptōcheuō*
2 COR. 8:9

4434. πτωχός *ptōchos*
MATT. 5:3; 11:5; 19:21; 26:9,11; MARK
10:21; 12:42,43; 14:5,7; LUKE 4:18; 6:20; 7:22;
14:13,21; 16:20,22; 18:22; 19:8; 21:3; JOHN
12:5,6,8; 13:29; ROM. 15:26; 2 COR. 6:10;
GAL. 2:10; 4:9; JAMES 2:2,3,5,6; REV. 3:17;
13:16

4435. πυγμή *pugmē*
MARK 7:3

4436. Πύθων *Puthōn*
ACTS 16:16

4437. πυκνός *puknos*
LUKE 5:33; ACTS 24:26; 1 TIM. 5:23

4438. πυκτεύω *pukteuō*
1 COR. 9:26

4439. πύλη *pulē*
MATT. 7:13,14; 16:18; LUKE 7:12; 13:24;
ACTS 3:10; 9:24; 12:10; HEB. 13:12

4440. πυλών *pulōn*
MATT. 26:71; LUKE 16:20; ACTS 10:17;
12:13,14; 14:13; REV. 21:12,13,15,21,25; 22:14

4441. πυνθάνομαι *punthanomai*
MATT. 2:4; LUKE 15:26; 18:36; JOHN 4:52;
13:24; ACTS 4:7; 10:18,29; 21:33; 23:19,20,34

4442. πῦρ *pur*
MATT. 3:10-12; 5:22; 7:19; 13:40,42,50; 17:15;
18:8,9; 25:41; MARK 9:22,43-49; LUKE
3:9,16,17; 9:54; 12:49; 17:29; 22:55; JOHN
15:6; ACTS 2:3,19; 7:30; 28:5; ROM. 12:20;
1 COR. 3:13,15; 2 THESS. 1:8; HEB. 1:7;
10:27; 11:34; 12:18,29; JAMES 3:5,6; 5:3;
1 PET. 1:7; 2 PET. 3:7; JUDE 1:7,23; REV.
1:14; 2:18; 3:18; 4:5; 8:5,7,8; 9:17,18; 10:1;
11:5; 13:13; 14:10,18; 15:2; 16:8; 17:16; 18:8;
19:12,20; 20:9,10,14,15; 21:8

4443. πυρά *pura*
ACTS 28:2,3

4444. πύργος *purgos*
MATT. 21:33; MARK 12:1; LUKE 13:4; 14:28

4445. πυρέσσω, πυρέττω
puressō, purettō
MATT. 8:14; MARK 1:30

4446. πυρετός *puretos*
MATT. 8:15; MARK 1:31; LUKE 4:38,39;
JOHN 4:52; ACTS 28:8

4447. πυρινός *purinos*
REV. 9:17

4448. πυρόω *puroō*
1 COR. 7:9; 2 COR. 11:29; EPH. 6:16; 2 PET.
3:12; REV. 1:15; 3:18

4449. πυρράζω *purrazō*
MATT. 16:2,3

4450. πυρρός *purros*
REV. 6:4; 12:3

4451. πύρωσις *purōsis*
1 PET. 4:12; REV. 18:9,18

4453. πωλέω *pōleō*
MATT. 10:29; 13:44; 19:21; 21:12; 25:9;
MARK 10:21; 11:15; LUKE 12:6,33; 17:28;
18:22; 19:45; 22:36; JOHN 2:14,16; ACTS
4:34,37; 5:1; 1 COR. 10:25; REV. 13:17

4454. πῶλος *pōlos*
MATT. 21:2,5,7; MARK 11:2,4,5,7; LUKE
19:30,33,35; JOHN 12:15

4455. πώποτε *pōpote*
LUKE 19:30; JOHN 1:18; 5:37; 6:35; 8:33;
1 JOHN 4:12

4456. πωρόω *pōroō*
MARK 6:52; 8:17; JOHN 12:40; ROM. 11:7;
2 COR. 3:14

4457. πώρωσις *pōrōsis*
MARK 3:5; ROM. 11:25; EPH. 4:18

4458. πώς *pōs* enclitic particle
ACTS 27:12,29; ROM. 1:10; 11:14,21; 1 COR.
8:9; 9:27; 2 COR. 2:7; 9:4; 11:3; 12:20; GAL.
2:2; 4:11; PHIL. 3:11; 1 THESS. 3:5

4459. πῶς *pōs* inter. particle
MATT. 6:28; 7:4; 10:19; 12:4,26,29,34; 16:11;
21:20; 22:12,43,45; 23:33; 26:54; MARK 2:26;
3:23; 4:13,40; 5:16; 8:21; 9:12; 10:23,24; 11:18;
12:35,41; 14:1,11; LUKE 1:34; 6:42; 8:18,36;
10:26; 11:18; 12:11,27,50,56; 14:7; 18:24; 20:41,
44; 22:2,4; JOHN 3:4,9,12; 4:9; 5:44,47; 6:42,
52; 7:15; 8:33; 9:10,15,16,19,21,26; 11:36;
12:34; 14:5,9; ACTS 2:8; 4:21; 8:31; 9:27;
11:13; 12:17; 15:36; 20:18; ROM. 3:6; 4:10; 6:2;
8:32; 10:14,15; 1 COR. 3:10; 7:32-34; 14:7,9,16;
15:12,35; 2 COR. 3:8; GAL. 4:9; EPH. 5:15;
COL. 4:6; 1 THESS. 1:9; 4:1; 2 THESS. 3:7;
1 TIM. 3:5,13; HEB. 2:3; 1 JOHN 3:17; 4:20;
REV. 3:3

P

4460. Ῥαάβ *Rhaab*
HEB. 11:31; JAMES 2:25

4461. ῥαββί *rhabbi*
MATT. 23:7,8; 26:25,49; MARK 9:5; 11:21;
14:45; JOHN 1:38,49; 3:2,26; 4:31; 6:25; 9:2;
11:8

4462. ῥαββονί, ῥαββουνί
rhabboni, rhabbouni
MARK 10:51; JOHN 20:16

4463. ῥαβδίζω *rhabdizō*
ACTS 16:22; 2 COR. 11:25

4464. ῥάβδος *rhabdos*
MATT. 10:10; MARK 6:8; LUKE 9:3; 1 COR.
4:21; HEB. 1:8; 9:4; 11:21; REV. 2:27; 11:1;
12:5; 19:15

4465. ῥαβδοῦχος *rhabdouchos*
ACTS 16:35,38

4466. Ῥαγαῦ *Rhagau*
LUKE 3:35

4467. ῥαδιούργημα *rhadiourgēma*
ACTS 18:4

4468. ῥαδιουργία *rhadiourgia*
ACTS 13:10

4469. ῥακά *rhaka*
MATT. 5:22

4470. ῥάκος *rhakos*
MATT. 9:16; MARK 2:21

4471. Ῥαμά *Rhama*
MATT. 2:18

4472. ῥαντίζω *rhantizō*
HEB. 9:13,19,21; 10:22

4473. ῥαντισμός *rhantismos*
HEB. 12:24; 1 PET. 1:2

4474. ῥαπίζω *rhapizō*
MATT. 5:39; 26:67

4475. ῥάπισμα *rhapisma*
MARK 14:65; JOHN 18:22; 19:3

4476. ῥαφίς *rhaphis*
MATT. 19:24; MARK 10:25; LUKE 18:25

4477. Ῥαχάβ *Rhachab*
MATT. 1:5

4478. Ῥαχήλ *Rhachēl*
MATT. 2:18

4479. Ῥεβέκκα *Rhebekka*
ROM. 9:10

4480. ῥέδα *rheda*
REV. 18:13

4481. Ῥεμφάν, Ῥεφάν
Rhemphan, Rhephan
ACTS 7:43

4482. ῥέω *rheō*
JOHN 7:38

4483. ῥέω *rheō*
(Obs. theme of ἐρέω)
MATT. 1:22; 2:15,17,23; 3:3; 4:14; 5:21,27,
31,33,38,43; 8:17; 12:17; 13:35; 21:4; 22:31;
24:15; 27:9,35; MARK 13:14; ROM. 9:12,26;
GAL. 3:16; REV. 6:11; 9:4

4484. Ῥήγιον *Rhēgion*
ACTS 28:13

4485. ῥῆγμα *rhēgma*
LUKE 6:49

4486. I. ῥήγνυμι *rhēgnumi*
MATT. 7:6; 9:17; LUKE 5:37; 9:42;
GAL. 4:27

II. ῥήσσω *rhēssō*
MARK 2:22; 9:18

4487. ῥῆμα *rhēma*
MATT. 4:4; 5:11; 12:36; 18:16; 26:75; 27:14;
MARK 9:32; 14:72; LUKE 1:37,38,65; 2:15,
17,19,29,50,51; 3:2; 4:4; 5:5; 7:1; 9:45; 18:34;
20:26; 24:8,11; JOHN 3:34; 5:47; 6:63,68; 8:20,
47; 10:21; 12:47,48; 14:10; 15:7; 17:8; ACTS
2:14; 5:20,32; 6:11,13; 10:22,37,44; 11:14,16;
13:42; 16:38; 26:25; 28:25; ROM. 10:8,17,18;
2 COR. 12:4; 13:1; EPH. 5:26; 6:17; HEB. 1:3;
6:5; 11:3; 12:19; 1 PET. 1:25; 2 PET. 3:2;
JUDE 1:17; REV. 17:17

4488. Ῥησά *Rhēsa*
LUKE 3:27

4489. ῥήτωρ *rhētōr*
ACTS 24:1

4490. ῥητῶς *rhētōs*
1 TIM. 4:1

4491. ῥίζα *rhiza*
MATT. 3:10; 13:6,21; MARK 4:6,17; 11:20;
LUKE 3:9; 8:13; ROM. 11:16,17,18; 15:12;
1 TIM. 6:10; HEB. 12:15; REV. 5:5; 22:16

4492. ῥιζόω *rhizoō*
EPH. 3:17; COL. 2:7

4493. ῥιπή *rhipē*
1 COR. 15:52

4494. ῥιπίζω *rhipizō*
JAMES 1:6

4495. ῥιπτέω *rhipteō*
ACTS 22:23

4496. ῥίπτω *rhiptō*
MATT. 9:36; 15:30; 27:5; LUKE 4:35; 17:2;
ACTS 27:19,29

4497. Ῥοβοάμ *Rhoboam*
MATT. 1:7

4498. Ῥόδη *Rhodē*
ACTS 12:13

4499. Ῥόδος Rhodos
ACTS 21:1

4500. ῥοιζηδόν rhoizēdon
2 PET. 3:10

4501. ῥομφαία rhomphaia
LUKE 2:35; REV. 1:16; 2:12,16; 6:8; 19:15,21

4502. Ῥουβήν Rhoubēn
REV. 7:5

4503. Ῥούθ Rhouth
MATT. 1:5

4504. Ῥοῦφος Rhouphos
MARK 15:21; ROM. 16:13

4505. ῥύμη rhumē
MATT. 6:2; LK 14:21; ACTS 9:11; 12:10

4506. ῥύομαι rhuomai
MATT. 6:13; 27:43; LUKE 1:74; 11:4; ROM.
7:24; 11:26; 15:31; 2 COR. 1:10; COL. 1:13;
1 THESS. 1:10; 2 THESS. 3:2; 2 TIM. 3:11;
4:17,18; 2 PET. 2:7,9

4507. ῥυπαρία rhuparia
JAMES 1:21

4508. ῥυπαρός rhuparos
JAMES 2:2

4509. ῥύπος rhupos
1 PET. 3:21

4510. ῥυπόω rhupoō
REV. 22:11

4511. ῥύσις rhusis
MARK 5:25; LUKE 8:43,44

4512. ῥυτίς rhutis
EPH. 5:27

4513. Ῥωμαϊκός Rhōmaikos
LUKE 23:38

4514. Ῥωμαῖος Rhōmaios
JOHN 11:48; ACTS 2:10; 16:21,37,38; 22:25-
27,29; 23:27; 25:16; 28:17

4515. Ῥωμαϊστί Rhōmaisti
JOHN 19:20

4516. Ῥώμη Rhōmē
ACTS 18:2; 19:21; 23:11; 28:14,16; ROM.
1:7,15; 2 TIM. 1:17

4517. ῥώννυμι rhōnnumai
ACTS 15:29; 23:30

Σ

4518. σαβαχθανί sabachthani
MATT. 27:46; MARK 15:34

4519. σαβαώθ sabaōth
ROM. 9:29; JAMES 5:4

4520. σαββατισμός sabbatismos
HEB. 4:9

4521. σάββατον sabbaton
MATT. 12:1,2,5,8,10-12; 24:20; 28:1; MARK
1:21; 2:23,24,27,28; 3:2,4; 6:2; 16:1,2,9; LUKE
4:16,31; 6:1,2,5-7,9; 13:10,14-16; 14:1,3,5;
18:12; 23:54,56; 24:1; JOHN 5:9,10,16,18;
7:22,23; 9:14,16; 19:31; 20:1,19; ACTS 1:12;
13:14,27,42,44; 15:21; 16:13; 17:2; 18:4; 20:7;
1 COR. 16:2; COL. 2:16

4522. σαγήνη sagēnē
MATT. 13:47

4523. Σαδδουκαῖος Saddoukaios
MATT. 3:7; 16:1,6,11,12; 22:23,34; MARK
12:18; LUKE 20:27; ACTS 4:1; 5:17; 23:6-8

4524. Σαδώκ Sadōk
MATT. 1:14

4525. σαίνω sainō
1 THESS. 3:3

4526. σάκκος *sakkos*
MATT. 11:21; LUKE 10:13; REV. 6:12; 11:3

4527. Σαλά *Sala*
LUKE 3:35

4528. Σαλαθιήλ *Salathiēl*
MATT. 1:12; LUKE 3:27

4529. Σαλαμίς *Salamis*
ACTS 13:5

4530. Σαλείμ *Saleim*
JOHN 3:23

4531. σαλεύω *saleuō*
MATT. 11:7; 24:29; MARK 13:25; LUKE 6:38,48; 7:24; 21:26; ACTS 2:25; 4:31; 16:26; 17:13; 2 THESS. 2:2; HEB. 12:26,27

4532. Σαλήμ *Salēm*
HEB. 7:1,2

4533. Σαλμών *Salmōn*
MATT. 1:4,5; LUKE 3:32

4534. Σαλμώνη *Salmōnē*
ACTS 27:7

4535. σάλος *salos*
LUKE 21:25

4536. σάλπιγξ *salpigx*
MATT. 24:31; 1 COR. 14:8; 15:52; 1 THESS. 4:16; HEB. 12:19; REV. 1:10; 4:1; 8:2,6,13; 9:14

4537. σαλπίζω *salpizō*
MATT. 6:2; 1 COR. 15:52; REV. 8:6-8,10,12,13; 9:1,13; 10:7; 11:15

4538. σαλπιστής *salpistēs*
REV. 18:22

4539. Σαλώμη *Salōmē*
MARK 15:40; 16:1

4540. Σαμάρεια *Samareia*
LUKE 17:11; JOHN 4:4,5,7; ACTS 1:8; 8:1,5,9,14; 9:31; 15:3

4541. Σαμαρείτης *Samareitēs*
MATT. 10:5; LUKE 9:52; 10:33; 17:16; JOHN 4:9,39,40; 8:48; ACTS 8:25

4542. Σαμαρεῖτις *Samareitis*
JOHN 4:9

4543. Σαμοθράκη *Samothrakē*
ACTS 16:11

4544. Σάμος *Samos*
ACTS 20:15

4545. Σαμουήλ *Samouēl*
ACTS 3:24; 13:20; HEB. 11:32

4546. Σαμψών *Sampsōn*
HEB. 11:32

4547. σανδάλιον *sandalion*
MARK 6:9; ACTS 12:8

4548. σανίς *sanis*
ACTS 27:44

4549. Σαούλ *Saoul*
ACTS 9:4,17; 13:21; 22:7,13; 26:14

4550. σαπρός *sapros*
MATT. 7:17,18; 12:33; 13:48; LUKE 6:43; EPH. 4:29

4551. Σαπφείρη *Sappheirē*
ACTS 5:1

4552. σάπφειρος *sappheiros*
REV. 21:19

4553. σαργάνη *sarganē*
2 COR. 11:33

4554. Σάρδεις *Sardeis*
REV. 1:11; 3:1,4

4555. σάρδινος *sardinos*
REV. 4:3

4556. σάρδιος *sardios*
REV. 21:20

4557. σαρδόνυξ *sardonux*
REV. 21:20

4558. Σάρεπτα *Sarepta*
LUKE 4:26

4559. σαρκικός *sarkikos*
ROM. 7:14; 15:27; **1 COR.** 3:1,3,4; 9:11;
2 COR. 1:12; 10:4; **HEB.** 7:16; **1 PET.** 2:11

4560. σάρκινος *sarkinos*
2 COR. 3:3

4561. σάρξ *sarx*
MATT. 16:17; 19:5,6; 24:22; 26:41; **MARK**
10:8; 13:20; 14:38; **LUKE** 3:6; 24:39; **JOHN**
1:13,14; 3:6; 6:51-56,63; 8:15; 17:2; **ACTS**
2:17,26,30,31; **ROM.** 1:3; 2:28; 3:20; 4:1; 6:19;
7:5,18,25; 8:1,3-9,12,13; 9:3,5,8; 11:14; 13:14;
1 COR. 1:26,29; 5:5; 6:16; 7:28; 10:18; 15:39,
50; **2 COR.** 1:17; 4:11; 5:16; 7:1,5; 10:2,3;
11:18; 12:7; **GAL.** 1:16; 2:16,20; 3:3; 4:13,14,
23,29; 5:13,16,17,19,24; 6:8,12,13; **EPH.**
2:3,11,15; 5:29-31; 6:5,12; **PHIL.** 1:22,24; 3:3,4;
COL. 1:22,24; 2:1,5,11,13,18,23; 3:22; **1 TIM.**
3:16; **PHILE.** 1:16; **HEB.** 2:14; 5:7; 9:10,13;
10:20; 12:9; **JAMES** 5:3; **1 PET.** 1:24; 3:18,21;
4:1,2,6; **2 PET.** 2:10,18; **1 JOHN** 2:16; 4:2,3;
2 JOHN 1:7; **JUDE** 1:7,8,23; **REV.** 17:16;
19:18,21

4562. Σαρούχ *Sarouch*
LUKE 3:35

4563. σαρόω *saroō*
MATT. 12:44; **LUKE** 11:25; 15:8

4564. Σάρρα *Sarra*
ROM. 4:19; 9:9; **HEB.** 11:11; **1 PET.** 3:6

4565. Σάρων *Sarōn*
ACTS 9:35

4566. Σατᾶν *Satan*
2 COR. 12:7

4567. Σατανᾶς *Satanas*
MATT. 4:10; 12:26; 16:23; **MARK** 1:13;
3:23,26; 4:15; 8:33; **LUKE** 4:8; 10:18; 11:18;
13:16; 22:3,31; **JOHN** 13:27; **ACTS** 5:3; 26:18;
ROM. 16:20; **1 COR.** 5:5; 7:5; **2 COR.** 2:11;
11:14; **1 THESS.** 2:18; **2 THESS.** 2:9; **1 TIM.**
1:20; 5:15; **REV.** 2:9,13,24; 3:9; 12:9; 20:2,7

4568. σάτον *saton*
MATT. 13:33; **LUKE** 13:21

4569. Σαῦλος *Saulos*
ACTS 7:58; 8:1,3; 9:1,8,11,19,22,24,26;
11:25,30; 12:25; 13:1,2,7,9

4570. σβέννυμι *sbennumi*
MATT. 12:20; 25:8; **MARK** 9:44,46,48; **EPH.**
6:16; **1 THESS.** 5:19; **HEB.** 11:34

4573. σεβάζομαι *sebazomai*
ROM. 1:25

4574. σέβασμα *sebasma*
ACTS 17:23; **2 THESS.** 2:4

4575. σεβαστός *sebastos*
ACTS 25:21,25; 27:1

4576. σέβομαι *sebomai*
MATT. 15:9; **MARK** 7:7; **ACTS** 13:43,50;
16:14; 17:4,17; 18:7,13; 19:27

4577. σειρά *seira*
2 PET. 2:4

4578. σεισμός *seismos*
MATT. 8:24; 24:7; 27:54; 28:2; **MARK** 13:8;
LUKE 21:11; **ACTS** 16:26; **REV.** 6:12; 8:5;
11:13,19; 16:18

4579. σείω *seiō*
MATT. 21:10; 27:51; 28:4; **HEB.** 12:26; **REV.**
6:13

4580. Σεκοῦνδος *Sekoundos*
ACTS 20:4

4581. Σελεύχεια Seleukeia
ACTS 13:4

4582. σελήνη selēnē
MATT. 24:29; MARK 13:24; LUKE 21:25;
ACTS 2:20; 1 COR. 15:41; REV. 6:12; 8:12;
12:1; 21:23

4583. σεληνιάζομαι selēniazomai
MATT. 4:24; 17:15

4584. Σεμεῖ Semei
LUKE 3:26

4585. σεμίδαλις semidalis
REV. 18:13

4586. σεμνός semnos
PHIL. 4:8; 1 TIM. 3:8,11; TITUS 2:2

4587. σεμνότης semnotēs
1 TIM. 2:2; 3:4; TITUS 2:7

4588. Σέργιος Sergios
ACTS 13:7

4589. Σήθ Sēth
LUKE 3:38

4590. Σήμ Sēm
LUKE 3:36

4591. σημαίνω sēmainō
JOHN 12:33; 18:32; 21:19; ACTS 11:28; 25:27;
REV. 1:1

4592. σημεῖον sēmeion
MATT. 12:38,39; 16:1,3,4; MATT. 24:3,24,30;
26:48; MARK 8:11,12; 13:4,22; 16:17,20;
LUKE 2:12,34; 11:16,29,30; 21:7,11,25; 23:8;
JOHN 2:11,18,23; 3:2; 4:48,54; 6:2,14,26,30;
7:31; 9:16; 10:41; 11:47; 12:18,37; 20:30; ACTS
2:19,22,43; 4:16,22,30; 5:12; 6:8; 7:36; 8:6,13;
14:3; 15:12; ROM. 4:11; 15:19; 1 COR. 1:22;
14:22; 2 COR. 12:12; 2 THESS. 2:9; 3:17;
HEB. 2:4; REV. 12:1,3; 13:13,14; 15:1; 16:14;
19:20

4593. σημειόω sēmeioō
2 THESS. 3:14

4594. σήμερον sēmeron
MATT. 6:11,30; 11:23; 16:3; 21:28; 27:8,19;
28:15; MARK 14:30; LUKE 2:11; 4:21; 5:26;
12:28; 13:32,33; 19:5,9; 22:34; 23:43; 24:21;
ACTS 4:9; 13:33; 19:40; 20:26; 22:3; 24:21;
26:2,29; 27:33; ROM. 11:8; 2 COR. 3:14,15;
HEB. 1:5; 3:7,13,15; 4:7; 5:5; 13:8; JAMES
4:13

4595. σήπω sēpō
JAMES 5:2

4596. σηριχός sērikos subst.
REV. 18:12

4597. σής sēs
MATT. 6:19,20; LUKE 12:33

4598. σητόβρωτος sētobrōtos
JAMES 5:2

4599. σθενόω sthenoō
1 PET. 5:10

4600. σιαγών siagōn
MATT. 5:39; LUKE 6:29

4601. σιγάω sigaō
LUKE 9:36; 20:26; ACTS 12:17; 15:12,13;
ROM. 16:25; 1 COR. 14:28,30,34

4602. σιγή sigē
ACTS 21:40; REV. 8:1

4603. σιδήρεος sidēreos
ACTS 12:10; REV. 2:27; 9:9; 12:5; 19:15

4604. σίδηρος sidēros
REV. 18:12

4605. Σιδών Sidōn
MATT. 11:21,22; 15:21; MARK 3:8; 7:24,31;
LUKE 4:26; 6:17; 10:13,14; ACTS 27:3

4606. Σιδώνιος Sidōnios
LUKE 4:26; ACTS 12:20

4607. σικάριος *sikarios*
ACTS 21:38

4608. σίκερα *sikera*
LUKE 1:15

4609. Σίλας *Silas*
ACTS 15:22,27,32,34,40; 16:19,25,29;
17:4,10,14,15; 18:5

4610. Σιλουανός *Silouanos*
2 COR. 1:19; **1 THESS.** 1:1; **2 THESS.** 1:1;
1 PET. 5:12

4611. Σιλωάμ *Siloam*
LUKE 13:4; JOHN 9:7,11

4612. σιμικίνθιον *simikinthion*
ACTS 19:12

4613. Σίμων *Simōn*
MATT. 4:18; 10:2,4; 13:55; 16:16,17; 17:25;
26:6; 27:32; **MARK** 1:16,29,30,36; 3:16,18; 6:3;
14:3,37; 15:21; **LUKE** 4:38; 5:3-5,8,10; 6:14,15;
7:40,43,44; 22:31; 23:26; 24:34; **JOHN** 1:40-42;
6:8,68,71; 12:4; 13:2,6,9,24,26,36; 18:10,15,25;
20:2,6; 21:2,3,7,11,15-17; **ACTS** 1:13; 8:9,13,
18,24; 9:43; 10:5,6,17,18,32; 11:13

4614. Σινᾶ *Sina*
ACTS 7:30,38; GAL. 4:24,25

4615. σίναπι *sinapi*
MATT. 13:31; 17:20; **MARK** 4:31; **LUKE**
13:19; 17:6

4616. σινδών *sindōn*
MATT. 27:59; **MARK** 14:51,52; 15:46; **LUKE**
23:53

4617. σινιάζω *siniazō*
LUKE 22:31

4618. σιτευτός *siteutos*
LUKE 15:23,27,30

4619. σιτιστός *sitistos*
MATT. 22:4

4620. σιτομέτριον *sitometrion*
LUKE 12:42

4621. σῖτος *sitos*
MATT. 3:12; 13:25,29,30; **MARK** 4:28;
LUKE 3:17; 16:7; 22:31; JOHN 12:24;
ACTS 7:12; 27:38; **1 COR.** 15:37; **REV.** 6:6;
18:13

4622. Σιών *Siōn*
MATT. 21:5; JOHN 12:15; **ROM.** 9:33; 11:26;
HEB. 12:22; **1 PET.** 2:6; **REV.** 14:1

4623. σιωπάω *siōpaō*
MATT. 20:31; 26:63; **MARK** 3:4; 4:39; 9:34;
10:48; 14:61; **LUKE** 1:20; 18:39; 19:40; **ACTS**
18:9

4624. σκανδαλίζω *skandalizō*
MATT. 5:29,30; 11:6; 13:21,57; 15:12; 17:27;
18:6,8,9; 24:10; 26:31,33; **MARK** 4:17; 6:3;
9:42,43,45,47; 14:27,29; **LUKE** 7:23; 17:2;
JOHN 6:61; 16:1; **ROM.** 14:21; **1 COR.** 8:13;
2 COR. 11:29

4625. σκάνδαλον *skandalon*
MATT. 13:41; 16:23; 18:7; **LUKE** 17:1;
ROM. 9:33; 11:9; 14:13; 16:17; **1 COR.** 1:23;
GAL. 5:11; **1 PET.** 2:8; **1 JOHN** 2:10; **REV.**
2:14

4626. σκάπτω *skaptō*
LUKE 6:48; 13:8; 16:3

4627. σκάφη *skaphē*
ACTS 27:16,30,32

4628. σκέλος *skelos*
JOHN 19:31-33

4629. σκέπασμα *skepasma*
1 TIM. 6:8

4630. Σκευᾶς *Skeuas*
ACTS 19:14

4631. σκευή *skeuē*
ACTS 27:19

4632. σκεῦος skeuos
MATT. 12:29; MARK 3:27; 11:16; LUKE
8:16; 17:31; JOHN 19:29; ACTS 9:15; 10:11,
16; 11:5; 27:17; ROM. 9:21-23; 2 COR. 4:7;
1 THESS. 4:4; 2 TIM. 2:20,21; HEB. 9:21;
1 PET. 3:7; REV. 2:27; 18:12

4633. σκηνή skēnē
MATT. 17:4; MARK 9:5; LUKE 9:33; 16:9;
ACTS 7:43,44; 15:16; HEB. 8:2,5; 9:1-3,6,8,11,
21; 11:9; 13:10; REV. 13:6; 15:5; 21:3

4634. σκηνοπηγία skēnopēgia
JOHN 7:2

4635. σκηνοποιός skēnopoios
ACTS 18:3

4636. σκῆνος skēnos
2 COR. 5:1,4

4637. σκηνόω skēnoō
JOHN 1:14; REV. 7:15; 12:12; 13:6; 21:3

4638. σκήνωμα skēnōma
ACTS 7:46; 2 PET. 1:13,14

4639. σκία skia
MATT. 4:16; MARK 4:32; LUKE 1:79; ACTS
5:15; COL. 2:17; HEB. 8:5; 10:1

4640. σκιρτάω skirtaō
LUKE 1:41,44; 6:23

4641. σκληροκαρδία sklērokardia
MATT. 19:8; MARK 10:5; 16:14

4642. σκληρός sklēros
MATT. 25:24; JOHN 6:60; ACTS 9:5; 26:14;
JAMES 3:4; JUDE 1:15

4643. σκληρότης sklērotēs
ROM. 2:5

**4644. σκληροτράχηλος
sklērotrachēlos**
ACTS 7:51

4645. σκληρύνω sklērunō
ACTS 19:9; ROM. 9:18; HEB. 3:8,13,15; 4:7

4646. σκολιός skolios
LUKE 3:5; ACTS 2:40; PHIL. 2:15; 1 PET.
2:18

4647. σκόλοψ skolops
2 COR. 12:7

4648. σκοπέω skopeō
LUKE 11:35; ROM. 16:17; 2 COR. 4:18; GAL.
6:1; PHIL. 2:4; 3:17

4649. σκοπός skopos
PHIL. 3:14

4650. σκορπίζω skorpizō
MATT. 12:30; LUKE 11:23; JOHN 10:12;
16:32; 2 COR. 9:9

4651. σκορπίος skorpios
LUKE 10:19; 11:12; REV. 9:3,5,10

4652. σκοτεινός skoteinos
MATT. 6:23; LUKE 11:34,36

4653. σκοτία skotia
MATT. 10:27; LUKE 12:3; JOHN 1:5; 6:17;
8:12; 12:35,46; 20:1; 1 JOHN 1:5; 2:8,9,11

4654. σκοτίζω skotizō
MATT. 24:29; MARK 13:24; LUKE 23:45;
ROM. 1:21; 11:10; EPH. 4:18; REV. 8:12;
9:2

4655. σκότος skotos
MATT. 4:16; 6:23; 8:12; 22:13; 25:30; 27:45;
MARK 15:33; LUKE 1:79; 11:35; 22:53; 23:44;
JOHN 3:19; ACTS 2:20; 13:11; 26:18; ROM.
2:19; 13:12; 1 COR. 4:5; 2 COR. 4:6; 6:14;
EPH. 5:8,11; 6:12; COL. 1:13; 1 THESS. 5:4,5;
HEB. 12:18; 1 PET. 2:9; 2 PET. 2:17; 1 JOHN
1:6; JUDE 1:13

4656. σκοτόω skotoō
REV. 16:10

4657. σκύβαλον *skubalon*
PHIL. 3:8

4658. Σκύθης *Skuthēs*
COL. 3:11

4659. σκυθρωπός *skuthrōpos*
MATT. 6:16; LUKE 24:17

4660. σκύλλω *skullō*
MARK 5:35; LUKE 7:6; 8:49

4661. σκῦλον *skulon*
LUKE 11:22

4662. σκωληκόβρωτος *skōlēkobrōtos*
ACTS 12:23

4663. σκώληξ *skōlēx*
MARK 9:44,46,48

4664. σμαράγδινος *smaragdinos*
REV. 4:3

4665. σμάραγδος *smaragdos*
REV. 21:19

4666. σμύρνα *smurna*
MATT. 2:11; JOHN 19:39

4667. Σμύρνα *Smurna*
REV. 1:11

4668. Σμυρναῖος *Smurnaios*
REV. 2:8

4669. σμυρνίζω *smurnizō*
MARK 15:23

4670. Σόδομα *Sodoma*
MATT. 10:15; 11:23,24; MARK 6:11; LUKE 10:12; 17:29; ROM. 9:29; 2 PET. 2:6; JUDE 1:7; REV. 11:8

4672. Σολομών *Solomōn*
MATT. 1:6,7; 6:29; 12:42; LUKE 11:31; 12:27; JOHN 10:23; ACTS 3:11; 5:12; 7:47

4673. σορός *soros*
LUKE 7:14

4674. σός *sos*
MATT. 7:3,22; 13:27; 20:14; 24:3; 25:25; MARK 2:18; 5:19; LUKE 5:33; 6:30; 15:31; 22:42; JOHN 4:42; 17:6,9,10,17; 18:35; ACTS 5:4; 24:2,4; 1 COR. 8:11; 14:16; PHILE. 1:14

4676. σουδάριον *soudarion*
LUKE 19:20; JOHN 11:44; 20:7; ACTS 19:12

4677. Σουσάννα *Sousanna*
LUKE 8:3

4678. σοφία *sophia*
MATT. 11:19; 12:42; 13:54; MARK 6:2; LUKE 2:40,52; 7:35; 11:31,49; 21:15; ACTS 6:3,10; 7:10,22; ROM. 11:33; 1 COR. 1:17,19-22,24,30; 2:1,4-7,13; 3:19; 12:8; 2 COR. 1:12; EPH. 1:8,17; 3:10; COL. 1:9,28; 2:3,23; 3:16; 4:5; JAMES 1:5; 3:13,15,17; 2 PET. 3:15; REV. 5:12; 7:12; 13:18; 17:9

4679. σοφίζω *sophizō*
2 TIM. 3:15; 2 PET. 1:16

4680. σοφός *sophos*
MATT. 11:25; 23:34; LUKE 10:21; ROM. 1:14,22; 16:19,27; 1 COR. 1:19,20,25-27; 3:10,18-20; 6:5; EPH. 5:15; 1 TIM. 1:17; JAMES 3:13; JUDE 1:25

4681. Σπανία *Spania*
ROM. 15:24,28

4682. σπαράσσω, σπαράττω
 sparassō, sparattō
MARK 1:26; 9:20; LUKE 9:39

4683. σπαργανόω *sparganoō*
LUKE 2:7,12

4684. σπαταλάω *spatalaō*
1 TIM. 5:6; JAMES 5:5

4685. σπάω *spaō*
MARK 14:47; ACTS 16:27

4686. σπεῖρα *speira*
MATT. 27:27; MARK 15:16; JOHN 18:3,12;
ACTS 10:1; 21:31; 27:1

4687. σπείρω *speirō*
MATT. 6:26; 13:3,4,18-20,22-25,27,31,37,39;
25:24,26; MARK 4:3,4,14-16,18,20,31,32;
LUKE 8:5; 12:24; 19:21,22; JOHN 4:36,37;
1 COR. 9:11; 15:36,37,42-44; 2 COR. 9:6,10;
GAL. 6:7,8; JAMES 3:18

4688. σπεκουλάτωρ *spekoulatōr*
MARK 6:27

4689. σπένδω *spendō*
PHIL. 2:17; 2 TIM. 4:6

4690. σπέρμα *sperma*
MATT. 13:24,27,32,37,38; 22:24,25; MARK
4:31; 12:19-22; LUKE 1:55; 20:28; JOHN 7:42;
8:33,37; ACTS 3:25; 7:5,6; 13:23; ROM. 1:3;
4:13,16,18; 9:7,8,29; 11:1; 1 COR. 15:38;
2 COR. 9:10; 11:22; GAL. 3:16,19,29; 2 TIM.
2:8; HEB. 2:16; 11:11,18; 1 JOHN 3:9; REV.
12:17

4691. σπερμολόγος *spermologos*
ACTS 17:18

4692. σπεύδω *speudō*
LUKE 2:16; 19:5,6; ACTS 20:16; 22:18;
2 PET. 3:12

4693. σπήλαιον *spēlaion*
MATT. 21:13; MARK 11:17; LUKE 19:46;
JOHN 11:38; HEB. 11:38; REV. 6:15

4694. σπιλάς *spilas*
JUDE 1:12

4695. σπιλόω *spiloō*
JAMES 3:6; JUDE 1:23

4696. σπῖλος *spilos*
EPH. 5:27; 2 PET. 2:13

4697. σπλαγχνίζομαι *splagchnizomai*
MATT. 9:36; 14:14; 15:32; 18:27; 20:34;
MARK 1:41; 6:34; 8:2; 9:22; LUKE 7:13;
10:33; 15:20

4698. σπλάγχνον *splagchnon*
LUKE 1:78; ACTS 1:18; 2 COR. 6:12; 7:15;
PHIL. 1:8; 2:1; COL. 3:12; PHILE. 1:7,12,20;
1 JOHN 3:17

4699. σπόγγος *spoggos*
MATT. 27:48; MARK 15:36; JOHN 19:29

4700. σποδός *spodos*
MATT. 11:21; LUKE 10:13; HEB. 9:13

4701. σπορά *spora*
1 PET. 1:23

4702. σπόριμος *sporimos*
MATT. 12:1; MARK 2:23; LUKE 6:1

4703. σπόρος *sporos*
MARK 4:26,27; LUKE 8:5,11; 2 COR. 9:10

4704. σπουδάζω *spoudazō*
GAL. 2:10; EPH. 4:3; 1 THESS. 2:17; 2 TIM.
2:15; 4:9,21; TITUS 3:12; HEB. 4:11; 2 PET.
1:10,15; 3:14

4705. σπουδαῖος *spoudaios*
2 COR. 8:22

4706. σπουδαιότερον
  spoudaioteron adv.
2 COR. 8:22; 2 TIM. 1:17

4707. σπουδαιότερος *spoudaioteros*
2 COR. 8:17,22

4708. σπουδαιοτέρως *spoudaioterōs*
PHIL. 2:28

4709. σπουδαίως *spoudaiōs*
LUKE 7:4; TITUS 3:13

4710. σπουδή *spoudē*
MARK 6:25; LUKE 1:39; ROM. 12:8,11;
2 COR. 7:11,12; 8:7,8,16; HEB. 6:11; 2 PET.
1:5; JUDE 1:3

4711. σπυρίς *spuris*
MATT. 15:37; 16:10; MARK 8:8,20; ACTS
9:25

4712. στάδιος *stadios*
MATT. 14:24 WH; **LUKE** 24:13; **JOHN** 6:19;
11:18; **1 COR.** 9:24; **REV.** 14:20; 21:16

4713. στάμνος *stamnos*
HEB. 9:4

4714. στάσις *stasis*
MARK 15:7; **LUKE** 23:19,25; **ACTS** 15:2;
19:40; 23:7,10; 24:5; **HEB.** 9:8

4715. στατήρ *statēr*
MATT. 17:27

4716. σταυρός *stauros*
MATT. 10:38; 16:24; 27:32,40,42; **MARK**
8:34; 10:21; 15:21,30,32; **LUKE** 9:23; 14:27;
23:26; **JOHN** 19:17,19,25,31; **1 COR.** 1:17,18;
GAL. 5:11; 6:12,14; **EPH.** 2:16; **PHIL.** 2:8;
3:18; **COL.** 1:20; 2:14; **HEB.** 12:2

4717. σταυρόω *stauroō*
MATT. 20:19; 23:34; 26:2;
27:22,23,26,31,35,38; 28:5; **MARK** 15:13-
15,20,24,25,27; 16:6; **LUKE** 23:21,23,33;
24:7,20; **JOHN** 19:6,10,15,16,18,20,23,41;
ACTS 2:36; 4:10; **1 COR.** 1:13,23; 2:2,8;
2 COR. 13:4; **GAL.** 3:1; 5:24; 6:14; **REV.**
11:8

4718. σταφυλή *staphulē*
MATT. 7:16; **LUKE** 6:44; **REV.** 14:18

4719. στάχυς *stachus*
MATT. 12:1; **MARK** 2:23; 4:28; **LUKE** 6:1

4720. Στάχυς *Stachus*
ROM. 16:9

4721. στέγη *stegē*
MATT. 8:8; **MARK** 2:4; **LUKE** 7:6

4722. στέγω *stegō*
1 COR. 9:12; 13:7; **1 THESS.** 3:1,5

4723. στεῖρος *steiros*
LUKE 1:7,36; 23:29; **GAL.** 4:27

4724. στέλλω *stellō*
2 COR. 8:20; **2 THESS.** 3:6

4725. στέμμα *stemma*
ACTS 14:13

4726. στεναγμός *stenagmos*
ACTS 7:34; **ROM.** 8:26

4727. στενάζω *stenazō*
MARK 7:34; **ROM.** 8:23; **2 COR.** 5:2,4; **HEB.**
13:17; **JAMES** 5:9

4728. στενός *stenos*
MATT. 7:13,14; **LUKE** 13:24

4729. στενοχωρέω *stenochōreō*
2 COR. 4:8; 6:12

4730. στενοχωρία *stenochōria*
ROM. 2:9; 8:35; **2 COR.** 6:4; 12:10

4731. στερεός *stereos*
2 TIM. 2:19; **HEB.** 5:12,14; **1 PET.** 5:9

4732. στερεόω *stereoō*
ACTS 3:7,16; 16:5

4733. στερέωμα *stereōma*
COL. 2:5

4734. Στεφανᾶς *Stephanas*
1 COR. 1:16; 16:15,17

4735. στέφανος *stephanos*
MATT. 27:29; **MARK** 15:17; **JOHN** 19:2,5;
1 COR. 9:25; **PHIL.** 4:1; **1 THESS.** 2:19;
2 TIM. 4:8; **JAMES** 1:12; **1 PET.** 5:4; **REV.**
2:10; 3:11; 4:4,10; 6:2; 9:7; 12:1; 14:14

4736. Στέφανος *Stephanos*
ACTS 6:5,8,9; 7:59; 8:2; 11:19; 22:20

4737. στεφανόω *stephanoō*
2 TIM. 2:5; **HEB.** 2:7,9

4738. στῆθος *stēthos*
LUKE 18:13; 23:48; **JOHN** 13:25; 21:20; **REV.** 15:6

4739. στήκω *stēkō*
MARK 11:25; **ROM.** 14:4; **1 COR.** 16:13; **GAL.** 5:1; **PHIL.** 1:27; 4:1; **1 THESS.** 3:8; **2 THESS.** 2:15

4740. στηριγμός *stērigmos*
2 PET. 3:17

4741. στηρίζω *stērizō*
LUKE 9:51; 16:26; 22:32; **ROM.** 1:11; 16:25; **1 THESS.** 3:2,13; **2 THESS.** 2:17; 3:3; **JAMES** 5:8; **1 PET.** 5:10; **2 PET.** 1:12; **REV.** 3:2

4742. στίγμα *stigma*
GAL. 6:17

4743. στιγμή *stigmē*
LUKE 4:5

4744. στίλβω *stilbō*
MARK 9:3

4745. στοά *stoa*
JOHN 5:2; 10:23; **ACTS** 3:11; 5:12

4746. στοιβάς *stoibas*
MARK 11:8

4747. στοιχεῖον *stoicheion*
GAL. 4:3,9; **COL.** 2:8,20; **HEB.** 5:12; **2 PET.** 3:10,12

4748. στοιχέω *stoicheō*
ACTS 21:24; **ROM.** 4:12; **GAL.** 5:25; 6:16; **PHIL.** 3:16

4749. στολή *stolē*
MARK 12:38; 16:5; **LUKE** 15:22; 20:46; **REV.** 6:11; 7:9,13,14

4750. στόμα *stoma*
MATT. 4:4; 5:2; 12:34; 13:35; 15:8,11,17,18; 17:27; 18:16; 21:16; **LUKE** 1:64,70; 4:22; 6:45;

11:54; 19:22; 21:15,24; 22:71; **JOHN** 19:29; **ACTS** 1:16; 3:18,21; 4:25; 8:32,35; 10:34; 11:8; 15:7; 18:14; 22:14; 23:2; **ROM.** 3:14,19; 10:8-10; 15:6; **2 COR.** 6:11; 13:1; **EPH.** 4:29; 6:19; **COL.** 3:8; **2 THESS.** 2:8; **2 TIM.** 4:17; **HEB.** 11:33,34; **JAMES** 3:3,10; **1 PET.** 2:22; **2 JOHN** 1:12; **3 JOHN** 1:14; **JUDE** 1:16; **REV.** 1:16; 2:16; 3:16; 9:17-19; 10:9,10; 11:5; 12:15,16; 13:2,5,6; 14:5; 16:13; 19:15,21

4751. στόμαχος *stomachos*
1 TIM. 5:23

4752. στρατεία *strateia*
2 COR. 10:4; **1 TIM.** 1:18

4753. στράτευμα *strateuma*
MATT. 22:7; **LUKE** 23:11; **ACTS** 23:10,27; **REV.** 9:16; 19:14,19

4754. στρατεύομαι *strateuomai*
LUKE 3:14; **1 COR.** 9:7; **2 COR.** 10:3; **1 TIM.** 1:18; **2 TIM.** 2:4; **JAMES** 4:1; **1 PET.** 2:11

4755. στρατηγός *stratēgos*
LUKE 22:4,52; **ACTS** 4:1; 5:24,26; 16:20,22,35,36,38

4756. στρατία *stratia*
LUKE 2:13; **ACTS** 7:42

4757. στρατιώτης *stratiōtēs*
MATT. 8:9; 27:27; 28:12; **MARK** 15:16; **LUKE** 7:8; 23:36; **JOHN** 19:2,23,24,32,34; **ACTS** 10:7; 12:4,6,18; 21:32,35; 23:23,31; 27:31,32,42; 28:16; **2 TIM.** 2:3

4758. στρατολογέω *stratologeō*
2 TIM. 2:4

4759. στρατοπεδάρχης *stratopedarchēs*
ACTS 28:16

4760. στρατόπεδον *stratopedon*
LUKE 21:20

4761. στρεβλόω *strebloō*
2 PET. 3:16

4762. στρέφω *strephō*
MATT. 5:39; 7:6; 16:23; 18:3; LUKE 7:9,44;
9:55; 10:23; 14:25; 22:61; 23:28; JOHN 1:38;
20:14,16; ACTS 7:39,42; 13:46; REV. 11:6

4763. στρηνιάω *strēniaō*
REV. 18:7,9

4764. στρῆνος *strēnos*
REV. 18:3

4765. στρουθίον *strouthion*
MATT. 10:29,31; LUKE 12:6,7

4766. I. στρώννυμι *strōnnumi*
MARK 14:15; LUKE 22:12

II. στρωννύω *strōnnuō*
MATT. 21:8; MARK 11:8; ACTS 9:34

4767. στυγητός *stugētos*
TITUS 3:3

4768. στυγνάζω *stugnazō*
MATT. 16:3; MARK 10:22

4769. στύλος *stulos*
GAL. 2:9; 1 TIM. 3:15; REV. 3:12; 10:1

4770. Στωϊκός *Stōikos*
ACTS 17:18

4772. συγγένεια *suggeneia*
LUKE 1:61; ACTS 7:3,14

4773. συγγενής *suggenēs*
MARK 6:4; LUKE 1:36,58; 2:44; 14:12; 21:16;
JOHN 18:26; ACTS 10:24; ROM. 9:3;
16:7,11,21

4774. συγγνώμη *suggnōmē*
1 COR. 7:6

4775. συγκάθημαι *sugkathēmai*
MARK 14:54; ACTS 26:30

4776. συγκαθίζω *sugkathizō*
LUKE 22:55; EPH. 2:6

4777. συγκακοπαθέω *sugkakopatheō*
2 TIM. 1:8

4778. συγκακουχέω *sugkakoucheō*
HEB. 11:25

4779. συγκαλέω *sugkaleō*
MARK 15:16; LUKE 9:1; 15:6,9; 23:13; ACTS
5:21; 10:24; 28:17

4780. συγκαλύπτω *sugkaluptō*
LUKE 12:2

4781. συγκάμπτω *sugkamptō*
ROM. 11:10

4782. συγκαταβαίνω *sugkatabainō*
ACTS 25:5

4783. συγκατάθεσις *sugkatathesis*
2 COR. 6:16

4784. συγκατατίθεμαι
sugkatatithemai
LUKE 23:51

4785. συγκαταψηφίζω
sugkatapsēphizō
ACTS 1:26

4786. συγκεράννυμι *sugkerannumi*
1 COR. 12:24; HEB. 4:2

4787. συγκινέω *sugkineō*
ACTS 6:12

4788. συγκλείω *sugkleiō*
LUKE 5:6; ROM. 11:32; GAL. 3:22,23

4789. συγκληρονόμος *sugklēronomos*
ROM. 8:17; EPH. 3:6; HEB. 11:9; 1 PET.
3:7

4790. συγκοινωνέω *sugkoinōneō*
EPH. 5:11; PHIL. 4:14; REV. 18:4

4791. συγκοινωνός *sugkoinōnos*
ROM. 11:17; 1 COR. 9:23; PHIL. 1:7; REV. 1:9

4792. συγκομίζω *sugkomizō*
ACTS 8:2

4793. συγκρίνω *sugkrinō*
1 COR. 2:13; 2 COR. 10:12

4794. συγκύπτω *sugkuptō*
LUKE 13:11

4795. συγκυρία *sugkuria*
LUKE 10:31

4796. συγχαίρω *sugchairō*
LUKE 1:58; 15:6,9; 1 COR. 12:26; 13:6; PHIL. 2:17,18

4797. I. συγχέω *sugcheō*
    ACTS 21:27

    II. συγχύννω *sugchunnō*
    ACTS 2:6; 9:22; 19:32; 21:31

4798. συγχράομαι *sugchraomai*
JOHN 4:9

4799. σύγχυσις *sugchusis*
ACTS 19:29

4800. συζάω *suzaō*
ROM. 6:8; 2 COR. 7:3; 2 TIM. 2:11

4801. συζευγνύμι *suzeugnumi*
MATT. 19:6; MARK 10:9

4802. συζητέω *suzēteō*
MARK 1:27; 8:11; 9:10,14,16; 12:28; LUKE 22:23; 24:15; ACTS 6:9; 9:29

4803. συζήτησις *suzētēsis*
ACTS 15:2,7; 28:29

4804. συζητητής *suzētētēs*
1 COR. 1:20

4805. σύζυγος *suzugos*
PHIL. 4:3

4806. συζωοποιέω *suzōopoieō*
EPH. 2:5; COL. 2:13

4807. συκάμινος *sukaminos*
LUKE 17:6

4808. συκῆ *sukē*
MATT. 21:19-21; 24:32; MARK 11:13,20,21; 13:28; LUKE 13:6,7; 21:29; JOHN 1:48,50; JAMES 3:12; 6:13

4809. συκομωραία, συκομορέα
sukomōraia, sukomorea
LUKE 19:4

4810. σῦκον *sukon*
MATT. 7:16; MARK 11:13; LUKE 6:44; JAMES 3:12

4811. συκοφαντέω *sukophanteō*
LUKE 3:14; 19:8

4812. συλαγωγέω *sulagōgeō*
COL. 2:8

4813. συλάω *sulaō*
2 COR. 11:8

4814. συλλαλέω *sullaleō*
MATT. 17:3; MARK 9:4; LUKE 4:36; 9:30; 22:4; ACTS 25:12

4815. συλλαμβάνω *sullambanō*
MATT. 26:55; MARK 14:48; LUKE 1:24,31,36; 2:21; 5:7,9; 22:54; JOHN 18:12; ACTS 1:16; 12:3; 23:27; 26:21; PHIL. 4:3; JAMES 1:15

4816. συλλέγω *sullegō*
MATT. 7:16; 13:28-30,40,41,48; LUKE 6:44

4817. συλλογίζομαι *sullogizomai*
LUKE 20:5

4818. συλλυπέω *sullupeō*
MARK 3:5

4819. συμβαίνω *sumbainō*
MARK 10:32; LUKE 24:14; ACTS 3:10;
20:19; 21:35; 1 COR. 10:11; 1 PET. 4:12;
2 PET. 2:22

4820. συμβάλλω *sumballō*
LUKE 2:19; 14:31; ACTS 4:15; 17:18; 18:27;
20:14

4821. συμβασιλεύω *sumbasileuō*
1 COR. 4:8; 2 TIM. 2:12

4822. συμβιβάζω *sumbibazō*
ACTS 9:22; 16:10; 1 COR. 2:16; EPH. 4:16;
COL. 2:2,19

4823. συμβουλεύω *sumbouleuō*
MATT. 26:4; JOHN 11:53; 18:14; ACTS 9:23;
REV. 3:18

4824. συμβούλιον *sumboulion*
MATT. 12:14; 22:15; 27:1,7; 28:12; MARK
3:6; 15:1; ACTS 25:12

4825. σύμβουλος *sumboulos*
ROM. 11:34

4826. Συμεών *Sumeōn*
LUKE 2:25,34; 3:30; ACTS 13:1; 15:14;
2 PET. 1:1; REV. 7:7

4827. συμμαθητής *summathētēs*
JOHN 11:16

4828. συμμαρτυρέω *summartureō*
ROM. 2:15; 8:16; 9:1; REV. 22:18

4829. συμμερίζω *summerizō*
1 COR. 9:13

4830. συμμέτοχος *summetochos*
EPH. 3:6; 5:7

4831. συμμιμητής *summimētēs*
PHIL. 3:17

4832. σύμμορφος *summorphos*
ROM. 8:29; PHIL. 3:21

4833. συμμορφόω *summorphoō*
PHIL. 3:10

4834. συμπαθέω *sumpatheō*
HEB. 4:15; 10:34

4835. συμπαθής *sumpathēs*
1 PET. 3:8

4836. συμπαραγίνομαι
sumparaginomai
LUKE 23:48; 2 TIM. 4:16

4837. συμπαρακαλέω *sumparakaleō*
ROM. 1:12

4838. συμπαραλαμβάνω
sumparalambanō
ACTS 12:25; 15:37,38; GAL. 2:1

4839. συμπαραμένω *sumparamenō*
PHIL. 1:25

4840. συμπάρειμι *sumpareimi*
ACTS 25:24

4841. συμπάσχω *sumpaschō*
ROM. 8:17; 1 COR. 12:26

4842. συμπέμπω *sumpempō*
2 COR. 8:18,22

4843. συμπεριλαμβάνω
sumperilambanō
ACTS 20:10

4844. συμπίνω *sumpinō*
ACTS 10:41

4845. συμπληρόω *sumplēroō*
LUKE 8:23; 9:51; ACTS 2:1

4846. συμπνίγω *sumpnigō*
MATT. 13:22; MARK 4:7,19; LUKE 8:14,42

4847. συμπολίτης *sumpolitēs*
EPH. 2:19

4848. συμπορεύομαι *sumporeuomai*
MARK 10:1; LUKE 7:11; 14:25; 24:15

4849. συμπόσιον *sumposion*
MARK 6:39

4850. συμπρεσβύτερος
sumpresbuteros
1 PET. 5:1

4851. συμφέρω *sumpherō*
MATT. 5:29,30; 18:6; 19:10; JOHN 11:50;
16:7; 18:14; ACTS 19:19; 20:20; 1 COR. 6:12;
7:35; 10:23,33; 12:7; 2 COR. 8:10; 12:1; HEB.
12:10

4852. σύμφημι *sumphēmi*
ROM. 7:16

4853. συμφυλέτης *sumphuletēs*
1 THESS. 2:14

4854. σύμφυτος *sumphutos*
ROM. 6:5

4855. συμφύω *sumphuō*
LUKE 8:7

4856. συμφωνέω *sumphōneō*
MATT. 18:19; 20:2,13; LUKE 5:36; ACTS 5:9;
15:15

4857. συμφώνησις *sumphōnēsis*
2 COR. 6:15

4858. συμφωνία *sumphōnia*
LUKE 15:25

4859. σύμφωνος *sumphōnos*
1 COR. 7:5

4860. συμψηφίζω *sumpsēphizō*
ACTS 19:19

4861. σύμψυχος *sumpsuchos*
PHIL. 2:2

4863. συνάγω *sunagō*
MATT. 2:4; 3:12; 6:26; 12:30; 13:2,30,47;
18:20; 22:10,34,41; 24:28; 25:24,26,32,35,38,43;
26:3,57; 27:17,27,62; 28:12; MARK 2:2; 4:1;
5:21; 6:30; 7:1; LUKE 3:17; 11:23; 12:17,18;
15:13; 17:37; 22:66; JOHN 4:36; 6:12,13; 11:47,
52; 15:6; 18:2; 20:19; ACTS 4:6,26,27,31;
11:26; 13:44; 14:27; 15:6,30; 20:7,8; 1 COR.
5:4; REV. 13:10; 16:14,16; 19:17,19; 20:8

4864. συναγωγή *sunagōgē*
MATT. 4:23; 6:2,5; 9:35; 10:17; 12:9; 13:54;
23:6,34; MARK 1:21,23,29,39; 3:1; 6:2; 12:39;
13:9; LUKE 4:15,16,20,28,33,38,44; 6:6; 7:5;
8:41; 11:43; 12:11; 13:10; 20:46; 21:12; JOHN
6:59; 18:20; ACTS 6:9; 9:2,20; 13:5,14,42,43;
14:1; 15:21; 17:1,10,17; 18:4,7,19,26; 19:8;
22:19; 24:12; 26:11; JAMES 2:2; REV. 2:9; 3:9

4865. συναγωνίζομαι *sunagōnizomai*
ROM. 15:30

4866. συναθλέω *sunathleō*
PHIL. 1:27; 4:3

4867. συναθροίζω *sunathroizō*
LUKE 24:33; ACTS 12:12; 19:25

4868. συναίρω *sunairō*
MATT. 18:23,24; 25:19

4869. συναιχμάλωτος *sunaichmalōtos*
ROM. 16:7; COL. 4:10; PHILE. 1:23

4870. συνακολουθέω *sunakoloutheō*
MARK 5:37; LUKE 23:49

4871. συναλίζω *sunalizō*
ACTS 1:4

4872. συναναβαίνω *sunanabainō*
MARK 15:41; ACTS 13:31

4873. συνανάκειμαι *sunanakeimai*
MATT. 9:10; 14:9; MARK 2:15; 6:22,26;
LUKE 7:49; 14:10,15; JOHN 12:2

4874. συναναμίγνυμι *sunanamignumi*
1 COR. 5:9,11; 2 THESS. 3:14

4875. συναναπαύω *sunanapauō*
ROM. 15:32

4876. συναντάω *sunantaō*
LUKE 9:37; 22:10; ACTS 10:25; 20:22; HEB.
7:1,10

4877. συνάντησις *sunantēsis*
MATT. 8:34

4878. συναντιλαμβάνω
  sunantilambanō
LUKE 10:40; ROM. 8:26

4879. συναπάγω *sunapagō*
ROM. 12:16; GAL. 2:13; 2 PET. 3:17

4880. συναποθνήσχω *sunapothnēschō*
MARK 14:31; 2 COR. 7:3; 2 TIM. 2:11

4881. συναπόλλυμι *sunapollumi*
HEB. 11:31

4882. συναποστέλλω *sunapostellō*
2 COR. 12:18

4883. συναρμολογέω *sunarmologeō*
EPH. 2:21; 4:16

4884. συναρπάζω *sunarpazō*
LUKE 8:29; ACTS 6:12; 19:29; 27:15

4885. συναυξάνω *sunauxanō*
MATT. 13:30

4886. σύνδεσμος *sundesmos*
ACTS 8:23; EPH. 4:3; COL. 2:19; 3:14

4887. συνδέω *sundeō*
HEB. 13:3

4888. συνδοξάζω *sundoxazō*
ROM. 8:17

4889. σύνδουλος *sundoulos*
MATT. 18:28,29,31,33; 24:49; COL. 1:7; 4:7;
REV. 6:11; 19:10; 22:9

4890. συνδρομή *sundromē*
ACTS 21:30

4891. συνεγείρω *sunegeirō*
EPH. 2:6; COL. 2:12; 3:1

4892. συνέδριον *sunedrion*
MATT. 5:22; 10:17; 26:59; MARK 13:9; 14:55;
15:1; LUKE 22:66; JOHN 11:47; ACTS 4:15;
5:21,27,34,41; 6:12,15; 22:30; 23:1,6,15,20,28;
24:20

4893. συνείδησις *suneidēsis*
JOHN 8:9; ACTS 23:1; 24:16; ROM. 2:15; 9:1;
13:5; 1 COR. 8:7,10,12; 10:25,27-29; 2 COR.
1:12; 4:2; 5:11; 1 TIM. 1:5,19; 3:9; 4:2; 2 TIM.
1:3; TITUS 1:15; HEB. 9:9,14; 10:2,22; 13:18;
1 PET. 2:19; 3:16,21

4894. συνείδω *suneidō*
ACTS 5:2; 12:12; 14:6; 1 COR. 4:4

4895. σύνειμι *suneimi*
LUKE 9:18; ACTS 22:11

4896. σύνειμι *suneimi*
LUKE 8:4

4897. συνεισέρχομαι *suneiserchomai*
JOHN 6:22; 18:15

4898. συνέκδημος *sunekdēmos*
ACTS 19:29; 2 COR. 8:19

4899. συνεκλεκτός *suneklektos*
1 PET. 5:13

4900. συνελαύνω *sunelaunō*
ACTS 7:26

4901. συνεπιμαρτυρέω
sunepimartureō
HEB. 2:4

4902. συνέπομαι *sunepomai*
ACTS 20:4

4903. συνεργέω *sunergeō*
MARK 16:20; ROM. 8:28; 1 COR. 16:16;
2 COR. 6:1; JAMES 2:22

4904. συνεργός *sunergos*
ROM. 16:3,9,21; 1 COR. 3:9; 2 COR. 1:24;
8:23; PHIL. 2:25; 4:3; COL. 4:11; 1 THESS.
3:2; PHILE. 1:1,24; 3 JOHN 1:8

4905. συνέρχομαι *sunerchomai*
MATT. 1:18; MARK 3:20; 6:33; 14:53; LUKE
5:15; 23:55; JOHN 11:33; 18:20; ACTS 1:6,21;
2:6; 5:16; 9:39; 10:23,27,45; 11:12; 15:38;
16:13; 19:32; 21:16,22; 25:17; 28:17; 1 COR.
7:5; 11:17,18,20,33,34; 14:23,26

4906. συνεσθίω *sunesthiō*
LUKE 15:2; ACTS 10:41; 11:3; 1 COR. 5:11;
GAL. 2:12

4907. σύνεσις *sunesis*
MARK 12:33; LUKE 2:47; 1 COR. 1:19; EPH.
3:4; COL. 1:9; 2:2; 2 TIM. 2:7

4908. συνετός *sunetos*
MATT. 11:25; LUKE 10:21; ACTS 13:7;
1 COR. 1:19

4909. συνευδοκέω *suneudokeō*
LUKE 11:48; ACTS 8:1; 22:20; ROM. 1:32;
1 COR. 7:12,13

4910. συνευωχέω *suneuōcheō*
2 PET. 22:13; JUDE 1:12

4911. συνεφίστημι *sunephistēmi*
ACTS 16:22

4912. συνέχω *sunechō*
MATT. 4:24; LUKE 4:38; 8:37,45; 12:50;
19:43; 22:63; ACTS 7:57; 18:5; 28:8; 2 COR.
5:14; PHIL. 1:23

4913. συνήδομαι *sunēdomai*
ROM. 7:22

4914. συνήθεια *sunētheia*
JOHN 18:39; 1 COR. 11:16

4915. συνηλικιώτης *sunēlikiōtēs*
GAL. 1:14

4916. συνθάπτω *sunthaptō*
ROM. 6:4; COL. 2:12

4917. συνθλάω *sunthlaō*
MATT. 21:44; LUKE 20:18

4918. συνθλίβω *sunthlibō*
MARK 5:24,31

4919. συνθρύπτω *sunthruptō*
ACTS 21:13

4920. συνίημι *suniēmi*
MATT. 13:13-15,19,23,51; 15:10; 16:12; 17:13;
MARK 4:12; 6:52; 7:14; 8:17,21; LUKE 2:50;
8:10; 18:34; 24:45; ACTS 7:25; 28:26,27;
ROM. 3:11; 15:21; 2 COR. 10:12; EPH. 5:17

4921. I. συνιστάνω *sunistanō*
2 COR. 3:1; 5:12; 10:12

II. συνιστάω *sunistaō*
2 COR. 4:2; 6:4; 10:18

III. συνίστημι *sunistēmi*
LUKE 9:32; ROM. 3:5; 5:8; 16:1;
2 COR. 7:11; 12:11; GAL. 2:18; COL.
1:17; 2 PET. 3:5

4922. συνοδεύω *sunodeuō*
ACTS 9:7

4923. συνοδία *sunodia*
LUKE 2:44

4924. συνοικέω *sunoikeō*
1 PET. 3:7

4925. συνοικοδομέω *sunoikodomeō*
EPH. 2:22

4926. συνομιλέω *sunomileō*
ACTS 10:27

4927. συνομορέω *sunomoreō*
ACTS 18:7

4928. συνοχή *sunochē*
LUKE 21:25; 2 COR. 2:4

4929. συντάσσω, συντάττω
suntassō, suntattō
MATT. 26:19; 27:10

4930. συντέλεια *sunteleia*
MATT. 13:39,40,49; 24:3; 28:20; HEB. 9:26

4931. συντελέω *sunteleō*
MATT. 7:28; MARK 13:4; LUKE 4:2,13;
ACTS 21:27; ROM. 9:28; HEB. 8:8

4932. συντέμνω *suntemnō*
ROM. 9:28

4933. συντηρέω *suntēreō*
MATT. 9:17; MARK 6:20; LUKE 2:19; 5:38

4934. συντίθημι *suntithēmi*
LUKE 22:5; JOHN 9:22; ACTS 23:20; 24:9

4935. συντόμως *suntomōs*
ACTS 24:4

4936. συντρέχω *suntrechō*
MARK 6:33; ACTS 3:11; 1 PET. 4:4

4937. συντρίβω *suntribō*
MATT. 12:20; MARK 5:4; 14:3; LUKE 4:18;
9:39; JOHN 19:36; ROM. 16:20; REV. 2:27

4938. σύντριμμα *suntrimma*
ROM. 3:16

4939. σύντροφος *suntrophos*
ACTS 13:1

4940. συντυγχάνω *suntugchanō*
LUKE 8:19

4941. Συντύχη *Suntuchē*
PHIL. 4:2

4942. συνυποκρίνομαι
sunupokrinomai
GAL. 2:13

4943. συνυπουργέω *sunupourgeō*
2 COR. 1:11

4944. συνωδίνω *sunōdinō*
ROM. 8:22

4945. συνωμοσία *sunōmosia*
ACTS 23:13

4946. Συράκουσαι *Surakousai*
ACTS 28:12

4947. Συρία *Suria*
MATT. 4:24; LUKE 2:2; ACTS 15:23,41;
18:18; 20:3; 21:3; GAL. 1:21

4948. Σύρος *Suros*
LUKE 4:27

4949. Συροφοίνισσα *Surophoinissa*
MARK 7:26

4950. σύρτις *surtis*
ACTS 27:17

4951. σύρω *surō*
JOHN 21:8; ACTS 8:3; 14:19; 17:6; REV.
12:4

4952. σvσπαράσσω, σvσπαράττω
susparassō, susparattō
LUKE 9:42

4953. σύσσημον sussēmon
MARK 14:44

4954. σύσσωμος sussōmos
EPH. 3:6

4955. σvστασιαστής sustasiastēs
MARK 15:7

4956. σvστατικός sustatikos
2 COR. 3:1

4957. σvσταυρόω sustauroō
MATT. 27:44; **MARK** 15:32; **JOHN** 19:32;
ROM. 6:6; **GAL.** 2:20

4958. σvστέλλω sustellō
ACTS 5:6; **1 COR.** 7:29

4959. σvστενάζω sustenazō
ROM. 8:22

4960. σvστοιχέω sustoicheō
GAL. 4:25

4961. σvστρατιώτης sustratiōtēs
PHIL. 2:25; **PHILE.** 1:2

4962. σvστρέφω sustrephō
ACTS 28:3

4963. σvστροφή sustrophē
ACTS 19:40; 23:12

4964. σvσχηματίζω suschēmatizō
ROM. 12:2; **1 PET.** 1:14

4965. Σvχάρ Suchar
JOHN 4:5

4966. Σvχέμ Suchem
ACTS 7:16

4967. σφαγή sphagē
ACTS 8:32; **ROM.** 8:36; **JAMES** 5:5

4968. σφάγιον sphagion
ACTS 7:42

4969. σφάζω sphazō
1 JOHN 3:12; **REV.** 5:6,9,12; 6:4,9; 13:3,8;
18:24

4970. σφόδρα sphodra
MATT. 2:10; 17:6,23; 18:31; 19:25; 26:22;
27:54; **MARK** 16:4; **LUKE** 18:23; **ACTS** 6:7;
REV. 16:21

4971. σφοδρῶς sphodrōs
ACTS 27:18

4972. σφραγίζω sphragizō
MATT. 27:66; **JOHN** 3:33; 6:27; **ROM.** 15:28;
2 COR. 1:22; 11:10; **EPH.** 1:13; 4:30; **REV.**
7:3-8; 10:4; 20:3; 22:10

4973. σφραγίς sphragis
ROM. 4:11; **1 COR.** 9:2; **2 TIM.** 2:19; **REV.**
5:1,2,5,9; 6:1,3,5,7,9,12; 7:2; 8:1; 9:4

4974. σφvρόν sphuron
ACTS 3:7

4975. σχεδόν schedon
ACTS 13:44; 19:26; **HEB.** 9:22

4976. σχῆμα schēma
1 COR. 7:31; **PHIL.** 2:8

4977. σχίζω schizō
MATT. 27:51; **MARK** 1:10; 15:38; **LUKE**
5:36; 23:45; **JOHN** 19:24; 21:11; **ACTS** 14:4;
23:7

4978. σχίσμα schisma
MATT. 9:16; **MARK** 2:21; **JOHN** 7:43; 9:16;
10:19; **1 COR.** 1:10; 11:18; 12:25

4979. σχοινίον schoinion
JOHN 2:15; **ACTS** 27:32

4980. σχολάζω *scholazō*
MATT. 12:44; 1 COR. 7:5

4981. σχολή *scholē*
ACTS 19:9

4982. σώζω *sōzō*
MATT. 1:21; 8:25; 9:21,22; 10:22; 14:30; 16:25;
18:11; 19:25; 24:13,22; 27:40,42,49; MARK
3:4; 5:23,28,34; 6:56; 8:35; 10:26,52; 13:13,20;
15:30,31; 16:16; LUKE 6:9; 7:50; 8:12,36,48,50;
9:24,56; 13:23; 17:19,33; 18:26,42; 19:10; 23:35,
37,39; JOHN 3:17; 5:34; 10:9; 11:12; 12:27,47;
ACTS 2:21,40,47; 4:9,12; 11:14; 14:9; 15:1,11;
16:30,31; 27:20,31; ROM. 5:9,10; 8:24; 9:27;
10:9,13; 11:14,26; 1 COR. 1:18,21; 3:15; 5:5;
7:16; 9:22; 10:33; 15:2; 2 COR. 2:15; EPH.
2:5,8; 1 THESS. 2:16; 2 THESS. 2:10; 1 TIM.
1:15; 2:4,15; 4:16; 2 TIM. 1:9; 4:18; TITUS 3:5;
HEB. 5:7; 7:25; JAMES 1:21; 2:14; 4:12;
5:15,20; 1 PET. 3:21; 4:18; JUDE 1:5,23; REV.
21:24

4983. σῶμα *sōma*
MATT. 5:29,30; 6:22,23,25; 10:28; 14:12;
26:12,26; 27:52,58,59; MARK 5:29; 14:8,22;
15:43,45; LUKE 11:34,36; 12:4,22,23; 17:37;
22:19; 23:52,55; 24:3,23; JOHN 2:21; 19:31,
38,40; 20:12; ACTS 9:40; ROM. 1:24; 4:19;
6:6,12; 7:4,24; 8:10,11,13,23; 12:1,4,5; 1 COR.
5:3; 6:13,15,16,18-20; 7:4,34; 9:27; 10:16,17;
11:24,27,29; 12:12-20,22-25,27; 13:3; 15:35,37,
38,40,44; 2 COR. 4:10; 5:6,8,10; 10:10; 12:2,3;
GAL. 6:17; EPH. 1:23; 2:16; 4:4,12,16; 5:23,
28,30; PHIL. 1:20; 3:21; COL. 1:18,22,24;
2:11,17,19,23; 3:15; 1 THESS. 5:23; HEB.
10:5,10,22; 13:3,11; JAMES 2:16,26; 3:2,3,6;
1 PET. 2:24; JUDE 1:9; REV. 18:13

4984. σωματικός *sōmatikos*
LUKE 3:22; 1 TIM. 4:8

4985. σωματικῶς *sōmatikōs*
COL. 2:9

4986. Σώπατρος *Sōpatros*
ACTS 20:4

4987. σωρεύω *sōreuō*
ROM. 12:20; 2 TIM. 3:6

4988. Σωσθένης *Sōsthenēs*
ACTS 18:17; 1 COR. 1:1

4989. Σωσίπατρος *Sōsipatros*
ROM. 16:21

4990. σωτήρ *sōtēr*
LUKE 1:47; 2:11; JOHN 4:42; ACTS 5:31;
13:23; EPH. 5:23; PHIL. 3:20; 1 TIM. 1:1; 2:3;
4:10; 2 TIM. 1:10; TITUS 1:3,4; 2:10,13; 3:4,6;
2 PET. 1:1,11; 2:20; 3:2,18; 1 JOHN 4:14;
JUDE 1:25

4991. σωτηρία *sōtēria*
LUKE 1:69,71,77; 19:9; JOHN 4:22; ACTS
4:12; 7:25; 13:26,47; 16:17; 27:34; ROM. 1:16;
10:1,10; 11:11; 13:11; 2 COR. 1:6; 6:2; 7:10;
EPH. 1:13; PHIL. 1:19,28; 2:12; 1 THESS.
5:8,9; 2 THESS. 2:13; 2 TIM. 2:10; 3:15; HEB.
1:14; 2:3,10; 5:9; 6:9; 9:28; 11:7; 1 PET.
1:5,9,10; 2 PET. 3:15; JUDE 1:3; REV. 7:10;
12:10; 19:1

4992. I. σωτήριος *sōtērios*
TITUS 2:11

    II. σωτήριον *sōtērion*   subst.
LUKE 2:30; 3:6; ACTS 28:28; EPH.
6:17

4993. σωφρονέω *sōphroneō*
MARK 5:15; LUKE 8:35; ROM. 12:3; 2 COR.
5:13; TITUS 2:6; 1 PET. 4:7

4994. σωφρονίζω *sōphronizō*
TITUS 2:4

4995. σωφρονισμός *sōphronismos*
2 TIM. 1:7

4996. σωφρόνως *sōphronōs*
TITUS 2:12

4997. σωφροσύνη *sōphrosunē*
ACTS 26:25; 1 TIM. 2:9,15

4998. σώφρων *sōphrōn*
1 TIM. 3:2; TITUS 1:8; 2:2,5

T

4999. Ταβέρναι Tabernai
ACTS 28:15

5000. Ταβιθά Tabitha
ACTS 9:36,40

5001. τάγμα tagma
1 COR. 15:23

5002. τακτός taktos
ACTS 12:21

5003. ταλαιπωρέω talaipōreō
JAMES 4:9

5004. ταλαιπωρία talaipōria
ROM. 3:16; JAMES 5:1

5005. ταλαίπωρος talaipōros
ROM. 7:24; REV. 3:17

5006. ταλαντιαῖος talantiaios
REV. 16:21

5007. τάλαντον talanton
MATT. 18:24; 25:15,16,20,22,24,25,28

5008. ταλιθά talitha
MARK 5:41

5009. ταμεῖον tameion
MATT. 6:6; 24:26; LUKE 12:3,24

5010. τάξις taxis
LUKE 1:8; 1 COR. 14:40; COL. 2:5; HEB.
5:6,10; 6:20; 7:11,17,21

5011. ταπεινός tapeinos
MATT. 11:29; LUKE 1:52; ROM. 12:16;
2 COR. 7:6; 10:1; JAMES 1:9; 4:6; 1 PET. 5:5

5012. ταπεινοφροσύνη
    tapeinophrosunē
ACTS 20:19; EPH. 4:2; PHIL. 2:3; COL.
2:18,23; 3:12; 1 PET. 5:5

5013. ταπεινόω tapeinoō
MATT. 18:4; 23:12; LUKE 3:5; 14:11; 18:14;
2 COR. 11:7; 12:21; PHIL. 2:8; 4:12; JAMES
4:10; 1 PET. 5:6

5014. ταπείνωσις tapeinōsis
LUKE 1:48; ACTS 8:33; PHIL. 3:21; JAMES
1:10

5015. ταράσσω, ταράττω
    tarassō, tarattō
MATT. 2:3; 14:26; MARK 6:50; LUKE 1:12;
24:38; JOHN 5:4,7; 11:33; 12:27; 13:21;
14:1,27; ACTS 15:24; 17:8; GAL. 1:7; 5:10;
1 PET. 3:14

5016. ταραχή tarachē
MARK 13:8; JOHN 5:4

5017. τάραχος tarachos
ACTS 12:18; 19:23

5018. Ταρσεύς Tarseus
ACTS 9:11; 21:39

5019. Τάρσος Tarsos
ACTS 9:30; 11:25; 22:3

5020. ταρταρόω tartaroō
2 PET. 2:4

5021. τάσσω, τάττω tassō, tattō
MATT. 28:16; LUKE 7:8; ACTS 13:48; 15:2;
22:10; 28:23; ROM. 13:1; 1 COR. 16:15

5022. ταῦρος tauros
MATT. 22:4; ACTS 14:13; HEB. 9:13; 10:4

5024. ταὐτά tauta
    (For τὰ αὐτά)
LUKE 6:23,26; 17:30; 1 THESS. 2:14

5027. ταφή taphē
MATT. 27:7

5028. τάφος taphos
MATT. 23:27,29; 27:61,64,66; 28:1; ROM.
3:13

5029. τάχα tacha
ROM. 5:7; PHILE. 1:15

5030. ταχέως tacheōs
LUKE 14:21; 16:6; JOHN 11:31; 1 COR. 4:19;
GAL. 1:6; PHIL. 2:19,24; 2 THESS. 2:2;
1 TIM. 5:22; 2 TIM. 4:9

5031. ταχινός tachinos
2 PET. 1:14; 2:1

5032. τάχιον tachion
JOHN 13:27; 20:4; 1 TIM. 3:14; HEB. 13:19,23

5033. τάχιστα tachista
ACTS 17:15

5034. τάχος tachos
LUKE 18:8; ACTS 12:7; 22:18; 25:4; ROM.
16:20; REV. 1:1; 22:6

5035. ταχύ tachu adv.
MATT. 5:25; 28:7,8; MARK 9:39; 16:8; JOHN
11:29; REV. 2:5,16; 3:11; 11:14; 22:7,12,20

5036. ταχύς tachus
JAMES 1:19

5038. τεῖχος teichos
ACTS 9:25; 2 COR. 11:33; HEB. 11:30; REV.
21:12,14,15,17-19

5039. τεκμήριον tekmērion
ACTS 1:3

5040. τεκνίον teknion
JOHN 13:33; GAL. 4:19; 1 JOHN 2:1,12,28;
3:7,18; 4:4; 5:21

5041. τεκνογονέω teknogoneō
1 TIM. 5:14

5042. τεκνογονια teknogonia
1 TIM. 2:15

5043. τέκνον teknon
MATT. 2:18; 3:9; 7:11; 9:2; 10:21; 11:19;

15:26; 18:25; 19:29; 21:28; 22:24; 23:37; 27:25;
MARK 2:5; 7:27; 10:24,29,30; 12:19; 13:12;
LUKE 1:7,17; 2:48; 3:8; 7:35; 11:13; 13:34;
14:26; 15:31; 16:25; 18:29; 19:44; 20:31; 23:28;
JOHN 1:12; 8:39; 11:52; ACTS 2:39; 7:5;
13:33; 21:5,21; ROM. 8:16,17,21; 9:7,8;
1 COR. 4:14,17; 7:14; 2 COR. 6:13; 12:14;
GAL. 4:25,27,28,31; EPH. 2:3; 5:1,8; 6:1,4;
PHIL. 2:15,22; COL. 3:20,21; 1 THESS. 2:7,
11; 1 TIM. 1:2,18; 3:4,12; 5:4; 2 TIM. 1:2; 2:1;
TITUS 1:4,6; PHILE. 1:10; 1 PET. 1:14; 3:6;
2 PET. 2:14; 1 JOHN 3:1,2,10; 5:2; 2 JOHN
1:1,4,13; 3 JOHN 1:4; REV. 2:23; 12:4,5

5044. τεκνοτροφέω teknotropheō
1 TIM. 5:10

5045. τέκτων tektōn
MATT. 13:55; MARK 6:3

5046. τέλειος teleios
MATT. 5:48; 19:21; ROM. 12:2; 1 COR. 2:6;
13:10; 14:20; EPH. 4:13; PHIL. 3:15; COL.
1:28; 4:12; HEB. 5:14; 9:11; JAMES 1:4,17,25;
3:2; 1 JOHN 4:18

5047. τελειότης teleiotēs
COL. 3:14; HEB. 6:1

5048. τελειόω teleioō
LUKE 2:43; 13:32; JOHN 4:34; 5:36; 17:4,23;
19:28; ACTS 20:24; 2 COR. 12:9; PHIL. 3:12;
HEB. 2:10; 5:9; 7:19,28; 9:9; 10:1,14; 11:40;
12:23; JAMES 2:22; 1 JOHN 2:5; 4:12,17,18

5049. τελείως teleiōs
1 PET. 1:13

5050. τελείωσις teleiōsis
LUKE 1:45; HEB. 7:11

5051. τελειωτής teleiōtēs
HEB. 12:2

5052. τελεσφορέω telesphoreō
LUKE 8:14

5053. τελευτάω teleutaō
MATT. 2:19; 9:18; 15:4; 22:25; MARK 7:10;

9:44,46,48; **LUKE** 7:2; **ACTS** 2:29; 7:15; **HEB.** 11:2

5054. τελευτή *teleutē*
MATT. 2:15

5055. τελέω *teleō*
MATT. 10:23; 11:1; 13:53; 17:24; 19:1; 26:1; **LUKE** 2:39; 12:50; 18:31; 22:37; **JOHN** 19:28,30; **ACTS** 13:29; **ROM.** 2:27; 13:6; **GAL.** 5:16; **2 TIM.** 4:7; **JAMES** 2:8; **REV.** 10:7; 11:7; 15:1,8; 17:17; 20:3,5,7

5056. τέλος *telos*
MATT. 10:22; 17:25; 24:6,13,14; 26:58; **MARK** 3:26; 13:7,13; **LUKE** 1:33; 18:5; 21:9; 22:37; **JOHN** 13:1; **ROM.** 6:21,22; 10:4; 13:7; **1 COR.** 1:8; 10:11; 15:24; **2 COR.** 1:13; 3:13; 11:15; **PHIL.** 3:19; **1 THESS.** 2:16; **1 TIM.** 1:5; **HEB.** 3:6,14; 6:8,11; 7:3; **JAMES** 5:11; **1 PET.** 1:9; 3:8; 4:7,17; **REV.** 1:8; 2:26; 21:6; 22:13

5057. τελώνης *telōnēs*
MATT. 5:46,47; 9:10,11; 10:3; 11:19; 18:17; 21:31,32; **MARK** 2:15,16; **LUKE** 3:12; 5:27,29,30; 7:29,34; 15:1; 18:10,11,13

5058. τελώνιον *telōnion*
MATT. 9:9; **MARK** 2:14; **LUKE** 5:27

5059. τέρας *teras*
MATT. 24:24; **MARK** 13:22; **JOHN** 4:48; **ACTS** 2:19,22,43; 4:30; 5:12; 6:8; 7:36; 14:3; 15:12; **ROM.** 15:19; **2 COR.** 12:12; **2 THESS.** 2:9; **HEB.** 2:4

5060. Τέρτιος *Tertios*
ROM. 16:22

5061. Τέρτυλλος *Tertullos*
ACTS 24:1,2

5062. τεσσαράκοντα *tessarakonta*
MATT. 4:2; **MARK** 1:13; **LUKE** 4:2; **JOHN** 2:20; **ACTS** 1:3; 4:22; 7:30,36,42; 13:21; 23:13,21; **2 COR.** 11:24; **HEB.** 3:9,17; **REV.** 7:4; 11:2; 13:5; 14:1,3; 21:17

5063. τεσσαρακονταετής *tessarakontaetēs*
ACTS 7:23; 13:18

5064. τέσσαρες *tessares*
MATT. 24:31; **MARK** 2:3; 13:27; **LUKE** 2:37; **JOHN** 11:17; 19:23; **ACTS** 10:11; 11:5; 12:4; 21:9,23; 27:29; **REV.** 4:4,6,8,10; 5:6,8,14; 6:1,6; 7:1,2,4,11; 9:13-15; 11:16; 14:1,3; 15:7; 19:4; 20:8; 21:17

5065. τεσσαρεσκαιδέκατος *tessareskaidekatos*
ACTS 27:27,33

5066. τεταρταῖος *tetartaios*
JOHN 11:39

5067. τέταρτος *tetartos*
MATT. 14:25; **MARK** 6:48; **ACTS** 10:30; **REV.** 4:7; 6:7,8; 8:12; 16:8; 21:19

5068. τετράγωνος *tetragōnos*
REV. 21:16

5069. τετράδιον *tetradion*
ACTS 12:4

5070. τετρακισχίλιοι *tetrakischilioi*
MATT. 15:38; 16:10; **MARK** 8:9,20; **ACTS** 21:38

5071. τετρακόσιοι *tetrakosioi*
ACTS 5:36; 7:6; 13:20; **GAL.** 3:17

5072. τετράμηνον *tetramēnon*
JOHN 4:35

5073. τετραπλόος *tetraploos*
LUKE 19:8

5074. τετράπους *tetrapous*
ACTS 10:12; 11:6; **ROM.** 1:23

5075. τετραρχέω *tetrarcheō*
LUKE 3:1

5076. τετράρχης *tetrarchēs*
MATT. 14:1; LUKE 3:19; 9:7; ACTS 13:1

5077. τεφρόω *tephroō*
2 PET. 2:6

5078. τέχνη *technē*
ACTS 17:29; 18:3; REV. 18:22

5079. τεχνίτης *technitēs*
ACTS 19:24,38; HEB. 11:10; REV. 18:22

5080. τήκω *tēkō*
2 PET. 3:12

5081. τηλαυγῶς *tēlaugōs*
MARK 8:25

5082. τηλικοῦτος *tēlikoutos*
2 COR. 1:10; HEB. 2:3; JAMES 3:4; REV. 16:18

5083. τηρέω *tēreō*
MATT. 19:17; 23:3; 27:36,54; 23:4,20; MARK 7:9; JOHN 2:10; 8:51,52,55; 9:16; 12:7; 14:15, 21,23,24; 15:10,20; 17:6,11,12,15; ACTS 12:5,6; 15:5,24; 16:23; 21:25; 24:23; 25:4,21; 1 COR. 7:37; 2 COR. 11:9; EPH. 4:3; 1 THESS. 5:23; 1 TIM. 5:22; 6:14; 2 TIM. 4:7; JAMES 1:27; 2:10; 1 PET. 1:4; 2 PET. 2:4,9,17; 3:7; 1 JOHN 2:3-5; 3:22,24; 5:2,3,18; JUDE 1:1,6,13,21; REV. 1:3; 2:26; 3:3,8,10; 12:17; 14:12; 16:15; 22:7,9

5084. τήρησις *tērēsis*
ACTS 4:3; 5:18; 1 COR. 7:19

5085. Τιβεριάς *Tiberias*
JOHN 6:1,23; 21:1

5086. Τιβέριος *Tiberios*
LUKE 3:1

5087. τίθημι *tithēmi*
MATT. 5:15; 12:18; 14:3; 22:4; 24:51; 27:60; MARK 4:21; 6:29,56; 10:16; 12:36; 15:19,47; 16:6; LUKE 1:66; 5:18; 6:48; 8:16; 9:44; 11:33; 12:46; 14:29; 19:21,22; 20:43; 21:14; 22:41;

23:53,55; JOHN 2:10; 10:11,15,17,18; 11:34; 13:4,37,38; 15:13,16; 19:19,41,42; 20:2,13,15; ACTS 1:7; 2:35; 3:2; 4:3,35,37; 5:2,4,15,18,25; 7:16,60; 9:37,40; 12:4; 13:29,47; 19:21; 20:28, 36; 21:5; 27:12; ROM. 4:17; 9:33; 14:13; 1 COR. 3:10,11; 9:18; 12:18,28; 15:25; 16:2; 2 COR. 3:13; 5:19; 1 THESS. 5:9; 1 TIM. 1:12; 2:7; 2 TIM. 1:11; HEB. 1:2,13; 10:13; 1 PET. 2:6,8; 2 PET. 2:6; 1 JOHN 3:16; REV. 10:2; 11:9

5088. τίκτω *tiktō*
MATT. 1:21,23,25; 2:2; LUKE 1:31,57; 2:6,7,11; JOHN 16:21; GAL. 4:27; HEB. 6:7; 11:11; JAMES 1:15; REV. 12:2,4,5,13

5089. τίλλω *tillō*
MATT. 12:1; MARK 2:23; LUKE 6:1

5090. Τιμαῖος *Timaios*
MARK 10:46

5091. τιμάω *timaō*
MATT. 15:4,6,8; 19:19; 27:9; MARK 7:6,10; 10:19; LUKE 18:20; JOHN 5:23; 8:49; 12:26; ACTS 28:10; EPH. 6:2; 1 TIM. 5:3; 1 PET. 2:17

5092. τιμή *timē*
MATT. 27:6,9; JOHN 4:44; ACTS 4:34; 5:2,3; 7:16; 19:19; 28:10; ROM. 2:7,10; 9:21; 12:10; 13:7; 1 COR. 6:20; 7:23; 12:23,24; COL. 2:23; 1 THESS. 4:4; 1 TIM. 1:17; 5:17; 6:1,16; 2 TIM. 2:20,21; HEB. 2:7,9; 3:3; 5:4; 1 PET. 1:7; 2:7; 3:7; 2 PET. 1:17; REV. 4:9,11; 5:12,13; 7:12; 19:1; 21:24,26

5093. I. τίμιος *timios*
ACTS 5:34; 20:24; 1 COR. 3:12; HEB. 13:4; JAMES 5:7; 1 PET. 1:7,19; 2 PET. 1:4; REV. 17:4; 18:12,16; 21:19

II. τιμιώτατος *timiōtatos*
REV. 18:12; 21:11

5094. τιμιότης *timiotēs*
REV. 18:19

5095. Τιμόθεος *Timotheos*
ACTS 16:1; 17:14,15; 18:5; 19:22; 20:4; ROM.

16:21; **1 COR.** 4:17; 16:10; **2 COR.** 1:1,19;
PHIL. 1:1; 2:19; **COL.** 1:1; **1 THESS.** 1:1;
3:2,6; **2 THESS.** 1:1; **1 TIM.** 1:2,18; 6:20;
2 TIM. 1:2; **PHILE.** 1:1; **HEB.** 13:23

5096. Τίμων Timōn
ACTS 6:5

5097. τιμωρέω timōreō
ACTS 22:5; 26:11

5098. τιμωρία timōria
HEB. 10:29

5099. τίνω tinō
2 THESS. 1:9

5102. τίτλος titlos
JOHN 19:19,20

5103. Τίτος Titos
2 COR. 2:13; 7:6,13,14; 8:6,16,23; 12:18; **GAL.**
2:1,3; **2 TIM.** 4:10; **TITUS** 1:4

5104. τοί toi
2 TIM. 2:19

5105. τοιγαροῦν toigaroun
1 THESS. 4:8; **HEB.** 12:1

5106. τοίνυν toinun
LUKE 20:25; **1 COR.** 9:26; **HEB.** 13:13;
JAMES 2:24

5107. τοιόσδε toiosde
2 PET. 1:17

5108. τοιοῦτος toioutos
MATT. 9:8; 18:5; 19:14; **MARK** 4:33; 6:2;
7:8,13; 9:37; 10:14; 13:19; **LUKE** 9:9; 13:2;
18:16; **JOHN** 4:23; 8:5; 9:16; **ACTS** 16:24;
19:25; 21:25; 22:22; 26:29; **ROM.** 1:32; 2:2,3;
16:18; **1 COR.** 5:1,5,11; 7:15,28; 11:16; 15:48;
16:16,18; **2 COR.** 2:6,7; 3:4,12; 10:11; 11:13;
12:2,3,5; **GAL.** 5:21,23; 6:1; **EPH.** 5:27; **PHIL.**
2:29; **2 THESS.** 3:12; **1 TIM.** 6:5; **TITUS** 3:11;
PHILE. 1:9; **HEB.** 7:26; 8:1; 11:14; 12:3; 13:16;
JAMES 4:16; **3 JOHN** 1:8

5109. τοῖχος toichos
ACTS 23:3

5110. τόκος tokos
MATT. 25:27; **LUKE** 19:23

5111. τολμάω tolmaō
MATT. 22:46; **MARK** 12:34; 15:43; **LUKE**
20:40; **JOHN** 21:12; **ACTS** 5:13; 7:32; **ROM.**
5:7; 15:18; **1 COR.** 6:1; **2 COR.** 10:2,12; 11:21;
PHIL. 1:14; **JUDE** 1:9

5112. τολμηρότερον tolmēroteron
ROM. 15:15

5113. τολμητής tolmētēs
2 PET. 2:10

5114. τομώτερος tomōteros
HEB. 4:12

5115. τόξον toxon
REV. 6:2

5116. τοπάζιον topazion
REV. 21:20

5117. τόπος topos
MATT. 12:43; 14:13,15,35; 24:7,15; 26:52;
27:33; 28:6; **MARK** 1:35,45; 6:31,32,35; 13:8;
15:22; 16:6; **LUKE** 2:7; 4:17,37,42; 6:17;
9:10,12; 10:1,32; 11:1,24; 14:9,10,22; 16:28;
19:5; 21:11; 22:40; 23:33; **JOHN** 4:20; 5:13;
6:10,23; 10:40; 11:6,30,48; 14:2,3; 18:2; 19:13,
17,20,41; 20:7; **ACTS** 1:25; 4:31; 6:13,14;
7:7,33,49; 12:17; 16:3; 21:28; 25:16; 27:2,8,
29,41; 28:7; **ROM.** 9:26; 12:19; 15:23; **1 COR.**
1:2; 14:16; **2 COR.** 2:14; **EPH.** 4:27; **1 THESS.**
1:8; **1 TIM.** 2:8; **HEB.** 8:7; 11:8; 12:17;
2 PET. 1:19; **REV.** 2:5; 6:14; 12:6,8,14; 16:16;
20:11

5118. τοσοῦτος tosoutos
MATT. 8:10; 15:33; **LUKE** 7:9; 15:29; **JOHN**
6:9; 12:37; 14:9; 21:11; **ACTS** 5:8; **1 COR.**
14:10; **GAL.** 3:4; **HEB.** 1:4; 4:7; 7:22; 10:25;
12:1; **REV.** 18:7,17; 21:16

5120. τοῦ tou
(For τούτου)
ACTS 17:28

5121. τοὐναντίον tounantion
2 COR. 2:7; GAL. 2:7; 1 PET. 3:9

5122. τοὔνομα tounoma
MATT. 27:57

5123. τουτέστι toutesti
MATT. 27:46; MARK 7:2; ACTS 1:19; 19:4;
ROM. 7:18; 9:8; 10:6-8; PHILE. 1:12; HEB.
2:14; 7:5; 9:11; 10:20; 11:16; 13:15; 1 PET. 3:20

5125. τούτοις toutois
LUKE 16:26; 24:21; ACTS 4:16; 5:35; ROM.
8:37; 14:18; 15:23; 1 COR. 12:23; GAL. 5:21;
COL. 3:14; 1 THESS. 4:18; 1 TIM. 4:15; 6:8;
HEB. 9:23; 2 PET. 2:20; 3 JOHN 1:10; JUDE
1:7,10,14

5131. τράγος tragos
HEB. 9:12,13,19; 10:4

5132. τράπεζα trapeza
MATT. 15:27; 21:12; MARK 7:28; 11:15;
LUKE 16:21; 19:23; 22:21,30; JOHN 2:15;
ACTS 6:2; 16:34; ROM. 11:9; 1 COR. 10:21;
HEB. 9:2

5133. τραπεζίτης trapezitēs
MATT. 25:27

5134. τραῦμα trauma
LUKE 10:34

5135. τραυματίζω traumatizō
LUKE 20:12; ACTS 19:16

5136. τραχηλίζω trachēlizō
HEB. 4:13

5137. τράχηλος trachēlos
MATT. 18:6; MARK 9:42; LUKE 15:20; 17:2;
ACTS 15:10; 20:37; ROM. 16:4

5138. τραχύς trachus
LUKE 3:5; ACTS 27:29

5139. Τραχωνῖτις Trachōnitis
LUKE 3:1

5140. A. τρεῖς treis
MATT. 12:40; 13:33; 15:32; 17:4;
18:16,20; 26:61; 27:40,63; MARK
8:2,31; 9:5; 14:58; 15:29; LUKE 1:56;
2:46; 4:25; 9:33; 10:36; 11:5; 12:52;
13:7,21; JOHN 2:6,19,20; 21:11; ACTS
5:7; 7:20; 9:9; 10:19; 11:11; 17:2; 19:8;
20:3; 25:1; 28:7,11,12,17; 1 COR. 10:8;
13:13; 14:27,29; 2 COR. 13:1; GAL.
1:18; 1 TIM. 5:19; HEB. 10:28; JAMES
5:17; 1 JOHN 5:7,8; REV. 6:6; 8:13;
9:18; 11:9,11; 16:13,19; 21:13

B. Τρεῖς Ταβέρναι
Treis Tabernai
ACTS 28:15

5141. τρέμω tremō
MARK 5:33; LUKE 8:47; ACTS 9:6; 2 PET.
2:10

5142. τρέφω trephō
MATT. 6:26; 25:37; LUKE 4:16; 12:24; ACTS
12:20; JAMES 5:5; REV. 12:6,14

5143. τρέχω trechō
MATT. 27:48; 28:8; MARK 5:6; 15:36; LUKE
15:20; 24:12; JOHN 20:2,4; ROM. 9:16;
1 COR. 9:24,26; GAL. 2:2; 5:7; PHIL. 2:16;
2 THESS. 3:1; HEB. 12:1; REV. 9:9

5144. τριάκοντα triakonta
MATT. 13:8,23; 26:15; 27:3,9; MARK 4:8,20;
LUKE 3:23; JOHN 5:5; 6:19; GAL. 3:17

5145. τριακόσιοι triakosioi
MARK 14:5; JOHN 12:5

5146. τρίβολος tribolos
MATT. 7:16; HEB. 6:8

5147. τρίβος tribos
MATT. 3:3; MARK 1:3; LUKE 3:4

5148. τριετία trietia
ACTS 20:31

5149. *τρίζω trizō*
MARK 9:18

5150. *τρίμηνον trimēnon*   subst.
HEB. 11:23

5151. *τρίς tris*
MATT. 26:34,75; MARK 14:30,72; LUKE 22:34,61; JOHN 13:38; ACTS 10:16; 11:10; 2 COR. 11:25; 12:8

5152. *τρίστεγον tristegon*   subst.
ACTS 20:9

5153. *τρισχίλιοι trischilioi*
ACTS 2:41

5154. *τρίτος tritos*
MATT. 16:21; 17:23; 20:3,19; 22:26; 26:44; 27:64; MARK 9:31; 10:34; 12:21; 14:41; 15:25; LUKE 9:22; 12:38; 13:32; 18:33; 20:12,31; 23:22; 24:7,21,46; JOHN 2:1; 21:14,17; ACTS 2:15; 10:40; 23:23; 27:19; 1 COR. 12:28; 15:4; 2 COR. 12:2,14; 13:1; REV. 4:7; 6:5; 8:7-12; 9:15,18; 11:14; 12:4; 14:9; 16:4; 21:19

5155. *τρίχινος trichinos*
REV. 6:12

5156. *τρόμος tromos*
MARK 16:8; 1 COR. 2:3; 2 COR. 7:15; EPH. 6:5; PHIL. 2:12

5157. *τροπή tropē*
JAMES 1:17

5158. *τρόπος tropos*
MATT. 23:37; LUKE 13:34; ACTS 1:11; 7:28; 15:11; 27:25; ROM. 3:2; PHIL. 1:18; 2 THESS. 2:3; 3:16; 2 TIM. 3:8; HEB. 13:5; JUDE 1:7

5159. *τροποφορέω tropophoreō*
ACTS 13:18

5160. *τροφή trophē*
MATT. 3:4; 6:25; 10:10; 24:45; LUKE 12:23; JOHN 4:8; ACTS 2:46; 9:19; 14:17; 27:33,34,36,38; HEB. 5:12,14; JAMES 2:15

5161. *Τρόφιμος Trophimos*
ACTS 20:4; 21:29; 2 TIM. 4:20

5162. *τροφός trophos*
1 THESS. 2:7

5163. *τροχιά trochia*
HEB. 12:13

5164. *τροχός trochos*
JAMES 3:6

5165. *τρυβλίον trublion*
MATT. 26:23; MARK 14:20

5166. *τρυγάω trugaō*
LUKE 6:44; REV. 14:18,19

5167. *τρυγών trugōn*
LUKE 2:24

5168. *τρυμαλιά trumalia*
MARK 10:25; LUKE 18:25

5169. *τρύπημα trupēma*
MATT. 19:24

5170. *Τρύφαινα Truphaina*
ROM. 16:12

5171. *τρυφάω truphaō*
JAMES 5:5

5172. *τρυφή truphē*
LUKE 7:25; 2 PET. 2:13

5173. *Τρυφῶσα Truphōsa*
ROM. 16:12

5174. *Τρωάς Trōas*
ACTS 16:8,11; 20:5,6; 2 COR. 2:12; 2 TIM. 4:13

5175. *Τρωγύλλιον Trōgullion*
ACTS 20:15

5176. τρώγω trōgō
MATT. 24:38; JOHN 6:54,56-58; 13:18

5177. τυγχάνω tugchanō
LUKE 10:30; 20:35; ACTS 19:11; 24:2; 26:22; 27:3; 28:2; 1 COR. 14:10; 15:37; 2 TIM. 2:10; HEB. 8:6; 11:35

5178. τυμπανίζω tumpanizō
HEB. 11:35

5179. τύπος tupos
JOHN 20:25; ACTS 7:43,44; 23:25; ROM. 5:14; 6:17; 1 COR. 10:6,11; PHIL. 3:17; 1 THESS. 1:7; 2 THESS. 3:9; 1 TIM. 4:12; TITUS 2:7; HEB. 8:5; 1 PET. 5:3

5180. τύπτω tuptō
MATT. 24:49; 27:30; MARK 15:19; LUKE 6:29; 12:45; 18:13; 22:64; 23:48; ACTS 18:17; 21:32; 23:2,3; 1 COR. 8:12

5181. Τύραννος Turannos
ACTS 19:9

5182. τυρβάζω turbazō
LUKE 10:41

5183. Τύριος Turios
ACTS 12:20

5184. Τύρος Turos
MATT. 11:21,22; 15:21; MARK 3:8; 7:24,31; LUKE 6:17; 10:13,14; ACTS 21:3,7

5185. τυφλός tuphlos
MATT. 9:27,28; 11:5; 12:22; 15:14,30,31; 20:30; 21:14; 23:16,17,19,24,26; MARK 8:22,23; 10:46,49,51; LUKE 4:18; 6:39; 7:21,22; 14:13,21; 18:35; JOHN 5:3; 9:1,2,6,8,13,17-20,24,25,32,39-41; 10:21; 11:37; ACTS 13:11; ROM. 2:19; 2 PET. 1:9; REV. 3:17

5186. τυφλόω tuphloō
JOHN 12:40; 2 COR. 4:4; 1 JOHN 2:11

5187. τυφόω tuphoō
1 TIM. 3:6; 6:4; 2 TIM. 3:4

5188. τύφω tuphō
MATT. 12:20

5189. τυφωνικός tuphōnikos
ACTS 27:14

5190. Τυχικός Tuchikos
ACTS 20:4; EPH. 6:21; COL. 4:7; 2 TIM. 4:12; TITUS 3:12

Y

5191. ὑακίνθινος huakinthinos
REV. 9:17

5192. ὑάκινθος huakinthos
REV. 21:20

5193. ὑάλινος hualinos
REV. 4:6; 15:2

5194. ὕαλος hualos
REV. 21:18,21

5195. ὑβρίζω hubrizō
MATT. 22:6; LUKE 11:45; 18:32; ACTS 14:5; 1 THESS. 2:2

5196. ὕβρις hubris
ACTS 27:10,21; 2 COR. 12:10

5197. ὑβριστής hubristēs
ROM. 1:30; 1 TIM. 1:13

5198. ὑγιαίνω hugiainō
LUKE 5:31; 7:10; 15:27; 1 TIM. 1:10; 6:3; 2 TIM. 1:13; 4:3; TITUS 1:9,13; 2:1,2; 3 JOHN 1:2

5199. ὑγιής hugiēs
MATT. 12:13; 15:31; MARK 3:5; 5:34; LUKE 6:10; JOHN 5:4,6,9,11,14,15; 7:23; ACTS 4:10; TITUS 2:8

5200. ὑγρός hugros
LUKE 23:31

5201. ὑδρία *hudria*
JOHN 2:6,7; 4:28

5202. ὑδροποτέω *hudropoteō*
1 TIM. 5:23

5203. ὑδρωπικός *hudrōpikos*
LUKE 14:2

5204. ὕδωρ *hudōr*
MATT. 3:11,16; 8:32; 14:28,29; 17:15; 27:24;
MARK 1:8,10; 9:22,41; 14:13; **LUKE** 3:16;
7:44; 8:24,25; 16:24; 22:10; **JOHN** 1:26,31,33;
2:7,9; 3:5,23; 4:7,10,11,13-15,46; 5:3,4,7; 7:38;
13:5; 19:34; **ACTS** 1:5; 8:36,38,39; 10:47;
11:16; **EPH.** 5:26; **HEB.** 9:19; 10:22; **JAMES**
3:12; **1 PET.** 3:20; **2 PET.** 3:5,6; **1 JOHN** 5:6,8;
REV. 1:15; 7:17; 8:10,11; 11:6; 12:15; 14:2,7;
16:4,5,12; 17:1,15; 19:6; 21:6; 22:1,17

5205. ὑετός *huetos*
ACTS 14:17; 28:2; **HEB.** 6:7; **JAMES** 5:7,18;
REV. 11:6

5206. υἱοθεσία *huiothesia*
ROM. 8:15,23; 9:4; **GAL.** 4:5; **EPH.** 1:5

5207. υἱός *huios*
MATT. 1:1,20,21,23,25; 2:15; 3:17; 4:3,6;
5:9,45; 7:9; 8:12,20,29; 9:6,15,27; 10:23,37;
11:19,27; 12:8,23,27,32,40; 13:37,38,41,55;
14:33; 15:22; 16:13,16,27,28; 17:5,9,12,15,
22,25,26; 18:11; 19:28; 20:18,20,21,28,30,31;
21:5,9,15,37,38; 22:2,42,45; 23:15,31,35;
24:27,30,37,39,44; 25:13,31; 26:2,24,37,45,63,
64; 27:9,40,43,54,56; 28:19; **MARK** 1:1,11;
2:10,19,28; 3:11,17,28; 5:7; 6:3; 8:31,38;
9:7,9,12,17,31; 10:33,35,45-48; 12:6,35,37;
13:26,32; 14:21,41,61,62; 15:39; **LUKE** 1:13,
16,31,32,35,36,57; 2:7; 3:2,22,23; 4:3,9,22,41;
5:10,24,34; 6:5,22,35; 7:12,34; 8:28; 9:22,26,
35,38,41,44,56,58; 10:6,22; 11:11,19,30; 12:8,
10,40,53; 15:11,13,19,21,24,25,30; 16:8; 17:22,
24,26,30; 18:8,31,38,39; 19:9,10; 20:13,34,36,
41,44; 21:27,36; 22:22,48,69,70; 24:7; **JOHN**
1:18,34,42,45,49,51; 3:13,14,16-18,35,36;
4:5,12,46,47,50,53; 5:19-23,25-27; 6:27,40,
42,53,62,69; 8:28,35,36; 9:19,20,35; 10:36;
11:4,27; 12:23,34,36; 13:31; 14:13; 17:1,12;
19:7,26; 20:31; **ACTS** 2:17; 3:25; 4:36; 5:21;

7:16,21,23,29,37,56; 8:37; 9:15,20; 10:36; 13:10,
21,26,33; 16:1; 19:14; 23:6,16; **ROM.** 1:3,4,9;
5:10; 8:3,14,19,29,32; 9:9,26,27; **1 COR.** 1:9;
15:28; **2 COR.** 1:19; 3:7,13; 6:18; **GAL.** 1:16;
2:20; 3:7,26; 4:4,6,7,22,30; **EPH.** 2:2; 3:5; 4:13;
5:6; **COL.** 1:13; 3:6; **1 THESS.** 1:10; 5:5;
2 THESS. 2:3; **HEB.** 1:2,5,8; 2:6,10; 3:6; 4:14;
5:5,8; 6:6; 7:3,5,28; 10:29; 11:21,22,24; 12:5-8;
JAMES 2:21; **1 PET.** 5:13; **2 PET.** 1:17;
1 JOHN 1:3,7; 2:22-24; 3:8,23; 4:9,10,14,15;
5:5,9-13,20; **2 JOHN** 1:3,9; **REV.** 1:13; 2:14,18;
7:4; 12:5; 14:14; 21:7,12

5208. ὕλη *hulē*
JAMES 3:5

5211. Ὑμεναῖος *Humenaios*
1 TIM. 1:20; **2 TIM.** 2:17

5212. ὑμέτερος *humeteros*
LUKE 6:20; 16:12; **JOHN** 7:6; 8:17; 15:20;
ACTS 27:34; **ROM.** 11:31; **1 COR.** 15:31;
2 COR. 8:8; **GAL.** 6:13

5214. ὑμνέω *humneō*
MATT. 26:30; **MARK** 14:26; **ACTS** 16:25;
HEB. 2:12

5215. ὕμνος *humnos*
EPH. 5:19; **COL.** 3:16

5217. ὑπάγω *hupagō*
MATT. 4:10; 5:24,41; 8:4,13,32; 9:6; 13:44;
16:23; 18:15; 19:21; 20:4,7,14; 21:28; 26:18,24;
27:65; 28:10; **MARK** 1:44; 2:11; 5:19,34; 6:31,
33,38; 7:29; 8:33; 10:21,52; 11:2; 14:13,21; 16:7;
LUKE 4:8; 8:42; 10:3; 12:58; 17:14; 19:30;
JOHN 3:8; 4:16; 6:21,67; 7:3,33; 8:14,21,22;
9:7,11; 11:8,31,44; 12:11,35; 13:3,33,36; 14:4,5,
28; 15:16; 16:5,10,16,17; 18:8; 21:3; **JAMES**
2:16; **1 JOHN** 2:11; **REV.** 10:8; 13:10; 14:4;
16:1; 17:8,11

5218. ὑπακοή *hupakoē*
ROM. 1:5; 5:19; 6:16; 15:18; 16:19,26; **2 COR.**
7:15; 10:5,6; **PHILE.** 1:21; **HEB.** 5:8; **1 PET.**
1:2,14,22

5219. ὑπακούω *hupakouō*
MATT. 8:27; **MARK** 1:27; 4:41; **LUKE** 8:25;

17:6; **ACTS** 6:7; 12:13; **ROM.** 6:12,16,17;
10:16; **EPH.** 6:1,5; **PHIL.** 2:12; **COL.** 3:20,22;
2 THESS. 1:8; 3:14; **HEB.** 5:9; 11:8; **1 PET.** 3:6

5220. ὕπανδρος hupandros
ROM. 7:2

5221. ὑπαντάω hupantaō
MATT. 8:28; **LUKE** 8:27; **JOHN** 11:20,30;
12:18

5222. ὑπάντησις hupantēsis
JOHN 12:13

5223. ὕπαρξις huparxis
ACTS 2:45; **HEB.** 10:34

5224. ὑπάρχοντα huparchonta
MATT. 19:21; 24:47; 25:14; **LUKE** 8:3; 11:21;
12:15,33,44; 14:33; 16:1; 19:8; **ACTS** 4:32;
1 COR. 13:3; **HEB.** 10:34

5225. ὑπάρχω huparchō
LUKE 7:25; 8:41; 9:48; 11:13; 16:14,23; 23:50;
ACTS 2:30; 3:2,6; 4:34,37; 5:4; 7:55; 8:16;
10:12; 14:8; 16:3,20,37; 17:24,27,29; 19:36,40;
21:20; 22:3; 27:12,21,34; 28:7,18; **ROM.** 4:19;
1 COR. 7:26; 11:7,18; 12:22; **2 COR.** 8:17;
12:16; **GAL.** 1:14; 2:14; **PHIL.** 2:6; 3:20;
JAMES 2:15; **2 PET.** 1:8; 2:19; 3:11

5226. ὑπείκω hupeikō
HEB. 13:17

5227. ὑπεναντίος hupenantios
COL. 2:14; **HEB.** 10:27

5229. ὑπεραίρω huperairō
2 COR. 12:7; **2 THESS.** 2:4

5230. ὑπέρακμος huperakmos
1 COR. 7:36

5231. ὑπεράνω huperanō
EPH. 1:21; 4:10; **HEB.** 9:5

5232. ὑπεραυξάνω huperauxanō
2 THESS. 1:3

5233. ὑπερβαίνω huperbainō
1 THESS. 4:6

5234. ὑπερβαλλόντως huperballontōs
2 COR. 11:23

5235. ὑπερβάλλω huperballō
2 COR. 3:10; 9:14; **EPH.** 1:19; 2:7; 3:19

5236. ὑπερβολή huperbolē
ROM. 7:13; **1 COR.** 12:31; **2 COR.** 1:8; 4:7,17;
12:7; **GAL.** 1:13

5237. ὑπερεῖδον hupereidon
(2 aor. of ὑπεροράω)
ACTS 17:30

5238. ὑπερέκεινα huperekeina
2 COR. 10:16

5239. ὑπερεκτείνω huperekteinō
2 COR. 10:14

5240. ὑπερεκχύνω huperekchunō
LUKE 6:38

5241. ὑπερεντυγχάνω
huperentugchanō
ROM. 8:26

5242. ὑπερέχω huperechō
ROM. 13:1; **PHIL.** 2:3; 3:8; 4:7; **1 PET.** 2:13

5243. ὑπερηφανία huperēphania
MARK 7:22

5244. ὑπερήφανος huperēphanos
LUKE 1:51; **ROM.** 1:30; **2 TIM.** 3:2; **JAMES**
4:6; **1 PET.** 5:5

5245. ὑπερνικάω hupernikaō
ROM. 8:37

5246. ὑπέρογκος huperogkos
2 PET. 2:18; **JUDE** 1:16

5247. ὑπεροχή *huperochē*
1 COR. 2:1; 1 TIM. 2:2

5248. ὑπερπερισσεύω *huperperisseuō*
ROM. 5:20; 2 COR. 7:4

5249. ὑπερπερισσῶς *huperperissōs*
MARK 7:37

5250. ὑπερπλεονάζω *huperpleonazō*
1 TIM. 1:14

5251. ὑπερυψόω *huperupsoō*
PHIL. 2:9

5252. ὑπερφρονέω *huperphroneō*
ROM. 12:3

5253. ὑπερῷον *huperōon* subst.
ACTS 1:13; 9:37,39; 20:8

5254. ὑπέχω *hupechō*
JUDE 1:7

5255. ὑπήκοος *hupēkoos*
ACTS 7:39; 2 COR. 2:9; PHIL. 2:8

5256. ὑπηρετέω *hupēreteō*
ACTS 13:36; 20:34; 24:23

5257. ὑπηρέτης *hupēretēs*
MATT. 5:25; 26:58; MARK 14:54,65; LUKE 1:2; 4:20; JOHN 7:32,45,46; 18:3,12,18,22,36; 19:6; ACTS 5:22,26; 13:5; 26:16; 1 COR. 4:1

5258. ὕπνος *hupnos*
MATT. 1:24; LUKE 9:32; JOHN 11:13; ACTS 20:9; ROM. 13:11

5260. ὑποβάλλω *hupoballō*
ACTS 6:11

5261. ὑπογραμμός *hupogrammos*
1 PET. 2:21

5262. ὑπόδειγμα *hupodeigma*
JOHN 13:15; HEB. 4:11; 8:5; 9:23; JAMES 5:10; 2 PET. 2:6

5263. ὑποδείκνυμι *hupodeiknumi*
MATT. 3:7; LUKE 3:7; 6:47; 12:5; ACTS 9:16; 20:35

5264. ὑποδέχομαι *hupodechomai*
LUKE 10:38; 19:6; ACTS 17:7; JAMES 2:25

5265. ὑποδέω *hupodeō*
MARK 6:9; ACTS 12:8; EPH. 6:15

5266. ὑπόδημα *hupodēma*
MATT. 3:11; 10:10; MARK 1:7; LUKE 3:16; 10:4; 15:22; 22:35; JOHN 1:27; ACTS 7:33; 18:25

5267. ὑπόδικος *hupodikos*
ROM. 3:19

5268. ὑποζύγιον *hupozugion*
MATT. 21:5; 2 PET. 2:16

5269. ὑποζώννυμι *hupozōnnumi*
ACTS 27:17

5270. ὑποκάτω *hupokatō*
MARK 6:11; 7:28; LUKE 8:16; JOHN 1:50; HEB. 2:8; REV. 5:3,13; 6:9; 12:1

5271. ὑποκρίνομαι *hupokrinomai*
LUKE 20:20

5272. ὑπόκρισις *hupokrisis*
MATT. 23:28; MARK 12:15; LUKE 12:1; GAL. 2:13; 1 TIM. 4:2; JAMES 5:12; 1 PET. 2:1

5273. ὑποκριτής *hupokritēs*
MATT. 6:2,5,16; 7:5; 15:7; 16:3; 22:18; 23:13-15,23,25,27,29; 24:51; MARK 7:6; LUKE 6:42; 11:44; 12:56; 13:15

5274. ὑπολαμβάνω *hupolambanō*
LUKE 7:43; 10:30; ACTS 1:9; 2:15

5275. ὑπολείπω *hupoleipō*
ROM. 11:3

5276. ὑπολήνιον *hupolēnion*
MARK 12:1

5277. ὑπολιμπάνω *hupolimpanō*
1 PET. 2:21

5278. ὑπομένω *hupomenō*
MATT. 10:22; 24:13; MARK 13:13; LUKE
2:43; ACTS 17:14; ROM. 12:12; 1 COR. 13:7;
2 TIM. 2:10,12; HEB. 10:32; 12:2,3,7; JAMES
1:12; 5:11; 1 PET. 2:20

5279. ὑπομιμνήσκω *hupomimnēskō*
LUKE 22:61; JOHN 14:26; 2 TIM. 2:14;
TITUS 3:1; 2 PET. 1:12; 3 JOHN 1:10; JUDE
1:5

5280. ὑπόμνησις *hupomnēsis*
2 TIM. 1:5; 2 PET. 1:13; 3:1

5281. ὑπομονή *hupomonē*
LUKE 8:15; 21:19; ROM. 2:7; 5:3,4; 8:25;
15:4,5; 2 COR. 1:6; 6:4; 12:12; COL. 1:11;
1 THESS. 1:3; 2 THESS. 1:4; 3:5; 1 TIM. 6:11;
2 TIM. 3:10; TITUS 2:2; HEB. 10:36; 12:1;
JAMES 1:3,4; 5:11; 2 PET. 1:6; REV. 1:9;
2:2,3,19; 3:10; 13:10; 14:12

5282. ὑπονοέω *huponoeō*
ACTS 13:25; 25:18; 27:27

5283. ὑπόνοια *huponoia*
1 TIM. 6:4

5284. ὑποπλέω *hupopleō*
ACTS 27:4,7

5285. ὑποπνέω *hupopneō*
ACTS 27:13

5286. ὑποπόδιον *hupopodion*
MATT. 5:35; 22:44; MARK 12:36; LUKE
20:43; ACTS 2:35; 7:49; HEB. 1:13; 10:13;
JAMES 2:3

5287. ὑπόστασις *hupostasis*
2 COR. 9:4; 11:17; HEB. 1:3; 3:14; 11:1

5288. ὑποστέλλω *hupostellō*
ACTS 20:20,27; GAL. 2:12; HEB. 10:38

5289. ὑποστολή *hupostolē*
HEB. 10:39

5290. ὑποστρέφω *hupostrephō*
MARK 14:40; LUKE 1:56; 2:39,43,45; 4:1,14;
7:10; 8:37,39,40; 9:10; 10:17; 11:24; 17:15,18;
19:12; 23:48,56; 24:9,33,52; ACTS 1:12;
8:25,28; 12:25; 13:13,34; 14:21; 20:3; 21:6;
22:17; 23:32; GAL. 1:17; HEB. 7:1

5291. ὑποστρώννυω, ὑποστρώννυμι
hupostrōnnuō, hupostrōnnumi
LUKE 19:36

5292. ὑποταγή *hupotagē*
2 COR. 9:13; GAL. 2:5; 1 TIM. 2:11; 3:4

5293. ὑποτάσσω, ὑποτάττω
hupotassō, hupotattō
LUKE 2:51; 10:17,20; ROM. 8:7,20; 10:3;
13:1,5; 1 COR. 14:32,34; 15:27,28; 16:16; EPH.
1:22; 5:21,22,24; PHIL. 3:21; COL. 3:18;
TITUS 2:5,9; 3:1; HEB. 2:5,8; 12:9; JAMES
4:7; 1 PET. 2:13,18; 3:1,5,22; 5:5

5294. ὑποτίθημι *hupotithēmi*
ROM. 16:4; 1 TIM. 4:6

5295. ὑποτρέχω *hupotrechō*
ACTS 27:16

5296. ὑποτύπωσις *hupotupōsis*
1 TIM. 1:16; 2 TIM. 1:13

5297. ὑποφέρω *hupopherō*
1 COR. 10:13; 2 TIM. 3:11; 1 PET. 2:19

5298. ὑποχωρέω *hupochōreo*
LUKE 5:16; 9:10

5299. ὑπωπιάζω *hupōpiazō*
LUKE 18:5; 1 COR. 9:27

5300. ὗς *hus*
2 PET. 2:22

5301. ὕσσωπος *hussōpos*
JOHN 19:29; HEB. 9:19

5302. ὑστερέω *hustereō*
MATT. 19:20; MARK 10:21; LUKE 15:14;
22:35; JOHN 2:3; ROM. 3:23; 1 COR. 1:7; 8:8;
12:24; 2 COR. 11:5,9; 12:11; PHIL. 4:12; HEB.
4:1; 11:37; 12:15

5303. ὑστέρημα *husterēma*
LUKE 21:4; 1 COR. 16:17; 2 COR. 8:14; 9:12;
11:9; PHIL. 2:30; COL. 1:24; 1 THESS. 3:10

5304. ὑστέρησις *husterēsis*
MARK 12:44; PHIL. 4:11

5305. ὕστερον *husteron* adv.
MATT. 4:2; 21:29,32,37; 22:27; 25:11; 26:60;
MARK 16:14; LUKE 4:2; 20:32; JOHN 13:36;
HEB. 12:11

5306. ὕστερος *husteros*
1 TIM. 4:1

5307. ὑφαντός *huphantos*
JOHN 19:23

5308. ὑψηλός *hupsēlos*
MATT. 4:8; 17:1; MARK 9:2; LUKE 4:5;
16:15; ACTS 13:17; ROM. 12:16; HEB. 1:3;
7:26; REV. 21:10,12

5309. ὑψηλοφρονέω *hupsēlophroneō*
ROM. 11:20; 1 TIM. 6:17

5310. ὕψιστος *hupsistos*
MATT. 21:9; MARK 5:7; 11:10; LUKE
1:32,35,76; 2:14; 6:35; 8:28; 19:38; ACTS 7:48;
16:17; HEB. 7:1

5311. ὕψος *hupsos*
LUKE 1:78; 24:49; EPH. 3:18; 4:8; JAMES
1:9; REV. 21:16

5312. ὑψόω *hupsoō*
MATT. 11:23; 23:12; LUKE 1:52; 10:15; 14:11;
18:14; JOHN 3:14; 8:28; 12:32,34; ACTS 2:33;
5:31; 13:17; 2 COR. 11:7; JAMES 4:10; 1 PET.
5:6

5313. ὕψωμα *hupsōma*
ROM. 8:39; 2 COR. 10:5

Φ

5314. φάγος *phagos*
MATT. 11:19; LUKE 7:34

5315. φάγω *phagō*
MATT. 6:25,31; 12:4; 14:16,20; 15:20,32,37;
25:35,42; 26:17,26; MARK 2:26; 3:20; 5:43;
6:31,36,37,42,44; 8:1,2,8,9; 11:14; 14:12,14,22;
LUKE 4:2; 6:4; 7:36; 8:55; 9:13,17; 12:19,22,
29; 13:26; 14:1,15; 15:23; 17:8; 22:8,11,15,16;
24:43; JOHN 4:31-33; 6:5,23,26,31,49-53,58;
18:28; ACTS 9:9; 10:13,14; 11:7; 23:12,21;
ROM. 14:2,21,23; 1 COR. 8:8,13; 9:4; 10:3,7;
11:20,21,24,33; 15:32; 2 THESS. 3:8; HEB.
13:10; JAMES 5:3; REV. 2:7,14,17,20; 10:10;
17:16; 19:18

5316. φαίνω *phainō*
MATT. 1:20; 2:7,13,19; 6:5,16,18; 9:33; 13:26;
23:27,28; 24:27,30; MARK 14:64; 16:9; LUKE
9:8; 24:11; JOHN 1:5; 5:35; ROM. 7:13;
2 COR. 13:7; PHIL. 2:15; HEB. 11:3; JAMES
4:14; 1 PET. 4:18; 2 PET. 1:19; 1 JOHN 2:8;
REV. 1:16; 8:12; 18:23; 21:23

5317. Φάλεκ *Phalek*
LUKE 3:35

5318. φανερός *phaneros*
MATT. 6:4,6,18; 12:16; MARK 3:12; 4:22;
6:14; LUKE 8:17; ACTS 4:16; 7:13; ROM.
1:19; 2:28; 1 COR. 3:13; 11:19; 14:25; GAL.
5:19; PHIL. 1:13; 1 TIM. 4:15; 1 JOHN 3:10

5319. φανερόω *phaneroō*
MARK 4:22; 16:12,14; JOHN 1:31; 2:11; 3:21;
7:4; 9:3; 17:6; 21:1,14; ROM. 1:19; 3:21; 16:26;
1 COR. 4:5; 2 COR. 2:14; 3:3; 4:10,11; 5:10,11;
7:12; 11:6; EPH. 5:13; COL. 1:26; 3:4; 4:4;
1 TIM. 3:16; 2 TIM. 1:10; TITUS 1:3; HEB.
9:8,26; 1 PET. 1:20; 5:4; 1 JOHN 1:2; 2:19,28;
3:2,5,8; 4:9; REV. 3:18; 15:4

5320. φανερῶς *phanerōs*
MARK 1:45; JOHN 7:10; ACTS 10:3

5321. φανέρωσις phanerōsis
1 COR. 12:7; 2 COR. 4:2

5322. φανός phanos
JOHN 18:3

5323. Φανουήλ Phanouēl
LUKE 2:36

5324. φαντάζω phantazō
HEB. 12:21

5325. φαντασία phantasia
ACTS 25:23

5326. φάντασμα phantasma
MATT. 14:26; MARK 6:49

5327. φάραγξ pharagx
LUKE 3:5

5328. Φαραώ Pharaō
ACTS 7:10,13,21; ROM. 9:17; HEB. 11:24

5329. Φαρές Phares
MATT. 1:3; LUKE 3:33

5330. Φαρισαῖος Pharisaios
MATT. 3:7; 5:20; 9:11,14,34; 12:2,14,24,38;
15:1,12; 16:1,6,11,12; 19:3; 21:45; 22:15,34,41;
23:2,13-15,23,25-27,29; 27:62; MARK
2:16,18,24; 3:6; 7:1,3,5; 8:11,15; 10:2; 12:13;
LUKE 5:17,21,30,33; 6:2,7; 7:30,36,37,39;
11:37-39,42-44,53; 12:1; 13:31; 14:1,3; 15:2;
16:14; 17:20; 18:10,11; 19:39; JOHN 1:24; 3:1;
4:1; 7:32,45,47,48; 8:3,13; 9:13,15,16,40;
11:46,47,57; 12:19,42; 18:3; ACTS 5:34; 15:5;
23:6-9; 26:5; PHIL. 3:5

5331. φαρμακεία pharmakeia
GAL. 5:20; REV. 9:21; 18:23

5332. φαρμακεύς pharmakeus
REV. 21:8

5333. φαρμακός pharmakos
REV. 22:15

5334. φάσις phasis
ACTS 21:31

5335. φάσκω phaskō
ACTS 24:9; 25:19; ROM. 1:22; REV. 2:2

5336. φάτνη phatnē
LUKE 2:7,12,16; 13:15

5337. φαῦλος phaulos
JOHN 3:20; 5:29; TITUS 2:8; JAMES 3:16

5338. φέγγος pheggos
MATT. 24:29; MARK 13:24; LUKE 11:33

5339. φείδομαι pheidomai
ACTS 20:29; ROM. 8:32; 11:21; 1 COR. 7:28;
2 COR. 1:23; 12:6; 13:2; 2 PET. 2:4,5

5340. φειδομένως pheidomenōs
2 COR. 9:6

5341. φελόνης, φαιλόνης
     phelonēs, phailonēs
2 TIM. 4:13

5342. φέρω pherō
MATT. 14:11,18; 17:17; MARK 1:32; 2:3; 4:8;
6:27,28; 7:32; 8:22; 9:17,19,20; 12:15,16; 15:22;
LUKE 5:18; 15:23; 23:26; 24:1; JOHN 2:8;
4:33; 12:24; 15:2,4,5,8,16; 18:29; 19:39; 20:27;
21:10,18; ACTS 2:2; 4:34,37; 5:2,16; 12:10;
14:13; 25:7; 27:15,17; ROM. 9:22; 2 TIM. 4:13;
HEB. 1:3; 6:1; 9:16; 12:20; 13:13; 1 PET. 1:13;
2 PET. 1:17,18,21; 2:11; 2 JOHN 1:10; REV.
21:24,26

5343. φεύγω pheugō
MATT. 2:13; 3:7; 8:33; 10:23; 23:33; 24:16;
26:56; MARK 5:14; 13:14; 14:50,52; 16:8;
LUKE 3:7; 8:34; 21:21; JOHN 10:5,12,13;
ACTS 7:29; 27:30; 1 COR. 6:18; 10:14; 1 TIM.
6:11; 2 TIM. 2:22; HEB. 11:34; 12:25; JAMES
4:7; REV. 9:6; 12:6; 16:20; 20:11

5344. Φῆλιξ Phēlix
ACTS 23:24,26; 24:3,22,24,25,27; 25:14

5345. φήμη phēmē
MATT. 9:26; LUKE 4:14

5346. φημί phēmi
MATT. 4:7; 8:8; 13:28,29; 14:8; 17:26; 19:21;
21:27; 25:21,23; 26:34,61; 27:11,23,65; **MARK**
14:29; **LUKE** 7:40,44; 22:58,70; 23:3; **JOHN**
1:23; 9:38; **ACTS** 2:38; 7:2; 8:36; 10:28,30,31;
16:30,37; 17:22; 19:35; 21:37; 22:2,27,28;
23:5,17,18,35; 25:5,22,24; 26:1,24,25,28,32;
ROM. 3:8; **1 COR.** 6:16; 7:29; 10:15,19; 15:50;
2 COR. 10:10; **HEB.** 8:5

5347. Φῆστος Phēstos
ACTS 24:27; 25:1,4,9,12-14,22-24; 26:24,25,32

5348. φθάνω phthanō
MATT. 12:28; LUKE 11:20; ROM. 9:31; 2
COR. 10:14; PHIL. 3:16; 1 THESS. 2:16; 4:15

5349. φθαρτός phthartos
ROM. 1:23; 1 COR. 9:25; 15:53,54; 1 PET.
1:18,23

5350. φθέγγομαι phtheggomai
ACTS 4:18; 2 PET. 2:16,18

5351. φθείρω phtheirō
1 COR. 3:17; 15:33; 2 COR. 7:2; 11:3; EPH.
4:22; JUDE 1:10; REV. 19:2

5352. φθινοπωρινός phthinopōrinos
JUDE 1:12

5353. φθόγγος phthoggos
ROM. 10:18; 1 COR. 14:7

5354. φθονέω phthoneō
GAL. 5:26

5355. φθόνος phthonos
MATT. 27:18; MARK 15:10; ROM. 1:29;
GAL. 5:21; PHIL. 1:15; 1 TIM. 6:4; TITUS
3:3; JAMES 4:5; 1 PET. 2:1

5356. φθορά phthora
ROM. 8:21; 1 COR. 15:42,50; GAL. 6:8; COL.
2:22; 2 PET. 1:4; 2:12,19

5357. φιάλη phialē
REV. 5:8; 15:7; 16:1-4,8,10,12,17; 17:1; 21:9

5358. φιλάγαθος philagathos
TITUS 1:8

5359. Φιλαδέλφια Philadelphia
REV. 1:11; 3:7

5360. φιλαδελφία philadelphia
ROM. 12:10; 1 THESS. 4:9; HEB. 13:1;
1 PET. 1:22; 2 PET. 1:7

5361. φιλάδελφος philadelphos
1 PET. 3:8

5362. φίλανδρος philandros
TITUS 2:4

5363. φιλανθρωπία philanthrōpia
ACTS 28:2; TITUS 3:4

5364. φιλανθρώπως philanthrōpōs
ACTS 27:3

5365. φιλαργυρία philarguria
1 TIM. 6:10

5366. φιλάργυρος philarguros
LUKE 16:14; 2 TIM. 3:2

5367. φίλαυτος philautos
2 TIM. 3:2

5368. φιλέω phileō
MATT. 6:5; 10:37; 23:6; 26:48; MARK 14:44;
LUKE 20:46; 22:47; JOHN 5:20; 11:3,36;
12:25; 15:19; 16:27; 20:2; 21:15-17; 1 COR.
16:22; TITUS 3:15; REV. 3:19; 22:15

5369. φιλήδονος philēdonos
2 TIM. 3:4

5370. φίλημα philēma
LUKE 7:45; 22:48; ROM. 16:16; 1 COR.
16:20; 2 COR. 13:12; 1 THESS. 5:26; 1 PET.
5:14

5371. Φιλήμων Philēmōn
PHILE. 1:1

5372. Φιλητός Philētos
2 TIM. 2:17

5373. φιλία philia
JAMES 4:4

5374. Φιλιππήσιος Philippēsios
PHIL. 4:15

5375. Φίλιπποι Philippoi
ACTS 16:12; 20:6; PHIL. 1:1; 1 THESS. 2:2

5376. Φίλιππος Philippos
MATT. 10:3; 14:3; 16:13; MARK 3:18; 6:17;
8:27; LUKE 3:1,19; 6:14; JOHN 1:43-46,48;
6:5,7; 12:21,22; 14:8,9; ACTS 1:13; 6:5;
8:5,6,12,13,26,29-31,34,35,37-40; 21:8

5377. φιλόθεος philotheos
2 TIM. 3:4

5378. Φιλόλογος Philologos
ROM. 16:15

5379. φιλονεικία philoneikia
LUKE 22:24

5380. φιλόνεικος philoneikos
1 COR. 11:16

5381. φιλοξενία philoxenia
ROM. 12:13; HEB. 13:2

5382. φιλόξενος philoxenos
1 TIM. 3:2; TITUS 1:8; 1 PET. 4:9

5383. φιλοπρωτεύω philoprōteuō
3 JOHN 1:9

5384. φίλος philos
MATT. 11:19; LUKE 7:6,34; 11:5,6,8; 12:4;
14:10,12; 15:6,9,29; 16:9; 21:16; 23:12; JOHN
3:29; 11:11; 15:13-15; 19:12; ACTS 10:24;
19:31; 27:3; JAMES 2:23; 4:4; 3 JOHN 1:14

5385. φιλοσοφία philosophia
COL. 2:8

5386. φιλόσοφος philosophos
ACTS 17:18

5387. φιλόστοργος philostorgos
ROM. 12:10

5388. φιλότεκνος philoteknos
TITUS 2:4

5389. φιλοτιμέομαι philotimeomai
ROM. 15:20; 2 COR. 5:9; 1 THESS. 4:11

5390. φιλοφρόνως philophronōs
ACTS 28:7

5391. φιλόφρων philophrōn
1 PET. 3:8

5392. φιμόω phimoō
MATT. 22:12,34; MARK 1:25; 4:39; LUKE
4:35; 1 COR. 9:9; 1 TIM. 5:18; 1 PET. 2:15

5393. Φλέγων Phlegōn
ROM. 16:14

5394. φλογίζω phlogizō
JAMES 3:6

5395. φλόξ phlox
LUKE 16:24; ACTS 7:30; 2 THESS. 1:8; HEB.
1:7; REV. 1:14; 2:18; 19:12

5396. φλυαρέω phluareō
3 JOHN 1:10

5397. φλύαρος phluaros
1 TIM. 5:13

5398. φοβερός phoberos
HEB. 10:27,31; 12:21

5399. φοβέω phobeō
MATT. 1:20; 2:22; 10:26,28,31; 14:5,27,30;
17:6,7; 21:26,46; 25:25; 27:54; 28:5,10; MARK

4:41; 5:15,33,36; 6:20,50; 9:32; 10:32; 11:18,32;
12:12; 16:8; **LUKE** 1:13,30,50; 2:9,10; 5:10;
8:25,35,50; 9:34,45; 12:4,5,7,32; 18:2,4; 19:21;
20:19; 22:2; 23:40; **JOHN** 6:19,20; 9:22; 12:15;
19:8; **ACTS** 5:26; 9:26; 10:2,22,35; 13:16,26;
16:38; 18:9; 22:29; 27:17,24,29; **ROM.** 11:20;
13:3,4; **2 COR.** 11:3; 12:20; **GAL.** 2:12; 4:11;
EPH. 5:33; **COL.** 3:22; **HEB.** 4:1; 11:23,27;
13:6; **1 PET.** 2:17; 3:6,14; **1 JOHN** 4:18; **REV.**
1:17; 2:10; 11:18; 14:7; 15:4; 19:5

5400. φόβητρον phobētron
LUKE 21:11

5401. φόβος phobos
MATT. 14:26; 28:4,8; **MARK** 4:41; **LUKE**
1:12,65; 2:9; 5:26; 7:16; 8:37; 21:26; **JOHN**
7:13; 19:38; 20:19; **ACTS** 2:43; 5:5,11; 9:31;
19:17; **ROM.** 3:18; 8:15; 13:3,7; **1 COR.** 2:3;
2 COR. 5:11; 7:1,5,11,15; **EPH.** 5:21; 6:5;
PHIL. 2:12; **1 TIM.** 5:20; **HEB.** 2:15; **1 PET.**
1:17; 2:18; 3:2,14,15; **1 JOHN** 4:18; **JUDE**
1:23; **REV.** 11:11; 18:10,15

5402. Φοίβη Phoibē
ROM. 16:1

5403. Φοινίκη Phoinikē
ACTS 11:19; 15:3; 21:2

5404. φοῖνιξ phoinix
JOHN 12:13; **REV.** 7:9

5405. Φοίνιξ Phoinix
ACTS 27:12

5406. φονεύς phoneus
MATT. 22:7; **ACTS** 3:14; 7:52; 28:4; **1 PET.**
4:15; **REV.** 21:8; 22:15

5407. φονεύω phoneuō
MATT. 5:21; 19:18; 23:31,35; **MARK** 10:19;
LUKE 18:20; **ROM.** 13:9; **JAMES** 2:11; 4:2;
5:6

5408. φόνος phonos
MATT. 15:19; **MARK** 7:21; 15:7; **LUKE**
23:19,25; **ACTS** 9:1; **ROM.** 1:29; **GAL.** 5:21;
HEB. 11:37; **REV.** 9:21

5409. φορέω phoreō
MATT. 11:8; **JOHN** 19:5; **ROM.** 13:4; **1 COR.**
15:49; **JAMES** 2:3

5410. Φόρον Phoron
(Only in Appii Forum)
ACTS 28:15

5411. φόρος phoros
LUKE 20:22; 23:2; **ROM.** 13:6,7

5412. φορτίζω phortizō
MATT. 11:28; **LUKE** 11:46

5413. φορτίον phortion
MATT. 11:30; 23:4; **LUKE** 11:46; **GAL.** 6:5

5414. φόρτος phortos
ACTS 27:10

5415. Φορτουνάτος Phortounatos
1 COR. 16:17

5416. φραγέλλιον phragellion
JOHN 2:15

5417. φραγελλόω phragelloō
MATT. 27:26; **MARK** 15:15

5418. φραγμός phragmos
MATT. 21:33; **MARK** 12:1; **LUKE** 14:23;
EPH. 2:14

5419. φράζω phrazō
MATT. 13:36; 15:15

5420. φράσσω, φράττω
phrassō, phrattō
ROM. 3:19; **2 COR.** 11:10; **HEB.** 11:33

5421. φρέαρ phrear
LUKE 14:5; **JOHN** 4:11,12; **REV.** 9:1,2

5422. φρεναπατάω phrenapataō
GAL. 6:3

5423. φρεναπάτης phrenapatēs
TITUS 1:10

5424. φρήν phrēn
1 COR. 14:20

5425. φρίσσω, φρίττω
phrissō, phrittō
JAMES 2:19

5426. φρονέω phroneō
MATT. 16:23; MARK 8:33; ACTS 28:22;
ROM. 8:5; 12:3,16; 14:6; 15:5; 1 COR. 4:6;
13:11; 2 COR. 13:11; GAL. 5:10; PHIL. 1:7;
2:2,5; 3:15,16,19; 4:2,10; COL. 3:2

5427. φρόνημα phronēma
ROM. 8:6,7,27

5428. φρόνησις phronēsis
LUKE 1:17; EPH. 1:8

5429. φρόνιμος phronimos
MATT. 7:24; 10:16; 24:45; 25:2,4,8,9; LUKE
12:42; 16:8; ROM. 11:25; 12:16; 1 COR. 4:10;
10:15; 2 COR. 11:19

5430. φρονίμως phronimōs
LUKE 16:8

5431. φροντίζω phrontizō
TITUS 3:8

5432. φρουρέω phroureō
2 COR. 11:32; GAL. 3:23; PHIL. 4:7; 1 PET.
1:5

5433. φρυάσσω, φρυάττω
phruassō, phruattō
ACTS 4:25

5434. φρύγανον phruganon
ACTS 28:3

5435. Φρυγία Phrugia
ACTS 2:10; 16:6; 18:23

5436. Φύγελλος Phugellos
2 TIM. 1:15

5437. φυγή phugē
MATT. 24:20; MARK 13:18

5438. φυλακή phulakē
MATT. 5:25; 14:3,10,25; 18:30; 24:43; 25:36,
39,43,44; MARK 6:17,27,48; LUKE 2:8; 3:20;
12:38,58; 21:12; 22:33; 23:19,25; JOHN 3:24;
ACTS 5:19,22,25; 8:3; 12:4-6,10,17; 16:23,
24,27,37,40; 22:4; 26:10; 2 COR. 6:5; 11:23;
HEB. 11:36; 1 PET. 3:19; REV. 2:10; 18:2;
20:7

5439. φυλακίζω phulakizō
ACTS 22:19

5440. φυλακτήριον phulaktērion
MATT. 23:5

5441. φύλαξ phulax
ACTS 5:23; 12:6,19

5442. φυλάσσω, φυλάττω
phulassō, phulattō
MATT. 19:20; MARK 10:20; LUKE 2:8; 8:29;
11:21,28; 12:15; 18:21; JOHN 12:25; 17:12;
ACTS 7:53; 12:4; 16:4; 21:24,25; 22:20; 23:35;
28:16; ROM. 2:26; GAL. 6:13; 2 THESS. 3:3;
1 TIM. 5:21; 6:20; 2 TIM. 1:12,14; 4:15; 2
PET. 2:5; 3:17; 1 JOHN 5:21; JUDE 1:24

5443. φυλή phulē
MATT. 19:28; 24:30; LUKE 2:36; 22:30;
ACTS 13:21; ROM. 11:1; PHIL. 3:5; HEB.
7:13,14; JAMES 1:1; REV. 1:7; 5:5,9; 7:4-9;
11:9; 13:7; 14:6; 21:12

5444. φύλλον phullon
MATT. 21:19; 24:32; MARK 11:13; 13:28;
REV. 22:2

5445. φύραμα phurama
ROM. 9:21; 11:16; 1 COR. 5:6,7; GAL. 5:9

5446. φυσικός phusikos
ROM. 1:26,27; 2 PET. 2:12

5447. φυσικῶς phusikōs
JUDE 1:10

5448. φυσιόω phusioō
1 COR. 4:6,18,19; 5:2; 8:1; 13:4; COL. 2:18

5449. φύσις phusis
ROM. 1:26; 2:14,27; 11:21,24; **1 COR.** 11:14;
GAL. 2:15; 4:8; **EPH.** 2:3; **JAMES** 3:7; **2 PET.**
1:4

5450. φυσίωσις phusiōsis
2 COR. 12:20

5451. φυτεία phuteia
MATT. 15:13

5452. φυτεύω phuteuō
MATT. 15:13; 21:33; **MARK** 12:1; **LUKE**
13:6; 17:6,28; 20:9; **1 COR.** 3:6-8; 9:7

5453. φύω phuō
LUKE 8:6,8; **HEB.** 12:15

5454. φωλεός phōleos
MATT. 8:20; **LUKE** 9:58

5455. φωνέω phōneō
MATT. 20:32; 26:34,74,75; 27:47; **MARK**
3:31; 9:35; 10:49; 14:30,68,72; 15:35; **LUKE**
8:8,54; 14:12; 16:2,24; 19:15; 22:34,60,61;
23:46; **JOHN** 1:48; 2:9; 4:16; 9:18,24; 11:28;
12:17; 13:13,38; 18:27,33; **ACTS** 9:41; 10:7,18;
16:28; **REV.** 14:18

5456. φωνή phōnē
MATT. 2:18; 3:3,17; 12:19; 17:5; 24:31;
27:46,50; **MARK** 1:3,11,26; 5:7; 9:7; 15:34,37;
LUKE 1:42,44; 3:4,22; 4:33; 8:28; 9:35,36;
11:27; 17:13,15; 19:37; 23:23,46; **JOHN** 1:23;
3:8,29; 5:25,28,37; 10:3-5,16,27; 11:43; 12:28,
30; 18:37; **ACTS** 2:6,14; 4:24; 7:31,57,60; 8:7;
9:4,7; 10:13,15; 11:7,9; 12:14,22; 13:27;
14:10,11; 16:28; 19:34; 22:7,9,14,22; 24:21;
26:14,24; **1 COR.** 14:7,8,10,11; **GAL.** 4:20;
1 THESS. 4:16; **HEB.** 3:7,15; 4:7; 12:19,26;
2 PET. 1:17,18; 2:16; **REV.** 1:10,12,15; 3:20;
4:1,5; 5:2,11,12; 6:1,6,7,10; 7:2,10; 8:5,13;
9:9,13; 10:3,4,7,8; 11:12,15,19; 12:10;

14:2,7,9,13,15; 16:1,17,18; 18:2,4,22,23;
19:1,5,6,17; 21:3

5457. φῶς phōs
MATT. 4:16; 5:14,16; 6:23; 10:27; 17:2;
MARK 14:54; **LUKE** 2:32; 8:16; 11:35; 12:3;
16:8; 22:56; **JOHN** 1:4,5,7-9; 3:19-21; 5:35;
8:12; 9:5; 11:9,10; 12:35,36,46; **ACTS** 9:3; 12:7;
13:47; 16:29; 22:6,9,11; 26:13,18,23; **ROM.**
2:19; 13:12; **2 COR.** 4:6; 6:14; 11:14; **EPH.**
5:8,13; **COL.** 1:12; **1 THESS.** 5:5; **1 TIM.** 6:16;
JAMES 1:17; **1 PET.** 2:9; **1 JOHN** 1:5,7; 2:8-
10; **REV.** 18:23; 21:24; 22:5

5458. φωστήρ phōstēr
PHIL. 2:15; **REV.** 21:11

5459. φωσφόρος phōsphoros
2 PET. 1:19

5460. φωτεινός phōteinos
MATT. 6:22; 17:5; **LUKE** 11:34,36

5461. φωτίζω phōtizō
LUKE 11:36; **JOHN** 1:9; **1 COR.** 4:5; **EPH.**
1:18; 3:9; **2 TIM.** 1:10; **HEB.** 6:4; 10:32; **REV.**
18:1; 21:23; 22:5

5462. φωτισμός phōtismos
2 COR. 4:4,6

X

5463. χαίρω chairō
MATT. 2:10; 5:12; 18:13; 26:49; 27:29; 28:9;
MARK 14:11; 15:18; **LUKE** 1:14,28; 6:23;
10:20; 13:17; 15:5,32; 19:6,37; 22:5; 23:8;
JOHN 3:29; 4:36; 8:56; 11:15; 14:28; 16:20,22;
19:3; 20:20; **ACTS** 5:41; 8:39; 11:23; 13:48;
15:23,31; 23:26; **ROM.** 12:12,15; 16:19;
1 COR. 7:30; 13:6; 16:17; **2 COR.** 2:3; 6:10;
7:7,9,13,16; 13:9,11; **PHIL.** 1:18; 2:17,18,28;
3:1; 4:4,10; **COL.** 1:24; 2:5; **1 THESS.** 3:9;
5:16; **JAMES** 1:1; **1 PET.** 4:13; **2 JOHN**
1:4,10,11; **3 JOHN** 1:3; **REV.** 11:10; 19:7

5464. χάλαζα chalaza
REV. 8:7; 11:19; 16:21

5465. χαλάω chalaō
MARK 2:4; LUKE 5:4,5; ACTS 9:25;
27:17,30; **2 COR.** 11:33

5466. Χαλδαῖος Chaldaios
ACTS 7:4

5467. χαλεπός chalepos
MATT. 8:28; **2 TIM.** 3:1

5468. χαλιναγωγέω chalinagōgeō
JAMES 1:26; 3:2

5469. χαλινός chalinos
JAMES 3:3; REV. 14:20

5470. χάλκεος chalkeos
REV. 9:20

5471. χαλκεύς chalkeus
2 TIM. 4:14

5472. χαλκηδών chalkēdōn
REV. 21:19

5473. χαλκίον chalkion
MARK 7:4

5474. χαλκολίβανον chalkolibanon
REV. 1:15; 2:18

5475. χαλκός chalkos
MATT. 10:9; MARK 6:8; 12:41; **1 COR.** 13:1;
REV. 18:12

5476. χαμαί chamai
JOHN 9:6; 18:6

5477. Χανάαν Chanaan
ACTS 7:11; 13:19

5478. Χαναναῖος Chananaios
MATT. 15:22

5479. χαρά chara
MATT. 2:10; 13:20,44; 25:21,23; 28:8; **MARK**

4:16; **LUKE** 1:14; 2:10; 8:13; 10:17; 15:7,10;
24:41,52; JOHN 3:29; 15:11; 16:20-22,24;
17:13; ACTS 8:8; 12:14; 13:52; 15:3; 20:24;
ROM. 14:17; 15:13,32; **2 COR.** 1:24; 2:3;
7:4,13; 8:2; GAL. 5:22; PHIL. 1:4,25; 2:2,29;
4:1; COL. 1:11; **1 THESS.** 1:6; 2:19,20; 3:9;
2 TIM. 1:4; HEB. 10:34; 12:2,11; 13:17;
JAMES 1:2; 4:9; **1 PET.** 1:8; **1 JOHN** 1:4;
2 JOHN 1:12; 3 JOHN 1:4

5480. χάραγμα charagma
ACTS 17:29; REV. 13:16,17; 14:9,11; 15:2;
16:2; 19:20; 20:4

5481. χαρακτήρ charaktēr
HEB. 1:3

5482. χάραξ charax
LUKE 19:43

5483. χαρίζομαι charizomai
LUKE 7:21,42,43; ACTS 3:14; 25:11,16; 27:24;
ROM. 8:32; **1 COR.** 2:12; **2 COR.** 2:7,10;
12:13; GAL. 3:18; EPH. 4:32; PHIL. 1:29; 2:9;
COL. 2:13; 3:13; PHILE. 1:22

5484. χάριν charin
LUKE 7:47; GAL. 3:19; EPH. 3:1,14; **1 TIM.**
5:14; TITUS 1:5,11; **1 JOHN** 3:12; JUDE 1:16

5485. χάρις charis
LUKE 1:30; 2:40,52; 4:22; 6:32-34; 17:9;
JOHN 1:14,16,17; ACTS 2:47; 4:33; 7:10,46;
11:23; 13:43; 14:3,26; 15:11,40; 18:27; 20:24,32;
24:27; 25:3,9; ROM. 1:5,7; 3:24; 4:4,16; 5:2,
15,17,20,21; 6:1,14,15,17; 11:5,6; 12:3,6; 15:15;
16:20,24; **1 COR.** 1:3,4; 3:10; 10:30; 15:10,57;
16:3,23; **2 COR.** 1:2,12,15; 2:14; 4:15; 6:1;
8:1,4,6,7,9,16,19; 9:8,14,15; 12:9; 13:4; GAL.
1:3,6,15; 2:9,21; 5:4; 6:18; EPH. 1:2,6,7; 2:5,
7,8; 3:2,7,8; 4:7,29; 6:24; PHIL. 1:2,7; 4:23;
COL. 1:2,6; 3:16; 4:6,18; **1 THESS.** 1:1; 5:28;
2 THESS. 1:2,12; 2:16; 3:18; **1 TIM.** 1:2,12,14;
6:21; **2 TIM.** 1:2,3,9; 2:1; 4:22; TITUS 1:4;
2:11; 3:7,15; PHILE. 1:3,7,25; HEB. 2:9; 4:16;
10:29; 12:15,28; 13:9,25; JAMES 4:6; **1 PET.**
1:2,10,13; 2:19,20; 3:7; 4:10; 5:5,10,12; **2 PET.**
1:2; 3:18; **2 JOHN** 1:3; JUDE 1:4; REV. 1:4;
22:21

5486. χάρισμα *charisma*
ROM. 1:11; 5:15,16; 6:23; 11:29; 12:6; **1 COR.**
1:7; 7:7; 12:4,9,28,30,31; **2 COR.** 1:11; **1 TIM.**
4:14; **2 TIM.** 1:6; **1 PET.** 4:10

5487. χαριτόω *charitoō*
LUKE 1:28; EPH. 1:6

5488. Χαρράν *Charran*
ACTS 7:2,4

5489. χάρτης *chartēs*
2 JOHN 1:12

5490. χάσμα *chasma*
LUKE 16:26

5491. χεῖλος *cheilos*
MATT. 15:8; MARK 7:6; ROM. 3:13; **1 COR.**
14:21; HEB. 11:12; 13:15; **1 PET.** 3:10

5492. χειμάζω *cheimazō*
ACTS 27:18

5493. χείμαρρος *cheimarros*
JOHN 18:1

5494. χειμών *cheimōn*
MATT. 16:3; 24:20; MARK 13:18; JOHN
10:22; ACTS 27:20; **2 TIM.** 4:21

5495. χείρ *cheir*
MATT. 3:12; 4:6; 5:30; 8:3,15; 9:18,25;
12:10,13,49; 14:31; 51:2,20; 17:22; 18:8;
19:13,15; 22:13; 26:23,45,50,51; 27:24; MARK
1:31,41; 3:1,3,5; 5:23,41; 6:2,5; 7:2,3,5,32;
8:23,25; 9:27,31,43; 10:16; 14:41,46; 16:18;
LUKE 1:66,71,74; 3:17; 4:11,40; 5:13;
6:1,6,8,10; 8:54; 9:44,62; 13:13; 15:22; 20:19;
21:12; 22:21,53; 23:46; 24:7,39,40,50; JOHN
3:35; 7:30,44; 10:28,29,39; 11:44; 13:3,9;
20:20,25,27; 21:18; ACTS 2:23; 3:7; 4:3,28,30;
5:12,18; 6:6; 7:25,35,41,50; 8:17-19; 9:12,17,41;
11:21,30; 12:1,7,11,17; 13:3,11,16; 14:3; 15:23;
17:25; 19:6,11,26,33; 20:34; 21:11,27,40; 23:19;
24:7; 26:1; 28:3,4,8,17; ROM. 10:21; **1 COR.**
4:12; 12:15,21; 16:21; **2 COR.** 11:33; GAL.
3:19; 6:11; EPH. 4:28; COL. 4:18; **1 THESS.**
4:11; **2 THESS.** 3:17; **1 TIM.** 2:8; 4:14; 5:22;

2 TIM. 1:6; PHILE. 1:19; HEB. 1:10; 2:7; 6:2;
8:9; 10:31; 12:12; JAMES 4:8; **1 PET.** 5:6;
1 JOHN 1:1; REV. 1:16,17; 6:5; 7:9; 8:4; 9:20;
10:2,5,8,10; 13:16; 14:9,14; 17:4; 19:2; 20:1,4

5496. χειραγωγέω *cheiragōgeō*
ACTS 9:8; 22:11

5497. χειραγωγός *cheiragōgos*
ACTS 13:11

5498. χειρόγραφον *cheirographon*
COL. 2:14

5499. χειροποίητος *cheiropoiētos*
MARK 14:58; ACTS 7:48; 17:24; EPH. 2:11;
HEB. 9:11,24

5500. χειροτονέω *cheirotoneō*
ACTS 14:23; **2 COR.** 8:19

5501. χείρων *cheirōn*
MATT. 9:16; 12:45; 27:64; MARK 2:21; 5:26;
LUKE 11:26; JOHN 5:14; **1 TIM.** 5:8; **2 TIM.**
3:13; HEB. 10:29; **2 PET.** 2:20

5502. Χερουβίμ *Cheroubim*
HEB. 9:5

5503. χήρα *chēra*
MATT. 23:14; MARK 12:40,42,43; LUKE
2:37; 4:25,26; 7:12; 18:3,5; 20:47; 21:2,3; ACTS
6:1; 9:39,41; **1 COR.** 7:8; **1 TIM.** 5:3-5,9,11,16;
JAMES 1:27; REV. 18:7

5504. χθές *chthes*
JOHN 4:52; ACTS 7:28; HEB. 13:8

5505. χιλιάς *chilias*
LUKE 14:31; ACTS 4:4; **1 COR.** 10:8; REV.
5:11; 7:4-8; 11:13; 14:1,3; 21:16

5506. χιλίαρχος *chiliarchos*
MARK 6:21; JOHN 18:12; ACTS 21:31-33,37;
22:24,26-29; 23:10,15,17-19,22; 24:7,22; 25:23;
REV. 6:15; 19:18

5507. χίλιοι *chilioi*
2 PET. 3:8; REV. 11:3; 12:6; 14:20; 20:2-7

5508. Χίος *Chios*
ACTS 20:15

5509. χιτών *chiton*
MATT. 5:40; 10:10; MARK 6:9; 14:63; LUKE
3:11; 6:29; 9:3; JOHN 19:23; ACTS 9:39;
JUDE 1:23

5510. χιών *chiōn*
MATT. 28:3; MARK 9:3; REV. 1:14

5511. χλαμύς *chlamus*
MATT. 27:28,31

5512. χλενάζω *chleuazō*
ACTS 2:13; 17:32

5513. χλιαρός *chliaros*
REV. 3:16

5514. Χλόη *Chloē*
1 COR. 1:11

5515. χλωρός *chlōros*
MARK 6:39; REV. 6:8; 8:7; 9:4

5516. χξς *chi xi sigma*
(The number 666)
REV. 13:18

5517. χοϊκός *choikos*
1 COR. 15:47-49

5518. χοῖνιξ *choinix*
REV. 6:6

5519. χοῖρος *choiros*
MATT. 7:6; 8:30-32; MARK 5:11-14,16;
LUKE 8:32,33; 15:15,16

5520. χολάω *cholaō*
JOHN 7:23

5521. χολή *cholē*
MATT. 27:34; ACTS 8:23

5522. χόος *choos*
MARK 6:11; REV. 18:19

5523. Χοραζίν *Chorazin*
MATT. 11:21; LUKE 10:13

5524. χορηγέω *chorēgeō*
2 COR. 9:10; 1 PET. 4:11

5525. χορός *choros*
LUKE 15:25

5526. χορτάζω *chortazō*
MATT. 5:6; 14:20; 15:33,37; MARK 6:42;
7:27; 8:4,8; LUKE 6:21; 9:17; 16:21; JOHN
6:26; PHIL. 4:12; JAMES 2:16; REV. 19:21

5527. χόρτασμα *chortasma*
ACTS 7:11

5528. χόρτος *chortos*
MATT. 6:30; 13:26; 14:19; MARK 4:28; 6:39;
LUKE 12:28; JOHN 6:10; 1 COR. 3:12;
JAMES 1:10,11; 1 PET. 1:24; REV. 8:7; 9:4

5529. Χουζᾶς *Chouzas*
LUKE 8:3

5530. χράομαι *chraomai*
ACTS 27:3,17; 1 COR. 7:21,31; 9:12,15; 2
COR. 1:17; 3:12; 13:10; 1 TIM. 1:8; 5:23

5531. χράω *chraō*
LUKE 11:5

5532. χρεία *chreia*
MATT. 3:14; 6:8; 9:12; 14:16; 21:3; 26:65;
MARK 2:17,25; 11:3; 14:63; LUKE 5:31; 9:11;
10:42; 15:7; 19:31,34; 22:71; JOHN 2:25;
13:10,29; 16:30; ACTS 2:45; 4:35; 6:3; 20:34;
28:10; ROM. 12:13; 1 COR. 12:21,24; EPH.
4:28,29; PHIL. 2:25; 4:16,19; 1 THESS. 1:8;
4:9,12; 5:1; TITUS 3:14; HEB. 5:12; 7:11;
10:36; 1 JOHN 2:27; 3:17; REV. 3:17; 21:23;
22:5

5533. χρεωφειλέτης *chreōpheiletēs*
LUKE 7:41; 16:5

5534. χρή *chrē*
JAMES 3:10

5535. χρήζω *chrēzō*
MATT. 6:32; LUKE 11:8; 12:30; ROM. 16:2; 2 COR. 3:1

5536. χρῆμα *chrēma*
MARK 10:23,24; LUKE 18:24; ACTS 4:37; 8:18,20; 24:26

5537. χρηματίζω *chrēmatizō*
MATT. 2:12,22; LUKE 2:26; ACTS 10:22; 11:26; ROM. 7:3; HEB. 8:5; 11:7; 12:25

5538. χρηματισμός *chrēmatismos*
ROM. 11:4

5539. χρήσιμος *chrēsimos*
2 TIM. 2:14

5540. χρῆσις *chrēsis*
ROM. 1:26,27

5541. χρηστεύομαι *chrēsteuomai*
1 COR. 13:4

5542. χρηστολογία *chrēstologia*
ROM. 16:18

5543. χρηστός *chrēstos*
MATT. 11:30; LUKE 5:39; 6:35; ROM. 2:4; 1 COR. 15:33; EPH. 4:32; 1 PET. 2:3

5544. χρηστότης *chrēstotēs*
ROM. 2:4; 3:12; 11:22; 2 COR. 6:6; GAL. 5:22; EPH. 2:7; COL. 3:12; TITUS 3:4

5545. χρίσμα *chrisma*
1 JOHN 2:20,27

5546. Χριστιανός *Christianos*
ACTS 11:26; 26:28; 1 PET. 4:16

5547. Χριστός *Christos*
MATT. 1:1,16-18; 2:4; 11:2; 16:16,20; 22:42;
23:8,10; 24:5,23; 26:63,68; 27:17,22; MARK
1:1; 8:29; 9:41; 12:35; 13:21; 14:61; 15:32;
LUKE 2:11,26; 3:15; 4:41; 9:20; 20:41; 22:67;
23:2,35,39; 24:26,46; JOHN 1:17,20,25,41;
3:28; 4:25,29,42; 6:69; 7:26,27,31,41,42; 9:22;
10:24; 11:27; 12:34; 17:3; 20:31; ACTS 2:30,
31,36,38; 3:6,18,20; 4:10,26; 5:42; 8:5,12,37;
9:20,22,34; 10:36; 11:17; 15:11,26; 16:18,31;
17:3; 18:5,28; 19:4; 20:21; 24:24; 26:23; 28:31;
ROM. 1:1,3,6-8,16; 2:16; 3:22,24; 5:1,6,8,11,
15,17,21; 6:3,4,8,9,11,23; 7:4,25; 8:1,2,9-
11,17,34,35,39; 9:1,3,5; 10:4,6,7; 12:5; 13:14;
14:9,10,15,18; 15:3,5-8,16-20,29,30; 16:3,5,
7,9,10,16,18,20,24,25,27; 1 COR. 1:1-4,6-
10,12,13,17,23,24,30; 2:2,16; 3:1,11,23;
4:1,10,15,17; 5:4,7; 6:15; 7:22; 8:6,11,12;
9:1,12,18,21; 10:4,9,16; 11:1,3; 12:12,27;
15:3,12-20,22,23,31,57; 16:22-24; 2 COR. 1:1-
3,5,19,21; 2:10,12,14,15,17; 3:3,4,14; 4:4-6;
5:10,14,16-20; 6:15; 8:9,23; 9:13; 10:1,5,7,14;
11:2,3,10,13,23,31; 12:2,9,10,19; 13:3,5,14;
GAL. 1:1,3,6,7,10,12,22; 2:4,16,17,20,21;
3:1,13,14,16,17,22,24,26-29; 4:7,14,19; 5:1,
2,4,6,24; 6:2,12,14,15,18; EPH. 1:1-3,5,10,
12,17,20; 2:5-7,10,12,13,20; 3:1,4,6,8,9,11,14,
17,19,21; 4:7,12,13,15,20,32; 5:2,5,14,20,23-
25,32; 6:5,6,23,24; PHIL. 1:1,2,6,8,10,11,
13,15,16,18-21,23,26,27,29; 2:1,5,11,16,21,30;
3:3,7-9,12,14,18,20; 4:7,13,19,21,23; COL. 1:1-
4,7,24,27,28; 2:2,5,6,8,11,17,20; 3:1,3,4,
11,13,16,24; 4:3,12; 1 THESS. 1:1,3; 2:6,14,19;
3:2,11,13; 4:16; 5:9,18,23,28; 2 THESS.
1:1,2,8,12; 2:1,2,14,16; 3:5,6,12,18; 1 TIM.
1:1,2,12,14-16; 2:5,7; 3:13; 4:6; 5:11,21;
6:3,13,14; 2 TIM. 1:1,2,9,10,13; 2:1,3,8,10,19;
3:12,15; 4:1,22; TITUS 1:1,4; 2:13; 3:6;
PHILE. 1:1,3,6,8,9,23,25; HEB. 3:1,6,14; 5:5;
6:1; 9:11,14,24,28; 10:10; 11:26; 13:8,21;
JAMES 1:1; 2:1; 1 PET. 1:1-3,7,11,13,19;
2:5,21; 3:16,18,21; 4:1,11,13,14; 5:1,10,14;
2 PET. 1:1,8,11,14,16; 2:20; 3:18; 1 JOHN
1:3,7; 2:1,22; 3:23; 4:2,3; 5:1,6,20; 2 JOHN
1:3,7,9; JUDE 1:1,4,17,21; REV. 1:1,2,5,9;
11:15; 12:10,17; 20:4,6; 22:21

5548. χρίω *chriō*
LUKE 4:18; ACTS 4:27; 10:38; 2 COR. 1:21;
HEB. 1:9

5549. χρονίζω *chronizō*
MATT. 24:48; 25:5; LUKE 1:21; 12:45; HEB.
10:37

5550. χρόνος chronos
MATT. 2:7,16; 25:19; MARK 2:19; 9:21;
LUKE 1:57; 4:5; 8:27,29; 18:4; 20:9; JOHN
5:6; 7:33; 12:35; 14:9; ACTS 1:6,7,21; 3:21;
7:17,23; 8:11; 13:18; 14:3,28; 15:33; 17:30;
18:20,23; 19:22; 20:18; 27:9; ROM. 7:1; 16:25;
1 COR. 7:39; 16:7; GAL. 4:1,4; 1 THESS. 5:1;
2 TIM. 1:9; TITUS 1:2; HEB. 4:7; 5:12; 11:32;
1 PET. 1:17,20; 4:2,3; JUDE 1:18; REV. 2:21;
6:11; 10:6; 20:3

5551. χρονοτριβέω chronotribeō
ACTS 20:16

5552. χρύσεος chruseos
2 TIM. 2:20; HEB. 9:4; REV. 1:12,13,20; 2:1;
4:4; 5:8; 8:3; 9:13,20; 14:14; 15:6,7; 17:4; 21:15

5553. χρυσίον chrusion
ACTS 3:6; 20:33; HEB. 9:4; 1 PET. 1:7,18; 3:3;
REV. 3:18; 21:18,21

5554. χρυσοδακτύλιος chrusodaktulios
JAMES 2:2

5555. χρυσόλιθος chrusolithos
REV. 21:20

5556. χρυσόπρασος chrusoprasos
REV. 21:20

5557. χρυσός chrusos
MATT. 2:11; 10:9; 23:16,17; ACTS 17:29;
1 COR. 3:12; 1 TIM. 2:9; JAMES 5:3; REV.
9:7; 17:4; 18:12,16

5558. χρυσόω chrusoō
REV. 17:4; 18:16

5559. χρώς chrōs
ACTS 19:12

5560. χωλός chōlos
MATT. 11:5; 15:30,31; 18:8; 21:14; MARK
9:45; LUKE 7:22; 14:13,21; JOHN 5:3; ACTS
3:2,11; 8:7; 14:8; HEB. 12:13

5561. χώρα chōra
MATT. 2:12; 4:16; 8:28; MARK 1:5; 5:1,10;
LUKE 2:8; 3:1; 8:26; 12:16; 15:13-15; 19:12;
21:21; JOHN 4:35; 11:54,55; ACTS 8:1; 10:39;
12:20; 13:49; 16:6; 18:23; 26:20; 27:27; JAMES
5:4

5562. χωρέω chōreō
MATT. 15:17; 19:11,12; MARK 2:2; JOHN
2:6; 8:37; 21:25; 2 COR. 7:2; 2 PET. 3:9

5563. χωρίζω chōrizo
MATT. 19:6; MARK 10:9; ACTS 1:4; 18:1,2;
ROM. 8:35,39; 1 COR. 7:10,11,15; PHILE.
1:15; HEB. 7:26

5564. χωρίον chōrion
MATT. 26:36; MARK 14:32; JOHN 4:5;
ACTS 1:18,19; 4:34; 5:3,8; 28:7

5565. χωρίς chōris
MATT. 13:34; 14:21; 15:38; MARK 4:34;
LUKE 6:49; JOHN 1:3; 15:5; 20:7; ROM.
3:21,28; 4:6; 7:8,9; 10:14; 1 COR. 4:8; 11:11;
2 COR. 11:28; EPH. 2:12; PHIL. 2:14; 1 TIM.
2:8; 5:21; PHILE. 1:14; HEB. 4:15; 7:7,20,21;
9:7,18,22,28; 10:28; 11:6,40; 12:8,14; JAMES
2:20,26

5566. χῶρος chōros
ACTS 27:12

Ψ

5567. ψάλλω psallō
ROM. 15:9; 1 COR. 14:15; EPH. 5:19; JAMES
5:13

5568. ψαλμός psalmos
LUKE 20:42; 24:44; ACTS 1:20; 13:33;
1 COR. 14:26; EPH. 5:19; COL. 3:16

5569. ψευδάδελφος pseudadelphos
2 COR. 11:26; GAL. 2:4

5570. ψευδαπόστολος pseudapostolos
2 COR. 11:13

5571. ψευδής *pseudēs*
ACTS 6:13; **REV.** 2:2; 21:8

5572. ψευδοδιδάσκαλος
pseudodidaskalos
2 PET. 2:1

5573. ψευδολόγος *pseudologos*
1 TIM. 4:2

5574. ψεύδομαι *pseudomai*
MATT. 5:11; **ACTS** 5:3,4; **ROM.** 9:1; **2 COR.**
11:31; **GAL.** 1:20; **COL.** 3:9; **1 TIM.** 2:7; **HEB.**
6:18; **JAMES** 3:14; **1 JOHN** 1:6; **REV.** 3:9

5575. ψευδομάρτυρ *pseudomartur*
MATT. 26:60; **1 COR.** 15:15

5576. ψευδομαρτυρέω
pseudomartureō
MATT. 19:18; **MARK** 10:19; 14:56,57; **LUKE**
18:20; **ROM.** 13:9

5577. ψευδομαρτυρία
pseudomarturia
MATT. 15:19; 26:59

5578. ψευδοπροφήτης
pseudoprophētēs
MATT. 7:15; 24:11,24; **MARK** 13:22; **LUKE**
6:26; **ACTS** 13:6; **2 PET.** 2:1; **1 JOHN** 4:1;
REV. 16:13; 19:20; 20:10

5579. ψεῦδος *pseudos*
JOHN 8:44; **ROM.** 1:25; **EPH.** 4:25; **2 THESS.**
2:9,11; **1 JOHN** 2:21,27; **REV.** 21:27; 22:15

5580. ψευδόχριστος *pseudochristos*
MATT. 24:24; **MARK** 13:22

5581. ψευδώνυμος *pseudōnumos*
1 TIM. 6:20

5582. ψεῦσμα *pseusma*
ROM. 3:7

5583. ψεύστης *pseustēs*
JOHN 8:44,55; **ROM.** 3:4; **1 TIM.** 1:10;
TITUS 1:12; **1 JOHN** 1:10; 2:4,22; 4:20; 5:10

5584. ψηλαφάω *psēlaphaō*
LUKE 24:39; **ACTS** 17:27; **HEB.** 12:18;
1 JOHN 1:1

5585. ψηφίζω *psēphizō*
LUKE 14:28; **REV.** 13:18

5586. ψῆφος *psēphos*
ACTS 26:10; **REV.** 2:17

5587. ψιθυρισμός *psithurismos*
2 COR. 12:20

5588. ψιθυριστής *psithuristēs*
ROM. 1:29

5589. ψιχίον *psichion*
MATT. 15:27; **MARK** 7:28; **LUKE** 16:21

5590. ψυχή *psuchē*
MATT. 2:20; 6:25; 10:28,39; 11:29; 12:18;
16:25,26; 20:28; 22:37; 26:38; **MARK** 3:4; 8:35-
37; 10:45; 12:30,33; 14:34; **LUKE** 1:46; 2:35;
6:9; 9:24,56; 10:27; 12:19,20,22,23; 14:26;
17:33; 21:19; **JOHN** 10:11,15,17,24; 12:25,27;
13:37,38; 15:13; **ACTS** 2:27,31,41,43; 3:23;
4:32; 7:14; 14:2,22; 15:24,26; 20:10,24; 27:10,
22,37; **ROM.** 2:9; 11:3; 13:1; 16:4; **1 COR.**
15:45; **2 COR.** 1:23; 12:15; **EPH.** 6:6; **PHIL.**
1:27; 2:30; **COL.** 3:23; **1 THESS.** 2:8; 5:23;
HEB. 4:12; 6:19; 10:38,39; 12:3; 13:17; **JAMES**
1:21; 5:20; **1 PET.** 1:9,22; 2:11,25; 3:20; 4:19;
2 PET. 2:8,14; **1 JOHN** 3:16; **3 JOHN** 1:2;
REV. 6:9; 8:9; 12:11; 16:3; 18:13,14; 20:4

5591. ψυχικός *psuchikos*
1 COR. 2:14; 15:44,46; **JAMES** 3:15; **JUDE**
1:19

5592. ψῦχος *psuchos*
JOHN 18:18; **ACTS** 28:2; **2 COR.** 11:27

5593. ψυχρός *psuchros*
MATT. 10:42; **REV.** 3:15,16

5594. ψύχω psuchō
MATT. 24:12

5595. ψωμίζω psōmizō
ROM. 12:20; 1 COR. 13:3

5596. ψωμίον psōmion
JOHN 13:26,27,30

5597. ψώχω psōchō
LUKE 6:1

Ω

5598. Ω Omega
REV. 1:8,11; 21:6; 22:13

5599. ὦ ō
MATT. 15:28; 17:17; MARK 9:19; LUKE 9:41; 24:25; ACTS 1:1; 13:10; 18:14; 27:21; ROM. 2:1,3; 9:20; 11:33; GAL. 3:1; 1 TIM. 6:20; JAMES 2:20

5600. ὦ ō
(All subj. forms of εἰμί)
MATT. 6:4,22,23; 10:13; 20:4,7; 24:28; MARK 3:14; 5:18; LUKE 10:6; 11:34; 14:8; JOHN 3:2,27; 6:65; 9:5,31; 14:3; 16:24; 17:11,19,21-24,26; ACTS 5:38; ROM. 2:25; 9:27; 11:25; 1 COR. 1:10; 2:5; 5:7; 7:29,34,36; 12:25; 14:28; 15:28; 16:4; 2 COR. 1:9,17; 4:7; 9:3; 13:7,9; GAL. 5:10; EPH. 4:14; 5:27; PHIL. 1:10; 2:28; 1 TIM. 4:15; 5:7; 2 TIM. 3:17; TITUS 1:9; 3:14; PHILE. 1:14; JAMES 1:4; 2:15; 5:15; 1 JOHN 1:4; 2 JOHN 1:12

5601. Ὠβήδ Obēd
MATT. 1:5; LUKE 3:32

5602. ὧδε hōde
MATT. 8:29; 12:6,41,42; 14:8,17,18; 16:28; 17:4,17; 20:6; 22:12; 24:2,23; 26:38; 28:6; MARK 6:3; 8:4; 9:1,5; 11:3; 13:21; 14:32,34; 16:6; LUKE 4:23; 9:12,27,33,41; 11:31,32; 14:21; 17:21,23; 19:27; 22:38; 23:5; 24:6; JOHN 6:9,25; 11:21,32; 20:27; ACTS 9:14,21; COL. 4:9; HEB. 7:8; 13:14; JAMES 2:3; REV. 4:1; 11:12; 13:10,18; 14:12; 17:9

5603. ὠδή ōdē
EPH. 5:19; COL. 3:16; REV. 5:9; 14:3; 15:3

5604. ὠδίν ōdin
MATT. 24:8; MARK 13:8; ACTS 2:24; 1 THESS. 5:3

5605. ὠδίνω ōdinō
GAL. 4:19,27; REV. 12:2

5606. ὦμος ōmos
MATT. 23:4; LUKE 15:5

5608. ὠνέομαι ōneomai
ACTS 7:16

5609. ὠόν ōon
LUKE 11:12

5610. ὥρα hōra
MATT. 8:13; 9:22; 10:19; 14:15; 15:28; 17:18; 18:1; 20:3,5,6,9,12; 24:36,42,44,50; 25:13; 26:40,45,55; 27:45,46; MARK 6:35; 11:11; 13:11,32; 14:35,37,41; 15:25,33,34; LUKE 1:10; 2:38; 7:21; 10:21; 12:12,39,40,46; 14:17; 20:19; 22:14,53,59; 23:44; 24:33; JOHN 1:39; 2:4; 4:6,21,23,52,53; 5:25,28,35; 7:30; 8:20; 11:9; 12:23,27; 13:1; 16:2,4,21,25,32; 17:1; 19:14,27; ACTS 2:15; 3:1; 5:7; 10:3,9,30; 16:18,33; 19:34; 22:13; 23:23; ROM. 13:11; 1 COR. 4:11; 15:30; 2 COR. 7:8; GAL. 2:5; 1 THESS. 2:17; PHILE. 1:15; 1 JOHN 2:18; REV. 3:3,10; 9:15; 11:13; 14:7,15; 17:12; 18:10,17,19

5611. ὡραῖος hōraios
MATT. 23:27; ACTS 3:2,10; ROM. 10:15

5612. ὠρύομαι ōruomai
1 PET. 5:8

5614. ὡσαννά hōsanna
MATT. 21:9,15; MARK 11:9,10; JOHN 12:13

5615. ὡσαύτως hōsautōs
MATT. 20:5; 21:30,36; 25:17; MARK 12:21; 14:31; LUKE 13:3; 20:31; 22:20; ROM. 8:26; 1 COR. 11:25; 1 TIM. 2:9; 3:8,11; 5:25; TITUS 2:3,6

5616. ὡσεί *hōsei*
MATT. 3:16; 9:36; 14:21; 28:3,4; **MARK** 1:10;
6:44; 9:26; **LUKE** 1:56; 3:22,23; 9:14,28;
22:41,44,59; 23:44; 24:11; **JOHN** 1:32; 4:6;
6:10; 19:14,39; **ACTS** 2:3,41; 4:4; 5:36; 6:15;
9:18; 10:3; 19:7; **HEB.** 1:12; 11:12; **REV.** 1:14

5617. Ὡσηέ *Hosēe*
ROM. 9:25

5618. ὥσπερ *hōsper*
MATT. 5:48; 6:2,5,7,16; 12:40; 13:40; 18:17;
20:28; 24:27,37,38; 25:14,32; **LUKE** 17:24;
18:11; **JOHN** 5:21,26; **ACTS** 2:2; 3:17; 11:15;
ROM. 5:12,19,21; 6:4,19; 11:30; **1 COR.** 8:5;
11:12; 15:22; 16:1; **2 COR.** 1:7; 8:7; 9:5; **GAL.**
4:29; **EPH.** 5:24; **1 THESS.** 5:3; **HEB.** 4:10;
7:27; 9:25; **JAMES** 2:26; **REV.** 10:3

5619. ὡσπερεί *hōsperei*
1 COR. 15:8

5620. ὥστε *hōste*
MATT. 8:24,28; 10:1; 12:12,22; 13:2,32,54;
15:31,33; 19:6; 23:31; 24:24; 27:1,14; **MARK**

1:27,45; 2:2,12,28; 3:10,20; 4:1,32,37; 9:26;
10:8; 15:5; **LUKE** 5:7; 9:52; 12:1; **JOHN** 3:16;
ACTS 1:19; 5:15; 14:1; 15:39; 16:26; 19:10,12,
16; **ROM.** 7:4,6,12; 13:2; 15:19; **1 COR.** 1:7;
3:7,21; 4:5; 5:1,8; 7:38; 10:12; 11:27,33; 13:2;
14:22,39; 15:58; **2 COR.** 1:8; 2:7; 3:7; 4:12;
5:16,17; 7:7; **GAL.** 2:13; 3:9,24; 4:7,16; **PHIL.**
1:13; 2:12; 4:1; **1 THESS.** 1:7,8; 4:18;
2 THESS. 1:4; 2:4; **HEB.** 13:6; **JAMES** 1:19;
1 PET. 1:21; 4:19

5621. ὠτίον *ōtion*
MATT. 26:51; **MARK** 14:47; **LUKE** 22:51;
JOHN 18:10,26

5622. ὠφέλεια *ōpheleia*
ROM. 3:1; **JUDE** 1:16

5623. ὠφελέω *ōpheleō*
MATT. 15:5; 16:26; 27:24; **MARK** 5:26; 7:11;
8:36; **LUKE** 9:25; **JOHN** 6:63; 12:19; **ROM.**
2:25; **1 COR.** 13:3; 14:6; **GAL.** 5:2; **HEB.** 4:2;
13:9

5624. ὠφέλιμος *ōphelimos*
1 TIM. 4:8; **2 TIM.** 3:16; **TITUS** 3:8

TRANSLATIONAL REFERENCE INDEX

This index lists certain of the English words used in the King James Version of the New Testament, along with their various forms and endings. Following the English word in each entry are the Strong's numbers for all the Greek words which that English word represents in this translation. Finally, sample scripture references are given in which the English word is used. Italicized references indicate that every reference in which the word appears has been included.

A

a; an — *1520, 3391:* John 1:6; Rev. 9:13

Aaron — *2:* Luke 1:5; Acts 7:40

Abaddon — *3: Rev. 9:11*

abased; abasing (see **humble; humilia-tion**) — *5013:* Luke 14:11; Phil. 4:12

Abba — *5: Mark 14:36; Rom. 8:15; Gal. 4:6*

Abel — *6:* Matt. 23:35; Heb. 11:4

abhor -rest (see **hate**) — *655, 948:* Rom. 2:22; 12:9

Abia; Abijah — *7: Matt. 1:7; Luke 1:5*

Abiathar — *8: Mark 2:26*

abide -eth -ing; abode — *63, 1304, 1961, 3306, 3887, 4357:* Luke 2:8; John 12:46

Abilene — *9: Luke 3:1*

ability; able — *1410, 1411, 1415, 1840, 2141, 2192, 2425, 2427, 2479, 2480:* Luke 14:31; Titus 1:9

Abiud — *10: Matt. 1:13*

aboard — *1910: Acts 21:2*

abolished — *2673: 2 Cor. 3:13; Eph. 2:15; 2 Tim. 1:10*

abominable; abomination -s — *111, 946, 947, 948:* Luke 16:15; Rev. 17:4

abound -ed -eth -ing (see **abundant**) — *4052, 4121, 4129, 5248:* Rom. 5:20; 2 Cor. 1:5

about — *1330, 1722, 1909, 1994, 2021, 2212, 2596, 2943, 2944, 2945, 3163, 3195, 4012, 4013, 4015, 4016, 4017, 4019, 4022, 4024, 4034, 4037, 4043, 4060, 4064, 4066, 4225, 4314, 4762, 5148, 5613, 5616:* Acts 9:3; Eph. 4:14

above — *507, 509, 511, 1883, 1909, 3844, 4012, 4117, 4253, 5228, 5231:* Matt. 10:24; Col. 3:1, 2*

Abraham — *11: Luke 1:55; Heb. 2:16*

abroad — *864, 1096/5456, 1232, 1255, 1287, 1289, 1290, 1310, 1330, 1519/5318, 1632, 1831, 4496, 4650:* Matt. 9:26; 1 Thess. 1:8

absence; absent — *548, 553, 666, 817:* 2 Cor. 5:6; Phil. 2:12

abstain; abstinence — *567, 776:* Acts 27:21; 1 Pet. 2:11

abundant -ly; abundance (see **abound**) —

100, 1411, 4050, 4051, 4052, 4053, 4054, 4055, 4056, 4121, 4146, 4183, 5236, 5250: John 10:10; 2 Cor. 8:2

abusers; abusing — *733, 2710: 1 Cor. 6:9; 7:31*

accept -able -ably -ation -ed — *587, 588, 594, 1184, 1209, 2101, 2102, 2144, 2983, 4327, 5487:* Luke 4:19; Rom. 12:1

access — *4318: Rom. 5:2; Eph. 2:18; 3:12*

accompany -ied — *2192, 4311, 4862, 4902, 4905:* Acts 10:23; Heb. 6:9

accomplish -ed -ing -ment — *1604, 1822, 2005, 4130, 4137, 5055:* Luke 2:61; Pet. 5:9

accord (see **agree; unite**) — *830, 844, 3661, 4861:* Acts 1:14; 2 Cor. 8:17

according — *2526, 2530, 2531, 2596, 4314, 5613:* John 7:24; Phil. 3:21

account -ed -ing — *1380, 1677, 2233, 2661, 3049, 3056:* 1 Cor. 4:1; Heb. 11:19

accursed — *331: Rom. 9:3; 1 Cor. 12:3; Gal. 1:8, 9*

accuse -ation -ed -er(s) — *156, 1225, 1228, 1458, 1722/2724, 1908, 2723, 2920, 4811:* 2 Pet. 2:11; Rev. 12:10

Aceldama — *184: Acts 1:19*

Achaia (see **Greece**) — *882: Acts 18:12; 1 Cor. 16:15*

Achaz — *881: Matt. 1:9*

Achim — *885: Matt. 1:14*

acknowledge -ed -eth -ing -ment — *1921, 1922: 2 Cor. 1:14; Phile. 1:6*

acquaintance — *1110, 2398: Luke 2:44; 23:49; Acts 24:23*

act — *1888: John 8:4*

Adam — *76: Luke 3:38; Jude 1:14*

add -ed -eth — *1928, 2007, 2018, 2023, 4323, 4369:* Matt. 6:27; Gal. 2:6

Addi — *78: Luke 3:28*

addicted — *5201: 1 Cor. 16:15*

administered; administration -s — *1247, 1248: 1 Cor. 8:19, 20; 12:5; 2 Cor. 9:12*

admired; admiration — *2295, 2296: 2 Thess. 1:10; Jude 1:16; Rev. 17:6*

admonish -ed -ing; admonition — *3559, 3560, 3867, 5537:* Rom. 15:14; 2 Thess. 3:15

ado — *2350: Mark 5:39*

adoption — *5206:* Rom. 8:23; Gal. 4:5

adorn -ed -ing — *2885, 2889:* 1 Tim. 2:9; Rev. 21:2

Adramyttium — *98: Acts 27:2*

Adria — *99: Acts 27:27*

adultery -ers -ess(es) -ies -ous (see **chaste; fornication**) — *3428, 3429, 3430, 3431:* John 8:3,4; Rom. 7:3

advantage -ed -eth — *3786, 4053, 4122, 5622, 5623:* Luke 9:25; 2 Cor. 2:11

adventure — *1325: Acts 19:31*

adversary -ies (see **enemy; foe**) — *476, 480, 5227:* Luke 13:17; 1 Tim. 5:14

adversity -ies — *2558:* Heb. 13:3

advice; advised — *1012/5087, 1106: Acts 27:12; 2 Cor. 8:10*

advocate — *3875: 1 John 2:1*

Aeneas — *132: Acts 9:33, 34*

Aenon — *137: John 3:23*

afar (see **far**) — *3112, 3113, 3467, 4207:* Mark 5:6; Heb. 11:13

affair -s — *2596, 4012, 4230:* Eph. 6:21; 2 Tim. 2:4

affect -ed — *2206, 2559: Acts 14:2; Gal. 4:17, 18*

affection -ately -ed -s — *794, 2442, 3804, 3806, 4698, 5387, 5426:* Rom. 1:26; Col. 3:2

affirm -ed — *1226, 1340, 5335, 5346:* Acts 12:15; Rom. 3:8; Titus 3:8

afflicted -est; affliction -s — *2346, 2347, 2552, 2553, 2561, 3804, 4777, 4797, 5003:* Matt. 24:9; 1 Pet. 5:9

affrighted (see **afraid**) — *1568, 1719: Mark 16:5, 6; Luke 24:37; Rev. 11:13*

afoot — *3978, 3979: Mark 6:33; Acts 20:13*

afore -hand -time (see **before**) — *4218, 4270, 4279, 4282, 4301:* John 9:13; Rom. 15:4

afraid (see **affright; fear**) — *1168, 1630, 1719, 5141, 5399:* Matt. 2:22; Mark 9:6

afresh — *388: Heb. 6:6*

after -ward -wards — *516, 1207, 1223, 1230, 1377, 1519/3195, 1534, 1567, 1722, 1836, 1887, 1894, 1899, 1909, 1934, 1938, 1971, 2089, 2517, 2596, 2614, 2628, 3195, 3326, 3326/5023, 3693, 3694, 3753, 3765, 3779, 4023, 4137, 4329, 4459, 5225, 5613, 5615:* Mark 4:17; 2 Thess. 2:9

Agabus — *13: Acts 11:28; 21:10*

again — *313, 321, 326, 330, 344, 364, 375, 386, 450, 467, 470, 479, 483, 488, 509, 518, 523, 560, 591, 600, 618, 654, 1208, 1364, 1453, 1515, 1537/1208, 1880, 1994, 3326, 3825, 3825/509, 4388, 4762, 5290:* Matt. 2:8; Rom. 4:25

against — *210, 368, 470, 471, 483, 495, 497, 561, 1519, 1537/1727, 1693, 1715, 1722,*

1909, 2018, 2019, 2596, 2620, 2649, 2691, 2702, 2713, 2729, 3326, 3844, 4012, 4314, 4366, 4814, 5396: Luke 12:52; Rev. 2:4

age -ed -s — *165, 1074, 2244, 2250, 4246, 4247, 5046, 5230:* Luke 2:36; Col. 1:26

ago — *575, 3819, 4253:* Acts 10:30; 2 Cor. 8:10

agony — *74: Luke 22:44*

agree -ed -eth (see **accord; unite**) — *800, 1106, 1526, 2470, 3662, 3982, 4783, 4856, 4934:* 2 Cor. 6:16; 1 John 5:8

Agrippa — *67:* Acts 25:13; 26:27

aground — *2027: Acts 27:41*

ah — *3758: Mark 15:29*

air — *109, 3722:* Eph. 2:2; Rev. 9:2

alabaster — *211:* Matt. 26:7; Mark 14:3; Luke 7:37

alas — *3759: Rev. 18:10, 16, 19*

albeit — *2443: Phile. 1:9*

Alexander — *223:* Mark 15:21; 1 Tim. 1:20

Alexandria -ns — *221: Acts 6:9; 18:24; 27:6; 28:11*

aliens — *245, 526:* Eph. 2:12; Heb. 11:34

alienated — *526: Eph. 4:18; Col. 1:21*

alike — *259: Rom. 14:5*

alive (see **quick**) — *326, 2198, 2227:* Mark 16:11; Acts 1:3

all — *537, 1273, 2178, 2527, 3122, 3364, 3367, 3650, 3654, 3745, 3762, 3779, 3829, 3832, 3837, 3843, 3908, 3956, 4219, 5033, 5613 :* Luke 1:3; 1 Tim. 1:15

alleging — *3908: Acts 17:3*

allegory — *238: Gal. 4:24*

alleluia — *239: Rev. 19:1, 3, 4, 6*

allow -ed -eth — *1097, 1381, 4327, 4909:* Luke 11:48; Rom. 7:15

allure (see **tempt**) — *1185: 2 Pet. 2:18*

almighty — *3841:* 2 Cor. 6:18; Rev. 1:8

almost — *1722/3641, 3195, 4975:* Acts 26:28; Heb. 9:22

alms; almsdeeds — *1654:* Matt. 6:1; Luke 11:41

aloes — *250: John 19:39*

alone — *863, 1439, 2596/1438, 2596/2398, 2651, 3440, 3441:* Matt. 4:4; James 2:17

aloud — *310: Mark 15:8*

Alpha — *1: Rev. 1:8, 11; 21:6; 22:13*

Alpheus — *256:* Matt. 10:3; Mark 2:14

already — *2235, 4258, 5348:* John 3:18; 2 Cor. 12:21

also (see **too**) — *260, 260/1161/2532, 1161, 1211, 2504, 2528, 2532, 2546, 2547, 2548, 4828, 4879, 4901, 5037:* Luke 1:3; Phile. 1:21

altar -s — *1041, 2379:* Matt. 5:23; Rom. 11:3

altered — *1096/2087: Luke 9:29*

although (see **nevertheless; though**) — *2532/1487, 2543: Mark 14:29; Heb. 4:3*

altogether (see **together**) — *1722/4183, 3650, 3843:* John 9:34; 1 Cor. 5:10

always — *104, 1223/3956, 1275, 1722/3956/ 2540, 3842, 3956/2250:* Matt. 28:20; 2 Thess. 1:3

am; art; be; been; being; is; was; wast; were — *1096, 1304, 1488, 1498, 1510, 1511, 1909, 2070, 2075, 2076, 2192, 2258, 3918, 4160, 4357, 5225, 5078, 5607:* Matt. 3:11; Rev. 11:17

amazed; amazement — *1096/2285, 1568, 1605, 1611, 1611/2983, 1839, 2284, 4423:* Luke 2:48; 1 Pet. 3:6

ambassador -s — *4242, 4243: Luke 14:32; 2 Cor. 5:20; Eph. 6:20*

Amen — *281:* Matt. 6:13; Gal. 1:5

amend — *2192/2866: John 4:52*

amethyst — *271: Rev. 21:20*

Aminadab — *284: Matt. 1:4; Luke 3:33*

amiss — *824, 2560: Luke 23:41; James 4:3*

Amon — *300: Matt. 1:10*

among — *303/3319, 1223, 1519, 1537, 1722, 1722/3319, 1909, 2596, 3319, 3326, 3844, 4045, 4314, 5216, 5259:* John 1:14; Acts 1:21

Amos — *301: Luke 3:25*

Amphipolis — *295: Acts 17:1*

Amplias — *291: Rom. 16:8*

Ananias — *367: Acts 5:1; 23:2*

anathema — *331:1 Cor. 16:22*

anchor -s — *45: Acts 27:29, 30, 40; Heb. 6:19*

Andrew — *406:* Mark 1:16; John 12:22

Andronicus — *408: Rom. 16:7*

angel -s (see **archangel**) — *32, 2465:* John 12:29; Rev. 1:1

anger; angry — *3709, 3710, 3711, 3949, 5520:* Eph. 4:31; Titus 1:7

anguish — *2347, 4730, 4928:* John 16:21; 2 Cor. 2:4

anise — *432: Matt. 23:23*

ankle — *4974: Acts 3:7*

Anna — *451: Luke 2:36*

Annas — *452: Luke 3:2; John 18:13, 24; Acts 4:6*

anoint -ed -ing — *218, 1472, 2025, 2025/ 1909, 3462, 5545, 5548:* Luke 4:18; 1 John 2:27

anon — (see **forthwith; immediately; straightway**) *2112, 2117: Matt. 13:20; Mark 1:30*

another (see **other**) — *240, 243, 245, 246, 1438, 1520, 2087, 3588, 3739, 4299, 4835:* Acts 1:20; Eph. 4:2

answer -ed -est -eth -ing — *38, 470, 611, 612, 626, 627, 1906, 2036, 4960, 5274, 5538:* Matt. 4:4; Gal. 4:25

antichrist -s — *500: 1 John 2:18, 22; 4:3; 2 John 1:7*

Antioch — *490, 491: Acts 6:5; 11:19*

Antipas — *493: Rev. 2:13*

Antipatris — *494: Acts 23:31*

any — *1520, 1536, 2089, 3361, 3364, 3367, 3379, 3387, 3588, 3762, 3763, 3765, 3956, 4218, 4455, 4458, 5100: Acts 4:12; 1 Cor. 1:15*

apart — *659, 2596/2398:* Matt. 14:13; James 1:21

Apelles — *559: Rom. 16:10*

apiece (see **each**) — *303: Luke 9:3; John 2:6*

Appolonia — *624: Acts 17:1*

Apollos — *625:* Acts 18:24; 1 Cor. 1:12

Apollyon — *623: Rev. 9:11*

apostle -s -ship — *651, 652, 5570:* Matt. 10:2; 2 Tim. 1:11

apparel -ed — *2066, 2440, 2441, 2689:* Luke 7:25; James 2:2

appeal -ed — *1941:Acts 25:11, 12, 21, 25; 26:32; 28:19*

appear -ance -ed -eth -ing — *82, 398, 602, 1718, 2014, 2015, 2064, 3700, 5316, 5318, 5319 :* Matt. 6:16; Titus 2:11

appeased — *2687: Acts 19:35*

Apphia — *682: Phile.2*

Appii — *675: Acts 28:15*

appoint -ed — *322, 606, 1299, 1303, 1935, 2476, 2525, 2749, 4160, 4287, 4384, 4929, 5021, 5087:* Matt. 26:19; Heb. 9:27

apprehend -ed — *2638, 4084: Acts 12:4; 2 Cor. 11:32; Phil 3:12, 13*

approach -eth -ing — *676, 1448:* Luke 12:33; 1 Tim. 6:6

approve -ed -est — *584, 1381, 1384, 4921:* Phil. 1:10; 2 Tim. 2:15

apron -s — *4612: Acts 19:12*

apt — *1317: 1 Tim. 3:2; 2 Tim. 2:24*

Aquila — *207:* Acts 18:2; Rom. 16:3

Arabia -ns — *688, 690: Acts 2:11; Gal. 1:17; 4:25*

Aram — *,689: Matt. 1:3, 4; Luke 3:33*

archangel (see **angel**) — *743: 1 Thess. 4:16; Jude 1:9*

Archelaus — *745: Mt. 2:22*

Archippus — *751: Col. 4:17; Phile. 1:2*

Areopagite — *698: Acts 17:34*

Areopagus — *697: Acts 17:19*

Aretas — *702: 2 Cor. 11:32*

Arimathea — *707:* Matt. 27:57; Mark 15:43

arise; arose; arouse; raise; rise; rouse — *305, 393, 450, 906, 1096, 1326, 1453:* Luke 1:39; 2 Pet. 1:19

ark — *2787:* Heb. 9:4; Rev. 11:19

arm -ed -s — *43, 1023, 1723, 3695:* Luke 2:28; Acts 13:17

Armageddon — *717: Rev. 16:16*

armor — *3696, 3833:* Luke 11:22; Eph. 6:11, 13

army -ies — *3925, 4753, 4760:* Matt. 22:7; Rev. 19:14

Arphaxad — *742:* Luke 3:36

array -ed — *1746, 2441, 4016:* 1 Tim. 2:9; Rev. 7:13

arrived — *2668, 3846:* Luke 8:26; Acts 20:15

arts — *4021:* Acts 19:19

Artemas — *734:* Titus 3:12

as — *5613:* Mark 1:2; 1 Pet. 1:14

Asa — *760:* Matt. 1:7, 8

ascend -ed -eth -ing — *305:* John 1:51; Rev. 17:8

ashamed (see **shame**) — *149, 152, 153, 422, 808, 819, 1788, 1791, 1870, 2617, 3856:* Mark 8:38; Titus 2:8

Asher — *768:* Luke 2:36; Rev. 7:6

Asia — *773, 775:* Acts 2:9; Rev. 1:4

aside — *402, 565, 659, 863, 1824, 2596/2398, 5087, 5298:* John 13:4; 1 Pet. 2:1

ask -ed -est -eth -ing (see **request**) — *154, 350, 523, 1905, 2065, 3004, 4441:* Mark 6:22; Rom. 10:20

asleep; sleep — *879, 1852, 1853, 2518, 2837, 5259:* Luke 8:23; 1 Thess. 4:13, 15

asps — *785:* Rom. 3:13

ass — *3678, 3688, 5268:* John 12:15; 2 Pet. 2:16

assault -ed — *2186, 3730:* Acts 14:5; 17:5

assembled; assembling; assemblies — *1096, 1997, 4863, 4871, 4905:* Acts 1:4; James 2:2

assented — *4934:* Acts 24:9

assist — *3936:* Rom. 16:12

Assos — *789:* Acts 20:13,14

assure -ance -ed -edly — *806, 3982, 4102, 4104, 4136, 4822:* 2 Tim. 3:14; Heb. 6:11

astonished; astonishment — *1605, 1611, 1839, 2284, 4023/2285:* Mark 5:42; Acts 9:6

astray — *4105:* Matt. 18:12; 2 Pet. 2:15

asunder — *673, 1288, 1371, 2997, 4249, 5562:* Acts 1:18; Heb. 4:12

Asyncritus — *799:* Rom. 16:14

at — *345, 575, 630, 1065, 1223, 1368, 1369, 1448, 1451, 1519, 1531, 1537, 1657, 1722, 1764, 1847, 1848, 1909, 2527, 2596, 2621, 2625, 2827, 2919, 3195, 3317, 3367, 3379, 3626, 3654, 3762, 3763, 3826, 3844, 4012, 4218, 4314, 4363, 4412, 4873:* Gal. 4:12; 1 John 1:5

Athens; Athenians — *116, 117:* Acts 17:21, 22; 1 Thess. 3:1

athirst (see **thirst**) — *1372:* Matt. 25:44; Rev. 21:6; 22:17

atonement (see **propitiation**) — *2643:* Rom. 5:11

attain -ed — *2638, 2658, 2983, 3877, 5348:* Acts 27:12; Phil. 3:11, 12

Attalia — *825:* Acts 14:25

attempted; attempting — *3984/2983, 3985; 3987:* Acts 9:26; 16:7; Heb. 11:29

attend -ance -ed -ing — *2145, 4337, 4342, 4612:* Rom. 13:6; 1 Cor. 7:35

attentive — *1582:* Luke 19:48

audience — *189, 191:* Luke 7:1; Acts 13:16

Augustus — *828:* Luke 2:1; Acts 25:21, 25; 27:1

austere — *840:* Luke 19:21, 22

author — *159, 747:* 1 Cor. 14:33; Heb. 5:9 ; 12:2

authority -ies — *831, 1413, 1849, 1850, 2003, 2715, 5247:* Matt. 7:29; Acts 8:27

availeth — *2480:* Gal. 5:6; 6:15; James 5:16

avenge -ed -er -eth -ing (see **revenge; vengeance**) — *1556, 1558, 2917, 2919,/3588/2917, 4160/1557, 4160/3588/1557:* Acts 7:24; 1 Thess. 4:6

avoid -ing — *1223, 1578, 1624, 3868, 4026, 4724:* 2 Cor. 8:20; 2 Tim. 2:23

await — *1917:* Acts 9:24

awake -ing; awoke — *1235, 1326, 1453, 1594, 1852, 1853:* Acts 16:27; Eph. 5:14

aware (see **ware**) — *1097, 1492:* Matt. 24:50; Luke 11:44; 12:46

away — *115, 142, 337, 343, 520, 565, 577, 580, 595, 617, 630, 646, 649, 657, 659, 665, 667, 683, 726, 803, 851, 863, 868, 1544, 1593, 1601, 1808, 1813, 1821, 1854, 2210, 2673, 3334, 3350, 3351, 3895, 3911, 3928, 4014, 4879, 5217:* Col. 1:23; 1 John 2:17

axe — *513:* Matt. 3:10; Luke 3:9

Azor — *107:* Matt. 1:13, 14

Azotus — *108:* Acts 8:40

B

Baal — *896:* Rom. 11:4

babbler; babblings — *2757, 4691:* Acts 17:18; 1 Tim. 6:20; 2 Tim. 2:16

babe -s (see **infants**) — *1025, 3516:* Luke 1:41; 1 Pet. 2:2

Babylon (see **Chaldeans**) — *897:* Matt. 1:11; Rev. 14:8

back — *617, 650, 3557, 3694, 4762, 5288, 5289, 5290:* John 18:6; Rom. 11:10

backbiters; backbitings — *2636, 2637:* Rom. 1:30; 2 Cor. 12:20

bag -s — *905, 1101:* Luke 12:33; John 12:6; 13:29

Balaam — *903:* 2 Pet. 2:15; Jude 1:11; Rev. 2:14

Balak — *904:* Rev. 2:14

band -ed -s — *1199, 2202, 4160/4963, 4886:* Acts 10:1; Col. 2:19

banquetings — *4224:* 1 Pet. 4:3

baptize -ed; baptism; Baptist — *907, 908, 909, 910:* Matt. 3:1; Gal. 3:27

Barabbas — *912:* Mark 15:7; John 18:40

Barachias — *914:* Matt. 23:35

Barak — *913: Heb. 11:32*

barbarian; barbarous — *915: Acts 28:2, 4; Rom. 1:14; 1 Cor. 14:11; Col. 3:11*

Bar-jesus — *919: Acts 13:6*

Bar-jona (see **Jona**) — *920: Matt. 16:17*

barley — *2915, 2916: John 6:9, 13; Rev. 6:6*

barn -s — *596: Matt. 6:26; 13:30; Luke 12:18, 24*

Barnabas — *921: Acts 4:36; Gal. 2:1*

barren — *692, 4723: Luke 1:7, 36; 23:29; Gal. 4:27; 2 Pet. 1:8*

Barsabas — *923: Acts 1:23; 15:22*

Bartholomew (see **Nathanael**) — *918: Matt. 10:3; Acts 1:13*

Bartimaeus (see **Timaeus**) — *924: Mark 10:46*

base -er (see **vile**) — *36, 60, 5011: Acts 17:5; 1 Cor. 1:28; 2 Cor. 10:1*

basin — *3537: John 13:5*

basket -s — *2894, 4553, 4711: Matt. 14:20; 2 Cor. 11:33*

bastards — *3541: Heb. 12:8*

battle — *4171: 1 Cor. 14:8; Rev. 9:7, 9; 16:14; 20:8*

beam — *1385: Matt. 7:3-5; Luke 6:41, 42*

bear -est -eth -ing; bare -est — *142, 399, 430, 503, 715, 941, 1080, 1131, 3114, 3140, 4160, 5041, 5297, 5342, 5409, 5576: 2 Cor. 11:1; Gal. 4:27*

beast -s — *2226, 2341, 2342, 2934, 4968, 5074: Luke 10:34; Jude 1:10*

beat -en -eth -ing — *1194, 1911, 4350, 4363, 4366, 4463, 5180: Acts 5:40; 1 Cor. 9:26*

beautiful — *5611: Matt. 23:27; Rom. 10:15*

became; become — *516, 889, 1096, 1402, 1519, 1986, 2289, 2412, 2673, 4241: Phil. 1:27; Heb. 5:9*

because — *473/3739, 575, 1063, 1223, 1360, 1537, 1722, 1893, 1894, 1909, 2443, 2530, 3704, 3739/1752, 3754, 3759, 4314, 5484: Matt. 2:18; Eph. 4:18*

beckoned; beckoning — *1269, 2656, 2678, 3506: Luke 1:22; Acts 13:16*

bed -s — *2825, 2845, 2895: Mark 6:55; Rev. 2:22*

Beelzebub — *954: Matt. 10:25; Luke 11:15*

befall -en; befell — *1096, 4819, 4876: Matt. 8:33; Mark 5:16; Acts 20:19, 22*

before -hand -time (see **afore; ere**) — *561, 575, 1519/4383, 1715, 1725, 1726, 1773, 1799, 1909, 2596, 2713, 2714, 3319, 3362/ 4386, 3764, 3844, 3908, 3936, 4250, 4250/ 2228, 4253, 4253/4383, 4254, 4256, 4257, 4264, 4267, 4270, 4271, 4275, 4277, 4278, 4280, 4281, 4282, 4283, 4293, 4294, 4295, 4296, 4299, 4300, 4301, 4302, 4303, 4305, 4308, 4309, 4310, 4313, 4314, 4315, 4363,*

4384, 4391, 4401, 4412, 4413: 1 Tim. 5:24; James 1:27

beg -gar -garly -ged -ging — *154, 1871, 4319, 4434: Luke 16:20; Gal. 4:9*

begat; begotten — *313, 616, 1080, 3439, 4416: Matt. 1:2; 1 John 4:9*

begin -ner -ning(s); began; begun — *746/ 2983, 756, 1728, 2020, 2691, 3195, 4278, 4413: Phil. 1:6; Rev. 1:8*

beguile -ed -ing (see **guile**) — *1185, 1818, 2603, 3884: 2 Cor. 11:3; Col. 2:4, 18; 2 Pet. 2:14*

behalf — *1909, 3313, 4012, 5228: Rom. 16:19; 1 Cor. 1:4*

behave -ed -eth -ior — *390, 807, 812, 1096: 1 Thess. 2:10; Titus 2:3*

behead -ed — *607, 3990: Matt. 14:10; Mark 6:16, 27; Luke 9:9; Rev. 20:4*

behind — *2641, 3693, 3694, 5278, 5302: 1 Cor. 1:7; Col. 1:24*

behold -est -eth -ing; beheld — *333, 816, 991, 1492, 1689, 1896, 2029, 2300, 2334, 2396, 2400, 2657, 2734, 3708: Luke 6:41; Jude 1:14*

behoove -ed (see **necessary; ought**) — *1163, 3784: Luke 24:46; Heb. 2:17*

Belial — *955: 2 Cor. 6:15*

believe -ing -rs; belief — *544, 569, 571, 1537, 1722, 1909, 3982, 4100, 4102, 4103, 4135: Acts 5:14; James 2:19*

belly -ies — *1064, 2836: Phil. 3:19; Titus 1:12*

belong -ed -eth -ing — *1510: Luke 9:10; Heb. 5:14*

beloved — *25, 27: Rom. 1:7; 2 Pet. 2:17*

beneath (see **under**) — *2736: Mark 14:66; John 8:23; Acts 2:19*

benefit; benefactors — *18, 210, 2108, 5485: Luke 22:25; 2 Cor. 1:15; 1 Tim. 6:2; Phile. 1:14*

benevolence — *2133: 1 Cor. 7:3*

Benjamin — *958: Acts 13:21; Rom. 11:1*

Bernice — *959: Acts 25:13, 23; 26:30*

berries — *1636: James 3:12*

beryl — *969: Rev. 21:20*

beseech -ing; besought — *1189, 2065, 3870: Luke 8:28; 1 Tim. 1:3*

beset — *2139: Heb. 12:1*

beside -s — *846, 1839, 1909, 3063, 3105, 4359, 4862, 5565: Matt. 25:20; 2 Pet. 1:5*

best (see **better -ed**) — *2909: Luke 15:22; 1 Cor. 12:31*

bestow -ed — *1325, 2872: Luke 12:17; 1 John 3:1*

Bethabara — *962: John 1:28*

Bethany — *963: Matt. 21:17; John 11:1*

Bethesda — *964: John 5:2*

Bethlehem — *965: Luke 2:4; John 7:42*

Bethphage — *967: Matt. 21:1; Mark 11:1; Luke 19:29*

Bethsaida — *966:* Matt. 11:21; John 1:44

betray -ed -eth -s -er — *1212/4160, 3860, 4273:* Mark 3:19; 1 Cor. 11:23

better -ed (see **best**) — *1308, 2570, 2573, 3081, 3123, 4851, 5242, 5543, 5623:* Mark 5:26; Heb. 1:4

between — *303/3319, 1537, 1537/3326, 1722, 3307, 3326, 3342, 4314:* Eph. 2:14; Phil. 1:23

bewail -ed — *2799, 2875, 3396:* Luke 8:52; Rev. 18:9

beware (see **ware**) — *991, 4337, 5442:* Mark 8:15; Col. 2:8

bewitched — *940, 1839: Acts 8:9, 11; Gal. 3:1*

beyond — *1900, 2596, 4008, 4058, 5228, 5233, 5236, 5239, 5249:* John 1:28; 1 Thess. 4:6

bid -den -deth; bade — *479, 657, 2036, 2564, 2753, 3004, 4367:* Matt. 16:12; 2 John 1:11

bier — *4673: Luke 7:14*

bill — *975, 1121: Mark 10:4; Luke 16:6*

bind -ing; bound (see **wound**) — *195, 332, 1196, 1210, 2611, 3734, 3784, 4019, 4029, 4385, 4887, 5265:* Acts 12:8; 2 Thess. 1:3

bird -s — *3732, 4071, 4421;* Rom. 1:23; James 3:7

birth — *1079, 1083, 5605:* John 9:1; Gal. 4:19

birthday — *1077: Matt. 14:6; Mark 6:21*

birthright — *4415: Heb. 12:16*

bishop -ric -s — *1984, 1985:* Phil. 1:1; 1 Tim. 3:1

bits — *5469: James 3:3*

bite — *1143: Gal. 5:15*

bitter -ly -ness — *4087, 4088, 4089, 4090:* Luke 26:62; Eph. 4:31

black -er -ish -ness — *3189:* Heb. 12:18; Rev. 6:5

blade — *5528: Matt. 13:26; Mark 4:28*

blame -ed -less — *273, 274, 298, 299, 338, 410, 483, 2607, 3469:* 2 Cor. 6:3; Eph. 1:4

blaspheme -ed -er -ing -ous -y — *987, 988, 989:* Rom. 2:24; Rev. 2:9

Blastus — *986: Acts 12:20*

blaze — *1310: Mark 1:45*

blemish -es — *299, 3470: Eph. 5:27; 1 Pet. 1:19; 2 Pet. 2:13*

bless -ed -edness -ing(s) (see **happy**) — *1757, 2127, 2128, 2129, 3106, 3107, 3108:* Matt. 5:3; Rom. 4:6

blind -ed -ness — *4456, 4457, 5185, 5186:* John 12:40; 1 John 2:11

blindfolded — *4028: Luke 22:64*

blood -y — *129, 131, 1420:* Matt. 9:20; Acts 28:8

blot -ted -ting — *1813: Acts 3:19; Col. 2:14; Rev. 3:5*

blow -eth; blew — *1920, 4154, 5285:* Luke 12:55; John 3:8

Boanerges — *993: Mark 3:17*

boards — *4548: Acts 27:44*

boast -ed -er(s) -eth -ful -ing(s) — *212, 213, 1431, 2620, 2744, 2745, 2746, 3004, 3166:* Rom. 1:30; 2 Tim. 3:2

boat -s — *4142, 4627: John 6:22, 23; Acts 27:16, 30, 32*

Boaz — *1003: Matt. 1:5; Luke 3:32*

body -ies -ily — *4430, 4954, 4983, 4984, 4985, 5559:* Col. 2:9; 1 Tim. 4:8

boisterous — *2478: Matt. 14:30*

bold -ly -ness (see **courage**; **embolden**) — *662, 2292, 3954, 3955, 5111, 5112:* Acts 4:31; Eph. 6:19

bond -age -s (see **bondman; slave**) — *254, 1198, 1199, 1210, 1397, 1398, 1401, 1402, 2615, 4886:* Acts 20:23; Gal. 2:4

bondman; bondmaid; bondwoman (see **bond**) — *1401, 3814: Gal. 4:22, 23, 30, 31; Rev. 6:15*

bone -s — *3747, 4974:* Matt. 23:27; Eph. 5:30

book -s — *974, 975, 976:* Luke 4:17; 2 Tim. 4:13

border -s — *2899, 3181, 3725:* Matt. 4:13; Mark 7:24

born — *313, 1080, 1084, 1085, 1626, 5088:* Acts 2:8; 1 John 2:29

borne — *142, 941, 1418, 5409:* John 5:37; 3 John 1:6

borrow — *1155: Matt. 5:42*

bosom — *2859:* Luke 6:38; John 1:18

Bosor — *1007: 2 Pet 2:15*

both — *297, 1417, 1538, 2532, 5037:* Phil. 4:12; Titus 1:9

bottle -s — *779: Matt. 5:17; Mark 2:22; Luke 5:37*

bottom -less — *12, 2736:* Mark 15:38; Rev. 9:1, 2

bounds — *3734: Acts 17:26*

bounty -ifully -ifulness — *572, 2129: 2 Cor. 9:5, 6, 11*

bow -ed -ing — *1120, 2578, 2827, 4781, 4794, 5087, 5115:* Matt. 27:29; Rom. 11:10

bowels — *4698: Acts 1:18; Phile. 1:7*

box — *211: Matt. 26:7; Mark 14:3; Luke 7:37*

braided — *4117: 1 Tim. 2:9*

bramble — *942: Luke 6:44*

branch -es — *902, 2798, 2814, 4746:* Matt. 24:32; John 12:13

brass; brazen — *5470, 5473, 5474, 5475:* Mark 7:4; 1 Cor. 13:1

brawler -s — *269: 1 Tim. 3:3; Titus 3:2*

bread (see **loaf**)- *740:* Matt. 4:3; 2 Thess. 3:8, 12

breadth (see **broad**) — *4114: Eph. 3:18; Rev. 20:9; 21:16*

break -er -ing; broke -en — *827, 1284, 1358, 1575, 1846, 2608, 2622, 2800, 2801, 2806, 3089, 3847, 3848, 4486, 4917, 4919, 4937, 4977:* Matt. 15:37; Acts 2:42

breast -s — *4738:* Luke 18:13; John 13:25

breastplate -s — *2382: Eph. 6:14; 1 Thess. 5:8; Rev. 9:9, 17*

breath -ed -ing — *1709, 1720, 4157: John 20:22; Acts 9:1; 17:25*

bride — *3565:* John 3:29; Rev. 18:23

bridechamber — *3567: Matt. 9:15; Mark 2:19; Luke 5:34*

bridegroom — *3566:* Matt. 9:15; Rev. 18:23

bridle -eth -s — *5468, 5469: James 1:26; 3:2; Rev. 14:20*

briefly — *346, 1223/3641: Rom. 13:9; 1 Pet. 5:12*

briers — *5146: Heb. 6:8*

bright -ness — *541, 796, 2015, 2986, 2987:* Luke 11:36; 2 Thess. 2:8

brim — *507: John 2:7*

brimstone — *2303, 2306:* Luke 17:29; Rev. 9:17

bring -est -eth -ing; brought — *71, 114, 163, 321, 363, 397, 399, 518, 520, 539, 616, 654, 667, 985, 1080, 1096, 1295, 1325, 1396, 1402, 1521, 1533, 1544, 1625, 1627, 1806, 1863, 1898, 2018, 2036, 2049, 2064, 2097, 2164, 2592, 2601, 2609, 2615, 2673, 2865, 2989, 3350, 3860, 3920, 3930, 3936, 4160, 4254, 4311, 4317, 4374, 4393, 4851, 4939, 4992, 5013, 5044, 5062, 5088, 5142, 5179, 5342, 5461:* Col. 1:6; Heb. 7:19

broad (see **breadth**) — *2149, 4115: Matt. 7:13; 23:5*

broiled — *3702: Luke 24:42*

brokenhearted — *4937/2588: Luke 4:18*

brood — *3555: Luke 13:34*

brook — *5493: John18:1*

brother -hood -ly -'s; brethren — *80, 81, 5360, 5361, 5569:* Matt. 1:2; 1 Pet. 2:17

brow — *3790: Luke 4:29*

bruise -ed -ing — *2352, 4937:* Matt. 12:20; Luke 4:18; 9:39; Rom. 16:20

brute — *249: 2 Pet. 2:12; Jude 1:10*

budded — *985: Heb. 9:4*

buffet -ed — *2852:* 2 Cor. 12:7; 1 Pet. 2:20

build -ed -er(s) -eth -ing; built (see **rear**) — *456, 2026, 2680, 2937, 3618, 3619, 4925, 5079:* 1 Cor. 3:10; Eph. 2:22

bulls — *5022: Heb. 9:13; 10:4*

bundle -s — *1197, 4128: Matt. 13:30; Acts 28:3*

burden -ed -s -some — *4, 916, 922, 1117,* 2347, 2599, 2655, 5413: 1 Thess. 2:6; Rev. 2:24

burn -ed -eth -ing -t — *1572, 1714, 2370, 2545, 2618, 2740, 2742, 4448, 4451:* Matt. 3:12; John 5:35

burst — *2997, 4486: Mark 2:22; Luke 5:37; Acts 1:18*

bury -ial -ied -ing — *1779, 1780, 2990, 4916, 5027:* John 19:40; Rom. 6:4

bush — *942:* Mark 12:26; Acts 7:30, 35

bushel — *3426: Matt. 5:15; Mark 4:21; Luke 11:33*

business — *2398, 4229, 4710, 5532:* Rom. 12:11; 1 Thess. 4:11

busybody -ies — *244, 4020, 4021: 2 Thess 3:11; 1 Tim. 5:13; 1 Pet. 1:15*

but (see **nevertheless**) — *235, 1161, 3305, 4133:* Phile. 1:11; 2 John 1:12

buy -eth — *59, 5608:* Matt. 13:46; James 4:13

by — *1223, 1537:* Phil. 1:11; Heb. 10:38

C

Caesar — *2541:* Matt. 22:17; Phil. 4:22

Caesarea — *2542:* Mark 8:27; Acts 8:40

cage — *5438: Rev. 18:2*

Caiaphas — *2533:* Matt. 26:57; Acts 4:6

Cain — *2503: Heb. 11:4; 1 John 3:12; Jude 1:11*

Cainan — *2536: Luke 3:36, 37*

calf; calves — *3447, 3448:* Luke 15:23; Heb. 9:12, 19

call -ed -est -eth -ing — *154, 363, 1458, 1528, 1941, 1951, 2028, 2036, 2046, 2564, 2821, 2822, 2840, 2919, 2983, 3004, 3106, 3333, 3343, 3686, 3687, 3739/2076, 3870, 4316, 4341, 4377, 4779, 4867, 5455, 5537, 5581:* Acts 10:7; Rom. 1:1

calm — *1055: Matt. 8:26; Mark 4:39; Luke 8:24*

Calvary — *2898: Luke 23:33*

camel — *2574: Matt. 19:24; 23:24; Mark 10:25; Luke 18:25*

camp — *3925: Heb. 13:11, 13; Rev. 20:9*

can -est; could -est (see **cannot**) — *102, 176, 180, 215, 368, 551, 761, 893, 1097, 1410, 1415, 1492, 1735, 2192, 2480, 2489, 3467, 5342:* Matt. 5:36; Phil. 4:13

Cana — *2580: John 2:1, 11; 4:46; 21:2*

Canaan; Canaanite — *2581, 5478: Matt. 10:4; 15:22; Mark 3:18; Acts 7:11*

Candace — *2582: Acts 8:27*

candle — *3088:* Matt. 5:15; Luke 8:16

candlestick -s — *3087:* Heb. 9:2; Rev. 1:12

canker -ed — *1044, 2728: 2 Tim. 2:17; James 5:3*

cannot (see **can -st**) — *3361, 3361/1410, 3756/1410, 3756/1492, 3756/1735, 3756/*

2076, 3756/2192, 3756/2480: Gal. 3:17; 2 Pet. 1:9

Capernaum — *2584:* Matt. 4:13; Luke 10:15

Cappadocia — *2587:* Acts 2:9; 1 Pet. 1:1

captain -s — *747, 4755, 4759, 5506:* John 18:12; Heb. 2:10

captive -ity -s — *161, 162, 163, 164, 2221:* Luke 4:18; Rev. 13:10

carcass -es — *2966, 4430: Matt. 24:28; Heb. 3:17*

care -ed -est -eth -s (see **careful**; **careless**) — *1959, 3199, 3308, 3309, 4710, 5426:* Luke 8:14; 1 Pet. 5:7

careful -ly -ness (see **care**; **careless**) — *275, 1567, 3309, 4708, 4710, 5426, 5431:* 1 Cor. 7:32; Phil. 4:6

carnal -ly — *4559, 4561:* Rom. 7:14; Heb. 7:16

carpenter -'s — *5045: Matt. 13:55; Mark 6:3*

Carpus — *2591: 2 Tim. 4:13*

carriages — *643: Acts 21:15*

carry -ed -eth -ing — *71, 142, 399, 520, 667, 941, 1308, 1580, 1627, 1643, 3346, 3350, 3351, 4046, 4064, 4216, 4792, 4879, 5342:* John 5:10; Jude 1:12

cases — *156: Matt. 5:20; 19:10; John 5:6; 1 Cor. 7:15*

cast -eth -ing — *114, 577, 641, 656, 683, 906, 1000, 1260, 1544, 1601, 1614, 1620, 1685, 1911, 1977, 2210, 2598, 2630, 2975, 3036, 3679, 3860, 4016, 4406, 4496, 5011, 5020:* Luke 1:29; 3 John 1:10

castaway — *96: 1 Cor. 9:27*

castle — *3925: Acts 21:34, 37; 22:24; 23:10, 16, 32*

Castor — *1359: Acts 28:11*

catch -eth; **caught** — *64, 726, 1949, 2221, 2340, 2983, 4084, 4815, 4884, 2983, 4084, 4815, 4884:* Matt. 13:19; Mark 12:3

cattle — *2353, 4165: Luke 17:7; John 4:12*

cause -ed -eth -s — *156, 158, 846, 873, 1223/ 5124, 1352, 1423, 1432, 1500, 1752, 2289, 2358, 2716, 3056, 3076, 3588/2596, 4160, 5484:* Matt. 5:22; 2 Cor. 2:14

cave -s — *3692, 4693: John 11:38; Heb. 11:38*

cease -ed -eth -ing — *83, 89, 180, 1257, 1618, 2270, 2308, 2664, 2673, 2869, 3973:* Rom. 1:9; 2 Tim. 1:3

Cedron — *2748: John 18:1*

Cenchrea — *2747: Acts 18:18; Rom. 16:1*

censer — *2369, 3031: Heb. 9:4; Rev. 8:3, 5*

centurion -s — *1543, 2760: Matt. 8:5; Luke 7:2*

Cephas (see **Peter**; **Simon**) — *2786:* John 1:42; Gal. 2:9

certain -ly -ty; certify (see **sure**) — *444, 790, 804, 1107, 1212, 1520, 3689, 4225, 5100:* Acts 3:2; Gal. 1:11

chaff — *892: Matt. 3:12; Luke 3:17*

chain -s — *254, 1199, 4577:* Mark 5:3; 2 Pet. 2:4

chalcedony — *5472: Rev. 21:19*

Chaldeans — *5466: Acts 7:4*

chamber -ing — *525, 2845, 5253: Acts 9:37, 39; 20:8; Rom. 13:13*

chamberlain -s — *3623: Acts 12:20; Rom. 16:23*

chance — *4795, 5177: Luke 10:31; 1 Cor. 15:37*

change -ed — *236, 3328, 3331, 3337, 3339, 3345, 3346:* Acts 6:14; 2 Cor. 3:18

changers (see **money**) — *2773, 2855: John 2:14, 15*

charge -able -ed -ing -s — *77, 916, 1159, 1263, 1291, 1462, 1690, 1781, 1909, 1912, 2004, 2008, 2476, 2655, 3049, 3146, 3726, 3800, 3852, 3853:* Acts 21:24; 1 Thess. 2:9

charger — *4094: Matt. 14:8, 11; Mark 6:25, 28*

chariot -s — *716, 4480: Acts 8:28, 29, 38; Rev. 9:9; 18:13*

charity; charitably (see **love**) — *26, 2596/26:* Rom. 14:15; 3 John 1:6

chaste — *53: 2 Cor. 11:2; Titus 2:5; 1 Pet. 3:2*

chasten -ed -eth -ing; chastise -ment (see **discipline**) — *53, 3809, 3811:* Luke 23:16; Heb. 12:8

cheek — *4600: Matt. 5:39; Luke 6:29*

cheer -ful -fully -fulness — *2114, 2115, 2293, 2431, 2432:* Rom. 12:8; 2 Cor. 9:7

cherished; cherisheth — *2282: Eph. 5:29; 1 Thess. 2:7*

cherubims — *5502: Heb. 9:5*

chicken -s — *3556: Matt. 23:37*

chief -est -ly — *204, 749, 750, 752, 754, 758, 775, 2233, 3122, 3390, 4410, 4411, 4412, 4413, 5228/3029, 5506:* Rom. 3:2; Rev. 6:15

child -ish -less; children; child-bearing — *815, 1025, 1471, 1722/1064/2192, 3439, 3515, 3516, 3808, 3812, 3813, 3816, 5040, 5041, 5042, 5043, 5044, 5207:* 1 Cor. 13:11; 1 Tim. 2:15

Chios — *5508: Acts 20:15*

Chloe — *5514: 1 Cor. 1:11*

choice; choose -ing; chose -en — *138, 140, 1586, 1588, 1589, 1951, 4400, 4401, , 4758, 5500:* Phil. 1:22; James 2:5

choke -ed — *638, 4155, 4846:* Matt. 13:7; Mark 5:13

Chorazin — *5523: Matt. 11:21; Luke 10:13*

Christ (see **God**; **Jesus**) — *5547:* Luke 20:41; Acts 8:37

Christian -s — *5546 : Acts 11:26; 26:28; 1 Pet 4:16*

chrysolite — *5555: Rev. 21:20*

chrysoprasus — *5556: Rev. 21:20*

church -es — *1577, 2417: Acts 9:31; Phile. 1:2*

Chuza — *5529: Luke 8:3*

Cilicia — *2791: Acts 6:9; Gal. 1:21*

cinnamon — *2792: Rev. 18:13*

circumcise -ed -ing -ion (see **concision**) — *203, 4059, 4061: Rom. 4:11; Col. 2:11*

circumspectly — *199: Eph. 5:15*

city -ies — *4172: Matt. 9:35; Titus 1:5*

citizen -s — *4177: Luke 15:15; 19:14; Acts 21:39*

clamor — *2906: Eph. 4:31*

Clauda — *2802: Acts 27:16*

Claudia — *2803: 2 Tim. 4:21*

Claudius — *2804: Acts 11:28; 18:2; 23:26*

clay — *4081: John 9:6, 11, 14, 15; Rom. 9:21*

clean; cleanse -ed -eth -ing — *2511, 2512, 2513, 3689: Luke 5:14; 1 John 1:7*

clear -ing -ly — *53, 627, 1227, 2513, 2529, 2929, 2986, 5081: Rom. 1:20; 2 Cor. 7:11*

cleave -ed -eth — *2853, 4347: Luke 10:11; Acts 17:34*

clemency — *1932: Acts 24:4*

Clement — *2815: Phil. 4:3*

Cleopas — *2810: Luke 24:18*

Cleophas — *2832: John 19:25*

climbed; climbeth — *305: Luke 19:4; John 10:1*

cloak — *1942, 2440, 4392, 5341: Matt. 5:40; 1 Pet. 2:16*

close -ed (see **inclose**) — *788, 2576, 4428, 4601: Luke 4:20; Acts 27:13*

closet -s — *5009: Matt. 6:6; Luke 12:3*

cloth — *4470, 4616: Matt. 9:16; 27:59; Mark 2:21; 14:51, 52*

clothe -ed -ing -s (see **raiment**) — *294, 1463, 1737, 1742, 1746, 1902, 2066, 2439, 2440, 3608, 4016, 4683, 4749, 5509: Acts 7:58; 1 Pet. 5:5*

cloud -s — *2385, 3507, 3509: Matt. 24:30; Jude 1:12*

cloven — *1266: Acts 2:3*

clusters — *1009: Rev. 14:18*

Cnidus — *2834: Acts 27:7*

coals — *439, 440: John 18:18; 21:9; Rom. 12:20*

coast -s — *3313, 3725, 3864, 3882, 5117, 5561: Matt. 4:13; Acts 13:50*

coat -s — *1903, 5509: Luke 6:29; John 19:23*

cock (see **crow**) — *220: Matt. 26:34; Luke 22:34*

cockcrowing — *219: Mark 13:35*

cold — *5592, 5593, 5594: 2 Cor. 11:27; Rev. 3:15, 16*

collection — *3048: 1 Cor. 16:1*

colony — *2862: Acts 16:12*

Colosse — *2857: Col. 1:2*

color -ed — *4392: Acts 27:30; Rev. 17:3, 4*

colt — *4454: Matt. 21:2; John 12:15*

come -ers -est -eth -ing; came — *191, 305, 565, 575, 576, 602, 864, 1096, 1204, 1205, 1224, 1237, 1330, 1448, 1511, 1525, 1529, 1531, 1607, 1660, 1684, 1764, 1831, 1834, 1880, 1904, 1910, 1975, 1998, 1999, 2049, 2064, 2113, 2186, 2240, 2597, 2638, 2658, 2673, 2718, 2983, 3195, 3415, 3719, 3854, 3918, 3928, 3936, 3952, 4130, 4301, 4137, 4331, 4334, 4365, 4370, 4845, 4863, 4872, 4905, 4940, 5302, 5342, 5348, 5562: Mark 1:9; Heb. 10:1*

comely -iness — *2157, 2158, 4241: 1 Cor. 7:35; 11:13; 12:23, 24*

comfort -ed -er -eth — *2174, 2293, 3870, 3874, 3875, 3888, 3889, 3890, 3931, 4837: Matt. 9:22; 2 Cor. 1:4*

comfortless — *3737: John 14:18*

command -ed -est -eth -ing -ment(s) — *1291, 1297, 1299, 1778, 1781, 1785, 2003, 2004, 2036, 2750, 2753, 3852, 3853, 4367, 4483: Mark 10:3; Acts 17:30*

commend -ation -ed -eth -ing — *1867, 3908, 3936, 4921, 4956: Luke 23:46; 2 Cor. 3:1*

commit -ted; commission — *764, 1325, 1439, 2011, 2038, 2416, 3429, 3431, 3860, 3866, 3872, 3908, 4100, 4160, 4203, 4238, 5087: Acts 26:12; Rom. 5:8*

commodious — *428: Acts 27:12*

common -ly — *442, 1219, 1310, 2839, 2840, 3654, 4183, 4232: Matt. 28:15; Jude 1:3*

commonwealth — *4174: Eph. 2:12*

commotions — *181: Luke 21:9*

communed; communion — *1255, 2842, 3656, 4814: Acts 24:26; 1 Cor. 10:16*

communicate -ed -ion(s) — *148, 394, 1697, 2841, 2842, 2843, 3056, 3657, 4790, 7879: Gal. 6:6; Phil. 4:14*

compacted — *4822: Eph. 4:16*

companion -s — *2844, 4791, 4898, 4904: Acts 19:29; Phil. 2:25; Heb. 10:33; Rev. 1:9*

company -ies — *2398, 2828, 2853, 3461, 3658, 3792, 3793, 4128, 4849, 4874, 4923: John 6:5; 2 Thess. 3:14*

compare -ed -ing -ison — *3846, 3850, 4793: Mark 4:30; Rom. 8:18*

compass -ed — *2944, 4013, 4029, 4033: Luke 21:20; Heb. 5:2*

compassion — *1653, 3356, 3627, 4697, 4834, 4835: Matt. 9:36; 1 John 3:17*

compel -led -lest — *29, 315: Mark 15:21; Gal. 2:14*

complainers; complaints — *157, 3202: Acts 25:7; Jude 1:16*

complete — *4137: Col. 2:10; 4.12*

comprehend -ed — *346, 2638: John 1:5; Rom. 13:9; Eph. 3:18*

conceits — *1438, 3844: Rom. 11:25; 12:16*

conceive -d — *1080, 2602, 2845/2192, 4815, 5087:* Matt. 1:20; Heb. 11:11

concern -ing — *1519/3056, 2596, 3754, 4012, 4314, 5228:* Acts 28:31; 2 Pet. 3:9

concision (see **circumcise**) — *2699: Phil. 3:2*

conclude -ed — *2919, 3049, 4788:* Acts 21:25; Rom. 11:32

concord — *4857: 2 Cor. 6:15*

concourse — *4963: Acts 19:40*

concupiscence — *1939: Rom. 7:8; Col. 3:5; 1 Thess. 4:5*

condemn -ation -ed -est -eth -ing (see **contemn**) — *176, 843, 1519/2917, 2613, 2631, 2632, 2633, 2919, 2920, 5272 :* Matt. 12:41; James 5:6, 9

condescend — *4879: Rom. 12:16*

conditions — *4314: Luke 14:32*

conduct -ed — *2525, 4311: Acts 17:15; 1 Cor. 16:11*

conferred; conference — *4323, 4814, 4820: Acts 4:15; 25:12; Gal. 1:16; 2:6*

confess -ed -eth -ing -ion — *1843, 3670, 3671: John 1:20; 1 Tim. 6:13*

confidence; confident -ly — *1340, 2292, 3954, 3982, 4006, 5287:* Acts 28:31; Phil. 1:6, 14

confirm -ation -ing — *950, 951, 1991, 2964, 3315, 4300:* Mark 16:20; Heb. 6:16

conflict — *73: Phil. 1:30; Col. 2:1*

conformed; conformable — *4832, 4964: Rom. 8:29; 12:2; Phil. 3:10*

confound -ed; confused; confusion — *181, 2617, 4797, 4799:* 1 Cor. 14:33; 1 Pet. 2:6

congregation — *4864: Acts 13:43*

conquer -ing -ors — *3528, 5245: Rom. 8:37; Rev. 6:2*

conscience -s — *4893:* John 8:9; 2 Cor. 5:11

consecrated — *1457, 5048: Heb. 7:28; 10:20*

consent -ed -eth -ing — *1962, 4334, 4787, 4852, 4859, 4909:* Acts 8:1; Rom. 7:16

consider -ed -est -eth -ing — *333, 357, 1260, 1492, 2334, 2648, 2657, 3539, 4648, 4894, 4920:* Mark 6:52; Rom. 4:19

consist -eth — *2076, 4921: Luke 12:15; Col. 1:17*

consolation — *3874:* Rom. 15:5; Phile. 1:7

consorted — *4345: Acts 17:4*

conspiracy — *4945: Acts 23:13*

constantly — *1226, 1340: Acts 12:15; Titus 3:8*

constrain -ed -eth -t — *315, 317, 3849, 4912:* Matt. 14:22; 2 Cor. 5:14

consultation; consulted; consulteth — *1011, 4823, 4824:* Mark 15:1; John 12:10

consume -ed -ing — *355, 1159, 2654:* Luke 9:54; James 4:3

contain -ed -ing — *1467, 4023, 5562:* John 2:6; 1 Cor. 7:9

contemptible — *1848: 2 Cor. 10:10*

contend -ed -ing (see **contention**) — *1252, 1864: Acts 11:2; Jude 1:3, 9*

content -ment — *714, 842, 2425/3588/4160:* Mark 15:15; 3 John 1:10

contentment — *841:* 1 Tim. 6:6

contention -s; contentious (see **contend**) — *73, 2052, 3948, 5380:* Rom. 2:8; 1 Thess. 2:2

continual -ly (see **continue**) — *88, 1275, 1519/5056, 1725, 4842:* Luke 18:5; Heb. 7:3

continue -ance -ed -eth -ing (see **continual**) — *1096, 1265, 1273, 1300, 1304, 1696, 1961, 2476, 2523, 3306, 3887, 3905, 4160, 4342, 4357, 4839, 5281:* Rom. 2:7; James 1:25

contradicting; contradiction — *483, 485: Acts 13:45; Heb. 7:7; 12:3*

contrariwise — *5121: 2 Cor. 2:7; Gal. 2:7; 1 Pet. 3:9*

contrary — *480, 561, 1727, 3844, 3891, 5227:* Mark 6:48; Titus 2:8

contribution — *2842: Rom. 15:26*

controversy — *3672: 1 Tim. 3:16*

convenient -ly — *433, 2119, 2121, 2122, 2520, 2540, 3477:* Mark 14:11; Phile. 1:8

conversation — *390, 391, 4175, 4176, 5158:* Eph. 2:3; 2 Pet. 3:11

convert -ed -eth; conversion — *1994, 1995, 4762:* Matt. 13:15; Acts 15:3

convey -ed — *1593: John 5:13*

convicted — *1651: John 8:9*

convince -ed -eth — *1246, 1651, 1827:* Acts 18:28; Jude 1:15

cool — *2711: Luke 16:24*

Coos — *2972: Acts 21:1*

coppersmith — *5471: 1 Tim. 4:14*

corban — *2878: Mark 7:11*

cords — *4979: John 2:15*

Corinth -ians — *2881, 2882:* Acts 18:8; 2 Tim. 4:20

corn — *2848, 4621, 4702, 4719:* Matt. 12:1; 1 Tim. 5:18

Cornelius — *2883:* Acts 10:1, 22

corner -s — *204, 746, 1137:* Matt. 21:42; Rev. 7:1

corpse — *4430: Mark 6:29*

corrected; correction — *1882, 3810: Heb. 12:9; 2 Tim. 3:16*

corrupt -eth -ible -ion — *853, 862, 1311, 1312, 2585, 2704, 4550, 4595, 5349, 5351, 5356:* Rom. 8:21; 1 Pet. 3:4

Cosam — *2973: Luke 3:28*

cost -liness -ly — *1160, 4185, 4186, 5094:*
Luke 14:28; John 12:3; 1 Tim. 2:9; Rev.
18:19

couch -es — *2826, 2895: Luke 5:19, 24; Acts*
5:15

council -s — *4824, 4892, 4894:* Matt. 5:22;
Mark 15:1

counsel -or -s — *1010, 1011, 1012, 4823,*
4824, 4825: Rom. 11:34; Eph. 1:11

count -ed -eth — *515, 1075, 2192, 2233,*
2661, 3049, 3106, 4860, 5585: Luke 14:28;
2 Pet. 2:13

countenance (see **face; visage**) — *2397,*
3799, 4383, 4659: 2 Cor. 3:7; Rev. 1:16

country -ies — *68, 589, 1085, 1093, 3968,*
4066, 5561: Luke 21:21; Acts 4:36

countrymen — *1085, 4853: 2 Cor. 11:26;*
1 Thess. 2:14

courage (see **bold; embolden**) — *2294: Acts*
28:15

course — *165, 1408, 2113, 2183, 3313, 4144,*
5143, 5164: Eph. 2:2; James 3:6

court -s — *833: Luke 7:25; Rev. 11:2*

cousin -s — *4773: Luke 1:36, 58*

covenant -ed -s — *1242:* Eph. 2:12; Heb. 8:6

covenant breakers — *802: Rom. 1:31*

cover -ed -ing — *1943, 2572, 2596, 2619,*
4018, 4028, 4780: Matt. 8:24; 1 Cor. 11:15

covet -ed -ous -ousness — *866, 1937, 2206,*
3713, 4123, 4124, 5366: Rom. 7:7; 1 Cor.
12:31

craft — *1388, 2039, 3313, 3673, 5078:* Acts
18:3; Rev. 18:22

craftsman; craftsmen — *5079:* Acts 19:24;
Rev. 18:22

crafty -iness — *3834, 3835: Luke 20:23; 1 Cor.*
3:19; 2 Cor. 4:2; 12:16; Eph. 4:14

craved — *1254: Mark 15:43*

created; creation; Creator; creature -s —
2936, 2937, 2938, 2939: Col. 1:16; 1 Pet.
4:19

creditor — *1157: Luke 7:41*

creek — *2859: Acts 27:39*

creep -ing; crept — *1744, 2062, 3921:* 2 Tim.
3:6; Jude 1:4

Crescens — *2913: 2 Tim. 4:10*

Crete -ians -s — *2912, 2914:* Acts 27:7; Tit:
1:12

crime -s — *156, 1462: Acts 25:16, 27*

cripple — *5560: Acts 14:8*

Crispus — *2921: Acts 18:8; 1 Cor. 1:14*

crooked — *4646: Luke 3:5; Phil. 2:15*

cross — *4716:* Mark 8:34; Col. 1:20

crow; crew (see **cock**) — *5455:* Matt. 26:34;
John 13:38

crown -ed -edst -s — *1238, 4735, 4737:* Phil.
4:1; Heb. 2:7, 9

crucify -ied — *388, 4362, 4717, 4957:* Mark
15:13; Gal. 2:20

crumbs — *5589: Matt. 15:27; Mark 7:28; Luke*
16:21

cry -eth -ied -ies -ing — *310, 349, 863, 994,*
995, 1916, 2019, 2896, 2905, 2906, 5455:
Rom. 9:27; James 5:4

crystal — *2929, 2930: Rev. 4:6; 21:11; 22:1*

cubit -s — *4083:* Matt. 6:27; John 21:8

cumbered; cumbereth — *2673, 4049: Luke*
10:40; 13:7

cumi — *2891: Mark 5:41*

cummin — *2951: Matt. 23:23*

cunning -ly — *4221: Eph. 4:14; 2 Pet. 1:16*

cup -s — *4221:* Matt. 10:42; 1 Cor. 10:16

cure -ed -s — *2323, 2392: Luke 9:1; 13:32;*
John 5:10

curious — *4021: Acts 19:19*

curse -ed -edst -eth -ing(s) — *332, 685,*
1944, 2551, 2652, 2653, 2671, 2672: Matt.
25:41; John 7:49

custom -s (see **accustomed**) — *1480, 1485,*
3588/1486, 4914, 5056, 5058: Luke 1:9; Acts
6:14

cut -ting, — *609, 851, 1282, 1371, 1581,*
2629, 2875, 4932: Mark 5:5; Gal. 5:12

cymbal — *2950: 1 Cor. 13:1*

Cyprus — *2954:* Acts 4:36; 27:4

Cyrene -ian(s) — *2956, 2957:* Matt. 27:32;
Luke 23:26

Cyrenius — *2958: Luke 2:2*

D

daily (see **day**) — *1967, 2184, 2522, 2596/*
2250, 2596/1538/2250, 2596/3956/2250:
Matt. 6:11; Luke 9:23

dainty — *3045: Rev. 18:14*

Dalmanutha — *1148: Mark 8:10*

Dalmatia — *1149: 2 Tim. 4:10*

damage (see **endamage**) — *2209, 2210: Acts*
27:10; 2 Cor. 7:9

Damaris — *1152: Acts 17:34*

Damascus; Damascenes — *1151, 1153:*
2 Cor. 11:32; Gal. 1:17

damnation; damnable; damned — *684,*
2917, 2919, 2920, 2632: Mark 3:20; 2 Pet.
2:1

damsel — *2877, 3813, 3814:* Matt. 14:11; Acts
12:13

danced; dancing — *3738, 5525:* Mark 6:22;
Luke 15:25

danger -ous — *1777, 2000, 2793:* Matt. 5:21,
22; Mark 3:29; Acts 19:27, 40; 27:9

Daniel — *1158: Matt. 24:15; Mark 13:14*

dare; durst — *5111:* Rom. 5:7; 2 Cor. 10:12

dark -ened -ly -ness — *135, 850, 1722, 2217,*

4652, 4653, 4654, 4655: Matt. 24:29; 2 Pet. 2:4

dart -s — 956, 1002: Eph. 6:16; Heb. 12:20

dash — 4350: Matt. 4:6; Luke 4:11

daughter -s — 2364, 2365, 5043: Mark 5:23; 1 Pet. 3:6

daughter-in-law — 3565: Matt. 10:35; Luke 12:53

David -'s — 1138: Luke 20:41; 2 Tim. 2:8

dawn — 1306, 2020: Matt. 28:1; 2 Pet. 1:19

day -s (see **daily; midday; today**) — 737, 827, 839, 1773, 1887, 2250, 4594: Luke 1:5; Jude 1:6

dayspring — 395: Luke 1:78

daystar — 5459: 2 Pet. 1:19

deacon -s — 1247, 1249: Phil. 1:1; 1 Tim. 3:8, 10, 12, 13

dead -ly -ness (see **death; die**) — 349, 581, 599, 2258, 2286, 2287, 2288, 2289, 2348, 2837, 3498, 3499, 3500, 4194, 4430, 4880, 5053, 5315: Rom. 4:19; James 3:8

deaf — 2974: Matt. 11:5; Mark 7:32, 37; 9:25; Luke 7:22

deal -eth -ings -t — 1793, 2686, 3307, 4054, 4160, 4374, 4798: John 4:9; Rom. 12:3

dear -ly — 26, 27, 1784, 5093: Luke 7:2; Phil. 4:1

dearth — 3042: Acts 7:11, 28

death -s (see **dead; die**) — 336, 337, 520, 599, 615, 1935, 2079, 2288, 2289: Col. 1:22; 2 Tim. 1:10

debate -s — 2054: Rom. 1:29; 2 Cor. 12:20

debt -or(s) -s — 1156, 3781, 3782, 3783, 3784, 5533: Luke 7:41; Gal. 5:3

Decapolis — 1179: Matt. 4:25; Mark 5:20; 7:31

decayeth — 3822: Heb. 8:13

decease -ed — 1841, 5053: Matt. 22:25; Luke 9:31; 2 Pet. 1:15

deceive -ableness -er(s) -eth -ing; deceit -ful -fully -fulness (see **lie -ed -ers**) — 538, 539, 1386, 1387, 1388, 1389, 1818, 3884, 4105, 4106, 4108, 5423: 2 Thess. 2:10; 2 John 1:7

decently — 2156: 1 Cor. 14:40

decked — 5558: Rev. 17:4; 18:16

declare -ation -ed -ing — 312, 394, 518, 1107, 1213, 1229, 1334, 1335, 1555, 1732, 1834, 2097, 2605, 3724, 3853, 5319, 5419: Acts 15:3; Col. 1:8

decreased — 1642: John 3:30

decree -ed -s — 1378, 2919: Acts 16:4; 1 Cor. 7:37

dedicated; dedication — 1456, 1457: John 10:22; Heb. 9:18

deed -s — 1411, 2041, 2108, 2735, 4162, 4234, 4238 , 4334: Luke 23:51; Jude 1:15

deemed — 5282: Acts 27:27

deep -ly -ness — 12, 389, 899, 900, 901, 1037: Matt. 13:5; Mark 8:12

defame -ed -ing — 987: 1 Cor. 4:13

defended; defense — 292, 626, 627: Acts 7:24; 19:33; 22:1; Phil. 1:7, 17

deferred — 306: Acts 24:22

defile -ed -eth — 733, 2839, 2840, 3392, 3435, 4695, 5351: Titus 1:15; James 3:6

defraud -ed — 650, 4122: 1 Cor. 6:7, 8; 7:5; 2 Cor. 7:2; 1 Thess. 4:6

degree — 898, 5011: Luke 1:52; 1 Tim. 3:13; James 1:9

delay -eth — 311, 3635, 5549: Matt. 24:48; Luke 12:45; Acts 9:38; 25:17

delicacies — 4764: Rev. 18:3

delicate — 5172: Luke 7:25

deliciously — 4763: Rev. 18:7, 9

delight — 4913: Rom. 7:22

deliver -ance -ed -edst -er -ing — 325, 525, 591, 629, 859, 1080, 1325, 1560, 1659, 1807, 1929, 2673, 3086, 3860, 4506, 5088, 5483: Matt. 11:27; Acts 7:35

delusion — 4106: 2 Thess. 2:11

demanded — 1905, 4441: Matt. 2:4; Luke 3:14; 17:20; Acts 21:33

Demas — 1214: Col. 4:14; 1 Tim. 4:10; Phile. 1:24

Demetrius — 1216: Acts 19:24, 28; 3 John 1:12

demonstration — 585: 1 Cor. 2:4

den -s — 4693: Matt. 21:13; Heb. 11:38

deny -ied -ing — 483, 533, 720: Titus 1:16; Jude 1:4

depart -ed -eth -ing -ure — 321, 359, 360, 402, 565, 630, 672, 673, 867, 868, 1316, 1330, 1607, 1633, 1826, 1831, 1841, 2718, 3327, 3332, 3855, 4198, 5217, 5562: Mark 6:33; 2 Tim. 4:6

depth -s — 899, 3989: Matt. 18:6; Eph. 3:18

deputy -ies — 446: Acts 13:7, 8, 12; 18:12; 19:38

Derbe — 1191: Acts 14:6, 20; 16:1; 20:4

derided — 1592: Luke 16:14; 23:35

descend -ed -eth -ing; descent — 35, 1075, 2597, 2600, 2718: Heb. 7:3; James 3:15

describeth — 1125, 3004: Rom. 4:6; 10:5

desert -s — 2047, 2048: Luke 1:80; Heb. 11:38

desire -able -ed -edst -est -eth -ing -ous -s — 154, 515, 1809, 1905, 1934, 1937, 1939, 1971, 1972, 1974, 2065, 2107, 2206, 2212, 2307, 2309, 2442, 2755, 3713, 3870: Acts 9:38; Gal. 5:26

desolate -ion — 2048, 2049, 2050, 3443: Luke 11:17; 1 Tim. 5:5

despair -ed — 1820: 2 Cor. 1:8; 4:8

despise -ed -er(s) -est -eth -ing (see **hate**) —

114, 818, 820, 865, 1848, 2706, 2707, 3643, 4065: Luke 18:9; Heb. 12:2

despite -ful -fully — *1796, 1908, 5195, 5197:* Matt. 5:44; Rom. 1:30

destitute — *650, 3007, 5302: 1 Tim. 6:5; Heb. 11:37; James 2:15*

destroy -er -est; destruction — *622, 684, 1311, 1842, 2506, 2507, 2647, 2673, 3089, 3639, 3644, 3645, 4199, 4938, 5351, 5356:* Matt. 7:13; 1 Cor. 10:10

determinate; determined — *1011, 1956, 2919, 3724, 4309, 5021:* Acts 2:23; Titus 3:12

device -s (see **devised**) — *1761, 3540:* Acts 17:29; 2 Cor. 2:11

devil -ish -s (see **Satan**) — *1139, 1140, 1142, 1228:* Matt. 4:1; James 3:15

devised (see **device**) — *4679: 2 Pet. 1:16*

devotions — *4574: Acts 17:23*

devour -ed -eth — *2068, 2666, 2719:* Mark 4:4; Rev. 11:5

devout — *2126, 2152, 4576:* Luke 2:25; Acts 10:2

Diana — *735: Acts 19:24, 27, 28, 34, 35*

Didymus (see **Thomas**) — *1324: John 11:16; 20:24; 21:2*

die -ed -eth; dying (see **dead; death**) — *599, 622, 684, 3500, 4880, 5053:* Mark 9:44; Acts 7:15

differ -ence(s) -ing — *914, 1243, 1252, 1293, 1308, 1313, 3307:* 1 Cor. 12:5; Gal. 4:1

dig -ged — *2679, 3736, 4626:* Luke 13:8; Rom. 11:3

dignities — *1391: 2 Pet. 2:10; Jude 1:8*

diligent -ly; diligence — *199, 1567, 1960, 2039, 4704, 4705, 4706, 4708, 4710:* Titus 3:12; Heb. 6:11

diminishing — *2275: Rom. 11:12*

dine -ed; dinner — *709, 712: Matt. 22:4; Luke 11:37, 38; 14:12; John 21:12, 15*

Dionysius — *1354: Acts 17:34*

Diotrephes — *1361: 3 John 1:9*

dip -ped -peth — *911, 1686:* Mark 14:20; Rev. 19:13

direct — *2720: 1 Thess. 3:11; 2 Thess. 3:5*

disallowed — *593: 1 Pet. 2:4, 7*

disannul -leth -ling — *114, 115, 208 , 3722: Gal. 3:15, 17; Heb. 7:18*

discern -ed -er -ing — *350, 1252, 1253, 1381, 2924:* Matt. 16:3; 1 Cor. 2:14

disciple -s — *3100, 3101, 3102:* John 4:2; Acts 1:15

discouraged — *120: Col. 3:21*

discovered — *98, 2657: Acts 21:3; 27:39*

discreet -ly — *3562, 4998: Mark 12:34; Titus 2:5*

disease -ed -s — *769, 770, 2560/2192, 3119, 3553, 3554:* Mark 1:32; Acts 28:9

disfigure — *853: Matt. 6:16*

dish — *5165, 5602 , 6747: Matt. 26:23; Mark 14:20*

dishonesty — *152: 2 Cor. 4:2*

dishonor -est -eth — *818, 819, 2617:* John 8:49; Rom. 2:23

dismissed — *630: Acts 15:30; 19:41*

disobedience; disobedient; disobeyed — *506, 543, 544, 545, 3876:* Rom. 5:19; 1 Tim. 1:9

disorderly — *812, 814: 2 Thess. 3:6, 7, 11*

dispensation — *3622: 1 Cor. 9:17; Eph. 1:10; 3:2; Col. 1:25*

dispersed — *1287, 1290, 4650: John 7:35; Acts 5:37; 2 Cor. 9:9*

displeased — *23, 2371: Matt. 21:15; Mark 10:14, 41; Acts 12:20*

disposed; disposition — *1014, 1296, 2309: Acts 7:53; 18:27; 1 Cor. 1:27*

disputed; disputer; disputing -s; disputation -s — *1253, 1256, 1260, 1261, 3198, 3859, 4802, 4803, 4804:* Rom. 14:1; 1 Cor. 1:20

dissembled — *4942: Gal. 2:13*

dissension — *4714: Acts 15:2; 23:7, 10*

dissimulation — *505, 5272: Rom. 12:9; Gal. 2:13*

dissolved — *2647, 3089: 2 Cor. 5:1; 2 Pet. 3:11, 12*

distinction — *1293: 1 Cor. 14:7*

distraction — *563: 1 Cor. 7:35*

distress -ed -es — *318, 4729, 4730, 4928:* Luke 21:23; 1 Thess. 3:7

distribute -ed -ing -ion — *1239, 2130, 2841, 2842, 3307:* Acts 4:35; 1 Tim. 6:18

ditch — *999: Matt. 15:14; Luke 6:39*

divers (see **diversities**) — *1313, 4164, 4187, 5100:* Mark 1:34; Acts 19:9

diversities (see **divers**) — *1243: 1 Cor. 12:4, 6, 28*

divide -ed -er -eth -ing (see **division**) — *873, 1096, 1239, 1244, 1266, 2624, 3307, 3311, 3312, 3718, 4977:* Matt. 12:25; Luke 12:14

divine -ation — *2304, 2999, 4436 , 4440:* Acts 16:16; Heb. 9:1

division -s (see **divide**) — *1267, 1370, 4978:* John 7:43; Rom. 16:17

divorced; divorcement — *630, 647: Matt. 5:31, 32; 19:7; Mark 10:4*

do -er(s) -es -est -eth -ing -ne -st -th; did -est (see **make; wrought**) — *14, 15, 16, 17, 91, 1096, 1107, 1286, 1398, 1731, 1754, 2005, 2038, 2041, 2109, 2192, 2480, 2554, 2557, 2569, 2673, 2698, 2716, 3000, 3056, 3930, 4160, 4163, 4233, 4374, 4704, 4982:* Rom. 2:13; Phile. 1:14

doctor -s — *1320, 3547: Luke 2:46; 5:17; Acts 5:34*

doctrine -s — *1319, 1322, 1819, 3056: Matt. 15:9; Eph. 4:14*

dog -s — *2952, 2965: Luke 16:21; 2 Pet. 2:22*

dominion -s — *2634, 2904, 2961, 2963: Col. 1:16; Jude 1:8*

door -s — *2374, 2377: Matt. 6:6; James 5:9*

Dorcas (see **Tabitha**) — *1393: Acts 9:36, 39*

doting — *3552: 1 Tim. 6:4*

double — *1362, 1363, 1374: 1 Tim. 5:17; James 1:8; 4:8; Rev. 18:6*

double-minded — *1374: James 1:8; 4:8*

double-tongued — *1351: 1 Tim. 3:8*

doubt -ed -eth -ful -ing — *142/5590, 639, 686, 1063, 1252, 1261, 1280, 1365, 3349, 3843: Matt. 28:17; Rom. 14:1*

doubtless — *1065, 1211, 3304: 1 Cor. 9:2; 2 Cor. 12:1; Phil. 3:8*

dove -s — *567, 4058, 5167: Matt. 10:16; John 2:14*

down — *345, 347, 377, 387, 1308, 1581, 1931, 2504, 2506, 2507, 2521, 2523, 2524, 2596, 2597, 2598, 2601, 2609, 2621, 2625, 2630, 2647, 2662, 2667, 2673, 2679, 2701, 2718, 2736, 2778, 2875, 3879, 3935, 4098, 4496, 4776, 4781, 4782, 4952, 5011, 5294, 5465: Mark 2:4; 1 John 3:16*

dragging — *4951: John 21:8*

dragon — *1404: Rev. 12:3; 20:2*

draught — *61, 856: Matt. 15:17; Mark 7:19; Luke 5:4, 9*

draw -eth -ing -n; drew — *385, 501, 502, 645, 1096, 1670, 1828, 4334, 5288, 5289: John 2:8; James 1:14*

dream -ers -s — *1797, 1798, 3677: Acts 2:17; Jude 1:8*

dressed; dresser — *289, 1090: Luke 13:7; Heb. 6:7*

drink -eth -ing -s; drank; drunk (see **drunken**) — *3182, 3184, 4095, 4188, 4213, 4222, 4608, 4844, 5202: Matt. 11:18; Eph. 5:18*

drive -en -eth; drove — *416, 556, 1308, 1643, 1856, 1929, 5342: John 2:15; Acts 7:45*

drops — *2361: Luke 22:44*

dropsy — *5203: Luke 14:2*

drown -ed — *1036, 2666, 2670: Matt. 18:6; 1 Tim. 6:9; Heb. 11:29*

drunken -ness; drunkard -s (see **drink**) — *3178, 3182, 3183, 3184, 4095, 5435: Gal. 5:21; 1 Thess. 5:7*

Drusilla — *1409: Acts 24:24*

dry -ied — *504, 3583, 3584: Luke 11:24; Rev. 16:12*

due -s — *514, 2398, 3782, 3784: Rom. 13:7; Gal. 6:9*

dull — *917, 3576: Matt. 13:15; Acts 28:27; Heb. 5:11*

dumb — *216, 880, 2974, 4623: Matt. 9:32; 2 Pet. 2:16*

dung (see **dunghill**)- *906/2874, 4657: Luke 13:8; Phil. 3:8*

dunghill (see **dung**) — *2874: Luke 14:35*

dureth (see **endure**) — *2076: Matt. 13:21*

dust — *2868, 5522, 6083: Acts 13:51; Rev. 18:19*

duty — *3784: Luke 17:10; Rom. 15:27*

dwell -ers -est -eth -ing -t — *790, 1460, 1774, 2521, 2730, 2731, 3306, 3611, 3940, 4039, 4637, 4924: Mark 5:3; Acts 1:9*

dwellingplace — *790: 1 Cor. 4:11*

E

each (see **every**) — *240, 303, 1538: Luke 13:15; 2 Thess. 1:3*

eagle -s — *105: Matt. 24:28; Luke 17:37; Rev. 4:7; 12:14*

ear -s — *189, 191, 3775, 4719, 5621: Mark 4:28; 1 Cor. 2:9*

early — *260/4404, 3719, 3722, 4404, 4405, 4406: Matt. 20:1; James 5:7*

earnest -ly — *603, 728, 816, 922, 1617, 1864, 1971, 2206, 4056, 4335, 4710: Acts 3:12; Eph. 1:14*

earth -en -ly -y — *1093, 1919, 2709, 3749, 5517: John 3:12; Phil. 3:19*

earthquake -s (see **quake**) — *4578, 5517: Matt. 24:7; Mark 13:8; Luke 21:11*

ease -ed (see **easy; easier**) — *373, 425: Luke 12:19; 2 Cor. 8:13*

east — *395: Matt. 2:1; Rev. 7:2*

Easter (see **Passover**) — *3957: Acts 12:4*

easy; easier (see **ease**) — *2123, 2138, 2154, 5543: Matt. 9:5; 1 Cor. 14:9*

eat -en -ing; ate — *977, 1035, 1089, 2068, 2192, 2719, 2880, 3335, 4662, 4906, 5176, 5315: 1 Cor. 8:4; 2 Tim. 2:17*

edge -s — *1366, 4750: Luke 21:24; Heb. 11:34; Rev. 2:12*

edify -ication -ied -ieth -ing — *3618, 3619: Acts 9:31; Eph. 4:29*

effect -ual -ually — *208, 1601, 1753, 1754, 1756, 2673, 2758: 1 Cor. 16:9; Gal. 2:8*

egg — *5609: Luke 11:12*

Egypt; Egyptian -s — *124, 125: Matt. 2:13; Acts 7:22*

eight; eighth — *3590, 3637, 3638: Phil. 3:5; 1 Pet. 3:20*

eighteen — *1176/2532/3638: Luke 13:4, 11, 16*

either — *1782/2532, 2228: Matt. 6:24; James 3:12*

Elamites — *1639: Acts 2:9*

elder -s; eldest (see **old**) — *3187, 4244, 4245, 4850:* Luke 15:25; 3 John 1:1

Eleazar — *1648: Matt. 1:15*

elect -ed -ion — *1588, 1589, 4899:* Rom. 11:7; 2 Tim. 2:10

elements — *4747: Gal. 4:3, 9; 2 Pet. 3:10, 12*

eleven -th — *1733, 1734:* Luke 24:9; Rev. 21:20

Eli (see **Eloi**) — *2241: Matt. 27:46*

Eliakim — *1662: Matt. 1:13*

Eliezer — *1663: Luke 3:29*

Elijah — *2243:* Matt. 17:3; Rom. 11:2

Elisabeth — *1665: Luke 1:5, 7, 13, 24, 36, 40, 41*

Elisha — *1666: Luke 4:27*

Eliud — *1664: Matt. 1:14, 15*

Elmodam — *1678: Luke 3:28*

Eloi (see **Eli**) — *1682: Mark 15:34*

eloquent — *3052: Acts 18:24*

else — *1490, 1893/686, 2087, 2532:* Matt. 9:17; Phil. 1:27

Elymas — *1681: Acts 13:8*

embolden (see **bold**)- *3618: 1 Cor. 8:10*

embraced; embracing — *782, 4843: Acts 20:1, 10; Heb. 11:13*

emerald — *4664: Rev. 4:3; 21:19*

Emmaus — *1695: Luke 24:13*

empty — *2756, 4980: Matt. 12:44; Mark 12:3; Luke 1:53; 20:10, 11*

emulation -s — *2205, 3863: Rom. 11:14; Gal. 5:20*

enabled — *1743: 1 Tim. 1:12*

enclosed — *4788: Luke 5:6*

encountered — *4820: Acts 17:18*

end -ed -ing -less — *165, 179, 206, 562, 1096, 1519, 1545, 2078, 2308, 3796, 4009, 4137, 4930, 4931, 5049, 5055, 5056:* Matt. 11:1; Heb. 7:16

endeavor -ed -ing — *2212, 4704: Acts 16:10; Eph. 4:4; 1 Thess. 2:17; 2 Pet. 1:15*

endued — *1746, 1990: Luke 24:49; James 3:13*

endure -ed -eth -ing — *430, 2076, 2553, 2594, 3114, 3306, 5278, 5281, 5297, 5342:* 2 Thess. 1:4; Heb. 6:15

enemy -ies; enmity (see **adversary; foe**) — *2189, 2190:* Matt. 5:43; James 4:4

engrafted (see **graft**) — *1721: James 1:21*

engraven; graven — *1795, 5480: Acts 17:29; 2 Cor. 3:7*

enjoin -ed — *1781, 2004: Phile. 1:8; Heb. 9:20*

enjoy — *619, 5177: Acts 24:2; 1 Tim. 6:17; Heb. 11:25*

enlarge -ed (see **large**) — *3170, 4115: Matt. 23:5; 2 Cor. 6:11, 13; 10:15*

enlightened (see **light**) — *5461: Eph. 1:18; Heb. 6:4*

Enoch — *1802: Luke 3:37*

Enos — *1800: Luke 3:38*

enough — *566, 713, 714, 2425, 2880, 4052:* Matt. 10:25; Acts 27:38

enriched (see **rich**) — *4148: 1 Cor. 1:5; 2 Cor. 9:11*

ensue (see **follow; pursue**) — *1377: 1 Pet. 3:11*

entangle -ed — *1707, 1758: Matt. 22:15; Gal. 5:1; 2 Tim. 2:4*

enter -ed -eth -ing; entrance — *305, 1524, 1525, 1529, 1531, 1684, 1910, 2064, 3922:* Mark 8:13; 1 Thess. 1:9

entertain -ed — *3579, 5381: Heb. 13:2*

enticed; enticing — *1185, 3981, 4086: 1 Cor. 2:4; Col. 2:4; James 1:14*

entire — *3648: James 1:4*

entreat -ed -ies -y (see **exhort**) — *818, 2138, 2559, 3868, 3870, 3874, 5195, 5530:* Luke 18:32; 2 Cor. 8:4

envy -ied -ies -ieth -ing(s) -ious — *2205, 2206, 5354, 5355:* 1 Cor. 3:3; Titus 3:3

Epaenetus — *1866: Rom. 16:5*

Epaphras — *1889: Col. 1:7; 4:12; Phile. 1:23*

Epaphroditus — *1891: Phil. 2:25; 4:18*

Ephesus; Ephesian -s — *2180, 2181:* Acts 19:28; 1 Cor. 15:32

ephphata — *2188: Mark 7:34*

Epicureans — *1946: Acts 17:18*

epistle -s — *1992: Acts 15:30; 2 Cor. 3:1*

equal -ity -ly -s — *2465, 2470, 2471, 4915:* 2 Cor. 8:14; Col. 4:1

Er — *2262: Luke 3:28*

Erastus — *2037: Acts 19:22; Rom. 16:23*

ere (see **afore; before**) — *4250: John 4:49*

err -ed -or(s) — *51, 635, 795, 4105, 4106:* Mark 12:24; Heb. 9:7

Esau — *2269: Rom. 9:13; Heb. 11:20; 12:16*

escape -ed — *575, 668, 1295, 1309, 1545, 1628, 1831, 5343:* 1 Thess. 5:3; 2 Pet. 1:4

eschew — *1578: 1 Pet. 3:11*

Esli — *2069: Luke 3:25*

especially — *3122: Gal. 6:10; Phile. 1:16*

espoused — *718, 3423: Matt. 1:18; Luke 1:27; 2:5; 2 Cor. 11:2*

Esrom — *2074: Matt. 1:3; Luke 3:33*

establish -ed -eth — *950, 2476, 3549, 4732, 4741:* Rom. 3:31; Col. 2:7

estate -s (see **state**) — *3588, 4012:* Col. 4:8; Jude 1:6

esteem -ed -eth -ing — *1848, 2233, 2919, 3049:* Rom. 14:5; Heb. 11:26

eternal (see **ever**) — *126, 165, 166:* Matt. 19:16; Eph. 3:11

Ethiopia -ns — *128: Acts 8:27*

Eubulus — *2108: 2 Tim. 4:21*

Eunice — *2131: 2 Tim. 1:5*

eunuch -s — *2134, 2135: Matt. 19:12; Acts 8:27, 34, 36, 38, 39*

Euodias — *2136: Phil. 4:2*
Euphrates — *2166: Rev. 9:14; 16:12*
Euroclydon — *2148: Acts 27:14*
Eutychus — *2161: Acts 20:9*
evangelist -s — *2099: Acts 21:8; Eph. 4:11; 2 Tim. 4:5*
Eve — *2096: 2 Cor. 11:3; 1 Tim. 2:13*
even — *737, 891, 1063, 1096, 1161, 2073, 2089, 2193, 2504, 2505, 2522, 2531, 2532, 2536, 2548, 3303, 3483, 3676, 3739/5158, 3761, 3779, 5037, 5613, 5615, 5618:* Gal. 2:16; Phile. 1:19
even -ing -tide — *3796, 3798, 3798/5610:* Luke 24:29; Acts 28:23
ever -lasting -more (see **eternal**) — *104, 126, 166, 1336, 3745, 3842, 4218, 4253:* Matt. 24:21; John 4:29
every — *303, 376, 537, 1330, 1520, 1538, 2596, 3650, 3837, 3840, 3956, 5100, 5101:* Col. 1:10; Rev. 1:7
evidence; evident -ly — *1212, 1650, 1732, 2612, 4270, 4271, 5320:* Acts 10:3; Gal. 3:1
evil -doer(s) -s — *92, 987, 988, 2549, 2551, 2554, 2555, 2556, 2557, 2559, 2560, 2635, 2636, 4190, 4487, 5337:* Luke 3:19; 1 Pet. 2:12, 14
exact — *4238: Luke 3:13*
exalt -ed -eth — *1869, 5229, 5251, 5311, 5312:* Luke 14:11; 2 Thess. 2:4
examine -ation -ed -ing — *350, 426, 1350, 1381, 3985:* Acts 4:9; 2 Cor. 13:5
example -s — *1164, 3856, 5179, 5261, 5262:* 1 Cor. 10:6, 11; 1 Pet. 2:21
exceed -ing -ingly — *1519/5236, 1613, 1630, 2316, 2596/5236, 3029, 3173, 3588/2316, 4036, 4052, 4056, 4057, 4086, 4970, 4971, 5228, 5228/1537/4053, 5235, 5248, 5250, 7235:* Matt. 2:10; 1 Thess. 3:10
excel -lency -lent -leth — *1308, 1313, 2903, 3619, 4052, 4119, 5235, 5236, 5242, 5247:* Phil. 1:10; Heb. 1:4
except -ed — *1508, 1509, 1622, 2228, 3362, 3923, 4133:* Rom. 7:7; 1 Cor. 15:27
excess — *192, 401, 810, 3632: Matt. 23:25; Eph. 5:18; 1 Pet. 4:3, 4*
exchange -rs — *465, 5133: Matt. 16:26; 25:27; Mark 8:37*
exclude -ed — *1576: Rom. 3:27; Gal. 4:17*
excuse -ed -ing — *379, 626, 3868:* Luke 14:18; 2 Cor. 12:19
execute -ed -ioner — *2407, 4160, 4688:* Mark 6:27; Jude 1:15
exercise -ed -eth — *778, 1128, 1129, 1855, 2634, 2715, 2961, 4160:* Heb. 5:14; Rev. 13:12
exhort -ation -ed -eth -ing (see **entreat**) — *3867, 3870, 3874, 4389:* Acts 2:40; Rom. 12:8
exorcists — *1845: Acts 19:13*

expectation; expecting — *603, 1551, 4328, 4329: Acts 3:5; 12:11; Rom. 8:19; Phil. 1:20; Heb. 10:13*
expedient — *4851: John 11:50; 2 Cor. 8:10*
expelled — *1544: Acts 13:50*
experience; experiment — *1382: Rom. 5:4; 2 Cor. 9:13*
expert — *1109: Acts 26:3*
expired — *4137, 5055: Acts 7:30; Rev. 20:7*
expounded — *1329, 1620, 1956: Mark 4:34; Luke 24:27; Acts 11:4; 18:6; 28:23*
express -ly — *4490, 5481: 1 Tim. 4:1; Heb. 1:3*
extortion -er(s) — *724, 727: Matt. 23:25; Luke 18:11; 1 Cor. 5:10, 11; 6:10*
eye -s — *3442, 3659, 3788, 5168, 5169:* Matt. 5:29; 1 John 1:1
eye salve — *2854: Rev. 3:18*
eyeservice — *3787: Eph. 6:6; Col. 3:22*
eyewitnesses — *845, 2030: Luke 1:2; 2 Pet. 1:16*
Ezekias — *1478: Matt. 1:9, 10*

F

fables — *3454: 1 Tim. 1:4; Titus 1:14*
face -s (see **countenance; visage**) — *1799, 3799, 4383, 4750:* Matt. 6:17; 2 John 1:12
fade -eth — *262, 263, 3133: James 1:11; 1 Pet. 1:4; 5:4*
fail -eth -ing — *413, 674, 1587, 1601, 1952, 2673, 4098, 5302:* Luke 16:9; 1 Cor. 13:8
fain — *1987: Luke 15:16*
faint -ed· — *1573, 1590, 2577:* Matt. 9:36; Eph. 3:13
fair — *791, 2105, 2129, 2146, 2568: Matt. 16:2; Acts 7:20; 27:8; Rom. 16:18; Gal. 6:12*
faith -ful -fully -less — *571, 1680, 3640, 4102, 4103:* Matt. 17:17; 3 John 1:5
fall -en -eth -ing; fell — *646, 679, 868, 1096, 1601, 1706, 1911, 1968, 2064, 2397, 2597, 2667, 2702, 2837, 3895, 3900, 4045, 4098, 4363, 4368, 4417, 4431, 4625, 8702:* Luke 1:12; James 1:11
false -ly — *1228, 4811, 5569, 5570, 5571, 5572, 5574, 5575, 5576, 5577, 5578, 5580, 5581:* Matt. 5:11; 1 Pet. 3:16
fame — *189, 1310, 2279, 3056, 5345:* Mark 1:28; Luke 4:14, 37
family — *3965: Eph. 3:15*
famine -s — *3042: Rom. 8:35; Rev. 18:8*
fan — *4425: Matt. 3:12; Luke 3:17*
far -ther (see **afar**) — *891, 2193, 2436, 3112, 3113, 3117, 3123, 4008, 4054, 4185, 4206, 4260, 4281, 5231, 5236:* Mark 1:19; Phil. 1:23
fare -ed -well — *657, 2165, 4517, 5468:* Luke 9:61; 2 Cor. 13:11

farm — *68: Matt. 22:5*

farthing -s — *787, 2835: Matt. 5:26; 10:29; Mark 12:42; Luke 12:6*

fashion -ed -ing — *1491, 3778, 4383, 4882, 4964, 4976, 5179:* Phil. 3:21; 1 Pet. 1:14

fast (see **steadfast**) — *472, 805, 2722:* 1 Cor. 16:13; Gal. 5:1

fast -ed -est -ing(s) — *3521, 3522:* Matt. 6:16; 2 Cor. 6:5

fastened; fastening — *816, 2510: Luke 4:20; Acts 3:4; 11:6; 28:3*

fatlings; fatness; fatted — *4096, 4618, 4619:* Matt. 22:4; Rom. 11:17

Father; father -less -s — *540, 3737, 3962, 3964, 3967, 3970, 3971, 3995:* Heb. 7:3; James 1:7

fathoms — *3712: Acts 27:28*

fault -less -s — *156, 158, 264, 273, 299, 816, 818, 1651, 2275, 3201, 3900:* Gal. 6:1; Jude 1:24

favor -ed — *5485, 5487: Luke 1:28, 30; 2:52; Acts 2:47; 7:10, 46; 25:3*

fear -ed -ful -fully -fulness -ing — *870, 1167, 1169, 1630/1510, 2124, 2125, 2192, 5398, 5399, 5400, 5401:* Matt. 8:26; 1 John 4:18

feast -s — *755, 1173, 1408, 1456, 1858, 1859, 4910: John 2:8, 9; 2 Pet. 2:13*

feeble — *772, 3886: 1 Cor. 12:22; Heb. 12:12*

feebleminded — *3642: 1 Thess. 5:14*

feed -eth -ing; fed — *1006, 4165, 4222, 5142, 5526, 5595:* Rom. 12:20; 1 Cor. 9:7

feel -ing; felt — *524, 1097, 3958, 4834, 5584:* Acts 28:5; Eph. 4:19

feign -ed — *4112, 5271: Luke 20:20; 2 Pet. 2:3*

Felix — *5344: Acts 23:24; 24:3*

fellow -s — *435, 2083, 3353: Luke 23:2;* Heb. 1:9

fellow citizens — *4847: Eph. 2:19*

fellow disciples — *4827: John 11:16*

fellow heirs — *4789: Eph. 3:6*

fellow helper -s; fellow laborer -s — *4904:* 1 Thess. 3:2; 3 John 1:8

fellow prisoner -s — *4869: Rom. 16:7; Col. 4:10; Phile. 1:23*

fellow servant -s — *4889:* Col. 1:7; Rev. 6:11

fellowship — *2842, 2844, 3852, 4790:* 2 Cor. 6:14; Eph. 5:11

fellow soldier — *4961: Phil. 2:25; Phile. 1:2*

fellow workers — *4904: Col. 4:11*

female — *2338: Matt. 19:4; Mark 10:6; Gal. 3:28*

fervent -ly — *1618, 1619, 2204, 2205:* James 5:16; 1 Pet. 1:22

Festus — *5347: Acts 24:27; 26:24*

fetch -ed — *1806: Acts 16:37; 28:13*

fetters — *3976: Mark 5:4; Luke 8:29*

fever — *4445, 4446:* Matt. 8:14; Acts 28:8

few — *1024, 3641, 4935:* Eph. 3:3; Rev. 2:14, 20

fidelity — *4102: Titus 2:10*

field -s — *68, 5561, 5564:* Matt. 6:28; Acts 1:18

fierce -ness — *434, 2001, 2372, 4642, 5467:* 2 Tim. 3:3; Rev. 16:19

fiery (see **fire**) — *4442, 4448, 4451: Eph. 6:16; Heb. 10:27; 1 Pet. 4:12*

fifteen -th — *1178, 1440, 4002, 4003:* Luke 3:1; John 11:18

fifty -ies — *4002/3461, 4004:* Mark 6:40; Acts 19:19

fig -s — *3653, 4808, 4810:* Matt. 21:19; James 3:12

fight -ings; fought — *73, 75, 119, 2313, 2314, 2163, 3164, 4170, 4171, 4438: John 18:36;* 2 Tim. 4:7

figure -s — *499, 3345, 3350, 5179:* Acts 7:43; Rom. 5:14

fill -ed -eth -ing (see **full**) — *378, 466, 1072, 1705, 2767, 4130, 4137, 4138, 4845, 5055, 5526:* Col. 1:9; 1 Thess. 2:6

filth -iness -y — *143, 147, 150, 151, 168, 766, 3436, 4037, 4507, 4509, 4510:* Eph. 5:4; 2 Pet. 2:7

finally — *3063, 5056:* Phil. 3:1; 1 Pet. 3:8

find -eth -ing; found — *75, 421, 429, 1096, 2147, 2638:* Matt. 7:8; Rom. 11:33

fine — *4585:* Mark 15:46; Rev. 1:15

finger -s — *1147:* Luke 11:20; John 8:6

finish -ed -er — *535, 658, 1096, 1274, 1615, 2005, 4931, 5047, 5048, 5055:* 2 Tim. 4:7; Heb. 12:2

fire — *4442, 4443, 4447, 4448, 5394, 5457:* Matt. 3:10; 2 Thess. 1:8

firkin -s — *3355: John 2:6*

firm — *949: Heb. 3:6*

first — *509, 746, 1207, 3391, 4276, 4295, 4386, 4412, 4413:* Matt. 5:24; Titus 3:10

first-begotten; firstborn — *4416:* Col. 1:15, 18; Heb. 1:6

firstfruit -s — *536:* Rom. 11:16; James 1:18

fish -er(s) -ermen -es -ing — *231, 232, 1903, 2485, 2486, 3795:* Luke 5:2; John 21:7

fit -ly -ted — *433, 2111, 2520, 2675, 4883:* Acts 22:22; Eph. 2:21

five; fifth — *3991, 3999, 4000, 4001, 4002:* Matt. 14:17; Rev. 6:9

fixed — *4741: Luke 16:26*

flame -ing — *5395:* 2 Thess. 1:8; Heb. 1:7

flattering — *2850: 1 Thess. 2:5*

flax — *3043: Matt. 12:20*

flee -eth; fled — *1628, 2703, 5343:* Matt. 2:13; John 10:12

flesh -ly — *2907, 4559, 4560, 4561:* 2 Cor. 1:12; 2 John 1:7

flock — *4167, 4168:* Luke 2:8; 1 Pet. 5:2, 3

flood -s — *2627, 4132, 4215, 4216:* Matt. 7:25; 2 Pet. 2:5

floor — *257: Matt. 3:12; Luke 3:17*

flour — *4585: Rev. 18:13*

flourished — *330: Phil. 4:10*

flow — *4482: John 7:38*

flower — *438, 5230: 1 Cor. 7:36; James 1:10, 11; 1 Pet. 1:24*

flux — *1420: Acts 28:8*

fly -ing; flight — *4072, 5437:* Heb. 11:34; Rev. 4:7

foal — *5207: Matt. 21:5*

foameth; foaming — *875, 876, 1890: Mark 9:18, 20; Luke 9:39; Jude 1:13*

foes (see **adversary; enemy**) — *2190: Matt. 10:36; Acts 2:35*

fold — *1667: Heb. 1:12*

fold (see **sheepfold**) — *833, 4167: John 10:16*

folk -s (see **kinsfolk**) — *3816, 5971: Mark 6:5; John 5:3; Acts 5:16*

follow -ed -ers -eth -ing — *190, 1096, 1205/ 3694, 1377, 1811, 1836, 1872, 1887, 1966, 2071, 2076/3326, 2192, 2517, 2614, 2628, 3326/5023, 3401, 3402, 3877, 4831, 4870:* Matt. 10:38; Eph. 5:1

food — *1035, 1304, 5160:* Acts 14:17; 1 Tim. 6:8

fool -ish -ishly -ishness -s; folly — *378, 453, 454, 781, 801, 876, 877, 878, 1722/877, 3471, 3472, 3473, 3474, 3912:* 1 Cor. 1:18; 2 Tim. 3:9

foot; feet — *939, 2662, 3979, 4158, 4228:* Mark 9:45; Eph. 1:22

footstool — *5286, 5286/3588/4228:* Luke 20:43; James 2:3

for — *1063, 5228:* 2 Cor. 13:8, 9; Jude 1:3

forasmuch (see **forsomuch; insomuch**) — *1487, 1893, 1894, 1895, 5607:* Acts 9:38; 2 Cor. 3:3

forbear -ance -ing — *430, 447, 463, 3361, 4722, 5339:* 1 Cor. 9:6; Eph. 4:2

forbid -den -deth -ding; forbade — *209, 1254, 2967, 3361/1096:* Luke 23:2; 3 John 1:10

force — *726, 949: Matt. 11:12; John 6:15; Acts 23:10; Heb. 9:17*

forehead -s — *3359:* Rev. 7:3; 17:5

foreigners — *3941: Eph. 2:19*

foreknow -ledge; foreknew — *4267, 4268: Acts 2:33; Rom. 8:29; 11:2; 1 Pet. 1:2*

foreordained — *4267: 1 Pet. 1:20*

forepart — *4408: Acts 27:41*

forerunner — *4274: Heb. 6:20*

foreship — *4408: Acts 27:30*

foretell; foretold — *4280, 4293, 4302: Matt. 13:23; Acts 3:24; 2 Cor. 13:2*

forewarn -ed — *4277, 5263: Luke 12:5; 1 Thess. 4:6*

forget -ful -teth -ting; forgotten — *1585, 1950, 1953, 2983, 3024:* Phil. 3:13; Heb. 13:2

forever -more — *165, 2250/165, 3588/165:* Rom. 1:25; Rev. 1:18

forgive -en -eth -ing -ness; forgave (see **pardon**) — *630, 859, 863, 5483:* Matt. 6:12; Col. 3:13

form -ed — *3444, 3445, 3446, 4110, 4111, 5179, 5296:* Mark 16:12; Phil. 2:6, 7

former — *4386, 4387, 4413:* Eph. 4:22; Rev. 21:4

fornication -s; fornicator — *1608, 4202, 4203, 4205:* Matt. 15:19; 1 Cor. 5:9

forsake -en -eth -ing; forsook -est — *575, 657, 863, 1459, 2641:* Luke 14:33; Heb. 10:25

forseeing; foresaw — *4275, 4308:* Acts 2:25; Gal. 3:8

forsomuch (see **forasmuch; insomuch**) — *2530:* Luke 19:9

forswear — *1964:* Matt. 5:33

forth — *321, 392, 584, 616, 649, 669, 985, 1032, 1080, 1544, 1554, 1584, 1599, 1600, 1607, 1614, 1627, 1631, 1632, 1731, 1754, 1804, 1806, 1821, 1831, 1854, 1901, 1907, 1911, 2164, 2564, 2592, 2604, 2609, 3004, 3318, 3319, 3855, 3860, 3908, 3928, 4160, 4198, 4254, 4261, 4270, 4311, 4388, 4393, 4486, 5087, 5088, 5319, 5348:* Mark 1:38; Phil. 2:16

forthwith (see **anon; immediately; straight-way**) — *2112, 2117, 3916:* Matt. 13:5; Acts 9:18

Fortunatus — *5415: 1 Cor. 16:17*

forty — *5062, 5063:* Matt. 4:2; Heb. 3:9, 17

forum — *675: Acts 28:15*

forward -ness — *2309, 4261, 4281, 4288, 4311, 4704, 4707, 4710:* 2 Cor. 8:8; 3 John 1:6

foul — *169, 4833, 5494: Matt. 16:3; Mark 9:25; Rev. 18:2*

founded; foundation -s — *2310, 2311, 2602:* Acts 16:26; 1 Pet. 1:20

fountain -s — *4077: James 3:11, 12; Rev. 7:17*

four -fold -th — *5064, 5066, 5067, 5070, 5071, 5072, 5073:* Mark 2:3; Luke 2:37

four-footed — *5074: Acts 10:12; 11:6; Rom. 1:23*

fourscore — *3589: Luke 2:37; 16:7*

foursquare — *5068: Rev. 21:16*

fourteen -th — *1180, 5065: Matt. 1:17; Acts 27:27, 33; 2 Cor. 12:2; Gal. 2:1*

fox -es — *258: Matt. 8:20; Luke 9:58; 13:32*

fragments — *2801: Mark 6:43; John 6:12*

framed — *2675, 4883: Eph. 2:21; Heb. 11:3*

frankincense — *3030: Matt. 2:11; Rev. 18:13*

frankly — *5435: Luke 7:42*

free -dom -ed -ly (see **freeman; freewoman; liberty**) — *1432, 1658, 1659, 3326/3954, 3955, 4174, 5486:* 2 Cor. 11:7; Gal. 3:28

freeman (see **free; liberty**) — *558: 1 Cor. 7:22*

freewoman (see **free; liberty**) — *1658: Gal. 4:22, 23, 30*

frequent — *4056: 2 Cor. 11:23*

fresh — *1099: James 3:12*

friend -s -ship — *2083, 3588/3844, 3982, 4674, 5373, 5384:* Mark 3:21; James 4:4

fro; from — *2831:* Matt. 1:17; Eph. 4:14

frogs — *944: Rev. 16:13*

froward — *4646: 1 Pet. 2:18*

fruit -ful -s — *175, 1081, 2590, 2592, 2593, 3703, 5062, 5352:* Matt. 7:20; Luke 1:42

frustrate — *114: Gal. 2:21*

fulfill -ed -ing — *378, 1096, 1603, 4137, 4138, 4160, 4931, 5048, 5055:* Eph. 2:3; 2 Thess. 1:11

full -ness -y (see **fill**) — *1072, 1073, 1705, 2880, 3324, 3325, 3877, 4130, 4134, 4135, 4136, 4137, 4138, 4845, 5046, 5460, 5526:* John 1:16; 2 Tim. 3:10

fuller — *1102: Mark 9:3*

furlongs — *4712:* John 6:19; Rev. 14:20

furnace — *2575:* Matt. 13:42, 50; Rev. 1:15; 9:2

furnished — *1822, 4130, 4766:* Matt. 22:10; Mark 14:15; Luke 22:12; 2 Tim. 3:17

further -ance -ed -more — *1161, 1339, 1534, 2089, 3063, 4118, 4206, 4297:* Acts 4:17; Phil. 1:12

G

Gabbatha — *1042: John 19:13*

Gabriel — *1043: Luke 1:19, 26*

Gad — *1045: Rev. 7:5*

Gadarenes — *1046: Mark 5:1; Luke 8:26, 37*

gain -ed -s — *1281, 2039, 2770, 2771, 4122, 4160, 4200, 4333:* Acts 16:19; 1 Tim. 6:5, 6

gainsay -ers -ing — *369, 471, 483, 485: Luke 21:15; Acts 10:29; Rom. 10:21; Titus 1:9; Jude 1:11*

Gaius — *1050: Acts 19:29; 20:4; Rom. 16:23; 1 Cor. 1:14; 3 John 1:1*

Galatia — *1053, 1054:* Acts 16:6; 2 Tim. 4:10

Galatians — *1052: Gal. 3:1*

Galilean -s — *1057:* Mark 14:70; Acts 2:7

Galilee — *1056:* Luke 1:26; John 1:43

gall — *5521:* Matt. 27:34; Acts 8:23

Gallio — *1058: Acts 18:12, 14, 17*

Gamaliel — *1059: Acts 5:34; 22:3*

garden -er — *2779, 2780: Luke 13:19; John 18:1, 26; 19:41; 20:15*

garlands — *4725: Acts 14:13*

garment -s — *1742, 2067, 2440, 4158, 4749, 5509:* Matt. 9:16; Jude 1:23

garner — *596: Matt. 3:12; Luke 3:17*

garnish -ed — *2885: Matt. 12:44; 23:29; Luke 11:25; Rev. 21:19*

garrison — *5432: 2 Cor. 11:32*

gate -s — *2374, 4439, 4440, 4489:* Matt. 16:18; Acts 3:2

gather -ed -eth -ing — *346, 1865, 1996, 1997, 3048, 3792, 4816, 4822, 4863, 4867, 4896, 4962, 5166:* Mark 13:27; Eph. 1:10

gay — *2986: James 2:3*

Gaza — *1048: Acts 8:26*

gazing — *1689: Acts 1:11*

gazingstock — *2301: Heb. 10:33*

gender -eth — *1080: Gal. 4:24; 2 Tim. 2:23*

genealogies — *1076: 1 Tim. 1:4; Titus 3:9*

general — *3831: Heb. 12:23*

generation -s — *1074, 1078, 1081, 1085:* Col. 1:26; 1 Pet. 2:9

Gennesaret (see **Chinnereth**) — *1082: Matt. 14:34; Mark 6:53; Luke 5:1*

Gentile -s — *1484, 1672:* Rom. 2:9; 3 John 1:7

gentle -ness — *1932, 1933, 2261, 5544:* 1 Thess. 2:7; Titus 3:2

Gergesenes — *1086: Matt. 8:28*

get; gotten — *645, 1684, 1826, 1831, 2147, 2597, 4122, 5217:* Acts 21:1; 2 Cor. 2:11

Gethsemane — *1068: Matt. 26:36; Mark 14:32*

Ghost; ghost — *1606, 1634, 4151:* John 19:30; Rom. 5:5

Gideon — *1066: Heb. 11:32*

gift -s (see **give**) — *334, 1390, 1394, 1431, 1434, 1445, 3311, 5485, 5486:* Matt. 2:11; Phil. 4:17

gird -ed -edst; girt; girdle -s — *328, 1241, 2223, 2224, 4024:* Luke 12:35; John 21:7

give -en -er -eth -ing -s; gave -est (see **gift; grant -ed**) — *402, 437, 591, 632, 1096, 1239, 1291, 1325, 1377, 1394, 1395, 1402, 1433, 1502, 1547, 1781, 1788, 1825, 1907, 1929, 2010, 2014, 2227, 2468, 2702, 2753, 3004, 3140, 3330, 3548, 3844, 3860, 3923, 3930, 3936, 3943, 4160, 4222, 4272, 4337, 4342, 4369, 4823, 4980, 5087, 5461, 5483, 5524:* 2 Cor. 9:7; 1 Pet. 3:7

glad -ly -ness — *20, 21, 780, 2097, 2165, 2167, 2234, 2236, 5463, 5479:* Mark 6:20; Rom. 10:15

glass — *2072, 2734, 5193, 5194:* 1 Cor. 13:12; James 1:23

glistering — *1823: Luke 9:29*

glorify -ied -ing (see **glory**) — *1392, 1740, 2744, 4888:* Gal. 1:24; 1 Pet. 2:12

glory -ieth -ing -ious (see **glorify**) — *1223/1391, 1391, 1392, 1722/1391, 1741, 2620,*

2744, 2745, 2746, 2755, 2811: 1 Cor. 5:6; 2 Cor. 7:4

gluttonous — *5314: Matt. 11:19; Luke 7:34*

gnashed; gnasheth; gnashing — *1030, 1031, 5149:* Mark 9:18; Acts 7:54

gnat — *2971: Matt. 23:2*

gnawed — *3145: Rev. 16:10*

go -est -eth -ing; gone; went -est — *33, 71, 305, 402, 424, 549, 565, 576, 589, 630, 863, 1136, 1276, 1279, 1330, 1339, 1353, 1524, 1525, 1578, 1607, 1681, 1684, 1821, 1826, 1831, 1910, 1994, 2021, 2064, 2212, 2597, 2718, 3327, 3596, 3597, 3854, 3899, 3928, 3985, 3987, 4013, 4043, 4105, 4108, 4160, 4198, 4254, 4260, 4281, 4313, 4320, 4334, 4344, 4570, 4782, 4848, 4897, 4905, 5055, 5217, 5221, 5233, 5298, 5342, 5562:* Acts 18:22; 3 John 1:7

goats — *2055, 2056, 5131: Matt. 25:32, 33; Heb. 9:12, 13, 19; 10:4*

goatskins — *122/1192: Heb. 11:37*

God; Godward; god -s (see **Jah**; **Jehovah**; **Jesus**; **spirit**) — *2316, 2962, 4314/2316:* Matt. 1:23; Acts 19:20

goddess — *2299: Acts 19:27, 35, 37*

Godhead — *2304, 2305, 2320: Acts 17:29; Rom. 1:20; Col. 2:9*

godly -iness — *516/2316, 2150, 2152, 2153, 2316, 2317, 2596/2316:* 1 Thess. 1:8; 1 Tim. 2:2

Godspeed — *5463: 2 John 1:10, 11*

Gog — *1136: Rev. 20:8*

gold -en — *5552, 5553, 5554, 5557:* 2 Tim. 2:20; Heb. 9:4

Golgotha — *1115: Matt. 27:33; Mark 15:22; John 19:17*

Gomorrah — *1116: Rom. 9:29; 2 Pet. 2:6; Jude 1:7*

good -ly -ness — *14, 15, 18, 515, 865, 979, 2095, 2097, 2106, 2107, 2133, 2108, 2109, 2140, 2162, 2163, 2425, 2480, 2565, 2567, 2570, 2573, 2750, 2986, 3112, 4851, 5358, 5542, 5543, 5544:* Phile. 1:6; James 2:2

goodman — *3611: Matt. 20:11; Mark 14:14; Luke 12:39; 22:11*

goods — *18, 3776, 4147, 4632, 4647, 5223, 5224:* Acts 2:45; 1 Cor. 13:3

gorgeous -ly — *1741, 2986: Luke 7:25; 23:11*

gospel -'s — *2097, 2098, 4283:* Gal. 3:8; Rev. 14:6

government -s — *2941, 2963: 1 Cor. 12:28; 2 Pet. 2:10*

governor -s — *755, 1481, 2116, 2230, 2232, 2233, 3623:* John 2:8, 1 Pet. 2:14

grace -ious — *2143, 5485, 5543:* Luke 2:40; 2 John 1:3

graft -ed (see **engrafted**) — *1461: Rom. 11:17, 19, 23, 24*

grain — *2848:* Matt. 13:31; 1 Cor. 15:37

grandmother — *3125: 2 Tim. 1:5*

grant -ed (see **give**) — *1325, 2036, 5483:* Acts 3:14; Eph. 3:16

grapes — *4713: Matt. 7:16; Luke 6:44; Rev. 14:18*

grass — *5528:* John 6:10; James 1:10, 11

grave -ity (see **sober**) — *4586, 4587: 1 Tim. 3:4, 8, 11; Titus 2:2, 7*

grave -s (see **sepulchre -s**) — *86, 3418, 3419:* Luke 11:44; 1 Cor. 15:55;

great -er -est -ly -ness — *1419, 1420, 1431, 1433, 1568, 1569, 1971, 1974, 1980, 2245, 2425, 3029, 3112, 3123, 3166, 3167, 3170, 3171, 3173, 3174, 3175, 3176, 3179, 3186, 3187, 3745, 3816, 3817, 3819, 3827, 4055, 4080, 4118, 4119, 4183, 4185, 4186, 4214, 4768, 4970, 5082, 5118, 5246, 5479:* John 3:29; Eph. 1:19

Greece; Grecians; Greek -s (see **Achaia**) — *1671, 1675:* Acts 20:2; Rom. 1:14

greedy -ily -iness — *146, 866, 1632, 4124: Eph. 4:19; 1 Tim. 3:3, 8; Jude 1:11*

green — *5200, 5515:* Mark 6:39; Rev. 8:7

greet -eth -ing — *782, 783, 5463:* Matt. 23:7; James 1:1

grieve -d -ous -ously; grief -s — *926, 1171, 1278, 1418, 2560, 3076, 3077, 3636, 4190, 4360, 4818:* 2 Cor. 2:5; 1 John 5:3

grind -ing — *229, 3030: Matt. 21:41, 44; Luke 17:35; 20:18*

groan -ed -eth -ing(s) — *1690, 4726, 4727, 4959:* John 11:33; Rom. 8:22

gross — *3975: Matt. 13:15; Acts 28:27*

ground -ed — *68, 1093, 1474, 1475, 2311, 5476, 5561, 5564:* Eph. 3:17; 1 Tim. 3:15

grow -eth -n; grew — *305, 837, 1096, 3373, 4886, 5232:* Acts 5:24; 2 Thess. 1:3

grudge -ing -ingly — *1112, 1537/3077, 4727:* 2 Cor. 9:7; James 5:9; 1 Pet. 4:9

guard — *4759: Acts 28:16*

guest -s — *345, 2647: Matt. 22:10, 11; Luke 19:7*

guestchamber — *2646: Mark 14:14; Luke 22:11*

guide -s — *2720, 3594, 3595, 3616:* Matt. 23:16, 24; Luke 1:29

guile (see **beguile**) — *1388: John 1:47; 1 Pet. 2:1*

guiltless; guilty — *338, 1777, 3784, 5267:* Matt. 12:7; Rom. 3:19

gulf — *5490: Luke 16:26*

gushed — *1632: Acts 1:18*

H

habitation -s — *1886, 2732, 2733, 3613, 4633:* Acts 1:20; Jude 1:6

Hagar — *28: Gal. 4:24, 25*

hail — *5464:* Luke 1:28; Rev. 8:7

hair -s — *2359, 2863, 2864, 4117, 5155:* Matt. 10:30; John 11:2

hale -ing — *2694, 4951: Luke 12:58; Acts 8:3*

half — *2253, 2255, 2256:* Mark 6:23; Luke 19:8

hall — *833, 4232:* Matt. 27:27; Mark 15:16; Acts 23:35

hallowed (see **sanctify -ed -eth**) — *37: Matt. 6:9; Luke 11:2*

halt (see **lame**) — *5560: Matt. 18:8; Mark 9:45; Luke 14:21; John 5:3*

Hamor — *1697: Acts 7:16*

hand -s — *849, 886, 1448, 1451, 1764, 2021, 2186, 2902, 4084, 4475, 5495, 5496, 5497, 5499:* Phile. 1:19; 1 Pet. 3:22

handkerchiefs (see **kerchiefs**) — *4676: Acts 19:12*

handle -ed -ing — *821, 1389, 2345, 5584:* 2 Cor. 4:2; 1 John 1:1

handmaid -en(s) (see **maid**) — *1399: Luke 1:38, 48; Acts 2:18*

handwriting — *5498: Col. 2:14*

hang -ed -eth — *519, 2910, 3935, 4029:* Gal. 3:13; Heb. 12:12

haply — *686, 3379, 3381: Mark 11:13; Luke 14:29; Acts 5:39; 17:27; 2 Cor. 9:4*

happen -ed — *1096, 4819:* Mark 10:32; Phil. 1:12

happy -ier (see **bless -ed -edness**) — *3106, 3107:* 1 Cor. 7:40; James 5:11

Haran — *5488: Acts 7:2*

hard -en -ened -eneth -er -ly -ness — *1421, 1422, 1423, 1425, 2553, 3425, 3433, 4456, 4457, 4641, 4642, 4643, 4645, 4927:* Matt. 19:8; Heb. 3:8

harlot -s — *4204:* Luke 15:30; 1 Cor. 6:15

harm -less — *172, 185, 824, 2556, 2559, 4190, 5196:* Phil. 2:15; 1 Pet. 3:13

harp -ed -ers -ing -s — *2788, 2789, 2790:* 1 Cor. 14:7; Rev. 14:2

harvest — *2326:* Mark 4:29; John 4:35

haste -ily -ing — *4692, 4710, 5030:* John 11:31; Acts 20:16

hate -ed -ers -est -eth -ful -ing; hatred (see **despise**) — *2189, 2319, 3404, 4767:* Matt. 5:43; Rev. 2:6

have -ing; had -st; hast; hath (see **retain -ed**) — *474, 568, 846, 1096, 1099, 1526, 1699, 1722, 1746, 1751, 2071, 2076, 2192, 2258, 2701, 2722, 2983, 3335, 3844, 3918, 4510, 5224, 5225, 5607:* Eph. 6:14; Jude 1:5

haven -s — *2568, 3040: Acts 27:8, 12*

havoc — *3075: Acts 8:3*

hay — *5528: 1 Cor. 3:12*

hazarded — *3860: Acts 15:26*

he; his; him -self (see **her -s -self**) — *846, 848, 1438:* Col. 3:4; Titus 2:14

head -s — *2776:* 2 Tim. 3:4; Rev. 4:4

headlong — *2630, 4248: Luke 4:29; Acts 1:18*

heady — *4312: 2 Tim. 3:4*

heal -ed -ing(s) -th — *1295, 2322, 2323, 2386, 2390, 2392, 4982, 4991, 5198:* 1 Cor. 12:28; 3 John 1:2

heap -ed — *2002, 2343, 4987: Rom. 12:20; 2 Tim. 4:3; James 5:3*

hear -d -er(s) -est -eth -ing (see **hearken; heed; listen; noise**) — *189, 191, 201, 202, 1233, 1251, 1522, 1873, 1874, 3878, 4257:* 1 Cor. 14:21; Heb. 5:11

hearken (see **hear; heed; listen**) — *191, 1801, 3980, 5219:* Mark 4:3; Acts 27:21

heart -s — *674, 1588, 2589, 4641, 5590:* Eph. 6:6; 1 John 3:19

heartily — *1537/5590: Col. 3:23*

heat — *2329, 2738, 2741, 2742:* Matt. 20:12; James 1:11

heathen — *1482, 1484:* Acts 4:25; Gal. 1:16

heaven -ly -s — *1537/3772, 2032, 3321, 3770, 3771, 3772:* 1 Thess. 1:10; Heb. 3:1

heavy -iness — *85, 916, 926, 2726, 3076, 3077:* Mark 14:33, 40; 1 Pet. 1:6

Heber (see **Eber**) — *1443: Luke 3:35*

Hebrew -s — *1145, 1444, 1446, 1447:* Acts 6:1; Phil. 3:5

hedge -ed -s — *5418, 5418/4060:* Matt. 21:33; *Mark 12:1; Luke 14:23*

heed (see **hear; hearken; listen**) — *433, 991, 1907, 3708, 4337, 4648:* Acts 3:5; Col. 4:17

heel — *4418: John 13:18*

heifer — *1151: Heb. 9:13*

height — *5311, 5313: Rom. 8:39; Eph. 3:18; Rev. 21:16*

heir -s — *2816, 2818, 4789:* Matt. 21:38; Heb. 11:9

hell — *86, 1067, 5020:* Luke 10:15; 2 Pet. 2:4

helm — *4079: James 3:4*

helmet — *4030: Eph. 6:17; 1 Thess. 5:8*

help -ed -er(s) -eth -ing -s — *482, 484, 996, 997, 998, 1947, 4815, 4820, 4878, 4903, 4904, 4943:* Luke 1:54; Acts 18:27

hem — *2899: Matt. 9:20; 14:36*

hen — *3733: Matt. 23:37; Luke 13:34*

hence -forth -forward — *534, 575/3588/ 3568, 737, 1782, 1821, 2089, 3063, 3371, 3568, 3765, 5025, 5217:* Acts 1:5; Eph. 4:14, 17

her -s -self (see **he**) — *844, 846, 1438:* Matt. 9:21; 2 John 1:1

herbs — *1008, 3001:* Luke 11:42; Heb. 6:7

herd — *34: Matt. 8:30-32; Mark 5:11, 13; Luke 8:32, 33*

here -after -by -in -of -tofore -unto -with — *575/737, 575/3568, 848, 1519, 1537, 1722/5129, 1759, 2089, 3195, 3326/5023, 3370, 3568, 3778, 3918, 3936, 4258, 4840, 5026, 5028, 5124, 5602:* 2 Cor. 13:2; 1 John 2:3

heresy -ies; heretic — *139, 141:* Gal. 5:20; Titus 3:10

heritage — *2819: 1 Pet. 5:3*

Hermas — *2057: Rom. 16:14*

Hermes — *2060: Rom. 16:14*

Hermogenes — *2061: 2 Tim. 1:15*

Herod -'s — *2264:* Matt. 2:1; Acts 23:35

Herodians — *2265: Matt. 22:16; Mark 3:6; 12:13*

Herodias — *2266:* Mark 6:17; Luke 3:19

Herodion — *2267: Rom. 16:11*

hewn — *1581, 2991, 2998:* Matt. 3:10; Mark 15:46

hide -eth -ing; hid -den — *613, 614, 1470, 2572, 2927, 2928, 2990, 3871, 4032:* 1 Cor. 2:7; James 5:20

Hierapolis — *2404: Col. 4:13*

high -er -est -ly -ness — *507, 511, 749, 1537/4053, 2032, 2371, 2409, 3173, 4410, 4411, 5242, 5251, 5252, 5308, 5310, 5311, 5313:* Luke 1:32; Rom. 11:20

highminded — *5187, 5309: Rom. 11:20; 1 Tim. 6:7; 2 Tim. 3:4*

highway -s — *1327/3598, 3598: Matt. 22:9, 10; Mark 10:46; Luke 14:23*

hill -s — *697, 1015, 3714, 3735:* Luke 23:30; Acts 17:22

hinder (see **rearward**) — *4403: Acts 27:41*

hinder -ed — *348, 1465, 1581, 2967, 5100/1464/1325:* Luke 11:52; Gal. 5:7

hire -ed -ling — *3407, 3408, 3409, 3410, 3411:* Matt. 20:7; Luke 10:7

hither — *1759, 3333, 5602:* Mark 11:3; Rev. 4:1

hitherto — *891/1204, 2193/737, 3768: John 5:17; 16:24; Rom. 1:13; 1 Cor. 3:2*

hoisted — *1869: Acts 27:40*

hold -en -est -eth -ing; held (see **stayed**) — *472, 1907, 1949, 2192, 2270, 2476, 2722, 2902, 2983, 4160, 4601, 4623, 4912, 5083, 5084, 5392, 5438:* Rom. 14:4; Rev. 2:1

holes — *5454: Matt. 8:20; Luke 9:58*

Holy; holy -iest -ily -iness — *39, 40, 1859, 2413, 3741, 3743:* Heb. 9:3; Jude 1:20

home; homeborn — *1438, 1736, 2398, 3614, 3624, 3626:* Matt. 8:6; Titus 2:5

honest -ly -y — *2156, 2570, 2573, 4586, 4587:* Rom. 13:13; 1 Tim. 2:2

honey — *3192: Matt. 3:4 Mark 1:6; Rev. 10;9, 10*

honeycomb — *3193/2781: Luke 24:42*

honor -able -ed -eth -s — *820, 1391, 1392, 1741, 1784, 2158, 5091, 5092, 5093:* Acts 28:10; Heb. 13:4

hook — *44: Matt. 17:27*

hope -ed -eth -ing -'s — *560, 1679, 1680:* 1 Cor. 13:7; 1 John 3:3

horn -s — *2768:* Luke 1:69; Rev. 5:6

horse -s — *2462:* James 3:3; Rev. 9:7

horsemen — *2460, 2461: Acts 23:23, 32; Rev. 9:16*

hosanna — *5614: Matt. 21:9, 15; Mark 11:9, 10; John 12:13*

Hosea — *5617: Rom. 9:25*

hospitality — *5381, 5382:* Titus 1:8; 1 Pet. 4:9

host — *3581, 3830, 4756: Luke 2:13; 10:35; Acts 7:42; Rom. 16:23*

hot — *2200, 2743: 1 Tim. 4:2; Rev. 3:15, 16*

hour -s — *734, 2256, 5610: John 11:9; 1 Cor. 8:7*

house -hold -holder -s -top(s) — *2322, 3609, 3610, 3613, 3614, 3615, 3616, 3617, 3624, 3832:* Matt. 13:27; Luke 12:3

how — *2193, 2245, 2531, 3704, 3745, 3754, 4012, 4080, 4212, 4214, 4459, 5101, 5613:* Acts 2:8; 2 Pet. 2:9

howbeit — *235, 1161, 3305:* John 16:13; Gal. 4:8

howl — *3649: James 5:1*

humble -ed -eth -ness (see **humility**) — *5011, 5012, 5013:* 2 Cor. 12:21; Col. 3:12

humility; humiliation (see **humble**) — *5012, 5014:* Acts 8:33; 1 Pet. 5:5

hundred -fold -s — *1250, 1540, 1541, 1542, 1812, 3461, 4001, 5071, 5145, 5516:* Mark 6:40; Rom. 4:19

hunger -ed; hungry — *3042, 3983, 4361:* Luke 1:53; 2 Cor. 11:27

hurt -ful — *91, 983, 984, 2559, 5196:* Mark 16:18; Rev. 2:11

husband -s — *435, 5220, 5362:* John 4:18; Eph. 5:23, 33

husbandman; husbandmen; husbandry — *1091, 1092:* 1 Cor. 3:9; James 5:7

husks — *2769: Luke 15:16*

Hymenaeus — *5211: 1 Tim. 1:20; 2 Tim. 2:17*

hymn -s — *5214, 5215: Matt. 26:30; Mark 14:26; Eph. 5:19; Col. 3:16*

hypocrisy -ies; hypocrite -s — *505, 5272, 5273:* Luke 11:44; James 3:17

hyssop — *5301: John 19:29; Heb. 9:19*

I

I; me; my, self (see **our**) — *1473, 1698, 1699, 1700, 3427, 3450:* Gal. 2:20; 1 Tim. 1:12

Iconium — *2430:* Acts 13:51; 2 Tim. 3:11
idle — *692, 1494, 1497, 3026, 3029:* Matt. 20:3; 1 Tim. 5:13
idol -ater(s) -atry -atries -s — *1493, 1494, 1495, 1496, 1497, 2712:* 1 Cor. 5:10; Rev. 21:8
Idumea — *2401: Mark 3:8*
if — *1437, 1487, 1489, 1490, 1499, 1512, 1513, 1535, 2579, 3379:* Rom. 10:9; Phile. 1:17, 18
ignorant -ly; ignorance — *50, 52, 56, 2399, 2990:* Acts 17:23; 2 Pet. 3:5
ill — *2536: Rom. 13:10*
illuminated — *5461: Heb. 10:32*
Illyricum — *2437: Rom. 15:19*
image — *1504, 5481:* Mark 12:16; 1 Cor. 15:49
imagine -ation(s) — *1261, 1271, 3053, 3191:* Luke 1:51; 2 Cor. 10:5
Immanuel — *1694: Matt. 1:23*
immediately (see **anon; straightway**) — *1824, 2112, 2117, 3916:* Luke 1:64; Acts 10:33
immortal -ity — *110, 861, 862:* Rom. 2:7; 1 Cor. 15:53, 54; 1 Tim. 1:17; 6:16; 2 Tim. 1:10
immutable; immutability — *276: Heb. 6:17, 18*
impart -ed — *3330:* Luke 3:11; Rom. 1:11; 1 Thess. 2:8
impediment — *3424: Mark 7:32*
impenitent — *279: Rom. 2:5*
implacable — *786: Rom. 1:31*
implead (see **plea**) — *1458: Acts 19:38*
importunity — *335: Luke 11:8*
imposed — *1945: Heb. 9:10*
impossible — *101, 102, 418:* Matt. 17:20; Luke 17:1
impotent — *102, 770, 772: John 5:3, 7; Acts 4:9; 14:8*
imprison -ed -ment(s) (see **prison**) — *5438, 5439: Acts 22:19; 2 Cor. 6:5; Heb. 11:36*
impute -ed -eth -ing — *1677, 3049:* Rom. 4:6; 2 Cor. 5:19
in (see **into**) — *1519, 1525, 1528, 1529, 1530, 1531, 1532, 1533, 1722, 1723, 1724, 1726, 1749, 1750, 1754, 1784, 1878, 1879, 1888, 1917, 1919, 1924, 1961, 3920:* Gal. 2:4; Titus 2:7
inasmuch — *1909/3745, 2526, 2596/3745:* Matt. 25:40; 1 Pet. 4:13
incense (see **frankincense**) — *2368, 2370: Luke 1:9-11; Rev. 8:3, 4*
incontinency; incontinent — *192, 193: 1 Cor. 7:5; 2 Tim. 3:3*
incorruptible; incorruption (see **uncorruptible**) — *861, 862:* 1 Cor. 9:25; 1 Pet. 1:4
increase -ed -ing -th — *837, 838, 1743, 4052,*

4121, 4147, 4298, 4369: John 3:30; Col. 1:10
incredible — *571: Acts 26:8*
indebted — *3784: Luke 11:4*
indeed — *230, 235, 1063, 2532, 3303, 3689:* Matt. 3:11; John 1:47
indigation — *23, 24, 2205, 2372, 3709:* Rom. 2:8; Heb. 10:27
inexcusable — *379: Rom. 2:1*
infants (see **babe**) — *1025: Luke 18:15*
inferior — *2274: 2 Cor. 12:13*
infidel — *571: 2 Cor. 6:15; 1 Tim. 5:8*
infirmity -ies — *769, 771, 3554:* Luke 7:21; Heb. 4:15
informed — *1718, 2727:* Acts 21:21, 24; 24:1; 25:2, 15
inhabitants; inhabiters — *2730:* Rev. 8:13; 12:12; 17:2
inherit -ance -ed — *2816, 2817, 2819, 2820:* Matt. 5:5; Eph. 1:11
iniquity -ies (see **sin**) — *92, 93, 458, 3892:* Luke 13:27; Rom. 4:7
injured; injurious — *91, 5197: Gal. 4:12; 1 Tim. 1:13*
ink — *3188: 2 Cor 3:3; 2 John 1:12; 3 John 1:13*
inn — *2646, 3829: Luke 2:7; 10:34*
inner — *2080, 2082: Acts 16:24; Eph. 3:16*
innocent — *121: Matt. 27:4, 24*
innumerable — *382, 3461: Luke 12:1; Heb. 11:12; 12:22*
inordinate — *3806: Col. 3:5*
inquire -ed -y — *198, 1231, 1331, 1567, 1833, 1934, 2212, 4441, 4802:* John 16:19; 1 Pet. 1:10
inscription — *1924: Acts 17:23*
insomuch (see **forasmuch; forsomuch**) — *1519, 5620:* Matt. 8:24; 2 Cor. 8:6
inspiration — *2315: 2 Tim. 3:16*
instant -ly — *1616, 1722, 1945, 2186, 4342, 4705, 5610:* Luke 7:4; Rom. 12:12
instruct -ed -ion -or — *2727, 3100, 3453, 3807, 3809, 3810, 3811, 4264, 4822:* 1 Cor. 4:15; 2 Tim. 2:25
instruments — *3696: Rom. 6:13*
insurrection — *2721, 4714, 4955: Mark 15:7; Acts 18:12*
intend -ing — *1011, 1014, 2309, 3195:* Luke 14:28; Acts 5:28, 35; 12:4; 20:13
intent -s — *1771, 2443, 3056:* Eph. 3:10; Heb. 4:12
intercession -s — *1783, 5241:* Rom. 8:26, 27, 34; 11:2; 1 Tim. 2:1; Heb. 7:25
interpret -ation -ed -er — *1328, 1329, 1377, 1955, 2058, 2059, 3177:* Mark 5:41; 1 Cor. 14:5
into (see **in**) — *891, 1519, 1531, 1722, 1909,*

2080, 2596, 3350, 5259: Matt. 1:17; Luke 23:42

intruding — *1687:* Col. 2:18

inventors — *2182:* Rom. 1:30

invisible — *517:* 1 Tim. 1:17; Heb. 11:27

inward -ly — *1722/2927, 2080, 2081, 4698:* Luke 11:39; Rom. 2:29

iron — *4603, 4604:* Acts 12:10; Rev. 2:27

Isaac — *2464:* Matt. 1:2; James 2:21

Isaiah — *2268:* Mark 7:6; Acts 28:25

Iscariot — *2469:* Matt. 10:4; Luke 22:3

island; isle — *3519, 3520:* Acts 13:6; Rev. 6:14

Israel -ite(s) — *2474, 2475:* Rom. 11:1; Eph. 2:12

Issachar — *2466:* Rev. 7:7

issue -ed — *131, 1607, 4511, 4690:* Mark 5:25; Rev. 9:17, 18

it -self — *846, 1438, 5565:* Matt. 1:22; 3 John 1:12

Italy -ian —*2482, 2483:* Acts 10:1; Heb. 13:24

itching — *2833:* 2 Tim. 4:3

Ituraea — *2484:* Luke 3:1

ivory — *1661:* Rev. 18:12

J

jacinth — *5191, 5192:* Rev. 9:17; 21:20

Jacob — *2384:* Matt. 1:2; Rom. 9:13

jailer — *1200:* Acts 16:23

Jairus — *2383:* Mark 5:22; Luke 8:41

Jambres — *2387:* 2 Tim. 3:8

James — *2385:* Acts 15:13; James 1:1

jangling — *3150:* 1 Tim. 1:6

Janna — *2388:* Luke 3:24

Jannes — *2389:* 2 Tim. 3:8

Jared — *2391:* Luke 3:37

Jason — *2394:* Acts 17:5-7, 9; Rom. 16:21

jasper — *2393:* Rev. 4:3; 21:11, 18, 19

jealous -y — *2205, 2206:* Rom. 10:19; 11:11; 1 Cor. 10:22; 2 Cor. 11:2

Jechonias — *2423:* Matt. 1:11, 12

jeopardy — *2793:* Luke 8:23; 1 Cor. 15:30

Jephthah — *2422:* Heb. 11:32

Jeremiah — *2408:* Matt. 2:17; 16:14; 27:9

Jericho — *2410:* Luke 10:30; Heb. 11:30

Jerusalem — *2414, 2419:* Mark 1:5; Gal. 1:17, 18

Jesse — *2421:* Matt. 1:5, 6; Luke 3:32; Acts 13:22; Rom. 15:12

jesting — *2160:* Eph. 5:4

Jesus (see **Christ**; **God**) — *2424:* Phile. 1:1; 1 John 4:2, 3

Jew -ess -ish -s — *2451, 2453:* Col. 3:11; Titus 1:14

Jewry (see **Judea**) — *2449:* Luke 23:5; John 7:1

Jezebel — *2403* :Rev. 2:20

Joanna — *2489:* Luke 3:27; 8:3; 24:10

Joatham — *2488:* Matt. 1:9

Job — *2492:* James 5:11

Joel — *2493:* Acts 2:16

John -'s — *2491:* John 1:6; Gal. 2:9

join -ed — *2675, 2853, 4347, 4801, 4883, 4927:* Acts 5:13; 1 Cor. 1:10

joint -s — *719, 860:* Eph. 4:16; Col. 2:9; Heb. 4:12

joint-heirs — *4789:* Rom. 8:17

Jona; Jonah (see **Bar-jona**) — *2495:* Matt. 12:39; John 1:42

Jonan — *2494:* Luke 3:30

Joppa — *2445:* Acts 9:36; 11:5

Joram — *2496:* Matt. 1:8

Jordan — *2446:* Mark 1:5, 9; John 1:28

Jorim — *2497:* Luke 3:29

Josaphat — *2498:* Matt. 1:8

Jose — *2499:* Luke 3:29

Joseph -'s — *2501:* Matt. 1:16; Heb. 11:21

Joses — *2500:* Mark 6:3; Acts 4:36

Josiah — *2502:* Matt. 1:10, 11

Joshua — *2424:* Heb. 4:8

jot — *2503:* Matt. 5:18

journey -ed -ing(s) — *589, 590, 1279, 2137, 3593, 3596, 3597, 3598, 4197/4160, 4198, 4922:* 2 Cor. 11:26; Titus 3:13

joy -ed -ing; joyful -ly -ness — *20, 21, 2167, 2744, 3326, 5463, 5479, 5485:* Col. 1:11; James 1:2

Judah; Judas; Jude — *2448, 2449, 2453, 2455:* Matt. 1:2; Jude 1:1

Judea (see **Jewry**) — *2449, 2453:* Acts 2:14; 1 Thess. 2:14

judge -ed -est -eth -ing -ment(s) -s (see **just; justify**) — *144, 350, 968, 1106, 1252, 1341, 1345, 1348, 1349, 2233, 2250, 2917, 2919, 2920, 2922, 2923, 4232:* Rom. 11:33; Phil. 1:9

Julia — *2456:* Rom. 16:15

Julius — *2457:* Acts 27:1, 3

Junia — *2458:* Rom. 16:7

Jupiter — *1356, 2203:* Acts 14:12, 13; 19:35

jurisdiction — *1849:* Luke 23:7

just -ice -ly (see **judge**; **justify**) — *1342, 1346, 1738:* Matt. 1:19; 1 Thess. 2:10

justify -ication -ied -ieth -ier (see **judge**; **just**) — *1344, 1345, 1347:* Rom. 3:26; Gal. 3:8

Justus — *2459:* Acts 1:23; 18:7; Col. 4:11

K

keep -er(s) -est -eth -ing -t — *71, 650, 1006, 1096, 1200, 1301, 1314, 1858, 2192, 2343, 2377, 2621, 2722, 2853, 2902, 2967, 3557,*

3626, 3930, 4160, 4238, 4601, 4874, 4933, 5083, 5288, 5299, 5432, 5441, 5442: Luke 2:8; Jude 1:6

key -s — *2807:* Matt. 16:19; Rev. 3:7

kick — *2979: Acts 9:5; 26:14*

kid — *2056: Luke 15:29*

kill -ed -est -eth -ing — *337, 615, 1315, 2289, 2380, 4969, 5407:* Rom. 13:9; James 5:6

kin -man -men -sfolk(s) (see **kindred**) — *4773:* Mark 6:4; Luke 14:12

kind -s — *1085, 5100, 5449, 5541:* Matt. 13:47; 1 Cor. 15:39

kind -ly -ness — *5360, 5363, 5387, 5543, 5544:* Rom. 12:10; 2 Pet. 1:7

kindled; kindleth — *381, 681: Luke 12:49; 22:55; Acts 28:2; James 3:5*

kindred -s (see **kin**) — *1085, 3965, 4772, 5443:* Luke 1:61; Rev. 7:9

king -dom(s) -s (see **royal**) — *932, 933, 935, 936, 937:* Col. 1:13; 1 Tim. 2:2

Kish — *2797: Acts 13:21*

kiss -ed — *2705, 5368, 5370:* Luke 7:38; 1 Thess. 5:26

knee -s — *1119:* Eph. 3:14; Phil. 2:10

kneeled; kneeling — *1120, 5087/1119:* Mark 1:40; Acts 21:5

knit — *1210, 4822: Acts 10:11; Col. 2:2, 19*

knock -ed -eth -ing — *2925:* Matt. 7:7,8; Rev. 3:20

know -est -eth -ing -ledge -n; knew -est (see **wist**) — *50, 56, 319, 1097, 1107, 1108, 1110, 1231, 1232, 1492, 1921, 1987, 1990, 2467, 2589, 4135, 4267, 4892, 4907, 5318:* Phile. 1:21; 2 John 1:1

Korah — *2879: Jude 1:11*

L

labor -ed -er(s) -eth -ing -s (see **work**) — *75, 2038, 2040, 2041, 2872, 2873, 4704, 4866, 4904, 5389:* Luke 10:7; 1 Thess. 2:9

lack -ed -est -eth -ing — *170, 1641, 1729, 3007, 3361/2192, 3361/3918, 5302, 5303, 5332:* 1 Cor. 16:17; 2 Pet. 1:9

lad — *3808: John 6:9*

lade -ed -en -ing — *2007, 4987, 5412: Matt. 11:28; Luke 11:46; Acts 27:10; 28:10; 2 Tim. 3:6*

lady — *2959: 2 John 1:1, 5*

lake — *3041:* Luke 8:22; Rev. 20:10

lama — *2982: Matt. 27:46; Mark 15:34*

lamb -s (see **sheep**) — *86, 704, 721:* John 1:29; 1 Pet. 1:19

lame (see **halt**) — *5560:* Acts 3:2, 11; Heb. 12:13

Lamech — *2984: Luke 3:36*

lament -ation -ed — *2354, 2355, 2870, 2875:* John 16:20; Acts 8:2

lamp -s — *2985:* Matt. 25:1; Rev. 8:10

land -s — *68, 1093, 3584, 5561, 5564:* Mark 10:29, 30; Jude 1:5

landed; landing — *2609, 2718: Acts 18:22; 21:3; 28:12*

lanes — *4505: Luke 14:21*

language — *1258: Acts 2:6*

lanterns — *5322: John 18:3*

Laodicea -ns — *2993, 2994:* Col. 2:1; Rev. 3:14

large (see **enlarge**) — *2425, 3173, 4080, 5118:* Mark 14:15; Gal. 6:11

lasciviousness — *766:* Eph. 4:19; 1 Pet. 4:3

Lasea — *2996: Acts 27:8*

last (see **late; latter**) — *2078, 4218, 5305:* John 6:39; 1 John 2:18

latchet — *2438: Mark 1:7; Luke 3:16; John 1:27*

late -ly (see **last; latter**) — *3568, 4373: John 11:8; Acts 18:2*

latter (see **last; late -ly**) — *2078, 3797, 5305: 1 Tim. 4:1; James 5:7; 2 Pet. 2:20*

Latin — *4513: Luke 23:38; John 19:20*

laud — *1867: Rom. 15:11*

laugh -ed -ter — *1070, 1071, 2606:* Matt. 9:24; James 4:9

launch -ed — *321, 1877: Luke 8:22; Acts 21:1; 27:2, 4*

law -ful -fully -giver -less -s -yer(s) — *60, 458, 459, 460, 1772, 1832, 1833, 2917, 2919, 2544, 3545, 3547, 3548, 3549, 3550, 3551, 3565, 3891, 3994, 3995:* 1 Tim. 1:8; Titus 3:13

lay -eth -ing; lie -eth; laid -st; lain — *347, 597, 606, 659, 863, 906, 991, 1462, 1474, 1748, 1911, 1917, 1936, 1945, 1968, 2007, 2192, 2343, 2476, 2598, 2621, 2698, 2749, 2827, 3049, 3180, 4160, 4369, 5087, 5294, 5342:* Eph. 4:14; 1 John 5:19

Lazarus — *2976:* Luke 16:20; John 11:1

lead -er -eth; led -dest — *71, 162, 163, 321, 399, 520, 1236, 1533, 1806, 3594, 3595, 4013, 4863, 4879, 5342, 5496, 5497:* Matt. 15:14; 1 Tim. 2:2

leaves — *5444: Matt. 21:19; 24:32; Mark 11:13; 13:28; Rev. 22:2*

leaned; leaning — *345, 377: John 13:23; 21:20; Heb. 11:21*

leap -ed -ing — *242, 1814, 2177, 4640:* Luke 1:41, 44; Acts 3:8

learn -ed -ing — *1121, 1319, 3129, 3928, 3811:* John 6:45; 2 Tim. 3:7, 14

least (see **less**) — *1646, 1647, 1848, 2534, 2579, 3398:* 1 Cor. 6:4; Eph. 3:8

leather — *1193: Matt. 3:4*

leave -eth -ing; left — *447, 620, 657, 710, 782, 863, 1439, 1459, 1544, 2010, 2176, 2641, 3973, 4051, 4052, 5275, 5277:* Acts 6:2; Titus 1:5

leaven -ed -eth — *2219, 2220:* Luke 12:1; Gal. 5:9

Lebbaeus (see **Thaddeus**) — *3002: Matt. 10:3*

legs — *4628: John 19:31 —33*

legion -s — *3003: Matt. 26:53; Mark 5:9, 15; Luke 8:30*

leisure — *2119: Mark 6:31*

lend — *1155, 5531: Luke 6:34, 35; 11:5*

length — *3372, 4218: Rom. 1:10; Eph. 3:18; Rev. 21:16*

leopard — *3917: Rev. 13:2*

leper -s; leprosy — *3014, 3015:* Matt. 10:8; Luke 5:12

less (see **least**) — *253, 820, 1640, 1647, 2276, 3398:* Mark 4:31; Phil. 2:28

lest — *1519/3588/3361, 3363, 3379, 3381:* Rom. 11:25; Heb. 2:1

let -test -teth — *630, 863, 1439, 1554, 1832, 1929, 2010, 2524, 2722, 2967, 5465:* Mark 1:24; 2 Thess. 2:7

letter -s — *1121, 1989, 1992:* Rom. 2:27, 29; 1 Cor. 16:3

Levi (see **Levite; Matthew**) — *3017, 3018:* Mark 2:14; Heb. 7:5

Levite -s -ical (see **Levi; priest**) — *3019, 3020: Luke 10:32; John 1:19; Acts 4:36; Heb. 7:11*

lewd -ness — *4190, 4467: Acts 17:5; 18:14*

liberal -ity -ly — *572, 574, 5485: 1 Cor. 16:3; 2 Cor. 8:2; 9:13; James 1:5*

liberty (see **free**) — *425, 630, 859, 1657, 1658, 1849, 2010:* Luke 4:18; Gal. 2:4

Libya — *3033: Acts 2:10*

license — *2010, 5117: Acts 21:40; 25:16*

licked — *621: Luke 16:21*

lie -ed -s; liars; lying (see **leasing**) — *5571, 5573, 5574, 5579, 5582, 5583:* Eph. 4:25; 1 Tim. 1:10

life -time (see **alive; live**) — *72, 326, 390, 895, 979, 980, 981, 982, 1514, 2068, 2071, 2198, 2222, 2225, 3118, 4151, 4800, 5225, 5590:* Luke 16:25; Jude 1:21

lift -ed -ing — *142, 352, 450, 461, 1453, 1458, 1869, 5188, 5312:* Matt. 12:11; Rev. 10:5

light -ed -eth -ing -s — *272, 681, 797, 1645, 2014, 2017, 2064, 2545, 2985, 2989, 3088, 4098, 5035, 5338, 5457, 5458, 5460, 5461, 5462:* John 1:4; Phil. 2:15

lighten -ed -eth — *602, 797, 1546/4160, 2893, 5461:* Acts 27:18; Rev. 18:1

lightly; lightness — *1644, 5035: Mark 9:39; 2 Cor. 1:17*

lightning -s — *796:* Matt. 24:27; Luke 10:18

like -en -ed -ness -wise — *36, 407, 437, 499, 871, 1381, 1503, 2470, 2472, 2473, 2504, 2532, 2596/3365, 3664, 3666, 3667, 3668, 3779, 3898, 3945, 3946, 4832, 5024, 5108,*

5613, 5615, 5616, 5618: 1 Pet. 3:21; Jude 1:7

likeminded — *2473, 3588/846/5426: Rom. 15:5; Phil. 2:2, 20*

lilies — *2918: Matt. 6:28; Luke 12:27*

limiteth — *3724: Heb. 4:7*

line — *2583: 2 Cor. 10:16*

lineage — *3965: Luke 2:4*

linen — *1039, 1040, 3043, 3608, 4616:* John 19:40; Rev. 15:6

lingereth — *691: 2 Pet. 2:3*

Linus — *3044: 2 Tim. 4:21*

lion — *3023: 2 Tim. 4:17; 1 Pet. 5:8; Rev. 4:7; 5:5; 10:3; 13:2*

lips — *5491:* Rom. 3:13; 1 Cor. 14:21

listed; listeth — *1014, 2309, 3730: Matt. 17:12; Mark 9:13; John 3:8; James 3:4*

little — *974, 1024, 1646, 2365, 2485, 3397, 3398, 3640, 3641, 3813, 4142, 5040, 5177:* Heb. 2:7; 1 John 5:21

live -ed -est -eth -ing -s (see **alive; life; lively; quick**) — *326, 390, 979, 980, 1236, 1514, 2068, 2071, 2198, 2225, 3118, 4176, 4800, 5171, 5225, 5590:* Luke 2:36; Gal. 2:14

lively (see **alive; live; quick**) — *2198: Acts 7:38; 1 Pet. 1:3; 2:5*

lo — *2396, 2400:* Matt. 2:9; John 7:26

loaf; loaves (see **bread**) — *740:* Mark 8:14; Luke 11:5

locusts — *200: Matt. 3:4; Mark 1:6; Rev. 9:3, 7*

lodge -ed -eth -ing — *835, 2647, 2681, 3578, 3579, 3580:* Acts 10:6; Phile. 1:22

loins — *3751:* Luke 12:35; 1 Pet. 1:13

Lois — *3090: 2 Tim. 1:5*

long -ed (see **desire**) — *1971, 1973:* Rom. 1:11; Phil. 2:26

long -er — *1909, 1909/4119, 2089, 2118, 2193, 2425, 2863, 3117, 3370, 3752, 3756/3641, 3819, 4183, 4214, 5118, 5550:* Luke 16:2; John 5:6

longsuffering — *3114, 3115:* 2 Cor. 6:6; 2 Pet. 3:9

look -ed -eth -ing — *308, 352, 553, 816, 872, 991, 1492, 1551, 1561, 1689, 1896, 1914, 1980, 1983, 2300, 2334, 3700, 3706, 3879, 4017, 4327, 4328, 4329, 4648:* Mark 3:5; Jude 1:21

loose -ed -ing — *142, 321, 447, 630, 2673, 3080, 3089:* Matt. 16:19; Rom. 7:2

Lord -'s; lord -s -ship — *1203, 2634, 2960, 2961, 2962, 3175, 4462:* Luke 22:25; Titus 1:4

lose -eth; loss; lost — *358, 580, 622, 1096, 2209, 2210, 3471:* Matt. 10:39; 2 John 1:8

lot -s — *2624, 2819, 2975:* John 19:24; Acts 1:26

Lot -'s — *3091: Luke 17:28, 29, 32; 2 Pet. 2:7*
loud — *3173:* Matt. 27:46; Acts 26:24
love -ed -er(s) -est -eth -ly — *25, 26, 2309, 4375, 5358, 5360, 5361, 5362, 5363, 5365, 5367, 5368, 5369, 5377, 5382, 5383, 5388:* Phil. 4:8; 2 Tim. 3:2, 4
low -er -ering -est -eth -liness -ly — *1642, 2078, 2737, 4768, 5011, 5012, 5013, 5014:* Luke 1:48; Eph. 4:2
lowering — *4768 Matt. 16:3*
Lucius — *3066: Acts 13:1; Rom. 16:21*
lucre -'s — *146, 147, 866, 2771: 1 Tim. 3:3, 8; Titus 1:7, 11; 1 Pet. 5:2*
Lydia — *3070: Acts 16:14, 40*
Luke — *3065:* Col. 4:14; Phile. 1:24
lukewarm — *5513: Rev. 3:16*
lump — *5445: Rom. 9:21; 11:16; 1 Cor. 5:6, 7; Gal. 5:9*
lunatic — *4583: Matt. 4:24; 17:15*
lust -ed -eth -s — *1511, 1937, 1938, 1939, 1971, 2237, 3715, 3806:* Gal. 5:17; Jude 1:16
Lycaonia — *3071: Acts 14:6, 11*
Lydda — *3069: Acts 9:32, 35, 38*
Lysanias — *3078: Luke 3:1*
Lysias — *3079: Acts 23:26; 24:7, 22*
Lystra — *3082: Acts 14:6, 8, 21; 16:1, 2; 2 Tim. 3:11*

M

Maath — *3092: Luke 3:26*
Macedonia -n — *3109, 3110:* Acts 16:9; 1 Thess. 1:7
mad -ness — *454, 1519/3130, 1693, 3105, 3913:* John 10:20; 1 Pet. 2:16
Magdala — *3093: Matt. 15:39*
Magdalene (see **Mary**) — *3094:* Mark 16:1; John 19:25
magistrate -s — *758, 796, 3980, 4755:* Luke 12:11; Titus 3:1
magnificence — *3168: Acts 19:27*
magnify -ied — *1392, 3170:* Rom. 11:13; Phil. 1:20
Magog — *3098: Rev. 20:8*
Mahalaleel — *3121: Luke 3:37*
maid -en(s) -s (see **handmaid**) — *2877, 3814, 3816:* Matt. 9:24, 25; Mark 14:66
maimed — *376, 2948: Matt. 15:30, 31; 18:8; Mark 9:43; Luke 14:13, 21*
mainsail — *736:* Acts 27:40
maintain — *4291: Titus 3:8, 14*
majesty — *3168, 3172: Heb. 1:3; 8:1; 2 Pet. 1:16; Jude 1:25*
Malchus — *3124: John 18:10*
male (see **man -kind**) — *730: Matt. 19:4; Mark 10:6; Luke 2:23; Gal. 3:28*

malefactor -s — *2555, 2557: Luke 23:32, 33, 39; John 18:30*
malice; malicious -ness — *2549, 4190:* Eph. 4:31; 3 John 1:10
malignity — *2550: Rom. 1:29*
man -kind; men (see **male**) — *245, 407, 435, 441, 442, 444, 730, 733, 1538, 2478, 3367, 3494, 3495, 3762, 3956, 4753, 5046, 5100, 5449:* Eph. 6:7; 1 Tim. 2:1
Manaen — *3127: Acts 13:1*
Manasseh; Manasses — *3128: Matt. 1:10; Rev. 7:6*
manger — *5336: Luke 2:7, 12, 16*
manifest -ation -ed -ly — *602, 852, 1212, 1552, 1717, 1718, 4271, 5318, 5319, 5321:* Rom. 8:19; 2 Cor. 3:3
manna — *3131: John 6:31, 49, 58; Heb. 9:4; Rev. 2:17*
manner -s — *72, 195, 442, 686, 981, 1483, 1485, 1486, 2239, 3592, 3634, 3697, 3779, 4012, 4169, 4187, 4217, 4458, 5158, 5159, 5179, 5615:* Acts 13:18; 1 John 3:1
menservants (see **man**) — *3816: Luke 12:45*
mansions — *3438: John 14:2*
manslayers (see **man**) — *409: 1 Tim. 1:9*
many; manifold — *2425, 3745, 4119, 4164, 4179, 4182, 4183, 4214, 5118:* Matt. 3:7; 1 Pet. 1:6
marred — *622: Mark 2:22*
Maranatha — *3134: 1 Cor. 16:22*
marble — *3139: Rev. 18:12*
Mark — *3138:* Acts 12:12; Col. 4:10
mark -ed — *1907, 3138, 4648, 4649, 4742, 5480:* Luke 14:7; Phil. 3:14, 17
market -place(s) -s (see **meat market**) — *58:* Matt. 20:3; John 5:2
marrow — *3452: Heb. 4:12*
marry -iage -ied -ieth -ing — *1060, 1061, 1062, 1096, 1447, 1448, 1547, 1548:* Mark 6:17; 1 Tim. 4:3
Mars'—697: Acts 17:22
Martha — *3136:* Luke 10:38; John 11:1
martyr -s — *3144: Acts 22:20; Rev. 2:13; 17:6*
marvel -ed -ous — *2296, 2298:* Matt. 21:42; 1 Pet. 2:9
Mary — *3137:* Luke 8:2; John 19:25
master -ies -s -y — *1203, 1320, 1988, 2519, 2942, 2962, 3617, 4461:* 2 Tim. 2:5; James 3:1
masterbuilder — *753: 1 Cor. 3:10*
Mattatha — *3160: Luke 3:31*
Mattathias — *3161: Luke 3:25, 26*
matter -s — *1308, 2596, 3056, 4229, 5208:* Mark 1:45; 1 Pet. 4:15
Matthan — *3157: Matt. 1:5*
Matthat — *3158: Luke 3:24, 29*
Matthew (see **Levi**) — *3156:* Matt. 9:9; Acts 1:13

Matthias — *3159: Acts 1:23, 26*
may -est; might -est (see **must**) — *1410, 1411, 1832, 2479, 2480, 2481:* Titus 2:14; 3 John 1:2
meal — *224: Matt. 13:33; Luke 13:21*
mean — *767, 3342:* John 4:31; Rom. 2:15
mean -eth -ing -t — *767, 1411, 1498, 2076, 2309/1511, 3195, 4160:* Acts 2:12; 2 Cor. 8:13
means — *1096, 3361, 3364, 3843, 4458, 4459, 5158:* John 9:21; 2 Thess. 2:3
measure -ed -ing -s — *280, 488, 942, 943, 2884, 3354, 3358, 4053, 4057, 4568, 5234, 5236, 5249, 5518:* Matt. 7:2; Rev. 6:6
meat -s — *1033, 1034, 1035, 4371, 4620, 5132, 5160, 5315:* Mark 7:19; Col. 2:16
meat market (see **market -s**) — *3111: 1 Cor. 10:25*
Medes — *3370: Acts 2:9*
mediator — *3316:* 1 Tim. 2:5; Gal. 3:19, 30
meditate — *3191, 4304: Luke 21:14; 1 Tim. 4:15*
meek -ness — *4235, 4236, 4239, 4240:* James 1:21; 1 Pet. 3:4
meet (see **fit**) — *1163, 1342, 2111, 2173, 2425, 2427, 2570:* Phil. 1:7; Col. 1:12
meet; met — *296, 528, 529, 4820, 4876, 4877, 5221, 5222:* Acts 10:25; 1 Thess. 4:17
Melchi — *3197: Luke 3:24, 28*
Melchizedek — *3198:* Heb. 5:6; 7:1
Melea — *3190: Luke 3:31*
Melita — *3194: Acts 28:1*
melody — *5567: Eph. 5:19*
melt — *3089, 5080: 2 Pet. 3:10, 12*
member -s — *3196:* Eph. 4:25; James 3:5
memory -ial — *3422: Matt. 26:13; Mark 14:9; Acts 10:4; 1 Cor. 15:2*
Menan — *3104: Luke 3:31*
mending — *2675: Matt. 4:21; Mark 1:19*
menpleasers (see **man**) — *441: Eph. 6:6; Col. 3:22*
menstealers (see **man**) — *405: 1 Tim. 1:10*
mention — *3417, 3421:* Rom. 1:9; Phile 4
merchant -s; merchandise — *1117, 1711, 1712, 1713:* Matt. 22:5; Rev. 18:3
Mercurius — *2060: Acts 14:12*
mercy -ful -ies — *448, 1653, 1655, 1656, 2433, 2436, 3628, 3629, 3741:* Rom. 12:1; Jude 1:2, 21
mercyseat — *2435: Heb. 9:5*
merry — *2114, 2165:* Luke 12:19; James 5:13
Mesopotamia (see **Aram**) — *3318: Acts 2:9; 7:2*
message; messenger -s — *31, 32, 652, 1860, 4242:* 2 Cor. 8:23; 1 John 1:5
Messiah — *3323: John 1:41; 4:25*
mete — *3354: Matt. 7:2; Mark 4:24; Luke 6:38*
Methuselah — *3103: Luke 3:37*

Michael — *3413: Jude 1:9; Rev. 12:7*
midday (see **day**) — *2250/3319: Acts 26:13*
middle; midst — *3319, 3320, 3321, 3322:* Eph. 2:14; Heb. 2:12
midnight — *3317, 3319/3571: Matt. 25:6; Mark 13:35; Luke 11:5; Acts 16:25; 20:7; 27:27*
Midian — *3099: Acts 7:29*
might -ier -ily -y — *972, 1411, 1413, 1414, 1415, 1722/1411, 1722/2479, 1754, 2159, 2478, 2596/2904, 2900, 3168, 3173, 5082:* Mark 1:7; Col. 1:29
mile — *3400: Matt. 5:41*
Miletum, Miletus — *3399: Acts 20:15, 17; 2 Tim. 4:20*
milk — *1051: 1 Cor. 3:2; 9:7; Heb. 5:12, 13; 1 Pet. 2:2*
mill — *3459: Matt. 24:41*
millstone — *3037/3457, 3458, 3458/3684:* Matt. 18:6; Rev. 18:21
mind -ed -ful -ing -s — *363, 1011, 1014, 1106, 1271, 1374, 1771, 1878, 3195, 3403, 3421, 3540, 3563, 3661, 3675, 4288, 4290, 4993, 4995, 5012, 5279, 5426, 5427, 5590:* Acts 20:13; Phile. 1:14
mingled — *3396: Matt. 27:34; Mark 15:23; Luke 13:1; Rev. 8:7; 15:2*
minister -ed -eth -ing -s; ministration; ministry — *1247, 1248, 1249, 1325, 2023, 2038, 2418, 3008, 3009, 3010, 3011, 3930, 5256, 5257, 5524:* Luke 1:23; Gal. 3:5
minstrels — *834: Matt. 9:23*
mint — *2238: Matt. 23:23; Luke 11:42*
miracle -s — *1411, 4592:* John 2:11; Acts 2:22
mire — *1004: 2 Pet. 2:22*
mischief — *4468: Acts 13:10*
misery -able -ably -ies — *1652, 2560, 5004:* Matt. 21:41; 1 Cor. 15:19
mist — *887, 2217: Acts 13:11; 2 Pet. 2:17*
mite -s — *3016: Mark 12:42; Luke 12:59; 21:2*
Mitylene — *3412: Acts 20:14*
mixed; mixture — *194, 3395, 4786: John 19:39; Heb. 4:2; Rev. 14:10*
Mnason — *3416: Acts 21:16*
mock -ed -ers -ing(s) — *1701, 1702, 1703, 3456, 5512:* Mark 10:34; Gal. 6:7
moderation — *1933: Phil. 4:5*
modest — *2887: 1 Tim. 2:9*
moisture — *2429: Luke 8:6*
Moloch — *3434: Acts 7:43*
moment — *823, 3901, 4743:* Luke 4:5; 1 Cor. 15:52; 2 Cor. 4:17
money — *694, 2772, 3546, 4715, 5365, 5475, 5536:* 1 Tim. 6:10
noneychangers — *2773, 2885:* Matt. 21:12
month -s — *3376, 5072, 5150:* Luke 1:26; James 5:17
moon — *3561, 4582:* Acts 2:20; Col. 2:16

more (see **most**) — *197, 243, 316, 414, 1065, 1308, 1508, 1617, 1833, 2001, 2115, 3122, 3123, 3185, 3187, 3370, 3745, 3761, 3765, 3844, 4053, 4054, 4055, 4056, 4057, 4119, 4179, 4325, 4369, 4707, 5112, 5228, 5236, 5245:* 1 Thess. 2:17; 1 Pet. 1:7

moreover — *235/2532, 1161/2532, 2089, 3739/1161/3063:* Rom. 5:20; 2 Pet. 1:15

morning — *3720, 4404, 4405:* Mark 1:35; Rev. 22:16

morrow; tomorrow — *839, 1836, 1887:* Acts 4:5; James 4:14

morsel — *1035: Heb. 12:16*

mortal -ity — *2349:* Rom. 6:12; 8:11; 1 Cor. 15:53, 54; 2 Cor. 4:11; 5:4

mortify — *2289, 3499:* Rom. 8:13; Col. 3:5

Moses — *3475:* Matt. 23:2; 2 Tim. 3:8

most (see **more**) — *40, 2236, 2903, 3122, 4118, 4119, 5310:* Mark 5:7; Jude 1:20

mote — *2595: Matt. 7:3-5; Luke 6:41, 42*

moth, eaten — *4597: Matt. 6:19, 20; Luke 12:33*

motheaten — *4598: James 5:2*

mother -s — *282, 3384, 3389, 3994:* Gal. 1:15; 1 Tim. 5:2

motions — *3804: Rom. 7:5*

mount -ain(s) -s — *3735:* Heb. 12:20; 2 Pet. 1:18

mourn -ed -ing — *2354, 2875, 3602, 3996, 3997:* Matt. 2:18; Rev. 18:11

mouth -s — *1993, 3056, 4750:* Eph. 6:19; Titus 1:11

move -ed -er -ing — *23, 383, 761, 2125, 2206, 2795, 2796, 3056/4160, 3334, 4525, 4531, 4579, 4697, 5342:* John 5:3; 2 Pet. 1:21

much — *23, 1280, 2425, 2470, 2579, 3123, 3366, 3383, 3433, 3588, 3745, 3761, 4055, 4056, 4124, 4180, 4183, 4214, 5118, 5248:* Matt. 6:7; Phile. 1:8

multiply -ied -ing — *4129:* Acts 6:1; Heb. 6:14

multitude -s (see **press**) — *2793, 3461, 3793, 4128:* Mark 14:43; Luke 5:15

murder -er(s) -s — *443, 3389, 3964, 4607, 5406, 5407, 5408:* Rom. 1:29; 1 John 3:15

murmur -ed; -ers -ing(s) — *1111, 1112, 1113, 1234, 1690:* Phil. 2:14; Jude 1:16

mused — *1260: Luke 3:15*

music -ians — *3451, 4858: Luke 15:25; Rev. 18:22*

must (see **may; ought**) — *318, 1163, 2192, 2443, 3784:* 2 Cor. 5:10; 2 Pet. 1:14

mustard — *4615:* Mark 4:31; Luke 13:19

mutual — *1722/240: Rom. 1:12*

muzzle — *5392: 1 Cor. 9:9; 1 Tim. 5:18*

my -self; mine (see **I; our**) — *846, 1683, 1691, 1698, 1699, 1700, 3427, 3450:* Matt. 7:24; Gal. 2:18

Myra — *3460: Acts 27:5*

myrrh — *4666, 4669: Matt. 2:11; Mark 15:23; John 19:39*

Mysia — *3465: Acts 16:7, 8*

mystery -ies — *3466:* 1 Cor. 13:2; Rev. 1:20

N

Naaman — *3497: Luke 4:27*

Naasson; Nahsson — *3476: Matt. 1:4; Luke 3:32*

Nagge — *3477: Luke 3:25*

Nahor — *3493: Luke 3:34*

nailing; nails — *2247, 4338: John 20:25; Col. 2:14*

Nain — *3484: Luke 7:11*

naked -ness — *1130, 1131, 1132:* Matt. 25:36; 2 Cor. 11:27

name -ed -eth -s — *2564, 3004, 3686, 3687:* Rom. 13:9; 2 Tim. 2:19

namely — *1722: Mark 12:31; Acts 15:22; Rom. 13:9*

Naphtali — *3508: Matt. 4:13, 15; Rev. 7:6*

napkin — *4676: Luke 19:20; John 11:44; 20:7*

Narcissus — *3488: Rom. 16:11*

narrow — *2346: Matt. 7:14*

Nathan — *3481: Luke 3:31*

Nathanael (see **Bartholomew**) — *3482: John 1:45-49; 21:2*

nation -s — *246, 1074, 1085, 1484:* Matt. 24:9; Acts 10:28

nature; natural -ly — *1078, 1083, 1103, 2596/5449, 5446, 5447, 5449, 5591:* Rom. 1:26; Jude 1:10

naughtiness — *2549: James 1:21*

Naum — *3486:Luke 3:25*

Nazarene -s — *3480: Matt. 2:23; Acts 24:5*

Nazareth — *3478:* Luke 1:26; John 1:45, 46

Neapolis — *3496: Acts 16:11*

near -er; nigh — *316, 1448, 1451, 1452, 3844, 3897, 4139, 4314, 4317, 4334:* Rom. 13:11; Eph. 2:13, 17

necessary; necessity -ies (see **need; ought**) — *316, 318, 1876, 2192, 4314/3588/5532, 5532:* 2 Cor. 6:4; Heb. 7:12

neck -s — *5137:* Matt. 18:6; Rom. 16:4

need -ed -est -eth -ful -s (see **necessary**) — *316, 422, 1163, 2006, 2121, 2192/318, 2192/5532, 3784, 3843, 4326, 5532, 5535:* John 2:25; Phil. 4:12

needle -'s — *4476: Matt. 19:24; Mark 10:25; Luke 18:25*

neglect -ed -ing; negligent — *272, 857, 3865, 3878:* Acts 6:1; Col. 2:23

neighbor -s — *1069, 4040, 4139:* Luke 10:27; Eph. 4:25

neither — *2228, 2532/3762, 3364, 3366,*

3383, 3761, 3777: Gal. 1:1; 2 John 1:10
nephews — *1549: 1 Tim. 5:4*
Nereus — *3517: Rom. 16:15*
Neri — *3518: Luke 3:27*
nests — *2682: Matt. 8:20; Luke 9:58*
net -s — *293, 1350, 4522:* Mark 1:18, 19; John 21:6
never (see **no; not**) — *3361, 3364/1519/ 3588/165, 3364/4219, 3364/4455, 3368, 3756, 3756/1519/3588/165, 3761/1520, 3762, 3762/4455, 3763, 3764:* 2 Tim. 3:7; 2 Pet. 1:10
nevertheless (see **although; but**) — *235, 1161, 2544, 3305, 3676/3305, 4133:* Gal. 2:20; Eph. 5:33
new -ness — *46, 1098, 2537, 2538, 3501, 3561, 4372:* Rom. 6:4; 1 Pet. 2:2
newborn — *738: 1 Pet. 2:2*
next — *839, 1206, 1836, 1887, 1966, 2064, 2087, 2192, 3342:* Mark 1:38; Acts 4:3
Nicanor — *3527: Acts 6:5*
Nicodemus — *3530:* John 3:1; 7:50
Nicolaitanes — *3531: Rev. 2:6, 15*
Nicolas — *3532: Acts 6:5*
Nicopolis — *3533: Tit 3:12*
Niger — *3526: Acts 13:1*
night -s — *1273, 3571, 3574:* Matt. 4:2; 1 Thess. 2:9
nine; ninth — *1767, 1768:* Luke 17:17; Rev. 21:20
ninety — *1768: Matt. 18:12, 13; Luke 15:4, 7*
Nineveh; Ninevites — *3535, 3536: Matt. 12:41; Luke 11:30, 32*
no; nay (see **naught; none; nor; not; nothing**) — *209, 235, 269, 686, 790, 1063, 1487, 3304, 3361, 3364, 3365/5100, 3367, 3756, 3761, 3762, 3765, 3777, 3780:* John 1:18; James 3:12
Noah — *3575: Heb. 11:7; 1 Pet. 3:20; 2 Pet. 2:5*
noble — *2903:* 1 Cor. 1:26
nobleman — *937, 2104/444:* Luke 19:12
noise -ed (see **hear; rumor -s**) — *191, 1096/ 5408, 1255, 2350, 4500, 5456:* Mark 2:1; 2 Pet. 3;10
noisome — *2556: Rev. 16:2*
Non, Nun — *5126: Ex. 33:11; 1 Chr. 7:27*
none (see **naught; no; nothing; nought**) — *208, 677, 1601, 2673, 2758, 3361, 3367, 3387, 3756, 3762, 3777, 5100/3756/3762:* 1 Thess. 5:15; 1 Pet. 4:15
noon — *3314: Acts 22:6*
nor (see **no**) — *2228, 2532/3756, 3361, 3364, 3366, 3383, 3756, 3761, 3777:* John 1:13; Rev. 14:11
north — *1005, 5566: Luke 13:29; Acts 27:17; Rev. 21:13*
not (see **no**) — *269, 3361, 3362, 3363, 3364,*

3367, 3369, 3370, 3378, 3380, 3385, 3386, 3756, 3761, 3764, 3765, 3777, 3780: Titus 1:6; 1 John 2:1, 2
note -able — *1110, 1978, 2016, 4593: Matt. 27:16; Acts 2:20; 4:16; Rom. 16:7; 2 Thess. 3:14*
nothing (see **no; naught; none; not; nought**) — *3114, 3361/848, 3367, 3385, 3756/3739, 3756/5100, 3762, 3777, 3956/ 3763, 4487:* Matt. 15:32; 1 Tim. 6:7
notice — *4293: 2 Cor. 9:5*
notwithstanding (see **but; no; not**) — *235, 4133:* Luke 10:11; Rev. 2:20
nought (see **naught; no; none; nothing**) — *557, 1432, 1847, 1848, 2049, 2647, 2673, 3762:* Acts 4:11; Rom. 14:10
nourished; nourisheth; nourishment — *397, 1625, 1789, 2023, 5142:* Eph. 5:29; James 5:5
novice — *3504: 1 Tim. 3:6*
now — *737, 1160, 1161, 1211, 2235, 2236, 2532, 3063, 3568, 3570, 3765, 3767:* 2 Cor. 1:21; 1 Pet. 1:6
number -ed — *705, 706, 1469, 2639, 2674, 3049, 3793, 4785:* Luke 12:7; 1 Tim. 5:9
nurse — *5162: 1 Thess. 2:7*
nurture — *3809: Eph. 6:4*
Nymphas — *3564: Col. 4:15*

O

oath -'s — *332, 3727, 3728:* Mark 6:26; Heb. 6:16, 17
Obed — *5601: Matt. 1:5; Luke 3:32*
obey -ed -ing; obedience; obedient — *544, 1036, 3980, 3982, 5218, 5219, 5255, 5293:* Acts 5:36; Titus 2:5, 9
object — *2723: Acts 24:19*
observe -ation -ed — *3906, 3907, 4160, 4933, 5083, 5442:* Mark 10:20; Gal. 4:10
obtain -ed -ing — *1653, 2013, 2147, 2638, 2816, 2902, 2932, 2975, 2983, 3140, 4047, 5177:* Rom. 11:31; 2 Thess. 2:14
occasion — *874, 1223, 4625:* 2 Cor. 8:8; 1 John 2:10
occupy -ied -ieth — *378, 4043, 4231:* 1 Cor. 14:16; Heb. 13:9
occupation — *5078: Acts 18:3; 19:25*
odor -s — *2368, 3744: John 12:3; Phil. 4:18; Rev. 5:8; 18:13*
off — *14, 554, 568, 575, 595, 609, 631, 659, 660, 851, 1537, 1562, 1575, 1581, 1601, 1621:* Col. 2:11; 2 Pet. 1:9
offend -ed -er; offense -s — *91, 264, 266, 677, 3900, 4348, 4349, 4624, 4625:* Rom. 5:15; James 2:10
offer -ed -ing(s) — *321, 399, 1325, 1435,*

1494, 1929, 3646, 3930, 4374, 4376, 4689: Acts 21:26; Phil. 2:17

office -er(s) — *1247, 1248, 1984, 2405, 2407, 4233, 4234, 5257:* Matt. 5:25; Rom. 11:13

offscouring — *4067: 1 Cor. 4:13*

offspring — *1085: Acts 17:28, 29; Rev. 22:16*

oft -en -ener -entimes -times — *3740, 4178, 4183/5550, 4212, 4435, 4437:* Mark 7:3; Acts 24:26

oil — *1637:* James 5:14; Rev. 6:6

ointment -s — *3464:* Matt. 26:7; John 11:2

old -ness (see **elder**) — *744, 1088, 1094, 1095, 1126, 1332, 1541, 1597, 3819, 3820, 3821, 3822, 4218, 4245, 4246, 5550:* Acts 2:17; Rom. 7:6

olive -s — *65, 1636, 2565:* Matt. 21:1; Rev. 11:4

Olympas — *3652: Rom. 16:15*

Omega — *5598: Rev. 1:8, 11; 21:6; 22:13*

omitted — *863: Matt. 23:23*

omnipotent — *3841: Rev. 19:6*

once (see **one**) — *530, 2178, 3366, 3826, 4218:* Heb. 6:4; Jude 1:3, 5

one -s (see **once; only**) — *240, 243, 848, 1438, 1520, 2087, 3391, 3442, 3538, 3588/ 846, 3588/3303, 3661, 3675, 3739/3303, 3956, 4861, 5100:* Matt. 20:12; 1 Cor. 3:4

Onesimus — *3682:* Col. 4:9; Phile. 1:10

Onesiphorus — *3683: 2 Tim. 1:16; 4:19*

only (see **one**) — *1520, 3439, 3440, 3441:* John 1:14; 1 Tim. 1:17

open -ed -eth -ing -ly — *71, 343, 380, 455, 457, 1272, 1722/3588/5318, 1722/3954, 3856, 4271, 4977, 5136:* Acts 17:3; Rev. 3:7

operation -s — *1753,1755: 1 Cor. 12:6; Col. 2:12*

opportunity — *170, 2120, 2540:* Gal. 6:10; Phil. 4:10

oppose -ed -eth -itions — *475, 477, 480, 498: Acts 18:6; 2 Thess. 2:4; 1 Tim. 6:20; 2 Tim. 2:25*

oppress -ed — *2616, 2669: Acts 7:24; 10:38; James 2:6*

oracles — *3051: Acts 7:38; Rom. 3:2; Heb. 5:12; 1 Pet. 4:11*

oration; orator — *1215, 4489: Acts 12:21; 24:1*

ordain -ed (see **ordinance**) — *1299, 2525, 2680, 2919, 3724, 4160, 4270, 4282, 4304, 5021, 5087, 5500:* Mark 3:14; Eph. 2:10

order -ly — *1299, 1930, 2517, 4748, 5001, 5010:* Luke 1:8; Acts 21:24

ordinance -s (see **ordain**) — *1296, 1345, 1378, 1379, 3862:* Rom. 13:2; Col. 2:14

other -s (see **another**) — *237, 240, 243, 244, 245, 492, 846, 1520, 1565, 1622, 2084, 2087, 2548, 3062, 3588, 3739, 4008:* Matt. 6:1; Phil. 2:4

otherwise — *243, 247, 1490, 1893, 2085, 2088:* Gal. 5:10; 1 Tim. 5:25

ought -est (see **must; necessary**) — *1163, 3784, 5534:* Acts 10:6; James 3:10

our -s; ourself -ves; us; we (see **I; my -self**) — *846, 1438, 2240, 2249, 2251, 2257:* Mark 12:7; 1 John 1:8

out -er -side -ward -wardly — *1623, 1722/ 3588/5318, 1722/5318, 1854, 1855, 1857, 4383:* Luke 11:39; Rom. 2:28

outrun — *4370/5032: John 20:4*

outwent — *4281: Mark 6:33*

oven — *2823: Matt. 6:30; Luke 12:28*

over — *481, 495, 561, 1224, 1276, 1277, 1330, 1537/1727, 1608, 1722, 1883, 1909, 1924, 2596, 2634, 2713, 3346, 3860, 3928, 4008, 4012, 4121, 4291, 5055, 5228, 5231, 5240:* Eph. 1:22; 1 Pet. 3:12

overcharge -ed — *925, 1912: Luke 21:34; 2 Cor. 2:5*

overcome -eth; overcame — *2274, 2634, 3528:* Acts 19:16; 2 Pet. 2:19, 20

overflowed — *2626: 2 Pet. 3:6*

overlaid — *4028: Heb. 9:4*

overmuch — *4055: 2 Cor. 2:7*

overseers; oversight — *1983, 1985: Acts 20:28; 1 Pet. 5:2*

overshadow -ed — *1982:* Matt. 17:5; Luke 1:35

overtake -n — *2638, 4301: Gal. 6:1; 1 Thess. 5:4*

overthrow, n; overthrew — *390, 396, 2647, 2690, 2692, 2693:* Acts 5:39; 2 Tim. 2:18

owe -ed -est -eth — *3781, 3784, 4359:* Rom. 13:8; Phile. 1:18

own — *830, 848, 849, 1103, 1438, 1683, 1699, 2398, 2596, 4572:* 2 Tim. 1:9; James 1:14

owneth; owner -s — *2076, 2962, 3490: Luke 19:33; Acts 21:11; 27:11*

ox; oxen — *1016, 5022:* 1 Cor. 9:9; 1 Tim. 5:18

Ozias — *3604: Matt. 1:8, 9*

P

pain -ed -fulness -s — *928, 3449, 4192, 5604:* 2 Cor. 11:27; Rev. 16:10

pair — *2201, 2218: Luke 2:24; Rev. 6:5*

palace — *833, 4232:* Matt. 26:3; Phil. 1:13

pale — *5515: Rev. 6:8*

palm -s (see **hand**) — *4474, 4475: Matt. 26:67; Mark 14:65; John 18:22*

palm -s (see **tree**) — *5404: John 12:13; Rev. 7:9*

palsy -ies — *3885, 3886:* Luke 5:18; Acts 8:7

Pamphylia — *3828:* Acts 2:10; 14:24; 27:5

paper — *5489: 2 John 1:12*

Paphos — *3974: Acts 13:6,13*

paps — *3149: Luke 11:27; 23:29; Rev. 1:13*

parable -s — *3850, 3942:* Matt. 13:34; John 10:6

paradise — *3857: Luke 23:43; 2 Cor. 12:4; Rev. 2:7*

parcel — *5564: John 4:5*

parchments — *3200: 2 Tim. 4:13*

parents — *1118, 3962, 4269:* John 9:2; 1 Tim. 5:4

Parmenas — *3937: Acts 6:5*

part -ly -s — *1161, 2819, 2825, 3307, 3310, 3313/5100, 3348, 4119, 5124/3303:* Luke 10:42; 1 Cor. 11:18

partakest; partaker -s — *482, 1096/4791, 2841, 2844, 3310, 3335, 3348, 3353, 4777, 4790, 4791, 4829, 4830:* Rom. 11:17; 2 Pet. 1:4

parted — *1266, 1339: Matt. 27:35; Mark 15:24; Luke 23:34; 24:51; John 19:24; Acts 2:45*

Parthians — *3934: Acts 2:9*

partial -ity — *87, 1252, 4346: 1 Tim. 5:21; James 2:4; 3:17*

particular -ly — *1520/1538/2596, 2596/ 3313, 3588/1520:* 1 Cor. 12:27; Heb. 9:5

partition — *5418: Eph. 2:14*

partner -s — *2844, 3353: Luke 5:7, 10; 2 Cor. 8:23; Phile. 1:17*

pass -ed -eth -ing; past — *390, 421, 492, 524, 565, 1096, 1224, 1230, 1276, 1279, 1330, 1353, 2064, 3327, 3819, 3844, 3855, 3881, 3899, 3928, 3944, 4266, 4281, 4302, 5230, 5235, 5242:* 2 Tim. 2:18; 1 John 2:17

passion -s — *3663, 3958: Acts 1:3; 14:15; James 5:17*

passover — *3957:* John 19:14; 1 Cor. 5:7

pastors — *4166: Eph. 4:11*

pasture — *3542: John 10:9*

Patara — *3959: Acts 21:1*

paths — *5147, 5163: Matt. 3:3; Mark 1:3; Luke 3:4; Heb. 12:13*

patient -ly; patience — *420, 1933, 3114, 3115, 3116, 5278, 5281:* Col. 1:11; 1 Pet. 2:20

Patmos — *3963: Rev. 1:9*

patriarch -s — *3966: Acts 2:29; 7:8, 9; Heb. 7:4*

Patrobas — *3969: Rom. 16:14*

pattern -s — *5179, 5262, 5296: 1 Tim. 1:16; Titus 2:7; Heb. 8:5; 9:23*

Paul; Paulus (see **Saul**) — *3972:* Acts 13:7; 2 Pet. 3:15

pavement — *3038: John 19:13*

pay -ment; paid — *586, 591, 1183, 5055:* Matt. 18:25; Heb. 7:9

peace -able -ably -makers — *1515, 1516, 1517, 1518, 2270, 2272, 4601, 4623, 5392:* 1 Cor. 1:3; Jude 1:2

pearl -s — *3135:* 1 Tim. 2:9; Rev. 17:4

peculiar — *1519/4047, 4041: Titus 2:14; 1 Pet. 2:9*

Peleg — *5317: Luke 3:35*

pen — *2563: 3 John 1:13*

pence; penny -worth — *1220:* Mark 6:37; John 12:5

Pentecost — *4005: Acts 2:1; 20:16; 1 Cor. 16:8*

penury — *5303: Luke 21:4*

people -s (see **person**) — *1218, 1484, 2992, 3793:* Acts 2:47; Jude 1:5

peradventure — *3379, 5029: Rom. 5:7; 2 Tim. 2:25*

perceive -ed -est -ing — *143, 991, 1097, 1492, 1921, 2147, 2334, 2638, 2657, 3539, 3708:* Acts 14:9; Gal. 2:9

perdition — *684:* 2 Thess. 2:3; Rev. 17:8

perfect -ed -ing -ion -ly -ness — *195, 197, 199, 739, 1295, 2005, 2675, 2676, 2677, 3647, 4137, 5046, 5047, 5048, 5050, 5051, 5052:* Matt. 5:48; 1 John 2:5

perform -ance -ed — *591, 1096, 2005, 2716, 4160, 5050, 5055:* Luke 1:20; 2 Cor. 8:11

Perga — *4011: Acts 13:13, 14; 14:25*

Pergamos — *4010: Rev. 1:11; 2:12*

perhaps — *686, 3381, 5029: Acts 8:22; 2 Cor. 2:7; Phile. 1:15*

peril -ous -s — *2794, 5467: Rom. 8:35; 2 Cor. 11:26; 2 Tim. 3:1*

perish -ed -eth — *599, 622, 684, 853, 1311, 1510, 1519, 2704, 4881, 5356:* John 6:27; Heb. 11:31

perjured — *1965: 1 Tim. 1:10*

permit -ted; permission — *2010, 4774:* 1 Cor. 7:6; Heb. 6:3

pernicious — *684: 2 Pet. 2:2*

perplexed; perplexity — *639, 640, 1280: Luke 9:7; 21:25; 24:4; 2 Cor. 4:8*

persecute -ed -est -ing -ion(s) -or — *1375, 1376, 1377, 1559, 2347:* John 5:16; 2 Tim. 3:12

perseverance — *4343: Eph. 6:18*

Persis — *4069: Rom. 16:12*

person -s (see **people**) — *678, 4380, 4381, 4382, 4383, 5287:* 1 Tim. 1:10; Heb. 1:3

persuade -ed -est -eth -ing; persuasion — *374, 3982, 3988, 4135:* Luke 16:31; Gal. 5:8

pertain -eth -ing — *3348, 4012: Acts 1:3; 1 Cor 6:3*

pervert -eth -ing; perverse — *654, 1294, 3344, 3859:* Luke 23:14; Phil. 2:15

pestilences; pestilent — *3061: Matt. 24:7; Luke 21:11; Acts 24:5*

Peter (see **Cephas; Simeon; Simon**) — *4074:* Mark 3:16; 1 Pet. 1:1

petitions — *155: 1 John 5:15*

Phanuel — *5323: Luke 2:36*

Pharaoh — *5328: Acts 7:10, 13; Rom. 9:17*

Phares — *5329: Matt. 1:3; Luke 3:33*

Pharisee -s — *5330:* Matt. 3:7; Acts 15:5

Phenice — *5405: Acts 27:12*
Phenicia; Phoenicia — *5403: Acts 11:19; 15:3; 21:2*
Philadelphia — *5359: Rev. 1:11; 3:7*
Philemon — *5371: Phile. 1:1*
Philetus — *5372: 2 Tim. 2:17*
Philip -'s — *5376:* Matt. 14:3; Mark 3:18; Acts 8:5
Philippi — *5375:* Matt. 16:13; Acts 16:12; Phil. 1:1
Philippians — *5374: Phil 4:15*
Philologus — *5378: Rom. 16:15*
philosophers; philosophy — *5385, 5386: Acts 17:18; Col. 2:8*
Phlegon — *5393: Rom. 16:14*
Phoebe — *5402: Rom. 16:1*
Phrygia — *5435: Acts 2:10; 16:6; 18:23*
Phygellus — *5436: 2 Tim. 1:15*
phylacteries — *5440: Matt. 23:5*
physician -s — *2395:* Luke 8:43; Col. 4:14
piece -s — *1288, 1406, 1915, 3313, 4138:* Mark 2:21; Acts 19:19
pierce -ed -ing — *1330, 1338, 1574, 3572, 4044:* Luke 2:35; Heb. 4:12
piety — *2151: 1 Tim. 5:4*
pigeons — *4058: Luke 2:24*
Pilate — *4091:* Mark 15:1; Acts 3:13
pilgrims — *3927: Heb. 11:13; 1 Pet. 2:11*
pillar -s — *4769: Gal. 2:9; 1 Tim. 3:15; Rev. 3:12; 10:1*
pillow — *4344: Mark 4:38*
pineth — *3583: Mark 9:18*
pinnacle — *4419: Matt. 4:5; Luke 4:9*
pipe -d -ers — *832, 834, 836: Matt. 11:17; Luke 7:32; 1 Cor. 14:7; Rev. 18:22*
Pisidia — *4099: Acts 13:14; 14:24*
pit -s — *999, 5421:* Luke 14:5; Rev. 17:8
pitched — *4078: Heb. 8:2*
pitcher — *2765: Mark 14:13; Luke 22:10*
pity -iful — *1653, 2155, 4184: Matt. 18:33; James 5:11; 1 Pet. 3:8*
place (see **yield -ed -eth**) — *402, 1502: Matt. 9:24; Gal. 2:5*
place -s — *201, 1564, 1786, 3692, 3699, 3837, 4042, 5117, 5562, 5564, 5602:* Mark 1:45; Phil. 1:13
plague -s — *3148, 4127:* Luke 7:21; Rev. 9:20
plain -ly -ness — *1718, 3123, 3954 :* Mark 7:35; 2 Cor. 3:12
plains — *5117/3977: Luke 6:17*
plaited; plaiting — *1708, 4120:* John 19:2; 1 Pet. 3:3
plant -ed -eth — *4854, 5451, 5452:* Matt. 15:13; Rom. 6:5
platter — *3953, 4094: Matt. 23:25, 26; Luke 11:39*
play — *3815: 1 Cor. 10:7*

please -ed -ing; pleasure -s — *699, 700, 701, 2100, 2101/1511, 2106, 2107, 2237, 2307, 2309, 3588/1380, 4684, 4909, 5171, 5485, 5569:* Titus 3:3; 2 Pet. 1:17
plentifully; plenteous — *2164, 4183: Matt. 9:37; Luke 12:16*
plow -eth -ing; plough — *722, 723: Luke 9:62; 17:7; 1 Cor. 9:10*
pluck -ed — *726, 1288, 1544, 1610, 1807, 1808, 1846, 5089: John 10:28, 29; Jude 1:12*
poets — *4163: Acts 17:28*
point -s — *2079, 3195: Mark 5:23; John 4:47; Heb. 4:15; James 2:10*
poison — *2447: Rom. 3:13; James 3:8*
polluted; pollutions — *234, 2840, 3393: Acts 15:20; 21:28; 2 Pet. 2:20*
Pollux — *1359: Acts 28:11*
pomp — *5325: Acts 25:23*
pondered — *4820 : Luke 2:19*
Pontius — *4194:* Matt. 27:2; Acts 4:27
Pontus — *4195: Acts 2:9; 18:2; 1 Pet. 1:1*
pool — *2861: John 5:2, 4, 7; 9:7, 11*
poor (see **poverty**) — *3993, 3998, 4433, 4434:* 1 Cor. 13:3; Gal. 2:10
porch -es — *4259, 4440, 4745:* John 5:2; Acts 3:11
Porcius — *4201: Acts 24:27*
porter — *2377: Mark 13:34; John 10:3*
portion — *3313, 4620: Matt. 24:51; Luke 12:42, 46; 15:12*
possess -ed -eth -ing -ion(s) -ors — *1139, 2192, 2697, 2722, 2932, 2933, 2935, 4047, 5224, 5564:* Acts 4:34; 2 Cor. 6:10
possible — *102, 1410, 1415:* Rom. 12:18; Heb. 10:4
pot -s; potter -'s — *2763, 2764, 3582, 4713:* Mark 7:4; Rom. 9:21
potentate — *1413: 1 Tim. 6:15*
pound -s — *3046, 3414:* Luke 19:13; John 12:3
pour -ed -eth -ing — *906, 1632, 2708, 2767:* Mark 14:3; Acts 10:45
poverty (see **poor**) — *4432: 2 Cor. 8:2, 9; Rev. 2:9*
powder — *3039: Matt. 21:44; Luke 20:18*
power -ful -s — *746, 1325, 1410, 1411, 1415, 1756, 1849, 1850, 2478, 2479, 2904, 3168:* Heb. 4:12; 1 Pet. 3:22
Praetorium — *4232: Mark 15:16*
praise -ed -ing -s — *133, 134, 136, 703, 1391, 1867, 1868, 2127, 5214:* Luke 1:64; Phil. 1:11
prating — *5396: 3 John 1:10*
pray -ed -er(s) -est -eth (see **supplication**) — *1162, 1189, 1783, 2065, 2171, 2172, 3870, 4335, 4336:* Col. 4:2; Jude 1:20
preach -ed -er -est -eth -ing — *189, 1229, 1256, 2097, 2605, 2782, 2783, 2784, 2980,*

3954, 4137, 4283, 4296: Rom. 10:14; Gal. 1:8

precept — *1785*: *Mark 10:5; Heb. 9:19*

precious — *927, 1784, 2472, 4185, 5092, 5093*: James 5:7; 2 Pet. 1:1, 4

predestinate -ed — *4309*: *Rom. 8:29, 30; Eph. 1:5, 11*

preeminence — *4409, 5383*: *Col. 1:18; 3 John 1:9*

preferred; preferring — *1096, 4285, 4299*: *John 1:15, 27, 30; Rom. 12:10; 1 Tim. 5:21*

premeditate — *3191*: *Mark 13:11*

prepare -ed -ing -ation — *2090, 2091, 2092, 2675, 2680, 3903, 3904, 4282*: John 19:14; Phile. 1:22

presbytery — *4244*: *1 Tim. 4:14*

presence — *1715, 1799, 2714, 3952, 4383*: Luke 1:19; 2 Thess. 1:9

present -ed — *2476, 4374, 4840*: Acts 9:41; Eph. 5:27;

present -ly — *737, 1736, 1764, 1824, 2186, 3306, 3568, 3854, 3873, 3916, 3918, 3936*: Matt. 21:19; Titus 2:12

preserve -ed — *2225, 4933, 4982, 5083*: Luke 17:33; 1 Thess. 5:23

press (see **multitude -s**) — *3793*: *Mark 2:4; 5:27, 30; Luke 8:19; 19:3*

press -ed -eth — *598, 916, 971, 1377, 1945, 1968, 4085, 4912*: Acts 18:5; Phil. 3:14

presumptuous — *5113*: *2 Pet. 2:10*

pretense — *4392*: *Matt. 23:14; Mark 12:40; Phil. 1:18*

prevail -ed — *2480, 2729, 3528, 5623*: John 12:19; Rev. 5:5

prevent -ed — *4399, 5348*: *Matt. 17:25; 1 Thess. 4:15*

price -s (see **prize**) — *4185, 4186, 5092*: 1 Cor. 6:20; 1 Pet. 3:4

pricked; pricks — *2669, 2759*: Acts 2:37; 9:5; 26:14

priest -hood -s (see **Levite**) — *748, 749, 2405, 2406, 2407, 2409, 2420*: Heb. 8:4; Rev. 1:6

prince -s — *747, 758, 2232*: 1 Cor. 2:6, 8; Eph. 2:2

principal -ities -ity — *746, 3588/2596/1851/ 5607*: Acts 25:23; Titus 3:1

principles — *746, 4747*: *Heb. 5:12; 6:1*

print — *5179*: *John 20:25*

Prisca — *4251*: *2 Tim. 4:19*

Priscilla — *4252*: Acts 18:2; Rom. 16:3

prison -er(s) -s — *1198, 1201, 1202, 3612, 3860, 5084, 5438*: Luke 21:12; Phile. 1:1, 9

private -ly (see **privy -ily**) — *2596/2398*: Gal. 2:2; 2 Pet. 1:20

privy -ily (see **private -ly**) — *2977, 3918, 3922, 4894*: Matt. 1:19; 2 Pet. 2:1

prize — *1017*: *1 Cor. 9:24; Phil. 3:14*

proceed -ed -eth -ing — *1607, 1831, 4298, 4369*: Eph. 4:29; Rev. 22:1

Prochorus — *4402*: Acts 6:5

proclaimed — *2784*: *Luke 12:3*

profane — *952, 953*: Matt. 12:5; 2 Tim. 2:16

profess -ed -ing -ion — *1861, 3670, 3671, 5335*: Titus 1:16; Heb. 3:1

profit -able -ed -eth -ing — *2076, 2173, 4297, 4298, 4851, 5539, 5622, 5623, 5624*: 1 Tim. 4:15; Heb. 13:9

promise -ed -s — *1843, 1860, 1861, 1862, 3670, 4279*: Rom. 9:4; 2 Pet. 2:19

proof -s — *1382, 1732, 4135, 5039*: 2 Cor. 2:9; Phil. 2:22

proper — *791, 2398*: Acts 1:19; 1 Cor. 7:7; Heb. 11:23

prophesy -ied -ieth -ing(s); prophecy -ies (see **prophet**) — *4394, 4395, 4397*: Mark 7:6; 1 Thess. 5:20

prophet -ess -s (see **prophesy**) — *4396, 4397, 4398, 5578*: Luke 2:36; Acts 13:6

propitiation — *2434, 2435*: *Rom. 3:25; 1 John 2:2; 4:10*

proportion — *356*: *Rom. 12:6*

proselyte -s — *4339*: *Matt. 23:15; Acts 2:10; 6:5; 13:43*

prosper -ed -eth -ous -ously — *2137*: Rom. 1:10; 3 John 1:2

protest — *3513*: *1 Cor. 15:31*

proud; pride — *212, 5187, 5243, 5244*: Luke 1:51; 1 John 2:16

prove -ed -ing — *584, 1381, 3936, 3985, 4256, 4822*: John 6:6; 1 Tim. 3:10

proverb -s — *3850, 3942*: *Luke 4:23; John 16:25, 29; 2 Pet. 2:22*

provide -ed -ing; provision; providence — *2090, 2932, 3936, 4160, 4265, 4306, 4307*: Acts 24:2; 2 Cor. 8:21

province — *1885*: Acts 23:34; 25:1

provoke -ed -ing; provocation — *653, 2042, 3863, 3893, 3894, 3947, 3948, 3949, 4292*: Gal. 5:26; Heb. 3:8, 15

prudent; prudence — *4908, 5428*: *Matt. 11:25; Luke 10:21; Acts 13:7; 1 Cor. 1:19; Eph. 1:8*

psalm -s — *5567, 5568*: Eph. 5:19; Col. 3:16

Ptolemais — *4424*: Acts 21:7

public -ly — *1219, 3856*: *Matt. 1:19; Acts 18:28; 20:20*

publican -s — *754, 5057*: Mark 2:15; Luke 7:29

publish -ed — *1096, 1308, 2784*: *Mark 1:45; 5:20; Acts 10:37; 13:49*

Publius — *4196*: Acts 28:7, 8

Pudens — *4227*: *2 Tim. 4:21*

puffed; puffeth — *5448*: 1 Cor. 4:6; Col. 2:18

pull -ed -ing — *385, 726, 1288, 1544, 2506, 2507: Luke 6:42; Jude 1:23*

punish -ed -ment — *1349, 1557, 2009, 2849, 2851, 5097, 5098, 5099: Matt. 25:46; Acts 22:5*

purchase -ed — *2932, 4046, 4047: Acts 1:18; 8:20; 20:28; Eph. 1:14; 1 Tim. 3:13*

pure -ity -ness — *47, 53, 54, 1506, 2513: 1 Tim. 4:12; 1 John 3:3*

purge -ed -eth -ing — *1245, 1571, 2508, 2511, 2512, 4160/2512: John 15:2; Heb. 9:14*

purify -ication -ied -ieth -ier -ing — *48, 49, 2511, 2512, 2514: James 4:8; 1 Pet. 1:22*

purloining — *3557: Titus 2:10*

purple — *4209, 4210, 4211: Mark 15:17; Rev. 17:4*

purpose -ed -eth -ing — *1011, 1013, 1096/1106, 4160, 4255, 4286, 4388, 5087: Rom. 8:28; 2 Cor. 9:7*

purse -s — *905, 2223: Matt. 10:9; Mark 6:8; Luke 10:4; 22:35, 36*

Puteoli — *4223: Acts 28:13*

Q

quake (see **earthquake -s**) — *1790, 4579: Matt. 27:51; Heb. 12:21*

quarrel — *1758, 3437: Mark 6:19; Col. 3:13*

quarter -s — *1137, 3836, 5117: Mark 1:45; Acts 9:32; 16:3; 28:7; Rev. 20:8*

Quartus — *2890: Rom. 16:23*

quaternions — *5069: Acts 12:4*

queen — *938: Matt. 12:42; Luke 11:31; Acts 8:27; Rev. 18:7*

quench -ed — *762, 4570: 1 Thess. 5:19; Heb. 11:34*

question -ed -ing -s — *1458, 1905, 2213, 2214, 2919, 3056, 4802: 1 Tim. 1:4; Titus 3:9*

quick -en -ed -eth -ing (see **alive; live; lively**) — *2198, 2227, 4806: 1 Cor. 15:45; 1 Pet. 4:5*

quickly — *1722/5034, 5030, 5032, 5035: John 13:27; Rev. 3:11*

quicksands — *4950: Acts 27:17*

quiet -ness — *1515, 2263, 2270, 2271, 2272, 2687: 1 Thess. 4:11; 2 Thess. 3:12*

quit (see **acquit**) — *407: 1 Cor. 16:13*

R

Rabbi (see **Rabboni**) — *4461: Matt. 23:7; John 3:2*

Rabboni (see **Rabbi**) — *4462: John 20:16*

Raca — *4469: Matt. 5:22*

race — *73, 4712: 1 Cor. 9:24; Heb. 12:1*

Rachab, Rahab — *4460, 4477: Matt. 1:5; Heb. 11:31; James 2:25*

Rachel — *4478: Matt. 2:18*

rage -ing — *66, 2830, 5433: Luke 8:24; Acts 4:25; Jude 1:13*

railed; railer; railing -s — *987, 988, 989, 3059, 3060: 1 Cor. 5:11; 1 Tim. 6:4*

raiment (see **clothe**) — *1742, 2066, 2440, 2441, 4629: John 19:24; James 2:2*

rain -ed — *1026, 1026/5025, 1028, 5205: Luke 17:29; Heb. 6:7*

rainbow — *2463: Rev. 4:3; 10:1*

raise -ed -eth -ing — *386, 450, 1326, 1453, 1817, 1825, 1892, 160/1999, 4891: John 5:21; Acts 24:12*

ranks — *4237: Mark 6:40*

ransom — *487, 3083: Matt. 20:28; Mark 10:45; 1 Tim. 2:6*

rashly — *4312: Acts 19:36*

rather — *2228, 2309, 3123, 3304, 4056, 4133: Matt. 10:6; Heb. 13:19*

ravening — *724, 727: Matt. 7:15; Luke 11:39*

ravens — *2876: Luke 12:24*

reach -ed -ing — *190, 1901, 2185, 5342: 2 Cor. 10:13; Rev. 18:5*

read -est -eth -ing — *314, 320, 6642: Luke 10:26; 1 Tim. 4:13*

ready -iness — *1451, 2090, 2092, 2093, 2130, 3195, 4288, 4289, 4689: Matt. 22:4; Acts 17:11*

reap -ed -ers -est -eth -ing — *270, 2325, 2327: Luke 19:22; John 4:36, 37*

rear (see **build**) — *1453: John 2:20*

reason -able -ed -ing — *701, 1223, 1256, 1260, 1261, 1537, 1752, 3049, 3050, 3056, 4802, 4803, 4817: Matt. 16:7; Rom. 12:1*

Rebecca — *4479: Rom. 9:10*

rebuke -ed -ing — *298, 1649, 1651, 1969, 2008, 2192: Luke 4:41; 2 Tim. 4:2*

receive -ed -edst -eth -ing; receipt — *308, 324, 353, 354, 568, 588, 618, 1183, 1209, 1325, 1523, 1653, 1926, 2210, 2865, 2983, 3028, 3336, 3549, 3858, 3880, 4327, 4355, 4356, 4687, 4732, 5058, 5264, 5274, 5562: James 2:25; 3 John 1:9*

reckon -ed -eth — *3049, 4868/3056: Matt. 25:19; Rom. 6:11*

recommended — *3860: Acts 14:26; 15:40*

recompense -ed -est -ing (see **reward**) — *467, 468, 489, 591, 3405: Luke 14:14; 2 Thess. 1:6*

reconcile -ed -iation -ing — *604, 1259, 2433, 2643, 2644: 2 Cor. 5:18, 19; Col. 1:20*

record — *3140, 3141, 3143, 3144: John 1:19; Phil. 1:8*

recover -ing — *309, 366, 2192/2573: Mark 16:18; Luke 4:18; 2 Tim. 2:26*

Red; red — *2281, 4449, 4450: Matt. 16:2, 3;*

Acts 7:36; Heb. 11:29; Rev. 6:4; 12:3

redeem -ed -ing; redemption — 59, 629, 1805, 3084, 3085, 4160/3085: Eph. 4:30; 1 Pet. 1:18

redound — 4052: 2 Cor. 4:15

reed — 2563: Matt. 11:7; Rev. 11:1

reformation — 1357: Heb. 9:10

refrain — 868, 3973: Acts 5:38; 1 Pet. 3:10

refresh -ed -eth -ing — 373, 403, 404, 1958, 4875, 5177: 2 Cor. 7:13; Phile. 1:7, 20

refuge — 2703: Heb. 6:18

refuse -ed — 579, 720, 3868: Acts 25:11; 1 Tim. 4:4

regard -ed -est -eth -ing — 272, 991, 1788, 1914, 3851, 4337, 5426: Mark 12:14; Rom. 14:6

regeneration — 3824: Matt. 19:28; Titus 3:5

region -s — 2825, 4066, 5561: Luke 3:1; Gal. 1:21

rehearsed — 312, 756: Acts 11:4; 14:27

reign -ed -eth — 757, 936, 2192/932, 2231, 4821: Rom. 5:14; 1 Cor. 4:8

reins — 3510: Rev. 2:23

reject -ed -eth — 96, 114, 593, 1609, 3868: Matt. 21:42; Gal. 4:14

rejoice -ed -eth -ing — 21, 2165, 2620, 2744, 2745, 2746, 4796, 5463: John 3:29; 2 John 1:4

release -ed — 630: Matt. 27:26; Mark 15:9, 11

relieve -ed; relief — 1248, 1884: Acts 11:29; 1 Tim. 5:10, 16

religion; religious — 2356, 2357, 2454, 4576: Gal. 1:13; James 1:26

remain -ed -est -eth -ing — 620, 1265, 3062, 3063, 3306, 3588, 4035, 4052: John 1:33; Heb. 1:11

remember -ed -est -eth -ing; remembrance — 363, 364, 3403, 3415, 3417, 3418, 3421, 5179, 5279, 5280, 5294: Matt. 5:23; Phil. 1:3

remit -ted; remission — 859, 863, 3929: John 20:23; Rom. 3:25

remnant — 2640, 3005, 3062: Matt. 22:6; Rom. 9:27; 11:5; Rev. 11:13; 12:17; 19:21

remove -ed -ing — 142, 2795, 3179, 3327, 3331, 3346, 3351, 3911: 1 Cor. 13:2; Heb. 12:27

Remphan — 4481: Acts 7:43

rend; rent — 1284, 4048, 4486, 4682, 4977, 4978: Matt. 7:6; John 19:24

render -ing (see **repay**) — 467, 591: 1 Thess. 5:15; 1 Pet. 3:9

renew -ed -ing — 340, 341, 342, 365: Rom. 12:2; Col. 3:10

renounced — 550: 2 Cor. 4:2

repay (see **render**) — 467, 591, 661: Luke 10:35; Rom. 12:19; Phile. 1:19

repetitions — 945: Matt. 6:7

repent -ance -ed -eth — 278, 3338, 3340, 3341: Heb. 6:1; 2 Pet. 3:9

repliest — 470: Rom. 9:20

report -ed — 189, 191, 312, 518, 987, 1310, 1426, 2162, 2163, 3140, 3141: Acts 4:23; 3 John 1:12

reproach -ed -es -est -fully — 819, 3059, 3679, 3680, 3681, 5195, 5196, 5484: Rom. 15:3; 1 Tim. 5:14

reprobate -s — 96: Rom. 1:28; 2 Cor. 13:5-7; 2 Tim. 3:8; Titus 1:16

reprove -ed; reproof — 1650, 1651: John 16:8; Eph. 5:11, 13

reputation — 1380, 1784, 2758, 5093: Acts 5:34; Gal. 2:2; Phil. 2:7, 29

request -s (see **ask**) — 155, 1162, 1189: Rom. 1:10; Phil. 1:4; 4:6

require -ed -ing — 154, 155, 523, 1096, 1567, 2212, 4238: Luke 23:24; 1 Cor. 4:2

requite — 287/591: 1 Tim. 5:4

rescued — 1807: Acts 23:27

resemble — 3666: Luke 13:18

reserve -ed (see **residue**) — 2641, 5083: 1 Pet. 1:4; 2 Peter 2:9

residue (see **reserve -ed**) — 2645, 3062: Mark 16:13; Acts 15:17

resist -ed -eth — 436, 478, 496, 498: Matt. 5:39; Rom. 13:2

resolved — 1097: Luke 16:4

resort -ed — 2064, 4848, 4863, 4905: Mark 2:13; John 18:20

respect -er — 578, 678, 1914, 2596, 3313, 3382, 4380, 4381, 4382: Acts 10:34; Col. 2:16

rest -ed -eth — 372, 373, 425, 1515, 1879, 1954, 1981, 2192/372, 2270, 2663, 2664, 2681, 2838, 3062, 4520: Matt. 11:28; Rom. 2:17

restitution (see **restore**) — 605: Acts 3:21

restore -ed -eth (see **restitution**) — 591, 600, 2675: Mark 9:12; Gal. 6:1

restrained — 2664: Acts 14:18

resurrection — 386, 1454, 1815: Phil. 3:11; Rev. 20:5

retain -ed (see **have -ing**) — 2192, 2722, 2902: John 20:23; Rom. 1:28; Phile. 1:13

return -ed -ing — 344, 360, 390, 844, 1877, 1880, 1994, 5290: Acts 8:28; 1 Pet. 2:25

Reu — 4466: Luke 3:35

Reuben — 4502: Rev. 7:5

reveal -ed; revelation -s — 601, 602, 5537: Luke 2:26; Eph. 3:3

revellings — 2970: Gal. 5:21; 1 Pet. 4:3

revenge -er (see **avenge; vengeance**) — 1556, 1557, 1558: Rom. 13:4; 2 Cor. 7:11; 10:6

reverence — *127, 1788, 5399:* Mark 12:6; Heb. 12:9, 28
revile -ed -ers -est — *486, 987, 3058, 3060, 3679:* Matt. 5:11; 1 Pet. 2:23
revived — *326:* Rom. *7:9; 14:9*
reward -ed -er (see **recompense**) — *469, 514, 591, 2603, 3405, 3406, 3408:* Heb. 11:6; Jude 1:11
Rhegium — *4484:* Acts 28:13
Rhesa — *4488:* Luke 3:27
Rhoda — *4498:* Acts 12:13
Rhodes — *4499:* Acts 21:1
rich -es -ly (see **enrich; wealth**) — *4145, 4146, 4147, 4148, 4149, 5536:* Col. 3:16; James 5:1
right — *1188:* Mark 10:37, 40; Gal. 2:9
right -ly (see **aright**) — *1342, 1849, 2117, 3723, 4993:* Luke 7:43; 2 Pet. 2:15
righteous -ly -ness(es) — *1341, 1343, 1344, 1345, 1346, 2118:* 1 Pet. 2:23; 1 John 2:29
ring — *1146, 5554:* Luke 15:22; James 2:2
ringleader — *4414:* Acts 24:5
riot -ing -ous — *810, 811, 2970, 5172:* Rom. 13:13; Titus 1:6
ripe — *187, 3583:* Rev. 14:15, 18
rise -en -eth -ing; rose (see **arise**) — *305, 386, 393, 450, 1453, 1817, 1881, 4891, 4911:* John 13:4; 1 Thess. 4:14
river -s — *4215:* Mark 1:5; Acts 16:13
roareth; roaring — *2278, 3455, 5612:* Luke 21:25; 1 Pet. 5:8; Rev. 10:3
robbed; robber -s -y — *725, 2417, 3027, 4813:* John 10:1; Phil. 2:6
robe -s — *2066, 2440, 4749, 5511:* Luke 15:22; Rev. 6:11
Roboam — *4497:* Matt. 1:7
Rock; rock -s — *4073, 5117, 5138:* Rom. 9:33; 1 Cor. 10:4
rod -s — *4463, 4464:* 2 Cor. 11:25; Heb. 9:4
roll -ed — *617, 1507, 4351:* Mark 16:3; Luke 24:2
Roman -s — *4514:* John 11:48; Acts 22:25
Rome — *4516:* Rom. 1:15; 2 Tim. 1:17
roof — *4721:* Matt. 8:8; Mark 2:4; Luke 7:6
room -s — *473, 508, 1240, 4411, 5117, 5253, 5562:* Matt. 23:6; 1 Cor. 14:16
root -ed -s — *1610, 4491, 4492:* Col. 2:7; Jude 1:12
ropes — *4979:* Acts 27:32
rough — *5138:* Luke 3:5
round — *2943, 2944, 3840, 4015, 4017, 4026, 4033, 4034, 4038, 4039, 4066:* Matt. 3:5; Rom. 15:19
rowed; rowing — *1643:* Mark 6:48; John 6:19
royal (see **king -s**) — *934, 937:* Acts 12:21; James 2:8; 1 Pet. 2:9
rubbing — *5597:* Luke 6:1

rudder — *4079:* Acts 27:40
rude — *2399:* 2 Cor. 11:6
rudiments — *4747:* Col. 2:8, 20
rue — *4076:* Luke 11:42
Rufus — *4504:* Mark 15:21; Rom. 16:13
ruin -s — *2679, 4485:* Luke 6:49; Acts 15:16
rule -eth -er(s) -ing — *746, 752, 757, 758, 1018, 2232, 2233, 2583, 2888, 4165, 4173, 4291:* Eph. 6:12; 1 Tim. 3:12
rumor -s (see **noise -d**) — *189, 3056:* Matt. 24:6; Mark 13:7; Luke 7:17
run -neth -ning; ran — *1530, 1532, 1632, 1998, 2027, 2701, 3729, 4063, 4370, 4390, 4890, 4936, 5143, 5240, 5295:* John 20:2; Rev. 9:9
rushed; rushing — *3729, 5342:* Acts 2:2; 19:29
rust — *1035, 2447:* Matt. 6:19, 20; James 5:3
Ruth — *4503:* Matt. 1:5

S

sabachthani — *4518:* Matt. 27:46; Mark 15:34
Sabaoth — *4519:* Rom. 9:29; James 5:4
sabbath — *4315, 4521:* Acts 1:2; Col. 2:16
sackcloth — *4526:* Matt. 11:21; Luke 10:13; Rev. 6:12; 11:3
sacrifice -ed -s — *1494, 2378, 2380:* 1 Cor. 5:7; Phil. 4:18
sacrilege — *2416:* Rom. 2:22
sad (see **sorrow**) — *4659, 4768:* Matt. 6:16; Mark 10:22; Luke 24:17
Sadducees — *4523:* Mark 12:18; Acts 23:6
Sadoc — *4524:* Matt. 1:14
safe -ly -ty — *803, 806, 809, 1295, 5198:* Acts 23:24; 1 Thess. 5:3
sail -ed -ing -ors — *321, 636, 1020, 1276, 1277, 1602, 3492, 3881, 3896, 4126, 4144, 4632, 5284:* Luke 8:23; Rev. 18:17
saint -s — *40:* Col. 1:2; 1 Tim. 5:10
sake -s — *1722, 1752:* Mark 6:26; 2 John 1:2
Salah — *4527:* Luke 3:35
Salamis — *4529:* Acts 13:5
Salem (see **Jerusalem**) — *4532:* Heb. 7:1, 2
Salim — *4530:* John 3:23
Salmon — *4533:* Matt. 1:4; Luke 3:32
Salmone — *4534:* Acts 27:7
Salome — *4539:* Mark 15:40; 16:1
salt -ed -ness — *217, 233, 251, 252, 358, 1096:* Mark 9:49, 50; Luke 14:34; Col. 4:6; James 3:12
salute -ation(s) -ed -eth — *782, 783:* 2 Thess. 3:17; 3 John 1:14
Samaria; Samaritan -s — *4540, 4541:* John 4:4; Acts 8:25
same (see **selfsame**) — *846, 1565, 2532, 3673, 3761, 3778, 4954, 5023, 5026, 5124,*

5126, 5129, 5615, 5718: Luke 6:33; 1 Cor. 11:23

Samos — *4544:* Acts 20:15
Samothracia — *4548:* Acts 16:11
Samson — *4546:* Heb. 11:32
Samuel — *4545:* Acts 3:24; 13:20; Heb. 11:32
sanctify -ication -ied -ieth (see **hallowed**) — *37, 38:* John 10:36; 1 Pet. 1:2
sanctuary — *39:* Heb. 8:2; 9:1, 2; 13:11
sand — *285:* Matt. 7:26; Rom. 9:27; Heb. 11:12; Rev. 13:1; 20:8
sandals — *4547:* Matt. 6:9; Acts 12:8
Sapphira — *4551:* Acts 5:1
sapphire — *4552:* Rev. 21:19
Sarah -'s — *4564:* Rom. 4:19; 9:9
sardine (see **sardius**) — *4555:* Rev. 4:3
Sardis — *4554:* Rev. 1:11; 3:1,4
sardius (see **sardine**) — *4556:* Rev. 21:20
sardonyx — *4557:* Rev. 21:20
Sarepta — *4558:* Luke 4:26
Satan -'s (see **devil**) — *4567:* 1 Thess. 2:18; 2 Thess. 2:9
satisfy -ing — *4140, 5526:* Mark 8:4; Col. 2:23
Saul (see **Paul**) — *4569:* Acts 7:58; 26:14
save -ing (see **except**) — *235, 1508, 2228, 3844, 4133:* Luke 4:27; Gal. 1:19
save -ed -ing; Savior; salvation — *1295, 3924, 4047, 4982, 4991, 4992, 5442:* Luke 1:69; Jude 1:5
savor -est — *2175, 3471, 3744, 5426:* Matt. 16:23; Eph. 5:2
sawn — *4249:* Heb. 11:37
say -est -ing(s); said; saith — *2036, 2046, 2980, 3004, 3007, 3056, 4280, 4483, 4487, 5335, 5346:* Luke 1:13; Titus 3:8
scales — *3013:* Acts 9:18
scarcely — *3433:* Rom. 5:7; 1 Pet. 4:18
scarlet — *2847:* Matt. 27:28; Heb. 9:19; Rev. 17:3, 4; 18:12, 16
scattered; scattereth — *1262, 1287, 1289, 1290, 4496, 4650:* John 10:12; Acts 5:36
scepter — *4464:* Heb. 1:8
Sceva — *4630:* Acts 19:14
schism — *4978:* 1 Cor. 12:25
school — *4981:* Acts 19:9
schoolmaster — *3807:* Gal. 3:24, 25
science — *1108:* 1 Tim. 6:20
scoffers — *1703:* 2 Pet. 3:3
scorch -ed — *2739:* Matt. 13:6; Mark 4:6; Rev. 16:8, 9
scorn — *2606:* Matt. 9:24; Mark 5:40; Luke 8:53
scorpion -s — *4651:* Luke 10:19; 11:12; Rev. 9:3, 5, 10
scourge -ed -eth -ing(s) — *3146, 3147, 3148, 3164, 5416, 5417:* Acts 22:25; Heb. 12:6

scribe -s — *1122:* Mark 1:22; 1 Cor. 1:20
scrip — *4082:* Matt. 10:10; Mark 6:8; Luke 9:3; 10:4; 22:35, 36
Scripture -s — *1121, 1124:* 2 Tim. 3:16; 2 Pet. 3:16
scroll — *975:* Rev. 6:14
Scythian — *4658:* Col. 3:11
sea -s — *1337, 1724, 2281, 3864, 3882, 3989:* Acts 27:41; James 1:6
seal -ed -ing -s — *2696, 4972, 4973:* Matt. 27:66; Rev. 5:1
seam — *729:* John 19:23
search -ed -eth -ing — *350, 1830, 1833, 2045:* Rom. 8:27; 1 Pet. 1:10, 11
seared — *2743:* 1 Tim. 4:2
season -ed -s — *171, 741, 2121, 2540, 3641, 4340, 5550, 5610:* Col. 4:6; 1 Thess. 5:1
seat -s — *968, 2362, 2382, 2515, 2615, 4410:* Matt. 21:12; 2 Cor. 5:10
second -arily (see **two-fold**) — *1207, 1208:* 1 Cor. 12:28; 2 Pet. 3:1
secret -ly -s — *614, 2926, 2927, 2928, 2931, 2977, 4601, 5009:* John 19:38; Rom. 2:16
sect — *139:* Acts 5:17; 15:5; 24:5; 26:5; 28:22
Secundus — *4580:* Acts 20:4
secure -ity — *2425, 4160/275:* Matt. 28:14; Acts 17:9
sedition -s — *1370, 4714:* Luke 23:19, 25; Acts 24:5; Gal. 5:20
seduce -ers -ing — *635, 1114, 4105, 4108:* 2 Tim. 3:13; 1 John 2:26
see -en -est -eth -ing; saw -est (see **sight -s**) — *308, 542, 990, 991, 1063, 1227, 1492, 1512, 1689, 1893, 1894, 1897, 2147, 2234, 2300, 2334, 2396, 2400, 2477, 2529, 3070, 3467, 3700, 3708, 3754, 4249, 4275, 4308, 5316, 5461:* Phil. 1:27; 3 John 1:11
seed -s — *4687, 4690, 4701, 4703:* Matt. 13:19; Mark 4:31
seek -est -eth -ing; sought — *327, 1567, 1934, 2212:* 1 Cor. 13:5; Col. 3:1
seem -ed -eth — *1096/2107, 1380, 5316:* Heb. 12:11; James 1:26
seize — *2722:* Matt. 21:38
Seleucia — *4581:* Acts 13:4
selfsame (see **same**) — *846/5124, 1565:* Matt. 8:13; 1 Cor. 12:11; 2 Cor. 5:5; 7:11
selfwilled — *829:* Titus 1:7; 2 Pet. 2:10
sell -er -eth; sold — *591, 1710, 4097, 4211, 4453:* John 12:5; Rev. 13:17
Semei — *4584:* Luke 3:26
senate — *1087:* Acts 5:21
send -eth -ing; sent — *375, 628, 630, 640, 649, 652, 657, 863, 906, 1032, 1524, 1544, 1599, 1821, 3343, 3992, 4882:* Eph. 6:22; Titus 3:12
senses — *145:* Heb. 5:14

sensual — *5591: James 3:15; Jude 1:19*

sentence — *610, 1948, 2919: Luke 23:24; Acts 15:19; 2 Cor. 1:9*

separate -ed — *873, 5562: Rom. 1:1; Heb. 7:26*

sepulcher -s (see **grave -s**) — *3418, 3419, 5028:* Matt. 27:60; Luke 11:47, 48

Sergius — *4588: Acts 13:7*

sergeants — *4465: Acts 16:35*

serpent -s — *2062, 3789:* Matt. 7:10; 1 Cor. 10:9

Serug — *4562: Luke 3:35*

servant -s (see **man; service**) — *1249, 1401, 1402, 3407, 3411, 3610, 3816, 5257:* Rom. 6:16; 2 Pet. 2:19

serve -eth -ice -ing (see **servant**) — *1247, 1248, 1398, 2999, 3000, 3009, 5256:* Gal. 4:8; Phil. 2:17, 30

set -ter -teth -ting — *321, 345, 377, 392, 461, 584, 630, 649, 816, 968, 1299, 1325, 1369, 1416, 1847, 1848, 1913, 1930, 1940, 2007, 2064, 2350, 2476, 2521, 2523, 2525, 2604, 2749, 3326, 3908, 5394:* Acts 17:18; James 3:6

Seth — *4589: Luke 3:38*

settle -ed — *1476, 2311, 5087: Luke 21:14; Col. 1:23; 1 Pet. 5:10*

seven -th — *1442, 2033, 2034, 2035:* Jude 1:14; Rev. 8:1

seventy — *1440, 1441: Matt. 18:22; Luke 10:1, 17*

sever — *873: Matt. 13:49*

several -ly — *303/1520, 2398: Matt. 25:15; 1 Cor. 12:11; Rev. 21:21*

severity — *663: Rom. 11:22*

seweth — *1976: Mark 2:21*

shadow -ing — *644, 2683, 4639:* Col. 2:17; Heb. 9:5

shake -n; shook — *660, 1621, 4531, 4579:* Acts 13:51; 2 Thess. 2:2

shame -facedness -fully (see **ashamed**) — *127, 149, 152, 808, 818, 819, 821, 1788, 1791, 2617, 3856, 5195, 8187:* Mark 12:4; 1 Tim. 2:9

shape -s — *1491, 3667: Luke 3:22; John 5:37; Rev. 9:7*

Sharon — *4565: Acts 9:35*

sharp -er -ly -ness — *664, 3691, 5114:* 2 Cor. 13:10; Heb. 4:12

shave -n — *3587: Acts 21:24; 1 Cor. 11:5, 6*

she (see **her -s -self**) — *846:* Gal. 4:27; Rev. 18:6

Shealtiel — *4528: Luke 3:27*

shearer; shorn — *2751: Acts 8:32; 1 Cor. 11:6*

sheath — *2336: John 18:11*

Shechem — *4966: Acts 7:16*

shed -ding — *130, 1632:* Titus 3:6; Heb. 9:22

sheep (see **lamb -s**) — *4262, 4263:* John 10:2; Heb. 11:37

sheepfold — *833/4263: John 10:1*

sheepskins — *3374: Heb. 11:37*

sheet — *3607: Acts 10:11; 11:5*

Shem — *4590: Luke 3:36*

shepherd -s — *4166:* Mark 14:27; 1 Pet. 5:4

shewbread — *740/4286; 4286/740: Matt. 12:4; Mark 2:26; Luke 6:4; Heb. 9:2*

shield — *2375: Eph. 6:16*

Simeon (see **Simon**) — *4826:* Luke 2:25; Acts 15:14

shine -ed -ing -eth; shone — *796, 797, 826, 1584, 2989, 4015, 4034, 4744, 5316:* John 1:5; 1 John 2:8

ship -ping -s — *3490, 3491, 3492, 4142, 4143:* Acts 27:27

shipmaster — *2942: Rev. 18:17*

shipwreck — *3489: 2 Cor. 11:25; 1 Tim. 1:19*

shivers — *4937: Rev. 2:27*

shoes; shod (see **latchet**) — *5265, 5266:* Matt. 3:11; Eph. 6:15

shoot -eth — *4160, 4261: Mark 4:32; Luke 21:30*

shore — *123, 4358, 5491:* John 21:4; Heb. 11:12

short -ened — *2856, 3641, 4932, 4958, 5302, 5610:* Mark 13:20; 1 Thess. 2:17

shortly — *1722/5034, 2112, 5030, 5031, 5032:* Phil. 2:19, 24; 3 John 1:14

should -est (see **ought**) — *1163, 3195, 3784:* John 18:32; Titus 1:5

shoulders — *5606:* Matt. 23:4; Luke 15:5

shout — *2019, 2752:* Acts 12:22; 1 Thess. 4:16

show -ed -est -eth -ing — *312, 322, 323, 518, 584, 1096, 1165, 1166, 1213, 1325, 1334, 1653, 1718, 1731, 1754, 1804, 1925, 2097, 2146, 2151, 2605, 2698, 3004, 3056, 3170, 3377, 3700, 3930, 3936, 4160, 4293, 4392, 5203, 5263, 5319:* Rom. 9:16; 1 John 1:2

shower — *3655: Luke 12:54*

shrines — *3485: Acts 19:24*

shun -ned — *4026, 5288: Acts 20:27; 2 Tim. 2:16*

shut -teth — *608, 2623, 2808, 4788:* Matt. 6:6; Gal. 3:23

sick -ly -ness(es) — *732, 769, 770, 772, 2192/2560, 2577, 3554, 3885, 4445:* John 11:4; 1 Cor. 11:30

sickle — *1407: Mark 4:29; Rev. 14:14-19*

side — *492, 1188, 1782, 3313, 3840, 3844, 4008, 4125:* Luke 1:11; 2 Cor. 4:8

Sidon — *4605:* Matt. 11:21; Acts 12:20

sift — *4617: Luke 22:31*

sighed — *389, 4727: Mark 7:34; 8:12*

sight -s (see **see**) — *308, 309, 991, 1491, 1715, 1726, 1799, 2714, 2335, 3705, 3706, 3788, 3844, 5324, 5400:* Luke 21:11; Acts 1:9

sign -s — *1770, 3902, 4592:* Rom. 4:11; Rev. 15:1

signify -ication -ied -ieth -ing — *880, 1213, 1229, 1718, 4591:* 1 Cor. 14:10; 1 Pet. 1:11

Silas (see **Silvanus**) — *4609:* Acts 15:22; 18:5

silence — *2271, 4601, 4602, 5392:* 1 Tim. 2:11, 12; 1 Pet. 2:15

silk — *4596: Rev. 18:12*

silly — *1133: 2 Tim. 3:6*

Siloam — *4611: Luke 13:4; John 9:7, 11*

Silvanus (see **Silas**) — *4610:* 2 Cor. 1:19; 1 Pet. 5:12

silver; silversmith — *693, 694, 695, 696, 1406:* Acts 19:24; James 5:3

Simeon (see **Peter; Simon**) — *3667:* Luke 2:25, 34; Rev. 7:7

similitude — *3665, 3666, 3669: Rom. 5:14; Heb. 7:15; James 3:9*

Simon (see **Peter; Simeon**) — *4613:* Matt. 4:18; Acts 1:13

simple; simplicity — *172, 185, 572: Rom. 12:8; 16:18, 19; 2 Cor. 1:12; 11:3*

sin -ful -ned -ner(s) -neth -s (see **transgress**) — *264, 265, 266, 268, 361, 3781, 3900, 4258:* Luke 5:8; Jude 1:15

Sinai — *4614: Acts 7:30, 38; Gal. 4:24, 25*

since — *575, 575/3739, 1537, 1893, 1894, 3326, 5613:* Luke 1:70; Heb. 7:28

sincere -ity -ly — *55, 97, 861, 1103, 1505, 1506:* Phil. 1:16; Eph. 6:24

sing -ing; sang; sung (see **song -s**) — *103, 524, 5214, 5567:* James 5:13; Rev. 5:9

single -ness — *572, 573, 858: Matt. 6:22; Luke 11:34; Acts 2:46; Eph. 6:5; Col. 3:22*

sink; sunk — *1036, 2670, 2702, 5087: Matt. 14:30; Luke 5:7; 9:44; Acts 20:9*

sir -s — *435, 2962:* John 20:15; Rev. 7:14

sister -s — *79, 431:* 1 Tim. 5:2; 2 John 1:13

sit -test -teth -ting; sat — *339, 345, 347, 377, 1910, 2516, 2521, 2523, 2621, 2625, 4775, 4776, 4873:* John 2:14; Heb. 1:3

six -th — *1803, 1812, 1835:* James 5:17; Rev. 6:12

sixteen — *1440/1803: Acts 27:37*

sixty -fold (see **threescore**) — *1835: Matt. 13:8; Mark 4:8, 20*

skin — *1193: Mark 1:6*

skull — *2898: Matt. 27:33; Mark 15:22; John 19:17*

sky — *3772: Matt. 16:2, 3; Luke 12:56; Heb. 11:12*

slack -ness — *1019, 1022: 2 Pet. 3:9*

slanderers; slanderously — *987, 1228: Rom. 3:8; 1 Tim. 3:11*

slaves (see **bondage**) — *4983: Rev. 18:13*

slay; slain; slew; slaughter — *337, 615, 1315, 1722/5408/599, 2380, 2695, 2871,*

4967, 4968, 4969, 5407: Heb. 7:1; 1 John 3:12

sleep -est -eth -ing; slept (see **slumber**) — *1852, 1853, 2518, 2837, 2838, 5258:* Luke 22:45, 46; 1 Thess. 4:14

sleight — *2940: Eph. 4:14*

slip — *3901: Heb. 2:1*

slothful — *3576, 3636: Matt. 25:26; Rom. 12:11; Heb. 6:12*

slow -ly — *692, 1021:* Acts 27:7; Titus 1:12

slumber -ed -eth (see **sleep**) — *2659, 3573: Matt. 25:5; Rom. 11:8; 2 Pet. 2:3*

small -est — *1646, 2485, 3398, 3641, 3795, 4142, 4979:* Mark 3:9; 1 Cor. 6:2

smell -ing — *2175, 3750: 1 Cor. 12:17; Phil. 4:18*

smite -est -eth -ing; smitten; smote (see **strike -eth**) — *851, 1194, 1325, 3817, 3960, 4141, 4474, 4475, 5180:* Luke 18:13; 2 Cor. 11:20

smoke -ing — *2586, 5187:* Matt. 12:20; Acts 2:19

smooth — *3006: Luke 3:5*

Smyrna — *4667, 4668: Rev. 1:11; 2:8*

snare — *1029, 3803:* Luke 21:35; 2 Tim. 2:26

snow — *5510: Matt. 28:3; Mark 9:3; Rev. 1:14*

so -ever — *686, 1161, 1437, 1519, 2443, 2504, 2532, 3123, 3303, 3365, 3366, 3368, 3383, 3483, 3704, 3745/302, 3761, 3767, 3779, 4819, 5023, 5037, 5082, 5118, 5124, 5613, 5615, 5620:* Rom. 3:19; 2 Pet. 1:11

sober -ly -ness; sobriety — *1519, 3524, 3525, 4993, 4994, 4996, 4997, 4998:* 1 Tim. 2:9; 1 Pet. 5:8

Sodom — *4670:* Rom. 9:29; Jude 1:7

soft -ly — *3120, 5285: Matt. 11:8; Luke 7:25; Acts 27:13*

sojourn -ed -ing — *1510/3941, 3939, 3940: Acts 7:6; Heb. 11:9; 1 Pet. 1:17*

soldier -s — *4753, 4754, 4757, 4758:* John 19:23; 2 Tim. 2:3

solitary — *2048: Mark 1:35*

Solomon — *4672:* Matt. 1:6; Luke 12:27

some -body -thing -time(s) -what — *243, 575, 1161, 1520, 2087, 3381, 3588/3303, 4218, 5100, 5207:* Luke 8:46; 1 Pet. 3:20

Son; son -s — *431, 3816, 5043, 5206:* Phile. 1:10; 1 John 3:1, 2

song -s (see **sing -ing**) — *5603: Eph. 5:19; Col. 3:16; Rev. 5:9; 14:3; 15:3*

soon -er — *1096, 2112, 3711, 3752, 3753, 3916, 5030, 5032:* Gal. 1:6; Heb. 13:19

soothsaying — *3132: Acts 16:16*

sop — *5596: John 13:26, 27, 30*

Sopater (see **Sosipater**) — *4986: Acts 20:4*

sorcerer -s; sorcery -ies — *3095, 3096, 3097, 5331, 5333:* Acts 13:6, 8; Rev. 9:21

sore -er — *23, 1568, 1630, 2425, 2560, 3029, 3173, 4183, 4970, 5501:* Mark 6:51; Heb. 10:29

sores — *1668, 1669: Luke 16:20, 21; Rev. 16:11*

sorrow -ed -ful -ing -s; sorry — *253, 3076, 3077, 3600, 3601, 3997, 4036, 5604:* 2 Cor. 2:2; Phil. 2:27

sort — *516, 3313, 3697:* 2 Tim. 3:6; 3 John 1:6

Sosipater (see **Sopater**) — *4989: Rom. 16:21*

Sosthenes — *4988: Acts 18:17; 1 Cor. 1:1*

soul -s — *5590:* 1 Thess. 5:23; 2 Pet. 2:14

sound -ness — *3647, 4995, 5198, 5199:* Acts 3:16; Titus 1:9, 13

sound -ed -ing -s — *1001, 1096, 1837, 2278, 2279, 4537, 5353, 5456, 5798:* Matt. 6:2; 1 Cor. 13:1

south — *3047, 3314, 3558:* Luke 11:31; Acts 8:26

sow -ed -er -est -eth -n — *4687, 5300:* 1 Cor. 9:11; Gal. 6:7, 8

space — *575, 1024, 1292, 1339, 1909, 4158, 5550:* Acts 5:7; James 5:17

Spain — *4681: Rom. 15:24,28*

spare -ed -ing — *4052, 5339:* Acts 20:29; 2 Pet. 2:4, 5

sparingly — *5340: 2 Cor. 9:6*

sparrows — *4765: Matt. 10:29, 31; Luke 12:6, 7*

speak -er -est -eth -ing(s); spake; spoken (see **speech**) — *226, 400, 483, 626, 653, 669, 987, 988, 1097, 1256, 2036, 2046, 2551, 2635, 2636, 2980, 3004, 3056, 4180, 4277, 4354, 4377, 4483, 4814, 5350, 5537, 5573:* 1 Pet. 2:1; Jude 1:16

spear — *3057: John 19:34*

spearmen — *1187: Acts 23:23*

special — *3756/3858/5177: Acts 19:11*

spectacle — *2302: 1 Cor. 4:9*

speech -es -less (see **speak**) — *1769, 2129, 2974, 2981, 3056, 3072, 3424, 5392:* Luke 1:22; Col. 4:6

speed -ily — *1722/5034, 5613/5033: Luke 18:8; Acts 17:5*

spend -est; spent — *1159, 1230, 1550, 2119, 2827, 4160, 4298, 4321, 4325, 5551:* Rom. 13:12; 2 Cor. 12:15

spew — *1692: Rev. 3:16*

spices — *759: Mark 16:1; Luke 23:56; 24:1; John 19:40*

spikenard — *3487/4101: Mark 14:3; John 12:3*

spilled — *1632: Mark 2:22; Luke 5:37*

spin — *3514: Matt. 6:28; Luke 12:27*

Spirit; spirit -s -ual -ually (see **God**) — *3588/ 4151, 4151, 4152, 4153, 5326:* 1 Cor. 2:14; 1 John 5:6, 8

spit -ted; spat; spittle — *1716, 4427, 4429:* Mark 7:33; John 9:6

spitefully — *5195: Matt. 22:6; Luke 18:32*

spoil -ed -ing -s — *205, 554, 724, 1283, 4661, 4812:* Col. 2:8; Heb. 7:4

sponge — *4699: Matt. 27:48; Mark 15:36; John 19:29*

sporting — *1792: 2 Pet. 2:13*

spot -s -ted — *299, 784, 4694, 4695, 4696:* 1 Tim. 6:14; Jude 1:23

spread — *1268, 1310, 1831, 4766, 5291:* Matt. 9:31; 1 Thess. 1:8

spring -ing; sprang; sprung — *242, 305, 393, 794, 1080, 1530, 1543, 1816, 4002, 4161, 4599, 4726, 4855, 5033, 5453:* Mark 4:5; Acts 16:29

sprinkled; sprinkling — *4378, 4472, 4473:* Heb. 9:13, 19, 21; 10:22; 11:28; 12:24; 1 Pet. 1:2

spy -ies (see **espy**) — *1455, 2684, 2685: Luke 20:20; Gal. 2:4; Heb. 11:31*

Stachys — *4720: Rom. 16:9*

staff; staves — *3586, 4464: Matt. 10:10; Mark 6:8*

staggered — *1252: Rom. 4:20*

stairs — *304: Acts 21:35, 40*

stall — *5336: Luke 13:15*

stanched — *2476: Luke 8:44*

stand -est -eth -ing; stood — *450, 639, 1453, 1510, 2186, 2192, 2476, 3306, 3936, 4026, 4714, 4739, 4921:* 2 Thess. 2:15; 2 Tim. 2:19

star -s — *792, 798:* Matt. 24:29; Acts 27:20

state (see **estate**) — *3588/2596, 3588/4012:* Phil. 4:11; Col. 4:7

stature — *2245: Matt. 6:27; Luke 2:52; 12:25; 19:3; Eph. 4:13*

stayed (see **hold**) — *1907, 2722: Luke 4:42; Acts 19:22*

stead — *5228: 2 Cor. 5:20; Phile. 1:13*

steadfast -ly -ness — *816, 949, 1476, 4342, 4731, 4733, 4740, 4741:* 2 Cor. 3:7, 13; 1 Pet. 5:9

steal; stole — *2813:* Matt. 28:13; Rom. 2:21

steep — *2911: Matt. 8:32; Mark 5:13; Luke 8:33*

stepped; steppeth; steps — *1684, 2487, 2597: John 5:4, 7; Rom. 4:12; 2 Cor. 12:18; 1 Pet. 2:21*

stern — *4403: Acts 27:29*

steward -ship -s — *2012, 3621, 3622, 3623:* Luke 16:2; Titus 1:7

sticks — *5434: Acts 28:3*

stiffnecked — *4644: Acts 7:51*

still — *2089, 2476, 4357, 5392:* Mark 4:39; 1 Tim. 1:3

sting -s — *2759: 1 Cor. 15:55, 56; Rev. 9:10*

stinketh — *3605: John 11:39*

stir -red -reth — *329, 383, 1326, 1892, 3947,*

3951, 4531, 4787, 4797, 5017: Luke 23:5;
2 Pet. 3:1

stock — *1085: Acts 13:26; Phil. 3:5*

stocks — *3586: Acts 16:24*

Stoics — *4770: Acts 17:18*

stomach's — *4751: 1 Tim. 5:23*

stone -ed -est -s -y — *2642, 2991, 3034, 3035, 3036, 3037, 4074, 4075, 5586: Matt. 13:5; 2 Cor. 3:7*

stoop -ed -ing — *2955, 3879: Mark 1:7; John 20:5*

stop -ped — *1993, 4912, 5420: 2 Cor. 11:10; Titus 1:11*

store — *597, 2343: 1 Cor. 16:2; 2 Pet. 3:7*

storehouse — *5009: Luke 12:24*

storm — *2978: Mark 4:37; Luke 8:23*

straight — *461, 2113, 2116, 2117, 3717: John 12:23; Heb. 12:13*

straightway — *1824, 2112, 2117, 3916: Acts 5:10; James 1:24*

strait -ened -est -ly — *196, 547, 4183, 4728, 4729, 4730, 4912: Mark 1:43; 2 Cor. 6:12*

strain — *1368: Matt. 23:24*

strange -er — *241, 245, 1722/3940, 1854, 1937, 2087, 3579, 3580, 3581, 3927, 3937, 3939, 3940, 3941, 5381: John 10:5; 1 Pet. 4:4, 12*

strangled — *4156: Acts 15:20, 29; 21:25*

stream — *4215: Luke 6:48, 49*

street -s — *58, 4113, 4505: Acts 5:15; Rev. 22:2*

strength -en -ened -eneth -ening (see **strong**) — *772, 1411, 1412, 1743, 1765, 1849, 1991, 2479, 2480, 2901, 2904, 4599, 4732, 4741: 2 Cor. 1:8; Eph. 3:16*

stretch -ed -ing — *1600, 1614, 1911, 5239:* Mark 3:5; Rom. 10:21

strewed — *1287, 4766: Matt. 21:8; 25:24, 26; Mark 11:8*

strike -er -eth; struck; stricken (see **smite**) — *906, 1325/4475, 3817, 3960, 4131, 4260, 5180, 5465:* Acts 27:17; Titus 1:7

string — *1199: Mark 7:35*

stripped — *1562: Matt. 27:28; Luke 10:30*

stripes — *3468, 4127: 2 Cor. 11:23, 24; 1 Pet. 2:24*

strive -ed -eth -ing(s); strove; strife -s — *75, 118, 464, 485, 1264, 2051, 2052, 2054, 3054, 3055, 3163, 3164, 4865, 4866, 5379, 5389:* John 6:52; Heb. 6:16

strong -er (see **strength**) — *1415, 1743, 1753, 2478, 2901, 3173, 3794, 4608, 4731, 4732:* Luke 11:22; 1 John 2:14

stubble — *2562: 1 Cor. 3:12*

study — *4704, 5389: 1 Thess. 4:11; 2 Tim. 2:15*

stuff — *4632: Luke 17:31*

stumble -ed -eth -ing -ingblock(s)

-ingstone — *3037, 4348, 4350, 4383, 4417, 4625:* Rom. 9:32; 1 Pet. 2:8

subdue -ed — *2610, 5293: 1 Cor. 15:28; Phil. 3:21; Heb. 11:33*

subject -ed -ion — *1379, 1396, 1777, 3663, 5292, 5293:* Rom. 8:20; James 5:17

submit -ted -ting — *5226, 5293:* Gal. 2:5; 1 Pet. 2:13

suborned — *5260: Acts 6:11*

substance — *3776, 5223, 5224, 5287: Luke 8:3; 15:13; Heb. 10:34; 11:1*

subtlely; subtlety — *1388, 2686, 3834: Matt. 26:4; Acts 7:19; 13:10; 2 Cor. 11:3*

subvert -ed -ing — *384, 396, 1612, 2692: Acts 15:24; 2 Tim. 2:14; Titus 1:11; 3:11*

succor -ed -er (see **help**) — *997, 4368: Rom. 16:2; 2 Cor. 6:2; Heb. 2:18*

such — *1170, 3588, 3592, 3634, 3748, 3778, 5023, 5107, 5108, 5125, 5128, 5130:* John 8:5; Phile. 1:9

suck -ed -lings — *2337:* Matt. 24:19; Mark 13:17

sudden -ly — *160, 869, 1810, 1819, 5030:* Luke 2:13; 1 Thess. 5:3, 22

sue — *2919: Matt. 5:40*

suffer -ed -est -ing(s) — *430, 818, 863, 971, 1325, 1377, 1439, 2010, 2210, 2552, 2553, 2558, 2967, 3114, 3804, 3805, 3905, 3958, 4310, 4330, 4722, 4778, 4841, 5159, 5254, 5278, 5302:* Phil. 3:8; 1 Pet. 1:11

suffice -eth -iency -ient — *713, 714, 841, 2425, 2426:* John 14:8; 2 Cor. 2:6

sum — *2774, 5092: Acts 7:16; 22:28; Heb. 8:1*

summer — *2330: Matt. 24:32; Mark 13:28; Luke 21:30*

sumptuously — *2983: Luke 16:19*

sun — *2246: Eph. 4:26; James 1:11*

sunder — *1371: Luke 12:46*

sundry — *4181: Heb. 1:1*

sup -ped -per — *1172, 1173:* 1 Cor. 11:25; Rev. 19:9

superfluity; superfluous — *4050, 4053: 2 Cor. 9:1; James 1:21*

superscription — *1923: Matt. 22:20; Mark 12:16; 15:26; ; Luke 20:24; 23:38*

superstition; superstitious — *1174, 1175: Acts 17:22; 25:19*

supplication -s (see **pray**) — *1162, 2428: Acts 1:14; Eph. 6:18; Phil. 4:6; 1 Tim. 2:1; 5:5; Heb. 5:7*

supply -ied -ieth — *378, 2024, 4137, 4322:* 1 Cor. 16:17; 2 Cor. 8:14

support — *472, 482: Acts 20:35; 1 Thess. 5:14*

suppose -ed -ing — *1380, 2233, 3049, 3543, 3633, 5274, 5282:* John 20:15; Heb. 10:29

supreme — *5242: 1 Pet. 2:13*

sure — *804, 805, 949, 1097, 1492, 4103, 4731*: John 6:69; 2 Tim. 2:19

surely — *230, 2229, 3483, 3843, 4135*: Mark 14:70; Rev. 22:20

surety — *230, 1450*: Acts 12:11; Heb. 7:22

surfeiting — *2897*: Luke 21:34

surmisings — *5283*: 1 Tim. 6:4

surname -ed — *1941, 2007/3686, 2564*: Mark 3:16; Acts 15:37

Susanna — *4677*: Luke 8:3

sustenance — *5527*: Acts 7:11

swaddling — *4683*: Luke 2:7, 12

swallow -ed — *2666*: Matt. 23:24; 1 Cor. 15:54; 2 Cor. 2:7; 5:4; Rev. 12:16

swear -eth; sware; sworn — *3660*: Heb. 4:3; James 5:12

sweat — *2402*: Luke 22:44

sweep; swept — *4563*: Matt. 12:44; Luke 11:25; 15:8

sweet — *1099*: Phil. 4:18; Rev. 10:9, 10

sweetsmelling — *2175*: Eph. 5:2

swelling -s; swollen — *5246, 5450*: Acts 28:6; 2 Cor. 12:20; 2 Pet. 2:18; Jude 1:16

swerved — *795*: 1 Tim. 1:6

swift — *3691, 5031, 5036*: Rom. 3:15; James 1:19; 2 Pet. 2:1

swim — *1579, 2860*: Acts 27:42, 43

swine — *5519*: Matt. 7:6; Luke 15:15, 16

sword -s — *3162, 4501*: Eph. 6:17; Rev. 1:16

sycamine — *4807*: Luke 17:6

sycamore — *4809*: Luke 19:4

Sychar — *4965*: John 4:5

synagogue -s — *656, 752, 4864*: John 9:22; Acts 15:21

Syntyche — *4941*: Phil. 4:2

Syracuse — *4946*: Acts 28:12

Syria -n — *4947, 4948*: Luke 4:27; Gal. 1:21

Syrophenician — *4949*: Mark 7:26

T

tabernacle -s — *4633, 4634, 4636, 4638*: John 7:2; Heb. 8:2

Tabitha (see **Dorcas**) — *5000*: Acts 9:36, 40

table -s — *345, 2825, 4093, 4109, 5132*: Rom. 11:9; 2 Cor. 3:3

tackling — *4631*: Acts 27:19

tail -s — *3769*: Rev. 9:10, 19; 12:4

tales — *3026*: Luke 24:11

talent -s — *5006, 5007*: Matt. 25:24; Rev. 16:21

Talitha — *5008*: Mark 5:41

talk -ed -ers -est -eth -ing — *2980, 3056, 3151, 3473, 3656, 4814, 4926*: Eph. 5:4; Titus 1:10

tame -ed — *1150*: Mark 5:4; James 3:7, 8

tanner — *1038*: Acts 9:43; 10:6, 32

tares — *2215*: Matt. 13:25-27, 29, 30, 36, 38, 40

tarry -ied -iest — *1019, 1304, 1551, 1961, 2523, 3195, 3306, 4160, 4328, 4357, 5278, 5549*: Acts 22:16; 1 Tim. 3:15

Tarsus — *5018, 5019*: Acts 9:11; 21:39

taste -ed — *1089*: John 2:9; Col. 2:21

tattlers — *5397*: 1 Tim. 5:13

taverns — *4999*: Acts 28:15

taxed; taxing — *582*: Luke 2:1-3, 5; Acts 5:37

teach -er(s) -est -eth -ing; taught — *1317, 1318, 1319, 1320, 1321, 1322, 2085, 2312, 2547, 2567, 2605, 2727, 3100, 3567, 3811, 4994, 5572*: Rom. 2:21; Titus 1:11

teareth; tore; torn — *4486, 4682, 4952*: Mark 1:26; Luke 9:39, 42

tears — *1144*: 2 Tim. 1:4; Rev. 21:4

tedious — *1465*: Acts 24:4

tell -eth; told — *226, 312, 518, 1334, 1492, 1583, 1650, 1834, 2036, 2046, 2980, 3004, 3377, 4280, 4302*: Gal. 4:16; Jude 1:18

temperance; temperate — *1466, 1467, 1468, 4998*: Titus 1:8; 2 Pet. 1:6

tempered — *4786*: 1 Cor. 12:24

tempest -uous — *2366, 2978, 4578, 5189, 5492*: Matt. 8:24; Heb. 12:18

temple -s — *2411, 3485, 3624*: Eph. 2:21; 2 Thess. 2:4

temporal — *4340*: 2 Cor. 4:18

tempt -ation(s) -ed, -er -eth -ing — *551, 1598, 3985, 3986*: Gal. 4:14; 1 Thess. 3:5

ten -th — *1176, 1181, 1182, 3461, 3463*: 1 Cor. 4:15; Rev. 11:13

tender -hearted — *527, 2155, 3629, 4698*: Matt. 24:32; Mark 13:28; Luke 1:78; Eph. 4:32; James 5:11

tentmakers — *4635*: Acts 18:3

Terah — *2291*: Luke 3:34

terrestrial — *1919*: 1 Cor. 15:40

terrible — *5398*: Heb. 12:21

terrify -ied; terror — *1629, 4422, 4426, 5401*: Luke 21:9; Phil. 1:28

Tertius — *5060*: Rom. 16:22

Tertullus — *5061*: Acts 24:1, 2

testament — *1242*: 2 Cor. 3:6; Rev. 11:19

testator — *1303*: Heb. 9:16, 17

testify -ied -ieth -ing — *1263, 1957, 3140, 3142, 3143, 4303, 4828*: Eph. 4:17; 3 John 1:3

testimony — *3140, 3141, 3142*: 2 Thess. 1:10; 2 Tim. 1:8

tetrarch — *5075, 5076*: Luke 3:1; Acts 13:1

Thaddaeus (see **Lebbaeus**) — *2280*: Matt. 10:3; Mark 3:18

Thamar — *2283*: Matt. 1:3

than — *1508, 1883, 2228, 2260, 3844, 4133, 5228, 5245*: Rom. 1:25; Heb. 4:12

thank -ed -ful -fulness -ing -s — *437, 1843, 2168, 2170, 2192/5485, 3670:* Acts 24:3; 1 Pet. 2:19

thanksgiving -s — *2169:* Phil. 4:6; Rev. 7:12

thankworthy — *5485: 1 Pet. 2:19*

that — *1565, 3754:* Col. 4:8; 2 John 1:1

theater — *2302: Acts 19:29, 31*

thee -ward; thine; thou; thy -self (see **ye**) — *846, 1438, 1519/5209, 2398, 4314/5209, 4571, 4572, 4671, 4674, 4675, 4771, 5209, 5210:* Eph. 3:2; Phile. 1:4

thefts (see **thief**) — *2809, 2829: Matt. 15:19; Mark 7:22; Rev. 9:21*

their -s; them -selves; they (see **he; she**) — *240, 846, 848, 1438, 1565, 3441, 3588:* Matt. 5:3; 1 Cor. 1:2

then — *686, 1161, 1534, 1899, 2532, 3063, 3303, 3766, 3767, 5037, 5119, 5119/1161/ 2532:* 2 Cor. 12:10; 1 Pet. 4:1

thence -forth — *1537/5127, 1564, 2089, 3606:* Mark 1:19; John 19:12

Theophilus — *2321: Luke 1:3; Acts 1:1*

there (see **thither; yonder**) — *847, 1563, 1722/846, 1759, 1927, 5602:* Titus 1:10; 1 John 2:10

thereabout — *4012/5127: Luke 24:4*

thereat; thereby — *1223/846, 1223/5026, 1722/846:* Matt. 7:13; Heb. 13:2

therefore — *235, 473/5607, 686/3767, 1063, 1160, 1211, 1223/5124, 1352, 1360, 1519/ 5124, 5106, 5620:* Acts 2:26; Rev. 2:5

therein -to — *1519/846, 1722/846, 1722/ 3739, 1722/5129, 5125:* Luke 21:21; Col. 2:7

thereof — *846, 1538/846, 4012/846:* Rom. 13:14; 2 Tim. 3:5

thereon; thereupon — *1722/846, 1883/846, 1909/846, 1911, 1913, 1924, 1945, 2026:* John 21:9; 1 Cor. 3:10, 14

thereto; thereunto — *1519/846, 5124, 1519/ 5124, 1928, 4334:* Gal. 3:15; 1 Thess. 3:3

therewith — *1722/846, 1909/5125, 5125:* 1 Tim. 6:8; James 3:9

these; this; those — *737, 1565, 2235, 2778, 3127, 3588/846, 3592, 3745, 3778, 3779, 4594, 5023, 5025, 5026, 5118, 5124, 5125, 5126, 5127, 5128, 5129, 5130, 5602:* Titus 3:8; 2 Pet. 1:5

Thessalonica; Thessalonians — *2331, 2332:* Phil. 4:16; 1 Thess. 1:1

Theudas — *2333: Acts 5:36*

thief; thieves (see **thefts**) — *2812, 3027:* Matt. 6:19; John 10:1

thigh — *3382: Rev. 19:16*

thing -s — *18, 846, 1520, 1697, 3056, 4110, 4229, 4406, 4487, 5023, 5313:* Heb. 10:1; 2 John 1:8, 12

think -est -eth -ing; thought -est -s — *1260, 1261, 1270, 1380, 1760, 1761, 1911, 1963, 2106, 2233, 2919, 3049, 3053, 3539, 3540, 3543, 3633, 4305, 5252, 5282, 5316, 5426:* Phil. 3:4; James 4:5

third -ly (see **three; thrice**) — *5152, 5154:* John 2:1; 1 Cor. 12:28

thirst -y — *1372, 1373:* Matt. 25:35, 37, 42; 2 Cor. 11:27

thirty -fold — *5144:* Mark 4:20; Gal. 3:17

thistles — *5146: Matt. 7:16*

thither -ward (see **there; yonder**) — *1563, 3854, 4370:* Acts 8:30; Rom. 15:24

Thomas (see **Didymus**) — *2381:* Mark 3:18; John 11:16

thongs — *2438: Acts 22:25*

thorn -s — *173, 174, 4647:* Luke 6:44; Heb. 6:8

though (see **although**) — *1223, 1437, 1499, 1512, 2532, 2539, 2544, 2579, 3676, 3754:* Phile. 1:8; 2 Pet. 1:12

thousand -s — *1367, 2035, 3461, 3463, 4000, 5070, 5153, 5505:* Mark 5:13; Jude 1:14

threaten -ed -ing(s) — *546, 547, 4324:* Eph. 6:9; 1 Pet. 2:23

three (see **third; thrice**) — *5140, 5145, 5148, 5150, 5151, 5153:* James 5:17; 1 John 5:7, 8

threescore (see **sixty**) — *1440, 1835:* Luke 24:13; 1 Tim. 5:9

thresheth — *248: 1 Cor. 9:10*

thrice (see **third; three**) — *5151:* John 13:38; 2 Cor. 11:25

throat — *2995, 4155: Matt. 18:28; Rom. 3:13*

throne -s — *968, 2362:* Heb. 1:8; Rev. 1:4

throng -ed -ing — *2346, 4846, 4912, 4918: Mark 3:9; 5:24, 31; Luke 8:42, 45*

through -ly -out — *303, 1223/3650, 1224, 1245, 1279, 1330, 1350, 1358, 1519, 1537, 1653, 1722/3956, 1822, 1909, 2596, 2700, 4044, 4063:* Eph. 1:7; 2 Tim. 3:17

throw -n; threw — *906, 2647, 4496, 4952:* Luke 4:35; Acts 22:23

thrust — *683, 906, 1544, 1856, 1877, 2601, 2700, 3992:* John 20:25; Heb. 12:20

thunder -ed -ings -s — *1027, 1096:* Mark 3:17; Rev. 4:5

thus — *2532, 2596, 3592, 3779, 5023, 5124, 5127:* Rom. 9:20; Phil. 3:15

Thyatira — *2363: Acts 16:14; Rev. 1:11; 2:18, 24*

thyine — *2367: Rev. 18:12*

Tiberias — *5085: John 6:1, 23; 21:1*

Tiberius — *5086: Luke 3:1*

tidings — *2097, 3056, 5334:* Acts 11:22; 1 Thess. 3:6

tied — *1210: Matt. 21:2; Mark 11:2, 4; Luke 19:30*

tiling — *2766: Luke 5:19*

till (see **until**) — *891/3757, 1508/3752, 1519, 2193, 3360: Gal. 3:19; Rev 2:25*

Timaeus (see **Bartimaeus**) — *5090: Mark 10:46*

time -s — *744, 1074, 1208, 1441, 1597, 1909, 2034, 2119, 2121, 2235, 2250, 2540, 3195, 3379, 3568, 3819, 3999, 4218, 4287, 4340, 4455, 5119, 5151, 5550, 5610: 1 Pet. 1:20; 1 John 2:18*

Timon — *5096: Acts 6:5*

Timothy — *5095: Rom. 16:21; 2 Thess. 1:1*

tinkling — *214: 1 Cor. 13:1*

tip — *206: Luke 16:24*

tithe -s — *586, 1181, 1183: Matt. 23:23; Luke 11:42; 18:12; Heb. 7:5, 6, 8, 9*

title — *5102: John 19:19, 20*

tittle — *2762: Matt. 5:18; Luke 16:17*

Titus — *5103: 2 Cor. 2:13; Gal. 2:1*

to -ward; unto — *1519, 1722, 1909, 2596, 4314, 4646, 5228: 1 Thess. 1:1; Titus 3:4*

today (see **day -s**) — *4594: Matt. 6:30; Heb. 4:7*

toil -ed -ing — *928, 2872: Matt. 6:28; Mark 6:48; Luke 5:5; 12:27*

token — *4592: Mark 14:44; Phil. 1:28; 2 Thess. 1:5; 3:17*

tolerable — *414: Matt. 10:15; 11:22, 24; Mark 6:11; Luke 10:12, 14*

tomb -s — *3418, 3419, 5028: Matt. 8:28; Luke 8:27*

tongue -s — *1100, 1258, 1447, 2084: 1 Cor. 12:10; Phil. 2:11*

too (see **also**) — *1174: Acts 17:22*

tooth; teeth — *3599, 3679: Matt. 5:38; Rev. 9:8*

top — *206, 509: Matt. 27:51; Mark 15:38; John 19:23; Heb. 11:21*

topaz — *5116: Rev. 21:20*

torches — *2985: John 18:3*

torment -ed -ors(s) — *928, 929, 930, 931, 2558, 2851, 3600: Luke 16:23; Heb. 11:37*

tortured — *5178: Heb. 11:35*

tossed — *928, 2831, 4494, 5492: Matt. 24:14; Acts 27:18; Eph. 4:14; James 1:6*

touch -ed -eth -ing — *680, 1909, 2345, 2596, 2609, 4012, 4379, 4834, 5584: Col. 4:10; 1 John 5:18*

towel — *3012: John 13:4, 5*

tower — *4444: Matt. 21:33; Mark 12:1; Luke 13:4; 14:28*

town -s — *2968, 2969: Mark 1:38; John 7:42*

town clerk — *1122: Acts 19:35*

Trachonitis — *5139: Luke 3:1*

trade -ed -ing — *1281, 2038: Matt. 25:16; Luke 19:15; Rev. 18:17*

tradition -s — *3862: Gal. 1:14; 1 Pet. 1:18*

traitor -s — *4273: Luke 6:16; 2 Tim. 3:4*

trample — *2662: Matt. 7:6*

trance — *1611: Acts 10:10; 11:5; 22:17*

transferred — *3345: 1 Cor. 4:6*

transfigured (see **transform**) — *3339: Matt. 17:2; Mark 9:2*

transform -ed -ing (see **transfigured**) — *3339, 3345: Rom. 12:2; 2 Cor. 11:13-15*

transgress -ed -eth -ion(s) -or(s) (see **sin**) — *458/4160, 459, 3845, 3847, 3848, 3928: 1 Tim. 2:14; 2 John 1:9*

translated; translation — *3179, 3331, 3346: Col. 1:13; Heb. 11:5*

transparent — *1307: Rev. 21:21*

trap — *2339: Rom. 11:9*

travail -est -eth -ing — *3449, 4944, 5088, 5604, 5605: 2 Thess. 3:8; Rev. 12:2*

travel -ed -ing — *589, 1330, 4898: Matt. 25:14; Acts 11:19; 19:29; 2 Cor. 8:19*

tread -eth; trode; trodden — *248, 2662, 3961: Luke 12:1; Rev. 11:2*

treasure -s -est; treasury — *1047, 1049, 2343, 2344, 2878: John 8:20; James 5:3*

treatise — *3056: Acts 1:1*

tree -s — *65, 1186, 2565, 3586, 4808, 4809: 1 Pet. 2:24; Jude 1:12*

tremble -ed -ing — *1719/1096, 1790/1096, 2192/5156, 5141, 5425: Mark 16:8; Acts 9:6*

trench — *5482: Luke 19:43*

trespass -es — *264, 3900: Matt. 18:15; Eph. 2:1*

trial (see **try**) — *1382, 1383, 3984: 2 Cor. 8:2; Heb. 11:36; 1 Pet. 1:7; 4:12*

tribe -s — *1429, 5443: Rom. 11:1; Rev. 21:12*

tribulation -s — *1429, 2346, 2347, 5443: Acts 14:22; 2 Thess. 1:4, 6*

tribute — *1323, 2778, 5411: Mark 12:14; Luke 20:22*

trimmed — *2885: Matt. 25:7*

triumph -ing — *2358: 2 Cor. 2:14; Col. 2:15*

Troas — *5174: Acts 16:8; 2 Tim. 4:13*

Trogyllium — *5175: Acts 20:15*

Trophimus — *5161: Acts 20:4; 21:29; 2 Tim. 4:20*

trouble -ed -est -eth -ing -s — *387, 1298, 1613, 1776, 2346, 2347, 2350, 2360, 2553, 2873/3930, 3926, 3930/2873, 4660, 5015, 5016, 5182: Mark 5:35; John 5:4*

trucebreakers — *786: 2 Tim. 3:3*

true -ly; truth -'s (see **verily; verity**) — *225, 226, 227, 228, 230, 258, 557, 558, 686, 1103, 1161, 1909/225, 3303, 3483, 3689, 4103: John 1:9; Titus 1:13*

trump; trumpet -s -ers — *4536, 4537, 4538: 1 Cor. 15:52; Rev. 18:22*

trust -ed -eth — *1679, 3982, 4006, 4100, 4276: Eph. 1:12, 13; Phile. 1:22*

try -ed -eth -ing (see **trial**) — *1381, 1383,*

1384, 3985, 3986, 4314, 4448: 1 Thess. 2:4;
James 1:3

Tryphena — *5170: Rom. 16:12*

Tryphosa — *5173: Rom. 16:12*

tumult -s — *181, 2351: Mark 5:38;* 2 Cor. 6:5

turn -ed -ing — *344, 387, 402, 576, 654, 665,
1096, 1294, 1624, 1824, 1994, 2827, 3179,
3329, 3344, 3346, 4672, 4762, 5077, 5290:*
Rom. 11:26; 1 Tim. 1:6

turtledoves — *5167: Luke 2:24*

tutors — *2012: Gal. 4:2*

twelve; twelfth — *1177, 1427, 1428, 1429:*
1 Cor. 15:5; Rev. 21:20

twenty — *1501:* John 6:19; Acts 27:28

twice (see **two, fold**) — *1364: Mark 14:30,
72; Luke 18:12; Jude 1:12*

twinkling — *4493:* 1 Cor. 15:52

two -fold; twain (see **second -arily; twice**) —
*296, 1250, 1322, 1333, 1337, 1366, 1367,
1417:* Matt. 23:15; Eph. 2:15

twoedged (see **two**) — *1366: Heb. 4:12; Rev.
1:16*

Tychicus — *5190:* Col. 4:7; Titus 3:12

Tyrannus — *5181: Acts 19:9*

Tyre — *5183, 5184, 5185:* Mark 3:8; Luke 10:13

U

unawares — *160, 2990, 3920, 3921: Luke
21:34; Gal. 2:4; Heb. 13:2; Jude 1:4*

unbelief; unbelievers; unbelieving — *543,
544, 570, 571:* Rom. 3:3; Titus 1:15

unblamable; unblamably — *274, 299: Col.
1:22;* 1 Thess. 2:10; 3:13

uncertain -ly — *82, 83:* 1 Cor. 9:26; 14:8;
1 Tim. 6:17

unchangeable — *531: Heb. 7:24*

uncircumcised; uncircumcision — *203/
2192, 564, 1722/3588/203:* 1 Cor. 7:18; Eph.
2:11

unclean -ness — *169, 2839, 2840, 3394:*
1 Thess. 4:7; Heb. 9:13

unclothed — *1562:* 2 Cor. 5:4

uncomely — *807, 809:* 1 Cor. 7:36; 12:23

uncondemned — *178: Acts 16:37; 22:25*

uncorruptible; uncorruptness (see **incorruptible**) — *90, 862: Rom. 1:23; Titus 2:7*

uncovered — *177, 648: Mark 2:4;* 1 Cor. 11:5,
13

unction — *5545:* 1 John 2:20

undefiled — *283: Heb. 7:26; 13:4; James 1:27;
1 Pet. 1:4*

under (see **beneath**) — *332, 506, 1640, 1722,
1909, 2662, 2709, 2736, 5259, 5270, 5273,
5284, 5293, 5295:* Rom. 7:14; Phil. 2:10

undergirding — *5269: Acts 27:17*

understand -est -eth -ing; understood —

*50, 191, 801, 1097, 1107, 1271, 1425, 1492,
1987, 2154, 3129, 3530, 3539, 3563, 3877,
4441, 4907, 4920, 5424, 5426:* Luke 18:34;
1 John 5:20

unequally — *2086:* 2 Cor. 6:14

unfeigned — *505:* 2 Cor. 6:6; 1 Tim. 1:5;
2 Tim. 1:5; 1 Pet. 1:22

unfruitful — *175:* Matt. 13:22; Mark 4:19

ungodly -iness — *763, 764, 765:* Rom. 1:18;
Jude 1:4, 15, 18

unholy — *462, 2839:* 1 Tim. 1:9; 2 Tim. 3:2;
Heb. 10:29

unity — *1775: Eph. 4:3, 13*

unjust — *91, 93, 94: Acts 24:15;* 2 Pet. 2:9

unknown — *50, 57:* 2 Cor. 6:9; Gal. 1:22

unlade — *670: Acts 21:3*

unlawful — *111, 459: Acts 10:28;* 2 Pet. 2:8

unlearned — *62, 261, 521, 2399: Acts 4:13;*
1 Cor. 14:16, 23, 24; 2 Tim. 2:23; 2 Pet.
3:16

unleavened — *106:* Matt. 26:17; Mark 14:1

unless — *1622/1508:* 1 Cor. 15:2

unloose — *3089: Mark 1:7; Luke 3:16; John
1:27*

unmarried — *22:* 1 Cor. 7:8, 11, 32, 34

unmerciful — *415: Rom. 1:31*

unmovable — *277, 761: Acts 27:41;* 1 Cor.
15:58

unprepared — *532:* 2 Cor. 9:4

unprofitable -ness — *255, 512, 888, 889,
890, 898: Luke 17:10;* Heb. 7:18

unquenchable — *762: Matt. 3:12; Luke 3:17*

unreasonable — *249, 824: Acts 25:27;* 2 Thess.
3:2

unrebukable — *423:* 1 Tim. 6:14

unreprovable — *410: Col. 1:22*

unrighteous -ness — *93, 94, 458: Luke 16:11;*
1 John 5:17

unruly — *183, 506, 814:* 1 Thess. 5:14; Titus
1:6, 10; James 3:8

unsearchable — *419, 421: Rom. 11:33; Eph.
3:8*

unseemly — *808: Rom. 1:27;* 1 Cor. 13:5

unskillful — *552: Heb. 5:13*

unspeakable — *411, 412, 731:* 2 Cor. 9:15;
12:4; 1 Pet. 1:8

unspotted — *784: James 1:27*

unstable — *182, 793: James 1:8;* 2 Pet. 2:14;
3:16

untaken — *3361/343:* 2 Cor. 3:14

unthankful — *884: Luke 6:35;* 2 Tim. 3:2

until (see **till**) — *891, 1519, 2193, 3360:* Acts
3:21; Phil. 1:5

untimely — *3653: Rev. 6:13*

untoward — *4646: Acts 2:40*

unwashen — *449:* Matt. 15:20; Mark 7:2, 5

unwise — *453, 878: Rom. 1:14; Eph. 5:17*

unworthy -ily — *370, 371, 3756/514: Acts 13:46; 1 Cor. 6:2; 11:27, 29*

up -on -side (see **on; upper**) — *507, 1909: Acts 17:6; Rev. 1:17*

upbraid -ed -eth — *3679: Matt. 11:20; Mark 16:14; James 1:5*

upholding — *5342: Heb. 1:3*

upper -most (see **up**) — *508, 510, 4410, 4411, 5250, 5253: Matt. 23:6; Luke 22:12*

upright -ly — *3716, 3717: Acts 14:10; Gal. 2:14*

uproar — *387, 2350, 2351, 4714, 4797: Mark 14:2; Acts 20:1*

Urbane — *3773: Rom. 16:9*

urge — *1758: Luke 11:53*

Uriah — *3774: Matt. 1:6*

us -ward (see **our; we**) — *1519, 2248: Mark 1:24; Eph. 1:19*

use -ed -ing -s — *390, 831, 1096/1722, 1247, 1838, 1908, 2192, 3348, 5195, 5382, 5383, 5530, 5532, 5540: Titus 3:14; 1 Pet. 2:16*

usury — *5110: Matt. 25:27; Luke 19:23*

utmost; uttermost — *206, 1231, 2075, 2078, 2556, 2596, 3833, 3838, 4009, 5056: Luke 11:31; Heb. 7:25*

utter -ance -ed (see **say; speak**) — *215, 669, 1325, 2044, 2075, 2556, 2980, 3004, 3056: Acts 2:4; 2 Cor. 12:4*

utterly — *2618, 2704, 3654: 1 Cor. 6:7; 2 Pet. 2:12; Rev. 18:8*

V

vagabond — *4022: Acts 19:13*

vain -glory -ly; vanity -ies — *1432, 1500, 2754, 2755, 2756, 2757, 2758, 2761, 2788, 3150, 3151, 3152, 3154, 3155: Gal. 5:26; Phil. 2:3*

valiant — *2478: Heb. 11:34*

valley — *5327: Luke 3:5*

value -ed — *1308, 5091: Matt. 10:31; 27:9; Luke 12:7*

vanish -ed -eth — *854, 1096/855, 2673: Luke 24:31; 1 Cor. 13:8; Heb. 8:13; James 4:14*

vapor — *822: Acts 2:19; James 4:14*

variableness — *3883: James 1:17*

variance — *1369, 2054: Matt. 10:35; Gal. 5:20*

vaunteth — *4068: 1 Cor. 13:4*

vehement -ly — *1171, 1722/4053, 1972, 2159, 2759, 4366: Luke 6:48, 49; 11:53; 23:10; 2 Cor. 7:11*

veil — *2571, 2665: Matt. 27:51; Heb. 6:19*

vengeance (see **avenge; revenge**) — *1349, 1557, 3709: Luke 21:22; Jude 1:7*

verily (see **amen; true -ly**) — *230, 281, 1063, 1222, 2532, 3303, 3304, 3483, 3689, 3767: Luke 12:37; Rom. 15:27*

verity (see **true -ly**) — *225: 1 Tim. 2:7*

very — *85, 230, 662, 846, 927, 957, 1565, 1582, 1646, 1888, 2236, 2532, 2566, 2735, 3029, 3827, 4036, 4118, 4119, 4184, 4185, 4186, 4708, 4970, 5228: Mark 8:1; Phil. 1:6*

vessel -s — *30, 4632: 2 Tim. 2:20; 1 Pet. 3:7*

vesture — *2440, 2441, 4018: Matt. 27:35; John 19:24; Heb. 1:12; Rev. 19:13, 16*

vex -ed — *928, 1139, 2559, 2669, 3791, 3958: Acts 12:1; 2 Pet. 2:7, 8*

vial -s — *5357: Rev. 5:8; 15:7*

victory — *3528, 3529, 3534: 1 Cor. 15:54, 55, 57; 1 John 5:4*

victuals — *1033, 1979: Matt. 14:15; Luke 9:12*

vigilant — *1127, 3524: 1 Tim. 3:2; 1 Pet. 5:8*

vile — *819, 4508, 5014: Rom. 1:26; Phil. 3:21; James 2:2*

village -s — *2864, 2968: Mark 11:2; Acts 8:25*

vine -yard — *288, 289, 290: John 15:1; 1 Cor. 9:7*

vinegar — *3690: Mark 15:36; Luke 23:36*

violence; violent -ly — *970, 971, 973, 1286, 1411, 3731: Matt. 11:12; Acts 5:26*

viper -s — *2191: Matt. 3:7; Acts 28:3*

virgin -ity -s — *3932, 3933: Luke 2:36; 2 Cor. 11:2*

virtue — *703, 1411: Mark 5:30; Luke 6:19; 8:46; Phil. 4:8; 2 Pet. 1:3, 5*

vision -s; visible — *3701, 3705, 3706, 3707: Acts 2:17; Col. 1:16*

visit -ed -est -ation — *1980, 1984: James 1:27; 1 Pet. 2:12*

vocation — *2821: Eph. 4:1*

voice -s — *5456, 5586: Gal. 4:20; Rev. 4:5*

void — *677, 2763, 2758: Acts 24:16; Rom. 4:14*

volume — *2777: Heb. 10:7*

voluntary (see **will**) — *2309: Col. 2:18*

vomit — *1829: 2 Pet. 2:22*

vow — *2171: Acts 18:18; 21:23*

voyage — *4144: Acts 27:10*

W

wagging — *2795: Matt. 27:39; Mark 15:29*

wages — *3408, 3800: Luke 3:14; 2 Pet. 2:15*

wail -ed -ing — *214, 2805, 2875, 3996: Matt. 13:42; Mark 5:38; Rev. 1:7; 18:15, 19*

wait -ed -eth -ing — *362, 553, 1096, 1551, 1747, 1748, 1917, 3180, 4037, 4160, 4327, 4328, 4332, 4342: John 5:3; Gal. 5:5*

wake — *1127: 1 Thess. 5:10*

walk -ed -edst -est -eth -ing — *1330, 1704, 3716, 4043, 4198, 4748: 1 John 2:6; 2 John 1:4*

wall -s — *5038, 5109: Eph. 2:14; Heb. 11:30*

wallowed; wallowing — *2946, 2947: Mark 9:20; 2 Pet. 2:22*

wandered; wandering — *4022, 4105, 4107: 1 Tim. 5:13; Heb. 11:37, 38; Jude 1:13*

want -ed -ing -s — *3007, 5302, 5303, 5304: Phil. 4:11; Titus 3:13*

wanton -ness — *766, 2691, 4684: Rom. 13:13; 1 Tim. 5:11; James 5:5; 2 Pet. 2:18*

war -fare -reth -ring -s — *497, 4170, 4171, 4752, 4753, 4754: Luke 14:31; 1 Cor. 9:7*

ward — *5438: Acts 12:10*

ware (see **aware**) — *4894, 5442: Acts 14:6; 2 Tim. 4:15*

warmed; warming — *2328: Mark 14:54, 67; John 18:18, 25; James 2:16*

warn -ed -ing — *3560, 5263, 5537:* Col. 1:28; 1 Thess. 5:14

wash -ed -ing — *628, 633, 637, 907, 909, 1026, 3067, 3068, 3538, 4150:* 1 Tim. 5:10; Heb. 9:10

waste -ed — *684, 1287, 4199: Matt. 26:8; Mark 14:4; Luke 15:13; 16:1; Gal. 1:13*

watch -ed -eth -ful -ing — *69, 70, 1127, 2892, 3525, 3906, 5083, 5438:* Luke 2:8; Rev. 3:2

water -ed -eth -ing -s — *504, 4215, 4222, 5202, 5203, 5204:* Eph. 5:26

waterpot -s — *5201: John 2:6,7*

wave -s — *2830, 2949, 4535:* Acts 27:41; James 1:6

wavereth; wavering — *186, 1252: Heb. 10:23; James 1:6*

wax -ed -eth -ing — *1095, 1096, 2691, 2901, 3822, 3955, 3975, 3982, 4147, 4298, 5594:* Phil. 1:14; 2 Tim. 3:13

way -s — *296, 684, 1545, 1624, 1722, 3112, 3319, 3598, 3938, 4197, 4105, 4206, 4311, 5158:* Mark 1:2; 2 Thess. 2:7

weak -er -ness — *102, 769, 770, 772:* Rom. 4:19; 1 Pet. 3:7

wealth (see **rich**) — *2142:* Acts 19:25; 1 Cor. 10:24

weapons — *3696: John 18:3; 2 Cor. 10:4*

wear -eth -ing — *2827, 4025, 5409:* Matt. 11:8; 1 Pet. 3:3

weary -ied — *1573, 2577, 2872, 2873, 5299:* John 4:6; 2 Thess. 3:13

weather — *2105, 5494: Matt. 16:2, 3*

wedding — *1062: Matt. 22:3, 8, 10-12; Luke 12:36; 14:8*

week — *4521: John 20:1, 19; Acts 20:7*

weep -est -ing; wept — *1145, 2799, 2805:* Mark 16:10; Rev. 18:15

weight -ier -y — *922, 926, 3591, 5006:* 2 Cor. 10:10; Heb. 12:1

well — *15, 16, 17, 18, 957, 1510/2101, 1921, 2095, 2100, 2101, 2106, 2509, 2532, 2569, 2573, 3140, 3184, 4077, 4260, 4982:, 5421:* Phil. 4:14; Titus 2:9

well -s — *4077, 5421:* John 4:6; 2 Pet. 2:17

wellbeloved — *27: Matt. 12:6; Rom. 16:3; 3 John 1:1*

wellpleasing — *2101: Phil. 4:18; Heb. 13:21*

west — *1424, 3047, 5566:* Luke 12:54; Acts 27:12

whale's — *2785: Matt. 12:40*

wheat — *4621:* Matt. 13:25; Rev. 6:6

when -soever — *1437, 1722/3588, 1722/3739, 1875, 1893, 2259, 2531, 3326, 3698, 3704, 3752, 3753/3588, 4218, 5613/1437, 5753:* Rom. 15:24; Eph. 2:5

whence (see **where -soever**) — *3606, 3739, 4158:* Heb. 11:15; James 4:1

where -soever (see **whence**) — *296, 1330, 1337, 1722/3739, 1722/3956, 1722/5117, 2596, 3606, 3699, 3699/302, 3699/1487, 3757, 3837, 4226:* Luke 17:37; 2 Pet. 3:4

whereas — *1722/3759, 3699, 3748:* 1 Cor. 3:3; 1 Pet. 2:12

whereby — *1223/3739, 1722/3739, 2596/5101, 4012/3757, 4314/3739:* Rom. 8:15; Phil. 3:21

wherefore (see **why**) — *686, 686/1065, 1161, 1223/3739, 1223/5124, 1302, 1352, 1355, 1519/3739, 1519/5101, 1909/3739, 2443/5101, 3606, 3739/5484, 3767, 5101, 5101/1752, 5105, 5484/5101, 5620:* Gal. 4:7; Phile. 1:8

wherein -soever; whereinto — *1223/3757, 1519/3739, 1519/3757, 1722/3739, 1722/3739/302, 1722/3757, 1909/3739, 1909/3757, 3757, 4012/3739:* 2 Cor. 11:21; Heb. 6:17

whereof — *1537/3739, 1909/3739, 3739, 4012/3739, 4012/5101:* Acts 2:32; 1 Tim. 1:7

whereon; whereupon — *1722/3739, 1909/3739, 3606:* Matt. 14:7; John 4:38

whereto; whereunto — *1519/3739, 3739, 5101:* Phil. 3:16; 2 Pet. 1:19

wherewith -al — *1722/5101, 3739, 3745, 5101:* Matt. 6:31; 1 Thess. 3:9

whether — *1487, 1535, 3379, 3739, 4220, 5037, 5101:* Luke 5:23; Rom. 14:8

which — *302, 846, 1352, 1520, 2076, 2532, 3588, 3739, 3748, 4169, 5101:* 1 Thess. 3:10; Titus 2:1

while -st — *1722, 2193, 2250, 2540, 3153, 3397, 3588, 3641, 3739, 3752, 3755, 3819, 4340, 5099, 5550, 5613:* Acts 5:4; Heb. 10:33

whisperers; whisperings — *5587, 5588: Rom. 1:29; 2 Cor. 12:20*

whit — *3367, 3650: John 7:23; 13:10; 2 Cor. 11:5*

white -ed — *2867, 2896, 3021, 3022: John 4:35; Acts 23:3*

who; whom -soever; whose; whoso -ever —

1437, 1437/5100, 1536, 2532/846, 3588, 3739, 3739/302, 3739/1437, 3745/302, 3746, 3748, 3748/302, 3778, 3956/3588, 3956/3739, 3956/3739/302, 5100, 5101: Mark 3:35; 2 John 1:9

whole -ly -some — *537, 1510/1722, 2480, 3390, 3648, 3650, 3651, 3956, 4982, 5198, 5199:* Mark 2:17; 1 Tim. 6:3

whore -monger(s) — *4204, 4205:* Eph. 5:5; Rev. 17:1

why (see **wherefore**) — *1063, 1302, 1519/ 5101, 2444, 3754:* Gal. 2:14; Col. 2:20

wicked -ness — *113, 459, 824, 2549, 2556, 4189, 4190, 4191, 5129:* Matt. 12:45; Eph. 6:12

wide — *4116: Matt. 7:13*

widow -s — *5503:* Mark 12:42, 43; Acts 6:1

wife -'s; wives — *1126, 1134, 1135, 3994:* 1 Cor. 7:29; 1 Tim. 4:7

wild — *66, 2342:* Matt. 3:4; Rom. 11:17, 24

wilderness — *2047, 2048:* Acts 13:18; Heb. 3:8, 17

wiles — *3180: Eph. 6:11*

will -eth -fully -ing -ingly; wilt; would -est (see **voluntary**) — *210, 830, 1012, 1013, 1014, 1096, 1106, 1497, 1595, 1596, 1635, 2106, 2107, 2133, 2172, 2307, 2309, 2596, 2843, 3106, 3195, 3785, 4288, 4289:* Rom. 9:16; Heb. 10:26

win; won — *2770: Phil. 3:8; 1 Pet. 3:1*

wind -s — *416, 417, 4151, 4154:* Matt. 7:25; Jude 1:12

window — *2376: Acts 20:9; 2 Cor. 11:33*

wine — *1098, 3631, 3632, 3943:* Mark 2:22; Titus 1:7

winebibber — *3630: Matt. 11:19; Luke 7:34*

wine vat — *5276: Mark 12:1*

winepress — *3025, 3025/3631: Matt. 21:33; Rev. 14:19, 20; 19:15*

wings — *4420: Matt. 23:37; Luke 13:34; Rev. 4:8; 9:9; 12:14*

winked — *5237: Acts 17:30*

winter -ed — *3914, 3915, 3916, 5494:* Matt. 24:20; 2 Tim. 4:21

wipe -ed — *631, 1591, 1813:* Luke 10:11; Rev. 7:17

wise -er -ly; wisdom — *3097, 3588, 3779, 3838, 3843, 4678, 4679, 4680, 4920, 5428, 5429, 5430:* Rom. 11:33; 1 Cor. 1:25

wish -ed — *2172: Acts 27:29; Rom. 9:3; 2 Cor. 13:9; 3 John 1:2*

wist; wit; wot (see **know**) — *1107, 1492, 5613:* Acts 3:17; Phil. 1:22

witchcraft — *5331: Gal. 5:20*

with -al — *260, 4862:* Mark 1:6; Col. 4:3

withdraw -n; withdrew — *402, 645, 868, 4724, 5288, 5298:* Mark 3:7; 2 Thess. 3:6

withered; withereth — *3583, 3584, 5352:* John 15:6; James 1:11

withholdeth — *2722: 2 Thess. 2:6*

within — *1223, 1722, 1787, 2080, 2081, 2082, 4314:* Matt. 3:9; 1 Cor. 5:12

withstand; withstood — *426, 2967:* Acts 11:17; Gal. 2:11

witness -ed -es -eth -ing — *267, 1263, 2649, 3140, 3141, 3142, 3144, 4828, 4901, 5576, 5577, 5707, 5749:* 1 John 1:2; Rev. 11:3

woe -s — *3759:* Luke 10:13; 1 Cor. 9:16

wolf; wolves — *3074: Matt. 7:15; 10:16; Luke 10:3; John 10:12; Acts 20:29*

woman; women — *1133, 1135, 2338, 4247:* Gal. 4:4; Titus 2:3

womb -s — *1064, 2836, 3388:* John 3:4; Rom. 4:19

wonder -ed -ful -ing -s — *1411, 1569, 1839, 2285, 2296, 2297, 3167, 4592, 5059:* Acts 2:11; Rev. 13:3

wont (see **custom**) — *1486, 2596/1485, 3543: Matt. 27:15; Mark 10:1; Luke 22:39; Acts 16:13*

wood — *3585, 3586: 1 Cor. 3:12; 2 Tim. 2:20; Rev. 9:20; 18:12*

wool — *2053: Heb. 9:19; Rev. 1:14*

word -s — *518, 2036, 3050, 3054, 3055, 3056, 4086, 4487, 5542:* Mark 4:17; 2 Pet. 1:19

work -ers -eth -ing -man -manmanship -men -s (see **labor**) — *1411, 1753, 1754, 1755, 2038, 2039, 2040, 2041, 2480, 2716, 3056, 3433, 3656, 4160, 4161, 4229, 4234, 4903:* Eph. 2:9, 10; Phil. 1:6

workfellow — *4904: Rom. 16:21*

world -ly -s — *165, 166, 1093, 2886, 2889, 3625:* Titus 2:12; Heb. 1:2

worm -s — *4662, 4663: Mark 9:44, 46, 48; Acts 12:23*

wormwood — *894: Rev. 8:11*

worse (see **bad**) — *1640, 2276, 5302, 5501:* Mark 2:21; 1 Tim. 5:8

worship -ed -er(s) -eth -ing — *1391, 1479, 1799, 2151, 2318, 2323, 2356, 3000, 3511, 4352, 4353, 4573, 4574, 4576:* John 9:31; Col. 2:18

wound (see **bind -ing**) — *1210, 4958: John 19:40; Acts 5:6*

wound -ed -s — *4127/2007, 4969, 5134, 5135, 5180:* Luke 10:30, 34; 1 Cor. 8:12

woven — *5307: John 19:23*

wrapped — *1750, 1794, 4683:* Matt. 27:59; Luke 2:7, 12

wrath -s; wroth — *2372, 2373, 3709, 3710, 3949, 3950:* Rom. 1:18; 2 Cor. 12:20

wrest — *4761: 2 Pet. 3:16*

wrestle — *2076/3823: Eph. 6:12*

wretched — *5005: Rom. 7:24; Rev. 3:17*

wrinkle — *4512: Eph. 5:27*

write -ing(s); written; wrote — *583, 975, 1123, 1125, 1449, 1722/1121, 1924, 1989, 4093, 4270:* Matt. 19:7; 2 John 1:5, 12

wrong -ed -fully — *91, 92, 93, 95:* Phile. 1:18; 1 Pet. 2:19

wrought (see **do; make; work**) — *1096, 1754, 2038, 2716, 4160, 4903:* Matt. 26:10; 2 Thess. 3:8

Y

ye; you -ward; your -self(-ves) (see **thee -ward**) — *240, 1438, 2398, 2596/5209, 3588, 3844/1438, 4314, 5209, 5210/846, 5212, 5213, 5213/846, 5216, 5216/846:* Luke 6:20; 1 Thess. 5:11

yea; yes — *235, 1161, 2228, 2532, 3304, 3483:* Matt. 5:37; Rom. 3:29

year -s — *1096/3173, 1332, 1333, 1541, 1763, 2094, 2250, 4070, 5063, 5148:* Gal. 4:10; James 4:13

yesterday — *5504: John 4:52; Acts 7:28; Heb. 13:8*

yet — *188, 235, 1063, 1065, 1161, 2089, 2236, 2532, 2579, 2596, 3195, 3305, 3364, 3369, 3380, 3764, 3765, 3768:* 1 Cor. 12:20; James 4:2

yield -ed -eth — *591, 863, 1325, 1634, 3936, 3982, 4160:* Mark 4:8; Acts 5:10

yoke -ed — *2086, 2201, 2218:* 2 Cor. 6:14; Gal. 5:1

yokefellow — *4805: Phil. 4:3*

yonder (see **there; thither**) — *1563: Matt. 17:20; 26:36*

young -er; youth -ful — *1025, 1640, 2365, 3494, 3495, 3501, 3502, 3512, 3678, 3813, 3816:* 2 Tim. 2:22; 1 John 2:13, 14

Z

Zacchaeus — *2195: Luke 19:2, 5, 8*

Zara — *2196: Matt. 1:3*

zeal -ous -ously — *2205, 2206, 2207:* Gal. 4:17; Col. 4:13

Zebedee — *2199:* Mark 1:19, 20; John 21:2

Zebulun — *2194: Matt. 4:13, 15; Rev. 7:8*

Zechariah — *2197:* Luke 1:5; 11:51

Zelotes — *2208: Luke 6:15; Acts 1:13*

Zenas — *2211: Titus 3:13*

Zion — *4622:* Rom. 9:33; Heb. 12:22

Zorobabel — *2216: Matt. 1:12, 13; Luke 3:27*

SCRIPTURE INDEX
To the Footnotes and Introductions

This is an index of the Scripture passages that are referenced in the footnotes and introductions. The left column displays the reference being referred to, while the right column denotes the footnote or book introduction where it is referenced. The references in bold type indicate passages where a footnote occurs. Even though a particular verse or passage may be referred to more than once in a given footnote or introduction, it will only be listed once in the index. Likewise, if a verse is a part of the passage on which a given footnote is appended (e.g., a reference to Acts 2:6 in the footnote on Acts 2:1–13), it will not be listed in the index.

Genesis

1:27	1 John 1:5–10
11:26	Acts 7:2–4
11:32	Acts 7:2–4
12:4	Acts 7:2–4

Exodus

4:21	Rom 9:17
5:2	Rom 9:17
7:13	Rom 9:17
7:22	2 Thess 2:9
8:15	Rom 9:17
8:32	Rom 9:17
9:12	Rom 9:17
9:34	Rom 9:17
33:19	Rom 9:17

Deuteronomy

11:14	James 5:7,8
22:21	Matt 19:3–9
23:15,16	Phile Intro
24:1–4	Matt 19:3–9

Joshua

24:2	Acts 7:2–4

1 Samuel

4:8	Rom 9:17

2 Samuel

7:14–17	Rev 20:1–15

1 Kings

14:25	John 7:52

Job

29:23	James 5:7,8

Psalms

24:1–10	Rev 20:1–15
51:12	Matt 5:1–12
68:18	Eph 4:8–10
113—118	John 10:22

Proverbs

16:15	James 5:7, 8

Ecclesiastes

3:11	Luke 11:9

Isaiah

2:1–4	Rev 20:1–15
2:12–24	1 Thess 5:2
11:5–12	Rev 20:1–15
13:6–9	1 Thess 5:2
34:1–8	Rev 14:14–20
35:1–10	Rev 20:1–15
55:6–8	Matt 13:10–17
63:1–6	Rev 14:14–20
63:7	Matt 21:18–22
64:12	Matt 21:18–22
65:3–7	Matt 21:18–22

Jeremiah

3:3	James 5:7,8
46:10	1 Thess 5:2

Ezekiel

13:5	1 Thess 5:2

Daniel

2:44	Rev 20:1–15
7:7,8	2 Thess 2:3–9
7:21	2 Thess 2:3–9

Hosea

6:3	James 5:7,8

Joel

1:15	1 Thess 5:2
2:1	1 Thess 5:2
2:1–11	Rev 14:14–20
2:11	1 Thess 5:2
2:23	James 5:7,8
2:31	1 Thess 5:2
3:9–13	Rev 14:14–20
3:14	1 Thess 5:2

Obadiah

1:8	1 Thess 5:2
1:15	1 Thess 5:2

Zephaniah

1:14	1 Thess 5:2
1:14–18	Rev 14:14–20
3:8	Rev 14:14–20

Zechariah

12:9–11	Rev 14:14–20
13:1	1 Thess 5:2
14:1–3	Rev 14:14–20
14:1–4	1 Thess 5:2

Matthew

3:11	Acts 1:5
5:1–12	
5:3–12	Matt 8:11,12
5:7	James 2:12,13
5:22	Matt 8:11,12
5:27–32	
5:29,30	Matt 8:11,12
5:31, 32	
5:32	Matt 19:3–9
6:13	
7:21–23	Matt 8:11,12
8:11,12	
9:9–13	Matt Intro
10:1–15	
10:3	Matt Intro
10:15	Matt 8:11,12
10:28	Matt 8:11,12
10:37	Luke 14:25–33
11:16	Matt 20:1–6
12:22–30	Mark 3:28,29
12:31,32	Mark 3:28,29
13:10–17	
13:24–30	Matt 13:47–50
13:30	Matt 8:11,12
13:31,32	
13:38	Matt 8:11,12
13:42,43	Matt 8:11,12
13:47–50	Matt 13:24–30
13:55	James Intro; Jude Intro
16:18,19	
16:23	Matt 8:11,12
17:1	John Intro
18:9	Matt 8:11,12
18:18	Matt 16:18,19
19:3–9	
19:27	Matt 20:1–6
20:1–16	
21:18–22	
21:31	Matt 8:11,12
22:1–14	Matt 8:11,12
22:12	Matt 20:1–6
22:13	Matt 8:11,12
24:1,2	Matt 24:4—25:46
24:3	Matt 24:4—25:46; 1 Thess 2:19

28:11
28:30, 31 — 2 Tim Intro

Romans

1:10 — 3 John 1:2
1:13 — Rom Intro

1:17

1:18
1:19 — Rom 1:20

1:20
1:20 — John 1:1–17
1:21 — Heb 10:26,27
1:23 — 2 Tim 1:12
1:25 — Heb 10:26,27
2:1–16 — Matt 8:11,12
2:13 — James 2:14–19
3:10–12 — 1 John 1:5–10
3:10–18 — Rom 3:19,20

3:19,20
3:20 — James 2:14–19
3:23 — 1 John 1:5–10
5:12 — 1 Cor 2:14; James 4:5; 1 John 1:5–10
5:19 — Luke 8:13
6:12 — 2 Tim 1:12
7:1–3 — 1 Tim 3:2
7:13 — Matt 13:10–17
7:15 — Rom 7:17–19

7:17–19

7:23
8:1 — Rom 3:19,20
8:11 — 2 Tim 1:12
8:23 — James 5:14,15; 1 Pet 1:5
8:28 — James 5:14,15
8:29 — Eph 1:4,5
8:33 — Eph 1:4,5
8:38,39 — 1 John 3:6–9
9:11 — Eph 1:4,5

9:17
12:3 — 1 Cor 4:6,7
12:6–8 — 1 Cor 12:1–11
12:16 — 1 Cor 4:6,7
13:11 — 1 Pet 1:5
14:10–23 — Matt 8:11,12
15:25 — Rom Intro
16:1–4 — 1 Tim 2:9–15
16:3 — 1 Tim 2:9–15
16:21 — 1 Tim 2:9–15
16:23 — 3 John 1:1

1 Corinthians

1:2 — 1 Cor 1:10–13
1:4–7 — 1 Cor 12:1–11
1:8 — 1 Cor 1:10–13; 1 Thess 5:2

1:10–13
1:11 — 1 Cor Intro
1:12 — 1 Cor Intro; 1 Pet Intro
1:14 — 3 John 1:1
1:18–13 — John 9:39
1:27 — Matt 13:10–17
2:1,2 — 1 Cor Intro

2:14
2:14 — Matt 13:10–17
3:4,5 — 1 Cor 10–13
3:10–15 — Matt 8:11,12
3:11 — Matt 16:18,19
3:13 — Matt 8:11,12
3:22 — 1 Pet Intro

4:1
4:1 — Luke 16:1–13
4:5 — Matt 8:11,12

4:6,7

4:7
4:17 — 1 Tim Intro
5:5 — 1 Thess 5:2
6:20 — 1 John 1:5–10
7:1 — 1 Cor 12:1–11
7:2 — 1 Tim 2:9–15
8:5 — 2 Cor 5:1
9:5 — 1 Pet Intro

10:2
10:18–31 — 1 Cor Intro

11:2–16 — 1 Cor Intro; 1 Tim 2:9–15
11:3 — 1 Cor 11:2–16; 1 Tim 2:9–15
11:4,5 — 1 Tim 2:9–15

11:14,15
11:17–34 — 1 Cor Intro

12:1–11 — 2 Tim 1:6

12:13 — Acts 10:44–48

12:28,29 — Matt 10:1–15

12:31
13:8 — 1 Cor 12:31

13:8–10

14:1–40 — 1 Cor Intro

14:1–3
14:1–14 — 1 Cor Intro
14:2 — Acts 2:1–13
14:4 — Acts 2:1–3; 1 Cor 14:1–3
14:13 — Acts 2:1–13; 1 Cor 14:1–3
14:19 — Acts 2:1–13; 1 Cor 14:1–3
14:23 — 1 Cor 14:1–3
14:26,27 — 1 Cor 14:1–3
14:27 — Acts 2:1–13
14:28 — 1 Cor 14:33–40
14:30 — 1 Cor 14:33–40

14:33–40 — 1 Tim 2:9–15
14:34–40 — Titus Intro
15:5 — 1 Pet Intro
15:7 — James Intro
15:50–57 — 2 Cor 5:1
15:51–54 — James 5:14,15
15:53,54 — 2 Tim 1:12
15:57 — 2 Cor 5:1
16:1–4 — Col 4:7; 2 Tim 4:20
16:2 — 3 John 1:2
16:5,6 — 2 Cor Intro
16:10 — 1 Tim 4:12
16:10,11 — 1 Tim Intro
16:12 — 1 Cor Intro
16:17 — 1 Thess 2:19
16:22 — 3 John 1:2

2 Corinthians

2:12,13 — Phil Intro
4:3,4 — Matt 13:10–17
4:11 — 2 Tim 1:12
4:17 — 2 Cor 5:1

5:1
5:2 — 2 Cor 5:1
5:4 — 2 Tim 1:12
5:10 — Matt 8:11,12; James 2:12,13
7:5–11 — 2 Cor Intro
7:7 — 1 Thess 2:19
7:13–15 — 1 Tim 4:12
7:15 — 1 Tim 4:12
8:16,17 — 2 Cor Intro
8:17 — 1 Tim 4:12
8:18 — Acts Intro
9:2–4 — 2 Cor Intro

11:5
11:7–9 — Phil Intro
11:13–15 — 2 Cor 11:5

11:26 — Gal 2:4

12:1–4 — 2 Cor Intro

12:1–10
12:2 — 2 Cor 5:1
12:7–9 — 2 Cor Intro
12:11 — 2 Cor 11:5
12:14 — 2 Cor Intro
12:18 — 1 Tim 4:12
13:1 — 2 Cor Intro

Galatians

1:6–8
1:11–19 — Gal Intro
1:18,19 — James Intro
1:18 — 1 Pet Intro
1:19 — Jude Intro
2:1 — Titus Intro
2:3 — Titus Intro
2:3–5 — Titus Intro

2:4
2:6 — 2 Cor 11:5
2:7–9 — 1 Pet Intro
2:11 — 1 Pet Intro
2:11–14 — Gal Intro
2:14 — 1 Pet Intro
2:15–4:15 — Gal Intro
3:28 — 1 Cor 11:2–16; 1 Tim 2:9–15
4:4 — 2 Cor 5:1

5:4
5:6 — James 2:14-19
5:16–6:10 — Gal Intro
6:17 — 2 Tim 1:12

Ephesians

1:1 — Eph Intro

1:4,5
1:6 — Heb 6:1–6
1:10 — Eph Intro

1:13,14
1:22,23 — Eph Intro
2:8 — Mark 16:16
2:15,16 — Eph Intro
2:20–22 — Eph Intro
3:10 — Eph 4:4

4:4

4:8–10
4:11,12 — 1 Cor 12:1–11
5:21–33 — Eph Intro
6:21,22 — Col 4:7

Philippians

1:1 — 1 Tim Intro
1:6,10 — 1 Thess 5:2
1:20,21 — Phil Intro

2:6–8
2:16 — 1 Thess 5:2
2:19 — 1 Tim Intro
2:25–30 — Phil Intro
4:16 — Phil Intro
4:18 — Phil Intro

Colossians

1:1 — 1 Tim Intro

1:7

1:9

1:9–2:19 — Col Intro

1:15–18
2:1 — Col Intro

2 John

1:1	2 John Intro
1:7	2 Thess 2:3–9
1:10,11	2 John Intro
1:12	2 John Intro

3 John

1:1	
1:2	
1:5–8	3 John Intro
1:9	
1:10	3 John Intro
1:11	1 John 3:6–9
1:14	3 John 1:1

Jude

1:1	Jude Intro
1:3–18	2 Pet Intro; Jude Intro
1:4	Jude Intro
1:7	Mark 3:28,29
1:7–11	Jude Intro
1:9	
1:14–16	

Revelation

1:1	Rev Intro
1:3	Rev Intro
1:9	Rev Intro
1:19	Rev Intro
2:1–3:22	
2:8–11	
2:12–17	
2:18–29	
3:1–6	
3:7–13	
3:14	
3:14–22	
3:21	1 Thess 2:19
4:1	Rev Intro
6:1–7	Rev 19:1–21
6:1–17	Rev 15:1–8
6:2	Rev 13:1–18
7:1–17	
7:17	Matt 8:11,12
8:1–7	

8:1–13	Rev 15:1–8
9:1–21	Rev 15:1–8
10:1–11	
11:1–12	
11:15–19	Rev 15:1–8
13:1–18	2 Thess 2:3–9
14:9–11	Rev 13:1–18
14:14–20	
15:1–8	
16:1–21	Rev 15:1–8
19:1–21	
19:11–21	Matt 24:4—25:46
20:1–15	
20:2	Jude 1:9
20:10	Jude 1:9
20:11–15	Matt 8:11,12
21:1—22:5	
21:2	Rev Intro
21:4	Matt 8:11,12
22:7	Rev 1:1
22:8	Rev Intro

A CONCISE

DICTIONARY

OF THE WORDS IN

THE GREEK TESTAMENT;

WITH THEIR RENDERINGS

IN THE

AUTHORIZED ENGLISH VERSION.

BY

JAMES STRONG, S.T.D., LL.D.

PLAN OF THE BOOK.

1. All the original words are treated in their alphabetical Greek order, and are numbered regularly from the first to the last, each being known throughout by its appropriate number. This renders reference easy without recourse to the Greek characters.

2. Immediately after each word is given its exact equivalent in English letters, according to the system of transliteration laid down in the scheme here following, which is substantially that adopted in the Common English Version, only more consistently and uniformly carried out; so that the word could readily be turned back again into Greek from the form thus given it.

3. Next follows the precise pronunciation, according to the usual English mode of sounding syllables, so plainly indicated that none can fail to apprehend and apply it. The most approved sounds are adopted, as laid down in the annexed scheme of articulation, and in such a way that any good Græcist would immediately recognise the word if so pronounced, notwithstanding the minor variations current among scholars in this respect.

4. Then ensues a tracing of the etymology, radical meaning, and applied significations of the word, justly but tersely analyzed and expressed, with any other important peculiarities in this regard.

5. In the case of proper names, the same method is pursued, and at this point the regular mode of Anglicizing it, after the general style of the Common English Version, is given, and a few words of explanation are added to identify it.

6. Finally (after the punctuation-mark :—) are given all the different renderings of the word in the Authorized English Version, arranged in the alphabetical order of the leading terms, and conveniently condensed according to the explanations given below.

By searching out these various renderings in the MAIN CONCORDANCE, to which this Dictionary is designed as a companion, and noting the passages to which the same number corresponding to that of any given Greek word is attached in the marginal column, the reader, whether acquainted with the original language or not, will obtain a complete *Greek Concordance* also, expressed in the words of the Common English Version. This is an advantage which no other Concordance or Lexicon affords.

GREEK ARTICULATION.

THE following explanations are sufficient to show the mode of writing and pronouncing Greek words in English adopted in this *Dictionary*.

1. The *Alphabet* is as follows:

No.	Form.		Name.	Transliteration and Power.
1.	A	α	Alpha (al'-fah)	**a**, as in ARM or [mAN*
2.	B	β	Bēta (bay'-tah)	**b**
3.	Γ	γ	Gamma (gam'-mah)	g hard †
4.	Δ	δ	Dĕlta (del'-tah)	**d**
5.	E	ε	Ĕpsilŏn (ep'-see-lon)	ĕ, as in MET
6.	Z	ζ	Zēta (dzay'-tah)	z, as in ADZE‡
7.	H	η	Ēta (ay'-tah)	ē, as in THEY
8.	Θ	θ or ϑ	Thēta (thay'-tah)	th, as in THIN§
9.	I	ι	Iōta (ee-o'-tah)	i, as in ma-
10.	K	κ or ϰ	Kappa (cap'-pah)	k [chINE‖
11.	Λ	λ	Lambda (lamb'-dah) l
12.	M	μ	Mu (moo)	m
13.	N	ν	Nu (noo)	n
14.	Ξ	ξ	Xi (ksee)	x = ks
15.	O	ο	Omikrŏn (om'-e-cron)	ŏ, as in NOT
16.	Π	π	Pi (pee)	p
17.	P	ρ	Rhō (hro)	r
18.	Σ	σ, final ς Sigma (sig'-mah)	s sharp
19.	T	τ	Tau (tŏw)	t ¶
20.	Υ	υ	Upsilŏn (u'-pse-lon)	u, as in fULL
21.	Φ	φ	Phi (fee)	ph = f
22.	X	χ	Chi (khee)	German ch *
23.	Ψ	ψ	Psi (psee)	ps
24.	Ω	ω	Omēga (o'-meg-ah)	ō, as in NO.

2. The mark ʽ, placed over the *initial* vowel of a word, is called the *Rough Breathing*, and is equivalent to the English *h*, by which we have accordingly represented it. Its *absence* over an initial vowel is indicated by the mark ʼ, called the *Smooth Breathing*, which is unappreciable or silent, and is therefore not represented in our method of transliteration.†

3. The following are the Greek *diphthongs*, properly so called :‡

Form.	Transliteration and Power.	Form.	Transliteration and Power.
αι	**ai** (ah'ee) [ă+ĕ]	αυ	**ow**, as in now
ει	**ei**, as in hEIGHT	ευ	**eu**, as in fEUd
οι	**oi**, as in OIl	ου	**ou**, as in thrOUgh.
υι	**we**, as in sWEet		

* From the difficulty of producing the true sound of χ, it is generally sounded like *k*.

† These signs are placed over the *second* vowel of a *diphthong*. The same is true of the accents.

The *Rough Breathing* always belongs to υ initial.

The Rough Breathing is always used with ρ, when it begins a word. If this letter be doubled in the middle of a word, the first takes the Smooth, and the second the Rough, Breathing.

As these signs cannot conveniently be written over the first letter of a word, when a *capital*, they are in such cases placed *before* it. This observation applies also to the *accents*. The aspiration *always* begins the syllable.

Occasionally, in consequence of a contraction (*crasis*), the Smooth Breathing is made to stand in the middle of a word, and is then called *Coro'nis*.

‡ The above are combinations of two *short* vowels, and are pronounced like their respective elements, but

4. The *accent* (stress of voice) falls on the syllable where it is written.* It is of three forms: the *acute* (ʹ), which is the only true accent; the *grave* (ˋ) which is its substitute; and the *circumflex* (ˆ or ˜), which is the union of the two. The acute may stand on any one of the last *three* syllables, and in case it occurs on the final syllable, before another word in the same sentence, it is written as a grave. The grave is understood (but never written as such) on every other syllable. The circumflex is written on any syllable (necessarily the last or next to the last one of a word), formed by the contraction of two syllables, of which the *first* would properly have the acute.

5. The following *punctuation*-marks are used: the comma (,), the semicolon (·), the colon or period (.), the interrogation-point (;), and, by some editors, also the exclamation-point, parentheses and quotation-marks.

---

in more rapid succession than otherwise. Thus αι is midway between *i* in *high*, and *ay* in SAY.

Besides these, there are what are called *improper* diphthongs, in which the former is a *long* vowel. In these,

ᾳ sounds like α	ηυ sounds like η+υ
ῃ " " η	ωυ " " ω+υ.
ῳ " " ω	

the second vowel, when ι, is written *under* the first (unless that be a capital), and is *silent*; when υ, it is sounded separately. When the initial is a capital, the ι is placed after it, but does not take the breathing nor accent.

The sign ¨, called *diær'esis*, placed over the *latter* of two vowels, indicates that they do *not* form a diphthong.

* Every word (except a few monosyllables, called *Aton'ics*) must have one accent; several small words (called *Enclit'ics*) throw their accent (always as an acute) on the last syllable of the preceding word (in addition to its own accent, which still has the principal stress), where this is possible.

* α, when *final*, or before ρ final or followed by any *other* consonant, is sounded like *a* in ARm; elsewhere like *a* in MAN.

† γ, when followed by γ, κ, χ, or ξ, is sounded like *ng* in kING.

ζ ζ is always sounded like *dz*.

§ θ never has the guttural sound, like *th* in THIs.

‖ ι has the sound of *ee* when it *ends* an *accented* syllable; in other situations a more obscure sound, like *i* in *amiable* or *imbecile*.

¶ τ never has a sibilant sound, like *t* in NATION, NATURE.

5

ABBREVIATIONS EMPLOYED.

abst. = abstract (-ly)
acc. = accusative (case)
adv. = adverb (-ial) (-ly)
aff. = affinity
alt. = alternate (-ly)
anal. = analogy
app. = apparent (-ly)
caus. = causative (-ly)

cer. = { ceremony
ceremonial (-ly)
Chald. = Chaldee
Chr. = Christian
coll. = collective (-ly)

comp. = { comparative
comparatively
compare
compound (-s)
concr. = concrete (-ly)
corr. = corresponding

dat. = dative (case)

der. = { derivation
derivative
derived
dim. = diminutive
dir. = direct (-ly)
E. = East
eccl. = ecclesiastical (-ly)
Eg. = Egypt (-ian)
ell. = { ellipsis
elliptical (-ly)
eq. = equivalent
esp. = especially

euph. = { euphemism
euphemistic
euphemistically
ext. = extension
fem. = feminine
fig. = figurative (-ly)

for. = foreign
gen. = genitive (case)
Gr. = Greek
Heb. = { Hebraism
Hebrew
i.e. = { id est
that is
imper. = imperative
imperf. = imperfect
impers. = impersonal (-ly)
impl. = { implication
implied
incl. = including
ind. = indicative (-ly)
indiv. = individual (-ly)
inf. = infinitive
inh. = inhabitant (-s)
intens. = intensive (-ly)
intr. = intransitive (-ly)

invol. = { involuntary
involuntarily
irr. = irregular (-ly)
Isr. = { Israelite (-s)
Israelitish
Jer. = Jerusalem
Lat. = Latin
lit. = literal (-ly)
mean. = meaning
ment. = mental (-ly)
mid. = middle (voice)
mor. = moral (-ly)
mult. = multiplicative
nat. = natural (-ly)
neg. = negative (-ly)
neut. = neuter
obj. = objective (-ly)
obs. = obsolete

or. = origin (-al) (-ly)
Pal. = Palestine
part. = participle
pass. = passive (-ly)
perh. = perhaps
pers. = person (-al) (-ly)
phys. = physical (-ly)
pl. = plural
pref. = prefix (-ed)
pos. = positive (-ly)
prim. = primary
prob. = probably
prol. = { prolongation
prolonged
pron. = { pronominal (-ly)
pronoun
prop. = properly
redupl. = { reduplicated
reduplication

refl. = reflexive (-ly)
rel. = relative (-ly)
Rom. = Roman
sing. = singular
spec. = special (-ly)
subj. = subjective (-ly)
sup. = superlative (-ly)
tech. = technical (-ly)
term. = termination
trans. = transitive (-ly)
transp. = { transposed
transposition
typ. = typical (-ly)
unc. = uncertain
var. = { variation
various
voc. = vocative
vol. = { voluntarily
voluntary

SIGNS EMPLOYED.

+ (addition) denotes a rendering in the A. V. of one or more Gr. words in connection with the one under consideration.

× (multiplication) denotes a rendering in the A. V. that results from an idiom peculiar to the Gr.

( ) (parenthesis), in the renderings from the A. V., denotes a word or syllable sometimes given in connection with the principal word to which it is annexed.

[ ] (bracket), in the rendering from the A. V., denotes the inclusion of an additional word in the Gr.

Italics, at the end of a rendering from the A. V., denote an explanation of the variations from the usual form.

NOTE.

Owing to changes in the enumeration while in progress, there were no words left for Nos. 2717 and 3203-3302, which were therefore silently dropped out of the vocabulary and references as redundant. This will occasion no practical mistake or inconvenience.

GREEK DICTIONARY OF THE NEW TESTAMENT.

A.

1. **A a**, *al-fah;* of Heb. or.; the first letter of the alphabet; fig. only (from its use as a numeral) the *first:*—Alpha. Often used (usually ἀν **an**, before a vowel) also in composition (as a contraction from *427*) in the sense of *privation;* so in many words beginning with this letter; occasionally in the sense of *union* (as a contraction of *200*).

2. **Ἀαρών Aarōn**, *ah-ar-ōhn';* of Heb. or. [175]; *Aaron,* the brother of Moses:—Aaron.

3. **Ἀβαδδών Abaddōn** *ab-ad-dōhn';* of Heb. or. [11]; a *destroying angel:*—Abaddon.

4. **ἀβαρής abarēs**, *ab-ar-ace';* from *1* (as a neg. particle) and *922; weightless,* i.e. (fig.) *not burdensome:*—from being burdensome.

5. **Ἀββᾶ Abba**, *ab-bah';* of Chald. or. [2]; *father* (as a voc.):—Abba.

6. **Ἄβελ Abĕl** *ab'-el;* of Heb. or. [1893]; *Abel,* the son of Adam:—Abel.

7. **Ἀβιά Abia**, *ab-ee-ah';* of Heb. or. [29]; *Abijah,* the name of two Isr.:—Abia.

8. **Ἀβιάθαρ Abiathar**, *ab-ee-ath'-ar;* of Heb. or. [54]; *Abiathar* an Isr.:—Abiathar.

9. **Ἀβιληνή Abilēnē**, *ab-ee-lay-nay';* of for. or. [comp. 58]; *Abilene,* a region of Syria:—Abilene.

10. **Ἀβιούδ Abiŏud**, *ab-ee-ood';* of Heb. or. [31]; *Abihud,* an Isr.:—Abiud.

11. **Ἀβραάμ Abraam**, *ab-rah-am';* of Heb. or. [85]; *Abraham,* the Heb. patriarch:—Abraham. [In Acts 7 : 16 the text should prob. read *Jacob.*]

12. **ἄβυσσος abussŏs**, *ab'-us-sos;* from *1* (as a neg. particle) and a var. of *1037; depthless,* i.e. (spec.) (infernal) *"abyss":*—deep, (bottomless) pit.

13. **Ἄγαβος Agabŏs**, *ag'-ab-os;* of Heb. or. [comp. 2285]; *Agabus,* an Isr.:—Agabus.

14. **ἀγαθοεργέω agathŏĕrgĕō**, *ag-ath-er-gheh'-o;* from *18* and *2041;* to *work good:*—do good.

15. **ἀγαθοποιέω agathŏpŏiĕō**, *ag-ath-op-oy-eh'-o;* from *17;* to *be a well-doer* (as a favor or a duty):—(when) do good (well).

16. **ἀγαθοποιΐα agathŏpŏiïa**, *ag-ath-op-oy-ee'-ah;* from *17; well-doing,* i.e. *virtue:*—well-doing.

17. **ἀγαθοποιός agathŏpŏiŏs**, *ag-ath-op-oy-os';* from *18* and *4160;* a *well-doer,* i.e. *virtuous:*—them that do well.

18. **ἀγαθός agathŏs**, *ag-ath-os';* a prim. word; *"good"* (in any sense, often as noun):—benefit, good (-s, things), well. Comp. *2570.*

19. **ἀγαθωσύνη agathōsunē**, *ag-ath-o-soo'-nay;* from *18; goodness,* i.e. *virtue* or *beneficence:*—goodness.

20. **ἀγαλλίασις agalliasis**, *ag-al-lee'-as-is;* from *21; exultation;* spec. *welcome:*—gladness, (exceeding) joy.

21. **ἀγαλλιάω agalliaō**, *ag-al-lee-ah'-o;* from *ἄγαν agan* (much) and *242;* prop. to *jump for joy,* i.e. *exult:*—be (exceeding) glad, with exceeding joy, rejoice (greatly).

22. **ἄγαμος agamŏs**, *ag'-am-os;* from *1* (as a neg. particle) and *1062; unmarried:*—unmarried.

23. **ἀγανακτέω aganaktĕō**, *ag-an-ak-teh'-o;* from *ἄγαν agan* (much) and *ἄχθος achthŏs* (grief; akin to the base of *43*) to be *greatly afflicted,* i.e. (fig.) *indignant:*—be much (sore) displeased, have (be moved with, with) indignation.

24. **ἀγανάκτησις aganaktēsis**, *ag-an-ak'-tay-sis;* from *23; indignation:*—indignation

25. **ἀγαπάω agapaō**, *ag-ap-ah'-o;* perh. from *ἄγαν agan* (much) [or comp. *5689*]; to *love* (in a social or moral sense):—(be-) love (-ed). Comp. *5368.*

26. **ἀγάπη agapē**, *ag-ah'-pay;* from *25; love,* i.e. *affection* or *benevolence;* spec. (plur.) a *love-feast:*—(feast of) charity ([-ably]), dear, love.

27. **ἀγαπητός agapētŏs**, *ag-ap-ay-tos';* from *25; beloved:*—(dearly, well) beloved, dear.

28. **Ἄγαρ Agar**, *ag'-ar;* of Heb. or. [1904]; *Hagar,* the concubine of Abraham:—Hagar.

29. **ἀγγαρεύω aggarĕuō**, *ang-ar-yew'-o;* of for. or. [comp. 104]; prop. to *be a courier,* i.e., (by impl.) to *press* into public service:—compel (to go).

30. **ἀγγεῖον aggĕiŏn**, *ang-eye'-on;* from *ἄγγος aggŏs* (a pail, perh. as *bent;* comp. the base of *43*); a *receptacle:*—vessel.

31. **ἀγγελία aggĕlia**, *ang-el-ee'-ah;* from *32;* an *announcement,* i.e. (by impl.) *precept:*—message.

32. **ἄγγελος aggĕlŏs**, *ang'-el-os;* from **ἀγγέλλω aggĕllō** [prob. der. from *71;* comp. *34*] (to *bring tidings*); a *messenger;* esp. an "*angel*"; by impl. a *pastor:*—angel, messenger.

33. **ἄγε agĕ**, *ag'-eh;* imper. of *71;* prop. *lead,* i.e. *come on:*—go to.

34. **ἀγέλη agĕlē**, *ag-el'-ay;* from *71* [comp. *32*]; a *drove:*—herd.

35. **ἀγενεαλόγητος agĕnĕalŏgētŏs**, *ag-en-eh-al-og'-ay-tos;* from *1* (as neg. particle) and *1075; unregistered* as to birth:—without descent.

36. **ἀγενής agĕnēs**, *ag-en-ace';* from *1* (as neg. particle) and *1085;* prop. *without kin,* i.e. (of unknown descent, and by impl.) *ignoble:*—base things.

37. **ἀγιάζω hagiazō**, *hag-ee-ad'-zo;* from *40;* to *make holy,* i.e. (cer.) *purify* or *consecrate;* (mentally) to *venerate:*—hallow, be holy, sanctify.

38. **ἁγιασμός hagiasmŏs**, *hag-ee-as-mos';* from *37;* prop. *purification,* i.e. (the state) *purity;* concr. (by Hebr.) a *purifier:*—holiness, sanctification.

39. **ἅγιον hagiŏn**, *hag'-ee-on;* neut. of *40;* a sacred thing (i.e. spot):—holiest (of all), holy place, sanctuary.

40. **ἅγιος hagiŏs**, *hag'-ee-os;* from *ἅγος hagŏs* (an *awful* thing) [comp. *53, 2282*]; *sacred* (phys. *pure,* mor. *blameless* or *religious,* cer. *consecrated):*—(most) holy (one, thing), saint.

41. **ἁγιότης hagiŏtēs**, *hag-ee-ot'-ace;* from *40; sanctity* (i.e. prop. the state):—holiness.

42. **ἁγιωσύνη hagiōsunē**, *hag-ee-o-soo'-nay;* from *40; sacredness* (i.e. prop. the quality):—holiness.

43. **ἀγκάλη agkalē**, *ang-kal'-ay;* from *ἄγκος agkŏs* (a bend, "ache"; an arm (as curved):—arm.

44. **ἄγκιστρον agkistrŏn**, *ang'-kis-tron;* from the same as *43;* a *hook* (as *bent*):—hook.

45. **ἄγκυρα agkura**, *ang'-koo-rah;* from the same as *43;* an "*anchor*" (as *crooked*):—anchor.

46. **ἄγναφος agnaphŏs**, *ag'-naf-os;* from *1* (as a neg. particle) and the same as *1102;* prop. *unfulled,* i.e. (by impl.) *new* (cloth):—new.

47. **ἀγνεία hagnĕia**, *hag-ni'-ah;* from *53; cleanliness* (the quality), i.e. (spec.) *chastity:*—purity.

48. **ἁγνίζω hagnizō**, *hag-nid'-zo;* from *53;* to *make clean,* i.e. (fig.) *sanctify* (cer. or mor.):—purify (self).

49. **ἁγνισμός hagnismŏs**, *hag-nis-mos';* from *48;* a *cleansing* (the act), i.e. (cer.) *lustration:*—purification.

50. **ἀγνοέω agnŏĕō**, *ag-no-eh'-o;* from *1* (as a neg. particle) and *3539; not to know* (through lack of information or intelligence); by impl. to *ignore* (through disinclination):—(be) ignorant (-ly), not know, not understand, unknown.

51. **ἀγνόημα agnŏēma**, *ag-no'-ay-mah;* from *50;* a thing *ignored,* i.e. *shortcoming:*—error.

52. **ἄγνοια agnŏia**, *ag'-noy-ah;* from *50; ignorance* (prop. the quality):—ignorance.

53. **ἁγνός hagnŏs**, *hag-nos';* from the same as *40;* prop. *clean,* i.e. (fig.) *innocent, modest, perfect:*—chaste, clean, pure.

54. **ἁγνότης hagnŏtēs**, *hag-not'-ace;* from *53; cleanness* (the state), i.e. (fig.) *blamelessness:*—pureness.

55. **ἁγνῶς hagnōs**, *hag-noce';* adv. from *53; purely,* i.e. *honestly:*—sincerely.

56. **ἀγνωσία agnōsia**, *ag-no-see'-ah;* from *1* (as neg. particle) and *1108; ignorance* (prop. the state):—ignorance, not the knowledge.

57. **ἄγνωστος agnōstŏs**, *ag'-noce-tos;* from *1* (as neg. particle) and *1110; unknown:*—unknown.

58. **ἀγορά agŏra**, *ag-or-ah';* from **ἀγείρω agĕirō** (to *gather;* prob. akin to *1453*); prop. the *town-square* (as a place of public resort); by impl. a *market* or *thoroughfare:*—market (-place), street.

59. **ἀγοράζω agŏrazō**, *ag-or-ad'-zo;* from *58;* prop. *to go to market,* i.e. (by impl.) to *purchase;* spec. to *redeem:*—buy, redeem.

60. **ἀγοραῖος agŏraiŏs**, *ag-or-ah'-yos;* from *58; relating to the market-place,* i.e. *forensic* (times); by impl. *vulgar:*—baser sort, low.

61. **ἄγρα agra**, *ag'-rah;* from *71;* (abstr.) a *catching* (of fish); also (concr.) a *haul* (of fish):—draught.

62. **ἀγράμματος agrammatŏs**, *ag-ram-mat-os;* from *1* (as neg. particle) and *1121; unlettered,* i.e. *illiterate:*—unlearned.

63. **ἀγραυλέω agraulĕō**, *ag-row-leh'-o;* from *68* and *832* (in the sense of *833*); to *camp out:*—abide in the field.

64. **ἀγρεύω agrĕuō**, *ag-rew'-o;* from *61;* to *hunt,* i.e. (fig.) to *entrap:*—catch.

65. **ἀγριέλαιος agriĕlaiŏs**, *ag-ree-el'-ah-yos;* from *66* and *1636;* an *oleaster:*—olive tree (which is) wild.

66. **ἄγριος agriŏs**, *ag'-ree-os;* from *68; wild* (as pertaining to the *country*), lit. (*natural*) or fig. (*fierce*):—wild, raging.

67. **Ἀγρίππας Agrippas**, *ag-rip'-pas;* appar. from *66* and *2462; wild-horse tamer; Agrippas,* one of the Herods:—Agrippa.

68. **ἀγρός agrŏs**, *ag-ros';* from *71;* a *field* (as a *drive* for cattle); gen. the *country;* spec. a *farm,* i.e. *hamlet:*—country, farm, piece of ground, land.

69. **ἀγρυπνέω agrupnĕō**, *ag-roop-neh'-o;* ultimately from *1* (as neg. particle) and *5258;* to be *sleepless,* i.e. *keep awake:*—watch.

70. **ἀγρυπνία agrupnia**, *ag-roop-nee'-ah;* from *69; sleeplessness,* i.e. a *keeping awake:*—watch.

71. **ἄγω agō**, *ag'-o;* a prim. verb; prop. to *lead;* by impl. to *bring, drive,* (reflex.) *go,* (spec.) *pass* (time), or (fig.) *induce:*—be, bring (forth), carry, (let) go, keep, lead away, be open.

72. **ἀγωγή agōgē**, *ag-o-gay';* redupl. from *71;* a *bringing up,* i.e. *mode of living:*—manner of life.

73. ἀγών **agōn,** *ag-one'*; from *71*; prop. a place of assembly (as if *led*), i.e. (by impl.) a *contest* (held there); fig. an *effort* or *anxiety*:—conflict, contention, fight, race.

74. ἀγωνία **agōnia,** *ag-o-nee'-ah*; from *73*; a *struggle* (prop. the state), i.e. (fig.) *anguish*:—agony.

75. ἀγωνίζομαι **agōnizŏmai,** *ag-o-nid'-zom-ahee*; from *73*; to struggle, lit. (to *compete* for a prize), fig. (to *contend* with an adversary), or gen. (to *endeavor* to accomplish something):—fight, labor fervently, strive.

76. Ἀδάμ **Adam,** *ad-am'*; of Heb. or. [121]; *Adam*, the first man; typ. (of Jesus) *man* (as his representative):—Adam.

77. ἀδάπανος **adapanŏs,** *ad-ap'-an-os*; from *1* (as neg. particle) and *1160*; *costless*, i.e. *gra'uitous*:—without expense.

78. Ἀδδί **Addi,** *ad-dee'*; prob. of Heb. or. [comp. 5716]; *Addi*, an Isr.:—Addi.

79. ἀδελφή **adelphē,** *ad-el-fay'*; fem. of *80*; a *sister* (nat. or eccles.):—sister.

80. ἀδελφός **adelphŏs,** *ad-el-fos'*; from *1* (as a connective particle) and δελφύς **delphus** (the *womb*); a *brother* (lit. or fig.) near or remote [much like 1]:—brother.

81. ἀδελφότης **adelphŏtēs,** *ad-el-fot'-ace*; from *80*; *brotherhood* (prop. the feeling of *brotherliness*), i.e. the (Christian) *fraternity*:—brethren, brotherhood.

82. ἄδηλος **adēlŏs,** *ad'-ay-los*; from *1* (as a neg. particle) and *1212*; *hidden*, fig. *indistinct*:—appear not, uncertain.

83. ἀδηλότης **adēlŏtēs,** *ad-ay-lot'-ace*; from *82*; *uncertainty*:— × uncertain.

84. ἀδήλως **adēlōs,** *ad-ay'-loce*; adv. from *82*; *uncertainly*:—uncertainly.

85. ἀδημονέω **adēmŏnĕō,** *ad-ay-mon-eh'-o*; from a der. of ἀδέω **adĕō,** (to be *sated* to loathing); to *be in distress* (of mind):—be full of heaviness, be very heavy.

86. ᾅδης **haidēs,** *hah'-dace*; from *1* (as a neg. particle) and *1492*; prop. *unseen*, i.e. "*Hades*" or the place (state) of departed souls:—grave, hell.

87. ἀδιάκριτος **adiakritŏs,** *ad-ee-ak'-ree-tos*; from *1* (as a neg. particle) and a der. of *1252*; prop. *undistinguished*, i.e. (act.) *impartial*:—without partiality.

88. ἀδιάλειπτος **adialĕiptŏs,** *ad-ee-al'-ipe-tos*; from *1* (as a neg. particle) and a der. of a compound of *1223* and *3007*; *unintermitted*, i.e. *permanent*:—without ceasing, continual.

89. ἀδιαλείπτως **adialĕiptōs,** *ad-ee-al-ipe'-toce*; adv. from *88*; *uninterruptedly*, i.e. *without omission* (on an appropriate occasion):—without ceasing.

90. ἀδιαφθορία **adiaphthŏria,** *ad-ee-af-thor-ee'-ah*; from a der. of a compound of *1* (as a neg. particle) and a der. of *1311*; *incorruptibleness*, i.e. (fig.) *purity* (of doctrine):—uncorruptness.

91. ἀδικέω **adikĕō,** *ad-ee-keh'-o*; from *94*; to be *unjust*, i.e. (act.) *do wrong* (mor., socially or phys.):—hurt, injure, be an offender, be unjust, (do, suffer, take) wrong.

92. ἀδίκημα **adikēma,** *ad-eek'-ay-mah*; from *91*; a *wrong done*:—evil doing, iniquity, matter of wrong.

93. ἀδικία **adikia,** *ad-ee-kee'-ah*; from *94*; (legal) *injustice* (prop. the quality, by impl. the act); mor. *wrongfulness* (of character, life or act):—iniquity, unjust, unrighteousness, wrong.

94. ἄδικος **adikŏs,** *ad'-ee-kos*; from *1* (as a neg. particle) and *1349*; *unjust*; by extens. *wicked*; by impl. *treacherous*; spec. *heathen*:—unjust, unrighteous.

95. ἀδίκως **adikōs,** *ad-ee'-koce*; adv. from *94*; *unjustly*:—wrongfully.

96. ἀδόκιμος **adŏkimŏs,** *ad-ok'-ee-mos*; from *1* (as a neg. particle) and *1384*; *unapproved*, i.e. *rejected*; by impl. *worthless* (lit. or mor.):—castaway, rejected, reprobate.

97. ἄδολος **adŏlŏs,** *ad'-ol-os*; from *1* (as a neg. particle) and *1388*; *undeceitful*, i.e. (fig.) *unadulterated*:—sincere.

98. Ἀδραμυττηνός **Adramuttēnŏs,** *ad-ram-oot-tay-nos'*; from Ἀδραμύττειον **Adramuttĕiŏn** (a place in Asia Minor); *Adramyttene* or belonging to Adramyttium:—of Adramyttium.

99. Ἀδρίας **Adrias,** *ad-ree'-as*; from Ἀδρία **Adria** (a place near its shore); the *Adriatic* sea (including the Ionian):—Adria.

100. ἁδρότης **hadrŏtēs,** *had-rot'-ace*; from ἁδρός **hadrŏs** (*stout*); *plumpness*, i.e. (fig.) *liberality*:—abundance.

101. ἀδυνατέω **adunatĕō,** *ad-oo-nat-eh'-o*; from *102*; to be *unable*, i.e. (pass.) *impossible*:—be impossible.

102. ἀδύνατος **adunatŏs,** *ad-oo'-nat-os*; from *1* (as a neg. particle) and *1415*; *unable*, i.e. *weak* (lit. or fig.); pass. *impossible*:—could not do, impossible, impotent, not possible, weak.

103. ᾄδω **a̧dō,** *ad'-o*; a prim. verb; to *sing*:—sing.

104. ἀεί **aĕi,** *ah-eye'*; from an obs. prim. noun (appar. mean. *continued duration*); "*ever*;" by qualification *regularly*; by impl. *earnestly*:—always, ever.

105. ἀετός **aĕtŏs,** *ah-et-os'*; from the same as *109*; an *eagle* (from its *wind*-like flight):—eagle.

106. ἄζυμος **azumŏs,** *ad'-zoo-mos*; from *1* (as a neg. particle) and *2219*; *unleavened*, i.e. (fig.) *uncorrupted*; (in the neut. plur.) spec. (by impl.) the *Passover week*:—unleavened (bread).

107. Ἀζώρ **Azōr,** *ad-zore'*; of Heb. or. [comp. 5809]; *Azor*, an Isr.:—Azor.

108. Ἄζωτος **Azōtŏs,** *ad'-zo-tos*; of Heb. or. [795]; *Azotus* (i.e. Ashdod), a place in Pal.:—Azotus.

109. ἀήρ **aēr,** *ah-ayr'*; from ἄημι **aēmi** (to *breathe* unconsciously, i.e. *respire*; by anal. to *blow*); "*air*" (as naturally *circumambient*):—air. Comp. *5594*.

ἀθά atha. See *3134*.

110. ἀθανασία **athanasia,** *ath-an-as-ee'-ah*; from a compound of *1* (as a neg. particle) and *2288*; *deathlessness*:—immortality.

111. ἀθέμιτος **athĕmitŏs,** *ath-em'-ee-tos*; from *1* (as a neg. particle) and a der. of θέμις **thĕmis** (*statute*; from the base of *5087*); *illegal*; by impl. *flagitious*:—abominable, unlawful thing.

112. ἄθεος **athĕŏs,** *ath'-eh-os*; from *1* (as a neg. particle) and *2316*; *godless*:—without God.

113. ἄθεσμος **athĕsmŏs,** *ath'-es-mos*; from *1* (as a neg. particle) and a der. of *5087* (in the sense of *enacting*); *lawless*, i.e. (by impl.) *criminal*:—wicked.

114. ἀθετέω **athĕtĕō,** *ath-et-eh'-o*; from a compound of *1* (as a neg. particle) and a der. of *5087*; to *set aside*, i.e. (by impl.) to *disesteem*, *neutralize* or *violate*:—cast off, despise, disannul, frustrate, bring to nought, reject.

115. ἀθέτησις **athĕtēsis,** *ath-et'-ay-sis*; from *114*; *cancellation* (lit. or fig.):—disannulling, put away.

116. Ἀθῆναι **Athēnai,** *ath-ay'-nahee*; plur. of Ἀθήνη **Athēnē** (the goddess of wisdom, who was reputed to have founded the city); *Athenæ*, the capital of Greece:—Athens.

117. Ἀθηναῖος **Athēnaiŏs,** *ath-ay-nah'-yos*; from *116*; an *Athenæan* or inhab. of Athenæ:—Athenian.

118. ἀθλέω **athlĕō,** *ath-leh'-o*; from ἆθλος **athlŏs** (a *contest* in the public lists); to *contend* in the competitive games:—strive.

119. ἄθλησις **athlēsis,** *ath'-lay-sis*; from *118*; a *struggle* (fig.):—fight.

120. ἀθυμέω **athumĕō,** *ath-oo-meh'-o*; from a comp. of *1* (as a neg. particle) and *2372*; to be *spiritless*, i.e. *disheartened*:—be dismayed.

121. ἄθωος **athōŏs,** *ath'-o-os*; from *1* (as a neg. particle) and a prob. der. of *5087* (mean. a *penalty*); *not guilty*:—innocent.

122. αἴγειος **aigĕiŏs,** *ah'ee-ghi-os*; from αἴξ **aix** (a *goat*); belonging to a *goat*:—goat.

123. αἰγιαλός **aigialŏs,** *ahee-ghee-al-os'*; from ἄϊσσω **aissō** (to *rush*) and *251* (in the sense of the *sea*); a *beach* (on which the *waves* dash):—shore.

124. Αἰγύπτιος **Aiguptiŏs,** *ahee-goop'-tee-os*; from *125*; an *Ægyptian* or inhab. of Ægyptus:—Egyptian.

125. Αἴγυπτος **Aiguptŏs,** *ah'ee-goop-tos*; of uncert. der.; *Ægyptus*, the land of the Nile:—Egypt.

126. ἀΐδιος **aïdiŏs,** *ah-id'-ee-os*; from *104*; *ever-during* (forward and backward, or forward only):—eternal, everlasting.

127. αἰδώς **aidōs,** *ahee-doce'*; perh. from *1* (as a neg. particle) and *1492* (through the idea of *downcast eyes*); *bashfulness*, i.e. (towards men), *modesty* or (towards God) *awe*:—reverence, shamefacedness.

128. Αἰθίοψ **Aithiŏps,** *ahee-thee'-ops*; from αἴθω **aithō** (to *scorch*) and ὤψ **ōps** (the *face*, from *3700*); an *Æthiopian* (as a *blackamoor*):—Ethiopian.

129. αἷμα **haima,** *hah'ee-mah*; of uncert. der.; *blood*, lit. (of men or animals), fig. (the *juice* of grapes) or spec. (the atoning *blood* of Christ); by impl. *bloodshed*, also *kindred*:—blood.

130. αἱματεκχυσία **haimatĕkchusia,** *hahee-mat-ek-khoo-see'-ah*; from *129* and a der. of *1632*; an *effusion of blood*:—shedding of blood.

131. αἱμορρέω **haimŏrrhĕō,** *hahee-mor-hreh'-o*; from *129* and *4482*; to *flow blood*, i.e. *have a hæmorrhage*:—diseased with an issue of blood.

132. Αἰνέας **Ainĕas,** *ahee-neh'-as*; of uncert. der.; *Æneas*, an Isr.:—Æneas.

133. αἴνεσις **ainĕsis,** *ah'ee-nes-is*; from *134*; a *praising* (the act), i.e. (spec.) a *thank* (-offering):—praise.

134. αἰνέω **ainĕō,** *ahee-neh'-o*; from *136*; to *praise* (God):—praise.

135. αἴνιγμα **ainigma,** *ah'ee-nig-ma*; from a der. of *136* (in its prim. sense); an *obscure saying* ("*enigma*"), i.e. (abstr.) *obscureness*:— × darkly.

136. αἶνος **ainŏs,** *ah'ee-nos*; appar. a prim. word; prop. a *story*, but used in the sense of *1868*; *praise* (of God):—praise.

137. Αἰνών **Ainōn,** *ahee-nohn'*; of Hebr. or. [a der. of 5869, *place of springs*]; *Ænon*, a place in Pal.:—Ænon.

138. αἱρέομαι **hairĕŏmai,** *hahee-reh'-om-ahee*; prob. akin to *142*; to *take for oneself*, i.e. to *prefer*:—choose. Some of the forms are borrowed from a cognate ἕλλομαι **hĕllŏmai,** *hel'-lom-ahee*; which is otherwise obsolete.

139. αἵρεσις **hairĕsis,** *hah'ee-res-is*; from *138*; prop. a *choice*, i.e. (spec.) a *party* or (abstr.) *disunion*:—heresy [*which is the Gr. word itself*], sect.

140. αἱρετίζω **hairĕtizō,** *hahee-ret-id'-zo*; from a der. of *138*; to *make a choice*:—choose.

141. αἱρετικός **hairĕtikŏs,** *hahee-ret-ee-kos'*; from the same as *140*; a *schismatic*:—heretic [*the Gr. word itself*].

142. αἴρω **airō,** *ah'ee-ro*; a prim. verb; to *lift*; by impl. to *take up* or *away*; fig. to *raise* (the voice), *keep in suspense* (the mind); spec. to *sail away* (i.e. *weigh anchor*); by Heb. [comp. 5375] to *expiate* sin:—away with, bear (up), carry, lift up, loose, make to doubt, put away, remove, take (away, up).

143. αἰσθάνομαι **aisthanŏmai,** *ahee-sthan'-om-ahee*; of uncert. der.; to *apprehend* (prop. by the senses):—perceive.

144. αἴσθησις **aisthēsis,** *ah'ee-sthay-sis*; from *143*; *perception*, i.e. (fig.) *discernment*:—judgment.

145. αἰσθητήριον **aisthētēriŏn,** *ahee-sthay-tay'-ree-on*; from a der. of *143*; prop. an *organ of perception*, i.e. (fig.) *judgment*:—senses.

146. αἰσχροκερδής **aischrŏkĕrdēs,** *ahee-skhrok-er-dace'*; from *150* and κέρδος **kĕrdos** (*gain*); *sordid*:—given to (greedy of) filthy lucre.

147. αἰσχροκερδῶς **aischrŏkĕrdōs,** *ahee-skhrok-er-doce'*; adv. from *146*; *sordidly*:—for filthy lucre's sake.

148. αἰσχρολογία **aischrŏlŏgia,** *ahee-skhrol-og-ee'-ah*; from *150* and *3056*; *vile conversation*:—filthy communication.

149. αἰσχρόν **aischrŏn,** *ahee-skhron'*; neut. of *150*; a *shameful thing*, i.e. *indecorum*:—shame.

150. **αἰσχρός aischrŏs**, *ahee-skhros'*; from the same as *153*; *shameful*, i.e. *base* (spec. *venal*):—filthy.

151. **αἰσχρότης aischrŏtēs**, *ahee-skhrot'-ace*; from *150*; *shamefulness*, i.e. *obscenity*:—filthiness.

152. **αἰσχύνη aischunē**, *ahee-skhoo'-nay*; from *153*; *shame* or *disgrace* (abstr. or concr.):—dishonesty, shame.

153. **αἰσχύνομαι aischunŏmai**, *ahee-skhoo'-nom-ahee*; from **αἶσχος aischŏs** (*disfigurement*, i.e. *disgrace*); to *feel shame* (for oneself):—be ashamed.

154. **αἰτέω aitĕō**, *ahee-teh'-o*; of uncert. der.; to *ask* (in gen.):—ask, beg, call for, crave, desire, require. Comp. *4441*.

155. **αἴτημα aitēma**, *ah'ee-tay-mah*; from *154*; a *thing asked* or (abstr.) an *asking*:—petition, request, required.

156. **αἰτία aitia**, *ahee-tee'-a*; from the same as *154*; a *cause* (as if *asked* for), i.e. (logical) *reason* (motive, matter), (legal) *crime* (alleged or proved):—accusation, case, cause, crime, fault, [wh-]ere [-fore].

157. **αἰτίαμα aitiama**, *ahee-tee'-am-ah*; from a der. of *156*; a *thing charged*:—complaint.

158. **αἴτιον aitiŏn**, *ah'ee-tee-on*; neut. of *159*; a *reason* or *crime* [like *156*]:—cause, fault.

159. **αἴτιος aitiŏs**, *ah'ee-tee-os*; from the same as *154*; causative, i.e. (concr.) a *causer*:—author.

160. **αἰφνίδιος aiphnidiŏs**, *aheef-nid'-ee-os*; from a comp. of *1* (as a neg. particle) and *5316* [comp. *1810*] (mean. *non-apparent*); *unexpected*, i.e. (adv.) *suddenly*:—sudden, unawares.

161. **αἰχμαλωσία aichmalŏsia**, *aheekh-mal-o-see'-ah*; from *164*; *captivity*:—captivity.

162. **αἰχμαλωτεύω aichmalŏtĕuō**, *aheekh-mal-o-tew'-o*; from *164*; to *capture* [like *163*]:—lead captive.

163. **αἰχμαλωτίζω aichmalŏtizō**, *aheekh-mal-o-tid'-zo*; from *164*; to *make captive*:—lead away captive, bring into captivity.

164. **αἰχμαλωτός aichmalŏtŏs**, *aheekh-mal-o-tos'*; from **αἰχμή aichmē** (a *spear*) and a der. of the same as *259*; prop. a *prisoner of war*, i.e. (gen.) a *captive*:—captive.

165. **αἰών aiōn**, *ah-ee-ohn'*; from the same as *104*; prop. an *age*; by extens. *perpetuity* (also past); by impl. the *world*; spec. (Jewish) a Messianic period (present or future):—age, course, eternal, (for) ever (-more), [n-]ever, (beginning of the, while the) world (began, without end). Comp. *5550*.

166. **αἰώνιος aiōniŏs**, *ahee-o'-nee-os*; from *165*; *perpetual* (also used of past time, or past and future as well):—eternal, for ever, everlasting, world (began).

167. **ἀκαθαρσία akatharsia**, *ak-ath-ar-see'-ah*; from *169*; *impurity* (the quality), phys. or mor.:—uncleanness.

168. **ἀκαθάρτης akathartēs**, *ak-ath-ar'-tace*; from *169*; *impurity* (the state), mor.:—filthiness.

169. **ἀκάθαρτος akathartŏs**, *ak-ath'-ar-tos*; from *1* (as a neg. particle) and a presumed der. of *2508* (mean. *cleansed*); *impure* (cer., mor. *lewd*) or spec. [*dæmonic*]):—foul, unclean.

170. **ἀκαιρέομαι akairĕŏmai**, *ak-ahee-reh'-om-ahee*; from a comp. of *1* (as a neg. particle) and *2540* (mean. *unseasonable*); to *be inopportune* (for oneself), i.e. to *fail* of a *proper occasion*:—lack opportunity.

171. **ἀκαίρως akairŏs**, *ak-ah'ee-roce*; adv. from the same as *170*; *inopportunely*:—out of season.

172. **ἄκακος akakŏs**, *ak'-ak-os*; from *1* (as a neg. particle) and *2556*; *not bad*, i.e. (obj.) *innocent* or (subj.) *unsuspecting*:—harmless, simple.

173. **ἄκανθα akantha**, *ak'-an-thah*; prob. from the same as *188*; a *thorn*:—thorn.

174. **ἀκάνθινος akanthinŏs**, *ak-an'-thee-nos*; from *173*; *thorny*:—of thorns.

175. **ἄκαρπος akarpŏs**, *ak'-ar-pos*; from *1* (as a neg. particle) and *2590*; *barren* (lit. or fig.):—without fruit, unfruitful.

176. **ἀκατάγνωστος akatagnōstŏs**, *ak-at-ag'-noce-tos*; from *1* (as a neg. particle) and a der. of *2607*; *unblamable*:—that cannot be condemned.

177. **ἀκατακάλυπτος akatakaluptŏs**, *ak-at-ak-al'-oop-tos*; from *1* (as a neg. particle) and a der. of a comp. of *2596* and *2572*; *unveiled*:—uncovered.

178. **ἀκατάκριτος akatakritŏs**, *ak-at-ak'-ree-tos*; from *1* (as a neg. particle) and a der. of *2632*; *without* (legal) *trial*:—uncondemned.

179. **ἀκατάλυτος akatalutŏs**, *ak-at-al'-oo-tos*; from *1* (as a neg. particle) and a der. of *2647*; *indissoluble*, i.e. (fig.) *permanent*:—endless.

180. **ἀκατάπαυστος akatapaustŏs**, *ak-at-ap'-ŏw-stos*; from *1* (as a neg. particle) and a der. of *2664*; *unrefraining*:—that cannot cease.

181. **ἀκαταστασία akatastasia**, *ak-at-as-tah-see'-ah*; from *182*; *instability*, i.e. *disorder*:—commotion, confusion, tumult.

182. **ἀκατάστατος akatastatŏs**, *ak-at-as'-tat-os*; from *1* (as a neg. particle) and a der. of *2525*; *inconstant*:—unstable.

183. **ἀκατάσχετος akataschĕtŏs**, *ak-at-as'-khet-os*; from *1* (as a neg. particle) and a der. of *2722*; *unrestrainable*:—unruly.

184. **Ἀκελδαμά Akeldama**, *ak-el-dam-ah'*; of Chald. or. [mean. *field of blood;* corresp. to *2506* and *1818*]; *Akeldama*, a place near Jerus.:—Aceldama.

185. **ἀκέραιος akĕraiŏs**, *ak-er'-ah-yos*; from *1* (as a neg. particle) and a presumed der. of *2767*; *unmixed*, i.e. (fig.) *innocent*:—harmless, s¹mple.

186. **ἀκλινής aklinēs**, *ak-lee-nace'*; from *1* (as a neg. particle) and *2827*; *not leaning*, i.e. (fig.) *firm*:—without wavering.

187. **ἀκμάζω akmazō**, *ak-mad'-zo*; from the same as *188*; to *make a point*, i.e. (fig.) *mature*:—be fully ripe.

188. **ἀκμήν akmēn**, *ak-mane'*; accus. of a noun ("*acme*") akin to **ἀκή akē** (a *point*) and mean. the same; adv. *just now*, i.e. *still*:—yet.

189. **ἀκοή akŏē**, *ak-ŏ-ay'*; from *191*; *hearing* (the act, the sense or the thing heard):—audience, ear, fame, which ye heard, hearing, preached, report, rumor.

190. **ἀκολουθέω akŏlŏuthĕō**, *ak-ol-oo-theh'-o*; from *1* (as a particle of union) and **κέλευθος kĕlĕuthŏs** (a *road*); prop. to *be in the same way with*, i.e. to *accompany* (spec. as a disciple):—follow, reach.

191. **ἀκούω akŏuō**, *ak-oo'-o*; a prim. verb; to *hear* (in various senses):—give (in the) audience (of), come (to the ears), ([shall]) hear (-er, -ken), be noised, be reported, understand.

192. **ἀκρασία akrasia**, *ak-ras-ee'-a*; from *193*; *want of self-restraint*:—excess, incontinency.

193. **ἀκρατής akratēs**, *ak-rat'-ace*; from *1* (as a neg. particle) and *2904*; *powerless*, i.e. *without self-control*:—incontinent.

194. **ἄκρατος akratŏs**, *ak'-rat-os*; from *1* (as a neg. particle) and a presumed der. of *2767*; *undiluted*:—without mixture.

195. **ἀκρίβεια akribĕia**, *ak-ree'-bi-ah*; from the same as *196*; *exactness*:—perfect manner.

196. **ἀκριβέστατος akribĕstatŏs**, *ak-ree-bes'-ta-tos*; superlative of **ἀκριβής akribēs** (a der. of the same as *206*); *most exact*:—most straitest.

197. **ἀκριβέστερον akribĕstĕrŏn**, *ak-ree-bes'-ter-on*; neut. of the comparative of the same as *196*; (adv.) *more exactly*:—more perfect (-ly).

198. **ἀκριβόω akribŏō**, *ak-ree-bŏ'-o*; from the same as *196*; to *be exact*, i.e. *ascertain*:—enquire diligently.

199. **ἀκριβῶς akribōs**, *ak-ree-boce'*; adv. from the same as *196*; *exactly*:—circumspectly, diligently, perfect (-ly).

200. **ἀκρίς akris**, *ak-rece'*; appar. from the same as *206*; a *locust* (as *pointed*, or as *lighting* on the top of vegetation):—locust.

201. **ἀκροατήριον akrŏatēriŏn**, *ak-rŏ-at-ay'-ree-on*; from *202*; an *audience-room*:—place of hearing.

202. **ἀκροατής akrŏatēs**, *ak-rŏ-at-ace'*; from **ἀκροάομαι akrŏaŏmai** (to *listen;* appar. an intens. of *191*); a *hearer* (merely):—hearer.

203. **ἀκροβυστία akrŏbustia**, *ak-rob-oos-tee'-ah*; from *206* and prob. a modified form of **πόσθη pŏsthē** (the *penis* or male sexual organ); the *prepuce;* by impl. an *uncircumcised* (i.e. *gentile*, fig. *unregenerate*) *state* or *person*:—not circumcised, uncircumcised [*with 2192*], uncircumcision.

204. **ἀκρογωνιαῖος akrŏgōniaiŏs**, *ak-rog-o-nee-ah'-yos*; from *206* and *1137*; *belonging to the extreme corner*:—chief corner.

205. **ἀκροθίνιον akrŏthiniŏn**, *ak-roth-in'-ee-on*; from *206* and **θίς this** (a *heap*); prop. (in the plur.) the *top of the heap*, i.e. (by impl.) *best of the booty*:—spoils.

206. **ἄκρον akrŏn**, *ak'-ron*; neut. of an adj. prob. akin to the base of *188*; the *extremity*:—one end . . . other, tip, top, uttermost part.

207. **Ἀκύλας Akulas**, *ak-oo'-las*; prob. for Lat. *aquila* (an *eagle*); *Akulas*, an Isr.:—Aquila.

208. **ἀκυρόω akurŏō**, *ak-oo-rŏ'-o*; from *1* (as a neg. particle) and *2964*; to *invalidate*:—disannul, make of none effect.

209. **ἀκωλύτως akōlutōs**, *ak-o-loo'-toce*; adv. from a compound of *1* (as a neg. particle) and a der. of *2967*; in an *unhindered manner*, i.e. *freely*:—no man forbidding him.

210. **ἄκων akōn**, *ak'-ohn*; from *1* (as a neg. particle) and *1635*; *unwilling*:—against the will.

211. **ἀλάβαστρον alabastrŏn**, *al-ab'-as-tron*; neut. of **ἀλάβαστρος alabastrŏs** (of uncert. der.), the name of a stone; prop. an "*alabaster*" box, i.e. (by extens.) a perfume *vase* (of any material):—(alabaster) box.

212. **ἀλαζονεία alazŏnĕia**, *al-ad-zon-i'-a*; from *213*; *braggadocio*, i.e. (by impl.) *self-confidence*:—boasting, pride.

213. **ἀλαζών alazōn**, *al-ad-zone'*; from **ἄλη alē** (*vagrancy*); *braggart*:—boaster.

214. **ἀλαλάζω alalazō**, *al-al-ad'-zo*; from **ἀλαλή alalē** (a *shout*, "*halloo*"); to *vociferate*, i.e. (by impl.) to *wail;* fig. to *clang*:—tinkle, wail.

215. **ἀλάλητος alalētŏs**, *al-al'-ay-tos*; from *1* (as a neg. particle) and a der. of *2980*; *unspeakable*:—unutterable, which cannot be uttered.

216. **ἄλαλος al'-al-os**; from *1* (as a neg. particle) and *2980*; *mute*:—dumb.

217. **ἅλας halas**, *hal'-as*; from *251*; *salt;* fig. *prudence*:—salt.

218. **ἀλείφω alĕiphō**, *al-i'-fo*; from *1* (as particle of union) and the base of *3045*; to *oil* (with perfume):—anoint.

219. **ἀλεκτοροφωνία alektŏrŏphōnia**, *al-ek-tor-of-o-nee'-ah*; from *220* and *5456*; *cock-crow*, i.e. the third night-watch:—cockcrowing.

220. **ἀλέκτωρ alēktōr**, *al-ek'-tore*; from **ἀλέκω** (to *ward off*); a cock or male fowl:—cock.

221. **Ἀλεξανδρεύς Alĕxandrĕus**, *al-ex-and-reuce'*; from **Ἀλεξάνδρεια** (the city so called); an *Alexandreian* or inhab. of Alexandria:—of Alexandria, Alexandrian.

222. **Ἀλεξανδρῖνος Alĕxandrinŏs**, *al-ex-andree'-nos*; from the same as *221*; *Alexandrine*, or belonging to Alexandria:—of Alexandria.

223. **Ἀλέξανδρος Alĕxandrŏs**, *al-ex'-and-ros*; from the same as (the first part of) *220* and *435*; *man-defender; Alexander*, the name of three Isr. and one other man:—Alexander.

224. **ἄλευρον alĕurŏn**, *al'-yoo-ron*; from **ἀλέω alĕō** (to *grind*); *flour*:—meal.

225. **ἀλήθεια alēthĕia**, *al-ay'-thi-a*; from *227*; *truth:*—true, X truly, truth, verity.

226. **ἀληθεύω alēthĕuō**, *al-ayth-yoo'-o*; from *227*; to *be true* (in doctrine and profession):—speak (tell) the truth.

227. **ἀληθής alēthēs**, *al-ay-thace'*; from *1* (as a neg. particle) and *2990*; *true* (as not *concealing*):—true, truly, truth.

228. ἀληθινός **alēthĭnŏs**, *al-ay-thee-nos'*; from *227; truthful:*—true.

229. ἀλήθω **alēthō**, *al-ay'-tho*; from the same as *224;* to *grind:*—grind.

230. ἀληθῶς **alēthōs**, *al-ay-thoce';* adv. from *227; truly:*—indeed, surely, of a surety, truly, of a (in) truth, verily, very

231. ἁλιεύς **haliĕus**, *hal-ee-yoos';* from *251;* a *sailor* (as engaged on the *salt* water), i.e. (by impl.) a *fisher:*—fisher (-man).

232. ἁλιεύω **haliĕuō**, *hal-ee-yoo'-o;* from *231;* to *be a fisher,* i.e. (by impl.) to *fish:*—go a-fishing.

233. ἁλίζω **halizō**, *hal-id'-zo;* from *251;* to *salt:*—salt.

234. ἀλίσγεμα **alisgĕma**, *al-is'-ghem-ah;* from ἀλισγέω **alisgĕō** (to *soil*); (cer.) *defilement:*—pollution.

235. ἀλλά **alla**, *al-lah';* neut. plur. of *243;* prop. *other things,* i.e. (adv.) *contrariwise* (in many relations):—and, but (even), howbeit, indeed, nay, nevertheless, no, notwithstanding, save, therefore, yea, yet.

236. ἀλλάσσω **allassō**, *al-las'-so;* from *243;* to *make different:*—change.

237. ἀλλαχόθεν **allachŏthĕn**, *al-lakh-oth'-en;* from *243; from elsewhere:*—some other way.

238. ἀλληγορέω **allēgŏrĕō**, *al-lay-gor-eh'-o;* from *243* and ἀγορέω **agŏrĕō** (to *harangue* [comp. *58*]); to *allegorize:*—be an allegory [*the Gr. word itself*].

239. ἀλληλουϊά **allēlŏuïa**, *al-lay-loo'-ee-ah;* of Heb. or. [imper. of 1984 and 3050]; *praise ye Jah!,* an adoring exclamation:—alleluia.

240. ἀλλήλων **allēlōn**, *al-lay'-lone;* Gen. plur. from *243* redupl.; *one another:*—each other, mutual, one another, (the other), (them-, your-) selves, (selves) together [*sometimes with 3326 or 4314*].

241. ἀλλογενής **allŏgĕnēs**, *al-log-en-ace';* from *243* and *1085; foreign,* i.e. not a Jew:—stranger.

242. ἅλλομαι **hallŏmai**, *hal'-lom-ahee;* mid. of appar. a prim. verb; to *jump;* fig. to *gush:*—leap, spring up.

243. ἄλλος **allŏs**, *al'-los;* a prim. word; "*else*," i.e. *different* (in many applications):—more, one (another), (an-, some an-) other (-s, -wise).

244. ἀλλοτριεπίσκοπος **allotriĕpiskŏpŏs**, *al-lot-ree-ep-is'-kop-os;* from *245* and *1985; overseeing others'* affairs, i.e. a *meddler* (spec. in Gentiles customs):—busybody in other men's matters.

245. ἀλλότριος **allŏtriŏs**, *al-lot'-ree-os;* from *243; another's,* i.e. not one's own; by extens. *foreign, not akin, hostile:*—alien, (an-) other (man's, men's), strange (-r).

246. ἀλλόφυλος **allŏphulŏs**, *al-lof-oo-los;* from *243* and *5443; foreign,* i.e. (spec.) *Gentile:*—one of another nation.

247. ἄλλως **allōs**, *al'-loce;* adv. from *243; differently:*—otherwise.

248. ἀλοάω **alŏaō**, *al-o-ah'-o;* from the same as *257;* to *tread out grain:*—thresh, tread out the corn.

249. ἄλογος **alŏgŏs**, *al'-og-os;* from *1* (as a neg. particle) and *3056; irrational:*—brute, unreasonable.

250. ἀλόη **alŏē**, *al-ŏ-ay';* of for. or. [comp. 174]; *aloes* (the gum):—aloes.

251. ἅλς **hals**, *halce;* a prim. word; "*salt*":—salt.

252. ἁλυκός **halukŏs**, *hal-oo-kos';* from *251; briny:*—salt.

253. ἀλυπότερος **alupŏtĕrŏs**, *al-oo-pot'-er-os;* compar. of a comp. of *1* (as a neg. particle) and *3077; more without grief:*—less sorrowful.

254. ἅλυσις **halusis**, *hal'-oo-sis;* of uncert. der.; a *fetter* or *manacle:*—bonds, chain.

255. ἀλυσιτελής **alusitĕlēs**, *al-oo-sit-el-ace';* from *1* (as a neg. particle) and the base of *3081; gainless,* i.e. (by impl.) *pernicious:*—unprofitable.

256. Ἀλφαῖος **Alphaiŏs**, *al-fah'-yos;* of Heb. or. [comp. 2501]; *Alphœus,* an Isr.:—Alpheus.

257. ἅλων **halōn**, *hal'-ohn;* prob. from the base of *1507;* a threshing-*floor* (as *rolled* hard), i.e. (fig.) the *grain* (and chaff, as just threshed):—floor.

258. ἀλώπηξ **alōpēx**, *al-o'-pakes;* of uncert. der.; a *fox,* i.e. (fig.) a *cunning* person:—fox.

259. ἅλωσις **halōsis**, *hal'-o-sis;* from a collateral form of *138; capture:*—be taken.

260. ἅμα **hama**, *ham'-ah;* a prim. particle; prop. *at the "same" time,* but freely used as a prep. or adv. denoting close association:—also, and, together, with (-al).

261. ἀμαθής **amathēs**, *am-ath-ace';* from *1* (as a neg. particle) and *3129; ignorant:*—unlearned.

262. ἀμαράντινος **amarantinŏs**, *am-ar-an'-tee-nos;* from *263;* "*amaranthine*," i.e. (by impl.) *fadeless:*—that fadeth not away.

263. ἀμάραντος **amarantŏs**, *am-ar'-an-tos;* from *1* (as a neg. particle) and a presumed der. of *3133; unfading,* i.e. (by impl.) *perpetual:*—that fadeth not away.

264. ἁμαρτάνω **hamartanō**, *ham-ar-tan'-o;* perh. from *1* (as a neg. particle) and the base of *3313;* prop. to *miss* the mark (and so *not share* in the prize), i.e. (fig.) to *err,* esp. (mor.) to *sin.*—for your faults, offend, sin, trespass.

265. ἁμάρτημα **hamartēma**, *ham-ar'-tay-mah;* from *264;* a *sin* (prop. concr.):—sin.

266. ἁμαρτία **hamartia**, *ham-ar-tee'-ah;* from *264; sin* (prop. abstr.):—offence, sin (-ful).

267. ἀμάρτυρος **amarturŏs**, *am-ar'-too-ros;* from *1* (as a neg. particle) and a form of *3144; unattested:*—without witness.

268. ἁμαρτωλός **hamartōlŏs**, *ham-ar-to-los';* from *264; sinful,* i.e. a *sinner:*—sinful, sinner.

269. ἄμαχος **amachŏs**, *am'-akh-os;* from *1* (as a neg. particle) and *3163; peaceable:*—not a brawler.

270. ἀμάω **amaō**, *am-ah'-o;* from *260;* prop. to *collect,* i.e. (by impl.) *reap:*—reap down.

271. ἀμέθυστος **amĕthustŏs**, *am-eth'-oos-tos;* from *1* (as a neg. particle) and a der. of *3184;* the "*amethyst*" (supposed to *prevent intoxication*):—amethyst.

272. ἀμελέω **amĕlĕō**, *am-el-eh'-o;* from *1* (as a neg. particle) and *3199;* to *be careless* of:—make light of, neglect, be negligent, not regard.

273. ἄμεμπτος **amĕmptŏs**, *am'-emp-tos;* from *1* (as a neg. particle) and a der. of *3201; irreproachable:*—blameless, faultless, unblamable.

274. ἀμέμπτως **amĕmptōs**, *am-emp'-toce;* adv. from *273; faultlessly:*—blameless, unblamably.

275. ἀμέριμνος **amĕrimnŏs**, *am-er'-im-nos;* from *1* (as a neg. particle) and *3308; not anxious:*—without care (-fulness), secure.

276. ἀμετάθετος **amĕtathĕtŏs**, *am-et-ath'-et-os;* from *1* (as a neg. particle) and a der. of *3346; unchangeable,* or (neut. as abstr.) *unchangeability:*—immutable (-ility).

277. ἀμετακίνητος **amĕtakinētŏs**, *am-et-ak-in'-ay-tos;* from *1* (as a neg. particle) and a der. of *3334; immovable:*—unmovable.

278. ἀμεταμέλητος **amĕtamĕlētŏs**, *am-et-am-el'-ay-tos;* from *1* (as a neg. particle) and a presumed der. of *3338; irrevocable:*—without repentance, not to be repented of.

279. ἀμετανόητος **amĕtanŏētŏs**, *am-et-an-ŏ'-ay-tos;* from *1* (as a neg. particle) and a presumed der. of *3340; unrepentant:*—impenitent.

280. ἄμετρος **amĕtrŏs**, *am'-et-ros;* from *1* (as a neg. particle) and *3358; immoderate:*—(thing) without measure.

281. ἀμήν **amēn**, *am-ane';* of Heb. or. [543]; prop. firm, i.e. (fig.) *trustworthy;* adv. *surely* (often as interj. *so be it*):—amen, verily.

282. ἀμήτωρ **amētōr**, *am-ay'-tore;* from *1* (as a neg. particle) and *3384; motherless,* i.e. *of unknown maternity:*—without mother.

283. ἀμίαντος **amiantŏs**, *am-ee'-an-tos;* from *1* (as a neg. particle) and a der. of *3392; unsoiled,* i.e. (fig.) *pure:*—undefiled.

284. Ἀμιναδάβ **Aminadab**, *am-ee-nad-ab';* of Heb. or. [5992]; *Aminadab,* an Isr.:—Aminadab.

285. ἄμμος **ammŏs**, *am'-mos;* perh. from *260; sand* (as *heaped* on the beach):—sand.

286. ἀμνός **amnŏs**, *am-nos';* appar. a prim. word; a *lamb:*—lamb.

287. ἀμοιβή **amŏibē**, *am-oy-bay';* from ἀμείβω **amĕibō** (to *exchange*); *requital:*—require.

288. ἄμπελος **ampĕlŏs**, *am'-pel-os;* prob. from the base of *207* and that of *257;* a *vine* (as *coiling about* a support):—vine.

289. ἀμπελουργός **ampĕlŏurgŏs**, *am-pel-oor-gos';* from *288* and *2041;* a *vine-worker,* i.e. *pruner:*—vine-dresser.

290. ἀμπελών **ampĕlōn**, *am-pel-ohn';* from *288;* a *vineyard:*—vineyard.

291. Ἀμπλίας **Amplias**, *am-plee'-as;* contr. for Lat. *ampliatus* [*enlarged*]; *Amplias,* a Rom. Chr.:—Amplias.

292. ἀμύνομαι **amunŏmai**, *am-oo'-nom-ahee;* mid. of a prim. verb; to *ward off* (for oneself), i.e. *protect:*—defend.

293. ἀμφίβληστρον **amphiblēstrŏn**, *am-fib'-lace-tron;* from a comp. of the base of *297* and *906;* a (fishing) *net* (as *thrown about* the fish):—net.

294. ἀμφιέννυμι **amphiĕnnumi**, *am-fee-en'-noo-mee;* from the base of *297* and ἕννυμι **hĕnnumi** (to *invest*); to *enrobe:*—clothe.

295. Ἀμφίπολις **Amphipŏlis**, *am-fip'-ol-is;* from the base of *297* and *4172;* a *city surrounded* by a river; *Amphipolis,* a place in Macedonia:—Amphipolis.

296. ἄμφοδον **amphŏdŏn**, *am'-fod-on;* from the base of *297* and *3598;* a *fork* in the road:—where two ways meet.

297. ἀμφότερος **amphŏtĕrŏs**, *am-fot'-er-os;* compar. of ἀμφί **amphi** (*around*); (in plur.) *both:*—both.

298. ἀμώμητος **amōmētŏs**, *am-o'-may-tos;* from *1* (as a neg. particle) and a der. of *3469; unblameable:*—blameless.

299. ἄμωμος **amōmŏs**, *am'-o-mos;* from *1* (as a neg. particle) and *3470; unblemished* (lit. or fig.):—without blame (blemish, fault, spot), faultless, unblameable.

300. Ἀμών **Amōn**, *am-one';* of Heb. or. [526]; *Amon,* an Isr.:—Amon.

301. Ἀμώς **Amōs**, *am-oce';* of Heb. or. [531]; *Amos,* an Isr.:—Amos.

302. ἄν **an**, *an;* a prim. particle, denoting a *supposition, wish, possibility* or *uncertainty*:—[what-, where-, whither-, who-]soever. Usually unexpressed except by the subjunctive or potential mood. Also contr. for *1437.*

303. ἀνά **ana**, *an-ah';* a prim. prep. and adv.; prop. *up;* but (by extens.) used (distributively) *severally,* or (locally) *at* (etc.):—and, apiece, by, each, every (man), in, through. In compounds (as a prefix) it often means (by impl.) *repetition, intensity, reversal,* etc.

304. ἀναβαθμός **anabathmŏs**, *an-ab-ath-mos';* from *305* [comp. *898*]; a *stairway:*—stairs.

305. ἀναβαίνω **anabainō**, *an-ab-ah'-ee-no;* from *303* and the base of *939;* to *go up* (lit. or fig.):—arise, ascend (up), climb (go, grow, rise, spring) up, come (up).

306. ἀναβάλλομαι **anaballŏmai**, *an-ab-al'-lom-ahee;* mid. from *303* and *906;* to *put off* (for oneself):—defer.

307. ἀναβιβάζω **anabibazō**, *an-ab-ee-bad'-zo;* from *303* and a der. of the base of *939;* to *cause to go up,* i.e. *haul* (a net):—draw.

308. ἀναβλέπω **anablĕpō**, *an-ab-lep'-o;* from *303* and *991;* to *look up;* by impl. to *recover* sight:—look (up), see, receive sight.

309. ἀνάβλεψις **anablĕpsis**, *an-ab'-lep-sis;* from *308; restoration* of sight:—recovering of sight.

310. ἀναβοάω **anabŏaō**, *an-ab-o-ah'-o;* from *303* and *994;* to *halloo:*—cry (aloud, out).

311. ἀναβολή **anabŏlē**, *an-ab-ol-ay';* from *906;* a *putting off:*—delay.

312. ἀναγγέλλω **anaggĕllō**, *an-ang-el'-lo;* from *303* and the base of *32;* to *announce* (in detail):—declare, rehearse, report, show, speak, tell.

313. ἀναγεννάω **anagĕnnaō**, *an-ag-en-nah'-o;* from *303* and *1080;* to *beget* or (by extens.) *bear* (again):—beget, (bear) × again.

314. ἀναγινώσκω **anaginōskō**, *an-ag-in-oce'-ko;* from *303* and *1097;* to *know again*, i. e. (by extens.) to *read*:—read.

315. ἀναγκάζω **anagkazō**, *an-ang-kad'-zo;* from *318;* to *necessitate;*—compel, constrain.

316. ἀναγκαῖος **anagkaiŏs**, *an-ang-kah'-yos;* from *318; necessary;* by impl. *close* (of kin):—near, necessary, necessity, needful.

317. ἀναγκαστῶς **anagkastōs**, *an-ang-kas-toce';* adv. from a der. of *315; compulsorily:*—by constraint.

318. ἀναγκή **anagkē**, *an-ang-kay';* from *303* and the base of *43; constraint* (lit. or fig.); by impl. *distress:*—distress, must needs, (of) necessity (-sary), needeth, needful.

319. ἀναγνωρίζομαι **anagnōrizŏmai**, *an-ag-no-rid'-zom-ahee;* mid. from *303* and *1107;* to *make* (oneself) *known:*—be made known.

320. ἀνάγνωσις **anagnōsis**, *an-ag'-no-sis;* from *314;* (the act of) *reading:*—reading.

321. ἀνάγω **anagō**, *an-ag'-o;* from *303* and *71;* to *lead up;* by extens. to *bring out;* spec. to *sail away:*—bring (again, forth, up again), depart, launch (forth), lead (up), loose, offer, sail, set forth, take up.

322. ἀναδείκνυμι **anadĕiknumi**, *an-ad-ike'-noo-mee;* from *303* and *1166;* to *exhibit*, i.e. (by impl.) to *indicate, appoint, shew.

323. ἀνάδειξις **anadĕixis**, *an-ad'-ike-sis;* from *322;* (the act of) *exhibition:*—shewing.

324. ἀναδέχομαι **anadĕchŏmai**, *an-ad-ekh'-om-ahee;* from *303* and *1209;* to *entertain* (as a guest):—receive.

325. ἀναδίδωμι **anadidōmi**, *an-ad-eed'-om-ee;* from *303* and *1325;* to *hand over:*—deliver.

326. ἀναζάω **anazaō**, *an-ad-zah'-o;* from *303* and *2198;* to *recover life* (lit. or fig.):—(be a-) live again, revive.

327. ἀναζητέω **anazētĕō**, *an-ad-zay-teh'-o;* from *303* and *2 12;* to *search out:*—seek.

328. ἀναζώννυμι **anazōnnumi**, *an-ad-zone'-noo-mee;* from *303* and *2224;* to *gird afresh:*—gird up.

329. ἀναζωπυρέω **anazōpurĕō**, *an-ad-zo-poor-eh'-o;* from *303* and a comp. of the base of *2226* and *4442;* to *re-enkindle:*—stir up.

330. ἀναθάλλω **anathallō**, *an-ath-al'-lo;* from *303* and θάλλω **thallō** (to *flourish*); to *revive:*—flourish again.

331. ἀνάθεμα **anathĕma**, *an-ath'-em-ah;* from *394;* a (religious) *ban* or (concr.) *excommunicated* (thing or person) :—accursed, anathema, curse, × great.

332. ἀναθεματίζω **anathĕmatizō**, *an-ath-em-at-id'-zo;* from *331;* to *declare* or *vow under penalty of execration:*—(bind under a) curse, bind with an oath.

333. ἀναθεωρέω **anathĕōrĕō**, *an-ath-eh-o-reh'-o;* from *303* and *2334;* to *look again* (i.e. attentively) at (lit. or fig.):—behold, consider.

334. ἀνάθημα **anathĕma**, *an-ath'-ay-mah;* from *304* [like *331,* but in a good sense]; a *votive offering:*—gift.

335. ἀναίδεια **anaidĕia**, *an-ah'ee-die-ah';* from a comp. of *1* (as a neg. particle [comp. *427*]) and *127; impudence*, i.e. (by impl.) *importunity:*—importunity.

336. ἀναίρεσις **anairĕsis**, *an-ah'ee-res-is;* from *337;* (the act of) *killing:*—death.

337. ἀναιρέω **anairĕō**, *an-ahee-reh'-o;* from *303* and (the act. of) *138;* to *take up;* by impl. to *take away* (violently), i.e. *abolish, murder:*—put to death, kill, slay, take away, take up.

338. ἀναίτιος **anaitiŏs**, *an-ah'ee-tee-os;* from *1* (as a neg. particle) and *159* (in the sense of *156*); *innocent:*—blameless, guiltless.

339. ἀνακαθίζω **anakathizō**, *an-ak-ath-id'-zo;* from *303* and *2523;* prop. to *set up*, i.e. (reflex.) to *sit up:*—sit up.

340. ἀνακαινίζω **anakainizō**, *an-ak-ahee-nid'-zo;* from *303* and a der. of *2537;* to *restore:*—renew.

341. ἀνακαινόω **anakainŏō**, *an-ak-ahee-nŏ'-o;* from *303* and a der. of *2537;* to *renovate:*—renew.

342. ἀνακαίνωσις **anakainōsis**, *an-ak-ah'ee-no-sis;* from *341; renovation:*—renewing.

343. ἀνακαλύπτω **anakaluptō**, *an-ak-al-oop'-to;* from *303* (in the sense of *reversal*) and *2572;* to *unveil:*—open, ([un-]) taken away.

344. ἀνακάμπτω **anakamptō**, *an-ak-amp'-to;* from *303* and *2578;* to *turn back:*—(re-) turn.

345. ἀνακεῖμαι **anakĕimai**, *an-ak-i'-mahee;* from *303* and *2749;* to *recline* (as a corpse or at a meal):—guest, lean, lie, sit (down, at meat), at the table.

346. ἀνακεφαλαίομαι **anakĕphalaiŏmai**, *an-ak-ef-al-ah'ee-om-ahee;* from *303* and *2775* (in its or. sense); to *sum up:*—briefly comprehend, gather together in one.

347. ἀνακλίνω **anaklinō**, *an-ak-lee'-no;* from *303* and *2827;* to *lean back:*—lay, (make) sit down.

348. ἀνακόπτω **anakŏptō**, *an-ak-op'-to;* from *303* and *2875;* to *beat back,* i.e. *check:*—hinder.

349. ἀνακράζω **anakrazō**, *an-ak-rad'-zo;* from *303* and *2896;* to *scream up* (aloud):—cry out.

350. ἀνακρίνω **anakrinō**, *an-ak-ree'-no;* from *303* and *2919;* prop. to *scrutinize,* i.e. (by impl.) *investigate, interrogate, determine:*—ask, question, discern, examine, judge, search.

351. ἀνάκρισις **anakrisis**, *an-ak'-ree-sis;* from *350;* a (judicial) *investigation:*—examination.

352. ἀνακύπτω **anakuptō**, *an-ak-oop'-to;* from *303* (in the sense of *reversal*) and *2955;* to *unbend,* i.e. *rise;* fig. *be elated,*—lift up, look up.

353. ἀναλαμβάνω **analambanō**, *an-al-am-ban'-o;* from *303* and *2983;* to *take up:*—receive up, take (in, unto, up).

354. ἀνάληψις **analēpsis**, *an-al'-ape-sis;* from *353; ascension:*—taking up.

355. ἀναλίσκω **analiskō**, *an-al-is'-ko;* from *303* and a form of the alternate of *138;* prop. to *use up,* i.e. *destroy:*—consume.

356. ἀναλογία **analŏgia**, *an-al-og-ee'-ah;* from a comp. of *303* and *3056; proportion:*—proportion.

357. ἀναλογίζομαι **analŏgizŏmai**, *an-al-og-id'-zom-ahee;* mid. from *356;* to *estimate,* i.e. (fig.) *contemplate:*—consider.

358. ἄναλος **analŏs**, *an'-al-os;* from *1* (as a neg. particle) and *251; saltless,* i.e. *insipid:*— × lose saltness.

359. ἀνάλυσις **analusis**, *an-al'-oo-sis;* from *360; departure:*—departure.

360. ἀναλύω **analuō**, *an-al-oo'-o;* from *303* and *3089;* to *break up,* i.e. *depart* (lit. or fig.):—depart, return.

361. ἀναμάρτητος **anamartētŏs**, *an-am-ar'-tay-tos;* from *1* (as a neg. particle) and a presumed der. of *264; sinless:*—that is without sin.

362. ἀναμένω **anamĕnō**, *an-am-en'-o;* from *303* and *3306;* to *await:*—wait for.

363. ἀναμιμνήσκω **anamimnēskō**, *an-am-im-nace'-ko;* from *303* and *3403;* to *remind;* reflex. to *recollect:*—call to mind, (bring to, call to, put in), remember (-brance).

364. ἀνάμνησις **anamnēsis**, *an-am'-nay-sis;* from *363; recollection:*—remembrance (again).

365. ἀνανεόω **ananĕŏō**, *an-an-neh-ŏ'-o;* from *303* and a der. of *3501;* to *renovate,* i.e. *reform:*—renew.

366. ἀνανήφω **ananēphō**, *an-an-ay'-fo;* from *303* and *3525;* to *become sober again,* i.e. (fig.) *regain* (one's) *senses:*—recover self.

367. Ἀνανίας **Ananias**, *an-an-ee'-as;* of Heb. or. [2608]; *Ananias,* the name of three Isr.:—Ananias.

368. ἀναντίῤῥητος **anantirrhētŏs**, *an-an-tir'-hray-tos;* from *1* (as a neg. particle) and a presumed

der. of a comp. of *473* and *4483; indisputable:*—cannot be spoken against.

369. ἀναντιῤῥήτως **anantirrhētōs**, *an-an-tir-hray'-toce;* adv. from *368; promptly:*—without gainsaying.

370. ἀνάξιος **anaxiŏs**, *an-ax'-ee-os;* from *1* (as a neg. particle) and *514; unfit:*—unworthy.

371. ἀναξίως **anaxiōs**, *an-ax-ee'-oce;* adv. from *370; irreverently:*—unworthily.

372. ἀνάπαυσις **anapausis**, *an-ap'-ŏw-sis;* from *373; intermission;* by impl. *recreation:*—rest.

373. ἀναπαύω **anapauō**, *an-up-ŏw'-o;* from *303* and *3973;* (reflex.) to *repose* (lit. or fig. [be *exempt*], *remain*); by impl. to *refresh:*—take ease, refresh, (give, take) rest.

374. ἀναπείθω **anapĕithō**, *an-ap-i'-tho;* from *303* and *3982;* to *incite:*—persuade.

375. ἀναπέμπω **anapĕmpō**, *an-ap-em'-po;* from *303* and *3992;* to *send up* or *back:*—send (again).

376. ἀνάπηρος **anapērŏs**, *an-ap'-ay-ros;* from *303* (in the sense of *intensity*) and πῆρος **pērŏs** (*maimed*); *crippled:*—maimed.

377. ἀναπίπτω **anapiptō**, *an-ap-ip'-to;* from *303* and *4098;* to *fall back,* i.e. *lie down, lean back:*—lean, sit down (to meat).

378. ἀναπληρόω **anaplērŏō**, *an-ap-lay-rŏ'-o;* from *303* and *4137;* to *complete;* by impl. to *occupy, supply;* fig. to *accomplish* (by coincidence or obedience):—fill up, fulfil, occupy, supply.

379. ἀναπολόγητος **anapŏlŏgētŏs**, *an-ap-ol-og'-ay-tos;* from *1* (as a neg. particle) and a presumed der. of *626; indefensible:*—without excuse, inexcusable.

380. ἀναπτύσσω **anaptussō**, *an-ap-toos'-so;* from *303* (in the sense of *reversal*) and *4428;* to *unroll* (a scroll or volume):—open.

381. ἀνάπτω **anaptō**, *an-ap'-to;* from *303* and *681;* to *enkindle:*—kindle, light.

382. ἀναρίθμητος **anarithmētŏs**, *an-ar-ith'-may-tos;* from *1* (as a neg. particle) and a der. of *705; innumerable,* i.e. *without number:*—innumerable.

383. ἀνασείω **anasĕiō**, *an-as-i'-o;* from *303* and *4579;* fig. to *excite:*—move, stir up.

384. ἀνασκευάζω **anaskĕuazō**, *an-ask-yoo-ad'-zo;* from *303* (in the sense of *reversal*) and a der. of *4632;* prop. to *pack up* (baggage), i.e. (by impl. and fig.) to *upset:*—subvert.

385. ἀνασπάω **anaspaō**, *an-as-pah'-o;* from *303* and *4685;* to *take up* or *extricate:*—draw up, pull out.

386. ἀνάστασις **anastasis**, *an-as'-tas-is;* from *450;* a *standing up again,* i.e. (lit.) a *resurrection* from death (individual, gen. or by impl.) [its author]), or (fig.) a (moral) *recovery* (of spiritual truth):—raised to life again, resurrection, rise from the dead, that should rise, rising again.

387. ἀναστατόω **anastatŏō**, *an-as-tat-ŏ'-o;* from a der. of *450* (in the sense of *removal*); prop. to *drive out of* home, i.e. (by impl.) to *disturb* (lit. or fig.):—trouble, turn upside down, make an uproar.

388. ἀνασταυρόω **anastaurŏō**, *an-as-tŏw-rŏ'-o;* from *303* and *4717;* to *recrucify* (fig.):—crucify afresh.

389. ἀναστενάζω **anastĕnazō**, *an-as-ten-ad'-zo;* from *303* and *4727;* to *sigh deeply:*—sigh deeply.

390. ἀναστρέφω **anastrĕphō**, *an-as-tref'-o;* from *303* and *4762;* to *overturn;* also to *return;* by impl. to *busy oneself,* i.e. *remain, live:*—abide, behave self, have conversation, live, overthrow, pass, return, be used.

391. ἀναστροφή **anastrŏphē**, *an-as-trof-ay';* from *390; behavior:*—conversation.

392. ἀνατάσσομαι **anatassŏmai**, *an-at-as'-som-ahee;* from *303* and the mid. of *5021;* to *arrange:*—set in order.

393. ἀνατέλλω **anatĕllō**, *an-at-el'-lo;* from *303* and the base of *5056;* to (cause to) *arise:*—(a-, make) to) *rise,* at the rising of, spring (up), be up.

394. ἀνατίθεμαι **anatithĕmai**, *an-at-ith'-em-ahee;* from *303* and the mid. of *5087;* to *set forth* (for oneself), i.e. *propound:*—communicate, declare.

395. **ἀνατολή anatŏlē**, *an-at-ol-ay´;* from *393;* a *rising* of light, i.e. *dawn* (fig.); by impl. the *east* (also in plur.):—dayspring, east, rising.

396. **ἀνατρέπω anatrĕpō**, *an-at-rep´-o;* from *303* and the base of *5157;* to *overturn* (fig.):—overthrow, subvert.

397. **ἀνατρέφω anatrĕphō**, *an-at-ref´-o;* from *303* and *5142;* to *rear* (phys. or ment.):—bring up, nourish (up).

398. **ἀναφαίνω anaphainō**, *an-af-ah´ee-no;* from *303* and *5316;* to *show*, i.e. (reflex.) *appear*, or (pass.) *have pointed out:*—(should) appear, discover.

399. **ἀναφέρω anaphĕrō**, *an-af-er´-o;* from *303* and *5342;* to *take up* (lit. or fig.):—bear, bring (carry, lead) up, offer (up).

400. **ἀναφωνέω anaphōnĕō**, *an-af-o-neh´-o;* from *303* and *5455;* to *exclaim:*—speak out.

401. **ἀνάχυσις anachusis**, *an-akh´-oo-sis;* from a comp. of *303* and χέω *chĕō* (to *pour*); prop. *effusion*, i.e. (fig.) *license:*—excess.

402. **ἀναχωρέω anachōrĕō**, *an-akh-o-reh´-o;* from *303* and *5562;* to *retire:*—depart, give place, go (turn) aside, withdraw self.

403. **ἀνάψυξις anapsuxis**, *an-aps´-ook-sis;* from *404;* prop. a *recovery of breath*, i.e. (fig.) *revival:*—revival.

404. **ἀναψύχω anapsuchō**, *an-aps-oo´-kho;* from *303* and *5594;* prop. to *cool off*, i.e. (fig.) *relieve:*—refresh.

405. **ἀνδραποδιστής andrapŏdistēs**, *an-drap-od-is-tace´;* from a der. of a comp. of *435* and *4228;* an *enslaver* (as bringing *men* to his *feet*):—menstealer.

406. **Ἀνδρέας Andrĕas**, *an-dreh´-as;* from *435;* manly; *Andreas*, an Isr.:—Andrew.

407. **ἀνδρίζομαι andrizŏmai**, *an-drid´-zom-ahee;* mid. from *435;* to *act manly:*—quit like men.

408. **Ἀνδρόνικος Andrŏnikŏs**, *an-dron´-ee-kos;* from *435* and *3534;* man *of victory; Andronicus*, an Isr.:—Andronicus.

409. **ἀνδροφόνος andrŏphŏnŏs**, *an-drof-on´-os;* from *435* and *5408;* a *murderer:*—manslayer.

410. **ἀνέγκλητος anĕgklētŏs**, *an-eng´-klay-tos;* from *1* (as a neg. particle) and a der. of *1458; unaccused*, i.e. (by impl.) *irreproachable:*—blameless.

411. **ἀνεκδιήγητος anĕkdiēgētŏs**, *an-ek-dee-ay´-gay-tos;* from *1* (as a neg. particle) and a presumed der. of *1555; not expounded in full*, i.e. *indescribable:*—unspeakable.

412. **ἀνεκλάλητος anĕklalētŏs**, *an-ek-lal´-ay-tos;* from *1* (as a neg. particle) and a presumed der. of *1583; not spoken out*, i.e. (by impl.) *unutterable:*—unspeakable.

413. **ἀνέκλειπτος anĕklĕiptŏs**, *an-ek´-lipe-tos;* from *1* (as a neg. particle) and a presumed der. of *1587; not left out*, i.e. (by impl.) *inexhaustible:*—that faileth not.

414. **ἀνεκτότερος anĕktŏtĕrŏs**, *an-ek-tot´-er-os;* compar. of a der. of *430; more endurable:*—more tolerable.

415. **ἀνελεήμων anĕlĕēmōn**, *an-eleh-ay´-mone;* from *1* (as a neg. particle) and *1655; merciless:*—unmerciful.

416. **ἀνεμίζω anemizō**, *an-em-id´-zo;* from *417;* to *toss with the wind:*—drive with the wind.

417. **ἄνεμος anĕmŏs**, *an´-em-os;* from the base of *109; wind;* (plur.) by impl. (the four) *quarters* (of the earth):—wind.

418. **ἀνένδεκτος anĕndĕktŏs**, *an-en´-dek-tos;* from *1* (as a neg. particle) and a der. of the same as *1735; unadmitted*, i.e. (by impl.) *not supposable:*—impossible.

419. **ἀνεξερεύνητος anĕxĕrĕunētŏs**, *an-ex-er-yoo´-nay-tos;* from *1* (as a neg. particle) and a presumed der. of *1830; not searched out*, i.e. (by impl.) *inscrutable:*—unsearchable.

420. **ἀνεξίκακος anĕxikakŏs**, *an-ex-ik´-ak-os;* from *430* and *2556; enduring of ill*, i.e. *forbearing:*—patient.

421. **ἀνεξιχνίαστος anĕxichniastŏs**, *an-ex-ikh-nee´-as-tos;* from *1* (as a neg. particle) and a presumed der. of a comp. of *1537* and a der. of *2487; not tracked out*, i.e. (by impl.) *untraceable:*—past finding out, unsearchable.

422. **ἀνεπαίσχυντος anĕpaischuntŏs**, *an-ep-ah´ee-skhoon-tos;* from *1* (as a neg. particle) and a presumed der. of a comp. of *1909* and *153; not ashamed*, i.e. (by impl.) *irreprehensible:*—that needeth not to be ashamed.

423. **ἀνεπίληπτος anĕpilēptŏs**, *an-ep-eel´-ape-tos;* from *1* (as a neg. particle) and a der. of *1949; not arrested*, i.e. (by impl.) *inculpable:*—blameless, unrebukeable.

424. **ἀνέρχομαι anĕrchŏmai**, *an-erkh´-om-ahee;* from *303* and *2064;* to *ascend:*—go up.

425. **ἄνεσις anĕsis**, *an´-es-is;* from *447; relaxation* or (fig.) *relief:*—eased, liberty, rest.

426. **ἀνετάζω anĕtazō**, *an-et-ad´-zo;* from *303* and ἐτάζω *ĕtazō* (to *test*); to *investigate* (judicially):—(should have) examine (-d).

427. **ἄνευ anĕu**, *an´-yoo;* a prim. particle; *without:*—without. Comp. *1.*

428. **ἀνεύθετος anĕuthĕtŏs**, *an-yoo´-the-tos;* from *1* (as a neg. particle) and *2111; not well set*, i.e. *inconvenient:*—not commodious.

429. **ἀνευρίσκω anĕuriskō**, *an-yoo-ris´-ko;* from *303* and *2147;* to *find out:*—find.

430. **ἀνέχομαι anĕchŏmai**, *an-ekh´-om-ahee;* mid. from *303* and *2192;* to *hold oneself up against*, i.e. (fig.) *put up with:*—bear with, endure, forbear, suffer.

431. **ἀνέψιος anĕpsiŏs**, *an-eps´-ee-os;* from *1* (as a particle of union) and an obsolete νέπος *nĕpŏs* (a *brood*); prop. *akin*, i.e. (spec.) a *cousin:*—sister's son.

432. **ἄνηθον anēthŏn**, *an´-ay-thon;* prob. of for. or.; *dill:*—anise.

433. **ἀνήκω anēkō**, *an-ay´-ko;* from *303* and *2240;* to *attain to*, i.e. (fig.) be *proper:*—convenient, be fit.

434. **ἀνήμερος anēmĕrŏs**, *an-ay´-mer-os;* from *1* (as a neg. particle) and ἥμερος *hēmĕrŏs* (*lame*); *savage:*—fierce.

435. **ἀνήρ anēr**, *an´-ayr;* a prim. word [comp. *444*]; a *man* (prop. as an individual male):—fellow, husband, man, sir.

436. **ἀνθίστημι anthistēmi**, *anth-is´-tay-mee;* from *473* and *2476;* to *stand against*, i.e. *oppose:*—resist, withstand.

437. **ἀνθομολογέομαι anthŏmŏlŏgĕŏmai**, *anth-om-ol-og-eh´-om-ahee;* from *473* and the mid. of *3670;* to *confess in turn*, i.e. *respond in praise:*—give thanks.

438. **ἄνθος anthŏs**, *anth´-os;* a prim. word; a *blossom:*—flower.

439. **ἀνθρακιά anthrakia**, *anth-rak-ee-ah´;* from *440;* a *bed of burning coals:*—fire of coals.

440. **ἄνθραξ anthrax**, *anth´-rax;* of uncert. der.; a *live coal:*—coal of fire.

441. **ἀνθρωπάρεσκος anthrōparĕskŏs**, *anth-ro-par´-es-kos;* from *444* and *700; man-courting*, i.e. *fawning:*—men-pleaser.

442. **ἀνθρώπινος anthrōpinŏs**, *anth-ro´-pee-nos;* from *444; human:*—human, common to man, man[-kind], [man-]kind, men's, after the manner of men.

443. **ἀνθρωποκτόνος anthrōpŏktŏnŏs**, *anth-ro-pok-ton´-os;* from *444* and κτείνω *ktĕinō* (to *kill*); a *manslayer:*—murderer. Comp. *5406.*

444. **ἄνθρωπος anthrōpŏs**, *anth´-ro-pos;* from *435* and ὤψ *ōps* (the *countenance;* from *3700*); *man-faced*, i.e. a *human being:*—certain, man.

445. **ἀνθυπατεύω anthupatĕuō**, *anth-oo-pat-yoo´-o;* from *446;* to *act as proconsul:*—be the deputy.

446. **ἀνθύπατος anthupatŏs**, *anth-oo´-pat-os;* from *473* and a superlative of *5228; instead of the highest* officer, i.e. (spec.) a Roman *proconsul:*—deputy.

447. **ἀνίημι aniēmi**, *an-ee´-ay-mee;* from *303* and ἵημι *hiĕmi* (to *send*); to *let up*, i.e. (lit.) *slacken*, or (fig.) *desert*, *desist* from:—forbear, leave, loose.

448. **ἀνίλεως anilĕōs**, *an-ee´-leh-oce;* from *1* (as a neg. particle) and *2436; inexorable:*—without mercy.

449. **ἄνιπτος aniptŏs**, *an´-ip-tos;* from *1* (as a neg. particle) and a presumed der. of *3538; without ablution:*—unwashen.

450. **ἀνίστημι anistēmi**, *an-is´-tay-mee;* from *303* and *2476;* to *stand up* (lit. or fig., trans. or intrans.):—arise, lift up, raise up (again), rise (again), stand up (-right).

451. **Ἄννα Anna**, *an´-nah;* of Heb. or. [*2584*]; *Anna*, an Israelitess:—Anna.

452. **Ἄννας Annas**, *an´-nas;* of Heb. or. [*2608*]; *Annas* (i.e. *307*), an Isr.:—Annas.

453. **ἀνόητος anŏētŏs**, *an-ŏ´-ay-tos;* from *1* (as a neg. particle) and a der. of *3539; unintelligent;* by impl. *sensual:*—fool (-ish), unwise.

454. **ἄνοια anŏia**, *an´-oy-ah;* from a comp. of *1* (as a neg. particle) and *3563; stupidity;* by impl. *rage:*—folly, madness.

455. **ἀνοίγω anŏigō**, *an-oy´-go;* from *303* and οἴγω *ŏigō* (to *open*); to *open up* (lit. or fig., in various applications):—open.

456. **ἀνοικοδομέω anŏikŏdŏmĕō**, *an-oy-kod-om-eh´-o;* from *303* and *3618;* to *rebuild:*—build again.

457. **ἄνοιξις anŏixis**, *an´-oix-is;* from *455; opening* (throat):— × open.

458. **ἀνομία anŏmia**, *an-om-ee´-ah;* from *459; illegality*, i.e. *violation of law* or (gen.) *wickedness:*—iniquity, × transgress (-ion of) the law, unrighteousness.

459. **ἄνομος anŏmŏs**, *an´-om-os;* from *1* (as a neg. particle) and *3551; lawless*, i.e. (neg.) *not subject to* (the Jewish) *law;* (by impl. a *Gentile*), or (pos.) *wicked:*—without law, lawless, transgressor, unlawful, wicked.

460. **ἀνόμως anŏmōs**, *an-om´-oce;* adv. from *459; lawlessly*, i.e. (spec.) *not amenable to* (the Jewish) *law:*—without law.

461. **ἀνορθόω anŏrthŏō**, *an-orth-ŏ´-o;* from *303* and a der. of the base of *3717;* to *straighten up:*—(set) up, make straight.

462. **ἀνόσιος anŏsiŏs**, *an-os´-ee-os;* from *1* (as a neg. particle) and *3741; wicked:*—unholy.

463. **ἀνοχή anŏchē**, *an-okh-ay´;* from *430; self-restraint*, i.e. *tolerance:*—forbearance.

464. **ἀνταγωνίζομαι antagōnizŏmai**, *an-tag-o-nid´-zom-ahee;* from *473* and *75;* to *struggle against* (fig.) [" antagonize"]:—strive against.

465. **ἀντάλλαγμα antallagma**, *an-tal´-ag-mah;* from a comp. of *473* and *236;* an *equivalent* or *ransom:*—in exchange.

466. **ἀνταναπληρόω antanaplērŏō**, *an-tan-ap-lay-rŏ´-o;* from *473* and *378;* to *supplement:*—fill up.

467. **ἀνταποδίδωμι antapŏdidōmi**, *an-tap-od-ee´-do-mee;* from *473* and *591;* to *requite* (good or evil):—recompense, render, repay.

468. **ἀνταπόδομα antapŏdŏma**, *an-tap-od´-om-ah;* from *467;* a *requital* (prop. the *thing*):—recompense.

469. **ἀνταπόδοσις antapŏdŏsis**, *an-tap-od´-os-is;* from *467; requital* (prop. the *act*):—reward.

470. **ἀνταποκρίνομαι antapŏkrinŏmai**, *an-tap-ok-ree´-nom-ahee;* from *473* and *611;* to *contradict* or *dispute:*—answer again, reply against.

471. **ἀντέπω antĕpō**, *an-tep´-o;* from *473* and *2036;* to *refute* or *deny:*—gainsay, say against.

472. **ἀντέχομαι antĕchŏmai**, *an-tekh´-om-ahee;* from *473* and the mid. of *2192;* to *hold oneself opposite to*, i.e. (by impl.) *adhere to;* by extens. to *care for:*—hold fast, hold to, support.

473. **ἀντί anti**, *an-tee´;* a prim. particle; *opposite*, i.e. *instead* or *because of* (rarely *in addition* to):—for, in the room of. Often used in composition to denote *contrast, requital, substitution, correspondence*, etc.

474. ἀντιβάλλω **antiballō**, *an-tee-bal'-lo;* from *473* and *906;* to *bandy:*—have.

475. ἀντιδιατίθεμαι **antidiatithěmai**, *an-tee-dee-at-eeth'-em-ahee;* from *473* and *1303;* to *set oneself opposite,* i.e. *be disputatious:*—that oppose themselves.

476. ἀντίδικος **antidikŏs**, *an-tid'-ee-kos;* from *473* and *1349;* an *opponent* (in a lawsuit); spec. Satan (as the arch-enemy):—*adversary.*

477. ἀντίθεσις **antithĕsis**, *an-tith'-es-is;* from a comp. of *473* and *5087; opposition,* i.e. a *conflict* (of theories):—opposition.

478. ἀντικαθίστημι **antikathistĕmi**, *an-tee-kath-is'-tay-mee;* from *473* and *2525;* to *set down* (troops) *against,* i.e. *withstand:*—resist.

479. ἀντικαλέω **antikalĕō**, *an-tee-kal-eh'-o;* from *473* and *2564;* to *invite in return:*—bid again.

480. ἀντίκειμαι **antikěimai**, *an-tik'-i-mahee;* from *473* and *2749;* to *lie opposite,* i.e. *be adverse* (fig. *repugnant*) to:—adversary, be contrary, oppose.

481. ἀντικρύ **antikru**, *an-tee-kroo';* prol. from *473; opposite:*—over against.

482. ἀντιλαμβάνομαι **antilambanŏmai**, *an-tee-lam-ban'-om-ahee;* from *473* and the mid. of *2983;* to *take hold of in turn,* i.e. *succor;* also to *participate:*—help, partaker, support.

483. ἀντιλέγω **antilěgō**, *an-til'-eg-o;* from *473* and *3004;* to *dispute, refuse;* answer again, contradict, deny, gainsay (-er), speak against.

484. ἀντίληψις **antilēpsis**, *an-til'-ape-sis;* from *482; relief:*—help.

485. ἀντιλογία **antilŏgia**, *an-tee-log-ee'-ah;* from a der. of *483; dispute, disobedience:*—contradiction, gainsaying, strife.

486. ἀντιλοιδορέω **antilŏidŏrěō**, *an-tee-loy-dor-eh'-o;* from *473* and *3058;* to *rail in reply:*—revile again.

487. ἀντίλυτρον **antilutrŏn**, *an-til'-oo-tron;* from *473* and *3083;* a *redemption-price:*—ransom.

488. ἀντιμετρέω **antimětrěō**, *an-tee-met-reh'-o;* from *473* and *3354;* to *mete in return:*—measure again.

489. ἀντιμισθία **antimisthia**, *an-tee-mis-thee'-ah;* from a comp. of *473* and *3408; requital,* correspondence:—recompense.

490. Ἀντιόχεια **Antiŏchĕia**, *an-tee-okh'-i-ah;* from Ἀντίοχος Antiochus (a Syrian king); Antiochia, a place in Syria:—Antioch.

491. Ἀντιοχεύς **Antiŏchĕus**, *an-tee-okh-yoos';* from *490;* an *Antiochian* or inhab. of Antiochia:—of Antioch.

492. ἀντιπαρέρχομαι **antiparěrchŏmai**, *an-tee-par-er'-khom-ahee;* from *473* and *3928;* to *go along opposite:*—pass by on the other side.

493. Ἀντίπας **Antipas**, *an-tee'-pas;* contr. for a comp. of *473* and a der. of *3962; Antipas,* a Chr.:—Antipas.

494. Ἀντιπατρίς **Antipatris**, *an-tip-at-rece';* from the same as *493; Antipatris,* a place in Pal.:—Antipatris.

495. ἀντιπέραν **antipěran**, *an-tee-per'-an;* from *473* and *4008;* on the *opposite side:*—over against.

496. ἀντιπίπτω **antipiptō**, *an-tee-pip'-to;* from *473* and *4098* (includ. its alt.); to *oppose:*—resist.

497. ἀντιστρατεύομαι **antistratěuŏmai**, *an-tee-strat-yoo'-om-ahee;* from *473* and *4754;* (fig.) to *attack,* i.e. (by impl.) *destroy:*—war against.

498. ἀντιτάσσομαι **antitassŏmai**, *an-tee-tas'-som-ahee;* from *473* and the mid. of *5021;* to *range oneself against,* i.e. *oppose:*—oppose themselves, resist.

499. ἀντίτυπον **antitupŏn**, *an-teet'-oo-pon;* neut. of a comp. of *473* and *5179;* corresponding ["an antitype"], i.e. a *representative, counterpart:*—(like) figure (whereunto).

500. ἀντίχριστος **antichristŏs**, *an-tee'-khris-tos;* from *473* and *5547;* an *opponent of the Messiah:*—antichrist.

501. ἀντλέω **antlěō**, *ant-leh'-o;* from ἄντλος antlŏs (the *hold* of a ship); to *bale* up (prop. bilge water), i.e. *dip* water (with a bucket, pitcher, etc.):—draw (out).

502. ἄντλημα **antlĕma**, *ant'-lay-mah;* from *501;* a *baling-vessel:*—thing to draw with.

503. ἀντοφθαλμέω **antŏphthalměō**, *ant-of-thal-meh'-o;* from a comp. of *473* and *3788;* to *face:*—bear up into.

504. ἄνυδρος **anudrŏs**, *an'-oo-dros;* from *1* (as a neg. particle) and *5204; waterless,* i.e. *dry:*—dry, without water.

505. ἀνυπόκριτος **anupŏkritŏs**, *an-oo-pok'-ree-tos;* from *1* (as a neg. particle) and a presumed der. of *5271; undissembled,* i.e. *sincere:*—without dissimulation (hypocrisy), unfeigned.

506. ἀνυπότακτος **anupŏtaktŏs**, *an-oo-pot'-ak-tos;* from *1* (as a neg. particle) and a presumed der. of *5293; unsubdued,* i.e. *insubordinate* (in fact or temper):—disobedient, that is not put under, unruly.

507. ἄνω **anō**, *an'-o;* adv. from *473; upward* or *on the top:*—above, brim, high, up.

508. ἀνώγεον **anōgĕŏn**, *an-ogue'-eh-on;* from *507* and *1093;* above the *ground,* i.e. (prop.) the *second floor* of a building; used for a *dome* or a *balcony* on the upper story:—upper room.

509. ἄνωθεν **anōthěn**, *an'-o-then;* from *507;* from *above;* by anal. from the *first;* by impl. *anew:*—from above, again, from the beginning (very first), the top.

510. ἀνωτερικός **anōtěrikŏs**, *an-o-ter-ee-kos';* from *511; superior,* i.e. (locally) *more remote:*—upper.

511. ἀνώτερος **anōtěrŏs**, *an-o'-ter-os;* comp. degree of *507; upper,* i.e. (neut. as adv.) to a *more conspicuous* place, in a *former* part of the book:—above, higher.

512. ἀνωφελές **anōphělěs**, *an-o-fel'-ace;* from *1* (as a neg. particle) and the base of *5624; useless* or (neut.) *inutility:*—unprofitable (-ness).

513. ἀξίνη **axinē**, *ax-ee'-nay;* prob. from ἄγνυμι agnumi (to *break;* comp. *4486*); an *axe:*—axe.

514. ἄξιος **axiŏs**, *ax'-ee-os;* prob. from *71; deserving, comparable* or *suitable* (as if *drawing* praise):—due reward, meet, [un-] worthy.

515. ἀξιόω **axiŏō**, *ax-ee-ŏ'-o;* from *514;* to *deem entitled* or *fit:*—desire, think good, count (think) worthy.

516. ἀξίως **axiōs**, *ax-ee'-oce;* adv. from *514; appropriately:*—as becometh, after a godly sort, worthily (-thy).

517. ἀόρατος **aŏratŏs**, *ah-or'-at-os;* from *1* (as a neg. particle) and *3707; invisible:*—invisible (thing).

518. ἀπαγγέλλω **apaggěllō**, *ap-ang-el'-lo;* from *575* and the base of *32;* to *announce:*—bring word (again), declare, report, shew (again), tell.

519. ἀπάγχομαι **apagchŏmai**, *ap-ang'-khom-ahee;* from *575* and ἄγχω agchō (to *choke;* akin to the base of *43*); to *strangle oneself off* (i.e. to death):—hang himself.

520. ἀπάγω **apagō**, *ap-ag'-o;* from *575* and *71;* to *take off* (in various senses):—bring, carry away, lead (away), put to death, take away.

521. ἀπαίδευτος **apaiděutŏs**, *ap-ah'ee-dyoo-tos;* from *1* (as a neg. particle) and der. of *3811; uninstructed,* i.e. (fig.) *stupid:*—unlearned.

522. ἀπαίρω **apairō**, *ap-ah'ee-ro;* from *575* and *142;* to *lift off,* i.e. *remove:*—take (away).

523. ἀπαιτέω **apaitěō**, *ap-ah'ee-teh-o;* from *575* and *154;* to *demand back:*—ask again, require.

524. ἀπαλγέω **apalgěō**, *ap-alg-eh'-o;* from *575* and ἀλγέω algěō (to *smart*); to *grieve out,* i.e. *become apathetic:*—be past feeling.

525. ἀπαλλάσσω **apallassō**, *ap-al-las'-so;* from *575* and *236;* to *change away,* i.e. *release* (reflex.) *remove:*—deliver, depart.

526. ἀπαλλοτριόω **apallŏtriŏō**, *ap-al-lot-ree-ŏ'-o;* from *575* and a der. of *245;* to *estrange away,* i.e. (pass. and fig.) to *be non-participant:*—alienate, be alien.

527. ἁπαλός **apalŏs**, *ap-al-os';* of uncert. der.; *soft:*—tender.

528. ἀπαντάω **apantaō**, *ap-an-tah'-o;* from *575* and a der. of *473;* to *meet away,* i.e. *encounter:*—meet.

529. ἀπάντησις **apantēsis**, *ap-an'-tay-sis;* from *528;* a (friendly) *encounter:*—meet.

530. ἅπαξ **hapax**, *hap'-ax;* prob. from *537; one* (or a *single*) *time* (numerically or conclusively):—once.

531. ἀπαράβατος **aparabatŏs**, *ap-ar-ab'-at-os;* from *1* (as a neg. particle) and a der. of *3845; not passing away,* i.e. *untransferable* (perpetual):—unchangeable.

532. ἀπαρασκεύαστος **aparaskěuastŏs**, *ap-ar-ask-yoo'-as-tos;* from *1* (as a neg. particle) and a der. of *3903; unready:*—unprepared.

533. ἀπαρνέομαι **aparněŏmai**, *ap-ar-neh'-om-ahee;* from *575* and *720;* to *deny utterly,* i.e. *disown, abstain:*—deny.

534. ἀπάρτι **aparti**, *ap-ar'-tee;* from *575* and *737;* *from now,* i.e. *henceforth* (*already*):—from henceforth.

535. ἀπαρτισμός **apartismŏs**, *ap-ar-tis-mos';* from a der. of *534; completion:*—finishing.

536. ἀπαρχή **aparchē**, *ap-ar-khay';* from a comp. of *575* and *756;* a *beginning* of sacrifice, i.e. the (Jewish) *first-fruit* (fig.):—first-fruits.

537. ἅπας **hapas**, *hap'-as;* from *1* (as a particle of union) and *3956;* absolutely *all* or (sing.) *every one:*—all (things), every (one), whole.

538. ἀπατάω **apataō**, *ap-at-ah'-o;* of uncert. der.; to *cheat,* i.e. *delude:*—deceive.

539. ἀπάτη **apatě**, *ap-at'-ay;* from *538; delusion:*—deceit (-ful, -fulness), deceivableness (-ving).

540. ἀπάτωρ **apatōr**, *ap-at'-ore;* from *1* (as a neg. particle) and *3962; fatherless,* i.e. *of unrecorded paternity:*—without father.

541. ἀπαύγασμα **apaugasma**, *ap-ŏw'-gas-mah;* from a comp. of *575* and *826;* an *off-flash,* i.e. *effulgence:*—brightness.

542. ἀπείδω **apěidō**, *ap-i'-do;* from *575* and the same as *1492;* to *see fully:*—see.

543. ἀπείθεια **apěithěia**, *ap-i'-thi-ah;* from *545; disbelief* (obstinate and rebellious):—disobedience, unbelief.

544. ἀπειθέω **apěithěō**, *ap-i-theh'-o;* from *545;* to *disbelieve* (wilfully and perversely):—not believe, disobedient, obey not, unbelieving.

545. ἀπειθής **apěithēs**, *ap-i-thace';* from *1* (as a neg. particle) and *3982; unpersuadable,* i.e. *contumacious:*—disobedient.

546. ἀπειλέω **apěilěō**, *ap-i-leh'-o;* of uncert. der.; to *menace;* by impl. to *forbid:*—threaten.

547. ἀπειλή **apěilē**, *ap-i-lay';* from *546;* a *menace:*—× straitly, threatening.

548. ἄπειμι **apěimi**, *ap'-i-mee;* from *575* and *1510,* to *be away:*—be absent. Comp. *540.*

549. ἄπειμι **apěimi**, *ap'-i-mee;* from *575* and εἶμι eimi (to *go*); to *go away:*—go. Comp. *548.*

550. ἀπειπόμην **apěipŏmēn**, *ap-i-pom'-ane;* reflex. past of a comp. of *575* and *2036;* to *say off* for oneself, i.e. *disown:*—renounce.

551. ἀπείραστος **apěirastŏs**, *ap-i'-ras-tos;* from *1* (as a neg. particle) and a presumed der. of *3987; untried,* i.e. *not temptable:*—not to be tempted.

552. ἄπειρος **apěirŏs**, *ap'-i-ros;* from *1* (as a neg. particle) and *3984; inexperienced,* i.e. *ignorant:*—unskilful.

553. ἀπεκδέχομαι **apěkděchŏmai**, *ap-ek-dekh'-om-ahee;* from *575* and *1551;* to *expect fully:*—look (wait) for.

554. ἀπεκδύομαι **apěkduŏmai**, *ap-ek-doo'-om-ahee;* mid. from *575* and *1562;* to *divest wholly* oneself, or (for oneself) *despoil:*—put off, spoil.

555. ἀπέκδυσις **apěkdusis**, *ap-ek'-doo-sis;* from *554; divestment:*—putting off.

556. ἀπελαύνω **apělaunō**, *ap-el-ŏw'-no;* from *575* and *1643;* to *dismiss:*—drive.

557. ἀπελεγμός **apĕlĕgmŏs,** *ap-el-eg-mos'*; from a comp. of *575* and *1651;* refutation, i.e. (by impl.) contempt:—nought.

558. ἀπελεύθερος **apĕlĕuthĕrŏs,** *ap-el-yoo'-ther-os;* from *575* and *1658;* one *freed away,* i.e. a *freedman:*—freeman.

559. Ἀπελλῆς **Apĕllēs,** *ap-el-lace';* of Lat. or.; *Apelles,* a Chr.:—Apelles.

560. ἀπελπίζω **apĕlpizō,** *ap-el-pid'-zo;* from *575* and *1679;* to *hope out,* i.e. *fully expect:*—hope for again.

561. ἀπέναντι **apĕnanti,** *ap-en'-an-tee;* from *575* and *1725;* from *in front,* i.e. *opposite, before* or *against:*—before, contrary, over against, in the presence of.

ἀπέπω **apĕpō.** See *550.*

562. ἀπέραντος **apĕrantŏs,** *ap-er'-an-tos;* from *1* (as a neg. particle) and a secondary der. of *4008; unfinished,* i.e. (by impl.) *interminable:*—endless.

563. ἀπερισπάστως **apĕrispastŏs,** *ap-er-is-pas-toce';* adv. from a comp. of *1* (as a neg. particle) and a presumed der. of *4049; undistractedly,* i.e. *free from* (domestic) *solicitude:*—without distraction.

564. ἀπερίτμητος **apĕritmētŏs,** *ap-er-eet'-may-tos;* from *1* (as a neg. particle) and a presumed der. of *4059; uncircumcised* (fig.):—uncircumcised.

565. ἀπέρχομαι **apĕrchŏmai,** *ap-erkh'-om-ahee;* from *575* and *2064;* to *go off* (i.e. *depart*), *aside* (i.e. *apart*) or *behind* (i.e. *follow*), lit. or fig.:—come, depart, go (aside, away, back, out, . . . ways), pass away, be past.

566. ἀπέχει **apĕchĕi,** *ap-ekh'-i;* 3d pers. sing. pres. indic. act. of *568* used impers.; *it is sufficient:*—it is enough.

567. ἀπέχομαι **apĕchŏmai,** *ap-ekh'-om-ahee;* mid. (reflex.) of *568;* to *hold oneself off,* i.e. *refrain:*—abstain.

568. ἀπέχω **apĕchō,** *ap-ekh'-o;* from *575* and *2192;* (act.) to *have out,* i.e. *receive in full;* (intrans.) to *keep* (oneself) *away,* i.e. *be distant* (lit. or fig.):—be, have, receive.

569. ἀπιστέω **apistĕō,** *ap-is-teh'-o;* from *571;* to be *unbelieving,* i.e. (trans.) *disbelieve,* or (by impl.) *disobey:*—believe not.

570. ἀπιστία **apistia,** *ap-is-tee'-ah;* from *571;* *faithlessness,* i.e. (neg.) *disbelief* (want of Chr. *faith*), or (pos.) *unfaithfulness* (disobedience):—unbelief.

571. ἄπιστος **apistŏs,** *ap'-is-tos;* from *1* (as a neg. particle) and *4103;* (act.) *disbelieving,* i.e. *without* Chr. *faith* (spec. a *heathen*); (pass.) *untrustworthy* (person), or *incredible* (thing):—that believeth not, faithless, incredible thing, infidel, unbeliever (-ing).

572. ἁπλότης **haplŏtēs,** *hap-lot'-ace;* from *573;* *singleness,* i.e. (subj.) *sincerity* (without dissimulation or self-seeking), or (obj.) *generosity* (copious bestowal):—bountifulness, liberal (-ity), simplicity, singleness.

573. ἁπλοῦς **haplŏus,** *hap-looce';* prob. from *1* (as a particle of union) and the base of *4120;* prop. *folded together,* i.e. *single* (fig. *clear*):—single.

574. ἁπλῶς **haplŏs,** *hap-loce';* adv. from *573* (in the obj. sense of *572*); *bountifully:*—liberally.

575. ἀπό **apŏ,** *apo';* a prim. particle; "*off,*" i.e. *away* (from something near), in various senses (of place, time, or relation; lit. or fig.):—(× here-) after, ago, at, because of, before, by (the space of), for (-th), from, in, (out) of, off, (up-) on (-cee), since, with. In composition (as a prefix) it usually denotes *separation, departure, cessation, completion, reversal,* etc.

576. ἀποβαίνω **apŏbainō,** *ap-ob-ah'ee-no;* from *575* and the base of *939;* lit. to *disembark;* fig. to *eventuate:*—become, go out, turn.

577. ἀποβάλλω **apŏballō,** *ap-ob-al'-lo;* from *575* and *906;* to *throw off;* fig. to *lose:*—cast away.

578. ἀποβλέπω **apŏblĕpō,** *ap-ob-lep'-o;* from *575* and *991;* to *look away* from everything else, i.e. (fig.) *intently regard:*—have respect.

579. ἀπόβλητος **apŏblētŏs,** *ap-ob'-lay-tos;* from *577; cast off,* i.e. (fig.) such as to *be rejected:*—be refused.

580. ἀποβολή **apŏbŏlē,** *ap-ob-ol-ay';* from *577; rejection;* fig. *loss:*—casting away, loss.

581. ἀπογενόμενος **apŏgĕnŏmĕnŏs,** *ap-og-en-om'-en-os;* past part. of a comp. of *575* and *1096; absent,* i.e. *deceased* (fig. *renounced*):—being dead.

582. ἀπογραφή **apŏgraphē,** *ap-og-raf-ay';* from *583;* an *enrollment;* by impl. an *assessment:*—taxing.

583. ἀπογράφω **apŏgraphō,** *ap-og-raf'-o;* from *575* and *1125;* to *write off* (a copy or list), i.e. *enrol:*—tax, write.

584. ἀποδείκνυμι **apŏdĕiknumi,** *ap-od-ike'-noo-mee;* from *575* and *1166;* to *show off,* i.e. *exhibit;* fig. to *demonstrate,* i.e. *accredit:*—(ap-) prove, set forth, shew.

585. ἀπόδειξις **apŏdĕixis,** *ap-od'-ike-sis;* from *584; manifestation:*—demonstration.

586. ἀποδεκατόω **apŏdĕkatŏō,** *ap-od-ek-at-ŏ'-o;* from *575* and *1183;* to *tithe* (as debtor or creditor):—(give, pay, take) tithe.

587. ἀπόδεκτος **apŏdĕktŏs,** *ap-od'-ek-tos;* from *588; accepted,* i.e. *agreeable:*—acceptable.

588. ἀποδέχομαι **apŏdĕchŏmai,** *ap-od-ekh'-om-ahee;* from *575* and *1209;* to *take fully,* i.e. *welcome* (persons), *approve* (things):—accept, receive (gladly).

589. ἀποδημέω **apŏdēmĕō,** *ap-od-ay-meh'-o;* from *590;* to *go abroad,* i.e. *visit a foreign land:*—go (travel) into a far country, journey.

590. ἀπόδημος **apŏdēmŏs,** *ap-od'-ay-mos;* from *575* and *1218; absent* from one's own people, i.e. a *foreign traveller:*—taking a far journey.

591. ἀποδίδωμι **apŏdidōmi,** *ap-od-eed'-o-mee;* from *575* and *1325;* to *give away,* i.e. *up, over, back,* etc. (in various applications):—deliver (again), give (again), (re-) pay (-ment be made), perform, recompense, render, requite, restore, reward, sell, yield.

592. ἀποδιορίζω **apŏdiŏrizō,** *ap-od-ee-or-id'-zo;* from *575* and a comp. of *1223* and *3724;* to *disjoin* (by a boundary, fig. a party):—separate.

593. ἀποδοκιμάζω **apŏdŏkimazō,** *ap-od-ok-ee-mad'-zo;* from *575* and *1381;* to *disapprove,* i.e. (by impl.) to *repudiate:*—disallow, reject.

594. ἀποδοχή **apŏdŏchē,** *ap-od-okh-ay';* from *588; acceptance:*—acceptation.

595. ἀπόθεσις **apŏthĕsis,** *ap-oth'-es-is;* from *659;* a *laying aside* (lit. or fig.):—putting away (off).

596. ἀποθήκη **apŏthēkē,** *ap-oth-ay'-kay;* from *659;* a *repository,* i.e. *granary:*—barn, garner.

597. ἀποθησαυρίζω **apŏthēsaurizō,** *ap-oth-ay-sŏw-rid'-zo;* from *575* and *2343;* to *treasure away:*—lay up in store.

598. ἀποθλίβω **apŏthlibō,** *ap-oth-lee'-bo;* from *575* and *2346;* to *crowd* from (every side):—press.

599. ἀποθνήσκω **apŏthnēskō,** *ap-oth-nace'-ko;* from *575* and *2348;* to *die off* (lit. or fig.):—be dead, death, die, lie a-dying, be slain (× with).

600. ἀποκαθίστημι **apŏkathistēmi,** *ap-ok-ath-is'-tay-mee;* from *575* and *2525;* to *reconstitute* (in health, home or organization):—restore (again).

601. ἀποκαλύπτω **apŏkaluptō,** *ap-ok-al-oop'-to;* from *575* and *2572;* to *take off the cover,* i.e. *disclose:*—reveal.

602. ἀποκάλυψις **apŏkalupsis,** *ap-ok-al'-oop-sis;* from *601; disclosure:*—appearing, coming, lighten, manifestation, be revealed, revelation.

603. ἀποκαραδοκία **apŏkaradŏkia,** *ap-ok-ar-ad-ok-ee'-ah;* from a comp. of *575* and a comp. of κάρα **kara** (the *head*) and *1380* (in the sense of *watching*); *intense anticipation:*—earnest expectation.

604. ἀποκαταλλάσσω **apŏkatallassō,** *ap-ok-at-al-las'-so;* from *575* and *2644;* to *reconcile fully:*—reconcile.

605. ἀποκατάστασις **apŏkatastasis,** *ap-ok-at-as'-tas-is;* from *600; reconstitution:*—restitution.

606. ἀπόκειμαι **apŏkĕimai,** *ap-ok'-i-mahee;* from *575* and *2749;* to be *reserved;* fig. to *await:*—be appointed, (be) laid up.

607. ἀποκεφαλίζω **apŏkĕphalizō,** *ap-ok-ef-al-id'-zo;* from *575* and *2776;* to *decapitate:*—behead.

608. ἀποκλείω **apŏklĕiō,** *ap-ok-li'-o;* from *575* and *2808;* to *close fully:*—shut up.

609. ἀποκόπτω **apŏkŏptō,** *ap-ok-op'-to;* from *575* and *2875;* to *amputate;* reflex. (by irony) to *mutilate* (the privy parts):—cut off. Comp. *2699.*

610. ἀπόκριμα **apŏkrima,** *ap-ok'-ree-mah;* from *611* (in its orig. sense of *judging*); a judicial *decision:*—sentence.

611. ἀποκρίνομαι **apŏkrinŏmai,** *ap-ok-ree'-nom-ahee;* from *575* and κρίνω **krino;** to *conclude for oneself,* i.e. (by impl.) to *respond;* by Hebr. [comp. *6030*] to *begin to speak* (where an address is expected):—answer.

612. ἀπόκρισις **apŏkrisis,** *ap-ok'-ree-sis;* from *611;* a *response:*—answer.

613. ἀποκρύπτω **apŏkruptō,** *ap-ok-roop'-to;* from *575* and *2928;* to *conceal away* (i.e. *fully*); fig. to *keep secret:*—hide.

614. ἀπόκρυφος **apŏkruphŏs,** *ap-ok'-roo-fos;* from *613; secret;* by impl. *treasured:*—hid, kept secret.

615. ἀποκτείνω **apŏktĕinō,** *ap-ok-ti'-no;* from *575* and κτείνω **ktĕinō** (to *slay*); to *kill* outright; fig. to *destroy:*—put to death, kill, slay.

616. ἀποκυέω **apŏkuĕō,** *ap-ok-oo-eh'o;* from *575* and the base of *2949;* to *breed forth,* i.e. (by transf.) to *generate* (fig.):—beget, bring forth.

617. ἀποκυλίω **apŏkuliō,** *ap-ok-oo-lee'-o;* from *575* and *2947;* to *roll away:*—roll away (back).

618. ἀπολαμβάνω **apŏlambanō,** *ap-ol-am-ban'-o;* from *575* and *2983;* to *receive* (spec. in *full,* or as a host); also to *take aside:*—receive, take.

619. ἀπόλαυσις **apŏlausis,** *ap-ol'-ŏw-sis;* from a comp. of *575* and λαύω **lauō** (to *enjoy*); *full enjoyment:*—enjoy (-ment).

620. ἀπολείπω **apŏlĕipō,** *ap-ol-ipe'-o;* from *575* and *3007;* to *leave behind* (pass. *remain*); by impl. to *forsake:*—leave, remain.

621. ἀπολείχω **apŏlĕichō,** *ap-ol-i'-kho;* from *575* and λείχω **lĕichō** (to "*lick*"); to *lick clean:*—lick.

622. ἀπόλλυμι **apŏllumi,** *ap-ol'-loo-mee;* from *575* and the base of *3639;* to *destroy fully* (reflex. to *perish,* or *lose*), lit. or fig.:—destroy, die, lose, mar, perish.

623. Ἀπολλύων **Apŏlluōn,** *ap-ol-loo'-ohn;* act. part. of *622;* a *destroyer* (i.e. *Satan*):—Apollyon.

624. Ἀπολλωνία **Apŏllōnia,** *ap-ol-lo-nee'-ah;* from the pagan deity Ἀπόλλων **Apŏllōn** (i.e. the *sun;* from *622*); *Apollonia,* a place in Macedonia:—Apollonia.

625. Ἀπολλῶς **Apŏllōs,** *ap-ol-loce';* prob. from the same as *624; Apollos,* an Isr.:—Apollos.

626. ἀπολογέομαι **apŏlŏgĕŏmai,** *ap-ol-og-eh'-om-ahee;* mid. from a comp. of *575* and *3056;* to *give an account* (legal *plea*) of oneself, i.e. *exculpate* (self):—answer (for self), make defence, excuse (self), speak for self.

627. ἀπολογία **apŏlŏgia,** *ap-ol-og-ee'-ah;* from the same as *626;* a *plea* ("apology"):—answer (for self), clearing of self, defence.

628. ἀπολούω **apŏlŏuō,** *ap-ol-oo'-o;* from *575* and *3068;* to *wash fully,* i.e. (fig.) *have remitted* (reflex.):—wash (away).

629. ἀπολύτρωσις **apŏlutrōsis,** *ap-ol-oo'-tro-sis;* from a comp. of *575* and *3083;* (the act) *ransom* in full, i.e. (fig.) *riddance,* or (spec.) Chr. *salvation:*—deliverance, redemption.

630. ἀπολύω **apŏluō,** *ap-ol-oo'-o;* from *575* and *3089;* to *free fully,* i.e. (lit.) *relieve, release, dismiss* (reflex. *depart*), or (fig.) *let die, pardon,* or (spec.) *divorce:*—(let) depart, dismiss, divorce, forgive, let go, loose, put (send) away, release, set at liberty.

631. ἀπομάσσομαι **apŏmassŏmai,** *ap-om-as'-som-ahee;* mid. from *575* and μάσσω **massō** (to *squeeze, knead, smear*); to *scrape away:*—wipe off.

632. ἀπονέμω **apŏnĕmō,** *ap-on-em'-o;* from *575* and the base of *3551;* to *apportion,* i.e. *bestow:*—give.

633. ἀπονίπτω **apŏniptŏ,** ap-on-ip'-to; from 575 and 3538; to wash off (reflex. one's own hands symbolically):—wash.

634. ἀπονίπτω **apŏpiptŏ,** ap-op-ip'-to; from 575 and 4098; to fall off:—fall.

635. ἀποπλανάω **apŏplanaŏ,** ap-op-lan-ah'-o; from 575 and 4105; to lead astray (fig.); pass. to stray (from truth):—err, seduce.

636. ἀποπλέω **apŏpleŏ,** ap-op-leh'-o; from 575 and 4126; to set sail:—sail away.

637. ἀποπλύνω **apŏplunŏ,** ap-op-loo'-no; from 575 and 4150; to rinse off:—wash.

638. ἀποπνίγω **apŏpnigŏ,** ap-op-nee'-go; from 575 and 4155; to stifle (by drowning or overgrowth):—choke.

639. ἀπορέω **apŏreŏ,** ap-or-eh'-o; from a comp. of 1 (as a neg. particle) and the base of 4198; to have no way out, i.e. be at a loss (mentally):—(stand in) doubt, be perplexed.

640. ἀπορία **apŏria,** ap-or-ee'-a; from the same as 639; a (state of) quandary:—perplexity.

641. ἀπορρίπτω **apŏrrhiptŏ,** ap-or-hrip'-to; from 575 and 4496; to hurl off, i.e. precipitate (oneself):—cast.

642. ἀπορφανίζω **apŏrphanizŏ,** ap-or-fan-id'-zo; from 575 and a der. of 3737; to bereave wholly, i.e. (fig.) separate (from intercourse):—take.

643. ἀποσκευάζω **apŏskĕuazŏ,** ap-osk-yoo-ad'-zo; from 575 and a der. of 4632; to pack up (one's baggage:—take up . . . carriages.

644. ἀποσκίασμα **apŏskiasma,** ap-os-kee'-as-mah; from a comp. of 575 and a der. of 4639; a shading off, i.e. obscuration:—shadow.

645. ἀποσπάω **apŏspaŏ,** ap-os-pah'-o; from 575 and 4685; to drag forth, i.e. (lit.) unsheathe (a sword), or rel. (with a degree of force implied) retire (pers. or factiously):—(with-) draw (away), after we were gotten from.

646. ἀποστασία **apŏstasia,** ap-os-tas-ee'-ah; fem. of the same as 647; defection from truth (prop. the state) [" apostasy "]:—falling away, forsake.

647. ἀποστάσιον **apŏstasiŏn,** ap-os-tas'-ee-on; neut. of a (presumed) adj. from a der. of 868; prop. something separative, i.e. (spec.) divorce:—(writing of) divorcement.

648. ἀποστεγάζω **apŏstĕgazŏ,** ap-os-teg-ad'-zo; from 575 and a der. of 4721; to unroof:—uncover.

649. ἀποστέλλω **apŏstĕllŏ,** ap-os-tel'-lo; from 575 and 4724; set apart, i.e. (by impl.) to send out (prop. on a mission) lit. or fig.:—put in, send (away, forth, out), set [at liberty].

650. ἀποστερέω **apŏstĕreŏ,** ap-os-ter-eh'-o; from 575 and στερέω stĕreŏ (to deprive); to despoil:—defraud, destitute, kept back by fraud.

651. ἀποστολή **apŏstŏlē,** ap-os-tol-ay'; from 649, commission, i.e. (spec.) apostolate:—apostleship.

652. ἀπόστολος **apŏstŏlŏs,** ap-os'-tol-os; from 649; a delegate; spec. an ambassador of the Gospel; officially a commissioner of Christ [" apostle "] (with miraculous powers):—apostle, messenger, he that is sent.

653. ἀποστοματίζω **apŏstŏmatizŏ,** ap-os-tom-at-id'-zo; from 575 and a (presumed) der. of 4750; to speak off-hand (prop. dictate), i.e. to catechize (in an invidious manner):—provoke to speak.

654. ἀποστρέφω **apŏstrĕphŏ,** ap-os-tref'-o; from 575 and 4762; to turn away or back (lit. or fig.):—bring again, pervert, turn away (from).

655. ἀποστυγέω **apŏstugeŏ,** ap-os-toog-eh'-o; from 575 and the base of 4767; to detest utterly:—abhor.

656. ἀποσυνάγωγος **apŏsunagōgŏs,** ap-os-oon-ag'-o-gos; from 575 and 4864; excommunicated:—(put) out of the synagogue (-s).

657. ἀποτάσσομαι **apŏtassŏmai,** ap-ot-as'-som-ahee; mid. from 575 and 5021; lit. to say adieu (by departing or dismissing); fig. to renounce:—bid farewell, forsake, take leave, send away.

658. ἀποτελέω **apŏtĕleŏ,** ap-ot-el-eh'-o; from 575 and 5055; to complete entirely, i.e. consummate:—finish.

659. ἀποτίθημι **apŏtithēmi,** ap-ot-eeth'-ay-mee; from 575 and 5087; to put away (lit. or fig.):—cast off, lay apart (aside, down), put away (off).

660. ἀποτινάσσω **apŏtinassŏ,** ap-ot-in-as'-so; from 575 and τινάσσω tinassŏ (to jostle); to brush off:—shake off.

661. ἀποτίνω **apŏtinŏ,** ap-ot-ee'-no; from 575 and 5099; to pay in full:—repay.

662. ἀποτολμάω **apŏtŏlmaŏ,** ap-ot-ol-mah'-o; from 575 and 5111; to venture plainly:—be very bold.

663. ἀποτομία **apŏtŏmia,** ap-ot-om-ee'-ah; from the base of 664; (fig.) decisiveness, i.e. rigor:—severity.

664. ἀποτόμως **apŏtŏmōs,** ap-ot-om'-oce; adv. from a der. of a comp. of 575 and τέμνω tĕmnŏ (to cut); abruptly, i.e. peremptorily:—sharply (-ness).

665. ἀποτρέπω **apŏtrĕpŏ,** ap-ot-rep'-o; from 575 and the base of 5157; to deflect, i.e. (reflex.) avoid:—turn away.

666. ἀπουσία **apŏusia,** ap-oo-see'-ah; from the part. of 548; a being away:—absence.

667. ἀποφέρω **apŏphĕrŏ,** ap-of-er'-o; from 575 and 5342; to bear off (lit. or rel.):—bring, carry (away).

668. ἀποφεύγω **apŏphĕugŏ,** ap-of-yoo'-go; from 575 and 5343; (fig.) to escape:—escape.

669. ἀποφθέγγομαι **apŏphthĕggŏmai,** ap-of-theng'-om-ahee; from 575 and 5350; to enunciate plainly, i.e. declare:—say, speak forth, utterance.

670. ἀποφορτίζομαι **apŏphŏrtizŏmai,** ap-of-or-tid'-zom-ahee; from 575 and the mid. of 5412; to unload:—unlade.

671. ἀπόχρησις **apŏchrēsis,** ap-okh'-ray-sis; from a comp. of 575 and 5530; the act of using up, i.e. consumption:—using.

672. ἀποχωρέω **apŏchōreŏ,** ap-okh-o-reh'-o; from 575 and 5562; to go away:—depart.

673. ἀποχωρίζω **apŏchōrizŏ,** ap-okh-o-rid'-zo; from 575 and 5563; to rend apart; reflex. to separate:—depart (asunder).

674. ἀποψύχω **apŏpsuchŏ,** ap-ops-oo'-kho; from 575 and 5594; to breathe out, i.e. faint:—hearts failing.

675. Ἄππιος **Appiŏs,** ap'-pee-os; of Lat. or.; (in the genitive, i.e. possessive case) of Appius, the name of a Roman:—Appii.

676. ἀπρόσιτος **aprŏsitŏs,** ap-ros'-ee-tos; from 1 (as a neg. particle) and a der. of a comp. of 4314 and εἶμι ĕimi (to go); inaccessible:—which no man can approach.

677. ἀπρόσκοπος **aprŏskŏpŏs,** ap-ros'-kop-os; from 1 (as a neg. particle) and a presumed der. of 4350; act. inoffensive, i.e. not leading into sin; pass. faultless, i.e. not led into sin:—none (void of, without) offence.

678. ἀπροσωπολήπτως **aprŏsōpŏlēptŏs,** ap-ros-o-pol-ape'-toce; adv. from a comp. of 1 (as a neg. particle) and a presumed der. of a presumed comp. of 4383 and 2983 [comp. 4381]; in a way not accepting the person, i.e. impartially:—without respect of persons.

679. ἄπταιστος **aptaistŏs,** ap-tah'ee-stos; from 1 (as a neg. particle) and a der. of 4417; not stumbling, i.e. (fig.) without sin:—from falling.

680. ἅπτομαι **haptŏmai,** hap'-tom-ahee; reflex. of 681; prop. to attach oneself to, i.e. to touch (in many implied relations):—touch.

681. ἅπτω **haptŏ,** hap'-to; a prim. verb; prop. to fasten to, i.e. (spec.) to set on fire:—kindle, light.

682. Ἀπφία **Apphia,** ap-fee'-a; prob. of for. or.; Apphia, a woman of Colossæ:—Apphia.

683. ἀπωθέομαι **apōthĕŏmai,** ap-o-theh'-om-ahee; or ἀπώθομαι **apōthŏmai,** ap-o'-thom-ahee; from 575 and the mid. of ὠθέω ōthĕŏ or ὤθω ōthŏ (to shove); to push off, fig. to reject:—cast away, put away (from), thrust away (from).

684. ἀπώλεια **apōlĕia,** ap-o'-li-a; from a presumed der. of 622; ruin or loss (phys., spiritual or eternal):—damnable (-nation), destruction, die, perdition, × perish, pernicious ways, waste.

685. ἀρά **ara,** ar-ah'; prob. from 142; prop. prayer (as lifted to Heaven), i.e. (by impl.) imprecation:—curse.

686. ἄρα **ara,** ar'-ah; prob. from 142 (through the idea of drawing a conclusion); a particle denoting an inference more or less decisive (as follows):—haply, (what) manner (of man), no doubt, perhaps, so be, then, therefore, truly, wherefore. Often used in connection with other particles, especially 1065 or 3767 (after) or 1487 (before). Comp. also 687.

687. ἆρα **ara,** ar'-ah; a form of 686, denoting an interrogation to which a negative answer is presumed:—therefore.

688. Ἀραβία **Arabia,** ar-ab-ee'-ah; of Heb. or. [6152]; Arabia, a region of Asia:—Arabia.

ἄραγε aragĕ. See 686 and 1065.

689. Ἀράμ **Aram,** ar-am'; of Heb. or. [7410]; Aram (i.e. Ram), an Isr.:—Aram.

690. Ἄραψ **Araps,** ar'-aps; from 688; an Arab or native of Arabia:—Arabian.

691. ἀργέω **argeŏ,** arg-eh'-o; from 692; to be idle, i.e. (fig.) to delay:—linger.

692. ἀργός **argŏs,** ar-gos'; from 1 (as a neg. particle) and 2041; inactive, i.e. unemployed; (by impl.) lazy, useless:—barren, idle, slow.

693. ἀργύρεος **argurĕŏs,** ar-goo'-reh-os; from 696; made of silver:—(of) silver.

694. ἀργύριον **arguriŏn,** ar-goo'-ree-on; neut. of a presumed der. of 696; silvery, i.e. (by impl.) cash; spec. a silverling (i.e. drachma or shekel):—money, (piece of) silver (piece).

695. ἀργυροκόπος **argurŏkŏpŏs,** ar-goo-rok-op'-os; from 696 and 2875; a beater (i.e. worker) of silver:—silversmith.

696. ἄργυρος **argurŏs,** ar'-goo-ros; from ἀργός argŏs (shining); silver (the metal, in the articles or coin):—silver.

697. Ἄρειος Πάγος **Arĕiŏs Pagŏs,** ar'-i-os pag'-os; from Ἄρης Arēs (the name of the Greek deity of war) and a der. of 4078; rock of Ares, a place in Athens:—Areopagus, Mars' Hill.

698. Ἀρεοπαγίτης **Arĕŏpagitēs,** ar-eh-op-ag-ee'-tace; from 697; an Areopagite or member of the court held on Mars' Hill:—Areopagite.

699. ἀρέσκεια **arĕskĕia,** ar-es'-ki-ah; from a der. of 700; complaisance:—pleasing.

700. ἀρέσκω **arĕskŏ,** ar-es'-ko; prob. from 142 (through the idea of exciting emotion); to be agreeable (or by impl. to seek to be so):—please.

701. ἀρεστός **arĕstŏs,** ar-es-tos'; from 700; agreeable; by impl. fit:—(things that) please (-ing), reason.

702. Ἀρέτας **Arĕtas,** ar-et'-as; of for. or.; Aretas, an Arabian:—Aretas.

703. ἀρετή **arĕtē,** ar-et'-ay; from the same as 730; prop. manliness (valor), i.e. excellence (intrinsic or attributed):—praise, virtue.

704. ἀρήν **arēn,** ar-ane'; perh. the same as 730; a lamb (as a male):—lamb.

705. ἀριθμέω **arithmeŏ,** ar-ith-meh'-o; from 706; to enumerate or count:—number.

706. ἀριθμός **arithmŏs,** ar-ith-mos'; from 142; a number (as reckoned up):—number.

707. Ἀριμαθαία **Arimathaia,** ar-ee-math-ah'ee-ah; of Heb. or. [7414]; Arimathæa (or Ramah), a place in Pal.:—Arimathæa.

708. Ἀρίσταρχος **Aristarchŏs,** ar-is'-tar-khos; from the same as 712 and 757; best ruling; Aristarchus, a Macedonian:—Aristarchus.

709. ἀριστάω **aristaŏ,** ar-is-tah'-o; from 712; to take the principal meal:—dine.

710. ἀριστερός **aristĕrŏs,** ar-is-ter-os'; appar. a comp. of the same as 712; the left hand (as second-best):—left [hand].

711. Ἀριστόβουλος **Aristŏbŏulŏs,** *ar-is-tob'-oo-los;* from the same as *712* and *1012; best counselling; Aristobulus,* a Chr.:—Aristobulus.

712. ἄριστον **aristŏn,** *ar'-is-ton;* appar. neut. of a superlative from the same as *730;* the *best meal* [or *breakfast;* perh. from ἦρι ἔρι ("*early*")], i.e. *luncheon:*—dinner.

713. ἀρκετός **arkĕtŏs,** *ar-ket-os';* from *714; satisfactory:*—enough, suffice (-ient).

714. ἀρκέω **arkĕō,** *ar-keh'-o;* appar. a prim. verb [but prob. akin to *142* through the idea of *raising* a barrier]; prop. to *ward off,* i.e. (by impl.) to *avail* (fig. be *satisfactory*):—be content, be enough, suffice, be sufficient.

715. ἄρκτος **arktŏs,** *ark'-tos;* prob. from *714;* a *bear* (as *obstructing* by ferocity):—bear.

716. ἅρμα **harma,** *har'-mah;* prob. from *142* [perh. with *1* (as a particle of union) prefixed]; a *chariot* (as *raised* or fitted *together* [comp. *719*]):—chariot.

717. Ἀρμαγεδδών **Armagĕddōn,** *ar-mag-ed-dohn';* of Heb. or. [*2022* and *4023*]; *Armageddon* (or *Har-Megiddon*), a symbol. name:—Armageddon.

718. ἁρμόζω **harmŏzō,** *har-mod'-zo;* from *719;* to *joint,* i.e. (fig.) to *woo* (reflex. to *betroth*):—espouse.

719. ἁρμός **harmŏs,** *har-mos';* from the same as *716;* an *articulation* (of the body):—joint.

720. ἀρνέομαι **arnĕŏmai.** *ar-neh'-om-ahee;* perh. from *1* (as a neg. particle) and the mid. of *4483;* to *contradict,* i.e. *disavow, reject, abnegate:*—deny, refuse.

721. ἀρνίον **arniŏn,** *ar-nee'-on;* diminutive from *704;* a *lambkin:*—lamb.

722. ἀροτριόω **arŏtriŏō,** *ar-ot-ree-ŏ'-o;* from *723;* to *plough:*—plow.

723. ἄροτρον **arŏtrŏn,** *ar'-ot-ron;* from ἀρόω **arŏō** (to *till*); a *plough:*—plow.

724. ἁρπαγή **harpagē,** *har-pag-ay';* from *726; pillage* (prop. abstr.):—extortion, ravening, spoiling.

725. ἁρπαγμός **harpagmŏs,** *har-pag-mos';* from *726; plunder* (prop. concr.):—robbery.

726. ἁρπάζω **harpazō,** *har-pad'-zo;* from a der. of *138;* to *seize* (in various applications):—catch (away, up), pluck, pull, take (by force).

727. ἅρπαξ **harpax,** *har'-pax;* from *726; rapacious:*—extortion, ravening.

728. ἀρραβών **arrhabŏn,** *ar-hrab-ohn';* of Heb. or. [*6162*]; a *pledge,* i.e. part of the purchase-money or property given in advance as *security* for the rest:—earnest.

729. ἄρραφος **arrhaphŏs,** *ar'-hhraf-os;* from *1* (as a neg. particle) and a presumed der. of the same as *4476; unsewed,* i.e. of a single piece:—without seam.

730. ἄρρην **arrhēn,** *ar'-hrane;* or ἄρσην **arsēn,** *ar'-sane;* prob. from *142; male* (as stronger for *lifting*):—male, man.

731. ἄρρητος **arrhētŏs,** *ar'-hray-tos;* from *1* (as a neg. particle) and the same as *4490; unsaid,* i.e. (by impl.) *inexpressible:*—unspeakable.

732. ἄρρωστος **arrhōstŏs,** *ar'-hroce-tos;* from *1* (as a neg. particle) and a presumed der. of *4517; infirm:*—sick (folk, -ly).

733. ἀρσενοκοίτης **arsĕnŏkŏitēs,** *ar-sen-ok-oy'-tace;* from *730* and *2845;* a *sodomite:*—abuser of (that defile) self with mankind.

734. Ἀρτεμάς **Artĕmas,** *ar-tem-as';* contr. from a comp. of *735* and *1435; gift of Artemis; Artemas* (or *Artemidorus*), a Chr.:—Artemas.

735. Ἄρτεμις **Artĕmis,** *ar'-tem-is;* prob. from the same as *730; prompt; Artemis,* the name of a Grecian goddess borrowed by the Asiatics for one of their deities:—Diana.

736. ἀρτέμων **artĕmōn,** *ar-tem'-ohn;* from a der. of *737;* prop. something *ready* [or else more remotely from *142* (comp. *740*); something *hung* up], i.e. (spec.) the *topsail* (rather *foresail* or *jib*) of a vessel:—mainsail.

737. ἄρτι **arti,** *ar'-tee;* adv. from a der. of *142* (comp. *740*) through the idea of *suspension;* just *now:*—this day (hour), hence [-forth], here [-after], hither [-to], (even) now, (this) present.

738. ἀρτιγέννητος **artigĕnnētŏs,** *ar-teeg-en'-nay-tos;* from *737* and *1084;* just *born,* i.e. (fig.) a *young convert:*—new born.

739. ἄρτιος **artiŏs,** *ar'-tee-os;* from *737; fresh,* i.e. (by impl.) *complete:*—perfect.

740. ἄρτος **artŏs,** *ar'-tos;* from *142; bread* (as *raised*) or a *loaf:*—(shew-) bread, loaf.

741. ἀρτύω **artuō,** *ar-too'-o;* from a presumed der. of *142;* to *prepare,* i.e. *spice* (with *stimulating* condiments):—season.

742. Ἀρφαξάδ **Arphaxad,** *ar-fax-ad';* of Heb. or. [*775*]; *Arphaxad,* a post-diluvian patriarch:—Arphaxad.

743. ἀρχάγγελος **archaggĕlŏs,** *ar-khang'-el-os;* from *757* and *32;* a *chief angel:*—archangel.

744. ἀρχαῖος **archaiŏs,** *ar-khah'-yos;* from *746; original* or *primeval:*—(them of) old (time).

745. Ἀρχέλαος **Archĕlaŏs,** *ar-khel'-ah-os;* from *757* and *2994; people-ruling; Archelaus,* a Jewish king:—Archelaus.

746. ἀρχή **archē,** *ar-khay';* from *756;* (prop. abstr.) a *commencement,* or (concr.) *chief* (in various applications of order, time, place or rank):—beginning, corner, (at the) first (estate), magistrate, power, principality, principle, rule.

747. ἀρχηγός **archēgŏs,** *ar-khay-gos';* from *746* and *71;* a *chief leader:*—author, captain, prince.

748. ἀρχιερατικός **archiĕratikŏs,** *ar-khee-er-at-ee-kos';* from *746* and a der. of *2413; high-priestly:*—of the high-priest.

749. ἀρχιερεύς **archiĕrĕus,** *ar-khee-er-yuce';* from *746* and *2409;* the *high-priest* (lit. of the Jews, typ. Christ); by extens. a *chief priest:*—chief (high) priest, chief of the priests.

750. ἀρχιποίμην **archipŏimēn.** *ar-khee-poy'-mane;* from *746* and *4166;* a *head shepherd:*—chief shepherd.

751. Ἀρχίππος **Archippŏs,** *ar'-khip-pos;* from *746* and *2462; horse-ruler; Archippus,* a Chr.:—Archippus.

752. ἀρχισυνάγωγος **archisunagōgŏs,** *ar-khee-soon-ag'-o-gos;* from *746* and *4864; director* of the *synagogue* services:—(chief) ruler of the synagogue.

753. ἀρχιτέκτων **architĕktōn,** *ar-khee-tek'-tone;* from *746* and *5045;* a *chief constructor,* i.e. "*architect*":—masterbuilder.

754. ἀρχιτελώνης **architĕlōnēs,** *ar-khee-tel-o'-nace;* from *746* and *5057;* a *principal tax-gatherer:*—chief among the publicans.

755. ἀρχιτρίκλινος **architriklinŏs,** *ar-khee-tree'-klee-nos;* from *746* and a comp. of *5140* and *2827* (a *dinner-bed,* because composed of three couches); *director* of the *entertainment:*—governor (ruler) of the feast.

756. ἄρχομαι **archŏmai,** *ar'-khom-ahee;* mid. of *757* (through the impl. of *precedence*); to *commence* (in order of time):—(rehearse from) begin (-ning).

757. ἄρχω **archō,** *ar'-kho;* a prim. verb; to be *first* (in political rank or power):—reign (rule) over.

758. ἄρχων **archōn,** *ar'-khone;* pres. part. of *757;* a *first* (in rank or power):—chief (ruler), magistrate, prince, ruler.

759. ἄρωμα **"arōma."** *ar'-o-mah;* from *142* (in the sense of *sending off* scent); an *aromatic:*—(sweet) spice.

760. Ἀσά **Asa,** *as-ah';* of Heb. or. [*609*]; *Asa,* an Isr.:—Asa.

761. ἀσάλευτος **asalĕutŏs,** *as-al'-yoo-tos;* from *1* (as a neg. particle) and a der. of *4531; unshaken,* i.e. (by impl.) *immovable* (fig.):—which cannot be moved, unmovable.

762. ἄσβεστος **asbĕstŏs,** *as'-bes-tos;* from *1* (as a neg. particle) and a der. of *4570; not extinguished,* i.e. (by impl.) *perpetual:*—not to be quenched, unquenchable.

763. ἀσέβεια **asĕbĕia,** *as-eb'-i-ah;* from *765; impiety,* i.e. (by impl.) *wickedness:*—ungodly (-liness).

764. ἀσεβέω **asĕbĕō,** *as-eb-eh'-o;* from *765;* to be (by impl. act) *impious* or *wicked:*—commit (live, that after should live) ungodly.

765. ἀσεβής **asĕbēs,** *as-eb-ace';* from *1* (as a neg. particle) and a presumed der. of *4576; irreverent,* i.e. (by extens.) *impious* or *wicked:*—ungodly (man).

766. ἀσέλγεια **asĕlgĕia,** *as-elg'-i-a;* from a comp. of *1* (as a neg. particle) and a presumed der. σελγής **sĕlgēs** (of uncert. der., but appar. mean. *continent*); *licentiousness* (sometimes including other vices):—filthy, lasciviousness, wantonness.

767. ἄσημος **asēmŏs,** *as'-ay-mos;* from *1* (as a neg. particle) and the base of *4591; unmarked,* i.e. (fig.) *ignoble:*—mean.

768. Ἀσήρ **Asēr,** *as-ayr';* of Heb. or. [*836*]; *Aser* (i.e. *Asher*), an Isr. tribe:—Aser.

769. ἀσθένεια **asthĕnĕia,** *as-then'-i-ah;* from *772; feebleness* (of body or mind); by impl. *malady;* mor. *frailty:*—disease, infirmity, sickness, weakness.

770. ἀσθενέω **asthĕnĕō,** *as-then-eh'-o;* from *772;* to be *feeble* (in any sense):—be diseased, impotent folk (man), (be) sick, (be, be made) weak.

771. ἀσθένημα **asthĕnēma,** *as-then'-ay-mah;* from *770;* a *scruple of conscience:*—infirmity.

772. ἀσθενής **asthĕnēs,** *as-then-ace';* from *1* (as a neg. particle) and the base of *4599; strengthless* (in various applications, lit., fig. and mor.):—more feeble, impotent, sick, without strength, weak (-er, -ness, thing).

773. Ἀσία **Asia,** *as-ee'-ah;* of uncert. der.; *Asia,* i.e. *Asia Minor,* or (usually) only its western shore:—Asia.

774. Ἀσιανός **Asianŏs,** *as-ee-an-os';* from *773;* an *Asian* (i.e. *Asiatic*) or inhab. of Asia:—of Asia.

775. Ἀσιάρχης **Asiarchēs,** *as-ee ar'-khace;* from *773* and *746;* an *Asiarch* or president of the public festivities in a city of Asia Minor:—chief of Asia.

776. ἀσιτία **asitia,** *as-ee-tee'-ah;* from *777; fasting* (the state):—abstinence.

777. ἄσιτος **asitŏs,** *as'-ee-tos;* from *1* (as a neg. particle) and *4621; without* (taking) *food:*—fasting.

778. ἀσκέω **askĕō,** *as-keh'-o;* prob. from the same as *4632;* to *elaborate,* i.e. (fig.) *train* (by impl. *strive*):—exercise.

779. ἀσκός **askŏs,** *as-kos';* from the same as *778;* a *leathern* (or skin) *bag* used as a bottle:—bottle.

780. ἀσμένως **asmĕnōs,** *as-men'-oce;* adv. from a der. of the base of *2237; with pleasure:*—gladly.

781. ἄσοφος **asŏphŏs,** *as'-of-os;* from *1* (as a neg. particle) and *4680; unwise:*—fool.

782. ἀσπάζομαι **aspazŏmai,** *as-pad'-zom-ahee;* from *1* (as a particle of union) and a presumed form of *4685;* to *enfold* in the arms, i.e. (by impl.) to *salute* (fig.) to *welcome:*—embrace, greet, salute, take leave.

783. ἀσπασμός **aspasmŏs,** *as-pas-mos';* from *782;* a *greeting* (in person or by letter):—greeting, salutation.

784. ἄσπιλος **aspilŏs,** *as'-pee-los;* from *1* (as a neg. particle) and *4695; unblemished* (phys. or mor.):—without spot, unspotted.

785. ἀσπίς **aspis,** *as-pece';* of uncert. der.; a *buckler* (or round shield); used of a serpent (as *coiling* itself), prob. the "*asp*":—asp.

786. ἄσπονδος **aspŏndŏs,** *as'-pon-dos;* from *1* (as a neg. particle) and a der. of *4689;* lit. *without libation* (which usually accompanied a treaty), i.e. (by impl.) *truceless;* figuratively *implacable:*—implacable, truce-breaker.

787. ἀσσάριον **assariŏn,** *as-sar'-ee-on;* of Lat. or.; an *assarius* or *as,* a Roman coin:—farthing.

788. ἄσσον **assŏn,** *as'-son;* neut. comparative of the base of *1451; more nearly,* i.e. *very near:*—close.

789. Ἄσσος **Assŏs,** *as'-sos;* prob. of for. or.; *Assus,* a city of Asia Minor:—Assos.

790. ἀστατέω **astatĕō,** *as-tat-eh'-o;* from *1* (as a neg. particle) and a der. of *2476;* to be *non-stationary,* i.e. (fig.) *homeless:*—have no certain dwelling-place.

791. ἀστεῖος **astĕiŏs,** *as-ti'-os;* from ἄστυ **astu** (a *city*); *urbane,* i.e. (by impl.) *handsome:*—fair.

792. ἀστήρ **astēr,** *as-tare';* prob. from the base of *4766;* a *star* (as *strown* over the sky), lit. or fig.:—star.

793. ἀστήρικτος **astēriktŏs**, *as-tay'-rik-tos;* from *1* (as a neg. particle) and a presumed der. of *4741; unfixed,* i.e. (fig.) *vacillating:*—unstable.

794. ἄστοργος **astŏrgŏs**, *as'-tor-gos;* from *1* (as a neg. particle) and a presumed der. of στέργω **stĕrgō** (to *cherish* affectionately); *hard-hearted* towards kindred:—without natural affection.

795. ἀστοχέω **astŏchĕō**, *as-tokh-eh'-o;* from a comp. of *1* (as a neg. particle) and στοῖχος **stŏichŏs** (an aim); to *miss* the mark, i.e. (fig.) *deviate* from truth:—err, swerve.

796. ἀστραπή **astrapē**, *as-trap-ay';* from *797; lightning;* by anal. *glare:*—lightning, bright shining.

797. ἀστράπτω **astraptō**, *as-trap'-to;* prob. from *792;* to *flash* as lightning:—lighten, shine.

798. ἄστρον **astrŏn**, *as'-tron;* neut. from *792;* prop. a *constellation;* put for a single *star* (nat. or artificial):—star.

799. Ἀσύγκριτος **Asugkritŏs**, *as-oong'-kree-tos;* from *1* (as a neg. particle) and a der. of *4793; incomparable;* Asyncritus, a Chr.:—Asyncritus.

800. ἀσύμφωνος **asumphōnŏs**, *as-oom'-fo-nos;* from *1* (as a neg. particle) and *4859; inharmonious* (fig.):—agree not.

801. ἀσύνετος **asunĕtŏs**, *as-oon'-ay-tos;* from *1* (as a neg. particle) and *4908; unintelligent;* by impl. *wicked:*—foolish, without understanding.

802. ἀσύνθετος **asunthĕtŏs**, *as-oon'-thet-os;* from *1* (as a neg. particle) and a der. of *4934;* prop. *not agreed,* i.e. *treacherous* to compacts:—covenant-breaker.

803. ἀσφάλεια **asphalĕia**, *as-fal'-i-ah;* from *804; security* (lit. or fig.):—certainty, safety.

804. ἀσφαλής **asphalēs**, *as-fal-ace';* from *1* (as a neg. particle) and σφάλλω **sphallō** (to "*fail*"); *secure* (lit. or fig.):—certain (-ty), safe, sure.

805. ἀσφαλίζω **asphalizō**, *as-fal-id'-zo;* from *804;* to *render secure:*—make fast (sure).

806. ἀσφαλῶς **asphalōs**, *as-fal-oce';* adv. from *804; securely* (lit. or fig.):—assuredly, safely.

807. ἀσχημονέω **aschēmŏnĕō**, *as-kay-mon-eh'-o;* from *809;* to *be* (i.e. *act*) *unbecoming:*—behave self uncomely (unseemly).

808. ἀσχημοσύνη **aschēmŏsunē**, *as-kay-mos-oo'-nay;* from *809;* an *indecency;* by impl. the *pudenda:*—shame, that which is unseemly.

809. ἀσχήμων **askēmōn**, *as-kay'-mone;* from *1* (as a neg. particle) and a presumed der. of *2192* (in the sense of its congener *4976*); prop. *shapeless,* i.e. (fig.) *inelegant:*—uncomely.

810. ἀσωτία **asōtia**, *as-o-tee'-ah;* from a comp. of *1* (as a neg. particle) and a presumed der. of *4982;* prop. *unsavedness,* i.e. (by impl.) *profligacy:*—excess, riot.

811. ἀσώτως **asōtōs**, *as-o'-toce;* adv. from the same as *810; dissolutely:*—riotous.

812. ἀτακτέω **ataktĕō**, *at-ak-teh'-o;* from *813;* to *be* (i.e. *act*) *irregular:*—behave self disorderly.

813. ἄτακτος **ataktŏs**, *at'-ak-tos;* from *1* (as a neg. particle) and a der. of *5021; unarranged,* i.e. (by impl.) *insubordinate* (religiously):—unruly.

814. ἀτάκτως **ataktōs**, *at-ak'-toce;* adv. from *813; irregularly* (mor.):—disorderly.

815. ἄτεκνος **atĕknŏs**, *at'-ek-nos;* from *1* (as a neg. particle) and *5043; childless:*—childless, without children.

816. ἀτενίζω **atĕnizō**, *at-en-id'-zo;* from a comp. of *1* (as a particle of union) and τείνω **tĕinō** (to *stretch*); to *gaze* intently:—behold earnestly (stedfastly), fasten (eyes), look (earnestly, stedfastly, up stedfastly), set eyes.

817. ἄτερ **atĕr**, *at'-er;* a particle prob. akin to *427; aloof,* i.e. *apart* from (lit. or fig.):—in the absence of, without.

818. ἀτιμάζω **atimazō**, *at-im-ad'-zo;* from *820;* to *render infamous,* i.e. (by impl.) *contemn* or *maltreat:*—despise, dishonour, suffer shame, entreat shamefully.

819. ἀτιμία **atimia**, *at-ee-mee'-ah;* from *820; infamy,* i.e. (subj.) *comparative indignity,* (obj.) *disgrace:*—dishonour, reproach, shame, vile.

820. ἄτιμος **atimŏs**, *at'-ee-mos;* from *1* (as a neg. particle) and *5092;* (neg.) *unhonoured* or (pos.) *dishonoured:*—despised, without honour, less honourable [*comparative degree*].

821. ἀτιμόω **atimŏō**, *at-ee-mŏ'-o;* from *820;* used like *818,* to *maltreat:*—handle shamefully.

822. ἀτμίς **atmis**, *at-mece';* from the same as *109; mist:*—vapour.

823. ἄτομος **atŏmŏs**, *at'-om-os;* from *1* (as a neg. particle) and the base of *5114; uncut,* i.e. (by impl.) *indivisible* [an "*atom*" of time]:—moment.

824. ἄτοπος **atŏpŏs**, *at'-op-os;* from *1* (as a neg. particle) and *5117; out of place,* i. e. (fig.) *improper, injurious, wicked:*—amiss, harm, unreasonable.

825. Ἀττάλεια **Attalĕia**, *at-tal'-i-ah;* from Ἄτταλος **Attalŏs** (a king of Pergamus); *Attaleia,* a place in Pamphylia:—Attalia.

826. αὐγάζω **augazō**, *ŏw-gad'-zo;* from *827;* to *beam* forth (fig.):—shine.

827. αὐγή **augē**, *ŏwg'-ay;* of uncert. der.; a *ray* of light, i.e. (by impl.) *radiance, dawn:*—break of day.

828. Αὔγουστος **Augŏustŏs**, *ŏw'-goos-tos;* from Lat. ["*august*"]; *Augustus,* a title of the Rom. emperor:—Augustus.

829. αὐθάδης **authadēs**, *ŏw-thad'-ace;* from *846* and the base of *2237; self-pleasing,* i.e. *arrogant:*—self-willed.

830. αὐθαίρετος **authairĕtŏs**, *ŏw-thah'-ee-ret-os;* from *846* and the same as *140; self-chosen,* i.e. (by impl.) *voluntary:*—of own accord, willing of self.

831. αὐθεντέω **authĕntĕō**, *ŏw-then-teh'-o;* from a comp. of *846* and an obsol. ἔντης **hĕntēs** (a *worker*); to *act of oneself,* i.e. (fig.) *dominate:*—usurp authority over.

832. αὐλέω **aulĕō**, *ŏw-leh'-o;* from *846;* to play the *flute:*—pipe.

833. αὐλή **aulē**, *ŏw-lay';* from the same as *109;* a *yard* (as open to the *wind*); by impl. a *mansion:*—court, ([sheep-]) fold, hall, palace.

834. αὐλητής **aulĕtēs**, *ŏw-lay-tace';* from *832;* a *flute-player:*—minstrel, piper.

835. αὐλίζομαι **aulizŏmai**, *ŏw-lid'-zom-ahee;* mid. from *833;* to *pass the night* (prop. in the open air):—abide, lodge.

836. αὐλός **aulŏs**, *ŏw-los';* from the same as *109,* a *flute* (as *blown*):—pipe.

837. αὐξάνω **auxanō**, *ŏwx-an'-o;* a prolonged form of a prim. verb; to *grow* ("*wax*"), i.e. *enlarge* (lit. or fig., act. or pass.):—grow (up), (give the) increase.

838. αὔξησις **auxēsis**, *ŏwx'-ay-sis;* from *837; growth:*—increase.

839. αὔριον **auriŏn**, *ŏw'-ree-on;* from a der. of the same as *109* (mean. a *breeze,* i.e. the *morning air*); prop. *fresh,* i.e. (adv. with ellipsis of *2250*) *to-morrow:*—(to-) morrow, next day.

840. αὐστηρός **austērŏs**, *ŏw-stay-ros';* from a (presumed) der. of the same as *109* (mean. *blown*); *rough* (prop. as a *gale*), i.e. (fig.) *severe:*—austere.

841. αὐτάρκεια **autarkeia**, *ŏw-tar'-ki-ah;* from *842; self-satisfaction,* i.e. (abstr.) *contentedness,* or (concr.) a *competence:*—contentment, sufficiency.

842. αὐτάρκης **autarkēs**, *ŏw-tar'-kace;* from *846* and *714; self-complacent,* i.e. *contented:*—content.

843. αὐτοκατάκριτος **autŏkatakritŏs**, *ŏw-tok-at-ak'-ree-tos;* from *846* and a der. of *2632; self-condemned:*—condemned of self.

844. αὐτόματος **autŏmatŏs**, *ŏw-tom'-at-os;* from *846* and the same as *3155; self-moved* ["automatic"], i.e. *spontaneous:*—of own accord, of self.

845. αὐτόπτης **autŏptēs**, *ŏw-top'-tace;* from *846* and *3700; self-seeing,* i.e. *eye-witness:*—eye-witness.

846. αὐτός **autŏs**, *ŏw-tos';* from the particle αὖ **au** [perh. akin to the base of *109* through the idea of a *baffling* wind] (*backward*); the reflex. pron. *self,* used (alone or in the comp. *1438*) of the third pers.,

and (with the prop. pers. pron.) of the other persons:—her, it (-self), one, the other, (mine) own, said, ([self-], the) same, ([him-, my-, thy-]) self, [your-] selves, she, that, their (-s), them ([-selves]), there [-at, -by, -in, -into, -of, -on, -with], they, (these) things, this (man), those, together, very, which. Comp. *848.*

847. αὐτοῦ **autŏu**, *ŏw-too';* genitive (i.e. possessive) of *846,* used as an adv. of location; prop. belonging to the *same* spot, i.e. *in this* (or *that*) *place:*—(t-) here.

848. αὑτοῦ **hautŏu**, *how-too';* contr. for *1438; self* (in some oblique case or reflex. relation):—her (own), (of) him (-self), his (own), of it, thee, their (own), them (-selves), they.

849. αὐτόχειρ **autŏchĕir**, *ŏw-tokh'-ire;* from *846* and *5495; self-handed,* i.e. doing *personally:*—with ... own hands.

850. αὐχμηρός **auchmērŏs**, *ŏwkh-may-ros';* from αὐχμός **auchmŏs** [prob. from a base akin to that of *109*] (*dust,* as dried by wind); prop. *dirty,* i.e. (by impl.) *obscure:*—dark.

851. ἀφαιρέω **aphairĕō**, *af-ahee-reh'-o;* from *575* and *138;* to *remove* (lit. or fig.):—cut (smite) off, take away.

852. ἀφανής **aphanēs**, *af-an-ace';* from *1* (as a neg. particle) and *5316; non-apparent:*—that is not manifest.

853. ἀφανίζω **aphanizō**, *af-an-id'-zo;* from *852;* to *render unapparent,* i.e. (act.) *consume* (becloud), or (pass.) *disappear* (be destroyed):—corrupt, disfigure, perish, vanish away.

854. ἀφανισμός **aphanismŏs**, *af-an-is-mos';* from *853; disappearance,* i.e. (fig.) *abrogation:*—vanish away.

855. ἄφαντος **aphantŏs**, *af'-an-tos;* from *1* (as a neg. particle) and a der. of *5316; non-manifested,* i.e. *invisible:*—vanished out of sight.

856. ἀφεδρών **aphĕdrōn**, *af-ed-rone';* from a comp. of *575* and the base of *1476;* a place of *sitting apart,* i.e. a *privy:*—draught.

857. ἀφειδία **aphĕidia**, *af-i-dee'-ah;* from a comp. of *1* (as a neg. particle) and *5339; unsparingness,* i.e. *austerity* (ascetism):—neglecting.

858. ἀφελότης **aphĕlŏtēs**, *af-el-ot'-ace;* from a comp. of *1* (as a neg. particle) and φέλλος **phĕllŏs** (in the sense of a *stone* as *stubbing* the foot); *smoothness,* i.e. (fig.) *simplicity:*—singleness.

859. ἄφεσις **aphĕsis**, *af'-es-is;* from *863; freedom;* (fig.) *pardon:*—deliverance, forgiveness, liberty, remission.

860. ἁφή **haphē**, *haf-ay';* from *680;* prob. a *ligament* (as *fastening*):—joint.

861. ἀφθαρσία **aphtharsia**, *af-thar-see'-ah;* from *862; incorruptibility;* gen. *unending existence;* (fig.) *genuineness:*—immortality, incorruption, sincerity.

862. ἄφθαρτος **aphthartŏs**, *af'-thar-tos;* from *1* (as a neg. particle) and a der. of *5351; undecaying* (in essence or continuance):—not (in-, un-) corruptible, immortal.

863. ἀφίημι **aphiēmi**, *af-ee'-ay-mee;* from *575* and ἵημι **hiĕmi** (to *send*); an intens. form of εἷμι **ĕimi** (to *go*); to *send forth,* in various applications (as follow):—cry, forgive, forsake, lay aside, leave, let (alone, be, go, have), omit, put (send) away, remit, suffer, yield up.

864. ἀφικνέομαι **aphiknĕŏmai**, *af-ik-neh'-om-ahee;* from *575* and the base of *2425;* to *go* (i.e. *spread*) *forth* (by rumor):—come abroad.

865. ἀφιλάγαθος **aphilagathŏs**, *af-il-ag'-ath-os;* from *1* (as a neg. particle) and *5358; hostile to virtue:*—despiser of those that are good.

866. ἀφιλάργυρος **aphilargurŏs**, *af-il-ar'-goo-ros;* from *1* (as a neg. particle) and *5366; unavaricious:*—without covetousness, not greedy of filthy lucre.

867. ἄφιξις **aphixis**, *af'-ix-is;* from *864;* prop. *arrival,* i.e. (by impl.) *departure:*—departing.

868. ἀφίστημι **aphistēmi**, *af-is'-tay-mee;* from *575* and *2476;* to *remove,* i.e. (act.) *instigate* to revolt;

usually (reflex.) to *desist, desert*, etc.:—depart, draw (fall) away, refrain, withdraw self.

869. ἄφνω **aphnō**, *af'-no*; adv. from *852* (contr.); *unawares*, i.e. *unexpectedly*:—suddenly.

870. ἄφοβος **aphŏbŏs**, *af-ob'-oce*; adv. from a comp. of *1* (as a neg. particle) and *5401*; *fearlessly*:—without fear.

871. ἀφομοιόω **aphŏmŏiŏō**, *af-om-oy-ŏ'-o*; from *575* and *3666*; to *assimilate* closely:—make like.

872. ἀφοράω **aphŏraō**, *af-or-ah'-o*; from *575* and *3708*; to *consider* attentively:—look.

873. ἀφορίζω **aphŏrizō**, *af-or-id'-zo*; from *575* and *3724*; to *set off* by boundary, i.e. (fig.) *limit, exclude, appoint*, etc.:—divide, separate, sever.

874. ἀφορμή **aphŏrmē**, *af-or-may'*; from a comp. of *575* and *3729*; a *starting-point*, i.e. (fig.) an *opportunity*:—occasion.

875. ἀφρίζω **aphrizō**, *af-rid'-zo*; from *876*; to *froth* at the mouth (in epilepsy):—foam.

876. ἀφρός **aphrŏs**, *af-ros'*; appar. a prim. word; *froth*, i.e. *slaver*:—foaming.

877. ἀφροσύνη **aphrŏsunē**, *af-ros-oo'-nay*; from *878*; *senselessness*, i.e. (euphem.) *egotism*; (mor.) *recklessness*:—folly, foolishly (-ness).

878. ἄφρων **aphrŏn**, *af'-rone*; from *1* (as a neg. particle) and *5424*; prop. *mindless*, i.e. *stupid*, (by impl.) *ignorant*, (spec.) *egotistic*, (practically) *rash*, or (mor.) *unbelieving*:—fool (-ish), unwise.

879. ἀφυπνόω **aphupnŏō**, *af-oop-nŏ'-o*; from a comp. of *575* and *5258*; prop. to *become awake*, i.e. (by impl.) to *drop* (off) in slumber:—fall asleep.

880. ἄφωνος **aphōnŏs**, *af'-o-nos*; from *1* (as a neg. particle) and *5456*; *voiceless*, i.e. *mute* (by nature or choice); fig. *unmeaning*:—dumb, without signification.

881. Ἀχάζ **Achaz**, *akh-adz'*; of Heb. or. [271]; *Achaz*, an Isr.:—Achaz.

882. Ἀχαΐα **Achaïa**, *ach-ah-ee'-ah*; of uncert. der.; *Achaïa* (i.e. *Greece*), a country of Europe:—Achaia.

883. Ἀχαϊκός **Achaïkŏs**, *ach-ah-ee-kos'*; from *882*; an *Achaïan*; *Achaïcus*, a Chr.:—Achaicus.

884. ἀχάριστος **acharistŏs**, *ach-ar'-is-tos*; from *1* (as a neg. particle) and a presumed der. of *5483*; *thankless*, i.e. *ungrateful*:—unthankful.

885. Ἀχείμ **Achĕim**, *akh-ime'*; prob. of Heb. or. [comp. 3137]; *Achim*, an Isr.:—Achim.

886. ἀχειροποίητος **achĕirŏpŏiētŏs**, *akh-i-rop-oy'-ay-tos*; from *1* (as a neg. particle) and *5499*; *unmanufactured*, i.e. *inartificial*:—made without (not made with) hands.

887. ἀχλύς **achlus**, *akh-looce'*; of uncert. der.; *dimness* of sight, i.e. (prob.) a *cataract*:—mist.

888. ἀχρεῖος **achrĕiŏs**, *akh-ri'-os*; from *1* (as a neg. particle) and a der. of *5534* [comp. *5532*]; *useless*, i.e. (euphem.) *unmeritorious*:—unprofitable.

889. ἀχρειόω **achrĕiŏō**, *akh-ri-ŏ'-o*; from *888*; to *render useless*, i.e. *spoil*:—become unprofitable.

890. ἄχρηστος **achrēstŏs**, *akh'-race-tos*; from *1* (as a neg. particle) and *5543*; *inefficient*, i.e. (by impl.) *detrimental*:—unprofitable.

891. ἄχρι **achri**, *akh'-ree*; or ἄχρις **achris**, *akh'-rece*; akin to *206* (through the idea of a *terminus*); (of time) *until* or (of place) *up to*:—as far as, for, in (-to), till, (even, un-) to, until, while.   Comp. *3360*.

892. ἄχυρον **achurŏn**, *akh'-oo-ron*; perh. remotely from χέω **chĕō** (to *shed forth*); *chaff* (as *diffusive*):—chaff.

893. ἀψευδής **apsĕudēs**, *aps-yoo-dace'*; from *1* (as a neg. particle) and *5579*; *veracious*:—that cannot lie.

894. ἄψινθος **apsinthŏs**, *ap'-sin-thos*; of uncert. der.; *wormwood* (as a type of *bitterness*, i.e. [fig.] *calamity*):—wormwood.

895. ἄψυχος **apsuchŏs**, *ap'-soo-khos*; from *1* (as a neg. particle) and *5590*; *lifeless*, i.e. *inanimate* (mechanical):—without life.

B

896. Βάαλ **Baal**, *bah'-al*; of Heb. or. [1168]; *Baal*, a Phœnician deity (used as a symbol of idolatry):—Baal.

897. Βαβυλών **Babulōn**, *bab-oo-lone'*; of Heb. or. [894]; *Babylon*, the capital of Chaldæa (lit. or fig. [as a type of tyranny]):—Babylon.

898. βαθμός **bathmŏs**, *bath-mos'*; from the same as *899*; a *step*, i.e. (fig.) *grade* (of dignity):—degree.

899. βάθος **bathŏs**, *bath'-os*; from the same as *901*; *profundity*, i.e. (by impl.) *extent*; (fig.) *mystery*:—deep (-ness, things), depth.

900. βαθύνω **bathunō**, *bath-oo'-no*; from *901*; to *deepen*:—deep.

901. βαθύς **bathus**, *bath-oos'*; from the base of *939*; *profound* (as *going down*), lit. or fig.:—deep, very early.

902. βαΐον **baïŏn**, *bah-ee'-on*; a diminutive of a der. prob. of the base of *939*; a palm *twig* (as *going out far*):—branch.

903. Βαλαάμ **Balaam**, *bal-ah-am'*; of Heb. or. [1109]; *Balaam*, a Mesopotamian (symb. of a false teacher):—Balaam.

904. Βαλάκ **Balak**, *bal-ak'*; of Heb. or. [1111]; *Balak*, a Moabite:—Balac.

905. βαλάντιον **balantiŏn**, *bal-an'-tee-on*; prob. remotely from *906* (as a *depository*); a *pouch* (for money):—bag, purse.

906. βάλλω **ballō**, *bal'-lo*; a prim. verb; to *throw* (in various applications, more or less violent or intense):—arise, cast (out), × dung, lay, lie, pour, put (up), send, strike, throw (down), thrust.   Comp. *4496*.

907. βαπτίζω **baptizō**, *bap-tid'-zo*; from a der. of *911*; to *make whelmed* (i.e. *fully wet*); used only (in the N. T.) of ceremonial *ablution*, espec. (techn.) of the ordinance of Chr. *baptism*:—baptist, baptize, wash.

908. βάπτισμα **baptisma**, *bap'-tis-mah*; from *907*; *baptism* (techn. or fig.):—baptism.

909. βαπτισμός **baptismŏs**, *bap-tis-mos'*; from *907*; *ablution* (cerem. or Chr.):—baptism, washing.

910. Βαπτιστής **Baptistēs**, *bap-tis-tace'*; from *907*; a *baptizer*, as an epithet of Christ's forerunner:—Baptist.

911. βάπτω **baptō**, *bap'-to*; a prim. verb; to *whelm*, i.e. *cover wholly* with a fluid; in the N. T. only in a qualified or spec. sense, i.e. (lit.) to *moisten* (a part of one's person), or (by impl.) to *stain* (as with dye):—dip.

912. Βαραββᾶς **Barabbas**, *bar-ab-bas'*; of Chald. or. [1247 and 5]; *son of Abba*; *Bar-abbas*, an Isr.:—Barabbas.

913. Βαράκ **Barak**, *bar-ak'*; of Heb. or. [1301]; *Barak*, an Isr.:—Barak.

914. Βαραχίας **Barachias**, *bar-akh-ee'-as*; of Heb. or. [1296]; *Barachias* (i.e. *Berechijah*), an Isr.:—Barachias.

915. βάρβαρος **barbarŏs**, *bar'-bar-os*; of uncert. der.; a *foreigner* (i.e. *non-Greek*):—barbarian (-rous).

916. βαρέω **barĕō**, *bar-eh'-o*; from *926*; to *weigh down* (fig.):—burden, charge, heavy, press.

917. βαρέως **barĕōs**, *bar-eh'-oce*; adv. from *926*; *heavily* (fig.):—dull.

918. Βαρθολομαῖος **Barthŏlŏmaiŏs**, *bar-thol-om-ah'-yos*; of Chald. or. [1247 and 8526]; *son of Tolmai*; *Bar-tholomæus*, a Chr. apostle:—Bartholomeus.

919. Βαριησοῦς **Bariēsŏus**, *bar-ee-ay-sooce'*; of Chald. or. [1247 and 3091]; *son of Jesus* (or *Joshua*); *Bar-jesus*, an Isr.:—Barjesus.

920. Βαριωνᾶς **Bariōnas**, *bar-ee-o-nas'*; of Chald. or. [1247 and 3124]; *son of Jonas* (or *Jonah*); *Bar-jonas*, an Isr.:—Bar-jona.

921. Βαρνάβας **Barnabas**, *bar-nab'-as*; of Chald. or. [1247 and 5029]; *son of Nabas* (i.e. *prophecy*); *Barnabas*, an Isr.:—Barnabas.

922. βάρος **barŏs**, *bar'-os*; prob. from the same as *939* (through the notion of *going down*; comp. *899*); *weight*; in the N. T. only fig. a *load, abundance, authority*:—burden (-some), weight.

923. Βαρσαβᾶς **Barsabas**, *bar-sab-as'*; of Chald. or. [1247 and prob. 6634]; *son of Sabas* (or *Tsaba*); *Bar-sabas*, the name of two Isr.:—Barsabas.

924. Βαρτιμαῖος **Bartimaiŏs**, *bar-tim-ah'-yos*; of Chald. or. [1247 and 2931]; *son of Timæus* (or *the unclean*); *Bar-timæus*, an Isr.:—Bartimæus.

925. βαρύνω **barunō**, *bar-oo'-no*; from *926*; to *burden* (fig.):—overcharge.

926. βαρύς **barus**, *bar-ooce'*; from the same as *922*; *weighty*, i.e. (fig.) *burdensome, grave*:—grievous, heavy, weightier.

927. βαρύτιμος **barutimŏs**, *bar-oo'-tim-os*; from *926* and *5092*; *highly valuable*:—very precious.

928. βασανίζω **basanizō**, *bas-an-id'-zo*; from *931*; to *torture*:—pain, toil, torment, toss, vex.

929. βασανισμός **basanismŏs**, *bas-an-is-mos'*; from *928*; *torture*:—torment.

930. βασανιστής **basanistēs**, *bas-an-is-tace'*; from *928*; a *torturer*:—tormentor.

931. βάσανος **basanŏs**, *bas'-an-os*; perh. remotely from the same as *939* (through the notion of *going to the bottom*); a *touch-stone*, i.e. (by anal.) *torture*:—torment.

932. βασιλεία **basilĕia**, *bas-il-i'-ah*; from *935*; prop. *royalty*, i.e. (abstr.) *rule*, or (concr.) a *realm* (lit. or fig.):—kingdom, + reign.

933. βασίλειον **basilĕiŏn**, *bas-il'-i-on*; neut. of *934*; a *palace*:—king's court.

934. βασίλειος **basilĕiŏs**, *bas-il'-i-os*; from *935*; *kingly* (in nature):—royal.

935. βασιλεύς **basilĕus**, *bas-il-yooce'*; prob. from *939* (through the notion of a *foundation* of power); a *sovereign* (abs., rel. or fig.):—king.

936. βασιλεύω **basilĕuō**, *bas-il-yoo'-o*; from *935*; to *rule* (lit. or fig.):—king, reign.

937. βασιλικός **basilikŏs**, *bas-il-ee-kos'*; from *935*; *regal* (in relation), i.e. (lit.) *belonging to* (or *befitting*) the *sovereign* (as land, dress, or a *courtier*), or (fig.) *preeminent*:—king's, nobleman, royal.

938. βασίλισσα **basilissa**, *bas-il'-is-sah*; fem. from *936*; a *queen*:—queen.

939. βάσις **basis**, *bas'-ece*; from βαίνω **bainō** (to *walk*); a *pace* (" base "), i.e. (by impl.) the *foot*:—foot.

940. βασκαίνω **baskainō**, *bas-kah'ee-no*; akin to *5335*; to *malign*, i.e. (by extens.) to *fascinate* (by false representations):—bewitch.

941. βαστάζω **bastazō**, *bas-tad'-zo*; perh. remotely der. from the base of *939* (through the idea of *removal*); to *lift*, lit. or fig. *endure, declare, sustain, receive*, etc.):—bear, carry, take up.

942. βάτος **batŏs**, *bat'-os*; of uncert. der.; a *brier shrub*:—bramble, bush.

943. βάτος **batŏs**, *bat'-os*; of Heb. or. [1324]; a *bath*, or measure for liquids:—measure.

944. βάτραχος **batrachŏs**, *bat'-rakh-os*; of uncert. der.; a *frog*:—frog.

945. βαττολογέω **battŏlŏgĕō**, *bat-tol-og-eh'-o*; from Βάττος **Battŏs** (a proverbial stammerer) and *3056*; to *stutter*, i.e. (by impl.) to *prate* tediously:—use vain repetitions.

946. βδέλυγμα **bdĕlugma**, *bdel'-oog-mah*; from *948*; a *detestation*, i.e. (spec.) *idolatry*:—abomination.

947. βδελυκτός **bdĕluktŏs**, *bdel-ook-tos'*; from *948*; *detestable*, i.e. (spec.) *idolatrous*:—abominable.

948. βδελύσσω **bdĕlussō**, *bdel-oos'-so*; from a (presumed) der. of βδέω **bdĕō** (to *stink*); to be *disgusted*, i.e. (by impl.) *detest* (espec. of idolatry):—abhor, abominable.

949. βέβαιος **bĕbaiŏs**, *beb'-ah-yos*; from the base of *939* (through the idea of *basality*); *stable* (lit. or fig.):—firm, of force, stedfast, sure.

950. βεβαιόω **bĕbaiŏō**, *beb-ah-yŏ'-o*; from *949*; to *stabilitate* (fig.):—confirm, (e-) stablish.

951. βεβαίωσις **bĕbaiōsis**, *beb-ah'-yo-sis*; from *950*; *stabiliment*:—confirmation.

952. βέβηλος **bĕbēlŏs**, *beb'-ay-los*; from the base of *939* and βηλός **bēlŏs** (a *threshold*); *accessible* (as by *crossing the door-way*), i.e. (by impl. of Jewish notions) *heathenish, wicked*:—profane (person).

953. βεβηλόω **bĕbēlŏō**, *beb-ay-lŏ'-o*; from 952; to *desecrate*:—profane.

954. Βεελζεβούλ **Bĕĕlzĕbŏul**, *beh-el-zeb-ool'*; of Chald. or. [by parody upon 1176]; *dung-god*; *Beelzebul*, a name of Satan:—Beelzebub.

955. Βελιάλ **Bĕlial**, *bel-ee'-al*; of Heb. or. [1100]; *worthlessness*; *Belial*, as an epithet of Satan:—Belial.

956. βέλος **bĕlŏs**, *bel'-os*; from 906; a *missile*, i.e. *spear* or *arrow*:—dart.

957. βελτίον **bĕltiŏn**, *bel-tee'-on*; neut. of a comp. of a der. of 906 (used for the comp. of 18); *better*:—very well.

958. Βενιαμίν **Bĕniamin**, *ben-ee-am-een'*; of Heb. or. [1144]; *Benjamin*, an Isr.:—Benjamin.

959. Βερνίκη **Bĕrnikĕ**, *ber-nee'-kay*; from a provincial form of 5342 and 3529; *victorious*; *Bernicè*, a member of the Herodian family:—Bernice.

960. Βέροια **Bĕrŏia**, *ber'-oy-ah*; perh. a provincial from a der. of 4008 [Perœa, i.e. the region *beyond* the coast-line]; *Berœa*, a place in Macedonia:—Berea.

961. Βεροιαῖος **Bĕrŏiaiŏs**, *ber-oy-ah'-yos*; from 960; a *Berœœan* or native of Berœa:—of Berea.

962. Βηθαβαρά **Bĕthabara**, *bay-thab-ar-ah'*; of Heb. or. [1004 and 5679]; *ferry-house*; *Bethabara* (i.e. *Bethabarah*), a place on the Jordan:—Bethabara.

963. Βηθανία **Bĕthania**, *bay-than-ee'-ah*; of Chald. or.; *date-house*; *Beth-any*, a place in Pal.:—Bethany.

964. Βηθεσδά **Bĕthĕsda**, *bay-thes-dah'*; of Chald. or. [comp. 1004 and 2617]; *house of kindness*; *Beth-esda*, a pool in Jerus.:—Bethesda.

965. Βηθλέεμ **Bĕthlĕĕm**, *bayth-leh-em'*; of Heb. or. [1036]; *Bethleem* (i.e. *Beth-lechem*), a place in Pal.:—Bethlehem.

966. Βηθσαϊδά **Bĕthsaïda**, *bayth-sahee-dah'*; of Chald. or. [comp. 1004 and 6719]; *fishing-house*; *Bethsaïda*, a place in Pal.:—Bethsaida.

967. Βηθφαγή **Bĕthphagĕ**, *bayth-fag-ay'*; of Chald. or. [comp. 1004 and 6291]; *fig-house*; *Bethphagè*, a place in Pal.:—Bethphage.

968. βῆμα **bĕma**, *bay'-ma*; from the base of 939; a *step*, i.e. *foot-breath*; by impl. a *rostrum*, i.e. *tribunal*:—judgment-seat, set [foot] on, throne.

969. βήρυλλος **bĕrullŏs**, *bay'-rool-los*; of uncert. der.; a "*beryl*":—beryl.

970. βία **bia**, *bee'-ah*; prob. akin to 979 (through the idea of *vital* activity); *force*:—violence.

971. βιάζω **biazō**, *bee-ad'-zo*; from 970; to *force*, i.e. (reflex.) to *crowd oneself* (into), or (pass.) to be *seized*:—press, suffer violence.

972. βίαιος **biaiŏs**, *bee'-ah-yos*; from 970; *violent*:—mighty.

973. βιαστής **biastĕs**, *bee-as-tace'*; from 971; a *forcer*, i.e. (fig.) *energetic*:—violent.

974. βιβλιαρίδιον **bibliaridiŏn**, *bib-lee-ar-id'-ee-on*; a dimin. of 975; a *booklet*:—little book.

975. βιβλίον **bibliŏn**, *bib-lee'-on*; a dimin. of 976; a *roll*:—bill, book, scroll, writing.

976. βίβλος **biblŏs**, *bib'-los*; prop. the inner *bark* of the papyrus plant, i.e. (by impl.) a *sheet* or *scroll* of writing:—book.

977. βιβρώσκω **bibrōskō**, *bib-ro'-sko*; a reduplicated and prolonged form of an obsol. prim. verb [perh. causative of 1006]; to *eat*:—eat.

978. Βιθυνία **Bithunia**, *bee-thoo-nee'-ah*; of uncert. der.; *Bithynia*, a region of Asia:—Bithynia.

979. βίος **biŏs**, *bee'-os*; a prim. word; *life*, i.e. (lit.) the present state of existence; by impl. the *means* of *livelihood*:—good, life, living.

980. βιόω **biŏō**, *bee-ŏ'-o*; from 979; to *spend existence*:—live.

981. βίωσις **biōsis**, *bee'-o-sis*; from 980; *living* (prop. the act, by impl. the mode):—manner of life.

982. βιωτικός **biōtikŏs**, *bee-o-tee-kos'*; from a der. of 980; *relating* to the present *existence*:—of (pertaining to, things that pertain to) this life.

983. βλαβερός **blabĕrŏs**, *blab-er-os'*; from 984; *injurious*:—hurtful.

984. βλάπτω **blaptō**, *blap'-to*; a prim. verb; prop. to *hinder*, i.e. (by impl.) to *injure*:—hurt.

985. βλαστάνω **blastanō**, *blas-tan'-o*; from βλαστός **blastŏs** (a *sprout*); to *germinate*; by impl. to *yield* fruit:—bring forth, bud, spring (up).

986. Βλάστος **Blastŏs**, *blas'-tos*; perh. the same as the base of 985; *Blastus*, an officer of Herod Agrippa:—Blastus.

987. βλασφημέω **blasphēmĕō**, *blas-fay-meh'-o*; from 989; to *vilify*; spec. to *speak impiously*:—(speak) blaspheme (-er, -mously, -my), defame, rail on, revile, speak evil.

988. βλασφημία **blasphēmia**, *blas-fay-me'-ah*; from 989; *vilification* (espec. against God):—blasphemy, evil speaking, railing.

989. βλάσφημος **blasphēmŏs**, *blas'-fay-mos*; from a der. of 984 and 5345; *scurrilous*, i.e. *calumnious* (against man), or (spec.) *impious* (against God):—blasphemer (-mous), railing.

990. βλέμμα **blemma**, *blem'-mah*; from 991; *vision* (prop. concr.; by impl. abstr.):—seeing.

991. βλέπω **blĕpō**, *blep'-o*; a prim. verb; to *look* at (lit. or fig.):—behold, beware, lie, look (on, to), perceive, regard, see, sight, take heed.   Comp. 3700.

992. βλητέος **blētĕŏs**, *blay-teh'-os*; from 906; *fit to be cast* (i.e. applied):—must be put.

993. Βοανεργές **Bŏanĕrgĕs**, *bŏ-an-erg-es'*; of Chald. or. [1123 and ⊤266]; *sons of commotion*; *Boänerges*, an epithet of two of the Apostles:—Boanerges.

994. βοάω **bŏaō**, *bŏ-ah'-o*; appar. a prol. form of a prim. verb; to *halloo*, i.e. *shout* (for help or in a tumultuous way):—cry.

995. βοή **bŏĕ**, *bŏ-ay'*; from 994; a *halloo*, i.e. *call* (for aid, etc.):—cry.

996. βοήθεια **bŏēthĕia**, *bŏ-ay'-thi-ah*; from 998; *aid*; spec. a *rope* or *chain* for *frapping* a vessel:—help.

997. βοηθέω **bŏēthĕō**, *bŏ-ay-theh'-o*; from 998; to *aid* or *relieve*:—help, succour.

998. βοηθός **bŏēthŏs**, *bŏ-ay-thos'*; from 995 and θέω **thĕō** (to *run*); a *succorer*:—helper.

999. βόθυνος **bŏthunŏs**, *both'-oo-nos*; akin to 900; a *hole* (in the ground); spec. a *cistern*:—ditch, pit.

1000. βολή **bŏlĕ**, *bol-ay'*; from 906; a *throw* (as a measure of distance):—cast.

1001. βολίζω **bŏlizō**, *bol-id'-zo*; from 1002; to *heave the lead*:—sound.

1002. βολίς **bŏlis**, *bol-ece'*; from 906; a *missile*, i.e. *javelin*:—dart.

1003. Βοόζ **Bŏŏz**, *bŏ-oz'*; of Heb. or. [1162]; *Boöz*, (i.e. *Boäz*), an Isr.:—Booz.

1004. βόρβορος **bŏrbŏrŏs**, *bor'-bor-os*; of uncert. der.; *mud*:—mire.

1005. βορρᾶς **bŏrrhas**, *bor-hras'*; of uncert. der.; the *north* (prop. wind):—north.

1006. βόσκω **bŏskō**, *bos'-ko*; a prol. form of a prim. verb [comp. 977, 1016]; to *pasture*; by extens. to *fodder*; reflex. to *graze*:—feed, keep.

1007. Βοσόρ **Bŏsŏr**, *bos-or'*; of Heb. or. [1160]; *Bosor* (i.e. *Beör*), a Moabite:—Bosor.

1008. βοτάνη **bŏtanĕ**, *bot-an'-ay*; from 1006; *herbage* (as if for *grazing*):—herb.

1009. βότρυς **bŏtrus**, *bot'-rooce*; of uncert. der.; a *bunch* (of grapes):—(vine) cluster (of the vine).

1010. βουλευτής **bŏulĕutĕs**, *bool-yoo-tace'*; from 1011; an *adviser*, i.e. (spec.) a *councillor* or *member* of the Jewish Sanhedrim:—counsellor.

1011. βουλεύω **bŏulĕuō**, *bool-yoo'-o*; from 1012; to *advise*, i.e. (reflex.) *deliberate*, or (by impl.) *resolve*:—consult, take counsel, determine, be minded, purpose.

1012. βουλή **bŏulĕ**, *boo-lay'*; from 1014; *volition*, i.e. (obj.) *advice*, or (by impl.) *purpose*:— + advise, counsel, will.

1013. βούλημα **bŏulēma**, *boo'-lay-mah*; from 1014; a *resolve*:—purpose, will.

1014. βούλομαι **bŏulŏmahĕĕ**; mid. of a prim. verb; to "*will*," i.e. (reflex.) be *willing*:—be disposed, minded, intend, list, (be, of own) will (-ing).   Comp. 2309.

1015. βουνός **bŏunŏs**, *boo-nos'*; prob. of for. or.; a *hillock*:—hill.

1016. βοῦς **bŏus**, *booce*; prob. from the base of 1006; an *ox* (as *grazing*), i.e. an animal of that species ("*beef*"):—ox.

1017. βραβεῖον **brabĕĭŏn**, *brab-i'-on*; from βραβεύς **brabĕus** (an *umpire*; of uncert. der.); an *award* (of arbitration), i.e. (spec.) a *prize* in the public games:—prize.

1018. βραβεύω **brabĕuō**, *brab-yoo'-o*; from the same as 1017; to *arbitrate*, i.e. (gen.) to *govern* (fig. prevail):—rule.

1019. βραδύνω **bradunō**, *brad-oo'-no*; from 1021; to *delay*:—be slack, tarry.

1020. βραδυπλοέω **braduplŏĕō**, *brad-oo-plŏ-eh'-o*; from 1021 and a prol. form of 4126; to *sail slowly*:—sail slowly.

1021. βραδύς **bradus**, *brad-ooce'*; of uncert. affin.; *slow*; fig. *dull*:—slow.

1022. βραδύτης **bradutēs**, *brad-oo'-tace*; from 1021; *tardiness*:—slackness.

1023. βραχίων **brachiōn**, *brakh-ee'-own*; prop. comp. of 1024, but appar. in the sense of βράσσω **brassō** (to *wield*); the *arm*, i.e. (fig.) *strength*:—arm.

1024. βραχύς **brachus**, *brakh-ooce'*; of uncert. affin.; *short* (of time, place, quantity, or number):—few words, little (space, while).

1025. βρέφος **brĕphŏs**, *bref'-os*; of uncert. affin.; an *infant* (prop. unborn) lit. or fig.:—babe, (young) child, infant.

1026. βρέχω **brĕchō**, *brekh'-o*; a prim. verb; to *moisten* (espec. by a shower):—(send) rain, wash.

1027. βροντή **brŏntĕ**, *bron-tay'*; akin to βρέμω **brĕmō** (to *roar*); *thunder*:—thunder (-ing).

1028. βροχή **brŏchĕ**, *brokh-ay'*; from 1026; *rain*:—rain.

1029. βρόχος **brŏchŏs**, *brokh'-os*; of uncert. der ; a *noose*:—snare.

1030. βρυγμός **brugmŏs**, *broog-mos'*; from 1031; a *grating* (of the teeth):—gnashing.

1031. βρύχω **bruchō**, *broo'-kho*; a prim. verb; to *grate* the teeth (in pain or rage):—gnash.

1032. βρύω **bruō**, *broo'-o*; a prim. verb; to *swell* out, i.e. (by impl.) to *gush*:—send forth.

1033. βρῶμα **brōma**, *bro'-mah*; from the base of 977; *food* (lit. or fig.), espec. (cer.) articles allowed or forbidden by the Jewish law:—meat, victuals.

1034. βρώσιμος **brōsimŏs**, *bro'-sim-os*; from 1035; *eatable*:—meat.

1035. βρῶσις **brōsis**, *bro'-sis*; from the base of 977; (abstr.) *eating* (lit. or fig.); by extens. (concr.) *food* (lit. or fig.):—eating, food, meat.

1036. βυθίζω **buthizō**, *boo-thid'-zo*; from 1037; to *sink*; by impl. to *drown*:—begin to sink, drown.

1037. βυθός **buthŏs**, *boo-thos'*; a var. of 899; *depth*, i.e. (by impl.) the *sea*:—deep.

1038. βυρσεύς **bursĕus**, *boorce-yooce'*; from βύρσα **bursa** (a *hide*); a *tanner*:—tanner.

1039. βύσσινος **bussinŏs**, *boos'-see-nos*; from 1040; made of *linen* (neut. a linen *cloth*):—fine linen.

1040. βύσσος **bussŏs**, *boos'-sos*; of Heb. or. [948]; white *linen*:—fine linen.

1041. βῶμος **bōmŏs**, *bo'-mos*; from the base of 939; prop. a *stand*, i.e. (spec.) an *altar*:—altar.

Γ

1042. γαββαθά **gabbatha**, *gab-bath-ah'*; of Chald. or. [comp. 1355]; *the knoll*; *gabbatha*, a vernacular term for the Roman tribunal in Jerus.:—Gabbatha.

1043. Γαβριήλ **Gabriēl**, *gab-ree-ale'*; of Heb. or. [1403]; *Gabriel*, an archangel:—Gabriel.

1044. γάγγραινα **gaggraina**, *gang'-grahee-nah*; from γραίνω **grainō** (to *gnaw*); an *ulcer* ("gangrene"):—canker.

1045. Γάδ **Gad**, *gad*; of Heb. or. [1410]; *Gad*, a tribe of Isr.:—Gad.

1046. Γαδαρηνός **Gadarēnŏs**, *gad-ar-ay-nos'*; from Γαδαρά (a town E. of the Jordan); a *Gadarene* or inhab. of Gadara:—Gadarene.

1047. γάζα **gaza**, *gad'-zah*; of for. or.; a *treasure*:—treasure.

1048. Γάζα **Gaza**, *gad'-zah*; of Heb. or. [5804]; *Gazah* (i.e. '*Azzah*), a place in Pal.:—Gaza.

1049. γαζοφυλάκιον **gazŏphulakiŏn**, *gad-zof-oo-lak'-ee-on*; from *1047* and *5438*; a *treasure-house*, i.e. a court in the temple for the collection-boxes:—treasury.

1050. Γάϊος **Gaiŏs**, *gah'-ee-os*; of Lat. or.; *Gaius* (i.e. *Caius*), a Chr.:—Gaius.

1051. γάλα **gala**, *gal'-ah*; of uncert. affin.; *milk* (fig.):—milk.

1052. Γαλάτης **Galatēs**, *gal-at'-ace*; from *1053*; a *Galatian* or inhab. of Galatia:—Galatian.

1053. Γαλατία **Galatia**, *gal-at-ee'-ah*; of for. or.; *Galatia*, a region of Asia:—Galatia.

1054. Γαλατικός **Galatikŏs**, *gal-at-ee-kos'*; from *1053*; *Galatic* or relating to Galatia:—of Galatia.

1055. γαλήνη **galēnē**, *gal-ay'-nay*; of uncert. der.; *tranquillity*:—calm.

1056. Γαλιλαία **Galilaia**, *gal-il-ah'-yah*; of Heb. or. [1551]; *Galilæa* (i.e. the heathen *circle*), a region of Pal.:—Galilee.

1057. Γαλιλαῖος **Galilaiŏs**, *gal-ee-lah'-yos*; from *1056*; *Galilæan* or belonging to Galilæa:—Galilæan, of Galilee.

1058. Γαλλίων **Galliōn**, *gal-lee'-own*; of Lat. or.; *Gallion* (i.e. *Gallio*), a Roman officer:—Gallio.

1059. Γαμαλιήλ **Gamaliēl**, *gam-al-ee-ale'*; of Heb. or. [1583]; *Gamaliel* (i.e. *Gamliel*), an Isr.:—Gamaliel.

1060. γαμέω **gamĕō**, *gam-eh'-o*; from *1062*; to *wed* (of either sex):—marry (a wife).

1061. γαμίσκω **gamiskō**, *gam-is'-ko*; from *1062*; to *espouse* (a daughter to a husband):—give in marriage.

1062. γάμος **gamŏs**, *gam'-os*; of uncert. affin.; *nuptials*:—marriage, wedding.

1063. γάρ **gar**, *gar*; a prim. particle; prop. assigning a *reason* (used in argument, explanation or intensification; often with other particles):—and, as, because (that), but, even, for, indeed, no doubt, seeing, then, therefore, verily, what, why, yet.

1064. γαστήρ **gastēr**, *gas-tare'*; of uncert. der.; the *stomach*; by anal. the *matrix*; fig. a *gourmand*:—belly, + with child, womb.

1065. γέ **gĕ**, *gheh*; a prim. particle of *emphasis* or *qualification* (often used with other particles prefixed):—and besides, doubtless, at least, yet.

1066. Γεδεών **Gĕdĕōn**, *ghed-eh-own'*; of Heb. or. [1439]; *Gedeon* (i.e. *Gid[e]on*), an Isr.:—Gedeon.

1067. γέεννα **gĕĕnna**, *gheh'-en-nah*; of Heb. or. [1516 and 2011]; *valley of (the son of) Hinnom*; *gehenna* (or *Ge-Hinnom*), a valley of Jerus., used (fig.) as a name for the place (or state) of everlasting punishment:—hell.

1068. Γεθσημανή **Gĕthsēmanē**, *gheth-say-man-ay'*; of Chald. or. [comp. 1660 and 8081]; *oil-press*; *Gethsemane*, a garden near Jerus.:—Gethsemane.

1069. γείτων **gĕitōn**, *ghi'-tone*; from *1093*; a *neighbor* (as adjoining one's *ground*); by impl. a *friend*:—neighbour.

1070. γελάω **gĕlaō**, *ghel-ah'-o*; of uncert. affin.; to *laugh* (as a sign of joy or satisfaction):—laugh.

1071. γέλως **gĕlŏs**, *ghel'-oce*; from *1070*; *laughter* (as a mark of gratification):—laughter.

1072. γεμίζω **gĕmizō**, *ghem-id'-zo*; trans. from *1073*, to *fill* entirely:—fill (be) full.

1073. γέμω **gĕmō**, *ghem'-o*; a prim. verb; to *swell* out, i.e. be *full*:—be full.

1074. γενεά **gĕnĕa**, *ghen-eh-ah'*; from (a presumed der. of) *1085*; a *generation*; by impl. an *age* (the period or the persons):—age, generation, nation, time.

1075. γενεαλογέω **gĕnĕalŏgĕō**, *ghen-eh-al-og-eh'-o*; from *1074* and *3056*; to *reckon by generations*, i.e. *trace in genealogy*:—count by descent.

1076. γενεαλογία **gĕnĕalŏgia**, *ghen-eh-al-og-ee'-ah*; from the same as *1075*; *tracing by generations*, i.e. "*genealogy*":—genealogy.

1077. γενέσια **gĕnĕsia**, *ghen-es'-ee-ah*; neut. plur. of a der. of *1078*; *birthday* ceremonies:—birthday.

1078. γένεσις **gĕnĕsis**, *ghen'-es-is*; from the same as *1074*; *nativity*; fig. *nature*:—generation, nature (-ral).

1079. γενετή **gĕnĕtē**, *ghen-et-ay'*; fem. of a presumed der. of the base of *1074*; *birth*:—birth.

1080. γεννάω **gĕnnaō**, *ghen-nah'-o*; from a var. of *1085*; to *procreate* (prop. of the father, but by extens. of the mother); fig. to *regenerate*:—bear, beget, be born, bring forth, conceive, be delivered of, gender, make, spring.

1081. γέννημα **gĕnnēma**, *ghen'-nay-mah*; from *1080*; *offspring*; by anal. *produce* (lit. or fig.):—fruit, generation.

1082. Γεννησαρέτ **Gĕnnēsarĕt**, *ghen-nay-sar-et'*; of Heb. or. [comp. 3672]; *Gennesaret* (i.e. *Kinnereth*), a lake and plain in Pal.:—Gennesaret.

1083. γέννησις **gĕnnēsis**, *ghen'-nay-sis*; from *1080*; *nativity*:—birth.

1084. γεννητός **gĕnnētŏs**, *ghen-nay-tos'*; from *1080*; *born*:—they that are born.

1085. γένος **gĕnŏs**, *ghen'-os*; from *1096*; "*kin*" (abstr. or concr., lit. or fig., indiv. or coll.):—born, country (-man), diversity, generation, kind (-red), nation, offspring, stock.

1086. Γεργεσηνός **Gĕrgĕsēnŏs**, *gher-ghes-ay-nos'*; of Heb. or. [1622]; a *Gergesene* (i.e. *Girgashite*) or one of the aborigines of Pal.:—Gergesene.

1087. γερουσία **gĕrŏusia**, *gher-oo-see'-ah*; from *1088*; the *eldership*, i.e. (collect.) the Jewish *Sanhedrim*:—senate.

1088. γέρων **gĕrōn**, *gher'-own*; of uncert. affin. [comp. *1094*]; *aged*:—old.

1089. γεύομαι **gĕuŏmai**, *ghyoo'-om-ahee*; a prim. verb; to *taste*; by impl. to *eat*; fig. to *experience* (good or ill):—eat, taste.

1090. γεωργέω **gĕōrgĕō**, *gheh-ore-gheh'-o*; from *1092*; to *till* (the soil):—dress.

1091. γεώργιον **gĕōrgiŏn**, *gheh-ore'-ghee-on*; neut. of a (presumed) der. of *1092*; *cultivable*, i.e. a *farm*:—husbandry.

1092. γεωργός **gĕōrgŏs**, *gheh-ore-gos'*; from *1093* and the base of *2041*; a *land-worker*, i.e. *farmer*:—husbandman.

1093. γῆ **gē**, *ghay*; contr. from a prim. word; *soil*; by extens. a *region*, or the solid part or the whole of the *terrene globe* (includ. the occupants in each application):—country, earth (-ly), ground, land, world.

1094. γῆρας **gēras**, *ghay'-ras*; akin to *1088*; *senility*:—old age.

1095. γηράσκω **gēraskō**, *ghay-ras'-ko*; from *1094*; to be *senescent*:—be (wax) old.

1096. γίνομαι **ginŏmai**, *ghin'-om-ahee*; a prol. and mid. form of a prim. verb; to *cause to be* ("*gen*'-*erate*), i.e. (reflex.) to *become* (come into being), used with great latitude (lit., fig., intens., etc.):—arise, be assembled, be (come, -fall, -have self), be brought (to pass), (be) come (to pass), continue, be divided, be done, draw, be ended, fall, be finished, follow, be found, be fulfilled, + God forbid, grow, happen, have, be kept, be made, be married, be ordained to be, partake, pass, be performed, be published, require, seem, be showed, × soon as it was, sound, be taken, be turned, use, wax, will, would, be wrought.

1097. γινώσκω **ginōskō**, *ghin-oce'-ko*; a prol. form of a prim. verb; to "*know*" (absol.), in a great variety of applications and with many impl. (as follow, with others not thus clearly expressed):—allow,

be aware (of), feel, (have) know (-ledge), perceive, be resolved, can speak, be sure, understand.

1098. γλεῦκος **glĕukŏs**, *glyoo'-kos*; akin to *1099*; *sweet wine*, i.e. (prop.) *must* (fresh juice), but used of the more saccharine (and therefore highly inebriating) fermented *wine*:—new wine.

1099. γλυκύς **glukus**, *gloo-koos'*; of uncert. affin.; *sweet* (i.e. not bitter nor salt):—sweet, fresh.

1100. γλῶσσα **glōssa**, *gloce-sah'*; of uncert. affin.; the *tongue*; by impl. a *language* (spec. one naturally unacquired):—tongue.

1101. γλωσσόκομον **glōssŏkŏmŏn**, *gloce-sok'-om-on*; from *1100* and the base of *2889*; prop. a *case* (to keep mouthpieces of wind-instruments in, i.e. (by extens.) a *casket* or (spec.) *purse*:—bag.

1102. γναφεύς **gnaphĕus**, *gnaf-yuce'*; by var. for a der. from κνάπτω **knaptō** (to *tease cloth*); a *cloth-dresser*:—fuller.

1103. γνήσιος **gnēsiŏs**, *gnay'-see-os*; from the same as *1077*; *legitimate* (of birth), i.e. *genuine*:—own, sincerity, true.

1104. γνησίως **gnēsiŏs**, *gnay-see'-oce*; adv. from *1103*; *genuinely*, i.e. *really*:—naturally.

1105. γνόφος **gnŏphŏs**, *gnof'-os*; akin to *3509*; *gloom* (as of a storm):—blackness.

1106. γνώμη **gnōmē**, *gno'-may*; from *1097*; *cognition*, i.e. (subj.) *opinion*, or (obj.) *resolve* (*counsel*, *consent*, etc.):—advice, + agree, judgment, mind, purpose, will.

1107. γνωρίζω **gnōrizō**, *gno-rid'-zo*; from a der. of *1097*; to *make known*; subj. to *know*:—certify, declare, make known, give to understand, do to wit, wot.

1108. γνῶσις **gnōsis**, *gno'-sis*; from *1097*; *knowing* (the act), i.e. (by impl.) *knowledge*:—knowledge, science.

1109. γνώστης **gnōstēs**, *gnoce'-tace*; from *1097*; a *knower*:—expert.

1110. γνωστός **gnōstŏs**, *gnoce-tos'*; from *1097*; well *known*:—acquaintance, (which may be) known, notable.

1111. γογγύζω **gŏgguzō**, *gong-good'-zo*; of uncert. der.; to *grumble*:—murmur.

1112. γογγυσμός **gŏggusmŏs**, *gong-goos-mos'*; from *1111*; a *grumbling*:—grudging, murmuring.

1113. γογγυστής **gŏggustēs**, *gong-goos-tace'*; from *1111*; a *grumbler*:—murmurer.

1114. γόης **gŏēs**, *gŏ'-ace*; from γοάω **gŏaō** (to *wail*); prop. a *wizard* (as *muttering* spells); by impl.) an *impostor*:—seducer.

1115. Γολγοθᾶ **Gŏlgŏtha**, *gol-goth-ah'*; of Chald. or. [comp. 1538]; the *skull*; *Golgotha*, a knoll near Jerus.:—Golgotha.

1116. Γόμορρα **Gŏmŏrrha**, *gom'-or-hrhah*; of Heb. or. [6017]; *Gomorrha* (i.e. '*Amorah*), a place near the Dead Sea:—Gomorrha.

1117. γόμος **gŏmŏs**, *gom'-os*; from *1073*; a *load* (as *filling*), i.e. (spec.) a *cargo*, or (by extens.) *wares*:—burden, merchandise.

1118. γονεύς **gŏnĕus**, *gon-yooce'*; from the base of *1096*; a *parent*:—parent.

1119. γόνυ **gŏnu**, *gon-oo'*; of uncert. affin.; the "*knee*":—knee (× -l).

1120. γονυπετέω **gŏnupĕtĕō**, *gon-oo-pet-eh'-o*; from a comp. of *1119* and the alt of *4098*; to *fall on the knee*:—bow the knee, kneel down.

1121. γράμμα **gramma**, *gram'-mah*; from *1125*; a *writing*, i.e. a *letter*, *note*, *epistle*, *book*, etc.; plur. *learning*:—bill, learning, letter, scripture, writing, written.

1122. γραμματεύς **grammatĕus**, *gram-mat-yooce'*; from *1121*; a *writer*, i.e. (professionally) *scribe* or *secretary*:—scribe, town-clerk.

1123. γραπτός **graptŏs**, *grap-tos'*; from *1125*; *inscribed* (fig.):—written.

1124. γραφή **graphē**, *graf-ay'*; from *1125*; a *document*, i.e. holy *Writ* (or its contents or a statement in it):—scripture.

125. γράφω **graphō**, *graf'-o*; a prim. verb; to write (-ing, -ten).

126. γραώδης **graōdēs**, *grah-o'-dace*; from γραῦς **graus** (an old woman) and *1491*; crone-like, -e. silly:—old wives'.

1127. γρηγορεύω **grēgŏreŭō**, *gray-gor-yoo'-o*; from *1453*; to keep awake, i.e. watch (lit. or fig.):—be vigilant, wake, (be) watch (-ful).

1128. γυμνάζω **gumnazō**, *goom-nad'-zo*; from *1131*; to practise naked (in the games), i.e. train (fig.):—exercise.

1129. γυμνασία **gumnasia**, *goom-nas-ee'-ah*; from *1128*; training, i.e. (fig.) asceticism:—exercise.

1130. γυμνητεύω **gumnētĕuō**, *goom-nayt-yoo'-o*; from a der. of *1131*; to strip, i.e. (reflex.) go poorly clad:—be naked.

1131. γυμνός **gumnŏs**, *goom-nos'*; of uncert. affin.; nude (absol. or rel., lit. or fig.):—naked.

1132. γυμνότης **gumnŏtēs**, *goom-not'-ace*; from *1131*; nudity (absol. or comp.):—nakedness.

1133. γυναικάριον **gunaikarion**, *goo-nahee-kar'-ee-on*; a dimin. from *1135*; a little (i.e. foolish) woman:—silly woman.

1134. γυναικεῖος **gunaikĕiŏs**, *goo-nahee-ki'-os*; from *1135*; feminine:—wife.

1135. γυνή **gunē**, *goo-nay'*; prob. from the base of *1096*; a woman; spec. a wife:—wife, woman.

1136. Γώγ **Gōg**, *gogue*; of Heb. or. [1463]; *Gog*, a symb. name for some future Antichrist:—Gog.

1137. γωνία **gōnia**, *go-nee'-ah*; prob. akin to *1119*; an angle:—corner, quarter.

Δ

1138. Δαβίδ **Dabid**, *dab-eed'*; of Heb. or. [1732]; *Dabid* (i.e. David), the Isr. king:—David.

1139. δαιμονίζομαι **daimŏnizŏmai**, *dahee-mon-id'-zom-ahee*; mid. from *1142*; to be exercised (by a dæmon:—have a (be vexed with, be possessed with) devil (-s).

1140. δαιμόνιον **daimŏniŏn**, *dahee-mon'-ee-on*; neut. of a der. of *1142*; a dæmonic being; by extens. a deity:—devil, god.

1141. δαιμονιώδης **daimŏniōdēs**, *dahee-mon-ee-o'-dace*; from *1140* and *1142*; dæmon-like:—devilish.

1142. δαίμων **daimōn**, *dah'ee-mown*; from δαίω **daiō** (to distribute fortunes); a dæmon or super-natural spirit (of a bad nature):—devil.

1143. δάκνω **daknō**, *dak'-no*; a prol. form of a prim. root: to bite, i.e. (fig.) thwart:—bite.

1144. δάκρυ **dakru**, *dak'-roo*; or

δάκρυον **dakruon**, *dak'-roo-on*; of uncert. affin.; a tear:—tear.

1145. δακρύω **dakruō**, *dak-roo'-o*; from 1144; to shed tears:—weep. Comp. *2799*.

1146. δακτύλιος **daktuliŏs**, *dak-too'-lee-os*; from *1147*; a finger-ring:—ring.

1147. δάκτυλος **daktulŏs**, *dak'-too-los*; prob. from *1176*; a finger:—finger.

1148. Δαλμανουθά **Dalmanŏutha**, *dal-man-oo-thah'*; prob. of Chald. or.; *Dalmanutha*, a place in Pal.:—Dalmanutha.

1149. Δαλματία **Dalmatia**, *dal-mat-ee'-ah*; prob. of for. der.; *Dalmatia*, a region of Europe:—Dalmatia.

1150. δαμάζω **damazō**, *dam-ad'-zo*; a var. of an obs. prim. of the same mean.; to tame:—tame.

1151. δάμαλις **damalis**, *dam'-al-is*; prob. from the base of *1150*; a heifer (as tame):—heifer.

1152. Δάμαρις **Damaris**, *dam'-ar-is*; prob. from the base of *1150*; perh. gentle; *Damaris*, an Athenian woman:—Damaris.

1153. Δαμασκηνός **Damaskēnŏs**, *dam-as-kay-nos'*; from *1154*; a Damascene or inhab. of Damascus:—Damascene.

1154. Δαμασκός **Damaskŏs**, *dam-as-kos'*; of Heb. or. [1834]; *Damascus*, a city of Syria:—Damascus.

1155. δανείζω **daneizō**, *dan-ide'-zo*; from *1156*; to loan on interest; reflex. to borrow:—borrow, lend.

1156. δάνειον **danĕiŏn**, *dan'-i-on*; from δάνος **danŏs** (a gift); prob. akin to the base of *1325*; a loan:—debt.

1157. δανειστής **danĕistēs**, *dan-ice-tace'*; from *1155*; a lender:—creditor.

1158. Δανιήλ **Daniēl**, *dan-ee-ale'*; of Heb. or. [1840]; *Daniel*, an Isr.:—Daniel.

1159. δαπανάω **dapanaō**, *dap-an-ah'-o*; from *1160*; to expend, i.e. (in a good sense) to incur cost, or (in a bad one) to waste:—be at charges, consume, spend.

1160. δαπάνη **dapanē**, *dap-an'-ay*; from δάπτω **daptō** (to devour); expense (as consuming):—cost.

1161. δέ **dĕ**, *deh*; a prim. particle (adversative or continuative); but, and, etc.:—also, and, but, more-over, now [often unexpressed in English].

1162. δέησις **dĕēsis**, *deh'-ay-sis*; from *1189*; a petition:—prayer, request, supplication.

1163. δεῖ **dĕi**, *die*; 3d pers. sing. act. pres. of *1210*; also δέον **dĕŏn**, *deh-on'*; neut. act. part. of the same; both used impers.; it is (was, etc.) necessary (as binding):—behoved, be meet, must (needs), (be) need (-ful), ought, should.

1164. δεῖγμα **dĕigma**, *digh'-mah*; from the base of *1166*; a specimen (as shown):—example.

1165. δειγματίζω **dĕigmatizō**, *digh-mat-id'-zo*; from *1164*; to exhibit:—make a shew.

1166. δεικνύω **dĕiknuō**, *dike-noo'-o*; a prol. form of an obs. prim. of the same mean.; to show (lit. or fig.):—shew.

1167. δειλία **dĕilia**, *di-lee'-ah*; from *1169*; timidity:—fear.

1168. δειλιάω **dĕiliaō**, *di-lee-ah'-o*; from *1167*; to be timid:—be afraid.

1169. δειλός **dĕilŏs**, *di-los'*; from δέος **dĕŏs** (dread); timid, i.e. (by impl.) faithless:—fearful.

1170. δεῖνα **dĕina**, *di'-nah*; prob. from the same as *1171* (through the idea of forgetting the name as fearful, i.e. strange); so and so (when the person is not specified):—such a man.

1171. δεινῶς **dĕinōs**, *di-noce'*; adv. from a der. of the same as *1169*; terribly, i.e. excessively:—grievously, vehemently.

1172. δειπνέω **dĕipnĕō**, *dipe-neh'-o*; from *1173*; to dine, i.e. take the principal (or evening) meal:—sup (X -per).

1173. δεῖπνον **dĕipnŏn**, *dipe'-non*; from the same as *1160*; dinner, i.e. the chief meal (usually in the evening):—feast, supper.

1174. δεισιδαιμονέστερος **dĕisidaimŏnĕstĕrŏs**, *dice-ee-dahee-mon-es'-ter-os*; the comp. of a der. of the base of *1169* and *1142*; more religious than others:—too superstitious.

1175. δεισιδαιμονία **dĕisidaimŏnia**, *dice-ee-dahee-mon-ee'-ah*; from the same as *1174*; religion:—superstition.

1176. δέκα **dĕka**, *dek'-ah*; a prim. number; ten:—[eight-] een, ten.

1177. δεκαδύο **dĕkaduŏ**, *dek-ad-oo'-o*; from *1176* and *1417*; two and ten, i.e. twelve:—twelve.

1178. δεκαπέντε **dĕkapĕntĕ**, *dek-ap-en'-teh*; from *1176* and *4002*; ten and five, i.e. fifteen:—fifteen.

1179. Δεκάπολις **Dĕkapŏlis**, *dek-ap'-ol-is*; from *1176* and *4172*; the ten-city region; the *Decapolis*, a district in Syria:—Decapolis.

1180. δεκατέσσαρες **dĕkatĕssarĕs**, *dek-at-es'-sar-es*; from *1176* and *5064*; ten and four, i.e. fourteen:—fourteen.

1181. δεκάτη **dĕkatē**, *dek-at'-ay*; fem. of *1182*; a tenth, i.e. as a percentage or (tech.) tithe:—tenth (part), tithe.

1182. δέκατος **dĕkatŏs**, *dek'-at-os*; ordinal from *1176*; tenth:—tenth.

1183. δεκατόω **dĕkatŏō**, *dek-at-ŏ'-o*; from *1181*; to tithe, i.e. to give or take a tenth:—pay (receive) tithes.

1184. δεκτός **dĕktŏs**, *dek-tos'*; from *1209*; approved; (fig.) propitious:—accepted (-table).

1185. δελεάζω **dĕlĕazō**, *del-eh-ad'-zo*; from the base of *1388*; to entrap, i.e. (fig.) delude:—allure, beguile, entice.

1186. δένδρον **dĕndrŏn**, *den'-dron*; prob. from δρῦς **drus** (an oak); a tree:—tree.

1187. δεξιολάβος **dĕxiŏlabŏs**, *dex-ee-ol-ab'-os*; from *1188* and *2983*; a guardsman (as if taking the right) or light-armed soldier:—spearman.

1188. δεξιός **dĕxiŏs**, *dex-ee-os'*; from *1209*; the right side or (fem.) hand (as that which usually takes):—right (hand, side).

1189. δέομαι **dĕŏmai**, *deh'-om-ahee*; mid. of *1210*; to beg (as binding oneself), i.e. petition:—beseech, pray (to), make request. Comp. *4441*.

1190. Δερβαῖος **Dĕrbaiŏs**, *der-bah'ee-os*; from *1191*; a Derbæan or inhab. of Derbe:—of Derbe.

1191. Δέρβη **Dĕrbē**, *der'-bay*; of for. or.; *Derbē*, a place in Asia Minor:—Derbe.

1192. δέρμα **dĕrma**, *der'-mah*; from *1194*; a hide:—skin.

1193. δερμάτινος **dĕrmatinŏs**, *der-mat'-ce-nos*; from *1192*; made of hide:—leathern, of a skin.

1194. δέρω **dĕrō**, *der'-o*; a prim. verb; prop. to flay, i.e. (by impl.) to scourge, or (by anal.) to thrash:—beat, smite.

1195. δεσμεύω **dĕsmĕuō**, *des-myoo'-o*; from a (presumed) der. of *1196*; to be a binder (captor), i.e. to enchain (a prisoner), to tie on (a load):—bind.

1196. δεσμέω **dĕsmĕō**, *des-meh'-o*; from *1199*; to tie, i.e. shackle:—bind.

1197. δεσμή **dĕsmē**, *des-may'*; from *1196*; a bundle:—bundle.

1198. δέσμιος **dĕsmiŏs**, *des'-mee-os*; from *1199*; a captive (as bound):—in bonds, prisoner.

1199. δεσμόν **dĕsmŏn**, *des-mon'*; or

δεσμός **dĕsmŏs**, *des-mos'*; neut. and masc. respectively from *1210*; a band, i.e. ligament (of the body) or shackle (of a prisoner); fig. an impediment or disability:—band, bond, chain, string.

1200. δεσμοφύλαξ **dĕsmŏphulax**, *des-mof-oo'-lax*; from *1199* and *5441*; a jailer (as guarding the prisoners):—jailor, keeper of the prison.

1201. δεσμωτήριον **dĕsmōtēriŏn**, *des-mo-tay'-ree-on*; from a der. of *1199* (equiv. to *1196*); a place of bondage, i.e. a dungeon:—prison.

1202. δεσμώτης **dĕsmōtēs**, *des-mo'-tace*; from the same as *1201*; (pass.) a captive:—prisoner.

1203. δεσπότης **dĕspŏtēs**, *des-pot'-ace*; perh. from *1210* and πόσις **pŏsis** (a husband); an absolute ruler ("despot"):—Lord, master.

1204. δεῦρο **dĕurŏ**, *dyoo'-ro*; of uncert. affin.; here; used also imper. hither!; and of time, hitherto:—come (hither), hither [-to].

1205. δεῦτε **dĕutĕ**, *dyoo'-teh*; from *1204* and an imper. form of εἶμι **ĕimi** (to go); come hither!:—come, X follow.

1206. δευτεραῖος **dĕutĕraiŏs**, *dyoo-ter-ah'-yos*; from *1208*; secondary, i.e. (spec.) on the second day:—next day.

1207. δευτερόπρωτος **dĕutĕrŏprōtŏs**, *dyoo-ter-op'-ro-tos*; from *1208* and *4413*; second-first, i.e. (spec.) a designation of the Sabbath immediately after the Paschal week (being the second after Passover day, and the first of the seven Sabbaths intervening before Pentecost):—second . . . after the first.

1208. δεύτερος **dĕutĕrŏs**, *dyoo'-ter-os*; as the comp. of *1417*; (ordinal) second (in time, place or rank; also adv.):—afterward, again, second (-arily, time).

1209. δέχομαι **dĕchŏmai**, *dekh'-om-ahee*; mid. of a prim. verb; to receive (in various applications, lit. or fig.):—accept, receive, take. Comp. *2983*.

1210. δέω **dĕō**, *deh'-o*; a prim. verb; to bind (in various applications, lit. or fig.):—bind, be in bonds, knit, tie, wind. See also *1163*, *1189*.

1211. δή **dĕ**, *day;* prob. akin to *1161;* a particle of emphasis or explicitness; *now, then,* etc.:—also, and, doubtless, now, therefore.

1212. δῆλος **dēlŏs**, *day'-los;* of uncert. der.; *clear:—* + bewray, certain, evident, manifest.

1213. δηλόω **dēlŏō**, *day-lŏ'-o;* from *1212; to make plain* (by words):—declare, shew, signify.

1214. Δημᾶς **Dēmas**, *day-mas';* prob. for *1216;* Demas, a Chr.:—Demas.

1215. δημηγορέω **dēmēgŏrĕō**, *day-may-gor-eh'-o;* from a comp. of *1218* and *58; to be a people-gatherer,* i.e. *to address* a public assembly:—make an oration.

1216. Δημήτριος **Dēmētriŏs**, *day-may'-tree-os;* from Δημήτηρ **Dēmētēr** (*Ceres*); *Demetrius,* the name of an Ephesian and of a Chr.:—Demetrius.

1217. δημιουργός **dēmiŏurgŏs**, *day-me-oor-gos';* from *1218* and *2041;* a *worker for the people,* i.e. *mechanic* (spoken of the *Creator*):—maker.

1218. δῆμος **dēmŏs**, *day'-mos;* from *1210;* the *public* (as *bound* together socially):—people.

1219. δημόσιος **dēmŏsiŏs**, *day-mos'-ee-os;* from *1218; public;* (fem. sing. dat. as adv.) *in public:*—common, openly, publickly.

1220. δηνάριον **dēnariŏn**, *day-nar'-ee-on;* of Lat. or.; a *denarius* (or *ten asses*):—pence, penny [-worth].

1221. δήποτε **dēpŏtĕ**, *day'-pot-eh;* from *1211* and *4218;* a particle of generalization; *indeed, at any time:—*(what-) soever.

1222. δήπου **dēpŏu**, *day'-poo;* from *1211* and *4225;* a particle of asseveration; *indeed doubtless:—*verily.

1223. διά **dia**, *dee-ah';* a prim. prep. denoting the *channel* of an act; *through* (in very wide applications, local, causal or occasional):—after, always, among, at, to avoid, because of (that), briefly, by, for (cause) . . . fore, from, in, by occasion of, of, by reason of, for sake, that, thereby, therefore, X though, through (-out), to, wherefore, with (-in). In composition it retains the same general import.

Δία Dia. See *2203.*

1224. διαβαίνω **diabainō**, *dee-ab-ah'ee-no;* from *1223* and the base of *939; to cross:*—come over, pass (through).

1225. διαβάλλω **diaballō**, *dee-ab-al'-lo;* from *1223* and *906;* (fig.) to *traduce:*—accuse.

1226. διαβεβαιόομαι **diabĕbaiŏŏmai**, *dee-ab-ahee-ŏ'-om-ahee;* mid. of a comp. of *1223* and *950;* to *confirm thoroughly* (by words), i.e. *asseverate:*—affirm constantly.

1227. διαβλέπω **diablĕpō**, *dee-ab-lep'-o;* from *1223* and *991;* to *look through,* i.e. *recover* full *vision:*—see clearly.

1228. διάβολος **diabŏlŏs**, *dee-ab'-ol-os;* from *1225;* a *traducer;* spec. *Satan* [comp. 7854]:—false accuser, devil, slanderer.

1229. διαγγέλλω **diaggĕllō**, *de-ang-gel'-lo;* from *1223* and the base of *32;* to *herald thoroughly,* i.e. *declare,* preach, signify.

1230. διαγίνομαι **diaginŏmai**, *dee-ag-in'-om-ahee;* from *1223* and *1096;* to *elapse meanwhile:*—X after, be past, be spent.

1231. διαγινώσκω **diaginŏskō**, *dee-ag-in-o'-sko;* from *1223* and *1097;* to *know thoroughly,* i.e. *ascertain exactly:*—(would) enquire, know the uttermost.

1232. διαγνωρίζω **diagnōrizō**, *dee-ag-no-rid'-zo;* from *1123* and *1107;* to *tell abroad:*—make known.

1233. διάγνωσις **diagnōsis**, *dee-ag'-no-sis;* from *1231;* (magisterial) *examination* ("diagnosis"):—hearing.

1234. διαγογγύζω **diagŏgguzō**, *dee-ag-ong-good'-zo;* from *1223* and *1111;* to *complain throughout* a crowd:—murmur.

1235. διαγρηγορέω **diagrēgŏrĕō**, *dee-ag-ray-gor-eh'-o;* from *1223* and *1127;* to *waken thoroughly:*—be awake.

1236. διάγω **diagō**, *dee-ag'-o;* from *1223* and *71;* to *pass* time or life:—lead life, living.

1237. διαδέχομαι **diadĕchŏmai**, *dee-ad-ekh'-om-ahee;* from *1223* and *1209;* to *receive in turn,* i.e. (fig.) *succeed to:*—come after.

1238. διάδημα **diadēma**, *dee-ad'-ay-mah;* from a comp. of *1223* and *1210;* a "*diadem*" (as *bound about* the head):—crown. Comp. *4735.*

1239. διαδίδωμι **diadidōmi**, *dee-ad-id'-o-mee;* from *1223* and *1325;* to *give throughout* a crowd, i.e. *deal out;* also to *deliver over* (as to a successor):—(make) distribute (-ion), divide, give.

1240. διάδοχος **diadŏchŏs**, *dee-ad'-okh-os;* from *1237;* a *successor* in office:—room.

1241. διαζώννυμι **diazōnnumi**, *dee-az-own'-noo-mee;* from *1223* and *2224;* to *gird tightly:*—gird.

1242. διαθήκη **diathēkē**, *dee-ath-ay'-kay;* from *1303;* prop. a *disposition,* i.e. (spec.) a *contract* (espec. a *devisory will*):—covenant, testament.

1243. διαίρεσις **diairĕsis**, *dee-ah'ee-res-is;* from *1244;* a *distinction* or (concr.) *variety:*—difference, diversity.

1244. διαιρέω **diairĕō**, *dee-ahee-reh'-o;* from *1223* and *138;* to *separate,* i.e. *distribute:*—divide.

1245. διακαθαρίζω **diakatharizō**, *dee-ak-ath-ar-id'-zo;* from *1223* and *2511;* to *cleanse perfectly,* i.e. (spec.) *winnow:*—throughly purge.

1246. διακατελέγχομαι **diakatĕlĕgchŏmai**, *dee-ak-at-el-eng'-khom-ahee;* mid. from *1223* and a comp. of *2596* and *1651;* to *prove downright,* i.e. *confute:*—convince.

1247. διακονέω **diakŏnĕō**, *dee-ak-on-eh'-o;* from *1249;* to *be an attendant,* i.e. *wait upon* (menially or as a host, friend or [fig.] teacher); techn. to *act as a* Chr. *deacon:*—(ad-) minister (unto), serve, use the office of a deacon.

1248. διακονία **diakŏnia**, *dee-ak-on-ee'-ah;* from *1249;* *attendance* (as a servant, etc.); fig. (eleemosynary) *aid,* (official) *service* (espec. of the Chr. teacher, or techn. of the *diaconate*):—(ad-) minister (-ing, -tra-tion, -try), office, relief, service (-ing).

1249. διάκονος **diakŏnŏs**, *dee-ak'-on-os;* prob. from an obs. διάκω **diakō** (to *run* on errands; comp. *1377*); an *attendant,* i.e. (gen.) a *waiter* (at table or in other menial duties); spec. a Chr. *teacher* and *pastor* (techn. a *deacon* or *deaconess*):—deacon, minister, servant.

1250. διακόσιοι **diakŏsiŏi**, *dee-ak-os'-ee-oy;* from *1364* and *1540; two hundred:*—two hundred.

1251. διακούομαι **diakŏuŏmai**, *dee-ak-oo'-om-ahee;* mid. from *1223* and *191;* to *hear throughout,* i.e. *patiently listen* (to a prisoner's plea):—hear.

1252. διακρίνω **diakrinō**, *dee-ak-ree'-no;* from *1223* and *2919;* to *separate thoroughly,* i.e. (lit. and reflex.) to *withdraw* from, or (by impl.) *oppose;* fig. to *discriminate* (by impl. *decide*), or (reflex.) *hesitate:*—contend, make (to) differ (-ence), discern, doubt, judge, be partial, stagger, waver.

1253. διάκρισις **diakrisis**, *dee-ak'-ree-sis;* from *1252;* judicial *estimation:*—discern (-ing), disputation.

1254. διακωλύω **diakōluō**, *dee-ak-o-loo'-o;* from *1223* and *2967;* to *hinder altogether,* i.e. *utterly prohibit:*—forbid.

1255. διαλαλέω **dialalĕō**, *dee-al-al-eh'-o;* from *1223* and *2980;* to *talk throughout* a company, i.e. *converse* or (gen.) *publish:*—commune, noise abroad.

1256. διαλέγομαι **dialĕgŏmai**, *dee-al-eg'-om-ahee;* mid. from *1223* and *3004;* to *say thoroughly,* i.e. *discuss* (in argument or exhortation):—dispute, preach (unto), reason (with), speak.

1257. διαλείπω **dialĕipō**, *dee-al-i'-po;* from *1223* and *3007;* to *leave off in the middle,* i.e. *intermit:*—cease.

1258. διάλεκτος **dialĕktŏs**, *dee-al'-ek-tos;* from *1256;* a (mode of) *discourse,* i.e. "*dialect*":—language, tongue.

1259. διαλλάσσω **diallassō**, *dee-al-las'-so;* from *1223* and *236;* to *change thoroughly,* i.e. (ment.) to *conciliate:*—reconcile.

1260. διαλογίζομαι **dialŏgizŏmai**, *dee-al-og-id'-zom-ahee;* from *1223* and *3049;* to *reckon thoroughly,* i.e. (gen.) to *deliberate* (by reflection or discussion):—cast in mind, consider, dispute, muse, reason, think.

1261. διαλογισμός **dialŏgismŏs**, *dee-al-og-is-mos';* from *1260;* *discussion,* i.e. (internal) *considera-*

tion (by impl. *purpose*), or (external) *debate:*—dispute, doubtful (-ing), imagination, reasoning, thought.

1262. διαλύω **dialuō**, *dee-al-oo'-o;* from *1223* an *3089;* to *dissolve utterly:*—scatter.

1263. διαμαρτύρομαι **diamarturŏmai**, *dee-am ar-too'-rom-ahee;* from *1223* and *3140;* to *attest* or *protest earnestly,* or (by impl.) *hortatively:*—charge, testify (unto), witness.

1264. διαμάχομαι **diamachŏmai**, *dee-am-akh'-om-ahee;* from *1223* and *3164;* to *fight fiercely* (in altercation):—strive.

1265. διαμένω **diamĕnō**, *dee-am-en'-o;* from *1223* and *3306;* to *stay constantly* (in being or relation):—continue, remain.

1266. διαμερίζω **diamĕrizō**, *dee-am-er-id'-zo;* from *1223* and *3307;* to *partition thoroughly* (lit. in distribution, fig. in dissension):—cloven, divide, part.

1267. διαμερισμός **diamĕrismŏs**, *dee-am-er-is-mos';* from *1266;* *disunion* (of opinion and conduct):—division.

1268. διανέμω **dianĕmō**, *dee-an-em'-o;* from *1223* and the base of *3551;* to *distribute,* i.e. (of information) to *disseminate:*—spread.

1269. διανεύω **dianĕuō**, *dee-an-yoo'-o;* from *1223* and *3506;* to *nod* (or express by signs) across an intervening space:—beckon.

1270. διανόημα **dianŏēma**, *dee-an-ŏ'-ay-mah;* from a comp. of *1223* and *3539;* something *thought through,* i.e. a *sentiment:*—thought.

1271. διάνοια **dianŏia**, *dee-an'-oy-ah;* from *1223* and *3563;* deep *thought,* prop. the *faculty* (*mind* or its *disposition*), by impl. its *exercise:*—imagination, mind, understanding.

1272. διανοίγω **dianŏigō**, *dee-an-oy'-go;* from *1223* and *455;* to *open thoroughly,* lit. (as a first-born) or fig. (to *expound*):—open.

1273. διανυκτερεύω **dianuktĕrĕuō**, *dee-an-ook-ter-yoo'-o;* from *1223* and a der. of *3571;* to *sit up* the whole *night:*—continue all night.

1274. διανύω **dianuō**, *dee-an-oo'-o;* from *1223* and ἀνύω **anuō** (to *effect*); to *accomplish thoroughly:*—finish.

1275. διαπαντός **diapantŏs**, *dee-ap-an-tos';* from *1223* and the genit. of *3956; through all time,* i.e. (adv.) *constantly:*—alway (-s), continually.

1276. διαπεράω **diapĕraō**, *dee-ap-er-ah'-o;* from *1223* and a der. of the base of *4008;* to *cross entirely:*—go over, pass (over), sail over.

1277. διαπλέω **diaplĕō**, *dee-ap-leh'-o;* from *1223* and *4126;* to *sail through:*—sail over.

1278. διαπονέω **diapŏnĕō**, *dee-ap-on-eh'-o;* from *1223* and a der. of *4192;* to *toil through,* i.e. (pass.) be *worried:*—be grieved.

1279. διαπορεύομαι **diapŏrĕuŏmai**, *dee-ap-or-yoo'-om-ahee;* from *1223* and *4198;* to *travel through:*—go through, journey in, pass by.

1280. διαπορέω **diapŏrĕō**, *dee-ap-or-eh'-o;* from *1223* and *639;* to *be thoroughly nonplussed:*—(be in) doubt, be (much) perplexed.

1281. διαπραγματεύομαι **diapragmatĕuŏmai**, *dee-ap-rag-mat-yoo'-om-ahee;* from *1223* and *4231;* to *thoroughly occupy oneself,* i.e. (trans. and by impl.) to *earn* in business:—gain by trading.

1282. διαπρίω **diapriō**, *dee-ap-ree'-o;* from *1223* and the base of *4249;* to *saw asunder,* i.e. (fig.) to *exasperate:*—cut (to the heart).

1283. διαρπάζω **diarpazō**, *dee-ar-pad'-zo;* from *1223* and *726;* to *seize asunder,* i.e. *plunder:*—spoil.

1284. διαῤῥήσσω **diarrhēssō**, *dee-ar-hrayce'-so;* from *1223* and *4486;* to *tear asunder:*—break, rend.

1285. διασαφέω **diasaphĕō**, *dee-as-af-eh'-o;* from *1223* and σαφής **saphēs** (*clear*); to *clear thoroughly,* i.e. (fig.) *declare:*—tell unto.

1286. διασείω **diasĕiō**, *dee-as-i'-o;* from *1223* and *4579;* to *shake thoroughly,* i.e. (fig.) to *intimidate:*—do violence to.

1287. διασκορπίζω **diaskŏrpizō**, *dee-as-kor-pid'-zo;* from *1223* and *4650;* to *dissipate,* i.e. (gen.) to *rout* or *separate;* spec. to *winnow;* fig. to *squander:*—disperse, scatter (abroad), strew, waste.

1288. διασπάω **diaspaō**, dee-as-pah'-o; from *1223* and *4685*; to draw apart, i.e. sever or dismember:—pluck asunder, pull in pieces.

1289. διασπείρω **diaspeirō**, dee-as-pi'-ro; from *1223* and *4687*; to sow throughout, i.e. (fig.) distribute n foreign lands:—scatter abroad.

1290. διασπορά **diaspŏra**, dee-as-por-ah'; from *1289*; dispersion, i.e. (spec. and concr.) the (converted) Isr. resident in Gentile countries:—(which are) scattered (abroad).

1291. διαστέλλομαι **diastĕllŏmai**, dee-as-tel'-lom-ahee; mid. from *1223* and *4724*; to set (oneself) apart (fig. distinguish), i.e. (by impl.) to enjoin:—charge, that which was (give) commanded (-ment).

1292. διάστημα **diastĕma**, dee-as'-tay-mah; from *1339*; an interval:—space.

1293. διαστολή **diastŏlē**, dee-as-tol-ay'; from *1291*; a variation:—difference, distinction.

1294. διαστρέφω **diastrĕphō**, dee-as-tref'-o; from *1223* and *4762*; to distort, i.e. (fig.) misinterpret, or (mor.) corrupt:—perverse (-rt), turn away.

1295. διασώζω **diasōzō**, dee-as-odze'-o; from *1223* and *4982*; to save thoroughly, i.e. (by impl. or anal.) to cure, preserve, rescue, etc.:—bring safe, escape (safe), heal, make perfectly whole, save.

1296. διαταγή **diatagē**, dee-at-ag-ay'; from *1299*; arrangement, i.e. institution:—instrumentality.

1297. διάταγμα **diatagma**, dee-at'-ag-mah; from *1299*; an arrangement, i.e. (authoritative) edict:—commandment.

1298. διαταράσσω **diatarassō**, dee-at-ar-as'-so; from *1223* and *5015*; to disturb wholly, i.e. agitate (with alarm):—trouble.

1299. διατάσσω **diatassō**, dee-at-as'-so; from *1223* and *5021*; to arrange thoroughly, i.e. (spec.) institute, prescribe, etc.:—appoint, command, give, (set in) order, ordain.

1300. διατελέω **diatelĕō**, dee-at-el-eh'-o; from *1223* and *5055*; to accomplish thoroughly, i.e. (subj.) to persist:—continue.

1301. διατηρέω **diatērĕō**, dee-at-ay-reh'-o; from *1223* and *5083*; to watch thoroughly, i.e. (pos. and trans.) to observe strictly, or (neg. and reflex.) to avoid wholly:—keep.

1302. διατί **diati**, dee-at-ee'; from *1223* and *5101*; through what cause ?, i.e. why?:—wherefore, why.

1303. διατίθεμαι **diatithĕmai**, dee-at-ith'-em-ahee; mid. from *1223* and *5087*; to put apart, i.e. (fig.) dispose by assignment, compact or bequest):—appoint, make, testator.

1304. διατρίβω **diatribō**, dee-at-ree'-bo; from *1223* and the base of *5147*; to wear through (time), i.e. remain:—abide, be, continue, tarry.

1305. διατροφή **diatrŏphē**, dee-at-rof-ay'; from a comp. of *1223* and *5142*; nourishment:—food.

1306. διαυγάζω **diaugazō**, dee-ŏw-gad'-zo; from *1223* and *826*; to glimmer through, i.e. break (as day):—dawn.

1307. διαφανής **diaphanēs**, dee-af-an-ace'; from *1223* and *5316*; appearing through, i.e. "diaphanous":—transparent.

1308. διαφέρω **diaphĕrō**, dee-af-er'-o; from *1223* and *5342*; to bear through, i.e. (lit.) transport; usually to bear apart, i.e. (obj.) to toss about (fig. report); subj. to "differ," or (by impl.) surpass:—be better, carry, differ from, drive up and down, be (more) excellent, make matter, publish, be of more value.

1309. διαφεύγω **diapheugō**, dee-af-yoo'-go; from *1223* and *5343*; to flee through, i.e. escape:—escape.

1310. διαφημίζω **diaphēmizō**, dee-af-ay-mid'-zo; from *1223* and a der. of *5345*; to report thoroughly, i.e. divulgate:—blaze abroad, commonly report, spread abroad, fame.

1311. διαφθείρω **diaphtheirō**, dee-af-thi'-ro; from *1223* and *5351*; to rot thoroughly, i.e. (by impl.) to ruin (pass. decay utterly, fig. pervert):—corrupt, destroy, perish.

1312. διαφθορά **diaphthŏra**, dee-af-thor-ah'; from *1311*; decay:—corruption.

1313. διάφορος **diaphŏrŏs**, dee-af'-or-os; from *1308*; varying; also surpassing:—differing, divers, more excellent.

1314. διαφυλάσσω **diaphulassō**, dee-af-oo-las'-so; from *1223* and *5442*; to guard thoroughly, i.e. protect:—keep.

1315. διαχειρίζομαι **diacheirizŏmai**, dee-akh-i-rid'-zom-ahee; from *1223* and a der. of *5495*; to handle thoroughly, i.e. lay violent hands upon:—kill, slay.

1316. διαχωρίζομαι **diachōrizŏmai**, dee-akh-o-rid'-zom-ahee; from *1223* and the mid. of *5563*; to remove (oneself) wholly, i.e. retire:—depart.

1317. διδακτός **didaktŏs**, did-ak-tik-os'; from *1318*; instructive (" didactic"):—apt to teach.

1318. διδακτός **didaktŏs**, did-ak-tos'; from *1321*; (subj.) instructed or (obj.) communicated by teaching:—taught, which . . . teacheth.

1319. διδασκαλία **didaskalia**, did-as-kal-ee'-ah; from *1320*; instruction (the function or the information):—doctrine, learning, teaching.

1320. διδάσκαλος **didaskalŏs**, did-as'-kal-os; from *1321*; an instructor (gen. or spec.):—doctor, master, teacher.

1321. διδάσκω **didaskō**, did-as'-ko; a prol. (caus.) form of a prim. verb δάω **daō** (to learn); to teach (in the same broad application):—teach.

1322. διδαχή **didachē**, did-akh-ay'; from *1321*; instruction (the act or the matter):—doctrine, hath been taught.

1323. δίδραχμον **didrachmŏn**, did'-rakh-mon; from *1364* and *1406*; a double drachma (didrachm):—tribute.

1324. Δίδυμος **Didumŏs**, did ʼo-mos; prol. from *1364*; double, i.e. twin; Didymus, a Chr.:—Didymus.

1325. δίδωμι **didŏmi**, did'-o-mee; a prol. form of a prim. verb (which is used as an altern. in most of the tenses); to give (used in a very wide application, prop. or by impl., lit. or fig.; greatly modified by the connection):—adventure, bestow, bring forth, commit, deliver (up), give, grant, hinder, make, minister, number, offer, have power, put, receive, set, shew, smite (+ with the hand), strike (+ with the palm of the hand), suffer, take, utter, yield.

1326. διεγείρω **diĕgeirō**, dee-eg-i'-ro; from *1223* and *1453*; to wake fully, i.e. arouse (lit. or fig.):—arise, awake, raise, stir up.

1327. διέξοδος **diĕxŏdŏs**, dee-ex'-od-os; from *1223* and *1841*; an outlet through, i.e. prob. an open square (from which roads diverge):—highway

1328. διερμηνευτής **diĕrmēnĕutēs**, dee-er-main-yoo-tace'; from *1329*; an explainer:—interpreter.

1329. διερμηνεύω **diĕrmēnĕuō**, dee-er-main-yoo' o; from *1223* and *2059*; to explain thoroughly; by impl. to translate:—expound, interpret (-ation).

1330. διέρχομαι **diĕrchŏmai**, dee-er'-khom-ahee; from *1223* and *2064*; to traverse (lit):—come, depart, go (about, abroad, every where, over, through, throughout), pass (by, over, through, throughout), pierce through, travel, walk through.

1331. διερωτάω **diĕrōtaō**, dee-er-o-tah'-o; from *1223* and *2065*; to question throughout, i.e. ascertain by interrogation:—make enquiry for.

1332. διετής **diĕtēs**, dee-et-ace'; from *1364* and *2094*; of two years (in age):—two years old.

1333. διετία **diĕtia**, dee-et-ee'-a; from *1332*; a space of two years (biennium):—two years.

1334. διηγέομαι **diēgĕŏmai**, dee-ayg-eh'-om-ahee; from *1223* and *2233*; to relate fully:—declare, shew, tell.

1335. διήγησις **diēgĕsis**, dee-ayg'-es-is; from *1334*; a recital:—declaration.

1336. διηνεκές **diēnĕkĕs**, dee-ay-nek-es'; neut. of a comp. of *1223* and a der. of an alt. of *5342*; carried through, i.e. (adv. with *1519* and *3588* pref.) perpetually:—+ continually, for ever.

1337. διθάλασσος **dithalassŏs**, dee-thal'-as-sos; from *1364* and *2281*; having two seas, i.e. a sound with a double outlet:—where two seas met.

1338. διϊκνέομαι **diïknĕŏmai**, dee-ik-neh'-om-ahee; from *1223* and the base of *2425*; to reach through, i.e. penetrate:—pierce.

1339. διΐστημι **diïstēmi**, dee-is'-tay-mee; from *1223* and *2476*; to stand apart, i.e. (reflex.) to remove, intervene:—go further, be parted, after the space ot.

1340. διϊσχυρίζομαι **diïschurizŏmai**, dee-is-khoo-rid'-zom-ahee; from *1223* and a der. of *2478*; to stout it through, i.e. asseverate:—confidently (constantly) affirm.

1341. δικαιοκρισία **dikaiŏkrisia**, dik-ah-yok-ris-ee'-ah; from *1342* and *2920*; a just sentence:—righteous judgment.

1342. δίκαιος **dikaiŏs**, dik'-ah-yos; from *1349*; equitable (in character or act); by impl. innocent, holy (absol. or rel.):—just, meet, right (-eous).

1343. δικαιοσύνη **dikaiŏsunē**, dik-ah-yos-oo'-nay; from *1342*; equity (of character or act); spec. (Chr.) justification:—righteousness.

1344. δικαιόω **dikaiŏō**, dik-ah-yŏ'-o; from *1342*; to render (i.e. show or regard as) just or innocent:—free, justify (-ier), be righteous.

1345. δικαίωμα **dikaiōma**, dik-ah'-yo-mah; from *1344*; an equitable deed; by impl. a statute or decision:—judgment, justification, ordinance, righteousness.

1346. δικαίως **dikaiōs**, dik-ah'-yoce; adv. from *1342*; equitably:—justly, (to) righteously (-ness).

1347. δικαίωσις **dikaiōsis**, dik-ah'-yo-sis; from *1344*; acquittal (for Christ's sake):—justification.

1348. δικαστής **dikastēs**, dik-as-tace'; from a der. of *1349*; a judger:—judge.

1349. δίκη **dikē**, dee'-kay; prob. from *1166*; right (as self-evident), i.e. justice (the principle, a decision, or its execution):—judgment, punish, vengeance.

1350. δίκτυον **diktuŏn**, dik'-too-on; prob. from a prim. verb δίκω **dikō** (to cast); a seine (for fishing):—net.

1351. δίλογος **dilŏgŏs**, dil'-og-os; from *1364* and *3056*; equivocal, i.e. telling a different story:—double tongued.

1352. διό **diŏ**, dee-ŏ'; from *1223* and *3739*; through which thing, i.e. consequently:—for which cause, therefore, wherefore.

1353. διοδεύω **diŏdĕuō**, dee-od-yoo'-o; from *1223* and *3593*; to travel through:—go throughout, pass through.

1354. Διονύσιος **Diŏnusiŏs**, dee-on-oo'-see-os; from Διόνυσος **Diŏnusŏs** (Bacchus); reveller; Dionysius, an Athenian:—Dionysius.

1355. διόπερ **diŏpĕr**, dee-op'-er; from *1352* and *4007*; on which very account:—wherefore.

1356. διοπετής **diŏpĕtēs**, dee-op-et'-ace; from the alt. of *2203* and the alt. of *4098*; sky-fallen (i.e. an aerolite):—which fell down from Jupiter.

1357. διόρθωσις **diŏrthōsis**, dee-or'-tho-sis; from a comp. of *1223* and a der. of *3717*, mean. to straighten thoroughly; rectification, i.e. (spec.) the Messianic restauration:—reformation.

1358. διορύσσω **diŏrussō**, dee-or-oos'-so; from *1223* and *3736*; to penetrate burglariously:—break through (up).

Διός Diŏs. See *2203*.

1359. Διόσκουροι **Diŏskŏurŏi**, dee-os'-koo-roy; from the alt. of *2203* and a form of the base of *2877*; sons of Jupiter, i.e. the twins Dioscuri:—Castor and Pollux.

1360. διότι **diŏti**, dee-ot'-ee; from *1223* and *3754*; on the very account that, or inasmuch as:—because (that), for, therefore.

1361. Διοτρεφής **Diŏtrĕphēs**, dee-ot-ref-ace'; from the alt. of *2203* and *5142*; Jove-nourished; Diotrephes, an opponent of Christianity:—Diotrephes.

1362. διπλοῦς **diplŏus**, dip-looce'; from *1364* and (prob.) the base of *4119*; two-fold:—double, two-fold more.

1363. διπλόω **diplŏō**, dip-lŏ'-o; from *1362*; to render two-fold:—double.

1364. **δίς dis,** *dece;* adv. from *1417; twice:*—again, twice.

Δίς Dis. See *2203.*

1365. **διστάζω distazō,** *dis-tad'-zo;* from *1364;* prop. to *duplicate,* i.e. (ment.) to *waver* (in opinion):—doubt.

1366. **δίστομος distŏmŏs,** *dis'-tom-os;* from *1364* and *4750; double-edged:*—with two edges, two-edged.

1367. **δισχίλιοι dischilioi,** *dis-khil'-ee-oy;* from *1364* and *5507; two thousand:*—two thousand.

1368. **διϋλίζω diulizō,** *dee-oo-lid'-zo;* from *1223* and **ὑλίζω hulizō,** *hoo-lid'-zo* (to *filter*); to *strain out:*—strain at [*prob. by misprint*].

1369. **διχάζω dichazō,** *dee-khad'-zo;* from a der. of *1364;* to *make apart,* i.e. *sunder* (fig. *alienate*):—set at variance.

1370. **διχοστασία dichŏstasia,** *dee-khos-tas-ee'-ah;* from a der. of *1364* and *4714; disunion,* i.e. (fig.) *dissension:*—division, sedition.

1371. **διχοτομέω dichŏtŏmeō,** *dee-khot-om-eh'-o;* from a comp. of a der. of *1364* and a der. of **τέμνω temnō** (to *cut*); to *bisect,* i.e. (by extens.) to *flog severely:*—cut asunder (in sunder).

1372. **διψάω dipsaō,** *dip-sah'-o;* from a var. of *1373;* to *thirst* for (lit. or fig.):—(be a-) thirst (-y).

1373. **δίψος dipsŏs,** *dip'-sos;* of uncert. affin.; *thirst:*—thirst.

1374. **δίψυχος dipsuchŏs,** *dip'-soo-khos;* from *1364* and *5590; two-spirited,* i.e. *vacillating* (in opinion or purpose):—double minded.

1375. **διωγμός diōgmŏs,** *dee-ogue-mos';* from *1377; persecution:*—persecution.

1376. **διώκτης diōktēs,** *dee-oke'-tace;* from *1377;* a *persecutor:*—persecutor.

1377. **διώκω diōkō,** *dee-o'-ko;* a prol. (and caus.) form of a prim. verb **δίω diō** (to *flee;* comp. the base of *1169* and *1249*); to *pursue* (lit. or fig.); by impl. to *persecute:*—ensue, follow (after), given to, (suffer) persecute (-ion), press toward.

1378. **δόγμα dŏgma,** *dog'-mah;* from the base of *1380;* a *law* (civil, cer. or eccl.):—decree, ordinance.

1379. **δογματίζω dŏgmatizō,** *dog-mat-id'-zo;* from *1378;* to *prescribe* by statute, i.e. (reflex.) to *submit* to cer. *rule:*—be subject to ordinances.

1380. **δοκέω dŏkeō,** *dok-eh'-o;* a prol. form of a prim. verb **δόκω dŏkō,** *dok'-o* (used only as an alt. in certain tenses; comp. the base of *1166*) of the same mean.; to *think;* by impl. to *seem* (truthfully or uncertainly):—be accounted, (of own) please (-ure), be of reputation, seem (good), suppose, think, trow.

1381. **δοκιμάζω dŏkimazō,** *dok-im-ad'-zo;* from *1384;* to *test* (lit. or fig.); by impl. to *approve:*—allow, discern, examine, × like, (ap-) prove, try.

1382. **δοκιμή dŏkimē,** *dok-ee-may';* from the same as *1384; test* (abstr. or concr.); by impl. *trustiness:*—experience (-riment), proof, trial.

1383. **δοκίμιον dŏkimiŏn,** *dok-im'-ee-on;* neut. of a presumed der. of *1382;* a *testing;* by impl. *trustworthiness:*—trial, trying.

1384. **δόκιμος dŏkimŏs,** *dok'-ee-mos;* from *1380;* prop. *acceptable* (current after assayal), i.e. *approved:*—approved, tried.

1385. **δοκός dŏkŏs,** *dok-os';* from *1209* (through the idea of *holding* up); a *stick* of timber:—beam.

δόκω dŏkō. See *1380.*

1386. **δόλιος dŏliŏs,** *dol'-ee-os;* from *1388; guileful:*—deceitful.

1387. **δολιόω dŏliŏō,** *dol-ee-ŏ'-o;* from *1386;* to *be guileful:*—use deceit.

1388. **δόλος dŏlŏs,** *dol'-os;* from an obs. prim. **δέλλω dellō** (prob. mean. to *decoy;* comp. *1185*); a *trick* (bait), i.e. (fig.) *wile:*—craft, deceit, guile, subtilty.

1389. **δολόω dŏlŏō,** *dol-ŏ'-o;* from *1388;* to *ensnare,* i.e. (fig.) *adulterate:*—handle deceitfully.

1390. **δόμα dŏma,** *dom'-ah;* from the base of *1325;* a *present:*—gift.

1391. **δόξα dŏxa,** *dox'-ah;* from the base of *1380; glory* (as very *apparent*), in a wide application (lit. or

fig., obj. or subj.):—*dignity, glory* (-ious), honour, praise, worship.

1392. **δοξάζω dŏxazō,** *dox-ad'-zo;* from *1391;* to *render* (or esteem) *glorious* (in a wide application):—(make) glorify (-ious), full of (have) glory, honour, magnify.

1393. **Δορκάς Dŏrkas,** *dor-kas';* gazelle; *Dorcas,* a Chr. woman:—Dorcas.

1394. **δόσις dŏsis,** *dos'-is;* from the base of *1325;* a *giving;* by impl. (concr.) a *gift:*—gift, giving.

1395. **δότης dŏtēs,** *dot'-ace;* from the base of *1325;* a *giver:*—giver.

1396. **δουλαγωγέω dŏulagōgeō,** *doo-lag-ogue-eh'-o;* from a presumed comp. of *1401* and *71;* to be a *slave-driver,* i.e. to *enslave* (fig. *subdue*):—bring into subjection.

1397. **δουλεία dŏuleia,** *doo-li'-ah;* from *1398; slavery* (cer. or fig.):—bondage.

1398. **δουλεύω dŏuleuō,** *dool-yoo'-o;* from *1401;* to be *a slave* (lit. or fig., invol. or vol.):—be in bondage, (do) serve (-ice).

1399. **δούλη dŏulē,** *doo'-lay;* fem. of *1401;* a *female slave* (invol. or vol.):—handmaid (-en).

1400. **δοῦλον dŏulŏn,** *doo'-lon;* neut. of *1401; subservient:*—servant.

1401. **δοῦλος dŏulŏs,** *doo'-los;* from *1210;* a *slave* (lit. or fig., invol. or vol.; frequently therefore in a qualified sense of *subjection* or *subserviency*):—bond (-man), servant.

1402. **δουλόω dŏulŏō,** *doo-lŏ'-o;* from *1401;* to *enslave* (lit. or fig.):—bring into (be under) bondage, × given, become (make) servant.

1403. **δοχή dŏchē,** *dokh-ay';* from *1209;* a *reception,* i.e. convivial *entertainment:*—feast.

1404. **δράκων drakōn,** *drak-own;* prob. from an alt. form of **δέρκομαι dĕrkŏmai** (to *look*); a *fabulous* kind of *serpent* (perh. as supposed to *fascinate*):—dragon.

1405. **δράσσομαι drassŏmai,** *dras'-som-ahee;* perh. akin to the base of *1404* (through the idea of *capturing*); to *grasp,* i.e. (fig.) *entrap:*—take.

1406. **δραχμή drachmē,** *drakh-may';* from *1405;* a *drachma* or (silver) *coin* (as *handled*):—piece (of silver).

δρέμω drĕmō. See *5143.*

1407. **δρέπανον drĕpanŏn,** *drep'-an-on;* from **δρέπω drĕpō** (to *pluck*); a *gathering hook* (espec. for harvesting):—sickle.

1408. **δρόμος drŏmŏs,** *drom'-os;* from the alt. of *5143;* a *race,* i.e. (fig.) *career:*—course.

1409. **Δρούσιλλα Drŏusilla,** *droo'-sil-lah;* a fem. dimin. of *Drusus* (a Rom. name); *Drusilla,* a member of the Herodian family:—Drusilla.

Δῦμι dumi. See *1416.*

1410. **δύναμαι dunamai,** *doo'-nam-ahee;* of uncert. affin.; to be *able* or *possible:*—be able, can (do, + -not), could, may, might, be possible, be of power.

1411. **δύναμις dunamis,** *doo'-nam-is;* from *1410; force* (lit. or fig.); spec. miraculous *power* (usually by impl. a *miracle* itself):—ability, abundance, meaning, might (-ily, -y, -y deed), (worker of) miracle (-s), power, strength, violence, mighty (wonderful) work.

1412. **δυναμόω dunamŏō,** *doo-nam-ŏ'-o;* from *1411;* to *enable:*—strengthen.

1413. **δυνάστης dunastēs,** *doo-nas'-tace;* from *1410;* a *ruler* or *officer:*—of great authority, mighty, potentate.

1414. **δυνατέω dunateō,** *doo-nat-eh'-o;* from *1415;* to be *efficient* (fig.):—be mighty.

1415. **δυνατός dunatŏs,** *doo-nat-os';* from *1410; powerful* or *capable* (lit. or fig.); neut. *possible:*—able, could, (that is) mighty (man), possible, power, strong.

1416. **δύνω dunō,** *doo'-no;* or

δῦμι dumi, *doo'-mee;* prol. forms of an obs. prim. **δύω duō,** *doo'-o* (to *sink*); to *go* 'down':—set.

1417. **δύο duŏ,** *doo'-ŏ;* a prim. numeral; "*two*":—both, twain, two.

1418. **δυσ- dus-,** *doos;* a prim. inseparable particle of uncert. der.; used only in composition as a pref.; *hard,* i.e. *with difficulty:*— + hard, + grievous, *etc.*

1419. **δυσβάστακτος dusbastaktŏs,** *doos-bas'-tak-tos;* from *1418* and a der. of *941; oppressive:*—grievous to be borne.

1420. **δυσεντερία dusĕnteria,** *doos-en-ter-ee'-ah;* from *1418* and a comp. of *1787* (mean. a *bowel*); a "*dysentery*":—bloody flux.

1421. **δυσερμήνευτος dusĕrmēnĕutŏs,** *doos-er-mane'-yoo-tos;* from *1418* and a presumed der. of *2059; difficult of explanation:*—hard to be uttered.

1422. **δύσκολος duskŏlŏs,** *doos'-kol-os;* from *1418* and **κόλον kŏlŏn** (*food*); prop. *fastidious about eating* (peevish), i.e. (gen.) *impracticable:*—hard.

1423. **δυσκόλως duskŏlōs,** *doos-kol'-oce;* adv. from *1422; impracticably:*—hardly.

1424. **δυσμή dusmē,** *doos-may';* from *1416;* the *sun-set,* i.e. (by impl.) the *western* region:—west.

1425. **δυσνόητος dusnŏētŏs,** *doos-nŏ'-ay-tos;* from *1418* and a der. of *3539; difficult of perception:*—hard to be understood.

1426. **δυσφημία dusphēmia,** *doos-fay-mee'-ah;* from a comp. of *1418* and *5345; defamation:*—evil report.

1427. **δύο duŏ.** See *1416.*

1427. **δώδεκα dōdeka,** *do'-dek-ah;* from *1417* and *1176; two* and *ten,* i.e. a *dozen:*—twelve.

1428. **δωδέκατος dōdĕkatŏs,** *do-dek'-at-os;* from *1427; twelfth:*—twelfth.

1429. **δωδεκάφυλον dōdĕkaphulŏn,** *do-dek-af'-oo-lon;* from *1427* and *5443;* the *commonwealth* of Israel:—twelve tribes.

1430. **δῶμα dōma,** *do'-mah;* from **δέμω dĕmō** (to *build*); prop. an *edifice,* i.e. (spec.) a *roof:*—housetop.

1431. **δωρεά dōrĕa,** *do-reh-ah';* from *1435;* a *gratuity:*—gift.

1432. **δωρεάν dōrĕan,** *do-reh-an';* acc. of *1431* as adv.; *gratuitously* (lit. or fig.):—without a cause, freely, for naught, in vain.

1433. **δωρέομαι dōrĕŏmai,** *do-reh'-om-ahee;* mid. from *1435;* to *bestow gratuitously:*—give.

1434. **δώρημα dōrēma,** *do'-ray-mah;* from *1433;* a *bestowment:*—gift.

1435. **δῶρον dōrŏn,** *do'-ron;* a *present;* spec. a *sacrifice:*—gift, offering.

E

1436. **ἔα ĕa,** *eh'-ah;* appar. imper. of *1439;* prop. *let it be,* i.e. (as interj.) *aha!:*—let alone.

1437. **ἐάν ĕan,** *eh-an';* from *1487* and *302;* a conditional particle; *in case that, provided,* etc.; often used in connection with other particles to denote *indefiniteness* or *uncertainty:*—before, but, except, (and) if, (if) so, (what-, whither-) soever, though, when (-soever), whether (or), to whom, [who-] so (-ever). See *3361.*

ἐὰν μή ĕan mē. See *3361.*

1438. **ἑαυτοῦ hĕautŏu,** *heh-ŏw-too'* (incl. all the other cases); from a reflex. pron. otherwise obsol. and the gen. (dat. or acc.) of *846; him-* (her-, it-, them-, also [in conjunction with the pers. pron. of the other persons] *my-, thy-, our-, your-*) *self* (*selves*), etc.:—alone, her (own, -self), (he) himself, his (own), itself, one (to) another, our (thine) own (-selves), + that she had, their (own, own selves), (of) them (-selves), they, thyself, you, your (own, own conceits, own selves, -selves).

1439. **ἐάω ĕaō,** *eh-ah'-o;* of uncert. affin.; to *let be,* i.e. *permit* or *leave alone:*—commit, leave, let (alone), suffer. See also *1436.*

1440. **ἑβδομήκοντα hĕbdomēkŏnta,** *heb-dom-ay'-kon-tah;* from *1442* and a modified form of *1176; seventy:*—seventy, three score and ten.

1441. **ἑβδομηκοντάκις hĕbdŏmēkŏntakis,** *heb-dom-ay-kon-tak-is';* multiple adv. from *1440; seventy times:*—seventy times.

1442. ἔβδομος **hĕbdŏmŏs**, *heb'-dom-os;* ordinal from 2033; *seventh:*—seventh.

1443. Ἐβέρ **Ĕbĕr**, *eb-er';* of Heb. or. [5677]; *Eber,* a patriarch:—Eber.

1444. Ἑβραϊκός **Hĕbraïkŏs**, *heb-rah-ee-kos';* from 1443; *Hebraïc* or the *Jewish* language:—Hebrew.

1445. Ἑβραῖος **Hĕbraiŏs**, *heb-rah'-yos;* from 1443; a *Hebrœan* (i.e. Hebrew) or *Jew:*—Hebrew.

1446. Ἑβραΐς **Hĕbraïs**, *heb-rah-is';* from 1443; the *Hebraistic* (i.e. *Hebrew*) or *Jewish* (Chaldee) language:—Hebrew.

1447. Ἑβραϊστί **Hĕbraïsti**, *heb-rah-is-tee';* adv. from 1446; *Hebraistically* or in the *Jewish* (Chaldee) language:—in (the) Hebrew (tongue).

1448. ἐγγίζω **ĕggizō**, *eng-id'-zo;* from 1451; to *make near,* i.e. (reflex.) *approach:*—approach, be at hand, come (draw) near, be (come, draw) nigh.

1449. ἐγγράφω **ĕggraphō**, *eng-graf'-o;* from 1722 and 1125; to "*engrave*", i.e. *inscribe:*—write (in).

1450. ἔγγυος **ĕgguŏs**, *eng'-goo-os;* from 1722 and γυῖον guiŏn (a *limb*); *pledged* (as if articulated by a member), i.e. a *bondsman:*—surety.

1451. ἐγγύς **ĕggus**, *eng-goos';* from a prim. verb ἄγχω **agchō** (to *squeeze* or *throttle;* akin to the base of 43); *near* (lit. or fig., of place or time):—from, at hand, near, nigh (at hand, unto), ready.

1452. ἐγγύτερον **ĕggutĕrŏn**, *eng-goo'-ter-on;* neut. of the comp. of 1451; *nearer:*—nearer.

1453. ἐγείρω **ĕgĕirō**, *eg-i'-ro;* prob. akin to the base of 58 (through the idea of *collecting* one's faculties); to *waken* (trans. or intrans.), i.e. *rouse* (lit. from sleep, from sitting or lying, from disease, from death; or fig. from obscurity, inactivity, ruins, nonexistence):—awake, lift (up), raise (again, up), rear up, (a-) rise (again, up), stand, take up.

1454. ἔγερσις **ĕgĕrsis**, *eg'-er-sis;* from 1453; a *resurgence* (from death):—resurrection.

1455. ἐγκάθετος **ĕgkathĕtŏs**, *eng-kath'-et-os;* from 1722 and a der. of 2524; *subinduced,* i.e. *surreptitiously suborned* as a lier-in-wait:—spy.

1456. ἐγκαίνια **ĕgkainia**, *eng-kah'ee-nee-ah;* neut. plur. of a presumed comp. from 1722 and 2537; *innovatives,* i.e. (spec.) *renewal* (of religious services after the Antiochian interruption):—dedication.

1457. ἐγκαινίζω **ĕgkainizō**, *eng-kahee-nid'-zo;* from 1456; to *renew,* i.e. *inaugurate:*—consecrate, dedicate.

1458. ἐγκαλέω **ĕgkalĕō**, *eng-kal-eh'-o;* from 1722 and 2564; to *call in* (as a debt or demand), i.e. *bring to account* (charge, criminate, etc.):—accuse, call in question, implead, lay to the charge.

1459. ἐγκαταλείπω **ĕgkatalĕipō**, *eng-kat-al-i'-po;* from 1722 and 2641; to *leave behind* in some place, i.e. (in a good sense) *let remain over,* or (in a bad one) to *desert:*—forsake, leave.

1460. ἐγκατοικέω **ĕgkatŏikĕō**, *eng-kat-oy-keh'-o;* from 1722 and 2730; to *settle down* in a place, i.e. *reside:*—dwell among.

1461. ἐγκεντρίζω **ĕgkĕntrizō**, *eng-ken-trid'-zo;* from 1722 and a der. of 2759; to *prick in,* i.e. *ingraft:*—graff in (-to).

1462. ἔγκλημα **ĕgklēma**, *eng'-klay-mah;* from 1458; an *accusation,* i.e. *offence alleged:*—crime laid against, laid to charge.

1463. ἐγκομβόομαι **ĕgkŏmbŏŏmai**, *eng-kom-bŏ'-om-ahee;* mid. from 1722 and κομβόω **kŏmbŏō** (to *gird*) to *engirdle* oneself (for labor), i.e. fig. (the apron being a badge of servitude) to *wear* (in token of mutual deference):—be clothed with.

1464. ἐγκοπή **ĕgkŏpē**, *eng-kop-ay';* from 1465; a *hindrance:*—× hinder.

1465. ἐγκόπτω **ĕgkŏptō**, *eng-kop'-to;* from 1722 and 2875; to *cut into,* i.e. (fig.) *impede, detain:*—hinder, be tedious unto.

1466. ἐγκράτεια **ĕgkratĕia**, *eng-krat'-i-ah;* from 1468; *self-control* (espec. *continence*):—temperance.

1467. ἐγκρατεύομαι **ĕgkratĕuŏmai**, *eng-krat-yoo'om-ahee;* mid. from 1468; to *exercise self-re-*

---

straint (in diet and chastity):—can ([-not]) contain, be temperate.

1468. ἐγκρατής **ĕgkratēs**, *eng-krat-ace';* from 1722 and 2904; *strong in a thing* (*masterful*), i.e. (fig. and reflex.) *self-controlled* (in appetite, etc.):—temperate.

1469. ἐγκρίνω **ĕgkrinō**, *eng-kree'-no;* from 1722 and 2919; to *judge in,* i.e. *count among:*—make of the number.

1470. ἐγκρύπτω **ĕgkruptō**, *eng-kroop'-to;* from 1722 and 2928; to *conceal in,* i.e. *incorporate with:*—hid in.

1471. ἔγκυος **ĕgkuŏs**, *eng'-koo-os;* from 1722 and the base of 2949; *swelling inside,* i.e. *pregnant:*—great with child.

1472. ἐγχρίω **ĕgchriō**, *eng-khree'-o;* from 1722 and 5548; to *rub in* (oil), i.e. *besmear:*—anoint.

1473. ἐγώ **ĕgō**, *eg-o';* a prim. pron. of the first pers. *I* (only expressed when emphatic):—I, me. For the other cases and the plur. see 1691, 1698, 1700, 2248, 2249, 2254, 2257, etc.

1474. ἐδαφίζω **ĕdaphizō**, *ed-af-id'-zo;* from 1475; to *raze:*—lay even with the ground.

1475. ἔδαφος **ĕdaphŏs**, *ed'-af-os;* from the base of 1476; a *basis* (bottom), i.e. the *soil:*—ground.

1476. ἑδραῖος **hĕdraiŏs**, *hed-rah'-yos;* from a der. of ἕζομαι **hĕzŏmai** (to *sit*); *sedentary,* i.e. (by impl.) *immovable:*—settled, stedfast.

1477. ἑδραίωμα **hĕdraiōma**, *hed-rah'-yo-mah;* from a der. of 1476; a *support,* i.e. (fig.) *basis:*—ground.

1478. Ἐζεκίας **Ĕzĕkias**, *ed-zek-ee'-as;* of Heb. or. [2396]; *Ezekias* (i.e. *Hezekiah*), an Isr.:—Ezekias.

1479. ἐθελοθρησκεία **ĕthĕlŏthrēskĕia**, *eth-el-oth-race-ki'-ah;* from 2309 and 2356; *voluntary* (*arbitrary* and *unwarranted*) *piety,* i.e. *sanctimony:*—will worship.

1480. ἐθίζω **ĕthizō**. See 2309.

1481. ἐθίζω **ĕthizō**, *eth-id'-zo;* from 1485; to *accustom,* i.e. (neut. pass. part.) *customary:*—custom.

1481. ἐθνάρχης **ĕthnarchēs**, *eth-nar'-khace;* from 1484 and 746; the *governor* [not king] *of a district:*—ethnarch.

1482. ἐθνικός **ĕthnikŏs**, *eth-nee-kos';* from 1484; *national* ("*ethnic*"), i.e. (spec.) a *Gentile:*—heathen (man).

1483. ἐθνικῶς **ĕthnikŏs**, *eth-nee-koce';* adv. from 1482; *as a Gentile:*—after the manner of Gentiles.

1484. ἔθνος **ĕthnŏs**, *eth-nos';* prob. from 1486; a *race* (as of the same *habit*), i.e. a *tribe;* spec. a *foreign* (non-Jewish) one (usually by impl. *pagan*):—Gentile, heathen, nation, people.

1485. ἔθος **ĕthŏs**, *eth'-os;* from 1486; a *usage* (prescribed by habit or law):—custom, manner, be wont.

1486. ἔθω **ĕthō**, *eth'-o;* a prim. verb; to *be used* (by habit or conventionality); neut. perf. part. *usage:*—be custom (manner, wont).

1487. εἰ **ĕi**, *i;* a prim. particle of conditionality; *if, whether, that,* etc.:—forasmuch as, if, that, ([al-]) though, whether. Often used in connection or composition with other particles, espec. as in 1489, 1490, 1499, 1508, 1509, 1512, 1513, 1536, 1537. See also 1437.

1488. εἶ **ĕi**, *i;* second pers. sing. pres. of 1510; thou *art:*—art, be.

1489. εἴγε **ĕigĕ**, *i'-gheh;* from 1487 and 1065; *if indeed, seeing that, unless,* (with neg.) *otherwise:*—if (so be that, yet).

1490. εἰ δὲ μή(γε) **ĕi dĕ mē(gĕ)**, *i deh may'-(gheh);* from 1487, 1161 and 3361 (sometimes with 1065 added); *but if not:*—(or) else, if (not, otherwise), otherwise.

1491. εἶδος **ĕidŏs**, *i'-dos,* from 1492; a *view,* i.e. *form* (lit. or fig.):—appearance, fashion, shape, sight.

1492. εἴδω **ĕidō**, *i'-do;* a prim. verb; used only in certain past tenses, the others being borrowed from the equiv. 3700 and 3708; prop. to *see* (lit. or fig.); by impl. (in the perf. only) to *know:*—be aware, behold, × can (+ not tell), consider, (have) know (-ledge), look (on), perceive, see, be sure, tell, understand, wist, wot. Comp. 3700.

1493. εἰδωλεῖον **ĕidōlĕiŏn**, *i-do-li'-on;* neut. of a presumed der. of 1497; an *image-fane:*—idol's temple.

1494. εἰδωλόθυτον **ĕidōlŏthutŏn**, *i-do-loth'-oo-ton;* neut. of a comp. of 1497 and a presumed der. of 2380; an *image-sacrifice,* i.e. part of an *idolatrous offering:*—(meat, thing that is) offered (in sacrifice, sacrificed) to (unto) idols.

1495. εἰδωλολατρεία **ĕidōlŏlatrĕia**, *i-do-lol-at-ri'-ah;* from 1497 and 2999; *image-worship* (lit. or fig.):—idolatry.

1496. εἰδωλολάτρης **ĕidōlŏlatrēs**, *i-do-lol-at'-race;* from 1497 and the base of 3000; an *image-* (*servant* or) *worshipper* (lit. or fig.):—idolater.

1497. εἴδωλον **ĕidōlŏn**, *i'-do-lon;* from 1491; an *image* (i.e. for worship); by impl. a *heathen god,* or (plur.) the *worship* of such:—idol.

1498. εἴην **ĕiēn**, *i'-ane;* optative (i.e. Eng. subjunctive) pres. of 1510 (includ. the other pers.); *might* (*could, would* or *should*) *be:*—mean, + perish, should be, was, were.

1499. εἰ καὶ **ĕi kai**, *i kahee;* from 1487 and 2532; *if also* (or *even*):—if (that), though.

1500. εἰκῆ **ĕikē**, *i-kay';* prob. from 1502 (through the idea of *failure*); *idly,* i.e. *without reason* (or *effect*):—without a cause, (in) vain (-ly).

1501. εἴκοσι **ĕikŏsi**, *i'-kos-ee;* of uncert. affin.; a *score:*—twenty.

1502. εἴκω **ĕikō**, *i'-ko;* appar. a prim. verb; prop. to *be weak,* i.e. *yield:*—give place.

1503. εἴκω **ĕikō**, *i'-ko;* appar. a prim. verb [perh. akin to 1502 through the idea of *faintness* as a copy]; to *resemble:*—be like.

1504. εἰκών **ĕikōn**, *i-kone';* from 1503; a *likeness,* i.e. (lit.) *statue, profile,* or (fig.) *representation, resemblance:*—image.

1505. εἰλικρίνεια **ĕilikrinĕia**, *i-lik-ree'-ni-ah;* from 1506; *clearness,* i.e. (by impl.) *purity* (fig.):—sincerity.

1506. εἰλικρινής **ĕilikrinēs**, *i-lik-ree-nace';* from εἵλη **hĕilē** (the sun's *ray*) and 2919; *judged by sunlight,* i.e. *tested* as *genuine* (fig.):—pure, sincere.

1507. εἱλίσσω **hĕilissō**, *hi-lis'-so;* a prol. form of a prim. but defective verb εἴλω **hĕilō** (of the same mean.); to *coil* or *wrap:*—roll together. See also 1667.

1508. εἰ μή **ĕi mē**, *i may;* from 1487 and 3361; *if not:*—but, except (that), if not, more than, save (only) that, saving, till.

1509. εἰ μή τι **ĕi mē ti**, *i may tee;* from 1508 and the neut. of 5100; *if not somewhat:*—except.

1510. εἰμί **ĕimi**, *i-mee';* first pers. sing. pres. indic.; a prol. form of a prim. and defective verb; I *exist* (used only when emphatic):—am, have been, × it is I, was. See also 1488, 1498, 1511, 1527, 2258, 2071, 2070, 2075, 2076, 2771, 2468, 5600.

1511. εἶναι **ĕinai**, *i'-nahee;* pres. infin. from 1510; to *exist:*—am, are, come, is, × lust after, × please well, there is, to be, was.

εἵνεκεν **hĕinĕkĕn**. See 1752.

1512. εἴ περ **ĕi pĕr**, *i per;* from 1487 and 4007; *if perhaps:*—if so be (that), seeing, though.

1513. εἴ πως **ĕi pōs**, *i poce;* from 1487 and 4458; *if somehow:*—if by any means.

1514. εἰρηνεύω **ĕirēnĕuō**, *i-rane-yoo'-o;* from 1515; to be (act) *peaceful:*—be at (have, live in) peace, live peaceably.

1515. εἰρήνη **ĕirēnē**, *i-ray-nay;* prob. from a prim. verb εἴρω **ĕirō** (to *join*); *peace* (lit. or fig.); by impl. *prosperity:*—one, peace, quietness, rest, + set at one again.

1516. εἰρηνικός **ĕirēnikŏs**, *i-ray-nee-kos';* from 1515; *pacific;* by impl. *salutary:*—peaceable.

1517. εἰρηνοποιέω **ĕirēnŏpŏiĕō**, *i-ray-nop-oy-eh'-o;* from 1518; to be a *peace-maker,* i.e. (fig.) to *harmonize:*—make peace.

1518. εἰρηνοποιός **ĕirēnŏpŏiŏs**, *i-ray-nop-oy-os';* from 1515 and 4160; *pacificatory,* i.e. (subj.) *peaceable:*—peacemaker.

εἴρω **ĕirō**. See 1515, 443, 5346.

1519. **εἰς ĕis**, *ice;* a prim. prep.; *to or into* (indicating the point reached or entered; of place, time, or (fig.) purpose (result, etc.); also in adv. phrases:— [abundant-] ly, against, among, as, at, [back-] ward, before, by, concerning, + continual, + far more exceeding, for [intent, purpose], fore, + forth, in (among, at, unto, -so much that, -to), to the intent that, + of one mind, + never, of, (up-) on, + perish, + set at one again, (so) that, therefore (-unto), throughout, till, to (be, the end, -ward), (here-) until (-to), . . . ward, [where-] fore, with. Often used in composition with the same general import, but only with verbs (etc.) expressing motion (lit. or fig.).

1520. **εἷς hĕis**, *hice;* (includ. the neut. [etc.] **ἕν hĕn**); a prim. numeral; *one:*—a (-n, -ny, certain), + abundantly, man, one (another), only, other, some. See also *1527, 3367, 3901, 3762.*

1521. **εἰσάγω ĕisagō**, *ice-ag'-o;* from *1519* and *71;* *to introduce* (lit. or fig.):—bring in (-to), (+ was to) lead into.

1522. **εἰσακούω ĕisakŏuō**, *ice-ak-oo'-o;* from *1519* and *191;* *to listen to:*—hear.

1523. **εἰσδέχομαι ĕisdĕchŏmai**, *ice-dekh'-om-ahee;* from *1519* and *1209;* *to take into* one's favor:—receive.

1524. **εἴσειμι ĕisĕimi**, *ice'-i-mee;* from *1519* and **εἶμι ĕimi** (to go); *to enter* (go) into.

1525. **εἰσέρχομαι ĕisĕrchŏmai**, *ice-er'-khom-ahee;* from *1519* and *2064;* *to enter* (lit. or fig.):— X arise, come (in, into), enter in (-to), go in (through).

1526. **εἰσί ĕisi**, *i-see';* 3d pers. plur. pres. indic. of *1510;* they are:—agree, are, be, dure, X is, were.

1527. **εἷς καθ' εἷς hĕis kath' hĕis**, *hice kath hice;* from *1520* repeated with *2596* inserted; severally:—one by one.

1528. **εἰσκαλέω ĕiskalĕō**, *ice-kal-eh'-o;* from *1519* and *2564;* *to invite* in:—call in.

1529. **εἴσοδος ĕisŏdŏs**, *ice'-od-os;* from. *1519* and *3598;* an *entrance* (lit. or fig.):—coming, enter (-ing) in (to).

1530. **εἰσπηδάω ĕispĕdaō**, *ice-pay-dah'-o;* from *1519* and **πηδάω pĕdaō** (to leap); *to rush in:*—run (spring) in.

1531. **εἰσπορεύομαι ĕispŏrĕuŏmai**, *ice-por-yoo'-om-ahee;* from *1519* and *4198;* *to enter* (lit. or fig.):—come (enter) in, go into.

1532. **εἰστρέχω ĕistrĕchō**, *ice-trekh'-o;* from *1519* and *5143;* *to hasten inward:*—run in.

1533. **εἰσφέρω ĕisphĕrō**, *ice-fer'-o;* from *1519* and *5342;* *to carry inward* (lit. or fig.):—bring (in), lead into.

1534. **εἶτα ĕita**, *i'-tah;* of uncert. affin.; a particle of *succession* (in time or logical enumeration), *then, moreover:*—after that (-ward), furthermore, then. See also *1899.*

1535. **εἴτε ĕitĕ**, *i'-teh;* from *1487* and *5037; if too:*—if, or, whether.

1536. **εἴ τις ĕi tis**, *i tis;* from *1487* and *5100; if any:*—he that, if a (-ny) man ('s, thing, from any, ought), whether any, whosoever.

1537. **ἐκ ĕk**, *ek;* or

ἐξ ĕx, *ex;* a prim. prep. denoting *origin* (the point *whence* motion or action proceeds), *from, out* (of place, time or cause; lit. or fig.; direct or remote):—after, among, X are, at, betwixt (-yond), by (the means of), exceedingly, (+ abundantly above), for (-th), from (among, forth, up), + grudgingly, + heartily, X heavenly, X hereby, + very highly, in, . . . ly, (because, by reason) of, off (from), on, out among (from, of), over, since, X thenceforth, through, X unto, X vehemently, with (-out). Often used in composition, with the same general import; often of *completion.*

1538. **ἕκαστος hĕkastŏs**, *hek'-as-tos;* as if a superlative of **ἕκας hĕkas** (afar); *each* or *every:*—any, both, each (one), every (man, one, woman), particularly.

1539. **ἑκάστοτε hĕkastŏtĕ**, *hek-as'-tot-eh;* as if from *1538* and *5119; at every time:*—always.

1540. **ἑκατόν hĕkatŏn**, *hek-at-on';* of uncert. affin.; a *hundred:*—hundred.

1541. **ἑκατονταέτης hĕkatŏntaĕtēs**, *hek-at-on-tah-et'-ace;* from *1540* and *2094; centenarian:*—hundred years old.

1542. **ἑκατονταπλασίων hĕkatŏntaplasiōn**, *hek-at-on-ta-plah-see'-own;* from *1540* and a presumed der. of *4111;* a *hundred times:*—hundredfold.

1543. **ἑκατοντάρχης hĕkatŏntarchēs**, *hek-at-on-tar'-khace;* or

ἑκατόνταρχος hĕkatŏntarchŏs, *hek-at-on'-tar-khos;* from *1540* and *757;* the *captain of one hundred men:*—centurion.

1544. **ἐκβάλλω ĕkballō**, *ek-bal'-lo;* from *1537* and *906; to eject* (lit. or fig.):—bring forth, cast (forth, out), drive (out), expel, leave, pluck (pull, take, thrust) out, put forth (out), send away (forth, out).

1545. **ἔκβασις ĕkbasis**, *ek'-bas-is;* from a comp. of *1537* and the base of *939* (mean. to *go out*); an *exit* (lit. or fig.):—end, way to escape.

1546. **ἐκβολή ĕkbŏlē**, *ek-bol-ay';* from *1544;* *ejection,* i.e. (spec.) a *throwing overboard of the cargo:*— + lighten the ship.

1547. **ἐκγαμίζω ĕkgamizō**, *ek-gam-id'-zo;* from *1537* and a form of *1061* [comp. *1548*]; *to marry off* a daughter:—give in marriage.

1548. **ἐκγαμίσκω ĕkgamiskō**, *ek-gam-is'-ko;* from *1537* and *1061;* the same as *1547:*—give in marriage.

1549. **ἔκγονον ĕkgŏnŏn**, *ek'-gon-on;* neut. of a der. of a comp. of *1537* and *1096;* a *descendant,* i.e. (spec.) *grandchild:*—nephew.

1550. **ἐκδαπανάω ĕkdapanaō**, *ek-dap-an-ah'-o;* from *1537* and *1159; to expend* (wholly), i.e. (fig.) *exhaust:*—spend.

1551. **ἐκδέχομαι ĕkdĕchŏmai**, *ek-dekh'-om-ahee;* from *1537* and *1209; to accept from* some source, i.e. (by impl.) *to await:*—expect, look (tarry) for, wait (for).

1552. **ἔκδηλος ĕkdēlŏs**, *ek'-day-los;* from *1537* and *1212; wholly evident:*—manifest.

1553. **ἐκδημέω ĕkdēmĕō**, *ek-day-meh'-o;* from a comp. of *1537* and *1218; to emigrate,* i.e. (fig.) *vacate* or *quit:*—be absent.

1554. **ἐκδίδωμι ĕkdidŏmi**, *ek-did-o'-mee;* from *1537* and *1325; to give forth,* i.e. (spec.) *to lease:*—let forth (out).

1555. **ἐκδιηγέομαι ĕkdiēgĕŏmai**, *ek-dee-ayg-eh'-om-ahee;* from *1537* and a comp. of *1223* and *2233;* to *narrate* through wholly:—declare.

1556. **ἐκδικέω ĕkdikĕō**, *ek-dik-eh'-o;* from *1558; to vindicate, retaliate, punish:*— a (re-) venge.

1557. **ἐκδίκησις ĕkdikēsis**, *ek-dik'-ay-sis;* from *1556; vindication, retribution:*—(a-, re-) venge (-ance), punishment.

1558. **ἔκδικος ĕkdikŏs**, *ek'-dik-os;* from *1537* and *1349;* carrying *justice out,* i.e. a *punisher:*—a (re-) venger.

1559. **ἐκδιώκω ĕkdiōkō**, *ek-dee-o'-ko;* from *1537* and *1377; to pursue out,* i.e. *expel* or *persecute* implacably:—persecute.

1560. **ἔκδοτος ĕkdŏtŏs**, *ek'-dot-os;* from *1537* and a der. of *1325; given out* or *over,* i.e. *surrendered:*—delivered.

1561. **ἐκδοχή ĕkdŏchē**, *ek-dokh-ay';* from *1551; expectation:*—looking for.

1562. **ἐκδύω ĕkduō**, *ek-doo'-o;* from *1537* and the base of *1416; to cause to sink out of,* i.e. (spec. as of clothing) *to divest:*—strip, take off from, unclothe.

1563. **ἐκεῖ ĕkĕi**, *ek-i';* of uncert. affin.; *there;* by extens. *thither:*—there, thither (-ward), (to) yonder (place).

1564. **ἐκεῖθεν ĕkĕithĕn**, *ek-i'-then;* from *1563; thence:*—from that place, (from) thence, there.

1565. **ἐκεῖνος ĕkĕinŏs**, *ek-i'-nos;* from *1563;* that one (or [neut.] thing); often intensified by the art. prefixed:—he, it, the other (same), selfsame, that (same, very), X their, X them, they, this, those. See also *3778.*

1566. **ἐκεῖσε ĕkĕisĕ**, *ek-i'-seh;* from *1563; thither:*—there.

1567. **ἐκζητέω ĕkzētĕō**, *ek-zay-teh'-o;* from *1537* and *2212; to search out,* i.e. (fig.) *investigate, crave, demand,* (by Hebr.) *worship:*—en- (re-) quire, seek after (carefully, diligently).

1568. **ἐκθαμβέω ĕkthambĕō**, *ek-tham-beh'-o;* from *1569; to astonish utterly:*—affright, greatly (sore) amaze.

1569. **ἔκθαμβος ĕkthambŏs**, *ek'-tham-bos;* from *1537* and *2285; utterly astounded:*—greatly wondering.

1570. **ἔκθετος ĕkthĕtŏs**, *ek'-thet-os;* from *1537* and a der. of *5087; put out,* i.e. *exposed to perish:*—cast out.

1571. **ἐκκαθαίρω ĕkkathairō**, *ek-kath-ah'ee-ro;* from *1537* and *2508; to cleanse thoroughly:*—purge (out).

1572. **ἐκκαίω ĕkkaiō**, *ek-kah'-yo;* from *1537* and *2545; to inflame deeply:*—burn.

1573. **ἐκκακέω ĕkkakĕō**, *ek-kak-eh'-o;* from *1537* and *2556; to be (bad or) weak,* i.e. (by impl.) *to fail* (in heart):—faint, be weary.

1574. **ἐκκεντέω ĕkkĕntĕō**, *ek-ken-teh'-o;* from *1537* and the base of *2759; to transfix:*—pierce.

1575. **ἐκκλάω ĕkklaō**, *ek-klah'-o;* from *1537* and *2806; to exscind:*—break off.

1576. **ἐκκλείω ĕkklĕiō**, *ek-kli'-o;* from *1537* and *2808; to shut out* (lit. or fig.):—exclude.

1577. **ἐκκλησία ĕkklēsia**, *ek-klay-see'-ah;* from a comp. of *1537* and a der. of *2564;* a *calling out,* i.e. (concr.) a *popular meeting,* espec. a religious congregation (Jewish *synagogue,* or Chr. community of members on earth or saints in heaven or both):—assembly, church.

1578. **ἐκκλίνω ĕkklinō**, *ek-klee'-no;* from *1537* and *2827; to deviate,* i.e. (absol.) *to shun* (lit. or fig.), or (rel.) *to decline* (from piety):—avoid, eschew, go out of the way.

1579. **ἐκκολυμβάω ĕkkŏlumbaō**, *ek-kol-oom-bah'-o;* from *1537* and *2860; to escape by swimming:*—swim out.

1580. **ἐκκομίζω ĕkkŏmizō**, *ek-kom-id'-zo;* from *1537* and *2875; to bear forth* (to burial):—carry out.

1581. **ἐκκόπτω ĕkkŏptō**, *ek-kop'-to;* from *1537* and *2875; to exscind;* fig. *to frustrate:*—cut down (off, out), hew down, hinder.

1582. **ἐκκρέμαμαι ĕkkrĕmamai**, *ek-krem'-am-ahee;* mid. from *1537* and *2910; to hang upon the lips* of a speaker, i.e. *listen closely:*—be very attentive.

1583. **ἐκλαλέω ĕklalĕō**, *ek-lal-eh'-o;* from *1537* and *2980; to divulge:*—tell.

1584. **ἐκλάμπω ĕklampō**, *ek-lam'-po;* from *1537* and *2989; to be resplendent:*—shine forth.

1585. **ἐκλανθάνομαι ĕklanthanŏmai**, *ek-lan-than'-om-ahee;* mid. from *1537* and *2990; to be utterly oblivious of:*—forget.

1586. **ἐκλέγομαι ĕklĕgŏmai**, *ek-leg'-om-ahee;* mid. from *1537* and *3004* (in its prim. sense); *to select:*—make choice, choose (out), chosen.

1587. **ἐκλείπω ĕklĕipō**, *ek-li'-po;* from *1537* and *3007; to omit,* i.e. (by impl.) *cease* (die):—fail.

1588. **ἐκλεκτός ĕklĕktŏs**, *ek-lek-tos';* from *1586; select;* by impl. *favorite:*—chosen, elect.

1589. **ἐκλογή ĕklŏgē**, *ek-log-ay';* from *1586;* (divine) *selection* (abstr. or concr.):—chosen, election.

1590. **ἐκλύω ĕkluō**, *ek-loo'-o;* from *1537* and *3089; to relax* (lit. or fig.):—faint.

1591. **ἐκμάσσω ĕkmassō**, *ek-mas'-so;* from *1537* and the base of *3145; to knead out,* i.e. (by anal.) *to wipe dry:*—wipe.

1592. **ἐκμυκτερίζω ĕkmuktĕrizō**, *ek-mook-ter-id'-zo;* from *1537* and *3456; to sneer outright at:*—deride.

1593. **ἐκνεύω ĕknĕuō**, *ek-nyoo'-o;* from *1537* and *3506;* (by anal.) *to slip off,* i.e. quietly *withdraw:*—convey self away.

1594. **ἐκνήφω ĕknēphō**, *ek-nay'-fo;* from *1537* and *3525;* (fig.) *to rouse* (oneself) *out of stupor:*—awake.

1595. **ἑκούσιον hĕkŏusiŏn**, *hek-oo'-see-on;* neut. of a der. from *1635; voluntariness:*—willingly.

596. ἐκουσίως **hĕkŏusiŏs**, *hek-oo-see'-oce;* adv. om the same as *1595;* *voluntarily:*—wilfully, willingly.

597. ἔκπαλαι **ĕkpalai**, *ek'-pal-ahee;* from *1537* and *3819; long ago, for a long while:*—of a long time, f old.

598. ἐκπειράζω **ĕkpĕirazō**, *ek-pi-rad'-zo;* from *1537* and *3985; to test thoroughly:*—tempt.

599. ἐκπέμπω **ĕkpĕmpō**, *ek-pem'-po;* from *1537* and *3992; to despatch:*—send away (forth).

ἐκπερισσοῦ **ĕkpĕrissŏu**. See *1537* and *4053.*

1600. ἐκπετάννυμι **ĕkpĕtannumi**, *ek-pet-an'-noo-mee;* from *1537* and a form of *4072; to fly out,* i.e. (by anal.) *extend:*—stretch forth.

1601. ἐκπίπτω **ĕkpiptō**, *ek-pip'-to;* from *1537* and *4098; to drop away;* spec. *be driven out* of one's *course;* fig. *to lose, become inefficient:*—be cast, fail, fall (away, off), take none effect.

1602. ἐκπλέω **ĕkplĕō**, *ek-pleh'-o;* from *1537* and *4126; to depart by ship:*—sail (away, thence).

1603. ἐκπληρόω **ĕkplērŏō**, *ek-play-rŏ'-o;* from *1537* and *4137; to accomplish entirely:*—fulfill.

1604. ἐκπλήρωσις **ĕkplērōsis**, *ek-play'-ro-sis;* from *1603; completion:*—accomplishment.

1605. ἐκπλήσσω **ĕkplēssō**, *ek-place'-so;* from *1537* and *4141; to strike with astonishment:*—amaze, astonish.

1606. ἐκπνέω **ĕkpnĕō**, *ek-pneh'-o;* from *1537* and *4154; to expire:*—give up the ghost.

1607. ἐκπορεύομαι **ĕkpŏrĕuŏmai**, *ek-por-yoo'-om-ahee;* from *1537* and *4108; to depart,* be discharged, proceed, project:*—come (forth, out of), depart, go (forth, out), issue, proceed (out of).

1608. ἐκπορνεύω **ĕkpŏrnĕuō**, *ek-porn-yoo'-o;* from *1537* and *4203; to be utterly unchaste:*—give self over to fornication.

1609. ἐκπτύω **ĕkptuō**, *ek-ptoo'-o;* from *1537* and *4429; to spit out,* i.e. (fig.) *spurn:*—reject.

1610. ἐκριζόω **ĕkrizŏō**, *ek-rid-zŏ'-o;* from *1537* and *4492; to uproot:*—pluck up by the root, root up.

1611. ἔκστασις **ĕkstasis**, *ek'-stas-is;* from *1839; a displacement* of the mind, i.e. *bewilderment,* "*ecstasy*"*;*— + be amazed, amazement, astonishment, trance.

1612. ἐκστρέφω **ĕkstrĕphō**, *ek-stref'-o;* from *1537* and *4762; to pervert* (fig.)*:*—subvert.

1613. ἐκταράσσω **ĕktarassō**, *ek-tar-as'-so;* from *1537* and *5015; to disturb wholly:*—exceedingly trouble.

1614. ἐκτείνω **ĕktĕinō**, *ek-ti'-no;* from *1537* and *τείνω* **tĕinō** (to stretch); *to extend:*—cast, put forth, stretch forth (out).

1615. ἐκτελέω **ĕktĕlĕō**, *ek-tel-eh'-o;* from *1537* and *5055; to complete fully:*—finish.

1616. ἐκτένεια **ĕktĕnĕia**, *ek-ten'-i-ah;* from *1618; intentness:*— × instantly.

1617. ἐκτενέστερον **ĕktĕnĕstĕrŏn**, *ek-ten-es'-ter-on;* neut. of the comp. of *1618; more intently:*—more earnestly.

1618. ἐκτενής **ĕktĕnēs**, *ek-ten-ace';* from *1614; intent:*—without ceasing, fervent.

1619. ἐκτενῶς **ĕktĕnōs**, *ek-ten-oce';* adv. from *1618; intently:*—fervently.

1620. ἐκτίθημι **ĕktithēmi**, *ek-tith'-ay-mee;* from *1537* and *5087; to expose;* fig. *to declare:*—cast out, expound.

1621. ἐκτινάσσω **ĕktinassō**, *ek-tin-as'-so;* from *1537* and *τινάσσω* **tinassō** (to swing); *to shake* violently:*—shake (off).

1622. ἐκτός **ĕktŏs**, *ek-tos';* from *1537;* the *exterior;* fig. (as a prep.) *aside from, besides:*—but, except (-ed), other than, out of, outside, unless, without.

1623. ἕκτος **hĕktŏs**, *hek'-tos;* ordinal from *1803; sixth:*—sixth.

1624. ἐκτρέπω **ĕktrĕpō**, *ek-trep'-o;* from *1537* and the base of *5157; to deflect,* i.e. *turn away* (lit. or fig.)*:*—avoid, turn (aside, out of the way).

1625. ἐκτρέφω **ĕktrĕphō**, *ek-tref'-o;* from *1537* and *5142; to rear up* to maturity, i.e. (gen.) *to cherish or train:*—bring up, nourish.

1626. ἔκτρωμα **ĕktrōma**, *ek'-tro-mah;* from a comp. of *1537* and *τιτρώσκω* **titrōskō** (to *wound*); a *miscarriage* (*abortion*), i.e. (by anal.) *untimely birth:*—born out of due time.

1627. ἐκφέρω **ĕkphĕrō**, *ek-fer'-o;* from *1537* and *5342; to bear out* (lit. or fig.)*:*—bear, bring forth, carry forth (out).

1628. ἐκφεύγω **ĕkphĕugō**, *ek-fyoo'-go;* from *1537* and *5343; to flee out:*—escape, flee.

1629. ἐκφοβέω **ĕkphŏbĕō**, *ek-fob-eh'-o;* from *1537* and *5399; to frighten utterly:*—terrify.

1630. ἔκφοβος **ĕkphŏbŏs**, *ek'-fob-os;* from *1537* and *5401; frightened out* of one's *wits:*—sore afraid, exceedingly fear.

1631. ἐκφύω **ĕkphuō**, *ek-foo'-o;* from *1537* and *5453; to sprout up:*—put forth.

1632. ἐκχέω **ĕkchĕō**, *ek-kheh'-o;* or (by var.)

ἐκχύνω **ĕkchunō**, *ek-khoo'-no;* from *1537* and χέω **chĕō** (to *pour*); *to pour forth;* fig. *to bestow:*—gush (pour) out, run greedily (out), shed (abroad, forth), spill.

1633. ἐκχωρέω **ĕkchōrĕō**, *ek-kho-reh'-o;* from *1537* and *5562; to depart:*—depart out.

1634. ἐκψύχω **ĕkpsuchō**, *ek-psoo'-kho;* from *1537* and *5594; to expire:*—give (yield) up the ghost.

1635. ἑκών **hĕkōn**, *hek-own';* of uncert. affin.; *voluntary:*—willingly.

1636. ἐλαία **ĕlaia**, *el-ah'-yah;* fem. of a presumed der. from an obsol. prim.; an *olive* (the tree or the fruit):*—olive (berry, tree).

1637. ἔλαιον **ĕlaiŏn**, *el'-ah-yon;* neut. of the same as *1636; olive oil:*—oil.

1638. ἐλαιών **ĕlaiōn**, *el-ah-yone';* from *1636;* an *olive-orchard,* i.e. (spec.) the *Mt. of Olives:*—Olivet.

1639. Ἐλαμίτης **Ĕlamitēs**, *el-am-ee'-tace;* of Heb. or. [5867]; an *Elamite* or Persian:*—Elamite.

1640. ἐλάσσων **ĕlassōn**, *el-as'-sone;* or

ἐλάττων **ĕlattōn**, *el-at-tone';* comp. of the same as *1646; smaller* (in size, quantity, age or quality):*—less, under, worse, younger.

1641. ἐλαττονέω **ĕlattŏnĕō**, *el-at-ton-eh-o;* from *1640; to diminish,* i.e. *fall short:*—have lack.

1642. ἐλαττόω **ĕlattŏō**, *el-at-tŏ'-o;* from *1640; to lessen* (in rank or influence):*—decrease, make lower.

1643. ἐλαύνω **ĕlaunō**, *el-ŏw'-no;* a prol. form of a prim. verb (obsol. except in certain tenses as an altern. of this) of uncert. affin.; *to push* (as wind, oars or dæmoniacal power):*—carry, drive, row.

1644. ἐλαφρία **ĕlaphria**, *el-af-ree'-ah;* from *1645; levity* (fig.), i.e. *fickleness:*—lightness.

1645. ἐλαφρός **ĕlaphrŏs**, *el-af-ros';* prob. akin to *1643* and the base of *1640; light,* i.e. *easy:*—light.

1646. ἐλάχιστος **ĕlachistŏs**, *el-akh'-is-tos;* superl. of ἐλαχύς **ĕlachus** (*short*); used as equiv. to *3398; least* (in size, amount, dignity, etc.):*—least, very little (small), smallest.

1647. ἐλαχιστότερος **ĕlachistŏtĕrŏs**, *el-akh-is-tot'-er-os;* comp. of *1646; far less:*—less than the least.

1648. Ἐλεάζαρ **Ĕlĕazar**, *el-eh-ad'-zar;* of Heb. or. [499]; *Eleazar,* an Isr.:*—Eleazar.

1649. ἔλεγξις **ĕlĕgxis**, *el'-eng-xis;* from *1651; refutation,* i.e. *reproof:*—rebuke.

1650. ἔλεγχος **ĕlĕgchŏs**, *el'-eng-khos;* from *1651; proof, conviction:*—evidence, reproof.

1651. ἐλέγχω **ĕlĕgchō**, *el-eng'-kho;* of uncert. affin.; *to confute, admonish:*—convict, convince, tell a fault, rebuke, reprove.

1652. ἐλεεινός **ĕlĕĕinŏs**, *el-eh-i-nos';* from *1656; pitiable:*—miserable.

1653. ἐλεέω **ĕlĕĕō**, *el-eh-eh'-o;* from *1656; to compassionate* (by word or deed, spec. by divine grace):*—have compassion (pity on), have (obtain, receive, shew) mercy (on).

1654. ἐλεημοσύνη **ĕlĕēmŏsunē**, *el-eh-ay-mos-oo'-nay;* from *1656; compassionateness,* i.e. (as exer-

cised towards the poor) *beneficence,* or (concr.) a *benefaction:*—alms (-deeds).

1655. ἐλεήμων **ĕlĕēmōn**, *el-eh-ay'-mone;* from *1653; compassionate* (actively):*—merciful.

1656. ἔλεος **ĕlĕŏs**, *el'-eh-os;* of uncert. affin.; *compassion* (human or divine, espec. active):*— (+ tender) mercy.

1657. ἐλευθερία **ĕlĕuthĕria**, *el-yoo-ther-ee'-ah;* from *1658; freedom* (legitimate or licentious, chiefly mor. or cer.):*—liberty.

1658. ἐλεύθερος **ĕlĕuthĕrŏs**, *el-yoo'-ther-os;* prob. from the alt. of *2064; unrestrained* (to go at pleasure), i.e. (as a citizen) *not a slave* (whether *freeborn* or *manumitted*), or (gen.) *exempt* (from obligation or liability):*—free (man, woman), at liberty.

1659. ἐλευθερόω **ĕlĕuthĕrŏō**, *el-yoo-ther-ŏ'-o;* from *1658; to liberate,* i.e. (fig.) *to exempt* (from mor., cer. or mortal liability):*—deliver, make free.

ἐλεύθω **ĕlĕuthō**. See *2064.*

1660. ἔλευσις **ĕlĕusis**, *el'-yoo-sis;* from the alt. of *2064;* an *advent:*—coming.

1661. ἐλεφάντινος **ĕlĕphantinŏs**, *el-ef-an'-tee-nos;* from ἔλεφας **ĕlĕphas** (an "*elephant*"); *elephantine,* i.e. (by impl.) *composed of ivory:*—of ivory.

1662. Ἐλιακείμ **Ĕliakĕim**, *el-ee-ak-ime';* of Heb. or. [471]; *Eliakim,* an Isr.:*—Eliakim.

1663. Ἐλιέζερ **Ĕliĕzĕr**, *el-ee-ed'-zer;* of Heb. or. [461]; *Eliezer,* an Isr.:*—Eliezer.

1664. Ἐλιούδ **Ĕliŏud**, *el-ee-ood';* of Heb. or. [410 and 1935]; *God of majesty; Eliud,* an Isr.:*—Eliud.

1665. Ἐλισάβετ **Ĕlisabĕt**, *el-ee-sab'-et;* of Heb. or. [472]; *Elisabet,* an Israelitess:*—Elisabeth.

1666. Ἐλισσαῖος **Ĕlissaiŏs**, *el-is-sah'-yos;* of Heb. or. [477]; *Elissæus,* an Isr.:*—Elissæus.

1667. ἑλίσσω **hĕlissō**, *hel-is'-so;* a form of *1507; to coil* or *wrap:*—fold up.

1668. ἕλκος **hĕlkŏs**, *hel'-kos;* prob. from *1670;* an *ulcer* (as if drawn together):*—sore.

1669. ἑλκόω **hĕlkŏō**, *hel-kŏ'-o;* from *1668; to cause to ulcerate,* i.e. (pass.) *be ulcerous:*—full of sores.

1670. ἕλκω **hĕlkō**, *hel'-ko;* prob. akin to *138; to drag* (lit. or fig.)*:*—draw. Comp. *1667.*

1671. Ἑλλάς **Hĕllas**, *hel-las';* of uncert. affin.; *Hellas* (or *Greece*), a country of Europe:*—Greece.

1672. Ἕλλην **Hĕllēn**, *hel'-lane;* from *1671;* a *Hellen* (Grecian) or inhab. of Hellas; by extens. a *Greek-speaking* person, espec. a *non-Jew:*—Gentile, Greek.

1673. Ἑλληνικός **Hĕllēnikŏs**, *hel-lay-nee-kos';* from *1672; Hellenic,* i.e. *Grecian* (in language):*—Greek.

1674. Ἑλληνίς **Hĕllēnis**, *hel-lay-nis';* fem. of *1672;* a *Grecian* (i.e. *non-Jewish*) woman:*—Greek.

1675. Ἑλληνιστής **Hĕllēnistēs**, *hel-lay-nis-tace';* from a der. of *1672;* a *Hellenist* or Greek-speaking Jew:*—Grecian.

1676. Ἑλληνιστί **Hĕllēnisti**, *hel-lay-nis-tee';* adv. from the same as *1675; Hellenistically,* i.e. in the Grecian language:*—Greek.

1677. ἐλλογέω **ĕllŏgĕō**, *el-log-eh'-o;* from *1722* and *3056* (in the sense of *account*); *to reckon in,* i.e. *attribute:*—impute, put on account.

1678. Ἐλμωδάμ **Ĕlmōdam**, *el-mo-dam';* of Heb. or. [perh. for 486]; *Elmodam,* an Isr.:*—Elmodam.

1679. ἐλπίζω **ĕlpizō**, *el-pid'-zo;* from *1680; to expect or confide:*—(have, thing) hope (-d) (for), trust.

1680. ἐλπίς **ĕlpis**, *el-pece';* from a prim. ἔλπω **ĕlpō** (to *anticipate,* usually with pleasure); *expectation* (abstr. or concr.) or *confidence:*—faith, hope.

1681. Ἐλύμας **Ĕlumas**, *el-oo'-mas;* of for. or.; *Elymas,* a *wizard:*—Elymas.

1682. ἠλί **ēli**, ἠλί **ēli**, *el-o-ee';* of Chald. or. [426 with pron. suff.]; *my God:*—Eloi.

1683. ἐμαυτοῦ **ĕmautŏu**, *em-ŏw-too'*; gen. comp. of *1700* and *846*; *of myself* (so likewise the dat.

ἐμαυτῷ **ĕmautōi**, *em-ow-tō'*; and acc.

ἐμαυτόν **ĕmautŏn**, *em-ow-ton')*:—me, mine own (self), myself.

1684. ἐμβαίνω **ĕmbainō**, *em-ba'-hee-no*; from *1722* and the base of *939*; to *walk on*, i.e. *embark* (aboard a vessel), *reach* (a pool):—come (get) into, enter (into), go (up) into, step in, take ship.

1685. ἐμβάλλω **ĕmballō**, *em-bal'-lo*; from *1722* and *906*; to *throw on*, i.e. (fig.) *subject to* (eternal punishment):—cast into.

1686. ἐμβάπτω **ĕmbaptō**, *em-bap'-to*; from *1722* and *911*; to *whelm on*, i.e. *wet* (a part of the person, etc.) by contact with a fluid:—dip.

1687. ἐμβατεύω **ĕmbatĕuō**, *em-bat-yoo'-o*; from *1722* and a presumed der. of the base of *939*; equiv. to *1684*; to *intrude on* (fig.):—intrude into.

1688. ἐμβιβάζω **ĕmbibazō**, *em-bib-ad'-zo*; from *1722* and βιβάζω **bibazō** (to *mount*; causat. of *1684*); to *place on*, i.e. *transfer* (aboard a vessel):—put in.

1689. ἐμβλέπω **ĕmblĕpō**, *em-blep'-o*; from *1722* and *991*; to *look on*, i.e. (rel.) to *observe* fixedly, or (absol.) to *discern* clearly:—behold, gaze up, look upon, (could) see.

1690. ἐμβριμάομαι **ĕmbrimaŏmai**, *em-brim-ah'-om-ahee*; from *1722* and βριμάομαι **brimaŏmai** (to *snort* with anger); to have *indignation on*, i.e. (trans.) to *blame*, (intrans.) to *sigh* with chagrin, (spec.) to sternly *enjoin*:—straitly charge, groan, murmur against.

1691. ἐμέ **ĕmĕ**, *em-eh'*; a prol. form of *3165*; *me*:—I, me, my (-self).

1692. ἐμέω **ĕmĕō**, *em-eh'-o*; of uncert. affin.; to *vomit*:—(will) spue.

1693. ἐμμαίνομαι **ĕmmainŏmai**, *em-mah'ee-nom-ahee*; from *1722* and *3105*; to *rave on*, i.e. *rage at*:—be mad against.

1694. Ἐμμανουήλ **Ĕmmanŏuēl**, *em-man-oo-ale'*; of Heb. or. [6005]; *God with us*; *Emmanuel*, a name of Christ:—Emmanuel.

1695. Ἐμμαοῦς **Ĕmmaŏus**, *em-mah-ooce'*; prob. of Heb. or. [comp. 3222]; *Emmaüs*, a place in Pal.:—Emmaus.

1696. ἐμμένω **ĕmmĕnō**, *em-men'-o*; from *1722* and *3306*; to *stay in the same place*, i.e. (fig.) to *persevere*:—continue.

1697. Ἐμμόρ **Ĕmmŏr**, *em-mor'*; of Heb. or. [2544]; *Emmor* (i.e. *Chamor*), a Canaanite:—Emmor.

1698. ἐμοί **ĕmŏi**, *em-oy'*; a prol. form of *3427*; to *me*:—I, me, mine, my.

1699. ἐμός **ĕmŏs**, *em-os'*; from the oblique cases of *1473* (*1698*, *1700*, *1691*); *my*:—of me, mine (own), my.

1700. ἐμοῦ **ĕmŏu**, *em-oo'*; a prol. form of *3450*; *of me*:—me, mine, my.

1701. ἐμπαιγμός **ĕmpaigmŏs**, *emp-aheeg-mos'*; from *1702*; *derision*:—mocking.

1702. ἐμπαίζω **ĕmpaizō**, *emp-aheed'-zo*; from *1722* and *3815*; to *jeer at*, i.e. *deride*:—mock.

1703. ἐμπαίκτης **ĕmpaiktēs**, *emp-aheek-tace'*; from *1702*; a *derider*, i.e. (by impl.) a *false teacher*:—mocker, scoffer.

1704. ἐμπεριπατέω **ĕmpĕripatĕō**, *em-per-ee-pat-eh'-o*; from *1722* and *4043*; to *perambulate on a place*, i.e. (fig.) to *be occupied among persons*:—walk in.

1705. ἐμπίπλημι **ĕmpiplēmi**, *em-pip'-lay-mee*; or

ἐμπλήθω **ĕmplēthō**, *em-play'-tho*; from *1722* and the base of *4118*; to *fill in* (up), i.e. (by impl.) to *satisfy* (lit. or fig.):—fill.

1706. ἐμπίπτω **ĕmpiptō**, *em-pip'-to*; from *1722* and *4098*; to *fall on*, i.e. (lit.) *be entrapped by*, or (fig.) *be overwhelmed with*:—fall among (into).

1707. ἐμπλέκω **ĕmplĕkō**, *em-plek'-o*; from *1722* and *4120*; to *entwine*, i.e. (fig.) *involve with*:—entangle (in, self with).

1708. ἐμπλήθω **ĕmplēthō**. See *1705*.

1708. ἐμπλοκή **ĕmplŏkē**, *em-plok-ay'*; from *1707*; elaborate *braiding* of the hair:—plaiting.

1709. ἐμπνέω **ĕmpnĕō**, *emp-neh'-o*; from *1722* and *4154*; to *inhale*, i.e. (fig.) to *be animated by* (bent upon):—breathe.

1710. ἐμπορεύομαι **ĕmpŏrĕuŏmai**, *em-por-yoo'-om-ahee*; from *1722* and *4198*; to *travel in* (a country as a pedlar), i.e. (by impl.) to *trade*:—buy and sell, make merchandise.

1711. ἐμπορία **ĕmpŏria**, *em-por-ee'-ah*; fem. from *1713*; *traffic*:—merchandise.

1712. ἐμπόριον **ĕmpŏriŏn**, *em-por'-ee-on*; neut. from *1713*; a *mart* (" emporium"):—merchandise.

1713. ἔμπορος **ĕmpŏrŏs**, *em'-por-os*; from *1722* and the base of *4198*; a (wholesale) *tradesman*:—merchant.

1714. ἐμπρήθω **ĕmprēthō**, *em-pray'-tho*; from *1722* and πρήθω **prēthō** (to *blow* a flame); to *enkindle*, i.e. *set on fire*:—burn up.

1715. ἔμπροσθεν **ĕmprŏsthĕn**, *em'-pros-then*; from *1722* and *4314*; *in front of* (in place [lit. or fig.] or time):—against, at, before, (in presence, sight) of.

1716. ἐμπτύω **ĕmptuō**, *emp-too'-o*; from *1722* and *4429*; to *spit at* or *on*:—spit (upon).

1717. ἐμφανής **ĕmphanēs**, *em-fan-ace'*; from a comp. of *1722* and *5316*; *apparent in self*:—manifest, openly.

1718. ἐμφανίζω **ĕmphanizō**, *em-fan-id'-zo*; from *1717*; to *exhibit* (in person) or *disclose* (by words):—appear, declare (plainly), inform, (will) manifest, shew, signify.

1719. ἔμφοβος **ĕmphŏbŏs**, *em'-fob-os*; from *1722* and *5401*; *in fear*, i.e. *alarmed*:—affrighted, afraid, tremble.

1720. ἐμφυσάω **ĕmphusaō**, *em-foo-sah'-o*; from *1722* and φυσάω **phusaō** (to *puff*) [comp. *5453*]; to *blow at* or *on*:—breathe on.

1721. ἔμφυτος **ĕmphutŏs**, *em'-foo-tos*; from *1722* and a der. of *5453*; *implanted* (fig.):—engrafted.

1722. ἐν **ĕn**, *en*; a prim. prep. denoting (fixed) position (in place, time or state), and (by impl.) *instrumentality* (medially or constructively), i.e. a relation of *rest* (intermediate between *1519* and *1537*); " *in*," *at*, (up-) *on*, *by*, etc.:—about, after, against, + almost, × altogether, among, × as, at, before, between, (here-) by (+ all means), for (. . . sake of), + give self wholly to, (here-) in (-to, -wardly), × mightily, (because) of, (up-) on, [open-] ly, × outwardly, one, × quickly, × shortly, [speedi-] ly, × that, × there (-in, -on), through (-out), (un-) to (-ward), under, when, where (-with), while, with (-in). Often used in compounds, with substantially the same import: rarely with verbs of motion, and then not to indicate direction, except (elliptically) by a separate (and different) prep.

1723. ἐναγκαλίζομαι **ĕnagkalizŏmai**, *en-ang-kal-id'-zom-ahee*; from *1722* and a der. of *43*; to *take in one's arms*, i.e. *embrace*:—take up in arms.

1724. ἐνάλιος **ĕnaliŏs**, *en-al'-ee-os*; from *1722* and *251*; *in the sea*, i.e. *marine*:—thing in the sea.

1725. ἔναντι **ĕnanti**, *en'-an-tee*; from *1722* and *473*; *in front* (i.e. fig. *presence*) *of*:—before.

1726. ἐναντίον **ĕnantiŏn**, *en-an-tee'-on*; neut. of *1727*; (adv.) *in the presence* (view) *of*:—before, in the presence of.

1727. ἐναντίος **ĕnantiŏs**, *en-an-tee'-os*; from *1725*; *opposite*; fig. *antagonistic*:—(over) against, contrary.

1728. ἐνάρχομαι **ĕnarchŏmai**, *en-ar'-khom-ahee*; from *1722* and *756*; to *commence on*:—rule [by mistake for *757*].

1729. ἐνδεής **ĕndĕēs**, *en-deh-ace'*; from a comp. of *1722* and *1210* (in the sense of *lacking*); *deficient in*:—lacking.

1730. ἔνδειγμα **ĕndĕigma**, *en'-dighe-mah*; from *1731*; an *indication* (concr.):—manifest token.

1731. ἐνδείκνυμι **ĕndĕiknumi**, *en-dike'-noo-mee*; from *1722* and *1166*; to *indicate* (by word or act):—do, show (forth).

1732. ἔνδειξις **ĕndĕixis**, *en'-dike-sis*; from *1731*; *indication* (abstr.):—declare, evident token, proof.

1733. ἕνδεκα **hĕndĕka**, *hen'-dek-ah*; from (the neut. of) *1520* and *1176*; *one and ten*, i.e. *eleven*:—eleven.

1734. ἑνδέκατος **hĕndĕkatŏs**, *hen-dek'-at-os*; ord. from *1733*; *eleventh*:—eleventh.

1735. ἐνδέχεται **ĕndĕchĕtai**, *en-dekh'-et-ahee*; third pers. sing. pres. of a comp. of *1722* and *1209* (impers.) *it is accepted in*, i.e. *admitted* (*possible*):—can (+ not) be.

1736. ἐνδημέω **ĕndēmĕō**, *en-day-meh'-o*; from comp. of *1722* and *1218*; to *be in one's own country* i.e. *home* (fig.):—be at home (present).

1737. ἐνδιδύσκω **ĕndiduskō**, *en-did-oos'-ko*; prol. form of *1746*; to *invest* (with a garment):—clothe in, wear.

1738. ἔνδικος **ĕndikŏs**, *en'-dee-kos*; from *1722* and *1349*; *in the right*, i.e. *equitable*:—just.

1739. ἐνδόμησις **ĕndŏmēsis**, *en-dom'-ay-sis* from a comp. of *1722* and a der. of the base of *1218* a *housing in* (residence), i.e. *structure*:—building.

1740. ἐνδοξάζω **ĕndŏxazō**, *en-dox-ad'-zo*; from *1741*; to *glorify*:—glorify.

1741. ἔνδοξος **ĕndŏxŏs**, *en'-dox-os*; from *1722* and *1391*; *in glory*, i.e. *splendid*, (fig.) *noble*:—glorious, gorgeous [-ly], honourable.

1742. ἔνδυμα **ĕnduma**, *en'-doo-mah*; from *1746* apparel (espec. the outer *robe*):—clothing, garment, raiment.

1743. ἐνδυναμόω **ĕndunamŏō**, *en-doo-nam-ŏ'-o* from *1722* and *1412*; to *empower*:—enable, (increase in) strength (-en), be (make) strong.

1744. ἐνδύνω **ĕndunō**, *en-doo'-no*; from *1722* and *1416*; to *sink* (by impl. *wrap* [comp. *1746*]) *on*, i.e. (fig. *sneak*:—creep.

1745. ἔνδυσις **ĕndusis**, *en'-doo-sis*; from *1746*; *investment* with clothing:—putting on.

1746. ἐνδύω **ĕnduō**, *en-doo'-o*; from *1722* and *1416* (in the sense of *sinking* into a garment); to *invest* with clothing (lit. or fig.):—array, clothe (with), en-due, have (put) on.

ἐνέγκω **ĕnĕgkō**. See *5342*.

1747. ἐνέδρα **ĕnĕdra**, *en-ed'-rah*; fem. from *1722* and the base of *1476*; an *ambuscade*, i.e. (fig.) murderous *purpose*:—lay wait. See also *1749*.

1748. ἐνεδρεύω **ĕnĕdrĕuō**, *en-ed-ryoo'-o*; from *1747*; to *lurk*, i.e. (fig.) *plot assassination*:—lay wait for.

1749. ἔνεδρον **ĕnĕdrŏn**, *en'-ed-ron*; neut. of the same as *1747*; an *ambush*, i.e. (fig.) *murderous design*:—lying in wait.

1750. ἐνειλέω **ĕnĕilĕō**, *en-i-leh'-o*; from *1722* and the base of *1507*; to *enwrap*:—wrap in.

1751. ἔνειμι **ĕnĕimi**, *en'-i-mee*; from *1722* and *1510*; to be *within* (neut. part. plur.):—such things as . . . have. See also *1762*.

1752. ἕνεκα **hĕnĕka**, *hen'-ek-ah*; or

ἕνεκεν **hĕnĕkĕn**, *hen'-ek-en*; or

εἵνεκεν **hĕinĕkĕn**, *hi'-nek-en*; of uncert. affin.; *on account of*:—because, for (cause, sake), (where-) fore, by reason of, that.

1753. ἐνέργεια **ĕnĕrgĕia**, *en-erg'-i-ah*; from *1756*; *efficiency* (" energy"):—operation, strong, (effectual) working.

1754. ἐνεργέω **ĕnĕrgĕō**, *en-erg-eh'-o*; from *1756*; to *be active*, *efficient*:—do, (be) effectual (fervent), be mighty in, shew forth self, work (effectually in).

1755. ἐνέργημα **ĕnĕrgēma,** *en-erg'-ay-mah;* from *1754:* an effect:—operation, working.

1756. ἐνεργής **ĕnĕrgēs**; *en-er-gace';* from *1722* and *2041;* active, operative:—effectual, powerful.

1757. ἐνευλογέω **ĕnĕulŏgĕō,** *en-yoo-log-eh'-o;* from *1722* and *2127;* to confer a benefit on:—bless.

1758. ἐνέχω **ĕnĕchō,** *en-ekh'-o;* from *1722* and *2192;* to hold in or upon, i.e. ensnare; by impl. to keep a grudge:—entangle with, have a quarrel against, urge.

1759. ἐνθάδε **ĕnthadĕ,** *en-thad'-eh;* from a prol. form of *1722;* prop. within, i.e. (of place) here, hither:—(t-) here, hither.

1760. ἐνθυμέομαι **ĕnthumĕŏmai,** *en-thoo-meh'-om-ahee;* from a comp. of *1722* and *2372;* to be inspirited, i.e. ponder:—think.

1761. ἐνθύμησις **ĕnthumēsis,** *en-thoo'-may-sis;* from *1760;* deliberation:—device, thought.

1762. ἔνι **ĕni,** *en'-ee;* contr. for third pers. sing. pres. indic. of *1751;* impers. there is in or among:—be, (there) is.

1763. ἐνιαυτός **ĕniautŏs,** *en-ee-ŏw-tos';* prol. from a prim. ἔνος ĕnŏs (a year); a year:—year.

1764. ἐνίστημι **ĕnistēmi,** *en-is'-tay-mee;* from *1722* and *2476;* to place on hand, i.e. (reflex.) impend, (part.) be instant:—come, be at hand, present.

1765. ἐνισχύω **ĕnischuō,** *en-is-khoo'-o;* from *1722* and *2480;* to invigorate (trans. or reflex.):—strengthen.

1766. ἔννατος **ĕnnatŏs,** *en'-nat-os;* ord. froai *1767;* ninth:—ninth.

1767. ἐννέα **ĕnnĕa,** *en-neh'-ah;* a prim. number; nine:—nine.

1768. ἐννενηκονταεννέα **ĕnnĕnēkŏntaĕnnĕa,** *en-nen-ay-kon-tah-en-neh'-ah;* from a (tenth) multiple of *1767* and *1767* itself; ninety-nine:—ninety and nine.

1769. ἐννεός **ĕnnĕŏs,** *en-neh-os';* from *1770;* dumb (as making signs), i.e. silent from astonishment:—speechless.

1770. ἐννεύω **ĕnnĕuō,** *en-nyoo'-o;* from *1722* and *3506;* to nod at, i.e. beckon or communicate by gesture:—make signs.

1771. ἔννοια **ĕnnŏia,** *en'-noy-ah;* from a comp. of *1722* and *3563;* thoughtfulness, i.e. moral understanding:—intent, mind.

1772. ἔννομος **ĕnnŏmŏs,** *en'-nom-os;* from *1722* and *3551;* (subj.) legal, or (obj.) subject to:—lawful, under law.

1773. ἔννυχον **ĕnnuchŏn,** *en'-noo-khon;* neut. of a comp. of *1722* and *3571;* (adv.) by night:—before day.

1774. ἐνοικέω **ĕnŏikĕō,** *en-oy-keh'-o;* from *1722* and *3611;* to inhabit (fig.):—dwell in.

1775. ἑνότης **hĕnŏtēs,** *hen-ot'-ace;* from *1520;* oneness, i.e. (fig.) unanimity:—unity.

1776. ἐνοχλέω **ĕnŏchlĕō,** *en-okh-leh'-o;* from *1722* and *3791;* to crowd in, i.e. (fig.) to annoy:—trouble.

1777. ἔνοχος **ĕnŏchŏs,** *en'-okh-os;* from *1758;* liable to (a condition, penalty or imputation):—in danger of, guilty of, subject to.

1778. ἔνταλμα **ĕntalma,** *en'-tal-mah;* from *1781;* an injunction, i.e. religious precept:—commandment.

1779. ἐνταφιάζω **ĕntaphiazō,** *en-taf-ee-ad'-zo;* from a comp. of *1722* and *5028;* to inswathe with cerements for interment:—bury.

1780. ἐνταφιασμός **ĕntaphiasmŏs,** *en-taf-ee-as-mos';* from *1779;* preparation for interment:—burying.

1781. ἐντέλλομαι **ĕntĕllŏmai,** *en-tel'-lom-ahee;* from *1722* and the base of *5056;* to enjoin:—(give) charge, (give) command (-ments), injoin.

1782. ἐντεῦθεν **ĕntĕuthĕn,** *ent-yoo'-then;* from the same as *1759;* hence (lit. or fig.); (repeated) on both sides:—(from) hence, on either side.

1783. ἔντευξις **ĕntĕuxis,** *ent'-yook-sis;* from *1793;* an interview, i.e. (spec.) supplication:—intercession, prayer.

1784. ἔντιμος **ĕntimŏs,** *en'-tee-mos;* from *1722* and *5092;* valued (fig.):—dear, more honourable, precious, in reputation.

1785. ἐντολή **ĕntŏlē,** *en-tol-ay';* from *1781;* injunction, i.e. an authoritative prescription:—commandment, precept.

1786. ἐντόπιος **ĕntŏpiŏs,** *en-top'-ee-os;* from *1722* and *5117;* a resident:—of that place.

1787. ἐντός **ĕntŏs,** *en-tos';* from *1722;* inside (adv. or noun):—within.

1788. ἐντρέπω **ĕntrĕpō,** *en-trep'-o;* from *1722* and the base of *5157;* to invert, i.e. (fig. and reflex.) in a good sense, to respect; or in a bad one, to confound:—regard, (give) reverence, shame.

1789. ἐντρέφω **ĕntrĕphō,** *en-tref'-o;* from *1722* and *5142;* (fig.) to educate:—nourish up in.

1790. ἔντρομος **ĕntrŏmŏs,** *en'-trom-os;* from *1722* and *5156;* terrified:— × quake, × trembled.

1791. ἐντροπή **ĕntrŏpē,** *en-trop-ay';* from *1788;* confusion:—shame.

1792. ἐντρυφάω **ĕntruphaŏ,** *en-troo-fah'-o;* from *1722* and *5171;* to revel in:—sporting selves.

1793. ἐντυγχάνω **ĕntugchanŏ,** *en-toong-khan'-o;* from *1722* and *5177;* to chance upon, i.e. (by impl.) confer with; by extens. to entreat (in favor or against):—deal with, make intercession.

1794. ἐντυλίσσω **ĕntulissō,** *en-too-lis'-so;* from *1722* and τυλίσσω **tulissō** (to twist; prob. akin to *1507*); to entwine, i.e. wind up in:—wrap in (together).

1795. ἐντυπόω **ĕntupŏō,** *en-too-pŏ'-o;* from *1722* and a der. of *5179;* to enstamp, i.e. engrave:—engrave.

1796. ἐνυβρίζω **ĕnubrizō,** *en-oo-brid'-zo;* from *1722* and *5195;* to insult:—do despite unto.

1797. ἐνυπνιάζομαι **ĕnupniazŏmai,** *en-oop-nee-ad'-zom-ahee;* mid. from *1798;* to dream (-er).

1798. ἐνύπνιον **ĕnupniŏn,** *en-oop'-nee-on;* from *1722* and *5258;* something seen in sleep, i.e. a dream (vision in a dream):—dream.

1799. ἐνώπιον **ĕnōpiŏn,** *en-o'-pee-on;* neut. of a comp. of *1722* and a der. of *3700;* in the face of (lit. or fig.):—before, in the presence (sight) of, to.

1800. Ἐνώς **Ĕnŏs,** *en-oce';* of Heb. or. [583]; Enos (i.e. Enosh), a patriarch:—Enos.

1801. ἐνωτίζομαι **ĕnōtizŏmai,** *en-o-tid'-zom-ahee;* mid. from a comp. of *1722* and *3775;* to take in one's ear, i.e. to listen:—hearken.

1802. Ἐνώχ **Ĕnōk,** *en-oke';* of Heb. or. [2585]; Enoch (i.e. Chanok), an antediluvian:—Enoch.

1803. ἕξ **hĕx,** *hex;* a prim. numeral; six:—six.

1804. ἐξαγγέλλω **ĕxaggĕllō,** *ex-ang-el'-lo;* from *1537* and the base of *32;* to publish, i.e. celebrate:—shew forth.

1805. ἐξαγοράζω **ĕxagŏrazō,** *ex-ag-or-ad'-zo;* from *1537* and *59;* to buy up, i.e. ransom; fig. to rescue from loss (improve opportunity):—redeem.

1806. ἐξάγω **ĕxagō,** *ex-ag'-o;* from *1537* and *71;* to lead forth:—bring forth (out), fetch (lead) out.

1807. ἐξαιρέω **ĕxairĕō,** *ex-ahee-reh'-o;* from *1537* and *138;* act. to tear out; mid. to select; fig. to release:—deliver, pluck out, rescue.

1808. ἐξαίρω **ĕxairō,** *ex-ah'ee-ro;* from *1537* and *142;* to remove:—put (take) away.

1809. ἐξαιτέομαι **ĕxaitĕŏmai,** *ex-ahee-teh'-om-ahee;* mid. from *1537* and *154;* to demand (for trial):—desire.

1810. ἐξαίφνης **ĕxaiphnēs,** *ex-ah'eef-nace;* from *1537* and the base of *160;* of a sudden (unexpectedly):—suddenly. Comp. *1819.*

1811. ἐξακολουθέω **ĕxakŏlŏuthĕō,** *ex-ak-ol-oo-theh'-o;* from *1537* and *190;* to follow out, i.e. (fig.) to imitate, obey, yield to:—follow.

1812. ἑξακόσιοι **hĕxakŏsiŏi,** *hex-ak-os'-ee-oy;* plur. ordinal from *1803* and *1540;* six hundred:—six hundred.

1813. ἐξαλείφω **ĕxalĕiphō,** *ex-al-i'-fo;* from *1537* and *218;* to smear out, i.e. obliterate (erase tears, fig. pardon sin):—blot out, wipe away.

1814. ἐξάλλομαι **ĕxallŏmai,** *ex-al'-lom-ahee;* from *1537* and *242;* to spring forth:—leap up.

1815. ἐξανάστασις **ĕxanastasis,** *ex-an-as'-tas-is;* from *1817;* a rising from death:—resurrection.

1816. ἐξανατέλλω **ĕxanatĕllō,** *ex-an-at-el'-lo;* from *1537* and *393;* to start up out of the ground, i.e. germinate:—spring up.

1817. ἐξανίστημι **ĕxanistēmi,** *ex-an-is'-tay-mee;* from *1537* and *450;* obj. to produce, i.e. (fig.) beget; subj. to arise, i.e. (fig.) object:—raise (rise) up.

1818. ἐξαπατάω **ĕxapataō,** *ex-ap-at-ah'-o;* from *1537* and *538;* to seduce wholly:—beguile, deceive.

1819. ἐξάπινα **ĕxapina,** *ex-ap'-ee-nah;* from *1537* and a der. of the same as *160;* of a sudden, i.e. unexpectedly:—suddenly. Comp. *1810.*

1820. ἐξαπορέομαι **ĕxapŏrĕŏmai,** *ex-ap-or-eh'-om-ahee;* mid. from *1537* and *639;* to be utterly at a loss, i.e. despond:—(in) despair.

1821. ἐξαποστέλλω **ĕxapŏstĕllō,** *ex-ap-os-tel'-lo;* frcm *1537* and *649;* to send away forth, i.e. (on a mission) to despatch, or (peremptorily) to dismiss:—send (away, forth, out).

1822. ἐξαρτίζω **ĕxartizō,** *ex-ar-tid'-zo;* from *1537* and a der. of *739;* to finish out (time); fig. to equip fully (a teacher):—accomplish, thoroughly furnish.

1823. ἐξαστράπτω **ĕxastraptō,** *ex-as-trap'-to;* from *1537* and *797;* to lighten forth, i.e. (fig.) to be radiant (of very white garments):—glistening.

1824. ἐξαυτῆς **ĕxautēs,** *ex-ŏw'-tace;* from *1537* and the gen. sing. fem. of *846* (*5610* being understood); from that hour, i.e. instantly:—by and by, immediately, presently, straightway.

1825. ἐξεγείρω **ĕxĕgĕirō,** *ex-eg-i'-ro;* from *1537* and *1453;* to rouse fully, i.e. (fig.) to resuscitate (from death), release (from infliction):—raise up.

1826. ἔξειμι **ĕxĕimi,** *ex'-i-mee;* from *1537* and εἶμι **ĕimi** (to go); to issue, i.e. leave (a place), escape (to the shore):—depart, get [to land], go out.

1827. ἐξελέγχω **ĕxĕlĕgchō,** *ex-el-eng'-kho;* from *1537* and *1651;* to convict fully, i.e. (by impl.) to punish:—convince.

1828. ἐξέλκω **ĕxĕlkō,** *ex-el'-ko;* from *1537* and *1670;* to drag forth, i.e. (fig.) to entice (to sin):—draw away.

1829. ἐξέραμα **ĕxĕrama,** *ex-er'-am-ah;* from a comp. of *1537* and a presumed ἐράω **ĕraō** (to spue); vomit, i.e. food disgorged:—vomit.

1830. ἐξερευνάω **ĕxĕrĕunaō,** *ex-er-yoo-nah'-o;* from *1537* and *2045;* to explore (fig.):—search diligently.

1831. ἐξέρχομαι **ĕxĕrchŏmai,** *ex-er'-khom-ahee;* from *1537* and *2064;* to issue (lit. or fig.):—come-(forth, out), depart (out of), escape, get out (abroad, away, forth, out, thence), proceed (forth), spread abroad.

1832. ἔξεστι **ĕxĕsti,** *ex'-es-tee;* third pers. sing. pres. indic. of a comp. of *1537* and *1510;* so also

ἐξόν **ĕxŏn,** *ex-on';* neut. pres. part. of the same (with or without some form of *1510* expressed); impers. it is right (through the fig. idea of being out in public):—be lawful, let, × may (-est).

1833. ἐξετάζω **ĕxĕtazō,** *ex-et-ad'-zo;* from *1537* and ἐτάζω **ĕtazō** (to examine); to test thoroughly (by questions), i.e. ascertain or interrogate:—ask, enquire, search.

1834. ἐξηγέομαι **ĕxēgĕŏmai,** *ex-ayg-eh'-om-ahee;* from *1537* and *2233;* to consider out (aloud), i.e. rehearse, unfold:—declare, tell.

1835. **ἑξήκοντα hĕxēkŏnta**, *hex-ay'-kon-tah;* the tenth multiple of *1803; sixty:*—sixty [-fold], threescore.

1836. **ἑξῆς hĕxēs**, *hex-ace';* from *2192* (in the sense of *taking hold of,* i.e. *adjoining*); *successive:*—after, following, ✕ morrow, next.

1837. **ἐξηχέομαι ĕxēchĕŏmai**, *ex-ay-kheh'-om-ahee;* mid. from *1537* and *2278;* to "*echo*" *forth,* i.e. *resound* (be generally reported):—sound forth.

1838. **ἕξις hĕxis**, *hex'-is;* from *2192; habit,* i.e. (by impl.) *practice:*—use.

1839. **ἐξίστημι ĕxistēmi**, *ex-is'-tay-mee;* from *1537* and *2476;* to *put* (*stand*) *out* of wits, i.e. *astound,* or (reflex.) *become astounded, insane:*—amaze, be (make) astonished, be beside self (selves), bewitch, wonder.

1840. **ἐξισχύω ĕxischuŏ**, *ex-is-khoo'-o;* from *1537* and *2480;* to *have full strength,* i.e. *be entirely competent:*—be able.

1841. **ἔξοδος ĕxŏdŏs**, *ex'-od-os;* from *1537* and *3598;* an *exit,* i.e. (fig.) *death:*—decease, departing.

1842. **ἐξολοθρεύω ĕxŏlŏthrĕuŏ**, *ex-ol-oth-ryoo'-o;* from *1537* and *3645;* to *extirpate:*—destroy.

1843. **ἐξομολογέω ĕxŏmŏlŏgĕō**, *ex-om-ol-og-eh'-o;* from *1537* and *3670;* to *acknowledge* or (by impl. of assent) *agree fully:*—confess, profess, promise.

ἐξόν ĕxŏn. See *1832.*

1844. **ἐξορκίζω ĕxŏrkizō**, *ex-or-kid'-zo;* from *1537* and *3726;* to *exact an oath,* i.e. *conjure:*—adjure.

1845. **ἐξορκιστής ĕxŏrkistēs**, *ex-or-kis-tace';* from *1844; one that binds by an oath* (or spell), i.e. (by impl.) an "*exorcist*" (*conjurer*):—exorcist.

1846. **ἐξορύσσω ĕxŏrussō**, *ex-or-oos'-so;* from *1537* and *3736;* to *dig out,* i.e. (by extens.) to *extract* (an eye), *remove* (a roofing):—break up, pluck out.

1847. **ἐξουδενόω ĕxŏudĕnŏō**, *ex-oo-den-ŏ'-o;* from *1537* and a der. of the neut. of *3762;* to *make utterly nothing of,* i.e. *despise:*—set at nought. See also *1848.*

1848. **ἐξουθενέω ĕxŏuthĕnĕō**, *ex-oo-then-eh'-o;* a var. of *1847* and mean. the same:—contemptible, despise, least esteemed, set at nought.

1849. **ἐξουσία ĕxŏusia**, *ex-oo-see'-ah;* from *1832* (in the sense of *ability*); *privilege,* i.e. (subj.) *force, capacity, competency, freedom,* or (obj.) *mastery* (concr. *magistrate, superhuman, potentate, token of control*), delegated *influence:*—authority, jurisdiction, liberty, power, right, strength.

1850. **ἐξουσιάζω ĕxŏusiazō**, *ex-oo-see-ad'-zo;* from *1849;* to *control:*—exercise authority upon, bring under the (have) power of.

1851. **ἐξοχή ĕxŏchē**, *ex-okh-ay';* from a comp. of *1537* and *2192* (mean. to *stand out*); *prominence* (fig.):—principal.

1852. **ἐξυπνίζω ĕxupnizō**, *ex-oop-nid'-zo;* from *1853;* to *waken:*—awake out of sleep.

1853. **ἔξυπνος ĕxupnŏs**, *ex'-oop-nos;* from *1537* and *5258; awake:*— ✕ out of sleep.

1854. **ἔξω ĕxō**, *ex'-o;* adv. from *1537; out* (-side, of doors), lit. or fig.:—away, forth, (with-) out (of, -ward), strange.

1855. **ἔξωθεν ĕxōthĕn**, *ex'-o-then;* from *1854; external* (-ly):—out (-side -ward, -wardly), (from) without.

1856. **ἐξωθέω ĕxōthĕō**, *ex-o-theh'-o;* or

ἐξώθω ĕxōthō, *ex-o'-tho;* from *1537* and **ὠθέω ōthĕō** (to *push*); to *expel;* by impl. to *propel:*—drive out, thrust in.

1857. **ἐξώτερος ĕxōtĕrŏs**, *ex-o'-ter-os;* comp. of *1854; exterior:*—outer.

1858. **ἑορτάζω hĕŏrtazō**, *heh-or-tad'-zo;* from *1859;* to *observe a festival:*—keep the feast.

1859. **ἑορτή hĕŏrtē**, *heh-or-tay';* of uncert. affin.; *a festival:*—feast, holyday.

1860. **ἐπαγγελία ĕpaggĕlia**, *ep-ang-el-ee'-ah;* from *1861;* an *announcement* (for information, assent or pledge; espec. a divine *assurance* of good):—message, promise.

1861. **ἐπαγγέλλω ĕpaggĕllō**, *ep-ang-el'-lo;* from *1909* and the base of *32;* to *announce upon* (reflex.),

1862. **ἐπάγγελμα ĕpaggĕlma**, *ep-ang'-el-mah;* from *1861;* a *self-committal* (by *assurance* of conferring some good):—promise.

1863. **ἐπάγω ĕpagō**, *ep-ag'-o;* from *1909* and *71;* to *superinduce,* i.e. *inflict* (an evil), *charge* (a crime):—bring upon.

1864. **ἐπαγωνίζομαι ĕpagōnizŏmai**, *ep-ag-o-nid'-zom-ahee;* from *1909* and *75;* to *struggle for:*—earnestly contend for.

1865. **ἐπαθροίζω ĕpathrŏizō**, *ep-ath-roid'-zo;* from *1909* and **ἀθροίζω athrŏizō** (to *assemble*); to *accumulate:*—gather thick together.

1866. **Ἐπαίνετος Ĕpainĕtŏs**, *ep-a'hee-net-os;* from *1867; praised;* Epaenetus, a Chr.:—Epenetus.

1867. **ἐπαινέω ĕpainĕō**, *ep-ahee-neh'-o;* from *1909* and *134;* to *applaud:*—commend, laud, praise.

1868. **ἔπαινος ĕpainŏs**, *ep'-ahee-nos;* from *1909* and the base of *134; laudation;* concr. a *commendable thing:*—praise.

1869. **ἐπαίρω ĕpairō**, *ep-ahee'-ro;* from *1909* and *142;* to *raise up* (lit. or fig.):—exalt self, poise (lift, take) up.

1870. **ἐπαισχύνομαι ĕpaischunŏmai**, *ep-ahee-skhoo'-nom-ahee;* from *1909* and *153;* to *feel shame for* something:—be ashamed.

1871. **ἐπαιτέω ĕpaitĕō**, *ep-ahee-teh'-o;* from *1909* and *154;* to *ask for:*—beg.

1872. **ἐπακολουθέω ĕpakŏlŏuthĕō**, *ep-ak-ol-oo-theh'-o;* from *1909* and *190;* to *accompany:*—follow (after).

1873. **ἐπακούω ĕpakŏuō**, *ep-ak-oo'-o;* from *1909* and *191;* to *hearken* (favorably) *to:*—hear.

1874. **ἐπακροάομαι ĕpakrŏaŏmai**, *ep-ak-ro-ah'-om-ahee;* from *1909* and the base of *202;* to *listen* (intently) *to:*—hear.

1875. **ἐπάν ĕpan**, *ep-an';* from *1909* and *302;* a particle of indef. contemporaneousness; *whenever, as soon as:*—when.

1876. **ἐπάναγκες ĕpanagkĕs**, *ep-an'-ang-kes;* neut. of a presumed comp. of *1909* and *318;* (adv.) *on necessity,* i.e. *necessarily:*—necessary.

1877. **ἐπανάγω ĕpanagō**, *ep-an-ag'-o;* from *1909* and *321;* to *lead up on,* i.e. (techn.) to *put out* (to sea); (intrans.) to *return:*—launch (thrust) out, return.

1878. **ἐπαναμιμνήσκω ĕpanamimnēskō**, *ep-an-ah-mim-nace'-ko;* from *1909* and *363;* to *remind of:*—put in mind.

1879. **ἐπαναπαύομαι ĕpanapauŏmai**, *ep-an-ah-pow'-om-ahee;* mid. from *1909* and *373;* to *settle on;* lit. (*remain*) or fig. (*rely*):—rest in (upon).

1880. **ἐπανέρχομαι ĕpanĕrchŏmai**, *ep-an-er'-khom-ahee;* from *1909* and *424;* to *come up on,* i.e. *return:*—come again, return.

1881. **ἐπανίσταμαι ĕpanistamai**, *ep-an-is'-tam-ahee;* mid. from *1909* and *450;* to *stand up on,* i.e. (fig.) to *attack:*—rise up against.

1882. **ἐπανόρθωσις ĕpanŏrthōsis**, *ep-an-or'-tho-sis;* from a comp. of *1909* and *461;* a *straightening up again,* i.e. (fig.) *rectification* (reformation):—correction.

1883. **ἐπάνω ĕpanō**, *ep-an'-o;* from *1909* and *507; up above,* i.e. *over* or *on* (of place, amount, rank, etc.):—above, more than, (up-) on, over.

1884. **ἐπαρκέω ĕparkĕō**, *ep-ar-keh'-o;* from *1909* and *714;* to *avail for,* i.e. *help:*—relieve.

1885. **ἐπαρχία ĕparchia**, *ep-ar-khee'-ah;* from a comp. of *1909* and *757* (mean. a *governor* of a district, "*eparch*"); a special *region* of government, i.e. a Roman *præfecture:*—province.

1886. **ἔπαυλις ĕpaulis**, *ep'-ow-lis;* from *1909* and an equiv. of *833; a hut over the head,* i.e. a *dwelling:*—habitation.

1887. **ἐπαύριον ĕpauriŏn**, *ep-ow'-ree-on;* from *1909* and *839;* occurring on the *succeeding* day, i.e. (*2250* being implied) *to-morrow:*—day following, morrow, next day (after).

1888. **ἐπαυτοφώρῳ ĕpautŏphōrŏi**, *ep-ow-tof-o'-ro;* from *1909* and *846* and (the dat. sing. of) a der. of

φώρ phōr (a *thief*); *in theft itself,* i.e. (by anal.) *in actual crime:*—in the very act.

1889. **Ἐπαφρᾶς Ĕpaphras**, *ep-af-ras';* contr. from *1891;* Epaphras, a Chr.:—Epaphras.

1890. **ἐπαφρίζω ĕpaphrizō**, *ep-af-rid'-zo;* from *1909* and *875;* to *foam upon,* i.e. (fig.) to *exhibit* (a vile passion):—foam out.

1891. **Ἐπαφρόδιτος Ĕpaphrŏditŏs**, *ep-af-rod'-ee-tos;* from *1909* (in the sense of *devoted* to) and **Ἀφροδίτη Aphrŏditē** (*Venus*); Epaphroditus, a Chr.:—Epaphroditus. Comp. *1889.*

1892. **ἐπεγείρω ĕpĕgĕirō**, *ep-eg-i'-ro;* from *1909* and *1453;* to *rouse upon,* i.e. (fig.) to *excite against:*—raise, stir up.

1893. **ἐπεί ĕpĕi**, *ep-i';* from *1909* and *1487; thereupon,* i.e. *since* (of time or cause):—because, else, for that (then, -asmuch as), otherwise, seeing that, since, when.

1894. **ἐπειδή ĕpĕidē**, *ep-i-day';* from *1893* and *1211; since now,* i.e. (of time) *when,* or (of cause) *whereas:*—after that, because, for (that, -asmuch as), seeing, since.

1895. **ἐπειδήπερ ĕpĕidēpĕr**, *ep-i-day'-per;* from *1894* and *4007; since indeed* (of cause):—forasmuch.

1896. **ἐπεῖδον ĕpĕidŏn**, *ep-i'-don;* and other moods and persons of the same tense; from *1909* and *1492;* to *regard* (favorably or otherwise):—behold, look upon.

1897. **ἐπείπερ ĕpĕipĕr**, *ep-i'-per;* from *1893* and *4007; since indeed* (of cause):—seeing.

1898. **ἐπεισαγωγή ĕpĕisagōgē**, *ep-ice-ag-o-gay';* from a comp. of *1909* and *1521;* a *superintroduction:*—bringing in.

1899. **ἔπειτα ĕpĕita**, *ep'-i-tah;* from *1909* and *1534; thereafter:*—after that (-ward), then.

1900. **ἐπέκεινα ĕpĕkĕina**, *ep-ek'-i-nah;* from *1909* and (the acc. plur. neut. of) *1565; upon those parts of,* i.e. *on the further side of:*—beyond.

1901. **ἐπεκτείνομαι ĕpĕktĕinŏmai**, *ep-ek-ti'-nom-ahee;* mid. from *1909* and *1614;* to *stretch* (oneself) *forward upon:*—reach forth.

1902. **ἐπενδύομαι ĕpĕnduŏmai**, *ep-en-doo'-om-ahee;* mid. from *1909* and *1746;* to *invest upon oneself:*—be clothed upon.

1903. **ἐπενδύτης ĕpĕndutēs**, *ep-en-doo'-tace;* from *1902;* a *wrapper,* i.e. outer garment:—fisher's coat.

1904. **ἐπέρχομαι ĕpĕrchŏmai**, *ep-er'-khom-ahee;* from *1909* and *2064;* to *supervene,* i.e. *arrive, occur, impend, attack,* (fig.) *influence:*—come (in, upon).

1905. **ἐπερωτάω ĕpĕrōtaō**, *ep-er-o-tah'-o;* from *1909* and *2065;* to *ask for,* i.e. *inquire, seek:*—ask (after, questions), demand, desire, question.

1906. **ἐπερώτημα ĕpĕrōtēma**, *ep-er-o'-tay-mah;* from *1905;* an *inquiry:*—answer.

1907. **ἐπέχω ĕpĕchō**, *ep-ekh'-o;* from *1909* and *2192;* to *hold upon,* i.e. (by impl.) to *retain;* (by extens.) to *detain;* (with impl. of *3563*) to *pay attention to:*—give (take) heed unto, hold forth, mark, stay.

1908. **ἐπηρεάζω ĕpērĕazō**, *ep-ay-reh-ad'-zo;* from a comp. of *1909* and (prob.) **ἀρειά arĕia** (*threats*); to *insult, slander:*—use despitefully, falsely accuse.

1909. **ἐπί ĕpi**, *ep-ee';* a prim. prep. prop. mean. *superimposition* (of time, place, order, etc.), as a relation of *distribution* [with the gen.], i.e. *over, upon,* etc.; of *rest* (with the dat.) *at, on,* etc.; of *direction* (with the acc.) *towards, upon,* etc.:—about (the times), above, after, against, among, as long as (touching), at, beside, ✕ have charge of, (be-, [where-] fore, in (a place, as much as, the time of, -to), (because) of, (up-) on (behalf of), over, (by, for) the space of, through (-out), (un-) to (-ward), with. In compounds it retains essentially the same import, *at, upon,* etc. (lit. or fig.).

1910. **ἐπιβαίνω ĕpibainō**, *ep-ee-bah'ee-no;* from *1909* and the base of *939;* to *walk upon,* i.e. *mount, ascend, embark, arrive:*—come (into), enter into, go abroad, sit upon, take ship.

1911. **ἐπιβάλλω ĕpiballō**, *ep-ee-bal'-lo;* from *1909* and *906;* to *throw upon* (lit. or fig., trans. or relex.; usually with more or less force): spec. (with *1438* implied) to *reflect*; impers. to *belong to*:—beat *into*, cast (up-) on, fall, lay (on), put (unto), stretch forth, think on.

1912. ἐπιβαρέω **ĕpibarĕō**, *ep-ee-bar-eh'-o*; from *1909* and *916*; to *be heavy upon*, i.e. (pecuniarily) to *be expensive to*; fig. to *be severe towards*:—be chargeable to, overcharge.

1913. ἐπιβιβάζω **ĕpibibazō**, *ep-ee-bee-bad'-zo*; from *1909* and a redupl. deriv. of the base of *939* comp. *307*]; to *cause to mount* (an animal):—set on.

1914. ἐπιβλέπω **ĕpiblĕpō**, *ep-ee-blep'-o*; from *1909* and *991*; to *gaze at* (with favor, pity or partiality):—look upon, regard, have respect to.

1915. ἐπίβλημα **ĕpiblēma**, *ep-ib'-lay-mah*; from *1911*; a *patch*:—piece.

1916. ἐπιβοάω **ĕpibŏaō**, *ep-ee-bo-ah'-o*; from *1909* and *994*; to *exclaim against*:—cry.

1917. ἐπιβουλή **ĕpibŏulē**, *ep-ee-boo-lay'*; from a presumed comp. of *1909* and *1014*; a *plan against* someone, i.e. a *plot*:—laying (lying) in wait.

1918. ἐπιγαμβρεύω **ĕpigambrĕuō**, *ep-ee-gam-bryoo'-o*; from *1909* and a der. of *1062*; to *form affinity with*, i.e. (spec.) in a levirate way:—marry.

1919. ἐπίγειος **ĕpigĕiŏs**, *ep-ig'-i-os*; from *1909* and *1093*; *worldly* (phys. or mor.):—earthly, in earth, terrestrial.

1920. ἐπιγίνομαι **ĕpiginŏmai**, *ep-ig-in'-om-ahee*; from *1909* and *1096*; to *arrive upon*, i.e. *spring up* (as a wind):—blow.

1921. ἐπιγινώσκω **ĕpiginŏskō**, *ep-ig-in-oce'-ko*; from *1909* and *1097*; to *know upon* some mark, i.e. *recognise*; by impl. to *become fully acquainted with*, to *acknowledge*:--(ac-, have, take) know (-ledge, -well), perceive.

1922. ἐπίγνωσις **ĕpignŏsis**, *ep-ig'-no-sis*; from *1921*; *recognition*, †.e. (by impl.) full *discernment*, *acknowledgment*:—(ac-) knowledge (-ing, -ment).

1923. ἐπιγραφή **ĕpigraphē**, *ep-ig-raf-ay'*; from *1924*; an *inscription*:—superscription.

1924. ἐπιγράφω **ĕpigraphō**, *ep-ee-graf'-o*; from *1909* and *1125*; to *inscribe* (phys. or ment.):—inscription, write in (over, thereon).

1925. ἐπιδείκνυμι **ĕpidĕiknumi**, *ep-ee-dike'-noo-mee*; from *1909* and *1166*; to *exhibit* (phys. or ment.):—shew.

1926. ἐπιδέχομαι **ĕpidĕchŏmai**, *ep-ee-dekh'-om-ahee*; from *1909* and *1209*; to *admit* (as a guest or [fig.] teacher):—receive.

1927. ἐπιδημέω **ĕpidēmĕō**, *ep-ee-day-meh'-o*; from a comp. of *1909* and *1218*; to *make oneself at home*, i.e. (by extens.) to *reside* (in a foreign country):—[be] dwelling (which were) there, stranger.

1928. ἐπιδιατάσσομαι **ĕpidiatassŏmai**, *ep-ee-dee-ah-tas'-som-ahee*; mid. from *1909* and *1299*; to *appoint besides*, i.e. *supplement* (as a codicil):—add to.

1929. ἐπιδίδωμι **ĕpididōmi**, *ep-ee-did'-o-mee*; from *1909* and *1325*; to *give over* (by hand or surrender):—deliver unto, give, let (+ [her drive]), offer.

1930. ἐπιδιορθόω **ĕpidiŏrthŏō**, *ep-ee-dee-or-thŏ'-o*; from *1909* and a der. of *3717*; to *straighten further*, i.e. (fig.) *arrange additionally*:—set in order.

1931. ἐπιδύω **ĕpiduō**, *ep-ee-doo'-o*; from *1909* and *1416*; to *set fully* (as the sun):—go down.

1932. ἐπιείκεια **ĕpiĕikĕia**, *ep-ee-i'-ki-ah*; from *1933*; *suitableness*, i.e. (by impl.) *equity*, *mildness*:—clemency, gentleness.

1933. ἐπιεικής **ĕpiĕikēs**, *ep-ee-i-kace'*; from *1909* and *1503*; *appropriate*, i.e. (by impl.) *mild*:—gentle, moderation, patient.

1934. ἐπιζητέω **ĕpizētĕō**, *ep-eed-zay-teh'-o*; from *1909* and *2212*; to *search (inquire) for*; intens to *demand*, to *crave*:—desire, enquire, seek (after, for).

1935. ἐπιθανάτιος **ĕpithanatiŏs**, *ep-ee-than-at'-ee-os*; from *1909* and *2288*; doomed to *death*:—appointed to death.

1936. ἐπίθεσις **ĕpithĕsis**, *ep-ith'-es-is*; from *2007*; an *imposition* (of hands officially):—laying (putting) on.

1937. ἐπιθυμέω **ĕpithumĕō**, *ep-ee-thoo-meh'-o*; from *1909* and *2372*; to *set the heart upon*, i.e. *long* for (rightfully or otherwise):—covet, desire, would fain, lust (after).

1938. ἐπιθυμητής **ĕpithumĕtēs**, *ep-ee-thoo-may-tace'*; from *1937*; a *craver*:— + lust after.

1939. ἐπιθυμία **ĕpithumia**, *ep-ee-thoo-mee'-ah*; from *1937*; a *longing* (espec. for what is forbidden):—concupiscence, desire, lust (after).

1940. ἐπικαθίζω **ĕpikathizō**, *ep-ee-kath-id'-zo*; from *1909* and *2523*; to *seat upon*:—set on.

1941. ἐπικαλέομαι **ĕpikalĕŏmai**, *ep-ee-kal-eh'-om-ahee*; mid. from *1909* and *2564*; to *entitle*; by impl. to *invoke* (for aid, worship, testimony, decision, etc.):—appeal (unto), call (on, upon), surname.

1942. ἐπικάλυμα **ĕpikaluma**, *ep-ee-kal'-oo-mah*; from *1943*; a *covering*, i.e. (fig.) *pretext*:—cloke.

1943. ἐπικαλύπτω **ĕpikaluptō**, *ep-ee-kal-oop'-to*; from *1909* and *2572*; to *conceal*, i.e. (fig.) *forgive*:—cover.

1944. ἐπικατάρατος **ĕpikataratŏs**, *ep-ee-kat-ar'-at-os*; from *1909* and a der. of *2672*; *imprecated*, i.e. *execrable*:—accursed.

1945. ἐπίκειμαι **ĕpikĕimai**, *ep-ik'-i-mahee*; from *1909* and *2749*; to *rest upon* (lit. or fig.):—impose, be instant, (be) laid (there-, up-) on, (when) lay (on), lie (on), press upon.

1946. Ἐπικούρειος **Ĕpikŏurĕiŏs**, *ep-ee-koo'-ri-os*; from Ἐπίκουρος **Ĕpikŏurŏs** [comp. *1947*] (a noted philosopher); an *Epicurean* or follower of Epicurus:—Epicurean.

1947. ἐπικουρία **ĕpikŏuria**, *ep-ee-koo-ree'-ah*; from a comp. of *1909* and a (prol.) form of the base of *2877* (in the sense of *servant*); *assistance*:—help.

1948. ἐπικρίνω **ĕpikrinō**, *ep-ee-kree'-no*; from *1909* and *2919*; to *adjudge*:—give sentence.

1949. ἐπιλαμβάνομαι **ĕpilambanŏmai**, *ep-ee-lam-ban'-om-ahee*; mid. from *1909* and *2983*; to *seize* (for help, injury, attainment or any other purpose; lit. or fig.):—catch, lay holà (up-) on, take (by, hold of, on).

1950. ἐπιλανθάνομαι **ĕpilanthanŏmai**, *ep-ee-lan-than'-om-ahee*; mid. from *1909* and *2990*; to *lose out of mind*; by impl. to *neglect*:—(be) forget (-ful of).

1951. ἐπιλέγομαι **ĕpilĕgŏmai**, *ep-ee-leg'-om-ahee*; mid. from *1909* and *3004*; to *surname*, *select*:—call, choose.

1952. ἐπιλείπω **ĕpilĕipō**, *ep-ee-li'-po*; from *1909* and *3007*; to *leave over*, i.e. (fig.) to *be insufficient for*:—fail.

1953. ἐπιλησμονή **ĕpilēsmŏnē**, *ep-ee-lace-mon-ay'*; from a der. of *1950*; *negligence*:— × forgetful.

1954. ἐπίλοιπος **ĕpilŏipŏs**, *ep-il'-oy-pos*; from *1909* and *3062*; *left over*, i.e. *remaining*:—rest.

1955. ἐπίλυσις **ĕpilusis**, *ep-il'-oo-sis*; from *1956*; *explanation*, i.e. *application*:—interpretation.

1956. ἐπιλύω **ĕpiluō**, *ep-ee-loo'-o*; from *1909* and *3080*; to *solve further*, i.e. (fig.) to *explain*, *decide*:—determine, expound.

1957. ἐπιμαρτυρέω **ĕpimarturĕō**, *ep-ee-mar-too-reh'-o*; from *1909* and *3140*; to *attest further*, i.e. *corroborate*:—testify.

1958. ἐπιμέλεια **ĕpimĕlĕia**, *ep-ee-mel'-i-ah*; from *1959*; *carefulness*, i.e. *kind attention* (hospitality):— + refresh self.

1959. ἐπιμελέομαι **ĕpimĕlĕŏmai**, *ep-ee-mel-eh'-om-ahee*; mid. from *1909* and the same as *3199*; to *care for* (phys. or otherwise):—take care of.

1960. ἐπιμελῶς **ĕpimĕlōs**, *ep-ee-mel-oce'*; adv. from a der. of *1959*; *carefully*:—diligently.

1961. ἐπιμένω **ĕpimĕnō**, *ep-ee-men'-o*; from *1909* and *3306*; to *stay over*, i.e. *remain* (fig. *persevere*):—abide (in), continue (in), tarry.

1962. ἐπινεύω **ĕpinĕuō**, *ep-een-yoo'-o*; from *1909* and *3506*; to *nod at*, i.e. (by impl.) to *assent*:—consent.

1963. ἐπίνοια **ĕpinŏia**, *ep-in'-oy-ah*; from *1909* and *3563*; *attention* (of the mind, i.e. (by impl.) *purpose*:—thought.

1964. ἐπιορκέω **ĕpiŏrkĕō**, *ep-ee-or-keh'-o*; from *1965*; to *commit perjury*:—forswear self.

1965. ἐπίορκος **ĕpiŏrkŏs**, *ep-ee'-or-kos*; from *1909* and *3727*; on *oath*, i.e. (falsely) a *forswearer*:—perjured person.

1966. ἐπιοῦσα **ĕpiŏusa**, *ep-ee-oo'-sah*; fem. sing. part. of a comp. of *1909* and εἰμί **hĕimi** (to *go*); *supervening*, i.e. (*2250* or *3571* being expressed or implied) the *ensuing day* or *night*:—following, next.

1967. ἐπιούσιος **ĕpiŏusiŏs**, *ep-ee-oo'-see-os*; perh. from the same as *1966*; *to-morrow's*; but more prob. from *1909* and a der. of the pres. part. fem. of *1510*; *for subsistence*, i.e. *needful*:—daily.

1968. ἐπιπίπτω **ĕpipiptō**, *ep-ee-pip'-to*; from *1909* and *4098*; to *embrace* (with *affection*) or *seize* (with more or less violence; lit. or fig.):—fall into (on, upon), lie on, press upon.

1969. ἐπιπλήσσω **ĕpiplēssō**, *ep-ee-place'-so*; from *1909* and *4141*; to *chastise*, i.e. (with words) to *upbraid*:—rebuke.

1970. ἐπιπνίγω **ĕpipnigō**, *ep-ee-pnee'-go*; from *1909* and *4155*; to *throttle upon*, i.e. (fig.) *overgrow*:—choke.

1971. ἐπιποθέω **ĕpipŏthĕō**, *ep-ee-poth-eh'-o*; from *1909* and ποθέω **pŏthĕō** (to *yearn*); to *dote upon*, i.e. *intensely crave possession* (lawfully or wrongfully):—(earnestly) desire (greatly), (greatly) long (after), lust.

1972. ἐπιπόθησις **ĕpipŏthēsis**, *ep-ee-poth'-ay-sis*; from *1971*; a *longing for*:—earnest (vehement) desire.

1973. ἐπιπόθητος **ĕpipŏthētŏs**, *ep-ee-poth'-ay-tos*; from *1909* and a der. of the latter part of *1971*; *yearned upon*, i.e. *greatly loved*:—longed for.

1974. ἐπιποθία **ĕpipŏthia**, *ep-ee-poth-ee'-ah*; from *1971*; *intense longing*:—great desire.

1975. ἐπιπορεύομαι **ĕpipŏrĕuŏmai**, *ep-ee-por-yoo'-om-ahee*; from *1909* and *4198*; to *journey further*, i.e. *travel on* (*reach*):—come.

1976. ἐπιρράπτω **ĕpirrhaptō**, *ep-ir-hrap'-to*; from *1909* and the base of *4476*; to *stitch upon*, i.e. *fasten* with the needle:—sew on.

1977. ἐπιρρίπτω **ĕpirrhiptō**, *ep-ir-hrip'-to*; from *1909* and *4496*; to *throw upon* (lit. or fig.):—cast upon.

1978. ἐπίσημος **ĕpisēmŏs**, *ep-is'-ay-mos*; from *1909* and some form of the base of *4591*; *remarkable*, i.e. (fig.) *eminent*:—notable, of note.

1979. ἐπισιτισμός **ĕpisitismŏs**, *ep-ee-sit-is-mos'*; from a comp. of *1909* and a der. of *4621*; a *provisioning*, i.e. (concr.) *food*:—victuals.

1980. ἐπισκέπτομαι **ĕpiskĕptŏmai**, *ep-ee-skep'-tom-ahee*; mid. from *1909* and the base of *4649*; to *inspect*, i.e. (by impl.) to *select*; by extens. to *go to see*, *relieve*:—look out, visit.

1981. ἐπισκηνόω **ĕpiskēnŏō**, *ep-ee-skay-nŏ'-o*; from *1909* and *4637*; to *tent upon*, i.e. (fig.) *abide with*:—rest upon.

1982. ἐπισκιάζω **ĕpiskiazō**, *ep-ee-skee-ad'-zo*; from *1909* and a der. of *4639*; to *cast a shade upon*, i.e. (by anal.) to *envelop in a haze of brilliancy*; fig. to *invest* with preternatural influence:—overshadow.

1983. ἐπισκοπέω **ĕpiskŏpĕō**, *ep-ee-skop-eh'-o*; from *1909* and *4648*; to *oversee*; by impl. to *beware*:—look diligently, take the oversight.

1984. ἐπισκοπή **ĕpiskŏpē**, *ep-is-kop-ay'*; from *1980*; *inspection* (for relief); by impl. *superintendence*; spec. the Chr. "*episcopate*":—the office of a "bishop", bishoprick, visitation.

1985. ἐπίσκοπος **ĕpiskŏpŏs**, *ep-is'-kop-os*; from *1909* and *4649* (in the sense of *1983*); a *superintendent*, i.e. Chr. officer in gen. charge of a (or the) church (lit. or fig.):—bishop, overseer.

1986. ἐπισπάομαι **ĕpispaŏmai**, *ep-ee-spah'-om-ahee*; from *1909* and *4685*; to *draw over*, i.e. (with *203* implied) *efface the mark of circumcision* (by recovering with the foreskin):—become uncircumcised.

1987. ἐπίσταμαι **ĕpistamai**, *ep-is'-tam-ahee*; appar. a mid. of *2186* (with *3563* implied); to *put the mind upon*, i.e. *comprehend*, or *be acquainted with*:—know, understand.

1988. ἐπιστάτης **ĕpistatĕs**, *ep-is-tat'-ace;* from *1909* and a presumed der. of *2476;* an appointee over, i.e. *commander* (*teacher*):—master.

1989. ἐπιστέλλω **ĕpistĕllō**, *ep-ee-stel'-lo;* from *1909* and *4724;* to enjoin (by writing), i.e. (gen.) to *communicate by letter* (for any purpose):—write (a letter, unto).

1990. ἐπιστήμων **ĕpistēmōn**, *ep-ee-stay'-mone;* from *1987; intelligent:*—endued with knowledge.

1991. ἐπιστηρίζω **ĕpistērizō**, *ep-ee-stay-rid'-zo;* from *1909* and *4741;* to support further, i.e. reëstablish:—confirm, strengthen.

1992. ἐπιστολή **ĕpistŏlē**, *ep-is-tol-ay';* from *1989;* a written message:—"epistle", letter.

1993. ἐπιστομίζω **ĕpistŏmizō**, *ep-ee-stom-id'-zo;* from *1909* and *4750;* to put something over the mouth, i.e. (fig.) to silence:—stop mouths.

1994. ἐπιστρέφω **ĕpistrĕphō**, *ep-ee-stref'-o;* from *1909* and *4762;* to revert (lit., fig. or mor.):—come (go) again, convert, (re-) turn (about, again).

1995. ἐπιστροφή **ĕpistrŏphē**, *ep-is-trof-ay';* from *1994; reversion,* i.e. mor. *revolution:*—conversion.

1996. ἐπισυνάγω **ĕpisunagō**, *ep-ee-soon-ag'-o;* from *1909* and *4863;* to collect upon the same place:—gather (together).

1997. ἐπισυναγωγή **ĕpisunagōgē**, *ep-ee-soon-ag-o-gay';* from *1996;* a complete collection; spec. a Chr. *meeting* (for worship):—assembling (gathering) together.

1998. ἐπισυντρέχω **ĕpisuntrĕchō**, *ep-ee-soon-trekh'-o;* from *1909* and *4936;* to hasten together upon one place (or a partic. occasion):—come running together.

1999. ἐπισύστασις **ĕpisustasis**, *ep-ee-soo'-stas-is;* from the mid. of a comp. of *1909* and *4921;* a conspiracy, i.e. concourse (riotous or friendly):—that which cometh upon, + raising up.

2000. ἐπισφαλής **ĕpisphalēs**, *ep-ee-sfal-ace';* from a comp. of *1909* and σφάλλω **sphallō** (to trip); fig. insecure:—dangerous.

2001. ἐπισχύω **ĕpischuō**, *ep-is-khoo'-o;* from *1909* and *2480;* to avail further, i.e. (fig.) insist stoutly:—be the more fierce.

2002. ἐπισωρεύω **ĕpisōrĕuō**, *ep-ee-so-ryoo'-o;* from *1909* and *4987;* to accumulate further, i.e. (fig.) seek additionally:—heap.

2003. ἐπιταγή **ĕpitagē**, *ep-ee-tag-ay';* from *2004;* an injunction or decree; by impl. authoritativeness:—authority, commandment.

2004. ἐπιτάσσω **ĕpitassō**, *ep-ee-tas'-so;* from *1909* and *5021;* to arrange upon, i.e. order:—charge, command, injoin.

2005. ἐπιτελέω **ĕpitĕlĕō**, *ep-ee-tel-eh'-o;* from *1909* and *5055;* to fulfill further (or completely), i.e. execute; by impl. to terminate, undergo:—accomplish, do, finish, (make) (perfect), perform (× -ance).

2006. ἐπιτήδειος **ĕpitēdĕiŏs**, *ep-ee-tay'-di-os;* from ἐπιτηδές **ĕpitēdĕs** (enough); serviceable, i.e. (by impl.) requisite:—things which are needful.

2007. ἐπιτίθημι **ĕpitithēmi**, *ep-ee-tith'-ay-mee;* from *1909* and *5087;* to impose (in a friendly or hostile sense):—add unto, lade, lay upon, put (up) on, set on (up), + surname, × wound.

2008. ἐπιτιμάω **ĕpitimaō**, *ep-ee-tee-mah'-o;* from *1909* and *5091;* to tax upon, i.e. censure or admonish; by impl. forbid:—(straitly) charge, rebuke.

2009. ἐπιτιμία **ĕpitimia**, *ep-ee-tee-mee'-ah;* from a comp. of *1909* and *5092;* prop. esteem, i.e. citizenship; used (in the sense of *2008*) of a penalty:—punishment.

2010. ἐπιτρέπω **ĕpitrĕpō**, *ep-ee-trep'-o;* from *1909* and the base of *5157;* to turn over (transfer), i.e. allow:—give leave (liberty, license), let, permit, suffer.

2011. ἐπιτροπή **ĕpitrŏpē**, *ep-ee-trop-ay';* from *2010;* permission, i.e. (by impl.) full power:—commission.

2012. ἐπίτροπος **ĕpitrŏpŏs**, *ep-it'-rop-os;* from *1909* and *5158* (in the sense of *2011*); a commissioner, i.e. domestic manager, guardian:—steward, tutor.

2013. ἐπιτυγχάνω **ĕpitugchanō**, *ep-ee-toongkhan'-o;* from *1909* and *5177;* to chance upon, i.e. (by impl.) attain:—obtain.

2014. ἐπιφαίνω **ĕpiphainō**, *ep-ee-fah'ee-no;* from *1909* and *5316;* to shine upon, i.e. become (lit.) visible or (fig.) known:—appear, give light.

2015. ἐπιφάνεια **ĕpiphanĕia**, *ep-if-an'-i-ah;* from *2016;* a manifestation, i.e. (spec.) the advent of Christ (past or fut.):—appearing, brightness.

2016. ἐπιφανής **ĕpiphanēs**, *ep-if-an-ace';* from *2014;* conspicuous, i.e. (fig.) memorable:—notable.

2017. ἐπιφαύω **ĕpiphauō**, *ep-ee-fŏw'-o;* a form of *2014;* to illuminate (fig.):—give light.

2018. ἐπιφέρω **ĕpiphĕrō**, *ep-ee-fer'-o;* from *1909* and *5342;* to bear upon (or further), i.e. adduce (pers. or judicially [accuse, inflict], superinduce:—add, bring (against), take.

2019. ἐπιφωνέω **ĕpiphōnĕō**, *ep-ee-fo-neh'-o;* from *1909* and *5455;* to call at something, i.e. exclaim:—cry (against), give a shout.

2020. ἐπιφώσκω **ĕpiphōskō**, *ep-ee-foce'-ko;* a form of *2017;* to begin to grow light:—begin to dawn, × draw on.

2021. ἐπιχειρέω **ĕpichĕirĕō**, *ep-ce-khi-reh'-o;* from *1909* and *5495;* to put the hand upon, i.e. undertake:—go about, take in hand (upon).

2022. ἐπιχέω **ĕpichĕō**, *ep-ee-kheh'-o;* from *1909* and χέω **chĕō** (to pour); to pour upon:—pour in.

2023. ἐπιχορηγέω **ĕpichŏrēgĕō**, *ep-ee-khorayg-eh'-o;* from *1909* and *5524;* to furnish besides, i.e. fully supply, (fig.) aid or contribute:—add, minister (nourishment, unto).

2024. ἐπιχορηγία **ĕpichŏrēgia**, *ep-ee-khor-aygee'-ah;* from *2023;* contribution:—supply.

2025. ἐπιχρίω **ĕpichriō**, *ep-ee-khree'-o;* from *1909* and *5548;* to smear over:—anoint.

2026. ἐποικοδομέω **ĕpŏikŏdŏmĕō**, *ep-oy-kodom-eh'-o;* from *1909* and *3618;* to build upon, i.e. (fig.) to rear up:—build thereon (thereupon, on, upon).

2027. ἐποκέλλω **ĕpŏkĕllō**, *ep-ok-el'-lo;* from *1909* and ὀκέλλω **ŏkĕllō** (to urge); to drive upon the shore, i.e. to beach a vessel:—run aground.

2028. ἐπονομάζω **ĕpŏnŏmazō**, *ep-on-om-ad'-zo;* from *1909* and *3687;* to name further, i.e. denominate:—call.

2029. ἐποπτεύω **ĕpŏptĕuō**, *ep-opt-yoo'-o;* from *1909* and a der. of *3700;* to inspect, i.e. watch:—behold.

2030. ἐπόπτης **ĕpŏptēs**, *ep-op'-tace;* from *1909* and a presumed der. of *3700;* a looker-on:—eye-witness.

2031. ἔπος **ĕpŏs**, *ep'-os;* from *2036;* a word:— × say.

2032. ἐπουράνιος **ĕpŏuranĭŏs**, *ep-oo-ran'-ee-os;* from *1909* and *3772;* above the sky:—celestial, (in) heaven (-ly), high.

2033. ἑπτά **hĕpta**, *hep-tah';* a prim. number; seven:—seven.

2034. ἑπτάκις **hĕptakis**, *hep-tak-is';* adv. from *2033;* seven times:—seven times.

2035. ἑπτακισχίλιοι **hĕptakischiliŏi**, *hep-tak-is-khil'-ee-oy;* from *2034* and *5507; seven times a thousand:*—seven thousand.

2036. ἔπω **ĕpō**, *ep'-o;* a prim. verb (used only in the def. past tense, the others being borrowed from *2046, 4483* and *5346*); to speak or say (by word or writing):—answer, bid, bring word, call, command, grant, say (on), speak, tell. Comp. *3004.*

2037. Ἔραστος **Ĕrastŏs**, *er'-as-tos;* from ἐράω **ĕraō** (to love); beloved; Erastus, a Chr.:—Erastus.

2038. ἐργάζομαι **ĕrgazŏmai**, *er-gad'-zom-ahee;* mid. from *2041;* to toil (as a task, occupation, etc.), (by impl.) effect, be engaged in or with, etc.:—commit, do, labor for, minister about, trade (by), work.

2039. ἐργασία **ĕrgasia**, *er-gas-ee'-ah;* from *2040;* occupation; by impl. profit, pains:—craft, diligence, gain, work.

2040. ἐργάτης **ĕrgatēs**, *er-gat'-ace;* from *2041;* a toiler; fig. a teacher:—labourer, worker (-men).

2041. ἔργον **ĕrgŏn**, *er'-gon;* from a prim. (but obsol.) ἔργω **ĕrgō** (to work); toil (as an effort or occupation); by impl. an act:—deed, doing, labour, work.

2042. ἐρεθίζω **ĕrĕthizō**, *er-eth-id'-zo;* from a presumed prol. form of *2054;* to stimulate (espec. to anger):—provoke.

2043. ἐρείδω **ĕrĕidō**, *er-i'-do;* of obscure affin.; to prop, i.e. (reflex.) get fast:—stick fast.

2044. ἐρεύγομαι **ĕrĕugŏmai**, *er-yoog'-om-ahee,* of uncert. affin.; to belch, i.e. (fig.) to speak out:—utter.

2045. ἐρευνάω **ĕrĕunaō**, *er-yoo-nah'-o;* appar. from *2046* (through the idea of inquiry); to seek, i.e. (fig.) to investigate:—search.

2046. ἐρέω **ĕrĕō**, *er-eh'-o;* prob. a fuller form of *4483;* an alt. for *2036* in cert. tenses; to utter, i.e. speak or say:—call, say, speak (of), tell.

2047. ἐρημία **ĕrēmia**, *er-ay-mee'-ah;* from *2048; solitude* (concr.):—desert, wilderness.

2048. ἔρημος **ĕrēmŏs**, *er'-ay-mos;* of uncert. affin.; lonesome, i.e. (by impl.) waste (usually as a noun, *5561* being implied):—desert, desolate, solitary, wilderness.

2049. ἐρημόω **ĕrēmŏō**, *er-ay-mŏ'-o;* from *2048;* to lay waste (lit. or fig.):—(bring to, make) desolate (-ion), come to nought.

2050. ἐρήμωσις **ĕrēmōsis**, *er-ay'-mo-sis;* from *2049; despoliation:*—desolation.

2051. ἐρίζω **ĕrizō**, *er-id'-zo;* from *2054;* to wrangle:—strive.

2052. ἐριθεία **ĕrithĕia**, *er-ith-i'-ah;* perh. from the same as *2042;* prop. intrigue, i.e. (by impl.) faction:—contention (-ious), strife.

2053. ἔριον **ĕriŏn**, *er'-ee-on;* of obscure affin.; wool:—wool.

2054. ἔρις **ĕris**, *er'-is;* of uncert. affin.; a quarrel, i.e. (by impl.) wrangling:—contention, debate, strife, variance.

2055. ἐρίφιον **ĕriphiŏn**, *er-if'-ee-on;* from *2056,* a kidling, i.e. (gen.) goat (symbol. wicked person):—goat.

2056. ἔριφος **ĕriphŏs**, *er'-if-os;* perh. from the same as *2053* (through the idea of hairiness); a kid or (gen.) goat:—goat, kid.

2057. Ἑρμᾶς **Hĕrmas**, *her-mas';* prob. from *2060; Hermas,* a Chr.:—Hermas.

2058. ἑρμηνεία **hĕrmēnĕia**, *her-may-ni'-ah;* from the same as *2059; translation:*—interpretation.

2059. ἑρμηνεύω **hĕrmēnĕuō**, *her-mayn-yoo'-o;* from a presumed der. of *2060* (as the god of language); to translate:—interpret.

2060. Ἑρμῆς **Hĕrmēs**, *her-mace';* perh. from *2046; Hermes,* the name of the messenger of the Gr. deities; also of a Chr.:—Hermes, Mercury.

2061. Ἑρμογένης **Hĕrmŏgĕnēs**, *her-mog-en'-ace;* from *2060* and *1096; born of Hermes; Hermogenes,* an apostate Chr.:—Hermogenes.

2062. ἑρπετόν **hĕrpĕtŏn**, *her-pet-on';* neut. of a der. of ἕρπω **hĕrpō** (to creep); a reptile, i.e. (by Hebr. [comp. 7431]) a small animal:—creeping thing, serpent.

2063. ἐρυθρός **ĕruthrŏs**, *er-oo-thros';* of uncert. affin.; red, i.e. (with *2281*) the Red Sea:—red.

2064. ἔρχομαι **ĕrchŏmai**, *er'-khom-ahee;* mid. of a prim. verb (used only in the pres. and imperf. tenses, the others being supplied by a kindred [mid.] ἐλεύθομαι **ĕlĕuthŏmai**, *el-yoo'-thom-ahee;* or [act.] ἔλθω **ĕlthō**, *el'-tho;* which do not otherwise occur); to come or go (in a great variety of applications, lit. and fig.):—accompany, appear, bring, come enter, fall out, go, grow, × light, × next, pass, resort, be set.

2065. ἐρωτάω **ĕrōtaō**, *er-o-tah'-o;* appar. from *2046* [comp. *2045*]; to interrogate; by impl. to request:—ask, beseech, desire, intreat, pray. Comp. *4441.*

2066. ἐσθής **ĕsthēs**, *es-thace';* from ἕννυμι **hĕnnumi** (to *clothe); dress:*—apparel, clothing, raiment, robe.

2067. ἔσθησις **ĕsthēsis**, *es'-thay-sis;* from a der. of *2066; clothing* (concr.):—garment.

2068. ἐσθίω **ĕsthiō**, *es-thee'-o;* strengthened for a prim. ἔδω **ĕdō** (to *eat);* used only in certain tenses, the rest being supplied by *5315;* to *eat* (usually lit.):—devour, eat, live.

2069. Ἐσλί **Ĕsli**, *es-lee';* of Heb. or. [prob. for 454]; *Esli,* an Isr.:—Esli.

2070. ἐσμέν **ĕsmĕn**, *es-men';* first pers. plur. indic. of *1510;* we *are:*—are, be, have our being, × have hope, + [the gospel] was [preached unto] us.

2071. ἔσομαι **ĕsŏmai**, *es'-om-ahee;* fut. of *1510; will be:*—shall (should) be (have), (shall) come (to pass), × may have, × fail, what would follow, × live long, × sojourn.

2072. ἔσοπτρον **ĕsŏptrŏn**, *es'-op-tron;* from *1519* and a presumed der. of *3700;* a *mirror* (for *looking into):*—glass. Comp. *2734.*

2073. ἑσπέρα **hĕspĕra**, *hes-per'-ah;* fem. of an adj. ἕσπερος **hĕspĕrŏs** *(evening);* the *eve* (*5610* being impl.):—evening (-tide).

2074. Ἐσρώμ **Ĕsrōm**, *es-rome';* of Heb. or. [2696]; *Esrom* (i.e. *Chetsron),* an Isr.:—Esrom.

2075. ἐστέ **ĕstĕ**, *es-teh';* second pers. plur. pres. indic. of *1510;* ye *are:*—be, have been, belong.

2076. ἐστί **ĕsti**, *es-tee';* third pers. sing. pres. indic. of *1510;* he (she or it) *is;* also (with neut. plur.) they *are:*—are, be (-long), call, × can [-not], come, consisteth, × dure for awhile, + follow, × have, (that) is (to say), make, meaneth, × must needs, + profit, + remaineth, + wrestle.

2077. ἔστω **ĕstō**, *es'-to;* second pers. sing. pres. imper. of *1510; be* thou; also
ἔστωσαν **ĕstōsan**, *es'-to-san;* third pers. of the same; *let* them *be:*—be.

2078. ἔσχατος **ĕschatŏs**, *es'-khat-os;* a superl. prob. from *2192* (in the sense of *contiguity); farthest, final* (of place or time):—ends of, last, latter end, lowest, uttermost.

2079. ἐσχάτως **ĕschatōs**, *es-khat'-oce;* adv. from *2078; finally,* i.e. (with *2192)* at the extremity of life:—point of death.

2080. ἔσω **ĕsō**, *es'-o;* from *1519; inside* (as prep. or adj.):—(with-) in (-ner, -to, -ward).

2081. ἔσωθεν **ĕsōthĕn**, *es'-o-then;* from *2080; from inside;* also used as equiv to *2080 (inside):*—inward (-ly), (from) within, without.

2082. ἐσώτερος **ĕsōtĕrŏs**, *es-o'-ter-os;* compar. of *2080; interior:*—inner, within.

2083. ἑταῖρος **hĕtairŏs**, *het-ah'ee-ros;* from ἔτης **ĕtēs** (a *clansman);* a comrade:—fellow, friend.

2084. ἑτερόγλωσσος **hĕtĕrŏglōssŏs**, *het-er-og'-loce-sos;* from *2087* and *1100; other-tongued,* i.e. a *foreigner:*—man of other tongue.

2085. ἑτεροδιδασκαλέω **hĕtĕrŏdidaskalĕō**, *het-er-od-id-as-kal-eh'-o;* from *2087* and *1320;* to *instruct differently:*—teach other doctrine (-wise).

2086. ἑτεροζυγέω **hĕtĕrŏzugĕō**, *het-er-od-zoog-eh'-o;* from a comp. of *2087* and *2218;* to *yoke up differently,* i.e. (fig.) to *associate discordantly:*—unequally yoke together with.

2087. ἕτερος **hĕtĕrŏs**, *het'-er-os;* of uncert. affin.; (an-, the) *other* or *different:*—altered, else, next (day), one, (an-) other, some, strange.

2088. ἑτέρως **hĕtĕrōs**, *het-er'-oce;* adv. from *2087; differently:*—otherwise.

2089. ἔτι **ĕti**, *et'-ee;* perh. akin to *2094;* "*yet*," *still* (of time or degree):—after that, also, ever, (any) further, (t-) henceforth (more), hereafter, (any) longer, (any) more (-one), now, still, yet.

2090. ἑτοιμάζω **hĕtŏimazō**, *het-oy-mad'-zo;* from *2092;* to *prepare:*—prepare, provide, make ready. Comp. *2680.*

2091. ἑτοιμασία **hĕtŏimasia**, *het-oy-mas-ee'-ah;* from *2090: preparation:*—preparation.

2092. ἕτοιμος **hĕtŏimŏs**, *het-oy'-mos;* from an old noun ἕτεος **hĕtĕŏs** *(fitness);* adjusted, i.e. *ready:*—prepared, (made) ready (-iness, to our hand).

2093. ἑτοίμως **hĕtŏimōs**, *het'-oy-moce;* adv. from *2092; in readiness:*—ready.

2094. ἔτος **ĕtŏs**, *et'-os;* appar. a prim. word; a *year:*—year.

2095. εὖ **ĕu**, *yoo;* neut. of a prim. εὖς **ĕus** *(good);* (adv.) *well:*—good, well (done).

2096. Εὖα **Ĕua**, *yoo'-ah;* of Heb. or. [2332]; *Eua* (or *Eva,* i.e. *Chavvah'),* the first woman:—Eve.

2097. εὐαγγελίζω **ĕuaggĕlizō**, *yoo-ang-ghel-id'-zo;* from *2095* and *32;* to *announce good news* ("evangelize") espec. the gospel:—declare, bring (declare, show) glad (good) tidings, preach (the gospel).

2098. εὐαγγέλιον **ĕuaggĕliŏn**, *yoo-ang-ghel'-ee-on;* from the same as *2097;* a *good message,* i.e. the *gospel:*—gospel.

2099. εὐαγγελιστής **ĕuaggĕlistēs**, *yoo-ang-ghel-is-tace';* from *2097;* a *preacher* of the gospel:—evangelist.

2100. εὐαρεστέω **ĕuarĕstĕō**, *yoo-ar-es-teh'-o;* from *2101;* to *gratify entirely:*—please (well).

2101. εὐάρεστος **ĕuarĕstŏs**, *yoo-ar'-es-tos;* from *2095* and *701; fully agreeable:*—acceptable (-ted), wellpleasing.

2102. εὐαρέστως **ĕuarĕstōs**, *yoo-ar-es'-toce;* adv. from *2101; quite agreeably:*—acceptably, + please well.

2103. Εὔβουλος **Ĕubŏulŏs**, *yoo'-boo-los;* from *2095* and *1014; good-willer; Eubulus,* a Chr.:—Eubulus.

2104. εὐγενής **ĕugĕnēs**, *yoog-en'-ace;* from *2095* and *1096; well born,* i.e. (lit.) *high* in rank, or (fig.) *generous:*—more noble, nobleman.

2105. εὐδία **ĕudia**, *yoo-dee'-ah;* fem. from *2095* and the alt. of *2203* (as the god of the weather); a *clear sky,* i.e. *fine weather:*—fair weather.

2106. εὐδοκέω **ĕudŏkĕō**, *yoo-dok-eh'-o;* from *2095* and *1380;* to *think well* of, i.e. *approve* (an act); spec. to *approbate* (a person or thing):—think good, (be well) please (-d), be the good (have, take) pleasure, be willing.

2107. εὐδοκία **ĕudŏkia**, *yoo-dok-ee'-ah;* from a presumed comp. of *2095* and the base of *1380; satisfaction,* i.e. (subj.) *delight,* or (obj.) *kindness, wish, purpose:*—desire, good pleasure (will), × seem good.

2108. εὐεργεσία **ĕuĕrgĕsia**, *yoo-erg-es-ee'-ah;* from *2110; beneficence* (gen. or spec.):—benefit, good deed done.

2109. εὐεργετέω **ĕuĕrgĕtĕō**, *yoo-erg-et-eh'-o;* from *2110;* to *be philanthropic:*—do good.

2110. εὐεργέτης **ĕuĕrgĕtēs**, *yoo-erg-et'-ace;* from *2095* and the base of *2041;* a *worker of good,* i.e. (spec.) a *philanthropist:*—benefactor.

2111. εὔθετος **ĕuthĕtŏs**, *yoo'-thet-os;* from *2095* and a der. of *5087; well placed,* i.e. (fig.) *appropriate:*—fit, meet.

2112. εὐθέως **ĕuthĕōs**, *yoo-theh'-oce;* adv. from *2117; directly,* i.e. *at once* or *soon:*—anon, as soon as, forthwith, immediately, shortly, straightway.

2113. εὐθυδρομέω **ĕuthudrŏmĕō**, *yoo-thoo-drom-eh'-o;* from *2117* and *1408;* to *lay a straight course,* i.e. *sail direct:*—(come) with a straight course.

2114. εὐθυμέω **ĕuthumĕō**, *yoo-thoo-meh'-o;* from *2115;* to *cheer up,* i.e. (intrans.) be *cheerful;* neut. comp. (adv.) *more cheerfully:*—be of good cheer (merry).

2115. εὔθυμος **ĕuthumŏs**, *yoo'-thoo-mos;* from *2095* and *2372;* in *fine spirits,* i.e. *cheerful:*—of good cheer, the more cheerfully.

2116. εὐθύνω **ĕuthunō**, *yoo-thoo'-no;* from *2117;* to *straighten* (level); tech. to *steer:*—governor, make straight.

2117. εὐθύς **ĕuthus**, *yoo-thoos';* perh. from *2095* and *5087; straight,* i.e. (lit.) *level,* or (fig.) *true;* adv. (of time) *at once:*—anon, by and by, forthwith, immediately, straightway.

2118. εὐθύτης **ĕuthutēs**, *yoo-thoo'-tace;* from *2117; rectitude:*—righteousness.

2119. εὐκαιρέω **ĕukairĕō**, *yoo-kahee-reh'-o;* from *2121;* to *have good time,* i.e. *opportunity* or *leisure:*—have leisure (convenient time), spend time.

2120. εὐκαιρία **ĕukairia**, *yoo-kahee-ree'-ah;* from *2121;* a *favorable occasion:*—opportunity.

2121. εὔκαιρος **ĕukairŏs**, *yoo'-kahee-ros;* from *2095* and *2540; well-timed,* i.e. *opportune:*—convenient, in time of need.

2122. εὐκαίρως **ĕukairōs**, *yoo-kah'ee-roce;* adv. from *2121; opportunely:*—conveniently, in season.

2123. εὐκοπώτερος **ĕukŏpōtĕrŏs**, *yoo-kop-o'-ter-os;* comp. of a comp. of *2095* and *2873; better for toil,* i.e. *more facile:*—easier.

2124. εὐλάβεια **ĕulabĕia**, *yoo-lab'-i-ah;* from *2126;* prop. *caution,* i.e. (religiously) *reverence (piety);* by impl. *dread* (concr.):—fear (-ed).

2125. εὐλαβέομαι **ĕulabĕŏmai**, *yoo-lab-eh'-om-ahee;* mid. from *2126;* to be *circumspect,* i.e. (by impl.) to *be apprehensive;* religiously, to *reverence:*—(moved with) fear.

2126. εὐλαβής **ĕulabēs**, *yoo-lab-ace';* from *2095* and *2983; taking well (carefully),* i.e. *circumspect* (religiously, *pious):*—devout.

2127. εὐλογέω **ĕulŏgĕō**, *yoo-log-eh'-o;* from a comp. of *2095* and *3056;* to *speak well of,* i.e. (religiously) to *bless* (thank or invoke a benediction upon, *prosper):*—bless, praise.

2128. εὐλογητός **ĕulŏgētŏs**, *yoo-log-ay-tos';* from *2127; adorable:*—blessed.

2129. εὐλογία **ĕulŏgia**, *yoo-log-ee'-ah;* from the same as *2127; fine speaking,* i.e. *elegance of language; commendation* ("*eulogy*"), i.e. (reverentially) *adoration;* religiously, *benediction;* by impl. *consecration;* by extens. *benefit* or *largess:*—blessing (a matter of) bounty (× -tifully), fair speech.

2130. εὐμετάδοτος **ĕumĕtadŏtŏs**, *yoo-met-ad'-ot-os;* from *2095* and a presumed der. of *3330; good at imparting,* i.e. *liberal:*—ready to distribute.

2131. Εὐνίκη **Ĕunikē**, *yoo-nee'-kay;* from *2095* and *3529; victorious; Eunice,* a Jewess:—Eunice.

2132. εὐνοέω **ĕunŏĕō**, *yoo-no-eh'-o;* from a comp. of *2095* and *3563;* to be *well-minded,* i.e. *reconcile:*—agree.

2133. εὔνοια **ĕunŏia**, *yoo'-noy-ah;* from the same as *2132; kindness;* euphem. *conjugal duty:*—benevolence, good will.

2134. εὐνουχίζω **ĕunŏuchizō**, *yoo-noo-khid'-zo,* from *2135;* to *castrate* (fig., *live unmarried):*—make + eunuch.

2135. εὐνοῦχος **ĕunŏuchŏs**, *yoo-noo'-khos;* from εὐνή **ĕunē** (a *bed)* and *2192;* a *castrated person* (such being employed in Oriental bed-chambers); by extens. an *impotent* or *unmarried* man; by impl. a *chamberlain* (state-*officer):*—eunuch.

2136. Εὐοδία **Ĕuŏdia**, *yoo-od-ee'-ah;* from the same as *2137; fine travelling; Euodia,* a Chr. woman:—Euodias.

2137. εὐοδόω **ĕuŏdŏō**, *yoo-od-o'-o;* from a comp. of *2095* and *3598;* to *help on the road,* i.e. (pass.) *succeed* in reaching; fig. to *succeed* in business affairs:—(have a) prosper (-ous journey).

2138. εὐπειθής **ĕupĕithēs**, *yoo-pi-thace';* from *2095* and *3982; good for persuasion,* i.e. (intrans.) *compliant:*—easy to be intreated.

2139. εὐπερίστατος **ĕupĕristatŏs**, *yoo-per-is'-tat-os;* from *2095* and a der. of a presumed comp. of *4012* and *2476; well standing around,* i.e. (a *competitor) thwarting* (a racer) in every direction (fig. of sin in gen.):—which doth so easily beset.

2140. εὐποιΐα **ĕupŏiïa**, *yoo-poy-ee'-ah;* from a comp. of *2095* and *4160; well doing,* i.e. *beneficence:*—to do good.

2141. εὐπορέω **ĕupŏrĕō**, *yoo-por-eh'-o;* from a comp. of *2090* and the base of *4197;* (intrans.) to *be good for passing through,* i.e. (fig.) *have* pecuniary *means:*—ability.

2142. εὐπορία **ĕupŏria**, *yoo-por-ee'-ah;* from the same as *2141;* pecuniary *resources:*—wealth.

2143. **εὐπρέπεια** **ĕuprĕpĕia**, *yoo-prep'-i-ah;* from a comp. of *2095* and *4241;* good suitableness, i.e. gracefulness:—grace.

2144. **εὐπρόσδεκτος** **ĕuprŏsdĕktŏs**, *yoo-pros'-dek-tos;* from *2095* and a der. of *4327;* well-received, i.e. approved, favorable:—acceptable (-ted).

2145. **εὐπρόσεδρος** **ĕuprŏsĕdrŏs**, *yoo-pros'-ed-ros;* from *2095* and the same as *4332; sitting well towards*, i.e. (fig.) assiduous (neut. diligent service):—✕ attend upon.

2146. **εὐπροσωπέω** **ĕuprŏsōpĕō**, *yoo-pros-o-peh'-o;* from a comp. of *2095* and *4383;* to be of good countenance, i.e. (fig.) to make a display:—make a fair show.

2147. **εὑρίσκω** **hĕuriskō**, *hyoo-ris'-ko;* a prol. form of a prim.

εὕρω **hĕurō**, *hyoo'-ro;* which (together with another cognate form

εὑρέω **hĕurĕō**, *hyoo-reh'-o*) is used for it in all the tenses except the pres. and imperf.; to find (lit. or fig.):—find, get, obtain, perceive, see.

2148. **Εὐροκλύδων** **Ēurokludōn**, *yoo-rok-loo'-dohn;* from **Εὖρος** **Ēurŏs** (the east wind) and *2830;* a storm from the East (or S.E.), i.e. (in modern phrase) a Levanter:—Euroclydon.

2149. **εὐρύχωρος** **ĕuruchōrŏs**, *yoo-roo'-kho-ros;* from **εὐρύς** **ĕurus** (wide) and *5561; spacious:—* broad.

2150. **εὐσέβεια** **ĕusĕbĕia**, *yoo-seb'-i-ah;* from *2152;* piety; spec. the gospel scheme:—godliness, holiness.

2151. **εὐσεβέω** **ĕusĕbĕō**, *yoo-seb-eh'-o;* from *2152;* to be pious, i.e. (towards God) to worship, or (towards parents) to respect (support):—show piety, worship.

2152. **εὐσεβής** **ĕusĕbēs**, *yoo-seb-ace';* from *2095* and *4576;* well-reverent, i.e. pious:—devout, godly.

2153. **εὐσεβῶς** **ĕusĕbōs**, *yoo-seb-oce';* adv. from *2152;* piously:—godly.

2154. **εὔσημος** **ĕusēmŏs**, *yoo'-say-mos;* from *2095* and the base of *4591;* well indicated, i.e. (fig.) significant:—easy to be understood.

2155. **εὔσπλαγχνος** **ĕusplagchnŏs**, *yoo'-splangkh-nos;* from *2095* and *4698;* well compassioned, i.e. sympathetic:—pitiful, tender-hearted.

2156. **εὐσχημόνως** **ĕuschēmŏnōs**, *yoo-skhay-mon'-oce;* adv. from *2158;* decorously:—decently, honestly.

2157. **εὐσχημοσύνη** **ĕuschēmŏsunē**, *yoo-skhay-mos-oo'-nay;* from *2158;* decorousness:—comeliness.

2158. **εὐσχήμων** **ĕuschēmōn**, *yoo-skhay'-mone;* from *2095* and *4976;* well-formed, i.e. (fig.) decorous, noble (in rank):—comely, honourable.

2159. **εὐτόνως** **ĕutŏnōs**, *yoo-ton'-oce;* adv. from a comp. of *2095* and a der. of **τείνω** **tĕinō** (to stretch); in a well-strung manner, i.e. (fig.) intensely (in a good sense, cogently; in a bad one, fiercely):—mightily, vehemently.

2160. **εὐτραπελία** **ĕutrapĕlia**, *yoo-trap-el-ee'-ah;* from a comp. of *2095* and a der. of the base of *5157* (mean. well-turned, i.e. ready at repartee, jocose); witticism, i.e. (in a vulgar sense) ribaldry:—jesting.

2161. **Εὔτυχος** **Ēutuchŏs**, *yoo'-too-khos;* from *2095* and a der. of *5177;* well-fated, i.e. fortunate; Eutychus, a young man:—Eutychus.

2162. **εὐφημία** **ĕuphēmia**, *yoo-fay-mee'-ah;* from *2163;* good language ("euphemy"), i.e. praise (repute):—good report.

2163. **εὔφημος** **ĕuphēmŏs**, *yoo'-fay-mos;* from *2095* and *5345;* well spoken of, i.e. reputable:—of good report.

2164. **εὐφορέω** **ĕuphŏrĕō**, *yoo-for-eh'-o;* from *2095* and *5409;* to bear well, i.e. be fertile:—bring forth abundantly.

2165. **εὐφραίνω** **ĕuphrainō**, *yoo-frah'ee-no;* from *2095* and *5424;* to put (mid. or pass. be) in a good frame of mind, i.e. rejoice:—fare, make glad, be (make) merry, rejoice.

2166. **Εὐφράτης** **Ēuphratēs**, *yoo-frat'-ace;* of for. or. [comp. 6578]; Euphrates, a river of Asia:—Euphrates.

2167. **εὐφροσύνη** **ĕuphrŏsunē**, *yoo-fros-oo'-nay;* from the same as *2165; joyfulness:—*gladness, joy.

2168. **εὐχαριστέω** **ĕucharistĕō**, *yoo-khar-is-teh'-o;* from *2170; to be grateful*, i.e. (act.) to express gratitude (towards); spec. to say grace at a meal:—(give) thank (-ful, -s).

2169. **εὐχαριστία** **ĕucharistia**, *yoo-khar-is-tee'-ah;* from *2170; gratitude;* act. grateful language (to God, as an act of worship):—thankfulness, (giving of) thanks (-giving).

2170. **εὐχάριστος** **ĕucharistŏs**, *yoo-khar'-is-tos;* from *2095* and a der. of *5483;* well favored, i.e. (by impl.) grateful:—thankful.

2171. **εὐχή** **ĕuchē**, *yoo-khay';* from *2172;* prop. a wish, expressed as a petition to God, or in votive obligation:—prayer, vow.

2172. **εὔχομαι** **ĕuchŏmai**, *yoo'-khom-ahee;* mid. of a prim. verb; to wish; by impl. to pray to God:—pray, will, wish.

2173. **εὔχρηστος** **ĕuchrēstŏs**, *yoo'-khrays-tos;* from *2095* and *5543;* easily used, i.e. useful:—profitable, meet for use.

2174. **εὐψυχέω** **ĕupsuchĕō**, *yoo-psoo-kheh'-o;* from a comp. of *2095* and *5590;* to be in good spirits, i.e. feel encouraged:—be of good comfort.

2175. **εὐωδία** **ĕuōdia**, *yoo-o-dee'-ah;* from a comp. of *2095* and a der. of *3605;* good-scentedness, i.e. fragrance:—sweet savour (smell, -smelling).

2176. **εὐώνυμος** **ĕuōnumŏs**, *yoo-o'-noo-mos;* from *2095* and *3686;* prop. well-named (good-omened), i.e. the left (which was the lucky side among the pagan Greeks); neut. as adv. at the left hand:—(on the) left.

2177. **ἐφάλλομαι** **ĕphallŏmai**, *ef-al'-lom-ahee;* from *1909* and *242;* to spring upon:—leap on.

2178. **ἐφάπαξ** **ĕphapax**, *ef-ap'-ax;* from *1909* and *530; upon one occasion* (only):—(at) once (for all).

2179. **Ἐφεσῖνος** **Ēphĕsinŏs**, *ef-es-ee'-nos;* from *2181; Ephesine*, or situated at Ephesus:—of Ephesus.

2180. **Ἐφέσιος** **Ēphĕsiŏs**, *ef-es'-ee-os;* from *2181;* an Ephesian or inhab. of Ephesus:—Ephesian, of Ephesus.

2181. **Ἔφεσος** **Ēphĕsŏs**, *ef'-es-os;* prob. of for. or.; Ephesus, a city of Asia Minor:—Ephesus.

2182. **ἐφευρετής** **ĕphĕurĕtēs**, *ef-yoo-ret'-ace;* from a comp. of *1909* and *2147;* a discoverer, i.e. contriver:—inventor.

2183. **ἐφημερία** **ĕphēmĕria**, *ef-ay-mer-ee'-ah;* from *2184; diurnality*, i.e. (spec.) the quotidian rotation or class of the Jewish priests' service at the Temple, as distributed by families:—course.

2184. **ἐφήμερος** **ĕphēmĕrŏs**, *ef-ay'-mer-os;* from *1909* and *2250; for a day* ("ephemeral"), i.e. diurnal:—daily.

2185. **ἐφικνέομαι** **ĕphiknĕŏmai**, *ef-ik-neh'-om-ahee;* from *1909* and a cognate of *2240;* to arrive upon, i.e. extend to:—reach.

2186. **ἐφίστημι** **ĕphistēmi**, *ef-is'-tay-mee;* from *1909* and *2476;* to stand upon, i.e. be present (in various applications, friendly or otherwise, usually lit.):—assault, come (in, to, unto, upon), be at hand (instant), present, stand (before, by, over).

2187. **Ἐφραΐμ** **Ēphraim**, *ef-rah-im';* of Heb. or. [669 or better 6085]; Ephraïm, a place in Pal.:—Ephraim.

2188. **ἐφφαθά** **ĕphphatha**, *ef-fath-ah';* of Chald. or. [6606]; be opened!:—Ephphatha.

2189. **ἔχθρα** **ĕchthra**, *ekh'-thrah;* fem. of *2190;* hostility; by impl. a reason for opposition:—enmity, hatred.

2190. **ἐχθρός** **ĕchthrŏs**, *ekh-thros';* from a prim. **ἔχθω** **ĕchthō** (to hate); hateful (pass. odious, or act. hostile); usually as a noun, an adversary (espec. Satan):—enemy, foe.

2191. **ἔχιδνα** **ĕchidna**, *ekh'-id-nah;* of uncert. or.; an adder or other poisonous snake (lit. or fig.):—viper.

2192. **ἔχω** **ĕchō**, *ekh'-o* (includ. an alt. form

σχέω **schŏō**, *skheh'-o;* used in certain tenses only); a prim. verb; to hold (used in very various applications, lit. or fig., direct or remote; such as possession, ability, contiguity, relation or condition):—be (able, ✕ hold, possessed with), accompany, + begin to amend, can (+ -not), ✕ conceive, count, diseased, do, + eat, + enjoy, + fear, following, have, hold, keep, + lack, + go to law, lie, + must needs, + of necessity, + need, next, + recover, + reign, + rest, return, ✕ sick, take for, + tremble, + uncircumcised, use.

2193. **ἕως** **hĕōs**, *heh'-oce;* of uncert. affin.; a conj., prep. and adv. of continuance, until (of time and place):—even (until, unto), (as) far (as), how long, (un-) til (-l), (hither-, un-, up) to, while (-s).

Z

2194. **Ζαβουλών** **Zabŏulōn**, *dzab-oo-lone';* of Heb. or. [2074]; Zabulon (i.e. Zebulon), a region of Pal.:—Zabulon.

2195. **Ζακχαῖος** **Zakchaiŏs**, *dzak-chah'ee-yos;* of Heb. or. [comp. 2140]; Zacchæus, an Isr.:—Zacchæus.

2196. **Ζαρά** **Zara**, *dzar-ah';* of Heb. or. [2226]; Zara (i.e. Zerach), an Isr.:—Zara.

2197. **Ζαχαρίας** **Zacharias**, *dzakh-ar-ee'-as;* of Heb. or. [2148]; Zacharias (i.e. Zechariah), the name of two Isr.:—Zacharias.

2198. **ζάω** **zaō**, *dzah'-o;* a prim. verb; to live (lit. or fig.):—life (-time), (a-) live (-ly), quick.

2199. **Ζεβεδαῖος** **Zĕbĕdaiŏs**, *dzeb-ed-ah'-yos;* of Heb. or. [comp. 2067]; Zebedæus, an Isr.:—Zebedee.

2200. **ζεστός** **zĕstŏs**, *dzes-tos';* from *2204;* boiled, i.e. (by impl.) calid (fig. fervent):—hot.

2201. **ζεῦγος** **zĕugŏs**, *dzyoo'-gos;* from the same as *2218;* a couple, i.e. a team (of oxen yoked together, or brace (of birds tied together):—yoke, pair.

2202. **ζευκτηρία** **zĕuktēria**, *dzyook-tay-ree'-ah,* fem. of a der. (at the second stage) from the same as *2218;* a fastening (tiller-rope):—band.

2203. **Ζεύς** **Zĕus**, *dzyooce;* of uncert. affin.; in the oblique cases there is used instead of it a (prob. cognate) name

Δίς **Dis**, *deece,* which is otherwise obsolete; Zeus or Dis (among the Latins Jupiter or Jove), the supreme deity of the Greeks:—Jupiter.

2204. **ζέω** **zĕō**, *dzeh'-o;* a prim. verb; to be hot (boil, of liquids; or glow, of solids), i.e. (fig.) be fervid (earnest):—be fervent.

2205. **ζῆλος** **zēlŏs**, *dzay'-los;* from *2204;* prop. heat, i.e. (fig.) "zeal" (in a favorable sense, ardor; in an unfavorable one, jealousy, as of a husband [fig. of God], or an enemy, malice):—emulation, envy (-ing), fervent mind, indignation, jealousy, zeal.

2206. **ζηλόω** **zēlŏō**, *dzay-lŏ'-o;* from *2205;* to have warmth of feeling for or against:—affect, covet (earnestly), (have) desire, (move with) envy, be jealous over, (be) zealous (-ly affect).

2207. **ζηλωτής** **zēlōtēs**, *dzay-lo-tace';* from *2206;* a "zealot":—zealous.

2208. **Ζηλωτής** **Zēlōtēs**, *dzay-lo-tace';* the same as *2207;* a Zealot, i.e. (spec.) partisan for Jewish political independence:—Zelotes.

2209. **ζημία** **zēmia**, *dzay-mee'-ah;* prob. akin to the base of *1150* (through the idea of violence); detriment:—damage, loss.

2210. **ζημιόω** **zēmiŏō**, *dzay-mee-ŏ'-o;* from *2209;* to injure, i.e. (reflex. or pass.) to experience detriment:—be cast away, receive damage, lose, suffer loss.

2211. **Ζηνᾶς** **Zēnas**, *dzay-nas';* prob. contr. from a poetic form of *2203* and *1435;* Jove-given; Zenas, a Chr.:—Zenas.

2212. **ζητέω** **zētĕō**, *dzay-teh'-o;* of uncert. affin.; to seek (lit. or fig.); spec. (by Heb.) to worship (God), or (in a bad sense) to plot (against life):—be (go) about, desire, endeavour, enquire (for), require, (✕ will) seek (after, for, means). Comp. *4441.*

2213. ζήτημα **zētēma,** dzay'-tay-mah; from *2212;* a search (prop. concr.), i.e. (in words) a debate:—question.

2214. ζήτησις **zētēsis,** dzay'-tay-sis; from *2212;* a searching (prop. the act), i.e. a dispute or its theme:—question.

2215. ζιζάνιον **zizanion,** dziz-an'-ee-on; of uncert. or.; darnel or false grain:—tares.

2216. Ζοροβάβελ **Zŏrŏbabĕl,** dzor-ob-ab'-el; of Heb, or. [2216]; Zorobabel (i.e. Zerubbabel) an Isr.:—Zorobabel.

2217. ζόφος **zŏphŏs,** dzof'-os; akin ˙ the base of *3509;* gloom (as shrouding like a cloud).—blackness, darkness, mist.

2218. ζυγός **zugŏs,** dzoo-gos'; from the root of ζεύγνυμι **zĕugnumi** (to join espec. by a "yoke"); a coupling, i.e. (fig.) servitude (a law or obligation); also (lit.) the beam of the balance (as connecting the scales).—pair of balances, yoke.

2219. ζύμη **zumē,** dzoo'-may; prob. from *2204;* ferment (as if boiling up):—leaven.

2220. ζυμόω **zumŏō,** dzoo-mŏ'-o; from *2219;* to cause to ferment:—leaven.

2221. ζωγρέω **zōgrĕō,** dzogue-reh'-o; from the same as *2226* and *64;* to take alive (make a prisoner of war), i.e. (fig.) to capture or ensnare:—take captive, catch.

2222. ζωή **zōē,** dzo-ay'; from *2198;* life (lit. or fig.):—life (-time). Comp. *5590.*

2223. ζώνη **zōnē,** dzo'-nay; prob. akin to the base of *2218;* a belt; by impl. a pocket:—girdle, purse.

2224. ζώννυμι **zōnnumi,** dzone'-noo-mi; from *2223;* to bind about (espec. with a belt):—gird.

2225. ζωογονέω **zōŏgŏnĕō,** dzo-og-on-eh'-o; from the same as *2226* and a der. of *1096;* to engender alive i.e. (by anal.) to rescue (pass. be saved) from death:—live, preserve.

2226. ζῶον **zōŏn,** dzo'-on; neut. of a der. of *2198;* a live thing, i.e. an animal:—beast.

2227. ζωοποιέω **zōŏpŏiĕō,** dzo-op-oy-eh'-o; from the same as *2226* and *4160;* to (re-) vitalize (lit. or fig.):—make alive, give life, quicken.

H

2228. ἤ **ē,** ay; a prim. particle of distinction between two connected terms; disjunctive, or; comparative, than:—and, but (either), (n-) either, except it be, (n-) or (else), rather, save, than, that, what, yea. Often used in connection with other particles. Comp. especially *2235, 2260, 2273.*

2229. ἤ **ē,** ay; an adv. of confirmation; perh. intens. of *2228;* used only (in the N. T.) before *3303;* assuredly:—surely.

ἦ **hē.** See *3588.*
ᾖ **hē.** See *3739.*
ᾗ **ē,** See *5600.*

2230. ἡγεμονεύω **hēgĕmŏnĕuō,** hayg-em-on-yoo'-o; from *2232;* to act as ruler:—be governor.

2231. ἡγεμονία **hēgĕmŏnia,** hayg-em-on-ee'-ah; from *2232;* government, i.e. (in time) official term:—reign.

2232. ἡγεμών **hēgĕmōn,** hayg-em-ohn'; from *2233;* a leader, i.e. chief person (or fig. place) of a province:—governor, prince, ruler.

2233. ἡγέομαι **hēgĕŏmai,** hayg-eh'-om-ahee; mid. of a (presumed) strengthened form of *71;* to lead, i.e. command (with official authority); fig. to deem, i.e. consider:—account, (be) chief, count, esteem, governor, judge, have the rule over, suppose, think.

2234. ἡδέως **hēdĕōs,** hay-deh'-oce; adv. from a der. of the base of *2237;* sweetly, i.e. (fig.) with pleasure:—gladly.

2235. ἤδη **ēdē,** ay'-day; appar. from *2228* (or possibly *2229*) and *1211;* even now:—already, (even) now (already), by this time.

2236. ἥδιστα **hēdista,** hay'-dis-tah; neut. plur. of the superl. of the same as *2234;* with great pleasure:—most (very) gladly.

2237. ἡδονή **hēdŏnē,** hay-don-ay'; from ἀνδάνω **handanō** (to please); sensual delight; by impl. desire:—lust, pleasure.

2238. ἡδύοσμον **hēduŏsmŏn,** hay-doo'-os-mon; neut. of a comp. of the same as *2234* and *3744;* a sweet-scented plant, i.e. mint:—mint.

2239. ἦθος **ēthŏs,** ay'-thos; a strengthened form of *1485;* usage, i.e. (plur.) moral habits:—manners.

2240. ἥκω **hēkō,** hay'-ko; a prim. verb; to arrive, i.e. be present (lit. or fig.):—come.

2241. ἠλί **ēli,** ay-lee'; of Heb. or. [410 with pron. suffix]; my God:—Eli.

2242. Ἠλί **Hēli,** hay-lee'; of Heb. or. [5941]; Heli (i.e. Eli), an Isr.:—Heli.

2243. Ἠλίας **Hēlias,** hay-lee'-as; of Heb. or. [452]; Helias (i.e. Elijah), an Isr.:—Elias.

2244. ἡλικία **hēlikia,** hay-lik-ee'-ah; from the same as *2245;* maturity (in years or size):—age, stature.

2245. ἡλίκος **hēlikŏs,** hay-lee'-kos; from ἧλιξ **hēlix** (a comrade, i.e. one of the same age); as big as, i.e. (interjectively) how much:—how (what) great.

2246. ἥλιος **hēliŏs,** hay'-lee-os; from ἕλη **hēlē** (a ray; perh. akin to the alt. of *138*); the sun; by impl. light:—+ east, sun.

2247. ἧλος **hēlŏs,** hay'-los; of uncert. affin.; a stud, i.e. spike:—nail.

2248. ἡμᾶς **hēmas,** hay-mas'; acc. plur. of *1473;* us:—our, us, we.

2249. ἡμεῖς **hēmĕis,** hay-mice'; nom. plur. of *1473;* we (only used when emphatic):—us, we (ourselves).

2250. ἡμέρα **hēmĕra,** hay-mer'-ah; fem. (with *5610* implied) of a der. of ἧμαι **hēmai** (to sit; akin to the base of *1476*) mean. tame, i.e. gentle; day, i.e. (lit.) the time space between dawn and dark, or the whole 24 hours (but several days were usually reckoned by the Jews as inclusive of the parts of both extremes); fig. a period (always defined more or less clearly by the context):—age, + alway, (mid-) day (by day, [-ly]), + for ever, judgment, (day) time, while, years.

2251. ἡμέτερος **hēmĕtĕrŏs,** hay-met'-er-os; from *2349;* our:—our, your [by a different reading].

2252. ἤμην **ēmēn,** ay'-mane; a prol. form of *2358;* I was:—be, was, [Sometimes unexpressed.]

2253. ἡμιθανής **hēmithanēs,** hay-mee-than-ace'; from a presumed comp. of the base of *2255* and *2348;* half dead, i.e. entirely exhausted:—half dead.

2254. ἡμῖν **hēmin,** hay-meen'; dat. plur. of *1473;* to (or for, with, by) us:—our, (for) us, we.

2255. ἥμισυ **hēmisu,** hay'-mee-soo; neut. of a der. from an inseparable pref. akin to *260* (through the idea of partition involved in connection) and mean. semi-; (as noun) half:—half.

2256. ἡμιώριον **hēmiōriŏn,** hay-mee-o'-ree-on; from the base of *2255* and *5610;* a half-hour:—half an hour.

2257. ἡμῶν **hēmōn,** hay-mone'; gen. plur. of *1473;* of (or from) us:—our (company), us, we.

2258. ἦν **ēn,** ane; imperf. of *1510;* I (thou, etc.) was (wast or were):—+ agree, be, × have (+ charge of), hold, use, was (-t), were.

2259. ἡνίκα **hēnika,** hay-nee'-kah; of uncert. affin.; at which time:—when.

2260. ἤπερ **ēpĕr,** ay'-per; from *2228* and *4007;* than at all (or than perhaps, than indeed):—than.

2261. ἤπιος **ēpiŏs,** ay'-pee-os; prob. from *2031;* prop. affable, i.e. mild or kind:—gentle.

2262. Ἤρ **Ēr,** ayr; of Heb. or. [6147]; Er, an Isr.:—Er.

2263. ἤρεμος **ērĕmŏs,** ay'-rem-os; perh. by transposition from *2048* (through the idea of stillness); tranquil:—quiet.

2264. Ἡρώδης **Hērōdēs,** hay-ro'-dace; comp. of ἥρως **hērōs** (a "hero") and *1491;* heroic; Herodes, the name of four Jewish kings:—Herod.

2265. Ἡρωδιανοί **Hērōdianŏi,** hay-ro-dee-an-oy'; plur. of a der. of *2264;* Herodians, i.e. partisans of Herodes:—Herodians.

2266. Ἡρωδιάς **Hērōdias,** hay-ro-dee-as'; from *2264;* Herodias, a woman of the Herodian family:—Herodias.

2267. Ἡρωδίων **Hērōdiōn,** hay-ro-dee'-ohn; from *2264;* Herodion, a Chr.:—Herodion.

2268. Ἡσαΐας **Hēsaias,** hay-sah-ee'-as; of Heb. or. [3470]; Hesaias (i.e. Jeshajah), an Isr.:—Esaias.

2269. Ἡσαῦ **Esau,** ay-sŏw'; of Heb. or. [6215]; Esau, an Edomite:—Esau.

2270. ἡσυχάζω **hēsuchazō,** hay-soo-khad'-zo; from the same as *2272;* to keep still (intrans.), i.e. refrain from labor, meddlesomeness or speech:—cease, hold peace, be quiet, rest.

2271. ἡσυχία **hēsuchia,** hay-soo-khee'-ah; fem. of *2272;* (as noun) stillness, i.e. desistance from bustle or language:—quietness, silence.

2272. ἡσύχιος **hēsuchiŏs,** hay-soo'-khee-os; a prol. form of a comp. prob. of a der. of the base of *1476* and perh. *2192;* prop. keeping one's seat (sedentary), i.e. (by impl.) still (undisturbed, undisturbing):—peaceable, quiet.

2273. ἤτοι **ētŏi,** ay'-toy; from *2228* and *5104;* either indeed:—whether.

2274. ἡττάω **hēttaō,** hayt-tah'-o; from the same as *2276;* to make worse, i.e. vanquish (lit. or fig.); by impl. to rate lower:—be inferior, overcome.

2275. ἥττημα **hēttēma,** hayt'-tay-mah; from *2274;* a deterioration, i.e. (obj.) failure or (subj.) loss:—diminishing, fault.

2276. ἧττον **hēttŏn,** hate'-ton; neut. of comp. of ἥκα **hēka** (slightly) used for that of *2556;* worse (as noun); by impl. less (as adv.):—less, worse.

2277. ἤτω **ētō,** ay'-to; third pers. sing. imperative of *1510;* let him (or it) be:—let . . . be.

2278. ἠχέω **ēchĕō,** ay-kheh'-o; from *2279;* to make a loud noise, i.e. reverberate:—roar, sound.

2279. ἦχος **ēchŏs,** ay'-khos; of uncert. affin.; a loud or confused noise ("echo"), i.e. roar; fig. a rumor:—fame, sound.

Θ

2280. Θαδδαῖος **Thaddaiŏs,** thad-dah'-yos; of uncert. or.; Thaddæus, one of the Apostles:—Thaddæus.

2281. θάλασσα **thalassa,** thal'-as-sah; prob. prol. from *251;* the sea (gen. or spec.):—sea.

2282. θάλπω **thalpō,** thal'-po; prob. akin to θάλλω **thallō** (to warm); to brood, i.e. (fig.) to foster:—cherish.

2283. Θάμαρ **Thamar,** tham'-ar; of Heb. or. [8559]; Thamar (i.e. Tamar), an Israelitess:—Thamar.

2284. θαμβέω **thambĕō,** tham-beh'-o; from *2285;* to stupefy (with surprise), i.e. astound:—amaze, astonish.

2285. θάμβος **thambŏs,** tham'-bos; akin to an obsol. τάφω **taphō** (to dumbfound); stupefaction (by surprise), i.e. astonishment:—× amazed, + astonished, wonder.

2286. θανάσιμος **thanasimŏs,** than-as'-ee-mos; from *2288;* fatal, i.e. poisonous:—deadly.

2287. θανατήφορος **thanatēphŏrŏs,** than-at-ay'-for-os; from (the fem. form of) *2288* and *5342;* death-bearing, i.e. fatal:—deadly.

2288. θάνατος **thanatŏs,** than'-at-os; from *2348;* (prop. an adj. used as a noun) death (lit. or fig.):—× deadly, (be . . .) death.

2289. θανατόω **thanatŏō,** than-at-ŏ'-o; from *2288;* to kill (lit. or fig.):—become dead, (cause to be) put to death, kill, mortify.

θάνω **thanō.** See *2348.*

2290. θάπτω **thaptō,** thap'-to; a prim. verb; to celebrate funeral rites, i.e. inter:—bury.

2291. Θάρα **Thara,** thar'-ah; of Heb. or. [8646]; Thara (i.e. Terach), the father of Abraham:—Thara.

2292. θαρρέω **tharrhĕō**, *thar-hreh'-o;* another form for *2293;* to *exercise courage:*—be bold, × boldly, have confidence, be confident. Comp. *5111.*

2293. θαρσέω **tharsĕō**, *thar-seh'-o;* from *2294;* to *have courage;*—be of good cheer (comfort). Comp. *2292.*

2294. θάρσος **tharsŏs**, *thar'-sos;* akin (by transp.) to θράσος **thrasŏs** (*daring*); boldness (subj.):— courage.

2295. θαῦμα '**thauma**, *thŏw'-mah;* appar. from a form of *2300;* wonder (prop. concr.; but by impl. abstr.):—admiration.

2296. θαυμάζω **thaumazō**, *thŏu-mad'-zo;* from *2295;* to *wonder;* by impl. to *admire:*—admire, have in admiration, marvel, wonder.

2297. θαυμάσιος **thaumasiŏs**, *thŏw-mas'-ee-os;* from *2295;* wondrous, i.e. (neut. as noun) a *miracle:*— wonderful thing.

2298. θαυμαστός **thaumastŏs**, *thŏw-mas-tos';* from *2296;* wondered at, i.e. (by impl.) wonderful:— marvel (-lous).

2299. θεά **thĕa**, *theh-ah';* fem. of *2316;* a female *deity:*—goddess.

2300. θεάομαι **thĕaŏmai**, *theh-ah'-om-ahee;* a prol. form of a prim. verb; to *look* closely at, i.e. (by impl.) to *perceive* (lit. or fig.); by extens. to *visit:*— behold, look (upon), see. Comp. *3700.*

2301. θεατρίζω **thĕatrizō**, *theh-at-rid'-zo;* from *2302;* to *expose as a spectacle:*—make a gazing stock.

2302. θέατρον **thĕatrŏn**, *theh'-at-ron;* from *2300;* a place for public show ("theatre"), i.e. general *audience-room;* by impl. a *show* itself (fig.):—spectacle, theatre.

2303. θεῖον **thĕiŏn**, *thi'-on;* prob. neut. of *2304* (in its or. sense of *flashing*); sulphur:—brimstone.

2304. θεῖος **thĕiŏs**, *thi'-os;* from *2316;* godlike (neut. as noun, *divinity*):—divine, godhead.

2305. θειότης **thĕiŏtēs**, *thi-ot'-ace;* from *2304;* divinity (abstr.):—godhead.

2306. θειώδης **thĕiōdēs**, *thi-o'-dace;* from *2303* and *1491;* sulphur-like, i.e. sulphurous:—brimstone.

2307. θέλημα **thĕlēma**, *thel'-ay-mah;* from the prol. form of *2309;* a determination (prop. the thing), i.e. (act.) choice (spec. purpose, decree); abstr. volition) or (pass.) inclination:—desire, pleasure, will.

2308. θέλησις **thĕlēsis**, *thel'-ay-sis;* from *2309;* determination (prop. the act), i.e. option:—will.

2309. θέλω **thĕlō**, *thel'-o;* or ἐθέλω **ĕthĕlō**, *eth-el'-o;* in certain tenses θελέω **thĕlĕō**, *thel-eh'-o;* and ἐθελέω **ĕthĕlĕō**, *eth-el-eh'-o,* which are otherwise obsol.; appar. strengthened from the alt. form of *138;* to determine (as an act. option from subj. impulse; whereas *1014* prop. denotes rather a pass. acquiescence in obj. considerations), i.e., choose or prefer (lit. or fig.); by impl. to wish, i.e. be inclined to (sometimes adv. gladly); impers. for the fut. tense, to be about to; by Heb. to delight in:—desire, be disposed (forward), intend, list, love, mean, please, have rather, (be) will (have, -ling, -ling [ly]).

2310. θεμέλιος **thĕmĕliŏs**, *them-el'-ee-os;* from a der. of *5087;* something put down, i.e. a substruction (of a building, etc.), (lit. or fig.):—foundation.

2311. θεμελιόω **thĕmĕliŏō**, *them-el-ee-ŏ'-o;* from *2310;* to lay a basis for, i.e. (lit.) erect, or (fig.) consolidate:—(lay the) found (-ation), ground, settle.

2312. θεοδίδακτος **thĕŏdidaktŏs**, *theh-od- d'-ak-tos;* from *2316* and *1321;* divinely instructed:— taught of God.

2312'. θεολόγος **thĕŏlŏgŏs**, *theh-ol-og'-os;* from *2316* and *3004;* a "theologian":—divine.

2313. θεομαχέω **thĕŏmachĕō**, *theh-o-makh- eh'-o;* from *2314;* to resist deity:—fight against God.

2314. θεόμαχος **thĕŏmachŏs**, *theh-om'-akh-os;* from *2316* and *3164;* an opponent of deity:—to fight against God.

2315. θεόπνευστος **thĕŏpnĕustŏs**, *theh-op'-nvoo-stos;* from *2316* and a presumed der. of *4154;* divinely breathed in:—given by inspiration of God.

2316. θεός **thĕŏs**, *theh'-os;* of uncert. affin.; a deity, espec. (with *3588*) the supreme *Divinity;* fig. a magistrate; by Heb. very:— × exceeding, God, god [-ly, -ward].

2317. θεοσέβεια **thĕŏsĕbĕia**, *theh-os-eb'-i-ah;* from *2318;* devoutness, i.e. piety:—godliness.

2318. θεοσεβής **thĕŏsĕbēs**, *theh-os-eb-ace';* from *2316* and *4576;* reverent of God, i.e. pious:—worshipper of God.

2319. θεοστυγής **thĕŏstugēs**, *theh-os-too-gace';* from *2316* and the base of *4767;* hateful to God, i.e. impious:—hater of God.

2320. θεότης **thĕŏtēs**, *theh-ot'-ace;* from *2316;* divinity (abstr.):—godhead.

2321. Θεόφιλος **Thĕŏphilŏs**, *theh-of'-il-os;* from *2316* and *5384;* friend of God; Theophilus, a Chr.:— Theophilus.

2322. θεραπεία **thĕrapĕia**, *ther-ap-i'-ah;* from *2323;* attendance (spec. medical, i.e. cure); fig. and collec. domestics:—healing, household.

2323. θεραπεύω **thĕrapĕuō**, *ther-ap-yoo'-o;* from the same as *2324;* to wait upon menially, i.e. (fig.) to adore (God), or (spec.) to relieve (of disease):—cure, heal, worship.

2324. θεράπων **thĕrapōn**, *ther-ap'-ohn;* appar. a part. from an otherwise obsol. der. of the base of *2330;* a menial attendant (as if cherishing):—servant.

2325. θερίζω **thĕrizō**, *ther-id'-zo;* from *2330* (in the sense of the crop); to harvest:—reap.

2326. θερισμός **thĕrismŏs**, *ther-is-mos';* from *2325;* reaping, i.e. the crop:—harvest.

2327. θεριστής **thĕristēs**, *ther-is-tace';* from *2325;* a harvester:—reaper.

2328. θερμαίνω **thĕrmainō**, *ther-mah'ee-no;* from *2329;* to heat (oneself):—(be) warm (-ed, self).

2329. θέρμη **thĕrmē**, *ther'-may;* from the base of *2330;* warmth:—heat.

2330. θέρος **thĕrŏs**, *ther'-os;* from a prim. θέρω **thĕrō** (to heat); prop. heat, i.e. summer:—summer.

2331. Θεσσαλονικεύς **Thĕssalŏnikĕus**, *thes-sal-on-ik-yoos';* from *2332;* a Thessalonican, i.e. inhab. of Thessalonice:—Thessalonian.

2332. Θεσσαλονίκη **Thĕssalŏnikē**, *thes-sal-on-ee'-kay;* from Θεσσαλός **Thĕssalŏs** (a Thessalian) and *3529;* Thessalonice, a place in Asia Minor:— Thessalonica.

2333. Θευδᾶς **Thĕudas**, *thyoo-das';* of uncert. or.; Theudas, an Isr.:—Theudas.

    θέω **thĕō**. See *5087.*

2334. θεωρέω **thĕōrĕō**, *theh-o-reh'-o;* from a der. of *2300* (perh. by add. of *3708*); to be a spectator of, i.e. discern, (lit., fig. [experience] or intens. [acknowledge]):—behold, consider, look on, perceive, see. Comp. *3700.*

2335. θεωρία **thĕōria**, *theh-o-ree'-ah;* from the same as *2334;* spectatorship, i.e. (concr.) a spectacle:—sight.

2336. θήκη **thēkē**, *thay'-kay;* from *5087;* a receptacle, i.e. scabbard:—sheath.

2337. θηλάζω **thēlazō**, *thay-lad'-zo;* from θηλή **thēlē** (the nipple); to suckle; by impl. to suck:— (give) suck (-ling).

2338. θῆλυς **thēlus**, *thay'-loos;* from the same as *2337;* female:—female, woman.

2339. θήρα **thēra**, *thay'-rah;* from θήρ **thēr** (a wild animal, as game); hunting, i.e. (fig.) destruction:—trap.

2340. θηρεύω **thērĕuō**, *thay-ryoo'-o;* from *2339;* to hunt (an animal), i.e. (fig.) to carp at:—catch.

2341. θηριομαχέω **thēriŏmachĕō**, *thay-ree-om-akh-eh'-o;* from a comp. of *2342* and *3164;* to be a beast-fighter (in the gladiatorial show), i.e. (fig.) to encounter (furious men):—fight with wild beasts.

2342. θηρίον **thēriŏn**, *thay-ree'-on;* dimin. from the same as *2339;* a dangerous animal:—(venomous, wild) beast.

2343. θησαυρίζω **thēsaurizō**, *thay-sŏw-rid'-zo;* from *2344;* to amass or reserve (lit. or fig.):—lay up (treasure), (keep) in store, (heap) treasure (together, up).

2344. θησαυρός **thēsaurŏs**, *thay-sow-ros';* from *5087;* a deposit, i.e. wealth (lit. or fig.):—treasure.

2345. θιγγάνω **thiggánō**, *thing-gan'-o;* a prol. form of an obsol. prim. θίγω **thigō** (to finger); to manipulate, i.e. have to do with; by impl. to injure:— handle, touch.

2346. θλίβω **thlibō**, *thlee'-bo;* akin to the base of *5147;* to crowd (lit. or fig.):—afflict, narrow, throng, suffer tribulation, trouble.

2347. θλῖψις **thlipsis**, *thlip'-sis;* from *2346;* pressure (lit. or fig.):—afflicted (-tion), anguish, burdened, persecution, tribulation, trouble.

2348. θνήσκω **thnēskō**, *thnay'-sko;* a strengthened form of a simpler prim. θάνω **thanō**, *than'-o* (which is used for it only in certain tenses); to die (lit. or fig.):—be dead, die.

2349. θνητός **thnētŏs**, *thnay-tos';* from *2348;* liable to die:—mortal (-ity).

2350. θορυβέω **thŏrubĕō**, *thor-oo-beh'-o;* from *2351;* to be in tumult, i.e. disturb, clamor:—make ado (a noise), trouble self, set on an uproar.

2351. θόρυβος **thŏrubŏs**, *thor'-oo-bos;* from the base of *2360;* a disturbance:—tumult, uproar.

2352. θραύω **thrauō**, *throw'-o;* a prim. verb; to crush:—bruise. Comp. *4486.*

2353. θρέμμα **thrĕmma**, *threm'-mah;* from *5142;* stock (as raised on a farm):—cattle.

2354. θρηνέω **thrēnĕō**, *thray-neh'-o;* from *2355;* to bewail:—lament, mourn.

2355. θρῆνος **thrēnŏs**, *thray'-nos;* from the base of *2360;* wailing:—lamentation.

2356. θρησκεία **thrēskĕia**, *thrace-ki'-ah;* from a der. of *2357;* ceremonial observance:—religion, worshipping.

2357. θρῆσκος **thrēskŏs**, *thrace'-kos;* prob. from the base of *2360;* ceremonious in worship (as demonstrative), i.e. pious:—religious.

2358. θριαμβεύω **thriambĕuō**, *three-am-byoo'-o;* from a prol. comp. of the base of *2360* and a der. of *680* (mean. a noisy iambus, sung in honor of Bacchus); to make an acclamatory procession, i.e. (fig.) to conquer or (by Hebr.) to give victory:—(cause) to triumph (over).

2359. θρίξ **thrix**, *threeks;* gen. τριχός **trichŏs**, etc.; of uncert. der.; hair:—hair. Comp. *2864.*

2360. θροέω **thrŏĕō**, *thrŏ-eh'-o;* from θρέομαι **thrĕŏmai** (to wail); to clamor, i.e. (by impl.) to frighten:—trouble.

2361. θρόμβος **thrŏmbŏs**, *throm'-bos;* perh. from *5142* (in the sense of thickening); a clot:—great drop.

2362. θρόνος **thrŏnŏs**, *thron'-os;* from θράω **thraō** (to sit); a stately seat ("throne"); by impl. power or (concr.) a potentate:—seat, throne.

2363. Θυάτειρα **Thuatĕira**, *thoo-at'-i-rah;* of uncert. der.; Thyatira, a place in Asia Minor:—Thyatira.

2364. θυγάτηρ **thugatēr**, *thoo-gat'-air;* appar. a prim. word [comp. "daughter"]; a female child, or (by Hebr.) descendant (or inhabitant):—daughter.

2365. θυγάτριον **thugatriŏn**, *thoo-gat'-ree-on;* from *2364;* a daughterling:—little (young) daughter.

2366. θύελλα **thuĕlla**, *thoo'-el-lah;* from *2380* (in the sense of blowing) a storm:—tempest.

2367. θύϊνος **thuïnŏs**, *thoo'-ee-nos;* from a der. of *2380;* (in the sense of blowing; denoting a certain fragrant tree); made of citron-wood:—thyine.

2368. θυμίαμα **thumiama**, *thoo-mee'-am-ah;* from *2370;* an aroma, i.e. fragrant powder burnt in religious service; by impl. the burning itself:—incense, odour.

2369. θυμιαστήριον **thumiastēriŏn**, *thoo-mee-as-tay'-ree-on;* from a der. of *2370;* a place of fumigation, i.e. the altar of incense (in the Temple):— censer.

2370. θυμιάω **thumiaō**, *thoo-mee-ah'-o;* from a der. of *2380* (in the sense of *smoking*); to *fumigate*, i.e. *offer* aromatic *fumes:*—burn incense.

2371. θυμομαχέω **thumŏmachĕō**, *thoo-mom-akh-eh'-o;* from a presumed comp. of *2372* and *3164;* to *be in a furious fight*, i.e. (fig.) to *be exasperated:*—be highly displeased.

2372. θυμός **thumŏs**, *thoo-mos';* from *2380;* passion (as if *breathing* hard):—fierceness, indignation, wrath. Comp. *5590.*

2373. θυμόω **thumŏō**, *thoo-mŏ'-o;* from *2372;* to put in a passion, i.e. *enrage:*—be wroth.

2374. θύρα **thura**, *thoo'-rah;* appar. a prim. word [comp. "door"]; a *portal* or entrance (the opening or the closure, lit. or fig.):—door, gate.

2375. θυρεός **thurĕŏs**, *thoo-reh-os';* from *2374;* a large *shield* (as *door*-shaped):—shield.

2376. θυρίς **thuris**, *thoo-rece';* from *2374;* an aperture, i.e. *window:*—window.

2377. θυρωρός **thurōrŏs**, *thoo-ro-ros';* from *2374* and οὖρος **ŏurŏs** (a *watcher*); a *gate-warden:*—that kept the door, porter.

2378. θυσία **thusia**, *thoo-see'-ah;* from *2380;* sacrifice (the act or the victim, lit. or fig.):—sacrifice.

2379. θυσιαστήριον **thusiastĕriŏn**, *thoo-see-as-tay'-ree-on;* from a der. of *2378;* a *place of sacrifice*, i.e. an *altar* (spec. or gen., lit. or fig.):—altar.

2380. θύω **thuō**, *thoo'-o;* a prim. verb; prop. to *rush* (breathe hard, blow, smoke), i.e. (by impl.) to *sacrifice* (prop. by fire, but gen.); by extens. to *immolate* (slaughter for any purpose):—kill, (do) sacrifice, slay.

2381. Θωμᾶς **Thōmas**, *tho-mas';* of Chald. or. [comp. 8380]; *the twin*; Thomas, a Chr.:—Thomas.

2382. θώραξ **thōrax**, *tho'-rax;* of uncert. affin.; the *chest* ("*thorax*"), i.e. (by impl.) a corslet:—breastplate.

I

2383. Ἰάειρος **Iaĕirŏs**, *ee-ah'-i-ros;* of Heb. or. [2971]; *Jairus* (i.e. *Jair*), an Isr.:—Jairus.

2384. Ἰακώβ **Iakōb**, *ee-ak-obe';* of Heb. or. [3290]; *Jacob* (i.e. Ja'akob), the progenitor of the Isr.; also an Isr.:—Jacob.

2385. Ἰάκωβος **Iakōbŏs**, *ee-ak'-o-bos;* the same as *2384* Græcized; *Jacobus*, the name of three Isr.:—James.

2386. ἴαμα **iama**, *ee'-am-ah;* from *2390;* a *cure* (the effect):—healing.

2387. Ἰαμβρῆς **Iambrēs**, *ee-am-brace';* of Eg. or.; *Jambres*, an Eg.:—Jambres.

2388. Ἰαννά **Ianna**, *ee-an-nah';* prob. of Heb. or. [comp. 3238]; *Janna*, an Isr.:—Janna.

2389. Ἰαννῆς **Iannēs**, *ee-an-nace';* of Eg. or.; *Jannes*, an Eg.:—Jannes.

2390. ἰάομαι **iaŏmai**, *ee-ah'-om-ahee;* mid. of appar. a prim. verb; to *cure* (lit. or fig.):—heal, make whole.

2391. Ἰάρεδ **Iarĕd**, *ee-ar'-ed;* of Heb. or. [3382]; *Jared* (i.e. *Jered*), an antediluvian:—Jared.

2392. ἴασις **iasis**, *ee'-as-is;* from *2390;* curing (the act):—cure, heal (-ing).

2393. ἴασπις **iaspis**, *ee'-as-pis;* prob. of for. or. [see 8471]; "*jasper*", a gem:—jasper.

2394. Ἰάσων **Iasōn**, *ee-as'-oan;* fut. act. part. masc. of *2390;* *about to cure*; *Jason*, a Chr.:—Jason.

2395. ἰατρός **iatrŏs**, *ee-at-ros';* from *2390;* a *physician:*—physician.

2396. ἴδε **idĕ**, *id'-eh;* second pers. sing. imper. act. of *1492;* used as interj. to denote surprise; lo!:—behold, lo, see.

2397. ἰδέα **idĕa**, *id-eh'-ah;* from *1492;* a *sight* [comp. fig. "idea"], i.e. *aspect:*—countenance.

2398. ἴδιος **idiŏs**, *id'-ee-os;* of uncert. affin.; pertaining to *self*, i.e. one's own; by impl. private or separate:— × his acquaintance, when they were

alone, apart, aside, due, his (own, proper, several), home, (her, our, thine, your) own (business), private (-ly), proper, severally, their (own).

2399. ἰδιώτης **idiōtēs**, *id-ee-o'-tace;* from *2398;* a private person, i.e. (by impl.) an *ignoramus* (comp. "idiot"):—ignorant, rude, unlearned.

2400. ἰδού **idŏu**, *id-oo';* second pers. sing. imper. mid. of *1492;* used as imper. lo!:—behold, lo, see.

2401. Ἰδουμαία **Idŏumaia**, *id-oo-mah'-yah;* of Heb. or. [123]; *Idumæa* (i.e. *Edom*), a region E. (and S.) of Pal.:—Idumæa.

2402. ἱδρώς **hidrŏs**, *hid-roce';* a strengthened form of a prim. ἴδος **idŏs** (*sweat*); perspiration:—sweat.

2403. Ἰεζαβήλ **Iĕzabēl**, *ee-ed-zab-ale';* of Heb. or. [348]; *Jezabel* (i.e. *Iezebel*), a Tyrian woman (used as a synonym of a termagant or false teacher):—Jezabel.

2404. Ἱεράπολις **Hiĕrapŏlis**, *hee-er-ap'-ol-is;* from *2413* and *4172;* *holy city*; *Hierapolis*, a place in Asia Minor:—Hierapolis.

2405. ἱερατεία **hiĕratĕia**, *hee-er-at-i'-ah;* from *2407;* priestliness, i.e. the *sacerdotal function:*—office of the priesthood, priest's office.

2406. ἱεράτευμα **hiĕratĕuma**, *hee-er-at'-yoo-mah;* from *2407;* the *priestly fraternity*, i.e. a *sacerdotal order* (fig.):—priesthood.

2407. ἱερατεύω **hiĕratĕuō**, *hee-er-at-yoo'-o;* prol. from *2409;* to be a priest, i.e. *perform his functions:*—execute the priest's office.

2408. Ἱερεμίας **Hiĕrĕmias**, *hee-er-em-ee'-as;* of Heb. or. [3414]; *Hieremias* (i.e. *Jermijah*), an Isr.:—Jeremiah.

2409. ἱερεύς **hiĕrĕus**, *hee-er-yooce';* from *2413;* a priest (lit. or fig.):—(high) priest.

2410. Ἱεριχώ **Hiĕrichŏ**, *hee-er-ee-kho';* of Heb. or. [3405]; *Jericho*, a place in Pal.:—Jericho.

2411. ἱερόν **hiĕrŏn**, *hee-er-on';* neut. of *2413;* a sacred place, i.e. the entire precincts (whereas *3485* denotes the central *sanctuary* itself) of the *Temple* (at Jerus. or elsewhere):—temple.

2412. ἱεροπρεπής **hiĕrŏprĕpēs**, *hee-er-op-rep-ace';* from *2413* and the same as *4241;* *reverent:*—as becometh holiness.

2413. ἱερός **hiĕrŏs**, *hee-er-os';* of uncert. affin.; sacred:—holy.

2414. Ἱεροσόλυμα **Hiĕrŏsŏluma**, *hee-er-os-ol'-oo-mah;* of Heb. or. [3389]; *Hierosolyma* (i.e. *Jerushalaïm*), the capital of Pal.:—Jerusalem. Comp. *2419.*

2415. Ἱεροσολυμίτης **Hiĕrŏsŏlumitēs**, *hee-er-os-ol-oo-mee'-tace;* from *2414;* a *Hierosolymite*, i.e. inhab. of Hierosolyma:—of Jerusalem.

2416. ἱεροσυλέω **hiĕrŏsulĕō**, *hee-er-os-ool-eh'-o;* from *2417;* to be a temple-robber (fig.):—commit sacrilege.

2417. ἱερόσυλος **hiĕrŏsulŏs**, *hee-er-os'-oo-los;* from *2411* and *4813;* a temple-despoiler:—robber of churches.

2418. ἱερουργέω **hiĕrŏurgĕō**, *hee-er-oorg-eh'-o;* from a comp. of *2411* and the base of *2041;* to be a temple-worker, i.e. *officiate as a priest* (fig.):—minister.

2419. Ἱερουσαλήμ **Hiĕrŏusalēm**, *hee-er-oo-sal-ame';* of Heb. or. [3389]; *Hierusalem* (i.e. *Jerushalem*), the capital of Pal.:—Jerusalem. Comp. *2414.*

2420. ἱερωσύνη **hiĕrŏsunē**, *hee-er-o-soo'-nay;* from *2413;* sacredness, i.e. (by impl.) the *priestly office:*—priesthood.

2421. Ἰεσσαί **Iĕssai**, *es-es-sah'ee;* of Heb. or. [3448]; *Jessæ* (i.e. *Jishai*), an Isr.:—Jesse.

2422. Ἰεφθάε **Iĕphthaĕ**, *ee-ef-thah'-eh;* of Heb. or. [3316]; *Jephthaë* (i.e. *Jiphtach*), an Isr.:—Jephthah.

2423. Ἰεχονίας **Iĕchŏnias**, *ee-ekh-on-ee'-as;* of Heb. or. [3204]; *Jechonias* (i.e. *Jekonjah*), an Isr.:—Jechonias.

2424. Ἰησοῦς **Iēsŏus**, *ee-ay-sooce';* of Heb. or. [3091]; *Jesus* (i.e. *Jehoshua*), the name of our Lord and two (three) other Isr.:—Jesus.

2425. ἱκανός **hikanŏs**, *hik-an-os';* from ἵκω **hikō** [ἱκάνω or ἱκνέομαι, akin to *2240*] (to *arrive*); competent (as if *coming* in season), i.e. *ample* (in amount) or *fit* (in character):—able, + content, enough, good, great, large, long (while), many, meet, much, security, sore, sufficient, worthy.

2426. ἱκανότης **hikanŏtēs**, *hik-an-ot'-ace;* from *2425;* *ability:*—sufficiency.

2427. ἱκανόω **hikanŏō**, *hik-an-ŏ'-o;* from *2425;* to *enable*, i.e. *qualify:*—make able (meet).

2428. ἱκετηρία **hikĕtēria**, *hik-et-ay-ree'-ah;* from a der. of the base of *2425* (through the idea of approaching for a favor); *intreaty:*—supplication.

2429. ἱκμάς **hikmas**, *hik-mas';* of uncert. affin.; dampness:—moisture.

2430. Ἰκόνιον **Ikŏniŏn**, *ee-kon'-ee-on;* perh. from *1504;* image-like; *Iconium*, a place in Asia Minor:—Iconium.

2431. ἱλαρός **hilarŏs**, *hil-ar-os';* from the same as *2436;* propitious or merry ("*hilarious*"), i.e. prompt or willing:—cheerful.

2432. ἱλαρότης **hilarŏtēs**, *hil-ar-ot'-ace;* from *2431;* alacrity:—cheerfulness.

2433. ἱλάσκομαι **hilaskŏmai**, *hil-as'-kom-ahee;* mid. from the same as *2436;* to conciliate, i.e. (trans.) to atone for (sin), or (intrans.) be propitious:—be merciful, make reconciliation for.

2434. ἱλασμός **hilasmŏs**, *hil-as-mos';* atonement, i.e. (concr.) an *expiator:*—propitiation.

2435. ἱλαστήριον **hilastĕriŏn**, *hil-as-tay'-ree-on;* neut. of a der. of *2433;* an *expiatory* (place or thing), i.e. (concr.) an atoning *victim*, or (spec.) the *lid* of the Ark (in the Temple):—mercyseat, propitiation.

2436. ἵλεως **hilĕōs**, *hil'-eh-oce;* perh. from the alt. form of *138;* cheerful (as *attractive*), i.e. *propitious*; adv. (by Hebr.) God be *gracious !*, i.e. (in averting some calamity) *far* be it:—be it far, merciful.

2437. Ἰλλυρικόν **Illurikŏn**, *il-loo-ree-kon';* neut. of an adj. from a name of uncert. der.; (the) *Illyrican* (shore), i.e. (as a name itself) *Illyricum*, a region of Europe:—Illyricum.

2438. ἱμάς **himas**, *hee-mas';* perh. from the same as *260;* a *strap*, i.e. (spec.) the *tie* (of a sandal) or the *lash* (of a scourge):—latchet, thong.

2439. ἱματίζω **himatizō**, *him-at-id'-zo;* from *2440;* to *dress:*—clothe.

2440. ἱμάτιον **himatiŏn**, *him-at'-ee-on;* neut. of a presumed der. of ἕννυμι **ĕnnumi** (to *put on*); a *dress* (inner or outer):—apparel, cloke, clothes, garment, raiment, robe, vesture.

2441. ἱματισμός **himatismŏs**, *him-at-is-mos';* from *2440;* clothing:—apparel (× -led), array, raiment, vesture.

2442. ἱμείρομαι **himĕirŏmai**, *him-i'-rom-ahee;* mid. from ἵμερος **himĕros** (a *yearning*; of uncert. affin.); to long for:—be affectionately desirous.

2443. ἵνα **hina**, *hin'-ah;* prob. from the same as the former part of *1438* (through the demonstrative idea; comp. *3588*); in order *that* (denoting the purpose or the result):—albeit, because, to the intent (that), lest, so as, (so) that. (for) to. Comp. *3363.*

ἵνα μή **hina mē**. See *3363.*

2444. ἱνατί **hinati**, *hin-at-ee';* from *2443* and *5101;* for what reason ?, i.e. why?:—wherefore, why.

2445. Ἰόππη **Iŏppē**, *ee-op'-pay;* of Heb. or. [3305]; *Joppa*, a place in Pal.:—Joppa.

2446. Ἰορδάνης **Iŏrdanēs**, *ee-or-dan'-ace;* of Heb. or. [3383]; the *Jordanes* (i.e. *Jarden*), a river of Pal.:—Jordan.

2447. ἰός **iŏs**, *ee-os';* perh. from εἶμι **ĕimi** (to *go*) or ἵημι **hiĕmi** (to *send*); rust (as if *emitted* by metals); also *venom* (as *emitted* by serpents):—poison, rust.

2448. Ἰουδά **Iŏuda**, ee-oo-dah'; of Heb. or. [3063 or perh. 3194]; Judah (i.e. Jehudah or Juttah), a part of (or place in) Pal.:—Judah.

2449. Ἰουδαία **Iŏudaia**, ee-oo-dah'-yah; fem. of 2453 (with 1093 impl.); the Judæan land (i.e. Judæa), a region of Pal.:—Judæa.

2450. Ἰουδαΐζω **Iŏudaizō**, ee-oo-dah-id'-zo; from 2453; to become a Judæan, i.e. "Judaize":—live as the Jews.

2451. Ἰουδαϊκός **Iŏudaïkŏs**, ee-oo-dah-ee-kos'; from 2453; Judaïc, i.e. resembling a Judæan:—Jewish.

2452. Ἰουδαϊκῶς **Iŏudaïkōs**, ee-oo-dah-ee-koce'; adv. from 2451; Judaïcally or in a manner resembling a Judæan:—as do the Jews.

2453. Ἰουδαῖος **Iŏudaiŏs**, ee-oo-dah'-yos; from 2448 (in the sense of 2455 as a country); Judæan, i.e. belonging to Jehudah:—Jew (-ess), of Judæa.

2454. Ἰουδαϊσμός **Iŏudaismŏs**, ee-oo-dah-is-mos'; from 2450; "Judaism", i.e. the Jewish faith and usages:—Jews' religion.

2455. Ἰουδάς **Iŏudas**, ee-oo-das'; of Heb. or. [3063]; Judas (i.e. Jehudah), the name of ten Isr.; also of the posterity of one of them and its region:—Juda (-h, -s); Jude.

2456. Ἰουλία **Iŏulia**, ee-oo-lee'-ah; fem. of the same as 2457; Julia, a Chr. woman:—Julia.

2457. Ἰούλιος **Iŏuliŏs**, ee-oo'-lee-os; of Lat. or.; Julius, a centurion:—Julius.

2458. Ἰουνίας **Iŏunias**, ee-oo-nee'-as; of Lat. or.; Junias, a Chr.:—Junias.

2459. Ἰοῦστος **Iŏustŏs**, ee-ooce'-tos; of Lat. or. ("just"); Justus, the name of three Chr.:—Justus.

2460. ἱππεύς **hippĕus**, hip-yooce'; from 2462; an equestrian, i.e. member of a cavalry corps:—horseman.

2461. ἱππικόν **hippikŏn**, hip-pee-kon'; neut. of a der. of 2462; the cavalry force:—horse [-men].

2462. ἵππος **hippŏs**, hip'-pos; of uncert. affin.; a horse:—horse.

2463. ἴρις **iris**, ee'-ris; perh. from 2046 (as a symb. of the female messenger of the pagan deities); a rainbow ("iris"):—rainbow.

2464. Ἰσαάκ **Isaak**, ee-sah-ak'; of Heb. or. [3327]; Isaac (i.e. Jitschak), the son of Abraham:—Isaac.

2465. ἰσάγγελος **isaggĕlŏs**, ee-sang'-el-los; from 2470 and 32; like an angel, i.e. angelic:—equal unto the angels.

2466. Ἰσαχάρ **Isachar**, ee-sakh-ar'; of Heb. or. [3485]; Isachar (i.e. Jissaskar), a son of Jacob (fig. his desc.):—Issachar.

2467. ἴσημι **isĕmi**, is'-ay-mee; assumed by some as the base of cert. irreg. forms of 1492; to know:—know.

2468. ἴσθι **isthi**, is'-thee; sec. pers. imper. pres. of 1510; be thou:— + agree, be, X give thyself wholly to.

2469. Ἰσκαριώτης **Iskariōtēs**, is-kar-ee-o'-tace; of Heb. or. [prob. 377 and 7149]; inhab. of Kerioth; Iscariotes (i.e. Keriothite), an epithet of Judas the traitor:—Iscariot.

2470. ἴσος **isŏs**, ee'-sos; prob. from 1492 (through the idea of seeming); similar (in amount or kind):— + agree, as much, equal, like.

2471. ἰσότης **isŏtēs**, ee-sot'-ace; likeness (in condition or proportion); by impl. equity:—equal (-ity).

2472. ἰσότιμος **isŏtimŏs**, ee-sot'-ee-mos; from 2470 and 5092; of equal value or honor:—like precious.

2473. ἰσόψυχος **isŏpsuchŏs**, ee-sop'-soo-khos; from 2470 and 5590; of similar spirit:—likeminded.

2474. Ἰσραήλ **Israēl**, is-rah-ale'; of Heb. or. [3478]; Israel (i.e. Jisrael), the adopted name of Jacob, includ. his desc. (lit. or fig.):—Israel.

2475. Ἰσραηλίτης **Israēlitēs**, is-rah-ale-ee'-tace; from 2474; an "Israelite", i.e. desc. of Israel (lit. or fig.):—Israelite.

2476. ἵστημι **histēmi**, his'-tay-mee; a prol. form of a prim. στάω **staō**, stah'-o (of the same mean.,

and used for it in certain tenses); to stand (trans. or intrans.), used in various applications (lit. or fig.):—abide, appoint, bring, continue, covenant, establish, hold up, lay, present, set (up), stanch, stand (by, forth, still, up). Comp. 5087.

2477. ἱστορέω **histŏrĕō**, his-tor-eh'-o; from a der. of 1492; to be knowing (learned), i.e. (by impl.) to visit for information (interview):—see.

2478. ἰσχυρός **ischurŏs**, is-khoo-ros'; from 2479; forcible (lit. or fig.):—boisterous, mighty (-ier), powerful, strong (-er, man), valiant.

2479. ἰσχύς **ischus**, is-khoos'; from a der. of ἴς **is** (force; comp. ἔσχον **ĕschŏn**, a form of 2192); forcefulness (lit. or fig.):—ability, might ([-ily]), power, strength.

2480. ἰσχύω **ischuō**, is-khoo'-o; from 2479; to have (or exercise) force (lit. or fig.):—be able, avail, can do ([-not]), could, be good, might, prevail, be of strength, be whole, + much work.

2481. ἴσως **isōs**, ee'-soce; adv. from 2470; likely, i.e. perhaps:—it may be.

2482. Ἰταλία **Italia**, ee-tal-ee'-ah; prob. of for. or.; Italia, a region of Europe:—Italy.

2483. Ἰταλικός **Italikŏs**, ee-tal-ee-kos'; from 2482; Italic, i.e. belonging to Italia:—Italian.

2484. Ἰτουραία **Itŏuraia**, ee-too-rah'-yah; of Heb. or. [3195]; Ituræa (i.e. Jetur), a region of Pal.:—Ituræa.

2485. ἰχθύδιον **ichthudiŏn**, ikh-thoo'-dee-on; dimin. from 2486; a petty fish:—little (small) fish.

2486. ἰχθύς **ichthus**, ikh-thoos'; of uncert. affin.; a fish:—fish.

2487. ἴχνος **ichnŏs**, ikh'-nos; from ἱκνέομαι **iknĕŏmai** (to arrive; comp. 2240); a track (fig.):—step.

2488. Ἰωάθαμ **Iŏatham**, ee-o-ath'-am; of Heb. or. [3147]; Joatham (i.e. Jotham), an Isr.:—Joatham.

2489. Ἰωάννα **Iŏanna**, ee-o-an'-nah; fem. of the same as 2491; Joanna, a Chr.:—Joanna.

2490. Ἰωαννᾶς **Iŏannas**, ee-o-an-nas'; a form of 2491; Joannas, an Isr.:—Joannas.

2491. Ἰωάννης **Iŏannēs**, ee-o-an'-nace; of Heb. or. [3110]; Joannes (i.e. Jochanan), the name of four Isr.:—John.

2492. Ἰώβ **Iŏb**, ee-obe'; of Heb. or. [347]; Job (i.e. Ijob), a patriarch:—Job.

2493. Ἰωήλ **Iŏēl**, ee-o-ale'; of Heb. or. [3100]; Joel, an Isr.:—Joel.

2494. Ἰωνάν **Iŏnan**, ee-o-nan'; prob. for 2491 or 2495; Jonan, an Isr.:—Jonan.

2495. Ἰωνᾶς **Iŏnas**, ee-o-nas'; of Heb. or. [3124]; Jonas (i.e. Jonah), the name of two Isr.:—Jonas.

2496. Ἰωράμ **Iŏram**, ee-o-ram'; of Heb. or. [3141]; Joram, an Isr.:—Joram.

2497. Ἰωρείμ **Iŏrĕim**, ee-o-rime'; perh. for 2496; Jorim, an Isr.:—Jorim.

2498. Ἰωσαφάτ **Iŏsaphat**, ee-o-saf-at'; of Heb. or. [3092]; Josaphat (i.e. Jehoshaphat), an Isr.:—Josaphat.

2499. Ἰωσή **Iŏsē**, ee-o-say'; gen. of 2500; Jose, an Isr.:—Jose.

2500. Ἰωσῆς **Iŏsēs**, ee-o-sace'; perh. for 2501; Joses, the name of two Isr.:—Joses. Comp. 2499.

2501. Ἰωσήφ **Iŏsēph**, ee-o-safe'; of Heb. or. [3130]; Joseph, the name of seven Isr.:—Joseph.

2502. Ἰωσίας **Iŏsias**, ee-o-see'-as; of Heb. or. [2977]; Josias (i.e. Joshiah), an Isr.:—Josias.

2503. ἰῶτα **iŏta**, ee-o'-tah; of Heb. or. [the tenth letter of the Heb. alphabet]; "iota", the name of the ninth letter of the Gr. alphabet, put (fig.) for a very small part of anything:—jot.

K

2504. κἀγώ **kagō**, kag-o'; from 2532 and 1473 (so also the dat.

κἀμοί **kamŏi**, kam-oy'; and acc.

κἀμέ **kamĕ**, kam-eh'; and (or also, even, etc.) I, (to) me:—(and, even, even so, so) I (also, in like wise), both me, me also.

2505. καθά **katha**, kath-ah'; from 2596 and the neut. plur. of 3739; according to which things, i.e. just as:—as.

2506. καθαίρεσις **kathairĕsis**, kath-ah'ee-res-is; from 2507; demolition; fig. extinction:—destruction, pulling down.

2507. καθαιρέω **kathairĕō**, kath-ahee-reh'-o; from 2596 and 138 (includ. its alt.); to lower (or with violence) demolish (lit. or fig.):—cast (pull, put, take) down, destroy.

2508. καθαίρω **kathairō**, kath-ah'ee-ro; from 2513; to cleanse, i.e. (spec.) to prune; fig. to expiate:—purge.

2509. καθάπερ **kathapĕr**, kath-ap'-er; from 2505 and 4007; exactly as:—(even, as well) as.

2510. καθάπτω **kathaptō**, kath-ap'-to; from 2596 and 680; to seize upon:—fasten on.

2511. καθαρίζω **katharizō**, kath-ar-id'-zo; from 2513; to cleanse (lit. or fig.):—(make) clean (-se), purge, purify.

2512. καθαρισμός **katharismŏs**, kath-ar-is-mos'; from 2511; a washing off, i.e. (cer.) ablution, (mor.) expiation:—cleansing, + purge, purification, (-fying).

2513. καθαρός **katharŏs**, kath-ar-os'; of uncert. affin.; clean (lit. or fig.):—clean, clear, pure.

2514. καθαρότης **katharŏtēs**, kath-ar-ot'-ace; from 2513; cleanness (cer.):—purification.

2515. καθέδρα **kathĕdra**, kath-ed'-rah; from 2596 and the base of 1476; a bench (lit. or fig.):—seat.

2516. καθέζομαι **kathĕzŏmai**, kath-ed'-zom-ahee; from 2596 and the base of 1476; to sit down:—sit.

2517. καθεξῆς **kathĕxēs**, kath-ex-ace'; from 2596 and 1836; thereafter, i.e. consecutively; as a noun (by ell. of noun) a subsequent person or time:—after (-ward), by (in) order.

2518. καθεύδω **kathĕudō**, kath-yoo'-do; from 2596 and εὕδω **hĕudō** (to sleep); to lie down to rest, i.e. (by impl.) to fall asleep (lit. or fig.):—(be a-) sleep.

2519. καθηγητής **kathēgētēs**, kath-ayg-ay-tace'; from a comp. of 2596 and 2233; a guide, i.e. (fig.) a teacher:—master.

2520. καθήκω **kathēkō**, kath-ay'-ko; from 2596 and 2240; to reach to, i.e. (neut. of pres. act. part., fig. as adj.) becoming:—convenient, fit.

2521. κάθημαι **kathēmai**, kath'-ay-mahee; from 2596 and ἧμαι **hēmai** (to sit; akin to the base of 1476); to sit down; fig. to remain, reside:—dwell, sit (by, down).

2522. καθημερινός **kathēmĕrinŏs**, kath-ay-mer-ee-nos'; from 2596 and 2250; quotidian:—daily.

2523. καθίζω **kathizō**, kath-id'-zo; another (act.) form for 2516; to seat down, i.e. set (fig. appoint); intrans. to sit (down); fig. to settle (hover, dwell):—continue, set, sit (down), tarry.

2524. καθίημι **kathiēmi**, kath-ee'-ay-mee; from 2596 and ἵημι **hiēmi** (to send); to lower:—let down.

2525. καθίστημι **kathistēmi**, kath-is'-tay-mee; from 2596 and 2476; to place down (permanently), i.e. (fig.) to designate, constitute, convoy:—appoint, be, conduct, make, ordain, set.

2526. καθό **kathŏ**, kath-o'; from 2596 and 3739; according to which thing, i.e. precisely as, in proportion as:—according to that, (inasmuch) as.

2526'. καθολικός **kathŏlikŏs**, kath-ol-ee-kos'; from 2527; universal:—general.

2527. καθόλου **kathŏlŏu**, kath-ol'-oo; from 2596 and 3650; on the whole, i.e. entirely:—at all.

2528. καθοπλίζω **kathŏplizō**, kath-op-lid'-zo; from 2596 and 3695; to equip fully with armor:—arm.

2529. καθοράω **kathŏraō**, kath-or-ah'-o; from 2596 and 3708; to behold fully, i.e. (fig.) distinctly apprehend:—clearly see.

2530. καθότι **kathŏti**, kath-ot'-ee; from 2596 and 3739 and 5100; according to which certain thing, i.e. as far (or inasmuch) as:—(according, forasmuch) as, because (that).

2531. καθώς **kathōs**, *kath-oce';* from *2596* and *5613; just* (or *inasmuch*) *as, that:*—according to, (according, even) as, how, when.

2532. καί **kai**, *kahee;* appar. a prim. particle, having a *copulative* and sometimes also a *cumulative* force ; *and, also, even, so, then, too,* etc. ; often used in connection (or composition) with other particles or small words :—and, also, both, but, even, for, if, indeed, likewise, moreover, or, so, that, then, therefore, when, yea, yet.

2533. Καϊάφας **Kaïaphas**, *kah-ee-af'-as;* of Chald. or.; *the dell; Caïapha* (i.e. *Cajepha*), an Isr.:—Caiaphas.

2534. καίγε **kaige**, *ka'hee-gheh;* from *2532* and *1065; and at least* (or *even, indeed*):—and, at least.

2535. Κάϊν **Kaïn**, *kah'-in;* of Heb. or. [7014]; *Caïn* (i.e. *Cajin*), the son of Adam:—Cain.

2536. Καϊνάν **Kaïnan**, *kah-ee-nan';* of Heb. or. [7018]; *Caïnan* (i.e. *Kenan*), the name of two patriarchs:—Cainan.

2537. καινός **kainŏs**, *kahee-nos';* of uncert. affin.; *new* (espec. in *freshness;* while *3501* is prop. so with respect to *age*):—new.

2538. καινότης **kainŏtēs**, *kahee-not'-ace;* from *2537;* renewal (fig.):—newness.

2539. καίπερ **kaipĕr**; from *2532* and *4007; and indeed,* i.e. *nevertheless* or *notwithstanding:*—and yet, although.

2540. καιρός **kairŏs**, *kahee-ros';* of uncert. affin.; an *occasion,* i.e. *set* or *proper time:*— × always, opportunity, (convenient, due) season, (due, short, while) time, a while. Comp. *5550.*

2541. Καίσαρ **Kaisar**, *kah'ee-sar;* of Lat. or.; *Cæsar,* a title of the Rom. emperor:—Cæsar.

2542. Καισάρεια **Kaisarĕia**, *kahee-sar'-i-a;* from *2541; Cæsaria,* the name of two places in Pal.:—Cæsarea.

2543. καίτοι **kaitŏi**, *kah'ee-toy;* from *2532* and *5104; and yet,* i.e. *nevertheless:*—although.

2544. καίτοιγε **kaitŏigĕ**, *kah'ee-toyg-eh;* from *2543* and *1065; and yet indeed,* i.e. *although really:*—nevertheless, though.

2545. καίω **kaiō**, *kah'-yo;* appar. a prim. verb; to *set on fire,* i.e. *kindle* or (by impl.) *consume:*—burn, light.

2546. κάκεῖ **kakĕi**, *kak-i';* from *2532* and *1563; likewise in that place:*—and there, there (thither) also.

2547. κάκεῖθεν **kakĕithĕn**, *kak-i'-then;* from *2532* and *1564; likewise from that place* (or *time*):—and afterward (from) (thence), thence also.

2548. κάκεῖνος **kakĕinŏs**, *kak-i'-nos;* from *2532* and *1565; likewise that* (or *those*):—and him (other, them), even he, him also, them (also), (and) they.

2549. κακία **kakia**, *kak-ee'-ah;* from *2556; badness,* i.e. (subj.) *depravity,* or (act.) *malignity,* or (pass.) *trouble:*—evil, malice (-iousness), naughtiness, wickedness.

2550. κακοήθεια **kakŏēthĕia**, *kak-ŏ-ay'-thi-ah;* from a comp. of *2556* and *2239; bad character,* i.e. (spec.) *mischievousness:*—malignity.

2551. κακολογέω **kakŏlŏgĕō**, *kak-ol-og-eh'-o;* from a comp. of *2556* and *3056;* to *revile:*—curse, speak evil of.

2552. κακοπάθεια **kakŏpathĕia**, *kak-op-ath'-i-ah;* from a comp. of *2556* and *3806; hardship:*—suffering affliction.

2553. κακοπαθέω **kakŏpathĕō**, *kak-op-ath-eh'-o;* from the same as *2552;* to *undergo hardship:*—be afflicted, endure afflictions (hardness), suffer trouble.

2554. κακοποιέω **kakŏpŏiĕō**, *kak-op-oy-eh'-o;* from *2555;* to *be a bad-doer,* i.e. (obj.) to *injure,* or (gen.) to *sin:*—do (-ing) evil.

2555. κακοποιός **kakŏpŏiŏs**, *kak-op-oy-os';* from *2556* and *4160;* a *bad-doer;* (spec.) a *criminal:*—evil-doer, malefactor.

2556. κακός **kakŏs**, *kak-os';* appar. a prim. word; *worthless* (intrinsically such; whereas *4190* prop. refers to *effects*), i.e. (subj.) *depraved,* or (obj.) *injurious:*—bad, evil, harm, ill, noisome, wicked.

2557. κακοῦργος **kakŏurgŏs**, *kak-oor'-gos;* from *2556* and the base of *2041;* a *wrong-doer,* i.e. *criminal:*—evil-doer, malefactor.

2558. κακουχέω **kakŏuchĕō**, *kak-oo-kheh'-o;* from a presumed comp. of *2556* and *2192;* to *maltreat:*—which suffer adversity, torment.

2559. κακόω **kakŏō**, *kak-ŏ'-o;* from *2556;* to *injure;* fig. to *exasperate:*—make evil affected, entreat evil, harm, hurt, vex.

2560. κακῶς **kakōs**, *kak-oce';* adv. from *2556; badly* (phys. or mor.):—amiss, diseased, evil, grievously, miserably, sick, sore.

2561. κάκωσις **kakōsis**, *kak'-o-sis;* from *2559; maltreatment:*—affliction.

2562. καλάμη **kalamē**, *kal-am'-ay;* fem. of *2563;* a *stalk* of grain, i.e. (collect.) *stubble:*—stubble.

2563. κάλαμος **kalamŏs**, *kal'-am-os;* of uncert. affin.; a *reed* (the plant or its stem, or that of a similar plant); by impl. a *pen:*—pen, reed.

2564. καλέω **kalĕō**, *kal-eh'-o;* akin to the base of *2753;* to "*call*" (prop. aloud, but used in a variety of applications, dir. or otherwise):—bid, call (forth), (whose, whose sur-) name (was [called]).

2565. καλλιέλαιος **kalliĕlaiŏs**, *kal-le-el'-ah-yos;* from the base of *2566* and *1636;* a *cultivated* olive tree, i.e. a *domesticated* or *improved* one:—good olive tree.

2566. καλλίον **kalliŏn**, *kal-lee'-on;* neut. of the (irreg.) comp. of *2570;* (adv.) *better* than many:—very well.

2567. καλοδιδάσκαλος **kalŏdidaskalŏs**, *kal-od-id-as'-kal-os;* from *2570* and *1320;* a *teacher* of the *right:*—teacher of good things.

2568. Καλοί Λιμένες **Kalŏi Limĕnĕs**, *kal-oy' lee-men'-es;* plur. of *2570* and *3040; Good Harbors,* i.e. *Fairhaven,* a bay of Crete:—fair havens.

2569. καλοποιέω **kalŏpŏiĕō**, *kal-op-oy-eh'-o;* from *2570* and *4160;* to *do well,* i.e. live *virtuously:*—well doing.

2570. καλός **kalŏs**, *kal-os';* of uncert. affin.; prop. *beautiful,* but chiefly (fig.) *good* (lit. or mor.), i.e. *valuable* or *virtuous* (for *appearance* or *use,* and thus distinguished from *18,* which is prop. *intrinsic*):— × better, fair, good (-ly), honest, meet, well, worthy.

2571. κάλυμα **kaluma**, *kal'-oo-mah;* from *2572;* a *cover,* i.e. *veil:*—vail.

2572. καλύπτω **kaluptō**, *kal-oop'-to;* akin to *2813* and *2928;* to *cover* up (lit. or fig.):—cover, hide.

2573. καλῶς **kalōs**, *kal-oce';* adv. from *2570; well* (usually mor.):—(in a) good (place), honestly, + recover, (full) well.

2574. κάμηλος **kamēlŏs**, *kam'-ay-los;* of Heb. or. [1581]; a "*camel*":—camel.

2575. κάμινος **kaminŏs**, *kam'-ee-nos;* prob. from *2545;* a *furnace:*—furnace.

2576. καμμύω **kammuō**, *kam-moo'-o;* for a comp. of *2596* and the base of *3466;* to *shut down,* i.e. *close* the eyes:—close.

2577. κάμνω **kamnō**, *kam'-no;* appar. a prim. verb; prop. to *toil,* i.e. (by impl.) to *tire* (fig. *faint, sicken*):—faint, sicken, be wearied.

2578. κάμπτω **kamptō**, *kamp'-to;* appar. a prim. verb; to *bend:*—bow.

2579. κάν **kan**, *kan;* from *2532* and *1437; and* (or *even*) *if:*—and (also) if (so much as), if but, at the least, though, yet.

2580. Κανᾶ **Kana**, *kan-ah';* of Heb. or. [comp. 7071]; *Cana,* a place in Pal.:—Cana.

2581. Κανανίτης **Kananitēs**, *kan-an-ee'-tace;* of Chald. or. [comp. 7067]; *zealous; Cananites,* an epithet:—Canaanite [by mistake for a der. from *5477*].

2582. Κανδάκη **Kandakē**, *kan-dak'-ay;* of for. or.; *Candace,* an Eg. queen:—Candace.

2583. κανών **kanōn**, *kan-ohn';* from κάνη **kanē** (a straight *reed,* i.e. *rod*); a *rule* ("*canon*"), i.e. (fig.) a *standard* (of faith and practice); by impl. a *boundary,* i.e. (fig.) a *sphere* (of activity):—line, rule.

2584. Καπερναούμ **Kapĕrnaŏum**, *cap-er-nah-oom';* of Heb. or. [prob. 3723 and 5151]; *Capernaüm* (i.e. *Caphanachum*), a place in Pal.:—Capernaum.

2585. καπηλεύω **kapēlĕuō**, *kap-ale-yoo'-o;* from κάπηλος **kapēlŏs** (a *huckster*); to *retail,* i.e. (by impl.) to *adulterate* (fig.):—corrupt.

2586. καπνός **kapnŏs**, *kap-nos';* of uncert. affin.; *smoke:*—smoke.

2587. Καππαδοκία **Kappadŏkia**, *kap-pad-ok-ee'-ah;* of for. or.; *Cappadocia,* a region of Asia Minor:—Cappadocia.

2588. καρδία **kardia**, *kar-dee'-ah;* prol. from a prim. κάρ **kar** (Lat. *cor,* "*heart*"); the *heart,* i.e. (fig.) the *thoughts* or *feelings* (*mind*); also (by anal.) the *middle:*—(+ broken-) heart (-ed).

2589. καρδιογνώστης **kardiŏgnōstēs**, *kar-dee-og-noce'-tace;* from *2588* and *1097;* a *heart-knower:*—which knowest the hearts.

2590. καρπός **karpŏs**, *kar-pos';* prob. from the base of *726; fruit* (as *plucked*), lit. or fig.:—fruit.

2591. Κάρπος **Karpŏs**, *kar'-pos;* perh. for *2590; Carpus,* prob. a Chr.:—Carpus.

2592. καρποφορέω **karpŏphŏrĕō**, *kar-pof-or-eh'-o;* from *2593;* to *be fertile* (lit. or fig.):—be (bear, bring forth) fruit (-ful).

2593. καρποφόρος **karpŏphŏrŏs**, *kar-pof-or'-os;* from *2590* and *5342; fruitbearing* (fig.):—fruitful.

2594. καρτερέω **kartĕrĕō**, *kar-ter-eh'-o;* from a der. of *2904* (transp.); to *be strong,* i.e. (fig.) *steadfast* (*patient*):—endure.

2595. κάρφος **karphŏs**, *kar'-fos;* from κάρφω **karphō** (to *wither*); a dry *twig* or *straw:*—mote.

2596. κατά **kata**, *kat-ah';* a prim. particle; (prep.) *down* (in place or time), in varied relations (according to the case [gen., dat. or acc.] with which it is joined):—about, according as (to), after, against, (when they were) × alone, among, and, × apart, (when), like) as (concerning, pertaining to, touching), × aside, at, before, beyond, by, to the charge of, [charita-] bly, concerning, + covered, [dai-] ly, down, every, (+ far more) exceeding, × more excellent, for, from . . . to, godly, in (-asmuch, divers, every, -to, respect of), . . . by, after the manner of, + by any means, beyond (out of) measure, × mightily, more, × natural, of (up-) on (× part), out (of every), over against, (+ your) × own, + particularly, so, through (-oughout, -oughout every), thus, (un-) to (-gether, -ward), × uttermost, where (-by), with. In composition it retains many of these applications, and frequently denotes *opposition, distribution* or *intensity.*

2597. καταβαίνω **katabainō**, *kat-ab-ah'ee-no;* from *2596* and *939;* to *descend* (lit. or fig.):—come (get, go, step) down, descend, fall (down).

2598. καταβάλλω **kataballō**, *kat-ab-al'-lo;* from *2596* and *906;* to *throw down:*—cast down, descend, fall (down).

2599. καταβαρέω **katabarĕō**, *kat-ab-ar-eh'-o;* from *2596* and *916;* to *impose upon:*—burden.

2600. κατάβασις **katabasis**, *kat-ab'-as-is;* from *2597;* a *declivity:*—descent.

2601. καταβιβάζω **katabibazō**, *kat-ab-ib-ad'-zo;* from *2596* and a der. of the base of *901;* to *cause to go down,* i.e. *precipitate:*—bring (thrust) down.

2602. καταβολή **katabŏlē**, *kat-ab-ol-ay';* from *2598;* a *deposition,* i.e. *founding;* fig. *conception:*—conceive, foundation.

2603. καταβραβεύω **katabrabĕuō**, *kat-ab-rab-yoo'-o;* from *2596* and *1018* (in its orig. sense); to *award the price against,* i.e. (fig.) to *defraud* (of salvation):—beguile of reward.

2604. καταγγελεύς **kataggĕlĕus**, *kat-ang-gel-yooce';* from *2605;* a *proclaimer:*—setter forth.

2605. καταγγέλλω **kataggĕllō**, *kat-ang-gel'-lo;* from *2596* and the base of *32;* to *proclaim, promulgate:*—declare, preach, shew, speak of, teach.

2606. καταγελάω **katagĕlaō**, *kat-ag-el-ah'-o;* to *laugh down,* i.e. *deride:*—laugh to scorn.

2607. καταγινώσκω **kataginōskō**, *kat-ag-in-o'-sko;* from *2596* and *1097;* to *note against,* i.e. *find fault with:*—blame, condemn.

2608. κατάγνυμι **katagnumi**, *kat-ag'-noo-mee;* from *2596* and the base of *4486;* to *rend in pieces,* i.e. *crack apart:*—break.

2609. κατάγω **katagō**, *kat-ag'-o;* from *2596* and *71;* to *lead down;* spec. to *moor* a vessel:—bring (down, forth), (bring to) land, touch.

2610. ματαγωνίζομαι **katagōnizŏmai**, *kat-ag-o-nid'-zom-ahee;* from *2596* and *75;* to *struggle against,* i.e. (by impl.) to *overcome:*—subdue.

2611. καταδέω **katadĕŏ**, *kat-ad-eh'-o;* from *2596* and *1210;* to *tie down,* i.e. *bandage* (a wound):—bind up.

2612. κατάδηλος **katadēlŏs**, *kat-ad'-ay-los;* from *2596* intens. and *1212; manifest:*—far more evident.

2613. καταδικάζω **katadĭkazō**, *kat-ad-ik-ad'-zo;* from *2596* and a der. of *1349;* to *adjudge against,* i.e. *pronounce guilty:*—condemn.

2614. καταδιώκω **katadĭōkō**, *kat-ad-ee-o'-ko;* from *2596* and *1377;* to *hunt down,* i.e. *search for:*—follow after.

2615. καταδουλόω **katadŏulŏō**, *kat-ad-oo-lŏ'-o;* from *2596* and *1402;* to *enslave utterly:*—bring into bondage.

2616. καταδυναστεύω **katadunastĕuō**, *kat-ad-oo-nas-tyoo'-o;* from *2596* and a der. of *1413;* to *exercise dominion against,* i.e. *oppress:*—oppress.

2617. καταισχύνω **kataischunō**, *kat-ahee-skhoo'-no;* from *2596* and *153;* to *shame down,* i.e. *disgrace* or (by impl.) *put to the blush:*—confound, dishonour, (be a-, make a-) shame (-d).

2618. κατακαίω **katakaiō**, *kat-ak-ah'ee-o;* from *2596* and *2545;* to *burn down* (to the ground), i.e. *consume wholly:*—burn (up, utterly).

2619. κατακαλύπτω **katakaluptō**, *kat-ak-al-oop'-to;* from *2596* and *2572;* to *cover wholly,* i.e. *veil:*—cover, hide.

2620. κατακαυχάομαι **katakauchaŏmai**, *kat-ak-ŏw-khah'-om-ahee;* from *2596* and *2744;* to *exult against* (i.e. *over*):—boast (against), glory, rejoice against.

2621. κατάκειμαι **katakĕimai**, *kat-ak'-i-mahee;* from *2596* and *2749;* to *lie down,* i.e. (by impl.) *be sick;* spec. to *recline* at a meal:—keep, lie, sit at meat (down).

2622. κατακλάω **kataklaō**, *kat-ak-lah'-o;* from *2596* and *2806;* to *break down,* i.e. *divide:*—break.

2623. κατακλείω **kataklĕiō**, *kat-ak-li'-o;* from *2596* and *2808;* to *shut down* (in a dungeon), i.e. *incarcerate:*—shut up.

2624. κατακληροδοτέω **kataklērŏdŏtĕō**, *kat-ak-lay-rod-ot-eh'-o;* from *2596* and a der. of a comp. of *2819* and *1325;* to *be a giver of lots to each,* i.e. (by impl.) to *apportion an estate:*—divide by lot.

2625. κατακλίνω **kataklĭnō**, *kat-ak-lee'-no;* from *2596* and *2827;* to *recline down,* i.e. (spec.) to *take a place at table:*—(make) sit down (at meat).

2626. κατακλύζω **katakluzō**, *kat-ak-lood'-zo;* from *2596* and the base of *2830;* to *dash* (wash) *down,* i.e. (by impl.) to *deluge:*—overflow.

2627. κατακλυσμός **kataklusmŏs**, *kat-ak-looce-mos';* from *2626;* an *inundation:*—flood.

2628. κατακολουθέω **katakŏlŏuthĕō**, *kat-ak-ol-oo-theh'-o;* from *2596* and *190;* to *accompany closely:*—follow (after).

2629. κατακόπτω **katakŏptō**, *kat-ak-op'-to;* from *2596* and *2875;* to *chop down,* i.e. *mangle:*—cut.

2630. κατακρημνίζω **katakrēmnizō**, *kat-ak-rame-nid'-zo;* from *2596* and a der. of *2911;* to *precipitate down:*—cast down headlong.

2631. κατάκριμα **katakrima**, *kat-ak'-ree-mah;* from *2632;* an *adverse sentence* (the verdict):—condemnation.

2632. κατακρίνω **katakrinō**, *kat-ak-ree'-no;* from *2596* and *2919;* to *judge against,* i.e. *sentence:*—condemn, damn.

2633. κατάκρισις **katakrisis**, *kat-ak'-ree-sis;* from *2632; sentencing adversely* (the act):—condemn (-ation).

2634. κατακυριεύω **katakurĭĕuō**, *kat-ak-oo-ree-yoo'-o;* from *2596* and *2961;* to *lord against,* i.e. *control, subjugate:*—exercise dominion over (lordship), be lord over, overcome.

2635. καταλαλέω **katalalĕō**, *kat-al-al-eh'-o;* from *2637;* to *be a traducer,* i.e. to *slander:*—speak against (evil of).

2636. καταλαλία **katalalia**, *kat-al-al-ee'-ah;* from *2637; defamation:*—backbiting, evil speaking.

2637. κατάλαλος **katalalŏs**, *kat-al'-al-os;* from *2596* and the base of *2980; talkative against,* i.e. a *slanderer:*—backbiter.

2638. καταλαμβάνω **katalambanō**, *kat-al-am-ban'-o;* from *2596* and *2983;* to *take eagerly,* i.e. *seize, possess,* etc. (lit. or fig.):—apprehend, attain, come upon, comprehend, find, obtain, perceive, (over-) take.

2639. καταλέγω **katalĕgō**, *kat-al-eg'-o;* from *2596* and *3004* (in its orig. mean.); to *lay down,* i.e. (fig.) to *enrol:*—take into the number.

2640. κατάλειμμα **katalĕimma**, *kat-al'-ime-mah;* from *2641;* a *remainder,* i.e. (by impl.) a *few:*—remnant.

2641. καταλείπω **katalĕipō**, *kat-al-i'-po;* from *2596* and *3007;* to *leave down,* i.e. *behind;* by impl. to *abandon, have remaining:*—forsake, leave, reserve.

2642. καταλιθάζω **katalithazō**, *kat-al-ith-ad'-zo;* from *2596* and *3034;* to *stone down,* i.e. to *death:*—stone.

2643. καταλλαγή **katallagē**, *kat-al-lag-ay';* from *2644; exchange* (fig. *adjustment*), i.e. *restoration* to (the divine) *favor:*—atonement, reconciliation (-ing).

2644. καταλλάσσω **katallassō**, *.kat-al-las'-so;* from *2596* and *236;* to *change mutually,* i.e. (fig.) to *compound a difference:*—reconcile.

2645. κατάλοιπος **katalŏipŏs**, *kat-al'-oy-pos;* from *2596* and *3062; left down* (behind), i.e. *remaining* (plur. the *rest*):—residue.

2646. κατάλυμα **kataluma**, *kat-al'-oo-mah;* from *2647;* prop. a *dissolution* (breaking up of a journey), i.e. (by impl.) a *lodging-place:*—guestchamber, inn.

2647. καταλύω **kataluō**, *kat-al-oo'-o;* from *2596* and *3089;* to *loosen down* (disintegrate), i.e. (by impl.) to *demolish* (lit. or fig.); spec. [comp. *2646*] to *halt for the night:*—destroy, dissolve, be guest, lodge, come to nought, overthrow, throw down.

2648. καταμανθάνω **katamanthanō**, *kat-am-an-than'-o;* from *2596* and *3129;* to *learn thoroughly,* i.e. (by impl.) to *note carefully:*—consider.

2649. καταμαρτυρέω **katamarturĕō**, *kat-am-ar-too-reh'-o;* from *2596* and *3140;* to *testify against:*—witness against.

2650. καταμένω **katamĕnō**, *kat-am-en'-o;* from *2596* and *3306;* to *stay fully,* i.e. *reside:*—abide.

2651. καταμόνας **katamŏnas**, *kat-am-on'-as;* from *2596* and acc. plur. fem. of *3441* (with *5561* impl.); *according to sole places,* i.e. (adv.) *separately:*—alone.

2652. κατανάθεμα **katanathĕma**, *kat-an-ath'-em-ah;* from *2596* (intens.) and *331;* an *imprecation:*—curse.

2653. καταναθεματίζω **katanathĕmatizō**, *kat-an-ath-em-at-id'-zo;* from *2596* (intens.) and *332;* to *imprecate:*—curse.

2654. καταναλίσκω **katanaliskō**, *kat-an-al-is'-ko;* from *2596* and *355;* to *consume utterly:*—consume.

2655. καταναρκάω **katanarkaō**, *kat-an-ar-kah'-o;* from *2596* and *ναρκάω* narkaō (to be *numb*); to *grow utterly torpid,* i.e. (by impl.) *slothful* (fig. *expensive*):—be burdensome (chargeable).

2656. κατανεύω **katanĕuō**, *kat-an-yoo'-o;* from *2596* and *3506;* to *nod down* (towards), i.e. (by anal.) to *make signs to:*—beckon.

2657. κατανοέω **katanŏĕō**, *kat-an-o-eh'-o;* from *2596* and *3539;* to *observe fully:*—behold, consider, discover, perceive.

2658. καταντάω **katantaō**, *kat-an-tah'-o;* from *2596* and a der. of *473;* to *meet against,* i.e. *arrive* at (lit. or fig.):—attain, come.

2659. κατάνυξις **katanuxis**, *kat-an'-oox-is;* from *2660;* a *prickling* (sensation, as of the limbs

asleep), i.e. (by impl. [perh. by some confusion with *3506* or even with *3571*]) *stupor* (*lethargy*):—slumber.

2660. κατανύσσω **katanussō**, *kat-an-oos'-so;* from *2596* and *3572;* to *pierce thoroughly,* i.e. (fig.) to *agitate violently* (" sting to the quick"):—prick.

2661. καταξιόω **kataxiŏō**, *kat-ax-ee-ŏ'-o;* from *2596* and *515;* to *deem entirely deserving:*—(ac-) count worthy.

2662. καταπατέω **katapatĕō**, *kat-ap-at-eh'-o;* from *2596* and *3961;* to *trample down;* fig. to *reject* with disdain:—trample, tread (down, underfoot).

2663. κατάπαυσις **katapausis**, *kat-ap'-ŏw-sis;* from *2664; reposing down,* i.e. (by Hebr.) *abode:*—rest.

2664. καταπαύω **katapauō**, *kat-ap-ŏw'-o;* from *2596* and *3973;* to *settle down,* i.e. (lit.) to *colonize,* or (fig.) to (*cause* to) *desist:*—cease, (give) rest (-rain).

2665. καταπέτασμα **katapĕtasma**, *kat-ap-et'-as-mah;* from a comp. of *2596* and a congener of *4072; something spread thoroughly,* i.e. (spec.) the *door screen* (to the Most Holy Place) in the Jewish Temple:—vail.

2666. καταπίνω **katapinō**, *kat-ap-ee'-no;* from *2596* and *4095;* to *drink down,* i.e. *gulp entire* (lit. or fig.):—devour, drown, swallow (up).

2667. καταπίπτω **katapiptō**, *kat-ap-ip'-to;* from *2596* and *4098;* to *fall down:*—fall (down).

2668. καταπλέω **kataplĕō**, *kat-ap-leh'-o;* from *2596* and *4126;* to *sail down* upon a place, i.e. to *land* at:—arrive.

2669. καταπονέω **kataponĕō**, *kat-ap-on-eh'-o;* from *2596* and a der. of *4102;* to *labor down,* i.e. *wear with toil* (fig. *harass*):—oppress, vex.

2670. καταποντίζω **katapontizō**, *kat-ap-on-tid'-zo;* from *2596* and a der. of the same as *4195;* to *plunge down,* i.e. *submerge:*—drown, sink.

2671. κατάρα **katara**, *kat-ar'-ah;* from *2596* (intens.) and *685; imprecation, execration:*—curse (-d, -ing).

2672. καταράομαι **kataraŏmai**, *kat-ar-ah'-om-ahee;* mid. from *2671;* to *execrate;* by anal. to *doom:*—curse.

2673. καταργέω **katargĕō**, *kat-arg-eh'-o;* from *2596* and *691;* to *be* (render) *entirely idle* (*useless*), lit. or fig.:—abolish, cease, cumber, deliver, destroy, do away, become (make) of no (none, without) effect, fail, loose, bring (come) to nought, put away (down), vanish away, make void.

2674. καταριθμέω **katarithmĕō**, *kat-ar-ith-meh'-o;* from *2596* and *705;* to *reckon among:*—number with.

2675. καταρτίζω **katartizō**, *kat-ar-tid'-zo;* from *2596* and a der. of *739;* to *complete thoroughly,* i.e. *repair* (lit. or fig.) or *adjust:*—fit, frame, mend, (make) perfect (-ly join together), prepare, restore.

2676. κατάρτισις **katartisis**, *kat-ar'-tis-is;* from *2675; thorough equipment* (subj.):—perfection.

2677. καταρτισμός **katartismŏs**, *kat-ar-tis-mos';* from *2675; complete furnishing* (obj.):—perfecting.

2678. κατασείω **katasĕiō**, *kat-as-i'-o;* from *2596* and *4579;* to *sway downward,* i.e. *make a signal:*—beckon.

2679. κατασκάπτω **kataskaptō**, *kat-as-kap'-to;* from *2596* and *4626;* to *undermine,* i.e. (by impl.) *destroy:*—dig down, ruin.

2680. κατασκευάζω **kataskĕuazō**, *kat-ask-yoo-ad'-zo;* from *2596* and a der. of *4632;* to *prepare thoroughly* (prop. by external *equipment;* whereas *2090* refers rather to internal *fitness*); by impl. to *construct, create:*—build, make, ordain, prepare.

2681. κατασκηνόω **kataskēnŏō**, *kat-as-kay-nŏ'-o;* from *2596* and *4637;* to *camp down,* i.e. *haunt;* fig. to *remain:*—lodge, rest.

2682. κατασκήνωσις **kataskēnōsis**, *kat-as-kay'-no-sis;* from *2681;* an *encamping,* i.e. (fig.) a *perch:*—nest.

2683. κατασκιάζω **kataskiazō**, *kat-as-kee-ad'-zo;* from *2596* and a der. of *4639;* to *overshade,* i.e. *cover:*—shadow.

2684. κατασκοπέω **kataskŏpĕō,** *kat-as-kop-eh'-o;* from *2685;* to be a sentinel, i.e. to inspect insidiously:—spy out.

2685. κατάσκοπος **kataskŏpŏs,** *kat-as'-kop-os;* from *2596* (intens.) and *4649* (in the sense of a watcher); a reconnoiterer:—spy.

2686. κατασοφίζομαι **katasŏphizŏmai,** *kat-as-of-id'-zom-ahee;* mid. from *2596* and *4679;* to be crafty against, i.e. circumvent:—deal subtilly with.

2687. κατασtέλλω **katastĕllō,** *kat-as-tel'-lo;* from *2596* and *4724;* to put down, i.e. quell:—appease, quiet.

2688. κατάστημα **katastēma,** *kat-as'-tay-mah;* from *2525;* prop. a position or condition, i.e. (subj.) demeanor:—behaviour.

2689. καταστολή **katastŏlē,** *kat-as-tol-ay';* from *2687;* a deposit, i.e. (spec.) costume:—apparel.

2690. καταστρέφω **katastrĕphō,** *kat-as-tref'-o;* from *2596* and *4762;* to turn upside down, i.e. upset:—overthrow.

2691. καταστρηνιάω **katastrēniaō,** *kat-as-tray-nee-ah'-o;* from *2596* and *4763;* to become voluptuous against:—begin to wax wanton against.

2692. καταστροφή **katastrŏphē,** *kat-as-trof-ay';* from *2690;* an overturn ("catastrophe"), i.e. demolition; fig. apostasy:—overthrow, subverting.

2693. καταστρώννυμι **katastrōnnumi,** *kat-as-trone'-noo-mee;* from *2596* and *4766;* to strew down, i.e. (by impl.) to prostrate (slay):—overthrow.

2694. κατασύρω **katasurō,** *kat-as-oo'-ro;* from *2596* and *4951;* to drag down, i.e. arrest judicially:—hale.

2695. κατασφάττω **katasphattō,** *kat-as-fat'-to;* from *2596* and *4969;* to kill down, i.e. slaughter:—slay.

2696. κατασφραγίζω **katasphragizō,** *kat-as-frag-id'-zo;* from *2596* and *4972;* to seal closely:—seal.

2697. κατάσχεσις **kataschĕsis,** *kat-as'-khes-is;* from *2722;* a holding down, i.e. occupancy:—possession.

2698. κατατίθημι **katatithēmi,** *kat-at-ith'-ay-mee;* from *2596* and *5087;* to place down, i.e. deposit (lit. or fig.):—do, lay, shew.

2699. κατατομή **katatŏmē,** *kat-at-om-ay';* from a comp. of *2596* and τέμνω **tĕmnō** (to cut); a cutting down (off), i.e. mutilation (ironically):—concision. Comp. *609.*

2700. κατατοξεύω **katatŏxĕuō,** *kat-at-ox-yoo'-o;* from *2596* and a der. of *5115;* to shoot down with an arrow or other missile:—thrust through.

2701. κατατρέχω **katatrĕchō,** *kat-at-rekh'-o;* from *2596* and *5143;* to run down, i.e. hasten from a tower:—run down.

καταφάγω **kataphagō.** See *2719.*

2702. καταφέρω **kataphĕrō,** *kat-af-er'-o;* from *2596* and *5342* (includ. its alt.); to bear down, i.e. (fig.) overcome (with drowsiness); spec. to cast a vote:—fall, give, sink down.

2703. καταφεύγω **kataphĕugō,** *kat-af-yoo'-go;* from *2596* and *5343;* to flee down (away):—flee.

2704. καταφθείρω **kataphthĕirō,** *kat-af-thi'-ro;* from *2596* and *5351;* to spoil entirely, i.e. (lit.) to destroy; or (fig.) to deprave:—corrupt, utterly perish.

2705. καταφιλέω **kataphilĕō,** *kat-af-ee-lch'-o;* from *2596* and *5368;* to kiss earnestly:—kiss.

2706. καταφρονέω **kataphrŏnĕō,** *kat-af-ron-eh'-o;* from *2596* and *5426;* to think against, i.e. disesteem:—despise.

2707. καταφροντής **kataphrŏntēs,** *kat-af-ron-tace';* from *2706;* a contemner:—despiser.

2708. καταχέω **katachĕō,** *kat-akh-eh'-o;* from *2596* and χέω **chĕō** (to pour); to pour down (out):—pour.

2709. καταχθόνιος **katachthŏniŏs,** *kat-akh-thon'-ee-os;* from *2596* and χθών **chthōn** (the ground); subterranean, i.e. infernal (belonging to the world of departed spirits):—under the earth.

2710. καταχράομαι **katachraŏmai,** *kat-akh-rah'-om-ahee;* from *2596* and *5530;* to overuse, i.e. misuse:—abuse.

2711. καταψύχω **katapsuchō,** *kat-ap-soo'-kho;* from *2596* and *5594;* to cool down (off), i.e. refresh:—cool.

2712. κατείδωλος **katĕidōlŏs,** *kat-i'-do-los;* from *2596* (intens.) and *1497;* utterly idolatrous:—wholly given to idolatry.

κατελεύθω **katĕlĕuthō.** See *2718.*

2713. κατέναντι **katĕnanti,** *kat-en'-an-tee;* from *2596* and *1725;* directly opposite:—before, over against.

κατενέγκω **katĕnĕgkō.** See *2702.*

2714. κατενώπιον **katĕnōpiŏn,** *kat-en-o'-pee-on;* from *2596* and *1799;* directly in front of:—before (the presence of), in the sight of.

2715. κατεξουσιάζω **katĕxŏusiazō,** *kat-ex-oo-see-ad'-zo;* from *2596* and *1850;* to have (wield) full privilege over:—exercise authority.

2716. κατεργάζομαι **katĕrgazŏmai,** *kat-er-gad'-zom-ahee;* from *2596* and *2038;* to work fully, i.e. accomplish; by impl. to finish, fashion:—cause, do (deed), perform, work (out).

2717. κατέρχομαι **katĕrchŏmai,** *kat-er'-khom-ahee;* from *2596* and *2064* (includ. its alt.); to come (or go) down (lit. or fig.):—come (down), depart, descend, go down, land.

2719. κατεσθίω **katĕsthiō,** *kat-es-thee'-o;* from *2596* and *2068* (includ. its alt.); to eat down, i.e. devour (lit. or fig.):—devour.

2720. κατευθύνω **katĕuthunō,** *kat-yoo-thoo'-no;* from *2596* and *2116;* to straighten fully, i.e. (fig.) direct:—guide, direct.

2721. κατεφίστημι **katĕphistēmi,** *kat-ef-is'-tay-mee;* from *2596* and *2186;* to stand over against, i.e. rush upon (assault):—make insurrection against.

2722. κατέχω **katĕchō,** *kat-ekh'-o;* from *2596* and *2192;* to hold down (fast), in various applications (lit. or fig.):—have, hold (fast), keep (in memory), let, × make toward, possess, retain, seize on, stay, take, withhold.

2723. κατηγορέω **katēgŏrĕō,** *kat-ay-gor-eh'-o;* from *2725;* to be a plaintiff, i.e. to charge with some offence:—accuse, object.

2724. κατηγορία **katēgŏria,** *kat-ay-gor-ee'-ah;* from *2725;* a complaint ("category"), i.e. criminal charge:—accusation (× -ed).

2725. κατήγορος **katēgŏrŏs,** *kat-ay'-gor-os;* from *2596* and *58;* against one in the assembly, i.e. a complainant at law; spec. Satan:—accuser.

2726. κατήφεια **katēphĕia,** *kat-ay'-fi-ah;* from a comp. of *2596* and perh. a der. of the base of *5316* (mean. downcast in look); demureness, i.e. (by impl.) sadness:—heaviness.

2727. κατηχέω **katēchĕō,** *kat-ay-kheh'-o;* from *2596* and *2279;* to sound down into the ears, i.e. (by impl.) to indoctrinate ("catechize") or (gen.) to apprise of:—inform, instruct, teach.

2728. κατιόω **katiŏō,** *kat-ee-ŏ'-o;* from *2596* and a der. of *2447;* to rust down, i.e. corrode:—canker.

2729. κατισχύω **katischuō,** *kat-is-khoo'-o;* from *2596* and *2480;* to overpower:—prevail (against).

2730. κατοικέω **katŏikĕō,** *kat-oy-keh'-o;* from *2596* and *3611;* to house permanently, i.e. reside (lit. or fig.):—dwell (-er), inhabitant (-ter).

2731. κατοίκησις **katŏikēsis,** *kat-oy'-kay-sis;* from *2730;* residence (prop. the act; but by impl. concr. the mansion):—dwelling.

2732. κατοικητήριον **katŏikētēriŏn,** *kat-oy-kay-tay'-ree-on;* from a der. of *2730;* a dwelling-place:—habitation.

2733. κατοικία **katŏikia,** *kat-oy-kee'-ah;* residence (prop. the condition; but by impl. the abode itself):—habitation.

2734. κατοπτρίζομαι **katŏptrizŏmai,** *kat-op-trid'-zom-ahee;* mid. from a comp. of *2596* and a der. of *3700* [comp. *2072*]; to mirror oneself, i.e. to see reflected (fig.):—behold as in a glass.

2735. κατόρθωμα **katŏrthōma,** *kat-or'-tho-mah;* from a comp. of *2596* and a der. of *3717* [comp. *1357*]; something made fully upright, i.e. (fig.) rectification (spec. good public administration):—very worthy deed.

2736. κάτω **katō,** *kat'-o;* also (comp.)
κατωτέρω **katōtĕrō,** *kat-o-ter'-o* [comp. *2737*]; adv. from *2596;* downwards:—beneath, bottom, down, under.

2737. κατώτερος **katōtĕrŏs,** *kat-o'-ter-os;* comp. from *2736;* inferior (locally, of Hades):—lower.

2738. καῦμα **kauma,** *kŏw'-mah;* from *2545;* prop. a burn (concr.), but used (abstr.) of a glow:—heat.

2739. καυματίζω **kaumatizō,** *kŏw-mat-id'-zo;* from *2738;* to burn:—scorch.

2740. καῦσις **kausis,** *kŏw'-sis;* from *2545;* burning (the act):—be burned.

2741. καυσόω **kausŏō,** *kŏw-sŏ'-o;* from *2740;* to set on fire:—with fervent heat.

2742. καύσων **kausōn,** *kŏw'-sone;* from *2741;* a glare:—(burning) heat.

2743. καυτηριάζω **kautēriazō,** *kŏw-tay-ree-ad'-zo;* from a der. of *2545;* to brand ("cauterize"), i.e. (by impl.) to render unsensitive (fig.):—sear with a hot iron.

2744. καυχάομαι **kauchaŏmai,** *kŏw-khah'-om-ahee;* from some (obsol.) base akin to that of αὐχέω **auchĕō** (to boast) and *2172;* to vaunt (in a good or a bad sense):—(make) boast, glory, joy, rejoice.

2745. καύχημα **kauchēma,** *kŏw'-khay-mah;* from *2744;* a boast (prop. the object; by impl. the act) in a good or a bad sense:—boasting, (whereof) to glory (of), glorying, rejoice (-ing).

2746. καύχησις **kauchēsis,** *kŏw'-khay-sis;* from *2744;* boasting (prop. the act; by impl. the object), in a good or a bad sense:—boasting, whereof I may glory, glorying, rejoicing.

2747. Κεγχρεαί **Kĕgchrĕai,** *keng-khreh-a'hee;* prob. from κέγχρος **kĕgchrŏs** (millet); Cenchreæ, a port of Corinth:—Cenchrea.

2748. Κεδρών **Kĕdrōn,** *ked-rone';* of Heb. or. [*6939*]; Cedron (i.e. Kidron), a brook near Jerus.:—Cedron.

2749. κεῖμαι **kĕimai,** *ki'-mahee;* mid. of a prim. verb; to lie outstretched (lit. or fig.):—be (appointed, laid up, made, set), lay, lie. Comp. *5087.*

2750. κειρία **kĕiria,** *ki-ree'-ah;* of uncert. affin.; a swathe, i.e. winding-sheet:—graveclothes.

2751. κείρω **kĕirō,** *ki'-ro;* a prim. verb; to shear:—shear (-er).

2752. κέλευμα **kĕlĕuma,** *kel'-yoo-mah;* from *2753;* a cry of incitement:—shout.

2753. κελεύω **kĕlĕuō,** *kel-yoo'-o;* from a prim. κέλλω **kĕllō** (to urge on); "hail"; to incite by word, i.e. order:—bid, (at, give) command (-ment).

2754. κενοδοξία **kĕnŏdŏxia,** *ken-od-ox-ee'-ah;* from *2755;* empty glorying, i.e. self-conceit:—vainglory.

2755. κενόδοξος **kĕnŏdŏxŏs,** *ken-od'-ox-os;* from *2756* and *1301;* vainly glorifying, i.e. self-conceited:—desirous of vain-glory.

2756. κενός **kĕnŏs,** *ken-os';* appar. a prim. word; empty (lit. or fig.):—empty, (in) vain.

2757. κενοφωνία **kĕnŏphōnia,** *ken-of-o-nee'-ah;* from a presumed comp. of *2756* and *5456;* empty sounding, i.e. fruitless discussion:—vain.

2758. κενόω **kĕnŏō,** *ken-ŏ'-o;* from *2756;* to make empty, i.e. (fig.) to abase, neutralize, falsify:—make (of none effect, of no reputation, void), be in vain.

2759. κέντρον **kĕntrŏn,** *ken'-tron;* from κεντέω **kĕntĕō** (to prick); a point ("centre"), i.e. a sting (fig. poison) or goad (fig. divine impulse):—prick, sting.

2760. κεντυρίων **kĕnturiōn,** *ken-too-ree'-ohn;* of Lat. or.; a centurion, i.e. captain of one hundred soldiers:—centurion.

2761. κενῶς **kĕnōs,** *ken-oce';* adv. from *2756;* vainly, i.e. to no purpose:—in vain.

2762. κεραία **kĕraia,** *ker-ah'-yah;* fem. of a presumed der. of the base of *2768;* something horn-like, i.e. (spec.) the apex of a Heb. letter (fig. the least particle):—tittle.

2763. κεραμεύς **kĕramĕus,** *ker-am-yooce';* from *2766;* a potter:—potter.

2764. κεραμικός **kĕramĭkŏs**, ker-am-ik-os'; from 2766; made of clay, i.e. earthen:—of a potter.

2765. κεράμιον **kĕramĭŏn**, ker-am'-ee-on; neut. of a presumed der. of 2766; an earthenware vessel, i.e. jar:—pitcher.

2766. κέραμος **kĕramŏs**, ker'-am-os; prob. from the base of 2767 (through the idea of mixing clay and water); earthenware, i.e. a tile (by anal. a thin roof or awning):—tiling.

2767. κεράννυμι **kĕrannumi**, ker-an'-noo-mee; a prol. form of a more prim. κεράω **kĕraō**, ker-ah'-o (which is used in certain tenses); to mingle, i.e. (by impl.) to pour out (for drinking):—fill, pour out. Comp. 3396.

2768. κέρας **kĕras**, ker'-as; from a prim. κάρ **kar** (the hair of the head; a horn (lit. or fig.):—horn.

2769. κεράτιον **kĕratĭŏn**, ker-at'-ee-on; neut of a presumed der. of 2768; something horned... ..e. (spec.) the pod of the carob-tree:—husk.
κεράω **kĕraō**. See 2767.

2770. κερδαίνω **kĕrdainō**, ker-dah'...o. from 2771; to gain (lit. or fig.):—(get) gain, wi

2771. κέρδος **kĕrdŏs**, ker'-dos; of uncert affin.; gain (pecuniary or gen.):—gain, lucre.

2772. κέρμα **kĕrma**, ker-mah; from 2751, a clipping (bit), i.e. (spec.) a coin:—money

2773. κερματιστής **kĕrmatĭstēs**, ker-mat-is-tace'; from a der. of 2772; a handler of coins, i.e. money-broker:—changer of money.

2774. κεφάλαιον **kĕphalaĭŏn**, kef-al'-ah-yon; neut. of a der. of 2776; a principal thing, i.e. main point; spec. an amount (of money):—sum.

2775. κεφαλαιόω **kĕphalaĭŏō**, kef-al-ahee-ŏ'-o; from the same as 2774; (spec.) to strike on the head:—wound in the head.

2776. κεφαλή **kĕphalē**, kef-al-ay'; prob. from the prim. κάπτω **kaptŏ** (in the sense of seizing); the head (as the part most readily taken hold of), lit. or fig.:—head.

2777. κεφαλίς **kĕphalĭs**, kef-al-is'; from 2776; prop. a knob, i.e. (by impl.) a roll (by extens. from the end of a stick on which the MS. was rolled):—volume.

2778. κῆνσος **kēnsŏs**, kane'-sos; of Lat. or.; prop. an enrolment ("census"), i.e. (by impl.) a tax:—tribute.

2779. κῆπος **kēpŏs**, kay'-pos; of uncert. affin.; a garden:—garden.

2780. κηπουρός **kēpŏurŏs**, kay-poo-ros'; from 2779 and οὖρος **ŏurŏs** (a warden); a garden-keeper, i.e. gardener:—gardener.

2781. κηρίον **kērĭŏn**, kay-ree'-on; dimin. from κηός **kĕŏs** (wax); a cell for honey, i.e. (collect.) the comb:—[honey-] comb.

2782. κήρυγμα **kērugma**, kay'-roog-mah; from 2784; a proclamation (espec. of the gospel; by impl. the gospel itself):—preaching.

2783. κῆρυξ **kērux**, kay'-roox; from 2784; a herald, i.e. of divine truth (espec. of the gospel):—preacher.

2784. κηρύσσω **kērussō**, kay-roos'-so; of uncert. affin.; to herald (as a public crier), espec. divine truth (the gospel):—preach (-er), proclaim, publish.

2785. κῆτος **kētŏs**, kay'-tos; prob. from the base of 5490; a huge fish (as gaping for prey):—whale.

2786. Κηφᾶς **Kēphas**, kay-fas'; of Chald. or. [comp. 3710]; the Rock; Cephas (i.e. Kepha), a surname of Peter:—Cephas.

2787. κιβωτός **kĭbōtŏs**, kib-o-tos'; of uncert. der.; a box, i.e. the sacred ark and that of Noah:—ark.

2788. κιθάρα **kĭthara**, kith-ar'-ah; of uncert. affin.; a lyre:—harp.

2789. κιθαρίζω **kĭtharĭzō**, kith-ar-id'-zo; from 2788; to play on a lyre:—harp.

2790. κιθαρῳδός **kĭtharōĭdŏs**, kith-ar-o'-dos; from 2788 and a der. of the same as 5603; a lyre-singer (-player), i.e. harpist:—harper.

2791. Κιλικία **Kĭlĭkĭa**, kil-ik-ee'-ah; prob. of for. or., Cilicia, a region of Asia Minor:—Cilicia.

2792. κινάμωμον **kĭnamōmŏn**, in-am'-o-mon; of for. or. [comp. 7076]; cinnamon.—cinnamon.

2793. κινδυνεύω **kĭndunĕuō**, in-doon-yoo'-o; from 2794; to undergo peril:—be in danger, be (stand) in jeopardy.

2794. κίνδυνος **kĭndunŏs**, kin'-doo-nos; of uncert. der.; danger:—peril.

2795. κινέω **kĭnĕō**, kin-eh'-o; from κίω **kĭō** (poetic for εἶμι **ĕimi**, to go); to stir (trans.), lit. or fig.:—(re-) move (-r), wag.

2796. κίνησις **kĭnēsĭs**, kin'-ay-sis; from 2795; a stirring:—moving.

2797. Κίς **Kĭs**, kis; of Heb. or. [7027]; Cis (i.e. Kish), an Isr.:—Cis.
κίχρημι **kĭchrēmĭ**. See 5531.

2798. κλάδος **kladŏs**, klad'-os; from 2806; a twig or bough (as if broken off):—branch.

2799. κλαίω **klaĭō**, klah'-yo; of uncert. affin.; to sob, i.e. wail aloud (whereas 1145 is rather to cry silently):—bewail, weep.

2800. κλάσις **klasĭs**, klas'-is; from 2806; fracture (the act):—breaking.

2801. κλάσμα **klasma**, klas'-mah; from 2806; a piece (bit):—broken, fragment.

2802. Κλαύδη **Klaudē**, klŏw'-day; of uncert. der.; Claude, an island near Crete:—Clauda.

2803. Κλαυδία **Klaudĭa**, klŏw-dee'-ah; fem. of 2804; Claudia, a Chr. woman:—Claudia.

2804. Κλαύδιος **Klaudĭŏs**, klŏw'-dee-os; of Lat. or.; Claudius, the name of two Romans:—Claudius.

2805. κλαυθμός **klauthmŏs**, klŏwth-mos'; from 2799; lamentation:—wailing, weeping, × wept.

2806. κλάω **klaō**, klah'-o; a prim. verb; to break (spec. of bread):—break.

2807. κλείς **klĕis**, klice; from 2808; a key (as shutting a lock), lit. or fig.:—key.

2808. κλείω **klĕiō**, kli'-o; a prim. verb; to close (lit. or fig.):—shut (up).

2809. κλέμμα **klĕmma**, klem'-mah; from 2813; stealing (prop. the thing stolen, but used of the act):—theft.

2810. Κλεόπας **Klĕŏpas**, kleh-op'-as; prob. contr. from Κλεόπατρος **Klĕŏpatrŏs** (comp. of 2811 and 3962); Cleopas, an Isr.:—Cleopas.

2811. κλέος **klĕŏs**, kleh'-os; from a shorter form of 2564; renown (as if being called):—glory.

2812. κλέπτης **klĕptēs**, klep'-tace; from 2813; a stealer (lit. or fig.):—thief. Comp. 3027.

2813. κλέπτω **klĕptō**, klep'-to; a prim. verb; to filch:—steal.

2814. κλῆμα **klēma**, klay'-mah; from 2806; a limb or shoot (as if broken off):—branch.

2815. Κλήμης **Klēmēs**, klay'-mace; of Lat. or.; merciful; Clemes (i.e. Clemens), a Chr.:—Clement.

2816. κληρονομέω **klērŏnŏmĕō**, klay-ron-om-eh'-o; from 2818; to be an heir to (lit. or fig.):—be heir, (obtain by) inherit (-ance).

2817. κληρονομία **klērŏnŏmĭa**, klay-ron-om-ee'-ah; from 2818; heirship, i.e. (concr.) a patrimony or (gen.) a possession:—inheritance.

2818. κληρονόμος **klērŏnŏmŏs**, klay-ron-om'-os; from 2819 and the base of 3551 (in its orig. sense of partitioning, i.e. [reflex.] getting by apportionment); a sharer by lot, i.e. an inheritor (lit. or fig.); by impl. a possessor:—heir.

2819. κλῆρος **klērŏs**, klay'-ros; prob. from 2806 (through the idea of using bits of wood, etc., for the purpose); a die (for drawing chances); by impl. a portion (as if so secured); by extens. an acquisition (espec. a patrimony, fig.):—heritage, inheritance, lot, part.

2820. κληρόω **klērŏō**, klay-ro'-o; from 2819; to allot (i.e. [fig.] to assign (a privilege):—obtain an inheritance.

2821. κλῆσις **klēsĭs**, klay'-sis; from a shorter form of 2564; an invitation (fig.):—calling, vocation.

2822. κλητός **klētŏs**, klay-tos'; from the same as 2821; invited, i.e. appointed, or (spec.) a saint:—called.

2823. κλίβανος **klĭbanŏs**, klib'-an-os; of uncert. der.; an earthen pot use. for baking in:—oven.

2824. κλίμα **klĭma**, klee'-mah; from 2827; a slope, i.e. (spec.) a "clime" or tract of country:—part, region.

2825. κλίνη **klĭnē**, klee'-nay; from 2827; a couch (for sleep, sickness, sitting or eating):—bed, table.

2826. κλινίδιον **klĭnĭdĭŏn**, klin-id'-ee-on; neut. of a presumed der. of 2825; a pallet or little couch:—bed.

2827. κλίνω **klĭnō**, klee'-no; a prim. verb; to slant or slope, i.e. incline or recline (lit. or fig.):—bow (down), be far spent, lay, turn to flight, wear away.

2828. κλισία **klĭsĭa**, klee-see'-ah; from a der. of 2827; prop. reclination, i.e. (concr. and spec.) a party at a meal:—company.

2829. κλοπή **klŏpē**, klop-ay'; from 2813; stealing:—theft.

2830. κλύδων **kludōn**, kloo'-dohn; from κλύζω **kluzō** (to billow or dash over); a surge of the sea (lit. or fig.):—raging, wave.

2831. κλυδωνίζομαι **kludōnĭzŏmai**, kloo-do-nid'-zom-ahee; mid. from 2830; to surge, i.e. (fig.) to fluctuate:—toss to and fro.

2832. Κλωπᾶς **Klōpas**, klo-pas'; of Chald. or. (corresp. to 256); Clopas, an Isr.:—Clopas.

2833. κνήθω **knēthō**, knay'-tho; from a prim. κνάω **knaō** (to scrape); to scratch, i.e. (by impl.) to tickle:— × itching.

2834. Κνίδος **Knĭdŏs**, knee'-dos; prob. of for. or.; Cnidus, a place in Asia Minor:—Cnidus.

2835. κοδράντης **kŏdrantēs**, kod-ran'-tace; of Lat. or.; a quadrans, i.e. the fourth part of an as:—farthing.

2836. κοιλία **kŏilĭa**, koy-lee'-ah; from κοῖλος **kŏilŏs** ("hollow"); a cavity, i.e. (spec.) the abdomen; by impl. the matrix; fig. the heart:—belly, womb.

2837. κοιμάω **kŏimaō**, koy-mah'-o; from 2749; to put to sleep, i.e. (pass. or reflex.) to slumber; fig. to decease:—(be a-, fall a-, fall on) sleep, be dead.

2838. κοίμησις **kŏimēsĭs**, koy'-may-sis; from 2837; sleeping, i.e. (by impl.) repose:—taking of rest.

2839. κοινός **kŏinŏs**, koy-nos'; prob. from 4862; common, i.e. (lit.) shared by all or several, or (cer.) profane:—common, defiled, unclean, unholy.

2840. κοινόω **kŏinŏō**, koy-nŏ'-o; from 2839; to make (or consider) profane (cer.):—call common, defile, pollute, unclean.

2841. κοινωνέω **kŏinōnĕō**, koy-no-neh'-o; from 2844; to share with others (obj. or subj.):—communicate, distribute, be partaker.

2842. κοινωνία **kŏinōnĭa**, koy-nohn-ee'-ah; from 2844; partnership, i.e. (lit.) participation, or (social) intercourse, or (pecuniary) benefaction:—(to) communicate (-ation), communion, (contri-) distribution, fellowship.

2843. κοινωνικός **kŏinōnĭkŏs**, koy-no-nee-kos'; from 2844; communicative, i.e. (pecuniarily) liberal:—willing to communicate.

2844. κοινωνός **kŏinōnŏs**, koy-no-nos'; from 2839; a sharer, i.e. associate:—companion, × fellowship, partaker, partner.

2845. κοίτη **kŏitē**, koy'-tay; from 2749; a couch; by extens. cohabitation; by impl. the male sperm:—bed, chambering, × conceive.

2846. κοιτών **kŏitōn**, koy-tone'; from 2845; a bed-room:— + chamberlain.

2847. κόκκινος **kŏkkĭnŏs**, kok'-kee-nos; from 2848 (from the kernel-shape of the insect); crimson-colored:—scarlet (colour, coloured).

2848. κόκκος **kŏkkŏs**, kok'-kos; appar. a prim. word; a kernel of seed:—corn, grain.

2849. κολάζω **kŏlazō**, kol-ad'-zo; from κόλος **kŏlŏs** (dwarf); prop. to curtail, i.e. (fig.) to chastise (or reserve for infliction).—punish.

2850. κολακεία **kŏlakĕía**, kol-ak-i'-ah; from a der. of κόλαξ **kŏlax** (a fawner); flattery:— × flattering.

2851. κόλασις **kŏlasis**, kol'-as-is; from 2849; penal infliction:—punishment, torment.

2852. κολαφίζω **kŏlaphízō**, kol-af-id'-zo; from a der. of the base of 2849; to rap with the fist:—buffet.

2853. κολλάω **kŏllaō**, kol-lah'-o; from κόλλα **kŏlla** (" glue"); to glue, i.e. (pass. or reflex.) to stick (fig.):—cleave, join (self), keep company.

2854. κολλούριον **kŏllóurĭŏn**, kol-loo'-ree-on; neut. of a presumed der. of κολλύρα **kŏllúra** (a cake; prob. akin to the base of 2853); prop. a poultice (as made of or in the form of crackers), i.e. (by anal.) a plaster:—eyesalve.

2855. κολλυβιστής **kŏllubĭstḗs**, kol-loo-bis-tace'; from a presumed der. of κόλλυβος **kŏllubŏs** (a small coin; prob. akin to 2854); a coin-dealer:—(money-) changer.

2856. κολοβόω **kŏlŏbóō**, kol-ob-ŏ'-o; from a der. of the base of 2849; to dock, i.e. (fig.) abridge:—shorten.

2857. Κολοσσαί **Kŏlŏssaí**, kol-os-sah'ee; appar. fem. plur. of κολοσσός **kŏlŏssŏs** (" colossal"); Colossæ, a place in Asia Minor:—Colosse.

2858. Κολοσσαεύς **Kŏlŏssaĕús**, kol-os-sayoos'; fr. 2857; a Colossæan, i.e. inh. of Colosse:—Colossian.

2859. κόλπος **kŏlpŏs**, kol'-pos; appar. a prim. word; the bosom; by anal. a bay:—bosom, creek.

2860. κολυμβάω **kŏlumbaō**, kol-oom-bah'-o; from κόλυμβος **kŏlumbŏs** (a diver); to plunge into water:—swim.

2861. κολυμβήθρα **kŏlumbḗthra**, kol-oom-bay'-thrah; from 2860; a diving-place, i.e. pond for bathing (or swimming):—pool.

2862. κολωνία **kŏlōnía**, kol-o-nee'-ah; of Lat. or.; a Roman " colony" for veterans:—colony.

2863. κομάω **kŏmaō**, kom-ah'-o; from 2864; to wear tresses of hair:—have long hair.

2864. κόμη **kŏmē**, kom'-ay; appar. from the same as 2865; the hair of the head (locks, as ornamental, and thus differing from 2359, which prop. denotes merely the scalp):—hair.

2865. κομίζω **kŏmízō**, kom-id'-zo; from a prim. κομέω **kŏmĕō** (to tend, i.e. take care of); prop. to provide for, i.e. (by impl.) to carry off (as if from harm; gen. obtain):—bring, receive.

2866. κομψότερον **kŏmpsŏtĕrŏn**, komp-sot'-er-on; neut. compar. of a der. of the base of 2865 (mean. prop. well dressed, i.e. nice); fig. convalescent:— + began to amend.

2867. κονιάω **kŏniaō**, kon-ee-ah'-o; from κονία **kŏnía** (dust; by anal. lime) to whitewash:—whiten.

2868. κονιορτός **kŏnĭŏrtŏs**, kon-ee-or-tos'; from the base of 2867 and ὄρνυμι **ŏrnumi** (to " rouse"); pulverulence (as blown about):—dust.

2869. κοπάζω **kŏpazō**, kop-ad'-zo; from 2873; to tire, i.e. (fig.) to relax:—cease.

2870. κοπετός **kŏpĕtŏs**, kop-et-os'; from 2875; mourning (prop. by beating the breast):—lamentation.

2871. κοπή **kŏpē**, kop-ay'; from 2875; cutting, i.e. carnage:—slaughter.

2872. κοπιάω **kŏpiaō**, kop-ee-ah'-o; from a der. of 2873; to feel fatigue; by impl. to work hard:—(bestow) labour, toil, be wearied.

2873. κόπος **kŏpŏs**, kop'-os; from 2875; a cut, i.e. (by anal.) toil (as reducing the strength), lit. or fig.; by impl. pains:—labour, + trouble, weariness.

2874. κοπρία **kŏpría**, kop-ree'-ah; from κόπρος **kŏprŏs** (ordure; perh. akin to 2875); manure:—dung (-hill).

2875. κόπτω **kŏptō**, kop'-to; a prim. verb; to " chop"; spec. to beat the breast in grief:—cut down, lament, mourn, (be-) wail. Comp. the base of 5114.

2876. κόραξ **kŏrax**, kor'-ax; perh. from 2880; a crow (from its voracity):—raven.

2877. κοράσιον **kŏrasĭŏn**, kor-as'-ee-o·., neut. ∫ a presumed der. of κόρη **kŏrē** (a maiden); a (little) girl:—damsel, maid.

2878. κορβᾶν **kŏrban**, kor-ban'; and κορβανᾶς **kŏrbanas**, kor-ban-as'; of Heb. and Chald. or. respectively [7133]; a votive offering and the offering; a consecrated present (to the Temple fund); by extens. (the latter term) the Treasury itself, i.e. the room where the contribution boxes stood:—Corban, treasury.

2879. Κορέ **Kŏrĕ**, kor-eh'; of Heb. or. [7141]; Corè (i.e. Korach), an Isr.:—Core.

2880. κορέννυμι **kŏrénnumi**, kor-en'-noo-mee; a prim. verb; to cram, i.e. glut or sate:—eat enough, full.

2881. Κορίνθιος **Kŏrínthĭŏs**, kor-in'-thee-os; from 2882; a Corinthian, i.e. inhab. of Corinth:—Corinthian.

2882. Κόρινθος **Kŏrínthŏs**, kor'-in-thos; of uncert. der.; Corinthus, a city of Greece:—Corinth.

2883. Κορνήλιος **Kŏrnḗlĭŏs**, kor-nay'-lee-os; of Lat. or.; Cornelius, a Roman:—Cornelius.

2884. κόρος **kŏrŏs**, kor'-os; of Heb. or. [3734]; a cor, i.e. a specific measure:—measure.

2885. κοσμέω **kŏsmĕō**, kos-meh'-o; from 2889; to put in proper order, i.e. decorate (lit. or fig.); spec. to snuff (a wick):—adorn, garnish, trim.

2886. κοσμικός **kŏsmĭkŏs**, kos-mee-kos'; from 2889 (in its secondary sense); terrene (" cosmic"), lit. (mundane) or fig. (corrupt):—worldly.

2887. κόσμιος **kŏsmĭŏs**, kos'-mee-os; from 2889 (in its prim. sense); orderly, i.e. decorous:—of good behaviour, modest.

2888. κοσμοκράτωρ **kŏsmŏkratōr**, kos-mok-rat'-ore; from 2889 and 2902; a world-ruler, an epithet of Satan:—ruler.

2889. κόσμος **kŏsmŏs**, kos'-mos; prob. from the base of 2865; orderly arrangement, i.e. decoration; by impl. the world (in a wide or narrow sense, includ. its inhab., lit. or fig. [mor.]):—adorning, world.

2890. Κούαρτος **Kŏuartŏs**, koo'-ar-tos; of Lat. or. (fourth); Quartus, a Chr.:—Quartus.

2891. κούμι **kŏumi**, koo'-mee; of Chald. or. [6966]; cumi (i.e. rise !):—cumi.

2892. κουστωδία **kŏustōdía**, koos-to-dee'-ah; of Lat. or.; " custody", i.e. a Roman sentry:—watch.

2893. κουφίζω **kŏuphízō**, koo-fid'-zo; from κοῦφος **kŏuphŏs** (light in weight); to unload:—lighten.

2894. κόφινος **kŏphĭnŏs**, kof'-ee-nos; of uncert. der.; a (small) basket:—basket.

2895. κράββατος **krabbatŏs**, krab'-bat-os; prob. of for. or.; a mattress:—bed.

2896. κράζω **krazō**, krad'-zo; a prim. verb; prop. to " croak" (as a raven) or scream, i.e. (gen.) to call aloud (shriek, exclaim, intreat):—cry (out).

2897. κραιπάλη **kraipalē**, krahee-pal'-ay; prob. from the same as 726; prop. a headache (as a seizure of pain) from drunkenness, i.e. (by impl.) a debauch (by anal. a glut):—surfeiting.

2898. κρανίον **kranĭŏn**, kran-ee'-on; dimin. of a der. of the base of 2768; a skull (" cranium"):—Calvary, skull.

2899. κράσπεδον **kraspĕdŏn**, kras'-ped-on; of uncert. der.; a margin, i.e. (spec.) a fringe or tassel:—border, hem.

2900. κραταιός **krataĭŏs**, krat-ah-yos'; from 2904; powerful:—mighty.

2901. κραταιόω **krataĭŏō**, krat-ah-yŏ'-o; from 2900; to empower, i.e. (pass.) increase in vigor:—be strenghtened, be (wax) strong.

2902. κρατέω **kratĕō**, krat-eh'-o; from 2904; to use strength, i.e. seize or retain (lit. or fig.):—hold (by, fast), keep, lay hand (hold) on, obtain, retain, take (by).

2903. κράτιστος **kratistŏs**, krat'-is-tos; superl. of a der. of 2904; strongest, i.e. (in dignity) very honorable:—most excellent (noble).

2904. κράτος **kratŏs**, krat'-os; perh. a prim. word; vigor [" great "] (lit. or fig.):—dominion, might [-ily], power, strength.

2905. κραυγάζω **kraugazō**, krŏw-gad'-zo; from 2906; to clamor:—cry out.

2906. κραυγή **kraugē**, krŏw-gay'; from 2896; an outcry (in notification, tumult or grief):—clamour, cry (-ing).

2907. κρέας **krĕas**, kreh'-as; perh. a prim. word; (butcher's) meat:—flesh.

2908. κρεῖσσον **krĕissŏn**, krice'-son; neut. of an alt. form of 2909; (as noun) better, i.e. greater advantage:—better.

2909. κρείττων **krĕíttōn**, krite'-tohn; compar. of a der. of 2904; stronger, i.e. (fig.) better, i.e. nobler:—best, better.

2910. κρεμάννυμι **krĕmannumi**, krem-an'-noo-mee; a prol. form of a prim. verb; to hang:—hang.

2911. κρημνός **krĕmnŏs**, krame-nos'; from 2910; overhanging, i.e. a precipice:—steep place.

2912. Κρής **Krēs**, krace; from 2914; a Cretan, i.e. inhab. of Crete:—Crete, Cretian.

2913. Κρήσκης **Krēskēs**, krace'-kace; of Lat. or.; growing; Cresces (i.e. Crescens), a Chr.:—Crescens.

2914. Κρήτη **Krētē**, kray'-tay; of uncert. der.; Cretè, an island in the Mediterranean:—Crete.

2915. κριθή **krithē**, kree-thay'; of uncert. der.; barley:—barley.

2916. κρίθινος **krithĭnŏs**, kree'-thee-nos; from 2915; consisting of barley:—barley.

2917. κρίμα **krima**, kree'-mah; from 2919; a decision (the function or the effect, for or against [" crime"]):—avenge, condemned, condemnation, damnation, + go to law, judgment.

2918. κρίνον **krinŏn**, kree'-non; perh. a prim. word; a lily:—lily.

2919. κρίνω **krinō**, kree'-no; prop. to distinguish, i.e. decide (mentally or judicially); by impl. to try, condemn, punish:—avenge, conclude, condemn, damn, decree, determine, esteem, judge, go to (sue at the) law, ordain, call in question, sentence to, think.

2920. κρίσις **krisis**, kree'-sis; decision (subj. or obj., for or against); by extens. a tribunal; by impl. justice (spec. divine law):—accusation, condemnation, damnation, judgment.

2921. Κρίσπος **Krispŏs**, kris'-pos; of Lat. or.; " crisp"; Crispus, a Corinthian:—Crispus.

2922. κριτήριον **kritḗrĭŏn**, kree-tay'-ree-on; neut. of a presumed der. of 2923; a rule of judging (" criterion"), i.e. (by impl.) a tribunal:—to judge, judgment (seat).

2923. κριτής **kritēs**, kree-tace'; from 2919; a judge (gen. or spec.):—judge.

2924. κριτικός **kritĭkŏs**, krit-ee-kos'; from 2923; decisive (" critical "), i.e. discriminative:—discerner.

2925. κρούω **krŏuō**, kroo'-o; appar. a prim. verb: to rap:—knock.

2926. κρυπτή **kruptē**, kroop-tay'; fem. of 2927; a hidden place, i.e. cellar (" crypt "):—secret.

2927. κρυπτός **kruptŏs**, kroop-tos'; from 2928; concealed, i.e. private:—hid (-den), inward [-ly], secret.

2928. κρύπτω **kruptō**, kroop'-to; a prim. verb; to conceal (prop. by covering):—hide (self), keep secret [-ly].

2929. κρυσταλλίζω **krustallizō**, kroos-tal-lid'-zo; from 2930; to make (i.e. intrans. resemble) ice (" crystallize"):—be clear as crystal.

2930. κρύσταλλος **krustallŏs**, kroos'-tal-los; from a der. of κρύος **kruŏs** (frost); ice, i.e. (by anal.) rock " crystal ":—crystal.

2931. κρυφῇ **kruphē**, kroo-fay'; adv. from 2928; privately:—in secret.

2932. κτάομαι **ktaŏmai**, ktah'-om-ahee; a prim. verb; to get, i.e. acquire (by any means; own):—obtain, possess, provide, purchase.

2933. κτῆμα **ktēma**, *ktay'-mah*; from *2932*; an acquirement, i.e. estate:—possession.

2934. κτῆνος **ktēnŏs**, *ktay'-nos*; from *2932*; property, i.e. (spec.) a domestic animal:—beast.

2935. κτήτωρ **ktētŏr**, *ktay'-tore*; from *2932*; an owner:—possessor.

2936. κτίζω **ktizō**, *ktid'-zo*; prob. akin to *2932* (through the idea of the proprietorship of the manufacturer); to fabricate, i.e. found (form originally):—create, Creator, make.

2937. κτίσις **ktisis**, *ktis'-is*; from *2936*; original formation (prop. the act; by impl. the thing, lit. or fig.):—building, creation, creature, ordinance.

2938. κτίσμα **ktisma**, *ktis'-mah*; from *2936*; an original formation (concr.), i.e. product (created thing):—creature.

2939. κτίστης **ktistēs**, *ktis-tace'*; from *2936*; a founder, i.e. God (as author of all things):—Creator.

2940. κυβεία **kubĕia**, *koo-bi'-ah*; from κύβος kubŏs (a "cube", i.e. die for playing); gambling, i.e. (fig.) artifice or fraud:--sleight.

2941. κυβέρνησις **kubĕrnēsis**, *koo-ber'-nay-sis*; from κυβερνάω kubĕrnaō (of Lat. or., to steer); pilotage, i.e. (fig.) directorship (in the church):—government.

2942. κυβερνήτης **kubĕrnētēs**, *koo-ber-nay'-tace*; from the same as *2941*; helmsman, i.e. (by impl.) captain:—(ship) master.

2943. κυκλόθεν **kuklŏthĕn**, *koo-kloth'-en*; adv. from the same as *2945*; from the circle, i.e. all around:—(round) about.

κυκλός **kuklŏs**. See *2945*.

2944. κυκλόω **kuklŏō**, *koo-klŏ'-o*; from the same as *2945*; to encircle, i.e. surround:—compass (about), come (stand) round about.

2945. κύκλῳ **kuklŏ̄**, *koo'-klo*; as if dat. of κύκλος kuklŏs (a ring, "cycle"; akin to *2947*); i.e. in a circle (by impl. of *1722*), i.e. (adv.) all around:—round about.

2946. κύλισμα **kulisma**, *koo'-lis-mah*; from *2947*; a wallow (the effect of rolling), i.e. filth:—wallowing.

2947. κυλιόω **kuliŏō**, *koo-lee-ŏ'-o*; from the base of *2949* (through the idea of circularity; comp. *2945*, *1507*); to roll about:—wallow.

2948. κυλλός **kullŏs**, *kool-los'*; from the same as *2947*; rocking about, i.e. crippled (maimed, in feet or hands):—maimed.

2949. κῦμα **kuma**, *koo'-mah*; from κύω kuō (to swell [with young], i.e. bend, curve); a billow (as bursting or toppling):—wave.

2950. κύμβαλον **kumbalŏn**, *koom'-bal-on*; from a der. of the base of *2949*; a "cymbal" (as hollow):—cymbal.

2951. κύμινον **kuminŏn**, *koo'-min-on*; of for. or. [comp. 8646]; dill or fennel ("cummin"):—cummin.

2952. κυνάριον **kunariŏn**, *koo-nar'-ee-on*; neut. of a presumed der. of *2965*; a puppy:—dog.

2953. Κύπριος **Kupriŏs**, *koo'-pree-os*; from *2954*; a Cyprian (Cypriot), i.e. inhab. of Cyprus:—of Cyprus.

2954. Κύπρος **Kuprŏs**, *koo'-pros*; of uncert. or.; Cyprus, an island in the Mediterranean:—Cyprus.

2955. κύπτω **kuptō**, *koop'-to*; prob. from the base of *2949*; to bend forward:—stoop (down).

2956. Κυρηναῖος **Kurēnaiŏs**, *koo-ray-nah'-yos*; from *2957*; a Cyrenæan, i.e. inhab. of Cyrene:—of Cyrene, Cyrenian.

2957. Κυρήνη **Kurēnē**, *koo-ray'-nay*; of uncert. der.; Cyrenè, a region of Africa:—Cyrene.

2958. Κυρήνιος **Kurēniŏs**, *koo-ray'-nee-os*; of Lat. or.; Cyrenius (i.e. Quirinus), a Roman:—Cyrenius.

2959. Κυρία **Kuria**, *koo-ree'-ah*; fem. of *2962*; Cyria, a Chr. woman:—lady.

2960. κυριακός **kuriakŏs**, *koo-ree-ak-os'*; from *2962*; belonging to the Lord (Jehovah or Jesus):—Lord's.

2961. κυριεύω **kuriĕuō**, *koo-ree-yoo'-o*; from *2962*; to rule:—have dominion over, lord, be lord of, exercise lordship over.

2962. κύριος **kuriŏs**, *koo'-ree-os*; from κῦρος kurŏs (supremacy); supreme in authority, i.e. (as noun) controller; by impl. Mr. (as a respectful title):—God, Lord, master, Sir.

2963. κυριότης **kuriŏtēs**, *koo-ree-ot'-ace*; from *2962*; mastery, i.e. (concr. and coll.) rulers:—dominion, government.

2964. κυρόω **kurŏō**, *koo-rŏ'-o*; from the same as *2962*; to make authoritative, i.e. ratify:—confirm.

2965. κύων **kuōn**, *koo'-ohn*; a prim. word; a dog ["hound"] (lit. or fig.):—dog.

2966. κῶλον **kōlŏn**, *ko'-lon*; from the base of *2849*; a limb of the body (as if lopped):—carcase.

2967. κωλύω **kōluō**, *ko-loo'-o*; from the base of *2849*; to estop, i.e. prevent (by word or act):—forbid, hinder, keep from, let, not suffer, withstand.

2968. κώμη **kōmē**, *ko'-may*; from *2749*; a hamlet (as if laid down):—town, village.

2969. κωμόπολις **kōmŏpŏlis**, *ko-mop'-ol-is*; from *2968* and *4172*; an unwalled city:—town.

2970. κῶμος **kōmŏs**, *ko'-mos*; from *2749*; a carousal (as if a letting loose):—revelling, rioting.

2971. κώνωψ **kōnōps**, *ko'-nopes*; appar. from a der. of the base of *2759* and a der. of *3700*; a mosquito (from its stinging proboscis):—gnat.

2972. Κῶς **Kōs**, *koce*; of uncert. or.; Cos, an island in the Mediterranean:—Cos.

2973. Κωσάμ **Kōsam**, *ko-sam'*; of Heb. or. [comp. 7081]; Cosam (i.e. Kosam), an Isr.:—Cosam.

2974. κωφός **kōphŏs**, *ko-fos'*; from *2875*; blunted, i.e. (fig.) of hearing (deaf) or speech (dumb):—deaf, dumb, speechless.

Λ

2975. λαγχάνω **lagchanō**, *lang-khan'-o*; a prol. form of a prim. verb, which is only used as an alt. in certain tenses; to lot, i.e. determine (by impl. receive) espec. by lot:—his lot be, cast lots, obtain.

2976. Λάζαρος **Lazarŏs**, *lad'-zar-os*; prob. of Heb. or. [499]; Lazarus (i.e. Elazar), the name of two Isr. (one imaginary):—Lazarus.

2977. λάθρα **lathra**, *lath'-rah*; adv. from *2990*; privately:—privily, secretly.

2978. λαῖλαψ **lailaps**, *lah'ee-laps*; of uncert. der.; a whirlwind (squall):—storm, tempest.

2979. λακτίζω **laktizō**, *lak-tid'-zo*; from adv. λάξ lax (heelwise); to recalcitrate:—kick.

2980. λαλέω **laleō**, *lal-eh'-o*; a prol. form of an otherwise obsol. verb; to talk, i.e. utter words:—preach, say, speak (after), talk, tell, utter. Comp. *3004*.

2981. λαλιά **lalia**, *lal-ee-ah'*; from *2980*; talk:—saying, speech.

2982. λαμά **lama**, *lam-ah'*; or

λαμμᾶ **lamma**, *lam-mah'*; of Heb. or. [4100 with prep. pref.]; lama (i.e. why):—lama.

2983. λαμβάνω **lambanō**, *lam-ban'-o*; a prol. form of a prim. verb, which is used only as an alt. in certain tenses; to take (in very many applications, lit. and fig. [prop. obj. or act., to get hold of; whereas *1209* is rather subj. or pass., to have offered to one; while *138* is more violent, to seize or remove]):—accept, + be amazed, assay, attain, bring, × when I call, catch, come on (× unto), + forget, have, hold, obtain, receive (× after), take (away, up).

2984. Λάμεχ **Lamĕch**, *lam'-ekh*; of Heb. or. [3929]; Lamech (i.e. Lemek), a patriarch:—Lamech.

λαμμᾶ **lamma**. See *2982*.

2985. λαμπάς **lampas**, *lam-pas'*; from *2989*; a "lamp" or flambeau:—lamp, light, torch.

2986. λαμπρός **lamprŏs**, *lam-pros'*; from the same as *2985*; radiant; by anal. limpid; fig. magnificent or sumptuous (in appearance):—bright, clear, gay, goodly, gorgeous, white.

2987. λαμπρότης **lamprŏtēs**, *lam-prot'-ace*; from *2986*; brilliancy:—brightness.

2988. λαμπρῶς **lamprŏs**, *lam-proce'*; adv. from *2986*; brilliantly, i.e. (fig.) luxuriously:—sumptuously.

2989. λάμπω **lampō**, *lam'-po*; a prim. verb; to beam, i.e. radiate brilliancy (lit. or fig.):—give light, shine.

2990. λανθάνω **lanthanō**, *lan-than'-o*; a prol. form of a prim. verb, which is used only as an alt. in certain tenses; to lie hid (lit. or fig.); often used adv. unwittingly:—be hid, be ignorant of, unawares.

2991. λαξευτός **laxĕutŏs**, *lax-yoo-tos'*; from a comp. of λᾶς las (a stone) and the base of *3584* (in its orig. sense of scraping); rock-quarried:—hewn in stone.

2992. λαός **laŏs**, *lah-os'*; appar. a prim. word; a people (in gen.; thus differing from *1218*, which denotes one's own populace):—people.

2993. Λαοδίκεια **Laŏdikĕia**, *lah-od-ik'-i-ah*; from a comp. of *2992* and *1349*; Laodicia, a place in Asia Minor:—Laodicea.

2994. Λαοδικεύς **Laŏdikĕus**, *lah-od-ik-yooce'*; from *2993*; a Laodicean, i.e. inhab. of Laodicia:—Laodicean.

2995. λάρυγξ **larugx**, *lar'-oongks*; of uncert. der.; the throat ("larynx"):—throat.

2996. Λασαία **Lasaia**, *las-ah'-yah*; of uncert. or.; Lasea, a place in Crete:—Lasea.

2997. λάσχω **laschō**, *las'-kho*; a strengthened form of a prim. verb, which only occurs in this and another prol. form as alt. in certain tenses; to crack open (from a fall):—burst asunder.

2998. λατομέω **latŏmĕō**, *lat-om-eh'-o*; from the same as the first part of *2991* and the base of *5114*; to quarry:—hew.

2999. λατρεία **latrĕia**, *lat-ri'-ah*; from *3000*; ministration of God, i.e. worship:—(divine) service.

3000. λατρεύω **latrĕuō**, *lat-ryoo'-o*; from λάτρις latris (a hired menial); to minister (to God), i.e. render religious homage:—serve, do the service, worship (-per).

3001. λάχανον **lachanŏn**, *lakh'-an-on*; from λαχαίνω lachainō (to dig); a vegetable:—herb.

3002. Λεββαῖος **Lĕbbaiŏs**, *leb-bah'-yos*; of uncert. or.; Lebbæus, a Chr.:—Lebbæus.

3003. λεγεών **lĕgĕōn**, *leg-eh-ohn'*; of Lat. or.; a "legion", i.e. Rom. regiment (fig.):—legion.

3004. λέγω **legō**, *leg'-o*; a prim. verb; prop. to "lay" forth, i.e. (fig.) relate (in words [usually of systematic or set discourse; whereas *2036* and *5346* generally refer to an individual expression or speech respectively; while *4483* is prop. to break silence merely, and *2980* means an extended or random harangue]); by impl. to mean:—ask, bid, boast, call, describe, give out, name, put forth, say (-ing, on), shew, speak, tell, utter.

3005. λεῖμμα **lĕimma**, *lime'-mah*; from *3007*; a remainder:—remnant.

3006. λεῖος **lĕiŏs**, *li'-os*; a prim. word; smooth, i.e. "level":—smooth.

3007. λείπω **lĕipō**, *li'-po*; a prim. verb; to leave, i.e. (intrans. or pass.) to fail or be absent:—be destitute (wanting), lack.

3008. λειτουργέω **lĕitŏurgĕō**, *li-toorg-eh'-o*; from *3011*; to be a public servant, i.e. (by anal.) to perform religious or charitable functions (worship, obey, relieve):—minister.

3009. λειτουργία **lĕitŏurgia**, *li-toorg-ee'-ah*; from *3008*; public function (as priest ["liturgy"] or almsgiver):—ministration (-try), service.

3010. λειτουργικός **lĕitŏurgikŏs**, *li-toorg-ik-os'*; from the same as *3008*; functional publicly ("liturgic"), i.e. beneficent:—ministering.

3011. λειτουργός **lĕitŏurgŏs**, *li-toorg-os'*; from a der. of *2992* and *2041*; a public servant, i.e. a functionary in the Temple or Gospel, or (gen.) a worshipper (of God) or benefactor (of man):—minister (-ed).

3012. λέντιον **lĕntiŏn**, *len'-tee-on*; of Lat. or.; a "linen" cloth, i.e. apron:—towel.

3013. λεπίς **lĕpis**, *lep-is'*; from λέπω lĕpō (to peel); a flake:—scale.

3014. λέπρα **lĕpra**, *lep'-rah;* from the same as *3013;* scaliness, i.e. "leprosy":—leprosy.

3015. λεπρός **lĕprŏs**, *lep-ros';* from the same as *3014;* scaly, i.e. leprous (a leper):—leper.

3016. λεπτόν **lĕptŏn**, *lep-ton';* neut. of a der. of the same as *3013;* something scaled (light), i.e. a small coin:—mite.

3017. Λευΐ **Lĕuï**, *lyoo-ee';* of Heb. or. [3878]; Levi, the name of three Isr.:—Levi. Comp. *3018.*

3018. Λευΐς **Lĕuïs**, *lyoo-is';* a form of *3017;* Lewis (i.e. Levi), a Chr.:—Levi.

3019. Λευΐτης **Lĕuïtēs**, *lyoo-ee'-tace;* from *3017;* a Levite, i.e. desc. of Levi:—Levite.

3020. Λευϊτικός **Lĕuïtikŏs**, *lyoo-it'-ee-kos;* from *3019;* Levitic, i.e. relating to the Levites:—Levitical.

3021. λευκαίνω **lĕukaïnō**, *lyoo-kah'ee-no;* from *3022;* to whiten:—make white, whiten.

3022. λευκός **lĕukŏs**, *lyoo-kos';* from λύκη **lukē** ("light"); white:—white.

3023. λεών **lĕōn**, *leh-ohn';* a prim. word; a "lion":—lion.

3024. λήθη **lēthē**, *lay'-thay;* from *2990;* forgetfulness:— + forget.

3025. ληνός **lēnŏs**, *lay-nos';* appar. a prim. word; a trough, i.e. wine-vat:—winepress.

3026. λῆρος **lērŏs**, *lay'-ros;* appar. a prim. word; twaddle, i.e. an incredible story:—idle tale.

3027. ληστής **lēstēs**, *lace-tace';* from ληΐζομαι **lēïzŏmai** (to plunder); a brigand:—robber, thief.

3028. λῆψις **lēpsis**, *lape'-sis;* from *2983;* receipt (the act):—receiving.

3029. λίαν **lian**, *lee'-an;* of uncert. affin.; much (adv.):—exceeding, great (-ly), sore, very (+ chiefest).

3030. λίβανος **libanŏs**, *lib'-an-os;* of for. or. [3828]; the incense-tree, i.e. (by impl.) incense itself:—frankincense.

3031. λιβανωτός **libanōtŏs**, *lib-an-o-tos';* from *3030;* frankincense, i.e. (by extens.) a censer for burning it:—censer.

3032. Λιβερτῖνος **Libĕrtinŏs**, *lib-er-tee'-nos;* of Lat. or.; a Rom. freedman:—Libertine.

3033. Λιβύη **Libuē**, *lib-oo'-ay;* prob. from *3047;* Libye, a region of Africa:—Libya.

3034. λιθάζω **lithazō**, *lith-ad'-zo;* from *3037;* to lapidate:—stone.

3035. λίθινος **lithinŏs**, *lith'-ee-nos;* from *3037;* stony, i.e. made of stone:—of stone.

3036. λιθοβολέω **lithŏbŏlĕō**, *lith-ob-ol-eh'-o;* from a comp. of *3037* and *906;* to throw stones, i.e. lapidate:—stone, cast stones.

3037. λίθος **lithŏs**, *lee'-thos;* appar. a prim. word; a stone (lit. or fig.):—(mill-, stumbling-) stone.

3038. λιθόστρωτος **lithŏstrōtŏs**, *lith-os'-tro-tos;* from *3037* and a der. of *4766;* stone-strewed, i.e. a tessellated mosaic on which the Rom. tribunal was placed:—Pavement.

3039. λικμάω **likmaō**, *lik-mah'-o;* from λικμός **likmŏs**, the equiv. of λίκνον **liknŏn** (a winnowing fan or basket); to winnow, i.e. (by anal.) to triturate:—grind to powder.

3040. λιμήν **limēn**, *lee-mane';* appar. a prim. word; a harbor:—haven. Comp. *2568.*

3041. λίμνη **limnē**, *lim'-nay;* prob. from *3040* (through the idea of the nearness of shore); a pond (large or small):—lake.

3042. λιμός **limŏs**, *lee-mos';* prob. from *3007* (through the idea of destitution); a scarcity of food:—dearth, famine, hunger.

3043. λίνον **linŏn**, *lee'-non;* prob. a prim. word; flax, i.e. (by impl.) "linen":—linen.

3044. Λίνος **Linŏs**, *lee'-nos;* perh. from *3043;* Linus, a Chr.:—Linus.

3045. λιπαρός **liparŏs**, *lip-ar-os';* from λίπος **lipŏs** (grease); fat, i.e. (fig.) sumptuous:—dainty.

3046. λίτρα **litra**, *lee'-trah;* of Lat. or. [libra]; a pound in weight:—pound.

3047. λίψ **lips**, *leeps;* prob. from λείβω **lĕibō** (to pour a "libation"); the south (-west) wind (as bringing rain, i.e. (by extens.) the south quarter:—southwest.

3048. λογία **lŏgia**, *log-ee'-ah;* from *3056* (in the commercial sense); a contribution:—collection, gathering.

3049. λογίζομαι **lŏgizŏmai**, *log-id'-zom-ahee;* mid. from *3056;* to take an inventory, i.e. estimate (lit. or fig.):—conclude, (ac-) count (of), + despise, esteem, impute, lay, number, reason, reckon, suppose, think (on).

3050. λογικός **lŏgikŏs**, *log-ik-os';* from *3056;* rational ("logical"):—reasonable, of the word.

3051. λόγιον **lŏgiŏn**, *log'-ee-on;* neut. of *3052;* an utterance (of God):—oracle.

3052. λόγιος **lŏgiŏs**, *log'-ee-os;* from *3056;* fluent, i.e. an orator:—eloquent.

3053. λογισμός **lŏgismŏs**, *log-is-mos';* from *3049;* computation, i.e. (fig.) reasoning (conscience, conceit):—imagination, thought.

3054. λογομαχέω **lŏgŏmachĕō**, *log-om-akh-eh'-o;* from a comp. of *3056* and *3164;* to be disputatious (on trifles):—strive about words.

3055. λογομαχία **lŏgŏmachia**, *log-om-akh-ee'-ah;* from the same as *3054;* disputation about trifles ("logomachy"):—strife of words.

3056. λόγος **lŏgŏs**, *log'-os;* from *3004;* something said (including the thought); by impl. a topic (subject of discourse), also reasoning (the mental faculty) or motive; by extens. a computation; spec. (with the art. in John) the Divine Expression (i.e. Christ):—account, cause, communication, × concerning, doctrine, fame, × have to do, intent, matter, mouth, preaching, question, reason, + reckon, remove, say (-ing), shew, × speaker, speech, talk, thing, + none of these things move me, tidings, treatise, utterance, word, work.

3057. λόγχη **lŏgchē**, *long'-khay;* perh. a prim. word; a "lance":—spear.

3058. λοιδορέω **lŏidŏrĕō**, *loy-dor-eh'-o;* from *3060;* to reproach, i.e. vilify:—revile.

3059. λοιδορία **lŏidŏria**, *loy-dor-ee'-ah;* from *3060;* slander or vituperation:—railing, reproach [-fully].

3060. λοίδορος **lŏidŏrŏs**, *loy'-dor-os;* from λοιδός **lŏidŏs** (mischief); abusive, i.e. a black-guard:—railer, reviler.

3061. λοιμός **lŏimŏs**, *loy-mos';* of uncert. affin.; a plague (lit. the disease, or fig. a pest):—pestilence (-t).

3062. λοιποί **lŏipŏy**, *loy-poy';* masc. plur. of a der. of *3007;* remaining ones:—other, which remain, remnant, residue, rest.

3063. λοιπόν **lŏipŏn**, *loy-pon';* neut. sing. of the same as *3062;* something remaining (adv.):—besides, finally, furthermore, (from) henceforth, moreover, now, + it remaineth, then.

3064. λοιποῦ **lŏipŏu**, *loy-poo';* gen. sing. of the same as *3062;* remaining time:—from henceforth.

3065. Λουκᾶς **Lŏukas**, *loo-kas';* contr. from Lat. Lucanus; Lucas, a Chr.:—Lucas, Luke.

3066. Λούκιος **Lŏukiŏs**, *loo'-kee-os;* of Lat. or.; illuminative; Lucius, a Chr.:—Lucius.

3067. λουτρόν **lŏutrŏn**, *loo-tron';* from *3068;* a bath, i.e. (fig.) baptism:—washing.

3068. λούω **lŏuō**, *loo'-o;* a prim. verb; to bathe (the whole person; whereas *3538* means to wet a part only, and *4150* to wash, cleanse garments exclusively):—wash.

3069. Λύδδα **Ludda**, *lud'-dah;* of Heb. or. [3850]; Lydda (i.e. Lod), a place in Pal.:—Lydda.

3070. Λυδία **Ludia**, *loo-dee'-ah;* prop. fem. of Λύδιος **Ludiŏs** [of for. or.] (a Lydian, in Asia Minor); Lydia, a Chr. woman:—Lydia.

3071. Λυκαονία **Lukaŏnia**, *loo-kah-on-ee'-ah;* perh. remotely from *3074;* Lycaonia, a region of Asia Minor:—Lycaonia.

3072. Λυκαονιστί **Lukaŏnisti**, *loo-kah-on-is-tee';* adv. from a der. of *3071;* Lycaonistically, i.e. in the language of the Lycaonians:—in the speech of Lycaonia.

3073. Λυκία **Lukia**, *loo-kee'-ah;* prob. remotely from *3074;* Lycia, a province of Asia Minor:—Lycia.

3074. λύκος **lukŏs**, *loo'-kos;* perh. akin to the base of *3022* (from the whitish hair); a wolf:—wolf.

3075. λυμαίνομαι **lumainŏmai**, *loo-mah'ee-nom-ahee;* mid. from a prob. der. of *3089* (mean. filth); prop. to soil, i.e. (fig.) insult (maltreat):—make havock of.

3076. λυπέω **lupĕō**, *loo-peh'-o;* from *3077;* to distress; reflex. or pass. to be sad:—cause grief, grieve, be in heaviness, (be) sorrow (-ful), be (make) sorry.

3077. λύπη **lupē**, *loo'-pay;* appar. a prim. word; sadness:—grief, grievous, + grudgingly, heaviness, sorrow.

3078. Λυσανίας **Lusanias**, *loo-san-ee'-as;* from *3080* and ἀνία **ania** (trouble); grief-dispelling; Ly sanias, a governor of Abilene:—Lysanias.

3079. Λυσίας **Lusias**, *loo-see'-as;* of uncert. affin.; Lysias, a Rom.:—Lysias.

3080. λύσις **lusis**, *loo'-sis;* from *3089;* a loosening, i.e. (spec.) divorce:—to be loosed.

3081. λυσιτελεῖ **lusitĕlĕi**, *loo-sit-el-i';* third pers. sing. pres. indic. act. of a der. of a comp. of *3080* and *5056;* impers. it answers the purpose, i.e. is advantageous:—it is better.

3082. Λύστρα **Lustra**, *loos'-trah;* of uncert. or.; Lystra, a place in Asia Minor:—Lystra.

3083. λύτρον **lutrŏn**, *loo'-tron;* from *3089;* something to loosen with, i.e. a redemption price (fig. atonement):—ransom.

3084. λυτρόω **lutrŏō**, *loo-trŏ'-o;* from *3083;* to ransom (lit. or fig.):—redeem.

3085. λύτρωσις **lutrōsis**, *loo'-tro-sis;* from *3084;* a ransoming (fig.):— + redeemed, redemption.

3086. λυτρωτής **lutrōtēs**, *loo-tro-tace';* from *3084;* a redeemer (fig.):—deliverer.

3087. λυχνία **luchnia**, *lookh-nee'-ah;* from *3088;* a lamp-stand (lit. or fig.):—candlestick.

3088. λύχνος **luchnŏs**, *lookh'-nos;* from the base of *3022;* a portable lamp or other illuminator (lit. or fig.):—candle, light.

3089. λύω **luō**, *loo'-o;* a prim. verb; to "loosen" (lit. or fig.):—break (up), destroy, dissolve, (un-) loose, melt, put off. Comp. *4486.*

3090. Λωΐς **Lōïs**, *lo-ece';* of uncert. or.; Loïs, a Chr. woman:—Lois.

3091. Λώτ **Lōt**, *lote;* of Heb. or. [3876]; Lot, a patriarch:—Lot.

M

3092. Μαάθ **Maath**, *mah-ath';* prob. of Heb. or.; Maath, an Isr.:—Maath.

3093. Μαγδαλά **Magdala**, *mag-dal-ah';* of Chald. or. [comp. 4026]; the tower; Magdala (i.e Migdala), a place in Pal.:—Magdala.

3094. Μαγδαληνή **Magdalēnē**, *mag-dal-ay-nay';* fem. of a der. of *3093;* a female Magdalene, i.e. inhab. of Magdala:—Magdalene.

3095. μαγεία **magĕia**, *mag-i'-ah;* from *3096;* "magic":—sorcery.

3096. μαγεύω **magĕuō**, *mag-yoo'-o;* from *3097;* to practice magic:—use sorcery.

3097. μάγος **magŏs**, *mag'-os;* of for. or. [7248]; a Magian, i.e. Oriental scientist; by impl. a magician:—sorcerer, wise man.

3098. Μαγώγ **Magōg**, *mag-ogue';* of Heb. or. [4031]; Magog, a for. nation, i.e. (fig.) an Antichristian party:—Magog.

3099. Μαδιάν **Madian**, *mad-ee-an';* of Heb. or. [4080]; Madian (i.e. Midian), a region of Arabia:—Madian.

3100. μαθητεύω **mathētĕuō**, *math-ayt-yoo'-o;* from *3101;* intrans. to become a pupil; trans. to disciple, i.e. enrol as scholar:—be disciple, instruct, teach.

3101. μαθητής **mathētēs**, *math-ay-tes';* from *3129;* a learner, i.e. pupil:—disciple.

3102. μαθήτρια **mathētria**, *math-ay'-tree-ah;* fem. from *3101;* a female pupil:—disciple.

3103. Μαθουσάλα **Mathŏusala**, *math-oo-sal'-ah;* of Heb. or. [4968]; *Mathusala* (i.e. *Methushelach*), an antediluvian:—Mathusala.

3104. Μαϊνάν **Mainan**, *mahee-nan';* prob. of Heb. or.; *Mainan*, an Isr.:—Mainan.

3105. μαίνομαι **mainŏmai**, *mah'ee-nom-ahee;* mid. from a prim. μάω (to *long* for); through the idea of insensate *craving*); to *rave* as a " maniac":—be beside self (mad).

3106. μακαρίζω **makarizō**, *mak-ar-id'-zo;* from *3107;* to *beatify,* i.e. *pronounce* (or esteem) *fortunate:*—call blessed, count happy.

3107. μακάριος **makariŏs**, *mak-ar'-ee-os;* a prol. form of the poetical μάκαρ **makar** (mean. the same); supremely *blest;* by extens. *fortunate, well off:*—blessed, happy (× -ier).

3108. μακαρισμός **makarismŏs**, *mak-ar-is-mos';* from *3106;* *beatification,* i.e. *attribution of good fortune:*—blessedness.

3109. Μακεδονία **Makĕdŏnia**, *mak-ed-on-ee'-ah;* from *3110;* *Macedonia,* a region of Greece:—Macedonia.

3110. Μακεδών **Makĕdōn**, *mak-ed'-ohn;* of uncert. der.; a *Macedon* (*Macedonian*), i.e. inhab. of Macedonia:—of Macedonia, Macedonian.

3111. μάκελλον **makĕllŏn**, *mak'-el-lon;* of Lat. or. [*macellum*]; a *butcher's stall,* meat market or *provision-shop:*—shambles.

3112. μακράν **makran**, *mak-ran';* fem. acc. sing. of *3117* (*3598* being implied); *at a distance* (lit. or fig.):—(a-) far (off), good (great) way off.

3113. μακρόθεν **makrŏthĕn**, *mak-roth'-en;* adv. from *3117;* *from a distance* or *afar:*—afar off, from far.

3114. μακροθυμέω **makrŏthumĕō**, *mak-roth-oo-meh'-o;* from the same as *3116;* to be *long-spirited,* i.e. (obj.) *forbearing* or (subj.) *patient:*—bear (suffer) long, be longsuffering, have (long) patience, be patient, patiently endure.

3115. μακροθυμία **makrŏthumia**, *mak-roth-oo-mee'-ah;* from the same as *3116;* *longanimity,* i.e. (obj.) *forbearance* or (subj.) *fortitude:*—longsuffering, patience.

3116. μακροθυμώς **makrŏthumōs**, *mak-roth-oo-moce';* adv. of a comp. of *3117* and *2372; with long* (*enduring*) *temper,* i.e. *leniently:*—patiently.

3117. μακρός **makrŏs**, *mak-ros';* from *3372; long* (in place [*distant*] or time [neut. plur.]):—far, long.

3118. μακροχρόνιος **makrŏchrŏniŏs**, *mak-rokh-ron'-ee-os;* from *3117* and *5550; long-timed,* i.e. *long-lived:*—live long.

3119. μαλακία **malakia**, *mal-ak-ee'-ah;* from *3120;* *softness,* i.e. *enervation* (*debility*):—disease.

3120. μαλακός **malakŏs**, *mal-ak-os';* of uncert. affin.; *soft,* i.e. *fine* (clothing); fig. a *catamite:*—effeminate, soft.

3121. Μαλελεήλ **Malĕlĕēl**, *mal-el-eh-ale';* of Heb. or [4111]; *Maleleël* (i.e. *Mahalalel*), an antediluvian:—Maleleel.

3122. μάλιστα **malista**, *mal'-is-tah;* neut. plur. of the superl. of an appar. prim. adv. μάλα **mala** (*very*); (adv.) *most* (*in the greatest degree*) or *particularly:*—chiefly, most of all, (e) specially.

3123. μᾶλλον **mallŏn**, *mal'-lon;* neut. of the compar. of the same as *3122;* (adv.) *more* (*in a greater degree*) or *rather:*—+ rather, × far, (the) more (and more), (so) much (the more), rather.

3124. Μάλχος **Malchŏs**, *mal'-khos;* of Heb. or. [4429]; *Malchus,* an Isr.:—Malchus.

3125. μάμμη **mammē**, *mam'-may;* of nat. or. [" mammy"]; a *grandmother:*—grandmother.

3126. μαμμωνᾶς **mammōnas**, *mam-mo-nas';* of Chald. or. (*confidence,* i.e. fig. *wealth,* personified); *mammonas,* i.e. *avarice* (deified):—mammon.

3127. Μαναήν **Manaēn**, *man-ah-ane';* of uncert. or.; *Manaën,* a Chr.:—Manaen.

3128. Μανασσῆς **Manassēs**, *man-as-sace';* of Heb. or. [4519]; *Manasses* (i.e. *Menashsheh*), an Isr.:—Manasses.

3129. μανθάνω **manthanō**, *man-than'-o;* prol. from a prim. verb, another form of which, μαθέω **mathĕō**, is used as an alt. in cert. tenses; to *learn* (in any way):—learn, understand.

3130. μανία **mania**, *man-ee'-ah;* from *3105;* *craziness:*—[+ make] × mad.

3131. μάννα **manna**, *man'-nah;* of Heb. or. [4478]; *manna* (i.e. *man*), an edible gum:—manna.

3132. μαντεύομαι **mantĕuŏmai**, *mant-yoo'-om-ahee;* from a der. of *3105* (mean. a *prophet,* as supposed to *rave* through *inspiration*); to *divine,* i.e. *utter spells* (under pretence of foretelling):—by soothsaying.

3133. μαραίνω **marainō**, *mar-ah'-ee-no;* of uncert. affin.; to *extinguish* (as fire), i.e. (fig. and pass.) to *pass away:*—fade away.

3134. μαρὰν ἀθά **maran atha**, *mar'-an ath'-ah;* of Chald. or. (mean. *our Lord has come*); *maranatha,* i.e. an exclamation of the approaching *divine judgment:*—Maran-atha.

3135. μαργαρίτης **margaritēs**, *mar-gar-ee'-tace;* from μάργαρος **margarŏs** (a *pearl-oyster*); a *pearl:*—pearl.

3136. Μάρθα **Martha**, *mar'-thah;* prob. of Chald. or. (mean. *mistress*); *Martha,* a Chr. woman:—Martha.

3137. Μαρία **Maria**, *mar-ee'-ah;* or

Μαριάμ **Mariam**, *mar-ee-am';* of Heb. or. [4813]; *Maria* or *Mariam* (i.e. *Mirjam*), the name of six Chr. females:—Mary.

3138. Μάρκος **Markŏs**, *mar'-kos;* of Lat. or.; *Marcus,* a Chr.:—Marcus, Mark.

3139. μάρμαρος **marmarŏs**, *mar'-mar-os;* from μαρμαίρω **marmairō** (to *glisten*); *marble* (as sparkling *white*):—marble.

μάρτυρ **martur**. See *3144.*

3140. μαρτυρέω **marturĕō**, *mar-too-reh'-o;* from *3144;* to be a *witness,* i.e. *testify* (lit. or fig.):—charge, give [*evidence*], bear record, have (obtain, of) good (honest) report, be well reported of, testify, give (have) testimony, (be, bear, give, obtain) witness.

3141. μαρτυρία **marturia**, *mar-too-ree'-ah;* from *3144;* *evidence* given (judicially or gen.):—record, report, testimony, witness.

3142. μαρτύριον **marturiŏn**, *mar-too'-ree-on;* neut. of a presumed der. of *3144;* something *evidential,* i.e. (gen.) *evidence* given or (spec.) the *Decalogue* (in the sacred *Tabernacle*):—to be testified, testimony, witness.

3143. μαρτύρομαι **marturŏmai**, *mar-too'-rom-ahee;* mid. from *3144;* to be *adduced* as a *witness,* i.e. (fig.) to *obtest* (in *affirmation* or *exhortation*):—take to record, testify.

3144. μάρτυς **martus**, *mar'-toos;* of uncert. affin.; a *witness* (lit. [judicially] or fig. [gen.]); by anal. a " martyr":—martyr, record, witness.

3145. μασσάομαι **massaŏmai**, *mas-sah'-om-ahee;* from a prim. μάσσω **massō** (to *handle* or *squeeze*); to *chew:*—gnaw.

3146. μαστιγόω **mastigŏō**, *mas-tig-ŏ'-o;* from *3148;* to *flog* (lit. or fig.):—scourge.

3147. μαστίζω **mastizō**, *mas-tid'-zo;* from *3149;* to *whip* (lit.):—scourge.

3148. μάστιξ **mastix**, *mas'-tix;* prob. from the base of *3145* (through the idea of *contact*); a *whip* (lit. the Roman *flagellum* for criminals; fig. a *disease*):—plague, scourging.

3149. μαστός **mastŏs**, *mas-tos';* from the base of *3145;* a (prop. female) *breast* (as if kneaded up):—pap.

3150. ματαιολογία **mataiŏlŏgia**, *mat-ah-yol-og-ee'-ah;* from *3151;* *random talk,* i.e. *babble:*—vain jangling.

3151. ματαιολόγος **mataiŏlŏgŏs**, *mat-ah-yol-og'-os;* from *3152* and *3004;* an *idle* (i.e. *senseless* or *mischievous*) *talker,* i.e. a *wrangler:*—vain talker.

3152. μάταιος **mataiŏs**, *mat'-ah-yos;* from the base of *3155;* *empty,* i.e. (lit.) *profitless,* or (spec.) an *idol:*—vain, vanity.

3153. ματαιότης **mataiŏtēs**, *mat-ah-yot'-ucez* from *3152;* *inutility;* fig. *transientness;* mor. *depravity:*—vanity.

3154. ματαιόω **mataiŏō**, *mat-ah-yŏ'-o;* from *3152;* to *render* (pass. *become*) *foolish,* i.e. (mor.) *wicked* or (spec.) *idolatrous:*—become vain.

3155. μάτην **matēn**, *mat'-ane;* accus. of a der. of the base of *3145* (through the idea of tentative *manipulation,* i.e. unsuccessful *search,* or else of *punishment*); *folly,* i.e. (adv.) *to no purpose:*—in vain.

3156. Ματθαῖος **Matthaiŏs**, *mat-thah'-yos;* a shorter form of *3161; Matthœus* (i.e. *Matthitjah*), an Isr. and Chr.:—Matthew.

3157. Ματθάν **Matthan**, *mat-than';* of Heb. or. [4977]; *Matthan* (i.e. *Mattan*), an Isr.:—Matthan.

3158. Ματθάτ **Matthat**, *mat-that';* prob. a shortened form of *3161; Matthat* (i.e. *Mattithjah*), the name of two Isr.:—Mathat.

3159. Ματθίας **Matthias**, *mat-thee'-as;* appar. a shortened form of *3161; Matthias* (i.e. *Mattithjah*), an Isr.:—Matthias.

3160. Ματταθά **Mattatha**, *mat-tath-ah';* prob. a shortened form of *3161* [comp. 4992]; *Mattatha* (i.e. *Mattithjah*), an Isr.:—Mattatha.

3161. Ματταθίας **Mattathias**, *mat-tath-ee'-as;* of Heb. or. [4993]; *Mattathias* (i.e. *Mattithjah*), an Isr. and Chr.:—Mattathias.

3162. μάχαιρα **machaira**, *makh'-ahee-rah;* prob. fem. of a presumed der. of *3163;* a *knife,* i.e. *dirk;* fig. *war,* judicial *punishment:*—sword.

3163. μάχη **machē**, *makh'-ay;* from *3164;* a *battle,* i.e. (fig.) *controversy:*—fighting, strive, striving.

3164. μάχομαι **machŏmai**, *makh'-om-ahee;* mid. of an appar. prim. verb; to *war,* i.e. (fig.) to *quarrel, dispute:*—fight, strive.

3165. μέ **mĕ**, *meh;* a shorter (and prob. orig.) form of *1691; me:*—I, me, my.

3166. μεγαλαυχέω **mĕgalauchĕō**, *meg-al-ŏw-kheh'-o;* from a comp. of *3173* and αὐχέω **auchĕō** (to *boast*; akin to *837* and *2744*); to *talk big,* i.e. be *grandiloquent* (*arrogant, egotistic*):—boast great things.

3167. μεγαλεῖος **mĕgalĕiŏs**, *meg-al-i'-os;* from *3173; magnificent,* i.e. (neut. plur. as noun) a conspicuous *favor,* or (subj.) *perfection:*—great things, wonderful works.

3168. μεγαλειότης **mĕgalĕiŏtēs**, *meg-al-i-ot'-ace;* from *3167; superbness,* i.e. *glory* or *splendor:*—magnificence, majesty, mighty power.

3169. μεγαλοπρεπής **mĕgalŏprĕpēs**, *meg-al-op-rep-ace';* from *3173* and *4241; befitting greatness* or *magnificence* (*majestic*):—excellent.

3170. μεγαλύνω **mĕgalunō**, *meg-al-oo'-no;* from *3173;* to *make* (or *declare*) *great,* i.e. *increase* or (fig.) *extol:*—enlarge, magnify, shew great.

3171. μεγάλως **mĕgalōs**, *meg-al'-oce;* adv. from *3173; much:*—greatly.

3172. μεγαλωσύνη **mĕgalōsunē**, *meg-al-o-soo'-nay;* from *3173; greatness,* i.e. (fig.) *divinity* (often God himself):—majesty.

3173. μέγας **mĕgas**, *meg'-as* [includ. the prol. forms, fem. μεγάλη **mĕgalē**, plur. μεγάλοι **mĕgalŏi**, etc.; comp. also *3176, 3187*]; *big* (lit. or fig., in a very wide application):—(+ fear) exceedingly, great (-est), high, large, loud, mighty, + (be) sore (afraid), strong, × to years.

3174. μέγεθος **mĕgĕthŏs**, *meg'-eth-os;* from *3173; magnitude* (fig.):—greatness.

3175. μεγιστᾶνες **mĕgistanĕs**, *meg-is-tan'-es;* plur. from *3176; grandees:*—great men, lords.

3176. μέγιστος **mĕgistŏs**, *meg'-is-tos;* superl. of *3173; greatest* or *very great:*—exceeding great.

3177. μεθερμηνεύω **mĕthĕrmēnĕuō**, *meth-er-mane-yoo'-o;* from *3326* and *2059;* to *explain over,* i.e. *translate:*—(by) interpret (-ation).

3178. μέθη **mĕthē**, *meth'-ay;* appar. a prim. word; an *intoxicant,* i.e. (by impl.) *intoxication:*—drunkenness.

3179. μεθίστημι **methistēmi,** *meth-is'-tay-mee;* or (1 Cor. 13 : 2)

μεθιστάνω **methistanō,** *meth-is-tan'-o;* from *3326* and *2476;* to transfer, i.e. *carry away, depose* or (fig.) *exchange, seduce:*—put out, remove, translate, turn away.

3180. μεθοδεία **methŏdĕia,** *meth-od-i'-ah;* from a comp. of *3326* and *3593* [comp. " method "]; *travelling over,* i.e. *travesty* (*trickery*):—wile, lie in wait.

3181. μεθόριος **methŏriŏs,** *meth-or'-ee-os;* from *3326* and *3725;* *bounded alongside,* i.e. *contiguous* (neut. plur. as noun, *frontier*):—border.

3182. μεθύσκω **methuskō,** *meth-oos'-ko;* a prol. (trans.) form of *3184;* to *intoxicate:*—be drunk (-en).

3183. μέθυσος **methusŏs,** *meth'-oo-sos;* from *3184;* *tipsy,* i.e. (as noun) a *sot:*—drunkard.

3184. μεθύω **methuō,** *meth-oo'-o;* from another form of *3178;* to *drink* to *intoxication,* i.e. *get drunk:*—drink well, make (be) drunk (-en).

3185. μεῖζον **meizŏn,** *mide'-zon;* neut. of *3187;* (adv.) in a *greater* degree:—the more.

3186. μειζότερος **meizŏtĕrŏs,** *mide-zot'-er-os;* continued compar. of *3187; still larger* (fig.):—greater.

3187. μείζων **meizōn,** *mide'-zone;* irreg. compar. of *3173; larger* (lit. or fig., spec. in age):—elder, greater (-est), more.

3188. μέλαν **melan,** *mel'-an;* neut. of *3189* as noun; *ink:*—ink.

3189. μέλας **melas,** *mel'-as;* appar. a prim. word; *black:*—black.

3190. Μελεᾶς **Mĕlĕas,** *mel-eh-as';* of uncert. or.; *Meleas,* an Isr.:—Meleas.

μέλει **melei.** See *3199.*

3191. μελετάω **meletaō,** *mel-et-ah'-o;* from a presumed der. of *3199;* to *take care of,* i.e. (by impl.) *revolve* in the mind:—imagine, (pre-) meditate.

3192. μέλι **meli,** *mel'-ee;* appar. a prim. word; *honey:*—honey.

3193. μελίσσιος ⟨**melissios,** *mel-is'-see-os;* from *3192;* *relating to honey,* i.e. *bee* (comb):—honeycomb.

3194. Μελίτη **Mĕlitē,** *mel-ee'-tay;* of uncert. or.; *Melita,* an island in the Mediterranean:—Melita.

3195. μέλλω **mĕllō,** *mel'-lo;* a strengthened form of *3199* (through the idea of *expectation*); to *intend,* i.e. *be about* to be, do, or suffer something (of persons or things, espec. events; in the sense of *purpose, duty, necessity, probability, possibility,* or *hesitation*):—about, after that, be (almost), (that which is, things, + which was for) to come, intend, was to (be), mean, mind, be at the point, (be) ready, + return, shall (begin), (which, that) should (after, afterwards, hereafter) tarry, which was for, will, would, be yet.

3196. μέλος **melŏs,** *mel'-os;* of uncert. affin.; a *limb* or *part* of the body:—member.

3197. Μελχί **Mĕlchi,** *mel-khee';* of Heb. or. [4428 with pron. suf., *my king*]; *Melchi* (i.e. *Malki*), the name of two Isr.:—Melchi.

3198. Μελχισεδέκ **Mĕlchisĕdĕk,** *mel-khis-ed-ek';* of Heb. or. [4442]; *Melchisedek* (i.e. *Malkitsedek*), a patriarch:—Melchisedec.

3199. μέλω **melō,** *mel'-o;* a prim. verb; to *be of interest* to, i.e. to *concern* (only third pers. sing. pres. indic. used impers. *it matters*):—(take) care.

3200. μεμβράνα **membrana,** *mem-bran'-ah;* of Lat. or. (" *membrane* "); a (written) *sheep-skin:*—parchment.

3201. μέμφομαι **memphŏmai,** *mem'-fom-ahee;* mid. of an appar. prim. verb; to *blame:*—find fault.

3202. μεμψίμοιρος **mempsimŏirŏs,** *mem-psim'-oy-ros;* from a presumed der. of *3201* and μοῖρα **mŏira** (*fate;* akin to the base of *3313*); *blaming fate,* i.e. *querulous* (*discontented*):—complainer.

3203. μέν **mĕn,** *men;* a prim. particle; prop. indic. of *affirmation* or *concession* (*in fact*); usually followed by a *contrasted* clause with *1161* (*this* one, the *former,* etc.):—even, indeed, so, some, truly, verily. Often compounded with other particles in an *intensive* or *asseverative* sense.

3204. μενοῦνγε **mĕnŏungĕ,** *men-oon'-geh;* from *3303* and *3767* and *1065; so then* at least:—nay but, yea doubtless (rather, verily).

3305. μέντοι **mĕntŏi,** *men'-toy;* from *3303* and *5104; indeed though,* i.e. *however:*—also, but, howbeit, nevertheless, yet.

3306. μένω **mĕnō,** *men'-o;* a prim. verb; to *stay* (in a given place, state, relation or expectancy):—abide, continue, dwell, endure, be present, remain, stand, tarry (for), × thine own.

3307. μερίζω **mĕrizō,** *mer-id'-zo;* from *3313;* to *part,* i.e. (lit.) to *apportion, bestow, share,* or (fig.) to *disunite, differ:*—deal, be difference between, distribute, divide, give part.

3308. μέριμνα **mĕrimna,** *mer'-im-nah;* from *3307* (through the idea of *distraction*); *solicitude:*—care.

3309. μεριμνάω **mĕrimnaō,** *mer-im-nah'-o;* from *3308;* to *be anxious* about:—(be, have) care (-ful), take thought.

3310. μερίς **mĕris,** *mer-ece';* fem. of *3313;* a *portion,* i.e. *province, share* or (abstr.) *participation:*—part (× -akers).

3311. μερισμός **mĕrismŏs,** *mer-is-mos';* from *3307;* a *separation* or *distribution:*—dividing asunder, gift.

3312. μεριστής **mĕristēs,** *mer-is-tace';* from *3307;* an *apportioner* (*administrator*):—divider.

3313. μέρος **mĕrŏs,** *mer'-os;* from an obsol. but more prim. form of μείρομαι **mĕirŏmai** (to *get* as a *section* or *allotment*); a *division* or *share* (lit. or fig., in a wide application):—behalf, coast, course, craft, particular (+ -ly), part (+ -ly), piece, portion, respect, side, some sort (-what).

3314. μεσημβρία **mĕsēmbria,** *mes-ame-bree'-ah;* from *3319* and *2250; midday;* by impl. the *south:*—noon, south.

3315. μεσιτεύω **mĕsitĕuō,** *mes-it-yoo'-o;* from *3316;* to *interpose* (as arbiter), i.e. (by impl.) to *ratify* (as surety):—confirm.

3316. μεσίτης **mĕsitēs,** *mes-ee'-tace;* from *3319;* a *go-between,* i.e. (simply) an *internunciator,* or (by impl.) a *reconciler* (*intercessor*):—mediator.

3317. μεσονύκτιον **mĕsŏnuktiŏn,** *mes-on-ook'-tee-on;* neut. of a comp. of *3319* and *3571; midnight* (espec. as a watch):—midnight.

3318. Μεσοποταμία **Mĕsŏpŏtamia,** *mes-op-ot-am-ee'-ah;* from *3319* and *4215; Mesopotamia* (as lying between the Euphrates and the Tigris; comp. 763), a region of Asia:—Mesopotamia.

3319. μέσος **mĕsŏs,** *mes'-os;* from *3326; middle* (as adj. or [neut.] noun):—among, × before them, between, + forth, mid [-day, -night], midst, way.

3320. μεσότοιχον **mĕsŏtŏichŏn,** *mes-ot'-oy-khon;* from *3319* and *5109;* a *partition* (fig.):—middle wall.

3321. μεσουράνημα **mĕsŏuranēma,** *mes-oo-ran'-ay-mah;* from a presumed comp. of *3319* and *3772; mid-sky:*—midst of heaven.

3322. μεσόω **mĕsŏō,** *mes-ŏ'-o;* from *3319;* to *form* the *middle,* i.e. (in point of time), to *be half-way over:*—be about the midst.

3323. Μεσσίας **Mĕssias,** *mes-see'-as;* of Heb. or. [4899]; the *Messias* (i.e. *Mashiach*), or *Christ:*—Messias.

3324. μεστός **mĕstŏs,** *mes-tos';* of uncert. der.; *replete* (lit. or fig.):—full.

3325. μεστόω **mĕstŏō,** *mes-tŏ'-o;* from *3324;* to *replenish,* i.e. (by impl.) to *intoxicate:*—fill.

3326. μετά **mĕta,** *met-ah';* a prim. prep. (often used adv.); prop. denoting *accompaniment;* " *amid* " (local or causal); modified variously according to the case (gen. *association,* or acc. *succession*) with which it is joined; occupying an intermediate position between *575* or *1537* and *1519* or *4314;* less intimate than *1722,* and less close than *4862*):—after (-ward), × that be again, against, among, × and, + follow, hence, hereafter, in, of, (up-) on, + our, × and setting, since, (un-) to, + together, when, with (+ -out). Often used in composition, in substantially the same

relations of *participation* or *proximity,* and *transfer* or *sequence.*

3327. μεταβαίνω **mĕtabainō,** *met-ab-ah'ee-no;* from *3326* and the base of *939;* to *change place:*—depart, go, pass, remove.

3328. μεταβάλλω **mĕtaballō,** *met-ab-al'-lo;* from *3326* and *906;* to *throw over,* i.e. (mid. fig.) to *turn about* in opinion:—change mind.

3329. μετάγω **mĕtagō,** *met-ag'-o;* from *3326* and *71;* to *lead over,* i.e. *transfer* (direct):—turn about.

3330. μεταδίδωμι **mĕtadidōmi,** *met-ad-id'-o-mee;* from *3326* and *1325;* to *give over,* i.e. *share:*—give, impart.

3331. μετάθεσις **mĕtathĕsis,** *met-ath'-es-is;* from *3346; transposition,* i.e. *transferral* (to heaven), *disestablishment* (of a law):—change, removing, translation.

3332. μεταίρω **mĕtairō,** *met-ah'ee-ro;* from *3326* and *142;* to *betake* oneself, i.e. *remove* (locally):—depart.

3333. μετακαλέω **mĕtakalĕō,** *met-ak-al-eh'-o;* from *3326* and *2564;* to *call elsewhere,* i.e. *summon:*—call (for, hither).

3334. μετακινέω **mĕtakinĕō,** *met-ak-ee-neh'-o;* from *3326* and *2795;* to *stir* to a *place elsewhere,* i.e. *remove* (fig.):—move away.

3335. μεταλαμβάνω **mĕtalambanō,** *met-al-am-ban'-o;* from *3326* and *2983;* to *participate;* gen. to *accept* (and use):—eat, have, be partaker, receive, take.

3336. μετάληψις **mĕtalēpsis,** *met-al'-ape-sis;* from *3335; participation:*—taking.

3337. μεταλλάσσω **mĕtallassō,** *met-al-las'-so;* from *3326* and *236;* to *exchange:*—change.

3338. μεταμέλλομαι **mĕtamĕllŏmai,** *met-am-el'-lom-ahee;* from *3326* and the mid. of *3199;* to *care* afterwards, i.e. *regret:*—repent (self).

3339. μεταμορφόω **mĕtamŏrphŏō,** *met-am-or-fŏ'-o;* from *3326* and *3445;* to *transform* (lit. or fig. " metamorphose"):—change, transfigure, transform.

3340. μετανοέω **mĕtanŏĕō,** *met-an-ŏ-eh'-o;* from *3326* and *3539;* to *think differently* or *afterwards,* i.e. *reconsider* (mor. *feel compunction*):—repent.

3341. μετάνοια **mĕtanŏia,** *met-an'-oy-ah;* from *3340;* (subj.) *compunction* (for guilt, includ. *reformation*); by impl. *reversal* (of [another's] decision):—repentance.

3342. μεταξύ **mĕtaxu,** *met-ax-oo';* from *3326* and a form of *4862; betwixt* (of place or person); (of time) as adj. *intervening,* or (by impl.) *adjoining:*—between, mean while, next.

3343. μεταπέμπω **mĕtapĕmpō,** *met-ap-emp'-o;* from *3326* and *3992;* to *send from elsewhere,* i.e. (mid.) to *summon* or *invite:*—call (send) for.

3344. μεταστρέφω **mĕtastrĕphō,** *met-as-tref'-o;* from *3326* and *4762;* to *turn across,* i.e. *transmute* or (fig.) *corrupt:*—pervert, turn about.

3345. μετασχηματίζω **mĕtaschēmatizō,** *met-askh-ay-mat-id'-zo;* from *3326* and a der. of *4976;* to *transfigure* or *disguise;* fig. to *apply* (by accommodation):—transfer, transform (self); to *change.*

3346. μετατίθημι **mĕtatithēmi,** *met-at-ith'-ay-mee;* from *3326* and *5087;* to *transfer* (i.e. (lit.) *transport,* (by impl.) *exchange,* (reflex.) *change sides,* or (fig.) *pervert:*—carry over, change, remove, translate, turn.

3347. μετέπειτα **mĕtĕpĕita,** *met-ep'-i-tah;* from *3326* and *1899; thereafter:*—afterward.

3348. μετέχω **mĕtĕchō,** *met-ekh'-o;* from *3326* and *2192;* to *share* or *participate;* by impl. *belong* to, *eat* (or *drink*):—be partaker, pertain, take part, use.

3349. μετεωρίζω **mĕtĕōrizō,** *met-eh-o-rid'-zo;* from a comp. of *3326* and a collat. form of *142* or perh. rather of *109* (comp. " meteor "); to *raise* in *mid-air,* i.e. (fig.) *suspend* (pass. *fluctuate* or be *anxious*):—be of doubtful mind.

3350. μετοικεσία **mĕtŏikĕsia,** *met-oy-kes-ee'-ah;* from a der. of a comp. of *3326* and *3624;* a *change of abode,* i.e. (spec.) *expatriation:*— × brought, carried (-ying) away (in-) to.

3351. μετοικίζω **mĕtŏikizō**, *met-oy-kid'-zo;* from the same as *3350;* to *transfer* as a *settler* or *captive,* i.e. *colonize* or *exile:*—carry away, remove into.

3352. μετοχή **mĕtŏchē**, *met-okh-ay';* from *3348;* participation, i.e. *intercourse:*—fellowship.

3353. μέτοχος **mĕtŏchŏs**, *met'-okh-os;* from *3348;* participant, i.e. (as noun) a *sharer;* by impl. an associate:—fellow, partaker, partner.

3354. μετρέω **mĕtrĕō**, *met-reh'-o;* from *3358;* to *measure* (i.e. ascertain in size by a fixed standard); by impl. to *admeasure* (i.e. allot by rule); fig. to *estimate:*—measure, mete.

3355. μετρητής **mĕtrĕtēs**, *met-ray-tace';* from *3354;* a *measurer,* i.e. (spec.) a certain standard measure of capacity for liquids:—firkin.

3356. μετριοπαθέω **mĕtriŏpathĕō**, *met-ree-op-ath-eh'-o;* from a comp. of the base of *3357* and *3806;* to *be moderate in passion,* i.e. *gentle* (to treat indulgently):—have compassion.

3357. μετρίως **mĕtriōs**, *met-ree'-oce;* adv. from a der. of *3358;* moderately, i.e. *slightly:*—a little.

3358. μέτρον **mĕtrŏn**, *met'-ron;* an appar. prim. word; a *measure* ("metre", lit. or fig.; by impl. a limited portion (degree):—measure.

3359. μέτωπον **mĕtōpŏn**, *met'-o-pon;* from *3326* and ὤψ **ōps** (the *face*); the *forehead* (as opposite the countenance):—forehead.

3360. μέχρι **mĕchri**, *mekh'-ree;* or

μέχρις **mĕchris**, *mekh-ris';* from *3372;* as *far as,* i.e. *up to* a certain point (as prep. of extent [denoting the *terminus,* whereas *891* refers espec. to the *space* of time or place intervening) or conj.):—till, (un-) to, until.

3361. μή **mē**, *may;* a prim. particle of qualified *negation* (whereas *3756* expresses an absolute denial); (adv.) *not,* (conj.) *lest;* also (as interrog. implying a neg. answer [whereas *3756* expects an *affirm.* one]) *whether:*—any, but (that), × forbear, + God forbid, + lack, lest, neither, never, no (× wise in), none, nor, [can-] not, nothing, that not, un (-taken), without. Often used in compounds in substantially the same relations. See also *3362, 3363, 3364, 3372, 3373, 3375, 3378.*

3362. ἐὰν μή **ĕan mē**, *eh-an' may;* i.e. *1437* and *3361; if not,* i.e. *unless:*— × before, but, except, if no, (if, + whosoever) not.

3363. ἵνα μή **hina mē**, *hin'-ah may;* i.e. *2443* and *3361; in order (or so) that not:*—albeit not, lest, that no (-t, [-thing]).

3364. οὐ μή **ŏu mē**, *oo may;* i.e. *3756* and *3361;* a double neg. strengthening the denial; *not at all:*—any more, at all, by any (no) means, neither, never, no (at all), in no case (wise), nor ever, not (at all, in any wise). Comp. *3378.*

3365. μηδαμῶς **mēdamōs**, *may-dam-oce';* adv. from a comp. of *3361* and ἀμός **amŏs** (somebody); *by no means:*—not so.

3366. μηδέ **mēdĕ**, *may-deh';* from *3361* and *1161; but not,* not even; in a continued negation, nor:—neither, nor (yet), (no) not (once, so much as).

3367. μηδείς **mēdĕis**, *may-dice';* includ. the irreg. fem. μηδεμία **mēdĕmia**, *may-dem-ee'-ah,* and the neut. μηδέν **mēdĕn**, *may-den';* from *3361* and *1520; not even one* (man, woman, thing):—any (man, thing), no (man), none, not (at all, any man, a whit), nothing, + without delay.

3368. μηδέποτε **mēdĕpŏtĕ**, *may-dep'-ot-eh;* from *3366* and *4218; not even ever:*—never.

3369. μηδέπω **mēdĕpō**, *may-dep'-o;* from *3366* and *4452; not even yet:*—not yet.

3370. Μῆδος **Mēdŏs**, *may'-dos;* of for. or. [comp. *4074*]; a *Median,* or inhab. of Media:—Mede.

3371. μηκέτι **mēkĕti**, *may-ket'-ee;* from *3361* and *2089; no further:*—any longer, (not) henceforth, hereafter, no henceforward (longer, more, soon), not any more.

3372. μῆκος **mēkŏs**, *may'-kos;* prob. akin to *3173;* length (lit. or fig.):—length.

3373. μηκύνω **mēkunō**, *may-koo'-no;* from *3372;* to *lengthen,* i.e. (mid.) to *enlarge:*—grow up.

3374. μηλωτή **mēlōtē**, *may-lo-tay';* from μῆλον **mēlŏn** (a *sheep*); a *sheep-skin:*—sheepskin.

3375. μήν **mēn**, *mane;* a stronger form of *3303;* a particle of affirmation (only with *2229*); assuredly:— + surely.

3376. μήν **mēn**, *mane;* a prim. word; a *month:*—month.

3377. μηνύω **mēnuō**, *may-noo'-o;* prob. from the same base as *3145* and *3415* (i.e. μάω **maŏ**, to *strive*); to *disclose* (through the idea of mental *effort* and thus *calling* to *mind*), i.e. *report, declare, intimate:*—shew, tell.

3378. μὴ οὐκ **mē ŏuk**, *may ook;* i.e. *3361* and *3756;* as interrog. and neg. *is it not that?:*—neither (followed by *no*), + never, not. Comp. *3364.*

3379. μήποτε **mēpŏtĕ**, *may'-pot-eh;* or

μὴ ποτε **mē pŏtĕ**, *may pot'-eh;* from *3361* and *4218; not ever;* also *if* (or *lest*) *ever* (or *perhaps*):—if peradventure, lest (at any time, haply), not at all, whether or not.

3380. μήπω **mēpō**, *may'-po;* from *3361* and *4452; not yet:*—not yet.

3381. μήπως **mēpōs**, *may'-poce;* or

μὴ πως **mē pōs**, *may poce;* from *3361* and *4458; lest somehow:*—lest (by any means, by some means, haply, perhaps).

3382. μηρός **mērŏs**, *may-ros';* perh. a prim. word; a *thigh:*—thigh.

3383. μήτε **mētĕ**, *may'-teh;* from *3361* and *5037; not too,* i.e. (in continued negation) *neither* or *nor;* also, *not even:*—neither, (n-) or, so much as.

3384. μήτηρ **mētēr**, *may'-tare;* appar. a prim. word; a "*mother*" (lit. or fig., immed. or remote):—mother.

3385. μήτι **mēti**, *may'-tee;* from *3361* and the neut. of *5100; whether at all:*—not [the particle usually not expressed, except by the form of the question].

3386. μήτιγε **mētigĕ**, *may'-tig-eh;* from *3385* and *1065; not at all then,* i.e. *not to say* (the rather still):—how much more.

3387. μήτις **mētis**, *may'-tis;* or

μή τις **mē tis**, *may tis;* from *3361* and *5100; whether any:*—any [sometimes unexpressed except by the simple interrogative form of the sentence].

3388. μήτρα **mētra**, *may'-trah;* from *3384;* the *matrix:*—womb.

3389. μητραλῴας **mētralōas**, *may-tral-o'-as;* from *3384* and the base of *257;* a *mother-thresher,* i.e. *matricide:*—murderer of mothers.

3390. μητρόπολις **mētrŏpŏlis**, *may-trop'-ol-is;* from *3384* and *4172;* a *mother city,* i.e. "*metropolis*":—chiefest city.

3391. μία **mia**, *mee'-ah;* irreg. fem. of *1520;* one or *first:*—a (certain), + agree, first, one, × other.

3392. μιαίνω **miainō**, *me-ah'ee-no;* perh. a prim. verb; to *sully* or *taint,* i.e. *contaminate* (cer. or mor.):—defile.

3393. μίασμα **miasma**, *mee'-as-mah;* from *3392* ("*miasma*"); (mor.) *foulness* (prop. the effect):—pollution.

3394. μιασμός **miasmŏs**, *mee-as-mos';* from *3392;* (mor.) *contamination* (prop. the act):—uncleanness.

3395. μίγμα **migma**, *mig'-mah;* from *3396;* a *compound:*—mixture.

3396. μίγνυμι **mignumi**, *mig'-noo-mee;* a prim. verb; to *mix:*—mingle.

3397. μικρόν **mikrŏn**, *mik-ron';* masc. or neut. sing. of *3398* (as noun); a *small space of time* or *degree:*—a (little) (while).

3398. μικρός **mikrŏs**, *mik-ros';* includ. the comp. μικρότερος **mikrŏtĕrŏs**, *mik-rot'-er-os;* appar. a prim. word; *small* (in size, quantity, number or (fig.) dignity):—least, less, little, small.

3399. Μίλητος **Milētŏs**, *mil'-ay-tos;* of uncert. or.; *Miletus,* a city of Asia Minor:—Miletus.

3400. μίλιον **miliŏn**, *mil'-ee-on;* of Lat. or.; a *thousand paces,* i.e. a "*mile*":—mile.

3401. μιμέομαι **mimĕŏmai**, *mim-eh'-om-ahee;* mid. from μίμος **mimŏs** (a "*mimic*"); to *imitate:*—follow.

3402. μιμητής **mimētēs**, *mim-ay-tace';* from *3401;* an *imitator:*—follower.

3403. μιμνήσκω **mimnēskō**, *mim-nace'-ko;* a prol. form of *3415* (from which some of the tenses are borrowed); to *remind,* i.e. (mid.) to *recall to mind:*—be mindful, remember.

3404. μισέω **misĕō**, *mis-eh'-o;* from a prim. μῖσος **misŏs** (*hatred*); to *detest* (espec. to *persecute*); by extens. to *love less:*—hate (-ful).

3405. μισθαποδοσία **misthapŏdŏsia**, *mis-thap-od-os-ee'-ah;* from *3406; requital* (good or bad):—recompence of reward.

3406. μισθαποδότης **misthapŏdŏtēs**, *mis-thap-od-ot'-ace;* from *3409* and *591;* a *remunerator:*—rewarder.

3407. μίσθιος **misthiŏs**, *mis'-thee-os;* from *3408;* a *wage-earner:*—hired servant.

3408. μισθός **misthŏs**, *mis-thos';* appar. a prim. word; *pay* for service (lit. or fig.), good or bad:—hire, reward, wages.

3409. μισθόω **misthŏō**, *mis-tho'-o;* from *3408;* to *let out for wages,* i.e. (mid.) to *hire:*—hire.

3410. μίσθωμα **misthōma**, *mis'-tho-mah;* from *3409;* a *rented building:*—hired house.

3411. μισθωτός **misthōtŏs**, *mis-tho-tos';* from *3409;* a *wage-worker* (good or bad):—hired servant, hireling.

3412. Μιτυλήνη **Mitulēnē**, *mit-oo-lay'-nay;* for μυτιλήνη **mutilēnē** (abounding in shell-fish); *Mitylene* (or *Mytilene*), a town in the island Lesbos:—Mitylene.

3413. Μιχαήλ **Michaēl**, *mikh-ah-ale';* of Heb. or. [4817]; *Michaël,* an archangel:—Michael.

3414. μνᾶ **mna**, *mnah;* of Lat. or.; a *mna* (i.e. *mina*), a certain *weight:*—pound.

3415. μνάομαι **mnaŏmai**, *mnah'-om-ahee;* mid. of a der. of *3306* or perh. of the base of *3145* (through the idea of *fixture* in the mind or of mental *grasp*); to *bear in mind,* i.e. *recollect;* by impl. to *reward* or *punish:*—be mindful, remember, come (have) in remembrance. Comp. *3403.*

3416. Μνάσων **Mnasōn**, *mnah'-sohn;* of uncert. or.; *Mnason,* a Chr.:—Mnason.

3417. μνεία **mnĕia**, *mni'-ah;* from *3415* or *3403; recollection;* by impl. *recital:*—mention, remembrance.

3418. μνῆμα **mnēma**, *mnay'-mah;* from *3415;* a *memorial,* i.e. sepulchral *monument* (burial-place):—grave, sepulchre, tomb.

3419. μνημεῖον **mnēmĕiŏn**, *mnay-mi'-on;* from *3420;* a *remembrance,* i.e. *cenotaph* (place of interment):—grave, sepulchre, tomb.

3420. μνήμη **mnēmē**, *mnay'-may;* from *3403; memory:*—remembrance.

3421. μνημονεύω **mnēmŏnĕuō**, *mnay-mon-yoo'-o;* from a der. of *3420;* to *exercise memory,* i.e. *recollect;* by impl. to *punish;* also to *rehearse:*—make mention, be mindful, remember.

3422. μνημόσυνον **mnēmŏsunŏn**, *mnay-mos'-oo-non;* from *3421;* a *reminder* (*memorandum*), i.e. *record:*—memorial.

3423. μνηστεύω **mnēstĕuō**, *mnace-tyoo'-o;* from a der. of *3415;* to *give* a *souvenir* (engagement present), i.e. *betroth:*—espouse.

3424. μογιλάλος **mŏgilalŏs**, *mog-il-al'-os;* from *3425* and *2980; hardly talking,* i.e. *dumb* (*tongue*-tied):—having an impediment in his speech.

3425. μόγις **mŏgis**, *mog'-is;* adv. from a prim. μόγος **mŏgŏs** (*toil*); with *difficulty:*—hardly.

3426. μόδιος **mŏdiŏs**, *mod'-ee-os;* of Lat. or.; a *modius,* i.e. certain *measure* for things dry (the quantity or the utensil):—bushel.

3427. μοί **mŏi**, *moy;* the simpler form of *1698; to me:*—I. me, mine, my.

3428. μοιχαλίς **mŏichalis,** *moy-khal-is'*; a prol. form of the fem. of *3432*; an *adulteress* (lit. or fig.):—adulteress (-ous, -y).

3429. μοιχάω **mŏichaō,** *moy-khah'-o*; from *3432*; (mid.) to *commit adultery*:—commit adultery.

3430. μοιχεία **mŏichĕia,** *moy-khi'-ah*; from *3431*; *adultery*:—adultery.

3431. μοιχεύω **mŏichĕuō,** *moy-khyoo'-o*; from *3432*; to *commit adultery*:—commit adultery.

3432. μοιχός **mŏichŏs,** *moy-khos'*; perh. a prim. word; a (male) *paramour*; fig. *apostate*:—adulterer.

3433. μόλις **mŏlis,** *mol'-is*; prob. by var. for *3425*; *with difficulty*:—hardly, scarce (-ly), + with much work.

3434. Μολόχ **Mŏlŏch,** *mol-okh'*; of Heb. or. [4432]; *Moloch* (i.e. *Molek*), an idol:—Moloch.

3435. μολύνω **mŏlunō,** *mol-oo'-no*; prob. from *3180*; to *soil* (fig.):—defile.

3436. μολυσμός **mŏlusmŏs,** *mol-oos-mos'*; from *3435*; a *stain*, i.e. (fig.) *immorality*:—filthiness.

3437. μομφή **mŏmphē,** *mom-fay'*; from *3201*; *blame*, i.e. (by impl.) a *fault*:—quarrel.

3438. μονή **mŏnē,** *mon-ay'*; from *3306*; a *staying*, i.e. *residence* (the act or the place):—abode, mansion.

3439. μονογενής **mŏnŏgĕnēs,** *mon-og-en-ace'*; from *3441* and *1096*; *only-born*, i.e. *sole*:—only (begotten, child).

3440. μόνον **mŏnŏn,** *mon'-on*; neut. of *3441* as adv.; *merely*:—alone, but, only.

3441. μόνος **mŏnŏs,** *mon'-os*; prob. from *3306*; *remaining*, i.e. *sole* or *single*; by impl. *mere*:—alone, only, by themselves.

3442. μονόφθαλμος **mŏnŏphthalmŏs,** *mon-of'-thal-mos*; from *3441* and *3788*; *one-eyed*:—with one eye.

3443. μονόω **mŏnŏō,** *mon-ŏ'-o*; from *3441*; to *isolate*, i.e. *bereave*:—be desolate.

3444. μορφή **mŏrphē,** *mor-fay'*; perh. from the base of *3313* (through the idea of *adjustment* of parts); *shape*; fig. *nature*:—form.

3445. μορφόω **mŏrphŏō,** *mor-fŏ'-o*; from the same as *3444*; to *fashion* (fig.):—form.

3446. μόρφωσις **mŏrphōsis,** *mor'-fo-sis*; from *3445*; *formation*, i.e. (by impl.) *appearance* (semblance o͞ [concr.] *formula*):—form.

3447. μοσχοποιέω **mŏschŏpŏiĕō,** *mos-khop-oy-eh'-o*; from *3448* and *4160*; to *fabricate* the image of a *bullock*:—make a calf.

3448. μόσχος **mŏschŏs,** *mos'-khos*; prob. strengthened for ὄσχος *ŏschŏs* (a *shoot*); a young *bullock*:—calf.

3449. μόχθος **mŏchthŏs,** *mokh'-thos*; from the base of *3425*; *toil*, i.e. (by impl.) *sadness*:—painfulness, travail.

3450. μοῦ **mŏu,** *moo*; the simpler form of *1700*; of *me*:—I, me, mine (own), my.

3451. μουσικός **mŏusikŏs,** *moo-sik-os'*; from Μοῦσα **Mŏusa** (a *Muse*); "musical", i.e. (as noun) a *minstrel*:—musician.

3452. μυελός **muĕlŏs,** *moo-el-os'*; perh. a prim. word; the *marrow*:—marrow.

3453. μυέω **muĕō,** *moo-eh'-o*; from the base of *3466*; to *initiate*, i.e. (by impl.) to *teach*:—instruct.

3454. μῦθος **muthŏs,** *moo'-thos*; perh. from the same as *3453* (through the idea of *tuition*); a *tale*, i.e. *fiction* ("*myth*"):—fable.

3455. μυκάομαι **mukaŏmai,** *moo-kah'-om-ahee*; from a presumed der. of μύζω *muzō* (to "*moo*"); to *bellow* (*roar*):—roar.

3456. μυκτηρίζω **muktērizō,** *mook-tay-rid'-zo*; from a der. of the base of *3455* (mean. *snout*, as that whence *lowing* proceeds); to *make mouths* at, i.e. *ridicule*:—mock.

3457. μυλικός **mulikŏs,** *moo-lee-kos'*; from *3458*; belonging to a *mill*:—mill [-stone].

3458. μύλος **mulŏs,** *moo'-los*; prob. ultimately from the base of *3433* (through the idea of *hardship*); a "*mill*", i.e. (by impl.) a *grinder* (*millstone*):—millstone.

3459. μύλων **mulōn,** *moo'-lone*; from *3458*; a *mill-house*:—mill.

3460. Μύρα **Mura,** *moo'-rah*; of uncert. der.; *Myra*, a place in Asia Minor:—Myra.

3461. μυρίας **murias,** *moo-ree'-as*; from *3463*; a *ten-thousand*; by extens. a "*myriad*" or indefinite number:—ten thousand.

3462. μυρίζω **murizō,** *moo-rid'-zo*; from *3464*; to *apply* (*perfumed*) *unguent* to:—anoint.

3463. μύριοι **muriŏi,** *moo'-ree-oi*; plur. of an appar. prim. word (prop. mean. *very many*); *ten thousand*; by extens. *innumerably* many:—ten thousand.

3464. μύρον **murŏn,** *moo'-ron*; prob. of for. or. [comp. 4753, 4666]; "*myrrh*", i.e. (by impl.) *perfumed oil*:—ointment.

3465. Μυσία **Musia,** *moo-see'-ah*; of uncert. or.; *Mysia*, a region of Asia Minor:—Mysia.

3466. μυστήριον **mustēriŏn,** *moos-tay'-ree-on*; from a der. of μύω *muō* (to *shut* the mouth); a *secret* or "*mystery*" (through the idea of *silence* imposed by *initiation* into religious rites):—mystery.

3467. μυωπάζω **muōpazō,** *moo-ope-ad'-zo*; from a comp. of the base of *3466* and ὤψ **ŏps** (the *face*: from *3700*); to *shut the eyes*, i.e. *blink* (*see indistinctly*):—cannot see afar off.

3468. μώλωψ **mōlōps,** *mo'-lopes*; from μῶλος **mōlŏs** ("*moil*"; prob. akin to the base of *3433*) and prob. ὤψ **ŏps** (the *face*; from *3700*); a *mole* ("black eye") or *blow-mark*:—stripe.

3469. μωμάομαι **mōmaŏmai,** *mo-mah'-om-ahee*; from *3470*; to *carp* at, i.e. *censure* (*discredit*):—blame.

3470. μῶμος **mōmŏs,** *mo'-mos*; perh. from *3201*; a *flaw* or *blot*, i.e. (fig.) *disgraceful* person:—blemish.

3471. μωραίνω **mōrainō,** *mo-rah'ee-no*; from *3474*; to *become insipid*; fig. to *make* (pass. *act*) as a *simpleton*:—become fool, make foolish, lose savour.

3472. μωρία **mōria,** *mo-ree'-ah*; from *3474*; *silliness*, i.e. *absurdity*:—foolishness.

3473. μωρολογία **mōrŏlŏgia,** *mo-rol-og-ee'-ah*; from a comp. of *3474* and *3004*; *silly talk*, i.e. *buffoonery*:—foolish talking.

3474. μωρός **mōrŏs,** *mo-ros'*; prob. from the base of *3466*; *dull* or *stupid* (as if *shut up*), i.e. *heedless*, (mor.) *blockhead*, (appar.) *absurd*:—fool (-ish, × -ishness).

3475. Μωσεύς **Mōsĕus,** *moce-yoos'*; or
    Μωσῆς **Mōsēs,** *mo-sace'*; or
    Μωϋσῆς **Mōüsēs** (i.e. *Mosheh*), the Heb. lawgiver:—Moses.

N

3476. Ναασσών **Naassōn,** *nah-as-sone'*; of Heb. or. [5177]; *Naasson* (i.e. *Nachshon*), an Isr.:—Naasson.

3477. Ναγγαί **Naggai,** *nang-gah'ee*; prob. of Heb. or. [comp. 5052]; *Nangæ* (i.e. perh. *Nogach*), an Isr.:—Nagge.

3478. Ναζαρέθ **Nazarĕth,** *nad-zar-eth'*; or
    Ναζαρέτ **Nazarĕt,** *nad-zar-et'*; of uncert. der.; *Nazareth* or *Nazaret*, a place in Pal.:—Nazareth.

3479. Ναζαρηνός **Nazarēnŏs,** *nad-zar-ay-nos'*; from *3478*; a *Nazarene*, i.e. inhab. of Nazareth:—of Nazareth.

3480. Ναζωραῖος **Nazōraiŏs,** *nad-zo-rah'-yos*; from *3478*; a *Nazoræan*, i.e. inhab. of Nazareth; by extens. a *Christian*:—Nazarene, of Nazareth.

3481. Ναθάν **Nathan,** *nath-an'*; of Heb. or. [5416]; *Nathan*, an Isr.:—Nathan.

3482. Ναθαναήλ **Nathanaēl,** *nath-an-ah-ale'*; of Heb. or. [5417]; *Nathanaël* (i.e. *Nathanel*), an Isr. and Chr.:—Nathanael.

3483. ναί **nai,** *nahee*; a prim. particle of strong affirmation; *yes*:—even so, surely, truth, verily, yea, yes.

3484. Ναΐν **Naïn,** *nah-in'*; prob. of Heb. or. [comp. 4999]; *Naïn*, a place in Pal.:—Nain.

3485. ναός **naŏs,** *nah-os'*; from a prim. ναίω **naiō** (to *dwell*); a *fane*, *shrine*, *temple*:—shrine, temple. Comp. *2411*.

3486. Ναούμ **Naŏum,** *nah-oom'*; of Heb. or. [5151]; *Naüm* (i.e. *Nachum*), an Isr.:—Naum.

3487. νάρδος **nardŏs,** *nar'-dos*; of for. or. [comp. 5878]; "*nard*":—[spike-] nard.

3488. Νάρκισσος **Narkissŏs,** *nar'-kis-sos*; a flower of the same name, from νάρκη **narkē** (*stupefaction*, as a "narcotic"); *Narcissus*, a Roman:—Narcissus.

3489. ναυαγέω **nauagĕō,** *now-ag-eh'-o*; from a comp. of *3491* and *71*; to *be shipwrecked* (*stranded*, "navigate"), lit. or fig.:—make (suffer) shipwreck.

3490. ναύκληρος **nauklērŏs,** *now'-klay-ros*; from *3491* and *2819* ("clerk"); a *captain*:—owner of a ship.

3491. ναῦς **naus,** *nŏwce*; from νάω **naō** or νέω **nĕō** (to *float*); a *boat* (of any size):—ship.

3492. ναύτης **nautēs,** *now'-tace*; from *3491*; a *boatman*, i.e. *seaman*:—sailor, shipman.

3493. Ναχώρ **Nachōr,** *nakh-ore'*; of Heb. or. [5152]; *Nachor*, the grandfather of Abraham:—Nachor.

3494. νεανίας **nĕanias,** *neh-an-ee'-as*; from a der. of *3501*; a *youth* (up to about forty years):—young man.

3495. νεανίσκος **nĕaniskŏs,** *neh-an-is'-kos*; from the same as *3494*; a *youth* (under forty):—young man.

3496. Νεάπολις **Nĕapŏlis,** *neh-ap'-ol-is*; from *3501* and *4172*; *new town*; *Neäpolis*, a place in Macedonia:—Neapolis.

3497. Νεεμάν **Nĕĕman,** *neh-eh-man'*; of Heb. or. [5283]; *Neëman* (i.e. *Naaman*), a Syrian:—Naaman.

3498. νεκρός **nĕkrŏs,** *nek-ros'*; from an appar. prim. νέκυς **nĕkus** (a *corpse*); *dead* (lit. or fig.; also as noun):—dead.

3499. νεκρόω **nĕkrŏō,** *nek-rŏ'-o*; from *3498*; to *deaden*, i.e. (fig.) to *subdue*:—be dead, mortify.

3500. νέκρωσις **nĕkrōsis,** *nek'-ro-sis*; from *3499*; *decease*; fig. *impotency*:—deadness, dying.

3501. νέος **nĕŏs,** *neh'-os*; includ. the comp. νεώτερος **nĕōtĕrŏs,** *neh-o'-ter-os*; a prim. word; "*new*", i.e. (of persons) *youthful*, or (of things) *fresh*; fig. *regenerate*:—new, young.

3502. νεοσσός **nĕŏssŏs,** *neh-os-sos'*; from *3501*; a *youngling* (*nestling*):—young.

3503. νεότης **nĕŏtēs,** *neh-ot'-ace*; from *3501*; *newness*, i.e. *youthfulness*:—youth.

3504. νεόφυτος **nĕŏphutŏs,** *neh-of'-oo-tos*; from *3501* and a der. of *5453*; *newly planted*, i.e. (fig.) a *young convert* ("*neophyte*"):—novice.

3505. Νέρων **Nĕrōn,** *ner'-ohn*; of Lat. or.; *Neron* (i.e. *Nero*), a Rom. emperor:—Nero.

3506. νεύω **nĕuō,** *nyoo'-o*; appar. a prim. verb; to "*nod*", i.e. (by anal.) to *signal*:—beckon.

3507. νεφέλη **nĕphĕlē,** *nef-el'-ay*; from *3509*; prop. *cloudiness*, i.e. (concr.) a *cloud*:—cloud.

3508. Νεφθαλείμ **Nĕphthalĕim,** *nef-thal-ime'*; of Heb. or. [5321]; *Nephthaleim* (i.e. *Naphthali*), a tribe in Pal.:—Nephthalim.

3509. νέφος **nĕphŏs,** *nef'-os*; appar. a prim. word; a *cloud*:—cloud.

3510. νεφρός **nĕphrŏs,** *nef-ros'*; of uncert. affin.; a *kidney* (plur.), i.e. (fig.) the inmost *mind*:—reins.

3511. νεωκόρος **nĕōkŏrŏs,** *neh-o-kor'-os*; from a form of *3485* and κορέω **kŏrĕō** (to *sweep*); a *temple-servant*, i.e. (by impl.) a *votary*:—worshipper.

3512. νεωτερικός **nĕōtĕrikŏs,** *neh-o-ter'-ik-os*; from the comp. of *3501*; *appertaining* to *younger* persons, i.e. *juvenile*:—youthful. νεώτερος **nĕōtĕrŏs.** See *3501*.

3513. νή **nē,** *nay*; prob. an intens. form of *3483*; a particle of attestation (accompanied by the object invoked or appealed to in confirmation); *as sure as*:—I protest by.

3514. νήθω **nēthō,** *nay'-tho*; from νέω **nĕō** (of like mean.); to *spin*:—spin.

3515. νηπιάζω **nēpiazō**, *nay-pee-ad'-zo;* from *3516;* to act as a babe, i.e. (fig.) innocently:—be a child.

3516. νήπιος **nēpiŏs**, *nay'-pee-os;* from an obsol. particle νη- nē- (implying *negation*) and *2031; not speaking,* i.e. an infant (*minor*); fig. a *simple-minded* person, an *immature* Christian:—babe, child (+ -ish).

3517. Νηρεύς **Nērĕus**, *nare-yoos';* appar. from a der. of the base of *3491* (mean. *wet*); *Nereus,* a Chr.:—Nereus.

3518. Νηρί **Nēri**, *nay-ree';* of Heb. or. [5374]; *Neri* (i.e. *Nerijah*), an Isr.:—Neri.

3519. νησίον **nēsiŏn**, *nay-see'-on;* dimin. of *3520;* an *islet:*—island.

3520. νῆσος **nēsŏs**, *nay'-sos;* prob. from the base of *3491;* an *island:*—island, isle.

3521. νηστεία **nēstĕia**, *nace-ti'-ah;* from *3522; abstinence* (from lack of food, or voluntary and religious); spec. the *fast* of the Day of Atonement:—fast (-ing.)

3522. νηστεύω **nēstĕuō**, *nace-tyoo'-o;* from *3523;* to *abstain* from food (religiously):—fast.

3523. νῆστις **nēstis**, *nace'-tis;* from the insep. neg. particle νη- nē- (*not*) and *2068; not eating,* i.e. *abstinent* from food (religiously):—fasting.

3524. νηφάλιος **nēphaliŏs**, *nay-fal'-eh-os;* or νηφάλιος **nēphaliŏs**, *nay-fal'-ee-os;* from *3525; sober,* i.e. (fig.) *circumspect* —sober, vigilant.

3525. νήφω **nēphō**, *nay'-fo;* of uncert. affin.; to *abstain* from wine (keep *sober*), i.e. (fig.) *be discreet:*—be sober, watch.

3526. Νίγερ **Nigĕr**, *neeg'-er;* of Lat. or.; *black; Niger,* a Chr.:—Niger.

3527. Νικάνωρ **Nikanōr**, *nik-an'-ore;* prob. from *3528; victorious; Nicanor,* a Chr.:—Nicanor.

3528. νικάω **nikaō**, *nik-ah'-o;* from *3529;* to *subdue* (lit. or fig.):—conquer, overcome, prevail, get the victory.

3529. νίκη **nikē**, *nee'-kay;* appar. a prim. word; *conquest* (abstr.), i.e. (fig.) the *means of success:*—victory.

3530. Νικόδημος **Nikŏdēmŏs**, *nik-od'-ay-mos;* from *3534* and *1218; victorious* among his people; *Nicodemus,* an Isr.:—Nicodemus.

3531. Νικολαΐτης **Nikŏlaïtēs**, *nik-ol-ah-ee'-tace;* from *3532;* a *Nicolaïte,* i.e. adherent of *Nicolaüs:*—Nicolaitane.

3532. Νικόλαος **Nikŏlaŏs**, *nik-ol'-ah-os;* from *3534* and *2992; victorious* over the *people; Nicolaüs,* a heretic:—Nicolaus.

3533. Νικόπολις **Nikŏpŏlis**, *nik-op'-ol-is;* from *3534* and *4172; victorious city; Nicopolis,* a place in Macedonia:—Nicopolis.

3534. νῖκος **nikŏs**, *nee'-kos;* from *3529;* a *conquest* (concr.), i.e. (by impl.) *triumph:*—victory.

3535. Νινευί **Ninĕui**, *nin-yoo-ee';* of Heb. or. [5210]; *Ninevi* (i.e. *Nineveh*), the capital of Assyria:—Nineve.

3536. Νινευίτης **Ninĕuitēs**, *nin-yoo-ee'-tace;* from *3535;* a *Ninevite,* i.e. inhab. of Nineveh:—of Nineve, Ninevite.

3537. νιπτήρ **niptēr**, *nip-tare';* from *3538;* a *ewer:*—bason.

3538. νίπτω **niptō**, *nip'-to;* to *cleanse* (espec. the hands or the feet or the face); cer. to *perform ablution:*—wash. Comp. *3068.*

3539. νοιέω **nŏiĕō**, *noy-eh'-o;* from *3563;* to *exercise the mind* (*observe*), i.e. (fig.) to *comprehend, heed:*—consider, perceive, think, understand.

3540. νόημα **nŏēma**, *nŏ'-ay-mah;* from *3539;* a *perception,* i.e. *purpose,* or (by impl.) the *intellect, disposition,* itself:—device, mind, thought.

3541. νόθος **nŏthŏs**, *noth'-os;* of uncert. affin.; a *spurious* or *illegitimate* son:—bastard.

3542. νομή **nŏmē**, *nom-ay';* fem. from the same as *3551; pasture,* i.e. (the act) *feeding* (fig. *spreading* of a gangrene), or (the food) *pasturage:*— × eat, pasture.

3543. νομίζω **nŏmizō**, *nom-id'-zo;* from *3551;* prop. to do by *law* (*usage*), i.e. to *accustom* (pass. be *usual*); by extens. to *deem* or *regard:*—suppose, think, be wont.

3544. νομικός **nŏmikŏs**, *nom-ik-os';* from *3551; according* (or *pertaining*) *to law,* i.e. *legal* (cer.); as noun, an *expert in* the (Mosaic) *law:*—about the law, lawyer.

3545. νομίμως **nŏmimōs**, *nom-im'-oce;* adv. from a der. of *3551; legitimately* (spec. *agreeably* to the rules of the lists):—lawfully.

3546. νόμισμα **nŏmisma**, *nom'-is-mah;* from *3543; what is reckoned* as of value (after the Lat. *numisma*), i.e. current *coin:*—money.

3547. νομοδιδάσκαλος **nŏmŏdidaskalŏs**, *nom-od-id-as'-kal-os;* from *3551* and *1320;* an *expounder of* the (Jewish) *law,* i.e. a *Rabbi:*—doctor (*teacher*) of the law.

3548. νομοθεσία **nŏmŏthĕsia**, *nom-oth-es-ee'-ah;* from *3550; legislation* (spec. the *institution* of the Mosaic code):—giving of the law.

3549. νομοθετέω **nŏmŏthĕtĕō**, *nom-oth-et'-eh'-o;* from *3550;* to *legislate,* i.e. (pass.) to *have* (the Mosaic) *enactments* injoined, be *sanctioned* (by them):—establish, receive the law.

3550. νομοθέτης **nŏmŏthĕtēs**, *nom-oth-et'-ace;* from *3551* and a der. of *5087;* a *legislator:*—lawgiver.

3551. νόμος **nŏmŏs**, *nom'-os;* from a prim. νέμω nĕmō (to *parcel* out, espec. *food* or *grazing* to animals); *law* (through the idea of prescriptive *usage*), gen. (*regulation*), spec. (of Moses [includ. the volume]; also of the Gospel), or fig. (a *principle*):—law.

3552. νοσέω **nŏsĕō**, *nos-eh'-o;* from *3554;* to be *sick,* i.e. (by impl. of a diseased appetite) to *hanker* after (fig. to *harp* upon):—dote.

3553. νόσημα **nŏsēma**, *nos'-ay-ma;* from *3552;* an *ailment:*—disease.

3554. νόσος **nŏsŏs**, *nos'-os;* of uncert. affin.; a *malady* (rarely fig. of mor. *disability*):—disease, infirmity, sickness.

3555. νοσσιά **nŏssia**, *nos-see-ah';* from *3502;* a *brood* (of chickens):—brood.

3556. νοσσίον **nŏssiŏn**, *nos-see'-on;* dimin. of *3502;* a *birdling:*—chicken.

3557. νοσφίζομαι **nŏsphizŏmai**, *nos-fid'-zom-ahee;* mid. from νόσφι **nŏsphi** (*apart* or *clandestinely*); to *sequestrate* for oneself, i.e. *embezzle:*—keep back, purloin.

3558. νότος **nŏtŏs**, *not'-os;* of uncert. affin.; the *south* (-*west*) *wind;* by extens. the *southern quarter* itself:—south (wind).

3559. νουθεσία **nŏuthĕsia**, *noo-thes-ee'-ah;* from *3563* and a der. of *5087; calling attention* 'to, i.e. (by impl.) mild *rebuke* or *warning:*—admonition.

3560. νουθετέω **nŏuthĕtĕō**, *noo-thet-eh'-o;* from the same as *3559;* to *put in mind,* i.e. (by impl.) to *caution* or *reprove* gently:—admonish, warn.

3561. νουμηνία **nŏumēnia**, *noo-may-nee'-ah;* fem. of a comp. of *3501* and *3376* (as noun by impl. of *2250*); the *festival* of *new moon:*—new moon.

3562. νουνεχῶς **nŏunĕchōs**, *noon-ekh-oce';* adv. from a comp. of the acc. of *3563* and *2192;* in a *mindhaving* way, i.e. *prudently:*—discreetly.

3563. νοῦς **nŏus**, *nooce;* prob. from the base of *1097;* the *intellect,* i.e. *mind* (divine or human; in thought, feeling, or will); by impl. *meaning:*—mind, understanding. Comp. *5590.*

3564. Νυμφᾶς **Numphas**, *noom-fas';* prob. contr. for a comp. of *3565* and *1435; nymph-given* (i.e. *-born*); *Nymphas,* a Chr.:—Nymphas.

3565. νύμφη **numphē**, *noom-fay';* from. a prim. but obsol. verb νύπτω **nuptō** (to *veil* as a bride; comp. Lat. "*nupto,*" to *marry*); a *young married* woman (as *veiled*), includ. a *betrothed* girl; by impl. a *son's wife:*—bride, daughter in law.

3566. νυμφίος **numphiŏs**, *noom-fee'-os;* from *3565;* a *bride-groom* (lit. or fig.):—bridegroom.

3567. νυμφών **numphōn**, *noom-fohn';* from *3565;* the *bridal room:*—bridechamber.

3568. νῦν **nun**, *noon;* a prim. particle of present time; "*now*" (as adv. of date, a transition or emphasis); also as noun or adj. *present* or *immediate:*—henceforth, + hereafter, of late, soon, present, this (time). See also *3569, 3570.*

3569. τανῦν **tanun**, *tan-oon';* or τὰ νῦν **ta nun**, *tah noon;* from neut. plur. of *3588* and *3568; the things now,* i.e. (adv.) *at present:*—(but) now.

3570. νυνί **nuni**, *noo-nee';* a prol. form of *3568* for emphasis; *just now:*—now.

3571. νύξ **nux**, *noox;* a prim. word; "*night*" (lit. or fig.):—(mid.-) night.

3572. νύσσω **nussō**, *noos'-so;* appar. a prim. word; to *prick* ("*nudge*"):—pierce.

3573. νυστάζω **nustazō**, *noos-tad'-zo;* from a presumed der. of *3506;* to *nod,* i.e. (by impl.) to *fall asleep;* fig. to *delay:*—slumber.

3574. νυχθήμερον **nuchthēmĕrŏn**, *nookhthay'-mer-on;* from *3571* and *2250;* a *day-and-night,* i.e. full *day* of twenty-four hours:—night and day.

3575. Νῶε **Nŏĕ**, *no'-eh;* of Heb. or. [5146]; *Noë,* (i.e. *Nŏäch*), a patriarch:—Noe.

3576. νωθρός **nōthrŏs**, *no-thros';* from a der. of *3541; sluggish,* i.e. (lit.) *lazy,* or (fig.) *stupid:*—dull, slothful.

3577. νῶτος **nōtŏs**, *no'-tos;* of uncert. affin.; the *back:*—back.

Ξ

3578. ξενία **xĕnia**, *xen-ee'-ah;* from *3581; hospitality,* i.e. (by impl.) a *place of entertainment:*—lodging.

3579. ξενίζω **xĕnizō**, *xen-id'-zo;* from *3581;* to be a *host* (pass. a *guest*); by impl. be (make, appear) *strange:*—entertain, lodge, (think it) strange.

3580. ξενοδοχέω **xĕnŏdŏchĕō**, *xen-od-okh-eh'-o;* from a comp. of *3581* and *1209;* to be *hospitable:*—lodge strangers.

3581. ξένος **xĕnŏs**, *xen'-os;* appar. a prim. word; *foreign* (lit. *alien,* or fig. *novel*); by impl. a *guest* or (vice-versa) *entertainer:*—host, strange (-r).

3582. ξέστης **xĕstēs**, *xes'-tace;* as if from ξέω **xĕō** (prop. to *smooth;* by impl. [of *friction*] to *boil* or *heat*); a *vessel* (as *fashioned* or for *cooking*) [or perh. by corruption from the Lat. *sextarius,* the *sixth* of a modius, i.e. about a *pint*], i.e. (spec.) a *measure* for liquids or solids, (by anal. a *pitcher*):—pot.

3583. ξηραίνω **xērainō**, *xay-rah'ee-no;* from *3584;* to *desiccate;* by impl. to *shrivel,* to *mature:*—dry up, pine away, be ripe, wither (away).

3584. ξηρός **xērŏs**, *xay-ros';* from the base of *3582* (through the idea of *scorching*); *arid;* by impl. *shrunken, earth* (as opposed to water):—dry, land, withered.

3585. ξύλινος **xulinŏs**, *xoo'-lin-os;* from *3586; wooden:*—of wood.

3586. ξύλον **xulŏn**, *xoo'-lon;* from another form of the base of *3582; timber* (as fuel or material); by impl. a *stick, club* or *tree* or other wooden article or substance:—staff, stocks, tree, wood.

3587. ξυράω **xuraō**, *xoo-rah'-o;* from a der. of the same as *3586* (mean. a *razor*); to *shave* or "*shear*" the hair:—shave.

Ο

3588. ὁ **hŏ**, *hŏ;* includ. the fem. ἡ **hē**, *hay;* and the neut. τό **tŏ**, *tŏ,* in all their inflections; the def. article; *the* (sometimes to be supplied, at others omitted in English idiom):—the, this, that, one, he, she, it, etc. ὁ **hŏ**. See *3739.*

3589. ὀγδοήκοντα **ŏgdŏēkŏnta**, *og-dŏ-ay'-kon-tah;* from *3590; ten times eight:*—fourscore.

3590. ὄγδοος **ŏgdŏŏs**, *og'-dŏ-os;* from *3638; the eighth:*—eighth.

3591. ὄγκος **ŏgkŏs**, *ong'-kos;* prob. from the same as *43;* a *mass* (as bending or bulging by its load), i.e. *burden* (*hindrance*):—weight.

3592. ὅδε **hŏdĕ**, *hod'-eh;* includ. the fem.
ἥδε **hēdĕ**, *hay'-deh;* and the neut.
τόδε **tŏdĕ**, *tod'-e;* from *3588* and *1161;* the *same,* i.e. *this* or *that* one (plur. *these* or *those);* often used as pers. pron.:—he, she, such, these, thus.

3593. ὁδεύω **hŏdĕuō**, *hod-yoo'-o;* from *3598;* to *travel:*—journey.

3594. ὁδηγέω **hŏdēgĕō**, *hod-ayg-eh'-o;* from *3595;* to *show the way* (lit. or fig. [*teach*]):—guide, lead.

3595. ὁδηγός **hŏdēgŏs**, *hod-ayg-os';* from *3598* and *2233;* a *conductor* (lit. or fig. [*teacher*]):—guide, leader.

3596. ὁδοιπορέω **hŏdŏipŏrĕō**, *hod-oy-por-eh'-o;* from a comp. of *3598* and *4198;* to *be a wayfarer,* i.e. *travel:*—go on a journey.

3597. ὁδοιπορία **hŏdŏipŏria**, *hod-oy-por-ee'-ah;* from the same as *3596; travel:*—journey (-ing).

3598. ὁδός **hŏdŏs**, *hod-os';* appar. a prim. word; a *road;* by impl. a *progress* (the route, act or distance); fig. a *mode* or *means:*—journey, (high-) way.

3599. ὀδούς **ŏdŏus**, *od-ooce ;* perh. from the base of *2068;* a "*tooth*":—tooth.

3600. ὀδυνάω **ŏdunaō**, *od-oo-nah'-o;* from *3601;* to *grieve:*—sorrow, torment.

3601. ὀδύνη **ŏdunē**, *od-oo'-nay;* from *1416; grief* (as *dejecting*):—sorrow.

3602. ὀδυρμός **ŏdurmŏs**, *od-oor-mos';* from a der. of the base of *1416; moaning,* i.e. *lamentation:*—mourning.

3603. ὅ ἐστι **hŏ esti**, *hŏ es-tee';* from the neut. of *3739* and the third pers. sing. pres. ind. of *1510;* which *is:*—called, which is (make), that is (to say).

3604. Ὀζίας **Ŏzias**, *od-zee'-as;* of Heb. or. [5818]; *Ozias* (i.e. *Uzzijah*), an Isr.:—Ozias.

3605. ὄζω **ŏzō**, *od'-zo;* a prim. verb (in a strengthened form); to *scent* (usually an ill " odor"):—stink.

3606. ὅθεν **hŏthĕn**, *hoth'-en;* from *3739* with the directive enclitic of source; *from which* place or source or cause (adv. or conj.):—from thence, (from) whence, where (-by, -fore, -upon).

3607. ὀθόνη **ŏthŏnē**, *oth-on'-ay;* of uncert. affin.; a *linen* cloth, i.e. (espec.) a *sail:*—sheet.

3608. ὀθόνιον **ŏthŏniŏn**, *oth-on'-ee-on;* neut. of a presumed der. of *3607;* a linen *bandage:*—linen clothes.

3609. οἰκεῖος **ŏikĕiŏs**, *oy-ki'-os;* from *3624;* *domestic,* i.e. (as noun), a *relative, adherent:*—(those) of the (his own) house (-hold).

3610. οἰκέτης **ŏikĕtēs**, *oy-ket'-ace;* from *3611;* a *fellow resident,* i.e. *menial domestic:*—(household) servant.

3611. οἰκέω **ŏikĕō**, *oy-keh'-o;* from *3624;* to *occupy a house,* i.e. *reside* (fig. *inhabit, remain, inhere*); by impl. to *cohabit:*—dwell. See also *3625.*

3612. οἴκημα **ŏikēma**, *oy'-kay-mah;* from *3611;* a *tenement,* i.e. (spec.) a *jail:*—prison.

3613. οἰκητήριον **ŏikētēriŏn**, *oy-kay-tay'-ree-on;* neut. of a presumed der. of *3611* (equiv. to *3612*); a *residence* (lit. or fig.):—habitation, house.

3614. οἰκία **ŏikia**, *oy-kee'-ah;* from *3624;* prop. *residence* (abstr.), but usually (concr.) an *abode* (lit. or fig.); by impl. a *family* (espec. *domestics*):—home, house (-hold).

3615. οἰκιακός **ŏikiakŏs**, *oy-kee-ak-os';* from *3614; familiar,* i.e. (as noun) *relatives:*—they (them) of (his own) household.

3616. οἰκοδεσποτέω **ŏikŏdĕspŏtĕō**, *oy-kod-es-pot-eh'-o;* from *3617;* to *be the head of* (i.e. *rule*) a *family:*—guide the house.

3617. οἰκοδεσπότης **ŏikŏdĕspŏtēs**, *oy-kod-es-pot'-ace;* from *3624* and *1203;* the *head of a family:*—goodman (of the house), householder, master of the house.

3618. οἰκοδομέω **ŏikŏdŏmĕō**, *oy-kod-om-eh'-o;* from the same as *3619;* to *be a house-builder,* i.e. *construct* or (fig.) *confirm:*—(be in) build (-er, -ing, up), edify, embolden.

3619. οἰκοδομή **ŏikŏdŏmē**, *oy-kod-om-ay';* fem. (abstr.) of a comp. of *3624* and the base of *1430;* architecture, i.e. (concr.) a *structure;* fig. *confirmation:*—building, edify (-ication, -ing).

3620. οἰκοδομία **ŏikŏdŏmia**, *oy-kod-om-ee'-ah;* from the same as *3619; confirmation:*—edifying.

3621. οἰκονομέω **ŏikŏnŏmĕō**, *oy-kon-om-eh'-o;* from *3623;* to *manage* (a house, i.e. an estate):—be steward.

3622. οἰκονομία **ŏikŏnŏmia**, *oy-kon-om-ee'-ah;* from *3623; administration* (of a household or estate); spec. a (religious) " *economy*":—dispensation, stewardship.

3623. οἰκονόμος **ŏikŏnŏmŏs**, *oy-kon-om'-os;* from *3624* and the base of *3551;* a *house-distributor* (i.e. *manager*), or *overseer,* i.e. an employee in that capacity; by extens. a fiscal *agent* (*treasurer*); fig. a *preacher* (of the Gospel):—chamberlain, governor, steward.

3624. οἶκος **ŏikŏs**, *oy'-kos;* of uncert. affin.; a *dwelling* (more or less extensive, lit. or fig.); by impl. a *family* (more or less related, lit. or fig.):—home, house (-hold), temple.

3625. οἰκουμένη **ŏikŏumĕnē**, *oy-kou-men'-ay;* fem. part. pres. pass. of *3611* (as noun, by impl. of *1093*); *land,* i.e. the (terrene part of the) *globe;* spec. the Roman *empire:*—earth, world.

3626. οἰκουρός **ŏikŏurŏs**, *oy-koo-ros';* from *3624* and οὖρος **ŏurŏs** (a *guard;* be " ware"); a *stayer at home,* i.e. *domestically inclined* (a " good housekeeper"):—keeper at home.

3627. οἰκτείρω **ŏiktĕirō**, *oyk-ti'-ro;* also (in certain tenses) prol.
οἰκτερέω **ŏiktĕrĕō**, *oyk-ter-eh'-o;* from οἶκτος **ŏiktŏs** (*pity*); to *exercise pity:*—have compassion on.

3628. οἰκτιρμός **ŏiktirmŏs**, *oyk-tir-mos';* from *3627; pity:*—mercy.

3629. οἰκτίρμων **ŏiktirmōn**, *oyk-tir'-mone;* from *3627; compassionate:*—merciful, of tender mercy.

3630. οἶμαι **ŏimai**. See *3633.*

3630. οἰνοπότης **ŏinŏpŏtēs**, *oy-nop-ot'-ace;* from *3631* and a der. of the alt. of *4095;* a *tippler:*—winebibber.

3631. οἶνος **ŏinŏs**, *oy'-nos;* a prim. word (or perh. of Heb. or. [3196]); " *wine*" (lit. or fig.):—wine.

3632. οἰνοφλυγία **ŏinŏphlugia**, *oy-nof-loog-ee'-ah;* from *3631* and a form of the base of *5397;* an *overflow* (or *surplus*) of *wine,* i.e. *vinolency* (drunkenness):—excess of wine.

3633. οἴομαι **ŏiŏmai**, *oy'-om-ahee;* or (shorter)
οἶμαι **ŏimai**, *oy'-mahee;* mid. appar. from *3634;* to *make like* (oneself), i.e. *imagine* (be *of the opinion*):—suppose, think.

3634. οἷος **ŏiŏs**, *hoy'-os;* prob. akin to *3588, 3739,* and *3745; such* or *what sort of* (as a correl. or exclamation): espec. the neut. (adv.) with neg. *not so*—so (as), such as, what (manner of), which.

3635. ὀκνέω **ŏknĕō**, *ok-neh'-o;* from ὄκνος **ŏknŏs** (*hesitation*); to *be slow* (fig. *loath*):—delay.

3636. ὀκνηρός **ŏknērŏs**, *ok-nay-ros';* from *3635; tardy,* i.e. *indolent;* (fig.) *irksome:*—grievous, slothful.

3637. ὀκταήμερος **ŏktaēmĕrŏs**, *ok-tah-ay'-mer-os;* from *3638* and *2250;* an *eight-day* old person or act:—the eighth day.

3638. ὀκτώ **ŏktō**, *ok-to';* a prim. numeral; " *eight* ":—eight.

3639. ὄλεθρος **ŏlĕthrŏs**, *ol'-eth-ros;* from a prim. ὄλλυμι **ŏllumi** (to *destroy;* a prol. form); *ruin,* i.e. *death, punishment:*—destruction.

3640. ὀλιγόπιστος **ŏligŏpistŏs**, *ol-ig-op'-is-tos;* from *3641* and *4102; incredulous,* i.e. *lacking confidence* (in Christ):—of little faith.

3641. ὀλίγος **ŏligŏs**, *ol-ee'-gos;* of uncert. affin.; *puny* (in extent, degree, number, duration or value); espec. neut. (adv.) *somewhat:*— + almost, brief [-ly], few, (a) little, + long, a season, short, small, a while.

3642. ὀλιγόψυχος **ŏligŏpsuchŏs**, *ol-ig-op'-soo-khos;* from *3641* and *5590; little-spirited,* i.e. *faint-hearted:*—feebleminded.

3643. ὀλιγωρέω **ŏligōrĕō**, *ol-ig-o-reh'-o;* from a comp. of *3641* and ὥρα **ŏra** (" *care*"); to *have little regard* for, i.e. to *disesteem:*—despise.

3644. ὀλοθρευτής **ŏlŏthrĕutēs**, *ol-oth-ryoo-tace';* from *3645;* a *ruiner,* i.e. (spec.) a venomous serpent:—destroyer.

3645. ὀλοθρεύω **ŏlŏthrĕuō**, *ol-oth-ryoo'-o;* from *3639;* to *spoil,* i.e. *slay:*—destroy.

3646. ὁλοκαύτωμα **hŏlŏkautōma**, *hol-ok-ow'-to-mah;* from a der. of a comp. of *3650* and a der. of *2545;* a *wholly-consumed* sacrifice (" holocaust "):—(whole) burnt offering.

3647. ὁλοκληρία **hŏlŏklēria**, *hol-ok-lay-ree'-ah;* from *3648; integrity,* i.e. *physical wholeness:*—perfect soundness.

3648. ὁλόκληρος **hŏlŏklērŏs**, *hol-ok'-lay-ros;* from *3650* and *2819; complete* in every *part,* i.e. *perfectly sound* (in body):—entire, whole.

3649. ὀλολύζω **ŏlŏluzō**, *ol-ol-ood'-zo;* a redupl. prim. verb; to " *howl*" or " *halloo*", i.e. *shriek:*—howl.

3650. ὅλος **hŏlŏs**, *hol'-os;* a prim. word; " *whole*" or " *all* ", i.e. *complete* (in extent, amount, time or degree), espec. (neut.) as noun or adv.:—all, altogether, every whit, + throughout, whole.

3651. ὁλοτελής **hŏlŏtĕlēs**, *hol-ot-el-ace';* from *3650* and *5056; complete* to the *end,* i.e. *absolutely perfect:*—wholly.

3652. Ὀλυμπᾶς **Ŏlumpas**, *ol-oom-pas';* prob. a contr. from Ὀλυμπιόδωρος **Ŏlumpiŏdōrŏs** (*Olympian-bestowed,* i.e. *heaven-descended*); *Olympas,* a Chr.:—Olympas.

3653. ὄλυνθος **ŏlunthŏs**, *ol'-oon-thos;* of uncert. der.; an *unripe* (because out of season) *fig:*—untimely fig.

3654. ὅλως **hŏlōs**, *hol'-oce;* adv. from *3650; completely,* i.e. *altogether;* (by anal.) *everywhere;* (neg.) *not by any means:*—at all, commonly, utterly.

3655. ὄμβρος **ŏmbrŏs**, *om'-bros;* of uncert. affin.; a *thunder storm:*—shower.

3656. ὁμιλέω **hŏmilĕō**, *hom-il-eh'-o;* from *3658;* to *be in company* with, i.e. (by impl.) to *converse:*—commune, talk.

3657. ὁμιλία **hŏmilia**, *hom-il-ee'-ah;* from *3658; companionship* (" *homily*"), i.e. (by impl.) *intercourse:*—communication.

3658. ὅμιλος **hŏmilŏs**, *hom'-il-os;* from the base of *3674* and a der. of the alt. of *138* (mean. a *crowd*); *association together,* i.e. a *multitude:*—company.

3659. ὄμμα **ŏmma**, *om'-mah;* from *3700;* a *sight,* i.e. (by impl.) the *eye:*—eye.

3660. ὀμνύω **ŏmnuō**, *om-noo'-o;* a prol. form of a prim. but obsol. ὄμω **ŏmō**, for which another prol. (ὀμόω **ŏmŏō**, *om-ŏ'-o*) is used in certain tenses; to *swear,* i.e. *take* (or *declare on*) *oath:*—swear.

3661. ὁμοθυμαδόν **hŏmŏthumadŏn**, *hom-oth-oo-mad-on';* adv. from a comp. of the base of *3674* and *2372; unanimously:*—with one accord (mind).

3662. ὁμοιάζω **hŏmŏiazō**, *hom-oy-ad'-zo;* from *3664;* to *resemble:*—agree.

3663. ὁμοιοπαθής **hŏmŏiŏpathēs**, *hom-oy-op-ath-ace';* from *3664* and the alt. of *3958; similarly affected:*—of (subject to) like passions.

3664. ὅμοιος **hŏmŏiŏs**, *hom'-oy-os;* from the base of *3674; similar* (in appearance or character):—like, + manner.

3665. ὁμοιότης **hŏmŏiŏtēs**, *hom-oy-ot'-ace;* from *3664; resemblance:*—like as, similitude.

3666. ὁμοιόω **hŏmŏiŏō**, *hom-oy-ŏ'-o;* from *3664;* to *assimilate,* i.e. *compare;* pass. to *become similar:*—be (made) like, (in the) liken (-ess), resemble.

3667. ὁμοίωμα **hŏmŏiōma**, *hom-oy'-o-mah;* from *3666;* a *form;* abstr. *resemblance:*—made like to, likeness, shape, similitude.

3668. ὁμοίως **hŏmŏiōs**, *hom-oy'-oce;* adv. from *3664; similarly:*—likewise, so.

3669. ὁμοίωσις **hŏmŏiōsis**, *hom-oy'-o-sis;* from *3666; assimilation,* i.e. *resemblance:*—similitude.

3670. ὁμολογέω **hŏmŏlŏgĕō**, *hom-ol-og-eh'-o;* from a comp. of the base of *3674* and *3056;* to *assent,* i.e. *covenant, acknowledge:*—con- (pro-) fess, confession is made, give thanks, promise.

3671. ὁμολογία **hŏmŏlŏgia**, *hom-ol-og-ee'-ah;* from the same as *3670; acknowledgment:*—con- (pro-) fession, professed.

3672. ὁμολογουμένως **hŏmŏlŏgŏumĕnōs**, *hom-ol-og-ŏw-men'-oce;* adv. of pres. pass. part. of *3670; confessedly:*—without controversy.

3673. ὁμότεχνος **hŏmŏtĕchnŏs**, *hom-ot'-ekh-nos;* from the base of *3674* and *5078;* a *fellow-artificer:*—of the same craft.

3674. ὁμοῦ **hŏmŏu**, *hom-oo';* gen. of ὁμός **hŏmŏs** (the *same;* akin to *260*) as adv.; *at the same* place or time:—together.

3675. ὁμόφρων **hŏmŏphrŏn**, *hom-of'-rone;* from the base of *3674* and *5424; like-minded,* i.e. *harmonious:*—of one mind.

ὁμόω **hŏmŏō**. See *3660.*

3676. ὅμως **hŏmōs**, *hom'-oce;* adv. from the base of *3674; at* the same time, i.e. (conj.) *notwithstanding, yet still:*—and even, nevertheless, though but.

3677. ὄναρ **ŏnar**, *on'-ar;* of uncert. der.; a *dream:*—dream.

3678. ὀνάριον **ŏnariŏn**, *on-ar'-ee-on;* neut. of a presumed der. of *3688;* a *little ass:*—young ass.

ὀνάω **ŏnaō**. See *3685.*

3679. ὀνειδίζω **ŏnĕidizō**, *on-i-did'-zo;* from *3681;* to *defame,* i.e. *rail at, chide, taunt:*—cast in teeth, (suffer) reproach, revile, upbraid.

3680. ὀνειδισμός **ŏnĕidismŏs**, *on-i-dis-mos';* from *3679; contumely:*—reproach.

3681. ὄνειδος **ŏnĕidŏs**, *on'-i-dos;* prob. akin to the base of *3686; notoriety,* i.e. a *taunt (disgrace):*—reproach.

3682. Ὀνήσιμος **Ŏnēsimŏs**, *on-ay'-sim-os;* from *3685; profitable;* Onesimus, a Chr.:—Onesimus.

3683. Ὀνησίφορος **Ŏnēsiphŏrŏs**, *on-ay-sif'-or-os;* from a der. of *3685* and *5411; profit-bearer;* Onesiphorus, a Chr.:—Onesiphorus.

3684. ὀνικός **ŏnikŏs**, *on-ik-os';* from *3688; belonging* to an ass, i.e. *large* (so as to be turned by an ass):—millstone.

3685. ὀνίνημι **ŏninēmi**, *on-in'-ay-mee;* a prol. form of an appar. prim. verb (ὄνομαι **ŏnŏmai**, to *slur*); for which another prol. form (ὀνάω **ŏnaō**) is used as an alt. in some tenses [unless indeed it be identical with the base of *3686* through the idea of *notoriety*]; to *gratify,* i.e. (mid.) to *derive pleasure* or *advantage* from:—have joy.

3686. ὄνομα **ŏnŏma**, *on'-om-ah;* from a presumed der. of the base of *1097* (comp. *3685*); a "*name*" (lit. or fig.) [*authority, character*]:—called, (+ sur-) name (-d).

3687. ὀνομάζω **ŏnŏmazō**, *on-om-ad'-zo;* from *3686;* to *name,* i.e. *assign* an *appellation;* by extens. to *utter, mention, profess:*—call, name.

3688. ὄνος **ŏnŏs**, *on'-os;* appar. a prim. word; a *donkey:*—ass.

3689. ὄντως **ŏntōs**, *on'-toce;* adv. of the oblique cases of *5607; really:*—certainly, clean, indeed, of a truth, verily.

3690. ὄξος **ŏxŏs**, *ox'-os;* from *3691; vinegar,* i.e. *sour wine:*—vinegar.

3691. ὀξύς **ŏxus**, *ox-oos';* prob. akin to the base of *188* ["*acid*"]; *keen;* by anal. *rapid:*—sharp, swift.

3692. ὀπή **ŏpē**, *op-ay';* prob. from *3700;* a *hole* (as if for *light*), i.e. *cavern;* by anal. a *spring* (of *water*):—cave, place.

3693. ὄπισθεν **ŏpisthĕn**, *op'-is-then;* from ὄπις **ŏpis** (*regard;* from *3700*) with enclitic of source; *from the rear* (as a *secure aspect*), i.e. *at the back*

3694. ὀπίσω **ŏpisō**, *op-is'-o;* from the same as *3693* with enclitic of direction; *to the back,* i.e. *aback* (as adv. or prep. of time or place; or as noun):—after, back (-ward), (+ get) behind, + follow.

3695. ὁπλίζω **hŏplizō**, *hop-lid'-zo;* from *3696;* to *equip* (with weapons [mid. and fig.]):—arm self.

3696. ὅπλον **hŏplŏn**, *hop'-lon;* prob. from a prim. ἕπω **hĕpō** (to be *busy* about); an *implement* or *utensil* or *tool* (lit. or fig., espec. offensive for war):—armour, instrument, weapon.

3697. ὁποῖος **hŏpŏiŏs**, *hop-oy'-os;* from *3739* and *4169;* of *what kind that,* i.e. *how* (as) *great (excellent)* (spec. as indef. correl. to anteced. def. *5108* of quality):—what manner (sort) of, such as, whatsoever.

3698. ὁπότε **hŏpŏtĕ**, *hop-ot'-eh;* from *3739* and *4218; what* (-ever) *then,* i.e. (of time) *as soon as:*—when.

3699. ὅπου **hŏpŏu**, *hop'-oo;* from *3739* and *4225; what* (-ever) *where,* i.e. *at whichever* spot:—in what place, where (-as, -soever), whither (+ soever).

3700. ὀπτάνομαι **ŏptanŏmai**, *op-tan'-om-ahee;* a (mid.) prol. form of the prim. (mid.)

ὄπτομαι **ŏptŏmai**, *op'-tom-ahee,* which is used for it in certain tenses; and both as alt. of *3708;* to *gaze* (i.e. with wide-open eyes, as at something remarkable; and thus differing from *991,* which denotes simply *voluntary* observation; and from *1492,* which expresses merely mechanical, passive or casual vision; while *2300,* and still more emphatically its intens. *2334,* signifies an earnest but more continued *inspection;* and *4648* a watching *from a distance*):—appear, look, see, shew self.

3701. ὀπτασία **ŏptasia**, *op-tas-ee'-ah;* from a presumed der. of *3700; visuality,* i.e. (concr.) an *apparition:*—vision.

ὄπτομαι **ŏptŏmai**. See *3700.*

3702. ὀπτός **ŏptŏs**, *op-tos';* from an obsol. verb akin to ἕψω **hĕpsō** (to "*steep*"); *cooked,* i.e. *roasted:*—broiled.

3703. ὀπώρα **ŏpōra**, *op-o'-rah;* appar. from the base of *3796* and *5610;* prop. *even-tide* of the (summer) season (*dog-days*), i.e. (by impl.) *ripe fruit:*—fruit.

3704. ὅπως **hŏpōs**, *hop'-oce;* from *3739* and *4459; what* (-ever) *how,* i.e. *in the manner that* (as adv. or conj. of coincidence, intentional or actual):—because, how, (so) that, to, when.

3705. ὅραμα **hŏrama**, *hor'-am-ah;* from *3708; something gazed at,* i.e. a *spectacle* (espec. supernat.):—sight, vision.

3706. ὅρασις **hŏrasis**, *hor'-as-is;* from *3708;* the act of *gazing,* i.e. (external) an *aspect* or (intern.) an inspired *appearance:*—sight, vision.

3707. ὁρατός **hŏratŏs**, *hor-at-os';* from *3708; gazed at,* i.e. (by impl.) *capable of being seen:*—visible.

3708. ὁράω **hŏraō**, *hor-ah'-o;* prop. to *stare at* [comp. *3700*], i.e. (by impl.) to *discern clearly* (phys. or ment.); by extens. to *attend to;* by Hebr. to *experience;* pass. to *appear:*—behold, perceive, see, take heed.

3709. ὀργή **ŏrgē**, *or-gay';* from *3713;* prop. *desire* (as a *reaching forth* or *excitement* of the mind), i.e. (by anal.) *violent passion (ire,* or [justifiable] *abhorrence);* by impl. *punishment:*—anger, indignation, vengeance, wrath.

3710. ὀργίζω **ŏrgizō**, *or-gid'-zo;* from *3709;* to *provoke* or *enrage,* i.e. (pass.) *become exasperated:*—be angry (wroth).

3711. ὀργίλος **ŏrgilŏs**, *org-ee'-los;* from *3709; irascible:*—soon angry.

3712. ὀργυιά **ŏrguia**, *org-wee-ah';* from *3713;* a *stretch* of the arms, i.e. a *fathom:*—fathom.

3713. ὀρέγομαι **ŏrĕgŏmai**, *or-eg'-om-ahee;* mid. of appar. a prol. form of an obsol. verb [comp. *3735*]; to *stretch* oneself, i.e. *reach out after* (long for):—covet after, desire.

3714. ὀρεινός **ŏrĕinŏs**, *or-i-nos';* from *3735; mountainous,* i.e. (fem. by impl. of *5561*) the *Highlands* (of Judæa):—hill country.

3715. ὄρεξις **ŏrĕxis**, *or'-ex-is;* from *3713; excitement* of the mind, i.e. *longing* after:—lust.

3716. ὀρθοποδέω **ŏrthŏpŏdĕō**, *or-thop-od-eh'-o;* from a comp. of *3717* and *4228;* to be *straight-footed,* i.e. (fig.) to *go directly* forward:—walk uprightly.

3717. ὀρθός **ŏrthŏs**, *or-thos';* prob. from the base of *3735; right* (as *rising*), i.e. (perpendicularly) *erect* (fig. *honest*), or (horizontally) *level* or *direct:*—straight, upright.

3718. ὀρθοτομέω **ŏrthŏtŏmĕō**, *or-thot-om-eh'-o;* from a comp. of *3717* and the base of *5114;* to *make a straight cut,* i.e. (fig.) to *dissect* (expound) correctly (the divine message):—rightly divide.

3719. ὀρθρίζω **ŏrthrizō**, *or-thrid'-zo;* from *3722,* to *use the dawn,* i.e. (by impl.) to *repair betimes:*—come early in the morning.

3720. ὀρθρινός **ŏrthrinŏs**, *or-thrin-os';* from *3722; relating to the dawn,* i.e. *matutinal* (as an epithet of Venus, espec. brilliant in the early day):—morning.

3721. ὄρθριος **ŏrthriŏs**, *or'-three-os;* from *3722;* in the *dawn,* i.e. *up at day-break:*—early.

3722. ὄρθρος **ŏrthrŏs**, *or'-thros;* from the same as *3735; dawn* (as *sun-rise, rising* of light); by extens. *morn:*—early in the morning.

3723. ὀρθῶς **ŏrthōs**, *or-thoce';* adv. from *3717;* in a *straight* manner, i.e. (fig.) *correctly* (also mor.):—plain, right (-ly).

3724. ὁρίζω **hŏrizō**, *hor-id'-zo;* from *3725;* to *mark out* or *bound* (" horizon"), i.e. (fig.) to *appoint, decree, specify:*—declare, determine, limit, ordain.

3725. ὅριον **hŏriŏn**, *hor'-ee-on;* neut. of a der. of an appar. prim. ὅρος **hŏrŏs** (a *bound* or *limit*); a *boundary*-line, i.e. (by impl.) a *frontier* (region):—border, coast.

3726. ὁρκίζω **hŏrkizō**, *hor-kid'-zo;* from *3727;* to *put* on oath, i.e. *make swear;* by anal. to solemnly *enjoin:*—adjure, charge.

3727. ὅρκος **hŏrkŏs**, *hor'-kos;* from ἕρκος **hĕrkŏs** (a *fence;* perh. akin to *3725*); a *limit,* i.e. (sacred) *restraint* (spec. *oath*):—oath.

3728. ὁρκωμοσία **hŏrkōmŏsia**, *hor-ko-mos-ee'-ah;* from a comp. of *3727* and a der. of *3660; asseveration on oath:*—oath.

3729. ὁρμάω **hŏrmaō**, *hor-mah'-o;* from *3730;* to *start, spur* or *urge on,* i.e. (reflex.) to *dash* or *plunge:*—run (violently), rush.

3730. ὁρμή **hŏrmē**, *hor-may';* of uncert. affin.; a *violent impulse,* i.e. *onset:*—assault.

3731. ὅρμημα **hŏrmēma**, *hor'-may-mah;* from *3730;* an *attack,* i.e. (abstr.) *precipitancy:*—violence.

3732. ὄρνεον **ŏrnĕŏn**, *or'-neh-on;* neut. of a presumed der. of *3733;* a *birdling:*—bird, fowl.

3733. ὄρνις **ŏrnis**, *or'-nis;* prob. from a prol. form of the base of *3735;* a *bird* (as *rising* in the air), i.e. (spec.) a *hen* (or female domestic fowl):—hen.

3734. ὁροθεσία **hŏrŏthĕsia**, *hor-oth-es-ee'-ah;* from a comp. of the base of *3725* and a der. of *5087;* a *limit*-placing, i.e. (concr.) *boundary*-line:—bound.

3735. ὄρος **ŏrŏs**, *or'-os;* prob. from an obsol. ὄρω **ŏrō** (to *rise* or "*rear*"; perh. akin to *142;* comp. *3733*); a *mountain* (as *lifting* itself above the plain):—hill, mount (-ain).

3736. ὀρύσσω **ŏrussō**, *or-oos'-so;* appar. a prim. verb; to "*burrow*" in the ground, i.e. *dig:*—dig.

3737. ὀρφανός **ŏrphanŏs**, *or-fan-os';* of uncert. affin.; *bereaved* ("*orphan*"), i.e. *parentless:*—comfortless, fatherless.

3738. ὀρχέομαι **ŏrchĕŏmai**, *or-kheh'-om-ahee;* mid. from ὄρχος **ŏrchŏs** (a *row* or *ring*); to *dance* (from the ranklike or regular motion):—dance.

3739. ὅς **hŏs**, *hos;* includ. fem.

ἥ **hē**, *hay;* and neut.

ὅ **hŏ**, *hŏ;* prob. a prim. word (or perh. a form of the art. *3588*); the rel. (sometimes demonstrative) pron., *who, which, what, that:*—one, (an-, the) other, some, that, what, which, who (-m, -se), etc. See also *3757.*

3740. ὁσάκις **hŏsakis**, *hos-ak'-is;* multiple adv. from *3739;* how (i.e. with *302,* so) many times as:—as oft (-en) as.

3741. ὅσιος **hŏsiŏs**, *hos'-ee-os;* of uncert. affin.; prop. *right* (by intrinsic or divine character; thus distinguished from *1342,* which refers rather to *human* statutes and relations; from *2413,* which denotes formal *consecration;* and from *40,* which relates to *purity* from defilement), i.e. *hallowed* (*pious, sacred, sure*):—holy, mercy, shalt be.

3742. ὁσιότης **hŏsiŏtēs**, *hos-ee-ot'-ace;* from *3741;* piety:—holiness.

3743. ὁσίως **hŏsiŏs**, *hos-ee-oce';* adv. from *3741;* piously:—holily.

3744. ὀσμή **ŏsmē**, *os-may';* from *3605; fragrance* (lit. or fig.):—odour, savour.

3745. ὅσος **hŏsŏs**, *hos-os;* by redupl. from *3739; as* (much, great, long, etc.) *as:*—all (that), as (long, many, much) (as), how great (many, much), [in-] asmuch as, so many as, that (ever), the more, those things, what (great, -soever), wheresoever, wherewithsoever, which, X while, who (-soever).

3746. ὅσπερ **hŏspĕr**, *hos'-per;* from *3739* and *4007; who especially:*—whomsoever.

3747. ὀστέον **ŏstĕŏn**, *os-teh'-on;* or contr.

ὀστοῦν **ŏstŏun**, *os-toon';* of uncert. affin.; a *bone:*—bone.

3748. ὅστις **hŏstis**, *hos'-tis;* includ. the fem.

ἥτις **hētis**, *hay'-tis;* and the neut.

ὅ,τι **hŏ,ti**, *hot'-ee;* from *3739* and *5100; which some,* i.e. *any that;* also (def.) *which same:*— X and (they), (such) as, (they) that, in that they, what (-soever), whereas ye, (they) which, who (-soever). Comp. *3754.*

3749. ὀστράκινος **ŏstrakinŏs**, *os-tra'-kin-os;* from ὄστρακον **ŏstrakŏn** ["oyster"] (a *tile,* i.e. *terra cotta); earthen-ware,* i.e. *clayey;* by impl. *frail:*—of earth, earthen.

3750. ὄσφρησις **ŏsphrēsis**, *os'-fray-sis;* from a der. of *3605; smell* (the sense):—smelling.

3751. ὀσφύς **ŏsphus**, *os-foos';* of uncert. affin.; the *loin* (extern.), i.e. the *hip;* intern. (by extens.) *procreative power:*—loin.

3752. ὅταν **hŏtan**, *hot'-an;* from *3753* and *302; whenever* (implying *hypothesis* or more or less *uncertainty*); also caus. (conj.) *inasmuch as:*—as long (soon) as, that, + till, when (-soever), while.

3753. ὅτε **hŏtĕ**, *hot'-eh;* from *3739* and *5037;* at *which* (thing) *too,* i.e. *when:*—after (that), as soon as, that, when, while.

ὅ,τε **hŏ,tĕ**, *hŏ,t'-eh;* also fem.

ἥ,τε **hē,tĕ**, *hay'-teh;* and neut.

τό,τε **tŏ,tĕ**, *tot'-eh;* simply the art. *3588* followed by *5037;* so written (in some editions) to distinguish them from *3752* and *5119.*

3754. ὅτι **hŏti**, *hot'-ee;* neut. of *3748* as conj.; demonst. *that* (sometimes redundant); caus. *because:*—as concerning that, as though, because (that), for (that), how (that), (in) that, though, why.

3755. ὅτου **hŏtŏu**, *hot'-oo;* for the gen. of *3748* (as adv.); *during which same time,* i.e. *whilst:*—whiles.

3756. οὐ **ŏu**, *oo;* also (before a vowel)

οὐκ **ŏuk**, *ook;* and (before an aspirate)

οὐχ **ŏuch**, *ookh;* a prim. word; the absol. neg. [comp. *3361*] adv.; *not* or *not:*—+ long, nay, neither, never, no (X man), none, [can-] not, + nothing, + special, un ([-worthy]), when, + without, + yet but. See also *3364, 3372.*

3757. οὗ **hŏu**, *hoo;* gen. of *3739* as adv.; at *which* place, i.e. *where:*—where (-in), whither [(-soever]).

3758. οὐά **ŏua**, *oo-ah';* a prim. *exclamation* of surprise; *" ah"*:—ah.

3759. οὐαί **ŏuai**, *oo-ah'ee;* a prim. *exclamation* of grief; *"woe"*:—alas, woe.

3760. οὐδαμῶς **ŏudamŏs**, *oo-dam-oce';* adv. from (the fem.) of *3762; by no means:*—not.

3761. οὐδέ **ŏudĕ**, *oo-deh';* from *3756* and *1161; not however,* i.e. *neither, nor, not even:*—neither (indeed),

---

never, no (more, nor, not), nor (yet), (also, even, then) not (even, so much as), + nothing, so much as.

3762. οὐδείς **ŏudĕis**, *oo-dice';* includ. fem.

οὐδεμία **ŏudĕmia**, *oo-dem-ee'-ah;* and neut.

οὐδέν **ŏudĕn**, *oo-den';* from *3761* and *1520; not even one* (man, woman or thing), i.e. *none, nobody, nothing:*—any (man), aught, man, neither any (thing), never (man), no (man), none (+ of these things), not (any, at all, -thing), nought.

3763. οὐδέποτε **ŏudĕpŏtĕ**, *oo-dep'-ot-eh;* from *3761* and *4218; not even at any time,* i.e. *never at all:*—neither at any time, never, nothing at any time.

3764. οὐδέπω **ŏudĕpō**, *oo-dep'-o;* from *3761* and *4452; not even yet:*—as yet not, never before (yet), (not) yet.

3765. οὐκέτι **ŏukĕti**, *ook-et'-ee;* also (separately)

οὐκ ἔτι **ŏuk ĕti**, *ook et'-ee;* from *3756* and *2089; not yet, no longer:*—after that (not), (not) any more, henceforth (hereafter) not, no longer (more), not as yet (now), now no more (not), yet (not).

3766. οὐκοῦν **ŏukŏun**, *ook-oon';* from *3756* and *3767;* is it *not therefore* that, i.e. (affirm.) *hence* or *so:*—then.

3767. οὖν **ŏun**, *oon;* appar. a prim. word; (adv.) *certainly,* or (conj.) *accordingly:*—and (so, truly), but, now (then), so (likewise then), then, therefore, verily, wherefore.

3768. οὔπω **ŏupō**, *oo'-po;* from *3756* and *4452; not yet:*—hitherto not, (no . . .) as yet, not yet.

3769. οὐρά **ŏura**, *oo-rah';* appar. a prim. word; a *tail:*—tail.

3770. οὐράνιος **ŏuraniŏs**, *oo-ran'-ee-os;* from *3772; celestial,* i.e. *belonging to* or *coming from the sky:*—heavenly.

3771. οὐρανόθεν **ŏuranŏthĕn**, *oo-ran-oth'-en;* from *3772* and the enclitic of source; *from the sky:*—from heaven.

3772. οὐρανός **ŏuranŏs**, *oo-ran-os';* perh. from the same as *3735* (through the idea of *elevation*); the *sky;* by extens. *heaven* (as the abode of God); by impl. *happiness, power, eternity;* spec. the *Gospel* (*Christianity*):—air, heaven ([-ly]), sky.

3773. Οὐρβανός **Ŏurbanŏs**, *oor-ban-os';* of Lat. or.; *Urbanus* (*of the city, "urbane"*), a Chr.:—Urbanus.

3774. Οὐρίας **Ŏurias**, *oo-ree'-as;* of Heb. or. [*223*]; *Urias* (i.e. *Urijah*), a Hittite:—Urias.

3775. οὖς **ŏus**, *ooce;* appar. a prim. word; the *ear* (phys. or ment.):—ear.

3776. οὐσία **ŏusia**, *oo-see'-ah;* from the fem. of *5607; substance,* i.e. *property* (*possessions*):—goods, substance.

3777. οὔτε **ŏutĕ**, *oo'-teh;* from *3756* and *5037; not too,* i.e. *neither* or *nor;* by anal. *not even:*—neither, none, nor (yet), (no, yet) not, nothing.

3778. οὗτος **hŏutŏs**, *hoo'-tos;* includ. nom. masc. plur.

οὗτοι **hŏutŏi**, *hoo'-toy;* nom. fem. sing.

αὕτη **hautē**, *hŏw'-tay;* and nom. fem. plur.

αὗται **hautai**, *hŏw'-tahee;* from the art. *3588* and *846;* the *he* (*she* or *it*), i.e. *this* or *that* (often with art. repeated):—he (it was that), hereof, it, she, such as, the same, these, they, this (man, same, woman), which, who.

3779. οὕτω **hŏutō**, *hoo'-to;* or (before a vowel)

οὕτως **hŏutōs**, *hoo'-toce;* adv. from *3778; in this way* (referring to what precedes or follows):—after that, after (in) this manner, as, even (so), for all that, like (-wise), no more, on this fashion (-wise), so (in like manner), thus, what.

3780. οὐχί **ŏuchi**, *oo-khee';* intens. of *3756; not indeed:*—nay, not.

3781. ὀφειλέτης **ŏphĕilĕtēs**, *of-i-let'-ace;* from *3784;* an *ower,* i.e. *person indebted;* fig. a *delinquent;* mor. a *transgressor* (against God):—debtor, which owed, sinner.

3782. ὀφειλή **ŏphĕilē**, *of-i-lay';* from *3784; indebtedness,* i.e. (concr.) a *sum owed;* fig. *obligation,* i.e. (conjugal) *duty:*—debt, due.

3783. ὀφείλημα **ŏphĕilēma**, *of-i'-lay-mah;* from (the alt. of) *3784; something owed,* i.e. (fig.) a *due;* mor. a *fault:*—debt.

3784. ὀφείλω **ŏphĕilō**, *of-i'-lo;* or (in cert. tenses) its prol. form

ὀφειλέω **ŏphĕilĕō**, *of-i-leh'-o;* prob. from the base of *3786* (through the idea of *accruing*); to *owe* (pecuniarily); fig. to be *under obligation* (*ought, must, should*); mor. to *fail* in duty:—behove, be bound, (be) debt (-or), (be) due (-ty), be guilty (indebted), (must) need (-s), ought, owe, should. See also *3785.*

3785. ὄφελον **ŏphĕlŏn**, *of'-el-on;* first pers. sing. of a past tense of *3784; I ought* (*wish*), i.e. (interj.) *oh that!*:—would (to God.)

3786. ὄφελος **ŏphĕlŏs**, *of'-el-os;* from ὀφέλλω **ŏphĕllō** (to *heap up,* i.e. *accumulate* or *benefit*); *gain:*—advantageth, profit.

3787. ὀφθαλμοδουλεία **ŏphthalmŏdŏulĕia**, *of-thal-mod-oo-li'-ah;* from *3788* and *1397; sightlabor,* i.e. that needs watching (*remissness*):—eyeservice.

3788. ὀφθαλμός **ŏphthalmŏs**, *of-thal-mos';* from *3700;* the *eye* (lit. or fig.); by impl. *vision;* fig. *envy* (from the jealous side-glance):—eye, sight.

3789. ὄφις **ŏphis**, *of'-is;* prob. from *3700* (through the idea of *sharpness* of vision); a *snake,* fig. (as a type of sly cunning) an artful *malicious* person, espec. *Satan:*—serpent.

3790. ὀφρύς **ŏphrus**, *of-roos';* perh. from *3700* (through the idea of the *shading* or proximity to the organ of *vision*); the *eye-" brow"* or *forehead,* i.e. (fig.) the *brink* of a precipice:—brow.

3791. ὀχλέω **ŏchlĕō**, *okh-leh'-o;* from *3793;* to *mob,* i.e. (by impl.) to *harass:*—vex.

3792. ὀχλοποιέω **ŏchlŏpŏiĕō**, *okh-lop-oy-eh'-o;* from *3793* and *4160;* to *make a crowd,* i.e. *raise a* public *disturbance:*—gather a company.

3793. ὄχλος **ŏchlŏs**, *okh'-los;* from a der. of *2192* (mean. a *vehicle*); a *throng* (as *borne* along); by impl. the *rabble;* by extens. a *class* of people; fig. a *riot:*—company, multitude, number (of people), people, press.

3794. ὀχύρωμα **ŏchurōma**, *okh-oo'-ro-mah;* from a remote der. of *2192* (mean. to *fortify,* through the idea of *holding* safely); a *castle* (fig. *argument*):—stronghold.

3795. ὀψάριον **ŏpsariŏn**, *op-sar'-ee-on;* neut. of a presumed der. of the base of *3702;* a *relish* to other food (as if cooked *sauce*), i.e. (spec.) *fish* (presumably salted and dried as a condiment):—fish.

3796. ὀψέ **ŏpsĕ**, *op-seh';* from the same as *3694* (through the idea of *backwardness*); (adv.) *late* in the day; by extens. *after the close of the day:*—(at) even, in the end.

3797. ὄψιμος **ŏpsimŏs**, *op'-sim-os;* from *3796; later,* i.e. *vernal* (showering):—latter.

3798. ὄψιος **ŏpsiŏs**, *op'-see-os;* from *3796; late;* fem. (as a noun) *afternoon* (early eve) or *nightfall* (later eve):—even (-ing, [-tide]).

3799. ὄψις **ŏpsis**, *op'-sis;* from *3700;* prop. *sight* (the act), i.e. (by impl.) the *visage,* an external *show:*—appearance, countenance, face.

3800. ὀψώνιον **ŏpsōniŏn**, *op-so'-nee-on;* neut. of a presumed der. of the same as *3795; rations* for a soldier, i.e. *stipend* or *pay:*—wages.

3801. ὁ ὢν καὶ ὁ ἦν καὶ ὁ ἐρχόμενος **hŏ ōn kai hŏ ēn kai hŏ ĕrchŏmĕnŏs**, *hŏ own kahee hŏ ane kahee hŏ er-khom'-en-os;* a phrase combining *3588* with the pres. part. and imperf. of *1510* and the pres. part. of *2064* by means of *2532;* the *one being and the one that was and the one coming,* i.e. the *Eternal,* as a divine epithet of Christ:—which art (is, was), and (which) wast (is, was), and art (is) to come (shalt be).

Π

3802. παγιδεύω **pagidĕuō**, *pag-id-yoo'-o;* from *3803;* to *ensnare* (fig.):—entangle.

3803. παγίς **pagis**, *pag-ece';* from *4078;* a *trap* (as *fastened* by a noose or notch); fig. a *trick* or *stratagem* (*temptation*):—snare.

Πάγος **Pagŏs.** See 697.

3804. πάθημα **pathēma,** *path'-ay-mah;* from a presumed der. of *3806;* something *undergone,* i.e. *hardship* or *pain;* subj. an *emotion* or *influence:*—affection, affliction, motion, suffering.

3805. παθητός **pathētŏs,** *path-ay-tos';* from the same as *3804;* *liable* (i.e. *doomed*) *to experience pain:*—suffer.

3806. πάθος **pathŏs,** *path'-os;* from the alt. of *3958;* prop. *suffering* ("*pathos*"), i.e. (subj.) a *passion* (espec. *concupiscence*):—(inordinate) affection, lust.

πάθω **pathō.** See *3958.*

3807. παιδαγωγός **paidagōgŏs,** *pahee-dag-o-gos';* from *3816* and a redupl. form of *71;* a *boy-leader,* i.e. a servant whose office it was to take the children to school; by impl. [fig.] a *tutor* ["*pœdagogue*"]):—instructor, schoolmaster.

3808. παιδάριον **paidariŏn,** *pahee-dar'-ee-on;* neut. of a presumed der. of *3816;* a *little boy:*—child, lad.

3809. παιδεία **paidĕia,** *pahee-di'-ah;* from *3811;* *tutorage,* i.e. *education* or *training;* by impl. disciplinary *correction:*—chastening, chastisement, instruction, nurture.

3810. παιδευτής **paidĕutēs,** *pahee-dyoo-tace';* from *3811;* a *trainer,* i.e. *teacher* or (by impl.) *discipliner:*—which corrected, instructor.

3811. παιδεύω **paidĕuō,** *pahee-dyoo'-o;* from *3816;* to *train* up a child, i.e. *educate,* or (by impl.) *discipline* (by punishment):—chasten (-ise), instruct, learn, teach.

3812. παιδιόθεν **paidiŏthĕn,** *pahee-dee-oth'-en;* adv. (of source) from *3813;* from *infancy:*—of a child.

3813. παιδίον **paidiŏn,** *pahee-dee'-on;* neut. dimin. of *3816;* a *childling* (of either sex), i.e. (prop.) an infant, or (by extens.) a half-grown *boy* or *girl;* fig. an *immature* Christian:—(little, young) child, damsel.

3814. παιδίσκη **paidiskē,** *pahee-dis'-kay;* fem. dimin. of *3816;* a *girl,* i.e. (spec.) a *female slave* or *servant:*—bondmaid (-woman), damsel, maid (-en).

3815. παίζω **paizō,** *paheed'-zo;* from *3816;* to *sport* (as a boy):—play.

3816. παῖς **pais,** *paheece;* perh. from *3817;* a *boy* (as often *beaten* with impunity), or (by anal.) a *girl,* and (gen.) a *child;* spec. a *slave* or *servant* (espec. a minister to a king; and by eminence to God):—child, maid (-en), (man) servant, son, young man.

3817. παίω **paiō,** *pah'-yo;* a prim. verb; to *hit* (as if by a single blow and less violently than *5180*); spec. to *sting* (as a scorpion):—smite, strike.

3818. Πακατιανή **Pakatianē,** *pak-at-ee-an-ay';* fem. of an adj. of uncert. der.; *Pacatianian,* a section of Phrygia:—Pacatiana.

3819. πάλαι **palai,** *pal'-ahee;* prob. another form for *3825* (through the idea of *retrocession*); (adv.) *formerly,* or (by rel.) *sometime since;* (ellipt. as adj.) *ancient:*—any while, a great while ago, (of) old, in time past.

3820. παλαιός **palaiŏs,** *pal-ah-yos';* from *3819;* *antique,* i.e. not *recent,* *worn out:*—old.

3821. παλαιότης **palaiŏtēs,** *pal-ah-yot'-ace;* from *3820;* *antiquatedness:*—oldness.

3822. παλαιόω **palaiŏō,** *pal-ah-yŏ'-o;* from *3820;* to make (pass. *become*) *worn out,* or *declare obsolete:*—decay, make (wax) old.

3823. πάλη **palē,** *pal'-ay;* from πάλλω **pallō** (to *vibrate;* another form for *906*); *wrestling:*—+ wrestle.

3824. παλιγγενεσία **paliggĕnĕsia,** *pal-ing-ghen-es-ee'-ah;* from *3825* and *1078;* (spiritual) *rebirth* (the state or the act), i.e. (fig.) spiritual *renovation;* spec. Messianic *restoration:*—regeneration.

3825. πάλιν **palin,** *pal'-in;* prob. from the same as *3823* (through the idea of *oscillatory repetition*); (adv.) *anew,* i.e. (of place) *back,* (of time) *once more,* or (conj.) *furthermore* or *on the other hand:*—again.

3826. παμπληθεί **pamplēthĕi,** *pam-play-thi';* dat. (adv.) of a comp. of *3956* and *4128; in full multitude,* i.e. *concertedly* or *simultaneously:*—all at once.

3827. πάμπολυς **pampŏlus,** *pam -pol-ooce;* from *3956* and *4183; full many,* i.e. *immense:*—very great.

3828. Παμφυλία **Pamphulia,** *pam-fool-ee'-ah;* from a comp. of *3956* and *5443; every-tribal,* i.e. *heterogeneous* (*5561* being impl.); *Pamphylia,* a region of Asia Minor:—Pamphylia.

3829. πανδοχεῖον **pandŏchĕiŏn,** *pan-dokh-i'-on;* neut. of a presumed comp. of *3956* and a der. of *1209; all-receptive,* i.e. a public *lodging*-place (*caravanserai* or *khan*):—inn.

3830. πανδοχεύς **pandŏchĕus,** *pan-dokh-yoos';* from the same as *3829;* an *innkeeper* (*warden of a caravanserai*):—host.

3831. πανήγυρις **panēguris,** *pan-ay'-goo-ris;* from *3956* and a der. of *58;* a *mass-meeting,* i.e. (fig.) *universal companionship:*—general assembly.

3832. πανοικί **panŏiki,** *pan-oy-kee';* adv. from *3956* and *3624; with the whole family:*—with all his house.

3833. πανοπλία **panŏplia,** *pan-op-lee'-ah;* from a comp. of *3956* and *3696; full armor* ("*panoply*"):—all (whole) armour.

3834. πανουργία **panŏurgia,** *pan-oorg-ee'-ah;* from *3835; adroitness,* i.e. (in a bad sense) *trickery* or *sophistry:*—(cunning) craftiness, subtilty.

3835. πανοῦργος **panŏurgŏs,** *pan-oor'-gos;* from *3956* and *2041; all-working,* i.e. *adroit* (*shrewd*):—crafty.

3836. πανταχόθεν **pantachŏthĕn,** *pan-takh-oth'-en;* ɩ dv. (of source) from *3837; from* all directions:—from every quarter.

3837. πανταχοῦ **pantachŏu,** *pan-takh-oo';* gen. (as adv. of *place*) of a presumed der. of *3956; universally:*—in all places, everywhere.

3838. παντελής **pantĕlēs,** *pan-tel-ace';* from *3956* and *5056; full-ended,* i.e. *entire* (neut. as noun, *completion*):— + in [no] wise, uttermost.

3839. πάντη **pantē,** *pan'-tay;* adv. (of *manner*) from *3956; wholly:*—always.

3840. παντόθεν **pantŏthĕn,** *pan-toth'-en;* adv. (of *source*) from *3956; from* (i.e. on) *all* sides:—on every side, round about.

3841. παντοκράτωρ **pantŏkratŏr,** *pan-tok-rat'-ore;* from *3956* and *2904; the all-ruling,* i.e. *God* (as absolute and universal *sovereign*):—Almighty, Omnipotent.

3842. πάντοτε **pantŏtĕ,** *pan'-tot-eh;* from *3956* and *3753; every when,* i.e. *at all* times:—alway (-s), ever (-more).

3843. πάντως **pantōs,** *pan'-toce;* adv. from *3956; entirely;* spec. *at all* events, (with neg. following) in *no event:*—by all means, altogether, at all, needs, no doubt, in [no] wise, surely.

3844. παρά **para,** *par-ah';* a prim. prep.; prop. *near,* i.e. (with gen.) *from beside* (lit. or fig.), (with dat.) *at* (or *in*) the *vicinity* of (obj. or subj.), (with acc.) to the *proximity* with (local [espec. *beyond* or *opposed* to] or causal [*on account of*]):—above, against, among, at, before, by, contrary to, × friend, from, + give [such things as they], + that [she] had, × his, in, more than, nigh unto, (out) of, past, save, side . . . by, in the sight of, than, [there-] fore, with.

In compounds it retains the same variety of application.

3845. παραβαίνω **parabainō,** *par-ab-ah'-ee-no;* from *3844* and the base of *939;* to *go contrary to,* i.e. *violate* a command:—(by) transgress (-ion).

3846. παραβάλλω **paraballō,** *par-ab-al'-lo;* from *3844* and *906;* to *throw alongside,* i.e. (reflex.) to *reach* a place, or (fig.) to *liken:*—arrive, compare.

3847. παράβασις **parabasis,** *par-ab'-as-is;* from *3845; violation:*—breaking, transgression.

3848. παραβάτης **parabatēs,** *par-ab-at'-ace;* from *3845;* a *violator:*—breaker, transgress (-or).

3849. παραβιάζομαι **parabiazŏmai,** *par-ab-ee-ad'-zom-ahee;* from *3844* and the mid. of *971;* to *force* contrary to (nature), i.e. *compel* (by entreaty):—constrain.

3850. παραβολή **parabŏlē,** *par-ab-ol-ay';* from *3846;* a *similitude* ("*parable*"), i.e. (symbol.) *fictitious narrative* (of common life conveying a moral), apothegm or adage:—comparison, figure, parable, proverb.

3851. παραβουλεύομαι **parabŏulĕuŏmai,** *par-ab-ool-yoo'-om-ahee;* from *3844* and the mid. of *1011;* to *misconsult,* i.e. *disregard:*—not (to) regard (-ing).

3852. παραγγελία **paraggĕlia,** *par-ang-gel-ee'-ah;* from *3853;* a *mandate:*—charge, command.

3853. παραγγέλλω **paraggĕllō,** *par-ang-gel'-lo;* from *3844* and the base of *32;* to *transmit* a message, i.e. (by impl.) to *enjoin:*—(give in) charge, (give) command (-ment), declare.

3854. παραγίνομαι **paraginŏmai,** *par-ag-in'-om-ahee;* from *3844* and *1096;* to *become near,* i.e. *approach* (*have arrived*); by impl. to *appear* publicly:—come, go, be present.

3855. παράγω **paragō,** *par-ag'-o;* from *3844* and *71;* to *lead near,* i.e. (reflex. or intrans.) to *go along* or *away:*—depart, pass (away, by, forth).

3856. παραδειγματίζω **paradĕigmatizō,** *par-ad-igue-mat-id'-zo;* from *3844* and *1165;* to *show alongside* (the public), i.e. *expose* to *infamy:*—make a public example, put to an open shame.

3857. παράδεισος **paradĕisŏs,** *par-ad'-i-sos;* of Oriental or. [comp. 6508]; a *park,* i.e. (spec.) an *Eden* (place of future happiness, "*paradise*"):—paradise.

3858. παραδέχομαι **paradĕchŏmai,** *par-ad-ekh'-om-ahee;* from *3844* and *1209;* to *accept* near, i.e. *admit* or (by impl.) *delight* in:—receive.

3859. παραδιατριβή **paradiatribē,** *par-ad-ee-at-ree-bay';* from a comp. of *3844* and *1304; misemployment,* i.e. *meddlesomeness:*—perverse disputing.

3860. παραδίδωμι **paradidōmi,** *par-ad-id'-o-mee;* from *3844* and *1325;* to *surrender,* i.e. *yield up, intrust, transmit:*—betray, bring forth, cast, commit, deliver (up), give (over, up), hazard, put in prison, recommend.

3861. παράδοξος **paradŏxŏs,** *par-ad'-ox-os;* from *3844* and *1391* (in the sense of *seeming*); *contrary to expectation,* i.e. *extraordinary* ("*paradox*"):—strange.

3862. παράδοσις **paradŏsis,** *par-ad'-os-is;* from *3860; transmission,* i.e. (concr.) a *precept;* spec. the Jewish traditionary *law:*—ordinance, tradition.

3863. παραζηλόω **parazēlŏō,** *par-ad-zay-lŏ'-o;* from *3844* and *2206;* to *stimulate alongside,* i.e. *excite to rivalry:*—provoke to emulation (jealousy).

3864. παραθαλάσσιος **parathalassiŏs,** *par-ath-al-as'-see-os;* from *3844* and *2281; along the sea,* i.e. *maritime* (*lacustrine*):—upon the sea coast.

3865. παραθεωρέω **parathĕōrĕō,** *par-ath-eh-o-reh'-o;* from *3844* and *2334;* to *overlook* or *disregard:*—neglect.

3866. παραθήκη **parathēkē,** *par-ath-ay'-kay;* from *3908;* a *deposit,* i.e. (fig.) *trust:*—committed unto.

3867. παραινέω **parainĕō,** *par-ahee-neh'-o;* from *3844* and *134;* to *mispraise,* i.e. *recommend* or *advise* (a different course):—admonish, exhort.

3868. παραιτέομαι **paraitĕŏmai,** *par-ahee-teh'-om-ahee;* from *3844* and the mid. of *154;* to *beg off,* i.e. *deprecate, decline, shun:*—avoid, (make) excuse, intreat, refuse, reject.

3869. παρακαθίζω **parakathizō,** *par-ak-ath-id'-zo;* from *3844* and *2523;* to *sit down* near:—sit.

3870. παρακαλέω **parakalĕō,** *par-ak-al-eh'-o;* from *3844* and *2564;* to *call* near, i.e. *invite, invoke* (by *imploration, hortation* or *consolation*):—beseech, call for, (be of good) comfort, desire, (give) exhort (-ation), intreat, pray.

3871. παρακαλύπτω **parakaluptō,** *par-ak-al-oop'-to;* from *3844* and *2572;* to *cover* all over, i.e. *veil* (fig.):—hide.

3872. παρακαταθήκη **parakatathēkē,** *par-ak-at-ath-ay'-kay;* from a comp. of *3844* and *2698;* something *put down alongside,* i.e. a *deposit* (sacred *trust*):—that (thing) which is committed (un-) to (trust).

3873. παράκειμαι **parakĕimai,** *par-ak'-i-mahee;* from *3844* and *2749;* to *lie near*, i.e. *be at hand* (fig. *be prompt* or *easy*):—be present.

3874. παράκλησις **paraklēsis,** *par-ak'-lay-sis;* from *3870; imploration, hortation, solace:*—comfort, consolation, exhortation, intreaty.

3875. παράκλητος **paraklētŏs,** *par-ak'-lay-tos;* an *intercessor, consoler:*—advocate, comforter.

3876. παρακοή **parakŏē,** *par-ak-ŏ-ay';* from *3878; inattention,* i.e. (by impl.) *disobedience:*—disobedience.

3877. παρακολουθέω **parakŏlŏuthĕō,** *par-ak-ol-oo-theh'-o;* from *3844* and *190;* to *follow near,* i.e. (fig.) *attend* (as a result), *trace out, conform* to:—attain, follow, fully know, have understanding.

3878. παρακούω **parakŏuō,** *par-ak-oo'-o;* from *3844* and *191;* to *mishear,* i.e. (by impl.) to *disobey:*—neglect to hear.

3879. παρακύπτω **parakuptō,** *par-ak-oop'-to;* from *3844* and *2955;* to *bend beside,* i.e. *lean over* (so as to *peer within*):—look (into), stoop down.

3880. παραλαμβάνω **paralambanō,** *par-al-am-ban'-o;* from *3844* and *2983;* to *receive near,* i.e. *associate with* oneself (in any familiar or intimate act or relation); by anal. to *assume* an office; fig. to *learn:*—receive, take (unto, with).

3881. παραλέγομαι **paralĕgŏmai,** *par-al-eg'-om-ahee;* from *3844* and the mid. of *3004* (in its orig. sense); (spec.) to *lay* one's course *near,* i.e. *sail past:*—pass, sail by.

3882. παράλιος **paraliŏs,** *par-al'-ee-os;* from *3844* and *251; beside the salt* (sea), i.e. *maritime:*—sea coast.

3883. παραλλαγή **parallagē,** *par-al-lag-ay';* from a comp. of *3844* and *236; transmutation* (of phase or orbit), i.e. (fig.) *fickleness:*—variableness.

3884. παραλογίζομαι **paralŏgizŏmai,** *par-al-og-id'-zom-ahee;* from *3844* and *3049;* to *misreckon,* i.e. *delude:*—beguile, deceive.

3885. παραλυτικός **paralutikŏs,** *par-al-oo-tee-kos';* from a der. of *3886;* as if *dissolved,* i.e. "*paralytic*":—that had (sick of) the palsy.

3886. παραλύω **paraluō,** *par-al-oo'-o;* from *3844* and *3089;* to *loosen beside,* i.e. *relax* (perf. pas. part. *paralyzed* or *enfeebled*):—feeble, sick of the (taken with) palsy.

3887. παραμένω **paramĕnō,** *par-am-en'-o;* from *3844* and *3306;* to *stay near,* i.e. *remain* (lit. *tarry;* or fig. *be permanent, persevere*):—abide, continue.

3888. παραμυθέομαι **paramuthĕŏmai,** *par-am-oo-theh'-om-ahee;* from *3844* and the mid. of der. of *3454;* to *relate near,* i.e. (by impl.) *encourage, console:*—comfort.

3889. παραμυθία **paramuthia,** *par-am-oo-thee'-ah;* from *3888; consolation* (prop. abstr.):—comfort.

3890. παραμύθιον **paramuthiŏn,** *par-am-oo'-thee-on;* neut. of *3889; consolation* (prop. concr.):—comfort.

3891. παρανομέω **paranŏmĕō,** *par-an-om-eh'-o;* from a comp. of *3844* and *3551;* to *be opposed to law,* i.e. to *transgress:*—contrary to law.

3892. παρανομία **paranŏmia,** *par-an-om-ee'-ah;* from the same as *3891; transgression:*—iniquity.

3893. παραπικραίνω **parapikrainō,** *par-ap-ik-rah'ee-no;* from *3844* and *4087;* to *embitter alongside,* i.e. (fig.) to *exasperate:*—provoke.

3894. παραπικρασμός **parapikrasmŏs,** *par-ap-ik-ras-mos';* from *3893; irritation:*—provocation.

3895. παραπίπτω **parapiptō,** *par-ap-ip'-to;* from *3844* and *4098;* to *fall aside,* i.e. (fig.) to *apostatize:*—fall away.

3896. παραπλέω **paraplĕō,** *par-ap-leh'-o;* from *3844* and *4126;* to *sail near:*—sail by.

3897. παραπλήσιον **paraplēsiŏn,** *par-ap-lay'-see-on;* neut. of a comp. of *3844* and the base of *4139* (as adv.); *close by,* i.e. (fig.) *almost:*—nigh unto.

3898. παραπλησίως **paraplēsiŏs,** *par-ap-lay-see'-oce;* adv. from the same as *3897; in a manner near by,* i.e. (fig.) *similarly:*—likewise.

3899. παραπορεύομαι **parapŏrĕuŏmai,** *par-ap-or-yoo'-om-ahee;* from *3844* and *4198;* to *travel near:*—go, pass (by).

3900. παράπτωμα **paraptōma,** *par-ap'-to-mah;* from *3895;* a *side-slip* (*lapse* or *deviation*), i.e. (unintentional) *error* or (wilful) *transgression:*—fall, fault, offence, sin, trespass.

3901. παραῤῥυέω **pararrhuĕō,** *par-ar-hroo-eh'-o;* from *3844* and the alt. of *4482;* to *flow by,* i.e. (fig.) carelessly *pass* (*miss*):—let slip.

3902. παράσημος **parasēmŏs,** *par-as'-ay-mos;* from *3844* and the base of *4591; side-marked,* i.e. *labelled* (with a *badge* [*figure-head*] of a ship):—sign.

3903. παρασκευάζω **paraskĕuazō,** *par-ask-yoo-ad'-zo;* from *3844* and a der. of *4632;* to *furnish aside,* i.e. *get ready:*—prepare self, be (make) ready.

3904. παρασκευή **paraskĕuē,** *par-ask-yoo-ay';* as if from *3903; readiness:*—preparation.

3905. παρατείνω **paratĕinō,** *par-at-i'-no;* from *3844* and τείνω **tĕinō** (to *stretch*); to *extend along,* i.e. *prolong* (in point of time):—continue.

3906. παρατηρέω **paratērĕō,** *par-at-ay-reh'-o;* from *3844* and *5083;* to *inspect alongside,* i.e. *note insidiously* or *scrupulously:*—observe, watch.

3907. παρατήρησις **paratērēsis,** *par-at-ay'-ray-sis;* from *3906; inspection,* i.e. *ocular evidence:*—observation

3908. παρατίθημι **paratithēmi,** *par-at-ith'-ay-mee;* from *3844* and *5087;* to *place alongside,* i.e. *present* (food, truth); by impl. to *deposit* (as a trust or for protection):—allege, commend, commit (the keeping of), put forth, set before.

3909. παρατυγχάνω **paratugchanō,** *par-at-oong-khan'-o;* from *3844* and *5177;* to *chance near,* i.e. *fall in with:*—meet with.

3910. παραυτίκα **parautika,** *par-ŏw-tee'-kah;* from *3844* and a der. of *846; at the very instant,* i.e. *momentary:*—but for a moment.

3911. παραφέρω **paraphĕrō,** *par-af-er'-o;* from *3844* and *5342* (includ. its alt. forms); to *bear along* or *aside,* i.e. *carry off* (lit. or fig.); by impl. to *avert:*—remove, take away.

3912. παραφρονέω **paraphrŏnĕō,** *par-af-ron-eh'-o;* from *3844* and *5426;* to *misthink,* i.e. *be insane* (*silly*):—as a fool.

3913. παραφρονία **paraphrŏnia,** *par-af-ron-ee'-ah;* from *3912; insanity,* i.e. *foolhardiness:*—madness.

3914. παραχειμάζω **parachĕimazō,** *par-akh-i-mad'-zo;* from *3844* and *5492;* to *winter near,* i.e. *stay* with over the *rainy* season:—winter.

3915. παραχειμασία **parachĕimasia,** *par-akh-i-mas-ee'-ah;* from *3914;* a *wintering over:*—winter in.

3916. παραχρῆμα **parachrēma,** *par-akh-ray'-mah;* from *3844* and *5536* (in its orig. sense); *at the thing* itself, i.e. *instantly:*—forthwith, immediately, presently, straightway, soon.

3917. πάρδαλις **pardalis,** *par'-dal-is;* fem. of πάρδος **pardŏs** (a *panther*); a *leopard:*—leopard.

3918. πάρειμι **parĕimi,** *par'-i-mee;* from *3844* and *1510* (includ. its various forms); to *be near,* i.e. *be at hand;* neut. pres. part. (sing.) *time being,* or (plur.) *property:*—come, × have, be here, + lack, (be here) present.

3919. παρεισάγω **parĕisagō,** *par-ice-ag'-o;* from *3844* and *1521;* to *lead in aside,* i.e. *introduce surreptitiously:*—privily bring in.

3920. παρείσακτος **parĕisaktŏs,** *par-ice'-ak-tos;* from *3919; smuggled in:*—unawares brought in.

3921. παρεισδύνω **parĕisdunō,** *par-ice-doo'-no;* from *3844* and a comp. of *1519* and *1416;* to *settle in alongside,* i.e. *lodge stealthily:*—creep in unawares.

3922. παρεισέρχομαι **parĕisĕrchŏmai,** *par-ice-er'-khom-ahee;* from *3844* and *1525;* to *come in alongside,* i.e. *supervene additionally* or *stealthily:*—come in privily, enter.

3923. παρεισφέρω **parĕisphĕrō,** *par-ice-fer'-o;* from *3844* and *1533;* to *bear in alongside,* i.e. *introduce simultaneously:*—give.

3924. παρεκτός **parĕktŏs,** *par-ek-tos';* from *3844* and *1622; near outside,* i.e. *besides:*—except, saving, without.

3925. παρεμβολή **parĕmbŏlē,** *par-em-bol-ay';* from a comp. of *3844* and *1685;* a *throwing in beside* (*juxtaposition*), i.e. (spec.) *battle-array, encampment* or *barracks* (tower Antonia):—army, camp, castle.

3926. παρενοχλέω **parĕnŏchlĕō,** *par-en-okh-leh'-o;* from *3844* and *1776;* to *harass further,* i.e. *annoy:*—trouble.

3927. παρεπίδημος **parĕpidēmŏs,** *par-ep-id'-ay-mos;* from *3844* and the base of *1927;* an *alien alongside,* i.e. a *resident foreigner:*—pilgrim, stranger.

3928. παρέρχομαι **parĕrchŏmai,** *par-er'-khom-ahee;* from *3844* and *2064;* to *come near* or *aside,* i.e. to *approach* (*arrive*), *go by* (or *away*), (fig.) *perish* or *neglect.* (caus.) *avert:*—come (forth), go, pass (away, by, over), past, transgress.

3929. πάρεσις **parēsis,** *par'-es-is;* from *3935; praetermission,* i.e. *toleration:*—remission.

3930. παρέχω **parĕchō,** *par-ekh'-o;* from *3844* and *2192;* to *hold near,* i.e. *present, afford, exhibit, furnish occasion:*—bring, do, give, keep, minister, offer, shew, + trouble.

3931. παρηγορία **parēgŏria,** *par-ay-gor-ee'-ah;* from a comp. of *3844* and a der. of *58* (mean. to *harangue* an assembly); an *address alongside,* i.e. (spec.) *consolation:*—comfort.

3932. παρθενία **parthĕnia,** *par-then-ee'-ah;* from *3933; maidenhood:*—virginity.

3933. παρθένος **parthĕnŏs,** *par-then'-os;* of unknown or. ; a *maiden;* by impl. an unmarried *daughter:*—virgin.

3934. Πάρθος **Parthŏs,** *par'-thos;* prob. of for. or.: a *Parthian,* i.e. inhab. of Parthia:—Parthian.

3935. παρίημι **pariēmi,** *par-ee'-ay-mi;* from *3844* and ἵημι **hiĕmi** (to *send*); to *let by,* i.e. *relax:*—hang down.

3936. παρίστημι **paristēmi,** *par-is'-tay-mee;* or prol. παριστάνω **paristanō,** *par-is-tan'-o;* from *3844* and *2476;* to *stand beside,* i.e. (trans.) to *exhibit, proffer,* (spec.) *recommend,* (fig.) *substantiate;* or (intrans.) to *be at hand* (or *ready*), *aid:*—assist, bring before, command, commend, give presently, present, prove, provide, shew, stand (before, by, here, up, with), yield.

3937. Παρμενᾶς **Parmĕnas,** *par-men-as';* prob. by contr. for Παρμενίδης **Parmĕnidēs** (a der. of a comp. of *3844* and *3306*); *constant; Parmenas,* a Chr.:—Parmenas.

3938. πάροδος **parŏdŏs,** *par'-od-os;* from *3844* and *3598;* a *by-road,* i.e. (act.) a *route:*—way.

3939. παροικέω **parŏikĕō,** *par-oy-keh'-o;* from *3844* and *3611;* to *dwell near,* i.e. *reside* as a *foreigner:*—sojourn in, be a stranger.

3940. παροικία **parŏikia,** *par-oy-kee'-ah;* from *3941; foreign residence:*—sojourning, × as strangers.

3941. πάροικος **parŏikŏs,** *par'-oy-kos;* from *3844* and *3624;* having a *home near,* i.e. (as noun) a *by-dweller* (*alien resident*):—foreigner, sojourn, stranger.

3942. παροιμία **parŏimia,** *par-oy-mee'-ah;* from a comp. of *3844* and perh. a der. of *3633;* appar. a state *alongside of supposition,* i.e. (concr.) an *adage;*

spec. an enigmatical or fictitious *illustration:*—parable, proverb.

3943. πάροινος **parŏinŏs**, *par'-oy-nos;* from *3844* and *3631;* staying *near* wine, i.e. *tippling* (a toper):—given to wine.

3944. παροίχομαι **parŏichŏmai**, *par-oy'-khom-ahee;* from *3844* and οἴχομαι **ŏichŏmai** (to *depart*); to *escape along*, i.e. *be gone:*—past.

3945. παρομοιάζω **parŏmŏiazō**, *par-om-oy-ad'-zo;* from *3946;* to *resemble:*—be like unto.

3946. παρόμοιος **parŏmŏiŏs**, *par-om'-oy-os;* from *3844* and *3664; alike* nearly, i.e. *similar:*—like.

3947. παροξύνω **parŏxunō**, *par-ox-oo'-no;* from *3844* and a der. of *3691;* to *sharpen alongside*, i.e. (fig.) to *exasperate:*—easily provoke, stir.

3948. παροξυσμός **parŏxusmŏs**, *par-ox-oos-mos';* from *3947* ("paroxysm"); *incitement* (to good), or *dispute* (in anger):—contention, provoke unto.

3949. παροργίζω **parŏrgizō**, *par-org-id'-zo;* from *3844* and *3710;* to *anger alongside*, i.e. *enrage:*—anger, provoke to wrath.

3950. παροργισμός **parŏrgismŏs**, *par-org-is-mos';* from *3949; rage:*—wrath.

3951. παροτρύνω **parŏtrunō**, *par-ot-roo'-no;* from *3844* and ὀτρύνω **ŏtrunō** (to *spur*); to *urge along*, i.e. *stimulate* (to hostility):—stir up.

3952. παρουσία **parŏusia**, *par-oo-see'-ah;* from the pres. part. of *3918; a being near*, i.e. *advent* (often, *return;* spec. of Christ to punish Jerusalem, or finally the wicked); (by impl.) phys. *aspect:*—coming, presence.

3953. παροψίς **parŏpsis**, *par-op-sis';* from *3844* and the base of *3795;* a *side-dish* (the receptacle):—platter.

3954. παρρησία **parrhēsia**, *par-rhay-see'-ah;* from *3956* and a der. of *4483; all out-spokenness*, i.e. *frankness, bluntness, publicity;* by impl. *assurance:*—bold (× -ly, -ness, -ness of speech), confidence, × freely, × openly, × plainly (-ness).

3955. παρρησιάζομαι **parrhēsiazŏmai**, *par-hray-see-ad'-zom-ahee;* mid. from *3954;* to *be frank* in utterance, or *confident* in spirit and demeanor:—be (wax) bold, (preach, speak) boldly.

3956. πᾶς **pas**, *pas;* includ. all the forms of declension; appar. a prim. word; *all, any, every*, the *whole:*—all (manner of, means), alway (-s), any (one), × daily, + ever, every (one, way), as many as, + no (-thing), × throughly, whatsoever, whole, whosoever.

3957. πάσχα **pascha**, *pas'-khah;* of Chald. or. [comp. 6453]; the *Passover* (the meal, the day, the festival or the special sacrifices connected with it):—Easter, Passover.

3958. πάσχω **paschō**, *pas'-kho;* includ. the forms πάθω (**pathō**, *path'-o*) and πένθω (**penthō**, *pen'-tho*), used only in certain tenses for it; appar. a prim. verb; to *experience* a sensation or impression (usually painful):—feel, passion, suffer, vex.

3959. Πάταρα **Patara**, *pat'-ar-ah;* prob. of for. or.; *Patara*, a place in Asia Minor:—Patara.

3960. πατάσσω **patassō**, *pat-as'-so;* prob. prol. from *3817;* to *knock* (gently or with a weapon or fatally):—smite, strike. Comp. *5180.*

3961. πατέω **patĕō**, *pat-eh'-o;* from a der. prob. of *3817* (mean. a "*path*"); to *trample* (lit. or fig.):—tread (down, under foot).

3962. πατήρ **patēr**, *pat-ayr';* appar. a prim. word; a "*father*" (lit. or fig., near or more remote):—father, parent.

3963. Πάτμος **Patmŏs**, *pat'-mos;* of uncert. der.; *Patmus*, an islet in the Mediterranean:—Patmos.

3964. πατραλῴας **patralŏias**, *pat-ral-o'-as;* from *3962* and the same as the latter part of *3389;* a *parricide:*—murderer of fathers.

3965. πατριά **patria**, *pat-ree-ah';* as if fem. of a der. of *3902;* paternal *descent*, i.e. (concr.) a *group* of families or a whole *race* (*nation*):—family, kindred, lineage.

3966. πατριάρχης **patriarchēs**, *pat-ree-arkh'-ace;* from *3965* and *757;* a *progenitor* ("patriarch"):—patriarch.

3967. πατρικός **patrikŏs**, *pat-ree-kos';* from *3962;* paternal, i.e. *ancestral:*—of fathers.

3968. πατρίς **patris**, *pat-rece';* from *3962;* a *father-land*, i.e. *native* town; (fig.) heavenly *home:*—(own) country.

3969. Πατρόβας **Patrŏbas**, *pat-rob'-as;* perh. contr. for Πατρόβιος **Patrŏbiŏs** (a comp. of *3962* and *979); father's life; Patrobas*, a Chr.:—Patrobas.

3970. πατροπαράδοτος **patrŏparadŏtŏs**, *pat-rop-ar-ad'-ot-os;* from *3962* and a der. of *3880* (in the sense of *handing over* or *down*); *traditionary:*—received by tradition from fathers.

3971. πατρῷος **patrŏiŏs**, *pat-ro'-os;* from *3962;* paternal, i.e. *hereditary:*—of fathers.

3972. Παῦλος **Paulŏs**, *pŏw'-los;* of Lat. or.; (*little;* but remotely from a der. of *3973*, mean. the same); *Paulus*, the name of a Rom. and of an apostle:—Paul, Paulus.

3973. παύω **pauō**, *pŏw'-o;* a prim. verb ("*pause*"); to *stop* (trans. or intrans.), i.e. *restrain, quit, desist, come to an end:*—cease, leave, refrain.

3974. Πάφος **Paphŏs**, *paf'-os;* of uncert. der.; *Paphus*, a place in Cyprus:—Paphos.

3975. παχύνω **pachunō**, *pakh-oo'-no;* from a der. of *4078* (mean. thick); to *thicken*, i.e. (by impl.) to *fatten* (fig. *stupefy* or render *callous*):—wax gross.

3976. πέδη **pĕdē**, *ped'-ay;* ultimately from *4228;* a *shackle* for the feet:—fetter.

3977. πεδινός **pĕdinŏs**, *ped-ee-nos';* from a der. of *4228* (mean. the *ground*); *level* (as easy for the *feet*):—plain.

3978. πεζεύω **pĕzĕuō**, *ped-zyoo'-o;* from the same as *3979;* to *foot* a journey, i.e. *travel* by land:—go afoot.

3979. πεζῇ **pĕzē**, *ped-zay';* dat. fem. of a der. of *4228* (as adv.); *foot-wise*, i.e. by *walking:*—a- (on) foot.

3980. πειθαρχέω **pĕitharchĕō**, *pi-tharkh-eh'-o;* from a comp. of *3982* and *757;* to *be persuaded by* a *ruler*, i.e. (gen.) to *submit* to authority; by anal. to *conform* to advice:—hearken, obey (magistrates).

3981. πειθός **pĕithŏs**, *pi-thos';* from *3982; persuasive:*—enticing.

3982. πείθω **pĕithō**, *pi'-tho;* a prim. verb; to *convince* (by argument, true or false); by anal. to *pacify* or *conciliate* (by other fair means); reflex. or pass. to *assent* (to evidence or authority), to *rely* (by inward certainty):—agree, assure, believe, have confidence, be (wax) confient, make friend, obey, persuade, trust, yield.

3983. πεινάω **pĕinaō**, *pi-nah'-o;* from the same as *3993* (through the idea of *pinching toil;* "*pine*"); to *famish* (absol. or comparatively); fig. to *crave:*—be an hungered.

3984. πεῖρα **pĕira**, *pi'-rah;* from the base of *4008* (through the idea of *piercing*); a *test*, i.e. *attempt, experience:*—assaying, trial.

3985. πειράζω **pĕirazō**, *pi-rad'-zo;* from *3984;* to *test* (obj.), i.e. *endeavor, scrutinize, entice, discipline:*—assay, examine, go about, prove, tempt (-er), try.

3986. πειρασμός **pĕirasmŏs**, *pi-ras-mos';* from *3985;* a *putting to proof* (by experiment [of good], *experience* [of evil], solicitation, discipline or provocation); by impl. *adversity:*—temptation, × try.

3987. πειράω **pĕiraō**, *pi-rah'-o;* from *3984;* to *test* (subj.), i.e. (reflex.) to *attempt:*—assay.

3988. πεισμονή **pĕismŏnē**, *pice-mon-ay';* from a presumed der. of *3982; persuadableness*, i.e. *credulity:*—persuasion.

3989. πέλαγος **pĕlagŏs**, *pel'-ag-os;* of uncert. affin.; *deep* or *open sea*, i.e. the *main:*—depth, sea.

3990. πελεκίζω **pĕlĕkizō**, *pel-ek-id'-zo;* from a der. of *4141* (mean. an *axe*); to *chop off* (the head), i.e. *truncate:*—behead.

3991. πέμπτος **pĕmptŏs**, *pemp'-tos;* from *4002; fifth:*—fifth.

3992. πέμπω **pĕmpō**, *pem'-po;* appar. a prim. verb; to *dispatch* (from the subj. view or point of *departure*, whereas ἵημι **hiĕmi** [as a stronger form of εἶμι **ĕimi**] refers rather to the obj. point or *terminus ad quem*, and *4724* denotes prop. the *orderly* motion involved; espec. on a temporary errand; also to *transmit, bestow*, or *wield*:—send, thrust in.

3993. πένης **pĕnēs**, *pen'-ace;* from a prim. πένω **pĕnō** (to *toil* for daily subsistence); *starving*, i.e. *indigent:*—poor. Comp. *4434.*

3994. πενθερά **pĕnthĕra**, *pen-ther-ah';* fem. of *3995;* a *wife's mother:*—mother in law, wife's mother.

3995. πενθερός **pĕnthĕrŏs**, *pen-ther-os';* of uncert. affin.; a *wife's father:*—father in law.

3996. πενθέω **pĕnthĕō**, *pen-theh'-o;* from *3997;* to *grieve* (the feeling or the act):—mourn, (be-) wail.

3997. πένθος **pĕnthŏs**, *pen'-thos;* strengthened from the alt. of *3958;* (prop.) *mourning, sorrow.*

3998. πεντιχρός **pĕntichrŏs**, *pen-tikh-ros';* prol. from the base of *3993; necessitous:*—poor.

3999. πεντάκις **pĕntakis**, *pen-tak-ece';* mult. adv. from *4002; five times:*—five times.

4000. πεντακισχίλιοι **pĕntakischiliŏi**, *pen-tak-is-khil'-ee-oy;* from *3999* and *5507; five times a thousand:*—five thousand.

4001. πεντακόσιοι **pĕntakŏsiŏi**, *pen-tak-os'-ee-oy;* from *4002* and *1540; five hundred:*—five hundred.

4002. πέντε **pĕntĕ**, *pen'-teh;* a prim. number; "*five*":—five.

4003. πεντεκαιδέκατος **pĕntĕkaidĕkatŏs**, *pen-tek-ahee-dek'-at-os;* from *4002* and *2532* and *1182; five and tenth:*—fifteenth.

4004. πεντήκοντα **pĕntēkŏnta**, *pen-tay'-kon-tah;* mult. of *4002; fifty:*—fifty.

4005. πεντηκοστή **pĕntēkŏstē**, *pen-tay-kos-tay';* fem. of the ord. of *4004; fiftieth* (*2250* being implied) from Passover, i.e. the festival of "*Pentecost*":—Pentecost.

4006. πεποίθησις **pĕpŏithēsis**, *pep-oy'-thay-sis;* from the perf. of the alt. of *3958; reliance:*—confidence, trust.

4007. περ **pĕr**, *per;* from the base of *4008;* an enclitic particle significant of *abundance* (*thoroughness*), i.e. *emphasis; much, very* or *ever:*—[whom-] soever.

4008. πέραν **pĕran**, *per'-an;* appar. acc. of an obsol. der. of πείρω **pĕirō** (to "*pierce*"); *through* (as adv. or prep.), i.e. *across:*—beyond, farther (other) side, over.

4009. πέρας **pĕras**, *per'-as;* from the same as *4008;* an *extremity:*—end, ut- (ter-) most part.

4010. Πέργαμος **Pĕrgamŏs**, *per'-gam-os;* from *4444; fortified; Pergamus*, a place in Asia Minor:—Pergamos.

4011. Πέργη **Pĕrgē**, *perg'-ay;* prob. from the same as *4010;* a *tower; Perga*, a place in Asia Minor:—Perga.

4012. περί **pĕri**, *per-ee';* from the base of *4008;* prop. *through* (all over), i.e. *around;* fig. *with respect to;* used in various applications, of place, cause or time (with the gen. denoting the *subject* or *occasion* or *superlative* point; with the acc. the *locality, circuit, matter, circumstance* or general *period*):—(there-) about, above, against, at, on behalf of, × and his company, which concern, (as) concerning, for, X how it will go with, ([there-, where-]) of, on, over, pertaining (to), for sake, X (e-) state, (as) touching. [where-] by (in), with. In comp. it retains substantially the same mean. of circuit (around), excess (beyond), or completeness (through).

4013. περιάγω **pĕriagō,** per-ee-ag'-o; from *4012* and *71;* to take around (as a companion); reflex. to walk around;—compass, go (round) about, lead about.

4014. περιαιρέω **pĕriairĕō,** per-ee-ahee-reh'-o; from *4012* and *138* (incl. its alt.); to remove all around, i.e. unveil, cast off (anchor); fig. to expiate:—take away (up).

4015. περιαστράπτω **pĕriastraptō,** per-ee-as-trap'-to; from *4012* and *797;* to flash all around, i.e. envelop in light:—shine round (about).

4016. περιβάλλω **pĕriballō,** per-ee-bal'-lo; from *4012* and *906;* to throw all around, i.e. invest (with a palisade or with clothing):—array, cast about, clothe (-d me), put on.

4017. περιβλέπω **pĕriblĕpō,** per-ee-blep'-o; from *4012* and *991;* to look all around:—look (round) about (on).

4018. περιβόλαιον **pĕribŏlaiŏn,** per-ib-ol'-ah-yon; neut. of a presumed der. of *4016;* something thrown around one, i.e. a mantle, veil:—covering, vesture.

4019. περιδέω **pĕridĕō,** per-ee-deh'-o; from *4012* and *1210;* to bind around one, i.e. enwrap:—bind about.

περιδρέμω **pĕridrĕmō.** See *4063.*

περιέλλω **pĕriĕllō.** See *4014.*

περιέλθω **pĕriĕlthō.** See *4022.*

4020. περιεργάζομαι **pĕriĕrgazŏmai,** per-ee-er-gad'-zom-ahee; from *4012* and *2038;* to work all around, i.e. bustle about (meddle):—be a busybody.

4021. περίεργος **pĕriĕrgŏs,** per-ee'-er-gos; from *4012* and *2041;* working all around, i.e. officious (meddlesome, neut. plur. magic):—busybody, curious arts.

4022. περιέρχομαι **pĕriĕrchŏmai,** per-ee-er'-khom-ahee; from *4012* and *2064* (includ. its alt.); to come all around, i.e. stroll, vacillate, veer:—fetch a compass, vagabond, wandering about.

4023. περιέχω **pĕriĕchō,** per-ee-ekh'-o; from *4012* and *2192;* to hold all around, i.e. include, clasp (fig.):— + astonished, contain, after [this manner].

4024. περιζώννυμι **pĕrizōnnumi,** per-id-zone'-.'oo-mee; from *4012* and *2224;* to gird all around, i.e. (m'.d. or pass.) to fasten on one's belt (lit. or fig.):—gird (about, self).

4025. περίθεσις **pĕrithĕsis,** per-ith'-es-is; from *4060;* a putting all around, i.e. decorating oneself with:—wearing.

4026. περιΐστημι **pĕristēmi,** per-ee-is'-tay-mee; from *4012* and *2476;* to stand all around, i.e. (near) to be a bystander, or (aloof) to keep away from:—avoid, shun, stand by (round about).

4027. περικάθαρμα **pĕrikatharma,** per-ee-kath'-ar-mah; from a comp. of *4012* and *2508;* something cleaned off all around, i.e. refuse (fig.):—filth.

4028. περικαλύπτω **pĕrikaluptō,** per-ee-kal-oop'-to; from *4012* and *2572;* to cover all around, i.e. entirely (the face, a surface):—blindfold, cover, overlay.

4029. περίκειμαι **pĕrikĕimai,** per-ik'-i-mahee; from *4012* and *2749;* to lie all around, i.e. inclose, encircle, hamper (lit. or fig.):—be bound (compassed) with, hang about.

4030. περικεφαλαία **pĕrikĕphalaia,** per-ee-kef-al-ah'-yah; fem. of a comp. of *4012* and *2776;* encirclement of the head, i.e. a helmet:—helmet.

4031. περικρατής **pĕrikratēs,** per-ee-krat-ace'; from *4012* and *2904;* strong all around, i.e. a master (manager):— + come by.

4032. περικρύπτω **pĕrikruptō,** per-ee-kroop'-to; from *4012* and *2928;* to conceal all around, i.e. entirely:—hide.

4033. περικυκλόω **pĕrikuklŏō,** per-ee-koo-klŏ'-o; from *4012* and *2944;* to encircle all around, i.e. blockade completely:—compass round.

4034. περιλάμπω **pĕrilampō,** per-ee-lam'-po; from *4012* and *2989;* to illuminate all around, i.e. invest with a halo:—shine round about.

4035. περιλείπω **pĕrilĕipō,** per-ee-li'-po; from *4012* and *3007;* to leave all around, i.e. (pass.) survive:—remain.

4036. περίλυπος **pĕrilupŏs,** per-il'-oo-pos; from *4012* and *3077;* grieved all around, i.e. intensely sad:—exceeding (very) sorry (-owful).

4037. περιμένω **pĕrimĕnō,** per-ee-men'-o; from *4012* and *3306;* to stay around, i.e. await:—wait for.

4038. περίξ **pĕrix,** per'-ix; adv. from *4012;* all around, i.e. (as adj.) circumjacent:—round about.

4039. περιοικέω **pĕriŏikĕō,** per-ee-oy-keh'-o; from *4012* and *3611;* to reside around, i.e. be a neighbor:—dwell round about.

4040. περίοικος **pĕriŏikŏs,** per-ee'-oy-kos; from *4012* and *3624;* housed around, i.e. neighboring (ellipt. as noun):—neighbour.

4041. περιούσιος **pĕriŏusiŏs,** per-ee-oo'-see-os; from the pres. part. fem. of a comp. of *4012* and *1510;* being beyond usual, i.e. special (one's own):—peculiar.

4042. περιοχή **pĕriŏchē,** per-ee-okh-ay'; from *4023;* a being held around, i.e. (concr.) a passage (of Scripture, as circumscribed):—place.

4043. περιπατέω **pĕripatĕō,** per-ee-pat-eh'-o; from *4012* and *3961;* to tread all around, i.e. walk at large (espec. as proof of ability); fig. to live, deport oneself, follow (as a companion or votary):—go, be occupied with, walk (about).

4044. περιπείρω **pĕripĕirō,** per-ee-pi'-ro; from *4012* and the base of *4008;* to penetrate entirely, i.e. transfix (fig.):—pierce through.

4045. περιπίπτω **pĕripiptō,** per-ee-pip'-to; from *4012* and *4098;* to fall into something that is all around, i.e. light among or upon, be surrounded with:—fall among (into).

4046. περιποιέομαι **pĕripŏiĕŏmai,** per-ee-poy-eh'-om-ahee; mid. from *4012* and *4160;* to make around oneself, i.e. acquire (buy):—purchase.

4047. περιποίησις **pĕripŏiēsis,** per-ee-poy'-ay-sis; from *4046;* acquisition (the act or the thing); by extens. preservation:—obtain (-ing), peculiar, purchased, possession, saving.

4048. περιρρήγνυμι **pĕrirrhēgnumi,** per-ir-hrayg'-noo-mee; from *4012* and *4486;* to tear all around, i.e. completely away:—rend off.

4049. περισπάω **pĕrispaō,** per-ee-spah'-o; from *4012* and *4685;* to drag all around, i.e. (fig.) to distract (with care):—cumber.

4050. περισσεία **pĕrissĕia,** per-is-si'-ah; from *4052;* surplusage, i.e. superabundance:—abundance (-ant, [-ly]), superfluity.

4051. περίσσευμα **pĕrissĕuma,** per-is'-syoo-mah; from *4052;* a surplus, or superabundance:—abundance, that was left, over and above.

4052. περισσεύω **pĕrissĕuō,** per-is-syoo'-o; from *4053;* to superabound (in quantity or quality), be in excess, be superfluous; also (trans.) to cause to superabound or excel:—(make, more) abound, (have, have more) abundance, (be more) abundant, be the better, enough and to spare, exceed, excel, increase, be left, redound, remain (over and above).

4053. περισσός **pĕrissŏs,** per-is-sos'; from *4012* (in the sense of beyond); superabundant (in quantity) or superior (in quality); by impl. excessive; adv. (with *1537*) violently; neut. (as noun) preeminence:—exceeding abundantly above, more abundantly, advantage, exceedingly, very highly, beyond measure, more, superfluous, vehement [-ly].

4054. περισσότερον **pĕrissŏtĕrŏn,** per-is-sot'-er-on; neut. of *4055* (as adv.); in a more superabundant way:—more abundantly, a great deal, far more.

4055. περισσότερος **pĕrissŏtĕrŏs,** per-is-sot'-er-os; comp. of *4053;* more superabundant (in number, degree or character):—more abundant, greater (much) more, overmuch.

4056. περισσοτέρως **pĕrissŏtĕrōs,** per-is-sot'-er'-oce; adv. from *4055;* more superabundantly:—

more abundant (-ly), X the more earnest, (more) exceedingly, more frequent, much more, the rather.

4057. περισσῶς **pĕrissōs,** per-is-soce'; adv. from *4053;* superabundantly:—exceedingly, out of measure, the more.

4058. περιστερά **pĕristĕra,** per-is-ter-ah'; of uncert. der.; a pigeon:—dove, pigeon.

4059. περιτέμνω **pĕritĕmnō,** per-ee-tem'-no; from *4012* and the base of *5114;* to cut around, i.e. (spec.) to circumcise:—circumcise.

4060. περιτίθημι **pĕritithēmi,** per-ee-tith'-ay-mee; from *4012* and *5087;* to place around; by impl. to present:—bestow upon, hedge round about, put about (on, upon), set about.

4061. περιτομή **pĕritŏmē,** per-it-om-ay'; from *4059;* circumcision (the rite, the condition or the people, lit. or fig.):— X circumcised, circumcision.

4062. περιτρέπω **pĕritrĕpō,** per-ee-trep'-o; from *4012* and the base of *5157;* to turn around, i.e. (ment.) to craze:— + make mad.

4063. περιτρέχω **pĕritrĕchō,** per-ee-trekh'-o; from *4012* and *5143* (includ. its alt.); to run around, i.e. traverse:—run through.

4064. περιφέρω **pĕriphĕrō,** per-ee-fer'-o; from *4012* and *5342;* to convey around, i.e. transport hither and thither:—bear (carry) about.

4065. περιφρονέω **pĕriphrŏnĕō,** per-ee-fron-eh'-o; from *4012* and *5426;* to think beyond, i.e. depreciate (contemn):—despise.

4066. περίχωρος **pĕrichōrŏs,** per-ikh'-o-ros; from *4012* and *5561;* around the region, i.e. circumjacent (as noun, with *1093* impl. vicinity):—country (round) about, region (that lieth) round about.

4067. περίψωμα **pĕripsōma,** per-ip'-so-mah; from a comp. of *4012* and ψάω **psaō** (to rub); something brushed all around, i.e. off-scrapings (fig. scum):—offscouring.

4068. περπερεύομαι **pĕrpĕrĕuŏmai,** per-per-yoo'-om-ahee; mid. from πέρπερος **pĕrpĕrŏs** (braggart; perh. by redupl. of the base of *4008*); to boast:—vaunt itself.

4069. Περσίς **Pĕrsis,** per-sece'; a Persian woman; Persis, a Chr. female:—Persis.

4070. πέρυσι **pĕrusi,** per'-oo-si; adv. from *4009;* the by-gone, i.e. (as noun) last year:— + a year ago.

4071. πετεινόν **pĕtĕinŏn,** pet-i-non'; neut. of a der. of *4072;* a flying animal, i.e. bird:—bird, fowl.

4072. πέτομαι **pĕtŏmai,** pet'-om-ahee; or prol. πετάομαι **pĕtaŏmai,** pet-ah'-om-ahee; or contr. πτάομαι **ptaŏmai,** ptah'-om-ahee; mid. of a prim. verb; to fly:—fly (-ing).

4073. πέτρα **pĕtra,** pet'-ra; fem. of the same as *4074;* a (mass of) rock (lit. or fig.):—rock.

4074. Πέτρος **Pĕtrŏs,** pet'-ros; appar. a prim. word; a (piece of) rock (larger than *3037*); as a name, Petrus, an apostle:—Peter, rock. Comp. *2786.*

4075. πετρώδης **pĕtrōdēs,** pet-ro'-dace; from *4073* and *1491;* rock-like, i.e. rocky:—stony.

4076. πήγανον **pēganŏn,** pay'-gan-on; from *4078;* rue (from its thick or fleshy leaves):—rue.

4077. πηγή **pēgē,** pay-gay'; prob. from *4078* (through the idea of gushing plumply); a fount (lit. or fig.), i.e. source or supply (of water, blood, enjoyment) (not necessarily the original spring):—fountain, well.

4078. πήγνυμι **pēgnumi,** payg'-noo-mee; a prol. form of a prim. verb (which in its simpler form occurs only as an alt. in certain tenses); to fix ("peg"), i.e. (spec.) to set up (a tent):—pitch.

4079. πηδάλιον **pēdaliŏn,** pay-dal'-ee-on; neut. of a (presumed) der. of πηδόν **pēdŏn** (the blade of an oar; from the same as *3976*); a "pedal", i.e. helm:—rudder.

4080. πηλίκος **pēlikŏs,** pay-lee'-kos; a quantitative form (the fem. of the base of *4225;* how much (as indef.), i.e. in size or (fig.) dignity:—how great (large).

4081. πηλός **pēlŏs,** pay-los'; perh. a prim. word; clay:—clay.

4082. πήρα **pēra**, *pay'-rah*; of uncert. affin.; a *wallet* or leather *pouch* for food:—scrip.

4083. πῆχυς **pēchus**, *pay'-khoos*; of uncert. affin.; the *fore-arm*, i.e. (as a measure) a *cubit*:—cubit.

4084. πιάζω **piazō**, *pee-ad'-zo*; prob. another form of *971*; to *squeeze*, i.e. *seize* (gently by the hand [*press*], or officially [*arrest*], or in hunting [*capture*]):—apprehend, catch, lay hand on, take. Comp. *4085*.

4085. πιέζω **piezō**, *pee-ed'-zo*; another form for *4084*; to *pack*:—press down.

4086. πιθανολογία **pithanologia**, *pith-an-ol-og-ee'-ah*; from a comp. of a der. of *3982* and *3056*; *persuasive language*:—enticing words.

4087. πικραίνω **pikrainō**, *pik-rah'ee-no*; from *4089*; to *embitter* (lit. or fig.):—be (make) bitter.

4088. πικρία **pikria**, *pik-ree'-ah*; from *4089*; *acridity* (espec. *poison*), lit. or fig.:—bitterness.

4089. πικρός **pikros**, *pik-ros'*; perh. from *4078* (through the idea of *piercing*); *sharp* (*pungent*), i.e. *acrid* (lit. or fig.):—bitter.

4090. πικρῶς **pikrōs**, *pik-roce'*; adv. from *4089*; *bitterly*, i.e. (fig.) *violently*:—bitterly.

4091. Πιλάτος **Pilatos**, *pil-at'-os*; of Lat. or.; *close-pressed*, i.e. *firm*; *Pilatus*, a Rom.:—Pilate.

πίμπλημι **pimplēmi.** See *4130*.

4092. πίμπρημι **pimprēmi**, *pim'-pray-mee*; a redupl. and prol. form of a prim.

πρέω **preō**, *preh'-o* (which occurs only as an alt. in certain tenses); to *fire*, i.e. *burn* (fig. and pass. *become inflamed* with fever):—be (× should have) swollen.

4093. πινακίδιον **pinakidion**, *pin-ak-id'-ee-on*; dimin. of *4094*; a *tablet* (for writing on):—writing table.

4094. πίναξ **pinax**, *pin'-ax*; appar. a form of *4109*; a *plate*:—charger, platter.

4095. πίνω **pinō**, *pee'-no*; a prol. form of

πίω **piō**, *pee'-o*, which (together with another form πόω **poō**, *pŏ'-o*) occurs only as an alt. in cert. tenses; to *imbibe* (lit. or fig.):—drink.

4096. πιότης **piotēs**, *pee-ot'-ace*; from πίων **piōn** (*fat*; perh. akin to the alt. of *4095* through the idea of *repletion*); *plumpness*, i.e. (by impl.) *richness* (*oiliness*):—fatness.

4097. πιπράσκω **piraskō**, *pip-ras'-ko*; a redupl. and prol. form of

πράω **praō**, *prah'-o* (which occurs only as an alt. in cert. tenses); contr. from περάω **peraō** (to *traverse*; from the base of *4008*); to *traffic* (by *travelling*), i.e. *dispose* of as merchandise or into slavery (lit. or fig.):—sell.

4098. πίπτω **piptō**, *pip'-to*; a redupl. and contr. form of πέτω **petō**, *pet'-o* (which occurs only as an alt. in cert. tenses); prob. akin to *4072* through the idea of *alighting*; to *fall* (lit or fig.):—fail, fall (down), light on.

4099. Πισιδία **Pisidia**, *pis-id-ee'-ah*; prob. of for. or.; *Pisidia*, a region of Asia Minor:—Pisidia.

4100. πιστεύω **pisteuō**, *pist-yoo'-o*; from *4102*; to *have faith* (in, upon, or with respect to, a person or thing), i.e. *credit*; by impl. to *entrust* (espec. one's spiritual well-being to Christ):—believe (-r), commit (to trust), put in trust with.

4101. πιστικός **pistikos**, *pis-tik-os'*; from *4102*; *trustworthy*, i.e. *genuine* (*unadulterated*):—spike-[nard].

4102. πίστις **pistis**, *pis'-tis*; from *3982*; *persuasion*, i.e. *credence*; mor. *conviction* (of *religious* truth, or the truthfulness of God or a religious teacher), espec. *reliance upon Christ* for salvation; abstr. *constancy* in such profession; by extens. the *system* of religious (Gospel) truth itself:—assurance, belief, believe, faith, fidelity.

4103. πιστός **pistos**, *pis-tos'*; from *3982*; obj. *trustworthy*; subj. *trustful*:—believe (-ing, -r), faithful (-ly), sure, true.

4104. πιστόω **pistoō**, *pis-tŏ'-o*; from *4103*; to *assure*:—assure of.

4105. πλανάω **planaō**, *plan-ah'-o*; from *4106*; to (prop. *cause* to) *roam* (from safety, truth, or virtue):—go astray, deceive, err, seduce, wander, be out of the way.

4106. πλάνη **planē**, *plan'-ay*; fem. of *4108* (as abstr.); obj. *fraudulence*; subj. a *straying* from orthodoxy or piety:—deceit, to deceive, delusion, error.

4107. πλανήτης **planētēs**, *plan-ay'-tace*; from *4108*; a *rover* ("planet"), i.e. (fig.) an *erratic* teacher:—wandering.

4108. πλάνος **planos**, *plan'-os*; of uncert. affin.; *roving* (as a *tramp*), i.e. (by impl.) an *impostor* or *misleader*:—deceiver, seducing.

4109. πλάξ **plax**, *plax*; from *4111*; a *moulding-board*, i.e. *flat surface* ("plate", or *tablet*, lit. or fig.):—table.

4110. πλάσμα **plasma**, *plas'-mah*; from *4111*; something *moulded*:—thing formed.

4111. πλάσσω **plassō**, *plas'-so*; a prim. verb; to *mould*, i.e. *shape* or *fabricate*:—form.

4112. πλαστός **plastos**, *plas-tos'*; from *4111*; *moulded*, i.e. (by impl.) *artificial* or (fig.) *fictitious* (*false*):—feigned.

4113. πλατεῖα **plateia**, *plat-i'-ah*; fem. of *4116*; a *wide "plat"* or *"place"*, i.e. open *square*:—street.

4114. πλάτος **platos**, *plat'-os*; from *4116*; *width*:—breadth.

4115. πλατύνω **platunō**, *plat-oo'-no*; from *4116*; to *widen* (lit. or fig.):—make broad, enlarge.

4116. πλατύς **platus**, *plat-oos'*; from *4111*; *spread out* ("flat" ("plot"), i.e. *broad*:—wide.

4117. πλέγμα **plegma**, *pleg'-mah*; from *4120*; a *plait* (of hair):—broidered hair.

πλεῖον **pleion.** See *4119*.

4118. πλεῖστος **pleistos**, *plice'-tos*; irreg. superl. of *4183*; the *largest number* or *very large*:—very great, most.

4119. πλείων **pleiōn**, *pli-own*; neut.

πλεῖον **pleion**, *pli'-on*; or

πλέον **pleon**, *pleh'-on*; compar. of *4183*; *more* in quantity, number, or quality; also (in plur.) the *major portion*;— × above, + exceed, more excellent, further, (very) great (-er), long (-er), (very) many, greater (more) part, + yet but.

4120. πλέκω **plekō**, *plek'-o*; a prim. word; to *twine* or *braid*:—plait.

πλέον **pleon.** See *4119*.

4121. πλεονάζω **pleonazō**, *pleh-on-ad'-zo*; from *4119*; to *do*, *make* or *be more*, i.e. *increase* (trans. or intrans.); by extens. to *superabound*:—abound, abundant, make to increase, have over.

4122. πλεονεκτέω **pleonekteō**, *pleh-on-ek-teh'-o*; from *4123*; to *be covetous*, i.e. (by impl.) to *overreach*:—get an advantage, defraud, make a gain.

4123. πλεονέκτης **pleonektēs**, *pleh-on-ek'-tace*; from *4119* and *2192*; *holding* (*desiring*) *more*, i.e. *eager for gain* (*avaricious*, hence a *defrauder*):—covetous.

4124. πλεονεξία **pleonexia**, *pleh-on-ex-ee'-ah*; from *4123*; *avarice*, i.e. (by impl.) *fraudulency*, *extortion*:—covetous (-ness) practices, greediness.

4125. πλευρά **pleura**, *plyoo-rah'*; of uncert. affin.; a *rib*, i.e. (by extens.) *side*:—side.

4126. πλέω **pleō**, *pleh'-o*; another form for

πλεύω **pleuō**, *plyoo'-o*, which is used as an alt. in certain tenses; prob. a form of *4150* (through the idea of *plunging* through the water); to *pass* in a vessel:—sail. See also *4130*.

4127. πληγή **plēgē**, *play-gay'*; from *4141*; a *stroke*; by impl. a *wound*; fig. a *calamity*:—plague, stripe, wound (-ed).

4128. πλῆθος **plēthos**, *play'-thos*; from *4130*; a *fulness*, i.e. a *large number*, *throng*, *populace*:—bundle, company, multitude.

4129. πληθύνω **plēthunō**, *play-thoo'-no*; from another form of *4128*; to *increase* (trans. or intrans.):—abound, multiply.

4130. πλήθω **plēthō**, *play'-tho*; a prol. form of a prim. πλέω **pleō**, *pleh'-o* (which appears only as an alt. in certain tenses and in the redupl.form πίμπλημι **pimplēmi**); to *"fill"* (lit. or fig. [*imbue*, *influence*, *supply*]); spec. to *fulfil* (time):—accomplish, full (... come), furnish.

4131. πλήκτης **plēktēs**, *plake'-tace*; from *4141*; a *smiter*, i.e. *pugnacious* (*quarrelsome*):—striker.

4132. πλημμύρα **plēmmura**, *plame-moo'-rah*; prol. from *4130*; *flood-tide*, i.e. (by anal.) a *freshet*:—flood.

4133. πλήν **plēn**, *plane*; from *4119*; *moreover* (*besides*), i.e. *albeit*, *save that*, *rather*, *yet*:—but (rather), except, nevertheless, notwithstanding, save, than.

4134. πλήρης **plērēs**, *play'-race*; from *4130*; *replete*, or *covered over*; by anal. *complete*:—full.

4135. πληροφορέω **plērophoreō**, *play-rof-or-eh'-o*; from *4134* and *5409*; to *carry out fully* (in evidence), i.e. *completely assure* (or *convince*), *entirely accomplish*:—most surely believe, fully know (persuade), make full proof of.

4136. πληροφορία **plērophoria**, *play-rof-or-ee'-ah*; from *4135*; *entire confidence*:—(full) assurance.

4137. πληρόω **plēroō**, *play-rŏ'-o*; from *4134*; to *make replete*, i.e. (lit.) to *cram* (a net), *level up* (a hollow), or (fig.) to *furnish* (or *imbue*, *diffuse*, *influence*), *satisfy*, *execute* (an office), *finish* (a period or task), *verify* (or *coincide* with a prediction), etc.:—accomplish, × after, (be) complete, end, expire, fill (up), fulfil, (be, make) full (come), fully preach, perfect, supply.

4138. πλήρωμα **plērōma**, *play'-ro-mah*; from *4137*; *repletion* or *completion*, i.e. (subj.) what *fills* (as contents, supplement, copiousness, multitude), or (obj.) what is *filled* (as container, performance, period):—which is put in to fill up, piece that filled up, fulfilling, full, fulness.

4139. πλησίον **plēsion**, *play-see'-on*; neut. of a der. of πέλας **pelas** (*near*); (adv.) *close* by; as noun, a *neighbor*, i.e. *fellow* (as man, countryman, Chr. or friend):—near, neighbour.

4140. πλησμονή **plēsmonē**, *place-mon-ay'*; from a presumed der. of *4130*; a *filling up*, i.e. (fig.) *gratification*:—satisfying.

4141. πλήσσω **plēssō**, *place'-so*; appar. another form of *4111* (through the idea of *flattening* out); to *pound*, i.e. (fig.) to *inflict* with (*calamity*):—smite. Comp. *4180*.

4142. πλοιάριον **ploiarion**, *ploy-ar'-ee-on*; neut. of a presumed der. of *4143*; a *boat*, *little* (*small*) *ship*.

4143. πλοῖον **ploion**, *ploy'-on*; from *4126*; a *sailer*, i.e. *vessel*:—ship (-ping).

4144. πλόος **ploos**, *plŏ'-os*; from *4126*; a *sail*, i.e. *navigation*:—course, sailing, voyage.

4145. πλούσιος **plousios**, *ploo'-see-os*; from *4149*; *wealthy*; fig. *abounding* with:—rich.

4146. πλουσίως **plousiōs**, *ploo-see'-oce*; adv. from *4145*; *copiously*:—abundantly, richly.

4147. πλουτέω **plouteō**, *ploo-teh'-o*; from *4148*; to *be* (or *become*) *wealthy* (lit. or fig.):—be increased with goods, (be, made, wax) rich.

4148. πλουτίζω **ploutizō**, *ploo-tid'-zo*; from *4149*; to *make wealthy* (fig.):—en- (make) rich.

4149. πλοῦτος **ploutos**, *ploo'-tos*; from the base of *4130*; *wealth* (as *fulness*), i.e. (lit.) *money*, *possessions*, or (fig.) *abundance*, *richness*, (spec.) *valuable bestowment*:—riches.

4150. πλύνω **plunō**, *ploo'-no*; a prol. form of an obsol. πλύω **pluō** (to "flow"); to "plunge", i.e. *launder clothing*:—wash. Comp. *3068*, *3538*.

4151. πνεῦμα **pneuma**, *pnyoo'-mah*; from *4154*; a *current* of air, i.e. *breath* (*blast*) or a *breeze*; by anal. or fig. a *spirit*, i.e. (human) the *rational soul*, (by impl.) *vital principle*, mental *disposition*, etc., or (superhuman) an *angel*, *dæmon*, or (divine) *God*, *Christ's spirit*, the *Holy Spirit*:—ghost, life, spirit (-ual, -ually), mind. Comp. *5590*.

4152. πνευματικός **pnĕumatikŏs**, *pnyoo-mat-ik-os'*; from *4151*; *non-carnal*, i.e. (humanly) *ethereal* (as opposed to gross), or (dæmoniacally) a *spirit* (concr.), or (divinely) *supernatural, regenerate, religious*:—spiritual. Comp. *5591*.

4153. πνευματικῶς **pnĕumatikōs**, *pnyoo-mat-ik-oce'*; adv. from *4152*; *non-physically*, i.e. *divinely, figuratively*:—spiritually.

4154. πνέω **pnĕō**, *pneh'-o*; a prim. word; to *breathe hard*, i.e. *breeze*:—blow. Comp. *5594*.

4155. πνίγω **pnigō**, *pnee'-go*; strengthened from *4154*; to *wheeze*, i.e. (caus. by impl.) to *throttle* or *strangle* (*drown*):—choke, take by the throat.

4156. πνικτός **pniktŏs**, *pnik-tos'*; from *4155*; *throttled*, i.e. (neut. concr.) an *animal choked* to death (*not bled*):—strangled.

4157. πνοή **pnŏē**, *pno-ay'*; from *4154*; *respiration*, a *breeze*:—breath, wind.

4158. ποδήρης **pŏdērēs**, *pod-ay'-race*; from *4228* and another element of uncert. affin.; a *dress* (*2066* implied) *reaching the ankles*:—garment down to the foot.

4159. πόθεν **pŏthĕn**, *poth'-en*; from the base of *4213* with enclitic adv. of origin; *from which* (as interrog.) or *what* (as rel.) place, state, source or cause:—whence.

4160. ποιέω **pŏiĕō**, *poy-eh'-o*; appar. a prol. form of an obsol. prim.; to *make* or *do* (in a very wide application, more or less direct):—abide, + agree, appoint, × avenge, + band together, be, bear, + bewray, bring (forth), cast out, cause, commit, + content, continue, deal, + without any delay, (would) do (-ing), execute, exercise, fulfil, gain, give, have, hold, × journeying, keep, + lay wait, + lighten the ship, make, × mean, + none of these things move me, observe, ordain, perform, provide, + have purged, purpose, put, + raising up, × secure, shew, × shoot out, spend, take, tarry, + transgress the law, work, yield. Comp. *4238*.

4161. ποίημα **pŏiēma**, *poy'-ay-mah*; from *4160*; a *product*, i.e. *fabric* (lit. or fig.):—thing that is made, workmanship.

4162. ποίησις **pŏiēsis**, *poy'-ay-sis*; from *4160*; *action*, i.e. *performance* (of the law):—deed.

4163. ποιητής **pŏiētēs**, *poy-ay-tace'*; from *4160*; a *performer*; spec. a "*poet*":—doer, poet.

4164. ποικίλος **pŏikilŏs**, *poy-kee'-los*; of uncert. der.; *motley*, i.e. *various in character*:—divers, manifold.

4165. ποιμαίνω **pŏimainō**, *poy-mah'-ee-no*; from *4166*; to *tend* as a shepherd (or fig. *superviser*):—feed (cattle), rule.

4166. ποιμήν **pŏimēn**, *poy-mane'*; of uncert. affin.; a *shepherd* (lit. or fig.):—shepherd, pastor.

4167. ποίμνη **pŏimnē**, *poym'-nay*; contr. from *4165*; a *flock* (lit. or fig.):—flock, fold.

4168. ποίμνιον **pŏimniŏn**, *poym'-nee-on*; neut. of a presumed der. of *4167*; a *flock*, i.e. (fig.) *group* (of believers):—flock.

4169. ποῖος **pŏiŏs**, *poy'-os*; from the base of *4226* and *3634*; individualizing interrog. (of character) *what sort of*, or (of number) *which one*:—what (manner of), which.

4170. πολεμέω **pŏlĕmĕō**, *pol-em-eh'-o*; from *4171*; to *be (engaged) in warfare*, i.e. to *battle* (lit. or fig.):—fight, (make) war.

4171. πόλεμος **pŏlĕmŏs**, *pol'-em-os*; from πέλομαι **pĕlŏmai** (to *bustle*); *warfare* (lit. or fig.; a single encounter or a series):—battle, fight, war.

4172. πόλις **pŏlis**, *pol'-is*; prob. from the same as *4171*, or perh. from *4183*; a *town* (prop. with walls, of greater or less size):—city.

4173. πολιτάρχης **pŏlitarchēs**, *pol-it-ar'-khace*; from *4172* and *757*; a *town-officer*, i.e. *magistrate*:—ruler of the city.

4174. πολιτεία **pŏlitĕia**, *pol-ee-ti'-ah*; from *4177* ("*polity*"); *citizenship*; concr. a *community*:—commonwealth, freedom.

4175. πολίτευμα **pŏlitĕuma**, *pol-it'-yoo-mah*; from *4176*; a *community*, i.e. (abstr.) *citizenship* (fig.):—conversation.

4176. πολιτεύομαι **pŏlitĕuŏmai**, *pol-it-yoo'-om-ahee*; mid. of a der. of *4177*; to *behave as a citizen* (fig.):—let conversation be, live.

4177. πολίτης **pŏlitēs**, *pol-ee'-tace*; from *4172*; a *townsman*:—citizen.

4178. πολλάκις **pŏllakis**, *pol-lak'-is*; mult. adv. from *4183*; *many times*, i.e. *frequently*:—oft (-en, -entimes, -times).

4179. πολλαπλασίων **pŏllaplasiōn**, *pol-lap-las-ee'-ohn*; from *4183* and prob. a der. of *4120*; *manifold*, i.e. (neut. as noun) *very much more*:—manifold more.

4180. πολυλογία **pŏlulŏgia**, *pol-oo-log-ee'-ah*; from a comp. of *4183* and *3056*; *loquacity*, i.e. *prolixity*:—much speaking.

4181. πολυμέρως **pŏlumĕrŏs**, *pol-oo-mer'-oce*; adv. from a comp. of *4183* and *3313*; *in many portions*, i.e. *variously* as to time and agency (*piecemeal*):—at sundry times.

4182. πολυποίκιλος **pŏlupŏikilŏs**, *pol-oo-poy'-kil-os*; from *4183* and *4164*; *much variegated*, i.e. *multifarious*:—manifold.

4183. πολύς **pŏlus**, *pol-oos'*; includ. the forms from the alt. πολλός **pŏllŏs**; (sing.) *much* (in any respect) or (plur.) *many*; neut. (sing.) as adv. *largely*; neut. (plur.) as adv. or noun *often, mostly, largely*:—abundant, + altogether, common, + far (passed, spent), (+ be of a) great (age, deal, -ly, while, long, many, much, oft (-en [-times]), plenteous, sore, straitly. Comp. *4118, 4119*.

4184. πολύσπλαγχνος **pŏlusplagchnŏs**, *pol-oo'-splankh-nos*; from *4183* and *4698* (fig.); *extremely compassionate*:—very pitiful.

4185. πολυτελής **pŏlutĕlēs**, *pol-oo-tel-ace'*; from *4183* and *5056*; *extremely expensive*:—costly, very precious, of great price.

4186. πολύτιμος **pŏlutimŏs**, *pol-oot'-ee-mos*; from *4183* and *5092*; *extremely valuable*:—very costly, of great price.

4187. πολυτρόπως **pŏlutrŏpŏs**, *pol-oot-rop'-oce*; adv. from a comp. of *4183* and *5158*; *in many ways*, i.e. *variously* as to method or form:—in divers manners.

4188. πόμα **pŏma**, *pom'-ah*; from the alt. of *4095*; a *beverage*:—drink.

4189. πονηρία **pŏnēria**, *pon-ay-ree'-ah*; from *4190*; *depravity*, i.e. (spec.) *malice*; plur. (concr.) *plots, sins*:—iniquity, wickedness.

4190. πονηρός **pŏnērŏs**, *pon-ay-ros'*; from a der. of *4192*; *hurtful*, i.e. *evil* (prop. in effect or influence, and thus differing from *2556*, which refers rather to *essential character*, as well as from *4550*, which indicates *degeneracy* from original virtue); fig. *calamitous*; also (pass.) *ill*, i.e. *diseased*; but espec. (mor.) *culpable*, i.e. *derelict, vicious, facinorous*; neut. (sing.) *mischief, malice*, or (plur.) *guilt*; masc. (sing.) the *devil*, or (plur.) *sinners*:—bad, evil, grievous, harm, lewd, malicious, wicked (-ness). See also *4191*.

4191. πονηρότερος **pŏnērŏtĕrŏs**, *pon-ay-rot'-er-os*; compar. of *4190*; *more evil*:—more wicked.

4192. πόνος **pŏnŏs**, *pon'-os*; from the base of *3993*; *toil*, i.e. (by impl.) *anguish*:—pain.

4193. Ποντικός **Pŏntikŏs**, *pon-tik-os'*; from *4195*; a *Pontican*, i.e. *native of Pontus*:—born in Pontus.

4194. Πόντιος **Pŏntiŏs**, *pon'-tee-os*; of Lat. or.; *appar. bridged*; *Pontius*, a Rom.:—Pontius.

4195. Πόντος **Pŏntŏs**, *pon'-tos*; a *sea*; *Pontus*, a region of Asia Minor:—Pontus.

4196. Πόπλιος **Pŏpliŏs**, *pop'-lee-os*; of Lat. or.; appar. "*popular*"; *Poplius* (i.e. *Publius*), a Rom.:—Publius.

4197. πορεία **pŏrĕia**, *por-i'-ah*; from *4198*; *travel* (by land); fig. (plur.) *proceedings*, i.e. *career*:—journey [-ing], ways.

4198. πορεύομαι **pŏrĕuŏmai**, *por-yoo'-om-ahee*; mid. from a der. of the same as *3984*; to *traverse*, i.e. *travel* (lit. or fig.; espec. to *remove* [fig. *die*], live,

etc.);—depart, *go* (away, forth, one's way, up), (make a, take a) journey, walk.

4199. πορθέω **pŏrthĕō**, *por-theh'-o*; prol. from πέρθω **pĕrthō** (to *sack*); to *ravage* (fig.):—destroy, waste.

4200. πορισμός **pŏrismŏs**, *por-is-mos'*; from a der. of πόρος **pŏrŏs** (a *way*, i.e. *means*); *furnishing* (*procuring*), i.e. (by impl.) *money-getting* (*acquisition*):—gain.

4201. Πόρκιος **Pŏrkiŏs**, *por'-kee-os*; of Lat. or.; appar. *swinish*; *Porcius*, a Rom.:—Porcius.

4202. πορνεία **pŏrnĕia**, *por-ni'-ah*; from *4203*; *harlotry* (includ. *adultery* and *incest*); fig. *idolatry*:—fornication.

4203. πορνεύω **pŏrnĕuō**, *porn-yoo'-o*; from *4204*; to *act the harlot*, i.e. (lit.) *indulge unlawful lust* (of either sex), or (fig.) *practise idolatry*:—commit (fornication).

4204. πόρνη **pŏrnē**, *por'-nay*; fem. of *4205*; a *strumpet*; fig. an *idolater*:—harlot, whore.

4205. πόρνος **pŏrnŏs**, *por'-nos*; from πέρνημι **pĕrnēmi** (to *sell*); akin to the base of *4097*); a (male) *prostitute* (as venal), i.e. (by anal.) a *debauchee* (*libertine*):—fornicator, whoremonger.

4206. πόρρω **pŏrrhō**, *por'-rho*; adv. from *4253*; *forwards*, i.e. *at a distance*:—far, a great way off. See also *4207*.

4207. πόρρωθεν **pŏrrhōthĕn**, *por'-rho-then*; from *4206* with adv. enclitic of source; *from far*, or (by impl.) *at a distance*, i.e. *distantly*:—afar off.

4208. πορρωτέρω **pŏrrhōtĕrō**, *por-rho-ter'-o*; adv. compar. of *4206*; *farther*, i.e. *a greater distance*:—further.

4209. πορφύρα **pŏrphura**, *por-foo'-rah*; of Lat. or.; the "*purple*" mussel, i.e. (by impl.) the *red-blue color itself*, and finally a *garment dyed* with it:—purple.

4210. πορφυροῦς **pŏrphurŏus**, *por-foo-rooce'*; from *4209*; *purpureal*, i.e. *bluish red*:—purple.

4211. πορφυρόπωλις **pŏrphurŏpŏlis**, *por-foo-rop'-o-lis*; fem. of a comp. of *4209* and *4453*; a *female trader in purple cloth*:—seller of purple.

4212. ποσάκις **pŏsakis**, *pos-ak'-is*; mult. from *4214*; *how many times*:—how oft (-en).

4213. πόσις **pŏsis**, *pos-is*; from the alt. of *4095*; a *drinking* (the act), i.e. (concr.) a *draught*:—drink.

4214. πόσος **pŏsŏs**, *pos'-os*; from an obsol. πός **pŏs** (*who, what*) and *3739*; interrog. pron. (of amount) *how much* (*large, long* or [plur.] *many*):—how great (long, many), what.

4215. ποταμός **pŏtamŏs**, *pot-am-os'*; prob. from a der. of the alt. of *4095* (comp. *4224*); a *current, brook* or *freshet* (as *drinkable*), i.e. *running water*:—flood, river, stream, water.

4216. ποταμοφόρητος **pŏtamŏphŏrētŏs**, *pot-am-of-or'-ay-tos*; from *4215* and a der. of *5409*; *river-borne*, i.e. *overwhelmed by a stream*:—carried away of the flood.

4217. ποταπός **pŏtapŏs**, *pot-ap-os'*; appar. from *4219* and the base of *4226*; interrog. *whatever*, i.e. of *what possible sort*:—what (manner of).

4218. ποτέ **pŏtĕ**, *pot-eh'*; from the base of *4225* and *5037*; indef. adv., at *some time, ever*:—afore- (any, some-) time (-s), at length (the last), (+ n-) ever, in the old time, in time past, once, when.

4219. πότε **pŏtĕ**, *pot'-eh*; from the base of *4226* and *5037*; interrog. adv., at *what time*:— + how long, when.

4220. πότερον **pŏtĕrŏn**, *pot'-er-on*; neut. of a compar. of the base of *4226*; interrog. as adv., *which* (of two), i.e. *is it* this or that:—whether.

4221. ποτήριον **pŏtērion**, *pot-ay'-ree-on*; neut. of a der. of the alt. of *4095*; a *drinking-vessel*; by extens. the *contents thereof*, i.e. a *cupful* (*draught*); fig. a *lot* or *fate*:—cup.

4222. ποτίζω **pŏtizō**, *pot-id'-zo*; from a der. of the alt. of *4095*; to *furnish drink, irrigate*:—give (make) to drink, feed, water.

4223. Ποτίολοι **Pŏtiŏlŏi**, *pot-ee'-ol-oy;* of Lat. or.; *little wells,* i.e. *mineral springs; Potioli* (i.e. *Puteoli*), a place in Italy:—Puteoli.

4224. πότος **pŏtŏs**, *pot'-os;* from the alt. of *4095;* a *drinking-bout* or *carousal:*—banqueting.

4225. πού **pŏu**, *poo;* gen. of an indef. pron. πός **pŏs** *(some)* otherwise obsol. (comp. *4214*); as adv. of place, *somewhere,* i.e. *nearly:*—about, a certain place.

4226. πού **pŏu**, *poo;* gen. of an interrog. pron. πός **pŏs** *(what)* otherwise obsol. (perh. the same as *4225* used with the rising slide of inquiry); as adv. of place; *at* (by impl. *to) what* locality:—where, whither.

4227. Πούδης **Pŏudēs**, *poo'-dace;* of Lat. or.; *modest; Pudes* (i.e. *Pudens*), a Chr.:—Pudens.

4228. πούς **pŏus**, *pooce;* a prim word; a *"foot"* (fig. or lit.):—foot (-stool).

4229. πρᾶγμα **pragma**, *prag'-mah;* from *4238;* a *deed;* by impl. an *affair;* by extens. an *object* (material):—business, matter, thing, work.

4230. πραγματεία **pragmatĕia**, *prag-mat-i'-ah;* from *4231;* a *transaction,* i.e. *negotiation:*—affair.

4231. πραγματεύομαι **pragmatĕuŏmai**, *pragmat-yoo'-om-ahee;* from *4229;* to *busy* oneself with, i.e. to *trade:*—occupy.

4232. πραιτώριον **praitōriŏn**, *prahee-to'-reeon;* of Lat. or.; the *prætorium* or governor's *courtroom* (sometimes includ. the whole *edifice* and *camp*):—(common, judgment) hall (of judgment), palace, prætorium.

4233. πράκτωρ **praktōr**, *prak'-tore;* from a der. of *4238;* a *practiser,* i.e. (spec.) an official *collector:*—officer.

4234. πρᾶξις **praxis**, *prax'-is;* from *4238; practice,* i.e. (concr.) an *act;* by extens. a *function:*—deed, office, work.

4235. πρᾶος **pra̯ŏs**, *prah'-os;* a form of *4239,* used in cert. parts; *gentle,* i.e. *humble:*—meek.

4236. πραότης **pra̯ŏtēs**, *prah-ot'-ace;* from *4235; gentleness;* by impl. *humility:*—meekness.

4237. πρασιά **prasia**, *pras-ee-ah';* perh. from πράσον **prasŏn** *(a leek,* and so an *onion-patch);* a *garden-plot,* i.e. (by impl. of regular beds) a *row* (repeated in plur. by Hebr. to indicate an arrangement):—in ranks.

4238. πράσσω **prassō**, *pras'-so;* a prim. verb; to "*practise*," i.e. *perform repeatedly* or *habitually* (thus differing from *4160,* which prop. refers to a *single* act); by impl. to *execute, accomplish,* etc.; spec. to *collect* (dues), *fare* (personally):—commit, deeds, do, exact, keep, require, use arts.

4239. πραΰς **praüs**, *prah-ooce';* appar. a prim. word; *mild,* i.e. (by impl.) *humble:*—meek. See also *4235.*

4240. πραΰτης **praütēs**, *prah-oo'-tace;* from *4239; mildness,* i.e. (by impl.) *humility:*—meekness.

4241. πρέπω **prepō**, *prep'-o;* appar. a prim. verb; to *tower up* (be conspicuous), i.e. (by impl.) to *be suitable* or *proper* (third pers. sing. pres. indic. often used impers., it is *fit* or *right*):—become, comely.

4242. πρεσβεία **presbĕia**, *pres-bi'-ah;* from *4243; seniority* (eldership), i.e. (by impl.) an *embassy* (concr. *ambassadors*):—ambassage, message.

4243. πρεσβεύω **presbĕuō**, *pres-byoo'-o;* from the base of *4245;* to be a *senior,* i.e. (by impl.) *act* as a *representative* (fig. *preacher*):—be an ambassador.

4244. πρεσβυτέριον **presbutĕriŏn**, *pres-booter'-ee-on;* neut. of a presumed der. of *4245;* the *order* of elders, i.e. (spec.) Isr. *Sanhedrim* or Chr. "*presbytery*":—(estate of) elder (-s), presbytery.

4245. πρεσβύτερος **presbutĕrŏs**, *pres-boo'-teros;* compar. of πρέσβυς **presbus** *(elderly); older;* as noun, a *senior;* spec. an Isr. *Sanhedrist* (lit. member of the celestial council) or Chr. "*presbyter*":—elder (-est), old.

4246. πρεσβύτης **presbutēs**, *pres-boo'-tace;* from the same as *4245;* an *old man:*—aged (man), old man.

4247. πρεσβῦτις **presbutis**, *pres-boo'-tis;* fem. of *4246;* an *old woman:*—aged woman.

πρήθω **prethō**. See *4092.*

4248. πρηνής **prēnēs**, *pray-nace';* from *4253; leaning (falling) forward* ("*prone*"), i.e. *head foremost:*—headlong.

4249. πρίζω **prizō**, *prid'-zo;* a strengthened form of a prim. πρίω **priō** (to *saw);* to *saw* in two:—saw asunder.

4250. πρίν **prin**, *prin;* adv. from *4253; prior, sooner:*—before (that), ere.

4251. Πρίσκα **Priska**, *pris'-kah;* of Lat. or.; fem. of *Priscus, ancient; Priska,* a Chr. woman:—Prisca. See also *4252.*

4252. Πρίσκιλλα **Priscilla**, *pris'-cil-lah;* dimin. of *4251; Priscilla* (i.e. *little Prisca*), a Chr. woman:—Priscilla.

4253. πρό **prŏ**, *pro;* a prim. prep.; "*fore*," i.e. *in front of, prior* (fig. *superior) to:*—above, ago, before, or ever. In comp. it retains the same significations.

4254. προάγω **prŏagō**, *pro-ag'-o;* from *4253* and *71;* to *lead forward* (magisterially); intrans. to *precede* (in place or time [part. *previous*]):—bring (forth, out), go before.

4255. προαιρέομαι **prŏairĕŏmai**, *pro-ahee-reh'-om-ahee;* from *4253* and *138;* to *choose* for oneself *before* another thing (*prefer*), i.e. (by impl.) to *propose* (*intend*):—purpose.

4256. προαιτιάομαι **prŏaitiaŏmai**, *pro-ahee-tee-ah'-om-ahee;* from *4253* and a der. of *150;* to *accuse* already, i.e. *previously charge:*—prove before.

4257. προακούω **prŏakŏuō**, *pro-ak-oo'-o;* from *4253* and *191;* to *hear* already, i.e. *anticipate:*—hear before.

4258. προαμαρτάνω **prŏamartanō**, *pro-am-ar-tan'-o;* from *4253* and *264;* to *sin* previously (to conversion):—sin already, heretofore sin.

4259. προαύλιον **prŏauliŏn**, *pro-ŏw'-lee-on;* neut. of a presumed comp. of *4253* and *833;* a *forecourt,* i.e. *vestibule* (*alley-way*):—porch.

4260. προβαίνω **prŏbainō**, *prob-ah'ee-no;* from *4253* and the base of *939;* to *walk forward,* i.e. *advance* (lit. or in years):— + be of a great age, go farther (on), be well stricken.

4261. προβάλλω **prŏballō**, *prob-al'-lo;* from *4253* and *906;* to *throw forward,* i.e. *push* to the front, *germinate:*—put forward, shoot forth.

4262. προβατικός **prŏbatikŏs**, *prob-at-ik-os';* from *4263; relating to sheep,* i.e. (a *gate*) through which they were led into Jerusalem:—sheep (market).

4263. πρόβατον **prŏbatŏn**, *prob'-at-on;* prop. neut. of a presumed der. of *4260; something that walks forward* (a quadruped), i.e. (spec.) a *sheep* (lit. or fig.):—sheep ([-fold]).

4264. προβιβάζω **prŏbibazō**, *prob-ib-ad'-zo;* from *4253* and a redupl. form of *971;* to *force forward,* i.e. *bring* to the *front, instigate:*—draw, before instruct.

4265. προβλέπω **prŏblepō**, *prob-lep'-o;* from *4253* and *991;* to *look out beforehand,* i.e. *furnish in advance:*—provide.

4266. προγίνομαι **prŏginŏmai**, *prog-in'-om-ahee;* from *4253* and *1096;* to *be already,* i.e. *have previously transpired:*—be past.

4267. προγινώσκω **prŏginōskō**, *prog-in-oce'-ko;* from *4253* and *1097;* to *know beforehand,* i.e. *foresee:*—foreknow (ordain), know (before).

4268. πρόγνωσις **prŏgnōsis**, *prog'-no-sis;* from *4267; forethought:*—foreknowledge.

4269. πρόγονος **prŏgŏnŏs**, *prog'-on-os;* from *4266;* an *ancestor,* (*grand-*) *parent:*—forefather, parent.

4270. προγράφω **prŏgraphō**, *prog-raf'-o;* from *4253* and *1125;* to *write previously,* fig. to *announce, prescribe:*—before ordain, evidently set forth, write (afore, aforetime).

4271. πρόδηλος **prŏdēlŏs**, *prod'-ay-los;* from *4253* and *1212;* *plain before* all men, i.e. *obvious:*—evident, manifest (open) beforehand.

4272. προδίδωμι **prŏdidōmi**, *prod-id'-o-mee;* from *4253* and *1325;* to *give before* the other party has given:—first give.

4273. προδότης **prŏdŏtēs**, *prod-ot'-ace;* from *4272* (in the sense of *giving forward* into another's [the enemy's] hands); a *surrender:*—betrayer, traitor.

προδρέμω **prŏdrĕmō**. See *4390.*

4274. πρόδρομος **prŏdrŏmŏs**, *prod'-rom-os;* from the alt. of *4390;* a *runner ahead,* i.e. *scout* (fig. *precursor*):—forerunner.

4275. προείδω **prŏeidō**, *pro-i'-do;* from *4253* and *1492; foresee:*—foresee, saw before.

προειρέω **prŏeirĕō**. See *4280.*

4276. προελπίζω **prŏelpizō**, *pro-el-pid'-zo;* from *4253* and *1679;* to *hope in advance* of other confirmation:—first trust.

4277. προέπω **prŏepō**, *pro-ep'-o;* from *4253* and *2036;* to *say already,* i.e. *predict:*—forewarn, say (speak, tell) before. Comp. *4280.*

4278. προενάρχομαι **prŏenarchŏmai**, *pro-enar'-khom-ahee;* from *4253* and *1728;* to *commence already:*—begin (before).

4279. προεπαγγέλλομαι **prŏepaggĕllŏmai**, *pro-ep-ang-ghel'-lom-ahee;* mid. from *4253* and *1861;* to *promise* of old:—promise before.

4280. προερέω **prŏerĕō**, *pro-er-eh'-o;* from *4253* and *2046;* used as alt. of *4277;* to *say already, predict:*—foretell, say (speak, tell) before.

4281. προέρχομαι **prŏerchŏmai**, *pro-er'-khom-ahee;* from *4253* and *2064* (includ. its alt.); to *go onward, precede* (in place or time):—go before (farther, forward), outgo, pass on.

4282. προετοιμάζω **prŏetŏimazō**, *pro-et-oy-mad'-zo;* from *4253* and *2090;* to *fit up in advance* (lit. or fig.):—ordain before, prepare afore.

4283. προευαγγελίζομαι **prŏeuaggĕlizŏmai**, *pro-yoo-ang-ghel-id'-zom-ahee;* mid. from *4253* and *2097;* to *announce* glad news *in advance:*—preach before the gospel.

4284. προέχομαι **prŏechŏmai**, *pro-ekh-om-ahee;* mid. from *4253* and *2192;* to *hold* oneself *before* others, i.e. (fig.) to *excel:*—be better.

4285. προηγέομαι **prŏēgĕŏmai**, *pro-ay-geh'-om-ahee;* from *4253* and *2233;* to *lead the way* for others, i.e. *show deference:*—prefer.

4286. πρόθεσις **prŏthĕsis**, *proth'-es-is;* from *4388;* a *setting forth,* i.e. (fig.) *proposal* (*intention*); spec. the *show-bread* in the Temple as *exposed* before God:—purpose, shew [-bread].

4287. προθεσμιος **prŏthĕsmiŏs**, *proth-es'-mee-os;* from *4253* and a der. of *5087;* *fixed beforehand,* i.e. (fem. with *2250* impl.) a *designated day:*—time appointed.

4288. προθυμία **prŏthumia**, *proth-oo-mee'-ah;* from *4289; predisposition,* i.e. *alacrity:*—forwardness of mind, readiness (of mind), ready (willing) mind.

4289. πρόθυμος **prŏthumŏs**, *proth'-oo-mos;* from *4253* and *2372; forward in spirit,* i.e. *predisposed;* neut. (as noun) *alacrity:*—ready, willing.

4290. προθύμως **prŏthumōs**, *proth-oo'-moce;* adv. from *4289; with alacrity:*—willingly.

4291. προΐστημι **prŏistēmi**, *pro-is'-tay-mee;* from *4253* and *2476;* to *stand before,* i.e. (in rank) to *preside,* or (by impl.) to *practise:*—maintain, be over, rule.

4292. προκαλέομαι **prŏkalĕŏmai**, *prok-al-eh'-om-ahee;* mid. from *4253* and *2564;* to *call forth* to oneself (*challenge*), i.e. (by impl.) to *irritate:*—provoke.

4293. προκαταγγέλλω **prŏkataggĕllō**, *prok-at-ang-ghel'-lo;* from *4253* and *2605;* to *announce beforehand,* i.e. *predict, promise:*—foretell, have notice (shew) before.

4294. προκαταρτίζω **prŏkatartizō**, *prok-at-artid'-zo;* from *4253* and *2675;* to *prepare in advance:*—make up beforehand.

4295. πρόκειμαι **prŏkĕimai**, *prok'-i-mahee;* from *4253* and *2749;* to *lie before* the mind, i.e. (fig.) to *be present* (to the mind), to *stand forth* (as an example or reward):—be first, set before (forth).

4296. προκηρύσσω **prŏkērussō**, *prok-ay-rooce'-so;* from *4253* and *2784;* to herald (i.e. proclaim) in advance:—before (first) preach.

4297. προκοπή **prŏkŏpē**, *prok-op-ay';* from *4298;* progress, i.e. advancement (subj. or obj.):—furtherance, profit.

4298. προκόπτω **prŏkŏptō**, *prok-op'-to;* from *4253* and *2875;* to drive forward (as if by beating), i.e. (fig. and intrans.) to advance (in amount, to grow; in time, to be well along):—increase, proceed, profit, be far spent, wax.

4299. πρόκριμα **prŏkrima**, *prok'-ree-mah;* from a comp. of *4253* and *2919;* a prejudgment (prejudice), i.e. prepossession:—prefer one before another.

4300. προκυρόω **prŏkurŏō**, *prok-oo-rŏ'-o;* from *4253* and *2964;* to ratify previously:—confirm before.

4301. προλαμβάνω **prŏlambanō**, *prol-am-ban'-o;* from *4253* and *2983;* to take in advance, i.e. (lit.) eat before others have an opportunity; (fig.) to anticipate, surprise:—come aforehand, overtake, take before.

4302. προλέγω **prŏlĕgō**, *prol-eg'-o;* from *4253* and *3004;* to say beforehand, i.e. predict, forewarn:—foretell, tell before.

4303. προμαρτύρομαι **prŏmarturŏmai**, *prom-ar-too'-rom-ahee;* from *4253* and *3143;* to be a witness in advance, i.e. predict:—testify beforehand.

4304. προμελετάω **prŏmĕlĕtaō**, *prom-el-et-ah'-o;* from *4253* and *3191;* to premeditate:—meditate before.

4305. προμεριμνάω **prŏmĕrimnaō**, *prom-er-im-nah'-o;* from *4253* and *3309;* to care (anxiously) in advance:—take thought beforehand.

4306. προνοέω **prŏnŏĕō**, *pron-ŏ-eh'-o;* from *4253* and *3539;* to consider in advance, i.e. look out for beforehand (act. by way of maintenance for others; mid. by way of circumspection for oneself):—provide (for).

4307. πρόνοια **prŏnŏia**, *pron'-oy-ah;* from *4306;* forethought, i.e. provident care or supply:—providence, provision.

4308. προοράω **prŏŏraō**, *prŏ-or-ah'-o;* from *4253* and *3708;* to behold in advance, i.e. (act.) to notice (another) previously, or (mid.) to keep in (one's own) view:—foresee, see before.

4309. προορίζω **prŏŏrizō**, *prŏ-or-id'-zo;* from *4253* and *3724;* to limit in advance, i.e. (fig.) predetermine:—determine before, ordain, predestinate.

4310. προπάσχω **prŏpaschō**, *prop-as'-kho;* from *4253* and *3958;* to undergo hardship previously:—suffer before.

4311. προπέμπω **prŏpĕmpō**, *prop-em'-po;* from *4253* and *3992;* to send forward, i.e. escort or aid in travel:—accompany, bring (forward) on journey (way), conduct forth.

4312. προπετής **prŏpĕtēs**, *prop-et-ace';* from a comp. of *4253* and *4098;* falling forward, i.e. headlong (fig. precipitate):—heady, rash [-ly].

4313. προπορεύομαι **prŏpŏrĕuŏmai**, *prop-or-yoo'-om-ahee;* from *4253* and *4198;* to precede (as guide or herald):—go before.

4314. πρός **prŏs**, *pros;* a strengthened form of *4253';* a prep. of direction; forward to, i.e. toward (with the genit. the side of, i.e. pertaining to; with the dat. by the side of, i.e. near to; usually with the accus. the place, time, occasion, or respect, which is the destination of the relation, i.e. whither or for which it is predicated):—about, according to, against, among, at, because of, before, between, ([where-]) by, for, × at thy house, in, for intent, nigh unto, of, which pertain to, that, to (the end that), + together to ([you]) -ward, unto, with (-in). In comp. it denotes essentially the same applications, namely, motion towards, accession to, or nearness at.

4315. προσάββατον **prŏsabbatŏn**, *pros-ab'-bat-on;* from *4253* and *4521;* a fore-sabbath, i.e. the Sabbath-eve:—day before the sabbath. Comp. *3904.*

4316. προσαγορεύω **prŏsagŏrĕuō**, *pros-ag-or-yoo'-o;* from *4314* and a der. of *58* (mean. to harangue); to address, i.e. salute by name:—call.

4317. προσάγω **prŏsagō**, *pros-ag'-o;* from *4314* and *71;* to lead towards, i.e. (trans.) to conduct near (summon, present), or (intrans.) to approach:—bring, draw near.

4318. προσαγωγή **prŏsagōgē**, *pros-ag-ogue-ay';* from *4317* (comp. *72*); admission:—access.

4319. προσαιτέω **prŏsaitĕō** *pros-ahee-teh'-o;* from *4314* and *154;* to ask repeatedly (importune), i.e. solicit:—beg.

4320. προσαναβαίνω **prŏsanabainō**, *pros-an-ab-ah'ee-no;* from *4314* and *305;* to ascend farther, i.e. be promoted (take an upper [more honorable] seat):—go up.

4321. προσαναλίσκω **prŏsanaliskō**, *pros-an-al-is'-ko;* from *4314* and *355;* to expend further:—spend.

4322. προσαναπληρόω **prŏsanaplērŏō**, *pros-an-ap-lay-rŏ'-o;* from *4314* and *378;* to fill up further, i.e. furnish fully:—supply.

4323. προσανατίθημι **prŏsanatithēmi**, *pros-an-at-ith'-ay-mee;* from *4314* and *394;* to lay up in addition, i.e. (mid. and fig.) to impart or (by impl.) to consult:—in conference add, confer.

4324. προσαπειλέω **prŏsapĕilĕō**, *pros-ap-i-leh'-o;* from *4314* and *546;* to menace additionally:—threaten further.

4325. προσδαπανάω **prŏsdapanaō**, *pros-dap-an-ah'-o;* from *4314* and *1159;* to expend additionally:—spend more.

4326. προσδέομαι **prŏsdĕŏmai**, *pros-deh'-om-ahee;* from *4314* and *1189;* to require additionally, i.e. want further:—need.

4327. προσδέχομαι **prŏsdĕchŏmai**, *pros-dekh'-om-ahee;* from *4314* and *1209;* to admit (to intercourse, hospitality, credence or [fig.] endurance); by impl. to await (with confidence or patience):—accept, allow, look (wait) for, take.

4328. προσδοκάω **prŏsdŏkaō**, *pros-dok-ah'-o;* from *4314* and δοκεύω **dŏkĕuō** (to watch); to anticipate (in thought, hope or fear); by impl. to await:—(be in) expect (-ation), look (for), when looked, tarry, wait for.

4329. προσδοκία **prŏsdŏkia**, *pros-dok-ee'-ah;* from *4328;* apprehension (of evil); by impl. infliction anticipated:—expectation, looking after.

προσδρέμω **prŏsdrĕmō**. See *4370.*

4330. προσεάω **prŏsĕaō**, *pros-eh-ah'-o;* from *4314* and *1439;* to permit further progress:—suffer.

4331. προσεγγίζω **prŏsĕggizō**, *pros-eng-ghid'-zo;* from *4314* and *1448;* to approach near:—come nigh.

4332. προσεδρεύω **prŏsĕdrĕuō**, *pros-ed-ryoo'-o;* from a comp. of *4314* and the base of *1476;* to sit near, i.e. attend as a servant:—wait at.

4333. προσεργάζομαι **prŏsĕrgazŏmai**, *pros-er-gad'-zom-ahee;* from *4314* and *2038;* to work additionally, i.e. (by impl.) acquire besides:—gain.

4334. προσέρχομαι **prŏsĕrchŏmai**, *pros-er'-khom-ahee;* from *4314* and *2064* (includ. its alt.); to approach, i.e. (by impl.) come near, visit, or (fig.) worship, assent to:—(as soon as he) come (unto), come thereunto, consent, draw near, go (near, to, unto).

4335. προσευχή **prŏsĕuchē**, *pros-yoo-khay';* from *4336;* prayer (worship); by impl. an oratory (chapel):— × pray earnestly, prayer.

4336. προσεύχομαι **prŏsĕuchŏmai**, *pros-yoo'-khom-ahee;* from *4314* and *2172;* to pray to God, i.e. supplicate, worship:—pray (× earnestly, for), make prayer.

4337. προσέχω **prŏsĕchō**, *pros-ekh'-o;* from *4314* and *2192;* (fig.) to hold the mind (*3563* impl.) towards, i.e. pay attention to, be cautious about, apply oneself to, adhere to:—(give) attend (-ance, -ance at, -ance to, unto), beware, be given to, give (take) heed (to, unto) have regard.

4338. προσηλόω **prŏsēlŏō**, *pros-ay-lŏ'-o;* from *4314* and a der. of *2247;* to peg to, i.e. spike fast:—nail to.

4339. προσήλυτος **prŏsēlutŏs**, *pros-ay'-loo-tos;* from the alt. of *4334;* an arriver from a foreign re-

gion, i.e. (spec.) an acceder (convert) to Judaism ("proselyte"):—proselyte.

4340. πρόσκαιρος **prŏskairŏs**, *pros'-kahee-ros;* from *4314* and *2540;* for the occasion only, i.e. temporary:—dur- [eth] for awhile, endure for a time, for a season, temporal.

4341. προσκαλέομαι **prŏskalĕŏmai**, *pros-kal-eh'-om-ahee;* mid. from *4314* and *2564;* to call toward oneself, i.e. summon, invite:—call (for, to, unto).

4342. προσκαρτερέω **prŏskartĕrĕō**, *pros-kar-ter-eh'-o;* from *4314* and *2594;* to be earnest towards, i.e. (to a thing) to persevere, be constantly diligent, or (in a place) to attend assiduously all the exercises, or (to a person) to adhere closely to (as a servitor):—attend (give self) continually (upon), continue (in, instant in, with), wait on (continually).

4343. προσκαρτέρησις **prŏskartĕrēsis**, *pros-kar-ter'-ay-sis;* from *4342;* persistency:—perseverance.

4344. προσκεφάλαιον **prŏskĕphalaiŏn**, *pros-kef-al'-ahee-on;* neut. of a presumed comp. of *4314* and *2776;* something for the head, i.e. a cushion:—pillow.

4345. προσκληρόω **prŏsklērŏō**, *pros-klay-rŏ'-o;* from *4314* and *2820;* to give a common lot to, i.e. (fig.) to associate with:—consort with.

4346. πρόσκλισις **prŏsklisis**, *pros'-klis-is;* from a comp. of *4314* and *2827;* a leaning towards, i.e. (fig.) proclivity (favoritism):—partiality.

4347. προσκολλάω **prŏskŏllaō**, *pros-kol-lah'-o;* from *4314* and *2853;* to glue to, i.e. (fig.) to adhere:—cleave, join (self).

4348. πρόσκομμα **prŏskŏmma**, *pros'-kom-mah;* from *4350;* a stub, i.e. (fig.) occasion of apostasy:—offence, stumbling (-block, [-stone]).

4349. προσκοπή **prŏskŏpē**, *pros-kop-ay';* from *4350;* a stumbling, i.e. (fig. and concr.) occasion of sin:—offence.

4350. προσκόπτω **prŏskŏptō**, *pros-kop'-to;* from *4314* and *2875;* to strike at, i.e. surge against (as water); spec. to stub on, i.e. trip up (lit. or fig.):—beat upon, dash, stumble (at).

4351. προσκυλίω **prŏskuliō**, *pros-koo-lee'-o;* from *4314* and *2947;* to roll towards, i.e. block against:—roll (to).

4352. προσκυνέω **prŏskunĕō**, *pros-koo-neh'-o;* from *4314* and a prob. der. of *2965* (mean. to kiss, like a dog licking his master's hand); to fawn or crouch to, i.e. (lit. or fig.) prostrate oneself in homage (do reverence to, adore):—worship.

4353. προσκυνητής **prŏskunētēs**, *pros-koo-nay-tace';* from *4352;* an adorer:—worshipper.

4354. προσλαλέω **prŏslalĕō**, *pros-lal-eh'-o;* from *4314* and *2980;* to talk to, i.e. converse with:—speak to (with).

4355. προσλαμβάνω **prŏslambanō**, *pros-lam-ban'-o;* from *4314* and *2983;* to take to oneself, i.e. use (food, lead (aside), admit (to friendship or hospitality):—receive, take (unto).

4356. πρόσληψις **prŏslēpsis**, *pros'-lape-sis;* from *4355;* admission:—receiving.

4357. προσμένω **prŏsmĕnō**, *pros-men'-o;* from *4314* and *3306;* to stay further, i.e. remain in a place, with a person; fig. to adhere to, persevere in:—abide still, be with, cleave unto, continue in (with).

4358. προσορμίζω **prŏsŏrmizō**, *pros-or-mid'-zo;* from *4314* and a der. of the same as *3730* (mean. to tie [anchor] or lull); to moor to, i.e. (by impl.) land at:—draw to the shore.

4359. προσοφείλω **prŏsŏphĕilō**, *pros-of-i'-lo;* from *4314* and *3784;* to be indebted additionally:—over besides.

4360. προσοχθίζω **prŏsŏchthizō**, *pros-okh-thid'-zo;* from *4314* and a form of *3976* **ŏchthĕō** (to be vexed with something irksome); to feel indignant at:—be grieved with.

4361. πρόσπεινος **prŏspĕinŏs**, *pros'-pi-nos;* from *4314* and the same as *3983;* hungering further, i.e. intensely hungry:—very hungry.

4362. προσπήγνυμι **prŏspēgnumi**, *pros-payg'-noo-mee*; from *4314* and *4078*; to *fasten to*, i.e. (spec.) to *impale* (on a cross):—crucify.

4363. προσπίπτω **prŏspiptō**, *pros-pip'-to*; from *4314* and *4098*; to *fall towards*, i.e. (gently) *prostrate oneself* (in supplication or homage), or (violently) to *rush* upon (in storm):—beat upon, fall (down) at (before).

4364. προσποιέομαι **prŏspŏiĕŏmai**, *pros-poy-eh'-om-ahee*; mid. from *4314* and *4160*; to *do forward for oneself*, i.e. *pretend* (as if about to do a thing):—make as though.

4365. προσπορεύομαι **prŏspŏrĕuŏmai**, *pros-por-yoo'-om-ahee*; from *4314* and *4198*; to *journey towards*, i.e. *approach* [not the same as *4313*]:—go before.

4366. προσρήγνυμι **prŏsrēgnumi**, *pros-rayg'-noo-mee*; from *4314* and *4486*; to *tear towards*, i.e. *burst upon* (as a tempest or flood):—beat vehemently against (upon).

4367. προστάσσω **prŏstassō**, *pros-tas'-so*; from *4314* and *5021*; to *arrange towards*, i.e. (fig.) *enjoin*:—bid, command.

4368. προστάτις **prŏstatis**, *pros-tat'-is*; fem. of a der. of *4291*; a *patroness*, i.e. *assistant*:—succourer.

4369. προστίθημι **prŏstithēmi**, *pros-tith'-ay-mee*; from *4314* and *5087*; to *place additionally*, i.e. *lay beside, annex, repeat*:—add, again, give more, increase, lay unto, proceed further, speak to any more.

4370. προστρέχω **prŏstrĕchō**, *pros-trekh'-o*; from *4314* and *5143* (includ. its alt.); to *run towards*, i.e. *hasten to meet* or join:—run (thither to, to).

4371. προσφάγιον **prŏsphagiŏn**, *pros-fag'-ee-on*; neut. of a presumed der. of a comp. of *4314* and *5315*; something *eaten in addition* to bread, i.e. a *relish* (spec. *fish*; comp. *3795*):—meat.

4372. πρόσφατος **prŏsphatŏs**, *pros'-fat-os*; from *4253* and a der. of *4160*; *previously* (*recently*) *slain* (*fresh*), i.e. (fig.) *lately made*:—new.

4373. προσφάτως **prŏsphatōs**, *pros-fat'-oce*; adv. from *4372*; *recently*:—lately.

4374. προσφέρω **prŏsphĕrō**, *pros-fer'-o*; from *4314* and *5342* (includ. its alt.); to *bear towards*, i.e. *lead to, tender* (espec. to God), *treat*:—bring (to, unto), deal with, do, offer (unto, up), present unto, put to.

4375. προσφιλής **prŏsphilēs**, *pros-fee-lace'*; from a presumed comp. of *4314* and *5368*; *friendly towards*, i.e. *acceptable*:—lovely.

4376. προσφορά **prŏsphŏra**, *pros-for-ah'*; from *4374*; *presentation*; concr. an *oblation* (bloodless) or *sacrifice*:—offering (up).

4377. προσφωνέω **prŏsphōnĕō**, *pros-fo-neh'-o*; from *4314* and *5455*; to *sound towards*, i.e. *address, exclaim, summon*:—call unto, speak (un-) to.

4378. πρόσχυσις **prŏschusis**, *pros'-khoo-sis*; from a comp. of *4314* and χέω **chĕō** (to *pour*); a *shedding forth*, i.e. *affusion*:—sprinkling.

4379. προσψαύω **prŏspsauō**, *pros-psŏw'-o*; from *4314* and ψαύω **psauō** (to *touch*); to *impinge*, i.e. *lay a finger on* (in order to relieve):—touch.

4380. προσωπολημπτέω **prŏsōpŏlēmptĕō**, *pros-o-pol-ape-teh'-o*; from *4381*; to *favor an individual*, i.e. *show partiality*:—have respect to persons.

4381. προσωπολήμπτης **prŏsōpŏlēmptēs**, *pros-o-pol-ape'-tace*; from *4383* and *2983*; an *accepter* of a *face* (individual), i.e. (spec.) one *exhibiting partiality*:—respecter of persons.

4382. προσωπολημψία **prŏsōpŏlēmpsia**, *pros-o-pol-ape-see'-ah*; from *4381*; *partiality*, i.e. *favoritism*:—respect of persons.

4383. πρόσωπον **prŏsōpŏn**, *pros'-o-pon*; from *4314* and ὤψ **ōps** (the *visage*; from *3700*); the *front* (as being *towards view*), i.e. the *countenance, aspect, appearance, surface*; by impl. *presence, person*:—(outward) appearance, X before, countenance, face, fashion, (men's) person, presence.

4384. προτάσσω **prŏtassō**, *prot-as'-so*; from *4253* and *5021*; to *pre-arrange*, i.e. *prescribe*:—before appoint.

4385. προτείνω **prŏtĕinō**, *prot-i'-no*; from *4253* and τείνω **tĕinō** (to *stretch*); to *protend*, i.e. *tie prostrate* (for scourging):—bind.

4386. πρότερον **prŏtĕrŏn**, *prot'-er-on*; neut. of *4387* as adv. (with or without the art.); *previously*:—before, (at the) first, former.

4387. πρότερος **prŏtĕrŏs**, *prot'-er-os*; compar. of *4253*; *prior* or *previous*:—former.

4388. προτίθεμαι **prŏtithĕmai**, *prot-ith'-em-ahee*; mid. from *4253* and *5087*; to *place before*, i.e. (for oneself) to *exhibit*; (to oneself) to *propose* (determine):—purpose, set forth.

4389. προτρέπομαι **prŏtrĕpŏmai**, *prot-rep'-om-ahee*; mid. from *4253* and the base of *5157*; to *turn forward* for oneself, i.e. *encourage*:—exhort.

4390. προτρέχω **prŏtrĕchō**, *prot-rekh'-o*; from *4253* and *5143* (includ. its alt.); to *run forward*, i.e. *outstrip, precede*:—outrun, run before.

4391. προϋπάρχω **prŏüparchō**, *pro-oop-ar'-kho*; from *4253* and *5225*; to *exist before*, i.e. (adv.) to be or do something *previously*:— + be before (-time).

4392. πρόφασις **prŏphasis**, *prof'-as-is*; from a comp. of *4253* and *5316*; an *outward showing*, i.e. *pretext*:—cloke, colour, pretence, show.

4393. προφέρω **prŏphĕrō**, *prof-er'-o*; from *4253* and *5342*; to *bear forward*, i.e. *produce*:—bring forth.

4394. προφητεία **prŏphētĕia**, *prof-ay-ti'-ah*; from *4396* ("*prophecy*"); *prediction* (scriptural or other):—prophecy, prophesying.

4395. προφητεύω **prŏphētĕuō**, *prof-ate-yoo'-o*; from *4396*; to *foretell* events, *divine, speak* under *inspiration, exercise* the *prophetic office*:—prophesy.

4396. προφήτης **prŏphētēs**, *prof-ay'-tace*; from a comp. of *4253* and *5346*; a *foreteller* ("*prophet*"); by anal. an *inspired speaker*; by extens. a *poet*:—prophet.

4397. προφητικός **prŏphētikŏs**, *prof-ay-tik-os'*; from *4396*; *pertaining to a foreteller* ("*prophetic*"):—of prophecy, of the prophets.

4398. προφῆτις **prŏphētis**, *prof-ay'-tis*; fem. of *4396*; a *female foreteller* or an *inspired woman*:—prophetess.

4399. προφθάνω **prŏphthanō**, *prof-than'-o*; from *4253* and *5348*; to *get an earlier start of*, i.e. *anticipate*:—prevent.

4400. προχειρίζομαι **prŏchĕirizŏmai**, *prokh-i-rid'-zom-ahee*; mid. from *4253* and a der. of *5495*; to *handle for oneself in advance*, i.e. (fig.) to *purpose*:—choose, make.

4401. προχειροτονέω **prŏchĕirŏtŏnĕō**, *prokh-i-rot-on-eh'-o*; from *4253* and *5500*; to *elect in advance*:—choose before.

4402. Πρόχορος **Prŏchŏrŏs**, *prokh'-or-os*; from *4253* and *5525*; *before the dance*; *Prochorus*, a Chr.:—Prochorus.

4403. πρύμνα **prumna**, *proom'-nah*; fem. of πρυμνύς **prumnus** (*hindmost*); the *stern* of a ship:—hinder part, stern.

4404. πρωΐ **prōi**, *pro-ee'*; adv. from *4253*; at *dawn*; by impl. the *day-break* watch:—early (in the morning), (in the) morning.

4405. πρωΐα **prōia**, *pro-ee'-ah*; fem. of a der. of *4404* as noun; *day-dawn*:—early, morning.

4406. πρώϊμος **prōïmŏs**, *pro'-ee-mos*; from *4404*; *dawning*, i.e. (by anal.) *autumnal* (showering, the first of the rainy season):—early.

4407. πρωϊνός **prōïnŏs**, *pro-ee-nos'*; from *4404*; *pertaining to the dawn*, i.e. *matutinal*:—morning.

4408. πρῶρα **prōra**, *pro'-ra*; fem. of a presumed der. of *4253* as noun; the *prow*, i.e. *forward part* of a vessel:—forepart (-ship).

4409. πρωτεύω **prōtĕuō**, *prote-yoo'-o*; from *4413*; to *be first* (in rank or influence):—have the preeminence.

4410. πρωτοκαθεδρία **prōtŏkathĕdria**, *pro-tok-ath-ed-ree'-ah*; from *4413* and *2515*; a *sitting first* (in the front row), i.e. *preeminence* in council:—chief (highest, uppermost) seat.

4411. πρωτοκλισία **prōtŏklisia**, *pro-tok-lis-ee'-ah*; from *4413* and *2828*; a *reclining first* (in the place of honor) at the dinner-bed, i.e. *preeminence* at meals:—chief (highest, uppermost) room.

4412. πρῶτον **prōtŏn**, *pro'-ton*; neut. of *4413* as adv. (with or without *3588*); *firstly* (in time, place, order, or importance):—before, at the beginning, chiefly, (at, at the) first (of all).

4413. πρῶτος **prōtŏs**, *pro'-tos*; contr. superl. of *4253*; *foremost* (in time, place, order or importance):—before, beginning, best, chief (-est), first (of all), former.

4414. πρωτοστάτης **prōtŏstatēs**, *pro-tos-tat'-ace*; from *4413* and *2476*; one *standing first* in the ranks, i.e. a *captain* (champion):—ringleader.

4415. πρωτοτόκια **prōtŏtŏkia**, *pro-tot-ok'-ee-ah*; from *4416*; *primogeniture* (as a privilege):—birthright.

4416. πρωτότοκος **prōtŏtŏkŏs**, *pro-tot-ok'-os*; from *4413* and the alt. of *5088*; *first-born* (usually as noun, lit. or fig.):—firstbegotten (-born).

4417. πταίω **ptaiō**, *ptah'-yo*; a form of *4098*; to *trip*, i.e. (fig.) to *err, sin, fail* (of salvation):—fall, offend, stumble.

4418. πτέρνα **ptĕrna**, *pter'-nah*; of uncert. der.; the *heel* (fig.):—heel.

4419. πτερύγιον **ptĕrugiŏn**, *pter-oog'-ee-on*; neut. of a presumed der. of *4420*; a *winglet*, i.e. (fig.) *extremity* (top corner):—pinnacle.

4420. πτέρυξ **ptĕrux**, *pter'-oox*; from a der. of *4072* (mean. a *feather*); a *wing*:—wing.

4421. πτηνόν **ptēnŏn**, *ptay-non'*; contr. for *4071*; a *bird*:—bird.

4422. πτοέω **ptŏĕō**, *ptŏ-eh'-o*; prob. akin to the alt. of *4098* (through the idea of *causing* to *fall*) or to *4072* (through that of causing to *fly* away); to *scare*:—frighten.

4423. πτόησις **ptŏēsis**, *ptŏ'-ay-sis*; from *4422*; *alarm*:—amazement.

4424. Πτολεμαΐς **Ptŏlĕmaïs**, *ptol-em-ah-is'*; from Πτολεμαῖος **Ptŏlĕmaiŏs** (*Ptolemy*, after whom it was named); *Ptolemaïs*, a place in Pal.:—Ptolemais.

4425. πτύον **ptuŏn**, *ptoo'-on*; from *4429*; a *winnowing-fork* (as *scattering* like spittle):—fan.

4426. πτύρω **pturō**, *ptoo'-ro*; from a presumed der. of *4429* (and thus akin to *4422*); to *frighten*:—terrify.

4427. πτύσμα **ptusma**, *ptoos'-mah*; from *4429*; *saliva*:—spittle.

4428. πτύσσω **ptussō**, *ptoos'-so*; prob. akin to πετάννυμι **pĕtannumi** (to *spread*; and thus appar. allied to *4072* through the idea of *expansion*, and to *4429* through that of *flattening*; comp. *3961*); to *fold*, i.e. *furl* a scroll:—close.

4429. πτύω **ptuō**, *ptoo'-o*; a prim. verb (comp. *4428*); to *spit*:—spit.

4430. πτῶμα **ptōma**, *pto'-mah*; from the alt. of *4098*; a *ruin*, i.e. (spec.) lifeless *body* (corpse, carrion):—dead body, carcase, corpse.

4431. πτῶσις **ptōsis**, *pto'-sis*; from the alt. of *4098*; a *crash*, i.e. *downfall* (lit. or fig.):—fall.

4432. πτωχεία **ptōchĕia**, *pto-khi'-ah*; from *4433*; *beggary*, i.e. *indigence* (lit. or fig.):—poverty.

4433. πτωχεύω **ptōchĕuō**, *pto-khyoo'-o*; from *4434*; to *be a beggar*, i.e. (by impl.) to *become indigent* (fig.):—become poor.

4434. πτωχός **ptōchŏs**, *pto-khos'*; from πτώσσω **ptōssō** (to *crouch*; akin to *4422* and the alt. of *4098*); a *beggar* (as *cringing*), i.e. *pauper* (strictly denoting absolute or public *mendicancy*, although also used in a qualified or relative sense; whereas *3993* prop. means only *straitened circumstances* in private), lit. (often as noun) or fig. (distressed):—beggar (-ly), poor.

4435. πυγμή **pugmē**, *poog-may'*; from a prim. πύξ **pux** (the *fist* as a weapon); the *clenched hand*,

ie. (only in dat. as adv.) *with the fist* (hard *scrubbing*):—oft.

4436. Πύθων **Puthōn,** *poo'-thone;* from Πυθώ **Puthō** (the name of the region where Delphi, the seat of the famous *oracle*, was located); a *Python*, i.e. (by anal. with the supposed *diviner* there) *inspiration* (*soothsaying*):—divination.

4437. πυκνός **puknŏs,** *pook-nos';* from the same as 4635; clasped (thick), i.e. (fig.) *frequent;* neut. plur. (as adv.) *frequently:*—often (-er).

4438. πυκτέω **puktĕō,** *pook-teh'-o;* from a der. of the same as 4435; to *box* (with the fist), i.e. *contend* (as a boxer) at the games (fig.):—fight.

4439. πύλη **pulē,** *poo'-lay;* appar. a prim. word; a *gate,* i.e. the leaf or wing of a folding *entrance* (lit. or fig.):—gate.

4440. πυλών **pulōn,** *poo-lone';* from 4439; a *gateway, door-way* of a building or city; by impl. a *portal* or *vestibule:*—gate, porch.

4441. πυνθάνομαι **punthanŏmai,** *poon-than'-om-ahee;* mid. prol. from a prim. πύθω **puthō** (which occurs only as an alt. in certain tenses); to *question,* i.e. *ascertain* by inquiry (as a matter of *information* merely; and thus differing from 2065, which prop. means a *request* as a favor; and from 154, which is strictly a *demand* of something due; as well as from 2212, which implies a *search* for something hidden; and from 1189, which involves the idea of urgent *need*); by impl. to *learn* (by casual intelligence):—ask, demand, enquire, understand.

4442. πῦρ **pur,** *poor;* a prim. word; *"fire"* (lit. or fig., spec. *lightning*):—fiery. fire.

4443. πυρά **pura,** *poo-rah';* from 4442; a *fire* (concr.):—fire.

4444. πύργος **purgŏs,** *poor'-gos;* appar. a prim. word *("burgh");* a *tower* or *castle:*—tower.

4445. πυρέσσω **puressō,** *poo-res'-so;* from 4443; to *be on fire,* i.e. (spec.) to *have a fever:*—be sick of a fever.

4446. πυρετός **purĕtŏs,** *poo-ret-os';* from 4445; *inflamed,* i.e. (by impl.) *feverish* (as noun, *fever*):—fever.

4447. πύρινος **purinŏs,** *poo'-ree-nos;* from 4443; *fiery,* i.e. (by impl.) *flaming:*—of fire.

4448. πυρόω **purŏō,** *poo-rŏ'-o;* from 4442; to *kindle,* i.e. (pass.) to *be ignited, glow* (lit.), *be refined* (by impl.), or (fig.) to *be inflamed* (with anger, grief, lust):—burn, fiery, be on fire, try.

4449. πυρράζω **purrhazō,** *poor-hrad'-zo;* from 4450; to *redden* (intrans.):—be red.

4450. πυρρός **purrhŏs,** *poor-hros';* from 4442; *fire-like,* i.e. (spec.) *flame-colored:*—red.

4451. πύρωσις **purōsis,** *poo'-ro-sis;* from 4448; *ignition,* i.e. (spec.) *smelting* (fig. *conflagration,* calamity as a *test*):—burning, trial.

4452. -πω **-pō,** *po;* another form of the base of 4458; an enclitic particle of indefiniteness; *yet, even;* used only in comp. See 3369, 3380, 3764, 3768, 4455.

4453. πωλέω **pōlĕō,** *po-leh'-o;* prob. ultimately from πέλομαι **pĕlŏmai** (to be busy, to trade); to *b*-*ter* (as a pedlar), i.e. to *sell:*—sell, whatever is sold.

4454. πῶλος **pōlŏs,** *po'-los;* appar. a prim. word; a *"foal"* or *"filly",* i.e. (spec.) a *young ass:*—colt.

4455. πώποτε **pōpŏte,** *po'-pot-e;* from 4452 and 4218; at *any time,* i.e. (with neg. particle) *at no time:*—at any time, + never (. . to any man), + yet never man.

4456. πωρόω **pōrŏō,** *po-rŏ'-o;* appar. from πῶρος **pōrŏs** (a kind of *stone*); to *petrify,* i.e. (fig.) to *indurate* (render stupid or callous):—blind, harden.

4457. πώρωσις **pōrōsis,** *po'-ro-sis;* from 4456; *stupidity* or *callousness:*—blindness, hardness.

4458. -πώς **-pōs,** *poce;* adv. from the base of 4225; an enclitic particle of indefiniteness of manner; *somehow* or *anyhow;* used only in comp.:—haply, by any (some) means, perhaps. See 1513, 3381. Comp. 4459.

4459. πῶς **pōs,** *poce;* adv. from the base of 4226; an interrog. particle of manner; *in what way?* (some-

---

times the question is indirect, *how?*); also as exclamation, *how* much!:—how, after (by) what manner (means), that. [*Occasionally unexpressed in English.*]

P

4460. 'Ραάβ **Rhaab,** *hrah-ab';* of Heb. or. [7343]; *Raab* (i.e. *Rachab*), a Canaanitess:—Rahab. See also 4477.

4461. ῥαββί **rhabbi,** *hrab-bee';* of Heb. or. [7227 with pron. suffix]; *my master,* i.e. *Rabbi,* as an official title of honor:—Master, Rabbi.

4462. ῥαββονί **rhabbŏni,** *hrab-bon-ee';* or ῥαββουνί **rhabbŏuni,** *hrab-boo-nee';* of Chald. or.; corresp. to 4461:—Lord, Rabboni.

4463. ῥαβδίζω **rhabdizō,** *hrab-did'-zo;* from 4464; to *strike with a stick,* i.e. *bastinado:*—beat (with rods).

4464. ῥάβδος **rhabdŏs,** *hrab'-dos;* from the base of 4474; a *stick* or *wand* (as a *cudgel,* a *cane* or a *baton* of royalty):—rod, sceptre, staff.

4465. ῥαβδοῦχος **rhabdŏuchŏs,** *hrab-doo'-khos;* from 4464 and 2192; a *rod-* (the Lat. *fasces*) *holder,* i.e. a Rom. *lictor* (constable or executioner):—serjeant.

4466. 'Ραγαῦ **Rhagau,** *hrag-ŏw';* of Heb. or. [7466]; *Ragau* (i.e. *Reü*), a patriarch:—Ragau.

4467. ῥᾳδιούργημα **rha͵diŏurgēma,** *hrad-ee-oorg'-ay-mah;* from a comp. of ῥᾴδιος **rha͵diŏs** (*easy,* i.e. *reckless*) and 2041; *easy-going behavior,* i.e. (by extens.) a *crime:*—lewdness.

4468. ῥᾳδιουργία **rha͵diŏurgia,** *hrad-ee-oorg-ee'-a;* from the same as 4467; *recklessness,* i.e. (by extens.) *malignity:*—mischief.

4469. ῥακά **rhaka,** *rhak-ah';* of Chald. or. [comp. 7386]; O *empty one,* i.e. thou *worthless* (as a term of utter vilification):—Raca.

4470. ῥάκος **rhakŏs,** *hrak'-os;* from 4486; a *"rag",* i.e. *piece* of cloth:—cloth.

4471. 'Ραμά **Rhama,** *hram-ah';* of Heb. or. [7414]; *Rama* (i.e. *Ramah*), a place in Pal.:—Rama.

4472. ῥαντίζω **rhantizō,** *hran-tid'-zo;* from a der. of ῥαίνω **rhainō** (to *sprinkle*); to *render besprinkled,* i.e. *asperse* (cer. or fig.):—sprinkle.

4473. ῥαντισμός **rhantismŏs,** *hran-tis-mos';* from 4472; *dispersion* (cer. or fig.):—sprinkling.

4474. ῥαπίζω **rhapizō,** *hrap-id'-zo;* from a der. of a prim. ῥέπω **rhĕpō** (to *let fall, "rap"*); to *slap:*—smite (with the palm of the hand). Comp. 5180.

4475. ῥάπισμα **rhapisma,** *hrap'-is-mah;* from 4474; a *slap:*—(+ strike with) palm of the hand, smite with the hand.

4476. ῥαφίς **rhaphis,** *hraf-ece';* from a prim. ῥάπτω **rhaptō** (to *sew;* perh. rather akin to the base of 4474 through the idea of *puncturing*); a *needle:*—needle.

4477. 'Ραχάβ **Rhachab,** *hrakh-ab';* from the same as 4460; *Rachab,* a Canaanitess:—Rachab.

4478. 'Ραχήλ **Rhachel,** *hrakh-ale';* of Heb. or. [7354]; *Rachel,* the wife of Jacob:—Rachel.

4479. 'Ρεβέκκα **Rhĕbĕkka,** *hreb-bek'-kah;* of Heb. or. [7259]; *Rebecca* (i.e. *Ribkah*), the wife of Isaac:—Rebecca.

4480. ῥέδα **rhĕda,** *hred'-ah;* of Lat. or.; a *rheda,* i.e. *four-wheeled carriage* (wagon for riding):—chariot.

4481. 'Ρεμφάν **Rhĕmphan,** *hrem-fan';* by incorrect transliteration for a word of Heb. or. [3594]; *Remphan* (i.e. *Kijun*), an Eg. idol:—Remphan.

4482. ῥέω **rhĕō,** *hreh'-o;* a prim. verb; for some tenses of which a prol. form
  ῥεύω **rhĕuō,** *hrĕyoo'-o,* is used; to *flow* (*"run",* as water):—flow.

4483. ῥέω **rhĕō,** *hreh'-o;* for certain tenses of which a prol. form
  ἐρέω **ĕrĕō,** *er-eh'-o,* is used; and both as alt. for 2036; perh. akin (or ident.) with 4482 (through the

---

idea of *pouring* forth); to *utter,* i.e. *speak* or *say:*—command, make, say, speak (of). Comp. 3004.

4484. 'Ρήγιον **Rhēgiŏn,** *hrayg'-ee-on;* of Lat. or.; *Rhegium,* a place in Italy:—Rhegium.

4485. ῥῆγμα **rhēgma,** *hrayg'-mah;* from 4486; something *torn,* i.e. a *fragment* (by impl. and abstr. a *fall*):—ruin.

4486. ῥήγνυμι **rhēgnumi,** *hrayg'-noo-mee;* or ῥήσσω **rhēssō,** *hrace'-so;* both prol. forms of ῥήκω **rhēkō** (which appears only in certain forms, and is itself prob. a strengthened form of ἄγνυμι **agnumi** [see in 2608]); to *"break", "wreck"* or *"crack",* i.e. (espec.) to *sunder* (by separation of the parts; 2608 being its intensive [with the prep. in comp.], and 2352 a *shattering* to minute fragments; but not a *reduction* to the constituent particles, like 3089) or *disrupt, lacerate;* by impl. to *convulse* (with *spasms*); fig. to *give vent* to joyful emotions:—break (forth), burst, rend, tear.

4487. ῥῆμα **rhēma,** *hray'-mah;* from 4483; an *utterance* (individ., collect. or spec.); by impl. a *matter* or *topic* (espec. of *narration, command* or *dispute*); with a neg. *naught* whatever:— + evil, + nothing, saying, word.

4488. 'Ρησά **Rhēsa,** *hray-sah';* prob. of Heb. or. [appar. for 7509]; *Resa* (i.e. *Rephajah*), an Isr.:—Rhesa.

4489. ῥήτωρ **rhētōr,** *hray'-tore;* from 4483; a *speaker,* i.e. (by impl.) a forensic *advocate:*—orator.

4490. ῥητῶς **rhētōs,** *hray-toce';* adv. from a der. of 4483; *out-spokenly,* i.e. *distinctly:*—expressly.

4491. ῥίζα **rhiza,** *hrid'-zah;* appar. a prim. word; a *"root"* (lit. or fig.):—root.

4492. ῥιζόω **rhizŏō,** *hrid-zŏ'-o;* from 4491; to *root* (fig. *become stable*):—root.

4493. ῥιπή **rhipē,** *hree-pay';* from 4496; a *jerk* (of the eye, i.e. [by anal.] an *instant*):—twinkling.

4494. ῥιπίζω **rhipizō,** *hrip-id'-zo;* from a der. of 4496 (mean. a *fan* or *bellows*); to *breeze up,* i.e. (by anal.) to *agitate* (into waves):—toss.

4495. ῥιπτέω **rhiptĕō,** *hrip-teh'-o;* from a der. of 4496; to *toss up:*—cast off.

4496. ῥίπτω **rhiptō,** *hrip'-to;* a prim. verb (perh. rather akin to the base of 4474, through the idea of sudden *motion*); to *fling* (prop. with a quick *toss,* thus differing from 906, which denotes a *deliberate* hurl; and from τείνω **tĕinō** [see in 1614], which indicates an *extended* projection); by qualification, to *deposit* (as if a load); by extens. to *disperse:*—cast (down, out), scatter abroad, throw.

4497. 'Ροβοάμ **Rhŏbŏam,** *hrob-ŏ-am';* of Heb. or. [7346]; *Roboäm* (i.e. *Rechabam*), an Isr.:—Roboam.

4498. 'Ρόδη **Rhŏdē,** *hrod'-ay;* prob. for ῥόδη **rhŏdē** (a *rose*); *Rodè,* a servant girl:—Rhoda.

4499. 'Ρόδος **Rhŏdŏs,** *hrod'-os;* prob. from ῥόδον **rhŏdŏn** (a *rose*); *Rhodus,* an island of the Mediterranean:—Rhodes.

4500. ῥοιζηδόν **rhŏizēdŏn,** *hroyd-zay-don';* adv. from a der. of ῥοῖζος **rhŏizŏs** (a *whir*); *whizzingly,* i.e. *with a crash:*—with a great noise.

4501. ῥομφαία **rhŏmphaia,** *hrom-fah'-yah;* prob. of for. or.: a *sabre,* i.e. a long and broad *cutlass* (any *weapon* of the kind, lit. or fig.):—sword.

4502. 'Ρουβήν **Rhŏubēn,** *hroo-bane';* of Heb. or. [7205]; *Ruben* (i.e. *Reuben*), an Isr.:—Reuben.

4503. 'Ρούθ **Rhŏuth,** *hrooth;* of Heb. or. [7327]; *Ruth,* a Moabitess:—Ruth.

4504. 'Ροῦφος **Rhŏuphŏs,** *hroo'-fos;* of Lat. or.; *red; Rufus,* a Chr.:—Rufus.

4505. ῥύμη **rhumē,** *hroo'-may;* prol. from 4506 in its orig. sense; an *alley* or *avenue* (as crowded):—lane, street.

4506. ῥύομαι **rhuŏmai,** *rhoo'-om-ahee;* mid. of an obsol. verb, akin to 4482 (through the idea of a *current;* comp. 4511); to *rush* or *draw* (for oneself), i.e. *rescue:*—deliver (-er).

4507. ῥυπαρία **rhuparia,** *hroo-par-ee'-ah;* from 4508; *dirtiness* (mor.):—filthiness.

4508. ῥυπαρός **rhuparŏs**, *rhoo-par-os'; from 4509; dirty,* i.e. (rel.) *cheap* or *shabby;* mor. *wicked;*—vile.

4509. ῥύπος **rhupŏs**, *hroo'-pos;* of uncert. affin.; *dirt,* i.e. (mor.) *depravity:*—filth.

4510. ῥυπόω **rhupŏō**, *rhoo-pŏ'-o; from 4509;* to *soil,* i.e. (intrans.) *to become dirty* (mor.):—be filthy.

4511. ῥύσις **rhusis**, *hroo'-sis; from 4506* in the sense of its congener *4482; a flux* (of blood):—issue.

4512. ῥυτίς **rhutis**, *hroo-tece'; from 4506; a fold* (as *drawing together*), i.e. a *wrinkle* (espec. on the face):—wrinkle.

4513. Ῥωμαϊκός **Rhōmaïkŏs**, *rho-mah-ee-kos'; from 4514; Romaïc,* i.e. *Latin:*—Latin.

4514. Ῥωμαῖος **Rhōmaïŏs**, *hro-mah'-yos; from 4516; Romæan,* i.e. *Roman* (as noun):—Roman, of Rome.

4515. Ῥωμαϊστί **Rhōmaïstï**, *hro-mah-is-tee'*; adv. from a presumed der. of *4516; Romaïstically,* i.e. *in the Latin* language:—Latin.

4516. Ῥώμη **Rhōmē**, *hro'-may; from the base of 4517; strength; Roma,* the capital of Italy:—Rome.

4517. ῥώννυμι **rhŏnnumi**, *hrone'-noo-mee;* prol. from ῥόομαι **rhŏŏmai** (to *dart;* prob. akin to *4506*); to *strengthen,* i.e. (imper. pass.) *have health* (as a parting exclamation, *good-bye*):—farewell.

Σ

4518. σαβαχθανί **sabachthani**, *sab-akh-than-ee'*; of Chald. or. [7662 with pron. suff.]; *thou hast left me; sabachthani* (i.e. *shebakthani*), a cry of distress:—sabachthani.

4519. σαβαώθ **sabaōth**, *sab-ah-owth';* of Heb. or. [6635 in fem. plur.]; *armies; sabaoth* (i.e. *tsebaoth*), a military epithet of God:—sabaoth.

4520. σαββατισμός **sabbatismŏs**, *sab-bat-is-mos'; from* a der. of *4521; a "sabbatism",* i.e. (fig.) the *repose* of Christianity (as a type of heaven):—rest.

4521. σάββατον **sabbatŏn**, *sab'-bat-on;* of Heb. or. [7676]; the *Sabbath* (i.e. *Shabbath*), or day of weekly *repose* from secular avocations (also the observance or institution itself); by extens. a *se'nnight,* i.e. the interval between two Sabbaths; likewise the plur. in all the above applications:—sabbath (day), week.

4522. σαγήνη **sagēnē**, *sag-ay'-nay;* from a der. of σάττω **sattō** (to *equip*) mean. *furniture,* espec. a *pack-saddle* (which in the East is merely a bag of netted rope); a "*seine*" for fishing:—net.

4523. Σαδδουκαῖος **Saddŏukaiŏs**, *sad-doo-kah'-yos;* prob. from *4524;* a *Sadducæan* (i.e. *Tsadokian*), or follower of a certain heretical Isr.:—Sadducee.

4524. Σαδώκ **Sadŏk**, *sad-oke';* of Heb. or. [6659]; *Sadoc* (i.e. *Tsadok*), an Isr.:—Sadoc.

4525. σαίνω **sainō**, *sah'ee-no;* akin to *4579;* to *wag* (as a dog its tail fawningly), i.e. (gen.) to *shake* (fig. *disturb*):—move.

4526. σάκκος **sakkŏs**, *sak'-kos;* of Heb. or. [8242]; "*sack*"-*cloth,* i.e. *mohair* (the material or garments made of it, worn as a sign of grief):—sackcloth.

4527. Σαλά **Sala**, *sal-ah´;* of Heb. or. [7974]; *Sala* (i.e. *Shelach*), a patriarch:—Sala.

4528. Σαλαθιήλ **Salathiēl**, *sal-ath-ee-ale';* of Heb. or. [7597]; *Salathiël* (i.e. *Shedltiël*), an Isr.:—Salathiel.

4529. Σαλαμίς **Salamis**, *sal-am-ece';* prob. from *4535* (from the *surge* on the shore); *Salamis,* a place in Cyprus:—Salamis.

4530. Σαλείμ **Salĕim**, *sal-ime';* prob. from the same as *4531; Salim,* a place in Pal.:—Salim.

4531. σαλεύω **salĕuō**, *sal-yoo'-o; from 4535;* to *waver,* i.e. *agitate, rock, topple* or (by impl.) *destroy;* fig. to *disturb, incite:*—move, shake (together), which cau [-not] be shaken, stir up.

4532. Σαλήμ **Salēm**, *sal-ame';* of Heb. or. [8004]; *Salem* (i.e. *Shalem*), a place in Pal.:—Salem.

4533. Σαλμών **Salmōn**, *sal-mone';* of Heb. or. [8012]; *Salmon,* an Isr.:—Salmon.

4534. Σαλμώνη **Salmōnē**, *sal-mo'-nay;* perh. of similar or. to *4529; Salmone,* a place in Crete:—Salmone.

4535. σάλος **salŏs**, *sal'-os;* prob. from the base of *4525;* a *vibration,* i.e. (spec.) *billow;*—wave.

4536. σάλπιγξ **salpigx**, *sal'-pinx;* perh. from *4535* (through the idea of *quavering* or *reverberation*): a *trumpet:*—trump (-et).

4537. σαλπίζω **salpizō**, *sal-pid'-zo; from 4536;* to *trumpet,* i.e. *sound a blast* (lit. or fig.):—(which are yet to) sound (a trumpet).

4538. σαλπιστής **salpistēs**, *sal-pis-tace';* from *4537;* a *trumpeter:*—trumpeter.

4539. Σαλώμη **Salōmē**, *sal-o'-may;* prob. of Heb. or. [fem. from 7965]; *Salomè* (i.e. *Shelomah*), an Israelitess:—Salome.

4540. Σαμάρεια **Samarĕia**, *sam-ar'-i-ah;* of Heb. or. [8111]; *Samaria* (i.e. *Shomeron*), a city and region of Pal.:—Samaria.

4541. Σαμαρείτης **Samarĕitēs**, *sam-ar-i'-tace; from 4540; a Samarite,* i.e. inhab. of Samaria:—Samaritan.

4542. Σαμαρεῖτις **Samarĕitis**, *sam-ar-i'-tis;* fem. of *4541; a Samaritess,* i.e. woman of Samaria:—of Samaria.

4543. Σαμοθρᾴκη **Samŏthra,kē**, *sam-oth-rak'-ay; from 4544* and Θρᾴκη **Thra,kē** (*Thrace*); *Samo-thracè* (*Samos of Thrace*), an island in the Mediterranean:—Samothrac'

4544. Σάμος **Samŏs**, *sam'-os;* of uncert. affin.; *Samus,* an island of the Mediterranean:—Samos.

4545. Σαμουήλ **Samŏuēl**, *sam-oo-ale';* of Heb. or. [8050]; *Samuel* (i.e. *Shemuel*), an Isr.:—Samuel.

4546. Σαμψών **Sampsōn**, *samp-sone';* of Heb. or. [8123]; *Sampson* (i.e. *Shimshon*), an Isr.:—Samson.

4547. σανδάλιον **sandaliŏn**, *san-dal'-ee-on;* neut. of a der. of σάνδαλον **sandalŏn** (a "*sandal*"; of uncert. or.); a *slipper* or *sole-pad*:—sandal.

4548. σανίς **sanis**, *san-ece';* of uncert. affin.; a *plank:*—board.

4549. Σαούλ **Saŏul**, *sah-ool';* of Heb. or. [7586]; *Saül* (i.e. *Shaül*), the Jewish name of Paul.—Saul. Comp. *4569.*

4550. σαπρός **saprŏs**, *sap-ros'; from 4595; rotten,* i.e. *worthless* (lit. or mor.):—bad, corrupt. Comp. *4190.*

4551. Σαπφείρη **Sapphĕirē**, *sap-fi'-ray;* fem. of *4552; Sapphirè,* an Israelitess:—Sapphira.

4552. σάπφειρος **sapphĕirŏs**, *sap'-fi-ros;* of Heb. or. [5601]; a "*sapphire*" or *lapis-lazuli* gem:—sapphire.

4553. σαργάνη **sarganē**, *sar-gan'-ay;* appar. of Heb. or. [8276]; a *basket* (as *interwoven* or *wicker*work):—basket.

4554. Σάρδεις **Sardĕis**, *sar'-dice;* plur. of uncert. der.; *Sardis,* a place in Asia Minor:—Sardis.

4555. σάρδινος **sardinŏs**, *sar'-dee-nos;* from the same as *4556; sardine* (*3037* being impl.), i.e. a gem, so called:—sardine.

4556. σάρδιος **sardiŏs**, *sar'-dee-os;* prop. adj. from an uncert. base; *sardian* (*3037* being impl.), i.e. (as noun) the gem so called:—sardius.

4557. σαρδόνυξ **sardŏnux**, *sar-don'-oox;* from the base of *4556* and ὄνυξ **ŏnux** (the *nail* of a finger; hence the "*onyx*" stone); a "*sardonyx*", i.e. the gem so called:—sardonyx.

4558. Σάρεπτα **Sarĕpta**, *sar'-ep-tah;* of Heb. or. [6886]; *Sarepta* (i.e. *Tsarephath*), a place in Pal.:—Sarepta.

4559. σαρκικός **sarkikŏs**, *sar-kee-kos'; from 4561; pertaining to flesh,* i.e. (by extens.) *bodily, temporal,* or (by impl.) *animal, unregenerate;*—carnal, fleshly.

4560. σάρκινος **sarkinŏs**, *sar'-kee-nos; from 4561; similar to flesh,* i.e. (by anal.) *soft:*—fleshly.

4561. σάρξ **sarx**, *sarz;* prob. from the base ot *4563; flesh* (as *stripped* of the skin), i.e. (strictly) the *meat* of an animal (as food), or (by extens.) the *body* (as opposed to the soul [or spirit], or as the symbol of what is external, or as the means of *kindred*), or (by impl.) *human nature* (with its frailties [phys. or mor.] and passions), or (spec.) a *human being* (as such):—carnal (-ly, + -ly minded), flesh ([-ly]).

4562. Σαρούχ **Sarŏuch**, *sar-ooch';* of Heb. or. [8286]; *Saruch* (i.e. *Serug*), a patriarch:—Saruch.

4563. σαρόω **sarŏō**, *sar-ŏ'-o; from* a der. of σαίρω **sairō** (to *brush* off; akin to *4951*) mean. a *broom;* to *sweep:*—sweep.

4564. Σάρρα **Sarrha**, *sar'-hrah;* of Heb. or. [8283]; *Sarra* (i.e. *Sarah*), the wife of Abraham:—Sara, Sarah.

4565. Σάρων **Sarōn**, *sar'-one;* of Heb. or. [8289]; *Saron* (i.e. *Sharon*), a district of Pal.:—Saron.

4566. Σατᾶν **Satan**, *sat-an';* of Heb. or. [7854]; *Satan,* i.e. the *devil:*—Satan. Comp. *4567.*

4567. Σατανᾶς **Satanas**, *sat-an-as';* of Chald. or. corresp. to *4566* (with the def. affix); the *accuser,* i.e. the *devil:*—Satan.

4568. σάτον **satŏn**, *sat'-on;* of Heb. or. [5429]; a certain *measure* for things dry:—measure.

4569. Σαῦλος **Saulŏs**, *sŏw'-los;* of Heb. or., the same as *4549; Saulus* (i.e. *Shaül*), the Jewish name of Paul:—Saul.

4570. σβέννυμι **sbĕnnumi**, *sben'-noo-mee;* a prol. form of an appar. prim. verb; to *extinguish* (lit. or fig.):—go out, quench.

4571. σέ **sĕ**, *seh;* accus. sing. of *4771; thee:*—thee, thou, × thy house.

4572. σεαυτοῦ **sĕautŏu**, *seh-ŏw-too';* gen. from *4571* and *846;* also dat. of the same,

σεαυτῷ **sĕautō**, *seh-ŏw-to';* and acc.

σεαυτόν **sĕautŏn**, *seh-ŏw-ton';* likewise contr. σαυτοῦ **sautŏu**, *sŏw-too';*

σαυτῷ **sautō**, *sŏw-to';* and

σαυτόν **sautŏn**, *sŏw-ton';* respectively; *of* (*with, to*) *thyself:*—thee, thine own self, (thou) thy (-self).

4573. σεβάζομαι **sĕbazŏmai**, *seb-ad'-zom-ahee;* mid. from a der. of *4576;* to *venerate,* i.e. *adore:*—worship.

4574. σέβασμα **sĕbasma**, *seb'-as-mah;* from *4573;* something *adored,* i.e. an *object of worship* (god, altar, etc.):—devotion, that is worshipped.

4575. σεβαστός **sĕbastŏs**, *seb-as-tos';* from *4573; venerable* (*august*), i.e. (as noun) a title of the Rom. *Emperor,* or (as adj.) *imperial:*—Augustus (-').

4576. σέβομαι **sĕbŏmai**, *seb'-om-ahee;* mid. of an appar. prim. verb; to *revere,* i.e. *adore:*—devout, religious, worship.

4577. σειρά **sĕira**, *si-rah';* prob. from *4951* through its congener εἴρω **ĕirō** (to *fasten;* akin to *138*); a *chain* (as *binding* or *drawing*):—chain.

4578. σεισμός **sĕismŏs**, *sice-mos'; from 4579;* a *commotion,* i.e. (of the air) a *gale,* (of the ground) an *earthquake:*—earthquake, tempest.

4579. σείω **sĕiō**, *si'-o;* appar. a prim. verb; to *rock* (*vibrate,* prop. *sideways* or *to and fro*), i.e. (gen.) to *agitate* (in any direction; *cause* to *tremble*); fig. to throw into a *tremor* (of fear or concern):—move, quake, shake.

4580. Σεκοῦνδος **Sĕkŏundŏs**, *sek-oon'-dos;* of Lat. or.; "*second*"; *Secundus,* a Chr.:—Secundus.

4581. Σελεύκεια **Sĕlĕukĕia**, *sel-yook'-i-ah;* from *4582;* Σέλευκος **Sĕlĕukŏs** (*Seleucus,* a Syrian king); *Seleuceia,* a place in Syria:—Seleucia.

4582. σελήνη **sĕlēnē**, *sel-ay'-nay;* from σέλας **sĕlas** (*brilliancy;* prob. akin to the alt. of *138,* through the idea of *attractiveness*); the *moon:*—moon.

4583. σεληνιάζομαι **sĕlēniazŏmai**, *sel-ay-noc-ad'-zom-ahee;* mid. or pass. from a presumed der. of *4582;* to be *moon-struck,* i.e. *crazy:*—be lunatic.

4584. Σεμεΐ **Sĕmĕï**, *sem-eh-ee'*; of Heb. or. [8096]; *Semeï* (i.e. *Shimi*), an Isr.:—Semei.

4585. σεμίδαλις **sĕmidalis**, *sem-id'-al-is*; prob. of for. or.; fine wheaten *flour*:—fine flour.

4586. σεμνός **sĕmnŏs**, *sem-nos'*; from *4576*; *venerable*, i.e. *honorable*:—grave, honest.

4587. σεμνότης **sĕmnŏtēs**, *sem-not'-ace*; from *4586*; *venerableness*, i.e. *probity*:—gravity, honesty.

4588. Σέργιος **Sĕrgiŏs**, *serg'-ee-os*; of Lat. or.; *Sergius*, a Rom.:—Sergius.

4589. Σήθ **Sēth**, *sayth*; of Heb. or. [8352]; *Seth* (i.e. *Sheth*), a patriarch:—Seth.

4590. Σήμ **Sēm**, *same*; of Heb. or. [8035]; *Sem* (i.e. *Shem*), a patriarch:—Sem.

4591. σημαίνω **sēmainō**, *say-mah'ee-no*; from σῆμα **sēma** (a *mark*; of uncert. der.); to *indicate*:—signify.

4592. σημεῖον **sēmĕiŏn**, *say-mi'-on*; neut. of a presumed der. of the base of *4591*; an *indication*, espec. cer. or supernat.:—miracle, sign, token, wonder.

4593. σημειόω **sēmĕiŏō**, *say-mi-ŏ'-o*; from *4592*; to *distinguish*, i.e. *mark* (for avoidance):—note.

4594. σήμερον **sēmĕrŏn**, *say'-mer-on*; neut. (as adv.) of a presumed comp. of the art. *3588* (τ changed to σ) and *2250*; on the (i.e. *this*) *day* (or *night* current or just passed); gen. *now* (i.e. at present, hitherto):—this (to-) day.

4595. σήπω **sēpō**, *say'-po*; appar. a prim. verb; to *putrefy*, i.e. (fig.) *perish*:—be corrupted.

4596. σηρικός **sērikŏs**, *say-ree-kos'*; from Σήρ **Sēr** (an Indian tribe from whom *silk* was procured; hence the name of the *silk-worm*); *Seric*, i.e. *silken* (neut. as noun, a *silky* fabric):—silk.

4597. σής **sēs**, *sace*; appar. of Heb. or. [5580], a *moth*:—moth.

4598. σητόβρωτος **sētŏbrŏtŏs**, *say-tob'-ro-tos*; from *4597* and a der. of *977*; *moth-eaten*:—motheaten.

4599. σθενόω **sthĕnŏō**, *sthen-ŏ'-o*; from σθένος **sthĕnŏs** (bodily *vigor*; prob. akin to the base of *2476*); to *strengthen*, i.e. (fig.) *confirm* (in spiritual knowledge and power):—strengthen.

4600. σιαγών **siagōn**, *see-ag-one'*; of uncert. der.; the *jaw-bone*, i.e. (by impl.) the *cheek* or side of the face:—cheek.

4601. σιγάω **sigaō**, *see-gah'-o*; from *4602*; to *keep silent* (trans. or intrans.):—keep close (secret, silence), hold peace.

4602. σιγή **sigē**, *see-gay'*; appar. from σίζω **sizō** (to *hiss*, i.e. *hist* or *hush*); *silence*:—silence. Comp. *4623*.

4603. σιδήρεος **sidērĕŏs**, *sid-ay'-reh-os*; from *4604*; made of *iron*:—(of) iron.

4604. σίδηρος **sidērŏs**, *sid'-ay-ros*; of uncert. der.; *iron*:—iron.

4605. Σιδών **Sidōn**, *sid-one'*; of Heb. or. [6721]; *Sidon* (i.e. *Tsidon*), a place in Pal.:—Sidon.

4606. Σιδώνιος **Sidōniŏs**, *sid-o'-nee-os*; from *4605*; a *Sidonian*, i.e. inhab. of Sidon:—of Sidon.

4607. σικάριος **sikariŏs**, *sik-ar'-ee-os*; of Lat. or.; a *dagger-man* or *assassin*; a *freebooter* (Jewish *fanatic* outlawed by the Romans):—murderer. Comp. *5406*.

4608. σίκερα **sikĕra**, *sik'-er-ah*; of Heb. or. [7941]; an *intoxicant*, i.e. intensely fermented *liquor*:—strong drink.

4609. Σίλας **Silas**, *see'-las*; contr. for *4610*; *Silas*, a Chr.:—Silas.

4610. Σιλουανός **Silŏuanŏs**, *sil-oo-an-os'*; of Lat. or.; "*silvan*;" *Silvanus*, a Chr.:—Silvanus. Comp. *4609*.

4611. Σιλωάμ **Silōam**, *sil-o-am'*; of Heb. or. [7975]; *Siloäm* (i.e. *Shilŏäch*), a pool of Jerus.:—Siloam.

4612. σιμικίνθιον **simikinthiŏn**, *sim-ee-kin'-thee-on*; of Lat. or.; a *semicinctium* or *half-girding*, i.e. narrow covering (*apron*):—apron.

4613. Σίμων **Simōn**, *see'-mone*; of Heb. or. [8095]; *Simon* (i.e. *Shimon*), the name of nine Isr.:—Simon. Comp. *4826*.

4614. Σινᾶ **Sina**, *see-nah'*; of Heb. or. [5514]; *Sina* (i.e. *Sinai*), a mountain in Arabia:—Sina.

4615. σίναπι **sinapi**, *sin'-ap-ee*; perh. from σίνομαι **sinŏmai** (to *hurt*, i.e. *sting*); *mustard* (the plant):—mustard.

4616. σινδών **sindōn**, *sin-done'*; of uncert. (perh. for.) or.; *byssos*, i.e. bleached *linen* (the cloth or a garment of it):—(fine) linen (cloth).

4617. σινιάζω **siniazō**, *sin-ee-ad'-zo*; from σινίον **siniŏn** (a *sieve*); to *riddle* (fig.):—sift.

σίτα **sita**. See *4621*.

4618. σιτευτός **sitĕutŏs**, *sit-yoo-tos'*; from a der. of *4621*; *grain-fed*, i.e. *fattened*:—fatted.

4619. σιτιστός **sitistŏs**, *sit-is-tos'*; from a der. of *4621*; *grained*, i.e. *fatted*:—fatling.

4620. σιτόμετρον **sitŏmĕtrŏn**, *sit-om'-et-ron*; from *4621* and *3358*; a *grain-measure*, i.e. (by impl.) *ration* (*allowance* of food):—portion of meat.

4621. σῖτος **sitŏs**, *see'-tos*; plur. irreg. neut. σῖτα **sita**, *see'-tah*; of uncert. der.; *grain*, espec. *wheat*:—corn, wheat.

4622. Σιών **Siōn**, *see-own'*; of Heb. or. [6726]; *Sion* (i.e. *Tsijon*), a hill of Jerus.; fig. the *Church* (militant or triumphant):—Sion.

4623. σιωπάω **siōpaō**, *see-o-pah'-o*; from σιωπή **siōpē** (*silence*, i.e. a *hush*; prop. *muteness*, i.e. *involuntary* stillness, or *inability* to speak; and thus differing from *4602*, which is rather a *voluntary refusal* or *indisposition* to speak, although the terms are often used synonymously); to *be dumb* (but not *deaf* also, like *2974* prop.) fig. to *be calm* (as *quiet water*):—dumb, (hold) peace.

4624. σκανδαλίζω **skandalizō**, *skan-dal-id'-zo* ("*scandalize*"); from *4625*; to *entrap*, i.e. *trip up* (fig. *stumble* [trans.] or *entice* to sin, apostasy or displeasure):—(make to) offend.

4625. σκάνδαλον **skandalŏn**, *skan'-dal-on* ("*scandal*"); prob. from a der. of *2578*; a *trap-stick* (*bent* sapling), i.e. *snare* (fig. *cause* of displeasure or sin):—occasion to fall (of stumbling), offence, thing that offends, stumblingblock.

4626. σκάπτω **skaptō**, *skap'-to*; appar. a prim. verb; to *dig*:—dig.

4627. σκάφη **skaphē**, *skaf'-ay*; a "*skiff*" (as if *dug* out), or *yawl* (carried aboard a large vessel for landing):—boat.

4628. σκέλος **skĕlŏs**, *skel'-os*; appar. from σκέλλω **skĕllō** (to *parch*; through the idea of *leanness*); the *leg* (as *lank*):—leg.

4629. σκέπασμα **skĕpasma**, *skep'-as-mah*; from a der. of σκέπας **skĕpas** (a *covering*; perh. akin to the base of *4649* through the idea of *noticeableness*); *clothing*:—raiment.

4630. Σκευᾶς **Skĕuas**, *skyoo-as'*; appar. of Lat. or.; *left-handed*; *Scevas* (i.e. *Scœvus*), an Isr.:—Sceva.

4631. σκευή **skĕuē**, *skyoo-ay'*; from *4632*; *furniture*, i.e. spare *tackle*:—tackling.

4632. σκεῦος **skĕuŏs**, *skyoo'-os*; of uncert. affin.; a *vessel*, *implement*, *equipment* or *apparatus* (lit. or fig. [spec. a *wife* as contributing to the usefulness of the husband]):—goods, sail, stuff, vessel.

4633. σκηνή **skēnē**, *skay-nay'*; appar. akin to *4632* and *4639*; a *tent* or cloth hut (lit. or fig.):—habitation, tabernacle.

4634. σκηνοπηγία **skēnŏpēgia**, *skay-nop-ayg-ee'-ah*; from *4636* and *4078*; the *Festival of Tabernacles* (so called from the custom of erecting booths for temporary homes):—tabernacles.

4635. σκηνοποιός **skēnŏpŏiŏs**, *skay-nop-oy-os'*; from *4633* and *4160*; a *manufacturer of tents*:—tentmaker.

4636. σκῆνος **skēnŏs**, *skay'-nos*; from *4633*; a *hut* or temporary residence, i.e. (fig.) the human *body* (as the abode of the spirit):—tabernacle.

4637. σκηνόω **skēnŏō**, *skay-nŏ'-o*; from *4636*; to *tent* or *encamp*, i.e. (fig.) to *occupy* (as a mansion) or (spec.) to *reside* (as God did in the Tabernacle of old, a symbol of protection and communion):—dwell.

4638. σκήνωμα **skēnōma**, *skay'-no-mah*; from *4637*; an *encampment*, i.e. (fig.) the *Temple* (as God's residence), the *body* (as a tenement for the soul):—tabernacle.

4639. σκία **skia**, *skee'-ah*; appar. a prim. word; "*shade*" or a shadow (lit. or fig. [darkness of *error* or an *adumbration*]):—shadow.

4640. σκιρτάω **skirtaō**, *skeer-tah'-o*; akin to σκαίρω **skairō** (to *skip*); to *jump*, i.e. sympathetically *move* (as the *quickening* of a *fœtus*):—leap (for joy).

4641. σκληροκαρδία **sklērŏkardia**, *sklay-rok-ar-dee'-ah*; fem. of a comp. of *4642* and *2588*; *hardheartedness*, i.e. (spec.) *destitution of* (spiritual) *perception*:—hardness of heart.

4642. σκληρός **sklērŏs**, *sklay-ros'*; from the base of *4628*; *dry*, i.e. *hard* or *tough* (fig. *harsh*, *severe*):—fierce, hard.

4643. σκληρότης **sklērŏtēs**, *sklay-rot'-ace*; from *4642*; *callousness*, i.e. (fig.) *stubbornness*:—hardness.

4644. σκληροτράχηλος **sklērŏtrachēlŏs**, *sklay-rot-rakh'-ay-los*; from *4642* and *5137*; *hardnaped*, i.e. (fig.) *obstinate*:—stiffnecked.

4645. σκληρύνω **sklērunō**, *sklay-roo'-no*; from *4642*; to *indurate*, i.e. (fig.) *render stubborn*:—harden.

4646. σκολιός **skŏliŏs**, *skol-ee-os'*; from the base of *4628*; *warped*, i.e. *winding*; fig. *perverse*:—crooked, froward, untoward.

4647. σκόλοψ **skŏlŏps**, *skol'-ops*; perh. from the base of *4628* and *3700*; *withered* at the *front*, i.e. a *point* or *prickle* (fig. a *bodily annoyance* or *disability*):—thorn.

4648. σκοπέω **skŏpĕō**, *skop-eh'-o*; from *4649*; to *take aim* at (*spy*), i.e. (fig.) *regard*:—consider, take heed, look at (on), mark. Comp. *3700*.

4649. σκοπός **skŏpŏs**, *skop-os'* ("*scope*"); from σκέπτομαι **skĕptŏmai** (to *peer about* ["*skeptic*"]; perh. akin to *4626* through the idea of *concealment*; comp. *4629*); a *watch* (*sentry* or *scout*), i.e. (by impl.) a *goal*:—mark.

4650. σκορπίζω **skŏrpizō**, *skor-pid'-zo*; appar. from the same as *4651* (through the idea of *penetrating*); to *dissipate*, i.e. (fig.) *put to flight*, *waste*, be *liberal*:—disperse abroad, scatter (abroad).

4651. σκορπίος **skŏrpiŏs**, *skor-pee'-os*; prob. from an obsol. σκέρπω **skĕrpō** (perh. strengthened from the base of *4649* and mean. to *pierce*); a "*scorpion*" (from its *sting*):—scorpion.

4652. σκοτεινός **skŏtĕinŏs**, *skot-i-nos'*; from *4655*; *opaque*, i.e. (fig.) *benighted*:—dark, full of darkness.

4653. σκοτία **skŏtia**, *skot-ee'-ah*; from *4655*; *dimness*, *obscurity* (lit. or fig.):—dark (-ness).

4654. σκοτίζω **skŏtizō**, *skot-id-zo*; from *4655*; to *obscure* (lit. or fig.):—darken.

4655. σκότος **skŏtŏs**, *skot'-os*; from the base of *4639*; *shadiness*, i.e. *obscurity* (lit. or fig.):—darkness.

4656. σκοτόω **skŏtŏō**, *skot-ŏ'-o*; from *4655*; to *obscure* or *blind* (lit. or fig.):—be full of darkness.

4657. σκύβαλον **skubalŏn**, *skoo'-bal-on*; neut. of a presumed der. of *1519* and *2965* and *906*; what is *thrown to the dogs*, i.e. *refuse* (*ordure*):—dung.

4658. Σκύθης **Skuthēs**, *skoo'-thace*; prob. of for. or.; a *Scythene* or *Scythian*, i.e. (by impl.) a *savage*:—Scythian.

4659. σκυθρωπός **skuthrōpŏs**, *skoo-thro-pos'*; from σκυθρός **skuthrŏs** (*sullen*) and a der. of *3700*; *angry-visaged*, i.e. *gloomy* or affecting a *mournful* appearance:—of a sad countenance.

4660. σκύλλω **skullō**, *skool'-lo*; appar. a prim. verb; to *flay*, i.e. (fig.) to *harass*:—trouble (self).

4661. σκῦλον **skulŏn**, *skoo'-lon*; neut. from *4660*; something *stripped* (as a *hide*), i.e. *booty*:—spoil.

4662. σκωληκόβρωτος **skōlēkŏbrōtŏs**, *sko-lay-kob'-ro-tos*; from *4663* and a der. of *977*; *worm-eaten*, i.e. *diseased with maggots*:—eaten of worms.

4663. σκώληξ **skōlēx**, *sko'-lakes;* of uncert. der.; a *grub,* maggot or earth-worm:—worm.

4664. σμαράγδινος **smaragdinŏs**, *smar-ag'-dee-nos;* from *4665;* consisting of emerald:—emerald.

4665. σμάραγδος **smaragdŏs**, *smar'-ag-dos;* of uncert. der.; the *emerald* or green gem so called:—emerald.

4666. σμύρνα **smurna**, *smoor'-nah;* appar. strengthened for *3464;* myrrh:—myrrh.

4667. Σμύρνα **Smurna**, *smoor'-nah;* the same as *4666; Smyrna,* a place in Asia Minor:—Smyrna.

4668. Σμυρναῖος **Smurnaiŏs**, *smoor-nah'-yos;* from *4667;* a *Smyrnœan:*—in Smyrna.

4669. σμυρνίζω **smurnizō**, *smoor-nid'-zo;* from *4667;* to *tincture with myrrh,* i.e. *embitter* (as a narcotic):—mingle with myrrh.

4670. Σόδομα **Sŏdŏma**, *sod'-om-ah;* plur. of Heb. or. [5467]; *Sodoma* (i.e. *Sedom*), a place in Pal.:—Sodom.

4671. σοί **sŏi**, *soy;* dat. of *4771;* to *thee:*—thee, thine own, thou, thy.

4672. Σολομών or Σολομῶν **Sŏlŏmōn**, *sol-om-one';* of Heb. or. [8010]; *Solomon* (i.e. *Shelomoh*), the son of David:—Solomon.

4673. σορός **sŏrŏs**, *sor-os';* prob. akin to the base of *4987;* a *funereal receptacle* (urn, coffin), i.e. (by anal.) a *bier:*—bier.

4674. σός **sŏs**, *sos;* from *4771; thine:*—thine (own), thy (friend).

4675. σοῦ **sŏu**, *soo;* gen. of *4771; of thee, thy:*—× home, thee, thine (own), thou, thy.

4676. σουδάριον **sŏudariŏn**, *soo-dar'-ee-on;* of Lat. or.; a *sudarium* (sweat-cloth), i.e. *towel* (for wiping the perspiration from the face, or binding the face of a corpse):—handkerchief, napkin.

4677. Σουσάννα **Sŏusanna**, *soo-san'-nah;* of Heb. or. [7799 fem.]; *lily; Susannah* (i.e. *Shoshannah*), an Israelitess:—Susanna.

4678. σοφία **sŏphia**, *sof-ee'-ah;* from *4680; wisdom* (higher or lower, worldly or spiritual):—wisdom.

4679. σοφίζω **sŏphizō**, *sof-id'-zo;* from *4680;* to *render wise;* in a sinister acceptation, to *form* "sophisms", i.e. *continue plausible error:*—cunningly devised, make wise.

4680. σοφός **sŏphŏs**, *sof-os';* akin to σαφής **saphēs** (clear); *wise* (in a most gen. application):—wise. Comp. *5429.*

4681. Σπανία **Spania**, *span-ee'-ah;* prob. of for. or.; *Spania,* a region of Europe:—Spain.

4682. σπαράσσω **sparassō**, *spar-as'-so;* prol. from σπαίρω **spairō** (to *gasp;* appar. strengthened from *4685* through the idea of *spasmodic* contraction); to *mangle,* i.e. *convulse* with epilepsy:—rend, tear.

4683. σπαργανόω **sparganŏō**, *spar-gan-ŏ'-o;* from σπάργανον **sparganŏn** (a *strip;* from a der. of the base of *4682* mean. to *strap* or *wrap* with strips); to *swathe* (an infant after the Oriental custom):—wrap in swaddling clothes.

4684. σπαταλάω **spatalaō**, *spat-al-ah'-o;* from σπατάλη **spatalē** (luxury); to *be voluptuous:*—live in pleasure, be wanton.

4685. σπάω **spaō**, *spah'-o;* a prim. verb; to *draw:*—draw (out).

4686. σπεῖρα **speira**, *spi'-rah;* of immed. Lat. or., but ultimately a der. of *138* in the sense of its cogn. *1507;* a *coil* (spira, "spire"), i.e. (fig.) a *mass* of men (a Rom. military *cohort;* also [by anal.] a *squad* of Levitical janitors):—band.

4687. σπείρω **speirō**, *spi'-ro;* prob. strengthened from *4685* (through the idea of *extending*); to *scatter,* i.e. *sow* (lit. or fig.):—sow (-er), receive seed.

4688. σπεκουλάτωρ **spĕkŏulatŏr**, *spek-oo-lat'-ore;* of Lat. or.; a *speculator,* i.e. *military scout* (spy or [by extens.] *life-guardsman*):—executioner.

4689. σπένδω **spĕndō**, *spen'-do;* appar. a prim. verb; to *pour out* as a libation, i.e. (fig.) to *devote* (one's life or blood, as a *sacrifice*) ("spend"):—(be ready to) be offered.

4690. σπέρμα **spĕrma**, *sper'-mah;* from *4687;* something *sown,* i.e. *seed* (includ. the male "sperm"); by impl. *offspring,* spec. a *remnant* (fig. as if kept over for planting):—issue, seed.

4691. σπερμολόγος **spĕrmŏlŏgŏs**, *sper-mol-og'-os;* from *4690* and *3004;* a *seed-picker* (as the crow), i.e. (fig.) a *sponger, loafer* (spec. a *gossip* or *trifler* in talk):—babbler.

4692. σπεύδω **spĕudō**, *spyoo'-do;* prob. strengthened from *4228;* to "speed" ("study"), i.e. *urge on* (diligently or earnestly); by impl. to *await eagerly:*—(make, with) haste unto.

4693. σπήλαιον **spēlaiŏn**, *spay'-lah-yon;* neut. of a presumed der. of σπέος **spĕŏs** (a *grotto*); a *cavern;* by impl. a *hiding-place* or *resort:*—cave, den.

4694. σπιλάς **spilas**, *spee-las';* of uncert. der.; a *ledge* or *reef* of rock in the sea:—spot [by confusion with *4696*].

4695. σπιλόω **spilŏō**, *spee-lŏ'-o;* from *4696;* to *stain* or *soil* (lit. or fig.):—defile, spot.

4696. σπίλος **spilŏs**, *spee'-los;* of uncert. der.; a *stain* or *blemish,* i.e. (fig.) *defect, disgrace:*—spot.

4697. σπλαγχνίζομαι **splagchnizŏmai**, *splangkh-nid'-zom-ahee;* mid. from *4698;* to have the *bowels yearn,* i.e. (fig.) *feel sympathy,* to *pity:*—have (be moved with) compassion.

4698. σπλάγχνον **splagchnŏn**, *splangkh'-non;* prob. strengthened from σπλήν **splēn** (the "spleen"); an *intestine* (plur.); fig. *pity* or *sympathy:*—bowels, inward affection, + tender mercy.

4699. σπόγγος **spŏggŏs**, *spong'-gos;* perh. of for. or.; a "sponge":—spunge.

4700. σπόδος **spŏdŏs**, *spod-os';* of uncert. der.; *ashes:*—ashes.

4701. σπορά **spŏra**, *spor-ah';* from *4687;* a *sowing,* i.e. (by impl.) *parentage:*—seed.

4702. σπόριμος **spŏrimŏs**, *spor'-ee-mos;* from *4703;* sown, i.e. (neut. plur.) a planted *field:*—corn (-field).

4703. σπόρος **spŏrŏs**, *spor'-os;* from *4687;* a *scattering* (of seed), i.e. (concr.) *seed* (as sown):—seed (× sown).

4704. σπουδάζω **spŏudazō**, *spoo-dad'-zo;* from *4710;* to *use speed,* i.e. to *make effort, be prompt* or *earnest:*—do (give) diligence, be diligent (forward), endeavour, labour, study.

4705. σπουδαῖος **spŏudaiŏs**, *spoo-dah'-yos;* from *4710;* prompt, energetic, earnest:—diligent.

4706. σπουδαιότερον **spŏudaiŏtĕrŏn**, *spoo-dah-yot'-er-on;* neut. of *4707* as adv.; more earnestly than others, i.e. very promptly:—very diligently.

4707. σπουδαιότερος **spŏudaiŏtĕrŏs**, *spoo-dah-yot'-er-os;* compar. of *4705;* more prompt, more earnest:—more diligent (forward).

4708. σπουδαιοτέρως **spŏudaiŏtĕrōs**, *spoo-dah-yot-er'-oce;* adv. from *4707;* more speedily, i.e. sooner than otherwise:—more carefully.

4709. σπουδαίως **spŏudaiōs**, *spoo-dah'-yoce;* adv. from *4705;* earnestly, promptly:—diligently, instantly.

4710. σπουδή **spŏudē**, *spoo-day';* from *4692;* "speed", i.e. (by impl.) *despatch, eagerness, earnestness:*—business, (earnest) care (-fulness), diligence, forwardness, haste.

4711. σπυρίς **spuris**, *spoo-rece';* from *4687* (as *woven*); a *hamper* or *lunch-receptacle:*—basket.

4712. στάδιον **stadiŏn**, *stad'-ee-on;* or masc. (in plur.) στάδιος **stadiŏs**, *stad'-ee-os;* from the base of *2476* (as *fixed*); a *stade* or certain measure of distance; by impl. a *stadium* or *race-course:*—furlong, race.

4713. στάμνος **stamnŏs**, *stam'-nos;* from the base of *2476* (as *stationary*); a *jar* or earthen *tank:*—pot.

4714. στάσις **stasis**, *stas'-is;* from the base of *2476;* a *standing* (prop. the act), i.e. (by anal.) *position* (existence); by impl. a popular *uprising;* fig. *controversy:*—dissension, insurrection, × standing, uproar.

4715. στατήρ **statēr**, *stat-air';* from the base or *2746;* a *stander* (standard of value), i.e. (spec.) a *stater* or certain coin:—piece of money.

4716. σταυρός **staurŏs**, *stŏw-ros';* from the base of *2476;* a *stake* or *post* (as set upright), i.e. (spec.) a *pole* or *cross* (as an instrument of capital punishment); fig. *exposure to death,* i.e. *self-denial;* by impl. the *atonement* of Christ:—cross.

4717. σταυρόω **staurŏō**, *stŏw-rŏ'-o;* from *4716;* to *impale* on the cross; fig. to *extinguish* (subdue) passion or selfishness:—crucify.

4718. σταφυλή **staphulē**, *staf-oo-lay';* prob. from the base of *4735;* a *cluster* of grapes (as if *intertwined*):—grapes.

4719. στάχυς **stachus**, *stakh'-oos;* from the base of *2476;* a *head* of grain (as *standing out* from the stalk):—ear (of corn).

4720. Στάχυς **Stachus**, *stakh'-oos;* the same as *4719; Stachys,* a Chr.:—Stachys.

4721. στέγη **stĕgē**, *steg'-ay;* strengthened from a prim. τέγος **tĕgŏs** (a "thatch" or "deck" of a building); a *roof:*—roof.

4722. στέγω **stĕgō**, *steg'-o;* from *4721;* to *roof* over, i.e. (fig.) to *cover* with silence (endure patiently):—(for-) bear, suffer.

4723. στεῖρος **steirŏs**, *sti'-ros;* a contr. from *4731* (as *stiff* and *unnatural*); "sterile":—barren.

4724. στέλλω **stĕllō**, *stel'-lo;* prob. strengthened from the base of *2476;* prop. to *set fast* ("stall"), i.e. (fig.) to *repress* (reflex. *abstain* from associating with):—avoid, withdraw self.

4725. στέμμα **stĕmma**, *stem'-mah;* from the base of *4735;* a *wreath* for show:—garland.

4726. στεναγμός **stĕnagmŏs**, *sten-ag-mos';* from *4727;* a *sigh:*—groaning.

4727. στενάζω **stĕnazō**, *sten-ad'-zo;* from *4728;* to *make* (intrans. be) *in straits,* i.e. (by impl.) to *sigh, murmur, pray* inaudibly:—with grief, groan, grudge, sigh.

4728. στενός **stĕnŏs**, *sten-os';* prob. from the base of *2476; narrow* (from obstacles *standing* close about):—strait.

4729. στενοχωρέω **stĕnŏchōrĕō**, *sten-okh-o-reh'-o;* from the same as *4730;* to *hem* in closely, i.e. (fig.) *cramp:*—distress, straiten.

4730. στενοχωρία **stĕnŏchōria**, *sten-okh-o-ree'-ah;* from a comp. of *4728* and *5561; narrowness* of room, i.e. (fig.) *calamity:*—anguish, distress.

4731. στερεός **stĕrĕŏs**, *ster-eh-os';* from *2476; stiff,* i.e. *solid, stable* (lit. or fig.):—stedfast, strong, sure.

4732. στερεόω **stĕrĕŏō**, *ster-eh-ŏ'-o;* from *4731;* to *solidify,* i.e. *confirm* (lit. or fig.):—establish, receive strength, make strong.

4733. στερέωμα **stĕrĕōma**, *ster-eh'-o-mah;* from *4732;* something *established,* i.e. (abstr.) *confirmation* (stability):—stedfastness.

4734. Στεφανᾶς **Stĕphanas**, *stef-an-as';* prob. contr. for στεφανωτός **stĕphanōtŏs** (crowned; from *4737*); *Stephanas,* a Chr.:—Stephanas.

4735. στέφανος **stĕphanŏs**, *stef-an-os';* from an appar. prim. στέφω **stĕphō** (to *twine* or *wreathe*); a *chaplet* (as a badge of royalty, a prize in the public games or a symbol of honor gen.; but more conspicuous and elaborate than the simple *fillet, 1238*), lit. or fig.:—crown.

4736. Στέφανος **Stĕphanŏs**, *stef'-an-os;* the same as *4735; Stephanus,* a Chr.:—Stephen.

4737. στεφανόω **stĕphanŏō**, *stef-an-ŏ'-o;* from *4735;* to *adorn with* an honorary *wreath* (lit. or fig.):—crown.

4738. στῆθος **stēthŏs**, *stay'-thos;* from *2476* (as *standing* prominently); the (entire extern.) *bosom,* i.e. *chest:*—breast.

4739. στήκω **stēkō**, *stay'-ko;* from the perf. tense of *2476;* to *be stationary,* i.e. (fig.) to *persevere:*—stand (fast).

4740. στηριγμός **stērigmŏs**, *stay-rig-mos';* from *4741; stability* (fig.):—stedfastness.

4741. στηρίζω **stērizō**, *stay-rid'-zo;* from a presumed der. of *2476* (like *4731*); to *set fast,* i.e. (lit.) to *turn resolutely* in a certain direction, or (fig.) to *confirm:*—fix, (e-) stablish, stedfastly set, strengthen.

4742. στίγμα **stigma**, *stig'-mah;* from a prim. στίζω **stizo** (to "*stick*", i.e. *prick*); a *mark* incised or punched (for recognition of ownership), i.e. (fig.) *scar* of service:—mark.

4743. στιγμή **stigmē**, *stig-may';* fem. of *4742;* a *point* of time, i.e. an *instant:*—moment.

4744. στίλβω **stilbō**, *stil'-bo;* appar. a prim. verb; to *gleam,* i.e. *flash* intensely:—shining.

4745. στοά **stŏa**, *stŏ-ah';* prob. from *2476;* a *colonnade* or interior *piazza:*—porch.

4746. στοιβάς **stŏibas**, *stoy-bas';* from a prim. στείβω **stěibō** (to "*step*" or "*stamp*"); a *spread* (as if *tramped flat*) of loose materials for a couch, i.e. (by impl.) a *bough* of a tree so employed:—branch.

4747. στοιχεῖον **stŏichěion**, *stoy-khi'-on;* neut. of a presumed der. of the base of *4748;* something *orderly* in arrangement, i.e. (by impl.) a *serial* (basal, *fundamental, initial*) constituent (lit.), proposition (fig.):—element, principle, rudiment.

4748. στοιχέω **stŏichěō**, *stoy-kheh'-o;* from a der. of στείχω **stěichō** (to *range* in regular line); to *march* in (military) rank (*keep step*), i.e. (fig.) to *conform* to virtue and piety:—walk (orderly).

4749. στολή **stŏlē**, *stol-ay';* from *4724;* equipment, i.e. (spec.) a "*stole*" or long-fitting *gown* (as a mark of dignity):—long clothing (garment), (long) robe.

4750. στόμα **stŏma**, *stom'-a;* prob. strengthened from a presumed der. of the base of *5114;* the *mouth* (as if a *gash* in the face); by impl. *language* (and its relations); fig. an *opening* (in the earth); spec. the *front* or *edge* (of a weapon):—edge, face, mouth.

4751. στόμαχος **stŏmachŏs**, *stom'-akh-os;* from *4750;* an *orifice* (the *gullet*), i.e. (spec.) the "*stomach*":—stomach.

4752. στρατεία **stratěia**, *strat-i'-ah;* from *4754;* military *service,* i.e. (fig.) the apostolic *career* (as one of hardship and danger):—warfare.

4753. στράτευμα **stratěuma**, *strat'-yoo-mah;* from *4754;* an *armament,* i.e. (by impl.) a *body* of *troops* (more or less extensive or comprehensive):—army, soldier, man of war.

4754. στρατεύομαι **stratěuŏmai**, *strat-yoo'-om-ahee;* mid. from the base of *4756;* to *serve* in a military campaign; fig. to *execute* the apostolate (with its arduous duties and functions), to *contend* with carnal inclinations:—soldier, (go to) war (-fare).

4755. στρατηγός **stratēgŏs**, *strat-ay-gos';* from the base of *4756* and *71* or *2233;* a *general,* i.e. (by impl. or anal.) a (military) *governor* (*prætor*), the *chief* (*præfect*) of the (Levitical) temple-wardens:—captain, magistrate.

4756. στρατιά **stratia**, *strat-ee'-ah;* fem. of a der. of *4758;* στρατός **stratŏs** (an *army;* from the base of *4766,* as encamped); *camp-likeness,* i.e. an *army,* i.e. (fig.) the *angels,* the celestial *luminaries:*—host.

4757. στρατιώτης **stratiōtēs**, *strat-ee-o'-tace;* from a presumed der. of the same as *4756;* a *camper-out,* i.e. a (common) *warrior* (lit. or fig.):—soldier.

4758. στρατολογέω **stratŏlŏgěō**, *strat-ol-og-eh'-o;* from a comp. of the base of *4756* and *3004* (in its orig. sense); to *gather* (or *select*) as a *warrior,* i.e. *enlist* in the army:—choose to be a soldier.

4759. στρατοπεδάρχης **stratŏpědarchēs**, *strat-op-ed-ar'-khace;* from *4760* and *757;* a *ruler* of an *army,* i.e. (spec.) a Prætorian *præfect:*—captain of the guard.

4760. στρατόπεδον **stratŏpědŏn**, *strat-op'-ed-on;* from the base of *4756* and the same as *3977;* a *camping-ground,* i.e. (by impl.) a *body* of *troops:*—army.

4761. στρεβλόω **strěblŏō**, *streb-lŏ'-o;* from a der. of *4762;* to *wrench,* i.e. (spec.) to *torture* (by the rack), but only fig. to *pervert:*—wrest.

4762. στρέφω **strěphō**, *stref'-o;* strengthened from the base of *5157;* to *twist,* i.e. *turn* quite around

---

or *reverse* (lit. or fig.):—convert, turn (again, back again, self, self about).

4763. στρηνιάω **strēniaō**, *stray-nee-ah'-o;* from a presumed der. of *4764;* to *be luxurious:*—live deliciously.

4764. στρῆνος **strēnŏs**, *stray'-nos;* akin to *4731;* a "*straining*", "*strenuousness*" or "*strength*", i.e. (fig.) *luxury* (*voluptuousness*):—delicacy.

4765. στρουθίον **strŏuthiŏn**, *stroo-thee'-on;* dimin. of στρουθός **strŏuthŏs** (a *sparrow*); a *little sparrow:*—sparrow.

4766. στρώννυμι **strōnnumi**, *strone'-noo-mee;* or simpler

στρωννύω **strōnnuō**, *strone-noo'-o;* prol. from a still simpler

στρόω **strŏō**, *strŏ'-o* (used only as an alt. in certain tenses; prob. akin to *4731* through the idea of *positing*); to "*strew*", i.e. *spread* (as a carpet or couch):—make bed, furnish, spread, strew.

4767. στυγνητός **stugnětŏs**, *stoog-nay-tos';* from a der. of an obsol. appar. prim. στύγω **stugō** (to *hate*); *hated,* i.e. *odious:*—hateful.

4768. στυγνάζω **stugnazō**, *stoog-nad'-zo;* from the same as *4767;* to *render gloomy,* i.e. (by impl.) *glower* (be overcast with clouds, or *sombreness* of speech):—lower, be sad.

4769. στῦλος **stulŏs**, *stoo'-los;* from στύω **stuō** (to *stiffen;* prob. akin to the base of *2476*); a *post* ("*style*"), i.e. (fig.) *support:*—pillar.

4770. Στωϊκός **Stŏikŏs**, *sto-ik-os';* from *4745;* a "*Stoic*" (as occupying a particular porch in Athens), i.e. adherent of a certain philosophy:—Stoick.

4771. σύ **su**, *soo;* the pers. pron. of the sec. pers. sing.; *thou:*—thou. See also *4571, 4671, 4675;* and for the plur. *5209, 5210, 5213, 5216.*

4772. συγγένεια **suggěněia**, *soong-ghen'-i-ah;* from *4773;* *relationship,* i.e. (concr.) *relatives:*—kindred.

4773. συγγενής **suggěnēs**, *soong-ghen-ace';* from *4862* and *1085;* a *relative* (by blood); by extens. a fellow *countryman:*—cousin, kin (-sfolk, -sman).

4774. συγγνώμη **suggnōmē**, *soong-gno'-may;* from a comp. of *4862* and *1097;* *fellow knowledge,* i.e. *concession:*—permission.

4775. συγκάθημαι **sugkathēmai**, *soong-kath'-ay-mahee;* from *4862* and *2521;* to *seat oneself* in company *with:*—sit with.

4776. συγκαθίζω **sugkathizō**, *soong-kath-id'-zo;* from *4862* and *2523;* to *give* (or *take*) a *seat* in company *with:*—(make) sit (down) together.

4777. συγκακοπαθέω **sugkakŏpathěō**, *soong-kak-op-ath-eh'-o;* from *4862* and *2553;* to *suffer hardship* in company *with:*—be partaker of afflictions.

4778. συγκακουχέω **sugkakŏuchěō**, *soong-kak-oo-kheh'-o;* from *4862* and *2558;* to *maltreat* in company *with,* i.e. (pass.) *endure persecution together:*—suffer affliction with.

4779. συγκαλέω **sugkalěō**, *soong-kal-eh'-o;* from *4862* and *2564;* to *convoke:*—call together.

4780. συγκαλύπτω **sugkaluptō**, *soong-kal-oop'-to;* from *4862* and *2572;* to *conceal altogether:*—cover.

4781. συγκάμπτω **sugkamptō**, *soong-kamp'-to;* from *4862* and *2578;* to *bend together,* i.e. (fig.) to *afflict:*—bow down.

4782. συγκαταβαίνω **sugkatabainō**, *soong-kat-ab-ah'ee-no;* from *4862* and *2597;* to *descend* in company *with:*—go down with.

4783. συγκατάθεσις **sugkatathěsis**, *soong-kat-ath'-es-is;* from *4784;* a *deposition* (of sentiment) in company *with,* i.e. (fig.) *accord with:*—agreement.

4784. συγκατατίθεμαι **sugkatatithěmai**, *soong-kat-at-ith'-em-ahee;* mid. from *4862* and *2698;* to *deposit* (one's vote or opinion) in company *with,* i.e. (fig.) to *accord with:*—consent.

4785. συγκαταψηφίζω **sugkatapsēphizō**, *soong-kat-aps-ay-fid'-zo;* from *4862* and a comp. of *2506* and *5585;* to *count down* in company *with,* i.e. *enroll among:*—number with.

4786. συγκεράννυμι **sugkěrannumi**, *soong-ker-an'-noo-mee;* from *4862* and *2767;* to *commingle,*

---

i.e. (fig.) to *combine* or *assimilate:*—mix with, temper together.

4787. συγκινέω **sugkiněō**, *soong-kin-eh'-o;* from *4862* and *2795;* to *move together,* i.e. (spec.) to *excite* as a mass (to sedition):—stir up.

4788. συγκλείω **sugklěiō**, *soong-kli'-o;* from *4862* and *2808;* to *shut together,* i.e. *include* or (fig.) *embrace* in a common subjection to:—conclude, inclose, shut up.

4789. συγκληρονόμος **sugklērŏnŏmŏs**, *soong-klay-ron-om'-os;* from *4862* and *2818;* a *co-heir,* i.e. (by anal.) *participant* in *common:*—fellow (joint) -heir, heir together, heir with.

4790. συγκοινωνέω **sugkŏinōněō**, *soong-koy-no-neh'-o;* from *4862* and *2841;* to *share* in company *with,* i.e. *co-participate* in:—communicate (have fellowship) with, be partaker of.

4791. συγκοινωνός **sugkŏinōnŏs**, *soong-koy-no-nos';* from *4862* and *2844;* a *co-participant:*—companion, partake (-r, -r with).

4792. συγκομίζω **sugkŏmizō**, *soong-kom-id'-zo;* from *4862* and *2865;* to *convey together,* i.e. *collect* or *bear away* in company *with* others:—carry.

4793. συγκρίνω **sugkrinō**, *soong-kree'-no;* from *4862* and *2919;* to *judge* of one thing in connection *with* another, i.e. *combine* (spiritual ideas with appropriate expressions) or *collate* (one person with another by way of contrast or resemblance):—compare among (with).

4794. συγκύπτω **sugkuptō**, *soong-koop'-to;* from *4862* and *2955;* to *stoop altogether,* i.e. *be completely overcome* by:—bow together.

4795. συγκυρία **sugkuria**, *soong-koo-ree'-ah;* from a comp. of *4862* and κυρέω **kurěō** (to *light* or *happen;* from the base of *2962*); *concurrence,* i.e. *accident:*—chance.

4796. συγχαίρω **sugchairō**, *soong-khah'ee-ro;* from *4862* and *5463;* to *sympathize* in gladness, *congratulate:*—rejoice in (with).

4797. συγχέω **sugchěō**, *soong-kheh'-o;* or

συγχύνω **sugchunō**, *soong-khoo'-no;* from *4862* and χέω **chěō** (to *pour*) or its alt.; to *commingle* promiscuously, i.e. (fig.) to *throw* (an assembly) *into disorder,* to *perplex* (the mind):—confound, confuse, stir up, be in an uproar.

4798. συγχράομαι **sugchraŏmai**, *soong-khrah'-om-ahee;* from *4862* and *5530;* to *use jointly,* i.e. (by impl.) to *hold intercourse* in common:—have dealings with.

4799. σύγχυσις **sugchusis**, *soong'-khoo-sis;* from *4797;* *commixture,* i.e. (fig.) *riotous disturbance:*—confusion.

4800. συζάω **suzaō**, *sood-zah'-o;* from *4862* and *2198;* to *continue* to *live* in common *with,* i.e. *co-survive* (lit. or fig.):—live with.

4801. συζεύγνυμι **suzěugnumi**, *sood-zyoog'-noo-mee;* from *4862* and the base of *2201;* to *yoke together,* i.e. (fig.) *conjoin* (in marriage):—join together.

4802. συζητέω **suzētěō**, *sood-zay-teh'-o;* from *4862* and *2212;* to *investigate jointly,* i.e. *discuss,* *controvert, cavil:*—dispute (with), enquire, question (with), reason (together).

4803. συζήτησις **suzētēsis**, *sood-zay'-tay-sis;* from *4802;* *mutual questioning,* i.e. *discussion:*—disputation (-ting), reasoning.

4804. συζητητής **suzētētēs**, *sood-zay-tay-tace';* from *4802;* a *disputant,* i.e. *sophist:*—disputer.

4805. σύζυγος **suzugŏs**, *sood'-zoo-gos;* from *4801;* *co-yoked,* i.e. (fig.) as noun, a *colleague;* prob. rather as prop. name; *Syzygus,* a Chr.:—yokefellow.

4806. συζωοποιέω **suzōŏpŏiěō**, *sood-zo-op-oy-eh'-o;* from *4862* and *2227;* to *reanimate conjointly* with (fig.):—quicken together with.

4807. συκάμινος **sukaminŏs**, *soo-kam'-ee-nos;* of Heb. or. [8256] in imitation of *4809;* a *sycamore-fig* tree:—sycamine tree.

4808. συκῆ **sukē**, *soo-kay';* from *4810;* a *fig-tree:*—fig tree.

4809. συκομωραία **sukŏmōraia**, *soo-kom-o-rah'-yah;* from *4810* and μόρον **mŏrŏn** (the *mul-*

berry); the "*sycamore*"-fig tree:—sycamore tree. Comp. *4807.*

4810. σῦκον **sukŏn**, *soo'-kon;* appar. a prim. word; a *fig:*—fig.

4811. συκοφαντέω **sukŏphantĕō**, *soo-kof-an-teh'-o;* from a comp. of *4810* and a der. of *5316;* to be a *fig-informer* (reporter of the law forbidding the exportation of figs from Greece), "*sycophant*", i.e. (gen. and by extens.) to *defraud* (exact unlawfully, *extort*):—accuse falsely, take by false accusation.

4812. συλαγωγέω **sulagŏgĕō**, *soo-lag-ogue-eh'-o;* from the base of *4813* and (the redupl. form of) *71;* to *lead* away as booty, i.e. (fig.) *seduce:*—spoil.

4813. συλάω **sulaō**, *soo-lah'-o;* from a der. of σύλλω **sullō** (to *strip;* prob. akin to *138;* comp. *4661*); to *despoil:*—rob.

4814. συλλαλέω **sullalĕō**, *sool-lal-eh'-o;* from *4862* and *2980;* to *talk together*, i.e. *converse:*—commune (confer, talk) with, speak among.

4815. συλλαμβάνω **sullambanō**, *sool-lam-ban'-o;* from *4862* and *2983;* to *clasp*, i.e. *seize* (arrest, *capture*); spec. to *conceive* (lit. or fig.); by impl. to *aid:*—catch, conceive, help, take.

4816. συλλέγω **sullĕgō**, *sool-leg'-o;* from *4862* and *3004* in its orig. sense; to *collect:*—gather (together, up).

4817. συλλογίζομαι **sullŏgizŏmai**, *sool-log-id'-zom-ahee;* from *4862* and *3049;* to *reckon together* (with oneself), i.e. *deliberate:*—reason with.

4818. συλλυπέω **sullupĕō**, *sool-loop-eh'-o;* from *4862* and *3076;* to *afflict jointly*, i.e. (pass.) *sorrow at* (on account of) some one:—be grieved.

4819. συμβαίνω **sumbainō**, *soom-bah'ee-no;* from *4862* and the base of *939;* to *walk* (fig. transpire) *together*, i.e. *concur* (take place):—be (-fall), happen (unto).

4820. συμβάλλω **sumballō**, *soom-bal'-lo;* from *4862* and *906;* to *combine*, i.e. (in speaking) to *converse*, *consult*, *dispute*, (mentally) to *consider*, (by impl.) to *aid*, (personally) to *join*, *attack:*—confer, encounter, help, make, meet with, ponder.

4821. συμβασιλεύω **sumbasilĕuō**, *soom-bas-il-yoo'-o;* from *4862* and *936;* to *be co-regent* (fig.):—reign with.

4822. συμβιβάζω **sumbibazō**, *soom-bib-ad'-zo;* from *4862* and βιβάζω **bibazō** (to *force;* caus. [by redupl.] of the base of *939*); to *drive together*, i.e. *unite* (in association or affection), (mentally) to *infer*, *show*, *teach:*—compact, assuredly gather, instruct, knit together, prove.

4823. συμβουλεύω **sumbŏulĕuō**, *soom-bool-yoo'-o;* from *4862* and *1011;* to *give* (or take) *advice jointly*, i.e. *recommend*, *deliberate* or *determine:*—consult, (give, take) counsel (together).

4824. συμβούλιον **sumbŏuliŏn**, *soom-boo'-lee-on;* neut. of a presumed der. of *4825;* *advisement;* spec. a *deliberative body*, i.e. the provincial assessors or lay-court:—consultation, counsel, council.

4825. σύμβουλος **sumbŏulŏs**, *soom'-boo-los;* from *4862* and *1012;* a *consultor*, i.e. *adviser:*—counsellor.

4826. Συμεών **Sumĕŏn**, *soom-eh-one';* from the same as *4613;* *Symeon* (i.e. *Shimon*), the name of five Isr.:—Simeon, Simon.

4827. συμμαθητής **summathĕtēs**, *soom-math-ay-tace';* from a comp. of *4862* and *3129;* a *co-learner* (of Christianity):—fellowdisciple.

4828. συμμαρτυρέω **summarturĕō**, *soom-mar-too-reh'-o;* from *4862* and *3140;* to *testify jointly*, i.e. *corroborate* by (concurrent) evidence:—testify unto, (also) bear witness (with).

4829. συμμερίζομαι **summĕrizŏmai**, *soom-mer-id'-zom-ahee;* mid. from *4862* and *3307;* to *share jointly*, i.e. *participate in:*—be partaker with.

4830. συμμέτοχος **summĕtŏchŏs**, *soom-met'-okh-os;* from *4862* and *3353;* a *co-participant:*—partaker.

4831. συμμιμητής **summimētēs**, *soom-mim-ay-tace';* from a presumed comp. of *4862* and *3401;* a *co-imitator*, i.e. *fellow votary:*—follower together.

4832. συμμορφός **summŏrphŏs**, *soom-mor-fos';* from *4862* and *3444;* *jointly formed*, i.e. (fig.) *similar:*—conformed to, fashioned like unto.

4833. συμμορφόω **summŏrphŏō**, *soom-mor-fŏ'-o;* from *4832;* to *render like*, i.e. (fig.) to *assimilate:*—make conformable unto.

4834. συμπαθέω **sumpathĕō**, *soom-path-eh'-o;* from *4835;* to *feel* "*sympathy*" with, i.e. (by impl.) to *commiserate:*—have compassion, be touched with a feeling of.

4835. συμπαθής **sumpathēs**, *soom-path-ace';* from *4841;* having a *fellow-feeling* ("*sympathetic*"), i.e. (by impl.) *mutually commiserative;*—having compassion one of another.

4836. συμπαραγίνομαι **sumparaginŏmai**, *soom-par-ag-in'-om-ahee;* from *4862* and *3854;* to be *present together*, i.e. to *convene;* by impl. to *appear in aid:*—come together, stand with.

4837. συμπαρακαλέω **sumparakalĕō**, *soom-par-ak-al-eh'-o;* from *4862* and *3870;* to *console jointly:*—comfort together.

4838. συμπαραλαμβάνω **sumparalambanō**, *soom-par-al-am-ban'-o;* from *4862* and *3880;* to *take along in company:*—take with.

4839. συμπαραμένω **sumparamĕnō**, *soom-par-am-en'-o;* from *4862* and *3887;* to *remain in company*, i.e. *still live:*—continue with.

4840. συμπάρειμι **sumparĕimi**, *soom-par'-i-mee;* from *4862* and *3918;* to be *at hand together*, i.e. *now present:*—be here present with.

4841. συμπάσχω **sumpaschō**, *soom-pas'-kho;* from *4862* and *3958* (includ. its alt.); to *experience pain jointly* or of the *same kind* (spec. *persecution*; to "*sympathize*"):—suffer with.

4842. συμπέμπω **sumpĕmpō**, *soom-pem'-po;* from *4862* and *3992;* to *despatch in company:*—send with.

4843. συμπεριλαμβάνω **sumpĕrilambanō**, *soom-per-ee-lam-ban'-o;* from *4862* and a comp. of *4012* and *2983;* to *take by inclosing altogether*, i.e. *earnestly throw the arms about one:*—embrace.

4844. συμπίνω **sumpinō**, *soom-pee'-no;* from *4862* and *4095;* to *partake a beverage in company:*—drink with.

4845. συμπληρόω **sumplērŏō**, *soom-play-rŏ'-o;* from *4862* and *4137;* to *implenish completely*, i.e. (of a vessel) to *swamp* (a boat), or (of time) to *accomplish* (pass. be *complete*):—(fully) come, fill up.

4846. συμπνίγω **sumpnigō**, *soom-pnee'-go;* from *4862* and *4155;* to *strangle completely*, i.e. (lit.) to *drown*, or (fig.) to *crowd:*—choke, throng.

4847. συμπολίτης **sumpŏlitēs**, *soom-pol-ee'-tace;* from *4862* and *4177;* a *native of the same town*, i.e. (fig.) *co-religionist* (*fellow-Christian*):—fellowcitizen.

4848. συμπορεύομαι **sumpŏrĕuŏmai**, *soom-por-yoo'-om-ahee;* from *4862* and *4198;* to *journey together;* by impl. to *assemble:*—go with, resort.

4849. συμπόσιον **sumpŏsiŏn**, *soom-pos'-ee-on;* neut. of a der. of the alt. of *4844;* a *drinking-party* ("*symposium*"), i.e. (by extens.) a *room of guests:*—company.

4850. συμπρεσβύτερος **sumprĕsbutĕrŏs**, *soom-pres-boo'-ter-os;* from *4862* and *4245;* a *co-presbyter:*—presbyter, also an elder.

συμφάγω **sumphagō**. See *4906.*

4851. συμφέρω **sumphĕrō**, *soom-fer'-o;* from *4862* and *5342* (includ. its alt.); to *bear together* (contribute), i.e. (lit.) to *collect*, or (fig.) to *conduce;* espec. (neut. part. as noun) *advantage:*—be better for, bring together, be expedient (for), be good, (be) profit (-able for).

4852. σύμφημι **sumphēmi**, *soom'-fay-mee;* from *4862* and *5346;* to *say jointly*, i.e. *assent to:*—consent unto.

4853. συμφυλέτης **sumphulĕtēs**, *soom-foo-let'-ace;* from *4862* and a der. of *5443;* a *co-tribesman*, i.e. *native of the same country:*—countryman.

4854. σύμφυτος **sumphutŏs**, *soom'-foo-tos;* from *4862* and a der. of *5453;* *grown* along *with* (*connate*), i.e. (fig.) closely *united to:*—planted together.

4855. συμφύω **sumphuō**, *soom-foo'-o;* from *4862* and *5453;* pass. to *grow jointly;*—spring up with.

4856. συμφωνέω **sumphōnĕō**, *soom-fo-neh'-o;* from *4859;* to be *harmonious*, i.e. (fig.) to *accord* (be *suitable*, *concur*) or *stipulate* (by compact):—agree (together, with).

4857. συμφώνησις **sumphōnēsis**, *soom-fo'-nay-sis;* from *4856;* *accordance:*—concord.

4858. συμφωνία **sumphōnia**, *soom-fo-nee'-ah;* from *4859;* *unison* of sound ("*symphony*"), i.e. a *concert* of instruments (harmonious *note*):—music.

4859. σύμφωνος **sumphōnŏs**, *soom'-fo-nos;* from *4862* and *5456;* *sounding together* (alike), i.e. (fig.) *accordant* (neut. as noun, *agreement*):—consent.

4860. συμψηφίζω **sumpsēphizō**, *soom-psay-fid'-zo;* from *4862* and *5585;* to *compute jointly:*—reckon.

4861. σύμψυχος **sumpsuchŏs**, *soom'-psoo-khos;* from *4862* and *5590;* *co-spirited*, i.e. *similar in sentiment:*—like-minded.

4862. σύν **sun**, *soon;* a prim. prep. denoting *union; with* or *together* (but much closer than *3326* or *3844*), i.e. by *association*, *companionship*, *process*, *resemblance*, *possession*, *instrumentality*, *addition* etc.:—beside, with. In comp. it has similar applications, includ. *completeness*.

4863. συνάγω **sunagō**, *soon-ag'-o;* from *4862* and *71;* to *lead together*, i.e. *collect* or *convene;* spec. to *entertain* (hospitably):— + *accompany*, assemble (selves, together), bestow, come together, gather (selves together, up, together), lead into, resort, take in.

4864. συναγωγή **sunagōgē**, *soon-ag-o-gay';* from (the redupl. form of) *4863;* an *assemblage* of persons; spec. a Jewish "*synagogue*" (the meeting or the place); by anal. a Christian *church:*—assembly, congregation, synagogue.

4865. συναγωνίζομαι **sunagōnizŏmai**, *soon-ag-o-nid'-zom-ahee;* from *4862* and *75;* to *struggle in company with*, i.e. (fig.) to be a *partner* (*assistant*):—strive together with.

4866. συναθλέω **sunathlĕō**, *soon-ath-leh'-o;* from *4862* and *118;* to *wrestle in company with*, i.e. (fig.) to *seek jointly:*—labour with, strive together for.

4867. συναθροίζω **sunathrŏizō**, *soon-ath-royd'-zo;* from *4862* and ἀθροίζω **athrŏizō** (to *hoard*); to *convene:*—call (gather) together.

4868. συναίρω **sunairō**, *soon-ah'ee-ro;* from *4862* and *142;* to *make up together*, i.e. (fig.) to *compute* (an account):—reckon, take.

4869. συναιχμάλωτος **sunaichmalōtŏs**, *soon-aheekh-mal'-o-tos;* from *4862* and *164;* a *co-captive:*—fellowprisoner.

4870. συνακολουθέω **sunakŏlŏuthĕō**, *soon-ak-ol-oo-theh'-o;* from *4862* and *190;* to *accompany:*—follow.

4871. συναλίζω **sunalizō**, *soon-al-id'-zo;* from *4862* and ἁλίζω **halizō** (to *throng*); to *accumulate*, i.e. *convene:*—assemble together.

4872. συναναβαίνω **sunanabainō**, *soon-an-ab-ah'ee-no;* from *4862* and *305;* to *ascend in company with:*—come up with.

4873. συνανάκειμαι **sunanakĕimai**, *soon-an-ak'-i-mahee;* from *4862* and *345;* to *recline in company with* (at a meal):—sit (down, at the table, together) with (at meat).

4874. συναναμίγνυμι **sunanamignumi**, *soon-an-am-ig'-noo-mee;* from *4862* and a comp. of *303* and *3396;* to *mix up together*, i.e. (fig.) *associate with:*—(have, keep) company (with).

4875. συναναπαύομαι **sunanapauŏmai**, *soon-an-ap-ŏw'-om-ahee;* mid. from *4862* and *373;* to *recruit oneself in company with:*—refresh with.

4876. συναντάω **sunantaō**, *soon-an-tah'-o;* from *4862* and a der. of *473;* to *meet with;* fig. to *occur:*—befall, meet.

4877. συνάντησις **sunantēsis,** *soon-an'-tay-sis;* from *4876;* a *meeting with:*—meet.

4878. συναντιλαμβάνομαι **sunantilambanŏmai,** *soon-an-tee-lam-ban'-om-ahee;* from *4862* and *482;* to take hold of *opposite together,* i.e. *co-operate* (assist):—help.

4879. συναπάγω **sunapagō,** *soon-ap-ag'-o;* from *4862* and *520;* to take off *together,* i.e. *transport with* (seduce, pass. *yield*):—carry (lead) away with, condescend.

4880. συναποθνήσκω **sunapŏthnēskō,** *soon-ap-oth-nace'-ko;* from *4862* and *599;* to *decease* (lit.) in company *with,* or (fig.) similarly *to:*—be dead (die) with.

4881. συναπόλλυμι **sunapŏllumi,** *soon-ap-ol'-loo-mee;* from *4862* and *622;* to *destroy* (mid. or pass. be *slain*) in company *with:*—perish with.

4882. συναποστέλλω **sunapŏstĕllō,** *soon-ap-os-tel'-lo;* from *4862* and *649;* to *despatch* (on an errand) in company *with:*—send with.

4883. συναρμολογέω **sunarmŏlŏgĕō,** *soon-armol-og-eh'-o;* from *4862* and a der. of a comp. of *719* and *3004* (in its orig. sense of *laying*); to *render close-jointed together,* i.e. *organize compactly:*—be fitly framed (joined) together.

4884. συναρπάζω **sunarpazō,** *soon-ar-pad'-zo;* from *4862* and *726;* to *snatch together,* i.e. *seize:*—catch.

4885. συναυξάνω **sunauxanō,** *soon-ŏwx-an'-o;* from *4862* and *837;* to *increase* (grow up) *together:*—grow together.

4886. σύνδεσμος **sundĕsmŏs,** *soon'-des-mos;* from *4862* and *1199;* a *joint tie,* i.e. *ligament,* (fig.) *uniting principle, control:*—band, bond.

4887. συνδέω **sundĕō,** *soon-deh'-o;* from *4862* and *1210;* to *bind with,* i.e. (pass.) be a *fellow-prisoner* (fig.):—be bound with.

4888. συνδοξάζω **sundŏxazō,** *soon-dox-ad'-zo;* from *4862* and *1392;* to *exalt* to dignity in company (i.e. *similarly*) *with:*—glorify together.

4889. σύνδουλος **sundŏulŏs,** *soon'-doo-los;* from *4862* and *1401;* a *co-slave,* i.e. *servitor* or *ministrant of the same master* (human or divine):—fellowservant.

4890. συνδρέμω **sundrĕmō.** See *4936.*

4890. συνδρομή **sundrŏmē,** *soon-drom-ay';* from (the alt. of) *4936;* a *running together,* i.e. (riotous) *concourse:*—run together.

4891. συνεγείρω **sunĕgĕirō,** *soon-eg-i'-ro;* from *4862* and *1453;* to *rouse* (from death) in company *with,* i.e. (fig.) to *revivify* (spiritually) in resemblance to:—raise up together, rise with.

4892. συνέδριον **sunĕdriŏn,** *soon-ed'-ree-on;* neut. of a presumed der. of a comp. of *4862* and the base of *1476;* a *joint session,* i.e. (spec.) the Jewish *Sanhedrim;* by anal. a subordinate *tribunal:*—council.

4893. συνείδησις **sunĕidēsis,** *soon-i'-day-sis;* from a prol. form of *4894;* co-perception, i.e. moral *consciousness:*—conscience.

4894. συνείδω **sunĕidō,** *soon-i'-do;* from *4862* and *1492;* to *see completely;* used (like its prim.) only in two past tenses, respectively mean. to *understand* or *become aware,* and to be *conscious* or (clandestinely) *informed of:*—consider, know, be privy, be ware of.

4895. σύνειμι **sunĕimi,** *soon'-i-mee;* from *4862* and *1510* (includ. its various inflections); to *be* in company *with,* i.e. *present* at the time:—be with.

4896. σύνειμι **sunĕimi,** *soon'-i-mee;* from *4862* and εἶμι **ĕimi** (to *go*); to *assemble:*—gather together.

4897. συνεισέρχομαι **sunĕisĕrchŏmai,** *soon-ice-er'-khom-ahee;* from *4862* and *1525;* to *enter* in company *with:*—go in with, go with into.

4898. συνέκδημος **sunĕkdēmŏs,** *soon-ek'-day-mos;* from *4862* and the base of *1553;* a *co-absentee* from home, i.e. *fellow-traveller:*—companion in travel, travel with.

4899. συνεκλεκτός **sunĕklĕktŏs,** *soon-ek-lek-tos';* from a comp. of *4862* and *1586;* chosen in company *with,* i.e. *co-elect* (*fellow Christian*):—elected together with.

4900. συνελαύνω **sunĕlaunō,** *soon-el-ow'-no;* from *4862* and *1643;* to *drive together,* i.e. (fig.) *exhort* (to reconciliation):— + set at one again.

4901. συνεπιμαρτυρέω **sunĕpimarturĕō,** *soon-ep-ee-mar-too-reh'-o;* from *4862* and *1957;* to *testify further jointly,* i.e. *unite in adding evidence:*—also bear witness.

4902. συνέπομαι **sunĕpŏmai,** *soon-ep'-om-ahee;* mid. from *4862* and a prim. ἕπω **hĕpō** (to *follow*); to *attend* (*travel*) in company *with:*—accompany.

4903. συνεργέω **sunĕrgĕō,** *soon-erg-eh'-o;* from *4904;* to be a *fellow-worker,* i.e. *co-operate:*—help (work) with, work (-er) together.

4904. συνεργός **sunĕrgŏs,** *soon-er-gos';* from a presumed comp. of *4862* and the base of *2041;* a *co-laborer,* i.e. *coadjutor:*—companion in labour, (fellow-) helper (-labourer, -worker), labourer together with, workfellow.

4905. συνέρχομαι **sunĕrchŏmai,** *soon-er'-khom-ahee;* from *4862* and *2064;* to *convene, depart* in company *with, associate with,* or (spec.) *cohabit* (conjugally):—accompany, assemble (with), come (together), come (company, go) with, resort.

4906. συνεσθίω **sunĕsthiō,** *soon-es-thee'-o;* from *4862* and *2068* (includ. its alt.); to *take food* in company *with:*—eat with.

4907. σύνεσις **sunĕsis,** *soon'-es-is;* from *4920;* a mental *putting together,* i.e. *intelligence* or (concr.) the *intellect:*—knowledge, understanding.

4908. συνετός **sunĕtŏs,** *soon-et'-os;* from *4920;* mentally *put* (or *putting*) *together,* i.e. *sagacious:*—prudent. Comp. *5429.*

4909. συνευδοκέω **sunĕudŏkĕō,** *soon-yoo-dok-eh'-o;* from *4862* and *2106;* to *think well of in common,* i.e. *assent* to, *feel gratified with:*—allow, assent, be pleased, have pleasure.

4910. συνευωχέω **sunĕuōchĕō,** *soon-yoo-o-kheh'-o;* from *4862* and a der. of a presumed comp. of *2095* and a der. of *2192* (mean. to *be in good condition,* i.e. [by impl.] to *fare well,* or *feast*); to *entertain* sumptuously in company *with,* i.e. (mid. or pass.) to *revel together:*—feast with.

4911. συνεφίστημι **sunĕphistēmi,** *soon-ef-is'-tay-mee;* from *4862* and *2186;* to *stand up together,* i.e. to *resist* (or *assault*) *jointly:*—rise up together.

4912. συνέχω **sunĕchō,** *soon-ekh'-o;* from *4862* and *2192;* to *hold together,* i.e. to *compress* (the ears, with a crowd or siege) or *arrest* (a prisoner); fig. to *compel, perplex, afflict, preoccupy:*—constrain, hold, keep in, press, lie sick of, stop, be in a strait, straiten, be taken with, throng.

4913. συνήδομαι **sunēdŏmai,** *soon-ay'-dom-ahee;* mid. from *4862* and the base of *2237;* to *rejoice in with* oneself, i.e. *feel satisfaction* concerning:—delight.

4914. συνήθεια **sunēthĕia,** *soon-ay'-thi-ah;* from a comp. of *4862* and *2239;* mutual *habitation,* i.e. *usage:*—custom.

4915. συνηλικιώτης **sunēlikiōtēs,** *soon-ay-lik-ee-o'-tace;* from *4862* and a der. of *2244;* a *co-aged* person, i.e. *alike* in years:—equal,

4916. συνθάπτω **sunthaptō,** *soon-thap'-to;* from *4862* and *2290;* to *inter* in company *with,* i.e. (fig.) to *assimilate* spiritually (to Christ by a sepulture as to sin):—bury with.

4917. συνθλάω **sunthlaō,** *soon-thlah'-o;* from *4862* and θλάω **thlaō** (to *crush*); to *dash together,* i.e. *shatter:*—break.

4918. συνθλίβω **sunthlibō,** *soon-thlee'-bo;* from *4862* and *2346;* to *compress,* i.e. *crowd on all sides:*—throng.

4919. συνθρύπτω **sunthruptō,** *soon-throop'-to;* from *4862* and θρύπτω **thruptō** (to *crumble*); to *crush together,* i.e. (fig.) to *dispirit:*—break.

4920. συνίημι **suniēmi,** *soon-ee'-ay-mee;* from *4862* and ἵημι **hiēmi** (to *send*); to *put together,* i.e. (mentally) to *comprehend;* by impl. to *act piously:*—consider, understand, be wise.

4921. συνιστάω **sunistaō,** *soon-is-tah'-o;* or (strengthened)

συνιστάνω **sunistanō,** *soon-is-tan'-o;* or

συνίστημι **sunistēmi,** *soon-is'-tay-mee;* from *4862* and *2476* (includ. its collat. forms); to *set together,* i.e. (by impl.) to *introduce* (favorably), or (fig.) to *exhibit;* intrans. to *stand near,* or (fig.) to *constitute:*—approve, commend, consist, make, stand (with).

4922. συνοδεύω **sunŏdĕuō,** *soon-od-yoo'-o;* from *4862* and *3593;* to *travel in company with:*—journey with.

4923. συνοδία **sunŏdia,** *soon-od-ee'-ah;* from a comp. of *4862* and *3598* ("*synod*"); *companionship* on a journey, i.e. (by impl.) a *caravan:*—company.

4924. συνοικέω **sunŏikĕō,** *soon-oy-keh'-o;* from *4862* and *3611;* to *reside together* (as a family):—dwell together.

4925. συνοικοδομέω **sunŏikŏdŏmĕō,** *soon-oy-kod-om-eh'-o;* from *4862* and *3618;* to *construct,* i.e. (pass.) to *compose* (in company with other Christians, fig.):—build together.

4926. συνομιλέω **sunŏmilĕō,** *soon-om-il-eh'-o;* from *4862* and *3656;* to *converse mutually:*—talk with.

4927. συνομορέω **sunŏmŏrĕō,** *soon-om-or-eh'-o;* from *4862* and a der. of a comp. of the base of *3674* and the base of *3725;* to *border together,* i.e. *adjoin:*—join hard.

4928. συνοχή **sunŏchē,** *soon-okh-ay';* from *4912;* *restraint,* i.e. (fig.) *anxiety:*—anguish, distress.

4929. συντάσσω **suntassō,** *soon-tas-so;* from *4862* and *5021;* to *arrange jointly,* i.e. (fig.) to *direct:*—appoint.

4930. συντέλεια **suntĕlĕia,** *soon-tel'-i-ah;* from *4931;* *entire completion,* i.e. *consummation* (of a dispensation):—end.

4931. συντελέω **suntĕlĕō,** *soon-tel-eh'-o;* from *4862* and *5055;* to *complete entirely;* gen. to *execute* (lit. or fig.):—end, finish, fulfil, make.

4932. συντέμνω **suntĕmnō,** *soon-tem'-no;* from *4862* and the base of *5114;* to *contract by cutting,* i.e. (fig.) do concisely (*speedily*):—(cut) short.

4933. συντηρέω **suntērĕō,** *soon-tay-reh'-o;* from *4862* and *5083;* to *keep closely together,* i.e. (by impl.) to *conserve* (from ruin); ment. to *remember* (and *obey*):—keep, observe, preserve.

4934. συντίθεμαι **suntithĕmai,** *soon-tith'-em-ahee;* mid. from *4862* and *5087;* to *place jointly,* i.e. (fig.) to *consent* (bargain, stipulate), *concur:*—agree, assent, covenant.

4935. συντόμως **suntŏmōs,** *soon-tom'-oce;* adv. from a der. of *4932;* concisely (*briefly*):—a few words.

4936. συντρέχω **suntrĕchō,** *soon-trekh'-o;* from *4862* and *5143* (includ. its alt.); to *rush together* (hastily assemble) or *headlong* (fig.):—run (together, with).

4937. συντρίβω **suntribō,** *soon-tree'-bo;* from *4862* and the base of *5147;* to *break* (in pieces), i.e. to *shatter* (lit. or fig.):—break (in pieces), broken to shivers (+ -hearted), bruise.

4938. σύντριμμα **suntrimma,** *soon-trim'-mah;* from *4937;* *concussion* or utter *fracture* (prop. concr.), i.e. complete *ruin:*—destruction.

4939. σύντροφος **suntrŏphŏs,** *soon'-trof-os;* from *4862* and *5162* (in a pass. sense); a *fellow-nursling,* i.e. *comrade:*—brought up with.

4940. συντυγχάνω **suntugchanō,** *soon-toong-khan'-o;* from *4862* and *5177;* to *chance together,* i.e. *meet with* (*reach*):—come at.

4941. Συντύχη **Suntuchē,** *soon-too'-khay;* from *4940;* an *accident;* Syntyche, a Chr. female:—Syntyche.

4942. συνυποκρίνομαι **sunupŏkrinŏmai,** *soon-oo-pok-rin'-om-ahee;* from *4862* and *5271;* to *act hypocritically* in concert with:—dissemble with.

4943. συνυπουργέω **sunupŏurgĕō,** *soon-oop-oorg-eh'-o;* from *4862* and a der. of a comp. of *5259* and the base of *2041;* to be a *co-auxiliary,* i.e. *assist:*—help together.

4944. συνωδίνω **sunōdinō**, *soon-o-dee'-no;* from *3602* and *5605;* to *have* (parturition) *pangs* in company (concert, simultaneously) *with,* i.e. (fig.) to *sympathize* (in expectation of relief from suffering):—travail in pain together.

4945. συνωμοσία **sunōmŏsia**, *soon-o-mos-ee'-ah,* from a comp. of *4862* and *3660;* a *swearing together,* i.e. (by impl.) a *plot:*—conspiracy.

4946. Συράκουσαι **Surakŏusai,** *soo-rak'-oo-sahee;* plur. of uncert. der.; *Syracusæ,* the capital of Sicily:—Syracuse.

4947. Συρία **Suria,** *soo-ree'-ah;* prob. of Heb. or. [6865]; *Syria* (i.e. *Tsyria* or *Tyre*), a region of Asia:—Syria.

4948. Σύρος **Surŏs,** *soo'-ros;* from the same as *4947;* a *Syran* (i.e. prob. *Tyrian*), a native of Syria:—Syrian.

4949. Συροφοίνισσα **Surŏphŏinissa,** *soo-rof-oy'-nis-sah;* fem. of a comp. of *4948* and the same as *5403;* a *Syro-phœnician* woman, i.e. a female native of Phœnicia in Syria:—Syrophenician.

4950. σύρτις **surtis,** *soor'-tis;* from *4951;* a *shoal* (from the sand *drawn* thither by the waves), i.e. the *Syrtis* Major or great bay on the N. coast of Africa:—quicksands.

4951. σύρω **surō,** *soo'-ro;* prob. akin to *138;* to *trail:*—drag, draw, hale.

4952. συσπαράσσω **susparassō,** *soos-par-as'-so;* from *4862* and *4682;* to *rend* completely, i.e. (by anal.) to *convulse* violently:—throw down.

4953. σύσσημον **sussēmŏn,** *soos'-say-mon;* neut. of a comp. of *4862* and the base of *4591;* a *sign* in common, i.e. preconcerted *signal:*—token.

4954. σύσσωμος **sussōmŏs,** *soos'-so-mos;* from *4862* and *4983;* of a *joint* body, i.e. (fig.) a *fellow-member* of the Christian community:—of the same body.

4955. συστασιαστής **sustasiastēs,** *soos-tas-ee-as-tace';* from a comp. of *4862* and a der. of *4714;* a *fellow-insurgent:*—make insurrection with.

4956. συστατικός **sustatikŏs,** *soos-tat-ee-kos';* from a der. of *4921;* introductory, i.e. *recommendatory:*—of commendation.

4957. συσταυρόω **sustaurŏō,** *soos-tow-rŏ'-o;* from *4862* and *4717;* to *impale* in company with (lit. or fig.):—crucify with.

4958. συστέλλω **sustĕllō,** *soos-tel'-lo;* from *4862* and *4724;* to *send* (draw) *together,* i.e. *enwrap* (enshroud a corpse for burial), *contract* (an interval):—short, wind up.

4959. συστενάζω **sustĕnazō,** *soos-ten-ad'-zo;* from *4862* and *4727;* to *moan* jointly, i.e. (fig.) experience a common calamity:—groan together.

4960. συστοιχέω **sustŏichĕō,** *soos-toy-kheh'-o;* from *4862* and *4748;* to *file together* (as soldiers in ranks), i.e. (fig.) to *correspond* to:—answer to.

4961. συστρατιώτης **sustratiōtēs,** *soos-trat-ee-o'-tace;* from *4862* and *4757;* a *co-campaigner,* i.e. (fig.) an *associate* in Christian toil:—fellowsoldier.

4962. συστρέφω **sustrĕphō,** *soos-tref'-o;* from *4862* and *4762;* to *twist together,* i.e. *collect* (a bundle, a crowd):—gather.

4963. συστροφή **sustrŏphē,** *soos-trof-ay';* from *4962;* a *twisting together,* i.e. (fig.) a secret *coalition,* riotous *crowd:*— + band together, concourse.

4964. συσχηματίζω **suschēmatizō,** *soos-khay-mat-id'-zo;* from *4862* and a der. of *4976;* to *fashion alike,* i.e. *conform* to the same pattern (fig.):—conform to, fashion self according to.

4965. Συχάρ **Suchar,** *soo-khar';* of Heb. or. [7941]; *Sychar* (i.e. *Shekar*), a place in Pal.:—Sychar.

4966. Συχέμ **Suchem,** *soo-khem';* of Heb. or. [7927]; *Sychem* (i.e. *Shekem*), the name of a Canaanite and of a place in Pal.:—Sychem.

4967. σφαγή **sphagē,** *sfag-ay';* from *4969;* *butchery* (of animals for food or sacrifice, or [fig.] of men [destruction]):—slaughter.

4968. σφάγιον **sphagiŏn,** *sfag'-ee-on;* neut. of a der. of *4967;* a *victim* (in sacrifice):—slain beast.

4969. σφάζω **sphazō,** *sfad'-zo;* a prim. verb; to *butcher* (espec. an animal for food or in sacrifice) or

(gen.) to *slaughter,* or (spec.) to *maim* (violently):—kill, slay, wound.

4970. σφόδρα **sphŏdra,** *sfod'-rah;* neut. plur. of *4971* (as adv.); *vehemently,* i.e. in a *high degree, much:*—exceeding (-ly), greatly, sore, very.

4971. σφοδρῶς **sphŏdrōs,** *sfod-roce';* adv. from the same as *4970; very much:*—exceedingly.

4972. σφραγίζω **sphragizō,** *sfrag-id'-zo;* from *4973;* to *stamp* (with a signet or private mark) for security or preservation (lit. or fig.); by impl. to *keep secret,* to *attest:*—(set a, set to) seal up.

4973. σφραγίς **sphragis,** *sfrag-ece';* prob. strengthened from *5420;* a *signet* (as fencing in or protecting from misappropriation); by impl. the *stamp* impressed (as a mark of privacy, or genuineness), lit. or fig.:—seal.

4974. σφυρόν **sphurŏn,** *sfoo-ron';* neut. of a presumed der. prob. of the same as σφαίρα **sphaira** (a *ball,* "*sphere*"; comp. the fem. σφῦρα **sphura,** a *hammer*); the *ankle* (as globular):—ancle bone.

4975. σχεδόν **schedŏn,** *sked-on';* neut. of a presumed der. of the alt. of *2192* as adv.; *nigh,* i.e. *nearly:*—almost.

4976. σχῆμα **schēma,** *skhay'-mah;* from the alt. of *2192;* a *figure* (as a mode or circumstance), i.e. (by impl.) external *condition:*—fashion.

4977. σχίζω **schizō,** *skhid'-zo;* appar. a prim. verb; to *split* or *sever* (lit. or fig.):—break, divide, open, rend, make a rent.

4978. σχίσμα **schisma,** *skhis'-mah;* from *4977;* a *split* or *gap* ("schism"), lit. or fig.:—division, rent, schism.

4979. σχοινίον **schoiniŏn,** *skhoy-nee'-on;* dimin. of σχοῖνος **schŏinŏs** (a *rush* or *flag*-plant; of uncert. der.); a *rushlet,* i.e. *grass-withe* or *tie* (gen.):—small cord, rope.

4980. σχολάζω **schŏlazō,** *skhol-ad'-zo;* from *4981;* to *take a holiday,* i.e. *be at leisure* for (by impl. *devote* oneself wholly to); fig. to *be vacant* (of a house):—empty, give self.

4981. σχολή **schŏlē,** *skhol-ay';* prob. fem. of a presumed der. of the alt. of *2192;* prop. *loitering* (as a *withholding* of oneself from work) or *leisure,* i.e. (by impl.) a "*school*" (as *vacation* from phys. employment):—school.

4982. σώζω **sōzō,** *sode'-zo;* from a prim. σῶς **sōs** (contr. for obsol. σάος **saŏs,** "*safe*"); to *save,* i.e. *deliver* or *protect* (lit. or fig.):—heal, preserve, save (self), do well, be (make) whole.

4983. σῶμα **sōma,** *so'-mah;* from *4982;* the *body* (as a *sound* whole), used in a very wide application, lit. or fig.:—bodily, body, slave.

4984. σωματικός **sōmatikŏs,** *so-mat-ee-kos';* from *4983;* *corporeal* or *physical:*—bodily.

4985. σωματικῶς **sōmatikōs,** *so-mat-ee-koce';* adv. from *4984;* *corporeally* or *physically:*—bodily.

4986. Σώπατρος **Sōpatrŏs,** *so'-pat-ros;* from the base of *4982* and *3962;* of a *safe father; Sopatrus,* a Chr.:—Sopater. Comp. *4986.*

4987. σωρεύω **sōreuō,** *sore-yoo'-o;* from another form of *4073;* to *pile up* (lit. or fig.):—heap, load.

4988. Σωσθένης **Sōsthĕnēs,** *soce-then'-ace;* from the base of *4982* and that of *4599;* of *safe strength; Sosthenes,* a Chr.:—Sosthenes.

4989. Σωσίπατρος **Sōsipatrŏs,** *so-sip'-at-ros;* prol. for *4986; Sosipatrus,* a Chr.:—Sosipater.

4990. σωτήρ **sōtēr,** *so-tare';* from *4982;* a *deliverer,* i.e. God or Christ:—saviour.

4991. σωτηρία **sōtēria,** *so-tay-ree'-ah;* fem. of a der. of *4990* as (prop. abstr.) noun; *rescue* or *safety* (phys. or mor.):—deliver, health, salvation, save, saving.

4992. σωτήριον **sōtēriŏn,** *so-tay'-ree-on;* neut. of the same as *4991* as (prop. concr.) noun; *defender* or (by impl.) *defence:*—salvation.

4993. σωφρονέω **sōphrŏnĕō,** *so-fron-eh'-o;* from *4998;* to be *of sound mind,* i.e. *sane,* (fig.) *moderate:*—be in right mind, be sober (minded), soberly.

4994. σωφρονίζω **sōphrŏnizō,** *so-fron-id'-zo;* from *4998;* to *make of sound mind,* i.e. (fig.) to *discipline* or *correct:*—teach to be sober.

4995. σωφρονισμός **sōphrŏnismŏs,** *so-fron-is-mos';* from *4994; discipline,* i.e. *self-control:*—sound mind.

4996. σωφρόνως **sōphrŏnōs,** *so-fron'-oce;* adv. from *4998; with* sound mind, i.e. *moderately:*—soberly.

4997. σωφροσύνη **sōphrŏsunē,** *so-fros-oo'-nay;* from *4998; soundness* of mind, i.e. (lit.) *sanity* or (fig.) *self-control:*—soberness, sobriety.

4998. σώφρων **sōphrōn,** *so'-frone;* from the base of *4982* and that of *5424; safe* (sound) in mind, i.e. *self-controlled* (moderate as to opinion or passion):—discreet, sober, temperate.

Τ

τά **ta.** See *3588.*

4999. Ταβέρναι **Tabĕrnai,** *tab-er'-nahee;* plur. of Lat. or.; *huts* or *wooden-walled* buildings; *Tabernœ:*—taverns.

5000. Ταβιθά **Tabitha,** *tab-ee-thah';* of Chald. or. [comp. 6646]; *the gazelle; Tabitha* (i.e. *Tabjetha*), a Chr. female:—Tabitha.

5001. τάγμα **tagma,** *tag'-mah;* from *5021;* something orderly in *arrangement* (a troop), i.e. (fig.) a *series* or *succession:*—order.

5002. τακτός **taktŏs,** *tak-tos';* from *5021;* arranged, i.e. *appointed* or *stated:*—set.

5003. ταλαιπωρέω **talaipōrĕō,** *tal-ahee-po-reh'-o,* from *5005;* to be *wretched,* i.e. realize one's own *misery:*—be afflicted.

5004. ταλαιπωρία **talaipōria,** *tal-ahee-po-ree'-ah;* from *5005; wretchedness,* i.e. *calamity:*—misery.

5005. ταλαίπωρος **talaipōrŏs,** *tal-ah'-ee-po-ros;* from the base of *5007* and a der. of the base of *3084; enduring trial,* i.e. *miserable:*—wretched.

5006. ταλαντιαῖος **talantiaiŏs,** *tal-an-tee-ah'-yos;* from *5007; talent-like* in weight:—weight of a talent.

5007. τάλαντον **talantŏn,** *tal'-an-ton;* neut. of a presumed der. of the orig. form of τλάω **tlaō** (to *bear;* equiv. to *5342*); a *balance* (as supporting weights), i.e. (by impl.) a certain *weight* (and thence a *coin* or rather *sum* of money) or "talent":—talent.

5008. ταλιθά **talitha,** *tal-ee-thah';* of Chald. or. [comp. 2924]; *the fresh,* i.e. *young girl; talitha* (O maiden):—talitha.

5009. ταμεῖον **tamĕiŏn,** *tam-i'-on;* neut. contr. of a presumed der. of ταμίας **tamias** (a *dispenser* or *distributor;* akin to τέμνω **tĕmnō,** to *cut*); a *dispensary* or *magazine,* i.e. a *chamber* on the ground-floor or interior of an Oriental house (gen. used for *storage* or *privacy,* a spot for retirement):—secret chamber, closet, storehouse.

τανῦν **tanun.** See *3568.*

5010. τάξις **taxis,** *tax'-is;* from *5021;* regular *arrangement,* i.e. (in time) fixed *succession* (of rank or character), official *dignity:*—order.

5011. ταπεινός **tapĕinŏs,** *tap-i-nos';* of uncert. der.; *depressed,* i.e. (fig.) *humiliated* (in circumstances or disposition):—base, cast down, humble, of low degree (estate), lowly.

5012. ταπεινοφροσύνη **tapĕinŏphrŏsunē,** *tap-i-nof-ros-oo'-nay;* from a comp. of *5011* and the base of *5424; humiliation* of mind, i.e. *modesty:*—humbleness of mind, humility (of mind), lowliness (of mind).

5013. ταπεινόω **tapĕinŏō,** *tap-i-nŏ'-o;* from *5011;* to *depress;* fig. to *humiliate* (in condition or heart):—abase, bring low, humble (self).

5014. ταπείνωσις **tapĕinōsis,** *tap-i'-no-sis;* from *5013; depression* in rank or feeling):—humiliation, made low, low estate, vile.

5015. ταράσσω **tarassō,** *tar-as'-so;* of uncert. affin.; to *stir* or *agitate* (roil water):—trouble.

5016. ταραχή **tarachē**, *tar-akh-ay'*; fem. from *5015*; *disturbance*, i.e. (of water) *roiling*, or (of a mob) *sedition*:—trouble (-ing).

5017. τάραχος **tarachŏs**, *tar'-akh-os*; masc. from *5015*; a *disturbance*, i.e. (popular) *tumult*:—stir.

5018. Ταρσεύς **Tarsĕus**, *tar-syoos'*; from *5019*; a *Tarsean*, i.e. native of Tarsus:—of Tarsus.

5019. Ταρσός **Tarsŏs**, *tar-sos'*; perh. the same as ταρσός **tarsŏs** (a *flat* basket); *Tarsus*, a place in Asia Minor:—Tarsus.

5020. ταρταρόω **tartarŏō**, *tar-tar-ŏ'-o*; from Τάρταρος **Tartarŏs** (the deepest *abyss* of Hades); to *incarcerate* in eternal torment:—cast down to hell.

5021. τάσσω **tassō**, *tas'-so*; a prol. form of a prim. verb (which latter appears only in certain tenses); to *arrange* in an orderly manner, i.e. *assign* or *dispose* (to a certain position or lot):—addict, appoint, determine, ordain, set.

5022. ταῦρος **taurŏs**, *tow'-ros*; appar. a prim. word [comp. *8450*, " *steer* "]; a *bullock*:—bull, ox.

5023. ταῦτα **tauta**, *tow'-tah*; nom. or acc. neut. plur. of *3778*; these *things*:— + afterward, follow, + hereafter, × him, the same, so, such, that, then, these, they, this, those, thus.

5024. ταὐτά **tauta**, *tow-tah'*; neut. plur. of *3588* and *846* as adv.; in *the same way*:—even thus, (manner) like, so.

5025. ταύταις **tautais**, *tow'-toheece*; and

ταύτας **tautas**, *tow'-tas*; dat. and acc. fem. plur. respectively of *3778*; (*to* or *with* or *by*, etc.) *these*:—hence, that, then, these, those.

5026. ταύτῃ **tautē**, *tow'-tay*; and

ταύτην **tautēn**, *tow'-tane*; and

ταύτης **tautēs**, *tow'-tace*; dat., acc. and gen. respectively of the fem. sing. of *3778*; (*towards* or *of*) *this*:—her, + hereof, it, that, + thereby, the (same), this (same).

5027. ταφή **taphē**, *taf-ay'*; fem. from *2290*; *burial* (the act):— × bury.

5028. τάφος **taphŏs**, *taf'-os*; masc. from *2290*; a *grave* (the place of interment):—sepulchre, tomb.

5029. τάχα **tacha**, *takh'-ah*; as if neut. plur. of *5036* (adv.); *shortly*, i.e. (fig.) *possibly*:—peradventure (-haps).

5030. ταχέως **tacheŏs**, *takh-eh'-oce*; adv. from *5036*; *briefly*, i.e. (in time) *speedily*, or (in manner) *rapidly*:—hastily, quickly, shortly, soon, suddenly.

5031. ταχινός **tachinŏs**, *takh-ee-nos'*; from *5034*; *curt*, i.e. *impending*:—shortly, swift.

5032. τάχιον **tachiŏn**, *takh'-ee-on*; neut. sing. of the compar. of *5036* (as adv.); *more swiftly*, i.e. (in manner) *more rapidly*, or (in time) *more speedily*:—out [run], quickly, shortly, sooner.

5033. τάχιστα **tachista**, *takh'-is-tah*; neut. plur. of the superl. of *5036* (as adv.); *most quickly*, i.e. (with *5613* pref.) *as soon as possible*:— + with all speed.

5034. τάχος **tachŏs**, *takh'-os*; from the same as *5036*; a *brief space* (of time), i.e. (with *1722* pref.) in *haste*:— + quickly, + shortly, + speedily.

5035. ταχύ **tachu**, *takh-oo'*; neut. sing. of *5036* (as adv.); *shortly*, i.e. *without delay*, *soon*, or (by surprise) *suddenly*, or (by impl. of ease) *readily*:—lightly, quickly.

5036. ταχύς **tachus**, *takh-oos'*; of uncert. affin.; *fleet*, i.e. (fig.) *prompt* or *ready*:—swift.

5037. τε **tĕ**, *teh*; a prim. particle (enclitic) of connection or addition; *both* or *also* (prop. as correl. of *2532*):—also, and, both, even, then, whether. Often used in comp., usually as the latter part.

5038. τεῖχος **tĕichŏs**, *ti'-khos*; akin to the base of *5088*; a *wall* (as formative of a house):—wall.

5039. τεκμήριον **tĕkmēriŏn**, *tek-may'-ree-on*; neut. of a presumed der. of τεκμάρ **tĕkmar** (a *goal* or fixed *limit*); a *token* (as *defining* a fact), i.e. *criterion* of certainty:—infallible proof.

5040. τεκνίον **tĕkniŏn**, *tek-nee'-on*; dimin. of *5043*; an *infant*, i.e. (plur. fig.) *darlings* (Christian converts):—little children.

5041. τεκνογονέω **tĕknŏgŏnĕō**, *tek-nog-on-eh'-o*; from a comp. of *5043* and the base of *1096*; to be a *child-bearer*, i.e. *parent* (mother):—bear children.

5042. τεκνογονία **tĕknŏgŏnia**, *tek-nog-on-ee'-ah*; from the same as *5041*; *childbirth* (parentage), i.e. (by impl.) *maternity* (the performance of maternal duties):—childbearing.

5043. τέκνον **tĕknŏn**, *tek'-non*; from the base of *5088*; a *child* (as produced):—child, daughter, son.

5044. τεκνοτροφέω **tĕknŏtrŏphĕō**, *tek-not-rof-eh'-o*; from a comp. of *5043* and *5142*; to be a *child-rearer*, i.e. *fulfil* the duties of a *female parent*:—bring up children.

5045. τέκτων **tĕktōn**, *tek'-tone*; from the base of *5088*; an *artificer* (as producer of fabrics), i.e. (spec.) a *craftsman* in wood:—carpenter.

5046. τέλειος **tĕlĕiŏs**, *tel'-i-os*; from *5056*; *complete* (in various applications of labor, growth, mental and moral character, etc.); neut. (as noun, with *3588*) *completeness*:—of full age, man, perfect.

5047. τελειότης **tĕlĕiŏtēs**, *tel-i-ot'-ace*; from *5046*; (the state) *completeness* (ment. or mor.):—perfection (-ness).

5048. τελειόω **tĕlĕiŏō**, *tel-i-ŏ'-o*; from *5046*; to *complete*, i.e. (lit.) *accomplish*, or (fig.) *consummate* (in character):—consecrate, finish, fulfil, (make) perfect.

5049. τελείως **tĕlĕiōs**, *tel-i'-oce*; adv. from *5046*; *completely*, i.e. (of hope) *without wavering*:—to the end.

5050. τελείωσις **tĕlĕiōsis**, *tel-i'-o-sis*; from *5448*; (the act) *completion*, i.e. (of prophecy) *verification*, or (of expiation) *absolution*:—perfection, performance.

5051. τελειωτής **tĕlĕiōtēs**, *tel-i-o-tace'*; from *5048*; a *completer*, i.e. *consummater*:—finisher.

5052. τελεσφορέω **tĕlĕsphŏrĕō**, *tel-es-for-eh'-o*; from a comp. of *5056* and *5342*; to be a *bearer* to completion (maturity), i.e. to *ripen* fruit (fig.):—bring fruit to perfection.

5053. τελευτάω **tĕlĕutaō**, *tel-yoo-tah'-o*; from a presumed der. of *5055*; to *finish* life (by impl. of *979*), i.e. *expire* (demise):—be dead, decease, die.

5054. τελευτή **tĕlĕutē**, *tel-yoo-tay'*; from *5053*; *decease*:—death.

5055. τελέω **tĕlĕō**, *tel-eh'-o*; from *5056*; to *end*, i.e. *complete*, *execute*, *conclude*, *discharge* (a debt):—accomplish, make an end, expire, fill up, finish, go over, pay, perform.

5056. τέλος **tĕlŏs**, *tel'-os*; from a prim. τέλλω **tĕllō** (to *set out* for a definite point or *goal*); prop. the point aimed at as a *limit*, i.e. (by impl.) the *conclusion* of an act or state (*termination* [lit., fig. or indef.], *result* [immed., ultimate or prophetic], *purpose*); spec. an *impost* or *levy* (as *paid*):— + continual, custom, end (-ing), finally, uttermost. Comp. *5411*.

5057. τελώνης **tĕlōnēs**, *tel-o'-nace*; from *5056* and *5608*; a *tax-farmer*, i.e. *collector* of public *revenue*:—publican.

5058. τελώνιον **tĕlōniŏn**, *tel-o'-nee-on*; neut. of a presumed der. of *5057*; a *tax-gatherer's* place of business:—receipt of custom.

5059. τέρας **tĕras**, *ter'-as*; of uncert. affin.; a *prodigy* or *omen*:—wonder.

5060. Τέρτιος **Tĕrtiŏs**, *ter'-tee-os*; of Lat. or.; *third*; *Tertius*, a Chr.:—Tertius.

5061. Τέρτυλλος **Tĕrtullŏs**, *ter'-tool-los*; of uncert. der.; *Tertullus*, a Rom.:—Tertullus.

5062. τεσσαρά **tĕssara**. See *5064*.

5063. τεσσαρακονταετής **tĕssarakŏntaĕtēs**, *tes-sar-ak-on-tah-et-ace'*; from *5062* and *2094*; of *forty years* of age:—(+ full, of) forty years (old).

5064. τέσσαρες **tĕssarĕs**, *tes'-sar-es*; neut.

τέσσαρα **tĕssara**, *tes'-sar-ah*; a plur. number; *four*:—four.

5065. τεσσαρεσκαιδέκατος **tĕssarĕskaidĕkatŏs**, *tes-sar-es-kahee-dek'-at-os*; from *5064* and *2532* and *1182*; *fourteenth*:—fourteenth.

5066. τεταρταῖος **tĕtartaiŏs**, *tet-ar-tah'-yos*; from *5064*; pertaining to the *fourth* day:—four days.

5067. τέταρτος **tĕtartŏs**, *tet'-ar-tos*; ord. from *5064*; *fourth*:—four (-th).

5068. τετράγωνος **tĕtragōnŏs**, *tet-rag'-o-nos*; from *5064* and *1137*; *four-cornered*, i.e. *square*:—foursquare.

5069. τετράδιον **tĕtradiŏn**, *tet-rad'-ee-on*; neut. of a presumed der. of τέτρας **tĕtras** (a *tetrad*; from *5064*); a *quaternion* or *squad* (picket) of four Rom. soldiers:—quaternion.

5070. τετρακισχίλιοι **tĕtrakischiliŏi**, *tet-rak-is-khil'-ee-oy*; from the mult. adv. of *5064* and *5507*; *four times a thousand*:—four thousand.

5071. τετρακόσιοι **tĕtrakŏsiŏi**, *tet-rak-os'-ee-oy*; neut. τετρακόσια **tĕtrakŏsia**, *tet-rak-os'-ee-ah*; plur. from *5064* and *1540*; *four hundred*:—four hundred.

5072. τετράμηνον **tĕtramēnŏn**, *tet-ram'-ay-non*; neut. of a comp. of *5064* and *3376*; a *four months'* space:—four months.

5073. τετραπλόος **tĕtraplŏŏs**, *tet-rap-lŏ'-os*; from *5064* and a der. of the base of *4118*; *quadruple*:—fourfold.

5074. τετράπους **tĕtrapŏus**, *tet-rap'-ooce*; from *5064* and *4228*; a *quadruped*:—fourfooted beast.

5075. τετραρχέω **tĕtrarchĕō**, *tet-rar-khch'-o*; from *5076*; to be a *tetrarch*:—(be) tetrarch.

5076. τετράρχης **tĕtrarchēs**, *tet-rar'-khace*; from *5064* and *757*; the *ruler* of a *fourth* part of a country (" *tetrarch* "):—tetrarch.

τεύχω **tĕuchō**. See *5177*.

5077. τεφρόω **tĕphrŏō**, *tef-rŏ'-o*; from τέφρα **tĕphra** (*ashes*); to *incinerate*, i.e. *consume*:—turn to ashes.

5078. τέχνη **tĕchnē**, *tekh'-nay*; from the base of *5088*; *art* (as productive), i.e. (spec.) a *trade*, or (gen.) *skill*:—art, craft, occupation.

5079. τεχνίτης **tĕchnitēs**, *tekh-nee'-tace*; from *5078*; an *artisan*; fig. a *founder* (*Creator*):—builder, craftsman.

5080. τήκω **tēkō**, *tay'-ko*; appar. a prim. verb; to *liquefy*:—melt.

5081. τηλαυγῶς **tēlaugōs**, *tay-lŏw-goce'*; adv. from a comp. of a der. of *5056* and *827*; in a *far-chining* manner, i.e. *plainly*:—clearly.

5082. τηλικοῦτος **tēlikŏutŏs**, *tay-lik-oo'-tos*; fem. τηλικαύτη **tēlikautē**, *tay-lik-ŏw'-tay*; from a comp. of *3588* with *2245* and *3778*; such as *this*, i.e. (in [fig.] magnitude) *so vast*:—so great, so mighty.

5083. τηρέω **tērĕō**, *tay-reh'-o*; from τηρός **tērŏs** (a *watch*; perh. akin to *2334*); to *guard* (from loss or *injury*, prop. by keeping the *eye* upon; and thus differing from *5442*, which is prop. to *prevent escaping*; and from *2892*, which implies a *fortress* or full military lines of apparatus), i.e. to *note* (a prophecy; fig. to *fulfil* a command); by impl. to *detain* (in custody; fig. to *maintain*); by extens. to *withhold* (for personal ends; fig. to *keep unmarried*):—hold fast, keep (-er), (ob-, pre-, re) serve, watch.

5084. τήρησις **tērēsis**, *tay'-ray-sis*; from *5083*; a *watching*, i.e. (fig.) *observance*, or (concr.) a *prison*:—hold.

τῇ τε **tē tĕ**, τὴν τόν **tēn tŏn**, τῆς τές **tēs tĕs**. See *3588*.

5085. Τιβεριάς **Tibĕrias**, *tib-er-ee-as'*; from *5086*; *Tiberias*, the name of a town and a lake in Pal.:—Tiberias.

5086. Τιβέριος **Tibĕriŏs**, *tib-er'-ee-os*; of Lat. or.; prob. *pertaining* to the *river Tiberis* or *Tiber*; *Tiberius*, a Rom. emperor:—Tiberius.

5087. τίθημι **tithēmi**, *tith'-ay-mee*; a prol. form of a prim.

θέω **thĕō**, *theh'-o* (which is used only as alt. in cert. tenses): to *place* (in the widest application, lit. and fig.; prop. in a passive or horizontal posture, and thus different from *2476*, which prop. denotes an upright and active position, while *2749* is prop. reflexive and utterly prostrate):— + advise, appoint, bow, commit, conceive, give, × kneel down, lay (aside, down, up), make, ordain, purpose, put, set (forth), settle, sink down.

5088. τίκτω **tiktō,** *tik'-to;* a strengthened form of a prim. τέκω **tĕkō,** *tek'-o* (which is used only as alt. in certain tenses); to *produce* (from seed, as a mother, a plant, the earth, etc.), lit. or fig.:—bear, be born, bring forth, be delivered, be in travail.

5089. τίλλω **tillō,** *til'-lo;* perh. akin to the alt. of *138,* and thus to *4951;* to *pull* off:—pluck.

5090. Τίμαιος **Timaiŏs,** *tim'-ah-yos;* prob. of Chald. or. [comp. 2931]; *Timæus* (i.e. *Timay*), an Isr.:—Timæus.

5091. τιμάω **timaō,** *tim-ah'-o;* from *5093;* to *prize,* i.e. *fix* a *valuation* upon; by impl. to *revere:*—honour, value.

5092. τιμή **timē,** *tee-may';* from *5099;* a *value,* i.e. *money* paid, or (concr. and collect.) *valuables;* by anal. *esteem* (espec. of the highest degree), or the *dignity* itself:—honour, precious, price, some.

5093. τίμιος **timiŏs,** *tim'-ee-os;* includ. the comp.

τιμιώτερος **timiōtĕrŏs,** *tim-ee-o'-ter-os;* and the superl.

τιμιώτατος **timiōtatŏs,** *tim-ee-o'-tat-os;* from *5092;* valuable, i.e. (obj.) *costly,* or (subj.) *honored, esteemed,* or (fig.) *beloved:*—dear, honourable, (more, most) precious, had in reputation.

5094. τιμιότης **timiŏtēs,** *tim-ee-ot'-ace;* from *5093;* expensiveness, i.e. (by impl.) *magnificence:*—costliness.

5095. Τιμόθεος **Timŏthĕŏs,** *tee-moth'-eh-os;* from *5092* and *2316; dear to God; Timotheus,* a Chr.:—Timotheus, Timothy.

5096. Τίμων **Timōn,** *tee'-mone;* from *5092;* valuable; *Timon,* a Chr.:—Timon.

5097. τιμωρέω **timōrĕō,** *tim-o-reh'-o;* from a comp. of *5092* and οὖρος **ŏurŏs** (a *guard*); prop. to *protect* one's *honor,* i.e. to *avenge* (*inflict* a *penalty*):—punish.

5098. τιμωρία **timōria,** *tee-mo-ree'-ah;* from *5097; vindication,* i.e. (by impl.) a *penalty:*—punishment.

5099. τίνω **tinō,** *tee'-no;* strengthened for a prim.

τίω **tiō,** *tee'-o* (which is only used as an alt. in certain tenses); to *pay* a price, i.e. as a *penalty:*—be punished with.

5100. τίς **tis,** *tis;* an enclit. indef. pron.; *some* or *any* person or object:—a (kind of), any (man, thing, thing at all), certain (thing), divers, he (every) man, one (× thing), ought, + partly, some (man, -body, -thing, -what), (+ that no -) thing, what (-soever), × wherewith, whom [-soever], whose ([-soever]).

5101. τίς **tis,** *tis;* prob. emphat. of *5100;* an interrog. pron., *who, which* or *what* (in direct or indirect questions):—every man, how (much), + no (-ne, thing), what (manner, thing), where ([-by, -fore, -of, unto, -with, -withal]), whether, which, who (-m, -se), why.

5102. τίτλος **titlŏs,** *tit'-los;* of Lat. or.; a *titulus* or "*title*" (*placard*):—title.

5103. Τίτος **Titŏs,** *tee'-tos;* of Lat. or. but uncert. signif.; *Titus,* a Chr.:—Titus.

τίω **tiō.** See *5099.*

τό **tŏ.** See *3588.*

5104. τοί **tŏi,** *toy;* prob. for the dat. of *3588;* an enclit. particle of *asseveration* by way of *contrast; in sooth:*—[used only with other particles in comp., as *2544, 3305, 5105, 5106,* etc.]

5105. τοιγαροῦν **tŏigarŏun,** *toy-gar-oon';* from *5104* and *1063* and *3767; truly for then,* i.e. consequently:—there- (where-) fore.

τοίγε **tŏigĕ.** See *2544.*

5106. τοίνυν **tŏinun,** *toy'-noon;* from *5104* and *3568; truly now,* i.e. *accordingly:*—then, therefore.

5107. τοιόσδε **tŏiŏsdĕ,** *toy-os'-deh* (includ. the other inflections); from a der. of *5104* and *1161; such-like* then, i.e. *so great:*—such.

5108. τοιοῦτος **tŏiŏutŏs,** *toy-oo'-tos* (includ. the other inflections); from *5104* and *3778; truly this,* i.e. *of this sort* (to denote *character* or *individuality*):—like, such (an one).

5109. τοῖχος **tŏichŏs,** *toy'-khos;* another form of *5038;* a *wall:*—wall.

5110. τόκος **tŏkŏs,** *tok'-os;* from the base of *5088; interest* on money loaned (as a *produce*):—usury.

5111. τολμάω **tŏlmaō,** *tol-mah'-o;* from τόλμα **tŏlma** (*boldness;* prob. itself from the base of *5056* through the idea of *extreme* conduct); to *venture* (obj. or in *act;* while *2292* is rather subj. or in *feeling*); by impl. to be *courageous:*—be bold, boldly, dare, durst.

5112. τολμηρότερον **tŏlmērŏtĕrŏn,** *tol-may-rot'-er-on;* neut. of the comp. of a der. of the base of *5111* (as adv.); *more daringly,* i.e. *with greater confidence* than otherwise:—the more boldly.

5113. τολμητής **tŏlmētēs,** *tol-may-tace';* from *5111;* a *daring* (*audacious*) man:—presumptuous.

5114. τομώτερος **tŏmōtĕrŏs,** *tom-o'-ter-os;* comp. of a der. of the prim. τέμνω **tĕmnō** (to *cut;* more comprehensive or decisive than *2875,* as if by a *single* stroke; whereas that implies repeated blows, like *hacking*); *more keen:*—sharper.

5115. τόξον **tŏxŏn,** *tox'-on;* from the base of *5088;* a *bow* (appar. as the simplest fabric):—bow.

5116. τοπάζιον **tŏpazion,** *top-ad'-zee-on;* neut. of a presumed der. (alt.) of τόπαζος **tŏpazŏs** (a "*topaz*"; of uncert. or.); a *gem,* prob. the *chrysolite:*—topaz.

5117. τόπος **tŏpŏs,** *top'-os;* appar. a prim. word; a *spot* (gen. in *space,* but limited by occupancy; whereas *5561* is a larger but partic. *locality*), i.e. *location* (as a position, home, tract, etc.); fig. *condition, opportunity;* spec. a *scabbard:*—coast, licence, place, × plain, quarter, + rock, room, where.

5118. τοσοῦτος **tŏsŏutŏs,** *tos-oo'-tos;* from τόσος **tŏsŏs** (*so much;* appar. from *3588* and *3739*) and *3778* (includ. its variations); so *vast as this,* i.e. *such* (in quantity, amount, number or space):—as large, so great (long, many, much), these many.

5119. τότε **tŏtĕ,** *tot'-eh;* from (the neut. of) *3588* and *3753; the when,* i.e. *at the time* that (of the past or future, also in consecution):—that time, then.

5120. τοῦ **tŏu,** *too;* prop. the gen. of *3588;* sometimes used for *5127;* of *this person:*—his.

5121. τοὐναντίον **tŏunantiŏn,** *too-nan-tee'-on;* contr. for the neut. of *3588* and *1726; on the contrary:*—contrariwise.

5122. τοὔνομα **tŏunŏma,** *too'-no-mah;* contr. for the neut. of *3588* and *3686; the name* (is):—named.

5123. τουτέστι **tŏutĕsti,** *toot-es'-tee;* contr. for *5124* and *2076; that is:*—that is (to say).

5124. τοῦτο **tŏutŏ,** *too'-to;* neut. sing. nom. or acc. of *3778; that thing:*—here [-unto], it, partly, self [-same], so, that (intent), the same, there [-fore, -unto], this, thus, where [-fore].

5125. τούτοις **tŏutŏis,** *too'-toice;* dat. plur. masc. or neut. of *3778;* to (*for, in, with* or *by*) *these* (persons or things):—such, them, there [-in, -with], these, this, those.

5126. τοῦτον **tŏutŏn,** *too'-ton;* acc. sing. masc. of *3778; this* (person, as obj. of verb or prep.):—him, the same, that, this.

5127. τούτου **tŏutŏu,** *too'-too;* gen. sing. masc. or neut. of *3778; of* (*from* or *concerning*) *this* (person or thing):—here [-by], him, it, + such manner of, that, thence [-forth], thereabout, this, thus.

5128. τούτους **tŏutŏus,** *too'-tooce;* acc. plur. masc. of *3778; these* (persons, as obj. of verb or prep.):—such, them, these, this.

5129. τούτῳ **tŏutō,** *too'-to;* dat. sing. masc. or neut. of *3778;* to (*in, with* or *by*) *this* (person or thing):—here [-by, -in], him, one, the same, there [-in], this.

5130. τούτων **tŏutōn,** *too'-tone;* gen. plur. masc. or neut. of *3778; of* (*from* or *concerning*) *these* (persons or things):—such, their, these (things), they, this sort, those.

5131. τράγος **tragŏs,** *trag'-os;* from the base of *5176;* a *he-goat* (as a *gnawer*):—goat.

5132. τράπεζα **trapĕza,** *trap'-ed-zah;* prob. contr. from *5064* and *3979;* a *table* or *stool* (as being *four-legged*), usually for food (fig. a *meal*); also a *counter* for money (fig. a broker's *office* for loans at interest):—bank, meat, table.

5133. τραπεζίτης **trapĕzitēs,** *trap-ed-zee'-tace;* from *5132;* a *money-broker* or *banker:*—exchanger.

5134. τραῦμα **trauma,** *trŏw'-mah;* from the base of τιτρώσκω **titrōskō** (to *wound;* akin to the base of *2352, 5147, 5149,* etc.); a *wound:*—wound.

5135. τραυματίζω **traumatizō,** *trŏw-mat-id'-zo;* from *5134;* to *inflict* a *wound:*—wound.

5136. τραχηλίζω **trachēlizō,** *trakh-ay-lid'-zo;* from *5137;* to *seize* by the *throat* or *neck,* i.e. to *expose* the *gullet* of a victim for killing (gen. to *lay bare*):—opened.

5137. τράχηλος **trachēlŏs,** *trakh'-ay-los;* prob. from *5143* (through the idea of *mobility*); the *throat* (*neck*), i.e. (fig.) *life:*—neck.

5138. τραχύς **trachus,** *trakh-oos';* perh. strengthened from the base of *4486* (as if *jagged* by rents); *uneven, rocky* (*reefy*):—rock, rough.

5139. Τραχωνῖτις **Trachōnitis,** *trakh-o-nee'-tis;* from a der. of *5138; rough* district; *Trachonitis,* a region of Syria:—Trachonitis.

5140. τρεῖς **trĕis,** *trice;* neut.

τρία **tria,** *tree'-ah;* a prim. (plur.) number; "*three*":—three.

5141. τρέμω **trĕmō,** *trem'-o;* strengthened from a prim. τρέω **trĕō** (to "*dread*", "*terrify*"); to "*tremble*" or *fear:*—be afraid, trembling.

5142. τρέφω **trĕphō,** *tref'-o;* a prim. verb (prop. θρέφω **thrĕphō**; but perh. strength. from the base of *5157* through the idea of *convolution*); prop. to *stiffen,* i.e. *fatten* (by impl. to *cherish* [with food, etc.], *pamper, rear*):—bring up, feed, nourish.

5143. τρέχω **trĕchō,** *trekh'-o;* appar. a prim. verb (prop. θρέχω **thrĕchō**; comp. *2359*); which uses δρέμω **drĕmō,** *drem'-o* (the base of *1408*) as alt. in certain tenses; to *run* or *walk hastily* (lit. or fig.):—have course, run.

5144. τριάκοντα **triakŏnta,** *tree-ak'-on-tah;* the decade of *5140; thirty:*—thirty.

5145. τριακόσιοι **triakŏsiŏi,** *tree-ak-os'-ee-oy;* plur. from *5140* and *1540; three hundred:*—three hundred.

5146. τρίβολος **tribŏlŏs,** *trib'-ol-os;* from *5140* and *956;* prop. a *crow-foot* (*three-pronged* obstruction in war), i.e. (by anal.) a *thorny* plant (*caltrop*):—brier, thistle.

5147. τρίβος **tribŏs,** *tree'-bos;* from τρίβω **tribō** (to *rub*"; akin to τείρω **tĕirō,** τρύω **truō,** and the base of *5131, 5134*); a *rut* or worn *track:*—path.

5148. τριετία **triĕtia,** *tree-et-ee'-ah;* from a comp. of *5140* and *2094;* a *three years'* period (*triennium*):—space of three years.

5149. τρίζω **trizō,** *trid'-zo;* appar. a prim. verb; to *creak* (*squeak*), i.e. (by anal.) to *grate* the teeth (in frenzy):—gnash.

5150. τρίμηνον **trimēnŏn,** *trim'-ay-non;* neut. of a comp. of *5140* and *3376* as noun; a *three months'* space:—three months.

5151. τρίς **tris,** *trece;* adv. from *5140; three times:*—three times, thrice.

5152. τρίστεγον **tristĕgŏn,** *tris'-teg-on;* neut. of a comp. of *5140* and *4721* as noun; a *third roof* (*story*):—third loft.

5153. τρισχίλιοι **trischiliŏi,** *tris-khil'-ee-oy;* from *5151* and *5507; three times a thousand:*—three thousand.

5154. τρίτος **tritŏs,** *tree'-tos;* ord. from *5140; third;* neut. (as noun) a *third part,* or (as adv.) a (or the) *third time,* or (fig.) a *third* (*-ly*).

τρίχες **trichĕs,** etc. See *2359.*

5155. τρίχινος **trichinŏs,** *trikh'-ee-nos;* from *2359; hairy,* i.e. made of *hair* (*mohair*):—of hair.

5156. τρόμος **trŏmŏs**, *trom'-os;* from *5141;* a "trembling", i.e. quaking with *fear:—* + tremble (-ing).

5157. τροπή **trŏpē**, *trop-ay';* from an appar. prim. τρέπω **trĕpō** (to *turn*); a *turn* ("trope"), i.e. revolution (fig. *variation*):—turning.

5158. τρόπος **trŏpŏs**, *trop'-os;* from the same as *5157;* a *turn*, i.e. (by impl.) *mode* or *style* (espec. with prep. or rel. pref. as adv. *like*); fig. *deportment* or *character:—*(even) as, conversation, [+ like] manner (+ by any) means, way.

5159. τροποφορέω **trŏpŏphŏrĕō**, *trop-of-or-eh'-o;* from *5158* and *5409;* to endure one's *habits:—* suffer the manners.

5160. τροφή **trŏphē**, *trof-ay';* from *5142;* nourishment (lit. or fig.); by impl. rations (*wages*):—food, meat.

5161. Τρόφιμος **Trŏphĭmŏs**, *trof'-ee-mos;* from *5160;* nutritive; Trophimus, a Chr.:—Trophimus.

5162. τροφός **trŏphŏs**, *trof-os';* from *5142;* a nourisher, i.e. *nurse:—*nurse.

5163. τροχιά **trŏchĭa**, *trokh-ee-ah';* from *5164;* a track (as a wheel-*rut*), i.e. (fig.) a *course* of conduct:—path.

5164. τροχός **trŏchŏs**, *trokh-os';* from *5143;* a wheel (as a *runner*), i.e. (fig.) a *circuit* of phys. effects:—course.

5165. τρύβλιον **trublĭŏn**, *troob'-lee-on;* neut. of a presumed der. of uncert. affin.; a *bowl:—*dish.

5166. τρυγάω **trugaō**, *troo-gah'-o;* from a der. of τρύγω **trugō** (to *dry*) mean. ripe *fruit* (as if *dry*); to *collect* the vintage:—gather.

5167. τρυγών **trugōn**, *troo-gone';* from τρύζω **truzō** (to *murmur*; akin to *5149*, but denoting a duller sound); a *turtle-dove* (as *cooing*):—turtle-dove.

5168. τρυμαλιά **trumalĭa**, *troo-mal-ee-ah';* from a der. of τρύω **truō** (to *wear* away; akin to the base of *5134, 5147* and *5176*); an *orifice*, i.e. a needle's *eye:—* eye. Comp. *5169.*

5169. τρύπημα **trupēma**, *troo'-pay-mah;* from a der. of the base of *5168;* an aperture, i.e. a needle's *eye:—*eye.

5170. Τρύφαινα **Truphaina**, *troo'-fahee-nah;* from *5172;* luxurious; Tryphœna, a Chr. woman:—Tryphena.

5171. τρυφάω **truphaō**, *troo-fah'-o;* from *5172;* to indulge in *luxury:—*live in pleasure.

5172. τρυφή **truphē**, *troo-fay';* from θρύπτω **thruptō** (to *break* up or [fig.] enfeeble, espec. the mind and body by indulgence); *effeminacy*, i.e. *luxury* or *debauchery:—*delicately, riot.

5173. Τρυφῶσα **Truphōsa**, *troo-fo'-sah;* from *5172;* luxuriating; Tryphosa, a Chr. female:—Tryphosa.

5174. Τρωάς **Trōas**, *tro-as';* from Τρός **Trŏs** (a *Trojan*); the *Troad* (or plain of Troy), i.e. *Troas*, a place in Asia Minor:—Troas.

5175. Τρωγύλλιον **Trōgullĭŏn**, *tro-gool'-lee-on;* of uncert. der.; *Trogyllium*, a place in Asia Minor:—Trogyllium.

5176. τρώγω **trōgō**, *tro'-go;* prob. strength. from a collat. form of the base of *5134* and *5147* through the idea of *corrosion* or *wear;* or perh. rather of a base of *5167* and *5149* through the idea of a *craunching* sound; to *gnaw* or *chew*, i.e. (gen.) to *eat:—*eat.

5177. τυγχάνω **tugchanō**, *toong-khan'-o;* prob. for an obsol. τύχω **tuchō** (for which the mid. of another alt. τεύχω **tĕuchō** [to *make ready* or *bring to pass*] is used in cert. tenses; akin to the base of *5088* through the idea of *effecting;* prop. to *affect;* or (spec.) to *hit* or *light upon* (as a mark to be reached), i.e. (trans.) to *attain* or *secure* an object or end, or (intrans.) to *happen* (as if *meeting* with); but in the latter application only impers. (with *1487*), i.e. *perchance;* or (pres. part.) as adj. *usual* (as if commonly *met* with, with *3756*, *extraordinary*), neut. (as adv.) *perhaps;* or (with aɴother verb) as by *accident* (as *it were*):—be, chance, enjoy, little, obtain, × refresh . . . self, + special. Comp. *5180.*

5178. τυμπανίζω **tumpanizō**, *toom-pan-id'-zo;* from a der. of *5180* (mean. a *drum*, "*tympanum*"); to stretch on an instrument of *torture* resembling a drum, and thus *beat* to death:—torture.

5179. τύπος **tupŏs**, *too'-pos;* from *5180;* a *die* (as struck), i.e. (by impl.) a *stamp* or *scar;* by anal. a *shape*, i.e. a *statue*, (fig.) *style* or *resemblance;* spec. a *sampler* ("*type*"), i.e. a *model* (for imitation) or *instance* (for warning):—en- (ex-) ample, fashion, figure, form, manner, pattern, print.

5180. τύπτω **tuptō**, *toop'-to;* a prim. verb (in a strength. form); to "*thump*", i.e. *cudgel* or *pummel* (prop. with a stick or *bastinado*), but in any case by *repeated* blows; thus differing from *3817* and *3060*, which denote a [usually single] blow with the hand or any instrument, or *4141* with the *fist* [or a *hammer*], or *4474* with the *palm;* as well as from *5177*, an *accidental* collision; by anal. to *punish;* fig. to *offend* (the conscience):—beat, smite, strike, wound.

5181. Τύραννος **Turannŏs**, *too'-ran-nos;* a provincial form of the der. of the base of *2962;* a "*tyrant*"; Tyrannus, an Ephesian:—Tyrannus.

5182. τυρβάζω **turbazō**, *toor-bad'-zo;* from τύρβη **turbē** (Lat. *turba*, a *crowd;* akin to *2351*); to make "*turbid* ", i.e. *disturb:—*trouble.

5183. Τύριος **Turĭŏs**, *too'-ree-os;* from *5184;* a Tyrian, i.e. inhab. of Tyrus:—of Tyre.

5184. Τύρος **Turŏs**, *too'-ros;* of Heb. or. [6865]: *Tyrus* (i.e. *Tsor*), a place in Pal.:—Tyre.

5185. τυφλός **tuphlŏs**, *toof-los';* from *5187;* opaque (as if *smoky*), i.e. (by anal.) *blind* (phys. or ment.):—blind.

5186. τυφλόω **tuphlŏō**, *toof-lŏ'-o;* from *5185;* to make *blind*, i.e. (fig.) to *obscure:—*blind.

5187. τυφόω **tuphŏō**, *toof-ŏ'-o;* from a der. of *5188;* to envelop with *smoke*, i.e. (fig.) to *inflate* with self-conceit:—high-minded, be lifted up with pride, be proud.

5188. τύφω **tuphō**, *too'-fo;* appar. a prim. verb; to make a *smoke*, i.e. slowly *consume* without flame:—smoke.

5189. τυφωνικός **tuphōnĭkŏs**, *too-fo-nee-kos';* from a der. of *5188;* stormy (as if *smoky*):—tempestuous.

5190. Τυχικός **Tuchĭkŏs**, *too-khee-kos';* from a der. of *5177;* fortuitous, i.e. *fortunate;* Tychicus, a Chr.:—Tychicus.

Υ

5191. ὑακίνθινος **huakinthĭnŏs**, *hoo-ak-in'-thee-nos;* from *5192;* "*hyacinthine*" or "*jacinthine*", i.e. deep *blue:—*jacinth.

5192. ὑάκινθος **huakinthŏs**, *hoo-ak'-in-thos;* of uncert. der.; the "*hyacinth*" or "*jacinth*", i.e. some gem of a deep *blue* color, prob. the *zirkon:—*jacinth.

5193. ὑάλινος **hualĭnŏs**, *hoo-al'-ee-nos;* from *5194;* glassy, i.e. *transparent:—*of glass.

5194. ὕαλος **hualŏs**, *hoo'-al-os;* perh. from the same as *5205* (as being transparent like *rain*); *glass:—*glass.

5195. ὑβρίζω **hubrizō**, *hoo-brid'-zo;* from *5196;* to *exercise violence*, i.e. *abuse:—*use despitefully, reproach, entreat shamefully (spitefully).

5196. ὕβρις **hubris**, *hoo'-bris;* from *5228;* insolence (as over-bearing), i.e. *insult*, *injury:—*harm, hurt, reproach.

5197. ὑβριστής **hubristēs**, *hoo-bris-tace';* from *5195;* an *insulter*, i.e. *maltreater:—*despiteful, injurious.

5198. ὑγιαίνω **hugiainō**, *hoog-ee-ah'-ee-no;* from *5199;* to *have* sound *health*, i.e. *be well* (in body); fig. to be *uncorrupt* (true in doctrine):—be in health, (be safe and) sound, (be) whole (-some).

5199. ὑγιής **hugĭēs**, *hoog-ee-ace';* from the base of *837;* healthy, i.e. *well* (in body); fig. *true* (in doctrine):—sound, whole.

5200. ὑγρός **hugrŏs**, *hoo-gros';* from the base of *5205;* wet (as if with *rain*), i.e. (by impl.) sappy (*fresh*):—green.

5201. ὑδρία **hudria**, *hoo-dree-ah';* from *5204;* a water-jar, i.e. receptacle for family supply:—waterpot.

5202. ὑδροποτέω **hudrŏpŏtĕō**, *hoo-drop-ot-eh'-o;* from a comp. of *5204* and a der. of *4095;* to be a *water-drinker*, i.e. to *abstain from vinous beverages:—*drink water.

5203. ὑδρωπικός **hudrōpĭkŏs**, *hoo-dro-pik-os';* from a comp. of *5204* and a der. of *3700* (as if *looking watery*); to be "*dropsical*":—have the dropsy.

5204. ὕδωρ **hudōr**, *hoo'-dore;* gen. ὕδατος **hudatŏs**, *hoo'-dat-os*, etc.; from the base of *5205;* water (as if *rainy*) lit. or fig.:—water.

5205. ὑετός **huĕtŏs**, *hoo-et-os';* from a prim. ὕω **huō** (to *rain*); rain, espec. a *shower:—*rain.

5206. υἱοθεσία **huĭŏthĕsĭa**, *hwee-oth-es-ee'-ah;* from a presumed comp. of *5207* and a der. of *5087;* the *placing* as a *son*, i.e. *adoption* (fig. Chr. *sonship* in respect to God):—adoption (of children, of sons).

5207. υἱός **huĭŏs**, *hwee-os';* appar. a prim. word; a "*son*" (sometimes of animals), used very widely of immed., remote or fig. kinship:—child, foal, son.

5208. ὕλη **hulē**, *hoo-lay';* perh. akin to *3586;* a forest, i.e. (by impl.) *fuel:—*matter.

5209. ὑμᾶς **humas**, *hoo-mas';* acc. of *5210;* you (as the obj. of a verb or prep.):—ye, you (+ -ward), your (+ own).

5210. ὑμεῖς **humĕis**, *hoo-mice';* irreg. plur. of *4771;* you (as subj. of verb):—ye (yourselves), you.

5211. Ὑμεναῖος **Humĕnaĭŏs**, *hoo-men-ah'-yos;* from Ὑμήν **Humēn** (the god of *weddings*); "*hymenœal*"; Hymenœus, an opponent of Christianity:—Hymenæus.

5212. ὑμέτερος **humĕtĕrŏs**, *hoo-met'-er-os;* from *5210;* yours, i.e. pertaining to *you:—*your (own).

5213. ὑμῖν **humin**, *hoo-min';* irreg. dat. of *5210;* to (with or by) *you:—*ye, you, your (-selves).

5214. ὑμνέω **humnĕō**, *hoom-neh'-o;* from *5215;* to *hymn*, i.e. sing a religious ode; by impl. to *celebrate* (God) in song:—sing an hymn (praise unto).

5215. ὕμνος **humnŏs**, *hoom'-nos;* appar. from a simpler (obsol.) form of ὕδέω **hudĕō** (to *celebrate;* prob. akin to *103;* comp. *5567*); a "*hymn*" or religious ode (one of the Psalms):—hymn.

5216. ὑμῶν **humōn**, *hoo-mone';* gen. of *5210;* of (*from* or *concerning*) *you:—*ye, you, your (own, -selves).

5217. ὑπάγω **hupagō**, *hoop-ag'-o;* from *5259* and *71;* to *lead* (oneself) *under*, i.e. *withdraw* or *retire* (as if *sinking* out of sight), lit. or fig.:—depart, get hence, go (a-) way.

5218. ὑπακοή **hupakŏē**, *hoop-ak-ŏ-ay';* from *5219;* attentive *hearkening*, i.e. (by impl.) compliance or *submission:—*obedience, (make) obedient, obey (-ing).

5219. ὑπακούω **hupakŏuō**, *hoop-ak-oo'-o;* from *5259* and *191;* to *hear under* (as a *subordinate*), i.e. to *listen attentively;* by impl. to *heed* or *conform* to a command or authority:—hearken, be obedient to, obey.

5220. ὕπανδρος **hupandrŏs**, *hoop'-an-dros;* from *5259* and *435;* in *subjection under* a *man*, i.e. a *married* woman:—which hath an husband.

5221. ὑπαντάω **hupantaō**, *hoop-an-tah'-o;* from *5259* and a der. of *473;* to *go opposite* (*meet*) under (*quietly*), i.e. to *encounter*, *fall in with:—*(go to) meet.

5222. ὑπάντησις **hupantēsis**, *hoop-an'-tay-sis;* from *5221;* an *encounter* or *concurrence* (with *1519* for infin., in order to *fall in with*):—meeting.

5223. ὕπαρξις **huparxis**, *hoop'-arx-is;* from *5225;* existency or proprietorship, i.e. (concr.) property, *wealth:—*goods, substance.

5224. ὑπάρχοντα **huparchŏnta**, *hoop-ar'-khon-tah;* neut. plur. of pres. part. act. of *5225* as noun; things *extant* or *in hand*, i.e. *property* or *possessions:—*goods, that which one has, things which (one) possesseth, substance, that hast.

5225. ὑπάρχω **hŭparchō**, *hoop-ar'-kho;* from *5259* and *756;* to begin under (quietly), i.e. come into existence (be present or at hand); expletively, to exist (as copula or subordinate to an adj., part., adv. or prep., or as auxil. to principal verb):—after, behave, live.

5226. ὑπείκω **hŭpĕikō**, *hoop-i'-ko;* from *5259* and εἴκω **ĕikō** (to yield, be "weak"); to surrender:—submit self.

5227. ὑπεναντίος **hŭpĕnantiŏs**, *hoop-en-an-tee'-os;* from *5259* and *1727;* under (covertly) contrary to, i.e. opposed or (as noun) an opponent:—adversary, against.

5228. ὑπέρ **hŭpĕr**, *hoop-er';* a prim. prep.; "over", i.e. (with the gen.) of place, above, beyond, across, or causal, for the sake of, instead, regarding; with the acc. superior to, more than:—(+ exceeding abundantly) above, in (on) behalf of, beyond, by, + very chiefest, concerning, exceeding (above, -ly), for, + very highly, more (than), of, over, on the part of, for sake of, in stead, than, to (-ward), very. In comp. it retains many of the above applications.

5229. ὑπεραίρομαι **hŭpĕrairŏmai**, *hoop-er-ah'ee-rom-ahee;* mid. from *5228* and *142;* to raise oneself over, i.e. (fig.) to become haughty:—exalt self, be exalted above measure.

5230. ὑπέρακμος **hŭpĕrakmŏs**, *hoop-er'-ak-mos;* from *5228* and the base of *188;* beyond the "acme", i.e. fig. (of a daughter) past the bloom (prime) of youth:—+ pass the flower of (her) age.

5231. ὑπεράνω **hŭpĕranō**, *hoop-er-an'-o;* from *5228* and *507;* above upward, i.e. greatly higher (in place or rank):—far above, over.

5232. ὑπεραυξάνω **hŭpĕrauxanō**, *hoop-er-owx-an'-o;* from *5228* and *837;* to increase above ordinary degree:—grow exceedingly.

5233. ὑπερβαίνω **hŭpĕrbainō**, *hoop-er-bah'ee-no;* from *5228* and the base of *939;* to transcend, i.e. (fig.) to overreach:—go beyond.

5234. ὑπερβαλλόντως **hŭpĕrballŏntōs**, *hoop-er-bal-lon'-toce;* adv. from pres. part. act. of *5235;* excessively:—beyond measure.

5235. ὑπερβάλλω **hŭpĕrballō**, *hoop-er-bal'-lo;* from *5228* and *906;* to throw beyond the usual mark, i.e. (fig.) to surpass (only act. part. supereminent):—exceeding, excel, pass.

5236. ὑπερβολή **hŭpĕrbŏlē**, *hoop-er-bol-ay';* from *5235;* a throwing beyond others, i.e. (fig.) supereminence; adv. (with *1519* or *2596*) pre-eminently:—abundance, (far more) exceeding, excellency, more excellent, beyond (out of) measure.

5237. ὑπερείδω **hŭpĕrĕidō**, *hoop-er-i'-do;* from *5228* and *1492;* to overlook, i.e. not punish:—wink at.

5238. ὑπερέκεινα **hŭpĕrĕkĕina**, *hoop-er-ek'-i-nah;* from *5228* and the neut. plur. of *1565;* above those parts, i.e. still farther:—beyond.

5239. ὑπερεκτείνω **hŭpĕrĕktĕinō**, *hoop-er-ek-ti'-no;* from *5228* and *1614;* to extend inordinately:—stretch beyond.

5240. ὑπερεκχύνω **hŭpĕrĕkchunō**, *hoop-er-ek-khoo'-no;* from *5228* and the alt. form of *1632;* to pour out over, i.e. (pass.) to overflow:—run over.

ὑπερεκπερισσοῦ **hŭpĕrĕkpĕrissŏu**. See *5228* and *1537* and *4053*.

5241. ὑπερεντυγχάνω **hŭpĕrĕntugchanō**, *hoop-er-en-toong-khan'-o;* from *5228* and *1793;* to intercede in behalf of:—make intercession for.

5242. ὑπερέχω **hŭpĕrĕchō**, *hoop-er-ekh'-o;* from *5228* and *2192;* to hold oneself above, i.e. (fig.) to excel; part. (as adj., or neut. as noun) superior, superiority:—better, excellency, higher, pass, supreme.

5243. ὑπερηφανία **hŭpĕrēphania**, *hoop-er-ay-fan-ee'-ah;* from *5244;* haughtiness:—pride.

5244. ὑπερήφανος **hŭpĕrēphanŏs**, *hoop-er-ay'-fan-os;* from *5228* and *5316;* appearing above others (conspicuous), i.e. (fig.) haughty:—proud.

ὑπερλίαν **hŭpĕrlian**. See *5228* and *3029.*

5245. ὑπερνικάω **hŭpĕrnikaō**, *hoop-er-nik-ah'-o;* from *5228* and *3528;* to vanquish beyond, i.e. gain a decisive victory:—more than conquer.

5246. ὑπέρογκος **hŭpĕrŏgkŏs**, *hoop-er'-ong-kos;* from *5228* and *3591;* bulging over, i.e. (fig.) insolent:—great swelling.

5247. ὑπεροχή **hŭpĕrŏchē**, *hoop-er-okh-ay';* from *5242;* prominence, i.e. (fig.) superiority (in rank or character):—authority, excellency.

5248. ὑπερπερισσεύω **hŭpĕrpĕrissĕuō**, *hoop-er-per-is-syoo'-o;* from *5228* and *4052;* to superabound:—abound much more, exceeding.

5249. ὑπερπερισσῶς **hŭpĕrpĕrissōs**, *hoop-er-per-is-soce';* from *5228* and *4057;* superabundantly, i.e. exceedingly:—beyond measure.

5250. ὑπερπλεονάζω **hŭpĕrplĕŏnazō**, *hoop-er-pleh-on-ad'-zo;* from *5228* and *4121;* to superabound:—be exceeding abundant.

5251. ὑπερυψόω **hŭpĕrupsŏō**, *hoop-er-oop-sŏ'-o;* from *5228* and *5312;* to elevate above others, i.e. raise to the highest position:—highly exalt.

5252. ὑπερφρονέω **hŭpĕrphrŏnĕō**, *hoop-er-fron-eh'-o;* from *5228* and *5426;* to esteem oneself overmuch, i.e. be vain or arrogant:—think more highly.

5253. ὑπερῷον **hŭpĕrō₂ŏn**, *hoop-er-o'-on;* neut. of a der. of *5228;* a higher part of the house, i.e. apartment in the third story:—upper chamber (room).

5254. ὑπέχω **hŭpĕchō**, *hoop-ekh'-o;* from *5259* and *2192;* to hold oneself under, i.e. endure with patience:—suffer.

5255. ὑπήκοος **hŭpēkŏŏs**, *hoop-ay'-kŏ-os;* from *5219;* attentively listening, i.e. (by impl.) submissive:—obedient.

5256. ὑπηρετέω **hŭpērĕtĕō**, *hoop-ay-ret-eh'-o;* from *5257;* to be a subordinate, i.e. (by impl.) subserve:—minister (unto), serve.

5257. ὑπηρέτης **hŭpērĕtēs**, *hoop-ay-ret'-ace;* from *5259* and a der. of ἐρέσσω **ĕrĕssō** (to row); an under-oarsman, i.e. (gen.) subordinate (assistant, sexton, constable):—minister, officer, servant.

5258. ὕπνος **hŭpnŏs**, *hoop'-nos;* from an obsol. prim. (perh. akin to *5259* through the idea of subsilience); sleep, i.e. (fig.) spiritual torpor:—sleep.

5259. ὑπό **hŭpŏ**, *hoop-ŏ';* a prim. prep.; under, i.e. (with the gen.) of place (beneath), or with verbs (the agency or means, through); (with the acc.) of place (whither [underneath] or where [below]) or time (when [at]):—among, by, from, in, of, under, with. In comp. it retains the same gen. applications, espec. of inferior position or condition, and spec. covertly or moderately.

5260. ὑποβάλλω **hŭpŏballō**, *hoop-ob-al'-lo;* from *5259* and *906;* to throw in stealthily, i.e. introduce by collusion:—suborn.

5261. ὑπογραμμός **hŭpŏgrammŏs**, *hoop-og-ram-mos';* from a comp. of *5259* and *1125;* an underwriting, i.e. copy for imitation (fig.):—example.

5262. ὑπόδειγμα **hŭpŏdĕigma**, *hoop-od'-igue-mah;* from *5263;* an exhibit for imitation or warning (fig. specimen, adumbration):—en- (ex-) ample, pattern.

5263. ὑποδείκνυμι **hŭpŏdĕiknumi**, *hoop-od-ike'-noo-mee;* from *5259* and *1166;* to exhibit under the eyes, i.e. (fig.) to exemplify (instruct, admonish):—show, (fore-) warn.

5264. ὑποδέχομαι **hŭpŏdĕchŏmai**, *hoop-od-ekh'-om-ahee;* from *5259* and *1209;* to admit under one's roof, i.e. entertain hospitably:—receive.

5265. ὑποδέω **hŭpŏdĕō**, *hoop-od-eh'-o;* from *5259* and *1210;* to bind under one's feet, i.e. put on shoes or sandals:—bind on, (be) shod.

5266. ὑπόδημα **hŭpŏdēma**, *hoop-od'-ay-mah;* from *5265;* something bound under the feet, i.e. a shoe or sandal:—shoe.

5267. ὑπόδικος **hŭpŏdikŏs**, *hoop-od'-ee-kos;* from *5259* and *1349;* under sentence, i.e. (by impl.) condemned:—guilty.

5268. ὑποζύγιον **hŭpŏzugiŏn**, *hoop-od-zoog'-ee-on;* neut. of a comp. of *5259* and *2218;* an animal under the yoke (draught-beast), i.e. (spec.) a donkey:—ass.

5269. ὑποζώννυμι **hŭpŏzōnnumi**, *hoop-od-zone'-noo-mee;* from *5259* and *2224;* to gird under, i.e. frap (a vessel with cables across the keel, sides and deck):—undergirt.

5270. ὑποκάτω **hŭpŏkatō**, *hoop-ok-at'-o;* from *5259* and *2736;* down under, i.e. beneath:—under.

5271. ὑποκρίνομαι **hŭpŏkrinŏmai**, *hoop-ok-rin'-om-ahee;* mid. from *5259* and *2919;* to decide (speak or act) under a false part, i.e. (fig.) dissemble (pretend):—feign.

5272. ὑπόκρισις **hŭpŏkrisis**, *hoop-ok'-ree-sis;* from *5271;* acting under a feigned part, i.e. (fig.) deceit ("hypocrisy"):—condemnation, dissimulation, hypocrisy.

5273. ὑποκριτής **hŭpŏkritēs**, *hoop-ok-ree-tace';* from *5271;* an actor under an assumed character (stage-player), i.e. (fig.) a dissembler ("hypocrite"):—hypocrite.

5274. ὑπολαμβάνω **hŭpŏlambanō**, *hoop-ol-am-ban'-o;* from *5259* and *2983;* to take from below, i.e. carry upward; fig. to take up, i.e. continue a discourse or topic; ment. to assume (presume):—answer, receive, suppose.

5275. ὑπολείπω **hŭpŏlĕipō**, *hoop-ol-i'-po;* from *5295* and *3007;* to leave under (behind), i.e. (pass.) to remain (survive):—be left.

5276. ὑπολήνιον **hŭpŏlēniŏn**, *hoop-ol-ay'-nee-on;* neut. of a presumed comp. of *5259* and *3025;* vessel or receptacle under the press, i.e. lower wine-vat:—winefat.

5277. ὑπολιμπάνω **hŭpŏlimpanō**, *hoop-ol-im-pan'-o;* a prol. form for *5275;* to leave behind, i.e. bequeath:—leave.

5278. ὑπομένω **hŭpŏmĕnō**, *hoop-om-en'-o;* from *5259* and *3306;* to stay under (behind), i.e. remain; fig. to undergo, i.e. bear (trials), have fortitude, persevere:—abide, endure, (take) patient (-ly), suffer, tarry behind.

5279. ὑπομιμνήσκω **hŭpŏmimnēskō**, *hoop-om-im-nace'-ko;* from *5259* and *3403;* to remind quietly, i.e. suggest to the (mid. one's own) memory:—put in mind, remember, bring to (put in) remembrance.

5280. ὑπόμνησις **hŭpŏmnēsis**, *hoop-om'-nay-sis;* from *5279;* a reminding or (reflex.) recollection:—remembrance.

5281. ὑπομονή **hŭpŏmŏnē**, *hoop-om-on-ay';* from *5278;* cheerful (or hopeful) endurance, constancy:—enduring, patience, patient continuance (waiting).

5282. ὑπονοέω **hŭpŏnŏĕō**, *hoop-on-ŏ-eh'-o;* from *5259* and *3539;* to think under (privately), i.e. to surmise or conjecture:—think, suppose, deem.

5283. ὑπόνοια **hŭpŏnŏia**, *hoop-on'-oy-ah;* from *5282;* suspicion:—surmising.

5284. ὑποπλέω **hŭpŏplĕō**, *hoop-op-leh'-o;* from *5259* and *4126;* to sail under the lee of:—sail under.

5285. ὑποπνέω **hŭpŏpnĕō**, *hoop-op-neh'-o;* from *5259* and *4154;* to breathe gently, i.e. breeze:—blow softly.

5286. ὑποπόδιον **hŭpŏpŏdiŏn**, *hoop-op-od'-ee-on;* neut. of a comp. of *5259* and *4228;* something under the feet, i.e. a foot-rest (fig.):—footstool.

5287. ὑπόστασις **hŭpŏstasis**, *hoop-os'-tas-is;* from a comp. of *5259* and *2476;* a setting under (support), i.e. (fig.) concr. essence, or abstr. assurance (obj. or subj.):—confidence, confident, person, substance.

5288. ὑποστέλλω **hŭpŏstĕllō**, *hoop-os-tel'-lo;* from *5259* and *4724;* to withhold under (out of sight), i.e. (reflex.) to cower or shrink, (fig.) to conceal (reserve):—draw (keep) back, shun, withdraw.

5289. ὑποστολή **hŭpŏstŏlē**, *hoop-os-tol-ay';* from *5288;* shrinkage (timidity), i.e. (by impl.) apostasy:—draw back.

5290. ὑποστρέφω **hŭpŏstrĕphō**, *hoop-os-tref'-o;* from *5259* and *4762;* to turn under (behind), i.e. to return (lit. or fig.):—come again, return (again, back again), turn back (again).

5291. ὑποστρώννυμι **hŭpŏstrōnnumi**, *hoop-os-trone'-noo-mee;* from *5259* and *4766;* to strew underneath (the feet as a carpet):—spread.

5292. ὑποταγή **hupŏtagē**, *hoop-ot-ag-ay'*; from *5293*; *subordination:*—subjection.

5293. ὑποτάσσω **hupŏtassō**, *hoop-ot-as'-so*; from *5259* and *5021*; *to subordinate*; reflex. *to obey:*—be under obedience (obedient), put under, subdue unto, (be, make) subject (to, unto), be (put) in subjection (to, under), submit self unto.

5294. ὑποτίθημι **hupŏtithēmi**, *hoop-ot-ith'-ay-mee*; from *5259* and *5087*; *to place underneath*, i.e. (fig.) *to hazard*, (reflex.) *to suggest:*—lay down, put in remembrance.

5295. ὑποτρέχω **hupŏtrĕchō**, *hoop-ot-rekh'-o*; from *5259* and *5143* (includ. its alt.); *to run under*, i.e. (spec.) *to sail past:*—run under.

5296. ὑποτύπωσις **hupŏtupōsis**, *hoop-ot-oop'-o-sis*; from a comp. of *5259* and a der. of *5179*; *typification under (after)*, i.e. (concr.) a *sketch* (fig.) for imitation:—form, pattern.

5297. ὑποφέρω **hupŏphĕrō**, *hoop-of-er'-o*; from *5259* and *5342*; *to bear from underneath*, i.e. (fig.) to *undergo hardship:*—bear, endure.

5298. ὑποχωρέω **hupŏchōrĕō**, *hoop-okh-o-reh'-o*; from *5259* and *5562*; *to vacate down*, i.e. *retire* quietly:—go aside, withdraw self.

5299. ὑπωπιάζω **hupōpiazō**, *hoop-o-pee-ad'-zo*; from a comp. of *5259* and a der. of *3700*; *to hit under the eye* (buffet or *disable* an antagonist as a pugilist), i.e. (fig.) to *tease* or *annoy* (into compliance), *subdue* (one's passions):—keep under, weary.

5300. ὗς **hus**, *hoos*; appar. a prim. word; a *hog* ("*swine*"):—sow.

5301. ὕσσωπος **hussōpos**, *hoos'-so-pos*; of for. or. [231]; "*hyssop*":—hyssop.

5302. ὑστερέω **hustĕrĕō**, *hoos-ter-eh'-o*; from *5306*; *to be later*, i.e. (by impl.) *to be inferior*; gen. *to fall short (be deficient):*—come behind (short), be destitute, fail, lack, suffer need, (be) in want, be the worse.

5303. ὑστέρημα **hustĕrēma**, *hoos-ter'-ay-mah*; from *5302*; a *deficit*; spec. *poverty:*—that which is behind, (that which was) lack (-ing), penury, want.

5304. ὑστέρησις **hustĕrēsis**, *hoos-ter'-ay-sis*; from *5302*; a *falling short*, i.e. (spec.) *penury:*—want.

5305. ὕστερον **hustĕrŏn**, *hoos'-ter-on*; neut. of *5306* as adv.; *more lately*, i.e. *eventually:*—afterward, (at the) last (of all).

5306. ὕστερος **hustĕrŏs**, *hoos'-ter-os*; compar. from *5259* (in the sense of *behind*); *later:*—latter.

5307. ὑφαντός **huphantŏs**, *hoo-fan-tos'*; from *5308*; *lofty* (in place or character):—high (-er, -ly) esteemed).

5309. ὑψηλοφρονέω **hupsĕlŏphrŏnĕō**, *hoop-say-lo-fron-eh'-o*; from a comp. of *5308* and *5424*; *to be lofty in mind*, i.e. *arrogant:*—be highminded.

5310. ὕψιστος **hupsistŏs**, *hoop-sis-tos*; superl. from the base of *5311*; *highest*, i.e. (masc. sing.) the *Supreme* (God), or (neut. plur.) the *heavens:*—most high, highest.

5311. ὕψος **hupsŏs**, *hoop'-sos*; from a der. of *5228*; *elevation*, i.e. (abstr.) *altitude*, (spec.) the *sky*, or (fig.) *dignity:*—be exalted, height, (on) high.

5312. ὑψόω **hupsŏō**, *hoop-sŏ'-o*; from *5311*; to *elevate* (lit. or fig.):—exalt, lift up.

5313. ὕψωμα **hupsōma**, *hoop'-so-mah*; from *5312*; an *elevated* place or thing, i.e. (abstr.) *altitude*, or (by impl.) a *barrier* (fig.):—height, high thing.

Φ

5314. φάγος **phagŏs**, *fag'-os*; from *5315*; a *glutton:*—gluttonous.

5315. φάγω **phagō**, *fag'-o*; a prim. verb (used as an alt. of *2068* in cert. tenses); *to eat* (lit. or fig.):—eat, meat.

5316. φαίνω **phainō**, *fah'ee-no*; prol. for the base of *5457*; *to lighten* (shine), i.e. *show* (trans. or intrans., lit. or fig.):—appear, seem, be seen, shine, ✕ think

5317. Φάλεκ **Phalĕk**, *fal'-ek*; of Heb. or. [6389]; *Phalek* (i.e. *Peleg*), a patriarch:—Phalec.

5318. φανερός **phanĕrŏs**, *fan-er-os'*; from *5316*; *shining*, i.e. *apparent* (lit. or fig.); neut. (as adv.) *publicly*, *externally:*—abroad, + appear, known, manifest, open ([+ -ly], outward ([+ -ly]).

5319. φανερόω **phanĕrŏō**, *fan-er-ŏ'-o*; from *5318*; *to render apparent* (lit. or fig.):—appear, manifestly declare, (make) manifest (forth), shew (self).

5320. φανερῶς **phanĕrŏs**, *fan-er-oce'*; adv. from *5318*; *plainly*, i.e. *clearly* or *publicly:*—evidently, openly.

5321. φανέρωσις **phanĕrōsis**, *fan-er'-o-sis*; from *5319*; *exhibition*, i.e. (fig.) *expression*, (by extens.) a *bestowment:*—manifestation.

5322. φανός **phanŏs**, *fan-os'*; from *5316*; a *lightener*, i.e. *light; lantern:*—lantern.

5323. Φανουήλ **Phanŏuēl**, *fan-oo-ale'*; of Heb. or. [6439]; *Phanuël* (i.e. *Penuël*), an Isr.:—Phanuel.

5324. φαντάζω **phantazō**, *fan-tad'-zo*; from a der. of *5316*; *to make apparent*, i.e. (pass.) *to appear* (neut. part. as noun, a *spectacle*):—sight.

5325. φαντασία **phantasia**, *fan-tas-ee'-ah*; from a der. of *5324*; (prop. abstr.) a (vain) *show* ("fantasy"):—pomp.

5326. φάντασμα **phantasma**, *fan'-tas-mah*; from *5324*; (prop. concr.) a (mere) *show* ("phantasm"), i.e. *spectre:*—spirit.

5327. φάραγξ **pharagx**, *far'-anx*; prop. *strength.* from the base of *4008* or rather of *4486*; a *gap* or *chasm*, i.e. *ravine* (winter-torrent):—valley.

5328. Φαραώ **Pharaō**, *far-ah-o'*; of for. or. [6547]; *Pharaō* (i.e. *Pharoh*), an Eg. king:—Pharaoh.

5329. Φαρές **Pharĕs**, *far-es'*; of Heb. or. [6557]; *Phares* (i.e. *Perets*), an Isr.:—Phares.

5330. Φαρισαῖος **Pharisaiŏs**, *far-is-ah'-yos*; of Heb. or. [comp. 6567]; a *separatist*, i.e. exclusively *religious*; a *Pharisæan*, i.e. Jewish sectary:—Pharisee.

5331. φαρμακεία **pharmakĕia**, *far-mak-i'-ah*; from *5332*; *medication* ("pharmacy"), i.e. (by extens.) *magic* (lit. or fig.):—sorcery, witchcraft.

5332. φαρμακεύς **pharmakĕus**, *far-mak-yoos'*; from φάρμακον **pharmakŏn** (a *drug*, i.e. *spell-giving potion*); a *druggist* ("pharmacist") or *poisoner*, i.e. (by extens.) a *magician:*—sorcerer.

5333. φαρμακός **pharmakŏs**, *far-mak-os'*; the same as *5332:*—sorcerer.

5334. φάσις **phasis**, *fas'-is*; from *5346* (not the same as "phase", which is from *5316*); a *saying*, i.e. *report:*—tidings.

5335. φάσκω **phaskō**, *fas'-ko*; prol. from the same as *5346*; *to assert:*—affirm, profess, say.

5336. φάτνη **phatnē**, *fat'-nay*; from πατέομαι **patĕŏmai** (*to eat*); a *crib* (for fodder):—manger, stall.

5337. φαῦλος **phaulŏs**, *fŏw'-los*; appar. a prim. word; "*foul*" or "*flawy*", i.e. (fig.) *wicked:*—evil.

5338. φέγγος **phĕggŏs**, *feng'-gos*; prob. akin to the base of *5457* [comp. *5350*]; *brilliancy:*—light.

5339. φείδομαι **phĕidŏmai**, *fi'-dom-ahee*; of uncert. affin.; *to be chary of*, i.e. (subj.) to *abstain* or (obj.) to *treat leniently:*—forbear, spare.

5340. φειδομένως **phĕidŏmĕnōs**, *fi-dom-en'-oce*; adv. from part. of *5339*; *abstemiously*, i.e. *stingily:*—sparingly.

5341. φελόνης **phĕlŏnēs**, *fel-on'-ace*; by transp. for a der. prob. of *5316* (as *showing* outside the other garments); a *mantle* (surtout):—cloke.

5342. φέρω **phĕrō**, *fer'-o*; a prim. verb (for which other and appar. not cognate ones are used in certain tenses only; namely,

οἴω **ŏiō**, *oy'-o*; and

ἐνέγκω **ĕnĕgkō**, *en-eng'-ko*); to "*bear*" or *carry* (in a very wide application, lit. and fig., as follows):—be, bear, ˈbring (forth), carry, come, + let be drive, be driven, endure, go on, lay, lead, move, reach, rushing, uphold.

5343. φεύγω **phĕugō**, *fyoo'-go*; appar. a prim. verb; *to run away* (lit. or fig.); by impl. to *shun*; by anal. *to vanish:*—escape, flee (away).

5344. Φῆλιξ **Phēlix**, *fay'-lix*; of Lat. or.; *happy*; *Phelix* (i.e. *Felix*), a Rom.:—Felix.

5345. φήμη **phēmē**, *fay'-may*; from *5346*; a *saying*, i.e. *rumor* ("fame"):—fame.

5346. φημί **phēmi**, *fay-mee'*; prop. the same as the base of *5457* and *5316*; *to show* or *make known* one's thoughts, i.e. *speak* or *say:*—affirm, say. Comp. *3004*.

5347. Φῆστος **Phēstŏs**, *face'-tos*; of Lat. der.; *festal*; *Phestus* (i.e. *Festus*), a Rom.:—Festus.

5348. φθάνω **phthanō**, *fthan'-o*; appar. a prim. verb; *to be beforehand*, i.e. *anticipate* or *precede*; by extens. *to have arrived at:*—(already) attain, come, prevent.

5349. φθαρτός **phthartŏs**, *fthar-tos'*; from *5351*; *decayed*, i.e. (by impl.) *perishable:*—corruptible.

5350. φθέγγομαι **phthĕggŏmai**, *ftheng'-gom-ahee*; prob. akin to *5338* and thus to *5346*; *to utter* a clear sound, i.e. (gen.) to *proclaim:*—speak.

5351. φθείρω **phthĕirō**, *fthi'-ro*; prob. strength. from φθίω **phthiō** (to *pine* or *waste*); prop. to *shrivel* or *wither*, i.e. to *spoil* (by any process) or (gen.) to *ruin* (espec. fig. by mor. influences, to *de prave*):—corrupt (self), defile, destroy.

5352. φθινοπωρινός **phthinŏpōrinŏs**, *fthin-op-o-ree-nos'*; from a der. of φθίω **phthinō** (to *wane*; akin to the base of *5351*) and *3703* (mean. *late autumn*); *autumnal* (as stripped of *leaves*):—whose fruit withereth.

5353. φθόγγος **phthŏggŏs**, *fthong'-gos*; from *5350*; *utterance*, i.e. a *musical* note (vocal or instrumental):—sound.

5354. φθονέω **phthŏnĕō**, *fthon-eh'-o*; from *5355*; *to be jealous* of:—envy.

5355. φθόνος **phthŏnŏs**, *fthon'-os*; prob. akin to the base of *5351*; *ill-will* (as *detraction*), i.e. *jealousy* (spite):—envy.

5356. φθορά **phthŏra**, *fthor-ah'*; from *5351*; *decay*, i.e. *ruin* (spontaneous or inflicted, lit. or fig.):—corruption, destroy, perish.

5357. φιάλη **phialē**, *fee-al'-ay*; of uncert. affin.; a *broad shallow cup* ("phial"):—vial.

5358. φιλάγαθος **philagathŏs**, *fil-ag'-ath-os*; from *5384* and *18*; *fond to good*, i.e. a *promoter of virtue:*—love of good men.

5359. Φιλαδέλφεια **Philadĕlphĕia**, *fil-ad-el'-fee-ah*; from Φιλάδελφος **Philadĕlphŏs** (the same as *5361*), a king of Pergamos; *Philadelphia*, a place in Asia Minor:—Philadelphia.

5360. φιλαδελφία **philadĕlphia**, *fil-ad-el-fee'-ah*; from *5361*; *fraternal affection:*—brotherly love (kindness), love of the brethren.

5361. φιλάδελφος **philadĕlphŏs**, *fil-ad'-el-fos*; from *5384* and *80*; *fond of brethren*, i.e. *fraternal:*—love as brethren.

5362. φίλανδρος **philandrŏs**, *fil'-an-dros*; from *5384* and *435*; *fond of man*, i.e. *affectionate* as a *wife:*—love their husbands.

5363. φιλανθρωπία **philanthrōpia**, *fil-an-thro-pee'-ah*; from the same as *5364*; *fondness of mankind*, i.e. *benevolence* ("philanthropy"):—kindness, love towards man.

5364. φιλανθρώπως **philanthrōpōs**, *fil-an-thrŏ'-poce*; adv. from a comp. of *5384* and *444*; *fondly to man* ("philanthropically"), i.e. *humanely:*—courteously.

5365. φιλαργυρία **philarguria**, *fil-ar-goo-ree'-ah*; from *5366*; *avarice:*—love of money.

5366. φιλάργυρος **philargurŏs**, *fil-ar'-goo-ros*; from *5384* and *696*; *fond of silver* (money), i.e. *avaricious:*—covetous.

5367. φίλαυτος **philautŏs**, *fil'-ŏw-tos*; from *5384* and *846*; *fond of self*, i.e. *selfish:*—lover of own self.

5368. φιλέω **philĕō**, *fil-eh'-o*; from *5384*; *to be a friend to* (*fond of* [an individual or an object]), i.e. *have affection for* (denoting *personal* attachment, as

76   Filaydonos
       Khlamoocc
      GREEK DICTIONARY OF THE NEW TESTAMENT.

a matter of sentiment or feeling; while *25* is wider, embracing espec. the judgment and the *deliberate* assent of the will as a matter of principle, duty and propriety: the two thus stand related very much as *2300* and *1014*, or as *2372* and *3563* respectively; the former being chiefly of the *heart* and the latter of the *head*); spec. to *kiss* (as a mark of tenderness):—kiss, love.

5369. φιλήδονος· **philēdŏnŏs**, *fil-ay'-don-os;* from *5384* and *2237; fond of pleasure,* i.e. *voluptuous:*—lover of pleasure.

5370. φίλημα **philēma**, *fil'-ay-mah;* from *5368;* a *kiss:*—kiss.

5371. Φιλήμων **Philēmōn**, *fil-ay'-mone;* from *5368; friendly; Philemon,* a Chr.:—Philemon.

5372. Φιλητός **Philētŏs**, *fil-ay-tos';* from *5368; amiable; Philetus,* an opposer of Christianity:—Philetus.

5373. φιλία **philia**, *fil-ee'-ah;* from *5384; fondness:*—friendship.

5374. Φιλιππήσιος **Philippēsiŏs**, *fil-ip-pay'-see-os;* from *5375;* a *Philippesian (Philippian),* i.e. native of Philippi:—Philippian.

5375. Φίλιπποι **Philippŏi**, *fil'-ip-poy;* plur. of *5376; Philippi,* a place in Macedonia:—Philippi.

5376. Φίλιππος **Philippŏs**, *fil'-ip-pos;* from *5384* and *2462; fond of horses; Philippus,* the name of four Isr.:—Philip.

5377. φιλόθεος **philŏthĕŏs**, *fil-oth'-eh-os;* from *5384* and *2316; fond of God,* i.e. *pious:*—lover of God.

5378. Φιλόλογος **Philŏlŏgŏs**, *fil-ol'-og-os;* from *5384* and *3056; fond of words,* i.e. *talkative (argumentative, learned, "philological"); Philologus,* a Chr.:—Philologus.

5379. φιλονεικία **philŏnĕikia**, *fil-on-i-kee'-ah;* from *5380; quarrelsomeness,* i.e. a *dispute:*—strife.

5380. φιλόνεικος **philŏnĕikŏs**, *fil-on'-i-kos;* from *5384* and *νεῖκος nĕikŏs* (a *quarrel;* prob. akin to *3534*); *fond of strife,* i.e. *disputatious:*—contentious.

5381. φιλονεξία **philŏnĕxia**, *fil-on-ex-ee'-ah;* from *5382; hospitableness:*—entertain strangers, hospitality.

5382. φιλόξενος **philŏxĕnŏs**, *fil-ox'-en-os;* from *5384* and *3581; fond of guests,* i.e. *hospitable:*—given to (lover of, use) hospitality.

5383. φιλοπρωτεύω **philŏprōtĕuō**, *fil-op-rote-yoo'-o;* from a comp. of *5384* and *4413;* to be *fond of being first,* i.e. *ambitious of distinction:*—love to have the preeminence.

5384. φίλος **philŏs**, *fee'-los;* prop. *dear,* i.e. a *friend;* act. *fond,* i.e. *friendly* (still as a noun, an *associate, neighbor,* etc.):—friend.

5385. φιλοσοφία **philŏsŏphia**, *fil-os-of-ee'-ah;* from *5386; "philosophy,"* i.e. (spec.) Jewish *sophistry:*—philosophy.

5386. φιλόσοφος **philŏsŏphŏs**, *fil-os'-of-os;* from *5384* and *4680; fond of wise* things, i.e. a *"philosopher":*—philosopher.

5387. φιλόστοργος **philŏstŏrgŏs**, *fil-os'-tor-gos;* from *5384* and στοργή **stŏrgē** (*cherishing* one's kindred, espec. parents or children); *fond of natural relatives,* i.e. *fraternal* towards fellow Chr.:—kindly affectioned.

5388. φιλότεκνος **philŏtĕknŏs**, *fil-ot'-ek-nos;* from *5384* and *5043; fond of one's children,* i.e. *maternal:*—love their children.

5389. φιλοτιμέομαι **philŏtimĕŏmai**, *fil-ot-im-eh'-om-ahee;* mid. from a comp. of *5384* and *5092;* to be *fond of honor,* i.e. *emulous (eager* or *earnest* to do something):—labour, strive, study.

5390. φιλοφρόνως **philŏphrŏnōs**, *fil-of-ron'-oce;* adv. from *5391; with friendliness of mind,* i.e. *kindly:*—courteously.

5391. φιλόφρων **philŏphrōn**, *fil-of'-rone;* from *5384* and *5424; friendly of mind,* i.e. *kind:*—courteous.

5392. φιμόω **phimŏō**, *fee-mŏ'-o;* from φιμός **phimŏs** (a *muzzle);* to *muzzle:*—muzzle.

5393. Φλέγων **Phlĕgōn**, *fleg'-one;* act. part. of the base of *5395; blazing; Phlegon,* a Chr.:—Phlegon.

5394. φλογίζω **phlŏgizō**, *flog-id'-zo;* from *5395;* to *cause a blaze,* i.e. *ignite* (fig. to *inflame* with passion):—set on fire.

5395. φλόξ **phlŏx**, *flox;* from a prim. φλέγω **phlĕgō** (to *"flash"* or *"flame");* a *blaze:*—flame (-ing).

5396. φλυαρέω **phluarĕō**, *floo-ar-eh'-o;* from *5397;* to be a *babbler* or *trifler,* i.e. (by impl.) to *berate* idly or mischievously:—prate against.

5397. φλύαρος **phluarŏs**, *floo'-ar-os;* from *prater:*—tattler.

5398. φοβερός **phŏbĕrŏs**, *fob-er-os';* from *5401; frightful,* i.e. (obj.) *formidable:*—fearful, terrible.

5399. φοβέω **phŏbĕō**, *fob-eh'-o;* from *5401;* to *frighten,* i.e. (pass.) to be *alarmed;* by anal. to be *in awe* of, i.e. *revere:*—be (+ sore) afraid, fear (exceedingly), reverence.

5400. φόβητρον **phŏbētrŏn**, *fob'-ay-tron;* neut. of a der. of *5399;* a *frightening thing,* i.e. *terrific portent:*—fearful sight.

5401. φόβος **phŏbŏs**, *fob'-os;* from a prim. φέβομαι **phĕbŏmai** (to be put in *fear); alarm* or *fright:*—be afraid, + exceedingly, fear, terror.

5402. Φοίβη **Phŏibē**, *foy'-bay;* fem. of φοῖβος **phŏibŏs** (*bright;* prob. akin to the base of *5457); Phœbe,* a Chr. woman:—Phebe.

5403. Φοινίκη **Phŏinikē**, *foy-nee'-kay;* from *5404; palm-country; Phœnice (or Phœnicia),* a region of Pal.:—Phenice, Phenicia.

5404. φοῖνιξ **phŏinix**, *foy'-nix;* of uncert. der.; a *palm-tree:*—palm (tree).

5405. Φοῖνιξ **Phŏinix**, *foy'-nix;* prob. the same as *5404; Phœnix,* a place in Crete:—Phenice.

5406. φονεύς **phŏnĕus**, *fon-yooce';* from *5408;* a *murderer* (always of *criminal* [or at least *intentional*] homicide; which *443* does not necessarily imply; while *4607* is a spec. term for a *public* bandit):—murderer.

5407. φονεύω **phŏnĕuō**, *fon-yoo'-o;* from *5406;* to be a *murderer* (of):—kill, do murder, slay.

5408. φόνος **phŏnŏs**, *fon'-os;* from an obsol. prim. φένω **phĕnō** (to *slay); murder:*—murder, + be slain with, slaughter.

5409. φορέω **phŏrĕō**, *for-eh'-o;* from *5411;* to have a *burden,* i.e. (by anal.) to *wear* as clothing or a constant accompaniment:—bear, wear.

5410. Φόρον **Phŏrŏn**, *for'-on;* of Lat. or.; a *forum* or market-place; only in comp. with *675;* a station on the Appian road:—forum.

5411. φόρος **phŏrŏs**, *for'-os;* from *5342;* a *load* (as borne), i.e. (fig.) a *tax* (prop. an individ. *assessment* on persons or property; whereas *5056* is usually a gen. *toll* on goods or travel):—tribute.

5412. φορτίζω **phŏrtizō**, *for-tid'-zo;* from *5414;* to *load* (up prop. as a *vessel* or animal), i.e. (fig.) to *overburden* with ceremony (or spiritual anxiety):—lade, be heavy laden.

5413. φορτίον **phŏrtiŏn**, *for-tee'-on;* dimin. of *5414;* an *invoice* (as part of *freight),* i.e. (fig.) a *task* or *service:*—burden.

5414. φόρτος **phŏrtŏs**, *for'-tos;* from *5342;* something *carried,* i.e. the *cargo* of a ship:—lading.

5415. Φορτουνᾶτος **Phŏrtŏunatŏs**, *for-too-nat'-os;* of Lat. or.; *"fortunate"; Fortunatus,* a Chr.:—Fortunatus.

5416. φραγέλλιον **phragĕlliŏn**, *frag-el'-le-on;* neut. of a der. from the base of *5417;* a *whip,* i.e. Rom. *lash* as a public punishment:—scourge.

5417. φραγελλόω **phragĕllŏō**, *frag-el-lŏ'-o;* from a presumed equiv. of the Lat. *flagellum;* to *whip,* i.e. *lash* as a public punishment:—scourge.

5418. φραγμός **phragmŏs**, *frag-mos';* from *5420;* a *fence,* or *inclosing barrier* (lit. or fig.):—hedge (+ round about), partition.

5419. φράζω **phrazō**, *frad'-zo;* prob. akin to *5420* through the idea of *defining;* to *indicate* (by word or act), i.e. (spec.) to *expound:*—declare.

5420. φράσσω **phrassō**, *fras'-so;* appar. a strength. form of the base of *5424;* to *fence* or *inclose,* i.e. (spec.) to *block up* (fig. to *silence):*—stop.

5421. φρέαρ **phrĕar**, *freh'-ar;* of uncert. der.; a *hole* in the ground (dug for obtaining or holding water or other purposes), i.e. a *cistern* or *well;* fig. an *abyss* (as a *prison):*—well, pit.

5422. φρεναπατάω **phrĕnapataō**, *fren-ap-at-ah'-o;* from *5423;* to be a *mind-misleader,* i.e. *delude:*—deceive.

5423. φρεναπάτης **phrĕnapatēs**, *fren-ap-at'-ace;* from *5424* and *539;* a *mind-misleader,* i.e. *seducer:*—deceiver.

5424. φρήν **phrēn**, *frane;* prob. from an obsol. φράω **phraō** (to *rein in* or *curb;* comp. *5420);* the *midrif* (as a *partition* of the *mind),* i.e. (fig. and by impl. of sympathy) the *feelings* (or sensitive nature: by extens. [also in the plur.] the *mind* or cognitive faculties):—understanding.

5425. φρίσσω **phrissō**, *fris'-so;* appar. a prim. verb; to *"bristle"* or *chill,* i.e. *shudder (fear):*—tremble.

5426. φρονέω **phrŏnĕō**, *fron-eh'-o;* from *5424;* to *exercise the mind,* i.e. *entertain* or have a *sentiment* or *opinion;* by impl. to be (mentally) *disposed* (more or less earnestly in a certain direction); intens. to *interest oneself in* (with concern or obedience):—set the *affection on,* (be) *care* (-ful), (be like-, + be of one, + be of the same, + let this) mind (-ed), regard, savour, think.

5427. φρόνημα **phrŏnēma**, *fron'-ay-mah;* from *5426;* (mental) *inclination* or *purpose:*—(be, + be carnally, + be spiritually) mind (-ed).

5428. φρόνησις **phrŏnēsis**, *fron'-ay-sis;* from *5426;* mental *action* or *activity,* i.e. intellectual or mor. *insight:*—prudence, wisdom.

5429. φρόνιμος **phrŏnimŏs**, *fron'-ee-mos;* from *5424; thoughtful,* i.e. *sagacious* or *discreet* (implying a *cautious* character; while *4680* denotes practical skill or acumen; and *4908* indicates rather *intelligence* or mental acquirement); in a bad sense *conceited* (also in the compar.):—wise (-r).

5430. φρονίμως **phrŏnimōs**, *fron-im'-oce;* adv. from *5429; prudently:*—wisely.

5431. φροντίζω **phrŏntizō**, *fron-tid'-zo;* from a der. of *5424;* to *exercise thought,* i.e. be *anxious:*—be careful.

5432. φρουρέω **phrŏurĕō**, *froo-reh'-o;* from a comp. of *4253* and *3708;* to be a *watcher* in advance, i.e. to *mount guard* as a sentinel (*post spies* at gates); fig. to *hem in, protect:*—keep (with a garrison). Comp. *5083.*

5433. φρυάσσω **phruassō**, *froo-as'-so;* akin to *1032, 1031;* to *snort* (as a spirited horse), i.e. (fig.) to *make a tumult:*—rage.

5434. φρύγανον **phruganŏn**, *froo'-gan-on;* neut. of a presumed der. of φρύγω **phrugō** (to *roast* or *parch;* akin to the base of *5395);* something *desiccated,* i.e. a *dry twig:*—stick.

5435. Φρυγία **Phrugia**, *froog-ee'-ah;* prob. of for. or.; *Phrygia,* a region of Asia Minor:—Phrygia.

5436. Φύγελλος **Phugĕllŏs**, *foog'-el-los;* prob. from *5343; fugitive; Phygellus,* an apostate Chr.:—Phygellus.

5437. φυγή **phugē**, *foog-ay';* from *5343;* a *fleeing,* i.e. *escape:*—flight.

5438. φυλακή **phulakē**, *foo-lak-ay';* from *5442; strength.* form of the base of *5424;* to *fence* or *imprison;* fig. the *place,* the *condition,* or (spec.) the *time* (as a *division* of day or night), lit. or fig.:—cage, hold, (imp-) prison (-ment), ward, watch.

5439. φυλακίζω **phulakizō**, *foo-lak-id'-zo;* from *5441;* to *incarcerate:*—imprison.

5440. φυλακτήριον **phulaktēriŏn**, *foo-lak-tay'-ree-on;* neut. of a der. of *5442;* a *guard-case,* i.e. *"phylactery"* for wearing slips of Scripture texts:—phylactery.

5441. φύλαξ **phulax**, *foo'-lax;* from *5442;* a *watcher* or *sentry:*—keeper.

5442. φυλάσσω **phulassō**, *foo-las'-so;* prob. from *5443* through the idea of *isolation;* to *watch,* i.e.

be on guard (lit. or fig.); by impl. to preserve, obey, avoid:—beware, keep (self), observe, save. Comp. 5083.

5443. φυλή phulē, foo-lay'; from 5453 (comp. 5444); an offshoot, i.e. race or clan:—kindred, tribe.

5444. φύλλον phullŏn, fool'-lon; from the same as 5443; a sprout, i.e. leaf:—leaf.

5445. φύραμα phurama, foo'-ram-ah; from a prol. form of φύρω phurō (to mix a liquid with a solid; perh. akin to 5453 through the idea of swelling in bulk), mean to knead; a mass of dough:—lump.

5446. φυσικός phusikŏs; from 5449; "physical", i.e. (by impl.) instinctive:—natural. Comp. 5591.

5447. φυσικῶς phusikŏs; adv. from 5446; "physically", i.e. (by impl.) instinctively:—naturally.

5448. φυσιόω phusiŏō, foo-see-ŏ'-o; from 5449 in the prim. sense of blowing; to inflate, i.e. (fig.) make proud (haughty):—puff up.

5449. φύσις phusis, foo'-sis; from 5453; growth (by germination or expansion), i.e. (by impl.) natural production (lineal descent); by extens. a genus or sort; fig. native disposition, constitution or usage:—([man-]) kind, nature ([-al]).

5450. φυσίωσις phusiŏsis, foo-see'-o-sis; from 5448; inflation, i.e. (fig.) haughtiness:—swelling.

5451. φυτεία phutĕia, foo-ti'-ah; from 5452; trans-planting, i.e. (concr.) a shrub or vegetable:—plant.

5452. φυτεύω phutĕuō, foot-yoo'-o; from a der. of 5453; to set out in the earth, i.e. implant; fig. to instil doctrine:—plant.

5453. φύω phuō, foo'-o; a prim. verb; prob. orig. to "puff" or blow, i.e. to swell up; but only used in the impl. sense, to germinate or grow (sprout, produce), lit. or fig.:—spring (up).

5454. φωλεός phōlĕŏs, fo-leh-os'; of uncert. der.; a burrow or lurking-place:—hole.

5455. φωνέω phōnĕō, fo-neh'-o; from 5456; to emit a sound (animal, human or instrumental); by impl. to address in words or by name, also in imitation:—call (for), crow, cry.

5456. φωνή phōnē, fo-nay'; prob. akin to 5316 through the idea of disclosure; a tone (articulate, bestial or artificial); by impl. an address (for any purpose), saying or language:—noise, sound, voice.

5457. φῶς phōs, foce; from an obsol. φάω phaō (to shine or make manifest, espec. by rays; comp. 5316, 5346); luminousness (in the widest application, nat. or artificial, abstr. or concr., lit. or fig.):—fire, light.

5458. φωστήρ phōstēr, foce-tare'; from 5457; an illuminator, i.e. (concr.) a luminary, or (abstr.) brilliancy:—light.

5459. φωσφόρος phōsphŏrŏs, foce-for'-os; from 5457 and 5342; light-bearing ("phosphorus"), i.e. (spec.) the morning-star (fig.):—day star.

5460. φωτεινός phōtĕinŏs; from 5457; lustrous, i.e. transparent or well-illuminated (fig.):—bright, full of light.

5461. φωτίζω phōtizō, fo-tid'-zo; from 5457; to shed rays, i.e. to shine or (trans.) to brighten up (lit. or fig.):—enlighten, illuminate, (bring to, give) light, make to see.

5462. φωτισμός phōtismŏs; from 5461; illumination (fig.):—light.

X

5463. χαίρω chairō, khah'ee-ro; a prim. verb; to be "cheer"ful, i.e. calmly happy or well-off; impers. espec. as salutation (on meeting or parting), be well:—farewell, be glad, God speed, greeting, hail, joy (-fully), rejoice.

5464. χάλαζα chalaza, khal'-ad-zah; prob. from 5465; hail:—hail.

5465. χαλάω chalaō, khal-ah'-o; from the base of 5490; to lower (as into a void):—let down, strike.

5466. Χαλδαῖος Chaldaiŏs, khal-dah'-yos; prob. of Heb. or. [3778]; a Chaldæan (i.e. Kasdi), or native of the region of the lower Euphrates:—Chaldæan.

5467. χαλεπός chalĕpŏs, khal-ep-os'; perh. from 5465 through the idea of reducing the strength; diffi-cult, i.e. dangerous, or (by impl.) furious:—fierce, perilous.

5468. χαλιναγωγέω chalinagōgĕō, khal-in-ag-ogue-eh'-o; from a comp. of 5469 and the redupl. form of 71; to be a bit-leader, i.e. to curb (fig.):—bridle.

5469. χαλινός chalinŏs, khal-ee-nos'; from 5465; a curb or head-stall (as curbing the spirit):—bit, bridle.

5470. χάλκεος chalkĕŏs, khal'-keh-os; from 5475; coppery:—brass.

5471. χαλκεύς chalkĕus, khalk-yooce'; from 5475; a copper-worker or brazier:—coppersmith.

5472. χαλκηδών chalkĕdōn, khal-kay-dohn'; from 5475 and perh. 1491; copper-like, i.e. "chalcedony":—chalcedony.

5473. χαλκίον chalkiŏn, khal-kee'-on; dimin. from 5475; a copper dish:—brazen vessel.

5474. χαλκολίβανον chalkŏlibanŏn, khal-kol-ib'-an-on; neut. of a comp. of 5475 and 3030 (in the impl. mean. of whiteness or brilliancy); burnished copper, an alloy of copper (or gold) and silver having a brilliant lustre:—fine brass.

5475. χαλκός chalkŏs, khal-kos'; perh. from 5465 through the idea of hollowing out as a vessel (this metal being chiefly used for that purpose); cop-per (the substance, or some implement or coin made of it):—brass, money.

5476. χαμαί chamai, kham-ah'ee; adv. perh. from the base of 5490 through the idea of a fissure in the soil; earthward, i.e. prostrate:—on (to) the ground.

5477. Χαναάν Chanaan, khan-ah-an'; of Heb. or. [3667]; Chanaan (i.e. Kenaan), the early name of Pal.:—Chanaan.

5478. Χαναναῖος Chananaiŏs, khan-ah-an-ah'-yos; from 5477; a Chanaanæan (i.e. Kenaanite), or native of gentile Pal.:—of Canaan.

5479. χαρά chara, khar-ah'; from 5463; cheerfulness, i.e. calm delight:—gladness, × greatly, (× be exceeding) joy (-ful, -fully, -fulness, -ous).

5480. χάραγμα charagma, khar'-ag-mah; from the same as 5482; a scratch or etching, i.e. stamp (as a badge of servitude), or sculptured figure (statue):—graven, mark.

5481. χαρακτήρ charaktēr, khar-ak-tare'; from the same as 5482; a graver (the tool or the person), i.e. (by impl.) engraving (["character"], the figure stamped, i.e. an exact copy or [fig.] representation):—express image.

5482. χάραξ charax, khar'-ax; from χαράσσω charassō (to sharpen to a point; akin to 1125 through the idea of scratching); a stake, i.e. (by impl.) a palisade or rampart (military mound for circumvallation in a siege):—trench.

5483. χαρίζομαι charizŏmai, khar-id'-zom-ahee; mid. from 5485; to grant as a favor, i.e. gra-tuitously, in kindness, pardon or rescue:—deliver, (frankly) forgive, (freely) give, grant.

5484. χάριν charin, khar'-in; acc. of 5485 as prep.; through favor of, i.e. on account of, be-(for) cause of, for sake of, + . . . fore, × reproachfully.

5485. χάρις charis, khar'-ece; from 5463; gra-ciousness (as gratifying), of manner or act (abstr. or concr.; lit., fig. or spiritual; espec. the divine influ-ence upon the heart, and its reflection in the life; in-cluding gratitude):—acceptable, benefit, favour, gift, grace (-ious), joy liberality, pleasure, thank (-s, -worthy).

5486. χάρισμα charisma, khar'-is-mah; from 5483; a (divine) gratuity, i.e. deliverance (from dan-ger or passion); (spec.) a (spiritual) endowment, i.e. (subj.) religious qualification, or (obj.) miraculous faculty:—(free) gift.

5487. χαριτόω charitŏō, khar-ee-tŏ'-o; from 5485; to grace, i.e. indue with special honor:—make accepted, be highly favoured.

5488. Χαρράν Charrhan, khar-hran'; of Heb. or. [2771]; Charrhan (i.e. Charan), a place in Meso-potamia:—Charran.

5489. χάρτης chartēs, khar'-tace; from the same as 5482; a sheet ("chart") of writing-material (as to be scribbled over):—paper.

5490. χάσμα chasma, khas'-mah; from a form of χάω chaō (to "gape" or "yawn"); a "chasm" or vacancy (impassable inter-val):—gulf.

5491. χεῖλος chĕilŏs, khi'-los; from a form of the same as 5490; a lip (as a pouring place); fig. a margin (of water):—lip, shore.

5492. χειμάζω chĕimazō, khi-mad'-zo; from the same as 5494; to storm, i.e. (pass.) to labor under a gale:—be tossed with tempest.

5493. χείμαρρος chĕimarrhŏs, khi'-mar-hros; from the base of 5494 and 4482; a storm-runlet, i.e. winter-torrent:—brook.

5494. χειμών chĕimōn, khi-mone'; from a der. of χέω chĕō (to pour; akin to the base of 5490 through the idea of a channel), mean. a storm (as pouring rain); by impl. the rainy season, i.e. winter:—tempest, foul weather, winter.

5495. χείρ chĕir, khire; perh. from the base of 5494 in the sense of its congener the base of 5490 (through the idea of hollowness for grasping); the hand (lit. or fig. [power]; espec. [by Heb.] a means or instrument):—hand.

5496. χειραγωγέω chĕiragōgĕō, khi-rag-ogue-eh'-o; from 5497; to be a hand-leader, i.e. to guide (a blind person):—lead by the hand.

5497. χειραγωγός chĕiragōgŏs, khi-rag-o-gos'; from 5495 and a redupl. form of 71; a hand-leader, i.e. personal conductor (of a blind person):—some to lead by the hand.

5498. χειρόγραφον chĕirŏgraphŏn, khi-rog'-raf-on; neut. of a comp. of 5495 and 1125; something hand-written ("chirograph"), i.e. a manuscript (spec. a legal document or bond [fig.]):—handwriting.

5499. χειροποίητος chĕirŏpŏiētŏs, khi-rop-oy'-ay-tos; from 5495 and a der. of 4160; manufactured, i.e. of human construction:—made by (make with) hands.

5500. χειροτονέω chĕirŏtŏnĕō, khi-rot-on-eh'-o; from a comp. of 5495 and τείνω tĕinō (to stretch); to be a hand-reacher or voter (by raising the hand), i.e. (gen.) to select or appoint:—choose, ordain.

5501. χείρων chĕirōn, khi'-rone; irreg. comp. of 2556; from an obsol. equiv. χέρης chĕrēs (of un-cert. der.); more evil or aggravated (phys., ment. or mor.):—sorer, worse.

5502. χερουβίμ chĕrŏubim, kher-oo-beem'; plur. of Heb. or. [3742]; "cherubim" (i.e. cherubs or kerubim):—cherubims.

5503. χήρα chēra, khay'-rah; fem. of a presumed der. appar. from the base of 5490 through the idea of deficiency; a widow (as lacking a husband), lit. or fig.:—widow.

5504. χθές chthĕs, khthes; of uncert. der.; "yes-terday"; by extens. in time past or hitherto:—yester-day.

5505. χιλιάς chilias, khil-ee-as'; from 5507; one thousand ("chiliad "):—thousand.

5506. χιλίαρχος chiliarchŏs, khil-ee'-ar-khos; from 5507 and 757; the commander of a thousand soldiers ("chiliarch"), i.e. colonel:—(chief, high) captain.

5507. χίλιοι chiliŏi, khil'-ee-oy; plur. of uncert. affin.; a thousand:—thousand.

5508. Χίος Chiŏs, khee'-os; of uncert. der.; Chios, an island in the Mediterranean:—Chios.

5509. χιτών chitōn, khee-tone'; of for. or. [8801]; a tunic or shirt:—clothes, coat, garment.

5510. χιών chiōn, khee-one'; perh. akin to the base of 5490 (5465) or 5494 (as descending or empty):—snow:—snow.

5511. χλαμύς chlamus, khlam-ooce'; of uncert. der.; a military cloak:—robe.

5512. χλευάζω **chleuazō,** *khlyoo-ad'-zo;* from a der. prob. of *5491;* to *throw out the lip,* i.e. *jeer* at:—mock.

5513. χλιαρός **chliarŏs,** *khlee-ar-os';* from χλίω **chliō** (to *warm*); *tepid:*—lukewarm.

5514. Χλόη **Chlŏē,** *khlŏ'-ay;* fem. of appar. a prim. word; "*green*"; *Chlŏē,* a Chr. female:—Chloe.

5515. χλωρός **chlōrŏs,** *khlo-ros';* from the same as *5514;* greenish, i.e. *verdant, dun-colored:*—green, pale.

5516. χ ξ ς **chi xi stigma,** *khee xee stig'-ma;* the 22d, 14th and an obsol. letter (*4742* as a *cross*) of the Greek alphabet (intermediate between the 5th and 6th), used as numbers; denoting respectively 600, 60 and 6; 666 as a numeral:—six hundred threescore and six.

5517. χοϊκός **chŏïkŏs,** *khŏ-ik-os';* from *5522;* dusty or dirty (soil-like), i.e. (by impl.) *terrene:*—earthy.

5518. χοῖνιξ **chŏïnix,** *khoy'-nix;* of uncert. der.; a *chœnix* or cert. dry measure:—measure.

5519. χοῖρος **chŏïrŏs,** *khoy'-ros;* of uncert. der.; a *hog:*—swine.

5520. χολάω **chŏlaō,** *khol-ah'-o;* from *5521;* to be *bilious,* i.e. (by impl.) *irritable* (*enraged,* "choleric"):—be angry.

5521. χολή **chŏlē,** *khol-ay';* fem. of an equiv. perh. akin to the same as *5514* (from the *greenish* hue); "*gall*" or *bile,* i.e. (by anal.) *poison* or an *anodyne* (wormwood, poppy, etc.):—gall.

5522. χόος **chŏŏs,** *khŏ'-os;* from the base of *5494;* a *heap* (as poured out), i.e. *rubbish;* loose *dirt:*—dust.

5523. Χοραζίν **Chŏrazin,** *khor-ad-zin';* of uncert. der.; *Chorazin,* a place in Pal.:—Chorazin.

5524. χορηγέω **chŏrēgĕō,** *khor-ayg-eh'-o;* from a comp. of *5525* and *71;* to be a *dance-leader,* i.e. (gen.) to *furnish:*—give, minister.

5525. χορός **chŏrŏs,** *khor-os';* of uncert. der.; a *ring,* i.e. *round dance* ("*choir*"):—dancing.

5526. χορτάζω **chŏrtazō,** *khor-tad'-zo;* from *5528;* to *fodder,* i.e. (gen.) to *gorge* (supply *food* in abundance):—feed, fill, satisfy.

5527. χόρτασμα **chŏrtasma,** *khor'-tas-mah;* from *5526;* forage, i.e. *food:*—sustenance.

5528. χόρτος **chŏrtŏs,** *khor'-tos;* appar. a prim. word; a "*court*" or "*garden*", i.e. (by impl. of *pasture*) *herbage* or *vegetation:*—blade, grass, hay.

5529. Χουζᾶς **Chŏuzas,** *khood-zas';* of uncert. or.; *Chuzas,* an officer of Herod:—Chuza.

5530. χράομαι **chraŏmai,** *khrah'-om-ahee;* mid. of a prim. verb (perh. rather from *5495,* to *handle*); to *furnish* what is needed; (give an *oracle,* "*graze*" [touch slightly], *light* upon, etc.), i.e. (by impl.) to *employ* or (by extens.) to *act towards* one in a given manner:—entreat, use. Comp. *5531, 5534.*

5531. χράω **chraō,** *khrah'-o;* prob. the same as the base of *5530;* to *loan:*—lend.

5532. χρεία **chrĕia,** *khri'-ah;* from the base of *5530* or *5534;* *employment,* i.e. an *affair;* also (by impl.) *occasion, demand, requirement* or *destitution:*—business, lack, necessary (-ity), need (-ful), use, want.

5533. χρεωφειλέτης **chrĕōphĕilĕtēs,** *khreh-o-fi-let'-ace;* from a der. of *5531* and *3781;* a *loan-ower,* i.e. *indebted* person:—debtor.

5534. χρή **chrē,** *khray;* third pers. sing. of the same as *5530* or *5531* used impers.; it *needs* (*must* or *should*) be:—ought.

5535. χρῄζω **chrēzō,** *khrade'-zo;* from *5532;* to *make* (i.e. *have*) *necessity,* i.e. be in *want* of:—(have) need.

5536. χρῆμα **chrēma,** *khray'-mah;* something *useful* or *needed,* i.e. *wealth, price:*—money, riches.

5537. χρηματίζω **chrēmatizō,** *khray-mat-id'-zo;* from *5530;* to *utter an oracle* (comp. the orig. sense of *5530*), i.e. divinely *intimate;* by impl. (comp. the secular sense of *5532*) to *constitute* a *firm* for business, i.e. (gen.) *bear* as a *title:*—be called, be admonished (warned) of God, reveal, speak.

5538. χρηματισμός **chrēmatismŏs,** *khray-mat-is-mos';* from *5537;* a divine *response* or *revelation:*—answer of God.

5539. χρήσιμος **chrēsimŏs,** *khray'-see-mos;* from *5540; serviceable:*—profit.

5540. χρῆσις **chrēsis,** *khray'-sis;* from *5530; employment,* i.e. (spec.) sexual *intercourse* (as an occupation of the body):—use.

5541. χρηστεύομαι **chrēstĕuŏmai,** *khraste-yoo'-om-ahee;* mid. from *5543;* to *show oneself useful,* i.e. *act benevolently:*—be kind.

5542. χρηστολογία **chrēstŏlŏgia,** *khrase-tol-og-ee'-ah;* from a comp. of *5543* and *3004; fair speech,* i.e. *plausibility:*—good words.

5543. χρηστός **chrēstŏs,** *khrase-tos';* from *5530; employed,* i.e. (by impl.) *useful* (in manner or morals):—better, easy, good (-ness), gracious, kind.

5544. χρηστότης **chrēstŏtēs,** *khray-stot'-ace;* from *5543; usefulness,* i.e. mor. *excellence* (in character or demeanor):—gentleness, good (-ness), kindness.

5545. χρῖσμα **chrisma,** *khris'-mah;* from *5548;* an *unguent* or *smearing,* i.e. (fig.) the spec. *endowment* ("chrism") of the Holy Spirit:—anointing, unction.

5546. Χριστιανός **Christianŏs,** *khris-tee-an-os';* from *5547;* a *Christian,* i.e. *follower* of *Christ:*—Christian.

5547. Χριστός **Christŏs,** *khris-tos';* from *5548; anointed,* i.e. the *Messiah,* an epithet of Jesus:—Christ.

5548. χρίω **chriō,** *khree'-o;* prob. akin to *5530* through the idea of *contact;* to *smear* or *rub* with oil, i.e. (by impl.) to *consecrate* to an office or religious service:—anoint.

5549. χρονίζω **chrŏnizō,** *khron-id'-zo;* from *5550;* to *take time,* i.e. *linger:*—delay, tarry.

5550. χρόνος **chrŏnŏs,** *khron'-os;* of uncert. der.; a space of *time* (in gen., and thus prop. distinguished from *2540,* which designates a *fixed* or special occasion; and from *165,* which denotes a *particular period*) or *interval;* by extens. an individ. *opportunity;* by impl. *delay:*—+ years old, season, space, (× often-) time (-s), (a) while.

5551. χρονοτριβέω **chrŏnŏtribĕō,** *khron-ot-rib-eh'-o;* from a presumed comp. of *5550* and the base of *5147;* to be a *time-wearer,* i.e. to *procrastinate* (*linger*):—spend time.

5552. χρύσεος **chrusĕŏs,** *khroo'-seh-os;* from *5557;* made of *gold:*—of gold, golden.

5553. χρυσίον **chrusiŏn,** *khroo-see'-on;* dimin. of *5557;* a *golden* article, i.e. *gold plating, ornament,* or *coin:*—gold.

5554. χρυσοδακτύλιος **chrusŏdaktuliŏs,** *khroo-sod-ak-too'-lee-os;* from *5557* and *1146; gold-ringed,* i.e. *wearing* a golden *finger-ring* or similar *jewelry:*—with a gold ring.

5555. χρυσόλιθος **chrusŏlithŏs,** *khroo-sol'-ee-thos;* from *5557* and *3037; gold-stone,* i.e. a *yellow* gem ("*chrysolite*"):—chrysolite.

5556. χρυσόπρασος **chrusŏprasŏs,** *khroo-sop'-ras-os;* from *5557* and πράσον **prason** (a leek); a *greenish-yellow* gem ("*chrysoprase*"):—chrysoprase.

5557. χρυσός **chrusŏs,** *khroo-sos';* perh. from the base of *5530* (through the idea of the *utility* of the metal); *gold;* by extens. a *golden* article, as an ornament or coin:—gold.

5558. χρυσόω **chrusŏō,** *khroo-sŏ'-o;* from *5557;* to *gild,* i.e. *bespangle* with golden ornaments:—deck.

5559. χρώς **chrōs,** *khroce;* prob. akin to the base of *5530* through the idea of *handling;* the *body* (prop. its *surface* or *skin*):—body.

5560. χωλός **chōlŏs,** *kho-los';* appar. a prim.word; "*halt*", i.e. *limping:*—cripple, halt, lame.

5561. χώρα **chōra,** *kho'-rah;* fem. of a der. of the base of *5490* through the idea of *empty expanse; room,* i.e. a *space* of *territory* (more or less extensive; often includ. its inhab.):—coast, county, fields, ground, land, region. Comp. *5117.*

5562. χωρέω **chōrĕō,** *kho-reh'-o;* from *5561;* to be in (*give*) *space,* i.e. (intrans.) to *pass, enter,* or (trans.)

to *hold, admit* (lit. or fig.):—come, contain, go, have place, (can, be room to) receive.

5563. χωρίζω **chōrizō,** *kho-rid'-zo;* from *5561;* to *place room* between, i.e. *part;* reflex. to *go away:*—depart, put asunder, separate.

5564. χωρίον **chōriŏn,** *kho-ree'-on;* dimin. of *5561;* a *spot* or *plot* of ground:—field, land, parcel of ground, place, possession.

5565. χωρίς **chōris,** *kho-rece';* adv. from *5561;* at a *space,* i.e. *separately* or *apart* from (often as prep.):—beside, by itself, without.

5566. χῶρος **chōrŏs,** *kho'-ros;* of Lat. or.; the *north-west* wind:—north west.

Ψ

5567. ψάλλω **psallō,** *psal'-lo;* prob. strengthened from ψάω **psaō** (to *rub* or *touch* the surface; comp. *5597*); to *twitch* or *twang,* i.e. to *play* on a stringed instrument (*celebrate* the divine worship *with music* and accompanying odes):—make melody, sing (psalms).

5568. ψαλμός **psalmŏs,** *psal-mos';* from *5567;* a set piece of *music,* i.e. a sacred *ode* (accompanied with the voice, harp or other instrument; a "*psalm*"); collect. the book of the *Psalms:*—psalm. Comp. *5603.*

5569. ψευδάδελφος **psĕudadĕlphŏs,** *psyoo-dad'-el-fos;* from *5571* and *80;* a *spurious brother,* i.e. *pretended associate:*—false brethren.

5570. ψευδαπόστολος **psĕudapŏstŏlŏs,** *psyoo-dap-os'-tol-os;* from *5571* and *652;* a *spurious apostle,* i.e. *pretended preacher:*—false teacher.

5571. ψευδής **psĕudēs,** *psyoo-dace';* from *5574; untrue,* i.e. *erroneous, deceitful, wicked:*—false, liar.

5572. ψευδοδιδάσκαλος **psĕudŏdidaskalŏs,** *psyoo-dod-id-as'-kal-os;* from *5571* and *1320;* a *spurious teacher,* i.e. *propagator* of *erroneous* Chr. doctrine:—false teacher.

5573. ψευδολόγος **psĕudŏlŏgŏs,** *psyoo-dol-og'-os;* from *5571* and *3004; mendacious,* i.e. *promulgating erroneous* Chr. doctrine:—speaking lies.

5574. ψεύδομαι **psĕudŏmai,** *psyoo'-dom-ahee;* mid. of an appar. prim. verb; to *utter* an *untruth* or attempt to *deceive* by falsehood:—falsely, lie.

5575. ψευδομάρτυρ **psĕudŏmartur,** *psyoo-dom-ar'-toor;* from *5571* and a kindred form of *3144;* a *spurious witness,* i.e. *bearer* of *untrue* testimony:—false witness.

5576. ψευδομαρτυρέω **psĕudŏmarturĕō,** *psyoo-dom-ar-too-reh'-o;* from *5575;* to *be an untrue* testifier, i.e. *offer* *falsehood* in *evidence:*—be a false witness.

5577. ψευδομαρτυρία **psĕudŏmarturia,** *psyoo-dom-ar-too-ree'-ah;* from *5575; untrue* testimony:—false witness.

5578. ψευδοπροφήτης **psĕudŏprŏphētēs,** *psyoo-dop-rof-ay'-tace;* from *5571* and *4396;* a *spurious prophet,* i.e. *pretended foreteller* or *religious impostor:*—false prophet.

5579. ψεῦδος **psĕudŏs,** *psyoo'-dos;* from *5574;* a *falsehood:*—lie, lying.

5580. ψευδόχριστος **psĕudŏchristŏs,** *psyoo-dokh'-ris-tos;* from *5571* and *5547;* a *spurious* *Messiah:*—false Christ.

5581. ψευδώνυμος **psĕudōnumŏs,** *psyoo-do'-noo-mos;* from *5571* and *3686; untruly named:*—falsely so called.

5582. ψεῦσμα **psĕusma,** *psyoos'-mah;* from *5574;* a *fabrication,* i.e. *falsehood:*—lie.

5583. ψεύστης **psĕustēs,** *psyoos-tace';* from *5574;* a *falsifier:*—liar.

5584. ψηλαφάω **psēlaphaō,** *psay-laf-ah'-o;* from the base of *5567* (comp. *5585*); to *manipulate,* i.e. *verify* by contact; fig. to *search* for:—feel after, handle, touch.

5585. ψηφίζω **psēphizō,** *psay-fid'-zo;* from *5586;* to *use pebbles* in enumeration, i.e. (gen.) to *compute:*—count.

5586. ψῆφος **psēphŏs,** *psay'-fos;* from the same as *5584;* a *pebble* (as worn smooth by *handling*), i.e.

(by impl. of use as a *counter* or *ballot*) a *verdict* (of acquittal) or *ticket* (of admission); a *vote*:—stone, voice.

5587. ψιθυρισμός **psithurismŏs**, *psith-oo-ris-mos'*; from a der. of ψίθος **psithŏs** (a *whisper*; by impl. a *slander*; prob. akin to *5574*); *whispering*, i.e. secret *detraction*:—whispering.

5588. ψιθυριστής **psithuristēs**, *psith-oo-ris-tace'*; from the same as *5587*; a secret *calumniator*:—whisperer.

5589. ψιχίον **psichiŏn**, *psikh-ee'-on*; dimin. from a der. of the base of *5567* (mean. a *crumb*); a *little bit* or *morsel*:—crumb.

5590. ψυχή **psuchē**, *psoo-khay'*; from *5594*; *breath*, i.e. (by impl.) *spirit*, abstr. or concr. (the *animal* sentient principle only; thus distinguished on the one hand from *4151*, which is the rational and immortal *soul*; and on the other from *2222*, which is mere *vitality*, even of plants: these terms thus exactly correspond respectively to the Heb. 5315, 7307 and 2416):—heart (+ -ily), life, mind, soul, + us, + you.

5591. ψυχικός **psuchikŏs**, *psoo-khee-kos'*; from *5590*; *sensitive*, i.e. *animate* (in distinction on the one hand from *4152*, which is the higher or *renovated* nature; and on the other from *5446*, which is the lower or *bestial* nature):—natural, sensual.

5592. ψῦχος **psuchŏs**, *psoo'-khos*; from *5594*; *coolness*:—cold.

5593. ψυχρός **psuchrŏs**, *psoo-chros'*; from *5592*; *chilly* (lit. or fig.):—cold.

5594. ψύχω **psuchō**, *psoo'-kho*; a prim. verb; to *breathe* (voluntarily but *gently*; thus differing on the one hand from *4154*, which denotes prop. a *forcible* respiration; and on the other from the base of *109*, which refers prop. to an inanimate *breeze*), i.e. (by impl. of reduction of temperature by evaporation) to *chill* (fig.):—wax cold.

5595. ψωμίζω **psōmizō**, *pso-mid'-zo*; from the base of *5596*; to *supply with bits*, i.e. (gen.) to *nourish*:—(bestow to) feed.

5596. ψωμίον **psōmiŏn**, *pso-mee'-on*; dim. from a der. of the base of *5597*; a *crumb* or *morsel* (as if *rubbed* off), i.e. a *mouthful*:—sop.

5597. ψώχω **psōchō**, *pso'-kho*; prol. from the same base as *5567*; to *triturate*, i.e. (by anal.) to *rub*

out (kernels from husks with the fingers or hand):—rub.

Ω

5598. Ω **ō**, i.e. ὤμεγα **ōměga**, *o'-meg-ah*; the last letter of the Gr. alphabet, i.e. (fig.) the *finality*:—Omega.

5599. ὦ **ō**, *o*; a prim. interj.; as a sign of the voc. *O*; as a note of exclamation, *oh*:—O.

5600. ὦ **ō**, *o*; includ. the oblique forms, as well as ἦς ἔα, *ace*; ἦ ἔ, *ay*, etc.; the subjunctive of *1510*; (may, might, can, could, would, should, must, etc.; also with *1487* and its comp., as well as with other particles) *be*:—+ appear, are, (may, might, should) be, × have, is, + pass the flower of her age, should stand, were.

5601. Ὠβήδ **Ōbēd**, *o-bade'*; of Heb. or. [5744]; *Obed*, an Isr.:—Obed.

5602. ὧδε **hōdĕ**, *ho'-deh*; from an adv. form of *3592*; in *this* same spot, i.e. *here* or *hither*:—here, hither, (in) this place, there.

5603. ᾠδή **ō,dē**, *o-day'*; from *103*; a *chant* or "*ode*" (the gen. term for any words sung; while *5215* denotes espec. a *religious* metrical composition, and *5.68* still more spec. a *Heb*. cantillation):—song.

5604. ὠδίν **ōdin**, *o-deen'*; akin to *3601*; a *pang* or *throe*, esp. of childbi.th:—pain, sorrow, travail.

5605. ὠδίνω **ōdinō**, *o-dee'-no*; from *5604*; to *experience* the *pains* of parturition (lit. or fig.):—travail in (birth).

5606. ὦμος **ōmŏs**, *o'-mos*; perh. from the alt. of *5342*; the *shoulder* (as that on which burdens are borne):—shoulder.

5607. ὤν **ōn**, *oan*; includ. the fem.

 οὖσα **ŏusa**, *oo'-sah*; and the neut.

ὄν **ŏn**, *on*; pres. part. of *1510*; *being*:—be, come, have.

5608. ὠνέομαι **ōnĕŏmai**, *o-neh'-om-ahee*; mid. from an appar. prim. ὦνος **ōnŏs** (a *sum* or *price*); to *purchase* (synon. with the earlier *4092*):—buy.

5609. ᾠόν **ōŏn**, *o-on'*; appar. a prim. word; an "*egg*":—egg.

5610. ὥρα **hōra**, *ho'-rah*; appar. a prim. word; an "*hour*" (lit. or fig.):—day, hour, instant, season, × short, [even-] tide, (high) time.

5611. ὡραῖος **hōraiŏs**, *ho-rah'-yos*; from *5610*; belonging to the right *hour* or *season* (*timely*), i.e. (by impl.) *flourishing* (*beauteous* [fig.]):—beautiful.

5612. ὠρύομαι **ōruŏmai**, *o-roo'-om-ahee*; mid. of an appar. prim. verb; to "*roar*":—roar.

5613. ὡς **hōs**, *hoce*; prob. adv. of comp. from *3739*; *which how*, i.e. *in that manner* (very variously used, as follows):—about, after (that), (according as) (it had been, it were), as soon (as), even as (like), for, how (greatly), like (as, unto), since, so (that), that, to wit, unto, when ([-soever]), while, × with all speed.

5614. ὡσαννά **hōsanna**, *ho-san-nah'*; of Heb. or. [8467 and 4994]; *oh save!*; *hosanna* (i.e. *hoshia-na*), an exclamation of adoration:—hosanna.

5615. ὡσαύτως **hōsautōs**, *ho-sŏw'-toce*; from *5613* and an adv. from *846*; as *thus*, i.e. in *the same way*:—even so, likewise, after the same (in like) manner.

5616. ὡσεί **hōsĕí**, *ho-si'*; from *5613* and *1487*; as *if*:—about, as (it had been, it were), like (as).

5617. Ὡσηέ **Hōsēĕ**, *ho-say-eh'*; of Heb. or. [1954]; *Hosee* (i.e. *Hosheä*), an Isr.:—Osee.

5618. ὥσπερ **hōspěr**, *hoce'-per*; from *5613* and *4007*; *just as*, i.e. *exactly like*:—(even, like) as.

5619. ὡσπερεί **hōspěrĕí**, *hoce-per-i'*; from *5618* and *1487*; *just as if*, i.e. *as it were*:—as.

5620. ὥστε **hōstĕ**, *hoce'-teh*; from *5613* and *5037*; so too, i.e. *thus therefore* (in various relations of consecution, as follow):—(insomuch) as, so that (then), (insomuch) that, therefore, to, wherefore.

5621. ὠτίον **ōtiŏn**, *o-tee'-on*; dimin. of *3775*; an *earlet*, i.e. *one* of the ears, or perh. the *lobe* of the ear:—ear.

5622. ὠφέλεια **ōphĕlĕia**, *o-fel'-i-ah*; from a der. of the base of *5624*; *usefulness*, i.e. *benefit*:—advantage, profit.

5623. ὠφελέω **ōphĕlĕō**, *o-fel-eh'-o*; from the same as *5622*; to *be useful*, i.e. to *benefit*:—advantage, better, prevail, profit.

5624. ὠφέλιμος **ōphĕlimŏs**, *o-fel'-ee-mos*; from a form of *3786*; *helpful* or *serviceable*, i.e. *advantageous*:—profit (-able).

VARIATIONS

IN THE NUMBERING OF VERSES IN THE GREEK AND ENGLISH NEW TESTAMENT.